Presented

To: ____________________

By: ____________________

On: ____________________

Special Note

The
Holy Bible

The Holy Bible

King James Version

Publisher's Note: In this edition of the King James Version Bible, occurrences of "Holy Ghost" have been changed to "Holy Spirit." No other changes have been made.

The Holy Bible – King James Version

Printed in China

Published and distributed by:
Zeiset
203 E. Birch Street
P.O. Box 652
Abbotsford, WI 54405

Help spread the Word. Learn more at www.zeiset.org.

Brown Cover ISBN: 978-1-62245-633-8
Black Cover ISBN: 978-1-62245-835-6
eBook ISBN: 978-1-62245-634-5

10 9 8 7 6 5 4 3 2

Table of Contents

The Old Testament

The New Testament

The
Old Testament

The First Book Of Moses Called

Genesis

Genesis 1

1 In the beginning God created the heaven
and the earth.
2 And the earth was without form, and void;
and darkness *was* upon the face of the deep.
And the Spirit of God moved upon the face
of the waters.
3 And God said, Let there be light: and there
was light.
4 And God saw the light, that *it was* good:
and God divided the light from the darkness.
5 And God called the light Day, and the
darkness he called Night. And the evening
and the morning were the first day.
6 ¶ And God said, Let there be a firmament
in the midst of the waters, and let it divide
the waters from the waters.
7 And God made the firmament, and divided
the waters which *were* under the firmament
from the waters which *were* above the firmament: and it was so.
8 And God called the firmament Heaven.
And the evening and the morning were the
second day.
9 ¶ And God said, Let the waters under
the heaven be gathered together unto one
place, and let the dry *land* appear: and it
was so.
10 And God called the dry *land* Earth; and
the gathering together of the waters called
he Seas: and God saw that *it was* good.
11 And God said, Let the earth bring forth
grass, the herb yielding seed, *and* the fruit
tree yielding fruit after his kind, whose seed
is in itself, upon the earth: and it was so.
12 And the earth brought forth grass, *and*
herb yielding seed after his kind, and the
tree yielding fruit, whose seed *was* in itself,
after his kind: and God saw that *it was* good.
13 And the evening and the morning were
the third day.
14 ¶ And God said, Let there be lights in the
firmament of the heaven to divide the day
from the night; and let them be for signs,
and for seasons, and for days, and years:
15 And let them be for lights in the firmament of the heaven to give light upon the
earth: and it was so.
16 And God made two great lights; the
greater light to rule the day, and the lesser
light to rule the night: *he made* the stars
also.
17 And God set them in the firmament of
the heaven to give light upon the earth,
18 And to rule over the day and over the
night, and to divide the light from the darkness: and God saw that *it was* good.
19 And the evening and the morning were
the fourth day.
20 And God said, Let the waters bring forth
abundantly the moving creature that hath
life, and fowl *that* may fly above the earth
in the open firmament of heaven.
21 And God created great whales, and
every living creature that moveth, which
the waters brought forth abundantly, after
their kind, and every winged fowl after his
kind: and God saw that *it was* good.
22 And God blessed them, saying, Be fruitful, and multiply, and fill the waters in the
seas, and let fowl multiply in the earth.
23 And the evening and the morning were
the fifth day.
24 ¶ And God said, Let the earth bring forth
the living creature after his kind, cattle, and
creeping thing, and beast of the earth after
his kind: and it was so.
25 And God made the beast of the earth
after his kind, and cattle after their kind, and

every thing that creepeth upon the earth
after his kind: and God saw that *it was* good.
26 ¶ And God said, Let us make man in our
image, after our likeness: and let them have
dominion over the fish of the sea, and over
the fowl of the air, and over the cattle, and
over all the earth, and over every creeping
thing that creepeth upon the earth.
27 So God created man in his *own* image,
in the image of God created he him; male
and female created he them.
28 And God blessed them, and God said
unto them, Be fruitful, and multiply, and
replenish the earth, and subdue it: and have
dominion over the fish of the sea, and over
the fowl of the air, and over every living
thing that moveth upon the earth.
29 ¶ And God said, Behold, I have given you
every herb bearing seed, which *is* upon the
face of all the earth, and every tree, in the
which *is* the fruit of a tree yielding seed; to
you it shall be for meat.
30 And to every beast of the earth, and to
every fowl of the air, and to every thing that
creepeth upon the earth, wherein *there is*
life, *I have given* every green herb for meat:
and it was so.
31 And God saw every thing that he had
made, and, behold, *it was* very good. And
the evening and the morning were the
sixth day.

Genesis 2

1 Thus the heavens and the earth were
finished, and all the host of them.
2 And on the seventh day God ended his
work which he had made; and he rested
on the seventh day from all his work which
he had made.
3 And God blessed the seventh day, and
sanctified it: because that in it he had
rested from all his work which God created
and made.
4 ¶ These *are* the generations of the heavens and of the earth when they were created, in the day that the LORD God made
the earth and the heavens,
5 And every plant of the field before it was
in the earth, and every herb of the field
before it grew: for the LORD God had not
caused it to rain upon the earth, and *there*
was not a man to till the ground.
6 But there went up a mist from the earth,
and watered the whole face of the ground.
7 And the LORD God formed man *of* the
dust of the ground, and breathed into his
nostrils the breath of life; and man became
a living soul.
8 ¶ And the LORD God planted a garden
eastward in Eden; and there he put the man
whom he had formed.
9 And out of the ground made the LORD
God to grow every tree that is pleasant to
the sight, and good for food; the tree of life
also in the midst of the garden, and the tree
of knowledge of good and evil.
10 And a river went out of Eden to water
the garden; and from thence it was parted,
and became into four heads.
11 The name of the first *is* Pison: that *is*
it which compasseth the whole land of
Havilah, where *there is* gold;
12 And the gold of that land *is* good: there
is bdellium and the onyx stone.
13 And the name of the second river *is*
Gihon: the same *is* it that compasseth the
whole land of Ethiopia.
14 And the name of the third river *is* Hiddekel: that *is* it which goeth toward the east of
Assyria. And the fourth river *is* Euphrates.
15 And the LORD God took the man, and
put him into the garden of Eden to dress it
and to keep it.
16 And the LORD God commanded the man,
saying, Of every tree of the garden thou
mayest freely eat:
17 But of the tree of the knowledge of good
and evil, thou shalt not eat of it: for in the
day that thou eatest thereof thou shalt
surely die.
18 ¶ And the LORD God said, *It is* not good
that the man should be alone; I will make
him an help meet for him.
19 And out of the ground the LORD God
formed every beast of the field, and every
fowl of the air; and brought *them* unto Adam
to see what he would call them: and whatsoever Adam called every living creature,
that *was* the name thereof.
20 And Adam gave names to all cattle, and
to the fowl of the air, and to every beast of
the field; but for Adam there was not found
an help meet for him.
21 And the LORD God caused a deep sleep
to fall upon Adam, and he slept: and he

took one of his ribs, and closed up the flesh
instead thereof;
22 And the rib, which the LORD God had
taken from man, made he a woman, and
brought her unto the man.
23 And Adam said, This *is* now bone of my
bones, and flesh of my flesh: she shall be
called Woman, because she was taken out
of Man.
24 Therefore shall a man leave his father
and his mother, and shall cleave unto his
wife: and they shall be one flesh.
25 And they were both naked, the man and
his wife, and were not ashamed.

Genesis 3

1 Now the serpent was more subtil than any
beast of the field which the LORD God had
made. And he said unto the woman, Yea,
hath God said, Ye shall not eat of every tree
of the garden?
2 And the woman said unto the serpent,
We may eat of the fruit of the trees of the
garden:
3 But of the fruit of the tree which *is* in
the midst of the garden, God hath said, Ye
shall not eat of it, neither shall ye touch it,
lest ye die.
4 And the serpent said unto the woman, Ye
shall not surely die:
5 For God doth know that in the day ye eat
thereof, then your eyes shall be opened, and
ye shall be as gods, knowing good and evil.
6 And when the woman saw that the tree
was good for food, and that it *was* pleasant
to the eyes, and a tree to be desired to make
one wise, she took of the fruit thereof, and
did eat, and gave also unto her husband
with her; and he did eat.
7 And the eyes of them both were opened,
and they knew that they *were* naked; and
they sewed fig leaves together, and made
themselves aprons.
8 And they heard the voice of the LORD God
walking in the garden in the cool of the day:
and Adam and his wife hid themselves from
the presence of the LORD God amongst the
trees of the garden.
9 And the LORD God called unto Adam, and
said unto him, Where *art* thou?
10 And he said, I heard thy voice in the garden, and I was afraid, because I *was* naked;
and I hid myself.
11 And he said, Who told thee that thou
wast naked? Hast thou eaten of the tree,
whereof I commanded thee that thou
shouldest not eat?
12 And the man said, The woman whom
thou gavest *to be* with me, she gave me of
the tree, and I did eat.
13 And the LORD God said unto the woman,
What *is* this *that* thou hast done? And the
woman said, The serpent beguiled me, and
I did eat.
14 And the LORD God said unto the serpent,
Because thou hast done this, thou *art* cursed
above all cattle, and above every beast of
the field; upon thy belly shalt thou go, and
dust shalt thou eat all the days of thy life:
15 And I will put enmity between thee and
the woman, and between thy seed and her
seed; it shall bruise thy head, and thou shalt
bruise his heel.
16 Unto the woman he said, I will greatly
multiply thy sorrow and thy conception; in
sorrow thou shalt bring forth children; and
thy desire *shall be* to thy husband, and he
shall rule over thee.
17 And unto Adam he said, Because thou
hast hearkened unto the voice of thy wife,
and hast eaten of the tree, of which I commanded thee, saying, Thou shalt not eat of
it: cursed *is* the ground for thy sake; in sorrow shalt thou eat *of* it all the days of thy life;
18 Thorns also and thistles shall it bring
forth to thee; and thou shalt eat the herb
of the field;
19 In the sweat of thy face shalt thou eat
bread, till thou return unto the ground; for
out of it wast thou taken: for dust thou *art*,
and unto dust shalt thou return.
20 And Adam called his wife's name Eve;
because she was the mother of all living.
21 Unto Adam also and to his wife did the
LORD God make coats of skins, and clothed
them.
22 ¶ And the LORD God said, Behold, the
man is become as one of us, to know good
and evil: and now, lest he put forth his hand,
and take also of the tree of life, and eat, and
live for ever:
23 Therefore the LORD God sent him forth
from the garden of Eden, to till the ground
from whence he was taken.
24 So he drove out the man; and he placed
at the east of the garden of Eden Cherubims,

and a flaming sword which turned every
way, to keep the way of the tree of life.

Genesis 4

1 And Adam knew Eve his wife; and she
conceived, and bare Cain, and said, I have
gotten a man from the LORD.
2 And she again bare his brother Abel. And
Abel was a keeper of sheep, but Cain was
a tiller of the ground.
3 And in process of time it came to pass,
that Cain brought of the fruit of the ground
an offering unto the LORD.
4 And Abel, he also brought of the firstlings
of his flock and of the fat thereof. And the
LORD had respect unto Abel and to his
offering:
5 But unto Cain and to his offering he had
not respect. And Cain was very wroth, and
his countenance fell.
6 And the LORD said unto Cain, Why art thou
wroth? and why is thy countenance fallen?
7 If thou doest well, shalt thou not be
accepted? and if thou doest not well, sin
lieth at the door. And unto thee *shall be* his
desire, and thou shalt rule over him.
8 And Cain talked with Abel his brother: and
it came to pass, when they were in the field,
that Cain rose up against Abel his brother,
and slew him.
9 ¶ And the LORD said unto Cain, Where *is*
Abel thy brother? And he said, I know not:
Am I my brother's keeper?
10 And he said, What hast thou done? the
voice of thy brother's blood crieth unto me
from the ground.
11 And now *art* thou cursed from the earth,
which hath opened her mouth to receive thy
brother's blood from thy hand;
12 When thou tillest the ground, it shall not
henceforth yield unto thee her strength; a
fugitive and a vagabond shalt thou be in
the earth.
13 And Cain said unto the LORD, My punishment *is* greater than I can bear.
14 Behold, thou hast driven me out this day
from the face of the earth; and from thy
face shall I be hid; and I shall be a fugitive
and a vagabond in the earth; and it shall
come to pass, *that* every one that findeth
me shall slay me.
15 And the LORD said unto him, Therefore
whosoever slayeth Cain, vengeance shall
be taken on him sevenfold. And the LORD
set a mark upon Cain, lest any finding him
should kill him.
16 ¶ And Cain went out from the presence
of the LORD, and dwelt in the land of Nod,
on the east of Eden.
17 And Cain knew his wife; and she conceived, and bare Enoch: and he builded a
city, and called the name of the city, after
the name of his son, Enoch.
18 And unto Enoch was born Irad: and
Irad begat Mehujael: and Mehujael begat
Methusael: and Methusael begat Lamech.
19 ¶ And Lamech took unto him two wives:
the name of the one *was* Adah, and the
name of the other Zillah.
20 And Adah bare Jabal: he was the father
of such as dwell in tents, and *of such as
have* cattle.
21 And his brother's name *was* Jubal: he
was the father of all such as handle the
harp and organ.
22 And Zillah, she also bare Tubal-cain, an
instructer of every artificer in brass and iron:
and the sister of Tubal-cain *was* Naamah.
23 And Lamech said unto his wives, Adah
and Zillah, Hear my voice; ye wives of
Lamech, hearken unto my speech: for I
have slain a man to my wounding, and a
young man to my hurt.
24 If Cain shall be avenged sevenfold, truly
Lamech seventy and sevenfold.
25 ¶ And Adam knew his wife again; and she
bare a son, and called his name Seth: For
God, *said she*, hath appointed me another
seed instead of Abel, whom Cain slew.
26 And to Seth, to him also there was born
a son; and he called his name Enos: then
began men to call upon the name of the
LORD.

Genesis 5

1 This *is* the book of the generations of
Adam. In the day that God created man, in
the likeness of God made he him;
2 Male and female created he them; and
blessed them, and called their name Adam,
in the day when they were created.
3 ¶ And Adam lived an hundred and thirty
years, and begat *a son* in his own likeness,
after his image; and called his name Seth:
4 And the days of Adam after he had begot-

ten Seth were eight hundred years: and he
begat sons and daughters:
5 And all the days that Adam lived were
nine hundred and thirty years: and he died.
6 And Seth lived an hundred and five years,
and begat Enos:
7 And Seth lived after he begat Enos eight
hundred and seven years, and begat sons
and daughters:
8 And all the days of Seth were nine hundred
and twelve years: and he died.
9 ¶ And Enos lived ninety years, and begat
Cainan:
10 And Enos lived after he begat Cainan
eight hundred and fifteen years, and begat
sons and daughters:
11 And all the days of Enos were nine hundred and five years: and he died.
12 ¶ And Cainan lived seventy years, and
begat Mahalaleel:
13 And Cainan lived after he begat Mahalaleel eight hundred and forty years, and
begat sons and daughters:
14 And all the days of Cainan were nine
hundred and ten years: and he died.
15 ¶ And Mahalaleel lived sixty and five
years, and begat Jared:
16 And Mahalaleel lived after he begat Jared
eight hundred and thirty years, and begat
sons and daughters:
17 And all the days of Mahalaleel were eight
hundred ninety and five years: and he died.
18 ¶ And Jared lived an hundred sixty and
two years, and he begat Enoch:
19 And Jared lived after he begat Enoch
eight hundred years, and begat sons and
daughters:
20 And all the days of Jared were nine
hundred sixty and two years: and he died.
21 ¶ And Enoch lived sixty and five years,
and begat Methuselah:
22 And Enoch walked with God after he
begat Methuselah three hundred years,
and begat sons and daughters:
23 And all the days of Enoch were three
hundred sixty and five years:
24 And Enoch walked with God: and he *was*
not; for God took him.
25 And Methuselah lived an hundred eighty
and seven years, and begat Lamech:
26 And Methuselah lived after he begat
Lamech seven hundred eighty and two
years, and begat sons and daughters:
27 And all the days of Methuselah were nine
hundred sixty and nine years: and he died.
28 ¶ And Lamech lived an hundred eighty
and two years, and begat a son:
29 And he called his name Noah, saying,
This *same* shall comfort us concerning our
work and toil of our hands, because of the
ground which the LORD hath cursed.
30 And Lamech lived after he begat Noah
five hundred ninety and five years, and
begat sons and daughters:
31 And all the days of Lamech were seven
hundred seventy and seven years: and he
died.
32 And Noah was five hundred years old:
and Noah begat Shem, Ham, and Japheth.

Genesis 6

1 And it came to pass, when men began
to multiply on the face of the earth, and
daughters were born unto them,
2 That the sons of God saw the daughters
of men that they *were* fair; and they took
them wives of all which they chose.
3 And the LORD said, My spirit shall not
always strive with man, for that he also *is*
flesh: yet his days shall be an hundred and
twenty years.
4 There were giants in the earth in those
days; and also after that, when the sons of
God came in unto the daughters of men,
and they bare *children* to them, the same
became mighty men which *were* of old,
men of renown.
5 ¶ And GOD saw that the wickedness of
man *was* great in the earth, and *that* every
imagination of the thoughts of his heart *was*
only evil continually.
6 And it repented the LORD that he had
made man on the earth, and it grieved him
at his heart.
7 And the LORD said, I will destroy man
whom I have created from the face of
the earth; both man, and beast, and the
creeping thing, and the fowls of the air; for
it repenteth me that I have made them.
8 But Noah found grace in the eyes of the
LORD.
9 ¶ These *are* the generations of Noah: Noah
was a just man *and* perfect in his generations, *and* Noah walked with God.
10 And Noah begat three sons, Shem, Ham,
and Japheth.

11 The earth also was corrupt before God, and the earth was filled with violence.

12 And God looked upon the earth, and, behold, it was corrupt; for all flesh had corrupted his way upon the earth.

13 And God said unto Noah, The end of all flesh is come before me; for the earth is filled with violence through them; and, behold, I will destroy them with the earth.

14 ¶ Make thee an ark of gopher wood; rooms shalt thou make in the ark, and shalt pitch it within and without with pitch.

15 And this *is the fashion* which thou shalt make it *of:* The length of the ark *shall be* three hundred cubits, the breadth of it fifty cubits, and the height of it thirty cubits.

16 A window shalt thou make to the ark, and in a cubit shalt thou finish it above; and the door of the ark shalt thou set in the side thereof; *with* lower, second, and third *stories* shalt thou make it.

17 And, behold, I, even I, do bring a flood of waters upon the earth, to destroy all flesh, wherein *is* the breath of life, from under heaven; *and* every thing that *is* in the earth shall die.

18 But with thee will I establish my covenant; and thou shalt come into the ark, thou, and thy sons, and thy wife, and thy sons' wives with thee.

19 And of every living thing of all flesh, two of every *sort* shalt thou bring into the ark, to keep *them* alive with thee; they shall be male and female.

20 Of fowls after their kind, and of cattle after their kind, of every creeping thing of the earth after his kind, two of every *sort* shall come unto thee, to keep *them* alive.

21 And take thou unto thee of all food that is eaten, and thou shalt gather *it* to thee; and it shall be for food for thee, and for them.

22 Thus did Noah; according to all that God commanded him, so did he.

Genesis 7

1 And the LORD said unto Noah, Come thou and all thy house into the ark; for thee have I seen righteous before me in this generation.

2 Of every clean beast thou shalt take to thee by sevens, the male and his female: and of beasts that *are* not clean by two, the male and his female.

3 Of fowls also of the air by sevens, the male and the female; to keep seed alive upon the face of all the earth.

4 For yet seven days, and I will cause it to rain upon the earth forty days and forty nights; and every living substance that I have made will I destroy from off the face of the earth.

5 And Noah did according unto all that the LORD commanded him.

6 And Noah *was* six hundred years old when the flood of waters was upon the earth.

7 ¶ And Noah went in, and his sons, and his wife, and his sons' wives with him, into the ark, because of the waters of the flood.

8 Of clean beasts, and of beasts that *are* not clean, and of fowls, and of every thing that creepeth upon the earth,

9 There went in two and two unto Noah into the ark, the male and the female, as God had commanded Noah.

10 And it came to pass after seven days, that the waters of the flood were upon the earth.

11 ¶ In the six hundredth year of Noah's life, in the second month, the seventeenth day of the month, the same day were all the fountains of the great deep broken up, and the windows of heaven were opened.

12 And the rain was upon the earth forty days and forty nights.

13 In the selfsame day entered Noah, and Shem, and Ham, and Japheth, the sons of Noah, and Noah's wife, and the three wives of his sons with them, into the ark;

14 They, and every beast after his kind, and all the cattle after their kind, and every creeping thing that creepeth upon the earth after his kind, and every fowl after his kind, every bird of every sort.

15 And they went in unto Noah into the ark, two and two of all flesh, wherein *is* the breath of life.

16 And they that went in, went in male and female of all flesh, as God had commanded him: and the LORD shut him in.

17 And the flood was forty days upon the earth; and the waters increased, and bare up the ark, and it was lift up above the earth.

18 And the waters prevailed, and were increased greatly upon the earth; and the ark went upon the face of the waters.

19 And the waters prevailed exceedingly upon the earth; and all the high hills, that

were under the whole heaven, were covered.

20 Fifteen cubits upward did the waters prevail; and the mountains were covered.

21 And all flesh died that moved upon the earth, both of fowl, and of cattle, and of beast, and of every creeping thing that creepeth upon the earth, and every man:

22 All in whose nostrils *was* the breath of life, of all that *was* in the dry *land*, died.

23 And every living substance was destroyed which was upon the face of the ground, both man, and cattle, and the creeping things, and the fowl of the heaven; and they were destroyed from the earth: and Noah only remained *alive*, and they that *were* with him in the ark.

24 And the waters prevailed upon the earth an hundred and fifty days.

Genesis 8

1 And God remembered Noah, and every living thing, and all the cattle that *was* with him in the ark: and God made a wind to pass over the earth, and the waters asswaged;

2 The fountains also of the deep and the windows of heaven were stopped, and the rain from heaven was restrained;

3 And the waters returned from off the earth continually: and after the end of the hundred and fifty days the waters were abated.

4 And the ark rested in the seventh month, on the seventeenth day of the month, upon the mountains of Ararat.

5 And the waters decreased continually until the tenth month: in the tenth *month*, on the first *day* of the month, were the tops of the mountains seen.

6 ¶ And it came to pass at the end of forty days, that Noah opened the window of the ark which he had made:

7 And he sent forth a raven, which went forth to and fro, until the waters were dried up from off the earth.

8 Also he sent forth a dove from him, to see if the waters were abated from off the face of the ground;

9 But the dove found no rest for the sole of her foot, and she returned unto him into the ark, for the waters *were* on the face of the whole earth: then he put forth his hand, and took her, and pulled her in unto him into the ark.

10 And he stayed yet other seven days; and again he sent forth the dove out of the ark;

11 And the dove came in to him in the evening; and, lo, in her mouth *was* an olive leaf pluckt off: so Noah knew that the waters were abated from off the earth.

12 And he stayed yet other seven days; and sent forth the dove; which returned not again unto him any more.

13 ¶ And it came to pass in the six hundredth and first year, in the first *month*, the first *day* of the month, the waters were dried up from off the earth: and Noah removed the covering of the ark, and looked, and, behold, the face of the ground was dry.

14 And in the second month, on the seven and twentieth day of the month, was the earth dried.

15 ¶ And God spake unto Noah, saying,

16 Go forth of the ark, thou, and thy wife, and thy sons, and thy sons' wives with thee.

17 Bring forth with thee every living thing that *is* with thee, of all flesh, *both* of fowl, and of cattle, and of every creeping thing that creepeth upon the earth; that they may breed abundantly in the earth, and be fruitful, and multiply upon the earth.

18 And Noah went forth, and his sons, and his wife, and his sons' wives with him:

19 Every beast, every creeping thing, and every fowl, *and* whatsoever creepeth upon the earth, after their kinds, went forth out of the ark.

20 ¶ And Noah builded an altar unto the LORD; and took of every clean beast, and of every clean fowl, and offered burnt offerings on the altar.

21 And the LORD smelled a sweet savour; and the LORD said in his heart, I will not again curse the ground any more for man's sake; for the imagination of man's heart *is* evil from his youth; neither will I again smite any more every thing living, as I have done.

22 While the earth remaineth, seedtime and harvest, and cold and heat, and summer and winter, and day and night shall not cease.

Genesis 9

1 And God blessed Noah and his sons, and said unto them, Be fruitful, and multiply, and replenish the earth.

2 And the fear of you and the dread of you
shall be upon every beast of the earth, and
upon every fowl of the air, upon all that
moveth *upon* the earth, and upon all the
fishes of the sea; into your hand are they
delivered.
3 Every moving thing that liveth shall be
meat for you; even as the green herb have
I given you all things.
4 But flesh with the life thereof, *which is* the
blood thereof, shall ye not eat.
5 And surely your blood of your lives will
I require; at the hand of every beast will I
require it, and at the hand of man; at the
hand of every man's brother will I require
the life of man.
6 Whoso sheddeth man's blood, by man
shall his blood be shed: for in the image of
God made he man.
7 And you, be ye fruitful, and multiply; bring
forth abundantly in the earth, and multiply
therein.
8 ¶ And God spake unto Noah, and to his
sons with him, saying,
9 And I, behold, I establish my covenant with
you, and with your seed after you;
10 And with every living creature that *is* with
you, of the fowl, of the cattle, and of every
beast of the earth with you; from all that go
out of the ark, to every beast of the earth.
11 And I will establish my covenant with you;
neither shall all flesh be cut off any more by
the waters of a flood; neither shall there
any more be a flood to destroy the earth.
12 And God said, This *is* the token of the
covenant which I make between me and
you and every living creature that *is* with
you, for perpetual generations:
13 I do set my bow in the cloud, and it shall
be for a token of a covenant between me
and the earth.
14 And it shall come to pass, when I bring
a cloud over the earth, that the bow shall
be seen in the cloud:
15 And I will remember my covenant, which
is between me and you and every living
creature of all flesh; and the waters shall no
more become a flood to destroy all flesh.
16 And the bow shall be in the cloud; and
I will look upon it, that I may remember
the everlasting covenant between God
and every living creature of all flesh that *is*
upon the earth.
17 And God said unto Noah, This *is* the token
of the covenant, which I have established
between me and all flesh that *is* upon the
earth.
18 ¶ And the sons of Noah, that went
forth of the ark, were Shem, and Ham, and
Japheth: and Ham *is* the father of Canaan.
19 These *are* the three sons of Noah: and
of them was the whole earth overspread.
20 And Noah began *to be* an husbandman,
and he planted a vineyard:
21 And he drank of the wine, and was
drunken; and he was uncovered within
his tent.
22 And Ham, the father of Canaan, saw the
nakedness of his father, and told his two
brethren without.
23 And Shem and Japheth took a garment,
and laid *it* upon both their shoulders, and
went backward, and covered the nakedness of their father; and their faces *were*
backward, and they saw not their father's
nakedness.
24 And Noah awoke from his wine, and
knew what his younger son had done unto
him.
25 And he said, Cursed *be* Canaan; a servant
of servants shall he be unto his brethren.
26 And he said, Blessed *be* the LORD God
of Shem; and Canaan shall be his servant.
27 God shall enlarge Japheth, and he shall
dwell in the tents of Shem; and Canaan shall
be his servant.
28 ¶ And Noah lived after the flood three
hundred and fifty years.
29 And all the days of Noah were nine hundred and fifty years: and he died.

Genesis 10

1 Now these *are* the generations of the sons
of Noah, Shem, Ham, and Japheth: and unto
them were sons born after the flood.
2 The sons of Japheth; Gomer, and Magog,
and Madai, and Javan, and Tubal, and
Meshech, and Tiras.
3 And the sons of Gomer; Ashkenaz, and
Riphath, and Togarmah.
4 And the sons of Javan; Elishah, and Tarshish, Kittim, and Dodanim.
5 By these were the isles of the Gentiles
divided in their lands; every one after his
tongue, after their families, in their nations.

6 ¶ And the sons of Ham; Cush, and Mizraim, and Phut, and Canaan.

7 And the sons of Cush; Seba, and Havilah, and Sabtah, and Raamah, and Sabtecha: and the sons of Raamah; Sheba, and Dedan.

8 And Cush begat Nimrod: he began to be a mighty one in the earth.

9 He was a mighty hunter before the LORD: wherefore it is said, Even as Nimrod the mighty hunter before the LORD.

10 And the beginning of his kingdom was Babel, and Erech, and Accad, and Calneh, in the land of Shinar.

11 Out of that land went forth Asshur, and builded Nineveh, and the city Rehoboth, and Calah,

12 And Resen between Nineveh and Calah: the same *is* a great city.

13 And Mizraim begat Ludim, and Anamim, and Lehabim, and Naphtuhim,

14 And Pathrusim, and Casluhim, (out of whom came Philistim,) and Caphtorim.

15 ¶ And Canaan begat Sidon his firstborn, and Heth,

16 And the Jebusite, and the Amorite, and the Girgasite,

17 And the Hivite, and the Arkite, and the Sinite,

18 And the Arvadite, and the Zemarite, and the Hamathite: and afterward were the families of the Canaanites spread abroad.

19 And the border of the Canaanites was from Sidon, as thou comest to Gerar, unto Gaza; as thou goest, unto Sodom, and Gomorrah, and Admah, and Zeboim, even unto Lasha.

20 These *are* the sons of Ham, after their families, after their tongues, in their countries, *and* in their nations.

21 ¶ Unto Shem also, the father of all the children of Eber, the brother of Japheth the elder, even to him were *children* born.

22 The children of Shem; Elam, and Asshur, and Arphaxad, and Lud, and Aram.

23 And the children of Aram; Uz, and Hul, and Gether, and Mash.

24 And Arphaxad begat Salah; and Salah begat Eber.

25 And unto Eber were born two sons: the name of one *was* Peleg; for in his days was the earth divided; and his brother's name *was* Joktan.

26 And Joktan begat Almodad, and Sheleph, and Hazarmaveth, and Jerah,

27 And Hadoram, and Uzal, and Diklah,

28 And Obal, and Abimael, and Sheba,

29 And Ophir, and Havilah, and Jobab: all these *were* the sons of Joktan.

30 And their dwelling was from Mesha, as thou goest unto Sephar a mount of the east.

31 These *are* the sons of Shem, after their families, after their tongues, in their lands, after their nations.

32 These *are* the families of the sons of Noah, after their generations, in their nations: and by these were the nations divided in the earth after the flood.

Genesis 11

1 And the whole earth was of one language, and of one speech.

2 And it came to pass, as they journeyed from the east, that they found a plain in the land of Shinar; and they dwelt there.

3 And they said one to another, Go to, let us make brick, and burn them throughly. And they had brick for stone, and slime had they for morter.

4 And they said, Go to, let us build us a city and a tower, whose top *may reach* unto heaven; and let us make us a name, lest we be scattered abroad upon the face of the whole earth.

5 And the LORD came down to see the city and the tower, which the children of men builded.

6 And the LORD said, Behold, the people *is* one, and they have all one language; and this they begin to do: and now nothing will be restrained from them, which they have imagined to do.

7 Go to, let us go down, and there confound their language, that they may not understand one another's speech.

8 So the LORD scattered them abroad from thence upon the face of all the earth: and they left off to build the city.

9 Therefore is the name of it called Babel; because the LORD did there confound the language of all the earth: and from thence did the LORD scatter them abroad upon the face of all the earth.

10 ¶ These *are* the generations of Shem: Shem *was* an hundred years old, and begat Arphaxad two years after the flood:

11 And Shem lived after he begat Arphaxad
five hundred years, and begat sons and
daughters.
12 And Arphaxad lived five and thirty years,
and begat Salah:
13 And Arphaxad lived after he begat Salah
four hundred and three years, and begat
sons and daughters.
14 And Salah lived thirty years, and begat
Eber:
15 And Salah lived after he begat Eber four
hundred and three years, and begat sons
and daughters.
16 And Eber lived four and thirty years, and
begat Peleg:
17 And Eber lived after he begat Peleg four
hundred and thirty years, and begat sons
and daughters.
18 And Peleg lived thirty years, and begat
Reu:
19 And Peleg lived after he begat Reu two
hundred and nine years, and begat sons
and daughters.
20 And Reu lived two and thirty years, and
begat Serug:
21 And Reu lived after he begat Serug two
hundred and seven years, and begat sons
and daughters.
22 And Serug lived thirty years, and begat
Nahor:
23 And Serug lived after he begat Nahor
two hundred years, and begat sons and
daughters.
24 And Nahor lived nine and twenty years,
and begat Terah:
25 And Nahor lived after he begat Terah
an hundred and nineteen years, and begat
sons and daughters.
26 And Terah lived seventy years, and begat
Abram, Nahor, and Haran.
27 ¶ Now these *are* the generations of
Terah: Terah begat Abram, Nahor, and
Haran; and Haran begat Lot.
28 And Haran died before his father Terah in
the land of his nativity, in Ur of the Chaldees.
29 And Abram and Nahor took them wives:
the name of Abram's wife *was* Sarai; and the
name of Nahor's wife, Milcah, the daughter of Haran, the father of Milcah, and the
father of Iscah.
30 But Sarai was barren; she *had* no child.
31 And Terah took Abram his son, and Lot
the son of Haran his son's son, and Sarai his
daughter in law, his son Abram's wife; and
they went forth with them from Ur of the
Chaldees, to go into the land of Canaan; and
they came unto Haran, and dwelt there.
32 And the days of Terah were two hundred
and five years: and Terah died in Haran.

Genesis 12

1 Now the LORD had said unto Abram, Get
thee out of thy country, and from thy kindred, and from thy father's house, unto a
land that I will shew thee:
2 And I will make of thee a great nation, and
I will bless thee, and make thy name great;
and thou shalt be a blessing:
3 And I will bless them that bless thee, and
curse him that curseth thee: and in thee
shall all families of the earth be blessed.
4 So Abram departed, as the LORD had
spoken unto him; and Lot went with him:
and Abram *was* seventy and five years old
when he departed out of Haran.
5 And Abram took Sarai his wife, and Lot his
brother's son, and all their substance that
they had gathered, and the souls that they
had gotten in Haran; and they went forth
to go into the land of Canaan; and into the
land of Canaan they came.
6 ¶ And Abram passed through the land
unto the place of Sichem, unto the plain
of Moreh. And the Canaanite *was* then in
the land.
7 And the LORD appeared unto Abram, and
said, Unto thy seed will I give this land: and
there builded he an altar unto the LORD,
who appeared unto him.
8 And he removed from thence unto a
mountain on the east of Beth-el, and pitched
his tent, *having* Beth-el on the west, and Hai
on the east: and there he builded an altar
unto the LORD, and called upon the name
of the LORD.
9 And Abram journeyed, going on still
toward the south.
10 ¶ And there was a famine in the land:
and Abram went down into Egypt to sojourn
there; for the famine *was* grievous in the
land.
11 And it came to pass, when he was come
near to enter into Egypt, that he said unto
Sarai his wife, Behold now, I know that thou
art a fair woman to look upon:
12 Therefore it shall come to pass, when

the Egyptians shall see thee, that they shall
say, This *is* his wife: and they will kill me, but
they will save thee alive.
13 Say, I pray thee, thou *art* my sister: that
it may be well with me for thy sake; and my
soul shall live because of thee.
14 ¶ And it came to pass, that, when Abram
was come into Egypt, the Egyptians beheld
the woman that she *was* very fair.
15 The princes also of Pharaoh saw her, and
commended her before Pharaoh: and the
woman was taken into Pharaoh's house.
16 And he entreated Abram well for her
sake: and he had sheep, and oxen, and he
asses, and menservants, and maidservants,
and she asses, and camels.
17 And the LORD plagued Pharaoh and his
house with great plagues because of Sarai
Abram's wife.
18 And Pharaoh called Abram, and said,
What *is* this *that* thou hast done unto me?
why didst thou not tell me that she *was*
thy wife?
19 Why saidst thou, She *is* my sister? so I
might have taken her to me to wife: now
therefore behold thy wife, take *her*, and
go thy way.
20 And Pharaoh commanded *his* men concerning him: and they sent him away, and
his wife, and all that he had.

Genesis 13

1 And Abram went up out of Egypt, he, and
his wife, and all that he had, and Lot with
him, into the south.
2 And Abram *was* very rich in cattle, in silver, and in gold.
3 And he went on his journeys from the
south even to Beth-el, unto the place where
his tent had been at the beginning, between
Beth-el and Hai;
4 Unto the place of the altar, which he had
made there at the first: and there Abram
called on the name of the LORD.
5 ¶ And Lot also, which went with Abram,
had flocks, and herds, and tents.
6 And the land was not able to bear them,
that they might dwell together: for their
substance was great, so that they could not
dwell together.
7 And there was a strife between the herdmen of Abram's cattle and the herdmen
of Lot's cattle: and the Canaanite and the
Perizzite dwelled then in the land.
8 And Abram said unto Lot, Let there be no
strife, I pray thee, between me and thee,
and between my herdmen and thy herdmen; for we *be* brethren.
9 *Is* not the whole land before thee? separate thyself, I pray thee, from me: if *thou
wilt take* the left hand, then I will go to the
right; or if *thou depart* to the right hand,
then I will go to the left.
10 And Lot lifted up his eyes, and beheld all
the plain of Jordan, that it *was* well watered
every where, before the LORD destroyed
Sodom and Gomorrah, *even* as the garden
of the LORD, like the land of Egypt, as thou
comest unto Zoar.
11 Then Lot chose him all the plain of Jordan;
and Lot journeyed east: and they separated
themselves the one from the other.
12 Abram dwelled in the land of Canaan,
and Lot dwelled in the cities of the plain,
and pitched *his* tent toward Sodom.
13 But the men of Sodom *were* wicked and
sinners before the LORD exceedingly.
14 ¶ And the LORD said unto Abram, after
that Lot was separated from him, Lift up now
thine eyes, and look from the place where
thou art northward, and southward, and
eastward, and westward:
15 For all the land which thou seest, to thee
will I give it, and to thy seed for ever.
16 And I will make thy seed as the dust of
the earth: so that if a man can number the
dust of the earth, *then* shall thy seed also
be numbered.
17 Arise, walk through the land in the length
of it and in the breadth of it; for I will give
it unto thee.
18 Then Abram removed *his* tent, and came
and dwelt in the plain of Mamre, which *is*
in Hebron, and built there an altar unto
the LORD.

Genesis 14

1 And it came to pass in the days of Am-
raphel king of Shinar, Arioch king of Ellasar,
Chedorlaomer king of Elam, and Tidal king
of nations;
2 *That these* made war with Bera king of
Sodom, and with Birsha king of Gomorrah,
Shinab king of Admah, and Shemeber king of
Zeboiim, and the king of Bela, which is Zoar.

3 All these were joined together in the vale of Siddim, which is the salt sea.

4 Twelve years they served Chedorlaomer, and in the thirteenth year they rebelled.

5 And in the fourteenth year came Chedorlaomer, and the kings that *were* with him, and smote the Rephaims in Ashteroth Karnaim, and the Zuzims in Ham, and the Emims in Shaveh Kiriathaim,

6 And the Horites in their mount Seir, unto El-paran, which *is* by the wilderness.

7 And they returned, and came to En-mishpat, which *is* Kadesh, and smote all the country of the Amalekites, and also the Amorites, that dwelt in Hazezon-tamar.

8 And there went out the king of Sodom, and the king of Gomorrah, and the king of Admah, and the king of Zeboiim, and the king of Bela (the same *is* Zoar;) and they joined battle with them in the vale of Siddim;

9 With Chedorlaomer the king of Elam, and with Tidal king of nations, and Amraphel king of Shinar, and Arioch king of Ellasar; four kings with five.

10 And the vale of Siddim *was full of* slimepits; and the kings of Sodom and Gomorrah fled, and fell there; and they that remained fled to the mountain.

11 And they took all the goods of Sodom and Gomorrah, and all their victuals, and went their way.

12 And they took Lot, Abram's brother's son, who dwelt in Sodom, and his goods, and departed.

13 ¶ And there came one that had escaped, and told Abram the Hebrew; for he dwelt in the plain of Mamre the Amorite, brother of Eshcol, and brother of Aner: and these *were* confederate with Abram.

14 And when Abram heard that his brother was taken captive, he armed his trained *servants*, born in his own house, three hundred and eighteen, and pursued *them* unto Dan.

15 And he divided himself against them, he and his servants, by night, and smote them, and pursued them unto Hobah, which *is* on the left hand of Damascus.

16 And he brought back all the goods, and also brought again his brother Lot, and his goods, and the women also, and the people.

17 ¶ And the king of Sodom went out to meet him after his return from the slaughter of Chedorlaomer, and of the kings that *were* with him, at the valley of Shaveh, which *is* the king's dale.

18 And Melchizedek king of Salem brought forth bread and wine: and he *was* the priest of the most high God.

19 And he blessed him, and said, Blessed *be* Abram of the most high God, possessor of heaven and earth:

20 And blessed be the most high God, which hath delivered thine enemies into thy hand. And he gave him tithes of all.

21 And the king of Sodom said unto Abram, Give me the persons, and take the goods to thyself.

22 And Abram said to the king of Sodom, I have lift up mine hand unto the LORD, the most high God, the possessor of heaven and earth,

23 That I will not *take* from a thread even to a shoelatchet, and that I will not take any thing that *is* thine, lest thou shouldest say, I have made Abram rich:

24 Save only that which the young men have eaten, and the portion of the men which went with me, Aner, Eshcol, and Mamre; let them take their portion.

Genesis 15

1 After these things the word of the LORD came unto Abram in a vision, saying, Fear not, Abram: I *am* thy shield, *and* thy exceeding great reward.

2 And Abram said, Lord GOD, what wilt thou give me, seeing I go childless, and the steward of my house *is* this Eliezer of Damascus?

3 And Abram said, Behold, to me thou hast given no seed: and, lo, one born in my house is mine heir.

4 And, behold, the word of the LORD *came* unto him, saying, This shall not be thine heir; but he that shall come forth out of thine own bowels shall be thine heir.

5 And he brought him forth abroad, and said, Look now toward heaven, and tell the stars, if thou be able to number them: and he said unto him, So shall thy seed be.

6 And he believed in the LORD; and he counted it to him for righteousness.

7 And he said unto him, I *am* the LORD that brought thee out of Ur of the Chaldees, to give thee this land to inherit it.

8 And he said, Lord GOD, whereby shall I know that I shall inherit it?

9 And he said unto him, Take me an heifer
of three years old, and a she goat of three
years old, and a ram of three years old, and
a turtledove, and a young pigeon.
10 And he took unto him all these, and
divided them in the midst, and laid each
piece one against another: but the birds
divided he not.
11 And when the fowls came down upon the
carcases, Abram drove them away.
12 And when the sun was going down, a
deep sleep fell upon Abram; and, lo, an
horror of great darkness fell upon him.
13 And he said unto Abram, Know of a
surety that thy seed shall be a stranger in
a land *that is* not theirs, and shall serve
them; and they shall afflict them four hundred years;
14 And also that nation, whom they shall
serve, will I judge: and afterward shall they
come out with great substance.
15 And thou shalt go to thy fathers in peace;
thou shalt be buried in a good old age.
16 But in the fourth generation they shall
come hither again: for the iniquity of the
Amorites *is* not yet full.
17 And it came to pass, that, when the
sun went down, and it was dark, behold a
smoking furnace, and a burning lamp that
passed between those pieces.
18 In the same day the LORD made a covenant with Abram, saying, Unto thy seed have
I given this land, from the river of Egypt unto
the great river, the river Euphrates:
19 The Kenites, and the Kenizzites, and the
Kadmonites,
20 And the Hittites, and the Perizzites, and
the Rephaims,
21 And the Amorites, and the Canaanites,
and the Girgashites, and the Jebusites.

Genesis 16

1 Now Sarai Abram's wife bare him no children: and she had an handmaid, an Egyptian, whose name *was* Hagar.
2 And Sarai said unto Abram, Behold now,
the LORD hath restrained me from bearing:
I pray thee, go in unto my maid; it may be
that I may obtain children by her. And Abram
hearkened to the voice of Sarai.
3 And Sarai Abram's wife took Hagar her
maid the Egyptian, after Abram had dwelt
ten years in the land of Canaan, and gave
her to her husband Abram to be his wife.
4 ¶ And he went in unto Hagar, and she
conceived: and when she saw that she had
conceived, her mistress was despised in
her eyes.
5 And Sarai said unto Abram, My wrong *be*
upon thee: I have given my maid into thy
bosom; and when she saw that she had
conceived, I was despised in her eyes: the
LORD judge between me and thee.
6 But Abram said unto Sarai, Behold, thy
maid *is* in thy hand; do to her as it pleaseth
thee. And when Sarai dealt hardly with her,
she fled from her face.
7 ¶ And the angel of the LORD found her by
a fountain of water in the wilderness, by the
fountain in the way to Shur.
8 And he said, Hagar, Sarai's maid, whence
camest thou? and whither wilt thou go?
And she said, I flee from the face of my
mistress Sarai.
9 And the angel of the LORD said unto her,
Return to thy mistress, and submit thyself
under her hands.
10 And the angel of the LORD said unto her,
I will multiply thy seed exceedingly, that it
shall not be numbered for multitude.
11 And the angel of the LORD said unto
her, Behold, thou *art* with child, and shalt
bear a son, and shalt call his name Ishmael;
because the LORD hath heard thy affliction.
12 And he will be a wild man; his hand *will*
be against every man, and every man's
hand against him; and he shall dwell in the
presence of all his brethren.
13 And she called the name of the LORD
that spake unto her, Thou God seest me:
for she said, Have I also here looked after
him that seeth me?
14 Wherefore the well was called Beer-lahai-
roi; behold, *it is* between Kadesh and Bered.
15 ¶ And Hagar bare Abram a son: and
Abram called his son's name, which Hagar
bare, Ishmael.
16 And Abram *was* fourscore and six years
old, when Hagar bare Ishmael to Abram.

Genesis 17

1 And when Abram was ninety years old
and nine, the LORD appeared to Abram, and
said unto him, I *am* the Almighty God; walk
before me, and be thou perfect.

2 And I will make my covenant between me and thee, and will multiply thee exceedingly.

3 And Abram fell on his face: and God talked with him, saying,

4 As for me, behold, my covenant *is* with thee, and thou shalt be a father of many nations.

5 Neither shall thy name any more be called Abram, but thy name shall be Abraham; for a father of many nations have I made thee.

6 And I will make thee exceeding fruitful, and I will make nations of thee, and kings shall come out of thee.

7 And I will establish my covenant between me and thee and thy seed after thee in their generations for an everlasting covenant, to be a God unto thee, and to thy seed after thee.

8 And I will give unto thee, and to thy seed after thee, the land wherein thou art a stranger, all the land of Canaan, for an everlasting possession; and I will be their God.

9 ¶ And God said unto Abraham, Thou shalt keep my covenant therefore, thou, and thy seed after thee in their generations.

10 This *is* my covenant, which ye shall keep, between me and you and thy seed after thee; Every man child among you shall be circumcised.

11 And ye shall circumcise the flesh of your foreskin; and it shall be a token of the covenant betwixt me and you.

12 And he that is eight days old shall be circumcised among you, every man child in your generations, he that is born in the house, or bought with money of any stranger, which *is* not of thy seed.

13 He that is born in thy house, and he that is bought with thy money, must needs be circumcised: and my covenant shall be in your flesh for an everlasting covenant.

14 And the uncircumcised man child whose flesh of his foreskin is not circumcised, that soul shall be cut off from his people; he hath broken my covenant.

15 ¶ And God said unto Abraham, As for Sarai thy wife, thou shalt not call her name Sarai, but Sarah *shall* her name *be*.

16 And I will bless her, and give thee a son also of her: yea, I will bless her, and she shall be *a mother* of nations; kings of people shall be of her.

17 Then Abraham fell upon his face, and laughed, and said in his heart, Shall *a child* be born unto him that is an hundred years old? and shall Sarah, that is ninety years old, bear?

18 And Abraham said unto God, O that Ishmael might live before thee!

19 And God said, Sarah thy wife shall bear thee a son indeed; and thou shalt call his name Isaac: and I will establish my covenant with him for an everlasting covenant, *and* with his seed after him.

20 And as for Ishmael, I have heard thee: Behold, I have blessed him, and will make him fruitful, and will multiply him exceedingly; twelve princes shall he beget, and I will make him a great nation.

21 But my covenant will I establish with Isaac, which Sarah shall bear unto thee at this set time in the next year.

22 And he left off talking with him, and God went up from Abraham.

23 ¶ And Abraham took Ishmael his son, and all that were born in his house, and all that were bought with his money, every male among the men of Abraham's house; and circumcised the flesh of their foreskin in the selfsame day, as God had said unto him.

24 And Abraham *was* ninety years old and nine, when he was circumcised in the flesh of his foreskin.

25 And Ishmael his son *was* thirteen years old, when he was circumcised in the flesh of his foreskin.

26 In the selfsame day was Abraham circumcised, and Ishmael his son.

27 And all the men of his house, born in the house, and bought with money of the stranger, were circumcised with him.

Genesis 18

1 And the LORD appeared unto him in the plains of Mamre: and he sat in the tent door in the heat of the day;

2 And he lift up his eyes and looked, and, lo, three men stood by him: and when he saw *them*, he ran to meet them from the tent door, and bowed himself toward the ground,

3 And said, My Lord, if now I have found favour in thy sight, pass not away, I pray thee, from thy servant:

4 Let a little water, I pray you, be fetched, and wash your feet, and rest yourselves under the tree:

5 And I will fetch a morsel of bread, and comfort ye your hearts; after that ye shall pass on: for therefore are ye come to your servant. And they said, So do, as thou hast said.

6 And Abraham hastened into the tent unto Sarah, and said, Make ready quickly three measures of fine meal, knead *it*, and make cakes upon the hearth.

7 And Abraham ran unto the herd, and fetcht a calf tender and good, and gave *it* unto a young man; and he hasted to dress it.

8 And he took butter, and milk, and the calf which he had dressed, and set *it* before them; and he stood by them under the tree, and they did eat.

9 ¶ And they said unto him, Where *is* Sarah thy wife? And he said, Behold, in the tent.

10 And he said, I will certainly return unto thee according to the time of life; and, lo, Sarah thy wife shall have a son. And Sarah heard *it* in the tent door, which *was* behind him.

11 Now Abraham and Sarah *were* old *and* well stricken in age; *and* it ceased to be with Sarah after the manner of women.

12 Therefore Sarah laughed within herself, saying, After I am waxed old shall I have pleasure, my lord being old also?

13 And the LORD said unto Abraham, Wherefore did Sarah laugh, saying, Shall I of a surety bear a child, which am old?

14 Is any thing too hard for the LORD? At the time appointed I will return unto thee, according to the time of life, and Sarah shall have a son.

15 Then Sarah denied, saying, I laughed not; for she was afraid. And he said, Nay; but thou didst laugh.

16 ¶ And the men rose up from thence, and looked toward Sodom: and Abraham went with them to bring them on the way.

17 And the LORD said, Shall I hide from Abraham that thing which I do;

18 Seeing that Abraham shall surely become a great and mighty nation, and all the nations of the earth shall be blessed in him?

19 For I know him, that he will command his children and his household after him, and they shall keep the way of the LORD, to do justice and judgment; that the LORD may bring upon Abraham that which he hath spoken of him.

20 And the LORD said, Because the cry of Sodom and Gomorrah is great, and because their sin is very grievous;

21 I will go down now, and see whether they have done altogether according to the cry of it, which is come unto me; and if not, I will know.

22 And the men turned their faces from thence, and went toward Sodom: but Abraham stood yet before the LORD.

23 ¶ And Abraham drew near, and said, Wilt thou also destroy the righteous with the wicked?

24 Peradventure there be fifty righteous within the city: wilt thou also destroy and not spare the place for the fifty righteous that *are* therein?

25 That be far from thee to do after this manner, to slay the righteous with the wicked: and that the righteous should be as the wicked, that be far from thee: Shall not the Judge of all the earth do right?

26 And the LORD said, If I find in Sodom fifty righteous within the city, then I will spare all the place for their sakes.

27 And Abraham answered and said, Behold now, I have taken upon me to speak unto the Lord, which *am but* dust and ashes:

28 Peradventure there shall lack five of the fifty righteous: wilt thou destroy all the city for *lack of* five? And he said, If I find there forty and five, I will not destroy *it*.

29 And he spake unto him yet again, and said, Peradventure there shall be forty found there. And he said, I will not do *it* for forty's sake.

30 And he said *unto him*, Oh let not the Lord be angry, and I will speak: Peradventure there shall thirty be found there. And he said, I will not do *it*, if I find thirty there.

31 And he said, Behold now, I have taken upon me to speak unto the Lord: Peradventure there shall be twenty found there. And he said, I will not destroy *it* for twenty's sake.

32 And he said, Oh let not the Lord be angry, and I will speak yet but this once: Peradventure ten shall be found there. And he said, I will not destroy *it* for ten's sake.

33 And the LORD went his way, as soon as he had left communing with Abraham: and Abraham returned unto his place.

Genesis 19

1 And there came two angels to Sodom at even; and Lot sat in the gate of Sodom: and Lot seeing *them* rose up to meet them; and he bowed himself with his face toward the ground;

2 And he said, Behold now, my lords, turn in, I pray you, into your servant's house, and tarry all night, and wash your feet, and ye shall rise up early, and go on your ways. And they said, Nay; but we will abide in the street all night.

3 And he pressed upon them greatly; and they turned in unto him, and entered into his house; and he made them a feast, and did bake unleavened bread, and they did eat.

4 ¶ But before they lay down, the men of the city, *even* the men of Sodom, compassed the house round, both old and young, all the people from every quarter:

5 And they called unto Lot, and said unto him, Where *are* the men which came in to thee this night? bring them out unto us, that we may know them.

6 And Lot went out at the door unto them, and shut the door after him,

7 And said, I pray you, brethren, do not so wickedly.

8 Behold now, I have two daughters which have not known man; let me, I pray you, bring them out unto you, and do ye to them as *is* good in your eyes: only unto these men do nothing; for therefore came they under the shadow of my roof.

9 And they said, Stand back. And they said *again*, This one *fellow* came in to sojourn, and he will needs be a judge: now will we deal worse with thee, than with them. And they pressed sore upon the man, *even* Lot, and came near to break the door.

10 But the men put forth their hand, and pulled Lot into the house to them, and shut to the door.

11 And they smote the men that *were* at the door of the house with blindness, both small and great: so that they wearied themselves to find the door.

12 ¶ And the men said unto Lot, Hast thou here any besides? son in law, and thy sons, and thy daughters, and whatsoever thou hast in the city, bring *them* out of this place:

13 For we will destroy this place, because the cry of them is waxen great before the face of the LORD; and the LORD hath sent us to destroy it.

14 And Lot went out, and spake unto his sons in law, which married his daughters, and said, Up, get you out of this place; for the LORD will destroy this city. But he seemed as one that mocked unto his sons in law.

15 ¶ And when the morning arose, then the angels hastened Lot, saying, Arise, take thy wife, and thy two daughters, which are here; lest thou be consumed in the iniquity of the city.

16 And while he lingered, the men laid hold upon his hand, and upon the hand of his wife, and upon the hand of his two daughters; the LORD being merciful unto him: and they brought him forth, and set him without the city.

17 ¶ And it came to pass, when they had brought them forth abroad, that he said, Escape for thy life; look not behind thee, neither stay thou in all the plain; escape to the mountain, lest thou be consumed.

18 And Lot said unto them, Oh, not so, my Lord:

19 Behold now, thy servant hath found grace in thy sight, and thou hast magnified thy mercy, which thou hast shewed unto me in saving my life; and I cannot escape to the mountain, lest some evil take me, and I die:

20 Behold now, this city *is* near to flee unto, and it *is* a little one: Oh, let me escape thither, (*is* it not a little one?) and my soul shall live.

21 And he said unto him, See, I have accepted thee concerning this thing also, that I will not overthrow this city, for the which thou hast spoken.

22 Haste thee, escape thither; for I cannot do any thing till thou be come thither. Therefore the name of the city was called Zoar.

23 ¶ The sun was risen upon the earth when Lot entered into Zoar.

24 Then the LORD rained upon Sodom and upon Gomorrah brimstone and fire from the LORD out of heaven;

25 And he overthrew those cities, and all the plain, and all the inhabitants of the cities, and that which grew upon the ground.

26 ¶ But his wife looked back from behind him, and she became a pillar of salt.

27 ¶ And Abraham gat up early in the morn-

ing to the place where he stood before
the LORD:
28 And he looked toward Sodom and
Gomorrah, and toward all the land of the
plain, and beheld, and, lo, the smoke of the
country went up as the smoke of a furnace.
29 ¶ And it came to pass, when God
destroyed the cities of the plain, that God
remembered Abraham, and sent Lot out
of the midst of the overthrow, when he
overthrew the cities in the which Lot dwelt.
30 ¶ And Lot went up out of Zoar, and dwelt
in the mountain, and his two daughters with
him; for he feared to dwell in Zoar: and he
dwelt in a cave, he and his two daughters.
31 And the firstborn said unto the younger,
Our father *is* old, and *there is* not a man
in the earth to come in unto us after the
manner of all the earth:
32 Come, let us make our father drink wine,
and we will lie with him, that we may preserve seed of our father.
33 And they made their father drink wine
that night: and the firstborn went in, and
lay with her father; and he perceived not
when she lay down, nor when she arose.
34 And it came to pass on the morrow, that
the firstborn said unto the younger, Behold,
I lay yesternight with my father: let us make
him drink wine this night also; and go thou
in, *and* lie with him, that we may preserve
seed of our father.
35 And they made their father drink wine
that night also: and the younger arose, and
lay with him; and he perceived not when she
lay down, nor when she arose.
36 Thus were both the daughters of Lot with
child by their father.
37 And the firstborn bare a son, and called
his name Moab: the same *is* the father of
the Moabites unto this day.
38 And the younger, she also bare a son,
and called his name Ben-ammi: the same
is the father of the children of Ammon
unto this day.

Genesis 20

1 And Abraham journeyed from thence
toward the south country, and dwelled
between Kadesh and Shur, and sojourned
in Gerar.
2 And Abraham said of Sarah his wife, She
is my sister: and Abimelech king of Gerar
sent, and took Sarah.
3 But God came to Abimelech in a dream
by night, and said to him, Behold, thou *art*
but a dead man, for the woman which thou
hast taken; for she *is* a man's wife.
4 But Abimelech had not come near her:
and he said, Lord, wilt thou slay also a righteous nation?
5 Said he not unto me, She *is* my sister? and
she, even she herself said, He *is* my brother:
in the integrity of my heart and innocency
of my hands have I done this.
6 And God said unto him in a dream, Yea,
I know that thou didst this in the integrity
of thy heart; for I also withheld thee from
sinning against me: therefore suffered I thee
not to touch her.
7 Now therefore restore the man *his* wife;
for he *is* a prophet, and he shall pray for
thee, and thou shalt live: and if thou restore
her not, know thou that thou shalt surely
die, thou, and all that *are* thine.
8 Therefore Abimelech rose early in the
morning, and called all his servants, and
told all these things in their ears: and the
men were sore afraid.
9 Then Abimelech called Abraham, and said
unto him, What hast thou done unto us?
and what have I offended thee, that thou
hast brought on me and on my kingdom a
great sin? thou hast done deeds unto me
that ought not to be done.
10 And Abimelech said unto Abraham, What
sawest thou, that thou hast done this thing?
11 And Abraham said, Because I thought,
Surely the fear of God *is* not in this place;
and they will slay me for my wife's sake.
12 And yet indeed *she is* my sister; she *is* the
daughter of my father, but not the daughter
of my mother; and she became my wife.
13 And it came to pass, when God caused
me to wander from my father's house, that I
said unto her, This *is* thy kindness which thou
shalt shew unto me; at every place whither
we shall come, say of me, He *is* my brother.
14 And Abimelech took sheep, and oxen,
and menservants, and womenservants, and
gave *them* unto Abraham, and restored him
Sarah his wife.
15 And Abimelech said, Behold, my land *is*
before thee: dwell where it pleaseth thee.
16 And unto Sarah he said, Behold, I have

given thy brother a thousand *pieces* of silver: behold, he *is* to thee a covering of the
eyes, unto all that *are* with thee, and with
all *other:* thus she was reproved.
17 ¶ So Abraham prayed unto God: and
God healed Abimelech, and his wife, and
his maidservants; and they bare *children*.
18 For the LORD had fast closed up all the
wombs of the house of Abimelech, because
of Sarah Abraham's wife.

Genesis 21

1 And the LORD visited Sarah as he had
said, and the LORD did unto Sarah as he
had spoken.
2 For Sarah conceived, and bare Abraham a
son in his old age, at the set time of which
God had spoken to him.
3 And Abraham called the name of his son
that was born unto him, whom Sarah bare
to him, Isaac.
4 And Abraham circumcised his son Isaac
being eight days old, as God had commanded him.
5 And Abraham was an hundred years old,
when his son Isaac was born unto him.
6 ¶ And Sarah said, God hath made me
to laugh, *so that* all that hear will laugh
with me.
7 And she said, Who would have said unto
Abraham, that Sarah should have given
children suck? for I have born *him* a son in
his old age.
8 And the child grew, and was weaned: and
Abraham made a great feast the *same* day
that Isaac was weaned.
9 ¶ And Sarah saw the son of Hagar the
Egyptian, which she had born unto Abraham, mocking.
10 Wherefore she said unto Abraham, Cast
out this bondwoman and her son: for the
son of this bondwoman shall not be heir
with my son, *even* with Isaac.
11 And the thing was very grievous in Abraham's sight because of his son.
12 ¶ And God said unto Abraham, Let it not
be grievous in thy sight because of the lad,
and because of thy bondwoman; in all that
Sarah hath said unto thee, hearken unto her
voice; for in Isaac shall thy seed be called.
13 And also of the son of the bondwoman
will I make a nation, because he *is* thy seed.
14 And Abraham rose up early in the morning, and took bread, and a bottle of water,
and gave *it* unto Hagar, putting *it* on her
shoulder, and the child, and sent her away:
and she departed, and wandered in the
wilderness of Beer-sheba.
15 And the water was spent in the bottle,
and she cast the child under one of the
shrubs.
16 And she went, and sat her down over
against *him* a good way off, as it were a
bowshot: for she said, Let me not see the
death of the child. And she sat over against
him, and lift up her voice, and wept.
17 And God heard the voice of the lad;
and the angel of God called to Hagar out
of heaven, and said unto her, What aileth
thee, Hagar? fear not; for God hath heard
the voice of the lad where he *is*.
18 Arise, lift up the lad, and hold him in thine
hand; for I will make him a great nation.
19 And God opened her eyes, and she saw
a well of water; and she went, and filled the
bottle with water, and gave the lad drink.
20 And God was with the lad; and he grew,
and dwelt in the wilderness, and became
an archer.
21 And he dwelt in the wilderness of Paran:
and his mother took him a wife out of the
land of Egypt.
22 ¶ And it came to pass at that time, that
Abimelech and Phichol the chief captain of
his host spake unto Abraham, saying, God
is with thee in all that thou doest:
23 Now therefore swear unto me here by
God that thou wilt not deal falsely with me,
nor with my son, nor with my son's son: *but*
according to the kindness that I have done
unto thee, thou shalt do unto me, and to the
land wherein thou hast sojourned.
24 And Abraham said, I will swear.
25 And Abraham reproved Abimelech
because of a well of water, which Abimelech's servants had violently taken away.
26 And Abimelech said, I wot not who hath
done this thing: neither didst thou tell me,
neither yet heard I *of it*, but to day.
27 And Abraham took sheep and oxen, and
gave them unto Abimelech; and both of
them made a covenant.
28 And Abraham set seven ewe lambs of
the flock by themselves.
29 And Abimelech said unto Abraham, What

mean these seven ewe lambs which thou
hast set by themselves?
30 And he said, For *these* seven ewe lambs
shalt thou take of my hand, that they may
be a witness unto me, that I have digged
this well.
31 Wherefore he called that place Beer-
sheba; because there they sware both of
them.
32 Thus they made a covenant at Beer-
sheba: then Abimelech rose up, and Phichol
the chief captain of his host, and they
returned into the land of the Philistines.
33 ¶ And *Abraham* planted a grove in Beer-
sheba, and called there on the name of the
LORD, the everlasting God.
34 And Abraham sojourned in the Philistines' land many days.

Genesis 22

1 And it came to pass after these things, that
God did tempt Abraham, and said unto him,
Abraham: and he said, Behold, *here* I *am*.
2 And he said, Take now thy son, thine only
son Isaac, whom thou lovest, and get thee
into the land of Moriah; and offer him there
for a burnt offering upon one of the mountains which I will tell thee of.
3 ¶ And Abraham rose up early in the morning, and saddled his ass, and took two of his
young men with him, and Isaac his son, and
clave the wood for the burnt offering, and
rose up, and went unto the place of which
God had told him.
4 Then on the third day Abraham lifted up
his eyes, and saw the place afar off.
5 And Abraham said unto his young men,
Abide ye here with the ass; and I and the
lad will go yonder and worship, and come
again to you.
6 And Abraham took the wood of the burnt
offering, and laid *it* upon Isaac his son; and
he took the fire in his hand, and a knife; and
they went both of them together.
7 And Isaac spake unto Abraham his father,
and said, My father: and he said, Here *am*
I, my son. And he said, Behold the fire and
the wood: but where *is* the lamb for a burnt
offering?
8 And Abraham said, My son, God will provide himself a lamb for a burnt offering: so
they went both of them together.
9 And they came to the place which God
had told him of; and Abraham built an altar
there, and laid the wood in order, and bound
Isaac his son, and laid him on the altar upon
the wood.
10 And Abraham stretched forth his hand,
and took the knife to slay his son.
11 And the angel of the LORD called unto him
out of heaven, and said, Abraham, Abraham:
and he said, Here *am* I.
12 And he said, Lay not thine hand upon the
lad, neither do thou any thing unto him: for
now I know that thou fearest God, seeing
thou hast not withheld thy son, thine only
son from me.
13 And Abraham lifted up his eyes, and
looked, and behold behind *him* a ram caught
in a thicket by his horns: and Abraham went
and took the ram, and offered him up for a
burnt offering in the stead of his son.
14 And Abraham called the name of that
place Jehovah-jireh: as it is said *to* this day,
In the mount of the LORD it shall be seen.
15 ¶ And the angel of the LORD called unto
Abraham out of heaven the second time,
16 And said, By myself have I sworn, saith
the LORD, for because thou hast done this
thing, and hast not withheld thy son, thine
only *son:*
17 That in blessing I will bless thee, and in
multiplying I will multiply thy seed as the
stars of the heaven, and as the sand which
is upon the sea shore; and thy seed shall
possess the gate of his enemies;
18 And in thy seed shall all the nations of
the earth be blessed; because thou hast
obeyed my voice.
19 So Abraham returned unto his young
men, and they rose up and went together
to Beer-sheba; and Abraham dwelt at Beer-
sheba.
20 ¶ And it came to pass after these things,
that it was told Abraham, saying, Behold,
Milcah, she hath also born children unto
thy brother Nahor;
21 Huz his firstborn, and Buz his brother,
and Kemuel the father of Aram,
22 And Chesed, and Hazo, and Pildash, and
Jidlaph, and Bethuel.
23 And Bethuel begat Rebekah: these
eight Milcah did bear to Nahor, Abraham's
brother.
24 And his concubine, whose name *was*

Reumah, she bare also Tebah, and Gaham, and Thahash, and Maachah.

Genesis 23

1 And Sarah was an hundred and seven and twenty years old: *these were* the years of the life of Sarah.

2 And Sarah died in Kirjath-arba; the same *is* Hebron in the land of Canaan: and Abraham came to mourn for Sarah, and to weep for her.

3 ¶ And Abraham stood up from before his dead, and spake unto the sons of Heth, saying,

4 I *am* a stranger and a sojourner with you: give me a possession of a buryingplace with you, that I may bury my dead out of my sight.

5 And the children of Heth answered Abraham, saying unto him,

6 Hear us, my lord: thou *art* a mighty prince among us: in the choice of our sepulchres bury thy dead; none of us shall withhold from thee his sepulchre, but that thou mayest bury thy dead.

7 And Abraham stood up, and bowed himself to the people of the land, *even* to the children of Heth.

8 And he communed with them, saying, If it be your mind that I should bury my dead out of my sight; hear me, and intreat for me to Ephron the son of Zohar,

9 That he may give me the cave of Machpelah, which he hath, which *is* in the end of his field; for as much money as it is worth he shall give it me for a possession of a buryingplace amongst you.

10 And Ephron dwelt among the children of Heth: and Ephron the Hittite answered Abraham in the audience of the children of Heth, *even* of all that went in at the gate of his city, saying,

11 Nay, my lord, hear me: the field give I thee, and the cave that *is* therein, I give it thee; in the presence of the sons of my people give I it thee: bury thy dead.

12 And Abraham bowed down himself before the people of the land.

13 And he spake unto Ephron in the audience of the people of the land, saying, But if thou *wilt give it*, I pray thee, hear me: I will give thee money for the field; take *it* of me, and I will bury my dead there.

14 And Ephron answered Abraham, saying unto him,

15 My lord, hearken unto me: the land *is worth* four hundred shekels of silver; what *is* that betwixt me and thee? bury therefore thy dead.

16 And Abraham hearkened unto Ephron; and Abraham weighed to Ephron the silver, which he had named in the audience of the sons of Heth, four hundred shekels of silver, current *money* with the merchant.

17 ¶ And the field of Ephron, which *was* in Machpelah, which *was* before Mamre, the field, and the cave which *was* therein, and all the trees that *were* in the field, that *were* in all the borders round about, were made sure

18 Unto Abraham for a possession in the presence of the children of Heth, before all that went in at the gate of his city.

19 And after this, Abraham buried Sarah his wife in the cave of the field of Machpelah before Mamre: the same *is* Hebron in the land of Canaan.

20 And the field, and the cave that *is* therein, were made sure unto Abraham for a possession of a buryingplace by the sons of Heth.

Genesis 24

1 And Abraham was old, *and* well stricken in age: and the LORD had blessed Abraham in all things.

2 And Abraham said unto his eldest servant of his house, that ruled over all that he had, Put, I pray thee, thy hand under my thigh:

3 And I will make thee swear by the LORD, the God of heaven, and the God of the earth, that thou shalt not take a wife unto my son of the daughters of the Canaanites, among whom I dwell:

4 But thou shalt go unto my country, and to my kindred, and take a wife unto my son Isaac.

5 And the servant said unto him, Peradventure the woman will not be willing to follow me unto this land: must I needs bring thy son again unto the land from whence thou camest?

6 And Abraham said unto him, Beware thou that thou bring not my son thither again.

7 ¶ The LORD God of heaven, which took me from my father's house, and from the land of my kindred, and which spake unto me, and that sware unto me, saying, Unto

thy seed will I give this land; he shall send his angel before thee, and thou shalt take a wife unto my son from thence.

8 And if the woman will not be willing to follow thee, then thou shalt be clear from this my oath: only bring not my son thither again.

9 And the servant put his hand under the thigh of Abraham his master, and sware to him concerning that matter.

10 ¶ And the servant took ten camels of the camels of his master, and departed; for all the goods of his master *were* in his hand: and he arose, and went to Mesopotamia, unto the city of Nahor.

11 And he made his camels to kneel down without the city by a well of water at the time of the evening, *even* the time that women go out to draw *water.*

12 And he said, O LORD God of my master Abraham, I pray thee, send me good speed this day, and shew kindness unto my master Abraham.

13 Behold, I stand *here* by the well of water; and the daughters of the men of the city come out to draw water:

14 And let it come to pass, that the damsel to whom I shall say, Let down thy pitcher, I pray thee, that I may drink; and she shall say, Drink, and I will give thy camels drink also: *let the same be* she *that* thou hast appointed for thy servant Isaac; and thereby shall I know that thou hast shewed kindness unto my master.

15 ¶ And it came to pass, before he had done speaking, that, behold, Rebekah came out, who was born to Bethuel, son of Milcah, the wife of Nahor, Abraham's brother, with her pitcher upon her shoulder.

16 And the damsel *was* very fair to look upon, a virgin, neither had any man known her: and she went down to the well, and filled her pitcher, and came up.

17 And the servant ran to meet her, and said, Let me, I pray thee, drink a little water of thy pitcher.

18 And she said, Drink, my lord: and she hasted, and let down her pitcher upon her hand, and gave him drink.

19 And when she had done giving him drink, she said, I will draw *water* for thy camels also, until they have done drinking.

20 And she hasted, and emptied her pitcher into the trough, and ran again unto the well to draw *water,* and drew for all his camels.

21 And the man wondering at her held his peace, to wit whether the LORD had made his journey prosperous or not.

22 And it came to pass, as the camels had done drinking, that the man took a golden earring of half a shekel weight, and two bracelets for her hands of ten *shekels* weight of gold;

23 And said, Whose daughter *art* thou? tell me, I pray thee: is there room *in* thy father's house for us to lodge in?

24 And she said unto him, I *am* the daughter of Bethuel the son of Milcah, which she bare unto Nahor.

25 She said moreover unto him, We have both straw and provender enough, and room to lodge in.

26 And the man bowed down his head, and worshipped the LORD.

27 And he said, Blessed *be* the LORD God of my master Abraham, who hath not left destitute my master of his mercy and his truth: I *being* in the way, the LORD led me to the house of my master's brethren.

28 And the damsel ran, and told *them of* her mother's house these things.

29 ¶ And Rebekah had a brother, and his name *was* Laban: and Laban ran out unto the man, unto the well.

30 And it came to pass, when he saw the earring and bracelets upon his sister's hands, and when he heard the words of Rebekah his sister, saying, Thus spake the man unto me; that he came unto the man; and, behold, he stood by the camels at the well.

31 And he said, Come in, thou blessed of the LORD; wherefore standest thou without? for I have prepared the house, and room for the camels.

32 ¶ And the man came into the house: and he ungirded his camels, and gave straw and provender for the camels, and water to wash his feet, and the men's feet that *were* with him.

33 And there was set *meat* before him to eat: but he said, I will not eat, until I have told mine errand. And he said, Speak on.

34 And he said, I *am* Abraham's servant.

35 And the LORD hath blessed my master greatly; and he is become great: and he hath

given him flocks, and herds, and silver, and
gold, and menservants, and maidservants,
and camels, and asses.
36 And Sarah my master's wife bare a son
to my master when she was old: and unto
him hath he given all that he hath.
37 And my master made me swear, saying,
Thou shalt not take a wife to my son of
the daughters of the Canaanites, in whose
land I dwell:
38 But thou shalt go unto my father's house,
and to my kindred, and take a wife unto
my son.
39 And I said unto my master, Peradventure
the woman will not follow me.
40 And he said unto me, The LORD, before
whom I walk, will send his angel with thee,
and prosper thy way; and thou shalt take a
wife for my son of my kindred, and of my
father's house:
41 Then shalt thou be clear from *this* my
oath, when thou comest to my kindred;
and if they give not thee *one*, thou shalt be
clear from my oath.
42 And I came this day unto the well, and
said, O LORD God of my master Abraham,
if now thou do prosper my way which I go:
43 Behold, I stand by the well of water; and
it shall come to pass, that when the virgin
cometh forth to draw *water*, and I say to
her, Give me, I pray thee, a little water of
thy pitcher to drink;
44 And she say to me, Both drink thou, and I
will also draw for thy camels: *let* the same *be*
the woman whom the LORD hath appointed
out for my master's son.
45 And before I had done speaking in mine
heart, behold, Rebekah came forth with
her pitcher on her shoulder; and she went
down unto the well, and drew *water:* and
I said unto her, Let me drink, I pray thee.
46 And she made haste, and let down her
pitcher from her *shoulder*, and said, Drink,
and I will give thy camels drink also: so I
drank, and she made the camels drink also.
47 And I asked her, and said, Whose daughter *art* thou? And she said, The daughter of
Bethuel, Nahor's son, whom Milcah bare
unto him: and I put the earring upon her
face, and the bracelets upon her hands.
48 And I bowed down my head, and worshipped the LORD, and blessed the LORD God
of my master Abraham, which had led me in
the right way to take my master's brother's
daughter unto his son.
49 And now if ye will deal kindly and truly
with my master, tell me: and if not, tell
me; that I may turn to the right hand, or
to the left.
50 Then Laban and Bethuel answered and
said, The thing proceedeth from the LORD:
we cannot speak unto thee bad or good.
51 Behold, Rebekah *is* before thee, take *her*,
and go, and let her be thy master's son's
wife, as the LORD hath spoken.
52 And it came to pass, that, when Abraham's servant heard their words, he worshipped the LORD, *bowing himself* to the
earth.
53 And the servant brought forth jewels of
silver, and jewels of gold, and raiment, and
gave *them* to Rebekah: he gave also to her
brother and to her mother precious things.
54 And they did eat and drink, he and the
men that *were* with him, and tarried all
night; and they rose up in the morning, and
he said, Send me away unto my master.
55 And her brother and her mother said, Let
the damsel abide with us *a few* days, at the
least ten; after that she shall go.
56 And he said unto them, Hinder me not,
seeing the LORD hath prospered my way;
send me away that I may go to my master.
57 And they said, We will call the damsel,
and inquire at her mouth.
58 And they called Rebekah, and said unto
her, Wilt thou go with this man? And she
said, I will go.
59 And they sent away Rebekah their sister, and her nurse, and Abraham's servant,
and his men.
60 And they blessed Rebekah, and said unto
her, Thou *art* our sister, be thou *the mother*
of thousands of millions, and let thy seed
possess the gate of those which hate them.
61 ¶ And Rebekah arose, and her damsels, and they rode upon the camels, and
followed the man: and the servant took
Rebekah, and went his way.
62 And Isaac came from the way of the well
Lahai-roi; for he dwelt in the south country.
63 And Isaac went out to meditate in the
field at the eventide: and he lifted up his
eyes, and saw, and, behold, the camels
were coming.
64 And Rebekah lifted up her eyes, and

when she saw Isaac, she lighted off the camel.
65 For she *had* said unto the servant, What man *is* this that walketh in the field to meet us? And the servant *had* said, It *is* my master: therefore she took a vail, and covered herself.
66 And the servant told Isaac all things that he had done.
67 And Isaac brought her into his mother Sarah's tent, and took Rebekah, and she became his wife; and he loved her: and Isaac was comforted after his mother's *death*.

Genesis 25

1 Then again Abraham took a wife, and her name *was* Keturah.
2 And she bare him Zimran, and Jokshan, and Medan, and Midian, and Ishbak, and Shuah.
3 And Jokshan begat Sheba, and Dedan. And the sons of Dedan were Asshurim, and Letushim, and Leummim.
4 And the sons of Midian; Ephah, and Epher, and Hanoch, and Abida, and Eldaah. All these *were* the children of Keturah.
5 ¶ And Abraham gave all that he had unto Isaac.
6 But unto the sons of the concubines, which Abraham had, Abraham gave gifts, and sent them away from Isaac his son, while he yet lived, eastward, unto the east country.
7 And these *are* the days of the years of Abraham's life which he lived, an hundred threescore and fifteen years.
8 Then Abraham gave up the ghost, and died in a good old age, an old man, and full *of years;* and was gathered to his people.
9 And his sons Isaac and Ishmael buried him in the cave of Machpelah, in the field of Ephron the son of Zohar the Hittite, which *is* before Mamre;
10 The field which Abraham purchased of the sons of Heth: there was Abraham buried, and Sarah his wife.
11 ¶ And it came to pass after the death of Abraham, that God blessed his son Isaac; and Isaac dwelt by the well Lahai-roi.
12 ¶ Now these *are* the generations of Ishmael, Abraham's son, whom Hagar the Egyptian, Sarah's handmaid, bare unto Abraham:
13 And these *are* the names of the sons of Ishmael, by their names, according to their generations: the firstborn of Ishmael, Nebajoth; and Kedar, and Adbeel, and Mibsam,
14 And Mishma, and Dumah, and Massa,
15 Hadar, and Tema, Jetur, Naphish, and Kedemah:
16 These *are* the sons of Ishmael, and these *are* their names, by their towns, and by their castles; twelve princes according to their nations.
17 And these *are* the years of the life of Ishmael, an hundred and thirty and seven years: and he gave up the ghost and died; and was gathered unto his people.
18 And they dwelt from Havilah unto Shur, that *is* before Egypt, as thou goest toward Assyria: *and* he died in the presence of all his brethren.
19 ¶ And these *are* the generations of Isaac, Abraham's son: Abraham begat Isaac:
20 And Isaac was forty years old when he took Rebekah to wife, the daughter of Bethuel the Syrian of Padan-aram, the sister to Laban the Syrian.
21 And Isaac intreated the LORD for his wife, because she *was* barren: and the LORD was intreated of him, and Rebekah his wife conceived.
22 And the children struggled together within her; and she said, If *it be* so, why *am* I thus? And she went to inquire of the LORD.
23 And the LORD said unto her, Two nations *are* in thy womb, and two manner of people shall be separated from thy bowels; and *the one* people shall be stronger than *the other* people; and the elder shall serve the younger.
24 ¶ And when her days to be delivered were fulfilled, behold, *there were* twins in her womb.
25 And the first came out red, all over like an hairy garment; and they called his name Esau.
26 And after that came his brother out, and his hand took hold on Esau's heel; and his name was called Jacob: and Isaac *was* threescore years old when she bare them.
27 And the boys grew: and Esau was a cunning hunter, a man of the field; and Jacob *was* a plain man, dwelling in tents.
28 And Isaac loved Esau, because he did eat of *his* venison: but Rebekah loved Jacob.

29 ¶ And Jacob sod pottage: and Esau came
from the field, and he *was* faint:
30 And Esau said to Jacob, Feed me, I pray
thee, with that same red *pottage;* for I *am*
faint: therefore was his name called Edom.
31 And Jacob said, Sell me this day thy
birthright.
32 And Esau said, Behold, I *am* at the point
to die: and what profit shall this birthright
do to me?
33 And Jacob said, Swear to me this day;
and he sware unto him: and he sold his
birthright unto Jacob.
34 Then Jacob gave Esau bread and pottage
of lentiles; and he did eat and drink, and rose
up, and went his way: thus Esau despised
his birthright.

Genesis 26

1 And there was a famine in the land, beside
the first famine that was in the days of Abraham. And Isaac went unto Abimelech king
of the Philistines unto Gerar.
2 And the LORD appeared unto him, and
said, Go not down into Egypt; dwell in the
land which I shall tell thee of:
3 Sojourn in this land, and I will be with thee,
and will bless thee; for unto thee, and unto
thy seed, I will give all these countries, and
I will perform the oath which I sware unto
Abraham thy father;
4 And I will make thy seed to multiply as the
stars of heaven, and will give unto thy seed
all these countries; and in thy seed shall all
the nations of the earth be blessed;
5 Because that Abraham obeyed my voice,
and kept my charge, my commandments,
my statutes, and my laws.
6 ¶ And Isaac dwelt in Gerar:
7 And the men of the place asked *him* of
his wife; and he said, She *is* my sister: for
he feared to say, *She is* my wife; lest, *said
he,* the men of the place should kill me for
Rebekah; because she *was* fair to look upon.
8 And it came to pass, when he had been
there a long time, that Abimelech king of
the Philistines looked out at a window, and
saw, and, behold, Isaac *was* sporting with
Rebekah his wife.
9 And Abimelech called Isaac, and said,
Behold, of a surety she *is* thy wife: and how
saidst thou, She *is* my sister? And Isaac said
unto him, Because I said, Lest I die for her.
10 And Abimelech said, What *is* this thou
hast done unto us? one of the people might
lightly have lien with thy wife, and thou
shouldest have brought guiltiness upon us.
11 And Abimelech charged all *his* people,
saying, He that toucheth this man or his
wife shall surely be put to death.
12 Then Isaac sowed in that land, and
received in the same year an hundredfold:
and the LORD blessed him.
13 And the man waxed great, and went forward, and grew until he became very great:
14 For he had possession of flocks, and possession of herds, and great store of servants:
and the Philistines envied him.
15 For all the wells which his father's servants had digged in the days of Abraham
his father, the Philistines had stopped them,
and filled them with earth.
16 And Abimelech said unto Isaac, Go from
us; for thou art much mightier than we.
17 ¶ And Isaac departed thence, and pitched
his tent in the valley of Gerar, and dwelt
there.
18 And Isaac digged again the wells of
water, which they had digged in the days of
Abraham his father; for the Philistines had
stopped them after the death of Abraham:
and he called their names after the names
by which his father had called them.
19 And Isaac's servants digged in the valley,
and found there a well of springing water.
20 And the herdmen of Gerar did strive with
Isaac's herdmen, saying, The water *is* ours:
and he called the name of the well Esek;
because they strove with him.
21 And they digged another well, and strove
for that also: and he called the name of it
Sitnah.
22 And he removed from thence, and digged
another well; and for that they strove not:
and he called the name of it Rehoboth; and
he said, For now the LORD hath made room
for us, and we shall be fruitful in the land.
23 And he went up from thence to Beer-
sheba.
24 And the LORD appeared unto him the
same night, and said, I *am* the God of Abraham thy father: fear not, for I *am* with thee,
and will bless thee, and multiply thy seed
for my servant Abraham's sake.
25 And he builded an altar there, and called
upon the name of the LORD, and pitched

his tent there: and there Isaac's servants digged a well.

26 ¶ Then Abimelech went to him from Gerar, and Ahuzzath one of his friends, and Phichol the chief captain of his army.

27 And Isaac said unto them, Wherefore come ye to me, seeing ye hate me, and have sent me away from you?

28 And they said, We saw certainly that the LORD was with thee: and we said, Let there be now an oath betwixt us, *even* betwixt us and thee, and let us make a covenant with thee;

29 That thou wilt do us no hurt, as we have not touched thee, and as we have done unto thee nothing but good, and have sent thee away in peace: thou *art* now the blessed of the LORD.

30 And he made them a feast, and they did eat and drink.

31 And they rose up betimes in the morning, and sware one to another: and Isaac sent them away, and they departed from him in peace.

32 And it came to pass the same day, that Isaac's servants came, and told him concerning the well which they had digged, and said unto him, We have found water.

33 And he called it Shebah: therefore the name of the city *is* Beer-sheba unto this day.

34 ¶ And Esau was forty years old when he took to wife Judith the daughter of Beeri the Hittite, and Bashemath the daughter of Elon the Hittite:

35 Which were a grief of mind unto Isaac and to Rebekah.

Genesis 27

1 And it came to pass, that when Isaac was old, and his eyes were dim, so that he could not see, he called Esau his eldest son, and said unto him, My son: and he said unto him, Behold, *here am* I.

2 And he said, Behold now, I am old, I know not the day of my death:

3 Now therefore take, I pray thee, thy weapons, thy quiver and thy bow, and go out to the field, and take me *some* venison;

4 And make me savoury meat, such as I love, and bring *it* to me, that I may eat; that my soul may bless thee before I die.

5 And Rebekah heard when Isaac spake to Esau his son. And Esau went to the field to hunt *for* venison, *and* to bring *it*.

6 ¶ And Rebekah spake unto Jacob her son, saying, Behold, I heard thy father speak unto Esau thy brother, saying,

7 Bring me venison, and make me savoury meat, that I may eat, and bless thee before the LORD before my death.

8 Now therefore, my son, obey my voice according to that which I command thee.

9 Go now to the flock, and fetch me from thence two good kids of the goats; and I will make them savoury meat for thy father, such as he loveth:

10 And thou shalt bring *it* to thy father, that he may eat, and that he may bless thee before his death.

11 And Jacob said to Rebekah his mother, Behold, Esau my brother *is* a hairy man, and I *am* a smooth man:

12 My father peradventure will feel me, and I shall seem to him as a deceiver; and I shall bring a curse upon me, and not a blessing.

13 And his mother said unto him, Upon me *be* thy curse, my son: only obey my voice, and go fetch me *them*.

14 And he went, and fetched, and brought *them* to his mother: and his mother made savoury meat, such as his father loved.

15 And Rebekah took goodly raiment of her eldest son Esau, which *were* with her in the house, and put them upon Jacob her younger son:

16 And she put the skins of the kids of the goats upon his hands, and upon the smooth of his neck:

17 And she gave the savoury meat and the bread, which she had prepared, into the hand of her son Jacob.

18 ¶ And he came unto his father, and said, My father: and he said, Here *am* I; who *art* thou, my son?

19 And Jacob said unto his father, I *am* Esau thy firstborn; I have done according as thou badest me: arise, I pray thee, sit and eat of my venison, that thy soul may bless me.

20 And Isaac said unto his son, How *is it* that thou hast found *it* so quickly, my son? And he said, Because the LORD thy God brought *it* to me.

21 And Isaac said unto Jacob, Come near, I pray thee, that I may feel thee, my son, whether thou *be* my very son Esau or not.

22 And Jacob went near unto Isaac his father; and he felt him, and said, The voice *is* Jacob's voice, but the hands *are* the hands of Esau.

23 And he discerned him not, because his hands were hairy, as his brother Esau's hands: so he blessed him.

24 And he said, *Art* thou my very son Esau? And he said, I *am*.

25 And he said, Bring *it* near to me, and I will eat of my son's venison, that my soul may bless thee. And he brought *it* near to him, and he did eat: and he brought him wine, and he drank.

26 And his father Isaac said unto him, Come near now, and kiss me, my son.

27 And he came near, and kissed him: and he smelled the smell of his raiment, and blessed him, and said, See, the smell of my son *is* as the smell of a field which the LORD hath blessed:

28 Therefore God give thee of the dew of heaven, and the fatness of the earth, and plenty of corn and wine:

29 Let people serve thee, and nations bow down to thee: be lord over thy brethren, and let thy mother's sons bow down to thee: cursed *be* every one that curseth thee, and blessed *be* he that blesseth thee.

30 ¶ And it came to pass, as soon as Isaac had made an end of blessing Jacob, and Jacob was yet scarce gone out from the presence of Isaac his father, that Esau his brother came in from his hunting.

31 And he also had made savoury meat, and brought it unto his father, and said unto his father, Let my father arise, and eat of his son's venison, that thy soul may bless me.

32 And Isaac his father said unto him, Who *art* thou? And he said, I *am* thy son, thy firstborn Esau.

33 And Isaac trembled very exceedingly, and said, Who? where *is* he that hath taken venison, and brought *it* me, and I have eaten of all before thou camest, and have blessed him? yea, *and* he shall be blessed.

34 And when Esau heard the words of his father, he cried with a great and exceeding bitter cry, and said unto his father, Bless me, *even* me also, O my father.

35 And he said, Thy brother came with subtilty, and hath taken away thy blessing.

36 And he said, Is not he rightly named Jacob? for he hath supplanted me these two times: he took away my birthright; and, behold, now he hath taken away my blessing. And he said, Hast thou not reserved a blessing for me?

37 And Isaac answered and said unto Esau, Behold, I have made him thy lord, and all his brethren have I given to him for servants; and with corn and wine have I sustained him: and what shall I do now unto thee, my son?

38 And Esau said unto his father, Hast thou but one blessing, my father? bless me, *even* me also, O my father. And Esau lifted up his voice, and wept.

39 And Isaac his father answered and said unto him, Behold, thy dwelling shall be the fatness of the earth, and of the dew of heaven from above;

40 And by thy sword shalt thou live, and shalt serve thy brother; and it shall come to pass when thou shalt have the dominion, that thou shalt break his yoke from off thy neck.

41 ¶ And Esau hated Jacob because of the blessing wherewith his father blessed him: and Esau said in his heart, The days of mourning for my father are at hand; then will I slay my brother Jacob.

42 And these words of Esau her elder son were told to Rebekah: and she sent and called Jacob her younger son, and said unto him, Behold, thy brother Esau, as touching thee, doth comfort himself, *purposing* to kill thee.

43 Now therefore, my son, obey my voice; and arise, flee thou to Laban my brother to Haran;

44 And tarry with him a few days, until thy brother's fury turn away;

45 Until thy brother's anger turn away from thee, and he forget *that* which thou hast done to him: then I will send, and fetch thee from thence: why should I be deprived also of you both in one day?

46 And Rebekah said to Isaac, I am weary of my life because of the daughters of Heth: if Jacob take a wife of the daughters of Heth, such as these *which are* of the daughters of the land, what good shall my life do me?

Genesis 28

1 And Isaac called Jacob, and blessed him,

and charged him, and said unto him, Thou
shalt not take a wife of the daughters of
Canaan.
2 Arise, go to Padan-aram, to the house of
Bethuel thy mother's father; and take thee a
wife from thence of the daughters of Laban
thy mother's brother.
3 And God Almighty bless thee, and make
thee fruitful, and multiply thee, that thou
mayest be a multitude of people;
4 And give thee the blessing of Abraham, to
thee, and to thy seed with thee; that thou
mayest inherit the land wherein thou art a
stranger, which God gave unto Abraham.
5 And Isaac sent away Jacob: and he went
to Padan-aram unto Laban, son of Bethuel
the Syrian, the brother of Rebekah, Jacob's
and Esau's mother.
6 ¶ When Esau saw that Isaac had blessed
Jacob, and sent him away to Padan-aram,
to take him a wife from thence; and that
as he blessed him he gave him a charge,
saying, Thou shalt not take a wife of the
daughters of Canaan;
7 And that Jacob obeyed his father and his
mother, and was gone to Padan-aram;
8 And Esau seeing that the daughters of
Canaan pleased not Isaac his father;
9 Then went Esau unto Ishmael, and took
unto the wives which he had Mahalath the
daughter of Ishmael Abraham's son, the
sister of Nebajoth, to be his wife.
10 ¶ And Jacob went out from Beer-sheba,
and went toward Haran.
11 And he lighted upon a certain place, and
tarried there all night, because the sun was
set; and he took of the stones of that place,
and put *them for* his pillows, and lay down
in that place to sleep.
12 And he dreamed, and behold a ladder set
up on the earth, and the top of it reached
to heaven: and behold the angels of God
ascending and descending on it.
13 And, behold, the LORD stood above it,
and said, I *am* the LORD God of Abraham
thy father, and the God of Isaac: the land
whereon thou liest, to thee will I give it,
and to thy seed;
14 And thy seed shall be as the dust of the
earth, and thou shalt spread abroad to the
west, and to the east, and to the north, and
to the south: and in thee and in thy seed
shall all the families of the earth be blessed.
15 And, behold, I *am* with thee, and will
keep thee in all *places* whither thou goest,
and will bring thee again into this land; for
I will not leave thee, until I have done *that*
which I have spoken to thee of.
16 ¶ And Jacob awaked out of his sleep, and
he said, Surely the LORD is in this place; and
I knew *it* not.
17 And he was afraid, and said, How dreadful *is* this place! this *is* none other but the
house of God, and this *is* the gate of heaven.
18 And Jacob rose up early in the morning,
and took the stone that he had put *for* his
pillows, and set it up *for* a pillar, and poured
oil upon the top of it.
19 And he called the name of that place
Beth-el: but the name of that city *was called*
Luz at the first.
20 And Jacob vowed a vow, saying, If God
will be with me, and will keep me in this way
that I go, and will give me bread to eat, and
raiment to put on,
21 So that I come again to my father's house
in peace; then shall the LORD be my God:
22 And this stone, which I have set *for* a
pillar, shall be God's house: and of all that
thou shalt give me I will surely give the
tenth unto thee.

Genesis 29

1 Then Jacob went on his journey, and came
into the land of the people of the east.
2 And he looked, and behold a well in the
field, and, lo, there *were* three flocks of
sheep lying by it; for out of that well they
watered the flocks: and a great stone *was*
upon the well's mouth.
3 And thither were all the flocks gathered:
and they rolled the stone from the well's
mouth, and watered the sheep, and put
the stone again upon the well's mouth in
his place.
4 And Jacob said unto them, My brethren,
whence *be* ye? And they said, Of Haran
are we.
5 And he said unto them, Know ye Laban the
son of Nahor? And they said, We know *him*.
6 And he said unto them, *Is* he well? And
they said, *He is* well: and, behold, Rachel his
daughter cometh with the sheep.
7 And he said, Lo, *it is* yet high day, neither
is it time that the cattle should be gathered

together: water ye the sheep, and go *and*
feed *them*.
8 And they said, We cannot, until all the
flocks be gathered together, and *till* they
roll the stone from the well's mouth; then
we water the sheep.
9 ¶ And while he yet spake with them,
Rachel came with her father's sheep: for
she kept them.
10 And it came to pass, when Jacob saw
Rachel the daughter of Laban his mother's
brother, and the sheep of Laban his mother's
brother, that Jacob went near, and rolled the
stone from the well's mouth, and watered
the flock of Laban his mother's brother.
11 And Jacob kissed Rachel, and lifted up
his voice, and wept.
12 And Jacob told Rachel that he *was* her
father's brother, and that he *was* Rebekah's
son: and she ran and told her father.
13 And it came to pass, when Laban heard
the tidings of Jacob his sister's son, that he
ran to meet him, and embraced him, and
kissed him, and brought him to his house.
And he told Laban all these things.
14 And Laban said to him, Surely thou *art*
my bone and my flesh. And he abode with
him the space of a month.
15 ¶ And Laban said unto Jacob, Because
thou *art* my brother, shouldest thou therefore serve me for nought? tell me, what *shall*
thy wages *be*?
16 And Laban had two daughters: the name
of the elder *was* Leah, and the name of the
younger *was* Rachel.
17 Leah *was* tender eyed; but Rachel was
beautiful and well favoured.
18 And Jacob loved Rachel; and said, I
will serve thee seven years for Rachel thy
younger daughter.
19 And Laban said, *It is* better that I give
her to thee, than that I should give her to
another man: abide with me.
20 And Jacob served seven years for Rachel;
and they seemed unto him *but* a few days,
for the love he had to her.
21 ¶ And Jacob said unto Laban, Give *me*
my wife, for my days are fulfilled, that I may
go in unto her.
22 And Laban gathered together all the men
of the place, and made a feast.
23 And it came to pass in the evening, that
he took Leah his daughter, and brought her
to him; and he went in unto her.
24 And Laban gave unto his daughter Leah
Zilpah his maid *for* an handmaid.
25 And it came to pass, that in the morning,
behold, it *was* Leah: and he said to Laban,
What *is* this thou hast done unto me? did
not I serve with thee for Rachel? wherefore
then hast thou beguiled me?
26 And Laban said, It must not be so done
in our country, to give the younger before
the firstborn.
27 Fulfil her week, and we will give thee this
also for the service which thou shalt serve
with me yet seven other years.
28 And Jacob did so, and fulfilled her week:
and he gave him Rachel his daughter to
wife also.
29 And Laban gave to Rachel his daughter
Bilhah his handmaid to be her maid.
30 And he went in also unto Rachel, and
he loved also Rachel more than Leah, and
served with him yet seven other years.
31 ¶ And when the LORD saw that Leah *was*
hated, he opened her womb: but Rachel
was barren.
32 And Leah conceived, and bare a son,
and she called his name Reuben: for she
said, Surely the LORD hath looked upon
my affliction; now therefore my husband
will love me.
33 And she conceived again, and bare a son;
and said, Because the LORD hath heard that
I *was* hated, he hath therefore given me this
son also: and she called his name Simeon.
34 And she conceived again, and bare a son;
and said, Now this time will my husband
be joined unto me, because I have born
him three sons: therefore was his name
called Levi.
35 And she conceived again, and bare a son:
and she said, Now will I praise the LORD:
therefore she called his name Judah; and
left bearing.

Genesis 30

1 And when Rachel saw that she bare Jacob
no children, Rachel envied her sister; and
said unto Jacob, Give me children, or else
I die.
2 And Jacob's anger was kindled against
Rachel: and he said, *Am* I in God's stead,

who hath withheld from thee the fruit of
the womb?
3 And she said, Behold my maid Bilhah, go
in unto her; and she shall bear upon my
knees, that I may also have children by her.
4 And she gave him Bilhah her handmaid to
wife: and Jacob went in unto her.
5 And Bilhah conceived, and bare Jacob
a son.
6 And Rachel said, God hath judged me, and
hath also heard my voice, and hath given me
a son: therefore called she his name Dan.
7 And Bilhah Rachel's maid conceived again,
and bare Jacob a second son.
8 And Rachel said, With great wrestlings
have I wrestled with my sister, and I have
prevailed: and she called his name Naphtali.
9 When Leah saw that she had left bearing,
she took Zilpah her maid, and gave her
Jacob to wife.
10 And Zilpah Leah's maid bare Jacob a son.
11 And Leah said, A troop cometh: and she
called his name Gad.
12 And Zilpah Leah's maid bare Jacob a
second son.
13 And Leah said, Happy am I, for the daughters will call me blessed: and she called his
name Asher.
14 ¶ And Reuben went in the days of wheat
harvest, and found mandrakes in the field,
and brought them unto his mother Leah.
Then Rachel said to Leah, Give me, I pray
thee, of thy son's mandrakes.
15 And she said unto her, *Is it* a small matter that thou hast taken my husband? and
wouldest thou take away my son's mandrakes also? And Rachel said, Therefore
he shall lie with thee to night for thy son's
mandrakes.
16 And Jacob came out of the field in the
evening, and Leah went out to meet him,
and said, Thou must come in unto me;
for surely I have hired thee with my son's
mandrakes. And he lay with her that night.
17 And God hearkened unto Leah, and she
conceived, and bare Jacob the fifth son.
18 And Leah said, God hath given me my
hire, because I have given my maiden to my
husband: and she called his name Issachar.
19 And Leah conceived again, and bare
Jacob the sixth son.
20 And Leah said, God hath endued me *with*
a good dowry; now will my husband dwell
with me, because I have born him six sons:
and she called his name Zebulun.
21 And afterwards she bare a daughter, and
called her name Dinah.
22 ¶ And God remembered Rachel, and God
hearkened to her, and opened her womb.
23 And she conceived, and bare a son; and
said, God hath taken away my reproach:
24 And she called his name Joseph; and
said, The LORD shall add to me another son.
25 ¶ And it came to pass, when Rachel had
born Joseph, that Jacob said unto Laban,
Send me away, that I may go unto mine own
place, and to my country.
26 Give *me* my wives and my children, for
whom I have served thee, and let me go:
for thou knowest my service which I have
done thee.
27 And Laban said unto him, I pray thee, if
I have found favour in thine eyes, *tarry: for*
I have learned by experience that the LORD
hath blessed me for thy sake.
28 And he said, Appoint me thy wages, and
I will give *it*.
29 And he said unto him, Thou knowest
how I have served thee, and how thy cattle
was with me.
30 For *it was* little which thou hadst before
I *came*, and it is *now* increased unto a multitude; and the LORD hath blessed thee since
my coming: and now when shall I provide
for mine own house also?
31 And he said, What shall I give thee? And
Jacob said, Thou shalt not give me any thing:
if thou wilt do this thing for me, I will again
feed *and* keep thy flock:
32 I will pass through all thy flock to day,
removing from thence all the speckled
and spotted cattle, and all the brown cattle among the sheep, and the spotted and
speckled among the goats: and *of such* shall
be my hire.
33 So shall my righteousness answer for
me in time to come, when it shall come for
my hire before thy face: every one that *is*
not speckled and spotted among the goats,
and brown among the sheep, that shall be
counted stolen with me.
34 And Laban said, Behold, I would it might
be according to thy word.
35 And he removed that day the he goats
that were ringstraked and spotted, and all
the she goats that were speckled and spot-

ted, *and* every one that had *some* white in it, and all the brown among the sheep, and gave *them* into the hand of his sons.

36 And he set three days' journey betwixt himself and Jacob: and Jacob fed the rest of Laban's flocks.

37 ¶ And Jacob took him rods of green poplar, and of the hazel and chesnut tree; and pilled white strakes in them, and made the white appear which *was* in the rods.

38 And he set the rods which he had pilled before the flocks in the gutters in the watering troughs when the flocks came to drink, that they should conceive when they came to drink.

39 And the flocks conceived before the rods, and brought forth cattle ringstraked, speckled, and spotted.

40 And Jacob did separate the lambs, and set the faces of the flocks toward the ringstraked, and all the brown in the flock of Laban; and he put his own flocks by themselves, and put them not unto Laban's cattle.

41 And it came to pass, whensoever the stronger cattle did conceive, that Jacob laid the rods before the eyes of the cattle in the gutters, that they might conceive among the rods.

42 But when the cattle were feeble, he put *them* not in: so the feebler were Laban's, and the stronger Jacob's.

43 And the man increased exceedingly, and had much cattle, and maidservants, and menservants, and camels, and asses.

Genesis 31

1 And he heard the words of Laban's sons, saying, Jacob hath taken away all that *was* our father's; and of *that* which *was* our father's hath he gotten all this glory.

2 And Jacob beheld the countenance of Laban, and, behold, it *was* not toward him as before.

3 And the LORD said unto Jacob, Return unto the land of thy fathers, and to thy kindred; and I will be with thee.

4 And Jacob sent and called Rachel and Leah to the field unto his flock,

5 And said unto them, I see your father's countenance, that it *is* not toward me as before; but the God of my father hath been with me.

6 And ye know that with all my power I have served your father.

7 And your father hath deceived me, and changed my wages ten times; but God suffered him not to hurt me.

8 If he said thus, The speckled shall be thy wages; then all the cattle bare speckled: and if he said thus, The ringstraked shall be thy hire; then bare all the cattle ringstraked.

9 Thus God hath taken away the cattle of your father, and given *them* to me.

10 And it came to pass at the time that the cattle conceived, that I lifted up mine eyes, and saw in a dream, and, behold, the rams which leaped upon the cattle *were* ringstraked, speckled, and grisled.

11 And the angel of God spake unto me in a dream, *saying*, Jacob: And I said, Here *am* I.

12 And he said, Lift up now thine eyes, and see, all the rams which leap upon the cattle *are* ringstraked, speckled, and grisled: for I have seen all that Laban doeth unto thee.

13 I *am* the God of Beth-el, where thou anointedst the pillar, *and* where thou vowedst a vow unto me: now arise, get thee out from this land, and return unto the land of thy kindred.

14 And Rachel and Leah answered and said unto him, *Is there* yet any portion or inheritance for us in our father's house?

15 Are we not counted of him strangers? for he hath sold us, and hath quite devoured also our money.

16 For all the riches which God hath taken from our father, that *is* ours, and our children's: now then, whatsoever God hath said unto thee, do.

17 ¶ Then Jacob rose up, and set his sons and his wives upon camels;

18 And he carried away all his cattle, and all his goods which he had gotten, the cattle of his getting, which he had gotten in Padanaram, for to go to Isaac his father in the land of Canaan.

19 And Laban went to shear his sheep: and Rachel had stolen the images that *were* her father's.

20 And Jacob stole away unawares to Laban the Syrian, in that he told him not that he fled.

21 So he fled with all that he had; and he rose up, and passed over the river, and set his face *toward* the mount Gilead.

22 And it was told Laban on the third day
that Jacob was fled.
23 And he took his brethren with him, and
pursued after him seven days' journey; and
they overtook him in the mount Gilead.
24 And God came to Laban the Syrian in
a dream by night, and said unto him, Take
heed that thou speak not to Jacob either
good or bad.
25 ¶ Then Laban overtook Jacob. Now
Jacob had pitched his tent in the mount:
and Laban with his brethren pitched in the
mount of Gilead.
26 And Laban said to Jacob, What hast thou
done, that thou hast stolen away unawares
to me, and carried away my daughters, as
captives *taken* with the sword?
27 Wherefore didst thou flee away secretly,
and steal away from me; and didst not tell
me, that I might have sent thee away with
mirth, and with songs, with tabret, and
with harp?
28 And hast not suffered me to kiss my sons
and my daughters? thou hast now done
foolishly in *so* doing.
29 It is in the power of my hand to do you
hurt: but the God of your father spake unto
me yesternight, saying, Take thou heed that
thou speak not to Jacob either good or bad.
30 And now, *though* thou wouldest needs
be gone, because thou sore longedst after
thy father's house, *yet* wherefore hast thou
stolen my gods?
31 And Jacob answered and said to Laban,
Because I was afraid: for I said, Peradventure
thou wouldest take by force thy daughters
from me.
32 With whomsoever thou findest thy gods,
let him not live: before our brethren discern
thou what *is* thine with me, and take *it* to
thee. For Jacob knew not that Rachel had
stolen them.
33 And Laban went into Jacob's tent, and
into Leah's tent, and into the two maidservants' tents; but he found *them* not. Then
went he out of Leah's tent, and entered into
Rachel's tent.
34 Now Rachel had taken the images, and
put them in the camel's furniture, and sat
upon them. And Laban searched all the tent,
but found *them* not.
35 And she said to her father, Let it not displease my lord that I cannot rise up before
thee; for the custom of women *is* upon me.
And he searched, but found not the images.
36 ¶ And Jacob was wroth, and chode with
Laban: and Jacob answered and said to
Laban, What *is* my trespass? what *is* my sin,
that thou hast so hotly pursued after me?
37 Whereas thou hast searched all my stuff,
what hast thou found of all thy household
stuff? set *it* here before my brethren and
thy brethren, that they may judge betwixt
us both.
38 This twenty years *have* I *been* with thee;
thy ewes and thy she goats have not cast
their young, and the rams of thy flock have
I not eaten.
39 That which was torn *of beasts* I brought
not unto thee; I bare the loss of it; of my
hand didst thou require it, *whether* stolen
by day, or stolen by night.
40 *Thus* I was; in the day the drought consumed me, and the frost by night; and my
sleep departed from mine eyes.
41 Thus have I been twenty years in thy
house; I served thee fourteen years for thy
two daughters, and six years for thy cattle:
and thou hast changed my wages ten times.
42 Except the God of my father, the God of
Abraham, and the fear of Isaac, had been
with me, surely thou hadst sent me away
now empty. God hath seen mine affliction
and the labour of my hands, and rebuked
thee yesternight.
43 ¶ And Laban answered and said unto
Jacob, *These* daughters *are* my daughters,
and *these* children *are* my children, and
these cattle *are* my cattle, and all that thou
seest *is* mine: and what can I do this day
unto these my daughters, or unto their
children which they have born?
44 Now therefore come thou, let us make
a covenant, I and thou; and let it be for a
witness between me and thee.
45 And Jacob took a stone, and set it up
for a pillar.
46 And Jacob said unto his brethren, Gather
stones; and they took stones, and made an
heap: and they did eat there upon the heap.
47 And Laban called it Jegar-sahadutha: but
Jacob called it Galeed.
48 And Laban said, This heap *is* a witness
between me and thee this day. Therefore
was the name of it called Galeed;
49 And Mizpah; for he said, The LORD watch

between me and thee, when we are absent
one from another.
50 If thou shalt afflict my daughters, or
if thou shalt take *other* wives beside my
daughters, no man *is* with us; see, God *is*
witness betwixt me and thee.
51 And Laban said to Jacob, Behold this
heap, and behold *this* pillar, which I have
cast betwixt me and thee;
52 This heap *be* witness, and *this* pillar *be*
witness, that I will not pass over this heap
to thee, and that thou shalt not pass over
this heap and this pillar unto me, for harm.
53 The God of Abraham, and the God
of Nahor, the God of their father, judge
betwixt us. And Jacob sware by the fear of
his father Isaac.
54 Then Jacob offered sacrifice upon the
mount, and called his brethren to eat bread:
and they did eat bread, and tarried all night
in the mount.
55 And early in the morning Laban rose up,
and kissed his sons and his daughters, and
blessed them: and Laban departed, and
returned unto his place.

Genesis 32

1 And Jacob went on his way, and the angels
of God met him.
2 And when Jacob saw them, he said, This *is*
God's host: and he called the name of that
place Mahanaim.
3 And Jacob sent messengers before him to
Esau his brother unto the land of Seir, the
country of Edom.
4 And he commanded them, saying, Thus
shall ye speak unto my lord Esau; Thy servant Jacob saith thus, I have sojourned with
Laban, and stayed there until now:
5 And I have oxen, and asses, flocks, and
menservants, and womenservants: and I
have sent to tell my lord, that I may find
grace in thy sight.
6 ¶ And the messengers returned to Jacob,
saying, We came to thy brother Esau, and
also he cometh to meet thee, and four hundred men with him.
7 Then Jacob was greatly afraid and distressed: and he divided the people that *was*
with him, and the flocks, and herds, and the
camels, into two bands;
8 And said, If Esau come to the one company, and smite it, then the other company
which is left shall escape.
9 ¶ And Jacob said, O God of my father
Abraham, and God of my father Isaac, the
LORD which saidst unto me, Return unto thy
country, and to thy kindred, and I will deal
well with thee:
10 I am not worthy of the least of all the
mercies, and of all the truth, which thou
hast shewed unto thy servant; for with my
staff I passed over this Jordan; and now I
am become two bands.
11 Deliver me, I pray thee, from the hand
of my brother, from the hand of Esau: for
I fear him, lest he will come and smite me,
and the mother with the children.
12 And thou saidst, I will surely do thee
good, and make thy seed as the sand of
the sea, which cannot be numbered for
multitude.
13 ¶ And he lodged there that same night;
and took of that which came to his hand a
present for Esau his brother;
14 Two hundred she goats, and twenty he
goats, two hundred ewes, and twenty rams,
15 Thirty milch camels with their colts,
forty kine, and ten bulls, twenty she asses,
and ten foals.
16 And he delivered *them* into the hand of
his servants, every drove by themselves; and
said unto his servants, Pass over before me,
and put a space betwixt drove and drove.
17 And he commanded the foremost, saying, When Esau my brother meeteth thee,
and asketh thee, saying, Whose *art* thou?
and whither goest thou? and whose *are*
these before thee?
18 Then thou shalt say, *They be* thy servant
Jacob's; it *is* a present sent unto my lord
Esau: and, behold, also he *is* behind us.
19 And so commanded he the second, and
the third, and all that followed the droves,
saying, On this manner shall ye speak unto
Esau, when ye find him.
20 And say ye moreover, Behold, thy servant Jacob *is* behind us. For he said, I will
appease him with the present that goeth
before me, and afterward I will see his face;
peradventure he will accept of me.
21 So went the present over before him: and
himself lodged that night in the company.
22 And he rose up that night, and took his
two wives, and his two womenservants,

and his eleven sons, and passed over the
ford Jabbok.
23 And he took them, and sent them over
the brook, and sent over that he had.
24 ¶ And Jacob was left alone; and there
wrestled a man with him until the breaking
of the day.
25 And when he saw that he prevailed not
against him, he touched the hollow of his
thigh; and the hollow of Jacob's thigh was
out of joint, as he wrestled with him.
26 And he said, Let me go, for the day
breaketh. And he said, I will not let thee go,
except thou bless me.
27 And he said unto him, What *is* thy name?
And he said, Jacob.
28 And he said, Thy name shall be called no
more Jacob, but Israel: for as a prince hast
thou power with God and with men, and
hast prevailed.
29 And Jacob asked *him*, and said, Tell *me*, I
pray thee, thy name. And he said, Wherefore
is it *that* thou dost ask after my name? And
he blessed him there.
30 And Jacob called the name of the place
Peniel: for I have seen God face to face, and
my life is preserved.
31 And as he passed over Penuel the sun
rose upon him, and he halted upon his thigh.
32 Therefore the children of Israel eat not *of*
the sinew which shrank, which *is* upon the
hollow of the thigh, unto this day: because
he touched the hollow of Jacob's thigh in
the sinew that shrank.

Genesis 33

1 And Jacob lifted up his eyes, and looked,
and, behold, Esau came, and with him four
hundred men. And he divided the children
unto Leah, and unto Rachel, and unto the
two handmaids.
2 And he put the handmaids and their children foremost, and Leah and her children
after, and Rachel and Joseph hindermost.
3 And he passed over before them, and
bowed himself to the ground seven times,
until he came near to his brother.
4 And Esau ran to meet him, and embraced
him, and fell on his neck, and kissed him:
and they wept.
5 And he lifted up his eyes, and saw the
women and the children; and said, Who *are*
those with thee? And he said, The children
which God hath graciously given thy servant.
6 Then the handmaidens came near, they
and their children, and they bowed themselves.
7 And Leah also with her children came near,
and bowed themselves: and after came
Joseph near and Rachel, and they bowed
themselves.
8 And he said, What *meanest* thou by all this
drove which I met? And he said, *These are*
to find grace in the sight of my lord.
9 And Esau said, I have enough, my brother;
keep that thou hast unto thyself.
10 And Jacob said, Nay, I pray thee, if now I
have found grace in thy sight, then receive
my present at my hand: for therefore I have
seen thy face, as though I had seen the face
of God, and thou wast pleased with me.
11 Take, I pray thee, my blessing that is
brought to thee; because God hath dealt
graciously with me, and because I have
enough. And he urged him, and he took *it*.
12 And he said, Let us take our journey, and
let us go, and I will go before thee.
13 And he said unto him, My lord knoweth
that the children *are* tender, and the flocks
and herds with young *are* with me: and if
men should overdrive them one day, all the
flock will die.
14 Let my lord, I pray thee, pass over before
his servant: and I will lead on softly, according as the cattle that goeth before me and
the children be able to endure, until I come
unto my lord unto Seir.
15 And Esau said, Let me now leave with
thee *some* of the folk that *are* with me. And
he said, What needeth it? let me find grace
in the sight of my lord.
16 ¶ So Esau returned that day on his way
unto Seir.
17 And Jacob journeyed to Succoth, and
built him an house, and made booths for
his cattle: therefore the name of the place
is called Succoth.
18 ¶ And Jacob came to Shalem, a city of
Shechem, which *is* in the land of Canaan,
when he came from Padan-aram; and
pitched his tent before the city.
19 And he bought a parcel of a field, where
he had spread his tent, at the hand of the
children of Hamor, Shechem's father, for an
hundred pieces of money.

20 And he erected there an altar, and called it El-elohe-Israel.

Genesis 34

1 And Dinah the daughter of Leah, which she bare unto Jacob, went out to see the daughters of the land.

2 And when Shechem the son of Hamor the Hivite, prince of the country, saw her, he took her, and lay with her, and defiled her.

3 And his soul clave unto Dinah the daughter of Jacob, and he loved the damsel, and spake kindly unto the damsel.

4 And Shechem spake unto his father Hamor, saying, Get me this damsel to wife.

5 And Jacob heard that he had defiled Dinah his daughter: now his sons were with his cattle in the field: and Jacob held his peace until they were come.

6 ¶ And Hamor the father of Shechem went out unto Jacob to commune with him.

7 And the sons of Jacob came out of the field when they heard *it:* and the men were grieved, and they were very wroth, because he had wrought folly in Israel in lying with Jacob's daughter; which thing ought not to be done.

8 And Hamor communed with them, saying, The soul of my son Shechem longeth for your daughter: I pray you give her him to wife.

9 And make ye marriages with us, *and* give your daughters unto us, and take our daughters unto you.

10 And ye shall dwell with us: and the land shall be before you; dwell and trade ye therein, and get you possessions therein.

11 And Shechem said unto her father and unto her brethren, Let me find grace in your eyes, and what ye shall say unto me I will give.

12 Ask me never so much dowry and gift, and I will give according as ye shall say unto me: but give me the damsel to wife.

13 And the sons of Jacob answered Shechem and Hamor his father deceitfully, and said, because he had defiled Dinah their sister:

14 And they said unto them, We cannot do this thing, to give our sister to one that is uncircumcised; for that *were* a reproach unto us:

15 But in this will we consent unto you: If ye will be as we *be*, that every male of you be circumcised;

16 Then will we give our daughters unto you, and we will take your daughters to us, and we will dwell with you, and we will become one people.

17 But if ye will not hearken unto us, to be circumcised; then will we take our daughter, and we will be gone.

18 And their words pleased Hamor, and Shechem Hamor's son.

19 And the young man deferred not to do the thing, because he had delight in Jacob's daughter: and he *was* more honourable than all the house of his father.

20 ¶ And Hamor and Shechem his son came unto the gate of their city, and communed with the men of their city, saying,

21 These men *are* peaceable with us; therefore let them dwell in the land, and trade therein; for the land, behold, *it is* large enough for them; let us take their daughters to us for wives, and let us give them our daughters.

22 Only herein will the men consent unto us for to dwell with us, to be one people, if every male among us be circumcised, as they *are* circumcised.

23 *Shall* not their cattle and their substance and every beast of theirs *be* ours? only let us consent unto them, and they will dwell with us.

24 And unto Hamor and unto Shechem his son hearkened all that went out of the gate of his city; and every male was circumcised, all that went out of the gate of his city.

25 ¶ And it came to pass on the third day, when they were sore, that two of the sons of Jacob, Simeon and Levi, Dinah's brethren, took each man his sword, and came upon the city boldly, and slew all the males.

26 And they slew Hamor and Shechem his son with the edge of the sword, and took Dinah out of Shechem's house, and went out.

27 The sons of Jacob came upon the slain, and spoiled the city, because they had defiled their sister.

28 They took their sheep, and their oxen, and their asses, and that which *was* in the city, and that which *was* in the field,

29 And all their wealth, and all their little

ones, and their wives took they captive,
and spoiled even all that *was* in the house.
30 And Jacob said to Simeon and Levi, Ye
have troubled me to make me to stink
among the inhabitants of the land, among
the Canaanites and the Perizzites: and I
being few in number, they shall gather
themselves together against me, and slay
me; and I shall be destroyed, I and my house.
31 And they said, Should he deal with our
sister as with an harlot?

Genesis 35

1 And God said unto Jacob, Arise, go up to
Beth-el, and dwell there: and make there
an altar unto God, that appeared unto thee
when thou fleddest from the face of Esau
thy brother.
2 Then Jacob said unto his household, and to
all that *were* with him, Put away the strange
gods that *are* among you, and be clean, and
change your garments:
3 And let us arise, and go up to Beth-el; and
I will make there an altar unto God, who
answered me in the day of my distress,
and was with me in the way which I went.
4 And they gave unto Jacob all the strange
gods which *were* in their hand, and *all*
their earrings which *were* in their ears; and
Jacob hid them under the oak which *was*
by Shechem.
5 And they journeyed: and the terror of
God was upon the cities that *were* round
about them, and they did not pursue after
the sons of Jacob.
6 ¶ So Jacob came to Luz, which *is* in the
land of Canaan, that *is*, Beth-el, he and all
the people that *were* with him.
7 And he built there an altar, and called
the place El-beth-el: because there God
appeared unto him, when he fled from the
face of his brother.
8 But Deborah Rebekah's nurse died, and
she was buried beneath Beth-el under an
oak: and the name of it was called Allon-ba-
chuth.
9 ¶ And God appeared unto Jacob again,
when he came out of Padan-aram, and
blessed him.
10 And God said unto him, Thy name *is*
Jacob: thy name shall not be called any more
Jacob, but Israel shall be thy name: and he
called his name Israel.
11 And God said unto him, I *am* God
Almighty: be fruitful and multiply; a nation
and a company of nations shall be of thee,
and kings shall come out of thy loins;
12 And the land which I gave Abraham and
Isaac, to thee I will give it, and to thy seed
after thee will I give the land.
13 And God went up from him in the place
where he talked with him.
14 And Jacob set up a pillar in the place
where he talked with him, *even* a pillar
of stone: and he poured a drink offering
thereon, and he poured oil thereon.
15 And Jacob called the name of the place
where God spake with him, Beth-el.
16 ¶ And they journeyed from Beth-el;
and there was but a little way to come to
Ephrath: and Rachel travailed, and she had
hard labour.
17 And it came to pass, when she was in
hard labour, that the midwife said unto
her, Fear not; thou shalt have this son also.
18 And it came to pass, as her soul was in
departing, (for she died) that she called his
name Ben-oni: but his father called him
Benjamin.
19 And Rachel died, and was buried in the
way to Ephrath, which *is* Beth-lehem.
20 And Jacob set a pillar upon her grave: that
is the pillar of Rachel's grave unto this day.
21 ¶ And Israel journeyed, and spread his
tent beyond the tower of Edar.
22 And it came to pass, when Israel dwelt
in that land, that Reuben went and lay with
Bilhah his father's concubine: and Israel
heard *it*. Now the sons of Jacob were twelve:
23 The sons of Leah; Reuben, Jacob's firstborn, and Simeon, and Levi, and Judah, and
Issachar, and Zebulun:
24 The sons of Rachel; Joseph, and Benjamin:
25 And the sons of Bilhah, Rachel's handmaid; Dan, and Naphtali:
26 And the sons of Zilpah, Leah's handmaid;
Gad, and Asher: these *are* the sons of Jacob,
which were born to him in Padan-aram.
27 ¶ And Jacob came unto Isaac his father
unto Mamre, unto the city of Arbah, which
is Hebron, where Abraham and Isaac
sojourned.
28 And the days of Isaac were an hundred
and fourscore years.
29 And Isaac gave up the ghost, and died,

and was gathered unto his people, *being*
old and full of days: and his sons Esau and
Jacob buried him.

Genesis 36

1 Now these *are* the generations of Esau,
who *is* Edom.
2 Esau took his wives of the daughters of
Canaan; Adah the daughter of Elon the Hittite, and Aholibamah the daughter of Anah
the daughter of Zibeon the Hivite;
3 And Bashemath Ishmael's daughter, sister
of Nebajoth.
4 And Adah bare to Esau Eliphaz; and Bashemath bare Reuel;
5 And Aholibamah bare Jeush, and Jaalam,
and Korah: these *are* the sons of Esau, which
were born unto him in the land of Canaan.
6 And Esau took his wives, and his sons,
and his daughters, and all the persons of his
house, and his cattle, and all his beasts, and
all his substance, which he had got in the
land of Canaan; and went into the country
from the face of his brother Jacob.
7 For their riches were more than that they
might dwell together; and the land wherein
they were strangers could not bear them
because of their cattle.
8 Thus dwelt Esau in mount Seir: Esau *is*
Edom.
9 ¶ And these *are* the generations of Esau
the father of the Edomites in mount Seir:
10 These *are* the names of Esau's sons; Eliphaz the son of Adah the wife of Esau, Reuel
the son of Bashemath the wife of Esau.
11 And the sons of Eliphaz were Teman,
Omar, Zepho, and Gatam, and Kenaz.
12 And Timna was concubine to Eliphaz
Esau's son; and she bare to Eliphaz Amalek:
these *were* the sons of Adah Esau's wife.
13 And these *are* the sons of Reuel; Nahath,
and Zerah, Shammah, and Mizzah: these
were the sons of Bashemath Esau's wife.
14 ¶ And these were the sons of Aholibamah, the daughter of Anah the daughter
of Zibeon, Esau's wife: and she bare to Esau
Jeush, and Jaalam, and Korah.
15 ¶ These *were* dukes of the sons of Esau:
the sons of Eliphaz the firstborn *son* of
Esau; duke Teman, duke Omar, duke Zepho,
duke Kenaz,
16 Duke Korah, duke Gatam, *and* duke
Amalek: these *are* the dukes *that came* of
Eliphaz in the land of Edom; these *were* the
sons of Adah.
17 ¶ And these *are* the sons of Reuel Esau's
son; duke Nahath, duke Zerah, duke Shammah, duke Mizzah: these *are* the dukes *that
came* of Reuel in the land of Edom; these *are*
the sons of Bashemath Esau's wife.
18 ¶ And these *are* the sons of Aholibamah
Esau's wife; duke Jeush, duke Jaalam, duke
Korah: these *were* the dukes *that came* of
Aholibamah the daughter of Anah, Esau's
wife.
19 These *are* the sons of Esau, who *is* Edom,
and these *are* their dukes.
20 ¶ These *are* the sons of Seir the Horite,
who inhabited the land; Lotan, and Shobal,
and Zibeon, and Anah,
21 And Dishon, and Ezer, and Dishan: these
are the dukes of the Horites, the children of
Seir in the land of Edom.
22 And the children of Lotan were Hori and
Hemam; and Lotan's sister *was* Timna.
23 And the children of Shobal *were* these;
Alvan, and Manahath, and Ebal, Shepho,
and Onam.
24 And these *are* the children of Zibeon;
both Ajah, and Anah: this *was that* Anah
that found the mules in the wilderness, as
he fed the asses of Zibeon his father.
25 And the children of Anah *were* these; Dishon, and Aholibamah the daughter of Anah.
26 And these *are* the children of Dishon;
Hemdan, and Eshban, and Ithran, and
Cheran.
27 The children of Ezer *are* these; Bilhan,
and Zaavan, and Akan.
28 The children of Dishan *are* these; Uz,
and Aran.
29 These *are* the dukes *that came* of the
Horites; duke Lotan, duke Shobal, duke
Zibeon, duke Anah,
30 Duke Dishon, duke Ezer, duke Dishan:
these *are* the dukes *that came* of Hori,
among their dukes in the land of Seir.
31 ¶ And these *are* the kings that reigned in
the land of Edom, before there reigned any
king over the children of Israel.
32 And Bela the son of Beor reigned in
Edom: and the name of his city *was* Din-
habah.
33 And Bela died, and Jobab the son of Zerah
of Bozrah reigned in his stead.

34 And Jobab died, and Husham of the land
of Temani reigned in his stead.
35 And Husham died, and Hadad the son
of Bedad, who smote Midian in the field of
Moab, reigned in his stead: and the name
of his city *was* Avith.
36 And Hadad died, and Samlah of Masrekah
reigned in his stead.
37 And Samlah died, and Saul of Rehoboth
by the river reigned in his stead.
38 And Saul died, and Baal-hanan the son
of Achbor reigned in his stead.
39 And Baal-hanan the son of Achbor died,
and Hadar reigned in his stead: and the
name of his city *was* Pau; and his wife's
name *was* Mehetabel, the daughter of
Matred, the daughter of Mezahab.
40 And these *are* the names of the dukes
that came of Esau, according to their families, after their places, by their names; duke
Timnah, duke Alvah, duke Jetheth,
41 Duke Aholibamah, duke Elah, duke Pinon,
42 Duke Kenaz, duke Teman, duke Mibzar,
43 Duke Magdiel, duke Iram: these *be* the
dukes of Edom, according to their habitations in the land of their possession: he *is*
Esau the father of the Edomites.

Genesis 37

1 And Jacob dwelt in the land wherein his
father was a stranger, in the land of Canaan.
2 These *are* the generations of Jacob.
Joseph, *being* seventeen years old, was
feeding the flock with his brethren; and the
lad *was* with the sons of Bilhah, and with the
sons of Zilpah, his father's wives: and Joseph
brought unto his father their evil report.
3 Now Israel loved Joseph more than all
his children, because he *was* the son of his
old age: and he made him a coat of *many*
colours.
4 And when his brethren saw that their
father loved him more than all his brethren, they hated him, and could not speak
peaceably unto him.
5 ¶ And Joseph dreamed a dream, and he
told *it* his brethren: and they hated him yet
the more.
6 And he said unto them, Hear, I pray you,
this dream which I have dreamed:
7 For, behold, we *were* binding sheaves in
the field, and, lo, my sheaf arose, and also
stood upright; and, behold, your sheaves
stood round about, and made obeisance
to my sheaf.
8 And his brethren said to him, Shalt thou
indeed reign over us? or shalt thou indeed
have dominion over us? And they hated
him yet the more for his dreams, and for
his words.
9 ¶ And he dreamed yet another dream,
and told it his brethren, and said, Behold, I
have dreamed a dream more; and, behold,
the sun and the moon and the eleven stars
made obeisance to me.
10 And he told *it* to his father, and to his
brethren: and his father rebuked him, and
said unto him, What *is* this dream that thou
hast dreamed? Shall I and thy mother and
thy brethren indeed come to bow down
ourselves to thee to the earth?
11 And his brethren envied him; but his
father observed the saying.
12 ¶ And his brethren went to feed their
father's flock in Shechem.
13 And Israel said unto Joseph, Do not thy
brethren feed *the flock* in Shechem? come,
and I will send thee unto them. And he said
to him, Here *am I*.
14 And he said to him, Go, I pray thee, see
whether it be well with thy brethren, and
well with the flocks; and bring me word
again. So he sent him out of the vale of
Hebron, and he came to Shechem.
15 ¶ And a certain man found him, and,
behold, *he was* wandering in the field: and
the man asked him, saying, What seekest
thou?
16 And he said, I seek my brethren: tell me,
I pray thee, where they feed *their flocks*.
17 And the man said, They are departed
hence; for I heard them say, Let us go to
Dothan. And Joseph went after his brethren,
and found them in Dothan.
18 And when they saw him afar off, even
before he came near unto them, they conspired against him to slay him.
19 And they said one to another, Behold,
this dreamer cometh.
20 Come now therefore, and let us slay him,
and cast him into some pit, and we will say,
Some evil beast hath devoured him: and we
shall see what will become of his dreams.
21 And Reuben heard *it*, and he delivered
him out of their hands; and said, Let us not
kill him.

22 And Reuben said unto them, Shed no blood, *but* cast him into this pit that *is* in the wilderness, and lay no hand upon him; that he might rid him out of their hands, to deliver him to his father again.

23 ¶ And it came to pass, when Joseph was come unto his brethren, that they stript Joseph out of his coat, *his* coat of *many* colours that *was* on him;

24 And they took him, and cast him into a pit: and the pit *was* empty, *there was* no water in it.

25 And they sat down to eat bread: and they lifted up their eyes and looked, and, behold, a company of Ishmeelites came from Gilead with their camels bearing spicery and balm and myrrh, going to carry *it* down to Egypt.

26 And Judah said unto his brethren, What profit *is it* if we slay our brother, and conceal his blood?

27 Come, and let us sell him to the Ishmeelites, and let not our hand be upon him; for he *is* our brother *and* our flesh. And his brethren were content.

28 Then there passed by Midianites merchantmen; and they drew and lifted up Joseph out of the pit, and sold Joseph to the Ishmeelites for twenty *pieces* of silver: and they brought Joseph into Egypt.

29 ¶ And Reuben returned unto the pit; and, behold, Joseph *was* not in the pit; and he rent his clothes.

30 And he returned unto his brethren, and said, The child *is* not; and I, whither shall I go?

31 And they took Joseph's coat, and killed a kid of the goats, and dipped the coat in the blood;

32 And they sent the coat of *many* colours, and they brought *it* to their father; and said, This have we found: know now whether it *be* thy son's coat or no.

33 And he knew it, and said, *It is* my son's coat; an evil beast hath devoured him; Joseph is without doubt rent in pieces.

34 And Jacob rent his clothes, and put sackcloth upon his loins, and mourned for his son many days.

35 And all his sons and all his daughters rose up to comfort him; but he refused to be comforted; and he said, For I will go down into the grave unto my son mourning. Thus his father wept for him.

36 And the Midianites sold him into Egypt unto Potiphar, an officer of Pharaoh's, *and* captain of the guard.

Genesis 38

1 And it came to pass at that time, that Judah went down from his brethren, and turned in to a certain Adullamite, whose name *was* Hirah.

2 And Judah saw there a daughter of a certain Canaanite, whose name *was* Shuah; and he took her, and went in unto her.

3 And she conceived, and bare a son; and he called his name Er.

4 And she conceived again, and bare a son; and she called his name Onan.

5 And she yet again conceived, and bare a son; and called his name Shelah: and he was at Chezib, when she bare him.

6 And Judah took a wife for Er his firstborn, whose name *was* Tamar.

7 And Er, Judah's firstborn, was wicked in the sight of the LORD; and the LORD slew him.

8 And Judah said unto Onan, Go in unto thy brother's wife, and marry her, and raise up seed to thy brother.

9 And Onan knew that the seed should not be his; and it came to pass, when he went in unto his brother's wife, that he spilled *it* on the ground, lest that he should give seed to his brother.

10 And the thing which he did displeased the LORD: wherefore he slew him also.

11 Then said Judah to Tamar his daughter in law, Remain a widow at thy father's house, till Shelah my son be grown: for he said, Lest peradventure he die also, as his brethren *did*. And Tamar went and dwelt in her father's house.

12 ¶ And in process of time the daughter of Shuah Judah's wife died; and Judah was comforted, and went up unto his sheepshearers to Timnath, he and his friend Hirah the Adullamite.

13 And it was told Tamar, saying, Behold thy father in law goeth up to Timnath to shear his sheep.

14 And she put her widow's garments off from her, and covered her with a vail, and wrapped herself, and sat in an open place, which *is* by the way to Timnath; for she saw that Shelah was grown, and she was not given unto him to wife.

15 When Judah saw her, he thought her
to be an harlot; because she had covered
her face.
16 And he turned unto her by the way,
and said, Go to, I pray thee, let me come in
unto thee; (for he knew not that she *was*
his daughter in law.) And she said, What
wilt thou give me, that thou mayest come
in unto me?
17 And he said, I will send *thee* a kid from
the flock. And she said, Wilt thou give *me*
a pledge, till thou send *it?*
18 And he said, What pledge shall I give
thee? And she said, Thy signet, and thy
bracelets, and thy staff that *is* in thine hand.
And he gave *it* her, and came in unto her,
and she conceived by him.
19 And she arose, and went away, and laid
by her vail from her, and put on the garments of her widowhood.
20 And Judah sent the kid by the hand of
his friend the Adullamite, to receive *his*
pledge from the woman's hand: but he
found her not.
21 Then he asked the men of that place,
saying, Where *is* the harlot, that *was* openly
by the way side? And they said, There was
no harlot in this *place*.
22 And he returned to Judah, and said, I cannot find her; and also the men of the place
said, *that* there was no harlot in this *place*.
23 And Judah said, Let her take *it* to her, lest
we be shamed: behold, I sent this kid, and
thou hast not found her.
24 ¶ And it came to pass about three
months after, that it was told Judah, saying,
Tamar thy daughter in law hath played the
harlot; and also, behold, she *is* with child by
whoredom. And Judah said, Bring her forth,
and let her be burnt.
25 When she *was* brought forth, she sent
to her father in law, saying, By the man,
whose these *are*, *am* I with child: and she
said, Discern, I pray thee, whose *are* these,
the signet, and bracelets, and staff.
26 And Judah acknowledged *them*, and
said, She hath been more righteous than
I; because that I gave her not to Shelah my
son. And he knew her again no more.
27 ¶ And it came to pass in the time of
her travail, that, behold, twins *were* in her
womb.
28 And it came to pass, when she travailed,
that *the one* put out *his* hand: and the midwife took and bound upon his hand a scarlet
thread, saying, This came out first.
29 And it came to pass, as he drew back his
hand, that, behold, his brother came out:
and she said, How hast thou broken forth?
this breach *be* upon thee: therefore his
name was called Pharez.
30 And afterward came out his brother, that
had the scarlet thread upon his hand: and
his name was called Zarah.

Genesis 39

1 And Joseph was brought down to Egypt;
and Potiphar, an officer of Pharaoh, captain
of the guard, an Egyptian, bought him of the
hands of the Ishmeelites, which had brought
him down thither.
2 And the LORD was with Joseph, and he
was a prosperous man; and he was in the
house of his master the Egyptian.
3 And his master saw that the LORD *was*
with him, and that the LORD made all that
he did to prosper in his hand.
4 And Joseph found grace in his sight, and
he served him: and he made him overseer
over his house, and all *that* he had he put
into his hand.
5 And it came to pass from the time *that* he
had made him overseer in his house, and
over all that he had, that the LORD blessed
the Egyptian's house for Joseph's sake; and
the blessing of the LORD was upon all that
he had in the house, and in the field.
6 And he left all that he had in Joseph's hand;
and he knew not ought he had, save the
bread which he did eat. And Joseph was *a*
goodly *person*, and well favoured.
7 ¶ And it came to pass after these things,
that his master's wife cast her eyes upon
Joseph; and she said, Lie with me.
8 But he refused, and said unto his master's
wife, Behold, my master wotteth not what
is with me in the house, and he hath committed all that he hath to my hand;
9 *There is* none greater in this house than
I; neither hath he kept back any thing from
me but thee, because thou *art* his wife: how
then can I do this great wickedness, and sin
against God?
10 And it came to pass, as she spake to
Joseph day by day, that he hearkened not
unto her, to lie by her, *or* to be with her.

11 And it came to pass about this time, that *Joseph* went into the house to do his business; and *there was* none of the men of the house there within.

12 And she caught him by his garment, saying, Lie with me: and he left his garment in her hand, and fled, and got him out.

13 And it came to pass, when she saw that he had left his garment in her hand, and was fled forth,

14 That she called unto the men of her house, and spake unto them, saying, See, he hath brought in an Hebrew unto us to mock us; he came in unto me to lie with me, and I cried with a loud voice:

15 And it came to pass, when he heard that I lifted up my voice and cried, that he left his garment with me, and fled, and got him out.

16 And she laid up his garment by her, until his lord came home.

17 And she spake unto him according to these words, saying, The Hebrew servant, which thou hast brought unto us, came in unto me to mock me:

18 And it came to pass, as I lifted up my voice and cried, that he left his garment with me, and fled out.

19 And it came to pass, when his master heard the words of his wife, which she spake unto him, saying, After this manner did thy servant to me; that his wrath was kindled.

20 And Joseph's master took him, and put him into the prison, a place where the king's prisoners *were* bound: and he was there in the prison.

21 ¶ But the LORD was with Joseph, and shewed him mercy, and gave him favour in the sight of the keeper of the prison.

22 And the keeper of the prison committed to Joseph's hand all the prisoners that *were* in the prison; and whatsoever they did there, he was the doer *of it*.

23 The keeper of the prison looked not to any thing *that was* under his hand; because the LORD was with him, and *that* which he did, the LORD made *it* to prosper.

Genesis 40

1 And it came to pass after these things, *that* the butler of the king of Egypt and *his* baker had offended their lord the king of Egypt.

2 And Pharaoh was wroth against two *of* his officers, against the chief of the butlers, and against the chief of the bakers.

3 And he put them in ward in the house of the captain of the guard, into the prison, the place where Joseph *was* bound.

4 And the captain of the guard charged Joseph with them, and he served them: and they continued a season in ward.

5 ¶ And they dreamed a dream both of them, each man his dream in one night, each man according to the interpretation of his dream, the butler and the baker of the king of Egypt, which *were* bound in the prison.

6 And Joseph came in unto them in the morning, and looked upon them, and, behold, they *were* sad.

7 And he asked Pharaoh's officers that *were* with him in the ward of his lord's house, saying, Wherefore look ye *so* sadly to day?

8 And they said unto him, We have dreamed a dream, and *there is* no interpreter of it. And Joseph said unto them, *Do* not interpretations *belong* to God? tell me *them*, I pray you.

9 And the chief butler told his dream to Joseph, and said to him, In my dream, behold, a vine *was* before me;

10 And in the vine *were* three branches: and it *was* as though it budded, *and* her blossoms shot forth; and the clusters thereof brought forth ripe grapes:

11 And Pharaoh's cup *was* in my hand: and I took the grapes, and pressed them into Pharaoh's cup, and I gave the cup into Pharaoh's hand.

12 And Joseph said unto him, This *is* the interpretation of it: The three branches *are* three days:

13 Yet within three days shall Pharaoh lift up thine head, and restore thee unto thy place: and thou shalt deliver Pharaoh's cup into his hand, after the former manner when thou wast his butler.

14 But think on me when it shall be well with thee, and shew kindness, I pray thee, unto me, and make mention of me unto Pharaoh, and bring me out of this house:

15 For indeed I was stolen away out of the land of the Hebrews: and here also have I done nothing that they should put me into the dungeon.

16 When the chief baker saw that the interpretation was good, he said unto Joseph, I

also *was* in my dream, and, behold, *I had*
three white baskets on my head:
17 And in the uppermost basket *there was*
of all manner of bakemeats for Pharaoh;
and the birds did eat them out of the basket
upon my head.
18 And Joseph answered and said, This *is* the
interpretation thereof: The three baskets
are three days:
19 Yet within three days shall Pharaoh lift
up thy head from off thee, and shall hang
thee on a tree; and the birds shall eat thy
flesh from off thee.
20 ¶ And it came to pass the third day, *which*
was Pharaoh's birthday, that he made a
feast unto all his servants: and he lifted up
the head of the chief butler and of the chief
baker among his servants.
21 And he restored the chief butler unto his
butlership again; and he gave the cup into
Pharaoh's hand:
22 But he hanged the chief baker: as Joseph
had interpreted to them.
23 Yet did not the chief butler remember
Joseph, but forgat him.

Genesis 41

1 And it came to pass at the end of two full
years, that Pharaoh dreamed: and, behold,
he stood by the river.
2 And, behold, there came up out of the
river seven well favoured kine and fatfleshed; and they fed in a meadow.
3 And, behold, seven other kine came up
after them out of the river, ill favoured and
leanfleshed; and stood by the *other* kine
upon the brink of the river.
4 And the ill favoured and leanfleshed kine
did eat up the seven well favoured and fat
kine. So Pharaoh awoke.
5 And he slept and dreamed the second
time: and, behold, seven ears of corn came
up upon one stalk, rank and good.
6 And, behold, seven thin ears and blasted
with the east wind sprung up after them.
7 And the seven thin ears devoured the
seven rank and full ears. And Pharaoh
awoke, and, behold, *it was* a dream.
8 And it came to pass in the morning that his
spirit was troubled; and he sent and called
for all the magicians of Egypt, and all the
wise men thereof: and Pharaoh told them
his dream; but *there was* none that could
interpret them unto Pharaoh.
9 ¶ Then spake the chief butler unto Pharaoh, saying, I do remember my faults this
day:
10 Pharaoh was wroth with his servants,
and put me in ward in the captain of the
guard's house, *both* me and the chief baker:
11 And we dreamed a dream in one night,
I and he; we dreamed each man according
to the interpretation of his dream.
12 And *there was* there with us a young man,
an Hebrew, servant to the captain of the
guard; and we told him, and he interpreted
to us our dreams; to each man according to
his dream he did interpret.
13 And it came to pass, as he interpreted
to us, so it was; me he restored unto mine
office, and him he hanged.
14 ¶ Then Pharaoh sent and called Joseph,
and they brought him hastily out of the dungeon: and he shaved *himself*, and changed
his raiment, and came in unto Pharaoh.
15 And Pharaoh said unto Joseph, I have
dreamed a dream, and *there is* none that
can interpret it: and I have heard say of
thee, *that* thou canst understand a dream
to interpret it.
16 And Joseph answered Pharaoh, saying,
It is not in me: God shall give Pharaoh an
answer of peace.
17 And Pharaoh said unto Joseph, In my
dream, behold, I stood upon the bank of
the river:
18 And, behold, there came up out of
the river seven kine, fatfleshed and well
favoured; and they fed in a meadow:
19 And, behold, seven other kine came up
after them, poor and very ill favoured and
leanfleshed, such as I never saw in all the
land of Egypt for badness:
20 And the lean and the ill favoured kine
did eat up the first seven fat kine:
21 And when they had eaten them up, it
could not be known that they had eaten
them; but they *were* still ill favoured, as at
the beginning. So I awoke.
22 And I saw in my dream, and, behold,
seven ears came up in one stalk, full and
good:
23 And, behold, seven ears, withered, thin,
and blasted with the east wind, sprung up
after them:

24 And the thin ears devoured the seven
good ears: and I told *this* unto the magicians; but *there was* none that could declare
it to me.
25 ¶ And Joseph said unto Pharaoh, The
dream of Pharaoh *is* one: God hath shewed
Pharaoh what he *is* about to do.
26 The seven good kine *are* seven years;
and the seven good ears *are* seven years:
the dream *is* one.
27 And the seven thin and ill favoured kine
that came up after them *are* seven years;
and the seven empty ears blasted with the
east wind shall be seven years of famine.
28 This *is* the thing which I have spoken
unto Pharaoh: What God *is* about to do he
sheweth unto Pharaoh.
29 Behold, there come seven years of great
plenty throughout all the land of Egypt:
30 And there shall arise after them seven
years of famine; and all the plenty shall
be forgotten in the land of Egypt; and the
famine shall consume the land;
31 And the plenty shall not be known in the
land by reason of that famine following; for
it *shall be* very grievous.
32 And for that the dream was doubled
unto Pharaoh twice; *it is* because the thing
is established by God, and God will shortly
bring it to pass.
33 Now therefore let Pharaoh look out a
man discreet and wise, and set him over
the land of Egypt.
34 Let Pharaoh do *this*, and let him appoint
officers over the land, and take up the fifth
part of the land of Egypt in the seven plenteous years.
35 And let them gather all the food of those
good years that come, and lay up corn under
the hand of Pharaoh, and let them keep
food in the cities.
36 And that food shall be for store to the
land against the seven years of famine,
which shall be in the land of Egypt; that the
land perish not through the famine.
37 ¶ And the thing was good in the eyes of
Pharaoh, and in the eyes of all his servants.
38 And Pharaoh said unto his servants, Can
we find *such a one* as this *is*, a man in whom
the Spirit of God *is?*
39 And Pharaoh said unto Joseph, Forasmuch as God hath shewed thee all this, *there*
is none so discreet and wise as thou *art:*
40 Thou shalt be over my house, and according unto thy word shall all my people be
ruled: only in the throne will I be greater
than thou.
41 And Pharaoh said unto Joseph, See, I have
set thee over all the land of Egypt.
42 And Pharaoh took off his ring from his
hand, and put it upon Joseph's hand, and
arrayed him in vestures of fine linen, and
put a gold chain about his neck;
43 And he made him to ride in the second
chariot which he had; and they cried before
him, Bow the knee: and he made him *ruler*
over all the land of Egypt.
44 And Pharaoh said unto Joseph, I *am*
Pharaoh, and without thee shall no man lift
up his hand or foot in all the land of Egypt.
45 And Pharaoh called Joseph's name
Zaphnath-paaneah; and he gave him to
wife Asenath the daughter of Poti-pherah
priest of On. And Joseph went out over *all*
the land of Egypt.
46 ¶ And Joseph *was* thirty years old when
he stood before Pharaoh king of Egypt.
And Joseph went out from the presence
of Pharaoh, and went throughout all the
land of Egypt.
47 And in the seven plenteous years the
earth brought forth by handfuls.
48 And he gathered up all the food of the
seven years, which were in the land of Egypt,
and laid up the food in the cities: the food
of the field, which *was* round about every
city, laid he up in the same.
49 And Joseph gathered corn as the sand of
the sea, very much, until he left numbering;
for *it was* without number.
50 And unto Joseph were born two sons
before the years of famine came, which
Asenath the daughter of Poti-pherah priest
of On bare unto him.
51 And Joseph called the name of the
firstborn Manasseh: For God, *said he*, hath
made me forget all my toil, and all my
father's house.
52 And the name of the second called he
Ephraim: For God hath caused me to be
fruitful in the land of my affliction.
53 ¶ And the seven years of plenteousness,
that was in the land of Egypt, were ended.
54 And the seven years of dearth began to
come, according as Joseph had said: and the

dearth was in all lands; but in all the land of
Egypt there was bread.
55 And when all the land of Egypt was famished, the people cried to Pharaoh for bread:
and Pharaoh said unto all the Egyptians,
Go unto Joseph; what he saith to you, do.
56 And the famine was over all the face of
the earth: And Joseph opened all the storehouses, and sold unto the Egyptians; and
the famine waxed sore in the land of Egypt.
57 And all countries came into Egypt to
Joseph for to buy *corn;* because that the
famine was *so* sore in all lands.

Genesis 42

1 Now when Jacob saw that there was corn
in Egypt, Jacob said unto his sons, Why do
ye look one upon another?
2 And he said, Behold, I have heard that
there is corn in Egypt: get you down thither,
and buy for us from thence; that we may
live, and not die.
3 ¶ And Joseph's ten brethren went down
to buy corn in Egypt.
4 But Benjamin, Joseph's brother, Jacob
sent not with his brethren; for he said, Lest
peradventure mischief befall him.
5 And the sons of Israel came to buy *corn*
among those that came: for the famine was
in the land of Canaan.
6 And Joseph *was* the governor over the
land, *and* he *it was* that sold to all the people
of the land: and Joseph's brethren came, and
bowed down themselves before him *with*
their faces to the earth.
7 And Joseph saw his brethren, and he knew
them, but made himself strange unto them,
and spake roughly unto them; and he said
unto them, Whence come ye? And they
said, From the land of Canaan to buy food.
8 And Joseph knew his brethren, but they
knew not him.
9 And Joseph remembered the dreams
which he dreamed of them, and said unto
them, Ye *are* spies; to see the nakedness of
the land ye are come.
10 And they said unto him, Nay, my lord, but
to buy food are thy servants come.
11 We *are* all one man's sons; we *are* true
men, thy servants are no spies.
12 And he said unto them, Nay, but to see
the nakedness of the land ye are come.
13 And they said, Thy servants *are* twelve
brethren, the sons of one man in the land
of Canaan; and, behold, the youngest *is* this
day with our father, and one *is* not.
14 And Joseph said unto them, That *is it*
that I spake unto you, saying, Ye *are* spies:
15 Hereby ye shall be proved: By the life of
Pharaoh ye shall not go forth hence, except
your youngest brother come hither.
16 Send one of you, and let him fetch your
brother, and ye shall be kept in prison, that
your words may be proved, whether *there*
be any truth in you: or else by the life of
Pharaoh surely ye *are* spies.
17 And he put them all together into ward
three days.
18 And Joseph said unto them the third day,
This do, and live; *for* I fear God:
19 If ye *be* true *men*, let one of your brethren
be bound in the house of your prison: go ye,
carry corn for the famine of your houses:
20 But bring your youngest brother unto
me; so shall your words be verified, and ye
shall not die. And they did so.
21 ¶ And they said one to another, We *are*
verily guilty concerning our brother, in that
we saw the anguish of his soul, when he
besought us, and we would not hear; therefore is this distress come upon us.
22 And Reuben answered them, saying,
Spake I not unto you, saying, Do not sin
against the child; and ye would not hear?
therefore, behold, also his blood is required.
23 And they knew not that Joseph understood *them;* for he spake unto them by an
interpreter.
24 And he turned himself about from them,
and wept; and returned to them again, and
communed with them, and took from them
Simeon, and bound him before their eyes.
25 ¶ Then Joseph commanded to fill their
sacks with corn, and to restore every man's
money into his sack, and to give them provision for the way: and thus did he unto them.
26 And they laded their asses with the corn,
and departed thence.
27 And as one of them opened his sack to
give his ass provender in the inn, he espied
his money; for, behold, it *was* in his sack's
mouth.
28 And he said unto his brethren, My money
is restored; and, lo, *it is* even in my sack:
and their heart failed *them*, and they were

afraid, saying one to another, What *is* this
that God hath done unto us?
29 ¶ And they came unto Jacob their father
unto the land of Canaan, and told him all
that befell unto them; saying,
30 The man, *who is* the lord of the land,
spake roughly to us, and took us for spies
of the country.
31 And we said unto him, We *are* true *men;*
we are no spies:
32 We *be* twelve brethren, sons of our
father; one *is* not, and the youngest *is* this
day with our father in the land of Canaan.
33 And the man, the lord of the country,
said unto us, Hereby shall I know that ye
are true *men;* leave one of your brethren
here with me, and take *food for* the famine
of your households, and be gone:
34 And bring your youngest brother unto
me: then shall I know that ye *are* no spies,
but *that* ye *are* true *men: so* will I deliver you
your brother, and ye shall traffick in the land.
35 ¶ And it came to pass as they emptied
their sacks, that, behold, every man's bundle
of money *was* in his sack: and when *both*
they and their father saw the bundles of
money, they were afraid.
36 And Jacob their father said unto them,
Me have ye bereaved *of my children:* Joseph
is not, and Simeon *is* not, and ye will take
Benjamin *away:* all these things are against
me.
37 And Reuben spake unto his father, saying,
Slay my two sons, if I bring him not to thee:
deliver him into my hand, and I will bring
him to thee again.
38 And he said, My son shall not go down
with you; for his brother is dead, and he is
left alone: if mischief befall him by the way
in the which ye go, then shall ye bring down
my gray hairs with sorrow to the grave.

Genesis 43

1 And the famine *was* sore in the land.
2 And it came to pass, when they had eaten
up the corn which they had brought out of
Egypt, their father said unto them, Go again,
buy us a little food.
3 And Judah spake unto him, saying, The
man did solemnly protest unto us, saying,
Ye shall not see my face, except your brother
be with you.
4 If thou wilt send our brother with us, we
will go down and buy thee food:
5 But if thou wilt not send *him,* we will not
go down: for the man said unto us, Ye shall
not see my face, except your brother *be*
with you.
6 And Israel said, Wherefore dealt ye *so* ill
with me, *as* to tell the man whether ye had
yet a brother?
7 And they said, The man asked us straitly of
our state, and of our kindred, saying, *Is* your
father yet alive? have ye *another* brother?
and we told him according to the tenor of
these words: could we certainly know that
he would say, Bring your brother down?
8 And Judah said unto Israel his father, Send
the lad with me, and we will arise and go;
that we may live, and not die, both we, and
thou, *and* also our little ones.
9 I will be surety for him; of my hand shalt
thou require him: if I bring him not unto
thee, and set him before thee, then let me
bear the blame for ever:
10 For except we had lingered, surely now
we had returned this second time.
11 And their father Israel said unto them, If
it must be so now, do this; take of the best
fruits in the land in your vessels, and carry
down the man a present, a little balm, and
a little honey, spices, and myrrh, nuts, and
almonds:
12 And take double money in your hand; and
the money that was brought again in the
mouth of your sacks, carry *it* again in your
hand; peradventure it *was* an oversight:
13 Take also your brother, and arise, go again
unto the man:
14 And God Almighty give you mercy before
the man, that he may send away your other
brother, and Benjamin. If I be bereaved *of*
my children, I am bereaved.
15 ¶ And the men took that present, and
they took double money in their hand, and
Benjamin; and rose up, and went down to
Egypt, and stood before Joseph.
16 And when Joseph saw Benjamin with
them, he said to the ruler of his house, Bring
these men home, and slay, and make ready;
for *these* men shall dine with me at noon.
17 And the man did as Joseph bade; and the
man brought the men into Joseph's house.
18 And the men were afraid, because they
were brought into Joseph's house; and

they said, Because of the money that was
returned in our sacks at the first time are
we brought in; that he may seek occasion
against us, and fall upon us, and take us for
bondmen, and our asses.
19 And they came near to the steward of
Joseph's house, and they communed with
him at the door of the house,
20 And said, O sir, we came indeed down
at the first time to buy food:
21 And it came to pass, when we came to
the inn, that we opened our sacks, and,
behold, *every* man's money *was* in the
mouth of his sack, our money in full weight:
and we have brought it again in our hand.
22 And other money have we brought down
in our hands to buy food: we cannot tell who
put our money in our sacks.
23 And he said, Peace *be* to you, fear not:
your God, and the God of your father, hath
given you treasure in your sacks: I had
your money. And he brought Simeon out
unto them.
24 And the man brought the men into
Joseph's house, and gave *them* water, and
they washed their feet; and he gave their
asses provender.
25 And they made ready the present against
Joseph came at noon: for they heard that
they should eat bread there.
26 ¶ And when Joseph came home, they
brought him the present which *was* in their
hand into the house, and bowed themselves
to him to the earth.
27 And he asked them of *their* welfare, and
said, *Is* your father well, the old man of
whom ye spake? *Is* he yet alive?
28 And they answered, Thy servant our
father *is* in good health, he *is* yet alive. And
they bowed down their heads, and made
obeisance.
29 And he lifted up his eyes, and saw his
brother Benjamin, his mother's son, and
said, *Is* this your younger brother, of whom
ye spake unto me? And he said, God be
gracious unto thee, my son.
30 And Joseph made haste; for his bowels
did yearn upon his brother: and he sought
where to weep; and he entered into *his*
chamber, and wept there.
31 And he washed his face, and went out,
and refrained himself, and said, Set on
bread.
32 And they set on for him by himself, and
for them by themselves, and for the Egyptians, which did eat with him, by themselves:
because the Egyptians might not eat bread
with the Hebrews; for that *is* an abomination
unto the Egyptians.
33 And they sat before him, the firstborn
according to his birthright, and the youngest
according to his youth: and the men marvelled one at another.
34 And he took *and sent* messes unto them
from before him: but Benjamin's mess was
five times so much as any of theirs. And they
drank, and were merry with him.

Genesis 44

1 And he commanded the steward of his
house, saying, Fill the men's sacks *with* food,
as much as they can carry, and put every
man's money in his sack's mouth.
2 And put my cup, the silver cup, in the
sack's mouth of the youngest, and his corn
money. And he did according to the word
that Joseph had spoken.
3 As soon as the morning was light, the
men were sent away, they and their asses.
4 *And* when they were gone out of the city,
and not *yet* far off, Joseph said unto his
steward, Up, follow after the men; and when
thou dost overtake them, say unto them,
Wherefore have ye rewarded evil for good?
5 *Is* not this *it* in which my lord drinketh, and
whereby indeed he divineth? ye have done
evil in so doing.
6 ¶ And he overtook them, and he spake
unto them these same words.
7 And they said unto him, Wherefore saith
my lord these words? God forbid that thy
servants should do according to this thing:
8 Behold, the money, which we found in
our sacks' mouths, we brought again unto
thee out of the land of Canaan: how then
should we steal out of thy lord's house silver or gold?
9 With whomsoever of thy servants it be
found, both let him die, and we also will be
my lord's bondmen.
10 And he said, Now also *let* it *be* according unto your words: he with whom it is
found shall be my servant; and ye shall be
blameless.
11 Then they speedily took down every man

his sack to the ground, and opened every
man his sack.
12 And he searched, *and* began at the
eldest, and left at the youngest: and the
cup was found in Benjamin's sack.
13 Then they rent their clothes, and laded
every man his ass, and returned to the city.
14 ¶ And Judah and his brethren came to
Joseph's house; for he *was* yet there: and
they fell before him on the ground.
15 And Joseph said unto them, What deed
is this that ye have done? wot ye not that
such a man as I can certainly divine?
16 And Judah said, What shall we say unto
my lord? what shall we speak? or how shall
we clear ourselves? God hath found out the
iniquity of thy servants: behold, we *are* my
lord's servants, both we, and *he* also with
whom the cup is found.
17 And he said, God forbid that I should do
so: *but* the man in whose hand the cup is
found, he shall be my servant; and as for
you, get you up in peace unto your father.
18 ¶ Then Judah came near unto him, and
said, Oh my lord, let thy servant, I pray thee,
speak a word in my lord's ears, and let not
thine anger burn against thy servant: for
thou *art* even as Pharaoh.
19 My lord asked his servants, saying, Have
ye a father, or a brother?
20 And we said unto my lord, We have a
father, an old man, and a child of his old
age, a little one; and his brother is dead,
and he alone is left of his mother, and his
father loveth him.
21 And thou saidst unto thy servants, Bring
him down unto me, that I may set mine
eyes upon him.
22 And we said unto my lord, The lad cannot
leave his father: for *if* he should leave his
father, *his father* would die.
23 And thou saidst unto thy servants, Except
your youngest brother come down with you,
ye shall see my face no more.
24 And it came to pass when we came up
unto thy servant my father, we told him the
words of my lord.
25 And our father said, Go again, *and* buy
us a little food.
26 And we said, We cannot go down: if our
youngest brother be with us, then will we
go down: for we may not see the man's face,
except our youngest brother *be* with us.
27 And thy servant my father said unto us,
Ye know that my wife bare me two *sons:*
28 And the one went out from me, and I
said, Surely he is torn in pieces; and I saw
him not since:
29 And if ye take this also from me, and
mischief befall him, ye shall bring down my
gray hairs with sorrow to the grave.
30 Now therefore when I come to thy
servant my father, and the lad *be* not with
us; seeing that his life is bound up in the
lad's life;
31 It shall come to pass, when he seeth
that the lad *is* not *with us,* that he will die:
and thy servants shall bring down the gray
hairs of thy servant our father with sorrow
to the grave.
32 For thy servant became surety for the
lad unto my father, saying, If I bring him
not unto thee, then I shall bear the blame
to my father for ever.
33 Now therefore, I pray thee, let thy servant abide instead of the lad a bondman
to my lord; and let the lad go up with his
brethren.
34 For how shall I go up to my father, and
the lad *be* not with me? lest peradventure
I see the evil that shall come on my father.

Genesis 45

1 Then Joseph could not refrain himself
before all them that stood by him; and
he cried, Cause every man to go out from
me. And there stood no man with him,
while Joseph made himself known unto
his brethren.
2 And he wept aloud: and the Egyptians and
the house of Pharaoh heard.
3 And Joseph said unto his brethren, I *am*
Joseph; doth my father yet live? And his
brethren could not answer him; for they
were troubled at his presence.
4 And Joseph said unto his brethren, Come
near to me, I pray you. And they came near.
And he said, I *am* Joseph your brother,
whom ye sold into Egypt.
5 Now therefore be not grieved, nor angry
with yourselves, that ye sold me hither: for
God did send me before you to preserve life.
6 For these two years *hath* the famine *been*
in the land: and yet *there are* five years, in
the which *there shall* neither *be* earing nor
harvest.

7 And God sent me before you to preserve
you a posterity in the earth, and to save
your lives by a great deliverance.
8 So now *it was* not you *that* sent me hither,
but God: and he hath made me a father to
Pharaoh, and lord of all his house, and a
ruler throughout all the land of Egypt.
9 Haste ye, and go up to my father, and say
unto him, Thus saith thy son Joseph, God
hath made me lord of all Egypt: come down
unto me, tarry not:
10 And thou shalt dwell in the land of Goshen, and thou shalt be near unto me, thou,
and thy children, and thy children's children,
and thy flocks, and thy herds, and all that
thou hast:
11 And there will I nourish thee; for yet
there are five years of famine; lest thou,
and thy household, and all that thou hast,
come to poverty.
12 And, behold, your eyes see, and the eyes
of my brother Benjamin, that *it is* my mouth
that speaketh unto you.
13 And ye shall tell my father of all my glory
in Egypt, and of all that ye have seen; and ye
shall haste and bring down my father hither.
14 And he fell upon his brother Benjamin's
neck, and wept; and Benjamin wept upon
his neck.
15 Moreover he kissed all his brethren, and
wept upon them: and after that his brethren
talked with him.
16 ¶ And the fame thereof was heard in
Pharaoh's house, saying, Joseph's brethren
are come: and it pleased Pharaoh well, and
his servants.
17 And Pharaoh said unto Joseph, Say unto
thy brethren, This do ye; lade your beasts,
and go, get you unto the land of Canaan;
18 And take your father and your households, and come unto me: and I will give
you the good of the land of Egypt, and ye
shall eat the fat of the land.
19 Now thou art commanded, this do ye;
take you wagons out of the land of Egypt
for your little ones, and for your wives, and
bring your father, and come.
20 Also regard not your stuff; for the good
of all the land of Egypt *is* yours.
21 And the children of Israel did so: and
Joseph gave them wagons, according to the
commandment of Pharaoh, and gave them
provision for the way.
22 To all of them he gave each man changes
of raiment; but to Benjamin he gave three
hundred *pieces* of silver, and five changes
of raiment.
23 And to his father he sent after this *manner;* ten asses laden with the good things of
Egypt, and ten she asses laden with corn and
bread and meat for his father by the way.
24 So he sent his brethren away, and they
departed: and he said unto them, See that
ye fall not out by the way.
25 ¶ And they went up out of Egypt, and
came into the land of Canaan unto Jacob
their father,
26 And told him, saying, Joseph *is* yet alive,
and he *is* governor over all the land of Egypt.
And Jacob's heart fainted, for he believed
them not.
27 And they told him all the words of Joseph,
which he had said unto them: and when he
saw the wagons which Joseph had sent to
carry him, the spirit of Jacob their father
revived:
28 And Israel said, *It is* enough; Joseph
my son *is* yet alive: I will go and see him
before I die.

Genesis 46

1 And Israel took his journey with all that he
had, and came to Beer-sheba, and offered
sacrifices unto the God of his father Isaac.
2 And God spake unto Israel in the visions
of the night, and said, Jacob, Jacob. And he
said, Here *am* I.
3 And he said, I *am* God, the God of thy
father: fear not to go down into Egypt; for
I will there make of thee a great nation:
4 I will go down with thee into Egypt; and
I will also surely bring thee up *again:* and
Joseph shall put his hand upon thine eyes.
5 And Jacob rose up from Beer-sheba: and
the sons of Israel carried Jacob their father,
and their little ones, and their wives, in the
wagons which Pharaoh had sent to carry
him.
6 And they took their cattle, and their goods,
which they had gotten in the land of Canaan,
and came into Egypt, Jacob, and all his seed
with him:
7 His sons, and his sons' sons with him, his
daughters, and his sons' daughters, and all
his seed brought he with him into Egypt.
8 ¶ And these *are* the names of the children

of Israel, which came into Egypt, Jacob and
his sons: Reuben, Jacob's firstborn.
9 And the sons of Reuben; Hanoch, and
Phallu, and Hezron, and Carmi.
10 ¶ And the sons of Simeon; Jemuel, and
Jamin, and Ohad, and Jachin, and Zohar,
and Shaul the son of a Canaanitish woman.
11 ¶ And the sons of Levi; Gershon, Kohath,
and Merari.
12 ¶ And the sons of Judah; Er, and Onan,
and Shelah, and Pharez, and Zerah: but Er
and Onan died in the land of Canaan. And
the sons of Pharez were Hezron and Hamul.
13 ¶ And the sons of Issachar; Tola, and
Phuvah, and Job, and Shimron.
14 ¶ And the sons of Zebulun; Sered, and
Elon, and Jahleel.
15 These *be* the sons of Leah, which she
bare unto Jacob in Padan-aram, with his
daughter Dinah: all the souls of his sons and
his daughters *were* thirty and three.
16 ¶ And the sons of Gad; Ziphion, and
Haggi, Shuni, and Ezbon, Eri, and Arodi,
and Areli.
17 ¶ And the sons of Asher; Jimnah, and
Ishuah, and Isui, and Beriah, and Serah
their sister: and the sons of Beriah; Heber,
and Malchiel.
18 These *are* the sons of Zilpah, whom Laban
gave to Leah his daughter, and these she
bare unto Jacob, *even* sixteen souls.
19 The sons of Rachel Jacob's wife; Joseph,
and Benjamin.
20 ¶ And unto Joseph in the land of Egypt
were born Manasseh and Ephraim, which
Asenath the daughter of Poti-pherah priest
of On bare unto him.
21 ¶ And the sons of Benjamin *were* Belah,
and Becher, and Ashbel, Gera, and Naaman,
Ehi, and Rosh, Muppim, and Huppim, and
Ard.
22 These *are* the sons of Rachel, which were
born to Jacob: all the souls *were* fourteen.
23 ¶ And the sons of Dan; Hushim.
24 ¶ And the sons of Naphtali; Jahzeel, and
Guni, and Jezer, and Shillem.
25 These *are* the sons of Bilhah, which Laban
gave unto Rachel his daughter, and she bare
these unto Jacob: all the souls *were* seven.
26 All the souls that came with Jacob into
Egypt, which came out of his loins, besides
Jacob's sons' wives, all the souls *were* threescore and six;
27 And the sons of Joseph, which were born
him in Egypt, *were* two souls: all the souls of
the house of Jacob, which came into Egypt,
were threescore and ten.
28 ¶ And he sent Judah before him unto
Joseph, to direct his face unto Goshen; and
they came into the land of Goshen.
29 And Joseph made ready his chariot, and
went up to meet Israel his father, to Goshen, and presented himself unto him; and
he fell on his neck, and wept on his neck a
good while.
30 And Israel said unto Joseph, Now let me
die, since I have seen thy face, because thou
art yet alive.
31 And Joseph said unto his brethren, and
unto his father's house, I will go up, and
shew Pharaoh, and say unto him, My brethren, and my father's house, which *were* in
the land of Canaan, are come unto me;
32 And the men *are* shepherds, for their
trade hath been to feed cattle; and they
have brought their flocks, and their herds,
and all that they have.
33 And it shall come to pass, when Pharaoh
shall call you, and shall say, What *is* your
occupation?
34 That ye shall say, Thy servants' trade
hath been about cattle from our youth even
until now, both we, *and* also our fathers:
that ye may dwell in the land of Goshen;
for every shepherd *is* an abomination unto
the Egyptians.

Genesis 47

1 Then Joseph came and told Pharaoh, and
said, My father and my brethren, and their
flocks, and their herds, and all that they
have, are come out of the land of Canaan;
and, behold, they *are* in the land of Goshen.
2 And he took some of his brethren, *even*
five men, and presented them unto Pharaoh.
3 And Pharaoh said unto his brethren, What
is your occupation? And they said unto Pharaoh, Thy servants *are* shepherds, both we,
and also our fathers.
4 They said moreover unto Pharaoh, For
to sojourn in the land are we come; for thy
servants have no pasture for their flocks; for
the famine *is* sore in the land of Canaan: now
therefore, we pray thee, let thy servants
dwell in the land of Goshen.

5 And Pharaoh spake unto Joseph, saying,
Thy father and thy brethren are come unto
thee:
6 The land of Egypt *is* before thee; in the
best of the land make thy father and brethren to dwell; in the land of Goshen let
them dwell: and if thou knowest *any* men
of activity among them, then make them
rulers over my cattle.
7 And Joseph brought in Jacob his father,
and set him before Pharaoh: and Jacob
blessed Pharaoh.
8 And Pharaoh said unto Jacob, How old
art thou?
9 And Jacob said unto Pharaoh, The days of
the years of my pilgrimage *are* an hundred
and thirty years: few and evil have the days
of the years of my life been, and have not
attained unto the days of the years of the life
of my fathers in the days of their pilgrimage.
10 And Jacob blessed Pharaoh, and went
out from before Pharaoh.
11 ¶ And Joseph placed his father and his
brethren, and gave them a possession in
the land of Egypt, in the best of the land,
in the land of Rameses, as Pharaoh had
commanded.
12 And Joseph nourished his father, and his
brethren, and all his father's household, with
bread, according to *their* families.
13 ¶ And *there was* no bread in all the land;
for the famine *was* very sore, so that the
land of Egypt and *all* the land of Canaan
fainted by reason of the famine.
14 And Joseph gathered up all the money
that was found in the land of Egypt, and in
the land of Canaan, for the corn which they
bought: and Joseph brought the money into
Pharaoh's house.
15 And when money failed in the land of
Egypt, and in the land of Canaan, all the
Egyptians came unto Joseph, and said,
Give us bread: for why should we die in thy
presence? for the money faileth.
16 And Joseph said, Give your cattle; and I
will give you for your cattle, if money fail.
17 And they brought their cattle unto
Joseph: and Joseph gave them bread *in*
exchange for horses, and for the flocks,
and for the cattle of the herds, and for the
asses: and he fed them with bread for all
their cattle for that year.
18 When that year was ended, they came
unto him the second year, and said unto
him, We will not hide *it* from my lord, how
that our money is spent; my lord also hath
our herds of cattle; there is not ought left
in the sight of my lord, but our bodies, and
our lands:
19 Wherefore shall we die before thine
eyes, both we and our land? buy us and our
land for bread, and we and our land will be
servants unto Pharaoh: and give *us* seed,
that we may live, and not die, that the land
be not desolate.
20 And Joseph bought all the land of Egypt
for Pharaoh; for the Egyptians sold every
man his field, because the famine prevailed
over them: so the land became Pharaoh's.
21 And as for the people, he removed them
to cities from *one* end of the borders of
Egypt even to the *other* end thereof.
22 Only the land of the priests bought he
not; for the priests had a portion *assigned*
them of Pharaoh, and did eat their portion
which Pharaoh gave them: wherefore they
sold not their lands.
23 Then Joseph said unto the people,
Behold, I have bought you this day and
your land for Pharaoh: lo, *here is* seed for
you, and ye shall sow the land.
24 And it shall come to pass in the increase,
that ye shall give the fifth *part* unto Pharaoh,
and four parts shall be your own, for seed
of the field, and for your food, and for them
of your households, and for food for your
little ones.
25 And they said, Thou hast saved our lives:
let us find grace in the sight of my lord, and
we will be Pharaoh's servants.
26 And Joseph made it a law over the land
of Egypt unto this day, *that* Pharaoh should
have the fifth *part;* except the land of the
priests only, *which* became not Pharaoh's.
27 ¶ And Israel dwelt in the land of Egypt,
in the country of Goshen; and they had possessions therein, and grew, and multiplied
exceedingly.
28 And Jacob lived in the land of Egypt seventeen years: so the whole age of Jacob was
an hundred forty and seven years.
29 And the time drew nigh that Israel must
die: and he called his son Joseph, and said
unto him, If now I have found grace in thy
sight, put, I pray thee, thy hand under my

thigh, and deal kindly and truly with me;
bury me not, I pray thee, in Egypt:
30 But I will lie with my fathers, and thou
shalt carry me out of Egypt, and bury me
in their buryingplace. And he said, I will do
as thou hast said.
31 And he said, Swear unto me. And he
sware unto him. And Israel bowed himself
upon the bed's head.

Genesis 48

1 And it came to pass after these things,
that *one* told Joseph, Behold, thy father
is sick: and he took with him his two sons,
Manasseh and Ephraim.
2 And *one* told Jacob, and said, Behold, thy
son Joseph cometh unto thee: and Israel
strengthened himself, and sat upon the bed.
3 And Jacob said unto Joseph, God Almighty
appeared unto me at Luz in the land of
Canaan, and blessed me,
4 And said unto me, Behold, I will make
thee fruitful, and multiply thee, and I will
make of thee a multitude of people; and
will give this land to thy seed after thee *for*
an everlasting possession.
5 ¶ And now thy two sons, Ephraim and
Manasseh, which were born unto thee in
the land of Egypt before I came unto thee
into Egypt, *are* mine; as Reuben and Simeon,
they shall be mine.
6 And thy issue, which thou begettest after
them, shall be thine, *and* shall be called
after the name of their brethren in their
inheritance.
7 And as for me, when I came from Padan,
Rachel died by me in the land of Canaan
in the way, when yet *there was* but a little
way to come unto Ephrath: and I buried
her there in the way of Ephrath; the same
is Beth-lehem.
8 And Israel beheld Joseph's sons, and said,
Who *are* these?
9 And Joseph said unto his father, They *are*
my sons, whom God hath given me in this
place. And he said, Bring them, I pray thee,
unto me, and I will bless them.
10 Now the eyes of Israel were dim for age,
so that he could not see. And he brought
them near unto him; and he kissed them,
and embraced them.
11 And Israel said unto Joseph, I had not
thought to see thy face: and, lo, God hath
shewed me also thy seed.
12 And Joseph brought them out from
between his knees, and he bowed himself
with his face to the earth.
13 And Joseph took them both, Ephraim in
his right hand toward Israel's left hand, and
Manasseh in his left hand toward Israel's
right hand, and brought *them* near unto him.
14 And Israel stretched out his right hand,
and laid *it* upon Ephraim's head, who
was the younger, and his left hand upon
Manasseh's head, guiding his hands wit-
tingly; for Manasseh *was* the firstborn.
15 ¶ And he blessed Joseph, and said, God,
before whom my fathers Abraham and Isaac
did walk, the God which fed me all my life
long unto this day,
16 The Angel which redeemed me from
all evil, bless the lads; and let my name be
named on them, and the name of my fathers
Abraham and Isaac; and let them grow into
a multitude in the midst of the earth.
17 And when Joseph saw that his father laid
his right hand upon the head of Ephraim, it
displeased him: and he held up his father's
hand, to remove it from Ephraim's head
unto Manasseh's head.
18 And Joseph said unto his father, Not so,
my father: for this *is* the firstborn; put thy
right hand upon his head.
19 And his father refused, and said, I know
it, my son, I know *it:* he also shall become a
people, and he also shall be great: but truly
his younger brother shall be greater than
he, and his seed shall become a multitude
of nations.
20 And he blessed them that day, saying,
In thee shall Israel bless, saying, God make
thee as Ephraim and as Manasseh: and he
set Ephraim before Manasseh.
21 And Israel said unto Joseph, Behold, I die:
but God shall be with you, and bring you
again unto the land of your fathers.
22 Moreover I have given to thee one portion above thy brethren, which I took out
of the hand of the Amorite with my sword
and with my bow.

Genesis 49

1 And Jacob called unto his sons, and said,
Gather yourselves together, that I may tell
you *that* which shall befall you in the last days.

2 Gather yourselves together, and hear, ye sons of Jacob; and hearken unto Israel your father.

3 ¶ Reuben, thou *art* my firstborn, my might, and the beginning of my strength, the excellency of dignity, and the excellency of power:

4 Unstable as water, thou shalt not excel; because thou wentest up to thy father's bed; then defiledst thou *it:* he went up to my couch.

5 ¶ Simeon and Levi *are* brethren; instruments of cruelty *are in* their habitations.

6 O my soul, come not thou into their secret; unto their assembly, mine honour, be not thou united: for in their anger they slew a man, and in their selfwill they digged down a wall.

7 Cursed *be* their anger, for *it was* fierce; and their wrath, for it was cruel: I will divide them in Jacob, and scatter them in Israel.

8 ¶ Judah, thou *art he* whom thy brethren shall praise: thy hand *shall be* in the neck of thine enemies; thy father's children shall bow down before thee.

9 Judah *is* a lion's whelp: from the prey, my son, thou art gone up: he stooped down, he couched as a lion, and as an old lion; who shall rouse him up?

10 The sceptre shall not depart from Judah, nor a lawgiver from between his feet, until Shiloh come; and unto him *shall* the gathering of the people *be.*

11 Binding his foal unto the vine, and his ass's colt unto the choice vine; he washed his garments in wine, and his clothes in the blood of grapes:

12 His eyes *shall be* red with wine, and his teeth white with milk.

13 ¶ Zebulun shall dwell at the haven of the sea; and he *shall be* for an haven of ships; and his border *shall be* unto Zidon.

14 ¶ Issachar *is* a strong ass couching down between two burdens:

15 And he saw that rest *was* good, and the land that *it was* pleasant; and bowed his shoulder to bear, and became a servant unto tribute.

16 ¶ Dan shall judge his people, as one of the tribes of Israel.

17 Dan shall be a serpent by the way, an adder in the path, that biteth the horse heels, so that his rider shall fall backward.

18 I have waited for thy salvation, O LORD.

19 ¶ Gad, a troop shall overcome him: but he shall overcome at the last.

20 ¶ Out of Asher his bread *shall be* fat, and he shall yield royal dainties.

21 ¶ Naphtali *is* a hind let loose: he giveth goodly words.

22 ¶ Joseph *is* a fruitful bough, *even* a fruitful bough by a well; *whose* branches run over the wall:

23 The archers have sorely grieved him, and shot *at him,* and hated him:

24 But his bow abode in strength, and the arms of his hands were made strong by the hands of the mighty *God* of Jacob; (from thence *is* the shepherd, the stone of Israel:)

25 *Even* by the God of thy father, who shall help thee; and by the Almighty, who shall bless thee with blessings of heaven above, blessings of the deep that lieth under, blessings of the breasts, and of the womb:

26 The blessings of thy father have prevailed above the blessings of my progenitors unto the utmost bound of the everlasting hills: they shall be on the head of Joseph, and on the crown of the head of him that was separate from his brethren.

27 ¶ Benjamin shall ravin *as* a wolf: in the morning he shall devour the prey, and at night he shall divide the spoil.

28 ¶ All these *are* the twelve tribes of Israel: and this *is it* that their father spake unto them, and blessed them; every one according to his blessing he blessed them.

29 And he charged them, and said unto them, I am to be gathered unto my people: bury me with my fathers in the cave that *is* in the field of Ephron the Hittite,

30 In the cave that *is* in the field of Machpelah, which *is* before Mamre, in the land of Canaan, which Abraham bought with the field of Ephron the Hittite for a possession of a buryingplace.

31 There they buried Abraham and Sarah his wife; there they buried Isaac and Rebekah his wife; and there I buried Leah.

32 The purchase of the field and of the cave that *is* therein *was* from the children of Heth.

33 And when Jacob had made an end of commanding his sons, he gathered up his feet into the bed, and yielded up the ghost, and was gathered unto his people.

Genesis 50

1 And Joseph fell upon his father's face, and
wept upon him, and kissed him.
2 And Joseph commanded his servants the
physicians to embalm his father: and the
physicians embalmed Israel.
3 And forty days were fulfilled for him; for
so are fulfilled the days of those which are
embalmed: and the Egyptians mourned for
him threescore and ten days.
4 And when the days of his mourning were
past, Joseph spake unto the house of Pharaoh, saying, If now I have found grace in
your eyes, speak, I pray you, in the ears of
Pharaoh, saying,
5 My father made me swear, saying, Lo, I
die: in my grave which I have digged for me
in the land of Canaan, there shalt thou bury
me. Now therefore let me go up, I pray thee,
and bury my father, and I will come again.
6 And Pharaoh said, Go up, and bury thy
father, according as he made thee swear.
7 ¶ And Joseph went up to bury his father:
and with him went up all the servants of
Pharaoh, the elders of his house, and all
the elders of the land of Egypt,
8 And all the house of Joseph, and his brethren, and his father's house: only their little
ones, and their flocks, and their herds, they
left in the land of Goshen.
9 And there went up with him both chariots and horsemen: and it was a very great
company.
10 And they came to the threshingfloor of
Atad, which *is* beyond Jordan, and there
they mourned with a great and very sore
lamentation: and he made a mourning for
his father seven days.
11 And when the inhabitants of the land,
the Canaanites, saw the mourning in the
floor of Atad, they said, This *is* a grievous
mourning to the Egyptians: wherefore the
name of it was called Abel-mizraim, which
is beyond Jordan.
12 And his sons did unto him according as
he commanded them:
13 For his sons carried him into the land of
Canaan, and buried him in the cave of the
field of Machpelah, which Abraham bought
with the field for a possession of a buryingplace of Ephron the Hittite, before Mamre.
14 ¶ And Joseph returned into Egypt, he,
and his brethren, and all that went up with
him to bury his father, after he had buried
his father.
15 ¶ And when Joseph's brethren saw that
their father was dead, they said, Joseph will
peradventure hate us, and will certainly
requite us all the evil which we did unto him.
16 And they sent a messenger unto Joseph,
saying, Thy father did command before he
died, saying,
17 So shall ye say unto Joseph, Forgive, I
pray thee now, the trespass of thy brethren,
and their sin; for they did unto thee evil: and
now, we pray thee, forgive the trespass of
the servants of the God of thy father. And
Joseph wept when they spake unto him.
18 And his brethren also went and fell down
before his face; and they said, Behold, we
be thy servants.
19 And Joseph said unto them, Fear not: for
am I in the place of God?
20 But as for you, ye thought evil against me;
but God meant it unto good, to bring to pass,
as *it is* this day, to save much people alive.
21 Now therefore fear ye not: I will nourish
you, and your little ones. And he comforted
them, and spake kindly unto them.
22 ¶ And Joseph dwelt in Egypt, he, and his
father's house: and Joseph lived an hundred
and ten years.
23 And Joseph saw Ephraim's children of
the third *generation:* the children also of
Machir the son of Manasseh were brought
up upon Joseph's knees.
24 And Joseph said unto his brethren, I
die: and God will surely visit you, and bring
you out of this land unto the land which he
sware to Abraham, to Isaac, and to Jacob.
25 And Joseph took an oath of the children
of Israel, saying, God will surely visit you,
and ye shall carry up my bones from hence.
26 So Joseph died, *being* an hundred and
ten years old: and they embalmed him, and
he was put in a coffin in Egypt.

The Second Book Of Moses Called

Exodus

Exodus 1

1 Now these *are* the names of the children
of Israel, which came into Egypt; every man
and his household came with Jacob.
2 Reuben, Simeon, Levi, and Judah,
3 Issachar, Zebulun, and Benjamin,
4 Dan, and Naphtali, Gad, and Asher.
5 And all the souls that came out of the loins
of Jacob were seventy souls: for Joseph was
in Egypt *already*.
6 And Joseph died, and all his brethren, and
all that generation.
7 ¶ And the children of Israel were fruitful,
and increased abundantly, and multiplied,
and waxed exceeding mighty; and the land
was filled with them.
8 Now there arose up a new king over Egypt,
which knew not Joseph.
9 And he said unto his people, Behold, the
people of the children of Israel *are* more
and mightier than we:
10 Come on, let us deal wisely with them;
lest they multiply, and it come to pass, that,
when there falleth out any war, they join
also unto our enemies, and fight against us,
and *so* get them up out of the land.
11 Therefore they did set over them taskmasters to afflict them with their burdens.
And they built for Pharaoh treasure cities,
Pithom and Raamses.
12 But the more they afflicted them, the
more they multiplied and grew. And they
were grieved because of the children of
Israel.
13 And the Egyptians made the children of
Israel to serve with rigour:
14 And they made their lives bitter with
hard bondage, in morter, and in brick, and
in all manner of service in the field: all their
service, wherein they made them serve,
was with rigour.
15 ¶ And the king of Egypt spake to the
Hebrew midwives, of which the name of
the one *was* Shiphrah, and the name of
the other Puah:
16 And he said, When ye do the office of
a midwife to the Hebrew women, and see
them upon the stools; if it *be* a son, then ye
shall kill him: but if it *be* a daughter, then
she shall live.
17 But the midwives feared God, and did
not as the king of Egypt commanded them,
but saved the men children alive.
18 And the king of Egypt called for the
midwives, and said unto them, Why have
ye done this thing, and have saved the men
children alive?
19 And the midwives said unto Pharaoh,
Because the Hebrew women *are* not as
the Egyptian women; for they *are* lively,
and are delivered ere the midwives come
in unto them.
20 Therefore God dealt well with the midwives: and the people multiplied, and waxed
very mighty.
21 And it came to pass, because the midwives feared God, that he made them
houses.
22 And Pharaoh charged all his people,
saying, Every son that is born ye shall cast
into the river, and every daughter ye shall
save alive.

Exodus 2

1 And there went a man of the house of
Levi, and took *to wife* a daughter of Levi.
2 And the woman conceived, and bare a son:
and when she saw him that he *was a* goodly
child, she hid him three months.
3 And when she could not longer hide him,
she took for him an ark of bulrushes, and
daubed it with slime and with pitch, and put
the child therein; and she laid *it* in the flags
by the river's brink.
4 And his sister stood afar off, to wit what
would be done to him.
5 ¶ And the daughter of Pharaoh came
down to wash *herself* at the river; and her
maidens walked along by the river's side;
and when she saw the ark among the flags,
she sent her maid to fetch it.
6 And when she had opened *it*, she saw the
child: and, behold, the babe wept. And she

had compassion on him, and said, This *is*
one of the Hebrews' children.
7 Then said his sister to Pharaoh's daughter, Shall I go and call to thee a nurse of the
Hebrew women, that she may nurse the
child for thee?
8 And Pharaoh's daughter said to her, Go.
And the maid went and called the child's
mother.
9 And Pharaoh's daughter said unto her,
Take this child away, and nurse it for me, and
I will give *thee* thy wages. And the woman
took the child, and nursed it.
10 And the child grew, and she brought him
unto Pharaoh's daughter, and he became
her son. And she called his name Moses:
and she said, Because I drew him out of
the water.
11 ¶ And it came to pass in those days, when
Moses was grown, that he went out unto
his brethren, and looked on their burdens:
and he spied an Egyptian smiting an Hebrew,
one of his brethren.
12 And he looked this way and that way,
and when he saw that *there was* no man, he
slew the Egyptian, and hid him in the sand.
13 And when he went out the second day,
behold, two men of the Hebrews strove
together: and he said to him that did the
wrong, Wherefore smitest thou thy fellow?
14 And he said, Who made thee a prince and
a judge over us? intendest thou to kill me,
as thou killedst the Egyptian? And Moses
feared, and said, Surely this thing is known.
15 Now when Pharaoh heard this thing, he
sought to slay Moses. But Moses fled from
the face of Pharaoh, and dwelt in the land
of Midian: and he sat down by a well.
16 Now the priest of Midian had seven
daughters: and they came and drew *water*,
and filled the troughs to water their father's
flock.
17 And the shepherds came and drove them
away: but Moses stood up and helped them,
and watered their flock.
18 And when they came to Reuel their
father, he said, How *is it that* ye are come
so soon to day?
19 And they said, An Egyptian delivered us
out of the hand of the shepherds, and also
drew *water* enough for us, and watered
the flock.
20 And he said unto his daughters, And
where *is* he? why *is* it *that* ye have left the
man? call him, that he may eat bread.
21 And Moses was content to dwell with
the man: and he gave Moses Zipporah his
daughter.
22 And she bare *him* a son, and he called
his name Gershom: for he said, I have been
a stranger in a strange land.
23 ¶ And it came to pass in process of time,
that the king of Egypt died: and the children
of Israel sighed by reason of the bondage,
and they cried, and their cry came up unto
God by reason of the bondage.
24 And God heard their groaning, and God
remembered his covenant with Abraham,
with Isaac, and with Jacob.
25 And God looked upon the children of
Israel, and God had respect unto *them*.

Exodus 3

1 Now Moses kept the flock of Jethro his
father in law, the priest of Midian: and he
led the flock to the backside of the desert,
and came to the mountain of God, *even*
to Horeb.
2 And the angel of the LORD appeared unto
him in a flame of fire out of the midst of
a bush: and he looked, and, behold, the
bush burned with fire, and the bush *was*
not consumed.
3 And Moses said, I will now turn aside,
and see this great sight, why the bush is
not burnt.
4 And when the LORD saw that he turned
aside to see, God called unto him out of the
midst of the bush, and said, Moses, Moses.
And he said, Here *am* I.
5 And he said, Draw not nigh hither: put off
thy shoes from off thy feet, for the place
whereon thou standest *is* holy ground.
6 Moreover he said, I *am* the God of thy
father, the God of Abraham, the God of
Isaac, and the God of Jacob. And Moses hid
his face; for he was afraid to look upon God.
7 ¶ And the LORD said, I have surely seen the
affliction of my people which *are* in Egypt,
and have heard their cry by reason of their
taskmasters; for I know their sorrows;
8 And I am come down to deliver them out
of the hand of the Egyptians, and to bring
them up out of that land unto a good land
and a large, unto a land flowing with milk
and honey; unto the place of the Canaanites,

and the Hittites, and the Amorites, and the
Perizzites, and the Hivites, and the Jebusites.
9 Now therefore, behold, the cry of the
children of Israel is come unto me: and I
have also seen the oppression wherewith
the Egyptians oppress them.
10 Come now therefore, and I will send thee
unto Pharaoh, that thou mayest bring forth
my people the children of Israel out of Egypt.
11 ¶ And Moses said unto God, Who *am*
I, that I should go unto Pharaoh, and that
I should bring forth the children of Israel
out of Egypt?
12 And he said, Certainly I will be with thee;
and this *shall be* a token unto thee, that I
have sent thee: When thou hast brought
forth the people out of Egypt, ye shall serve
God upon this mountain.
13 And Moses said unto God, Behold, *when*
I come unto the children of Israel, and shall
say unto them, The God of your fathers
hath sent me unto you; and they shall say
to me, What *is* his name? what shall I say
unto them?
14 And God said unto Moses, I AM THAT I
AM: and he said, Thus shalt thou say unto
the children of Israel, I AM hath sent me
unto you.
15 And God said moreover unto Moses,
Thus shalt thou say unto the children of
Israel, The LORD God of your fathers, the
God of Abraham, the God of Isaac, and the
God of Jacob, hath sent me unto you: this *is*
my name for ever, and this *is* my memorial
unto all generations.
16 Go, and gather the elders of Israel
together, and say unto them, The LORD
God of your fathers, the God of Abraham,
of Isaac, and of Jacob, appeared unto me,
saying, I have surely visited you, and *seen*
that which is done to you in Egypt:
17 And I have said, I will bring you up out
of the affliction of Egypt unto the land of
the Canaanites, and the Hittites, and the
Amorites, and the Perizzites, and the Hivites,
and the Jebusites, unto a land flowing with
milk and honey.
18 And they shall hearken to thy voice: and
thou shalt come, thou and the elders of
Israel, unto the king of Egypt, and ye shall
say unto him, The LORD God of the Hebrews
hath met with us: and now let us go, we
beseech thee, three days' journey into the
wilderness, that we may sacrifice to the
LORD our God.
19 ¶ And I am sure that the king of Egypt
will not let you go, no, not by a mighty hand.
20 And I will stretch out my hand, and smite
Egypt with all my wonders which I will do
in the midst thereof: and after that he will
let you go.
21 And I will give this people favour in the
sight of the Egyptians: and it shall come
to pass, that, when ye go, ye shall not go
empty:
22 But every woman shall borrow of her
neighbour, and of her that sojourneth in her
house, jewels of silver, and jewels of gold,
and raiment: and ye shall put *them* upon
your sons, and upon your daughters; and
ye shall spoil the Egyptians.

Exodus 4

1 And Moses answered and said, But,
behold, they will not believe me, nor hearken unto my voice: for they will say, The
LORD hath not appeared unto thee.
2 And the LORD said unto him, What *is* that
in thine hand? And he said, A rod.
3 And he said, Cast it on the ground. And
he cast it on the ground, and it became a
serpent; and Moses fled from before it.
4 And the LORD said unto Moses, Put forth
thine hand, and take it by the tail. And he
put forth his hand, and caught it, and it
became a rod in his hand:
5 That they may believe that the LORD God
of their fathers, the God of Abraham, the
God of Isaac, and the God of Jacob, hath
appeared unto thee.
6 ¶ And the LORD said furthermore unto
him, Put now thine hand into thy bosom.
And he put his hand into his bosom: and
when he took it out, behold, his hand *was*
leprous as snow.
7 And he said, Put thine hand into thy
bosom again. And he put his hand into
his bosom again; and plucked it out of his
bosom, and, behold, it was turned again as
his *other* flesh.
8 And it shall come to pass, if they will not
believe thee, neither hearken to the voice
of the first sign, that they will believe the
voice of the latter sign.
9 And it shall come to pass, if they will not
believe also these two signs, neither hear-

ken unto thy voice, that thou shalt take of the water of the river, and pour *it* upon the dry *land:* and the water which thou takest out of the river shall become blood upon the dry *land*.

10 ¶ And Moses said unto the LORD, O my Lord, I *am* not eloquent, neither heretofore, nor since thou hast spoken unto thy servant: but I *am* slow of speech, and of a slow tongue.

11 And the LORD said unto him, Who hath made man's mouth? or who maketh the dumb, or deaf, or the seeing, or the blind? have not I the LORD?

12 Now therefore go, and I will be with thy mouth, and teach thee what thou shalt say.

13 And he said, O my Lord, send, I pray thee, by the hand *of him whom* thou wilt send.

14 And the anger of the LORD was kindled against Moses, and he said, *Is* not Aaron the Levite thy brother? I know that he can speak well. And also, behold, he cometh forth to meet thee: and when he seeth thee, he will be glad in his heart.

15 And thou shalt speak unto him, and put words in his mouth: and I will be with thy mouth, and with his mouth, and will teach you what ye shall do.

16 And he shall be thy spokesman unto the people: and he shall be, *even* he shall be to thee instead of a mouth, and thou shalt be to him instead of God.

17 And thou shalt take this rod in thine hand, wherewith thou shalt do signs.

18 ¶ And Moses went and returned to Jethro his father in law, and said unto him, Let me go, I pray thee, and return unto my brethren which *are* in Egypt, and see whether they be yet alive. And Jethro said to Moses, Go in peace.

19 And the LORD said unto Moses in Midian, Go, return into Egypt: for all the men are dead which sought thy life.

20 And Moses took his wife and his sons, and set them upon an ass, and he returned to the land of Egypt: and Moses took the rod of God in his hand.

21 And the LORD said unto Moses, When thou goest to return into Egypt, see that thou do all those wonders before Pharaoh, which I have put in thine hand: but I will harden his heart, that he shall not let the people go.

22 And thou shalt say unto Pharaoh, Thus saith the LORD, Israel *is* my son, *even* my firstborn:

23 And I say unto thee, Let my son go, that he may serve me: and if thou refuse to let him go, behold, I will slay thy son, *even* thy firstborn.

24 ¶ And it came to pass by the way in the inn, that the LORD met him, and sought to kill him.

25 Then Zipporah took a sharp stone, and cut off the foreskin of her son, and cast *it* at his feet, and said, Surely a bloody husband *art* thou to me.

26 So he let him go: then she said, A bloody husband *thou art*, because of the circumcision.

27 ¶ And the LORD said to Aaron, Go into the wilderness to meet Moses. And he went, and met him in the mount of God, and kissed him.

28 And Moses told Aaron all the words of the LORD who had sent him, and all the signs which he had commanded him.

29 ¶ And Moses and Aaron went and gathered together all the elders of the children of Israel:

30 And Aaron spake all the words which the LORD had spoken unto Moses, and did the signs in the sight of the people.

31 And the people believed: and when they heard that the LORD had visited the children of Israel, and that he had looked upon their affliction, then they bowed their heads and worshipped.

Exodus 5

1 And afterward Moses and Aaron went in, and told Pharaoh, Thus saith the LORD God of Israel, Let my people go, that they may hold a feast unto me in the wilderness.

2 And Pharaoh said, Who *is* the LORD, that I should obey his voice to let Israel go? I know not the LORD, neither will I let Israel go.

3 And they said, The God of the Hebrews hath met with us: let us go, we pray thee, three days' journey into the desert, and sacrifice unto the LORD our God; lest he fall upon us with pestilence, or with the sword.

4 And the king of Egypt said unto them, Wherefore do ye, Moses and Aaron, let the people from their works? get you unto your burdens.

5 And Pharaoh said, Behold, the people of the land now *are* many, and ye make them rest from their burdens.

6 And Pharaoh commanded the same day the taskmasters of the people, and their officers, saying,

7 Ye shall no more give the people straw to make brick, as heretofore: let them go and gather straw for themselves.

8 And the tale of the bricks, which they did make heretofore, ye shall lay upon them; ye shall not diminish *ought* thereof: for they *be* idle; therefore they cry, saying, Let us go *and* sacrifice to our God.

9 Let there more work be laid upon the men, that they may labour therein; and let them not regard vain words.

10 ¶ And the taskmasters of the people went out, and their officers, and they spake to the people, saying, Thus saith Pharaoh, I will not give you straw.

11 Go ye, get you straw where ye can find it: yet not ought of your work shall be diminished.

12 So the people were scattered abroad throughout all the land of Egypt to gather stubble instead of straw.

13 And the taskmasters hasted *them*, saying, Fulfil your works, *your* daily tasks, as when there was straw.

14 And the officers of the children of Israel, which Pharaoh's taskmasters had set over them, were beaten, *and* demanded, Wherefore have ye not fulfilled your task in making brick both yesterday and to day, as heretofore?

15 ¶ Then the officers of the children of Israel came and cried unto Pharaoh, saying, Wherefore dealest thou thus with thy servants?

16 There is no straw given unto thy servants, and they say to us, Make brick: and, behold, thy servants *are* beaten; but the fault *is* in thine own people.

17 But he said, Ye *are* idle, *ye are* idle: therefore ye say, Let us go *and* do sacrifice to the LORD.

18 Go therefore now, *and* work; for there shall no straw be given you, yet shall ye deliver the tale of bricks.

19 And the officers of the children of Israel did see *that* they *were* in evil *case*, after it was said, Ye shall not minish *ought* from your bricks of your daily task.

20 ¶ And they met Moses and Aaron, who stood in the way, as they came forth from Pharaoh:

21 And they said unto them, The LORD look upon you, and judge; because ye have made our savour to be abhorred in the eyes of Pharaoh, and in the eyes of his servants, to put a sword in their hand to slay us.

22 And Moses returned unto the LORD, and said, Lord, wherefore hast thou *so* evil entreated this people? why *is* it *that* thou hast sent me?

23 For since I came to Pharaoh to speak in thy name, he hath done evil to this people; neither hast thou delivered thy people at all.

Exodus 6

1 Then the LORD said unto Moses, Now shalt thou see what I will do to Pharaoh: for with a strong hand shall he let them go, and with a strong hand shall he drive them out of his land.

2 And God spake unto Moses, and said unto him, I *am* the LORD:

3 And I appeared unto Abraham, unto Isaac, and unto Jacob, by *the name of* God Almighty, but by my name JEHOVAH was I not known to them.

4 And I have also established my covenant with them, to give them the land of Canaan, the land of their pilgrimage, wherein they were strangers.

5 And I have also heard the groaning of the children of Israel, whom the Egyptians keep in bondage; and I have remembered my covenant.

6 Wherefore say unto the children of Israel, I *am* the LORD, and I will bring you out from under the burdens of the Egyptians, and I will rid you out of their bondage, and I will redeem you with a stretched out arm, and with great judgments:

7 And I will take you to me for a people, and I will be to you a God: and ye shall know that I *am* the LORD your God, which bringeth you out from under the burdens of the Egyptians.

8 And I will bring you in unto the land, concerning the which I did swear to give it to Abraham, to Isaac, and to Jacob; and I will give it you for an heritage: I *am* the LORD.

9 ¶ And Moses spake so unto the children of
Israel: but they hearkened not unto Moses
for anguish of spirit, and for cruel bondage.
10 And the LORD spake unto Moses, saying,
11 Go in, speak unto Pharaoh king of Egypt,
that he let the children of Israel go out of
his land.
12 And Moses spake before the LORD, saying, Behold, the children of Israel have not
hearkened unto me; how then shall Pharaoh
hear me, who *am* of uncircumcised lips?
13 And the LORD spake unto Moses and
unto Aaron, and gave them a charge unto
the children of Israel, and unto Pharaoh king
of Egypt, to bring the children of Israel out
of the land of Egypt.
14 ¶ These *be* the heads of their fathers'
houses: The sons of Reuben the firstborn of
Israel; Hanoch, and Pallu, Hezron, and Carmi:
these *be* the families of Reuben.
15 And the sons of Simeon; Jemuel, and
Jamin, and Ohad, and Jachin, and Zohar,
and Shaul the son of a Canaanitish woman:
these *are* the families of Simeon.
16 ¶ And these *are* the names of the sons
of Levi according to their generations; Gershon, and Kohath, and Merari: and the years
of the life of Levi *were* an hundred thirty
and seven years.
17 The sons of Gershon; Libni, and Shimi,
according to their families.
18 And the sons of Kohath; Amram, and
Izhar, and Hebron, and Uzziel: and the years
of the life of Kohath *were* an hundred thirty
and three years.
19 And the sons of Merari; Mahali and
Mushi: these *are* the families of Levi according to their generations.
20 And Amram took him Jochebed his
father's sister to wife; and she bare him
Aaron and Moses: and the years of the life
of Amram *were* an hundred and thirty and
seven years.
21 ¶ And the sons of Izhar; Korah, and
Nepheg, and Zichri.
22 And the sons of Uzziel; Mishael, and
Elzaphan, and Zithri.
23 And Aaron took him Elisheba, daughter
of Amminadab, sister of Naashon, to wife;
and she bare him Nadab, and Abihu, Eleazar,
and Ithamar.
24 And the sons of Korah; Assir, and Elkanah,
and Abiasaph: these *are* the families of the
Korhites.
25 And Eleazar Aaron's son took him *one*
of the daughters of Putiel to wife; and she
bare him Phinehas: these *are* the heads
of the fathers of the Levites according to
their families.
26 These *are* that Aaron and Moses, to
whom the LORD said, Bring out the children
of Israel from the land of Egypt according
to their armies.
27 These *are* they which spake to Pharaoh
king of Egypt, to bring out the children of
Israel from Egypt: these *are* that Moses
and Aaron.
28 ¶ And it came to pass on the day *when*
the LORD spake unto Moses in the land of
Egypt,
29 That the LORD spake unto Moses, saying,
I *am* the LORD: speak thou unto Pharaoh king
of Egypt all that I say unto thee.
30 And Moses said before the LORD, Behold,
I *am* of uncircumcised lips, and how shall
Pharaoh hearken unto me?

Exodus 7

1 And the LORD said unto Moses, See, I have
made thee a god to Pharaoh: and Aaron thy
brother shall be thy prophet.
2 Thou shalt speak all that I command thee:
and Aaron thy brother shall speak unto
Pharaoh, that he send the children of Israel
out of his land.
3 And I will harden Pharaoh's heart, and
multiply my signs and my wonders in the
land of Egypt.
4 But Pharaoh shall not hearken unto you,
that I may lay my hand upon Egypt, and
bring forth mine armies, *and* my people the
children of Israel, out of the land of Egypt
by great judgments.
5 And the Egyptians shall know that I *am*
the LORD, when I stretch forth mine hand
upon Egypt, and bring out the children of
Israel from among them.
6 And Moses and Aaron did as the LORD
commanded them, so did they.
7 And Moses *was* fourscore years old, and
Aaron fourscore and three years old, when
they spake unto Pharaoh.
8 ¶ And the LORD spake unto Moses and
unto Aaron, saying,
9 When Pharaoh shall speak unto you,

saying, Shew a miracle for you: then thou
shalt say unto Aaron, Take thy rod, and
cast *it* before Pharaoh, *and* it shall become
a serpent.
10 ¶ And Moses and Aaron went in unto
Pharaoh, and they did so as the LORD had
commanded: and Aaron cast down his rod
before Pharaoh, and before his servants,
and it became a serpent.
11 Then Pharaoh also called the wise men
and the sorcerers: now the magicians of
Egypt, they also did in like manner with
their enchantments.
12 For they cast down every man his rod,
and they became serpents: but Aaron's rod
swallowed up their rods.
13 And he hardened Pharaoh's heart, that
he hearkened not unto them; as the LORD
had said.
14 ¶ And the LORD said unto Moses, Pharaoh's heart *is* hardened, he refuseth to let
the people go.
15 Get thee unto Pharaoh in the morning; lo,
he goeth out unto the water; and thou shalt
stand by the river's brink against he come;
and the rod which was turned to a serpent
shalt thou take in thine hand.
16 And thou shalt say unto him, The LORD
God of the Hebrews hath sent me unto thee,
saying, Let my people go, that they may
serve me in the wilderness: and, behold,
hitherto thou wouldest not hear.
17 Thus saith the LORD, In this thou shalt
know that I *am* the LORD: behold, I will smite
with the rod that *is* in mine hand upon the
waters which *are* in the river, and they shall
be turned to blood.
18 And the fish that *is* in the river shall die,
and the river shall stink; and the Egyptians
shall lothe to drink of the water of the river.
19 ¶ And the LORD spake unto Moses, Say
unto Aaron, Take thy rod, and stretch out
thine hand upon the waters of Egypt, upon
their streams, upon their rivers, and upon
their ponds, and upon all their pools of
water, that they may become blood; and
that there may be blood throughout all the
land of Egypt, both in *vessels of* wood, and
in *vessels of* stone.
20 And Moses and Aaron did so, as the LORD
commanded; and he lifted up the rod, and
smote the waters that *were* in the river, in
the sight of Pharaoh, and in the sight of his
servants; and all the waters that *were* in the
river were turned to blood.
21 And the fish that *was* in the river died;
and the river stank, and the Egyptians could
not drink of the water of the river; and there
was blood throughout all the land of Egypt.
22 And the magicians of Egypt did so with
their enchantments: and Pharaoh's heart
was hardened, neither did he hearken unto
them; as the LORD had said.
23 And Pharaoh turned and went into his
house, neither did he set his heart to this
also.
24 And all the Egyptians digged round about
the river for water to drink; for they could
not drink of the water of the river.
25 And seven days were fulfilled, after that
the LORD had smitten the river.

Exodus 8

1 And the LORD spake unto Moses, Go unto
Pharaoh, and say unto him, Thus saith the
LORD, Let my people go, that they may
serve me.
2 And if thou refuse to let *them* go, behold,
I will smite all thy borders with frogs:
3 And the river shall bring forth frogs abundantly, which shall go up and come into
thine house, and into thy bedchamber, and
upon thy bed, and into the house of thy
servants, and upon thy people, and into
thine ovens, and into thy kneadingtroughs:
4 And the frogs shall come up both on
thee, and upon thy people, and upon all
thy servants.
5 ¶ And the LORD spake unto Moses, Say
unto Aaron, Stretch forth thine hand with
thy rod over the streams, over the rivers,
and over the ponds, and cause frogs to
come up upon the land of Egypt.
6 And Aaron stretched out his hand over
the waters of Egypt; and the frogs came up,
and covered the land of Egypt.
7 And the magicians did so with their
enchantments, and brought up frogs upon
the land of Egypt.
8 ¶ Then Pharaoh called for Moses and
Aaron, and said, Intreat the LORD, that he
may take away the frogs from me, and from
my people; and I will let the people go, that
they may do sacrifice unto the LORD.
9 And Moses said unto Pharaoh, Glory over
me: when shall I intreat for thee, and for thy

servants, and for thy people, to destroy the
frogs from thee and thy houses, *that* they
may remain in the river only?
10 And he said, To morrow. And he said, *Be*
it according to thy word: that thou mayest
know that *there is* none like unto the LORD
our God.
11 And the frogs shall depart from thee, and
from thy houses, and from thy servants,
and from thy people; they shall remain in
the river only.
12 And Moses and Aaron went out from
Pharaoh: and Moses cried unto the LORD
because of the frogs which he had brought
against Pharaoh.
13 And the LORD did according to the word
of Moses; and the frogs died out of the
houses, out of the villages, and out of the
fields.
14 And they gathered them together upon
heaps: and the land stank.
15 But when Pharaoh saw that there was
respite, he hardened his heart, and hearkened not unto them; as the LORD had said.
16 ¶ And the LORD said unto Moses, Say
unto Aaron, Stretch out thy rod, and smite
the dust of the land, that it may become lice
throughout all the land of Egypt.
17 And they did so; for Aaron stretched out
his hand with his rod, and smote the dust of
the earth, and it became lice in man, and in
beast; all the dust of the land became lice
throughout all the land of Egypt.
18 And the magicians did so with their
enchantments to bring forth lice, but they
could not: so there were lice upon man,
and upon beast.
19 Then the magicians said unto Pharaoh,
This *is* the finger of God: and Pharaoh's heart
was hardened, and he hearkened not unto
them; as the LORD had said.
20 ¶ And the LORD said unto Moses, Rise
up early in the morning, and stand before
Pharaoh; lo, he cometh forth to the water;
and say unto him, Thus saith the LORD, Let
my people go, that they may serve me.
21 Else, if thou wilt not let my people go,
behold, I will send swarms *of flies* upon
thee, and upon thy servants, and upon thy
people, and into thy houses: and the houses
of the Egyptians shall be full of swarms *of*
flies, and also the ground whereon they *are*.
22 And I will sever in that day the land of
Goshen, in which my people dwell, that no
swarms *of flies* shall be there; to the end
thou mayest know that I *am* the LORD in
the midst of the earth.
23 And I will put a division between my
people and thy people: to morrow shall
this sign be.
24 And the LORD did so; and there came
a grievous swarm *of flies* into the house
of Pharaoh, and *into* his servants' houses,
and into all the land of Egypt: the land was
corrupted by reason of the swarm *of flies*.
25 ¶ And Pharaoh called for Moses and for
Aaron, and said, Go ye, sacrifice to your
God in the land.
26 And Moses said, It is not meet so to do;
for we shall sacrifice the abomination of the
Egyptians to the LORD our God: lo, shall we
sacrifice the abomination of the Egyptians
before their eyes, and will they not stone us?
27 We will go three days' journey into the
wilderness, and sacrifice to the LORD our
God, as he shall command us.
28 And Pharaoh said, I will let you go, that
ye may sacrifice to the LORD your God in
the wilderness; only ye shall not go very far
away: intreat for me.
29 And Moses said, Behold, I go out from
thee, and I will intreat the LORD that the
swarms *of flies* may depart from Pharaoh,
from his servants, and from his people, to
morrow: but let not Pharaoh deal deceitfully any more in not letting the people go
to sacrifice to the LORD.
30 And Moses went out from Pharaoh, and
intreated the LORD.
31 And the LORD did according to the word
of Moses; and he removed the swarms *of*
flies from Pharaoh, from his servants, and
from his people; there remained not one.
32 And Pharaoh hardened his heart at this
time also, neither would he let the people go.

Exodus 9

1 Then the LORD said unto Moses, Go in
unto Pharaoh, and tell him, Thus saith the
LORD God of the Hebrews, Let my people
go, that they may serve me.
2 For if thou refuse to let *them* go, and wilt
hold them still,
3 Behold, the hand of the LORD is upon thy
cattle which *is* in the field, upon the horses,
upon the asses, upon the camels, upon the

oxen, and upon the sheep: *there shall be* a very grievous murrain.

4 And the LORD shall sever between the cattle of Israel and the cattle of Egypt: and there shall nothing die of all *that is* the children's of Israel.

5 And the LORD appointed a set time, saying, To morrow the LORD shall do this thing in the land.

6 And the LORD did that thing on the morrow, and all the cattle of Egypt died: but of the cattle of the children of Israel died not one.

7 And Pharaoh sent, and, behold, there was not one of the cattle of the Israelites dead. And the heart of Pharaoh was hardened, and he did not let the people go.

8 ¶ And the LORD said unto Moses and unto Aaron, Take to you handfuls of ashes of the furnace, and let Moses sprinkle it toward the heaven in the sight of Pharaoh.

9 And it shall become small dust in all the land of Egypt, and shall be a boil breaking forth *with* blains upon man, and upon beast, throughout all the land of Egypt.

10 And they took ashes of the furnace, and stood before Pharaoh; and Moses sprinkled it up toward heaven; and it became a boil breaking forth *with* blains upon man, and upon beast.

11 And the magicians could not stand before Moses because of the boils; for the boil was upon the magicians, and upon all the Egyptians.

12 And the LORD hardened the heart of Pharaoh, and he hearkened not unto them; as the LORD had spoken unto Moses.

13 ¶ And the LORD said unto Moses, Rise up early in the morning, and stand before Pharaoh, and say unto him, Thus saith the LORD God of the Hebrews, Let my people go, that they may serve me.

14 For I will at this time send all my plagues upon thine heart, and upon thy servants, and upon thy people; that thou mayest know that *there is* none like me in all the earth.

15 For now I will stretch out my hand, that I may smite thee and thy people with pestilence; and thou shalt be cut off from the earth.

16 And in very deed for this *cause* have I raised thee up, for to shew *in* thee my power; and that my name may be declared throughout all the earth.

17 As yet exaltest thou thyself against my people, that thou wilt not let them go?

18 Behold, to morrow about this time I will cause it to rain a very grievous hail, such as hath not been in Egypt since the foundation thereof even until now.

19 Send therefore now, *and* gather thy cattle, and all that thou hast in the field; *for upon* every man and beast which shall be found in the field, and shall not be brought home, the hail shall come down upon them, and they shall die.

20 He that feared the word of the LORD among the servants of Pharaoh made his servants and his cattle flee into the houses:

21 And he that regarded not the word of the LORD left his servants and his cattle in the field.

22 ¶ And the LORD said unto Moses, Stretch forth thine hand toward heaven, that there may be hail in all the land of Egypt, upon man, and upon beast, and upon every herb of the field, throughout the land of Egypt.

23 And Moses stretched forth his rod toward heaven: and the LORD sent thunder and hail, and the fire ran along upon the ground; and the LORD rained hail upon the land of Egypt.

24 So there was hail, and fire mingled with the hail, very grievous, such as there was none like it in all the land of Egypt since it became a nation.

25 And the hail smote throughout all the land of Egypt all that *was* in the field, both man and beast; and the hail smote every herb of the field, and brake every tree of the field.

26 Only in the land of Goshen, where the children of Israel *were*, was there no hail.

27 ¶ And Pharaoh sent, and called for Moses and Aaron, and said unto them, I have sinned this time: the LORD *is* righteous, and I and my people *are* wicked.

28 Intreat the LORD (for *it is* enough) that there be no *more* mighty thunderings and hail; and I will let you go, and ye shall stay no longer.

29 And Moses said unto him, As soon as I am gone out of the city, I will spread abroad my hands unto the LORD; *and* the thunder shall cease, neither shall there be any more

hail; that thou mayest know how that the earth *is* the LORD's.

30 But as for thee and thy servants, I know that ye will not yet fear the LORD God.

31 And the flax and the barley was smitten: for the barley *was* in the ear, and the flax *was* bolled.

32 But the wheat and the rie were not smitten: for they *were* not grown up.

33 And Moses went out of the city from Pharaoh, and spread abroad his hands unto the LORD: and the thunders and hail ceased, and the rain was not poured upon the earth.

34 And when Pharaoh saw that the rain and the hail and the thunders were ceased, he sinned yet more, and hardened his heart, he and his servants.

35 And the heart of Pharaoh was hardened, neither would he let the children of Israel go; as the LORD had spoken by Moses.

Exodus 10

1 And the LORD said unto Moses, Go in unto Pharaoh: for I have hardened his heart, and the heart of his servants, that I might shew these my signs before him:

2 And that thou mayest tell in the ears of thy son, and of thy son's son, what things I have wrought in Egypt, and my signs which I have done among them; that ye may know how that I *am* the LORD.

3 And Moses and Aaron came in unto Pharaoh, and said unto him, Thus saith the LORD God of the Hebrews, How long wilt thou refuse to humble thyself before me? let my people go, that they may serve me.

4 Else, if thou refuse to let my people go, behold, to morrow will I bring the locusts into thy coast:

5 And they shall cover the face of the earth, that one cannot be able to see the earth: and they shall eat the residue of that which is escaped, which remaineth unto you from the hail, and shall eat every tree which groweth for you out of the field:

6 And they shall fill thy houses, and the houses of all thy servants, and the houses of all the Egyptians; which neither thy fathers, nor thy fathers' fathers have seen, since the day that they were upon the earth unto this day. And he turned himself, and went out from Pharaoh.

7 And Pharaoh's servants said unto him, How long shall this man be a snare unto us? let the men go, that they may serve the LORD their God: knowest thou not yet that Egypt is destroyed?

8 And Moses and Aaron were brought again unto Pharaoh: and he said unto them, Go, serve the LORD your God: *but* who *are* they that shall go?

9 And Moses said, We will go with our young and with our old, with our sons and with our daughters, with our flocks and with our herds will we go; for we *must hold* a feast unto the LORD.

10 And he said unto them, Let the LORD be so with you, as I will let you go, and your little ones: look *to it;* for evil *is* before you.

11 Not so: go now ye *that are* men, and serve the LORD; for that ye did desire. And they were driven out from Pharaoh's presence.

12 ¶ And the LORD said unto Moses, Stretch out thine hand over the land of Egypt for the locusts, that they may come up upon the land of Egypt, and eat every herb of the land, *even* all that the hail hath left.

13 And Moses stretched forth his rod over the land of Egypt, and the LORD brought an east wind upon the land all that day, and all *that* night; *and* when it was morning, the east wind brought the locusts.

14 And the locusts went up over all the land of Egypt, and rested in all the coasts of Egypt: very grievous *were they;* before them there were no such locusts as they, neither after them shall be such.

15 For they covered the face of the whole earth, so that the land was darkened; and they did eat every herb of the land, and all the fruit of the trees which the hail had left: and there remained not any green thing in the trees, or in the herbs of the field, through all the land of Egypt.

16 ¶ Then Pharaoh called for Moses and Aaron in haste; and he said, I have sinned against the LORD your God, and against you.

17 Now therefore forgive, I pray thee, my sin only this once, and intreat the LORD your God, that he may take away from me this death only.

18 And he went out from Pharaoh, and intreated the LORD.

19 And the LORD turned a mighty strong west wind, which took away the locusts, and

cast them into the Red sea; there remained
not one locust in all the coasts of Egypt.
20 But the LORD hardened Pharaoh's heart,
so that he would not let the children of
Israel go.
21 ¶ And the LORD said unto Moses, Stretch
out thine hand toward heaven, that there
may be darkness over the land of Egypt,
even darkness *which* may be felt.
22 And Moses stretched forth his hand
toward heaven; and there was a thick
darkness in all the land of Egypt three days:
23 They saw not one another, neither rose
any from his place for three days: but all the
children of Israel had light in their dwellings.
24 ¶ And Pharaoh called unto Moses, and
said, Go ye, serve the LORD; only let your
flocks and your herds be stayed: let your
little ones also go with you.
25 And Moses said, Thou must give us also
sacrifices and burnt offerings, that we may
sacrifice unto the LORD our God.
26 Our cattle also shall go with us; there
shall not an hoof be left behind; for thereof
must we take to serve the LORD our God;
and we know not with what we must serve
the LORD, until we come thither.
27 ¶ But the LORD hardened Pharaoh's
heart, and he would not let them go.
28 And Pharaoh said unto him, Get thee
from me, take heed to thyself, see my face
no more; for in *that* day thou seest my face
thou shalt die.
29 And Moses said, Thou hast spoken well,
I will see thy face again no more.

Exodus 11

1 And the LORD said unto Moses, Yet will I
bring one plague *more* upon Pharaoh, and
upon Egypt; afterwards he will let you go
hence: when he shall let *you* go, he shall
surely thrust you out hence altogether.
2 Speak now in the ears of the people, and
let every man borrow of his neighbour, and
every woman of her neighbour, jewels of
silver, and jewels of gold.
3 And the LORD gave the people favour in
the sight of the Egyptians. Moreover the
man Moses *was* very great in the land of
Egypt, in the sight of Pharaoh's servants,
and in the sight of the people.
4 And Moses said, Thus saith the LORD,
About midnight will I go out into the midst
of Egypt:
5 And all the firstborn in the land of Egypt
shall die, from the firstborn of Pharaoh that
sitteth upon his throne, even unto the firstborn of the maidservant that *is* behind the
mill; and all the firstborn of beasts.
6 And there shall be a great cry throughout
all the land of Egypt, such as there was none
like it, nor shall be like it any more.
7 But against any of the children of Israel
shall not a dog move his tongue, against
man or beast: that ye may know how that
the LORD doth put a difference between the
Egyptians and Israel.
8 And all these thy servants shall come
down unto me, and bow down themselves
unto me, saying, Get thee out, and all the
people that follow thee: and after that I will
go out. And he went out from Pharaoh in
a great anger.
9 And the LORD said unto Moses, Pharaoh
shall not hearken unto you; that my wonders may be multiplied in the land of Egypt.
10 And Moses and Aaron did all these wonders before Pharaoh: and the LORD hardened Pharaoh's heart, so that he would not
let the children of Israel go out of his land.

Exodus 12

1 And the LORD spake unto Moses and Aaron
in the land of Egypt, saying,
2 This month *shall be* unto you the beginning of months: it *shall be* the first month
of the year to you.
3 ¶ Speak ye unto all the congregation of
Israel, saying, In the tenth *day* of this month
they shall take to them every man a lamb,
according to the house of *their* fathers, a
lamb for an house:
4 And if the household be too little for the
lamb, let him and his neighbour next unto
his house take *it* according to the number
of the souls; every man according to his
eating shall make your count for the lamb.
5 Your lamb shall be without blemish, a male
of the first year: ye shall take *it* out from the
sheep, or from the goats:
6 And ye shall keep it up until the fourteenth
day of the same month: and the whole
assembly of the congregation of Israel shall
kill it in the evening.
7 And they shall take of the blood, and

strike *it* on the two side posts and on the upper door post of the houses, wherein they shall eat it.

8 And they shall eat the flesh in that night, roast with fire, and unleavened bread; *and* with bitter *herbs* they shall eat it.

9 Eat not of it raw, nor sodden at all with water, but roast *with* fire; his head with his legs, and with the purtenance thereof.

10 And ye shall let nothing of it remain until the morning; and that which remaineth of it until the morning ye shall burn with fire.

11 ¶ And thus shall ye eat it; *with* your loins girded, your shoes on your feet, and your staff in your hand; and ye shall eat it in haste: it *is* the LORD's passover.

12 For I will pass through the land of Egypt this night, and will smite all the firstborn in the land of Egypt, both man and beast; and against all the gods of Egypt I will execute judgment: I *am* the LORD.

13 And the blood shall be to you for a token upon the houses where ye *are:* and when I see the blood, I will pass over you, and the plague shall not be upon you to destroy *you*, when I smite the land of Egypt.

14 And this day shall be unto you for a memorial; and ye shall keep it a feast to the LORD throughout your generations; ye shall keep it a feast by an ordinance for ever.

15 Seven days shall ye eat unleavened bread; even the first day ye shall put away leaven out of your houses: for whosoever eateth leavened bread from the first day until the seventh day, that soul shall be cut off from Israel.

16 And in the first day *there shall be* an holy convocation, and in the seventh day there shall be an holy convocation to you; no manner of work shall be done in them, save *that* which every man must eat, that only may be done of you.

17 And ye shall observe *the feast of* unleavened bread; for in this selfsame day have I brought your armies out of the land of Egypt: therefore shall ye observe this day in your generations by an ordinance for ever.

18 ¶ In the first *month*, on the fourteenth day of the month at even, ye shall eat unleavened bread, until the one and twentieth day of the month at even.

19 Seven days shall there be no leaven found in your houses: for whosoever eateth that which is leavened, even that soul shall be cut off from the congregation of Israel, whether he be a stranger, or born in the land.

20 Ye shall eat nothing leavened; in all your habitations shall ye eat unleavened bread.

21 ¶ Then Moses called for all the elders of Israel, and said unto them, Draw out and take you a lamb according to your families, and kill the passover.

22 And ye shall take a bunch of hyssop, and dip *it* in the blood that *is* in the bason, and strike the lintel and the two side posts with the blood that *is* in the bason; and none of you shall go out at the door of his house until the morning.

23 For the LORD will pass through to smite the Egyptians; and when he seeth the blood upon the lintel, and on the two side posts, the LORD will pass over the door, and will not suffer the destroyer to come in unto your houses to smite *you*.

24 And ye shall observe this thing for an ordinance to thee and to thy sons for ever.

25 And it shall come to pass, when ye be come to the land which the LORD will give you, according as he hath promised, that ye shall keep this service.

26 And it shall come to pass, when your children shall say unto you, What mean ye by this service?

27 That ye shall say, It *is* the sacrifice of the LORD's passover, who passed over the houses of the children of Israel in Egypt, when he smote the Egyptians, and delivered our houses. And the people bowed the head and worshipped.

28 And the children of Israel went away, and did as the LORD had commanded Moses and Aaron, so did they.

29 ¶ And it came to pass, that at midnight the LORD smote all the firstborn in the land of Egypt, from the firstborn of Pharaoh that sat on his throne unto the firstborn of the captive that *was* in the dungeon; and all the firstborn of cattle.

30 And Pharaoh rose up in the night, he, and all his servants, and all the Egyptians; and there was a great cry in Egypt; for *there was* not a house where *there was* not one dead.

31 ¶ And he called for Moses and Aaron by night, and said, Rise up, *and* get you forth from among my people, both ye and the

children of Israel; and go, serve the LORD,
as ye have said.
32 Also take your flocks and your herds, as
ye have said, and be gone; and bless me also.
33 And the Egyptians were urgent upon
the people, that they might send them out
of the land in haste; for they said, We *be*
all dead *men*.
34 And the people took their dough before
it was leavened, their kneadingtroughs
being bound up in their clothes upon their
shoulders.
35 And the children of Israel did according
to the word of Moses; and they borrowed
of the Egyptians jewels of silver, and jewels
of gold, and raiment:
36 And the LORD gave the people favour in
the sight of the Egyptians, so that they lent
unto them *such things as they required*. And
they spoiled the Egyptians.
37 ¶ And the children of Israel journeyed
from Rameses to Succoth, about six hundred thousand on foot *that were* men,
beside children.
38 And a mixed multitude went up also
with them; and flocks, and herds, *even* very
much cattle.
39 And they baked unleavened cakes of
the dough which they brought forth out
of Egypt, for it was not leavened; because
they were thrust out of Egypt, and could
not tarry, neither had they prepared for
themselves any victual.
40 ¶ Now the sojourning of the children of
Israel, who dwelt in Egypt, *was* four hundred
and thirty years.
41 And it came to pass at the end of the four
hundred and thirty years, even the selfsame
day it came to pass, that all the hosts of the
LORD went out from the land of Egypt.
42 It *is* a night to be much observed unto
the LORD for bringing them out from the
land of Egypt: this *is* that night of the LORD
to be observed of all the children of Israel
in their generations.
43 ¶ And the LORD said unto Moses and
Aaron, This *is* the ordinance of the passover:
There shall no stranger eat thereof:
44 But every man's servant that is bought
for money, when thou hast circumcised him,
then shall he eat thereof.
45 A foreigner and an hired servant shall
not eat thereof.
46 In one house shall it be eaten; thou shalt
not carry forth ought of the flesh abroad
out of the house; neither shall ye break a
bone thereof.
47 All the congregation of Israel shall keep it.
48 And when a stranger shall sojourn with
thee, and will keep the passover to the
LORD, let all his males be circumcised, and
then let him come near and keep it; and he
shall be as one that is born in the land: for
no uncircumcised person shall eat thereof.
49 One law shall be to him that is homeborn, and unto the stranger that sojourneth
among you.
50 Thus did all the children of Israel; as
the LORD commanded Moses and Aaron,
so did they.
51 And it came to pass the selfsame day,
that the LORD did bring the children of Israel
out of the land of Egypt by their armies.

Exodus 13

1 And the LORD spake unto Moses, saying,
2 Sanctify unto me all the firstborn, whatsoever openeth the womb among the children
of Israel, *both* of man and of beast: it *is* mine.
3 ¶ And Moses said unto the people,
Remember this day, in which ye came out
from Egypt, out of the house of bondage; for
by strength of hand the LORD brought you
out from this *place:* there shall no leavened
bread be eaten.
4 This day came ye out in the month Abib.
5 ¶ And it shall be when the LORD shall
bring thee into the land of the Canaanites,
and the Hittites, and the Amorites, and the
Hivites, and the Jebusites, which he sware
unto thy fathers to give thee, a land flowing
with milk and honey, that thou shalt keep
this service in this month.
6 Seven days thou shalt eat unleavened
bread, and in the seventh day *shall be* a
feast to the LORD.
7 Unleavened bread shall be eaten seven
days; and there shall no leavened bread be
seen with thee, neither shall there be leaven
seen with thee in all thy quarters.
8 ¶ And thou shalt shew thy son in that day,
saying, *This is done* because of that *which*
the LORD did unto me when I came forth
out of Egypt.
9 And it shall be for a sign unto thee upon
thine hand, and for a memorial between

thine eyes, that the LORD's law may be in
thy mouth: for with a strong hand hath the
LORD brought thee out of Egypt.
10 Thou shalt therefore keep this ordinance
in his season from year to year.
11 ¶ And it shall be when the LORD shall
bring thee into the land of the Canaanites,
as he sware unto thee and to thy fathers,
and shall give it thee,
12 That thou shalt set apart unto the LORD
all that openeth the matrix, and every firstling that cometh of a beast which thou hast;
the males *shall be* the LORD's.
13 And every firstling of an ass thou shalt
redeem with a lamb; and if thou wilt not
redeem it, then thou shalt break his neck:
and all the firstborn of man among thy children shalt thou redeem.
14 ¶ And it shall be when thy son asketh
thee in time to come, saying, What *is* this?
that thou shalt say unto him, By strength of
hand the LORD brought us out from Egypt,
from the house of bondage:
15 And it came to pass, when Pharaoh
would hardly let us go, that the LORD slew
all the firstborn in the land of Egypt, both
the firstborn of man, and the firstborn of
beast: therefore I sacrifice to the LORD all
that openeth the matrix, being males; but
all the firstborn of my children I redeem.
16 And it shall be for a token upon thine
hand, and for frontlets between thine eyes:
for by strength of hand the LORD brought
us forth out of Egypt.
17 ¶ And it came to pass, when Pharaoh had
let the people go, that God led them not
through the way of the land of the Philistines, although that *was* near; for God said,
Lest peradventure the people repent when
they see war, and they return to Egypt:
18 But God led the people about, *through*
the way of the wilderness of the Red sea:
and the children of Israel went up harnessed
out of the land of Egypt.
19 And Moses took the bones of Joseph
with him: for he had straitly sworn the children of Israel, saying, God will surely visit
you; and ye shall carry up my bones away
hence with you.
20 ¶ And they took their journey from Succoth, and encamped in Etham, in the edge
of the wilderness.
21 And the LORD went before them by day
in a pillar of a cloud, to lead them the way;
and by night in a pillar of fire, to give them
light; to go by day and night:
22 He took not away the pillar of the cloud
by day, nor the pillar of fire by night, *from*
before the people.

Exodus 14

1 And the LORD spake unto Moses, saying,
2 Speak unto the children of Israel, that
they turn and encamp before Pi-hahiroth,
between Migdol and the sea, over against
Baal-zephon: before it shall ye encamp by
the sea.
3 For Pharaoh will say of the children of
Israel, They *are* entangled in the land, the
wilderness hath shut them in.
4 And I will harden Pharaoh's heart, that he
shall follow after them; and I will be honoured upon Pharaoh, and upon all his host;
that the Egyptians may know that I *am* the
LORD. And they did so.
5 ¶ And it was told the king of Egypt that the
people fled: and the heart of Pharaoh and of
his servants was turned against the people,
and they said, Why have we done this, that
we have let Israel go from serving us?
6 And he made ready his chariot, and took
his people with him:
7 And he took six hundred chosen chariots,
and all the chariots of Egypt, and captains
over every one of them.
8 And the LORD hardened the heart of Pharaoh king of Egypt, and he pursued after the
children of Israel: and the children of Israel
went out with an high hand.
9 But the Egyptians pursued after them, all
the horses *and* chariots of Pharaoh, and his
horsemen, and his army, and overtook them
encamping by the sea, beside Pi-hahiroth,
before Baal-zephon.
10 ¶ And when Pharaoh drew nigh, the
children of Israel lifted up their eyes, and,
behold, the Egyptians marched after them;
and they were sore afraid: and the children
of Israel cried out unto the LORD.
11 And they said unto Moses, Because *there*
were no graves in Egypt, hast thou taken us
away to die in the wilderness? wherefore
hast thou dealt thus with us, to carry us
forth out of Egypt?
12 *Is* not this the word that we did tell thee
in Egypt, saying, Let us alone, that we may

serve the Egyptians? For *it had been* better
for us to serve the Egyptians, than that we
should die in the wilderness.
13 ¶ And Moses said unto the people, Fear
ye not, stand still, and see the salvation of
the LORD, which he will shew to you to day:
for the Egyptians whom ye have seen to day,
ye shall see them again no more for ever.
14 The LORD shall fight for you, and ye shall
hold your peace.
15 ¶ And the LORD said unto Moses, Wherefore criest thou unto me? speak unto the
children of Israel, that they go forward:
16 But lift thou up thy rod, and stretch out
thine hand over the sea, and divide it: and
the children of Israel shall go on dry *ground*
through the midst of the sea.
17 And I, behold, I will harden the hearts of
the Egyptians, and they shall follow them:
and I will get me honour upon Pharaoh,
and upon all his host, upon his chariots, and
upon his horsemen.
18 And the Egyptians shall know that I *am*
the LORD, when I have gotten me honour
upon Pharaoh, upon his chariots, and upon
his horsemen.
19 ¶ And the angel of God, which went
before the camp of Israel, removed and
went behind them; and the pillar of the
cloud went from before their face, and
stood behind them:
20 And it came between the camp of the
Egyptians and the camp of Israel; and it was
a cloud and darkness *to them,* but it gave
light by night *to these:* so that the one came
not near the other all the night.
21 And Moses stretched out his hand over
the sea; and the LORD caused the sea to go
back by a strong east wind all that night,
and made the sea dry *land,* and the waters
were divided.
22 And the children of Israel went into the
midst of the sea upon the dry *ground:* and
the waters *were* a wall unto them on their
right hand, and on their left.
23 ¶ And the Egyptians pursued, and went
in after them to the midst of the sea, *even*
all Pharaoh's horses, his chariots, and his
horsemen.
24 And it came to pass, that in the morning watch the LORD looked unto the host
of the Egyptians through the pillar of fire
and of the cloud, and troubled the host of
the Egyptians,
25 And took off their chariot wheels, that
they drave them heavily: so that the Egyptians said, Let us flee from the face of Israel;
for the LORD fighteth for them against the
Egyptians.
26 ¶ And the LORD said unto Moses, Stretch
out thine hand over the sea, that the waters
may come again upon the Egyptians, upon
their chariots, and upon their horsemen.
27 And Moses stretched forth his hand over
the sea, and the sea returned to his strength
when the morning appeared; and the Egyptians fled against it; and the LORD overthrew
the Egyptians in the midst of the sea.
28 And the waters returned, and covered
the chariots, and the horsemen, *and* all
the host of Pharaoh that came into the sea
after them; there remained not so much as
one of them.
29 But the children of Israel walked upon dry
land in the midst of the sea; and the waters
were a wall unto them on their right hand,
and on their left.
30 Thus the LORD saved Israel that day out
of the hand of the Egyptians; and Israel saw
the Egyptians dead upon the sea shore.
31 And Israel saw that great work which
the LORD did upon the Egyptians: and the
people feared the LORD, and believed the
LORD, and his servant Moses.

Exodus 15

1 Then sang Moses and the children of
Israel this song unto the LORD, and spake,
saying, I will sing unto the LORD, for he hath
triumphed gloriously: the horse and his rider
hath he thrown into the sea.
2 The LORD *is* my strength and song, and he
is become my salvation: he *is* my God, and I
will prepare him an habitation; my father's
God, and I will exalt him.
3 The LORD *is* a man of war: the LORD *is*
his name.
4 Pharaoh's chariots and his host hath he
cast into the sea: his chosen captains also
are drowned in the Red sea.
5 The depths have covered them: they sank
into the bottom as a stone.
6 Thy right hand, O LORD, is become glorious in power: thy right hand, O LORD, hath
dashed in pieces the enemy.

7 And in the greatness of thine excellency
thou hast overthrown them that rose up
against thee: thou sentest forth thy wrath,
which consumed them as stubble.
8 And with the blast of thy nostrils the
waters were gathered together, the floods
stood upright as an heap, *and* the depths
were congealed in the heart of the sea.
9 The enemy said, I will pursue, I will overtake, I will divide the spoil; my lust shall be
satisfied upon them; I will draw my sword,
my hand shall destroy them.
10 Thou didst blow with thy wind, the sea
covered them: they sank as lead in the
mighty waters.
11 Who *is* like unto thee, O LORD, among the
gods? who *is* like thee, glorious in holiness,
fearful *in* praises, doing wonders?
12 Thou stretchedst out thy right hand, the
earth swallowed them.
13 Thou in thy mercy hast led forth the
people *which* thou hast redeemed: thou
hast guided *them* in thy strength unto thy
holy habitation.
14 The people shall hear, *and* be afraid:
sorrow shall take hold on the inhabitants
of Palestina.
15 Then the dukes of Edom shall be amazed;
the mighty men of Moab, trembling shall
take hold upon them; all the inhabitants of
Canaan shall melt away.
16 Fear and dread shall fall upon them; by
the greatness of thine arm they shall be *as*
still as a stone; till thy people pass over, O
LORD, till the people pass over, *which* thou
hast purchased.
17 Thou shalt bring them in, and plant them
in the mountain of thine inheritance, *in* the
place, O LORD, *which* thou hast made for
thee to dwell in, *in* the Sanctuary, O Lord,
which thy hands have established.
18 The LORD shall reign for ever and ever.
19 For the horse of Pharaoh went in with his
chariots and with his horsemen into the sea,
and the LORD brought again the waters of
the sea upon them; but the children of Israel
went on dry *land* in the midst of the sea.
20 ¶ And Miriam the prophetess, the sister
of Aaron, took a timbrel in her hand; and all
the women went out after her with timbrels
and with dances.
21 And Miriam answered them, Sing ye to
the LORD, for he hath triumphed gloriously;
the horse and his rider hath he thrown into
the sea.
22 So Moses brought Israel from the Red
sea, and they went out into the wilderness
of Shur; and they went three days in the
wilderness, and found no water.
23 ¶ And when they came to Marah, they
could not drink of the waters of Marah, for
they *were* bitter: therefore the name of it
was called Marah.
24 And the people murmured against
Moses, saying, What shall we drink?
25 And he cried unto the LORD; and the
LORD shewed him a tree, *which* when he had
cast into the waters, the waters were made
sweet: there he made for them a statute and
an ordinance, and there he proved them,
26 And said, If thou wilt diligently hearken
to the voice of the LORD thy God, and wilt
do that which is right in his sight, and wilt
give ear to his commandments, and keep
all his statutes, I will put none of these
diseases upon thee, which I have brought
upon the Egyptians: for I *am* the LORD that
healeth thee.
27 ¶ And they came to Elim, where *were*
twelve wells of water, and threescore and
ten palm trees: and they encamped there
by the waters.

Exodus 16

1 And they took their journey from Elim, and
all the congregation of the children of Israel
came unto the wilderness of Sin, which *is*
between Elim and Sinai, on the fifteenth day
of the second month after their departing
out of the land of Egypt.
2 And the whole congregation of the children of Israel murmured against Moses and
Aaron in the wilderness:
3 And the children of Israel said unto them,
Would to God we had died by the hand of
the LORD in the land of Egypt, when we sat
by the flesh pots, *and* when we did eat bread
to the full; for ye have brought us forth into
this wilderness, to kill this whole assembly
with hunger.
4 ¶ Then said the LORD unto Moses, Behold,
I will rain bread from heaven for you; and
the people shall go out and gather a certain rate every day, that I may prove them,
whether they will walk in my law, or no.
5 And it shall come to pass, that on the sixth

day they shall prepare *that* which they bring in; and it shall be twice as much as they gather daily.

6 And Moses and Aaron said unto all the children of Israel, At even, then ye shall know that the LORD hath brought you out from the land of Egypt:

7 And in the morning, then ye shall see the glory of the LORD; for that he heareth your murmurings against the LORD: and what *are* we, that ye murmur against us?

8 And Moses said, *This shall be*, when the LORD shall give you in the evening flesh to eat, and in the morning bread to the full; for that the LORD heareth your murmurings which ye murmur against him: and what *are* we? your murmurings *are* not against us, but against the LORD.

9 ¶ And Moses spake unto Aaron, Say unto all the congregation of the children of Israel, Come near before the LORD: for he hath heard your murmurings.

10 And it came to pass, as Aaron spake unto the whole congregation of the children of Israel, that they looked toward the wilderness, and, behold, the glory of the LORD appeared in the cloud.

11 ¶ And the LORD spake unto Moses, saying,

12 I have heard the murmurings of the children of Israel: speak unto them, saying, At even ye shall eat flesh, and in the morning ye shall be filled with bread; and ye shall know that I *am* the LORD your God.

13 And it came to pass, that at even the quails came up, and covered the camp: and in the morning the dew lay round about the host.

14 And when the dew that lay was gone up, behold, upon the face of the wilderness *there lay* a small round thing, *as* small as the hoar frost on the ground.

15 And when the children of Israel saw *it*, they said one to another, It *is* manna: for they wist not what it *was*. And Moses said unto them, This *is* the bread which the LORD hath given you to eat.

16 ¶ This *is* the thing which the LORD hath commanded, Gather of it every man according to his eating, an omer for every man, *according to* the number of your persons; take ye every man for *them* which *are* in his tents.

17 And the children of Israel did so, and gathered, some more, some less.

18 And when they did mete *it* with an omer, he that gathered much had nothing over, and he that gathered little had no lack; they gathered every man according to his eating.

19 And Moses said, Let no man leave of it till the morning.

20 Notwithstanding they hearkened not unto Moses; but some of them left of it until the morning, and it bred worms, and stank: and Moses was wroth with them.

21 And they gathered it every morning, every man according to his eating: and when the sun waxed hot, it melted.

22 ¶ And it came to pass, *that* on the sixth day they gathered twice as much bread, two omers for one *man:* and all the rulers of the congregation came and told Moses.

23 And he said unto them, This *is that* which the LORD hath said, To morrow *is* the rest of the holy sabbath unto the LORD: bake *that* which ye will bake *to day*, and seethe that ye will seethe; and that which remaineth over lay up for you to be kept until the morning.

24 And they laid it up till the morning, as Moses bade: and it did not stink, neither was there any worm therein.

25 And Moses said, Eat that to day; for to day *is* a sabbath unto the LORD: to day ye shall not find it in the field.

26 Six days ye shall gather it; but on the seventh day, *which is* the sabbath, in it there shall be none.

27 ¶ And it came to pass, *that* there went out *some* of the people on the seventh day for to gather, and they found none.

28 And the LORD said unto Moses, How long refuse ye to keep my commandments and my laws?

29 See, for that the LORD hath given you the sabbath, therefore he giveth you on the sixth day the bread of two days; abide ye every man in his place, let no man go out of his place on the seventh day.

30 So the people rested on the seventh day.

31 And the house of Israel called the name thereof Manna: and it *was* like coriander seed, white; and the taste of it *was* like wafers *made* with honey.

32 ¶ And Moses said, This *is* the thing which the LORD commandeth, Fill an omer of it to be kept for your generations; that they may

see the bread wherewith I have fed you in
the wilderness, when I brought you forth
from the land of Egypt.
33 And Moses said unto Aaron, Take a pot,
and put an omer full of manna therein, and
lay it up before the LORD, to be kept for your
generations.
34 As the LORD commanded Moses, so
Aaron laid it up before the Testimony, to
be kept.
35 And the children of Israel did eat manna
forty years, until they came to a land inhabited; they did eat manna, until they came
unto the borders of the land of Canaan.
36 Now an omer *is* the tenth *part* of an
ephah.

Exodus 17

1 And all the congregation of the children
of Israel journeyed from the wilderness of
Sin, after their journeys, according to the
commandment of the LORD, and pitched in
Rephidim: and *there was* no water for the
people to drink.
2 Wherefore the people did chide with
Moses, and said, Give us water that we
may drink. And Moses said unto them, Why
chide ye with me? wherefore do ye tempt
the LORD?
3 And the people thirsted there for water;
and the people murmured against Moses,
and said, Wherefore *is* this *that* thou hast
brought us up out of Egypt, to kill us and our
children and our cattle with thirst?
4 And Moses cried unto the LORD, saying,
What shall I do unto this people? they be
almost ready to stone me.
5 And the LORD said unto Moses, Go on
before the people, and take with thee of the
elders of Israel; and thy rod, wherewith thou
smotest the river, take in thine hand, and go.
6 Behold, I will stand before thee there upon
the rock in Horeb; and thou shalt smite the
rock, and there shall come water out of it,
that the people may drink. And Moses did
so in the sight of the elders of Israel.
7 And he called the name of the place Massah, and Meribah, because of the chiding
of the children of Israel, and because they
tempted the LORD, saying, Is the LORD
among us, or not?
8 ¶ Then came Amalek, and fought with
Israel in Rephidim.
9 And Moses said unto Joshua, Choose us
out men, and go out, fight with Amalek: to
morrow I will stand on the top of the hill
with the rod of God in mine hand.
10 So Joshua did as Moses had said to him,
and fought with Amalek: and Moses, Aaron,
and Hur went up to the top of the hill.
11 And it came to pass, when Moses held
up his hand, that Israel prevailed: and when
he let down his hand, Amalek prevailed.
12 But Moses' hands *were* heavy; and they
took a stone, and put *it* under him, and he
sat thereon; and Aaron and Hur stayed up
his hands, the one on the one side, and the
other on the other side; and his hands were
steady until the going down of the sun.
13 And Joshua discomfited Amalek and his
people with the edge of the sword.
14 And the LORD said unto Moses, Write this
for a memorial in a book, and rehearse *it* in
the ears of Joshua: for I will utterly put out
the remembrance of Amalek from under
heaven.
15 And Moses built an altar, and called the
name of it Jehovah-nissi:
16 For he said, Because the LORD hath sworn
that the LORD *will have* war with Amalek
from generation to generation.

Exodus 18

1 When Jethro, the priest of Midian, Moses'
father in law, heard of all that God had done
for Moses, and for Israel his people, *and* that
the LORD had brought Israel out of Egypt;
2 Then Jethro, Moses' father in law, took
Zipporah, Moses' wife, after he had sent
her back,
3 And her two sons; of which the name of
the one *was* Gershom; for he said, I have
been an alien in a strange land:
4 And the name of the other *was* Eliezer;
for the God of my father, *said he*, *was* mine
help, and delivered me from the sword of
Pharaoh:
5 And Jethro, Moses' father in law, came
with his sons and his wife unto Moses into
the wilderness, where he encamped at the
mount of God:
6 And he said unto Moses, I thy father in law
Jethro am come unto thee, and thy wife,
and her two sons with her.
7 ¶ And Moses went out to meet his father
in law, and did obeisance, and kissed him;

and they asked each other of *their* welfare;
and they came into the tent.
8 And Moses told his father in law all that
the LORD had done unto Pharaoh and to the
Egyptians for Israel's sake, *and* all the travail
that had come upon them by the way, and
how the LORD delivered them.
9 And Jethro rejoiced for all the goodness
which the LORD had done to Israel, whom
he had delivered out of the hand of the
Egyptians.
10 And Jethro said, Blessed *be* the LORD,
who hath delivered you out of the hand of
the Egyptians, and out of the hand of Pharaoh, who hath delivered the people from
under the hand of the Egyptians.
11 Now I know that the LORD *is* greater than
all gods: for in the thing wherein they dealt
proudly *he was* above them.
12 And Jethro, Moses' father in law, took a
burnt offering and sacrifices for God: and
Aaron came, and all the elders of Israel, to
eat bread with Moses' father in law before
God.
13 ¶ And it came to pass on the morrow,
that Moses sat to judge the people: and the
people stood by Moses from the morning
unto the evening.
14 And when Moses' father in law saw all
that he did to the people, he said, What *is*
this thing that thou doest to the people?
why sittest thou thyself alone, and all the
people stand by thee from morning unto
even?
15 And Moses said unto his father in law,
Because the people come unto me to
inquire of God:
16 When they have a matter, they come
unto me; and I judge between one and
another, and I do make *them* know the
statutes of God, and his laws.
17 And Moses' father in law said unto him,
The thing that thou doest *is* not good.
18 Thou wilt surely wear away, both thou,
and this people that *is* with thee: for this
thing *is* too heavy for thee; thou art not
able to perform it thyself alone.
19 Hearken now unto my voice, I will give
thee counsel, and God shall be with thee:
Be thou for the people to God-ward, that
thou mayest bring the causes unto God:
20 And thou shalt teach them ordinances
and laws, and shalt shew them the way
wherein they must walk, and the work that
they must do.
21 Moreover thou shalt provide out of all
the people able men, such as fear God, men
of truth, hating covetousness; and place
such over them, *to be* rulers of thousands,
and rulers of hundreds, rulers of fifties, and
rulers of tens:
22 And let them judge the people at all
seasons: and it shall be, *that* every great
matter they shall bring unto thee, but every
small matter they shall judge: so shall it be
easier for thyself, and they shall bear *the
burden* with thee.
23 If thou shalt do this thing, and God command thee *so*, then thou shalt be able to
endure, and all this people shall also go to
their place in peace.
24 So Moses hearkened to the voice of his
father in law, and did all that he had said.
25 And Moses chose able men out of all
Israel, and made them heads over the people, rulers of thousands, rulers of hundreds,
rulers of fifties, and rulers of tens.
26 And they judged the people at all seasons: the hard causes they brought unto
Moses, but every small matter they judged
themselves.
27 ¶ And Moses let his father in law depart;
and he went his way into his own land.

Exodus 19

1 In the third month, when the children of
Israel were gone forth out of the land of
Egypt, the same day came they *into* the
wilderness of Sinai.
2 For they were departed from Rephidim,
and were come *to* the desert of Sinai, and
had pitched in the wilderness; and there
Israel camped before the mount.
3 And Moses went up unto God, and the
LORD called unto him out of the mountain,
saying, Thus shalt thou say to the house of
Jacob, and tell the children of Israel;
4 Ye have seen what I did unto the Egyptians,
and *how* I bare you on eagles' wings, and
brought you unto myself.
5 Now therefore, if ye will obey my voice
indeed, and keep my covenant, then ye
shall be a peculiar treasure unto me above
all people: for all the earth *is* mine:
6 And ye shall be unto me a kingdom of
priests, and an holy nation. These *are* the

words which thou shalt speak unto the
children of Israel.
7 ¶ And Moses came and called for the
elders of the people, and laid before their
faces all these words which the LORD commanded him.
8 And all the people answered together,
and said, All that the LORD hath spoken we
will do. And Moses returned the words of
the people unto the LORD.
9 And the LORD said unto Moses, Lo, I come
unto thee in a thick cloud, that the people
may hear when I speak with thee, and
believe thee for ever. And Moses told the
words of the people unto the LORD.
10 ¶ And the LORD said unto Moses, Go unto
the people, and sanctify them to day and to
morrow, and let them wash their clothes,
11 And be ready against the third day: for
the third day the LORD will come down in
the sight of all the people upon mount Sinai.
12 And thou shalt set bounds unto the people round about, saying, Take heed to yourselves, *that ye* go *not* up into the mount, or
touch the border of it: whosoever toucheth
the mount shall be surely put to death:
13 There shall not an hand touch it, but
he shall surely be stoned, or shot through;
whether *it be* beast or man, it shall not live:
when the trumpet soundeth long, they shall
come up to the mount.
14 ¶ And Moses went down from the mount
unto the people, and sanctified the people;
and they washed their clothes.
15 And he said unto the people, Be ready
against the third day: come not at *your*
wives.
16 ¶ And it came to pass on the third day
in the morning, that there were thunders
and lightnings, and a thick cloud upon the
mount, and the voice of the trumpet exceeding loud; so that all the people that *was* in
the camp trembled.
17 And Moses brought forth the people
out of the camp to meet with God; and
they stood at the nether part of the mount.
18 And mount Sinai was altogether on a
smoke, because the LORD descended upon
it in fire: and the smoke thereof ascended
as the smoke of a furnace, and the whole
mount quaked greatly.
19 And when the voice of the trumpet
sounded long, and waxed louder and louder,
Moses spake, and God answered him by
a voice.
20 And the LORD came down upon mount
Sinai, on the top of the mount: and the LORD
called Moses *up* to the top of the mount;
and Moses went up.
21 And the LORD said unto Moses, Go down,
charge the people, lest they break through
unto the LORD to gaze, and many of them
perish.
22 And let the priests also, which come near
to the LORD, sanctify themselves, lest the
LORD break forth upon them.
23 And Moses said unto the LORD, The people cannot come up to mount Sinai: for thou
chargedst us, saying, Set bounds about the
mount, and sanctify it.
24 And the LORD said unto him, Away, get
thee down, and thou shalt come up, thou,
and Aaron with thee: but let not the priests
and the people break through to come up
unto the LORD, lest he break forth upon
them.
25 So Moses went down unto the people,
and spake unto them.

Exodus 20

1 And God spake all these words, saying,
2 I *am* the LORD thy God, which have brought
thee out of the land of Egypt, out of the
house of bondage.
3 Thou shalt have no other gods before me.
4 Thou shalt not make unto thee any graven
image, or any likeness *of any thing* that
is in heaven above, or that *is* in the earth
beneath, or that *is* in the water under the
earth:
5 Thou shalt not bow down thyself to them,
nor serve them: for I the LORD thy God *am*
a jealous God, visiting the iniquity of the
fathers upon the children unto the third
and fourth *generation* of them that hate me;
6 And shewing mercy unto thousands of
them that love me, and keep my commandments.
7 Thou shalt not take the name of the LORD
thy God in vain; for the LORD will not hold
him guiltless that taketh his name in vain.
8 Remember the sabbath day, to keep it
holy.
9 Six days shalt thou labour, and do all thy
work:
10 But the seventh day *is* the sabbath of the

LORD thy God: *in it* thou shalt not do any
work, thou, nor thy son, nor thy daughter,
thy manservant, nor thy maidservant, nor
thy cattle, nor thy stranger that *is* within
thy gates:
11 For *in* six days the LORD made heaven and
earth, the sea, and all that in them *is*, and
rested the seventh day: wherefore the LORD
blessed the sabbath day, and hallowed it.
12 ¶ Honour thy father and thy mother: that
thy days may be long upon the land which
the LORD thy God giveth thee.
13 Thou shalt not kill.
14 Thou shalt not commit adultery.
15 Thou shalt not steal.
16 Thou shalt not bear false witness against
thy neighbour.
17 Thou shalt not covet thy neighbour's
house, thou shalt not covet thy neighbour's
wife, nor his manservant, nor his maidservant, nor his ox, nor his ass, nor any thing
that *is* thy neighbour's.
18 ¶ And all the people saw the thunderings, and the lightnings, and the noise of
the trumpet, and the mountain smoking:
and when the people saw *it*, they removed,
and stood afar off.
19 And they said unto Moses, Speak thou
with us, and we will hear: but let not God
speak with us, lest we die.
20 And Moses said unto the people, Fear
not: for God is come to prove you, and that
his fear may be before your faces, that ye
sin not.
21 And the people stood afar off, and Moses
drew near unto the thick darkness where
God *was*.
22 ¶ And the LORD said unto Moses, Thus
thou shalt say unto the children of Israel,
Ye have seen that I have talked with you
from heaven.
23 Ye shall not make with me gods of silver,
neither shall ye make unto you gods of gold.
24 ¶ An altar of earth thou shalt make unto
me, and shalt sacrifice thereon thy burnt
offerings, and thy peace offerings, thy sheep,
and thine oxen: in all places where I record
my name I will come unto thee, and I will
bless thee.
25 And if thou wilt make me an altar of
stone, thou shalt not build it of hewn stone:
for if thou lift up thy tool upon it, thou hast
polluted it.
26 Neither shalt thou go up by steps unto
mine altar, that thy nakedness be not discovered thereon.

Exodus 21

1 Now these *are* the judgments which thou
shalt set before them.
2 If thou buy an Hebrew servant, six years
he shall serve: and in the seventh he shall
go out free for nothing.
3 If he came in by himself, he shall go out
by himself: if he were married, then his wife
shall go out with him.
4 If his master have given him a wife, and
she have born him sons or daughters; the
wife and her children shall be her master's,
and he shall go out by himself.
5 And if the servant shall plainly say, I love
my master, my wife, and my children; I will
not go out free:
6 Then his master shall bring him unto the
judges; he shall also bring him to the door,
or unto the door post; and his master shall
bore his ear through with an aul; and he
shall serve him for ever.
7 ¶ And if a man sell his daughter to be a
maidservant, she shall not go out as the
menservants do.
8 If she please not her master, who hath
betrothed her to himself, then shall he let
her be redeemed: to sell her unto a strange
nation he shall have no power, seeing he
hath dealt deceitfully with her.
9 And if he have betrothed her unto his son,
he shall deal with her after the manner of
daughters.
10 If he take him another *wife;* her food, her
raiment, and her duty of marriage, shall he
not diminish.
11 And if he do not these three unto her,
then shall she go out free without money.
12 ¶ He that smiteth a man, so that he die,
shall be surely put to death.
13 And if a man lie not in wait, but God
deliver *him* into his hand; then I will appoint
thee a place whither he shall flee.
14 But if a man come presumptuously
upon his neighbour, to slay him with guile;
thou shalt take him from mine altar, that
he may die.
15 ¶ And he that smiteth his father, or his
mother, shall be surely put to death.
16 ¶ And he that stealeth a man, and selleth

him, or if he be found in his hand, he shall
surely be put to death.
17 ¶ And he that curseth his father, or his
mother, shall surely be put to death.
18 ¶ And if men strive together, and one
smite another with a stone, or with *his* fist,
and he die not, but keepeth *his* bed:
19 If he rise again, and walk abroad upon his
staff, then shall he that smote *him* be quit:
only he shall pay *for* the loss of his time, and
shall cause *him* to be thoroughly healed.
20 ¶ And if a man smite his servant, or his
maid, with a rod, and he die under his hand;
he shall be surely punished.
21 Notwithstanding, if he continue a day
or two, he shall not be punished: for he *is*
his money.
22 ¶ If men strive, and hurt a woman with
child, so that her fruit depart *from her*, and
yet no mischief follow: he shall be surely
punished, according as the woman's husband will lay upon him; and he shall pay as
the judges *determine*.
23 And if *any* mischief follow, then thou
shalt give life for life,
24 Eye for eye, tooth for tooth, hand for
hand, foot for foot,
25 Burning for burning, wound for wound,
stripe for stripe.
26 ¶ And if a man smite the eye of his servant, or the eye of his maid, that it perish;
he shall let him go free for his eye's sake.
27 And if he smite out his manservant's
tooth, or his maidservant's tooth; he shall
let him go free for his tooth's sake.
28 ¶ If an ox gore a man or a woman, that
they die: then the ox shall be surely stoned,
and his flesh shall not be eaten; but the
owner of the ox *shall be* quit.
29 But if the ox were wont to push with his
horn in time past, and it hath been testified
to his owner, and he hath not kept him in,
but that he hath killed a man or a woman;
the ox shall be stoned, and his owner also
shall be put to death.
30 If there be laid on him a sum of money,
then he shall give for the ransom of his life
whatsoever is laid upon him.
31 Whether he have gored a son, or have
gored a daughter, according to this judgment shall it be done unto him.
32 If the ox shall push a manservant or a
maidservant; he shall give unto their master thirty shekels of silver, and the ox shall
be stoned.
33 ¶ And if a man shall open a pit, or if a
man shall dig a pit, and not cover it, and an
ox or an ass fall therein;
34 The owner of the pit shall make *it* good,
and give money unto the owner of them;
and the dead *beast* shall be his.
35 ¶ And if one man's ox hurt another's,
that he die; then they shall sell the live ox,
and divide the money of it; and the dead *ox*
also they shall divide.
36 Or if it be known that the ox hath used
to push in time past, and his owner hath
not kept him in; he shall surely pay ox for
ox; and the dead shall be his own.

Exodus 22

1 If a man shall steal an ox, or a sheep, and
kill it, or sell it; he shall restore five oxen for
an ox, and four sheep for a sheep.
2 ¶ If a thief be found breaking up, and be
smitten that he die, *there shall* no blood *be*
shed for him.
3 If the sun be risen upon him, *there shall*
be blood *shed* for him; *for* he should make
full restitution; if he have nothing, then he
shall be sold for his theft.
4 If the theft be certainly found in his hand
alive, whether it be ox, or ass, or sheep; he
shall restore double.
5 ¶ If a man shall cause a field or vineyard
to be eaten, and shall put in his beast, and
shall feed in another man's field; of the best
of his own field, and of the best of his own
vineyard, shall he make restitution.
6 ¶ If fire break out, and catch in thorns, so
that the stacks of corn, or the standing corn,
or the field, be consumed *therewith;* he that
kindled the fire shall surely make restitution.
7 ¶ If a man shall deliver unto his neighbour
money or stuff to keep, and it be stolen out
of the man's house; if the thief be found, let
him pay double.
8 If the thief be not found, then the master of the house shall be brought unto the
judges, *to see* whether he have put his hand
unto his neighbour's goods.
9 For all manner of trespass, *whether it be*
for ox, for ass, for sheep, for raiment, *or* for
any manner of lost thing, which *another*
challengeth to be his, the cause of both
parties shall come before the judges; *and*

whom the judges shall condemn, he shall
pay double unto his neighbour.
10 If a man deliver unto his neighbour an
ass, or an ox, or a sheep, or any beast, to
keep; and it die, or be hurt, or driven away,
no man seeing *it:*
11 *Then* shall an oath of the LORD be
between them both, that he hath not put
his hand unto his neighbour's goods; and
the owner of it shall accept *thereof,* and he
shall not make *it* good.
12 And if it be stolen from him, he shall
make restitution unto the owner thereof.
13 If it be torn in pieces, *then* let him bring
it *for* witness, *and* he shall not make good
that which was torn.
14 ¶ And if a man borrow *ought* of his
neighbour, and it be hurt, or die, the owner
thereof *being* not with it, he shall surely
make *it* good.
15 *But* if the owner thereof *be* with it, he
shall not make *it* good: if it *be* an hired *thing,*
it came for his hire.
16 ¶ And if a man entice a maid that is not
betrothed, and lie with her, he shall surely
endow her to be his wife.
17 If her father utterly refuse to give her
unto him, he shall pay money according to
the dowry of virgins.
18 ¶ Thou shalt not suffer a witch to live.
19 ¶ Whosoever lieth with a beast shall
surely be put to death.
20 ¶ He that sacrificeth unto *any* god, save
unto the LORD only, he shall be utterly
destroyed.
21 ¶ Thou shalt neither vex a stranger, nor
oppress him: for ye were strangers in the
land of Egypt.
22 ¶ Ye shall not afflict any widow, or
fatherless child.
23 If thou afflict them in any wise, and they
cry at all unto me, I will surely hear their cry;
24 And my wrath shall wax hot, and I will
kill you with the sword; and your wives shall
be widows, and your children fatherless.
25 ¶ If thou lend money to *any of* my people *that is* poor by thee, thou shalt not be
to him as an usurer, neither shalt thou lay
upon him usury.
26 If thou at all take thy neighbour's raiment
to pledge, thou shalt deliver it unto him by
that the sun goeth down:
27 For that *is* his covering only, it *is* his raiment for his skin: wherein shall he sleep?
and it shall come to pass, when he crieth
unto me, that I will hear; for I *am* gracious.
28 ¶ Thou shalt not revile the gods, nor
curse the ruler of thy people.
29 ¶ Thou shalt not delay *to offer* the first of
thy ripe fruits, and of thy liquors: the firstborn of thy sons shalt thou give unto me.
30 Likewise shalt thou do with thine oxen,
and with thy sheep: seven days it shall be
with his dam; on the eighth day thou shalt
give it me.
31 ¶ And ye shall be holy men unto me:
neither shall ye eat *any* flesh *that is* torn of
beasts in the field; ye shall cast it to the dogs.

Exodus 23

1 Thou shalt not raise a false report: put
not thine hand with the wicked to be an
unrighteous witness.
2 ¶ Thou shalt not follow a multitude to
do evil; neither shalt thou speak in a cause
to decline after many to wrest *judgment:*
3 ¶ Neither shalt thou countenance a poor
man in his cause.
4 ¶ If thou meet thine enemy's ox or his ass
going astray, thou shalt surely bring it back
to him again.
5 If thou see the ass of him that hateth
thee lying under his burden, and wouldest
forbear to help him, thou shalt surely help
with him.
6 Thou shalt not wrest the judgment of thy
poor in his cause.
7 Keep thee far from a false matter; and the
innocent and righteous slay thou not: for I
will not justify the wicked.
8 ¶ And thou shalt take no gift: for the gift
blindeth the wise, and perverteth the words
of the righteous.
9 ¶ Also thou shalt not oppress a stranger:
for ye know the heart of a stranger, seeing
ye were strangers in the land of Egypt.
10 And six years thou shalt sow thy land, and
shalt gather in the fruits thereof:
11 But the seventh *year* thou shalt let it rest
and lie still; that the poor of thy people may
eat: and what they leave the beasts of the
field shall eat. In like manner thou shalt deal
with thy vineyard, *and* with thy oliveyard.
12 Six days thou shalt do thy work, and on
the seventh day thou shalt rest: that thine
ox and thine ass may rest, and the son of

thy handmaid, and the stranger, may be refreshed.

13 And in all *things* that I have said unto you be circumspect: and make no mention of the name of other gods, neither let it be heard out of thy mouth.

14 ¶ Three times thou shalt keep a feast unto me in the year.

15 Thou shalt keep the feast of unleavened bread: (thou shalt eat unleavened bread seven days, as I commanded thee, in the time appointed of the month Abib; for in it thou camest out from Egypt: and none shall appear before me empty:)

16 And the feast of harvest, the firstfruits of thy labours, which thou hast sown in the field: and the feast of ingathering, *which is* in the end of the year, when thou hast gathered in thy labours out of the field.

17 Three times in the year all thy males shall appear before the Lord GOD.

18 Thou shalt not offer the blood of my sacrifice with leavened bread; neither shall the fat of my sacrifice remain until the morning.

19 The first of the firstfruits of thy land thou shalt bring into the house of the LORD thy God. Thou shalt not seethe a kid in his mother's milk.

20 ¶ Behold, I send an Angel before thee, to keep thee in the way, and to bring thee into the place which I have prepared.

21 Beware of him, and obey his voice, provoke him not; for he will not pardon your transgressions: for my name *is* in him.

22 But if thou shalt indeed obey his voice, and do all that I speak; then I will be an enemy unto thine enemies, and an adversary unto thine adversaries.

23 For mine Angel shall go before thee, and bring thee in unto the Amorites, and the Hittites, and the Perizzites, and the Canaanites, *and* the Hivites, and the Jebusites: and I will cut them off.

24 Thou shalt not bow down to their gods, nor serve them, nor do after their works: but thou shalt utterly overthrow them, and quite break down their images.

25 And ye shall serve the LORD your God, and he shall bless thy bread, and thy water; and I will take sickness away from the midst of thee.

26 ¶ There shall nothing cast their young, nor be barren, in thy land: the number of thy days I will fulfil.

27 I will send my fear before thee, and will destroy all the people to whom thou shalt come, and I will make all thine enemies turn their backs unto thee.

28 And I will send hornets before thee, which shall drive out the Hivite, the Canaanite, and the Hittite, from before thee.

29 I will not drive them out from before thee in one year; lest the land become desolate, and the beast of the field multiply against thee.

30 By little and little I will drive them out from before thee, until thou be increased, and inherit the land.

31 And I will set thy bounds from the Red sea even unto the sea of the Philistines, and from the desert unto the river: for I will deliver the inhabitants of the land into your hand; and thou shalt drive them out before thee.

32 Thou shalt make no covenant with them, nor with their gods.

33 They shall not dwell in thy land, lest they make thee sin against me: for if thou serve their gods, it will surely be a snare unto thee.

Exodus 24

1 And he said unto Moses, Come up unto the LORD, thou, and Aaron, Nadab, and Abihu, and seventy of the elders of Israel; and worship ye afar off.

2 And Moses alone shall come near the LORD: but they shall not come nigh; neither shall the people go up with him.

3 ¶ And Moses came and told the people all the words of the LORD, and all the judgments: and all the people answered with one voice, and said, All the words which the LORD hath said will we do.

4 And Moses wrote all the words of the LORD, and rose up early in the morning, and builded an altar under the hill, and twelve pillars, according to the twelve tribes of Israel.

5 And he sent young men of the children of Israel, which offered burnt offerings, and sacrificed peace offerings of oxen unto the LORD.

6 And Moses took half of the blood, and put *it* in basons; and half of the blood he sprinkled on the altar.

7 And he took the book of the covenant, and
read in the audience of the people: and they
said, All that the LORD hath said will we do,
and be obedient.
8 And Moses took the blood, and sprinkled
it on the people, and said, Behold the blood
of the covenant, which the LORD hath made
with you concerning all these words.
9 ¶ Then went up Moses, and Aaron, Nadab,
and Abihu, and seventy of the elders of
Israel:
10 And they saw the God of Israel: and *there
was* under his feet as it were a paved work
of a sapphire stone, and as it were the body
of heaven in *his* clearness.
11 And upon the nobles of the children of
Israel he laid not his hand: also they saw
God, and did eat and drink.
12 ¶ And the LORD said unto Moses, Come
up to me into the mount, and be there: and
I will give thee tables of stone, and a law,
and commandments which I have written;
that thou mayest teach them.
13 And Moses rose up, and his minister
Joshua: and Moses went up into the mount
of God.
14 And he said unto the elders, Tarry ye
here for us, until we come again unto you:
and, behold, Aaron and Hur *are* with you:
if any man have any matters to do, let him
come unto them.
15 And Moses went up into the mount, and
a cloud covered the mount.
16 And the glory of the LORD abode upon
mount Sinai, and the cloud covered it six
days: and the seventh day he called unto
Moses out of the midst of the cloud.
17 And the sight of the glory of the LORD
was like devouring fire on the top of the
mount in the eyes of the children of Israel.
18 And Moses went into the midst of the
cloud, and gat him up into the mount: and
Moses was in the mount forty days and
forty nights.

Exodus 25

1 And the LORD spake unto Moses, saying,
2 Speak unto the children of Israel, that
they bring me an offering: of every man
that giveth it willingly with his heart ye shall
take my offering.
3 And this *is* the offering which ye shall take
of them; gold, and silver, and brass,
4 And blue, and purple, and scarlet, and fine
linen, and goats' *hair,*
5 And rams' skins dyed red, and badgers'
skins, and shittim wood,
6 Oil for the light, spices for anointing oil,
and for sweet incense,
7 Onyx stones, and stones to be set in the
ephod, and in the breastplate.
8 And let them make me a sanctuary; that
I may dwell among them.
9 According to all that I shew thee, *after* the
pattern of the tabernacle, and the pattern
of all the instruments thereof, even so shall
ye make *it.*
10 ¶ And they shall make an ark *of* shittim
wood: two cubits and a half *shall be* the
length thereof, and a cubit and a half the
breadth thereof, and a cubit and a half the
height thereof.
11 And thou shalt overlay it with pure gold,
within and without shalt thou overlay it,
and shalt make upon it a crown of gold
round about.
12 And thou shalt cast four rings of gold for
it, and put *them* in the four corners thereof;
and two rings *shall be* in the one side of it,
and two rings in the other side of it.
13 And thou shalt make staves *of* shittim
wood, and overlay them with gold.
14 And thou shalt put the staves into the
rings by the sides of the ark, that the ark
may be borne with them.
15 The staves shall be in the rings of the ark:
they shall not be taken from it.
16 And thou shalt put into the ark the testimony which I shall give thee.
17 And thou shalt make a mercy seat *of*
pure gold: two cubits and a half *shall be* the
length thereof, and a cubit and a half the
breadth thereof.
18 And thou shalt make two cherubims *of*
gold, *of* beaten work shalt thou make them,
in the two ends of the mercy seat.
19 And make one cherub on the one end,
and the other cherub on the other end:
even of the mercy seat shall ye make the
cherubims on the two ends thereof.
20 And the cherubims shall stretch forth
their wings on high, covering the mercy seat
with their wings, and their faces *shall look*
one to another; toward the mercy seat shall
the faces of the cherubims be.
21 And thou shalt put the mercy seat above

upon the ark; and in the ark thou shalt put
the testimony that I shall give thee.
22 And there I will meet with thee, and I will
commune with thee from above the mercy
seat, from between the two cherubims
which *are* upon the ark of the testimony, of
all *things* which I will give thee in commandment unto the children of Israel.
23 ¶ Thou shalt also make a table *of* shittim
wood: two cubits *shall be* the length thereof,
and a cubit the breadth thereof, and a cubit
and a half the height thereof.
24 And thou shalt overlay it with pure gold,
and make thereto a crown of gold round
about.
25 And thou shalt make unto it a border
of an hand breadth round about, and thou
shalt make a golden crown to the border
thereof round about.
26 And thou shalt make for it four rings of
gold, and put the rings in the four corners
that *are* on the four feet thereof.
27 Over against the border shall the rings
be for places of the staves to bear the table.
28 And thou shalt make the staves *of* shittim
wood, and overlay them with gold, that the
table may be borne with them.
29 And thou shalt make the dishes thereof,
and spoons thereof, and covers thereof, and
bowls thereof, to cover withal: *of* pure gold
shalt thou make them.
30 And thou shalt set upon the table shewbread before me alway.
31 ¶ And thou shalt make a candlestick *of*
pure gold: *of* beaten work shall the candlestick be made: his shaft, and his branches,
his bowls, his knops, and his flowers, shall
be of the same.
32 And six branches shall come out of the
sides of it; three branches of the candlestick
out of the one side, and three branches of
the candlestick out of the other side:
33 Three bowls made like unto almonds,
with a knop and a flower in one branch;
and three bowls made like almonds in the
other branch, *with* a knop and a flower: so
in the six branches that come out of the
candlestick.
34 And in the candlestick *shall be* four bowls
made like unto almonds, *with* their knops
and their flowers.
35 And *there shall be* a knop under two
branches of the same, and a knop under
two branches of the same, and a knop
under two branches of the same, according
to the six branches that proceed out of the
candlestick.
36 Their knops and their branches shall be
of the same: all it *shall be* one beaten work
of pure gold.
37 And thou shalt make the seven lamps
thereof: and they shall light the lamps
thereof, that they may give light over against
it.
38 And the tongs thereof, and the snuffdishes thereof, *shall be of* pure gold.
39 *Of* a talent of pure gold shall he make it,
with all these vessels.
40 And look that thou make *them* after
their pattern, which was shewed thee in
the mount.

Exodus 26

1 Moreover thou shalt make the tabernacle
with ten curtains *of* fine twined linen, and
blue, and purple, and scarlet: *with* cherubims of cunning work shalt thou make them.
2 The length of one curtain *shall be* eight
and twenty cubits, and the breadth of one
curtain four cubits: and every one of the
curtains shall have one measure.
3 The five curtains shall be coupled together
one to another; and *other* five curtains *shall*
be coupled one to another.
4 And thou shalt make loops of blue upon
the edge of the one curtain from the selvedge in the coupling; and likewise shalt
thou make in the uttermost edge of *another*
curtain, in the coupling of the second.
5 Fifty loops shalt thou make in the one curtain, and fifty loops shalt thou make in the
edge of the curtain that *is* in the coupling
of the second; that the loops may take hold
one of another.
6 And thou shalt make fifty taches of gold,
and couple the curtains together with the
taches: and it shall be one tabernacle.
7 ¶ And thou shalt make curtains *of* goats'
hair to be a covering upon the tabernacle:
eleven curtains shalt thou make.
8 The length of one curtain *shall be* thirty
cubits, and the breadth of one curtain four
cubits: and the eleven curtains *shall be all*
of one measure.
9 And thou shalt couple five curtains by
themselves, and six curtains by themselves,

and shalt double the sixth curtain in the forefront of the tabernacle.

10 And thou shalt make fifty loops on the edge of the one curtain *that is* outmost in the coupling, and fifty loops in the edge of the curtain which coupleth the second.

11 And thou shalt make fifty taches of brass, and put the taches into the loops, and couple the tent together, that it may be one.

12 And the remnant that remaineth of the curtains of the tent, the half curtain that remaineth, shall hang over the backside of the tabernacle.

13 And a cubit on the one side, and a cubit on the other side of that which remaineth in the length of the curtains of the tent, it shall hang over the sides of the tabernacle on this side and on that side, to cover it.

14 And thou shalt make a covering for the tent *of* rams' skins dyed red, and a covering above *of* badgers' skins.

15 ¶ And thou shalt make boards for the tabernacle *of* shittim wood standing up.

16 Ten cubits *shall be* the length of a board, and a cubit and a half *shall be* the breadth of one board.

17 Two tenons *shall there be* in one board, set in order one against another: thus shalt thou make for all the boards of the tabernacle.

18 And thou shalt make the boards for the tabernacle, twenty boards on the south side southward.

19 And thou shalt make forty sockets of silver under the twenty boards; two sockets under one board for his two tenons, and two sockets under another board for his two tenons.

20 And for the second side of the tabernacle on the north side *there shall be* twenty boards:

21 And their forty sockets *of* silver; two sockets under one board, and two sockets under another board.

22 And for the sides of the tabernacle westward thou shalt make six boards.

23 And two boards shalt thou make for the corners of the tabernacle in the two sides.

24 And they shall be coupled together beneath, and they shall be coupled together above the head of it unto one ring: thus shall it be for them both; they shall be for the two corners.

25 And they shall be eight boards, and their sockets *of* silver, sixteen sockets; two sockets under one board, and two sockets under another board.

26 ¶ And thou shalt make bars *of* shittim wood; five for the boards of the one side of the tabernacle,

27 And five bars for the boards of the other side of the tabernacle, and five bars for the boards of the side of the tabernacle, for the two sides westward.

28 And the middle bar in the midst of the boards shall reach from end to end.

29 And thou shalt overlay the boards with gold, and make their rings *of* gold *for* places for the bars: and thou shalt overlay the bars with gold.

30 And thou shalt rear up the tabernacle according to the fashion thereof which was shewed thee in the mount.

31 ¶ And thou shalt make a vail *of* blue, and purple, and scarlet, and fine twined linen of cunning work: with cherubims shall it be made:

32 And thou shalt hang it upon four pillars of shittim *wood* overlaid with gold: their hooks *shall be of* gold, upon the four sockets of silver.

33 ¶ And thou shalt hang up the vail under the taches, that thou mayest bring in thither within the vail the ark of the testimony: and the vail shall divide unto you between the holy *place* and the most holy.

34 And thou shalt put the mercy seat upon the ark of the testimony in the most holy *place*.

35 And thou shalt set the table without the vail, and the candlestick over against the table on the side of the tabernacle toward the south: and thou shalt put the table on the north side.

36 And thou shalt make an hanging for the door of the tent, *of* blue, and purple, and scarlet, and fine twined linen, wrought with needlework.

37 And thou shalt make for the hanging five pillars *of* shittim *wood*, and overlay them with gold, *and* their hooks *shall be of* gold: and thou shalt cast five sockets of brass for them.

Exodus 27

1 And thou shalt make an altar *of* shittim

wood, five cubits long, and five cubits broad; the altar shall be foursquare: and the height thereof *shall be* three cubits.

2 And thou shalt make the horns of it upon the four corners thereof: his horns shall be of the same: and thou shalt overlay it with brass.

3 And thou shalt make his pans to receive his ashes, and his shovels, and his basons, and his fleshhooks, and his firepans: all the vessels thereof thou shalt make *of* brass.

4 And thou shalt make for it a grate of network *of* brass; and upon the net shalt thou make four brasen rings in the four corners thereof.

5 And thou shalt put it under the compass of the altar beneath, that the net may be even to the midst of the altar.

6 And thou shalt make staves for the altar, staves *of* shittim wood, and overlay them with brass.

7 And the staves shall be put into the rings, and the staves shall be upon the two sides of the altar, to bear it.

8 Hollow with boards shalt thou make it: as it was shewed thee in the mount, so shall they make *it*.

9 ¶ And thou shalt make the court of the tabernacle: for the south side southward *there shall be* hangings for the court *of* fine twined linen of an hundred cubits long for one side:

10 And the twenty pillars thereof and their twenty sockets *shall be of* brass; the hooks of the pillars and their fillets *shall be of* silver.

11 And likewise for the north side in length *there shall be* hangings of an hundred *cubits* long, and his twenty pillars and their twenty sockets *of* brass; the hooks of the pillars and their fillets *of* silver.

12 ¶ And *for* the breadth of the court on the west side *shall be* hangings of fifty cubits: their pillars ten, and their sockets ten.

13 And the breadth of the court on the east side eastward *shall be* fifty cubits.

14 The hangings of one side *of the gate shall be* fifteen cubits: their pillars three, and their sockets three.

15 And on the other side *shall be* hangings fifteen *cubits:* their pillars three, and their sockets three.

16 ¶ And for the gate of the court *shall be* an hanging of twenty cubits, *of* blue, and purple, and scarlet, and fine twined linen, wrought with needlework: *and* their pillars *shall be* four, and their sockets four.

17 All the pillars round about the court *shall be* filleted with silver; their hooks *shall be of* silver, and their sockets *of* brass.

18 ¶ The length of the court *shall be* an hundred cubits, and the breadth fifty every where, and the height five cubits *of* fine twined linen, and their sockets *of* brass.

19 All the vessels of the tabernacle in all the service thereof, and all the pins thereof, and all the pins of the court, *shall be of* brass.

20 ¶ And thou shalt command the children of Israel, that they bring thee pure oil olive beaten for the light, to cause the lamp to burn always.

21 In the tabernacle of the congregation without the vail, which *is* before the testimony, Aaron and his sons shall order it from evening to morning before the LORD: *it shall be* a statute for ever unto their generations on the behalf of the children of Israel.

Exodus 28

1 And take thou unto thee Aaron thy brother, and his sons with him, from among the children of Israel, that he may minister unto me in the priest's office, *even* Aaron, Nadab and Abihu, Eleazar and Ithamar, Aaron's sons.

2 And thou shalt make holy garments for Aaron thy brother for glory and for beauty.

3 And thou shalt speak unto all *that are* wise hearted, whom I have filled with the spirit of wisdom, that they may make Aaron's garments to consecrate him, that he may minister unto me in the priest's office.

4 And these *are* the garments which they shall make; a breastplate, and an ephod, and a robe, and a broidered coat, a mitre, and a girdle: and they shall make holy garments for Aaron thy brother, and his sons, that he may minister unto me in the priest's office.

5 And they shall take gold, and blue, and purple, and scarlet, and fine linen.

6 ¶ And they shall make the ephod *of* gold, *of* blue, and *of* purple, *of* scarlet, and fine twined linen, with cunning work.

7 It shall have the two shoulderpieces thereof joined at the two edges thereof; and *so* it shall be joined together.

8 And the curious girdle of the ephod, which

is upon it, shall be of the same, according to the work thereof; *even of* gold, *of* blue, and purple, and scarlet, and fine twined linen.

9 And thou shalt take two onyx stones, and grave on them the names of the children of Israel:

10 Six of their names on one stone, and *the other* six names of the rest on the other stone, according to their birth.

11 With the work of an engraver in stone, *like* the engravings of a signet, shalt thou engrave the two stones with the names of the children of Israel: thou shalt make them to be set in ouches of gold.

12 And thou shalt put the two stones upon the shoulders of the ephod *for* stones of memorial unto the children of Israel: and Aaron shall bear their names before the LORD upon his two shoulders for a memorial.

13 ¶ And thou shalt make ouches *of* gold;

14 And two chains *of* pure gold at the ends; *of* wreathen work shalt thou make them, and fasten the wreathen chains to the ouches.

15 ¶ And thou shalt make the breastplate of judgment with cunning work; after the work of the ephod thou shalt make it; *of* gold, *of* blue, and *of* purple, and *of* scarlet, and *of* fine twined linen, shalt thou make it.

16 Foursquare it shall be *being* doubled; a span *shall be* the length thereof, and a span *shall be* the breadth thereof.

17 And thou shalt set in it settings of stones, *even* four rows of stones: *the first* row *shall be* a sardius, a topaz, and a carbuncle: *this shall be* the first row.

18 And the second row *shall be* an emerald, a sapphire, and a diamond.

19 And the third row a ligure, an agate, and an amethyst.

20 And the fourth row a beryl, and an onyx, and a jasper: they shall be set in gold in their inclosings.

21 And the stones shall be with the names of the children of Israel, twelve, according to their names, *like* the engravings of a signet; every one with his name shall they be according to the twelve tribes.

22 ¶ And thou shalt make upon the breastplate chains at the ends *of* wreathen work *of* pure gold.

23 And thou shalt make upon the breastplate two rings of gold, and shalt put the two rings on the two ends of the breastplate.

24 And thou shalt put the two wreathen *chains* of gold in the two rings *which are* on the ends of the breastplate.

25 And *the other* two ends of the two wreathen *chains* thou shalt fasten in the two ouches, and put *them* on the shoulderpieces of the ephod before it.

26 ¶ And thou shalt make two rings of gold, and thou shalt put them upon the two ends of the breastplate in the border thereof, which *is* in the side of the ephod inward.

27 And two *other* rings of gold thou shalt make, and shalt put them on the two sides of the ephod underneath, toward the forepart thereof, over against the *other* coupling thereof, above the curious girdle of the ephod.

28 And they shall bind the breastplate by the rings thereof unto the rings of the ephod with a lace of blue, that *it* may be above the curious girdle of the ephod, and that the breastplate be not loosed from the ephod.

29 And Aaron shall bear the names of the children of Israel in the breastplate of judgment upon his heart, when he goeth in unto the holy *place*, for a memorial before the LORD continually.

30 ¶ And thou shalt put in the breastplate of judgment the Urim and the Thummim; and they shall be upon Aaron's heart, when he goeth in before the LORD: and Aaron shall bear the judgment of the children of Israel upon his heart before the LORD continually.

31 ¶ And thou shalt make the robe of the ephod all *of* blue.

32 And there shall be an hole in the top of it, in the midst thereof: it shall have a binding of woven work round about the hole of it, as it were the hole of an habergeon, that it be not rent.

33 ¶ And *beneath* upon the hem of it thou shalt make pomegranates *of* blue, and *of* purple, and *of* scarlet, round about the hem thereof; and bells of gold between them round about:

34 A golden bell and a pomegranate, a golden bell and a pomegranate, upon the hem of the robe round about.

35 And it shall be upon Aaron to minister: and his sound shall be heard when he goeth

in unto the holy *place* before the LORD, and
when he cometh out, that he die not.
36 ¶ And thou shalt make a plate *of* pure
gold, and grave upon it, *like* the engravings
of a signet, HOLINESS TO THE LORD.
37 And thou shalt put it on a blue lace, that
it may be upon the mitre; upon the forefront
of the mitre it shall be.
38 And it shall be upon Aaron's forehead,
that Aaron may bear the iniquity of the holy
things, which the children of Israel shall
hallow in all their holy gifts; and it shall be
always upon his forehead, that they may be
accepted before the LORD.
39 ¶ And thou shalt embroider the coat of
fine linen, and thou shalt make the mitre *of*
fine linen, and thou shalt make the girdle *of*
needlework.
40 ¶ And for Aaron's sons thou shalt make
coats, and thou shalt make for them girdles,
and bonnets shalt thou make for them, for
glory and for beauty.
41 And thou shalt put them upon Aaron thy
brother, and his sons with him; and shalt
anoint them, and consecrate them, and
sanctify them, that they may minister unto
me in the priest's office.
42 And thou shalt make them linen breeches
to cover their nakedness; from the loins
even unto the thighs they shall reach:
43 And they shall be upon Aaron, and upon
his sons, when they come in unto the tabernacle of the congregation, or when they
come near unto the altar to minister in the
holy *place;* that they bear not iniquity, and
die: *it shall be* a statute for ever unto him
and his seed after him.

Exodus 29

1 And this *is* the thing that thou shalt do unto
them to hallow them, to minister unto me in
the priest's office: Take one young bullock,
and two rams without blemish,
2 And unleavened bread, and cakes unleavened tempered with oil, and wafers unleavened anointed with oil: *of* wheaten flour
shalt thou make them.
3 And thou shalt put them into one basket,
and bring them in the basket, with the bullock and the two rams.
4 And Aaron and his sons thou shalt bring
unto the door of the tabernacle of the congregation, and shalt wash them with water.
5 And thou shalt take the garments, and
put upon Aaron the coat, and the robe of
the ephod, and the ephod, and the breastplate, and gird him with the curious girdle
of the ephod:
6 And thou shalt put the mitre upon his
head, and put the holy crown upon the
mitre.
7 Then shalt thou take the anointing oil,
and pour *it* upon his head, and anoint him.
8 And thou shalt bring his sons, and put
coats upon them.
9 And thou shalt gird them with girdles,
Aaron and his sons, and put the bonnets on
them: and the priest's office shall be theirs
for a perpetual statute: and thou shalt consecrate Aaron and his sons.
10 And thou shalt cause a bullock to be
brought before the tabernacle of the congregation: and Aaron and his sons shall put
their hands upon the head of the bullock.
11 And thou shalt kill the bullock before the
LORD, *by* the door of the tabernacle of the
congregation.
12 And thou shalt take of the blood of the
bullock, and put *it* upon the horns of the
altar with thy finger, and pour all the blood
beside the bottom of the altar.
13 And thou shalt take all the fat that
covereth the inwards, and the caul *that is*
above the liver, and the two kidneys, and
the fat that *is* upon them, and burn *them*
upon the altar.
14 But the flesh of the bullock, and his skin,
and his dung, shalt thou burn with fire without the camp: it *is* a sin offering.
15 ¶ Thou shalt also take one ram; and
Aaron and his sons shall put their hands
upon the head of the ram.
16 And thou shalt slay the ram, and thou
shalt take his blood, and sprinkle *it* round
about upon the altar.
17 And thou shalt cut the ram in pieces, and
wash the inwards of him, and his legs, and
put *them* unto his pieces, and unto his head.
18 And thou shalt burn the whole ram upon
the altar: it *is* a burnt offering unto the LORD:
it *is* a sweet savour, an offering made by fire
unto the LORD.
19 ¶ And thou shalt take the other ram; and
Aaron and his sons shall put their hands
upon the head of the ram.
20 Then shalt thou kill the ram, and take

of his blood, and put *it* upon the tip of the
right ear of Aaron, and upon the tip of the
right ear of his sons, and upon the thumb
of their right hand, and upon the great toe
of their right foot, and sprinkle the blood
upon the altar round about.
21 And thou shalt take of the blood that
is upon the altar, and of the anointing oil,
and sprinkle *it* upon Aaron, and upon his
garments, and upon his sons, and upon the
garments of his sons with him: and he shall
be hallowed, and his garments, and his sons,
and his sons' garments with him.
22 Also thou shalt take of the ram the fat
and the rump, and the fat that covereth the
inwards, and the caul *above* the liver, and
the two kidneys, and the fat that *is* upon
them, and the right shoulder; for it *is* a ram
of consecration:
23 And one loaf of bread, and one cake of
oiled bread, and one wafer out of the basket of the unleavened bread that *is* before
the LORD:
24 And thou shalt put all in the hands of
Aaron, and in the hands of his sons; and
shalt wave them *for* a wave offering before
the LORD.
25 And thou shalt receive them of their
hands, and burn *them* upon the altar for a
burnt offering, for a sweet savour before
the LORD: it *is* an offering made by fire unto
the LORD.
26 And thou shalt take the breast of the
ram of Aaron's consecration, and wave it
for a wave offering before the LORD: and it
shall be thy part.
27 And thou shalt sanctify the breast of
the wave offering, and the shoulder of the
heave offering, which is waved, and which is
heaved up, of the ram of the consecration,
even of *that* which *is* for Aaron, and of *that*
which is for his sons:
28 And it shall be Aaron's and his sons' by a
statute for ever from the children of Israel:
for it *is* an heave offering: and it shall be an
heave offering from the children of Israel of
the sacrifice of their peace offerings, *even*
their heave offering unto the LORD.
29 ¶ And the holy garments of Aaron shall
be his sons' after him, to be anointed
therein, and to be consecrated in them.
30 *And* that son that is priest in his stead
shall put them on seven days, when he cometh into the tabernacle of the congregation
to minister in the holy *place*.
31 ¶ And thou shalt take the ram of the
consecration, and seethe his flesh in the
holy place.
32 And Aaron and his sons shall eat the
flesh of the ram, and the bread that *is* in
the basket, *by* the door of the tabernacle
of the congregation.
33 And they shall eat those things wherewith the atonement was made, to consecrate *and* to sanctify them: but a stranger
shall not eat *thereof*, because they *are* holy.
34 And if ought of the flesh of the consecrations, or of the bread, remain unto the
morning, then thou shalt burn the remainder with fire: it shall not be eaten, because
it *is* holy.
35 And thus shalt thou do unto Aaron, and
to his sons, according to all *things* which I
have commanded thee: seven days shalt
thou consecrate them.
36 And thou shalt offer every day a bullock
for a sin offering for atonement: and thou
shalt cleanse the altar, when thou hast made
an atonement for it, and thou shalt anoint
it, to sanctify it.
37 Seven days thou shalt make an atonement for the altar, and sanctify it; and it shall
be an altar most holy: whatsoever toucheth
the altar shall be holy.
38 ¶ Now this *is that* which thou shalt offer
upon the altar; two lambs of the first year
day by day continually.
39 The one lamb thou shalt offer in the
morning; and the other lamb thou shalt
offer at even:
40 And with the one lamb a tenth deal of
flour mingled with the fourth part of an hin
of beaten oil; and the fourth part of an hin
of wine *for* a drink offering.
41 And the other lamb thou shalt offer
at even, and shalt do thereto according
to the meat offering of the morning, and
according to the drink offering thereof, for
a sweet savour, an offering made by fire
unto the LORD.
42 *This shall be* a continual burnt offering
throughout your generations *at* the door of
the tabernacle of the congregation before
the LORD: where I will meet you, to speak
there unto thee.
43 And there I will meet with the children of

Israel, and *the tabernacle* shall be sanctified by my glory.

44 And I will sanctify the tabernacle of the congregation, and the altar: I will sanctify also both Aaron and his sons, to minister to me in the priest's office.

45 ¶ And I will dwell among the children of Israel, and will be their God.

46 And they shall know that I *am* the LORD their God, that brought them forth out of the land of Egypt, that I may dwell among them: I *am* the LORD their God.

Exodus 30

1 And thou shalt make an altar to burn incense upon: *of* shittim wood shalt thou make it.

2 A cubit *shall be* the length thereof, and a cubit the breadth thereof; foursquare shall it be: and two cubits *shall be* the height thereof: the horns thereof *shall be* of the same.

3 And thou shalt overlay it with pure gold, the top thereof, and the sides thereof round about, and the horns thereof; and thou shalt make unto it a crown of gold round about.

4 And two golden rings shalt thou make to it under the crown of it, by the two corners thereof, upon the two sides of it shalt thou make *it;* and they shall be for places for the staves to bear it withal.

5 And thou shalt make the staves *of* shittim wood, and overlay them with gold.

6 And thou shalt put it before the vail that *is* by the ark of the testimony, before the mercy seat that *is* over the testimony, where I will meet with thee.

7 And Aaron shall burn thereon sweet incense every morning: when he dresseth the lamps, he shall burn incense upon it.

8 And when Aaron lighteth the lamps at even, he shall burn incense upon it, a perpetual incense before the LORD throughout your generations.

9 Ye shall offer no strange incense thereon, nor burnt sacrifice, nor meat offering; neither shall ye pour drink offering thereon.

10 And Aaron shall make an atonement upon the horns of it once in a year with the blood of the sin offering of atonements: once in the year shall he make atonement upon it throughout your generations: it *is* most holy unto the LORD.

11 ¶ And the LORD spake unto Moses, saying,

12 When thou takest the sum of the children of Israel after their number, then shall they give every man a ransom for his soul unto the LORD, when thou numberest them; that there be no plague among them, when *thou* numberest them.

13 This they shall give, every one that passeth among them that are numbered, half a shekel after the shekel of the sanctuary: (a shekel *is* twenty gerahs:) an half shekel *shall be* the offering of the LORD.

14 Every one that passeth among them that are numbered, from twenty years old and above, shall give an offering unto the LORD.

15 The rich shall not give more, and the poor shall not give less than half a shekel, when *they* give an offering unto the LORD, to make an atonement for your souls.

16 And thou shalt take the atonement money of the children of Israel, and shalt appoint it for the service of the tabernacle of the congregation; that it may be a memorial unto the children of Israel before the LORD, to make an atonement for your souls.

17 ¶ And the LORD spake unto Moses, saying,

18 Thou shalt also make a laver *of* brass, and his foot *also of* brass, to wash *withal:* and thou shalt put it between the tabernacle of the congregation and the altar, and thou shalt put water therein.

19 For Aaron and his sons shall wash their hands and their feet thereat:

20 When they go into the tabernacle of the congregation, they shall wash with water, that they die not; or when they come near to the altar to minister, to burn offering made by fire unto the LORD:

21 So they shall wash their hands and their feet, that they die not: and it shall be a statute for ever to them, *even* to him and to his seed throughout their generations.

22 ¶ Moreover the LORD spake unto Moses, saying,

23 Take thou also unto thee principal spices, of pure myrrh five hundred *shekels*, and of sweet cinnamon half so much, *even* two hundred and fifty *shekels*, and of sweet calamus two hundred and fifty *shekels*,

24 And of cassia five hundred *shekels*, after

the shekel of the sanctuary, and of oil olive
an hin:
25 And thou shalt make it an oil of holy
ointment, an ointment compound after the
art of the apothecary: it shall be an holy
anointing oil.
26 And thou shalt anoint the tabernacle of
the congregation therewith, and the ark of
the testimony,
27 And the table and all his vessels, and the
candlestick and his vessels, and the altar
of incense,
28 And the altar of burnt offering with all his
vessels, and the laver and his foot.
29 And thou shalt sanctify them, that they
may be most holy: whatsoever toucheth
them shall be holy.
30 And thou shalt anoint Aaron and his sons,
and consecrate them, that *they* may minister
unto me in the priest's office.
31 And thou shalt speak unto the children of
Israel, saying, This shall be an holy anointing
oil unto me throughout your generations.
32 Upon man's flesh shall it not be poured,
neither shall ye make *any other* like it, after
the composition of it: it *is* holy, *and* it shall
be holy unto you.
33 Whosoever compoundeth *any* like it, or
whosoever putteth *any* of it upon a stranger,
shall even be cut off from his people.
34 ¶ And the LORD said unto Moses, Take
unto thee sweet spices, stacte, and onycha,
and galbanum; *these* sweet spices with
pure frankincense: of each shall there be
a like *weight:*
35 And thou shalt make it a perfume, a
confection after the art of the apothecary,
tempered together, pure *and* holy:
36 And thou shalt beat *some* of it very
small, and put of it before the testimony in
the tabernacle of the congregation, where
I will meet with thee: it shall be unto you
most holy.
37 And *as for* the perfume which thou
shalt make, ye shall not make to yourselves
according to the composition thereof: it
shall be unto thee holy for the LORD.
38 Whosoever shall make like unto that,
to smell thereto, shall even be cut off from
his people.

Exodus 31

1 And the LORD spake unto Moses, saying,
2 See, I have called by name Bezaleel the son
of Uri, the son of Hur, of the tribe of Judah:
3 And I have filled him with the spirit of
God, in wisdom, and in understanding,
and in knowledge, and in all manner of
workmanship,
4 To devise cunning works, to work in gold,
and in silver, and in brass,
5 And in cutting of stones, to set *them*, and
in carving of timber, to work in all manner
of workmanship.
6 And I, behold, I have given with him Aholiab, the son of Ahisamach, of the tribe of
Dan: and in the hearts of all that are wise
hearted I have put wisdom, that they may
make all that I have commanded thee;
7 The tabernacle of the congregation, and
the ark of the testimony, and the mercy seat
that *is* thereupon, and all the furniture of
the tabernacle,
8 And the table and his furniture, and the
pure candlestick with all his furniture, and
the altar of incense,
9 And the altar of burnt offering with all his
furniture, and the laver and his foot,
10 And the cloths of service, and the holy
garments for Aaron the priest, and the
garments of his sons, to minister in the
priest's office,
11 And the anointing oil, and sweet incense
for the holy *place:* according to all that I have
commanded thee shall they do.
12 ¶ And the LORD spake unto Moses,
saying,
13 Speak thou also unto the children of
Israel, saying, Verily my sabbaths ye shall
keep: for it *is* a sign between me and you
throughout your generations; that *ye* may
know that I *am* the LORD that doth sanctify you.
14 Ye shall keep the sabbath therefore; for
it *is* holy unto you: every one that defileth it
shall surely be put to death: for whosoever
doeth *any* work therein, that soul shall be
cut off from among his people.
15 Six days may work be done; but in the
seventh *is* the sabbath of rest, holy to the
LORD: whosoever doeth *any* work in the
sabbath day, he shall surely be put to death.
16 Wherefore the children of Israel shall
keep the sabbath, to observe the sabbath
throughout their generations, *for* a perpetual covenant.

17 It *is* a sign between me and the children
of Israel for ever: for *in* six days the LORD
made heaven and earth, and on the seventh
day he rested, and was refreshed.
18 ¶ And he gave unto Moses, when he had
made an end of communing with him upon
mount Sinai, two tables of testimony, tables
of stone, written with the finger of God.

Exodus 32

1 And when the people saw that Moses
delayed to come down out of the mount,
the people gathered themselves together
unto Aaron, and said unto him, Up, make
us gods, which shall go before us; for *as for*
this Moses, the man that brought us up
out of the land of Egypt, we wot not what
is become of him.
2 And Aaron said unto them, Break off the
golden earrings, which *are* in the ears of
your wives, of your sons, and of your daughters, and bring *them* unto me.
3 And all the people brake off the golden
earrings which *were* in their ears, and
brought *them* unto Aaron.
4 And he received *them* at their hand, and
fashioned it with a graving tool, after he had
made it a molten calf: and they said, These
be thy gods, O Israel, which brought thee
up out of the land of Egypt.
5 And when Aaron saw *it*, he built an altar
before it; and Aaron made proclamation,
and said, To morrow *is* a feast to the LORD.
6 And they rose up early on the morrow, and
offered burnt offerings, and brought peace
offerings; and the people sat down to eat
and to drink, and rose up to play.
7 ¶ And the LORD said unto Moses, Go,
get thee down; for thy people, which thou
broughtest out of the land of Egypt, have
corrupted *themselves:*
8 They have turned aside quickly out of
the way which I commanded them: they
have made them a molten calf, and have
worshipped it, and have sacrificed thereunto, and said, These *be* thy gods, O Israel,
which have brought thee up out of the land
of Egypt.
9 And the LORD said unto Moses, I have
seen this people, and, behold, it *is* a stiffnecked people:
10 Now therefore let me alone, that my
wrath may wax hot against them, and that I
may consume them: and I will make of thee
a great nation.
11 And Moses besought the LORD his God,
and said, LORD, why doth thy wrath wax hot
against thy people, which thou hast brought
forth out of the land of Egypt with great
power, and with a mighty hand?
12 Wherefore should the Egyptians speak,
and say, For mischief did he bring them
out, to slay them in the mountains, and to
consume them from the face of the earth?
Turn from thy fierce wrath, and repent of
this evil against thy people.
13 Remember Abraham, Isaac, and Israel,
thy servants, to whom thou swarest by
thine own self, and saidst unto them, I will
multiply your seed as the stars of heaven,
and all this land that I have spoken of will I
give unto your seed, and they shall inherit
it for ever.
14 And the LORD repented of the evil which
he thought to do unto his people.
15 ¶ And Moses turned, and went down
from the mount, and the two tables of the
testimony *were* in his hand: the tables *were*
written on both their sides; on the one side
and on the other *were* they written.
16 And the tables *were* the work of God, and
the writing *was* the writing of God, graven
upon the tables.
17 And when Joshua heard the noise of the
people as they shouted, he said unto Moses,
There is a noise of war in the camp.
18 And he said, *It is* not the voice of *them*
that shout for mastery, neither *is it* the voice
of *them that* cry for being overcome: *but* the
noise of *them that* sing do I hear.
19 ¶ And it came to pass, as soon as he came
nigh unto the camp, that he saw the calf, and
the dancing: and Moses' anger waxed hot,
and he cast the tables out of his hands, and
brake them beneath the mount.
20 And he took the calf which they had
made, and burnt *it* in the fire, and ground *it*
to powder, and strawed *it* upon the water,
and made the children of Israel drink *of it*.
21 And Moses said unto Aaron, What
did this people unto thee, that thou hast
brought so great a sin upon them?
22 And Aaron said, Let not the anger of my
lord wax hot: thou knowest the people, that
they *are set* on mischief.
23 For they said unto me, Make us gods,

which shall go before us: for *as for* this
Moses, the man that brought us up out
of the land of Egypt, we wot not what is
become of him.
24 And I said unto them, Whosoever hath
any gold, let them break *it* off. So they gave
it me: then I cast it into the fire, and there
came out this calf.
25 ¶ And when Moses saw that the people
were naked (for Aaron had made them
naked unto *their* shame among their enemies);
26 Then Moses stood in the gate of the
camp, and said, Who *is* on the LORD's side?
let him come unto me. And all the sons of
Levi gathered themselves together unto
him.
27 And he said unto them, Thus saith the
LORD God of Israel, Put every man his sword
by his side, *and* go in and out from gate to
gate throughout the camp, and slay every
man his brother, and every man his companion, and every man his neighbour.
28 And the children of Levi did according
to the word of Moses: and there fell of the
people that day about three thousand men.
29 For Moses had said, Consecrate yourselves to day to the LORD, even every man
upon his son, and upon his brother; that he
may bestow upon you a blessing this day.
30 ¶ And it came to pass on the morrow,
that Moses said unto the people, Ye have
sinned a great sin: and now I will go up
unto the LORD; peradventure I shall make
an atonement for your sin.
31 And Moses returned unto the LORD, and
said, Oh, this people have sinned a great sin,
and have made them gods of gold.
32 Yet now, if thou wilt forgive their sin—;
and if not, blot me, I pray thee, out of thy
book which thou hast written.
33 And the LORD said unto Moses, Whosoever hath sinned against me, him will I blot
out of my book.
34 Therefore now go, lead the people unto
the place of which I have spoken unto thee:
behold, mine Angel shall go before thee:
nevertheless in the day when I visit I will
visit their sin upon them.
35 And the LORD plagued the people,
because they made the calf, which Aaron
made.

Exodus 33

1 And the LORD said unto Moses, Depart,
and go up hence, thou and the people
which thou hast brought up out of the land
of Egypt, unto the land which I sware unto
Abraham, to Isaac, and to Jacob, saying,
Unto thy seed will I give it:
2 And I will send an angel before thee; and
I will drive out the Canaanite, the Amorite,
and the Hittite, and the Perizzite, the Hivite,
and the Jebusite:
3 Unto a land flowing with milk and honey:
for I will not go up in the midst of thee; for
thou *art* a stiffnecked people: lest I consume
thee in the way.
4 ¶ And when the people heard these evil
tidings, they mourned: and no man did put
on him his ornaments.
5 For the LORD had said unto Moses, Say
unto the children of Israel, Ye *are* a stiffnecked people: I will come up into the midst
of thee in a moment, and consume thee:
therefore now put off thy ornaments from
thee, that I may know what to do unto thee.
6 And the children of Israel stripped themselves of their ornaments by the mount
Horeb.
7 And Moses took the tabernacle, and
pitched it without the camp, afar off from
the camp, and called it the Tabernacle of
the congregation. And it came to pass, *that*
every one which sought the LORD went out
unto the tabernacle of the congregation,
which *was* without the camp.
8 And it came to pass, when Moses went
out unto the tabernacle, *that* all the people
rose up, and stood every man *at* his tent
door, and looked after Moses, until he was
gone into the tabernacle.
9 And it came to pass, as Moses entered into
the tabernacle, the cloudy pillar descended,
and stood *at* the door of the tabernacle, and
the LORD talked with Moses.
10 And all the people saw the cloudy pillar
stand *at* the tabernacle door: and all the
people rose up and worshipped, every man
in his tent door.
11 And the LORD spake unto Moses face
to face, as a man speaketh unto his friend.
And he turned again into the camp: but his
servant Joshua, the son of Nun, a young
man, departed not out of the tabernacle.
12 ¶ And Moses said unto the LORD, See,

thou sayest unto me, Bring up this people: and thou hast not let me know whom thou wilt send with me. Yet thou hast said, I know thee by name, and thou hast also found grace in my sight.

13 Now therefore, I pray thee, if I have found grace in thy sight, shew me now thy way, that I may know thee, that I may find grace in thy sight: and consider that this nation *is* thy people.

14 And he said, My presence shall go *with thee*, and I will give thee rest.

15 And he said unto him, If thy presence go not *with me*, carry us not up hence.

16 For wherein shall it be known here that I and thy people have found grace in thy sight? *is it* not in that thou goest with us? so shall we be separated, I and thy people, from all the people that *are* upon the face of the earth.

17 And the LORD said unto Moses, I will do this thing also that thou hast spoken: for thou hast found grace in my sight, and I know thee by name.

18 And he said, I beseech thee, shew me thy glory.

19 And he said, I will make all my goodness pass before thee, and I will proclaim the name of the LORD before thee; and will be gracious to whom I will be gracious, and will shew mercy on whom I will shew mercy.

20 And he said, Thou canst not see my face: for there shall no man see me, and live.

21 And the LORD said, Behold, *there is* a place by me, and thou shalt stand upon a rock:

22 And it shall come to pass, while my glory passeth by, that I will put thee in a clift of the rock, and will cover thee with my hand while I pass by:

23 And I will take away mine hand, and thou shalt see my back parts: but my face shall not be seen.

Exodus 34

1 And the LORD said unto Moses, Hew thee two tables of stone like unto the first: and I will write upon *these* tables the words that were in the first tables, which thou brakest.

2 And be ready in the morning, and come up in the morning unto mount Sinai, and present thyself there to me in the top of the mount.

3 And no man shall come up with thee, neither let any man be seen throughout all the mount; neither let the flocks nor herds feed before that mount.

4 ¶ And he hewed two tables of stone like unto the first; and Moses rose up early in the morning, and went up unto mount Sinai, as the LORD had commanded him, and took in his hand the two tables of stone.

5 And the LORD descended in the cloud, and stood with him there, and proclaimed the name of the LORD.

6 And the LORD passed by before him, and proclaimed, The LORD, The LORD God, merciful and gracious, longsuffering, and abundant in goodness and truth,

7 Keeping mercy for thousands, forgiving iniquity and transgression and sin, and that will by no means clear *the guilty;* visiting the iniquity of the fathers upon the children, and upon the children's children, unto the third and to the fourth *generation*.

8 And Moses made haste, and bowed his head toward the earth, and worshipped.

9 And he said, If now I have found grace in thy sight, O Lord, let my Lord, I pray thee, go among us; for it *is* a stiffnecked people; and pardon our iniquity and our sin, and take us for thine inheritance.

10 ¶ And he said, Behold, I make a covenant: before all thy people I will do marvels, such as have not been done in all the earth, nor in any nation: and all the people among which thou *art* shall see the work of the LORD: for it *is* a terrible thing that I will do with thee.

11 Observe thou that which I command thee this day: behold, I drive out before thee the Amorite, and the Canaanite, and the Hittite, and the Perizzite, and the Hivite, and the Jebusite.

12 Take heed to thyself, lest thou make a covenant with the inhabitants of the land whither thou goest, lest it be for a snare in the midst of thee:

13 But ye shall destroy their altars, break their images, and cut down their groves:

14 For thou shalt worship no other god: for the LORD, whose name *is* Jealous, *is* a jealous God:

15 Lest thou make a covenant with the inhabitants of the land, and they go a whoring after their gods, and do sacrifice unto

their gods, and *one* call thee, and thou eat of his sacrifice;

16 And thou take of their daughters unto thy sons, and their daughters go a whoring after their gods, and make thy sons go a whoring after their gods.

17 Thou shalt make thee no molten gods.

18 ¶ The feast of unleavened bread shalt thou keep. Seven days thou shalt eat unleavened bread, as I commanded thee, in the time of the month Abib: for in the month Abib thou camest out from Egypt.

19 All that openeth the matrix *is* mine; and every firstling among thy cattle, *whether* ox or sheep, *that is male*.

20 But the firstling of an ass thou shalt redeem with a lamb: and if thou redeem *him* not, then shalt thou break his neck. All the firstborn of thy sons thou shalt redeem. And none shall appear before me empty.

21 ¶ Six days thou shalt work, but on the seventh day thou shalt rest: in earing time and in harvest thou shalt rest.

22 ¶ And thou shalt observe the feast of weeks, of the firstfruits of wheat harvest, and the feast of ingathering at the year's end.

23 ¶ Thrice in the year shall all your men children appear before the Lord GOD, the God of Israel.

24 For I will cast out the nations before thee, and enlarge thy borders: neither shall any man desire thy land, when thou shalt go up to appear before the LORD thy God thrice in the year.

25 Thou shalt not offer the blood of my sacrifice with leaven; neither shall the sacrifice of the feast of the passover be left unto the morning.

26 The first of the firstfruits of thy land thou shalt bring unto the house of the LORD thy God. Thou shalt not seethe a kid in his mother's milk.

27 And the LORD said unto Moses, Write thou these words: for after the tenor of these words I have made a covenant with thee and with Israel.

28 And he was there with the LORD forty days and forty nights; he did neither eat bread, nor drink water. And he wrote upon the tables the words of the covenant, the ten commandments.

29 ¶ And it came to pass, when Moses came down from mount Sinai with the two tables of testimony in Moses' hand, when he came down from the mount, that Moses wist not that the skin of his face shone while he talked with him.

30 And when Aaron and all the children of Israel saw Moses, behold, the skin of his face shone; and they were afraid to come nigh him.

31 And Moses called unto them; and Aaron and all the rulers of the congregation returned unto him: and Moses talked with them.

32 And afterward all the children of Israel came nigh: and he gave them in commandment all that the LORD had spoken with him in mount Sinai.

33 And *till* Moses had done speaking with them, he put a vail on his face.

34 But when Moses went in before the LORD to speak with him, he took the vail off, until he came out. And he came out, and spake unto the children of Israel *that* which he was commanded.

35 And the children of Israel saw the face of Moses, that the skin of Moses' face shone: and Moses put the vail upon his face again, until he went in to speak with him.

Exodus 35

1 And Moses gathered all the congregation of the children of Israel together, and said unto them, These *are* the words which the LORD hath commanded, that *ye* should do them.

2 Six days shall work be done, but on the seventh day there shall be to you an holy day, a sabbath of rest to the LORD: whosoever doeth work therein shall be put to death.

3 Ye shall kindle no fire throughout your habitations upon the sabbath day.

4 ¶ And Moses spake unto all the congregation of the children of Israel, saying, This *is* the thing which the LORD commanded, saying,

5 Take ye from among you an offering unto the LORD: whosoever *is* of a willing heart, let him bring it, an offering of the LORD; gold, and silver, and brass,

6 And blue, and purple, and scarlet, and fine linen, and goats' *hair*,

7 And rams' skins dyed red, and badgers' skins, and shittim wood,

8 And oil for the light, and spices for anointing oil, and for the sweet incense,
9 And onyx stones, and stones to be set for
the ephod, and for the breastplate.
10 And every wise hearted among you
shall come, and make all that the LORD hath
commanded;
11 The tabernacle, his tent, and his covering, his taches, and his boards, his bars, his
pillars, and his sockets,
12 The ark, and the staves thereof, *with* the
mercy seat, and the vail of the covering,
13 The table, and his staves, and all his vessels, and the shewbread,
14 The candlestick also for the light, and
his furniture, and his lamps, with the oil
for the light,
15 And the incense altar, and his staves, and
the anointing oil, and the sweet incense, and
the hanging for the door at the entering in
of the tabernacle,
16 The altar of burnt offering, with his
brasen grate, his staves, and all his vessels,
the laver and his foot,
17 The hangings of the court, his pillars,
and their sockets, and the hanging for the
door of the court,
18 The pins of the tabernacle, and the pins
of the court, and their cords,
19 The cloths of service, to do service in
the holy *place*, the holy garments for Aaron
the priest, and the garments of his sons, to
minister in the priest's office.
20 ¶ And all the congregation of the children of Israel departed from the presence
of Moses.
21 And they came, every one whose heart
stirred him up, and every one whom his
spirit made willing, *and* they brought the
LORD's offering to the work of the tabernacle
of the congregation, and for all his service,
and for the holy garments.
22 And they came, both men and women, as
many as were willing hearted, *and* brought
bracelets, and earrings, and rings, and tablets, all jewels of gold: and every man that
offered *offered* an offering of gold unto
the LORD.
23 And every man, with whom was found
blue, and purple, and scarlet, and fine linen,
and goats' *hair*, and red skins of rams, and
badgers' skins, brought *them*.
24 Every one that did offer an offering of
silver and brass brought the LORD's offering: and every man, with whom was found
shittim wood for any work of the service,
brought *it*.
25 And all the women that were wise
hearted did spin with their hands, and
brought that which they had spun, *both* of
blue, and of purple, *and* of scarlet, and of
fine linen.
26 And all the women whose heart stirred
them up in wisdom spun goats' *hair*.
27 And the rulers brought onyx stones, and
stones to be set, for the ephod, and for the
breastplate;
28 And spice, and oil for the light, and for
the anointing oil, and for the sweet incense.
29 The children of Israel brought a willing
offering unto the LORD, every man and
woman, whose heart made them willing
to bring for all manner of work, which the
LORD had commanded to be made by the
hand of Moses.
30 ¶ And Moses said unto the children of
Israel, See, the LORD hath called by name
Bezaleel the son of Uri, the son of Hur, of
the tribe of Judah;
31 And he hath filled him with the spirit
of God, in wisdom, in understanding, and
in knowledge, and in all manner of workmanship;
32 And to devise curious works, to work in
gold, and in silver, and in brass,
33 And in the cutting of stones, to set *them*,
and in carving of wood, to make any manner
of cunning work.
34 And he hath put in his heart that he
may teach, *both* he, and Aholiab, the son
of Ahisamach, of the tribe of Dan.
35 Them hath he filled with wisdom of
heart, to work all manner of work, of the
engraver, and of the cunning workman, and
of the embroiderer, in blue, and in purple, in
scarlet, and in fine linen, and of the weaver,
even of them that do any work, and of those
that devise cunning work.

Exodus 36

1 Then wrought Bezaleel and Aholiab, and
every wise hearted man, in whom the LORD
put wisdom and understanding to know
how to work all manner of work for the
service of the sanctuary, according to all
that the LORD had commanded.

2 And Moses called Bezaleel and Aholiab,
and every wise hearted man, in whose heart
the LORD had put wisdom, *even* every one
whose heart stirred him up to come unto
the work to do it:
3 And they received of Moses all the offering, which the children of Israel had brought
for the work of the service of the sanctuary,
to make it *withal*. And they brought yet unto
him free offerings every morning.
4 And all the wise men, that wrought all
the work of the sanctuary, came every man
from his work which they made;
5 ¶ And they spake unto Moses, saying,
The people bring much more than enough
for the service of the work, which the LORD
commanded to make.
6 And Moses gave commandment, and they
caused it to be proclaimed throughout the
camp, saying, Let neither man nor woman
make any more work for the offering of the
sanctuary. So the people were restrained
from bringing.
7 For the stuff they had was sufficient for all
the work to make it, and too much.
8 ¶ And every wise hearted man among
them that wrought the work of the tabernacle made ten curtains *of* fine twined
linen, and blue, and purple, and scarlet: *with*
cherubims of cunning work made he them.
9 The length of one curtain *was* twenty and
eight cubits, and the breadth of one curtain
four cubits: the curtains *were* all of one size.
10 And he coupled the five curtains one
unto another: and *the other* five curtains
he coupled one unto another.
11 And he made loops of blue on the edge
of one curtain from the selvedge in the
coupling: likewise he made in the uttermost
side of *another* curtain, in the coupling of
the second.
12 Fifty loops made he in one curtain, and
fifty loops made he in the edge of the curtain which *was* in the coupling of the second:
the loops held one *curtain* to another.
13 And he made fifty taches of gold, and
coupled the curtains one unto another with
the taches: so it became one tabernacle.
14 ¶ And he made curtains *of* goats' *hair* for
the tent over the tabernacle: eleven curtains
he made them.
15 The length of one curtain *was* thirty
cubits, and four cubits *was* the breadth
of one curtain: the eleven curtains *were*
of one size.
16 And he coupled five curtains by themselves, and six curtains by themselves.
17 And he made fifty loops upon the uttermost edge of the curtain in the coupling, and
fifty loops made he upon the edge of the
curtain which coupleth the second.
18 And he made fifty taches *of* brass to couple the tent together, that it might be one.
19 And he made a covering for the tent
of rams' skins dyed red, and a covering *of*
badgers' skins above *that*.
20 ¶ And he made boards for the tabernacle
of shittim wood, standing up.
21 The length of a board *was* ten cubits, and
the breadth of a board one cubit and a half.
22 One board had two tenons, equally dis-
tant one from another: thus did he make for
all the boards of the tabernacle.
23 And he made boards for the tabernacle;
twenty boards for the south side southward:
24 And forty sockets of silver he made under
the twenty boards; two sockets under one
board for his two tenons, and two sockets
under another board for his two tenons.
25 And for the other side of the tabernacle,
which is toward the north corner, he made
twenty boards,
26 And their forty sockets of silver; two
sockets under one board, and two sockets
under another board.
27 And for the sides of the tabernacle westward he made six boards.
28 And two boards made he for the corners
of the tabernacle in the two sides.
29 And they were coupled beneath, and
coupled together at the head thereof, to
one ring: thus he did to both of them in
both the corners.
30 And there were eight boards; and their
sockets *were* sixteen sockets of silver, under
every board two sockets.
31 ¶ And he made bars of shittim wood;
five for the boards of the one side of the
tabernacle,
32 And five bars for the boards of the other
side of the tabernacle, and five bars for
the boards of the tabernacle for the sides
westward.
33 And he made the middle bar to shoot
through the boards from the one end to
the other.

34 And he overlaid the boards with gold, and made their rings *of* gold *to be* places for the bars, and overlaid the bars with gold.

35 ¶ And he made a vail *of* blue, and purple, and scarlet, and fine twined linen: *with* cherubims made he it of cunning work.

36 And he made thereunto four pillars *of* shittim *wood*, and overlaid them with gold: their hooks *were of* gold; and he cast for them four sockets of silver.

37 ¶ And he made an hanging for the tabernacle door *of* blue, and purple, and scarlet, and fine twined linen, of needlework;

38 And the five pillars of it with their hooks: and he overlaid their chapiters and their fillets with gold: but their five sockets *were of* brass.

Exodus 37

1 And Bezaleel made the ark *of* shittim wood: two cubits and a half *was* the length of it, and a cubit and a half the breadth of it, and a cubit and a half the height of it:

2 And he overlaid it with pure gold within and without, and made a crown of gold to it round about.

3 And he cast for it four rings of gold, *to be set* by the four corners of it; even two rings upon the one side of it, and two rings upon the other side of it.

4 And he made staves *of* shittim wood, and overlaid them with gold.

5 And he put the staves into the rings by the sides of the ark, to bear the ark.

6 ¶ And he made the mercy seat *of* pure gold: two cubits and a half *was* the length thereof, and one cubit and a half the breadth thereof.

7 And he made two cherubims *of* gold, beaten out of one piece made he them, on the two ends of the mercy seat;

8 One cherub on the end on this side, and another cherub on the *other* end on that side: out of the mercy seat made he the cherubims on the two ends thereof.

9 And the cherubims spread out *their* wings on high, *and* covered with their wings over the mercy seat, with their faces one to another; *even* to the mercy seatward were the faces of the cherubims.

10 ¶ And he made the table *of* shittim wood: two cubits *was* the length thereof, and a cubit the breadth thereof, and a cubit and a half the height thereof:

11 And he overlaid it with pure gold, and made thereunto a crown of gold round about.

12 Also he made thereunto a border of an handbreadth round about; and made a crown of gold for the border thereof round about.

13 And he cast for it four rings of gold, and put the rings upon the four corners that *were* in the four feet thereof.

14 Over against the border were the rings, the places for the staves to bear the table.

15 And he made the staves *of* shittim wood, and overlaid them with gold, to bear the table.

16 And he made the vessels which *were* upon the table, his dishes, and his spoons, and his bowls, and his covers to cover withal, *of* pure gold.

17 ¶ And he made the candlestick *of* pure gold: *of* beaten work made he the candlestick; his shaft, and his branch, his bowls, his knops, and his flowers, were of the same:

18 And six branches going out of the sides thereof; three branches of the candlestick out of the one side thereof, and three branches of the candlestick out of the other side thereof:

19 Three bowls made after the fashion of almonds in one branch, a knop and a flower; and three bowls made like almonds in another branch, a knop and a flower: so throughout the six branches going out of the candlestick.

20 And in the candlestick *were* four bowls made like almonds, his knops, and his flowers:

21 And a knop under two branches of the same, and a knop under two branches of the same, and a knop under two branches of the same, according to the six branches going out of it.

22 Their knops and their branches were of the same: all of it *was* one beaten work *of* pure gold.

23 And he made his seven lamps, and his snuffers, and his snuffdishes, *of* pure gold.

24 *Of* a talent of pure gold made he it, and all the vessels thereof.

25 ¶ And he made the incense altar *of* shittim wood: the length of it *was* a cubit, and

the breadth of it a cubit; *it was* foursquare;
and two cubits *was* the height of it; the
horns thereof were of the same.
26 And he overlaid it with pure gold, *both*
the top of it, and the sides thereof round
about, and the horns of it: also he made
unto it a crown of gold round about.
27 And he made two rings of gold for it
under the crown thereof, by the two corners of it, upon the two sides thereof, to
be places for the staves to bear it withal.
28 And he made the staves *of* shittim wood,
and overlaid them with gold.
29 ¶ And he made the holy anointing oil, and
the pure incense of sweet spices, according
to the work of the apothecary.

Exodus 38

1 And he made the altar of burnt offering
of shittim wood: five cubits *was* the length
thereof, and five cubits the breadth thereof;
it was foursquare; and three cubits the
height thereof.
2 And he made the horns thereof on the
four corners of it; the horns thereof were
of the same: and he overlaid it with brass.
3 And he made all the vessels of the altar,
the pots, and the shovels, and the basons,
and the fleshhooks, and the firepans: all the
vessels thereof made he *of* brass.
4 And he made for the altar a brasen grate
of network under the compass thereof
beneath unto the midst of it.
5 And he cast four rings for the four ends
of the grate of brass, *to be* places for the
staves.
6 And he made the staves *of* shittim wood,
and overlaid them with brass.
7 And he put the staves into the rings on the
sides of the altar, to bear it withal; he made
the altar hollow with boards.
8 ¶ And he made the laver *of* brass, and the
foot of it *of* brass, of the lookingglasses of
the women assembling, which assembled
at the door of the tabernacle of the congregation.
9 ¶ And he made the court: on the south
side southward the hangings of the court
were of fine twined linen, an hundred cubits:
10 Their pillars *were* twenty, and their
brasen sockets twenty; the hooks of the
pillars and their fillets *were of* silver.
11 And for the north side *the hangings were*
an hundred cubits, their pillars *were* twenty,
and their sockets of brass twenty; the hooks
of the pillars and their fillets *of* silver.
12 And for the west side *were* hangings of
fifty cubits, their pillars ten, and their sockets ten; the hooks of the pillars and their
fillets *of* silver.
13 And for the east side eastward fifty
cubits.
14 The hangings of the one side *of the gate*
were fifteen cubits; their pillars three, and
their sockets three.
15 And for the other side of the court gate,
on this hand and that hand, *were* hangings
of fifteen cubits; their pillars three, and their
sockets three.
16 All the hangings of the court round about
were of fine twined linen.
17 And the sockets for the pillars *were of*
brass; the hooks of the pillars and their
fillets *of* silver; and the overlaying of their
chapiters *of* silver; and all the pillars of the
court *were* filleted with silver.
18 And the hanging for the gate of the court
was needlework, *of* blue, and purple, and
scarlet, and fine twined linen: and twenty
cubits *was* the length, and the height in the
breadth *was* five cubits, answerable to the
hangings of the court.
19 And their pillars *were* four, and their
sockets *of* brass four; their hooks *of* silver,
and the overlaying of their chapiters and
their fillets *of* silver.
20 And all the pins of the tabernacle, and
of the court round about, *were of* brass.
21 ¶ This is the sum of the tabernacle, *even*
of the tabernacle of testimony, as it was
counted, according to the commandment
of Moses, *for* the service of the Levites, by
the hand of Ithamar, son to Aaron the priest.
22 And Bezaleel the son of Uri, the son of
Hur, of the tribe of Judah, made all that the
LORD commanded Moses.
23 And with him *was* Aholiab, son of Ahisamach, of the tribe of Dan, an engraver, and
a cunning workman, and an embroiderer
in blue, and in purple, and in scarlet, and
fine linen.
24 All the gold that was occupied for the
work in all the work of the holy *place*, even
the gold of the offering, was twenty and
nine talents, and seven hundred and thirty
shekels, after the shekel of the sanctuary.

25 And the silver of them that were numbered of the congregation *was* an hundred
talents, and a thousand seven hundred and
threescore and fifteen shekels, after the
shekel of the sanctuary:
26 A bekah for every man, *that is*, half a
shekel, after the shekel of the sanctuary,
for every one that went to be numbered,
from twenty years old and upward, for six
hundred thousand and three thousand and
five hundred and fifty *men*.
27 And of the hundred talents of silver were
cast the sockets of the sanctuary, and the
sockets of the vail; an hundred sockets of
the hundred talents, a talent for a socket.
28 And of the thousand seven hundred
seventy and five *shekels* he made hooks
for the pillars, and overlaid their chapiters,
and filleted them.
29 And the brass of the offering *was* seventy talents, and two thousand and four
hundred shekels.
30 And therewith he made the sockets to
the door of the tabernacle of the congregation, and the brasen altar, and the brasen
grate for it, and all the vessels of the altar,
31 And the sockets of the court round about,
and the sockets of the court gate, and all
the pins of the tabernacle, and all the pins
of the court round about.

Exodus 39

1 And of the blue, and purple, and scarlet,
they made cloths of service, to do service in
the holy *place*, and made the holy garments
for Aaron; as the LORD commanded Moses.
2 And he made the ephod *of* gold, blue, and
purple, and scarlet, and fine twined linen.
3 And they did beat the gold into thin plates,
and cut *it into* wires, to work *it* in the blue,
and in the purple, and in the scarlet, and in
the fine linen, *with* cunning work.
4 They made shoulderpieces for it, to couple
it together: by the two edges was it coupled
together.
5 And the curious girdle of his ephod, that
was upon it, *was* of the same, according to
the work thereof; *of* gold, blue, and purple,
and scarlet, and fine twined linen; as the
LORD commanded Moses.
6 ¶ And they wrought onyx stones inclosed
in ouches of gold, graven, as signets are
graven, with the names of the children of
Israel.
7 And he put them on the shoulders of the
ephod, *that they should be* stones for a
memorial to the children of Israel; as the
LORD commanded Moses.
8 ¶ And he made the breastplate *of* cunning work, like the work of the ephod; *of*
gold, blue, and purple, and scarlet, and fine
twined linen.
9 It was foursquare; they made the breastplate double: a span *was* the length thereof,
and a span the breadth thereof, *being*
doubled.
10 And they set in it four rows of stones:
the first row *was* a sardius, a topaz, and a
carbuncle: this *was* the first row.
11 And the second row, an emerald, a sapphire, and a diamond.
12 And the third row, a ligure, an agate, and
an amethyst.
13 And the fourth row, a beryl, an onyx,
and a jasper: *they were* inclosed in ouches
of gold in their inclosings.
14 And the stones *were* according to the
names of the children of Israel, twelve,
according to their names, *like* the engravings of a signet, every one with his name,
according to the twelve tribes.
15 And they made upon the breastplate
chains at the ends, *of* wreathen work *of*
pure gold.
16 And they made two ouches *of* gold, and
two gold rings; and put the two rings in the
two ends of the breastplate.
17 And they put the two wreathen chains
of gold in the two rings on the ends of the
breastplate.
18 And the two ends of the two wreathen
chains they fastened in the two ouches,
and put them on the shoulderpieces of the
ephod, before it.
19 And they made two rings of gold, and put
them on the two ends of the breastplate,
upon the border of it, which *was* on the side
of the ephod inward.
20 And they made two *other* golden rings,
and put them on the two sides of the ephod
underneath, toward the forepart of it, over
against the *other* coupling thereof, above
the curious girdle of the ephod.
21 And they did bind the breastplate by his
rings unto the rings of the ephod with a lace

of blue, that it might be above the curious
girdle of the ephod, and that the breastplate
might not be loosed from the ephod; as the
LORD commanded Moses.
22 ¶ And he made the robe of the ephod
of woven work, all *of* blue.
23 And *there was* an hole in the midst of the
robe, as the hole of an habergeon, *with* a
band round about the hole, that it should
not rend.
24 And they made upon the hems of the
robe pomegranates *of* blue, and purple,
and scarlet, *and* twined *linen*.
25 And they made bells *of* pure gold, and put
the bells between the pomegranates upon
the hem of the robe, round about between
the pomegranates;
26 A bell and a pomegranate, a bell and
a pomegranate, round about the hem of
the robe to minister *in;* as the LORD commanded Moses.
27 ¶ And they made coats *of* fine linen *of*
woven work for Aaron, and for his sons,
28 And a mitre *of* fine linen, and goodly
bonnets *of* fine linen, and linen breeches
of fine twined linen,
29 And a girdle *of* fine twined linen, and
blue, and purple, and scarlet, *of* needlework;
as the LORD commanded Moses.
30 ¶ And they made the plate of the holy
crown *of* pure gold, and wrote upon it a
writing, *like to* the engravings of a signet,
HOLINESS TO THE LORD.
31 And they tied unto it a lace of blue, to
fasten *it* on high upon the mitre; as the LORD
commanded Moses.
32 ¶ Thus was all the work of the tabernacle
of the tent of the congregation finished: and
the children of Israel did according to all that
the LORD commanded Moses, so did they.
33 ¶ And they brought the tabernacle unto
Moses, the tent, and all his furniture, his
taches, his boards, his bars, and his pillars,
and his sockets,
34 And the covering of rams' skins dyed red,
and the covering of badgers' skins, and the
vail of the covering,
35 The ark of the testimony, and the staves
thereof, and the mercy seat,
36 The table, *and* all the vessels thereof,
and the shewbread,
37 The pure candlestick, *with* the lamps
thereof, *even with* the lamps to be set in
order, and all the vessels thereof, and the
oil for light,
38 And the golden altar, and the anointing
oil, and the sweet incense, and the hanging
for the tabernacle door,
39 The brasen altar, and his grate of brass,
his staves, and all his vessels, the laver and
his foot,
40 The hangings of the court, his pillars,
and his sockets, and the hanging for the
court gate, his cords, and his pins, and all
the vessels of the service of the tabernacle,
for the tent of the congregation,
41 The cloths of service to do service in
the holy *place*, and the holy garments for
Aaron the priest, and his sons' garments,
to minister in the priest's office.
42 According to all that the LORD commanded Moses, so the children of Israel
made all the work.
43 And Moses did look upon all the work,
and, behold, they had done it as the LORD
had commanded, even so had they done it:
and Moses blessed them.

Exodus 40

1 And the LORD spake unto Moses, saying,
2 On the first day of the first month shalt
thou set up the tabernacle of the tent of
the congregation.
3 And thou shalt put therein the ark of the
testimony, and cover the ark with the vail.
4 And thou shalt bring in the table, and
set in order the things that are to be set in
order upon it; and thou shalt bring in the
candlestick, and light the lamps thereof.
5 And thou shalt set the altar of gold for the
incense before the ark of the testimony,
and put the hanging of the door to the
tabernacle.
6 And thou shalt set the altar of the burnt
offering before the door of the tabernacle
of the tent of the congregation.
7 And thou shalt set the laver between the
tent of the congregation and the altar, and
shalt put water therein.
8 And thou shalt set up the court round
about, and hang up the hanging at the
court gate.
9 And thou shalt take the anointing oil,
and anoint the tabernacle, and all that *is*
therein, and shalt hallow it, and all the vessels thereof: and it shall be holy.

10 And thou shalt anoint the altar of the
burnt offering, and all his vessels, and
sanctify the altar: and it shall be an altar
most holy.
11 And thou shalt anoint the laver and his
foot, and sanctify it.
12 And thou shalt bring Aaron and his sons
unto the door of the tabernacle of the
congregation, and wash them with water.
13 And thou shalt put upon Aaron the holy
garments, and anoint him, and sanctify
him; that he may minister unto me in the
priest's office.
14 And thou shalt bring his sons, and clothe
them with coats:
15 And thou shalt anoint them, as thou
didst anoint their father, that they may
minister unto me in the priest's office: for
their anointing shall surely be an everlasting
priesthood throughout their generations.
16 Thus did Moses: according to all that the
LORD commanded him, so did he.
17 ¶ And it came to pass in the first month
in the second year, on the first *day* of the
month, *that* the tabernacle was reared up.
18 And Moses reared up the tabernacle, and
fastened his sockets, and set up the boards
thereof, and put in the bars thereof, and
reared up his pillars.
19 And he spread abroad the tent over the tabernacle, and put the covering of the tent above
upon it; as the LORD commanded Moses.
20 ¶ And he took and put the testimony
into the ark, and set the staves on the ark,
and put the mercy seat above upon the ark:
21 And he brought the ark into the tabernacle, and set up the vail of the covering,
and covered the ark of the testimony; as
the LORD commanded Moses.
22 ¶ And he put the table in the tent of the
congregation, upon the side of the tabernacle northward, without the vail.
23 And he set the bread in order upon it
before the LORD; as the LORD had commanded Moses.
24 ¶ And he put the candlestick in the tent
of the congregation, over against the table,
on the side of the tabernacle southward.
25 And he lighted the lamps before the
LORD; as the LORD commanded Moses.
26 ¶ And he put the golden altar in the tent
of the congregation before the vail:
27 And he burnt sweet incense thereon; as
the LORD commanded Moses.
28 ¶ And he set up the hanging *at* the door
of the tabernacle.
29 And he put the altar of burnt offering *by*
the door of the tabernacle of the tent of the
congregation, and offered upon it the burnt
offering and the meat offering; as the LORD
commanded Moses.
30 ¶ And he set the laver between the tent
of the congregation and the altar, and put
water there, to wash *withal*.
31 And Moses and Aaron and his sons
washed their hands and their feet thereat:
32 When they went into the tent of the
congregation, and when they came near
unto the altar, they washed; as the LORD
commanded Moses.
33 And he reared up the court round about
the tabernacle and the altar, and set up
the hanging of the court gate. So Moses
finished the work.
34 ¶ Then a cloud covered the tent of the
congregation, and the glory of the LORD
filled the tabernacle.
35 And Moses was not able to enter into
the tent of the congregation, because the
cloud abode thereon, and the glory of the
LORD filled the tabernacle.
36 And when the cloud was taken up from
over the tabernacle, the children of Israel
went onward in all their journeys:
37 But if the cloud were not taken up, then
they journeyed not till the day that it was
taken up.
38 For the cloud of the LORD *was* upon the
tabernacle by day, and fire was on it by
night, in the sight of all the house of Israel,
throughout all their journeys.

The Third Book Of Moses Called

Leviticus

Leviticus 1

1 And the LORD called unto Moses, and
spake unto him out of the tabernacle of the
congregation, saying,
2 Speak unto the children of Israel, and
say unto them, If any man of you bring an
offering unto the LORD, ye shall bring your
offering of the cattle, *even* of the herd, and
of the flock.
3 If his offering *be* a burnt sacrifice of the
herd, let him offer a male without blemish:
he shall offer it of his own voluntary will at
the door of the tabernacle of the congregation before the LORD.
4 And he shall put his hand upon the head of
the burnt offering; and it shall be accepted
for him to make atonement for him.
5 And he shall kill the bullock before the
LORD: and the priests, Aaron's sons, shall
bring the blood, and sprinkle the blood
round about upon the altar that *is by* the
door of the tabernacle of the congregation.
6 And he shall flay the burnt offering, and
cut it into his pieces.
7 And the sons of Aaron the priest shall
put fire upon the altar, and lay the wood in
order upon the fire:
8 And the priests, Aaron's sons, shall lay
the parts, the head, and the fat, in order
upon the wood that *is* on the fire which *is*
upon the altar:
9 But his inwards and his legs shall he wash
in water: and the priest shall burn all on
the altar, *to be* a burnt sacrifice, an offering made by fire, of a sweet savour unto
the LORD.
10 ¶ And if his offering *be* of the flocks,
namely, of the sheep, or of the goats, for
a burnt sacrifice; he shall bring it a male
without blemish.
11 And he shall kill it on the side of the altar
northward before the LORD: and the priests,
Aaron's sons, shall sprinkle his blood round
about upon the altar.
12 And he shall cut it into his pieces, with
his head and his fat: and the priest shall lay
them in order on the wood that *is* on the
fire which *is* upon the altar:
13 But he shall wash the inwards and the
legs with water: and the priest shall bring *it*
all, and burn *it* upon the altar: it *is* a burnt
sacrifice, an offering made by fire, of a sweet
savour unto the LORD.
14 ¶ And if the burnt sacrifice for his offering to the LORD *be* of fowls, then he shall
bring his offering of turtledoves, or of young
pigeons.
15 And the priest shall bring it unto the altar,
and wring off his head, and burn *it* on the
altar; and the blood thereof shall be wrung
out at the side of the altar:
16 And he shall pluck away his crop with his
feathers, and cast it beside the altar on the
east part, by the place of the ashes:
17 And he shall cleave it with the wings
thereof, *but* shall not divide *it* asunder: and
the priest shall burn it upon the altar, upon
the wood that *is* upon the fire: it *is* a burnt
sacrifice, an offering made by fire, of a sweet
savour unto the LORD.

Leviticus 2

1 And when any will offer a meat offering
unto the LORD, his offering shall be *of* fine
flour; and he shall pour oil upon it, and put
frankincense thereon:
2 And he shall bring it to Aaron's sons the
priests: and he shall take thereout his
handful of the flour thereof, and of the oil
thereof, with all the frankincense thereof;
and the priest shall burn the memorial of
it upon the altar, *to be* an offering made by
fire, of a sweet savour unto the LORD:
3 And the remnant of the meat offering
shall be Aaron's and his sons': *it is* a thing
most holy of the offerings of the LORD
made by fire.
4 ¶ And if thou bring an oblation of a meat
offering baken in the oven, *it shall be* unleavened cakes of fine flour mingled with oil, or
unleavened wafers anointed with oil.
5 ¶ And if thy oblation *be* a meat offer-

ing *baken* in a pan, it shall be *of* fine flour unleavened, mingled with oil.

6 Thou shalt part it in pieces, and pour oil thereon: it *is* a meat offering.

7 ¶ And if thy oblation *be* a meat offering *baken* in the fryingpan, it shall be made *of* fine flour with oil.

8 And thou shalt bring the meat offering that is made of these things unto the LORD: and when it is presented unto the priest, he shall bring it unto the altar.

9 And the priest shall take from the meat offering a memorial thereof, and shall burn *it* upon the altar: *it is* an offering made by fire, of a sweet savour unto the LORD.

10 And that which is left of the meat offering *shall be* Aaron's and his sons': *it is* a thing most holy of the offerings of the LORD made by fire.

11 No meat offering, which ye shall bring unto the LORD, shall be made with leaven: for ye shall burn no leaven, nor any honey, in any offering of the LORD made by fire.

12 ¶ As for the oblation of the firstfruits, ye shall offer them unto the LORD: but they shall not be burnt on the altar for a sweet savour.

13 And every oblation of thy meat offering shalt thou season with salt; neither shalt thou suffer the salt of the covenant of thy God to be lacking from thy meat offering: with all thine offerings thou shalt offer salt.

14 And if thou offer a meat offering of thy firstfruits unto the LORD, thou shalt offer for the meat offering of thy firstfruits green ears of corn dried by the fire, *even* corn beaten out of full ears.

15 And thou shalt put oil upon it, and lay frankincense thereon: it *is* a meat offering.

16 And the priest shall burn the memorial of it, *part* of the beaten corn thereof, and *part* of the oil thereof, with all the frankincense thereof: *it is* an offering made by fire unto the LORD.

Leviticus 3

1 And if his oblation *be* a sacrifice of peace offering, if he offer *it* of the herd; whether *it be* a male or female, he shall offer it without blemish before the LORD.

2 And he shall lay his hand upon the head of his offering, and kill it *at* the door of the tabernacle of the congregation: and Aaron's sons the priests shall sprinkle the blood upon the altar round about.

3 And he shall offer of the sacrifice of the peace offering an offering made by fire unto the LORD; the fat that covereth the inwards, and all the fat that *is* upon the inwards,

4 And the two kidneys, and the fat that *is* on them, which *is* by the flanks, and the caul above the liver, with the kidneys, it shall he take away.

5 And Aaron's sons shall burn it on the altar upon the burnt sacrifice, which *is* upon the wood that *is* on the fire: *it is* an offering made by fire, of a sweet savour unto the LORD.

6 ¶ And if his offering for a sacrifice of peace offering unto the LORD *be* of the flock; male or female, he shall offer it without blemish.

7 If he offer a lamb for his offering, then shall he offer it before the LORD.

8 And he shall lay his hand upon the head of his offering, and kill it before the tabernacle of the congregation: and Aaron's sons shall sprinkle the blood thereof round about upon the altar.

9 And he shall offer of the sacrifice of the peace offering an offering made by fire unto the LORD; the fat thereof, *and* the whole rump, it shall he take off hard by the backbone; and the fat that covereth the inwards, and all the fat that *is* upon the inwards,

10 And the two kidneys, and the fat that *is* upon them, which *is* by the flanks, and the caul above the liver, with the kidneys, it shall he take away.

11 And the priest shall burn it upon the altar: *it is* the food of the offering made by fire unto the LORD.

12 ¶ And if his offering *be* a goat, then he shall offer it before the LORD.

13 And he shall lay his hand upon the head of it, and kill it before the tabernacle of the congregation: and the sons of Aaron shall sprinkle the blood thereof upon the altar round about.

14 And he shall offer thereof his offering, *even* an offering made by fire unto the LORD; the fat that covereth the inwards, and all the fat that *is* upon the inwards,

15 And the two kidneys, and the fat that *is* upon them, which *is* by the flanks, and the caul above the liver, with the kidneys, it shall he take away.

16 And the priest shall burn them upon the altar: *it is* the food of the offering made by fire for a sweet savour: all the fat *is* the LORD's.
17 *It shall be* a perpetual statute for your generations throughout all your dwellings, that ye eat neither fat nor blood.

Leviticus 4

1 And the LORD spake unto Moses, saying,
2 Speak unto the children of Israel, saying, If a soul shall sin through ignorance against any of the commandments of the LORD *concerning things* which ought not to be done, and shall do against any of them:
3 If the priest that is anointed do sin according to the sin of the people; then let him bring for his sin, which he hath sinned, a young bullock without blemish unto the LORD for a sin offering.
4 And he shall bring the bullock unto the door of the tabernacle of the congregation before the LORD; and shall lay his hand upon the bullock's head, and kill the bullock before the LORD.
5 And the priest that is anointed shall take of the bullock's blood, and bring it to the tabernacle of the congregation:
6 And the priest shall dip his finger in the blood, and sprinkle of the blood seven times before the LORD, before the vail of the sanctuary.
7 And the priest shall put *some* of the blood upon the horns of the altar of sweet incense before the LORD, which *is* in the tabernacle of the congregation; and shall pour all the blood of the bullock at the bottom of the altar of the burnt offering, which *is at* the door of the tabernacle of the congregation.
8 And he shall take off from it all the fat of the bullock for the sin offering; the fat that covereth the inwards, and all the fat that *is* upon the inwards,
9 And the two kidneys, and the fat that *is* upon them, which *is* by the flanks, and the caul above the liver, with the kidneys, it shall he take away,
10 As it was taken off from the bullock of the sacrifice of peace offerings: and the priest shall burn them upon the altar of the burnt offering.
11 And the skin of the bullock, and all his flesh, with his head, and with his legs, and his inwards, and his dung,
12 Even the whole bullock shall he carry forth without the camp unto a clean place, where the ashes are poured out, and burn him on the wood with fire: where the ashes are poured out shall he be burnt.
13 ¶ And if the whole congregation of Israel sin through ignorance, and the thing be hid from the eyes of the assembly, and they have done *somewhat against* any of the commandments of the LORD *concerning things* which should not be done, and are guilty;
14 When the sin, which they have sinned against it, is known, then the congregation shall offer a young bullock for the sin, and bring him before the tabernacle of the congregation.
15 And the elders of the congregation shall lay their hands upon the head of the bullock before the LORD: and the bullock shall be killed before the LORD.
16 And the priest that is anointed shall bring of the bullock's blood to the tabernacle of the congregation:
17 And the priest shall dip his finger *in some* of the blood, and sprinkle *it* seven times before the LORD, *even* before the vail.
18 And he shall put *some* of the blood upon the horns of the altar which *is* before the LORD, that *is* in the tabernacle of the congregation, and shall pour out all the blood at the bottom of the altar of the burnt offering, which *is at* the door of the tabernacle of the congregation.
19 And he shall take all his fat from him, and burn *it* upon the altar.
20 And he shall do with the bullock as he did with the bullock for a sin offering, so shall he do with this: and the priest shall make an atonement for them, and it shall be forgiven them.
21 And he shall carry forth the bullock without the camp, and burn him as he burned the first bullock: it *is* a sin offering for the congregation.
22 ¶ When a ruler hath sinned, and done *somewhat* through ignorance *against* any of the commandments of the LORD his God *concerning things* which should not be done, and is guilty;
23 Or if his sin, wherein he hath sinned,

come to his knowledge; he shall bring his
offering, a kid of the goats, a male without
blemish:
24 And he shall lay his hand upon the head
of the goat, and kill it in the place where
they kill the burnt offering before the LORD:
it *is* a sin offering.
25 And the priest shall take of the blood of
the sin offering with his finger, and put *it*
upon the horns of the altar of burnt offering,
and shall pour out his blood at the bottom
of the altar of burnt offering.
26 And he shall burn all his fat upon the altar,
as the fat of the sacrifice of peace offerings:
and the priest shall make an atonement for
him as concerning his sin, and it shall be
forgiven him.
27 ¶ And if any one of the common people
sin through ignorance, while he doeth *somewhat against* any of the commandments of
the LORD *concerning things* which ought not
to be done, and be guilty;
28 Or if his sin, which he hath sinned, come
to his knowledge: then he shall bring his
offering, a kid of the goats, a female without
blemish, for his sin which he hath sinned.
29 And he shall lay his hand upon the head
of the sin offering, and slay the sin offering
in the place of the burnt offering.
30 And the priest shall take of the blood
thereof with his finger, and put *it* upon the
horns of the altar of burnt offering, and
shall pour out all the blood thereof at the
bottom of the altar.
31 And he shall take away all the fat thereof,
as the fat is taken away from off the sacrifice
of peace offerings; and the priest shall burn
it upon the altar for a sweet savour unto the
LORD; and the priest shall make an atonement for him, and it shall be forgiven him.
32 And if he bring a lamb for a sin offering,
he shall bring it a female without blemish.
33 And he shall lay his hand upon the
head of the sin offering, and slay it for a
sin offering in the place where they kill the
burnt offering.
34 And the priest shall take of the blood of
the sin offering with his finger, and put *it*
upon the horns of the altar of burnt offering,
and shall pour out all the blood thereof at
the bottom of the altar:
35 And he shall take away all the fat thereof,
as the fat of the lamb is taken away from
the sacrifice of the peace offerings; and
the priest shall burn them upon the altar,
according to the offerings made by fire
unto the LORD: and the priest shall make an
atonement for his sin that he hath committed, and it shall be forgiven him.

Leviticus 5

1 And if a soul sin, and hear the voice of
swearing, and *is* a witness, whether he hath
seen or known *of it;* if he do not utter *it*, then
he shall bear his iniquity.
2 Or if a soul touch any unclean thing,
whether *it be* a carcase of an unclean beast,
or a carcase of unclean cattle, or the carcase of unclean creeping things, and *if* it be
hidden from him; he also shall be unclean,
and guilty.
3 Or if he touch the uncleanness of man,
whatsoever uncleanness *it be* that a man
shall be defiled withal, and it be hid from
him; when he knoweth *of it*, then he shall
be guilty.
4 Or if a soul swear, pronouncing with *his*
lips to do evil, or to do good, whatsoever *it
be* that a man shall pronounce with an oath,
and it be hid from him; when he knoweth
of it, then he shall be guilty in one of these.
5 And it shall be, when he shall be guilty in
one of these *things*, that he shall confess
that he hath sinned in that *thing:*
6 And he shall bring his trespass offering
unto the LORD for his sin which he hath
sinned, a female from the flock, a lamb or
a kid of the goats, for a sin offering; and
the priest shall make an atonement for him
concerning his sin.
7 And if he be not able to bring a lamb, then
he shall bring for his trespass, which he
hath committed, two turtledoves, or two
young pigeons, unto the LORD; one for a sin
offering, and the other for a burnt offering.
8 And he shall bring them unto the priest,
who shall offer *that* which *is* for the sin
offering first, and wring off his head from
his neck, but shall not divide *it* asunder:
9 And he shall sprinkle of the blood of the
sin offering upon the side of the altar; and
the rest of the blood shall be wrung out at
the bottom of the altar: it *is* a sin offering.
10 And he shall offer the second *for* a burnt
offering, according to the manner: and the
priest shall make an atonement for him for

his sin which he hath sinned, and it shall be
forgiven him.
11 ¶ But if he be not able to bring two turtledoves, or two young pigeons, then he
that sinned shall bring for his offering the
tenth part of an ephah of fine flour for a sin
offering; he shall put no oil upon it, neither
shall he put *any* frankincense thereon: for
it *is* a sin offering.
12 Then shall he bring it to the priest, and
the priest shall take his handful of it, *even* a
memorial thereof, and burn *it* on the altar,
according to the offerings made by fire unto
the LORD: it *is* a sin offering.
13 And the priest shall make an atonement for him as touching his sin that he
hath sinned in one of these, and it shall be
forgiven him: and *the remnant* shall be the
priest's, as a meat offering.
14 ¶ And the LORD spake unto Moses,
saying,
15 If a soul commit a trespass, and sin
through ignorance, in the holy things of the
LORD; then he shall bring for his trespass
unto the LORD a ram without blemish out
of the flocks, with thy estimation by shekels
of silver, after the shekel of the sanctuary,
for a trespass offering:
16 And he shall make amends for the harm
that he hath done in the holy thing, and
shall add the fifth part thereto, and give it
unto the priest: and the priest shall make an
atonement for him with the ram of the trespass offering, and it shall be forgiven him.
17 ¶ And if a soul sin, and commit any of
these things which are forbidden to be done
by the commandments of the LORD; though
he wist *it* not, yet is he guilty, and shall bear
his iniquity.
18 And he shall bring a ram without blemish
out of the flock, with thy estimation, for a
trespass offering, unto the priest: and the
priest shall make an atonement for him
concerning his ignorance wherein he erred
and wist *it* not, and it shall be forgiven him.
19 It *is* a trespass offering: he hath certainly
trespassed against the LORD.

Leviticus 6

1 And the LORD spake unto Moses, saying,
2 If a soul sin, and commit a trespass against
the LORD, and lie unto his neighbour in
that which was delivered him to keep, or
in fellowship, or in a thing taken away by
violence, or hath deceived his neighbour;
3 Or have found that which was lost, and
lieth concerning it, and sweareth falsely; in
any of all these that a man doeth, sinning
therein:
4 Then it shall be, because he hath sinned,
and is guilty, that he shall restore that which
he took violently away, or the thing which
he hath deceitfully gotten, or that which
was delivered him to keep, or the lost thing
which he found,
5 Or all that about which he hath sworn
falsely; he shall even restore it in the principal, and shall add the fifth part more
thereto, *and* give it unto him to whom it
appertaineth, in the day of his trespass
offering.
6 And he shall bring his trespass offering
unto the LORD, a ram without blemish out of
the flock, with thy estimation, for a trespass
offering, unto the priest:
7 And the priest shall make an atonement
for him before the LORD: and it shall be forgiven him for any thing of all that he hath
done in trespassing therein.
8 ¶ And the LORD spake unto Moses, saying,
9 Command Aaron and his sons, saying, This
is the law of the burnt offering: It *is* the burnt
offering, because of the burning upon the
altar all night unto the morning, and the fire
of the altar shall be burning in it.
10 And the priest shall put on his linen
garment, and his linen breeches shall he
put upon his flesh, and take up the ashes
which the fire hath consumed with the burnt
offering on the altar, and he shall put them
beside the altar.
11 And he shall put off his garments, and
put on other garments, and carry forth the
ashes without the camp unto a clean place.
12 And the fire upon the altar shall be burning in it; it shall not be put out: and the priest
shall burn wood on it every morning, and
lay the burnt offering in order upon it; and
he shall burn thereon the fat of the peace
offerings.
13 The fire shall ever be burning upon the
altar; it shall never go out.
14 ¶ And this *is* the law of the meat offering:
the sons of Aaron shall offer it before the
LORD, before the altar.
15 And he shall take of it his handful, of

the flour of the meat offering, and of the
oil thereof, and all the frankincense which
is upon the meat offering, and shall burn *it*
upon the altar *for* a sweet savour, *even* the
memorial of it, unto the LORD.
16 And the remainder thereof shall Aaron
and his sons eat: with unleavened bread
shall it be eaten in the holy place; in the
court of the tabernacle of the congregation
they shall eat it.
17 It shall not be baken with leaven. I have
given it *unto them for* their portion of my
offerings made by fire; it *is* most holy, as *is*
the sin offering, and as the trespass offering.
18 All the males among the children of
Aaron shall eat of it. *It shall be* a statute for
ever in your generations concerning the
offerings of the LORD made by fire: every
one that toucheth them shall be holy.
19 ¶ And the LORD spake unto Moses,
saying,
20 This *is* the offering of Aaron and of his
sons, which they shall offer unto the LORD in
the day when he is anointed; the tenth part
of an ephah of fine flour for a meat offering
perpetual, half of it in the morning, and half
thereof at night.
21 In a pan it shall be made with oil; *and
when it is* baken, thou shalt bring it in: *and*
the baken pieces of the meat offering shalt
thou offer *for* a sweet savour unto the LORD.
22 And the priest of his sons that is anointed
in his stead shall offer it: *it is* a statute for
ever unto the LORD; it shall be wholly burnt.
23 For every meat offering for the priest
shall be wholly burnt: it shall not be eaten.
24 ¶ And the LORD spake unto Moses,
saying,
25 Speak unto Aaron and to his sons, saying, This *is* the law of the sin offering: In the
place where the burnt offering is killed shall
the sin offering be killed before the LORD:
it *is* most holy.
26 The priest that offereth it for sin shall eat
it: in the holy place shall it be eaten, in the
court of the tabernacle of the congregation.
27 Whatsoever shall touch the flesh thereof
shall be holy: and when there is sprinkled of
the blood thereof upon any garment, thou
shalt wash that whereon it was sprinkled
in the holy place.
28 But the earthen vessel wherein it is sodden shall be broken: and if it be sodden in
a brasen pot, it shall be both scoured, and
rinsed in water.
29 All the males among the priests shall eat
thereof: it *is* most holy.
30 And no sin offering, whereof *any* of the
blood is brought into the tabernacle of the
congregation to reconcile *withal* in the
holy *place*, shall be eaten: it shall be burnt
in the fire.

Leviticus 7

1 Likewise this *is* the law of the trespass
offering: it *is* most holy.
2 In the place where they kill the burnt offering shall they kill the trespass offering: and
the blood thereof shall he sprinkle round
about upon the altar.
3 And he shall offer of it all the fat thereof;
the rump, and the fat that covereth the
inwards,
4 And the two kidneys, and the fat that *is* on
them, which *is* by the flanks, and the caul
that is above the liver, with the kidneys, it
shall he take away:
5 And the priest shall burn them upon the
altar *for* an offering made by fire unto the
LORD: it *is* a trespass offering.
6 Every male among the priests shall eat
thereof: it shall be eaten in the holy place:
it *is* most holy.
7 As the sin offering *is*, so *is* the trespass
offering: *there is* one law for them: the
priest that maketh atonement therewith
shall have *it*.
8 And the priest that offereth any man's
burnt offering, *even* the priest shall have to
himself the skin of the burnt offering which
he hath offered.
9 And all the meat offering that is baken in
the oven, and all that is dressed in the fryingpan, and in the pan, shall be the priest's
that offereth it.
10 And every meat offering, mingled with
oil, and dry, shall all the sons of Aaron have,
one *as much* as another.
11 And this *is* the law of the sacrifice of
peace offerings, which he shall offer unto
the LORD.
12 If he offer it for a thanksgiving, then he
shall offer with the sacrifice of thanksgiving
unleavened cakes mingled with oil, and
unleavened wafers anointed with oil, and
cakes mingled with oil, of fine flour, fried.

13 Besides the cakes, he shall offer *for* his
offering leavened bread with the sacrifice of
thanksgiving of his peace offerings.
14 And of it he shall offer one out of the
whole oblation *for* an heave offering unto
the LORD, *and* it shall be the priest's that
sprinkleth the blood of the peace offerings.
15 And the flesh of the sacrifice of his peace
offerings for thanksgiving shall be eaten the
same day that it is offered; he shall not leave
any of it until the morning.
16 But if the sacrifice of his offering *be* a
vow, or a voluntary offering, it shall be eaten
the same day that he offereth his sacrifice:
and on the morrow also the remainder of
it shall be eaten:
17 But the remainder of the flesh of the
sacrifice on the third day shall be burnt
with fire.
18 And if *any* of the flesh of the sacrifice of
his peace offerings be eaten at all on the
third day, it shall not be accepted, neither
shall it be imputed unto him that offereth
it: it shall be an abomination, and the soul
that eateth of it shall bear his iniquity.
19 And the flesh that toucheth any unclean
thing shall not be eaten; it shall be burnt
with fire: and as for the flesh, all that be
clean shall eat thereof.
20 But the soul that eateth *of* the flesh of
the sacrifice of peace offerings, that *pertain* unto the LORD, having his uncleanness
upon him, even that soul shall be cut off
from his people.
21 Moreover the soul that shall touch any
unclean *thing, as* the uncleanness of man,
or *any* unclean beast, or any abominable
unclean *thing,* and eat of the flesh of the
sacrifice of peace offerings, which *pertain*
unto the LORD, even that soul shall be cut
off from his people.
22 ¶ And the LORD spake unto Moses,
saying,
23 Speak unto the children of Israel, saying,
Ye shall eat no manner of fat, of ox, or of
sheep, or of goat.
24 And the fat of the beast that dieth of
itself, and the fat of that which is torn with
beasts, may be used in any other use: but
ye shall in no wise eat of it.
25 For whosoever eateth the fat of the
beast, of which men offer an offering made
by fire unto the LORD, even the soul that
eateth *it* shall be cut off from his people.
26 Moreover ye shall eat no manner of
blood, *whether it be* of fowl or of beast, in
any of your dwellings.
27 Whatsoever soul *it be* that eateth any
manner of blood, even that soul shall be
cut off from his people.
28 ¶ And the LORD spake unto Moses,
saying,
29 Speak unto the children of Israel, saying,
He that offereth the sacrifice of his peace
offerings unto the LORD shall bring his oblation unto the LORD of the sacrifice of his
peace offerings.
30 His own hands shall bring the offerings
of the LORD made by fire, the fat with the
breast, it shall he bring, that the breast
may be waved *for* a wave offering before
the LORD.
31 And the priest shall burn the fat upon
the altar: but the breast shall be Aaron's
and his sons'.
32 And the right shoulder shall ye give unto
the priest *for* an heave offering of the sacrifices of your peace offerings.
33 He among the sons of Aaron, that
offereth the blood of the peace offerings,
and the fat, shall have the right shoulder
for *his* part.
34 For the wave breast and the heave shoulder have I taken of the children of Israel from
off the sacrifices of their peace offerings,
and have given them unto Aaron the priest
and unto his sons by a statute for ever from
among the children of Israel.
35 ¶ This *is the portion* of the anointing of
Aaron, and of the anointing of his sons, out
of the offerings of the LORD made by fire, in
the day *when* he presented them to minister
unto the LORD in the priest's office;
36 Which the LORD commanded to be given
them of the children of Israel, in the day
that he anointed them, *by* a statute for ever
throughout their generations.
37 This *is* the law of the burnt offering, of
the meat offering, and of the sin offering,
and of the trespass offering, and of the
consecrations, and of the sacrifice of the
peace offerings;
38 Which the LORD commanded Moses in
mount Sinai, in the day that he commanded

the children of Israel to offer their oblations
unto the LORD, in the wilderness of Sinai.

Leviticus 8

1 And the LORD spake unto Moses, saying,
2 Take Aaron and his sons with him, and
the garments, and the anointing oil, and a
bullock for the sin offering, and two rams,
and a basket of unleavened bread;
3 And gather thou all the congregation
together unto the door of the tabernacle
of the congregation.
4 And Moses did as the LORD commanded
him; and the assembly was gathered
together unto the door of the tabernacle
of the congregation.
5 And Moses said unto the congregation,
This *is* the thing which the LORD commanded
to be done.
6 And Moses brought Aaron and his sons,
and washed them with water.
7 And he put upon him the coat, and girded
him with the girdle, and clothed him with
the robe, and put the ephod upon him, and
he girded him with the curious girdle of the
ephod, and bound *it* unto him therewith.
8 And he put the breastplate upon him: also
he put in the breastplate the Urim and the
Thummim.
9 And he put the mitre upon his head; also
upon the mitre, *even* upon his forefront, did
he put the golden plate, the holy crown; as
the LORD commanded Moses.
10 And Moses took the anointing oil, and
anointed the tabernacle and all that *was*
therein, and sanctified them.
11 And he sprinkled thereof upon the altar
seven times, and anointed the altar and all
his vessels, both the laver and his foot, to
sanctify them.
12 And he poured of the anointing oil
upon Aaron's head, and anointed him, to
sanctify him.
13 And Moses brought Aaron's sons, and
put coats upon them, and girded them with
girdles, and put bonnets upon them; as the
LORD commanded Moses.
14 And he brought the bullock for the sin
offering: and Aaron and his sons laid their
hands upon the head of the bullock for the
sin offering.
15 And he slew *it;* and Moses took the blood,
and put *it* upon the horns of the altar round
about with his finger, and purified the altar,
and poured the blood at the bottom of the
altar, and sanctified it, to make reconciliation upon it.
16 And he took all the fat that *was* upon the
inwards, and the caul *above* the liver, and
the two kidneys, and their fat, and Moses
burned *it* upon the altar.
17 But the bullock, and his hide, his flesh,
and his dung, he burnt with fire without
the camp; as the LORD commanded Moses.
18 ¶ And he brought the ram for the burnt
offering: and Aaron and his sons laid their
hands upon the head of the ram.
19 And he killed *it;* and Moses sprinkled the
blood upon the altar round about.
20 And he cut the ram into pieces; and
Moses burnt the head, and the pieces, and
the fat.
21 And he washed the inwards and the legs
in water; and Moses burnt the whole ram
upon the altar: it *was* a burnt sacrifice for a
sweet savour, *and* an offering made by fire
unto the LORD; as the LORD commanded
Moses.
22 ¶ And he brought the other ram, the ram
of consecration: and Aaron and his sons
laid their hands upon the head of the ram.
23 And he slew *it;* and Moses took of the
blood of it, and put *it* upon the tip of Aaron's right ear, and upon the thumb of his
right hand, and upon the great toe of his
right foot.
24 And he brought Aaron's sons, and Moses
put of the blood upon the tip of their right
ear, and upon the thumbs of their right
hands, and upon the great toes of their right
feet: and Moses sprinkled the blood upon
the altar round about.
25 And he took the fat, and the rump, and all
the fat that *was* upon the inwards, and the
caul *above* the liver, and the two kidneys,
and their fat, and the right shoulder:
26 And out of the basket of unleavened
bread, that *was* before the LORD, he took
one unleavened cake, and a cake of oiled
bread, and one wafer, and put *them* on the
fat, and upon the right shoulder:
27 And he put all upon Aaron's hands, and
upon his sons' hands, and waved them *for*
a wave offering before the LORD.
28 And Moses took them from off their
hands, and burnt *them* on the altar upon

the burnt offering: they *were* consecrations
for a sweet savour: it *is* an offering made by
fire unto the LORD.
29 And Moses took the breast, and waved
it *for* a wave offering before the LORD: *for* of
the ram of consecration it was Moses' part;
as the LORD commanded Moses.
30 And Moses took of the anointing oil,
and of the blood which *was* upon the altar,
and sprinkled *it* upon Aaron, *and* upon his
garments, and upon his sons, and upon his
sons' garments with him; and sanctified
Aaron, *and* his garments, and his sons, and
his sons' garments with him.
31 ¶ And Moses said unto Aaron and to
his sons, Boil the flesh *at* the door of the
tabernacle of the congregation: and there
eat it with the bread that *is* in the basket
of consecrations, as I commanded, saying,
Aaron and his sons shall eat it.
32 And that which remaineth of the flesh
and of the bread shall ye burn with fire.
33 And ye shall not go out of the door of
the tabernacle of the congregation *in* seven
days, until the days of your consecration
be at an end: for seven days shall he consecrate you.
34 As he hath done this day, *so* the LORD
hath commanded to do, to make an atonement for you.
35 Therefore shall ye abide *at* the door of
the tabernacle of the congregation day
and night seven days, and keep the charge
of the LORD, that ye die not: for so I am
commanded.
36 So Aaron and his sons did all things which
the LORD commanded by the hand of Moses.

Leviticus 9

1 And it came to pass on the eighth day,
that Moses called Aaron and his sons, and
the elders of Israel;
2 And he said unto Aaron, Take thee a young
calf for a sin offering, and a ram for a burnt
offering, without blemish, and offer *them*
before the LORD.
3 And unto the children of Israel thou shalt
speak, saying, Take ye a kid of the goats
for a sin offering; and a calf and a lamb,
both of the first year, without blemish, for
a burnt offering;
4 Also a bullock and a ram for peace offerings, to sacrifice before the LORD; and a
meat offering mingled with oil: for to day
the LORD will appear unto you.
5 ¶ And they brought *that* which Moses
commanded before the tabernacle of the
congregation: and all the congregation drew
near and stood before the LORD.
6 And Moses said, This *is* the thing which
the LORD commanded that ye should do: and
the glory of the LORD shall appear unto you.
7 And Moses said unto Aaron, Go unto the
altar, and offer thy sin offering, and thy burnt
offering, and make an atonement for thyself,
and for the people: and offer the offering
of the people, and make an atonement for
them; as the LORD commanded.
8 ¶ Aaron therefore went unto the altar,
and slew the calf of the sin offering, which
was for himself.
9 And the sons of Aaron brought the blood
unto him: and he dipped his finger in the
blood, and put *it* upon the horns of the altar,
and poured out the blood at the bottom
of the altar:
10 But the fat, and the kidneys, and the caul
above the liver of the sin offering, he burnt
upon the altar; as the LORD commanded
Moses.
11 And the flesh and the hide he burnt with
fire without the camp.
12 And he slew the burnt offering; and
Aaron's sons presented unto him the blood,
which he sprinkled round about upon the
altar.
13 And they presented the burnt offering
unto him, with the pieces thereof, and the
head: and he burnt *them* upon the altar.
14 And he did wash the inwards and the
legs, and burnt *them* upon the burnt offering on the altar.
15 ¶ And he brought the people's offering,
and took the goat, which *was* the sin offering for the people, and slew it, and offered
it for sin, as the first.
16 And he brought the burnt offering, and
offered it according to the manner.
17 And he brought the meat offering, and
took an handful thereof, and burnt *it* upon
the altar, beside the burnt sacrifice of the
morning.
18 He slew also the bullock and the ram *for*
a sacrifice of peace offerings, which *was* for
the people: and Aaron's sons presented unto

him the blood, which he sprinkled upon the
altar round about,
19 And the fat of the bullock and of the
ram, the rump, and that which covereth
the inwards, and the kidneys, and the caul
above the liver:
20 And they put the fat upon the breasts,
and he burnt the fat upon the altar:
21 And the breasts and the right shoulder
Aaron waved *for* a wave offering before the
LORD; as Moses commanded.
22 And Aaron lifted up his hand toward the
people, and blessed them, and came down
from offering of the sin offering, and the
burnt offering, and peace offerings.
23 And Moses and Aaron went into the
tabernacle of the congregation, and came
out, and blessed the people: and the glory
of the LORD appeared unto all the people.
24 And there came a fire out from before
the LORD, and consumed upon the altar the
burnt offering and the fat: *which* when all
the people saw, they shouted, and fell on
their faces.

Leviticus 10

1 And Nadab and Abihu, the sons of Aaron,
took either of them his censer, and put
fire therein, and put incense thereon, and
offered strange fire before the LORD, which
he commanded them not.
2 And there went out fire from the LORD,
and devoured them, and they died before
the LORD.
3 Then Moses said unto Aaron, This *is it* that
the LORD spake, saying, I will be sanctified
in them that come nigh me, and before all
the people I will be glorified. And Aaron
held his peace.
4 And Moses called Mishael and Elzaphan,
the sons of Uzziel the uncle of Aaron, and
said unto them, Come near, carry your
brethren from before the sanctuary out
of the camp.
5 So they went near, and carried them in
their coats out of the camp; as Moses had
said.
6 And Moses said unto Aaron, and unto
Eleazar and unto Ithamar, his sons, Uncover
not your heads, neither rend your clothes;
lest ye die, and lest wrath come upon all the
people: but let your brethren, the whole
house of Israel, bewail the burning which
the LORD hath kindled.
7 And ye shall not go out from the door of
the tabernacle of the congregation, lest
ye die: for the anointing oil of the LORD *is*
upon you. And they did according to the
word of Moses.
8 ¶ And the LORD spake unto Aaron, saying,
9 Do not drink wine nor strong drink, thou,
nor thy sons with thee, when ye go into the
tabernacle of the congregation, lest ye die:
it shall be a statute for ever throughout your
generations:
10 And that ye may put difference between
holy and unholy, and between unclean
and clean;
11 And that ye may teach the children of
Israel all the statutes which the LORD hath
spoken unto them by the hand of Moses.
12 ¶ And Moses spake unto Aaron, and unto
Eleazar and unto Ithamar, his sons that were
left, Take the meat offering that remaineth
of the offerings of the LORD made by fire,
and eat it without leaven beside the altar:
for it *is* most holy:
13 And ye shall eat it in the holy place,
because it *is* thy due, and thy sons' due, of
the sacrifices of the LORD made by fire: for
so I am commanded.
14 And the wave breast and heave shoulder
shall ye eat in a clean place; thou, and thy
sons, and thy daughters with thee: for *they*
be thy due, and thy sons' due, *which* are
given out of the sacrifices of peace offerings
of the children of Israel.
15 The heave shoulder and the wave breast
shall they bring with the offerings made by
fire of the fat, to wave *it for* a wave offering
before the LORD; and it shall be thine, and
thy sons' with thee, by a statute for ever;
as the LORD hath commanded.
16 ¶ And Moses diligently sought the goat
of the sin offering, and, behold, it was
burnt: and he was angry with Eleazar and
Ithamar, the sons of Aaron *which were* left
alive, saying,
17 Wherefore have ye not eaten the sin
offering in the holy place, seeing it *is* most
holy, and *God* hath given it you to bear the
iniquity of the congregation, to make atonement for them before the LORD?
18 Behold, the blood of it was not brought in

within the holy *place:* ye should indeed have
eaten it in the holy *place*, as I commanded.
19 And Aaron said unto Moses, Behold, this
day have they offered their sin offering and
their burnt offering before the LORD; and
such things have befallen me: and *if* I had
eaten the sin offering to day, should it have
been accepted in the sight of the LORD?
20 And when Moses heard *that*, he was
content.

Leviticus 11

1 And the LORD spake unto Moses and to
Aaron, saying unto them,
2 Speak unto the children of Israel, saying,
These *are* the beasts which ye shall eat
among all the beasts that *are* on the earth.
3 Whatsoever parteth the hoof, and is clovenfooted, *and* cheweth the cud, among the
beasts, that shall ye eat.
4 Nevertheless these shall ye not eat of
them that chew the cud, or of them that
divide the hoof: *as* the camel, because he
cheweth the cud, but divideth not the hoof;
he *is* unclean unto you.
5 And the coney, because he cheweth the
cud, but divideth not the hoof; he *is* unclean
unto you.
6 And the hare, because he cheweth the
cud, but divideth not the hoof; he *is* unclean
unto you.
7 And the swine, though he divide the hoof,
and be clovenfooted, yet he cheweth not
the cud; he *is* unclean to you.
8 Of their flesh shall ye not eat, and their
carcase shall ye not touch; they *are* unclean
to you.
9 ¶ These shall ye eat of all that *are* in the
waters: whatsoever hath fins and scales in
the waters, in the seas, and in the rivers,
them shall ye eat.
10 And all that have not fins and scales in
the seas, and in the rivers, of all that move
in the waters, and of any living thing which
is in the waters, they *shall be* an abomination unto you:
11 They shall be even an abomination unto
you; ye shall not eat of their flesh, but ye
shall have their carcases in abomination.
12 Whatsoever hath no fins nor scales in
the waters, that *shall be* an abomination
unto you.
13 ¶ And these *are they which* ye shall have
in abomination among the fowls; they shall
not be eaten, they *are* an abomination: the
eagle, and the ossifrage, and the ospray,
14 And the vulture, and the kite after his
kind;
15 Every raven after his kind;
16 And the owl, and the night hawk, and
the cuckow, and the hawk after his kind,
17 And the little owl, and the cormorant,
and the great owl,
18 And the swan, and the pelican, and the
gier eagle,
19 And the stork, the heron after her kind,
and the lapwing, and the bat.
20 All fowls that creep, going upon *all* four,
shall be an abomination unto you.
21 Yet these may ye eat of every flying
creeping thing that goeth upon *all* four,
which have legs above their feet, to leap
withal upon the earth;
22 *Even* these of them ye may eat; the locust
after his kind, and the bald locust after his
kind, and the beetle after his kind, and the
grasshopper after his kind.
23 But all *other* flying creeping things, which
have four feet, *shall be* an abomination
unto you.
24 And for these ye shall be unclean: whosoever toucheth the carcase of them shall
be unclean until the even.
25 And whosoever beareth *ought* of the
carcase of them shall wash his clothes, and
be unclean until the even.
26 *The carcases* of every beast which divideth the hoof, and *is* not clovenfooted,
nor cheweth the cud, *are* unclean unto
you: every one that toucheth them shall
be unclean.
27 And whatsoever goeth upon his paws,
among all manner of beasts that go on *all*
four, those *are* unclean unto you: whoso
toucheth their carcase shall be unclean
until the even.
28 And he that beareth the carcase of them
shall wash his clothes, and be unclean until
the even: they *are* unclean unto you.
29 ¶ These also *shall be* unclean unto you
among the creeping things that creep upon
the earth; the weasel, and the mouse, and
the tortoise after his kind,
30 And the ferret, and the chameleon, and
the lizard, and the snail, and the mole.
31 These *are* unclean to you among all

that creep: whosoever doth touch them,
when they be dead, shall be unclean until
the even.
32 And upon whatsoever *any* of them, when
they are dead, doth fall, it shall be unclean;
whether *it be* any vessel of wood, or raiment, or skin, or sack, whatsoever vessel
it be, wherein *any* work is done, it must be
put into water, and it shall be unclean until
the even; so it shall be cleansed.
33 And every earthen vessel, whereinto *any*
of them falleth, whatsoever *is* in it shall be
unclean; and ye shall break it.
34 Of all meat which may be eaten, *that* on
which *such* water cometh shall be unclean:
and all drink that may be drunk in every *such*
vessel shall be unclean.
35 And every *thing* whereupon *any part*
of their carcase falleth shall be unclean;
whether it be oven, or ranges for pots, they
shall be broken down: *for* they *are* unclean,
and shall be unclean unto you.
36 Nevertheless a fountain or pit, *wherein*
there is plenty of water, shall be clean: but
that which toucheth their carcase shall be
unclean.
37 And if *any part* of their carcase fall upon
any sowing seed which is to be sown, it
shall be clean.
38 But if *any* water be put upon the seed,
and *any part* of their carcase fall thereon,
it *shall be* unclean unto you.
39 And if any beast, of which ye may eat,
die; he that toucheth the carcase thereof
shall be unclean until the even.
40 And he that eateth of the carcase of it
shall wash his clothes, and be unclean until
the even: he also that beareth the carcase
of it shall wash his clothes, and be unclean
until the even.
41 And every creeping thing that creepeth
upon the earth *shall be* an abomination; it
shall not be eaten.
42 Whatsoever goeth upon the belly, and
whatsoever goeth upon *all* four, or whatsoever hath more feet among all creeping
things that creep upon the earth, them ye
shall not eat; for they *are* an abomination.
43 Ye shall not make yourselves abominable
with any creeping thing that creepeth, neither shall ye make yourselves unclean with
them, that ye should be defiled thereby.
44 For I *am* the LORD your God: ye shall
therefore sanctify yourselves, and ye shall
be holy; for I *am* holy: neither shall ye defile
yourselves with any manner of creeping
thing that creepeth upon the earth.
45 For I *am* the LORD that bringeth you up
out of the land of Egypt, to be your God: ye
shall therefore be holy, for I *am* holy.
46 This *is* the law of the beasts, and of
the fowl, and of every living creature that
moveth in the waters, and of every creature
that creepeth upon the earth:
47 To make a difference between the
unclean and the clean, and between the
beast that may be eaten and the beast that
may not be eaten.

Leviticus 12

1 And the LORD spake unto Moses, saying,
2 Speak unto the children of Israel, saying, If
a woman have conceived seed, and born a
man child: then she shall be unclean seven
days; according to the days of the separation for her infirmity shall she be unclean.
3 And in the eighth day the flesh of his foreskin shall be circumcised.
4 And she shall then continue in the blood
of her purifying three and thirty days; she
shall touch no hallowed thing, nor come
into the sanctuary, until the days of her
purifying be fulfilled.
5 But if she bear a maid child, then she shall
be unclean two weeks, as in her separation:
and she shall continue in the blood of her
purifying threescore and six days.
6 And when the days of her purifying are
fulfilled, for a son, or for a daughter, she
shall bring a lamb of the first year for a
burnt offering, and a young pigeon, or a
turtledove, for a sin offering, unto the door
of the tabernacle of the congregation, unto
the priest:
7 Who shall offer it before the LORD, and
make an atonement for her; and she shall
be cleansed from the issue of her blood.
This *is* the law for her that hath born a male
or a female.
8 And if she be not able to bring a lamb, then
she shall bring two turtles, or two young
pigeons; the one for the burnt offering, and
the other for a sin offering: and the priest
shall make an atonement for her, and she
shall be clean.

Leviticus 13

1 And the LORD spake unto Moses and Aaron, saying,

2 When a man shall have in the skin of his flesh a rising, a scab, or bright spot, and it be in the skin of his flesh *like* the plague of leprosy; then he shall be brought unto Aaron the priest, or unto one of his sons the priests:

3 And the priest shall look on the plague in the skin of the flesh: and *when* the hair in the plague is turned white, and the plague in sight *be* deeper than the skin of his flesh, it *is* a plague of leprosy: and the priest shall look on him, and pronounce him unclean.

4 If the bright spot *be* white in the skin of his flesh, and in sight *be* not deeper than the skin, and the hair thereof be not turned white; then the priest shall shut up *him that hath* the plague seven days:

5 And the priest shall look on him the seventh day: and, behold, *if* the plague in his sight be at a stay, *and* the plague spread not in the skin; then the priest shall shut him up seven days more:

6 And the priest shall look on him again the seventh day: and, behold, *if* the plague *be* somewhat dark, *and* the plague spread not in the skin, the priest shall pronounce him clean: it *is but* a scab: and he shall wash his clothes, and be clean.

7 But if the scab spread much abroad in the skin, after that he hath been seen of the priest for his cleansing, he shall be seen of the priest again:

8 And *if* the priest see that, behold, the scab spreadeth in the skin, then the priest shall pronounce him unclean: it *is* a leprosy.

9 ¶ When the plague of leprosy is in a man, then he shall be brought unto the priest;

10 And the priest shall see *him:* and, behold, *if* the rising *be* white in the skin, and it have turned the hair white, and *there be* quick raw flesh in the rising;

11 It *is* an old leprosy in the skin of his flesh, and the priest shall pronounce him unclean, and shall not shut him up: for he *is* unclean.

12 And if a leprosy break out abroad in the skin, and the leprosy cover all the skin of *him that hath* the plague from his head even to his foot, wheresoever the priest looketh;

13 Then the priest shall consider: and, behold, *if* the leprosy have covered all his flesh, he shall pronounce *him* clean *that hath* the plague: it is all turned white: he *is* clean.

14 But when raw flesh appeareth in him, he shall be unclean.

15 And the priest shall see the raw flesh, and pronounce him to be unclean: *for* the raw flesh *is* unclean: it *is* a leprosy.

16 Or if the raw flesh turn again, and be changed unto white, he shall come unto the priest;

17 And the priest shall see him: and, behold, *if* the plague be turned into white; then the priest shall pronounce *him* clean *that hath* the plague: he *is* clean.

18 ¶ The flesh also, in which, *even* in the skin thereof, was a boil, and is healed,

19 And in the place of the boil there be a white rising, or a bright spot, white, and somewhat reddish, and it be shewed to the priest;

20 And if, when the priest seeth it, behold, it *be* in sight lower than the skin, and the hair thereof be turned white; the priest shall pronounce him unclean: it *is* a plague of leprosy broken out of the boil.

21 But if the priest look on it, and, behold, *there be* no white hairs therein, and *if* it *be* not lower than the skin, but *be* somewhat dark; then the priest shall shut him up seven days:

22 And if it spread much abroad in the skin, then the priest shall pronounce him unclean: it *is* a plague.

23 But if the bright spot stay in his place, *and* spread not, it *is* a burning boil; and the priest shall pronounce him clean.

24 ¶ Or if there be *any* flesh, in the skin whereof *there is* a hot burning, and the quick *flesh* that burneth have a white bright spot, somewhat reddish, or white;

25 Then the priest shall look upon it: and, behold, *if* the hair in the bright spot be turned white, and it *be in* sight deeper than the skin; it *is* a leprosy broken out of the burning: wherefore the priest shall pronounce him unclean: it *is* the plague of leprosy.

26 But if the priest look on it, and, behold, *there be* no white hair in the bright spot, and it *be* no lower than the *other* skin, but *be* somewhat dark; then the priest shall shut him up seven days:

27 And the priest shall look upon him the seventh day: *and* if it be spread much abroad in the skin, then the priest shall pronounce him unclean: it *is* the plague of leprosy.

28 And if the bright spot stay in his place, *and* spread not in the skin, but it *be* somewhat dark; it *is* a rising of the burning, and the priest shall pronounce him clean: for it *is* an inflammation of the burning.

29 ¶ If a man or woman have a plague upon the head or the beard;

30 Then the priest shall see the plague: and, behold, if it *be* in sight deeper than the skin; *and there be* in it a yellow thin hair; then the priest shall pronounce him unclean: it *is* a dry scall, *even* a leprosy upon the head or beard.

31 And if the priest look on the plague of the scall, and, behold, it *be* not in sight deeper than the skin, and *that there is* no black hair in it; then the priest shall shut up *him that hath* the plague of the scall seven days:

32 And in the seventh day the priest shall look on the plague: and, behold, *if* the scall spread not, and there be in it no yellow hair, and the scall *be* not in sight deeper than the skin;

33 He shall be shaven, but the scall shall he not shave; and the priest shall shut up *him that hath* the scall seven days more:

34 And in the seventh day the priest shall look on the scall: and, behold, *if* the scall be not spread in the skin, nor *be* in sight deeper than the skin; then the priest shall pronounce him clean: and he shall wash his clothes, and be clean.

35 But if the scall spread much in the skin after his cleansing;

36 Then the priest shall look on him: and, behold, if the scall be spread in the skin, the priest shall not seek for yellow hair; he *is* unclean.

37 But if the scall be in his sight at a stay, and *that* there is black hair grown up therein; the scall is healed, he *is* clean: and the priest shall pronounce him clean.

38 ¶ If a man also or a woman have in the skin of their flesh bright spots, *even* white bright spots;

39 Then the priest shall look: and, behold, *if* the bright spots in the skin of their flesh *be* darkish white; it *is* a freckled spot *that* groweth in the skin; he *is* clean.

40 And the man whose hair is fallen off his head, he *is* bald; *yet is* he clean.

41 And he that hath his hair fallen off from the part of his head toward his face, he *is* forehead bald: *yet is* he clean.

42 And if there be in the bald head, or bald forehead, a white reddish sore; it *is* a leprosy sprung up in his bald head, or his bald forehead.

43 Then the priest shall look upon it: and, behold, *if* the rising of the sore *be* white reddish in his bald head, or in his bald forehead, as the leprosy appeareth in the skin of the flesh;

44 He is a leprous man, he *is* unclean: the priest shall pronounce him utterly unclean; his plague *is* in his head.

45 And the leper in whom the plague *is*, his clothes shall be rent, and his head bare, and he shall put a covering upon his upper lip, and shall cry, Unclean, unclean.

46 All the days wherein the plague *shall be* in him he shall be defiled; he *is* unclean: he shall dwell alone; without the camp *shall* his habitation *be*.

47 ¶ The garment also that the plague of leprosy is in, *whether it be* a woollen garment, or a linen garment;

48 Whether *it be* in the warp, or woof; of linen, or of woollen; whether in a skin, or in any thing made of skin;

49 And if the plague be greenish or reddish in the garment, or in the skin, either in the warp, or in the woof, or in any thing of skin; it *is* a plague of leprosy, and shall be shewed unto the priest:

50 And the priest shall look upon the plague, and shut up *it that hath* the plague seven days:

51 And he shall look on the plague on the seventh day: if the plague be spread in the garment, either in the warp, or in the woof, or in a skin, *or* in any work that is made of skin; the plague *is* a fretting leprosy; it *is* unclean.

52 He shall therefore burn that garment, whether warp or woof, in woollen or in linen, or any thing of skin, wherein the plague is: for it *is* a fretting leprosy; it shall be burnt in the fire.

53 And if the priest shall look, and, behold, the plague be not spread in the garment,

either in the warp, or in the woof, or in any
thing of skin;
54 Then the priest shall command that they
wash *the thing* wherein the plague *is*, and
he shall shut it up seven days more:
55 And the priest shall look on the plague,
after that it is washed: and, behold, *if* the
plague have not changed his colour, and
the plague be not spread; it *is* unclean; thou
shalt burn it in the fire; it *is* fret inward,
whether it *be* bare within or without.
56 And if the priest look, and, behold, the
plague *be* somewhat dark after the washing
of it; then he shall rend it out of the garment,
or out of the skin, or out of the warp, or out
of the woof:
57 And if it appear still in the garment, either
in the warp, or in the woof, or in any thing
of skin; it *is* a spreading *plague:* thou shalt
burn that wherein the plague *is* with fire.
58 And the garment, either warp, or woof,
or whatsoever thing of skin *it be*, which thou
shalt wash, if the plague be departed from
them, then it shall be washed the second
time, and shall be clean.
59 This *is* the law of the plague of leprosy in
a garment of woollen or linen, either in the
warp, or woof, or any thing of skins, to pronounce it clean, or to pronounce it unclean.

Leviticus 14

1 And the LORD spake unto Moses, saying,
2 This shall be the law of the leper in the
day of his cleansing: He shall be brought
unto the priest:
3 And the priest shall go forth out of the
camp; and the priest shall look, and, behold,
if the plague of leprosy be healed in the
leper;
4 Then shall the priest command to take for
him that is to be cleansed two birds alive
and clean, and cedar wood, and scarlet,
and hyssop:
5 And the priest shall command that one of
the birds be killed in an earthen vessel over
running water:
6 As for the living bird, he shall take it, and
the cedar wood, and the scarlet, and the
hyssop, and shall dip them and the living
bird in the blood of the bird *that was* killed
over the running water:
7 And he shall sprinkle upon him that is to
be cleansed from the leprosy seven times,
and shall pronounce him clean, and shall
let the living bird loose into the open field.
8 And he that is to be cleansed shall wash his
clothes, and shave off all his hair, and wash
himself in water, that he may be clean: and
after that he shall come into the camp, and
shall tarry abroad out of his tent seven days.
9 But it shall be on the seventh day, that he
shall shave all his hair off his head and his
beard and his eyebrows, even all his hair he
shall shave off: and he shall wash his clothes,
also he shall wash his flesh in water, and he
shall be clean.
10 And on the eighth day he shall take two
he lambs without blemish, and one ewe
lamb of the first year without blemish, and
three tenth deals of fine flour *for* a meat
offering, mingled with oil, and one log of oil.
11 And the priest that maketh *him* clean
shall present the man that is to be made
clean, and those things, before the LORD,
at the door of the tabernacle of the congregation:
12 And the priest shall take one he lamb,
and offer him for a trespass offering, and
the log of oil, and wave them *for* a wave
offering before the LORD:
13 And he shall slay the lamb in the place
where he shall kill the sin offering and the
burnt offering, in the holy place: for as the
sin offering *is* the priest's, *so is* the trespass
offering: it *is* most holy:
14 And the priest shall take *some* of the
blood of the trespass offering, and the
priest shall put *it* upon the tip of the right
ear of him that is to be cleansed, and upon
the thumb of his right hand, and upon the
great toe of his right foot:
15 And the priest shall take *some* of the
log of oil, and pour *it* into the palm of his
own left hand:
16 And the priest shall dip his right finger
in the oil that *is* in his left hand, and shall
sprinkle of the oil with his finger seven times
before the LORD:
17 And of the rest of the oil that *is* in his hand
shall the priest put upon the tip of the right
ear of him that is to be cleansed, and upon
the thumb of his right hand, and upon the
great toe of his right foot, upon the blood
of the trespass offering:
18 And the remnant of the oil that *is* in the
priest's hand he shall pour upon the head

of him that is to be cleansed: and the priest
shall make an atonement for him before
the LORD.
19 And the priest shall offer the sin offering, and make an atonement for him that
is to be cleansed from his uncleanness; and
afterward he shall kill the burnt offering:
20 And the priest shall offer the burnt offering and the meat offering upon the altar:
and the priest shall make an atonement for
him, and he shall be clean.
21 And if he *be* poor, and cannot get so
much; then he shall take one lamb *for* a
trespass offering to be waved, to make an
atonement for him, and one tenth deal of
fine flour mingled with oil for a meat offering, and a log of oil;
22 And two turtledoves, or two young
pigeons, such as he is able to get; and the
one shall be a sin offering, and the other a
burnt offering.
23 And he shall bring them on the eighth day
for his cleansing unto the priest, unto the
door of the tabernacle of the congregation,
before the LORD.
24 And the priest shall take the lamb of the
trespass offering, and the log of oil, and the
priest shall wave them *for* a wave offering
before the LORD:
25 And he shall kill the lamb of the trespass
offering, and the priest shall take *some* of
the blood of the trespass offering, and put
it upon the tip of the right ear of him that
is to be cleansed, and upon the thumb of
his right hand, and upon the great toe of
his right foot:
26 And the priest shall pour of the oil into
the palm of his own left hand:
27 And the priest shall sprinkle with his right
finger *some* of the oil that *is* in his left hand
seven times before the LORD:
28 And the priest shall put of the oil that *is* in
his hand upon the tip of the right ear of him
that is to be cleansed, and upon the thumb
of his right hand, and upon the great toe of
his right foot, upon the place of the blood
of the trespass offering:
29 And the rest of the oil that *is* in the
priest's hand he shall put upon the head
of him that is to be cleansed, to make an
atonement for him before the LORD.
30 And he shall offer the one of the turtledoves, or of the young pigeons, such as
he can get;
31 *Even* such as he is able to get, the one
for a sin offering, and the other *for* a burnt
offering, with the meat offering: and the
priest shall make an atonement for him that
is to be cleansed before the LORD.
32 This *is* the law *of him* in whom *is* the
plague of leprosy, whose hand is not able to
get *that which pertaineth* to his cleansing.
33 ¶ And the LORD spake unto Moses and
unto Aaron, saying,
34 When ye be come into the land of
Canaan, which I give to you for a possession,
and I put the plague of leprosy in a house
of the land of your possession;
35 And he that owneth the house shall come
and tell the priest, saying, It seemeth to me
there is as it were a plague in the house:
36 Then the priest shall command that they
empty the house, before the priest go *into*
it to see the plague, that all that *is* in the
house be not made unclean: and afterward
the priest shall go in to see the house:
37 And he shall look on the plague, and,
behold, *if* the plague *be* in the walls of the
house with hollow strakes, greenish or reddish, which in sight *are* lower than the wall;
38 Then the priest shall go out of the house
to the door of the house, and shut up the
house seven days:
39 And the priest shall come again the seventh day, and shall look: and, behold, *if* the
plague be spread in the walls of the house;
40 Then the priest shall command that they
take away the stones in which the plague
is, and they shall cast them into an unclean
place without the city:
41 And he shall cause the house to be
scraped within round about, and they shall
pour out the dust that they scrape off without the city into an unclean place:
42 And they shall take other stones, and put
them in the place of those stones; and he
shall take other morter, and shall plaister
the house.
43 And if the plague come again, and break
out in the house, after that he hath taken
away the stones, and after he hath scraped
the house, and after it is plaistered;
44 Then the priest shall come and look,
and, behold, *if* the plague be spread in the

house, it *is* a fretting leprosy in the house:
it *is* unclean.
45 And he shall break down the house, the
stones of it, and the timber thereof, and
all the morter of the house; and he shall
carry *them* forth out of the city into an
unclean place.
46 Moreover he that goeth into the house all
the while that it is shut up shall be unclean
until the even.
47 And he that lieth in the house shall wash
his clothes; and he that eateth in the house
shall wash his clothes.
48 And if the priest shall come in, and look
upon it, and, behold, the plague hath not
spread in the house, after the house was
plaistered: then the priest shall pronounce
the house clean, because the plague is
healed.
49 And he shall take to cleanse the house
two birds, and cedar wood, and scarlet,
and hyssop:
50 And he shall kill the one of the birds in an
earthen vessel over running water:
51 And he shall take the cedar wood, and
the hyssop, and the scarlet, and the living
bird, and dip them in the blood of the slain
bird, and in the running water, and sprinkle
the house seven times:
52 And he shall cleanse the house with the
blood of the bird, and with the running
water, and with the living bird, and with
the cedar wood, and with the hyssop, and
with the scarlet:
53 But he shall let go the living bird out of
the city into the open fields, and make an
atonement for the house: and it shall be
clean.
54 This *is* the law for all manner of plague
of leprosy, and scall,
55 And for the leprosy of a garment, and
of a house,
56 And for a rising, and for a scab, and for
a bright spot:
57 To teach when *it is* unclean, and when *it
is* clean: this *is* the law of leprosy.

Leviticus 15

1 And the LORD spake unto Moses and to
Aaron, saying,
2 Speak unto the children of Israel, and say
unto them, When any man hath a running
issue out of his flesh, *because of* his issue
he *is* unclean.
3 And this shall be his uncleanness in his
issue: whether his flesh run with his issue,
or his flesh be stopped from his issue, it *is*
his uncleanness.
4 Every bed, whereon he lieth that hath the
issue, is unclean: and every thing, whereon
he sitteth, shall be unclean.
5 And whosoever toucheth his bed shall
wash his clothes, and bathe *himself* in water,
and be unclean until the even.
6 And he that sitteth on *any* thing whereon
he sat that hath the issue shall wash his
clothes, and bathe *himself* in water, and be
unclean until the even.
7 And he that toucheth the flesh of him
that hath the issue shall wash his clothes,
and bathe *himself* in water, and be unclean
until the even.
8 And if he that hath the issue spit upon him
that is clean; then he shall wash his clothes,
and bathe *himself* in water, and be unclean
until the even.
9 And what saddle soever he rideth upon
that hath the issue shall be unclean.
10 And whosoever toucheth any thing
that was under him shall be unclean until
the even: and he that beareth *any of* those
things shall wash his clothes, and bathe *himself* in water, and be unclean until the even.
11 And whomsoever he toucheth that hath
the issue, and hath not rinsed his hands in
water, he shall wash his clothes, and bathe
himself in water, and be unclean until the
even.
12 And the vessel of earth, that he toucheth
which hath the issue, shall be broken: and
every vessel of wood shall be rinsed in
water.
13 And when he that hath an issue is
cleansed of his issue; then he shall number
to himself seven days for his cleansing, and
wash his clothes, and bathe his flesh in running water, and shall be clean.
14 And on the eighth day he shall take to
him two turtledoves, or two young pigeons,
and come before the LORD unto the door
of the tabernacle of the congregation, and
give them unto the priest:
15 And the priest shall offer them, the one
for a sin offering, and the other *for* a burnt

offering; and the priest shall make an atonement for him before the LORD for his issue.
16 And if any man's seed of copulation go
out from him, then he shall wash all his flesh
in water, and be unclean until the even.
17 And every garment, and every skin,
whereon is the seed of copulation, shall
be washed with water, and be unclean
until the even.
18 The woman also with whom man shall
lie *with* seed of copulation, they shall *both*
bathe *themselves* in water, and be unclean
until the even.
19 ¶ And if a woman have an issue, *and* her
issue in her flesh *be* blood, she shall be put
apart seven days: and whosoever toucheth
her shall be unclean until the even.
20 And every *thing* that she lieth upon in
her separation shall be unclean: every thing
also that she sitteth upon shall be unclean.
21 And whosoever toucheth her bed shall
wash his clothes, and bathe *himself* in water,
and be unclean until the even.
22 And whosoever toucheth any thing that
she sat upon shall wash his clothes, and
bathe *himself* in water, and be unclean
until the even.
23 And if it *be* on *her* bed, or on any thing
whereon she sitteth, when he toucheth it,
he shall be unclean until the even.
24 And if any man lie with her at all, and her
flowers be upon him, he shall be unclean
seven days; and all the bed whereon he
lieth shall be unclean.
25 And if a woman have an issue of her
blood many days out of the time of her
separation, or if it run beyond the time of
her separation; all the days of the issue of
her uncleanness shall be as the days of her
separation: she *shall be* unclean.
26 Every bed whereon she lieth all the days
of her issue shall be unto her as the bed of
her separation: and whatsoever she sitteth
upon shall be unclean, as the uncleanness
of her separation.
27 And whosoever toucheth those things
shall be unclean, and shall wash his clothes,
and bathe *himself* in water, and be unclean
until the even.
28 But if she be cleansed of her issue, then
she shall number to herself seven days, and
after that she shall be clean.
29 And on the eighth day she shall take unto
her two turtles, or two young pigeons, and
bring them unto the priest, to the door of
the tabernacle of the congregation.
30 And the priest shall offer the one *for* a sin
offering, and the other *for* a burnt offering;
and the priest shall make an atonement
for her before the LORD for the issue of her
uncleanness.
31 Thus shall ye separate the children of
Israel from their uncleanness; that they die
not in their uncleanness, when they defile
my tabernacle that *is* among them.
32 This *is* the law of him that hath an issue,
and *of him* whose seed goeth from him, and
is defiled therewith;
33 And of her that is sick of her flowers, and
of him that hath an issue, of the man, and
of the woman, and of him that lieth with
her that is unclean.

Leviticus 16

1 And the LORD spake unto Moses after the
death of the two sons of Aaron, when they
offered before the LORD, and died;
2 And the LORD said unto Moses, Speak
unto Aaron thy brother, that he come not
at all times into the holy *place* within the
vail before the mercy seat, which *is* upon
the ark; that he die not: for I will appear in
the cloud upon the mercy seat.
3 Thus shall Aaron come into the holy *place:*
with a young bullock for a sin offering, and
a ram for a burnt offering.
4 He shall put on the holy linen coat, and
he shall have the linen breeches upon his
flesh, and shall be girded with a linen girdle,
and with the linen mitre shall he be attired:
these *are* holy garments; therefore shall he
wash his flesh in water, and *so* put them on.
5 And he shall take of the congregation of
the children of Israel two kids of the goats
for a sin offering, and one ram for a burnt
offering.
6 And Aaron shall offer his bullock of the sin
offering, which *is* for himself, and make an
atonement for himself, and for his house.
7 And he shall take the two goats, and present them before the LORD *at* the door of the
tabernacle of the congregation.
8 And Aaron shall cast lots upon the two
goats; one lot for the LORD, and the other
lot for the scapegoat.
9 And Aaron shall bring the goat upon

which the LORD's lot fell, and offer him *for*
a sin offering.
10 But the goat, on which the lot fell to
be the scapegoat, shall be presented alive
before the LORD, to make an atonement
with him, *and* to let him go for a scapegoat
into the wilderness.
11 And Aaron shall bring the bullock of the
sin offering, which *is* for himself, and shall
make an atonement for himself, and for his
house, and shall kill the bullock of the sin
offering which *is* for himself:
12 And he shall take a censer full of burning
coals of fire from off the altar before the
LORD, and his hands full of sweet incense
beaten small, and bring *it* within the vail:
13 And he shall put the incense upon the
fire before the LORD, that the cloud of the
incense may cover the mercy seat that *is*
upon the testimony, that he die not:
14 And he shall take of the blood of the bullock, and sprinkle *it* with his finger upon the
mercy seat eastward; and before the mercy
seat shall he sprinkle of the blood with his
finger seven times.
15 ¶ Then shall he kill the goat of the sin
offering, that *is* for the people, and bring his
blood within the vail, and do with that blood
as he did with the blood of the bullock, and
sprinkle it upon the mercy seat, and before
the mercy seat:
16 And he shall make an atonement for the
holy *place*, because of the uncleanness of
the children of Israel, and because of their
transgressions in all their sins: and so shall
he do for the tabernacle of the congregation, that remaineth among them in the
midst of their uncleanness.
17 And there shall be no man in the tabernacle of the congregation when he goeth in to
make an atonement in the holy *place*, until
he come out, and have made an atonement
for himself, and for his household, and for
all the congregation of Israel.
18 And he shall go out unto the altar that *is*
before the LORD, and make an atonement
for it; and shall take of the blood of the bullock, and of the blood of the goat, and put
it upon the horns of the altar round about.
19 And he shall sprinkle of the blood upon
it with his finger seven times, and cleanse
it, and hallow it from the uncleanness of the
children of Israel.
20 ¶ And when he hath made an end of reconciling the holy *place*, and the tabernacle
of the congregation, and the altar, he shall
bring the live goat:
21 And Aaron shall lay both his hands upon
the head of the live goat, and confess over
him all the iniquities of the children of Israel,
and all their transgressions in all their sins,
putting them upon the head of the goat,
and shall send *him* away by the hand of a
fit man into the wilderness:
22 And the goat shall bear upon him all their
iniquities unto a land not inhabited: and he
shall let go the goat in the wilderness.
23 And Aaron shall come into the tabernacle of the congregation, and shall put off
the linen garments, which he put on when
he went into the holy *place*, and shall leave
them there:
24 And he shall wash his flesh with water
in the holy place, and put on his garments,
and come forth, and offer his burnt offering, and the burnt offering of the people,
and make an atonement for himself, and
for the people.
25 And the fat of the sin offering shall he
burn upon the altar.
26 And he that let go the goat for the scapegoat shall wash his clothes, and bathe his
flesh in water, and afterward come into
the camp.
27 And the bullock *for* the sin offering, and
the goat *for* the sin offering, whose blood
was brought in to make atonement in the
holy *place*, shall *one* carry forth without the
camp; and they shall burn in the fire their
skins, and their flesh, and their dung.
28 And he that burneth them shall wash
his clothes, and bathe his flesh in water,
and afterward he shall come into the camp.
29 ¶ And *this* shall be a statute for ever
unto you: *that* in the seventh month, on
the tenth *day* of the month, ye shall afflict
your souls, and do no work at all, *whether
it be* one of your own country, or a stranger
that sojourneth among you:
30 For on that day shall *the priest* make an
atonement for you, to cleanse you, *that*
ye may be clean from all your sins before
the LORD.
31 It *shall be* a sabbath of rest unto you,
and ye shall afflict your souls, by a statute
for ever.

32 And the priest, whom he shall anoint, and whom he shall consecrate to minister in the priest's office in his father's stead, shall make the atonement, and shall put on the linen clothes, *even* the holy garments:

33 And he shall make an atonement for the holy sanctuary, and he shall make an atonement for the tabernacle of the congregation, and for the altar, and he shall make an atonement for the priests, and for all the people of the congregation.

34 And this shall be an everlasting statute unto you, to make an atonement for the children of Israel for all their sins once a year. And he did as the LORD commanded Moses.

Leviticus 17

1 And the LORD spake unto Moses, saying,

2 Speak unto Aaron, and unto his sons, and unto all the children of Israel, and say unto them; This *is* the thing which the LORD hath commanded, saying,

3 What man soever *there be* of the house of Israel, that killeth an ox, or lamb, or goat, in the camp, or that killeth *it* out of the camp,

4 And bringeth it not unto the door of the tabernacle of the congregation, to offer an offering unto the LORD before the tabernacle of the LORD; blood shall be imputed unto that man; he hath shed blood; and that man shall be cut off from among his people:

5 To the end that the children of Israel may bring their sacrifices, which they offer in the open field, even that they may bring them unto the LORD, unto the door of the tabernacle of the congregation, unto the priest, and offer them *for* peace offerings unto the LORD.

6 And the priest shall sprinkle the blood upon the altar of the LORD *at* the door of the tabernacle of the congregation, and burn the fat for a sweet savour unto the LORD.

7 And they shall no more offer their sacrifices unto devils, after whom they have gone a whoring. This shall be a statute for ever unto them throughout their generations.

8 ¶ And thou shalt say unto them, Whatsoever man *there be* of the house of Israel, or of the strangers which sojourn among you, that offereth a burnt offering or sacrifice,

9 And bringeth it not unto the door of the tabernacle of the congregation, to offer it unto the LORD; even that man shall be cut off from among his people.

10 ¶ And whatsoever man *there be* of the house of Israel, or of the strangers that sojourn among you, that eateth any manner of blood; I will even set my face against that soul that eateth blood, and will cut him off from among his people.

11 For the life of the flesh *is* in the blood: and I have given it to you upon the altar to make an atonement for your souls: for it *is* the blood *that* maketh an atonement for the soul.

12 Therefore I said unto the children of Israel, No soul of you shall eat blood, neither shall any stranger that sojourneth among you eat blood.

13 And whatsoever man *there be* of the children of Israel, or of the strangers that sojourn among you, which hunteth and catcheth any beast or fowl that may be eaten; he shall even pour out the blood thereof, and cover it with dust.

14 For *it is* the life of all flesh; the blood of it *is* for the life thereof: therefore I said unto the children of Israel, Ye shall eat the blood of no manner of flesh: for the life of all flesh *is* the blood thereof: whosoever eateth it shall be cut off.

15 And every soul that eateth that which died *of itself*, or that which was torn *with beasts, whether it be* one of your own country, or a stranger, he shall both wash his clothes, and bathe *himself* in water, and be unclean until the even: then shall he be clean.

16 But if he wash *them* not, nor bathe his flesh; then he shall bear his iniquity.

Leviticus 18

1 And the LORD spake unto Moses, saying,

2 Speak unto the children of Israel, and say unto them, I am the LORD your God.

3 After the doings of the land of Egypt, wherein ye dwelt, shall ye not do: and after the doings of the land of Canaan, whither I bring you, shall ye not do: neither shall ye walk in their ordinances.

4 Ye shall do my judgments, and keep mine ordinances, to walk therein: I *am* the LORD your God.

5 Ye shall therefore keep my statutes, and

my judgments: which if a man do, he shall
live in them: I *am* the LORD.
6 ¶ None of you shall approach to any that
is near of kin to him, to uncover *their* nakedness: I *am* the LORD.
7 The nakedness of thy father, or the nakedness of thy mother, shalt thou not uncover:
she *is* thy mother; thou shalt not uncover
her nakedness.
8 The nakedness of thy father's wife shalt
thou not uncover: it *is* thy father's nakedness.
9 The nakedness of thy sister, the daughter
of thy father, or daughter of thy mother,
whether she be born at home, or born
abroad, *even* their nakedness thou shalt
not uncover.
10 The nakedness of thy son's daughter,
or of thy daughter's daughter, *even* their
nakedness thou shalt not uncover: for theirs
is thine own nakedness.
11 The nakedness of thy father's wife's
daughter, begotten of thy father, she *is* thy
sister, thou shalt not uncover her nakedness.
12 Thou shalt not uncover the nakedness
of thy father's sister: she *is* thy father's near
kinswoman.
13 Thou shalt not uncover the nakedness of
thy mother's sister: for she *is* thy mother's
near kinswoman.
14 Thou shalt not uncover the nakedness of
thy father's brother, thou shalt not approach
to his wife: she *is* thine aunt.
15 Thou shalt not uncover the nakedness
of thy daughter in law: she *is* thy son's wife;
thou shalt not uncover her nakedness.
16 Thou shalt not uncover the nakedness
of thy brother's wife: it *is* thy brother's
nakedness.
17 Thou shalt not uncover the nakedness
of a woman and her daughter, neither
shalt thou take her son's daughter, or her
daughter's daughter, to uncover her nakedness; *for* they *are* her near kinswomen: it *is*
wickedness.
18 Neither shalt thou take a wife to her sister, to vex *her*, to uncover her nakedness,
beside the other in her life *time*.
19 Also thou shalt not approach unto a
woman to uncover her nakedness, as long
as she is put apart for her uncleanness.
20 Moreover thou shalt not lie carnally
with thy neighbour's wife, to defile thyself
with her.
21 And thou shalt not let any of thy seed
pass through *the fire* to Molech, neither
shalt thou profane the name of thy God: I
am the LORD.
22 Thou shalt not lie with mankind, as with
womankind: it *is* abomination.
23 Neither shalt thou lie with any beast to
defile thyself therewith: neither shall any
woman stand before a beast to lie down
thereto: it *is* confusion.
24 Defile not ye yourselves in any of these
things: for in all these the nations are defiled
which I cast out before you:
25 And the land is defiled: therefore I do
visit the iniquity thereof upon it, and the
land itself vomiteth out her inhabitants.
26 Ye shall therefore keep my statutes and
my judgments, and shall not commit *any*
of these abominations; *neither* any of your
own nation, nor any stranger that sojourneth among you:
27 (For all these abominations have the men
of the land done, which *were* before you,
and the land is defiled;)
28 That the land spue not you out also, when
ye defile it, as it spued out the nations that
were before you.
29 For whosoever shall commit any of
these abominations, even the souls that
commit *them* shall be cut off from among
their people.
30 Therefore shall ye keep mine ordinance,
that *ye* commit not *any one* of these abominable customs, which were committed
before you, and that ye defile not yourselves
therein: I *am* the LORD your God.

Leviticus 19

1 And the LORD spake unto Moses, saying,
2 Speak unto all the congregation of the
children of Israel, and say unto them, Ye shall
be holy: for I the LORD your God *am* holy.
3 ¶ Ye shall fear every man his mother, and
his father, and keep my sabbaths: I *am* the
LORD your God.
4 ¶ Turn ye not unto idols, nor make to yourselves molten gods: I *am* the LORD your God.
5 ¶ And if ye offer a sacrifice of peace
offerings unto the LORD, ye shall offer it at
your own will.
6 It shall be eaten the same day ye offer it,

and on the morrow: and if ought remain
until the third day, it shall be burnt in the
fire.
7 And if it be eaten at all on the third day,
it *is* abominable; it shall not be accepted.
8 Therefore *every one* that eateth it shall
bear his iniquity, because he hath profaned
the hallowed thing of the LORD: and that
soul shall be cut off from among his people.
9 ¶ And when ye reap the harvest of your
land, thou shalt not wholly reap the corners
of thy field, neither shalt thou gather the
gleanings of thy harvest.
10 And thou shalt not glean thy vineyard,
neither shalt thou gather *every* grape of
thy vineyard; thou shalt leave them for the
poor and stranger: I *am* the LORD your God.
11 ¶ Ye shall not steal, neither deal falsely,
neither lie one to another.
12 ¶ And ye shall not swear by my name
falsely, neither shalt thou profane the name
of thy God: I *am* the LORD.
13 ¶ Thou shalt not defraud thy neighbour,
neither rob *him:* the wages of him that is
hired shall not abide with thee all night until
the morning.
14 ¶ Thou shalt not curse the deaf, nor put
a stumblingblock before the blind, but shalt
fear thy God: I *am* the LORD.
15 ¶ Ye shall do no unrighteousness in
judgment: thou shalt not respect the person of the poor, nor honour the person of
the mighty: *but* in righteousness shalt thou
judge thy neighbour.
16 ¶ Thou shalt not go up and down *as* a
talebearer among thy people: neither shalt
thou stand against the blood of thy neighbour: I *am* the LORD.
17 ¶ Thou shalt not hate thy brother in
thine heart: thou shalt in any wise rebuke
thy neighbour, and not suffer sin upon him.
18 ¶ Thou shalt not avenge, nor bear any
grudge against the children of thy people,
but thou shalt love thy neighbour as thyself:
I *am* the LORD.
19 ¶ Ye shall keep my statutes. Thou shalt
not let thy cattle gender with a diverse kind:
thou shalt not sow thy field with mingled
seed: neither shall a garment mingled of
linen and woollen come upon thee.
20 ¶ And whosoever lieth carnally with a
woman, that *is* a bondmaid, betrothed to
an husband, and not at all redeemed, nor
freedom given her; she shall be scourged;
they shall not be put to death, because she
was not free.
21 And he shall bring his trespass offering
unto the LORD, unto the door of the tabernacle of the congregation, *even* a ram for
a trespass offering.
22 And the priest shall make an atonement
for him with the ram of the trespass offering
before the LORD for his sin which he hath
done: and the sin which he hath done shall
be forgiven him.
23 ¶ And when ye shall come into the
land, and shall have planted all manner of
trees for food, then ye shall count the fruit
thereof as uncircumcised: three years shall
it be as uncircumcised unto you: it shall not
be eaten of.
24 But in the fourth year all the fruit thereof
shall be holy to praise the LORD *withal.*
25 And in the fifth year shall ye eat of the
fruit thereof, that it may yield unto you the
increase thereof: I *am* the LORD your God.
26 ¶ Ye shall not eat *any thing* with the
blood: neither shall ye use enchantment,
nor observe times.
27 Ye shall not round the corners of your
heads, neither shalt thou mar the corners
of thy beard.
28 Ye shall not make any cuttings in your
flesh for the dead, nor print any marks upon
you: I *am* the LORD.
29 ¶ Do not prostitute thy daughter, to
cause her to be a whore; lest the land fall
to whoredom, and the land become full of
wickedness.
30 ¶ Ye shall keep my sabbaths, and reverence my sanctuary: I *am* the LORD.
31 ¶ Regard not them that have familiar
spirits, neither seek after wizards, to be
defiled by them: I *am* the LORD your God.
32 ¶ Thou shalt rise up before the hoary
head, and honour the face of the old man,
and fear thy God: I *am* the LORD.
33 ¶ And if a stranger sojourn with thee in
your land, ye shall not vex him.
34 *But* the stranger that dwelleth with you
shall be unto you as one born among you,
and thou shalt love him as thyself; for ye
were strangers in the land of Egypt: I *am*
the LORD your God.
35 ¶ Ye shall do no unrighteousness in judgment, in meteyard, in weight, or in measure.

36 Just balances, just weights, a just ephah,
and a just hin, shall ye have: I *am* the LORD
your God, which brought you out of the
land of Egypt.
37 Therefore shall ye observe all my statutes, and all my judgments, and do them:
I *am* the LORD.

Leviticus 20

1 And the LORD spake unto Moses, saying,
2 Again, thou shalt say to the children of
Israel, Whosoever *he be* of the children
of Israel, or of the strangers that sojourn
in Israel, that giveth *any* of his seed unto
Molech; he shall surely be put to death:
the people of the land shall stone him with
stones.
3 And I will set my face against that man,
and will cut him off from among his people;
because he hath given of his seed unto
Molech, to defile my sanctuary, and to
profane my holy name.
4 And if the people of the land do any
ways hide their eyes from the man, when
he giveth of his seed unto Molech, and kill
him not:
5 Then I will set my face against that man,
and against his family, and will cut him off,
and all that go a whoring after him, to commit whoredom with Molech, from among
their people.
6 ¶ And the soul that turneth after such as
have familiar spirits, and after wizards, to
go a whoring after them, I will even set my
face against that soul, and will cut him off
from among his people.
7 ¶ Sanctify yourselves therefore, and be ye
holy: for I *am* the LORD your God.
8 And ye shall keep my statutes, and do
them: I *am* the LORD which sanctify you.
9 ¶ For every one that curseth his father
or his mother shall be surely put to death:
he hath cursed his father or his mother; his
blood *shall be* upon him.
10 ¶ And the man that committeth adultery
with *another* man's wife, *even he* that committeth adultery with his neighbour's wife,
the adulterer and the adulteress shall surely
be put to death.
11 And the man that lieth with his father's
wife hath uncovered his father's nakedness:
both of them shall surely be put to death;
their blood *shall be* upon them.
12 And if a man lie with his daughter in law,
both of them shall surely be put to death:
they have wrought confusion; their blood
shall be upon them.
13 If a man also lie with mankind, as he lieth
with a woman, both of them have committed an abomination: they shall surely be put
to death; their blood *shall be* upon them.
14 And if a man take a wife and her mother,
it *is* wickedness: they shall be burnt with
fire, both he and they; that there be no
wickedness among you.
15 And if a man lie with a beast, he shall
surely be put to death: and ye shall slay
the beast.
16 And if a woman approach unto any beast,
and lie down thereto, thou shalt kill the
woman, and the beast: they shall surely be
put to death; their blood *shall be* upon them.
17 And if a man shall take his sister, his
father's daughter, or his mother's daughter, and see her nakedness, and she see
his nakedness; it *is* a wicked thing; and they
shall be cut off in the sight of their people:
he hath uncovered his sister's nakedness;
he shall bear his iniquity.
18 And if a man shall lie with a woman
having her sickness, and shall uncover her
nakedness; he hath discovered her fountain,
and she hath uncovered the fountain of her
blood: and both of them shall be cut off from
among their people.
19 And thou shalt not uncover the nakedness of thy mother's sister, nor of thy
father's sister: for he uncovereth his near
kin: they shall bear their iniquity.
20 And if a man shall lie with his uncle's
wife, he hath uncovered his uncle's nakedness: they shall bear their sin; they shall
die childless.
21 And if a man shall take his brother's wife,
it *is* an unclean thing: he hath uncovered his
brother's nakedness; they shall be childless.
22 ¶ Ye shall therefore keep all my statutes,
and all my judgments, and do them: that the
land, whither I bring you to dwell therein,
spue you not out.
23 And ye shall not walk in the manners of
the nation, which I cast out before you: for
they committed all these things, and therefore I abhorred them.
24 But I have said unto you, Ye shall inherit
their land, and I will give it unto you to pos-

sess it, a land that floweth with milk and
honey: I *am* the LORD your God, which have
separated you from *other* people.
25 Ye shall therefore put difference between
clean beasts and unclean, and between
unclean fowls and clean: and ye shall not
make your souls abominable by beast, or
by fowl, or by any manner of living thing
that creepeth on the ground, which I have
separated from you as unclean.
26 And ye shall be holy unto me: for I the
LORD *am* holy, and have severed you from
other people, that ye should be mine.
27 ¶ A man also or woman that hath a familiar spirit, or that is a wizard, shall surely be
put to death: they shall stone them with
stones: their blood *shall be* upon them.

Leviticus 21

1 And the LORD said unto Moses, Speak
unto the priests the sons of Aaron, and say
unto them, There shall none be defiled for
the dead among his people:
2 But for his kin, that is near unto him, *that
is*, for his mother, and for his father, and
for his son, and for his daughter, and for
his brother,
3 And for his sister a virgin, that is nigh unto
him, which hath had no husband; for her
may he be defiled.
4 *But* he shall not defile himself, *being* a chief
man among his people, to profane himself.
5 They shall not make baldness upon their
head, neither shall they shave off the corner of their beard, nor make any cuttings
in their flesh.
6 They shall be holy unto their God, and
not profane the name of their God: for the
offerings of the LORD made by fire, *and* the
bread of their God, they do offer: therefore
they shall be holy.
7 They shall not take a wife *that is* a whore,
or profane; neither shall they take a woman
put away from her husband: for he *is* holy
unto his God.
8 Thou shalt sanctify him therefore; for he
offereth the bread of thy God: he shall be
holy unto thee: for I the LORD, which sanctify
you, *am* holy.
9 ¶ And the daughter of any priest, if she
profane herself by playing the whore, she
profaneth her father: she shall be burnt
with fire.
10 And *he that is* the high priest among his
brethren, upon whose head the anointing
oil was poured, and that is consecrated to
put on the garments, shall not uncover his
head, nor rend his clothes;
11 Neither shall he go in to any dead body,
nor defile himself for his father, or for his
mother;
12 Neither shall he go out of the sanctuary,
nor profane the sanctuary of his God; for
the crown of the anointing oil of his God *is*
upon him: I *am* the LORD.
13 And he shall take a wife in her virginity.
14 A widow, or a divorced woman, or profane, *or* an harlot, these shall he not take:
but he shall take a virgin of his own people
to wife.
15 Neither shall he profane his seed among
his people: for I the LORD do sanctify him.
16 ¶ And the LORD spake unto Moses,
saying,
17 Speak unto Aaron, saying, Whosoever
he be of thy seed in their generations that
hath *any* blemish, let him not approach to
offer the bread of his God.
18 For whatsoever man *he be* that hath a
blemish, he shall not approach: a blind man,
or a lame, or he that hath a flat nose, or any
thing superfluous,
19 Or a man that is brokenfooted, or bro-
kenhanded,
20 Or crookbackt, or a dwarf, or that hath a
blemish in his eye, or be scurvy, or scabbed,
or hath his stones broken;
21 No man that hath a blemish of the seed
of Aaron the priest shall come nigh to offer
the offerings of the LORD made by fire: he
hath a blemish; he shall not come nigh to
offer the bread of his God.
22 He shall eat the bread of his God, *both*
of the most holy, and of the holy.
23 Only he shall not go in unto the vail, nor
come nigh unto the altar, because he hath a
blemish; that he profane not my sanctuaries:
for I the LORD do sanctify them.
24 And Moses told *it* unto Aaron, and to
his sons, and unto all the children of Israel.

Leviticus 22

1 And the LORD spake unto Moses, saying,
2 Speak unto Aaron and to his sons, that
they separate themselves from the holy
things of the children of Israel, and that they

profane not my holy name *in those things*
which they hallow unto me: I *am* the LORD.
3 Say unto them, Whosoever *he be* of all
your seed among your generations, that
goeth unto the holy things, which the children of Israel hallow unto the LORD, having
his uncleanness upon him, that soul shall
be cut off from my presence: I *am* the LORD.
4 What man soever of the seed of Aaron *is*
a leper, or hath a running issue; he shall not
eat of the holy things, until he be clean. And
whoso toucheth any thing *that is* unclean
by the dead, or a man whose seed goeth
from him;
5 Or whosoever toucheth any creeping
thing, whereby he may be made unclean, or
a man of whom he may take uncleanness,
whatsoever uncleanness he hath;
6 The soul which hath touched any such
shall be unclean until even, and shall not
eat of the holy things, unless he wash his
flesh with water.
7 And when the sun is down, he shall be
clean, and shall afterward eat of the holy
things; because it *is* his food.
8 That which dieth of itself, or is torn *with*
beasts, he shall not eat to defile himself
therewith: I *am* the LORD.
9 They shall therefore keep mine ordinance,
lest they bear sin for it, and die therefore, if
they profane it: I the LORD do sanctify them.
10 There shall no stranger eat *of* the holy
thing: a sojourner of the priest, or an hired
servant, shall not eat *of* the holy thing.
11 But if the priest buy *any* soul with his
money, he shall eat of it, and he that is born
in his house: they shall eat of his meat.
12 If the priest's daughter also be *married*
unto a stranger, she may not eat of an offering of the holy things.
13 But if the priest's daughter be a widow, or
divorced, and have no child, and is returned
unto her father's house, as in her youth, she
shall eat of her father's meat: but there shall
no stranger eat thereof.
14 ¶ And if a man eat *of* the holy thing
unwittingly, then he shall put the fifth *part*
thereof unto it, and shall give *it* unto the
priest with the holy thing.
15 And they shall not profane the holy things
of the children of Israel, which they offer
unto the LORD;
16 Or suffer them to bear the iniquity of
trespass, when they eat their holy things:
for I the LORD do sanctify them.
17 ¶ And the LORD spake unto Moses,
saying,
18 Speak unto Aaron, and to his sons, and
unto all the children of Israel, and say unto
them, Whatsoever *he be* of the house of
Israel, or of the strangers in Israel, that will
offer his oblation for all his vows, and for all
his freewill offerings, which they will offer
unto the LORD for a burnt offering;
19 *Ye shall offer* at your own will a male without blemish, of the beeves, of the sheep, or
of the goats.
20 *But* whatsoever hath a blemish, *that* shall
ye not offer: for it shall not be acceptable
for you.
21 And whosoever offereth a sacrifice of
peace offerings unto the LORD to accomplish
his vow, or a freewill offering in beeves or
sheep, it shall be perfect to be accepted;
there shall be no blemish therein.
22 Blind, or broken, or maimed, or having a
wen, or scurvy, or scabbed, ye shall not offer
these unto the LORD, nor make an offering
by fire of them upon the altar unto the LORD.
23 Either a bullock or a lamb that hath any
thing superfluous or lacking in his parts, that
mayest thou offer *for* a freewill offering; but
for a vow it shall not be accepted.
24 Ye shall not offer unto the LORD that
which is bruised, or crushed, or broken,
or cut; neither shall ye make *any offering*
thereof in your land.
25 Neither from a stranger's hand shall
ye offer the bread of your God of any of
these; because their corruption *is* in them,
and blemishes *be* in them: they shall not be
accepted for you.
26 ¶ And the LORD spake unto Moses,
saying,
27 When a bullock, or a sheep, or a goat, is
brought forth, then it shall be seven days
under the dam; and from the eighth day
and thenceforth it shall be accepted for an
offering made by fire unto the LORD.
28 And *whether it be* cow or ewe, ye shall
not kill it and her young both in one day.
29 And when ye will offer a sacrifice of
thanksgiving unto the LORD, offer *it* at your
own will.
30 On the same day it shall be eaten up;

ye shall leave none of it until the morrow:
I *am* the LORD.
31 Therefore shall ye keep my commandments, and do them: I *am* the LORD.
32 Neither shall ye profane my holy name;
but I will be hallowed among the children
of Israel: I *am* the LORD which hallow you,
33 That brought you out of the land of Egypt,
to be your God: I *am* the LORD.

Leviticus 23

1 And the LORD spake unto Moses, saying,
2 Speak unto the children of Israel, and say
unto them, *Concerning* the feasts of the
LORD, which ye shall proclaim *to be* holy
convocations, *even* these *are* my feasts.
3 Six days shall work be done: but the
seventh day *is* the sabbath of rest, an holy
convocation; ye shall do no work *therein:* it *is*
the sabbath of the LORD in all your dwellings.
4 ¶ These *are* the feasts of the LORD, *even*
holy convocations, which ye shall proclaim
in their seasons.
5 In the fourteenth *day* of the first month
at even *is* the LORD's passover.
6 And on the fifteenth day of the same
month *is* the feast of unleavened bread
unto the LORD: seven days ye must eat
unleavened bread.
7 In the first day ye shall have an holy convocation: ye shall do no servile work therein.
8 But ye shall offer an offering made by fire
unto the LORD seven days: in the seventh
day *is* an holy convocation: ye shall do no
servile work *therein.*
9 ¶ And the LORD spake unto Moses, saying,
10 Speak unto the children of Israel, and
say unto them, When ye be come into the
land which I give unto you, and shall reap
the harvest thereof, then ye shall bring a
sheaf of the firstfruits of your harvest unto
the priest:
11 And he shall wave the sheaf before the
LORD, to be accepted for you: on the morrow
after the sabbath the priest shall wave it.
12 And ye shall offer that day when ye wave
the sheaf an he lamb without blemish of the
first year for a burnt offering unto the LORD.
13 And the meat offering thereof *shall be*
two tenth deals of fine flour mingled with
oil, an offering made by fire unto the LORD
for a sweet savour: and the drink offering
thereof *shall be* of wine, the fourth *part*
of an hin.
14 And ye shall eat neither bread, nor
parched corn, nor green ears, until the selfsame day that ye have brought an offering
unto your God: *it shall be* a statute for ever
throughout your generations in all your
dwellings.
15 ¶ And ye shall count unto you from the
morrow after the sabbath, from the day that
ye brought the sheaf of the wave offering;
seven sabbaths shall be complete:
16 Even unto the morrow after the seventh
sabbath shall ye number fifty days; and ye
shall offer a new meat offering unto the
LORD.
17 Ye shall bring out of your habitations two
wave loaves of two tenth deals: they shall
be of fine flour; they shall be baken with
leaven; *they are* the firstfruits unto the LORD.
18 And ye shall offer with the bread seven
lambs without blemish of the first year,
and one young bullock, and two rams: they
shall be *for* a burnt offering unto the LORD,
with their meat offering, and their drink
offerings, *even* an offering made by fire, of
sweet savour unto the LORD.
19 Then ye shall sacrifice one kid of the goats
for a sin offering, and two lambs of the first
year for a sacrifice of peace offerings.
20 And the priest shall wave them with the
bread of the firstfruits *for* a wave offering
before the LORD, with the two lambs: they
shall be holy to the LORD for the priest.
21 And ye shall proclaim on the selfsame
day, *that* it may be an holy convocation unto
you: ye shall do no servile work *therein: it
shall be* a statute for ever in all your dwellings throughout your generations.
22 ¶ And when ye reap the harvest of your
land, thou shalt not make clean riddance
of the corners of thy field when thou reapest, neither shalt thou gather any gleaning
of thy harvest: thou shalt leave them unto
the poor, and to the stranger: I *am* the LORD
your God.
23 ¶ And the LORD spake unto Moses,
saying,
24 Speak unto the children of Israel, saying,
In the seventh month, in the first *day* of the
month, shall ye have a sabbath, a memorial
of blowing of trumpets, an holy convocation.
25 Ye shall do no servile work *therein:* but

ye shall offer an offering made by fire unto
the LORD.
26 ¶ And the LORD spake unto Moses,
saying,
27 Also on the tenth *day* of this seventh
month *there shall be* a day of atonement:
it shall be an holy convocation unto you;
and ye shall afflict your souls, and offer an
offering made by fire unto the LORD.
28 And ye shall do no work in that same
day: for it *is* a day of atonement, to make
an atonement for you before the LORD
your God.
29 For whatsoever soul *it be* that shall not
be afflicted in that same day, he shall be cut
off from among his people.
30 And whatsoever soul *it be* that doeth any
work in that same day, the same soul will I
destroy from among his people.
31 Ye shall do no manner of work: *it shall
be* a statute for ever throughout your generations in all your dwellings.
32 It *shall be* unto you a sabbath of rest, and
ye shall afflict your souls: in the ninth *day* of
the month at even, from even unto even,
shall ye celebrate your sabbath.
33 ¶ And the LORD spake unto Moses,
saying,
34 Speak unto the children of Israel, saying,
The fifteenth day of this seventh month *shall
be* the feast of tabernacles *for* seven days
unto the LORD.
35 On the first day *shall be* an holy convocation: ye shall do no servile work *therein*.
36 Seven days ye shall offer an offering
made by fire unto the LORD: on the eighth
day shall be an holy convocation unto you;
and ye shall offer an offering made by fire
unto the LORD: it *is* a solemn assembly; *and*
ye shall do no servile work *therein*.
37 These *are* the feasts of the LORD, which
ye shall proclaim *to be* holy convocations,
to offer an offering made by fire unto the
LORD, a burnt offering, and a meat offering,
a sacrifice, and drink offerings, every thing
upon his day:
38 Beside the sabbaths of the LORD, and
beside your gifts, and beside all your vows,
and beside all your freewill offerings, which
ye give unto the LORD.
39 Also in the fifteenth day of the seventh
month, when ye have gathered in the fruit
of the land, ye shall keep a feast unto the
LORD seven days: on the first day *shall be*
a sabbath, and on the eighth day *shall be*
a sabbath.
40 And ye shall take you on the first day the
boughs of goodly trees, branches of palm
trees, and the boughs of thick trees, and
willows of the brook; and ye shall rejoice
before the LORD your God seven days.
41 And ye shall keep it a feast unto the LORD
seven days in the year. *It shall be* a statute
for ever in your generations: ye shall celebrate it in the seventh month.
42 Ye shall dwell in booths seven days; all
that are Israelites born shall dwell in booths:
43 That your generations may know that
I made the children of Israel to dwell in
booths, when I brought them out of the land
of Egypt: I *am* the LORD your God.
44 And Moses declared unto the children
of Israel the feasts of the LORD.

Leviticus 24

1 And the LORD spake unto Moses, saying,
2 Command the children of Israel, that they
bring unto thee pure oil olive beaten for the
light, to cause the lamps to burn continually.
3 Without the vail of the testimony, in the
tabernacle of the congregation, shall Aaron
order it from the evening unto the morning
before the LORD continually: *it shall be* a
statute for ever in your generations.
4 He shall order the lamps upon the pure
candlestick before the LORD continually.
5 ¶ And thou shalt take fine flour, and bake
twelve cakes thereof: two tenth deals shall
be in one cake.
6 And thou shalt set them in two rows, six on
a row, upon the pure table before the LORD.
7 And thou shalt put pure frankincense upon
each row, that it may be on the bread for
a memorial, *even* an offering made by fire
unto the LORD.
8 Every sabbath he shall set it in order
before the LORD continually, *being taken*
from the children of Israel by an everlasting
covenant.
9 And it shall be Aaron's and his sons'; and
they shall eat it in the holy place: for it *is*
most holy unto him of the offerings of the
LORD made by fire by a perpetual statute.
10 ¶ And the son of an Israelitish woman,
whose father *was* an Egyptian, went out
among the children of Israel: and this son

of the Israelitish *woman* and a man of Israel
strove together in the camp;
11 And the Israelitish woman's son blasphemed the name *of the* LORD, and cursed.
And they brought him unto Moses: (and his
mother's name *was* Shelomith, the daughter
of Dibri, of the tribe of Dan:)
12 And they put him in ward, that the mind
of the LORD might be shewed them.
13 And the LORD spake unto Moses, saying,
14 Bring forth him that hath cursed without
the camp; and let all that heard *him* lay their
hands upon his head, and let all the congregation stone him.
15 And thou shalt speak unto the children
of Israel, saying, Whosoever curseth his God
shall bear his sin.
16 And he that blasphemeth the name of
the LORD, he shall surely be put to death,
and all the congregation shall certainly stone
him: as well the stranger, as he that is born
in the land, when he blasphemeth the name
of the LORD, shall be put to death.
17 ¶ And he that killeth any man shall surely
be put to death.
18 And he that killeth a beast shall make it
good; beast for beast.
19 And if a man cause a blemish in his
neighbour; as he hath done, so shall it be
done to him;
20 Breach for breach, eye for eye, tooth for
tooth: as he hath caused a blemish in a man,
so shall it be done to him *again*.
21 And he that killeth a beast, he shall
restore it: and he that killeth a man, he shall
be put to death.
22 Ye shall have one manner of law, as well
for the stranger, as for one of your own
country: for I *am* the LORD your God.
23 ¶ And Moses spake to the children of
Israel, that they should bring forth him that
had cursed out of the camp, and stone him
with stones. And the children of Israel did
as the LORD commanded Moses.

Leviticus 25

1 And the LORD spake unto Moses in mount
Sinai, saying,
2 Speak unto the children of Israel, and say
unto them, When ye come into the land
which I give you, then shall the land keep a
sabbath unto the LORD.
3 Six years thou shalt sow thy field, and six
years thou shalt prune thy vineyard, and
gather in the fruit thereof;
4 But in the seventh year shall be a sabbath
of rest unto the land, a sabbath for the LORD:
thou shalt neither sow thy field, nor prune
thy vineyard.
5 That which groweth of its own accord
of thy harvest thou shalt not reap, neither
gather the grapes of thy vine undressed: *for*
it is a year of rest unto the land.
6 And the sabbath of the land shall be meat
for you; for thee, and for thy servant, and
for thy maid, and for thy hired servant, and
for thy stranger that sojourneth with thee,
7 And for thy cattle, and for the beast that
are in thy land, shall all the increase thereof
be meat.
8 ¶ And thou shalt number seven sabbaths
of years unto thee, seven times seven years;
and the space of the seven sabbaths of years
shall be unto thee forty and nine years.
9 Then shalt thou cause the trumpet of the
jubile to sound on the tenth *day* of the seventh month, in the day of atonement shall
ye make the trumpet sound throughout all
your land.
10 And ye shall hallow the fiftieth year, and
proclaim liberty throughout *all* the land
unto all the inhabitants thereof: it shall be
a jubile unto you; and ye shall return every
man unto his possession, and ye shall return
every man unto his family.
11 A jubile shall that fiftieth year be unto
you: ye shall not sow, neither reap that
which groweth of itself in it, nor gather *the*
grapes in it of thy vine undressed.
12 For it *is* the jubile; it shall be holy unto
you: ye shall eat the increase thereof out
of the field.
13 In the year of this jubile ye shall return
every man unto his possession.
14 And if thou sell ought unto thy neighbour,
or buyest *ought* of thy neighbour's hand, ye
shall not oppress one another:
15 According to the number of years after
the jubile thou shalt buy of thy neighbour,
and according unto the number of years of
the fruits he shall sell unto thee:
16 According to the multitude of years
thou shalt increase the price thereof, and
according to the fewness of years thou shalt
diminish the price of it: for *according* to the

number *of the years* of the fruits doth he
sell unto thee.
17 Ye shall not therefore oppress one
another; but thou shalt fear thy God: for I
am the LORD your God.
18 ¶ Wherefore ye shall do my statutes, and
keep my judgments, and do them; and ye
shall dwell in the land in safety.
19 And the land shall yield her fruit, and ye
shall eat your fill, and dwell therein in safety.
20 And if ye shall say, What shall we eat the
seventh year? behold, we shall not sow, nor
gather in our increase:
21 Then I will command my blessing upon
you in the sixth year, and it shall bring forth
fruit for three years.
22 And ye shall sow the eighth year, and eat
yet of old fruit until the ninth year; until her
fruits come in ye shall eat *of* the old *store.*
23 ¶ The land shall not be sold for ever: for
the land *is* mine; for ye *are* strangers and
sojourners with me.
24 And in all the land of your possession ye
shall grant a redemption for the land.
25 ¶ If thy brother be waxen poor, and hath
sold away *some* of his possession, and if any
of his kin come to redeem it, then shall he
redeem that which his brother sold.
26 And if the man have none to redeem it,
and himself be able to redeem it;
27 Then let him count the years of the sale
thereof, and restore the overplus unto the
man to whom he sold it; that he may return
unto his possession.
28 But if he be not able to restore *it* to him,
then that which is sold shall remain in the
hand of him that hath bought it until the
year of jubile: and in the jubile it shall go
out, and he shall return unto his possession.
29 And if a man sell a dwelling house in a
walled city, then he may redeem it within a
whole year after it is sold; *within* a full year
may he redeem it.
30 And if it be not redeemed within the
space of a full year, then the house that *is*
in the walled city shall be established for
ever to him that bought it throughout his
generations: it shall not go out in the jubile.
31 But the houses of the villages which
have no wall round about them shall be
counted as the fields of the country: they
may be redeemed, and they shall go out
in the jubile.
32 Notwithstanding the cities of the Levites,
and the houses of the cities of their possession, may the Levites redeem at any time.
33 And if a man purchase of the Levites,
then the house that was sold, and the city
of his possession, shall go out in *the year
of* jubile: for the houses of the cities of the
Levites *are* their possession among the
children of Israel.
34 But the field of the suburbs of their cities may not be sold; for it *is* their perpetual
possession.
35 ¶ And if thy brother be waxen poor, and
fallen in decay with thee; then thou shalt
relieve him: *yea, though he be* a stranger,
or a sojourner; that he may live with thee.
36 Take thou no usury of him, or increase:
but fear thy God; that thy brother may live
with thee.
37 Thou shalt not give him thy money upon
usury, nor lend him thy victuals for increase.
38 I *am* the LORD your God, which brought
you forth out of the land of Egypt, to give
you the land of Canaan, *and* to be your God.
39 ¶ And if thy brother *that dwelleth* by
thee be waxen poor, and be sold unto thee;
thou shalt not compel him to serve as a
bondservant:
40 *But* as an hired servant, *and* as a
sojourner, he shall be with thee, *and* shall
serve thee unto the year of jubile:
41 And *then* shall he depart from thee,
both he and his children with him, and shall
return unto his own family, and unto the
possession of his fathers shall he return.
42 For they *are* my servants, which I brought
forth out of the land of Egypt: they shall not
be sold as bondmen.
43 Thou shalt not rule over him with rigour;
but shalt fear thy God.
44 Both thy bondmen, and thy bondmaids,
which thou shalt have, *shall be* of the heathen that are round about you; of them shall
ye buy bondmen and bondmaids.
45 Moreover of the children of the strangers
that do sojourn among you, of them shall
ye buy, and of their families that *are* with
you, which they begat in your land: and they
shall be your possession.
46 And ye shall take them as an inheritance
for your children after you, to inherit *them
for* a possession; they shall be your bondmen for ever: but over your brethren the

children of Israel, ye shall not rule one over another with rigour.

47 ¶ And if a sojourner or stranger wax rich by thee, and thy brother *that dwelleth* by him wax poor, and sell himself unto the stranger *or* sojourner by thee, or to the stock of the stranger's family:

48 After that he is sold he may be redeemed again; one of his brethren may redeem him:

49 Either his uncle, or his uncle's son, may redeem him, or *any* that is nigh of kin unto him of his family may redeem him; or if he be able, he may redeem himself.

50 And he shall reckon with him that bought him from the year that he was sold to him unto the year of jubile: and the price of his sale shall be according unto the number of years, according to the time of an hired servant shall it be with him.

51 If *there be* yet many years *behind*, according unto them he shall give again the price of his redemption out of the money that he was bought for.

52 And if there remain but few years unto the year of jubile, then he shall count with him, *and* according unto his years shall he give him again the price of his redemption.

53 *And* as a yearly hired servant shall he be with him: *and the other* shall not rule with rigour over him in thy sight.

54 And if he be not redeemed in these *years*, then he shall go out in the year of jubile, *both* he, and his children with him.

55 For unto me the children of Israel *are* servants; they *are* my servants whom I brought forth out of the land of Egypt: I *am* the LORD your God.

Leviticus 26

1 Ye shall make you no idols nor graven image, neither rear you up a standing image, neither shall ye set up *any* image of stone in your land, to bow down unto it: for I *am* the LORD your God.

2 ¶ Ye shall keep my sabbaths, and reverence my sanctuary: I *am* the LORD.

3 ¶ If ye walk in my statutes, and keep my commandments, and do them;

4 Then I will give you rain in due season, and the land shall yield her increase, and the trees of the field shall yield their fruit.

5 And your threshing shall reach unto the vintage, and the vintage shall reach unto the sowing time: and ye shall eat your bread to the full, and dwell in your land safely.

6 And I will give peace in the land, and ye shall lie down, and none shall make *you* afraid: and I will rid evil beasts out of the land, neither shall the sword go through your land.

7 And ye shall chase your enemies, and they shall fall before you by the sword.

8 And five of you shall chase an hundred, and an hundred of you shall put ten thousand to flight: and your enemies shall fall before you by the sword.

9 For I will have respect unto you, and make you fruitful, and multiply you, and establish my covenant with you.

10 And ye shall eat old store, and bring forth the old because of the new.

11 And I will set my tabernacle among you: and my soul shall not abhor you.

12 And I will walk among you, and will be your God, and ye shall be my people.

13 I *am* the LORD your God, which brought you forth out of the land of Egypt, that ye should not be their bondmen; and I have broken the bands of your yoke, and made you go upright.

14 ¶ But if ye will not hearken unto me, and will not do all these commandments;

15 And if ye shall despise my statutes, or if your soul abhor my judgments, so that ye will not do all my commandments, *but* that ye break my covenant:

16 I also will do this unto you; I will even appoint over you terror, consumption, and the burning ague, that shall consume the eyes, and cause sorrow of heart: and ye shall sow your seed in vain, for your enemies shall eat it.

17 And I will set my face against you, and ye shall be slain before your enemies: they that hate you shall reign over you; and ye shall flee when none pursueth you.

18 And if ye will not yet for all this hearken unto me, then I will punish you seven times more for your sins.

19 And I will break the pride of your power; and I will make your heaven as iron, and your earth as brass:

20 And your strength shall be spent in vain: for your land shall not yield her increase, neither shall the trees of the land yield their fruits.

21 ¶ And if ye walk contrary unto me, and
will not hearken unto me; I will bring seven
times more plagues upon you according to
your sins.
22 I will also send wild beasts among you,
which shall rob you of your children, and
destroy your cattle, and make you few
in number; and your *high* ways shall be
desolate.
23 And if ye will not be reformed by me by
these things, but will walk contrary unto me;
24 Then will I also walk contrary unto you,
and will punish you yet seven times for
your sins.
25 And I will bring a sword upon you, that
shall avenge the quarrel of *my* covenant:
and when ye are gathered together within
your cities, I will send the pestilence among
you; and ye shall be delivered into the hand
of the enemy.
26 *And* when I have broken the staff of your
bread, ten women shall bake your bread in
one oven, and they shall deliver *you* your
bread again by weight: and ye shall eat, and
not be satisfied.
27 And if ye will not for all this hearken unto
me, but walk contrary unto me;
28 Then I will walk contrary unto you also
in fury; and I, even I, will chastise you seven
times for your sins.
29 And ye shall eat the flesh of your sons,
and the flesh of your daughters shall ye eat.
30 And I will destroy your high places, and
cut down your images, and cast your carcases upon the carcases of your idols, and
my soul shall abhor you.
31 And I will make your cities waste, and
bring your sanctuaries unto desolation, and
I will not smell the savour of your sweet
odours.
32 And I will bring the land into desolation:
and your enemies which dwell therein shall
be astonished at it.
33 And I will scatter you among the heathen, and will draw out a sword after you:
and your land shall be desolate, and your
cities waste.
34 Then shall the land enjoy her sabbaths,
as long as it lieth desolate, and ye *be* in your
enemies' land; *even* then shall the land rest,
and enjoy her sabbaths.
35 As long as it lieth desolate it shall rest;
because it did not rest in your sabbaths,
when ye dwelt upon it.
36 And upon them that are left *alive* of you I
will send a faintness into their hearts in the
lands of their enemies; and the sound of a
shaken leaf shall chase them; and they shall
flee, as fleeing from a sword; and they shall
fall when none pursueth.
37 And they shall fall one upon another, as it
were before a sword, when none pursueth:
and ye shall have no power to stand before
your enemies.
38 And ye shall perish among the heathen,
and the land of your enemies shall eat
you up.
39 And they that are left of you shall pine
away in their iniquity in your enemies' lands;
and also in the iniquities of their fathers shall
they pine away with them.
40 If they shall confess their iniquity, and the
iniquity of their fathers, with their trespass
which they trespassed against me, and that
also they have walked contrary unto me;
41 And *that* I also have walked contrary unto
them, and have brought them into the land
of their enemies; if then their uncircumcised
hearts be humbled, and they then accept of
the punishment of their iniquity:
42 Then will I remember my covenant with
Jacob, and also my covenant with Isaac,
and also my covenant with Abraham will I
remember; and I will remember the land.
43 The land also shall be left of them, and
shall enjoy her sabbaths, while she lieth
desolate without them: and they shall
accept of the punishment of their iniquity:
because, even because they despised my
judgments, and because their soul abhorred
my statutes.
44 And yet for all that, when they be in the
land of their enemies, I will not cast them
away, neither will I abhor them, to destroy
them utterly, and to break my covenant with
them: for I *am* the LORD their God.
45 But I will for their sakes remember the
covenant of their ancestors, whom I brought
forth out of the land of Egypt in the sight
of the heathen, that I might be their God:
I *am* the LORD.
46 These *are* the statutes and judgments
and laws, which the LORD made between
him and the children of Israel in mount Sinai
by the hand of Moses.

Leviticus 27

1 And the LORD spake unto Moses, saying,
2 Speak unto the children of Israel, and say
unto them, When a man shall make a sin-
gular vow, the persons *shall be* for the LORD
by thy estimation.
3 And thy estimation shall be of the male
from twenty years old even unto sixty years
old, even thy estimation shall be fifty shekels
of silver, after the shekel of the sanctuary.
4 And if it *be* a female, then thy estimation
shall be thirty shekels.
5 And if *it be* from five years old even unto
twenty years old, then thy estimation shall
be of the male twenty shekels, and for the
female ten shekels.
6 And if *it be* from a month old even unto
five years old, then thy estimation shall be
of the male five shekels of silver, and for
the female thy estimation *shall be* three
shekels of silver.
7 And if *it be* from sixty years old and
above; if *it be* a male, then thy estimation
shall be fifteen shekels, and for the female
ten shekels.
8 But if he be poorer than thy estimation,
then he shall present himself before the
priest, and the priest shall value him; according to his ability that vowed shall the priest
value him.
9 And if *it be* a beast, whereof men bring
an offering unto the LORD, all that *any man*
giveth of such unto the LORD shall be holy.
10 He shall not alter it, nor change it, a good
for a bad, or a bad for a good: and if he shall
at all change beast for beast, then it and the
exchange thereof shall be holy.
11 And if *it be* any unclean beast, of which
they do not offer a sacrifice unto the LORD,
then he shall present the beast before the
priest:
12 And the priest shall value it, whether it
be good or bad: as thou valuest it, *who art*
the priest, so shall it be.
13 But if he will at all redeem it, then he shall
add a fifth *part* thereof unto thy estimation.
14 ¶ And when a man shall sanctify his
house *to be* holy unto the LORD, then the
priest shall estimate it, whether it be good
or bad: as the priest shall estimate it, so
shall it stand.
15 And if he that sanctified it will redeem
his house, then he shall add the fifth *part*
of the money of thy estimation unto it, and
it shall be his.
16 And if a man shall sanctify unto the LORD
some part of a field of his possession, then
thy estimation shall be according to the seed
thereof: an homer of barley seed *shall be*
valued at fifty shekels of silver.
17 If he sanctify his field from the year of
jubile, according to thy estimation it shall
stand.
18 But if he sanctify his field after the jubile,
then the priest shall reckon unto him the
money according to the years that remain,
even unto the year of the jubile, and it shall
be abated from thy estimation.
19 And if he that sanctified the field will in
any wise redeem it, then he shall add the
fifth *part* of the money of thy estimation
unto it, and it shall be assured to him.
20 And if he will not redeem the field, or
if he have sold the field to another man, it
shall not be redeemed any more.
21 But the field, when it goeth out in the
jubile, shall be holy unto the LORD, as a
field devoted; the possession thereof shall
be the priest's.
22 And if *a man* sanctify unto the LORD a
field which he hath bought, which *is* not of
the fields of his possession;
23 Then the priest shall reckon unto him
the worth of thy estimation, *even* unto the
year of the jubile: and he shall give thine
estimation in that day, *as* a holy thing unto
the LORD.
24 In the year of the jubile the field shall
return unto him of whom it was bought,
even to him to whom the possession of the
land *did belong*.
25 And all thy estimations shall be according to the shekel of the sanctuary: twenty
gerahs shall be the shekel.
26 ¶ Only the firstling of the beasts, which
should be the LORD's firstling, no man shall
sanctify it; whether *it be* ox, or sheep: it *is*
the LORD's.
27 And if *it be* of an unclean beast, then he
shall redeem *it* according to thine estimation, and shall add a fifth *part* of it thereto:
or if it be not redeemed, then it shall be sold
according to thy estimation.
28 Notwithstanding no devoted thing, that
a man shall devote unto the LORD of all
that he hath, *both* of man and beast, and

of the field of his possession, shall be sold
or redeemed: every devoted thing *is* most
holy unto the LORD.
29 None devoted, which shall be devoted
of men, shall be redeemed; *but* shall surely
be put to death.
30 And all the tithe of the land, *whether* of
the seed of the land, *or* of the fruit of the
tree, *is* the LORD's: *it is* holy unto the LORD.
31 And if a man will at all redeem *ought*
of his tithes, he shall add thereto the fifth
part thereof.
32 And concerning the tithe of the herd, or
of the flock, *even* of whatsoever passeth
under the rod, the tenth shall be holy unto
the LORD.
33 He shall not search whether it be good
or bad, neither shall he change it: and if
he change it at all, then both it and the
change thereof shall be holy; it shall not
be redeemed.
34 These *are* the commandments, which the
LORD commanded Moses for the children
of Israel in mount Sinai.

The Fourth Book Of Moses Called

Numbers

Numbers 1

1 And the LORD spake unto Moses in the
wilderness of Sinai, in the tabernacle of the
congregation, on the first *day* of the second
month, in the second year after they were
come out of the land of Egypt, saying,
2 Take ye the sum of all the congregation of
the children of Israel, after their families, by
the house of their fathers, with the number
of *their* names, every male by their polls;
3 From twenty years old and upward, all that
are able to go forth to war in Israel: thou and
Aaron shall number them by their armies.
4 And with you there shall be a man of
every tribe; every one head of the house
of his fathers.
5 ¶ And these *are* the names of the men that
shall stand with you: of *the tribe of* Reuben;
Elizur the son of Shedeur.
6 Of Simeon; Shelumiel the son of Zurishaddai.
7 Of Judah; Nahshon the son of Amminadab.
8 Of Issachar; Nethaneel the son of Zuar.
9 Of Zebulun; Eliab the son of Helon.
10 Of the children of Joseph: of Ephraim;
Elishama the son of Ammihud: of Manasseh;
Gamaliel the son of Pedahzur.
11 Of Benjamin; Abidan the son of Gideoni.
12 Of Dan; Ahiezer the son of Ammishaddai.
13 Of Asher; Pagiel the son of Ocran.
14 Of Gad; Eliasaph the son of Deuel.
15 Of Naphtali; Ahira the son of Enan.
16 These *were* the renowned of the congregation, princes of the tribes of their fathers,
heads of thousands in Israel.
17 ¶ And Moses and Aaron took these men
which are expressed by *their* names:
18 And they assembled all the congregation together on the first *day* of the second
month, and they declared their pedigrees
after their families, by the house of their
fathers, according to the number of the
names, from twenty years old and upward,
by their polls.
19 As the LORD commanded Moses, so he
numbered them in the wilderness of Sinai.
20 And the children of Reuben, Israel's
eldest son, by their generations, after their
families, by the house of their fathers,
according to the number of the names, by
their polls, every male from twenty years
old and upward, all that were able to go
forth to war;
21 Those that were numbered of them, *even*
of the tribe of Reuben, *were* forty and six
thousand and five hundred.
22 ¶ Of the children of Simeon, by their
generations, after their families, by the
house of their fathers, those that were numbered of them, according to the number of
the names, by their polls, every male from
twenty years old and upward, all that were
able to go forth to war;
23 Those that were numbered of them, *even*

of the tribe of Simeon, *were* fifty and nine
thousand and three hundred.
24 ¶ Of the children of Gad, by their generations, after their families, by the house of
their fathers, according to the number of the
names, from twenty years old and upward,
all that were able to go forth to war;
25 Those that were numbered of them,
even of the tribe of Gad, *were* forty and five
thousand six hundred and fifty.
26 ¶ Of the children of Judah, by their generations, after their families, by the house
of their fathers, according to the number
of the names, from twenty years old and
upward, all that were able to go forth to war;
27 Those that were numbered of them, *even*
of the tribe of Judah, *were* threescore and
fourteen thousand and six hundred.
28 ¶ Of the children of Issachar, by their generations, after their families, by the house
of their fathers, according to the number
of the names, from twenty years old and
upward, all that were able to go forth to war;
29 Those that were numbered of them, *even*
of the tribe of Issachar, *were* fifty and four
thousand and four hundred.
30 ¶ Of the children of Zebulun, by their generations, after their families, by the house
of their fathers, according to the number
of the names, from twenty years old and
upward, all that were able to go forth to war;
31 Those that were numbered of them, *even*
of the tribe of Zebulun, *were* fifty and seven
thousand and four hundred.
32 ¶ Of the children of Joseph, *namely*, of
the children of Ephraim, by their generations, after their families, by the house of
their fathers, according to the number of the
names, from twenty years old and upward,
all that were able to go forth to war;
33 Those that were numbered of them, *even*
of the tribe of Ephraim, *were* forty thousand
and five hundred.
34 ¶ Of the children of Manasseh, by their
generations, after their families, by the
house of their fathers, according to the
number of the names, from twenty years
old and upward, all that were able to go
forth to war;
35 Those that were numbered of them, *even*
of the tribe of Manasseh, *were* thirty and
two thousand and two hundred.
36 ¶ Of the children of Benjamin, by their
generations, after their families, by the
house of their fathers, according to the
number of the names, from twenty years
old and upward, all that were able to go
forth to war;
37 Those that were numbered of them, *even*
of the tribe of Benjamin, *were* thirty and five
thousand and four hundred.
38 ¶ Of the children of Dan, by their generations, after their families, by the house of
their fathers, according to the number of the
names, from twenty years old and upward,
all that were able to go forth to war;
39 Those that were numbered of them, *even*
of the tribe of Dan, *were* threescore and two
thousand and seven hundred.
40 ¶ Of the children of Asher, by their generations, after their families, by the house
of their fathers, according to the number
of the names, from twenty years old and
upward, all that were able to go forth to war;
41 Those that were numbered of them,
even of the tribe of Asher, *were* forty and
one thousand and five hundred.
42 ¶ Of the children of Naphtali, throughout their generations, after their families,
by the house of their fathers, according
to the number of the names, from twenty
years old and upward, all that were able to
go forth to war;
43 Those that were numbered of them, *even*
of the tribe of Naphtali, *were* fifty and three
thousand and four hundred.
44 These *are* those that were numbered,
which Moses and Aaron numbered, and
the princes of Israel, *being* twelve men:
each one was for the house of his fathers.
45 So were all those that were numbered of
the children of Israel, by the house of their
fathers, from twenty years old and upward,
all that were able to go forth to war in Israel;
46 Even all they that were numbered were
six hundred thousand and three thousand
and five hundred and fifty.
47 ¶ But the Levites after the tribe of their
fathers were not numbered among them.
48 For the LORD had spoken unto Moses,
saying,
49 Only thou shalt not number the tribe of
Levi, neither take the sum of them among
the children of Israel:
50 But thou shalt appoint the Levites over
the tabernacle of testimony, and over all

the vessels thereof, and over all things that
belong to it: they shall bear the tabernacle,
and all the vessels thereof; and they shall
minister unto it, and shall encamp round
about the tabernacle.
51 And when the tabernacle setteth forward, the Levites shall take it down: and
when the tabernacle is to be pitched, the
Levites shall set it up: and the stranger that
cometh nigh shall be put to death.
52 And the children of Israel shall pitch their
tents, every man by his own camp, and
every man by his own standard, throughout
their hosts.
53 But the Levites shall pitch round about
the tabernacle of testimony, that there be
no wrath upon the congregation of the
children of Israel: and the Levites shall keep
the charge of the tabernacle of testimony.
54 And the children of Israel did according
to all that the LORD commanded Moses,
so did they.

Numbers 2

1 And the LORD spake unto Moses and unto
Aaron, saying,
2 Every man of the children of Israel shall
pitch by his own standard, with the ensign
of their father's house: far off about the tabernacle of the congregation shall they pitch.
3 And on the east side toward the rising
of the sun shall they of the standard of
the camp of Judah pitch throughout their
armies: and Nahshon the son of Amminadab
shall be captain of the children of Judah.
4 And his host, and those that were numbered of them, *were* threescore and fourteen thousand and six hundred.
5 And those that do pitch next unto him *shall*
be the tribe of Issachar: and Nethaneel the
son of Zuar *shall be* captain of the children
of Issachar.
6 And his host, and those that were numbered thereof, *were* fifty and four thousand
and four hundred.
7 *Then* the tribe of Zebulun: and Eliab the
son of Helon *shall be* captain of the children
of Zebulun.
8 And his host, and those that were numbered thereof, *were* fifty and seven thousand and four hundred.
9 All that were numbered in the camp of
Judah *were* an hundred thousand and fourscore thousand and six thousand and four
hundred, throughout their armies. These
shall first set forth.
10 ¶ On the south side *shall be* the standard
of the camp of Reuben according to their
armies: and the captain of the children of
Reuben *shall be* Elizur the son of Shedeur.
11 And his host, and those that were numbered thereof, *were* forty and six thousand
and five hundred.
12 And those which pitch by him *shall be*
the tribe of Simeon: and the captain of the
children of Simeon *shall be* Shelumiel the
son of Zurishaddai.
13 And his host, and those that were numbered of them, *were* fifty and nine thousand
and three hundred.
14 Then the tribe of Gad: and the captain
of the sons of Gad *shall be* Eliasaph the son
of Reuel.
15 And his host, and those that were numbered of them, *were* forty and five thousand
and six hundred and fifty.
16 All that were numbered in the camp of
Reuben *were* an hundred thousand and
fifty and one thousand and four hundred
and fifty, throughout their armies. And they
shall set forth in the second rank.
17 ¶ Then the tabernacle of the congregation shall set forward with the camp of the
Levites in the midst of the camp: as they
encamp, so shall they set forward, every
man in his place by their standards.
18 ¶ On the west side *shall be* the standard of the camp of Ephraim according to
their armies: and the captain of the sons
of Ephraim *shall be* Elishama the son of
Ammihud.
19 And his host, and those that were numbered of them, *were* forty thousand and
five hundred.
20 And by him *shall be* the tribe of
Manasseh: and the captain of the children
of Manasseh *shall be* Gamaliel the son of
Pedahzur.
21 And his host, and those that were numbered of them, *were* thirty and two thousand and two hundred.
22 Then the tribe of Benjamin: and the captain of the sons of Benjamin *shall be* Abidan
the son of Gideoni.
23 And his host, and those that were num-

bered of them, *were* thirty and five thousand and four hundred.

24 All that were numbered of the camp of Ephraim *were* an hundred thousand and eight thousand and an hundred, throughout their armies. And they shall go forward in the third rank.

25 ¶ The standard of the camp of Dan *shall be* on the north side by their armies: and the captain of the children of Dan *shall be* Ahiezer the son of Ammishaddai.

26 And his host, and those that were numbered of them, *were* threescore and two thousand and seven hundred.

27 And those that encamp by him *shall be* the tribe of Asher: and the captain of the children of Asher *shall be* Pagiel the son of Ocran.

28 And his host, and those that were numbered of them, *were* forty and one thousand and five hundred.

29 ¶ Then the tribe of Naphtali: and the captain of the children of Naphtali *shall be* Ahira the son of Enan.

30 And his host, and those that were numbered of them, *were* fifty and three thousand and four hundred.

31 All they that were numbered in the camp of Dan *were* an hundred thousand and fifty and seven thousand and six hundred. They shall go hindmost with their standards.

32 ¶ These *are* those which were numbered of the children of Israel by the house of their fathers: all those that were numbered of the camps throughout their hosts *were* six hundred thousand and three thousand and five hundred and fifty.

33 But the Levites were not numbered among the children of Israel; as the LORD commanded Moses.

34 And the children of Israel did according to all that the LORD commanded Moses: so they pitched by their standards, and so they set forward, every one after their families, according to the house of their fathers.

Numbers 3

1 These also *are* the generations of Aaron and Moses in the day *that* the LORD spake with Moses in mount Sinai.

2 And these *are* the names of the sons of Aaron; Nadab the firstborn, and Abihu, Eleazar, and Ithamar.

3 These *are* the names of the sons of Aaron, the priests which were anointed, whom he consecrated to minister in the priest's office.

4 And Nadab and Abihu died before the LORD, when they offered strange fire before the LORD, in the wilderness of Sinai, and they had no children: and Eleazar and Ithamar ministered in the priest's office in the sight of Aaron their father.

5 ¶ And the LORD spake unto Moses, saying,

6 Bring the tribe of Levi near, and present them before Aaron the priest, that they may minister unto him.

7 And they shall keep his charge, and the charge of the whole congregation before the tabernacle of the congregation, to do the service of the tabernacle.

8 And they shall keep all the instruments of the tabernacle of the congregation, and the charge of the children of Israel, to do the service of the tabernacle.

9 And thou shalt give the Levites unto Aaron and to his sons: they *are* wholly given unto him out of the children of Israel.

10 And thou shalt appoint Aaron and his sons, and they shall wait on their priest's office: and the stranger that cometh nigh shall be put to death.

11 And the LORD spake unto Moses, saying,

12 And I, behold, I have taken the Levites from among the children of Israel instead of all the firstborn that openeth the matrix among the children of Israel: therefore the Levites shall be mine;

13 Because all the firstborn *are* mine; *for* on the day that I smote all the firstborn in the land of Egypt I hallowed unto me all the firstborn in Israel, both man and beast: mine shall they be: I *am* the LORD.

14 ¶ And the LORD spake unto Moses in the wilderness of Sinai, saying,

15 Number the children of Levi after the house of their fathers, by their families: every male from a month old and upward shalt thou number them.

16 And Moses numbered them according to the word of the LORD, as he was commanded.

17 And these were the sons of Levi by their names; Gershon, and Kohath, and Merari.

18 And these *are* the names of the sons of Gershon by their families; Libni, and Shimei.

19 And the sons of Kohath by their families;
Amram, and Izehar, Hebron, and Uzziel.
20 And the sons of Merari by their families;
Mahli, and Mushi. These *are* the families
of the Levites according to the house of
their fathers.
21 Of Gershon *was* the family of the Libnites,
and the family of the Shimites: these *are* the
families of the Gershonites.
22 Those that were numbered of them,
according to the number of all the males,
from a month old and upward, *even* those
that were numbered of them *were* seven
thousand and five hundred.
23 The families of the Gershonites shall pitch
behind the tabernacle westward.
24 And the chief of the house of the father
of the Gershonites *shall be* Eliasaph the
son of Lael.
25 And the charge of the sons of Gershon in
the tabernacle of the congregation *shall be*
the tabernacle, and the tent, the covering
thereof, and the hanging for the door of the
tabernacle of the congregation,
26 And the hangings of the court, and the
curtain for the door of the court, which *is*
by the tabernacle, and by the altar round
about, and the cords of it for all the service
thereof.
27 ¶ And of Kohath *was* the family of the
Amramites, and the family of the Izeharites,
and the family of the Hebronites, and the
family of the Uzzielites: these *are* the families of the Kohathites.
28 In the number of all the males, from a
month old and upward, *were* eight thousand and six hundred, keeping the charge
of the sanctuary.
29 The families of the sons of Kohath shall
pitch on the side of the tabernacle southward.
30 And the chief of the house of the father
of the families of the Kohathites *shall be*
Elizaphan the son of Uzziel.
31 And their charge *shall be* the ark, and the
table, and the candlestick, and the altars,
and the vessels of the sanctuary wherewith
they minister, and the hanging, and all the
service thereof.
32 And Eleazar the son of Aaron the priest
shall be chief over the chief of the Levites,
and have the oversight of them that keep
the charge of the sanctuary.
33 ¶ Of Merari *was* the family of the Mahlites, and the family of the Mushites: these
are the families of Merari.
34 And those that were numbered of them,
according to the number of all the males,
from a month old and upward, *were* six
thousand and two hundred.
35 And the chief of the house of the father
of the families of Merari *was* Zuriel the son
of Abihail: *these* shall pitch on the side of
the tabernacle northward.
36 And *under* the custody and charge of
the sons of Merari *shall be* the boards of
the tabernacle, and the bars thereof, and
the pillars thereof, and the sockets thereof,
and all the vessels thereof, and all that serveth thereto,
37 And the pillars of the court round about,
and their sockets, and their pins, and their
cords.
38 ¶ But those that encamp before the
tabernacle toward the east, *even* before
the tabernacle of the congregation eastward, *shall be* Moses, and Aaron and his
sons, keeping the charge of the sanctuary
for the charge of the children of Israel; and
the stranger that cometh nigh shall be put
to death.
39 All that were numbered of the Levites,
which Moses and Aaron numbered at the
commandment of the LORD, throughout
their families, all the males from a month
old and upward, *were* twenty and two
thousand.
40 ¶ And the LORD said unto Moses, Number
all the firstborn of the males of the children
of Israel from a month old and upward, and
take the number of their names.
41 And thou shalt take the Levites for me
(I *am* the LORD) instead of all the firstborn
among the children of Israel; and the cattle
of the Levites instead of all the firstlings
among the cattle of the children of Israel.
42 And Moses numbered, as the LORD
commanded him, all the firstborn among
the children of Israel.
43 And all the firstborn males by the number
of names, from a month old and upward, of
those that were numbered of them, were
twenty and two thousand two hundred and
threescore and thirteen.
44 ¶ And the LORD spake unto Moses,
saying,

45 Take the Levites instead of all the firstborn among the children of Israel, and the
cattle of the Levites instead of their cattle;
and the Levites shall be mine: I *am* the LORD.
46 And for those that are to be redeemed
of the two hundred and threescore and
thirteen of the firstborn of the children of
Israel, which are more than the Levites;
47 Thou shalt even take five shekels apiece
by the poll, after the shekel of the sanctuary
shalt thou take *them:* (the shekel *is* twenty
gerahs:)
48 And thou shalt give the money, wherewith the odd number of them is to be
redeemed, unto Aaron and to his sons.
49 And Moses took the redemption money
of them that were over and above them that
were redeemed by the Levites:
50 Of the firstborn of the children of Israel
took he the money; a thousand three hundred and threescore and five *shekels*, after
the shekel of the sanctuary:
51 And Moses gave the money of them that
were redeemed unto Aaron and to his sons,
according to the word of the LORD, as the
LORD commanded Moses.

Numbers 4

1 And the LORD spake unto Moses and unto
Aaron, saying,
2 Take the sum of the sons of Kohath from
among the sons of Levi, after their families,
by the house of their fathers,
3 From thirty years old and upward even
until fifty years old, all that enter into the
host, to do the work in the tabernacle of
the congregation.
4 This *shall be* the service of the sons of
Kohath in the tabernacle of the congregation, *about* the most holy things:
5 ¶ And when the camp setteth forward,
Aaron shall come, and his sons, and they
shall take down the covering vail, and cover
the ark of testimony with it:
6 And shall put thereon the covering of
badgers' skins, and shall spread over *it* a
cloth wholly of blue, and shall put in the
staves thereof.
7 And upon the table of shewbread they
shall spread a cloth of blue, and put thereon
the dishes, and the spoons, and the bowls,
and covers to cover withal: and the continual
bread shall be thereon:
8 And they shall spread upon them a cloth
of scarlet, and cover the same with a covering of badgers' skins, and shall put in the
staves thereof.
9 And they shall take a cloth of blue, and
cover the candlestick of the light, and his
lamps, and his tongs, and his snuffdishes,
and all the oil vessels thereof, wherewith
they minister unto it:
10 And they shall put it and all the vessels
thereof within a covering of badgers' skins,
and shall put *it* upon a bar.
11 And upon the golden altar they shall
spread a cloth of blue, and cover it with a
covering of badgers' skins, and shall put to
the staves thereof:
12 And they shall take all the instruments
of ministry, wherewith they minister in the
sanctuary, and put *them* in a cloth of blue,
and cover them with a covering of badgers'
skins, and shall put *them* on a bar:
13 And they shall take away the ashes from
the altar, and spread a purple cloth thereon:
14 And they shall put upon it all the vessels
thereof, wherewith they minister about it,
even the censers, the fleshhooks, and the
shovels, and the basons, all the vessels of
the altar; and they shall spread upon it a
covering of badgers' skins, and put to the
staves of it.
15 And when Aaron and his sons have made
an end of covering the sanctuary, and all the
vessels of the sanctuary, as the camp is to
set forward; after that, the sons of Kohath
shall come to bear *it:* but they shall not
touch *any* holy thing, lest they die. These
things are the burden of the sons of Kohath
in the tabernacle of the congregation.
16 ¶ And to the office of Eleazar the son of
Aaron the priest *pertaineth* the oil for the
light, and the sweet incense, and the daily
meat offering, and the anointing oil, *and*
the oversight of all the tabernacle, and of
all that therein *is*, in the sanctuary, and in
the vessels thereof.
17 ¶ And the LORD spake unto Moses and
unto Aaron, saying,
18 Cut ye not off the tribe of the families
of the Kohathites from among the Levites:
19 But thus do unto them, that they may
live, and not die, when they approach unto
the most holy things: Aaron and his sons

shall go in, and appoint them every one to
his service and to his burden:
20 But they shall not go in to see when the
holy things are covered, lest they die.
21 ¶ And the LORD spake unto Moses,
saying,
22 Take also the sum of the sons of Gershon,
throughout the houses of their fathers, by
their families;
23 From thirty years old and upward until
fifty years old shalt thou number them; all
that enter in to perform the service, to do
the work in the tabernacle of the congregation.
24 This *is* the service of the families of the
Gershonites, to serve, and for burdens:
25 And they shall bear the curtains of the
tabernacle, and the tabernacle of the congregation, his covering, and the covering of
the badgers' skins that *is* above upon it, and
the hanging for the door of the tabernacle
of the congregation,
26 And the hangings of the court, and the
hanging for the door of the gate of the court,
which *is* by the tabernacle and by the altar
round about, and their cords, and all the
instruments of their service, and all that is
made for them: so shall they serve.
27 At the appointment of Aaron and his
sons shall be all the service of the sons of
the Gershonites, in all their burdens, and in
all their service: and ye shall appoint unto
them in charge all their burdens.
28 This *is* the service of the families of the
sons of Gershon in the tabernacle of the
congregation: and their charge *shall be*
under the hand of Ithamar the son of Aaron
the priest.
29 ¶ As for the sons of Merari, thou shalt
number them after their families, by the
house of their fathers;
30 From thirty years old and upward even
unto fifty years old shalt thou number them,
every one that entereth into the service,
to do the work of the tabernacle of the
congregation.
31 And this *is* the charge of their burden,
according to all their service in the tabernacle of the congregation; the boards of the
tabernacle, and the bars thereof, and the
pillars thereof, and sockets thereof,
32 And the pillars of the court round about,
and their sockets, and their pins, and their
cords, with all their instruments, and with
all their service: and by name ye shall reckon
the instruments of the charge of their
burden.
33 This *is* the service of the families of the
sons of Merari, according to all their service, in the tabernacle of the congregation,
under the hand of Ithamar the son of Aaron
the priest.
34 ¶ And Moses and Aaron and the chief
of the congregation numbered the sons of
the Kohathites after their families, and after
the house of their fathers,
35 From thirty years old and upward even
unto fifty years old, every one that entereth
into the service, for the work in the tabernacle of the congregation:
36 And those that were numbered of them
by their families were two thousand seven
hundred and fifty.
37 These *were* they that were numbered
of the families of the Kohathites, all that
might do service in the tabernacle of the
congregation, which Moses and Aaron did
number according to the commandment of
the LORD by the hand of Moses.
38 And those that were numbered of the
sons of Gershon, throughout their families,
and by the house of their fathers,
39 From thirty years old and upward even
unto fifty years old, every one that entereth
into the service, for the work in the tabernacle of the congregation,
40 Even those that were numbered of them,
throughout their families, by the house of
their fathers, were two thousand and six
hundred and thirty.
41 These *are* they that were numbered of
the families of the sons of Gershon, of all
that might do service in the tabernacle of
the congregation, whom Moses and Aaron
did number according to the commandment
of the LORD.
42 ¶ And those that were numbered of the
families of the sons of Merari, throughout
their families, by the house of their fathers,
43 From thirty years old and upward even
unto fifty years old, every one that entereth
into the service, for the work in the tabernacle of the congregation,
44 Even those that were numbered of them
after their families, were three thousand
and two hundred.

45 These *be* those that were numbered of
the families of the sons of Merari, whom
Moses and Aaron numbered according to
the word of the LORD by the hand of Moses.
46 All those that were numbered of the Levites, whom Moses and Aaron and the chief
of Israel numbered, after their families, and
after the house of their fathers,
47 From thirty years old and upward even
unto fifty years old, every one that came
to do the service of the ministry, and the
service of the burden in the tabernacle of
the congregation,
48 Even those that were numbered of them,
were eight thousand and five hundred and
fourscore.
49 According to the commandment of the
LORD they were numbered by the hand of
Moses, every one according to his service,
and according to his burden: thus were they
numbered of him, as the LORD commanded
Moses.

Numbers 5

1 And the LORD spake unto Moses, saying,
2 Command the children of Israel, that they
put out of the camp every leper, and every
one that hath an issue, and whosoever is
defiled by the dead:
3 Both male and female shall ye put out,
without the camp shall ye put them; that
they defile not their camps, in the midst
whereof I dwell.
4 And the children of Israel did so, and put
them out without the camp: as the LORD
spake unto Moses, so did the children of
Israel.
5 ¶ And the LORD spake unto Moses, saying,
6 Speak unto the children of Israel, When
a man or woman shall commit any sin that
men commit, to do a trespass against the
LORD, and that person be guilty;
7 Then they shall confess their sin which
they have done: and he shall recompense
his trespass with the principal thereof, and
add unto it the fifth *part* thereof, and give *it*
unto *him* against whom he hath trespassed.
8 But if the man have no kinsman to recompense the trespass unto, let the trespass be
recompensed unto the LORD, *even* to the
priest; beside the ram of the atonement,
whereby an atonement shall be made for
him.
9 And every offering of all the holy things
of the children of Israel, which they bring
unto the priest, shall be his.
10 And every man's hallowed things shall be
his: whatsoever any man giveth the priest,
it shall be his.
11 ¶ And the LORD spake unto Moses,
saying,
12 Speak unto the children of Israel, and say
unto them, If any man's wife go aside, and
commit a trespass against him,
13 And a man lie with her carnally, and it be
hid from the eyes of her husband, and be
kept close, and she be defiled, and *there be*
no witness against her, neither she be taken
with the manner;
14 And the spirit of jealousy come upon
him, and he be jealous of his wife, and she
be defiled: or if the spirit of jealousy come
upon him, and he be jealous of his wife, and
she be not defiled:
15 Then shall the man bring his wife unto
the priest, and he shall bring her offering
for her, the tenth *part* of an ephah of barley
meal; he shall pour no oil upon it, nor put
frankincense thereon; for it *is* an offering of
jealousy, an offering of memorial, bringing
iniquity to remembrance.
16 And the priest shall bring her near, and
set her before the LORD:
17 And the priest shall take holy water in an
earthen vessel; and of the dust that is in the
floor of the tabernacle the priest shall take,
and put *it* into the water:
18 And the priest shall set the woman before
the LORD, and uncover the woman's head,
and put the offering of memorial in her
hands, which *is* the jealousy offering: and
the priest shall have in his hand the bitter
water that causeth the curse:
19 And the priest shall charge her by an
oath, and say unto the woman, If no man
have lain with thee, and if thou hast not
gone aside to uncleanness *with another*
instead of thy husband, be thou free from
this bitter water that causeth the curse:
20 But if thou hast gone aside *to another*
instead of thy husband, and if thou be
defiled, and some man have lain with thee
beside thine husband:
21 Then the priest shall charge the woman
with an oath of cursing, and the priest shall
say unto the woman, The LORD make thee a

curse and an oath among thy people, when
the LORD doth make thy thigh to rot, and
thy belly to swell;
22 And this water that causeth the curse
shall go into thy bowels, to make *thy* belly to
swell, and *thy* thigh to rot: And the woman
shall say, Amen, amen.
23 And the priest shall write these curses
in a book, and he shall blot *them* out with
the bitter water:
24 And he shall cause the woman to drink
the bitter water that causeth the curse: and
the water that causeth the curse shall enter
into her, *and become* bitter.
25 Then the priest shall take the jealousy
offering out of the woman's hand, and shall
wave the offering before the LORD, and offer
it upon the altar:
26 And the priest shall take an handful of
the offering, *even* the memorial thereof,
and burn *it* upon the altar, and afterward
shall cause the woman to drink the water.
27 And when he hath made her to drink
the water, then it shall come to pass, *that*,
if she be defiled, and have done trespass
against her husband, that the water that
causeth the curse shall enter into her, *and
become* bitter, and her belly shall swell, and
her thigh shall rot: and the woman shall be
a curse among her people.
28 And if the woman be not defiled, but
be clean; then she shall be free, and shall
conceive seed.
29 This *is* the law of jealousies, when a wife
goeth aside *to another* instead of her husband, and is defiled;
30 Or when the spirit of jealousy cometh
upon him, and he be jealous over his wife,
and shall set the woman before the LORD,
and the priest shall execute upon her all
this law.
31 Then shall the man be guiltless from iniquity, and this woman shall bear her iniquity.

Numbers 6

1 And the LORD spake unto Moses, saying,
2 Speak unto the children of Israel, and say
unto them, When either man or woman
shall separate *themselves* to vow a vow of
a Nazarite, to separate *themselves* unto
the LORD:
3 He shall separate *himself* from wine and
strong drink, and shall drink no vinegar of
wine, or vinegar of strong drink, neither
shall he drink any liquor of grapes, nor eat
moist grapes, or dried.
4 All the days of his separation shall he eat
nothing that is made of the vine tree, from
the kernels even to the husk.
5 All the days of the vow of his separation
there shall no rasor come upon his head:
until the days be fulfilled, in the which he
separateth *himself* unto the LORD, he shall
be holy, *and* shall let the locks of the hair
of his head grow.
6 All the days that he separateth *himself*
unto the LORD he shall come at no dead
body.
7 He shall not make himself unclean for his
father, or for his mother, for his brother, or
for his sister, when they die: because the
consecration of his God *is* upon his head.
8 All the days of his separation he *is* holy
unto the LORD.
9 And if any man die very suddenly by him,
and he hath defiled the head of his consecration; then he shall shave his head in the
day of his cleansing, on the seventh day
shall he shave it.
10 And on the eighth day he shall bring
two turtles, or two young pigeons, to the
priest, to the door of the tabernacle of the
congregation:
11 And the priest shall offer the one for a sin
offering, and the other for a burnt offering,
and make an atonement for him, for that
he sinned by the dead, and shall hallow his
head that same day.
12 And he shall consecrate unto the LORD
the days of his separation, and shall bring a
lamb of the first year for a trespass offering:
but the days that were before shall be lost,
because his separation was defiled.
13 ¶ And this *is* the law of the Nazarite,
when the days of his separation are fulfilled:
he shall be brought unto the door of the
tabernacle of the congregation:
14 And he shall offer his offering unto the
LORD, one he lamb of the first year without
blemish for a burnt offering, and one ewe
lamb of the first year without blemish for a
sin offering, and one ram without blemish
for peace offerings,
15 And a basket of unleavened bread, cakes
of fine flour mingled with oil, and wafers of

unleavened bread anointed with oil, and their meat offering, and their drink offerings.

16 And the priest shall bring *them* before the LORD, and shall offer his sin offering, and his burnt offering:

17 And he shall offer the ram *for* a sacrifice of peace offerings unto the LORD, with the basket of unleavened bread: the priest shall offer also his meat offering, and his drink offering.

18 And the Nazarite shall shave the head of his separation *at* the door of the tabernacle of the congregation, and shall take the hair of the head of his separation, and put *it* in the fire which *is* under the sacrifice of the peace offerings.

19 And the priest shall take the sodden shoulder of the ram, and one unleavened cake out of the basket, and one unleavened wafer, and shall put *them* upon the hands of the Nazarite, after *the hair of* his separation is shaven:

20 And the priest shall wave them *for* a wave offering before the LORD: this *is* holy for the priest, with the wave breast and heave shoulder: and after that the Nazarite may drink wine.

21 This *is* the law of the Nazarite who hath vowed, *and of* his offering unto the LORD for his separation, beside *that* that his hand shall get: according to the vow which he vowed, so he must do after the law of his separation.

22 ¶ And the LORD spake unto Moses, saying,

23 Speak unto Aaron and unto his sons, saying, On this wise ye shall bless the children of Israel, saying unto them,

24 The LORD bless thee, and keep thee:

25 The LORD make his face shine upon thee, and be gracious unto thee:

26 The LORD lift up his countenance upon thee, and give thee peace.

27 And they shall put my name upon the children of Israel; and I will bless them.

Numbers 7

1 And it came to pass on the day that Moses had fully set up the tabernacle, and had anointed it, and sanctified it, and all the instruments thereof, both the altar and all the vessels thereof, and had anointed them, and sanctified them;

2 That the princes of Israel, heads of the house of their fathers, who *were* the princes of the tribes, and were over them that were numbered, offered:

3 And they brought their offering before the LORD, six covered wagons, and twelve oxen; a wagon for two of the princes, and for each one an ox: and they brought them before the tabernacle.

4 And the LORD spake unto Moses, saying,

5 Take *it* of them, that they may be to do the service of the tabernacle of the congregation; and thou shalt give them unto the Levites, to every man according to his service.

6 And Moses took the wagons and the oxen, and gave them unto the Levites.

7 Two wagons and four oxen he gave unto the sons of Gershon, according to their service:

8 And four wagons and eight oxen he gave unto the sons of Merari, according unto their service, under the hand of Ithamar the son of Aaron the priest.

9 But unto the sons of Kohath he gave none: because the service of the sanctuary belonging unto them *was that* they should bear upon their shoulders.

10 ¶ And the princes offered for dedicating of the altar in the day that it was anointed, even the princes offered their offering before the altar.

11 And the LORD said unto Moses, They shall offer their offering, each prince on his day, for the dedicating of the altar.

12 ¶ And he that offered his offering the first day was Nahshon the son of Amminadab, of the tribe of Judah:

13 And his offering *was* one silver charger, the weight thereof *was* an hundred and thirty *shekels*, one silver bowl of seventy shekels, after the shekel of the sanctuary; both of them *were* full of fine flour mingled with oil for a meat offering:

14 One spoon of ten *shekels* of gold, full of incense:

15 One young bullock, one ram, one lamb of the first year, for a burnt offering:

16 One kid of the goats for a sin offering:

17 And for a sacrifice of peace offerings, two oxen, five rams, five he goats, five lambs of the first year: this *was* the offering of Nahshon the son of Amminadab.

18 ¶ On the second day Nethaneel the son
of Zuar, prince of Issachar, did offer:
19 He offered *for* his offering one silver charger, the weight whereof *was* an hundred and
thirty *shekels*, one silver bowl of seventy
shekels, after the shekel of the sanctuary;
both of them full of fine flour mingled with
oil for a meat offering:
20 One spoon of gold of ten *shekels*, full
of incense:
21 One young bullock, one ram, one lamb
of the first year, for a burnt offering:
22 One kid of the goats for a sin offering:
23 And for a sacrifice of peace offerings, two
oxen, five rams, five he goats, five lambs of
the first year: this *was* the offering of Nethaneel the son of Zuar.
24 ¶ On the third day Eliab the son of Helon,
prince of the children of Zebulun, *did offer:*
25 His offering *was* one silver charger, the
weight whereof *was* an hundred and thirty
shekels, one silver bowl of seventy shekels,
after the shekel of the sanctuary; both of
them full of fine flour mingled with oil for
a meat offering:
26 One golden spoon of ten *shekels*, full
of incense:
27 One young bullock, one ram, one lamb
of the first year, for a burnt offering:
28 One kid of the goats for a sin offering:
29 And for a sacrifice of peace offerings, two
oxen, five rams, five he goats, five lambs of
the first year: this *was* the offering of Eliab
the son of Helon.
30 ¶ On the fourth day Elizur the son of
Shedeur, prince of the children of Reuben,
did offer:
31 His offering *was* one silver charger of the
weight of an hundred and thirty *shekels*,
one silver bowl of seventy shekels, after
the shekel of the sanctuary; both of them
full of fine flour mingled with oil for a meat
offering:
32 One golden spoon of ten *shekels*, full
of incense:
33 One young bullock, one ram, one lamb
of the first year, for a burnt offering:
34 One kid of the goats for a sin offering:
35 And for a sacrifice of peace offerings, two
oxen, five rams, five he goats, five lambs of
the first year: this *was* the offering of Elizur
the son of Shedeur.
36 ¶ On the fifth day Shelumiel the son of
Zurishaddai, prince of the children of Simeon, *did offer:*
37 His offering *was* one silver charger, the
weight whereof *was* an hundred and thirty
shekels, one silver bowl of seventy shekels,
after the shekel of the sanctuary; both of
them full of fine flour mingled with oil for
a meat offering:
38 One golden spoon of ten *shekels*, full
of incense:
39 One young bullock, one ram, one lamb
of the first year, for a burnt offering:
40 One kid of the goats for a sin offering:
41 And for a sacrifice of peace offerings, two
oxen, five rams, five he goats, five lambs of
the first year: this *was* the offering of Shelumiel the son of Zurishaddai.
42 ¶ On the sixth day Eliasaph the son of
Deuel, prince of the children of Gad, *offered:*
43 His offering *was* one silver charger of
the weight of an hundred and thirty *shekels*, a silver bowl of seventy shekels, after
the shekel of the sanctuary; both of them
full of fine flour mingled with oil for a meat
offering:
44 One golden spoon of ten *shekels*, full
of incense:
45 One young bullock, one ram, one lamb
of the first year, for a burnt offering:
46 One kid of the goats for a sin offering:
47 And for a sacrifice of peace offerings, two
oxen, five rams, five he goats, five lambs
of the first year: this *was* the offering of
Eliasaph the son of Deuel.
48 ¶ On the seventh day Elishama the
son of Ammihud, prince of the children of
Ephraim, *offered:*
49 His offering *was* one silver charger, the
weight whereof *was* an hundred and thirty
shekels, one silver bowl of seventy shekels,
after the shekel of the sanctuary; both of
them full of fine flour mingled with oil for
a meat offering:
50 One golden spoon of ten *shekels*, full
of incense:
51 One young bullock, one ram, one lamb
of the first year, for a burnt offering:
52 One kid of the goats for a sin offering:
53 And for a sacrifice of peace offerings, two
oxen, five rams, five he goats, five lambs
of the first year: this *was* the offering of
Elishama the son of Ammihud.
54 ¶ On the eighth day *offered* Gamaliel

the son of Pedahzur, prince of the children
of Manasseh:
55 His offering *was* one silver charger of the
weight of an hundred and thirty *shekels*,
one silver bowl of seventy shekels, after
the shekel of the sanctuary; both of them
full of fine flour mingled with oil for a meat
offering:
56 One golden spoon of ten *shekels*, full
of incense:
57 One young bullock, one ram, one lamb
of the first year, for a burnt offering:
58 One kid of the goats for a sin offering:
59 And for a sacrifice of peace offerings, two
oxen, five rams, five he goats, five lambs
of the first year: this *was* the offering of
Gamaliel the son of Pedahzur.
60 ¶ On the ninth day Abidan the son of
Gideoni, prince of the children of Benjamin, *offered:*
61 His offering *was* one silver charger, the
weight whereof *was* an hundred and thirty
shekels, one silver bowl of seventy shekels,
after the shekel of the sanctuary; both of
them full of fine flour mingled with oil for
a meat offering:
62 One golden spoon of ten *shekels*, full
of incense:
63 One young bullock, one ram, one lamb
of the first year, for a burnt offering:
64 One kid of the goats for a sin offering:
65 And for a sacrifice of peace offerings, two
oxen, five rams, five he goats, five lambs of
the first year: this *was* the offering of Abidan
the son of Gideoni.
66 ¶ On the tenth day Ahiezer the son of
Ammishaddai, prince of the children of
Dan, *offered:*
67 His offering *was* one silver charger, the
weight whereof *was* an hundred and thirty
shekels, one silver bowl of seventy shekels,
after the shekel of the sanctuary; both of
them full of fine flour mingled with oil for
a meat offering:
68 One golden spoon of ten *shekels*, full
of incense:
69 One young bullock, one ram, one lamb
of the first year, for a burnt offering:
70 One kid of the goats for a sin offering:
71 And for a sacrifice of peace offerings, two
oxen, five rams, five he goats, five lambs of
the first year: this *was* the offering of Ahiezer
the son of Ammishaddai.
72 ¶ On the eleventh day Pagiel the son
of Ocran, prince of the children of Asher,
offered:
73 His offering *was* one silver charger, the
weight whereof *was* an hundred and thirty
shekels, one silver bowl of seventy shekels,
after the shekel of the sanctuary; both of
them full of fine flour mingled with oil for
a meat offering:
74 One golden spoon of ten *shekels*, full
of incense:
75 One young bullock, one ram, one lamb
of the first year, for a burnt offering:
76 One kid of the goats for a sin offering:
77 And for a sacrifice of peace offerings, two
oxen, five rams, five he goats, five lambs of
the first year: this *was* the offering of Pagiel
the son of Ocran.
78 ¶ On the twelfth day Ahira the son of
Enan, prince of the children of Naphtali,
offered:
79 His offering *was* one silver charger, the
weight whereof *was* an hundred and thirty
shekels, one silver bowl of seventy shekels,
after the shekel of the sanctuary; both of
them full of fine flour mingled with oil for
a meat offering:
80 One golden spoon of ten *shekels*, full
of incense:
81 One young bullock, one ram, one lamb
of the first year, for a burnt offering:
82 One kid of the goats for a sin offering:
83 And for a sacrifice of peace offerings, two
oxen, five rams, five he goats, five lambs of
the first year: this *was* the offering of Ahira
the son of Enan.
84 This *was* the dedication of the altar, in
the day when it was anointed, by the princes
of Israel: twelve chargers of silver, twelve
silver bowls, twelve spoons of gold:
85 Each charger of silver *weighing* an hundred and thirty *shekels*, each bowl seventy:
all the silver vessels *weighed* two thousand
and four hundred *shekels*, after the shekel
of the sanctuary:
86 The golden spoons *were* twelve, full of
incense, *weighing* ten *shekels* apiece, after
the shekel of the sanctuary: all the gold of
the spoons *was* an hundred and twenty
shekels.
87 All the oxen for the burnt offering *were*
twelve bullocks, the rams twelve, the lambs
of the first year twelve, with their meat

offering: and the kids of the goats for sin
offering twelve.
88 And all the oxen for the sacrifice of the
peace offerings *were* twenty and four bullocks, the rams sixty, the he goats sixty, the
lambs of the first year sixty. This *was* the
dedication of the altar, after that it was
anointed.
89 And when Moses was gone into the tabernacle of the congregation to speak with
him, then he heard the voice of one speaking
unto him from off the mercy seat that *was*
upon the ark of testimony, from between
the two cherubims: and he spake unto him.

Numbers 8

1 And the LORD spake unto Moses, saying,
2 Speak unto Aaron, and say unto him,
When thou lightest the lamps, the seven
lamps shall give light over against the candlestick.
3 And Aaron did so; he lighted the lamps
thereof over against the candlestick, as the
LORD commanded Moses.
4 And this work of the candlestick *was of*
beaten gold, unto the shaft thereof, unto the
flowers thereof, *was* beaten work: according unto the pattern which the LORD had
shewed Moses, so he made the candlestick.
5 ¶ And the LORD spake unto Moses, saying,
6 Take the Levites from among the children
of Israel, and cleanse them.
7 And thus shalt thou do unto them, to
cleanse them: Sprinkle water of purifying
upon them, and let them shave all their
flesh, and let them wash their clothes, and
so make themselves clean.
8 Then let them take a young bullock with
his meat offering, *even* fine flour mingled
with oil, and another young bullock shalt
thou take for a sin offering.
9 And thou shalt bring the Levites before
the tabernacle of the congregation: and
thou shalt gather the whole assembly of
the children of Israel together:
10 And thou shalt bring the Levites before
the LORD: and the children of Israel shall put
their hands upon the Levites:
11 And Aaron shall offer the Levites before
the LORD *for* an offering of the children of
Israel, that they may execute the service
of the LORD.
12 And the Levites shall lay their hands upon
the heads of the bullocks: and thou shalt
offer the one *for* a sin offering, and the other
for a burnt offering, unto the LORD, to make
an atonement for the Levites.
13 And thou shalt set the Levites before
Aaron, and before his sons, and offer them
for an offering unto the LORD.
14 Thus shalt thou separate the Levites
from among the children of Israel: and the
Levites shall be mine.
15 And after that shall the Levites go in
to do the service of the tabernacle of the
congregation: and thou shalt cleanse them,
and offer them *for* an offering.
16 For they *are* wholly given unto me from
among the children of Israel; instead of such
as open every womb, *even instead of* the
firstborn of all the children of Israel, have I
taken them unto me.
17 For all the firstborn of the children of
Israel *are* mine, *both* man and beast: on
the day that I smote every firstborn in the
land of Egypt I sanctified them for myself.
18 And I have taken the Levites for all the
firstborn of the children of Israel.
19 And I have given the Levites *as* a gift
to Aaron and to his sons from among the
children of Israel, to do the service of the
children of Israel in the tabernacle of the
congregation, and to make an atonement
for the children of Israel: that there be no
plague among the children of Israel, when
the children of Israel come nigh unto the
sanctuary.
20 And Moses, and Aaron, and all the congregation of the children of Israel, did to
the Levites according unto all that the LORD
commanded Moses concerning the Levites,
so did the children of Israel unto them.
21 And the Levites were purified, and they
washed their clothes; and Aaron offered
them *as* an offering before the LORD; and
Aaron made an atonement for them to
cleanse them.
22 And after that went the Levites in to do
their service in the tabernacle of the congregation before Aaron, and before his sons:
as the LORD had commanded Moses concerning the Levites, so did they unto them.
23 ¶ And the LORD spake unto Moses,
saying,
24 This *is it* that *belongeth* unto the Levites:
from twenty and five years old and upward

they shall go in to wait upon the service of
the tabernacle of the congregation:
25 And from the age of fifty years they shall
cease waiting upon the service *thereof*, and
shall serve no more:
26 But shall minister with their brethren
in the tabernacle of the congregation, to
keep the charge, and shall do no service.
Thus shalt thou do unto the Levites touching their charge.

Numbers 9

1 And the LORD spake unto Moses in the
wilderness of Sinai, in the first month of
the second year after they were come out
of the land of Egypt, saying,
2 Let the children of Israel also keep the
passover at his appointed season.
3 In the fourteenth day of this month,
at even, ye shall keep it in his appointed
season: according to all the rites of it, and
according to all the ceremonies thereof,
shall ye keep it.
4 And Moses spake unto the children of
Israel, that they should keep the passover.
5 And they kept the passover on the fourteenth day of the first month at even in the
wilderness of Sinai: according to all that
the LORD commanded Moses, so did the
children of Israel.
6 ¶ And there were certain men, who were
defiled by the dead body of a man, that they
could not keep the passover on that day:
and they came before Moses and before
Aaron on that day:
7 And those men said unto him, We *are*
defiled by the dead body of a man: wherefore are we kept back, that we may not offer
an offering of the LORD in his appointed
season among the children of Israel?
8 And Moses said unto them, Stand still,
and I will hear what the LORD will command
concerning you.
9 ¶ And the LORD spake unto Moses, saying,
10 Speak unto the children of Israel, saying,
If any man of you or of your posterity shall
be unclean by reason of a dead body, or *be*
in a journey afar off, yet he shall keep the
passover unto the LORD.
11 The fourteenth day of the second month
at even they shall keep it, *and* eat it with
unleavened bread and bitter *herbs*.
12 They shall leave none of it unto the
morning, nor break any bone of it: according
to all the ordinances of the passover they
shall keep it.
13 But the man that *is* clean, and is not in a
journey, and forbeareth to keep the passover, even the same soul shall be cut off
from among his people: because he brought
not the offering of the LORD in his appointed
season, that man shall bear his sin.
14 And if a stranger shall sojourn among
you, and will keep the passover unto the
LORD; according to the ordinance of the
passover, and according to the manner
thereof, so shall he do: ye shall have one
ordinance, both for the stranger, and for
him that was born in the land.
15 ¶ And on the day that the tabernacle
was reared up the cloud covered the tabernacle, *namely*, the tent of the testimony:
and at even there was upon the tabernacle
as it were the appearance of fire, until the
morning.
16 So it was alway: the cloud covered it *by*
day, and the appearance of fire by night.
17 And when the cloud was taken up from
the tabernacle, then after that the children
of Israel journeyed: and in the place where
the cloud abode, there the children of Israel
pitched their tents.
18 At the commandment of the LORD the
children of Israel journeyed, and at the
commandment of the LORD they pitched: as
long as the cloud abode upon the tabernacle
they rested in their tents.
19 And when the cloud tarried long upon
the tabernacle many days, then the children
of Israel kept the charge of the LORD, and
journeyed not.
20 And *so* it was, when the cloud was a few
days upon the tabernacle; according to the
commandment of the LORD they abode in
their tents, and according to the commandment of the LORD they journeyed.
21 And *so* it was, when the cloud abode
from even unto the morning, and *that* the
cloud was taken up in the morning, then
they journeyed: whether *it was* by day or
by night that the cloud was taken up, they
journeyed.
22 Or *whether it were* two days, or a month,
or a year, that the cloud tarried upon the
tabernacle, remaining thereon, the children of Israel abode in their tents, and

journeyed not: but when it was taken up,
they journeyed.
23 At the commandment of the LORD they
rested in the tents, and at the commandment of the LORD they journeyed: they kept
the charge of the LORD, at the commandment of the LORD by the hand of Moses.

Numbers 10

1 And the LORD spake unto Moses, saying,
2 Make thee two trumpets of silver; of a
whole piece shalt thou make them: that
thou mayest use them for the calling of
the assembly, and for the journeying of
the camps.
3 And when they shall blow with them, all
the assembly shall assemble themselves to
thee at the door of the tabernacle of the
congregation.
4 And if they blow *but* with one *trumpet*,
then the princes, *which are* heads of the
thousands of Israel, shall gather themselves
unto thee.
5 When ye blow an alarm, then the camps
that lie on the east parts shall go forward.
6 When ye blow an alarm the second time,
then the camps that lie on the south side
shall take their journey: they shall blow an
alarm for their journeys.
7 But when the congregation is to be gathered together, ye shall blow, but ye shall not
sound an alarm.
8 And the sons of Aaron, the priests, shall
blow with the trumpets; and they shall be
to you for an ordinance for ever throughout
your generations.
9 And if ye go to war in your land against
the enemy that oppresseth you, then ye
shall blow an alarm with the trumpets;
and ye shall be remembered before the
LORD your God, and ye shall be saved from
your enemies.
10 Also in the day of your gladness, and in
your solemn days, and in the beginnings of
your months, ye shall blow with the trumpets over your burnt offerings, and over the
sacrifices of your peace offerings; that they
may be to you for a memorial before your
God: I *am* the LORD your God.
11 ¶ And it came to pass on the twentieth
day of the second month, in the second
year, that the cloud was taken up from off
the tabernacle of the testimony.
12 And the children of Israel took their
journeys out of the wilderness of Sinai; and
the cloud rested in the wilderness of Paran.
13 And they first took their journey according to the commandment of the LORD by the
hand of Moses.
14 ¶ In the first *place* went the standard of
the camp of the children of Judah according to their armies: and over his host *was*
Nahshon the son of Amminadab.
15 And over the host of the tribe of the
children of Issachar *was* Nethaneel the
son of Zuar.
16 And over the host of the tribe of the children of Zebulun *was* Eliab the son of Helon.
17 And the tabernacle was taken down; and
the sons of Gershon and the sons of Merari
set forward, bearing the tabernacle.
18 ¶ And the standard of the camp of Reuben set forward according to their armies:
and over his host *was* Elizur the son of
Shedeur.
19 And over the host of the tribe of the
children of Simeon *was* Shelumiel the son
of Zurishaddai.
20 And over the host of the tribe of the children of Gad *was* Eliasaph the son of Deuel.
21 And the Kohathites set forward, bearing
the sanctuary: and *the other* did set up the
tabernacle against they came.
22 ¶ And the standard of the camp of the
children of Ephraim set forward according to
their armies: and over his host *was* Elishama
the son of Ammihud.
23 And over the host of the tribe of the
children of Manasseh *was* Gamaliel the son
of Pedahzur.
24 And over the host of the tribe of the
children of Benjamin *was* Abidan the son
of Gideoni.
25 ¶ And the standard of the camp of the
children of Dan set forward, *which was* the
rereward of all the camps throughout their
hosts: and over his host *was* Ahiezer the son
of Ammishaddai.
26 And over the host of the tribe of the children of Asher *was* Pagiel the son of Ocran.
27 And over the host of the tribe of the children of Naphtali *was* Ahira the son of Enan.
28 Thus *were* the journeyings of the children
of Israel according to their armies, when
they set forward.
29 ¶ And Moses said unto Hobab, the son of

Raguel the Midianite, Moses' father in law,
We are journeying unto the place of which
the LORD said, I will give it you: come thou
with us, and we will do thee good: for the
LORD hath spoken good concerning Israel.
30 And he said unto him, I will not go; but
I will depart to mine own land, and to my
kindred.
31 And he said, Leave us not, I pray thee;
forasmuch as thou knowest how we are to
encamp in the wilderness, and thou mayest
be to us instead of eyes.
32 And it shall be, if thou go with us, yea, it
shall be, that what goodness the LORD shall
do unto us, the same will we do unto thee.
33 ¶ And they departed from the mount of
the LORD three days' journey: and the ark
of the covenant of the LORD went before
them in the three days' journey, to search
out a resting place for them.
34 And the cloud of the LORD *was* upon
them by day, when they went out of the
camp.
35 And it came to pass, when the ark set
forward, that Moses said, Rise up, LORD,
and let thine enemies be scattered; and let
them that hate thee flee before thee.
36 And when it rested, he said, Return, O
LORD, unto the many thousands of Israel.

Numbers 11

1 And *when* the people complained, it displeased the LORD: and the LORD heard *it;*
and his anger was kindled; and the fire of
the LORD burnt among them, and consumed
them that were in the uttermost parts of
the camp.
2 And the people cried unto Moses; and
when Moses prayed unto the LORD, the fire
was quenched.
3 And he called the name of the place
Taberah: because the fire of the LORD burnt
among them.
4 ¶ And the mixt multitude that *was* among
them fell a lusting: and the children of Israel
also wept again, and said, Who shall give us
flesh to eat?
5 We remember the fish, which we did eat
in Egypt freely; the cucumbers, and the
melons, and the leeks, and the onions, and
the garlick:
6 But now our soul *is* dried away: *there is*
nothing at all, beside this manna, *before*
our eyes.
7 And the manna *was* as coriander seed, and
the colour thereof as the colour of bdellium.
8 *And* the people went about, and gathered *it*, and ground *it* in mills, or beat *it* in
a mortar, and baked *it* in pans, and made
cakes of it: and the taste of it was as the
taste of fresh oil.
9 And when the dew fell upon the camp in
the night, the manna fell upon it.
10 ¶ Then Moses heard the people weep
throughout their families, every man in
the door of his tent: and the anger of the
LORD was kindled greatly; Moses also was
displeased.
11 And Moses said unto the LORD, Wherefore hast thou afflicted thy servant? and
wherefore have I not found favour in thy
sight, that thou layest the burden of all this
people upon me?
12 Have I conceived all this people? have I
begotten them, that thou shouldest say unto
me, Carry them in thy bosom, as a nursing
father beareth the sucking child, unto the
land which thou swarest unto their fathers?
13 Whence should I have flesh to give unto
all this people? for they weep unto me, saying, Give us flesh, that we may eat.
14 I am not able to bear all this people alone,
because *it is* too heavy for me.
15 And if thou deal thus with me, kill me,
I pray thee, out of hand, if I have found
favour in thy sight; and let me not see my
wretchedness.
16 ¶ And the LORD said unto Moses, Gather
unto me seventy men of the elders of Israel,
whom thou knowest to be the elders of the
people, and officers over them; and bring
them unto the tabernacle of the congregation, that they may stand there with thee.
17 And I will come down and talk with thee
there: and I will take of the spirit which *is*
upon thee, and will put *it* upon them; and
they shall bear the burden of the people
with thee, that thou bear *it* not thyself alone.
18 And say thou unto the people, Sanctify
yourselves against to morrow, and ye shall
eat flesh: for ye have wept in the ears of the
LORD, saying, Who shall give us flesh to eat?
for *it was* well with us in Egypt: therefore
the LORD will give you flesh, and ye shall eat.
19 Ye shall not eat one day, nor two days,

nor five days, neither ten days, nor twenty
days;
20 *But* even a whole month, until it come
out at your nostrils, and it be loathsome
unto you: because that ye have despised
the LORD which *is* among you, and have
wept before him, saying, Why came we
forth out of Egypt?
21 And Moses said, The people, among
whom I *am, are* six hundred thousand footmen; and thou hast said, I will give them
flesh, that they may eat a whole month.
22 Shall the flocks and the herds be slain for
them, to suffice them? or shall all the fish
of the sea be gathered together for them,
to suffice them?
23 And the LORD said unto Moses, Is the
LORD's hand waxed short? thou shalt see
now whether my word shall come to pass
unto thee or not.
24 ¶ And Moses went out, and told the
people the words of the LORD, and gathered
the seventy men of the elders of the people,
and set them round about the tabernacle.
25 And the LORD came down in a cloud, and
spake unto him, and took of the spirit that
was upon him, and gave *it* unto the seventy
elders: and it came to pass, *that*, when the
spirit rested upon them, they prophesied,
and did not cease.
26 But there remained two *of the* men in
the camp, the name of the one *was* Eldad,
and the name of the other Medad: and the
spirit rested upon them; and they *were* of
them that were written, but went not out
unto the tabernacle: and they prophesied
in the camp.
27 And there ran a young man, and told
Moses, and said, Eldad and Medad do
prophesy in the camp.
28 And Joshua the son of Nun, the servant
of Moses, *one* of his young men, answered
and said, My lord Moses, forbid them.
29 And Moses said unto him, Enviest thou
for my sake? would God that all the LORD's
people were prophets, *and* that the LORD
would put his spirit upon them!
30 And Moses gat him into the camp, he
and the elders of Israel.
31 ¶ And there went forth a wind from the
LORD, and brought quails from the sea, and
let *them* fall by the camp, as it were a day's
journey on this side, and as it were a day's
journey on the other side, round about the
camp, and as it were two cubits *high* upon
the face of the earth.
32 And the people stood up all that day,
and all *that* night, and all the next day, and
they gathered the quails: he that gathered
least gathered ten homers: and they spread
them all abroad for themselves round about
the camp.
33 And while the flesh *was* yet between
their teeth, ere it was chewed, the wrath
of the LORD was kindled against the people,
and the LORD smote the people with a very
great plague.
34 And he called the name of that place
Kibroth-hattaavah: because there they
buried the people that lusted.
35 *And* the people journeyed from
Kibroth-hattaavah unto Hazeroth; and
abode at Hazeroth.

Numbers 12

1 And Miriam and Aaron spake against
Moses because of the Ethiopian woman
whom he had married: for he had married
an Ethiopian woman.
2 And they said, Hath the LORD indeed spoken only by Moses? hath he not spoken also
by us? And the LORD heard *it*.
3 (Now the man Moses *was* very meek,
above all the men which *were* upon the
face of the earth.)
4 And the LORD spake suddenly unto Moses,
and unto Aaron, and unto Miriam, Come out
ye three unto the tabernacle of the congregation. And they three came out.
5 And the LORD came down in the pillar
of the cloud, and stood *in* the door of the
tabernacle, and called Aaron and Miriam:
and they both came forth.
6 And he said, Hear now my words: If there
be a prophet among you, *I* the LORD will
make myself known unto him in a vision,
and will speak unto him in a dream.
7 My servant Moses *is* not so, who *is* faithful
in all mine house.
8 With him will I speak mouth to mouth,
even apparently, and not in dark speeches;
and the similitude of the LORD shall he
behold: wherefore then were ye not afraid
to speak against my servant Moses?
9 And the anger of the LORD was kindled
against them; and he departed.

10 And the cloud departed from off the
tabernacle; and, behold, Miriam *became*
leprous, *white* as snow: and Aaron looked
upon Miriam, and, behold, *she was* leprous.
11 And Aaron said unto Moses, Alas, my
lord, I beseech thee, lay not the sin upon
us, wherein we have done foolishly, and
wherein we have sinned.
12 Let her not be as one dead, of whom the
flesh is half consumed when he cometh out
of his mother's womb.
13 And Moses cried unto the LORD, saying,
Heal her now, O God, I beseech thee.
14 ¶ And the LORD said unto Moses, If her
father had but spit in her face, should she
not be ashamed seven days? let her be shut
out from the camp seven days, and after
that let her be received in *again*.
15 And Miriam was shut out from the camp
seven days: and the people journeyed not
till Miriam was brought in *again*.
16 And afterward the people removed from
Hazeroth, and pitched in the wilderness
of Paran.

Numbers 13

1 And the LORD spake unto Moses, saying,
2 Send thou men, that they may search
the land of Canaan, which I give unto the
children of Israel: of every tribe of their
fathers shall ye send a man, every one a
ruler among them.
3 And Moses by the commandment of
the LORD sent them from the wilderness
of Paran: all those men *were* heads of the
children of Israel.
4 And these *were* their names: of the tribe
of Reuben, Shammua the son of Zaccur.
5 Of the tribe of Simeon, Shaphat the son
of Hori.
6 Of the tribe of Judah, Caleb the son of
Jephunneh.
7 Of the tribe of Issachar, Igal the son of
Joseph.
8 Of the tribe of Ephraim, Oshea the son
of Nun.
9 Of the tribe of Benjamin, Palti the son
of Raphu.
10 Of the tribe of Zebulun, Gaddiel the son
of Sodi.
11 Of the tribe of Joseph, *namely*, of the
tribe of Manasseh, Gaddi the son of Susi.
12 Of the tribe of Dan, Ammiel the son of
Gemalli.
13 Of the tribe of Asher, Sethur the son of
Michael.
14 Of the tribe of Naphtali, Nahbi the son
of Vophsi.
15 Of the tribe of Gad, Geuel the son of
Machi.
16 These *are* the names of the men which
Moses sent to spy out the land. And Moses
called Oshea the son of Nun Jehoshua.
17 ¶ And Moses sent them to spy out the
land of Canaan, and said unto them, Get
you up this *way* southward, and go up into
the mountain:
18 And see the land, what it *is;* and the people that dwelleth therein, whether they *be*
strong or weak, few or many;
19 And what the land *is* that they dwell in,
whether it *be* good or bad; and what cities
they be that they dwell in, whether in tents,
or in strong holds;
20 And what the land *is*, whether it *be* fat
or lean, whether there be wood therein, or
not. And be ye of good courage, and bring
of the fruit of the land. Now the time *was*
the time of the firstripe grapes.
21 ¶ So they went up, and searched the land
from the wilderness of Zin unto Rehob, as
men come to Hamath.
22 And they ascended by the south, and
came unto Hebron; where Ahiman, Sheshai, and Talmai, the children of Anak, *were*.
(Now Hebron was built seven years before
Zoan in Egypt.)
23 And they came unto the brook of Eshcol, and cut down from thence a branch
with one cluster of grapes, and they bare it
between two upon a staff; and *they brought*
of the pomegranates, and of the figs.
24 The place was called the brook Eshcol,
because of the cluster of grapes which the
children of Israel cut down from thence.
25 And they returned from searching of the
land after forty days.
26 ¶ And they went and came to Moses,
and to Aaron, and to all the congregation
of the children of Israel, unto the wilderness
of Paran, to Kadesh; and brought back word
unto them, and unto all the congregation,
and shewed them the fruit of the land.
27 And they told him, and said, We came
unto the land whither thou sentest us, and

surely it floweth with milk and honey; and
this *is* the fruit of it.
28 Nevertheless the people *be* strong that
dwell in the land, and the cities *are* walled,
and very great: and moreover we saw the
children of Anak there.
29 The Amalekites dwell in the land of the
south: and the Hittites, and the Jebusites,
and the Amorites, dwell in the mountains:
and the Canaanites dwell by the sea, and
by the coast of Jordan.
30 And Caleb stilled the people before
Moses, and said, Let us go up at once, and
possess it; for we are well able to overcome it.
31 But the men that went up with him said,
We be not able to go up against the people;
for they *are* stronger than we.
32 And they brought up an evil report of
the land which they had searched unto the
children of Israel, saying, The land, through
which we have gone to search it, *is* a land
that eateth up the inhabitants thereof; and
all the people that we saw in it *are* men of
a great stature.
33 And there we saw the giants, the sons
of Anak, *which come* of the giants: and we
were in our own sight as grasshoppers, and
so we were in their sight.

Numbers 14

1 And all the congregation lifted up their
voice, and cried; and the people wept that
night.
2 And all the children of Israel murmured
against Moses and against Aaron: and the
whole congregation said unto them, Would
God that we had died in the land of Egypt! or
would God we had died in this wilderness!
3 And wherefore hath the LORD brought
us unto this land, to fall by the sword, that
our wives and our children should be a
prey? were it not better for us to return
into Egypt?
4 And they said one to another, Let us make
a captain, and let us return into Egypt.
5 Then Moses and Aaron fell on their faces
before all the assembly of the congregation
of the children of Israel.
6 ¶ And Joshua the son of Nun, and Caleb
the son of Jephunneh, *which were* of them
that searched the land, rent their clothes:
7 And they spake unto all the company
of the children of Israel, saying, The land,
which we passed through to search it, *is* an
exceeding good land.
8 If the LORD delight in us, then he will bring
us into this land, and give it us; a land which
floweth with milk and honey.
9 Only rebel not ye against the LORD, neither
fear ye the people of the land; for they *are*
bread for us: their defence is departed from
them, and the LORD *is* with us: fear them not.
10 But all the congregation bade stone
them with stones. And the glory of the LORD
appeared in the tabernacle of the congregation before all the children of Israel.
11 ¶ And the LORD said unto Moses, How
long will this people provoke me? and how
long will it be ere they believe me, for all the
signs which I have shewed among them?
12 I will smite them with the pestilence,
and disinherit them, and will make of thee
a greater nation and mightier than they.
13 ¶ And Moses said unto the LORD, Then
the Egyptians shall hear *it*, (for thou broughtest up this people in thy might from among
them;)
14 And they will tell *it* to the inhabitants of
this land: *for* they have heard that thou LORD
art among this people, that thou LORD art
seen face to face, and *that* thy cloud standeth over them, and *that* thou goest before
them, by day time in a pillar of a cloud, and
in a pillar of fire by night.
15 ¶ Now *if* thou shalt kill *all* this people
as one man, then the nations which have
heard the fame of thee will speak, saying,
16 Because the LORD was not able to bring
this people into the land which he sware
unto them, therefore he hath slain them in
the wilderness.
17 And now, I beseech thee, let the power
of my Lord be great, according as thou hast
spoken, saying,
18 The LORD *is* longsuffering, and of great
mercy, forgiving iniquity and transgression,
and by no means clearing *the guilty*, visiting
the iniquity of the fathers upon the children
unto the third and fourth *generation*.
19 Pardon, I beseech thee, the iniquity of
this people according unto the greatness
of thy mercy, and as thou hast forgiven this
people, from Egypt even until now.
20 And the LORD said, I have pardoned
according to thy word:

21 But *as* truly *as* I live, all the earth shall be
filled with the glory of the LORD.
22 Because all those men which have seen
my glory, and my miracles, which I did
in Egypt and in the wilderness, and have
tempted me now these ten times, and have
not hearkened to my voice;
23 Surely they shall not see the land which
I sware unto their fathers, neither shall any
of them that provoked me see it:
24 But my servant Caleb, because he had
another spirit with him, and hath followed
me fully, him will I bring into the land whereinto he went; and his seed shall possess it.
25 (Now the Amalekites and the Canaanites
dwelt in the valley.) To morrow turn you,
and get you into the wilderness by the way
of the Red sea.
26 ¶ And the LORD spake unto Moses and
unto Aaron, saying,
27 How long *shall I bear with* this evil congregation, which murmur against me? I
have heard the murmurings of the children
of Israel, which they murmur against me.
28 Say unto them, *As truly as* I live, saith
the LORD, as ye have spoken in mine ears,
so will I do to you:
29 Your carcases shall fall in this wilderness; and all that were numbered of you,
according to your whole number, from
twenty years old and upward, which have
murmured against me,
30 Doubtless ye shall not come into the land,
concerning which I sware to make you dwell
therein, save Caleb the son of Jephunneh,
and Joshua the son of Nun.
31 But your little ones, which ye said should
be a prey, them will I bring in, and they shall
know the land which ye have despised.
32 But *as for* you, your carcases, they shall
fall in this wilderness.
33 And your children shall wander in the wilderness forty years, and bear your whoredoms, until your carcases be wasted in the
wilderness.
34 After the number of the days in which
ye searched the land, *even* forty days, each
day for a year, shall ye bear your iniquities,
even forty years, and ye shall know my
breach of promise.
35 I the LORD have said, I will surely do it
unto all this evil congregation, that are
gathered together against me: in this wilderness they shall be consumed, and there
they shall die.
36 And the men, which Moses sent to search
the land, who returned, and made all the
congregation to murmur against him, by
bringing up a slander upon the land,
37 Even those men that did bring up the evil
report upon the land, died by the plague
before the LORD.
38 But Joshua the son of Nun, and Caleb
the son of Jephunneh, *which were* of the
men that went to search the land, lived *still*.
39 And Moses told these sayings unto all the
children of Israel: and the people mourned
greatly.
40 ¶ And they rose up early in the morning, and gat them up into the top of the
mountain, saying, Lo, we *be here*, and will
go up unto the place which the LORD hath
promised: for we have sinned.
41 And Moses said, Wherefore now do ye
transgress the commandment of the LORD?
but it shall not prosper.
42 Go not up, for the LORD *is* not among you;
that ye be not smitten before your enemies.
43 For the Amalekites and the Canaanites
are there before you, and ye shall fall by
the sword: because ye are turned away
from the LORD, therefore the LORD will not
be with you.
44 But they presumed to go up unto the hill
top: nevertheless the ark of the covenant
of the LORD, and Moses, departed not out
of the camp.
45 Then the Amalekites came down, and
the Canaanites which dwelt in that hill, and
smote them, and discomfited them, *even*
unto Hormah.

Numbers 15

1 And the LORD spake unto Moses, saying,
2 Speak unto the children of Israel, and say
unto them, When ye be come into the land
of your habitations, which I give unto you,
3 And will make an offering by fire unto the
LORD, a burnt offering, or a sacrifice in per-
forming a vow, or in a freewill offering, or in
your solemn feasts, to make a sweet savour
unto the LORD, of the herd, or of the flock:
4 Then shall he that offereth his offering
unto the LORD bring a meat offering of a
tenth deal of flour mingled with the fourth
part of an hin of oil.

5 And the fourth *part* of an hin of wine for
a drink offering shalt thou prepare with the
burnt offering or sacrifice, for one lamb.
6 Or for a ram, thou shalt prepare *for* a meat
offering two tenth deals of flour mingled
with the third *part* of an hin of oil.
7 And for a drink offering thou shalt offer
the third *part* of an hin of wine, *for* a sweet
savour unto the LORD.
8 And when thou preparest a bullock *for* a
burnt offering, or *for* a sacrifice in perform-
ing a vow, or peace offerings unto the LORD:
9 Then shall he bring with a bullock a meat
offering of three tenth deals of flour mingled
with half an hin of oil.
10 And thou shalt bring for a drink offering
half an hin of wine, *for* an offering made by
fire, of a sweet savour unto the LORD.
11 Thus shall it be done for one bullock, or
for one ram, or for a lamb, or a kid.
12 According to the number that ye shall
prepare, so shall ye do to every one according to their number.
13 All that are born of the country shall do
these things after this manner, in offering
an offering made by fire, of a sweet savour
unto the LORD.
14 And if a stranger sojourn with you, or
whosoever *be* among you in your generations, and will offer an offering made by
fire, of a sweet savour unto the LORD; as ye
do, so he shall do.
15 One ordinance *shall be both* for you of
the congregation, and also for the stranger
that sojourneth *with you*, an ordinance for
ever in your generations: as ye *are*, so shall
the stranger be before the LORD.
16 One law and one manner shall be for
you, and for the stranger that sojourneth
with you.
17 ¶ And the LORD spake unto Moses,
saying,
18 Speak unto the children of Israel, and
say unto them, When ye come into the land
whither I bring you,
19 Then it shall be, that, when ye eat of the
bread of the land, ye shall offer up an heave
offering unto the LORD.
20 Ye shall offer up a cake of the first of
your dough *for* an heave offering: as *ye do*
the heave offering of the threshingfloor, so
shall ye heave it.
21 Of the first of your dough ye shall give
unto the LORD an heave offering in your
generations.
22 ¶ And if ye have erred, and not observed
all these commandments, which the LORD
hath spoken unto Moses,
23 *Even* all that the LORD hath commanded
you by the hand of Moses, from the day that
the LORD commanded *Moses*, and henceforward among your generations;
24 Then it shall be, if *ought* be committed
by ignorance without the knowledge of the
congregation, that all the congregation shall
offer one young bullock for a burnt offering,
for a sweet savour unto the LORD, with his
meat offering, and his drink offering, according to the manner, and one kid of the goats
for a sin offering.
25 And the priest shall make an atonement
for all the congregation of the children of
Israel, and it shall be forgiven them; for it *is*
ignorance: and they shall bring their offering, a sacrifice made by fire unto the LORD,
and their sin offering before the LORD, for
their ignorance:
26 And it shall be forgiven all the congregation of the children of Israel, and the
stranger that sojourneth among them;
seeing all the people *were* in ignorance.
27 ¶ And if any soul sin through ignorance,
then he shall bring a she goat of the first
year for a sin offering.
28 And the priest shall make an atonement
for the soul that sinneth ignorantly, when
he sinneth by ignorance before the LORD,
to make an atonement for him; and it shall
be forgiven him.
29 Ye shall have one law for him that sinneth through ignorance, *both for* him that
is born among the children of Israel, and for
the stranger that sojourneth among them.
30 ¶ But the soul that doeth *ought* presumptuously, *whether he be* born in the
land, or a stranger, the same reproacheth
the LORD; and that soul shall be cut off from
among his people.
31 Because he hath despised the word of the
LORD, and hath broken his commandment,
that soul shall utterly be cut off; his iniquity
shall be upon him.
32 ¶ And while the children of Israel were
in the wilderness, they found a man that
gathered sticks upon the sabbath day.
33 And they that found him gathering sticks

brought him unto Moses and Aaron, and unto all the congregation.

34 And they put him in ward, because it was not declared what should be done to him.

35 And the LORD said unto Moses, The man shall be surely put to death: all the congregation shall stone him with stones without the camp.

36 And all the congregation brought him without the camp, and stoned him with stones, and he died; as the LORD commanded Moses.

37 ¶ And the LORD spake unto Moses, saying,

38 Speak unto the children of Israel, and bid them that they make them fringes in the borders of their garments throughout their generations, and that they put upon the fringe of the borders a ribband of blue:

39 And it shall be unto you for a fringe, that ye may look upon it, and remember all the commandments of the LORD, and do them; and that ye seek not after your own heart and your own eyes, after which ye use to go a whoring:

40 That ye may remember, and do all my commandments, and be holy unto your God.

41 I *am* the LORD your God, which brought you out of the land of Egypt, to be your God: I *am* the LORD your God.

Numbers 16

1 Now Korah, the son of Izhar, the son of Kohath, the son of Levi, and Dathan and Abiram, the sons of Eliab, and On, the son of Peleth, sons of Reuben, took *men:*

2 And they rose up before Moses, with certain of the children of Israel, two hundred and fifty princes of the assembly, famous in the congregation, men of renown:

3 And they gathered themselves together against Moses and against Aaron, and said unto them, *Ye take* too much upon you, seeing all the congregation *are* holy, every one of them, and the LORD *is* among them: wherefore then lift ye up yourselves above the congregation of the LORD?

4 And when Moses heard *it*, he fell upon his face:

5 And he spake unto Korah and unto all his company, saying, Even to morrow the LORD will shew who *are* his, and *who is* holy; and will cause *him* to come near unto him: even *him* whom he hath chosen will he cause to come near unto him.

6 This do; Take you censers, Korah, and all his company;

7 And put fire therein, and put incense in them before the LORD to morrow: and it shall be *that* the man whom the LORD doth choose, he *shall be* holy: *ye take* too much upon you, ye sons of Levi.

8 And Moses said unto Korah, Hear, I pray you, ye sons of Levi:

9 *Seemeth it but* a small thing unto you, that the God of Israel hath separated you from the congregation of Israel, to bring you near to himself to do the service of the tabernacle of the LORD, and to stand before the congregation to minister unto them?

10 And he hath brought thee near *to him*, and all thy brethren the sons of Levi with thee: and seek ye the priesthood also?

11 For which cause *both* thou and all thy company *are* gathered together against the LORD: and what *is* Aaron, that ye murmur against him?

12 ¶ And Moses sent to call Dathan and Abiram, the sons of Eliab: which said, We will not come up:

13 *Is it* a small thing that thou hast brought us up out of a land that floweth with milk and honey, to kill us in the wilderness, except thou make thyself altogether a prince over us?

14 Moreover thou hast not brought us into a land that floweth with milk and honey, or given us inheritance of fields and vineyards: wilt thou put out the eyes of these men? we will not come up.

15 And Moses was very wroth, and said unto the LORD, Respect not thou their offering: I have not taken one ass from them, neither have I hurt one of them.

16 And Moses said unto Korah, Be thou and all thy company before the LORD, thou, and they, and Aaron, to morrow:

17 And take every man his censer, and put incense in them, and bring ye before the LORD every man his censer, two hundred and fifty censers; thou also, and Aaron, each *of you* his censer.

18 And they took every man his censer, and put fire in them, and laid incense thereon,

and stood in the door of the tabernacle of
the congregation with Moses and Aaron.
19 And Korah gathered all the congregation
against them unto the door of the tabernacle of the congregation: and the glory of the
LORD appeared unto all the congregation.
20 And the LORD spake unto Moses and
unto Aaron, saying,
21 Separate yourselves from among this
congregation, that I may consume them
in a moment.
22 And they fell upon their faces, and said,
O God, the God of the spirits of all flesh,
shall one man sin, and wilt thou be wroth
with all the congregation?
23 ¶ And the LORD spake unto Moses,
saying,
24 Speak unto the congregation, saying, Get
you up from about the tabernacle of Korah,
Dathan, and Abiram.
25 And Moses rose up and went unto
Dathan and Abiram; and the elders of Israel
followed him.
26 And he spake unto the congregation,
saying, Depart, I pray you, from the tents
of these wicked men, and touch nothing of
theirs, lest ye be consumed in all their sins.
27 So they gat up from the tabernacle of
Korah, Dathan, and Abiram, on every side:
and Dathan and Abiram came out, and stood
in the door of their tents, and their wives,
and their sons, and their little children.
28 And Moses said, Hereby ye shall know
that the LORD hath sent me to do all these
works; for *I have* not *done them* of mine
own mind.
29 If these men die the common death of all
men, or if they be visited after the visitation
of all men; *then* the LORD hath not sent me.
30 But if the LORD make a new thing, and
the earth open her mouth, and swallow
them up, with all that *appertain* unto them,
and they go down quick into the pit; then
ye shall understand that these men have
provoked the LORD.
31 ¶ And it came to pass, as he had made
an end of speaking all these words, that the
ground clave asunder that *was* under them:
32 And the earth opened her mouth, and
swallowed them up, and their houses, and
all the men that *appertained* unto Korah,
and all *their* goods.
33 They, and all that *appertained* to them,
went down alive into the pit, and the earth
closed upon them: and they perished from
among the congregation.
34 And all Israel that *were* round about them
fled at the cry of them: for they said, Lest
the earth swallow us up *also*.
35 And there came out a fire from the LORD,
and consumed the two hundred and fifty
men that offered incense.
36 ¶ And the LORD spake unto Moses,
saying,
37 Speak unto Eleazar the son of Aaron the
priest, that he take up the censers out of the
burning, and scatter thou the fire yonder;
for they are hallowed.
38 The censers of these sinners against their
own souls, let them make them broad plates
for a covering of the altar: for they offered
them before the LORD, therefore they are
hallowed: and they shall be a sign unto the
children of Israel.
39 And Eleazar the priest took the brasen
censers, wherewith they that were burnt
had offered; and they were made broad
plates for a covering of the altar:
40 *To be* a memorial unto the children of
Israel, that no stranger, which *is* not of the
seed of Aaron, come near to offer incense
before the LORD; that he be not as Korah,
and as his company: as the LORD said to him
by the hand of Moses.
41 ¶ But on the morrow all the congregation
of the children of Israel murmured against
Moses and against Aaron, saying, Ye have
killed the people of the LORD.
42 And it came to pass, when the congregation was gathered against Moses and
against Aaron, that they looked toward the
tabernacle of the congregation: and, behold,
the cloud covered it, and the glory of the
LORD appeared.
43 And Moses and Aaron came before the
tabernacle of the congregation.
44 ¶ And the LORD spake unto Moses,
saying,
45 Get you up from among this congregation, that I may consume them as in a
moment. And they fell upon their faces.
46 ¶ And Moses said unto Aaron, Take a censer, and put fire therein from off the altar,
and put on incense, and go quickly unto the
congregation, and make an atonement for

them: for there is wrath gone out from the
LORD; the plague is begun.
47 And Aaron took as Moses commanded,
and ran into the midst of the congregation;
and, behold, the plague was begun among
the people: and he put on incense, and
made an atonement for the people.
48 And he stood between the dead and the
living; and the plague was stayed.
49 Now they that died in the plague were
fourteen thousand and seven hundred,
beside them that died about the matter
of Korah.
50 And Aaron returned unto Moses unto the
door of the tabernacle of the congregation:
and the plague was stayed.

Numbers 17

1 And the LORD spake unto Moses, saying,
2 Speak unto the children of Israel, and take
of every one of them a rod according to the
house of *their* fathers, of all their princes
according to the house of their fathers
twelve rods: write thou every man's name
upon his rod.
3 And thou shalt write Aaron's name upon
the rod of Levi: for one rod *shall be* for the
head of the house of their fathers.
4 And thou shalt lay them up in the tabernacle of the congregation before the testimony, where I will meet with you.
5 And it shall come to pass, *that* the man's
rod, whom I shall choose, shall blossom:
and I will make to cease from me the murmurings of the children of Israel, whereby
they murmur against you.
6 ¶ And Moses spake unto the children of
Israel, and every one of their princes gave
him a rod apiece, for each prince one,
according to their fathers' houses, *even*
twelve rods: and the rod of Aaron *was*
among their rods.
7 And Moses laid up the rods before the
LORD in the tabernacle of witness.
8 And it came to pass, that on the morrow
Moses went into the tabernacle of witness;
and, behold, the rod of Aaron for the house
of Levi was budded, and brought forth
buds, and bloomed blossoms, and yielded
almonds.
9 And Moses brought out all the rods from
before the LORD unto all the children of
Israel: and they looked, and took every
man his rod.
10 ¶ And the LORD said unto Moses, Bring
Aaron's rod again before the testimony, to
be kept for a token against the rebels; and
thou shalt quite take away their murmurings
from me, that they die not.
11 And Moses did *so:* as the LORD commanded him, so did he.
12 And the children of Israel spake unto
Moses, saying, Behold, we die, we perish,
we all perish.
13 Whosoever cometh any thing near unto
the tabernacle of the LORD shall die: shall
we be consumed with dying?

Numbers 18

1 And the LORD said unto Aaron, Thou and
thy sons and thy father's house with thee
shall bear the iniquity of the sanctuary: and
thou and thy sons with thee shall bear the
iniquity of your priesthood.
2 And thy brethren also of the tribe of Levi,
the tribe of thy father, bring thou with thee,
that they may be joined unto thee, and minister unto thee: but thou and thy sons with
thee *shall minister* before the tabernacle
of witness.
3 And they shall keep thy charge, and the
charge of all the tabernacle: only they shall
not come nigh the vessels of the sanctuary and the altar, that neither they, nor ye
also, die.
4 And they shall be joined unto thee, and
keep the charge of the tabernacle of the
congregation, for all the service of the
tabernacle: and a stranger shall not come
nigh unto you.
5 And ye shall keep the charge of the sanctuary, and the charge of the altar: that there
be no wrath any more upon the children
of Israel.
6 And I, behold, I have taken your brethren
the Levites from among the children of
Israel: to you *they are* given *as* a gift for the
LORD, to do the service of the tabernacle of
the congregation.
7 Therefore thou and thy sons with thee
shall keep your priest's office for every thing
of the altar, and within the vail; and ye shall
serve: I have given your priest's office *unto
you as* a service of gift: and the stranger that
cometh nigh shall be put to death.

8 ¶ And the LORD spake unto Aaron, Behold,
I also have given thee the charge of mine
heave offerings of all the hallowed things of
the children of Israel; unto thee have I given
them by reason of the anointing, and to thy
sons, by an ordinance for ever.
9 This shall be thine of the most holy things,
reserved from the fire: every oblation of
theirs, every meat offering of theirs, and
every sin offering of theirs, and every trespass offering of theirs, which they shall
render unto me, *shall be* most holy for thee
and for thy sons.
10 In the most holy *place* shalt thou eat
it; every male shall eat it: it shall be holy
unto thee.
11 And this *is* thine; the heave offering of
their gift, with all the wave offerings of the
children of Israel: I have given them unto
thee, and to thy sons and to thy daughters
with thee, by a statute for ever: every one
that is clean in thy house shall eat of it.
12 All the best of the oil, and all the best of
the wine, and of the wheat, the firstfruits of
them which they shall offer unto the LORD,
them have I given thee.
13 *And* whatsoever is first ripe in the land,
which they shall bring unto the LORD, shall
be thine; every one that is clean in thine
house shall eat *of* it.
14 Every thing devoted in Israel shall be
thine.
15 Every thing that openeth the matrix in
all flesh, which they bring unto the LORD,
whether it be of men or beasts, shall be
thine: nevertheless the firstborn of man
shalt thou surely redeem, and the firstling
of unclean beasts shalt thou redeem.
16 And those that are to be redeemed from
a month old shalt thou redeem, according
to thine estimation, for the money of five
shekels, after the shekel of the sanctuary,
which *is* twenty gerahs.
17 But the firstling of a cow, or the firstling
of a sheep, or the firstling of a goat, thou
shalt not redeem; they *are* holy: thou shalt
sprinkle their blood upon the altar, and shalt
burn their fat *for* an offering made by fire,
for a sweet savour unto the LORD.
18 And the flesh of them shall be thine, as
the wave breast and as the right shoulder
are thine.
19 All the heave offerings of the holy things,
which the children of Israel offer unto the
LORD, have I given thee, and thy sons and thy
daughters with thee, by a statute for ever:
it *is* a covenant of salt for ever before the
LORD unto thee and to thy seed with thee.
20 ¶ And the LORD spake unto Aaron, Thou
shalt have no inheritance in their land, neither shalt thou have any part among them:
I *am* thy part and thine inheritance among
the children of Israel.
21 And, behold, I have given the children
of Levi all the tenth in Israel for an inheritance, for their service which they serve,
even the service of the tabernacle of the
congregation.
22 Neither must the children of Israel
henceforth come nigh the tabernacle of the
congregation, lest they bear sin, and die.
23 But the Levites shall do the service of the
tabernacle of the congregation, and they
shall bear their iniquity: *it shall be* a statute
for ever throughout your generations, that
among the children of Israel they have no
inheritance.
24 But the tithes of the children of Israel,
which they offer *as* an heave offering unto
the LORD, I have given to the Levites to
inherit: therefore I have said unto them,
Among the children of Israel they shall have
no inheritance.
25 ¶ And the LORD spake unto Moses,
saying,
26 Thus speak unto the Levites, and say unto
them, When ye take of the children of Israel
the tithes which I have given you from them
for your inheritance, then ye shall offer up
an heave offering of it for the LORD, *even* a
tenth *part* of the tithe.
27 And *this* your heave offering shall be
reckoned unto you, as though *it were* the
corn of the threshingfloor, and as the fulness
of the winepress.
28 Thus ye also shall offer an heave offering unto the LORD of all your tithes, which
ye receive of the children of Israel; and ye
shall give thereof the LORD's heave offering
to Aaron the priest.
29 Out of all your gifts ye shall offer every
heave offering of the LORD, of all the best
thereof, *even* the hallowed part thereof
out of it.
30 Therefore thou shalt say unto them,
When ye have heaved the best thereof from

it, then it shall be counted unto the Levites
as the increase of the threshingfloor, and
as the increase of the winepress.
31 And ye shall eat it in every place, ye
and your households: for it *is* your reward
for your service in the tabernacle of the
congregation.
32 And ye shall bear no sin by reason of it,
when ye have heaved from it the best of it:
neither shall ye pollute the holy things of
the children of Israel, lest ye die.

Numbers 19

1 And the LORD spake unto Moses and unto
Aaron, saying,
2 This *is* the ordinance of the law which the
LORD hath commanded, saying, Speak unto
the children of Israel, that they bring thee
a red heifer without spot, wherein *is* no
blemish, *and* upon which never came yoke:
3 And ye shall give her unto Eleazar the
priest, that he may bring her forth without
the camp, and *one* shall slay her before
his face:
4 And Eleazar the priest shall take of her
blood with his finger, and sprinkle of her
blood directly before the tabernacle of the
congregation seven times:
5 And *one* shall burn the heifer in his sight;
her skin, and her flesh, and her blood, with
her dung, shall he burn:
6 And the priest shall take cedar wood, and
hyssop, and scarlet, and cast *it* into the midst
of the burning of the heifer.
7 Then the priest shall wash his clothes,
and he shall bathe his flesh in water, and
afterward he shall come into the camp, and
the priest shall be unclean until the even.
8 And he that burneth her shall wash his
clothes in water, and bathe his flesh in water,
and shall be unclean until the even.
9 And a man *that is* clean shall gather up
the ashes of the heifer, and lay *them* up
without the camp in a clean place, and it
shall be kept for the congregation of the
children of Israel for a water of separation:
it *is* a purification for sin.
10 And he that gathereth the ashes of
the heifer shall wash his clothes, and be
unclean until the even: and it shall be unto
the children of Israel, and unto the stranger
that sojourneth among them, for a statute
for ever.
11 ¶ He that toucheth the dead body of any
man shall be unclean seven days.
12 He shall purify himself with it on the
third day, and on the seventh day he shall
be clean: but if he purify not himself the
third day, then the seventh day he shall
not be clean.
13 Whosoever toucheth the dead body
of any man that is dead, and purifieth not
himself, defileth the tabernacle of the LORD;
and that soul shall be cut off from Israel:
because the water of separation was not
sprinkled upon him, he shall be unclean;
his uncleanness *is* yet upon him.
14 This *is* the law, when a man dieth in a
tent: all that come into the tent, and all that
is in the tent, shall be unclean seven days.
15 And every open vessel, which hath no
covering bound upon it, *is* unclean.
16 And whosoever toucheth one that is slain
with a sword in the open fields, or a dead
body, or a bone of a man, or a grave, shall
be unclean seven days.
17 And for an unclean *person* they shall take
of the ashes of the burnt heifer of purification for sin, and running water shall be put
thereto in a vessel:
18 And a clean person shall take hyssop,
and dip *it* in the water, and sprinkle *it* upon
the tent, and upon all the vessels, and upon
the persons that were there, and upon him
that touched a bone, or one slain, or one
dead, or a grave:
19 And the clean *person* shall sprinkle upon
the unclean on the third day, and on the
seventh day: and on the seventh day he
shall purify himself, and wash his clothes,
and bathe himself in water, and shall be
clean at even.
20 But the man that shall be unclean, and
shall not purify himself, that soul shall be cut
off from among the congregation, because
he hath defiled the sanctuary of the LORD:
the water of separation hath not been sprinkled upon him; he *is* unclean.
21 And it shall be a perpetual statute unto
them, that he that sprinkleth the water of
separation shall wash his clothes; and he
that toucheth the water of separation shall
be unclean until even.
22 And whatsoever the unclean *person*
toucheth shall be unclean; and the soul
that toucheth *it* shall be unclean until even.

Numbers 20

1 Then came the children of Israel, *even* the whole congregation, into the desert of Zin in the first month: and the people abode in Kadesh; and Miriam died there, and was buried there.

2 And there was no water for the congregation: and they gathered themselves together against Moses and against Aaron.

3 And the people chode with Moses, and spake, saying, Would God that we had died when our brethren died before the LORD!

4 And why have ye brought up the congregation of the LORD into this wilderness, that we and our cattle should die there?

5 And wherefore have ye made us to come up out of Egypt, to bring us in unto this evil place? it *is* no place of seed, or of figs, or of vines, or of pomegranates; neither *is* there any water to drink.

6 And Moses and Aaron went from the presence of the assembly unto the door of the tabernacle of the congregation, and they fell upon their faces: and the glory of the LORD appeared unto them.

7 ¶ And the LORD spake unto Moses, saying,

8 Take the rod, and gather thou the assembly together, thou, and Aaron thy brother, and speak ye unto the rock before their eyes; and it shall give forth his water, and thou shalt bring forth to them water out of the rock: so thou shalt give the congregation and their beasts drink.

9 And Moses took the rod from before the LORD, as he commanded him.

10 And Moses and Aaron gathered the congregation together before the rock, and he said unto them, Hear now, ye rebels; must we fetch you water out of this rock?

11 And Moses lifted up his hand, and with his rod he smote the rock twice: and the water came out abundantly, and the congregation drank, and their beasts *also*.

12 ¶ And the LORD spake unto Moses and Aaron, Because ye believed me not, to sanctify me in the eyes of the children of Israel, therefore ye shall not bring this congregation into the land which I have given them.

13 This *is* the water of Meribah; because the children of Israel strove with the LORD, and he was sanctified in them.

14 ¶ And Moses sent messengers from Kadesh unto the king of Edom, Thus saith thy brother Israel, Thou knowest all the travail that hath befallen us:

15 How our fathers went down into Egypt, and we have dwelt in Egypt a long time; and the Egyptians vexed us, and our fathers:

16 And when we cried unto the LORD, he heard our voice, and sent an angel, and hath brought us forth out of Egypt: and, behold, we *are* in Kadesh, a city in the uttermost of thy border:

17 Let us pass, I pray thee, through thy country: we will not pass through the fields, or through the vineyards, neither will we drink *of* the water of the wells: we will go by the king's *high* way, we will not turn to the right hand nor to the left, until we have passed thy borders.

18 And Edom said unto him, Thou shalt not pass by me, lest I come out against thee with the sword.

19 And the children of Israel said unto him, We will go by the high way: and if I and my cattle drink of thy water, then I will pay for it: I will only, without *doing* any thing *else*, go through on my feet.

20 And he said, Thou shalt not go through. And Edom came out against him with much people, and with a strong hand.

21 Thus Edom refused to give Israel passage through his border: wherefore Israel turned away from him.

22 ¶ And the children of Israel, *even* the whole congregation, journeyed from Kadesh, and came unto mount Hor.

23 And the LORD spake unto Moses and Aaron in mount Hor, by the coast of the land of Edom, saying,

24 Aaron shall be gathered unto his people: for he shall not enter into the land which I have given unto the children of Israel, because ye rebelled against my word at the water of Meribah.

25 Take Aaron and Eleazar his son, and bring them up unto mount Hor:

26 And strip Aaron of his garments, and put them upon Eleazar his son: and Aaron shall be gathered *unto his people*, and shall die there.

27 And Moses did as the LORD commanded: and they went up into mount Hor in the sight of all the congregation.

28 And Moses stripped Aaron of his garments, and put them upon Eleazar his son;

and Aaron died there in the top of the
mount: and Moses and Eleazar came down
from the mount.
29 And when all the congregation saw that
Aaron was dead, they mourned for Aaron
thirty days, *even* all the house of Israel.

Numbers 21

1 And *when* king Arad the Canaanite, which
dwelt in the south, heard tell that Israel
came by the way of the spies; then he
fought against Israel, and took *some* of
them prisoners.
2 And Israel vowed a vow unto the LORD,
and said, If thou wilt indeed deliver this
people into my hand, then I will utterly
destroy their cities.
3 And the LORD hearkened to the voice of
Israel, and delivered up the Canaanites; and
they utterly destroyed them and their cities:
and he called the name of the place Hormah.
4 ¶ And they journeyed from mount Hor
by the way of the Red sea, to compass the
land of Edom: and the soul of the people
was much discouraged because of the way.
5 And the people spake against God, and
against Moses, Wherefore have ye brought
us up out of Egypt to die in the wilderness?
for *there is* no bread, neither *is there any*
water; and our soul loatheth this light bread.
6 And the LORD sent fiery serpents among
the people, and they bit the people; and
much people of Israel died.
7 ¶ Therefore the people came to Moses,
and said, We have sinned, for we have
spoken against the LORD, and against thee;
pray unto the LORD, that he take away the
serpents from us. And Moses prayed for
the people.
8 And the LORD said unto Moses, Make thee
a fiery serpent, and set it upon a pole: and
it shall come to pass, that every one that is
bitten, when he looketh upon it, shall live.
9 And Moses made a serpent of brass, and
put it upon a pole, and it came to pass, that
if a serpent had bitten any man, when he
beheld the serpent of brass, he lived.
10 ¶ And the children of Israel set forward,
and pitched in Oboth.
11 And they journeyed from Oboth, and
pitched at Ije-abarim, in the wilderness
which *is* before Moab, toward the sunrising.
12 ¶ From thence they removed, and
pitched in the valley of Zared.
13 From thence they removed, and pitched
on the other side of Arnon, which *is* in the
wilderness that cometh out of the coasts
of the Amorites: for Arnon *is* the border of
Moab, between Moab and the Amorites.
14 Wherefore it is said in the book of the
wars of the LORD, What he did in the Red
sea, and in the brooks of Arnon,
15 And at the stream of the brooks that
goeth down to the dwelling of Ar, and lieth
upon the border of Moab.
16 And from thence *they went* to Beer: that
is the well whereof the LORD spake unto
Moses, Gather the people together, and I
will give them water.
17 ¶ Then Israel sang this song, Spring up,
O well; sing ye unto it:
18 The princes digged the well, the nobles
of the people digged it, by *the direction of*
the lawgiver, with their staves. And from the
wilderness *they went* to Mattanah:
19 And from Mattanah to Nahaliel: and from
Nahaliel to Bamoth:
20 And from Bamoth *in* the valley, that *is* in
the country of Moab, to the top of Pisgah,
which looketh toward Jeshimon.
21 ¶ And Israel sent messengers unto Sihon
king of the Amorites, saying,
22 Let me pass through thy land: we will not
turn into the fields, or into the vineyards;
we will not drink *of* the waters of the well:
but we will go along by the king's *high* way,
until we be past thy borders.
23 And Sihon would not suffer Israel to pass
through his border: but Sihon gathered all
his people together, and went out against
Israel into the wilderness: and he came to
Jahaz, and fought against Israel.
24 And Israel smote him with the edge of
the sword, and possessed his land from
Arnon unto Jabbok, even unto the children
of Ammon: for the border of the children of
Ammon *was* strong.
25 And Israel took all these cities: and Israel
dwelt in all the cities of the Amorites, in
Heshbon, and in all the villages thereof.
26 For Heshbon *was* the city of Sihon the
king of the Amorites, who had fought against
the former king of Moab, and taken all his
land out of his hand, even unto Arnon.
27 Wherefore they that speak in proverbs

say, Come into Heshbon, let the city of Sihon be built and prepared:

28 For there is a fire gone out of Heshbon, a flame from the city of Sihon: it hath consumed Ar of Moab, *and* the lords of the high places of Arnon.

29 Woe to thee, Moab! thou art undone, O people of Chemosh: he hath given his sons that escaped, and his daughters, into captivity unto Sihon king of the Amorites.

30 We have shot at them; Heshbon is perished even unto Dibon, and we have laid them waste even unto Nophah, which *reacheth* unto Medeba.

31 ¶ Thus Israel dwelt in the land of the Amorites.

32 And Moses sent to spy out Jaazer, and they took the villages thereof, and drove out the Amorites that *were* there.

33 ¶ And they turned and went up by the way of Bashan: and Og the king of Bashan went out against them, he, and all his people, to the battle at Edrei.

34 And the LORD said unto Moses, Fear him not: for I have delivered him into thy hand, and all his people, and his land; and thou shalt do to him as thou didst unto Sihon king of the Amorites, which dwelt at Heshbon.

35 So they smote him, and his sons, and all his people, until there was none left him alive: and they possessed his land.

Numbers 22

1 And the children of Israel set forward, and pitched in the plains of Moab on this side Jordan *by* Jericho.

2 ¶ And Balak the son of Zippor saw all that Israel had done to the Amorites.

3 And Moab was sore afraid of the people, because they *were* many: and Moab was distressed because of the children of Israel.

4 And Moab said unto the elders of Midian, Now shall this company lick up all *that are* round about us, as the ox licketh up the grass of the field. And Balak the son of Zippor *was* king of the Moabites at that time.

5 He sent messengers therefore unto Balaam the son of Beor to Pethor, which *is* by the river of the land of the children of his people, to call him, saying, Behold, there is a people come out from Egypt: behold, they cover the face of the earth, and they abide over against me:

6 Come now therefore, I pray thee, curse me this people; for they *are* too mighty for me: peradventure I shall prevail, *that* we may smite them, and *that* I may drive them out of the land: for I wot that he whom thou blessest *is* blessed, and he whom thou cursest is cursed.

7 And the elders of Moab and the elders of Midian departed with the rewards of divination in their hand; and they came unto Balaam, and spake unto him the words of Balak.

8 And he said unto them, Lodge here this night, and I will bring you word again, as the LORD shall speak unto me: and the princes of Moab abode with Balaam.

9 And God came unto Balaam, and said, What men *are* these with thee?

10 And Balaam said unto God, Balak the son of Zippor, king of Moab, hath sent unto me, *saying*,

11 Behold, *there is* a people come out of Egypt, which covereth the face of the earth: come now, curse me them; peradventure I shall be able to overcome them, and drive them out.

12 And God said unto Balaam, Thou shalt not go with them; thou shalt not curse the people: for they *are* blessed.

13 And Balaam rose up in the morning, and said unto the princes of Balak, Get you into your land: for the LORD refuseth to give me leave to go with you.

14 And the princes of Moab rose up, and they went unto Balak, and said, Balaam refuseth to come with us.

15 ¶ And Balak sent yet again princes, more, and more honourable than they.

16 And they came to Balaam, and said to him, Thus saith Balak the son of Zippor, Let nothing, I pray thee, hinder thee from coming unto me:

17 For I will promote thee unto very great honour, and I will do whatsoever thou sayest unto me: come therefore, I pray thee, curse me this people.

18 And Balaam answered and said unto the servants of Balak, If Balak would give me his house full of silver and gold, I cannot go beyond the word of the LORD my God, to do less or more.

19 Now therefore, I pray you, tarry ye also

here this night, that I may know what the
LORD will say unto me more.
20 And God came unto Balaam at night,
and said unto him, If the men come to call
thee, rise up, *and* go with them; but yet
the word which I shall say unto thee, that
shalt thou do.
21 And Balaam rose up in the morning, and
saddled his ass, and went with the princes
of Moab.
22 ¶ And God's anger was kindled because
he went: and the angel of the LORD stood
in the way for an adversary against him.
Now he was riding upon his ass, and his two
servants *were* with him.
23 And the ass saw the angel of the LORD
standing in the way, and his sword drawn
in his hand: and the ass turned aside out of
the way, and went into the field: and Balaam
smote the ass, to turn her into the way.
24 But the angel of the LORD stood in a path
of the vineyards, a wall *being* on this side,
and a wall on that side.
25 And when the ass saw the angel of the
LORD, she thrust herself unto the wall, and
crushed Balaam's foot against the wall: and
he smote her again.
26 And the angel of the LORD went further,
and stood in a narrow place, where *was*
no way to turn either to the right hand or
to the left.
27 And when the ass saw the angel of the
LORD, she fell down under Balaam: and
Balaam's anger was kindled, and he smote
the ass with a staff.
28 And the LORD opened the mouth of the
ass, and she said unto Balaam, What have I
done unto thee, that thou hast smitten me
these three times?
29 And Balaam said unto the ass, Because
thou hast mocked me: I would there were
a sword in mine hand, for now would I kill
thee.
30 And the ass said unto Balaam, *Am* not I
thine ass, upon which thou hast ridden ever
since *I was* thine unto this day? was I ever
wont to do so unto thee? And he said, Nay.
31 Then the LORD opened the eyes of
Balaam, and he saw the angel of the LORD
standing in the way, and his sword drawn
in his hand: and he bowed down his head,
and fell flat on his face.
32 And the angel of the LORD said unto
him, Wherefore hast thou smitten thine
ass these three times? behold, I went out
to withstand thee, because *thy* way is perverse before me:
33 And the ass saw me, and turned from me
these three times: unless she had turned
from me, surely now also I had slain thee,
and saved her alive.
34 And Balaam said unto the angel of the
LORD, I have sinned; for I knew not that
thou stoodest in the way against me: now
therefore, if it displease thee, I will get me
back again.
35 And the angel of the LORD said unto
Balaam, Go with the men: but only the word
that I shall speak unto thee, that thou shalt
speak. So Balaam went with the princes
of Balak.
36 ¶ And when Balak heard that Balaam was
come, he went out to meet him unto a city
of Moab, which *is* in the border of Arnon,
which *is* in the utmost coast.
37 And Balak said unto Balaam, Did I not
earnestly send unto thee to call thee?
wherefore camest thou not unto me? am I
not able indeed to promote thee to honour?
38 And Balaam said unto Balak, Lo, I am
come unto thee: have I now any power at all
to say any thing? the word that God putteth
in my mouth, that shall I speak.
39 And Balaam went with Balak, and they
came unto Kirjath-huzoth.
40 And Balak offered oxen and sheep, and
sent to Balaam, and to the princes that
were with him.
41 And it came to pass on the morrow, that
Balak took Balaam, and brought him up into
the high places of Baal, that thence he might
see the utmost *part* of the people.

Numbers 23

1 And Balaam said unto Balak, Build me here
seven altars, and prepare me here seven
oxen and seven rams.
2 And Balak did as Balaam had spoken; and
Balak and Balaam offered on *every* altar a
bullock and a ram.
3 And Balaam said unto Balak, Stand by thy
burnt offering, and I will go: peradventure
the LORD will come to meet me: and whatsoever he sheweth me I will tell thee. And
he went to an high place.
4 And God met Balaam: and he said unto

him, I have prepared seven altars, and I have
offered upon *every* altar a bullock and a ram.
5 And the LORD put a word in Balaam's
mouth, and said, Return unto Balak, and
thus thou shalt speak.
6 And he returned unto him, and, lo, he
stood by his burnt sacrifice, he, and all the
princes of Moab.
7 And he took up his parable, and said,
Balak the king of Moab hath brought me
from Aram, out of the mountains of the
east, *saying*, Come, curse me Jacob, and
come, defy Israel.
8 How shall I curse, whom God hath not
cursed? or how shall I defy, *whom* the LORD
hath not defied?
9 For from the top of the rocks I see him, and
from the hills I behold him: lo, the people
shall dwell alone, and shall not be reckoned
among the nations.
10 Who can count the dust of Jacob, and the
number of the fourth *part* of Israel? Let me
die the death of the righteous, and let my
last end be like his!
11 And Balak said unto Balaam, What hast
thou done unto me? I took thee to curse
mine enemies, and, behold, thou hast
blessed *them* altogether.
12 And he answered and said, Must I not
take heed to speak that which the LORD hath
put in my mouth?
13 And Balak said unto him, Come, I pray
thee, with me unto another place, from
whence thou mayest see them: thou shalt
see but the utmost part of them, and shalt
not see them all: and curse me them from
thence.
14 ¶ And he brought him into the field of
Zophim, to the top of Pisgah, and built seven
altars, and offered a bullock and a ram on
every altar.
15 And he said unto Balak, Stand here by thy
burnt offering, while I meet *the LORD* yonder.
16 And the LORD met Balaam, and put a
word in his mouth, and said, Go again unto
Balak, and say thus.
17 And when he came to him, behold, he
stood by his burnt offering, and the princes
of Moab with him. And Balak said unto him,
What hath the LORD spoken?
18 And he took up his parable, and said,
Rise up, Balak, and hear; hearken unto me,
thou son of Zippor:
19 God *is* not a man, that he should lie; neither the son of man, that he should repent:
hath he said, and shall he not do *it*? or hath
he spoken, and shall he not make it good?
20 Behold, I have received *commandment*
to bless: and he hath blessed; and I cannot
reverse it.
21 He hath not beheld iniquity in Jacob,
neither hath he seen perverseness in Israel:
the LORD his God *is* with him, and the shout
of a king *is* among them.
22 God brought them out of Egypt; he hath
as it were the strength of an unicorn.
23 Surely *there is* no enchantment against
Jacob, neither *is there* any divination against
Israel: according to this time it shall be
said of Jacob and of Israel, What hath God
wrought!
24 Behold, the people shall rise up as a great
lion, and lift up himself as a young lion: he
shall not lie down until he eat *of* the prey,
and drink the blood of the slain.
25 ¶ And Balak said unto Balaam, Neither
curse them at all, nor bless them at all.
26 But Balaam answered and said unto
Balak, Told not I thee, saying, All that the
LORD speaketh, that I must do?
27 ¶ And Balak said unto Balaam, Come,
I pray thee, I will bring thee unto another
place; peradventure it will please God that
thou mayest curse me them from thence.
28 And Balak brought Balaam unto the top
of Peor, that looketh toward Jeshimon.
29 And Balaam said unto Balak, Build me
here seven altars, and prepare me here
seven bullocks and seven rams.
30 And Balak did as Balaam had said, and
offered a bullock and a ram on *every* altar.

Numbers 24

1 And when Balaam saw that it pleased the
LORD to bless Israel, he went not, as at other
times, to seek for enchantments, but he set
his face toward the wilderness.
2 And Balaam lifted up his eyes, and he saw
Israel abiding *in his tents* according to their
tribes; and the spirit of God came upon him.
3 And he took up his parable, and said,
Balaam the son of Beor hath said, and the
man whose eyes are open hath said:
4 He hath said, which heard the words of
God, which saw the vision of the Almighty,

falling *into a trance*, but having his eyes open:

5 How goodly are thy tents, O Jacob, *and* thy tabernacles, O Israel!

6 As the valleys are they spread forth, as gardens by the river's side, as the trees of lign aloes which the LORD hath planted, *and* as cedar trees beside the waters.

7 He shall pour the water out of his buckets, and his seed *shall be* in many waters, and his king shall be higher than Agag, and his kingdom shall be exalted.

8 God brought him forth out of Egypt; he hath as it were the strength of an unicorn: he shall eat up the nations his enemies, and shall break their bones, and pierce *them* through with his arrows.

9 He couched, he lay down as a lion, and as a great lion: who shall stir him up? Blessed *is* he that blesseth thee, and cursed *is* he that curseth thee.

10 ¶ And Balak's anger was kindled against Balaam, and he smote his hands together: and Balak said unto Balaam, I called thee to curse mine enemies, and, behold, thou hast altogether blessed *them* these three times.

11 Therefore now flee thou to thy place: I thought to promote thee unto great honour; but, lo, the LORD hath kept thee back from honour.

12 And Balaam said unto Balak, Spake I not also to thy messengers which thou sentest unto me, saying,

13 If Balak would give me his house full of silver and gold, I cannot go beyond the commandment of the LORD, to do *either* good or bad of mine own mind; *but* what the LORD saith, that will I speak?

14 And now, behold, I go unto my people: come *therefore, and* I will advertise thee what this people shall do to thy people in the latter days.

15 ¶ And he took up his parable, and said, Balaam the son of Beor hath said, and the man whose eyes are open hath said:

16 He hath said, which heard the words of God, and knew the knowledge of the most High, *which* saw the vision of the Almighty, falling *into a trance*, but having his eyes open:

17 I shall see him, but not now: I shall behold him, but not nigh: there shall come a Star out of Jacob, and a Sceptre shall rise out of Israel, and shall smite the corners of Moab, and destroy all the children of Sheth.

18 And Edom shall be a possession, Seir also shall be a possession for his enemies; and Israel shall do valiantly.

19 Out of Jacob shall come he that shall have dominion, and shall destroy him that remaineth of the city.

20 ¶ And when he looked on Amalek, he took up his parable, and said, Amalek *was* the first of the nations; but his latter end *shall be* that he perish for ever.

21 And he looked on the Kenites, and took up his parable, and said, Strong is thy dwellingplace, and thou puttest thy nest in a rock.

22 Nevertheless the Kenite shall be wasted, until Asshur shall carry thee away captive.

23 And he took up his parable, and said, Alas, who shall live when God doeth this!

24 And ships *shall come* from the coast of Chittim, and shall afflict Asshur, and shall afflict Eber, and he also shall perish for ever.

25 And Balaam rose up, and went and returned to his place: and Balak also went his way.

Numbers 25

1 And Israel abode in Shittim, and the people began to commit whoredom with the daughters of Moab.

2 And they called the people unto the sacrifices of their gods: and the people did eat, and bowed down to their gods.

3 And Israel joined himself unto Baal-peor: and the anger of the LORD was kindled against Israel.

4 And the LORD said unto Moses, Take all the heads of the people, and hang them up before the LORD against the sun, that the fierce anger of the LORD may be turned away from Israel.

5 And Moses said unto the judges of Israel, Slay ye every one his men that were joined unto Baal-peor.

6 ¶ And, behold, one of the children of Israel came and brought unto his brethren a Midianitish woman in the sight of Moses, and in the sight of all the congregation of the children of Israel, who *were* weeping *before* the door of the tabernacle of the congregation.

7 And when Phinehas, the son of Eleazar, the son of Aaron the priest, saw *it*, he rose

up from among the congregation, and took
a javelin in his hand;
8 And he went after the man of Israel into
the tent, and thrust both of them through,
the man of Israel, and the woman through
her belly. So the plague was stayed from
the children of Israel.
9 And those that died in the plague were
twenty and four thousand.
10 ¶ And the LORD spake unto Moses,
saying,
11 Phinehas, the son of Eleazar, the son of
Aaron the priest, hath turned my wrath
away from the children of Israel, while he
was zealous for my sake among them, that
I consumed not the children of Israel in my
jealousy.
12 Wherefore say, Behold, I give unto him
my covenant of peace:
13 And he shall have it, and his seed after
him, *even* the covenant of an everlasting
priesthood; because he was zealous for
his God, and made an atonement for the
children of Israel.
14 Now the name of the Israelite that
was slain, *even* that was slain with the
Midianitish woman, *was* Zimri, the son of
Salu, a prince of a chief house among the
Simeonites.
15 And the name of the Midianitish woman
that was slain *was* Cozbi, the daughter of
Zur; he *was* head over a people, *and* of a
chief house in Midian.
16 ¶ And the LORD spake unto Moses,
saying,
17 Vex the Midianites, and smite them:
18 For they vex you with their wiles, wherewith they have beguiled you in the matter
of Peor, and in the matter of Cozbi, the
daughter of a prince of Midian, their sister,
which was slain in the day of the plague for
Peor's sake.

Numbers 26

1 And it came to pass after the plague, that
the LORD spake unto Moses and unto Eleazar
the son of Aaron the priest, saying,
2 Take the sum of all the congregation of
the children of Israel, from twenty years
old and upward, throughout their fathers'
house, all that are able to go to war in Israel.
3 And Moses and Eleazar the priest spake
with them in the plains of Moab by Jordan
near Jericho, saying,
4 *Take the sum of the people*, from twenty
years old and upward; as the LORD commanded Moses and the children of Israel,
which went forth out of the land of Egypt.
5 ¶ Reuben, the eldest son of Israel: the children of Reuben; Hanoch, *of whom cometh*
the family of the Hanochites: of Pallu, the
family of the Palluites:
6 Of Hezron, the family of the Hezronites: of
Carmi, the family of the Carmites.
7 These *are* the families of the Reubenites:
and they that were numbered of them
were forty and three thousand and seven
hundred and thirty.
8 And the sons of Pallu; Eliab.
9 And the sons of Eliab; Nemuel, and Dathan,
and Abiram. This *is that* Dathan and Abiram,
which were famous in the congregation,
who strove against Moses and against Aaron
in the company of Korah, when they strove
against the LORD:
10 And the earth opened her mouth, and
swallowed them up together with Korah,
when that company died, what time the
fire devoured two hundred and fifty men:
and they became a sign.
11 Notwithstanding the children of Korah
died not.
12 ¶ The sons of Simeon after their families:
of Nemuel, the family of the Nemuelites: of
Jamin, the family of the Jaminites: of Jachin,
the family of the Jachinites:
13 Of Zerah, the family of the Zarhites: of
Shaul, the family of the Shaulites.
14 These *are* the families of the Simeonites,
twenty and two thousand and two hundred.
15 ¶ The children of Gad after their families:
of Zephon, the family of the Zephonites: of
Haggi, the family of the Haggites: of Shuni,
the family of the Shunites:
16 Of Ozni, the family of the Oznites: of Eri,
the family of the Erites:
17 Of Arod, the family of the Arodites: of
Areli, the family of the Arelites.
18 These *are* the families of the children of
Gad according to those that were numbered
of them, forty thousand and five hundred.
19 ¶ The sons of Judah *were* Er and Onan:
and Er and Onan died in the land of Canaan.
20 And the sons of Judah after their families
were; of Shelah, the family of the Shelanites:

of Pharez, the family of the Pharzites: of
Zerah, the family of the Zarhites.
21 And the sons of Pharez were; of Hezron,
the family of the Hezronites: of Hamul, the
family of the Hamulites.
22 These *are* the families of Judah according
to those that were numbered of them,
threescore and sixteen thousand and five
hundred.
23 ¶ *Of* the sons of Issachar after their
families: *of* Tola, the family of the Tolaites:
of Pua, the family of the Punites:
24 Of Jashub, the family of the Jashubites:
of Shimron, the family of the Shimronites.
25 These *are* the families of Issachar according
to those that were numbered of them,
threescore and four thousand and three
hundred.
26 ¶ *Of* the sons of Zebulun after their families:
of Sered, the family of the Sardites: of
Elon, the family of the Elonites: of Jahleel,
the family of the Jahleelites.
27 These *are* the families of the Zebulunites
according to those that were numbered
of them, threescore thousand and five
hundred.
28 ¶ The sons of Joseph after their families
were Manasseh and Ephraim.
29 Of the sons of Manasseh: of Machir,
the family of the Machirites: and Machir
begat Gilead: of Gilead *come* the family of
the Gileadites.
30 These *are* the sons of Gilead: *of* Jeezer,
the family of the Jeezerites: of Helek, the
family of the Helekites:
31 And *of* Asriel, the family of the Asrielites:
and *of* Shechem, the family of the
Shechemites:
32 And *of* Shemida, the family of the Shemidaites:
and *of* Hepher, the family of the
Hepherites.
33 ¶ And Zelophehad the son of Hepher had
no sons, but daughters: and the names of
the daughters of Zelophehad *were* Mahlah,
and Noah, Hoglah, Milcah, and Tirzah.
34 These *are* the families of Manasseh, and
those that were numbered of them, fifty and
two thousand and seven hundred.
35 ¶ These *are* the sons of Ephraim after
their families: of Shuthelah, the family of
the Shuthalhites: of Becher, the family of
the Bachrites: of Tahan, the family of the
Tahanites.
36 And these *are* the sons of Shuthelah: of
Eran, the family of the Eranites.
37 These *are* the families of the sons of
Ephraim according to those that were numbered
of them, thirty and two thousand and
five hundred. These *are* the sons of Joseph
after their families.
38 ¶ The sons of Benjamin after their families:
of Bela, the family of the Belaites: of
Ashbel, the family of the Ashbelites: of Ahiram,
the family of the Ahiramites:
39 Of Shupham, the family of the Shuphamites:
of Hupham, the family of the Huphamites.
40 And the sons of Bela were Ard and
Naaman: *of Ard*, the family of the Ardites:
and of Naaman, the family of the Naamites.
41 These *are* the sons of Benjamin after
their families: and they that were numbered
of them *were* forty and five thousand and
six hundred.
42 ¶ These *are* the sons of Dan after their
families: of Shuham, the family of the Shuhamites.
These *are* the families of Dan after
their families.
43 All the families of the Shuhamites,
according to those that were numbered of
them, *were* threescore and four thousand
and four hundred.
44 ¶ *Of* the children of Asher after their
families: of Jimna, the family of the Jimnites:
of Jesui, the family of the Jesuites: of Beriah,
the family of the Beriites.
45 Of the sons of Beriah: of Heber, the family
of the Heberites: of Malchiel, the family of
the Malchielites.
46 And the name of the daughter of Asher
was Sarah.
47 These *are* the families of the sons of
Asher according to those that were numbered
of them; *who were* fifty and three
thousand and four hundred.
48 ¶ *Of* the sons of Naphtali after their families:
of Jahzeel, the family of the Jahzeelites:
of Guni, the family of the Gunites:
49 Of Jezer, the family of the Jezerites: of
Shillem, the family of the Shillemites.
50 These *are* the families of Naphtali according
to their families: and they that were
numbered of them *were* forty and five
thousand and four hundred.
51 These *were* the numbered of the children

of Israel, six hundred thousand and a thousand seven hundred and thirty.
52 ¶ And the LORD spake unto Moses,
saying,
53 Unto these the land shall be divided for
an inheritance according to the number
of names.
54 To many thou shalt give the more inheritance, and to few thou shalt give the less
inheritance: to every one shall his inheritance be given according to those that were
numbered of him.
55 Notwithstanding the land shall be divided
by lot: according to the names of the tribes
of their fathers they shall inherit.
56 According to the lot shall the possession
thereof be divided between many and few.
57 ¶ And these *are* they that were numbered of the Levites after their families:
of Gershon, the family of the Gershonites:
of Kohath, the family of the Kohathites: of
Merari, the family of the Merarites.
58 These *are* the families of the Levites:
the family of the Libnites, the family of the
Hebronites, the family of the Mahlites, the
family of the Mushites, the family of the
Korathites. And Kohath begat Amram.
59 And the name of Amram's wife *was*
Jochebed, the daughter of Levi, whom *her
mother* bare to Levi in Egypt: and she bare
unto Amram Aaron and Moses, and Miriam
their sister.
60 And unto Aaron was born Nadab, and
Abihu, Eleazar, and Ithamar.
61 And Nadab and Abihu died, when they
offered strange fire before the LORD.
62 And those that were numbered of them
were twenty and three thousand, all males
from a month old and upward: for they were
not numbered among the children of Israel,
because there was no inheritance given
them among the children of Israel.
63 ¶ These *are* they that were numbered
by Moses and Eleazar the priest, who numbered the children of Israel in the plains of
Moab by Jordan *near* Jericho.
64 But among these there was not a man
of them whom Moses and Aaron the priest
numbered, when they numbered the children of Israel in the wilderness of Sinai.
65 For the LORD had said of them, They shall
surely die in the wilderness. And there was
not left a man of them, save Caleb the son
of Jephunneh, and Joshua the son of Nun.

Numbers 27

1 Then came the daughters of Zelophehad,
the son of Hepher, the son of Gilead, the
son of Machir, the son of Manasseh, of the
families of Manasseh the son of Joseph:
and these *are* the names of his daughters;
Mahlah, Noah, and Hoglah, and Milcah,
and Tirzah.
2 And they stood before Moses, and before
Eleazar the priest, and before the princes
and all the congregation, *by* the door of
the tabernacle of the congregation, saying,
3 Our father died in the wilderness, and
he was not in the company of them that
gathered themselves together against the
LORD in the company of Korah; but died in
his own sin, and had no sons.
4 Why should the name of our father be
done away from among his family, because
he hath no son? Give unto us *therefore*
a possession among the brethren of our
father.
5 And Moses brought their cause before
the LORD.
6 ¶ And the LORD spake unto Moses, saying,
7 The daughters of Zelophehad speak right:
thou shalt surely give them a possession of
an inheritance among their father's brethren; and thou shalt cause the inheritance of
their father to pass unto them.
8 And thou shalt speak unto the children of
Israel, saying, If a man die, and have no son,
then ye shall cause his inheritance to pass
unto his daughter.
9 And if he have no daughter, then ye shall
give his inheritance unto his brethren.
10 And if he have no brethren, then ye
shall give his inheritance unto his father's
brethren.
11 And if his father have no brethren, then
ye shall give his inheritance unto his kinsman
that is next to him of his family, and he shall
possess it: and it shall be unto the children
of Israel a statute of judgment, as the LORD
commanded Moses.
12 ¶ And the LORD said unto Moses, Get
thee up into this mount Abarim, and see
the land which I have given unto the children of Israel.
13 And when thou hast seen it, thou also

shalt be gathered unto thy people, as Aaron thy brother was gathered.
14 For ye rebelled against my commandment in the desert of Zin, in the strife of the congregation, to sanctify me at the water before their eyes: that *is* the water of Meribah in Kadesh in the wilderness of Zin.
15 ¶ And Moses spake unto the LORD, saying,
16 Let the LORD, the God of the spirits of all flesh, set a man over the congregation,
17 Which may go out before them, and which may go in before them, and which may lead them out, and which may bring them in; that the congregation of the LORD be not as sheep which have no shepherd.
18 ¶ And the LORD said unto Moses, Take thee Joshua the son of Nun, a man in whom *is* the spirit, and lay thine hand upon him;
19 And set him before Eleazar the priest, and before all the congregation; and give him a charge in their sight.
20 And thou shalt put *some* of thine honour upon him, that all the congregation of the children of Israel may be obedient.
21 And he shall stand before Eleazar the priest, who shall ask *counsel* for him after the judgment of Urim before the LORD: at his word shall they go out, and at his word they shall come in, *both* he, and all the children of Israel with him, even all the congregation.
22 And Moses did as the LORD commanded him: and he took Joshua, and set him before Eleazar the priest, and before all the congregation:
23 And he laid his hands upon him, and gave him a charge, as the LORD commanded by the hand of Moses.

Numbers 28

1 And the LORD spake unto Moses, saying,
2 Command the children of Israel, and say unto them, My offering, *and* my bread for my sacrifices made by fire, *for* a sweet savour unto me, shall ye observe to offer unto me in their due season.
3 And thou shalt say unto them, This *is* the offering made by fire which ye shall offer unto the LORD; two lambs of the first year without spot day by day, *for* a continual burnt offering.
4 The one lamb shalt thou offer in the morning, and the other lamb shalt thou offer at even;
5 And a tenth *part* of an ephah of flour for a meat offering, mingled with the fourth *part* of an hin of beaten oil.
6 *It is* a continual burnt offering, which was ordained in mount Sinai for a sweet savour, a sacrifice made by fire unto the LORD.
7 And the drink offering thereof *shall be* the fourth *part* of an hin for the one lamb: in the holy *place* shalt thou cause the strong wine to be poured unto the LORD *for* a drink offering.
8 And the other lamb shalt thou offer at even: as the meat offering of the morning, and as the drink offering thereof, thou shalt offer *it*, a sacrifice made by fire, of a sweet savour unto the LORD.
9 ¶ And on the sabbath day two lambs of the first year without spot, and two tenth deals of flour *for* a meat offering, mingled with oil, and the drink offering thereof:
10 *This is* the burnt offering of every sabbath, beside the continual burnt offering, and his drink offering.
11 ¶ And in the beginnings of your months ye shall offer a burnt offering unto the LORD; two young bullocks, and one ram, seven lambs of the first year without spot;
12 And three tenth deals of flour *for* a meat offering, mingled with oil, for one bullock; and two tenth deals of flour *for* a meat offering, mingled with oil, for one ram;
13 And a several tenth deal of flour mingled with oil *for* a meat offering unto one lamb; *for* a burnt offering of a sweet savour, a sacrifice made by fire unto the LORD.
14 And their drink offerings shall be half an hin of wine unto a bullock, and the third *part* of an hin unto a ram, and a fourth *part* of an hin unto a lamb: this *is* the burnt offering of every month throughout the months of the year.
15 And one kid of the goats for a sin offering unto the LORD shall be offered, beside the continual burnt offering, and his drink offering.
16 And in the fourteenth day of the first month *is* the passover of the LORD.
17 And in the fifteenth day of this month *is* the feast: seven days shall unleavened bread be eaten.
18 In the first day *shall be* an holy convo-

cation; ye shall do no manner of servile
work *therein:*
19 But ye shall offer a sacrifice made by
fire *for* a burnt offering unto the LORD; two
young bullocks, and one ram, and seven
lambs of the first year: they shall be unto
you without blemish:
20 And their meat offering *shall be of* flour
mingled with oil: three tenth deals shall
ye offer for a bullock, and two tenth deals
for a ram;
21 A several tenth deal shalt thou offer for
every lamb, throughout the seven lambs:
22 And one goat *for* a sin offering, to make
an atonement for you.
23 Ye shall offer these beside the burnt
offering in the morning, which *is* for a continual burnt offering.
24 After this manner ye shall offer daily,
throughout the seven days, the meat of
the sacrifice made by fire, of a sweet savour
unto the LORD: it shall be offered beside
the continual burnt offering, and his drink
offering.
25 And on the seventh day ye shall have
an holy convocation; ye shall do no servile
work.
26 ¶ Also in the day of the firstfruits, when
ye bring a new meat offering unto the
LORD, after your weeks *be out*, ye shall
have an holy convocation; ye shall do no
servile work:
27 But ye shall offer the burnt offering for a
sweet savour unto the LORD; two young bullocks, one ram, seven lambs of the first year;
28 And their meat offering of flour mingled
with oil, three tenth deals unto one bullock,
two tenth deals unto one ram,
29 A several tenth deal unto one lamb,
throughout the seven lambs;
30 *And* one kid of the goats, to make an
atonement for you.
31 Ye shall offer *them* beside the continual
burnt offering, and his meat offering, (they
shall be unto you without blemish) and their
drink offerings.

Numbers 29

1 And in the seventh month, on the first
day of the month, ye shall have an holy
convocation; ye shall do no servile work: it
is a day of blowing the trumpets unto you.
2 And ye shall offer a burnt offering for a
sweet savour unto the LORD; one young
bullock, one ram, *and* seven lambs of the
first year without blemish:
3 And their meat offering *shall be of* flour
mingled with oil, three tenth deals for a
bullock, *and* two tenth deals for a ram,
4 And one tenth deal for one lamb, throughout the seven lambs:
5 And one kid of the goats *for* a sin offering,
to make an atonement for you:
6 Beside the burnt offering of the month,
and his meat offering, and the daily burnt
offering, and his meat offering, and their
drink offerings, according unto their manner,
for a sweet savour, a sacrifice made by fire
unto the LORD.
7 ¶ And ye shall have on the tenth *day* of
this seventh month an holy convocation;
and ye shall afflict your souls: ye shall not
do any work *therein:*
8 But ye shall offer a burnt offering unto the
LORD *for* a sweet savour; one young bullock,
one ram, *and* seven lambs of the first year;
they shall be unto you without blemish:
9 And their meat offering *shall be of* flour
mingled with oil, three tenth deals to a
bullock, *and* two tenth deals to one ram,
10 A several tenth deal for one lamb,
throughout the seven lambs:
11 One kid of the goats *for* a sin offering;
beside the sin offering of atonement, and
the continual burnt offering, and the meat
offering of it, and their drink offerings.
12 ¶ And on the fifteenth day of the seventh
month ye shall have an holy convocation; ye
shall do no servile work, and ye shall keep a
feast unto the LORD seven days:
13 And ye shall offer a burnt offering, a
sacrifice made by fire, of a sweet savour
unto the LORD; thirteen young bullocks, two
rams, *and* fourteen lambs of the first year;
they shall be without blemish:
14 And their meat offering *shall be of* flour
mingled with oil, three tenth deals unto
every bullock of the thirteen bullocks, two
tenth deals to each ram of the two rams,
15 And a several tenth deal to each lamb of
the fourteen lambs:
16 And one kid of the goats *for* a sin offering;
beside the continual burnt offering, his meat
offering, and his drink offering.
17 ¶ And on the second day *ye shall offer*

twelve young bullocks, two rams, fourteen
lambs of the first year without spot:
18 And their meat offering and their drink
offerings for the bullocks, for the rams, and
for the lambs, *shall be* according to their
number, after the manner:
19 And one kid of the goats *for* a sin offering; beside the continual burnt offering,
and the meat offering thereof, and their
drink offerings.
20 ¶ And on the third day eleven bullocks,
two rams, fourteen lambs of the first year
without blemish;
21 And their meat offering and their drink
offerings for the bullocks, for the rams, and
for the lambs, *shall be* according to their
number, after the manner:
22 And one goat *for* a sin offering; beside
the continual burnt offering, and his meat
offering, and his drink offering.
23 ¶ And on the fourth day ten bullocks,
two rams, *and* fourteen lambs of the first
year without blemish:
24 Their meat offering and their drink offerings for the bullocks, for the rams, and for
the lambs, *shall be* according to their number, after the manner:
25 And one kid of the goats *for* a sin offering;
beside the continual burnt offering, his meat
offering, and his drink offering.
26 ¶ And on the fifth day nine bullocks, two
rams, *and* fourteen lambs of the first year
without spot:
27 And their meat offering and their drink
offerings for the bullocks, for the rams, and
for the lambs, *shall be* according to their
number, after the manner:
28 And one goat *for* a sin offering; beside
the continual burnt offering, and his meat
offering, and his drink offering.
29 ¶ And on the sixth day eight bullocks,
two rams, *and* fourteen lambs of the first
year without blemish:
30 And their meat offering and their drink
offerings for the bullocks, for the rams, and
for the lambs, *shall be* according to their
number, after the manner:
31 And one goat *for* a sin offering; beside the
continual burnt offering, his meat offering,
and his drink offering.
32 ¶ And on the seventh day seven bullocks,
two rams, *and* fourteen lambs of the first
year without blemish:
33 And their meat offering and their drink
offerings for the bullocks, for the rams, and
for the lambs, *shall be* according to their
number, after the manner:
34 And one goat *for* a sin offering; beside the
continual burnt offering, his meat offering,
and his drink offering.
35 ¶ On the eighth day ye shall have a solemn assembly: ye shall do no servile work
therein:
36 But ye shall offer a burnt offering, a sacrifice made by fire, of a sweet savour unto
the LORD: one bullock, one ram, seven lambs
of the first year without blemish:
37 Their meat offering and their drink offerings for the bullock, for the ram, and for the
lambs, *shall be* according to their number,
after the manner:
38 And one goat *for* a sin offering; beside
the continual burnt offering, and his meat
offering, and his drink offering.
39 These *things* ye shall do unto the LORD in
your set feasts, beside your vows, and your
freewill offerings, for your burnt offerings,
and for your meat offerings, and for your
drink offerings, and for your peace offerings.
40 And Moses told the children of Israel
according to all that the LORD commanded
Moses.

Numbers 30

1 And Moses spake unto the heads of the
tribes concerning the children of Israel, saying, This *is* the thing which the LORD hath
commanded.
2 If a man vow a vow unto the LORD, or
swear an oath to bind his soul with a bond;
he shall not break his word, he shall do
according to all that proceedeth out of his
mouth.
3 If a woman also vow a vow unto the LORD,
and bind *herself* by a bond, *being* in her
father's house in her youth;
4 And her father hear her vow, and her bond
wherewith she hath bound her soul, and her
father shall hold his peace at her: then all her
vows shall stand, and every bond wherewith
she hath bound her soul shall stand.
5 But if her father disallow her in the day
that he heareth; not any of her vows, or of
her bonds wherewith she hath bound her
soul, shall stand: and the LORD shall forgive
her, because her father disallowed her.

6 And if she had at all an husband, when
she vowed, or uttered ought out of her lips,
wherewith she bound her soul;
7 And her husband heard *it*, and held his
peace at her in the day that he heard *it:*
then her vows shall stand, and her bonds
wherewith she bound her soul shall stand.
8 But if her husband disallowed her on the
day that he heard *it;* then he shall make her
vow which she vowed, and that which she
uttered with her lips, wherewith she bound
her soul, of none effect: and the LORD shall
forgive her.
9 But every vow of a widow, and of her that
is divorced, wherewith they have bound
their souls, shall stand against her.
10 And if she vowed in her husband's house,
or bound her soul by a bond with an oath;
11 And her husband heard *it*, and held his
peace at her, *and* disallowed her not: then
all her vows shall stand, and every bond
wherewith she bound her soul shall stand.
12 But if her husband hath utterly made
them void on the day he heard *them; then*
whatsoever proceeded out of her lips concerning her vows, or concerning the bond
of her soul, shall not stand: her husband
hath made them void; and the LORD shall
forgive her.
13 Every vow, and every binding oath to
afflict the soul, her husband may establish
it, or her husband may make it void.
14 But if her husband altogether hold his
peace at her from day to day; then he
establisheth all her vows, or all her bonds,
which *are* upon her: he confirmeth them,
because he held his peace at her in the day
that he heard *them*.
15 But if he shall any ways make them void
after that he hath heard *them;* then he shall
bear her iniquity.
16 These *are* the statutes, which the LORD
commanded Moses, between a man and his
wife, between the father and his daughter,
being yet in her youth in her father's house.

Numbers 31

1 And the LORD spake unto Moses, saying,
2 Avenge the children of Israel of the Midianites: afterward shalt thou be gathered
unto thy people.
3 And Moses spake unto the people, saying,
Arm some of yourselves unto the war, and
let them go against the Midianites, and
avenge the LORD of Midian.
4 Of every tribe a thousand, throughout all
the tribes of Israel, shall ye send to the war.
5 So there were delivered out of the thousands of Israel, a thousand of *every* tribe,
twelve thousand armed for war.
6 And Moses sent them to the war, a thousand of *every* tribe, them and Phinehas the
son of Eleazar the priest, to the war, with
the holy instruments, and the trumpets to
blow in his hand.
7 And they warred against the Midianites,
as the LORD commanded Moses; and they
slew all the males.
8 And they slew the kings of Midian, beside
the rest of them that were slain; *namely*, Evi,
and Rekem, and Zur, and Hur, and Reba, five
kings of Midian: Balaam also the son of Beor
they slew with the sword.
9 And the children of Israel took *all* the
women of Midian captives, and their little
ones, and took the spoil of all their cattle,
and all their flocks, and all their goods.
10 And they burnt all their cities wherein
they dwelt, and all their goodly castles,
with fire.
11 And they took all the spoil, and all the
prey, *both* of men and of beasts.
12 And they brought the captives, and the
prey, and the spoil, unto Moses, and Eleazar the priest, and unto the congregation
of the children of Israel, unto the camp at
the plains of Moab, which *are* by Jordan
near Jericho.
13 ¶ And Moses, and Eleazar the priest, and
all the princes of the congregation, went
forth to meet them without the camp.
14 And Moses was wroth with the officers of
the host, *with* the captains over thousands,
and captains over hundreds, which came
from the battle.
15 And Moses said unto them, Have ye
saved all the women alive?
16 Behold, these caused the children of
Israel, through the counsel of Balaam, to
commit trespass against the LORD in the
matter of Peor, and there was a plague
among the congregation of the LORD.
17 Now therefore kill every male among the
little ones, and kill every woman that hath
known man by lying with him.
18 But all the women children, that have

not known a man by lying with him, keep
alive for yourselves.
19 And do ye abide without the camp seven
days: whosoever hath killed any person, and
whosoever hath touched any slain, purify
both yourselves and your captives on the
third day, and on the seventh day.
20 And purify all *your* raiment, and all that
is made of skins, and all work of goats' *hair*,
and all things made of wood.
21 ¶ And Eleazar the priest said unto the
men of war which went to the battle, This
is the ordinance of the law which the LORD
commanded Moses;
22 Only the gold, and the silver, the brass,
the iron, the tin, and the lead,
23 Every thing that may abide the fire, ye
shall make *it* go through the fire, and it shall
be clean: nevertheless it shall be purified
with the water of separation: and all that
abideth not the fire ye shall make go through
the water.
24 And ye shall wash your clothes on the
seventh day, and ye shall be clean, and afterward ye shall come into the camp.
25 ¶ And the LORD spake unto Moses,
saying,
26 Take the sum of the prey that was taken,
both of man and of beast, thou, and Eleazar the priest, and the chief fathers of the
congregation:
27 And divide the prey into two parts;
between them that took the war upon them,
who went out to battle, and between all the
congregation:
28 And levy a tribute unto the LORD of the
men of war which went out to battle: one
soul of five hundred, *both* of the persons,
and of the beeves, and of the asses, and of
the sheep:
29 Take *it* of their half, and give *it* unto
Eleazar the priest, *for* an heave offering of
the LORD.
30 And of the children of Israel's half, thou
shalt take one portion of fifty, of the persons, of the beeves, of the asses, and of
the flocks, of all manner of beasts, and
give them unto the Levites, which keep the
charge of the tabernacle of the LORD.
31 And Moses and Eleazar the priest did as
the LORD commanded Moses.
32 And the booty, *being* the rest of the prey
which the men of war had caught, was six
hundred thousand and seventy thousand
and five thousand sheep,
33 And threescore and twelve thousand
beeves,
34 And threescore and one thousand asses,
35 And thirty and two thousand persons in
all, of women that had not known man by
lying with him.
36 And the half, *which was* the portion of
them that went out to war, was in number
three hundred thousand and seven and
thirty thousand and five hundred sheep:
37 And the LORD's tribute of the sheep was
six hundred and threescore and fifteen.
38 And the beeves *were* thirty and six
thousand; of which the LORD's tribute *was*
threescore and twelve.
39 And the asses *were* thirty thousand and
five hundred; of which the LORD's tribute
was threescore and one.
40 And the persons *were* sixteen thousand;
of which the LORD's tribute *was* thirty and
two persons.
41 And Moses gave the tribute, *which was*
the LORD's heave offering, unto Eleazar the
priest, as the LORD commanded Moses.
42 And of the children of Israel's half, which
Moses divided from the men that warred,
43 (Now the half *that pertained unto* the
congregation was three hundred thousand
and thirty thousand *and* seven thousand
and five hundred sheep,
44 And thirty and six thousand beeves,
45 And thirty thousand asses and five
hundred,
46 And sixteen thousand persons;)
47 Even of the children of Israel's half, Moses
took one portion of fifty, *both* of man and
of beast, and gave them unto the Levites,
which kept the charge of the tabernacle of
the LORD; as the LORD commanded Moses.
48 ¶ And the officers which *were* over thousands of the host, the captains of thousands,
and captains of hundreds, came near unto
Moses:
49 And they said unto Moses, Thy servants
have taken the sum of the men of war which
are under our charge, and there lacketh not
one man of us.
50 We have therefore brought an oblation
for the LORD, what every man hath gotten, of
jewels of gold, chains, and bracelets, rings,

earrings, and tablets, to make an atonement
for our souls before the LORD.
51 And Moses and Eleazar the priest took
the gold of them, *even* all wrought jewels.
52 And all the gold of the offering that they
offered up to the LORD, of the captains of
thousands, and of the captains of hundreds,
was sixteen thousand seven hundred and
fifty shekels.
53 (*For* the men of war had taken spoil,
every man for himself.)
54 And Moses and Eleazar the priest took
the gold of the captains of thousands and of
hundreds, and brought it into the tabernacle
of the congregation, *for* a memorial for the
children of Israel before the LORD.

Numbers 32

1 Now the children of Reuben and the children of Gad had a very great multitude of
cattle: and when they saw the land of Jazer,
and the land of Gilead, that, behold, the
place *was* a place for cattle;
2 The children of Gad and the children of
Reuben came and spake unto Moses, and
to Eleazar the priest, and unto the princes
of the congregation, saying,
3 Ataroth, and Dibon, and Jazer, and Nimrah,
and Heshbon, and Elealeh, and Shebam, and
Nebo, and Beon,
4 *Even* the country which the LORD smote
before the congregation of Israel, *is* a land
for cattle, and thy servants have cattle:
5 Wherefore, said they, if we have found
grace in thy sight, let this land be given unto
thy servants for a possession, *and* bring us
not over Jordan.
6 ¶ And Moses said unto the children of Gad
and to the children of Reuben, Shall your
brethren go to war, and shall ye sit here?
7 And wherefore discourage ye the heart of
the children of Israel from going over into
the land which the LORD hath given them?
8 Thus did your fathers, when I sent them
from Kadesh-barnea to see the land.
9 For when they went up unto the valley of
Eshcol, and saw the land, they discouraged
the heart of the children of Israel, that they
should not go into the land which the LORD
had given them.
10 And the LORD's anger was kindled the
same time, and he sware, saying,
11 Surely none of the men that came up
out of Egypt, from twenty years old and
upward, shall see the land which I sware
unto Abraham, unto Isaac, and unto Jacob;
because they have not wholly followed me:
12 Save Caleb the son of Jephunneh the
Kenezite, and Joshua the son of Nun: for
they have wholly followed the LORD.
13 And the LORD's anger was kindled against
Israel, and he made them wander in the wilderness forty years, until all the generation,
that had done evil in the sight of the LORD,
was consumed.
14 And, behold, ye are risen up in your
fathers' stead, an increase of sinful men, to
augment yet the fierce anger of the LORD
toward Israel.
15 For if ye turn away from after him, he will
yet again leave them in the wilderness; and
ye shall destroy all this people.
16 ¶ And they came near unto him, and said,
We will build sheepfolds here for our cattle,
and cities for our little ones:
17 But we ourselves will go ready armed
before the children of Israel, until we have
brought them unto their place: and our little
ones shall dwell in the fenced cities because
of the inhabitants of the land.
18 We will not return unto our houses, until
the children of Israel have inherited every
man his inheritance.
19 For we will not inherit with them on
yonder side Jordan, or forward; because
our inheritance is fallen to us on this side
Jordan eastward.
20 ¶ And Moses said unto them, If ye will
do this thing, if ye will go armed before the
LORD to war,
21 And will go all of you armed over Jordan
before the LORD, until he hath driven out his
enemies from before him,
22 And the land be subdued before the
LORD: then afterward ye shall return, and
be guiltless before the LORD, and before
Israel; and this land shall be your possession
before the LORD.
23 But if ye will not do so, behold, ye have
sinned against the LORD: and be sure your
sin will find you out.
24 Build you cities for your little ones, and
folds for your sheep; and do that which hath
proceeded out of your mouth.
25 And the children of Gad and the children

of Reuben spake unto Moses, saying, Thy servants will do as my lord commandeth.

26 Our little ones, our wives, our flocks, and all our cattle, shall be there in the cities of Gilead:

27 But thy servants will pass over, every man armed for war, before the LORD to battle, as my lord saith.

28 So concerning them Moses commanded Eleazar the priest, and Joshua the son of Nun, and the chief fathers of the tribes of the children of Israel:

29 And Moses said unto them, If the children of Gad and the children of Reuben will pass with you over Jordan, every man armed to battle, before the LORD, and the land shall be subdued before you; then ye shall give them the land of Gilead for a possession:

30 But if they will not pass over with you armed, they shall have possessions among you in the land of Canaan.

31 And the children of Gad and the children of Reuben answered, saying, As the LORD hath said unto thy servants, so will we do.

32 We will pass over armed before the LORD into the land of Canaan, that the possession of our inheritance on this side Jordan *may be* ours.

33 And Moses gave unto them, *even* to the children of Gad, and to the children of Reuben, and unto half the tribe of Manasseh the son of Joseph, the kingdom of Sihon king of the Amorites, and the kingdom of Og king of Bashan, the land, with the cities thereof in the coasts, *even* the cities of the country round about.

34 ¶ And the children of Gad built Dibon, and Ataroth, and Aroer,

35 And Atroth, Shophan, and Jaazer, and Jogbehah,

36 And Beth-nimrah, and Beth-haran, fenced cities: and folds for sheep.

37 And the children of Reuben built Heshbon, and Elealeh, and Kirjathaim,

38 And Nebo, and Baal-meon, (their names being changed,) and Shibmah: and gave other names unto the cities which they builded.

39 And the children of Machir the son of Manasseh went to Gilead, and took it, and dispossessed the Amorite which *was* in it.

40 And Moses gave Gilead unto Machir the son of Manasseh; and he dwelt therein.

41 And Jair the son of Manasseh went and took the small towns thereof, and called them Havoth-jair.

42 And Nobah went and took Kenath, and the villages thereof, and called it Nobah, after his own name.

Numbers 33

1 These *are* the journeys of the children of Israel, which went forth out of the land of Egypt with their armies under the hand of Moses and Aaron.

2 And Moses wrote their goings out according to their journeys by the commandment of the LORD: and these *are* their journeys according to their goings out.

3 And they departed from Rameses in the first month, on the fifteenth day of the first month; on the morrow after the passover the children of Israel went out with an high hand in the sight of all the Egyptians.

4 For the Egyptians buried all *their* firstborn, which the LORD had smitten among them: upon their gods also the LORD executed judgments.

5 And the children of Israel removed from Rameses, and pitched in Succoth.

6 And they departed from Succoth, and pitched in Etham, which *is* in the edge of the wilderness.

7 And they removed from Etham, and turned again unto Pi-hahiroth, which *is* before Baal-zephon: and they pitched before Migdol.

8 And they departed from before Pi-hahiroth, and passed through the midst of the sea into the wilderness, and went three days' journey in the wilderness of Etham, and pitched in Marah.

9 And they removed from Marah, and came unto Elim: and in Elim *were* twelve fountains of water, and threescore and ten palm trees; and they pitched there.

10 And they removed from Elim, and encamped by the Red sea.

11 And they removed from the Red sea, and encamped in the wilderness of Sin.

12 And they took their journey out of the wilderness of Sin, and encamped in Dophkah.

13 And they departed from Dophkah, and encamped in Alush.

14 And they removed from Alush, and

encamped at Rephidim, where was no water
for the people to drink.
15 And they departed from Rephidim, and
pitched in the wilderness of Sinai.
16 And they removed from the desert of
Sinai, and pitched at Kibroth-hattaavah.
17 And they departed from Kibroth-hattaavah, and encamped at Hazeroth.
18 And they departed from Hazeroth, and
pitched in Rithmah.
19 And they departed from Rithmah, and
pitched at Rimmon-parez.
20 And they departed from Rimmon-parez,
and pitched in Libnah.
21 And they removed from Libnah, and
pitched at Rissah.
22 And they journeyed from Rissah, and
pitched in Kehelathah.
23 And they went from Kehelathah, and
pitched in mount Shapher.
24 And they removed from mount Shapher,
and encamped in Haradah.
25 And they removed from Haradah, and
pitched in Makheloth.
26 And they removed from Makheloth, and
encamped at Tahath.
27 And they departed from Tahath, and
pitched at Tarah.
28 And they removed from Tarah, and
pitched in Mithcah.
29 And they went from Mithcah, and
pitched in Hashmonah.
30 And they departed from Hashmonah,
and encamped at Moseroth.
31 And they departed from Moseroth, and
pitched in Bene-jaakan.
32 And they removed from Bene-jaakan,
and encamped at Hor-hagidgad.
33 And they went from Hor-hagidgad, and
pitched in Jotbathah.
34 And they removed from Jotbathah, and
encamped at Ebronah.
35 And they departed from Ebronah, and
encamped at Ezion-gaber.
36 And they removed from Ezion-gaber,
and pitched in the wilderness of Zin, which
is Kadesh.
37 And they removed from Kadesh, and
pitched in mount Hor, in the edge of the
land of Edom.
38 And Aaron the priest went up into mount
Hor at the commandment of the LORD, and
died there, in the fortieth year after the
children of Israel were come out of the land
of Egypt, in the first *day* of the fifth month.
39 And Aaron *was* an hundred and twenty
and three years old when he died in mount
Hor.
40 And king Arad the Canaanite, which dwelt
in the south in the land of Canaan, heard of
the coming of the children of Israel.
41 And they departed from mount Hor, and
pitched in Zalmonah.
42 And they departed from Zalmonah, and
pitched in Punon.
43 And they departed from Punon, and
pitched in Oboth.
44 And they departed from Oboth, and
pitched in Ije-abarim, in the border of Moab.
45 And they departed from Iim, and pitched
in Dibon-gad.
46 And they removed from Dibon-gad, and
encamped in Almon-diblathaim.
47 And they removed from Almon-diblathaim, and pitched in the mountains of
Abarim, before Nebo.
48 And they departed from the mountains
of Abarim, and pitched in the plains of Moab
by Jordan *near* Jericho.
49 And they pitched by Jordan, from
Beth-jesimoth *even* unto Abel-shittim in
the plains of Moab.
50 ¶ And the LORD spake unto Moses in
the plains of Moab by Jordan *near* Jericho,
saying,
51 Speak unto the children of Israel, and
say unto them, When ye are passed over
Jordan into the land of Canaan;
52 Then ye shall drive out all the inhabitants
of the land from before you, and destroy all
their pictures, and destroy all their molten
images, and quite pluck down all their high
places:
53 And ye shall dispossess *the inhabitants of*
the land, and dwell therein: for I have given
you the land to possess it.
54 And ye shall divide the land by lot for
an inheritance among your families: *and*
to the more ye shall give the more inheritance, and to the fewer ye shall give the less
inheritance: every man's *inheritance* shall be
in the place where his lot falleth; according
to the tribes of your fathers ye shall inherit.
55 But if ye will not drive out the inhabitants of the land from before you; then it
shall come to pass, that those which ye let

remain of them *shall be* pricks in your eyes, and thorns in your sides, and shall vex you in the land wherein ye dwell.
56 Moreover it shall come to pass, *that* I shall do unto you, as I thought to do unto them.

Numbers 34

1 And the LORD spake unto Moses, saying,
2 Command the children of Israel, and say unto them, When ye come into the land of Canaan; (this *is* the land that shall fall unto you for an inheritance, *even* the land of Canaan with the coasts thereof:)
3 Then your south quarter shall be from the wilderness of Zin along by the coast of Edom, and your south border shall be the outmost coast of the salt sea eastward:
4 And your border shall turn from the south to the ascent of Akrabbim, and pass on to Zin: and the going forth thereof shall be from the south to Kadesh-barnea, and shall go on to Hazar-addar, and pass on to Azmon:
5 And the border shall fetch a compass from Azmon unto the river of Egypt, and the goings out of it shall be at the sea.
6 And *as for* the western border, ye shall even have the great sea for a border: this shall be your west border.
7 And this shall be your north border: from the great sea ye shall point out for you mount Hor:
8 From mount Hor ye shall point out *your border* unto the entrance of Hamath; and the goings forth of the border shall be to Zedad:
9 ¶ And the border shall go on to Ziphron, and the goings out of it shall be at Hazar-enan: this shall be your north border.
10 And ye shall point out your east border from Hazar-enan to Shepham:
11 And the coast shall go down from Shepham to Riblah, on the east side of Ain; and the border shall descend, and shall reach unto the side of the sea of Chinnereth eastward:
12 And the border shall go down to Jordan, and the goings out of it shall be at the salt sea: this shall be your land with the coasts thereof round about.
13 And Moses commanded the children of Israel, saying, This *is* the land which ye shall inherit by lot, which the LORD commanded to give unto the nine tribes, and to the half tribe:
14 For the tribe of the children of Reuben according to the house of their fathers, and the tribe of the children of Gad according to the house of their fathers, have received *their inheritance;* and half the tribe of Manasseh have received their inheritance:
15 The two tribes and the half tribe have received their inheritance on this side Jordan *near* Jericho eastward, toward the sunrising.
16 And the LORD spake unto Moses, saying,
17 These *are* the names of the men which shall divide the land unto you: Eleazar the priest, and Joshua the son of Nun.
18 And ye shall take one prince of every tribe, to divide the land by inheritance.
19 And the names of the men *are* these: Of the tribe of Judah, Caleb the son of Jephunneh.
20 And of the tribe of the children of Simeon, Shemuel the son of Ammihud.
21 Of the tribe of Benjamin, Elidad the son of Chislon.
22 And the prince of the tribe of the children of Dan, Bukki the son of Jogli.
23 The prince of the children of Joseph, for the tribe of the children of Manasseh, Hanniel the son of Ephod.
24 And the prince of the tribe of the children of Ephraim, Kemuel the son of Shiphtan.
25 And the prince of the tribe of the children of Zebulun, Elizaphan the son of Parnach.
26 And the prince of the tribe of the children of Issachar, Paltiel the son of Azzan.
27 And the prince of the tribe of the children of Asher, Ahihud the son of Shelomi.
28 And the prince of the tribe of the children of Naphtali, Pedahel the son of Ammihud.
29 These *are they* whom the LORD commanded to divide the inheritance unto the children of Israel in the land of Canaan.

Numbers 35

1 And the LORD spake unto Moses in the plains of Moab by Jordan *near* Jericho, saying,
2 Command the children of Israel, that they give unto the Levites of the inheritance of their possession cities to dwell in; and ye shall give *also* unto the Levites suburbs for the cities round about them.

3 And the cities shall they have to dwell in;
and the suburbs of them shall be for their
cattle, and for their goods, and for all their
beasts.
4 And the suburbs of the cities, which ye
shall give unto the Levites, *shall reach* from
the wall of the city and outward a thousand
cubits round about.
5 And ye shall measure from without the
city on the east side two thousand cubits,
and on the south side two thousand cubits,
and on the west side two thousand cubits,
and on the north side two thousand cubits;
and the city *shall be* in the midst: this shall
be to them the suburbs of the cities.
6 And among the cities which ye shall give
unto the Levites *there shall be* six cities for
refuge, which ye shall appoint for the manslayer, that he may flee thither: and to them
ye shall add forty and two cities.
7 *So* all the cities which ye shall give to the
Levites *shall be* forty and eight cities: them
shall ye give with their suburbs.
8 And the cities which ye shall give *shall be*
of the possession of the children of Israel:
from *them that have* many ye shall give
many; but from *them that have* few ye shall
give few: every one shall give of his cities
unto the Levites according to his inheritance
which he inheriteth.
9 ¶ And the LORD spake unto Moses, saying,
10 Speak unto the children of Israel, and say
unto them, When ye be come over Jordan
into the land of Canaan;
11 Then ye shall appoint you cities to be
cities of refuge for you; that the slayer may
flee thither, which killeth any person at
unawares.
12 And they shall be unto you cities for refuge from the avenger; that the manslayer
die not, until he stand before the congregation in judgment.
13 And of these cities which ye shall give six
cities shall ye have for refuge.
14 Ye shall give three cities on this side Jordan, and three cities shall ye give in the land
of Canaan, *which* shall be cities of refuge.
15 These six cities shall be a refuge, *both* for
the children of Israel, and for the stranger,
and for the sojourner among them: that
every one that killeth any person unawares
may flee thither.
16 And if he smite him with an instrument
of iron, so that he die, he *is* a murderer:
the murderer shall surely be put to death.
17 And if he smite him with throwing a
stone, wherewith he may die, and he die,
he *is* a murderer: the murderer shall surely
be put to death.
18 Or *if* he smite him with an hand weapon
of wood, wherewith he may die, and he die,
he *is* a murderer: the murderer shall surely
be put to death.
19 The revenger of blood himself shall slay
the murderer: when he meeteth him, he
shall slay him.
20 But if he thrust him of hatred, or hurl at
him by laying of wait, that he die;
21 Or in enmity smite him with his hand,
that he die: he that smote *him* shall surely
be put to death; *for* he *is* a murderer: the
revenger of blood shall slay the murderer,
when he meeteth him.
22 But if he thrust him suddenly without
enmity, or have cast upon him any thing
without laying of wait,
23 Or with any stone, wherewith a man may
die, seeing *him* not, and cast *it* upon him,
that he die, and *was* not his enemy, neither
sought his harm:
24 Then the congregation shall judge
between the slayer and the revenger of
blood according to these judgments:
25 And the congregation shall deliver the
slayer out of the hand of the revenger of
blood, and the congregation shall restore
him to the city of his refuge, whither he was
fled: and he shall abide in it unto the death
of the high priest, which was anointed with
the holy oil.
26 But if the slayer shall at any time come
without the border of the city of his refuge,
whither he was fled;
27 And the revenger of blood find him without the borders of the city of his refuge, and
the revenger of blood kill the slayer; he shall
not be guilty of blood:
28 Because he should have remained in
the city of his refuge until the death of the
high priest: but after the death of the high
priest the slayer shall return into the land
of his possession.
29 So these *things* shall be for a statute of
judgment unto you throughout your generations in all your dwellings.
30 Whoso killeth any person, the murderer

shall be put to death by the mouth of witnesses: but one witness shall not testify
against any person *to cause him* to die.
31 Moreover ye shall take no satisfaction
for the life of a murderer, which *is* guilty of
death: but he shall be surely put to death.
32 And ye shall take no satisfaction for him
that is fled to the city of his refuge, that he
should come again to dwell in the land, until
the death of the priest.
33 So ye shall not pollute the land wherein
ye *are:* for blood it defileth the land: and
the land cannot be cleansed of the blood
that is shed therein, but by the blood of
him that shed it.
34 Defile not therefore the land which ye
shall inhabit, wherein I dwell: for I the LORD
dwell among the children of Israel.

Numbers 36

1 And the chief fathers of the families of the
children of Gilead, the son of Machir, the son
of Manasseh, of the families of the sons of
Joseph, came near, and spake before Moses,
and before the princes, the chief fathers of
the children of Israel:
2 And they said, The LORD commanded my
lord to give the land for an inheritance by
lot to the children of Israel: and my lord
was commanded by the LORD to give the
inheritance of Zelophehad our brother unto
his daughters.
3 And if they be married to any of the sons
of the *other* tribes of the children of Israel,
then shall their inheritance be taken from
the inheritance of our fathers, and shall be
put to the inheritance of the tribe whereunto they are received: so shall it be taken
from the lot of our inheritance.
4 And when the jubile of the children of
Israel shall be, then shall their inheritance
be put unto the inheritance of the tribe
whereunto they are received: so shall their
inheritance be taken away from the inheritance of the tribe of our fathers.
5 And Moses commanded the children of
Israel according to the word of the LORD,
saying, The tribe of the sons of Joseph hath
said well.
6 This *is* the thing which the LORD doth command concerning the daughters of Zelophehad, saying, Let them marry to whom they
think best; only to the family of the tribe of
their father shall they marry.
7 So shall not the inheritance of the children of Israel remove from tribe to tribe:
for every one of the children of Israel shall
keep himself to the inheritance of the tribe
of his fathers.
8 And every daughter, that possesseth an
inheritance in any tribe of the children of
Israel, shall be wife unto one of the family
of the tribe of her father, that the children of
Israel may enjoy every man the inheritance
of his fathers.
9 Neither shall the inheritance remove from
one tribe to another tribe; but every one of
the tribes of the children of Israel shall keep
himself to his own inheritance.
10 Even as the LORD commanded Moses, so
did the daughters of Zelophehad:
11 For Mahlah, Tirzah, and Hoglah, and
Milcah, and Noah, the daughters of Zelophehad, were married unto their father's
brothers' sons:
12 *And* they were married into the families
of the sons of Manasseh the son of Joseph,
and their inheritance remained in the tribe
of the family of their father.
13 These *are* the commandments and the
judgments, which the LORD commanded by
the hand of Moses unto the children of Israel
in the plains of Moab by Jordan *near* Jericho.

The Fifth Book Of Moses Called

Deuteronomy

Deuteronomy 1

1 These *be* the words which Moses spake
unto all Israel on this side Jordan in the wilderness, in the plain over against the Red
sea, between Paran, and Tophel, and Laban,
and Hazeroth, and Dizahab.
2 (*There are* eleven days' *journey* from
Horeb by the way of mount Seir unto
Kadesh-barnea.)
3 And it came to pass in the fortieth year, in
the eleventh month, on the first *day* of the
month, *that* Moses spake unto the children
of Israel, according unto all that the LORD
had given him in commandment unto them;
4 After he had slain Sihon the king of the
Amorites, which dwelt in Heshbon, and Og
the king of Bashan, which dwelt at Astaroth
in Edrei:
5 On this side Jordan, in the land of Moab,
began Moses to declare this law, saying,
6 The LORD our God spake unto us in Horeb,
saying, Ye have dwelt long enough in this
mount:
7 Turn you, and take your journey, and go
to the mount of the Amorites, and unto all
the places nigh thereunto, in the plain, in the
hills, and in the vale, and in the south, and by
the sea side, to the land of the Canaanites,
and unto Lebanon, unto the great river, the
river Euphrates.
8 Behold, I have set the land before you:
go in and possess the land which the LORD
sware unto your fathers, Abraham, Isaac,
and Jacob, to give unto them and to their
seed after them.
9 ¶ And I spake unto you at that time, saying, I am not able to bear you myself alone:
10 The LORD your God hath multiplied you,
and, behold, ye *are* this day as the stars of
heaven for multitude.
11 (The LORD God of your fathers make you
a thousand times so many more as ye *are*,
and bless you, as he hath promised you!)
12 How can I myself alone bear your cum-
brance, and your burden, and your strife?
13 Take you wise men, and understanding,
and known among your tribes, and I will
make them rulers over you.
14 And ye answered me, and said, The thing
which thou hast spoken *is* good *for us* to do.
15 So I took the chief of your tribes, wise
men, and known, and made them heads
over you, captains over thousands, and
captains over hundreds, and captains over
fifties, and captains over tens, and officers
among your tribes.
16 And I charged your judges at that time,
saying, Hear *the causes* between your brethren, and judge righteously between *every*
man and his brother, and the stranger *that*
is with him.
17 Ye shall not respect persons in judgment;
but ye shall hear the small as well as the
great; ye shall not be afraid of the face of
man; for the judgment *is* God's: and the
cause that is too hard for you, bring *it* unto
me, and I will hear it.
18 And I commanded you at that time all
the things which ye should do.
19 ¶ And when we departed from Horeb,
we went through all that great and terrible
wilderness, which ye saw by the way of
the mountain of the Amorites, as the LORD
our God commanded us; and we came to
Kadesh-barnea.
20 And I said unto you, Ye are come unto
the mountain of the Amorites, which the
LORD our God doth give unto us.
21 Behold, the LORD thy God hath set the
land before thee: go up *and* possess *it*, as
the LORD God of thy fathers hath said unto
thee; fear not, neither be discouraged.
22 ¶ And ye came near unto me every one
of you, and said, We will send men before
us, and they shall search us out the land, and
bring us word again by what way we must
go up, and into what cities we shall come.
23 And the saying pleased me well: and
I took twelve men of you, one of a tribe:
24 And they turned and went up into the
mountain, and came unto the valley of Eshcol, and searched it out.
25 And they took of the fruit of the land

in their hands, and brought *it* down unto
us, and brought us word again, and said,
It is a good land which the LORD our God
doth give us.
26 Notwithstanding ye would not go up, but
rebelled against the commandment of the
LORD your God:
27 And ye murmured in your tents, and
said, Because the LORD hated us, he hath
brought us forth out of the land of Egypt,
to deliver us into the hand of the Amorites,
to destroy us.
28 Whither shall we go up? our brethren
have discouraged our heart, saying, The
people *is* greater and taller than we; the
cities *are* great and walled up to heaven;
and moreover we have seen the sons of
the Anakims there.
29 Then I said unto you, Dread not, neither
be afraid of them.
30 The LORD your God which goeth before
you, he shall fight for you, according to all
that he did for you in Egypt before your eyes;
31 And in the wilderness, where thou hast
seen how that the LORD thy God bare thee,
as a man doth bear his son, in all the way
that ye went, until ye came into this place.
32 Yet in this thing ye did not believe the
LORD your God,
33 Who went in the way before you, to
search you out a place to pitch your tents
in, in fire by night, to shew you by what way
ye should go, and in a cloud by day.
34 And the LORD heard the voice of your
words, and was wroth, and sware, saying,
35 Surely there shall not one of these men
of this evil generation see that good land,
which I sware to give unto your fathers,
36 Save Caleb the son of Jephunneh; he shall
see it, and to him will I give the land that
he hath trodden upon, and to his children,
because he hath wholly followed the LORD.
37 Also the LORD was angry with me for
your sakes, saying, Thou also shalt not go
in thither.
38 *But* Joshua the son of Nun, which standeth before thee, he shall go in thither:
encourage him: for he shall cause Israel to
inherit it.
39 Moreover your little ones, which ye said
should be a prey, and your children, which in
that day had no knowledge between good
and evil, they shall go in thither, and unto
them will I give it, and they shall possess it.
40 But *as for* you, turn you, and take your
journey into the wilderness by the way of
the Red sea.
41 Then ye answered and said unto me, We
have sinned against the LORD, we will go
up and fight, according to all that the LORD
our God commanded us. And when ye had
girded on every man his weapons of war, ye
were ready to go up into the hill.
42 And the LORD said unto me, Say unto
them, Go not up, neither fight; for I *am* not
among you; lest ye be smitten before your
enemies.
43 So I spake unto you; and ye would not
hear, but rebelled against the commandment of the LORD, and went presumptuously
up into the hill.
44 And the Amorites, which dwelt in that
mountain, came out against you, and chased
you, as bees do, and destroyed you in Seir,
even unto Hormah.
45 And ye returned and wept before the
LORD; but the LORD would not hearken to
your voice, nor give ear unto you.
46 So ye abode in Kadesh many days,
according unto the days that ye abode *there*.

Deuteronomy 2

1 Then we turned, and took our journey into
the wilderness by the way of the Red sea, as
the LORD spake unto me: and we compassed
mount Seir many days.
2 And the LORD spake unto me, saying,
3 Ye have compassed this mountain long
enough: turn you northward.
4 And command thou the people, saying,
Ye *are* to pass through the coast of your
brethren the children of Esau, which dwell
in Seir; and they shall be afraid of you: take
ye good heed unto yourselves therefore:
5 Meddle not with them; for I will not give
you of their land, no, not so much as a foot
breadth; because I have given mount Seir
unto Esau *for* a possession.
6 Ye shall buy meat of them for money, that
ye may eat; and ye shall also buy water of
them for money, that ye may drink.
7 For the LORD thy God hath blessed thee in
all the works of thy hand: he knoweth thy
walking through this great wilderness: these

forty years the LORD thy God *hath been* with
thee; thou hast lacked nothing.
8 And when we passed by from our brethren
the children of Esau, which dwelt in Seir,
through the way of the plain from Elath, and
from Ezion-gaber, we turned and passed by
the way of the wilderness of Moab.
9 And the LORD said unto me, Distress not
the Moabites, neither contend with them
in battle: for I will not give thee of their land
for a possession; because I have given Ar
unto the children of Lot *for* a possession.
10 The Emims dwelt therein in times past,
a people great, and many, and tall, as the
Anakims;
11 Which also were accounted giants, as the
Anakims; but the Moabites call them Emims.
12 The Horims also dwelt in Seir beforetime;
but the children of Esau succeeded them,
when they had destroyed them from before
them, and dwelt in their stead; as Israel did
unto the land of his possession, which the
LORD gave unto them.
13 Now rise up, *said I*, and get you over
the brook Zered. And we went over the
brook Zered.
14 And the space in which we came from
Kadesh-barnea, until we were come over
the brook Zered, *was* thirty and eight years;
until all the generation of the men of war
were wasted out from among the host, as
the LORD sware unto them.
15 For indeed the hand of the LORD was
against them, to destroy them from among
the host, until they were consumed.
16 ¶ So it came to pass, when all the men of
war were consumed and dead from among
the people,
17 That the LORD spake unto me, saying,
18 Thou art to pass over through Ar, the
coast of Moab, this day:
19 And *when* thou comest nigh over against
the children of Ammon, distress them not,
nor meddle with them: for I will not give
thee of the land of the children of Ammon
any possession; because I have given it unto
the children of Lot *for* a possession.
20 (That also was accounted a land of giants:
giants dwelt therein in old time; and the
Ammonites call them Zamzummims;
21 A people great, and many, and tall, as
the Anakims; but the LORD destroyed them
before them; and they succeeded them, and
dwelt in their stead:
22 As he did to the children of Esau, which
dwelt in Seir, when he destroyed the Horims
from before them; and they succeeded
them, and dwelt in their stead even unto
this day:
23 And the Avims which dwelt in Hazerim,
even unto Azzah, the Caphtorims, which
came forth out of Caphtor, destroyed them,
and dwelt in their stead.)
24 ¶ Rise ye up, take your journey, and pass
over the river Arnon: behold, I have given
into thine hand Sihon the Amorite, king of
Heshbon, and his land: begin to possess *it*,
and contend with him in battle.
25 This day will I begin to put the dread of
thee and the fear of thee upon the nations
that are under the whole heaven, who shall
hear report of thee, and shall tremble, and
be in anguish because of thee.
26 ¶ And I sent messengers out of the wilderness of Kedemoth unto Sihon king of
Heshbon with words of peace, saying,
27 Let me pass through thy land: I will go
along by the high way, I will neither turn
unto the right hand nor to the left.
28 Thou shalt sell me meat for money, that
I may eat; and give me water for money,
that I may drink: only I will pass through
on my feet;
29 (As the children of Esau which dwell in
Seir, and the Moabites which dwell in Ar, did
unto me;) until I shall pass over Jordan into
the land which the LORD our God giveth us.
30 But Sihon king of Heshbon would not
let us pass by him: for the LORD thy God
hardened his spirit, and made his heart
obstinate, that he might deliver him into
thy hand, as *appeareth* this day.
31 And the LORD said unto me, Behold, I
have begun to give Sihon and his land before
thee: begin to possess, that thou mayest
inherit his land.
32 Then Sihon came out against us, he and
all his people, to fight at Jahaz.
33 And the LORD our God delivered him
before us; and we smote him, and his sons,
and all his people.
34 And we took all his cities at that time,
and utterly destroyed the men, and the
women, and the little ones, of every city,
we left none to remain:

35 Only the cattle we took for a prey unto ourselves, and the spoil of the cities which we took.

36 From Aroer, which *is* by the brink of the river of Arnon, and *from* the city that *is* by the river, even unto Gilead, there was not one city too strong for us: the LORD our God delivered all unto us:

37 Only unto the land of the children of Ammon thou camest not, *nor* unto any place of the river Jabbok, nor unto the cities in the mountains, nor unto whatsoever the LORD our God forbad us.

Deuteronomy 3

1 Then we turned, and went up the way to Bashan: and Og the king of Bashan came out against us, he and all his people, to battle at Edrei.

2 And the LORD said unto me, Fear him not: for I will deliver him, and all his people, and his land, into thy hand; and thou shalt do unto him as thou didst unto Sihon king of the Amorites, which dwelt at Heshbon.

3 So the LORD our God delivered into our hands Og also, the king of Bashan, and all his people: and we smote him until none was left to him remaining.

4 And we took all his cities at that time, there was not a city which we took not from them, threescore cities, all the region of Argob, the kingdom of Og in Bashan.

5 All these cities *were* fenced with high walls, gates, and bars; beside unwalled towns a great many.

6 And we utterly destroyed them, as we did unto Sihon king of Heshbon, utterly destroying the men, women, and children, of every city.

7 But all the cattle, and the spoil of the cities, we took for a prey to ourselves.

8 And we took at that time out of the hand of the two kings of the Amorites the land that *was* on this side Jordan, from the river of Arnon unto mount Hermon;

9 (*Which* Hermon the Sidonians call Sirion; and the Amorites call it Shenir;)

10 All the cities of the plain, and all Gilead, and all Bashan, unto Salchah and Edrei, cities of the kingdom of Og in Bashan.

11 For only Og king of Bashan remained of the remnant of giants; behold, his bedstead *was* a bedstead of iron; *is* it not in Rabbath of the children of Ammon? nine cubits *was* the length thereof, and four cubits the breadth of it, after the cubit of a man.

12 And this land, *which* we possessed at that time, from Aroer, which *is* by the river Arnon, and half mount Gilead, and the cities thereof, gave I unto the Reubenites and to the Gadites.

13 And the rest of Gilead, and all Bashan, *being* the kingdom of Og, gave I unto the half tribe of Manasseh; all the region of Argob, with all Bashan, which was called the land of giants.

14 Jair the son of Manasseh took all the country of Argob unto the coasts of Geshuri and Maachathi; and called them after his own name, Bashan-havoth-jair, unto this day.

15 And I gave Gilead unto Machir.

16 And unto the Reubenites and unto the Gadites I gave from Gilead even unto the river Arnon half the valley, and the border even unto the river Jabbok, *which is* the border of the children of Ammon;

17 The plain also, and Jordan, and the coast *thereof*, from Chinnereth even unto the sea of the plain, *even* the salt sea, under Ashdoth-pisgah eastward.

18 ¶ And I commanded you at that time, saying, The LORD your God hath given you this land to possess it: ye shall pass over armed before your brethren the children of Israel, all *that are* meet for the war.

19 But your wives, and your little ones, and your cattle, (*for* I know that ye have much cattle,) shall abide in your cities which I have given you;

20 Until the LORD have given rest unto your brethren, as well as unto you, and *until* they also possess the land which the LORD your God hath given them beyond Jordan: and *then* shall ye return every man unto his possession, which I have given you.

21 ¶ And I commanded Joshua at that time, saying, Thine eyes have seen all that the LORD your God hath done unto these two kings: so shall the LORD do unto all the kingdoms whither thou passest.

22 Ye shall not fear them: for the LORD your God he shall fight for you.

23 And I besought the LORD at that time, saying,

24 O Lord GOD, thou hast begun to shew

thy servant thy greatness, and thy mighty hand: for what God *is there* in heaven or in earth, that can do according to thy works, and according to thy might?

25 I pray thee, let me go over, and see the good land that *is* beyond Jordan, that goodly mountain, and Lebanon.

26 But the LORD was wroth with me for your sakes, and would not hear me: and the LORD said unto me, Let it suffice thee; speak no more unto me of this matter.

27 Get thee up into the top of Pisgah, and lift up thine eyes westward, and northward, and southward, and eastward, and behold *it* with thine eyes: for thou shalt not go over this Jordan.

28 But charge Joshua, and encourage him, and strengthen him: for he shall go over before this people, and he shall cause them to inherit the land which thou shalt see.

29 So we abode in the valley over against Beth-peor.

Deuteronomy 4

1 Now therefore hearken, O Israel, unto the statutes and unto the judgments, which I teach you, for to do *them*, that ye may live, and go in and possess the land which the LORD God of your fathers giveth you.

2 Ye shall not add unto the word which I command you, neither shall ye diminish *ought* from it, that ye may keep the commandments of the LORD your God which I command you.

3 Your eyes have seen what the LORD did because of Baal-peor: for all the men that followed Baal-peor, the LORD thy God hath destroyed them from among you.

4 But ye that did cleave unto the LORD your God *are* alive every one of you this day.

5 Behold, I have taught you statutes and judgments, even as the LORD my God commanded me, that ye should do so in the land whither ye go to possess it.

6 Keep therefore and do *them;* for this *is* your wisdom and your understanding in the sight of the nations, which shall hear all these statutes, and say, Surely this great nation *is* a wise and understanding people.

7 For what nation *is there so* great, who *hath* God *so* nigh unto them, as the LORD our God *is* in all *things that* we call upon him *for?*

8 And what nation *is there so* great, that hath statutes and judgments *so* righteous as all this law, which I set before you this day?

9 Only take heed to thyself, and keep thy soul diligently, lest thou forget the things which thine eyes have seen, and lest they depart from thy heart all the days of thy life: but teach them thy sons, and thy sons' sons;

10 *Specially* the day that thou stoodest before the LORD thy God in Horeb, when the LORD said unto me, Gather me the people together, and I will make them hear my words, that they may learn to fear me all the days that they shall live upon the earth, and *that* they may teach their children.

11 And ye came near and stood under the mountain; and the mountain burned with fire unto the midst of heaven, with darkness, clouds, and thick darkness.

12 And the LORD spake unto you out of the midst of the fire: ye heard the voice of the words, but saw no similitude; only *ye heard* a voice.

13 And he declared unto you his covenant, which he commanded you to perform, *even* ten commandments; and he wrote them upon two tables of stone.

14 ¶ And the LORD commanded me at that time to teach you statutes and judgments, that ye might do them in the land whither ye go over to possess it.

15 Take ye therefore good heed unto yourselves; for ye saw no manner of similitude on the day *that* the LORD spake unto you in Horeb out of the midst of the fire:

16 Lest ye corrupt *yourselves*, and make you a graven image, the similitude of any figure, the likeness of male or female,

17 The likeness of any beast that *is* on the earth, the likeness of any winged fowl that flieth in the air,

18 The likeness of any thing that creepeth on the ground, the likeness of any fish that *is* in the waters beneath the earth:

19 And lest thou lift up thine eyes unto heaven, and when thou seest the sun, and the moon, and the stars, *even* all the host of heaven, shouldest be driven to worship them, and serve them, which the LORD thy God hath divided unto all nations under the whole heaven.

20 But the LORD hath taken you, and brought you forth out of the iron furnace, *even* out

of Egypt, to be unto him a people of inheritance, as *ye are* this day.
21 Furthermore the LORD was angry with
me for your sakes, and sware that I should
not go over Jordan, and that I should not go
in unto that good land, which the LORD thy
God giveth thee *for* an inheritance:
22 But I must die in this land, I must not go
over Jordan: but ye shall go over, and possess that good land.
23 Take heed unto yourselves, lest ye forget
the covenant of the LORD your God, which
he made with you, and make you a graven
image, *or* the likeness of any *thing*, which the
LORD thy God hath forbidden thee.
24 For the LORD thy God *is* a consuming fire,
even a jealous God.
25 ¶ When thou shalt beget children,
and children's children, and ye shall have
remained long in the land, and shall corrupt
yourselves, and make a graven image, *or*
the likeness of any *thing*, and shall do evil
in the sight of the LORD thy God, to provoke
him to anger:
26 I call heaven and earth to witness against
you this day, that ye shall soon utterly perish
from off the land whereunto ye go over Jordan to possess it; ye shall not prolong *your*
days upon it, but shall utterly be destroyed.
27 And the LORD shall scatter you among the
nations, and ye shall be left few in number
among the heathen, whither the LORD shall
lead you.
28 And there ye shall serve gods, the work
of men's hands, wood and stone, which
neither see, nor hear, nor eat, nor smell.
29 But if from thence thou shalt seek the
LORD thy God, thou shalt find *him*, if thou
seek him with all thy heart and with all
thy soul.
30 When thou art in tribulation, and all
these things are come upon thee, *even* in
the latter days, if thou turn to the LORD thy
God, and shalt be obedient unto his voice;
31 (For the LORD thy God *is* a merciful God;)
he will not forsake thee, neither destroy
thee, nor forget the covenant of thy fathers
which he sware unto them.
32 For ask now of the days that are past,
which were before thee, since the day that
God created man upon the earth, and *ask*
from the one side of heaven unto the other,
whether there hath been *any such thing* as
this great thing *is*, or hath been heard like it?
33 Did *ever* people hear the voice of God
speaking out of the midst of the fire, as thou
hast heard, and live?
34 Or hath God assayed to go *and* take him
a nation from the midst of *another* nation,
by temptations, by signs, and by wonders,
and by war, and by a mighty hand, and by
a stretched out arm, and by great terrors,
according to all that the LORD your God did
for you in Egypt before your eyes?
35 Unto thee it was shewed, that thou
mightest know that the LORD he *is* God;
there is none else beside him.
36 Out of heaven he made thee to hear
his voice, that he might instruct thee: and
upon earth he shewed thee his great fire;
and thou heardest his words out of the
midst of the fire.
37 And because he loved thy fathers, therefore he chose their seed after them, and
brought thee out in his sight with his mighty
power out of Egypt;
38 To drive out nations from before thee
greater and mightier than thou *art*, to bring
thee in, to give thee their land *for* an inheritance, as *it is* this day.
39 Know therefore this day, and consider
it in thine heart, that the LORD he *is* God in
heaven above, and upon the earth beneath:
there is none else.
40 Thou shalt keep therefore his statutes,
and his commandments, which I command
thee this day, that it may go well with thee,
and with thy children after thee, and that
thou mayest prolong *thy* days upon the
earth, which the LORD thy God giveth thee,
for ever.
41 ¶ Then Moses severed three cities on this
side Jordan toward the sunrising;
42 That the slayer might flee thither, which
should kill his neighbour unawares, and
hated him not in times past; and that fleeing unto one of these cities he might live:
43 *Namely*, Bezer in the wilderness, in
the plain country, of the Reubenites; and
Ramoth in Gilead, of the Gadites; and Golan
in Bashan, of the Manassites.
44 ¶ And this *is* the law which Moses set
before the children of Israel:
45 These *are* the testimonies, and the statutes, and the judgments, which Moses spake

unto the children of Israel, after they came
forth out of Egypt,
46 On this side Jordan, in the valley over
against Beth-peor, in the land of Sihon king
of the Amorites, who dwelt at Heshbon,
whom Moses and the children of Israel
smote, after they were come forth out of
Egypt:
47 And they possessed his land, and the
land of Og king of Bashan, two kings of the
Amorites, which *were* on this side Jordan
toward the sunrising;
48 From Aroer, which *is* by the bank of the
river Arnon, even unto mount Sion, which
is Hermon,
49 And all the plain on this side Jordan eastward, even unto the sea of the plain, under
the springs of Pisgah.

Deuteronomy 5

1 And Moses called all Israel, and said
unto them, Hear, O Israel, the statutes and
judgments which I speak in your ears this
day, that ye may learn them, and keep, and
do them.
2 The LORD our God made a covenant with
us in Horeb.
3 The LORD made not this covenant with
our fathers, but with us, *even* us, who *are*
all of us here alive this day.
4 The LORD talked with you face to face in
the mount out of the midst of the fire,
5 (I stood between the LORD and you at that
time, to shew you the word of the LORD: for
ye were afraid by reason of the fire, and
went not up into the mount;) saying,
6 ¶ I *am* the LORD thy God, which brought
thee out of the land of Egypt, from the
house of bondage.
7 Thou shalt have none other gods before
me.
8 Thou shalt not make thee *any* graven
image, *or* any likeness *of any thing* that
is in heaven above, or that *is* in the earth
beneath, or that *is* in the waters beneath
the earth:
9 Thou shalt not bow down thyself unto
them, nor serve them: for I the LORD thy God
am a jealous God, visiting the iniquity of the
fathers upon the children unto the third and
fourth *generation* of them that hate me,
10 And shewing mercy unto thousands
of them that love me and keep my commandments.
11 Thou shalt not take the name of the LORD
thy God in vain: for the LORD will not hold
him guiltless that taketh his name in vain.
12 Keep the sabbath day to sanctify it, as
the LORD thy God hath commanded thee.
13 Six days thou shalt labour, and do all
thy work:
14 But the seventh day *is* the sabbath of the
LORD thy God: *in it* thou shalt not do any
work, thou, nor thy son, nor thy daughter,
nor thy manservant, nor thy maidservant,
nor thine ox, nor thine ass, nor any of thy
cattle, nor thy stranger that *is* within thy
gates; that thy manservant and thy maidservant may rest as well as thou.
15 And remember that thou wast a servant
in the land of Egypt, and *that* the LORD thy
God brought thee out thence through a
mighty hand and by a stretched out arm:
therefore the LORD thy God commanded
thee to keep the sabbath day.
16 ¶ Honour thy father and thy mother, as
the LORD thy God hath commanded thee;
that thy days may be prolonged, and that
it may go well with thee, in the land which
the LORD thy God giveth thee.
17 Thou shalt not kill.
18 Neither shalt thou commit adultery.
19 Neither shalt thou steal.
20 Neither shalt thou bear false witness
against thy neighbour.
21 Neither shalt thou desire thy neighbour's
wife, neither shalt thou covet thy neighbour's house, his field, or his manservant,
or his maidservant, his ox, or his ass, or any
thing that *is* thy neighbour's.
22 ¶ These words the LORD spake unto all
your assembly in the mount out of the midst
of the fire, of the cloud, and of the thick
darkness, with a great voice: and he added
no more. And he wrote them in two tables
of stone, and delivered them unto me.
23 And it came to pass, when ye heard the
voice out of the midst of the darkness, (for
the mountain did burn with fire,) that ye
came near unto me, *even* all the heads of
your tribes, and your elders;
24 And ye said, Behold, the LORD our God
hath shewed us his glory and his greatness,
and we have heard his voice out of the midst

of the fire: we have seen this day that God
doth talk with man, and he liveth.
25 Now therefore why should we die? for
this great fire will consume us: if we hear
the voice of the LORD our God any more,
then we shall die.
26 For who *is there of* all flesh, that hath
heard the voice of the living God speaking
out of the midst of the fire, as we *have*,
and lived?
27 Go thou near, and hear all that the LORD
our God shall say: and speak thou unto us
all that the LORD our God shall speak unto
thee; and we will hear *it*, and do *it*.
28 And the LORD heard the voice of your
words, when ye spake unto me; and the
LORD said unto me, I have heard the voice
of the words of this people, which they have
spoken unto thee: they have well said all
that they have spoken.
29 O that there were such an heart in them,
that they would fear me, and keep all my
commandments always, that it might be
well with them, and with their children
for ever!
30 Go say to them, Get you into your tents
again.
31 But as for thee, stand thou here by me,
and I will speak unto thee all the commandments, and the statutes, and the judgments,
which thou shalt teach them, that they may
do *them* in the land which I give them to
possess it.
32 Ye shall observe to do therefore as the
LORD your God hath commanded you: ye
shall not turn aside to the right hand or to
the left.
33 Ye shall walk in all the ways which the
LORD your God hath commanded you, that
ye may live, and *that it may be* well with
you, and *that* ye may prolong *your* days in
the land which ye shall possess.

Deuteronomy 6

1 Now these *are* the commandments, the
statutes, and the judgments, which the
LORD your God commanded to teach you,
that ye might do *them* in the land whither
ye go to possess it:
2 That thou mightest fear the LORD thy God,
to keep all his statutes and his commandments, which I command thee, thou, and
thy son, and thy son's son, all the days of
thy life; and that thy days may be prolonged.
3 ¶ Hear therefore, O Israel, and observe
to do *it;* that it may be well with thee, and
that ye may increase mightily, as the LORD
God of thy fathers hath promised thee, in
the land that floweth with milk and honey.
4 Hear, O Israel: The LORD our God *is* one
LORD:
5 And thou shalt love the LORD thy God
with all thine heart, and with all thy soul,
and with all thy might.
6 And these words, which I command thee
this day, shall be in thine heart:
7 And thou shalt teach them diligently unto
thy children, and shalt talk of them when
thou sittest in thine house, and when thou
walkest by the way, and when thou liest
down, and when thou risest up.
8 And thou shalt bind them for a sign upon
thine hand, and they shall be as frontlets
between thine eyes.
9 And thou shalt write them upon the posts
of thy house, and on thy gates.
10 And it shall be, when the LORD thy God
shall have brought thee into the land which
he sware unto thy fathers, to Abraham, to
Isaac, and to Jacob, to give thee great and
goodly cities, which thou buildedst not,
11 And houses full of all good *things*, which
thou filledst not, and wells digged, which
thou diggedst not, vineyards and olive trees,
which thou plantedst not; when thou shalt
have eaten and be full;
12 *Then* beware lest thou forget the LORD,
which brought thee forth out of the land of
Egypt, from the house of bondage.
13 Thou shalt fear the LORD thy God, and
serve him, and shalt swear by his name.
14 Ye shall not go after other gods, of the
gods of the people which *are* round about
you;
15 (For the LORD thy God *is* a jealous God
among you) lest the anger of the LORD thy
God be kindled against thee, and destroy
thee from off the face of the earth.
16 ¶ Ye shall not tempt the LORD your God,
as ye tempted *him* in Massah.
17 Ye shall diligently keep the commandments of the LORD your God, and his testimonies, and his statutes, which he hath
commanded thee.
18 And thou shalt do *that which is* right and

good in the sight of the LORD: that it may be
well with thee, and that thou mayest go in
and possess the good land which the LORD
sware unto thy fathers,
19 To cast out all thine enemies from before
thee, as the LORD hath spoken.
20 *And* when thy son asketh thee in time to
come, saying, What *mean* the testimonies,
and the statutes, and the judgments, which
the LORD our God hath commanded you?
21 Then thou shalt say unto thy son, We
were Pharaoh's bondmen in Egypt; and
the LORD brought us out of Egypt with a
mighty hand:
22 And the LORD shewed signs and wonders,
great and sore, upon Egypt, upon Pharaoh,
and upon all his household, before our eyes:
23 And he brought us out from thence, that
he might bring us in, to give us the land
which he sware unto our fathers.
24 And the LORD commanded us to do all
these statutes, to fear the LORD our God, for
our good always, that he might preserve us
alive, as *it is* at this day.
25 And it shall be our righteousness, if we
observe to do all these commandments
before the LORD our God, as he hath commanded us.

Deuteronomy 7

1 When the LORD thy God shall bring thee
into the land whither thou goest to possess
it, and hath cast out many nations before
thee, the Hittites, and the Girgashites, and
the Amorites, and the Canaanites, and the
Perizzites, and the Hivites, and the Jebusites, seven nations greater and mightier
than thou;
2 And when the LORD thy God shall deliver
them before thee; thou shalt smite them,
and utterly destroy them; thou shalt make
no covenant with them, nor shew mercy
unto them:
3 Neither shalt thou make marriages with
them; thy daughter thou shalt not give unto
his son, nor his daughter shalt thou take
unto thy son.
4 For they will turn away thy son from following me, that they may serve other gods:
so will the anger of the LORD be kindled
against you, and destroy thee suddenly.
5 But thus shall ye deal with them; ye shall
destroy their altars, and break down their
images, and cut down their groves, and burn
their graven images with fire.
6 For thou *art* an holy people unto the LORD
thy God: the LORD thy God hath chosen thee
to be a special people unto himself, above all
people that *are* upon the face of the earth.
7 The LORD did not set his love upon you,
nor choose you, because ye were more in
number than any people; for ye *were* the
fewest of all people:
8 But because the LORD loved you, and
because he would keep the oath which
he had sworn unto your fathers, hath the
LORD brought you out with a mighty hand,
and redeemed you out of the house of
bondmen, from the hand of Pharaoh king
of Egypt.
9 Know therefore that the LORD thy God,
he *is* God, the faithful God, which keepeth
covenant and mercy with them that love him
and keep his commandments to a thousand
generations;
10 And repayeth them that hate him to
their face, to destroy them: he will not be
slack to him that hateth him, he will repay
him to his face.
11 Thou shalt therefore keep the commandments, and the statutes, and the judgments,
which I command thee this day, to do them.
12 ¶ Wherefore it shall come to pass, if
ye hearken to these judgments, and keep,
and do them, that the LORD thy God shall
keep unto thee the covenant and the mercy
which he sware unto thy fathers:
13 And he will love thee, and bless thee,
and multiply thee: he will also bless the
fruit of thy womb, and the fruit of thy land,
thy corn, and thy wine, and thine oil, the
increase of thy kine, and the flocks of thy
sheep, in the land which he sware unto thy
fathers to give thee.
14 Thou shalt be blessed above all people:
there shall not be male or female barren
among you, or among your cattle.
15 And the LORD will take away from thee
all sickness, and will put none of the evil
diseases of Egypt, which thou knowest,
upon thee; but will lay them upon all *them*
that hate thee.
16 And thou shalt consume all the people
which the LORD thy God shall deliver thee;
thine eye shall have no pity upon them:

neither shalt thou serve their gods; for that
will be a snare unto thee.
17 If thou shalt say in thine heart, These
nations *are* more than I; how can I dispossess them?
18 Thou shalt not be afraid of them: *but*
shalt well remember what the LORD thy
God did unto Pharaoh, and unto all Egypt;
19 The great temptations which thine eyes
saw, and the signs, and the wonders, and
the mighty hand, and the stretched out arm,
whereby the LORD thy God brought thee
out: so shall the LORD thy God do unto all
the people of whom thou art afraid.
20 Moreover the LORD thy God will send
the hornet among them, until they that
are left, and hide themselves from thee,
be destroyed.
21 Thou shalt not be affrighted at them: for
the LORD thy God *is* among you, a mighty
God and terrible.
22 And the LORD thy God will put out those
nations before thee by little and little: thou
mayest not consume them at once, lest the
beasts of the field increase upon thee.
23 But the LORD thy God shall deliver them
unto thee, and shall destroy them with a
mighty destruction, until they be destroyed.
24 And he shall deliver their kings into thine
hand, and thou shalt destroy their name
from under heaven: there shall no man be
able to stand before thee, until thou have
destroyed them.
25 The graven images of their gods shall
ye burn with fire: thou shalt not desire the
silver or gold *that is* on them, nor take *it*
unto thee, lest thou be snared therein: for
it *is* an abomination to the LORD thy God.
26 Neither shalt thou bring an abomination into thine house, lest thou be a cursed
thing like it: *but* thou shalt utterly detest
it, and thou shalt utterly abhor it; for it *is*
a cursed thing.

Deuteronomy 8

1 All the commandments which I command
thee this day shall ye observe to do, that ye
may live, and multiply, and go in and possess the land which the LORD sware unto
your fathers.
2 And thou shalt remember all the way
which the LORD thy God led thee these
forty years in the wilderness, to humble
thee, *and* to prove thee, to know what *was*
in thine heart, whether thou wouldest keep
his commandments, or no.
3 And he humbled thee, and suffered thee
to hunger, and fed thee with manna, which
thou knewest not, neither did thy fathers
know; that he might make thee know that
man doth not live by bread only, but by
every *word* that proceedeth out of the
mouth of the LORD doth man live.
4 Thy raiment waxed not old upon thee,
neither did thy foot swell, these forty years.
5 Thou shalt also consider in thine heart,
that, as a man chasteneth his son, *so* the
LORD thy God chasteneth thee.
6 Therefore thou shalt keep the commandments of the LORD thy God, to walk in his
ways, and to fear him.
7 For the LORD thy God bringeth thee into
a good land, a land of brooks of water, of
fountains and depths that spring out of
valleys and hills;
8 A land of wheat, and barley, and vines,
and fig trees, and pomegranates; a land of
oil olive, and honey;
9 A land wherein thou shalt eat bread without scarceness, thou shalt not lack any *thing*
in it; a land whose stones *are* iron, and out
of whose hills thou mayest dig brass.
10 When thou hast eaten and art full, then
thou shalt bless the LORD thy God for the
good land which he hath given thee.
11 Beware that thou forget not the LORD
thy God, in not keeping his commandments,
and his judgments, and his statutes, which
I command thee this day:
12 Lest *when* thou hast eaten and art full,
and hast built goodly houses, and dwelt
therein;
13 And *when* thy herds and thy flocks multiply, and thy silver and thy gold is multiplied,
and all that thou hast is multiplied;
14 Then thine heart be lifted up, and thou
forget the LORD thy God, which brought
thee forth out of the land of Egypt, from
the house of bondage;
15 Who led thee through that great and
terrible wilderness, *wherein were* fiery serpents, and scorpions, and drought, where
there was no water; who brought thee forth
water out of the rock of flint;
16 Who fed thee in the wilderness with
manna, which thy fathers knew not, that

he might humble thee, and that he might
prove thee, to do thee good at thy latter end;
17 And thou say in thine heart, My power
and the might of *mine* hand hath gotten
me this wealth.
18 But thou shalt remember the LORD thy
God: for *it is* he that giveth thee power to
get wealth, that he may establish his covenant which he sware unto thy fathers, as
it is this day.
19 And it shall be, if thou do at all forget
the LORD thy God, and walk after other
gods, and serve them, and worship them,
I testify against you this day that ye shall
surely perish.
20 As the nations which the LORD destroyeth
before your face, so shall ye perish; because
ye would not be obedient unto the voice of
the LORD your God.

Deuteronomy 9

1 Hear, O Israel: Thou *art* to pass over Jordan
this day, to go in to possess nations greater
and mightier than thyself, cities great and
fenced up to heaven,
2 A people great and tall, the children of
the Anakims, whom thou knowest, and *of
whom* thou hast heard *say*, Who can stand
before the children of Anak!
3 Understand therefore this day, that the
LORD thy God *is* he which goeth over before
thee; *as* a consuming fire he shall destroy
them, and he shall bring them down before
thy face: so shalt thou drive them out, and
destroy them quickly, as the LORD hath said
unto thee.
4 Speak not thou in thine heart, after that
the LORD thy God hath cast them out from
before thee, saying, For my righteousness
the LORD hath brought me in to possess
this land: but for the wickedness of these
nations the LORD doth drive them out from
before thee.
5 Not for thy righteousness, or for the
uprightness of thine heart, dost thou go to
possess their land: but for the wickedness of
these nations the LORD thy God doth drive
them out from before thee, and that he may
perform the word which the LORD sware
unto thy fathers, Abraham, Isaac, and Jacob.
6 Understand therefore, that the LORD thy
God giveth thee not this good land to possess it for thy righteousness; for thou *art* a
stiffnecked people.
7 ¶ Remember, *and* forget not, how thou
provokedst the LORD thy God to wrath in
the wilderness: from the day that thou didst
depart out of the land of Egypt, until ye
came unto this place, ye have been rebellious against the LORD.
8 Also in Horeb ye provoked the LORD to
wrath, so that the LORD was angry with you
to have destroyed you.
9 When I was gone up into the mount to
receive the tables of stone, *even* the tables
of the covenant which the LORD made with
you, then I abode in the mount forty days
and forty nights, I neither did eat bread nor
drink water:
10 And the LORD delivered unto me two
tables of stone written with the finger of
God; and on them *was written* according
to all the words, which the LORD spake with
you in the mount out of the midst of the fire
in the day of the assembly.
11 And it came to pass at the end of forty
days and forty nights, *that* the LORD gave
me the two tables of stone, *even* the tables
of the covenant.
12 And the LORD said unto me, Arise, get
thee down quickly from hence; for thy people which thou hast brought forth out of
Egypt have corrupted *themselves;* they are
quickly turned aside out of the way which
I commanded them; they have made them
a molten image.
13 Furthermore the LORD spake unto me,
saying, I have seen this people, and, behold,
it *is* a stiffnecked people:
14 Let me alone, that I may destroy them,
and blot out their name from under heaven:
and I will make of thee a nation mightier and
greater than they.
15 So I turned and came down from the
mount, and the mount burned with fire:
and the two tables of the covenant *were* in
my two hands.
16 And I looked, and, behold, ye had sinned
against the LORD your God, *and* had made
you a molten calf: ye had turned aside
quickly out of the way which the LORD had
commanded you.
17 And I took the two tables, and cast them
out of my two hands, and brake them before
your eyes.

18 And I fell down before the LORD, as at
the first, forty days and forty nights: I did
neither eat bread, nor drink water, because
of all your sins which ye sinned, in doing
wickedly in the sight of the LORD, to provoke
him to anger.
19 For I was afraid of the anger and hot
displeasure, wherewith the LORD was wroth
against you to destroy you. But the LORD
hearkened unto me at that time also.
20 And the LORD was very angry with Aaron
to have destroyed him: and I prayed for
Aaron also the same time.
21 And I took your sin, the calf which ye had
made, and burnt it with fire, and stamped it,
and ground *it* very small, *even* until it was as
small as dust: and I cast the dust thereof into
the brook that descended out of the mount.
22 And at Taberah, and at Massah, and at
Kibroth-hattaavah, ye provoked the LORD
to wrath.
23 Likewise when the LORD sent you from
Kadesh-barnea, saying, Go up and possess
the land which I have given you; then ye
rebelled against the commandment of the
LORD your God, and ye believed him not,
nor hearkened to his voice.
24 Ye have been rebellious against the LORD
from the day that I knew you.
25 Thus I fell down before the LORD forty
days and forty nights, as I fell down *at the
first;* because the LORD had said he would
destroy you.
26 I prayed therefore unto the LORD, and
said, O Lord GOD, destroy not thy people
and thine inheritance, which thou hast
redeemed through thy greatness, which
thou hast brought forth out of Egypt with
a mighty hand.
27 Remember thy servants, Abraham, Isaac,
and Jacob; look not unto the stubbornness
of this people, nor to their wickedness, nor
to their sin:
28 Lest the land whence thou broughtest
us out say, Because the LORD was not able
to bring them into the land which he promised them, and because he hated them, he
hath brought them out to slay them in the
wilderness.
29 Yet they *are* thy people and thine inheritance, which thou broughtest out by thy
mighty power and by thy stretched out arm.

Deuteronomy 10

1 At that time the LORD said unto me, Hew
thee two tables of stone like unto the first,
and come up unto me into the mount, and
make thee an ark of wood.
2 And I will write on the tables the words
that were in the first tables which thou
brakest, and thou shalt put them in the ark.
3 And I made an ark *of* shittim wood, and
hewed two tables of stone like unto the
first, and went up into the mount, having
the two tables in mine hand.
4 And he wrote on the tables, according to
the first writing, the ten commandments,
which the LORD spake unto you in the mount
out of the midst of the fire in the day of the
assembly: and the LORD gave them unto me.
5 And I turned myself and came down from
the mount, and put the tables in the ark
which I had made; and there they be, as
the LORD commanded me.
6 ¶ And the children of Israel took their journey from Beeroth of the children of Jaakan
to Mosera: there Aaron died, and there he
was buried; and Eleazar his son ministered
in the priest's office in his stead.
7 From thence they journeyed unto Gudgodah; and from Gudgodah to Jotbath, a
land of rivers of waters.
8 ¶ At that time the LORD separated the
tribe of Levi, to bear the ark of the covenant
of the LORD, to stand before the LORD to
minister unto him, and to bless in his name,
unto this day.
9 Wherefore Levi hath no part nor inheritance with his brethren; the LORD *is* his
inheritance, according as the LORD thy God
promised him.
10 And I stayed in the mount, according to
the first time, forty days and forty nights;
and the LORD hearkened unto me at that
time also, *and* the LORD would not destroy
thee.
11 And the LORD said unto me, Arise, take
thy journey before the people, that they
may go in and possess the land, which I
sware unto their fathers to give unto them.
12 ¶ And now, Israel, what doth the LORD
thy God require of thee, but to fear the LORD
thy God, to walk in all his ways, and to love
him, and to serve the LORD thy God with all
thy heart and with all thy soul,
13 To keep the commandments of the LORD,

and his statutes, which I command thee this
day for thy good?
14 Behold, the heaven and the heaven of
heavens *is* the LORD's thy God, the earth
also, with all that therein *is*.
15 Only the LORD had a delight in thy fathers
to love them, and he chose their seed after
them, *even* you above all people, as *it is*
this day.
16 Circumcise therefore the foreskin of your
heart, and be no more stiffnecked.
17 For the LORD your God *is* God of gods, and
Lord of lords, a great God, a mighty, and a
terrible, which regardeth not persons, nor
taketh reward:
18 He doth execute the judgment of the
fatherless and widow, and loveth the
stranger, in giving him food and raiment.
19 Love ye therefore the stranger: for ye
were strangers in the land of Egypt.
20 Thou shalt fear the LORD thy God; him
shalt thou serve, and to him shalt thou
cleave, and swear by his name.
21 He *is* thy praise, and he *is* thy God, that
hath done for thee these great and terrible
things, which thine eyes have seen.
22 Thy fathers went down into Egypt with
threescore and ten persons; and now the
LORD thy God hath made thee as the stars
of heaven for multitude.

Deuteronomy 11

1 Therefore thou shalt love the LORD thy
God, and keep his charge, and his statutes,
and his judgments, and his commandments,
alway.
2 And know ye this day: for *I speak* not with
your children which have not known, and
which have not seen the chastisement of
the LORD your God, his greatness, his mighty
hand, and his stretched out arm,
3 And his miracles, and his acts, which he
did in the midst of Egypt unto Pharaoh the
king of Egypt, and unto all his land;
4 And what he did unto the army of Egypt,
unto their horses, and to their chariots;
how he made the water of the Red sea to
overflow them as they pursued after you,
and *how* the LORD hath destroyed them
unto this day;
5 And what he did unto you in the wilderness, until ye came into this place;
6 And what he did unto Dathan and Abiram,
the sons of Eliab, the son of Reuben: how
the earth opened her mouth, and swallowed them up, and their households, and
their tents, and all the substance that *was*
in their possession, in the midst of all Israel:
7 But your eyes have seen all the great acts
of the LORD which he did.
8 Therefore shall ye keep all the commandments which I command you this day, that
ye may be strong, and go in and possess the
land, whither ye go to possess it;
9 And that ye may prolong *your* days in
the land, which the LORD sware unto your
fathers to give unto them and to their seed,
a land that floweth with milk and honey.
10 ¶ For the land, whither thou goest in to
possess it, *is* not as the land of Egypt, from
whence ye came out, where thou sowedst
thy seed, and wateredst *it* with thy foot, as
a garden of herbs:
11 But the land, whither ye go to possess
it, *is* a land of hills and valleys, *and* drinketh
water of the rain of heaven:
12 A land which the LORD thy God careth
for: the eyes of the LORD thy God *are* always
upon it, from the beginning of the year even
unto the end of the year.
13 ¶ And it shall come to pass, if ye shall
hearken diligently unto my commandments
which I command you this day, to love the
LORD your God, and to serve him with all
your heart and with all your soul,
14 That I will give *you* the rain of your land
in his due season, the first rain and the latter
rain, that thou mayest gather in thy corn,
and thy wine, and thine oil.
15 And I will send grass in thy fields for thy
cattle, that thou mayest eat and be full.
16 Take heed to yourselves, that your heart
be not deceived, and ye turn aside, and
serve other gods, and worship them;
17 And *then* the LORD's wrath be kindled
against you, and he shut up the heaven, that
there be no rain, and that the land yield not
her fruit; and *lest* ye perish quickly from off
the good land which the LORD giveth you.
18 ¶ Therefore shall ye lay up these my
words in your heart and in your soul, and
bind them for a sign upon your hand, that
they may be as frontlets between your eyes.
19 And ye shall teach them your children,
speaking of them when thou sittest in
thine house, and when thou walkest by

the way, when thou liest down, and when thou risest up.

20 And thou shalt write them upon the door posts of thine house, and upon thy gates:

21 That your days may be multiplied, and the days of your children, in the land which the LORD sware unto your fathers to give them, as the days of heaven upon the earth.

22 ¶ For if ye shall diligently keep all these commandments which I command you, to do them, to love the LORD your God, to walk in all his ways, and to cleave unto him;

23 Then will the LORD drive out all these nations from before you, and ye shall possess greater nations and mightier than yourselves.

24 Every place whereon the soles of your feet shall tread shall be yours: from the wilderness and Lebanon, from the river, the river Euphrates, even unto the uttermost sea shall your coast be.

25 There shall no man be able to stand before you: *for* the LORD your God shall lay the fear of you and the dread of you upon all the land that ye shall tread upon, as he hath said unto you.

26 ¶ Behold, I set before you this day a blessing and a curse;

27 A blessing, if ye obey the commandments of the LORD your God, which I command you this day:

28 And a curse, if ye will not obey the commandments of the LORD your God, but turn aside out of the way which I command you this day, to go after other gods, which ye have not known.

29 And it shall come to pass, when the LORD thy God hath brought thee in unto the land whither thou goest to possess it, that thou shalt put the blessing upon mount Gerizim, and the curse upon mount Ebal.

30 *Are* they not on the other side Jordan, by the way where the sun goeth down, in the land of the Canaanites, which dwell in the champaign over against Gilgal, beside the plains of Moreh?

31 For ye shall pass over Jordan to go in to possess the land which the LORD your God giveth you, and ye shall possess it, and dwell therein.

32 And ye shall observe to do all the statutes and judgments which I set before you this day.

Deuteronomy 12

1 These *are* the statutes and judgments, which ye shall observe to do in the land, which the LORD God of thy fathers giveth thee to possess it, all the days that ye live upon the earth.

2 Ye shall utterly destroy all the places, wherein the nations which ye shall possess served their gods, upon the high mountains, and upon the hills, and under every green tree:

3 And ye shall overthrow their altars, and break their pillars, and burn their groves with fire; and ye shall hew down the graven images of their gods, and destroy the names of them out of that place.

4 Ye shall not do so unto the LORD your God.

5 But unto the place which the LORD your God shall choose out of all your tribes to put his name there, *even* unto his habitation shall ye seek, and thither thou shalt come:

6 And thither ye shall bring your burnt offerings, and your sacrifices, and your tithes, and heave offerings of your hand, and your vows, and your freewill offerings, and the firstlings of your herds and of your flocks:

7 And there ye shall eat before the LORD your God, and ye shall rejoice in all that ye put your hand unto, ye and your households, wherein the LORD thy God hath blessed thee.

8 Ye shall not do after all *the things* that we do here this day, every man whatsoever *is* right in his own eyes.

9 For ye are not as yet come to the rest and to the inheritance, which the LORD your God giveth you.

10 But *when* ye go over Jordan, and dwell in the land which the LORD your God giveth you to inherit, and *when* he giveth you rest from all your enemies round about, so that ye dwell in safety;

11 Then there shall be a place which the LORD your God shall choose to cause his name to dwell there; thither shall ye bring all that I command you; your burnt offerings, and your sacrifices, your tithes, and the heave offering of your hand, and all your choice vows which ye vow unto the LORD:

12 And ye shall rejoice before the LORD your God, ye, and your sons, and your daughters, and your menservants, and your maidservants, and the Levite that *is* within your

gates; forasmuch as he hath no part nor inheritance with you.

13 Take heed to thyself that thou offer not thy burnt offerings in every place that thou seest:

14 But in the place which the LORD shall choose in one of thy tribes, there thou shalt offer thy burnt offerings, and there thou shalt do all that I command thee.

15 Notwithstanding thou mayest kill and eat flesh in all thy gates, whatsoever thy soul lusteth after, according to the blessing of the LORD thy God which he hath given thee: the unclean and the clean may eat thereof, as of the roebuck, and as of the hart.

16 Only ye shall not eat the blood; ye shall pour it upon the earth as water.

17 ¶ Thou mayest not eat within thy gates the tithe of thy corn, or of thy wine, or of thy oil, or the firstlings of thy herds or of thy flock, nor any of thy vows which thou vowest, nor thy freewill offerings, or heave offering of thine hand:

18 But thou must eat them before the LORD thy God in the place which the LORD thy God shall choose, thou, and thy son, and thy daughter, and thy manservant, and thy maidservant, and the Levite that *is* within thy gates: and thou shalt rejoice before the LORD thy God in all that thou puttest thine hands unto.

19 Take heed to thyself that thou forsake not the Levite as long as thou livest upon the earth.

20 ¶ When the LORD thy God shall enlarge thy border, as he hath promised thee, and thou shalt say, I will eat flesh, because thy soul longeth to eat flesh; thou mayest eat flesh, whatsoever thy soul lusteth after.

21 If the place which the LORD thy God hath chosen to put his name there be too far from thee, then thou shalt kill of thy herd and of thy flock, which the LORD hath given thee, as I have commanded thee, and thou shalt eat in thy gates whatsoever thy soul lusteth after.

22 Even as the roebuck and the hart is eaten, so thou shalt eat them: the unclean and the clean shall eat *of* them alike.

23 Only be sure that thou eat not the blood: for the blood *is* the life; and thou mayest not eat the life with the flesh.

24 Thou shalt not eat it; thou shalt pour it upon the earth as water.

25 Thou shalt not eat it; that it may go well with thee, and with thy children after thee, when thou shalt do *that which is* right in the sight of the LORD.

26 Only thy holy things which thou hast, and thy vows, thou shalt take, and go unto the place which the LORD shall choose:

27 And thou shalt offer thy burnt offerings, the flesh and the blood, upon the altar of the LORD thy God: and the blood of thy sacrifices shall be poured out upon the altar of the LORD thy God, and thou shalt eat the flesh.

28 Observe and hear all these words which I command thee, that it may go well with thee, and with thy children after thee for ever, when thou doest *that which is* good and right in the sight of the LORD thy God.

29 ¶ When the LORD thy God shall cut off the nations from before thee, whither thou goest to possess them, and thou succeedest them, and dwellest in their land;

30 Take heed to thyself that thou be not snared by following them, after that they be destroyed from before thee; and that thou inquire not after their gods, saying, How did these nations serve their gods? even so will I do likewise.

31 Thou shalt not do so unto the LORD thy God: for every abomination to the LORD, which he hateth, have they done unto their gods; for even their sons and their daughters they have burnt in the fire to their gods.

32 What thing soever I command you, observe to do it: thou shalt not add thereto, nor diminish from it.

Deuteronomy 13

1 If there arise among you a prophet, or a dreamer of dreams, and giveth thee a sign or a wonder,

2 And the sign or the wonder come to pass, whereof he spake unto thee, saying, Let us go after other gods, which thou hast not known, and let us serve them;

3 Thou shalt not hearken unto the words of that prophet, or that dreamer of dreams: for the LORD your God proveth you, to know whether ye love the LORD your God with all your heart and with all your soul.

4 Ye shall walk after the LORD your God, and fear him, and keep his commandments, and

obey his voice, and ye shall serve him, and
cleave unto him.
5 And that prophet, or that dreamer of
dreams, shall be put to death; because he
hath spoken to turn *you* away from the LORD
your God, which brought you out of the
land of Egypt, and redeemed you out of the
house of bondage, to thrust thee out of the
way which the LORD thy God commanded
thee to walk in. So shalt thou put the evil
away from the midst of thee.
6 ¶ If thy brother, the son of thy mother, or
thy son, or thy daughter, or the wife of thy
bosom, or thy friend, which *is* as thine own
soul, entice thee secretly, saying, Let us go
and serve other gods, which thou hast not
known, thou, nor thy fathers;
7 *Namely*, of the gods of the people which
are round about you, nigh unto thee, or
far off from thee, from the *one* end of the
earth even unto the *other* end of the earth;
8 Thou shalt not consent unto him, nor
hearken unto him; neither shall thine eye
pity him, neither shalt thou spare, neither
shalt thou conceal him:
9 But thou shalt surely kill him; thine hand
shall be first upon him to put him to death,
and afterwards the hand of all the people.
10 And thou shalt stone him with stones,
that he die; because he hath sought to thrust
thee away from the LORD thy God, which
brought thee out of the land of Egypt, from
the house of bondage.
11 And all Israel shall hear, and fear, and
shall do no more any such wickedness as
this is among you.
12 ¶ If thou shalt hear *say* in one of thy
cities, which the LORD thy God hath given
thee to dwell there, saying,
13 *Certain* men, the children of Belial, are
gone out from among you, and have withdrawn the inhabitants of their city, saying,
Let us go and serve other gods, which ye
have not known;
14 Then shalt thou inquire, and make search,
and ask diligently; and, behold, *if it be* truth,
and the thing certain, *that* such abomination
is wrought among you;
15 Thou shalt surely smite the inhabitants
of that city with the edge of the sword,
destroying it utterly, and all that *is* therein,
and the cattle thereof, with the edge of
the sword.
16 And thou shalt gather all the spoil of it
into the midst of the street thereof, and
shalt burn with fire the city, and all the spoil
thereof every whit, for the LORD thy God:
and it shall be an heap for ever; it shall not
be built again.
17 And there shall cleave nought of the
cursed thing to thine hand: that the LORD
may turn from the fierceness of his anger,
and shew thee mercy, and have compassion
upon thee, and multiply thee, as he hath
sworn unto thy fathers;
18 When thou shalt hearken to the voice
of the LORD thy God, to keep all his commandments which I command thee this
day, to do *that which is* right in the eyes of
the LORD thy God.

Deuteronomy 14

1 Ye *are* the children of the LORD your God:
ye shall not cut yourselves, nor make any
baldness between your eyes for the dead.
2 For thou *art* an holy people unto the LORD
thy God, and the LORD hath chosen thee to
be a peculiar people unto himself, above all
the nations that *are* upon the earth.
3 ¶ Thou shalt not eat any abominable thing.
4 These *are* the beasts which ye shall eat:
the ox, the sheep, and the goat,
5 The hart, and the roebuck, and the fallow
deer, and the wild goat, and the pygarg, and
the wild ox, and the chamois.
6 And every beast that parteth the hoof,
and cleaveth the cleft into two claws, *and*
cheweth the cud among the beasts, that
ye shall eat.
7 Nevertheless these ye shall not eat of
them that chew the cud, or of them that
divide the cloven hoof; *as* the camel, and
the hare, and the coney: for they chew the
cud, but divide not the hoof; *therefore* they
are unclean unto you.
8 And the swine, because it divideth the
hoof, yet cheweth not the cud, it *is* unclean
unto you: ye shall not eat of their flesh, nor
touch their dead carcase.
9 ¶ These ye shall eat of all that *are* in the
waters: all that have fins and scales shall
ye eat:
10 And whatsoever hath not fins and scales
ye may not eat; it *is* unclean unto you.
11 ¶ *Of* all clean birds ye shall eat.
12 But these *are they* of which ye shall not

eat: the eagle, and the ossifrage, and the
ospray,
13 And the glede, and the kite, and the vulture after his kind,
14 And every raven after his kind,
15 And the owl, and the night hawk, and
the cuckow, and the hawk after his kind,
16 The little owl, and the great owl, and
the swan,
17 And the pelican, and the gier eagle, and
the cormorant,
18 And the stork, and the heron after her
kind, and the lapwing, and the bat.
19 And every creeping thing that flieth *is*
unclean unto you: they shall not be eaten.
20 *But of* all clean fowls ye may eat.
21 ¶ Ye shall not eat *of* any thing that dieth
of itself: thou shalt give it unto the stranger
that *is* in thy gates, that he may eat it; or
thou mayest sell it unto an alien: for thou *art*
an holy people unto the LORD thy God. Thou
shalt not seethe a kid in his mother's milk.
22 Thou shalt truly tithe all the increase
of thy seed, that the field bringeth forth
year by year.
23 And thou shalt eat before the LORD thy
God, in the place which he shall choose to
place his name there, the tithe of thy corn, of
thy wine, and of thine oil, and the firstlings
of thy herds and of thy flocks; that thou mayest learn to fear the LORD thy God always.
24 And if the way be too long for thee, so
that thou art not able to carry it; *or* if the
place be too far from thee, which the LORD
thy God shall choose to set his name there,
when the LORD thy God hath blessed thee:
25 Then shalt thou turn *it* into money, and
bind up the money in thine hand, and shalt
go unto the place which the LORD thy God
shall choose:
26 And thou shalt bestow that money for
whatsoever thy soul lusteth after, for oxen,
or for sheep, or for wine, or for strong
drink, or for whatsoever thy soul desireth:
and thou shalt eat there before the LORD
thy God, and thou shalt rejoice, thou, and
thine household,
27 And the Levite that *is* within thy gates;
thou shalt not forsake him; for he hath no
part nor inheritance with thee.
28 ¶ At the end of three years thou shalt
bring forth all the tithe of thine increase
the same year, and shalt lay *it* up within
thy gates:
29 And the Levite, (because he hath no part
nor inheritance with thee,) and the stranger,
and the fatherless, and the widow, which
are within thy gates, shall come, and shall
eat and be satisfied; that the LORD thy God
may bless thee in all the work of thine hand
which thou doest.

Deuteronomy 15

1 At the end of *every* seven years thou shalt
make a release.
2 And this *is* the manner of the release:
Every creditor that lendeth *ought* unto his
neighbour shall release *it;* he shall not exact
it of his neighbour, or of his brother; because
it is called the LORD's release.
3 Of a foreigner thou mayest exact *it again:*
but *that* which is thine with thy brother thine
hand shall release;
4 Save when there shall be no poor among
you; for the LORD shall greatly bless thee in
the land which the LORD thy God giveth thee
for an inheritance to possess it:
5 Only if thou carefully hearken unto the
voice of the LORD thy God, to observe to do
all these commandments which I command
thee this day.
6 For the LORD thy God blesseth thee, as
he promised thee: and thou shalt lend unto
many nations, but thou shalt not borrow;
and thou shalt reign over many nations, but
they shall not reign over thee.
7 ¶ If there be among you a poor man of
one of thy brethren within any of thy gates
in thy land which the LORD thy God giveth
thee, thou shalt not harden thine heart,
nor shut thine hand from thy poor brother:
8 But thou shalt open thine hand wide unto
him, and shalt surely lend him sufficient for
his need, *in that* which he wanteth.
9 Beware that there be not a thought in thy
wicked heart, saying, The seventh year, the
year of release, is at hand; and thine eye
be evil against thy poor brother, and thou
givest him nought; and he cry unto the LORD
against thee, and it be sin unto thee.
10 Thou shalt surely give him, and thine
heart shall not be grieved when thou givest
unto him: because that for this thing the
LORD thy God shall bless thee in all thy

works, and in all that thou puttest thine
hand unto.
11 For the poor shall never cease out of
the land: therefore I command thee, saying, Thou shalt open thine hand wide unto
thy brother, to thy poor, and to thy needy,
in thy land.
12 ¶ *And* if thy brother, an Hebrew man, or
an Hebrew woman, be sold unto thee, and
serve thee six years; then in the seventh
year thou shalt let him go free from thee.
13 And when thou sendest him out free
from thee, thou shalt not let him go away
empty:
14 Thou shalt furnish him liberally out of
thy flock, and out of thy floor, and out of
thy winepress: *of that* wherewith the LORD
thy God hath blessed thee thou shalt give
unto him.
15 And thou shalt remember that thou wast
a bondman in the land of Egypt, and the
LORD thy God redeemed thee: therefore I
command thee this thing to day.
16 And it shall be, if he say unto thee, I will
not go away from thee; because he loveth
thee and thine house, because he is well
with thee;
17 Then thou shalt take an aul, and thrust *it*
through his ear unto the door, and he shall
be thy servant for ever. And also unto thy
maidservant thou shalt do likewise.
18 It shall not seem hard unto thee, when
thou sendest him away free from thee; for
he hath been worth a double hired servant
to thee, in serving thee six years: and the
LORD thy God shall bless thee in all that
thou doest.
19 ¶ All the firstling males that come of thy
herd and of thy flock thou shalt sanctify
unto the LORD thy God: thou shalt do no
work with the firstling of thy bullock, nor
shear the firstling of thy sheep.
20 Thou shalt eat *it* before the LORD thy
God year by year in the place which the
LORD shall choose, thou and thy household.
21 And if there be *any* blemish therein, *as if
it be* lame, or blind, *or have* any ill blemish,
thou shalt not sacrifice it unto the LORD
thy God.
22 Thou shalt eat it within thy gates: the
unclean and the clean *person shall eat it*
alike, as the roebuck, and as the hart.
23 Only thou shalt not eat the blood thereof;
thou shalt pour it upon the ground as water.

Deuteronomy 16

1 Observe the month of Abib, and keep the
passover unto the LORD thy God: for in the
month of Abib the LORD thy God brought
thee forth out of Egypt by night.
2 Thou shalt therefore sacrifice the passover
unto the LORD thy God, of the flock and
the herd, in the place which the LORD shall
choose to place his name there.
3 Thou shalt eat no leavened bread with it;
seven days shalt thou eat unleavened bread
therewith, *even* the bread of affliction; for
thou camest forth out of the land of Egypt
in haste: that thou mayest remember the
day when thou camest forth out of the land
of Egypt all the days of thy life.
4 And there shall be no leavened bread seen
with thee in all thy coast seven days; neither
shall there *any thing* of the flesh, which thou
sacrificedst the first day at even, remain all
night until the morning.
5 Thou mayest not sacrifice the passover
within any of thy gates, which the LORD thy
God giveth thee:
6 But at the place which the LORD thy God
shall choose to place his name in, there thou
shalt sacrifice the passover at even, at the
going down of the sun, at the season that
thou camest forth out of Egypt.
7 And thou shalt roast and eat *it* in the place
which the LORD thy God shall choose: and
thou shalt turn in the morning, and go unto
thy tents.
8 Six days thou shalt eat unleavened bread:
and on the seventh day *shall be* a solemn
assembly to the LORD thy God: thou shalt
do no work *therein*.
9 ¶ Seven weeks shalt thou number unto
thee: begin to number the seven weeks
from *such time as* thou beginnest *to put*
the sickle to the corn.
10 And thou shalt keep the feast of weeks
unto the LORD thy God with a tribute of a
freewill offering of thine hand, which thou
shalt give *unto the LORD thy God*, according
as the LORD thy God hath blessed thee:
11 And thou shalt rejoice before the LORD
thy God, thou, and thy son, and thy daughter, and thy manservant, and thy maidservant, and the Levite that *is* within thy

gates, and the stranger, and the fatherless,
and the widow, that *are* among you, in the
place which the LORD thy God hath chosen
to place his name there.
12 And thou shalt remember that thou wast
a bondman in Egypt: and thou shalt observe
and do these statutes.
13 ¶ Thou shalt observe the feast of tabernacles seven days, after that thou hast
gathered in thy corn and thy wine:
14 And thou shalt rejoice in thy feast, thou,
and thy son, and thy daughter, and thy
manservant, and thy maidservant, and the
Levite, the stranger, and the fatherless, and
the widow, that *are* within thy gates.
15 Seven days shalt thou keep a solemn
feast unto the LORD thy God in the place
which the LORD shall choose: because the
LORD thy God shall bless thee in all thine
increase, and in all the works of thine hands,
therefore thou shalt surely rejoice.
16 ¶ Three times in a year shall all thy males
appear before the LORD thy God in the place
which he shall choose; in the feast of unleavened bread, and in the feast of weeks, and
in the feast of tabernacles: and they shall
not appear before the LORD empty:
17 Every man *shall give* as he is able, according to the blessing of the LORD thy God
which he hath given thee.
18 ¶ Judges and officers shalt thou make
thee in all thy gates, which the LORD thy God
giveth thee, throughout thy tribes: and they
shall judge the people with just judgment.
19 Thou shalt not wrest judgment; thou
shalt not respect persons, neither take a gift:
for a gift doth blind the eyes of the wise, and
pervert the words of the righteous.
20 That which is altogether just shalt thou
follow, that thou mayest live, and inherit the
land which the LORD thy God giveth thee.
21 ¶ Thou shalt not plant thee a grove of
any trees near unto the altar of the LORD thy
God, which thou shalt make thee.
22 Neither shalt thou set thee up *any* image;
which the LORD thy God hateth.

Deuteronomy 17

1 Thou shalt not sacrifice unto the LORD
thy God *any* bullock, or sheep, wherein is
blemish, *or* any evilfavouredness: for that
is an abomination unto the LORD thy God.
2 ¶ If there be found among you, within any
of thy gates which the LORD thy God giveth
thee, man or woman, that hath wrought
wickedness in the sight of the LORD thy God,
in transgressing his covenant,
3 And hath gone and served other gods, and
worshipped them, either the sun, or moon,
or any of the host of heaven, which I have
not commanded;
4 And it be told thee, and thou hast heard
of it, and inquired diligently, and, behold,
it be true, *and* the thing certain, *that* such
abomination is wrought in Israel:
5 Then shalt thou bring forth that man or
that woman, which have committed that
wicked thing, unto thy gates, *even* that man
or that woman, and shalt stone them with
stones, till they die.
6 At the mouth of two witnesses, or three
witnesses, shall he that is worthy of death
be put to death; *but* at the mouth of one
witness he shall not be put to death.
7 The hands of the witnesses shall be first
upon him to put him to death, and afterward
the hands of all the people. So thou shalt
put the evil away from among you.
8 ¶ If there arise a matter too hard for thee
in judgment, between blood and blood,
between plea and plea, and between stroke
and stroke, *being* matters of controversy
within thy gates: then shalt thou arise, and
get thee up into the place which the LORD
thy God shall choose;
9 And thou shalt come unto the priests the
Levites, and unto the judge that shall be in
those days, and inquire; and they shall shew
thee the sentence of judgment:
10 And thou shalt do according to the sentence, which they of that place which the
LORD shall choose shall shew thee; and thou
shalt observe to do according to all that they
inform thee:
11 According to the sentence of the law
which they shall teach thee, and according
to the judgment which they shall tell thee,
thou shalt do: thou shalt not decline from
the sentence which they shall shew thee,
to the right hand, nor *to* the left.
12 And the man that will do presumptuously, and will not hearken unto the priest
that standeth to minister there before the
LORD thy God, or unto the judge, even that
man shall die: and thou shalt put away the
evil from Israel.

13 And all the people shall hear, and fear,
and do no more presumptuously.
14 ¶ When thou art come unto the land
which the LORD thy God giveth thee, and
shalt possess it, and shalt dwell therein, and
shalt say, I will set a king over me, like as all
the nations that *are* about me;
15 Thou shalt in any wise set *him* king over
thee, whom the LORD thy God shall choose:
one from among thy brethren shalt thou
set king over thee: thou mayest not set a
stranger over thee, which *is* not thy brother.
16 But he shall not multiply horses to himself, nor cause the people to return to Egypt,
to the end that he should multiply horses:
forasmuch as the LORD hath said unto you,
Ye shall henceforth return no more that way.
17 Neither shall he multiply wives to himself,
that his heart turn not away: neither shall he
greatly multiply to himself silver and gold.
18 And it shall be, when he sitteth upon the
throne of his kingdom, that he shall write
him a copy of this law in a book out of *that
which is* before the priests the Levites:
19 And it shall be with him, and he shall
read therein all the days of his life: that he
may learn to fear the LORD his God, to keep
all the words of this law and these statutes,
to do them:
20 That his heart be not lifted up above his
brethren, and that he turn not aside from
the commandment, *to* the right hand, or *to*
the left: to the end that he may prolong *his*
days in his kingdom, he, and his children, in
the midst of Israel.

Deuteronomy 18

1 The priests the Levites, *and* all the tribe
of Levi, shall have no part nor inheritance
with Israel: they shall eat the offerings of
the LORD made by fire, and his inheritance.
2 Therefore shall they have no inheritance
among their brethren: the LORD *is* their
inheritance, as he hath said unto them.
3 ¶ And this shall be the priest's due from
the people, from them that offer a sacrifice,
whether *it be* ox or sheep; and they shall
give unto the priest the shoulder, and the
two cheeks, and the maw.
4 The firstfruit *also* of thy corn, of thy wine,
and of thine oil, and the first of the fleece
of thy sheep, shalt thou give him.
5 For the LORD thy God hath chosen him out
of all thy tribes, to stand to minister in the
name of the LORD, him and his sons for ever.
6 ¶ And if a Levite come from any of thy
gates out of all Israel, where he sojourned,
and come with all the desire of his mind
unto the place which the LORD shall choose;
7 Then he shall minister in the name of the
LORD his God, as all his brethren the Levites
do, which stand there before the LORD.
8 They shall have like portions to eat, beside
that which cometh of the sale of his patri-
mony.
9 ¶ When thou art come into the land which
the LORD thy God giveth thee, thou shalt
not learn to do after the abominations of
those nations.
10 There shall not be found among you
any one that maketh his son or his daughter to pass through the fire, *or* that useth
divination, *or* an observer of times, or an
enchanter, or a witch,
11 Or a charmer, or a consulter with familiar
spirits, or a wizard, or a necromancer.
12 For all that do these things *are* an abomination unto the LORD: and because of these
abominations the LORD thy God doth drive
them out from before thee.
13 Thou shalt be perfect with the LORD
thy God.
14 For these nations, which thou shalt possess, hearkened unto observers of times,
and unto diviners: but as for thee, the LORD
thy God hath not suffered thee so *to do*.
15 ¶ The LORD thy God will raise up unto
thee a Prophet from the midst of thee, of
thy brethren, like unto me; unto him ye
shall hearken;
16 According to all that thou desiredst of
the LORD thy God in Horeb in the day of the
assembly, saying, Let me not hear again the
voice of the LORD my God, neither let me
see this great fire any more, that I die not.
17 And the LORD said unto me, They have
well *spoken that* which they have spoken.
18 I will raise them up a Prophet from
among their brethren, like unto thee, and
will put my words in his mouth; and he
shall speak unto them all that I shall command him.
19 And it shall come to pass, *that* whosoever will not hearken unto my words which
he shall speak in my name, I will require *it*
of him.

20 But the prophet, which shall presume
to speak a word in my name, which I have
not commanded him to speak, or that shall
speak in the name of other gods, even that
prophet shall die.
21 And if thou say in thine heart, How shall
we know the word which the LORD hath
not spoken?
22 When a prophet speaketh in the name
of the LORD, if the thing follow not, nor
come to pass, that *is* the thing which the
LORD hath not spoken, *but* the prophet hath
spoken it presumptuously: thou shalt not
be afraid of him.

Deuteronomy 19

1 When the LORD thy God hath cut off the
nations, whose land the LORD thy God
giveth thee, and thou succeedest them, and
dwellest in their cities, and in their houses;
2 Thou shalt separate three cities for thee
in the midst of thy land, which the LORD thy
God giveth thee to possess it.
3 Thou shalt prepare thee a way, and divide
the coasts of thy land, which the LORD thy
God giveth thee to inherit, into three parts,
that every slayer may flee thither.
4 ¶ And this *is* the case of the slayer, which
shall flee thither, that he may live: Whoso
killeth his neighbour ignorantly, whom he
hated not in time past;
5 As when a man goeth into the wood with
his neighbour to hew wood, and his hand
fetcheth a stroke with the axe to cut down
the tree, and the head slippeth from the
helve, and lighteth upon his neighbour,
that he die; he shall flee unto one of those
cities, and live:
6 Lest the avenger of the blood pursue the
slayer, while his heart is hot, and overtake
him, because the way is long, and slay
him; whereas he *was* not worthy of death,
inasmuch as he hated him not in time past.
7 Wherefore I command thee, saying, Thou
shalt separate three cities for thee.
8 And if the LORD thy God enlarge thy coast,
as he hath sworn unto thy fathers, and give
thee all the land which he promised to give
unto thy fathers;
9 If thou shalt keep all these commandments
to do them, which I command thee this day,
to love the LORD thy God, and to walk ever
in his ways; then shalt thou add three cities
more for thee, beside these three:
10 That innocent blood be not shed in thy
land, which the LORD thy God giveth thee *for*
an inheritance, and *so* blood be upon thee.
11 ¶ But if any man hate his neighbour, and
lie in wait for him, and rise up against him,
and smite him mortally that he die, and
fleeth into one of these cities:
12 Then the elders of his city shall send
and fetch him thence, and deliver him into
the hand of the avenger of blood, that he
may die.
13 Thine eye shall not pity him, but thou
shalt put away *the guilt of* innocent blood
from Israel, that it may go well with thee.
14 ¶ Thou shalt not remove thy neighbour's
landmark, which they of old time have set in
thine inheritance, which thou shalt inherit
in the land that the LORD thy God giveth
thee to possess it.
15 ¶ One witness shall not rise up against
a man for any iniquity, or for any sin, in any
sin that he sinneth: at the mouth of two witnesses, or at the mouth of three witnesses,
shall the matter be established.
16 ¶ If a false witness rise up against any
man to testify against him *that which is*
wrong;
17 Then both the men, between whom the
controversy *is*, shall stand before the LORD,
before the priests and the judges, which
shall be in those days;
18 And the judges shall make diligent inquisition: and, behold, *if* the witness *be* a false
witness, *and* hath testified falsely against
his brother;
19 Then shall ye do unto him, as he had
thought to have done unto his brother: so
shalt thou put the evil away from among
you.
20 And those which remain shall hear, and
fear, and shall henceforth commit no more
any such evil among you.
21 And thine eye shall not pity; *but* life *shall*
go for life, eye for eye, tooth for tooth, hand
for hand, foot for foot.

Deuteronomy 20

1 When thou goest out to battle against
thine enemies, and seest horses, and chariots, *and* a people more than thou, be not
afraid of them: for the LORD thy God *is* with

thee, which brought thee up out of the land
of Egypt.
2 And it shall be, when ye are come nigh unto
the battle, that the priest shall approach and
speak unto the people,
3 And shall say unto them, Hear, O Israel, ye
approach this day unto battle against your
enemies: let not your hearts faint, fear not,
and do not tremble, neither be ye terrified
because of them;
4 For the LORD your God *is* he that goeth
with you, to fight for you against your enemies, to save you.
5 ¶ And the officers shall speak unto the
people, saying, What man *is there* that hath
built a new house, and hath not dedicated
it? let him go and return to his house, lest
he die in the battle, and another man dedicate it.
6 And what man *is he* that hath planted
a vineyard, and hath not *yet* eaten of it?
let him *also* go and return unto his house,
lest he die in the battle, and another man
eat of it.
7 And what man *is there* that hath betrothed
a wife, and hath not taken her? let him go
and return unto his house, lest he die in the
battle, and another man take her.
8 And the officers shall speak further unto
the people, and they shall say, What man
is there that is fearful and fainthearted? let
him go and return unto his house, lest his
brethren's heart faint as well as his heart.
9 And it shall be, when the officers have
made an end of speaking unto the people,
that they shall make captains of the armies
to lead the people.
10 ¶ When thou comest nigh unto a city to
fight against it, then proclaim peace unto it.
11 And it shall be, if it make thee answer
of peace, and open unto thee, then it shall
be, *that* all the people *that is* found therein
shall be tributaries unto thee, and they shall
serve thee.
12 And if it will make no peace with thee,
but will make war against thee, then thou
shalt besiege it:
13 And when the LORD thy God hath delivered it into thine hands, thou shalt smite
every male thereof with the edge of the
sword:
14 But the women, and the little ones,
and the cattle, and all that is in the city,
even all the spoil thereof, shalt thou take
unto thyself; and thou shalt eat the spoil
of thine enemies, which the LORD thy God
hath given thee.
15 Thus shalt thou do unto all the cities
which are very far off from thee, which *are*
not of the cities of these nations.
16 But of the cities of these people, which
the LORD thy God doth give thee *for* an
inheritance, thou shalt save alive nothing
that breatheth:
17 But thou shalt utterly destroy them;
namely, the Hittites, and the Amorites, the
Canaanites, and the Perizzites, the Hivites,
and the Jebusites; as the LORD thy God hath
commanded thee:
18 That they teach you not to do after all
their abominations, which they have done
unto their gods; so should ye sin against the
LORD your God.
19 ¶ When thou shalt besiege a city a long
time, in making war against it to take it, thou
shalt not destroy the trees thereof by forcing
an axe against them: for thou mayest eat of
them, and thou shalt not cut them down (for
the tree of the field *is* man's *life*) to employ
them in the siege:
20 Only the trees which thou knowest
that they *be* not trees for meat, thou shalt
destroy and cut them down; and thou shalt
build bulwarks against the city that maketh
war with thee, until it be subdued.

Deuteronomy 21

1 If *one* be found slain in the land which
the LORD thy God giveth thee to possess it,
lying in the field, *and* it be not known who
hath slain him:
2 Then thy elders and thy judges shall come
forth, and they shall measure unto the cities
which *are* round about him that is slain:
3 And it shall be, *that* the city *which is* next
unto the slain man, even the elders of that
city shall take an heifer, which hath not
been wrought with, *and* which hath not
drawn in the yoke;
4 And the elders of that city shall bring down
the heifer unto a rough valley, which is neither eared nor sown, and shall strike off the
heifer's neck there in the valley:
5 And the priests the sons of Levi shall come
near; for them the LORD thy God hath chosen to minister unto him, and to bless in the

name of the LORD; and by their word shall every controversy and every stroke be *tried:*

6 And all the elders of that city, *that are* next unto the slain *man*, shall wash their hands over the heifer that is beheaded in the valley:

7 And they shall answer and say, Our hands have not shed this blood, neither have our eyes seen *it*.

8 Be merciful, O LORD, unto thy people Israel, whom thou hast redeemed, and lay not innocent blood unto thy people of Israel's charge. And the blood shall be forgiven them.

9 So shalt thou put away the *guilt of* innocent blood from among you, when thou shalt do *that which is* right in the sight of the LORD.

10 ¶ When thou goest forth to war against thine enemies, and the LORD thy God hath delivered them into thine hands, and thou hast taken them captive,

11 And seest among the captives a beautiful woman, and hast a desire unto her, that thou wouldest have her to thy wife;

12 Then thou shalt bring her home to thine house; and she shall shave her head, and pare her nails;

13 And she shall put the raiment of her captivity from off her, and shall remain in thine house, and bewail her father and her mother a full month: and after that thou shalt go in unto her, and be her husband, and she shall be thy wife.

14 And it shall be, if thou have no delight in her, then thou shalt let her go whither she will; but thou shalt not sell her at all for money, thou shalt not make merchandise of her, because thou hast humbled her.

15 ¶ If a man have two wives, one beloved, and another hated, and they have born him children, *both* the beloved and the hated; and *if* the firstborn son be hers that was hated:

16 Then it shall be, when he maketh his sons to inherit *that* which he hath, *that* he may not make the son of the beloved firstborn before the son of the hated, *which is indeed* the firstborn:

17 But he shall acknowledge the son of the hated *for* the firstborn, by giving him a double portion of all that he hath: for he *is* the beginning of his strength; the right of the firstborn *is* his.

18 ¶ If a man have a stubborn and rebellious son, which will not obey the voice of his father, or the voice of his mother, and *that*, when they have chastened him, will not hearken unto them:

19 Then shall his father and his mother lay hold on him, and bring him out unto the elders of his city, and unto the gate of his place;

20 And they shall say unto the elders of his city, This our son *is* stubborn and rebellious, he will not obey our voice; *he is* a glutton, and a drunkard.

21 And all the men of his city shall stone him with stones, that he die: so shalt thou put evil away from among you; and all Israel shall hear, and fear.

22 ¶ And if a man have committed a sin worthy of death, and he be to be put to death, and thou hang him on a tree:

23 His body shall not remain all night upon the tree, but thou shalt in any wise bury him that day; (for he that is hanged *is* accursed of God;) that thy land be not defiled, which the LORD thy God giveth thee *for* an inheritance.

Deuteronomy 22

1 Thou shalt not see thy brother's ox or his sheep go astray, and hide thyself from them: thou shalt in any case bring them again unto thy brother.

2 And if thy brother *be* not nigh unto thee, or if thou know him not, then thou shalt bring it unto thine own house, and it shall be with thee until thy brother seek after it, and thou shalt restore it to him again.

3 In like manner shalt thou do with his ass; and so shalt thou do with his raiment; and with all lost thing of thy brother's, which he hath lost, and thou hast found, shalt thou do likewise: thou mayest not hide thyself.

4 ¶ Thou shalt not see thy brother's ass or his ox fall down by the way, and hide thyself from them: thou shalt surely help him to lift *them* up again.

5 ¶ The woman shall not wear that which pertaineth unto a man, neither shall a man put on a woman's garment: for all that do so *are* abomination unto the LORD thy God.

6 ¶ If a bird's nest chance to be before thee in the way in any tree, or on the ground,

whether they be young ones, or eggs, and
the dam sitting upon the young, or upon
the eggs, thou shalt not take the dam with
the young:
7 *But* thou shalt in any wise let the dam go,
and take the young to thee; that it may be
well with thee, and *that* thou mayest prolong *thy* days.
8 ¶ When thou buildest a new house, then
thou shalt make a battlement for thy roof,
that thou bring not blood upon thine house,
if any man fall from thence.
9 ¶ Thou shalt not sow thy vineyard with
divers seeds: lest the fruit of thy seed which
thou hast sown, and the fruit of thy vineyard, be defiled.
10 ¶ Thou shalt not plow with an ox and an
ass together.
11 ¶ Thou shalt not wear a garment of divers sorts, *as* of woollen and linen together.
12 ¶ Thou shalt make thee fringes upon the
four quarters of thy vesture, wherewith thou
coverest *thyself*.
13 ¶ If any man take a wife, and go in unto
her, and hate her,
14 And give occasions of speech against her,
and bring up an evil name upon her, and say,
I took this woman, and when I came to her,
I found her not a maid:
15 Then shall the father of the damsel, and
her mother, take and bring forth *the tokens
of* the damsel's virginity unto the elders of
the city in the gate:
16 And the damsel's father shall say unto the
elders, I gave my daughter unto this man to
wife, and he hateth her;
17 And, lo, he hath given occasions of
speech *against her*, saying, I found not thy
daughter a maid; and yet these *are the
tokens of* my daughter's virginity. And they
shall spread the cloth before the elders of
the city.
18 And the elders of that city shall take that
man and chastise him;
19 And they shall amerce him in an hundred *shekels* of silver, and give *them* unto
the father of the damsel, because he hath
brought up an evil name upon a virgin of
Israel: and she shall be his wife; he may not
put her away all his days.
20 But if this thing be true, *and the tokens
of* virginity be not found for the damsel:
21 Then they shall bring out the damsel to
the door of her father's house, and the men
of her city shall stone her with stones that
she die: because she hath wrought folly
in Israel, to play the whore in her father's
house: so shalt thou put evil away from
among you.
22 ¶ If a man be found lying with a woman
married to an husband, then they shall both
of them die, *both* the man that lay with the
woman, and the woman: so shalt thou put
away evil from Israel.
23 ¶ If a damsel *that is* a virgin be betrothed
unto an husband, and a man find her in the
city, and lie with her;
24 Then ye shall bring them both out unto
the gate of that city, and ye shall stone
them with stones that they die; the damsel,
because she cried not, *being* in the city;
and the man, because he hath humbled his
neighbour's wife: so thou shalt put away evil
from among you.
25 ¶ But if a man find a betrothed damsel
in the field, and the man force her, and lie
with her: then the man only that lay with
her shall die:
26 But unto the damsel thou shalt do nothing; *there is* in the damsel no sin *worthy* of
death: for as when a man riseth against
his neighbour, and slayeth him, even so *is*
this matter:
27 For he found her in the field, *and* the
betrothed damsel cried, and *there was*
none to save her.
28 ¶ If a man find a damsel *that is* a virgin,
which is not betrothed, and lay hold on her,
and lie with her, and they be found;
29 Then the man that lay with her shall
give unto the damsel's father fifty *shekels*
of silver, and she shall be his wife; because
he hath humbled her, he may not put her
away all his days.
30 ¶ A man shall not take his father's wife,
nor discover his father's skirt.

Deuteronomy 23

1 He that is wounded in the stones, or hath
his privy member cut off, shall not enter into
the congregation of the LORD.
2 A bastard shall not enter into the congregation of the LORD; even to his tenth
generation shall he not enter into the congregation of the LORD.
3 An Ammonite or Moabite shall not enter

into the congregation of the LORD; even to
their tenth generation shall they not enter
into the congregation of the LORD for ever:
4 Because they met you not with bread and
with water in the way, when ye came forth
out of Egypt; and because they hired against
thee Balaam the son of Beor of Pethor of
Mesopotamia, to curse thee.
5 Nevertheless the LORD thy God would not
hearken unto Balaam; but the LORD thy God
turned the curse into a blessing unto thee,
because the LORD thy God loved thee.
6 Thou shalt not seek their peace nor their
prosperity all thy days for ever.
7 ¶ Thou shalt not abhor an Edomite; for
he *is* thy brother: thou shalt not abhor an
Egyptian; because thou wast a stranger in
his land.
8 The children that are begotten of them
shall enter into the congregation of the
LORD in their third generation.
9 ¶ When the host goeth forth against
thine enemies, then keep thee from every
wicked thing.
10 ¶ If there be among you any man, that
is not clean by reason of uncleanness that
chanceth him by night, then shall he go
abroad out of the camp, he shall not come
within the camp:
11 But it shall be, when evening cometh
on, he shall wash *himself* with water: and
when the sun is down, he shall come into
the camp *again*.
12 ¶ Thou shalt have a place also without
the camp, whither thou shalt go forth
abroad:
13 And thou shalt have a paddle upon thy
weapon; and it shall be, when thou wilt ease
thyself abroad, thou shalt dig therewith,
and shalt turn back and cover that which
cometh from thee:
14 For the LORD thy God walketh in the
midst of thy camp, to deliver thee, and to
give up thine enemies before thee; therefore shall thy camp be holy: that he see
no unclean thing in thee, and turn away
from thee.
15 ¶ Thou shalt not deliver unto his master the servant which is escaped from his
master unto thee:
16 He shall dwell with thee, *even* among
you, in that place which he shall choose in
one of thy gates, where it liketh him best:
thou shalt not oppress him.
17 ¶ There shall be no whore of the daughters of Israel, nor a sodomite of the sons
of Israel.
18 Thou shalt not bring the hire of a whore,
or the price of a dog, into the house of the
LORD thy God for any vow: for even both
these *are* abomination unto the LORD thy
God.
19 ¶ Thou shalt not lend upon usury to thy
brother; usury of money, usury of victuals,
usury of any thing that is lent upon usury:
20 Unto a stranger thou mayest lend upon
usury; but unto thy brother thou shalt not
lend upon usury: that the LORD thy God
may bless thee in all that thou settest thine
hand to in the land whither thou goest to
possess it.
21 ¶ When thou shalt vow a vow unto the
LORD thy God, thou shalt not slack to pay it:
for the LORD thy God will surely require it of
thee; and it would be sin in thee.
22 But if thou shalt forbear to vow, it shall
be no sin in thee.
23 That which is gone out of thy lips thou
shalt keep and perform; *even* a freewill
offering, according as thou hast vowed unto
the LORD thy God, which thou hast promised
with thy mouth.
24 ¶ When thou comest into thy neighbour's
vineyard, then thou mayest eat grapes thy
fill at thine own pleasure; but thou shalt not
put *any* in thy vessel.
25 When thou comest into the standing
corn of thy neighbour, then thou mayest
pluck the ears with thine hand; but thou
shalt not move a sickle unto thy neighbour's
standing corn.

Deuteronomy 24

1 When a man hath taken a wife, and married her, and it come to pass that she find
no favour in his eyes, because he hath found
some uncleanness in her: then let him write
her a bill of divorcement, and give *it* in her
hand, and send her out of his house.
2 And when she is departed out of his house,
she may go and be another man's *wife*.
3 And *if* the latter husband hate her, and
write her a bill of divorcement, and giveth
it in her hand, and sendeth her out of his

house; or if the latter husband die, which
took her *to be* his wife;
4 Her former husband, which sent her away,
may not take her again to be his wife, after
that she is defiled; for that *is* abomination
before the LORD: and thou shalt not cause
the land to sin, which the LORD thy God
giveth thee *for* an inheritance.
5 ¶ When a man hath taken a new wife, he
shall not go out to war, neither shall he be
charged with any business: *but* he shall be
free at home one year, and shall cheer up
his wife which he hath taken.
6 ¶ No man shall take the nether or the
upper millstone to pledge: for he taketh *a*
man's life to pledge.
7 ¶ If a man be found stealing any of his
brethren of the children of Israel, and
maketh merchandise of him, or selleth him;
then that thief shall die; and thou shalt put
evil away from among you.
8 ¶ Take heed in the plague of leprosy, that
thou observe diligently, and do according to
all that the priests the Levites shall teach
you: as I commanded them, *so* ye shall
observe to do.
9 Remember what the LORD thy God did
unto Miriam by the way, after that ye were
come forth out of Egypt.
10 ¶ When thou dost lend thy brother any
thing, thou shalt not go into his house to
fetch his pledge.
11 Thou shalt stand abroad, and the man
to whom thou dost lend shall bring out the
pledge abroad unto thee.
12 And if the man *be* poor, thou shalt not
sleep with his pledge:
13 In any case thou shalt deliver him the
pledge again when the sun goeth down,
that he may sleep in his own raiment, and
bless thee: and it shall be righteousness unto
thee before the LORD thy God.
14 ¶ Thou shalt not oppress an hired servant
that is poor and needy, *whether he be* of thy
brethren, or of thy strangers that *are* in thy
land within thy gates:
15 At his day thou shalt give *him* his hire,
neither shall the sun go down upon it; for
he *is* poor, and setteth his heart upon it:
lest he cry against thee unto the LORD, and
it be sin unto thee.
16 The fathers shall not be put to death for
the children, neither shall the children be
put to death for the fathers: every man shall
be put to death for his own sin.
17 ¶ Thou shalt not pervert the judgment
of the stranger, *nor* of the fatherless; nor
take a widow's raiment to pledge:
18 But thou shalt remember that thou wast
a bondman in Egypt, and the LORD thy God
redeemed thee thence: therefore I command thee to do this thing.
19 ¶ When thou cuttest down thine harvest
in thy field, and hast forgot a sheaf in the
field, thou shalt not go again to fetch it: it
shall be for the stranger, for the fatherless,
and for the widow: that the LORD thy God
may bless thee in all the work of thine hands.
20 When thou beatest thine olive tree, thou
shalt not go over the boughs again: it shall
be for the stranger, for the fatherless, and
for the widow.
21 When thou gatherest the grapes of thy
vineyard, thou shalt not glean *it* afterward:
it shall be for the stranger, for the fatherless,
and for the widow.
22 And thou shalt remember that thou wast
a bondman in the land of Egypt: therefore I
command thee to do this thing.

Deuteronomy 25

1 If there be a controversy between men,
and they come unto judgment, that *the*
judges may judge them; then they shall justify the righteous, and condemn the wicked.
2 And it shall be, if the wicked man *be*
worthy to be beaten, that the judge shall
cause him to lie down, and to be beaten
before his face, according to his fault, by a
certain number.
3 Forty stripes he may give him, *and* not
exceed: lest, *if* he should exceed, and beat
him above these with many stripes, then thy
brother should seem vile unto thee.
4 ¶ Thou shalt not muzzle the ox when he
treadeth out *the corn*.
5 ¶ If brethren dwell together, and one of
them die, and have no child, the wife of
the dead shall not marry without unto a
stranger: her husband's brother shall go in
unto her, and take her to him to wife, and
perform the duty of an husband's brother
unto her.
6 And it shall be, *that* the firstborn which
she beareth shall succeed in the name of his

brother *which is* dead, that his name be not
put out of Israel.
7 And if the man like not to take his brother's
wife, then let his brother's wife go up to the
gate unto the elders, and say, My husband's
brother refuseth to raise up unto his brother
a name in Israel, he will not perform the
duty of my husband's brother.
8 Then the elders of his city shall call him,
and speak unto him: and *if* he stand *to it*,
and say, I like not to take her;
9 Then shall his brother's wife come unto
him in the presence of the elders, and loose
his shoe from off his foot, and spit in his
face, and shall answer and say, So shall it
be done unto that man that will not build
up his brother's house.
10 And his name shall be called in Israel,
The house of him that hath his shoe loosed.
11 ¶ When men strive together one with
another, and the wife of the one draweth
near for to deliver her husband out of the
hand of him that smiteth him, and putteth
forth her hand, and taketh him by the
secrets:
12 Then thou shalt cut off her hand, thine
eye shall not pity *her*.
13 ¶ Thou shalt not have in thy bag divers
weights, a great and a small.
14 Thou shalt not have in thine house divers
measures, a great and a small.
15 *But* thou shalt have a perfect and just
weight, a perfect and just measure shalt
thou have: that thy days may be length-
ened in the land which the LORD thy God
giveth thee.
16 For all that do such things, *and* all that
do unrighteously, *are* an abomination unto
the LORD thy God.
17 ¶ Remember what Amalek did unto thee
by the way, when ye were come forth out
of Egypt;
18 How he met thee by the way, and smote
the hindmost of thee, *even* all *that were*
feeble behind thee, when thou *wast* faint
and weary; and he feared not God.
19 Therefore it shall be, when the LORD
thy God hath given thee rest from all thine
enemies round about, in the land which
the LORD thy God giveth thee *for* an inheritance to possess it, *that* thou shalt blot out
the remembrance of Amalek from under
heaven; thou shalt not forget *it*.

Deuteronomy 26

1 And it shall be, when thou *art* come in
unto the land which the LORD thy God giveth
thee *for* an inheritance, and possessest it,
and dwellest therein;
2 That thou shalt take of the first of all the
fruit of the earth, which thou shalt bring
of thy land that the LORD thy God giveth
thee, and shalt put *it* in a basket, and shalt
go unto the place which the LORD thy God
shall choose to place his name there.
3 And thou shalt go unto the priest that
shall be in those days, and say unto him,
I profess this day unto the LORD thy God,
that I am come unto the country which the
LORD sware unto our fathers for to give us.
4 And the priest shall take the basket out
of thine hand, and set it down before the
altar of the LORD thy God.
5 And thou shalt speak and say before the
LORD thy God, A Syrian ready to perish *was*
my father, and he went down into Egypt, and
sojourned there with a few, and became
there a nation, great, mighty, and populous:
6 And the Egyptians evil entreated us, and
afflicted us, and laid upon us hard bondage:
7 And when we cried unto the LORD God of
our fathers, the LORD heard our voice, and
looked on our affliction, and our labour, and
our oppression:
8 And the LORD brought us forth out of
Egypt with a mighty hand, and with an outstretched arm, and with great terribleness,
and with signs, and with wonders:
9 And he hath brought us into this place,
and hath given us this land, *even* a land that
floweth with milk and honey.
10 And now, behold, I have brought the
firstfruits of the land, which thou, O LORD,
hast given me. And thou shalt set it before
the LORD thy God, and worship before the
LORD thy God:
11 And thou shalt rejoice in every good *thing*
which the LORD thy God hath given unto
thee, and unto thine house, thou, and the
Levite, and the stranger that *is* among you.
12 ¶ When thou hast made an end of tithing all the tithes of thine increase the third
year, *which is* the year of tithing, and hast
given *it* unto the Levite, the stranger, the
fatherless, and the widow, that they may
eat within thy gates, and be filled;
13 Then thou shalt say before the LORD

thy God, I have brought away the hallowed things out of *mine* house, and also
have given them unto the Levite, and unto
the stranger, to the fatherless, and to the
widow, according to all thy commandments
which thou hast commanded me: I have not
transgressed thy commandments, neither
have I forgotten *them:*
14 I have not eaten thereof in my mourning,
neither have I taken away *ought* thereof for
any unclean *use*, nor given *ought* thereof for
the dead: *but* I have hearkened to the voice
of the LORD my God, *and* have done according to all that thou hast commanded me.
15 Look down from thy holy habitation,
from heaven, and bless thy people Israel,
and the land which thou hast given us, as
thou swarest unto our fathers, a land that
floweth with milk and honey.
16 ¶ This day the LORD thy God hath commanded thee to do these statutes and
judgments: thou shalt therefore keep and
do them with all thine heart, and with all
thy soul.
17 Thou hast avouched the LORD this day
to be thy God, and to walk in his ways, and
to keep his statutes, and his commandments, and his judgments, and to hearken
unto his voice:
18 And the LORD hath avouched thee this
day to be his peculiar people, as he hath
promised thee, and that *thou* shouldest
keep all his commandments;
19 And to make thee high above all nations
which he hath made, in praise, and in name,
and in honour; and that thou mayest be an
holy people unto the LORD thy God, as he
hath spoken.

Deuteronomy 27

1 And Moses with the elders of Israel commanded the people, saying, Keep all the
commandments which I command you
this day.
2 And it shall be on the day when ye shall
pass over Jordan unto the land which the
LORD thy God giveth thee, that thou shalt
set thee up great stones, and plaister them
with plaister:
3 And thou shalt write upon them all the
words of this law, when thou art passed
over, that thou mayest go in unto the land
which the LORD thy God giveth thee, a land
that floweth with milk and honey; as the
LORD God of thy fathers hath promised thee.
4 Therefore it shall be when ye be gone
over Jordan, *that* ye shall set up these
stones, which I command you this day, in
mount Ebal, and thou shalt plaister them
with plaister.
5 And there shalt thou build an altar unto
the LORD thy God, an altar of stones: thou
shalt not lift up *any* iron *tool* upon them.
6 Thou shalt build the altar of the LORD thy
God of whole stones: and thou shalt offer
burnt offerings thereon unto the LORD thy
God:
7 And thou shalt offer peace offerings, and
shalt eat there, and rejoice before the LORD
thy God.
8 And thou shalt write upon the stones all
the words of this law very plainly.
9 ¶ And Moses and the priests the Levites
spake unto all Israel, saying, Take heed, and
hearken, O Israel; this day thou art become
the people of the LORD thy God.
10 Thou shalt therefore obey the voice of
the LORD thy God, and do his commandments and his statutes, which I command
thee this day.
11 ¶ And Moses charged the people the
same day, saying,
12 These shall stand upon mount Gerizim
to bless the people, when ye are come over
Jordan; Simeon, and Levi, and Judah, and
Issachar, and Joseph, and Benjamin:
13 And these shall stand upon mount Ebal
to curse; Reuben, Gad, and Asher, and Zebulun, Dan, and Naphtali.
14 ¶ And the Levites shall speak, and say
unto all the men of Israel with a loud voice,
15 Cursed *be* the man that maketh *any*
graven or molten image, an abomination
unto the LORD, the work of the hands of
the craftsman, and putteth *it* in *a* secret
place. And all the people shall answer and
say, Amen.
16 Cursed *be* he that setteth light by his
father or his mother. And all the people
shall say, Amen.
17 Cursed *be* he that removeth his neighbour's landmark. And all the people shall
say, Amen.
18 Cursed *be* he that maketh the blind to
wander out of the way. And all the people
shall say, Amen.

19 Cursed *be* he that perverteth the judgment of the stranger, fatherless, and widow.
And all the people shall say, Amen.
20 Cursed *be* he that lieth with his father's
wife; because he uncovereth his father's
skirt. And all the people shall say, Amen.
21 Cursed *be* he that lieth with any manner
of beast. And all the people shall say, Amen.
22 Cursed *be* he that lieth with his sister, the
daughter of his father, or the daughter of his
mother. And all the people shall say, Amen.
23 Cursed *be* he that lieth with his mother
in law. And all the people shall say, Amen.
24 Cursed *be* he that smiteth his neighbour
secretly. And all the people shall say, Amen.
25 Cursed *be* he that taketh reward to slay
an innocent person. And all the people shall
say, Amen.
26 Cursed *be* he that confirmeth not *all* the
words of this law to do them. And all the
people shall say, Amen.

Deuteronomy 28

1 And it shall come to pass, if thou shalt
hearken diligently unto the voice of the
LORD thy God, to observe *and* to do all his
commandments which I command thee this
day, that the LORD thy God will set thee on
high above all nations of the earth:
2 And all these blessings shall come on thee,
and overtake thee, if thou shalt hearken
unto the voice of the LORD thy God.
3 Blessed *shalt* thou *be* in the city, and
blessed *shalt* thou *be* in the field.
4 Blessed *shall be* the fruit of thy body,
and the fruit of thy ground, and the fruit of
thy cattle, the increase of thy kine, and the
flocks of thy sheep.
5 Blessed *shall be* thy basket and thy store.
6 Blessed *shalt* thou *be* when thou comest
in, and blessed *shalt* thou *be* when thou
goest out.
7 The LORD shall cause thine enemies that
rise up against thee to be smitten before
thy face: they shall come out against thee
one way, and flee before thee seven ways.
8 The LORD shall command the blessing
upon thee in thy storehouses, and in all that
thou settest thine hand unto; and he shall
bless thee in the land which the LORD thy
God giveth thee.
9 The LORD shall establish thee an holy
people unto himself, as he hath sworn unto
thee, if thou shalt keep the commandments
of the LORD thy God, and walk in his ways.
10 And all people of the earth shall see that
thou art called by the name of the LORD; and
they shall be afraid of thee.
11 And the LORD shall make thee plenteous
in goods, in the fruit of thy body, and in
the fruit of thy cattle, and in the fruit of thy
ground, in the land which the LORD sware
unto thy fathers to give thee.
12 The LORD shall open unto thee his good
treasure, the heaven to give the rain unto
thy land in his season, and to bless all the
work of thine hand: and thou shalt lend unto
many nations, and thou shalt not borrow.
13 And the LORD shall make thee the head,
and not the tail; and thou shalt be above
only, and thou shalt not be beneath; if that
thou hearken unto the commandments of
the LORD thy God, which I command thee
this day, to observe and to do *them:*
14 And thou shalt not go aside from any of
the words which I command thee this day,
to the right hand, or *to* the left, to go after
other gods to serve them.
15 ¶ But it shall come to pass, if thou wilt
not hearken unto the voice of the LORD thy
God, to observe to do all his commandments
and his statutes which I command thee this
day; that all these curses shall come upon
thee, and overtake thee:
16 Cursed *shalt* thou *be* in the city, and
cursed *shalt* thou *be* in the field.
17 Cursed *shall be* thy basket and thy store.
18 Cursed *shall be* the fruit of thy body, and
the fruit of thy land, the increase of thy kine,
and the flocks of thy sheep.
19 Cursed *shalt* thou *be* when thou comest
in, and cursed *shalt* thou *be* when thou
goest out.
20 The LORD shall send upon thee cursing,
vexation, and rebuke, in all that thou settest
thine hand unto for to do, until thou be
destroyed, and until thou perish quickly;
because of the wickedness of thy doings,
whereby thou hast forsaken me.
21 The LORD shall make the pestilence
cleave unto thee, until he have consumed
thee from off the land, whither thou goest
to possess it.
22 The LORD shall smite thee with a consumption, and with a fever, and with an
inflammation, and with an extreme burning,

and with the sword, and with blasting, and
with mildew; and they shall pursue thee
until thou perish.
23 And thy heaven that *is* over thy head
shall be brass, and the earth that *is* under
thee *shall be* iron.
24 The LORD shall make the rain of thy land
powder and dust: from heaven shall it come
down upon thee, until thou be destroyed.
25 The LORD shall cause thee to be smitten
before thine enemies: thou shalt go out
one way against them, and flee seven ways
before them: and shalt be removed into all
the kingdoms of the earth.
26 And thy carcase shall be meat unto all
fowls of the air, and unto the beasts of the
earth, and no man shall fray *them* away.
27 The LORD will smite thee with the botch
of Egypt, and with the emerods, and with
the scab, and with the itch, whereof thou
canst not be healed.
28 The LORD shall smite thee with madness,
and blindness, and astonishment of heart:
29 And thou shalt grope at noonday, as the
blind gropeth in darkness, and thou shalt
not prosper in thy ways: and thou shalt be
only oppressed and spoiled evermore, and
no man shall save *thee*.
30 Thou shalt betroth a wife, and another
man shall lie with her: thou shalt build an
house, and thou shalt not dwell therein:
thou shalt plant a vineyard, and shalt not
gather the grapes thereof.
31 Thine ox *shall be* slain before thine eyes,
and thou shalt not eat thereof: thine ass
shall be violently taken away from before
thy face, and shall not be restored to thee:
thy sheep *shall be* given unto thine enemies,
and thou shalt have none to rescue *them*.
32 Thy sons and thy daughters *shall be*
given unto another people, and thine eyes
shall look, and fail *with longing* for them all
the day long: and *there shall be* no might in
thine hand.
33 The fruit of thy land, and all thy labours,
shall a nation which thou knowest not eat
up; and thou shalt be only oppressed and
crushed alway:
34 So that thou shalt be mad for the sight
of thine eyes which thou shalt see.
35 The LORD shall smite thee in the knees,
and in the legs, with a sore botch that cannot be healed, from the sole of thy foot unto
the top of thy head.
36 The LORD shall bring thee, and thy king
which thou shalt set over thee, unto a nation
which neither thou nor thy fathers have
known; and there shalt thou serve other
gods, wood and stone.
37 And thou shalt become an astonishment,
a proverb, and a byword, among all nations
whither the LORD shall lead thee.
38 Thou shalt carry much seed out into the
field, and shalt gather *but* little in; for the
locust shall consume it.
39 Thou shalt plant vineyards, and dress
them, but shalt neither drink *of* the wine,
nor gather *the grapes;* for the worms shall
eat them.
40 Thou shalt have olive trees throughout all
thy coasts, but thou shalt not anoint *thyself*
with the oil; for thine olive shall cast *his fruit*.
41 Thou shalt beget sons and daughters, but
thou shalt not enjoy them; for they shall go
into captivity.
42 All thy trees and fruit of thy land shall
the locust consume.
43 The stranger that *is* within thee shall get
up above thee very high; and thou shalt
come down very low.
44 He shall lend to thee, and thou shalt not
lend to him: he shall be the head, and thou
shalt be the tail.
45 Moreover all these curses shall come
upon thee, and shall pursue thee, and overtake thee, till thou be destroyed; because
thou hearkenedst not unto the voice of the
LORD thy God, to keep his commandments
and his statutes which he commanded thee:
46 And they shall be upon thee for a sign and
for a wonder, and upon thy seed for ever.
47 Because thou servedst not the LORD thy
God with joyfulness, and with gladness of
heart, for the abundance of all *things;*
48 Therefore shalt thou serve thine enemies
which the LORD shall send against thee, in
hunger, and in thirst, and in nakedness,
and in want of all *things:* and he shall put
a yoke of iron upon thy neck, until he have
destroyed thee.
49 The LORD shall bring a nation against thee
from far, from the end of the earth, *as swift*
as the eagle flieth; a nation whose tongue
thou shalt not understand;
50 A nation of fierce countenance, which

shall not regard the person of the old, nor shew favour to the young:

51 And he shall eat the fruit of thy cattle, and the fruit of thy land, until thou be destroyed: which *also* shall not leave thee *either* corn, wine, or oil, *or* the increase of thy kine, or flocks of thy sheep, until he have destroyed thee.

52 And he shall besiege thee in all thy gates, until thy high and fenced walls come down, wherein thou trustedst, throughout all thy land: and he shall besiege thee in all thy gates throughout all thy land, which the LORD thy God hath given thee.

53 And thou shalt eat the fruit of thine own body, the flesh of thy sons and of thy daughters, which the LORD thy God hath given thee, in the siege, and in the straitness, wherewith thine enemies shall distress thee:

54 *So that* the man *that is* tender among you, and very delicate, his eye shall be evil toward his brother, and toward the wife of his bosom, and toward the remnant of his children which he shall leave:

55 So that he will not give to any of them of the flesh of his children whom he shall eat: because he hath nothing left him in the siege, and in the straitness, wherewith thine enemies shall distress thee in all thy gates.

56 The tender and delicate woman among you, which would not adventure to set the sole of her foot upon the ground for delicateness and tenderness, her eye shall be evil toward the husband of her bosom, and toward her son, and toward her daughter,

57 And toward her young one that cometh out from between her feet, and toward her children which she shall bear: for she shall eat them for want of all *things* secretly in the siege and straitness, wherewith thine enemy shall distress thee in thy gates.

58 If thou wilt not observe to do all the words of this law that are written in this book, that thou mayest fear this glorious and fearful name, THE LORD THY GOD;

59 Then the LORD will make thy plagues wonderful, and the plagues of thy seed, *even* great plagues, and of long continuance, and sore sicknesses, and of long continuance.

60 Moreover he will bring upon thee all the diseases of Egypt, which thou wast afraid of; and they shall cleave unto thee.

61 Also every sickness, and every plague, which *is* not written in the book of this law, them will the LORD bring upon thee, until thou be destroyed.

62 And ye shall be left few in number, whereas ye were as the stars of heaven for multitude; because thou wouldest not obey the voice of the LORD thy God.

63 And it shall come to pass, *that* as the LORD rejoiced over you to do you good, and to multiply you; so the LORD will rejoice over you to destroy you, and to bring you to nought; and ye shall be plucked from off the land whither thou goest to possess it.

64 And the LORD shall scatter thee among all people, from the one end of the earth even unto the other; and there thou shalt serve other gods, which neither thou nor thy fathers have known, *even* wood and stone.

65 And among these nations shalt thou find no ease, neither shall the sole of thy foot have rest: but the LORD shall give thee there a trembling heart, and failing of eyes, and sorrow of mind:

66 And thy life shall hang in doubt before thee; and thou shalt fear day and night, and shalt have none assurance of thy life:

67 In the morning thou shalt say, Would God it were even! and at even thou shalt say, Would God it were morning! for the fear of thine heart wherewith thou shalt fear, and for the sight of thine eyes which thou shalt see.

68 And the LORD shall bring thee into Egypt again with ships, by the way whereof I spake unto thee, Thou shalt see it no more again: and there ye shall be sold unto your enemies for bondmen and bondwomen, and no man shall buy *you*.

Deuteronomy 29

1 These *are* the words of the covenant, which the LORD commanded Moses to make with the children of Israel in the land of Moab, beside the covenant which he made with them in Horeb.

2 ¶ And Moses called unto all Israel, and said unto them, Ye have seen all that the LORD did before your eyes in the land of Egypt unto Pharaoh, and unto all his servants, and unto all his land;

3 The great temptations which thine eyes have seen, the signs, and those great miracles:

4 Yet the LORD hath not given you an heart
to perceive, and eyes to see, and ears to
hear, unto this day.
5 And I have led you forty years in the wilderness: your clothes are not waxen old
upon you, and thy shoe is not waxen old
upon thy foot.
6 Ye have not eaten bread, neither have ye
drunk wine or strong drink: that ye might
know that I *am* the LORD your God.
7 And when ye came unto this place, Sihon
the king of Heshbon, and Og the king of
Bashan, came out against us unto battle,
and we smote them:
8 And we took their land, and gave it for an
inheritance unto the Reubenites, and to the
Gadites, and to the half tribe of Manasseh.
9 Keep therefore the words of this covenant, and do them, that ye may prosper in
all that ye do.
10 ¶ Ye stand this day all of you before the
LORD your God; your captains of your tribes,
your elders, and your officers, *with* all the
men of Israel,
11 Your little ones, your wives, and thy
stranger that *is* in thy camp, from the hewer
of thy wood unto the drawer of thy water:
12 That thou shouldest enter into covenant
with the LORD thy God, and into his oath,
which the LORD thy God maketh with thee
this day:
13 That he may establish thee to day for a
people unto himself, and *that* he may be
unto thee a God, as he hath said unto thee,
and as he hath sworn unto thy fathers, to
Abraham, to Isaac, and to Jacob.
14 Neither with you only do I make this
covenant and this oath;
15 But with *him* that standeth here with us
this day before the LORD our God, and also
with *him* that *is* not here with us this day:
16 (For ye know how we have dwelt in the
land of Egypt; and how we came through
the nations which ye passed by;
17 And ye have seen their abominations,
and their idols, wood and stone, silver and
gold, which *were* among them:)
18 Lest there should be among you man, or
woman, or family, or tribe, whose heart turneth away this day from the LORD our God,
to go *and* serve the gods of these nations;
lest there should be among you a root that
beareth gall and wormwood;
19 And it come to pass, when he heareth the
words of this curse, that he bless himself in
his heart, saying, I shall have peace, though
I walk in the imagination of mine heart, to
add drunkenness to thirst:
20 The LORD will not spare him, but then
the anger of the LORD and his jealousy shall
smoke against that man, and all the curses
that are written in this book shall lie upon
him, and the LORD shall blot out his name
from under heaven.
21 And the LORD shall separate him unto
evil out of all the tribes of Israel, according
to all the curses of the covenant that are
written in this book of the law:
22 So that the generation to come of your
children that shall rise up after you, and
the stranger that shall come from a far
land, shall say, when they see the plagues
of that land, and the sicknesses which the
LORD hath laid upon it;
23 *And that* the whole land thereof *is* brimstone, and salt, *and* burning, *that* it is not
sown, nor beareth, nor any grass groweth
therein, like the overthrow of Sodom, and
Gomorrah, Admah, and Zeboim, which
the LORD overthrew in his anger, and in
his wrath:
24 Even all nations shall say, Wherefore
hath the LORD done thus unto this land?
what *meaneth* the heat of this great anger?
25 Then men shall say, Because they have
forsaken the covenant of the LORD God of
their fathers, which he made with them
when he brought them forth out of the
land of Egypt:
26 For they went and served other gods, and
worshipped them, gods whom they knew
not, and *whom* he had not given unto them:
27 And the anger of the LORD was kindled
against this land, to bring upon it all the
curses that are written in this book:
28 And the LORD rooted them out of their
land in anger, and in wrath, and in great
indignation, and cast them into another
land, as *it is* this day.
29 The secret *things belong* unto the LORD
our God: but those *things which are* revealed
belong unto us and to our children for ever,
that *we* may do all the words of this law.

Deuteronomy 30

1 And it shall come to pass, when all these

things are come upon thee, the blessing and the curse, which I have set before thee, and thou shalt call *them* to mind among all the nations, whither the LORD thy God hath driven thee,

2 And shalt return unto the LORD thy God, and shalt obey his voice according to all that I command thee this day, thou and thy children, with all thine heart, and with all thy soul;

3 That then the LORD thy God will turn thy captivity, and have compassion upon thee, and will return and gather thee from all the nations, whither the LORD thy God hath scattered thee.

4 If *any* of thine be driven out unto the outmost *parts* of heaven, from thence will the LORD thy God gather thee, and from thence will he fetch thee:

5 And the LORD thy God will bring thee into the land which thy fathers possessed, and thou shalt possess it; and he will do thee good, and multiply thee above thy fathers.

6 And the LORD thy God will circumcise thine heart, and the heart of thy seed, to love the LORD thy God with all thine heart, and with all thy soul, that thou mayest live.

7 And the LORD thy God will put all these curses upon thine enemies, and on them that hate thee, which persecuted thee.

8 And thou shalt return and obey the voice of the LORD, and do all his commandments which I command thee this day.

9 And the LORD thy God will make thee plenteous in every work of thine hand, in the fruit of thy body, and in the fruit of thy cattle, and in the fruit of thy land, for good: for the LORD will again rejoice over thee for good, as he rejoiced over thy fathers:

10 If thou shalt hearken unto the voice of the LORD thy God, to keep his commandments and his statutes which are written in this book of the law, *and* if thou turn unto the LORD thy God with all thine heart, and with all thy soul.

11 ¶ For this commandment which I command thee this day, it *is* not hidden from thee, neither *is* it far off.

12 It *is* not in heaven, that thou shouldest say, Who shall go up for us to heaven, and bring it unto us, that we may hear it, and do it?

13 Neither *is* it beyond the sea, that thou shouldest say, Who shall go over the sea for us, and bring it unto us, that we may hear it, and do it?

14 But the word *is* very nigh unto thee, in thy mouth, and in thy heart, that thou mayest do it.

15 ¶ See, I have set before thee this day life and good, and death and evil;

16 In that I command thee this day to love the LORD thy God, to walk in his ways, and to keep his commandments and his statutes and his judgments, that thou mayest live and multiply: and the LORD thy God shall bless thee in the land whither thou goest to possess it.

17 But if thine heart turn away, so that thou wilt not hear, but shalt be drawn away, and worship other gods, and serve them;

18 I denounce unto you this day, that ye shall surely perish, *and that* ye shall not prolong *your* days upon the land, whither thou passest over Jordan to go to possess it.

19 I call heaven and earth to record this day against you, *that* I have set before you life and death, blessing and cursing: therefore choose life, that both thou and thy seed may live:

20 That thou mayest love the LORD thy God, *and* that thou mayest obey his voice, and that thou mayest cleave unto him: for he *is* thy life, and the length of thy days: that thou mayest dwell in the land which the LORD sware unto thy fathers, to Abraham, to Isaac, and to Jacob, to give them.

Deuteronomy 31

1 And Moses went and spake these words unto all Israel.

2 And he said unto them, I *am* an hundred and twenty years old this day; I can no more go out and come in: also the LORD hath said unto me, Thou shalt not go over this Jordan.

3 The LORD thy God, he will go over before thee, *and* he will destroy these nations from before thee, and thou shalt possess them: *and* Joshua, he shall go over before thee, as the LORD hath said.

4 And the LORD shall do unto them as he did to Sihon and to Og, kings of the Amorites, and unto the land of them, whom he destroyed.

5 And the LORD shall give them up before your face, that ye may do unto them accord-

ing unto all the commandments which I have
commanded you.
6 Be strong and of a good courage, fear not,
nor be afraid of them: for the LORD thy God,
he *it is* that doth go with thee; he will not
fail thee, nor forsake thee.
7 ¶ And Moses called unto Joshua, and said
unto him in the sight of all Israel, Be strong
and of a good courage: for thou must go
with this people unto the land which the
LORD hath sworn unto their fathers to
give them; and thou shalt cause them to
inherit it.
8 And the LORD, he *it is* that doth go before
thee; he will be with thee, he will not fail
thee, neither forsake thee: fear not, neither
be dismayed.
9 ¶ And Moses wrote this law, and delivered
it unto the priests the sons of Levi, which
bare the ark of the covenant of the LORD,
and unto all the elders of Israel.
10 And Moses commanded them, saying, At
the end of *every* seven years, in the solemnity of the year of release, in the feast of
tabernacles,
11 When all Israel is come to appear before
the LORD thy God in the place which he shall
choose, thou shalt read this law before all
Israel in their hearing.
12 Gather the people together, men, and
women, and children, and thy stranger
that *is* within thy gates, that they may hear,
and that they may learn, and fear the LORD
your God, and observe to do all the words
of this law:
13 And *that* their children, which have not
known *any thing*, may hear, and learn to fear
the LORD your God, as long as ye live in the
land whither ye go over Jordan to possess it.
14 ¶ And the LORD said unto Moses, Behold,
thy days approach that thou must die: call
Joshua, and present yourselves in the tabernacle of the congregation, that I may give
him a charge. And Moses and Joshua went,
and presented themselves in the tabernacle
of the congregation.
15 And the LORD appeared in the tabernacle
in a pillar of a cloud: and the pillar of the
cloud stood over the door of the tabernacle.
16 ¶ And the LORD said unto Moses, Behold,
thou shalt sleep with thy fathers; and this
people will rise up, and go a whoring after
the gods of the strangers of the land,
whither they go *to be* among them, and
will forsake me, and break my covenant
which I have made with them.
17 Then my anger shall be kindled against
them in that day, and I will forsake them,
and I will hide my face from them, and they
shall be devoured, and many evils and troubles shall befall them; so that they will say in
that day, Are not these evils come upon us,
because our God *is* not among us?
18 And I will surely hide my face in that
day for all the evils which they shall have
wrought, in that they are turned unto
other gods.
19 Now therefore write ye this song for
you, and teach it the children of Israel: put
it in their mouths, that this song may be a
witness for me against the children of Israel.
20 For when I shall have brought them into
the land which I sware unto their fathers,
that floweth with milk and honey; and they
shall have eaten and filled themselves, and
waxen fat; then will they turn unto other
gods, and serve them, and provoke me, and
break my covenant.
21 And it shall come to pass, when many
evils and troubles are befallen them, that
this song shall testify against them as a
witness; for it shall not be forgotten out of
the mouths of their seed: for I know their
imagination which they go about, even now,
before I have brought them into the land
which I sware.
22 ¶ Moses therefore wrote this song the
same day, and taught it the children of Israel.
23 And he gave Joshua the son of Nun a
charge, and said, Be strong and of a good
courage: for thou shalt bring the children
of Israel into the land which I sware unto
them: and I will be with thee.
24 ¶ And it came to pass, when Moses had
made an end of writing the words of this law
in a book, until they were finished,
25 That Moses commanded the Levites,
which bare the ark of the covenant of the
LORD, saying,
26 Take this book of the law, and put it in
the side of the ark of the covenant of the
LORD your God, that it may be there for a
witness against thee.
27 For I know thy rebellion, and thy stiff
neck: behold, while I am yet alive with you

this day, ye have been rebellious against the
LORD; and how much more after my death?
28 ¶ Gather unto me all the elders of your
tribes, and your officers, that I may speak
these words in their ears, and call heaven
and earth to record against them.
29 For I know that after my death ye will
utterly corrupt *yourselves*, and turn aside
from the way which I have commanded
you; and evil will befall you in the latter
days; because ye will do evil in the sight of
the LORD, to provoke him to anger through
the work of your hands.
30 And Moses spake in the ears of all the
congregation of Israel the words of this
song, until they were ended.

Deuteronomy 32

1 Give ear, O ye heavens, and I will speak;
and hear, O earth, the words of my mouth.
2 My doctrine shall drop as the rain, my
speech shall distil as the dew, as the small
rain upon the tender herb, and as the showers upon the grass:
3 Because I will publish the name of the
LORD: ascribe ye greatness unto our God.
4 *He is* the Rock, his work *is* perfect: for all
his ways *are* judgment: a God of truth and
without iniquity, just and right *is* he.
5 They have corrupted themselves, their
spot *is* not *the spot* of his children: *they are*
a perverse and crooked generation.
6 Do ye thus requite the LORD, O foolish
people and unwise? *is* not he thy father *that*
hath bought thee? hath he not made thee,
and established thee?
7 ¶ Remember the days of old, consider the
years of many generations: ask thy father,
and he will shew thee; thy elders, and they
will tell thee.
8 When the most High divided to the nations
their inheritance, when he separated the
sons of Adam, he set the bounds of the
people according to the number of the
children of Israel.
9 For the LORD's portion *is* his people; Jacob
is the lot of his inheritance.
10 He found him in a desert land, and in
the waste howling wilderness; he led him
about, he instructed him, he kept him as
the apple of his eye.
11 As an eagle stirreth up her nest, flutter-
eth over her young, spreadeth abroad her
wings, taketh them, beareth them on her
wings:
12 *So* the LORD alone did lead him, and *there*
was no strange god with him.
13 He made him ride on the high places of
the earth, that he might eat the increase of
the fields; and he made him to suck honey
out of the rock, and oil out of the flinty rock;
14 Butter of kine, and milk of sheep, with fat
of lambs, and rams of the breed of Bashan,
and goats, with the fat of kidneys of wheat;
and thou didst drink the pure blood of the
grape.
15 ¶ But Jeshurun waxed fat, and kicked:
thou art waxen fat, thou art grown thick,
thou art covered *with fatness;* then he
forsook God *which* made him, and lightly
esteemed the Rock of his salvation.
16 They provoked him to jealousy with
strange *gods*, with abominations provoked
they him to anger.
17 They sacrificed unto devils, not to God;
to gods whom they knew not, to new *gods*
that came newly up, whom your fathers
feared not.
18 Of the Rock *that* begat thee thou art
unmindful, and hast forgotten God that
formed thee.
19 And when the LORD saw *it*, he abhorred
them, because of the provoking of his sons,
and of his daughters.
20 And he said, I will hide my face from
them, I will see what their end *shall be:* for
they *are* a very froward generation, children
in whom *is* no faith.
21 They have moved me to jealousy with
that which is not God; they have provoked
me to anger with their vanities: and I will
move them to jealousy with *those which are*
not a people; I will provoke them to anger
with a foolish nation.
22 For a fire is kindled in mine anger, and
shall burn unto the lowest hell, and shall
consume the earth with her increase, and
set on fire the foundations of the mountains.
23 I will heap mischiefs upon them; I will
spend mine arrows upon them.
24 *They shall be* burnt with hunger, and
devoured with burning heat, and with bitter destruction: I will also send the teeth
of beasts upon them, with the poison of
serpents of the dust.
25 The sword without, and terror within,

shall destroy both the young man and the
virgin, the suckling *also* with the man of
gray hairs.
26 I said, I would scatter them into corners,
I would make the remembrance of them to
cease from among men:
27 Were it not that I feared the wrath of the
enemy, lest their adversaries should behave
themselves strangely, *and* lest they should
say, Our hand *is* high, and the LORD hath
not done all this.
28 For they *are* a nation void of counsel,
neither *is there any* understanding in them.
29 O that they were wise, *that* they understood this, *that* they would consider their
latter end!
30 How should one chase a thousand, and
two put ten thousand to flight, except their
Rock had sold them, and the LORD had shut
them up?
31 For their rock *is* not as our Rock, even our
enemies themselves *being* judges.
32 For their vine *is* of the vine of Sodom,
and of the fields of Gomorrah: their grapes
are grapes of gall, their clusters *are* bitter:
33 Their wine *is* the poison of dragons, and
the cruel venom of asps.
34 *Is* not this laid up in store with me, *and*
sealed up among my treasures?
35 To me *belongeth* vengeance, and recompence; their foot shall slide in *due* time:
for the day of their calamity *is* at hand,
and the things that shall come upon them
make haste.
36 For the LORD shall judge his people, and
repent himself for his servants, when he
seeth that *their* power is gone, and *there is*
none shut up, or left.
37 And he shall say, Where *are* their gods,
their rock in whom they trusted,
38 Which did eat the fat of their sacrifices,
and drank the wine of their drink offerings?
let them rise up and help you, *and* be your
protection.
39 See now that I, *even* I, *am* he, and *there*
is no god with me: I kill, and I make alive; I
wound, and I heal: neither *is there any* that
can deliver out of my hand.
40 For I lift up my hand to heaven, and say,
I live for ever.
41 If I whet my glittering sword, and mine
hand take hold on judgment; I will render
vengeance to mine enemies, and will reward
them that hate me.
42 I will make mine arrows drunk with blood,
and my sword shall devour flesh; *and that*
with the blood of the slain and of the captives, from the beginning of revenges upon
the enemy.
43 Rejoice, O ye nations, *with* his people:
for he will avenge the blood of his servants,
and will render vengeance to his adversaries, and will be merciful unto his land, *and*
to his people.
44 ¶ And Moses came and spake all the
words of this song in the ears of the people,
he, and Hoshea the son of Nun.
45 And Moses made an end of speaking all
these words to all Israel:
46 And he said unto them, Set your hearts
unto all the words which I testify among
you this day, which ye shall command your
children to observe to do, all the words of
this law.
47 For it *is* not a vain thing for you; because
it *is* your life: and through this thing ye shall
prolong *your* days in the land, whither ye go
over Jordan to possess it.
48 And the LORD spake unto Moses that
selfsame day, saying,
49 Get thee up into this mountain Abarim,
unto mount Nebo, which *is* in the land of
Moab, that *is* over against Jericho; and
behold the land of Canaan, which I give
unto the children of Israel for a possession:
50 And die in the mount whither thou goest
up, and be gathered unto thy people; as
Aaron thy brother died in mount Hor, and
was gathered unto his people:
51 Because ye trespassed against me among
the children of Israel at the waters of Merib-
ah-Kadesh, in the wilderness of Zin; because
ye sanctified me not in the midst of the
children of Israel.
52 Yet thou shalt see the land before *thee;*
but thou shalt not go thither unto the land
which I give the children of Israel.

Deuteronomy 33

1 And this *is* the blessing, wherewith Moses
the man of God blessed the children of Israel
before his death.
2 And he said, The LORD came from Sinai,
and rose up from Seir unto them; he shined
forth from mount Paran, and he came with

ten thousands of saints: from his right hand
went a fiery law for them.
3 Yea, he loved the people; all his saints *are*
in thy hand: and they sat down at thy feet;
every one shall receive of thy words.
4 Moses commanded us a law, *even* the
inheritance of the congregation of Jacob.
5 And he was king in Jeshurun, when the
heads of the people *and* the tribes of Israel
were gathered together.
6 ¶ Let Reuben live, and not die; and let *not*
his men be few.
7 ¶ And this *is the blessing* of Judah: and
he said, Hear, LORD, the voice of Judah, and
bring him unto his people: let his hands be
sufficient for him; and be thou an help *to*
him from his enemies.
8 ¶ And of Levi he said, *Let* thy Thummim
and thy Urim *be* with thy holy one, whom
thou didst prove at Massah, *and with* whom
thou didst strive at the waters of Meribah;
9 Who said unto his father and to his
mother, I have not seen him; neither did
he acknowledge his brethren, nor knew his
own children: for they have observed thy
word, and kept thy covenant.
10 They shall teach Jacob thy judgments,
and Israel thy law: they shall put incense
before thee, and whole burnt sacrifice upon
thine altar.
11 Bless, LORD, his substance, and accept
the work of his hands: smite through the
loins of them that rise against him, and of
them that hate him, that they rise not again.
12 ¶ *And* of Benjamin he said, The beloved
of the LORD shall dwell in safety by him; *and*
the LORD shall cover him all the day long,
and he shall dwell between his shoulders.
13 ¶ And of Joseph he said, Blessed of the
LORD *be* his land, for the precious things of
heaven, for the dew, and for the deep that
coucheth beneath,
14 And for the precious fruits *brought forth*
by the sun, and for the precious things put
forth by the moon,
15 And for the chief things of the ancient
mountains, and for the precious things of
the lasting hills,
16 And for the precious things of the earth
and fulness thereof, and *for* the good will of
him that dwelt in the bush: let *the blessing*
come upon the head of Joseph, and upon
the top of the head of him *that was* separated from his brethren.
17 His glory *is like* the firstling of his bullock,
and his horns *are like* the horns of unicorns:
with them he shall push the people together
to the ends of the earth: and they *are* the
ten thousands of Ephraim, and they *are* the
thousands of Manasseh.
18 ¶ And of Zebulun he said, Rejoice, Zebulun, in thy going out; and, Issachar, in thy
tents.
19 They shall call the people unto the
mountain; there they shall offer sacrifices
of righteousness: for they shall suck *of* the
abundance of the seas, and *of* treasures
hid in the sand.
20 ¶ And of Gad he said, Blessed *be* he that
enlargeth Gad: he dwelleth as a lion, and
teareth the arm with the crown of the head.
21 And he provided the first part for himself,
because there, *in* a portion of the lawgiver,
was he seated; and he came with the heads
of the people, he executed the justice of the
LORD, and his judgments with Israel.
22 ¶ And of Dan he said, Dan *is* a lion's
whelp: he shall leap from Bashan.
23 ¶ And of Naphtali he said, O Naphtali,
satisfied with favour, and full with the blessing of the LORD: possess thou the west and
the south.
24 ¶ And of Asher he said, *Let* Asher *be*
blessed with children; let him be acceptable
to his brethren, and let him dip his foot in oil.
25 Thy shoes *shall be* iron and brass; and as
thy days, *so shall* thy strength *be*.
26 ¶ *There is* none like unto the God of
Jeshurun, *who* rideth upon the heaven in
thy help, and in his excellency on the sky.
27 The eternal God *is thy* refuge, and underneath *are* the everlasting arms: and he shall
thrust out the enemy from before thee; and
shall say, Destroy *them*.
28 Israel then shall dwell in safety alone:
the fountain of Jacob *shall be* upon a land
of corn and wine; also his heavens shall
drop down dew.
29 Happy *art* thou, O Israel: who *is* like
unto thee, O people saved by the LORD, the
shield of thy help, and who *is* the sword of
thy excellency! and thine enemies shall be
found liars unto thee; and thou shalt tread
upon their high places.

Deuteronomy 34

1 And Moses went up from the plains of Moab unto the mountain of Nebo, to the top of Pisgah, that *is* over against Jericho. And the LORD shewed him all the land of Gilead, unto Dan,

2 And all Naphtali, and the land of Ephraim, and Manasseh, and all the land of Judah, unto the utmost sea,

3 And the south, and the plain of the valley of Jericho, the city of palm trees, unto Zoar.

4 And the LORD said unto him, This *is* the land which I sware unto Abraham, unto Isaac, and unto Jacob, saying, I will give it unto thy seed: I have caused thee to see *it* with thine eyes, but thou shalt not go over thither.

5 ¶ So Moses the servant of the LORD died there in the land of Moab, according to the word of the LORD.

6 And he buried him in a valley in the land of Moab, over against Beth-peor: but no man knoweth of his sepulchre unto this day.

7 ¶ And Moses *was* an hundred and twenty years old when he died: his eye was not dim, nor his natural force abated.

8 ¶ And the children of Israel wept for Moses in the plains of Moab thirty days: so the days of weeping *and* mourning for Moses were ended.

9 ¶ And Joshua the son of Nun was full of the spirit of wisdom; for Moses had laid his hands upon him: and the children of Israel hearkened unto him, and did as the LORD commanded Moses.

10 ¶ And there arose not a prophet since in Israel like unto Moses, whom the LORD knew face to face,

11 In all the signs and the wonders, which the LORD sent him to do in the land of Egypt to Pharaoh, and to all his servants, and to all his land,

12 And in all that mighty hand, and in all the great terror which Moses shewed in the sight of all Israel.

The Book Of

Joshua

Joshua 1

1 Now after the death of Moses the servant of the LORD it came to pass, that the LORD spake unto Joshua the son of Nun, Moses' minister, saying,

2 Moses my servant is dead; now therefore arise, go over this Jordan, thou, and all this people, unto the land which I do give to them, *even* to the children of Israel.

3 Every place that the sole of your foot shall tread upon, that have I given unto you, as I said unto Moses.

4 From the wilderness and this Lebanon even unto the great river, the river Euphrates, all the land of the Hittites, and unto the great sea toward the going down of the sun, shall be your coast.

5 There shall not any man be able to stand before thee all the days of thy life: as I was with Moses, *so* I will be with thee: I will not fail thee, nor forsake thee.

6 Be strong and of a good courage: for unto this people shalt thou divide for an inheritance the land, which I sware unto their fathers to give them.

7 Only be thou strong and very courageous, that thou mayest observe to do according to all the law, which Moses my servant commanded thee: turn not from it *to* the right hand or *to* the left, that thou mayest prosper whithersoever thou goest.

8 This book of the law shall not depart out of thy mouth; but thou shalt meditate therein day and night, that thou mayest observe to do according to all that is written therein: for then thou shalt make thy way prosperous, and then thou shalt have good success.

9 Have not I commanded thee? Be strong and of a good courage; be not afraid, neither be thou dismayed: for the LORD thy God *is* with thee whithersoever thou goest.

10 ¶ Then Joshua commanded the officers of the people, saying,

11 Pass through the host, and command the people, saying, Prepare you victuals; for within three days ye shall pass over this Jordan, to go in to possess the land, which the LORD your God giveth you to possess it.

12 ¶ And to the Reubenites, and to the Gadites, and to half the tribe of Manasseh, spake Joshua, saying,

13 Remember the word which Moses the servant of the LORD commanded you, saying, The LORD your God hath given you rest, and hath given you this land.

14 Your wives, your little ones, and your cattle, shall remain in the land which Moses gave you on this side Jordan; but ye shall pass before your brethren armed, all the mighty men of valour, and help them;

15 Until the LORD have given your brethren rest, as *he hath given* you, and they also have possessed the land which the LORD your God giveth them: then ye shall return unto the land of your possession, and enjoy it, which Moses the LORD's servant gave you on this side Jordan toward the sunrising.

16 ¶ And they answered Joshua, saying, All that thou commandest us we will do, and whithersoever thou sendest us, we will go.

17 According as we hearkened unto Moses in all things, so will we hearken unto thee: only the LORD thy God be with thee, as he was with Moses.

18 Whosoever *he be* that doth rebel against thy commandment, and will not hearken unto thy words in all that thou commandest him, he shall be put to death: only be strong and of a good courage.

Joshua 2

1 And Joshua the son of Nun sent out of Shittim two men to spy secretly, saying, Go view the land, even Jericho. And they went, and came into an harlot's house, named Rahab, and lodged there.

2 And it was told the king of Jericho, saying, Behold, there came men in hither to night of the children of Israel to search out the country.

3 And the king of Jericho sent unto Rahab, saying, Bring forth the men that are come to thee, which are entered into thine house: for they be come to search out all the country.

4 And the woman took the two men, and hid them, and said thus, There came men unto me, but I wist not whence they *were:*

5 And it came to pass *about the time* of shutting of the gate, when it was dark, that the men went out: whither the men went I wot not: pursue after them quickly; for ye shall overtake them.

6 But she had brought them up to the roof of the house, and hid them with the stalks of flax, which she had laid in order upon the roof.

7 And the men pursued after them the way to Jordan unto the fords: and as soon as they which pursued after them were gone out, they shut the gate.

8 ¶ And before they were laid down, she came up unto them upon the roof;

9 And she said unto the men, I know that the LORD hath given you the land, and that your terror is fallen upon us, and that all the inhabitants of the land faint because of you.

10 For we have heard how the LORD dried up the water of the Red sea for you, when ye came out of Egypt; and what ye did unto the two kings of the Amorites, that *were* on the other side Jordan, Sihon and Og, whom ye utterly destroyed.

11 And as soon as we had heard *these things*, our hearts did melt, neither did there remain any more courage in any man, because of you: for the LORD your God, he *is* God in heaven above, and in earth beneath.

12 Now therefore, I pray you, swear unto me by the LORD, since I have shewed you kindness, that ye will also shew kindness unto my father's house, and give me a true token:

13 And *that* ye will save alive my father, and my mother, and my brethren, and my sisters, and all that they have, and deliver our lives from death.

14 And the men answered her, Our life for yours, if ye utter not this our business. And it shall be, when the LORD hath given us the land, that we will deal kindly and truly with thee.

15 Then she let them down by a cord through the window: for her house *was* upon the town wall, and she dwelt upon the wall.

16 And she said unto them, Get you to the mountain, lest the pursuers meet you; and hide yourselves there three days, until the

pursuers be returned: and afterward may
ye go your way.
17 And the men said unto her, We *will be*
blameless of this thine oath which thou hast
made us swear.
18 Behold, *when* we come into the land,
thou shalt bind this line of scarlet thread in
the window which thou didst let us down
by: and thou shalt bring thy father, and
thy mother, and thy brethren, and all thy
father's household, home unto thee.
19 And it shall be, *that* whosoever shall go
out of the doors of thy house into the street,
his blood *shall be* upon his head, and we *will*
be guiltless: and whosoever shall be with
thee in the house, his blood *shall be* on our
head, if *any* hand be upon him.
20 And if thou utter this our business, then
we will be quit of thine oath which thou hast
made us to swear.
21 And she said, According unto your words,
so *be* it. And she sent them away, and they
departed: and she bound the scarlet line
in the window.
22 And they went, and came unto the mountain, and abode there three days, until the
pursuers were returned: and the pursuers
sought *them* throughout all the way, but
found *them* not.
23 ¶ So the two men returned, and
descended from the mountain, and passed
over, and came to Joshua the son of Nun,
and told him all *things* that befell them:
24 And they said unto Joshua, Truly the LORD
hath delivered into our hands all the land;
for even all the inhabitants of the country
do faint because of us.

Joshua 3

1 And Joshua rose early in the morning;
and they removed from Shittim, and came
to Jordan, he and all the children of Israel,
and lodged there before they passed over.
2 And it came to pass after three days, that
the officers went through the host;
3 And they commanded the people, saying,
When ye see the ark of the covenant of the
LORD your God, and the priests the Levites
bearing it, then ye shall remove from your
place, and go after it.
4 Yet there shall be a space between you and
it, about two thousand cubits by measure:
come not near unto it, that ye may know
the way by which ye must go: for ye have
not passed *this* way heretofore.
5 And Joshua said unto the people, Sanctify
yourselves: for to morrow the LORD will do
wonders among you.
6 And Joshua spake unto the priests, saying,
Take up the ark of the covenant, and pass
over before the people. And they took up
the ark of the covenant, and went before
the people.
7 ¶ And the LORD said unto Joshua, This day
will I begin to magnify thee in the sight of
all Israel, that they may know that, as I was
with Moses, *so* I will be with thee.
8 And thou shalt command the priests that
bear the ark of the covenant, saying, When
ye are come to the brink of the water of
Jordan, ye shall stand still in Jordan.
9 ¶ And Joshua said unto the children of
Israel, Come hither, and hear the words of
the LORD your God.
10 And Joshua said, Hereby ye shall know
that the living God *is* among you, and *that*
he will without fail drive out from before
you the Canaanites, and the Hittites, and the
Hivites, and the Perizzites, and the Girgashites, and the Amorites, and the Jebusites.
11 Behold, the ark of the covenant of the
Lord of all the earth passeth over before
you into Jordan.
12 Now therefore take you twelve men
out of the tribes of Israel, out of every
tribe a man.
13 And it shall come to pass, as soon as the
soles of the feet of the priests that bear the
ark of the LORD, the Lord of all the earth,
shall rest in the waters of Jordan, *that* the
waters of Jordan shall be cut off *from* the
waters that come down from above; and
they shall stand upon an heap.
14 ¶ And it came to pass, when the people
removed from their tents, to pass over Jordan, and the priests bearing the ark of the
covenant before the people;
15 And as they that bare the ark were come
unto Jordan, and the feet of the priests that
bare the ark were dipped in the brim of the
water, (for Jordan overfloweth all his banks
all the time of harvest,)
16 That the waters which came down from
above stood *and* rose up upon an heap very
far from the city Adam, that *is* beside Zare-
tan: and those that came down toward the

sea of the plain, *even* the salt sea, failed, *and*
were cut off: and the people passed over
right against Jericho.
17 And the priests that bare the ark of the
covenant of the LORD stood firm on dry
ground in the midst of Jordan, and all the
Israelites passed over on dry ground, until all
the people were passed clean over Jordan.

Joshua 4

1 And it came to pass, when all the people
were clean passed over Jordan, that the
LORD spake unto Joshua, saying,
2 Take you twelve men out of the people,
out of every tribe a man,
3 And command ye them, saying, Take
you hence out of the midst of Jordan, out
of the place where the priests' feet stood
firm, twelve stones, and ye shall carry them
over with you, and leave them in the lodging
place, where ye shall lodge this night.
4 Then Joshua called the twelve men, whom
he had prepared of the children of Israel,
out of every tribe a man:
5 And Joshua said unto them, Pass over
before the ark of the LORD your God into
the midst of Jordan, and take ye up every
man of you a stone upon his shoulder,
according unto the number of the tribes of
the children of Israel:
6 That this may be a sign among you, *that*
when your children ask *their fathers* in
time to come, saying, What *mean* ye by
these stones?
7 Then ye shall answer them, That the
waters of Jordan were cut off before the ark
of the covenant of the LORD; when it passed
over Jordan, the waters of Jordan were cut
off: and these stones shall be for a memorial
unto the children of Israel for ever.
8 And the children of Israel did so as Joshua
commanded, and took up twelve stones out
of the midst of Jordan, as the LORD spake
unto Joshua, according to the number of the
tribes of the children of Israel, and carried
them over with them unto the place where
they lodged, and laid them down there.
9 And Joshua set up twelve stones in the
midst of Jordan, in the place where the feet
of the priests which bare the ark of the covenant stood: and they are there unto this day.
10 ¶ For the priests which bare the ark stood
in the midst of Jordan, until every thing was
finished that the LORD commanded Joshua
to speak unto the people, according to all
that Moses commanded Joshua: and the
people hasted and passed over.
11 And it came to pass, when all the people
were clean passed over, that the ark of the
LORD passed over, and the priests, in the
presence of the people.
12 And the children of Reuben, and the children of Gad, and half the tribe of Manasseh,
passed over armed before the children of
Israel, as Moses spake unto them:
13 About forty thousand prepared for war
passed over before the LORD unto battle, to
the plains of Jericho.
14 ¶ On that day the LORD magnified Joshua
in the sight of all Israel; and they feared him,
as they feared Moses, all the days of his life.
15 And the LORD spake unto Joshua, saying,
16 Command the priests that bear the ark
of the testimony, that they come up out
of Jordan.
17 Joshua therefore commanded the priests,
saying, Come ye up out of Jordan.
18 And it came to pass, when the priests
that bare the ark of the covenant of the
LORD were come up out of the midst of Jordan, *and* the soles of the priests' feet were
lifted up unto the dry land, that the waters
of Jordan returned unto their place, and
flowed over all his banks, as *they did* before.
19 ¶ And the people came up out of Jordan
on the tenth *day* of the first month, and
encamped in Gilgal, in the east border of
Jericho.
20 And those twelve stones, which they
took out of Jordan, did Joshua pitch in Gilgal.
21 And he spake unto the children of Israel,
saying, When your children shall ask their
fathers in time to come, saying, What *mean*
these stones?
22 Then ye shall let your children know, saying, Israel came over this Jordan on dry land.
23 For the LORD your God dried up the
waters of Jordan from before you, until ye
were passed over, as the LORD your God
did to the Red sea, which he dried up from
before us, until we were gone over:
24 That all the people of the earth might
know the hand of the LORD, that it *is* mighty:
that ye might fear the LORD your God for
ever.

Joshua 5

1 And it came to pass, when all the kings
of the Amorites, which *were* on the side of
Jordan westward, and all the kings of the
Canaanites, which *were* by the sea, heard
that the LORD had dried up the waters of
Jordan from before the children of Israel,
until we were passed over, that their heart
melted, neither was there spirit in them
any more, because of the children of Israel.
2 ¶ At that time the LORD said unto Joshua,
Make thee sharp knives, and circumcise
again the children of Israel the second time.
3 And Joshua made him sharp knives, and
circumcised the children of Israel at the hill
of the foreskins.
4 And this *is* the cause why Joshua did circumcise: All the people that came out of
Egypt, *that were* males, *even* all the men
of war, died in the wilderness by the way,
after they came out of Egypt.
5 Now all the people that came out were
circumcised: but all the people *that were*
born in the wilderness by the way as they
came forth out of Egypt, *them* they had not
circumcised.
6 For the children of Israel walked forty
years in the wilderness, till all the people
that were men of war, which came out
of Egypt, were consumed, because they
obeyed not the voice of the LORD: unto
whom the LORD sware that he would not
shew them the land, which the LORD sware
unto their fathers that he would give us, a
land that floweth with milk and honey.
7 And their children, *whom* he raised up in
their stead, them Joshua circumcised: for
they were uncircumcised, because they had
not circumcised them by the way.
8 And it came to pass, when they had
done circumcising all the people, that they
abode in their places in the camp, till they
were whole.
9 And the LORD said unto Joshua, This day
have I rolled away the reproach of Egypt
from off you. Wherefore the name of the
place is called Gilgal unto this day.
10 ¶ And the children of Israel encamped
in Gilgal, and kept the passover on the
fourteenth day of the month at even in the
plains of Jericho.
11 And they did eat of the old corn of the
land on the morrow after the passover,
unleavened cakes, and parched *corn* in the
selfsame day.
12 ¶ And the manna ceased on the morrow after they had eaten of the old corn of
the land; neither had the children of Israel
manna any more; but they did eat of the
fruit of the land of Canaan that year.
13 ¶ And it came to pass, when Joshua was
by Jericho, that he lifted up his eyes and
looked, and, behold, there stood a man
over against him with his sword drawn in
his hand: and Joshua went unto him, and
said unto him, *Art* thou for us, or for our
adversaries?
14 And he said, Nay; but *as* captain of the
host of the LORD am I now come. And Joshua
fell on his face to the earth, and did worship,
and said unto him, What saith my lord unto
his servant?
15 And the captain of the LORD's host said
unto Joshua, Loose thy shoe from off thy
foot; for the place whereon thou standest
is holy. And Joshua did so.

Joshua 6

1 Now Jericho was straitly shut up because
of the children of Israel: none went out, and
none came in.
2 And the LORD said unto Joshua, See, I have
given into thine hand Jericho, and the king
thereof, *and* the mighty men of valour.
3 And ye shall compass the city, all *ye* men
of war, *and* go round about the city once.
Thus shalt thou do six days.
4 And seven priests shall bear before the
ark seven trumpets of rams' horns: and
the seventh day ye shall compass the city
seven times, and the priests shall blow with
the trumpets.
5 And it shall come to pass, that when they
make a long *blast* with the ram's horn, *and*
when ye hear the sound of the trumpet, all
the people shall shout with a great shout;
and the wall of the city shall fall down flat,
and the people shall ascend up every man
straight before him.
6 ¶ And Joshua the son of Nun called the
priests, and said unto them, Take up the ark
of the covenant, and let seven priests bear
seven trumpets of rams' horns before the
ark of the LORD.
7 And he said unto the people, Pass on, and

compass the city, and let him that is armed
pass on before the ark of the LORD.
8 ¶ And it came to pass, when Joshua had
spoken unto the people, that the seven
priests bearing the seven trumpets of rams'
horns passed on before the LORD, and blew
with the trumpets: and the ark of the covenant of the LORD followed them.
9 ¶ And the armed men went before the
priests that blew with the trumpets, and
the rereward came after the ark, *the priests*
going on, and blowing with the trumpets.
10 And Joshua had commanded the people,
saying, Ye shall not shout, nor make any
noise with your voice, neither shall *any* word
proceed out of your mouth, until the day I
bid you shout; then shall ye shout.
11 So the ark of the LORD compassed the
city, going about *it* once: and they came into
the camp, and lodged in the camp.
12 ¶ And Joshua rose early in the morning,
and the priests took up the ark of the LORD.
13 And seven priests bearing seven trumpets of rams' horns before the ark of the
LORD went on continually, and blew with
the trumpets: and the armed men went
before them; but the rereward came after
the ark of the LORD, *the priests* going on,
and blowing with the trumpets.
14 And the second day they compassed the
city once, and returned into the camp: so
they did six days.
15 And it came to pass on the seventh day,
that they rose early about the dawning of
the day, and compassed the city after the
same manner seven times: only on that
day they compassed the city seven times.
16 And it came to pass at the seventh time,
when the priests blew with the trumpets,
Joshua said unto the people, Shout; for the
LORD hath given you the city.
17 ¶ And the city shall be accursed, *even* it,
and all that *are* therein, to the LORD: only
Rahab the harlot shall live, she and all that
are with her in the house, because she hid
the messengers that we sent.
18 And ye, in any wise keep *yourselves* from
the accursed thing, lest ye make *yourselves*
accursed, when ye take of the accursed
thing, and make the camp of Israel a curse,
and trouble it.
19 But all the silver, and gold, and vessels
of brass and iron, *are* consecrated unto the
LORD: they shall come into the treasury of
the LORD.
20 So the people shouted when *the priests*
blew with the trumpets: and it came to
pass, when the people heard the sound of
the trumpet, and the people shouted with
a great shout, that the wall fell down flat,
so that the people went up into the city,
every man straight before him, and they
took the city.
21 And they utterly destroyed all that *was*
in the city, both man and woman, young
and old, and ox, and sheep, and ass, with
the edge of the sword.
22 But Joshua had said unto the two men
that had spied out the country, Go into the
harlot's house, and bring out thence the
woman, and all that she hath, as ye sware
unto her.
23 And the young men that were spies
went in, and brought out Rahab, and her
father, and her mother, and her brethren,
and all that she had; and they brought out
all her kindred, and left them without the
camp of Israel.
24 And they burnt the city with fire, and all
that *was* therein: only the silver, and the
gold, and the vessels of brass and of iron,
they put into the treasury of the house of
the LORD.
25 And Joshua saved Rahab the harlot alive,
and her father's household, and all that she
had; and she dwelleth in Israel *even* unto this
day; because she hid the messengers, which
Joshua sent to spy out Jericho.
26 ¶ And Joshua adjured *them* at that time,
saying, Cursed *be* the man before the LORD,
that riseth up and buildeth this city Jericho:
he shall lay the foundation thereof in his
firstborn, and in his youngest *son* shall he
set up the gates of it.
27 So the LORD was with Joshua; and his
fame was *noised* throughout all the country.

Joshua 7

1 But the children of Israel committed a
trespass in the accursed thing: for Achan,
the son of Carmi, the son of Zabdi, the son
of Zerah, of the tribe of Judah, took of the
accursed thing: and the anger of the LORD
was kindled against the children of Israel.
2 And Joshua sent men from Jericho to Ai,
which *is* beside Beth-aven, on the east side

of Beth-el, and spake unto them, saying, Go up and view the country. And the men went up and viewed Ai.

3 And they returned to Joshua, and said unto him, Let not all the people go up; but let about two or three thousand men go up and smite Ai; *and* make not all the people to labour thither; for they *are but* few.

4 So there went up thither of the people about three thousand men: and they fled before the men of Ai.

5 And the men of Ai smote of them about thirty and six men: for they chased them *from* before the gate *even* unto Shebarim, and smote them in the going down: wherefore the hearts of the people melted, and became as water.

6 ¶ And Joshua rent his clothes, and fell to the earth upon his face before the ark of the LORD until the eventide, he and the elders of Israel, and put dust upon their heads.

7 And Joshua said, Alas, O Lord GOD, wherefore hast thou at all brought this people over Jordan, to deliver us into the hand of the Amorites, to destroy us? would to God we had been content, and dwelt on the other side Jordan!

8 O Lord, what shall I say, when Israel turneth their backs before their enemies!

9 For the Canaanites and all the inhabitants of the land shall hear *of it,* and shall environ us round, and cut off our name from the earth: and what wilt thou do unto thy great name?

10 ¶ And the LORD said unto Joshua, Get thee up; wherefore liest thou thus upon thy face?

11 Israel hath sinned, and they have also transgressed my covenant which I commanded them: for they have even taken of the accursed thing, and have also stolen, and dissembled also, and they have put *it* even among their own stuff.

12 Therefore the children of Israel could not stand before their enemies, *but* turned *their* backs before their enemies, because they were accursed: neither will I be with you any more, except ye destroy the accursed from among you.

13 Up, sanctify the people, and say, Sanctify yourselves against to morrow: for thus saith the LORD God of Israel, *There is* an accursed thing in the midst of thee, O Israel: thou canst not stand before thine enemies, until ye take away the accursed thing from among you.

14 In the morning therefore ye shall be brought according to your tribes: and it shall be, *that* the tribe which the LORD taketh shall come according to the families *thereof;* and the family which the LORD shall take shall come by households; and the household which the LORD shall take shall come man by man.

15 And it shall be, *that* he that is taken with the accursed thing shall be burnt with fire, he and all that he hath: because he hath transgressed the covenant of the LORD, and because he hath wrought folly in Israel.

16 ¶ So Joshua rose up early in the morning, and brought Israel by their tribes; and the tribe of Judah was taken:

17 And he brought the family of Judah; and he took the family of the Zarhites: and he brought the family of the Zarhites man by man; and Zabdi was taken:

18 And he brought his household man by man; and Achan, the son of Carmi, the son of Zabdi, the son of Zerah, of the tribe of Judah, was taken.

19 And Joshua said unto Achan, My son, give, I pray thee, glory to the LORD God of Israel, and make confession unto him; and tell me now what thou hast done; hide *it* not from me.

20 And Achan answered Joshua, and said, Indeed I have sinned against the LORD God of Israel, and thus and thus have I done:

21 When I saw among the spoils a goodly Babylonish garment, and two hundred shekels of silver, and a wedge of gold of fifty shekels weight, then I coveted them, and took them; and, behold, they *are* hid in the earth in the midst of my tent, and the silver under it.

22 ¶ So Joshua sent messengers, and they ran unto the tent; and, behold, *it was* hid in his tent, and the silver under it.

23 And they took them out of the midst of the tent, and brought them unto Joshua, and unto all the children of Israel, and laid them out before the LORD.

24 And Joshua, and all Israel with him, took Achan the son of Zerah, and the silver, and the garment, and the wedge of gold, and his sons, and his daughters, and his oxen,

and his asses, and his sheep, and his tent,
and all that he had: and they brought them
unto the valley of Achor.
25 And Joshua said, Why hast thou troubled
us? the LORD shall trouble thee this day. And
all Israel stoned him with stones, and burned
them with fire, after they had stoned them
with stones.
26 And they raised over him a great heap
of stones unto this day. So the LORD turned
from the fierceness of his anger. Wherefore
the name of that place was called, The valley
of Achor, unto this day.

Joshua 8

1 And the LORD said unto Joshua, Fear not,
neither be thou dismayed: take all the people of war with thee, and arise, go up to Ai:
see, I have given into thy hand the king of
Ai, and his people, and his city, and his land:
2 And thou shalt do to Ai and her king as
thou didst unto Jericho and her king: only
the spoil thereof, and the cattle thereof,
shall ye take for a prey unto yourselves:
lay thee an ambush for the city behind it.
3 ¶ So Joshua arose, and all the people of
war, to go up against Ai: and Joshua chose
out thirty thousand mighty men of valour,
and sent them away by night.
4 And he commanded them, saying, Behold,
ye shall lie in wait against the city, *even*
behind the city: go not very far from the
city, but be ye all ready:
5 And I, and all the people that *are* with me,
will approach unto the city: and it shall come
to pass, when they come out against us, as
at the first, that we will flee before them,
6 (For they will come out after us) till we
have drawn them from the city; for they
will say, They flee before us, as at the first:
therefore we will flee before them.
7 Then ye shall rise up from the ambush,
and seize upon the city: for the LORD your
God will deliver it into your hand.
8 And it shall be, when ye have taken the
city, *that* ye shall set the city on fire: according to the commandment of the LORD shall
ye do. See, I have commanded you.
9 ¶ Joshua therefore sent them forth: and
they went to lie in ambush, and abode
between Beth-el and Ai, on the west side
of Ai: but Joshua lodged that night among
the people.
10 And Joshua rose up early in the morning, and numbered the people, and went
up, he and the elders of Israel, before the
people to Ai.
11 And all the people, *even the people* of war
that *were* with him, went up, and drew nigh,
and came before the city, and pitched on
the north side of Ai: now *there was* a valley
between them and Ai.
12 And he took about five thousand men,
and set them to lie in ambush between
Beth-el and Ai, on the west side of the city.
13 And when they had set the people,
even all the host that *was* on the north of
the city, and their liers in wait on the west
of the city, Joshua went that night into the
midst of the valley.
14 ¶ And it came to pass, when the king of
Ai saw *it*, that they hasted and rose up early,
and the men of the city went out against
Israel to battle, he and all his people, at a
time appointed, before the plain; but he wist
not that *there were* liers in ambush against
him behind the city.
15 And Joshua and all Israel made as if they
were beaten before them, and fled by the
way of the wilderness.
16 And all the people that *were* in Ai were
called together to pursue after them: and
they pursued after Joshua, and were drawn
away from the city.
17 And there was not a man left in Ai or
Beth-el, that went not out after Israel: and
they left the city open, and pursued after
Israel.
18 And the LORD said unto Joshua, Stretch
out the spear that *is* in thy hand toward Ai;
for I will give it into thine hand. And Joshua
stretched out the spear that *he had* in his
hand toward the city.
19 And the ambush arose quickly out of
their place, and they ran as soon as he had
stretched out his hand: and they entered
into the city, and took it, and hasted and
set the city on fire.
20 And when the men of Ai looked behind
them, they saw, and, behold, the smoke of
the city ascended up to heaven, and they
had no power to flee this way or that way:
and the people that fled to the wilderness
turned back upon the pursuers.
21 And when Joshua and all Israel saw that
the ambush had taken the city, and that

the smoke of the city ascended, then they
turned again, and slew the men of Ai.
22 And the other issued out of the city
against them; so they were in the midst of
Israel, some on this side, and some on that
side: and they smote them, so that they let
none of them remain or escape.
23 And the king of Ai they took alive, and
brought him to Joshua.
24 And it came to pass, when Israel had
made an end of slaying all the inhabitants
of Ai in the field, in the wilderness wherein
they chased them, and when they were
all fallen on the edge of the sword, until
they were consumed, that all the Israelites
returned unto Ai, and smote it with the edge
of the sword.
25 And *so* it was, *that* all that fell that day,
both of men and women, *were* twelve thousand, *even* all the men of Ai.
26 For Joshua drew not his hand back,
wherewith he stretched out the spear, until
he had utterly destroyed all the inhabitants
of Ai.
27 Only the cattle and the spoil of that city
Israel took for a prey unto themselves,
according unto the word of the LORD which
he commanded Joshua.
28 And Joshua burnt Ai, and made it an heap
for ever, *even* a desolation unto this day.
29 And the king of Ai he hanged on a tree
until eventide: and as soon as the sun was
down, Joshua commanded that they should
take his carcase down from the tree, and
cast it at the entering of the gate of the city,
and raise thereon a great heap of stones,
that remaineth unto this day.
30 ¶ Then Joshua built an altar unto the
LORD God of Israel in mount Ebal,
31 As Moses the servant of the LORD commanded the children of Israel, as it is written
in the book of the law of Moses, an altar
of whole stones, over which no man hath
lift up *any* iron: and they offered thereon
burnt offerings unto the LORD, and sacrificed
peace offerings.
32 ¶ And he wrote there upon the stones a
copy of the law of Moses, which he wrote
in the presence of the children of Israel.
33 And all Israel, and their elders, and officers, and their judges, stood on this side the
ark and on that side before the priests the
Levites, which bare the ark of the covenant
of the LORD, as well the stranger, as he that
was born among them; half of them over
against mount Gerizim, and half of them
over against mount Ebal; as Moses the servant of the LORD had commanded before,
that they should bless the people of Israel.
34 And afterward he read all the words
of the law, the blessings and cursings,
according to all that is written in the book
of the law.
35 There was not a word of all that Moses
commanded, which Joshua read not before
all the congregation of Israel, with the
women, and the little ones, and the strangers that were conversant among them.

Joshua 9

1 And it came to pass, when all the kings
which *were* on this side Jordan, in the hills,
and in the valleys, and in all the coasts of
the great sea over against Lebanon, the
Hittite, and the Amorite, the Canaanite,
the Perizzite, the Hivite, and the Jebusite,
heard *thereof;*
2 That they gathered themselves together,
to fight with Joshua and with Israel, with
one accord.
3 ¶ And when the inhabitants of Gibeon
heard what Joshua had done unto Jericho
and to Ai,
4 They did work wilily, and went and made
as if they had been ambassadors, and took
old sacks upon their asses, and wine bottles,
old, and rent, and bound up;
5 And old shoes and clouted upon their feet,
and old garments upon them; and all the
bread of their provision was dry *and* mouldy.
6 And they went to Joshua unto the camp
at Gilgal, and said unto him, and to the men
of Israel, We be come from a far country:
now therefore make ye a league with us.
7 And the men of Israel said unto the Hivites,
Peradventure ye dwell among us; and how
shall we make a league with you?
8 And they said unto Joshua, We *are* thy
servants. And Joshua said unto them, Who
are ye? and from whence come ye?
9 And they said unto him, From a very far
country thy servants are come because of
the name of the LORD thy God: for we have
heard the fame of him, and all that he did
in Egypt,
10 And all that he did to the two kings of

the Amorites, that *were* beyond Jordan, to Sihon king of Heshbon, and to Og king of Bashan, which *was* at Ashtaroth.

11 Wherefore our elders and all the inhabitants of our country spake to us, saying, Take victuals with you for the journey, and go to meet them, and say unto them, We *are* your servants: therefore now make ye a league with us.

12 This our bread we took hot *for* our provision out of our houses on the day we came forth to go unto you; but now, behold, it is dry, and it is mouldy:

13 And these bottles of wine, which we filled, *were* new; and, behold, they be rent: and these our garments and our shoes are become old by reason of the very long journey.

14 And the men took of their victuals, and asked not *counsel* at the mouth of the LORD.

15 And Joshua made peace with them, and made a league with them, to let them live: and the princes of the congregation sware unto them.

16 ¶ And it came to pass at the end of three days after they had made a league with them, that they heard that they *were* their neighbours, and *that* they dwelt among them.

17 And the children of Israel journeyed, and came unto their cities on the third day. Now their cities *were* Gibeon, and Chephirah, and Beeroth, and Kirjath-jearim.

18 And the children of Israel smote them not, because the princes of the congregation had sworn unto them by the LORD God of Israel. And all the congregation murmured against the princes.

19 But all the princes said unto all the congregation, We have sworn unto them by the LORD God of Israel: now therefore we may not touch them.

20 This we will do to them; we will even let them live, lest wrath be upon us, because of the oath which we sware unto them.

21 And the princes said unto them, Let them live; but let them be hewers of wood and drawers of water unto all the congregation; as the princes had promised them.

22 ¶ And Joshua called for them, and he spake unto them, saying, Wherefore have ye beguiled us, saying, We *are* very far from you; when ye dwell among us?

23 Now therefore ye *are* cursed, and there shall none of you be freed from being bondmen, and hewers of wood and drawers of water for the house of my God.

24 And they answered Joshua, and said, Because it was certainly told thy servants, how that the LORD thy God commanded his servant Moses to give you all the land, and to destroy all the inhabitants of the land from before you, therefore we were sore afraid of our lives because of you, and have done this thing.

25 And now, behold, we *are* in thine hand: as it seemeth good and right unto thee to do unto us, do.

26 And so did he unto them, and delivered them out of the hand of the children of Israel, that they slew them not.

27 And Joshua made them that day hewers of wood and drawers of water for the congregation, and for the altar of the LORD, even unto this day, in the place which he should choose.

Joshua 10

1 Now it came to pass, when Adoni-zedek king of Jerusalem had heard how Joshua had taken Ai, and had utterly destroyed it; as he had done to Jericho and her king, so he had done to Ai and her king; and how the inhabitants of Gibeon had made peace with Israel, and were among them;

2 That they feared greatly, because Gibeon *was* a great city, as one of the royal cities, and because it *was* greater than Ai, and all the men thereof *were* mighty.

3 Wherefore Adoni-zedek king of Jerusalem sent unto Hoham king of Hebron, and unto Piram king of Jarmuth, and unto Japhia king of Lachish, and unto Debir king of Eglon, saying,

4 Come up unto me, and help me, that we may smite Gibeon: for it hath made peace with Joshua and with the children of Israel.

5 Therefore the five kings of the Amorites, the king of Jerusalem, the king of Hebron, the king of Jarmuth, the king of Lachish, the king of Eglon, gathered themselves together, and went up, they and all their hosts, and encamped before Gibeon, and made war against it.

6 ¶ And the men of Gibeon sent unto Joshua to the camp to Gilgal, saying, Slack not thy

hand from thy servants; come up to us
quickly, and save us, and help us: for all
the kings of the Amorites that dwell in the
mountains are gathered together against us.
7 So Joshua ascended from Gilgal, he, and
all the people of war with him, and all the
mighty men of valour.
8 ¶ And the LORD said unto Joshua, Fear
them not: for I have delivered them into
thine hand; there shall not a man of them
stand before thee.
9 Joshua therefore came unto them suddenly, *and* went up from Gilgal all night.
10 And the LORD discomfited them before
Israel, and slew them with a great slaughter
at Gibeon, and chased them along the way
that goeth up to Beth-horon, and smote
them to Azekah, and unto Makkedah.
11 And it came to pass, as they fled from
before Israel, *and* were in the going down
to Beth-horon, that the LORD cast down
great stones from heaven upon them unto
Azekah, and they died: *they were* more
which died with hailstones than *they* whom
the children of Israel slew with the sword.
12 ¶ Then spake Joshua to the LORD in the
day when the LORD delivered up the Amorites before the children of Israel, and he
said in the sight of Israel, Sun, stand thou
still upon Gibeon; and thou, Moon, in the
valley of Ajalon.
13 And the sun stood still, and the moon
stayed, until the people had avenged themselves upon their enemies. *Is* not this written
in the book of Jasher? So the sun stood still
in the midst of heaven, and hasted not to
go down about a whole day.
14 And there was no day like that before it
or after it, that the LORD hearkened unto
the voice of a man: for the LORD fought
for Israel.
15 ¶ And Joshua returned, and all Israel with
him, unto the camp to Gilgal.
16 But these five kings fled, and hid themselves in a cave at Makkedah.
17 And it was told Joshua, saying, The five
kings are found hid in a cave at Makkedah.
18 And Joshua said, Roll great stones upon
the mouth of the cave, and set men by it
for to keep them:
19 And stay ye not, *but* pursue after your
enemies, and smite the hindmost of them;
suffer them not to enter into their cities:
for the LORD your God hath delivered them
into your hand.
20 And it came to pass, when Joshua and
the children of Israel had made an end of
slaying them with a very great slaughter, till
they were consumed, that the rest *which*
remained of them entered into fenced cities.
21 And all the people returned to the camp
to Joshua at Makkedah in peace: none
moved his tongue against any of the children of Israel.
22 Then said Joshua, Open the mouth of the
cave, and bring out those five kings unto me
out of the cave.
23 And they did so, and brought forth those
five kings unto him out of the cave, the king
of Jerusalem, the king of Hebron, the king
of Jarmuth, the king of Lachish, *and* the
king of Eglon.
24 And it came to pass, when they brought
out those kings unto Joshua, that Joshua
called for all the men of Israel, and said unto
the captains of the men of war which went
with him, Come near, put your feet upon the
necks of these kings. And they came near,
and put their feet upon the necks of them.
25 And Joshua said unto them, Fear not, nor
be dismayed, be strong and of good courage: for thus shall the LORD do to all your
enemies against whom ye fight.
26 And afterward Joshua smote them, and
slew them, and hanged them on five trees:
and they were hanging upon the trees until
the evening.
27 And it came to pass at the time of the
going down of the sun, *that* Joshua commanded, and they took them down off the
trees, and cast them into the cave wherein
they had been hid, and laid great stones in
the cave's mouth, *which remain* until this
very day.
28 ¶ And that day Joshua took Makkedah,
and smote it with the edge of the sword,
and the king thereof he utterly destroyed,
them, and all the souls that *were* therein; he
let none remain: and he did to the king of
Makkedah as he did unto the king of Jericho.
29 Then Joshua passed from Makkedah, and
all Israel with him, unto Libnah, and fought
against Libnah:
30 And the LORD delivered it also, and the
king thereof, into the hand of Israel; and he
smote it with the edge of the sword, and

all the souls that *were* therein; he let none
remain in it; but did unto the king thereof
as he did unto the king of Jericho.
31 ¶ And Joshua passed from Libnah, and all
Israel with him, unto Lachish, and encamped
against it, and fought against it:
32 And the LORD delivered Lachish into the
hand of Israel, which took it on the second
day, and smote it with the edge of the
sword, and all the souls that *were* therein,
according to all that he had done to Libnah.
33 ¶ Then Horam king of Gezer came up
to help Lachish; and Joshua smote him
and his people, until he had left him none
remaining.
34 ¶ And from Lachish Joshua passed unto
Eglon, and all Israel with him; and they
encamped against it, and fought against it:
35 And they took it on that day, and smote
it with the edge of the sword, and all the
souls that *were* therein he utterly destroyed
that day, according to all that he had done
to Lachish.
36 And Joshua went up from Eglon, and
all Israel with him, unto Hebron; and they
fought against it:
37 And they took it, and smote it with the
edge of the sword, and the king thereof,
and all the cities thereof, and all the souls
that *were* therein; he left none remaining,
according to all that he had done to Eglon;
but destroyed it utterly, and all the souls
that *were* therein.
38 ¶ And Joshua returned, and all Israel with
him, to Debir; and fought against it:
39 And he took it, and the king thereof, and
all the cities thereof; and they smote them
with the edge of the sword, and utterly
destroyed all the souls that *were* therein;
he left none remaining: as he had done to
Hebron, so he did to Debir, and to the king
thereof; as he had done also to Libnah, and
to her king.
40 ¶ So Joshua smote all the country of
the hills, and of the south, and of the vale,
and of the springs, and all their kings: he
left none remaining, but utterly destroyed
all that breathed, as the LORD God of Israel
commanded.
41 And Joshua smote them from Kadesh-barnea even unto Gaza, and all the country of
Goshen, even unto Gibeon.
42 And all these kings and their land did
Joshua take at one time, because the LORD
God of Israel fought for Israel.
43 And Joshua returned, and all Israel with
him, unto the camp to Gilgal.

Joshua 11

1 And it came to pass, when Jabin king of
Hazor had heard *those things*, that he sent
to Jobab king of Madon, and to the king of
Shimron, and to the king of Achshaph,
2 And to the kings that *were* on the north
of the mountains, and of the plains south
of Chinneroth, and in the valley, and in the
borders of Dor on the west,
3 *And to* the Canaanite on the east and
on the west, and *to* the Amorite, and the
Hittite, and the Perizzite, and the Jebusite
in the mountains, and *to* the Hivite under
Hermon in the land of Mizpeh.
4 And they went out, they and all their hosts
with them, much people, even as the sand
that *is* upon the sea shore in multitude, with
horses and chariots very many.
5 And when all these kings were met
together, they came and pitched together at
the waters of Merom, to fight against Israel.
6 ¶ And the LORD said unto Joshua, Be not
afraid because of them: for to morrow
about this time will I deliver them up all
slain before Israel: thou shalt hough their
horses, and burn their chariots with fire.
7 So Joshua came, and all the people of war
with him, against them by the waters of
Merom suddenly; and they fell upon them.
8 And the LORD delivered them into the
hand of Israel, who smote them, and chased
them unto great Zidon, and unto Misrephoth-maim, and unto the valley of Mizpeh
eastward; and they smote them, until they
left them none remaining.
9 And Joshua did unto them as the LORD
bade him: he houghed their horses, and
burnt their chariots with fire.
10 ¶ And Joshua at that time turned back,
and took Hazor, and smote the king thereof
with the sword: for Hazor beforetime was
the head of all those kingdoms.
11 And they smote all the souls that *were*
therein with the edge of the sword, utterly
destroying *them:* there was not any left to
breathe: and he burnt Hazor with fire.
12 And all the cities of those kings, and
all the kings of them, did Joshua take, and

smote them with the edge of the sword,
and he utterly destroyed them, as Moses
the servant of the LORD commanded.
13 But *as for* the cities that stood still in their
strength, Israel burned none of them, save
Hazor only; *that* did Joshua burn.
14 And all the spoil of these cities, and the
cattle, the children of Israel took for a prey
unto themselves; but every man they smote
with the edge of the sword, until they had
destroyed them, neither left they any to
breathe.
15 ¶ As the LORD commanded Moses his
servant, so did Moses command Joshua,
and so did Joshua; he left nothing undone
of all that the LORD commanded Moses.
16 So Joshua took all that land, the hills,
and all the south country, and all the land
of Goshen, and the valley, and the plain,
and the mountain of Israel, and the valley
of the same;
17 *Even* from the mount Halak, that goeth
up to Seir, even unto Baal-gad in the valley
of Lebanon under mount Hermon: and all
their kings he took, and smote them, and
slew them.
18 Joshua made war a long time with all
those kings.
19 There was not a city that made peace
with the children of Israel, save the Hivites
the inhabitants of Gibeon: all *other* they
took in battle.
20 For it was of the LORD to harden their
hearts, that they should come against Israel
in battle, that he might destroy them utterly,
and that they might have no favour, but
that he might destroy them, as the LORD
commanded Moses.
21 ¶ And at that time came Joshua, and cut
off the Anakims from the mountains, from
Hebron, from Debir, from Anab, and from
all the mountains of Judah, and from all the
mountains of Israel: Joshua destroyed them
utterly with their cities.
22 There was none of the Anakims left in the
land of the children of Israel: only in Gaza,
in Gath, and in Ashdod, there remained.
23 So Joshua took the whole land, according
to all that the LORD said unto Moses; and
Joshua gave it for an inheritance unto Israel
according to their divisions by their tribes.
And the land rested from war.

Joshua 12

1 Now these *are* the kings of the land, which
the children of Israel smote, and possessed
their land on the other side Jordan toward
the rising of the sun, from the river Arnon
unto mount Hermon, and all the plain on
the east:
2 Sihon king of the Amorites, who dwelt
in Heshbon, *and* ruled from Aroer, which
is upon the bank of the river Arnon, and
from the middle of the river, and from half
Gilead, even unto the river Jabbok, *which*
is the border of the children of Ammon;
3 And from the plain to the sea of Chinneroth on the east, and unto the sea of
the plain, *even* the salt sea on the east, the
way to Beth-jeshimoth; and from the south,
under Ashdoth-pisgah:
4 ¶ And the coast of Og king of Bashan,
which was of the remnant of the giants, that
dwelt at Ashtaroth and at Edrei,
5 And reigned in mount Hermon, and in
Salcah, and in all Bashan, unto the border
of the Geshurites and the Maachathites,
and half Gilead, the border of Sihon king
of Heshbon.
6 Them did Moses the servant of the LORD
and the children of Israel smite: and Moses
the servant of the LORD gave it *for* a possession unto the Reubenites, and the Gadites,
and the half tribe of Manasseh.
7 ¶ And these *are* the kings of the country
which Joshua and the children of Israel
smote on this side Jordan on the west, from
Baal-gad in the valley of Lebanon even unto
the mount Halak, that goeth up to Seir;
which Joshua gave unto the tribes of Israel
for a possession according to their divisions;
8 In the mountains, and in the valleys, and
in the plains, and in the springs, and in the
wilderness, and in the south country; the
Hittites, the Amorites, and the Canaanites,
the Perizzites, the Hivites, and the Jebusites:
9 ¶ The king of Jericho, one; the king of Ai,
which *is* beside Beth-el, one;
10 The king of Jerusalem, one; the king of
Hebron, one;
11 The king of Jarmuth, one; the king of
Lachish, one;
12 The king of Eglon, one; the king of Gezer,
one;
13 The king of Debir, one; the king of Geder,
one;

14 The king of Hormah, one; the king of
Arad, one;
15 The king of Libnah, one; the king of
Adullam, one;
16 The king of Makkedah, one; the king of
Beth-el, one;
17 The king of Tappuah, one; the king of
Hepher, one;
18 The king of Aphek, one; the king of
Lasharon, one;
19 The king of Madon, one; the king of
Hazor, one;
20 The king of Shimron-meron, one; the
king of Achshaph, one;
21 The king of Taanach, one; the king of
Megiddo, one;
22 The king of Kedesh, one; the king of Jokneam of Carmel, one;
23 The king of Dor in the coast of Dor, one;
the king of the nations of Gilgal, one;
24 The king of Tirzah, one: all the kings
thirty and one.

Joshua 13

1 Now Joshua was old *and* stricken in years;
and the LORD said unto him, Thou art old
and stricken in years, and there remaineth
yet very much land to be possessed.
2 This *is* the land that yet remaineth: all the
borders of the Philistines, and all Geshuri,
3 From Sihor, which *is* before Egypt, even
unto the borders of Ekron northward, *which*
is counted to the Canaanite: five lords of the
Philistines; the Gazathites, and the Ashdo-
thites, the Eshkalonites, the Gittites, and
the Ekronites; also the Avites:
4 From the south, all the land of the Canaanites, and Mearah that *is* beside the Sidonians, unto Aphek, to the borders of the
Amorites:
5 And the land of the Giblites, and all Lebanon, toward the sunrising, from Baal-gad
under mount Hermon unto the entering
into Hamath.
6 All the inhabitants of the hill country from
Lebanon unto Misrephoth-maim, *and* all the
Sidonians, them will I drive out from before
the children of Israel: only divide thou it by
lot unto the Israelites for an inheritance, as
I have commanded thee.
7 Now therefore divide this land for an
inheritance unto the nine tribes, and the
half tribe of Manasseh,
8 With whom the Reubenites and the
Gadites have received their inheritance,
which Moses gave them, beyond Jordan
eastward, *even* as Moses the servant of the
LORD gave them;
9 From Aroer, that *is* upon the bank of the
river Arnon, and the city that *is* in the midst
of the river, and all the plain of Medeba
unto Dibon;
10 And all the cities of Sihon king of the
Amorites, which reigned in Heshbon, unto
the border of the children of Ammon;
11 And Gilead, and the border of the Geshurites and Maachathites, and all mount Hermon, and all Bashan unto Salcah;
12 All the kingdom of Og in Bashan, which
reigned in Ashtaroth and in Edrei, who
remained of the remnant of the giants: for
these did Moses smite, and cast them out.
13 Nevertheless the children of Israel
expelled not the Geshurites, nor the Maachathites: but the Geshurites and the Maachathites dwell among the Israelites until
this day.
14 Only unto the tribe of Levi he gave none
inheritance; the sacrifices of the LORD God
of Israel made by fire *are* their inheritance,
as he said unto them.
15 ¶ And Moses gave unto the tribe of the
children of Reuben *inheritance* according
to their families.
16 And their coast was from Aroer, that *is*
on the bank of the river Arnon, and the city
that *is* in the midst of the river, and all the
plain by Medeba;
17 Heshbon, and all her cities that *are* in
the plain; Dibon, and Bamoth-baal, and
Beth-baal-meon,
18 And Jahazah, and Kedemoth, and
Mephaath,
19 And Kirjathaim, and Sibmah, and
Zareth-shahar in the mount of the valley,
20 And Beth-peor, and Ashdoth-pisgah, and
Beth-jeshimoth,
21 And all the cities of the plain, and all the
kingdom of Sihon king of the Amorites,
which reigned in Heshbon, whom Moses
smote with the princes of Midian, Evi, and
Rekem, and Zur, and Hur, and Reba, *which*
were dukes of Sihon, dwelling in the country.
22 ¶ Balaam also the son of Beor, the sooth-
sayer, did the children of Israel slay with the
sword among them that were slain by them.

23 And the border of the children of Reuben was Jordan, and the border *thereof*. This *was* the inheritance of the children of Reuben after their families, the cities and the villages thereof.

24 And Moses gave *inheritance* unto the tribe of Gad, *even* unto the children of Gad according to their families.

25 And their coast was Jazer, and all the cities of Gilead, and half the land of the children of Ammon, unto Aroer that *is* before Rabbah;

26 And from Heshbon unto Ramath-mizpeh, and Betonim; and from Mahanaim unto the border of Debir;

27 And in the valley, Beth-aram, and Beth-nimrah, and Succoth, and Zaphon, the rest of the kingdom of Sihon king of Heshbon, Jordan and *his* border, *even* unto the edge of the sea of Chinnereth on the other side Jordan eastward.

28 This *is* the inheritance of the children of Gad after their families, the cities, and their villages.

29 ¶ And Moses gave *inheritance* unto the half tribe of Manasseh: and *this* was *the possession* of the half tribe of the children of Manasseh by their families.

30 And their coast was from Mahanaim, all Bashan, all the kingdom of Og king of Bashan, and all the towns of Jair, which *are* in Bashan, threescore cities:

31 And half Gilead, and Ashtaroth, and Edrei, cities of the kingdom of Og in Bashan, *were pertaining* unto the children of Machir the son of Manasseh, *even* to the one half of the children of Machir by their families.

32 These *are the countries* which Moses did distribute for inheritance in the plains of Moab, on the other side Jordan, by Jericho, eastward.

33 But unto the tribe of Levi Moses gave not *any* inheritance: the LORD God of Israel *was* their inheritance, as he said unto them.

Joshua 14

1 And these *are the countries* which the children of Israel inherited in the land of Canaan, which Eleazar the priest, and Joshua the son of Nun, and the heads of the fathers of the tribes of the children of Israel, distributed for inheritance to them.

2 By lot *was* their inheritance, as the LORD commanded by the hand of Moses, for the nine tribes, and *for* the half tribe.

3 For Moses had given the inheritance of two tribes and an half tribe on the other side Jordan: but unto the Levites he gave none inheritance among them.

4 For the children of Joseph were two tribes, Manasseh and Ephraim: therefore they gave no part unto the Levites in the land, save cities to dwell *in*, with their suburbs for their cattle and for their substance.

5 As the LORD commanded Moses, so the children of Israel did, and they divided the land.

6 ¶ Then the children of Judah came unto Joshua in Gilgal: and Caleb the son of Jephunneh the Kenezite said unto him, Thou knowest the thing that the LORD said unto Moses the man of God concerning me and thee in Kadesh-barnea.

7 Forty years old *was* I when Moses the servant of the LORD sent me from Kadesh-barnea to espy out the land; and I brought him word again as *it was* in mine heart.

8 Nevertheless my brethren that went up with me made the heart of the people melt: but I wholly followed the LORD my God.

9 And Moses sware on that day, saying, Surely the land whereon thy feet have trodden shall be thine inheritance, and thy children's for ever, because thou hast wholly followed the LORD my God.

10 And now, behold, the LORD hath kept me alive, as he said, these forty and five years, even since the LORD spake this word unto Moses, while *the children of* Israel wandered in the wilderness: and now, lo, I *am* this day fourscore and five years old.

11 As yet I *am as* strong this day as *I was* in the day that Moses sent me: as my strength *was* then, even so *is* my strength now, for war, both to go out, and to come in.

12 Now therefore give me this mountain, whereof the LORD spake in that day; for thou heardest in that day how the Anakims *were* there, and *that* the cities *were* great *and* fenced: if so be the LORD *will be* with me, then I shall be able to drive them out, as the LORD said.

13 And Joshua blessed him, and gave unto Caleb the son of Jephunneh Hebron for an inheritance.

14 Hebron therefore became the inheri-

tance of Caleb the son of Jephunneh the Kenezite unto this day, because that he wholly followed the LORD God of Israel.

15 And the name of Hebron before *was* Kirjath-arba; *which Arba was* a great man among the Anakims. And the land had rest from war.

Joshua 15

1 *This* then was the lot of the tribe of the children of Judah by their families; *even* to the border of Edom the wilderness of Zin southward *was* the uttermost part of the south coast.

2 And their south border was from the shore of the salt sea, from the bay that looketh southward:

3 And it went out to the south side to Maaleh-acrabbim, and passed along to Zin, and ascended up on the south side unto Kadesh-barnea, and passed along to Hezron, and went up to Adar, and fetched a compass to Karkaa:

4 *From thence* it passed toward Azmon, and went out unto the river of Egypt; and the goings out of that coast were at the sea: this shall be your south coast.

5 And the east border *was* the salt sea, *even* unto the end of Jordan. And *their* border in the north quarter *was* from the bay of the sea at the uttermost part of Jordan:

6 And the border went up to Beth-hogla, and passed along by the north of Beth-arabah; and the border went up to the stone of Bohan the son of Reuben:

7 And the border went up toward Debir from the valley of Achor, and so northward, looking toward Gilgal, that *is* before the going up to Adummim, which *is* on the south side of the river: and the border passed toward the waters of En-shemesh, and the goings out thereof were at En-rogel:

8 And the border went up by the valley of the son of Hinnom unto the south side of the Jebusite; the same *is* Jerusalem: and the border went up to the top of the mountain that *lieth* before the valley of Hinnom westward, which *is* at the end of the valley of the giants northward:

9 And the border was drawn from the top of the hill unto the fountain of the water of Nephtoah, and went out to the cities of mount Ephron; and the border was drawn to Baalah, which *is* Kirjath-jearim:

10 And the border compassed from Baalah westward unto mount Seir, and passed along unto the side of mount Jearim, which *is* Chesalon, on the north side, and went down to Beth-shemesh, and passed on to Timnah:

11 And the border went out unto the side of Ekron northward: and the border was drawn to Shicron, and passed along to mount Baalah, and went out unto Jabneel; and the goings out of the border were at the sea.

12 And the west border *was* to the great sea, and the coast *thereof*. This *is* the coast of the children of Judah round about according to their families.

13 ¶ And unto Caleb the son of Jephunneh he gave a part among the children of Judah, according to the commandment of the LORD to Joshua, *even* the city of Arba the father of Anak, which *city is* Hebron.

14 And Caleb drove thence the three sons of Anak, Sheshai, and Ahiman, and Talmai, the children of Anak.

15 And he went up thence to the inhabitants of Debir: and the name of Debir before *was* Kirjath-sepher.

16 ¶ And Caleb said, He that smiteth Kirjath-sepher, and taketh it, to him will I give Achsah my daughter to wife.

17 And Othniel the son of Kenaz, the brother of Caleb, took it: and he gave him Achsah his daughter to wife.

18 And it came to pass, as she came *unto him*, that she moved him to ask of her father a field: and she lighted off *her* ass; and Caleb said unto her, What wouldest thou?

19 Who answered, Give me a blessing; for thou hast given me a south land; give me also springs of water. And he gave her the upper springs, and the nether springs.

20 This *is* the inheritance of the tribe of the children of Judah according to their families.

21 And the uttermost cities of the tribe of the children of Judah toward the coast of Edom southward were Kabzeel, and Eder, and Jagur,

22 And Kinah, and Dimonah, and Adadah,

23 And Kedesh, and Hazor, and Ithnan,

24 Ziph, and Telem, and Bealoth,

25 And Hazor, Hadattah, and Kerioth, *and* Hezron, which *is* Hazor,

26 Amam, and Shema, and Moladah,
27 And Hazar-gaddah, and Heshmon, and Beth-palet,
28 And Hazar-shual, and Beer-sheba, and Bizjothjah,
29 Baalah, and Iim, and Azem,
30 And Eltolad, and Chesil, and Hormah,
31 And Ziklag, and Madmannah, and Sansannah,
32 And Lebaoth, and Shilhim, and Ain, and Rimmon: all the cities *are* twenty and nine, with their villages:
33 *And* in the valley, Eshtaol, and Zoreah, and Ashnah,
34 And Zanoah, and En-gannim, Tappuah, and Enam,
35 Jarmuth, and Adullam, Socoh, and Azekah,
36 And Sharaim, and Adithaim, and Gederah, and Gederothaim; fourteen cities with their villages:
37 Zenan, and Hadashah, and Migdal-gad,
38 And Dilean, and Mizpeh, and Joktheel,
39 Lachish, and Bozkath, and Eglon,
40 And Cabbon, and Lahmam, and Kithlish,
41 And Gederoth, Beth-dagon, and Naamah, and Makkedah; sixteen cities with their villages:
42 Libnah, and Ether, and Ashan,
43 And Jiphtah, and Ashnah, and Nezib,
44 And Keilah, and Achzib, and Mareshah; nine cities with their villages:
45 Ekron, with her towns and her villages:
46 From Ekron even unto the sea, all that *lay* near Ashdod, with their villages:
47 Ashdod with her towns and her villages, Gaza with her towns and her villages, unto the river of Egypt, and the great sea, and the border *thereof:*
48 ¶ And in the mountains, Shamir, and Jattir, and Socoh,
49 And Dannah, and Kirjath-sannah, which *is* Debir,
50 And Anab, and Eshtemoh, and Anim,
51 And Goshen, and Holon, and Giloh; eleven cities with their villages:
52 Arab, and Dumah, and Eshean,
53 And Janum, and Beth-tappuah, and Aphekah,
54 And Humtah, and Kirjath-arba, which *is* Hebron, and Zior; nine cities with their villages:
55 Maon, Carmel, and Ziph, and Juttah,
56 And Jezreel, and Jokdeam, and Zanoah,
57 Cain, Gibeah, and Timnah; ten cities with their villages:
58 Halhul, Beth-zur, and Gedor,
59 And Maarath, and Beth-anoth, and Eltekon; six cities with their villages:
60 Kirjath-baal, which *is* Kirjath-jearim, and Rabbah; two cities with their villages:
61 In the wilderness, Beth-arabah, Middin, and Secacah,
62 And Nibshan, and the city of Salt, and En-gedi; six cities with their villages.
63 ¶ As for the Jebusites the inhabitants of Jerusalem, the children of Judah could not drive them out: but the Jebusites dwell with the children of Judah at Jerusalem unto this day.

Joshua 16

1 And the lot of the children of Joseph fell from Jordan by Jericho, unto the water of Jericho on the east, to the wilderness that goeth up from Jericho throughout mount Beth-el,
2 And goeth out from Beth-el to Luz, and passeth along unto the borders of Archi to Ataroth,
3 And goeth down westward to the coast of Japhleti, unto the coast of Beth-horon the nether, and to Gezer: and the goings out thereof are at the sea.
4 So the children of Joseph, Manasseh and Ephraim, took their inheritance.
5 ¶ And the border of the children of Ephraim according to their families was *thus:* even the border of their inheritance on the east side was Ataroth-addar, unto Beth-horon the upper;
6 And the border went out toward the sea to Michmethah on the north side; and the border went about eastward unto Taanath-shiloh, and passed by it on the east to Janohah;
7 And it went down from Janohah to Ataroth, and to Naarath, and came to Jericho, and went out at Jordan.
8 The border went out from Tappuah westward unto the river Kanah; and the goings out thereof were at the sea. This *is* the inheritance of the tribe of the children of Ephraim by their families.
9 And the separate cities for the children of Ephraim *were* among the inheritance of

the children of Manasseh, all the cities with
their villages.
10 And they drave not out the Canaanites
that dwelt in Gezer: but the Canaanites
dwell among the Ephraimites unto this day,
and serve under tribute.

Joshua 17

1 There was also a lot for the tribe of Manasseh; for he *was* the firstborn of Joseph; *to
wit*, for Machir the firstborn of Manasseh,
the father of Gilead: because he was a man
of war, therefore he had Gilead and Bashan.
2 There was also *a lot* for the rest of the
children of Manasseh by their families;
for the children of Abiezer, and for the
children of Helek, and for the children of
Asriel, and for the children of Shechem,
and for the children of Hepher, and for the
children of Shemida: these *were* the male
children of Manasseh the son of Joseph by
their families.
3 ¶ But Zelophehad, the son of Hepher, the
son of Gilead, the son of Machir, the son
of Manasseh, had no sons, but daughters:
and these *are* the names of his daughters,
Mahlah, and Noah, Hoglah, Milcah, and
Tirzah.
4 And they came near before Eleazar the
priest, and before Joshua the son of Nun,
and before the princes, saying, The LORD
commanded Moses to give us an inheritance
among our brethren. Therefore according
to the commandment of the LORD he gave
them an inheritance among the brethren
of their father.
5 And there fell ten portions to Manasseh,
beside the land of Gilead and Bashan, which
were on the other side Jordan;
6 Because the daughters of Manasseh had
an inheritance among his sons: and the rest
of Manasseh's sons had the land of Gilead.
7 ¶ And the coast of Manasseh was from
Asher to Michmethah, that *lieth* before
Shechem; and the border went along on
the right hand unto the inhabitants of
En-tappuah.
8 *Now* Manasseh had the land of Tappuah:
but Tappuah on the border of Manasseh
belonged to the children of Ephraim;
9 And the coast descended unto the river
Kanah, southward of the river: these cities of
Ephraim *are* among the cities of Manasseh:
the coast of Manasseh also *was* on the
north side of the river, and the outgoings
of it were at the sea:
10 Southward *it was* Ephraim's, and northward *it was* Manasseh's, and the sea is his
border; and they met together in Asher on
the north, and in Issachar on the east.
11 And Manasseh had in Issachar and in
Asher Beth-shean and her towns, and
Ibleam and her towns, and the inhabitants
of Dor and her towns, and the inhabitants
of Endor and her towns, and the inhabitants of Taanach and her towns, and the
inhabitants of Megiddo and her towns, *even*
three countries.
12 Yet the children of Manasseh could not
drive out *the inhabitants of* those cities; but
the Canaanites would dwell in that land.
13 Yet it came to pass, when the children
of Israel were waxen strong, that they put
the Canaanites to tribute; but did not utterly
drive them out.
14 And the children of Joseph spake unto
Joshua, saying, Why hast thou given me *but*
one lot and one portion to inherit, seeing I
am a great people, forasmuch as the LORD
hath blessed me hitherto?
15 And Joshua answered them, If thou *be* a
great people, *then* get thee up to the wood
country, and cut down for thyself there in
the land of the Perizzites and of the giants,
if mount Ephraim be too narrow for thee.
16 And the children of Joseph said, The hill
is not enough for us: and all the Canaanites
that dwell in the land of the valley have
chariots of iron, *both they* who *are* of Beth-
shean and her towns, and *they* who *are* of
the valley of Jezreel.
17 And Joshua spake unto the house of
Joseph, *even* to Ephraim and to Manasseh,
saying, Thou *art* a great people, and hast
great power: thou shalt not have one lot
only:
18 But the mountain shall be thine; for it *is*
a wood, and thou shalt cut it down: and the
outgoings of it shall be thine: for thou shalt
drive out the Canaanites, though they have
iron chariots, *and* though they *be* strong.

Joshua 18

1 And the whole congregation of the children of Israel assembled together at Shiloh,
and set up the tabernacle of the congre-

gation there. And the land was subdued
before them.
2 And there remained among the children
of Israel seven tribes, which had not yet
received their inheritance.
3 And Joshua said unto the children of Israel,
How long *are* ye slack to go to possess the
land, which the LORD God of your fathers
hath given you?
4 Give out from among you three men for
each tribe: and I will send them, and they
shall rise, and go through the land, and
describe it according to the inheritance of
them; and they shall come *again* to me.
5 And they shall divide it into seven parts:
Judah shall abide in their coast on the south,
and the house of Joseph shall abide in their
coasts on the north.
6 Ye shall therefore describe the land *into*
seven parts, and bring *the description* hither
to me, that I may cast lots for you here
before the LORD our God.
7 But the Levites have no part among you;
for the priesthood of the LORD *is* their
inheritance: and Gad, and Reuben, and
half the tribe of Manasseh, have received
their inheritance beyond Jordan on the
east, which Moses the servant of the LORD
gave them.
8 ¶ And the men arose, and went away: and
Joshua charged them that went to describe
the land, saying, Go and walk through the
land, and describe it, and come again to me,
that I may here cast lots for you before the
LORD in Shiloh.
9 And the men went and passed through the
land, and described it by cities into seven
parts in a book, and came *again* to Joshua
to the host at Shiloh.
10 ¶ And Joshua cast lots for them in Shiloh
before the LORD: and there Joshua divided
the land unto the children of Israel according
to their divisions.
11 ¶ And the lot of the tribe of the children
of Benjamin came up according to their
families: and the coast of their lot came
forth between the children of Judah and
the children of Joseph.
12 And their border on the north side was
from Jordan; and the border went up to the
side of Jericho on the north side, and went
up through the mountains westward; and
the goings out thereof were at the wilderness of Beth-aven.
13 And the border went over from thence
toward Luz, to the side of Luz, which
is Beth-el, southward; and the border
descended to Ataroth-adar, near the hill
that *lieth* on the south side of the nether
Beth-horon.
14 And the border was drawn *thence*, and
compassed the corner of the sea southward,
from the hill that *lieth* before Beth-horon
southward; and the goings out thereof were
at Kirjath-baal, which *is* Kirjath-jearim, a
city of the children of Judah: this *was* the
west quarter.
15 And the south quarter *was* from the end
of Kirjath-jearim, and the border went out
on the west, and went out to the well of
waters of Nephtoah:
16 And the border came down to the end of
the mountain that *lieth* before the valley of
the son of Hinnom, *and* which *is* in the valley
of the giants on the north, and descended
to the valley of Hinnom, to the side of Jebusi
on the south, and descended to En-rogel,
17 And was drawn from the north, and went
forth to En-shemesh, and went forth toward
Geliloth, which *is* over against the going up
of Adummim, and descended to the stone
of Bohan the son of Reuben,
18 And passed along toward the side over
against Arabah northward, and went down
unto Arabah:
19 And the border passed along to the side
of Beth-hoglah northward: and the outgoings of the border were at the north bay of
the salt sea at the south end of Jordan: this
was the south coast.
20 And Jordan was the border of it on the
east side. This *was* the inheritance of the
children of Benjamin, by the coasts thereof
round about, according to their families.
21 Now the cities of the tribe of the children
of Benjamin according to their families
were Jericho, and Beth-hoglah, and the
valley of Keziz,
22 And Beth-arabah, and Zemaraim, and
Beth-el,
23 And Avim, and Parah, and Ophrah,
24 And Chephar-haammonai, and Ophni,
and Gaba; twelve cities with their villages:
25 Gibeon, and Ramah, and Beeroth,
26 And Mizpeh, and Chephirah, and Mozah,

27 And Rekem, and Irpeel, and Taralah,
28 And Zelah, Eleph, and Jebusi, which *is*
Jerusalem, Gibeath, *and* Kirjath; fourteen
cities with their villages. This *is* the inheritance of the children of Benjamin according
to their families.

Joshua 19

1 And the second lot came forth to Simeon,
even for the tribe of the children of Simeon
according to their families: and their inheritance was within the inheritance of the
children of Judah.
2 And they had in their inheritance Beer-
sheba, or Sheba, and Moladah,
3 And Hazar-shual, and Balah, and Azem,
4 And Eltolad, and Bethul, and Hormah,
5 And Ziklag, and Beth-marcaboth, and
Hazar-susah,
6 And Beth-lebaoth, and Sharuhen; thirteen
cities and their villages:
7 Ain, Remmon, and Ether, and Ashan; four
cities and their villages:
8 And all the villages that *were* round about
these cities to Baalath-beer, Ramath of the
south. This *is* the inheritance of the tribe of
the children of Simeon according to their
families.
9 Out of the portion of the children of Judah
was the inheritance of the children of Simeon: for the part of the children of Judah was
too much for them: therefore the children
of Simeon had their inheritance within the
inheritance of them.
10 ¶ And the third lot came up for the children of Zebulun according to their families:
and the border of their inheritance was
unto Sarid:
11 And their border went up toward the
sea, and Maralah, and reached to Dab-
basheth, and reached to the river that *is*
before Jokneam;
12 And turned from Sarid eastward toward
the sunrising unto the border of Chisloth-ta-
bor, and then goeth out to Daberath, and
goeth up to Japhia,
13 And from thence passeth on along on the
east to Gittah-hepher, to Ittah-kazin, and
goeth out to Remmon-methoar to Neah;
14 And the border compasseth it on the
north side to Hannathon: and the outgoings thereof are in the valley of Jiphthah-el:
15 And Kattath, and Nahallal, and Shimron,
and Idalah, and Beth-lehem: twelve cities
with their villages.
16 This *is* the inheritance of the children of
Zebulun according to their families, these
cities with their villages.
17 ¶ *And* the fourth lot came out to Issachar,
for the children of Issachar according to
their families.
18 And their border was toward Jezreel, and
Chesulloth, and Shunem,
19 And Hapharaim, and Shion, and Ana-
harath,
20 And Rabbith, and Kishion, and Abez,
21 And Remeth, and En-gannim, and
En-haddah, and Beth-pazzez;
22 And the coast reacheth to Tabor, and
Shahazimah, and Beth-shemesh; and the
outgoings of their border were at Jordan:
sixteen cities with their villages.
23 This *is* the inheritance of the tribe of the
children of Issachar according to their families, the cities and their villages.
24 ¶ And the fifth lot came out for the tribe
of the children of Asher according to their
families.
25 And their border was Helkath, and Hali,
and Beten, and Achshaph,
26 And Alammelech, and Amad, and Mis-
heal; and reacheth to Carmel westward,
and to Shihor-libnath;
27 And turneth toward the sunrising to
Beth-dagon, and reacheth to Zebulun, and
to the valley of Jiphthah-el toward the north
side of Beth-emek, and Neiel, and goeth out
to Cabul on the left hand,
28 And Hebron, and Rehob, and Hammon,
and Kanah, *even* unto great Zidon;
29 And *then* the coast turneth to Ramah,
and to the strong city Tyre; and the coast
turneth to Hosah; and the outgoings thereof
are at the sea from the coast to Achzib:
30 Ummah also, and Aphek, and Rehob:
twenty and two cities with their villages.
31 This *is* the inheritance of the tribe of the
children of Asher according to their families,
these cities with their villages.
32 ¶ The sixth lot came out to the children
of Naphtali, *even* for the children of Naphtali
according to their families.
33 And their coast was from Heleph, from
Allon to Zaanannim, and Adami, Nekeb, and
Jabneel, unto Lakum; and the outgoings
thereof were at Jordan:

34 And *then* the coast turneth westward to
Aznoth-tabor, and goeth out from thence
to Hukkok, and reacheth to Zebulun on the
south side, and reacheth to Asher on the
west side, and to Judah upon Jordan toward
the sunrising.
35 And the fenced cities *are* Ziddim, Zer,
and Hammath, Rakkath, and Chinnereth,
36 And Adamah, and Ramah, and Hazor,
37 And Kedesh, and Edrei, and En-hazor,
38 And Iron, and Migdal-el, Horem, and
Beth-anath, and Beth-shemesh; nineteen
cities with their villages.
39 This *is* the inheritance of the tribe of the
children of Naphtali according to their families, the cities and their villages.
40 ¶ *And* the seventh lot came out for the
tribe of the children of Dan according to
their families.
41 And the coast of their inheritance was
Zorah, and Eshtaol, and Ir-shemesh,
42 And Shaalabbin, and Ajalon, and Jethlah,
43 And Elon, and Thimnathah, and Ekron,
44 And Eltekeh, and Gibbethon, and Baalath,
45 And Jehud, and Bene-berak, and
Gath-rimmon,
46 And Me-jarkon, and Rakkon, with the
border before Japho.
47 And the coast of the children of Dan went
out *too little* for them: therefore the children
of Dan went up to fight against Leshem, and
took it, and smote it with the edge of the
sword, and possessed it, and dwelt therein,
and called Leshem, Dan, after the name of
Dan their father.
48 This *is* the inheritance of the tribe of the
children of Dan according to their families,
these cities with their villages.
49 ¶ When they had made an end of dividing the land for inheritance by their coasts,
the children of Israel gave an inheritance to
Joshua the son of Nun among them:
50 According to the word of the LORD they
gave him the city which he asked, *even*
Timnath-serah in mount Ephraim: and he
built the city, and dwelt therein.
51 These *are* the inheritances, which Eleazar
the priest, and Joshua the son of Nun, and
the heads of the fathers of the tribes of the
children of Israel, divided for an inheritance
by lot in Shiloh before the LORD, at the door
of the tabernacle of the congregation. So
they made an end of dividing the country.

Joshua 20

1 The LORD also spake unto Joshua, saying,
2 Speak to the children of Israel, saying,
Appoint out for you cities of refuge, whereof
I spake unto you by the hand of Moses:
3 That the slayer that killeth *any* person
unawares *and* unwittingly may flee thither:
and they shall be your refuge from the
avenger of blood.
4 And when he that doth flee unto one of
those cities shall stand at the entering of the
gate of the city, and shall declare his cause in
the ears of the elders of that city, they shall
take him into the city unto them, and give
him a place, that he may dwell among them.
5 And if the avenger of blood pursue after
him, then they shall not deliver the slayer
up into his hand; because he smote his
neighbour unwittingly, and hated him not
beforetime.
6 And he shall dwell in that city, until he
stand before the congregation for judgment,
and until the death of the high priest that
shall be in those days: then shall the slayer
return, and come unto his own city, and
unto his own house, unto the city from
whence he fled.
7 ¶ And they appointed Kedesh in Galilee
in mount Naphtali, and Shechem in mount
Ephraim, and Kirjath-arba, which *is* Hebron,
in the mountain of Judah.
8 And on the other side Jordan by Jericho
eastward, they assigned Bezer in the wilderness upon the plain out of the tribe of
Reuben, and Ramoth in Gilead out of the
tribe of Gad, and Golan in Bashan out of
the tribe of Manasseh.
9 These were the cities appointed for all
the children of Israel, and for the stranger
that sojourneth among them, that whosoever killeth *any* person at unawares might
flee thither, and not die by the hand of the
avenger of blood, until he stood before the
congregation.

Joshua 21

1 Then came near the heads of the fathers
of the Levites unto Eleazar the priest, and
unto Joshua the son of Nun, and unto the
heads of the fathers of the tribes of the
children of Israel;
2 And they spake unto them at Shiloh in
the land of Canaan, saying, The LORD com-

manded by the hand of Moses to give us
cities to dwell in, with the suburbs thereof
for our cattle.
3 And the children of Israel gave unto the
Levites out of their inheritance, at the commandment of the LORD, these cities and
their suburbs.
4 And the lot came out for the families of
the Kohathites: and the children of Aaron
the priest, *which were* of the Levites, had
by lot out of the tribe of Judah, and out of
the tribe of Simeon, and out of the tribe of
Benjamin, thirteen cities.
5 And the rest of the children of Kohath
had by lot out of the families of the tribe of
Ephraim, and out of the tribe of Dan, and
out of the half tribe of Manasseh, ten cities.
6 And the children of Gershon *had* by lot
out of the families of the tribe of Issachar,
and out of the tribe of Asher, and out of the
tribe of Naphtali, and out of the half tribe of
Manasseh in Bashan, thirteen cities.
7 The children of Merari by their families
had out of the tribe of Reuben, and out
of the tribe of Gad, and out of the tribe of
Zebulun, twelve cities.
8 And the children of Israel gave by lot unto
the Levites these cities with their suburbs, as
the LORD commanded by the hand of Moses.
9 ¶ And they gave out of the tribe of the
children of Judah, and out of the tribe of
the children of Simeon, these cities which
are *here* mentioned by name,
10 Which the children of Aaron, *being* of
the families of the Kohathites, *who were*
of the children of Levi, had: for theirs was
the first lot.
11 And they gave them the city of Arba
the father of Anak, which *city is* Hebron, in
the hill *country* of Judah, with the suburbs
thereof round about it.
12 But the fields of the city, and the villages thereof, gave they to Caleb the son
of Jephunneh for his possession.
13 ¶ Thus they gave to the children of Aaron
the priest Hebron with her suburbs, *to be*
a city of refuge for the slayer; and Libnah
with her suburbs,
14 And Jattir with her suburbs, and Eshtemoa with her suburbs,
15 And Holon with her suburbs, and Debir
with her suburbs,
16 And Ain with her suburbs, and Juttah with
her suburbs, *and* Beth-shemesh with her
suburbs; nine cities out of those two tribes.
17 And out of the tribe of Benjamin, Gibeon
with her suburbs, Geba with her suburbs,
18 Anathoth with her suburbs, and Almon
with her suburbs; four cities.
19 All the cities of the children of Aaron,
the priests, *were* thirteen cities with their
suburbs.
20 ¶ And the families of the children of
Kohath, the Levites which remained of the
children of Kohath, even they had the cities
of their lot out of the tribe of Ephraim.
21 For they gave them Shechem with her
suburbs in mount Ephraim, *to be* a city of
refuge for the slayer; and Gezer with her
suburbs,
22 And Kibzaim with her suburbs, and Beth-
horon with her suburbs; four cities.
23 And out of the tribe of Dan, Eltekeh with
her suburbs, Gibbethon with her suburbs,
24 Aijalon with her suburbs, Gath-rimmon
with her suburbs; four cities.
25 And out of the half tribe of Manasseh,
Tanach with her suburbs, and Gath-rimmon
with her suburbs; two cities.
26 All the cities *were* ten with their suburbs
for the families of the children of Kohath
that remained.
27 ¶ And unto the children of Gershon, of
the families of the Levites, out of the *other*
half tribe of Manasseh *they gave* Golan in
Bashan with her suburbs, *to be* a city of
refuge for the slayer; and Beesh-terah with
her suburbs; two cities.
28 And out of the tribe of Issachar, Kishon
with her suburbs, Dabareh with her suburbs,
29 Jarmuth with her suburbs, En-gannim
with her suburbs; four cities.
30 And out of the tribe of Asher, Mishal
with her suburbs, Abdon with her suburbs,
31 Helkath with her suburbs, and Rehob
with her suburbs; four cities.
32 And out of the tribe of Naphtali, Kedesh
in Galilee with her suburbs, *to be* a city of
refuge for the slayer; and Hammoth-dor
with her suburbs, and Kartan with her suburbs; three cities.
33 All the cities of the Gershonites according
to their families *were* thirteen cities with
their suburbs.
34 ¶ And unto the families of the children
of Merari, the rest of the Levites, out of the

tribe of Zebulun, Jokneam with her suburbs,
and Kartah with her suburbs,
35 Dimnah with her suburbs, Nahalal with
her suburbs; four cities.
36 And out of the tribe of Reuben, Bezer
with her suburbs, and Jahazah with her
suburbs,
37 Kedemoth with her suburbs, and
Mephaath with her suburbs; four cities.
38 And out of the tribe of Gad, Ramoth
in Gilead with her suburbs, *to be* a city of
refuge for the slayer; and Mahanaim with
her suburbs,
39 Heshbon with her suburbs, Jazer with
her suburbs; four cities in all.
40 So all the cities for the children of Merari
by their families, which were remaining of
the families of the Levites, were *by* their lot
twelve cities.
41 All the cities of the Levites within the
possession of the children of Israel *were*
forty and eight cities with their suburbs.
42 These cities were every one with their
suburbs round about them: thus *were* all
these cities.
43 ¶ And the LORD gave unto Israel all the
land which he sware to give unto their
fathers; and they possessed it, and dwelt
therein.
44 And the LORD gave them rest round
about, according to all that he sware unto
their fathers: and there stood not a man
of all their enemies before them; the LORD
delivered all their enemies into their hand.
45 There failed not ought of any good thing
which the LORD had spoken unto the house
of Israel; all came to pass.

Joshua 22

1 Then Joshua called the Reubenites, and
the Gadites, and the half tribe of Manasseh,
2 And said unto them, Ye have kept all that
Moses the servant of the LORD commanded
you, and have obeyed my voice in all that I
commanded you:
3 Ye have not left your brethren these many
days unto this day, but have kept the charge
of the commandment of the LORD your God.
4 And now the LORD your God hath given
rest unto your brethren, as he promised
them: therefore now return ye, and get you
unto your tents, *and* unto the land of your
possession, which Moses the servant of the
LORD gave you on the other side Jordan.
5 But take diligent heed to do the commandment and the law, which Moses the servant
of the LORD charged you, to love the LORD
your God, and to walk in all his ways, and
to keep his commandments, and to cleave
unto him, and to serve him with all your
heart and with all your soul.
6 So Joshua blessed them, and sent them
away: and they went unto their tents.
7 ¶ Now to the *one* half of the tribe of
Manasseh Moses had given *possession* in
Bashan: but unto the *other* half thereof
gave Joshua among their brethren on this
side Jordan westward. And when Joshua
sent them away also unto their tents, then
he blessed them,
8 And he spake unto them, saying, Return
with much riches unto your tents, and with
very much cattle, with silver, and with gold,
and with brass, and with iron, and with very
much raiment: divide the spoil of your enemies with your brethren.
9 ¶ And the children of Reuben and the children of Gad and the half tribe of Manasseh
returned, and departed from the children of
Israel out of Shiloh, which *is* in the land of
Canaan, to go unto the country of Gilead, to
the land of their possession, whereof they
were possessed, according to the word of
the LORD by the hand of Moses.
10 ¶ And when they came unto the borders
of Jordan, that *are* in the land of Canaan, the
children of Reuben and the children of Gad
and the half tribe of Manasseh built there
an altar by Jordan, a great altar to see to.
11 ¶ And the children of Israel heard say,
Behold, the children of Reuben and the children of Gad and the half tribe of Manasseh
have built an altar over against the land of
Canaan, in the borders of Jordan, at the
passage of the children of Israel.
12 And when the children of Israel heard *of
it*, the whole congregation of the children
of Israel gathered themselves together at
Shiloh, to go up to war against them.
13 And the children of Israel sent unto the
children of Reuben, and to the children of
Gad, and to the half tribe of Manasseh,
into the land of Gilead, Phinehas the son
of Eleazar the priest,
14 And with him ten princes, of each chief

house a prince throughout all the tribes of Israel; and each one *was* an head of the house of their fathers among the thousands of Israel.

15 ¶ And they came unto the children of Reuben, and to the children of Gad, and to the half tribe of Manasseh, unto the land of Gilead, and they spake with them, saying,

16 Thus saith the whole congregation of the LORD, What trespass *is* this that ye have committed against the God of Israel, to turn away this day from following the LORD, in that ye have builded you an altar, that ye might rebel this day against the LORD?

17 *Is* the iniquity of Peor too little for us, from which we are not cleansed until this day, although there was a plague in the congregation of the LORD,

18 But that ye must turn away this day from following the LORD? and it will be, *seeing* ye rebel to day against the LORD, that to morrow he will be wroth with the whole congregation of Israel.

19 Notwithstanding, if the land of your possession *be* unclean, *then* pass ye over unto the land of the possession of the LORD, wherein the LORD's tabernacle dwelleth, and take possession among us: but rebel not against the LORD, nor rebel against us, in building you an altar beside the altar of the LORD our God.

20 Did not Achan the son of Zerah commit a trespass in the accursed thing, and wrath fell on all the congregation of Israel? and that man perished not alone in his iniquity.

21 ¶ Then the children of Reuben and the children of Gad and the half tribe of Manasseh answered, and said unto the heads of the thousands of Israel,

22 The LORD God of gods, the LORD God of gods, he knoweth, and Israel he shall know; if *it be* in rebellion, or if in transgression against the LORD, (save us not this day,)

23 That we have built us an altar to turn from following the LORD, or if to offer thereon burnt offering or meat offering, or if to offer peace offerings thereon, let the LORD himself require *it;*

24 And if we have not *rather* done it for fear of *this* thing, saying, In time to come your children might speak unto our children, saying, What have ye to do with the LORD God of Israel?

25 For the LORD hath made Jordan a border between us and you, ye children of Reuben and children of Gad; ye have no part in the LORD: so shall your children make our children cease from fearing the LORD.

26 Therefore we said, Let us now prepare to build us an altar, not for burnt offering, nor for sacrifice:

27 But *that* it *may be* a witness between us, and you, and our generations after us, that we might do the service of the LORD before him with our burnt offerings, and with our sacrifices, and with our peace offerings; that your children may not say to our children in time to come, Ye have no part in the LORD.

28 Therefore said we, that it shall be, when they should *so* say to us or to our generations in time to come, that we may say *again*, Behold the pattern of the altar of the LORD, which our fathers made, not for burnt offerings, nor for sacrifices; but it *is* a witness between us and you.

29 God forbid that we should rebel against the LORD, and turn this day from following the LORD, to build an altar for burnt offerings, for meat offerings, or for sacrifices, beside the altar of the LORD our God that *is* before his tabernacle.

30 ¶ And when Phinehas the priest, and the princes of the congregation and heads of the thousands of Israel which *were* with him, heard the words that the children of Reuben and the children of Gad and the children of Manasseh spake, it pleased them.

31 And Phinehas the son of Eleazar the priest said unto the children of Reuben, and to the children of Gad, and to the children of Manasseh, This day we perceive that the LORD *is* among us, because ye have not committed this trespass against the LORD: now ye have delivered the children of Israel out of the hand of the LORD.

32 ¶ And Phinehas the son of Eleazar the priest, and the princes, returned from the children of Reuben, and from the children of Gad, out of the land of Gilead, unto the land of Canaan, to the children of Israel, and brought them word again.

33 And the thing pleased the children of Israel; and the children of Israel blessed God, and did not intend to go up against them in battle, to destroy the land wherein the children of Reuben and Gad dwelt.

34 And the children of Reuben and the children of Gad called the altar *Ed:* for it *shall be*
a witness between us that the LORD *is* God.

Joshua 23

1 And it came to pass a long time after that
the LORD had given rest unto Israel from
all their enemies round about, that Joshua
waxed old *and* stricken in age.
2 And Joshua called for all Israel, *and* for
their elders, and for their heads, and for
their judges, and for their officers, and said
unto them, I am old *and* stricken in age:
3 And ye have seen all that the LORD your
God hath done unto all these nations
because of you; for the LORD your God *is*
he that hath fought for you.
4 Behold, I have divided unto you by lot
these nations that remain, to be an inheritance for your tribes, from Jordan, with all
the nations that I have cut off, even unto
the great sea westward.
5 And the LORD your God, he shall expel
them from before you, and drive them from
out of your sight; and ye shall possess their
land, as the LORD your God hath promised
unto you.
6 Be ye therefore very courageous to keep
and to do all that is written in the book of
the law of Moses, that ye turn not aside
therefrom *to* the right hand or *to* the left;
7 That ye come not among these nations,
these that remain among you; neither make
mention of the name of their gods, nor
cause to swear *by them*, neither serve them,
nor bow yourselves unto them:
8 But cleave unto the LORD your God, as ye
have done unto this day.
9 For the LORD hath driven out from before
you great nations and strong: but *as for* you,
no man hath been able to stand before you
unto this day.
10 One man of you shall chase a thousand:
for the LORD your God, he *it is* that fighteth
for you, as he hath promised you.
11 Take good heed therefore unto yourselves, that ye love the LORD your God.
12 Else if ye do in any wise go back, and
cleave unto the remnant of these nations,
even these that remain among you, and shall
make marriages with them, and go in unto
them, and they to you:
13 Know for a certainty that the LORD your
God will no more drive out *any of* these
nations from before you; but they shall be
snares and traps unto you, and scourges in
your sides, and thorns in your eyes, until
ye perish from off this good land which the
LORD your God hath given you.
14 And, behold, this day I *am* going the
way of all the earth: and ye know in all
your hearts and in all your souls, that not
one thing hath failed of all the good things
which the LORD your God spake concerning
you; all are come to pass unto you, *and* not
one thing hath failed thereof.
15 Therefore it shall come to pass, *that* as all
good things are come upon you, which the
LORD your God promised you; so shall the
LORD bring upon you all evil things, until he
have destroyed you from off this good land
which the LORD your God hath given you.
16 When ye have transgressed the covenant
of the LORD your God, which he commanded
you, and have gone and served other gods,
and bowed yourselves to them; then shall
the anger of the LORD be kindled against
you, and ye shall perish quickly from off the
good land which he hath given unto you.

Joshua 24

1 And Joshua gathered all the tribes of
Israel to Shechem, and called for the elders
of Israel, and for their heads, and for their
judges, and for their officers; and they presented themselves before God.
2 And Joshua said unto all the people, Thus
saith the LORD God of Israel, Your fathers
dwelt on the other side of the flood in old
time, *even* Terah, the father of Abraham,
and the father of Nachor: and they served
other gods.
3 And I took your father Abraham from the
other side of the flood, and led him throughout all the land of Canaan, and multiplied
his seed, and gave him Isaac.
4 And I gave unto Isaac Jacob and Esau: and
I gave unto Esau mount Seir, to possess it;
but Jacob and his children went down into
Egypt.
5 I sent Moses also and Aaron, and I plagued
Egypt, according to that which I did among
them: and afterward I brought you out.
6 And I brought your fathers out of Egypt:
and ye came unto the sea; and the Egyptians

pursued after your fathers with chariots and
horsemen unto the Red sea.
7 And when they cried unto the LORD, he put
darkness between you and the Egyptians,
and brought the sea upon them, and covered them; and your eyes have seen what
I have done in Egypt: and ye dwelt in the
wilderness a long season.
8 And I brought you into the land of the
Amorites, which dwelt on the other side
Jordan; and they fought with you: and I
gave them into your hand, that ye might
possess their land; and I destroyed them
from before you.
9 Then Balak the son of Zippor, king of
Moab, arose and warred against Israel, and
sent and called Balaam the son of Beor to
curse you:
10 But I would not hearken unto Balaam;
therefore he blessed you still: so I delivered
you out of his hand.
11 And ye went over Jordan, and came
unto Jericho: and the men of Jericho fought
against you, the Amorites, and the Perizzites, and the Canaanites, and the Hittites,
and the Girgashites, the Hivites, and the Jebusites; and I delivered them into your hand.
12 And I sent the hornet before you, which
drave them out from before you, *even* the
two kings of the Amorites; *but* not with thy
sword, nor with thy bow.
13 And I have given you a land for which ye
did not labour, and cities which ye built not,
and ye dwell in them; of the vineyards and
oliveyards which ye planted not do ye eat.
14 ¶ Now therefore fear the LORD, and serve
him in sincerity and in truth: and put away
the gods which your fathers served on the
other side of the flood, and in Egypt; and
serve ye the LORD.
15 And if it seem evil unto you to serve the
LORD, choose you this day whom ye will
serve; whether the gods which your fathers
served that *were* on the other side of the
flood, or the gods of the Amorites, in whose
land ye dwell: but as for me and my house,
we will serve the LORD.
16 And the people answered and said, God
forbid that we should forsake the LORD, to
serve other gods;
17 For the LORD our God, he *it is* that
brought us up and our fathers out of the
land of Egypt, from the house of bondage,
and which did those great signs in our sight,
and preserved us in all the way wherein we
went, and among all the people through
whom we passed:
18 And the LORD drave out from before us all
the people, even the Amorites which dwelt
in the land: *therefore* will we also serve the
LORD; for he *is* our God.
19 And Joshua said unto the people, Ye cannot serve the LORD: for he *is* an holy God;
he *is* a jealous God; he will not forgive your
transgressions nor your sins.
20 If ye forsake the LORD, and serve strange
gods, then he will turn and do you hurt,
and consume you, after that he hath done
you good.
21 And the people said unto Joshua, Nay;
but we will serve the LORD.
22 And Joshua said unto the people, Ye *are*
witnesses against yourselves that ye have
chosen you the LORD, to serve him. And they
said, *We are* witnesses.
23 Now therefore put away, *said he*, the
strange gods which *are* among you, and
incline your heart unto the LORD God of
Israel.
24 And the people said unto Joshua, The
LORD our God will we serve, and his voice
will we obey.
25 So Joshua made a covenant with the
people that day, and set them a statute and
an ordinance in Shechem.
26 ¶ And Joshua wrote these words in the
book of the law of God, and took a great
stone, and set it up there under an oak, that
was by the sanctuary of the LORD.
27 And Joshua said unto all the people,
Behold, this stone shall be a witness unto us;
for it hath heard all the words of the LORD
which he spake unto us: it shall be therefore
a witness unto you, lest ye deny your God.
28 So Joshua let the people depart, every
man unto his inheritance.
29 ¶ And it came to pass after these things,
that Joshua the son of Nun, the servant of
the LORD, died, *being* an hundred and ten
years old.
30 And they buried him in the border of
his inheritance in Timnath-serah, which *is*
in mount Ephraim, on the north side of the
hill of Gaash.
31 And Israel served the LORD all the days
of Joshua, and all the days of the elders that

overlived Joshua, and which had known all the works of the LORD, that he had done for Israel.

32 ¶ And the bones of Joseph, which the children of Israel brought up out of Egypt, buried they in Shechem, in a parcel of ground which Jacob bought of the sons of Hamor the father of Shechem for an hundred pieces of silver: and it became the inheritance of the children of Joseph.

33 And Eleazar the son of Aaron died; and they buried him in a hill *that pertained to* Phinehas his son, which was given him in mount Ephraim.

The Book Of

Judges

Judges 1

1 Now after the death of Joshua it came to pass, that the children of Israel asked the LORD, saying, Who shall go up for us against the Canaanites first, to fight against them?

2 And the LORD said, Judah shall go up: behold, I have delivered the land into his hand.

3 And Judah said unto Simeon his brother, Come up with me into my lot, that we may fight against the Canaanites; and I likewise will go with thee into thy lot. So Simeon went with him.

4 And Judah went up; and the LORD delivered the Canaanites and the Perizzites into their hand: and they slew of them in Bezek ten thousand men.

5 And they found Adoni-bezek in Bezek: and they fought against him, and they slew the Canaanites and the Perizzites.

6 But Adoni-bezek fled; and they pursued after him, and caught him, and cut off his thumbs and his great toes.

7 And Adoni-bezek said, Threescore and ten kings, having their thumbs and their great toes cut off, gathered *their meat* under my table: as I have done, so God hath requited me. And they brought him to Jerusalem, and there he died.

8 Now the children of Judah had fought against Jerusalem, and had taken it, and smitten it with the edge of the sword, and set the city on fire.

9 ¶ And afterward the children of Judah went down to fight against the Canaanites, that dwelt in the mountain, and in the south, and in the valley.

10 And Judah went against the Canaanites that dwelt in Hebron: (now the name of Hebron before *was* Kirjath-arba:) and they slew Sheshai, and Ahiman, and Talmai.

11 And from thence he went against the inhabitants of Debir: and the name of Debir before *was* Kirjath-sepher:

12 And Caleb said, He that smiteth Kirjath-sepher, and taketh it, to him will I give Achsah my daughter to wife.

13 And Othniel the son of Kenaz, Caleb's younger brother, took it: and he gave him Achsah his daughter to wife.

14 And it came to pass, when she came *to him*, that she moved him to ask of her father a field: and she lighted from off *her* ass; and Caleb said unto her, What wilt thou?

15 And she said unto him, Give me a blessing: for thou hast given me a south land; give me also springs of water. And Caleb gave her the upper springs and the nether springs.

16 ¶ And the children of the Kenite, Moses' father in law, went up out of the city of palm trees with the children of Judah into the wilderness of Judah, which *lieth* in the south of Arad; and they went and dwelt among the people.

17 And Judah went with Simeon his brother, and they slew the Canaanites that inhabited Zephath, and utterly destroyed it. And the name of the city was called Hormah.

18 Also Judah took Gaza with the coast thereof, and Askelon with the coast thereof, and Ekron with the coast thereof.

19 And the LORD was with Judah; and he drave out *the inhabitants of* the mountain;

but could not drive out the inhabitants of
the valley, because they had chariots of iron.
20 And they gave Hebron unto Caleb, as
Moses said: and he expelled thence the
three sons of Anak.
21 And the children of Benjamin did not
drive out the Jebusites that inhabited Jerusalem;
but the Jebusites dwell with the children
of Benjamin in Jerusalem unto this day.
22 ¶ And the house of Joseph, they also
went up against Beth-el: and the LORD *was*
with them.
23 And the house of Joseph sent to descry
Beth-el. (Now the name of the city before
was Luz.)
24 And the spies saw a man come forth out
of the city, and they said unto him, Shew us,
we pray thee, the entrance into the city, and
we will shew thee mercy.
25 And when he shewed them the entrance
into the city, they smote the city with the
edge of the sword; but they let go the man
and all his family.
26 And the man went into the land of the
Hittites, and built a city, and called the name
thereof Luz: which *is* the name thereof unto
this day.
27 ¶ Neither did Manasseh drive out *the
inhabitants of* Beth-shean and her towns,
nor Taanach and her towns, nor the inhabitants
of Dor and her towns, nor the inhabitants
of Ibleam and her towns, nor the
inhabitants of Megiddo and her towns: but
the Canaanites would dwell in that land.
28 And it came to pass, when Israel was
strong, that they put the Canaanites to
tribute, and did not utterly drive them out.
29 ¶ Neither did Ephraim drive out the
Canaanites that dwelt in Gezer; but the
Canaanites dwelt in Gezer among them.
30 ¶ Neither did Zebulun drive out the
inhabitants of Kitron, nor the inhabitants of
Nahalol; but the Canaanites dwelt among
them, and became tributaries.
31 ¶ Neither did Asher drive out the inhabitants
of Accho, nor the inhabitants of Zidon,
nor of Ahlab, nor of Achzib, nor of Helbah,
nor of Aphik, nor of Rehob:
32 But the Asherites dwelt among the
Canaanites, the inhabitants of the land: for
they did not drive them out.
33 ¶ Neither did Naphtali drive out the
inhabitants of Beth-shemesh, nor the
inhabitants of Beth-anath; but he dwelt
among the Canaanites, the inhabitants of
the land: nevertheless the inhabitants of
Beth-shemesh and of Beth-anath became
tributaries unto them.
34 And the Amorites forced the children of
Dan into the mountain: for they would not
suffer them to come down to the valley:
35 But the Amorites would dwell in mount
Heres in Aijalon, and in Shaalbim: yet the
hand of the house of Joseph prevailed, so
that they became tributaries.
36 And the coast of the Amorites *was* from
the going up to Akrabbim, from the rock,
and upward.

Judges 2

1 And an angel of the LORD came up from
Gilgal to Bochim, and said, I made you to go
up out of Egypt, and have brought you unto
the land which I sware unto your fathers;
and I said, I will never break my covenant
with you.
2 And ye shall make no league with the
inhabitants of this land; ye shall throw
down their altars: but ye have not obeyed
my voice: why have ye done this?
3 Wherefore I also said, I will not drive them
out from before you; but they shall be *as
thorns* in your sides, and their gods shall be
a snare unto you.
4 And it came to pass, when the angel of
the LORD spake these words unto all the
children of Israel, that the people lifted up
their voice, and wept.
5 And they called the name of that place
Bochim: and they sacrificed there unto
the LORD.
6 ¶ And when Joshua had let the people go,
the children of Israel went every man unto
his inheritance to possess the land.
7 And the people served the LORD all the
days of Joshua, and all the days of the
elders that outlived Joshua, who had seen
all the great works of the LORD, that he did
for Israel.
8 And Joshua the son of Nun, the servant
of the LORD, died, *being* an hundred and
ten years old.
9 And they buried him in the border of
his inheritance in Timnath-heres, in the
mount of Ephraim, on the north side of
the hill Gaash.

10 And also all that generation were gathered unto their fathers: and there arose
another generation after them, which knew
not the LORD, nor yet the works which he
had done for Israel.
11 ¶ And the children of Israel did evil in
the sight of the LORD, and served Baalim:
12 And they forsook the LORD God of their
fathers, which brought them out of the land
of Egypt, and followed other gods, of the
gods of the people that *were* round about
them, and bowed themselves unto them,
and provoked the LORD to anger.
13 And they forsook the LORD, and served
Baal and Ashtaroth.
14 ¶ And the anger of the LORD was hot
against Israel, and he delivered them into
the hands of spoilers that spoiled them,
and he sold them into the hands of their
enemies round about, so that they could
not any longer stand before their enemies.
15 Whithersoever they went out, the hand
of the LORD was against them for evil, as the
LORD had said, and as the LORD had sworn
unto them: and they were greatly distressed.
16 ¶ Nevertheless the LORD raised up
judges, which delivered them out of the
hand of those that spoiled them.
17 And yet they would not hearken unto
their judges, but they went a whoring after
other gods, and bowed themselves unto
them: they turned quickly out of the way
which their fathers walked in, obeying the
commandments of the LORD; *but* they did
not so.
18 And when the LORD raised them up
judges, then the LORD was with the judge,
and delivered them out of the hand of their
enemies all the days of the judge: for it
repented the LORD because of their groanings by reason of them that oppressed them
and vexed them.
19 And it came to pass, when the judge was
dead, *that* they returned, and corrupted
themselves more than their fathers, in following other gods to serve them, and to bow
down unto them; they ceased not from their
own doings, nor from their stubborn way.
20 ¶ And the anger of the LORD was hot
against Israel; and he said, Because that
this people hath transgressed my covenant
which I commanded their fathers, and have
not hearkened unto my voice;
21 I also will not henceforth drive out any
from before them of the nations which
Joshua left when he died:
22 That through them I may prove Israel,
whether they will keep the way of the
LORD to walk therein, as their fathers did
keep *it*, or not.
23 Therefore the LORD left those nations,
without driving them out hastily; neither
delivered he them into the hand of Joshua.

Judges 3

1 Now these *are* the nations which the LORD
left, to prove Israel by them, *even* as many
of Israel as had not known all the wars of
Canaan;
2 Only that the generations of the children
of Israel might know, to teach them war,
at the least such as before knew nothing
thereof;
3 *Namely*, five lords of the Philistines, and
all the Canaanites, and the Sidonians, and
the Hivites that dwelt in mount Lebanon,
from mount Baal-hermon unto the entering
in of Hamath.
4 And they were to prove Israel by them, to
know whether they would hearken unto the
commandments of the LORD, which he commanded their fathers by the hand of Moses.
5 ¶ And the children of Israel dwelt among
the Canaanites, Hittites, and Amorites, and
Perizzites, and Hivites, and Jebusites:
6 And they took their daughters to be their
wives, and gave their daughters to their
sons, and served their gods.
7 And the children of Israel did evil in the
sight of the LORD, and forgat the LORD their
God, and served Baalim and the groves.
8 ¶ Therefore the anger of the LORD was
hot against Israel, and he sold them into the
hand of Chushan-rishathaim king of Mesopotamia: and the children of Israel served
Chushan-rishathaim eight years.
9 And when the children of Israel cried unto
the LORD, the LORD raised up a deliverer to
the children of Israel, who delivered them,
even Othniel the son of Kenaz, Caleb's
younger brother.
10 And the Spirit of the LORD came upon
him, and he judged Israel, and went out to
war: and the LORD delivered Chushan-rishathaim king of Mesopotamia into his hand;

and his hand prevailed against Chushan-rishathaim.
11 And the land had rest forty years. And
Othniel the son of Kenaz died.
12 ¶ And the children of Israel did evil
again in the sight of the LORD: and the
LORD strengthened Eglon the king of Moab
against Israel, because they had done evil
in the sight of the LORD.
13 And he gathered unto him the children of
Ammon and Amalek, and went and smote
Israel, and possessed the city of palm trees.
14 So the children of Israel served Eglon the
king of Moab eighteen years.
15 But when the children of Israel cried
unto the LORD, the LORD raised them up a
deliverer, Ehud the son of Gera, a Benjamite,
a man lefthanded: and by him the children
of Israel sent a present unto Eglon the king
of Moab.
16 But Ehud made him a dagger which had
two edges, of a cubit length; and he did gird
it under his raiment upon his right thigh.
17 And he brought the present unto Eglon
king of Moab: and Eglon *was* a very fat man.
18 And when he had made an end to offer
the present, he sent away the people that
bare the present.
19 But he himself turned again from the
quarries that *were* by Gilgal, and said, I have
a secret errand unto thee, O king: who said,
Keep silence. And all that stood by him went
out from him.
20 And Ehud came unto him; and he was
sitting in a summer parlour, which he had
for himself alone. And Ehud said, I have a
message from God unto thee. And he arose
out of *his* seat.
21 And Ehud put forth his left hand, and
took the dagger from his right thigh, and
thrust it into his belly:
22 And the haft also went in after the blade;
and the fat closed upon the blade, so that he
could not draw the dagger out of his belly;
and the dirt came out.
23 Then Ehud went forth through the porch,
and shut the doors of the parlour upon him,
and locked them.
24 When he was gone out, his servants
came; and when they saw that, behold, the
doors of the parlour *were* locked, they said,
Surely he covereth his feet in his summer
chamber.
25 And they tarried till they were ashamed:
and, behold, he opened not the doors of
the parlour; therefore they took a key, and
opened *them:* and, behold, their lord *was*
fallen down dead on the earth.
26 And Ehud escaped while they tarried, and
passed beyond the quarries, and escaped
unto Seirath.
27 And it came to pass, when he was come,
that he blew a trumpet in the mountain of
Ephraim, and the children of Israel went
down with him from the mount, and he
before them.
28 And he said unto them, Follow after me:
for the LORD hath delivered your enemies
the Moabites into your hand. And they
went down after him, and took the fords
of Jordan toward Moab, and suffered not
a man to pass over.
29 And they slew of Moab at that time about
ten thousand men, all lusty, and all men of
valour; and there escaped not a man.
30 So Moab was subdued that day under
the hand of Israel. And the land had rest
fourscore years.
31 ¶ And after him was Shamgar the son
of Anath, which slew of the Philistines six
hundred men with an ox goad: and he also
delivered Israel.

Judges 4

1 And the children of Israel again did evil in
the sight of the LORD, when Ehud was dead.
2 And the LORD sold them into the hand of
Jabin king of Canaan, that reigned in Hazor;
the captain of whose host *was* Sisera, which
dwelt in Harosheth of the Gentiles.
3 And the children of Israel cried unto
the LORD: for he had nine hundred chariots of iron; and twenty years he mightily
oppressed the children of Israel.
4 ¶ And Deborah, a prophetess, the wife
of Lapidoth, she judged Israel at that time.
5 And she dwelt under the palm tree of
Deborah between Ramah and Beth-el in
mount Ephraim: and the children of Israel
came up to her for judgment.
6 And she sent and called Barak the son of
Abinoam out of Kedesh-naphtali, and said
unto him, Hath not the LORD God of Israel
commanded, *saying,* Go and draw toward
mount Tabor, and take with thee ten thou-

sand men of the children of Naphtali and of
the children of Zebulun?
7 And I will draw unto thee to the river
Kishon Sisera, the captain of Jabin's army,
with his chariots and his multitude; and I
will deliver him into thine hand.
8 And Barak said unto her, If thou wilt go
with me, then I will go: but if thou wilt not
go with me, *then* I will not go.
9 And she said, I will surely go with thee:
notwithstanding the journey that thou
takest shall not be for thine honour; for
the LORD shall sell Sisera into the hand of a
woman. And Deborah arose, and went with
Barak to Kedesh.
10 ¶ And Barak called Zebulun and Naphtali
to Kedesh; and he went up with ten thousand men at his feet: and Deborah went
up with him.
11 Now Heber the Kenite, *which was* of
the children of Hobab the father in law
of Moses, had severed himself from the
Kenites, and pitched his tent unto the plain
of Zaanaim, which *is* by Kedesh.
12 And they shewed Sisera that Barak the
son of Abinoam was gone up to mount
Tabor.
13 And Sisera gathered together all his
chariots, *even* nine hundred chariots of
iron, and all the people that *were* with him,
from Harosheth of the Gentiles unto the
river of Kishon.
14 And Deborah said unto Barak, Up; for
this *is* the day in which the LORD hath delivered Sisera into thine hand: is not the LORD
gone out before thee? So Barak went down
from mount Tabor, and ten thousand men
after him.
15 And the LORD discomfited Sisera, and all
his chariots, and all *his* host, with the edge
of the sword before Barak; so that Sisera
lighted down off *his* chariot, and fled away
on his feet.
16 But Barak pursued after the chariots,
and after the host, unto Harosheth of the
Gentiles: and all the host of Sisera fell upon
the edge of the sword; *and* there was not
a man left.
17 Howbeit Sisera fled away on his feet to
the tent of Jael the wife of Heber the Kenite:
for *there was* peace between Jabin the king
of Hazor and the house of Heber the Kenite.
18 ¶ And Jael went out to meet Sisera, and
said unto him, Turn in, my lord, turn in to
me; fear not. And when he had turned in
unto her into the tent, she covered him
with a mantle.
19 And he said unto her, Give me, I pray
thee, a little water to drink; for I am thirsty.
And she opened a bottle of milk, and gave
him drink, and covered him.
20 Again he said unto her, Stand in the door
of the tent, and it shall be, when any man
doth come and inquire of thee, and say, Is
there any man here? that thou shalt say, No.
21 Then Jael Heber's wife took a nail of the
tent, and took an hammer in her hand, and
went softly unto him, and smote the nail
into his temples, and fastened it into the
ground: for he was fast asleep and weary.
So he died.
22 And, behold, as Barak pursued Sisera, Jael
came out to meet him, and said unto him,
Come, and I will shew thee the man whom
thou seekest. And when he came into her
tent, behold, Sisera lay dead, and the nail
was in his temples.
23 So God subdued on that day Jabin the
king of Canaan before the children of Israel.
24 And the hand of the children of Israel
prospered, and prevailed against Jabin the
king of Canaan, until they had destroyed
Jabin king of Canaan.

Judges 5

1 Then sang Deborah and Barak the son of
Abinoam on that day, saying,
2 Praise ye the LORD for the avenging of
Israel, when the people willingly offered
themselves.
3 Hear, O ye kings; give ear, O ye princes;
I, *even* I, will sing unto the LORD; I will sing
praise to the LORD God of Israel.
4 LORD, when thou wentest out of Seir, when
thou marchedst out of the field of Edom, the
earth trembled, and the heavens dropped,
the clouds also dropped water.
5 The mountains melted from before the
LORD, *even* that Sinai from before the LORD
God of Israel.
6 In the days of Shamgar the son of Anath,
in the days of Jael, the highways were unoc-
cupied, and the travellers walked through
byways.
7 *The inhabitants of* the villages ceased, they

ceased in Israel, until that I Deborah arose,
that I arose a mother in Israel.
8 They chose new gods; then *was* war in
the gates: was there a shield or spear seen
among forty thousand in Israel?
9 My heart *is* toward the governors of Israel,
that offered themselves willingly among the
people. Bless ye the LORD.
10 Speak, ye that ride on white asses, ye
that sit in judgment, and walk by the way.
11 *They that are delivered* from the noise
of archers in the places of drawing water,
there shall they rehearse the righteous acts
of the LORD, *even* the righteous acts *toward*
the inhabitants of his villages in Israel: then
shall the people of the LORD go down to
the gates.
12 Awake, awake, Deborah: awake, awake,
utter a song: arise, Barak, and lead thy captivity captive, thou son of Abinoam.
13 Then he made him that remaineth have
dominion over the nobles among the people: the LORD made me have dominion over
the mighty.
14 Out of Ephraim *was there* a root of
them against Amalek; after thee, Benjamin,
among thy people; out of Machir came
down governors, and out of Zebulun they
that handle the pen of the writer.
15 And the princes of Issachar *were* with
Deborah; even Issachar, and also Barak:
he was sent on foot into the valley. For
the divisions of Reuben *there were* great
thoughts of heart.
16 Why abodest thou among the sheepfolds, to hear the bleatings of the flocks?
For the divisions of Reuben *there were* great
searchings of heart.
17 Gilead abode beyond Jordan: and why
did Dan remain in ships? Asher continued
on the sea shore, and abode in his breaches.
18 Zebulun and Naphtali *were* a people *that*
jeoparded their lives unto the death in the
high places of the field.
19 The kings came *and* fought, then fought
the kings of Canaan in Taanach by the waters
of Megiddo; they took no gain of money.
20 They fought from heaven; the stars in
their courses fought against Sisera.
21 The river of Kishon swept them away,
that ancient river, the river Kishon. O my
soul, thou hast trodden down strength.
22 Then were the horsehoofs broken by
the means of the pransings, the pransings
of their mighty ones.
23 Curse ye Meroz, said the angel of the
LORD, curse ye bitterly the inhabitants
thereof; because they came not to the help
of the LORD, to the help of the LORD against
the mighty.
24 Blessed above women shall Jael the wife
of Heber the Kenite be, blessed shall she be
above women in the tent.
25 He asked water, *and* she gave *him* milk;
she brought forth butter in a lordly dish.
26 She put her hand to the nail, and her right
hand to the workmen's hammer; and with
the hammer she smote Sisera, she smote off
his head, when she had pierced and stricken
through his temples.
27 At her feet he bowed, he fell, he lay
down: at her feet he bowed, he fell: where
he bowed, there he fell down dead.
28 The mother of Sisera looked out at a
window, and cried through the lattice, Why
is his chariot *so* long in coming? why tarry
the wheels of his chariots?
29 Her wise ladies answered her, yea, she
returned answer to herself,
30 Have they not sped? have they *not*
divided the prey; to every man a damsel *or*
two; to Sisera a prey of divers colours, a prey
of divers colours of needlework, of divers
colours of needlework on both sides, *meet*
for the necks of *them that take* the spoil?
31 So let all thine enemies perish, O LORD:
but *let* them that love him *be* as the sun
when he goeth forth in his might. And the
land had rest forty years.

Judges 6

1 And the children of Israel did evil in the
sight of the LORD: and the LORD delivered
them into the hand of Midian seven years.
2 And the hand of Midian prevailed against
Israel: *and* because of the Midianites the
children of Israel made them the dens
which *are* in the mountains, and caves, and
strong holds.
3 And *so* it was, when Israel had sown, that
the Midianites came up, and the Amalekites,
and the children of the east, even they came
up against them;
4 And they encamped against them, and
destroyed the increase of the earth, till thou

come unto Gaza, and left no sustenance for Israel, neither sheep, nor ox, nor ass.

5 For they came up with their cattle and their tents, and they came as grasshoppers for multitude; *for* both they and their camels were without number: and they entered into the land to destroy it.

6 And Israel was greatly impoverished because of the Midianites; and the children of Israel cried unto the LORD.

7 ¶ And it came to pass, when the children of Israel cried unto the LORD because of the Midianites,

8 That the LORD sent a prophet unto the children of Israel, which said unto them, Thus saith the LORD God of Israel, I brought you up from Egypt, and brought you forth out of the house of bondage;

9 And I delivered you out of the hand of the Egyptians, and out of the hand of all that oppressed you, and drave them out from before you, and gave you their land;

10 And I said unto you, I *am* the LORD your God; fear not the gods of the Amorites, in whose land ye dwell: but ye have not obeyed my voice.

11 ¶ And there came an angel of the LORD, and sat under an oak which *was* in Ophrah, that *pertained* unto Joash the Abi-ezrite: and his son Gideon threshed wheat by the winepress, to hide *it* from the Midianites.

12 And the angel of the LORD appeared unto him, and said unto him, The LORD *is* with thee, thou mighty man of valour.

13 And Gideon said unto him, Oh my Lord, if the LORD be with us, why then is all this befallen us? and where *be* all his miracles which our fathers told us of, saying, Did not the LORD bring us up from Egypt? but now the LORD hath forsaken us, and delivered us into the hands of the Midianites.

14 And the LORD looked upon him, and said, Go in this thy might, and thou shalt save Israel from the hand of the Midianites: have not I sent thee?

15 And he said unto him, Oh my Lord, wherewith shall I save Israel? behold, my family *is* poor in Manasseh, and I *am* the least in my father's house.

16 And the LORD said unto him, Surely I will be with thee, and thou shalt smite the Midianites as one man.

17 And he said unto him, If now I have found grace in thy sight, then shew me a sign that thou talkest with me.

18 Depart not hence, I pray thee, until I come unto thee, and bring forth my present, and set *it* before thee. And he said, I will tarry until thou come again.

19 ¶ And Gideon went in, and made ready a kid, and unleavened cakes of an ephah of flour: the flesh he put in a basket, and he put the broth in a pot, and brought *it* out unto him under the oak, and presented *it*.

20 And the angel of God said unto him, Take the flesh and the unleavened cakes, and lay *them* upon this rock, and pour out the broth. And he did so.

21 ¶ Then the angel of the LORD put forth the end of the staff that *was* in his hand, and touched the flesh and the unleavened cakes; and there rose up fire out of the rock, and consumed the flesh and the unleavened cakes. Then the angel of the LORD departed out of his sight.

22 And when Gideon perceived that he *was* an angel of the LORD, Gideon said, Alas, O Lord GOD! for because I have seen an angel of the LORD face to face.

23 And the LORD said unto him, Peace *be* unto thee; fear not: thou shalt not die.

24 Then Gideon built an altar there unto the LORD, and called it Jehovah-shalom: unto this day it *is* yet in Ophrah of the Abi-ezrites.

25 ¶ And it came to pass the same night, that the LORD said unto him, Take thy father's young bullock, even the second bullock of seven years old, and throw down the altar of Baal that thy father hath, and cut down the grove that *is* by it:

26 And build an altar unto the LORD thy God upon the top of this rock, in the ordered place, and take the second bullock, and offer a burnt sacrifice with the wood of the grove which thou shalt cut down.

27 Then Gideon took ten men of his servants, and did as the LORD had said unto him: and *so* it was, because he feared his father's household, and the men of the city, that he could not do *it* by day, that he did *it* by night.

28 ¶ And when the men of the city arose early in the morning, behold, the altar of Baal was cast down, and the grove was cut down that *was* by it, and the second bullock was offered upon the altar *that was* built.

29 And they said one to another, Who hath done this thing? And when they inquired and asked, they said, Gideon the son of Joash hath done this thing.

30 Then the men of the city said unto Joash, Bring out thy son, that he may die: because he hath cast down the altar of Baal, and because he hath cut down the grove that *was* by it.

31 And Joash said unto all that stood against him, Will ye plead for Baal? will ye save him? he that will plead for him, let him be put to death whilst *it is yet* morning: if he *be* a god, let him plead for himself, because *one* hath cast down his altar.

32 Therefore on that day he called him Jerubbaal, saying, Let Baal plead against him, because he hath thrown down his altar.

33 ¶ Then all the Midianites and the Amalekites and the children of the east were gathered together, and went over, and pitched in the valley of Jezreel.

34 But the Spirit of the LORD came upon Gideon, and he blew a trumpet; and Abiezer was gathered after him.

35 And he sent messengers throughout all Manasseh; who also was gathered after him: and he sent messengers unto Asher, and unto Zebulun, and unto Naphtali; and they came up to meet them.

36 ¶ And Gideon said unto God, If thou wilt save Israel by mine hand, as thou hast said,

37 Behold, I will put a fleece of wool in the floor; *and* if the dew be on the fleece only, and *it be* dry upon all the earth *beside*, then shall I know that thou wilt save Israel by mine hand, as thou hast said.

38 And it was so: for he rose up early on the morrow, and thrust the fleece together, and wringed the dew out of the fleece, a bowl full of water.

39 And Gideon said unto God, Let not thine anger be hot against me, and I will speak but this once: let me prove, I pray thee, but this once with the fleece; let it now be dry only upon the fleece, and upon all the ground let there be dew.

40 And God did so that night: for it was dry upon the fleece only, and there was dew on all the ground.

Judges 7

1 Then Jerubbaal, who *is* Gideon, and all the people that *were* with him, rose up early, and pitched beside the well of Harod: so that the host of the Midianites were on the north side of them, by the hill of Moreh, in the valley.

2 And the LORD said unto Gideon, The people that *are* with thee *are* too many for me to give the Midianites into their hands, lest Israel vaunt themselves against me, saying, Mine own hand hath saved me.

3 Now therefore go to, proclaim in the ears of the people, saying, Whosoever *is* fearful and afraid, let him return and depart early from mount Gilead. And there returned of the people twenty and two thousand; and there remained ten thousand.

4 And the LORD said unto Gideon, The people *are* yet *too* many; bring them down unto the water, and I will try them for thee there: and it shall be, *that* of whom I say unto thee, This shall go with thee, the same shall go with thee; and of whomsoever I say unto thee, This shall not go with thee, the same shall not go.

5 So he brought down the people unto the water: and the LORD said unto Gideon, Every one that lappeth of the water with his tongue, as a dog lappeth, him shalt thou set by himself; likewise every one that boweth down upon his knees to drink.

6 And the number of them that lapped, *putting* their hand to their mouth, were three hundred men: but all the rest of the people bowed down upon their knees to drink water.

7 And the LORD said unto Gideon, By the three hundred men that lapped will I save you, and deliver the Midianites into thine hand: and let all the *other* people go every man unto his place.

8 So the people took victuals in their hand, and their trumpets: and he sent all *the rest of* Israel every man unto his tent, and retained those three hundred men: and the host of Midian was beneath him in the valley.

9 ¶ And it came to pass the same night, that the LORD said unto him, Arise, get thee down unto the host; for I have delivered it into thine hand.

10 But if thou fear to go down, go thou with Phurah thy servant down to the host:

11 And thou shalt hear what they say; and

afterward shall thine hands be strengthened
to go down unto the host. Then went he
down with Phurah his servant unto the outside of the armed men that *were* in the host.
12 And the Midianites and the Amalekites
and all the children of the east lay along in
the valley like grasshoppers for multitude;
and their camels *were* without number, as
the sand by the sea side for multitude.
13 And when Gideon was come, behold,
there was a man that told a dream unto his
fellow, and said, Behold, I dreamed a dream,
and, lo, a cake of barley bread tumbled into
the host of Midian, and came unto a tent,
and smote it that it fell, and overturned it,
that the tent lay along.
14 And his fellow answered and said, This
is nothing else save the sword of Gideon
the son of Joash, a man of Israel: *for* into
his hand hath God delivered Midian, and
all the host.
15 ¶ And it was *so*, when Gideon heard the
telling of the dream, and the interpretation
thereof, that he worshipped, and returned
into the host of Israel, and said, Arise; for
the LORD hath delivered into your hand the
host of Midian.
16 And he divided the three hundred men
into three companies, and he put a trumpet
in every man's hand, with empty pitchers,
and lamps within the pitchers.
17 And he said unto them, Look on me, and
do likewise: and, behold, when I come to
the outside of the camp, it shall be *that*, as
I do, so shall ye do.
18 When I blow with a trumpet, I and all that
are with me, then blow ye the trumpets also
on every side of all the camp, and say, *The
sword* of the LORD, and of Gideon.
19 ¶ So Gideon, and the hundred men that
were with him, came unto the outside of the
camp in the beginning of the middle watch;
and they had but newly set the watch: and
they blew the trumpets, and brake the
pitchers that *were* in their hands.
20 And the three companies blew the trumpets, and brake the pitchers, and held the
lamps in their left hands, and the trumpets
in their right hands to blow *withal:* and they
cried, The sword of the LORD, and of Gideon.
21 And they stood every man in his place
round about the camp: and all the host ran,
and cried, and fled.
22 And the three hundred blew the trumpets, and the LORD set every man's sword
against his fellow, even throughout all the
host: and the host fled to Beth-shittah in
Zererath, *and* to the border of Abel-meholah, unto Tabbath.
23 And the men of Israel gathered themselves together out of Naphtali, and out of
Asher, and out of all Manasseh, and pursued
after the Midianites.
24 ¶ And Gideon sent messengers throughout all mount Ephraim, saying, Come down
against the Midianites, and take before
them the waters unto Beth-barah and Jordan. Then all the men of Ephraim gathered
themselves together, and took the waters
unto Beth-barah and Jordan.
25 And they took two princes of the Midianites, Oreb and Zeeb; and they slew Oreb
upon the rock Oreb, and Zeeb they slew at
the winepress of Zeeb, and pursued Midian,
and brought the heads of Oreb and Zeeb to
Gideon on the other side Jordan.

Judges 8

1 And the men of Ephraim said unto him,
Why hast thou served us thus, that thou
calledst us not, when thou wentest to fight
with the Midianites? And they did chide
with him sharply.
2 And he said unto them, What have I done
now in comparison of you? *Is* not the gleaning of the grapes of Ephraim better than the
vintage of Abi-ezer?
3 God hath delivered into your hands the
princes of Midian, Oreb and Zeeb: and what
was I able to do in comparison of you? Then
their anger was abated toward him, when
he had said that.
4 ¶ And Gideon came to Jordan, *and* passed
over, he, and the three hundred men that
were with him, faint, yet pursuing *them*.
5 And he said unto the men of Succoth, Give,
I pray you, loaves of bread unto the people
that follow me; for they *be* faint, and I am
pursuing after Zebah and Zalmunna, kings
of Midian.
6 ¶ And the princes of Succoth said, *Are*
the hands of Zebah and Zalmunna now in
thine hand, that we should give bread unto
thine army?
7 And Gideon said, Therefore when the LORD
hath delivered Zebah and Zalmunna into

mine hand, then I will tear your flesh with
the thorns of the wilderness and with briers.
8 ¶ And he went up thence to Penuel, and
spake unto them likewise: and the men of
Penuel answered him as the men of Succoth
had answered *him*.
9 And he spake also unto the men of Penuel,
saying, When I come again in peace, I will
break down this tower.
10 ¶ Now Zebah and Zalmunna *were* in
Karkor, and their hosts with them, about
fifteen thousand *men*, all that were left of
all the hosts of the children of the east: for
there fell an hundred and twenty thousand
men that drew sword.
11 ¶ And Gideon went up by the way of
them that dwelt in tents on the east of
Nobah and Jogbehah, and smote the host:
for the host was secure.
12 And when Zebah and Zalmunna fled,
he pursued after them, and took the two
kings of Midian, Zebah and Zalmunna, and
discomfited all the host.
13 ¶ And Gideon the son of Joash returned
from battle before the sun *was up*,
14 And caught a young man of the men
of Succoth, and inquired of him: and he
described unto him the princes of Succoth,
and the elders thereof, *even* threescore and
seventeen men.
15 And he came unto the men of Succoth,
and said, Behold Zebah and Zalmunna, with
whom ye did upbraid me, saying, *Are* the
hands of Zebah and Zalmunna now in thine
hand, that we should give bread unto thy
men *that are* weary?
16 And he took the elders of the city, and
thorns of the wilderness and briers, and
with them he taught the men of Succoth.
17 And he beat down the tower of Penuel,
and slew the men of the city.
18 ¶ Then said he unto Zebah and Zalmunna,
What manner of men *were they* whom ye
slew at Tabor? And they answered, As thou
art, so *were* they; each one resembled the
children of a king.
19 And he said, They *were* my brethren,
even the sons of my mother: *as* the LORD
liveth, if ye had saved them alive, I would
not slay you.
20 And he said unto Jether his firstborn,
Up, *and* slay them. But the youth drew not
his sword: for he feared, because he *was*
yet a youth.
21 Then Zebah and Zalmunna said, Rise
thou, and fall upon us: for as the man *is*, *so*
is his strength. And Gideon arose, and slew
Zebah and Zalmunna, and took away the
ornaments that *were* on their camels' necks.
22 ¶ Then the men of Israel said unto
Gideon, Rule thou over us, both thou, and
thy son, and thy son's son also: for thou
hast delivered us from the hand of Midian.
23 And Gideon said unto them, I will not rule
over you, neither shall my son rule over you:
the LORD shall rule over you.
24 ¶ And Gideon said unto them, I would
desire a request of you, that ye would give
me every man the earrings of his prey. (For
they had golden earrings, because they *were*
Ishmaelites.)
25 And they answered, We will willingly
give *them*. And they spread a garment, and
did cast therein every man the earrings of
his prey.
26 And the weight of the golden earrings
that he requested was a thousand and seven
hundred *shekels* of gold; beside ornaments,
and collars, and purple raiment that *was* on
the kings of Midian, and beside the chains
that *were* about their camels' necks.
27 And Gideon made an ephod thereof,
and put it in his city, *even* in Ophrah: and
all Israel went thither a whoring after it:
which thing became a snare unto Gideon,
and to his house.
28 ¶ Thus was Midian subdued before the
children of Israel, so that they lifted up their
heads no more. And the country was in
quietness forty years in the days of Gideon.
29 ¶ And Jerubbaal the son of Joash went
and dwelt in his own house.
30 And Gideon had threescore and ten sons
of his body begotten: for he had many wives.
31 And his concubine that *was* in Shechem,
she also bare him a son, whose name he
called Abimelech.
32 ¶ And Gideon the son of Joash died in a
good old age, and was buried in the sepulchre of Joash his father, in Ophrah of the
Abi-ezrites.
33 And it came to pass, as soon as Gideon
was dead, that the children of Israel turned
again, and went a whoring after Baalim, and
made Baal-berith their god.

34 And the children of Israel remembered not the LORD their God, who had delivered them out of the hands of all their enemies on every side:

35 Neither shewed they kindness to the house of Jerubbaal, *namely*, Gideon, according to all the goodness which he had shewed unto Israel.

Judges 9

1 And Abimelech the son of Jerubbaal went to Shechem unto his mother's brethren, and communed with them, and with all the family of the house of his mother's father, saying,

2 Speak, I pray you, in the ears of all the men of Shechem, Whether *is* better for you, either that all the sons of Jerubbaal, *which are* threescore and ten persons, reign over you, or that one reign over you? remember also that I *am* your bone and your flesh.

3 And his mother's brethren spake of him in the ears of all the men of Shechem all these words: and their hearts inclined to follow Abimelech; for they said, He *is* our brother.

4 And they gave him threescore and ten *pieces* of silver out of the house of Baal-berith, wherewith Abimelech hired vain and light persons, which followed him.

5 And he went unto his father's house at Ophrah, and slew his brethren the sons of Jerubbaal, *being* threescore and ten persons, upon one stone: notwithstanding yet Jotham the youngest son of Jerubbaal was left; for he hid himself.

6 And all the men of Shechem gathered together, and all the house of Millo, and went, and made Abimelech king, by the plain of the pillar that *was* in Shechem.

7 ¶ And when they told *it* to Jotham, he went and stood in the top of mount Gerizim, and lifted up his voice, and cried, and said unto them, Hearken unto me, ye men of Shechem, that God may hearken unto you.

8 The trees went forth *on a time* to anoint a king over them; and they said unto the olive tree, Reign thou over us.

9 But the olive tree said unto them, Should I leave my fatness, wherewith by me they honour God and man, and go to be promoted over the trees?

10 And the trees said to the fig tree, Come thou, *and* reign over us.

11 But the fig tree said unto them, Should I forsake my sweetness, and my good fruit, and go to be promoted over the trees?

12 Then said the trees unto the vine, Come thou, *and* reign over us.

13 And the vine said unto them, Should I leave my wine, which cheereth God and man, and go to be promoted over the trees?

14 Then said all the trees unto the bramble, Come thou, *and* reign over us.

15 And the bramble said unto the trees, If in truth ye anoint me king over you, *then* come *and* put your trust in my shadow: and if not, let fire come out of the bramble, and devour the cedars of Lebanon.

16 Now therefore, if ye have done truly and sincerely, in that ye have made Abimelech king, and if ye have dealt well with Jerubbaal and his house, and have done unto him according to the deserving of his hands;

17 (For my father fought for you, and adventured his life far, and delivered you out of the hand of Midian:

18 And ye are risen up against my father's house this day, and have slain his sons, threescore and ten persons, upon one stone, and have made Abimelech, the son of his maidservant, king over the men of Shechem, because he *is* your brother;)

19 If ye then have dealt truly and sincerely with Jerubbaal and with his house this day, *then* rejoice ye in Abimelech, and let him also rejoice in you:

20 But if not, let fire come out from Abimelech, and devour the men of Shechem, and the house of Millo; and let fire come out from the men of Shechem, and from the house of Millo, and devour Abimelech.

21 And Jotham ran away, and fled, and went to Beer, and dwelt there, for fear of Abimelech his brother.

22 ¶ When Abimelech had reigned three years over Israel,

23 Then God sent an evil spirit between Abimelech and the men of Shechem; and the men of Shechem dealt treacherously with Abimelech:

24 That the cruelty *done* to the threescore and ten sons of Jerubbaal might come, and their blood be laid upon Abimelech their brother, which slew them; and upon the men of Shechem, which aided him in the killing of his brethren.

25 And the men of Shechem set liers in wait for him in the top of the mountains, and they robbed all that came along that way by them: and it was told Abimelech.

26 And Gaal the son of Ebed came with his brethren, and went over to Shechem: and the men of Shechem put their confidence in him.

27 And they went out into the fields, and gathered their vineyards, and trode *the grapes*, and made merry, and went into the house of their god, and did eat and drink, and cursed Abimelech.

28 And Gaal the son of Ebed said, Who *is* Abimelech, and who *is* Shechem, that we should serve him? *is* not *he* the son of Jerubbaal? and Zebul his officer? serve the men of Hamor the father of Shechem: for why should we serve him?

29 And would to God this people were under my hand! then would I remove Abimelech. And he said to Abimelech, Increase thine army, and come out.

30 ¶ And when Zebul the ruler of the city heard the words of Gaal the son of Ebed, his anger was kindled.

31 And he sent messengers unto Abimelech privily, saying, Behold, Gaal the son of Ebed and his brethren be come to Shechem; and, behold, they fortify the city against thee.

32 Now therefore up by night, thou and the people that *is* with thee, and lie in wait in the field:

33 And it shall be, *that* in the morning, as soon as the sun is up, thou shalt rise early, and set upon the city: and, behold, *when* he and the people that *is* with him come out against thee, then mayest thou do to them as thou shalt find occasion.

34 ¶ And Abimelech rose up, and all the people that *were* with him, by night, and they laid wait against Shechem in four companies.

35 And Gaal the son of Ebed went out, and stood in the entering of the gate of the city: and Abimelech rose up, and the people that *were* with him, from lying in wait.

36 And when Gaal saw the people, he said to Zebul, Behold, there come people down from the top of the mountains. And Zebul said unto him, Thou seest the shadow of the mountains as *if they were* men.

37 And Gaal spake again and said, See there come people down by the middle of the land, and another company come along by the plain of Meonenim.

38 Then said Zebul unto him, Where *is* now thy mouth, wherewith thou saidst, Who *is* Abimelech, that we should serve him? *is* not this the people that thou hast despised? go out, I pray now, and fight with them.

39 And Gaal went out before the men of Shechem, and fought with Abimelech.

40 And Abimelech chased him, and he fled before him, and many were overthrown *and* wounded, *even* unto the entering of the gate.

41 And Abimelech dwelt at Arumah: and Zebul thrust out Gaal and his brethren, that they should not dwell in Shechem.

42 And it came to pass on the morrow, that the people went out into the field; and they told Abimelech.

43 And he took the people, and divided them into three companies, and laid wait in the field, and looked, and, behold, the people *were* come forth out of the city; and he rose up against them, and smote them.

44 And Abimelech, and the company that *was* with him, rushed forward, and stood in the entering of the gate of the city: and the two *other* companies ran upon all *the people* that *were* in the fields, and slew them.

45 And Abimelech fought against the city all that day; and he took the city, and slew the people that *was* therein, and beat down the city, and sowed it with salt.

46 ¶ And when all the men of the tower of Shechem heard *that*, they entered into an hold of the house of the god Berith.

47 And it was told Abimelech, that all the men of the tower of Shechem were gathered together.

48 And Abimelech gat him up to mount Zalmon, he and all the people that *were* with him; and Abimelech took an axe in his hand, and cut down a bough from the trees, and took it, and laid *it* on his shoulder, and said unto the people that *were* with him, What ye have seen me do, make haste, *and* do as I *have done*.

49 And all the people likewise cut down every man his bough, and followed Abimelech, and put *them* to the hold, and set the hold on fire upon them; so that all the men

of the tower of Shechem died also, about a
thousand men and women.
50 ¶ Then went Abimelech to Thebez, and
encamped against Thebez, and took it.
51 But there was a strong tower within the
city, and thither fled all the men and women,
and all they of the city, and shut *it* to them,
and gat them up to the top of the tower.
52 And Abimelech came unto the tower,
and fought against it, and went hard unto
the door of the tower to burn it with fire.
53 And a certain woman cast a piece of a
millstone upon Abimelech's head, and all
to brake his skull.
54 Then he called hastily unto the young
man his armourbearer, and said unto him,
Draw thy sword, and slay me, that men
say not of me, A woman slew him. And his
young man thrust him through, and he died.
55 And when the men of Israel saw that
Abimelech was dead, they departed every
man unto his place.
56 ¶ Thus God rendered the wickedness of
Abimelech, which he did unto his father, in
slaying his seventy brethren:
57 And all the evil of the men of Shechem
did God render upon their heads: and upon
them came the curse of Jotham the son of
Jerubbaal.

Judges 10

1 And after Abimelech there arose to defend
Israel Tola the son of Puah, the son of Dodo,
a man of Issachar; and he dwelt in Shamir
in mount Ephraim.
2 And he judged Israel twenty and three
years, and died, and was buried in Shamir.
3 ¶ And after him arose Jair, a Gileadite, and
judged Israel twenty and two years.
4 And he had thirty sons that rode on thirty
ass colts, and they had thirty cities, which
are called Havoth-jair unto this day, which
are in the land of Gilead.
5 And Jair died, and was buried in Camon.
6 ¶ And the children of Israel did evil again
in the sight of the LORD, and served Baalim,
and Ashtaroth, and the gods of Syria, and
the gods of Zidon, and the gods of Moab,
and the gods of the children of Ammon, and
the gods of the Philistines, and forsook the
LORD, and served not him.
7 And the anger of the LORD was hot against
Israel, and he sold them into the hands of
the Philistines, and into the hands of the
children of Ammon.
8 And that year they vexed and oppressed
the children of Israel: eighteen years, all the
children of Israel that *were* on the other side
Jordan in the land of the Amorites, which
is in Gilead.
9 Moreover the children of Ammon passed
over Jordan to fight also against Judah, and
against Benjamin, and against the house of
Ephraim; so that Israel was sore distressed.
10 ¶ And the children of Israel cried unto
the LORD, saying, We have sinned against
thee, both because we have forsaken our
God, and also served Baalim.
11 And the LORD said unto the children of
Israel, *Did* not *I deliver you* from the Egyptians, and from the Amorites, from the children of Ammon, and from the Philistines?
12 The Zidonians also, and the Amalekites,
and the Maonites, did oppress you; and
ye cried to me, and I delivered you out of
their hand.
13 Yet ye have forsaken me, and served
other gods: wherefore I will deliver you
no more.
14 Go and cry unto the gods which ye have
chosen; let them deliver you in the time of
your tribulation.
15 ¶ And the children of Israel said unto
the LORD, We have sinned: do thou unto
us whatsoever seemeth good unto thee;
deliver us only, we pray thee, this day.
16 And they put away the strange gods from
among them, and served the LORD: and his
soul was grieved for the misery of Israel.
17 Then the children of Ammon were gathered together, and encamped in Gilead. And
the children of Israel assembled themselves
together, and encamped in Mizpeh.
18 And the people *and* princes of Gilead
said one to another, What man *is he* that
will begin to fight against the children of
Ammon? he shall be head over all the inhabitants of Gilead.

Judges 11

1 Now Jephthah the Gileadite was a mighty
man of valour, and he *was* the son of an
harlot: and Gilead begat Jephthah.
2 And Gilead's wife bare him sons; and his
wife's sons grew up, and they thrust out
Jephthah, and said unto him, Thou shalt

28 Howbeit the king of the children of
Ammon hearkened not unto the words of
Jephthah which he sent him.
29 ¶ Then the Spirit of the LORD came upon
Jephthah, and he passed over Gilead, and
Manasseh, and passed over Mizpeh of Gilead, and from Mizpeh of Gilead he passed
over *unto* the children of Ammon.
30 And Jephthah vowed a vow unto the
LORD, and said, If thou shalt without fail
deliver the children of Ammon into mine
hands,
31 Then it shall be, that whatsoever cometh
forth of the doors of my house to meet me,
when I return in peace from the children of
Ammon, shall surely be the LORD's, and I will
offer it up for a burnt offering.
32 ¶ So Jephthah passed over unto the
children of Ammon to fight against them;
and the LORD delivered them into his hands.
33 And he smote them from Aroer, even till
thou come to Minnith, *even* twenty cities,
and unto the plain of the vineyards, with a
very great slaughter. Thus the children of
Ammon were subdued before the children
of Israel.
34 ¶ And Jephthah came to Mizpeh unto his
house, and, behold, his daughter came out
to meet him with timbrels and with dances:
and she *was his* only child; beside her he had
neither son nor daughter.
35 And it came to pass, when he saw her,
that he rent his clothes, and said, Alas, my
daughter! thou hast brought me very low,
and thou art one of them that trouble me:
for I have opened my mouth unto the LORD,
and I cannot go back.
36 And she said unto him, My father, *if* thou
hast opened thy mouth unto the LORD, do to
me according to that which hath proceeded
out of thy mouth; forasmuch as the LORD
hath taken vengeance for thee of thine
enemies, *even* of the children of Ammon.
37 And she said unto her father, Let this
thing be done for me: let me alone two
months, that I may go up and down upon
the mountains, and bewail my virginity, I
and my fellows.
38 And he said, Go. And he sent her away
for two months: and she went with her
companions, and bewailed her virginity
upon the mountains.
39 And it came to pass at the end of two
months, that she returned unto her father,
who did with her *according* to his vow which
he had vowed: and she knew no man. And
it was a custom in Israel,
40 *That* the daughters of Israel went yearly
to lament the daughter of Jephthah the
Gileadite four days in a year.

Judges 12

1 And the men of Ephraim gathered themselves together, and went northward, and
said unto Jephthah, Wherefore passedst
thou over to fight against the children of
Ammon, and didst not call us to go with
thee? we will burn thine house upon thee
with fire.
2 And Jephthah said unto them, I and my
people were at great strife with the children
of Ammon; and when I called you, ye delivered me not out of their hands.
3 And when I saw that ye delivered *me* not,
I put my life in my hands, and passed over
against the children of Ammon, and the
LORD delivered them into my hand: wherefore then are ye come up unto me this day,
to fight against me?
4 Then Jephthah gathered together all the
men of Gilead, and fought with Ephraim:
and the men of Gilead smote Ephraim,
because they said, Ye Gileadites *are* fugitives of Ephraim among the Ephraimites,
and among the Manassites.
5 And the Gileadites took the passages of
Jordan before the Ephraimites: and it was
so, that when those Ephraimites which
were escaped said, Let me go over; that
the men of Gilead said unto him, *Art* thou
an Ephraimite? If he said, Nay;
6 Then said they unto him, Say now Shib-
boleth: and he said Sibboleth: for he could
not frame to pronounce *it* right. Then they
took him, and slew him at the passages of
Jordan: and there fell at that time of the
Ephraimites forty and two thousand.
7 And Jephthah judged Israel six years. Then
died Jephthah the Gileadite, and was buried
in *one of* the cities of Gilead.
8 ¶ And after him Ibzan of Beth-lehem
judged Israel.
9 And he had thirty sons, and thirty daughters, *whom* he sent abroad, and took in
thirty daughters from abroad for his sons.
And he judged Israel seven years.

10 Then died Ibzan, and was buried at
Beth-lehem.
11 ¶ And after him Elon, a Zebulonite,
judged Israel; and he judged Israel ten years.
12 And Elon the Zebulonite died, and was
buried in Aijalon in the country of Zebulun.
13 ¶ And after him Abdon the son of Hillel,
a Pirathonite, judged Israel.
14 And he had forty sons and thirty nephews, that rode on threescore and ten ass
colts: and he judged Israel eight years.
15 And Abdon the son of Hillel the Pirathonite died, and was buried in Pirathon
in the land of Ephraim, in the mount of the
Amalekites.

Judges 13

1 And the children of Israel did evil again in
the sight of the LORD; and the LORD delivered them into the hand of the Philistines
forty years.
2 ¶ And there was a certain man of Zorah,
of the family of the Danites, whose name
was Manoah; and his wife *was* barren, and
bare not.
3 And the angel of the LORD appeared unto
the woman, and said unto her, Behold now,
thou *art* barren, and bearest not: but thou
shalt conceive, and bear a son.
4 Now therefore beware, I pray thee, and
drink not wine nor strong drink, and eat not
any unclean *thing:*
5 For, lo, thou shalt conceive, and bear a son;
and no rasor shall come on his head: for the
child shall be a Nazarite unto God from the
womb: and he shall begin to deliver Israel
out of the hand of the Philistines.
6 ¶ Then the woman came and told her
husband, saying, A man of God came unto
me, and his countenance *was* like the countenance of an angel of God, very terrible:
but I asked him not whence he *was*, neither
told he me his name:
7 But he said unto me, Behold, thou shalt
conceive, and bear a son; and now drink
no wine nor strong drink, neither eat any
unclean *thing:* for the child shall be a
Nazarite to God from the womb to the day
of his death.
8 ¶ Then Manoah intreated the LORD, and
said, O my Lord, let the man of God which
thou didst send come again unto us, and
teach us what we shall do unto the child
that shall be born.
9 And God hearkened to the voice of
Manoah; and the angel of God came again
unto the woman as she sat in the field: but
Manoah her husband *was* not with her.
10 And the woman made haste, and ran,
and shewed her husband, and said unto him,
Behold, the man hath appeared unto me,
that came unto me the *other* day.
11 And Manoah arose, and went after his
wife, and came to the man, and said unto
him, *Art* thou the man that spakest unto the
woman? And he said, I *am*.
12 And Manoah said, Now let thy words
come to pass. How shall we order the child,
and *how* shall we do unto him?
13 And the angel of the LORD said unto
Manoah, Of all that I said unto the woman
let her beware.
14 She may not eat of any *thing* that cometh of the vine, neither let her drink wine
or strong drink, nor eat any unclean *thing:*
all that I commanded her let her observe.
15 ¶ And Manoah said unto the angel of the
LORD, I pray thee, let us detain thee, until
we shall have made ready a kid for thee.
16 And the angel of the LORD said unto
Manoah, Though thou detain me, I will not
eat of thy bread: and if thou wilt offer a
burnt offering, thou must offer it unto the
LORD. For Manoah knew not that he *was* an
angel of the LORD.
17 And Manoah said unto the angel of the
LORD, What *is* thy name, that when thy sayings come to pass we may do thee honour?
18 And the angel of the LORD said unto
him, Why askest thou thus after my name,
seeing it *is* secret?
19 So Manoah took a kid with a meat offering, and offered *it* upon a rock unto the
LORD: and *the angel* did wondrously; and
Manoah and his wife looked on.
20 For it came to pass, when the flame went
up toward heaven from off the altar, that the
angel of the LORD ascended in the flame of
the altar. And Manoah and his wife looked
on *it*, and fell on their faces to the ground.
21 But the angel of the LORD did no more
appear to Manoah and to his wife. Then
Manoah knew that he *was* an angel of the
LORD.

22 And Manoah said unto his wife, We shall surely die, because we have seen God.

23 But his wife said unto him, If the LORD were pleased to kill us, he would not have received a burnt offering and a meat offering at our hands, neither would he have shewed us all these *things*, nor would as at this time have told us *such things* as these.

24 ¶ And the woman bare a son, and called his name Samson: and the child grew, and the LORD blessed him.

25 And the Spirit of the LORD began to move him at times in the camp of Dan between Zorah and Eshtaol.

Judges 14

1 And Samson went down to Timnath, and saw a woman in Timnath of the daughters of the Philistines.

2 And he came up, and told his father and his mother, and said, I have seen a woman in Timnath of the daughters of the Philistines: now therefore get her for me to wife.

3 Then his father and his mother said unto him, *Is there* never a woman among the daughters of thy brethren, or among all my people, that thou goest to take a wife of the uncircumcised Philistines? And Samson said unto his father, Get her for me; for she pleaseth me well.

4 But his father and his mother knew not that it *was* of the LORD, that he sought an occasion against the Philistines: for at that time the Philistines had dominion over Israel.

5 ¶ Then went Samson down, and his father and his mother, to Timnath, and came to the vineyards of Timnath: and, behold, a young lion roared against him.

6 And the Spirit of the LORD came mightily upon him, and he rent him as he would have rent a kid, and *he had* nothing in his hand: but he told not his father or his mother what he had done.

7 And he went down, and talked with the woman; and she pleased Samson well.

8 ¶ And after a time he returned to take her, and he turned aside to see the carcase of the lion: and, behold, *there was* a swarm of bees and honey in the carcase of the lion.

9 And he took thereof in his hands, and went on eating, and came to his father and mother, and he gave them, and they did eat: but he told not them that he had taken the honey out of the carcase of the lion.

10 ¶ So his father went down unto the woman: and Samson made there a feast; for so used the young men to do.

11 And it came to pass, when they saw him, that they brought thirty companions to be with him.

12 ¶ And Samson said unto them, I will now put forth a riddle unto you: if ye can certainly declare it me within the seven days of the feast, and find *it* out, then I will give you thirty sheets and thirty change of garments:

13 But if ye cannot declare *it* me, then shall ye give me thirty sheets and thirty change of garments. And they said unto him, Put forth thy riddle, that we may hear it.

14 And he said unto them, Out of the eater came forth meat, and out of the strong came forth sweetness. And they could not in three days expound the riddle.

15 And it came to pass on the seventh day, that they said unto Samson's wife, Entice thy husband, that he may declare unto us the riddle, lest we burn thee and thy father's house with fire: have ye called us to take that we have? *is it* not *so?*

16 And Samson's wife wept before him, and said, Thou dost but hate me, and lovest me not: thou hast put forth a riddle unto the children of my people, and hast not told *it* me. And he said unto her, Behold, I have not told *it* my father nor my mother, and shall I tell *it* thee?

17 And she wept before him the seven days, while their feast lasted: and it came to pass on the seventh day, that he told her, because she lay sore upon him: and she told the riddle to the children of her people.

18 And the men of the city said unto him on the seventh day before the sun went down, What *is* sweeter than honey? and what *is* stronger than a lion? And he said unto them, If ye had not plowed with my heifer, ye had not found out my riddle.

19 ¶ And the Spirit of the LORD came upon him, and he went down to Ashkelon, and slew thirty men of them, and took their spoil, and gave change of garments unto them which expounded the riddle. And his anger was kindled, and he went up to his father's house.

27 Now the house was full of men and
women; and all the lords of the Philistines
were there; and *there were* upon the roof
about three thousand men and women, that
beheld while Samson made sport.
28 And Samson called unto the LORD, and
said, O Lord GOD, remember me, I pray thee,
and strengthen me, I pray thee, only this
once, O God, that I may be at once avenged
of the Philistines for my two eyes.
29 And Samson took hold of the two middle
pillars upon which the house stood, and on
which it was borne up, of the one with his
right hand, and of the other with his left.
30 And Samson said, Let me die with the
Philistines. And he bowed himself with *all
his* might; and the house fell upon the lords,
and upon all the people that *were* therein.
So the dead which he slew at his death were
more than *they* which he slew in his life.
31 Then his brethren and all the house of
his father came down, and took him, and
brought *him* up, and buried him between
Zorah and Eshtaol in the buryingplace of
Manoah his father. And he judged Israel
twenty years.

Judges 17

1 And there was a man of mount Ephraim,
whose name *was* Micah.
2 And he said unto his mother, The eleven
hundred *shekels* of silver that were taken
from thee, about which thou cursedst, and
spakest of also in mine ears, behold, the
silver *is* with me; I took it. And his mother
said, Blessed *be thou* of the LORD, my son.
3 And when he had restored the eleven
hundred *shekels* of silver to his mother, his
mother said, I had wholly dedicated the silver unto the LORD from my hand for my son,
to make a graven image and a molten image:
now therefore I will restore it unto thee.
4 Yet he restored the money unto his
mother; and his mother took two hundred
shekels of silver, and gave them to the
founder, who made thereof a graven image
and a molten image: and they were in the
house of Micah.
5 And the man Micah had an house of gods,
and made an ephod, and teraphim, and
consecrated one of his sons, who became
his priest.
6 In those days *there was* no king in Israel,
but every man did *that which was* right in
his own eyes.
7 ¶ And there was a young man out of
Beth-lehem-judah of the family of Judah,
who *was* a Levite, and he sojourned there.
8 And the man departed out of the city
from Beth-lehem-judah to sojourn where
he could find *a place:* and he came to
mount Ephraim to the house of Micah, as
he journeyed.
9 And Micah said unto him, Whence comest
thou? And he said unto him, I *am* a Levite
of Beth-lehem-judah, and I go to sojourn
where I may find *a place.*
10 And Micah said unto him, Dwell with me,
and be unto me a father and a priest, and
I will give thee ten *shekels* of silver by the
year, and a suit of apparel, and thy victuals.
So the Levite went in.
11 And the Levite was content to dwell with
the man; and the young man was unto him
as one of his sons.
12 And Micah consecrated the Levite; and
the young man became his priest, and was
in the house of Micah.
13 Then said Micah, Now know I that the
LORD will do me good, seeing I have a Levite
to *my* priest.

Judges 18

1 In those days *there was* no king in Israel:
and in those days the tribe of the Danites
sought them an inheritance to dwell in; for
unto that day *all their* inheritance had not
fallen unto them among the tribes of Israel.
2 And the children of Dan sent of their family
five men from their coasts, men of valour,
from Zorah, and from Eshtaol, to spy out
the land, and to search it; and they said
unto them, Go, search the land: who when
they came to mount Ephraim, to the house
of Micah, they lodged there.
3 When they *were* by the house of Micah,
they knew the voice of the young man the
Levite: and they turned in thither, and said
unto him, Who brought thee hither? and
what makest thou in this *place?* and what
hast thou here?
4 And he said unto them, Thus and thus
dealeth Micah with me, and hath hired me,
and I am his priest.
5 And they said unto him, Ask counsel,
we pray thee, of God, that we may know

whether our way which we go shall be
prosperous.
6 And the priest said unto them, Go in
peace: before the LORD *is* your way wherein
ye go.
7 ¶ Then the five men departed, and came
to Laish, and saw the people that *were*
therein, how they dwelt careless, after the
manner of the Zidonians, quiet and secure;
and *there was* no magistrate in the land, that
might put *them* to shame in *any* thing; and
they *were* far from the Zidonians, and had
no business with *any* man.
8 And they came unto their brethren to
Zorah and Eshtaol: and their brethren said
unto them, What *say* ye?
9 And they said, Arise, that we may go up
against them: for we have seen the land,
and, behold, it *is* very good: and *are* ye
still? be not slothful to go, *and* to enter to
possess the land.
10 When ye go, ye shall come unto a people
secure, and to a large land: for God hath
given it into your hands; a place where *there*
is no want of any thing that *is* in the earth.
11 ¶ And there went from thence of the
family of the Danites, out of Zorah and out
of Eshtaol, six hundred men appointed with
weapons of war.
12 And they went up, and pitched in Kirjath-jearim, in Judah: wherefore they called
that place Mahaneh-dan unto this day:
behold, *it is* behind Kirjath-jearim.
13 And they passed thence unto mount
Ephraim, and came unto the house of Micah.
14 ¶ Then answered the five men that went
to spy out the country of Laish, and said
unto their brethren, Do ye know that there
is in these houses an ephod, and teraphim,
and a graven image, and a molten image?
now therefore consider what ye have to do.
15 And they turned thitherward, and came
to the house of the young man the Levite,
even unto the house of Micah, and saluted
him.
16 And the six hundred men appointed
with their weapons of war, which *were* of
the children of Dan, stood by the entering
of the gate.
17 And the five men that went to spy out the
land went up, *and* came in thither, *and* took
the graven image, and the ephod, and the
teraphim, and the molten image: and the
priest stood in the entering of the gate with
the six hundred men *that were* appointed
with weapons of war.
18 And these went into Micah's house, and
fetched the carved image, the ephod, and
the teraphim, and the molten image. Then
said the priest unto them, What do ye?
19 And they said unto him, Hold thy peace,
lay thine hand upon thy mouth, and go with
us, and be to us a father and a priest: *is it*
better for thee to be a priest unto the house
of one man, or that thou be a priest unto a
tribe and a family in Israel?
20 And the priest's heart was glad, and he
took the ephod, and the teraphim, and the
graven image, and went in the midst of
the people.
21 So they turned and departed, and put the
little ones and the cattle and the carriage
before them.
22 ¶ *And* when they were a good way from
the house of Micah, the men that *were* in
the houses near to Micah's house were
gathered together, and overtook the children of Dan.
23 And they cried unto the children of Dan.
And they turned their faces, and said unto
Micah, What aileth thee, that thou comest
with such a company?
24 And he said, Ye have taken away my gods
which I made, and the priest, and ye are
gone away: and what have I more? and what
is this *that* ye say unto me, What aileth thee?
25 And the children of Dan said unto him,
Let not thy voice be heard among us, lest
angry fellows run upon thee, and thou lose
thy life, with the lives of thy household.
26 And the children of Dan went their way:
and when Micah saw that they *were* too
strong for him, he turned and went back
unto his house.
27 And they took *the things* which Micah
had made, and the priest which he had, and
came unto Laish, unto a people *that were*
at quiet and secure: and they smote them
with the edge of the sword, and burnt the
city with fire.
28 And *there was* no deliverer, because it
was far from Zidon, and they had no business with *any* man; and it was in the valley
that *lieth* by Beth-rehob. And they built a
city, and dwelt therein.
29 And they called the name of the city Dan,

after the name of Dan their father, who was
born unto Israel: howbeit the name of the
city *was* Laish at the first.
30 ¶ And the children of Dan set up the
graven image: and Jonathan, the son of
Gershom, the son of Manasseh, he and his
sons were priests to the tribe of Dan until
the day of the captivity of the land.
31 And they set them up Micah's graven
image, which he made, all the time that the
house of God was in Shiloh.

Judges 19

1 And it came to pass in those days, when
there was no king in Israel, that there was
a certain Levite sojourning on the side of
mount Ephraim, who took to him a concubine out of Beth-lehem-judah.
2 And his concubine played the whore
against him, and went away from him unto
her father's house to Beth-lehem-judah, and
was there four whole months.
3 And her husband arose, and went after
her, to speak friendly unto her, *and* to bring
her again, having his servant with him,
and a couple of asses: and she brought
him into her father's house: and when the
father of the damsel saw him, he rejoiced
to meet him.
4 And his father in law, the damsel's father,
retained him; and he abode with him three
days: so they did eat and drink, and lodged
there.
5 ¶ And it came to pass on the fourth day,
when they arose early in the morning, that
he rose up to depart: and the damsel's
father said unto his son in law, Comfort
thine heart with a morsel of bread, and
afterward go your way.
6 And they sat down, and did eat and drink
both of them together: for the damsel's
father had said unto the man, Be content,
I pray thee, and tarry all night, and let thine
heart be merry.
7 And when the man rose up to depart,
his father in law urged him: therefore he
lodged there again.
8 And he arose early in the morning on the
fifth day to depart: and the damsel's father
said, Comfort thine heart, I pray thee. And
they tarried until afternoon, and they did
eat both of them.
9 And when the man rose up to depart,
he, and his concubine, and his servant, his
father in law, the damsel's father, said unto
him, Behold, now the day draweth toward
evening, I pray you tarry all night: behold,
the day groweth to an end, lodge here, that
thine heart may be merry; and to morrow
get you early on your way, that thou mayest go home.
10 But the man would not tarry that night,
but he rose up and departed, and came
over against Jebus, which *is* Jerusalem; and
there were with him two asses saddled, his
concubine also *was* with him.
11 *And* when they *were* by Jebus, the day
was far spent; and the servant said unto his
master, Come, I pray thee, and let us turn in
into this city of the Jebusites, and lodge in it.
12 And his master said unto him, We will not
turn aside hither into the city of a stranger,
that *is* not of the children of Israel; we will
pass over to Gibeah.
13 And he said unto his servant, Come, and
let us draw near to one of these places to
lodge all night, in Gibeah, or in Ramah.
14 And they passed on and went their way;
and the sun went down upon them *when
they were* by Gibeah, which *belongeth* to
Benjamin.
15 And they turned aside thither, to go in
and to lodge in Gibeah: and when he went
in, he sat him down in a street of the city:
for *there was* no man that took them into
his house to lodging.
16 ¶ And, behold, there came an old man
from his work out of the field at even,
which *was* also of mount Ephraim; and he
sojourned in Gibeah: but the men of the
place *were* Benjamites.
17 And when he had lifted up his eyes, he
saw a wayfaring man in the street of the
city: and the old man said, Whither goest
thou? and whence comest thou?
18 And he said unto him, We *are* passing
from Beth-lehem-judah toward the side
of mount Ephraim; from thence *am* I: and
I went to Beth-lehem-judah, but I *am now*
going to the house of the LORD; and there *is*
no man that receiveth me to house.
19 Yet there is both straw and provender
for our asses; and there is bread and wine
also for me, and for thy handmaid, and for
the young man *which is* with thy servants:
there is no want of any thing.

20 And the old man said, Peace *be* with
thee; howsoever *let* all thy wants *lie* upon
me; only lodge not in the street.
21 So he brought him into his house, and
gave provender unto the asses: and they
washed their feet, and did eat and drink.
22 ¶ *Now* as they were making their hearts
merry, behold, the men of the city, certain
sons of Belial, beset the house round about,
and beat at the door, and spake to the master of the house, the old man, saying, Bring
forth the man that came into thine house,
that we may know him.
23 And the man, the master of the house,
went out unto them, and said unto them,
Nay, my brethren, *nay*, I pray you, do not *so*
wickedly; seeing that this man is come into
mine house, do not this folly.
24 Behold, *here is* my daughter a maiden,
and his concubine; them I will bring out now,
and humble ye them, and do with them
what seemeth good unto you: but unto this
man do not so vile a thing.
25 But the men would not hearken to him:
so the man took his concubine, and brought
her forth unto them; and they knew her, and
abused her all the night until the morning:
and when the day began to spring, they
let her go.
26 Then came the woman in the dawning
of the day, and fell down at the door of
the man's house where her lord *was*, till
it was light.
27 And her lord rose up in the morning, and
opened the doors of the house, and went
out to go his way: and, behold, the woman
his concubine was fallen down *at* the door
of the house, and her hands *were* upon the
threshold.
28 And he said unto her, Up, and let us be
going. But none answered. Then the man
took her *up* upon an ass, and the man rose
up, and gat him unto his place.
29 ¶ And when he was come into his house,
he took a knife, and laid hold on his concubine, and divided her, *together* with her
bones, into twelve pieces, and sent her into
all the coasts of Israel.
30 And it was so, that all that saw it said,
There was no such deed done nor seen
from the day that the children of Israel
came up out of the land of Egypt unto this
day: consider of it, take advice, and speak
your minds.

Judges 20

1 Then all the children of Israel went out,
and the congregation was gathered together
as one man, from Dan even to Beer-sheba,
with the land of Gilead, unto the LORD in
Mizpeh.
2 And the chief of all the people, *even* of all
the tribes of Israel, presented themselves in
the assembly of the people of God, four hundred thousand footmen that drew sword.
3 (Now the children of Benjamin heard that
the children of Israel were gone up to Mizpeh.) Then said the children of Israel, Tell
us, how was this wickedness?
4 And the Levite, the husband of the woman
that was slain, answered and said, I came
into Gibeah that *belongeth* to Benjamin, I
and my concubine, to lodge.
5 And the men of Gibeah rose against me,
and beset the house round about upon
me by night, *and* thought to have slain me:
and my concubine have they forced, that
she is dead.
6 And I took my concubine, and cut her
in pieces, and sent her throughout all the
country of the inheritance of Israel: for they
have committed lewdness and folly in Israel.
7 Behold, ye *are* all children of Israel; give
here your advice and counsel.
8 ¶ And all the people arose as one man,
saying, We will not any *of us* go to his tent,
neither will we any *of us* turn into his house.
9 But now this *shall be* the thing which
we will do to Gibeah; *we will go up* by lot
against it;
10 And we will take ten men of an hundred
throughout all the tribes of Israel, and an
hundred of a thousand, and a thousand
out of ten thousand, to fetch victual for the
people, that they may do, when they come
to Gibeah of Benjamin, according to all the
folly that they have wrought in Israel.
11 So all the men of Israel were gathered
against the city, knit together as one man.
12 ¶ And the tribes of Israel sent men
through all the tribe of Benjamin, saying,
What wickedness *is* this that is done among
you?
13 Now therefore deliver *us* the men, the
children of Belial, which *are* in Gibeah, that

we may put them to death, and put away
evil from Israel. But the children of Benjamin would not hearken to the voice of their
brethren the children of Israel:
14 But the children of Benjamin gathered
themselves together out of the cities unto
Gibeah, to go out to battle against the children of Israel.
15 And the children of Benjamin were
numbered at that time out of the cities
twenty and six thousand men that drew
sword, beside the inhabitants of Gibeah,
which were numbered seven hundred
chosen men.
16 Among all this people *there were* seven
hundred chosen men lefthanded; every
one could sling stones at an hair *breadth*,
and not miss.
17 And the men of Israel, beside Benjamin,
were numbered four hundred thousand
men that drew sword: all these *were* men
of war.
18 ¶ And the children of Israel arose, and
went up to the house of God, and asked
counsel of God, and said, Which of us shall
go up first to the battle against the children
of Benjamin? And the LORD said, Judah *shall
go up* first.
19 And the children of Israel rose up in the
morning, and encamped against Gibeah.
20 And the men of Israel went out to battle
against Benjamin; and the men of Israel put
themselves in array to fight against them
at Gibeah.
21 And the children of Benjamin came forth
out of Gibeah, and destroyed down to the
ground of the Israelites that day twenty and
two thousand men.
22 And the people the men of Israel encouraged themselves, and set their battle again
in array in the place where they put themselves in array the first day.
23 (And the children of Israel went up and
wept before the LORD until even, and asked
counsel of the LORD, saying, Shall I go up
again to battle against the children of Benjamin my brother? And the LORD said, Go
up against him.)
24 And the children of Israel came near
against the children of Benjamin the second day.
25 And Benjamin went forth against them
out of Gibeah the second day, and destroyed
down to the ground of the children of Israel
again eighteen thousand men; all these
drew the sword.
26 ¶ Then all the children of Israel, and all
the people, went up, and came unto the
house of God, and wept, and sat there
before the LORD, and fasted that day until
even, and offered burnt offerings and peace
offerings before the LORD.
27 And the children of Israel inquired of the
LORD, (for the ark of the covenant of God
was there in those days,
28 And Phinehas, the son of Eleazar, the son
of Aaron, stood before it in those days,) saying, Shall I yet again go out to battle against
the children of Benjamin my brother, or shall
I cease? And the LORD said, Go up; for to
morrow I will deliver them into thine hand.
29 And Israel set liers in wait round about
Gibeah.
30 And the children of Israel went up against
the children of Benjamin on the third day,
and put themselves in array against Gibeah,
as at other times.
31 And the children of Benjamin went out
against the people, *and* were drawn away
from the city; and they began to smite of
the people, *and* kill, as at other times, in
the highways, of which one goeth up to the
house of God, and the other to Gibeah in
the field, about thirty men of Israel.
32 And the children of Benjamin said, They
are smitten down before us, as at the first.
But the children of Israel said, Let us flee,
and draw them from the city unto the
highways.
33 And all the men of Israel rose up out of
their place, and put themselves in array at
Baal-tamar: and the liers in wait of Israel
came forth out of their places, *even* out of
the meadows of Gibeah.
34 And there came against Gibeah ten
thousand chosen men out of all Israel, and
the battle was sore: but they knew not that
evil *was* near them.
35 And the LORD smote Benjamin before
Israel: and the children of Israel destroyed
of the Benjamites that day twenty and five
thousand and an hundred men: all these
drew the sword.
36 So the children of Benjamin saw that
they were smitten: for the men of Israel
gave place to the Benjamites, because they

trusted unto the liers in wait which they had
set beside Gibeah.
37 And the liers in wait hasted, and rushed
upon Gibeah; and the liers in wait drew
themselves along, and smote all the city
with the edge of the sword.
38 Now there was an appointed sign
between the men of Israel and the liers in
wait, that they should make a great flame
with smoke rise up out of the city.
39 And when the men of Israel retired in
the battle, Benjamin began to smite *and* kill
of the men of Israel about thirty persons:
for they said, Surely they are smitten down
before us, as *in* the first battle.
40 But when the flame began to arise up out
of the city with a pillar of smoke, the Benjamites looked behind them, and, behold,
the flame of the city ascended up to heaven.
41 And when the men of Israel turned again,
the men of Benjamin were amazed: for they
saw that evil was come upon them.
42 Therefore they turned *their backs* before
the men of Israel unto the way of the wilderness; but the battle overtook them; and
them which *came* out of the cities they
destroyed in the midst of them.
43 *Thus* they inclosed the Benjamites round
about, *and* chased them, *and* trode them
down with ease over against Gibeah toward
the sunrising.
44 And there fell of Benjamin eighteen
thousand men; all these *were* men of valour.
45 And they turned and fled toward the
wilderness unto the rock of Rimmon: and
they gleaned of them in the highways five
thousand men; and pursued hard after
them unto Gidom, and slew two thousand
men of them.
46 So that all which fell that day of Benjamin were twenty and five thousand men
that drew the sword; all these *were* men
of valour.
47 But six hundred men turned and fled to
the wilderness unto the rock Rimmon, and
abode in the rock Rimmon four months.
48 And the men of Israel turned again upon
the children of Benjamin, and smote them
with the edge of the sword, as well the men
of *every* city, as the beast, and all that came
to hand: also they set on fire all the cities
that they came to.

Judges 21

1 Now the men of Israel had sworn in Mizpeh, saying, There shall not any of us give
his daughter unto Benjamin to wife.
2 And the people came to the house of God,
and abode there till even before God, and
lifted up their voices, and wept sore;
3 And said, O LORD God of Israel, why is this
come to pass in Israel, that there should be
to day one tribe lacking in Israel?
4 And it came to pass on the morrow, that
the people rose early, and built there an
altar, and offered burnt offerings and peace
offerings.
5 And the children of Israel said, Who *is*
there among all the tribes of Israel that
came not up with the congregation unto
the LORD? For they had made a great oath
concerning him that came not up to the
LORD to Mizpeh, saying, He shall surely be
put to death.
6 And the children of Israel repented them
for Benjamin their brother, and said, There
is one tribe cut off from Israel this day.
7 How shall we do for wives for them that
remain, seeing we have sworn by the LORD
that we will not give them of our daughters
to wives?
8 ¶ And they said, What one *is there* of the
tribes of Israel that came not up to Mizpeh
to the LORD? And, behold, there came
none to the camp from Jabesh-gilead to
the assembly.
9 For the people were numbered, and,
behold, *there were* none of the inhabitants
of Jabesh-gilead there.
10 And the congregation sent thither twelve
thousand men of the valiantest, and commanded them, saying, Go and smite the
inhabitants of Jabesh-gilead with the edge
of the sword, with the women and the
children.
11 And this *is* the thing that ye shall do, Ye
shall utterly destroy every male, and every
woman that hath lain by man.
12 And they found among the inhabitants
of Jabesh-gilead four hundred young virgins,
that had known no man by lying with any
male: and they brought them unto the camp
to Shiloh, which *is* in the land of Canaan.
13 And the whole congregation sent *some* to
speak to the children of Benjamin that *were*

in the rock Rimmon, and to call peaceably
unto them.
14 And Benjamin came again at that time;
and they gave them wives which they had
saved alive of the women of Jabesh-gilead:
and yet so they sufficed them not.
15 And the people repented them for Benjamin, because that the LORD had made a
breach in the tribes of Israel.
16 ¶ Then the elders of the congregation
said, How shall we do for wives for them that
remain, seeing the women are destroyed
out of Benjamin?
17 And they said, *There must be* an inheritance for them that be escaped of Benjamin,
that a tribe be not destroyed out of Israel.
18 Howbeit we may not give them wives
of our daughters: for the children of Israel
have sworn, saying, Cursed *be* he that giveth
a wife to Benjamin.
19 Then they said, Behold, *there is* a feast of
the LORD in Shiloh yearly *in a place* which *is*
on the north side of Beth-el, on the east side
of the highway that goeth up from Beth-el
to Shechem, and on the south of Lebonah.
20 Therefore they commanded the children
of Benjamin, saying, Go and lie in wait in
the vineyards;
21 And see, and, behold, if the daughters of
Shiloh come out to dance in dances, then
come ye out of the vineyards, and catch
you every man his wife of the daughters
of Shiloh, and go to the land of Benjamin.
22 And it shall be, when their fathers or their
brethren come unto us to complain, that
we will say unto them, Be favourable unto
them for our sakes: because we reserved
not to each man his wife in the war: for ye
did not give unto them at this time, *that* ye
should be guilty.
23 And the children of Benjamin did so,
and took *them* wives, according to their
number, of them that danced, whom they
caught: and they went and returned unto
their inheritance, and repaired the cities,
and dwelt in them.
24 And the children of Israel departed
thence at that time, every man to his tribe
and to his family, and they went out from
thence every man to his inheritance.
25 In those days *there was* no king in Israel:
every man did *that which was* right in his
own eyes.

The Book Of

Ruth

Ruth 1

1 Now it came to pass in the days when the
judges ruled, that there was a famine in the
land. And a certain man of Beth-lehem-judah went to sojourn in the country of Moab,
he, and his wife, and his two sons.
2 And the name of the man *was* Elimelech,
and the name of his wife Naomi, and the
name of his two sons Mahlon and Chilion,
Ephrathites of Beth-lehem-judah. And they
came into the country of Moab, and continued there.
3 And Elimelech Naomi's husband died; and
she was left, and her two sons.
4 And they took them wives of the women
of Moab; the name of the one *was* Orpah,
and the name of the other Ruth: and they
dwelled there about ten years.
5 And Mahlon and Chilion died also both of
them; and the woman was left of her two
sons and her husband.
6 ¶ Then she arose with her daughters in
law, that she might return from the country
of Moab: for she had heard in the country
of Moab how that the LORD had visited his
people in giving them bread.
7 Wherefore she went forth out of the place
where she was, and her two daughters in
law with her; and they went on the way to
return unto the land of Judah.
8 And Naomi said unto her two daughters in
law, Go, return each to her mother's house:

the LORD deal kindly with you, as ye have
dealt with the dead, and with me.
9 The LORD grant you that ye may find rest,
each *of you* in the house of her husband.
Then she kissed them; and they lifted up
their voice, and wept.
10 And they said unto her, Surely we will
return with thee unto thy people.
11 And Naomi said, Turn again, my daughters: why will ye go with me? *are* there yet
any more sons in my womb, that they may
be your husbands?
12 Turn again, my daughters, go *your way;*
for I am too old to have an husband. If I
should say, I have hope, *if* I should have
an husband also to night, and should also
bear sons;
13 Would ye tarry for them till they were
grown? would ye stay for them from having
husbands? nay, my daughters; for it grieveth
me much for your sakes that the hand of the
LORD is gone out against me.
14 And they lifted up their voice, and wept
again: and Orpah kissed her mother in law;
but Ruth clave unto her.
15 And she said, Behold, thy sister in law is
gone back unto her people, and unto her
gods: return thou after thy sister in law.
16 And Ruth said, Intreat me not to leave
thee, *or* to return from following after thee:
for whither thou goest, I will go; and where
thou lodgest, I will lodge: thy people *shall be*
my people, and thy God my God:
17 Where thou diest, will I die, and there will
I be buried: the LORD do so to me, and more
also, *if ought* but death part thee and me.
18 When she saw that she was stedfastly
minded to go with her, then she left speaking unto her.
19 ¶ So they two went until they came to
Beth-lehem. And it came to pass, when they
were come to Beth-lehem, that all the city
was moved about them, and they said, *Is*
this Naomi?
20 And she said unto them, Call me not
Naomi, call me Mara: for the Almighty hath
dealt very bitterly with me.
21 I went out full, and the LORD hath brought
me home again empty: why *then* call ye
me Naomi, seeing the LORD hath testified
against me, and the Almighty hath afflicted
me?
22 So Naomi returned, and Ruth the Moabitess, her daughter in law, with her, which
returned out of the country of Moab: and
they came to Beth-lehem in the beginning
of barley harvest.

Ruth 2

1 And Naomi had a kinsman of her husband's, a mighty man of wealth, of the
family of Elimelech; and his name *was* Boaz.
2 And Ruth the Moabitess said unto Naomi,
Let me now go to the field, and glean ears
of corn after *him* in whose sight I shall
find grace. And she said unto her, Go, my
daughter.
3 And she went, and came, and gleaned in
the field after the reapers: and her hap was
to light on a part of the field *belonging* unto
Boaz, who *was* of the kindred of Elimelech.
4 ¶ And, behold, Boaz came from Beth-lehem, and said unto the reapers, The LORD
be with you. And they answered him, The
LORD bless thee.
5 Then said Boaz unto his servant that was
set over the reapers, Whose damsel *is* this?
6 And the servant that was set over the
reapers answered and said, It *is* the Moabit-
ish damsel that came back with Naomi out
of the country of Moab:
7 And she said, I pray you, let me glean and
gather after the reapers among the sheaves:
so she came, and hath continued even from
the morning until now, that she tarried a
little in the house.
8 Then said Boaz unto Ruth, Hearest thou
not, my daughter? Go not to glean in
another field, neither go from hence, but
abide here fast by my maidens:
9 *Let* thine eyes *be* on the field that they
do reap, and go thou after them: have I not
charged the young men that they shall not
touch thee? and when thou art athirst, go
unto the vessels, and drink of *that* which
the young men have drawn.
10 Then she fell on her face, and bowed herself to the ground, and said unto him, Why
have I found grace in thine eyes, that thou
shouldest take knowledge of me, seeing I
am a stranger?
11 And Boaz answered and said unto her,
It hath fully been shewed me, all that thou
hast done unto thy mother in law since the
death of thine husband: and *how* thou hast
left thy father and thy mother, and the land

of thy nativity, and art come unto a people
which thou knewest not heretofore.
12 The LORD recompense thy work, and a
full reward be given thee of the LORD God
of Israel, under whose wings thou art come
to trust.
13 Then she said, Let me find favour in thy
sight, my lord; for that thou hast comforted
me, and for that thou hast spoken friendly
unto thine handmaid, though I be not like
unto one of thine handmaidens.
14 And Boaz said unto her, At mealtime
come thou hither, and eat of the bread,
and dip thy morsel in the vinegar. And she
sat beside the reapers: and he reached her
parched *corn*, and she did eat, and was
sufficed, and left.
15 And when she was risen up to glean,
Boaz commanded his young men, saying,
Let her glean even among the sheaves, and
reproach her not:
16 And let fall also *some* of the handfuls of
purpose for her, and leave *them*, that she
may glean *them*, and rebuke her not.
17 So she gleaned in the field until even,
and beat out that she had gleaned: and it
was about an ephah of barley.
18 ¶ And she took *it* up, and went into the
city: and her mother in law saw what she
had gleaned: and she brought forth, and
gave to her that she had reserved after she
was sufficed.
19 And her mother in law said unto her,
Where hast thou gleaned to day? and where
wroughtest thou? blessed be he that did
take knowledge of thee. And she shewed
her mother in law with whom she had
wrought, and said, The man's name with
whom I wrought to day *is* Boaz.
20 And Naomi said unto her daughter in law,
Blessed *be* he of the LORD, who hath not
left off his kindness to the living and to the
dead. And Naomi said unto her, The man *is*
near of kin unto us, one of our next kinsmen.
21 And Ruth the Moabitess said, He said
unto me also, Thou shalt keep fast by my
young men, until they have ended all my
harvest.
22 And Naomi said unto Ruth her daughter
in law, *It is* good, my daughter, that thou go
out with his maidens, that they meet thee
not in any other field.
23 So she kept fast by the maidens of Boaz
to glean unto the end of barley harvest
and of wheat harvest; and dwelt with her
mother in law.

Ruth 3

1 Then Naomi her mother in law said unto
her, My daughter, shall I not seek rest for
thee, that it may be well with thee?
2 And now *is* not Boaz of our kindred, with
whose maidens thou wast? Behold, he win-
noweth barley to night in the threshingfloor.
3 Wash thyself therefore, and anoint thee,
and put thy raiment upon thee, and get
thee down to the floor: *but* make not thyself known unto the man, until he shall have
done eating and drinking.
4 And it shall be, when he lieth down, that
thou shalt mark the place where he shall lie,
and thou shalt go in, and uncover his feet,
and lay thee down; and he will tell thee what
thou shalt do.
5 And she said unto her, All that thou sayest
unto me I will do.
6 ¶ And she went down unto the floor, and
did according to all that her mother in law
bade her.
7 And when Boaz had eaten and drunk, and
his heart was merry, he went to lie down
at the end of the heap of corn: and she
came softly, and uncovered his feet, and
laid her down.
8 ¶ And it came to pass at midnight, that the
man was afraid, and turned himself: and,
behold, a woman lay at his feet.
9 And he said, Who *art* thou? And she
answered, I *am* Ruth thine handmaid: spread
therefore thy skirt over thine handmaid; for
thou *art* a near kinsman.
10 And he said, Blessed *be* thou of the
LORD, my daughter: *for* thou hast shewed
more kindness in the latter end than at the
beginning, inasmuch as thou followedst not
young men, whether poor or rich.
11 And now, my daughter, fear not; I will
do to thee all that thou requirest: for all the
city of my people doth know that thou *art*
a virtuous woman.
12 And now it is true that I *am thy* near
kinsman: howbeit there is a kinsman nearer
than I.
13 Tarry this night, and it shall be in the
morning, *that* if he will perform unto thee
the part of a kinsman, well; let him do the

kinsman's part: but if he will not do the part
of a kinsman to thee, then will I do the part
of a kinsman to thee, *as* the LORD liveth: lie
down until the morning.
14 ¶ And she lay at his feet until the morning: and she rose up before one could know
another. And he said, Let it not be known
that a woman came into the floor.
15 Also he said, Bring the vail that *thou hast*
upon thee, and hold it. And when she held
it, he measured six *measures* of barley, and
laid *it* on her: and she went into the city.
16 And when she came to her mother in
law, she said, Who *art* thou, my daughter?
And she told her all that the man had done
to her.
17 And she said, These six *measures* of barley gave he me; for he said to me, Go not
empty unto thy mother in law.
18 Then said she, Sit still, my daughter, until
thou know how the matter will fall: for the
man will not be in rest, until he have finished
the thing this day.

Ruth 4

1 Then went Boaz up to the gate, and sat
him down there: and, behold, the kinsman
of whom Boaz spake came by; unto whom
he said, Ho, such a one! turn aside, sit down
here. And he turned aside, and sat down.
2 And he took ten men of the elders of the
city, and said, Sit ye down here. And they
sat down.
3 And he said unto the kinsman, Naomi,
that is come again out of the country of
Moab, selleth a parcel of land, which *was*
our brother Elimelech's:
4 And I thought to advertise thee, saying,
Buy *it* before the inhabitants, and before
the elders of my people. If thou wilt redeem
it, redeem *it:* but if thou wilt not redeem
it, then tell me, that I may know: for *there
is* none to redeem *it* beside thee; and I *am*
after thee. And he said, I will redeem *it*.
5 Then said Boaz, What day thou buyest the
field of the hand of Naomi, thou must buy
it also of Ruth the Moabitess, the wife of
the dead, to raise up the name of the dead
upon his inheritance.
6 ¶ And the kinsman said, I cannot redeem
it for myself, lest I mar mine own inheritance: redeem thou my right to thyself; for
I cannot redeem *it*.
7 Now this *was the manner* in former time
in Israel concerning redeeming and concerning changing, for to confirm all things;
a man plucked off his shoe, and gave *it* to
his neighbour: and this *was* a testimony
in Israel.
8 Therefore the kinsman said unto Boaz, Buy
it for thee. So he drew off his shoe.
9 ¶ And Boaz said unto the elders, and *unto*
all the people, Ye *are* witnesses this day,
that I have bought all that *was* Elimelech's,
and all that *was* Chilion's and Mahlon's, of
the hand of Naomi.
10 Moreover Ruth the Moabitess, the wife
of Mahlon, have I purchased to be my wife,
to raise up the name of the dead upon his
inheritance, that the name of the dead be
not cut off from among his brethren, and
from the gate of his place: ye *are* witnesses
this day.
11 And all the people that *were* in the gate,
and the elders, said, *We are* witnesses. The
LORD make the woman that is come into
thine house like Rachel and like Leah, which
two did build the house of Israel: and do
thou worthily in Ephratah, and be famous
in Beth-lehem:
12 And let thy house be like the house of
Pharez, whom Tamar bare unto Judah, of
the seed which the LORD shall give thee of
this young woman.
13 ¶ So Boaz took Ruth, and she was his
wife: and when he went in unto her, the
LORD gave her conception, and she bare
a son.
14 And the women said unto Naomi, Blessed
be the LORD, which hath not left thee this
day without a kinsman, that his name may
be famous in Israel.
15 And he shall be unto thee a restorer of
thy life, and a nourisher of thine old age:
for thy daughter in law, which loveth thee,
which is better to thee than seven sons,
hath born him.
16 And Naomi took the child, and laid it in
her bosom, and became nurse unto it.
17 And the women her neighbours gave it a
name, saying, There is a son born to Naomi;
and they called his name Obed: he *is* the
father of Jesse, the father of David.
18 ¶ Now these *are* the generations of
Pharez: Pharez begat Hezron,

19 And Hezron begat Ram, and Ram begat
Amminadab,
20 And Amminadab begat Nahshon, and
Nahshon begat Salmon,
21 And Salmon begat Boaz, and Boaz begat
Obed,
22 And Obed begat Jesse, and Jesse begat
David.

The First Book Of

Samuel

1 Samuel 1

1 Now there was a certain man of Rama-
thaim-zophim, of mount Ephraim, and his
name *was* Elkanah, the son of Jeroham,
the son of Elihu, the son of Tohu, the son
of Zuph, an Ephrathite:
2 And he had two wives; the name of the
one *was* Hannah, and the name of the other
Peninnah: and Peninnah had children, but
Hannah had no children.
3 And this man went up out of his city yearly
to worship and to sacrifice unto the LORD
of hosts in Shiloh. And the two sons of Eli,
Hophni and Phinehas, the priests of the
LORD, *were* there.
4 ¶ And when the time was that Elkanah
offered, he gave to Peninnah his wife, and
to all her sons and her daughters, portions:
5 But unto Hannah he gave a worthy portion; for he loved Hannah: but the LORD had
shut up her womb.
6 And her adversary also provoked her sore,
for to make her fret, because the LORD had
shut up her womb.
7 And *as* he did so year by year, when she
went up to the house of the LORD, so she
provoked her; therefore she wept, and did
not eat.
8 Then said Elkanah her husband to her,
Hannah, why weepest thou? and why eatest
thou not? and why is thy heart grieved? *am*
not I better to thee than ten sons?
9 ¶ So Hannah rose up after they had eaten
in Shiloh, and after they had drunk. Now Eli
the priest sat upon a seat by a post of the
temple of the LORD.
10 And she *was* in bitterness of soul, and
prayed unto the LORD, and wept sore.
11 And she vowed a vow, and said, O LORD
of hosts, if thou wilt indeed look on the
affliction of thine handmaid, and remember me, and not forget thine handmaid,
but wilt give unto thine handmaid a man
child, then I will give him unto the LORD all
the days of his life, and there shall no rasor
come upon his head.
12 And it came to pass, as she continued
praying before the LORD, that Eli marked
her mouth.
13 Now Hannah, she spake in her heart; only
her lips moved, but her voice was not heard:
therefore Eli thought she had been drunken.
14 And Eli said unto her, How long wilt thou
be drunken? put away thy wine from thee.
15 And Hannah answered and said, No, my
lord, I *am* a woman of a sorrowful spirit: I
have drunk neither wine nor strong drink,
but have poured out my soul before the
LORD.
16 Count not thine handmaid for a daughter
of Belial: for out of the abundance of my
complaint and grief have I spoken hitherto.
17 Then Eli answered and said, Go in peace:
and the God of Israel grant *thee* thy petition
that thou hast asked of him.
18 And she said, Let thine handmaid find
grace in thy sight. So the woman went her
way, and did eat, and her countenance was
no more *sad*.
19 ¶ And they rose up in the morning
early, and worshipped before the LORD,
and returned, and came to their house to
Ramah: and Elkanah knew Hannah his wife;
and the LORD remembered her.
20 Wherefore it came to pass, when the
time was come about after Hannah had
conceived, that she bare a son, and called
his name Samuel, *saying*, Because I have
asked him of the LORD.
21 And the man Elkanah, and all his house,

went up to offer unto the LORD the yearly sacrifice, and his vow.

22 But Hannah went not up; for she said unto her husband, *I will not go up* until the child be weaned, and *then* I will bring him, that he may appear before the LORD, and there abide for ever.

23 And Elkanah her husband said unto her, Do what seemeth thee good; tarry until thou have weaned him; only the LORD establish his word. So the woman abode, and gave her son suck until she weaned him.

24 ¶ And when she had weaned him, she took him up with her, with three bullocks, and one ephah of flour, and a bottle of wine, and brought him unto the house of the LORD in Shiloh: and the child *was* young.

25 And they slew a bullock, and brought the child to Eli.

26 And she said, Oh my lord, *as* thy soul liveth, my lord, I *am* the woman that stood by thee here, praying unto the LORD.

27 For this child I prayed; and the LORD hath given me my petition which I asked of him:

28 Therefore also I have lent him to the LORD; as long as he liveth he shall be lent to the LORD. And he worshipped the LORD there.

1 Samuel 2

1 And Hannah prayed, and said, My heart rejoiceth in the LORD, mine horn is exalted in the LORD: my mouth is enlarged over mine enemies; because I rejoice in thy salvation.

2 *There is* none holy as the LORD: for *there is* none beside thee: neither *is there* any rock like our God.

3 Talk no more so exceeding proudly; let *not* arrogancy come out of your mouth: for the LORD *is* a God of knowledge, and by him actions are weighed.

4 The bows of the mighty men *are* broken, and they that stumbled are girded with strength.

5 *They that were* full have hired out themselves for bread; and *they that were* hungry ceased: so that the barren hath born seven; and she that hath many children is waxed feeble.

6 The LORD killeth, and maketh alive: he bringeth down to the grave, and bringeth up.

7 The LORD maketh poor, and maketh rich: he bringeth low, and lifteth up.

8 He raiseth up the poor out of the dust, *and* lifteth up the beggar from the dunghill, to set *them* among princes, and to make them inherit the throne of glory: for the pillars of the earth *are* the LORD's, and he hath set the world upon them.

9 He will keep the feet of his saints, and the wicked shall be silent in darkness; for by strength shall no man prevail.

10 The adversaries of the LORD shall be broken to pieces; out of heaven shall he thunder upon them: the LORD shall judge the ends of the earth; and he shall give strength unto his king, and exalt the horn of his anointed.

11 And Elkanah went to Ramah to his house. And the child did minister unto the LORD before Eli the priest.

12 ¶ Now the sons of Eli *were* sons of Belial; they knew not the LORD.

13 And the priests' custom with the people *was, that,* when any man offered sacrifice, the priest's servant came, while the flesh was in seething, with a fleshhook of three teeth in his hand;

14 And he struck *it* into the pan, or kettle, or caldron, or pot; all that the fleshhook brought up the priest took for himself. So they did in Shiloh unto all the Israelites that came thither.

15 Also before they burnt the fat, the priest's servant came, and said to the man that sacrificed, Give flesh to roast for the priest; for he will not have sodden flesh of thee, but raw.

16 And *if* any man said unto him, Let them not fail to burn the fat presently, and *then* take *as much* as thy soul desireth; then he would answer him, *Nay;* but thou shalt give *it me* now: and if not, I will take *it* by force.

17 Wherefore the sin of the young men was very great before the LORD: for men abhorred the offering of the LORD.

18 ¶ But Samuel ministered before the LORD, *being* a child, girded with a linen ephod.

19 Moreover his mother made him a little coat, and brought *it* to him from year to year, when she came up with her husband to offer the yearly sacrifice.

20 ¶ And Eli blessed Elkanah and his wife, and said, The LORD give thee seed of this woman for the loan which is lent to the LORD. And they went unto their own home.

21 And the LORD visited Hannah, so that
she conceived, and bare three sons and
two daughters. And the child Samuel grew
before the LORD.
22 ¶ Now Eli was very old, and heard all that
his sons did unto all Israel; and how they
lay with the women that assembled *at* the
door of the tabernacle of the congregation.
23 And he said unto them, Why do ye such
things? for I hear of your evil dealings by
all this people.
24 Nay, my sons; for *it is* no good report
that I hear: ye make the LORD's people to
transgress.
25 If one man sin against another, the judge
shall judge him: but if a man sin against the
LORD, who shall intreat for him? Notwithstanding they hearkened not unto the voice
of their father, because the LORD would
slay them.
26 And the child Samuel grew on, and was
in favour both with the LORD, and also
with men.
27 ¶ And there came a man of God unto
Eli, and said unto him, Thus saith the LORD,
Did I plainly appear unto the house of thy
father, when they were in Egypt in Pharaoh's house?
28 And did I choose him out of all the tribes
of Israel *to be* my priest, to offer upon mine
altar, to burn incense, to wear an ephod
before me? and did I give unto the house
of thy father all the offerings made by fire
of the children of Israel?
29 Wherefore kick ye at my sacrifice and
at mine offering, which I have commanded
in my habitation; and honourest thy sons
above me, to make yourselves fat with
the chiefest of all the offerings of Israel
my people?
30 Wherefore the LORD God of Israel saith,
I said indeed *that* thy house, and the house
of thy father, should walk before me for
ever: but now the LORD saith, Be it far from
me; for them that honour me I will honour,
and they that despise me shall be lightly
esteemed.
31 Behold, the days come, that I will cut
off thine arm, and the arm of thy father's
house, that there shall not be an old man
in thine house.
32 And thou shalt see an enemy *in my* habitation, in all *the wealth* which *God* shall give
Israel: and there shall not be an old man in
thine house for ever.
33 And the man of thine, *whom* I shall not
cut off from mine altar, *shall be* to consume
thine eyes, and to grieve thine heart: and
all the increase of thine house shall die in
the flower of their age.
34 And this *shall be* a sign unto thee, that
shall come upon thy two sons, on Hophni
and Phinehas; in one day they shall die
both of them.
35 And I will raise me up a faithful priest,
that shall do according to *that* which *is* in
mine heart and in my mind: and I will build
him a sure house; and he shall walk before
mine anointed for ever.
36 And it shall come to pass, *that* every
one that is left in thine house shall come
and crouch to him for a piece of silver and
a morsel of bread, and shall say, Put me, I
pray thee, into one of the priests' offices,
that I may eat a piece of bread.

1 Samuel 3

1 And the child Samuel ministered unto the
LORD before Eli. And the word of the LORD
was precious in those days; *there was* no
open vision.
2 And it came to pass at that time, when
Eli *was* laid down in his place, and his eyes
began to wax dim, *that* he could not see;
3 And ere the lamp of God went out in the
temple of the LORD, where the ark of God
was, and Samuel was laid down *to sleep;*
4 That the LORD called Samuel: and he
answered, Here *am* I.
5 And he ran unto Eli, and said, Here *am* I; for
thou calledst me. And he said, I called not;
lie down again. And he went and lay down.
6 And the LORD called yet again, Samuel.
And Samuel arose and went to Eli, and
said, Here *am* I; for thou didst call me.
And he answered, I called not, my son; lie
down again.
7 Now Samuel did not yet know the LORD,
neither was the word of the LORD yet
revealed unto him.
8 And the LORD called Samuel again the
third time. And he arose and went to Eli,
and said, Here *am* I; for thou didst call me.
And Eli perceived that the LORD had called
the child.
9 Therefore Eli said unto Samuel, Go, lie

down: and it shall be, if he call thee, that thou shalt say, Speak, LORD; for thy servant heareth. So Samuel went and lay down in his place.

10 And the LORD came, and stood, and called as at other times, Samuel, Samuel. Then Samuel answered, Speak; for thy servant heareth.

11 ¶ And the LORD said to Samuel, Behold, I will do a thing in Israel, at which both the ears of every one that heareth it shall tingle.

12 In that day I will perform against Eli all *things* which I have spoken concerning his house: when I begin, I will also make an end.

13 For I have told him that I will judge his house for ever for the iniquity which he knoweth; because his sons made themselves vile, and he restrained them not.

14 And therefore I have sworn unto the house of Eli, that the iniquity of Eli's house shall not be purged with sacrifice nor offering for ever.

15 ¶ And Samuel lay until the morning, and opened the doors of the house of the LORD. And Samuel feared to shew Eli the vision.

16 Then Eli called Samuel, and said, Samuel, my son. And he answered, Here *am* I.

17 And he said, What *is* the thing that *the LORD* hath said unto thee? I pray thee hide *it* not from me: God do so to thee, and more also, if thou hide *any* thing from me of all the things that he said unto thee.

18 And Samuel told him every whit, and hid nothing from him. And he said, It *is* the LORD: let him do what seemeth him good.

19 ¶ And Samuel grew, and the LORD was with him, and did let none of his words fall to the ground.

20 And all Israel from Dan even to Beer-sheba knew that Samuel *was* established *to be* a prophet of the LORD.

21 And the LORD appeared again in Shiloh: for the LORD revealed himself to Samuel in Shiloh by the word of the LORD.

1 Samuel 4

1 And the word of Samuel came to all Israel. Now Israel went out against the Philistines to battle, and pitched beside Eben-ezer: and the Philistines pitched in Aphek.

2 And the Philistines put themselves in array against Israel: and when they joined battle, Israel was smitten before the Philistines: and they slew of the army in the field about four thousand men.

3 ¶ And when the people were come into the camp, the elders of Israel said, Wherefore hath the LORD smitten us to day before the Philistines? Let us fetch the ark of the covenant of the LORD out of Shiloh unto us, that, when it cometh among us, it may save us out of the hand of our enemies.

4 So the people sent to Shiloh, that they might bring from thence the ark of the covenant of the LORD of hosts, which dwelleth *between* the cherubims: and the two sons of Eli, Hophni and Phinehas, *were* there with the ark of the covenant of God.

5 And when the ark of the covenant of the LORD came into the camp, all Israel shouted with a great shout, so that the earth rang again.

6 And when the Philistines heard the noise of the shout, they said, What *meaneth* the noise of this great shout in the camp of the Hebrews? And they understood that the ark of the LORD was come into the camp.

7 And the Philistines were afraid, for they said, God is come into the camp. And they said, Woe unto us! for there hath not been such a thing heretofore.

8 Woe unto us! who shall deliver us out of the hand of these mighty Gods? these *are* the Gods that smote the Egyptians with all the plagues in the wilderness.

9 Be strong, and quit yourselves like men, O ye Philistines, that ye be not servants unto the Hebrews, as they have been to you: quit yourselves like men, and fight.

10 ¶ And the Philistines fought, and Israel was smitten, and they fled every man into his tent: and there was a very great slaughter; for there fell of Israel thirty thousand footmen.

11 And the ark of God was taken; and the two sons of Eli, Hophni and Phinehas, were slain.

12 ¶ And there ran a man of Benjamin out of the army, and came to Shiloh the same day with his clothes rent, and with earth upon his head.

13 And when he came, lo, Eli sat upon a seat by the wayside watching: for his heart trembled for the ark of God. And when the man came into the city, and told *it*, all the city cried out.

14 And when Eli heard the noise of the
crying, he said, What *meaneth* the noise of
this tumult? And the man came in hastily,
and told Eli.
15 Now Eli was ninety and eight years old;
and his eyes were dim, that he could not see.
16 And the man said unto Eli, I *am* he that
came out of the army, and I fled to day out
of the army. And he said, What is there
done, my son?
17 And the messenger answered and said,
Israel is fled before the Philistines, and there
hath been also a great slaughter among the
people, and thy two sons also, Hophni and
Phinehas, are dead, and the ark of God is
taken.
18 And it came to pass, when he made mention of the ark of God, that he fell from off
the seat backward by the side of the gate,
and his neck brake, and he died: for he was
an old man, and heavy. And he had judged
Israel forty years.
19 ¶ And his daughter in law, Phinehas'
wife, was with child, *near* to be delivered:
and when she heard the tidings that the
ark of God was taken, and that her father
in law and her husband were dead, she
bowed herself and travailed; for her pains
came upon her.
20 And about the time of her death the
women that stood by her said unto her,
Fear not; for thou hast born a son. But she
answered not, neither did she regard *it*.
21 And she named the child I-chabod,
saying, The glory is departed from Israel:
because the ark of God was taken, and
because of her father in law and her husband.
22 And she said, The glory is departed from
Israel: for the ark of God is taken.

1 Samuel 5

1 And the Philistines took the ark of God,
and brought it from Eben-ezer unto Ashdod.
2 When the Philistines took the ark of God,
they brought it into the house of Dagon, and
set it by Dagon.
3 ¶ And when they of Ashdod arose early
on the morrow, behold, Dagon *was* fallen
upon his face to the earth before the ark
of the LORD. And they took Dagon, and set
him in his place again.
4 And when they arose early on the morrow
morning, behold, Dagon *was* fallen upon
his face to the ground before the ark of the
LORD; and the head of Dagon and both the
palms of his hands *were* cut off upon the
threshold; only *the stump of* Dagon was
left to him.
5 Therefore neither the priests of Dagon,
nor any that come into Dagon's house,
tread on the threshold of Dagon in Ashdod
unto this day.
6 But the hand of the LORD was heavy upon
them of Ashdod, and he destroyed them,
and smote them with emerods, *even* Ashdod and the coasts thereof.
7 And when the men of Ashdod saw that
it was so, they said, The ark of the God of
Israel shall not abide with us: for his hand
is sore upon us, and upon Dagon our god.
8 They sent therefore and gathered all the
lords of the Philistines unto them, and said,
What shall we do with the ark of the God
of Israel? And they answered, Let the ark
of the God of Israel be carried about unto
Gath. And they carried the ark of the God
of Israel about *thither*.
9 And it was *so*, that, after they had carried
it about, the hand of the LORD was against
the city with a very great destruction: and
he smote the men of the city, both small
and great, and they had emerods in their
secret parts.
10 ¶ Therefore they sent the ark of God
to Ekron. And it came to pass, as the ark
of God came to Ekron, that the Ekronites
cried out, saying, They have brought about
the ark of the God of Israel to us, to slay us
and our people.
11 So they sent and gathered together all
the lords of the Philistines, and said, Send
away the ark of the God of Israel, and let
it go again to his own place, that it slay us
not, and our people: for there was a deadly
destruction throughout all the city; the hand
of God was very heavy there.
12 And the men that died not were smitten
with the emerods: and the cry of the city
went up to heaven.

1 Samuel 6

1 And the ark of the LORD was in the country
of the Philistines seven months.
2 And the Philistines called for the priests
and the diviners, saying, What shall we do

to the ark of the LORD? tell us wherewith
we shall send it to his place.
3 And they said, If ye send away the ark of
the God of Israel, send it not empty; but in
any wise return him a trespass offering: then
ye shall be healed, and it shall be known to
you why his hand is not removed from you.
4 Then said they, What *shall be* the trespass
offering which we shall return to him? They
answered, Five golden emerods, and five
golden mice, *according to* the number of
the lords of the Philistines: for one plague
was on you all, and on your lords.
5 Wherefore ye shall make images of your
emerods, and images of your mice that mar
the land; and ye shall give glory unto the
God of Israel: peradventure he will lighten
his hand from off you, and from off your
gods, and from off your land.
6 Wherefore then do ye harden your hearts,
as the Egyptians and Pharaoh hardened
their hearts? when he had wrought wonderfully among them, did they not let the
people go, and they departed?
7 Now therefore make a new cart, and take
two milch kine, on which there hath come
no yoke, and tie the kine to the cart, and
bring their calves home from them:
8 And take the ark of the LORD, and lay it
upon the cart; and put the jewels of gold,
which ye return him *for* a trespass offering,
in a coffer by the side thereof; and send it
away, that it may go.
9 And see, if it goeth up by the way of his
own coast to Beth-shemesh, *then* he hath
done us this great evil: but if not, then we
shall know that *it is* not his hand *that* smote
us; it *was* a chance *that* happened to us.
10 ¶ And the men did so; and took two milch
kine, and tied them to the cart, and shut up
their calves at home:
11 And they laid the ark of the LORD upon
the cart, and the coffer with the mice of gold
and the images of their emerods.
12 And the kine took the straight way to the
way of Beth-shemesh, *and* went along the
highway, lowing as they went, and turned
not aside *to* the right hand or *to* the left; and
the lords of the Philistines went after them
unto the border of Beth-shemesh.
13 And *they of* Beth-shemesh *were* reaping
their wheat harvest in the valley: and they
lifted up their eyes, and saw the ark, and
rejoiced to see *it*.
14 And the cart came into the field of
Joshua, a Beth-shemite, and stood there,
where *there was* a great stone: and they
clave the wood of the cart, and offered the
kine a burnt offering unto the LORD.
15 And the Levites took down the ark of
the LORD, and the coffer that *was* with it,
wherein the jewels of gold *were*, and put
them on the great stone: and the men of
Beth-shemesh offered burnt offerings and
sacrificed sacrifices the same day unto the
LORD.
16 And when the five lords of the Philistines had seen *it*, they returned to Ekron
the same day.
17 And these *are* the golden emerods
which the Philistines returned *for* a trespass
offering unto the LORD; for Ashdod one, for
Gaza one, for Askelon one, for Gath one,
for Ekron one;
18 And the golden mice, *according to* the
number of all the cities of the Philistines
belonging to the five lords, *both* of fenced
cities, and of country villages, even unto the
great *stone of* Abel, whereon they set down
the ark of the LORD: *which stone remaineth*
unto this day in the field of Joshua, the
Beth-shemite.
19 ¶ And he smote the men of Beth-
shemesh, because they had looked into
the ark of the LORD, even he smote of the
people fifty thousand and threescore and
ten men: and the people lamented, because
the LORD had smitten *many* of the people
with a great slaughter.
20 And the men of Beth-shemesh said, Who
is able to stand before this holy LORD God?
and to whom shall he go up from us?
21 ¶ And they sent messengers to the
inhabitants of Kirjath-jearim, saying, The
Philistines have brought again the ark of the
LORD; come ye down, *and* fetch it up to you.

1 Samuel 7

1 And the men of Kirjath-jearim came, and
fetched up the ark of the LORD, and brought
it into the house of Abinadab in the hill, and
sanctified Eleazar his son to keep the ark
of the LORD.
2 And it came to pass, while the ark abode
in Kirjath-jearim, that the time was long;

for it was twenty years: and all the house
of Israel lamented after the LORD.
3 ¶ And Samuel spake unto all the house
of Israel, saying, If ye do return unto the
LORD with all your hearts, *then* put away
the strange gods and Ashtaroth from among
you, and prepare your hearts unto the LORD,
and serve him only: and he will deliver you
out of the hand of the Philistines.
4 Then the children of Israel did put away
Baalim and Ashtaroth, and served the
LORD only.
5 And Samuel said, Gather all Israel to Mizpeh, and I will pray for you unto the LORD.
6 And they gathered together to Mizpeh,
and drew water, and poured *it* out before
the LORD, and fasted on that day, and said
there, We have sinned against the LORD.
And Samuel judged the children of Israel
in Mizpeh.
7 And when the Philistines heard that the
children of Israel were gathered together
to Mizpeh, the lords of the Philistines went
up against Israel. And when the children
of Israel heard *it*, they were afraid of the
Philistines.
8 And the children of Israel said to Samuel,
Cease not to cry unto the LORD our God for
us, that he will save us out of the hand of
the Philistines.
9 ¶ And Samuel took a sucking lamb, and
offered *it for* a burnt offering wholly unto
the LORD: and Samuel cried unto the LORD
for Israel; and the LORD heard him.
10 And as Samuel was offering up the burnt
offering, the Philistines drew near to battle
against Israel: but the LORD thundered with
a great thunder on that day upon the Philistines, and discomfited them; and they were
smitten before Israel.
11 And the men of Israel went out of Mizpeh, and pursued the Philistines, and smote
them, until *they came* under Beth-car.
12 Then Samuel took a stone, and set *it*
between Mizpeh and Shen, and called the
name of it Eben-ezer, saying, Hitherto hath
the LORD helped us.
13 ¶ So the Philistines were subdued, and
they came no more into the coast of Israel:
and the hand of the LORD was against the
Philistines all the days of Samuel.
14 And the cities which the Philistines had
taken from Israel were restored to Israel,
from Ekron even unto Gath; and the coasts
thereof did Israel deliver out of the hands
of the Philistines. And there was peace
between Israel and the Amorites.
15 And Samuel judged Israel all the days
of his life.
16 And he went from year to year in circuit
to Beth-el, and Gilgal, and Mizpeh, and
judged Israel in all those places.
17 And his return *was* to Ramah; for there
was his house; and there he judged Israel;
and there he built an altar unto the LORD.

1 Samuel 8

1 And it came to pass, when Samuel was
old, that he made his sons judges over Israel.
2 Now the name of his firstborn was Joel;
and the name of his second, Abiah: *they
were* judges in Beer-sheba.
3 And his sons walked not in his ways, but
turned aside after lucre, and took bribes,
and perverted judgment.
4 Then all the elders of Israel gathered
themselves together, and came to Samuel
unto Ramah,
5 And said unto him, Behold, thou art old,
and thy sons walk not in thy ways: now make
us a king to judge us like all the nations.
6 ¶ But the thing displeased Samuel, when
they said, Give us a king to judge us. And
Samuel prayed unto the LORD.
7 And the LORD said unto Samuel, Hearken
unto the voice of the people in all that they
say unto thee: for they have not rejected
thee, but they have rejected me, that I
should not reign over them.
8 According to all the works which they have
done since the day that I brought them up
out of Egypt even unto this day, wherewith
they have forsaken me, and served other
gods, so do they also unto thee.
9 Now therefore hearken unto their voice:
howbeit yet protest solemnly unto them,
and shew them the manner of the king that
shall reign over them.
10 ¶ And Samuel told all the words of the
LORD unto the people that asked of him
a king.
11 And he said, This will be the manner of
the king that shall reign over you: He will
take your sons, and appoint *them* for himself, for his chariots, and *to be* his horsemen;
and *some* shall run before his chariots.

12 And he will appoint him captains over
thousands, and captains over fifties; and
will set them to ear his ground, and to reap
his harvest, and to make his instruments of
war, and instruments of his chariots.
13 And he will take your daughters *to be*
confectionaries, and *to be* cooks, and *to*
be bakers.
14 And he will take your fields, and your
vineyards, and your oliveyards, *even* the
best *of them*, and give *them* to his servants.
15 And he will take the tenth of your seed,
and of your vineyards, and give to his officers, and to his servants.
16 And he will take your menservants, and
your maidservants, and your goodliest
young men, and your asses, and put *them*
to his work.
17 He will take the tenth of your sheep: and
ye shall be his servants.
18 And ye shall cry out in that day because
of your king which ye shall have chosen you;
and the LORD will not hear you in that day.
19 ¶ Nevertheless the people refused to
obey the voice of Samuel; and they said,
Nay; but we will have a king over us;
20 That we also may be like all the nations;
and that our king may judge us, and go out
before us, and fight our battles.
21 And Samuel heard all the words of the
people, and he rehearsed them in the ears
of the LORD.
22 And the LORD said to Samuel, Hearken
unto their voice, and make them a king. And
Samuel said unto the men of Israel, Go ye
every man unto his city.

1 Samuel 9

1 Now there was a man of Benjamin, whose
name *was* Kish, the son of Abiel, the son
of Zeror, the son of Bechorath, the son of
Aphiah, a Benjamite, a mighty man of power.
2 And he had a son, whose name *was* Saul,
a choice young man, and a goodly: and
there was not among the children of Israel
a goodlier person than he: from his shoulders and upward *he was* higher than any
of the people.
3 And the asses of Kish Saul's father were
lost. And Kish said to Saul his son, Take now
one of the servants with thee, and arise, go
seek the asses.
4 And he passed through mount Ephraim,
and passed through the land of Shalisha,
but they found *them* not: then they passed
through the land of Shalim, and *there they*
were not: and he passed through the land
of the Benjamites, but they found *them* not.
5 *And* when they were come to the land
of Zuph, Saul said to his servant that *was*
with him, Come, and let us return; lest my
father leave *caring* for the asses, and take
thought for us.
6 And he said unto him, Behold now, *there*
is in this city a man of God, and *he is* an honourable man; all that he saith cometh surely
to pass: now let us go thither; peradventure
he can shew us our way that we should go.
7 Then said Saul to his servant, But, behold,
if we go, what shall we bring the man? for
the bread is spent in our vessels, and *there*
is not a present to bring to the man of God:
what have we?
8 And the servant answered Saul again, and
said, Behold, I have here at hand the fourth
part of a shekel of silver: *that* will I give to
the man of God, to tell us our way.
9 (Beforetime in Israel, when a man went to
inquire of God, thus he spake, Come, and let
us go to the seer: for *he that is* now *called*
a Prophet was beforetime called a Seer.)
10 Then said Saul to his servant, Well said;
come, let us go. So they went unto the city
where the man of God *was*.
11 ¶ *And* as they went up the hill to the city,
they found young maidens going out to draw
water, and said unto them, Is the seer here?
12 And they answered them, and said, He
is; behold, *he is* before you: make haste
now, for he came to day to the city; for
there is a sacrifice of the people to day in
the high place:
13 As soon as ye be come into the city, ye
shall straightway find him, before he go up
to the high place to eat: for the people will
not eat until he come, because he doth bless
the sacrifice; *and* afterwards they eat that
be bidden. Now therefore get you up; for
about this time ye shall find him.
14 And they went up into the city: *and* when
they were come into the city, behold, Samuel came out against them, for to go up to
the high place.
15 ¶ Now the LORD had told Samuel in his
ear a day before Saul came, saying,
16 To morrow about this time I will send

thee a man out of the land of Benjamin, and
thou shalt anoint him *to be* captain over my
people Israel, that he may save my people
out of the hand of the Philistines: for I have
looked upon my people, because their cry
is come unto me.
17 And when Samuel saw Saul, the LORD
said unto him, Behold the man whom I
spake to thee of! this same shall reign over
my people.
18 Then Saul drew near to Samuel in the
gate, and said, Tell me, I pray thee, where
the seer's house *is*.
19 And Samuel answered Saul, and said, I
am the seer: go up before me unto the high
place; for ye shall eat with me to day, and to
morrow I will let thee go, and will tell thee
all that *is* in thine heart.
20 And as for thine asses that were lost
three days ago, set not thy mind on them;
for they are found. And on whom *is* all the
desire of Israel? *Is it* not on thee, and on all
thy father's house?
21 And Saul answered and said, *Am* not I
a Benjamite, of the smallest of the tribes
of Israel? and my family the least of all the
families of the tribe of Benjamin? wherefore
then speakest thou so to me?
22 And Samuel took Saul and his servant,
and brought them into the parlour, and
made them sit in the chiefest place among
them that were bidden, which *were* about
thirty persons.
23 And Samuel said unto the cook, Bring
the portion which I gave thee, of which I
said unto thee, Set it by thee.
24 And the cook took up the shoulder, and
that which *was* upon it, and set *it* before
Saul. And *Samuel* said, Behold that which
is left! set *it* before thee, *and* eat: for unto
this time hath it been kept for thee since I
said, I have invited the people. So Saul did
eat with Samuel that day.
25 ¶ And when they were come down from
the high place into the city, *Samuel* communed with Saul upon the top of the house.
26 And they arose early: and it came to pass
about the spring of the day, that Samuel
called Saul to the top of the house, saying,
Up, that I may send thee away. And Saul
arose, and they went out both of them, he
and Samuel, abroad.
27 *And* as they were going down to the end
of the city, Samuel said to Saul, Bid the servant pass on before us, (and he passed on,)
but stand thou still a while, that I may shew
thee the word of God.

1 Samuel 10

1 Then Samuel took a vial of oil, and poured
it upon his head, and kissed him, and said, *Is
it* not because the LORD hath anointed thee
to be captain over his inheritance?
2 When thou art departed from me to day,
then thou shalt find two men by Rachel's
sepulchre in the border of Benjamin at Zel-
zah; and they will say unto thee, The asses
which thou wentest to seek are found: and,
lo, thy father hath left the care of the asses,
and sorroweth for you, saying, What shall
I do for my son?
3 Then shalt thou go on forward from
thence, and thou shalt come to the plain
of Tabor, and there shall meet thee three
men going up to God to Beth-el, one carrying three kids, and another carrying three
loaves of bread, and another carrying a
bottle of wine:
4 And they will salute thee, and give thee
two *loaves* of bread; which thou shalt
receive of their hands.
5 After that thou shalt come to the hill of
God, where *is* the garrison of the Philistines:
and it shall come to pass, when thou art
come thither to the city, that thou shalt
meet a company of prophets coming down
from the high place with a psaltery, and a
tabret, and a pipe, and a harp, before them;
and they shall prophesy:
6 And the Spirit of the LORD will come upon
thee, and thou shalt prophesy with them,
and shalt be turned into another man.
7 And let it be, when these signs are come
unto thee, *that* thou do as occasion serve
thee; for God *is* with thee.
8 And thou shalt go down before me to
Gilgal; and, behold, I will come down unto
thee, to offer burnt offerings, *and* to sacrifice sacrifices of peace offerings: seven days
shalt thou tarry, till I come to thee, and shew
thee what thou shalt do.
9 ¶ And it was *so*, that when he had turned
his back to go from Samuel, God gave him
another heart: and all those signs came to
pass that day.
10 And when they came thither to the hill,

behold, a company of prophets met him; and the Spirit of God came upon him, and he prophesied among them.
11 And it came to pass, when all that knew him beforetime saw that, behold, he prophesied among the prophets, then the people said one to another, What *is* this *that* is come unto the son of Kish? *Is* Saul also among the prophets?
12 And one of the same place answered and said, But who *is* their father? Therefore it became a proverb, *Is* Saul also among the prophets?
13 And when he had made an end of prophesying, he came to the high place.
14 ¶ And Saul's uncle said unto him and to his servant, Whither went ye? And he said, To seek the asses: and when we saw that *they were* no where, we came to Samuel.
15 And Saul's uncle said, Tell me, I pray thee, what Samuel said unto you.
16 And Saul said unto his uncle, He told us plainly that the asses were found. But of the matter of the kingdom, whereof Samuel spake, he told him not.
17 ¶ And Samuel called the people together unto the LORD to Mizpeh;
18 And said unto the children of Israel, Thus saith the LORD God of Israel, I brought up Israel out of Egypt, and delivered you out of the hand of the Egyptians, and out of the hand of all kingdoms, *and* of them that oppressed you:
19 And ye have this day rejected your God, who himself saved you out of all your adversities and your tribulations; and ye have said unto him, *Nay,* but set a king over us. Now therefore present yourselves before the LORD by your tribes, and by your thousands.
20 And when Samuel had caused all the tribes of Israel to come near, the tribe of Benjamin was taken.
21 When he had caused the tribe of Benjamin to come near by their families, the family of Matri was taken, and Saul the son of Kish was taken: and when they sought him, he could not be found.
22 Therefore they inquired of the LORD further, if the man should yet come thither. And the LORD answered, Behold, he hath hid himself among the stuff.
23 And they ran and fetched him thence: and when he stood among the people, he was higher than any of the people from his shoulders and upward.
24 And Samuel said to all the people, See ye him whom the LORD hath chosen, that *there is* none like him among all the people? And all the people shouted, and said, God save the king.
25 Then Samuel told the people the manner of the kingdom, and wrote *it* in a book, and laid *it* up before the LORD. And Samuel sent all the people away, every man to his house.
26 ¶ And Saul also went home to Gibeah; and there went with him a band of men, whose hearts God had touched.
27 But the children of Belial said, How shall this man save us? And they despised him, and brought him no presents. But he held his peace.

1 Samuel 11

1 Then Nahash the Ammonite came up, and encamped against Jabesh-gilead: and all the men of Jabesh said unto Nahash, Make a covenant with us, and we will serve thee.
2 And Nahash the Ammonite answered them, On this *condition* will I make *a covenant* with you, that I may thrust out all your right eyes, and lay it *for* a reproach upon all Israel.
3 And the elders of Jabesh said unto him, Give us seven days' respite, that we may send messengers unto all the coasts of Israel: and then, if *there be* no man to save us, we will come out to thee.
4 ¶ Then came the messengers to Gibeah of Saul, and told the tidings in the ears of the people: and all the people lifted up their voices, and wept.
5 And, behold, Saul came after the herd out of the field; and Saul said, What *aileth* the people that they weep? And they told him the tidings of the men of Jabesh.
6 And the Spirit of God came upon Saul when he heard those tidings, and his anger was kindled greatly.
7 And he took a yoke of oxen, and hewed them in pieces, and sent *them* throughout all the coasts of Israel by the hands of messengers, saying, Whosoever cometh not forth after Saul and after Samuel, so shall it be done unto his oxen. And the fear of the LORD fell on the people, and they came out with one consent.

8 And when he numbered them in Bezek,
the children of Israel were three hundred
thousand, and the men of Judah thirty
thousand.
9 And they said unto the messengers that
came, Thus shall ye say unto the men of
Jabesh-gilead, To morrow, by *that time*
the sun be hot, ye shall have help. And the
messengers came and shewed *it* to the men
of Jabesh; and they were glad.
10 Therefore the men of Jabesh said, To
morrow we will come out unto you, and
ye shall do with us all that seemeth good
unto you.
11 And it was *so* on the morrow, that Saul
put the people in three companies; and
they came into the midst of the host in the
morning watch, and slew the Ammonites
until the heat of the day: and it came to pass,
that they which remained were scattered,
so that two of them were not left together.
12 ¶ And the people said unto Samuel, Who
is he that said, Shall Saul reign over us? bring
the men, that we may put them to death.
13 And Saul said, There shall not a man be
put to death this day: for to day the LORD
hath wrought salvation in Israel.
14 Then said Samuel to the people, Come,
and let us go to Gilgal, and renew the kingdom there.
15 And all the people went to Gilgal; and
there they made Saul king before the LORD
in Gilgal; and there they sacrificed sacrifices of peace offerings before the LORD;
and there Saul and all the men of Israel
rejoiced greatly.

1 Samuel 12

1 And Samuel said unto all Israel, Behold, I
have hearkened unto your voice in all that
ye said unto me, and have made a king
over you.
2 And now, behold, the king walketh before
you: and I am old and grayheaded; and,
behold, my sons *are* with you: and I have
walked before you from my childhood
unto this day.
3 Behold, here I *am:* witness against me
before the LORD, and before his anointed:
whose ox have I taken? or whose ass have
I taken? or whom have I defrauded? whom
have I oppressed? or of whose hand have I
received *any* bribe to blind mine eyes therewith? and I will restore it you.
4 And they said, Thou hast not defrauded us,
nor oppressed us, neither hast thou taken
ought of any man's hand.
5 And he said unto them, The LORD *is* witness against you, and his anointed *is* witness
this day, that ye have not found ought in my
hand. And they answered, *He is* witness.
6 ¶ And Samuel said unto the people, *It is*
the LORD that advanced Moses and Aaron,
and that brought your fathers up out of the
land of Egypt.
7 Now therefore stand still, that I may
reason with you before the LORD of all the
righteous acts of the LORD, which he did to
you and to your fathers.
8 When Jacob was come into Egypt, and
your fathers cried unto the LORD, then the
LORD sent Moses and Aaron, which brought
forth your fathers out of Egypt, and made
them dwell in this place.
9 And when they forgat the LORD their God,
he sold them into the hand of Sisera, captain
of the host of Hazor, and into the hand of
the Philistines, and into the hand of the king
of Moab, and they fought against them.
10 And they cried unto the LORD, and said,
We have sinned, because we have forsaken
the LORD, and have served Baalim and
Ashtaroth: but now deliver us out of the
hand of our enemies, and we will serve thee.
11 And the LORD sent Jerubbaal, and Bedan,
and Jephthah, and Samuel, and delivered
you out of the hand of your enemies on
every side, and ye dwelled safe.
12 And when ye saw that Nahash the king of
the children of Ammon came against you, ye
said unto me, Nay; but a king shall reign over
us: when the LORD your God *was* your king.
13 Now therefore behold the king whom ye
have chosen, *and* whom ye have desired!
and, behold, the LORD hath set a king over
you.
14 If ye will fear the LORD, and serve him,
and obey his voice, and not rebel against
the commandment of the LORD, then shall
both ye and also the king that reigneth over
you continue following the LORD your God:
15 But if ye will not obey the voice of the
LORD, but rebel against the commandment of the LORD, then shall the hand of

the LORD be against you, as *it was* against
your fathers.
16 ¶ Now therefore stand and see this
great thing, which the LORD will do before
your eyes.
17 *Is it* not wheat harvest to day? I will call
unto the LORD, and he shall send thunder
and rain; that ye may perceive and see that
your wickedness *is* great, which ye have
done in the sight of the LORD, in asking
you a king.
18 So Samuel called unto the LORD; and
the LORD sent thunder and rain that day:
and all the people greatly feared the LORD
and Samuel.
19 And all the people said unto Samuel, Pray
for thy servants unto the LORD thy God, that
we die not: for we have added unto all our
sins *this* evil, to ask us a king.
20 ¶ And Samuel said unto the people, Fear
not: ye have done all this wickedness: yet
turn not aside from following the LORD, but
serve the LORD with all your heart;
21 And turn ye not aside: for *then should
ye go* after vain *things*, which cannot profit
nor deliver; for they *are* vain.
22 For the LORD will not forsake his people
for his great name's sake: because it hath
pleased the LORD to make you his people.
23 Moreover as for me, God forbid that I
should sin against the LORD in ceasing to
pray for you: but I will teach you the good
and the right way:
24 Only fear the LORD, and serve him in truth
with all your heart: for consider how great
things he hath done for you.
25 But if ye shall still do wickedly, ye shall be
consumed, both ye and your king.

1 Samuel 13

1 Saul reigned one year; and when he had
reigned two years over Israel,
2 Saul chose him three thousand *men* of
Israel; *whereof* two thousand were with
Saul in Michmash and in mount Beth-el, and
a thousand were with Jonathan in Gibeah
of Benjamin: and the rest of the people he
sent every man to his tent.
3 And Jonathan smote the garrison of the
Philistines that *was* in Geba, and the Philistines heard *of it*. And Saul blew the trumpet throughout all the land, saying, Let the
Hebrews hear.
4 And all Israel heard say *that* Saul had
smitten a garrison of the Philistines, and
that Israel also was had in abomination with
the Philistines. And the people were called
together after Saul to Gilgal.
5 ¶ And the Philistines gathered themselves
together to fight with Israel, thirty thousand
chariots, and six thousand horsemen, and
people as the sand which *is* on the sea shore
in multitude: and they came up, and pitched
in Michmash, eastward from Beth-aven.
6 When the men of Israel saw that they were
in a strait, (for the people were distressed,)
then the people did hide themselves in
caves, and in thickets, and in rocks, and in
high places, and in pits.
7 And *some of* the Hebrews went over Jordan to the land of Gad and Gilead. As for
Saul, he *was* yet in Gilgal, and all the people
followed him trembling.
8 ¶ And he tarried seven days, according to
the set time that Samuel *had appointed:* but
Samuel came not to Gilgal; and the people
were scattered from him.
9 And Saul said, Bring hither a burnt offering
to me, and peace offerings. And he offered
the burnt offering.
10 And it came to pass, that as soon as he
had made an end of offering the burnt offering, behold, Samuel came; and Saul went
out to meet him, that he might salute him.
11 ¶ And Samuel said, What hast thou done?
And Saul said, Because I saw that the people were scattered from me, and *that* thou
camest not within the days appointed, and
that the Philistines gathered themselves
together at Michmash;
12 Therefore said I, The Philistines will
come down now upon me to Gilgal, and I
have not made supplication unto the LORD:
I forced myself therefore, and offered a
burnt offering.
13 And Samuel said to Saul, Thou hast
done foolishly: thou hast not kept the commandment of the LORD thy God, which he
commanded thee: for now would the LORD
have established thy kingdom upon Israel
for ever.
14 But now thy kingdom shall not continue:
the LORD hath sought him a man after his
own heart, and the LORD hath commanded
him *to be* captain over his people, because

thou hast not kept *that* which the LORD
commanded thee.
15 And Samuel arose, and gat him up from
Gilgal unto Gibeah of Benjamin. And Saul
numbered the people *that were* present
with him, about six hundred men.
16 And Saul, and Jonathan his son, and the
people *that were* present with them, abode
in Gibeah of Benjamin: but the Philistines
encamped in Michmash.
17 ¶ And the spoilers came out of the camp
of the Philistines in three companies: one
company turned unto the way *that leadeth*
to Ophrah, unto the land of Shual:
18 And another company turned the way *to*
Beth-horon: and another company turned
to the way of the border that looketh to the
valley of Zeboim toward the wilderness.
19 ¶ Now there was no smith found throughout all the land of Israel: for the Philistines
said, Lest the Hebrews make *them* swords
or spears:
20 But all the Israelites went down to the
Philistines, to sharpen every man his share,
and his coulter, and his axe, and his mattock.
21 Yet they had a file for the mattocks, and
for the coulters, and for the forks, and for
the axes, and to sharpen the goads.
22 So it came to pass in the day of battle,
that there was neither sword nor spear
found in the hand of any of the people that
were with Saul and Jonathan: but with Saul
and with Jonathan his son was there found.
23 And the garrison of the Philistines went
out to the passage of Michmash.

1 Samuel 14

1 Now it came to pass upon a day, that Jonathan the son of Saul said unto the young
man that bare his armour, Come, and let us
go over to the Philistines' garrison, that *is*
on the other side. But he told not his father.
2 And Saul tarried in the uttermost part of
Gibeah under a pomegranate tree which *is*
in Migron: and the people that *were* with
him *were* about six hundred men;
3 And Ahiah, the son of Ahitub, I-chabod's
brother, the son of Phinehas, the son of
Eli, the LORD's priest in Shiloh, wearing an
ephod. And the people knew not that Jonathan was gone.
4 ¶ And between the passages, by which
Jonathan sought to go over unto the Philistines' garrison, *there was* a sharp rock on
the one side, and a sharp rock on the other
side: and the name of the one *was* Bozez,
and the name of the other Seneh.
5 The forefront of the one *was* situate northward over against Michmash, and the other
southward over against Gibeah.
6 And Jonathan said to the young man that
bare his armour, Come, and let us go over
unto the garrison of these uncircumcised:
it may be that the LORD will work for us: for
there is no restraint to the LORD to save by
many or by few.
7 And his armourbearer said unto him, Do
all that *is* in thine heart: turn thee; behold,
I *am* with thee according to thy heart.
8 Then said Jonathan, Behold, we will pass
over unto *these* men, and we will discover
ourselves unto them.
9 If they say thus unto us, Tarry until we
come to you; then we will stand still in our
place, and will not go up unto them.
10 But if they say thus, Come up unto us;
then we will go up: for the LORD hath delivered them into our hand: and this *shall be*
a sign unto us.
11 And both of them discovered themselves
unto the garrison of the Philistines: and the
Philistines said, Behold, the Hebrews come
forth out of the holes where they had hid
themselves.
12 And the men of the garrison answered
Jonathan and his armourbearer, and said,
Come up to us, and we will shew you a thing.
And Jonathan said unto his armourbearer,
Come up after me: for the LORD hath delivered them into the hand of Israel.
13 And Jonathan climbed up upon his hands
and upon his feet, and his armourbearer
after him: and they fell before Jonathan; and
his armourbearer slew after him.
14 And that first slaughter, which Jonathan
and his armourbearer made, was about
twenty men, within as it were an half acre
of land, *which* a yoke *of oxen might plow.*
15 And there was trembling in the host,
in the field, and among all the people: the
garrison, and the spoilers, they also trembled, and the earth quaked: so it was a very
great trembling.
16 And the watchmen of Saul in Gibeah of
Benjamin looked; and, behold, the multitude

melted away, and they went on beating
down *one another.*
17 Then said Saul unto the people that *were*
with him, Number now, and see who is gone
from us. And when they had numbered,
behold, Jonathan and his armourbearer
were not *there.*
18 And Saul said unto Ahiah, Bring hither the
ark of God. For the ark of God was at that
time with the children of Israel.
19 ¶ And it came to pass, while Saul talked
unto the priest, that the noise that *was*
in the host of the Philistines went on and
increased: and Saul said unto the priest,
Withdraw thine hand.
20 And Saul and all the people that *were*
with him assembled themselves, and they
came to the battle: and, behold, every man's
sword was against his fellow, *and there was*
a very great discomfiture.
21 Moreover the Hebrews *that* were with
the Philistines before that time, which went
up with them into the camp *from the country* round about, even they also *turned* to
be with the Israelites that *were* with Saul
and Jonathan.
22 Likewise all the men of Israel which had
hid themselves in mount Ephraim, *when*
they heard that the Philistines fled, even
they also followed hard after them in the
battle.
23 So the LORD saved Israel that day: and the
battle passed over unto Beth-aven.
24 ¶ And the men of Israel were distressed
that day: for Saul had adjured the people,
saying, Cursed *be* the man that eateth *any*
food until evening, that I may be avenged
on mine enemies. So none of the people
tasted *any* food.
25 And all *they of* the land came to a wood;
and there was honey upon the ground.
26 And when the people were come into
the wood, behold, the honey dropped; but
no man put his hand to his mouth: for the
people feared the oath.
27 But Jonathan heard not when his father
charged the people with the oath: wherefore he put forth the end of the rod that *was*
in his hand, and dipped it in an honeycomb,
and put his hand to his mouth; and his eyes
were enlightened.
28 Then answered one of the people, and
said, Thy father straitly charged the people
with an oath, saying, Cursed *be* the man that
eateth *any* food this day. And the people
were faint.
29 Then said Jonathan, My father hath troubled the land: see, I pray you, how mine eyes
have been enlightened, because I tasted a
little of this honey.
30 How much more, if haply the people
had eaten freely to day of the spoil of their
enemies which they found? for had there
not been now a much greater slaughter
among the Philistines?
31 And they smote the Philistines that day
from Michmash to Aijalon: and the people
were very faint.
32 And the people flew upon the spoil, and
took sheep, and oxen, and calves, and slew
them on the ground: and the people did eat
them with the blood.
33 ¶ Then they told Saul, saying, Behold, the
people sin against the LORD, in that they eat
with the blood. And he said, Ye have transgressed: roll a great stone unto me this day.
34 And Saul said, Disperse yourselves among
the people, and say unto them, Bring me
hither every man his ox, and every man his
sheep, and slay *them* here, and eat; and
sin not against the LORD in eating with the
blood. And all the people brought every
man his ox with him that night, and slew
them there.
35 And Saul built an altar unto the LORD:
the same was the first altar that he built
unto the LORD.
36 ¶ And Saul said, Let us go down after the
Philistines by night, and spoil them until the
morning light, and let us not leave a man
of them. And they said, Do whatsoever
seemeth good unto thee. Then said the
priest, Let us draw near hither unto God.
37 And Saul asked counsel of God, Shall
I go down after the Philistines? wilt thou
deliver them into the hand of Israel? But
he answered him not that day.
38 And Saul said, Draw ye near hither, all
the chief of the people: and know and see
wherein this sin hath been this day.
39 For, *as* the LORD liveth, which saveth
Israel, though it be in Jonathan my son, he
shall surely die. But *there was* not a man
among all the people *that* answered him.
40 Then said he unto all Israel, Be ye on one
side, and I and Jonathan my son will be on

the other side. And the people said unto
Saul, Do what seemeth good unto thee.
41 Therefore Saul said unto the LORD God of
Israel, Give a perfect *lot*. And Saul and Jonathan were taken: but the people escaped.
42 And Saul said, Cast *lots* between me and
Jonathan my son. And Jonathan was taken.
43 Then Saul said to Jonathan, Tell me what
thou hast done. And Jonathan told him, and
said, I did but taste a little honey with the
end of the rod that *was* in mine hand, *and*,
lo, I must die.
44 And Saul answered, God do so and more
also: for thou shalt surely die, Jonathan.
45 And the people said unto Saul, Shall
Jonathan die, who hath wrought this great
salvation in Israel? God forbid: *as* the LORD
liveth, there shall not one hair of his head
fall to the ground; for he hath wrought with
God this day. So the people rescued Jonathan, that he died not.
46 Then Saul went up from following the
Philistines: and the Philistines went to their
own place.
47 ¶ So Saul took the kingdom over Israel,
and fought against all his enemies on every
side, against Moab, and against the children
of Ammon, and against Edom, and against
the kings of Zobah, and against the Philistines: and whithersoever he turned himself,
he vexed *them*.
48 And he gathered an host, and smote the
Amalekites, and delivered Israel out of the
hands of them that spoiled them.
49 Now the sons of Saul were Jonathan, and
Ishui, and Melchi-shua: and the names of
his two daughters *were these;* the name of
the firstborn Merab, and the name of the
younger Michal:
50 And the name of Saul's wife *was* Ahinoam, the daughter of Ahimaaz: and the
name of the captain of his host *was* Abner,
the son of Ner, Saul's uncle.
51 And Kish *was* the father of Saul; and Ner
the father of Abner *was* the son of Abiel.
52 And there was sore war against the Philistines all the days of Saul: and when Saul
saw any strong man, or any valiant man, he
took him unto him.

1 Samuel 15

1 Samuel also said unto Saul, The LORD sent
me to anoint thee *to be* king over his people,
over Israel: now therefore hearken thou
unto the voice of the words of the LORD.
2 Thus saith the LORD of hosts, I remember
that which Amalek did to Israel, how he laid
wait for him in the way, when he came up
from Egypt.
3 Now go and smite Amalek, and utterly
destroy all that they have, and spare them
not; but slay both man and woman, infant
and suckling, ox and sheep, camel and ass.
4 And Saul gathered the people together,
and numbered them in Telaim, two hundred
thousand footmen, and ten thousand men
of Judah.
5 And Saul came to a city of Amalek, and
laid wait in the valley.
6 ¶ And Saul said unto the Kenites, Go,
depart, get you down from among the
Amalekites, lest I destroy you with them:
for ye shewed kindness to all the children
of Israel, when they came up out of Egypt.
So the Kenites departed from among the
Amalekites.
7 And Saul smote the Amalekites from
Havilah *until* thou comest to Shur, that *is*
over against Egypt.
8 And he took Agag the king of the Amalekites alive, and utterly destroyed all the
people with the edge of the sword.
9 But Saul and the people spared Agag, and
the best of the sheep, and of the oxen, and
of the fatlings, and the lambs, and all *that*
was good, and would not utterly destroy
them: but every thing *that was* vile and
refuse, that they destroyed utterly.
10 ¶ Then came the word of the LORD unto
Samuel, saying,
11 It repenteth me that I have set up Saul *to*
be king: for he is turned back from following
me, and hath not performed my commandments. And it grieved Samuel; and he cried
unto the LORD all night.
12 And when Samuel rose early to meet
Saul in the morning, it was told Samuel,
saying, Saul came to Carmel, and, behold,
he set him up a place, and is gone about,
and passed on, and gone down to Gilgal.
13 And Samuel came to Saul: and Saul said
unto him, Blessed *be* thou of the LORD:
I have performed the commandment of
the LORD.
14 And Samuel said, What *meaneth* then this

bleating of the sheep in mine ears, and the
lowing of the oxen which I hear?
15 And Saul said, They have brought them
from the Amalekites: for the people spared
the best of the sheep and of the oxen, to
sacrifice unto the LORD thy God; and the
rest we have utterly destroyed.
16 Then Samuel said unto Saul, Stay, and I
will tell thee what the LORD hath said to me
this night. And he said unto him, Say on.
17 And Samuel said, When thou *wast* little
in thine own sight, *wast* thou not *made* the
head of the tribes of Israel, and the LORD
anointed thee king over Israel?
18 And the LORD sent thee on a journey,
and said, Go and utterly destroy the sinners
the Amalekites, and fight against them until
they be consumed.
19 Wherefore then didst thou not obey the
voice of the LORD, but didst fly upon the
spoil, and didst evil in the sight of the LORD?
20 And Saul said unto Samuel, Yea, I have
obeyed the voice of the LORD, and have gone
the way which the LORD sent me, and have
brought Agag the king of Amalek, and have
utterly destroyed the Amalekites.
21 But the people took of the spoil, sheep
and oxen, the chief of the things which
should have been utterly destroyed, to
sacrifice unto the LORD thy God in Gilgal.
22 And Samuel said, Hath the LORD *as great*
delight in burnt offerings and sacrifices, as
in obeying the voice of the LORD? Behold, to
obey *is* better than sacrifice, *and* to hearken
than the fat of rams.
23 For rebellion *is as* the sin of witchcraft,
and stubbornness *is as* iniquity and idolatry. Because thou hast rejected the word of
the LORD, he hath also rejected thee from
being king.
24 ¶ And Saul said unto Samuel, I have
sinned: for I have transgressed the commandment of the LORD, and thy words:
because I feared the people, and obeyed
their voice.
25 Now therefore, I pray thee, pardon my
sin, and turn again with me, that I may worship the LORD.
26 And Samuel said unto Saul, I will not
return with thee: for thou hast rejected
the word of the LORD, and the LORD hath
rejected thee from being king over Israel.
27 And as Samuel turned about to go away,
he laid hold upon the skirt of his mantle,
and it rent.
28 And Samuel said unto him, The LORD
hath rent the kingdom of Israel from thee
this day, and hath given it to a neighbour of
thine, *that is* better than thou.
29 And also the Strength of Israel will not
lie nor repent: for he *is* not a man, that he
should repent.
30 Then he said, I have sinned: *yet* honour
me now, I pray thee, before the elders of
my people, and before Israel, and turn
again with me, that I may worship the LORD
thy God.
31 So Samuel turned again after Saul; and
Saul worshipped the LORD.
32 ¶ Then said Samuel, Bring ye hither to
me Agag the king of the Amalekites. And
Agag came unto him delicately. And Agag
said, Surely the bitterness of death is past.
33 And Samuel said, As thy sword hath made
women childless, so shall thy mother be
childless among women. And Samuel hewed
Agag in pieces before the LORD in Gilgal.
34 ¶ Then Samuel went to Ramah; and Saul
went up to his house to Gibeah of Saul.
35 And Samuel came no more to see Saul
until the day of his death: nevertheless
Samuel mourned for Saul: and the LORD
repented that he had made Saul king over
Israel.

1 Samuel 16

1 And the LORD said unto Samuel, How
long wilt thou mourn for Saul, seeing I have
rejected him from reigning over Israel? fill
thine horn with oil, and go, I will send thee
to Jesse the Beth-lehemite: for I have provided me a king among his sons.
2 And Samuel said, How can I go? if Saul hear
it, he will kill me. And the LORD said, Take
an heifer with thee, and say, I am come to
sacrifice to the LORD.
3 And call Jesse to the sacrifice, and I will
shew thee what thou shalt do: and thou
shalt anoint unto me *him* whom I name
unto thee.
4 And Samuel did that which the LORD spake,
and came to Beth-lehem. And the elders of
the town trembled at his coming, and said,
Comest thou peaceably?
5 And he said, Peaceably: I am come to
sacrifice unto the LORD: sanctify yourselves,

and come with me to the sacrifice. And he
sanctified Jesse and his sons, and called
them to the sacrifice.
6 ¶ And it came to pass, when they were
come, that he looked on Eliab, and said,
Surely the LORD's anointed *is* before him.
7 But the LORD said unto Samuel, Look not
on his countenance, or on the height of his
stature; because I have refused him: for
the LORD seeth not as man seeth; for man
looketh on the outward appearance, but
the LORD looketh on the heart.
8 Then Jesse called Abinadab, and made him
pass before Samuel. And he said, Neither
hath the LORD chosen this.
9 Then Jesse made Shammah to pass by. And
he said, Neither hath the LORD chosen this.
10 Again, Jesse made seven of his sons to
pass before Samuel. And Samuel said unto
Jesse, The LORD hath not chosen these.
11 And Samuel said unto Jesse, Are here all
thy children? And he said, There remaineth
yet the youngest, and, behold, he keepeth
the sheep. And Samuel said unto Jesse, Send
and fetch him: for we will not sit down till
he come hither.
12 And he sent, and brought him in. Now
he *was* ruddy, *and* withal of a beautiful
countenance, and goodly to look to. And the
LORD said, Arise, anoint him: for this *is* he.
13 Then Samuel took the horn of oil, and
anointed him in the midst of his brethren:
and the Spirit of the LORD came upon David
from that day forward. So Samuel rose up,
and went to Ramah.
14 ¶ But the Spirit of the LORD departed
from Saul, and an evil spirit from the LORD
troubled him.
15 And Saul's servants said unto him, Behold
now, an evil spirit from God troubleth thee.
16 Let our lord now command thy servants,
which are before thee, to seek out a man,
who is a cunning player on an harp: and it
shall come to pass, when the evil spirit from
God is upon thee, that he shall play with his
hand, and thou shalt be well.
17 And Saul said unto his servants, Provide
me now a man that can play well, and bring
him to me.
18 Then answered one of the servants, and
said, Behold, I have seen a son of Jesse the
Beth-lehemite, *that is* cunning in playing,
and a mighty valiant man, and a man of
war, and prudent in matters, and a comely
person, and the LORD *is* with him.
19 ¶ Wherefore Saul sent messengers unto
Jesse, and said, Send me David thy son,
which *is* with the sheep.
20 And Jesse took an ass *laden* with bread,
and a bottle of wine, and a kid, and sent
them by David his son unto Saul.
21 And David came to Saul, and stood
before him: and he loved him greatly; and
he became his armourbearer.
22 And Saul sent to Jesse, saying, Let David,
I pray thee, stand before me; for he hath
found favour in my sight.
23 And it came to pass, when the *evil* spirit
from God was upon Saul, that David took
an harp, and played with his hand: so Saul
was refreshed, and was well, and the evil
spirit departed from him.

1 Samuel 17

1 Now the Philistines gathered together
their armies to battle, and were gathered
together at Shochoh, which *belongeth* to
Judah, and pitched between Shochoh and
Azekah, in Ephes-dammim.
2 And Saul and the men of Israel were gathered together, and pitched by the valley of
Elah, and set the battle in array against the
Philistines.
3 And the Philistines stood on a mountain on
the one side, and Israel stood on a mountain
on the other side: and *there was* a valley
between them.
4 ¶ And there went out a champion out of
the camp of the Philistines, named Goliath, of Gath, whose height *was* six cubits
and a span.
5 And *he had* an helmet of brass upon his
head, and he *was* armed with a coat of
mail; and the weight of the coat *was* five
thousand shekels of brass.
6 And *he had* greaves of brass upon his legs,
and a target of brass between his shoulders.
7 And the staff of his spear *was* like a weaver's beam; and his spear's head *weighed* six
hundred shekels of iron: and one bearing a
shield went before him.
8 And he stood and cried unto the armies
of Israel, and said unto them, Why are ye
come out to set *your* battle in array? *am*
not I a Philistine, and ye servants to Saul?

choose you a man for you, and let him come
down to me.
9 If he be able to fight with me, and to kill
me, then will we be your servants: but if I
prevail against him, and kill him, then shall
ye be our servants, and serve us.
10 And the Philistine said, I defy the armies
of Israel this day; give me a man, that we
may fight together.
11 When Saul and all Israel heard those
words of the Philistine, they were dismayed,
and greatly afraid.
12 ¶ Now David *was* the son of that Ephrathite of Beth-lehem-judah, whose name
was Jesse; and he had eight sons: and the
man went among men *for* an old man in
the days of Saul.
13 And the three eldest sons of Jesse went
and followed Saul to the battle: and the
names of his three sons that went to the
battle *were* Eliab the firstborn, and next
unto him Abinadab, and the third Shammah.
14 And David *was* the youngest: and the
three eldest followed Saul.
15 But David went and returned from Saul
to feed his father's sheep at Beth-lehem.
16 And the Philistine drew near morning and
evening, and presented himself forty days.
17 And Jesse said unto David his son, Take
now for thy brethren an ephah of this
parched *corn*, and these ten loaves, and run
to the camp to thy brethren;
18 And carry these ten cheeses unto the
captain of *their* thousand, and look how
thy brethren fare, and take their pledge.
19 Now Saul, and they, and all the men of
Israel, *were* in the valley of Elah, fighting
with the Philistines.
20 ¶ And David rose up early in the morning, and left the sheep with a keeper, and
took, and went, as Jesse had commanded
him; and he came to the trench, as the host
was going forth to the fight, and shouted
for the battle.
21 For Israel and the Philistines had put the
battle in array, army against army.
22 And David left his carriage in the hand of
the keeper of the carriage, and ran into the
army, and came and saluted his brethren.
23 And as he talked with them, behold,
there came up the champion, the Philistine
of Gath, Goliath by name, out of the armies
of the Philistines, and spake according to the
same words: and David heard *them*.
24 And all the men of Israel, when they
saw the man, fled from him, and were
sore afraid.
25 And the men of Israel said, Have ye
seen this man that is come up? surely to
defy Israel is he come up: and it shall be,
that the man who killeth him, the king will
enrich him with great riches, and will give
him his daughter, and make his father's
house free in Israel.
26 And David spake to the men that stood
by him, saying, What shall be done to the
man that killeth this Philistine, and taketh
away the reproach from Israel? for who *is*
this uncircumcised Philistine, that he should
defy the armies of the living God?
27 And the people answered him after this
manner, saying, So shall it be done to the
man that killeth him.
28 ¶ And Eliab his eldest brother heard
when he spake unto the men; and Eliab's
anger was kindled against David, and he
said, Why camest thou down hither? and
with whom hast thou left those few sheep
in the wilderness? I know thy pride, and
the naughtiness of thine heart; for thou
art come down that thou mightest see
the battle.
29 And David said, What have I now done?
Is there not a cause?
30 ¶ And he turned from him toward
another, and spake after the same manner: and the people answered him again
after the former manner.
31 And when the words were heard which
David spake, they rehearsed *them* before
Saul: and he sent for him.
32 ¶ And David said to Saul, Let no man's
heart fail because of him; thy servant will
go and fight with this Philistine.
33 And Saul said to David, Thou art not able
to go against this Philistine to fight with him:
for thou *art but* a youth, and he a man of
war from his youth.
34 And David said unto Saul, Thy servant
kept his father's sheep, and there came
a lion, and a bear, and took a lamb out of
the flock:
35 And I went out after him, and smote
him, and delivered *it* out of his mouth: and

when he arose against me, I caught *him* by
his beard, and smote him, and slew him.
36 Thy servant slew both the lion and the
bear: and this uncircumcised Philistine shall
be as one of them, seeing he hath defied
the armies of the living God.
37 David said moreover, The LORD that delivered me out of the paw of the lion, and out
of the paw of the bear, he will deliver me out
of the hand of this Philistine. And Saul said
unto David, Go, and the LORD be with thee.
38 ¶ And Saul armed David with his armour,
and he put an helmet of brass upon his head;
also he armed him with a coat of mail.
39 And David girded his sword upon his
armour, and he assayed to go; for he had
not proved *it*. And David said unto Saul, I
cannot go with these; for I have not proved
them. And David put them off him.
40 And he took his staff in his hand, and
chose him five smooth stones out of the
brook, and put them in a shepherd's bag
which he had, even in a scrip; and his sling
was in his hand: and he drew near to the
Philistine.
41 And the Philistine came on and drew
near unto David; and the man that bare the
shield *went* before him.
42 And when the Philistine looked about,
and saw David, he disdained him: for he
was *but* a youth, and ruddy, and of a fair
countenance.
43 And the Philistine said unto David, *Am* I
a dog, that thou comest to me with staves?
And the Philistine cursed David by his gods.
44 And the Philistine said to David, Come to
me, and I will give thy flesh unto the fowls
of the air, and to the beasts of the field.
45 Then said David to the Philistine, Thou
comest to me with a sword, and with a
spear, and with a shield: but I come to thee
in the name of the LORD of hosts, the God of
the armies of Israel, whom thou hast defied.
46 This day will the LORD deliver thee into
mine hand; and I will smite thee, and take
thine head from thee; and I will give the
carcases of the host of the Philistines this
day unto the fowls of the air, and to the wild
beasts of the earth; that all the earth may
know that there is a God in Israel.
47 And all this assembly shall know that the
LORD saveth not with sword and spear: for
the battle *is* the LORD's, and he will give you
into our hands.
48 And it came to pass, when the Philistine
arose, and came and drew nigh to meet
David, that David hasted, and ran toward
the army to meet the Philistine.
49 And David put his hand in his bag, and
took thence a stone, and slang *it*, and smote
the Philistine in his forehead, that the stone
sunk into his forehead; and he fell upon his
face to the earth.
50 So David prevailed over the Philistine
with a sling and with a stone, and smote
the Philistine, and slew him; but *there was*
no sword in the hand of David.
51 Therefore David ran, and stood upon the
Philistine, and took his sword, and drew it
out of the sheath thereof, and slew him,
and cut off his head therewith. And when
the Philistines saw their champion was
dead, they fled.
52 And the men of Israel and of Judah arose,
and shouted, and pursued the Philistines,
until thou come to the valley, and to the
gates of Ekron. And the wounded of the
Philistines fell down by the way to Shaaraim,
even unto Gath, and unto Ekron.
53 And the children of Israel returned
from chasing after the Philistines, and they
spoiled their tents.
54 And David took the head of the Philistine,
and brought it to Jerusalem; but he put his
armour in his tent.
55 ¶ And when Saul saw David go forth
against the Philistine, he said unto Abner,
the captain of the host, Abner, whose son
is this youth? And Abner said, *As* thy soul
liveth, O king, I cannot tell.
56 And the king said, Inquire thou whose
son the stripling *is*.
57 And as David returned from the slaughter of the Philistine, Abner took him, and
brought him before Saul with the head of
the Philistine in his hand.
58 And Saul said to him, Whose son *art* thou,
thou young man? And David answered, *I am*
the son of thy servant Jesse the Beth-lehemite.

1 Samuel 18

1 And it came to pass, when he had made
an end of speaking unto Saul, that the soul

of Jonathan was knit with the soul of David,
and Jonathan loved him as his own soul.
2 And Saul took him that day, and would let
him go no more home to his father's house.
3 Then Jonathan and David made a covenant, because he loved him as his own soul.
4 And Jonathan stripped himself of the robe
that *was* upon him, and gave it to David, and
his garments, even to his sword, and to his
bow, and to his girdle.
5 ¶ And David went out whithersoever Saul
sent him, *and* behaved himself wisely: and
Saul set him over the men of war, and he
was accepted in the sight of all the people,
and also in the sight of Saul's servants.
6 And it came to pass as they came, when
David was returned from the slaughter of
the Philistine, that the women came out of
all cities of Israel, singing and dancing, to
meet king Saul, with tabrets, with joy, and
with instruments of musick.
7 And the women answered *one another*
as they played, and said, Saul hath slain his
thousands, and David his ten thousands.
8 And Saul was very wroth, and the saying
displeased him; and he said, They have
ascribed unto David ten thousands, and to
me they have ascribed *but* thousands: and
what can he have more but the kingdom?
9 And Saul eyed David from that day and
forward.
10 ¶ And it came to pass on the morrow,
that the evil spirit from God came upon Saul,
and he prophesied in the midst of the house:
and David played with his hand, as at other
times: and *there was* a javelin in Saul's hand.
11 And Saul cast the javelin; for he said, I
will smite David even to the wall *with it*. And
David avoided out of his presence twice.
12 ¶ And Saul was afraid of David, because
the LORD was with him, and was departed
from Saul.
13 Therefore Saul removed him from him,
and made him his captain over a thousand;
and he went out and came in before the
people.
14 And David behaved himself wisely in all
his ways; and the LORD *was* with him.
15 Wherefore when Saul saw that he
behaved himself very wisely, he was afraid
of him.
16 But all Israel and Judah loved David,
because he went out and came in before
them.
17 ¶ And Saul said to David, Behold my elder
daughter Merab, her will I give thee to wife:
only be thou valiant for me, and fight the
LORD's battles. For Saul said, Let not mine
hand be upon him, but let the hand of the
Philistines be upon him.
18 And David said unto Saul, Who *am* I?
and what *is* my life, *or* my father's family in
Israel, that I should be son in law to the king?
19 But it came to pass at the time when
Merab Saul's daughter should have been
given to David, that she was given unto
Adriel the Meholathite to wife.
20 And Michal Saul's daughter loved David:
and they told Saul, and the thing pleased
him.
21 And Saul said, I will give him her, that she
may be a snare to him, and that the hand of
the Philistines may be against him. Wherefore Saul said to David, Thou shalt this day
be my son in law in *the one of* the twain.
22 ¶ And Saul commanded his servants,
saying, Commune with David secretly, and
say, Behold, the king hath delight in thee,
and all his servants love thee: now therefore
be the king's son in law.
23 And Saul's servants spake those words in
the ears of David. And David said, Seemeth
it to you *a* light *thing* to be a king's son in
law, seeing that I *am* a poor man, and lightly
esteemed?
24 And the servants of Saul told him, saying,
On this manner spake David.
25 And Saul said, Thus shall ye say to David,
The king desireth not any dowry, but an
hundred foreskins of the Philistines, to be
avenged of the king's enemies. But Saul
thought to make David fall by the hand of
the Philistines.
26 And when his servants told David these
words, it pleased David well to be the king's
son in law: and the days were not expired.
27 Wherefore David arose and went, he and
his men, and slew of the Philistines two hundred men; and David brought their foreskins,
and they gave them in full tale to the king,
that he might be the king's son in law. And
Saul gave him Michal his daughter to wife.
28 ¶ And Saul saw and knew that the LORD
was with David, and *that* Michal Saul's
daughter loved him.

29 And Saul was yet the more afraid of
David; and Saul became David's enemy
continually.
30 Then the princes of the Philistines went
forth: and it came to pass, after they went
forth, *that* David behaved himself more
wisely than all the servants of Saul; so that
his name was much set by.

1 Samuel 19

1 And Saul spake to Jonathan his son, and to
all his servants, that they should kill David.
2 But Jonathan Saul's son delighted much
in David: and Jonathan told David, saying,
Saul my father seeketh to kill thee: now
therefore, I pray thee, take heed to thyself
until the morning, and abide in a secret
place, and hide thyself:
3 And I will go out and stand beside my
father in the field where thou *art*, and I will
commune with my father of thee; and what
I see, that I will tell thee.
4 ¶ And Jonathan spake good of David unto
Saul his father, and said unto him, Let not
the king sin against his servant, against
David; because he hath not sinned against
thee, and because his works *have been* to
thee-ward very good:
5 For he did put his life in his hand, and slew
the Philistine, and the LORD wrought a great
salvation for all Israel: thou sawest *it*, and
didst rejoice: wherefore then wilt thou sin
against innocent blood, to slay David without a cause?
6 And Saul hearkened unto the voice of Jonathan: and Saul sware, *As* the LORD liveth,
he shall not be slain.
7 And Jonathan called David, and Jonathan
shewed him all those things. And Jonathan
brought David to Saul, and he was in his
presence, as in times past.
8 ¶ And there was war again: and David
went out, and fought with the Philistines,
and slew them with a great slaughter; and
they fled from him.
9 And the evil spirit from the LORD was upon
Saul, as he sat in his house with his javelin
in his hand: and David played with *his* hand.
10 And Saul sought to smite David even
to the wall with the javelin; but he slipped
away out of Saul's presence, and he smote
the javelin into the wall: and David fled, and
escaped that night.
11 Saul also sent messengers unto David's
house, to watch him, and to slay him in the
morning: and Michal David's wife told him,
saying, If thou save not thy life to night, to
morrow thou shalt be slain.
12 ¶ So Michal let David down through
a window: and he went, and fled, and
escaped.
13 And Michal took an image, and laid *it*
in the bed, and put a pillow of goats' *hair*
for his bolster, and covered *it* with a cloth.
14 And when Saul sent messengers to take
David, she said, He *is* sick.
15 And Saul sent the messengers *again* to
see David, saying, Bring him up to me in the
bed, that I may slay him.
16 And when the messengers were come
in, behold, *there was* an image in the bed,
with a pillow of goats' *hair* for his bolster.
17 And Saul said unto Michal, Why hast
thou deceived me so, and sent away mine
enemy, that he is escaped? And Michal
answered Saul, He said unto me, Let me
go; why should I kill thee?
18 ¶ So David fled, and escaped, and came
to Samuel to Ramah, and told him all that
Saul had done to him. And he and Samuel
went and dwelt in Naioth.
19 And it was told Saul, saying, Behold,
David *is* at Naioth in Ramah.
20 And Saul sent messengers to take David:
and when they saw the company of the
prophets prophesying, and Samuel standing
as appointed over them, the Spirit of God
was upon the messengers of Saul, and they
also prophesied.
21 And when it was told Saul, he sent other
messengers, and they prophesied likewise.
And Saul sent messengers again the third
time, and they prophesied also.
22 Then went he also to Ramah, and came
to a great well that *is* in Sechu: and he asked
and said, Where *are* Samuel and David?
And *one* said, Behold, *they be* at Naioth
in Ramah.
23 And he went thither to Naioth in Ramah:
and the Spirit of God was upon him also, and
he went on, and prophesied, until he came
to Naioth in Ramah.
24 And he stripped off his clothes also, and
prophesied before Samuel in like manner,
and lay down naked all that day and all

that night. Wherefore they say, *Is* Saul also among the prophets?

1 Samuel 20

1 And David fled from Naioth in Ramah, and came and said before Jonathan, What have I done? what *is* mine iniquity? and what *is* my sin before thy father, that he seeketh my life?
2 And he said unto him, God forbid; thou shalt not die: behold, my father will do nothing either great or small, but that he will shew it me: and why should my father hide this thing from me? it *is* not *so*.
3 And David sware moreover, and said, Thy father certainly knoweth that I have found grace in thine eyes; and he saith, Let not Jonathan know this, lest he be grieved: but truly *as* the LORD liveth, and *as* thy soul liveth, *there is* but a step between me and death.
4 Then said Jonathan unto David, Whatsoever thy soul desireth, I will even do *it* for thee.
5 And David said unto Jonathan, Behold, to morrow *is* the new moon, and I should not fail to sit with the king at meat: but let me go, that I may hide myself in the field unto the third *day* at even.
6 If thy father at all miss me, then say, David earnestly asked *leave* of me that he might run to Beth-lehem his city: for *there is* a yearly sacrifice there for all the family.
7 If he say thus, *It is* well; thy servant shall have peace: but if he be very wroth, *then* be sure that evil is determined by him.
8 Therefore thou shalt deal kindly with thy servant; for thou hast brought thy servant into a covenant of the LORD with thee: notwithstanding, if there be in me iniquity, slay me thyself; for why shouldest thou bring me to thy father?
9 And Jonathan said, Far be it from thee: for if I knew certainly that evil were determined by my father to come upon thee, then would not I tell it thee?
10 Then said David to Jonathan, Who shall tell me? or what *if* thy father answer thee roughly?
11 ¶ And Jonathan said unto David, Come, and let us go out into the field. And they went out both of them into the field.
12 And Jonathan said unto David, O LORD God of Israel, when I have sounded my father about to morrow any time, *or* the third *day*, and, behold, *if there be* good toward David, and I then send not unto thee, and shew it thee;
13 The LORD do so and much more to Jonathan: but if it please my father *to do* thee evil, then I will shew it thee, and send thee away, that thou mayest go in peace: and the LORD be with thee, as he hath been with my father.
14 And thou shalt not only while yet I live shew me the kindness of the LORD, that I die not:
15 But *also* thou shalt not cut off thy kindness from my house for ever: no, not when the LORD hath cut off the enemies of David every one from the face of the earth.
16 So Jonathan made *a covenant* with the house of David, *saying*, Let the LORD even require *it* at the hand of David's enemies.
17 And Jonathan caused David to swear again, because he loved him: for he loved him as he loved his own soul.
18 Then Jonathan said to David, To morrow *is* the new moon: and thou shalt be missed, because thy seat will be empty.
19 And *when* thou hast stayed three days, *then* thou shalt go down quickly, and come to the place where thou didst hide thyself when the business was *in hand*, and shalt remain by the stone Ezel.
20 And I will shoot three arrows on the side *thereof*, as though I shot at a mark.
21 And, behold, I will send a lad, *saying*, Go, find out the arrows. If I expressly say unto the lad, Behold, the arrows *are* on this side of thee, take them; then come thou: for *there is* peace to thee, and no hurt; *as* the LORD liveth.
22 But if I say thus unto the young man, Behold, the arrows *are* beyond thee; go thy way: for the LORD hath sent thee away.
23 And *as touching* the matter which thou and I have spoken of, behold, the LORD *be* between thee and me for ever.
24 ¶ So David hid himself in the field: and when the new moon was come, the king sat him down to eat meat.
25 And the king sat upon his seat, as at other times, *even* upon a seat by the wall: and Jonathan arose, and Abner sat by Saul's side, and David's place was empty.
26 Nevertheless Saul spake not any thing

that day: for he thought, Something hath
befallen him, he *is* not clean; surely he *is*
not clean.
27 And it came to pass on the morrow,
which was the second *day* of the month,
that David's place was empty: and Saul said
unto Jonathan his son, Wherefore cometh
not the son of Jesse to meat, neither yesterday, nor to day?
28 And Jonathan answered Saul, David earnestly asked *leave* of me *to go* to Beth-lehem:
29 And he said, Let me go, I pray thee; for
our family hath a sacrifice in the city; and
my brother, he hath commanded me *to be
there:* and now, if I have found favour in
thine eyes, let me get away, I pray thee, and
see my brethren. Therefore he cometh not
unto the king's table.
30 Then Saul's anger was kindled against
Jonathan, and he said unto him, Thou son
of the perverse rebellious *woman*, do not I
know that thou hast chosen the son of Jesse
to thine own confusion, and unto the confusion of thy mother's nakedness?
31 For as long as the son of Jesse liveth upon
the ground, thou shalt not be established,
nor thy kingdom. Wherefore now send and
fetch him unto me, for he shall surely die.
32 And Jonathan answered Saul his father,
and said unto him, Wherefore shall he be
slain? what hath he done?
33 And Saul cast a javelin at him to smite
him: whereby Jonathan knew that it was
determined of his father to slay David.
34 So Jonathan arose from the table in fierce
anger, and did eat no meat the second day
of the month: for he was grieved for David,
because his father had done him shame.
35 ¶ And it came to pass in the morning,
that Jonathan went out into the field at
the time appointed with David, and a little
lad with him.
36 And he said unto his lad, Run, find out
now the arrows which I shoot. *And* as the
lad ran, he shot an arrow beyond him.
37 And when the lad was come to the place
of the arrow which Jonathan had shot, Jonathan cried after the lad, and said, *Is* not the
arrow beyond thee?
38 And Jonathan cried after the lad, Make
speed, haste, stay not. And Jonathan's lad
gathered up the arrows, and came to his
master.
39 But the lad knew not any thing: only Jonathan and David knew the matter.
40 And Jonathan gave his artillery unto his
lad, and said unto him, Go, carry *them* to
the city.
41 ¶ *And* as soon as the lad was gone, David
arose out of *a place* toward the south, and
fell on his face to the ground, and bowed
himself three times: and they kissed one
another, and wept one with another, until
David exceeded.
42 And Jonathan said to David, Go in peace,
forasmuch as we have sworn both of us in
the name of the LORD, saying, The LORD be
between me and thee, and between my
seed and thy seed for ever. And he arose and
departed: and Jonathan went into the city.

1 Samuel 21

1 Then came David to Nob to Ahimelech
the priest: and Ahimelech was afraid at
the meeting of David, and said unto him,
Why *art* thou alone, and no man with thee?
2 And David said unto Ahimelech the priest,
The king hath commanded me a business,
and hath said unto me, Let no man know
any thing of the business whereabout I send
thee, and what I have commanded thee:
and I have appointed *my* servants to such
and such a place.
3 Now therefore what is under thine hand?
give *me* five *loaves of* bread in mine hand,
or what there is present.
4 And the priest answered David, and said,
There is no common bread under mine
hand, but there is hallowed bread; if the
young men have kept themselves at least
from women.
5 And David answered the priest, and said
unto him, Of a truth women *have been*
kept from us about these three days, since
I came out, and the vessels of the young
men are holy, and *the bread is* in a manner
common, yea, though it were sanctified this
day in the vessel.
6 So the priest gave him hallowed *bread:*
for there was no bread there but the shewbread, that was taken from before the LORD,
to put hot bread in the day when it was
taken away.
7 Now a certain man of the servants of Saul

was there that day, detained before the
LORD; and his name *was* Doeg, an Edomite,
the chiefest of the herdmen that *belonged*
to Saul.
8 ¶ And David said unto Ahimelech, And is
there not here under thine hand spear or
sword? for I have neither brought my sword
nor my weapons with me, because the king's
business required haste.
9 And the priest said, The sword of Goliath
the Philistine, whom thou slewest in the
valley of Elah, behold, it *is here* wrapped in
a cloth behind the ephod: if thou wilt take
that, take *it:* for *there is* no other save that
here. And David said, *There is* none like
that; give it me.
10 ¶ And David arose, and fled that day for
fear of Saul, and went to Achish the king
of Gath.
11 And the servants of Achish said unto
him, *Is* not this David the king of the land?
did they not sing one to another of him in
dances, saying, Saul hath slain his thousands, and David his ten thousands?
12 And David laid up these words in his
heart, and was sore afraid of Achish the
king of Gath.
13 And he changed his behaviour before
them, and feigned himself mad in their
hands, and scrabbled on the doors of the
gate, and let his spittle fall down upon his
beard.
14 Then said Achish unto his servants, Lo,
ye see the man is mad: wherefore *then* have
ye brought him to me?
15 Have I need of mad men, that ye have
brought this *fellow* to play the mad man in
my presence? shall this *fellow* come into
my house?

1 Samuel 22

1 David therefore departed thence, and
escaped to the cave Adullam: and when his
brethren and all his father's house heard *it*,
they went down thither to him.
2 And every one *that was* in distress, and
every one that *was* in debt, and every one
that was discontented, gathered themselves
unto him; and he became a captain over
them: and there were with him about four
hundred men.
3 ¶ And David went thence to Mizpeh of
Moab: and he said unto the king of Moab,
Let my father and my mother, I pray thee,
come forth, *and be* with you, till I know what
God will do for me.
4 And he brought them before the king of
Moab: and they dwelt with him all the while
that David was in the hold.
5 ¶ And the prophet Gad said unto David,
Abide not in the hold; depart, and get thee
into the land of Judah. Then David departed,
and came into the forest of Hareth.
6 ¶ When Saul heard that David was discovered, and the men that *were* with him,
(now Saul abode in Gibeah under a tree in
Ramah, having his spear in his hand, and
all his servants *were* standing about him;)
7 Then Saul said unto his servants that stood
about him, Hear now, ye Benjamites; will
the son of Jesse give every one of you fields
and vineyards, *and* make you all captains of
thousands, and captains of hundreds;
8 That all of you have conspired against me,
and *there is* none that sheweth me that my
son hath made a league with the son of
Jesse, and *there is* none of you that is sorry
for me, or sheweth unto me that my son
hath stirred up my servant against me, to
lie in wait, as at this day?
9 ¶ Then answered Doeg the Edomite, which
was set over the servants of Saul, and said,
I saw the son of Jesse coming to Nob, to
Ahimelech the son of Ahitub.
10 And he inquired of the LORD for him, and
gave him victuals, and gave him the sword
of Goliath the Philistine.
11 Then the king sent to call Ahimelech the
priest, the son of Ahitub, and all his father's
house, the priests that *were* in Nob: and they
came all of them to the king.
12 And Saul said, Hear now, thou son of
Ahitub. And he answered, Here I *am*, my
lord.
13 And Saul said unto him, Why have ye
conspired against me, thou and the son of
Jesse, in that thou hast given him bread,
and a sword, and hast inquired of God for
him, that he should rise against me, to lie
in wait, as at this day?
14 Then Ahimelech answered the king,
and said, And who *is so* faithful among all
thy servants as David, which is the king's
son in law, and goeth at thy bidding, and is
honourable in thine house?
15 Did I then begin to inquire of God for

him? be it far from me: let not the king
impute *any* thing unto his servant, *nor* to
all the house of my father: for thy servant
knew nothing of all this, less or more.
16 And the king said, Thou shalt surely die,
Ahimelech, thou, and all thy father's house.
17 ¶ And the king said unto the footmen that
stood about him, Turn, and slay the priests
of the LORD; because their hand also *is* with
David, and because they knew when he fled,
and did not shew it to me. But the servants
of the king would not put forth their hand
to fall upon the priests of the LORD.
18 And the king said to Doeg, Turn thou, and
fall upon the priests. And Doeg the Edomite
turned, and he fell upon the priests, and
slew on that day fourscore and five persons
that did wear a linen ephod.
19 And Nob, the city of the priests, smote
he with the edge of the sword, both men
and women, children and sucklings, and
oxen, and asses, and sheep, with the edge
of the sword.
20 ¶ And one of the sons of Ahimelech the
son of Ahitub, named Abiathar, escaped,
and fled after David.
21 And Abiathar shewed David that Saul
had slain the LORD's priests.
22 And David said unto Abiathar, I knew
it that day, when Doeg the Edomite *was*
there, that he would surely tell Saul: I have
occasioned *the death* of all the persons of
thy father's house.
23 Abide thou with me, fear not: for he that
seeketh my life seeketh thy life: but with me
thou *shalt be* in safeguard.

1 Samuel 23

1 Then they told David, saying, Behold, the
Philistines fight against Keilah, and they rob
the threshingfloors.
2 Therefore David inquired of the LORD,
saying, Shall I go and smite these Philistines?
And the LORD said unto David, Go, and smite
the Philistines, and save Keilah.
3 And David's men said unto him, Behold,
we be afraid here in Judah: how much more
then if we come to Keilah against the armies
of the Philistines?
4 Then David inquired of the LORD yet again.
And the LORD answered him and said, Arise,
go down to Keilah; for I will deliver the Philistines into thine hand.
5 So David and his men went to Keilah, and
fought with the Philistines, and brought
away their cattle, and smote them with a
great slaughter. So David saved the inhabitants of Keilah.
6 And it came to pass, when Abiathar the
son of Ahimelech fled to David to Keilah,
that he came down *with* an ephod in his
hand.
7 ¶ And it was told Saul that David was
come to Keilah. And Saul said, God hath
delivered him into mine hand; for he is
shut in, by entering into a town that hath
gates and bars.
8 And Saul called all the people together to
war, to go down to Keilah, to besiege David
and his men.
9 ¶ And David knew that Saul secretly practised mischief against him; and he said to
Abiathar the priest, Bring hither the ephod.
10 Then said David, O LORD God of Israel,
thy servant hath certainly heard that Saul
seeketh to come to Keilah, to destroy the
city for my sake.
11 Will the men of Keilah deliver me up
into his hand? will Saul come down, as thy
servant hath heard? O LORD God of Israel, I
beseech thee, tell thy servant. And the LORD
said, He will come down.
12 Then said David, Will the men of Keilah
deliver me and my men into the hand of
Saul? And the LORD said, They will deliver
thee up.
13 ¶ Then David and his men, *which were*
about six hundred, arose and departed out
of Keilah, and went whithersoever they
could go. And it was told Saul that David
was escaped from Keilah; and he forbare
to go forth.
14 And David abode in the wilderness in
strong holds, and remained in a mountain
in the wilderness of Ziph. And Saul sought
him every day, but God delivered him not
into his hand.
15 And David saw that Saul was come out to
seek his life: and David *was* in the wilderness
of Ziph in a wood.
16 ¶ And Jonathan Saul's son arose, and
went to David into the wood, and strengthened his hand in God.
17 And he said unto him, Fear not: for the
hand of Saul my father shall not find thee;
and thou shalt be king over Israel, and I

shall be next unto thee; and that also Saul
my father knoweth.
18 And they two made a covenant before
the LORD: and David abode in the wood, and
Jonathan went to his house.
19 ¶ Then came up the Ziphites to Saul to
Gibeah, saying, Doth not David hide himself with us in strong holds in the wood, in
the hill of Hachilah, which *is* on the south
of Jeshimon?
20 Now therefore, O king, come down
according to all the desire of thy soul to
come down; and our part *shall be* to deliver
him into the king's hand.
21 And Saul said, Blessed *be* ye of the LORD;
for ye have compassion on me.
22 Go, I pray you, prepare yet, and know
and see his place where his haunt is, *and*
who hath seen him there: for it is told me
that he dealeth very subtilly.
23 See therefore, and take knowledge of all
the lurking places where he hideth himself,
and come ye again to me with the certainty,
and I will go with you: and it shall come to
pass, if he be in the land, that I will search
him out throughout all the thousands of
Judah.
24 And they arose, and went to Ziph before
Saul: but David and his men *were* in the wilderness of Maon, in the plain on the south
of Jeshimon.
25 Saul also and his men went to seek *him*.
And they told David: wherefore he came
down into a rock, and abode in the wilderness of Maon. And when Saul heard *that*,
he pursued after David in the wilderness
of Maon.
26 And Saul went on this side of the mountain, and David and his men on that side of
the mountain: and David made haste to get
away for fear of Saul; for Saul and his men
compassed David and his men round about
to take them.
27 ¶ But there came a messenger unto
Saul, saying, Haste thee, and come; for the
Philistines have invaded the land.
28 Wherefore Saul returned from pursuing
after David, and went against the Philistines:
therefore they called that place Sela-ham-
mahlekoth.
29 ¶ And David went up from thence, and
dwelt in strong holds at En-gedi.

1 Samuel 24

1 And it came to pass, when Saul was
returned from following the Philistines, that
it was told him, saying, Behold, David *is* in
the wilderness of En-gedi.
2 Then Saul took three thousand chosen
men out of all Israel, and went to seek
David and his men upon the rocks of the
wild goats.
3 And he came to the sheepcotes by the
way, where *was* a cave; and Saul went in
to cover his feet: and David and his men
remained in the sides of the cave.
4 And the men of David said unto him,
Behold the day of which the LORD said unto
thee, Behold, I will deliver thine enemy
into thine hand, that thou mayest do to
him as it shall seem good unto thee. Then
David arose, and cut off the skirt of Saul's
robe privily.
5 And it came to pass afterward, that David's
heart smote him, because he had cut off
Saul's skirt.
6 And he said unto his men, The LORD forbid
that I should do this thing unto my master,
the LORD's anointed, to stretch forth mine
hand against him, seeing he *is* the anointed
of the LORD.
7 So David stayed his servants with these
words, and suffered them not to rise against
Saul. But Saul rose up out of the cave, and
went on *his* way.
8 David also arose afterward, and went out
of the cave, and cried after Saul, saying, My
lord the king. And when Saul looked behind
him, David stooped with his face to the
earth, and bowed himself.
9 ¶ And David said to Saul, Wherefore hearest thou men's words, saying, Behold, David
seeketh thy hurt?
10 Behold, this day thine eyes have seen
how that the LORD had delivered thee to day
into mine hand in the cave: and *some* bade
me kill thee: but *mine eye* spared thee; and
I said, I will not put forth mine hand against
my lord; for he *is* the LORD's anointed.
11 Moreover, my father, see, yea, see the
skirt of thy robe in my hand: for in that I cut
off the skirt of thy robe, and killed thee not,
know thou and see that *there is* neither evil
nor transgression in mine hand, and I have
not sinned against thee; yet thou huntest
my soul to take it.

12 The LORD judge between me and thee,
and the LORD avenge me of thee: but mine
hand shall not be upon thee.
13 As saith the proverb of the ancients,
Wickedness proceedeth from the wicked:
but mine hand shall not be upon thee.
14 After whom is the king of Israel come
out? after whom dost thou pursue? after a
dead dog, after a flea.
15 The LORD therefore be judge, and judge
between me and thee, and see, and plead
my cause, and deliver me out of thine hand.
16 ¶ And it came to pass, when David had
made an end of speaking these words
unto Saul, that Saul said, *Is* this thy voice,
my son David? And Saul lifted up his voice,
and wept.
17 And he said to David, Thou *art* more
righteous than I: for thou hast rewarded me
good, whereas I have rewarded thee evil.
18 And thou hast shewed this day how that
thou hast dealt well with me: forasmuch as
when the LORD had delivered me into thine
hand, thou killedst me not.
19 For if a man find his enemy, will he let
him go well away? wherefore the LORD
reward thee good for that thou hast done
unto me this day.
20 And now, behold, I know well that thou
shalt surely be king, and that the kingdom
of Israel shall be established in thine hand.
21 Swear now therefore unto me by the
LORD, that thou wilt not cut off my seed
after me, and that thou wilt not destroy my
name out of my father's house.
22 And David sware unto Saul. And Saul
went home; but David and his men gat them
up unto the hold.

1 Samuel 25

1 And Samuel died; and all the Israelites
were gathered together, and lamented him,
and buried him in his house at Ramah. And
David arose, and went down to the wilderness of Paran.
2 And *there was* a man in Maon, whose
possessions *were* in Carmel; and the man
was very great, and he had three thousand
sheep, and a thousand goats: and he was
shearing his sheep in Carmel.
3 Now the name of the man *was* Nabal; and
the name of his wife Abigail: and *she was*
a woman of good understanding, and of a
beautiful countenance: but the man *was*
churlish and evil in his doings; and he *was*
of the house of Caleb.
4 ¶ And David heard in the wilderness that
Nabal did shear his sheep.
5 And David sent out ten young men, and
David said unto the young men, Get you up
to Carmel, and go to Nabal, and greet him
in my name:
6 And thus shall ye say to him that liveth
in prosperity, Peace *be* both to thee, and
peace *be* to thine house, and peace *be* unto
all that thou hast.
7 And now I have heard that thou hast
shearers: now thy shepherds which were
with us, we hurt them not, neither was there
ought missing unto them, all the while they
were in Carmel.
8 Ask thy young men, and they will shew
thee. Wherefore let the young men find
favour in thine eyes: for we come in a good
day: give, I pray thee, whatsoever cometh
to thine hand unto thy servants, and to thy
son David.
9 And when David's young men came, they
spake to Nabal according to all those words
in the name of David, and ceased.
10 ¶ And Nabal answered David's servants,
and said, Who *is* David? and who *is* the son
of Jesse? there be many servants now a days
that break away every man from his master.
11 Shall I then take my bread, and my water,
and my flesh that I have killed for my shearers, and give *it* unto men, whom I know not
whence they *be*?
12 So David's young men turned their way,
and went again, and came and told him all
those sayings.
13 And David said unto his men, Gird ye on
every man his sword. And they girded on
every man his sword; and David also girded
on his sword: and there went up after David
about four hundred men; and two hundred
abode by the stuff.
14 ¶ But one of the young men told Abigail,
Nabal's wife, saying, Behold, David sent
messengers out of the wilderness to salute
our master; and he railed on them.
15 But the men *were* very good unto us, and
we were not hurt, neither missed we any
thing, as long as we were conversant with
them, when we were in the fields:
16 They were a wall unto us both by night

and day, all the while we were with them
keeping the sheep.
17 Now therefore know and consider what
thou wilt do; for evil is determined against
our master, and against all his household:
for he *is such* a son of Belial, that *a man*
cannot speak to him.
18 ¶ Then Abigail made haste, and took
two hundred loaves, and two bottles of
wine, and five sheep ready dressed, and five
measures of parched *corn*, and an hundred
clusters of raisins, and two hundred cakes
of figs, and laid *them* on asses.
19 And she said unto her servants, Go on
before me; behold, I come after you. But
she told not her husband Nabal.
20 And it was *so, as* she rode on the ass,
that she came down by the covert of the
hill, and, behold, David and his men came
down against her; and she met them.
21 Now David had said, Surely in vain have
I kept all that this *fellow* hath in the wilderness, so that nothing was missed of all that
pertained unto him: and he hath requited
me evil for good.
22 So and more also do God unto the enemies of David, if I leave of all that *pertain* to
him by the morning light any that pisseth
against the wall.
23 And when Abigail saw David, she hasted,
and lighted off the ass, and fell before
David on her face, and bowed herself to
the ground,
24 And fell at his feet, and said, Upon me,
my lord, *upon* me *let this* iniquity *be:* and
let thine handmaid, I pray thee, speak in
thine audience, and hear the words of thine
handmaid.
25 Let not my lord, I pray thee, regard this
man of Belial, *even* Nabal: for as his name *is,*
so *is* he; Nabal *is* his name, and folly *is* with
him: but I thine handmaid saw not the young
men of my lord, whom thou didst send.
26 Now therefore, my lord, *as* the LORD
liveth, and *as* thy soul liveth, seeing the
LORD hath withholden thee from coming to
shed blood, and from avenging thyself with
thine own hand, now let thine enemies, and
they that seek evil to my lord, be as Nabal.
27 And now this blessing which thine handmaid hath brought unto my lord, let it even
be given unto the young men that follow
my lord.
28 I pray thee, forgive the trespass of thine
handmaid: for the LORD will certainly make
my lord a sure house; because my lord
fighteth the battles of the LORD, and evil
hath not been found in thee *all* thy days.
29 Yet a man is risen to pursue thee, and
to seek thy soul: but the soul of my lord
shall be bound in the bundle of life with
the LORD thy God; and the souls of thine
enemies, them shall he sling out, *as out* of
the middle of a sling.
30 And it shall come to pass, when the LORD
shall have done to my lord according to all
the good that he hath spoken concerning
thee, and shall have appointed thee ruler
over Israel;
31 That this shall be no grief unto thee, nor
offence of heart unto my lord, either that
thou hast shed blood causeless, or that my
lord hath avenged himself: but when the
LORD shall have dealt well with my lord,
then remember thine handmaid.
32 ¶ And David said to Abigail, Blessed *be*
the LORD God of Israel, which sent thee this
day to meet me:
33 And blessed *be* thy advice, and blessed
be thou, which hast kept me this day from
coming to *shed* blood, and from avenging
myself with mine own hand.
34 For in very deed, *as* the LORD God of
Israel liveth, which hath kept me back from
hurting thee, except thou hadst hasted and
come to meet me, surely there had not been
left unto Nabal by the morning light any that
pisseth against the wall.
35 So David received of her hand *that* which
she had brought him, and said unto her,
Go up in peace to thine house; see, I have
hearkened to thy voice, and have accepted
thy person.
36 ¶ And Abigail came to Nabal; and, behold,
he held a feast in his house, like the feast of
a king; and Nabal's heart *was* merry within
him, for he *was* very drunken: wherefore
she told him nothing, less or more, until
the morning light.
37 But it came to pass in the morning, when
the wine was gone out of Nabal, and his wife
had told him these things, that his heart
died within him, and he became *as* a stone.
38 And it came to pass about ten days *after,*
that the LORD smote Nabal, that he died.
39 ¶ And when David heard that Nabal was

dead, he said, Blessed *be* the LORD, that hath
pleaded the cause of my reproach from the
hand of Nabal, and hath kept his servant
from evil: for the LORD hath returned the
wickedness of Nabal upon his own head.
And David sent and communed with Abigail,
to take her to him to wife.
40 And when the servants of David were
come to Abigail to Carmel, they spake unto
her, saying, David sent us unto thee, to take
thee to him to wife.
41 And she arose, and bowed herself on *her*
face to the earth, and said, Behold, *let* thine
handmaid *be* a servant to wash the feet of
the servants of my lord.
42 And Abigail hasted, and arose, and rode
upon an ass, with five damsels of hers that
went after her; and she went after the
messengers of David, and became his wife.
43 David also took Ahinoam of Jezreel; and
they were also both of them his wives.
44 ¶ But Saul had given Michal his daughter, David's wife, to Phalti the son of Laish,
which *was* of Gallim.

1 Samuel 26

1 And the Ziphites came unto Saul to Gibeah,
saying, Doth not David hide himself in the
hill of Hachilah, *which is* before Jeshimon?
2 Then Saul arose, and went down to the
wilderness of Ziph, having three thousand
chosen men of Israel with him, to seek David
in the wilderness of Ziph.
3 And Saul pitched in the hill of Hachilah,
which *is* before Jeshimon, by the way. But
David abode in the wilderness, and he saw
that Saul came after him into the wilderness.
4 David therefore sent out spies, and understood that Saul was come in very deed.
5 ¶ And David arose, and came to the place
where Saul had pitched: and David beheld
the place where Saul lay, and Abner the son
of Ner, the captain of his host: and Saul lay
in the trench, and the people pitched round
about him.
6 Then answered David and said to Ahimelech the Hittite, and to Abishai the son of
Zeruiah, brother to Joab, saying, Who will
go down with me to Saul to the camp? And
Abishai said, I will go down with thee.
7 So David and Abishai came to the people
by night: and, behold, Saul lay sleeping
within the trench, and his spear stuck in
the ground at his bolster: but Abner and
the people lay round about him.
8 Then said Abishai to David, God hath delivered thine enemy into thine hand this day:
now therefore let me smite him, I pray thee,
with the spear even to the earth at once,
and I will not *smite* him the second time.
9 And David said to Abishai, Destroy him not:
for who can stretch forth his hand against
the LORD's anointed, and be guiltless?
10 David said furthermore, *As* the LORD
liveth, the LORD shall smite him; or his day
shall come to die; or he shall descend into
battle, and perish.
11 The LORD forbid that I should stretch forth
mine hand against the LORD's anointed: but,
I pray thee, take thou now the spear that *is*
at his bolster, and the cruse of water, and
let us go.
12 So David took the spear and the cruse
of water from Saul's bolster; and they gat
them away, and no man saw *it*, nor knew
it, neither awaked: for they *were* all asleep;
because a deep sleep from the LORD was
fallen upon them.
13 ¶ Then David went over to the other side,
and stood on the top of an hill afar off; a
great space *being* between them:
14 And David cried to the people, and to
Abner the son of Ner, saying, Answerest
thou not, Abner? Then Abner answered and
said, Who *art* thou *that* criest to the king?
15 And David said to Abner, *Art* not thou
a *valiant* man? and who *is* like to thee in
Israel? wherefore then hast thou not kept
thy lord the king? for there came one of
the people in to destroy the king thy lord.
16 This thing *is* not good that thou hast
done. *As* the LORD liveth, ye *are* worthy to
die, because ye have not kept your master,
the LORD's anointed. And now see where
the king's spear *is*, and the cruse of water
that *was* at his bolster.
17 And Saul knew David's voice, and said,
Is this thy voice, my son David? And David
said, *It is* my voice, my lord, O king.
18 And he said, Wherefore doth my lord
thus pursue after his servant? for what have
I done? or what evil *is* in mine hand?
19 Now therefore, I pray thee, let my lord
the king hear the words of his servant. If
the LORD have stirred thee up against me,
let him accept an offering: but if *they be* the

children of men, cursed *be* they before the
LORD; for they have driven me out this day
from abiding in the inheritance of the LORD,
saying, Go, serve other gods.
20 Now therefore, let not my blood fall to
the earth before the face of the LORD: for
the king of Israel is come out to seek a flea,
as when one doth hunt a partridge in the
mountains.
21 ¶ Then said Saul, I have sinned: return,
my son David: for I will no more do thee
harm, because my soul was precious in thine
eyes this day: behold, I have played the fool,
and have erred exceedingly.
22 And David answered and said, Behold
the king's spear! and let one of the young
men come over and fetch it.
23 The LORD render to every man his righteousness and his faithfulness: for the LORD
delivered thee into *my* hand to day, but I
would not stretch forth mine hand against
the LORD's anointed.
24 And, behold, as thy life was much set by
this day in mine eyes, so let my life be much
set by in the eyes of the LORD, and let him
deliver me out of all tribulation.
25 Then Saul said to David, Blessed *be*
thou, my son David: thou shalt both do
great *things*, and also shalt still prevail. So
David went on his way, and Saul returned
to his place.

1 Samuel 27

1 And David said in his heart, I shall now
perish one day by the hand of Saul: *there
is* nothing better for me than that I should
speedily escape into the land of the Philistines; and Saul shall despair of me, to seek
me any more in any coast of Israel: so shall
I escape out of his hand.
2 And David arose, and he passed over with
the six hundred men that *were* with him
unto Achish, the son of Maoch, king of Gath.
3 And David dwelt with Achish at Gath, he
and his men, every man with his household,
even David with his two wives, Ahinoam the
Jezreelitess, and Abigail the Carmelitess,
Nabal's wife.
4 And it was told Saul that David was fled to
Gath: and he sought no more again for him.
5 ¶ And David said unto Achish, If I have now
found grace in thine eyes, let them give me
a place in some town in the country, that I
may dwell there: for why should thy servant
dwell in the royal city with thee?
6 Then Achish gave him Ziklag that day:
wherefore Ziklag pertaineth unto the kings
of Judah unto this day.
7 And the time that David dwelt in the
country of the Philistines was a full year
and four months.
8 ¶ And David and his men went up, and
invaded the Geshurites, and the Gezrites,
and the Amalekites: for those *nations were*
of old the inhabitants of the land, as thou
goest to Shur, even unto the land of Egypt.
9 And David smote the land, and left neither
man nor woman alive, and took away the
sheep, and the oxen, and the asses, and the
camels, and the apparel, and returned, and
came to Achish.
10 And Achish said, Whither have ye made
a road to day? And David said, Against the
south of Judah, and against the south of
the Jerahmeelites, and against the south
of the Kenites.
11 And David saved neither man nor woman
alive, to bring *tidings* to Gath, saying, Lest
they should tell on us, saying, So did David,
and so *will be* his manner all the while he
dwelleth in the country of the Philistines.
12 And Achish believed David, saying,
He hath made his people Israel utterly to
abhor him; therefore he shall be my servant for ever.

1 Samuel 28

1 And it came to pass in those days, that the
Philistines gathered their armies together
for warfare, to fight with Israel. And Achish
said unto David, Know thou assuredly, that
thou shalt go out with me to battle, thou
and thy men.
2 And David said to Achish, Surely thou shalt
know what thy servant can do. And Achish
said to David, Therefore will I make thee
keeper of mine head for ever.
3 ¶ Now Samuel was dead, and all Israel had
lamented him, and buried him in Ramah,
even in his own city. And Saul had put away
those that had familiar spirits, and the wizards, out of the land.
4 And the Philistines gathered themselves
together, and came and pitched in Shunem:
and Saul gathered all Israel together, and
they pitched in Gilboa.

5 And when Saul saw the host of the Philistines, he was afraid, and his heart greatly
trembled.
6 And when Saul inquired of the LORD, the
LORD answered him not, neither by dreams,
nor by Urim, nor by prophets.
7 ¶ Then said Saul unto his servants, Seek
me a woman that hath a familiar spirit, that
I may go to her, and inquire of her. And
his servants said to him, Behold, *there is* a
woman that hath a familiar spirit at En-dor.
8 And Saul disguised himself, and put on
other raiment, and he went, and two men
with him, and they came to the woman by
night: and he said, I pray thee, divine unto
me by the familiar spirit, and bring me *him*
up, whom I shall name unto thee.
9 And the woman said unto him, Behold,
thou knowest what Saul hath done, how he
hath cut off those that have familiar spirits,
and the wizards, out of the land: wherefore
then layest thou a snare for my life, to cause
me to die?
10 And Saul sware to her by the LORD,
saying, *As* the LORD liveth, there shall no
punishment happen to thee for this thing.
11 Then said the woman, Whom shall I
bring up unto thee? And he said, Bring me
up Samuel.
12 And when the woman saw Samuel, she
cried with a loud voice: and the woman
spake to Saul, saying, Why hast thou
deceived me? for thou *art* Saul.
13 And the king said unto her, Be not afraid:
for what sawest thou? And the woman
said unto Saul, I saw gods ascending out
of the earth.
14 And he said unto her, What form *is* he of?
And she said, An old man cometh up; and he
is covered with a mantle. And Saul perceived
that it *was* Samuel, and he stooped with
his face to the ground, and bowed himself.
15 ¶ And Samuel said to Saul, Why hast
thou disquieted me, to bring me up? And
Saul answered, I am sore distressed; for the
Philistines make war against me, and God is
departed from me, and answereth me no
more, neither by prophets, nor by dreams:
therefore I have called thee, that thou mayest make known unto me what I shall do.
16 Then said Samuel, Wherefore then dost
thou ask of me, seeing the LORD is departed
from thee, and is become thine enemy?
17 And the LORD hath done to him, as he
spake by me: for the LORD hath rent the
kingdom out of thine hand, and given it to
thy neighbour, *even* to David:
18 Because thou obeyedst not the voice of
the LORD, nor executedst his fierce wrath
upon Amalek, therefore hath the LORD done
this thing unto thee this day.
19 Moreover the LORD will also deliver Israel
with thee into the hand of the Philistines:
and to morrow *shalt* thou and thy sons *be*
with me: the LORD also shall deliver the host
of Israel into the hand of the Philistines.
20 Then Saul fell straightway all along on
the earth, and was sore afraid, because
of the words of Samuel: and there was no
strength in him; for he had eaten no bread
all the day, nor all the night.
21 ¶ And the woman came unto Saul, and
saw that he was sore troubled, and said unto
him, Behold, thine handmaid hath obeyed
thy voice, and I have put my life in my hand,
and have hearkened unto thy words which
thou spakest unto me.
22 Now therefore, I pray thee, hearken thou
also unto the voice of thine handmaid, and
let me set a morsel of bread before thee;
and eat, that thou mayest have strength,
when thou goest on thy way.
23 But he refused, and said, I will not eat.
But his servants, together with the woman,
compelled him; and he hearkened unto their
voice. So he arose from the earth, and sat
upon the bed.
24 And the woman had a fat calf in the
house; and she hasted, and killed it, and
took flour, and kneaded *it*, and did bake
unleavened bread thereof:
25 And she brought *it* before Saul, and
before his servants; and they did eat. Then
they rose up, and went away that night.

1 Samuel 29

1 Now the Philistines gathered together all
their armies to Aphek: and the Israelites
pitched by a fountain which *is* in Jezreel.
2 And the lords of the Philistines passed on
by hundreds, and by thousands: but David
and his men passed on in the rereward
with Achish.
3 Then said the princes of the Philistines,
What *do* these Hebrews *here*? And Achish
said unto the princes of the Philistines, *Is* not

this David, the servant of Saul the king of
Israel, which hath been with me these days,
or these years, and I have found no fault
in him since he fell *unto me* unto this day?
4 And the princes of the Philistines were
wroth with him; and the princes of the Philistines said unto him, Make this fellow return,
that he may go again to his place which thou
hast appointed him, and let him not go down
with us to battle, lest in the battle he be an
adversary to us: for wherewith should he
reconcile himself unto his master? *should it*
not *be* with the heads of these men?
5 *Is* not this David, of whom they sang one
to another in dances, saying, Saul slew his
thousands, and David his ten thousands?
6 ¶ Then Achish called David, and said unto
him, Surely, *as* the LORD liveth, thou hast
been upright, and thy going out and thy
coming in with me in the host *is* good in my
sight: for I have not found evil in thee since
the day of thy coming unto me unto this
day: nevertheless the lords favour thee not.
7 Wherefore now return, and go in peace,
that thou displease not the lords of the
Philistines.
8 ¶ And David said unto Achish, But what
have I done? and what hast thou found in
thy servant so long as I have been with thee
unto this day, that I may not go fight against
the enemies of my lord the king?
9 And Achish answered and said to David, I
know that thou *art* good in my sight, as an
angel of God: notwithstanding the princes
of the Philistines have said, He shall not go
up with us to the battle.
10 Wherefore now rise up early in the morning with thy master's servants that are come
with thee: and as soon as ye be up early in
the morning, and have light, depart.
11 So David and his men rose up early to
depart in the morning, to return into the
land of the Philistines. And the Philistines
went up to Jezreel.

1 Samuel 30

1 And it came to pass, when David and his
men were come to Ziklag on the third day,
that the Amalekites had invaded the south,
and Ziklag, and smitten Ziklag, and burned
it with fire;
2 And had taken the women captives, that
were therein: they slew not any, either great
or small, but carried *them* away, and went
on their way.
3 ¶ So David and his men came to the city,
and, behold, *it was* burned with fire; and
their wives, and their sons, and their daughters, were taken captives.
4 Then David and the people that *were* with
him lifted up their voice and wept, until they
had no more power to weep.
5 And David's two wives were taken captives, Ahinoam the Jezreelitess, and Abigail
the wife of Nabal the Carmelite.
6 And David was greatly distressed; for the
people spake of stoning him, because the
soul of all the people was grieved, every man
for his sons and for his daughters: but David
encouraged himself in the LORD his God.
7 And David said to Abiathar the priest,
Ahimelech's son, I pray thee, bring me hither
the ephod. And Abiathar brought thither the
ephod to David.
8 And David inquired at the LORD, saying,
Shall I pursue after this troop? shall I overtake them? And he answered him, Pursue:
for thou shalt surely overtake *them*, and
without fail recover *all*.
9 So David went, he and the six hundred
men that *were* with him, and came to the
brook Besor, where those that were left
behind stayed.
10 But David pursued, he and four hundred
men: for two hundred abode behind, which
were so faint that they could not go over
the brook Besor.
11 ¶ And they found an Egyptian in the
field, and brought him to David, and gave
him bread, and he did eat; and they made
him drink water;
12 And they gave him a piece of a cake of
figs, and two clusters of raisins: and when
he had eaten, his spirit came again to him:
for he had eaten no bread, nor drunk *any*
water, three days and three nights.
13 And David said unto him, To whom
belongest thou? and whence *art* thou? And
he said, I *am* a young man of Egypt, servant
to an Amalekite; and my master left me,
because three days agone I fell sick.
14 We made an invasion *upon* the south of
the Cherethites, and upon *the coast* which
belongeth to Judah, and upon the south of
Caleb; and we burned Ziklag with fire.
15 And David said to him, Canst thou bring

me down to this company? And he said,
Swear unto me by God, that thou wilt neither kill me, nor deliver me into the hands
of my master, and I will bring thee down to
this company.
16 ¶ And when he had brought him down,
behold, *they were* spread abroad upon all
the earth, eating and drinking, and dancing,
because of all the great spoil that they had
taken out of the land of the Philistines, and
out of the land of Judah.
17 And David smote them from the twilight
even unto the evening of the next day: and
there escaped not a man of them, save
four hundred young men, which rode upon
camels, and fled.
18 And David recovered all that the Amalekites had carried away: and David rescued
his two wives.
19 And there was nothing lacking to them,
neither small nor great, neither sons nor
daughters, neither spoil, nor any *thing* that
they had taken to them: David recovered all.
20 And David took all the flocks and the
herds, *which* they drave before those *other*
cattle, and said, This *is* David's spoil.
21 ¶ And David came to the two hundred
men, which were so faint that they could
not follow David, whom they had made
also to abide at the brook Besor: and they
went forth to meet David, and to meet the
people that *were* with him: and when David
came near to the people, he saluted them.
22 Then answered all the wicked men and
men of Belial, of those that went with David,
and said, Because they went not with us, we
will not give them *ought* of the spoil that we
have recovered, save to every man his wife
and his children, that they may lead *them*
away, and depart.
23 Then said David, Ye shall not do so,
my brethren, with that which the LORD
hath given us, who hath preserved us, and
delivered the company that came against
us into our hand.
24 For who will hearken unto you in this
matter? but as his part *is* that goeth down
to the battle, so *shall* his part *be* that tarrieth
by the stuff: they shall part alike.
25 And it was *so* from that day forward, that
he made it a statute and an ordinance for
Israel unto this day.
26 ¶ And when David came to Ziklag, he sent
of the spoil unto the elders of Judah, *even*
to his friends, saying, Behold a present for
you of the spoil of the enemies of the LORD;
27 To *them* which *were* in Beth-el, and to
them which *were* in south Ramoth, and to
them which *were* in Jattir,
28 And to *them* which *were* in Aroer, and to
them which *were* in Siphmoth, and to *them*
which *were* in Eshtemoa,
29 And to *them* which *were* in Rachal, and
to *them* which *were* in the cities of the Jerahmeelites, and to *them* which *were* in the
cities of the Kenites,
30 And to *them* which *were* in Hormah, and
to *them* which *were* in Chor-ashan, and to
them which *were* in Athach,
31 And to *them* which *were* in Hebron, and
to all the places where David himself and
his men were wont to haunt.

1 Samuel 31

1 Now the Philistines fought against Israel:
and the men of Israel fled from before the
Philistines, and fell down slain in mount
Gilboa.
2 And the Philistines followed hard upon
Saul and upon his sons; and the Philistines
slew Jonathan, and Abinadab, and Malchi-shua, Saul's sons.
3 And the battle went sore against Saul,
and the archers hit him; and he was sore
wounded of the archers.
4 Then said Saul unto his armourbearer,
Draw thy sword, and thrust me through
therewith; lest these uncircumcised come
and thrust me through, and abuse me. But
his armourbearer would not; for he was
sore afraid. Therefore Saul took a sword,
and fell upon it.
5 And when his armourbearer saw that Saul
was dead, he fell likewise upon his sword,
and died with him.
6 So Saul died, and his three sons, and his
armourbearer, and all his men, that same
day together.
7 ¶ And when the men of Israel that *were*
on the other side of the valley, and *they* that
were on the other side Jordan, saw that the
men of Israel fled, and that Saul and his sons
were dead, they forsook the cities, and fled;
and the Philistines came and dwelt in them.
8 And it came to pass on the morrow, when
the Philistines came to strip the slain, that

they found Saul and his three sons fallen in
mount Gilboa.
9 And they cut off his head, and stripped
off his armour, and sent into the land of the
Philistines round about, to publish *it in* the
house of their idols, and among the people.
10 And they put his armour in the house of
Ashtaroth: and they fastened his body to
the wall of Beth-shan.
11 ¶ And when the inhabitants of Jabesh-gilead heard of that which the Philistines had
done to Saul;
12 All the valiant men arose, and went all
night, and took the body of Saul and the
bodies of his sons from the wall of Beth-shan, and came to Jabesh, and burnt them
there.
13 And they took their bones, and buried
them under a tree at Jabesh, and fasted
seven days.

The Second Book Of

Samuel

2 Samuel 1

1 Now it came to pass after the death of
Saul, when David was returned from the
slaughter of the Amalekites, and David had
abode two days in Ziklag;
2 It came even to pass on the third day, that,
behold, a man came out of the camp from
Saul with his clothes rent, and earth upon his
head: and *so* it was, when he came to David,
that he fell to the earth, and did obeisance.
3 And David said unto him, From whence
comest thou? And he said unto him, Out of
the camp of Israel am I escaped.
4 And David said unto him, How went
the matter? I pray thee, tell me. And he
answered, That the people are fled from
the battle, and many of the people also are
fallen and dead; and Saul and Jonathan his
son are dead also.
5 And David said unto the young man that
told him, How knowest thou that Saul and
Jonathan his son be dead?
6 And the young man that told him said, As
I happened by chance upon mount Gilboa,
behold, Saul leaned upon his spear; and, lo,
the chariots and horsemen followed hard
after him.
7 And when he looked behind him, he saw
me, and called unto me. And I answered,
Here *am* I.
8 And he said unto me, Who *art* thou? And
I answered him, I *am* an Amalekite.
9 He said unto me again, Stand, I pray thee,
upon me, and slay me: for anguish is come
upon me, because my life *is* yet whole in me.
10 So I stood upon him, and slew him,
because I was sure that he could not live
after that he was fallen: and I took the crown
that *was* upon his head, and the bracelet
that *was* on his arm, and have brought them
hither unto my lord.
11 Then David took hold on his clothes, and
rent them; and likewise all the men that
were with him:
12 And they mourned, and wept, and fasted
until even, for Saul, and for Jonathan his son,
and for the people of the LORD, and for the
house of Israel; because they were fallen
by the sword.
13 ¶ And David said unto the young man
that told him, Whence *art* thou? And he
answered, I *am* the son of a stranger, an
Amalekite.
14 And David said unto him, How wast thou
not afraid to stretch forth thine hand to
destroy the LORD's anointed?
15 And David called one of the young men,
and said, Go near, *and* fall upon him. And
he smote him that he died.
16 And David said unto him, Thy blood *be*
upon thy head; for thy mouth hath testified
against thee, saying, I have slain the LORD's
anointed.
17 ¶ And David lamented with this lamentation over Saul and over Jonathan his son:
18 (Also he bade them teach the children

of Judah *the use of* the bow: behold, *it is*
written in the book of Jasher.)
19 The beauty of Israel is slain upon thy high
places: how are the mighty fallen!
20 Tell *it* not in Gath, publish *it* not in the
streets of Askelon; lest the daughters of the
Philistines rejoice, lest the daughters of the
uncircumcised triumph.
21 Ye mountains of Gilboa, *let there be* no
dew, neither *let there be* rain, upon you, nor
fields of offerings: for there the shield of the
mighty is vilely cast away, the shield of Saul,
as though he had not *been* anointed with oil.
22 From the blood of the slain, from the fat
of the mighty, the bow of Jonathan turned
not back, and the sword of Saul returned
not empty.
23 Saul and Jonathan *were* lovely and
pleasant in their lives, and in their death
they were not divided: they were swifter
than eagles, they were stronger than lions.
24 Ye daughters of Israel, weep over Saul,
who clothed you in scarlet, with *other*
delights, who put on ornaments of gold
upon your apparel.
25 How are the mighty fallen in the midst
of the battle! O Jonathan, *thou wast* slain
in thine high places.
26 I am distressed for thee, my brother Jonathan: very pleasant hast thou been unto
me: thy love to me was wonderful, passing
the love of women.
27 How are the mighty fallen, and the weapons of war perished!

2 Samuel 2

1 And it came to pass after this, that David
inquired of the LORD, saying, Shall I go up
into any of the cities of Judah? And the
LORD said unto him, Go up. And David said,
Whither shall I go up? And he said, Unto
Hebron.
2 So David went up thither, and his two
wives also, Ahinoam the Jezreelitess, and
Abigail Nabal's wife the Carmelite.
3 And his men that *were* with him did David
bring up, every man with his household: and
they dwelt in the cities of Hebron.
4 And the men of Judah came, and there
they anointed David king over the house
of Judah. And they told David, saying, *That*
the men of Jabesh-gilead *were they* that
buried Saul.
5 ¶ And David sent messengers unto the
men of Jabesh-gilead, and said unto them,
Blessed *be* ye of the LORD, that ye have
shewed this kindness unto your lord, *even*
unto Saul, and have buried him.
6 And now the LORD shew kindness and
truth unto you: and I also will requite you
this kindness, because ye have done this
thing.
7 Therefore now let your hands be strengthened, and be ye valiant: for your master Saul
is dead, and also the house of Judah have
anointed me king over them.
8 ¶ But Abner the son of Ner, captain of
Saul's host, took Ish-bosheth the son of
Saul, and brought him over to Mahanaim;
9 And made him king over Gilead, and over
the Ashurites, and over Jezreel, and over
Ephraim, and over Benjamin, and over all
Israel.
10 Ish-bosheth Saul's son *was* forty years
old when he began to reign over Israel, and
reigned two years. But the house of Judah
followed David.
11 And the time that David was king in
Hebron over the house of Judah was seven
years and six months.
12 ¶ And Abner the son of Ner, and the servants of Ish-bosheth the son of Saul, went
out from Mahanaim to Gibeon.
13 And Joab the son of Zeruiah, and the servants of David, went out, and met together
by the pool of Gibeon: and they sat down,
the one on the one side of the pool, and the
other on the other side of the pool.
14 And Abner said to Joab, Let the young
men now arise, and play before us. And Joab
said, Let them arise.
15 Then there arose and went over by number twelve of Benjamin, which *pertained* to
Ish-bosheth the son of Saul, and twelve of
the servants of David.
16 And they caught every one his fellow by
the head, and *thrust* his sword in his fellow's
side; so they fell down together: wherefore
that place was called Helkath-hazzurim,
which *is* in Gibeon.
17 And there was a very sore battle that
day; and Abner was beaten, and the men of
Israel, before the servants of David.
18 ¶ And there were three sons of Zeruiah
there, Joab, and Abishai, and Asahel: and
Asahel *was as* light of foot as a wild roe.

19 And Asahel pursued after Abner; and in
going he turned not to the right hand nor
to the left from following Abner.
20 Then Abner looked behind him, and said,
Art thou Asahel? And he answered, I *am*.
21 And Abner said to him, Turn thee aside
to thy right hand or to thy left, and lay thee
hold on one of the young men, and take thee
his armour. But Asahel would not turn aside
from following of him.
22 And Abner said again to Asahel, Turn thee
aside from following me: wherefore should I
smite thee to the ground? how then should
I hold up my face to Joab thy brother?
23 Howbeit he refused to turn aside: wherefore Abner with the hinder end of the
spear smote him under the fifth *rib*, that
the spear came out behind him; and he fell
down there, and died in the same place:
and it came to pass, *that* as many as came
to the place where Asahel fell down and
died stood still.
24 Joab also and Abishai pursued after
Abner: and the sun went down when they
were come to the hill of Ammah, that *lieth*
before Giah by the way of the wilderness
of Gibeon.
25 ¶ And the children of Benjamin gathered themselves together after Abner, and
became one troop, and stood on the top
of an hill.
26 Then Abner called to Joab, and said,
Shall the sword devour for ever? knowest
thou not that it will be bitterness in the
latter end? how long shall it be then, ere
thou bid the people return from following
their brethren?
27 And Joab said, *As* God liveth, unless thou
hadst spoken, surely then in the morning
the people had gone up every one from
following his brother.
28 So Joab blew a trumpet, and all the people stood still, and pursued after Israel no
more, neither fought they any more.
29 And Abner and his men walked all that
night through the plain, and passed over
Jordan, and went through all Bithron, and
they came to Mahanaim.
30 And Joab returned from following Abner:
and when he had gathered all the people
together, there lacked of David's servants
nineteen men and Asahel.
31 But the servants of David had smitten
of Benjamin, and of Abner's men, *so that*
three hundred and threescore men died.
32 ¶ And they took up Asahel, and buried
him in the sepulchre of his father, which
was in Beth-lehem. And Joab and his men
went all night, and they came to Hebron at
break of day.

2 Samuel 3

1 Now there was long war between the
house of Saul and the house of David: but
David waxed stronger and stronger, and the
house of Saul waxed weaker and weaker.
2 ¶ And unto David were sons born in
Hebron: and his firstborn was Amnon, of
Ahinoam the Jezreelitess;
3 And his second, Chileab, of Abigail the
wife of Nabal the Carmelite; and the third,
Absalom the son of Maacah the daughter
of Talmai king of Geshur;
4 And the fourth, Adonijah the son of Haggith; and the fifth, Shephatiah the son of
Abital;
5 And the sixth, Ithream, by Eglah David's
wife. These were born to David in Hebron.
6 ¶ And it came to pass, while there was war
between the house of Saul and the house
of David, that Abner made himself strong
for the house of Saul.
7 And Saul had a concubine, whose name
was Rizpah, the daughter of Aiah: and *Ish-
bosheth* said to Abner, Wherefore hast thou
gone in unto my father's concubine?
8 Then was Abner very wroth for the words
of Ish-bosheth, and said, *Am* I a dog's head,
which against Judah do shew kindness this
day unto the house of Saul thy father, to
his brethren, and to his friends, and have
not delivered thee into the hand of David,
that thou chargest me to day with a fault
concerning this woman?
9 So do God to Abner, and more also, except,
as the LORD hath sworn to David, even so
I do to him;
10 To translate the kingdom from the house
of Saul, and to set up the throne of David
over Israel and over Judah, from Dan even
to Beer-sheba.
11 And he could not answer Abner a word
again, because he feared him.
12 ¶ And Abner sent messengers to David
on his behalf, saying, Whose *is* the land?
saying *also*, Make thy league with me, and,

behold, my hand *shall be* with thee, to bring
about all Israel unto thee.
13 ¶ And he said, Well; I will make a league
with thee: but one thing I require of thee,
that is, Thou shalt not see my face, except
thou first bring Michal Saul's daughter, when
thou comest to see my face.
14 And David sent messengers to Ish-
bosheth Saul's son, saying, Deliver *me* my
wife Michal, which I espoused to me for an
hundred foreskins of the Philistines.
15 And Ish-bosheth sent, and took her
from *her* husband, *even* from Phaltiel the
son of Laish.
16 And her husband went with her along
weeping behind her to Bahurim. Then
said Abner unto him, Go, return. And he
returned.
17 ¶ And Abner had communication with
the elders of Israel, saying, Ye sought for
David in times past *to be* king over you:
18 Now then do *it:* for the LORD hath spoken
of David, saying, By the hand of my servant
David I will save my people Israel out of the
hand of the Philistines, and out of the hand
of all their enemies.
19 And Abner also spake in the ears of
Benjamin: and Abner went also to speak in
the ears of David in Hebron all that seemed
good to Israel, and that seemed good to the
whole house of Benjamin.
20 So Abner came to David to Hebron, and
twenty men with him. And David made
Abner and the men that *were* with him a
feast.
21 And Abner said unto David, I will arise
and go, and will gather all Israel unto my
lord the king, that they may make a league
with thee, and that thou mayest reign over
all that thine heart desireth. And David sent
Abner away; and he went in peace.
22 ¶ And, behold, the servants of David
and Joab came from *pursuing* a troop, and
brought in a great spoil with them: but
Abner *was* not with David in Hebron; for
he had sent him away, and he was gone
in peace.
23 When Joab and all the host that *was*
with him were come, they told Joab, saying, Abner the son of Ner came to the king,
and he hath sent him away, and he is gone
in peace.
24 Then Joab came to the king, and said,
What hast thou done? behold, Abner came
unto thee; why *is* it *that* thou hast sent him
away, and he is quite gone?
25 Thou knowest Abner the son of Ner, that
he came to deceive thee, and to know thy
going out and thy coming in, and to know
all that thou doest.
26 And when Joab was come out from
David, he sent messengers after Abner,
which brought him again from the well of
Sirah: but David knew *it* not.
27 And when Abner was returned to
Hebron, Joab took him aside in the gate
to speak with him quietly, and smote him
there under the fifth *rib,* that he died, for
the blood of Asahel his brother.
28 ¶ And afterward when David heard *it,* he
said, I and my kingdom *are* guiltless before
the LORD for ever from the blood of Abner
the son of Ner:
29 Let it rest on the head of Joab, and on
all his father's house; and let there not fail
from the house of Joab one that hath an
issue, or that is a leper, or that leaneth on
a staff, or that falleth on the sword, or that
lacketh bread.
30 So Joab and Abishai his brother slew
Abner, because he had slain their brother
Asahel at Gibeon in the battle.
31 ¶ And David said to Joab, and to all
the people that *were* with him, Rend your
clothes, and gird you with sackcloth, and
mourn before Abner. And king David *himself*
followed the bier.
32 And they buried Abner in Hebron: and
the king lifted up his voice, and wept at the
grave of Abner; and all the people wept.
33 And the king lamented over Abner, and
said, Died Abner as a fool dieth?
34 Thy hands *were* not bound, nor thy feet
put into fetters: as a man falleth before
wicked men, *so* fellest thou. And all the
people wept again over him.
35 And when all the people came to cause
David to eat meat while it was yet day, David
sware, saying, So do God to me, and more
also, if I taste bread, or ought else, till the
sun be down.
36 And all the people took notice *of it,* and
it pleased them: as whatsoever the king did
pleased all the people.
37 For all the people and all Israel under-

stood that day that it was not of the king to slay Abner the son of Ner.

38 And the king said unto his servants, Know ye not that there is a prince and a great man fallen this day in Israel?

39 And I *am* this day weak, though anointed king; and these men the sons of Zeruiah *be* too hard for me: the LORD shall reward the doer of evil according to his wickedness.

2 Samuel 4

1 And when Saul's son heard that Abner was dead in Hebron, his hands were feeble, and all the Israelites were troubled.

2 And Saul's son had two men *that were* captains of bands: the name of the one *was* Baanah, and the name of the other Rechab, the sons of Rimmon a Beerothite, of the children of Benjamin: (for Beeroth also was reckoned to Benjamin:

3 And the Beerothites fled to Gittaim, and were sojourners there until this day.)

4 And Jonathan, Saul's son, had a son *that was* lame of *his* feet. He was five years old when the tidings came of Saul and Jonathan out of Jezreel, and his nurse took him up, and fled: and it came to pass, as she made haste to flee, that he fell, and became lame. And his name *was* Mephibosheth.

5 And the sons of Rimmon the Beerothite, Rechab and Baanah, went, and came about the heat of the day to the house of Ish-bosheth, who lay on a bed at noon.

6 And they came thither into the midst of the house, *as though* they would have fetched wheat; and they smote him under the fifth *rib:* and Rechab and Baanah his brother escaped.

7 For when they came into the house, he lay on his bed in his bedchamber, and they smote him, and slew him, and beheaded him, and took his head, and gat them away through the plain all night.

8 And they brought the head of Ish-bosheth unto David to Hebron, and said to the king, Behold the head of Ish-bosheth the son of Saul thine enemy, which sought thy life; and the LORD hath avenged my lord the king this day of Saul, and of his seed.

9 ¶ And David answered Rechab and Baanah his brother, the sons of Rimmon the Beerothite, and said unto them, *As* the LORD liveth, who hath redeemed my soul out of all adversity,

10 When one told me, saying, Behold, Saul is dead, thinking to have brought good tidings, I took hold of him, and slew him in Ziklag, who *thought* that I would have given him a reward for his tidings:

11 How much more, when wicked men have slain a righteous person in his own house upon his bed? shall I not therefore now require his blood of your hand, and take you away from the earth?

12 And David commanded his young men, and they slew them, and cut off their hands and their feet, and hanged *them* up over the pool in Hebron. But they took the head of Ish-bosheth, and buried *it* in the sepulchre of Abner in Hebron.

2 Samuel 5

1 Then came all the tribes of Israel to David unto Hebron, and spake, saying, Behold, we *are* thy bone and thy flesh.

2 Also in time past, when Saul was king over us, thou wast he that leddest out and broughtest in Israel: and the LORD said to thee, Thou shalt feed my people Israel, and thou shalt be a captain over Israel.

3 So all the elders of Israel came to the king to Hebron; and king David made a league with them in Hebron before the LORD: and they anointed David king over Israel.

4 ¶ David *was* thirty years old when he began to reign, *and* he reigned forty years.

5 In Hebron he reigned over Judah seven years and six months: and in Jerusalem he reigned thirty and three years over all Israel and Judah.

6 ¶ And the king and his men went to Jerusalem unto the Jebusites, the inhabitants of the land: which spake unto David, saying, Except thou take away the blind and the lame, thou shalt not come in hither: thinking, David cannot come in hither.

7 Nevertheless David took the strong hold of Zion: the same *is* the city of David.

8 And David said on that day, Whosoever getteth up to the gutter, and smiteth the Jebusites, and the lame and the blind, *that are* hated of David's soul, *he shall be chief and captain.* Wherefore they said, The blind and the lame shall not come into the house.

9 So David dwelt in the fort, and called it the

city of David. And David built round about
from Millo and inward.
10 And David went on, and grew great, and
the LORD God of hosts *was* with him.
11 ¶ And Hiram king of Tyre sent messengers to David, and cedar trees, and carpenters, and masons: and they built David
an house.
12 And David perceived that the LORD had
established him king over Israel, and that
he had exalted his kingdom for his people
Israel's sake.
13 ¶ And David took *him* more concubines
and wives out of Jerusalem, after he was
come from Hebron: and there were yet sons
and daughters born to David.
14 And these *be* the names of those that
were born unto him in Jerusalem; Shammua,
and Shobab, and Nathan, and Solomon,
15 Ibhar also, and Elishua, and Nepheg,
and Japhia,
16 And Elishama, and Eliada, and Eliphalet.
17 ¶ But when the Philistines heard that
they had anointed David king over Israel,
all the Philistines came up to seek David;
and David heard *of it*, and went down to
the hold.
18 The Philistines also came and spread
themselves in the valley of Rephaim.
19 And David inquired of the LORD, saying,
Shall I go up to the Philistines? wilt thou
deliver them into mine hand? And the LORD
said unto David, Go up: for I will doubtless
deliver the Philistines into thine hand.
20 And David came to Baal-perazim, and
David smote them there, and said, The
LORD hath broken forth upon mine enemies before me, as the breach of waters.
Therefore he called the name of that place
Baal-perazim.
21 And there they left their images, and
David and his men burned them.
22 ¶ And the Philistines came up yet again,
and spread themselves in the valley of
Rephaim.
23 And when David inquired of the LORD,
he said, Thou shalt not go up; *but* fetch a
compass behind them, and come upon them
over against the mulberry trees.
24 And let it be, when thou hearest the
sound of a going in the tops of the mulberry
trees, that then thou shalt bestir thyself: for
then shall the LORD go out before thee, to
smite the host of the Philistines.
25 And David did so, as the LORD had commanded him; and smote the Philistines from
Geba until thou come to Gazer.

2 Samuel 6

1 Again, David gathered together all *the*
chosen *men* of Israel, thirty thousand.
2 And David arose, and went with all the
people that *were* with him from Baale of
Judah, to bring up from thence the ark of
God, whose name is called by the name of
the LORD of hosts that dwelleth *between*
the cherubims.
3 And they set the ark of God upon a new
cart, and brought it out of the house of
Abinadab that *was* in Gibeah: and Uzzah
and Ahio, the sons of Abinadab, drave the
new cart.
4 And they brought it out of the house of
Abinadab which *was* at Gibeah, accompa-
nying the ark of God: and Ahio went before
the ark.
5 And David and all the house of Israel
played before the LORD on all manner of
instruments made of fir wood, even on
harps, and on psalteries, and on timbrels,
and on cornets, and on cymbals.
6 ¶ And when they came to Nachon's
threshingfloor, Uzzah put forth *his hand* to
the ark of God, and took hold of it; for the
oxen shook *it*.
7 And the anger of the LORD was kindled
against Uzzah; and God smote him there
for *his* error; and there he died by the ark
of God.
8 And David was displeased, because the
LORD had made a breach upon Uzzah: and
he called the name of the place Perez-uzzah
to this day.
9 And David was afraid of the LORD that
day, and said, How shall the ark of the LORD
come to me?
10 So David would not remove the ark of
the LORD unto him into the city of David:
but David carried it aside into the house of
Obed-edom the Gittite.
11 And the ark of the LORD continued in
the house of Obed-edom the Gittite three
months: and the LORD blessed Obed-edom,
and all his household.
12 ¶ And it was told king David, saying, The

LORD hath blessed the house of Obed-edom, and all that *pertaineth* unto him, because of the ark of God. So David went and brought up the ark of God from the house of Obed-edom into the city of David with gladness.

13 And it was *so*, that when they that bare the ark of the LORD had gone six paces, he sacrificed oxen and fatlings.

14 And David danced before the LORD with all *his* might; and David *was* girded with a linen ephod.

15 So David and all the house of Israel brought up the ark of the LORD with shouting, and with the sound of the trumpet.

16 And as the ark of the LORD came into the city of David, Michal Saul's daughter looked through a window, and saw king David leaping and dancing before the LORD; and she despised him in her heart.

17 ¶ And they brought in the ark of the LORD, and set it in his place, in the midst of the tabernacle that David had pitched for it: and David offered burnt offerings and peace offerings before the LORD.

18 And as soon as David had made an end of offering burnt offerings and peace offerings, he blessed the people in the name of the LORD of hosts.

19 And he dealt among all the people, *even* among the whole multitude of Israel, as well to the women as men, to every one a cake of bread, and a good piece *of flesh*, and a flagon *of wine*. So all the people departed every one to his house.

20 ¶ Then David returned to bless his household. And Michal the daughter of Saul came out to meet David, and said, How glorious was the king of Israel to day, who uncovered himself to day in the eyes of the handmaids of his servants, as one of the vain fellows shamelessly uncovereth himself!

21 And David said unto Michal, *It was* before the LORD, which chose me before thy father, and before all his house, to appoint me ruler over the people of the LORD, over Israel: therefore will I play before the LORD.

22 And I will yet be more vile than thus, and will be base in mine own sight: and of the maidservants which thou hast spoken of, of them shall I be had in honour.

23 Therefore Michal the daughter of Saul had no child unto the day of her death.

2 Samuel 7

1 And it came to pass, when the king sat in his house, and the LORD had given him rest round about from all his enemies;

2 That the king said unto Nathan the prophet, See now, I dwell in an house of cedar, but the ark of God dwelleth within curtains.

3 And Nathan said to the king, Go, do all that *is* in thine heart; for the LORD *is* with thee.

4 ¶ And it came to pass that night, that the word of the LORD came unto Nathan, saying,

5 Go and tell my servant David, Thus saith the LORD, Shalt thou build me an house for me to dwell in?

6 Whereas I have not dwelt in *any* house since the time that I brought up the children of Israel out of Egypt, even to this day, but have walked in a tent and in a tabernacle.

7 In all *the places* wherein I have walked with all the children of Israel spake I a word with any of the tribes of Israel, whom I commanded to feed my people Israel, saying, Why build ye not me an house of cedar?

8 Now therefore so shalt thou say unto my servant David, Thus saith the LORD of hosts, I took thee from the sheepcote, from following the sheep, to be ruler over my people, over Israel:

9 And I was with thee whithersoever thou wentest, and have cut off all thine enemies out of thy sight, and have made thee a great name, like unto the name of the great *men* that *are* in the earth.

10 Moreover I will appoint a place for my people Israel, and will plant them, that they may dwell in a place of their own, and move no more; neither shall the children of wickedness afflict them any more, as beforetime,

11 And as since the time that I commanded judges *to be* over my people Israel, and have caused thee to rest from all thine enemies. Also the LORD telleth thee that he will make thee an house.

12 ¶ And when thy days be fulfilled, and thou shalt sleep with thy fathers, I will set up thy seed after thee, which shall proceed out of thy bowels, and I will establish his kingdom.

13 He shall build an house for my name, and I will stablish the throne of his kingdom for ever.

14 I will be his father, and he shall be my

son. If he commit iniquity, I will chasten him
with the rod of men, and with the stripes of
the children of men:
15 But my mercy shall not depart away from
him, as I took *it* from Saul, whom I put away
before thee.
16 And thine house and thy kingdom shall be
established for ever before thee: thy throne
shall be established for ever.
17 According to all these words, and according
to all this vision, so did Nathan speak
unto David.
18 ¶ Then went king David in, and sat before
the LORD, and he said, Who *am* I, O Lord
GOD? and what *is* my house, that thou hast
brought me hitherto?
19 And this was yet a small thing in thy sight,
O Lord GOD; but thou hast spoken also of thy
servant's house for a great while to come.
And *is* this the manner of man, O Lord GOD?
20 And what can David say more unto thee?
for thou, Lord GOD, knowest thy servant.
21 For thy word's sake, and according to
thine own heart, hast thou done all these
great things, to make thy servant know
them.
22 Wherefore thou art great, O LORD God:
for *there is* none like thee, neither *is there*
any God beside thee, according to all that
we have heard with our ears.
23 And what one nation in the earth *is* like
thy people, *even* like Israel, whom God went
to redeem for a people to himself, and to
make him a name, and to do for you great
things and terrible, for thy land, before thy
people, which thou redeemedst to thee
from Egypt, *from* the nations and their gods?
24 For thou hast confirmed to thyself thy
people Israel *to be* a people unto thee for
ever: and thou, LORD, art become their God.
25 And now, O LORD God, the word that
thou hast spoken concerning thy servant,
and concerning his house, establish *it* for
ever, and do as thou hast said.
26 And let thy name be magnified for ever,
saying, The LORD of hosts *is* the God over
Israel: and let the house of thy servant David
be established before thee.
27 For thou, O LORD of hosts, God of Israel,
hast revealed to thy servant, saying, I will
build thee an house: therefore hath thy servant
found in his heart to pray this prayer
unto thee.
28 And now, O Lord GOD, thou *art* that
God, and thy words be true, and thou hast
promised this goodness unto thy servant:
29 Therefore now let it please thee to bless
the house of thy servant, that it may continue
for ever before thee: for thou, O Lord
GOD, hast spoken *it*: and with thy blessing let
the house of thy servant be blessed for ever.

2 Samuel 8

1 And after this it came to pass, that David
smote the Philistines, and subdued them:
and David took Metheg-ammah out of the
hand of the Philistines.
2 And he smote Moab, and measured
them with a line, casting them down to the
ground; even with two lines measured he to
put to death, and with one full line to keep
alive. And *so* the Moabites became David's
servants, *and* brought gifts.
3 ¶ David smote also Hadadezer, the son of
Rehob, king of Zobah, as he went to recover
his border at the river Euphrates.
4 And David took from him a thousand
chariots, and seven hundred horsemen,
and twenty thousand footmen: and David
houghed all the chariot *horses*, but reserved
of them *for* an hundred chariots.
5 And when the Syrians of Damascus came
to succour Hadadezer king of Zobah, David
slew of the Syrians two and twenty thousand
men.
6 Then David put garrisons in Syria of
Damascus: and the Syrians became servants
to David, *and* brought gifts. And the LORD
preserved David whithersoever he went.
7 And David took the shields of gold that
were on the servants of Hadadezer, and
brought them to Jerusalem.
8 And from Betah, and from Berothai, cities
of Hadadezer, king David took exceeding
much brass.
9 ¶ When Toi king of Hamath heard that
David had smitten all the host of Hadadezer,
10 Then Toi sent Joram his son unto king
David, to salute him, and to bless him,
because he had fought against Hadadezer,
and smitten him: for Hadadezer had wars
with Toi. And *Joram* brought with him
vessels of silver, and vessels of gold, and
vessels of brass:
11 Which also king David did dedicate unto
the LORD, with the silver and gold that

he had dedicated of all nations which he
subdued;
12 Of Syria, and of Moab, and of the children of Ammon, and of the Philistines, and
of Amalek, and of the spoil of Hadadezer,
son of Rehob, king of Zobah.
13 And David gat *him* a name when he
returned from smiting of the Syrians in the
valley of salt, *being* eighteen thousand *men.*
14 ¶ And he put garrisons in Edom; throughout all Edom put he garrisons, and all they
of Edom became David's servants. And
the LORD preserved David whithersoever
he went.
15 And David reigned over all Israel; and
David executed judgment and justice unto
all his people.
16 And Joab the son of Zeruiah *was* over
the host; and Jehoshaphat the son of Ahilud
was recorder;
17 And Zadok the son of Ahitub, and Ahimelech the son of Abiathar, *were* the priests;
and Seraiah *was* the scribe;
18 And Benaiah the son of Jehoiada *was over*
both the Cherethites and the Pelethites; and
David's sons were chief rulers.

2 Samuel 9

1 And David said, Is there yet any that is left
of the house of Saul, that I may shew him
kindness for Jonathan's sake?
2 And *there was* of the house of Saul a
servant whose name *was* Ziba. And when
they had called him unto David, the king
said unto him, *Art* thou Ziba? And he said,
Thy servant *is he.*
3 And the king said, *Is* there not yet any of
the house of Saul, that I may shew the kindness of God unto him? And Ziba said unto
the king, Jonathan hath yet a son, *which is*
lame on *his* feet.
4 And the king said unto him, Where *is* he?
And Ziba said unto the king, Behold, he *is*
in the house of Machir, the son of Ammiel,
in Lo-debar.
5 ¶ Then king David sent, and fetched him
out of the house of Machir, the son of
Ammiel, from Lo-debar.
6 Now when Mephibosheth, the son of
Jonathan, the son of Saul, was come unto
David, he fell on his face, and did reverence.
And David said, Mephibosheth. And he
answered, Behold thy servant!
7 ¶ And David said unto him, Fear not: for I
will surely shew thee kindness for Jonathan
thy father's sake, and will restore thee all
the land of Saul thy father; and thou shalt
eat bread at my table continually.
8 And he bowed himself, and said, What *is*
thy servant, that thou shouldest look upon
such a dead dog as I *am?*
9 ¶ Then the king called to Ziba, Saul's servant, and said unto him, I have given unto
thy master's son all that pertained to Saul
and to all his house.
10 Thou therefore, and thy sons, and thy
servants, shall till the land for him, and thou
shalt bring in *the fruits,* that thy master's son
may have food to eat: but Mephibosheth
thy master's son shall eat bread alway at
my table. Now Ziba had fifteen sons and
twenty servants.
11 Then said Ziba unto the king, According
to all that my lord the king hath commanded
his servant, so shall thy servant do. As for
Mephibosheth, *said the king,* he shall eat at
my table, as one of the king's sons.
12 And Mephibosheth had a young son,
whose name *was* Micha. And all that dwelt
in the house of Ziba *were* servants unto
Mephibosheth.
13 So Mephibosheth dwelt in Jerusalem:
for he did eat continually at the king's table;
and was lame on both his feet.

2 Samuel 10

1 And it came to pass after this, that the king
of the children of Ammon died, and Hanun
his son reigned in his stead.
2 Then said David, I will shew kindness unto
Hanun the son of Nahash, as his father
shewed kindness unto me. And David sent
to comfort him by the hand of his servants
for his father. And David's servants came
into the land of the children of Ammon.
3 And the princes of the children of Ammon
said unto Hanun their lord, Thinkest thou
that David doth honour thy father, that he
hath sent comforters unto thee? hath not
David *rather* sent his servants unto thee,
to search the city, and to spy it out, and to
overthrow it?
4 Wherefore Hanun took David's servants,
and shaved off the one half of their beards,
and cut off their garments in the middle,
even to their buttocks, and sent them away.

5 When they told *it* unto David, he sent to meet them, because the men were greatly ashamed: and the king said, Tarry at Jericho until your beards be grown, and *then* return.
6 ¶ And when the children of Ammon saw that they stank before David, the children of Ammon sent and hired the Syrians of Beth-rehob, and the Syrians of Zoba, twenty thousand footmen, and of king Maacah a thousand men, and of Ish-tob twelve thousand men.
7 And when David heard of *it*, he sent Joab, and all the host of the mighty men.
8 And the children of Ammon came out, and put the battle in array at the entering in of the gate: and the Syrians of Zoba, and of Rehob, and Ish-tob, and Maacah, *were* by themselves in the field.
9 When Joab saw that the front of the battle was against him before and behind, he chose of all the choice *men* of Israel, and put *them* in array against the Syrians:
10 And the rest of the people he delivered into the hand of Abishai his brother, that he might put *them* in array against the children of Ammon.
11 And he said, If the Syrians be too strong for me, then thou shalt help me: but if the children of Ammon be too strong for thee, then I will come and help thee.
12 Be of good courage, and let us play the men for our people, and for the cities of our God: and the LORD do that which seemeth him good.
13 And Joab drew nigh, and the people that *were* with him, unto the battle against the Syrians: and they fled before him.
14 And when the children of Ammon saw that the Syrians were fled, then fled they also before Abishai, and entered into the city. So Joab returned from the children of Ammon, and came to Jerusalem.
15 ¶ And when the Syrians saw that they were smitten before Israel, they gathered themselves together.
16 And Hadarezer sent, and brought out the Syrians that *were* beyond the river: and they came to Helam; and Shobach the captain of the host of Hadarezer *went* before them.
17 And when it was told David, he gathered all Israel together, and passed over Jordan, and came to Helam. And the Syrians set themselves in array against David, and fought with him.
18 And the Syrians fled before Israel; and David slew *the men of* seven hundred chariots of the Syrians, and forty thousand horsemen, and smote Shobach the captain of their host, who died there.
19 And when all the kings *that were* servants to Hadarezer saw that they were smitten before Israel, they made peace with Israel, and served them. So the Syrians feared to help the children of Ammon any more.

2 Samuel 11

1 And it came to pass, after the year was expired, at the time when kings go forth *to battle*, that David sent Joab, and his servants with him, and all Israel; and they destroyed the children of Ammon, and besieged Rabbah. But David tarried still at Jerusalem.
2 ¶ And it came to pass in an eveningtide, that David arose from off his bed, and walked upon the roof of the king's house: and from the roof he saw a woman washing herself; and the woman *was* very beautiful to look upon.
3 And David sent and inquired after the woman. And *one* said, *Is* not this Bath-sheba, the daughter of Eliam, the wife of Uriah the Hittite?
4 And David sent messengers, and took her; and she came in unto him, and he lay with her; for she was purified from her uncleanness: and she returned unto her house.
5 And the woman conceived, and sent and told David, and said, I *am* with child.
6 ¶ And David sent to Joab, *saying*, Send me Uriah the Hittite. And Joab sent Uriah to David.
7 And when Uriah was come unto him, David demanded *of him* how Joab did, and how the people did, and how the war prospered.
8 And David said to Uriah, Go down to thy house, and wash thy feet. And Uriah departed out of the king's house, and there followed him a mess *of meat* from the king.
9 But Uriah slept at the door of the king's house with all the servants of his lord, and went not down to his house.
10 And when they had told David, saying, Uriah went not down unto his house, David said unto Uriah, Camest thou not from *thy*

journey? why *then* didst thou not go down
unto thine house?
11 And Uriah said unto David, The ark, and
Israel, and Judah, abide in tents; and my
lord Joab, and the servants of my lord, are
encamped in the open fields; shall I then go
into mine house, to eat and to drink, and to
lie with my wife? *as* thou livest, and *as* thy
soul liveth, I will not do this thing.
12 And David said to Uriah, Tarry here to day
also, and to morrow I will let thee depart.
So Uriah abode in Jerusalem that day, and
the morrow.
13 And when David had called him, he did
eat and drink before him; and he made him
drunk: and at even he went out to lie on his
bed with the servants of his lord, but went
not down to his house.
14 ¶ And it came to pass in the morning,
that David wrote a letter to Joab, and sent
it by the hand of Uriah.
15 And he wrote in the letter, saying, Set ye
Uriah in the forefront of the hottest battle,
and retire ye from him, that he may be
smitten, and die.
16 And it came to pass, when Joab observed
the city, that he assigned Uriah unto a place
where he knew that valiant men *were*.
17 And the men of the city went out, and
fought with Joab: and there fell *some* of the
people of the servants of David; and Uriah
the Hittite died also.
18 ¶ Then Joab sent and told David all the
things concerning the war;
19 And charged the messenger, saying,
When thou hast made an end of telling the
matters of the war unto the king,
20 And if so be that the king's wrath
arise, and he say unto thee, Wherefore
approached ye so nigh unto the city when
ye did fight? knew ye not that they would
shoot from the wall?
21 Who smote Abimelech the son of Jerub-
besheth? did not a woman cast a piece of a
millstone upon him from the wall, that he
died in Thebez? why went ye nigh the wall?
then say thou, Thy servant Uriah the Hittite
is dead also.
22 ¶ So the messenger went, and came and
shewed David all that Joab had sent him for.
23 And the messenger said unto David,
Surely the men prevailed against us, and
came out unto us into the field, and we
were upon them even unto the entering
of the gate.
24 And the shooters shot from off the wall
upon thy servants; and *some* of the king's
servants be dead, and thy servant Uriah the
Hittite is dead also.
25 Then David said unto the messenger,
Thus shalt thou say unto Joab, Let not this
thing displease thee, for the sword devoureth one as well as another: make thy
battle more strong against the city, and
overthrow it: and encourage thou him.
26 ¶ And when the wife of Uriah heard that
Uriah her husband was dead, she mourned
for her husband.
27 And when the mourning was past, David
sent and fetched her to his house, and she
became his wife, and bare him a son. But
the thing that David had done displeased
the LORD.

2 Samuel 12

1 And the LORD sent Nathan unto David.
And he came unto him, and said unto him,
There were two men in one city; the one
rich, and the other poor.
2 The rich *man* had exceeding many flocks
and herds:
3 But the poor *man* had nothing, save one
little ewe lamb, which he had bought and
nourished up: and it grew up together with
him, and with his children; it did eat of his
own meat, and drank of his own cup, and
lay in his bosom, and was unto him as a
daughter.
4 And there came a traveller unto the rich
man, and he spared to take of his own flock
and of his own herd, to dress for the wayfaring man that was come unto him; but took
the poor man's lamb, and dressed it for the
man that was come to him.
5 And David's anger was greatly kindled
against the man; and he said to Nathan, *As*
the LORD liveth, the man that hath done this
thing shall surely die:
6 And he shall restore the lamb fourfold,
because he did this thing, and because he
had no pity.
7 ¶ And Nathan said to David, Thou *art* the
man. Thus saith the LORD God of Israel, I
anointed thee king over Israel, and I delivered thee out of the hand of Saul;
8 And I gave thee thy master's house, and

thy master's wives into thy bosom, and gave
thee the house of Israel and of Judah; and if
that had been too little, I would moreover
have given unto thee such and such things.
9 Wherefore hast thou despised the commandment of the LORD, to do evil in his
sight? thou hast killed Uriah the Hittite with
the sword, and hast taken his wife *to be* thy
wife, and hast slain him with the sword of
the children of Ammon.
10 Now therefore the sword shall never
depart from thine house; because thou
hast despised me, and hast taken the wife
of Uriah the Hittite to be thy wife.
11 Thus saith the LORD, Behold, I will raise up
evil against thee out of thine own house, and
I will take thy wives before thine eyes, and
give *them* unto thy neighbour, and he shall
lie with thy wives in the sight of this sun.
12 For thou didst *it* secretly: but I will do this
thing before all Israel, and before the sun.
13 And David said unto Nathan, I have
sinned against the LORD. And Nathan said
unto David, The LORD also hath put away
thy sin; thou shalt not die.
14 Howbeit, because by this deed thou hast
given great occasion to the enemies of the
LORD to blaspheme, the child also *that is*
born unto thee shall surely die.
15 ¶ And Nathan departed unto his house.
And the LORD struck the child that Uriah's
wife bare unto David, and it was very sick.
16 David therefore besought God for the
child; and David fasted, and went in, and
lay all night upon the earth.
17 And the elders of his house arose, *and*
went to him, to raise him up from the earth:
but he would not, neither did he eat bread
with them.
18 And it came to pass on the seventh day,
that the child died. And the servants of
David feared to tell him that the child was
dead: for they said, Behold, while the child
was yet alive, we spake unto him, and he
would not hearken unto our voice: how will
he then vex himself, if we tell him that the
child is dead?
19 But when David saw that his servants
whispered, David perceived that the child
was dead: therefore David said unto his
servants, Is the child dead? And they said,
He is dead.
20 Then David arose from the earth, and
washed, and anointed *himself*, and changed
his apparel, and came into the house of the
LORD, and worshipped: then he came to his
own house; and when he required, they set
bread before him, and he did eat.
21 Then said his servants unto him, What
thing *is* this that thou hast done? thou didst
fast and weep for the child, *while it was*
alive; but when the child was dead, thou
didst rise and eat bread.
22 And he said, While the child was yet alive,
I fasted and wept: for I said, Who can tell
whether GOD will be gracious to me, that
the child may live?
23 But now he is dead, wherefore should I
fast? can I bring him back again? I shall go to
him, but he shall not return to me.
24 ¶ And David comforted Bath-sheba his
wife, and went in unto her, and lay with her:
and she bare a son, and he called his name
Solomon: and the LORD loved him.
25 And he sent by the hand of Nathan the
prophet; and he called his name Jedidiah,
because of the LORD.
26 ¶ And Joab fought against Rabbah of the
children of Ammon, and took the royal city.
27 And Joab sent messengers to David, and
said, I have fought against Rabbah, and have
taken the city of waters.
28 Now therefore gather the rest of the
people together, and encamp against the
city, and take it: lest I take the city, and it
be called after my name.
29 And David gathered all the people
together, and went to Rabbah, and fought
against it, and took it.
30 And he took their king's crown from off
his head, the weight whereof *was* a talent
of gold with the precious stones: and it was
set on David's head. And he brought forth
the spoil of the city in great abundance.
31 And he brought forth the people that
were therein, and put *them* under saws,
and under harrows of iron, and under axes
of iron, and made them pass through the
brickkiln: and thus did he unto all the cities
of the children of Ammon. So David and all
the people returned unto Jerusalem.

2 Samuel 13

1 And it came to pass after this, that Absalom the son of David had a fair sister, whose

name *was* Tamar; and Amnon the son of
David loved her.
2 And Amnon was so vexed, that he fell sick
for his sister Tamar; for she *was* a virgin;
and Amnon thought it hard for him to do
any thing to her.
3 But Amnon had a friend, whose name
was Jonadab, the son of Shimeah David's
brother: and Jonadab *was* a very subtil man.
4 And he said unto him, Why *art* thou, *being*
the king's son, lean from day to day? wilt
thou not tell me? And Amnon said unto him,
I love Tamar, my brother Absalom's sister.
5 And Jonadab said unto him, Lay thee down
on thy bed, and make thyself sick: and when
thy father cometh to see thee, say unto him,
I pray thee, let my sister Tamar come, and
give me meat, and dress the meat in my
sight, that I may see *it*, and eat *it* at her hand.
6 ¶ So Amnon lay down, and made himself
sick: and when the king was come to see
him, Amnon said unto the king, I pray thee,
let Tamar my sister come, and make me a
couple of cakes in my sight, that I may eat
at her hand.
7 Then David sent home to Tamar, saying,
Go now to thy brother Amnon's house, and
dress him meat.
8 So Tamar went to her brother Amnon's
house; and he was laid down. And she took
flour, and kneaded *it*, and made cakes in his
sight, and did bake the cakes.
9 And she took a pan, and poured *them*
out before him; but he refused to eat. And
Amnon said, Have out all men from me. And
they went out every man from him.
10 And Amnon said unto Tamar, Bring the
meat into the chamber, that I may eat of
thine hand. And Tamar took the cakes which
she had made, and brought *them* into the
chamber to Amnon her brother.
11 And when she had brought *them* unto
him to eat, he took hold of her, and said unto
her, Come lie with me, my sister.
12 And she answered him, Nay, my brother,
do not force me; for no such thing ought
to be done in Israel: do not thou this folly.
13 And I, whither shall I cause my shame
to go? and as for thee, thou shalt be as one
of the fools in Israel. Now therefore, I pray
thee, speak unto the king; for he will not
withhold me from thee.
14 Howbeit he would not hearken unto her
voice: but, being stronger than she, forced
her, and lay with her.
15 ¶ Then Amnon hated her exceedingly;
so that the hatred wherewith he hated her
was greater than the love wherewith he
had loved her. And Amnon said unto her,
Arise, be gone.
16 And she said unto him, *There is* no cause:
this evil in sending me away *is* greater than
the other that thou didst unto me. But he
would not hearken unto her.
17 Then he called his servant that ministered
unto him, and said, Put now this *woman*
out from me, and bolt the door after her.
18 And *she had* a garment of divers colours
upon her: for with such robes were the
king's daughters *that were* virgins apparelled. Then his servant brought her out, and
bolted the door after her.
19 ¶ And Tamar put ashes on her head, and
rent her garment of divers colours that *was*
on her, and laid her hand on her head, and
went on crying.
20 And Absalom her brother said unto
her, Hath Amnon thy brother been with
thee? but hold now thy peace, my sister:
he *is* thy brother; regard not this thing. So
Tamar remained desolate in her brother
Absalom's house.
21 ¶ But when king David heard of all these
things, he was very wroth.
22 And Absalom spake unto his brother
Amnon neither good nor bad: for Absalom
hated Amnon, because he had forced his
sister Tamar.
23 ¶ And it came to pass after two full
years, that Absalom had sheepshearers in
Baal-hazor, which *is* beside Ephraim: and
Absalom invited all the king's sons.
24 And Absalom came to the king, and said,
Behold now, thy servant hath sheepshearers; let the king, I beseech thee, and his
servants go with thy servant.
25 And the king said to Absalom, Nay,
my son, let us not all now go, lest we be
chargeable unto thee. And he pressed him:
howbeit he would not go, but blessed him.
26 Then said Absalom, If not, I pray thee, let
my brother Amnon go with us. And the king
said unto him, Why should he go with thee?
27 But Absalom pressed him, that he let
Amnon and all the king's sons go with him.
28 ¶ Now Absalom had commanded his ser-

vants, saying, Mark ye now when Amnon's
heart is merry with wine, and when I say
unto you, Smite Amnon; then kill him, fear
not: have not I commanded you? be courageous, and be valiant.
29 And the servants of Absalom did unto
Amnon as Absalom had commanded. Then
all the king's sons arose, and every man gat
him up upon his mule, and fled.
30 ¶ And it came to pass, while they were in
the way, that tidings came to David, saying,
Absalom hath slain all the king's sons, and
there is not one of them left.
31 Then the king arose, and tare his garments, and lay on the earth; and all his
servants stood by with their clothes rent.
32 And Jonadab, the son of Shimeah David's
brother, answered and said, Let not my lord
suppose *that* they have slain all the young
men the king's sons; for Amnon only is dead:
for by the appointment of Absalom this
hath been determined from the day that
he forced his sister Tamar.
33 Now therefore let not my lord the king
take the thing to his heart, to think that all
the king's sons are dead: for Amnon only
is dead.
34 But Absalom fled. And the young man
that kept the watch lifted up his eyes, and
looked, and, behold, there came much people by the way of the hill side behind him.
35 And Jonadab said unto the king, Behold,
the king's sons come: as thy servant said,
so it is.
36 And it came to pass, as soon as he had
made an end of speaking, that, behold, the
king's sons came, and lifted up their voice
and wept: and the king also and all his servants wept very sore.
37 ¶ But Absalom fled, and went to Talmai,
the son of Ammihud, king of Geshur. And
David mourned for his son every day.
38 So Absalom fled, and went to Geshur,
and was there three years.
39 And *the soul of* king David longed to go
forth unto Absalom: for he was comforted
concerning Amnon, seeing he was dead.

2 Samuel 14

1 Now Joab the son of Zeruiah perceived
that the king's heart *was* toward Absalom.
2 And Joab sent to Tekoah, and fetched
thence a wise woman, and said unto her, I
pray thee, feign thyself to be a mourner, and
put on now mourning apparel, and anoint
not thyself with oil, but be as a woman that
had a long time mourned for the dead:
3 And come to the king, and speak on this
manner unto him. So Joab put the words
in her mouth.
4 ¶ And when the woman of Tekoah spake to
the king, she fell on her face to the ground,
and did obeisance, and said, Help, O king.
5 And the king said unto her, What aileth
thee? And she answered, I *am* indeed a
widow woman, and mine husband is dead.
6 And thy handmaid had two sons, and they
two strove together in the field, and *there
was* none to part them, but the one smote
the other, and slew him.
7 And, behold, the whole family is risen
against thine handmaid, and they said,
Deliver him that smote his brother, that we
may kill him, for the life of his brother whom
he slew; and we will destroy the heir also:
and so they shall quench my coal which is
left, and shall not leave to my husband *neither* name nor remainder upon the earth.
8 And the king said unto the woman, Go
to thine house, and I will give charge concerning thee.
9 And the woman of Tekoah said unto the
king, My lord, O king, the iniquity *be* on me,
and on my father's house: and the king and
his throne *be* guiltless.
10 And the king said, Whosoever saith *ought*
unto thee, bring him to me, and he shall not
touch thee any more.
11 Then said she, I pray thee, let the king
remember the LORD thy God, that thou
wouldest not suffer the revengers of blood
to destroy any more, lest they destroy my
son. And he said, *As* the LORD liveth, there
shall not one hair of thy son fall to the earth.
12 Then the woman said, Let thine handmaid, I pray thee, speak *one* word unto my
lord the king. And he said, Say on.
13 And the woman said, Wherefore then
hast thou thought such a thing against the
people of God? for the king doth speak this
thing as one which is faulty, in that the king
doth not fetch home again his banished.
14 For we must needs die, and *are* as water
spilt on the ground, which cannot be gathered up again; neither doth God respect *any*

person: yet doth he devise means, that his
banished be not expelled from him.
15 Now therefore that I am come to speak of
this thing unto my lord the king, *it is* because
the people have made me afraid: and thy
handmaid said, I will now speak unto the
king; it may be that the king will perform
the request of his handmaid.
16 For the king will hear, to deliver his handmaid out of the hand of the man *that would*
destroy me and my son together out of the
inheritance of God.
17 Then thine handmaid said, The word of
my lord the king shall now be comfortable:
for as an angel of God, so *is* my lord the king
to discern good and bad: therefore the LORD
thy God will be with thee.
18 Then the king answered and said unto the
woman, Hide not from me, I pray thee, the
thing that I shall ask thee. And the woman
said, Let my lord the king now speak.
19 And the king said, *Is not* the hand of
Joab with thee in all this? And the woman
answered and said, *As* thy soul liveth, my
lord the king, none can turn to the right
hand or to the left from ought that my lord
the king hath spoken: for thy servant Joab,
he bade me, and he put all these words in
the mouth of thine handmaid:
20 To fetch about this form of speech hath
thy servant Joab done this thing: and my
lord *is* wise, according to the wisdom of an
angel of God, to know all *things* that *are* in
the earth.
21 ¶ And the king said unto Joab, Behold
now, I have done this thing: go therefore,
bring the young man Absalom again.
22 And Joab fell to the ground on his face,
and bowed himself, and thanked the king:
and Joab said, To day thy servant knoweth
that I have found grace in thy sight, my lord,
O king, in that the king hath fulfilled the
request of his servant.
23 So Joab arose and went to Geshur, and
brought Absalom to Jerusalem.
24 And the king said, Let him turn to his
own house, and let him not see my face.
So Absalom returned to his own house, and
saw not the king's face.
25 ¶ But in all Israel there was none to be
so much praised as Absalom for his beauty:
from the sole of his foot even to the crown
of his head there was no blemish in him.
26 And when he polled his head, (for it was
at every year's end that he polled *it:* because
the hair was heavy on him, therefore he
polled it:) he weighed the hair of his head at
two hundred shekels after the king's weight.
27 And unto Absalom there were born three
sons, and one daughter, whose name *was*
Tamar: she was a woman of a fair countenance.
28 ¶ So Absalom dwelt two full years in
Jerusalem, and saw not the king's face.
29 Therefore Absalom sent for Joab, to have
sent him to the king; but he would not come
to him: and when he sent again the second
time, he would not come.
30 Therefore he said unto his servants, See,
Joab's field is near mine, and he hath barley
there; go and set it on fire. And Absalom's
servants set the field on fire.
31 Then Joab arose, and came to Absalom
unto *his* house, and said unto him, Wherefore have thy servants set my field on fire?
32 And Absalom answered Joab, Behold, I
sent unto thee, saying, Come hither, that I
may send thee to the king, to say, Wherefore am I come from Geshur? *it had been*
good for me *to have been* there still: now
therefore let me see the king's face; and if
there be *any* iniquity in me, let him kill me.
33 So Joab came to the king, and told him:
and when he had called for Absalom, he
came to the king, and bowed himself on
his face to the ground before the king: and
the king kissed Absalom.

2 Samuel 15

1 And it came to pass after this, that Absalom prepared him chariots and horses, and
fifty men to run before him.
2 And Absalom rose up early, and stood
beside the way of the gate: and it was *so*,
that when any man that had a controversy
came to the king for judgment, then Absalom called unto him, and said, Of what city
art thou? And he said, Thy servant *is* of one
of the tribes of Israel.
3 And Absalom said unto him, See, thy matters *are* good and right; but *there is* no man
deputed of the king to hear thee.
4 Absalom said moreover, Oh that I were
made judge in the land, that every man
which hath any suit or cause might come
unto me, and I would do him justice!

5 And it was *so*, that when any man came nigh *to him* to do him obeisance, he put forth his hand, and took him, and kissed him.
6 And on this manner did Absalom to all Israel that came to the king for judgment: so Absalom stole the hearts of the men of Israel.
7 ¶ And it came to pass after forty years, that Absalom said unto the king, I pray thee, let me go and pay my vow, which I have vowed unto the LORD, in Hebron.
8 For thy servant vowed a vow while I abode at Geshur in Syria, saying, If the LORD shall bring me again indeed to Jerusalem, then I will serve the LORD.
9 And the king said unto him, Go in peace. So he arose, and went to Hebron.
10 ¶ But Absalom sent spies throughout all the tribes of Israel, saying, As soon as ye hear the sound of the trumpet, then ye shall say, Absalom reigneth in Hebron.
11 And with Absalom went two hundred men out of Jerusalem, *that were* called; and they went in their simplicity, and they knew not any thing.
12 And Absalom sent for Ahithophel the Gilonite, David's counseller, from his city, *even* from Giloh, while he offered sacrifices. And the conspiracy was strong; for the people increased continually with Absalom.
13 ¶ And there came a messenger to David, saying, The hearts of the men of Israel are after Absalom.
14 And David said unto all his servants that *were* with him at Jerusalem, Arise, and let us flee; for we shall not *else* escape from Absalom: make speed to depart, lest he overtake us suddenly, and bring evil upon us, and smite the city with the edge of the sword.
15 And the king's servants said unto the king, Behold, thy servants *are ready to do* whatsoever my lord the king shall appoint.
16 And the king went forth, and all his household after him. And the king left ten women, *which were* concubines, to keep the house.
17 And the king went forth, and all the people after him, and tarried in a place that was far off.
18 And all his servants passed on beside him; and all the Cherethites, and all the Pelethites, and all the Gittites, six hundred men which came after him from Gath, passed on before the king.
19 ¶ Then said the king to Ittai the Gittite, Wherefore goest thou also with us? return to thy place, and abide with the king: for thou *art* a stranger, and also an exile.
20 Whereas thou camest *but* yesterday, should I this day make thee go up and down with us? seeing I go whither I may, return thou, and take back thy brethren: mercy and truth *be* with thee.
21 And Ittai answered the king, and said, *As* the LORD liveth, and *as* my lord the king liveth, surely in what place my lord the king shall be, whether in death or life, even there also will thy servant be.
22 And David said to Ittai, Go and pass over. And Ittai the Gittite passed over, and all his men, and all the little ones that *were* with him.
23 And all the country wept with a loud voice, and all the people passed over: the king also himself passed over the brook Kidron, and all the people passed over, toward the way of the wilderness.
24 ¶ And lo Zadok also, and all the Levites *were* with him, bearing the ark of the covenant of God: and they set down the ark of God; and Abiathar went up, until all the people had done passing out of the city.
25 And the king said unto Zadok, Carry back the ark of God into the city: if I shall find favour in the eyes of the LORD, he will bring me again, and shew me *both* it, and his habitation:
26 But if he thus say, I have no delight in thee; behold, *here am* I, let him do to me as seemeth good unto him.
27 The king said also unto Zadok the priest, *Art not* thou a seer? return into the city in peace, and your two sons with you, Ahimaaz thy son, and Jonathan the son of Abiathar.
28 See, I will tarry in the plain of the wilderness, until there come word from you to certify me.
29 Zadok therefore and Abiathar carried the ark of God again to Jerusalem: and they tarried there.
30 ¶ And David went up by the ascent of *mount* Olivet, and wept as he went up, and had his head covered, and he went barefoot: and all the people that *was* with

him covered every man his head, and they
went up, weeping as they went up.
31 ¶ And *one* told David, saying, Ahithophel
is among the conspirators with Absalom.
And David said, O LORD, I pray thee, turn
the counsel of Ahithophel into foolishness.
32 ¶ And it came to pass, that *when* David
was come to the top *of the mount*, where he
worshipped God, behold, Hushai the Archite
came to meet him with his coat rent, and
earth upon his head:
33 Unto whom David said, If thou passest
on with me, then thou shalt be a burden
unto me:
34 But if thou return to the city, and say
unto Absalom, I will be thy servant, O king;
as I *have been* thy father's servant hitherto, so *will* I now also *be* thy servant: then
mayest thou for me defeat the counsel of
Ahithophel.
35 And *hast thou* not there with thee Zadok
and Abiathar the priests? therefore it shall
be, *that* what thing soever thou shalt hear
out of the king's house, thou shalt tell *it* to
Zadok and Abiathar the priests.
36 Behold, *they have* there with them their
two sons, Ahimaaz Zadok's *son*, and Jonathan Abiathar's *son;* and by them ye shall
send unto me every thing that ye can hear.
37 So Hushai David's friend came into the
city, and Absalom came into Jerusalem.

2 Samuel 16

1 And when David was a little past the
top *of the hill*, behold, Ziba the servant of
Mephibosheth met him, with a couple of
asses saddled, and upon them two hundred
loaves of bread, and an hundred bunches of
raisins, and an hundred of summer fruits,
and a bottle of wine.
2 And the king said unto Ziba, What meanest
thou by these? And Ziba said, The asses *be*
for the king's household to ride on; and the
bread and summer fruit for the young men
to eat; and the wine, that such as be faint
in the wilderness may drink.
3 And the king said, And where *is* thy master's son? And Ziba said unto the king,
Behold, he abideth at Jerusalem: for he said,
To day shall the house of Israel restore me
the kingdom of my father.
4 Then said the king to Ziba, Behold, thine
are all that *pertained* unto Mephibosheth.
And Ziba said, I humbly beseech thee *that* I
may find grace in thy sight, my lord, O king.
5 ¶ And when king David came to Bahurim,
behold, thence came out a man of the family of the house of Saul, whose name *was*
Shimei, the son of Gera: he came forth, and
cursed still as he came.
6 And he cast stones at David, and at all the
servants of king David: and all the people
and all the mighty men *were* on his right
hand and on his left.
7 And thus said Shimei when he cursed,
Come out, come out, thou bloody man, and
thou man of Belial:
8 The LORD hath returned upon thee all the
blood of the house of Saul, in whose stead
thou hast reigned; and the LORD hath delivered the kingdom into the hand of Absalom
thy son: and, behold, thou *art taken* in thy
mischief, because thou *art* a bloody man.
9 ¶ Then said Abishai the son of Zeruiah
unto the king, Why should this dead dog
curse my lord the king? let me go over, I
pray thee, and take off his head.
10 And the king said, What have I to do with
you, ye sons of Zeruiah? so let him curse,
because the LORD hath said unto him, Curse
David. Who shall then say, Wherefore hast
thou done so?
11 And David said to Abishai, and to all his
servants, Behold, my son, which came forth
of my bowels, seeketh my life: how much
more now *may this* Benjamite *do it?* let him
alone, and let him curse; for the LORD hath
bidden him.
12 It may be that the LORD will look on mine
affliction, and that the LORD will requite me
good for his cursing this day.
13 And as David and his men went by the
way, Shimei went along on the hill's side
over against him, and cursed as he went,
and threw stones at him, and cast dust.
14 And the king, and all the people that
were with him, came weary, and refreshed
themselves there.
15 ¶ And Absalom, and all the people the
men of Israel, came to Jerusalem, and
Ahithophel with him.
16 And it came to pass, when Hushai the
Archite, David's friend, was come unto
Absalom, that Hushai said unto Absalom,
God save the king, God save the king.
17 And Absalom said to Hushai, *Is* this thy

kindness to thy friend? why wentest thou
not with thy friend?
18 And Hushai said unto Absalom, Nay; but
whom the LORD, and this people, and all the
men of Israel, choose, his will I be, and with
him will I abide.
19 And again, whom should I serve? *should*
I not *serve* in the presence of his son? as I
have served in thy father's presence, so will
I be in thy presence.
20 ¶ Then said Absalom to Ahithophel, Give
counsel among you what we shall do.
21 And Ahithophel said unto Absalom, Go
in unto thy father's concubines, which he
hath left to keep the house; and all Israel
shall hear that thou art abhorred of thy
father: then shall the hands of all that *are*
with thee be strong.
22 So they spread Absalom a tent upon
the top of the house; and Absalom went
in unto his father's concubines in the sight
of all Israel.
23 And the counsel of Ahithophel, which he
counselled in those days, *was* as if a man
had inquired at the oracle of God: so *was* all
the counsel of Ahithophel both with David
and with Absalom.

2 Samuel 17

1 Moreover Ahithophel said unto Absalom,
Let me now choose out twelve thousand
men, and I will arise and pursue after David
this night:
2 And I will come upon him while he *is* weary
and weak handed, and will make him afraid:
and all the people that *are* with him shall
flee; and I will smite the king only:
3 And I will bring back all the people unto
thee: the man whom thou seekest *is* as if all
returned: *so* all the people shall be in peace.
4 And the saying pleased Absalom well, and
all the elders of Israel.
5 Then said Absalom, Call now Hushai the
Archite also, and let us hear likewise what
he saith.
6 And when Hushai was come to Absalom,
Absalom spake unto him, saying, Ahithophel
hath spoken after this manner: shall we do
after his saying? if not; speak thou.
7 And Hushai said unto Absalom, The counsel that Ahithophel hath given *is* not good
at this time.
8 For, said Hushai, thou knowest thy father
and his men, that they *be* mighty men, and
they *be* chafed in their minds, as a bear
robbed of her whelps in the field: and thy
father *is* a man of war, and will not lodge
with the people.
9 Behold, he is hid now in some pit, or in
some *other* place: and it will come to pass,
when some of them be overthrown at the
first, that whosoever heareth it will say,
There is a slaughter among the people that
follow Absalom.
10 And he also *that is* valiant, whose heart
is as the heart of a lion, shall utterly melt:
for all Israel knoweth that thy father *is* a
mighty man, and *they* which *be* with him
are valiant men.
11 Therefore I counsel that all Israel be
generally gathered unto thee, from Dan
even to Beer-sheba, as the sand that *is* by
the sea for multitude; and that thou go to
battle in thine own person.
12 So shall we come upon him in some place
where he shall be found, and we will light
upon him as the dew falleth on the ground:
and of him and of all the men that *are* with
him there shall not be left so much as one.
13 Moreover, if he be gotten into a city, then
shall all Israel bring ropes to that city, and
we will draw it into the river, until there be
not one small stone found there.
14 And Absalom and all the men of Israel
said, The counsel of Hushai the Archite *is*
better than the counsel of Ahithophel. For
the LORD had appointed to defeat the good
counsel of Ahithophel, to the intent that the
LORD might bring evil upon Absalom.
15 ¶ Then said Hushai unto Zadok and
to Abiathar the priests, Thus and thus
did Ahithophel counsel Absalom and the
elders of Israel; and thus and thus have I
counselled.
16 Now therefore send quickly, and tell
David, saying, Lodge not this night in the
plains of the wilderness, but speedily pass
over; lest the king be swallowed up, and all
the people that *are* with him.
17 Now Jonathan and Ahimaaz stayed by
En-rogel; for they might not be seen to come
into the city: and a wench went and told
them; and they went and told king David.
18 Nevertheless a lad saw them, and told
Absalom: but they went both of them
away quickly, and came to a man's house

in Bahurim, which had a well in his court;
whither they went down.
19 And the woman took and spread a covering over the well's mouth, and spread
ground corn thereon; and the thing was
not known.
20 And when Absalom's servants came to
the woman to the house, they said, Where *is*
Ahimaaz and Jonathan? And the woman said
unto them, They be gone over the brook of
water. And when they had sought and could
not find *them*, they returned to Jerusalem.
21 And it came to pass, after they were
departed, that they came up out of the
well, and went and told king David, and said
unto David, Arise, and pass quickly over the
water: for thus hath Ahithophel counselled
against you.
22 Then David arose, and all the people that
were with him, and they passed over Jordan:
by the morning light there lacked not one of
them that was not gone over Jordan.
23 ¶ And when Ahithophel saw that his
counsel was not followed, he saddled *his*
ass, and arose, and gat him home to his
house, to his city, and put his household in
order, and hanged himself, and died, and
was buried in the sepulchre of his father.
24 Then David came to Mahanaim. And
Absalom passed over Jordan, he and all the
men of Israel with him.
25 ¶ And Absalom made Amasa captain of
the host instead of Joab: which Amasa *was*
a man's son, whose name *was* Ithra an Israelite, that went in to Abigail the daughter
of Nahash, sister to Zeruiah Joab's mother.
26 So Israel and Absalom pitched in the
land of Gilead.
27 ¶ And it came to pass, when David was
come to Mahanaim, that Shobi the son
of Nahash of Rabbah of the children of
Ammon, and Machir the son of Ammiel
of Lo-debar, and Barzillai the Gileadite of
Rogelim,
28 Brought beds, and basons, and earthen
vessels, and wheat, and barley, and flour,
and parched *corn*, and beans, and lentiles,
and parched *pulse*,
29 And honey, and butter, and sheep, and
cheese of kine, for David, and for the people
that *were* with him, to eat: for they said, The
people *is* hungry, and weary, and thirsty, in
the wilderness.

2 Samuel 18

1 And David numbered the people that *were*
with him, and set captains of thousands and
captains of hundreds over them.
2 And David sent forth a third part of the
people under the hand of Joab, and a third
part under the hand of Abishai the son of
Zeruiah, Joab's brother, and a third part
under the hand of Ittai the Gittite. And the
king said unto the people, I will surely go
forth with you myself also.
3 But the people answered, Thou shalt not
go forth: for if we flee away, they will not
care for us; neither if half of us die, will they
care for us: but now *thou art* worth ten
thousand of us: therefore now *it is* better
that thou succour us out of the city.
4 And the king said unto them, What
seemeth you best I will do. And the king
stood by the gate side, and all the people
came out by hundreds and by thousands.
5 And the king commanded Joab and Abishai
and Ittai, saying, *Deal* gently for my sake
with the young man, *even* with Absalom.
And all the people heard when the king gave
all the captains charge concerning Absalom.
6 ¶ So the people went out into the field
against Israel: and the battle was in the
wood of Ephraim;
7 Where the people of Israel were slain
before the servants of David, and there was
there a great slaughter that day of twenty
thousand *men*.
8 For the battle was there scattered over
the face of all the country: and the wood
devoured more people that day than the
sword devoured.
9 ¶ And Absalom met the servants of David.
And Absalom rode upon a mule, and the
mule went under the thick boughs of a great
oak, and his head caught hold of the oak,
and he was taken up between the heaven
and the earth; and the mule that *was* under
him went away.
10 And a certain man saw *it*, and told Joab,
and said, Behold, I saw Absalom hanged
in an oak.
11 And Joab said unto the man that told
him, And, behold, thou sawest *him*, and
why didst thou not smite him there to the
ground? and I would have given thee ten
shekels of silver, and a girdle.
12 And the man said unto Joab, Though I

should receive a thousand *shekels* of silver
in mine hand, *yet* would I not put forth
mine hand against the king's son: for in our
hearing the king charged thee and Abishai
and Ittai, saying, Beware that none *touch*
the young man Absalom.
13 Otherwise I should have wrought falsehood against mine own life: for there is no
matter hid from the king, and thou thyself
wouldest have set thyself against *me*.
14 Then said Joab, I may not tarry thus
with thee. And he took three darts in his
hand, and thrust them through the heart
of Absalom, while he *was* yet alive in the
midst of the oak.
15 And ten young men that bare Joab's
armour compassed about and smote Absalom, and slew him.
16 And Joab blew the trumpet, and the
people returned from pursuing after Israel:
for Joab held back the people.
17 And they took Absalom, and cast him
into a great pit in the wood, and laid a very
great heap of stones upon him: and all Israel
fled every one to his tent.
18 ¶ Now Absalom in his lifetime had taken
and reared up for himself a pillar, which *is*
in the king's dale: for he said, I have no son
to keep my name in remembrance: and he
called the pillar after his own name: and
it is called unto this day, Absalom's place.
19 ¶ Then said Ahimaaz the son of Zadok,
Let me now run, and bear the king tidings,
how that the LORD hath avenged him of
his enemies.
20 And Joab said unto him, Thou shalt not
bear tidings this day, but thou shalt bear
tidings another day: but this day thou
shalt bear no tidings, because the king's
son is dead.
21 Then said Joab to Cushi, Go tell the king
what thou hast seen. And Cushi bowed
himself unto Joab, and ran.
22 Then said Ahimaaz the son of Zadok yet
again to Joab, But howsoever, let me, I pray
thee, also run after Cushi. And Joab said,
Wherefore wilt thou run, my son, seeing
that thou hast no tidings ready?
23 But howsoever, *said he*, let me run. And
he said unto him, Run. Then Ahimaaz ran
by the way of the plain, and overran Cushi.
24 And David sat between the two gates:
and the watchman went up to the roof
over the gate unto the wall, and lifted up
his eyes, and looked, and behold a man
running alone.
25 And the watchman cried, and told the
king. And the king said, If he *be* alone, *there*
is tidings in his mouth. And he came apace,
and drew near.
26 And the watchman saw another man
running: and the watchman called unto
the porter, and said, Behold *another* man
running alone. And the king said, He also
bringeth tidings.
27 And the watchman said, Me thinketh the
running of the foremost is like the running
of Ahimaaz the son of Zadok. And the king
said, He *is* a good man, and cometh with
good tidings.
28 And Ahimaaz called, and said unto the
king, All is well. And he fell down to the
earth upon his face before the king, and
said, Blessed *be* the LORD thy God, which
hath delivered up the men that lifted up
their hand against my lord the king.
29 And the king said, *Is* the young man
Absalom safe? And Ahimaaz answered,
When Joab sent the king's servant, and *me*
thy servant, I saw a great tumult, but I knew
not what *it was*.
30 And the king said *unto him*, Turn aside,
and stand here. And he turned aside, and
stood still.
31 And, behold, Cushi came; and Cushi said,
Tidings, my lord the king: for the LORD hath
avenged thee this day of all them that rose
up against thee.
32 And the king said unto Cushi, *Is* the young
man Absalom safe? And Cushi answered,
The enemies of my lord the king, and all
that rise against thee to do *thee* hurt, be
as *that* young man *is*.
33 ¶ And the king was much moved, and
went up to the chamber over the gate, and
wept: and as he went, thus he said, O my
son Absalom, my son, my son Absalom!
would God I had died for thee, O Absalom,
my son, my son!

2 Samuel 19

1 And it was told Joab, Behold, the king
weepeth and mourneth for Absalom.
2 And the victory that day was *turned* into
mourning unto all the people: for the peo-

ple heard say that day how the king was
grieved for his son.
3 And the people gat them by stealth that
day into the city, as people being ashamed
steal away when they flee in battle.
4 But the king covered his face, and the king
cried with a loud voice, O my son Absalom,
O Absalom, my son, my son!
5 And Joab came into the house to the king,
and said, Thou hast shamed this day the
faces of all thy servants, which this day have
saved thy life, and the lives of thy sons and
of thy daughters, and the lives of thy wives,
and the lives of thy concubines;
6 In that thou lovest thine enemies, and
hatest thy friends. For thou hast declared
this day, that thou regardest neither princes
nor servants: for this day I perceive, that if
Absalom had lived, and all we had died this
day, then it had pleased thee well.
7 Now therefore arise, go forth, and speak
comfortably unto thy servants: for I swear
by the LORD, if thou go not forth, there will
not tarry one with thee this night: and that
will be worse unto thee than all the evil that
befell thee from thy youth until now.
8 Then the king arose, and sat in the gate.
And they told unto all the people, saying,
Behold, the king doth sit in the gate. And all
the people came before the king: for Israel
had fled every man to his tent.
9 ¶ And all the people were at strife throughout all the tribes of Israel, saying, The king
saved us out of the hand of our enemies,
and he delivered us out of the hand of the
Philistines; and now he is fled out of the
land for Absalom.
10 And Absalom, whom we anointed over
us, is dead in battle. Now therefore why
speak ye not a word of bringing the king
back?
11 ¶ And king David sent to Zadok and to
Abiathar the priests, saying, Speak unto the
elders of Judah, saying, Why are ye the last
to bring the king back to his house? seeing
the speech of all Israel is come to the king,
even to his house.
12 Ye *are* my brethren, ye *are* my bones and
my flesh: wherefore then are ye the last to
bring back the king?
13 And say ye to Amasa, *Art* thou not of my
bone, and of my flesh? God do so to me, and
more also, if thou be not captain of the host
before me continually in the room of Joab.
14 And he bowed the heart of all the men
of Judah, even as *the heart of* one man;
so that they sent *this word* unto the king,
Return thou, and all thy servants.
15 So the king returned, and came to Jordan.
And Judah came to Gilgal, to go to meet
the king, to conduct the king over Jordan.
16 ¶ And Shimei the son of Gera, a Benjamite, which *was* of Bahurim, hasted and
came down with the men of Judah to meet
king David.
17 And *there were* a thousand men of Benjamin with him, and Ziba the servant of the
house of Saul, and his fifteen sons and his
twenty servants with him; and they went
over Jordan before the king.
18 And there went over a ferry boat to carry
over the king's household, and to do what
he thought good. And Shimei the son of
Gera fell down before the king, as he was
come over Jordan;
19 And said unto the king, Let not my lord
impute iniquity unto me, neither do thou
remember that which thy servant did perversely the day that my lord the king went
out of Jerusalem, that the king should take
it to his heart.
20 For thy servant doth know that I have
sinned: therefore, behold, I am come the
first this day of all the house of Joseph to
go down to meet my lord the king.
21 But Abishai the son of Zeruiah answered
and said, Shall not Shimei be put to death for
this, because he cursed the LORD's anointed?
22 And David said, What have I to do with
you, ye sons of Zeruiah, that ye should this
day be adversaries unto me? shall there any
man be put to death this day in Israel? for do
not I know that I *am* this day king over Israel?
23 Therefore the king said unto Shimei, Thou
shalt not die. And the king sware unto him.
24 ¶ And Mephibosheth the son of Saul
came down to meet the king, and had
neither dressed his feet, nor trimmed his
beard, nor washed his clothes, from the
day the king departed until the day he came
again in peace.
25 And it came to pass, when he was come
to Jerusalem to meet the king, that the king
said unto him, Wherefore wentest not thou
with me, Mephibosheth?

26 And he answered, My lord, O king, my servant deceived me: for thy servant said, I will saddle me an ass, that I may ride thereon, and go to the king; because thy servant *is* lame.

27 And he hath slandered thy servant unto my lord the king; but my lord the king *is* as an angel of God: do therefore *what is* good in thine eyes.

28 For all *of* my father's house were but dead men before my lord the king: yet didst thou set thy servant among them that did eat at thine own table. What right therefore have I yet to cry any more unto the king?

29 And the king said unto him, Why speakest thou any more of thy matters? I have said, Thou and Ziba divide the land.

30 And Mephibosheth said unto the king, Yea, let him take all, forasmuch as my lord the king is come again in peace unto his own house.

31 ¶ And Barzillai the Gileadite came down from Rogelim, and went over Jordan with the king, to conduct him over Jordan.

32 Now Barzillai was a very aged man, *even* fourscore years old: and he had provided the king of sustenance while he lay at Mahanaim; for he *was* a very great man.

33 And the king said unto Barzillai, Come thou over with me, and I will feed thee with me in Jerusalem.

34 And Barzillai said unto the king, How long have I to live, that I should go up with the king unto Jerusalem?

35 I *am* this day fourscore years old: *and* can I discern between good and evil? can thy servant taste what I eat or what I drink? can I hear any more the voice of singing men and singing women? wherefore then should thy servant be yet a burden unto my lord the king?

36 Thy servant will go a little way over Jordan with the king: and why should the king recompense it me with such a reward?

37 Let thy servant, I pray thee, turn back again, that I may die in mine own city, *and be buried* by the grave of my father and of my mother. But behold thy servant Chimham; let him go over with my lord the king; and do to him what shall seem good unto thee.

38 And the king answered, Chimham shall go over with me, and I will do to him that which shall seem good unto thee: and whatsoever thou shalt require of me, *that* will I do for thee.

39 And all the people went over Jordan. And when the king was come over, the king kissed Barzillai, and blessed him; and he returned unto his own place.

40 Then the king went on to Gilgal, and Chimham went on with him: and all the people of Judah conducted the king, and also half the people of Israel.

41 ¶ And, behold, all the men of Israel came to the king, and said unto the king, Why have our brethren the men of Judah stolen thee away, and have brought the king, and his household, and all David's men with him, over Jordan?

42 And all the men of Judah answered the men of Israel, Because the king *is* near of kin to us: wherefore then be ye angry for this matter? have we eaten at all of the king's *cost?* or hath he given us any gift?

43 And the men of Israel answered the men of Judah, and said, We have ten parts in the king, and we have also more *right* in David than ye: why then did ye despise us, that our advice should not be first had in bringing back our king? And the words of the men of Judah were fiercer than the words of the men of Israel.

2 Samuel 20

1 And there happened to be there a man of Belial, whose name *was* Sheba, the son of Bichri, a Benjamite: and he blew a trumpet, and said, We have no part in David, neither have we inheritance in the son of Jesse: every man to his tents, O Israel.

2 So every man of Israel went up from after David, *and* followed Sheba the son of Bichri: but the men of Judah clave unto their king, from Jordan even to Jerusalem.

3 ¶ And David came to his house at Jerusalem; and the king took the ten women *his* concubines, whom he had left to keep the house, and put them in ward, and fed them, but went not in unto them. So they were shut up unto the day of their death, living in widowhood.

4 ¶ Then said the king to Amasa, Assemble me the men of Judah within three days, and be thou here present.

5 So Amasa went to assemble *the men of*

Judah: but he tarried longer than the set
time which he had appointed him.
6 And David said to Abishai, Now shall Sheba
the son of Bichri do us more harm than *did*
Absalom: take thou thy lord's servants, and
pursue after him, lest he get him fenced
cities, and escape us.
7 And there went out after him Joab's men,
and the Cherethites, and the Pelethites, and
all the mighty men: and they went out of
Jerusalem, to pursue after Sheba the son
of Bichri.
8 When they *were* at the great stone which
is in Gibeon, Amasa went before them. And
Joab's garment that he had put on was
girded unto him, and upon it a girdle *with* a
sword fastened upon his loins in the sheath
thereof; and as he went forth it fell out.
9 And Joab said to Amasa, *Art* thou in health,
my brother? And Joab took Amasa by the
beard with the right hand to kiss him.
10 But Amasa took no heed to the sword
that *was* in Joab's hand: so he smote him
therewith in the fifth *rib*, and shed out his
bowels to the ground, and struck him not
again; and he died. So Joab and Abishai
his brother pursued after Sheba the son
of Bichri.
11 And one of Joab's men stood by him, and
said, He that favoureth Joab, and he that *is*
for David, *let him go* after Joab.
12 And Amasa wallowed in blood in the
midst of the highway. And when the man
saw that all the people stood still, he
removed Amasa out of the highway into
the field, and cast a cloth upon him, when
he saw that every one that came by him
stood still.
13 When he was removed out of the highway, all the people went on after Joab, to
pursue after Sheba the son of Bichri.
14 ¶ And he went through all the tribes
of Israel unto Abel, and to Beth-maachah,
and all the Berites: and they were gathered
together, and went also after him.
15 And they came and besieged him in Abel
of Beth-maachah, and they cast up a bank
against the city, and it stood in the trench:
and all the people that *were* with Joab bat-
tered the wall, to throw it down.
16 ¶ Then cried a wise woman out of the
city, Hear, hear; say, I pray you, unto Joab,
Come near hither, that I may speak with
thee.
17 And when he was come near unto her,
the woman said, *Art* thou Joab? And he
answered, I *am he*. Then she said unto him,
Hear the words of thine handmaid. And he
answered, I do hear.
18 Then she spake, saying, They were wont
to speak in old time, saying, They shall surely
ask *counsel* at Abel: and so they ended *the
matter*.
19 I *am one of them that are* peaceable *and*
faithful in Israel: thou seekest to destroy a
city and a mother in Israel: why wilt thou
swallow up the inheritance of the LORD?
20 And Joab answered and said, Far be it,
far be it from me, that I should swallow up
or destroy.
21 The matter *is* not so: but a man of mount
Ephraim, Sheba the son of Bichri by name,
hath lifted up his hand against the king, *even*
against David: deliver him only, and I will
depart from the city. And the woman said
unto Joab, Behold, his head shall be thrown
to thee over the wall.
22 Then the woman went unto all the
people in her wisdom. And they cut off the
head of Sheba the son of Bichri, and cast *it*
out to Joab. And he blew a trumpet, and
they retired from the city, every man to
his tent. And Joab returned to Jerusalem
unto the king.
23 ¶ Now Joab *was* over all the host of Israel:
and Benaiah the son of Jehoiada *was* over
the Cherethites and over the Pelethites:
24 And Adoram *was* over the tribute: and
Jehoshaphat the son of Ahilud *was* recorder:
25 And Sheva *was* scribe: and Zadok and
Abiathar *were* the priests:
26 And Ira also the Jairite was a chief ruler
about David.

2 Samuel 21

1 Then there was a famine in the days of
David three years, year after year; and
David inquired of the LORD. And the LORD
answered, *It is* for Saul, and for *his* bloody
house, because he slew the Gibeonites.
2 And the king called the Gibeonites, and
said unto them; (now the Gibeonites *were*
not of the children of Israel, but of the remnant of the Amorites; and the children of
Israel had sworn unto them: and Saul sought

to slay them in his zeal to the children of
Israel and Judah.)
3 Wherefore David said unto the Gibeonites,
What shall I do for you? and wherewith shall
I make the atonement, that ye may bless the
inheritance of the LORD?
4 And the Gibeonites said unto him, We
will have no silver nor gold of Saul, nor of
his house; neither for us shalt thou kill any
man in Israel. And he said, What ye shall
say, *that* will I do for you.
5 And they answered the king, The man that
consumed us, and that devised against us
that we should be destroyed from remaining
in any of the coasts of Israel,
6 Let seven men of his sons be delivered
unto us, and we will hang them up unto the
LORD in Gibeah of Saul, *whom* the LORD did
choose. And the king said, I will give *them*.
7 But the king spared Mephibosheth, the
son of Jonathan the son of Saul, because
of the LORD's oath that *was* between them,
between David and Jonathan the son of
Saul.
8 But the king took the two sons of Rizpah
the daughter of Aiah, whom she bare unto
Saul, Armoni and Mephibosheth; and the
five sons of Michal the daughter of Saul,
whom she brought up for Adriel the son of
Barzillai the Meholathite:
9 And he delivered them into the hands of
the Gibeonites, and they hanged them in
the hill before the LORD: and they fell *all*
seven together, and were put to death in
the days of harvest, in the first *days*, in the
beginning of barley harvest.
10 ¶ And Rizpah the daughter of Aiah took
sackcloth, and spread it for her upon the
rock, from the beginning of harvest until
water dropped upon them out of heaven,
and suffered neither the birds of the air to
rest on them by day, nor the beasts of the
field by night.
11 And it was told David what Rizpah the
daughter of Aiah, the concubine of Saul,
had done.
12 ¶ And David went and took the bones of
Saul and the bones of Jonathan his son from
the men of Jabesh-gilead, which had stolen
them from the street of Beth-shan, where
the Philistines had hanged them, when the
Philistines had slain Saul in Gilboa:
13 And he brought up from thence the
bones of Saul and the bones of Jonathan his
son; and they gathered the bones of them
that were hanged.
14 And the bones of Saul and Jonathan his
son buried they in the country of Benjamin
in Zelah, in the sepulchre of Kish his father:
and they performed all that the king commanded. And after that God was intreated
for the land.
15 ¶ Moreover the Philistines had yet war
again with Israel; and David went down, and
his servants with him, and fought against the
Philistines: and David waxed faint.
16 And Ishbi-benob, which *was* of the sons
of the giant, the weight of whose spear
weighed three hundred *shekels* of brass in
weight, he being girded with a new *sword*,
thought to have slain David.
17 But Abishai the son of Zeruiah succoured
him, and smote the Philistine, and killed
him. Then the men of David sware unto
him, saying, Thou shalt go no more out
with us to battle, that thou quench not the
light of Israel.
18 And it came to pass after this, that there
was again a battle with the Philistines at
Gob: then Sibbechai the Hushathite slew
Saph, which *was* of the sons of the giant.
19 And there was again a battle in Gob with
the Philistines, where Elhanan the son of
Jaare-oregim, a Beth-lehemite, slew *the
brother of* Goliath the Gittite, the staff of
whose spear *was* like a weaver's beam.
20 And there was yet a battle in Gath, where
was a man of *great* stature, that had on
every hand six fingers, and on every foot
six toes, four and twenty in number; and
he also was born to the giant.
21 And when he defied Israel, Jonathan the
son of Shimea the brother of David slew him.
22 These four were born to the giant in
Gath, and fell by the hand of David, and by
the hand of his servants.

2 Samuel 22

1 And David spake unto the LORD the words
of this song in the day *that* the LORD had
delivered him out of the hand of all his enemies, and out of the hand of Saul:
2 And he said, The LORD *is* my rock, and my
fortress, and my deliverer;
3 The God of my rock; in him will I trust: *he
is* my shield, and the horn of my salvation,

my high tower, and my refuge, my saviour;
thou savest me from violence.
4 I will call on the LORD, *who is* worthy to
be praised: so shall I be saved from mine
enemies.
5 When the waves of death compassed me,
the floods of ungodly men made me afraid;
6 The sorrows of hell compassed me about;
the snares of death prevented me;
7 In my distress I called upon the LORD, and
cried to my God: and he did hear my voice
out of his temple, and my cry *did enter* into
his ears.
8 Then the earth shook and trembled; the
foundations of heaven moved and shook,
because he was wroth.
9 There went up a smoke out of his nostrils,
and fire out of his mouth devoured: coals
were kindled by it.
10 He bowed the heavens also, and came
down; and darkness *was* under his feet.
11 And he rode upon a cherub, and did fly:
and he was seen upon the wings of the wind.
12 And he made darkness pavilions round
about him, dark waters, *and* thick clouds
of the skies.
13 Through the brightness before him were
coals of fire kindled.
14 The LORD thundered from heaven, and
the most High uttered his voice.
15 And he sent out arrows, and scattered
them; lightning, and discomfited them.
16 And the channels of the sea appeared,
the foundations of the world were discovered, at the rebuking of the LORD, at the
blast of the breath of his nostrils.
17 He sent from above, he took me; he drew
me out of many waters;
18 He delivered me from my strong enemy,
and from them that hated me: for they were
too strong for me.
19 They prevented me in the day of my
calamity: but the LORD was my stay.
20 He brought me forth also into a large
place: he delivered me, because he
delighted in me.
21 The LORD rewarded me according to my
righteousness: according to the cleanness of
my hands hath he recompensed me.
22 For I have kept the ways of the LORD, and
have not wickedly departed from my God.
23 For all his judgments *were* before me:
and *as for* his statutes, I did not depart
from them.
24 I was also upright before him, and have
kept myself from mine iniquity.
25 Therefore the LORD hath recompensed
me according to my righteousness; according to my cleanness in his eye sight.
26 With the merciful thou wilt shew thyself
merciful, *and* with the upright man thou wilt
shew thyself upright.
27 With the pure thou wilt shew thyself
pure; and with the froward thou wilt shew
thyself unsavoury.
28 And the afflicted people thou wilt save:
but thine eyes *are* upon the haughty, *that*
thou mayest bring *them* down.
29 For thou *art* my lamp, O LORD: and the
LORD will lighten my darkness.
30 For by thee I have run through a troop:
by my God have I leaped over a wall.
31 *As for* God, his way *is* perfect; the word
of the LORD *is* tried: he *is* a buckler to all
them that trust in him.
32 For who *is* God, save the LORD? and who
is a rock, save our God?
33 God *is* my strength *and* power: and he
maketh my way perfect.
34 He maketh my feet like hinds' *feet:* and
setteth me upon my high places.
35 He teacheth my hands to war; so that a
bow of steel is broken by mine arms.
36 Thou hast also given me the shield of thy
salvation: and thy gentleness hath made
me great.
37 Thou hast enlarged my steps under me;
so that my feet did not slip.
38 I have pursued mine enemies, and
destroyed them; and turned not again
until I had consumed them.
39 And I have consumed them, and
wounded them, that they could not arise:
yea, they are fallen under my feet.
40 For thou hast girded me with strength to
battle: them that rose up against me hast
thou subdued under me.
41 Thou hast also given me the necks of
mine enemies, that I might destroy them
that hate me.
42 They looked, but *there was* none to
save; *even* unto the LORD, but he answered
them not.
43 Then did I beat them as small as the dust

of the earth, I did stamp them as the mire
of the street, *and* did spread them abroad.
44 Thou also hast delivered me from the
strivings of my people, thou hast kept me
to be head of the heathen: a people *which*
I knew not shall serve me.
45 Strangers shall submit themselves unto
me: as soon as they hear, they shall be obedient unto me.
46 Strangers shall fade away, and they shall
be afraid out of their close places.
47 The LORD liveth; and blessed *be* my rock;
and exalted be the God of the rock of my
salvation.
48 It *is* God that avengeth me, and that
bringeth down the people under me,
49 And that bringeth me forth from mine
enemies: thou also hast lifted me up on high
above them that rose up against me: thou
hast delivered me from the violent man.
50 Therefore I will give thanks unto thee,
O LORD, among the heathen, and I will sing
praises unto thy name.
51 *He is* the tower of salvation for his king:
and sheweth mercy to his anointed, unto
David, and to his seed for evermore.

2 Samuel 23

1 Now these *be* the last words of David.
David the son of Jesse said, and the man
who was raised up on high, the anointed of
the God of Jacob, and the sweet psalmist
of Israel, said,
2 The Spirit of the LORD spake by me, and
his word *was* in my tongue.
3 The God of Israel said, the Rock of Israel
spake to me, He that ruleth over men *must*
be just, ruling in the fear of God.
4 And *he shall be* as the light of the morning,
when the sun riseth, *even* a morning without
clouds; *as* the tender grass *springing* out of
the earth by clear shining after rain.
5 Although my house *be* not so with God;
yet he hath made with me an everlasting
covenant, ordered in all *things*, and sure:
for *this is* all my salvation, and all *my* desire,
although he make *it* not to grow.
6 ¶ But *the sons* of Belial *shall be* all of them
as thorns thrust away, because they cannot
be taken with hands:
7 But the man *that* shall touch them must
be fenced with iron and the staff of a spear;
and they shall be utterly burned with fire in
the *same* place.
8 ¶ These *be* the names of the mighty men
whom David had: The Tachmonite that sat
in the seat, chief among the captains; the
same *was* Adino the Eznite: *he lift up his*
spear against eight hundred, whom he slew
at one time.
9 And after him *was* Eleazar the son of Dodo
the Ahohite, *one* of the three mighty men
with David, when they defied the Philistines
that were there gathered together to battle, and the men of Israel were gone away:
10 He arose, and smote the Philistines until
his hand was weary, and his hand clave unto
the sword: and the LORD wrought a great
victory that day; and the people returned
after him only to spoil.
11 And after him *was* Shammah the son of
Agee the Hararite. And the Philistines were
gathered together into a troop, where was
a piece of ground full of lentiles: and the
people fled from the Philistines.
12 But he stood in the midst of the ground,
and defended it, and slew the Philistines:
and the LORD wrought a great victory.
13 And three of the thirty chief went down,
and came to David in the harvest time unto
the cave of Adullam: and the troop of the
Philistines pitched in the valley of Rephaim.
14 And David *was* then in an hold, and
the garrison of the Philistines *was* then *in*
Beth-lehem.
15 And David longed, and said, Oh that one
would give me drink of the water of the well
of Beth-lehem, which *is* by the gate!
16 And the three mighty men brake through
the host of the Philistines, and drew water
out of the well of Beth-lehem, that *was* by
the gate, and took *it*, and brought *it* to David:
nevertheless he would not drink thereof,
but poured it out unto the LORD.
17 And he said, Be it far from me, O LORD,
that I should do this: *is not this* the blood
of the men that went in jeopardy of their
lives? therefore he would not drink it. These
things did these three mighty men.
18 And Abishai, the brother of Joab, the son
of Zeruiah, was chief among three. And he
lifted up his spear against three hundred,
and slew *them*, and had the name among
three.
19 Was he not most honourable of three?

therefore he was their captain: howbeit he
attained not unto the *first* three.
20 And Benaiah the son of Jehoiada, the
son of a valiant man, of Kabzeel, who had
done many acts, he slew two lionlike men
of Moab: he went down also and slew a lion
in the midst of a pit in time of snow:
21 And he slew an Egyptian, a goodly man:
and the Egyptian had a spear in his hand;
but he went down to him with a staff, and
plucked the spear out of the Egyptian's
hand, and slew him with his own spear.
22 These *things* did Benaiah the son of
Jehoiada, and had the name among three
mighty men.
23 He was more honourable than the thirty,
but he attained not to the *first* three. And
David set him over his guard.
24 Asahel the brother of Joab *was* one
of the thirty; Elhanan the son of Dodo of
Beth-lehem,
25 Shammah the Harodite, Elika the
Harodite,
26 Helez the Paltite, Ira the son of Ikkesh
the Tekoite,
27 Abiezer the Anethothite, Mebunnai the
Hushathite,
28 Zalmon the Ahohite, Maharai the Netophathite,
29 Heleb the son of Baanah, a Netophathite,
Ittai the son of Ribai out of Gibeah of the
children of Benjamin,
30 Benaiah the Pirathonite, Hiddai of the
brooks of Gaash,
31 Abi-albon the Arbathite, Azmaveth the
Barhumite,
32 Eliahba the Shaalbonite, of the sons of
Jashen, Jonathan,
33 Shammah the Hararite, Ahiam the son
of Sharar the Hararite,
34 Eliphelet the son of Ahasbai, the son of
the Maachathite, Eliam the son of Ahithophel the Gilonite,
35 Hezrai the Carmelite, Paarai the Arbite,
36 Igal the son of Nathan of Zobah, Bani
the Gadite,
37 Zelek the Ammonite, Naharai the Beerothite, armourbearer to Joab the son of
Zeruiah,
38 Ira an Ithrite, Gareb an Ithrite,
39 Uriah the Hittite: thirty and seven in all.

2 Samuel 24

1 And again the anger of the LORD was
kindled against Israel, and he moved David
against them to say, Go, number Israel and
Judah.
2 For the king said to Joab the captain of the
host, which *was* with him, Go now through
all the tribes of Israel, from Dan even to
Beer-sheba, and number ye the people,
that I may know the number of the people.
3 And Joab said unto the king, Now the LORD
thy God add unto the people, how many
soever they be, an hundredfold, and that the
eyes of my lord the king may see *it:* but why
doth my lord the king delight in this thing?
4 Notwithstanding the king's word prevailed
against Joab, and against the captains of the
host. And Joab and the captains of the host
went out from the presence of the king, to
number the people of Israel.
5 ¶ And they passed over Jordan, and
pitched in Aroer, on the right side of the city
that *lieth* in the midst of the river of Gad,
and toward Jazer:
6 Then they came to Gilead, and to the land
of Tahtim-hodshi; and they came to Dan-
jaan, and about to Zidon,
7 And came to the strong hold of Tyre, and
to all the cities of the Hivites, and of the
Canaanites: and they went out to the south
of Judah, *even* to Beer-sheba.
8 So when they had gone through all the
land, they came to Jerusalem at the end of
nine months and twenty days.
9 And Joab gave up the sum of the number
of the people unto the king: and there were
in Israel eight hundred thousand valiant men
that drew the sword; and the men of Judah
were five hundred thousand men.
10 ¶ And David's heart smote him after that
he had numbered the people. And David
said unto the LORD, I have sinned greatly in
that I have done: and now, I beseech thee, O
LORD, take away the iniquity of thy servant;
for I have done very foolishly.
11 For when David was up in the morning,
the word of the LORD came unto the prophet
Gad, David's seer, saying,
12 Go and say unto David, Thus saith the
LORD, I offer thee three *things;* choose thee
one of them, that I may *do it* unto thee.
13 So Gad came to David, and told him, and
said unto him, Shall seven years of famine

come unto thee in thy land? or wilt thou flee
three months before thine enemies, while
they pursue thee? or that there be three
days' pestilence in thy land? now advise,
and see what answer I shall return to him
that sent me.
14 And David said unto Gad, I am in a great
strait: let us fall now into the hand of the
LORD; for his mercies *are* great: and let me
not fall into the hand of man.
15 ¶ So the LORD sent a pestilence upon
Israel from the morning even to the time
appointed: and there died of the people
from Dan even to Beer-sheba seventy
thousand men.
16 And when the angel stretched out his
hand upon Jerusalem to destroy it, the
LORD repented him of the evil, and said to
the angel that destroyed the people, It is
enough: stay now thine hand. And the angel
of the LORD was by the threshingplace of
Araunah the Jebusite.
17 And David spake unto the LORD when
he saw the angel that smote the people,
and said, Lo, I have sinned, and I have done
wickedly: but these sheep, what have they
done? let thine hand, I pray thee, be against
me, and against my father's house.
18 ¶ And Gad came that day to David, and
said unto him, Go up, rear an altar unto
the LORD in the threshingfloor of Araunah
the Jebusite.
19 And David, according to the saying of
Gad, went up as the LORD commanded.
20 And Araunah looked, and saw the king
and his servants coming on toward him:
and Araunah went out, and bowed himself
before the king on his face upon the ground.
21 And Araunah said, Wherefore is my lord
the king come to his servant? And David
said, To buy the threshingfloor of thee, to
build an altar unto the LORD, that the plague
may be stayed from the people.
22 And Araunah said unto David, Let my lord
the king take and offer up what *seemeth*
good unto him: behold, *here be* oxen for
burnt sacrifice, and threshing instruments
and *other* instruments of the oxen for wood.
23 All these *things* did Araunah, *as* a king,
give unto the king. And Araunah said unto
the king, The LORD thy God accept thee.
24 And the king said unto Araunah, Nay; but
I will surely buy *it* of thee at a price: neither
will I offer burnt offerings unto the LORD my
God of that which doth cost me nothing. So
David bought the threshingfloor and the
oxen for fifty shekels of silver.
25 And David built there an altar unto the
LORD, and offered burnt offerings and peace
offerings. So the LORD was intreated for the
land, and the plague was stayed from Israel.

The First Book Of The

Kings

1 Kings 1

1 Now king David was old *and* stricken in
years; and they covered him with clothes,
but he gat no heat.
2 Wherefore his servants said unto him, Let
there be sought for my lord the king a young
virgin: and let her stand before the king,
and let her cherish him, and let her lie in thy
bosom, that my lord the king may get heat.
3 So they sought for a fair damsel throughout all the coasts of Israel, and found
Abishag a Shunammite, and brought her
to the king.
4 And the damsel *was* very fair, and cher-
ished the king, and ministered to him: but
the king knew her not.
5 ¶ Then Adonijah the son of Haggith
exalted himself, saying, I will be king: and
he prepared him chariots and horsemen,
and fifty men to run before him.
6 And his father had not displeased him at
any time in saying, Why hast thou done so?
and he also *was a* very goodly *man;* and *his
mother* bare him after Absalom.
7 And he conferred with Joab the son of

Zeruiah, and with Abiathar the priest: and
they following Adonijah helped *him*.
8 But Zadok the priest, and Benaiah the son
of Jehoiada, and Nathan the prophet, and
Shimei, and Rei, and the mighty men which
belonged to David, were not with Adonijah.
9 And Adonijah slew sheep and oxen and
fat cattle by the stone of Zoheleth, which *is*
by En-rogel, and called all his brethren the
king's sons, and all the men of Judah the
king's servants:
10 But Nathan the prophet, and Benaiah,
and the mighty men, and Solomon his
brother, he called not.
11 ¶ Wherefore Nathan spake unto Bath-
sheba the mother of Solomon, saying,
Hast thou not heard that Adonijah the son
of Haggith doth reign, and David our lord
knoweth *it* not?
12 Now therefore come, let me, I pray
thee, give thee counsel, that thou mayest
save thine own life, and the life of thy son
Solomon.
13 Go and get thee in unto king David, and
say unto him, Didst not thou, my lord, O
king, swear unto thine handmaid, saying,
Assuredly Solomon thy son shall reign after
me, and he shall sit upon my throne? why
then doth Adonijah reign?
14 Behold, while thou yet talkest there with
the king, I also will come in after thee, and
confirm thy words.
15 ¶ And Bath-sheba went in unto the king
into the chamber: and the king was very old;
and Abishag the Shunammite ministered
unto the king.
16 And Bath-sheba bowed, and did obeisance unto the king. And the king said, What
wouldest thou?
17 And she said unto him, My lord, thou
swarest by the LORD thy God unto thine
handmaid, *saying*, Assuredly Solomon thy
son shall reign after me, and he shall sit
upon my throne.
18 And now, behold, Adonijah reigneth; and
now, my lord the king, thou knowest *it* not:
19 And he hath slain oxen and fat cattle and
sheep in abundance, and hath called all the
sons of the king, and Abiathar the priest, and
Joab the captain of the host: but Solomon
thy servant hath he not called.
20 And thou, my lord, O king, the eyes of
all Israel *are* upon thee, that thou shouldest
tell them who shall sit on the throne of my
lord the king after him.
21 Otherwise it shall come to pass, when
my lord the king shall sleep with his fathers,
that I and my son Solomon shall be counted
offenders.
22 ¶ And, lo, while she yet talked with the
king, Nathan the prophet also came in.
23 And they told the king, saying, Behold
Nathan the prophet. And when he was
come in before the king, he bowed himself
before the king with his face to the ground.
24 And Nathan said, My lord, O king, hast
thou said, Adonijah shall reign after me, and
he shall sit upon my throne?
25 For he is gone down this day, and hath
slain oxen and fat cattle and sheep in abundance, and hath called all the king's sons,
and the captains of the host, and Abiathar
the priest; and, behold, they eat and drink
before him, and say, God save king Adonijah.
26 But me, *even* me thy servant, and Zadok
the priest, and Benaiah the son of Jehoiada,
and thy servant Solomon, hath he not called.
27 Is this thing done by my lord the king, and
thou hast not shewed *it* unto thy servant,
who should sit on the throne of my lord the
king after him?
28 ¶ Then king David answered and said,
Call me Bath-sheba. And she came into the
king's presence, and stood before the king.
29 And the king sware, and said, *As* the
LORD liveth, that hath redeemed my soul
out of all distress,
30 Even as I sware unto thee by the LORD
God of Israel, saying, Assuredly Solomon
thy son shall reign after me, and he shall sit
upon my throne in my stead; even so will I
certainly do this day.
31 Then Bath-sheba bowed with *her* face
to the earth, and did reverence to the king,
and said, Let my lord king David live for ever.
32 ¶ And king David said, Call me Zadok
the priest, and Nathan the prophet, and
Benaiah the son of Jehoiada. And they came
before the king.
33 The king also said unto them, Take with
you the servants of your lord, and cause
Solomon my son to ride upon mine own
mule, and bring him down to Gihon:
34 And let Zadok the priest and Nathan the
prophet anoint him there king over Israel:

and blow ye with the trumpet, and say, God
save king Solomon.
35 Then ye shall come up after him, that
he may come and sit upon my throne; for
he shall be king in my stead: and I have
appointed him to be ruler over Israel and
over Judah.
36 And Benaiah the son of Jehoiada
answered the king, and said, Amen: the
LORD God of my lord the king say so *too*.
37 As the LORD hath been with my lord the
king, even so be he with Solomon, and make
his throne greater than the throne of my
lord king David.
38 So Zadok the priest, and Nathan the
prophet, and Benaiah the son of Jehoiada,
and the Cherethites, and the Pelethites,
went down, and caused Solomon to ride
upon king David's mule, and brought him
to Gihon.
39 And Zadok the priest took an horn of oil
out of the tabernacle, and anointed Solomon. And they blew the trumpet; and all
the people said, God save king Solomon.
40 And all the people came up after him, and
the people piped with pipes, and rejoiced
with great joy, so that the earth rent with
the sound of them.
41 ¶ And Adonijah and all the guests that
were with him heard *it* as they had made
an end of eating. And when Joab heard the
sound of the trumpet, he said, Wherefore
is this noise of the city being in an uproar?
42 And while he yet spake, behold, Jonathan
the son of Abiathar the priest came: and
Adonijah said unto him, Come in; for thou
art a valiant man, and bringest good tidings.
43 And Jonathan answered and said to
Adonijah, Verily our lord king David hath
made Solomon king.
44 And the king hath sent with him Zadok
the priest, and Nathan the prophet, and
Benaiah the son of Jehoiada, and the Cherethites, and the Pelethites, and they have
caused him to ride upon the king's mule:
45 And Zadok the priest and Nathan the
prophet have anointed him king in Gihon:
and they are come up from thence rejoicing,
so that the city rang again. This *is* the noise
that ye have heard.
46 And also Solomon sitteth on the throne
of the kingdom.
47 And moreover the king's servants came
to bless our lord king David, saying, God
make the name of Solomon better than thy
name, and make his throne greater than
thy throne. And the king bowed himself
upon the bed.
48 And also thus said the king, Blessed *be*
the LORD God of Israel, which hath given
one to sit on my throne this day, mine eyes
even seeing *it*.
49 And all the guests that *were* with Adonijah were afraid, and rose up, and went every
man his way.
50 ¶ And Adonijah feared because of Solomon, and arose, and went, and caught hold
on the horns of the altar.
51 And it was told Solomon, saying, Behold,
Adonijah feareth king Solomon: for, lo, he
hath caught hold on the horns of the altar,
saying, Let king Solomon swear unto me
to day that he will not slay his servant with
the sword.
52 And Solomon said, If he will shew himself
a worthy man, there shall not an hair of him
fall to the earth: but if wickedness shall be
found in him, he shall die.
53 So king Solomon sent, and they brought
him down from the altar. And he came
and bowed himself to king Solomon: and
Solomon said unto him, Go to thine house.

1 Kings 2

1 Now the days of David drew nigh that he
should die; and he charged Solomon his
son, saying,
2 I go the way of all the earth: be thou strong
therefore, and shew thyself a man;
3 And keep the charge of the LORD thy God,
to walk in his ways, to keep his statutes, and
his commandments, and his judgments,
and his testimonies, as it is written in the
law of Moses, that thou mayest prosper in
all that thou doest, and whithersoever thou
turnest thyself:
4 That the LORD may continue his word
which he spake concerning me, saying, If
thy children take heed to their way, to walk
before me in truth with all their heart and
with all their soul, there shall not fail thee
(said he) a man on the throne of Israel.
5 Moreover thou knowest also what Joab
the son of Zeruiah did to me, *and* what he
did to the two captains of the hosts of Israel,
unto Abner the son of Ner, and unto Amasa

the son of Jether, whom he slew, and shed
the blood of war in peace, and put the blood
of war upon his girdle that *was* about his
loins, and in his shoes that *were* on his feet.
6 Do therefore according to thy wisdom,
and let not his hoar head go down to the
grave in peace.
7 But shew kindness unto the sons of Barzillai the Gileadite, and let them be of those
that eat at thy table: for so they came to me
when I fled because of Absalom thy brother.
8 And, behold, *thou hast* with thee Shimei
the son of Gera, a Benjamite of Bahurim,
which cursed me with a grievous curse in
the day when I went to Mahanaim: but he
came down to meet me at Jordan, and I
sware to him by the LORD, saying, I will not
put thee to death with the sword.
9 Now therefore hold him not guiltless: for
thou *art* a wise man, and knowest what thou
oughtest to do unto him; but his hoar head
bring thou down to the grave with blood.
10 So David slept with his fathers, and was
buried in the city of David.
11 And the days that David reigned over
Israel *were* forty years: seven years reigned
he in Hebron, and thirty and three years
reigned he in Jerusalem.
12 ¶ Then sat Solomon upon the throne
of David his father; and his kingdom was
established greatly.
13 ¶ And Adonijah the son of Haggith came
to Bath-sheba the mother of Solomon. And
she said, Comest thou peaceably? And he
said, Peaceably.
14 He said moreover, I have somewhat to
say unto thee. And she said, Say on.
15 And he said, Thou knowest that the kingdom was mine, and *that* all Israel set their
faces on me, that I should reign: howbeit
the kingdom is turned about, and is become
my brother's: for it was his from the LORD.
16 And now I ask one petition of thee, deny
me not. And she said unto him, Say on.
17 And he said, Speak, I pray thee, unto
Solomon the king, (for he will not say thee
nay,) that he give me Abishag the Shunammite to wife.
18 And Bath-sheba said, Well; I will speak
for thee unto the king.
19 ¶ Bath-sheba therefore went unto king
Solomon, to speak unto him for Adonijah.
And the king rose up to meet her, and
bowed himself unto her, and sat down on his
throne, and caused a seat to be set for the
king's mother; and she sat on his right hand.
20 Then she said, I desire one small petition
of thee; *I pray thee*, say me not nay. And the
king said unto her, Ask on, my mother: for I
will not say thee nay.
21 And she said, Let Abishag the Shunammite be given to Adonijah thy brother to
wife.
22 And king Solomon answered and said
unto his mother, And why dost thou ask
Abishag the Shunammite for Adonijah? ask
for him the kingdom also; for he *is* mine
elder brother; even for him, and for Abiathar
the priest, and for Joab the son of Zeruiah.
23 Then king Solomon sware by the LORD,
saying, God do so to me, and more also, if
Adonijah have not spoken this word against
his own life.
24 Now therefore, *as* the LORD liveth, which
hath established me, and set me on the
throne of David my father, and who hath
made me an house, as he promised, Adonijah shall be put to death this day.
25 And king Solomon sent by the hand of
Benaiah the son of Jehoiada; and he fell
upon him that he died.
26 ¶ And unto Abiathar the priest said the
king, Get thee to Anathoth, unto thine own
fields; for thou *art* worthy of death: but
I will not at this time put thee to death,
because thou barest the ark of the Lord
GOD before David my father, and because
thou hast been afflicted in all wherein my
father was afflicted.
27 So Solomon thrust out Abiathar from
being priest unto the LORD; that he might
fulfil the word of the LORD, which he spake
concerning the house of Eli in Shiloh.
28 ¶ Then tidings came to Joab: for Joab had
turned after Adonijah, though he turned
not after Absalom. And Joab fled unto the
tabernacle of the LORD, and caught hold on
the horns of the altar.
29 And it was told king Solomon that Joab
was fled unto the tabernacle of the LORD;
and, behold, *he is* by the altar. Then Solomon
sent Benaiah the son of Jehoiada, saying,
Go, fall upon him.
30 And Benaiah came to the tabernacle of
the LORD, and said unto him, Thus saith the
king, Come forth. And he said, Nay; but I

will die here. And Benaiah brought the king
word again, saying, Thus said Joab, and thus
he answered me.
31 And the king said unto him, Do as he hath
said, and fall upon him, and bury him; that
thou mayest take away the innocent blood,
which Joab shed, from me, and from the
house of my father.
32 And the LORD shall return his blood upon
his own head, who fell upon two men more
righteous and better than he, and slew them
with the sword, my father David not knowing *thereof, to wit,* Abner the son of Ner,
captain of the host of Israel, and Amasa the
son of Jether, captain of the host of Judah.
33 Their blood shall therefore return upon
the head of Joab, and upon the head of his
seed for ever: but upon David, and upon
his seed, and upon his house, and upon his
throne, shall there be peace for ever from
the LORD.
34 So Benaiah the son of Jehoiada went up,
and fell upon him, and slew him: and he was
buried in his own house in the wilderness.
35 ¶ And the king put Benaiah the son of
Jehoiada in his room over the host: and
Zadok the priest did the king put in the
room of Abiathar.
36 ¶ And the king sent and called for Shimei,
and said unto him, Build thee an house in
Jerusalem, and dwell there, and go not forth
thence any whither.
37 For it shall be, *that* on the day thou goest
out, and passest over the brook Kidron, thou
shalt know for certain that thou shalt surely
die: thy blood shall be upon thine own head.
38 And Shimei said unto the king, The saying *is* good: as my lord the king hath said,
so will thy servant do. And Shimei dwelt in
Jerusalem many days.
39 And it came to pass at the end of three
years, that two of the servants of Shimei ran
away unto Achish son of Maachah king of
Gath. And they told Shimei, saying, Behold,
thy servants *be* in Gath.
40 And Shimei arose, and saddled his ass,
and went to Gath to Achish to seek his servants: and Shimei went, and brought his
servants from Gath.
41 And it was told Solomon that Shimei
had gone from Jerusalem to Gath, and was
come again.
42 And the king sent and called for Shimei,
and said unto him, Did I not make thee to
swear by the LORD, and protested unto thee,
saying, Know for a certain, on the day thou
goest out, and walkest abroad any whither,
that thou shalt surely die? and thou saidst
unto me, The word *that* I have heard *is* good.
43 Why then hast thou not kept the oath
of the LORD, and the commandment that I
have charged thee with?
44 The king said moreover to Shimei, Thou
knowest all the wickedness which thine
heart is privy to, that thou didst to David my
father: therefore the LORD shall return thy
wickedness upon thine own head;
45 And king Solomon *shall be* blessed, and
the throne of David shall be established
before the LORD for ever.
46 So the king commanded Benaiah the
son of Jehoiada; which went out, and fell
upon him, that he died. And the kingdom
was established in the hand of Solomon.

1 Kings 3

1 And Solomon made affinity with Pharaoh
king of Egypt, and took Pharaoh's daughter,
and brought her into the city of David, until
he had made an end of building his own
house, and the house of the LORD, and the
wall of Jerusalem round about.
2 Only the people sacrificed in high places,
because there was no house built unto the
name of the LORD, until those days.
3 And Solomon loved the LORD, walking
in the statutes of David his father: only he
sacrificed and burnt incense in high places.
4 And the king went to Gibeon to sacrifice
there; for that *was* the great high place: a
thousand burnt offerings did Solomon offer
upon that altar.
5 ¶ In Gibeon the LORD appeared to Solomon in a dream by night: and God said, Ask
what I shall give thee.
6 And Solomon said, Thou hast shewed unto
thy servant David my father great mercy,
according as he walked before thee in truth,
and in righteousness, and in uprightness of
heart with thee; and thou hast kept for him
this great kindness, that thou hast given him
a son to sit on his throne, as *it is* this day.
7 And now, O LORD my God, thou hast made
thy servant king instead of David my father:
and I *am but* a little child: I know not *how*
to go out or come in.

8 And thy servant *is* in the midst of thy people which thou hast chosen, a great people,
that cannot be numbered nor counted for
multitude.
9 Give therefore thy servant an understanding heart to judge thy people, that I may
discern between good and bad: for who
is able to judge this thy so great a people?
10 And the speech pleased the Lord, that
Solomon had asked this thing.
11 And God said unto him, Because thou
hast asked this thing, and hast not asked for
thyself long life; neither hast asked riches
for thyself, nor hast asked the life of thine
enemies; but hast asked for thyself understanding to discern judgment;
12 Behold, I have done according to thy
words: lo, I have given thee a wise and an
understanding heart; so that there was none
like thee before thee, neither after thee shall
any arise like unto thee.
13 And I have also given thee that which
thou hast not asked, both riches, and honour: so that there shall not be any among
the kings like unto thee all thy days.
14 And if thou wilt walk in my ways, to keep
my statutes and my commandments, as thy
father David did walk, then I will lengthen
thy days.
15 And Solomon awoke; and, behold, *it was*
a dream. And he came to Jerusalem, and
stood before the ark of the covenant of the
LORD, and offered up burnt offerings, and
offered peace offerings, and made a feast
to all his servants.
16 ¶ Then came there two women, *that*
were harlots, unto the king, and stood
before him.
17 And the one woman said, O my lord, I and
this woman dwell in one house; and I was
delivered of a child with her in the house.
18 And it came to pass the third day after
that I was delivered, that this woman was
delivered also: and we *were* together; *there*
was no stranger with us in the house, save
we two in the house.
19 And this woman's child died in the night;
because she overlaid it.
20 And she arose at midnight, and took my
son from beside me, while thine handmaid
slept, and laid it in her bosom, and laid her
dead child in my bosom.
21 And when I rose in the morning to give
my child suck, behold, it was dead: but when
I had considered it in the morning, behold,
it was not my son, which I did bear.
22 And the other woman said, Nay; but the
living *is* my son, and the dead *is* thy son.
And this said, No; but the dead *is* thy son,
and the living *is* my son. Thus they spake
before the king.
23 Then said the king, The one saith, This *is*
my son that liveth, and thy son *is* the dead:
and the other saith, Nay; but thy son *is* the
dead, and my son *is* the living.
24 And the king said, Bring me a sword.
And they brought a sword before the king.
25 And the king said, Divide the living child
in two, and give half to the one, and half
to the other.
26 Then spake the woman whose the living child *was* unto the king, for her bowels
yearned upon her son, and she said, O my
lord, give her the living child, and in no wise
slay it. But the other said, Let it be neither
mine nor thine, *but* divide *it*.
27 Then the king answered and said, Give
her the living child, and in no wise slay it:
she *is* the mother thereof.
28 And all Israel heard of the judgment
which the king had judged; and they feared
the king: for they saw that the wisdom of
God *was* in him, to do judgment.

1 Kings 4

1 So king Solomon was king over all Israel.
2 And these *were* the princes which he had;
Azariah the son of Zadok the priest,
3 Elihoreph and Ahiah, the sons of Shisha,
scribes; Jehoshaphat the son of Ahilud, the
recorder.
4 And Benaiah the son of Jehoiada *was* over
the host: and Zadok and Abiathar *were* the
priests:
5 And Azariah the son of Nathan *was* over
the officers: and Zabud the son of Nathan
was principal officer, *and* the king's friend:
6 And Ahishar *was* over the household:
and Adoniram the son of Abda *was* over
the tribute.
7 ¶ And Solomon had twelve officers over all
Israel, which provided victuals for the king
and his household: each man his month in
a year made provision.
8 And these *are* their names: The son of Hur,
in mount Ephraim:

9 The son of Dekar, in Makaz, and in Shaalbim, and Beth-shemesh, and Elon-beth-
hanan:
10 The son of Hesed, in Aruboth; to him *pertained* Sochoh, and all the land of Hepher:
11 The son of Abinadab, in all the region
of Dor; which had Taphath the daughter of
Solomon to wife:
12 Baana the son of Ahilud; *to him pertained*
Taanach and Megiddo, and all Beth-shean,
which *is* by Zartanah beneath Jezreel, from
Beth-shean to Abel-meholah, *even* unto *the
place that is* beyond Jokneam:
13 The son of Geber, in Ramoth-gilead; to
him *pertained* the towns of Jair the son of
Manasseh, which *are* in Gilead; to him *also
pertained* the region of Argob, which *is* in
Bashan, threescore great cities with walls
and brasen bars:
14 Ahinadab the son of Iddo *had* Mahanaim:
15 Ahimaaz *was* in Naphtali; he also took
Basmath the daughter of Solomon to wife:
16 Baanah the son of Hushai *was* in Asher
and in Aloth:
17 Jehoshaphat the son of Paruah, in
Issachar:
18 Shimei the son of Elah, in Benjamin:
19 Geber the son of Uri *was* in the country
of Gilead, *in* the country of Sihon king of the
Amorites, and of Og king of Bashan; and *he
was* the only officer which *was* in the land.
20 ¶ Judah and Israel *were* many, as the sand
which *is* by the sea in multitude, eating and
drinking, and making merry.
21 And Solomon reigned over all kingdoms
from the river unto the land of the Philistines, and unto the border of Egypt: they
brought presents, and served Solomon all
the days of his life.
22 ¶ And Solomon's provision for one day
was thirty measures of fine flour, and threescore measures of meal,
23 Ten fat oxen, and twenty oxen out of the
pastures, and an hundred sheep, beside
harts, and roebucks, and fallowdeer, and
fatted fowl.
24 For he had dominion over all *the region*
on this side the river, from Tiphsah even
to Azzah, over all the kings on this side the
river: and he had peace on all sides round
about him.
25 And Judah and Israel dwelt safely, every
man under his vine and under his fig tree,
from Dan even to Beer-sheba, all the days
of Solomon.
26 ¶ And Solomon had forty thousand stalls
of horses for his chariots, and twelve thousand horsemen.
27 And those officers provided victual for
king Solomon, and for all that came unto
king Solomon's table, every man in his
month: they lacked nothing.
28 Barley also and straw for the horses and
dromedaries brought they unto the place
where *the officers* were, every man according to his charge.
29 ¶ And God gave Solomon wisdom and
understanding exceeding much, and large-
ness of heart, even as the sand that *is* on
the sea shore.
30 And Solomon's wisdom excelled the wisdom of all the children of the east country,
and all the wisdom of Egypt.
31 For he was wiser than all men; than Ethan
the Ezrahite, and Heman, and Chalcol, and
Darda, the sons of Mahol: and his fame was
in all nations round about.
32 And he spake three thousand proverbs:
and his songs were a thousand and five.
33 And he spake of trees, from the cedar
tree that *is* in Lebanon even unto the hyssop that springeth out of the wall: he spake
also of beasts, and of fowl, and of creeping
things, and of fishes.
34 And there came of all people to hear
the wisdom of Solomon, from all kings of
the earth, which had heard of his wisdom.

1 Kings 5

1 And Hiram king of Tyre sent his servants
unto Solomon; for he had heard that they
had anointed him king in the room of his
father: for Hiram was ever a lover of David.
2 And Solomon sent to Hiram, saying,
3 Thou knowest how that David my father
could not build an house unto the name of
the LORD his God for the wars which were
about him on every side, until the LORD put
them under the soles of his feet.
4 But now the LORD my God hath given me
rest on every side, *so that there is* neither
adversary nor evil occurrent.
5 And, behold, I purpose to build an house
unto the name of the LORD my God, as the
LORD spake unto David my father, saying,
Thy son, whom I will set upon thy throne

in thy room, he shall build an house unto
my name.
6 Now therefore command thou that they
hew me cedar trees out of Lebanon; and
my servants shall be with thy servants: and
unto thee will I give hire for thy servants
according to all that thou shalt appoint:
for thou knowest that *there is* not among
us any that can skill to hew timber like unto
the Sidonians.
7 ¶ And it came to pass, when Hiram heard
the words of Solomon, that he rejoiced
greatly, and said, Blessed *be* the LORD this
day, which hath given unto David a wise son
over this great people.
8 And Hiram sent to Solomon, saying, I have
considered the things which thou sentest to
me for: *and* I will do all thy desire concerning
timber of cedar, and concerning timber of fir.
9 My servants shall bring *them* down from
Lebanon unto the sea: and I will convey
them by sea in floats unto the place that
thou shalt appoint me, and will cause them
to be discharged there, and thou shalt
receive *them:* and thou shalt accomplish
my desire, in giving food for my household.
10 So Hiram gave Solomon cedar trees and
fir trees *according to* all his desire.
11 And Solomon gave Hiram twenty thousand measures of wheat *for* food to his
household, and twenty measures of pure oil:
thus gave Solomon to Hiram year by year.
12 And the LORD gave Solomon wisdom,
as he promised him: and there was peace
between Hiram and Solomon; and they two
made a league together.
13 ¶ And king Solomon raised a levy out
of all Israel; and the levy was thirty thousand men.
14 And he sent them to Lebanon, ten thousand a month by courses: a month they were
in Lebanon, *and* two months at home: and
Adoniram *was* over the levy.
15 And Solomon had threescore and ten
thousand that bare burdens, and fourscore
thousand hewers in the mountains;
16 Beside the chief of Solomon's officers
which *were* over the work, three thousand
and three hundred, which ruled over the
people that wrought in the work.
17 And the king commanded, and they
brought great stones, costly stones, *and*
hewed stones, to lay the foundation of
the house.
18 And Solomon's builders and Hiram's
builders did hew *them*, and the stonesquar-
ers: so they prepared timber and stones to
build the house.

1 Kings 6

1 And it came to pass in the four hundred
and eightieth year after the children of
Israel were come out of the land of Egypt,
in the fourth year of Solomon's reign over
Israel, in the month Zif, which *is* the second
month, that he began to build the house
of the LORD.
2 And the house which king Solomon
built for the LORD, the length thereof *was*
threescore cubits, and the breadth thereof
twenty *cubits*, and the height thereof thirty
cubits.
3 And the porch before the temple of the
house, twenty cubits *was* the length thereof,
according to the breadth of the house; *and*
ten cubits *was* the breadth thereof before
the house.
4 And for the house he made windows of
narrow lights.
5 ¶ And against the wall of the house he
built chambers round about, *against* the
walls of the house round about, *both* of
the temple and of the oracle: and he made
chambers round about:
6 The nethermost chamber *was* five cubits
broad, and the middle *was* six cubits broad,
and the third *was* seven cubits broad: for
without *in the wall* of the house he made
narrowed rests round about, that *the beams*
should not be fastened in the walls of the
house.
7 And the house, when it was in building,
was built of stone made ready before it was
brought thither: so that there was neither
hammer nor axe *nor* any tool of iron heard
in the house, while it was in building.
8 The door for the middle chamber *was* in
the right side of the house: and they went up
with winding stairs into the middle *chamber*,
and out of the middle into the third.
9 So he built the house, and finished it; and
covered the house with beams and boards
of cedar.
10 And *then* he built chambers against all

the house, five cubits high: and they rested
on the house with timber of cedar.
11 ¶ And the word of the LORD came to
Solomon, saying,
12 *Concerning* this house which thou art in
building, if thou wilt walk in my statutes,
and execute my judgments, and keep all
my commandments to walk in them; then
will I perform my word with thee, which I
spake unto David thy father:
13 And I will dwell among the children of
Israel, and will not forsake my people Israel.
14 So Solomon built the house, and finished it.
15 And he built the walls of the house within
with boards of cedar, both the floor of the
house, and the walls of the cieling: *and* he
covered *them* on the inside with wood,
and covered the floor of the house with
planks of fir.
16 And he built twenty cubits on the sides
of the house, both the floor and the walls
with boards of cedar: he even built *them* for
it within, *even* for the oracle, *even* for the
most holy *place*.
17 And the house, that *is*, the temple before
it, was forty cubits *long*.
18 And the cedar of the house within *was*
carved with knops and open flowers: all *was*
cedar; there was no stone seen.
19 And the oracle he prepared in the house
within, to set there the ark of the covenant
of the LORD.
20 And the oracle in the forepart *was*
twenty cubits in length, and twenty cubits
in breadth, and twenty cubits in the height
thereof: and he overlaid it with pure gold;
and *so* covered the altar *which was of* cedar.
21 So Solomon overlaid the house within
with pure gold: and he made a partition by
the chains of gold before the oracle; and he
overlaid it with gold.
22 And the whole house he overlaid with
gold, until he had finished all the house: also
the whole altar that *was* by the oracle he
overlaid with gold.
23 ¶ And within the oracle he made two
cherubims *of* olive tree, *each* ten cubits high.
24 And five cubits *was* the one wing of the
cherub, and five cubits the other wing of the
cherub: from the uttermost part of the one
wing unto the uttermost part of the other
were ten cubits.
25 And the other cherub *was* ten cubits:
both the cherubims *were* of one measure
and one size.
26 The height of the one cherub *was* ten
cubits, and so *was it* of the other cherub.
27 And he set the cherubims within the
inner house: and they stretched forth the
wings of the cherubims, so that the wing of
the one touched the *one* wall, and the wing
of the other cherub touched the other wall;
and their wings touched one another in the
midst of the house.
28 And he overlaid the cherubims with gold.
29 And he carved all the walls of the house
round about with carved figures of cherubims and palm trees and open flowers,
within and without.
30 And the floor of the house he overlaid
with gold, within and without.
31 ¶ And for the entering of the oracle he
made doors *of* olive tree: the lintel *and* side
posts *were* a fifth part *of the wall*.
32 The two doors also *were of* olive tree; and
he carved upon them carvings of cherubims
and palm trees and open flowers, and overlaid *them* with gold, and spread gold upon
the cherubims, and upon the palm trees.
33 So also made he for the door of the
temple posts *of* olive tree, a fourth part
of the wall.
34 And the two doors *were of* fir tree: the
two leaves of the one door *were* folding,
and the two leaves of the other door *were*
folding.
35 And he carved *thereon* cherubims and
palm trees and open flowers: and covered
them with gold fitted upon the carved work.
36 ¶ And he built the inner court with three
rows of hewed stone, and a row of cedar
beams.
37 ¶ In the fourth year was the foundation of
the house of the LORD laid, in the month Zif:
38 And in the eleventh year, in the month
Bul, which *is* the eighth month, was the
house finished throughout all the parts
thereof, and according to all the fashion
of it. So was he seven years in building it.

1 Kings 7

1 But Solomon was building his own house
thirteen years, and he finished all his house.
2 ¶ He built also the house of the forest of
Lebanon; the length thereof *was* an hundred

cubits, and the breadth thereof fifty cubits, and the height thereof thirty cubits, upon four rows of cedar pillars, with cedar beams upon the pillars.

3 And *it was* covered with cedar above upon the beams, that *lay* on forty five pillars, fifteen *in* a row.

4 And *there were* windows *in* three rows, and light *was* against light *in* three ranks.

5 And all the doors and posts *were* square, with the windows: and light *was* against light *in* three ranks.

6 ¶ And he made a porch of pillars; the length thereof *was* fifty cubits, and the breadth thereof thirty cubits: and the porch *was* before them: and the *other* pillars and the thick beam *were* before them.

7 ¶ Then he made a porch for the throne where he might judge, *even* the porch of judgment: and *it was* covered with cedar from one side of the floor to the other.

8 ¶ And his house where he dwelt *had* another court within the porch, *which* was of the like work. Solomon made also an house for Pharaoh's daughter, whom he had taken *to wife*, like unto this porch.

9 All these *were of* costly stones, according to the measures of hewed stones, sawed with saws, within and without, even from the foundation unto the coping, and *so* on the outside toward the great court.

10 And the foundation *was of* costly stones, even great stones, stones of ten cubits, and stones of eight cubits.

11 And above *were* costly stones, after the measures of hewed stones, and cedars.

12 And the great court round about *was* with three rows of hewed stones, and a row of cedar beams, both for the inner court of the house of the LORD, and for the porch of the house.

13 ¶ And king Solomon sent and fetched Hiram out of Tyre.

14 He *was* a widow's son of the tribe of Naphtali, and his father *was* a man of Tyre, a worker in brass: and he was filled with wisdom, and understanding, and cunning to work all works in brass. And he came to king Solomon, and wrought all his work.

15 For he cast two pillars of brass, of eighteen cubits high apiece: and a line of twelve cubits did compass either of them about.

16 And he made two chapiters *of* molten brass, to set upon the tops of the pillars: the height of the one chapiter *was* five cubits, and the height of the other chapiter *was* five cubits:

17 *And* nets of checker work, and wreaths of chain work, for the chapiters which *were* upon the top of the pillars; seven for the one chapiter, and seven for the other chapiter.

18 And he made the pillars, and two rows round about upon the one network, to cover the chapiters that *were* upon the top, with pomegranates: and so did he for the other chapiter.

19 And the chapiters that *were* upon the top of the pillars *were* of lily work in the porch, four cubits.

20 And the chapiters upon the two pillars *had pomegranates* also above, over against the belly which *was* by the network: and the pomegranates *were* two hundred in rows round about upon the other chapiter.

21 And he set up the pillars in the porch of the temple: and he set up the right pillar, and called the name thereof Jachin: and he set up the left pillar, and called the name thereof Boaz.

22 And upon the top of the pillars *was* lily work: so was the work of the pillars finished.

23 ¶ And he made a molten sea, ten cubits from the one brim to the other: *it was* round all about, and his height *was* five cubits: and a line of thirty cubits did compass it round about.

24 And under the brim of it round about *there were* knops compassing it, ten in a cubit, compassing the sea round about: the knops *were* cast in two rows, when it was cast.

25 It stood upon twelve oxen, three looking toward the north, and three looking toward the west, and three looking toward the south, and three looking toward the east: and the sea *was set* above upon them, and all their hinder parts *were* inward.

26 And it *was* an hand breadth thick, and the brim thereof was wrought like the brim of a cup, with flowers of lilies: it contained two thousand baths.

27 ¶ And he made ten bases of brass; four cubits *was* the length of one base, and four cubits the breadth thereof, and three cubits the height of it.

28 And the work of the bases *was* on this

manner: they had borders, and the borders
were between the ledges:
29 And on the borders that *were* between
the ledges *were* lions, oxen, and cherubims:
and upon the ledges *there was* a base above:
and beneath the lions and oxen *were* certain
additions made of thin work.
30 And every base had four brasen wheels,
and plates of brass: and the four corners
thereof had undersetters: under the laver
were undersetters molten, at the side of
every addition.
31 And the mouth of it within the chapiter and above *was* a cubit: but the mouth
thereof *was* round *after* the work of the
base, a cubit and an half: and also upon the
mouth of it *were* gravings with their borders,
foursquare, not round.
32 And under the borders *were* four wheels;
and the axletrees of the wheels *were joined*
to the base: and the height of a wheel *was*
a cubit and half a cubit.
33 And the work of the wheels *was* like the
work of a chariot wheel: their axletrees,
and their naves, and their felloes, and their
spokes, *were* all molten.
34 And *there were* four undersetters to the
four corners of one base: *and* the undersetters *were* of the very base itself.
35 And in the top of the base *was there* a
round compass of half a cubit high: and on
the top of the base the ledges thereof and
the borders thereof *were* of the same.
36 For on the plates of the ledges thereof,
and on the borders thereof, he graved cherubims, lions, and palm trees, according to
the proportion of every one, and additions
round about.
37 After this *manner* he made the ten bases:
all of them had one casting, one measure,
and one size.
38 ¶ Then made he ten lavers of brass: one
laver contained forty baths: *and* every laver
was four cubits: *and* upon every one of the
ten bases one laver.
39 And he put five bases on the right side
of the house, and five on the left side of the
house: and he set the sea on the right side of
the house eastward over against the south.
40 ¶ And Hiram made the lavers, and the
shovels, and the basons. So Hiram made an
end of doing all the work that he made king
Solomon for the house of the LORD:
41 The two pillars, and the *two* bowls of the
chapiters that *were* on the top of the two
pillars; and the two networks, to cover the
two bowls of the chapiters which *were* upon
the top of the pillars;
42 And four hundred pomegranates for
the two networks, *even* two rows of pomegranates for one network, to cover the two
bowls of the chapiters that *were* upon the
pillars;
43 And the ten bases, and ten lavers on
the bases;
44 And one sea, and twelve oxen under
the sea;
45 And the pots, and the shovels, and the
basons: and all these vessels, which Hiram
made to king Solomon for the house of the
LORD, *were of* bright brass.
46 In the plain of Jordan did the king cast
them, in the clay ground between Succoth
and Zarthan.
47 And Solomon left all the vessels
unweighed, because they were exceeding
many: neither was the weight of the brass
found out.
48 And Solomon made all the vessels that
pertained unto the house of the LORD: the
altar of gold, and the table of gold, whereupon the shewbread *was,*
49 And the candlesticks of pure gold, five
on the right *side,* and five on the left, before
the oracle, with the flowers, and the lamps,
and the tongs *of* gold,
50 And the bowls, and the snuffers, and the
basons, and the spoons, and the censers
of pure gold; and the hinges *of* gold, *both*
for the doors of the inner house, the most
holy *place, and* for the doors of the house,
to wit, of the temple.
51 So was ended all the work that king Solomon made for the house of the LORD. And
Solomon brought in the things which David
his father had dedicated; *even* the silver, and
the gold, and the vessels, did he put among
the treasures of the house of the LORD.

1 Kings 8

1 Then Solomon assembled the elders of
Israel, and all the heads of the tribes, the
chief of the fathers of the children of Israel,
unto king Solomon in Jerusalem, that they
might bring up the ark of the covenant of the
LORD out of the city of David, which *is* Zion.

2 And all the men of Israel assembled themselves unto king Solomon at the feast in the
month Ethanim, which *is* the seventh month.
3 And all the elders of Israel came, and the
priests took up the ark.
4 And they brought up the ark of the LORD,
and the tabernacle of the congregation,
and all the holy vessels that *were* in the
tabernacle, even those did the priests and
the Levites bring up.
5 And king Solomon, and all the congregation of Israel, that were assembled unto him,
were with him before the ark, sacrificing
sheep and oxen, that could not be told nor
numbered for multitude.
6 And the priests brought in the ark of the
covenant of the LORD unto his place, into the
oracle of the house, to the most holy *place*,
even under the wings of the cherubims.
7 For the cherubims spread forth *their* two
wings over the place of the ark, and the
cherubims covered the ark and the staves
thereof above.
8 And they drew out the staves, that the
ends of the staves were seen out in the
holy *place* before the oracle, and they were
not seen without: and there they are unto
this day.
9 *There was* nothing in the ark save the two
tables of stone, which Moses put there at
Horeb, when the LORD made *a covenant*
with the children of Israel, when they came
out of the land of Egypt.
10 And it came to pass, when the priests
were come out of the holy *place*, that the
cloud filled the house of the LORD,
11 So that the priests could not stand to
minister because of the cloud: for the glory
of the LORD had filled the house of the LORD.
12 ¶ Then spake Solomon, The LORD said
that he would dwell in the thick darkness.
13 I have surely built thee an house to
dwell in, a settled place for thee to abide
in for ever.
14 And the king turned his face about, and
blessed all the congregation of Israel: (and
all the congregation of Israel stood;)
15 And he said, Blessed *be* the LORD God
of Israel, which spake with his mouth unto
David my father, and hath with his hand
fulfilled *it*, saying,
16 Since the day that I brought forth my
people Israel out of Egypt, I chose no city out
of all the tribes of Israel to build an house,
that my name might be therein; but I chose
David to be over my people Israel.
17 And it was in the heart of David my father
to build an house for the name of the LORD
God of Israel.
18 And the LORD said unto David my father,
Whereas it was in thine heart to build an
house unto my name, thou didst well that
it was in thine heart.
19 Nevertheless thou shalt not build the
house; but thy son that shall come forth
out of thy loins, he shall build the house
unto my name.
20 And the LORD hath performed his word
that he spake, and I am risen up in the room
of David my father, and sit on the throne
of Israel, as the LORD promised, and have
built an house for the name of the LORD
God of Israel.
21 And I have set there a place for the ark,
wherein *is* the covenant of the LORD, which
he made with our fathers, when he brought
them out of the land of Egypt.
22 ¶ And Solomon stood before the altar of
the LORD in the presence of all the congregation of Israel, and spread forth his hands
toward heaven:
23 And he said, LORD God of Israel, *there*
is no God like thee, in heaven above, or on
earth beneath, who keepest covenant and
mercy with thy servants that walk before
thee with all their heart:
24 Who hast kept with thy servant David my
father that thou promisedst him: thou spakest also with thy mouth, and hast fulfilled
it with thine hand, as *it is* this day.
25 Therefore now, LORD God of Israel, keep
with thy servant David my father that thou
promisedst him, saying, There shall not fail
thee a man in my sight to sit on the throne
of Israel; so that thy children take heed to
their way, that they walk before me as thou
hast walked before me.
26 And now, O God of Israel, let thy word, I
pray thee, be verified, which thou spakest
unto thy servant David my father.
27 But will God indeed dwell on the earth?
behold, the heaven and heaven of heavens
cannot contain thee; how much less this
house that I have builded?
28 Yet have thou respect unto the prayer
of thy servant, and to his supplication, O

LORD my God, to hearken unto the cry and
to the prayer, which thy servant prayeth
before thee to day:
29 That thine eyes may be open toward this
house night and day, *even* toward the place
of which thou hast said, My name shall be
there: that thou mayest hearken unto the
prayer which thy servant shall make toward
this place.
30 And hearken thou to the supplication of
thy servant, and of thy people Israel, when
they shall pray toward this place: and hear
thou in heaven thy dwelling place: and when
thou hearest, forgive.
31 ¶ If any man trespass against his neighbour, and an oath be laid upon him to cause
him to swear, and the oath come before
thine altar in this house:
32 Then hear thou in heaven, and do, and
judge thy servants, condemning the wicked,
to bring his way upon his head; and justifying the righteous, to give him according to
his righteousness.
33 ¶ When thy people Israel be smitten
down before the enemy, because they have
sinned against thee, and shall turn again to
thee, and confess thy name, and pray, and
make supplication unto thee in this house:
34 Then hear thou in heaven, and forgive
the sin of thy people Israel, and bring them
again unto the land which thou gavest unto
their fathers.
35 ¶ When heaven is shut up, and there is
no rain, because they have sinned against
thee; if they pray toward this place, and
confess thy name, and turn from their sin,
when thou afflictest them:
36 Then hear thou in heaven, and forgive
the sin of thy servants, and of thy people
Israel, that thou teach them the good way
wherein they should walk, and give rain
upon thy land, which thou hast given to thy
people for an inheritance.
37 ¶ If there be in the land famine, if there
be pestilence, blasting, mildew, locust, *or* if
there be caterpiller; if their enemy besiege
them in the land of their cities; whatsoever
plague, whatsoever sickness *there be;*
38 What prayer and supplication soever be
made by any man, *or* by all thy people Israel,
which shall know every man the plague of
his own heart, and spread forth his hands
toward this house:
39 Then hear thou in heaven thy dwelling
place, and forgive, and do, and give to
every man according to his ways, whose
heart thou knowest; (for thou, *even* thou
only, knowest the hearts of all the children
of men;)
40 That they may fear thee all the days that
they live in the land which thou gavest unto
our fathers.
41 Moreover concerning a stranger, that *is*
not of thy people Israel, but cometh out of
a far country for thy name's sake;
42 (For they shall hear of thy great name,
and of thy strong hand, and of thy stretched
out arm;) when he shall come and pray
toward this house;
43 Hear thou in heaven thy dwelling place,
and do according to all that the stranger
calleth to thee for: that all people of the
earth may know thy name, to fear thee,
as *do* thy people Israel; and that they may
know that this house, which I have builded,
is called by thy name.
44 ¶ If thy people go out to battle against
their enemy, whithersoever thou shalt send
them, and shall pray unto the LORD toward
the city which thou hast chosen, and *toward*
the house that I have built for thy name:
45 Then hear thou in heaven their prayer
and their supplication, and maintain their
cause.
46 If they sin against thee, (for *there is* no
man that sinneth not,) and thou be angry
with them, and deliver them to the enemy,
so that they carry them away captives unto
the land of the enemy, far or near;
47 *Yet* if they shall bethink themselves in the
land whither they were carried captives, and
repent, and make supplication unto thee in
the land of them that carried them captives,
saying, We have sinned, and have done
perversely, we have committed wickedness;
48 And *so* return unto thee with all their
heart, and with all their soul, in the land of
their enemies, which led them away captive, and pray unto thee toward their land,
which thou gavest unto their fathers, the
city which thou hast chosen, and the house
which I have built for thy name:
49 Then hear thou their prayer and their
supplication in heaven thy dwelling place,
and maintain their cause,
50 And forgive thy people that have sinned

against thee, and all their transgressions
wherein they have transgressed against
thee, and give them compassion before
them who carried them captive, that they
may have compassion on them:
51 For they *be* thy people, and thine inheritance, which thou broughtest forth out of
Egypt, from the midst of the furnace of iron:
52 That thine eyes may be open unto the
supplication of thy servant, and unto the
supplication of thy people Israel, to hearken
unto them in all that they call for unto thee.
53 For thou didst separate them from
among all the people of the earth, *to be*
thine inheritance, as thou spakest by the
hand of Moses thy servant, when thou
broughtest our fathers out of Egypt, O
Lord GOD.
54 And it was *so*, that when Solomon had
made an end of praying all this prayer and
supplication unto the LORD, he arose from
before the altar of the LORD, from kneeling
on his knees with his hands spread up to
heaven.
55 And he stood, and blessed all the congregation of Israel with a loud voice, saying,
56 Blessed *be* the LORD, that hath given rest
unto his people Israel, according to all that
he promised: there hath not failed one word
of all his good promise, which he promised
by the hand of Moses his servant.
57 The LORD our God be with us, as he was
with our fathers: let him not leave us, nor
forsake us:
58 That he may incline our hearts unto him,
to walk in all his ways, and to keep his commandments, and his statutes, and his judgments, which he commanded our fathers.
59 And let these my words, wherewith I
have made supplication before the LORD, be
nigh unto the LORD our God day and night,
that he maintain the cause of his servant,
and the cause of his people Israel at all
times, as the matter shall require:
60 That all the people of the earth may
know that the LORD *is* God, *and that there
is* none else.
61 Let your heart therefore be perfect with
the LORD our God, to walk in his statutes,
and to keep his commandments, as at this
day.
62 ¶ And the king, and all Israel with him,
offered sacrifice before the LORD.
63 And Solomon offered a sacrifice of peace
offerings, which he offered unto the LORD,
two and twenty thousand oxen, and an
hundred and twenty thousand sheep. So the
king and all the children of Israel dedicated
the house of the LORD.
64 The same day did the king hallow the
middle of the court that *was* before the
house of the LORD: for there he offered
burnt offerings, and meat offerings, and
the fat of the peace offerings: because the
brasen altar that *was* before the LORD *was*
too little to receive the burnt offerings, and
meat offerings, and the fat of the peace
offerings.
65 And at that time Solomon held a feast,
and all Israel with him, a great congregation,
from the entering in of Hamath unto the
river of Egypt, before the LORD our God,
seven days and seven days, *even* fourteen
days.
66 On the eighth day he sent the people
away: and they blessed the king, and went
unto their tents joyful and glad of heart for
all the goodness that the LORD had done for
David his servant, and for Israel his people.

1 Kings 9

1 And it came to pass, when Solomon had
finished the building of the house of the
LORD, and the king's house, and all Solomon's desire which he was pleased to do,
2 That the LORD appeared to Solomon the
second time, as he had appeared unto him
at Gibeon.
3 And the LORD said unto him, I have heard
thy prayer and thy supplication, that thou
hast made before me: I have hallowed this
house, which thou hast built, to put my
name there for ever; and mine eyes and
mine heart shall be there perpetually.
4 And if thou wilt walk before me, as David
thy father walked, in integrity of heart, and
in uprightness, to do according to all that I
have commanded thee, *and* wilt keep my
statutes and my judgments:
5 Then I will establish the throne of thy
kingdom upon Israel for ever, as I promised
to David thy father, saying, There shall not
fail thee a man upon the throne of Israel.
6 *But* if ye shall at all turn from following
me, ye or your children, and will not keep
my commandments *and* my statutes which I

have set before you, but go and serve other
gods, and worship them:
7 Then will I cut off Israel out of the land
which I have given them; and this house,
which I have hallowed for my name, will
I cast out of my sight; and Israel shall be a
proverb and a byword among all people:
8 And at this house, *which* is high, every
one that passeth by it shall be astonished,
and shall hiss; and they shall say, Why hath
the LORD done thus unto this land, and to
this house?
9 And they shall answer, Because they
forsook the LORD their God, who brought
forth their fathers out of the land of Egypt,
and have taken hold upon other gods, and
have worshipped them, and served them:
therefore hath the LORD brought upon them
all this evil.
10 ¶ And it came to pass at the end of
twenty years, when Solomon had built the
two houses, the house of the LORD, and the
king's house,
11 (*Now* Hiram the king of Tyre had furnished Solomon with cedar trees and fir
trees, and with gold, according to all his
desire,) that then king Solomon gave Hiram
twenty cities in the land of Galilee.
12 And Hiram came out from Tyre to see
the cities which Solomon had given him;
and they pleased him not.
13 And he said, What cities *are* these which
thou hast given me, my brother? And he
called them the land of Cabul unto this day.
14 And Hiram sent to the king sixscore talents of gold.
15 ¶ And this *is* the reason of the levy which
king Solomon raised; for to build the house
of the LORD, and his own house, and Millo,
and the wall of Jerusalem, and Hazor, and
Megiddo, and Gezer.
16 *For* Pharaoh king of Egypt had gone up,
and taken Gezer, and burnt it with fire, and
slain the Canaanites that dwelt in the city,
and given it *for* a present unto his daughter,
Solomon's wife.
17 And Solomon built Gezer, and Beth-horon
the nether,
18 And Baalath, and Tadmor in the wilderness, in the land,
19 And all the cities of store that Solomon
had, and cities for his chariots, and cities
for his horsemen, and that which Solomon
desired to build in Jerusalem, and in Lebanon, and in all the land of his dominion.
20 *And* all the people *that were* left of the
Amorites, Hittites, Perizzites, Hivites, and
Jebusites, which *were* not of the children
of Israel,
21 Their children that were left after them
in the land, whom the children of Israel also
were not able utterly to destroy, upon those
did Solomon levy a tribute of bondservice
unto this day.
22 But of the children of Israel did Solomon
make no bondmen: but they *were* men of
war, and his servants, and his princes, and
his captains, and rulers of his chariots, and
his horsemen.
23 These *were* the chief of the officers that
were over Solomon's work, five hundred and
fifty, which bare rule over the people that
wrought in the work.
24 ¶ But Pharaoh's daughter came up out
of the city of David unto her house which
Solomon had built for her: then did he
build Millo.
25 ¶ And three times in a year did Solomon
offer burnt offerings and peace offerings
upon the altar which he built unto the LORD,
and he burnt incense upon the altar that *was*
before the LORD. So he finished the house.
26 ¶ And king Solomon made a navy of ships
in Ezion-geber, which *is* beside Eloth, on the
shore of the Red sea, in the land of Edom.
27 And Hiram sent in the navy his servants,
shipmen that had knowledge of the sea,
with the servants of Solomon.
28 And they came to Ophir, and fetched
from thence gold, four hundred and twenty
talents, and brought *it* to king Solomon.

1 Kings 10

1 And when the queen of Sheba heard of
the fame of Solomon concerning the name
of the LORD, she came to prove him with
hard questions.
2 And she came to Jerusalem with a very
great train, with camels that bare spices, and
very much gold, and precious stones: and
when she was come to Solomon, she communed with him of all that was in her heart.
3 And Solomon told her all her questions:
there was not *any* thing hid from the king,
which he told her not.
4 And when the queen of Sheba had seen

all Solomon's wisdom, and the house that
he had built,
5 And the meat of his table, and the sitting
of his servants, and the attendance of his
ministers, and their apparel, and his cupbearers, and his ascent by which he went
up unto the house of the LORD; there was
no more spirit in her.
6 And she said to the king, It was a true
report that I heard in mine own land of thy
acts and of thy wisdom.
7 Howbeit I believed not the words, until
I came, and mine eyes had seen *it:* and,
behold, the half was not told me: thy wisdom and prosperity exceedeth the fame
which I heard.
8 Happy *are* thy men, happy *are* these thy
servants, which stand continually before
thee, *and* that hear thy wisdom.
9 Blessed be the LORD thy God, which
delighted in thee, to set thee on the throne
of Israel: because the LORD loved Israel for
ever, therefore made he thee king, to do
judgment and justice.
10 And she gave the king an hundred and
twenty talents of gold, and of spices very
great store, and precious stones: there
came no more such abundance of spices
as these which the queen of Sheba gave to
king Solomon.
11 And the navy also of Hiram, that brought
gold from Ophir, brought in from Ophir great
plenty of almug trees, and precious stones.
12 And the king made of the almug trees
pillars for the house of the LORD, and for
the king's house, harps also and psalteries
for singers: there came no such almug trees,
nor were seen unto this day.
13 And king Solomon gave unto the queen
of Sheba all her desire, whatsoever she
asked, beside *that* which Solomon gave her
of his royal bounty. So she turned and went
to her own country, she and her servants.
14 ¶ Now the weight of gold that came to
Solomon in one year was six hundred threescore and six talents of gold,
15 Beside *that he had* of the merchantmen,
and of the traffick of the spice merchants,
and of all the kings of Arabia, and of the
governors of the country.
16 ¶ And king Solomon made two hundred
targets *of* beaten gold: six hundred *shekels*
of gold went to one target.
17 And *he made* three hundred shields *of*
beaten gold; three pound of gold went to
one shield: and the king put them in the
house of the forest of Lebanon.
18 ¶ Moreover the king made a great throne
of ivory, and overlaid it with the best gold.
19 The throne had six steps, and the top
of the throne *was* round behind: and *there
were* stays on either side on the place of the
seat, and two lions stood beside the stays.
20 And twelve lions stood there on the one
side and on the other upon the six steps:
there was not the like made in any kingdom.
21 ¶ And all king Solomon's drinking vessels *were of* gold, and all the vessels of the
house of the forest of Lebanon *were of* pure
gold; none *were of* silver: it was nothing
accounted of in the days of Solomon.
22 For the king had at sea a navy of Tharshish with the navy of Hiram: once in three
years came the navy of Tharshish, bringing gold, and silver, ivory, and apes, and
peacocks.
23 So king Solomon exceeded all the kings
of the earth for riches and for wisdom.
24 ¶ And all the earth sought to Solomon,
to hear his wisdom, which God had put in
his heart.
25 And they brought every man his present,
vessels of silver, and vessels of gold, and
garments, and armour, and spices, horses,
and mules, a rate year by year.
26 ¶ And Solomon gathered together chariots and horsemen: and he had a thousand
and four hundred chariots, and twelve
thousand horsemen, whom he bestowed
in the cities for chariots, and with the king
at Jerusalem.
27 And the king made silver *to be* in Jerusalem as stones, and cedars made he *to be*
as the sycomore trees that *are* in the vale,
for abundance.
28 ¶ And Solomon had horses brought out
of Egypt, and linen yarn: the king's merchants received the linen yarn at a price.
29 And a chariot came up and went out of
Egypt for six hundred *shekels* of silver, and
an horse for an hundred and fifty: and so
for all the kings of the Hittites, and for the
kings of Syria, did they bring *them* out by
their means.

1 Kings 11

1 But king Solomon loved many strange
women, together with the daughter of Pharaoh, women of the Moabites, Ammonites,
Edomites, Zidonians, *and* Hittites;
2 Of the nations *concerning* which the LORD
said unto the children of Israel, Ye shall not
go in to them, neither shall they come in
unto you: *for* surely they will turn away your
heart after their gods: Solomon clave unto
these in love.
3 And he had seven hundred wives, prin-
cesses, and three hundred concubines: and
his wives turned away his heart.
4 For it came to pass, when Solomon was
old, *that* his wives turned away his heart
after other gods: and his heart was not
perfect with the LORD his God, as *was* the
heart of David his father.
5 For Solomon went after Ashtoreth the
goddess of the Zidonians, and after Milcom
the abomination of the Ammonites.
6 And Solomon did evil in the sight of the
LORD, and went not fully after the LORD, as
did David his father.
7 Then did Solomon build an high place for
Chemosh, the abomination of Moab, in the
hill that *is* before Jerusalem, and for Molech,
the abomination of the children of Ammon.
8 And likewise did he for all his strange
wives, which burnt incense and sacrificed
unto their gods.
9 ¶ And the LORD was angry with Solomon,
because his heart was turned from the
LORD God of Israel, which had appeared
unto him twice,
10 And had commanded him concerning
this thing, that he should not go after other
gods: but he kept not that which the LORD
commanded.
11 Wherefore the LORD said unto Solomon,
Forasmuch as this is done of thee, and thou
hast not kept my covenant and my statutes,
which I have commanded thee, I will surely
rend the kingdom from thee, and will give
it to thy servant.
12 Notwithstanding in thy days I will not do
it for David thy father's sake: *but* I will rend
it out of the hand of thy son.
13 Howbeit I will not rend away all the kingdom; *but* will give one tribe to thy son for
David my servant's sake, and for Jerusalem's
sake which I have chosen.
14 ¶ And the LORD stirred up an adversary
unto Solomon, Hadad the Edomite: he *was*
of the king's seed in Edom.
15 For it came to pass, when David was
in Edom, and Joab the captain of the host
was gone up to bury the slain, after he had
smitten every male in Edom;
16 (For six months did Joab remain there
with all Israel, until he had cut off every
male in Edom:)
17 That Hadad fled, he and certain Edomites
of his father's servants with him, to go into
Egypt; Hadad *being* yet a little child.
18 And they arose out of Midian, and came
to Paran: and they took men with them out
of Paran, and they came to Egypt, unto
Pharaoh king of Egypt; which gave him an
house, and appointed him victuals, and
gave him land.
19 And Hadad found great favour in the
sight of Pharaoh, so that he gave him to
wife the sister of his own wife, the sister of
Tahpenes the queen.
20 And the sister of Tahpenes bare him
Genubath his son, whom Tahpenes weaned
in Pharaoh's house: and Genubath was in
Pharaoh's household among the sons of
Pharaoh.
21 And when Hadad heard in Egypt that
David slept with his fathers, and that Joab
the captain of the host was dead, Hadad
said to Pharaoh, Let me depart, that I may
go to mine own country.
22 Then Pharaoh said unto him, But what
hast thou lacked with me, that, behold,
thou seekest to go to thine own country?
And he answered, Nothing: howbeit let me
go in any wise.
23 ¶ And God stirred him up *another* adversary, Rezon the son of Eliadah, which fled
from his lord Hadadezer king of Zobah:
24 And he gathered men unto him, and
became captain over a band, when David
slew them *of Zobah:* and they went to
Damascus, and dwelt therein, and reigned
in Damascus.
25 And he was an adversary to Israel all
the days of Solomon, beside the mischief
that Hadad *did:* and he abhorred Israel, and
reigned over Syria.
26 ¶ And Jeroboam the son of Nebat, an
Ephrathite of Zereda, Solomon's servant,
whose mother's name *was* Zeruah, a widow

woman, even he lifted up *his* hand against the king.

27 And this *was* the cause that he lifted up *his* hand against the king: Solomon built Millo, *and* repaired the breaches of the city of David his father.

28 And the man Jeroboam *was* a mighty man of valour: and Solomon seeing the young man that he was industrious, he made him ruler over all the charge of the house of Joseph.

29 And it came to pass at that time when Jeroboam went out of Jerusalem, that the prophet Ahijah the Shilonite found him in the way; and he had clad himself with a new garment; and they two *were* alone in the field:

30 And Ahijah caught the new garment that *was* on him, and rent it *in* twelve pieces:

31 And he said to Jeroboam, Take thee ten pieces: for thus saith the LORD, the God of Israel, Behold, I will rend the kingdom out of the hand of Solomon, and will give ten tribes to thee:

32 (But he shall have one tribe for my servant David's sake, and for Jerusalem's sake, the city which I have chosen out of all the tribes of Israel:)

33 Because that they have forsaken me, and have worshipped Ashtoreth the goddess of the Zidonians, Chemosh the god of the Moabites, and Milcom the god of the children of Ammon, and have not walked in my ways, to do *that which is* right in mine eyes, and *to keep* my statutes and my judgments, as *did* David his father.

34 Howbeit I will not take the whole kingdom out of his hand: but I will make him prince all the days of his life for David my servant's sake, whom I chose, because he kept my commandments and my statutes:

35 But I will take the kingdom out of his son's hand, and will give it unto thee, *even* ten tribes.

36 And unto his son will I give one tribe, that David my servant may have a light alway before me in Jerusalem, the city which I have chosen me to put my name there.

37 And I will take thee, and thou shalt reign according to all that thy soul desireth, and shalt be king over Israel.

38 And it shall be, if thou wilt hearken unto all that I command thee, and wilt walk in my ways, and do *that is* right in my sight, to keep my statutes and my commandments, as David my servant did; that I will be with thee, and build thee a sure house, as I built for David, and will give Israel unto thee.

39 And I will for this afflict the seed of David, but not for ever.

40 Solomon sought therefore to kill Jeroboam. And Jeroboam arose, and fled into Egypt, unto Shishak king of Egypt, and was in Egypt until the death of Solomon.

41 ¶ And the rest of the acts of Solomon, and all that he did, and his wisdom, *are* they not written in the book of the acts of Solomon?

42 And the time that Solomon reigned in Jerusalem over all Israel *was* forty years.

43 And Solomon slept with his fathers, and was buried in the city of David his father: and Rehoboam his son reigned in his stead.

1 Kings 12

1 And Rehoboam went to Shechem: for all Israel were come to Shechem to make him king.

2 And it came to pass, when Jeroboam the son of Nebat, who was yet in Egypt, heard *of it*, (for he was fled from the presence of king Solomon, and Jeroboam dwelt in Egypt;)

3 That they sent and called him. And Jeroboam and all the congregation of Israel came, and spake unto Rehoboam, saying,

4 Thy father made our yoke grievous: now therefore make thou the grievous service of thy father, and his heavy yoke which he put upon us, lighter, and we will serve thee.

5 And he said unto them, Depart yet *for* three days, then come again to me. And the people departed.

6 ¶ And king Rehoboam consulted with the old men, that stood before Solomon his father while he yet lived, and said, How do ye advise that I may answer this people?

7 And they spake unto him, saying, If thou wilt be a servant unto this people this day, and wilt serve them, and answer them, and speak good words to them, then they will be thy servants for ever.

8 But he forsook the counsel of the old men, which they had given him, and consulted with the young men that were grown up with him, *and* which stood before him:

9 And he said unto them, What counsel give

ye that we may answer this people, who
have spoken to me, saying, Make the yoke
which thy father did put upon us lighter?
10 And the young men that were grown
up with him spake unto him, saying, Thus
shalt thou speak unto this people that spake
unto thee, saying, Thy father made our yoke
heavy, but make thou *it* lighter unto us; thus
shalt thou say unto them, My little *finger*
shall be thicker than my father's loins.
11 And now whereas my father did lade you
with a heavy yoke, I will add to your yoke:
my father hath chastised you with whips,
but I will chastise you with scorpions.
12 ¶ So Jeroboam and all the people came
to Rehoboam the third day, as the king had
appointed, saying, Come to me again the
third day.
13 And the king answered the people
roughly, and forsook the old men's counsel
that they gave him;
14 And spake to them after the counsel of
the young men, saying, My father made your
yoke heavy, and I will add to your yoke: my
father *also* chastised you with whips, but I
will chastise you with scorpions.
15 Wherefore the king hearkened not unto
the people; for the cause was from the LORD,
that he might perform his saying, which the
LORD spake by Ahijah the Shilonite unto
Jeroboam the son of Nebat.
16 ¶ So when all Israel saw that the king
hearkened not unto them, the people
answered the king, saying, What portion
have we in David? neither *have we* inheritance in the son of Jesse: to your tents, O
Israel: now see to thine own house, David.
So Israel departed unto their tents.
17 But *as for* the children of Israel which
dwelt in the cities of Judah, Rehoboam
reigned over them.
18 Then king Rehoboam sent Adoram, who
was over the tribute; and all Israel stoned
him with stones, that he died. Therefore
king Rehoboam made speed to get him up
to his chariot, to flee to Jerusalem.
19 So Israel rebelled against the house of
David unto this day.
20 And it came to pass, when all Israel heard
that Jeroboam was come again, that they
sent and called him unto the congregation,
and made him king over all Israel: there was
none that followed the house of David, but
the tribe of Judah only.
21 ¶ And when Rehoboam was come to
Jerusalem, he assembled all the house of
Judah, with the tribe of Benjamin, an hundred and fourscore thousand chosen men,
which were warriors, to fight against the
house of Israel, to bring the kingdom again
to Rehoboam the son of Solomon.
22 But the word of God came unto Shemaiah the man of God, saying,
23 Speak unto Rehoboam, the son of Solomon, king of Judah, and unto all the house
of Judah and Benjamin, and to the remnant
of the people, saying,
24 Thus saith the LORD, Ye shall not go up,
nor fight against your brethren the children
of Israel: return every man to his house;
for this thing is from me. They hearkened
therefore to the word of the LORD, and
returned to depart, according to the word
of the LORD.
25 ¶ Then Jeroboam built Shechem in
mount Ephraim, and dwelt therein; and
went out from thence, and built Penuel.
26 And Jeroboam said in his heart, Now shall
the kingdom return to the house of David:
27 If this people go up to do sacrifice in the
house of the LORD at Jerusalem, then shall
the heart of this people turn again unto
their lord, *even* unto Rehoboam king of
Judah, and they shall kill me, and go again
to Rehoboam king of Judah.
28 Whereupon the king took counsel, and
made two calves *of* gold, and said unto
them, It is too much for you to go up to
Jerusalem: behold thy gods, O Israel, which
brought thee up out of the land of Egypt.
29 And he set the one in Beth-el, and the
other put he in Dan.
30 And this thing became a sin: for the
people went *to worship* before the one,
even unto Dan.
31 And he made an house of high places, and
made priests of the lowest of the people,
which were not of the sons of Levi.
32 And Jeroboam ordained a feast in the
eighth month, on the fifteenth day of the
month, like unto the feast that *is* in Judah,
and he offered upon the altar. So did he
in Beth-el, sacrificing unto the calves that
he had made: and he placed in Beth-el the

priests of the high places which he had
made.
33 So he offered upon the altar which he
had made in Beth-el the fifteenth day of the
eighth month, *even* in the month which he
had devised of his own heart; and ordained
a feast unto the children of Israel: and he
offered upon the altar, and burnt incense.

1 Kings 13

1 And, behold, there came a man of God
out of Judah by the word of the LORD unto
Beth-el: and Jeroboam stood by the altar
to burn incense.
2 And he cried against the altar in the word
of the LORD, and said, O altar, altar, thus saith
the LORD; Behold, a child shall be born unto
the house of David, Josiah by name; and
upon thee shall he offer the priests of the
high places that burn incense upon thee,
and men's bones shall be burnt upon thee.
3 And he gave a sign the same day, saying,
This *is* the sign which the LORD hath spoken;
Behold, the altar shall be rent, and the ashes
that *are* upon it shall be poured out.
4 And it came to pass, when king Jeroboam
heard the saying of the man of God, which
had cried against the altar in Beth-el, that
he put forth his hand from the altar, saying,
Lay hold on him. And his hand, which he put
forth against him, dried up, so that he could
not pull it in again to him.
5 The altar also was rent, and the ashes
poured out from the altar, according to the
sign which the man of God had given by the
word of the LORD.
6 And the king answered and said unto the
man of God, Intreat now the face of the
LORD thy God, and pray for me, that my
hand may be restored me again. And the
man of God besought the LORD, and the
king's hand was restored him again, and
became as *it was* before.
7 And the king said unto the man of God,
Come home with me, and refresh thyself,
and I will give thee a reward.
8 And the man of God said unto the king,
If thou wilt give me half thine house, I will
not go in with thee, neither will I eat bread
nor drink water in this place:
9 For so was it charged me by the word of
the LORD, saying, Eat no bread, nor drink
water, nor turn again by the same way that
thou camest.
10 So he went another way, and returned
not by the way that he came to Beth-el.
11 ¶ Now there dwelt an old prophet in
Beth-el; and his sons came and told him all
the works that the man of God had done
that day in Beth-el: the words which he had
spoken unto the king, them they told also
to their father.
12 And their father said unto them, What
way went he? For his sons had seen what
way the man of God went, which came
from Judah.
13 And he said unto his sons, Saddle me
the ass. So they saddled him the ass: and
he rode thereon,
14 And went after the man of God, and
found him sitting under an oak: and he
said unto him, *Art* thou the man of God
that camest from Judah? And he said, I *am*.
15 Then he said unto him, Come home with
me, and eat bread.
16 And he said, I may not return with thee,
nor go in with thee: neither will I eat bread
nor drink water with thee in this place:
17 For it was said to me by the word of the
LORD, Thou shalt eat no bread nor drink
water there, nor turn again to go by the
way that thou camest.
18 He said unto him, I *am* a prophet also as
thou *art;* and an angel spake unto me by the
word of the LORD, saying, Bring him back
with thee into thine house, that he may eat
bread and drink water. *But* he lied unto him.
19 So he went back with him, and did eat
bread in his house, and drank water.
20 ¶ And it came to pass, as they sat at the
table, that the word of the LORD came unto
the prophet that brought him back:
21 And he cried unto the man of God that
came from Judah, saying, Thus saith the
LORD, Forasmuch as thou hast disobeyed
the mouth of the LORD, and hast not kept
the commandment which the LORD thy God
commanded thee,
22 But camest back, and hast eaten bread
and drunk water in the place, of the which
the LORD did say to thee, Eat no bread, and
drink no water; thy carcase shall not come
unto the sepulchre of thy fathers.
23 ¶ And it came to pass, after he had eaten
bread, and after he had drunk, that he sad-

dled for him the ass, *to wit*, for the prophet
whom he had brought back.
24 And when he was gone, a lion met him
by the way, and slew him: and his carcase
was cast in the way, and the ass stood by it,
the lion also stood by the carcase.
25 And, behold, men passed by, and saw the
carcase cast in the way, and the lion standing by the carcase: and they came and told
it in the city where the old prophet dwelt.
26 And when the prophet that brought him
back from the way heard *thereof*, he said,
It *is* the man of God, who was disobedient
unto the word of the LORD: therefore the
LORD hath delivered him unto the lion, which
hath torn him, and slain him, according
to the word of the LORD, which he spake
unto him.
27 And he spake to his sons, saying, Saddle
me the ass. And they saddled *him*.
28 And he went and found his carcase cast
in the way, and the ass and the lion standing
by the carcase: the lion had not eaten the
carcase, nor torn the ass.
29 And the prophet took up the carcase of
the man of God, and laid it upon the ass,
and brought it back: and the old prophet
came to the city, to mourn and to bury him.
30 And he laid his carcase in his own grave;
and they mourned over him, *saying*, Alas,
my brother!
31 And it came to pass, after he had buried
him, that he spake to his sons, saying, When
I am dead, then bury me in the sepulchre
wherein the man of God *is* buried; lay my
bones beside his bones:
32 For the saying which he cried by the word
of the LORD against the altar in Beth-el, and
against all the houses of the high places
which *are* in the cities of Samaria, shall
surely come to pass.
33 ¶ After this thing Jeroboam returned
not from his evil way, but made again of
the lowest of the people priests of the high
places: whosoever would, he consecrated
him, and he became *one* of the priests of
the high places.
34 And this thing became sin unto the
house of Jeroboam, even to cut *it* off, and
to destroy *it* from off the face of the earth.

1 Kings 14

1 At that time Abijah the son of Jeroboam
fell sick.
2 And Jeroboam said to his wife, Arise, I pray
thee, and disguise thyself, that thou be not
known to be the wife of Jeroboam; and get
thee to Shiloh: behold, there *is* Ahijah the
prophet, which told me that *I should be* king
over this people.
3 And take with thee ten loaves, and crack-
nels, and a cruse of honey, and go to him: he
shall tell thee what shall become of the child.
4 And Jeroboam's wife did so, and arose,
and went to Shiloh, and came to the house
of Ahijah. But Ahijah could not see; for his
eyes were set by reason of his age.
5 ¶ And the LORD said unto Ahijah, Behold,
the wife of Jeroboam cometh to ask a thing
of thee for her son; for he *is* sick: thus and
thus shalt thou say unto her: for it shall be,
when she cometh in, that she shall feign
herself *to be* another *woman*.
6 And it was *so*, when Ahijah heard the
sound of her feet, as she came in at the
door, that he said, Come in, thou wife of
Jeroboam; why feignest thou thyself *to be*
another? for I *am* sent to thee *with* heavy
tidings.
7 Go, tell Jeroboam, Thus saith the LORD God
of Israel, Forasmuch as I exalted thee from
among the people, and made thee prince
over my people Israel,
8 And rent the kingdom away from the
house of David, and gave it thee: and *yet*
thou hast not been as my servant David,
who kept my commandments, and who
followed me with all his heart, to do *that*
only *which was* right in mine eyes;
9 But hast done evil above all that were
before thee: for thou hast gone and made
thee other gods, and molten images, to
provoke me to anger, and hast cast me
behind thy back:
10 Therefore, behold, I will bring evil upon
the house of Jeroboam, and will cut off from
Jeroboam him that pisseth against the wall,
and him that is shut up and left in Israel, and
will take away the remnant of the house of
Jeroboam, as a man taketh away dung, till
it be all gone.
11 Him that dieth of Jeroboam in the city
shall the dogs eat; and him that dieth in the

field shall the fowls of the air eat: for the
LORD hath spoken *it*.
12 Arise thou therefore, get thee to thine
own house: *and* when thy feet enter into
the city, the child shall die.
13 And all Israel shall mourn for him, and
bury him: for he only of Jeroboam shall
come to the grave, because in him there
is found *some* good thing toward the LORD
God of Israel in the house of Jeroboam.
14 Moreover the LORD shall raise him up a
king over Israel, who shall cut off the house
of Jeroboam that day: but what? even now.
15 For the LORD shall smite Israel, as a reed
is shaken in the water, and he shall root up
Israel out of this good land, which he gave
to their fathers, and shall scatter them
beyond the river, because they have made
their groves, provoking the LORD to anger.
16 And he shall give Israel up because of
the sins of Jeroboam, who did sin, and who
made Israel to sin.
17 ¶ And Jeroboam's wife arose, and
departed, and came to Tirzah: *and* when
she came to the threshold of the door, the
child died;
18 And they buried him; and all Israel
mourned for him, according to the word of
the LORD, which he spake by the hand of his
servant Ahijah the prophet.
19 And the rest of the acts of Jeroboam,
how he warred, and how he reigned, behold,
they *are* written in the book of the chronicles of the kings of Israel.
20 And the days which Jeroboam reigned
were two and twenty years: and he slept
with his fathers, and Nadab his son reigned
in his stead.
21 ¶ And Rehoboam the son of Solomon
reigned in Judah. Rehoboam *was* forty and
one years old when he began to reign, and
he reigned seventeen years in Jerusalem,
the city which the LORD did choose out
of all the tribes of Israel, to put his name
there. And his mother's name *was* Naamah
an Ammonitess.
22 And Judah did evil in the sight of the
LORD, and they provoked him to jealousy
with their sins which they had committed,
above all that their fathers had done.
23 For they also built them high places, and
images, and groves, on every high hill, and
under every green tree.
24 And there were also sodomites in the
land: *and* they did according to all the abominations of the nations which the LORD cast
out before the children of Israel.
25 ¶ And it came to pass in the fifth year of
king Rehoboam, *that* Shishak king of Egypt
came up against Jerusalem:
26 And he took away the treasures of the
house of the LORD, and the treasures of the
king's house; he even took away all: and
he took away all the shields of gold which
Solomon had made.
27 And king Rehoboam made in their stead
brasen shields, and committed *them* unto
the hands of the chief of the guard, which
kept the door of the king's house.
28 And it was *so*, when the king went into
the house of the LORD, that the guard bare
them, and brought them back into the
guard chamber.
29 ¶ Now the rest of the acts of Rehoboam,
and all that he did, *are* they not written in
the book of the chronicles of the kings of
Judah?
30 And there was war between Rehoboam
and Jeroboam all *their* days.
31 And Rehoboam slept with his fathers,
and was buried with his fathers in the city of
David. And his mother's name *was* Naamah
an Ammonitess. And Abijam his son reigned
in his stead.

1 Kings 15

1 Now in the eighteenth year of king
Jeroboam the son of Nebat reigned Abijam over Judah.
2 Three years reigned he in Jerusalem.
And his mother's name *was* Maachah, the
daughter of Abishalom.
3 And he walked in all the sins of his father,
which he had done before him: and his heart
was not perfect with the LORD his God, as
the heart of David his father.
4 Nevertheless for David's sake did the LORD
his God give him a lamp in Jerusalem, to
set up his son after him, and to establish
Jerusalem:
5 Because David did *that which was* right in
the eyes of the LORD, and turned not aside
from any *thing* that he commanded him all
the days of his life, save only in the matter
of Uriah the Hittite.

6 And there was war between Rehoboam
and Jeroboam all the days of his life.
7 Now the rest of the acts of Abijam, and
all that he did, *are* they not written in the
book of the chronicles of the kings of Judah?
And there was war between Abijam and
Jeroboam.
8 And Abijam slept with his fathers; and they
buried him in the city of David: and Asa his
son reigned in his stead.
9 ¶ And in the twentieth year of Jeroboam
king of Israel reigned Asa over Judah.
10 And forty and one years reigned he in
Jerusalem. And his mother's name *was*
Maachah, the daughter of Abishalom.
11 And Asa did *that which was* right in the
eyes of the LORD, as *did* David his father.
12 And he took away the sodomites out of
the land, and removed all the idols that his
fathers had made.
13 And also Maachah his mother, even her
he removed from *being* queen, because
she had made an idol in a grove; and Asa
destroyed her idol, and burnt *it* by the
brook Kidron.
14 But the high places were not removed:
nevertheless Asa's heart was perfect with
the LORD all his days.
15 And he brought in the things which his
father had dedicated, and the things which
himself had dedicated, into the house of the
LORD, silver, and gold, and vessels.
16 ¶ And there was war between Asa and
Baasha king of Israel all their days.
17 And Baasha king of Israel went up against
Judah, and built Ramah, that he might not
suffer any to go out or come in to Asa king
of Judah.
18 Then Asa took all the silver and the gold
that were left in the treasures of the house
of the LORD, and the treasures of the king's
house, and delivered them into the hand
of his servants: and king Asa sent them
to Ben-hadad, the son of Tabrimon, the
son of Hezion, king of Syria, that dwelt at
Damascus, saying,
19 *There is* a league between me and thee,
and between my father and thy father:
behold, I have sent unto thee a present of
silver and gold; come and break thy league
with Baasha king of Israel, that he may
depart from me.
20 So Ben-hadad hearkened unto king Asa,
and sent the captains of the hosts which he
had against the cities of Israel, and smote
Ijon, and Dan, and Abel-beth-maachah, and
all Cinneroth, with all the land of Naphtali.
21 And it came to pass, when Baasha heard
thereof, that he left off building of Ramah,
and dwelt in Tirzah.
22 Then king Asa made a proclamation
throughout all Judah; none *was* exempted:
and they took away the stones of Ramah,
and the timber thereof, wherewith Baasha
had builded; and king Asa built with them
Geba of Benjamin, and Mizpah.
23 The rest of all the acts of Asa, and all
his might, and all that he did, and the cities
which he built, *are* they not written in the
book of the chronicles of the kings of Judah?
Nevertheless in the time of his old age he
was diseased in his feet.
24 And Asa slept with his fathers, and was
buried with his fathers in the city of David
his father: and Jehoshaphat his son reigned
in his stead.
25 ¶ And Nadab the son of Jeroboam began
to reign over Israel in the second year of
Asa king of Judah, and reigned over Israel
two years.
26 And he did evil in the sight of the LORD,
and walked in the way of his father, and
in his sin wherewith he made Israel to sin.
27 ¶ And Baasha the son of Ahijah, of the
house of Issachar, conspired against him;
and Baasha smote him at Gibbethon, which
belonged to the Philistines; for Nadab and
all Israel laid siege to Gibbethon.
28 Even in the third year of Asa king of Judah
did Baasha slay him, and reigned in his stead.
29 And it came to pass, when he reigned,
that he smote all the house of Jeroboam;
he left not to Jeroboam any that breathed,
until he had destroyed him, according unto
the saying of the LORD, which he spake by
his servant Ahijah the Shilonite:
30 Because of the sins of Jeroboam which
he sinned, and which he made Israel sin, by
his provocation wherewith he provoked the
LORD God of Israel to anger.
31 ¶ Now the rest of the acts of Nadab, and
all that he did, *are* they not written in the
book of the chronicles of the kings of Israel?
32 And there was war between Asa and
Baasha king of Israel all their days.
33 In the third year of Asa king of Judah

began Baasha the son of Ahijah to reign over
all Israel in Tirzah, twenty and four years.
34 And he did evil in the sight of the LORD,
and walked in the way of Jeroboam, and
in his sin wherewith he made Israel to sin.

1 Kings 16

1 Then the word of the LORD came to Jehu
the son of Hanani against Baasha, saying,
2 Forasmuch as I exalted thee out of the
dust, and made thee prince over my people Israel; and thou hast walked in the way
of Jeroboam, and hast made my people
Israel to sin, to provoke me to anger with
their sins;
3 Behold, I will take away the posterity of
Baasha, and the posterity of his house;
and will make thy house like the house of
Jeroboam the son of Nebat.
4 Him that dieth of Baasha in the city shall
the dogs eat; and him that dieth of his in the
fields shall the fowls of the air eat.
5 Now the rest of the acts of Baasha, and
what he did, and his might, *are* they not
written in the book of the chronicles of the
kings of Israel?
6 So Baasha slept with his fathers, and was
buried in Tirzah: and Elah his son reigned
in his stead.
7 And also by the hand of the prophet Jehu
the son of Hanani came the word of the
LORD against Baasha, and against his house,
even for all the evil that he did in the sight
of the LORD, in provoking him to anger with
the work of his hands, in being like the house
of Jeroboam; and because he killed him.
8 ¶ In the twenty and sixth year of Asa king
of Judah began Elah the son of Baasha to
reign over Israel in Tirzah, two years.
9 And his servant Zimri, captain of half *his*
chariots, conspired against him, as he was in
Tirzah, drinking himself drunk in the house
of Arza steward of *his* house in Tirzah.
10 And Zimri went in and smote him, and
killed him, in the twenty and seventh year of
Asa king of Judah, and reigned in his stead.
11 ¶ And it came to pass, when he began to
reign, as soon as he sat on his throne, *that*
he slew all the house of Baasha: he left him
not one that pisseth against a wall, neither
of his kinsfolks, nor of his friends.
12 Thus did Zimri destroy all the house of
Baasha, according to the word of the LORD,
which he spake against Baasha by Jehu the
prophet,
13 For all the sins of Baasha, and the sins of
Elah his son, by which they sinned, and by
which they made Israel to sin, in provoking
the LORD God of Israel to anger with their
vanities.
14 Now the rest of the acts of Elah, and all
that he did, *are* they not written in the book
of the chronicles of the kings of Israel?
15 ¶ In the twenty and seventh year of Asa
king of Judah did Zimri reign seven days
in Tirzah. And the people *were* encamped
against Gibbethon, which *belonged* to the
Philistines.
16 And the people *that were* encamped
heard say, Zimri hath conspired, and hath
also slain the king: wherefore all Israel made
Omri, the captain of the host, king over
Israel that day in the camp.
17 And Omri went up from Gibbethon, and
all Israel with him, and they besieged Tirzah.
18 And it came to pass, when Zimri saw that
the city was taken, that he went into the
palace of the king's house, and burnt the
king's house over him with fire, and died,
19 For his sins which he sinned in doing evil
in the sight of the LORD, in walking in the
way of Jeroboam, and in his sin which he
did, to make Israel to sin.
20 Now the rest of the acts of Zimri, and
his treason that he wrought, *are* they not
written in the book of the chronicles of the
kings of Israel?
21 ¶ Then were the people of Israel divided
into two parts: half of the people followed
Tibni the son of Ginath, to make him king;
and half followed Omri.
22 But the people that followed Omri prevailed against the people that followed
Tibni the son of Ginath: so Tibni died, and
Omri reigned.
23 ¶ In the thirty and first year of Asa king
of Judah began Omri to reign over Israel,
twelve years: six years reigned he in Tirzah.
24 And he bought the hill Samaria of Shemer
for two talents of silver, and built on the
hill, and called the name of the city which
he built, after the name of Shemer, owner
of the hill, Samaria.
25 ¶ But Omri wrought evil in the eyes of
the LORD, and did worse than all that *were*
before him.

26 For he walked in all the way of Jeroboam
the son of Nebat, and in his sin wherewith
he made Israel to sin, to provoke the LORD
God of Israel to anger with their vanities.
27 Now the rest of the acts of Omri which he
did, and his might that he shewed, *are* they
not written in the book of the chronicles of
the kings of Israel?
28 So Omri slept with his fathers, and was
buried in Samaria: and Ahab his son reigned
in his stead.
29 ¶ And in the thirty and eighth year of Asa
king of Judah began Ahab the son of Omri
to reign over Israel: and Ahab the son of
Omri reigned over Israel in Samaria twenty
and two years.
30 And Ahab the son of Omri did evil in
the sight of the LORD above all that *were*
before him.
31 And it came to pass, as if it had been
a light thing for him to walk in the sins of
Jeroboam the son of Nebat, that he took to
wife Jezebel the daughter of Ethbaal king of
the Zidonians, and went and served Baal,
and worshipped him.
32 And he reared up an altar for Baal in the
house of Baal, which he had built in Samaria.
33 And Ahab made a grove; and Ahab did
more to provoke the LORD God of Israel to
anger than all the kings of Israel that were
before him.
34 ¶ In his days did Hiel the Beth-elite build
Jericho: he laid the foundation thereof in
Abiram his firstborn, and set up the gates
thereof in his youngest *son* Segub, according
to the word of the LORD, which he spake by
Joshua the son of Nun.

1 Kings 17

1 And Elijah the Tishbite, *who was* of the
inhabitants of Gilead, said unto Ahab, *As*
the LORD God of Israel liveth, before whom I
stand, there shall not be dew nor rain these
years, but according to my word.
2 And the word of the LORD came unto
him, saying,
3 Get thee hence, and turn thee eastward,
and hide thyself by the brook Cherith, that
is before Jordan.
4 And it shall be, *that* thou shalt drink of the
brook; and I have commanded the ravens
to feed thee there.
5 So he went and did according unto the
word of the LORD: for he went and dwelt
by the brook Cherith, that *is* before Jordan.
6 And the ravens brought him bread and
flesh in the morning, and bread and flesh
in the evening; and he drank of the brook.
7 And it came to pass after a while, that the
brook dried up, because there had been no
rain in the land.
8 ¶ And the word of the LORD came unto
him, saying,
9 Arise, get thee to Zarephath, which *belongeth* to Zidon, and dwell there: behold, I
have commanded a widow woman there
to sustain thee.
10 So he arose and went to Zarephath.
And when he came to the gate of the city,
behold, the widow woman *was* there gathering of sticks: and he called to her, and
said, Fetch me, I pray thee, a little water in
a vessel, that I may drink.
11 And as she was going to fetch *it*, he called
to her, and said, Bring me, I pray thee, a
morsel of bread in thine hand.
12 And she said, *As* the LORD thy God liveth,
I have not a cake, but an handful of meal
in a barrel, and a little oil in a cruse: and,
behold, I *am* gathering two sticks, that I
may go in and dress it for me and my son,
that we may eat it, and die.
13 And Elijah said unto her, Fear not; go *and*
do as thou hast said: but make me thereof
a little cake first, and bring *it* unto me, and
after make for thee and for thy son.
14 For thus saith the LORD God of Israel, The
barrel of meal shall not waste, neither shall
the cruse of oil fail, until the day *that* the
LORD sendeth rain upon the earth.
15 And she went and did according to the
saying of Elijah: and she, and he, and her
house, did eat *many* days.
16 *And* the barrel of meal wasted not, neither did the cruse of oil fail, according to the
word of the LORD, which he spake by Elijah.
17 ¶ And it came to pass after these things,
that the son of the woman, the mistress of
the house, fell sick; and his sickness was so
sore, that there was no breath left in him.
18 And she said unto Elijah, What have I to
do with thee, O thou man of God? art thou
come unto me to call my sin to remembrance, and to slay my son?
19 And he said unto her, Give me thy son.
And he took him out of her bosom, and

carried him up into a loft, where he abode,
and laid him upon his own bed.
20 And he cried unto the LORD, and said, O
LORD my God, hast thou also brought evil
upon the widow with whom I sojourn, by
slaying her son?
21 And he stretched himself upon the child
three times, and cried unto the LORD, and
said, O LORD my God, I pray thee, let this
child's soul come into him again.
22 And the LORD heard the voice of Elijah;
and the soul of the child came into him
again, and he revived.
23 And Elijah took the child, and brought
him down out of the chamber into the
house, and delivered him unto his mother:
and Elijah said, See, thy son liveth.
24 ¶ And the woman said to Elijah, Now
by this I know that thou *art* a man of God,
and that the word of the LORD in thy mouth
is truth.

1 Kings 18

1 And it came to pass *after* many days, that
the word of the LORD came to Elijah in the
third year, saying, Go, shew thyself unto
Ahab; and I will send rain upon the earth.
2 And Elijah went to shew himself unto
Ahab. And *there was* a sore famine in
Samaria.
3 And Ahab called Obadiah, which *was* the
governor of *his* house. (Now Obadiah feared
the LORD greatly:
4 For it was *so*, when Jezebel cut off the
prophets of the LORD, that Obadiah took an
hundred prophets, and hid them by fifty in a
cave, and fed them with bread and water.)
5 And Ahab said unto Obadiah, Go into the
land, unto all fountains of water, and unto
all brooks: peradventure we may find grass
to save the horses and mules alive, that we
lose not all the beasts.
6 So they divided the land between them
to pass throughout it: Ahab went one way
by himself, and Obadiah went another way
by himself.
7 ¶ And as Obadiah was in the way, behold,
Elijah met him: and he knew him, and fell
on his face, and said, *Art* thou that my lord
Elijah?
8 And he answered him, I *am:* go, tell thy
lord, Behold, Elijah *is here.*
9 And he said, What have I sinned, that thou
wouldest deliver thy servant into the hand
of Ahab, to slay me?
10 *As* the LORD thy God liveth, there is no
nation or kingdom, whither my lord hath not
sent to seek thee: and when they said, *He is*
not *there;* he took an oath of the kingdom
and nation, that they found thee not.
11 And now thou sayest, Go, tell thy lord,
Behold, Elijah *is here.*
12 And it shall come to pass, *as soon as* I am
gone from thee, that the Spirit of the LORD
shall carry thee whither I know not; and *so*
when I come and tell Ahab, and he cannot
find thee, he shall slay me: but I thy servant
fear the LORD from my youth.
13 Was it not told my lord what I did when
Jezebel slew the prophets of the LORD, how I
hid an hundred men of the LORD's prophets
by fifty in a cave, and fed them with bread
and water?
14 And now thou sayest, Go, tell thy lord,
Behold, Elijah *is here:* and he shall slay me.
15 And Elijah said, *As* the LORD of hosts
liveth, before whom I stand, I will surely
shew myself unto him to day.
16 So Obadiah went to meet Ahab, and told
him: and Ahab went to meet Elijah.
17 ¶ And it came to pass, when Ahab saw
Elijah, that Ahab said unto him, *Art* thou he
that troubleth Israel?
18 And he answered, I have not troubled
Israel; but thou, and thy father's house, in
that ye have forsaken the commandments
of the LORD, and thou hast followed Baalim.
19 Now therefore send, *and* gather to me all
Israel unto mount Carmel, and the prophets of Baal four hundred and fifty, and the
prophets of the groves four hundred, which
eat at Jezebel's table.
20 So Ahab sent unto all the children of
Israel, and gathered the prophets together
unto mount Carmel.
21 And Elijah came unto all the people,
and said, How long halt ye between two
opinions? if the LORD *be* God, follow him:
but if Baal, *then* follow him. And the people
answered him not a word.
22 Then said Elijah unto the people, I, *even*
I only, remain a prophet of the LORD; but
Baal's prophets *are* four hundred and fifty
men.
23 Let them therefore give us two bullocks; and let them choose one bullock for

themselves, and cut it in pieces, and lay *it*
on wood, and put no fire *under:* and I will
dress the other bullock, and lay *it* on wood,
and put no fire *under:*
24 And call ye on the name of your gods,
and I will call on the name of the LORD: and
the God that answereth by fire, let him be
God. And all the people answered and said,
It is well spoken.
25 And Elijah said unto the prophets of Baal,
Choose you one bullock for yourselves, and
dress *it* first; for ye *are* many; and call on the
name of your gods, but put no fire *under.*
26 And they took the bullock which was
given them, and they dressed *it*, and called
on the name of Baal from morning even
until noon, saying, O Baal, hear us. But *there*
was no voice, nor any that answered. And
they leaped upon the altar which was made.
27 And it came to pass at noon, that Elijah
mocked them, and said, Cry aloud: for he *is*
a god; either he is talking, or he is pursuing,
or he is in a journey, *or* peradventure he
sleepeth, and must be awaked.
28 And they cried aloud, and cut themselves
after their manner with knives and lancets,
till the blood gushed out upon them.
29 And it came to pass, when midday was
past, and they prophesied until the *time* of
the offering of the *evening* sacrifice, that
there was neither voice, nor any to answer,
nor any that regarded.
30 And Elijah said unto all the people, Come
near unto me. And all the people came near
unto him. And he repaired the altar of the
LORD *that was* broken down.
31 And Elijah took twelve stones, according
to the number of the tribes of the sons of
Jacob, unto whom the word of the LORD
came, saying, Israel shall be thy name:
32 And with the stones he built an altar in
the name of the LORD: and he made a trench
about the altar, as great as would contain
two measures of seed.
33 And he put the wood in order, and cut
the bullock in pieces, and laid *him* on the
wood, and said, Fill four barrels with water,
and pour *it* on the burnt sacrifice, and on
the wood.
34 And he said, Do *it* the second time. And
they did *it* the second time. And he said,
Do *it* the third time. And they did *it* the
third time.
35 And the water ran round about the altar;
and he filled the trench also with water.
36 And it came to pass at *the time of* the
offering of the *evening* sacrifice, that Elijah
the prophet came near, and said, LORD God
of Abraham, Isaac, and of Israel, let it be
known this day that thou *art* God in Israel,
and *that* I *am* thy servant, and *that* I have
done all these things at thy word.
37 Hear me, O LORD, hear me, that this
people may know that thou *art* the LORD
God, and *that* thou hast turned their heart
back again.
38 Then the fire of the LORD fell, and consumed the burnt sacrifice, and the wood,
and the stones, and the dust, and licked up
the water that *was* in the trench.
39 And when all the people saw *it*, they fell
on their faces: and they said, The LORD, he
is the God; the LORD, he *is* the God.
40 And Elijah said unto them, Take the
prophets of Baal; let not one of them
escape. And they took them: and Elijah
brought them down to the brook Kishon,
and slew them there.
41 ¶ And Elijah said unto Ahab, Get thee
up, eat and drink; for *there is* a sound of
abundance of rain.
42 So Ahab went up to eat and to drink. And
Elijah went up to the top of Carmel; and he
cast himself down upon the earth, and put
his face between his knees,
43 And said to his servant, Go up now, look
toward the sea. And he went up, and looked,
and said, *There is* nothing. And he said, Go
again seven times.
44 And it came to pass at the seventh time,
that he said, Behold, there ariseth a little
cloud out of the sea, like a man's hand. And
he said, Go up, say unto Ahab, Prepare *thy*
chariot, and get thee down, that the rain
stop thee not.
45 And it came to pass in the mean while,
that the heaven was black with clouds and
wind, and there was a great rain. And Ahab
rode, and went to Jezreel.
46 And the hand of the LORD was on Elijah;
and he girded up his loins, and ran before
Ahab to the entrance of Jezreel.

1 Kings 19

1 And Ahab told Jezebel all that Elijah had

done, and withal how he had slain all the
prophets with the sword.
2 Then Jezebel sent a messenger unto Elijah,
saying, So let the gods do *to me*, and more
also, if I make not thy life as the life of one
of them by to morrow about this time.
3 And when he saw *that*, he arose, and
went for his life, and came to Beer-sheba,
which *belongeth* to Judah, and left his servant there.
4 ¶ But he himself went a day's journey into
the wilderness, and came and sat down
under a juniper tree: and he requested for
himself that he might die; and said, It is
enough; now, O LORD, take away my life; for
I *am* not better than my fathers.
5 And as he lay and slept under a juniper
tree, behold, then an angel touched him,
and said unto him, Arise *and* eat.
6 And he looked, and, behold, *there was*
a cake baken on the coals, and a cruse of
water at his head. And he did eat and drink,
and laid him down again.
7 And the angel of the LORD came again the
second time, and touched him, and said,
Arise *and* eat; because the journey *is* too
great for thee.
8 And he arose, and did eat and drink, and
went in the strength of that meat forty days
and forty nights unto Horeb the mount of
God.
9 ¶ And he came thither unto a cave, and
lodged there; and, behold, the word of the
LORD *came* to him, and he said unto him,
What doest thou here, Elijah?
10 And he said, I have been very jealous for
the LORD God of hosts: for the children of
Israel have forsaken thy covenant, thrown
down thine altars, and slain thy prophets
with the sword; and I, *even* I only, am left;
and they seek my life, to take it away.
11 And he said, Go forth, and stand upon
the mount before the LORD. And, behold,
the LORD passed by, and a great and strong
wind rent the mountains, and brake in
pieces the rocks before the LORD; *but* the
LORD *was* not in the wind: and after the
wind an earthquake; *but* the LORD *was* not
in the earthquake:
12 And after the earthquake a fire; *but* the
LORD *was* not in the fire: and after the fire
a still small voice.
13 And it was *so*, when Elijah heard *it*, that
he wrapped his face in his mantle, and went
out, and stood in the entering in of the cave.
And, behold, *there came* a voice unto him,
and said, What doest thou here, Elijah?
14 And he said, I have been very jealous for
the LORD God of hosts: because the children
of Israel have forsaken thy covenant, thrown
down thine altars, and slain thy prophets
with the sword; and I, *even* I only, am left;
and they seek my life, to take it away.
15 And the LORD said unto him, Go, return
on thy way to the wilderness of Damascus:
and when thou comest, anoint Hazael *to be*
king over Syria:
16 And Jehu the son of Nimshi shalt thou
anoint *to be* king over Israel: and Elisha the
son of Shaphat of Abel-meholah shalt thou
anoint *to be* prophet in thy room.
17 And it shall come to pass, *that* him that
escapeth the sword of Hazael shall Jehu slay:
and him that escapeth from the sword of
Jehu shall Elisha slay.
18 Yet I have left *me* seven thousand in
Israel, all the knees which have not bowed
unto Baal, and every mouth which hath not
kissed him.
19 ¶ So he departed thence, and found Elisha the son of Shaphat, who *was* plowing
with twelve yoke *of oxen* before him, and he
with the twelfth: and Elijah passed by him,
and cast his mantle upon him.
20 And he left the oxen, and ran after Elijah,
and said, Let me, I pray thee, kiss my father
and my mother, and *then* I will follow thee.
And he said unto him, Go back again: for
what have I done to thee?
21 And he returned back from him, and took
a yoke of oxen, and slew them, and boiled
their flesh with the instruments of the oxen,
and gave unto the people, and they did eat.
Then he arose, and went after Elijah, and
ministered unto him.

1 Kings 20

1 And Ben-hadad the king of Syria gathered
all his host together: and *there were* thirty
and two kings with him, and horses, and
chariots: and he went up and besieged
Samaria, and warred against it.
2 And he sent messengers to Ahab king of
Israel into the city, and said unto him, Thus
saith Ben-hadad,
3 Thy silver and thy gold *is* mine; thy wives

also and thy children, *even* the goodliest,
are mine.
4 And the king of Israel answered and said,
My lord, O king, according to thy saying, I
am thine, and all that I have.
5 And the messengers came again, and said,
Thus speaketh Ben-hadad, saying, Although
I have sent unto thee, saying, Thou shalt
deliver me thy silver, and thy gold, and thy
wives, and thy children;
6 Yet I will send my servants unto thee to
morrow about this time, and they shall
search thine house, and the houses of thy
servants; and it shall be, *that* whatsoever
is pleasant in thine eyes, they shall put *it* in
their hand, and take *it* away.
7 Then the king of Israel called all the elders
of the land, and said, Mark, I pray you, and
see how this *man* seeketh mischief: for
he sent unto me for my wives, and for my
children, and for my silver, and for my gold;
and I denied him not.
8 And all the elders and all the people
said unto him, Hearken not *unto him*, nor
consent.
9 Wherefore he said unto the messengers
of Ben-hadad, Tell my lord the king, All that
thou didst send for to thy servant at the
first I will do: but this thing I may not do.
And the messengers departed, and brought
him word again.
10 And Ben-hadad sent unto him, and said,
The gods do so unto me, and more also, if
the dust of Samaria shall suffice for handfuls
for all the people that follow me.
11 And the king of Israel answered and said,
Tell *him*, Let not him that girdeth on *his harness*
boast himself as he that putteth it off.
12 And it came to pass, when *Ben-hadad*
heard this message, as he *was* drinking, he
and the kings in the pavilions, that he said
unto his servants, Set *yourselves in array*.
And they set *themselves in array* against
the city.
13 ¶ And, behold, there came a prophet
unto Ahab king of Israel, saying, Thus saith
the LORD, Hast thou seen all this great multitude?
behold, I will deliver it into thine
hand this day; and thou shalt know that I
am the LORD.
14 And Ahab said, By whom? And he said,
Thus saith the LORD, *Even* by the young
men of the princes of the provinces. Then
he said, Who shall order the battle? And he
answered, Thou.
15 Then he numbered the young men of
the princes of the provinces, and they were
two hundred and thirty two: and after them
he numbered all the people, *even* all the
children of Israel, *being* seven thousand.
16 And they went out at noon. But Ben-hadad
was drinking himself drunk in the pavilions,
he and the kings, the thirty and two
kings that helped him.
17 And the young men of the princes of the
provinces went out first; and Ben-hadad
sent out, and they told him, saying, There
are men come out of Samaria.
18 And he said, Whether they be come out
for peace, take them alive; or whether they
be come out for war, take them alive.
19 So these young men of the princes of
the provinces came out of the city, and the
army which followed them.
20 And they slew every one his man: and
the Syrians fled; and Israel pursued them:
and Ben-hadad the king of Syria escaped on
an horse with the horsemen.
21 And the king of Israel went out, and
smote the horses and chariots, and slew
the Syrians with a great slaughter.
22 ¶ And the prophet came to the king of
Israel, and said unto him, Go, strengthen
thyself, and mark, and see what thou doest:
for at the return of the year the king of Syria
will come up against thee.
23 And the servants of the king of Syria said
unto him, Their gods *are* gods of the hills;
therefore they were stronger than we; but
let us fight against them in the plain, and
surely we shall be stronger than they.
24 And do this thing, Take the kings away,
every man out of his place, and put captains
in their rooms:
25 And number thee an army, like the army
that thou hast lost, horse for horse, and
chariot for chariot: and we will fight against
them in the plain, *and* surely we shall be
stronger than they. And he hearkened unto
their voice, and did so.
26 And it came to pass at the return of the
year, that Ben-hadad numbered the Syrians,
and went up to Aphek, to fight against Israel.
27 And the children of Israel were numbered,
and were all present, and went
against them: and the children of Israel

pitched before them like two little flocks
of kids; but the Syrians filled the country.
28 ¶ And there came a man of God, and
spake unto the king of Israel, and said,
Thus saith the LORD, Because the Syrians
have said, The LORD *is* God of the hills, but
he *is* not God of the valleys, therefore will
I deliver all this great multitude into thine
hand, and ye shall know that I *am* the LORD.
29 And they pitched one over against the
other seven days. And *so* it was, that in the
seventh day the battle was joined: and the
children of Israel slew of the Syrians an hundred thousand footmen in one day.
30 But the rest fled to Aphek, into the city;
and *there* a wall fell upon twenty and seven
thousand of the men *that were* left. And
Ben-hadad fled, and came into the city, into
an inner chamber.
31 ¶ And his servants said unto him, Behold
now, we have heard that the kings of the
house of Israel *are* merciful kings: let us, I
pray thee, put sackcloth on our loins, and
ropes upon our heads, and go out to the king
of Israel: peradventure he will save thy life.
32 So they girded sackcloth on their loins,
and *put* ropes on their heads, and came
to the king of Israel, and said, Thy servant
Ben-hadad saith, I pray thee, let me live.
And he said, *Is* he yet alive? he *is* my brother.
33 Now the men did diligently observe
whether *any thing would come* from him,
and did hastily catch *it:* and they said, Thy
brother Ben-hadad. Then he said, Go ye,
bring him. Then Ben-hadad came forth to
him; and he caused him to come up into
the chariot.
34 And *Ben-hadad* said unto him, The cities,
which my father took from thy father, I will
restore; and thou shalt make streets for thee
in Damascus, as my father made in Samaria.
Then *said Ahab*, I will send thee away with
this covenant. So he made a covenant with
him, and sent him away.
35 ¶ And a certain man of the sons of the
prophets said unto his neighbour in the
word of the LORD, Smite me, I pray thee.
And the man refused to smite him.
36 Then said he unto him, Because thou
hast not obeyed the voice of the LORD,
behold, as soon as thou art departed from
me, a lion shall slay thee. And as soon as he
was departed from him, a lion found him,
and slew him.
37 Then he found another man, and said,
Smite me, I pray thee. And the man smote
him, so that in smiting he wounded *him*.
38 So the prophet departed, and waited for
the king by the way, and disguised himself
with ashes upon his face.
39 And as the king passed by, he cried unto
the king: and he said, Thy servant went out
into the midst of the battle; and, behold, a
man turned aside, and brought a man unto
me, and said, Keep this man: if by any means
he be missing, then shall thy life be for his
life, or else thou shalt pay a talent of silver.
40 And as thy servant was busy here and
there, he was gone. And the king of Israel
said unto him, So *shall* thy judgment *be;*
thyself hast decided *it*.
41 And he hasted, and took the ashes
away from his face; and the king of Israel
discerned him that he *was* of the prophets.
42 And he said unto him, Thus saith the
LORD, Because thou hast let go out of *thy*
hand a man whom I appointed to utter
destruction, therefore thy life shall go for
his life, and thy people for his people.
43 And the king of Israel went to his house
heavy and displeased, and came to Samaria.

1 Kings 21

1 And it came to pass after these things,
that Naboth the Jezreelite had a vineyard,
which *was* in Jezreel, hard by the palace of
Ahab king of Samaria.
2 And Ahab spake unto Naboth, saying,
Give me thy vineyard, that I may have it for
a garden of herbs, because it *is* near unto
my house: and I will give thee for it a better
vineyard than it; *or,* if it seem good to thee,
I will give thee the worth of it in money.
3 And Naboth said to Ahab, The LORD forbid
it me, that I should give the inheritance of
my fathers unto thee.
4 And Ahab came into his house heavy
and displeased because of the word which
Naboth the Jezreelite had spoken to him: for
he had said, I will not give thee the inheritance of my fathers. And he laid him down
upon his bed, and turned away his face, and
would eat no bread.
5 ¶ But Jezebel his wife came to him, and

said unto him, Why is thy spirit so sad, that
thou eatest no bread?
6 And he said unto her, Because I spake
unto Naboth the Jezreelite, and said unto
him, Give me thy vineyard for money; or
else, if it please thee, I will give thee *another*
vineyard for it: and he answered, I will not
give thee my vineyard.
7 And Jezebel his wife said unto him, Dost
thou now govern the kingdom of Israel?
arise, *and* eat bread, and let thine heart
be merry: I will give thee the vineyard of
Naboth the Jezreelite.
8 So she wrote letters in Ahab's name, and
sealed *them* with his seal, and sent the
letters unto the elders and to the nobles
that *were* in his city, dwelling with Naboth.
9 And she wrote in the letters, saying, Proclaim a fast, and set Naboth on high among
the people:
10 And set two men, sons of Belial, before
him, to bear witness against him, saying,
Thou didst blaspheme God and the king.
And *then* carry him out, and stone him,
that he may die.
11 And the men of his city, *even* the elders
and the nobles who were the inhabitants in
his city, did as Jezebel had sent unto them,
and as it *was* written in the letters which
she had sent unto them.
12 They proclaimed a fast, and set Naboth
on high among the people.
13 And there came in two men, children of
Belial, and sat before him: and the men of
Belial witnessed against him, *even* against
Naboth, in the presence of the people, saying, Naboth did blaspheme God and the king.
Then they carried him forth out of the city,
and stoned him with stones, that he died.
14 Then they sent to Jezebel, saying, Naboth
is stoned, and is dead.
15 ¶ And it came to pass, when Jezebel
heard that Naboth was stoned, and was
dead, that Jezebel said to Ahab, Arise, take
possession of the vineyard of Naboth the
Jezreelite, which he refused to give thee for
money: for Naboth is not alive, but dead.
16 And it came to pass, when Ahab heard
that Naboth was dead, that Ahab rose up
to go down to the vineyard of Naboth the
Jezreelite, to take possession of it.
17 ¶ And the word of the LORD came to
Elijah the Tishbite, saying,
18 Arise, go down to meet Ahab king of
Israel, which *is* in Samaria: behold, *he is* in
the vineyard of Naboth, whither he is gone
down to possess it.
19 And thou shalt speak unto him, saying,
Thus saith the LORD, Hast thou killed, and
also taken possession? And thou shalt speak
unto him, saying, Thus saith the LORD, In
the place where dogs licked the blood of
Naboth shall dogs lick thy blood, even thine.
20 And Ahab said to Elijah, Hast thou found
me, O mine enemy? And he answered, I have
found *thee:* because thou hast sold thyself
to work evil in the sight of the LORD.
21 Behold, I will bring evil upon thee, and
will take away thy posterity, and will cut off
from Ahab him that pisseth against the wall,
and him that is shut up and left in Israel,
22 And will make thine house like the house
of Jeroboam the son of Nebat, and like the
house of Baasha the son of Ahijah, for the
provocation wherewith thou hast provoked
me to anger, and made Israel to sin.
23 And of Jezebel also spake the LORD,
saying, The dogs shall eat Jezebel by the
wall of Jezreel.
24 Him that dieth of Ahab in the city the
dogs shall eat; and him that dieth in the
field shall the fowls of the air eat.
25 ¶ But there was none like unto Ahab,
which did sell himself to work wickedness
in the sight of the LORD, whom Jezebel his
wife stirred up.
26 And he did very abominably in following idols, according to all *things* as did the
Amorites, whom the LORD cast out before
the children of Israel.
27 And it came to pass, when Ahab heard
those words, that he rent his clothes, and
put sackcloth upon his flesh, and fasted, and
lay in sackcloth, and went softly.
28 And the word of the LORD came to Elijah
the Tishbite, saying,
29 Seest thou how Ahab humbleth himself
before me? because he humbleth himself
before me, I will not bring the evil in his
days: *but* in his son's days will I bring the
evil upon his house.

1 Kings 22

1 And they continued three years without
war between Syria and Israel.
2 And it came to pass in the third year, that

Jehoshaphat the king of Judah came down
to the king of Israel.
3 And the king of Israel said unto his servants, Know ye that Ramoth in Gilead *is*
ours, and we *be* still, *and* take it not out of
the hand of the king of Syria?
4 And he said unto Jehoshaphat, Wilt thou
go with me to battle to Ramoth-gilead? And
Jehoshaphat said to the king of Israel, I *am*
as thou *art*, my people as thy people, my
horses as thy horses.
5 And Jehoshaphat said unto the king of
Israel, Inquire, I pray thee, at the word of
the LORD to day.
6 Then the king of Israel gathered the
prophets together, about four hundred
men, and said unto them, Shall I go against
Ramoth-gilead to battle, or shall I forbear?
And they said, Go up; for the Lord shall
deliver *it* into the hand of the king.
7 And Jehoshaphat said, *Is there* not here a
prophet of the LORD besides, that we might
inquire of him?
8 And the king of Israel said unto Jehoshaphat, *There is* yet one man, Micaiah the
son of Imlah, by whom we may inquire of
the LORD: but I hate him; for he doth not
prophesy good concerning me, but evil. And
Jehoshaphat said, Let not the king say so.
9 Then the king of Israel called an officer, and
said, Hasten *hither* Micaiah the son of Imlah.
10 And the king of Israel and Jehoshaphat
the king of Judah sat each on his throne,
having put on their robes, in a void place
in the entrance of the gate of Samaria; and
all the prophets prophesied before them.
11 And Zedekiah the son of Chenaanah
made him horns of iron: and he said, Thus
saith the LORD, With these shalt thou push
the Syrians, until thou have consumed them.
12 And all the prophets prophesied so,
saying, Go up to Ramoth-gilead, and prosper: for the LORD shall deliver *it* into the
king's hand.
13 And the messenger that was gone to call
Micaiah spake unto him, saying, Behold now,
the words of the prophets *declare* good unto
the king with one mouth: let thy word, I pray
thee, be like the word of one of them, and
speak *that which is* good.
14 And Micaiah said, *As* the LORD liveth,
what the LORD saith unto me, that will I
speak.
15 ¶ So he came to the king. And the king
said unto him, Micaiah, shall we go against
Ramoth-gilead to battle, or shall we forbear?
And he answered him, Go, and prosper:
for the LORD shall deliver *it* into the hand
of the king.
16 And the king said unto him, How many
times shall I adjure thee that thou tell me
nothing but *that which is* true in the name
of the LORD?
17 And he said, I saw all Israel scattered
upon the hills, as sheep that have not a
shepherd: and the LORD said, These have
no master: let them return every man to
his house in peace.
18 And the king of Israel said unto
Jehoshaphat, Did I not tell thee that he
would prophesy no good concerning me,
but evil?
19 And he said, Hear thou therefore the
word of the LORD: I saw the LORD sitting on
his throne, and all the host of heaven standing by him on his right hand and on his left.
20 And the LORD said, Who shall persuade Ahab, that he may go up and fall
at Ramoth-gilead? And one said on this
manner, and another said on that manner.
21 And there came forth a spirit, and stood
before the LORD, and said, I will persuade
him.
22 And the LORD said unto him, Wherewith?
And he said, I will go forth, and I will be a
lying spirit in the mouth of all his prophets.
And he said, Thou shalt persuade *him*, and
prevail also: go forth, and do so.
23 Now therefore, behold, the LORD hath
put a lying spirit in the mouth of all these
thy prophets, and the LORD hath spoken evil
concerning thee.
24 But Zedekiah the son of Chenaanah went
near, and smote Micaiah on the cheek, and
said, Which way went the Spirit of the LORD
from me to speak unto thee?
25 And Micaiah said, Behold, thou shalt see
in that day, when thou shalt go into an inner
chamber to hide thyself.
26 And the king of Israel said, Take Micaiah,
and carry him back unto Amon the governor of the city, and to Joash the king's son;
27 And say, Thus saith the king, Put this *fellow* in the prison, and feed him with bread
of affliction and with water of affliction,
until I come in peace.

28 And Micaiah said, If thou return at all
in peace, the LORD hath not spoken by me.
And he said, Hearken, O people, every one
of you.
29 So the king of Israel and Jehoshaphat the
king of Judah went up to Ramoth-gilead.
30 And the king of Israel said unto
Jehoshaphat, I will disguise myself, and
enter into the battle; but put thou on thy
robes. And the king of Israel disguised himself, and went into the battle.
31 But the king of Syria commanded his
thirty and two captains that had rule over
his chariots, saying, Fight neither with small
nor great, save only with the king of Israel.
32 And it came to pass, when the captains
of the chariots saw Jehoshaphat, that they
said, Surely it *is* the king of Israel. And
they turned aside to fight against him: and
Jehoshaphat cried out.
33 And it came to pass, when the captains
of the chariots perceived that it *was* not the
king of Israel, that they turned back from
pursuing him.
34 And a *certain* man drew a bow at a venture, and smote the king of Israel between
the joints of the harness: wherefore he said
unto the driver of his chariot, Turn thine
hand, and carry me out of the host; for I
am wounded.
35 And the battle increased that day: and
the king was stayed up in his chariot against
the Syrians, and died at even: and the blood
ran out of the wound into the midst of the
chariot.
36 And there went a proclamation throughout the host about the going down of the
sun, saying, Every man to his city, and every
man to his own country.
37 ¶ So the king died, and was brought
to Samaria; and they buried the king in
Samaria.
38 And *one* washed the chariot in the pool
of Samaria; and the dogs licked up his blood;
and they washed his armour; according
unto the word of the LORD which he spake.
39 Now the rest of the acts of Ahab, and all
that he did, and the ivory house which he
made, and all the cities that he built, *are*
they not written in the book of the chronicles of the kings of Israel?
40 So Ahab slept with his fathers; and Ahaziah his son reigned in his stead.
41 ¶ And Jehoshaphat the son of Asa began
to reign over Judah in the fourth year of
Ahab king of Israel.
42 Jehoshaphat *was* thirty and five years
old when he began to reign; and he reigned
twenty and five years in Jerusalem. And his
mother's name *was* Azubah the daughter
of Shilhi.
43 And he walked in all the ways of Asa his
father; he turned not aside from it, doing
that which was right in the eyes of the LORD:
nevertheless the high places were not taken
away; *for* the people offered and burnt
incense yet in the high places.
44 And Jehoshaphat made peace with the
king of Israel.
45 Now the rest of the acts of Jehoshaphat,
and his might that he shewed, and how he
warred, *are* they not written in the book of
the chronicles of the kings of Judah?
46 And the remnant of the sodomites, which
remained in the days of his father Asa, he
took out of the land.
47 *There was* then no king in Edom: a deputy *was* king.
48 Jehoshaphat made ships of Tharshish
to go to Ophir for gold: but they went not;
for the ships were broken at Ezion-geber.
49 Then said Ahaziah the son of Ahab unto
Jehoshaphat, Let my servants go with thy
servants in the ships. But Jehoshaphat
would not.
50 ¶ And Jehoshaphat slept with his fathers,
and was buried with his fathers in the city
of David his father: and Jehoram his son
reigned in his stead.
51 ¶ Ahaziah the son of Ahab began to reign
over Israel in Samaria the seventeenth year
of Jehoshaphat king of Judah, and reigned
two years over Israel.
52 And he did evil in the sight of the LORD,
and walked in the way of his father, and
in the way of his mother, and in the way
of Jeroboam the son of Nebat, who made
Israel to sin:
53 For he served Baal, and worshipped
him, and provoked to anger the LORD God
of Israel, according to all that his father
had done.

The Second Book Of The

Kings

2 Kings 1

1 Then Moab rebelled against Israel after
the death of Ahab.
2 And Ahaziah fell down through a lattice
in his upper chamber that *was* in Samaria,
and was sick: and he sent messengers, and
said unto them, Go, inquire of Baal-zebub
the god of Ekron whether I shall recover of
this disease.
3 But the angel of the LORD said to Elijah the
Tishbite, Arise, go up to meet the messengers of the king of Samaria, and say unto
them, *Is it* not because *there is* not a God
in Israel, *that* ye go to inquire of Baal-zebub
the god of Ekron?
4 Now therefore thus saith the LORD, Thou
shalt not come down from that bed on
which thou art gone up, but shalt surely
die. And Elijah departed.
5 ¶ And when the messengers turned back
unto him, he said unto them, Why are ye
now turned back?
6 And they said unto him, There came a
man up to meet us, and said unto us, Go,
turn again unto the king that sent you, and
say unto him, Thus saith the LORD, *Is it* not
because *there is* not a God in Israel, *that*
thou sendest to inquire of Baal-zebub the
god of Ekron? therefore thou shalt not come
down from that bed on which thou art gone
up, but shalt surely die.
7 And he said unto them, What manner of
man *was he* which came up to meet you,
and told you these words?
8 And they answered him, *He was* an hairy
man, and girt with a girdle of leather about
his loins. And he said, It *is* Elijah the Tishbite.
9 Then the king sent unto him a captain of
fifty with his fifty. And he went up to him:
and, behold, he sat on the top of an hill. And
he spake unto him, Thou man of God, the
king hath said, Come down.
10 And Elijah answered and said to the captain of fifty, If I *be* a man of God, then let fire
come down from heaven, and consume thee
and thy fifty. And there came down fire from
heaven, and consumed him and his fifty.
11 Again also he sent unto him another captain of fifty with his fifty. And he answered
and said unto him, O man of God, thus hath
the king said, Come down quickly.
12 And Elijah answered and said unto them,
If I *be* a man of God, let fire come down
from heaven, and consume thee and thy
fifty. And the fire of God came down from
heaven, and consumed him and his fifty.
13 ¶ And he sent again a captain of the third
fifty with his fifty. And the third captain of
fifty went up, and came and fell on his knees
before Elijah, and besought him, and said
unto him, O man of God, I pray thee, let my
life, and the life of these fifty thy servants,
be precious in thy sight.
14 Behold, there came fire down from
heaven, and burnt up the two captains of
the former fifties with their fifties: therefore
let my life now be precious in thy sight.
15 And the angel of the LORD said unto
Elijah, Go down with him: be not afraid of
him. And he arose, and went down with
him unto the king.
16 And he said unto him, Thus saith the
LORD, Forasmuch as thou hast sent messengers to inquire of Baal-zebub the god
of Ekron, *is it* not because *there is* no God
in Israel to inquire of his word? therefore
thou shalt not come down off that bed on
which thou art gone up, but shalt surely die.
17 ¶ So he died according to the word of the
LORD which Elijah had spoken. And Jehoram
reigned in his stead in the second year of
Jehoram the son of Jehoshaphat king of
Judah; because he had no son.
18 Now the rest of the acts of Ahaziah which
he did, *are* they not written in the book of
the chronicles of the kings of Israel?

2 Kings 2

1 And it came to pass, when the LORD would
take up Elijah into heaven by a whirlwind,
that Elijah went with Elisha from Gilgal.
2 And Elijah said unto Elisha, Tarry here,
I pray thee; for the LORD hath sent me to
Beth-el. And Elisha said *unto him*, *As* the

LORD liveth, and *as* thy soul liveth, I will not
leave thee. So they went down to Beth-el.
3 And the sons of the prophets that *were* at
Beth-el came forth to Elisha, and said unto
him, Knowest thou that the LORD will take
away thy master from thy head to day? And
he said, Yea, I know *it;* hold ye your peace.
4 And Elijah said unto him, Elisha, tarry here,
I pray thee; for the LORD hath sent me to
Jericho. And he said, *As* the LORD liveth, and
as thy soul liveth, I will not leave thee. So
they came to Jericho.
5 And the sons of the prophets that *were* at
Jericho came to Elisha, and said unto him,
Knowest thou that the LORD will take away
thy master from thy head to day? And he
answered, Yea, I know *it;* hold ye your peace.
6 And Elijah said unto him, Tarry, I pray thee,
here; for the LORD hath sent me to Jordan.
And he said, *As* the LORD liveth, and *as* thy
soul liveth, I will not leave thee. And they
two went on.
7 And fifty men of the sons of the prophets
went, and stood to view afar off: and they
two stood by Jordan.
8 And Elijah took his mantle, and wrapped
it together, and smote the waters, and they
were divided hither and thither, so that they
two went over on dry ground.
9 ¶ And it came to pass, when they were
gone over, that Elijah said unto Elisha, Ask
what I shall do for thee, before I be taken
away from thee. And Elisha said, I pray thee,
let a double portion of thy spirit be upon me.
10 And he said, Thou hast asked a hard
thing: *nevertheless,* if thou see me *when I
am* taken from thee, it shall be so unto thee;
but if not, it shall not be *so.*
11 And it came to pass, as they still went on,
and talked, that, behold, *there appeared* a
chariot of fire, and horses of fire, and parted
them both asunder; and Elijah went up by
a whirlwind into heaven.
12 ¶ And Elisha saw *it*, and he cried, My
father, my father, the chariot of Israel, and
the horsemen thereof. And he saw him no
more: and he took hold of his own clothes,
and rent them in two pieces.
13 He took up also the mantle of Elijah that
fell from him, and went back, and stood by
the bank of Jordan;
14 And he took the mantle of Elijah that fell
from him, and smote the waters, and said,
Where *is* the LORD God of Elijah? and when
he also had smitten the waters, they parted
hither and thither: and Elisha went over.
15 And when the sons of the prophets which
were to view at Jericho saw him, they said,
The spirit of Elijah doth rest on Elisha. And
they came to meet him, and bowed themselves to the ground before him.
16 ¶ And they said unto him, Behold now,
there be with thy servants fifty strong men;
let them go, we pray thee, and seek thy
master: lest peradventure the Spirit of the
LORD hath taken him up, and cast him upon
some mountain, or into some valley. And he
said, Ye shall not send.
17 And when they urged him till he was
ashamed, he said, Send. They sent therefore
fifty men; and they sought three days, but
found him not.
18 And when they came again to him, (for
he tarried at Jericho,) he said unto them,
Did I not say unto you, Go not?
19 ¶ And the men of the city said unto Elisha,
Behold, I pray thee, the situation of this city
is pleasant, as my lord seeth: but the water
is naught, and the ground barren.
20 And he said, Bring me a new cruse, and
put salt therein. And they brought *it* to him.
21 And he went forth unto the spring of the
waters, and cast the salt in there, and said,
Thus saith the LORD, I have healed these
waters; there shall not be from thence any
more death or barren *land.*
22 So the waters were healed unto this
day, according to the saying of Elisha which
he spake.
23 ¶ And he went up from thence unto
Beth-el: and as he was going up by the way,
there came forth little children out of the
city, and mocked him, and said unto him, Go
up, thou bald head; go up, thou bald head.
24 And he turned back, and looked on them,
and cursed them in the name of the LORD.
And there came forth two she bears out of
the wood, and tare forty and two children
of them.
25 And he went from thence to mount
Carmel, and from thence he returned to
Samaria.

2 Kings 3

1 Now Jehoram the son of Ahab began to
reign over Israel in Samaria the eighteenth

year of Jehoshaphat king of Judah, and
reigned twelve years.
2 And he wrought evil in the sight of the
LORD; but not like his father, and like his
mother: for he put away the image of Baal
that his father had made.
3 Nevertheless he cleaved unto the sins of
Jeroboam the son of Nebat, which made
Israel to sin; he departed not therefrom.
4 ¶ And Mesha king of Moab was a sheep-
master, and rendered unto the king of Israel
an hundred thousand lambs, and an hundred thousand rams, with the wool.
5 But it came to pass, when Ahab was dead,
that the king of Moab rebelled against the
king of Israel.
6 ¶ And king Jehoram went out of Samaria
the same time, and numbered all Israel.
7 And he went and sent to Jehoshaphat the
king of Judah, saying, The king of Moab hath
rebelled against me: wilt thou go with me
against Moab to battle? And he said, I will
go up: I *am* as thou *art*, my people as thy
people, *and* my horses as thy horses.
8 And he said, Which way shall we go up?
And he answered, The way through the
wilderness of Edom.
9 So the king of Israel went, and the king
of Judah, and the king of Edom: and they
fetched a compass of seven days' journey:
and there was no water for the host, and
for the cattle that followed them.
10 And the king of Israel said, Alas! that the
LORD hath called these three kings together,
to deliver them into the hand of Moab!
11 But Jehoshaphat said, *Is there* not here
a prophet of the LORD, that we may inquire
of the LORD by him? And one of the king of
Israel's servants answered and said, Here
is Elisha the son of Shaphat, which poured
water on the hands of Elijah.
12 And Jehoshaphat said, The word of the
LORD is with him. So the king of Israel and
Jehoshaphat and the king of Edom went
down to him.
13 And Elisha said unto the king of Israel,
What have I to do with thee? get thee to the
prophets of thy father, and to the prophets
of thy mother. And the king of Israel said
unto him, Nay: for the LORD hath called
these three kings together, to deliver them
into the hand of Moab.
14 And Elisha said, *As* the LORD of hosts
liveth, before whom I stand, surely,
were it not that I regard the presence of
Jehoshaphat the king of Judah, I would not
look toward thee, nor see thee.
15 But now bring me a minstrel. And it came
to pass, when the minstrel played, that the
hand of the LORD came upon him.
16 And he said, Thus saith the LORD, Make
this valley full of ditches.
17 For thus saith the LORD, Ye shall not see
wind, neither shall ye see rain; yet that valley
shall be filled with water, that ye may drink,
both ye, and your cattle, and your beasts.
18 And this is *but* a light thing in the sight of
the LORD: he will deliver the Moabites also
into your hand.
19 And ye shall smite every fenced city,
and every choice city, and shall fell every
good tree, and stop all wells of water, and
mar every good piece of land with stones.
20 And it came to pass in the morning, when
the meat offering was offered, that, behold,
there came water by the way of Edom, and
the country was filled with water.
21 ¶ And when all the Moabites heard that
the kings were come up to fight against
them, they gathered all that were able to
put on armour, and upward, and stood in
the border.
22 And they rose up early in the morning,
and the sun shone upon the water, and the
Moabites saw the water on the other side
as red as blood:
23 And they said, This *is* blood: the kings
are surely slain, and they have smitten one
another: now therefore, Moab, to the spoil.
24 And when they came to the camp of
Israel, the Israelites rose up and smote the
Moabites, so that they fled before them: but
they went forward smiting the Moabites,
even in *their* country.
25 And they beat down the cities, and on
every good piece of land cast every man his
stone, and filled it; and they stopped all the
wells of water, and felled all the good trees:
only in Kir-haraseth left they the stones
thereof; howbeit the slingers went about
it, and smote it.
26 ¶ And when the king of Moab saw that
the battle was too sore for him, he took
with him seven hundred men that drew
swords, to break through *even* unto the
king of Edom: but they could not.

27 Then he took his eldest son that should
have reigned in his stead, and offered him
for a burnt offering upon the wall. And there
was great indignation against Israel: and
they departed from him, and returned to
their own land.

2 Kings 4

1 Now there cried a certain woman of the
wives of the sons of the prophets unto
Elisha, saying, Thy servant my husband is
dead; and thou knowest that thy servant did
fear the LORD: and the creditor is come to
take unto him my two sons to be bondmen.
2 And Elisha said unto her, What shall I do for
thee? tell me, what hast thou in the house?
And she said, Thine handmaid hath not any
thing in the house, save a pot of oil.
3 Then he said, Go, borrow thee vessels
abroad of all thy neighbours, *even* empty
vessels; borrow not a few.
4 And when thou art come in, thou shalt
shut the door upon thee and upon thy sons,
and shalt pour out into all those vessels,
and thou shalt set aside that which is full.
5 So she went from him, and shut the door
upon her and upon her sons, who brought
the vessels to her; and she poured out.
6 And it came to pass, when the vessels
were full, that she said unto her son, Bring
me yet a vessel. And he said unto her, *There
is* not a vessel more. And the oil stayed.
7 Then she came and told the man of God.
And he said, Go, sell the oil, and pay thy
debt, and live thou and thy children of
the rest.
8 ¶ And it fell on a day, that Elisha passed
to Shunem, where *was* a great woman; and
she constrained him to eat bread. And *so* it
was, *that* as oft as he passed by, he turned
in thither to eat bread.
9 And she said unto her husband, Behold
now, I perceive that this *is* an holy man of
God, which passeth by us continually.
10 Let us make a little chamber, I pray thee,
on the wall; and let us set for him there a
bed, and a table, and a stool, and a candlestick: and it shall be, when he cometh to us,
that he shall turn in thither.
11 And it fell on a day, that he came thither,
and he turned into the chamber, and lay
there.
12 And he said to Gehazi his servant, Call
this Shunammite. And when he had called
her, she stood before him.
13 And he said unto him, Say now unto
her, Behold, thou hast been careful for us
with all this care; what *is* to be done for
thee? wouldest thou be spoken for to the
king, or to the captain of the host? And she
answered, I dwell among mine own people.
14 And he said, What then *is* to be done for
her? And Gehazi answered, Verily she hath
no child, and her husband is old.
15 And he said, Call her. And when he had
called her, she stood in the door.
16 And he said, About this season, according
to the time of life, thou shalt embrace a son.
And she said, Nay, my lord, *thou* man of God,
do not lie unto thine handmaid.
17 And the woman conceived, and bare a
son at that season that Elisha had said unto
her, according to the time of life.
18 ¶ And when the child was grown, it fell
on a day, that he went out to his father to
the reapers.
19 And he said unto his father, My head,
my head. And he said to a lad, Carry him
to his mother.
20 And when he had taken him, and brought
him to his mother, he sat on her knees till
noon, and *then* died.
21 And she went up, and laid him on the
bed of the man of God, and shut *the door*
upon him, and went out.
22 And she called unto her husband, and
said, Send me, I pray thee, one of the young
men, and one of the asses, that I may run to
the man of God, and come again.
23 And he said, Wherefore wilt thou go to
him to day? *it is* neither new moon, nor sabbath. And she said, *It shall be* well.
24 Then she saddled an ass, and said to her
servant, Drive, and go forward; slack not *thy*
riding for me, except I bid thee.
25 So she went and came unto the man of
God to mount Carmel. And it came to pass,
when the man of God saw her afar off, that
he said to Gehazi his servant, Behold, *yonder
is* that Shunammite:
26 Run now, I pray thee, to meet her, and
say unto her, *Is it* well with thee? *is it* well
with thy husband? *is it* well with the child?
And she answered, *It is* well.
27 And when she came to the man of God
to the hill, she caught him by the feet: but

Gehazi came near to thrust her away. And the man of God said, Let her alone; for her soul *is* vexed within her: and the LORD hath hid *it* from me, and hath not told me.

28 Then she said, Did I desire a son of my lord? did I not say, Do not deceive me?

29 Then he said to Gehazi, Gird up thy loins, and take my staff in thine hand, and go thy way: if thou meet any man, salute him not; and if any salute thee, answer him not again: and lay my staff upon the face of the child.

30 And the mother of the child said, *As* the LORD liveth, and *as* thy soul liveth, I will not leave thee. And he arose, and followed her.

31 And Gehazi passed on before them, and laid the staff upon the face of the child; but *there was* neither voice, nor hearing. Wherefore he went again to meet him, and told him, saying, The child is not awaked.

32 And when Elisha was come into the house, behold, the child was dead, *and* laid upon his bed.

33 He went in therefore, and shut the door upon them twain, and prayed unto the LORD.

34 And he went up, and lay upon the child, and put his mouth upon his mouth, and his eyes upon his eyes, and his hands upon his hands: and he stretched himself upon the child; and the flesh of the child waxed warm.

35 Then he returned, and walked in the house to and fro; and went up, and stretched himself upon him: and the child sneezed seven times, and the child opened his eyes.

36 And he called Gehazi, and said, Call this Shunammite. So he called her. And when she was come in unto him, he said, Take up thy son.

37 Then she went in, and fell at his feet, and bowed herself to the ground, and took up her son, and went out.

38 ¶ And Elisha came again to Gilgal: and *there was* a dearth in the land; and the sons of the prophets *were* sitting before him: and he said unto his servant, Set on the great pot, and seethe pottage for the sons of the prophets.

39 And one went out into the field to gather herbs, and found a wild vine, and gathered thereof wild gourds his lap full, and came and shred *them* into the pot of pottage: for they knew *them* not.

40 So they poured out for the men to eat. And it came to pass, as they were eating of the pottage, that they cried out, and said, O *thou* man of God, *there is* death in the pot. And they could not eat *thereof*.

41 But he said, Then bring meal. And he cast *it* into the pot; and he said, Pour out for the people, that they may eat. And there was no harm in the pot.

42 ¶ And there came a man from Baal-shalisha, and brought the man of God bread of the firstfruits, twenty loaves of barley, and full ears of corn in the husk thereof. And he said, Give unto the people, that they may eat.

43 And his servitor said, What, should I set this before an hundred men? He said again, Give the people, that they may eat: for thus saith the LORD, They shall eat, and shall leave *thereof*.

44 So he set *it* before them, and they did eat, and left *thereof*, according to the word of the LORD.

2 Kings 5

1 Now Naaman, captain of the host of the king of Syria, was a great man with his master, and honourable, because by him the LORD had given deliverance unto Syria: he was also a mighty man in valour, *but he was* a leper.

2 And the Syrians had gone out by companies, and had brought away captive out of the land of Israel a little maid; and she waited on Naaman's wife.

3 And she said unto her mistress, Would God my lord *were* with the prophet that *is* in Samaria! for he would recover him of his leprosy.

4 And *one* went in, and told his lord, saying, Thus and thus said the maid that *is* of the land of Israel.

5 And the king of Syria said, Go to, go, and I will send a letter unto the king of Israel. And he departed, and took with him ten talents of silver, and six thousand *pieces* of gold, and ten changes of raiment.

6 And he brought the letter to the king of Israel, saying, Now when this letter is come unto thee, behold, I have *therewith* sent Naaman my servant to thee, that thou mayest recover him of his leprosy.

7 And it came to pass, when the king of Israel had read the letter, that he rent his clothes, and said, *Am* I God, to kill and to make alive,

that this man doth send unto me to recover
a man of his leprosy? wherefore consider, I
pray you, and see how he seeketh a quarrel
against me.
8 ¶ And it was *so,* when Elisha the man of
God had heard that the king of Israel had
rent his clothes, that he sent to the king, saying, Wherefore hast thou rent thy clothes?
let him come now to me, and he shall know
that there is a prophet in Israel.
9 So Naaman came with his horses and
with his chariot, and stood at the door of
the house of Elisha.
10 And Elisha sent a messenger unto him,
saying, Go and wash in Jordan seven times,
and thy flesh shall come again to thee, and
thou shalt be clean.
11 But Naaman was wroth, and went away,
and said, Behold, I thought, He will surely
come out to me, and stand, and call on the
name of the LORD his God, and strike his
hand over the place, and recover the leper.
12 *Are* not Abana and Pharpar, rivers of
Damascus, better than all the waters of
Israel? may I not wash in them, and be
clean? So he turned and went away in a rage.
13 And his servants came near, and spake
unto him, and said, My father, *if* the prophet
had bid thee *do some* great thing, wouldest
thou not have done *it?* how much rather
then, when he saith to thee, Wash, and
be clean?
14 Then went he down, and dipped himself
seven times in Jordan, according to the saying of the man of God: and his flesh came
again like unto the flesh of a little child, and
he was clean.
15 ¶ And he returned to the man of God, he
and all his company, and came, and stood
before him: and he said, Behold, now I know
that *there is* no God in all the earth, but in
Israel: now therefore, I pray thee, take a
blessing of thy servant.
16 But he said, *As* the LORD liveth, before
whom I stand, I will receive none. And he
urged him to take *it;* but he refused.
17 And Naaman said, Shall there not then,
I pray thee, be given to thy servant two
mules' burden of earth? for thy servant will
henceforth offer neither burnt offering nor
sacrifice unto other gods, but unto the LORD.
18 In this thing the LORD pardon thy servant,
that when my master goeth into the house
of Rimmon to worship there, and he leaneth
on my hand, and I bow myself in the house
of Rimmon: when I bow down myself in
the house of Rimmon, the LORD pardon thy
servant in this thing.
19 And he said unto him, Go in peace. So he
departed from him a little way.
20 ¶ But Gehazi, the servant of Elisha the
man of God, said, Behold, my master hath
spared Naaman this Syrian, in not receiving
at his hands that which he brought: but, *as*
the LORD liveth, I will run after him, and take
somewhat of him.
21 So Gehazi followed after Naaman. And
when Naaman saw *him* running after him,
he lighted down from the chariot to meet
him, and said, *Is* all well?
22 And he said, All *is* well. My master hath
sent me, saying, Behold, even now there
be come to me from mount Ephraim two
young men of the sons of the prophets: give
them, I pray thee, a talent of silver, and two
changes of garments.
23 And Naaman said, Be content, take
two talents. And he urged him, and bound
two talents of silver in two bags, with two
changes of garments, and laid *them* upon
two of his servants; and they bare *them*
before him.
24 And when he came to the tower, he took
them from their hand, and bestowed *them*
in the house: and he let the men go, and
they departed.
25 But he went in, and stood before his
master. And Elisha said unto him, Whence
comest thou, Gehazi? And he said, Thy servant went no whither.
26 And he said unto him, Went not mine
heart *with thee,* when the man turned
again from his chariot to meet thee? *Is it*
a time to receive money, and to receive
garments, and oliveyards, and vineyards,
and sheep, and oxen, and menservants,
and maidservants?
27 The leprosy therefore of Naaman shall
cleave unto thee, and unto thy seed for ever.
And he went out from his presence a leper
as white as snow.

2 Kings 6

1 And the sons of the prophets said unto
Elisha, Behold now, the place where we
dwell with thee is too strait for us.

2 Let us go, we pray thee, unto Jordan, and
take thence every man a beam, and let us
make us a place there, where we may dwell.
And he answered, Go ye.
3 And one said, Be content, I pray thee, and
go with thy servants. And he answered, I
will go.
4 So he went with them. And when they
came to Jordan, they cut down wood.
5 But as one was felling a beam, the axe
head fell into the water: and he cried, and
said, Alas, master! for it was borrowed.
6 And the man of God said, Where fell it?
And he shewed him the place. And he cut
down a stick, and cast *it* in thither; and the
iron did swim.
7 Therefore said he, Take *it* up to thee. And
he put out his hand, and took it.
8 ¶ Then the king of Syria warred against
Israel, and took counsel with his servants,
saying, In such and such a place *shall be*
my camp.
9 And the man of God sent unto the king
of Israel, saying, Beware that thou pass
not such a place; for thither the Syrians are
come down.
10 And the king of Israel sent to the place
which the man of God told him and warned
him of, and saved himself there, not once
nor twice.
11 Therefore the heart of the king of Syria
was sore troubled for this thing; and he
called his servants, and said unto them,
Will ye not shew me which of us *is* for the
king of Israel?
12 And one of his servants said, None, my
lord, O king: but Elisha, the prophet that *is*
in Israel, telleth the king of Israel the words
that thou speakest in thy bedchamber.
13 ¶ And he said, Go and spy where he *is*,
that I may send and fetch him. And it was
told him, saying, Behold, *he is* in Dothan.
14 Therefore sent he thither horses, and
chariots, and a great host: and they came
by night, and compassed the city about.
15 And when the servant of the man of God
was risen early, and gone forth, behold, an
host compassed the city both with horses
and chariots. And his servant said unto him,
Alas, my master! how shall we do?
16 And he answered, Fear not: for they
that *be* with us *are* more than they that *be*
with them.
17 And Elisha prayed, and said, LORD, I pray
thee, open his eyes, that he may see. And
the LORD opened the eyes of the young
man; and he saw: and, behold, the mountain *was* full of horses and chariots of fire
round about Elisha.
18 And when they came down to him, Elisha
prayed unto the LORD, and said, Smite this
people, I pray thee, with blindness. And he
smote them with blindness according to the
word of Elisha.
19 ¶ And Elisha said unto them, This *is* not
the way, neither *is* this the city: follow me,
and I will bring you to the man whom ye
seek. But he led them to Samaria.
20 And it came to pass, when they were
come into Samaria, that Elisha said, LORD,
open the eyes of these *men*, that they may
see. And the LORD opened their eyes, and
they saw; and, behold, *they were* in the
midst of Samaria.
21 And the king of Israel said unto Elisha,
when he saw them, My father, shall I smite
them? shall I smite *them?*
22 And he answered, Thou shalt not smite
them: wouldest thou smite those whom
thou hast taken captive with thy sword and
with thy bow? set bread and water before
them, that they may eat and drink, and go
to their master.
23 And he prepared great provision for
them: and when they had eaten and drunk,
he sent them away, and they went to their
master. So the bands of Syria came no more
into the land of Israel.
24 ¶ And it came to pass after this, that
Ben-hadad king of Syria gathered all his
host, and went up, and besieged Samaria.
25 And there was a great famine in Samaria:
and, behold, they besieged it, until an ass's
head was *sold* for fourscore *pieces* of silver,
and the fourth part of a cab of dove's dung
for five *pieces* of silver.
26 And as the king of Israel was passing by
upon the wall, there cried a woman unto
him, saying, Help, my lord, O king.
27 And he said, If the LORD do not help
thee, whence shall I help thee? out of the
barnfloor, or out of the winepress?
28 And the king said unto her, What aileth
thee? And she answered, This woman said
unto me, Give thy son, that we may eat him
to day, and we will eat my son to morrow.

29 So we boiled my son, and did eat him:
and I said unto her on the next day, Give
thy son, that we may eat him: and she hath
hid her son.
30 ¶ And it came to pass, when the king
heard the words of the woman, that he rent
his clothes; and he passed by upon the wall,
and the people looked, and, behold, *he had*
sackcloth within upon his flesh.
31 Then he said, God do so and more also to
me, if the head of Elisha the son of Shaphat
shall stand on him this day.
32 But Elisha sat in his house, and the elders
sat with him; and *the king* sent a man from
before him: but ere the messenger came to
him, he said to the elders, See ye how this
son of a murderer hath sent to take away
mine head? look, when the messenger
cometh, shut the door, and hold him fast
at the door: *is* not the sound of his master's
feet behind him?
33 And while he yet talked with them,
behold, the messenger came down unto
him: and he said, Behold, this evil *is* of the
LORD; what should I wait for the LORD any
longer?

2 Kings 7

1 Then Elisha said, Hear ye the word of the
LORD; Thus saith the LORD, To morrow about
this time *shall* a measure of fine flour *be sold*
for a shekel, and two measures of barley for
a shekel, in the gate of Samaria.
2 Then a lord on whose hand the king leaned
answered the man of God, and said, Behold,
if the LORD would make windows in heaven,
might this thing be? And he said, Behold,
thou shalt see *it* with thine eyes, but shalt
not eat thereof.
3 ¶ And there were four leprous men at the
entering in of the gate: and they said one
to another, Why sit we here until we die?
4 If we say, We will enter into the city, then
the famine *is* in the city, and we shall die
there: and if we sit still here, we die also.
Now therefore come, and let us fall unto the
host of the Syrians: if they save us alive, we
shall live; and if they kill us, we shall but die.
5 And they rose up in the twilight, to go
unto the camp of the Syrians: and when
they were come to the uttermost part of
the camp of Syria, behold, *there was* no
man there.
6 For the Lord had made the host of the Syrians to hear a noise of chariots, and a noise
of horses, *even* the noise of a great host:
and they said one to another, Lo, the king
of Israel hath hired against us the kings of
the Hittites, and the kings of the Egyptians,
to come upon us.
7 Wherefore they arose and fled in the twilight, and left their tents, and their horses,
and their asses, even the camp as it *was*,
and fled for their life.
8 And when these lepers came to the
uttermost part of the camp, they went
into one tent, and did eat and drink, and
carried thence silver, and gold, and raiment,
and went and hid *it;* and came again, and
entered into another tent, and carried
thence *also*, and went and hid *it*.
9 Then they said one to another, We do not
well: this day *is* a day of good tidings, and we
hold our peace: if we tarry till the morning
light, some mischief will come upon us: now
therefore come, that we may go and tell the
king's household.
10 So they came and called unto the porter of the city: and they told them, saying,
We came to the camp of the Syrians, and,
behold, *there was* no man there, neither
voice of man, but horses tied, and asses
tied, and the tents as they *were*.
11 And he called the porters; and they told
it to the king's house within.
12 ¶ And the king arose in the night, and said
unto his servants, I will now shew you what
the Syrians have done to us. They know that
we *be* hungry; therefore are they gone out
of the camp to hide themselves in the field,
saying, When they come out of the city, we
shall catch them alive, and get into the city.
13 And one of his servants answered and
said, Let *some* take, I pray thee, five of the
horses that remain, which are left in the
city, (behold, they *are* as all the multitude
of Israel that are left in it: behold, *I say*, they
are even as all the multitude of the Israelites
that are consumed:) and let us send and see.
14 They took therefore two chariot horses;
and the king sent after the host of the Syrians, saying, Go and see.
15 And they went after them unto Jordan:
and, lo, all the way *was* full of garments and
vessels, which the Syrians had cast away in

their haste. And the messengers returned, and told the king.

16 And the people went out, and spoiled the tents of the Syrians. So a measure of fine flour was *sold* for a shekel, and two measures of barley for a shekel, according to the word of the LORD.

17 ¶ And the king appointed the lord on whose hand he leaned to have the charge of the gate: and the people trode upon him in the gate, and he died, as the man of God had said, who spake when the king came down to him.

18 And it came to pass as the man of God had spoken to the king, saying, Two measures of barley for a shekel, and a measure of fine flour for a shekel, shall be to morrow about this time in the gate of Samaria:

19 And that lord answered the man of God, and said, Now, behold, *if* the LORD should make windows in heaven, might such a thing be? And he said, Behold, thou shalt see it with thine eyes, but shalt not eat thereof.

20 And so it fell out unto him: for the people trode upon him in the gate, and he died.

2 Kings 8

1 Then spake Elisha unto the woman, whose son he had restored to life, saying, Arise, and go thou and thine household, and sojourn wheresoever thou canst sojourn: for the LORD hath called for a famine; and it shall also come upon the land seven years.

2 And the woman arose, and did after the saying of the man of God: and she went with her household, and sojourned in the land of the Philistines seven years.

3 And it came to pass at the seven years' end, that the woman returned out of the land of the Philistines: and she went forth to cry unto the king for her house and for her land.

4 And the king talked with Gehazi the servant of the man of God, saying, Tell me, I pray thee, all the great things that Elisha hath done.

5 And it came to pass, as he was telling the king how he had restored a dead body to life, that, behold, the woman, whose son he had restored to life, cried to the king for her house and for her land. And Gehazi said, My lord, O king, this *is* the woman, and this *is* her son, whom Elisha restored to life.

6 And when the king asked the woman, she told him. So the king appointed unto her a certain officer, saying, Restore all that *was* hers, and all the fruits of the field since the day that she left the land, even until now.

7 ¶ And Elisha came to Damascus; and Ben-hadad the king of Syria was sick; and it was told him, saying, The man of God is come hither.

8 And the king said unto Hazael, Take a present in thine hand, and go, meet the man of God, and inquire of the LORD by him, saying, Shall I recover of this disease?

9 So Hazael went to meet him, and took a present with him, even of every good thing of Damascus, forty camels' burden, and came and stood before him, and said, Thy son Ben-hadad king of Syria hath sent me to thee, saying, Shall I recover of this disease?

10 And Elisha said unto him, Go, say unto him, Thou mayest certainly recover: howbeit the LORD hath shewed me that he shall surely die.

11 And he settled his countenance stedfastly, until he was ashamed: and the man of God wept.

12 And Hazael said, Why weepeth my lord? And he answered, Because I know the evil that thou wilt do unto the children of Israel: their strong holds wilt thou set on fire, and their young men wilt thou slay with the sword, and wilt dash their children, and rip up their women with child.

13 And Hazael said, But what, *is* thy servant a dog, that he should do this great thing? And Elisha answered, The LORD hath shewed me that thou *shalt be* king over Syria.

14 So he departed from Elisha, and came to his master; who said to him, What said Elisha to thee? And he answered, He told me *that* thou shouldest surely recover.

15 And it came to pass on the morrow, that he took a thick cloth, and dipped *it* in water, and spread *it* on his face, so that he died: and Hazael reigned in his stead.

16 ¶ And in the fifth year of Joram the son of Ahab king of Israel, Jehoshaphat *being* then king of Judah, Jehoram the son of Jehoshaphat king of Judah began to reign.

17 Thirty and two years old was he when he began to reign; and he reigned eight years in Jerusalem.

18 And he walked in the way of the kings

of Israel, as did the house of Ahab: for the
daughter of Ahab was his wife: and he did
evil in the sight of the LORD.
19 Yet the LORD would not destroy Judah for
David his servant's sake, as he promised him
to give him alway a light, *and* to his children.
20 ¶ In his days Edom revolted from under
the hand of Judah, and made a king over
themselves.
21 So Joram went over to Zair, and all the
chariots with him: and he rose by night, and
smote the Edomites which compassed him
about, and the captains of the chariots: and
the people fled into their tents.
22 Yet Edom revolted from under the hand
of Judah unto this day. Then Libnah revolted
at the same time.
23 And the rest of the acts of Joram, and
all that he did, *are* they not written in the
book of the chronicles of the kings of Judah?
24 And Joram slept with his fathers, and was
buried with his fathers in the city of David:
and Ahaziah his son reigned in his stead.
25 ¶ In the twelfth year of Joram the son
of Ahab king of Israel did Ahaziah the son
of Jehoram king of Judah begin to reign.
26 Two and twenty years old *was* Ahaziah
when he began to reign; and he reigned
one year in Jerusalem. And his mother's
name *was* Athaliah, the daughter of Omri
king of Israel.
27 And he walked in the way of the house of
Ahab, and did evil in the sight of the LORD,
as *did* the house of Ahab: for he *was* the
son in law of the house of Ahab.
28 ¶ And he went with Joram the son of
Ahab to the war against Hazael king of
Syria in Ramoth-gilead; and the Syrians
wounded Joram.
29 And king Joram went back to be healed
in Jezreel of the wounds which the Syrians
had given him at Ramah, when he fought
against Hazael king of Syria. And Ahaziah the
son of Jehoram king of Judah went down
to see Joram the son of Ahab in Jezreel,
because he was sick.

2 Kings 9

1 And Elisha the prophet called one of the
children of the prophets, and said unto him,
Gird up thy loins, and take this box of oil in
thine hand, and go to Ramoth-gilead:
2 And when thou comest thither, look out
there Jehu the son of Jehoshaphat the son
of Nimshi, and go in, and make him arise up
from among his brethren, and carry him to
an inner chamber;
3 Then take the box of oil, and pour *it* on his
head, and say, Thus saith the LORD, I have
anointed thee king over Israel. Then open
the door, and flee, and tarry not.
4 ¶ So the young man, *even* the young man
the prophet, went to Ramoth-gilead.
5 And when he came, behold, the captains
of the host *were* sitting; and he said, I have
an errand to thee, O captain. And Jehu said,
Unto which of all us? And he said, To thee,
O captain.
6 And he arose, and went into the house;
and he poured the oil on his head, and said
unto him, Thus saith the LORD God of Israel,
I have anointed thee king over the people
of the LORD, *even* over Israel.
7 And thou shalt smite the house of Ahab
thy master, that I may avenge the blood of
my servants the prophets, and the blood
of all the servants of the LORD, at the hand
of Jezebel.
8 For the whole house of Ahab shall perish:
and I will cut off from Ahab him that pisseth
against the wall, and him that is shut up and
left in Israel:
9 And I will make the house of Ahab like the
house of Jeroboam the son of Nebat, and
like the house of Baasha the son of Ahijah:
10 And the dogs shall eat Jezebel in the portion of Jezreel, and *there shall be* none to
bury *her*. And he opened the door, and fled.
11 ¶ Then Jehu came forth to the servants
of his lord: and *one* said unto him, *Is* all well?
wherefore came this mad *fellow* to thee?
And he said unto them, Ye know the man,
and his communication.
12 And they said, *It is* false; tell us now.
And he said, Thus and thus spake he to me,
saying, Thus saith the LORD, I have anointed
thee king over Israel.
13 Then they hasted, and took every man
his garment, and put *it* under him on the
top of the stairs, and blew with trumpets,
saying, Jehu is king.
14 So Jehu the son of Jehoshaphat the son
of Nimshi conspired against Joram. (Now
Joram had kept Ramoth-gilead, he and all
Israel, because of Hazael king of Syria.
15 But king Joram was returned to be healed

in Jezreel of the wounds which the Syrians had given him, when he fought with Hazael king of Syria.) And Jehu said, If it be your minds, *then* let none go forth *nor* escape out of the city to go to tell *it* in Jezreel.

16 So Jehu rode in a chariot, and went to Jezreel; for Joram lay there. And Ahaziah king of Judah was come down to see Joram.

17 And there stood a watchman on the tower in Jezreel, and he spied the company of Jehu as he came, and said, I see a company. And Joram said, Take an horseman, and send to meet them, and let him say, *Is it* peace?

18 So there went one on horseback to meet him, and said, Thus saith the king, *Is it* peace? And Jehu said, What hast thou to do with peace? turn thee behind me. And the watchman told, saying, The messenger came to them, but he cometh not again.

19 Then he sent out a second on horseback, which came to them, and said, Thus saith the king, *Is it* peace? And Jehu answered, What hast thou to do with peace? turn thee behind me.

20 And the watchman told, saying, He came even unto them, and cometh not again: and the driving *is* like the driving of Jehu the son of Nimshi; for he driveth furiously.

21 And Joram said, Make ready. And his chariot was made ready. And Joram king of Israel and Ahaziah king of Judah went out, each in his chariot, and they went out against Jehu, and met him in the portion of Naboth the Jezreelite.

22 And it came to pass, when Joram saw Jehu, that he said, *Is it* peace, Jehu? And he answered, What peace, so long as the whoredoms of thy mother Jezebel and her witchcrafts *are so* many?

23 And Joram turned his hands, and fled, and said to Ahaziah, *There is* treachery, O Ahaziah.

24 And Jehu drew a bow with his full strength, and smote Jehoram between his arms, and the arrow went out at his heart, and he sunk down in his chariot.

25 Then said *Jehu* to Bidkar his captain, Take up, *and* cast him in the portion of the field of Naboth the Jezreelite: for remember how that, when I and thou rode together after Ahab his father, the LORD laid this burden upon him;

26 Surely I have seen yesterday the blood of Naboth, and the blood of his sons, saith the LORD; and I will requite thee in this plat, saith the LORD. Now therefore take *and* cast him into the plat *of ground*, according to the word of the LORD.

27 ¶ But when Ahaziah the king of Judah saw *this*, he fled by the way of the garden house. And Jehu followed after him, and said, Smite him also in the chariot. *And they did so* at the going up to Gur, which *is* by Ibleam. And he fled to Megiddo, and died there.

28 And his servants carried him in a chariot to Jerusalem, and buried him in his sepulchre with his fathers in the city of David.

29 And in the eleventh year of Joram the son of Ahab began Ahaziah to reign over Judah.

30 ¶ And when Jehu was come to Jezreel, Jezebel heard *of it;* and she painted her face, and tired her head, and looked out at a window.

31 And as Jehu entered in at the gate, she said, *Had* Zimri peace, who slew his master?

32 And he lifted up his face to the window, and said, Who *is* on my side? who? And there looked out to him two *or* three eunuchs.

33 And he said, Throw her down. So they threw her down: and *some* of her blood was sprinkled on the wall, and on the horses: and he trode her under foot.

34 And when he was come in, he did eat and drink, and said, Go, see now this cursed *woman*, and bury her: for she *is* a king's daughter.

35 And they went to bury her: but they found no more of her than the skull, and the feet, and the palms of *her* hands.

36 Wherefore they came again, and told him. And he said, This *is* the word of the LORD, which he spake by his servant Elijah the Tishbite, saying, In the portion of Jezreel shall dogs eat the flesh of Jezebel:

37 And the carcase of Jezebel shall be as dung upon the face of the field in the portion of Jezreel; *so* that they shall not say, This *is* Jezebel.

2 Kings 10

1 And Ahab had seventy sons in Samaria. And Jehu wrote letters, and sent to Samaria, unto the rulers of Jezreel, to the elders, and

to them that brought up Ahab's *children*,
saying,
2 Now as soon as this letter cometh to you,
seeing your master's sons *are* with you, and
there are with you chariots and horses, a
fenced city also, and armour;
3 Look even out the best and meetest of
your master's sons, and set *him* on his
father's throne, and fight for your master's
house.
4 But they were exceedingly afraid, and
said, Behold, two kings stood not before
him: how then shall we stand?
5 And he that *was* over the house, and
he that *was* over the city, the elders also,
and the bringers up *of the children*, sent to
Jehu, saying, We *are* thy servants, and will
do all that thou shalt bid us; we will not
make any king: do thou *that which is* good
in thine eyes.
6 Then he wrote a letter the second time
to them, saying, If ye *be* mine, and *if* ye will
hearken unto my voice, take ye the heads
of the men your master's sons, and come
to me to Jezreel by to morrow this time.
Now the king's sons, *being* seventy persons,
were with the great men of the city, which
brought them up.
7 And it came to pass, when the letter came
to them, that they took the king's sons, and
slew seventy persons, and put their heads
in baskets, and sent him *them* to Jezreel.
8 ¶ And there came a messenger, and told
him, saying, They have brought the heads
of the king's sons. And he said, Lay ye them
in two heaps at the entering in of the gate
until the morning.
9 And it came to pass in the morning, that
he went out, and stood, and said to all the
people, Ye *be* righteous: behold, I conspired
against my master, and slew him: but who
slew all these?
10 Know now that there shall fall unto the
earth nothing of the word of the LORD, which
the LORD spake concerning the house of
Ahab: for the LORD hath done *that* which
he spake by his servant Elijah.
11 So Jehu slew all that remained of the
house of Ahab in Jezreel, and all his great
men, and his kinsfolks, and his priests, until
he left him none remaining.
12 ¶ And he arose and departed, and came
to Samaria. *And* as he *was* at the shearing
house in the way,
13 Jehu met with the brethren of Ahaziah
king of Judah, and said, Who *are* ye? And
they answered, We *are* the brethren of Ahaziah; and we go down to salute the children
of the king and the children of the queen.
14 And he said, Take them alive. And they
took them alive, and slew them at the pit
of the shearing house, *even* two and forty
men; neither left he any of them.
15 ¶ And when he was departed thence,
he lighted on Jehonadab the son of Rechab
coming to meet him: and he saluted him,
and said to him, Is thine heart right, as my
heart *is* with thy heart? And Jehonadab
answered, It is. If it be, give *me* thine hand.
And he gave *him* his hand; and he took him
up to him into the chariot.
16 And he said, Come with me, and see my
zeal for the LORD. So they made him ride
in his chariot.
17 And when he came to Samaria, he slew
all that remained unto Ahab in Samaria,
till he had destroyed him, according to the
saying of the LORD, which he spake to Elijah.
18 ¶ And Jehu gathered all the people
together, and said unto them, Ahab served
Baal a little; *but* Jehu shall serve him much.
19 Now therefore call unto me all the
prophets of Baal, all his servants, and all
his priests; let none be wanting: for I have
a great sacrifice *to do* to Baal; whosoever
shall be wanting, he shall not live. But Jehu
did *it* in subtilty, to the intent that he might
destroy the worshippers of Baal.
20 And Jehu said, Proclaim a solemn assembly for Baal. And they proclaimed *it*.
21 And Jehu sent through all Israel: and all
the worshippers of Baal came, so that there
was not a man left that came not. And they
came into the house of Baal; and the house
of Baal was full from one end to another.
22 And he said unto him that *was* over the
vestry, Bring forth vestments for all the
worshippers of Baal. And he brought them
forth vestments.
23 And Jehu went, and Jehonadab the son
of Rechab, into the house of Baal, and said
unto the worshippers of Baal, Search, and
look that there be here with you none of the
servants of the LORD, but the worshippers
of Baal only.

24 And when they went in to offer sacrifices
and burnt offerings, Jehu appointed fourscore men without, and said, *If* any of the
men whom I have brought into your hands
escape, *he that letteth him go*, his life *shall*
be for the life of him.
25 And it came to pass, as soon as he had
made an end of offering the burnt offering,
that Jehu said to the guard and to the captains, Go in, *and* slay them; let none come
forth. And they smote them with the edge
of the sword; and the guard and the captains
cast *them* out, and went to the city of the
house of Baal.
26 And they brought forth the images out of
the house of Baal, and burned them.
27 And they brake down the image of Baal,
and brake down the house of Baal, and
made it a draught house unto this day.
28 Thus Jehu destroyed Baal out of Israel.
29 ¶ Howbeit *from* the sins of Jeroboam
the son of Nebat, who made Israel to sin,
Jehu departed not from after them, *to wit*,
the golden calves that *were* in Beth-el, and
that *were* in Dan.
30 And the LORD said unto Jehu, Because
thou hast done well in executing *that which*
is right in mine eyes, *and* hast done unto
the house of Ahab according to all that *was*
in mine heart, thy children of the fourth
generation shall sit on the throne of Israel.
31 But Jehu took no heed to walk in the
law of the LORD God of Israel with all his
heart: for he departed not from the sins of
Jeroboam, which made Israel to sin.
32 ¶ In those days the LORD began to cut
Israel short: and Hazael smote them in all
the coasts of Israel;
33 From Jordan eastward, all the land of
Gilead, the Gadites, and the Reubenites,
and the Manassites, from Aroer, which *is*
by the river Arnon, even Gilead and Bashan.
34 Now the rest of the acts of Jehu, and all
that he did, and all his might, *are* they not
written in the book of the chronicles of the
kings of Israel?
35 And Jehu slept with his fathers: and they
buried him in Samaria. And Jehoahaz his son
reigned in his stead.
36 And the time that Jehu reigned over Israel
in Samaria *was* twenty and eight years.

2 Kings 11

1 And when Athaliah the mother of Ahaziah
saw that her son was dead, she arose and
destroyed all the seed royal.
2 But Jehosheba, the daughter of king
Joram, sister of Ahaziah, took Joash the
son of Ahaziah, and stole him from among
the king's sons *which were* slain; and they
hid him, *even* him and his nurse, in the
bedchamber from Athaliah, so that he was
not slain.
3 And he was with her hid in the house of
the LORD six years. And Athaliah did reign
over the land.
4 ¶ And the seventh year Jehoiada sent and
fetched the rulers over hundreds, with the
captains and the guard, and brought them
to him into the house of the LORD, and made
a covenant with them, and took an oath of
them in the house of the LORD, and shewed
them the king's son.
5 And he commanded them, saying, This
is the thing that ye shall do; A third part of
you that enter in on the sabbath shall even
be keepers of the watch of the king's house;
6 And a third part *shall be* at the gate of
Sur; and a third part at the gate behind the
guard: so shall ye keep the watch of the
house, that it be not broken down.
7 And two parts of all you that go forth on
the sabbath, even they shall keep the watch
of the house of the LORD about the king.
8 And ye shall compass the king round
about, every man with his weapons in his
hand: and he that cometh within the ranges,
let him be slain: and be ye with the king as
he goeth out and as he cometh in.
9 And the captains over the hundreds did
according to all *things* that Jehoiada the
priest commanded: and they took every
man his men that were to come in on the
sabbath, with them that should go out on
the sabbath, and came to Jehoiada the
priest.
10 And to the captains over hundreds did
the priest give king David's spears and
shields, that *were* in the temple of the LORD.
11 And the guard stood, every man with his
weapons in his hand, round about the king,
from the right corner of the temple to the
left corner of the temple, *along* by the altar
and the temple.
12 And he brought forth the king's son, and

put the crown upon him, and *gave him* the
testimony; and they made him king, and
anointed him; and they clapped their hands,
and said, God save the king.
13 ¶ And when Athaliah heard the noise
of the guard *and* of the people, she came
to the people into the temple of the LORD.
14 And when she looked, behold, the king
stood by a pillar, as the manner *was*, and
the princes and the trumpeters by the king,
and all the people of the land rejoiced, and
blew with trumpets: and Athaliah rent her
clothes, and cried, Treason, Treason.
15 But Jehoiada the priest commanded
the captains of the hundreds, the officers
of the host, and said unto them, Have her
forth without the ranges: and him that
followeth her kill with the sword. For the
priest had said, Let her not be slain in the
house of the LORD.
16 And they laid hands on her; and she
went by the way by the which the horses
came into the king's house: and there was
she slain.
17 ¶ And Jehoiada made a covenant
between the LORD and the king and the
people, that they should be the LORD's people; between the king also and the people.
18 And all the people of the land went into
the house of Baal, and brake it down; his
altars and his images brake they in pieces
thoroughly, and slew Mattan the priest
of Baal before the altars. And the priest
appointed officers over the house of the
LORD.
19 And he took the rulers over hundreds,
and the captains, and the guard, and all the
people of the land; and they brought down
the king from the house of the LORD, and
came by the way of the gate of the guard to
the king's house. And he sat on the throne
of the kings.
20 And all the people of the land rejoiced,
and the city was in quiet: and they slew
Athaliah with the sword *beside* the king's
house.
21 Seven years old *was* Jehoash when he
began to reign.

2 Kings 12

1 In the seventh year of Jehu Jehoash began
to reign; and forty years reigned he in Jerusalem. And his mother's name *was* Zibiah
of Beer-sheba.
2 And Jehoash did *that which was* right in
the sight of the LORD all his days wherein
Jehoiada the priest instructed him.
3 But the high places were not taken away:
the people still sacrificed and burnt incense
in the high places.
4 ¶ And Jehoash said to the priests, All
the money of the dedicated things that is
brought into the house of the LORD, *even*
the money of every one that passeth *the
account*, the money that every man is set
at, *and* all the money that cometh into any
man's heart to bring into the house of the
LORD,
5 Let the priests take *it* to them, every man
of his acquaintance: and let them repair the
breaches of the house, wheresoever any
breach shall be found.
6 But it was *so, that* in the three and twentieth year of king Jehoash the priests had
not repaired the breaches of the house.
7 Then king Jehoash called for Jehoiada the
priest, and the *other* priests, and said unto
them, Why repair ye not the breaches of
the house? now therefore receive no *more*
money of your acquaintance, but deliver it
for the breaches of the house.
8 And the priests consented to receive no
more money of the people, neither to repair
the breaches of the house.
9 But Jehoiada the priest took a chest, and
bored a hole in the lid of it, and set it beside
the altar, on the right side as one cometh
into the house of the LORD: and the priests
that kept the door put therein all the money
that was brought into the house of the LORD.
10 And it was *so*, when they saw that *there
was* much money in the chest, that the
king's scribe and the high priest came up,
and they put up in bags, and told the money
that was found in the house of the LORD.
11 And they gave the money, being told,
into the hands of them that did the work,
that had the oversight of the house of the
LORD: and they laid it out to the carpenters
and builders, that wrought upon the house
of the LORD,
12 And to masons, and hewers of stone, and
to buy timber and hewed stone to repair the
breaches of the house of the LORD, and for
all that was laid out for the house to repair *it*.

13 Howbeit there were not made for the
house of the LORD bowls of silver, snuffers,
basons, trumpets, any vessels of gold, or
vessels of silver, of the money *that was*
brought into the house of the LORD:
14 But they gave that to the workmen, and
repaired therewith the house of the LORD.
15 Moreover they reckoned not with the
men, into whose hand they delivered the
money to be bestowed on workmen: for
they dealt faithfully.
16 The trespass money and sin money was
not brought into the house of the LORD: it
was the priests'.
17 ¶ Then Hazael king of Syria went up, and
fought against Gath, and took it: and Hazael
set his face to go up to Jerusalem.
18 And Jehoash king of Judah took all the
hallowed things that Jehoshaphat, and
Jehoram, and Ahaziah, his fathers, kings of
Judah, had dedicated, and his own hallowed
things, and all the gold *that was* found in the
treasures of the house of the LORD, and in
the king's house, and sent *it* to Hazael king
of Syria: and he went away from Jerusalem.
19 ¶ And the rest of the acts of Joash, and
all that he did, *are* they not written in the
book of the chronicles of the kings of Judah?
20 And his servants arose, and made a
conspiracy, and slew Joash in the house of
Millo, which goeth down to Silla.
21 For Jozachar the son of Shimeath, and
Jehozabad the son of Shomer, his servants,
smote him, and he died; and they buried
him with his fathers in the city of David:
and Amaziah his son reigned in his stead.

2 Kings 13

1 In the three and twentieth year of Joash
the son of Ahaziah king of Judah Jehoahaz
the son of Jehu began to reign over Israel
in Samaria, *and reigned* seventeen years.
2 And he did *that which was* evil in the
sight of the LORD, and followed the sins of
Jeroboam the son of Nebat, which made
Israel to sin; he departed not therefrom.
3 ¶ And the anger of the LORD was kindled
against Israel, and he delivered them into
the hand of Hazael king of Syria, and into
the hand of Ben-hadad the son of Hazael,
all *their* days.
4 And Jehoahaz besought the LORD, and
the LORD hearkened unto him: for he saw
the oppression of Israel, because the king
of Syria oppressed them.
5 (And the LORD gave Israel a saviour, so that
they went out from under the hand of the
Syrians: and the children of Israel dwelt in
their tents, as beforetime.
6 Nevertheless they departed not from the
sins of the house of Jeroboam, who made
Israel sin, *but* walked therein: and there
remained the grove also in Samaria.)
7 Neither did he leave of the people to Jehoahaz but fifty horsemen, and ten chariots,
and ten thousand footmen; for the king of
Syria had destroyed them, and had made
them like the dust by threshing.
8 ¶ Now the rest of the acts of Jehoahaz,
and all that he did, and his might, *are* they
not written in the book of the chronicles of
the kings of Israel?
9 And Jehoahaz slept with his fathers; and
they buried him in Samaria: and Joash his
son reigned in his stead.
10 ¶ In the thirty and seventh year of Joash
king of Judah began Jehoash the son of
Jehoahaz to reign over Israel in Samaria,
and reigned sixteen years.
11 And he did *that which was* evil in the
sight of the LORD; he departed not from
all the sins of Jeroboam the son of Nebat,
who made Israel sin: *but* he walked therein.
12 And the rest of the acts of Joash, and
all that he did, and his might wherewith he
fought against Amaziah king of Judah, *are*
they not written in the book of the chronicles of the kings of Israel?
13 And Joash slept with his fathers; and
Jeroboam sat upon his throne: and Joash
was buried in Samaria with the kings of
Israel.
14 ¶ Now Elisha was fallen sick of his sickness whereof he died. And Joash the king of
Israel came down unto him, and wept over
his face, and said, O my father, my father, the
chariot of Israel, and the horsemen thereof.
15 And Elisha said unto him, Take bow and
arrows. And he took unto him bow and
arrows.
16 And he said to the king of Israel, Put
thine hand upon the bow. And he put his
hand *upon it:* and Elisha put his hands upon
the king's hands.
17 And he said, Open the window eastward. And he opened *it*. Then Elisha said,

Shoot. And he shot. And he said, The arrow
of the LORD's deliverance, and the arrow
of deliverance from Syria: for thou shalt
smite the Syrians in Aphek, till thou have
consumed *them*.
18 And he said, Take the arrows. And he
took *them*. And he said unto the king of
Israel, Smite upon the ground. And he smote
thrice, and stayed.
19 And the man of God was wroth with him,
and said, Thou shouldest have smitten five
or six times; then hadst thou smitten Syria
till thou hadst consumed *it:* whereas now
thou shalt smite Syria *but* thrice.
20 ¶ And Elisha died, and they buried him.
And the bands of the Moabites invaded the
land at the coming in of the year.
21 And it came to pass, as they were burying
a man, that, behold, they spied a band *of*
men; and they cast the man into the sepulchre of Elisha: and when the man was let
down, and touched the bones of Elisha, he
revived, and stood up on his feet.
22 ¶ But Hazael king of Syria oppressed
Israel all the days of Jehoahaz.
23 And the LORD was gracious unto them,
and had compassion on them, and had
respect unto them, because of his covenant
with Abraham, Isaac, and Jacob, and would
not destroy them, neither cast he them from
his presence as yet.
24 So Hazael king of Syria died; and Ben-hadad his son reigned in his stead.
25 And Jehoash the son of Jehoahaz took
again out of the hand of Ben-hadad the son
of Hazael the cities, which he had taken out
of the hand of Jehoahaz his father by war.
Three times did Joash beat him, and recovered the cities of Israel.

2 Kings 14

1 In the second year of Joash son of Jehoahaz king of Israel reigned Amaziah the son
of Joash king of Judah.
2 He was twenty and five years old when
he began to reign, and reigned twenty and
nine years in Jerusalem. And his mother's
name *was* Jehoaddan of Jerusalem.
3 And he did *that which was* right in the sight
of the LORD, yet not like David his father:
he did according to all things as Joash his
father did.
4 Howbeit the high places were not taken
away: as yet the people did sacrifice and
burnt incense on the high places.
5 ¶ And it came to pass, as soon as the
kingdom was confirmed in his hand, that
he slew his servants which had slain the
king his father.
6 But the children of the murderers he slew
not: according unto that which is written
in the book of the law of Moses, wherein
the LORD commanded, saying, The fathers
shall not be put to death for the children,
nor the children be put to death for the
fathers; but every man shall be put to death
for his own sin.
7 He slew of Edom in the valley of salt ten
thousand, and took Selah by war, and called
the name of it Joktheel unto this day.
8 ¶ Then Amaziah sent messengers to
Jehoash, the son of Jehoahaz son of Jehu,
king of Israel, saying, Come, let us look one
another in the face.
9 And Jehoash the king of Israel sent to
Amaziah king of Judah, saying, The thistle
that *was* in Lebanon sent to the cedar that
was in Lebanon, saying, Give thy daughter
to my son to wife: and there passed by a
wild beast that *was* in Lebanon, and trode
down the thistle.
10 Thou hast indeed smitten Edom, and
thine heart hath lifted thee up: glory *of this*,
and tarry at home: for why shouldest thou
meddle to *thy* hurt, that thou shouldest fall,
even thou, and Judah with thee?
11 But Amaziah would not hear. Therefore
Jehoash king of Israel went up; and he and
Amaziah king of Judah looked one another
in the face at Beth-shemesh, which *belon-*
geth to Judah.
12 And Judah was put to the worse before
Israel; and they fled every man to their tents.
13 And Jehoash king of Israel took Amaziah
king of Judah, the son of Jehoash the son
of Ahaziah, at Beth-shemesh, and came
to Jerusalem, and brake down the wall of
Jerusalem from the gate of Ephraim unto
the corner gate, four hundred cubits.
14 And he took all the gold and silver, and
all the vessels that were found in the house
of the LORD, and in the treasures of the
king's house, and hostages, and returned
to Samaria.
15 ¶ Now the rest of the acts of Jehoash
which he did, and his might, and how he

fought with Amaziah king of Judah, *are* they not written in the book of the chronicles of the kings of Israel?

16 And Jehoash slept with his fathers, and was buried in Samaria with the kings of Israel; and Jeroboam his son reigned in his stead.

17 ¶ And Amaziah the son of Joash king of Judah lived after the death of Jehoash son of Jehoahaz king of Israel fifteen years.

18 And the rest of the acts of Amaziah, *are* they not written in the book of the chronicles of the kings of Judah?

19 Now they made a conspiracy against him in Jerusalem: and he fled to Lachish; but they sent after him to Lachish, and slew him there.

20 And they brought him on horses: and he was buried at Jerusalem with his fathers in the city of David.

21 ¶ And all the people of Judah took Azariah, which *was* sixteen years old, and made him king instead of his father Amaziah.

22 He built Elath, and restored it to Judah, after that the king slept with his fathers.

23 ¶ In the fifteenth year of Amaziah the son of Joash king of Judah Jeroboam the son of Joash king of Israel began to reign in Samaria, *and reigned* forty and one years.

24 And he did *that which was* evil in the sight of the LORD: he departed not from all the sins of Jeroboam the son of Nebat, who made Israel to sin.

25 He restored the coast of Israel from the entering of Hamath unto the sea of the plain, according to the word of the LORD God of Israel, which he spake by the hand of his servant Jonah, the son of Amittai, the prophet, which *was* of Gath-hepher.

26 For the LORD saw the affliction of Israel, *that it was* very bitter: for *there was* not any shut up, nor any left, nor any helper for Israel.

27 And the LORD said not that he would blot out the name of Israel from under heaven: but he saved them by the hand of Jeroboam the son of Joash.

28 ¶ Now the rest of the acts of Jeroboam, and all that he did, and his might, how he warred, and how he recovered Damascus, and Hamath, *which belonged* to Judah, for Israel, *are* they not written in the book of the chronicles of the kings of Israel?

29 And Jeroboam slept with his fathers, *even* with the kings of Israel; and Zachariah his son reigned in his stead.

2 Kings 15

1 In the twenty and seventh year of Jeroboam king of Israel began Azariah son of Amaziah king of Judah to reign.

2 Sixteen years old was he when he began to reign, and he reigned two and fifty years in Jerusalem. And his mother's name *was* Jecholiah of Jerusalem.

3 And he did *that which was* right in the sight of the LORD, according to all that his father Amaziah had done;

4 Save that the high places were not removed: the people sacrificed and burnt incense still on the high places.

5 ¶ And the LORD smote the king, so that he was a leper unto the day of his death, and dwelt in a several house. And Jotham the king's son *was* over the house, judging the people of the land.

6 And the rest of the acts of Azariah, and all that he did, *are* they not written in the book of the chronicles of the kings of Judah?

7 So Azariah slept with his fathers; and they buried him with his fathers in the city of David: and Jotham his son reigned in his stead.

8 ¶ In the thirty and eighth year of Azariah king of Judah did Zachariah the son of Jeroboam reign over Israel in Samaria six months.

9 And he did *that which was* evil in the sight of the LORD, as his fathers had done: he departed not from the sins of Jeroboam the son of Nebat, who made Israel to sin.

10 And Shallum the son of Jabesh conspired against him, and smote him before the people, and slew him, and reigned in his stead.

11 And the rest of the acts of Zachariah, behold, they *are* written in the book of the chronicles of the kings of Israel.

12 This *was* the word of the LORD which he spake unto Jehu, saying, Thy sons shall sit on the throne of Israel unto the fourth *generation*. And so it came to pass.

13 ¶ Shallum the son of Jabesh began to reign in the nine and thirtieth year of Uzziah king of Judah; and he reigned a full month in Samaria.

14 For Menahem the son of Gadi went up

from Tirzah, and came to Samaria, and
smote Shallum the son of Jabesh in Samaria,
and slew him, and reigned in his stead.
15 And the rest of the acts of Shallum, and
his conspiracy which he made, behold, they
are written in the book of the chronicles of
the kings of Israel.
16 ¶ Then Menahem smote Tiphsah, and all
that *were* therein, and the coasts thereof
from Tirzah: because they opened not
to him, therefore he smote *it; and* all the
women therein that were with child he
ripped up.
17 In the nine and thirtieth year of Azariah
king of Judah began Menahem the son of
Gadi to reign over Israel, *and reigned* ten
years in Samaria.
18 And he did *that which was* evil in the
sight of the LORD: he departed not all his
days from the sins of Jeroboam the son of
Nebat, who made Israel to sin.
19 *And* Pul the king of Assyria came against
the land: and Menahem gave Pul a thousand
talents of silver, that his hand might be with
him to confirm the kingdom in his hand.
20 And Menahem exacted the money
of Israel, *even* of all the mighty men of
wealth, of each man fifty shekels of silver,
to give to the king of Assyria. So the king of
Assyria turned back, and stayed not there
in the land.
21 ¶ And the rest of the acts of Menahem,
and all that he did, *are* they not written in
the book of the chronicles of the kings of
Israel?
22 And Menahem slept with his fathers;
and Pekahiah his son reigned in his stead.
23 ¶ In the fiftieth year of Azariah king of
Judah Pekahiah the son of Menahem began
to reign over Israel in Samaria, *and reigned*
two years.
24 And he did *that which was* evil in the sight
of the LORD: he departed not from the sins
of Jeroboam the son of Nebat, who made
Israel to sin.
25 But Pekah the son of Remaliah, a captain
of his, conspired against him, and smote
him in Samaria, in the palace of the king's
house, with Argob and Arieh, and with him
fifty men of the Gileadites: and he killed him,
and reigned in his room.
26 And the rest of the acts of Pekahiah, and
all that he did, behold, they *are* written in
the book of the chronicles of the kings of
Israel.
27 ¶ In the two and fiftieth year of Azariah
king of Judah Pekah the son of Remaliah
began to reign over Israel in Samaria, *and
reigned* twenty years.
28 And he did *that which was* evil in the sight
of the LORD: he departed not from the sins
of Jeroboam the son of Nebat, who made
Israel to sin.
29 In the days of Pekah king of Israel came
Tiglath-pileser king of Assyria, and took Ijon,
and Abel-beth-maachah, and Janoah, and
Kedesh, and Hazor, and Gilead, and Galilee,
all the land of Naphtali, and carried them
captive to Assyria.
30 And Hoshea the son of Elah made a conspiracy against Pekah the son of Remaliah,
and smote him, and slew him, and reigned
in his stead, in the twentieth year of Jotham
the son of Uzziah.
31 And the rest of the acts of Pekah, and all
that he did, behold, they *are* written in the
book of the chronicles of the kings of Israel.
32 ¶ In the second year of Pekah the son
of Remaliah king of Israel began Jotham the
son of Uzziah king of Judah to reign.
33 Five and twenty years old was he when
he began to reign, and he reigned sixteen
years in Jerusalem. And his mother's name
was Jerusha, the daughter of Zadok.
34 And he did *that which was* right in the
sight of the LORD: he did according to all
that his father Uzziah had done.
35 ¶ Howbeit the high places were not
removed: the people sacrificed and burned
incense still in the high places. He built the
higher gate of the house of the LORD.
36 ¶ Now the rest of the acts of Jotham, and
all that he did, *are* they not written in the
book of the chronicles of the kings of Judah?
37 In those days the LORD began to send
against Judah Rezin the king of Syria, and
Pekah the son of Remaliah.
38 And Jotham slept with his fathers, and
was buried with his fathers in the city of
David his father: and Ahaz his son reigned
in his stead.

2 Kings 16

1 In the seventeenth year of Pekah the son
of Remaliah Ahaz the son of Jotham king of
Judah began to reign.

2 Twenty years old *was* Ahaz when he began to reign, and reigned sixteen years in Jerusalem, and did not *that which was* right in the sight of the LORD his God, like David his father.
3 But he walked in the way of the kings of Israel, yea, and made his son to pass through the fire, according to the abominations of the heathen, whom the LORD cast out from before the children of Israel.
4 And he sacrificed and burnt incense in the high places, and on the hills, and under every green tree.
5 ¶ Then Rezin king of Syria and Pekah son of Remaliah king of Israel came up to Jerusalem to war: and they besieged Ahaz, but could not overcome *him*.
6 At that time Rezin king of Syria recovered Elath to Syria, and drave the Jews from Elath: and the Syrians came to Elath, and dwelt there unto this day.
7 So Ahaz sent messengers to Tiglath-pileser king of Assyria, saying, I *am* thy servant and thy son: come up, and save me out of the hand of the king of Syria, and out of the hand of the king of Israel, which rise up against me.
8 And Ahaz took the silver and gold that was found in the house of the LORD, and in the treasures of the king's house, and sent *it for* a present to the king of Assyria.
9 And the king of Assyria hearkened unto him: for the king of Assyria went up against Damascus, and took it, and carried *the people of* it captive to Kir, and slew Rezin.
10 ¶ And king Ahaz went to Damascus to meet Tiglath-pileser king of Assyria, and saw an altar that *was* at Damascus: and king Ahaz sent to Urijah the priest the fashion of the altar, and the pattern of it, according to all the workmanship thereof.
11 And Urijah the priest built an altar according to all that king Ahaz had sent from Damascus: so Urijah the priest made *it* against king Ahaz came from Damascus.
12 And when the king was come from Damascus, the king saw the altar: and the king approached to the altar, and offered thereon.
13 And he burnt his burnt offering and his meat offering, and poured his drink offering, and sprinkled the blood of his peace offerings, upon the altar.
14 And he brought also the brasen altar, which *was* before the LORD, from the forefront of the house, from between the altar and the house of the LORD, and put it on the north side of the altar.
15 And king Ahaz commanded Urijah the priest, saying, Upon the great altar burn the morning burnt offering, and the evening meat offering, and the king's burnt sacrifice, and his meat offering, with the burnt offering of all the people of the land, and their meat offering, and their drink offerings; and sprinkle upon it all the blood of the burnt offering, and all the blood of the sacrifice: and the brasen altar shall be for me to inquire *by*.
16 Thus did Urijah the priest, according to all that king Ahaz commanded.
17 ¶ And king Ahaz cut off the borders of the bases, and removed the laver from off them; and took down the sea from off the brasen oxen that *were* under it, and put it upon a pavement of stones.
18 And the covert for the sabbath that they had built in the house, and the king's entry without, turned he from the house of the LORD for the king of Assyria.
19 ¶ Now the rest of the acts of Ahaz which he did, *are* they not written in the book of the chronicles of the kings of Judah?
20 And Ahaz slept with his fathers, and was buried with his fathers in the city of David: and Hezekiah his son reigned in his stead.

2 Kings 17

1 In the twelfth year of Ahaz king of Judah began Hoshea the son of Elah to reign in Samaria over Israel nine years.
2 And he did *that which was* evil in the sight of the LORD, but not as the kings of Israel that were before him.
3 ¶ Against him came up Shalmaneser king of Assyria; and Hoshea became his servant, and gave him presents.
4 And the king of Assyria found conspiracy in Hoshea: for he had sent messengers to So king of Egypt, and brought no present to the king of Assyria, as *he had done* year by year: therefore the king of Assyria shut him up, and bound him in prison.
5 ¶ Then the king of Assyria came up throughout all the land, and went up to Samaria, and besieged it three years.

6 ¶ In the ninth year of Hoshea the king
of Assyria took Samaria, and carried Israel
away into Assyria, and placed them in Halah
and in Habor *by* the river of Gozan, and in
the cities of the Medes.
7 For *so* it was, that the children of Israel
had sinned against the LORD their God,
which had brought them up out of the land
of Egypt, from under the hand of Pharaoh
king of Egypt, and had feared other gods,
8 And walked in the statutes of the heathen,
whom the LORD cast out from before the
children of Israel, and of the kings of Israel,
which they had made.
9 And the children of Israel did secretly
those things that *were* not right against the
LORD their God, and they built them high
places in all their cities, from the tower of
the watchmen to the fenced city.
10 And they set them up images and groves
in every high hill, and under every green
tree:
11 And there they burnt incense in all the
high places, as *did* the heathen whom
the LORD carried away before them; and
wrought wicked things to provoke the LORD
to anger:
12 For they served idols, whereof the LORD
had said unto them, Ye shall not do this
thing.
13 Yet the LORD testified against Israel, and
against Judah, by all the prophets, *and by*
all the seers, saying, Turn ye from your evil
ways, and keep my commandments *and*
my statutes, according to all the law which
I commanded your fathers, and which I sent
to you by my servants the prophets.
14 Notwithstanding they would not hear,
but hardened their necks, like to the neck
of their fathers, that did not believe in the
LORD their God.
15 And they rejected his statutes, and his
covenant that he made with their fathers,
and his testimonies which he testified
against them; and they followed vanity, and
became vain, and went after the heathen
that *were* round about them, *concerning*
whom the LORD had charged them, that
they should not do like them.
16 And they left all the commandments of
the LORD their God, and made them molten
images, *even* two calves, and made a grove,
and worshipped all the host of heaven, and
served Baal.
17 And they caused their sons and their
daughters to pass through the fire, and
used divination and enchantments, and
sold themselves to do evil in the sight of
the LORD, to provoke him to anger.
18 Therefore the LORD was very angry
with Israel, and removed them out of his
sight: there was none left but the tribe of
Judah only.
19 Also Judah kept not the commandments
of the LORD their God, but walked in the
statutes of Israel which they made.
20 And the LORD rejected all the seed of
Israel, and afflicted them, and delivered
them into the hand of spoilers, until he had
cast them out of his sight.
21 For he rent Israel from the house of
David; and they made Jeroboam the son
of Nebat king: and Jeroboam drave Israel
from following the LORD, and made them
sin a great sin.
22 For the children of Israel walked in all
the sins of Jeroboam which he did; they
departed not from them;
23 Until the LORD removed Israel out of his
sight, as he had said by all his servants the
prophets. So was Israel carried away out
of their own land to Assyria unto this day.
24 ¶ And the king of Assyria brought *men*
from Babylon, and from Cuthah, and from
Ava, and from Hamath, and from Sepharvaim, and placed *them* in the cities of
Samaria instead of the children of Israel:
and they possessed Samaria, and dwelt in
the cities thereof.
25 And *so* it was at the beginning of their
dwelling there, *that* they feared not the
LORD: therefore the LORD sent lions among
them, which slew *some* of them.
26 Wherefore they spake to the king of
Assyria, saying, The nations which thou
hast removed, and placed in the cities of
Samaria, know not the manner of the God
of the land: therefore he hath sent lions
among them, and, behold, they slay them,
because they know not the manner of the
God of the land.
27 Then the king of Assyria commanded,
saying, Carry thither one of the priests
whom ye brought from thence; and let them

go and dwell there, and let him teach them
the manner of the God of the land.
28 Then one of the priests whom they had
carried away from Samaria came and dwelt
in Beth-el, and taught them how they should
fear the LORD.
29 Howbeit every nation made gods of
their own, and put *them* in the houses of
the high places which the Samaritans had
made, every nation in their cities wherein
they dwelt.
30 And the men of Babylon made Succoth-benoth, and the men of Cuth made
Nergal, and the men of Hamath made
Ashima,
31 And the Avites made Nibhaz and Tartak,
and the Sepharvites burnt their children in
fire to Adrammelech and Anammelech, the
gods of Sepharvaim.
32 So they feared the LORD, and made unto
themselves of the lowest of them priests of
the high places, which sacrificed for them
in the houses of the high places.
33 They feared the LORD, and served their
own gods, after the manner of the nations
whom they carried away from thence.
34 Unto this day they do after the former
manners: they fear not the LORD, neither do
they after their statutes, or after their ordinances, or after the law and commandment
which the LORD commanded the children of
Jacob, whom he named Israel;
35 With whom the LORD had made a covenant, and charged them, saying, Ye shall
not fear other gods, nor bow yourselves to
them, nor serve them, nor sacrifice to them:
36 But the LORD, who brought you up out
of the land of Egypt with great power and
a stretched out arm, him shall ye fear, and
him shall ye worship, and to him shall ye
do sacrifice.
37 And the statutes, and the ordinances,
and the law, and the commandment, which
he wrote for you, ye shall observe to do for
evermore; and ye shall not fear other gods.
38 And the covenant that I have made with
you ye shall not forget; neither shall ye fear
other gods.
39 But the LORD your God ye shall fear; and
he shall deliver you out of the hand of all
your enemies.
40 Howbeit they did not hearken, but they
did after their former manner.
41 So these nations feared the LORD, and
served their graven images, both their
children, and their children's children: as
did their fathers, so do they unto this day.

2 Kings 18

1 Now it came to pass in the third year
of Hoshea son of Elah king of Israel, *that*
Hezekiah the son of Ahaz king of Judah
began to reign.
2 Twenty and five years old was he when he
began to reign; and he reigned twenty and
nine years in Jerusalem. His mother's name
also *was* Abi, the daughter of Zachariah.
3 And he did *that which was* right in the
sight of the LORD, according to all that David
his father did.
4 ¶ He removed the high places, and brake
the images, and cut down the groves, and
brake in pieces the brasen serpent that
Moses had made: for unto those days the
children of Israel did burn incense to it: and
he called it Nehushtan.
5 He trusted in the LORD God of Israel; so
that after him was none like him among
all the kings of Judah, nor *any* that were
before him.
6 For he clave to the LORD, *and* departed not
from following him, but kept his commandments, which the LORD commanded Moses.
7 And the LORD was with him; *and* he prospered whithersoever he went forth: and
he rebelled against the king of Assyria, and
served him not.
8 He smote the Philistines, *even* unto Gaza,
and the borders thereof, from the tower of
the watchmen to the fenced city.
9 ¶ And it came to pass in the fourth year
of king Hezekiah, which *was* the seventh
year of Hoshea son of Elah king of Israel,
that Shalmaneser king of Assyria came up
against Samaria, and besieged it.
10 And at the end of three years they took
it: *even* in the sixth year of Hezekiah, that
is the ninth year of Hoshea king of Israel,
Samaria was taken.
11 And the king of Assyria did carry away
Israel unto Assyria, and put them in Halah
and in Habor *by* the river of Gozan, and in
the cities of the Medes:
12 Because they obeyed not the voice of
the LORD their God, but transgressed his
covenant, *and* all that Moses the servant of

the LORD commanded, and would not hear *them*, nor do *them*.

13 ¶ Now in the fourteenth year of king Hezekiah did Sennacherib king of Assyria come up against all the fenced cities of Judah, and took them.

14 And Hezekiah king of Judah sent to the king of Assyria to Lachish, saying, I have offended; return from me: that which thou puttest on me will I bear. And the king of Assyria appointed unto Hezekiah king of Judah three hundred talents of silver and thirty talents of gold.

15 And Hezekiah gave *him* all the silver that was found in the house of the LORD, and in the treasures of the king's house.

16 At that time did Hezekiah cut off *the gold from* the doors of the temple of the LORD, and *from* the pillars which Hezekiah king of Judah had overlaid, and gave it to the king of Assyria.

17 ¶ And the king of Assyria sent Tartan and Rabsaris and Rab-shakeh from Lachish to king Hezekiah with a great host against Jerusalem. And they went up and came to Jerusalem. And when they were come up, they came and stood by the conduit of the upper pool, which *is* in the highway of the fuller's field.

18 And when they had called to the king, there came out to them Eliakim the son of Hilkiah, which *was* over the household, and Shebna the scribe, and Joah the son of Asaph the recorder.

19 And Rab-shakeh said unto them, Speak ye now to Hezekiah, Thus saith the great king, the king of Assyria, What confidence *is* this wherein thou trustest?

20 Thou sayest, (but *they are but* vain words,) *I have* counsel and strength for the war. Now on whom dost thou trust, that thou rebellest against me?

21 Now, behold, thou trustest upon the staff of this bruised reed, *even* upon Egypt, on which if a man lean, it will go into his hand, and pierce it: so *is* Pharaoh king of Egypt unto all that trust on him.

22 But if ye say unto me, We trust in the LORD our God: *is* not that he, whose high places and whose altars Hezekiah hath taken away, and hath said to Judah and Jerusalem, Ye shall worship before this altar in Jerusalem?

23 Now therefore, I pray thee, give pledges to my lord the king of Assyria, and I will deliver thee two thousand horses, if thou be able on thy part to set riders upon them.

24 How then wilt thou turn away the face of one captain of the least of my master's servants, and put thy trust on Egypt for chariots and for horsemen?

25 Am I now come up without the LORD against this place to destroy it? The LORD said to me, Go up against this land, and destroy it.

26 Then said Eliakim the son of Hilkiah, and Shebna, and Joah, unto Rab-shakeh, Speak, I pray thee, to thy servants in the Syrian language; for we understand *it:* and talk not with us in the Jews' language in the ears of the people that *are* on the wall.

27 But Rab-shakeh said unto them, Hath my master sent me to thy master, and to thee, to speak these words? *hath he* not *sent me* to the men which sit on the wall, that they may eat their own dung, and drink their own piss with you?

28 Then Rab-shakeh stood and cried with a loud voice in the Jews' language, and spake, saying, Hear the word of the great king, the king of Assyria:

29 Thus saith the king, Let not Hezekiah deceive you: for he shall not be able to deliver you out of his hand:

30 Neither let Hezekiah make you trust in the LORD, saying, The LORD will surely deliver us, and this city shall not be delivered into the hand of the king of Assyria.

31 Hearken not to Hezekiah: for thus saith the king of Assyria, Make *an agreement* with me by a present, and come out to me, and *then* eat ye every man of his own vine, and every one of his fig tree, and drink ye every one the waters of his cistern:

32 Until I come and take you away to a land like your own land, a land of corn and wine, a land of bread and vineyards, a land of oil olive and of honey, that ye may live, and not die: and hearken not unto Hezekiah, when he persuadeth you, saying, The LORD will deliver us.

33 Hath any of the gods of the nations delivered at all his land out of the hand of the king of Assyria?

34 Where *are* the gods of Hamath, and of Arpad? where *are* the gods of Sepharvaim,

Hena, and Ivah? have they delivered Samaria out of mine hand?

35 Who *are* they among all the gods of the countries, that have delivered their country out of mine hand, that the LORD should deliver Jerusalem out of mine hand?

36 But the people held their peace, and answered him not a word: for the king's commandment was, saying, Answer him not.

37 Then came Eliakim the son of Hilkiah, which *was* over the household, and Shebna the scribe, and Joah the son of Asaph the recorder, to Hezekiah with *their* clothes rent, and told him the words of Rab-shakeh.

2 Kings 19

1 And it came to pass, when king Hezekiah heard *it*, that he rent his clothes, and covered himself with sackcloth, and went into the house of the LORD.

2 And he sent Eliakim, which *was* over the household, and Shebna the scribe, and the elders of the priests, covered with sackcloth, to Isaiah the prophet the son of Amoz.

3 And they said unto him, Thus saith Hezekiah, This day *is* a day of trouble, and of rebuke, and blasphemy: for the children are come to the birth, and *there is* not strength to bring forth.

4 It may be the LORD thy God will hear all the words of Rab-shakeh, whom the king of Assyria his master hath sent to reproach the living God; and will reprove the words which the LORD thy God hath heard: wherefore lift up *thy* prayer for the remnant that are left.

5 So the servants of king Hezekiah came to Isaiah.

6 ¶ And Isaiah said unto them, Thus shall ye say to your master, Thus saith the LORD, Be not afraid of the words which thou hast heard, with which the servants of the king of Assyria have blasphemed me.

7 Behold, I will send a blast upon him, and he shall hear a rumour, and shall return to his own land; and I will cause him to fall by the sword in his own land.

8 ¶ So Rab-shakeh returned, and found the king of Assyria warring against Libnah: for he had heard that he was departed from Lachish.

9 And when he heard say of Tirhakah king of Ethiopia, Behold, he is come out to fight against thee: he sent messengers again unto Hezekiah, saying,

10 Thus shall ye speak to Hezekiah king of Judah, saying, Let not thy God in whom thou trustest deceive thee, saying, Jerusalem shall not be delivered into the hand of the king of Assyria.

11 Behold, thou hast heard what the kings of Assyria have done to all lands, by destroying them utterly: and shalt thou be delivered?

12 Have the gods of the nations delivered them which my fathers have destroyed; *as* Gozan, and Haran, and Rezeph, and the children of Eden which *were* in Thelasar?

13 Where *is* the king of Hamath, and the king of Arpad, and the king of the city of Sepharvaim, of Hena, and Ivah?

14 ¶ And Hezekiah received the letter of the hand of the messengers, and read it: and Hezekiah went up into the house of the LORD, and spread it before the LORD.

15 And Hezekiah prayed before the LORD, and said, O LORD God of Israel, which dwellest *between* the cherubims, thou art the God, *even* thou alone, of all the kingdoms of the earth; thou hast made heaven and earth.

16 LORD, bow down thine ear, and hear: open, LORD, thine eyes, and see: and hear the words of Sennacherib, which hath sent him to reproach the living God.

17 Of a truth, LORD, the kings of Assyria have destroyed the nations and their lands,

18 And have cast their gods into the fire: for they *were* no gods, but the work of men's hands, wood and stone: therefore they have destroyed them.

19 Now therefore, O LORD our God, I beseech thee, save thou us out of his hand, that all the kingdoms of the earth may know that thou *art* the LORD God, *even* thou only.

20 ¶ Then Isaiah the son of Amoz sent to Hezekiah, saying, Thus saith the LORD God of Israel, *That* which thou hast prayed to me against Sennacherib king of Assyria I have heard.

21 This *is* the word that the LORD hath spoken concerning him; The virgin the daughter of Zion hath despised thee, *and* laughed thee to scorn; the daughter of Jerusalem hath shaken her head at thee.

22 Whom hast thou reproached and blasphemed? and against whom hast thou

exalted *thy* voice, and lifted up thine eyes
on high? *even* against the Holy *One* of Israel.
23 By thy messengers thou hast reproached
the Lord, and hast said, With the multitude
of my chariots I am come up to the height of
the mountains, to the sides of Lebanon, and
will cut down the tall cedar trees thereof,
and the choice fir trees thereof: and I will
enter into the lodgings of his borders, *and*
into the forest of his Carmel.
24 I have digged and drunk strange waters,
and with the sole of my feet have I dried up
all the rivers of besieged places.
25 Hast thou not heard long ago *how* I have
done it, *and* of ancient times that I have
formed it? now have I brought it to pass,
that thou shouldest be to lay waste fenced
cities *into* ruinous heaps.
26 Therefore their inhabitants were of
small power, they were dismayed and confounded;
they were *as* the grass of the field,
and *as* the green herb, *as* the grass on the
housetops, and *as corn* blasted before it
be grown up.
27 But I know thy abode, and thy going out,
and thy coming in, and thy rage against me.
28 Because thy rage against me and thy
tumult is come up into mine ears, therefore
I will put my hook in thy nose, and my bridle
in thy lips, and I will turn thee back by the
way by which thou camest.
29 And this *shall be* a sign unto thee, Ye shall
eat this year such things as grow of themselves,
and in the second year that which
springeth of the same; and in the third year
sow ye, and reap, and plant vineyards, and
eat the fruits thereof.
30 And the remnant that is escaped of the
house of Judah shall yet again take root
downward, and bear fruit upward.
31 For out of Jerusalem shall go forth a
remnant, and they that escape out of mount
Zion: the zeal of the LORD *of hosts* shall do
this.
32 Therefore thus saith the LORD concerning
the king of Assyria, He shall not come
into this city, nor shoot an arrow there, nor
come before it with shield, nor cast a bank
against it.
33 By the way that he came, by the same
shall he return, and shall not come into this
city, saith the LORD.
34 For I will defend this city, to save it, for
mine own sake, and for my servant David's
sake.
35 ¶ And it came to pass that night, that
the angel of the LORD went out, and smote
in the camp of the Assyrians an hundred
fourscore and five thousand: and when
they arose early in the morning, behold,
they *were* all dead corpses.
36 So Sennacherib king of Assyria departed,
and went and returned, and dwelt at
Nineveh.
37 And it came to pass, as he was worshipping
in the house of Nisroch his god, that
Adrammelech and Sharezer his sons smote
him with the sword: and they escaped into
the land of Armenia. And Esarhaddon his
son reigned in his stead.

2 Kings 20

1 In those days was Hezekiah sick unto
death. And the prophet Isaiah the son of
Amoz came to him, and said unto him, Thus
saith the LORD, Set thine house in order; for
thou shalt die, and not live.
2 Then he turned his face to the wall, and
prayed unto the LORD, saying,
3 I beseech thee, O LORD, remember now
how I have walked before thee in truth and
with a perfect heart, and have done *that*
which is good in thy sight. And Hezekiah
wept sore.
4 And it came to pass, afore Isaiah was gone
out into the middle court, that the word of
the LORD came to him, saying,
5 Turn again, and tell Hezekiah the captain
of my people, Thus saith the LORD, the God
of David thy father, I have heard thy prayer, I
have seen thy tears: behold, I will heal thee:
on the third day thou shalt go up unto the
house of the LORD.
6 And I will add unto thy days fifteen years;
and I will deliver thee and this city out of
the hand of the king of Assyria; and I will
defend this city for mine own sake, and for
my servant David's sake.
7 And Isaiah said, Take a lump of figs. And
they took and laid *it* on the boil, and he
recovered.
8 ¶ And Hezekiah said unto Isaiah, What
shall be the sign that the LORD will heal me,
and that I shall go up into the house of the
LORD the third day?
9 And Isaiah said, This sign shalt thou have of

the LORD, that the LORD will do the thing that he hath spoken: shall the shadow go forward ten degrees, or go back ten degrees?

10 And Hezekiah answered, It is a light thing for the shadow to go down ten degrees: nay, but let the shadow return backward ten degrees.

11 And Isaiah the prophet cried unto the LORD: and he brought the shadow ten degrees backward, by which it had gone down in the dial of Ahaz.

12 ¶ At that time Berodach-baladan, the son of Baladan, king of Babylon, sent letters and a present unto Hezekiah: for he had heard that Hezekiah had been sick.

13 And Hezekiah hearkened unto them, and shewed them all the house of his precious things, the silver, and the gold, and the spices, and the precious ointment, and *all* the house of his armour, and all that was found in his treasures: there was nothing in his house, nor in all his dominion, that Hezekiah shewed them not.

14 ¶ Then came Isaiah the prophet unto king Hezekiah, and said unto him, What said these men? and from whence came they unto thee? And Hezekiah said, They are come from a far country, *even* from Babylon.

15 And he said, What have they seen in thine house? And Hezekiah answered, All *the things* that *are* in mine house have they seen: there is nothing among my treasures that I have not shewed them.

16 And Isaiah said unto Hezekiah, Hear the word of the LORD.

17 Behold, the days come, that all that *is* in thine house, and that which thy fathers have laid up in store unto this day, shall be carried into Babylon: nothing shall be left, saith the LORD.

18 And of thy sons that shall issue from thee, which thou shalt beget, shall they take away; and they shall be eunuchs in the palace of the king of Babylon.

19 Then said Hezekiah unto Isaiah, Good *is* the word of the LORD which thou hast spoken. And he said, *Is it* not *good*, if peace and truth be in my days?

20 ¶ And the rest of the acts of Hezekiah, and all his might, and how he made a pool, and a conduit, and brought water into the city, *are* they not written in the book of the chronicles of the kings of Judah?

21 And Hezekiah slept with his fathers: and Manasseh his son reigned in his stead.

2 Kings 21

1 Manasseh *was* twelve years old when he began to reign, and reigned fifty and five years in Jerusalem. And his mother's name *was* Hephzi-bah.

2 And he did *that which was* evil in the sight of the LORD, after the abominations of the heathen, whom the LORD cast out before the children of Israel.

3 For he built up again the high places which Hezekiah his father had destroyed; and he reared up altars for Baal, and made a grove, as did Ahab king of Israel; and worshipped all the host of heaven, and served them.

4 And he built altars in the house of the LORD, of which the LORD said, In Jerusalem will I put my name.

5 And he built altars for all the host of heaven in the two courts of the house of the LORD.

6 And he made his son pass through the fire, and observed times, and used enchantments, and dealt with familiar spirits and wizards: he wrought much wickedness in the sight of the LORD, to provoke *him* to anger.

7 And he set a graven image of the grove that he had made in the house, of which the LORD said to David, and to Solomon his son, In this house, and in Jerusalem, which I have chosen out of all tribes of Israel, will I put my name for ever:

8 Neither will I make the feet of Israel move any more out of the land which I gave their fathers; only if they will observe to do according to all that I have commanded them, and according to all the law that my servant Moses commanded them.

9 But they hearkened not: and Manasseh seduced them to do more evil than did the nations whom the LORD destroyed before the children of Israel.

10 ¶ And the LORD spake by his servants the prophets, saying,

11 Because Manasseh king of Judah hath done these abominations, *and* hath done wickedly above all that the Amorites did, which *were* before him, and hath made Judah also to sin with his idols:

12 Therefore thus saith the LORD God of Israel, Behold, I *am* bringing *such* evil upon

Jerusalem and Judah, that whosoever
heareth of it, both his ears shall tingle.
13 And I will stretch over Jerusalem the
line of Samaria, and the plummet of the
house of Ahab: and I will wipe Jerusalem as
a man wipeth a dish, wiping *it*, and turning
it upside down.
14 And I will forsake the remnant of mine
inheritance, and deliver them into the hand
of their enemies; and they shall become a
prey and a spoil to all their enemies;
15 Because they have done *that which was*
evil in my sight, and have provoked me to
anger, since the day their fathers came forth
out of Egypt, even unto this day.
16 Moreover Manasseh shed innocent
blood very much, till he had filled Jerusalem from one end to another; beside his sin
wherewith he made Judah to sin, in doing
that which was evil in the sight of the LORD.
17 ¶ Now the rest of the acts of Manasseh,
and all that he did, and his sin that he sinned,
are they not written in the book of the
chronicles of the kings of Judah?
18 And Manasseh slept with his fathers, and
was buried in the garden of his own house,
in the garden of Uzza: and Amon his son
reigned in his stead.
19 ¶ Amon *was* twenty and two years old
when he began to reign, and he reigned
two years in Jerusalem. And his mother's
name *was* Meshullemeth, the daughter of
Haruz of Jotbah.
20 And he did *that which was* evil in the sight
of the LORD, as his father Manasseh did.
21 And he walked in all the way that his
father walked in, and served the idols that
his father served, and worshipped them:
22 And he forsook the LORD God of his
fathers, and walked not in the way of the
LORD.
23 ¶ And the servants of Amon conspired
against him, and slew the king in his own
house.
24 And the people of the land slew all them
that had conspired against king Amon; and
the people of the land made Josiah his son
king in his stead.
25 Now the rest of the acts of Amon which
he did, *are* they not written in the book of
the chronicles of the kings of Judah?
26 And he was buried in his sepulchre in the
garden of Uzza: and Josiah his son reigned
in his stead.

2 Kings 22

1 Josiah *was* eight years old when he began
to reign, and he reigned thirty and one years
in Jerusalem. And his mother's name *was*
Jedidah, the daughter of Adaiah of Boscath.
2 And he did *that which was* right in the
sight of the LORD, and walked in all the way
of David his father, and turned not aside to
the right hand or to the left.
3 ¶ And it came to pass in the eighteenth
year of king Josiah, *that* the king sent
Shaphan the son of Azaliah, the son of
Meshullam, the scribe, to the house of the
LORD, saying,
4 Go up to Hilkiah the high priest, that he
may sum the silver which is brought into
the house of the LORD, which the keepers
of the door have gathered of the people:
5 And let them deliver it into the hand of the
doers of the work, that have the oversight
of the house of the LORD: and let them give
it to the doers of the work which *is* in the
house of the LORD, to repair the breaches
of the house,
6 Unto carpenters, and builders, and
masons, and to buy timber and hewn stone
to repair the house.
7 Howbeit there was no reckoning made
with them of the money that was delivered
into their hand, because they dealt faithfully.
8 ¶ And Hilkiah the high priest said unto
Shaphan the scribe, I have found the book of
the law in the house of the LORD. And Hilkiah
gave the book to Shaphan, and he read it.
9 And Shaphan the scribe came to the king,
and brought the king word again, and said,
Thy servants have gathered the money that
was found in the house, and have delivered
it into the hand of them that do the work,
that have the oversight of the house of
the LORD.
10 And Shaphan the scribe shewed the king,
saying, Hilkiah the priest hath delivered me
a book. And Shaphan read it before the king.
11 And it came to pass, when the king had
heard the words of the book of the law, that
he rent his clothes.
12 And the king commanded Hilkiah the
priest, and Ahikam the son of Shaphan, and
Achbor the son of Michaiah, and Shaphan

the scribe, and Asahiah a servant of the
king's, saying,
13 Go ye, inquire of the LORD for me, and for
the people, and for all Judah, concerning the
words of this book that is found: for great *is*
the wrath of the LORD that is kindled against
us, because our fathers have not hearkened
unto the words of this book, to do according
unto all that which is written concerning us.
14 So Hilkiah the priest, and Ahikam, and
Achbor, and Shaphan, and Asahiah, went
unto Huldah the prophetess, the wife of
Shallum the son of Tikvah, the son of Harhas,
keeper of the wardrobe; (now she dwelt in
Jerusalem in the college;) and they communed with her.
15 ¶ And she said unto them, Thus saith
the LORD God of Israel, Tell the man that
sent you to me,
16 Thus saith the LORD, Behold, I will bring
evil upon this place, and upon the inhabitants thereof, *even* all the words of the book
which the king of Judah hath read:
17 Because they have forsaken me, and
have burned incense unto other gods, that
they might provoke me to anger with all the
works of their hands; therefore my wrath
shall be kindled against this place, and shall
not be quenched.
18 But to the king of Judah which sent you
to inquire of the LORD, thus shall ye say to
him, Thus saith the LORD God of Israel, *As
touching* the words which thou hast heard;
19 Because thine heart was tender, and thou
hast humbled thyself before the LORD, when
thou heardest what I spake against this
place, and against the inhabitants thereof,
that they should become a desolation and
a curse, and hast rent thy clothes, and wept
before me; I also have heard *thee*, saith
the LORD.
20 Behold therefore, I will gather thee unto
thy fathers, and thou shalt be gathered into
thy grave in peace; and thine eyes shall not
see all the evil which I will bring upon this
place. And they brought the king word again.

2 Kings 23

1 And the king sent, and they gathered unto
him all the elders of Judah and of Jerusalem.
2 And the king went up into the house of
the LORD, and all the men of Judah and all
the inhabitants of Jerusalem with him, and
the priests, and the prophets, and all the
people, both small and great: and he read
in their ears all the words of the book of the
covenant which was found in the house of
the LORD.
3 ¶ And the king stood by a pillar, and made
a covenant before the LORD, to walk after
the LORD, and to keep his commandments
and his testimonies and his statutes with
all *their* heart and all *their* soul, to perform
the words of this covenant that were written in this book. And all the people stood
to the covenant.
4 And the king commanded Hilkiah the high
priest, and the priests of the second order,
and the keepers of the door, to bring forth
out of the temple of the LORD all the vessels that were made for Baal, and for the
grove, and for all the host of heaven: and
he burned them without Jerusalem in the
fields of Kidron, and carried the ashes of
them unto Beth-el.
5 And he put down the idolatrous priests,
whom the kings of Judah had ordained to
burn incense in the high places in the cities
of Judah, and in the places round about
Jerusalem; them also that burned incense
unto Baal, to the sun, and to the moon, and
to the planets, and to all the host of heaven.
6 And he brought out the grove from the
house of the LORD, without Jerusalem, unto
the brook Kidron, and burned it at the brook
Kidron, and stamped *it* small to powder, and
cast the powder thereof upon the graves of
the children of the people.
7 And he brake down the houses of the
sodomites, that *were* by the house of the
LORD, where the women wove hangings
for the grove.
8 And he brought all the priests out of the
cities of Judah, and defiled the high places
where the priests had burned incense, from
Geba to Beer-sheba, and brake down the
high places of the gates that *were* in the
entering in of the gate of Joshua the governor of the city, which *were* on a man's left
hand at the gate of the city.
9 Nevertheless the priests of the high places
came not up to the altar of the LORD in Jerusalem, but they did eat of the unleavened
bread among their brethren.
10 And he defiled Topheth, which *is* in the
valley of the children of Hinnom, that no

man might make his son or his daughter to
pass through the fire to Molech.
11 And he took away the horses that the
kings of Judah had given to the sun, at the
entering in of the house of the LORD, by the
chamber of Nathan-melech the chamberlain, which *was* in the suburbs, and burned
the chariots of the sun with fire.
12 And the altars that *were* on the top of
the upper chamber of Ahaz, which the kings
of Judah had made, and the altars which
Manasseh had made in the two courts of the
house of the LORD, did the king beat down,
and brake *them* down from thence, and
cast the dust of them into the brook Kidron.
13 And the high places that *were* before
Jerusalem, which *were* on the right hand of
the mount of corruption, which Solomon the
king of Israel had builded for Ashtoreth the
abomination of the Zidonians, and for Chemosh the abomination of the Moabites, and
for Milcom the abomination of the children
of Ammon, did the king defile.
14 And he brake in pieces the images, and
cut down the groves, and filled their places
with the bones of men.
15 ¶ Moreover the altar that *was* at Beth-el,
and the high place which Jeroboam the
son of Nebat, who made Israel to sin, had
made, both that altar and the high place
he brake down, and burned the high place,
and stamped *it* small to powder, and burned
the grove.
16 And as Josiah turned himself, he spied
the sepulchres that *were* there in the mount,
and sent, and took the bones out of the
sepulchres, and burned *them* upon the altar,
and polluted it, according to the word of the
LORD which the man of God proclaimed,
who proclaimed these words.
17 Then he said, What title *is* that that I
see? And the men of the city told him, *It*
is the sepulchre of the man of God, which
came from Judah, and proclaimed these
things that thou hast done against the altar
of Beth-el.
18 And he said, Let him alone; let no man
move his bones. So they let his bones alone,
with the bones of the prophet that came
out of Samaria.
19 And all the houses also of the high places
that *were* in the cities of Samaria, which
the kings of Israel had made to provoke *the*
LORD to anger, Josiah took away, and did to
them according to all the acts that he had
done in Beth-el.
20 And he slew all the priests of the high
places that *were* there upon the altars,
and burned men's bones upon them, and
returned to Jerusalem.
21 ¶ And the king commanded all the people, saying, Keep the passover unto the
LORD your God, as *it is* written in the book
of this covenant.
22 Surely there was not holden such a
passover from the days of the judges that
judged Israel, nor in all the days of the kings
of Israel, nor of the kings of Judah;
23 But in the eighteenth year of king Josiah,
wherein this passover was holden to the
LORD in Jerusalem.
24 ¶ Moreover the *workers with* familiar
spirits, and the wizards, and the images, and
the idols, and all the abominations that were
spied in the land of Judah and in Jerusalem,
did Josiah put away, that he might perform
the words of the law which were written in
the book that Hilkiah the priest found in the
house of the LORD.
25 And like unto him was there no king
before him, that turned to the LORD with all
his heart, and with all his soul, and with all
his might, according to all the law of Moses;
neither after him arose there *any* like him.
26 ¶ Notwithstanding the LORD turned
not from the fierceness of his great wrath,
wherewith his anger was kindled against
Judah, because of all the provocations that
Manasseh had provoked him withal.
27 And the LORD said, I will remove Judah
also out of my sight, as I have removed
Israel, and will cast off this city Jerusalem
which I have chosen, and the house of which
I said, My name shall be there.
28 Now the rest of the acts of Josiah, and
all that he did, *are* they not written in the
book of the chronicles of the kings of Judah?
29 ¶ In his days Pharaoh-nechoh king of
Egypt went up against the king of Assyria
to the river Euphrates: and king Josiah went
against him; and he slew him at Megiddo,
when he had seen him.
30 And his servants carried him in a chariot dead from Megiddo, and brought him
to Jerusalem, and buried him in his own
sepulchre. And the people of the land took

Jehoahaz the son of Josiah, and anointed
him, and made him king in his father's stead.
31 ¶ Jehoahaz *was* twenty and three years
old when he began to reign; and he reigned
three months in Jerusalem. And his mother's name *was* Hamutal, the daughter of
Jeremiah of Libnah.
32 And he did *that which was* evil in the
sight of the LORD, according to all that his
fathers had done.
33 And Pharaoh-nechoh put him in bands at
Riblah in the land of Hamath, that he might
not reign in Jerusalem; and put the land to a
tribute of an hundred talents of silver, and
a talent of gold.
34 And Pharaoh-nechoh made Eliakim the
son of Josiah king in the room of Josiah his
father, and turned his name to Jehoiakim,
and took Jehoahaz away: and he came to
Egypt, and died there.
35 And Jehoiakim gave the silver and the
gold to Pharaoh; but he taxed the land to
give the money according to the commandment of Pharaoh: he exacted the silver and
the gold of the people of the land, of every
one according to his taxation, to give *it* unto
Pharaoh-nechoh.
36 ¶ Jehoiakim *was* twenty and five years
old when he began to reign; and he reigned
eleven years in Jerusalem. And his mother's
name *was* Zebudah, the daughter of Pedaiah
of Rumah.
37 And he did *that which was* evil in the
sight of the LORD, according to all that his
fathers had done.

2 Kings 24

1 In his days Nebuchadnezzar king of Babylon came up, and Jehoiakim became his
servant three years: then he turned and
rebelled against him.
2 And the LORD sent against him bands of
the Chaldees, and bands of the Syrians, and
bands of the Moabites, and bands of the
children of Ammon, and sent them against
Judah to destroy it, according to the word
of the LORD, which he spake by his servants
the prophets.
3 Surely at the commandment of the LORD
came *this* upon Judah, to remove *them*
out of his sight, for the sins of Manasseh,
according to all that he did;
4 And also for the innocent blood that he
shed: for he filled Jerusalem with innocent
blood; which the LORD would not pardon.
5 ¶ Now the rest of the acts of Jehoiakim,
and all that he did, *are* they not written in
the book of the chronicles of the kings of
Judah?
6 So Jehoiakim slept with his fathers: and
Jehoiachin his son reigned in his stead.
7 And the king of Egypt came not again any
more out of his land: for the king of Babylon
had taken from the river of Egypt unto the
river Euphrates all that pertained to the
king of Egypt.
8 ¶ Jehoiachin *was* eighteen years old when
he began to reign, and he reigned in Jerusalem three months. And his mother's name
was Nehushta, the daughter of Elnathan
of Jerusalem.
9 And he did *that which was* evil in the sight
of the LORD, according to all that his father
had done.
10 ¶ At that time the servants of Nebuchadnezzar king of Babylon came up against
Jerusalem, and the city was besieged.
11 And Nebuchadnezzar king of Babylon
came against the city, and his servants did
besiege it.
12 And Jehoiachin the king of Judah went
out to the king of Babylon, he, and his
mother, and his servants, and his princes,
and his officers: and the king of Babylon took
him in the eighth year of his reign.
13 And he carried out thence all the treasures of the house of the LORD, and the
treasures of the king's house, and cut in
pieces all the vessels of gold which Solomon
king of Israel had made in the temple of the
LORD, as the LORD had said.
14 And he carried away all Jerusalem, and
all the princes, and all the mighty men of
valour, *even* ten thousand captives, and all
the craftsmen and smiths: none remained,
save the poorest sort of the people of the
land.
15 And he carried away Jehoiachin to Babylon, and the king's mother, and the king's
wives, and his officers, and the mighty of
the land, *those* carried he into captivity from
Jerusalem to Babylon.
16 And all the men of might, *even* seven
thousand, and craftsmen and smiths a
thousand, all *that were* strong *and* apt for

war, even them the king of Babylon brought
captive to Babylon.
17 ¶ And the king of Babylon made Mattaniah his father's brother king in his stead,
and changed his name to Zedekiah.
18 Zedekiah *was* twenty and one years old
when he began to reign, and he reigned
eleven years in Jerusalem. And his mother's name *was* Hamutal, the daughter of
Jeremiah of Libnah.
19 And he did *that which was* evil in the sight
of the LORD, according to all that Jehoiakim
had done.
20 For through the anger of the LORD it
came to pass in Jerusalem and Judah, until
he had cast them out from his presence,
that Zedekiah rebelled against the king of
Babylon.

2 Kings 25

1 And it came to pass in the ninth year of his
reign, in the tenth month, in the tenth *day*
of the month, *that* Nebuchadnezzar king of
Babylon came, he, and all his host, against
Jerusalem, and pitched against it; and they
built forts against it round about.
2 And the city was besieged unto the eleventh year of king Zedekiah.
3 And on the ninth *day* of the *fourth* month
the famine prevailed in the city, and there
was no bread for the people of the land.
4 ¶ And the city was broken up, and all
the men of war *fled* by night by the way of
the gate between two walls, which *is* by
the king's garden: (now the Chaldees *were*
against the city round about:) and *the king*
went the way toward the plain.
5 And the army of the Chaldees pursued
after the king, and overtook him in the plains
of Jericho: and all his army were scattered
from him.
6 So they took the king, and brought him up
to the king of Babylon to Riblah; and they
gave judgment upon him.
7 And they slew the sons of Zedekiah before
his eyes, and put out the eyes of Zedekiah,
and bound him with fetters of brass, and
carried him to Babylon.
8 ¶ And in the fifth month, on the seventh
day of the month, which *is* the nineteenth
year of king Nebuchadnezzar king of Babylon, came Nebuzar-adan, captain of the
guard, a servant of the king of Babylon,
unto Jerusalem:
9 And he burnt the house of the LORD, and
the king's house, and all the houses of Jerusalem, and every great *man's* house burnt
he with fire.
10 And all the army of the Chaldees, that
were with the captain of the guard, brake
down the walls of Jerusalem round about.
11 Now the rest of the people *that were* left
in the city, and the fugitives that fell away
to the king of Babylon, with the remnant of
the multitude, did Nebuzar-adan the captain
of the guard carry away.
12 But the captain of the guard left of the
poor of the land *to be* vinedressers and
husbandmen.
13 And the pillars of brass that *were* in the
house of the LORD, and the bases, and the
brasen sea that *was* in the house of the
LORD, did the Chaldees break in pieces, and
carried the brass of them to Babylon.
14 And the pots, and the shovels, and the
snuffers, and the spoons, and all the vessels
of brass wherewith they ministered, took
they away.
15 And the firepans, and the bowls, *and* such
things as *were* of gold, *in* gold, and of silver,
in silver, the captain of the guard took away.
16 The two pillars, one sea, and the bases
which Solomon had made for the house of
the LORD; the brass of all these vessels was
without weight.
17 The height of the one pillar *was* eighteen
cubits, and the chapiter upon it *was* brass:
and the height of the chapiter three cubits;
and the wreathen work, and pomegranates
upon the chapiter round about, all of brass:
and like unto these had the second pillar
with wreathen work.
18 ¶ And the captain of the guard took
Seraiah the chief priest, and Zephaniah
the second priest, and the three keepers
of the door:
19 And out of the city he took an officer
that was set over the men of war, and five
men of them that were in the king's presence, which were found in the city, and the
principal scribe of the host, which mustered
the people of the land, and threescore men
of the people of the land *that were* found
in the city:
20 And Nebuzar-adan captain of the guard

took these, and brought them to the king
of Babylon to Riblah:
21 And the king of Babylon smote them, and
slew them at Riblah in the land of Hamath.
So Judah was carried away out of their land.
22 ¶ And *as for* the people that remained in
the land of Judah, whom Nebuchadnezzar
king of Babylon had left, even over them he
made Gedaliah the son of Ahikam, the son
of Shaphan, ruler.
23 And when all the captains of the armies,
they and their men, heard that the king of
Babylon had made Gedaliah governor, there
came to Gedaliah to Mizpah, even Ishmael
the son of Nethaniah, and Johanan the son
of Careah, and Seraiah the son of Tanhumeth the Netophathite, and Jaazaniah the
son of a Maachathite, they and their men.
24 And Gedaliah sware to them, and to their
men, and said unto them, Fear not to be the
servants of the Chaldees: dwell in the land,
and serve the king of Babylon; and it shall
be well with you.
25 But it came to pass in the seventh month,
that Ishmael the son of Nethaniah, the son
of Elishama, of the seed royal, came, and
ten men with him, and smote Gedaliah, that
he died, and the Jews and the Chaldees that
were with him at Mizpah.
26 And all the people, both small and great,
and the captains of the armies, arose, and
came to Egypt: for they were afraid of the
Chaldees.
27 ¶ And it came to pass in the seven and
thirtieth year of the captivity of Jehoiachin
king of Judah, in the twelfth month, on the
seven and twentieth *day* of the month, *that*
Evil-merodach king of Babylon in the year
that he began to reign did lift up the head
of Jehoiachin king of Judah out of prison;
28 And he spake kindly to him, and set his
throne above the throne of the kings that
were with him in Babylon;
29 And changed his prison garments: and
he did eat bread continually before him all
the days of his life.
30 And his allowance *was* a continual allowance given him of the king, a daily rate for
every day, all the days of his life.

The First Book Of The

Chronicles

1 Chronicles 1

1 Adam, Sheth, Enosh,
2 Kenan, Mahalaleel, Jered,
3 Henoch, Methuselah, Lamech,
4 Noah, Shem, Ham, and Japheth.
5 ¶ The sons of Japheth; Gomer, and Magog,
and Madai, and Javan, and Tubal, and
Meshech, and Tiras.
6 And the sons of Gomer; Ashchenaz, and
Riphath, and Togarmah.
7 And the sons of Javan; Elishah, and Tarshish, Kittim, and Dodanim.
8 ¶ The sons of Ham; Cush, and Mizraim,
Put, and Canaan.
9 And the sons of Cush; Seba, and Havilah,
and Sabta, and Raamah, and Sabtecha. And
the sons of Raamah; Sheba, and Dedan.
10 And Cush begat Nimrod: he began to be
mighty upon the earth.
11 And Mizraim begat Ludim, and Anamim,
and Lehabim, and Naphtuhim,
12 And Pathrusim, and Casluhim, (of whom
came the Philistines,) and Caphthorim.
13 And Canaan begat Zidon his firstborn,
and Heth,
14 The Jebusite also, and the Amorite, and
the Girgashite,
15 And the Hivite, and the Arkite, and the
Sinite,
16 And the Arvadite, and the Zemarite, and
the Hamathite.
17 ¶ The sons of Shem; Elam, and Asshur,
and Arphaxad, and Lud, and Aram, and Uz,
and Hul, and Gether, and Meshech.
18 And Arphaxad begat Shelah, and Shelah
begat Eber.
19 And unto Eber were born two sons: the
name of the one *was* Peleg; because in his

days the earth was divided: and his brother's
name *was* Joktan.
20 And Joktan begat Almodad, and Sheleph,
and Hazarmaveth, and Jerah,
21 Hadoram also, and Uzal, and Diklah,
22 And Ebal, and Abimael, and Sheba,
23 And Ophir, and Havilah, and Jobab. All
these *were* the sons of Joktan.
24 ¶ Shem, Arphaxad, Shelah,
25 Eber, Peleg, Reu,
26 Serug, Nahor, Terah,
27 Abram; the same *is* Abraham.
28 The sons of Abraham; Isaac, and Ishmael.
29 ¶ These *are* their generations: The firstborn of Ishmael, Nebaioth; then Kedar, and
Adbeel, and Mibsam,
30 Mishma, and Dumah, Massa, Hadad,
and Tema,
31 Jetur, Naphish, and Kedemah. These are
the sons of Ishmael.
32 ¶ Now the sons of Keturah, Abraham's
concubine: she bare Zimran, and Jokshan,
and Medan, and Midian, and Ishbak, and
Shuah. And the sons of Jokshan; Sheba,
and Dedan.
33 And the sons of Midian; Ephah, and
Epher, and Henoch, and Abida, and Eldaah.
All these *are* the sons of Keturah.
34 And Abraham begat Isaac. The sons of
Isaac; Esau and Israel.
35 ¶ The sons of Esau; Eliphaz, Reuel, and
Jeush, and Jaalam, and Korah.
36 The sons of Eliphaz; Teman, and Omar,
Zephi, and Gatam, Kenaz, and Timna, and
Amalek.
37 The sons of Reuel; Nahath, Zerah, Shammah, and Mizzah.
38 And the sons of Seir; Lotan, and Shobal,
and Zibeon, and Anah, and Dishon, and
Ezer, and Dishan.
39 And the sons of Lotan; Hori, and Homam:
and Timna *was* Lotan's sister.
40 The sons of Shobal; Alian, and Manahath,
and Ebal, Shephi, and Onam. And the sons
of Zibeon; Aiah, and Anah.
41 The sons of Anah; Dishon. And the sons
of Dishon; Amram, and Eshban, and Ithran,
and Cheran.
42 The sons of Ezer; Bilhan, and Zavan, *and*
Jakan. The sons of Dishan; Uz, and Aran.
43 ¶ Now these *are* the kings that reigned
in the land of Edom before *any* king reigned
over the children of Israel; Bela the son of
Beor: and the name of his city *was* Din-
habah.
44 And when Bela was dead, Jobab the
son of Zerah of Bozrah reigned in his stead.
45 And when Jobab was dead, Husham of
the land of the Temanites reigned in his
stead.
46 And when Husham was dead, Hadad the
son of Bedad, which smote Midian in the
field of Moab, reigned in his stead: and the
name of his city *was* Avith.
47 And when Hadad was dead, Samlah of
Masrekah reigned in his stead.
48 And when Samlah was dead, Shaul of
Rehoboth by the river reigned in his stead.
49 And when Shaul was dead, Baal-hanan
the son of Achbor reigned in his stead.
50 And when Baal-hanan was dead, Hadad
reigned in his stead: and the name of his city
was Pai; and his wife's name *was* Mehetabel, the daughter of Matred, the daughter
of Mezahab.
51 ¶ Hadad died also. And the dukes of
Edom were; duke Timnah, duke Aliah, duke
Jetheth,
52 Duke Aholibamah, duke Elah, duke Pinon,
53 Duke Kenaz, duke Teman, duke Mibzar,
54 Duke Magdiel, duke Iram. These *are* the
dukes of Edom.

1 Chronicles 2

1 These *are* the sons of Israel; Reuben, Simeon, Levi, and Judah, Issachar, and Zebulun,
2 Dan, Joseph, and Benjamin, Naphtali,
Gad, and Asher.
3 ¶ The sons of Judah; Er, and Onan, and
Shelah: *which* three were born unto him of
the daughter of Shua the Canaanitess. And
Er, the firstborn of Judah, was evil in the
sight of the LORD; and he slew him.
4 And Tamar his daughter in law bare him
Pharez and Zerah. All the sons of Judah
were five.
5 The sons of Pharez; Hezron, and Hamul.
6 And the sons of Zerah; Zimri, and Ethan,
and Heman, and Calcol, and Dara: five of
them in all.
7 And the sons of Carmi; Achar, the troubler
of Israel, who transgressed in the thing
accursed.
8 And the sons of Ethan; Azariah.
9 The sons also of Hezron, that were born

unto him; Jerahmeel, and Ram, and Che-
lubai.
10 And Ram begat Amminadab; and Amminadab begat Nahshon, prince of the children
of Judah;
11 And Nahshon begat Salma, and Salma
begat Boaz,
12 And Boaz begat Obed, and Obed begat
Jesse,
13 ¶ And Jesse begat his firstborn Eliab, and
Abinadab the second, and Shimma the third,
14 Nethaneel the fourth, Raddai the fifth,
15 Ozem the sixth, David the seventh:
16 Whose sisters *were* Zeruiah, and Abigail.
And the sons of Zeruiah; Abishai, and Joab,
and Asahel, three.
17 And Abigail bare Amasa: and the father
of Amasa *was* Jether the Ishmeelite.
18 ¶ And Caleb the son of Hezron begat
children of Azubah *his* wife, and of Jerioth:
her sons *are* these; Jesher, and Shobab,
and Ardon.
19 And when Azubah was dead, Caleb took
unto him Ephrath, which bare him Hur.
20 And Hur begat Uri, and Uri begat Bezaleel.
21 ¶ And afterward Hezron went in to the
daughter of Machir the father of Gilead,
whom he married when he *was* threescore
years old; and she bare him Segub.
22 And Segub begat Jair, who had three and
twenty cities in the land of Gilead.
23 And he took Geshur, and Aram, with the
towns of Jair, from them, with Kenath, and
the towns thereof, *even* threescore cities.
All these *belonged to* the sons of Machir the
father of Gilead.
24 And after that Hezron was dead in
Caleb-ephratah, then Abiah Hezron's wife
bare him Ashur the father of Tekoa.
25 ¶ And the sons of Jerahmeel the firstborn
of Hezron were, Ram the firstborn, and
Bunah, and Oren, and Ozem, *and* Ahijah.
26 Jerahmeel had also another wife, whose
name *was* Atarah; she *was* the mother of
Onam.
27 And the sons of Ram the firstborn of
Jerahmeel were, Maaz, and Jamin, and Eker.
28 And the sons of Onam were, Shammai,
and Jada. And the sons of Shammai; Nadab,
and Abishur.
29 And the name of the wife of Abishur *was*
Abihail, and she bare him Ahban, and Molid.
30 And the sons of Nadab; Seled, and
Appaim: but Seled died without children.
31 And the sons of Appaim; Ishi. And the
sons of Ishi; Sheshan. And the children of
Sheshan; Ahlai.
32 And the sons of Jada the brother of
Shammai; Jether, and Jonathan: and Jether
died without children.
33 And the sons of Jonathan; Peleth, and
Zaza. These were the sons of Jerahmeel.
34 ¶ Now Sheshan had no sons, but daughters. And Sheshan had a servant, an Egyptian, whose name *was* Jarha.
35 And Sheshan gave his daughter to Jarha
his servant to wife; and she bare him Attai.
36 And Attai begat Nathan, and Nathan
begat Zabad,
37 And Zabad begat Ephlal, and Ephlal
begat Obed,
38 And Obed begat Jehu, and Jehu begat
Azariah,
39 And Azariah begat Helez, and Helez
begat Eleasah,
40 And Eleasah begat Sisamai, and Sisamai
begat Shallum,
41 And Shallum begat Jekamiah, and Jekamiah begat Elishama.
42 ¶ Now the sons of Caleb the brother
of Jerahmeel *were*, Mesha his firstborn,
which *was* the father of Ziph; and the sons
of Mareshah the father of Hebron.
43 And the sons of Hebron; Korah, and
Tappuah, and Rekem, and Shema.
44 And Shema begat Raham, the father of
Jorkoam: and Rekem begat Shammai.
45 And the son of Shammai *was* Maon: and
Maon *was* the father of Beth-zur.
46 And Ephah, Caleb's concubine, bare
Haran, and Moza, and Gazez: and Haran
begat Gazez.
47 And the sons of Jahdai; Regem, and
Jotham, and Geshan, and Pelet, and Ephah,
and Shaaph.
48 Maachah, Caleb's concubine, bare She-
ber, and Tirhanah.
49 She bare also Shaaph the father of Madmannah, Sheva the father of Machbenah,
and the father of Gibea: and the daughter
of Caleb *was* Achsah.
50 ¶ These were the sons of Caleb the son
of Hur, the firstborn of Ephratah; Shobal the
father of Kirjath-jearim,

51 Salma the father of Beth-lehem, Hareph
the father of Beth-gader.
52 And Shobal the father of Kirjath-jearim
had sons; Haroeh, *and* half of the Manahethites.
53 And the families of Kirjath-jearim; the Ith-
rites, and the Puhites, and the Shumathites,
and the Mishraites; of them came the
Zareathites, and the Eshtaulites.
54 The sons of Salma; Beth-lehem, and the
Netophathites, Ataroth, the house of Joab,
and half of the Manahethites, the Zorites.
55 And the families of the scribes which
dwelt at Jabez; the Tirathites, the Shimeath-
ites, *and* Suchathites. These *are* the Kenites
that came of Hemath, the father of the
house of Rechab.

1 Chronicles 3

1 Now these were the sons of David, which
were born unto him in Hebron; the firstborn
Amnon, of Ahinoam the Jezreelitess; the
second Daniel, of Abigail the Carmelitess:
2 The third, Absalom the son of Maachah
the daughter of Talmai king of Geshur: the
fourth, Adonijah the son of Haggith:
3 The fifth, Shephatiah of Abital: the sixth,
Ithream by Eglah his wife.
4 *These* six were born unto him in Hebron;
and there he reigned seven years and six
months: and in Jerusalem he reigned thirty
and three years.
5 And these were born unto him in Jerusalem; Shimea, and Shobab, and Nathan, and
Solomon, four, of Bath-shua the daughter
of Ammiel:
6 Ibhar also, and Elishama, and Eliphelet,
7 And Nogah, and Nepheg, and Japhia,
8 And Elishama, and Eliada, and Eliphelet,
nine.
9 *These were* all the sons of David, beside
the sons of the concubines, and Tamar
their sister.
10 ¶ And Solomon's son *was* Rehoboam,
Abia his son, Asa his son, Jehoshaphat his
son,
11 Joram his son, Ahaziah his son, Joash
his son,
12 Amaziah his son, Azariah his son, Jotham
his son,
13 Ahaz his son, Hezekiah his son, Manasseh
his son,
14 Amon his son, Josiah his son.
15 And the sons of Josiah *were*, the firstborn
Johanan, the second Jehoiakim, the third
Zedekiah, the fourth Shallum.
16 And the sons of Jehoiakim: Jeconiah his
son, Zedekiah his son.
17 ¶ And the sons of Jeconiah; Assir, Salathiel his son,
18 Malchiram also, and Pedaiah, and
Shenazar, Jecamiah, Hoshama, and Ned-
abiah.
19 And the sons of Pedaiah *were*, Zerubbabel, and Shimei: and the sons of Zerubbabel;
Meshullam, and Hananiah, and Shelomith
their sister:
20 And Hashubah, and Ohel, and Berechiah,
and Hasadiah, Jushab-hesed, five.
21 And the sons of Hananiah; Pelatiah, and
Jesaiah: the sons of Rephaiah, the sons of
Arnan, the sons of Obadiah, the sons of
Shechaniah.
22 And the sons of Shechaniah; Shemaiah: and the sons of Shemaiah; Hattush,
and Igeal, and Bariah, and Neariah, and
Shaphat, six.
23 And the sons of Neariah; Elioenai, and
Hezekiah, and Azrikam, three.
24 And the sons of Elioenai *were*, Hodaiah,
and Eliashib, and Pelaiah, and Akkub, and
Johanan, and Dalaiah, and Anani, seven.

1 Chronicles 4

1 The sons of Judah; Pharez, Hezron, and
Carmi, and Hur, and Shobal.
2 And Reaiah the son of Shobal begat Jahath;
and Jahath begat Ahumai, and Lahad. These
are the families of the Zorathites.
3 And these *were of* the father of Etam; Jezreel, and Ishma, and Idbash: and the name
of their sister *was* Hazelelponi:
4 And Penuel the father of Gedor, and Ezer
the father of Hushah. These *are* the sons of
Hur, the firstborn of Ephratah, the father of
Beth-lehem.
5 ¶ And Ashur the father of Tekoa had two
wives, Helah and Naarah.
6 And Naarah bare him Ahuzam, and Hepher, and Temeni, and Haahashtari. These
were the sons of Naarah.
7 And the sons of Helah *were*, Zereth, and
Jezoar, and Ethnan.
8 And Coz begat Anub, and Zobebah, and
the families of Aharhel the son of Harum.
9 ¶ And Jabez was more honourable than

his brethren: and his mother called his
name Jabez, saying, Because I bare him
with sorrow.
10 And Jabez called on the God of Israel,
saying, Oh that thou wouldest bless me
indeed, and enlarge my coast, and that
thine hand might be with me, and that thou
wouldest keep *me* from evil, that it may not
grieve me! And God granted him that which
he requested.
11 ¶ And Chelub the brother of Shuah begat
Mehir, which *was* the father of Eshton.
12 And Eshton begat Beth-rapha, and
Paseah, and Tehinnah the father of Ir-na-
hash. These *are* the men of Rechah.
13 And the sons of Kenaz; Othniel, and
Seraiah: and the sons of Othniel; Hathath.
14 And Meonothai begat Ophrah: and
Seraiah begat Joab, the father of the valley
of Charashim; for they were craftsmen.
15 And the sons of Caleb the son of Jephunneh; Iru, Elah, and Naam: and the sons of
Elah, even Kenaz.
16 And the sons of Jehaleleel; Ziph, and
Ziphah, Tiria, and Asareel.
17 And the sons of Ezra *were*, Jether, and
Mered, and Epher, and Jalon: and she bare
Miriam, and Shammai, and Ishbah the father
of Eshtemoa.
18 And his wife Jehudijah bare Jered the
father of Gedor, and Heber the father of
Socho, and Jekuthiel the father of Zanoah.
And these *are* the sons of Bithiah the daughter of Pharaoh, which Mered took.
19 And the sons of *his* wife Hodiah the sister
of Naham, the father of Keilah the Garmite,
and Eshtemoa the Maachathite.
20 And the sons of Shimon *were*, Amnon,
and Rinnah, Ben-hanan, and Tilon. And the
sons of Ishi *were*, Zoheth, and Ben-zoheth.
21 ¶ The sons of Shelah the son of Judah
were, Er the father of Lecah, and Laadah the
father of Mareshah, and the families of the
house of them that wrought fine linen, of
the house of Ashbea,
22 And Jokim, and the men of Chozeba, and
Joash, and Saraph, who had the dominion
in Moab, and Jashubi-lehem. And *these are*
ancient things.
23 These *were* the potters, and those that
dwelt among plants and hedges: there they
dwelt with the king for his work.
24 ¶ The sons of Simeon *were*, Nemuel, and
Jamin, Jarib, Zerah, *and* Shaul:
25 Shallum his son, Mibsam his son, Mishma
his son.
26 And the sons of Mishma; Hamuel his son,
Zacchur his son, Shimei his son.
27 And Shimei had sixteen sons and six
daughters; but his brethren had not many
children, neither did all their family multiply,
like to the children of Judah.
28 And they dwelt at Beer-sheba, and Moladah, and Hazar-shual,
29 And at Bilhah, and at Ezem, and at Tolad,
30 And at Bethuel, and at Hormah, and at
Ziklag,
31 And at Beth-marcaboth, and Hazar-susim,
and at Beth-birei, and at Shaaraim. These
were their cities unto the reign of David.
32 And their villages *were*, Etam, and Ain,
Rimmon, and Tochen, and Ashan, five cities:
33 And all their villages that *were* round
about the same cities, unto Baal. These
were their habitations, and their genealogy.
34 And Meshobab, and Jamlech, and Joshah
the son of Amaziah,
35 And Joel, and Jehu the son of Josibiah,
the son of Seraiah, the son of Asiel,
36 And Elioenai, and Jaakobah, and Jesho-
haiah, and Asaiah, and Adiel, and Jesimiel,
and Benaiah,
37 And Ziza the son of Shiphi, the son of
Allon, the son of Jedaiah, the son of Shimri,
the son of Shemaiah;
38 These mentioned by *their* names *were*
princes in their families: and the house of
their fathers increased greatly.
39 ¶ And they went to the entrance of
Gedor, *even* unto the east side of the valley,
to seek pasture for their flocks.
40 And they found fat pasture and good, and
the land *was* wide, and quiet, and peaceable; for *they* of Ham had dwelt there of old.
41 And these written by name came in the
days of Hezekiah king of Judah, and smote
their tents, and the habitations that were
found there, and destroyed them utterly
unto this day, and dwelt in their rooms:
because *there was* pasture there for their
flocks.
42 And *some* of them, *even* of the sons of
Simeon, five hundred men, went to mount
Seir, having for their captains Pelatiah, and

Neariah, and Rephaiah, and Uzziel, the
sons of Ishi.
43 And they smote the rest of the Amalekites that were escaped, and dwelt there
unto this day.

1 Chronicles 5

1 Now the sons of Reuben the firstborn of
Israel, (for he *was* the firstborn; but, forasmuch as he defiled his father's bed, his
birthright was given unto the sons of Joseph
the son of Israel: and the genealogy is not
to be reckoned after the birthright.
2 For Judah prevailed above his brethren,
and of him *came* the chief ruler; but the
birthright *was* Joseph's:)
3 The sons, *I say*, of Reuben the firstborn
of Israel *were*, Hanoch, and Pallu, Hezron,
and Carmi.
4 The sons of Joel; Shemaiah his son, Gog
his son, Shimei his son,
5 Micah his son, Reaia his son, Baal his son,
6 Beerah his son, whom Tilgath-pilneser
king of Assyria carried away *captive:* he *was*
prince of the Reubenites.
7 And his brethren by their families, when
the genealogy of their generations was reckoned, *were* the chief, Jeiel, and Zechariah,
8 And Bela the son of Azaz, the son of
Shema, the son of Joel, who dwelt in Aroer,
even unto Nebo and Baal-meon:
9 And eastward he inhabited unto the
entering in of the wilderness from the river
Euphrates: because their cattle were multiplied in the land of Gilead.
10 And in the days of Saul they made war
with the Hagarites, who fell by their hand:
and they dwelt in their tents throughout all
the east *land* of Gilead.
11 ¶ And the children of Gad dwelt over
against them, in the land of Bashan unto
Salchah:
12 Joel the chief, and Shapham the next,
and Jaanai, and Shaphat in Bashan.
13 And their brethren of the house of their
fathers *were*, Michael, and Meshullam, and
Sheba, and Jorai, and Jachan, and Zia, and
Heber, seven.
14 These *are* the children of Abihail the son
of Huri, the son of Jaroah, the son of Gilead,
the son of Michael, the son of Jeshishai, the
son of Jahdo, the son of Buz;
15 Ahi the son of Abdiel, the son of Guni,
chief of the house of their fathers.
16 And they dwelt in Gilead in Bashan, and in
her towns, and in all the suburbs of Sharon,
upon their borders.
17 All these were reckoned by genealogies
in the days of Jotham king of Judah, and in
the days of Jeroboam king of Israel.
18 ¶ The sons of Reuben, and the Gadites,
and half the tribe of Manasseh, of valiant
men, men able to bear buckler and sword,
and to shoot with bow, and skilful in war,
were four and forty thousand seven hundred and threescore, that went out to the
war.
19 And they made war with the Hagarites,
with Jetur, and Nephish, and Nodab.
20 And they were helped against them, and
the Hagarites were delivered into their hand,
and all that *were* with them: for they cried
to God in the battle, and he was intreated
of them; because they put their trust in him.
21 And they took away their cattle; of their
camels fifty thousand, and of sheep two
hundred and fifty thousand, and of asses
two thousand, and of men an hundred
thousand.
22 For there fell down many slain, because
the war *was* of God. And they dwelt in their
steads until the captivity.
23 ¶ And the children of the half tribe of
Manasseh dwelt in the land: they increased
from Bashan unto Baal-hermon and Senir,
and unto mount Hermon.
24 And these *were* the heads of the house of
their fathers, even Epher, and Ishi, and Eliel,
and Azriel, and Jeremiah, and Hodaviah, and
Jahdiel, mighty men of valour, famous men,
and heads of the house of their fathers.
25 ¶ And they transgressed against the God
of their fathers, and went a whoring after
the gods of the people of the land, whom
God destroyed before them.
26 And the God of Israel stirred up the spirit
of Pul king of Assyria, and the spirit of Tilgath-pilneser king of Assyria, and he carried
them away, even the Reubenites, and the
Gadites, and the half tribe of Manasseh, and
brought them unto Halah, and Habor, and
Hara, and to the river Gozan, unto this day.

1 Chronicles 6

1 The sons of Levi; Gershon, Kohath, and Merari.

2 And the sons of Kohath; Amram, Izhar, and Hebron, and Uzziel.

3 And the children of Amram; Aaron, and Moses, and Miriam. The sons also of Aaron; Nadab, and Abihu, Eleazar, and Ithamar.

4 ¶ Eleazar begat Phinehas, Phinehas begat Abishua,

5 And Abishua begat Bukki, and Bukki begat Uzzi,

6 And Uzzi begat Zerahiah, and Zerahiah begat Meraioth,

7 Meraioth begat Amariah, and Amariah begat Ahitub,

8 And Ahitub begat Zadok, and Zadok begat Ahimaaz,

9 And Ahimaaz begat Azariah, and Azariah begat Johanan,

10 And Johanan begat Azariah, (he *it is* that executed the priest's office in the temple that Solomon built in Jerusalem:)

11 And Azariah begat Amariah, and Amariah begat Ahitub,

12 And Ahitub begat Zadok, and Zadok begat Shallum,

13 And Shallum begat Hilkiah, and Hilkiah begat Azariah,

14 And Azariah begat Seraiah, and Seraiah begat Jehozadak,

15 And Jehozadak went *into captivity*, when the LORD carried away Judah and Jerusalem by the hand of Nebuchadnezzar.

16 ¶ The sons of Levi; Gershom, Kohath, and Merari.

17 And these *be* the names of the sons of Gershom; Libni, and Shimei.

18 And the sons of Kohath *were*, Amram, and Izhar, and Hebron, and Uzziel.

19 The sons of Merari; Mahli, and Mushi. And these *are* the families of the Levites according to their fathers.

20 Of Gershom; Libni his son, Jahath his son, Zimmah his son,

21 Joah his son, Iddo his son, Zerah his son, Jeaterai his son.

22 The sons of Kohath; Amminadab his son, Korah his son, Assir his son,

23 Elkanah his son, and Ebiasaph his son, and Assir his son,

24 Tahath his son, Uriel his son, Uzziah his son, and Shaul his son.

25 And the sons of Elkanah; Amasai, and Ahimoth.

26 *As for* Elkanah: the sons of Elkanah; Zophai his son, and Nahath his son,

27 Eliab his son, Jeroham his son, Elkanah his son.

28 And the sons of Samuel; the firstborn Vashni, and Abiah.

29 The sons of Merari; Mahli, Libni his son, Shimei his son, Uzza his son,

30 Shimea his son, Haggiah his son, Asaiah his son.

31 And these *are they* whom David set over the service of song in the house of the LORD, after that the ark had rest.

32 And they ministered before the dwelling place of the tabernacle of the congregation with singing, until Solomon had built the house of the LORD in Jerusalem: and *then* they waited on their office according to their order.

33 And these *are* they that waited with their children. Of the sons of the Kohathites: Heman a singer, the son of Joel, the son of Shemuel,

34 The son of Elkanah, the son of Jeroham, the son of Eliel, the son of Toah,

35 The son of Zuph, the son of Elkanah, the son of Mahath, the son of Amasai,

36 The son of Elkanah, the son of Joel, the son of Azariah, the son of Zephaniah,

37 The son of Tahath, the son of Assir, the son of Ebiasaph, the son of Korah,

38 The son of Izhar, the son of Kohath, the son of Levi, the son of Israel.

39 And his brother Asaph, who stood on his right hand, *even* Asaph the son of Berachiah, the son of Shimea,

40 The son of Michael, the son of Baaseiah, the son of Malchiah,

41 The son of Ethni, the son of Zerah, the son of Adaiah,

42 The son of Ethan, the son of Zimmah, the son of Shimei,

43 The son of Jahath, the son of Gershom, the son of Levi.

44 And their brethren the sons of Merari *stood* on the left hand: Ethan the son of Kishi, the son of Abdi, the son of Malluch,

45 The son of Hashabiah, the son of Amaziah, the son of Hilkiah,

46 The son of Amzi, the son of Bani, the son of Shamer,

47 The son of Mahli, the son of Mushi, the
son of Merari, the son of Levi.
48 Their brethren also the Levites *were*
appointed unto all manner of service of the
tabernacle of the house of God.
49 ¶ But Aaron and his sons offered upon
the altar of the burnt offering, and on the
altar of incense, *and were appointed* for
all the work of the *place* most holy, and to
make an atonement for Israel, according
to all that Moses the servant of God had
commanded.
50 And these *are* the sons of Aaron; Eleazar
his son, Phinehas his son, Abishua his son,
51 Bukki his son, Uzzi his son, Zerahiah
his son,
52 Meraioth his son, Amariah his son,
Ahitub his son,
53 Zadok his son, Ahimaaz his son.
54 ¶ Now these *are* their dwelling places
throughout their castles in their coasts, of
the sons of Aaron, of the families of the
Kohathites: for theirs was the lot.
55 And they gave them Hebron in the land
of Judah, and the suburbs thereof round
about it.
56 But the fields of the city, and the villages thereof, they gave to Caleb the son
of Jephunneh.
57 And to the sons of Aaron they gave the
cities of Judah, *namely*, Hebron, *the city* of
refuge, and Libnah with her suburbs, and
Jattir, and Eshtemoa, with their suburbs,
58 And Hilen with her suburbs, Debir with
her suburbs,
59 And Ashan with her suburbs, and Beth-
shemesh with her suburbs:
60 And out of the tribe of Benjamin; Geba
with her suburbs, and Alemeth with her
suburbs, and Anathoth with her suburbs. All
their cities throughout their families *were*
thirteen cities.
61 And unto the sons of Kohath, *which were*
left of the family of that tribe, *were cities*
given out of the half tribe, *namely, out of*
the half *tribe* of Manasseh, by lot, ten cities.
62 And to the sons of Gershom throughout
their families out of the tribe of Issachar,
and out of the tribe of Asher, and out of
the tribe of Naphtali, and out of the tribe of
Manasseh in Bashan, thirteen cities.
63 Unto the sons of Merari *were given* by lot,
throughout their families, out of the tribe
of Reuben, and out of the tribe of Gad, and
out of the tribe of Zebulun, twelve cities.
64 And the children of Israel gave to the
Levites *these* cities with their suburbs.
65 And they gave by lot out of the tribe of
the children of Judah, and out of the tribe of
the children of Simeon, and out of the tribe
of the children of Benjamin, these cities,
which are called by *their* names.
66 And *the residue* of the families of the sons
of Kohath had cities of their coasts out of
the tribe of Ephraim.
67 And they gave unto them, *of* the cities
of refuge, Shechem in mount Ephraim with
her suburbs; *they gave* also Gezer with her
suburbs,
68 And Jokmeam with her suburbs, and
Beth-horon with her suburbs,
69 And Aijalon with her suburbs, and
Gath-rimmon with her suburbs:
70 And out of the half tribe of Manasseh;
Aner with her suburbs, and Bileam with her
suburbs, for the family of the remnant of
the sons of Kohath.
71 Unto the sons of Gershom *were given* out
of the family of the half tribe of Manasseh,
Golan in Bashan with her suburbs, and
Ashtaroth with her suburbs:
72 And out of the tribe of Issachar; Kedesh
with her suburbs, Daberath with her suburbs,
73 And Ramoth with her suburbs, and Anem
with her suburbs:
74 And out of the tribe of Asher; Mashal with
her suburbs, and Abdon with her suburbs,
75 And Hukok with her suburbs, and Rehob
with her suburbs:
76 And out of the tribe of Naphtali; Kedesh
in Galilee with her suburbs, and Hammon
with her suburbs, and Kirjathaim with her
suburbs.
77 Unto the rest of the children of Merari
were given out of the tribe of Zebulun,
Rimmon with her suburbs, Tabor with her
suburbs:
78 And on the other side Jordan by Jericho,
on the east side of Jordan, *were given them*
out of the tribe of Reuben, Bezer in the wilderness with her suburbs, and Jahzah with
her suburbs,
79 Kedemoth also with her suburbs, and
Mephaath with her suburbs:
80 And out of the tribe of Gad; Ramoth in

Gilead with her suburbs, and Mahanaim
with her suburbs,
81 And Heshbon with her suburbs, and Jazer
with her suburbs.

1 Chronicles 7

1 Now the sons of Issachar *were*, Tola, and
Puah, Jashub, and Shimron, four.
2 And the sons of Tola; Uzzi, and Rephaiah,
and Jeriel, and Jahmai, and Jibsam, and
Shemuel, heads of their father's house, *to
wit*, of Tola: *they were* valiant men of might
in their generations; whose number *was* in
the days of David two and twenty thousand
and six hundred.
3 And the sons of Uzzi; Izrahiah: and the sons
of Izrahiah; Michael, and Obadiah, and Joel,
Ishiah, five: all of them chief men.
4 And with them, by their generations, after
the house of their fathers, *were* bands of
soldiers for war, six and thirty thousand
men: for they had many wives and sons.
5 And their brethren among all the families
of Issachar *were* valiant men of might, reckoned in all by their genealogies fourscore
and seven thousand.
6 ¶ *The sons* of Benjamin; Bela, and Becher,
and Jediael, three.
7 And the sons of Bela; Ezbon, and Uzzi, and
Uzziel, and Jerimoth, and Iri, five; heads of
the house of *their* fathers, mighty men of
valour; and were reckoned by their genealogies twenty and two thousand and thirty
and four.
8 And the sons of Becher; Zemira, and Joash,
and Eliezer, and Elioenai, and Omri, and
Jerimoth, and Abiah, and Anathoth, and
Alameth. All these *are* the sons of Becher.
9 And the number of them, after their genealogy by their generations, heads of the
house of their fathers, mighty men of valour,
was twenty thousand and two hundred.
10 The sons also of Jediael; Bilhan: and the
sons of Bilhan; Jeush, and Benjamin, and
Ehud, and Chenaanah, and Zethan, and
Tharshish, and Ahishahar.
11 All these the sons of Jediael, by the heads
of their fathers, mighty men of valour, *were*
seventeen thousand and two hundred *soldiers*, fit to go out for war *and* battle.
12 Shuppim also, and Huppim, the children
of Ir, *and* Hushim, the sons of Aher.
13 ¶ The sons of Naphtali; Jahziel, and Guni,
and Jezer, and Shallum, the sons of Bilhah.
14 ¶ The sons of Manasseh; Ashriel, whom
she bare: (*but* his concubine the Aramitess
bare Machir the father of Gilead:
15 And Machir took to wife *the sister* of
Huppim and Shuppim, whose sister's name
was Maachah;) and the name of the second *was* Zelophehad: and Zelophehad had
daughters.
16 And Maachah the wife of Machir bare
a son, and she called his name Peresh; and
the name of his brother *was* Sheresh; and
his sons *were* Ulam and Rakem.
17 And the sons of Ulam; Bedan. These *were*
the sons of Gilead, the son of Machir, the
son of Manasseh.
18 And his sister Hammoleketh bare Ishod,
and Abiezer, and Mahalah.
19 And the sons of Shemida were, Ahian,
and Shechem, and Likhi, and Aniam.
20 ¶ And the sons of Ephraim; Shuthelah,
and Bered his son, and Tahath his son, and
Eladah his son, and Tahath his son,
21 ¶ And Zabad his son, and Shuthelah his
son, and Ezer, and Elead, whom the men
of Gath *that were* born in *that* land slew,
because they came down to take away
their cattle.
22 And Ephraim their father mourned many
days, and his brethren came to comfort him.
23 ¶ And when he went in to his wife, she
conceived, and bare a son, and he called
his name Beriah, because it went evil with
his house.
24 (And his daughter *was* Sherah, who built
Beth-horon the nether, and the upper, and
Uzzen-sherah.)
25 And Rephah *was* his son, also Resheph,
and Telah his son, and Tahan his son,
26 Laadan his son, Ammihud his son,
Elishama his son,
27 Non his son, Jehoshua his son.
28 ¶ And their possessions and habitations
were, Beth-el and the towns thereof, and
eastward Naaran, and westward Gezer,
with the towns thereof; Shechem also
and the towns thereof, unto Gaza and the
towns thereof:
29 And by the borders of the children of
Manasseh, Beth-shean and her towns,
Taanach and her towns, Megiddo and her

towns, Dor and her towns. In these dwelt
the children of Joseph the son of Israel.
30 ¶ The sons of Asher; Imnah, and Isuah,
and Ishuai, and Beriah, and Serah their sister.
31 And the sons of Beriah; Heber, and Malchiel, who *is* the father of Birzavith.
32 And Heber begat Japhlet, and Shomer,
and Hotham, and Shua their sister.
33 And the sons of Japhlet; Pasach, and
Bimhal, and Ashvath. These *are* the children
of Japhlet.
34 And the sons of Shamer; Ahi, and Rohgah,
Jehubbah, and Aram.
35 And the sons of his brother Helem;
Zophah, and Imna, and Shelesh, and Amal.
36 The sons of Zophah; Suah, and Harnep-
her, and Shual, and Beri, and Imrah,
37 Bezer, and Hod, and Shamma, and
Shilshah, and Ithran, and Beera.
38 And the sons of Jether; Jephunneh, and
Pispah, and Ara.
39 And the sons of Ulla; Arah, and Haniel,
and Rezia.
40 All these *were* the children of Asher,
heads of *their* father's house, choice *and*
mighty men of valour, chief of the princes.
And the number throughout the genealogy
of them that were apt to the war *and* to
battle *was* twenty and six thousand men.

1 Chronicles 8

1 Now Benjamin begat Bela his firstborn,
Ashbel the second, and Aharah the third,
2 Nohah the fourth, and Rapha the fifth.
3 And the sons of Bela were, Addar, and
Gera, and Abihud,
4 And Abishua, and Naaman, and Ahoah,
5 And Gera, and Shephuphan, and Huram.
6 And these *are* the sons of Ehud: these are
the heads of the fathers of the inhabitants of
Geba, and they removed them to Manahath:
7 And Naaman, and Ahiah, and Gera, he
removed them, and begat Uzza, and Ahihud.
8 And Shaharaim begat *children* in the country of Moab, after he had sent them away;
Hushim and Baara *were* his wives.
9 And he begat of Hodesh his wife, Jobab,
and Zibia, and Mesha, and Malcham,
10 And Jeuz, and Shachia, and Mirma. These
were his sons, heads of the fathers.
11 And of Hushim he begat Abitub, and
Elpaal.
12 The sons of Elpaal; Eber, and Misham,
and Shamed, who built Ono, and Lod, with
the towns thereof:
13 Beriah also, and Shema, who *were* heads
of the fathers of the inhabitants of Aijalon,
who drove away the inhabitants of Gath:
14 And Ahio, Shashak, and Jeremoth,
15 And Zebadiah, and Arad, and Ader,
16 And Michael, and Ispah, and Joha, the
sons of Beriah;
17 And Zebadiah, and Meshullam, and
Hezeki, and Heber,
18 Ishmerai also, and Jezliah, and Jobab,
the sons of Elpaal;
19 And Jakim, and Zichri, and Zabdi,
20 And Elienai, and Zilthai, and Eliel,
21 And Adaiah, and Beraiah, and Shimrath,
the sons of Shimhi;
22 And Ishpan, and Heber, and Eliel,
23 And Abdon, and Zichri, and Hanan,
24 And Hananiah, and Elam, and Antothijah,
25 And Iphedeiah, and Penuel, the sons of
Shashak;
26 And Shamsherai, and Shehariah, and
Athaliah,
27 And Jaresiah, and Eliah, and Zichri, the
sons of Jeroham.
28 These *were* heads of the fathers, by
their generations, chief *men*. These dwelt
in Jerusalem.
29 And at Gibeon dwelt the father of
Gibeon; whose wife's name *was* Maachah:
30 And his firstborn son Abdon, and Zur,
and Kish, and Baal, and Nadab,
31 And Gedor, and Ahio, and Zacher.
32 And Mikloth begat Shimeah. And these
also dwelt with their brethren in Jerusalem,
over against them.
33 ¶ And Ner begat Kish, and Kish begat
Saul, and Saul begat Jonathan, and Malchi-shua, and Abinadab, and Esh-baal.
34 And the son of Jonathan *was* Merib-baal;
and Merib-baal begat Micah.
35 And the sons of Micah *were*, Pithon, and
Melech, and Tarea, and Ahaz.
36 And Ahaz begat Jehoadah; and Jehoadah
begat Alemeth, and Azmaveth, and Zimri;
and Zimri begat Moza,
37 And Moza begat Binea: Rapha *was* his
son, Eleasah his son, Azel his son:
38 And Azel had six sons, whose names *are*
these, Azrikam, Bocheru, and Ishmael, and
Sheariah, and Obadiah, and Hanan. All these
were the sons of Azel.

39 And the sons of Eshek his brother *were*,
Ulam his firstborn, Jehush the second, and
Eliphelet the third.
40 And the sons of Ulam were mighty men
of valour, archers, and had many sons, and
sons' sons, an hundred and fifty. All these
are of the sons of Benjamin.

1 Chronicles 9

1 So all Israel were reckoned by genealogies; and, behold, they *were* written in the
book of the kings of Israel and Judah, *who*
were carried away to Babylon for their
transgression.
2 ¶ Now the first inhabitants that *dwelt*
in their possessions in their cities *were*,
the Israelites, the priests, Levites, and the
Nethinims.
3 And in Jerusalem dwelt of the children of
Judah, and of the children of Benjamin, and
of the children of Ephraim, and Manasseh;
4 Uthai the son of Ammihud, the son of
Omri, the son of Imri, the son of Bani, of the
children of Pharez the son of Judah.
5 And of the Shilonites; Asaiah the firstborn,
and his sons.
6 And of the sons of Zerah; Jeuel, and their
brethren, six hundred and ninety.
7 And of the sons of Benjamin; Sallu the son
of Meshullam, the son of Hodaviah, the son
of Hasenuah,
8 And Ibneiah the son of Jeroham, and
Elah the son of Uzzi, the son of Michri, and
Meshullam the son of Shephathiah, the son
of Reuel, the son of Ibnijah;
9 And their brethren, according to their
generations, nine hundred and fifty and
six. All these men *were* chief of the fathers
in the house of their fathers.
10 ¶ And of the priests; Jedaiah, and
Jehoiarib, and Jachin,
11 And Azariah the son of Hilkiah, the son
of Meshullam, the son of Zadok, the son of
Meraioth, the son of Ahitub, the ruler of
the house of God;
12 And Adaiah the son of Jeroham, the son
of Pashur, the son of Malchijah, and Maasiai
the son of Adiel, the son of Jahzerah, the son
of Meshullam, the son of Meshillemith, the
son of Immer;
13 And their brethren, heads of the house of
their fathers, a thousand and seven hundred
and threescore; very able men for the work
of the service of the house of God.
14 And of the Levites; Shemaiah the son
of Hasshub, the son of Azrikam, the son of
Hashabiah, of the sons of Merari;
15 And Bakbakkar, Heresh, and Galal, and
Mattaniah the son of Micah, the son of
Zichri, the son of Asaph;
16 And Obadiah the son of Shemaiah, the
son of Galal, the son of Jeduthun, and Berechiah the son of Asa, the son of Elkanah, that
dwelt in the villages of the Netophathites.
17 And the porters *were*, Shallum, and
Akkub, and Talmon, and Ahiman, and their
brethren: Shallum *was* the chief;
18 Who hitherto *waited* in the king's gate
eastward: they *were* porters in the companies of the children of Levi.
19 And Shallum the son of Kore, the son of
Ebiasaph, the son of Korah, and his brethren,
of the house of his father, the Korahites,
were over the work of the service, keepers
of the gates of the tabernacle: and their
fathers, *being* over the host of the LORD,
were keepers of the entry.
20 And Phinehas the son of Eleazar was the
ruler over them in time past, *and* the LORD
was with him.
21 *And* Zechariah the son of Meshelemiah
was porter of the door of the tabernacle of
the congregation.
22 All these *which were* chosen to be porters
in the gates *were* two hundred and twelve.
These were reckoned by their genealogy in
their villages, whom David and Samuel the
seer did ordain in their set office.
23 So they and their children *had* the oversight of the gates of the house of the LORD,
namely, the house of the tabernacle, by
wards.
24 In four quarters were the porters, toward
the east, west, north, and south.
25 And their brethren, *which were* in their
villages, *were* to come after seven days from
time to time with them.
26 For these Levites, the four chief porters,
were in *their* set office, and were over the
chambers and treasuries of the house of
God.
27 ¶ And they lodged round about the house
of God, because the charge *was* upon them,
and the opening thereof every morning
pertained to them.

28 And *certain* of them had the charge of
the ministering vessels, that they should
bring them in and out by tale.
29 *Some* of them also *were* appointed to
oversee the vessels, and all the instruments
of the sanctuary, and the fine flour, and the
wine, and the oil, and the frankincense, and
the spices.
30 And *some* of the sons of the priests made
the ointment of the spices.
31 And Mattithiah, *one* of the Levites, who
was the firstborn of Shallum the Korahite,
had the set office over the things that were
made in the pans.
32 And *other* of their brethren, of the sons
of the Kohathites, *were* over the shewbread,
to prepare *it* every sabbath.
33 And these *are* the singers, chief of the
fathers of the Levites, *who remaining* in
the chambers *were* free: for they were
employed in *that* work day and night.
34 These chief fathers of the Levites *were*
chief throughout their generations; these
dwelt at Jerusalem.
35 ¶ And in Gibeon dwelt the father of
Gibeon, Jehiel, whose wife's name *was*
Maachah:
36 And his firstborn son Abdon, then Zur,
and Kish, and Baal, and Ner, and Nadab,
37 And Gedor, and Ahio, and Zechariah,
and Mikloth.
38 And Mikloth begat Shimeam. And they
also dwelt with their brethren at Jerusalem,
over against their brethren.
39 And Ner begat Kish; and Kish begat Saul;
and Saul begat Jonathan, and Malchi-shua,
and Abinadab, and Esh-baal.
40 And the son of Jonathan *was* Merib-baal:
and Merib-baal begat Micah.
41 And the sons of Micah *were*, Pithon, and
Melech, and Tahrea, *and Ahaz*.
42 And Ahaz begat Jarah; and Jarah begat
Alemeth, and Azmaveth, and Zimri; and
Zimri begat Moza;
43 And Moza begat Binea; and Rephaiah his
son, Eleasah his son, Azel his son.
44 And Azel had six sons, whose names *are*
these, Azrikam, Bocheru, and Ishmael, and
Sheariah, and Obadiah, and Hanan: these
were the sons of Azel.

1 Chronicles 10

1 Now the Philistines fought against Israel;
and the men of Israel fled from before the
Philistines, and fell down slain in mount
Gilboa.
2 And the Philistines followed hard after
Saul, and after his sons; and the Philistines
slew Jonathan, and Abinadab, and Malchi-shua, the sons of Saul.
3 And the battle went sore against Saul, and
the archers hit him, and he was wounded
of the archers.
4 Then said Saul to his armourbearer, Draw
thy sword, and thrust me through therewith;
lest these uncircumcised come and abuse
me. But his armourbearer would not; for
he was sore afraid. So Saul took a sword,
and fell upon it.
5 And when his armourbearer saw that Saul
was dead, he fell likewise on the sword,
and died.
6 So Saul died, and his three sons, and all
his house died together.
7 And when all the men of Israel that *were*
in the valley saw that they fled, and that Saul
and his sons were dead, then they forsook
their cities, and fled: and the Philistines
came and dwelt in them.
8 ¶ And it came to pass on the morrow,
when the Philistines came to strip the slain,
that they found Saul and his sons fallen in
mount Gilboa.
9 And when they had stripped him, they
took his head, and his armour, and sent
into the land of the Philistines round about,
to carry tidings unto their idols, and to the
people.
10 And they put his armour in the house
of their gods, and fastened his head in the
temple of Dagon.
11 ¶ And when all Jabesh-gilead heard all
that the Philistines had done to Saul,
12 They arose, all the valiant men, and took
away the body of Saul, and the bodies of
his sons, and brought them to Jabesh, and
buried their bones under the oak in Jabesh,
and fasted seven days.
13 ¶ So Saul died for his transgression which
he committed against the LORD, *even* against
the word of the LORD, which he kept not,
and also for asking *counsel* of *one that had*
a familiar spirit, to inquire *of it*;
14 And inquired not of the LORD: therefore
he slew him, and turned the kingdom unto
David the son of Jesse.

1 Chronicles 11

1 Then all Israel gathered themselves to
David unto Hebron, saying, Behold, we *are*
thy bone and thy flesh.
2 And moreover in time past, even when
Saul was king, thou *wast* he that leddest
out and broughtest in Israel: and the LORD
thy God said unto thee, Thou shalt feed my
people Israel, and thou shalt be ruler over
my people Israel.
3 Therefore came all the elders of Israel
to the king to Hebron; and David made a
covenant with them in Hebron before the
LORD; and they anointed David king over
Israel, according to the word of the LORD
by Samuel.
4 ¶ And David and all Israel went to Jerusalem, which *is* Jebus; where the Jebusites
were, the inhabitants of the land.
5 And the inhabitants of Jebus said to David,
Thou shalt not come hither. Nevertheless
David took the castle of Zion, which *is* the
city of David.
6 And David said, Whosoever smiteth the
Jebusites first shall be chief and captain.
So Joab the son of Zeruiah went first up,
and was chief.
7 And David dwelt in the castle; therefore
they called it the city of David.
8 And he built the city round about, even
from Millo round about: and Joab repaired
the rest of the city.
9 So David waxed greater and greater: for
the LORD of hosts *was* with him.
10 ¶ These also *are* the chief of the mighty
men whom David had, who strengthened
themselves with him in his kingdom, *and*
with all Israel, to make him king, according
to the word of the LORD concerning Israel.
11 And this *is* the number of the mighty
men whom David had; Jashobeam, an
Hachmonite, the chief of the captains: he
lifted up his spear against three hundred
slain *by him* at one time.
12 And after him *was* Eleazar the son of
Dodo, the Ahohite, who *was one* of the
three mighties.
13 He was with David at Pas-dammim, and
there the Philistines were gathered together
to battle, where was a parcel of ground full
of barley; and the people fled from before
the Philistines.
14 And they set themselves in the midst of
that parcel, and delivered it, and slew the
Philistines; and the LORD saved *them* by a
great deliverance.
15 ¶ Now three of the thirty captains went
down to the rock to David, into the cave
of Adullam; and the host of the Philistines
encamped in the valley of Rephaim.
16 And David *was* then in the hold, and the
Philistines' garrison *was* then at Beth-lehem.
17 And David longed, and said, Oh that one
would give me drink of the water of the well
of Beth-lehem, that *is* at the gate!
18 And the three brake through the host of
the Philistines, and drew water out of the
well of Beth-lehem, that *was* by the gate,
and took *it*, and brought *it* to David: but
David would not drink *of* it, but poured it
out to the LORD,
19 And said, My God forbid it me, that I
should do this thing: shall I drink the blood
of these men that have put their lives in
jeopardy? for with *the jeopardy of* their
lives they brought it. Therefore he would
not drink it. These things did these three
mightiest.
20 ¶ And Abishai the brother of Joab, he
was chief of the three: for lifting up his spear
against three hundred, he slew *them*, and
had a name among the three.
21 Of the three, he was more honourable
than the two; for he was their captain:
howbeit he attained not to the *first* three.
22 Benaiah the son of Jehoiada, the son of a
valiant man of Kabzeel, who had done many
acts; he slew two lionlike men of Moab:
also he went down and slew a lion in a pit
in a snowy day.
23 And he slew an Egyptian, a man of
great stature, five cubits high; and in the
Egyptian's hand *was* a spear like a weaver's
beam; and he went down to him with a staff,
and plucked the spear out of the Egyptian's
hand, and slew him with his own spear.
24 These *things* did Benaiah the son of
Jehoiada, and had the name among the
three mighties.
25 Behold, he was honourable among the
thirty, but attained not to the *first* three:
and David set him over his guard.
26 ¶ Also the valiant men of the armies
were, Asahel the brother of Joab, Elhanan
the son of Dodo of Beth-lehem,

27 Shammoth the Harorite, Helez the Pelonite,

28 Ira the son of Ikkesh the Tekoite, Abi-ezer the Antothite,

29 Sibbecai the Hushathite, Ilai the Ahohite,

30 Maharai the Netophathite, Heled the son of Baanah the Netophathite,

31 Ithai the son of Ribai of Gibeah, *that pertained* to the children of Benjamin, Benaiah the Pirathonite,

32 Hurai of the brooks of Gaash, Abiel the Arbathite,

33 Azmaveth the Baharumite, Eliahba the Shaalbonite,

34 The sons of Hashem the Gizonite, Jonathan the son of Shage the Hararite,

35 Ahiam the son of Sacar the Hararite, Eliphal the son of Ur,

36 Hepher the Mecherathite, Ahijah the Pelonite,

37 Hezro the Carmelite, Naarai the son of Ezbai,

38 Joel the brother of Nathan, Mibhar the son of Haggeri,

39 Zelek the Ammonite, Naharai the Berothite, the armourbearer of Joab the son of Zeruiah,

40 Ira the Ithrite, Gareb the Ithrite,

41 Uriah the Hittite, Zabad the son of Ahlai,

42 Adina the son of Shiza the Reubenite, a captain of the Reubenites, and thirty with him,

43 Hanan the son of Maachah, and Joshaphat the Mithnite,

44 Uzzia the Ashterathite, Shama and Jehiel the sons of Hothan the Aroerite,

45 Jediael the son of Shimri, and Joha his brother, the Tizite,

46 Eliel the Mahavite, and Jeribai, and Joshaviah, the sons of Elnaam, and Ithmah the Moabite,

47 Eliel, and Obed, and Jasiel the Mesobaite.

1 Chronicles 12

1 Now these *are* they that came to David to Ziklag, while he yet kept himself close because of Saul the son of Kish: and they *were* among the mighty men, helpers of the war.

2 *They were* armed with bows, and could use both the right hand and the left in *hurling* stones and *shooting* arrows out of a bow, *even* of Saul's brethren of Benjamin.

3 The chief *was* Ahiezer, then Joash, the sons of Shemaah the Gibeathite; and Jeziel, and Pelet, the sons of Azmaveth; and Berachah, and Jehu the Antothite,

4 And Ismaiah the Gibeonite, a mighty man among the thirty, and over the thirty; and Jeremiah, and Jahaziel, and Johanan, and Josabad the Gederathite,

5 Eluzai, and Jerimoth, and Bealiah, and Shemariah, and Shephatiah the Haruphite,

6 Elkanah, and Jesiah, and Azareel, and Joezer, and Jashobeam, the Korhites,

7 And Joelah, and Zebadiah, the sons of Jeroham of Gedor.

8 And of the Gadites there separated themselves unto David into the hold to the wilderness men of might, *and* men of war *fit* for the battle, that could handle shield and buckler, whose faces *were like* the faces of lions, and *were* as swift as the roes upon the mountains;

9 Ezer the first, Obadiah the second, Eliab the third,

10 Mishmannah the fourth, Jeremiah the fifth,

11 Attai the sixth, Eliel the seventh,

12 Johanan the eighth, Elzabad the ninth,

13 Jeremiah the tenth, Machbanai the eleventh.

14 These *were* of the sons of Gad, captains of the host: one of the least *was* over an hundred, and the greatest over a thousand.

15 These *are* they that went over Jordan in the first month, when it had overflown all his banks; and they put to flight all *them* of the valleys, *both* toward the east, and toward the west.

16 And there came of the children of Benjamin and Judah to the hold unto David.

17 And David went out to meet them, and answered and said unto them, If ye be come peaceably unto me to help me, mine heart shall be knit unto you: but if *ye be come* to betray me to mine enemies, seeing *there is* no wrong in mine hands, the God of our fathers look *thereon*, and rebuke *it*.

18 Then the spirit came upon Amasai, *who was* chief of the captains, *and he said*, Thine *are we*, David, and on thy side, thou son of Jesse: peace, peace *be* unto thee, and peace *be* to thine helpers; for thy God helpeth thee. Then David received them, and made them captains of the band.

19 And there fell *some* of Manasseh to
David, when he came with the Philistines
against Saul to battle: but they helped them
not: for the lords of the Philistines upon
advisement sent him away, saying, He will
fall to his master Saul to *the jeopardy of*
our heads.
20 As he went to Ziklag, there fell to him of
Manasseh, Adnah, and Jozabad, and Jediael, and Michael, and Jozabad, and Elihu,
and Zilthai, captains of the thousands that
were of Manasseh.
21 And they helped David against the band
of the rovers: for they *were* all mighty men
of valour, and were captains in the host.
22 For at *that* time day by day there came to
David to help him, until *it was* a great host,
like the host of God.
23 ¶ And these *are* the numbers of the
bands *that were* ready armed to the war,
and came to David to Hebron, to turn the
kingdom of Saul to him, according to the
word of the LORD.
24 The children of Judah that bare shield and
spear *were* six thousand and eight hundred,
ready armed to the war.
25 Of the children of Simeon, mighty men
of valour for the war, seven thousand and
one hundred.
26 Of the children of Levi four thousand
and six hundred.
27 And Jehoiada *was* the leader of the Aaronites, and with him *were* three thousand
and seven hundred;
28 And Zadok, a young man mighty of
valour, and of his father's house twenty
and two captains.
29 And of the children of Benjamin, the kindred of Saul, three thousand: for hitherto
the greatest part of them had kept the ward
of the house of Saul.
30 And of the children of Ephraim twenty
thousand and eight hundred, mighty men
of valour, famous throughout the house of
their fathers.
31 And of the half tribe of Manasseh eighteen thousand, which were expressed by
name, to come and make David king.
32 And of the children of Issachar, *which*
were men that had understanding of the
times, to know what Israel ought to do; the
heads of them *were* two hundred; and all
their brethren *were* at their commandment.
33 Of Zebulun, such as went forth to battle,
expert in war, with all instruments of war,
fifty thousand, which could keep rank: *they*
were not of double heart.
34 And of Naphtali a thousand captains, and
with them with shield and spear thirty and
seven thousand.
35 And of the Danites expert in war twenty
and eight thousand and six hundred.
36 And of Asher, such as went forth to battle, expert in war, forty thousand.
37 And on the other side of Jordan, of the
Reubenites, and the Gadites, and of the
half tribe of Manasseh, with all manner of
instruments of war for the battle, an hundred and twenty thousand.
38 All these men of war, that could keep
rank, came with a perfect heart to Hebron,
to make David king over all Israel: and all
the rest also of Israel *were* of one heart to
make David king.
39 And there they were with David three
days, eating and drinking: for their brethren
had prepared for them.
40 Moreover they that were nigh them, *even*
unto Issachar and Zebulun and Naphtali,
brought bread on asses, and on camels,
and on mules, and on oxen, *and* meat, meal,
cakes of figs, and bunches of raisins, and
wine, and oil, and oxen, and sheep abundantly: for *there was* joy in Israel.

1 Chronicles 13

1 And David consulted with the captains of
thousands and hundreds, *and* with every
leader.
2 And David said unto all the congregation
of Israel, If *it seem* good unto you, and *that*
it be of the LORD our God, let us send abroad
unto our brethren every where, *that are* left
in all the land of Israel, and with them *also*
to the priests and Levites *which are* in their
cities *and* suburbs, that they may gather
themselves unto us:
3 And let us bring again the ark of our God
to us: for we inquired not at it in the days
of Saul.
4 And all the congregation said that they
would do so: for the thing was right in the
eyes of all the people.
5 So David gathered all Israel together, from
Shihor of Egypt even unto the entering of

Hemath, to bring the ark of God from Kirjath-jearim.
6 And David went up, and all Israel, to Baalah, *that is*, to Kirjath-jearim, which *belonged*
to Judah, to bring up thence the ark of God
the LORD, that dwelleth *between* the cherubims, whose name is called *on it*.
7 And they carried the ark of God in a new
cart out of the house of Abinadab: and Uzza
and Ahio drave the cart.
8 And David and all Israel played before
God with all *their* might, and with singing,
and with harps, and with psalteries, and
with timbrels, and with cymbals, and with
trumpets.
9 ¶ And when they came unto the threshingfloor of Chidon, Uzza put forth his hand
to hold the ark; for the oxen stumbled.
10 And the anger of the LORD was kindled
against Uzza, and he smote him, because
he put his hand to the ark: and there he
died before God.
11 And David was displeased, because
the LORD had made a breach upon Uzza:
wherefore that place is called Perez-uzza
to this day.
12 And David was afraid of God that day,
saying, How shall I bring the ark of God
home to me?
13 So David brought not the ark *home* to
himself to the city of David, but carried it
aside into the house of Obed-edom the
Gittite.
14 And the ark of God remained with the
family of Obed-edom in his house three
months. And the LORD blessed the house
of Obed-edom, and all that he had.

1 Chronicles 14

1 Now Hiram king of Tyre sent messengers
to David, and timber of cedars, with masons
and carpenters, to build him an house.
2 And David perceived that the LORD had
confirmed him king over Israel, for his kingdom was lifted up on high, because of his
people Israel.
3 ¶ And David took more wives at Jerusalem:
and David begat more sons and daughters.
4 Now these *are* the names of *his* children
which he had in Jerusalem; Shammua, and
Shobab, Nathan, and Solomon,
5 And Ibhar, and Elishua, and Elpalet,
6 And Nogah, and Nepheg, and Japhia,
7 And Elishama, and Beeliada, and Eliphalet.
8 ¶ And when the Philistines heard that
David was anointed king over all Israel, all
the Philistines went up to seek David. And
David heard *of it*, and went out against
them.
9 And the Philistines came and spread themselves in the valley of Rephaim.
10 And David inquired of God, saying, Shall
I go up against the Philistines? and wilt thou
deliver them into mine hand? And the LORD
said unto him, Go up; for I will deliver them
into thine hand.
11 So they came up to Baal-perazim; and
David smote them there. Then David said,
God hath broken in upon mine enemies by
mine hand like the breaking forth of waters:
therefore they called the name of that place
Baal-perazim.
12 And when they had left their gods there,
David gave a commandment, and they were
burned with fire.
13 And the Philistines yet again spread
themselves abroad in the valley.
14 Therefore David inquired again of God;
and God said unto him, Go not up after
them; turn away from them, and come
upon them over against the mulberry trees.
15 And it shall be, when thou shalt hear a
sound of going in the tops of the mulberry
trees, *that* then thou shalt go out to battle:
for God is gone forth before thee to smite
the host of the Philistines.
16 David therefore did as God commanded
him: and they smote the host of the Philistines from Gibeon even to Gazer.
17 And the fame of David went out into all
lands; and the LORD brought the fear of him
upon all nations.

1 Chronicles 15

1 And *David* made him houses in the city of
David, and prepared a place for the ark of
God, and pitched for it a tent.
2 Then David said, None ought to carry the
ark of God but the Levites: for them hath
the LORD chosen to carry the ark of God,
and to minister unto him for ever.
3 And David gathered all Israel together to
Jerusalem, to bring up the ark of the LORD
unto his place, which he had prepared for it.
4 And David assembled the children of
Aaron, and the Levites:

5 Of the sons of Kohath; Uriel the chief, and
his brethren an hundred and twenty:
6 Of the sons of Merari; Asaiah the chief,
and his brethren two hundred and twenty:
7 Of the sons of Gershom; Joel the chief, and
his brethren an hundred and thirty:
8 Of the sons of Elizaphan; Shemaiah the
chief, and his brethren two hundred:
9 Of the sons of Hebron; Eliel the chief, and
his brethren fourscore:
10 Of the sons of Uzziel; Amminadab the
chief, and his brethren an hundred and
twelve.
11 And David called for Zadok and Abiathar
the priests, and for the Levites, for Uriel,
Asaiah, and Joel, Shemaiah, and Eliel, and
Amminadab,
12 And said unto them, Ye *are* the chief of
the fathers of the Levites: sanctify yourselves, *both* ye and your brethren, that ye
may bring up the ark of the LORD God of
Israel unto *the place that* I have prepared
for it.
13 For because ye *did it* not at the first, the
LORD our God made a breach upon us, for
that we sought him not after the due order.
14 So the priests and the Levites sanctified
themselves to bring up the ark of the LORD
God of Israel.
15 And the children of the Levites bare
the ark of God upon their shoulders with
the staves thereon, as Moses commanded
according to the word of the LORD.
16 And David spake to the chief of the Levites to appoint their brethren *to be* the singers with instruments of musick, psalteries
and harps and cymbals, sounding, by lifting
up the voice with joy.
17 So the Levites appointed Heman the
son of Joel; and of his brethren, Asaph the
son of Berechiah; and of the sons of Merari
their brethren, Ethan the son of Kushaiah;
18 And with them their brethren of the second *degree*, Zechariah, Ben, and Jaaziel, and
Shemiramoth, and Jehiel, and Unni, Eliab,
and Benaiah, and Maaseiah, and Mattithiah,
and Elipheleh, and Mikneiah, and Obed-
edom, and Jeiel, the porters.
19 So the singers, Heman, Asaph, and Ethan,
were appointed to sound with cymbals of
brass;
20 And Zechariah, and Aziel, and Shemiramoth, and Jehiel, and Unni, and Eliab, and
Maaseiah, and Benaiah, with psalteries on
Alamoth;
21 And Mattithiah, and Elipheleh, and
Mikneiah, and Obed-edom, and Jeiel, and
Azaziah, with harps on the Sheminith to
excel.
22 And Chenaniah, chief of the Levites, *was*
for song: he instructed about the song,
because he *was* skilful.
23 And Berechiah and Elkanah *were* door-
keepers for the ark.
24 And Shebaniah, and Jehoshaphat, and
Nethaneel, and Amasai, and Zechariah, and
Benaiah, and Eliezer, the priests, did blow
with the trumpets before the ark of God:
and Obed-edom and Jehiah *were* doorkeep-
ers for the ark.
25 ¶ So David, and the elders of Israel, and
the captains over thousands, went to bring
up the ark of the covenant of the LORD out
of the house of Obed-edom with joy.
26 And it came to pass, when God helped
the Levites that bare the ark of the covenant
of the LORD, that they offered seven bullocks
and seven rams.
27 And David *was* clothed with a robe of fine
linen, and all the Levites that bare the ark,
and the singers, and Chenaniah the master
of the song with the singers: David also *had*
upon him an ephod of linen.
28 Thus all Israel brought up the ark of the
covenant of the LORD with shouting, and
with sound of the cornet, and with trumpets, and with cymbals, making a noise with
psalteries and harps.
29 ¶ And it came to pass, *as* the ark of the
covenant of the LORD came to the city of
David, that Michal the daughter of Saul
looking out at a window saw king David
dancing and playing: and she despised him
in her heart.

1 Chronicles 16

1 So they brought the ark of God, and set
it in the midst of the tent that David had
pitched for it: and they offered burnt sacrifices and peace offerings before God.
2 And when David had made an end of
offering the burnt offerings and the peace
offerings, he blessed the people in the name
of the LORD.
3 And he dealt to every one of Israel, both
man and woman, to every one a loaf of

bread, and a good piece of flesh, and a
flagon *of wine*.
4 ¶ And he appointed *certain* of the Levites
to minister before the ark of the LORD, and
to record, and to thank and praise the LORD
God of Israel:
5 Asaph the chief, and next to him Zechariah, Jeiel, and Shemiramoth, and Jehiel,
and Mattithiah, and Eliab, and Benaiah,
and Obed-edom: and Jeiel with psalteries
and with harps; but Asaph made a sound
with cymbals;
6 Benaiah also and Jahaziel the priests with
trumpets continually before the ark of the
covenant of God.
7 ¶ Then on that day David delivered first
this psalm to thank the LORD into the hand
of Asaph and his brethren.
8 Give thanks unto the LORD, call upon his
name, make known his deeds among the
people.
9 Sing unto him, sing psalms unto him, talk
ye of all his wondrous works.
10 Glory ye in his holy name: let the heart
of them rejoice that seek the LORD.
11 Seek the LORD and his strength, seek his
face continually.
12 Remember his marvellous works that he
hath done, his wonders, and the judgments
of his mouth;
13 O ye seed of Israel his servant, ye children
of Jacob, his chosen ones.
14 He *is* the LORD our God; his judgments
are in all the earth.
15 Be ye mindful always of his covenant; the
word *which* he commanded to a thousand
generations;
16 *Even of the covenant* which he made
with Abraham, and of his oath unto Isaac;
17 And hath confirmed the same to Jacob
for a law, *and* to Israel *for* an everlasting
covenant,
18 Saying, Unto thee will I give the land of
Canaan, the lot of your inheritance;
19 When ye were but few, even a few, and
strangers in it.
20 And *when* they went from nation to
nation, and from *one* kingdom to another
people;
21 He suffered no man to do them wrong:
yea, he reproved kings for their sakes,
22 *Saying*, Touch not mine anointed, and
do my prophets no harm.
23 Sing unto the LORD, all the earth; shew
forth from day to day his salvation.
24 Declare his glory among the heathen; his
marvellous works among all nations.
25 For great *is* the LORD, and greatly to
be praised: he also *is* to be feared above
all gods.
26 For all the gods of the people *are* idols:
but the LORD made the heavens.
27 Glory and honour *are* in his presence;
strength and gladness *are* in his place.
28 Give unto the LORD, ye kindreds of
the people, give unto the LORD glory and
strength.
29 Give unto the LORD the glory *due* unto his
name: bring an offering, and come before
him: worship the LORD in the beauty of
holiness.
30 Fear before him, all the earth: the world
also shall be stable, that it be not moved.
31 Let the heavens be glad, and let the earth
rejoice: and let *men* say among the nations,
The LORD reigneth.
32 Let the sea roar, and the fulness thereof:
let the fields rejoice, and all that *is* therein.
33 Then shall the trees of the wood sing
out at the presence of the LORD, because
he cometh to judge the earth.
34 O give thanks unto the LORD; for *he is*
good; for his mercy *endureth* for ever.
35 And say ye, Save us, O God of our salvation, and gather us together, and deliver us
from the heathen, that we may give thanks
to thy holy name, *and* glory in thy praise.
36 Blessed *be* the LORD God of Israel for ever
and ever. And all the people said, Amen, and
praised the LORD.
37 ¶ So he left there before the ark of the
covenant of the LORD Asaph and his brethren, to minister before the ark continually,
as every day's work required:
38 And Obed-edom with their brethren,
threescore and eight; Obed-edom also the
son of Jeduthun and Hosah *to be* porters:
39 And Zadok the priest, and his brethren
the priests, before the tabernacle of the
LORD in the high place that *was* at Gibeon,
40 To offer burnt offerings unto the LORD
upon the altar of the burnt offering continually morning and evening, and *to do*
according to all that is written in the law
of the LORD, which he commanded Israel;
41 And with them Heman and Jeduthun,

and the rest that were chosen, who were
expressed by name, to give thanks to the
LORD, because his mercy *endureth* for ever;
42 And with them Heman and Jeduthun with
trumpets and cymbals for those that should
make a sound, and with musical instruments of God. And the sons of Jeduthun
were porters.
43 And all the people departed every man
to his house: and David returned to bless
his house.

1 Chronicles 17

1 Now it came to pass, as David sat in
his house, that David said to Nathan the
prophet, Lo, I dwell in an house of cedars,
but the ark of the covenant of the LORD
remaineth under curtains.
2 Then Nathan said unto David, Do all that
is in thine heart; for God *is* with thee.
3 ¶ And it came to pass the same night, that
the word of God came to Nathan, saying,
4 Go and tell David my servant, Thus saith
the LORD, Thou shalt not build me an house
to dwell in:
5 For I have not dwelt in an house since the
day that I brought up Israel unto this day;
but have gone from tent to tent, and from
one tabernacle *to another.*
6 Wheresoever I have walked with all Israel,
spake I a word to any of the judges of Israel,
whom I commanded to feed my people,
saying, Why have ye not built me an house
of cedars?
7 Now therefore thus shalt thou say unto my
servant David, Thus saith the LORD of hosts,
I took thee from the sheepcote, *even* from
following the sheep, that thou shouldest be
ruler over my people Israel:
8 And I have been with thee whithersoever
thou hast walked, and have cut off all thine
enemies from before thee, and have made
thee a name like the name of the great men
that *are* in the earth.
9 Also I will ordain a place for my people
Israel, and will plant them, and they shall
dwell in their place, and shall be moved no
more; neither shall the children of wickedness waste them any more, as at the
beginning,
10 And since the time that I commanded
judges *to be* over my people Israel. Moreover I will subdue all thine enemies. Furthermore I tell thee that the LORD will build
thee an house.
11 ¶ And it shall come to pass, when thy
days be expired that thou must go *to be*
with thy fathers, that I will raise up thy seed
after thee, which shall be of thy sons; and I
will establish his kingdom.
12 He shall build me an house, and I will
stablish his throne for ever.
13 I will be his father, and he shall be my son:
and I will not take my mercy away from him,
as I took *it* from *him* that was before thee:
14 But I will settle him in mine house and in
my kingdom for ever: and his throne shall
be established for evermore.
15 According to all these words, and according to all this vision, so did Nathan speak
unto David.
16 ¶ And David the king came and sat before
the LORD, and said, Who *am* I, O LORD God,
and what *is* mine house, that thou hast
brought me hitherto?
17 And *yet* this was a small thing in thine
eyes, O God; for thou hast *also* spoken of thy
servant's house for a great while to come,
and hast regarded me according to the
estate of a man of high degree, O LORD God.
18 What can David *speak* more to thee for
the honour of thy servant? for thou knowest
thy servant.
19 O LORD, for thy servant's sake, and
according to thine own heart, hast thou
done all this greatness, in making known
all *these* great things.
20 O LORD, *there is* none like thee, neither *is*
there any God beside thee, according to all
that we have heard with our ears.
21 And what one nation in the earth *is*
like thy people Israel, whom God went to
redeem *to be* his own people, to make thee
a name of greatness and terribleness, by
driving out nations from before thy people,
whom thou hast redeemed out of Egypt?
22 For thy people Israel didst thou make
thine own people for ever; and thou, LORD,
becamest their God.
23 Therefore now, LORD, let the thing that
thou hast spoken concerning thy servant
and concerning his house be established
for ever, and do as thou hast said.
24 Let it even be established, that thy name
may be magnified for ever, saying, The LORD
of hosts *is* the God of Israel, *even* a God to

Israel: and *let* the house of David thy servant
be established before thee.
25 For thou, O my God, hast told thy servant
that thou wilt build him an house: therefore
thy servant hath found *in his heart* to pray
before thee.
26 And now, LORD, thou art God, and hast
promised this goodness unto thy servant:
27 Now therefore let it please thee to bless
the house of thy servant, that it may be
before thee for ever: for thou blessest, O
LORD, and *it shall be* blessed for ever.

1 Chronicles 18

1 Now after this it came to pass, that David
smote the Philistines, and subdued them,
and took Gath and her towns out of the
hand of the Philistines.
2 And he smote Moab; and the Moabites
became David's servants, *and* brought gifts.
3 ¶ And David smote Hadarezer king of
Zobah unto Hamath, as he went to stablish
his dominion by the river Euphrates.
4 And David took from him a thousand
chariots, and seven thousand horsemen,
and twenty thousand footmen: David also
houghed all the chariot *horses*, but reserved
of them an hundred chariots.
5 And when the Syrians of Damascus came
to help Hadarezer king of Zobah, David
slew of the Syrians two and twenty thousand men.
6 Then David put *garrisons* in Syria-da-
mascus; and the Syrians became David's
servants, *and* brought gifts. Thus the LORD
preserved David whithersoever he went.
7 And David took the shields of gold that
were on the servants of Hadarezer, and
brought them to Jerusalem.
8 Likewise from Tibhath, and from Chun, cities of Hadarezer, brought David very much
brass, wherewith Solomon made the brasen
sea, and the pillars, and the vessels of brass.
9 ¶ Now when Tou king of Hamath heard
how David had smitten all the host of
Hadarezer king of Zobah;
10 He sent Hadoram his son to king David,
to inquire of his welfare, and to congrat-
ulate him, because he had fought against
Hadarezer, and smitten him; (for Hadarezer
had war with Tou;) and *with him* all manner
of vessels of gold and silver and brass.
11 ¶ Them also king David dedicated unto
the LORD, with the silver and the gold that
he brought from all *these* nations; from
Edom, and from Moab, and from the children of Ammon, and from the Philistines,
and from Amalek.
12 Moreover Abishai the son of Zeruiah
slew of the Edomites in the valley of salt
eighteen thousand.
13 ¶ And he put garrisons in Edom; and
all the Edomites became David's servants.
Thus the LORD preserved David whithersoever he went.
14 ¶ So David reigned over all Israel, and
executed judgment and justice among all
his people.
15 And Joab the son of Zeruiah *was* over
the host; and Jehoshaphat the son of Ahilud, recorder.
16 And Zadok the son of Ahitub, and Abimelech the son of Abiathar, *were* the priests;
and Shavsha was scribe;
17 And Benaiah the son of Jehoiada *was*
over the Cherethites and the Pelethites; and
the sons of David *were* chief about the king.

1 Chronicles 19

1 Now it came to pass after this, that Nahash
the king of the children of Ammon died, and
his son reigned in his stead.
2 And David said, I will shew kindness unto
Hanun the son of Nahash, because his father
shewed kindness to me. And David sent
messengers to comfort him concerning his
father. So the servants of David came into
the land of the children of Ammon to Hanun,
to comfort him.
3 But the princes of the children of Ammon
said to Hanun, Thinkest thou that David
doth honour thy father, that he hath sent
comforters unto thee? are not his servants
come unto thee for to search, and to overthrow, and to spy out the land?
4 Wherefore Hanun took David's servants,
and shaved them, and cut off their garments
in the midst hard by their buttocks, and sent
them away.
5 Then there went *certain*, and told David
how the men were served. And he sent
to meet them: for the men were greatly
ashamed. And the king said, Tarry at Jericho
until your beards be grown, and *then* return.
6 ¶ And when the children of Ammon saw
that they had made themselves odious to

David, Hanun and the children of Ammon
sent a thousand talents of silver to hire them
chariots and horsemen out of Mesopotamia,
and out of Syria-maachah, and out of Zobah.
7 So they hired thirty and two thousand
chariots, and the king of Maachah and
his people; who came and pitched before
Medeba. And the children of Ammon gathered themselves together from their cities,
and came to battle.
8 And when David heard *of it*, he sent Joab,
and all the host of the mighty men.
9 And the children of Ammon came out,
and put the battle in array before the gate
of the city: and the kings that were come
were by themselves in the field.
10 Now when Joab saw that the battle was
set against him before and behind, he chose
out of all the choice of Israel, and put *them*
in array against the Syrians.
11 And the rest of the people he delivered
unto the hand of Abishai his brother, and
they set *themselves* in array against the
children of Ammon.
12 And he said, If the Syrians be too strong
for me, then thou shalt help me: but if the
children of Ammon be too strong for thee,
then I will help thee.
13 Be of good courage, and let us behave
ourselves valiantly for our people, and for
the cities of our God: and let the LORD do
that which is good in his sight.
14 So Joab and the people that *were* with
him drew nigh before the Syrians unto the
battle; and they fled before him.
15 And when the children of Ammon saw
that the Syrians were fled, they likewise
fled before Abishai his brother, and entered
into the city. Then Joab came to Jerusalem.
16 ¶ And when the Syrians saw that they
were put to the worse before Israel, they
sent messengers, and drew forth the Syrians
that *were* beyond the river: and Shophach
the captain of the host of Hadarezer *went*
before them.
17 And it was told David; and he gathered
all Israel, and passed over Jordan, and came
upon them, and set *the battle* in array
against them. So when David had put the
battle in array against the Syrians, they
fought with him.
18 But the Syrians fled before Israel; and
David slew of the Syrians seven thousand
men which fought in chariots, and forty
thousand footmen, and killed Shophach
the captain of the host.
19 And when the servants of Hadarezer
saw that they were put to the worse before
Israel, they made peace with David, and
became his servants: neither would the Syrians help the children of Ammon any more.

1 Chronicles 20

1 And it came to pass, that after the year
was expired, at the time that kings go out *to*
battle, Joab led forth the power of the army,
and wasted the country of the children of
Ammon, and came and besieged Rabbah.
But David tarried at Jerusalem. And Joab
smote Rabbah, and destroyed it.
2 And David took the crown of their king
from off his head, and found it to weigh
a talent of gold, and *there were* precious
stones in it; and it was set upon David's
head: and he brought also exceeding much
spoil out of the city.
3 And he brought out the people that *were*
in it, and cut *them* with saws, and with harrows of iron, and with axes. Even so dealt
David with all the cities of the children
of Ammon. And David and all the people
returned to Jerusalem.
4 ¶ And it came to pass after this, that there
arose war at Gezer with the Philistines; at
which time Sibbechai the Hushathite slew
Sippai, *that was* of the children of the giant:
and they were subdued.
5 And there was war again with the Philistines; and Elhanan the son of Jair slew Lahmi
the brother of Goliath the Gittite, whose
spear staff *was* like a weaver's beam.
6 And yet again there was war at Gath,
where was a man of *great* stature, whose
fingers and toes *were* four and twenty, six
on each hand, and six *on each foot:* and he
also was the son of the giant.
7 But when he defied Israel, Jonathan the
son of Shimea David's brother slew him.
8 These were born unto the giant in Gath;
and they fell by the hand of David, and by
the hand of his servants.

1 Chronicles 21

1 And Satan stood up against Israel, and
provoked David to number Israel.
2 And David said to Joab and to the rulers

of the people, Go, number Israel from Beer-sheba even to Dan; and bring the number of them to me, that I may know *it*.

3 And Joab answered, The LORD make his people an hundred times so many more as they *be:* but, my lord the king, *are* they not all my lord's servants? why then doth my lord require this thing? why will he be a cause of trespass to Israel?

4 Nevertheless the king's word prevailed against Joab. Wherefore Joab departed, and went throughout all Israel, and came to Jerusalem.

5 ¶ And Joab gave the sum of the number of the people unto David. And all *they of* Israel were a thousand thousand and an hundred thousand men that drew sword: and Judah *was* four hundred threescore and ten thousand men that drew sword.

6 But Levi and Benjamin counted he not among them: for the king's word was abominable to Joab.

7 And God was displeased with this thing; therefore he smote Israel.

8 And David said unto God, I have sinned greatly, because I have done this thing: but now, I beseech thee, do away the iniquity of thy servant; for I have done very foolishly.

9 ¶ And the LORD spake unto Gad, David's seer, saying,

10 Go and tell David, saying, Thus saith the LORD, I offer thee three *things:* choose thee one of them, that I may do *it* unto thee.

11 So Gad came to David, and said unto him, Thus saith the LORD, Choose thee

12 Either three years' famine; or three months to be destroyed before thy foes, while that the sword of thine enemies overtaketh *thee;* or else three days the sword of the LORD, even the pestilence, in the land, and the angel of the LORD destroying throughout all the coasts of Israel. Now therefore advise thyself what word I shall bring again to him that sent me.

13 And David said unto Gad, I am in a great strait: let me fall now into the hand of the LORD; for very great *are* his mercies: but let me not fall into the hand of man.

14 ¶ So the LORD sent pestilence upon Israel: and there fell of Israel seventy thousand men.

15 And God sent an angel unto Jerusalem to destroy it: and as he was destroying, the LORD beheld, and he repented him of the evil, and said to the angel that destroyed, It is enough, stay now thine hand. And the angel of the LORD stood by the threshingfloor of Ornan the Jebusite.

16 And David lifted up his eyes, and saw the angel of the LORD stand between the earth and the heaven, having a drawn sword in his hand stretched out over Jerusalem. Then David and the elders *of Israel, who were* clothed in sackcloth, fell upon their faces.

17 And David said unto God, *Is it* not I *that* commanded the people to be numbered? even I it is that have sinned and done evil indeed; but *as for* these sheep, what have they done? let thine hand, I pray thee, O LORD my God, be on me, and on my father's house; but not on thy people, that they should be plagued.

18 ¶ Then the angel of the LORD commanded Gad to say to David, that David should go up, and set up an altar unto the LORD in the threshingfloor of Ornan the Jebusite.

19 And David went up at the saying of Gad, which he spake in the name of the LORD.

20 And Ornan turned back, and saw the angel; and his four sons with him hid themselves. Now Ornan was threshing wheat.

21 And as David came to Ornan, Ornan looked and saw David, and went out of the threshingfloor, and bowed himself to David with *his* face to the ground.

22 Then David said to Ornan, Grant me the place of *this* threshingfloor, that I may build an altar therein unto the LORD: thou shalt grant it me for the full price: that the plague may be stayed from the people.

23 And Ornan said unto David, Take *it* to thee, and let my lord the king do *that which is* good in his eyes: lo, I give *thee* the oxen *also* for burnt offerings, and the threshing instruments for wood, and the wheat for the meat offering; I give it all.

24 And king David said to Ornan, Nay; but I will verily buy it for the full price: for I will not take *that* which *is* thine for the LORD, nor offer burnt offerings without cost.

25 So David gave to Ornan for the place six hundred shekels of gold by weight.

26 And David built there an altar unto the LORD, and offered burnt offerings and peace offerings, and called upon the LORD; and he

answered him from heaven by fire upon the altar of burnt offering.

27 And the LORD commanded the angel; and he put up his sword again into the sheath thereof.

28 ¶ At that time when David saw that the LORD had answered him in the threshingfloor of Ornan the Jebusite, then he sacrificed there.

29 For the tabernacle of the LORD, which Moses made in the wilderness, and the altar of the burnt offering, *were* at that season in the high place at Gibeon.

30 But David could not go before it to inquire of God: for he was afraid because of the sword of the angel of the LORD.

1 Chronicles 22

1 Then David said, This *is* the house of the LORD God, and this *is* the altar of the burnt offering for Israel.

2 And David commanded to gather together the strangers that *were* in the land of Israel; and he set masons to hew wrought stones to build the house of God.

3 And David prepared iron in abundance for the nails for the doors of the gates, and for the joinings; and brass in abundance without weight;

4 Also cedar trees in abundance: for the Zidonians and they of Tyre brought much cedar wood to David.

5 And David said, Solomon my son *is* young and tender, and the house *that is* to be builded for the LORD *must be* exceeding magnifical, of fame and of glory throughout all countries: I will *therefore* now make preparation for it. So David prepared abundantly before his death.

6 ¶ Then he called for Solomon his son, and charged him to build an house for the LORD God of Israel.

7 And David said to Solomon, My son, as for me, it was in my mind to build an house unto the name of the LORD my God:

8 But the word of the LORD came to me, saying, Thou hast shed blood abundantly, and hast made great wars: thou shalt not build an house unto my name, because thou hast shed much blood upon the earth in my sight.

9 Behold, a son shall be born to thee, who shall be a man of rest; and I will give him rest from all his enemies round about: for his name shall be Solomon, and I will give peace and quietness unto Israel in his days.

10 He shall build an house for my name; and he shall be my son, and I *will be* his father; and I will establish the throne of his kingdom over Israel for ever.

11 Now, my son, the LORD be with thee; and prosper thou, and build the house of the LORD thy God, as he hath said of thee.

12 Only the LORD give thee wisdom and understanding, and give thee charge concerning Israel, that thou mayest keep the law of the LORD thy God.

13 Then shalt thou prosper, if thou takest heed to fulfil the statutes and judgments which the LORD charged Moses with concerning Israel: be strong, and of good courage; dread not, nor be dismayed.

14 Now, behold, in my trouble I have prepared for the house of the LORD an hundred thousand talents of gold, and a thousand thousand talents of silver; and of brass and iron without weight; for it is in abundance: timber also and stone have I prepared; and thou mayest add thereto.

15 Moreover *there are* workmen with thee in abundance, hewers and workers of stone and timber, and all manner of cunning men for every manner of work.

16 Of the gold, the silver, and the brass, and the iron, *there is* no number. Arise *therefore,* and be doing, and the LORD be with thee.

17 ¶ David also commanded all the princes of Israel to help Solomon his son, *saying,*

18 *Is* not the LORD your God with you? and hath he *not* given you rest on every side? for he hath given the inhabitants of the land into mine hand; and the land is subdued before the LORD, and before his people.

19 Now set your heart and your soul to seek the LORD your God; arise therefore, and build ye the sanctuary of the LORD God, to bring the ark of the covenant of the LORD, and the holy vessels of God, into the house that is to be built to the name of the LORD.

1 Chronicles 23

1 So when David was old and full of days, he made Solomon his son king over Israel.

2 ¶ And he gathered together all the princes of Israel, with the priests and the Levites.

3 Now the Levites were numbered from the age of thirty years and upward: and their

not inherit in our father's house; for thou
art the son of a strange woman.
3 Then Jephthah fled from his brethren, and
dwelt in the land of Tob: and there were
gathered vain men to Jephthah, and went
out with him.
4 ¶ And it came to pass in process of time,
that the children of Ammon made war
against Israel.
5 And it was so, that when the children of
Ammon made war against Israel, the elders
of Gilead went to fetch Jephthah out of the
land of Tob:
6 And they said unto Jephthah, Come, and
be our captain, that we may fight with the
children of Ammon.
7 And Jephthah said unto the elders of
Gilead, Did not ye hate me, and expel me
out of my father's house? and why are ye
come unto me now when ye are in distress?
8 And the elders of Gilead said unto
Jephthah, Therefore we turn again to thee
now, that thou mayest go with us, and fight
against the children of Ammon, and be our
head over all the inhabitants of Gilead.
9 And Jephthah said unto the elders of
Gilead, If ye bring me home again to fight
against the children of Ammon, and the
LORD deliver them before me, shall I be
your head?
10 And the elders of Gilead said unto
Jephthah, The LORD be witness between
us, if we do not so according to thy words.
11 Then Jephthah went with the elders of
Gilead, and the people made him head and
captain over them: and Jephthah uttered all
his words before the LORD in Mizpeh.
12 ¶ And Jephthah sent messengers unto
the king of the children of Ammon, saying,
What hast thou to do with me, that thou
art come against me to fight in my land?
13 And the king of the children of Ammon
answered unto the messengers of Jephthah,
Because Israel took away my land, when
they came up out of Egypt, from Arnon even
unto Jabbok, and unto Jordan: now therefore restore those *lands* again peaceably.
14 And Jephthah sent messengers again
unto the king of the children of Ammon:
15 And said unto him, Thus saith Jephthah,
Israel took not away the land of Moab, nor
the land of the children of Ammon:
16 But when Israel came up from Egypt,
and walked through the wilderness unto
the Red sea, and came to Kadesh;
17 Then Israel sent messengers unto the
king of Edom, saying, Let me, I pray thee,
pass through thy land: but the king of Edom
would not hearken *thereto*. And in like
manner they sent unto the king of Moab:
but he would not *consent:* and Israel abode
in Kadesh.
18 Then they went along through the wilderness, and compassed the land of Edom,
and the land of Moab, and came by the
east side of the land of Moab, and pitched
on the other side of Arnon, but came not
within the border of Moab: for Arnon *was*
the border of Moab.
19 And Israel sent messengers unto Sihon
king of the Amorites, the king of Heshbon;
and Israel said unto him, Let us pass, we
pray thee, through thy land into my place.
20 But Sihon trusted not Israel to pass
through his coast: but Sihon gathered all
his people together, and pitched in Jahaz,
and fought against Israel.
21 And the LORD God of Israel delivered
Sihon and all his people into the hand
of Israel, and they smote them: so Israel
possessed all the land of the Amorites, the
inhabitants of that country.
22 And they possessed all the coasts of the
Amorites, from Arnon even unto Jabbok,
and from the wilderness even unto Jordan.
23 So now the LORD God of Israel hath dispossessed the Amorites from before his
people Israel, and shouldest thou possess it?
24 Wilt not thou possess that which Chemosh thy god giveth thee to possess? So
whomsoever the LORD our God shall drive
out from before us, them will we possess.
25 And now *art* thou any thing better than
Balak the son of Zippor, king of Moab? did
he ever strive against Israel, or did he ever
fight against them,
26 While Israel dwelt in Heshbon and her
towns, and in Aroer and her towns, and in
all the cities that *be* along by the coasts of
Arnon, three hundred years? why therefore
did ye not recover *them* within that time?
27 Wherefore I have not sinned against
thee, but thou doest me wrong to war
against me: the LORD the Judge be judge
this day between the children of Israel and
the children of Ammon.

number by their polls, man by man, was
thirty and eight thousand.
4 Of which, twenty and four thousand *were*
to set forward the work of the house of
the LORD; and six thousand *were* officers
and judges:
5 Moreover four thousand *were* porters;
and four thousand praised the LORD with
the instruments which I made, *said David,*
to praise *therewith.*
6 And David divided them into courses
among the sons of Levi, *namely,* Gershon,
Kohath, and Merari.
7 ¶ Of the Gershonites *were,* Laadan, and
Shimei.
8 The sons of Laadan; the chief *was* Jehiel,
and Zetham, and Joel, three.
9 The sons of Shimei; Shelomith, and Haziel,
and Haran, three. These *were* the chief of
the fathers of Laadan.
10 And the sons of Shimei *were,* Jahath, Zina,
and Jeush, and Beriah. These four *were* the
sons of Shimei.
11 And Jahath was the chief, and Zizah the
second: but Jeush and Beriah had not many
sons; therefore they were in one reckoning,
according to *their* father's house.
12 ¶ The sons of Kohath; Amram, Izhar,
Hebron, and Uzziel, four.
13 The sons of Amram; Aaron and Moses:
and Aaron was separated, that he should
sanctify the most holy things, he and his
sons for ever, to burn incense before the
LORD, to minister unto him, and to bless in
his name for ever.
14 Now *concerning* Moses the man of God,
his sons were named of the tribe of Levi.
15 The sons of Moses *were,* Gershom, and
Eliezer.
16 Of the sons of Gershom, Shebuel *was*
the chief.
17 And the sons of Eliezer *were,* Rehabiah
the chief. And Eliezer had none other sons;
but the sons of Rehabiah were very many.
18 Of the sons of Izhar; Shelomith the chief.
19 Of the sons of Hebron; Jeriah the first,
Amariah the second, Jahaziel the third, and
Jekameam the fourth.
20 Of the sons of Uzziel; Michah the first,
and Jesiah the second.
21 ¶ The sons of Merari; Mahli, and Mushi.
The sons of Mahli; Eleazar, and Kish.
22 And Eleazar died, and had no sons, but
daughters: and their brethren the sons of
Kish took them.
23 The sons of Mushi; Mahli, and Eder, and
Jeremoth, three.
24 ¶ These *were* the sons of Levi after the
house of their fathers; *even* the chief of the
fathers, as they were counted by number
of names by their polls, that did the work
for the service of the house of the LORD,
from the age of twenty years and upward.
25 For David said, The LORD God of Israel
hath given rest unto his people, that they
may dwell in Jerusalem for ever:
26 And also unto the Levites; they shall no
more carry the tabernacle, nor any vessels
of it for the service thereof.
27 For by the last words of David the Levites *were* numbered from twenty years old
and above:
28 Because their office *was* to wait on the
sons of Aaron for the service of the house of
the LORD, in the courts, and in the chambers,
and in the purifying of all holy things, and
the work of the service of the house of God;
29 Both for the shewbread, and for the fine
flour for meat offering, and for the unleavened cakes, and for *that which is baked in*
the pan, and for that which is fried, and for
all manner of measure and size;
30 And to stand every morning to thank
and praise the LORD, and likewise at even;
31 And to offer all burnt sacrifices unto the
LORD in the sabbaths, in the new moons, and
on the set feasts, by number, according to
the order commanded unto them, continually before the LORD:
32 And that they should keep the charge
of the tabernacle of the congregation, and
the charge of the holy *place,* and the charge
of the sons of Aaron their brethren, in the
service of the house of the LORD.

1 Chronicles 24

1 Now *these are* the divisions of the sons
of Aaron. The sons of Aaron; Nadab, and
Abihu, Eleazar, and Ithamar.
2 But Nadab and Abihu died before their
father, and had no children: therefore Eleazar and Ithamar executed the priest's office.
3 And David distributed them, both Zadok
of the sons of Eleazar, and Ahimelech of the
sons of Ithamar, according to their offices
in their service.

4 And there were more chief men found
of the sons of Eleazar than of the sons of
Ithamar; and *thus* were they divided. Among
the sons of Eleazar *there were* sixteen chief
men of the house of *their* fathers, and eight
among the sons of Ithamar according to the
house of their fathers.
5 Thus were they divided by lot, one sort
with another; for the governors of the sanctuary, and governors *of the house* of God,
were of the sons of Eleazar, and of the sons
of Ithamar.
6 And Shemaiah the son of Nethaneel the
scribe, *one* of the Levites, wrote them before
the king, and the princes, and Zadok the
priest, and Ahimelech the son of Abiathar,
and *before* the chief of the fathers of the
priests and Levites: one principal household
being taken for Eleazar, and *one* taken for
Ithamar.
7 Now the first lot came forth to Jehoiarib,
the second to Jedaiah,
8 The third to Harim, the fourth to Seorim,
9 The fifth to Malchijah, the sixth to Mijamin,
10 The seventh to Hakkoz, the eighth to
Abijah,
11 The ninth to Jeshua, the tenth to Shecaniah,
12 The eleventh to Eliashib, the twelfth
to Jakim,
13 The thirteenth to Huppah, the fourteenth
to Jeshebeab,
14 The fifteenth to Bilgah, the sixteenth
to Immer,
15 The seventeenth to Hezir, the eighteenth
to Aphses,
16 The nineteenth to Pethahiah, the twentieth to Jehezekel,
17 The one and twentieth to Jachin, the two
and twentieth to Gamul,
18 The three and twentieth to Delaiah, the
four and twentieth to Maaziah.
19 These *were* the orderings of them in their
service to come into the house of the LORD,
according to their manner, under Aaron
their father, as the LORD God of Israel had
commanded him.
20 ¶ And the rest of the sons of Levi *were
these:* Of the sons of Amram; Shubael: of
the sons of Shubael; Jehdeiah.
21 Concerning Rehabiah: of the sons of
Rehabiah, the first *was* Isshiah.
22 Of the Izharites; Shelomoth: of the sons
of Shelomoth; Jahath.
23 And the sons *of Hebron;* Jeriah *the first,*
Amariah the second, Jahaziel the third,
Jekameam the fourth.
24 *Of* the sons of Uzziel; Michah: of the sons
of Michah; Shamir.
25 The brother of Michah *was* Isshiah: of
the sons of Isshiah; Zechariah.
26 The sons of Merari *were* Mahli and
Mushi: the sons of Jaaziah; Beno.
27 ¶ The sons of Merari by Jaaziah; Beno,
and Shoham, and Zaccur, and Ibri.
28 Of Mahli *came* Eleazar, who had no sons.
29 Concerning Kish: the son of Kish *was*
Jerahmeel.
30 The sons also of Mushi; Mahli, and Eder,
and Jerimoth. These *were* the sons of the
Levites after the house of their fathers.
31 These likewise cast lots over against
their brethren the sons of Aaron in the
presence of David the king, and Zadok, and
Ahimelech, and the chief of the fathers of
the priests and Levites, even the principal
fathers over against their younger brethren.

1 Chronicles 25

1 Moreover David and the captains of the
host separated to the service of the sons of
Asaph, and of Heman, and of Jeduthun, who
should prophesy with harps, with psalteries,
and with cymbals: and the number of the
workmen according to their service was:
2 Of the sons of Asaph; Zaccur, and Joseph,
and Nethaniah, and Asarelah, the sons of
Asaph under the hands of Asaph, which
prophesied according to the order of the
king.
3 Of Jeduthun: the sons of Jeduthun; Gedaliah, and Zeri, and Jeshaiah, Hashabiah, and
Mattithiah, six, under the hands of their
father Jeduthun, who prophesied with a
harp, to give thanks and to praise the LORD.
4 Of Heman: the sons of Heman; Bukkiah,
Mattaniah, Uzziel, Shebuel, and Jerimoth,
Hananiah, Hanani, Eliathah, Giddalti, and
Romamti-ezer, Joshbekashah, Mallothi,
Hothir, *and* Mahazioth:
5 All these *were* the sons of Heman the
king's seer in the words of God, to lift up
the horn. And God gave to Heman fourteen
sons and three daughters.
6 All these *were* under the hands of their

father for song *in* the house of the LORD,
with cymbals, psalteries, and harps, for the
service of the house of God, according to
the king's order to Asaph, Jeduthun, and
Heman.
7 So the number of them, with their brethren that were instructed in the songs of the
LORD, *even* all that were cunning, was two
hundred fourscore and eight.
8 ¶ And they cast lots, ward against *ward*,
as well the small as the great, the teacher
as the scholar.
9 Now the first lot came forth for Asaph to
Joseph: the second to Gedaliah, who with
his brethren and sons *were* twelve:
10 The third to Zaccur, *he*, his sons, and his
brethren, *were* twelve:
11 The fourth to Izri, *he*, his sons, and his
brethren, *were* twelve:
12 The fifth to Nethaniah, *he*, his sons, and
his brethren, *were* twelve:
13 The sixth to Bukkiah, *he*, his sons, and
his brethren, *were* twelve:
14 The seventh to Jesharelah, *he*, his sons,
and his brethren, *were* twelve:
15 The eighth to Jeshaiah, *he*, his sons, and
his brethren, *were* twelve:
16 The ninth to Mattaniah, *he*, his sons, and
his brethren, *were* twelve:
17 The tenth to Shimei, *he*, his sons, and his
brethren, *were* twelve:
18 The eleventh to Azareel, *he*, his sons, and
his brethren, *were* twelve:
19 The twelfth to Hashabiah, *he*, his sons,
and his brethren, *were* twelve:
20 The thirteenth to Shubael, *he*, his sons,
and his brethren, *were* twelve:
21 The fourteenth to Mattithiah, *he*, his
sons, and his brethren, *were* twelve:
22 The fifteenth to Jeremoth, *he*, his sons,
and his brethren, *were* twelve:
23 The sixteenth to Hananiah, *he*, his sons,
and his brethren, *were* twelve:
24 The seventeenth to Joshbekashah, *he*,
his sons, and his brethren, *were* twelve:
25 The eighteenth to Hanani, *he*, his sons,
and his brethren, *were* twelve:
26 The nineteenth to Mallothi, *he*, his sons,
and his brethren, *were* twelve:
27 The twentieth to Eliathah, *he*, his sons,
and his brethren, *were* twelve:
28 The one and twentieth to Hothir, *he*, his
sons, and his brethren, *were* twelve:
29 The two and twentieth to Giddalti, *he*,
his sons, and his brethren, *were* twelve:
30 The three and twentieth to Mahazioth,
he, his sons, and his brethren, *were* twelve:
31 The four and twentieth to Romamti-ezer,
he, his sons, and his brethren, *were* twelve.

1 Chronicles 26

1 Concerning the divisions of the porters:
Of the Korhites *was* Meshelemiah the son
of Kore, of the sons of Asaph.
2 And the sons of Meshelemiah *were*, Zechariah the firstborn, Jediael the second, Zebadiah the third, Jathniel the fourth,
3 Elam the fifth, Jehohanan the sixth, Elioenai the seventh.
4 Moreover the sons of Obed-edom *were*,
Shemaiah the firstborn, Jehozabad the second, Joah the third, and Sacar the fourth,
and Nethaneel the fifth,
5 Ammiel the sixth, Issachar the seventh,
Peulthai the eighth: for God blessed him.
6 Also unto Shemaiah his son were sons
born, that ruled throughout the house of
their father: for they *were* mighty men of
valour.
7 The sons of Shemaiah; Othni, and Rephael,
and Obed, Elzabad, whose brethren *were*
strong men, Elihu, and Semachiah.
8 All these of the sons of Obed-edom: they
and their sons and their brethren, able men
for strength for the service, *were* threescore
and two of Obed-edom.
9 And Meshelemiah had sons and brethren,
strong men, eighteen.
10 Also Hosah, of the children of Merari,
had sons; Simri the chief, (for *though* he
was not the firstborn, yet his father made
him the chief;)
11 Hilkiah the second, Tebaliah the third,
Zechariah the fourth: all the sons and brethren of Hosah *were* thirteen.
12 Among these *were* the divisions of the
porters, *even* among the chief men, *having*
wards one against another, to minister in
the house of the LORD.
13 ¶ And they cast lots, as well the small as
the great, according to the house of their
fathers, for every gate.
14 And the lot eastward fell to Shelemiah.
Then for Zechariah his son, a wise counseller, they cast lots; and his lot came out
northward.

15 To Obed-edom southward; and to his
sons the house of Asuppim.
16 To Shuppim and Hosah *the lot came*
forth westward, with the gate Shallecheth,
by the causeway of the going up, ward
against ward.
17 Eastward *were* six Levites, northward
four a day, southward four a day, and toward
Asuppim two *and* two.
18 At Parbar westward, four at the causeway, *and* two at Parbar.
19 These *are* the divisions of the porters
among the sons of Kore, and among the
sons of Merari.
20 ¶ And of the Levites, Ahijah *was* over the
treasures of the house of God, and over the
treasures of the dedicated things.
21 *As concerning* the sons of Laadan; the
sons of the Gershonite Laadan, chief fathers,
even of Laadan the Gershonite, *were* Jehieli.
22 The sons of Jehieli; Zetham, and Joel his
brother, *which were* over the treasures of
the house of the LORD.
23 Of the Amramites, *and* the Izharites, the
Hebronites, *and* the Uzzielites:
24 And Shebuel the son of Gershom, the
son of Moses, *was* ruler of the treasures.
25 And his brethren by Eliezer; Rehabiah his
son, and Jeshaiah his son, and Joram his son,
and Zichri his son, and Shelomith his son.
26 Which Shelomith and his brethren *were*
over all the treasures of the dedicated
things, which David the king, and the chief
fathers, the captains over thousands and
hundreds, and the captains of the host,
had dedicated.
27 Out of the spoils won in battles did they
dedicate to maintain the house of the LORD.
28 And all that Samuel the seer, and Saul
the son of Kish, and Abner the son of Ner,
and Joab the son of Zeruiah, had dedicated;
and whosoever had dedicated *any thing, it*
was under the hand of Shelomith, and of
his brethren.
29 ¶ Of the Izharites, Chenaniah and his sons
were for the outward business over Israel,
for officers and judges.
30 *And* of the Hebronites, Hashabiah and
his brethren, men of valour, a thousand and
seven hundred, *were* officers among them
of Israel on this side Jordan westward in all
the business of the LORD, and in the service
of the king.
31 Among the Hebronites *was* Jerijah the
chief, *even* among the Hebronites, according to the generations of his fathers. In
the fortieth year of the reign of David they
were sought for, and there were found
among them mighty men of valour at Jazer
of Gilead.
32 And his brethren, men of valour, *were*
two thousand and seven hundred chief
fathers, whom king David made rulers
over the Reubenites, the Gadites, and the
half tribe of Manasseh, for every matter
pertaining to God, and affairs of the king.

1 Chronicles 27

1 Now the children of Israel after their number, *to wit*, the chief fathers and captains of
thousands and hundreds, and their officers
that served the king in any matter of the
courses, which came in and went out month
by month throughout all the months of the
year, of every course *were* twenty and four
thousand.
2 Over the first course for the first month
was Jashobeam the son of Zabdiel: and in
his course *were* twenty and four thousand.
3 Of the children of Perez *was* the chief of all
the captains of the host for the first month.
4 And over the course of the second month
was Dodai an Ahohite, and of his course *was*
Mikloth also the ruler: in his course likewise
were twenty and four thousand.
5 The third captain of the host for the third
month *was* Benaiah the son of Jehoiada, a
chief priest: and in his course *were* twenty
and four thousand.
6 This *is that* Benaiah, *who was* mighty
among the thirty, and above the thirty:
and in his course *was* Ammizabad his son.
7 The fourth *captain* for the fourth month
was Asahel the brother of Joab, and Zebadiah his son after him: and in his course *were*
twenty and four thousand.
8 The fifth captain for the fifth month *was*
Shamhuth the Izrahite: and in his course
were twenty and four thousand.
9 The sixth *captain* for the sixth month *was*
Ira the son of Ikkesh the Tekoite: and in his
course *were* twenty and four thousand.
10 The seventh *captain* for the seventh
month *was* Helez the Pelonite, of the children of Ephraim: and in his course *were*
twenty and four thousand.

11 The eighth *captain* for the eighth month *was* Sibbecai the Hushathite, of the Zarhites: and in his course *were* twenty and four thousand.

12 The ninth *captain* for the ninth month *was* Abiezer the Anetothite, of the Benjamites: and in his course *were* twenty and four thousand.

13 The tenth *captain* for the tenth month *was* Maharai the Netophathite, of the Zarhites: and in his course *were* twenty and four thousand.

14 The eleventh *captain* for the eleventh month *was* Benaiah the Pirathonite, of the children of Ephraim: and in his course *were* twenty and four thousand.

15 The twelfth *captain* for the twelfth month *was* Heldai the Netophathite, of Othniel: and in his course *were* twenty and four thousand.

16 ¶ Furthermore over the tribes of Israel: the ruler of the Reubenites *was* Eliezer the son of Zichri: of the Simeonites, Shephatiah the son of Maachah:

17 Of the Levites, Hashabiah the son of Kemuel: of the Aaronites, Zadok:

18 Of Judah, Elihu, *one* of the brethren of David: of Issachar, Omri the son of Michael:

19 Of Zebulun, Ishmaiah the son of Obadiah: of Naphtali, Jerimoth the son of Azriel:

20 Of the children of Ephraim, Hoshea the son of Azaziah: of the half tribe of Manasseh, Joel the son of Pedaiah:

21 Of the half *tribe* of Manasseh in Gilead, Iddo the son of Zechariah: of Benjamin, Jaasiel the son of Abner:

22 Of Dan, Azareel the son of Jeroham. These *were* the princes of the tribes of Israel.

23 ¶ But David took not the number of them from twenty years old and under: because the LORD had said he would increase Israel like to the stars of the heavens.

24 Joab the son of Zeruiah began to number, but he finished not, because there fell wrath for it against Israel; neither was the number put in the account of the chronicles of king David.

25 ¶ And over the king's treasures *was* Azmaveth the son of Adiel: and over the storehouses in the fields, in the cities, and in the villages, and in the castles, *was* Jehonathan the son of Uzziah:

26 And over them that did the work of the field for tillage of the ground *was* Ezri the son of Chelub:

27 And over the vineyards *was* Shimei the Ramathite: over the increase of the vineyards for the wine cellars *was* Zabdi the Shiphmite:

28 And over the olive trees and the sycomore trees that *were* in the low plains *was* Baal-hanan the Gederite: and over the cellars of oil *was* Joash:

29 And over the herds that fed in Sharon *was* Shitrai the Sharonite: and over the herds *that were* in the valleys *was* Shaphat the son of Adlai:

30 Over the camels also *was* Obil the Ishmaelite: and over the asses *was* Jehdeiah the Meronothite:

31 And over the flocks *was* Jaziz the Hagerite. All these *were* the rulers of the substance which *was* king David's.

32 Also Jonathan David's uncle was a counseller, a wise man, and a scribe: and Jehiel the son of Hachmoni *was* with the king's sons:

33 And Ahithophel *was* the king's counseller: and Hushai the Archite *was* the king's companion:

34 And after Ahithophel *was* Jehoiada the son of Benaiah, and Abiathar: and the general of the king's army *was* Joab.

1 Chronicles 28

1 And David assembled all the princes of Israel, the princes of the tribes, and the captains of the companies that ministered to the king by course, and the captains over the thousands, and captains over the hundreds, and the stewards over all the substance and possession of the king, and of his sons, with the officers, and with the mighty men, and with all the valiant men, unto Jerusalem.

2 Then David the king stood up upon his feet, and said, Hear me, my brethren, and my people: *As for me,* I *had* in mine heart to build an house of rest for the ark of the covenant of the LORD, and for the footstool of our God, and had made ready for the building:

3 But God said unto me, Thou shalt not build an house for my name, because thou *hast been* a man of war, and hast shed blood.

4 Howbeit the LORD God of Israel chose

me before all the house of my father to be
king over Israel for ever: for he hath chosen
Judah *to be* the ruler; and of the house of
Judah, the house of my father; and among
the sons of my father he liked me to make
me king over all Israel:
5 And of all my sons, (for the LORD hath given
me many sons,) he hath chosen Solomon my
son to sit upon the throne of the kingdom
of the LORD over Israel.
6 And he said unto me, Solomon thy son,
he shall build my house and my courts: for
I have chosen him *to be* my son, and I will
be his father.
7 Moreover I will establish his kingdom for
ever, if he be constant to do my commandments and my judgments, as at this day.
8 Now therefore in the sight of all Israel the
congregation of the LORD, and in the audience of our God, keep and seek for all the
commandments of the LORD your God: that
ye may possess this good land, and leave *it*
for an inheritance for your children after
you for ever.
9 ¶ And thou, Solomon my son, know thou
the God of thy father, and serve him with a
perfect heart and with a willing mind: for the
LORD searcheth all hearts, and understandeth all the imaginations of the thoughts:
if thou seek him, he will be found of thee;
but if thou forsake him, he will cast thee
off for ever.
10 Take heed now; for the LORD hath chosen
thee to build an house for the sanctuary: be
strong, and do *it*.
11 ¶ Then David gave to Solomon his son
the pattern of the porch, and of the houses
thereof, and of the treasuries thereof, and
of the upper chambers thereof, and of the
inner parlours thereof, and of the place of
the mercy seat,
12 And the pattern of all that he had by the
spirit, of the courts of the house of the LORD,
and of all the chambers round about, of the
treasuries of the house of God, and of the
treasuries of the dedicated things:
13 Also for the courses of the priests and the
Levites, and for all the work of the service
of the house of the LORD, and for all the
vessels of service in the house of the LORD.
14 *He gave* of gold by weight for *things* of
gold, for all instruments of all manner of
service; *silver also* for all instruments of
silver by weight, for all instruments of every
kind of service:
15 Even the weight for the candlesticks of
gold, and for their lamps of gold, by weight
for every candlestick, and for the lamps
thereof: and for the candlesticks of silver
by weight, *both* for the candlestick, and *also*
for the lamps thereof, according to the use
of every candlestick.
16 And by weight *he gave* gold for the tables
of shewbread, for every table; and *likewise*
silver for the tables of silver:
17 Also pure gold for the fleshhooks, and
the bowls, and the cups: and for the golden
basons *he gave gold* by weight for every
bason; and *likewise silver* by weight for every
bason of silver:
18 And for the altar of incense refined gold
by weight; and gold for the pattern of the
chariot of the cherubims, that spread out
their wings, and covered the ark of the covenant of the LORD.
19 All *this, said David*, the LORD made me
understand in writing by *his* hand upon me,
even all the works of this pattern.
20 And David said to Solomon his son, Be
strong and of good courage, and do *it:* fear
not, nor be dismayed: for the LORD God,
even my God, *will be* with thee; he will not
fail thee, nor forsake thee, until thou hast
finished all the work for the service of the
house of the LORD.
21 And, behold, the courses of the priests
and the Levites, *even they shall be with
thee* for all the service of the house of God:
and *there shall be* with thee for all manner
of workmanship every willing skilful man,
for any manner of service: also the princes
and all the people *will be* wholly at thy
commandment.

1 Chronicles 29

1 Furthermore David the king said unto all
the congregation, Solomon my son, whom
alone God hath chosen, *is yet* young and
tender, and the work *is* great: for the palace
is not for man, but for the LORD God.
2 Now I have prepared with all my might for
the house of my God the gold for *things to
be made* of gold, and the silver for *things* of
silver, and the brass for *things* of brass, the
iron for *things* of iron, and wood for *things*
of wood; onyx stones, and *stones* to be set,

glistering stones, and of divers colours, and all manner of precious stones, and marble stones in abundance.

3 Moreover, because I have set my affection to the house of my God, I have of mine own proper good, of gold and silver, *which* I have given to the house of my God, over and above all that I have prepared for the holy house,

4 *Even* three thousand talents of gold, of the gold of Ophir, and seven thousand talents of refined silver, to overlay the walls of the houses *withal:*

5 The gold for *things* of gold, and the silver for *things* of silver, and for all manner of work *to be made* by the hands of artificers. And who *then* is willing to consecrate his service this day unto the LORD?

6 ¶ Then the chief of the fathers and princes of the tribes of Israel, and the captains of thousands and of hundreds, with the rulers of the king's work, offered willingly,

7 And gave for the service of the house of God of gold five thousand talents and ten thousand drams, and of silver ten thousand talents, and of brass eighteen thousand talents, and one hundred thousand talents of iron.

8 And they with whom *precious* stones were found gave *them* to the treasure of the house of the LORD, by the hand of Jehiel the Gershonite.

9 Then the people rejoiced, for that they offered willingly, because with perfect heart they offered willingly to the LORD: and David the king also rejoiced with great joy.

10 ¶ Wherefore David blessed the LORD before all the congregation: and David said, Blessed *be* thou, LORD God of Israel our father, for ever and ever.

11 Thine, O LORD, *is* the greatness, and the power, and the glory, and the victory, and the majesty: for all *that is* in the heaven and in the earth *is thine;* thine *is* the kingdom, O LORD, and thou art exalted as head above all.

12 Both riches and honour *come* of thee, and thou reignest over all; and in thine hand *is* power and might; and in thine hand *it is* to make great, and to give strength unto all.

13 Now therefore, our God, we thank thee, and praise thy glorious name.

14 But who *am* I, and what *is* my people, that we should be able to offer so willingly after this sort? for all things *come* of thee, and of thine own have we given thee.

15 For we *are* strangers before thee, and sojourners, as *were* all our fathers: our days on the earth *are* as a shadow, and *there is* none abiding.

16 O LORD our God, all this store that we have prepared to build thee an house for thine holy name *cometh* of thine hand, and *is* all thine own.

17 I know also, my God, that thou triest the heart, and hast pleasure in uprightness. As for me, in the uprightness of mine heart I have willingly offered all these things: and now have I seen with joy thy people, which are present here, to offer willingly unto thee.

18 O LORD God of Abraham, Isaac, and of Israel, our fathers, keep this for ever in the imagination of the thoughts of the heart of thy people, and prepare their heart unto thee:

19 And give unto Solomon my son a perfect heart, to keep thy commandments, thy testimonies, and thy statutes, and to do all *these things,* and to build the palace, *for* the which I have made provision.

20 ¶ And David said to all the congregation, Now bless the LORD your God. And all the congregation blessed the LORD God of their fathers, and bowed down their heads, and worshipped the LORD, and the king.

21 And they sacrificed sacrifices unto the LORD, and offered burnt offerings unto the LORD, on the morrow after that day, *even* a thousand bullocks, a thousand rams, *and* a thousand lambs, with their drink offerings, and sacrifices in abundance for all Israel:

22 And did eat and drink before the LORD on that day with great gladness. And they made Solomon the son of David king the second time, and anointed *him* unto the LORD *to be* the chief governor, and Zadok *to be* priest.

23 Then Solomon sat on the throne of the LORD as king instead of David his father, and prospered; and all Israel obeyed him.

24 And all the princes, and the mighty men, and all the sons likewise of king David, submitted themselves unto Solomon the king.

25 And the LORD magnified Solomon exceedingly in the sight of all Israel, and bestowed upon him *such* royal majesty as had not been on any king before him in Israel.

26 ¶ Thus David the son of Jesse reigned over all Israel.

27 And the time that he reigned over Israel *was* forty years; seven years reigned he in Hebron, and thirty and three *years* reigned he in Jerusalem.

28 And he died in a good old age, full of days, riches, and honour: and Solomon his son reigned in his stead.

29 Now the acts of David the king, first and last, behold, they *are* written in the book of Samuel the seer, and in the book of Nathan the prophet, and in the book of Gad the seer,

30 With all his reign and his might, and the times that went over him, and over Israel, and over all the kingdoms of the countries.

The Second Book Of The

Chronicles

2 Chronicles 1

1 And Solomon the son of David was strengthened in his kingdom, and the LORD his God *was* with him, and magnified him exceedingly.

2 Then Solomon spake unto all Israel, to the captains of thousands and of hundreds, and to the judges, and to every governor in all Israel, the chief of the fathers.

3 So Solomon, and all the congregation with him, went to the high place that *was* at Gibeon; for there was the tabernacle of the congregation of God, which Moses the servant of the LORD had made in the wilderness.

4 But the ark of God had David brought up from Kirjath-jearim to *the place which* David had prepared for it: for he had pitched a tent for it at Jerusalem.

5 Moreover the brasen altar, that Bezaleel the son of Uri, the son of Hur, had made, he put before the tabernacle of the LORD: and Solomon and the congregation sought unto it.

6 And Solomon went up thither to the brasen altar before the LORD, which *was* at the tabernacle of the congregation, and offered a thousand burnt offerings upon it.

7 ¶ In that night did God appear unto Solomon, and said unto him, Ask what I shall give thee.

8 And Solomon said unto God, Thou hast shewed great mercy unto David my father, and hast made me to reign in his stead.

9 Now, O LORD God, let thy promise unto David my father be established: for thou hast made me king over a people like the dust of the earth in multitude.

10 Give me now wisdom and knowledge, that I may go out and come in before this people: for who can judge this thy people, *that is so* great?

11 And God said to Solomon, Because this was in thine heart, and thou hast not asked riches, wealth, or honour, nor the life of thine enemies, neither yet hast asked long life; but hast asked wisdom and knowledge for thyself, that thou mayest judge my people, over whom I have made thee king:

12 Wisdom and knowledge *is* granted unto thee; and I will give thee riches, and wealth, and honour, such as none of the kings have had that *have been* before thee, neither shall there any after thee have the like.

13 ¶ Then Solomon came *from his journey* to the high place that *was* at Gibeon to Jerusalem, from before the tabernacle of the congregation, and reigned over Israel.

14 And Solomon gathered chariots and horsemen: and he had a thousand and four hundred chariots, and twelve thousand horsemen, which he placed in the chariot cities, and with the king at Jerusalem.

15 And the king made silver and gold at Jerusalem *as plenteous* as stones, and cedar trees made he as the sycomore trees that *are* in the vale for abundance.

16 And Solomon had horses brought out of Egypt, and linen yarn: the king's merchants received the linen yarn at a price.

17 And they fetched up, and brought forth
out of Egypt a chariot for six hundred *shekels*
of silver, and an horse for an hundred and
fifty: and so brought they out *horses* for all
the kings of the Hittites, and for the kings
of Syria, by their means.

2 Chronicles 2

1 And Solomon determined to build an
house for the name of the LORD, and an
house for his kingdom.
2 And Solomon told out threescore and
ten thousand men to bear burdens, and
fourscore thousand to hew in the mountain, and three thousand and six hundred
to oversee them.
3 ¶ And Solomon sent to Huram the king of
Tyre, saying, As thou didst deal with David
my father, and didst send him cedars to
build him an house to dwell therein, *even
so deal with me.*
4 Behold, I build an house to the name of
the LORD my God, to dedicate *it* to him, *and*
to burn before him sweet incense, and for
the continual shewbread, and for the burnt
offerings morning and evening, on the sabbaths, and on the new moons, and on the
solemn feasts of the LORD our God. This *is
an ordinance* for ever to Israel.
5 And the house which I build *is* great: for
great *is* our God above all gods.
6 But who is able to build him an house,
seeing the heaven and heaven of heavens
cannot contain him? who *am* I then, that
I should build him an house, save only to
burn sacrifice before him?
7 Send me now therefore a man cunning to
work in gold, and in silver, and in brass, and
in iron, and in purple, and crimson, and blue,
and that can skill to grave with the cunning
men that *are* with me in Judah and in Jerusalem, whom David my father did provide.
8 Send me also cedar trees, fir trees, and
algum trees, out of Lebanon: for I know
that thy servants can skill to cut timber in
Lebanon; and, behold, my servants *shall be*
with thy servants,
9 Even to prepare me timber in abundance:
for the house which I am about to build *shall
be* wonderful great.
10 And, behold, I will give to thy servants,
the hewers that cut timber, twenty thousand measures of beaten wheat, and twenty
thousand measures of barley, and twenty
thousand baths of wine, and twenty thousand baths of oil.
11 ¶ Then Huram the king of Tyre answered
in writing, which he sent to Solomon,
Because the LORD hath loved his people,
he hath made thee king over them.
12 Huram said moreover, Blessed *be* the
LORD God of Israel, that made heaven and
earth, who hath given to David the king a
wise son, endued with prudence and understanding, that might build an house for the
LORD, and an house for his kingdom.
13 And now I have sent a cunning man,
endued with understanding, of Huram my
father's,
14 The son of a woman of the daughters
of Dan, and his father *was* a man of Tyre,
skilful to work in gold, and in silver, in brass,
in iron, in stone, and in timber, in purple, in
blue, and in fine linen, and in crimson; also
to grave any manner of graving, and to find
out every device which shall be put to him,
with thy cunning men, and with the cunning
men of my lord David thy father.
15 Now therefore the wheat, and the barley,
the oil, and the wine, which my lord hath
spoken of, let him send unto his servants:
16 And we will cut wood out of Lebanon, as
much as thou shalt need: and we will bring
it to thee in floats by sea to Joppa; and thou
shalt carry it up to Jerusalem.
17 ¶ And Solomon numbered all the strangers that *were* in the land of Israel, after the
numbering wherewith David his father had
numbered them; and they were found an
hundred and fifty thousand and three thousand and six hundred.
18 And he set threescore and ten thousand
of them *to be* bearers of burdens, and fourscore thousand *to be* hewers in the mountain, and three thousand and six hundred
overseers to set the people a work.

2 Chronicles 3

1 Then Solomon began to build the house
of the LORD at Jerusalem in mount Moriah,
where *the LORD* appeared unto David his
father, in the place that David had prepared
in the threshingfloor of Ornan the Jebusite.
2 And he began to build in the second *day*
of the second month, in the fourth year of
his reign.

3 ¶ Now these *are the things wherein* Solomon was instructed for the building of the house of God. The length by cubits after the first measure *was* threescore cubits, and the breadth twenty cubits.

4 And the porch that *was* in the front *of the house*, the length *of it was* according to the breadth of the house, twenty cubits, and the height *was* an hundred and twenty: and he overlaid it within with pure gold.

5 And the greater house he cieled with fir tree, which he overlaid with fine gold, and set thereon palm trees and chains.

6 And he garnished the house with precious stones for beauty: and the gold *was* gold of Parvaim.

7 He overlaid also the house, the beams, the posts, and the walls thereof, and the doors thereof, with gold; and graved cherubims on the walls.

8 And he made the most holy house, the length whereof *was* according to the breadth of the house, twenty cubits, and the breadth thereof twenty cubits: and he overlaid it with fine gold, *amounting* to six hundred talents.

9 And the weight of the nails *was* fifty shekels of gold. And he overlaid the upper chambers with gold.

10 And in the most holy house he made two cherubims of image work, and overlaid them with gold.

11 ¶ And the wings of the cherubims *were* twenty cubits long: one wing *of the one cherub was* five cubits, reaching to the wall of the house: and the other wing *was likewise* five cubits, reaching to the wing of the other cherub.

12 And *one* wing of the other cherub *was* five cubits, reaching to the wall of the house: and the other wing *was* five cubits *also*, joining to the wing of the other cherub.

13 The wings of these cherubims spread themselves forth twenty cubits: and they stood on their feet, and their faces *were* inward.

14 ¶ And he made the vail *of* blue, and purple, and crimson, and fine linen, and wrought cherubims thereon.

15 Also he made before the house two pillars of thirty and five cubits high, and the chapiter that *was* on the top of each of them *was* five cubits.

16 And he made chains, *as* in the oracle, and put *them* on the heads of the pillars; and made an hundred pomegranates, and put *them* on the chains.

17 And he reared up the pillars before the temple, one on the right hand, and the other on the left; and called the name of that on the right hand Jachin, and the name of that on the left Boaz.

2 Chronicles 4

1 Moreover he made an altar of brass, twenty cubits the length thereof, and twenty cubits the breadth thereof, and ten cubits the height thereof.

2 ¶ Also he made a molten sea of ten cubits from brim to brim, round in compass, and five cubits the height thereof; and a line of thirty cubits did compass it round about.

3 And under it *was* the similitude of oxen, which did compass it round about: ten in a cubit, compassing the sea round about. Two rows of oxen *were* cast, when it was cast.

4 It stood upon twelve oxen, three looking toward the north, and three looking toward the west, and three looking toward the south, and three looking toward the east: and the sea *was set* above upon them, and all their hinder parts *were* inward.

5 And the thickness of it *was* an handbreadth, and the brim of it like the work of the brim of a cup, with flowers of lilies; *and* it received and held three thousand baths.

6 ¶ He made also ten lavers, and put five on the right hand, and five on the left, to wash in them: such things as they offered for the burnt offering they washed in them; but the sea *was* for the priests to wash in.

7 And he made ten candlesticks of gold according to their form, and set *them* in the temple, five on the right hand, and five on the left.

8 He made also ten tables, and placed *them* in the temple, five on the right side, and five on the left. And he made an hundred basons of gold.

9 ¶ Furthermore he made the court of the priests, and the great court, and doors for the court, and overlaid the doors of them with brass.

10 And he set the sea on the right side of the east end, over against the south.

11 And Huram made the pots, and the shov-

els, and the basons. And Huram finished the
work that he was to make for king Solomon
for the house of God;
12 *To wit,* the two pillars, and the pommels,
and the chapiters *which were* on the top of
the two pillars, and the two wreaths to cover
the two pommels of the chapiters which
were on the top of the pillars;
13 And four hundred pomegranates on the
two wreaths; two rows of pomegranates on
each wreath, to cover the two pommels of
the chapiters which *were* upon the pillars.
14 He made also bases, and lavers made he
upon the bases;
15 One sea, and twelve oxen under it.
16 The pots also, and the shovels, and the
fleshhooks, and all their instruments, did
Huram his father make to king Solomon
for the house of the LORD of bright brass.
17 In the plain of Jordan did the king cast
them, in the clay ground between Succoth
and Zeredathah.
18 Thus Solomon made all these vessels in
great abundance: for the weight of the brass
could not be found out.
19 ¶ And Solomon made all the vessels that
were for the house of God, the golden altar
also, and the tables whereon the shewbread
was set;
20 Moreover the candlesticks with their
lamps, that they should burn after the manner before the oracle, of pure gold;
21 And the flowers, and the lamps, and
the tongs, *made he of* gold, *and* that perfect gold;
22 And the snuffers, and the basons, and
the spoons, and the censers, *of* pure gold:
and the entry of the house, the inner doors
thereof for the most holy *place,* and the
doors of the house of the temple, *were*
of gold.

2 Chronicles 5

1 Thus all the work that Solomon made for
the house of the LORD was finished: and
Solomon brought in *all* the things that David
his father had dedicated; and the silver, and
the gold, and all the instruments, put he
among the treasures of the house of God.
2 ¶ Then Solomon assembled the elders
of Israel, and all the heads of the tribes,
the chief of the fathers of the children of
Israel, unto Jerusalem, to bring up the ark
of the covenant of the LORD out of the city
of David, which *is* Zion.
3 Wherefore all the men of Israel assembled
themselves unto the king in the feast which
was in the seventh month.
4 And all the elders of Israel came; and the
Levites took up the ark.
5 And they brought up the ark, and the tabernacle of the congregation, and all the holy
vessels that *were* in the tabernacle, these
did the priests *and* the Levites bring up.
6 Also king Solomon, and all the congregation of Israel that were assembled unto him
before the ark, sacrificed sheep and oxen,
which could not be told nor numbered for
multitude.
7 And the priests brought in the ark of
the covenant of the LORD unto his place,
to the oracle of the house, into the most
holy *place, even* under the wings of the
cherubims:
8 For the cherubims spread forth *their*
wings over the place of the ark, and the
cherubims covered the ark and the staves
thereof above.
9 And they drew out the staves *of the ark,*
that the ends of the staves were seen from
the ark before the oracle; but they were not
seen without. And there it is unto this day.
10 *There was* nothing in the ark save the
two tables which Moses put *therein* at
Horeb, when the LORD made *a covenant*
with the children of Israel, when they came
out of Egypt.
11 ¶ And it came to pass, when the priests
were come out of the holy *place:* (for all the
priests *that were* present were sanctified,
and did not *then* wait by course:
12 Also the Levites *which were* the singers,
all of them of Asaph, of Heman, of Jeduthun,
with their sons and their brethren, *being*
arrayed in white linen, having cymbals and
psalteries and harps, stood at the east end
of the altar, and with them an hundred and
twenty priests sounding with trumpets:)
13 It came even to pass, as the trumpeters
and singers *were* as one, to make one sound
to be heard in praising and thanking the
LORD; and when they lifted up *their* voice
with the trumpets and cymbals and instruments of musick, and praised the LORD, *say-*
ing, For *he is* good; for his mercy *endureth*

for ever: that *then* the house was filled with a cloud, *even* the house of the LORD;

14 So that the priests could not stand to minister by reason of the cloud: for the glory of the LORD had filled the house of God.

2 Chronicles 6

1 Then said Solomon, The LORD hath said that he would dwell in the thick darkness.

2 But I have built an house of habitation for thee, and a place for thy dwelling for ever.

3 And the king turned his face, and blessed the whole congregation of Israel: and all the congregation of Israel stood.

4 And he said, Blessed *be* the LORD God of Israel, who hath with his hands fulfilled *that* which he spake with his mouth to my father David, saying,

5 Since the day that I brought forth my people out of the land of Egypt I chose no city among all the tribes of Israel to build an house in, that my name might be there; neither chose I any man to be a ruler over my people Israel:

6 But I have chosen Jerusalem, that my name might be there; and have chosen David to be over my people Israel.

7 Now it was in the heart of David my father to build an house for the name of the LORD God of Israel.

8 But the LORD said to David my father, Forasmuch as it was in thine heart to build an house for my name, thou didst well in that it was in thine heart:

9 Notwithstanding thou shalt not build the house; but thy son which shall come forth out of thy loins, he shall build the house for my name.

10 The LORD therefore hath performed his word that he hath spoken: for I am risen up in the room of David my father, and am set on the throne of Israel, as the LORD promised, and have built the house for the name of the LORD God of Israel.

11 And in it have I put the ark, wherein *is* the covenant of the LORD, that he made with the children of Israel.

12 ¶ And he stood before the altar of the LORD in the presence of all the congregation of Israel, and spread forth his hands:

13 For Solomon had made a brasen scaffold, of five cubits long, and five cubits broad, and three cubits high, and had set it in the midst of the court: and upon it he stood, and kneeled down upon his knees before all the congregation of Israel, and spread forth his hands toward heaven,

14 And said, O LORD God of Israel, *there is* no God like thee in the heaven, nor in the earth; which keepest covenant, and *shewest* mercy unto thy servants, that walk before thee with all their hearts:

15 Thou which hast kept with thy servant David my father that which thou hast promised him; and spakest with thy mouth, and hast fulfilled *it* with thine hand, as *it is* this day.

16 Now therefore, O LORD God of Israel, keep with thy servant David my father that which thou hast promised him, saying, There shall not fail thee a man in my sight to sit upon the throne of Israel; yet so that thy children take heed to their way to walk in my law, as thou hast walked before me.

17 Now then, O LORD God of Israel, let thy word be verified, which thou hast spoken unto thy servant David.

18 But will God in very deed dwell with men on the earth? behold, heaven and the heaven of heavens cannot contain thee; how much less this house which I have built!

19 Have respect therefore to the prayer of thy servant, and to his supplication, O LORD my God, to hearken unto the cry and the prayer which thy servant prayeth before thee:

20 That thine eyes may be open upon this house day and night, upon the place whereof thou hast said that thou wouldest put thy name there; to hearken unto the prayer which thy servant prayeth toward this place.

21 Hearken therefore unto the supplications of thy servant, and of thy people Israel, which they shall make toward this place: hear thou from thy dwelling place, *even* from heaven; and when thou hearest, forgive.

22 ¶ If a man sin against his neighbour, and an oath be laid upon him to make him swear, and the oath come before thine altar in this house;

23 Then hear thou from heaven, and do, and judge thy servants, by requiting the wicked, by recompensing his way upon his

own head; and by justifying the righteous,
by giving him according to his righteousness.
24 ¶ And if thy people Israel be put to the
worse before the enemy, because they
have sinned against thee; and shall return
and confess thy name, and pray and make
supplication before thee in this house;
25 Then hear thou from the heavens, and
forgive the sin of thy people Israel, and bring
them again unto the land which thou gavest
to them and to their fathers.
26 ¶ When the heaven is shut up, and there
is no rain, because they have sinned against
thee; *yet* if they pray toward this place, and
confess thy name, and turn from their sin,
when thou dost afflict them;
27 Then hear thou from heaven, and forgive
the sin of thy servants, and of thy people
Israel, when thou hast taught them the good
way, wherein they should walk; and send
rain upon thy land, which thou hast given
unto thy people for an inheritance.
28 ¶ If there be dearth in the land, if there
be pestilence, if there be blasting, or mildew, locusts, or caterpillers; if their enemies
besiege them in the cities of their land;
whatsoever sore or whatsoever sickness
there be:
29 *Then* what prayer *or* what supplication
soever shall be made of any man, or of all
thy people Israel, when every one shall
know his own sore and his own grief, and
shall spread forth his hands in this house:
30 Then hear thou from heaven thy dwelling
place, and forgive, and render unto every
man according unto all his ways, whose
heart thou knowest; (for thou only knowest
the hearts of the children of men:)
31 That they may fear thee, to walk in thy
ways, so long as they live in the land which
thou gavest unto our fathers.
32 ¶ Moreover concerning the stranger,
which is not of thy people Israel, but is come
from a far country for thy great name's sake,
and thy mighty hand, and thy stretched out
arm; if they come and pray in this house;
33 Then hear thou from the heavens, *even*
from thy dwelling place, and do according
to all that the stranger calleth to thee for;
that all people of the earth may know thy
name, and fear thee, as *doth* thy people
Israel, and may know that this house which
I have built is called by thy name.
34 If thy people go out to war against their
enemies by the way that thou shalt send
them, and they pray unto thee toward this
city which thou hast chosen, and the house
which I have built for thy name;
35 Then hear thou from the heavens their
prayer and their supplication, and maintain
their cause.
36 If they sin against thee, (for *there is* no
man which sinneth not,) and thou be angry
with them, and deliver them over before
their enemies, and they carry them away
captives unto a land far off or near;
37 Yet *if* they bethink themselves in the
land whither they are carried captive, and
turn and pray unto thee in the land of their
captivity, saying, We have sinned, we have
done amiss, and have dealt wickedly;
38 If they return to thee with all their heart
and with all their soul in the land of their
captivity, whither they have carried them
captives, and pray toward their land, which
thou gavest unto their fathers, and *toward*
the city which thou hast chosen, and toward
the house which I have built for thy name:
39 Then hear thou from the heavens, *even*
from thy dwelling place, their prayer and
their supplications, and maintain their
cause, and forgive thy people which have
sinned against thee.
40 Now, my God, let, I beseech thee, thine
eyes be open, and *let* thine ears *be* attent
unto the prayer *that is made* in this place.
41 Now therefore arise, O LORD God, into
thy resting place, thou, and the ark of thy
strength: let thy priests, O LORD God, be
clothed with salvation, and let thy saints
rejoice in goodness.
42 O LORD God, turn not away the face of
thine anointed: remember the mercies of
David thy servant.

2 Chronicles 7

1 Now when Solomon had made an end of
praying, the fire came down from heaven,
and consumed the burnt offering and the
sacrifices; and the glory of the LORD filled
the house.
2 And the priests could not enter into the
house of the LORD, because the glory of the
LORD had filled the LORD's house.
3 And when all the children of Israel saw
how the fire came down, and the glory

of the LORD upon the house, they bowed
themselves with their faces to the ground
upon the pavement, and worshipped, and
praised the LORD, *saying*, For *he is* good; for
his mercy *endureth* for ever.
4 ¶ Then the king and all the people offered
sacrifices before the LORD.
5 And king Solomon offered a sacrifice of
twenty and two thousand oxen, and an
hundred and twenty thousand sheep: so
the king and all the people dedicated the
house of God.
6 And the priests waited on their offices: the
Levites also with instruments of musick of
the LORD, which David the king had made to
praise the LORD, because his mercy *endureth*
for ever, when David praised by their ministry; and the priests sounded trumpets
before them, and all Israel stood.
7 Moreover Solomon hallowed the middle
of the court that *was* before the house of
the LORD: for there he offered burnt offerings, and the fat of the peace offerings,
because the brasen altar which Solomon
had made was not able to receive the
burnt offerings, and the meat offerings,
and the fat.
8 ¶ Also at the same time Solomon kept the
feast seven days, and all Israel with him, a
very great congregation, from the entering
in of Hamath unto the river of Egypt.
9 And in the eighth day they made a solemn
assembly: for they kept the dedication of the
altar seven days, and the feast seven days.
10 And on the three and twentieth day of
the seventh month he sent the people away
into their tents, glad and merry in heart for
the goodness that the LORD had shewed
unto David, and to Solomon, and to Israel
his people.
11 Thus Solomon finished the house of the
LORD, and the king's house: and all that
came into Solomon's heart to make in the
house of the LORD, and in his own house,
he prosperously effected.
12 ¶ And the LORD appeared to Solomon
by night, and said unto him, I have heard
thy prayer, and have chosen this place to
myself for an house of sacrifice.
13 If I shut up heaven that there be no
rain, or if I command the locusts to devour
the land, or if I send pestilence among my
people;
14 If my people, which are called by my
name, shall humble themselves, and pray,
and seek my face, and turn from their
wicked ways; then will I hear from heaven,
and will forgive their sin, and will heal their
land.
15 Now mine eyes shall be open, and mine
ears attent unto the prayer *that is made* in
this place.
16 For now have I chosen and sanctified
this house, that my name may be there for
ever: and mine eyes and mine heart shall
be there perpetually.
17 And as for thee, if thou wilt walk before
me, as David thy father walked, and do
according to all that I have commanded
thee, and shalt observe my statutes and
my judgments;
18 Then will I stablish the throne of thy kingdom, according as I have covenanted with
David thy father, saying, There shall not fail
thee a man *to be* ruler in Israel.
19 But if ye turn away, and forsake my statutes and my commandments, which I have
set before you, and shall go and serve other
gods, and worship them;
20 Then will I pluck them up by the roots
out of my land which I have given them;
and this house, which I have sanctified for
my name, will I cast out of my sight, and
will make it *to be* a proverb and a byword
among all nations.
21 And this house, which is high, shall be
an astonishment to every one that passeth by it; so that he shall say, Why hath the
LORD done thus unto this land, and unto
this house?
22 And it shall be answered, Because they
forsook the LORD God of their fathers, which
brought them forth out of the land of Egypt,
and laid hold on other gods, and worshipped
them, and served them: therefore hath he
brought all this evil upon them.

2 Chronicles 8

1 And it came to pass at the end of twenty
years, wherein Solomon had built the house
of the LORD, and his own house,
2 That the cities which Huram had restored
to Solomon, Solomon built them, and
caused the children of Israel to dwell there.
3 And Solomon went to Hamath-zobah, and
prevailed against it.

4 And he built Tadmor in the wilderness, and all the store cities, which he built in Hamath.
5 Also he built Beth-horon the upper, and Beth-horon the nether, fenced cities, with walls, gates, and bars;
6 And Baalath, and all the store cities that Solomon had, and all the chariot cities, and the cities of the horsemen, and all that Solomon desired to build in Jerusalem, and in Lebanon, and throughout all the land of his dominion.
7 ¶ *As for* all the people *that were* left of the Hittites, and the Amorites, and the Perizzites, and the Hivites, and the Jebusites, which *were* not of Israel,
8 *But* of their children, who were left after them in the land, whom the children of Israel consumed not, them did Solomon make to pay tribute until this day.
9 But of the children of Israel did Solomon make no servants for his work; but they *were* men of war, and chief of his captains, and captains of his chariots and horsemen.
10 And these *were* the chief of king Solomon's officers, *even* two hundred and fifty, that bare rule over the people.
11 ¶ And Solomon brought up the daughter of Pharaoh out of the city of David unto the house that he had built for her: for he said, My wife shall not dwell in the house of David king of Israel, because *the places are* holy, whereunto the ark of the LORD hath come.
12 ¶ Then Solomon offered burnt offerings unto the LORD on the altar of the LORD, which he had built before the porch,
13 Even after a certain rate every day, offering according to the commandment of Moses, on the sabbaths, and on the new moons, and on the solemn feasts, three times in the year, *even* in the feast of unleavened bread, and in the feast of weeks, and in the feast of tabernacles.
14 ¶ And he appointed, according to the order of David his father, the courses of the priests to their service, and the Levites to their charges, to praise and minister before the priests, as the duty of every day required: the porters also by their courses at every gate: for so had David the man of God commanded.
15 And they departed not from the commandment of the king unto the priests and Levites concerning any matter, or concerning the treasures.
16 Now all the work of Solomon was prepared unto the day of the foundation of the house of the LORD, and until it was finished. *So* the house of the LORD was perfected.
17 ¶ Then went Solomon to Ezion-geber, and to Eloth, at the sea side in the land of Edom.
18 And Huram sent him by the hands of his servants ships, and servants that had knowledge of the sea; and they went with the servants of Solomon to Ophir, and took thence four hundred and fifty talents of gold, and brought *them* to king Solomon.

2 Chronicles 9

1 And when the queen of Sheba heard of the fame of Solomon, she came to prove Solomon with hard questions at Jerusalem, with a very great company, and camels that bare spices, and gold in abundance, and precious stones: and when she was come to Solomon, she communed with him of all that was in her heart.
2 And Solomon told her all her questions: and there was nothing hid from Solomon which he told her not.
3 And when the queen of Sheba had seen the wisdom of Solomon, and the house that he had built,
4 And the meat of his table, and the sitting of his servants, and the attendance of his ministers, and their apparel; his cupbearers also, and their apparel; and his ascent by which he went up into the house of the LORD; there was no more spirit in her.
5 And she said to the king, *It was* a true report which I heard in mine own land of thine acts, and of thy wisdom:
6 Howbeit I believed not their words, until I came, and mine eyes had seen *it:* and, behold, the one half of the greatness of thy wisdom was not told me: *for* thou exceedest the fame that I heard.
7 Happy *are* thy men, and happy *are* these thy servants, which stand continually before thee, and hear thy wisdom.
8 Blessed be the LORD thy God, which delighted in thee to set thee on his throne, *to be* king for the LORD thy God: because thy God loved Israel, to establish them for ever,

therefore made he thee king over them, to
do judgment and justice.
9 And she gave the king an hundred and
twenty talents of gold, and of spices great
abundance, and precious stones: neither
was there any such spice as the queen of
Sheba gave king Solomon.
10 And the servants also of Huram, and
the servants of Solomon, which brought
gold from Ophir, brought algum trees and
precious stones.
11 And the king made *of* the algum trees
terraces to the house of the LORD, and to
the king's palace, and harps and psalteries
for singers: and there were none such seen
before in the land of Judah.
12 And king Solomon gave to the queen of
Sheba all her desire, whatsoever she asked,
beside *that* which she had brought unto the
king. So she turned, and went away to her
own land, she and her servants.
13 ¶ Now the weight of gold that came to
Solomon in one year was six hundred and
threescore and six talents of gold;
14 Beside *that which* chapmen and merchants brought. And all the kings of Arabia
and governors of the country brought gold
and silver to Solomon.
15 ¶ And king Solomon made two hundred
targets *of* beaten gold: six hundred *shekels*
of beaten gold went to one target.
16 And three hundred shields *made he of*
beaten gold: three hundred *shekels* of gold
went to one shield. And the king put them
in the house of the forest of Lebanon.
17 Moreover the king made a great throne
of ivory, and overlaid it with pure gold.
18 And *there were* six steps to the throne,
with a footstool of gold, *which were* fastened to the throne, and stays on each side
of the sitting place, and two lions standing
by the stays:
19 And twelve lions stood there on the one
side and on the other upon the six steps.
There was not the like made in any kingdom.
20 ¶ And all the drinking vessels of king
Solomon *were of* gold, and all the vessels of
the house of the forest of Lebanon *were of*
pure gold: none *were of* silver; it was *not* any
thing accounted of in the days of Solomon.
21 For the king's ships went to Tarshish
with the servants of Huram: every three
years once came the ships of Tarshish
bringing gold, and silver, ivory, and apes,
and peacocks.
22 And king Solomon passed all the kings of
the earth in riches and wisdom.
23 ¶ And all the kings of the earth sought the
presence of Solomon, to hear his wisdom,
that God had put in his heart.
24 And they brought every man his present,
vessels of silver, and vessels of gold, and
raiment, harness, and spices, horses, and
mules, a rate year by year.
25 ¶ And Solomon had four thousand
stalls for horses and chariots, and twelve
thousand horsemen; whom he bestowed
in the chariot cities, and with the king at
Jerusalem.
26 ¶ And he reigned over all the kings from
the river even unto the land of the Philistines, and to the border of Egypt.
27 And the king made silver in Jerusalem
as stones, and cedar trees made he as the
sycomore trees that *are* in the low plains
in abundance.
28 And they brought unto Solomon horses
out of Egypt, and out of all lands.
29 ¶ Now the rest of the acts of Solomon,
first and last, *are* they not written in the
book of Nathan the prophet, and in the
prophecy of Ahijah the Shilonite, and in the
visions of Iddo the seer against Jeroboam
the son of Nebat?
30 And Solomon reigned in Jerusalem over
all Israel forty years.
31 And Solomon slept with his fathers, and
he was buried in the city of David his father:
and Rehoboam his son reigned in his stead.

2 Chronicles 10

1 And Rehoboam went to Shechem: for
to Shechem were all Israel come to make
him king.
2 And it came to pass, when Jeroboam the
son of Nebat, who *was* in Egypt, whither
he had fled from the presence of Solomon
the king, heard *it*, that Jeroboam returned
out of Egypt.
3 And they sent and called him. So Jeroboam
and all Israel came and spake to Rehoboam,
saying,
4 Thy father made our yoke grievous: now
therefore ease thou somewhat the grievous
servitude of thy father, and his heavy yoke
that he put upon us, and we will serve thee.

5 And he said unto them, Come again
unto me after three days. And the people
departed.
6 ¶ And king Rehoboam took counsel with
the old men that had stood before Solomon his father while he yet lived, saying,
What counsel give ye *me* to return answer
to this people?
7 And they spake unto him, saying, If thou
be kind to this people, and please them, and
speak good words to them, they will be thy
servants for ever.
8 But he forsook the counsel which the old
men gave him, and took counsel with the
young men that were brought up with him,
that stood before him.
9 And he said unto them, What advice
give ye that we may return answer to this
people, which have spoken to me, saying,
Ease somewhat the yoke that thy father did
put upon us?
10 And the young men that were brought
up with him spake unto him, saying, Thus
shalt thou answer the people that spake
unto thee, saying, Thy father made our
yoke heavy, but make thou *it* somewhat
lighter for us; thus shalt thou say unto
them, My little *finger* shall be thicker than
my father's loins.
11 For whereas my father put a heavy yoke
upon you, I will put more to your yoke: my
father chastised you with whips, but I *will
chastise you* with scorpions.
12 So Jeroboam and all the people came
to Rehoboam on the third day, as the king
bade, saying, Come again to me on the
third day.
13 And the king answered them roughly;
and king Rehoboam forsook the counsel
of the old men,
14 And answered them after the advice of
the young men, saying, My father made
your yoke heavy, but I will add thereto: my
father chastised you with whips, but I *will
chastise you* with scorpions.
15 So the king hearkened not unto the people: for the cause was of God, that the LORD
might perform his word, which he spake by
the hand of Ahijah the Shilonite to Jeroboam
the son of Nebat.
16 ¶ And when all Israel *saw* that the king
would not hearken unto them, the people
answered the king, saying, What portion
have we in David? and *we have* none inheritance in the son of Jesse: every man to your
tents, O Israel: *and* now, David, see to thine
own house. So all Israel went to their tents.
17 But *as for* the children of Israel that dwelt
in the cities of Judah, Rehoboam reigned
over them.
18 Then king Rehoboam sent Hadoram that
was over the tribute; and the children of
Israel stoned him with stones, that he died.
But king Rehoboam made speed to get him
up to *his* chariot, to flee to Jerusalem.
19 And Israel rebelled against the house of
David unto this day.

2 Chronicles 11

1 And when Rehoboam was come to Jerusalem, he gathered of the house of Judah
and Benjamin an hundred and fourscore
thousand chosen *men*, which were warriors,
to fight against Israel, that he might bring
the kingdom again to Rehoboam.
2 But the word of the LORD came to Shemaiah the man of God, saying,
3 Speak unto Rehoboam the son of Solomon, king of Judah, and to all Israel in Judah
and Benjamin, saying,
4 Thus saith the LORD, Ye shall not go up,
nor fight against your brethren: return every
man to his house: for this thing is done of
me. And they obeyed the words of the LORD,
and returned from going against Jeroboam.
5 ¶ And Rehoboam dwelt in Jerusalem, and
built cities for defence in Judah.
6 He built even Beth-lehem, and Etam,
and Tekoa,
7 And Beth-zur, and Shoco, and Adullam,
8 And Gath, and Mareshah, and Ziph,
9 And Adoraim, and Lachish, and Azekah,
10 And Zorah, and Aijalon, and Hebron,
which *are* in Judah and in Benjamin fenced
cities.
11 And he fortified the strong holds, and
put captains in them, and store of victual,
and of oil and wine.
12 And in every several city *he put* shields
and spears, and made them exceeding
strong, having Judah and Benjamin on his
side.
13 ¶ And the priests and the Levites that
were in all Israel resorted to him out of all
their coasts.
14 For the Levites left their suburbs and

their possession, and came to Judah and
Jerusalem: for Jeroboam and his sons had
cast them off from executing the priest's
office unto the LORD:
15 And he ordained him priests for the high
places, and for the devils, and for the calves
which he had made.
16 And after them out of all the tribes of
Israel such as set their hearts to seek the
LORD God of Israel came to Jerusalem, to
sacrifice unto the LORD God of their fathers.
17 So they strengthened the kingdom of
Judah, and made Rehoboam the son of Solomon strong, three years: for three years they
walked in the way of David and Solomon.
18 ¶ And Rehoboam took him Mahalath
the daughter of Jerimoth the son of David
to wife, *and* Abihail the daughter of Eliab
the son of Jesse;
19 Which bare him children; Jeush, and
Shamariah, and Zaham.
20 And after her he took Maachah the
daughter of Absalom; which bare him
Abijah, and Attai, and Ziza, and Shelomith.
21 And Rehoboam loved Maachah the
daughter of Absalom above all his wives
and his concubines: (for he took eighteen
wives, and threescore concubines; and
begat twenty and eight sons, and threescore
daughters.)
22 And Rehoboam made Abijah the son of
Maachah the chief, *to be* ruler among his
brethren: for *he thought* to make him king.
23 And he dealt wisely, and dispersed of all
his children throughout all the countries of
Judah and Benjamin, unto every fenced city:
and he gave them victual in abundance. And
he desired many wives.

2 Chronicles 12

1 And it came to pass, when Rehoboam
had established the kingdom, and had
strengthened himself, he forsook the law
of the LORD, and all Israel with him.
2 And it came to pass, *that* in the fifth year
of king Rehoboam Shishak king of Egypt
came up against Jerusalem, because they
had transgressed against the LORD,
3 With twelve hundred chariots, and threescore thousand horsemen: and the people
were without number that came with him
out of Egypt; the Lubims, the Sukkiims, and
the Ethiopians.
4 And he took the fenced cities which *pertained* to Judah, and came to Jerusalem.
5 ¶ Then came Shemaiah the prophet to
Rehoboam, and *to* the princes of Judah,
that were gathered together to Jerusalem
because of Shishak, and said unto them,
Thus saith the LORD, Ye have forsaken me,
and therefore have I also left you in the
hand of Shishak.
6 Whereupon the princes of Israel and the
king humbled themselves; and they said,
The LORD *is* righteous.
7 And when the LORD saw that they humbled
themselves, the word of the LORD came to
Shemaiah, saying, They have humbled themselves; *therefore* I will not destroy them, but
I will grant them some deliverance; and my
wrath shall not be poured out upon Jerusalem by the hand of Shishak.
8 Nevertheless they shall be his servants;
that they may know my service, and the
service of the kingdoms of the countries.
9 So Shishak king of Egypt came up against
Jerusalem, and took away the treasures of
the house of the LORD, and the treasures
of the king's house; he took all: he carried
away also the shields of gold which Solomon
had made.
10 Instead of which king Rehoboam made
shields of brass, and committed *them* to the
hands of the chief of the guard, that kept
the entrance of the king's house.
11 And when the king entered into the
house of the LORD, the guard came and
fetched them, and brought them again into
the guard chamber.
12 And when he humbled himself, the
wrath of the LORD turned from him, that
he would not destroy *him* altogether: and
also in Judah things went well.
13 ¶ So king Rehoboam strengthened
himself in Jerusalem, and reigned: for
Rehoboam *was* one and forty years old
when he began to reign, and he reigned
seventeen years in Jerusalem, the city which
the LORD had chosen out of all the tribes of
Israel, to put his name there. And his mother's name *was* Naamah an Ammonitess.
14 And he did evil, because he prepared not
his heart to seek the LORD.
15 Now the acts of Rehoboam, first and last,
are they not written in the book of Shemaiah
the prophet, and of Iddo the seer concerning

genealogies? And *there were* wars between
Rehoboam and Jeroboam continually.
16 And Rehoboam slept with his fathers, and
was buried in the city of David: and Abijah
his son reigned in his stead.

2 Chronicles 13

1 Now in the eighteenth year of king
Jeroboam began Abijah to reign over Judah.
2 He reigned three years in Jerusalem.
His mother's name also *was* Michaiah the
daughter of Uriel of Gibeah. And there was
war between Abijah and Jeroboam.
3 And Abijah set the battle in array with
an army of valiant men of war, *even* four
hundred thousand chosen men: Jeroboam
also set the battle in array against him with
eight hundred thousand chosen men, *being*
mighty men of valour.
4 ¶ And Abijah stood up upon mount Zemaraim, which *is* in mount Ephraim, and said,
Hear me, thou Jeroboam, and all Israel;
5 Ought ye not to know that the LORD God
of Israel gave the kingdom over Israel to
David for ever, *even* to him and to his sons
by a covenant of salt?
6 Yet Jeroboam the son of Nebat, the servant of Solomon the son of David, is risen
up, and hath rebelled against his lord.
7 And there are gathered unto him vain men,
the children of Belial, and have strengthened themselves against Rehoboam the
son of Solomon, when Rehoboam was
young and tenderhearted, and could not
withstand them.
8 And now ye think to withstand the kingdom of the LORD in the hand of the sons of
David; and ye *be* a great multitude, and *there
are* with you golden calves, which Jeroboam
made you for gods.
9 Have ye not cast out the priests of the
LORD, the sons of Aaron, and the Levites,
and have made you priests after the manner
of the nations of *other* lands? so that whosoever cometh to consecrate himself with
a young bullock and seven rams, *the same*
may be a priest of *them that are* no gods.
10 But as for us, the LORD *is* our God, and
we have not forsaken him; and the priests,
which minister unto the LORD, *are* the sons
of Aaron, and the Levites *wait* upon *their*
business:
11 And they burn unto the LORD every
morning and every evening burnt sacrifices
and sweet incense: the shewbread also *set
they in order* upon the pure table; and the
candlestick of gold with the lamps thereof,
to burn every evening: for we keep the
charge of the LORD our God; but ye have
forsaken him.
12 And, behold, God himself *is* with us for
our captain, and his priests with sounding
trumpets to cry alarm against you. O children of Israel, fight ye not against the LORD
God of your fathers; for ye shall not prosper.
13 ¶ But Jeroboam caused an ambushment
to come about behind them: so they were
before Judah, and the ambushment *was*
behind them.
14 And when Judah looked back, behold,
the battle *was* before and behind: and
they cried unto the LORD, and the priests
sounded with the trumpets.
15 Then the men of Judah gave a shout:
and as the men of Judah shouted, it came
to pass, that God smote Jeroboam and all
Israel before Abijah and Judah.
16 And the children of Israel fled before
Judah: and God delivered them into their
hand.
17 And Abijah and his people slew them with
a great slaughter: so there fell down slain of
Israel five hundred thousand chosen men.
18 Thus the children of Israel were brought
under at that time, and the children of Judah
prevailed, because they relied upon the
LORD God of their fathers.
19 And Abijah pursued after Jeroboam,
and took cities from him, Beth-el with the
towns thereof, and Jeshanah with the towns
thereof, and Ephrain with the towns thereof.
20 Neither did Jeroboam recover strength
again in the days of Abijah: and the LORD
struck him, and he died.
21 ¶ But Abijah waxed mighty, and married
fourteen wives, and begat twenty and two
sons, and sixteen daughters.
22 And the rest of the acts of Abijah, and
his ways, and his sayings, *are* written in the
story of the prophet Iddo.

2 Chronicles 14

1 So Abijah slept with his fathers, and they
buried him in the city of David: and Asa his
son reigned in his stead. In his days the land
was quiet ten years.

2 And Asa did *that which was* good and right
in the eyes of the LORD his God:
3 For he took away the altars of the strange
gods, and the high places, and brake down
the images, and cut down the groves:
4 And commanded Judah to seek the LORD
God of their fathers, and to do the law and
the commandment.
5 Also he took away out of all the cities of
Judah the high places and the images: and
the kingdom was quiet before him.
6 ¶ And he built fenced cities in Judah: for
the land had rest, and he had no war in
those years; because the LORD had given
him rest.
7 Therefore he said unto Judah, Let us build
these cities, and make about *them* walls,
and towers, gates, and bars, *while* the land
is yet before us; because we have sought
the LORD our God, we have sought *him*, and
he hath given us rest on every side. So they
built and prospered.
8 And Asa had an army *of men* that bare targets and spears, out of Judah three hundred
thousand; and out of Benjamin, that bare
shields and drew bows, two hundred and
fourscore thousand: all these *were* mighty
men of valour.
9 ¶ And there came out against them Zerah
the Ethiopian with an host of a thousand
thousand, and three hundred chariots; and
came unto Mareshah.
10 Then Asa went out against him, and
they set the battle in array in the valley of
Zephathah at Mareshah.
11 And Asa cried unto the LORD his God, and
said, LORD, *it is* nothing with thee to help,
whether with many, or with them that have
no power: help us, O LORD our God; for we
rest on thee, and in thy name we go against
this multitude. O LORD, thou *art* our God;
let not man prevail against thee.
12 So the LORD smote the Ethiopians before
Asa, and before Judah; and the Ethiopians
fled.
13 And Asa and the people that *were* with
him pursued them unto Gerar: and the
Ethiopians were overthrown, that they
could not recover themselves; for they were
destroyed before the LORD, and before his
host; and they carried away very much spoil.
14 And they smote all the cities round about
Gerar; for the fear of the LORD came upon
them: and they spoiled all the cities; for
there was exceeding much spoil in them.
15 They smote also the tents of cattle, and
carried away sheep and camels in abundance, and returned to Jerusalem.

2 Chronicles 15

1 And the Spirit of God came upon Azariah
the son of Oded:
2 And he went out to meet Asa, and said
unto him, Hear ye me, Asa, and all Judah
and Benjamin; The LORD *is* with you, while
ye be with him; and if ye seek him, he will
be found of you; but if ye forsake him, he
will forsake you.
3 Now for a long season Israel *hath been*
without the true God, and without a teaching priest, and without law.
4 But when they in their trouble did turn
unto the LORD God of Israel, and sought
him, he was found of them.
5 And in those times *there was* no peace
to him that went out, nor to him that came
in, but great vexations *were* upon all the
inhabitants of the countries.
6 And nation was destroyed of nation, and
city of city: for God did vex them with all
adversity.
7 Be ye strong therefore, and let not your
hands be weak: for your work shall be
rewarded.
8 And when Asa heard these words, and
the prophecy of Oded the prophet, he took
courage, and put away the abominable idols
out of all the land of Judah and Benjamin,
and out of the cities which he had taken
from mount Ephraim, and renewed the
altar of the LORD, that *was* before the porch
of the LORD.
9 And he gathered all Judah and Benjamin,
and the strangers with them out of Ephraim
and Manasseh, and out of Simeon: for
they fell to him out of Israel in abundance,
when they saw that the LORD his God *was*
with him.
10 So they gathered themselves together
at Jerusalem in the third month, in the fifteenth year of the reign of Asa.
11 And they offered unto the LORD the same
time, of the spoil *which* they had brought,
seven hundred oxen and seven thousand
sheep.
12 And they entered into a covenant to seek

the LORD God of their fathers with all their heart and with all their soul;
13 That whosoever would not seek the LORD God of Israel should be put to death, whether small or great, whether man or woman.
14 And they sware unto the LORD with a loud voice, and with shouting, and with trumpets, and with cornets.
15 And all Judah rejoiced at the oath: for they had sworn with all their heart, and sought him with their whole desire; and he was found of them: and the LORD gave them rest round about.
16 ¶ And also *concerning* Maachah the mother of Asa the king, he removed her from *being* queen, because she had made an idol in a grove: and Asa cut down her idol, and stamped *it*, and burnt *it* at the brook Kidron.
17 But the high places were not taken away out of Israel: nevertheless the heart of Asa was perfect all his days.
18 ¶ And he brought into the house of God the things that his father had dedicated, and that he himself had dedicated, silver, and gold, and vessels.
19 And there was no *more* war unto the five and thirtieth year of the reign of Asa.

2 Chronicles 16

1 In the six and thirtieth year of the reign of Asa Baasha king of Israel came up against Judah, and built Ramah, to the intent that he might let none go out or come in to Asa king of Judah.
2 Then Asa brought out silver and gold out of the treasures of the house of the LORD and of the king's house, and sent to Ben-hadad king of Syria, that dwelt at Damascus, saying,
3 *There is* a league between me and thee, as *there was* between my father and thy father: behold, I have sent thee silver and gold; go, break thy league with Baasha king of Israel, that he may depart from me.
4 And Ben-hadad hearkened unto king Asa, and sent the captains of his armies against the cities of Israel; and they smote Ijon, and Dan, and Abel-maim, and all the store cities of Naphtali.
5 And it came to pass, when Baasha heard *it*, that he left off building of Ramah, and let his work cease.
6 Then Asa the king took all Judah; and they carried away the stones of Ramah, and the timber thereof, wherewith Baasha was building; and he built therewith Geba and Mizpah.
7 ¶ And at that time Hanani the seer came to Asa king of Judah, and said unto him, Because thou hast relied on the king of Syria, and not relied on the LORD thy God, therefore is the host of the king of Syria escaped out of thine hand.
8 Were not the Ethiopians and the Lubims a huge host, with very many chariots and horsemen? yet, because thou didst rely on the LORD, he delivered them into thine hand.
9 For the eyes of the LORD run to and fro throughout the whole earth, to shew himself strong in the behalf of *them* whose heart *is* perfect toward him. Herein thou hast done foolishly: therefore from henceforth thou shalt have wars.
10 Then Asa was wroth with the seer, and put him in a prison house; for *he was* in a rage with him because of this *thing*. And Asa oppressed *some* of the people the same time.
11 ¶ And, behold, the acts of Asa, first and last, lo, they *are* written in the book of the kings of Judah and Israel.
12 And Asa in the thirty and ninth year of his reign was diseased in his feet, until his disease *was* exceeding *great:* yet in his disease he sought not to the LORD, but to the physicians.
13 ¶ And Asa slept with his fathers, and died in the one and fortieth year of his reign.
14 And they buried him in his own sepulchres, which he had made for himself in the city of David, and laid him in the bed which was filled with sweet odours and divers kinds *of spices* prepared by the apothecaries' art: and they made a very great burning for him.

2 Chronicles 17

1 And Jehoshaphat his son reigned in his stead, and strengthened himself against Israel.
2 And he placed forces in all the fenced cities of Judah, and set garrisons in the land of Judah, and in the cities of Ephraim, which Asa his father had taken.
3 And the LORD was with Jehoshaphat,

because he walked in the first ways of his
father David, and sought not unto Baalim;
4 But sought to the *LORD* God of his father,
and walked in his commandments, and not
after the doings of Israel.
5 Therefore the LORD stablished the kingdom in his hand; and all Judah brought to
Jehoshaphat presents; and he had riches
and honour in abundance.
6 And his heart was lifted up in the ways of
the LORD: moreover he took away the high
places and groves out of Judah.
7 ¶ Also in the third year of his reign he
sent to his princes, *even* to Ben-hail, and
to Obadiah, and to Zechariah, and to Nethaneel, and to Michaiah, to teach in the cities
of Judah.
8 And with them *he sent* Levites, *even* Shemaiah, and Nethaniah, and Zebadiah, and
Asahel, and Shemiramoth, and Jehonathan,
and Adonijah, and Tobijah, and Tob-adon-
ijah, Levites; and with them Elishama and
Jehoram, priests.
9 And they taught in Judah, and *had* the
book of the law of the LORD with them,
and went about throughout all the cities
of Judah, and taught the people.
10 ¶ And the fear of the LORD fell upon all
the kingdoms of the lands that *were* round
about Judah, so that they made no war
against Jehoshaphat.
11 Also *some* of the Philistines brought
Jehoshaphat presents, and tribute silver;
and the Arabians brought him flocks, seven
thousand and seven hundred rams, and
seven thousand and seven hundred he
goats.
12 ¶ And Jehoshaphat waxed great exceedingly; and he built in Judah castles, and
cities of store.
13 And he had much business in the cities
of Judah: and the men of war, mighty men
of valour, *were* in Jerusalem.
14 And these *are* the numbers of them
according to the house of their fathers: Of
Judah, the captains of thousands; Adnah the
chief, and with him mighty men of valour
three hundred thousand.
15 And next to him *was* Jehohanan the
captain, and with him two hundred and
fourscore thousand.
16 And next him *was* Amasiah the son of
Zichri, who willingly offered himself unto the
LORD; and with him two hundred thousand
mighty men of valour.
17 And of Benjamin; Eliada a mighty man of
valour, and with him armed men with bow
and shield two hundred thousand.
18 And next him *was* Jehozabad, and with
him an hundred and fourscore thousand
ready prepared for the war.
19 These waited on the king, beside *those*
whom the king put in the fenced cities
throughout all Judah.

2 Chronicles 18

1 Now Jehoshaphat had riches and honour
in abundance, and joined affinity with Ahab.
2 And after *certain* years he went down to
Ahab to Samaria. And Ahab killed sheep
and oxen for him in abundance, and for the
people that *he had* with him, and persuaded
him to go up *with him* to Ramoth-gilead.
3 And Ahab king of Israel said unto
Jehoshaphat king of Judah, Wilt thou go with
me to Ramoth-gilead? And he answered
him, I *am* as thou *art*, and my people as thy
people; and *we will be* with thee in the war.
4 ¶ And Jehoshaphat said unto the king of
Israel, Inquire, I pray thee, at the word of
the LORD to day.
5 Therefore the king of Israel gathered
together of prophets four hundred men, and
said unto them, Shall we go to Ramoth-gilead to battle, or shall I forbear? And they
said, Go up; for God will deliver *it* into the
king's hand.
6 But Jehoshaphat said, *Is there* not here a
prophet of the LORD besides, that we might
inquire of him?
7 And the king of Israel said unto
Jehoshaphat, *There is* yet one man, by
whom we may inquire of the LORD: but I
hate him; for he never prophesied good unto
me, but always evil: the same *is* Micaiah the
son of Imla. And Jehoshaphat said, Let not
the king say so.
8 And the king of Israel called for one *of his*
officers, and said, Fetch quickly Micaiah the
son of Imla.
9 And the king of Israel and Jehoshaphat
king of Judah sat either of them on his
throne, clothed in *their* robes, and they sat
in a void place at the entering in of the gate
of Samaria; and all the prophets prophesied
before them.

10 And Zedekiah the son of Chenaanah had made him horns of iron, and said, Thus saith the LORD, With these thou shalt push Syria until they be consumed.
11 And all the prophets prophesied so, saying, Go up to Ramoth-gilead, and prosper: for the LORD shall deliver *it* into the hand of the king.
12 And the messenger that went to call Micaiah spake to him, saying, Behold, the words of the prophets *declare* good to the king with one assent; let thy word therefore, I pray thee, be like one of theirs, and speak thou good.
13 And Micaiah said, *As* the LORD liveth, even what my God saith, that will I speak.
14 And when he was come to the king, the king said unto him, Micaiah, shall we go to Ramoth-gilead to battle, or shall I forbear? And he said, Go ye up, and prosper, and they shall be delivered into your hand.
15 And the king said to him, How many times shall I adjure thee that thou say nothing but the truth to me in the name of the LORD?
16 Then he said, I did see all Israel scattered upon the mountains, as sheep that have no shepherd: and the LORD said, These have no master; let them return *therefore* every man to his house in peace.
17 And the king of Israel said to Jehoshaphat, Did I not tell thee *that* he would not prophesy good unto me, but evil?
18 Again he said, Therefore hear the word of the LORD; I saw the LORD sitting upon his throne, and all the host of heaven standing on his right hand and *on* his left.
19 And the LORD said, Who shall entice Ahab king of Israel, that he may go up and fall at Ramoth-gilead? And one spake saying after this manner, and another saying after that manner.
20 Then there came out a spirit, and stood before the LORD, and said, I will entice him. And the LORD said unto him, Wherewith?
21 And he said, I will go out, and be a lying spirit in the mouth of all his prophets. And *the LORD* said, Thou shalt entice *him*, and thou shalt also prevail: go out, and do *even* so.
22 Now therefore, behold, the LORD hath put a lying spirit in the mouth of these thy prophets, and the LORD hath spoken evil against thee.
23 Then Zedekiah the son of Chenaanah came near, and smote Micaiah upon the cheek, and said, Which way went the Spirit of the LORD from me to speak unto thee?
24 And Micaiah said, Behold, thou shalt see on that day when thou shalt go into an inner chamber to hide thyself.
25 Then the king of Israel said, Take ye Micaiah, and carry him back to Amon the governor of the city, and to Joash the king's son;
26 And say, Thus saith the king, Put this *fellow* in the prison, and feed him with bread of affliction and with water of affliction, until I return in peace.
27 And Micaiah said, If thou certainly return in peace, *then* hath not the LORD spoken by me. And he said, Hearken, all ye people.
28 So the king of Israel and Jehoshaphat the king of Judah went up to Ramoth-gilead.
29 And the king of Israel said unto Jehoshaphat, I will disguise myself, and will go to the battle; but put thou on thy robes. So the king of Israel disguised himself; and they went to the battle.
30 Now the king of Syria had commanded the captains of the chariots that *were* with him, saying, Fight ye not with small or great, save only with the king of Israel.
31 And it came to pass, when the captains of the chariots saw Jehoshaphat, that they said, It *is* the king of Israel. Therefore they compassed about him to fight: but Jehoshaphat cried out, and the LORD helped him; and God moved them *to depart* from him.
32 For it came to pass, that, when the captains of the chariots perceived that it was not the king of Israel, they turned back again from pursuing him.
33 And a *certain* man drew a bow at a venture, and smote the king of Israel between the joints of the harness: therefore he said to his chariot man, Turn thine hand, that thou mayest carry me out of the host; for I am wounded.
34 And the battle increased that day: howbeit the king of Israel stayed *himself* up in *his* chariot against the Syrians until the even: and about the time of the sun going down he died.

2 Chronicles 19

1 And Jehoshaphat the king of Judah
returned to his house in peace to Jerusalem.
2 And Jehu the son of Hanani the seer
went out to meet him, and said to king
Jehoshaphat, Shouldest thou help the
ungodly, and love them that hate the LORD?
therefore *is* wrath upon thee from before
the LORD.
3 Nevertheless there are good things found
in thee, in that thou hast taken away the
groves out of the land, and hast prepared
thine heart to seek God.
4 And Jehoshaphat dwelt at Jerusalem:
and he went out again through the people
from Beer-sheba to mount Ephraim, and
brought them back unto the LORD God of
their fathers.
5 ¶ And he set judges in the land throughout
all the fenced cities of Judah, city by city,
6 And said to the judges, Take heed what
ye do: for ye judge not for man, but for the
LORD, who *is* with you in the judgment.
7 Wherefore now let the fear of the LORD
be upon you; take heed and do *it:* for *there*
is no iniquity with the LORD our God, nor
respect of persons, nor taking of gifts.
8 ¶ Moreover in Jerusalem did Jehoshaphat
set of the Levites, and *of* the priests, and
of the chief of the fathers of Israel, for the
judgment of the LORD, and for controversies,
when they returned to Jerusalem.
9 And he charged them, saying, Thus shall
ye do in the fear of the LORD, faithfully, and
with a perfect heart.
10 And what cause soever shall come to you
of your brethren that dwell in their cities,
between blood and blood, between law and
commandment, statutes and judgments, ye
shall even warn them that they trespass not
against the LORD, and *so* wrath come upon
you, and upon your brethren: this do, and
ye shall not trespass.
11 And, behold, Amariah the chief priest
is over you in all matters of the LORD; and
Zebadiah the son of Ishmael, the ruler of the
house of Judah, for all the king's matters:
also the Levites *shall be* officers before you.
Deal courageously, and the LORD shall be
with the good.

2 Chronicles 20

1 It came to pass after this also, *that* the children of Moab, and the children of Ammon,
and with them *other* beside the Ammonites,
came against Jehoshaphat to battle.
2 Then there came some that told Jehosh
aphat, saying, There cometh a great multitude against thee from beyond the sea
on this side Syria; and, behold, they *be* in
Hazazon-tamar, which *is* En-gedi.
3 And Jehoshaphat feared, and set himself
to seek the LORD, and proclaimed a fast
throughout all Judah.
4 And Judah gathered themselves together,
to ask *help* of the LORD: even out of all the
cities of Judah they came to seek the LORD.
5 ¶ And Jehoshaphat stood in the congregation of Judah and Jerusalem, in the house
of the LORD, before the new court,
6 And said, O LORD God of our fathers, *art*
not thou God in heaven? and rulest *not* thou
over all the kingdoms of the heathen? and in
thine hand *is there not* power and might, so
that none is able to withstand thee?
7 *Art* not thou our God, *who* didst drive
out the inhabitants of this land before thy
people Israel, and gavest it to the seed of
Abraham thy friend for ever?
8 And they dwelt therein, and have built
thee a sanctuary therein for thy name,
saying,
9 If, *when* evil cometh upon us, *as* the sword,
judgment, or pestilence, or famine, we stand
before this house, and in thy presence, (for
thy name *is* in this house,) and cry unto
thee in our affliction, then thou wilt hear
and help.
10 And now, behold, the children of Ammon
and Moab and mount Seir, whom thou
wouldest not let Israel invade, when they
came out of the land of Egypt, but they
turned from them, and destroyed them not;
11 Behold, *I say, how* they reward us, to
come to cast us out of thy possession, which
thou hast given us to inherit.
12 O our God, wilt thou not judge them? for
we have no might against this great company that cometh against us; neither know
we what to do: but our eyes *are* upon thee.
13 And all Judah stood before the LORD,
with their little ones, their wives, and their
children.
14 ¶ Then upon Jahaziel the son of Zechariah, the son of Benaiah, the son of Jeiel,
the son of Mattaniah, a Levite of the sons

of Asaph, came the Spirit of the LORD in the
midst of the congregation;
15 And he said, Hearken ye, all Judah, and
ye inhabitants of Jerusalem, and thou king
Jehoshaphat, Thus saith the LORD unto
you, Be not afraid nor dismayed by reason
of this great multitude; for the battle *is* not
yours, but God's.
16 To morrow go ye down against them:
behold, they come up by the cliff of Ziz; and
ye shall find them at the end of the brook,
before the wilderness of Jeruel.
17 Ye shall not *need* to fight in this *battle:*
set yourselves, stand ye *still*, and see the
salvation of the LORD with you, O Judah and
Jerusalem: fear not, nor be dismayed; to
morrow go out against them: for the LORD
will be with you.
18 And Jehoshaphat bowed his head with
his face to the ground: and all Judah and
the inhabitants of Jerusalem fell before the
LORD, worshipping the LORD.
19 And the Levites, of the children of the
Kohathites, and of the children of the
Korhites, stood up to praise the LORD God
of Israel with a loud voice on high.
20 ¶ And they rose early in the morning, and
went forth into the wilderness of Tekoa: and
as they went forth, Jehoshaphat stood and
said, Hear me, O Judah, and ye inhabitants of
Jerusalem; Believe in the LORD your God, so
shall ye be established; believe his prophets,
so shall ye prosper.
21 And when he had consulted with the
people, he appointed singers unto the
LORD, and that should praise the beauty of
holiness, as they went out before the army,
and to say, Praise the LORD; for his mercy
endureth for ever.
22 ¶ And when they began to sing and to
praise, the LORD set ambushments against
the children of Ammon, Moab, and mount
Seir, which were come against Judah; and
they were smitten.
23 For the children of Ammon and Moab
stood up against the inhabitants of mount
Seir, utterly to slay and destroy *them:* and
when they had made an end of the inhabitants of Seir, every one helped to destroy
another.
24 And when Judah came toward the watch
tower in the wilderness, they looked unto
the multitude, and, behold, they *were*
dead bodies fallen to the earth, and none
escaped.
25 And when Jehoshaphat and his people
came to take away the spoil of them, they
found among them in abundance both
riches with the dead bodies, and precious
jewels, which they stripped off for themselves, more than they could carry away:
and they were three days in gathering of
the spoil, it was so much.
26 ¶ And on the fourth day they assembled
themselves in the valley of Berachah; for
there they blessed the LORD: therefore the
name of the same place was called, The
valley of Berachah, unto this day.
27 Then they returned, every man of Judah
and Jerusalem, and Jehoshaphat in the forefront of them, to go again to Jerusalem with
joy; for the LORD had made them to rejoice
over their enemies.
28 And they came to Jerusalem with psalteries and harps and trumpets unto the
house of the LORD.
29 And the fear of God was on all the kingdoms of *those* countries, when they had
heard that the LORD fought against the
enemies of Israel.
30 So the realm of Jehoshaphat was quiet:
for his God gave him rest round about.
31 ¶ And Jehoshaphat reigned over Judah:
he was thirty and five years old when he
began to reign, and he reigned twenty and
five years in Jerusalem. And his mother's
name *was* Azubah the daughter of Shilhi.
32 And he walked in the way of Asa his
father, and departed not from it, doing *that
which was* right in the sight of the LORD.
33 Howbeit the high places were not taken
away: for as yet the people had not prepared their hearts unto the God of their
fathers.
34 Now the rest of the acts of Jehoshaphat,
first and last, behold, they *are* written in
the book of Jehu the son of Hanani, who *is*
mentioned in the book of the kings of Israel.
35 ¶ And after this did Jehoshaphat king
of Judah join himself with Ahaziah king of
Israel, who did very wickedly:
36 And he joined himself with him to make
ships to go to Tarshish: and they made the
ships in Ezion-geber.
37 Then Eliezer the son of Dodavah of Mareshah prophesied against Jehoshaphat, say-

ing, Because thou hast joined thyself with
Ahaziah, the LORD hath broken thy works.
And the ships were broken, that they were
not able to go to Tarshish.

2 Chronicles 21

1 Now Jehoshaphat slept with his fathers,
and was buried with his fathers in the city
of David. And Jehoram his son reigned in
his stead.
2 And he had brethren the sons of
Jehoshaphat, Azariah, and Jehiel, and Zechariah, and Azariah, and Michael, and Shephatiah: all these *were* the sons of Jehoshaphat
king of Israel.
3 And their father gave them great gifts of
silver, and of gold, and of precious things,
with fenced cities in Judah: but the kingdom gave he to Jehoram; because he *was*
the firstborn.
4 Now when Jehoram was risen up to the
kingdom of his father, he strengthened
himself, and slew all his brethren with the
sword, and *divers* also of the princes of
Israel.
5 ¶ Jehoram *was* thirty and two years old
when he began to reign, and he reigned
eight years in Jerusalem.
6 And he walked in the way of the kings of
Israel, like as did the house of Ahab: for he
had the daughter of Ahab to wife: and he
wrought *that which was* evil in the eyes of
the LORD.
7 Howbeit the LORD would not destroy the
house of David, because of the covenant
that he had made with David, and as he
promised to give a light to him and to his
sons for ever.
8 ¶ In his days the Edomites revolted from
under the dominion of Judah, and made
themselves a king.
9 Then Jehoram went forth with his princes,
and all his chariots with him: and he rose
up by night, and smote the Edomites which
compassed him in, and the captains of the
chariots.
10 So the Edomites revolted from under
the hand of Judah unto this day. The same
time *also* did Libnah revolt from under his
hand; because he had forsaken the LORD
God of his fathers.
11 Moreover he made high places in the
mountains of Judah, and caused the inhabitants of Jerusalem to commit fornication,
and compelled Judah *thereto*.
12 ¶ And there came a writing to him from
Elijah the prophet, saying, Thus saith the
LORD God of David thy father, Because thou
hast not walked in the ways of Jehoshaphat
thy father, nor in the ways of Asa king of
Judah,
13 But hast walked in the way of the kings of
Israel, and hast made Judah and the inhabitants of Jerusalem to go a whoring, like to
the whoredoms of the house of Ahab, and
also hast slain thy brethren of thy father's
house, *which were* better than thyself:
14 Behold, with a great plague will the LORD
smite thy people, and thy children, and thy
wives, and all thy goods:
15 And thou *shalt have* great sickness by
disease of thy bowels, until thy bowels fall
out by reason of the sickness day by day.
16 ¶ Moreover the LORD stirred up against
Jehoram the spirit of the Philistines, and of
the Arabians, that *were* near the Ethiopians:
17 And they came up into Judah, and brake
into it, and carried away all the substance
that was found in the king's house, and his
sons also, and his wives; so that there was
never a son left him, save Jehoahaz, the
youngest of his sons.
18 ¶ And after all this the LORD smote him
in his bowels with an incurable disease.
19 And it came to pass, that in process of
time, after the end of two years, his bowels fell out by reason of his sickness: so he
died of sore diseases. And his people made
no burning for him, like the burning of his
fathers.
20 Thirty and two years old was he when
he began to reign, and he reigned in Jerusalem eight years, and departed without
being desired. Howbeit they buried him in
the city of David, but not in the sepulchres
of the kings.

2 Chronicles 22

1 And the inhabitants of Jerusalem made
Ahaziah his youngest son king in his stead:
for the band of men that came with the
Arabians to the camp had slain all the
eldest. So Ahaziah the son of Jehoram king
of Judah reigned.
2 Forty and two years old *was* Ahaziah when
he began to reign, and he reigned one year

in Jerusalem. His mother's name also *was*
Athaliah the daughter of Omri.
3 He also walked in the ways of the house
of Ahab: for his mother was his counseller
to do wickedly.
4 Wherefore he did evil in the sight of the
LORD like the house of Ahab: for they were
his counsellers after the death of his father
to his destruction.
5 ¶ He walked also after their counsel, and
went with Jehoram the son of Ahab king
of Israel to war against Hazael king of Syria
at Ramoth-gilead: and the Syrians smote
Joram.
6 And he returned to be healed in Jezreel
because of the wounds which were given
him at Ramah, when he fought with Hazael king of Syria. And Azariah the son of
Jehoram king of Judah went down to see
Jehoram the son of Ahab at Jezreel, because
he was sick.
7 And the destruction of Ahaziah was of God
by coming to Joram: for when he was come,
he went out with Jehoram against Jehu the
son of Nimshi, whom the LORD had anointed
to cut off the house of Ahab.
8 And it came to pass, that, when Jehu
was executing judgment upon the house
of Ahab, and found the princes of Judah,
and the sons of the brethren of Ahaziah,
that ministered to Ahaziah, he slew them.
9 And he sought Ahaziah: and they caught
him, (for he was hid in Samaria,) and brought
him to Jehu: and when they had slain him,
they buried him: Because, said they, he *is* the
son of Jehoshaphat, who sought the LORD
with all his heart. So the house of Ahaziah
had no power to keep still the kingdom.
10 ¶ But when Athaliah the mother of
Ahaziah saw that her son was dead, she
arose and destroyed all the seed royal of
the house of Judah.
11 But Jehoshabeath, the daughter of the
king, took Joash the son of Ahaziah, and
stole him from among the king's sons that
were slain, and put him and his nurse in a
bedchamber. So Jehoshabeath, the daughter
of king Jehoram, the wife of Jehoiada the
priest, (for she was the sister of Ahaziah,) hid
him from Athaliah, so that she slew him not.
12 And he was with them hid in the house
of God six years: and Athaliah reigned over
the land.

2 Chronicles 23

1 And in the seventh year Jehoiada strengthened himself, and took the captains of
hundreds, Azariah the son of Jeroham, and
Ishmael the son of Jehohanan, and Azariah
the son of Obed, and Maaseiah the son of
Adaiah, and Elishaphat the son of Zichri, into
covenant with him.
2 And they went about in Judah, and gathered the Levites out of all the cities of Judah,
and the chief of the fathers of Israel, and
they came to Jerusalem.
3 And all the congregation made a covenant with the king in the house of God.
And he said unto them, Behold, the king's
son shall reign, as the LORD hath said of the
sons of David.
4 This *is* the thing that ye shall do; A third
part of you entering on the sabbath, of the
priests and of the Levites, *shall be* porters
of the doors;
5 And a third part *shall be* at the king's
house; and a third part at the gate of the
foundation: and all the people *shall be* in
the courts of the house of the LORD.
6 But let none come into the house of the
LORD, save the priests, and they that minister of the Levites; they shall go in, for they
are holy: but all the people shall keep the
watch of the LORD.
7 And the Levites shall compass the king
round about, every man with his weapons
in his hand; and whosoever *else* cometh into
the house, he shall be put to death: but be
ye with the king when he cometh in, and
when he goeth out.
8 So the Levites and all Judah did according
to all things that Jehoiada the priest had
commanded, and took every man his men
that were to come in on the sabbath, with
them that were to go *out* on the sabbath:
for Jehoiada the priest dismissed not the
courses.
9 Moreover Jehoiada the priest delivered
to the captains of hundreds spears, and
bucklers, and shields, that *had been* king
David's, which *were* in the house of God.
10 And he set all the people, every man
having his weapon in his hand, from the
right side of the temple to the left side of the
temple, along by the altar and the temple,
by the king round about.
11 Then they brought out the king's son, and

put upon him the crown, and *gave him* the
testimony, and made him king. And Jehoiada
and his sons anointed him, and said, God
save the king.
12 ¶ Now when Athaliah heard the noise of
the people running and praising the king,
she came to the people into the house of
the LORD:
13 And she looked, and, behold, the king
stood at his pillar at the entering in, and
the princes and the trumpets by the king:
and all the people of the land rejoiced, and
sounded with trumpets, also the singers
with instruments of musick, and such as
taught to sing praise. Then Athaliah rent her
clothes, and said, Treason, Treason.
14 Then Jehoiada the priest brought out the
captains of hundreds that were set over the
host, and said unto them, Have her forth of
the ranges: and whoso followeth her, let
him be slain with the sword. For the priest
said, Slay her not in the house of the LORD.
15 So they laid hands on her; and when she
was come to the entering of the horse gate
by the king's house, they slew her there.
16 ¶ And Jehoiada made a covenant
between him, and between all the people,
and between the king, that they should be
the LORD's people.
17 Then all the people went to the house of
Baal, and brake it down, and brake his altars
and his images in pieces, and slew Mattan
the priest of Baal before the altars.
18 Also Jehoiada appointed the offices of
the house of the LORD by the hand of the
priests the Levites, whom David had distributed in the house of the LORD, to offer the
burnt offerings of the LORD, as *it is* written
in the law of Moses, with rejoicing and with
singing, *as it was ordained* by David.
19 And he set the porters at the gates of
the house of the LORD, that none *which
was* unclean in any thing should enter in.
20 And he took the captains of hundreds,
and the nobles, and the governors of the
people, and all the people of the land, and
brought down the king from the house of
the LORD: and they came through the high
gate into the king's house, and set the king
upon the throne of the kingdom.
21 And all the people of the land rejoiced:
and the city was quiet, after that they had
slain Athaliah with the sword.

2 Chronicles 24

1 Joash *was* seven years old when he began
to reign, and he reigned forty years in Jerusalem. His mother's name also *was* Zibiah
of Beer-sheba.
2 And Joash did *that which was* right in the
sight of the LORD all the days of Jehoiada
the priest.
3 And Jehoiada took for him two wives; and
he begat sons and daughters.
4 ¶ And it came to pass after this, *that* Joash
was minded to repair the house of the LORD.
5 And he gathered together the priests and
the Levites, and said to them, Go out unto
the cities of Judah, and gather of all Israel
money to repair the house of your God from
year to year, and see that ye hasten the
matter. Howbeit the Levites hastened *it* not.
6 And the king called for Jehoiada the
chief, and said unto him, Why hast thou
not required of the Levites to bring in out
of Judah and out of Jerusalem the collection, *according to the commandment* of
Moses the servant of the LORD, and of the
congregation of Israel, for the tabernacle
of witness?
7 For the sons of Athaliah, that wicked
woman, had broken up the house of God;
and also all the dedicated things of the
house of the LORD did they bestow upon
Baalim.
8 And at the king's commandment they
made a chest, and set it without at the gate
of the house of the LORD.
9 And they made a proclamation through
Judah and Jerusalem, to bring in to the LORD
the collection *that* Moses the servant of God
laid upon Israel in the wilderness.
10 And all the princes and all the people
rejoiced, and brought in, and cast into the
chest, until they had made an end.
11 Now it came to pass, that at what time
the chest was brought unto the king's office
by the hand of the Levites, and when they
saw that *there was* much money, the king's
scribe and the high priest's officer came and
emptied the chest, and took it, and carried
it to his place again. Thus they did day by
day, and gathered money in abundance.
12 And the king and Jehoiada gave it to
such as did the work of the service of the
house of the LORD, and hired masons and
carpenters to repair the house of the LORD,

and also such as wrought iron and brass to
mend the house of the LORD.
13 So the workmen wrought, and the work
was perfected by them, and they set the
house of God in his state, and strengthened it.
14 And when they had finished *it*, they
brought the rest of the money before the
king and Jehoiada, whereof were made vessels for the house of the LORD, *even* vessels
to minister, and to offer *withal*, and spoons,
and vessels of gold and silver. And they
offered burnt offerings in the house of the
LORD continually all the days of Jehoiada.
15 ¶ But Jehoiada waxed old, and was full of
days when he died; an hundred and thirty
years old *was he* when he died.
16 And they buried him in the city of David
among the kings, because he had done good
in Israel, both toward God, and toward his
house.
17 Now after the death of Jehoiada came the
princes of Judah, and made obeisance to the
king. Then the king hearkened unto them.
18 And they left the house of the LORD God
of their fathers, and served groves and idols:
and wrath came upon Judah and Jerusalem
for this their trespass.
19 Yet he sent prophets to them, to bring
them again unto the LORD; and they testified
against them: but they would not give ear.
20 And the Spirit of God came upon Zechariah the son of Jehoiada the priest, which
stood above the people, and said unto
them, Thus saith God, Why transgress ye
the commandments of the LORD, that ye
cannot prosper? because ye have forsaken
the LORD, he hath also forsaken you.
21 And they conspired against him, and
stoned him with stones at the commandment of the king in the court of the house
of the LORD.
22 Thus Joash the king remembered not
the kindness which Jehoiada his father had
done to him, but slew his son. And when
he died, he said, The LORD look upon *it*,
and require *it*.
23 ¶ And it came to pass at the end of the
year, *that* the host of Syria came up against
him: and they came to Judah and Jerusalem,
and destroyed all the princes of the people
from among the people, and sent all the
spoil of them unto the king of Damascus.
24 For the army of the Syrians came with
a small company of men, and the LORD
delivered a very great host into their hand,
because they had forsaken the LORD God
of their fathers. So they executed judgment
against Joash.
25 And when they were departed from him,
(for they left him in great diseases,) his own
servants conspired against him for the blood
of the sons of Jehoiada the priest, and slew
him on his bed, and he died: and they buried
him in the city of David, but they buried him
not in the sepulchres of the kings.
26 And these are they that conspired against
him; Zabad the son of Shimeath an Ammonitess, and Jehozabad the son of Shimrith
a Moabitess.
27 ¶ Now *concerning* his sons, and the
greatness of the burdens *laid* upon him, and
the repairing of the house of God, behold,
they *are* written in the story of the book
of the kings. And Amaziah his son reigned
in his stead.

2 Chronicles 25

1 Amaziah *was* twenty and five years old
when he began to reign, and he reigned
twenty and nine years in Jerusalem. And
his mother's name *was* Jehoaddan of Jerusalem.
2 And he did *that which was* right in the sight
of the LORD, but not with a perfect heart.
3 ¶ Now it came to pass, when the kingdom
was established to him, that he slew his
servants that had killed the king his father.
4 But he slew not their children, but *did* as
it is written in the law in the book of Moses,
where the LORD commanded, saying, The
fathers shall not die for the children, neither
shall the children die for the fathers, but
every man shall die for his own sin.
5 ¶ Moreover Amaziah gathered Judah
together, and made them captains over
thousands, and captains over hundreds,
according to the houses of *their* fathers,
throughout all Judah and Benjamin: and
he numbered them from twenty years old
and above, and found them three hundred
thousand choice *men*, *able* to go forth to
war, that could handle spear and shield.
6 He hired also an hundred thousand mighty
men of valour out of Israel for an hundred
talents of silver.

7 But there came a man of God to him, saying, O king, let not the army of Israel go with
thee; for the LORD *is* not with Israel, *to wit*,
with all the children of Ephraim.
8 But if thou wilt go, do *it*, be strong for the
battle: God shall make thee fall before the
enemy: for God hath power to help, and
to cast down.
9 And Amaziah said to the man of God, But
what shall we do for the hundred talents
which I have given to the army of Israel?
And the man of God answered, The LORD
is able to give thee much more than this.
10 Then Amaziah separated them, *to wit*, the
army that was come to him out of Ephraim,
to go home again: wherefore their anger
was greatly kindled against Judah, and they
returned home in great anger.
11 ¶ And Amaziah strengthened himself,
and led forth his people, and went to the
valley of salt, and smote of the children of
Seir ten thousand.
12 And *other* ten thousand *left* alive did the
children of Judah carry away captive, and
brought them unto the top of the rock, and
cast them down from the top of the rock,
that they all were broken in pieces.
13 ¶ But the soldiers of the army which
Amaziah sent back, that they should not
go with him to battle, fell upon the cities of
Judah, from Samaria even unto Beth-horon,
and smote three thousand of them, and
took much spoil.
14 ¶ Now it came to pass, after that Amaziah was come from the slaughter of the
Edomites, that he brought the gods of the
children of Seir, and set them up *to be* his
gods, and bowed down himself before them,
and burned incense unto them.
15 Wherefore the anger of the LORD was kindled against Amaziah, and he sent unto him
a prophet, which said unto him, Why hast
thou sought after the gods of the people,
which could not deliver their own people
out of thine hand?
16 And it came to pass, as he talked with
him, that *the king* said unto him, Art thou
made of the king's counsel? forbear; why
shouldest thou be smitten? Then the
prophet forbare, and said, I know that God
hath determined to destroy thee, because
thou hast done this, and hast not hearkened
unto my counsel.
17 ¶ Then Amaziah king of Judah took
advice, and sent to Joash, the son of Jehoahaz, the son of Jehu, king of Israel, saying,
Come, let us see one another in the face.
18 And Joash king of Israel sent to Amaziah
king of Judah, saying, The thistle that *was* in
Lebanon sent to the cedar that *was* in Lebanon, saying, Give thy daughter to my son to
wife: and there passed by a wild beast that
was in Lebanon, and trode down the thistle.
19 Thou sayest, Lo, thou hast smitten the
Edomites; and thine heart lifteth thee up to
boast: abide now at home; why shouldest
thou meddle to *thine* hurt, that thou shouldest fall, *even* thou, and Judah with thee?
20 But Amaziah would not hear; for it *came*
of God, that he might deliver them into the
hand *of their enemies*, because they sought
after the gods of Edom.
21 So Joash the king of Israel went up; and
they saw one another in the face, *both*
he and Amaziah king of Judah, at Beth-
shemesh, which *belongeth* to Judah.
22 And Judah was put to the worse before
Israel, and they fled every man to his tent.
23 And Joash the king of Israel took Amaziah
king of Judah, the son of Joash, the son of
Jehoahaz, at Beth-shemesh, and brought
him to Jerusalem, and brake down the wall
of Jerusalem from the gate of Ephraim to
the corner gate, four hundred cubits.
24 And *he took* all the gold and the silver,
and all the vessels that were found in the
house of God with Obed-edom, and the
treasures of the king's house, the hostages
also, and returned to Samaria.
25 ¶ And Amaziah the son of Joash king of
Judah lived after the death of Joash son of
Jehoahaz king of Israel fifteen years.
26 Now the rest of the acts of Amaziah, first
and last, behold, *are* they not written in the
book of the kings of Judah and Israel?
27 ¶ Now after the time that Amaziah did
turn away from following the LORD they
made a conspiracy against him in Jerusalem; and he fled to Lachish: but they sent
to Lachish after him, and slew him there.
28 And they brought him upon horses,
and buried him with his fathers in the city
of Judah.

2 Chronicles 26

1 Then all the people of Judah took Uzziah,

who *was* sixteen years old, and made him king in the room of his father Amaziah.
2 He built Eloth, and restored it to Judah, after that the king slept with his fathers.
3 Sixteen years old *was* Uzziah when he began to reign, and he reigned fifty and two years in Jerusalem. His mother's name also *was* Jecoliah of Jerusalem.
4 And he did *that which was* right in the sight of the LORD, according to all that his father Amaziah did.
5 And he sought God in the days of Zechariah, who had understanding in the visions of God: and as long as he sought the LORD, God made him to prosper.
6 And he went forth and warred against the Philistines, and brake down the wall of Gath, and the wall of Jabneh, and the wall of Ashdod, and built cities about Ashdod, and among the Philistines.
7 And God helped him against the Philistines, and against the Arabians that dwelt in Gur-baal, and the Mehunims.
8 And the Ammonites gave gifts to Uzziah: and his name spread abroad *even* to the entering in of Egypt; for he strengthened *himself* exceedingly.
9 Moreover Uzziah built towers in Jerusalem at the corner gate, and at the valley gate, and at the turning *of the wall*, and fortified them.
10 Also he built towers in the desert, and digged many wells: for he had much cattle, both in the low country, and in the plains: husbandmen *also*, and vine dressers in the mountains, and in Carmel: for he loved husbandry.
11 Moreover Uzziah had an host of fighting men, that went out to war by bands, according to the number of their account by the hand of Jeiel the scribe and Maaseiah the ruler, under the hand of Hananiah, *one* of the king's captains.
12 The whole number of the chief of the fathers of the mighty men of valour *were* two thousand and six hundred.
13 And under their hand *was* an army, three hundred thousand and seven thousand and five hundred, that made war with mighty power, to help the king against the enemy.
14 And Uzziah prepared for them throughout all the host shields, and spears, and helmets, and habergeons, and bows, and slings *to cast* stones.
15 And he made in Jerusalem engines, invented by cunning men, to be on the towers and upon the bulwarks, to shoot arrows and great stones withal. And his name spread far abroad; for he was marvellously helped, till he was strong.
16 ¶ But when he was strong, his heart was lifted up to *his* destruction: for he transgressed against the LORD his God, and went into the temple of the LORD to burn incense upon the altar of incense.
17 And Azariah the priest went in after him, and with him fourscore priests of the LORD, *that were* valiant men:
18 And they withstood Uzziah the king, and said unto him, *It appertaineth* not unto thee, Uzziah, to burn incense unto the LORD, but to the priests the sons of Aaron, that are consecrated to burn incense: go out of the sanctuary; for thou hast trespassed; neither *shall it be* for thine honour from the LORD God.
19 Then Uzziah was wroth, and *had* a censer in his hand to burn incense: and while he was wroth with the priests, the leprosy even rose up in his forehead before the priests in the house of the LORD, from beside the incense altar.
20 And Azariah the chief priest, and all the priests, looked upon him, and, behold, he *was* leprous in his forehead, and they thrust him out from thence; yea, himself hasted also to go out, because the LORD had smitten him.
21 And Uzziah the king was a leper unto the day of his death, and dwelt in a several house, *being* a leper; for he was cut off from the house of the LORD: and Jotham his son *was* over the king's house, judging the people of the land.
22 ¶ Now the rest of the acts of Uzziah, first and last, did Isaiah the prophet, the son of Amoz, write.
23 So Uzziah slept with his fathers, and they buried him with his fathers in the field of the burial which *belonged* to the kings; for they said, He *is* a leper: and Jotham his son reigned in his stead.

2 Chronicles 27

1 Jotham *was* twenty and five years old

when he began to reign, and he reigned sixteen years in Jerusalem. His mother's name
also *was* Jerushah, the daughter of Zadok.
2 And he did *that which was* right in the
sight of the LORD, according to all that his
father Uzziah did: howbeit he entered not
into the temple of the LORD. And the people
did yet corruptly.
3 He built the high gate of the house of
the LORD, and on the wall of Ophel he built
much.
4 Moreover he built cities in the mountains
of Judah, and in the forests he built castles
and towers.
5 ¶ He fought also with the king of the
Ammonites, and prevailed against them.
And the children of Ammon gave him the
same year an hundred talents of silver, and
ten thousand measures of wheat, and ten
thousand of barley. So much did the children
of Ammon pay unto him, both the second
year, and the third.
6 So Jotham became mighty, because he
prepared his ways before the LORD his God.
7 ¶ Now the rest of the acts of Jotham, and
all his wars, and his ways, lo, they *are* written
in the book of the kings of Israel and Judah.
8 He was five and twenty years old when he
began to reign, and reigned sixteen years
in Jerusalem.
9 ¶ And Jotham slept with his fathers, and
they buried him in the city of David: and
Ahaz his son reigned in his stead.

2 Chronicles 28

1 Ahaz *was* twenty years old when he began
to reign, and he reigned sixteen years in
Jerusalem: but he did not *that which was*
right in the sight of the LORD, like David
his father:
2 For he walked in the ways of the kings
of Israel, and made also molten images
for Baalim.
3 Moreover he burnt incense in the valley
of the son of Hinnom, and burnt his children in the fire, after the abominations of
the heathen whom the LORD had cast out
before the children of Israel.
4 He sacrificed also and burnt incense in
the high places, and on the hills, and under
every green tree.
5 Wherefore the LORD his God delivered him
into the hand of the king of Syria; and they
smote him, and carried away a great multitude of them captives, and brought *them* to
Damascus. And he was also delivered into
the hand of the king of Israel, who smote
him with a great slaughter.
6 ¶ For Pekah the son of Remaliah slew in
Judah an hundred and twenty thousand
in one day, *which were* all valiant men;
because they had forsaken the LORD God
of their fathers.
7 And Zichri, a mighty man of Ephraim, slew
Maaseiah the king's son, and Azrikam the
governor of the house, and Elkanah *that
was* next to the king.
8 And the children of Israel carried away
captive of their brethren two hundred
thousand, women, sons, and daughters,
and took also away much spoil from them,
and brought the spoil to Samaria.
9 But a prophet of the LORD was there,
whose name *was* Oded: and he went out
before the host that came to Samaria, and
said unto them, Behold, because the LORD
God of your fathers was wroth with Judah,
he hath delivered them into your hand, and
ye have slain them in a rage *that* reacheth
up unto heaven.
10 And now ye purpose to keep under
the children of Judah and Jerusalem for
bondmen and bondwomen unto you: *but
are there* not with you, even with you, sins
against the LORD your God?
11 Now hear me therefore, and deliver the
captives again, which ye have taken captive
of your brethren: for the fierce wrath of the
LORD *is* upon you.
12 Then certain of the heads of the children
of Ephraim, Azariah the son of Johanan,
Berechiah the son of Meshillemoth, and
Jehizkiah the son of Shallum, and Amasa
the son of Hadlai, stood up against them
that came from the war,
13 And said unto them, Ye shall not bring
in the captives hither: for whereas we have
offended against the LORD *already*, ye intend
to add *more* to our sins and to our trespass:
for our trespass is great, and *there is* fierce
wrath against Israel.
14 So the armed men left the captives and
the spoil before the princes and all the
congregation.
15 And the men which were expressed by
name rose up, and took the captives, and

with the spoil clothed all that were naked
among them, and arrayed them, and shod
them, and gave them to eat and to drink,
and anointed them, and carried all the feeble of them upon asses, and brought them
to Jericho, the city of palm trees, to their
brethren: then they returned to Samaria.
16 ¶ At that time did king Ahaz send unto
the kings of Assyria to help him.
17 For again the Edomites had come and
smitten Judah, and carried away captives.
18 The Philistines also had invaded the cities of the low country, and of the south of
Judah, and had taken Beth-shemesh, and
Ajalon, and Gederoth, and Shocho with
the villages thereof, and Timnah with the
villages thereof, Gimzo also and the villages
thereof: and they dwelt there.
19 For the LORD brought Judah low because
of Ahaz king of Israel; for he made Judah
naked, and transgressed sore against the
LORD.
20 And Tilgath-pilneser king of Assyria came
unto him, and distressed him, but strengthened him not.
21 For Ahaz took away a portion *out* of the
house of the LORD, and *out* of the house of
the king, and of the princes, and gave *it* unto
the king of Assyria: but he helped him not.
22 ¶ And in the time of his distress did he
trespass yet more against the LORD: this *is*
that king Ahaz.
23 For he sacrificed unto the gods of Damascus, which smote him: and he said, Because
the gods of the kings of Syria help them,
therefore will I sacrifice to them, that they
may help me. But they were the ruin of him,
and of all Israel.
24 And Ahaz gathered together the vessels
of the house of God, and cut in pieces the
vessels of the house of God, and shut up the
doors of the house of the LORD, and he made
him altars in every corner of Jerusalem.
25 And in every several city of Judah he
made high places to burn incense unto other
gods, and provoked to anger the LORD God
of his fathers.
26 ¶ Now the rest of his acts and of all his
ways, first and last, behold, they *are* written
in the book of the kings of Judah and Israel.
27 And Ahaz slept with his fathers, and they
buried him in the city, *even* in Jerusalem: but
they brought him not into the sepulchres
of the kings of Israel: and Hezekiah his son
reigned in his stead.

2 Chronicles 29

1 Hezekiah began to reign *when he was*
five and twenty years old, and he reigned
nine and twenty years in Jerusalem. And his
mother's name *was* Abijah, the daughter
of Zechariah.
2 And he did *that which was* right in the sight
of the LORD, according to all that David his
father had done.
3 ¶ He in the first year of his reign, in the
first month, opened the doors of the house
of the LORD, and repaired them.
4 And he brought in the priests and the
Levites, and gathered them together into
the east street,
5 And said unto them, Hear me, ye Levites,
sanctify now yourselves, and sanctify the
house of the LORD God of your fathers,
and carry forth the filthiness out of the
holy *place*.
6 For our fathers have trespassed, and done
that which was evil in the eyes of the LORD
our God, and have forsaken him, and have
turned away their faces from the habitation
of the LORD, and turned *their* backs.
7 Also they have shut up the doors of the
porch, and put out the lamps, and have not
burned incense nor offered burnt offerings
in the holy *place* unto the God of Israel.
8 Wherefore the wrath of the LORD was
upon Judah and Jerusalem, and he hath
delivered them to trouble, to astonishment,
and to hissing, as ye see with your eyes.
9 For, lo, our fathers have fallen by the
sword, and our sons and our daughters and
our wives *are* in captivity for this.
10 Now *it is* in mine heart to make a covenant with the LORD God of Israel, that his
fierce wrath may turn away from us.
11 My sons, be not now negligent: for the
LORD hath chosen you to stand before him,
to serve him, and that ye should minister
unto him, and burn incense.
12 ¶ Then the Levites arose, Mahath the
son of Amasai, and Joel the son of Azariah,
of the sons of the Kohathites: and of the
sons of Merari, Kish the son of Abdi, and
Azariah the son of Jehalelel: and of the
Gershonites; Joah the son of Zimmah, and
Eden the son of Joah:

13 And of the sons of Elizaphan; Shimri, and
Jeiel: and of the sons of Asaph; Zechariah,
and Mattaniah:
14 And of the sons of Heman; Jehiel, and
Shimei: and of the sons of Jeduthun; Shemaiah, and Uzziel.
15 And they gathered their brethren, and
sanctified themselves, and came, according
to the commandment of the king, by the
words of the LORD, to cleanse the house
of the LORD.
16 And the priests went into the inner part
of the house of the LORD, to cleanse *it*, and
brought out all the uncleanness that they
found in the temple of the LORD into the
court of the house of the LORD. And the
Levites took *it*, to carry *it* out abroad into
the brook Kidron.
17 Now they began on the first *day* of the
first month to sanctify, and on the eighth
day of the month came they to the porch
of the LORD: so they sanctified the house of
the LORD in eight days; and in the sixteenth
day of the first month they made an end.
18 Then they went in to Hezekiah the king,
and said, We have cleansed all the house
of the LORD, and the altar of burnt offering,
with all the vessels thereof, and the shewbread table, with all the vessels thereof.
19 Moreover all the vessels, which king
Ahaz in his reign did cast away in his transgression, have we prepared and sanctified,
and, behold, they *are* before the altar of
the LORD.
20 ¶ Then Hezekiah the king rose early, and
gathered the rulers of the city, and went up
to the house of the LORD.
21 And they brought seven bullocks, and
seven rams, and seven lambs, and seven
he goats, for a sin offering for the kingdom,
and for the sanctuary, and for Judah. And he
commanded the priests the sons of Aaron to
offer *them* on the altar of the LORD.
22 So they killed the bullocks, and the
priests received the blood, and sprinkled *it*
on the altar: likewise, when they had killed
the rams, they sprinkled the blood upon the
altar: they killed also the lambs, and they
sprinkled the blood upon the altar.
23 And they brought forth the he goats
for the sin offering before the king and the
congregation; and they laid their hands
upon them:
24 And the priests killed them, and they
made reconciliation with their blood upon
the altar, to make an atonement for all
Israel: for the king commanded *that* the
burnt offering and the sin offering *should
be made* for all Israel.
25 And he set the Levites in the house of
the LORD with cymbals, with psalteries, and
with harps, according to the commandment
of David, and of Gad the king's seer, and
Nathan the prophet: for *so was* the commandment of the LORD by his prophets.
26 And the Levites stood with the instruments of David, and the priests with the
trumpets.
27 And Hezekiah commanded to offer the
burnt offering upon the altar. And when the
burnt offering began, the song of the LORD
began *also* with the trumpets, and with the
instruments *ordained* by David king of Israel.
28 And all the congregation worshipped,
and the singers sang, and the trumpeters
sounded: *and* all *this continued* until the
burnt offering was finished.
29 And when they had made an end of offering, the king and all that were present with
him bowed themselves, and worshipped.
30 Moreover Hezekiah the king and the
princes commanded the Levites to sing
praise unto the LORD with the words of
David, and of Asaph the seer. And they sang
praises with gladness, and they bowed their
heads and worshipped.
31 Then Hezekiah answered and said, Now
ye have consecrated yourselves unto the
LORD, come near and bring sacrifices and
thank offerings into the house of the LORD.
And the congregation brought in sacrifices
and thank offerings; and as many as were
of a free heart burnt offerings.
32 And the number of the burnt offerings,
which the congregation brought, was threescore and ten bullocks, an hundred rams,
and two hundred lambs: all these *were* for
a burnt offering to the LORD.
33 And the consecrated things *were* six
hundred oxen and three thousand sheep.
34 But the priests were too few, so that
they could not flay all the burnt offerings:
wherefore their brethren the Levites did
help them, till the work was ended, and until
the *other* priests had sanctified themselves:

for the Levites *were* more upright in heart
to sanctify themselves than the priests.
35 And also the burnt offerings *were* in
abundance, with the fat of the peace offerings, and the drink offerings for *every* burnt
offering. So the service of the house of the
LORD was set in order.
36 And Hezekiah rejoiced, and all the people, that God had prepared the people: for
the thing was *done* suddenly.

2 Chronicles 30

1 And Hezekiah sent to all Israel and Judah,
and wrote letters also to Ephraim and
Manasseh, that they should come to the
house of the LORD at Jerusalem, to keep
the passover unto the LORD God of Israel.
2 For the king had taken counsel, and his
princes, and all the congregation in Jerusalem, to keep the passover in the second
month.
3 For they could not keep it at that time,
because the priests had not sanctified themselves sufficiently, neither had the people
gathered themselves together to Jerusalem.
4 And the thing pleased the king and all the
congregation.
5 So they established a decree to make
proclamation throughout all Israel, from
Beer-sheba even to Dan, that they should
come to keep the passover unto the LORD
God of Israel at Jerusalem: for they had
not done *it* of a long *time in such sort* as it
was written.
6 So the posts went with the letters from the
king and his princes throughout all Israel and
Judah, and according to the commandment
of the king, saying, Ye children of Israel, turn
again unto the LORD God of Abraham, Isaac,
and Israel, and he will return to the remnant
of you, that are escaped out of the hand of
the kings of Assyria.
7 And be not ye like your fathers, and like
your brethren, which trespassed against the
LORD God of their fathers, *who* therefore
gave them up to desolation, as ye see.
8 Now be ye not stiffnecked, as your fathers
were, but yield yourselves unto the LORD,
and enter into his sanctuary, which he hath
sanctified for ever: and serve the LORD your
God, that the fierceness of his wrath may
turn away from you.
9 For if ye turn again unto the LORD, your
brethren and your children *shall find* compassion before them that lead them captive,
so that they shall come again into this land:
for the LORD your God *is* gracious and merciful, and will not turn away *his* face from
you, if ye return unto him.
10 So the posts passed from city to city
through the country of Ephraim and
Manasseh even unto Zebulun: but they
laughed them to scorn, and mocked them.
11 Nevertheless divers of Asher and
Manasseh and of Zebulun humbled themselves, and came to Jerusalem.
12 Also in Judah the hand of God was to give
them one heart to do the commandment
of the king and of the princes, by the word
of the LORD.
13 ¶ And there assembled at Jerusalem
much people to keep the feast of unleavened bread in the second month, a very
great congregation.
14 And they arose and took away the altars
that *were* in Jerusalem, and all the altars for
incense took they away, and cast *them* into
the brook Kidron.
15 Then they killed the passover on the fourteenth *day* of the second month: and the
priests and the Levites were ashamed, and
sanctified themselves, and brought in the
burnt offerings into the house of the LORD.
16 And they stood in their place after their
manner, according to the law of Moses
the man of God: the priests sprinkled the
blood, *which they received* of the hand of
the Levites.
17 For *there were* many in the congregation that were not sanctified: therefore the
Levites had the charge of the killing of the
passovers for every one *that was* not clean,
to sanctify *them* unto the LORD.
18 For a multitude of the people, *even* many
of Ephraim, and Manasseh, Issachar, and
Zebulun, had not cleansed themselves, yet
did they eat the passover otherwise than it
was written. But Hezekiah prayed for them,
saying, The good LORD pardon every one
19 *That* prepareth his heart to seek God,
the LORD God of his fathers, though *he be*
not *cleansed* according to the purification
of the sanctuary.
20 And the LORD hearkened to Hezekiah,
and healed the people.
21 And the children of Israel that were

present at Jerusalem kept the feast of
unleavened bread seven days with great
gladness: and the Levites and the priests
praised the LORD day by day, *singing* with
loud instruments unto the LORD.
22 And Hezekiah spake comfortably unto all
the Levites that taught the good knowledge
of the LORD: and they did eat throughout the
feast seven days, offering peace offerings,
and making confession to the LORD God of
their fathers.
23 And the whole assembly took counsel to
keep other seven days: and they kept *other*
seven days with gladness.
24 For Hezekiah king of Judah did give to
the congregation a thousand bullocks and
seven thousand sheep; and the princes gave
to the congregation a thousand bullocks and
ten thousand sheep: and a great number of
priests sanctified themselves.
25 And all the congregation of Judah, with
the priests and the Levites, and all the congregation that came out of Israel, and the
strangers that came out of the land of Israel,
and that dwelt in Judah, rejoiced.
26 So there was great joy in Jerusalem:
for since the time of Solomon the son of
David king of Israel *there was* not the like
in Jerusalem.
27 ¶ Then the priests the Levites arose and
blessed the people: and their voice was
heard, and their prayer came *up* to his holy
dwelling place, *even* unto heaven.

2 Chronicles 31

1 Now when all this was finished, all Israel
that were present went out to the cities
of Judah, and brake the images in pieces,
and cut down the groves, and threw down
the high places and the altars out of all
Judah and Benjamin, in Ephraim also and
Manasseh, until they had utterly destroyed
them all. Then all the children of Israel
returned, every man to his possession, into
their own cities.
2 ¶ And Hezekiah appointed the courses
of the priests and the Levites after their
courses, every man according to his service,
the priests and Levites for burnt offerings
and for peace offerings, to minister, and to
give thanks, and to praise in the gates of the
tents of the LORD.
3 *He appointed* also the king's portion of his
substance for the burnt offerings, *to wit*, for
the morning and evening burnt offerings,
and the burnt offerings for the sabbaths,
and for the new moons, and for the set
feasts, as *it is* written in the law of the LORD.
4 Moreover he commanded the people that
dwelt in Jerusalem to give the portion of the
priests and the Levites, that they might be
encouraged in the law of the LORD.
5 ¶ And as soon as the commandment
came abroad, the children of Israel brought
in abundance the firstfruits of corn, wine,
and oil, and honey, and of all the increase of
the field; and the tithe of all *things* brought
they in abundantly.
6 And *concerning* the children of Israel and
Judah, that dwelt in the cities of Judah, they
also brought in the tithe of oxen and sheep,
and the tithe of holy things which were
consecrated unto the LORD their God, and
laid *them* by heaps.
7 In the third month they began to lay the
foundation of the heaps, and finished *them*
in the seventh month.
8 And when Hezekiah and the princes came
and saw the heaps, they blessed the LORD,
and his people Israel.
9 Then Hezekiah questioned with the priests
and the Levites concerning the heaps.
10 And Azariah the chief priest of the house
of Zadok answered him, and said, Since *the
people* began to bring the offerings into the
house of the LORD, we have had enough to
eat, and have left plenty: for the LORD hath
blessed his people; and that which is left *is*
this great store.
11 ¶ Then Hezekiah commanded to prepare
chambers in the house of the LORD; and they
prepared *them*,
12 And brought in the offerings and the
tithes and the dedicated *things* faithfully:
over which Cononiah the Levite *was* ruler,
and Shimei his brother *was* the next.
13 And Jehiel, and Azaziah, and Nahath,
and Asahel, and Jerimoth, and Jozabad,
and Eliel, and Ismachiah, and Mahath, and
Benaiah, *were* overseers under the hand
of Cononiah and Shimei his brother, at the
commandment of Hezekiah the king, and
Azariah the ruler of the house of God.
14 And Kore the son of Imnah the Levite, the
porter toward the east, *was* over the freewill

offerings of God, to distribute the oblations
of the LORD, and the most holy things.
15 And next him *were* Eden, and Miniamin,
and Jeshua, and Shemaiah, Amariah, and
Shecaniah, in the cities of the priests, in
their set office, to give to their brethren by
courses, as well to the great as to the small:
16 Beside their genealogy of males, from
three years old and upward, *even* unto
every one that entereth into the house of
the LORD, his daily portion for their service
in their charges according to their courses;
17 Both to the genealogy of the priests by
the house of their fathers, and the Levites
from twenty years old and upward, in their
charges by their courses;
18 And to the genealogy of all their little
ones, their wives, and their sons, and their
daughters, through all the congregation: for
in their set office they sanctified themselves
in holiness:
19 Also of the sons of Aaron the priests,
which were in the fields of the suburbs of
their cities, in every several city, the men
that were expressed by name, to give portions
to all the males among the priests, and
to all that were reckoned by genealogies
among the Levites.
20 ¶ And thus did Hezekiah throughout all
Judah, and wrought *that which was* good
and right and truth before the LORD his God.
21 And in every work that he began in the
service of the house of God, and in the law,
and in the commandments, to seek his God,
he did *it* with all his heart, and prospered.

2 Chronicles 32

1 After these things, and the establishment
thereof, Sennacherib king of Assyria came,
and entered into Judah, and encamped
against the fenced cities, and thought to
win them for himself.
2 And when Hezekiah saw that Sennacherib
was come, and that he was purposed to fight
against Jerusalem,
3 He took counsel with his princes and his
mighty men to stop the waters of the fountains
which *were* without the city: and they
did help him.
4 So there was gathered much people
together, who stopped all the fountains,
and the brook that ran through the midst
of the land, saying, Why should the kings of
Assyria come, and find much water?
5 Also he strengthened himself, and built
up all the wall that was broken, and raised
it up to the towers, and another wall without,
and repaired Millo *in* the city of David,
and made darts and shields in abundance.
6 And he set captains of war over the people,
and gathered them together to him in
the street of the gate of the city, and spake
comfortably to them, saying,
7 Be strong and courageous, be not afraid
nor dismayed for the king of Assyria, nor for
all the multitude that *is* with him: for *there
be* more with us than with him:
8 With him *is* an arm of flesh; but with us *is*
the LORD our God to help us, and to fight our
battles. And the people rested themselves
upon the words of Hezekiah king of Judah.
9 ¶ After this did Sennacherib king of Assyria
send his servants to Jerusalem, (but he
himself laid siege against Lachish, and all
his power with him,) unto Hezekiah king
of Judah, and unto all Judah that *were* at
Jerusalem, saying,
10 Thus saith Sennacherib king of Assyria,
Whereon do ye trust, that ye abide in the
siege in Jerusalem?
11 Doth not Hezekiah persuade you to give
over yourselves to die by famine and by
thirst, saying, The LORD our God shall deliver
us out of the hand of the king of Assyria?
12 Hath not the same Hezekiah taken away
his high places and his altars, and commanded
Judah and Jerusalem, saying, Ye
shall worship before one altar, and burn
incense upon it?
13 Know ye not what I and my fathers have
done unto all the people of *other* lands?
were the gods of the nations of those lands
any ways able to deliver their lands out of
mine hand?
14 Who *was there* among all the gods
of those nations that my fathers utterly
destroyed, that could deliver his people out
of mine hand, that your God should be able
to deliver you out of mine hand?
15 Now therefore let not Hezekiah deceive
you, nor persuade you on this manner,
neither yet believe him: for no god of any
nation or kingdom was able to deliver his
people out of mine hand, and out of the

hand of my fathers: how much less shall
your God deliver you out of mine hand?
16 And his servants spake yet *more* against
the LORD God, and against his servant
Hezekiah.
17 He wrote also letters to rail on the LORD
God of Israel, and to speak against him,
saying, As the gods of the nations of *other*
lands have not delivered their people out of
mine hand, so shall not the God of Hezekiah
deliver his people out of mine hand.
18 Then they cried with a loud voice in the
Jews' speech unto the people of Jerusalem
that *were* on the wall, to affright them,
and to trouble them; that they might take
the city.
19 And they spake against the God of Jerusalem, as against the gods of the people
of the earth, *which were* the work of the
hands of man.
20 And for this *cause* Hezekiah the king, and
the prophet Isaiah the son of Amoz, prayed
and cried to heaven.
21 ¶ And the LORD sent an angel, which cut
off all the mighty men of valour, and the
leaders and captains in the camp of the
king of Assyria. So he returned with shame
of face to his own land. And when he was
come into the house of his god, they that
came forth of his own bowels slew him there
with the sword.
22 Thus the LORD saved Hezekiah and the
inhabitants of Jerusalem from the hand of
Sennacherib the king of Assyria, and from
the hand of all *other*, and guided them on
every side.
23 And many brought gifts unto the LORD to
Jerusalem, and presents to Hezekiah king of
Judah: so that he was magnified in the sight
of all nations from thenceforth.
24 ¶ In those days Hezekiah was sick to
the death, and prayed unto the LORD: and
he spake unto him, and he gave him a sign.
25 But Hezekiah rendered not again according to the benefit *done* unto him; for his
heart was lifted up: therefore there was
wrath upon him, and upon Judah and
Jerusalem.
26 Notwithstanding Hezekiah humbled
himself for the pride of his heart, *both* he
and the inhabitants of Jerusalem, so that the
wrath of the LORD came not upon them in
the days of Hezekiah.
27 ¶ And Hezekiah had exceeding much
riches and honour: and he made himself
treasuries for silver, and for gold, and for
precious stones, and for spices, and for
shields, and for all manner of pleasant
jewels;
28 Storehouses also for the increase of corn,
and wine, and oil; and stalls for all manner
of beasts, and cotes for flocks.
29 Moreover he provided him cities, and
possessions of flocks and herds in abundance: for God had given him substance
very much.
30 This same Hezekiah also stopped the
upper watercourse of Gihon, and brought
it straight down to the west side of the
city of David. And Hezekiah prospered in
all his works.
31 ¶ Howbeit in *the business of* the ambassadors of the princes of Babylon, who sent
unto him to inquire of the wonder that was
done in the land, God left him, to try him,
that he might know all *that was* in his heart.
32 ¶ Now the rest of the acts of Hezekiah,
and his goodness, behold, they *are* written
in the vision of Isaiah the prophet, the son
of Amoz, *and* in the book of the kings of
Judah and Israel.
33 And Hezekiah slept with his fathers, and
they buried him in the chiefest of the sepulchres of the sons of David: and all Judah and
the inhabitants of Jerusalem did him honour
at his death. And Manasseh his son reigned
in his stead.

2 Chronicles 33

1 Manasseh *was* twelve years old when he
began to reign, and he reigned fifty and five
years in Jerusalem:
2 But did *that which was* evil in the sight
of the LORD, like unto the abominations of
the heathen, whom the LORD had cast out
before the children of Israel.
3 ¶ For he built again the high places which
Hezekiah his father had broken down, and
he reared up altars for Baalim, and made
groves, and worshipped all the host of
heaven, and served them.
4 Also he built altars in the house of the
LORD, whereof the LORD had said, In Jerusalem shall my name be for ever.
5 And he built altars for all the host of

heaven in the two courts of the house of
the LORD.
6 And he caused his children to pass through
the fire in the valley of the son of Hinnom:
also he observed times, and used enchantments, and used witchcraft, and dealt with a
familiar spirit, and with wizards: he wrought
much evil in the sight of the LORD, to provoke him to anger.
7 And he set a carved image, the idol which
he had made, in the house of God, of which
God had said to David and to Solomon his
son, In this house, and in Jerusalem, which
I have chosen before all the tribes of Israel,
will I put my name for ever:
8 Neither will I any more remove the foot
of Israel from out of the land which I have
appointed for your fathers; so that they will
take heed to do all that I have commanded
them, according to the whole law and the
statutes and the ordinances by the hand
of Moses.
9 So Manasseh made Judah and the inhabitants of Jerusalem to err, *and* to do worse
than the heathen, whom the LORD had
destroyed before the children of Israel.
10 And the LORD spake to Manasseh, and
to his people: but they would not hearken.
11 ¶ Wherefore the LORD brought upon
them the captains of the host of the king of
Assyria, which took Manasseh among the
thorns, and bound him with fetters, and
carried him to Babylon.
12 And when he was in affliction, he
besought the LORD his God, and humbled
himself greatly before the God of his fathers,
13 And prayed unto him: and he was
intreated of him, and heard his supplication, and brought him again to Jerusalem
into his kingdom. Then Manasseh knew
that the LORD he *was* God.
14 Now after this he built a wall without the
city of David, on the west side of Gihon, in
the valley, even to the entering in at the
fish gate, and compassed about Ophel, and
raised it up a very great height, and put captains of war in all the fenced cities of Judah.
15 And he took away the strange gods, and
the idol out of the house of the LORD, and
all the altars that he had built in the mount
of the house of the LORD, and in Jerusalem,
and cast *them* out of the city.
16 And he repaired the altar of the LORD,
and sacrificed thereon peace offerings and
thank offerings, and commanded Judah to
serve the LORD God of Israel.
17 Nevertheless the people did sacrifice
still in the high places, *yet* unto the LORD
their God only.
18 ¶ Now the rest of the acts of Manasseh,
and his prayer unto his God, and the words
of the seers that spake to him in the name
of the LORD God of Israel, behold, they *are*
written in the book of the kings of Israel.
19 His prayer also, and *how God* was
intreated of him, and all his sin, and his
trespass, and the places wherein he built
high places, and set up groves and graven
images, before he was humbled: behold,
they *are* written among the sayings of the
seers.
20 ¶ So Manasseh slept with his fathers,
and they buried him in his own house: and
Amon his son reigned in his stead.
21 ¶ Amon *was* two and twenty years old
when he began to reign, and reigned two
years in Jerusalem.
22 But he did *that which was* evil in the sight
of the LORD, as did Manasseh his father: for
Amon sacrificed unto all the carved images
which Manasseh his father had made, and
served them;
23 And humbled not himself before the
LORD, as Manasseh his father had humbled himself; but Amon trespassed more
and more.
24 And his servants conspired against him,
and slew him in his own house.
25 ¶ But the people of the land slew all them
that had conspired against king Amon; and
the people of the land made Josiah his son
king in his stead.

2 Chronicles 34

1 Josiah *was* eight years old when he began
to reign, and he reigned in Jerusalem one
and thirty years.
2 And he did *that which was* right in the
sight of the LORD, and walked in the ways
of David his father, and declined *neither* to
the right hand, nor to the left.
3 ¶ For in the eighth year of his reign, while
he was yet young, he began to seek after the
God of David his father: and in the twelfth
year he began to purge Judah and Jerusalem

from the high places, and the groves, and
the carved images, and the molten images.
4 And they brake down the altars of Baalim
in his presence; and the images, that *were*
on high above them, he cut down; and the
groves, and the carved images, and the molten images, he brake in pieces, and made
dust *of them*, and strowed *it* upon the graves
of them that had sacrificed unto them.
5 And he burnt the bones of the priests
upon their altars, and cleansed Judah and
Jerusalem.
6 And *so did he* in the cities of Manasseh,
and Ephraim, and Simeon, even unto Naphtali, with their mattocks round about.
7 And when he had broken down the altars
and the groves, and had beaten the graven
images into powder, and cut down all the
idols throughout all the land of Israel, he
returned to Jerusalem.
8 ¶ Now in the eighteenth year of his reign,
when he had purged the land, and the
house, he sent Shaphan the son of Azaliah,
and Maaseiah the governor of the city,
and Joah the son of Joahaz the recorder,
to repair the house of the LORD his God.
9 And when they came to Hilkiah the high
priest, they delivered the money that was
brought into the house of God, which the
Levites that kept the doors had gathered of
the hand of Manasseh and Ephraim, and of
all the remnant of Israel, and of all Judah and
Benjamin; and they returned to Jerusalem.
10 And they put *it* in the hand of the workmen that had the oversight of the house of
the LORD, and they gave it to the workmen
that wrought in the house of the LORD, to
repair and amend the house:
11 Even to the artificers and builders gave
they *it*, to buy hewn stone, and timber for
couplings, and to floor the houses which
the kings of Judah had destroyed.
12 And the men did the work faithfully:
and the overseers of them *were* Jahath and
Obadiah, the Levites, of the sons of Merari;
and Zechariah and Meshullam, of the sons
of the Kohathites, to set *it* forward; and
other of the Levites, all that could skill of
instruments of musick.
13 Also *they were* over the bearers of burdens, and *were* overseers of all that wrought
the work in any manner of service: and of
the Levites *there were* scribes, and officers,
and porters.
14 ¶ And when they brought out the money
that was brought into the house of the LORD,
Hilkiah the priest found a book of the law
of the LORD *given* by Moses.
15 And Hilkiah answered and said to
Shaphan the scribe, I have found the book
of the law in the house of the LORD. And
Hilkiah delivered the book to Shaphan.
16 And Shaphan carried the book to the
king, and brought the king word back again,
saying, All that was committed to thy servants, they do *it*.
17 And they have gathered together the
money that was found in the house of the
LORD, and have delivered it into the hand
of the overseers, and to the hand of the
workmen.
18 Then Shaphan the scribe told the king,
saying, Hilkiah the priest hath given me a
book. And Shaphan read it before the king.
19 And it came to pass, when the king had
heard the words of the law, that he rent
his clothes.
20 And the king commanded Hilkiah, and
Ahikam the son of Shaphan, and Abdon
the son of Micah, and Shaphan the scribe,
and Asaiah a servant of the king's, saying,
21 Go, inquire of the LORD for me, and for
them that are left in Israel and in Judah,
concerning the words of the book that is
found: for great *is* the wrath of the LORD that
is poured out upon us, because our fathers
have not kept the word of the LORD, to do
after all that is written in this book.
22 And Hilkiah, and *they* that the king *had
appointed*, went to Huldah the prophetess,
the wife of Shallum the son of Tikvath, the
son of Hasrah, keeper of the wardrobe; (now
she dwelt in Jerusalem in the college:) and
they spake to her to that *effect*.
23 ¶ And she answered them, Thus saith
the LORD God of Israel, Tell ye the man that
sent you to me,
24 Thus saith the LORD, Behold, I will bring
evil upon this place, and upon the inhabitants thereof, *even* all the curses that are
written in the book which they have read
before the king of Judah:
25 Because they have forsaken me, and
have burned incense unto other gods, that
they might provoke me to anger with all the

works of their hands; therefore my wrath
shall be poured out upon this place, and
shall not be quenched.
26 And as for the king of Judah, who sent
you to inquire of the LORD, so shall ye
say unto him, Thus saith the LORD God of
Israel *concerning* the words which thou
hast heard;
27 Because thine heart was tender, and thou
didst humble thyself before God, when thou
heardest his words against this place, and
against the inhabitants thereof, and hum-
bledst thyself before me, and didst rend thy
clothes, and weep before me; I have even
heard *thee* also, saith the LORD.
28 Behold, I will gather thee to thy fathers,
and thou shalt be gathered to thy grave in
peace, neither shall thine eyes see all the
evil that I will bring upon this place, and
upon the inhabitants of the same. So they
brought the king word again.
29 ¶ Then the king sent and gathered
together all the elders of Judah and Jerusalem.
30 And the king went up into the house of
the LORD, and all the men of Judah, and the
inhabitants of Jerusalem, and the priests,
and the Levites, and all the people, great
and small: and he read in their ears all the
words of the book of the covenant that was
found in the house of the LORD.
31 And the king stood in his place, and made
a covenant before the LORD, to walk after
the LORD, and to keep his commandments,
and his testimonies, and his statutes, with
all his heart, and with all his soul, to perform
the words of the covenant which are written
in this book.
32 And he caused all that were present in
Jerusalem and Benjamin to stand *to it*. And
the inhabitants of Jerusalem did according
to the covenant of God, the God of their
fathers.
33 And Josiah took away all the abominations out of all the countries that *pertained*
to the children of Israel, and made all that
were present in Israel to serve, *even* to serve
the LORD their God. *And* all his days they
departed not from following the LORD, the
God of their fathers.

2 Chronicles 35

1 Moreover Josiah kept a passover unto
the LORD in Jerusalem: and they killed the
passover on the fourteenth *day* of the first
month.
2 And he set the priests in their charges,
and encouraged them to the service of the
house of the LORD,
3 And said unto the Levites that taught all
Israel, which were holy unto the LORD, Put
the holy ark in the house which Solomon
the son of David king of Israel did build; *it*
shall not *be* a burden upon *your* shoulders:
serve now the LORD your God, and his people Israel,
4 And prepare *yourselves* by the houses of
your fathers, after your courses, according
to the writing of David king of Israel, and
according to the writing of Solomon his son.
5 And stand in the holy *place* according to
the divisions of the families of the fathers
of your brethren the people, and *after* the
division of the families of the Levites.
6 So kill the passover, and sanctify yourselves, and prepare your brethren, that *they*
may do according to the word of the LORD
by the hand of Moses.
7 And Josiah gave to the people, of the flock,
lambs and kids, all for the passover offerings,
for all that were present, to the number of
thirty thousand, and three thousand bullocks: these *were* of the king's substance.
8 And his princes gave willingly unto the
people, to the priests, and to the Levites:
Hilkiah and Zechariah and Jehiel, rulers of
the house of God, gave unto the priests
for the passover offerings two thousand
and six hundred *small cattle*, and three
hundred oxen.
9 Conaniah also, and Shemaiah and Nethaneel, his brethren, and Hashabiah and Jeiel
and Jozabad, chief of the Levites, gave unto
the Levites for passover offerings five thousand *small cattle*, and five hundred oxen.
10 So the service was prepared, and the
priests stood in their place, and the Levites
in their courses, according to the king's
commandment.
11 And they killed the passover, and the
priests sprinkled *the blood* from their hands,
and the Levites flayed *them*.
12 And they removed the burnt offerings,
that they might give according to the divisions of the families of the people, to offer

unto the LORD, as *it is* written in the book of Moses. And so *did they* with the oxen.
13 And they roasted the passover with fire according to the ordinance: but the *other* holy *offerings* sod they in pots, and in caldrons, and in pans, and divided *them* speedily among all the people.
14 And afterward they made ready for themselves, and for the priests: because the priests the sons of Aaron *were busied* in offering of burnt offerings and the fat until night; therefore the Levites prepared for themselves, and for the priests the sons of Aaron.
15 And the singers the sons of Asaph *were* in their place, according to the commandment of David, and Asaph, and Heman, and Jeduthun the king's seer; and the porters *waited* at every gate; they might not depart from their service; for their brethren the Levites prepared for them.
16 So all the service of the LORD was prepared the same day, to keep the passover, and to offer burnt offerings upon the altar of the LORD, according to the commandment of king Josiah.
17 And the children of Israel that were present kept the passover at that time, and the feast of unleavened bread seven days.
18 And there was no passover like to that kept in Israel from the days of Samuel the prophet; neither did all the kings of Israel keep such a passover as Josiah kept, and the priests, and the Levites, and all Judah and Israel that were present, and the inhabitants of Jerusalem.
19 In the eighteenth year of the reign of Josiah was this passover kept.
20 ¶ After all this, when Josiah had prepared the temple, Necho king of Egypt came up to fight against Carchemish by Euphrates: and Josiah went out against him.
21 But he sent ambassadors to him, saying, What have I to do with thee, thou king of Judah? *I come* not against thee this day, but against the house wherewith I have war: for God commanded me to make haste: forbear thee from *meddling with* God, who *is* with me, that he destroy thee not.
22 Nevertheless Josiah would not turn his face from him, but disguised himself, that he might fight with him, and hearkened not unto the words of Necho from the mouth of God, and came to fight in the valley of Megiddo.
23 And the archers shot at king Josiah; and the king said to his servants, Have me away; for I am sore wounded.
24 His servants therefore took him out of that chariot, and put him in the second chariot that he had; and they brought him to Jerusalem, and he died, and was buried in *one of* the sepulchres of his fathers. And all Judah and Jerusalem mourned for Josiah.
25 ¶ And Jeremiah lamented for Josiah: and all the singing men and the singing women spake of Josiah in their lamentations to this day, and made them an ordinance in Israel: and, behold, they *are* written in the lamentations.
26 Now the rest of the acts of Josiah, and his goodness, according to *that which was* written in the law of the LORD,
27 And his deeds, first and last, behold, they *are* written in the book of the kings of Israel and Judah.

2 Chronicles 36

1 Then the people of the land took Jehoahaz the son of Josiah, and made him king in his father's stead in Jerusalem.
2 Jehoahaz *was* twenty and three years old when he began to reign, and he reigned three months in Jerusalem.
3 And the king of Egypt put him down at Jerusalem, and condemned the land in an hundred talents of silver and a talent of gold.
4 And the king of Egypt made Eliakim his brother king over Judah and Jerusalem, and turned his name to Jehoiakim. And Necho took Jehoahaz his brother, and carried him to Egypt.
5 ¶ Jehoiakim *was* twenty and five years old when he began to reign, and he reigned eleven years in Jerusalem: and he did *that which was* evil in the sight of the LORD his God.
6 Against him came up Nebuchadnezzar king of Babylon, and bound him in fetters, to carry him to Babylon.
7 Nebuchadnezzar also carried of the vessels of the house of the LORD to Babylon, and put them in his temple at Babylon.
8 Now the rest of the acts of Jehoiakim, and his abominations which he did, and that which was found in him, behold, they

are written in the book of the kings of Israel
and Judah: and Jehoiachin his son reigned
in his stead.
9 ¶ Jehoiachin *was* eight years old when he
began to reign, and he reigned three months
and ten days in Jerusalem: and he did *that
which was* evil in the sight of the LORD.
10 And when the year was expired, king
Nebuchadnezzar sent, and brought him
to Babylon, with the goodly vessels of the
house of the LORD, and made Zedekiah his
brother king over Judah and Jerusalem.
11 ¶ Zedekiah *was* one and twenty years
old when he began to reign, and reigned
eleven years in Jerusalem.
12 And he did *that which was* evil in the sight
of the LORD his God, *and* humbled not himself before Jeremiah the prophet *speaking*
from the mouth of the LORD.
13 And he also rebelled against king Nebuchadnezzar, who had made him swear by
God: but he stiffened his neck, and hardened his heart from turning unto the LORD
God of Israel.
14 ¶ Moreover all the chief of the priests,
and the people, transgressed very much
after all the abominations of the heathen;
and polluted the house of the LORD which
he had hallowed in Jerusalem.
15 And the LORD God of their fathers sent to
them by his messengers, rising up betimes,
and sending; because he had compassion
on his people, and on his dwelling place:
16 But they mocked the messengers of God,
and despised his words, and misused his
prophets, until the wrath of the LORD arose
against his people, till *there was* no remedy.
17 Therefore he brought upon them the
king of the Chaldees, who slew their young
men with the sword in the house of their
sanctuary, and had no compassion upon
young man or maiden, old man, or him
that stooped for age: he gave *them* all into
his hand.
18 And all the vessels of the house of God,
great and small, and the treasures of the
house of the LORD, and the treasures of the
king, and of his princes; all *these* he brought
to Babylon.
19 And they burnt the house of God, and
brake down the wall of Jerusalem, and
burnt all the palaces thereof with fire, and
destroyed all the goodly vessels thereof.
20 And them that had escaped from the
sword carried he away to Babylon; where
they were servants to him and his sons until
the reign of the kingdom of Persia:
21 To fulfil the word of the LORD by the
mouth of Jeremiah, until the land had
enjoyed her sabbaths: *for* as long as she lay
desolate she kept sabbath, to fulfil threescore and ten years.
22 ¶ Now in the first year of Cyrus king of
Persia, that the word of the LORD *spoken*
by the mouth of Jeremiah might be accomplished, the LORD stirred up the spirit of
Cyrus king of Persia, that he made a proclamation throughout all his kingdom, and
put it also in writing, saying,
23 Thus saith Cyrus king of Persia, All the
kingdoms of the earth hath the LORD God of
heaven given me; and he hath charged me
to build him an house in Jerusalem, which
is in Judah. Who *is there* among you of all
his people? The LORD his God *be* with him,
and let him go up.

The Book Of

Ezra

Ezra 1

1 Now in the first year of Cyrus king of
Persia, that the word of the LORD by the
mouth of Jeremiah might be fulfilled, the
LORD stirred up the spirit of Cyrus king
of Persia, that he made a proclamation
throughout all his kingdom, and *put it* also
in writing, saying,
2 Thus saith Cyrus king of Persia, The LORD
God of heaven hath given me all the kingdoms of the earth; and he hath charged me

to build him an house at Jerusalem, which
is in Judah.
3 Who *is there* among you of all his people?
his God be with him, and let him go up to
Jerusalem, which *is* in Judah, and build the
house of the LORD God of Israel, (he *is* the
God,) which *is* in Jerusalem.
4 And whosoever remaineth in any place
where he sojourneth, let the men of his
place help him with silver, and with gold,
and with goods, and with beasts, beside
the freewill offering for the house of God
that *is* in Jerusalem.
5 ¶ Then rose up the chief of the fathers of
Judah and Benjamin, and the priests, and
the Levites, with all *them* whose spirit God
had raised, to go up to build the house of
the LORD which *is* in Jerusalem.
6 And all they that *were* about them
strengthened their hands with vessels
of silver, with gold, with goods, and with
beasts, and with precious things, beside all
that was willingly offered.
7 ¶ Also Cyrus the king brought forth the
vessels of the house of the LORD, which
Nebuchadnezzar had brought forth out of
Jerusalem, and had put them in the house
of his gods;
8 Even those did Cyrus king of Persia bring
forth by the hand of Mithredath the treasurer, and numbered them unto Sheshbazzar, the prince of Judah.
9 And this *is* the number of them: thirty
chargers of gold, a thousand chargers of
silver, nine and twenty knives,
10 Thirty basons of gold, silver basons of
a second *sort* four hundred and ten, *and*
other vessels a thousand.
11 All the vessels of gold and of silver *were*
five thousand and four hundred. All *these*
did Sheshbazzar bring up with *them of* the
captivity that were brought up from Babylon
unto Jerusalem.

Ezra 2

1 Now these *are* the children of the province that went up out of the captivity, of
those which had been carried away, whom
Nebuchadnezzar the king of Babylon had
carried away unto Babylon, and came again
unto Jerusalem and Judah, every one unto
his city;
2 Which came with Zerubbabel: Jeshua,
Nehemiah, Seraiah, Reelaiah, Mordecai,
Bilshan, Mispar, Bigvai, Rehum, Baanah. The
number of the men of the people of Israel:
3 The children of Parosh, two thousand an
hundred seventy and two.
4 The children of Shephatiah, three hundred
seventy and two.
5 The children of Arah, seven hundred seventy and five.
6 The children of Pahath-moab, of the children of Jeshua *and* Joab, two thousand eight
hundred and twelve.
7 The children of Elam, a thousand two
hundred fifty and four.
8 The children of Zattu, nine hundred forty
and five.
9 The children of Zaccai, seven hundred
and threescore.
10 The children of Bani, six hundred forty
and two.
11 The children of Bebai, six hundred twenty
and three.
12 The children of Azgad, a thousand two
hundred twenty and two.
13 The children of Adonikam, six hundred
sixty and six.
14 The children of Bigvai, two thousand
fifty and six.
15 The children of Adin, four hundred fifty
and four.
16 The children of Ater of Hezekiah, ninety
and eight.
17 The children of Bezai, three hundred
twenty and three.
18 The children of Jorah, an hundred and
twelve.
19 The children of Hashum, two hundred
twenty and three.
20 The children of Gibbar, ninety and five.
21 The children of Beth-lehem, an hundred
twenty and three.
22 The men of Netophah, fifty and six.
23 The men of Anathoth, an hundred twenty
and eight.
24 The children of Azmaveth, forty and two.
25 The children of Kirjath-arim, Chephirah,
and Beeroth, seven hundred and forty and
three.
26 The children of Ramah and Geba, six
hundred twenty and one.
27 The men of Michmas, an hundred twenty
and two.

28 The men of Beth-el and Ai, two hundred
twenty and three.
29 The children of Nebo, fifty and two.
30 The children of Magbish, an hundred
fifty and six.
31 The children of the other Elam, a thousand two hundred fifty and four.
32 The children of Harim, three hundred
and twenty.
33 The children of Lod, Hadid, and Ono,
seven hundred twenty and five.
34 The children of Jericho, three hundred
forty and five.
35 The children of Senaah, three thousand
and six hundred and thirty.
36 ¶ The priests: the children of Jedaiah, of
the house of Jeshua, nine hundred seventy
and three.
37 The children of Immer, a thousand fifty
and two.
38 The children of Pashur, a thousand two
hundred forty and seven.
39 The children of Harim, a thousand and
seventeen.
40 ¶ The Levites: the children of Jeshua
and Kadmiel, of the children of Hodaviah,
seventy and four.
41 ¶ The singers: the children of Asaph, an
hundred twenty and eight.
42 ¶ The children of the porters: the children
of Shallum, the children of Ater, the children
of Talmon, the children of Akkub, the children of Hatita, the children of Shobai, *in* all
an hundred thirty and nine.
43 ¶ The Nethinims: the children of Ziha,
the children of Hasupha, the children of
Tabbaoth,
44 The children of Keros, the children of
Siaha, the children of Padon,
45 The children of Lebanah, the children of
Hagabah, the children of Akkub,
46 The children of Hagab, the children of
Shalmai, the children of Hanan,
47 The children of Giddel, the children of
Gahar, the children of Reaiah,
48 The children of Rezin, the children of
Nekoda, the children of Gazzam,
49 The children of Uzza, the children of
Paseah, the children of Besai,
50 The children of Asnah, the children of
Mehunim, the children of Nephusim,
51 The children of Bakbuk, the children of
Hakupha, the children of Harhur,
52 The children of Bazluth, the children of
Mehida, the children of Harsha,
53 The children of Barkos, the children of
Sisera, the children of Thamah,
54 The children of Neziah, the children of
Hatipha.
55 ¶ The children of Solomon's servants: the
children of Sotai, the children of Sophereth,
the children of Peruda,
56 The children of Jaalah, the children of
Darkon, the children of Giddel,
57 The children of Shephatiah, the children of Hattil, the children of Pochereth of
Zebaim, the children of Ami.
58 All the Nethinims, and the children of
Solomon's servants, *were* three hundred
ninety and two.
59 And these *were* they which went up
from Tel-melah, Tel-harsa, Cherub, Addan,
and Immer: but they could not shew their
father's house, and their seed, whether they
were of Israel:
60 The children of Delaiah, the children of
Tobiah, the children of Nekoda, six hundred
fifty and two.
61 ¶ And of the children of the priests: the
children of Habaiah, the children of Koz,
the children of Barzillai; which took a wife
of the daughters of Barzillai the Gileadite,
and was called after their name:
62 These sought their register *among* those
that were reckoned by genealogy, but they
were not found: therefore were they, as
polluted, put from the priesthood.
63 And the Tirshatha said unto them, that
they should not eat of the most holy things,
till there stood up a priest with Urim and
with Thummim.
64 ¶ The whole congregation together *was*
forty and two thousand three hundred *and*
threescore,
65 Beside their servants and their maids,
of whom *there were* seven thousand three
hundred thirty and seven: and *there were*
among them two hundred singing men and
singing women.
66 Their horses *were* seven hundred thirty
and six; their mules, two hundred forty
and five;
67 Their camels, four hundred thirty and
five; *their* asses, six thousand seven hundred
and twenty.
68 ¶ And *some* of the chief of the fathers,

when they came to the house of the LORD
which *is* at Jerusalem, offered freely for the
house of God to set it up in his place:
69 They gave after their ability unto the
treasure of the work threescore and one
thousand drams of gold, and five thousand
pound of silver, and one hundred priests'
garments.
70 So the priests, and the Levites, and *some*
of the people, and the singers, and the porters, and the Nethinims, dwelt in their cities,
and all Israel in their cities.

Ezra 3

1 And when the seventh month was come,
and the children of Israel *were* in the cities,
the people gathered themselves together
as one man to Jerusalem.
2 Then stood up Jeshua the son of Jozadak,
and his brethren the priests, and Zerubbabel
the son of Shealtiel, and his brethren, and
builded the altar of the God of Israel, to offer
burnt offerings thereon, as *it is* written in
the law of Moses the man of God.
3 And they set the altar upon his bases; for
fear *was* upon them because of the people
of those countries: and they offered burnt
offerings thereon unto the LORD, *even* burnt
offerings morning and evening.
4 They kept also the feast of tabernacles,
as *it is* written, and *offered* the daily burnt
offerings by number, according to the custom, as the duty of every day required;
5 And afterward *offered* the continual burnt
offering, both of the new moons, and of all
the set feasts of the LORD that were consecrated, and of every one that willingly
offered a freewill offering unto the LORD.
6 From the first day of the seventh month
began they to offer burnt offerings unto the
LORD. But the foundation of the temple of
the LORD was not *yet* laid.
7 They gave money also unto the masons,
and to the carpenters; and meat, and drink,
and oil, unto them of Zidon, and to them of
Tyre, to bring cedar trees from Lebanon to
the sea of Joppa, according to the grant that
they had of Cyrus king of Persia.
8 ¶ Now in the second year of their coming
unto the house of God at Jerusalem, in the
second month, began Zerubbabel the son of
Shealtiel, and Jeshua the son of Jozadak, and
the remnant of their brethren the priests
and the Levites, and all they that were come
out of the captivity unto Jerusalem; and
appointed the Levites, from twenty years
old and upward, to set forward the work
of the house of the LORD.
9 Then stood Jeshua *with* his sons and his
brethren, Kadmiel and his sons, the sons
of Judah, together, to set forward the
workmen in the house of God: the sons of
Henadad, *with* their sons and their brethren
the Levites.
10 And when the builders laid the foundation of the temple of the LORD, they set the
priests in their apparel with trumpets, and
the Levites the sons of Asaph with cymbals,
to praise the LORD, after the ordinance of
David king of Israel.
11 And they sang together by course in
praising and giving thanks unto the LORD;
because *he is* good, for his mercy *endureth*
for ever toward Israel. And all the people
shouted with a great shout, when they
praised the LORD, because the foundation
of the house of the LORD was laid.
12 But many of the priests and Levites and
chief of the fathers, *who were* ancient men,
that had seen the first house, when the
foundation of this house was laid before
their eyes, wept with a loud voice; and many
shouted aloud for joy:
13 So that the people could not discern the
noise of the shout of joy from the noise of
the weeping of the people: for the people
shouted with a loud shout, and the noise
was heard afar off.

Ezra 4

1 Now when the adversaries of Judah and
Benjamin heard that the children of the
captivity builded the temple unto the LORD
God of Israel;
2 Then they came to Zerubbabel, and to the
chief of the fathers, and said unto them, Let
us build with you: for we seek your God, as
ye *do;* and we do sacrifice unto him since
the days of Esar-haddon king of Assur, which
brought us up hither.
3 But Zerubbabel, and Jeshua, and the rest
of the chief of the fathers of Israel, said unto
them, Ye have nothing to do with us to build
an house unto our God; but we ourselves
together will build unto the LORD God of

Israel, as king Cyrus the king of Persia hath
commanded us.
4 Then the people of the land weakened the
hands of the people of Judah, and troubled
them in building,
5 And hired counsellers against them, to
frustrate their purpose, all the days of Cyrus
king of Persia, even until the reign of Darius
king of Persia.
6 And in the reign of Ahasuerus, in the
beginning of his reign, wrote they *unto him*
an accusation against the inhabitants of
Judah and Jerusalem.
7 ¶ And in the days of Artaxerxes wrote
Bishlam, Mithredath, Tabeel, and the rest
of their companions, unto Artaxerxes king
of Persia; and the writing of the letter *was*
written in the Syrian tongue, and interpreted
in the Syrian tongue.
8 Rehum the chancellor and Shimshai the
scribe wrote a letter against Jerusalem to
Artaxerxes the king in this sort:
9 Then *wrote* Rehum the chancellor, and
Shimshai the scribe, and the rest of their
companions; the Dinaites, the Apharsath-
chites, the Tarpelites, the Apharsites, the
Archevites, the Babylonians, the Susanchites,
the Dehavites, *and* the Elamites,
10 And the rest of the nations whom the
great and noble Asnappar brought over, and
set in the cities of Samaria, and the rest *that*
are on this side the river, and at such a time.
11 ¶ This *is* the copy of the letter that they
sent unto him, *even* unto Artaxerxes the
king; Thy servants the men on this side the
river, and at such a time.
12 Be it known unto the king, that the Jews
which came up from thee to us are come
unto Jerusalem, building the rebellious
and the bad city, and have set up the walls
thereof, and joined the foundations.
13 Be it known now unto the king, that, if
this city be builded, and the walls set up
again, *then* will they not pay toll, tribute,
and custom, and *so* thou shalt endamage
the revenue of the kings.
14 Now because we have maintenance from
the king's palace, and it was not meet for us
to see the king's dishonour, therefore have
we sent and certified the king;
15 That search may be made in the book
of the records of thy fathers: so shalt thou
find in the book of the records, and know
that this city *is* a rebellious city, and hurtful
unto kings and provinces, and that they have
moved sedition within the same of old time:
for which cause was this city destroyed.
16 We certify the king that, if this city be
builded *again*, and the walls thereof set up,
by this means thou shalt have no portion on
this side the river.
17 ¶ *Then* sent the king an answer unto
Rehum the chancellor, and *to* Shimshai the
scribe, and *to* the rest of their companions
that dwell in Samaria, and *unto* the rest
beyond the river, Peace, and at such a time.
18 The letter which ye sent unto us hath
been plainly read before me.
19 And I commanded, and search hath been
made, and it is found that this city of old
time hath made insurrection against kings,
and *that* rebellion and sedition have been
made therein.
20 There have been mighty kings also over
Jerusalem, which have ruled over all *coun-*
tries beyond the river; and toll, tribute, and
custom, was paid unto them.
21 Give ye now commandment to cause
these men to cease, and that this city be
not builded, until *another* commandment
shall be given from me.
22 Take heed now that ye fail not to do
this: why should damage grow to the hurt
of the kings?
23 ¶ Now when the copy of king Artaxerxes'
letter *was* read before Rehum, and Shimshai
the scribe, and their companions, they went
up in haste to Jerusalem unto the Jews, and
made them to cease by force and power.
24 Then ceased the work of the house of
God which *is* at Jerusalem. So it ceased
unto the second year of the reign of Darius
king of Persia.

Ezra 5

1 Then the prophets, Haggai the prophet,
and Zechariah the son of Iddo, prophesied
unto the Jews that *were* in Judah and Jerusalem in the name of the God of Israel, *even*
unto them.
2 Then rose up Zerubbabel the son of Shealtiel, and Jeshua the son of Jozadak, and
began to build the house of God which *is* at
Jerusalem: and with them *were* the prophets
of God helping them.
3 ¶ At the same time came to them Tatnai,

governor on this side the river, and Shethar-boznai, and their companions, and said thus unto them, Who hath commanded you to build this house, and to make up this wall?

4 Then said we unto them after this manner, What are the names of the men that make this building?

5 But the eye of their God was upon the elders of the Jews, that they could not cause them to cease, till the matter came to Darius: and then they returned answer by letter concerning this *matter*.

6 ¶ The copy of the letter that Tatnai, governor on this side the river, and Shethar-boznai, and his companions the Apharsachites, which *were* on this side the river, sent unto Darius the king:

7 They sent a letter unto him, wherein was written thus; Unto Darius the king, all peace.

8 Be it known unto the king, that we went into the province of Judea, to the house of the great God, which is builded with great stones, and timber is laid in the walls, and this work goeth fast on, and prospereth in their hands.

9 Then asked we those elders, *and* said unto them thus, Who commanded you to build this house, and to make up these walls?

10 We asked their names also, to certify thee, that we might write the names of the men that *were* the chief of them.

11 And thus they returned us answer, saying, We are the servants of the God of heaven and earth, and build the house that was builded these many years ago, which a great king of Israel builded and set up.

12 But after that our fathers had provoked the God of heaven unto wrath, he gave them into the hand of Nebuchadnezzar the king of Babylon, the Chaldean, who destroyed this house, and carried the people away into Babylon.

13 But in the first year of Cyrus the king of Babylon *the same* king Cyrus made a decree to build this house of God.

14 And the vessels also of gold and silver of the house of God, which Nebuchadnezzar took out of the temple that *was* in Jerusalem, and brought them into the temple of Babylon, those did Cyrus the king take out of the temple of Babylon, and they were delivered unto *one*, whose name *was* Sheshbazzar, whom he had made governor;

15 And said unto him, Take these vessels, go, carry them into the temple that *is* in Jerusalem, and let the house of God be builded in his place.

16 Then came the same Sheshbazzar, *and* laid the foundation of the house of God which *is* in Jerusalem: and since that time even until now hath it been in building, and *yet* it is not finished.

17 Now therefore, if *it seem* good to the king, let there be search made in the king's treasure house, which *is* there at Babylon, whether it be *so*, that a decree was made of Cyrus the king to build this house of God at Jerusalem, and let the king send his pleasure to us concerning this matter.

Ezra 6

1 Then Darius the king made a decree, and search was made in the house of the rolls, where the treasures were laid up in Babylon.

2 And there was found at Achmetha, in the palace that *is* in the province of the Medes, a roll, and therein *was* a record thus written:

3 In the first year of Cyrus the king *the same* Cyrus the king made a decree *concerning* the house of God at Jerusalem, Let the house be builded, the place where they offered sacrifices, and let the foundations thereof be strongly laid; the height thereof threescore cubits, *and* the breadth thereof threescore cubits;

4 *With* three rows of great stones, and a row of new timber: and let the expences be given out of the king's house:

5 And also let the golden and silver vessels of the house of God, which Nebuchadnezzar took forth out of the temple which *is* at Jerusalem, and brought unto Babylon, be restored, and brought again unto the temple which *is* at Jerusalem, *every one* to his place, and place *them* in the house of God.

6 Now *therefore*, Tatnai, governor beyond the river, Shethar-boznai, and your companions the Apharsachites, which *are* beyond the river, be ye far from thence:

7 Let the work of this house of God alone; let the governor of the Jews and the elders of the Jews build this house of God in his place.

8 Moreover I make a decree what ye shall do to the elders of these Jews for the building of this house of God: that of the king's goods, *even* of the tribute beyond the river,

forthwith expences be given unto these
men, that they be not hindered.
9 And that which they have need of, both
young bullocks, and rams, and lambs, for
the burnt offerings of the God of heaven,
wheat, salt, wine, and oil, according to the
appointment of the priests which *are* at
Jerusalem, let it be given them day by day
without fail:
10 That they may offer sacrifices of sweet
savours unto the God of heaven, and pray
for the life of the king, and of his sons.
11 Also I have made a decree, that whosoever shall alter this word, let timber be
pulled down from his house, and being set
up, let him be hanged thereon; and let his
house be made a dunghill for this.
12 And the God that hath caused his name
to dwell there destroy all kings and people,
that shall put to their hand to alter *and* to
destroy this house of God which *is* at Jerusalem. I Darius have made a decree; let it
be done with speed.
13 ¶ Then Tatnai, governor on this side the
river, Shethar-boznai, and their companions,
according to that which Darius the king had
sent, so they did speedily.
14 And the elders of the Jews builded, and
they prospered through the prophesying of
Haggai the prophet and Zechariah the son
of Iddo. And they builded, and finished *it*,
according to the commandment of the God
of Israel, and according to the commandment of Cyrus, and Darius, and Artaxerxes
king of Persia.
15 And this house was finished on the third
day of the month Adar, which was in the
sixth year of the reign of Darius the king.
16 ¶ And the children of Israel, the priests,
and the Levites, and the rest of the children
of the captivity, kept the dedication of this
house of God with joy,
17 And offered at the dedication of this
house of God an hundred bullocks, two
hundred rams, four hundred lambs; and
for a sin offering for all Israel, twelve he
goats, according to the number of the
tribes of Israel.
18 And they set the priests in their divisions,
and the Levites in their courses, for the
service of God, which *is* at Jerusalem; as it
is written in the book of Moses.
19 And the children of the captivity kept
the passover upon the fourteenth *day* of
the first month.
20 For the priests and the Levites were
purified together, all of them *were* pure,
and killed the passover for all the children
of the captivity, and for their brethren the
priests, and for themselves.
21 And the children of Israel, which were
come again out of captivity, and all such as
had separated themselves unto them from
the filthiness of the heathen of the land, to
seek the LORD God of Israel, did eat,
22 And kept the feast of unleavened bread
seven days with joy: for the LORD had made
them joyful, and turned the heart of the king
of Assyria unto them, to strengthen their
hands in the work of the house of God, the
God of Israel.

Ezra 7

1 Now after these things, in the reign of
Artaxerxes king of Persia, Ezra the son
of Seraiah, the son of Azariah, the son of
Hilkiah,
2 The son of Shallum, the son of Zadok, the
son of Ahitub,
3 The son of Amariah, the son of Azariah,
the son of Meraioth,
4 The son of Zerahiah, the son of Uzzi, the
son of Bukki,
5 The son of Abishua, the son of Phinehas,
the son of Eleazar, the son of Aaron the
chief priest:
6 This Ezra went up from Babylon; and he
was a ready scribe in the law of Moses,
which the LORD God of Israel had given:
and the king granted him all his request,
according to the hand of the LORD his God
upon him.
7 And there went up *some* of the children
of Israel, and of the priests, and the Levites,
and the singers, and the porters, and the
Nethinims, unto Jerusalem, in the seventh
year of Artaxerxes the king.
8 And he came to Jerusalem in the fifth
month, which *was* in the seventh year of
the king.
9 For upon the first *day* of the first month
began he to go up from Babylon, and on
the first *day* of the fifth month came he to
Jerusalem, according to the good hand of
his God upon him.
10 For Ezra had prepared his heart to seek

the law of the LORD, and to do *it*, and to
teach in Israel statutes and judgments.
11 ¶ Now this *is* the copy of the letter that
the king Artaxerxes gave unto Ezra the
priest, the scribe, *even* a scribe of the words
of the commandments of the LORD, and of
his statutes to Israel.
12 Artaxerxes, king of kings, unto Ezra the
priest, a scribe of the law of the God of
heaven, perfect *peace*, and at such a time.
13 I make a decree, that all they of the people of Israel, and *of* his priests and Levites,
in my realm, which are minded of their own
freewill to go up to Jerusalem, go with thee.
14 Forasmuch as thou art sent of the king,
and of his seven counsellers, to inquire concerning Judah and Jerusalem, according to
the law of thy God which *is* in thine hand;
15 And to carry the silver and gold, which
the king and his counsellers have freely
offered unto the God of Israel, whose habitation *is* in Jerusalem,
16 And all the silver and gold that thou canst
find in all the province of Babylon, with the
freewill offering of the people, and of the
priests, offering willingly for the house of
their God which *is* in Jerusalem:
17 That thou mayest buy speedily with this
money bullocks, rams, lambs, with their
meat offerings and their drink offerings, and
offer them upon the altar of the house of
your God which *is* in Jerusalem.
18 And whatsoever shall seem good to thee,
and to thy brethren, to do with the rest of
the silver and the gold, that do after the
will of your God.
19 The vessels also that are given thee for
the service of the house of thy God, *those*
deliver thou before the God of Jerusalem.
20 And whatsoever more shall be needful
for the house of thy God, which thou shalt
have occasion to bestow, bestow *it* out of
the king's treasure house.
21 And I, *even* I Artaxerxes the king, do
make a decree to all the treasurers which
are beyond the river, that whatsoever Ezra
the priest, the scribe of the law of the God
of heaven, shall require of you, it be done
speedily,
22 Unto an hundred talents of silver, and to
an hundred measures of wheat, and to an
hundred baths of wine, and to an hundred
baths of oil, and salt without prescribing
how much.
23 Whatsoever is commanded by the God
of heaven, let it be diligently done for the
house of the God of heaven: for why should
there be wrath against the realm of the king
and his sons?
24 Also we certify you, that touching any
of the priests and Levites, singers, porters,
Nethinims, or ministers of this house of God,
it shall not be lawful to impose toll, tribute,
or custom, upon them.
25 And thou, Ezra, after the wisdom of thy
God, that *is* in thine hand, set magistrates
and judges, which may judge all the people
that *are* beyond the river, all such as know
the laws of thy God; and teach ye them that
know *them* not.
26 And whosoever will not do the law of thy
God, and the law of the king, let judgment
be executed speedily upon him, whether
it be unto death, or to banishment, or to
confiscation of goods, or to imprisonment.
27 ¶ Blessed *be* the LORD God of our fathers,
which hath put *such a thing* as this in the
king's heart, to beautify the house of the
LORD which *is* in Jerusalem:
28 And hath extended mercy unto me
before the king, and his counsellers, and
before all the king's mighty princes. And I
was strengthened as the hand of the LORD
my God *was* upon me, and I gathered
together out of Israel chief men to go up
with me.

Ezra 8

1 These *are* now the chief of their fathers,
and *this is* the genealogy of them that went
up with me from Babylon, in the reign of
Artaxerxes the king.
2 Of the sons of Phinehas; Gershom: of
the sons of Ithamar; Daniel: of the sons of
David; Hattush.
3 Of the sons of Shechaniah, of the sons
of Pharosh; Zechariah: and with him were
reckoned by genealogy of the males an
hundred and fifty.
4 Of the sons of Pahath-moab; Elihoenai
the son of Zerahiah, and with him two
hundred males.
5 Of the sons of Shechaniah; the son of
Jahaziel, and with him three hundred males.

6 Of the sons also of Adin; Ebed the son of
Jonathan, and with him fifty males.
7 And of the sons of Elam; Jeshaiah the son
of Athaliah, and with him seventy males.
8 And of the sons of Shephatiah; Zebadiah
the son of Michael, and with him fourscore
males.
9 Of the sons of Joab; Obadiah the son
of Jehiel, and with him two hundred and
eighteen males.
10 And of the sons of Shelomith; the son
of Josiphiah, and with him an hundred and
threescore males.
11 And of the sons of Bebai; Zechariah the
son of Bebai, and with him twenty and
eight males.
12 And of the sons of Azgad; Johanan the
son of Hakkatan, and with him an hundred
and ten males.
13 And of the last sons of Adonikam, whose
names *are* these, Eliphelet, Jeiel, and Shemaiah, and with them threescore males.
14 Of the sons also of Bigvai; Uthai, and
Zabbud, and with them seventy males.
15 ¶ And I gathered them together to the
river that runneth to Ahava; and there
abode we in tents three days: and I viewed
the people, and the priests, and found there
none of the sons of Levi.
16 Then sent I for Eliezer, for Ariel, for
Shemaiah, and for Elnathan, and for Jarib,
and for Elnathan, and for Nathan, and for
Zechariah, and for Meshullam, chief men;
also for Joiarib, and for Elnathan, men of
understanding.
17 And I sent them with commandment
unto Iddo the chief at the place Casiphia,
and I told them what they should say unto
Iddo, *and* to his brethren the Nethinims, at
the place Casiphia, that they should bring
unto us ministers for the house of our God.
18 And by the good hand of our God upon
us they brought us a man of understanding,
of the sons of Mahli, the son of Levi, the son
of Israel; and Sherebiah, with his sons and
his brethren, eighteen;
19 And Hashabiah, and with him Jeshaiah
of the sons of Merari, his brethren and their
sons, twenty;
20 Also of the Nethinims, whom David and
the princes had appointed for the service of
the Levites, two hundred and twenty Nethinims: all of them were expressed by name.
21 ¶ Then I proclaimed a fast there, at the
river of Ahava, that we might afflict ourselves before our God, to seek of him a right
way for us, and for our little ones, and for
all our substance.
22 For I was ashamed to require of the king
a band of soldiers and horsemen to help
us against the enemy in the way: because
we had spoken unto the king, saying, The
hand of our God *is* upon all them for good
that seek him; but his power and his wrath
is against all them that forsake him.
23 So we fasted and besought our God for
this: and he was intreated of us.
24 ¶ Then I separated twelve of the chief of
the priests, Sherebiah, Hashabiah, and ten
of their brethren with them,
25 And weighed unto them the silver, and
the gold, and the vessels, *even* the offering
of the house of our God, which the king, and
his counsellers, and his lords, and all Israel
there present, had offered:
26 I even weighed unto their hand six hundred and fifty talents of silver, and silver
vessels an hundred talents, *and* of gold an
hundred talents;
27 Also twenty basons of gold, of a thousand drams; and two vessels of fine copper,
precious as gold.
28 And I said unto them, Ye *are* holy unto
the LORD; the vessels *are* holy also; and the
silver and the gold *are* a freewill offering
unto the LORD God of your fathers.
29 Watch ye, and keep *them*, until ye weigh
them before the chief of the priests and the
Levites, and chief of the fathers of Israel, at
Jerusalem, in the chambers of the house
of the LORD.
30 So took the priests and the Levites the
weight of the silver, and the gold, and the
vessels, to bring *them* to Jerusalem unto
the house of our God.
31 ¶ Then we departed from the river of
Ahava on the twelfth *day* of the first month,
to go unto Jerusalem: and the hand of our
God was upon us, and he delivered us from
the hand of the enemy, and of such as lay
in wait by the way.
32 And we came to Jerusalem, and abode
there three days.
33 ¶ Now on the fourth day was the silver
and the gold and the vessels weighed in the
house of our God by the hand of Meremoth

the son of Uriah the priest; and with him *was* Eleazar the son of Phinehas; and with them *was* Jozabad the son of Jeshua, and Noadiah the son of Binnui, Levites;
34 By number *and* by weight of every one: and all the weight was written at that time.
35 *Also* the children of those that had been carried away, which were come out of the captivity, offered burnt offerings unto the God of Israel, twelve bullocks for all Israel, ninety and six rams, seventy and seven lambs, twelve he goats *for* a sin offering: all *this was* a burnt offering unto the LORD.
36 ¶ And they delivered the king's commissions unto the king's lieutenants, and to the governors on this side the river: and they furthered the people, and the house of God.

Ezra 9

1 Now when these things were done, the princes came to me, saying, The people of Israel, and the priests, and the Levites, have not separated themselves from the people of the lands, *doing* according to their abominations, *even* of the Canaanites, the Hittites, the Perizzites, the Jebusites, the Ammonites, the Moabites, the Egyptians, and the Amorites.
2 For they have taken of their daughters for themselves, and for their sons: so that the holy seed have mingled themselves with the people of *those* lands: yea, the hand of the princes and rulers hath been chief in this trespass.
3 And when I heard this thing, I rent my garment and my mantle, and plucked off the hair of my head and of my beard, and sat down astonied.
4 Then were assembled unto me every one that trembled at the words of the God of Israel, because of the transgression of those that had been carried away; and I sat astonied until the evening sacrifice.
5 ¶ And at the evening sacrifice I arose up from my heaviness; and having rent my garment and my mantle, I fell upon my knees, and spread out my hands unto the LORD my God,
6 And said, O my God, I am ashamed and blush to lift up my face to thee, my God: for our iniquities are increased over *our* head, and our trespass is grown up unto the heavens.
7 Since the days of our fathers *have* we *been* in a great trespass unto this day; and for our iniquities have we, our kings, *and* our priests, been delivered into the hand of the kings of the lands, to the sword, to captivity, and to a spoil, and to confusion of face, as *it is* this day.
8 And now for a little space grace hath been *shewed* from the LORD our God, to leave us a remnant to escape, and to give us a nail in his holy place, that our God may lighten our eyes, and give us a little reviving in our bondage.
9 For we *were* bondmen; yet our God hath not forsaken us in our bondage, but hath extended mercy unto us in the sight of the kings of Persia, to give us a reviving, to set up the house of our God, and to repair the desolations thereof, and to give us a wall in Judah and in Jerusalem.
10 And now, O our God, what shall we say after this? for we have forsaken thy commandments,
11 Which thou hast commanded by thy servants the prophets, saying, The land, unto which ye go to possess it, is an unclean land with the filthiness of the people of the lands, with their abominations, which have filled it from one end to another with their uncleanness.
12 Now therefore give not your daughters unto their sons, neither take their daughters unto your sons, nor seek their peace or their wealth for ever: that ye may be strong, and eat the good of the land, and leave *it* for an inheritance to your children for ever.
13 And after all that is come upon us for our evil deeds, and for our great trespass, seeing that thou our God hast punished us less than our iniquities *deserve*, and hast given us *such* deliverance as this;
14 Should we again break thy commandments, and join in affinity with the people of these abominations? wouldest not thou be angry with us till thou hadst consumed *us*, so that *there should be* no remnant nor escaping?
15 O LORD God of Israel, thou *art* righteous: for we remain yet escaped, as *it is* this day: behold, we *are* before thee in our trespasses: for we cannot stand before thee because of this.

Ezra 10

1 Now when Ezra had prayed, and when
he had confessed, weeping and casting
himself down before the house of God,
there assembled unto him out of Israel a
very great congregation of men and women
and children: for the people wept very sore.
2 And Shechaniah the son of Jehiel, *one* of
the sons of Elam, answered and said unto
Ezra, We have trespassed against our God,
and have taken strange wives of the people
of the land: yet now there is hope in Israel
concerning this thing.
3 Now therefore let us make a covenant
with our God to put away all the wives, and
such as are born of them, according to the
counsel of my lord, and of those that tremble at the commandment of our God; and
let it be done according to the law.
4 Arise; for *this* matter *belongeth* unto thee:
we also *will be* with thee: be of good courage, and do *it*.
5 Then arose Ezra, and made the chief
priests, the Levites, and all Israel, to swear
that they should do according to this word.
And they sware.
6 ¶ Then Ezra rose up from before the
house of God, and went into the chamber
of Johanan the son of Eliashib: and *when*
he came thither, he did eat no bread, nor
drink water: for he mourned because of
the transgression of them that had been
carried away.
7 And they made proclamation throughout
Judah and Jerusalem unto all the children
of the captivity, that they should gather
themselves together unto Jerusalem;
8 And that whosoever would not come
within three days, according to the counsel of the princes and the elders, all his
substance should be forfeited, and himself
separated from the congregation of those
that had been carried away.
9 ¶ Then all the men of Judah and Benjamin gathered themselves together unto
Jerusalem within three days. It *was* the
ninth month, on the twentieth *day* of the
month; and all the people sat in the street
of the house of God, trembling because of
this matter, and for the great rain.
10 And Ezra the priest stood up, and said
unto them, Ye have transgressed, and have
taken strange wives, to increase the trespass of Israel.
11 Now therefore make confession unto the
LORD God of your fathers, and do his pleasure: and separate yourselves from the people of the land, and from the strange wives.
12 Then all the congregation answered and
said with a loud voice, As thou hast said, so
must we do.
13 But the people *are* many, and *it is* a time
of much rain, and we are not able to stand
without, neither *is this* a work of one day or
two: for we are many that have transgressed
in this thing.
14 Let now our rulers of all the congregation stand, and let all them which have
taken strange wives in our cities come at
appointed times, and with them the elders
of every city, and the judges thereof, until
the fierce wrath of our God for this matter
be turned from us.
15 ¶ Only Jonathan the son of Asahel and
Jahaziah the son of Tikvah were employed
about this *matter:* and Meshullam and Shabbethai the Levite helped them.
16 And the children of the captivity did so.
And Ezra the priest, *with* certain chief of the
fathers, after the house of their fathers, and
all of them by *their* names, were separated,
and sat down in the first day of the tenth
month to examine the matter.
17 And they made an end with all the men
that had taken strange wives by the first
day of the first month.
18 ¶ And among the sons of the priests
there were found that had taken strange
wives: *namely*, of the sons of Jeshua the son
of Jozadak, and his brethren; Maaseiah, and
Eliezer, and Jarib, and Gedaliah.
19 And they gave their hands that they
would put away their wives; and *being*
guilty, *they offered* a ram of the flock for
their trespass.
20 And of the sons of Immer; Hanani, and
Zebadiah.
21 And of the sons of Harim; Maaseiah, and
Elijah, and Shemaiah, and Jehiel, and Uzziah.
22 And of the sons of Pashur; Elioenai,
Maaseiah, Ishmael, Nethaneel, Jozabad,
and Elasah.
23 Also of the Levites; Jozabad, and Shimei,
and Kelaiah, (the same *is* Kelita,) Pethahiah,
Judah, and Eliezer.

24 Of the singers also; Eliashib: and of the porters; Shallum, and Telem, and Uri.

25 Moreover of Israel: of the sons of Parosh; Ramiah, and Jeziah, and Malchiah, and Miamin, and Eleazar, and Malchijah, and Benaiah.

26 And of the sons of Elam; Mattaniah, Zechariah, and Jehiel, and Abdi, and Jeremoth, and Eliah.

27 And of the sons of Zattu; Elioenai, Eliashib, Mattaniah, and Jeremoth, and Zabad, and Aziza.

28 Of the sons also of Bebai; Jehohanan, Hananiah, Zabbai, *and* Athlai.

29 And of the sons of Bani; Meshullam, Malluch, and Adaiah, Jashub, and Sheal, and Ramoth.

30 And of the sons of Pahath-moab; Adna, and Chelal, Benaiah, Maaseiah, Mattaniah, Bezaleel, and Binnui, and Manasseh.

31 And *of* the sons of Harim; Eliezer, Ishijah, Malchiah, Shemaiah, Shimeon,

32 Benjamin, Malluch, *and* Shemariah.

33 Of the sons of Hashum; Mattenai, Mattathah, Zabad, Eliphelet, Jeremai, Manasseh, *and* Shimei.

34 Of the sons of Bani; Maadai, Amram, and Uel,

35 Benaiah, Bedeiah, Chelluh,

36 Vaniah, Meremoth, Eliashib,

37 Mattaniah, Mattenai, and Jaasau,

38 And Bani, and Binnui, Shimei,

39 And Shelemiah, and Nathan, and Adaiah,

40 Machnadebai, Shashai, Sharai,

41 Azareel, and Shelemiah, Shemariah,

42 Shallum, Amariah, *and* Joseph.

43 Of the sons of Nebo; Jeiel, Mattithiah, Zabad, Zebina, Jadau, and Joel, Benaiah.

44 All these had taken strange wives: and *some* of them had wives by whom they had children.

The Book Of

Nehemiah

Nehemiah 1

1 The words of Nehemiah the son of Hachaliah. And it came to pass in the month Chisleu, in the twentieth year, as I was in Shushan the palace,

2 That Hanani, one of my brethren, came, he and *certain* men of Judah; and I asked them concerning the Jews that had escaped, which were left of the captivity, and concerning Jerusalem.

3 And they said unto me, The remnant that are left of the captivity there in the province *are* in great affliction and reproach: the wall of Jerusalem also *is* broken down, and the gates thereof are burned with fire.

4 ¶ And it came to pass, when I heard these words, that I sat down and wept, and mourned *certain* days, and fasted, and prayed before the God of heaven,

5 And said, I beseech thee, O LORD God of heaven, the great and terrible God, that keepeth covenant and mercy for them that love him and observe his commandments:

6 Let thine ear now be attentive, and thine eyes open, that thou mayest hear the prayer of thy servant, which I pray before thee now, day and night, for the children of Israel thy servants, and confess the sins of the children of Israel, which we have sinned against thee: both I and my father's house have sinned.

7 We have dealt very corruptly against thee, and have not kept the commandments, nor the statutes, nor the judgments, which thou commandedst thy servant Moses.

8 Remember, I beseech thee, the word that thou commandedst thy servant Moses, saying, *If* ye transgress, I will scatter you abroad among the nations:

9 But *if* ye turn unto me, and keep my commandments, and do them; though there were of you cast out unto the uttermost part of the heaven, *yet* will I gather them from thence, and will bring them unto the place that I have chosen to set my name there.

10 Now these *are* thy servants and thy peo-

ple, whom thou hast redeemed by thy great
power, and by thy strong hand.
11 O Lord, I beseech thee, let now thine ear
be attentive to the prayer of thy servant, and
to the prayer of thy servants, who desire
to fear thy name: and prosper, I pray thee,
thy servant this day, and grant him mercy
in the sight of this man. For I was the king's
cupbearer.

Nehemiah 2

1 And it came to pass in the month Nisan, in
the twentieth year of Artaxerxes the king,
that wine *was* before him: and I took up the
wine, and gave *it* unto the king. Now I had
not been *beforetime* sad in his presence.
2 Wherefore the king said unto me, Why *is*
thy countenance sad, seeing thou *art* not
sick? this *is* nothing *else* but sorrow of heart.
Then I was very sore afraid,
3 And said unto the king, Let the king live
for ever: why should not my countenance
be sad, when the city, the place of my
fathers' sepulchres, *lieth* waste, and the
gates thereof are consumed with fire?
4 Then the king said unto me, For what dost
thou make request? So I prayed to the God
of heaven.
5 And I said unto the king, If it please the
king, and if thy servant have found favour
in thy sight, that thou wouldest send me
unto Judah, unto the city of my fathers'
sepulchres, that I may build it.
6 And the king said unto me, (the queen
also sitting by him,) For how long shall thy
journey be? and when wilt thou return? So
it pleased the king to send me; and I set
him a time.
7 Moreover I said unto the king, If it please
the king, let letters be given me to the governors beyond the river, that they may convey
me over till I come into Judah;
8 And a letter unto Asaph the keeper of the
king's forest, that he may give me timber
to make beams for the gates of the palace
which *appertained* to the house, and for the
wall of the city, and for the house that I shall
enter into. And the king granted me, according to the good hand of my God upon me.
9 ¶ Then I came to the governors beyond
the river, and gave them the king's letters.
Now the king had sent captains of the army
and horsemen with me.
10 When Sanballat the Horonite, and Tobiah
the servant, the Ammonite, heard *of it*, it
grieved them exceedingly that there was
come a man to seek the welfare of the
children of Israel.
11 So I came to Jerusalem, and was there
three days.
12 ¶ And I arose in the night, I and some
few men with me; neither told I *any* man
what my God had put in my heart to do at
Jerusalem: neither *was there any* beast with
me, save the beast that I rode upon.
13 And I went out by night by the gate of
the valley, even before the dragon well, and
to the dung port, and viewed the walls of
Jerusalem, which were broken down, and
the gates thereof were consumed with fire.
14 Then I went on to the gate of the fountain, and to the king's pool: but *there was*
no place for the beast *that was* under me
to pass.
15 Then went I up in the night by the brook,
and viewed the wall, and turned back, and
entered by the gate of the valley, and *so*
returned.
16 And the rulers knew not whither I went,
or what I did; neither had I as yet told *it*
to the Jews, nor to the priests, nor to the
nobles, nor to the rulers, nor to the rest
that did the work.
17 ¶ Then said I unto them, Ye see the distress that we *are* in, how Jerusalem *lieth*
waste, and the gates thereof are burned
with fire: come, and let us build up the
wall of Jerusalem, that we be no more a
reproach.
18 Then I told them of the hand of my God
which was good upon me; as also the king's
words that he had spoken unto me. And
they said, Let us rise up and build. So they
strengthened their hands for *this* good *work*.
19 But when Sanballat the Horonite, and
Tobiah the servant, the Ammonite, and
Geshem the Arabian, heard *it*, they laughed
us to scorn, and despised us, and said, What
is this thing that ye do? will ye rebel against
the king?
20 Then answered I them, and said unto
them, The God of heaven, he will prosper
us; therefore we his servants will arise and
build: but ye have no portion, nor right, nor
memorial, in Jerusalem.

Nehemiah 3

1 Then Eliashib the high priest rose up with his brethren the priests, and they builded the sheep gate; they sanctified it, and set up the doors of it; even unto the tower of Meah they sanctified it, unto the tower of Hananeel.

2 And next unto him builded the men of Jericho. And next to them builded Zaccur the son of Imri.

3 But the fish gate did the sons of Hassenaah build, who *also* laid the beams thereof, and set up the doors thereof, the locks thereof, and the bars thereof.

4 And next unto them repaired Meremoth the son of Urijah, the son of Koz. And next unto them repaired Meshullam the son of Berechiah, the son of Meshezabeel. And next unto them repaired Zadok the son of Baana.

5 And next unto them the Tekoites repaired; but their nobles put not their necks to the work of their Lord.

6 Moreover the old gate repaired Jehoiada the son of Paseah, and Meshullam the son of Besodeiah; they laid the beams thereof, and set up the doors thereof, and the locks thereof, and the bars thereof.

7 And next unto them repaired Melatiah the Gibeonite, and Jadon the Meronothite, the men of Gibeon, and of Mizpah, unto the throne of the governor on this side the river.

8 Next unto him repaired Uzziel the son of Harhaiah, of the goldsmiths. Next unto him also repaired Hananiah the son of *one of* the apothecaries, and they fortified Jerusalem unto the broad wall.

9 And next unto them repaired Rephaiah the son of Hur, the ruler of the half part of Jerusalem.

10 And next unto them repaired Jedaiah the son of Harumaph, even over against his house. And next unto him repaired Hattush the son of Hashabniah.

11 Malchijah the son of Harim, and Hashub the son of Pahath-moab, repaired the other piece, and the tower of the furnaces.

12 And next unto him repaired Shallum the son of Halohesh, the ruler of the half part of Jerusalem, he and his daughters.

13 The valley gate repaired Hanun, and the inhabitants of Zanoah; they built it, and set up the doors thereof, the locks thereof, and the bars thereof, and a thousand cubits on the wall unto the dung gate.

14 But the dung gate repaired Malchiah the son of Rechab, the ruler of part of Beth-haccerem; he built it, and set up the doors thereof, the locks thereof, and the bars thereof.

15 But the gate of the fountain repaired Shallun the son of Col-hozeh, the ruler of part of Mizpah; he built it, and covered it, and set up the doors thereof, the locks thereof, and the bars thereof, and the wall of the pool of Siloah by the king's garden, and unto the stairs that go down from the city of David.

16 After him repaired Nehemiah the son of Azbuk, the ruler of the half part of Beth-zur, unto *the place* over against the sepulchres of David, and to the pool that was made, and unto the house of the mighty.

17 After him repaired the Levites, Rehum the son of Bani. Next unto him repaired Hashabiah, the ruler of the half part of Keilah, in his part.

18 After him repaired their brethren, Bavai the son of Henadad, the ruler of the half part of Keilah.

19 And next to him repaired Ezer the son of Jeshua, the ruler of Mizpah, another piece over against the going up to the armoury at the turning *of the wall*.

20 After him Baruch the son of Zabbai earnestly repaired the other piece, from the turning *of the wall* unto the door of the house of Eliashib the high priest.

21 After him repaired Meremoth the son of Urijah the son of Koz another piece, from the door of the house of Eliashib even to the end of the house of Eliashib.

22 And after him repaired the priests, the men of the plain.

23 After him repaired Benjamin and Hashub over against their house. After him repaired Azariah the son of Maaseiah the son of Ananiah by his house.

24 After him repaired Binnui the son of Henadad another piece, from the house of Azariah unto the turning *of the wall*, even unto the corner.

25 Palal the son of Uzai, over against the turning *of the wall*, and the tower which lieth out from the king's high house, that

was by the court of the prison. After him
Pedaiah the son of Parosh.
26 Moreover the Nethinims dwelt in Ophel,
unto *the place* over against the water gate
toward the east, and the tower that lieth
out.
27 After them the Tekoites repaired another
piece, over against the great tower that lieth
out, even unto the wall of Ophel.
28 From above the horse gate repaired the
priests, every one over against his house.
29 After them repaired Zadok the son of
Immer over against his house. After him
repaired also Shemaiah the son of Shechaniah, the keeper of the east gate.
30 After him repaired Hananiah the son
of Shelemiah, and Hanun the sixth son of
Zalaph, another piece. After him repaired
Meshullam the son of Berechiah over
against his chamber.
31 After him repaired Malchiah the goldsmith's son unto the place of the Nethinims,
and of the merchants, over against the gate
Miphkad, and to the going up of the corner.
32 And between the going up of the corner
unto the sheep gate repaired the goldsmiths
and the merchants.

Nehemiah 4

1 But it came to pass, that when Sanballat
heard that we builded the wall, he was
wroth, and took great indignation, and
mocked the Jews.
2 And he spake before his brethren and the
army of Samaria, and said, What do these
feeble Jews? will they fortify themselves?
will they sacrifice? will they make an end
in a day? will they revive the stones out of
the heaps of the rubbish which are burned?
3 Now Tobiah the Ammonite *was* by him,
and he said, Even that which they build, if
a fox go up, he shall even break down their
stone wall.
4 Hear, O our God; for we are despised:
and turn their reproach upon their own
head, and give them for a prey in the land
of captivity:
5 And cover not their iniquity, and let not
their sin be blotted out from before thee:
for they have provoked *thee* to anger before
the builders.
6 So built we the wall; and all the wall was
joined together unto the half thereof: for
the people had a mind to work.
7 ¶ But it came to pass, *that* when Sanballat, and Tobiah, and the Arabians, and the
Ammonites, and the Ashdodites, heard that
the walls of Jerusalem were made up, *and*
that the breaches began to be stopped, then
they were very wroth,
8 And conspired all of them together to
come *and* to fight against Jerusalem, and
to hinder it.
9 Nevertheless we made our prayer unto
our God, and set a watch against them day
and night, because of them.
10 And Judah said, The strength of the
bearers of burdens is decayed, and *there
is* much rubbish; so that we are not able to
build the wall.
11 And our adversaries said, They shall not
know, neither see, till we come in the midst
among them, and slay them, and cause the
work to cease.
12 And it came to pass, that when the Jews
which dwelt by them came, they said unto
us ten times, From all places whence ye
shall return unto us *they will be upon you.*
13 ¶ Therefore set I in the lower places
behind the wall, *and* on the higher places, I
even set the people after their families with
their swords, their spears, and their bows.
14 And I looked, and rose up, and said
unto the nobles, and to the rulers, and to
the rest of the people, Be not ye afraid of
them: remember the Lord, *which is* great
and terrible, and fight for your brethren,
your sons, and your daughters, your wives,
and your houses.
15 And it came to pass, when our enemies
heard that it was known unto us, and God
had brought their counsel to nought, that
we returned all of us to the wall, every one
unto his work.
16 And it came to pass from that time forth,
that the half of my servants wrought in the
work, and the other half of them held both
the spears, the shields, and the bows, and
the habergeons; and the rulers *were* behind
all the house of Judah.
17 They which builded on the wall, and they
that bare burdens, with those that laded,
every one with one of his hands wrought
in the work, and with the other *hand* held
a weapon.

18 For the builders, every one had his sword
girded by his side, and *so* builded. And he
that sounded the trumpet *was* by me.
19 ¶ And I said unto the nobles, and to the
rulers, and to the rest of the people, The
work *is* great and large, and we are separated upon the wall, one far from another.
20 In what place *therefore* ye hear the sound
of the trumpet, resort ye thither unto us:
our God shall fight for us.
21 So we laboured in the work: and half of
them held the spears from the rising of the
morning till the stars appeared.
22 Likewise at the same time said I unto the
people, Let every one with his servant lodge
within Jerusalem, that in the night they may
be a guard to us, and labour on the day.
23 So neither I, nor my brethren, nor my
servants, nor the men of the guard which
followed me, none of us put off our clothes,
saving that every one put them off for
washing.

Nehemiah 5

1 And there was a great cry of the people
and of their wives against their brethren
the Jews.
2 For there were that said, We, our sons, and
our daughters, *are* many: therefore we take
up corn *for them*, that we may eat, and live.
3 *Some* also there were that said, We
have mortgaged our lands, vineyards, and
houses, that we might buy corn, because
of the dearth.
4 There were also that said, We have borrowed money for the king's tribute, *and that
upon* our lands and vineyards.
5 Yet now our flesh *is* as the flesh of our
brethren, our children as their children:
and, lo, we bring into bondage our sons
and our daughters to be servants, and
some of our daughters are brought unto
bondage *already:* neither *is it* in our power
to redeem them; for other men have our
lands and vineyards.
6 ¶ And I was very angry when I heard their
cry and these words.
7 Then I consulted with myself, and I
rebuked the nobles, and the rulers, and
said unto them, Ye exact usury, every one
of his brother. And I set a great assembly
against them.
8 And I said unto them, We after our ability have redeemed our brethren the Jews,
which were sold unto the heathen; and will
ye even sell your brethren? or shall they be
sold unto us? Then held they their peace,
and found nothing *to answer.*
9 Also I said, It *is* not good that ye do: ought
ye not to walk in the fear of our God because
of the reproach of the heathen our enemies?
10 I likewise, *and* my brethren, and my
servants, might exact of them money and
corn: I pray you, let us leave off this usury.
11 Restore, I pray you, to them, even this
day, their lands, their vineyards, their oliveyards, and their houses, also the hundredth
part of the money, and of the corn, the wine,
and the oil, that ye exact of them.
12 Then said they, We will restore *them,*
and will require nothing of them; so will we
do as thou sayest. Then I called the priests,
and took an oath of them, that they should
do according to this promise.
13 Also I shook my lap, and said, So God
shake out every man from his house, and
from his labour, that performeth not this
promise, even thus be he shaken out, and
emptied. And all the congregation said,
Amen, and praised the LORD. And the people
did according to this promise.
14 ¶ Moreover from the time that I was
appointed to be their governor in the land
of Judah, from the twentieth year even unto
the two and thirtieth year of Artaxerxes the
king, *that is,* twelve years, I and my brethren
have not eaten the bread of the governor.
15 But the former governors that *had been*
before me were chargeable unto the people, and had taken of them bread and wine,
beside forty shekels of silver; yea, even their
servants bare rule over the people: but so
did not I, because of the fear of God.
16 Yea, also I continued in the work of this
wall, neither bought we any land: and all
my servants *were* gathered thither unto
the work.
17 Moreover *there were* at my table an hundred and fifty of the Jews and rulers, beside
those that came unto us from among the
heathen that *are* about us.
18 Now *that* which was prepared *for me*
daily *was* one ox *and* six choice sheep; also
fowls were prepared for me, and once
in ten days store of all sorts of wine: yet
for all this required not I the bread of the

governor, because the bondage was heavy
upon this people.
19 Think upon me, my God, for good,
according to all that I have done for this
people.

Nehemiah 6

1 Now it came to pass, when Sanballat, and
Tobiah, and Geshem the Arabian, and the
rest of our enemies, heard that I had builded
the wall, and *that* there was no breach left
therein; (though at that time I had not set
up the doors upon the gates;)
2 That Sanballat and Geshem sent unto me,
saying, Come, let us meet together in *some*
one of the villages in the plain of Ono. But
they thought to do me mischief.
3 And I sent messengers unto them, saying,
I *am* doing a great work, so that I cannot
come down: why should the work cease,
whilst I leave it, and come down to you?
4 Yet they sent unto me four times after
this sort; and I answered them after the
same manner.
5 Then sent Sanballat his servant unto me
in like manner the fifth time with an open
letter in his hand;
6 Wherein *was* written, It is reported among
the heathen, and Gashmu saith *it, that* thou
and the Jews think to rebel: for which cause
thou buildest the wall, that thou mayest be
their king, according to these words.
7 And thou hast also appointed prophets
to preach of thee at Jerusalem, saying,
There is a king in Judah: and now shall it
be reported to the king according to these
words. Come now therefore, and let us take
counsel together.
8 Then I sent unto him, saying, There are
no such things done as thou sayest, but
thou feignest them out of thine own heart.
9 For they all made us afraid, saying, Their
hands shall be weakened from the work,
that it be not done. Now therefore, *O God*,
strengthen my hands.
10 Afterward I came unto the house of
Shemaiah the son of Delaiah the son of
Mehetabeel, who *was* shut up; and he
said, Let us meet together in the house of
God, within the temple, and let us shut the
doors of the temple: for they will come to
slay thee; yea, in the night will they come
to slay thee.
11 And I said, Should such a man as I flee?
and who *is there*, that, *being* as I *am*, would
go into the temple to save his life? I will
not go in.
12 And, lo, I perceived that God had not sent
him; but that he pronounced this prophecy
against me: for Tobiah and Sanballat had
hired him.
13 Therefore *was* he hired, that I should
be afraid, and do so, and sin, and *that* they
might have *matter* for an evil report, that
they might reproach me.
14 My God, think thou upon Tobiah and
Sanballat according to these their works,
and on the prophetess Noadiah, and the
rest of the prophets, that would have put
me in fear.
15 ¶ So the wall was finished in the twenty
and fifth *day* of *the month* Elul, in fifty and
two days.
16 And it came to pass, that when all our
enemies heard *thereof*, and all the heathen
that *were* about us saw *these things*, they
were much cast down in their own eyes: for
they perceived that this work was wrought
of our God.
17 ¶ Moreover in those days the nobles of
Judah sent many letters unto Tobiah, and
the letters of Tobiah came unto them.
18 For *there were* many in Judah sworn
unto him, because he *was* the son in law
of Shechaniah the son of Arah; and his son
Johanan had taken the daughter of Meshullam the son of Berechiah.
19 Also they reported his good deeds before
me, and uttered my words to him. *And*
Tobiah sent letters to put me in fear.

Nehemiah 7

1 Now it came to pass, when the wall was
built, and I had set up the doors, and the
porters and the singers and the Levites
were appointed,
2 That I gave my brother Hanani, and Hananiah the ruler of the palace, charge over
Jerusalem: for he *was* a faithful man, and
feared God above many.
3 And I said unto them, Let not the gates of
Jerusalem be opened until the sun be hot;
and while they stand by, let them shut the
doors, and bar *them:* and appoint watches
of the inhabitants of Jerusalem, every one in

his watch, and every one *to be* over against his house.

4 Now the city *was* large and great: but the people *were* few therein, and the houses *were* not builded.

5 ¶ And my God put into mine heart to gather together the nobles, and the rulers, and the people, that they might be reckoned by genealogy. And I found a register of the genealogy of them which came up at the first, and found written therein,

6 These *are* the children of the province, that went up out of the captivity, of those that had been carried away, whom Nebuchadnezzar the king of Babylon had carried away, and came again to Jerusalem and to Judah, every one unto his city;

7 Who came with Zerubbabel, Jeshua, Nehemiah, Azariah, Raamiah, Nahamani, Mordecai, Bilshan, Mispereth, Bigvai, Nehum, Baanah. The number, *I say*, of the men of the people of Israel *was this;*

8 The children of Parosh, two thousand an hundred seventy and two.

9 The children of Shephatiah, three hundred seventy and two.

10 The children of Arah, six hundred fifty and two.

11 The children of Pahath-moab, of the children of Jeshua and Joab, two thousand and eight hundred *and* eighteen.

12 The children of Elam, a thousand two hundred fifty and four.

13 The children of Zattu, eight hundred forty and five.

14 The children of Zaccai, seven hundred and threescore.

15 The children of Binnui, six hundred forty and eight.

16 The children of Bebai, six hundred twenty and eight.

17 The children of Azgad, two thousand three hundred twenty and two.

18 The children of Adonikam, six hundred threescore and seven.

19 The children of Bigvai, two thousand threescore and seven.

20 The children of Adin, six hundred fifty and five.

21 The children of Ater of Hezekiah, ninety and eight.

22 The children of Hashum, three hundred twenty and eight.

23 The children of Bezai, three hundred twenty and four.

24 The children of Hariph, an hundred and twelve.

25 The children of Gibeon, ninety and five.

26 The men of Beth-lehem and Netophah, an hundred fourscore and eight.

27 The men of Anathoth, an hundred twenty and eight.

28 The men of Beth-azmaveth, forty and two.

29 The men of Kirjath-jearim, Chephirah, and Beeroth, seven hundred forty and three.

30 The men of Ramah and Geba, six hundred twenty and one.

31 The men of Michmas, an hundred and twenty and two.

32 The men of Beth-el and Ai, an hundred twenty and three.

33 The men of the other Nebo, fifty and two.

34 The children of the other Elam, a thousand two hundred fifty and four.

35 The children of Harim, three hundred and twenty.

36 The children of Jericho, three hundred forty and five.

37 The children of Lod, Hadid, and Ono, seven hundred twenty and one.

38 The children of Senaah, three thousand nine hundred and thirty.

39 ¶ The priests: the children of Jedaiah, of the house of Jeshua, nine hundred seventy and three.

40 The children of Immer, a thousand fifty and two.

41 The children of Pashur, a thousand two hundred forty and seven.

42 The children of Harim, a thousand and seventeen.

43 ¶ The Levites: the children of Jeshua, of Kadmiel, *and* of the children of Hodevah, seventy and four.

44 ¶ The singers: the children of Asaph, an hundred forty and eight.

45 ¶ The porters: the children of Shallum, the children of Ater, the children of Talmon, the children of Akkub, the children of Hatita, the children of Shobai, an hundred thirty and eight.

46 ¶ The Nethinims: the children of Ziha, the children of Hashupha, the children of Tabbaoth,

47 The children of Keros, the children of Sia,
the children of Padon,
48 The children of Lebana, the children of
Hagaba, the children of Shalmai,
49 The children of Hanan, the children of
Giddel, the children of Gahar,
50 The children of Reaiah, the children of
Rezin, the children of Nekoda,
51 The children of Gazzam, the children of
Uzza, the children of Phaseah,
52 The children of Besai, the children of
Meunim, the children of Nephishesim,
53 The children of Bakbuk, the children of
Hakupha, the children of Harhur,
54 The children of Bazlith, the children of
Mehida, the children of Harsha,
55 The children of Barkos, the children of
Sisera, the children of Tamah,
56 The children of Neziah, the children of
Hatipha.
57 ¶ The children of Solomon's servants: the
children of Sotai, the children of Sophereth,
the children of Perida,
58 The children of Jaala, the children of
Darkon, the children of Giddel,
59 The children of Shephatiah, the children of Hattil, the children of Pochereth of
Zebaim, the children of Amon.
60 All the Nethinims, and the children of
Solomon's servants, *were* three hundred
ninety and two.
61 And these *were* they which went up
also from Tel-melah, Tel-haresha, Cherub,
Addon, and Immer: but they could not shew
their father's house, nor their seed, whether
they *were* of Israel.
62 The children of Delaiah, the children of
Tobiah, the children of Nekoda, six hundred
forty and two.
63 ¶ And of the priests: the children of
Habaiah, the children of Koz, the children of
Barzillai, which took *one* of the daughters
of Barzillai the Gileadite to wife, and was
called after their name.
64 These sought their register *among* those
that were reckoned by genealogy, but it was
not found: therefore were they, as polluted,
put from the priesthood.
65 And the Tirshatha said unto them, that
they should not eat of the most holy things,
till there stood *up* a priest with Urim and
Thummim.
66 ¶ The whole congregation together *was*
forty and two thousand three hundred and
threescore,
67 Beside their manservants and their
maidservants, of whom *there were* seven
thousand three hundred thirty and seven:
and they had two hundred forty and five
singing men and singing women.
68 Their horses, seven hundred thirty and
six: their mules, two hundred forty and five:
69 *Their* camels, four hundred thirty and
five: six thousand seven hundred and twenty
asses.
70 ¶ And some of the chief of the fathers
gave unto the work. The Tirshatha gave
to the treasure a thousand drams of gold,
fifty basons, five hundred and thirty priests'
garments.
71 And *some* of the chief of the fathers gave
to the treasure of the work twenty thousand
drams of gold, and two thousand and two
hundred pound of silver.
72 And *that* which the rest of the people
gave *was* twenty thousand drams of gold,
and two thousand pound of silver, and
threescore and seven priests' garments.
73 So the priests, and the Levites, and the
porters, and the singers, and *some* of the
people, and the Nethinims, and all Israel,
dwelt in their cities; and when the seventh
month came, the children of Israel *were* in
their cities.

Nehemiah 8

1 And all the people gathered themselves
together as one man into the street that *was*
before the water gate; and they spake unto
Ezra the scribe to bring the book of the law
of Moses, which the LORD had commanded
to Israel.
2 And Ezra the priest brought the law before
the congregation both of men and women,
and all that could hear with understanding,
upon the first day of the seventh month.
3 And he read therein before the street that
was before the water gate from the morning until midday, before the men and the
women, and those that could understand;
and the ears of all the people *were attentive*
unto the book of the law.
4 And Ezra the scribe stood upon a pulpit
of wood, which they had made for the purpose; and beside him stood Mattithiah, and
Shema, and Anaiah, and Urijah, and Hilkiah,

and Maaseiah, on his right hand; and on his left hand, Pedaiah, and Mishael, and Malchiah, and Hashum, and Hashbadana, Zechariah, *and* Meshullam.

5 And Ezra opened the book in the sight of all the people; (for he was above all the people;) and when he opened it, all the people stood up:

6 And Ezra blessed the LORD, the great God. And all the people answered, Amen, Amen, with lifting up their hands: and they bowed their heads, and worshipped the LORD with *their* faces to the ground.

7 Also Jeshua, and Bani, and Sherebiah, Jamin, Akkub, Shabbethai, Hodijah, Maaseiah, Kelita, Azariah, Jozabad, Hanan, Pelaiah, and the Levites, caused the people to understand the law: and the people *stood* in their place.

8 So they read in the book in the law of God distinctly, and gave the sense, and caused *them* to understand the reading.

9 ¶ And Nehemiah, which *is* the Tirshatha, and Ezra the priest the scribe, and the Levites that taught the people, said unto all the people, This day *is* holy unto the LORD your God; mourn not, nor weep. For all the people wept, when they heard the words of the law.

10 Then he said unto them, Go your way, eat the fat, and drink the sweet, and send portions unto them for whom nothing is prepared: for *this* day *is* holy unto our Lord: neither be ye sorry; for the joy of the LORD is your strength.

11 So the Levites stilled all the people, saying, Hold your peace, for the day *is* holy; neither be ye grieved.

12 And all the people went their way to eat, and to drink, and to send portions, and to make great mirth, because they had understood the words that were declared unto them.

13 ¶ And on the second day were gathered together the chief of the fathers of all the people, the priests, and the Levites, unto Ezra the scribe, even to understand the words of the law.

14 And they found written in the law which the LORD had commanded by Moses, that the children of Israel should dwell in booths in the feast of the seventh month:

15 And that they should publish and proclaim in all their cities, and in Jerusalem, saying, Go forth unto the mount, and fetch olive branches, and pine branches, and myrtle branches, and palm branches, and branches of thick trees, to make booths, as *it is* written.

16 ¶ So the people went forth, and brought *them*, and made themselves booths, every one upon the roof of his house, and in their courts, and in the courts of the house of God, and in the street of the water gate, and in the street of the gate of Ephraim.

17 And all the congregation of them that were come again out of the captivity made booths, and sat under the booths: for since the days of Jeshua the son of Nun unto that day had not the children of Israel done so. And there was very great gladness.

18 Also day by day, from the first day unto the last day, he read in the book of the law of God. And they kept the feast seven days; and on the eighth day *was* a solemn assembly, according unto the manner.

Nehemiah 9

1 Now in the twenty and fourth day of this month the children of Israel were assembled with fasting, and with sackclothes, and earth upon them.

2 And the seed of Israel separated themselves from all strangers, and stood and confessed their sins, and the iniquities of their fathers.

3 And they stood up in their place, and read in the book of the law of the LORD their God *one* fourth part of the day; and *another* fourth part they confessed, and worshipped the LORD their God.

4 ¶ Then stood up upon the stairs, of the Levites, Jeshua, and Bani, Kadmiel, Shebaniah, Bunni, Sherebiah, Bani, *and* Chenani, and cried with a loud voice unto the LORD their God.

5 Then the Levites, Jeshua, and Kadmiel, Bani, Hashabniah, Sherebiah, Hodijah, Shebaniah, *and* Pethahiah, said, Stand up *and* bless the LORD your God for ever and ever: and blessed be thy glorious name, which is exalted above all blessing and praise.

6 Thou, *even* thou, *art* LORD alone; thou hast made heaven, the heaven of heavens, with all their host, the earth, and all *things* that *are* therein, the seas, and all that *is* therein,

and thou preservest them all; and the host
of heaven worshippeth thee.
7 Thou *art* the LORD the God, who didst
choose Abram, and broughtest him forth
out of Ur of the Chaldees, and gavest him
the name of Abraham;
8 And foundest his heart faithful before
thee, and madest a covenant with him to
give the land of the Canaanites, the Hittites,
the Amorites, and the Perizzites, and the
Jebusites, and the Girgashites, to give *it*,
I say, to his seed, and hast performed thy
words; for thou *art* righteous:
9 And didst see the affliction of our fathers
in Egypt, and heardest their cry by the
Red sea;
10 And shewedst signs and wonders upon
Pharaoh, and on all his servants, and on all
the people of his land: for thou knewest
that they dealt proudly against them. So
didst thou get thee a name, as *it is* this day.
11 And thou didst divide the sea before
them, so that they went through the midst
of the sea on the dry land; and their persecutors thou threwest into the deeps, as a
stone into the mighty waters.
12 Moreover thou leddest them in the day
by a cloudy pillar; and in the night by a pillar
of fire, to give them light in the way wherein
they should go.
13 Thou camest down also upon mount
Sinai, and spakest with them from heaven,
and gavest them right judgments, and true
laws, good statutes and commandments:
14 And madest known unto them thy holy
sabbath, and commandedst them precepts,
statutes, and laws, by the hand of Moses
thy servant:
15 And gavest them bread from heaven for
their hunger, and broughtest forth water
for them out of the rock for their thirst, and
promisedst them that they should go in to
possess the land which thou hadst sworn
to give them.
16 But they and our fathers dealt proudly,
and hardened their necks, and hearkened
not to thy commandments,
17 And refused to obey, neither were mindful of thy wonders that thou didst among
them; but hardened their necks, and in their
rebellion appointed a captain to return to
their bondage: but thou *art* a God ready
to pardon, gracious and merciful, slow to
anger, and of great kindness, and forsookest
them not.
18 Yea, when they had made them a molten
calf, and said, This *is* thy God that brought
thee up out of Egypt, and had wrought great
provocations;
19 Yet thou in thy manifold mercies forsookest them not in the wilderness: the
pillar of the cloud departed not from them
by day, to lead them in the way; neither the
pillar of fire by night, to shew them light, and
the way wherein they should go.
20 Thou gavest also thy good spirit to
instruct them, and withheldest not thy
manna from their mouth, and gavest them
water for their thirst.
21 Yea, forty years didst thou sustain them
in the wilderness, *so that* they lacked nothing; their clothes waxed not old, and their
feet swelled not.
22 Moreover thou gavest them kingdoms
and nations, and didst divide them into corners: so they possessed the land of Sihon,
and the land of the king of Heshbon, and
the land of Og king of Bashan.
23 Their children also multipliedst thou as
the stars of heaven, and broughtest them
into the land, concerning which thou hadst
promised to their fathers, that they should
go in to possess *it*.
24 So the children went in and possessed
the land, and thou subduedst before them
the inhabitants of the land, the Canaanites,
and gavest them into their hands, with their
kings, and the people of the land, that they
might do with them as they would.
25 And they took strong cities, and a fat
land, and possessed houses full of all goods,
wells digged, vineyards, and oliveyards, and
fruit trees in abundance: so they did eat, and
were filled, and became fat, and delighted
themselves in thy great goodness.
26 Nevertheless they were disobedient,
and rebelled against thee, and cast thy law
behind their backs, and slew thy prophets
which testified against them to turn them to
thee, and they wrought great provocations.
27 Therefore thou deliveredst them into the
hand of their enemies, who vexed them: and
in the time of their trouble, when they cried
unto thee, thou heardest *them* from heaven;
and according to thy manifold mercies thou

gavest them saviours, who saved them out
of the hand of their enemies.
28 But after they had rest, they did evil again
before thee: therefore leftest thou them in
the hand of their enemies, so that they had
the dominion over them: yet when they
returned, and cried unto thee, thou heardest *them* from heaven; and many times didst
thou deliver them according to thy mercies;
29 And testifiedst against them, that thou
mightest bring them again unto thy law: yet
they dealt proudly, and hearkened not unto
thy commandments, but sinned against thy
judgments, (which if a man do, he shall live
in them;) and withdrew the shoulder, and
hardened their neck, and would not hear.
30 Yet many years didst thou forbear them,
and testifiedst against them by thy spirit in
thy prophets: yet would they not give ear:
therefore gavest thou them into the hand
of the people of the lands.
31 Nevertheless for thy great mercies' sake
thou didst not utterly consume them, nor
forsake them; for thou *art* a gracious and
merciful God.
32 Now therefore, our God, the great, the
mighty, and the terrible God, who keepest
covenant and mercy, let not all the trouble
seem little before thee, that hath come
upon us, on our kings, on our princes, and
on our priests, and on our prophets, and on
our fathers, and on all thy people, since the
time of the kings of Assyria unto this day.
33 Howbeit thou *art* just in all that is brought
upon us; for thou hast done right, but we
have done wickedly:
34 Neither have our kings, our princes, our
priests, nor our fathers, kept thy law, nor
hearkened unto thy commandments and
thy testimonies, wherewith thou didst testify against them.
35 For they have not served thee in their
kingdom, and in thy great goodness that
thou gavest them, and in the large and fat
land which thou gavest before them, neither turned they from their wicked works.
36 Behold, we *are* servants this day, and *for*
the land that thou gavest unto our fathers to
eat the fruit thereof and the good thereof,
behold, we *are* servants in it:
37 And it yieldeth much increase unto the
kings whom thou hast set over us because
of our sins: also they have dominion over our
bodies, and over our cattle, at their pleasure,
and we *are* in great distress.
38 And because of all this we make a sure
covenant, and write *it;* and our princes,
Levites, *and* priests, seal *unto it*.

Nehemiah 10

1 Now those that sealed *were*, Nehemiah,
the Tirshatha, the son of Hachaliah, and
Zidkijah,
2 Seraiah, Azariah, Jeremiah,
3 Pashur, Amariah, Malchijah,
4 Hattush, Shebaniah, Malluch,
5 Harim, Meremoth, Obadiah,
6 Daniel, Ginnethon, Baruch,
7 Meshullam, Abijah, Mijamin,
8 Maaziah, Bilgai, Shemaiah: these *were*
the priests.
9 And the Levites: both Jeshua the son of
Azaniah, Binnui of the sons of Henadad,
Kadmiel;
10 And their brethren, Shebaniah, Hodijah,
Kelita, Pelaiah, Hanan,
11 Micha, Rehob, Hashabiah,
12 Zaccur, Sherebiah, Shebaniah,
13 Hodijah, Bani, Beninu.
14 The chief of the people; Parosh, Pahath-
moab, Elam, Zatthu, Bani,
15 Bunni, Azgad, Bebai,
16 Adonijah, Bigvai, Adin,
17 Ater, Hizkijah, Azzur,
18 Hodijah, Hashum, Bezai,
19 Hariph, Anathoth, Nebai,
20 Magpiash, Meshullam, Hezir,
21 Meshezabeel, Zadok, Jaddua,
22 Pelatiah, Hanan, Anaiah,
23 Hoshea, Hananiah, Hashub,
24 Hallohesh, Pileha, Shobek,
25 Rehum, Hashabnah, Maaseiah,
26 And Ahijah, Hanan, Anan,
27 Malluch, Harim, Baanah.
28 ¶ And the rest of the people, the priests,
the Levites, the porters, the singers, the
Nethinims, and all they that had separated
themselves from the people of the lands
unto the law of God, their wives, their
sons, and their daughters, every one having knowledge, and having understanding;
29 They clave to their brethren, their nobles,
and entered into a curse, and into an oath,
to walk in God's law, which was given by
Moses the servant of God, and to observe

and do all the commandments of the LORD
our Lord, and his judgments and his statutes;
30 And that we would not give our daughters unto the people of the land, nor take
their daughters for our sons:
31 And *if* the people of the land bring ware
or any victuals on the sabbath day to sell,
that we would not buy it of them on the
sabbath, or on the holy day: and *that* we
would leave the seventh year, and the exac-
tion of every debt.
32 Also we made ordinances for us, to
charge ourselves yearly with the third part
of a shekel for the service of the house of
our God;
33 For the shewbread, and for the continual meat offering, and for the continual
burnt offering, of the sabbaths, of the new
moons, for the set feasts, and for the holy
things, and for the sin offerings to make an
atonement for Israel, and *for* all the work
of the house of our God.
34 And we cast the lots among the priests,
the Levites, and the people, for the wood
offering, to bring *it* into the house of our
God, after the houses of our fathers, at times
appointed year by year, to burn upon the
altar of the LORD our God, as *it is* written
in the law:
35 And to bring the firstfruits of our ground,
and the firstfruits of all fruit of all trees, year
by year, unto the house of the LORD:
36 Also the firstborn of our sons, and of
our cattle, as *it is* written in the law, and
the firstlings of our herds and of our flocks,
to bring to the house of our God, unto the
priests that minister in the house of our God:
37 And *that* we should bring the firstfruits of
our dough, and our offerings, and the fruit of
all manner of trees, of wine and of oil, unto
the priests, to the chambers of the house of
our God; and the tithes of our ground unto
the Levites, that the same Levites might
have the tithes in all the cities of our tillage.
38 And the priest the son of Aaron shall
be with the Levites, when the Levites take
tithes: and the Levites shall bring up the
tithe of the tithes unto the house of our God,
to the chambers, into the treasure house.
39 For the children of Israel and the children of Levi shall bring the offering of the
corn, of the new wine, and the oil, unto
the chambers, where *are* the vessels of the
sanctuary, and the priests that minister, and
the porters, and the singers: and we will not
forsake the house of our God.

Nehemiah 11

1 And the rulers of the people dwelt at
Jerusalem: the rest of the people also cast
lots, to bring one of ten to dwell in Jerusalem the holy city, and nine parts *to dwell*
in *other* cities.
2 And the people blessed all the men, that
willingly offered themselves to dwell at
Jerusalem.
3 ¶ Now these *are* the chief of the province
that dwelt in Jerusalem: but in the cities of
Judah dwelt every one in his possession in
their cities, *to wit*, Israel, the priests, and the
Levites, and the Nethinims, and the children
of Solomon's servants.
4 And at Jerusalem dwelt *certain* of the
children of Judah, and of the children of
Benjamin. Of the children of Judah; Athaiah
the son of Uzziah, the son of Zechariah, the
son of Amariah, the son of Shephatiah, the
son of Mahalaleel, of the children of Perez;
5 And Maaseiah the son of Baruch, the son
of Col-hozeh, the son of Hazaiah, the son of
Adaiah, the son of Joiarib, the son of Zechariah, the son of Shiloni.
6 All the sons of Perez that dwelt at Jerusalem *were* four hundred threescore and
eight valiant men.
7 And these *are* the sons of Benjamin; Sallu
the son of Meshullam, the son of Joed, the
son of Pedaiah, the son of Kolaiah, the son
of Maaseiah, the son of Ithiel, the son of
Jesaiah.
8 And after him Gabbai, Sallai, nine hundred
twenty and eight.
9 And Joel the son of Zichri *was* their overseer: and Judah the son of Senuah *was*
second over the city.
10 Of the priests: Jedaiah the son of Joiarib,
Jachin.
11 Seraiah the son of Hilkiah, the son of
Meshullam, the son of Zadok, the son of
Meraioth, the son of Ahitub, *was* the ruler
of the house of God.
12 And their brethren that did the work of
the house *were* eight hundred twenty and
two: and Adaiah the son of Jeroham, the
son of Pelaliah, the son of Amzi, the son

of Zechariah, the son of Pashur, the son of
Malchiah,
13 And his brethren, chief of the fathers,
two hundred forty and two: and Amashai
the son of Azareel, the son of Ahasai, the
son of Meshillemoth, the son of Immer,
14 And their brethren, mighty men of
valour, an hundred twenty and eight: and
their overseer *was* Zabdiel, the son of *one*
of the great men.
15 Also of the Levites: Shemaiah the son
of Hashub, the son of Azrikam, the son of
Hashabiah, the son of Bunni;
16 And Shabbethai and Jozabad, of the
chief of the Levites, *had* the oversight of
the outward business of the house of God.
17 And Mattaniah the son of Micha, the son
of Zabdi, the son of Asaph, *was* the principal to begin the thanksgiving in prayer: and
Bakbukiah the second among his brethren,
and Abda the son of Shammua, the son of
Galal, the son of Jeduthun.
18 All the Levites in the holy city *were* two
hundred fourscore and four.
19 Moreover the porters, Akkub, Talmon,
and their brethren that kept the gates, *were*
an hundred seventy and two.
20 ¶ And the residue of Israel, of the priests,
and the Levites, *were* in all the cities of
Judah, every one in his inheritance.
21 But the Nethinims dwelt in Ophel: and
Ziha and Gispa *were* over the Nethinims.
22 The overseer also of the Levites at Jerusalem *was* Uzzi the son of Bani, the son of
Hashabiah, the son of Mattaniah, the son
of Micha. Of the sons of Asaph, the singers
were over the business of the house of God.
23 For *it was* the king's commandment concerning them, that a certain portion should
be for the singers, due for every day.
24 And Pethahiah the son of Meshezabeel,
of the children of Zerah the son of Judah,
was at the king's hand in all matters concerning the people.
25 And for the villages, with their fields,
some of the children of Judah dwelt at Kirjath-arba, and *in* the villages thereof, and
at Dibon, and *in* the villages thereof, and
at Jekabzeel, and *in* the villages thereof,
26 And at Jeshua, and at Moladah, and at
Beth-phelet,
27 And at Hazar-shual, and at Beer-sheba,
and *in* the villages thereof,
28 And at Ziklag, and at Mekonah, and in
the villages thereof,
29 And at En-rimmon, and at Zareah, and
at Jarmuth,
30 Zanoah, Adullam, and *in* their villages, at
Lachish, and the fields thereof, at Azekah,
and *in* the villages thereof. And they dwelt
from Beer-sheba unto the valley of Hinnom.
31 The children also of Benjamin from Geba
dwelt at Michmash, and Aija, and Beth-el,
and *in* their villages,
32 *And* at Anathoth, Nob, Ananiah,
33 Hazor, Ramah, Gittaim,
34 Hadid, Zeboim, Neballat,
35 Lod, and Ono, the valley of craftsmen.
36 And of the Levites *were* divisions *in* Judah,
and in Benjamin.

Nehemiah 12

1 Now these *are* the priests and the Levites
that went up with Zerubbabel the son of
Shealtiel, and Jeshua: Seraiah, Jeremiah,
Ezra,
2 Amariah, Malluch, Hattush,
3 Shechaniah, Rehum, Meremoth,
4 Iddo, Ginnetho, Abijah,
5 Miamin, Maadiah, Bilgah,
6 Shemaiah, and Joiarib, Jedaiah,
7 Sallu, Amok, Hilkiah, Jedaiah. These *were*
the chief of the priests and of their brethren
in the days of Jeshua.
8 Moreover the Levites: Jeshua, Binnui,
Kadmiel, Sherebiah, Judah, *and* Mattaniah,
which was over the thanksgiving, he and
his brethren.
9 Also Bakbukiah and Unni, their brethren,
were over against them in the watches.
10 ¶ And Jeshua begat Joiakim, Joiakim also
begat Eliashib, and Eliashib begat Joiada,
11 And Joiada begat Jonathan, and Jonathan
begat Jaddua.
12 And in the days of Joiakim were priests,
the chief of the fathers: of Seraiah, Meraiah;
of Jeremiah, Hananiah;
13 Of Ezra, Meshullam; of Amariah, Jehohanan;
14 Of Melicu, Jonathan; of Shebaniah,
Joseph;
15 Of Harim, Adna; of Meraioth, Helkai;
16 Of Iddo, Zechariah; of Ginnethon,
Meshullam;
17 Of Abijah, Zichri; of Miniamin, of Moa-
diah, Piltai;

18 Of Bilgah, Shammua; of Shemaiah, Jehonathan;
19 And of Joiarib, Mattenai; of Jedaiah, Uzzi;
20 Of Sallai, Kallai; of Amok, Eber;
21 Of Hilkiah, Hashabiah; of Jedaiah, Nethaneel.
22 ¶ The Levites in the days of Eliashib,
Joiada, and Johanan, and Jaddua, *were*
recorded chief of the fathers: also the
priests, to the reign of Darius the Persian.
23 The sons of Levi, the chief of the fathers,
were written in the book of the chronicles,
even until the days of Johanan the son of
Eliashib.
24 And the chief of the Levites: Hashabiah,
Sherebiah, and Jeshua the son of Kadmiel,
with their brethren over against them, to
praise *and* to give thanks, according to the
commandment of David the man of God,
ward over against ward.
25 Mattaniah, and Bakbukiah, Obadiah,
Meshullam, Talmon, Akkub, *were* porters
keeping the ward at the thresholds of the
gates.
26 These *were* in the days of Joiakim the
son of Jeshua, the son of Jozadak, and in
the days of Nehemiah the governor, and of
Ezra the priest, the scribe.
27 ¶ And at the dedication of the wall of
Jerusalem they sought the Levites out of
all their places, to bring them to Jerusalem,
to keep the dedication with gladness, both
with thanksgivings, and with singing, *with*
cymbals, psalteries, and with harps.
28 And the sons of the singers gathered
themselves together, both out of the plain
country round about Jerusalem, and from
the villages of Netophathi;
29 Also from the house of Gilgal, and out
of the fields of Geba and Azmaveth: for the
singers had builded them villages round
about Jerusalem.
30 And the priests and the Levites purified
themselves, and purified the people, and
the gates, and the wall.
31 Then I brought up the princes of Judah
upon the wall, and appointed two great
companies of them that gave thanks,
whereof one went on the right hand upon
the wall toward the dung gate:
32 And after them went Hoshaiah, and half
of the princes of Judah,
33 And Azariah, Ezra, and Meshullam,
34 Judah, and Benjamin, and Shemaiah,
and Jeremiah,
35 And *certain* of the priests' sons with
trumpets; *namely*, Zechariah the son of
Jonathan, the son of Shemaiah, the son of
Mattaniah, the son of Michaiah, the son of
Zaccur, the son of Asaph:
36 And his brethren, Shemaiah, and Azarael,
Milalai, Gilalai, Maai, Nethaneel, and Judah,
Hanani, with the musical instruments of
David the man of God, and Ezra the scribe
before them.
37 And at the fountain gate, which was over
against them, they went up by the stairs
of the city of David, at the going up of the
wall, above the house of David, even unto
the water gate eastward.
38 And the other *company of them that gave*
thanks went over against *them*, and I after
them, and the half of the people upon the
wall, from beyond the tower of the furnaces
even unto the broad wall;
39 And from above the gate of Ephraim, and
above the old gate, and above the fish gate,
and the tower of Hananeel, and the tower of
Meah, even unto the sheep gate: and they
stood still in the prison gate.
40 So stood the two *companies of them that*
gave thanks in the house of God, and I, and
the half of the rulers with me:
41 And the priests; Eliakim, Maaseiah, Miniamin, Michaiah, Elioenai, Zechariah, *and*
Hananiah, with trumpets;
42 And Maaseiah, and Shemaiah, and Eleazar, and Uzzi, and Jehohanan, and Malchijah,
and Elam, and Ezer. And the singers sang
loud, with Jezrahiah *their* overseer.
43 Also that day they offered great sacrifices, and rejoiced: for God had made
them rejoice with great joy: the wives also
and the children rejoiced: so that the joy of
Jerusalem was heard even afar off.
44 ¶ And at that time were some appointed
over the chambers for the treasures, for
the offerings, for the firstfruits, and for the
tithes, to gather into them out of the fields
of the cities the portions of the law for the
priests and Levites: for Judah rejoiced for
the priests and for the Levites that waited.
45 And both the singers and the porters
kept the ward of their God, and the ward
of the purification, according to the commandment of David, *and* of Solomon his son.

46 For in the days of David and Asaph of old
there were chief of the singers, and songs of
praise and thanksgiving unto God.
47 And all Israel in the days of Zerubbabel,
and in the days of Nehemiah, gave the
portions of the singers and the porters,
every day his portion: and they sanctified
holy things unto the Levites; and the Levites
sanctified *them* unto the children of Aaron.

Nehemiah 13

1 On that day they read in the book of Moses
in the audience of the people; and therein
was found written, that the Ammonite and
the Moabite should not come into the congregation of God for ever;
2 Because they met not the children of
Israel with bread and with water, but hired
Balaam against them, that he should curse
them: howbeit our God turned the curse
into a blessing.
3 Now it came to pass, when they had heard
the law, that they separated from Israel all
the mixed multitude.
4 ¶ And before this, Eliashib the priest,
having the oversight of the chamber of the
house of our God, *was* allied unto Tobiah:
5 And he had prepared for him a great
chamber, where aforetime they laid the
meat offerings, the frankincense, and the
vessels, and the tithes of the corn, the new
wine, and the oil, which was commanded *to
be given* to the Levites, and the singers, and
the porters; and the offerings of the priests.
6 But in all this *time* was not I at Jerusalem:
for in the two and thirtieth year of Artaxerxes king of Babylon came I unto the king,
and after certain days obtained I leave of
the king:
7 And I came to Jerusalem, and understood
of the evil that Eliashib did for Tobiah, in
preparing him a chamber in the courts of
the house of God.
8 And it grieved me sore: therefore I cast
forth all the household stuff of Tobiah out
of the chamber.
9 Then I commanded, and they cleansed the
chambers: and thither brought I again the
vessels of the house of God, with the meat
offering and the frankincense.
10 ¶ And I perceived that the portions of
the Levites had not been given *them:* for the
Levites and the singers, that did the work,
were fled every one to his field.
11 Then contended I with the rulers, and
said, Why is the house of God forsaken?
And I gathered them together, and set them
in their place.
12 Then brought all Judah the tithe of the
corn and the new wine and the oil unto the
treasuries.
13 And I made treasurers over the treasuries, Shelemiah the priest, and Zadok the
scribe, and of the Levites, Pedaiah: and next
to them *was* Hanan the son of Zaccur, the
son of Mattaniah: for they were counted
faithful, and their office *was* to distribute
unto their brethren.
14 Remember me, O my God, concerning
this, and wipe not out my good deeds that
I have done for the house of my God, and
for the offices thereof.
15 ¶ In those days saw I in Judah *some*
treading wine presses on the sabbath, and
bringing in sheaves, and lading asses; as also
wine, grapes, and figs, and all *manner of*
burdens, which they brought into Jerusalem
on the sabbath day: and I testified *against
them* in the day wherein they sold victuals.
16 There dwelt men of Tyre also therein,
which brought fish, and all manner of ware,
and sold on the sabbath unto the children
of Judah, and in Jerusalem.
17 Then I contended with the nobles of
Judah, and said unto them, What evil thing
is this that ye do, and profane the sabbath
day?
18 Did not your fathers thus, and did not our
God bring all this evil upon us, and upon this
city? yet ye bring more wrath upon Israel
by profaning the sabbath.
19 And it came to pass, that when the gates
of Jerusalem began to be dark before the
sabbath, I commanded that the gates should
be shut, and charged that they should not
be opened till after the sabbath: and *some*
of my servants set I at the gates, *that* there
should no burden be brought in on the
sabbath day.
20 So the merchants and sellers of all kind
of ware lodged without Jerusalem once
or twice.
21 Then I testified against them, and said
unto them, Why lodge ye about the wall?
if ye do *so* again, I will lay hands on you.

From that time forth came they no *more*
on the sabbath.
22 And I commanded the Levites that they
should cleanse themselves, and *that* they
should come *and* keep the gates, to sanctify
the sabbath day. Remember me, O my God,
concerning this also, and spare me according
to the greatness of thy mercy.
23 ¶ In those days also saw I Jews *that* had
married wives of Ashdod, of Ammon, *and*
of Moab:
24 And their children spake half in the
speech of Ashdod, and could not speak in
the Jews' language, but according to the
language of each people.
25 And I contended with them, and cursed
them, and smote certain of them, and
plucked off their hair, and made them swear
by God, *saying*, Ye shall not give your daughters unto their sons, nor take their daughters
unto your sons, or for yourselves.
26 Did not Solomon king of Israel sin by
these things? yet among many nations was
there no king like him, who was beloved of
his God, and God made him king over all
Israel: nevertheless even him did outlandish
women cause to sin.
27 Shall we then hearken unto you to do all
this great evil, to transgress against our God
in marrying strange wives?
28 And *one* of the sons of Joiada, the son
of Eliashib the high priest, *was* son in law to
Sanballat the Horonite: therefore I chased
him from me.
29 Remember them, O my God, because
they have defiled the priesthood, and the
covenant of the priesthood, and of the
Levites.
30 Thus cleansed I them from all strangers,
and appointed the wards of the priests and
the Levites, every one in his business;
31 And for the wood offering, at times
appointed, and for the firstfruits. Remember
me, O my God, for good.

The Book Of

Esther

Esther 1

1 Now it came to pass in the days of Ahasuerus, (this *is* Ahasuerus which reigned,
from India even unto Ethiopia, *over* an
hundred and seven and twenty provinces:)
2 *That* in those days, when the king Ahasuerus sat on the throne of his kingdom,
which *was* in Shushan the palace,
3 In the third year of his reign, he made a
feast unto all his princes and his servants;
the power of Persia and Media, the nobles
and princes of the provinces, *being* before
him:
4 When he shewed the riches of his glorious
kingdom and the honour of his excellent
majesty many days, *even* an hundred and
fourscore days.
5 And when these days were expired, the
king made a feast unto all the people that
were present in Shushan the palace, both
unto great and small, seven days, in the
court of the garden of the king's palace;
6 *Where were* white, green, and blue, *hangings*, fastened with cords of fine linen and
purple to silver rings and pillars of marble:
the beds *were of* gold and silver, upon a
pavement of red, and blue, and white, and
black, marble.
7 And they gave *them* drink in vessels of
gold, (the vessels being diverse one from
another,) and royal wine in abundance,
according to the state of the king.
8 And the drinking *was* according to the
law; none did compel: for so the king had
appointed to all the officers of his house,
that they should do according to every
man's pleasure.
9 Also Vashti the queen made a feast for the
women *in* the royal house which *belonged*
to king Ahasuerus.
10 ¶ On the seventh day, when the heart
of the king was merry with wine, he commanded Mehuman, Biztha, Harbona, Bigtha,
and Abagtha, Zethar, and Carcas, the seven

chamberlains that served in the presence of Ahasuerus the king,

11 To bring Vashti the queen before the king with the crown royal, to shew the people and the princes her beauty: for she *was* fair to look on.

12 But the queen Vashti refused to come at the king's commandment by *his* chamberlains: therefore was the king very wroth, and his anger burned in him.

13 ¶ Then the king said to the wise men, which knew the times, (for so *was* the king's manner toward all that knew law and judgment:

14 And the next unto him *was* Carshena, Shethar, Admatha, Tarshish, Meres, Marsena, *and* Memucan, the seven princes of Persia and Media, which saw the king's face, *and* which sat the first in the kingdom;)

15 What shall we do unto the queen Vashti according to law, because she hath not performed the commandment of the king Ahasuerus by the chamberlains?

16 And Memucan answered before the king and the princes, Vashti the queen hath not done wrong to the king only, but also to all the princes, and to all the people that *are* in all the provinces of the king Ahasuerus.

17 For *this* deed of the queen shall come abroad unto all women, so that they shall despise their husbands in their eyes, when it shall be reported, The king Ahasuerus commanded Vashti the queen to be brought in before him, but she came not.

18 *Likewise* shall the ladies of Persia and Media say this day unto all the king's princes, which have heard of the deed of the queen. Thus *shall there arise* too much contempt and wrath.

19 If it please the king, let there go a royal commandment from him, and let it be written among the laws of the Persians and the Medes, that it be not altered, That Vashti come no more before king Ahasuerus; and let the king give her royal estate unto another that is better than she.

20 And when the king's decree which he shall make shall be published throughout all his empire, (for it is great,) all the wives shall give to their husbands honour, both to great and small.

21 And the saying pleased the king and the princes; and the king did according to the word of Memucan:

22 For he sent letters into all the king's provinces, into every province according to the writing thereof, and to every people after their language, that every man should bear rule in his own house, and that *it* should be published according to the language of every people.

Esther 2

1 After these things, when the wrath of king Ahasuerus was appeased, he remembered Vashti, and what she had done, and what was decreed against her.

2 Then said the king's servants that ministered unto him, Let there be fair young virgins sought for the king:

3 And let the king appoint officers in all the provinces of his kingdom, that they may gather together all the fair young virgins unto Shushan the palace, to the house of the women, unto the custody of Hege the king's chamberlain, keeper of the women; and let their things for purification be given *them:*

4 And let the maiden which pleaseth the king be queen instead of Vashti. And the thing pleased the king; and he did so.

5 ¶ *Now* in Shushan the palace there was a certain Jew, whose name *was* Mordecai, the son of Jair, the son of Shimei, the son of Kish, a Benjamite;

6 Who had been carried away from Jerusalem with the captivity which had been carried away with Jeconiah king of Judah, whom Nebuchadnezzar the king of Babylon had carried away.

7 And he brought up Hadassah, that *is,* Esther, his uncle's daughter: for she had neither father nor mother, and the maid *was* fair and beautiful; whom Mordecai, when her father and mother were dead, took for his own daughter.

8 ¶ So it came to pass, when the king's commandment and his decree was heard, and when many maidens were gathered together unto Shushan the palace, to the custody of Hegai, that Esther was brought also unto the king's house, to the custody of Hegai, keeper of the women.

9 And the maiden pleased him, and she obtained kindness of him; and he speedily gave her her things for purification, with

such things as belonged to her, and seven
maidens, *which were* meet to be given her,
out of the king's house: and he preferred
her and her maids unto the best *place* of
the house of the women.
10 Esther had not shewed her people nor
her kindred: for Mordecai had charged her
that she should not shew *it*.
11 And Mordecai walked every day before
the court of the women's house, to know
how Esther did, and what should become
of her.
12 ¶ Now when every maid's turn was come
to go in to king Ahasuerus, after that she
had been twelve months, according to the
manner of the women, (for so were the days
of their purifications accomplished, *to wit*,
six months with oil of myrrh, and six months
with sweet odours, and with *other* things
for the purifying of the women;)
13 Then thus came *every* maiden unto the
king; whatsoever she desired was given
her to go with her out of the house of the
women unto the king's house.
14 In the evening she went, and on the morrow she returned into the second house of
the women, to the custody of Shaashgaz,
the king's chamberlain, which kept the
concubines: she came in unto the king no
more, except the king delighted in her, and
that she were called by name.
15 ¶ Now when the turn of Esther, the
daughter of Abihail the uncle of Mordecai,
who had taken her for his daughter, was
come to go in unto the king, she required
nothing but what Hegai the king's chamberlain, the keeper of the women, appointed.
And Esther obtained favour in the sight of
all them that looked upon her.
16 So Esther was taken unto king Ahasuerus
into his house royal in the tenth month,
which *is* the month Tebeth, in the seventh
year of his reign.
17 And the king loved Esther above all the
women, and she obtained grace and favour
in his sight more than all the virgins; so that
he set the royal crown upon her head, and
made her queen instead of Vashti.
18 Then the king made a great feast unto all
his princes and his servants, *even* Esther's
feast; and he made a release to the provinces, and gave gifts, according to the state
of the king.
19 And when the virgins were gathered
together the second time, then Mordecai
sat in the king's gate.
20 Esther had not *yet* shewed her kindred
nor her people; as Mordecai had charged
her: for Esther did the commandment of
Mordecai, like as when she was brought
up with him.
21 ¶ In those days, while Mordecai sat in the
king's gate, two of the king's chamberlains,
Bigthan and Teresh, of those which kept the
door, were wroth, and sought to lay hand
on the king Ahasuerus.
22 And the thing was known to Mordecai,
who told *it* unto Esther the queen; and
Esther certified the king *thereof* in Mordecai's name.
23 And when inquisition was made of the
matter, it was found out; therefore they
were both hanged on a tree: and it was
written in the book of the chronicles before
the king.

Esther 3

1 After these things did king Ahasuerus promote Haman the son of Hammedatha the
Agagite, and advanced him, and set his seat
above all the princes that *were* with him.
2 And all the king's servants, that *were* in
the king's gate, bowed, and reverenced
Haman: for the king had so commanded
concerning him. But Mordecai bowed not,
nor did *him* reverence.
3 Then the king's servants, which *were* in the
king's gate, said unto Mordecai, Why trans-
gressest thou the king's commandment?
4 Now it came to pass, when they spake
daily unto him, and he hearkened not unto
them, that they told Haman, to see whether
Mordecai's matters would stand: for he had
told them that he *was* a Jew.
5 And when Haman saw that Mordecai
bowed not, nor did him reverence, then
was Haman full of wrath.
6 And he thought scorn to lay hands on
Mordecai alone; for they had shewed him
the people of Mordecai: wherefore Haman
sought to destroy all the Jews that *were*
throughout the whole kingdom of Ahasuerus, *even* the people of Mordecai.
7 ¶ In the first month, that *is*, the month
Nisan, in the twelfth year of king Ahasuerus, they cast Pur, that *is*, the lot, before

Haman from day to day, and from month
to month, *to* the twelfth *month*, that *is*, the
month Adar.
8 ¶ And Haman said unto king Ahasuerus,
There is a certain people scattered abroad
and dispersed among the people in all the
provinces of thy kingdom; and their laws
are diverse from all people; neither keep
they the king's laws: therefore it *is* not for
the king's profit to suffer them.
9 If it please the king, let it be written that
they may be destroyed: and I will pay ten
thousand talents of silver to the hands of
those that have the charge of the business,
to bring *it* into the king's treasuries.
10 And the king took his ring from his hand,
and gave it unto Haman the son of Hammedatha the Agagite, the Jews' enemy.
11 And the king said unto Haman, The silver
is given to thee, the people also, to do with
them as it seemeth good to thee.
12 Then were the king's scribes called on the
thirteenth day of the first month, and there
was written according to all that Haman had
commanded unto the king's lieutenants,
and to the governors that *were* over every
province, and to the rulers of every people
of every province according to the writing
thereof, and *to* every people after their language; in the name of king Ahasuerus was
it written, and sealed with the king's ring.
13 And the letters were sent by posts into all
the king's provinces, to destroy, to kill, and
to cause to perish, all Jews, both young and
old, little children and women, in one day,
even upon the thirteenth *day* of the twelfth
month, which *is* the month Adar, and *to take*
the spoil of them for a prey.
14 The copy of the writing for a commandment to be given in every province was
published unto all people, that they should
be ready against that day.
15 The posts went out, being hastened by
the king's commandment, and the decree
was given in Shushan the palace. And the
king and Haman sat down to drink; but the
city Shushan was perplexed.

Esther 4

1 When Mordecai perceived all that was
done, Mordecai rent his clothes, and put
on sackcloth with ashes, and went out into
the midst of the city, and cried with a loud
and a bitter cry;
2 And came even before the king's gate:
for none *might* enter into the king's gate
clothed with sackcloth.
3 And in every province, whithersoever the
king's commandment and his decree came,
there was great mourning among the Jews,
and fasting, and weeping, and wailing; and
many lay in sackcloth and ashes.
4 ¶ So Esther's maids and her chamberlains
came and told *it* her. Then was the queen
exceedingly grieved; and she sent raiment
to clothe Mordecai, and to take away his
sackcloth from him: but he received *it* not.
5 Then called Esther for Hatach, *one* of
the king's chamberlains, whom he had
appointed to attend upon her, and gave
him a commandment to Mordecai, to know
what it *was*, and why it *was*.
6 So Hatach went forth to Mordecai unto
the street of the city, which *was* before the
king's gate.
7 And Mordecai told him of all that had
happened unto him, and of the sum of the
money that Haman had promised to pay
to the king's treasuries for the Jews, to
destroy them.
8 Also he gave him the copy of the writing
of the decree that was given at Shushan to
destroy them, to shew *it* unto Esther, and
to declare *it* unto her, and to charge her
that she should go in unto the king, to make
supplication unto him, and to make request
before him for her people.
9 And Hatach came and told Esther the
words of Mordecai.
10 ¶ Again Esther spake unto Hatach, and
gave him commandment unto Mordecai;
11 All the king's servants, and the people of
the king's provinces, do know, that whosoever, whether man or woman, shall come
unto the king into the inner court, who is not
called, *there is* one law of his to put *him* to
death, except such to whom the king shall
hold out the golden sceptre, that he may
live: but I have not been called to come in
unto the king these thirty days.
12 And they told to Mordecai Esther's
words.
13 Then Mordecai commanded to answer
Esther, Think not with thyself that thou

shalt escape in the king's house, more than
all the Jews.
14 For if thou altogether holdest thy peace
at this time, *then* shall there enlargement
and deliverance arise to the Jews from
another place; but thou and thy father's
house shall be destroyed: and who knoweth
whether thou art come to the kingdom for
such a time as this?
15 ¶ Then Esther bade *them* return Mordecai *this answer*,
16 Go, gather together all the Jews that are
present in Shushan, and fast ye for me, and
neither eat nor drink three days, night or
day: I also and my maidens will fast likewise;
and so will I go in unto the king, which *is* not
according to the law: and if I perish, I perish.
17 So Mordecai went his way, and did
according to all that Esther had commanded
him.

Esther 5

1 Now it came to pass on the third day, that
Esther put on *her* royal *apparel*, and stood
in the inner court of the king's house, over
against the king's house: and the king sat
upon his royal throne in the royal house,
over against the gate of the house.
2 And it was so, when the king saw Esther
the queen standing in the court, *that* she
obtained favour in his sight: and the king
held out to Esther the golden sceptre that
was in his hand. So Esther drew near, and
touched the top of the sceptre.
3 Then said the king unto her, What wilt
thou, queen Esther? and what *is* thy
request? it shall be even given thee to the
half of the kingdom.
4 And Esther answered, If *it seem* good unto
the king, let the king and Haman come this
day unto the banquet that I have prepared
for him.
5 Then the king said, Cause Haman to make
haste, that he may do as Esther hath said. So
the king and Haman came to the banquet
that Esther had prepared.
6 ¶ And the king said unto Esther at the
banquet of wine, What *is* thy petition? and
it shall be granted thee: and what *is* thy
request? even to the half of the kingdom it
shall be performed.
7 Then answered Esther, and said, My petition and my request *is;*
8 If I have found favour in the sight of the
king, and if it please the king to grant my
petition, and to perform my request, let
the king and Haman come to the banquet
that I shall prepare for them, and I will do
to morrow as the king hath said.
9 ¶ Then went Haman forth that day joyful
and with a glad heart: but when Haman saw
Mordecai in the king's gate, that he stood
not up, nor moved for him, he was full of
indignation against Mordecai.
10 Nevertheless Haman refrained himself:
and when he came home, he sent and called
for his friends, and Zeresh his wife.
11 And Haman told them of the glory of his
riches, and the multitude of his children,
and all *the things* wherein the king had promoted him, and how he had advanced him
above the princes and servants of the king.
12 Haman said moreover, Yea, Esther the
queen did let no man come in with the king
unto the banquet that she had prepared but
myself; and to morrow am I invited unto her
also with the king.
13 Yet all this availeth me nothing, so long
as I see Mordecai the Jew sitting at the
king's gate.
14 ¶ Then said Zeresh his wife and all his
friends unto him, Let a gallows be made
of fifty cubits high, and to morrow speak
thou unto the king that Mordecai may be
hanged thereon: then go thou in merrily
with the king unto the banquet. And the
thing pleased Haman; and he caused the
gallows to be made.

Esther 6

1 On that night could not the king sleep,
and he commanded to bring the book of
records of the chronicles; and they were
read before the king.
2 And it was found written, that Mordecai
had told of Bigthana and Teresh, two of
the king's chamberlains, the keepers of the
door, who sought to lay hand on the king
Ahasuerus.
3 And the king said, What honour and dignity hath been done to Mordecai for this?
Then said the king's servants that ministered
unto him, There is nothing done for him.
4 ¶ And the king said, Who *is* in the court?
Now Haman was come into the outward
court of the king's house, to speak unto the

king to hang Mordecai on the gallows that
he had prepared for him.
5 And the king's servants said unto him,
Behold, Haman standeth in the court. And
the king said, Let him come in.
6 So Haman came in. And the king said
unto him, What shall be done unto the
man whom the king delighteth to honour?
Now Haman thought in his heart, To whom
would the king delight to do honour more
than to myself?
7 And Haman answered the king, For the
man whom the king delighteth to honour,
8 Let the royal apparel be brought which
the king *useth* to wear, and the horse that
the king rideth upon, and the crown royal
which is set upon his head:
9 And let this apparel and horse be delivered
to the hand of one of the king's most noble
princes, that they may array the man *withal*
whom the king delighteth to honour, and
bring him on horseback through the street
of the city, and proclaim before him, Thus
shall it be done to the man whom the king
delighteth to honour.
10 Then the king said to Haman, Make haste,
and take the apparel and the horse, as thou
hast said, and do even so to Mordecai the
Jew, that sitteth at the king's gate: let nothing fail of all that thou hast spoken.
11 Then took Haman the apparel and the
horse, and arrayed Mordecai, and brought
him on horseback through the street of the
city, and proclaimed before him, Thus shall
it be done unto the man whom the king
delighteth to honour.
12 ¶ And Mordecai came again to the king's
gate. But Haman hasted to his house mourning, and having his head covered.
13 And Haman told Zeresh his wife and all
his friends every *thing* that had befallen him.
Then said his wise men and Zeresh his wife
unto him, If Mordecai *be* of the seed of the
Jews, before whom thou hast begun to fall,
thou shalt not prevail against him, but shalt
surely fall before him.
14 And while they *were* yet talking with him,
came the king's chamberlains, and hasted to
bring Haman unto the banquet that Esther
had prepared.

Esther 7

1 So the king and Haman came to banquet
with Esther the queen.
2 And the king said again unto Esther on the
second day at the banquet of wine, What
is thy petition, queen Esther? and it shall
be granted thee: and what *is* thy request?
and it shall be performed, *even* to the half
of the kingdom.
3 Then Esther the queen answered and
said, If I have found favour in thy sight, O
king, and if it please the king, let my life be
given me at my petition, and my people at
my request:
4 For we are sold, I and my people, to be
destroyed, to be slain, and to perish. But if
we had been sold for bondmen and bondwomen, I had held my tongue, although
the enemy could not countervail the king's
damage.
5 ¶ Then the king Ahasuerus answered and
said unto Esther the queen, Who is he, and
where is he, that durst presume in his heart
to do so?
6 And Esther said, The adversary and enemy
is this wicked Haman. Then Haman was
afraid before the king and the queen.
7 ¶ And the king arising from the banquet of
wine in his wrath *went* into the palace garden: and Haman stood up to make request
for his life to Esther the queen; for he saw
that there was evil determined against him
by the king.
8 Then the king returned out of the palace
garden into the place of the banquet of
wine; and Haman was fallen upon the bed
whereon Esther *was*. Then said the king, Will
he force the queen also before me in the
house? As the word went out of the king's
mouth, they covered Haman's face.
9 And Harbonah, one of the chamberlains, said before the king, Behold also,
the gallows fifty cubits high, which Haman
had made for Mordecai, who had spoken
good for the king, standeth in the house
of Haman. Then the king said, Hang him
thereon.
10 So they hanged Haman on the gallows
that he had prepared for Mordecai. Then
was the king's wrath pacified.

Esther 8

1 On that day did the king Ahasuerus give
the house of Haman the Jews' enemy unto
Esther the queen. And Mordecai came
before the king; for Esther had told what
he *was* unto her.
2 And the king took off his ring, which he
had taken from Haman, and gave it unto
Mordecai. And Esther set Mordecai over
the house of Haman.
3 ¶ And Esther spake yet again before the
king, and fell down at his feet, and besought
him with tears to put away the mischief of
Haman the Agagite, and his device that he
had devised against the Jews.
4 Then the king held out the golden sceptre
toward Esther. So Esther arose, and stood
before the king,
5 And said, If it please the king, and if I have
found favour in his sight, and the thing *seem*
right before the king, and I *be* pleasing in his
eyes, let it be written to reverse the letters
devised by Haman the son of Hammedatha
the Agagite, which he wrote to destroy the
Jews which *are* in all the king's provinces:
6 For how can I endure to see the evil
that shall come unto my people? or how
can I endure to see the destruction of my
kindred?
7 ¶ Then the king Ahasuerus said unto
Esther the queen and to Mordecai the Jew,
Behold, I have given Esther the house of
Haman, and him they have hanged upon
the gallows, because he laid his hand upon
the Jews.
8 Write ye also for the Jews, as it liketh you,
in the king's name, and seal *it* with the king's
ring: for the writing which is written in the
king's name, and sealed with the king's ring,
may no man reverse.
9 Then were the king's scribes called at
that time in the third month, that *is*, the
month Sivan, on the three and twentieth
day thereof; and it was written according
to all that Mordecai commanded unto the
Jews, and to the lieutenants, and the deputies and rulers of the provinces which *are*
from India unto Ethiopia, an hundred twenty
and seven provinces, unto every province
according to the writing thereof, and unto
every people after their language, and to
the Jews according to their writing, and
according to their language.
10 And he wrote in the king Ahasuerus'
name, and sealed *it* with the king's ring,
and sent letters by posts on horseback,
and riders on mules, camels, *and* young
dromedaries:
11 Wherein the king granted the Jews
which *were* in every city to gather themselves together, and to stand for their life,
to destroy, to slay, and to cause to perish,
all the power of the people and province
that would assault them, *both* little ones
and women, and *to take* the spoil of them
for a prey,
12 Upon one day in all the provinces of king
Ahasuerus, *namely*, upon the thirteenth
day of the twelfth month, which *is* the
month Adar.
13 The copy of the writing for a commandment to be given in every province *was*
published unto all people, and that the Jews
should be ready against that day to avenge
themselves on their enemies.
14 *So* the posts that rode upon mules
and camels went out, being hastened and
pressed on by the king's commandment.
And the decree was given at Shushan the
palace.
15 ¶ And Mordecai went out from the presence of the king in royal apparel of blue and
white, and with a great crown of gold, and
with a garment of fine linen and purple: and
the city of Shushan rejoiced and was glad.
16 The Jews had light, and gladness, and
joy, and honour.
17 And in every province, and in every city,
whithersoever the king's commandment
and his decree came, the Jews had joy and
gladness, a feast and a good day. And many
of the people of the land became Jews; for
the fear of the Jews fell upon them.

Esther 9

1 Now in the twelfth month, that *is*, the
month Adar, on the thirteenth day of the
same, when the king's commandment and
his decree drew near to be put in execution,
in the day that the enemies of the Jews
hoped to have power over them, (though
it was turned to the contrary, that the Jews
had rule over them that hated them;)
2 The Jews gathered themselves together
in their cities throughout all the provinces
of the king Ahasuerus, to lay hand on such

as sought their hurt: and no man could
withstand them; for the fear of them fell
upon all people.
3 And all the rulers of the provinces, and the
lieutenants, and the deputies, and officers
of the king, helped the Jews; because the
fear of Mordecai fell upon them.
4 For Mordecai *was* great in the king's
house, and his fame went out throughout
all the provinces: for this man Mordecai
waxed greater and greater.
5 Thus the Jews smote all their enemies with
the stroke of the sword, and slaughter, and
destruction, and did what they would unto
those that hated them.
6 And in Shushan the palace the Jews slew
and destroyed five hundred men.
7 And Parshandatha, and Dalphon, and
Aspatha,
8 And Poratha, and Adalia, and Aridatha,
9 And Parmashta, and Arisai, and Aridai,
and Vajezatha,
10 The ten sons of Haman the son of Hammedatha, the enemy of the Jews, slew they;
but on the spoil laid they not their hand.
11 On that day the number of those that
were slain in Shushan the palace was
brought before the king.
12 ¶ And the king said unto Esther the
queen, The Jews have slain and destroyed
five hundred men in Shushan the palace,
and the ten sons of Haman; what have they
done in the rest of the king's provinces? now
what *is* thy petition? and it shall be granted
thee: or what *is* thy request further? and it
shall be done.
13 Then said Esther, If it please the king,
let it be granted to the Jews which *are* in
Shushan to do to morrow also according
unto this day's decree, and let Haman's ten
sons be hanged upon the gallows.
14 And the king commanded it so to be
done: and the decree was given at Shushan;
and they hanged Haman's ten sons.
15 For the Jews that *were* in Shushan gathered themselves together on the fourteenth
day also of the month Adar, and slew three
hundred men at Shushan; but on the prey
they laid not their hand.
16 But the other Jews that *were* in the king's
provinces gathered themselves together,
and stood for their lives, and had rest from
their enemies, and slew of their foes seventy
and five thousand, but they laid not their
hands on the prey,
17 On the thirteenth day of the month Adar;
and on the fourteenth day of the same
rested they, and made it a day of feasting
and gladness.
18 But the Jews that *were* at Shushan assembled together on the thirteenth *day* thereof,
and on the fourteenth thereof; and on the
fifteenth *day* of the same they rested, and
made it a day of feasting and gladness.
19 Therefore the Jews of the villages, that
dwelt in the unwalled towns, made the
fourteenth day of the month Adar *a day of*
gladness and feasting, and a good day, and
of sending portions one to another.
20 ¶ And Mordecai wrote these things, and
sent letters unto all the Jews that *were* in all
the provinces of the king Ahasuerus, *both*
nigh and far,
21 To stablish *this* among them, that they
should keep the fourteenth day of the
month Adar, and the fifteenth day of the
same, yearly,
22 As the days wherein the Jews rested from
their enemies, and the month which was
turned unto them from sorrow to joy, and
from mourning into a good day: that they
should make them days of feasting and joy,
and of sending portions one to another, and
gifts to the poor.
23 And the Jews undertook to do as they
had begun, and as Mordecai had written
unto them;
24 Because Haman the son of Hammedatha,
the Agagite, the enemy of all the Jews, had
devised against the Jews to destroy them,
and had cast Pur, that *is*, the lot, to consume
them, and to destroy them;
25 But when *Esther* came before the king,
he commanded by letters that his wicked
device, which he devised against the Jews,
should return upon his own head, and that
he and his sons should be hanged on the
gallows.
26 Wherefore they called these days Purim
after the name of Pur. Therefore for all the
words of this letter, and *of that* which they
had seen concerning this matter, and which
had come unto them,
27 The Jews ordained, and took upon them,
and upon their seed, and upon all such as
joined themselves unto them, so as it should

not fail, that they would keep these two days
according to their writing, and according to
their *appointed* time every year;
28 And *that* these days *should be* remembered and kept throughout every generation, every family, every province, and every
city; and *that* these days of Purim should not
fail from among the Jews, nor the memorial
of them perish from their seed.
29 Then Esther the queen, the daughter of
Abihail, and Mordecai the Jew, wrote with
all authority, to confirm this second letter
of Purim.
30 And he sent the letters unto all the Jews,
to the hundred twenty and seven provinces
of the kingdom of Ahasuerus, *with* words of
peace and truth,
31 To confirm these days of Purim in their
times *appointed*, according as Mordecai
the Jew and Esther the queen had enjoined
them, and as they had decreed for themselves and for their seed, the matters of the
fastings and their cry.
32 And the decree of Esther confirmed
these matters of Purim; and it was written
in the book.

Esther 10

1 And the king Ahasuerus laid a tribute upon
the land, and *upon* the isles of the sea.
2 And all the acts of his power and of his
might, and the declaration of the greatness
of Mordecai, whereunto the king advanced
him, *are* they not written in the book of the
chronicles of the kings of Media and Persia?
3 For Mordecai the Jew *was* next unto king
Ahasuerus, and great among the Jews, and
accepted of the multitude of his brethren,
seeking the wealth of his people, and speaking peace to all his seed.

The Book Of

Job

Job 1

1 There was a man in the land of Uz, whose
name *was* Job; and that man was perfect
and upright, and one that feared God, and
eschewed evil.
2 And there were born unto him seven sons
and three daughters.
3 His substance also was seven thousand
sheep, and three thousand camels, and five
hundred yoke of oxen, and five hundred she
asses, and a very great household; so that
this man was the greatest of all the men
of the east.
4 And his sons went and feasted *in their*
houses, every one his day; and sent and
called for their three sisters to eat and to
drink with them.
5 And it was so, when the days of *their*
feasting were gone about, that Job sent
and sanctified them, and rose up early in
the morning, and offered burnt offerings
according to the number of them all: for Job
said, It may be that my sons have sinned,
and cursed God in their hearts. Thus did
Job continually.
6 ¶ Now there was a day when the sons of
God came to present themselves before the
LORD, and Satan came also among them.
7 And the LORD said unto Satan, Whence
comest thou? Then Satan answered the
LORD, and said, From going to and fro in the
earth, and from walking up and down in it.
8 And the LORD said unto Satan, Hast thou
considered my servant Job, that *there is*
none like him in the earth, a perfect and
an upright man, one that feareth God, and
escheweth evil?
9 Then Satan answered the LORD, and said,
Doth Job fear God for nought?
10 Hast not thou made an hedge about him,
and about his house, and about all that he
hath on every side? thou hast blessed the
work of his hands, and his substance is
increased in the land.
11 But put forth thine hand now, and touch
all that he hath, and he will curse thee to
thy face.

12 And the LORD said unto Satan, Behold, all that he hath *is* in thy power; only upon himself put not forth thine hand. So Satan went forth from the presence of the LORD.
13 ¶ And there was a day when his sons and his daughters *were* eating and drinking wine in their eldest brother's house:
14 And there came a messenger unto Job, and said, The oxen were plowing, and the asses feeding beside them:
15 And the Sabeans fell *upon them*, and took them away; yea, they have slain the servants with the edge of the sword; and I only am escaped alone to tell thee.
16 While he *was* yet speaking, there came also another, and said, The fire of God is fallen from heaven, and hath burned up the sheep, and the servants, and consumed them; and I only am escaped alone to tell thee.
17 While he *was* yet speaking, there came also another, and said, The Chaldeans made out three bands, and fell upon the camels, and have carried them away, yea, and slain the servants with the edge of the sword; and I only am escaped alone to tell thee.
18 While he *was* yet speaking, there came also another, and said, Thy sons and thy daughters *were* eating and drinking wine in their eldest brother's house:
19 And, behold, there came a great wind from the wilderness, and smote the four corners of the house, and it fell upon the young men, and they are dead; and I only am escaped alone to tell thee.
20 Then Job arose, and rent his mantle, and shaved his head, and fell down upon the ground, and worshipped,
21 And said, Naked came I out of my mother's womb, and naked shall I return thither: the LORD gave, and the LORD hath taken away; blessed be the name of the LORD.
22 In all this Job sinned not, nor charged God foolishly.

Job 2

1 Again there was a day when the sons of God came to present themselves before the LORD, and Satan came also among them to present himself before the LORD.
2 And the LORD said unto Satan, From whence comest thou? And Satan answered the LORD, and said, From going to and fro in the earth, and from walking up and down in it.
3 And the LORD said unto Satan, Hast thou considered my servant Job, that *there is* none like him in the earth, a perfect and an upright man, one that feareth God, and escheweth evil? and still he holdeth fast his integrity, although thou movedst me against him, to destroy him without cause.
4 And Satan answered the LORD, and said, Skin for skin, yea, all that a man hath will he give for his life.
5 But put forth thine hand now, and touch his bone and his flesh, and he will curse thee to thy face.
6 And the LORD said unto Satan, Behold, he *is* in thine hand; but save his life.
7 ¶ So went Satan forth from the presence of the LORD, and smote Job with sore boils from the sole of his foot unto his crown.
8 And he took him a potsherd to scrape himself withal; and he sat down among the ashes.
9 ¶ Then said his wife unto him, Dost thou still retain thine integrity? curse God, and die.
10 But he said unto her, Thou speakest as one of the foolish women speaketh. What? shall we receive good at the hand of God, and shall we not receive evil? In all this did not Job sin with his lips.
11 ¶ Now when Job's three friends heard of all this evil that was come upon him, they came every one from his own place; Eliphaz the Temanite, and Bildad the Shuhite, and Zophar the Naamathite: for they had made an appointment together to come to mourn with him and to comfort him.
12 And when they lifted up their eyes afar off, and knew him not, they lifted up their voice, and wept; and they rent every one his mantle, and sprinkled dust upon their heads toward heaven.
13 So they sat down with him upon the ground seven days and seven nights, and none spake a word unto him: for they saw that *his* grief was very great.

Job 3

1 After this opened Job his mouth, and cursed his day.
2 And Job spake, and said,
3 Let the day perish wherein I was born,

and the night *in which* it was said, There is
a man child conceived.
4 Let that day be darkness; let not God
regard it from above, neither let the light
shine upon it.
5 Let darkness and the shadow of death
stain it; let a cloud dwell upon it; let the
blackness of the day terrify it.
6 *As for* that night, let darkness seize upon
it; let it not be joined unto the days of the
year, let it not come into the number of
the months.
7 Lo, let that night be solitary, let no joyful
voice come therein.
8 Let them curse it that curse the day, who
are ready to raise up their mourning.
9 Let the stars of the twilight thereof be
dark; let it look for light, but *have* none;
neither let it see the dawning of the day:
10 Because it shut not up the doors of
my *mother's* womb, nor hid sorrow from
mine eyes.
11 Why died I not from the womb? *why* did
I *not* give up the ghost when I came out of
the belly?
12 Why did the knees prevent me? or why
the breasts that I should suck?
13 For now should I have lain still and been
quiet, I should have slept: then had I been
at rest,
14 With kings and counsellers of the earth,
which built desolate places for themselves;
15 Or with princes that had gold, who filled
their houses with silver:
16 Or as an hidden untimely birth I had not
been; as infants *which* never saw light.
17 There the wicked cease *from* troubling;
and there the weary be at rest.
18 *There* the prisoners rest together; they
hear not the voice of the oppressor.
19 The small and great are there; and the
servant *is* free from his master.
20 Wherefore is light given to him that is
in misery, and life unto the bitter *in* soul;
21 Which long for death, but it *cometh* not;
and dig for it more than for hid treasures;
22 Which rejoice exceedingly, *and* are glad,
when they can find the grave?
23 *Why is light given* to a man whose way is
hid, and whom God hath hedged in?
24 For my sighing cometh before I eat, and
my roarings are poured out like the waters.
25 For the thing which I greatly feared is
come upon me, and that which I was afraid
of is come unto me.
26 I was not in safety, neither had I rest,
neither was I quiet; yet trouble came.

Job 4

1 Then Eliphaz the Temanite answered
and said,
2 *If* we assay to commune with thee, wilt
thou be grieved? but who can withhold
himself from speaking?
3 Behold, thou hast instructed many, and
thou hast strengthened the weak hands.
4 Thy words have upholden him that was
falling, and thou hast strengthened the
feeble knees.
5 But now it is come upon thee, and thou
faintest; it toucheth thee, and thou art
troubled.
6 *Is* not *this* thy fear, thy confidence, thy
hope, and the uprightness of thy ways?
7 Remember, I pray thee, who *ever* perished, being innocent? or where were the
righteous cut off?
8 Even as I have seen, they that plow iniquity, and sow wickedness, reap the same.
9 By the blast of God they perish, and by the
breath of his nostrils are they consumed.
10 The roaring of the lion, and the voice of
the fierce lion, and the teeth of the young
lions, are broken.
11 The old lion perisheth for lack of prey,
and the stout lion's whelps are scattered
abroad.
12 Now a thing was secretly brought to me,
and mine ear received a little thereof.
13 In thoughts from the visions of the night,
when deep sleep falleth on men,
14 Fear came upon me, and trembling,
which made all my bones to shake.
15 Then a spirit passed before my face; the
hair of my flesh stood up:
16 It stood still, but I could not discern the
form thereof: an image *was* before mine
eyes, *there was* silence, and I heard a voice,
saying,
17 Shall mortal man be more just than God?
shall a man be more pure than his maker?
18 Behold, he put no trust in his servants;
and his angels he charged with folly:
19 How much less *in* them that dwell in
houses of clay, whose foundation *is* in the
dust, *which* are crushed before the moth?

20 They are destroyed from morning to evening: they perish for ever without any regarding *it*.
21 Doth not their excellency *which is* in them go away? they die, even without wisdom.

Job 5

1 Call now, if there be any that will answer thee; and to which of the saints wilt thou turn?
2 For wrath killeth the foolish man, and envy slayeth the silly one.
3 I have seen the foolish taking root: but suddenly I cursed his habitation.
4 His children are far from safety, and they are crushed in the gate, neither *is there* any to deliver *them*.
5 Whose harvest the hungry eateth up, and taketh it even out of the thorns, and the robber swalloweth up their substance.
6 Although affliction cometh not forth of the dust, neither doth trouble spring out of the ground;
7 Yet man is born unto trouble, as the sparks fly upward.
8 I would seek unto God, and unto God would I commit my cause:
9 Which doeth great things and unsearchable; marvellous things without number:
10 Who giveth rain upon the earth, and sendeth waters upon the fields:
11 To set up on high those that be low; that those which mourn may be exalted to safety.
12 He disappointeth the devices of the crafty, so that their hands cannot perform *their* enterprise.
13 He taketh the wise in their own craftiness: and the counsel of the froward is carried headlong.
14 They meet with darkness in the daytime, and grope in the noonday as in the night.
15 But he saveth the poor from the sword, from their mouth, and from the hand of the mighty.
16 So the poor hath hope, and iniquity stoppeth her mouth.
17 Behold, happy *is* the man whom God correcteth: therefore despise not thou the chastening of the Almighty:
18 For he maketh sore, and bindeth up: he woundeth, and his hands make whole.
19 He shall deliver thee in six troubles: yea, in seven there shall no evil touch thee.
20 In famine he shall redeem thee from death: and in war from the power of the sword.
21 Thou shalt be hid from the scourge of the tongue: neither shalt thou be afraid of destruction when it cometh.
22 At destruction and famine thou shalt laugh: neither shalt thou be afraid of the beasts of the earth.
23 For thou shalt be in league with the stones of the field: and the beasts of the field shall be at peace with thee.
24 And thou shalt know that thy tabernacle *shall be* in peace; and thou shalt visit thy habitation, and shalt not sin.
25 Thou shalt know also that thy seed *shall be* great, and thine offspring as the grass of the earth.
26 Thou shalt come to *thy* grave in a full age, like as a shock of corn cometh in in his season.
27 Lo this, we have searched it, so it *is;* hear it, and know thou *it* for thy good.

Job 6

1 But Job answered and said,
2 Oh that my grief were throughly weighed, and my calamity laid in the balances together!
3 For now it would be heavier than the sand of the sea: therefore my words are swallowed up.
4 For the arrows of the Almighty *are* within me, the poison whereof drinketh up my spirit: the terrors of God do set themselves in array against me.
5 Doth the wild ass bray when he hath grass? or loweth the ox over his fodder?
6 Can that which is unsavoury be eaten without salt? or is there *any* taste in the white of an egg?
7 The things *that* my soul refused to touch *are* as my sorrowful meat.
8 Oh that I might have my request; and that God would grant *me* the thing that I long for!
9 Even that it would please God to destroy me; that he would let loose his hand, and cut me off!
10 Then should I yet have comfort; yea, I would harden myself in sorrow: let him not

spare; for I have not concealed the words
of the Holy One.
11 What *is* my strength, that I should hope?
and what *is* mine end, that I should prolong
my life?
12 *Is* my strength the strength of stones?
or *is* my flesh of brass?
13 *Is* not my help in me? and is wisdom
driven quite from me?
14 To him that is afflicted pity *should be*
shewed from his friend; but he forsaketh
the fear of the Almighty.
15 My brethren have dealt deceitfully as
a brook, *and* as the stream of brooks they
pass away;
16 Which are blackish by reason of the ice,
and wherein the snow is hid:
17 What time they wax warm, they vanish:
when it is hot, they are consumed out of
their place.
18 The paths of their way are turned aside;
they go to nothing, and perish.
19 The troops of Tema looked, the companies of Sheba waited for them.
20 They were confounded because they
had hoped; they came thither, and were
ashamed.
21 For now ye are nothing; ye see *my* casting
down, and are afraid.
22 Did I say, Bring unto me? or, Give a
reward for me of your substance?
23 Or, Deliver me from the enemy's hand?
or, Redeem me from the hand of the mighty?
24 Teach me, and I will hold my tongue:
and cause me to understand wherein I
have erred.
25 How forcible are right words! but what
doth your arguing reprove?
26 Do ye imagine to reprove words, and the
speeches of one that is desperate, *which*
are as wind?
27 Yea, ye overwhelm the fatherless, and
ye dig *a pit* for your friend.
28 Now therefore be content, look upon
me; for *it is* evident unto you if I lie.
29 Return, I pray you, let it not be iniquity;
yea, return again, my righteousness *is* in it.
30 Is there iniquity in my tongue? cannot
my taste discern perverse things?

Job 7

1 *Is there* not an appointed time to man
upon earth? *are not* his days also like the
days of an hireling?
2 As a servant earnestly desireth the
shadow, and as an hireling looketh for *the*
reward of his work:
3 So am I made to possess months of vanity,
and wearisome nights are appointed to me.
4 When I lie down, I say, When shall I arise,
and the night be gone? and I am full of toss-
ings to and fro unto the dawning of the day.
5 My flesh is clothed with worms and clods
of dust; my skin is broken, and become
loathsome.
6 My days are swifter than a weaver's shut-
tle, and are spent without hope.
7 O remember that my life *is* wind: mine
eye shall no more see good.
8 The eye of him that hath seen me shall
see me no *more:* thine eyes *are* upon me,
and I *am* not.
9 *As* the cloud is consumed and vanisheth
away: so he that goeth down to the grave
shall come up no *more.*
10 He shall return no more to his house,
neither shall his place know him any more.
11 Therefore I will not refrain my mouth; I
will speak in the anguish of my spirit; I will
complain in the bitterness of my soul.
12 *Am* I a sea, or a whale, that thou settest
a watch over me?
13 When I say, My bed shall comfort me,
my couch shall ease my complaint;
14 Then thou scarest me with dreams, and
terrifiest me through visions:
15 So that my soul chooseth strangling, *and*
death rather than my life.
16 I loathe *it;* I would not live alway: let me
alone; for my days *are* vanity.
17 What *is* man, that thou shouldest magnify him? and that thou shouldest set thine
heart upon him?
18 And *that* thou shouldest visit him every
morning, *and* try him every moment?
19 How long wilt thou not depart from
me, nor let me alone till I swallow down
my spittle?
20 I have sinned; what shall I do unto thee,
O thou preserver of men? why hast thou
set me as a mark against thee, so that I am
a burden to myself?
21 And why dost thou not pardon my transgression, and take away mine iniquity? for

now shall I sleep in the dust; and thou shalt
seek me in the morning, but I *shall* not *be.*

Job 8

1 Then answered Bildad the Shuhite, and
said,
2 How long wilt thou speak these *things?*
and *how long shall* the words of thy mouth
be like a strong wind?
3 Doth God pervert judgment? or doth the
Almighty pervert justice?
4 If thy children have sinned against him,
and he have cast them away for their transgression;
5 If thou wouldest seek unto God betimes,
and make thy supplication to the Almighty;
6 If thou *wert* pure and upright; surely now
he would awake for thee, and make the
habitation of thy righteousness prosperous.
7 Though thy beginning was small, yet thy
latter end should greatly increase.
8 For inquire, I pray thee, of the former
age, and prepare thyself to the search of
their fathers:
9 (For we *are but of* yesterday, and know
nothing, because our days upon earth *are*
a shadow:)
10 Shall not they teach thee, *and* tell thee,
and utter words out of their heart?
11 Can the rush grow up without mire? can
the flag grow without water?
12 Whilst it *is* yet in his greenness, *and* not
cut down, it withereth before any *other*
herb.
13 So *are* the paths of all that forget God;
and the hypocrite's hope shall perish:
14 Whose hope shall be cut off, and whose
trust *shall be* a spider's web.
15 He shall lean upon his house, but it shall
not stand: he shall hold it fast, but it shall
not endure.
16 He *is* green before the sun, and his branch
shooteth forth in his garden.
17 His roots are wrapped about the heap,
and seeth the place of stones.
18 If he destroy him from his place, then *it*
shall deny him, *saying,* I have not seen thee.
19 Behold, this *is* the joy of his way, and out
of the earth shall others grow.
20 Behold, God will not cast away a perfect
man, neither will he help the evil doers:
21 Till he fill thy mouth with laughing, and
thy lips with rejoicing.
22 They that hate thee shall be clothed with
shame; and the dwelling place of the wicked
shall come to nought.

Job 9

1 Then Job answered and said,
2 I know *it is* so of a truth: but how should
man be just with God?
3 If he will contend with him, he cannot
answer him one of a thousand.
4 *He is* wise in heart, and mighty in strength:
who hath hardened *himself* against him, and
hath prospered?
5 Which removeth the mountains, and
they know not: which overturneth them
in his anger.
6 Which shaketh the earth out of her place,
and the pillars thereof tremble.
7 Which commandeth the sun, and it riseth
not; and sealeth up the stars.
8 Which alone spreadeth out the heavens,
and treadeth upon the waves of the sea.
9 Which maketh Arcturus, Orion, and Pleiades, and the chambers of the south.
10 Which doeth great things past finding
out; yea, and wonders without number.
11 Lo, he goeth by me, and I see *him* not:
he passeth on also, but I perceive him not.
12 Behold, he taketh away, who can hinder
him? who will say unto him, What doest
thou?
13 *If* God will not withdraw his anger, the
proud helpers do stoop under him.
14 How much less shall I answer him, *and*
choose out my words *to reason* with him?
15 Whom, though I were righteous, *yet*
would I not answer, *but* I would make supplication to my judge.
16 If I had called, and he had answered me;
yet would I not believe that he had hearkened unto my voice.
17 For he breaketh me with a tempest, and
multiplieth my wounds without cause.
18 He will not suffer me to take my breath,
but filleth me with bitterness.
19 If *I speak* of strength, lo, *he is* strong:
and if of judgment, who shall set me a time
to plead?
20 If I justify myself, mine own mouth shall
condemn me: *if I say,* I *am* perfect, it shall
also prove me perverse.
21 *Though* I *were* perfect, *yet* would I not
know my soul: I would despise my life.

22 This *is* one *thing*, therefore I said *it*, He
destroyeth the perfect and the wicked.
23 If the scourge slay suddenly, he will laugh
at the trial of the innocent.
24 The earth is given into the hand of the
wicked: he covereth the faces of the judges
thereof; if not, where, *and* who *is* he?
25 Now my days are swifter than a post:
they flee away, they see no good.
26 They are passed away as the swift ships:
as the eagle *that* hasteth to the prey.
27 If I say, I will forget my complaint, I will
leave off my heaviness, and comfort *myself:*
28 I am afraid of all my sorrows, I know that
thou wilt not hold me innocent.
29 *If* I be wicked, why then labour I in vain?
30 If I wash myself with snow water, and
make my hands never so clean;
31 Yet shalt thou plunge me in the ditch, and
mine own clothes shall abhor me.
32 For *he is* not a man, as I *am*, *that* I should
answer him, *and* we should come together
in judgment.
33 Neither is there any daysman betwixt
us, *that* might lay his hand upon us both.
34 Let him take his rod away from me, and
let not his fear terrify me:
35 *Then* would I speak, and not fear him;
but *it is* not so with me.

Job 10

1 My soul is weary of my life; I will leave my
complaint upon myself; I will speak in the
bitterness of my soul.
2 I will say unto God, Do not condemn
me; shew me wherefore thou contendest
with me.
3 *Is it* good unto thee that thou shouldest
oppress, that thou shouldest despise the
work of thine hands, and shine upon the
counsel of the wicked?
4 Hast thou eyes of flesh? or seest thou as
man seeth?
5 *Are* thy days as the days of man? *are* thy
years as man's days,
6 That thou inquirest after mine iniquity,
and searchest after my sin?
7 Thou knowest that I am not wicked; and
there is none that can deliver out of thine
hand.
8 Thine hands have made me and fashioned
me together round about; yet thou dost
destroy me.
9 Remember, I beseech thee, that thou hast
made me as the clay; and wilt thou bring me
into dust again?
10 Hast thou not poured me out as milk,
and curdled me like cheese?
11 Thou hast clothed me with skin and flesh,
and hast fenced me with bones and sinews.
12 Thou hast granted me life and favour,
and thy visitation hath preserved my spirit.
13 And these *things* hast thou hid in thine
heart: I know that this *is* with thee.
14 If I sin, then thou markest me, and thou
wilt not acquit me from mine iniquity.
15 If I be wicked, woe unto me; and *if* I be
righteous, *yet* will I not lift up my head. *I*
am full of confusion; therefore see thou
mine affliction;
16 For it increaseth. Thou huntest me as a
fierce lion: and again thou shewest thyself
marvellous upon me.
17 Thou renewest thy witnesses against me,
and increasest thine indignation upon me;
changes and war *are* against me.
18 Wherefore then hast thou brought me
forth out of the womb? Oh that I had given
up the ghost, and no eye had seen me!
19 I should have been as though I had not
been; I should have been carried from the
womb to the grave.
20 *Are* not my days few? cease *then, and* let
me alone, that I may take comfort a little,
21 Before I go *whence* I shall not return,
even to the land of darkness and the shadow
of death;
22 A land of darkness, as darkness *itself; and*
of the shadow of death, without any order,
and *where* the light *is* as darkness.

Job 11

1 Then answered Zophar the Naamathite,
and said,
2 Should not the multitude of words be
answered? and should a man full of talk
be justified?
3 Should thy lies make men hold their
peace? and when thou mockest, shall no
man make thee ashamed?
4 For thou hast said, My doctrine *is* pure,
and I am clean in thine eyes.
5 But oh that God would speak, and open
his lips against thee;
6 And that he would shew thee the secrets
of wisdom, that *they are* double to that

which is! Know therefore that God exacteth
of thee *less* than thine iniquity *deserveth*.
7 Canst thou by searching find out God?
canst thou find out the Almighty unto
perfection?
8 *It is* as high as heaven; what canst thou do?
deeper than hell; what canst thou know?
9 The measure thereof *is* longer than the
earth, and broader than the sea.
10 If he cut off, and shut up, or gather
together, then who can hinder him?
11 For he knoweth vain men: he seeth wickedness also; will he not then consider *it?*
12 For vain man would be wise, though man
be born *like* a wild ass's colt.
13 If thou prepare thine heart, and stretch
out thine hands toward him;
14 If iniquity *be* in thine hand, put it far
away, and let not wickedness dwell in thy
tabernacles.
15 For then shalt thou lift up thy face without spot; yea, thou shalt be stedfast, and
shalt not fear:
16 Because thou shalt forget *thy* misery,
and remember *it* as waters *that* pass away:
17 And *thine* age shall be clearer than the
noonday; thou shalt shine forth, thou shalt
be as the morning.
18 And thou shalt be secure, because there
is hope; yea, thou shalt dig *about thee, and*
thou shalt take thy rest in safety.
19 Also thou shalt lie down, and none shall
make *thee* afraid; yea, many shall make suit
unto thee.
20 But the eyes of the wicked shall fail, and
they shall not escape, and their hope *shall*
be as the giving up of the ghost.

Job 12

1 And Job answered and said,
2 No doubt but ye *are* the people, and wisdom shall die with you.
3 But I have understanding as well as you;
I *am* not inferior to you: yea, who knoweth
not such things as these?
4 I am *as* one mocked of his neighbour, who
calleth upon God, and he answereth him:
the just upright *man is* laughed to scorn.
5 He that is ready to slip with *his* feet *is as*
a lamp despised in the thought of him that
is at ease.
6 The tabernacles of robbers prosper, and
they that provoke God are secure; into
whose hand God bringeth *abundantly*.
7 But ask now the beasts, and they shall
teach thee; and the fowls of the air, and
they shall tell thee:
8 Or speak to the earth, and it shall teach
thee: and the fishes of the sea shall declare
unto thee.
9 Who knoweth not in all these that the
hand of the LORD hath wrought this?
10 In whose hand *is* the soul of every living
thing, and the breath of all mankind.
11 Doth not the ear try words? and the
mouth taste his meat?
12 With the ancient *is* wisdom; and in length
of days understanding.
13 With him *is* wisdom and strength, he
hath counsel and understanding.
14 Behold, he breaketh down, and it cannot
be built again: he shutteth up a man, and
there can be no opening.
15 Behold, he withholdeth the waters, and
they dry up: also he sendeth them out, and
they overturn the earth.
16 With him *is* strength and wisdom: the
deceived and the deceiver *are* his.
17 He leadeth counsellers away spoiled, and
maketh the judges fools.
18 He looseth the bond of kings, and girdeth
their loins with a girdle.
19 He leadeth princes away spoiled, and
overthroweth the mighty.
20 He removeth away the speech of the
trusty, and taketh away the understanding
of the aged.
21 He poureth contempt upon princes, and
weakeneth the strength of the mighty.
22 He discovereth deep things out of darkness, and bringeth out to light the shadow
of death.
23 He increaseth the nations, and destroyeth
them: he enlargeth the nations, and strait-
eneth them *again*.
24 He taketh away the heart of the chief of
the people of the earth, and causeth them
to wander in a wilderness *where there is*
no way.
25 They grope in the dark without light, and
he maketh them to stagger like *a* drunken
man.

Job 13

1 Lo, mine eye hath seen all *this*, mine ear hath heard and understood it.
2 What ye know, *the same* do I know also: I *am* not inferior unto you.
3 Surely I would speak to the Almighty, and I desire to reason with God.
4 But ye *are* forgers of lies, ye *are* all physicians of no value.
5 O that ye would altogether hold your peace! and it should be your wisdom.
6 Hear now my reasoning, and hearken to the pleadings of my lips.
7 Will ye speak wickedly for God? and talk deceitfully for him?
8 Will ye accept his person? will ye contend for God?
9 Is it good that he should search you out? or as one man mocketh another, do ye *so* mock him?
10 He will surely reprove you, if ye do secretly accept persons.
11 Shall not his excellency make you afraid? and his dread fall upon you?
12 Your remembrances *are* like unto ashes, your bodies to bodies of clay.
13 Hold your peace, let me alone, that I may speak, and let come on me what *will*.
14 Wherefore do I take my flesh in my teeth, and put my life in mine hand?
15 Though he slay me, yet will I trust in him: but I will maintain mine own ways before him.
16 He also *shall be* my salvation: for an hypocrite shall not come before him.
17 Hear diligently my speech, and my declaration with your ears.
18 Behold now, I have ordered *my* cause; I know that I shall be justified.
19 Who *is* he *that* will plead with me? for now, if I hold my tongue, I shall give up the ghost.
20 Only do not two *things* unto me: then will I not hide myself from thee.
21 Withdraw thine hand far from me: and let not thy dread make me afraid.
22 Then call thou, and I will answer: or let me speak, and answer thou me.
23 How many *are* mine iniquities and sins? make me to know my transgression and my sin.
24 Wherefore hidest thou thy face, and holdest me for thine enemy?
25 Wilt thou break a leaf driven to and fro? and wilt thou pursue the dry stubble?
26 For thou writest bitter things against me, and makest me to possess the iniquities of my youth.
27 Thou puttest my feet also in the stocks, and lookest narrowly unto all my paths; thou settest a print upon the heels of my feet.
28 And he, as a rotten thing, consumeth, as a garment that is moth eaten.

Job 14

1 MAN *that is* born of a woman *is* of few days, and full of trouble.
2 He cometh forth like a flower, and is cut down: he fleeth also as a shadow, and continueth not.
3 And dost thou open thine eyes upon such an one, and bringest me into judgment with thee?
4 Who can bring a clean *thing* out of an unclean? not one.
5 Seeing his days *are* determined, the number of his months *are* with thee, thou hast appointed his bounds that he cannot pass;
6 Turn from him, that he may rest, till he shall accomplish, as an hireling, his day.
7 For there is hope of a tree, if it be cut down, that it will sprout again, and that the tender branch thereof will not cease.
8 Though the root thereof wax old in the earth, and the stock thereof die in the ground;
9 *Yet* through the scent of water it will bud, and bring forth boughs like a plant.
10 But man dieth, and wasteth away: yea, man giveth up the ghost, and where *is* he?
11 *As* the waters fail from the sea, and the flood decayeth and drieth up:
12 So man lieth down, and riseth not: till the heavens *be* no more, they shall not awake, nor be raised out of their sleep.
13 O that thou wouldest hide me in the grave, that thou wouldest keep me secret, until thy wrath be past, that thou wouldest appoint me a set time, and remember me!
14 If a man die, shall he live *again?* all the days of my appointed time will I wait, till my change come.
15 Thou shalt call, and I will answer thee: thou wilt have a desire to the work of thine hands.

16 For now thou numberest my steps: dost
thou not watch over my sin?
17 My transgression *is* sealed up in a bag,
and thou sewest up mine iniquity.
18 And surely the mountain falling cometh
to nought, and the rock is removed out of
his place.
19 The waters wear the stones: thou wash-
est away the things which grow *out* of the
dust of the earth; and thou destroyest the
hope of man.
20 Thou prevailest for ever against him, and
he passeth: thou changest his countenance,
and sendest him away.
21 His sons come to honour, and he knoweth
it not; and they are brought low, but he
perceiveth *it* not of them.
22 But his flesh upon him shall have pain,
and his soul within him shall mourn.

Job 15

1 Then answered Eliphaz the Temanite,
and said,
2 Should a wise man utter vain knowledge,
and fill his belly with the east wind?
3 Should he reason with unprofitable talk?
or with speeches wherewith he can do no
good?
4 Yea, thou castest off fear, and restrainest
prayer before God.
5 For thy mouth uttereth thine iniquity,
and thou choosest the tongue of the crafty.
6 Thine own mouth condemneth thee, and
not I: yea, thine own lips testify against thee.
7 *Art* thou the first man *that* was born? or
wast thou made before the hills?
8 Hast thou heard the secret of God? and
dost thou restrain wisdom to thyself?
9 What knowest thou, that we know not?
what understandest thou, which *is* not in us?
10 With us *are* both the grayheaded and
very aged men, much elder than thy father.
11 *Are* the consolations of God small with
thee? is there any secret thing with thee?
12 Why doth thine heart carry thee away?
and what do thy eyes wink at,
13 That thou turnest thy spirit against God,
and lettest *such* words go out of thy mouth?
14 What *is* man, that he should be clean?
and *he which is* born of a woman, that he
should be righteous?
15 Behold, he putteth no trust in his saints;
yea, the heavens are not clean in his sight.
16 How much more abominable and filthy
is man, which drinketh iniquity like water?
17 I will shew thee, hear me; and that *which*
I have seen I will declare;
18 Which wise men have told from their
fathers, and have not hid *it:*
19 Unto whom alone the earth was given,
and no stranger passed among them.
20 The wicked man travaileth with pain all
his days, and the number of years is hidden
to the oppressor.
21 A dreadful sound *is* in his ears: in prosperity the destroyer shall come upon him.
22 He believeth not that he shall return
out of darkness, and he is waited for of
the sword.
23 He wandereth abroad for bread, *saying,*
Where *is it?* he knoweth that the day of
darkness is ready at his hand.
24 Trouble and anguish shall make him
afraid; they shall prevail against him, as a
king ready to the battle.
25 For he stretcheth out his hand against
God, and strengtheneth himself against
the Almighty.
26 He runneth upon him, *even* on *his* neck,
upon the thick bosses of his bucklers:
27 Because he covereth his face with his fatness, and maketh collops of fat on *his* flanks.
28 And he dwelleth in desolate cities, *and*
in houses which no man inhabiteth, which
are ready to become heaps.
29 He shall not be rich, neither shall his substance continue, neither shall he prolong the
perfection thereof upon the earth.
30 He shall not depart out of darkness; the
flame shall dry up his branches, and by the
breath of his mouth shall he go away.
31 Let not him that is deceived trust in
vanity: for vanity shall be his recompence.
32 It shall be accomplished before his time,
and his branch shall not be green.
33 He shall shake off his unripe grape as the
vine, and shall cast off his flower as the olive.
34 For the congregation of hypocrites *shall*
be desolate, and fire shall consume the tabernacles of bribery.
35 They conceive mischief, and bring forth
vanity, and their belly prepareth deceit.

Job 16

1 Then Job answered and said,

2 I have heard many such things: miserable comforters *are* ye all.

3 Shall vain words have an end? or what emboldeneth thee that thou answerest?

4 I also could speak as ye *do:* if your soul were in my soul's stead, I could heap up words against you, and shake mine head at you.

5 *But* I would strengthen you with my mouth, and the moving of my lips should asswage *your grief.*

6 Though I speak, my grief is not asswaged: and *though* I forbear, what am I eased?

7 But now he hath made me weary: thou hast made desolate all my company.

8 And thou hast filled me with wrinkles, *which* is a witness *against me:* and my leanness rising up in me beareth witness to my face.

9 He teareth *me* in his wrath, who hateth me: he gnasheth upon me with his teeth; mine enemy sharpeneth his eyes upon me.

10 They have gaped upon me with their mouth; they have smitten me upon the cheek reproachfully; they have gathered themselves together against me.

11 God hath delivered me to the ungodly, and turned me over into the hands of the wicked.

12 I was at ease, but he hath broken me asunder: he hath also taken *me* by my neck, and shaken me to pieces, and set me up for his mark.

13 His archers compass me round about, he cleaveth my reins asunder, and doth not spare; he poureth out my gall upon the ground.

14 He breaketh me with breach upon breach, he runneth upon me like a giant.

15 I have sewed sackcloth upon my skin, and defiled my horn in the dust.

16 My face is foul with weeping, and on my eyelids *is* the shadow of death;

17 Not for *any* injustice in mine hands: also my prayer *is* pure.

18 O earth, cover not thou my blood, and let my cry have no place.

19 Also now, behold, my witness *is* in heaven, and my record *is* on high.

20 My friends scorn me: *but* mine eye poureth out *tears* unto God.

21 O that one might plead for a man with God, as a man *pleadeth* for his neighbour!

22 When a few years are come, then I shall go the way *whence* I shall not return.

Job 17

1 My breath is corrupt, my days are extinct, the graves *are ready* for me.

2 *Are there* not mockers with me? and doth not mine eye continue in their provocation?

3 Lay down now, put me in a surety with thee; who *is* he *that* will strike hands with me?

4 For thou hast hid their heart from understanding: therefore shalt thou not exalt *them.*

5 He that speaketh flattery to *his* friends, even the eyes of his children shall fail.

6 He hath made me also a byword of the people; and aforetime I was as a tabret.

7 Mine eye also is dim by reason of sorrow, and all my members *are* as a shadow.

8 Upright *men* shall be astonied at this, and the innocent shall stir up himself against the hypocrite.

9 The righteous also shall hold on his way, and he that hath clean hands shall be stronger and stronger.

10 But as for you all, do ye return, and come now: for I cannot find *one* wise *man* among you.

11 My days are past, my purposes are broken off, *even* the thoughts of my heart.

12 They change the night into day: the light *is* short because of darkness.

13 If I wait, the grave *is* mine house: I have made my bed in the darkness.

14 I have said to corruption, Thou *art* my father: to the worm, *Thou art* my mother, and my sister.

15 And where *is* now my hope? as for my hope, who shall see it?

16 They shall go down to the bars of the pit, when *our* rest together *is* in the dust.

Job 18

1 Then answered Bildad the Shuhite, and said,

2 How long *will it be ere* ye make an end of words? mark, and afterwards we will speak.

3 Wherefore are we counted as beasts, *and* reputed vile in your sight?

4 He teareth himself in his anger: shall the earth be forsaken for thee? and shall the rock be removed out of his place?

5 Yea, the light of the wicked shall be put
out, and the spark of his fire shall not shine.
6 The light shall be dark in his tabernacle,
and his candle shall be put out with him.
7 The steps of his strength shall be straitened, and his own counsel shall cast him
down.
8 For he is cast into a net by his own feet,
and he walketh upon a snare.
9 The gin shall take *him* by the heel, *and* the
robber shall prevail against him.
10 The snare *is* laid for him in the ground,
and a trap for him in the way.
11 Terrors shall make him afraid on every
side, and shall drive him to his feet.
12 His strength shall be hungerbitten, and
destruction *shall be* ready at his side.
13 It shall devour the strength of his skin:
even the firstborn of death shall devour
his strength.
14 His confidence shall be rooted out of
his tabernacle, and it shall bring him to the
king of terrors.
15 It shall dwell in his tabernacle, because *it*
is none of his: brimstone shall be scattered
upon his habitation.
16 His roots shall be dried up beneath, and
above shall his branch be cut off.
17 His remembrance shall perish from the
earth, and he shall have no name in the
street.
18 He shall be driven from light into darkness, and chased out of the world.
19 He shall neither have son nor nephew
among his people, nor any remaining in
his dwellings.
20 They that come after *him* shall be astonied at his day, as they that went before were
affrighted.
21 Surely such *are* the dwellings of the
wicked, and this *is* the place *of him that*
knoweth not God.

Job 19

1 Then Job answered and said,
2 How long will ye vex my soul, and break
me in pieces with words?
3 These ten times have ye reproached me:
ye are not ashamed *that* ye make yourselves
strange to me.
4 And be it indeed *that* I have erred, mine
error remaineth with myself.
5 If indeed ye will magnify *yourselves* against
me, and plead against me my reproach:
6 Know now that God hath overthrown me,
and hath compassed me with his net.
7 Behold, I cry out of wrong, but I am not
heard: I cry aloud, but *there is* no judgment.
8 He hath fenced up my way that I cannot
pass, and he hath set darkness in my paths.
9 He hath stripped me of my glory, and taken
the crown *from* my head.
10 He hath destroyed me on every side, and
I am gone: and mine hope hath he removed
like a tree.
11 He hath also kindled his wrath against
me, and he counteth me unto him as *one*
of his enemies.
12 His troops come together, and raise up
their way against me, and encamp round
about my tabernacle.
13 He hath put my brethren far from me,
and mine acquaintance are verily estranged
from me.
14 My kinsfolk have failed, and my familiar
friends have forgotten me.
15 They that dwell in mine house, and my
maids, count me for a stranger: I am an alien
in their sight.
16 I called my servant, and he gave *me* no
answer; I intreated him with my mouth.
17 My breath is strange to my wife, though
I intreated for the children's *sake* of mine
own body.
18 Yea, young children despised me; I arose,
and they spake against me.
19 All my inward friends abhorred me: and
they whom I loved are turned against me.
20 My bone cleaveth to my skin and to my
flesh, and I am escaped with the skin of
my teeth.
21 Have pity upon me, have pity upon me,
O ye my friends; for the hand of God hath
touched me.
22 Why do ye persecute me as God, and
are not satisfied with my flesh?
23 Oh that my words were now written! oh
that they were printed in a book!
24 That they were graven with an iron pen
and lead in the rock for ever!
25 For I know *that* my redeemer liveth, and
that he shall stand at the latter *day* upon
the earth:
26 And *though* after my skin *worms* destroy
this *body*, yet in my flesh shall I see God:

27 Whom I shall see for myself, and mine
eyes shall behold, and not another; *though*
my reins be consumed within me.
28 But ye should say, Why persecute we
him, seeing the root of the matter is found
in me?
29 Be ye afraid of the sword: for wrath *brin-*
geth the punishments of the sword, that ye
may know *there is* a judgment.

Job 20

1 Then answered Zophar the Naamathite,
and said,
2 Therefore do my thoughts cause me to
answer, and for *this* I make haste.
3 I have heard the check of my reproach,
and the spirit of my understanding causeth
me to answer.
4 Knowest thou *not* this of old, since man
was placed upon earth,
5 That the triumphing of the wicked *is*
short, and the joy of the hypocrite *but* for
a moment?
6 Though his excellency mount up to the
heavens, and his head reach unto the clouds;
7 *Yet* he shall perish for ever like his own
dung: they which have seen him shall say,
Where *is* he?
8 He shall fly away as a dream, and shall not
be found: yea, he shall be chased away as a
vision of the night.
9 The eye also *which* saw him shall *see him*
no more; neither shall his place any more
behold him.
10 His children shall seek to please the poor,
and his hands shall restore their goods.
11 His bones are full *of the sin* of his youth,
which shall lie down with him in the dust.
12 Though wickedness be sweet in his
mouth, *though* he hide it under his tongue;
13 *Though* he spare it, and forsake it not;
but keep it still within his mouth:
14 *Yet* his meat in his bowels is turned, *it is*
the gall of asps within him.
15 He hath swallowed down riches, and he
shall vomit them up again: God shall cast
them out of his belly.
16 He shall suck the poison of asps: the
viper's tongue shall slay him.
17 He shall not see the rivers, the floods,
the brooks of honey and butter.
18 That which he laboured for shall he
restore, and shall not swallow *it* down:
according to *his* substance *shall* the restitution *be*, and he shall not rejoice *therein*.
19 Because he hath oppressed *and* hath
forsaken the poor; *because* he hath violently
taken away an house which he builded not;
20 Surely he shall not feel quietness in his
belly, he shall not save of that which he
desired.
21 There shall none of his meat be left;
therefore shall no man look for his goods.
22 In the fulness of his sufficiency he shall
be in straits: every hand of the wicked shall
come upon him.
23 *When* he is about to fill his belly, *God*
shall cast the fury of his wrath upon him,
and shall rain *it* upon him while he is eating.
24 He shall flee from the iron weapon, *and*
the bow of steel shall strike him through.
25 It is drawn, and cometh out of the body;
yea, the glittering sword cometh out of his
gall: terrors *are* upon him.
26 All darkness *shall be* hid in his secret
places: a fire not blown shall consume
him; it shall go ill with him that is left in his
tabernacle.
27 The heaven shall reveal his iniquity; and
the earth shall rise up against him.
28 The increase of his house shall depart,
and his goods shall flow away in the day of
his wrath.
29 This *is* the portion of a wicked man from
God, and the heritage appointed unto him
by God.

Job 21

1 But Job answered and said,
2 Hear diligently my speech, and let this be
your consolations.
3 Suffer me that I may speak; and after that
I have spoken, mock on.
4 As for me, *is* my complaint to man? and
if *it were so*, why should not my spirit be
troubled?
5 Mark me, and be astonished, and lay *your*
hand upon *your* mouth.
6 Even when I remember I am afraid, and
trembling taketh hold on my flesh.
7 Wherefore do the wicked live, become
old, yea, are mighty in power?
8 Their seed is established in their sight with
them, and their offspring before their eyes.
9 Their houses *are* safe from fear, neither
is the rod of God upon them.

10 Their bull gendereth, and faileth not;
their cow calveth, and casteth not her calf.
11 They send forth their little ones like a
flock, and their children dance.
12 They take the timbrel and harp, and
rejoice at the sound of the organ.
13 They spend their days in wealth, and in
a moment go down to the grave.
14 Therefore they say unto God, Depart
from us; for we desire not the knowledge
of thy ways.
15 What *is* the Almighty, that we should
serve him? and what profit should we have,
if we pray unto him?
16 Lo, their good *is* not in their hand: the
counsel of the wicked is far from me.
17 How oft is the candle of the wicked put
out! and *how oft* cometh their destruction
upon them! *God* distributeth sorrows in
his anger.
18 They are as stubble before the wind,
and as chaff that the storm carrieth away.
19 God layeth up his iniquity for his children:
he rewardeth him, and he shall know *it*.
20 His eyes shall see his destruction, and
he shall drink of the wrath of the Almighty.
21 For what pleasure *hath* he in his house
after him, when the number of his months
is cut off in the midst?
22 Shall *any* teach God knowledge? seeing
he judgeth those that are high.
23 One dieth in his full strength, being
wholly at ease and quiet.
24 His breasts are full of milk, and his bones
are moistened with marrow.
25 And another dieth in the bitterness of
his soul, and never eateth with pleasure.
26 They shall lie down alike in the dust, and
the worms shall cover them.
27 Behold, I know your thoughts, and
the devices *which* ye wrongfully imagine
against me.
28 For ye say, Where *is* the house of the
prince? and where *are* the dwelling places
of the wicked?
29 Have ye not asked them that go by the
way? and do ye not know their tokens,
30 That the wicked is reserved to the day
of destruction? they shall be brought forth
to the day of wrath.
31 Who shall declare his way to his face? and
who shall repay him *what* he hath done?
32 Yet shall he be brought to the grave, and
shall remain in the tomb.
33 The clods of the valley shall be sweet
unto him, and every man shall draw after
him, as *there are* innumerable before him.
34 How then comfort ye me in vain, seeing
in your answers there remaineth falsehood?

Job 22

1 Then Eliphaz the Temanite answered
and said,
2 Can a man be profitable unto God, as he
that is wise may be profitable unto himself?
3 *Is it* any pleasure to the Almighty, that
thou art righteous? or *is it* gain *to him*, that
thou makest thy ways perfect?
4 Will he reprove thee for fear of thee? will
he enter with thee into judgment?
5 *Is* not thy wickedness great? and thine
iniquities infinite?
6 For thou hast taken a pledge from thy
brother for nought, and stripped the naked
of their clothing.
7 Thou hast not given water to the weary
to drink, and thou hast withholden bread
from the hungry.
8 But *as for* the mighty man, he had the
earth; and the honourable man dwelt in it.
9 Thou hast sent widows away empty, and
the arms of the fatherless have been broken.
10 Therefore snares *are* round about thee,
and sudden fear troubleth thee;
11 Or darkness, *that* thou canst not see; and
abundance of waters cover thee.
12 *Is* not God in the height of heaven? and
behold the height of the stars, how high
they are!
13 And thou sayest, How doth God know?
can he judge through the dark cloud?
14 Thick clouds *are* a covering to him, that
he seeth not; and he walketh in the circuit
of heaven.
15 Hast thou marked the old way which
wicked men have trodden?
16 Which were cut down out of time, whose
foundation was overflown with a flood:
17 Which said unto God, Depart from us:
and what can the Almighty do for them?
18 Yet he filled their houses with good
things: but the counsel of the wicked is far
from me.
19 The righteous see *it*, and are glad: and
the innocent laugh them to scorn.

20 Whereas our substance is not cut down,
but the remnant of them the fire consumeth.
21 Acquaint now thyself with him, and be at
peace: thereby good shall come unto thee.
22 Receive, I pray thee, the law from his
mouth, and lay up his words in thine heart.
23 If thou return to the Almighty, thou shalt
be built up, thou shalt put away iniquity far
from thy tabernacles.
24 Then shalt thou lay up gold as dust,
and the *gold* of Ophir as the stones of the
brooks.
25 Yea, the Almighty shall be thy defence,
and thou shalt have plenty of silver.
26 For then shalt thou have thy delight in the
Almighty, and shalt lift up thy face unto God.
27 Thou shalt make thy prayer unto him,
and he shall hear thee, and thou shalt pay
thy vows.
28 Thou shalt also decree a thing, and it shall
be established unto thee: and the light shall
shine upon thy ways.
29 When *men* are cast down, then thou shalt
say, *There is* lifting up; and he shall save the
humble person.
30 He shall deliver the island of the innocent: and it is delivered by the pureness of
thine hands.

Job 23

1 Then Job answered and said,
2 Even to day *is* my complaint bitter: my
stroke is heavier than my groaning.
3 Oh that I knew where I might find him!
that I might come *even* to his seat!
4 I would order *my* cause before him, and
fill my mouth with arguments.
5 I would know the words *which* he would
answer me, and understand what he would
say unto me.
6 Will he plead against me with *his* great
power? No; but he would put *strength* in me.
7 There the righteous might dispute with
him; so should I be delivered for ever from
my judge.
8 Behold, I go forward, but he *is* not *there;*
and backward, but I cannot perceive him:
9 On the left hand, where he doth work,
but I cannot behold *him:* he hideth himself
on the right hand, that I cannot see *him:*
10 But he knoweth the way that I take: *when*
he hath tried me, I shall come forth as gold.
11 My foot hath held his steps, his way have
I kept, and not declined.
12 Neither have I gone back from the commandment of his lips; I have esteemed the
words of his mouth more than my necessary *food.*
13 But he *is* in one *mind,* and who can turn
him? and *what* his soul desireth, even *that*
he doeth.
14 For he performeth *the thing that is*
appointed for me: and many such *things*
are with him.
15 Therefore am I troubled at his presence:
when I consider, I am afraid of him.
16 For God maketh my heart soft, and the
Almighty troubleth me:
17 Because I was not cut off before the darkness, *neither* hath he covered the darkness
from my face.

Job 24

1 Why, seeing times are not hidden from
the Almighty, do they that know him not
see his days?
2 *Some* remove the landmarks; they violently take away flocks, and feed *thereof.*
3 They drive away the ass of the fatherless,
they take the widow's ox for a pledge.
4 They turn the needy out of the way: the
poor of the earth hide themselves together.
5 Behold, *as* wild asses in the desert, go they
forth to their work; rising betimes for a prey:
the wilderness *yieldeth* food for them *and*
for *their* children.
6 They reap *every one* his corn in the field:
and they gather the vintage of the wicked.
7 They cause the naked to lodge without
clothing, that *they have* no covering in
the cold.
8 They are wet with the showers of the
mountains, and embrace the rock for want
of a shelter.
9 They pluck the fatherless from the breast,
and take a pledge of the poor.
10 They cause *him* to go naked without
clothing, and they take away the sheaf *from*
the hungry;
11 *Which* make oil within their walls, *and*
tread *their* winepresses, and suffer thirst.
12 Men groan from out of the city, and the
soul of the wounded crieth out: yet God
layeth not folly *to them.*
13 They are of those that rebel against the

light; they know not the ways thereof, nor
abide in the paths thereof.
14 The murderer rising with the light killeth
the poor and needy, and in the night is as
a thief.
15 The eye also of the adulterer waiteth for
the twilight, saying, No eye shall see me: and
disguiseth *his* face.
16 In the dark they dig through houses,
which they had marked for themselves in
the daytime: they know not the light.
17 For the morning *is* to them even as the
shadow of death: if *one* know *them, they*
are in the terrors of the shadow of death.
18 He *is* swift as the waters; their portion is
cursed in the earth: he beholdeth not the
way of the vineyards.
19 Drought and heat consume the snow
waters: *so doth* the grave *those which* have
sinned.
20 The womb shall forget him; the worm
shall feed sweetly on him; he shall be no
more remembered; and wickedness shall
be broken as a tree.
21 He evil entreateth the barren *that*
beareth not: and doeth not good to the
widow.
22 He draweth also the mighty with his
power: he riseth up, and no *man* is sure
of life.
23 *Though* it be given him *to be* in safety,
whereon he resteth; yet his eyes *are* upon
their ways.
24 They are exalted for a little while, but are
gone and brought low; they are taken out of
the way as all *other,* and cut off as the tops
of the ears of corn.
25 And if *it be* not *so* now, who will make me
a liar, and make my speech nothing worth?

Job 25

1 Then answered Bildad the Shuhite, and
said,
2 Dominion and fear *are* with him, he
maketh peace in his high places.
3 Is there any number of his armies? and
upon whom doth not his light arise?
4 How then can man be justified with God?
or how can he be clean *that is* born of a
woman?
5 Behold even to the moon, and it shineth
not; yea, the stars are not pure in his sight.
6 How much less man, *that is* a worm? and
the son of man, *which is* a worm?

Job 26

1 But Job answered and said,
2 How hast thou helped *him that is* without
power? *how* savest thou the arm *that hath*
no strength?
3 How hast thou counselled *him that hath*
no wisdom? and *how* hast thou plentifully
declared the thing as it is?
4 To whom hast thou uttered words? and
whose spirit came from thee?
5 Dead *things* are formed from under the
waters, and the inhabitants thereof.
6 Hell *is* naked before him, and destruction
hath no covering.
7 He stretcheth out the north over the
empty place, *and* hangeth the earth upon
nothing.
8 He bindeth up the waters in his thick
clouds; and the cloud is not rent under
them.
9 He holdeth back the face of his throne,
and spreadeth his cloud upon it.
10 He hath compassed the waters with
bounds, until the day and night come to
an end.
11 The pillars of heaven tremble and are
astonished at his reproof.
12 He divideth the sea with his power, and
by his understanding he smiteth through
the proud.
13 By his spirit he hath garnished the heavens; his hand hath formed the crooked
serpent.
14 Lo, these *are* parts of his ways: but how
little a portion is heard of him? but the
thunder of his power who can understand?

Job 27

1 Moreover Job continued his parable,
and said,
2 *As* God liveth, *who* hath taken away my
judgment; and the Almighty, *who* hath
vexed my soul;
3 All the while my breath *is* in me, and the
spirit of God *is* in my nostrils;
4 My lips shall not speak wickedness, nor
my tongue utter deceit.
5 God forbid that I should justify you: till I
die I will not remove mine integrity from me.
6 My righteousness I hold fast, and will not

let it go: my heart shall not reproach *me* so
long as I live.
7 Let mine enemy be as the wicked, and he
that riseth up against me as the unrighteous.
8 For what *is* the hope of the hypocrite,
though he hath gained, when God taketh
away his soul?
9 Will God hear his cry when trouble cometh upon him?
10 Will he delight himself in the Almighty?
will he always call upon God?
11 I will teach you by the hand of God: *that*
which *is* with the Almighty will I not conceal.
12 Behold, all ye yourselves have seen *it;*
why then are ye thus altogether vain?
13 This *is* the portion of a wicked man with
God, and the heritage of oppressors, *which*
they shall receive of the Almighty.
14 If his children be multiplied, *it is* for the
sword: and his offspring shall not be satisfied with bread.
15 Those that remain of him shall be buried
in death: and his widows shall not weep.
16 Though he heap up silver as the dust,
and prepare raiment as the clay;
17 He may prepare *it*, but the just shall put *it*
on, and the innocent shall divide the silver.
18 He buildeth his house as a moth, and as
a booth *that* the keeper maketh.
19 The rich man shall lie down, but he shall
not be gathered: he openeth his eyes, and
he *is* not.
20 Terrors take hold on him as waters, a
tempest stealeth him away in the night.
21 The east wind carrieth him away, and
he departeth: and as a storm hurleth him
out of his place.
22 For *God* shall cast upon him, and not
spare: he would fain flee out of his hand.
23 *Men* shall clap their hands at him, and
shall hiss him out of his place.

Job 28

1 Surely there is a vein for the silver, and a
place for gold *where* they fine *it*.
2 Iron is taken out of the earth, and brass
is molten *out of* the stone.
3 He setteth an end to darkness, and searcheth out all perfection: the stones of darkness, and the shadow of death.
4 The flood breaketh out from the inhabitant; *even the waters* forgotten of the foot:
they are dried up, they are gone away from
men.
5 *As for* the earth, out of it cometh bread:
and under it is turned up as it were fire.
6 The stones of it *are* the place of sapphires:
and it hath dust of gold.
7 *There is* a path which no fowl knoweth,
and which the vulture's eye hath not seen:
8 The lion's whelps have not trodden it, nor
the fierce lion passed by it.
9 He putteth forth his hand upon the rock;
he overturneth the mountains by the roots.
10 He cutteth out rivers among the rocks;
and his eye seeth every precious thing.
11 He bindeth the floods from overflowing;
and *the thing that is* hid bringeth he forth
to light.
12 But where shall wisdom be found? and
where *is* the place of understanding?
13 Man knoweth not the price thereof;
neither is it found in the land of the living.
14 The depth saith, It *is* not in me: and the
sea saith, *It is* not with me.
15 It cannot be gotten for gold, neither shall
silver be weighed *for* the price thereof.
16 It cannot be valued with the gold of
Ophir, with the precious onyx, or the sapphire.
17 The gold and the crystal cannot equal
it: and the exchange of it *shall not be for*
jewels of fine gold.
18 No mention shall be made of coral, or
of pearls: for the price of wisdom *is* above
rubies.
19 The topaz of Ethiopia shall not equal it,
neither shall it be valued with pure gold.
20 Whence then cometh wisdom? and
where *is* the place of understanding?
21 Seeing it is hid from the eyes of all living,
and kept close from the fowls of the air.
22 Destruction and death say, We have
heard the fame thereof with our ears.
23 God understandeth the way thereof, and
he knoweth the place thereof.
24 For he looketh to the ends of the earth,
and seeth under the whole heaven;
25 To make the weight for the winds; and
he weigheth the waters by measure.
26 When he made a decree for the rain,
and a way for the lightning of the thunder:
27 Then did he see it, and declare it; he
prepared it, yea, and searched it out.
28 And unto man he said, Behold, the fear

of the Lord, that *is* wisdom; and to depart
from evil *is* understanding.

Job 29

1 Moreover Job continued his parable,
and said,
2 Oh that I were as *in* months past, as *in* the
days *when* God preserved me;
3 When his candle shined upon my head,
and when by his light I walked *through*
darkness;
4 As I was in the days of my youth, when
the secret of God *was* upon my tabernacle;
5 When the Almighty *was* yet with me, *when*
my children *were* about me;
6 When I washed my steps with butter, and
the rock poured me out rivers of oil;
7 When I went out to the gate through the
city, *when* I prepared my seat in the street!
8 The young men saw me, and hid themselves: and the aged arose, *and* stood up.
9 The princes refrained talking, and laid *their*
hand on their mouth.
10 The nobles held their peace, and their
tongue cleaved to the roof of their mouth.
11 When the ear heard *me*, then it blessed
me; and when the eye saw *me*, it gave witness to me:
12 Because I delivered the poor that cried,
and the fatherless, and *him that had* none
to help him.
13 The blessing of him that was ready to
perish came upon me: and I caused the
widow's heart to sing for joy.
14 I put on righteousness, and it clothed me:
my judgment *was* as a robe and a diadem.
15 I was eyes to the blind, and feet *was* I
to the lame.
16 I *was* a father to the poor: and the cause
which I knew not I searched out.
17 And I brake the jaws of the wicked, and
plucked the spoil out of his teeth.
18 Then I said, I shall die in my nest, and I
shall multiply *my* days as the sand.
19 My root *was* spread out by the waters,
and the dew lay all night upon my branch.
20 My glory *was* fresh in me, and my bow
was renewed in my hand.
21 Unto me *men* gave ear, and waited, and
kept silence at my counsel.
22 After my words they spake not again; and
my speech dropped upon them.
23 And they waited for me as for the rain;
and they opened their mouth wide *as* for
the latter rain.
24 *If* I laughed on them, they believed *it*
not; and the light of my countenance they
cast not down.
25 I chose out their way, and sat chief, and
dwelt as a king in the army, as one *that*
comforteth the mourners.

Job 30

1 But now *they that are* younger than I
have me in derision, whose fathers I would
have disdained to have set with the dogs
of my flock.
2 Yea, whereto *might* the strength of their
hands *profit* me, in whom old age was
perished?
3 For want and famine *they were* solitary;
fleeing into the wilderness in former time
desolate and waste.
4 Who cut up mallows by the bushes, and
juniper roots *for* their meat.
5 They were driven forth from among *men*,
(they cried after them as *after* a thief;)
6 To dwell in the clifts of the valleys, *in* caves
of the earth, and *in* the rocks.
7 Among the bushes they brayed; under
the nettles they were gathered together.
8 *They were* children of fools, yea, children
of base men: they were viler than the earth.
9 And now am I their song, yea, I am their
byword.
10 They abhor me, they flee far from me,
and spare not to spit in my face.
11 Because he hath loosed my cord, and
afflicted me, they have also let loose the
bridle before me.
12 Upon *my* right *hand* rise the youth; they
push away my feet, and they raise up against
me the ways of their destruction.
13 They mar my path, they set forward my
calamity, they have no helper.
14 They came *upon me* as a wide breaking
in *of waters:* in the desolation they rolled
themselves *upon me*.
15 Terrors are turned upon me: they pursue
my soul as the wind: and my welfare passeth
away as a cloud.
16 And now my soul is poured out upon
me; the days of affliction have taken hold
upon me.
17 My bones are pierced in me in the night
season: and my sinews take no rest.

18 By the great force *of my disease* is my
garment changed: it bindeth me about as
the collar of my coat.
19 He hath cast me into the mire, and I am
become like dust and ashes.
20 I cry unto thee, and thou dost not hear
me: I stand up, and thou regardest me *not*.
21 Thou art become cruel to me: with thy
strong hand thou opposest thyself against
me.
22 Thou liftest me up to the wind; thou
causest me to ride *upon it*, and dissolvest
my substance.
23 For I know *that* thou wilt bring me *to*
death, and *to* the house appointed for all
living.
24 Howbeit he will not stretch out *his*
hand to the grave, though they cry in his
destruction.
25 Did not I weep for him that was in trouble? was *not* my soul grieved for the poor?
26 When I looked for good, then evil came
unto me: and when I waited for light, there
came darkness.
27 My bowels boiled, and rested not: the
days of affliction prevented me.
28 I went mourning without the sun: I stood
up, *and* I cried in the congregation.
29 I am a brother to dragons, and a companion to owls.
30 My skin is black upon me, and my bones
are burned with heat.
31 My harp also is *turned* to mourning, and
my organ into the voice of them that weep.

Job 31

1 I made a covenant with mine eyes; why
then should I think upon a maid?
2 For what portion of God *is there* from
above? and *what* inheritance of the Almighty
from on high?
3 *Is* not destruction to the wicked? and
a strange *punishment* to the workers of
iniquity?
4 Doth not he see my ways, and count all
my steps?
5 If I have walked with vanity, or if my foot
hath hasted to deceit;
6 Let me be weighed in an even balance,
that God may know mine integrity.
7 If my step hath turned out of the way, and
mine heart walked after mine eyes, and if
any blot hath cleaved to mine hands;
8 *Then* let me sow, and let another eat; yea,
let my offspring be rooted out.
9 If mine heart have been deceived by a
woman, or *if* I have laid wait at my neighbour's door;
10 *Then* let my wife grind unto another, and
let others bow down upon her.
11 For this *is* an heinous crime; yea, it *is* an
iniquity *to be punished by* the judges.
12 For it *is* a fire *that* consumeth to destruction, and would root out all mine increase.
13 If I did despise the cause of my manservant or of my maidservant, when they
contended with me;
14 What then shall I do when God riseth
up? and when he visiteth, what shall I
answer him?
15 Did not he that made me in the womb
make him? and did not one fashion us in
the womb?
16 If I have withheld the poor from *their*
desire, or have caused the eyes of the
widow to fail;
17 Or have eaten my morsel myself alone,
and the fatherless hath not eaten thereof;
18 (For from my youth he was brought up
with me, as *with* a father, and I have guided
her from my mother's womb;)
19 If I have seen any perish for want of clothing, or any poor without covering;
20 If his loins have not blessed me, and
if he were *not* warmed with the fleece of
my sheep;
21 If I have lifted up my hand against the
fatherless, when I saw my help in the gate:
22 *Then* let mine arm fall from my shoulder blade, and mine arm be broken from
the bone.
23 For destruction *from* God *was* a terror
to me, and by reason of his highness I could
not endure.
24 If I have made gold my hope, or have said
to the fine gold, *Thou art* my confidence;
25 If I rejoiced because my wealth *was* great,
and because mine hand had gotten much;
26 If I beheld the sun when it shined, or the
moon walking *in* brightness;
27 And my heart hath been secretly enticed,
or my mouth hath kissed my hand:
28 This also *were* an iniquity *to be punished*
by the judge: for I should have denied the
God *that is* above.
29 If I rejoiced at the destruction of him

that hated me, or lifted up myself when
evil found him:
30 Neither have I suffered my mouth to sin
by wishing a curse to his soul.
31 If the men of my tabernacle said not,
Oh that we had of his flesh! we cannot be
satisfied.
32 The stranger did not lodge in the street:
but I opened my doors to the traveller.
33 If I covered my transgressions as Adam,
by hiding mine iniquity in my bosom:
34 Did I fear a great multitude, or did the
contempt of families terrify me, that I kept
silence, *and* went not out of the door?
35 Oh that one would hear me! behold, my
desire *is*, *that* the Almighty would answer
me, and *that* mine adversary had written
a book.
36 Surely I would take it upon my shoulder,
and bind it *as* a crown to me.
37 I would declare unto him the number
of my steps; as a prince would I go near
unto him.
38 If my land cry against me, or that the
furrows likewise thereof complain;
39 If I have eaten the fruits thereof without
money, or have caused the owners thereof
to lose their life:
40 Let thistles grow instead of wheat, and
cockle instead of barley. The words of Job
are ended.

Job 32

1 So these three men ceased to answer Job,
because he *was* righteous in his own eyes.
2 Then was kindled the wrath of Elihu the
son of Barachel the Buzite, of the kindred
of Ram: against Job was his wrath kindled,
because he justified himself rather than
God.
3 Also against his three friends was his wrath
kindled, because they had found no answer,
and *yet* had condemned Job.
4 Now Elihu had waited till Job had spoken,
because they *were* elder than he.
5 When Elihu saw that *there was* no answer
in the mouth of *these* three men, then his
wrath was kindled.
6 And Elihu the son of Barachel the Buzite
answered and said, I *am* young, and ye *are*
very old; wherefore I was afraid, and durst
not shew you mine opinion.
7 I said, Days should speak, and multitude
of years should teach wisdom.
8 But *there is* a spirit in man: and the inspiration of the Almighty giveth them understanding.
9 Great men are not *always* wise: neither
do the aged understand judgment.
10 Therefore I said, Hearken to me; I also
will shew mine opinion.
11 Behold, I waited for your words; I gave
ear to your reasons, whilst ye searched out
what to say.
12 Yea, I attended unto you, and, behold,
there was none of you that convinced Job,
or that answered his words:
13 Lest ye should say, We have found out
wisdom: God thrusteth him down, not man.
14 Now he hath not directed *his* words
against me: neither will I answer him with
your speeches.
15 They were amazed, they answered no
more: they left off speaking.
16 When I had waited, (for they spake not,
but stood still, *and* answered no more;)
17 *I said*, I will answer also my part, I also
will shew mine opinion.
18 For I am full of matter, the spirit within
me constraineth me.
19 Behold, my belly *is* as wine *which* hath
no vent; it is ready to burst like new bottles.
20 I will speak, that I may be refreshed: I
will open my lips and answer.
21 Let me not, I pray you, accept any man's
person, neither let me give flattering titles
unto man.
22 For I know not to give flattering titles;
in so doing my maker would soon take me
away.

Job 33

1 Wherefore, Job, I pray thee, hear my
speeches, and hearken to all my words.
2 Behold, now I have opened my mouth, my
tongue hath spoken in my mouth.
3 My words *shall be of* the uprightness of
my heart: and my lips shall utter knowledge
clearly.
4 The Spirit of God hath made me, and the
breath of the Almighty hath given me life.
5 If thou canst answer me, set *thy words* in
order before me, stand up.
6 Behold, I *am* according to thy wish in God's
stead: I also am formed out of the clay.

7 Behold, my terror shall not make thee
afraid, neither shall my hand be heavy
upon thee.
8 Surely thou hast spoken in mine hearing,
and I have heard the voice of *thy* words,
saying,
9 I am clean without transgression, I *am*
innocent; neither *is there* iniquity in me.
10 Behold, he findeth occasions against me,
he counteth me for his enemy,
11 He putteth my feet in the stocks, he
marketh all my paths.
12 Behold, *in* this thou art not just: I will
answer thee, that God is greater than man.
13 Why dost thou strive against him? for
he giveth not account of any of his matters.
14 For God speaketh once, yea twice, *yet*
man perceiveth it not.
15 In a dream, in a vision of the night, when
deep sleep falleth upon men, in slumberings
upon the bed;
16 Then he openeth the ears of men, and
sealeth their instruction,
17 That he may withdraw man *from his*
purpose, and hide pride from man.
18 He keepeth back his soul from the pit,
and his life from perishing by the sword.
19 He is chastened also with pain upon his
bed, and the multitude of his bones with
strong *pain:*
20 So that his life abhorreth bread, and his
soul dainty meat.
21 His flesh is consumed away, that it cannot be seen; and his bones *that* were not
seen stick out.
22 Yea, his soul draweth near unto the grave,
and his life to the destroyers.
23 If there be a messenger with him, an
interpreter, one among a thousand, to shew
unto man his uprightness:
24 Then he is gracious unto him, and saith,
Deliver him from going down to the pit: I
have found a ransom.
25 His flesh shall be fresher than a child's: he
shall return to the days of his youth:
26 He shall pray unto God, and he will be
favourable unto him: and he shall see his
face with joy: for he will render unto man
his righteousness.
27 He looketh upon men, and *if any* say, I
have sinned, and perverted *that which was*
right, and it profited me not;
28 He will deliver his soul from going into
the pit, and his life shall see the light.
29 Lo, all these *things* worketh God oftentimes with man,
30 To bring back his soul from the pit, to
be enlightened with the light of the living.
31 Mark well, O Job, hearken unto me: hold
thy peace, and I will speak.
32 If thou hast any thing to say, answer me:
speak, for I desire to justify thee.
33 If not, hearken unto me: hold thy peace,
and I shall teach thee wisdom.

Job 34

1 Furthermore Elihu answered and said,
2 Hear my words, O ye wise *men;* and give
ear unto me, ye that have knowledge.
3 For the ear trieth words, as the mouth
tasteth meat.
4 Let us choose to us judgment: let us know
among ourselves what *is* good.
5 For Job hath said, I am righteous: and God
hath taken away my judgment.
6 Should I lie against my right? my wound *is*
incurable without transgression.
7 What man *is* like Job, *who* drinketh up
scorning like water?
8 Which goeth in company with the workers
of iniquity, and walketh with wicked men.
9 For he hath said, It profiteth a man nothing
that he should delight himself with God.
10 Therefore hearken unto me, ye men
of understanding: far be it from God, *that*
he should do wickedness; and *from* the
Almighty, *that he should commit* iniquity.
11 For the work of a man shall he render
unto him, and cause every man to find
according to *his* ways.
12 Yea, surely God will not do wickedly,
neither will the Almighty pervert judgment.
13 Who hath given him a charge over the
earth? or who hath disposed the whole
world?
14 If he set his heart upon man, *if* he gather
unto himself his spirit and his breath;
15 All flesh shall perish together, and man
shall turn again unto dust.
16 If now *thou hast* understanding, hear this:
hearken to the voice of my words.
17 Shall even he that hateth right govern?
and wilt thou condemn him that is most
just?

18 *Is it fit* to say to a king, *Thou art* wicked? *and* to princes, *Ye are* ungodly?

19 *How much less to him* that accepteth not the persons of princes, nor regardeth the rich more than the poor? for they all *are* the work of his hands.

20 In a moment shall they die, and the people shall be troubled at midnight, and pass away: and the mighty shall be taken away without hand.

21 For his eyes *are* upon the ways of man, and he seeth all his goings.

22 *There is* no darkness, nor shadow of death, where the workers of iniquity may hide themselves.

23 For he will not lay upon man more *than right;* that he should enter into judgment with God.

24 He shall break in pieces mighty men without number, and set others in their stead.

25 Therefore he knoweth their works, and he overturneth *them* in the night, so that they are destroyed.

26 He striketh them as wicked men in the open sight of others;

27 Because they turned back from him, and would not consider any of his ways:

28 So that they cause the cry of the poor to come unto him, and he heareth the cry of the afflicted.

29 When he giveth quietness, who then can make trouble? and when he hideth *his* face, who then can behold him? whether *it be done* against a nation, or against a man only:

30 That the hypocrite reign not, lest the people be ensnared.

31 Surely it is meet to be said unto God, I have borne *chastisement,* I will not offend *any more:*

32 *That which* I see not teach thou me: if I have done iniquity, I will do no more.

33 *Should it be* according to thy mind? he will recompense it, whether thou refuse, or whether thou choose; and not I: therefore speak what thou knowest.

34 Let men of understanding tell me, and let a wise man hearken unto me.

35 Job hath spoken without knowledge, and his words *were* without wisdom.

36 My desire *is that* Job may be tried unto the end because of *his* answers for wicked men.

37 For he addeth rebellion unto his sin, he clappeth *his hands* among us, and multiplieth his words against God.

Job 35

1 Elihu spake moreover, and said,

2 Thinkest thou this to be right, *that* thou saidst, My righteousness *is* more than God's?

3 For thou saidst, What advantage will it be unto thee? *and,* What profit shall I have, *if I be cleansed* from my sin?

4 I will answer thee, and thy companions with thee.

5 Look unto the heavens, and see; and behold the clouds *which* are higher than thou.

6 If thou sinnest, what doest thou against him? or *if* thy transgressions be multiplied, what doest thou unto him?

7 If thou be righteous, what givest thou him? or what receiveth he of thine hand?

8 Thy wickedness *may hurt* a man as thou *art;* and thy righteousness *may profit* the son of man.

9 By reason of the multitude of oppressions they make *the oppressed* to cry: they cry out by reason of the arm of the mighty.

10 But none saith, Where *is* God my maker, who giveth songs in the night;

11 Who teacheth us more than the beasts of the earth, and maketh us wiser than the fowls of heaven?

12 There they cry, but none giveth answer, because of the pride of evil men.

13 Surely God will not hear vanity, neither will the Almighty regard it.

14 Although thou sayest thou shalt not see him, *yet* judgment *is* before him; therefore trust thou in him.

15 But now, because *it is* not *so,* he hath visited in his anger; yet he knoweth *it* not in great extremity:

16 Therefore doth Job open his mouth in vain; he multiplieth words without knowledge.

Job 36

1 Elihu also proceeded, and said,

2 Suffer me a little, and I will shew thee that *I have* yet to speak on God's behalf.

3 I will fetch my knowledge from afar, and will ascribe righteousness to my Maker.

4 For truly my words *shall* not *be* false: he
that is perfect in knowledge *is* with thee.
5 Behold, God *is* mighty, and despiseth not
any: he is mighty in strength *and* wisdom.
6 He preserveth not the life of the wicked:
but giveth right to the poor.
7 He withdraweth not his eyes from the
righteous: but with kings *are they* on the
throne; yea, he doth establish them for ever,
and they are exalted.
8 And if *they be* bound in fetters, *and* be
holden in cords of affliction;
9 Then he sheweth them their work,
and their transgressions that they have
exceeded.
10 He openeth also their ear to discipline,
and commandeth that they return from
iniquity.
11 If they obey and serve *him*, they shall
spend their days in prosperity, and their
years in pleasures.
12 But if they obey not, they shall perish
by the sword, and they shall die without
knowledge.
13 But the hypocrites in heart heap up
wrath: they cry not when he bindeth them.
14 They die in youth, and their life *is* among
the unclean.
15 He delivereth the poor in his affliction,
and openeth their ears in oppression.
16 Even so would he have removed thee
out of the strait *into* a broad place, where
there is no straitness; and that which should
be set on thy table *should be* full of fatness.
17 But thou hast fulfilled the judgment
of the wicked: judgment and justice take
hold *on thee.*
18 Because *there is* wrath, *beware* lest he
take thee away with *his* stroke: then a great
ransom cannot deliver thee.
19 Will he esteem thy riches? *no,* not gold,
nor all the forces of strength.
20 Desire not the night, when people are
cut off in their place.
21 Take heed, regard not iniquity: for this
hast thou chosen rather than affliction.
22 Behold, God exalteth by his power: who
teacheth like him?
23 Who hath enjoined him his way? or who
can say, Thou hast wrought iniquity?
24 Remember that thou magnify his work,
which men behold.
25 Every man may see it; man may behold
it afar off.
26 Behold, God *is* great, and we know *him*
not, neither can the number of his years be
searched out.
27 For he maketh small the drops of water:
they pour down rain according to the vapour
thereof:
28 Which the clouds do drop *and* distil upon
man abundantly.
29 Also can *any* understand the spreadings
of the clouds, *or* the noise of his tabernacle?
30 Behold, he spreadeth his light upon it,
and covereth the bottom of the sea.
31 For by them judgeth he the people; he
giveth meat in abundance.
32 With clouds he covereth the light; and
commandeth it *not to shine* by *the cloud*
that cometh betwixt.
33 The noise thereof sheweth concerning
it, the cattle also concerning the vapour.

Job 37

1 At this also my heart trembleth, and is
moved out of his place.
2 Hear attentively the noise of his voice,
and the sound *that* goeth out of his mouth.
3 He directeth it under the whole heaven,
and his lightning unto the ends of the earth.
4 After it a voice roareth: he thundereth with
the voice of his excellency; and he will not
stay them when his voice is heard.
5 God thundereth marvellously with his
voice; great things doeth he, which we
cannot comprehend.
6 For he saith to the snow, Be thou *on* the
earth; likewise to the small rain, and to the
great rain of his strength.
7 He sealeth up the hand of every man; that
all men may know his work.
8 Then the beasts go into dens, and remain
in their places.
9 Out of the south cometh the whirlwind:
and cold out of the north.
10 By the breath of God frost is given: and
the breadth of the waters is straitened.
11 Also by watering he wearieth the thick
cloud: he scattereth his bright cloud:
12 And it is turned round about by his
counsels: that they may do whatsoever he
commandeth them upon the face of the
world in the earth.

13 He causeth it to come, whether for correction, or for his land, or for mercy.
14 Hearken unto this, O Job: stand still, and
consider the wondrous works of God.
15 Dost thou know when God disposed
them, and caused the light of his cloud to
shine?
16 Dost thou know the balancings of the
clouds, the wondrous works of him which
is perfect in knowledge?
17 How thy garments *are* warm, when he
quieteth the earth by the south *wind?*
18 Hast thou with him spread out the sky,
which is strong, *and* as a molten looking
glass?
19 Teach us what we shall say unto him;
for we cannot order *our speech* by reason
of darkness.
20 Shall it be told him that I speak? if a man
speak, surely he shall be swallowed up.
21 And now *men* see not the bright light
which *is* in the clouds: but the wind passeth,
and cleanseth them.
22 Fair weather cometh out of the north:
with God *is* terrible majesty.
23 *Touching* the Almighty, we cannot find
him out: *he is* excellent in power, and in
judgment, and in plenty of justice: he will
not afflict.
24 Men do therefore fear him: he respecteth
not any *that are* wise of heart.

Job 38

1 Then the LORD answered Job out of the
whirlwind, and said,
2 Who *is* this that darkeneth counsel by
words without knowledge?
3 Gird up now thy loins like a man; for I will
demand of thee, and answer thou me.
4 Where wast thou when I laid the foundations of the earth? declare, if thou hast
understanding.
5 Who hath laid the measures thereof, if
thou knowest? or who hath stretched the
line upon it?
6 Whereupon are the foundations thereof
fastened? or who laid the corner stone
thereof;
7 When the morning stars sang together,
and all the sons of God shouted for joy?
8 Or *who* shut up the sea with doors, when
it brake forth, *as if* it had issued out of the
womb?
9 When I made the cloud the garment
thereof, and thick darkness a swaddling-
band for it,
10 And brake up for it my decreed *place,*
and set bars and doors,
11 And said, Hitherto shalt thou come, but
no further: and here shall thy proud waves
be stayed?
12 Hast thou commanded the morning
since thy days; *and* caused the dayspring
to know his place;
13 That it might take hold of the ends of
the earth, that the wicked might be shaken
out of it?
14 It is turned as clay *to* the seal; and they
stand as a garment.
15 And from the wicked their light is withholden, and the high arm shall be broken.
16 Hast thou entered into the springs of
the sea? or hast thou walked in the search
of the depth?
17 Have the gates of death been opened
unto thee? or hast thou seen the doors of
the shadow of death?
18 Hast thou perceived the breadth of the
earth? declare if thou knowest it all.
19 Where *is* the way *where* light dwelleth?
and *as for* darkness, where *is* the place
thereof,
20 That thou shouldest take it to the bound
thereof, and that thou shouldest know the
paths *to* the house thereof?
21 Knowest thou *it,* because thou wast
then born? or *because* the number of thy
days *is* great?
22 Hast thou entered into the treasures of
the snow? or hast thou seen the treasures
of the hail,
23 Which I have reserved against the time of
trouble, against the day of battle and war?
24 By what way is the light parted, *which*
scattereth the east wind upon the earth?
25 Who hath divided a watercourse for
the overflowing of waters, or a way for the
lightning of thunder;
26 To cause it to rain on the earth, *where*
no man *is; on* the wilderness, wherein *there*
is no man;
27 To satisfy the desolate and waste *ground;*
and to cause the bud of the tender herb to
spring forth?
28 Hath the rain a father? or who hath
begotten the drops of dew?

29 Out of whose womb came the ice? and
the hoary frost of heaven, who hath gen-
dered it?
30 The waters are hid as *with* a stone, and
the face of the deep is frozen.
31 Canst thou bind the sweet influences of
Pleiades, or loose the bands of Orion?
32 Canst thou bring forth Mazzaroth in his
season? or canst thou guide Arcturus with
his sons?
33 Knowest thou the ordinances of heaven?
canst thou set the dominion thereof in the
earth?
34 Canst thou lift up thy voice to the clouds,
that abundance of waters may cover thee?
35 Canst thou send lightnings, that they may
go, and say unto thee, Here we *are?*
36 Who hath put wisdom in the inward
parts? or who hath given understanding
to the heart?
37 Who can number the clouds in wisdom?
or who can stay the bottles of heaven,
38 When the dust groweth into hardness,
and the clods cleave fast together?
39 Wilt thou hunt the prey for the lion? or
fill the appetite of the young lions,
40 When they couch in *their* dens, *and* abide
in the covert to lie in wait?
41 Who provideth for the raven his food?
when his young ones cry unto God, they
wander for lack of meat.

Job 39

1 Knowest thou the time when the wild
goats of the rock bring forth? *or* canst thou
mark when the hinds do calve?
2 Canst thou number the months *that* they
fulfil? or knowest thou the time when they
bring forth?
3 They bow themselves, they bring forth
their young ones, they cast out their sorrows.
4 Their young ones are in good liking, they
grow up with corn; they go forth, and return
not unto them.
5 Who hath sent out the wild ass free? or
who hath loosed the bands of the wild ass?
6 Whose house I have made the wilderness,
and the barren land his dwellings.
7 He scorneth the multitude of the city, neither regardeth he the crying of the driver.
8 The range of the mountains *is* his pasture,
and he searcheth after every green thing.
9 Will the unicorn be willing to serve thee,
or abide by thy crib?
10 Canst thou bind the unicorn with his
band in the furrow? or will he harrow the
valleys after thee?
11 Wilt thou trust him, because his strength
is great? or wilt thou leave thy labour to him?
12 Wilt thou believe him, that he will bring
home thy seed, and gather *it into* thy barn?
13 *Gavest thou* the goodly wings unto the
peacocks? or wings and feathers unto the
ostrich?
14 Which leaveth her eggs in the earth, and
warmeth them in dust,
15 And forgetteth that the foot may crush
them, or that the wild beast may break
them.
16 She is hardened against her young ones,
as though *they were* not hers: her labour is
in vain without fear;
17 Because God hath deprived her of wisdom, neither hath he imparted to her
understanding.
18 What time she lifteth up herself on high,
she scorneth the horse and his rider.
19 Hast thou given the horse strength? hast
thou clothed his neck with thunder?
20 Canst thou make him afraid as a grasshopper? the glory of his nostrils *is* terrible.
21 He paweth in the valley, and rejoiceth
in *his* strength: he goeth on to meet the
armed men.
22 He mocketh at fear, and is not affrighted;
neither turneth he back from the sword.
23 The quiver rattleth against him, the glittering spear and the shield.
24 He swalloweth the ground with fierceness and rage: neither believeth he that *it*
is the sound of the trumpet.
25 He saith among the trumpets, Ha, ha; and
he smelleth the battle afar off, the thunder
of the captains, and the shouting.
26 Doth the hawk fly by thy wisdom, *and*
stretch her wings toward the south?
27 Doth the eagle mount up at thy command, and make her nest on high?
28 She dwelleth and abideth on the rock,
upon the crag of the rock, and the strong
place.
29 From thence she seeketh the prey, *and*
her eyes behold afar off.
30 Her young ones also suck up blood: and
where the slain *are*, there *is* she.

Job 40

1 Moreover the LORD answered Job, and said,

2 Shall he that contendeth with the Almighty instruct *him?* he that reproveth God, let him answer it.

3 ¶ Then Job answered the LORD, and said,

4 Behold, I am vile; what shall I answer thee? I will lay mine hand upon my mouth.

5 Once have I spoken; but I will not answer: yea, twice; but I will proceed no further.

6 ¶ Then answered the LORD unto Job out of the whirlwind, and said,

7 Gird up thy loins now like a man: I will demand of thee, and declare thou unto me.

8 Wilt thou also disannul my judgment? wilt thou condemn me, that thou mayest be righteous?

9 Hast thou an arm like God? or canst thou thunder with a voice like him?

10 Deck thyself now *with* majesty and excellency; and array thyself with glory and beauty.

11 Cast abroad the rage of thy wrath: and behold every one *that is* proud, and abase him.

12 Look on every one *that is* proud, *and* bring him low; and tread down the wicked in their place.

13 Hide them in the dust together; *and* bind their faces in secret.

14 Then will I also confess unto thee that thine own right hand can save thee.

15 ¶ Behold now behemoth, which I made with thee; he eateth grass as an ox.

16 Lo now, his strength *is* in his loins, and his force *is* in the navel of his belly.

17 He moveth his tail like a cedar: the sinews of his stones are wrapped together.

18 His bones *are as* strong pieces of brass; his bones *are* like bars of iron.

19 He *is* the chief of the ways of God: he that made him can make his sword to approach *unto him*.

20 Surely the mountains bring him forth food, where all the beasts of the field play.

21 He lieth under the shady trees, in the covert of the reed, and fens.

22 The shady trees cover him *with* their shadow; the willows of the brook compass him about.

23 Behold, he drinketh up a river, *and* hasteth not: he trusteth that he can draw up Jordan into his mouth.

24 He taketh it with his eyes: *his* nose pierceth through snares.

Job 41

1 Canst thou draw out leviathan with an hook? or his tongue with a cord *which* thou lettest down?

2 Canst thou put an hook into his nose? or bore his jaw through with a thorn?

3 Will he make many supplications unto thee? will he speak soft *words* unto thee?

4 Will he make a covenant with thee? wilt thou take him for a servant for ever?

5 Wilt thou play with him as *with* a bird? or wilt thou bind him for thy maidens?

6 Shall the companions make a banquet of him? shall they part him among the merchants?

7 Canst thou fill his skin with barbed irons? or his head with fish spears?

8 Lay thine hand upon him, remember the battle, do no more.

9 Behold, the hope of him is in vain: shall not *one* be cast down even at the sight of him?

10 None *is so* fierce that dare stir him up: who then is able to stand before me?

11 Who hath prevented me, that I should repay *him? whatsoever is* under the whole heaven is mine.

12 I will not conceal his parts, nor his power, nor his comely proportion.

13 Who can discover the face of his garment? *or* who can come *to him* with his double bridle?

14 Who can open the doors of his face? his teeth *are* terrible round about.

15 *His* scales *are his* pride, shut up together *as with* a close seal.

16 One is so near to another, that no air can come between them.

17 They are joined one to another, they stick together, that they cannot be sundered.

18 By his neesings a light doth shine, and his eyes *are* like the eyelids of the morning.

19 Out of his mouth go burning lamps, *and* sparks of fire leap out.

20 Out of his nostrils goeth smoke, as *out* of a seething pot or caldron.

21 His breath kindleth coals, and a flame goeth out of his mouth.

22 In his neck remaineth strength, and sorrow is turned into joy before him.
23 The flakes of his flesh are joined together:
they are firm in themselves; they cannot
be moved.
24 His heart is as firm as a stone; yea, as hard
as a piece of the nether *millstone.*
25 When he raiseth up himself, the mighty
are afraid: by reason of breakings they purify
themselves.
26 The sword of him that layeth at him
cannot hold: the spear, the dart, nor the
habergeon.
27 He esteemeth iron as straw, *and* brass
as rotten wood.
28 The arrow cannot make him flee: sling-
stones are turned with him into stubble.
29 Darts are counted as stubble: he laugheth
at the shaking of a spear.
30 Sharp stones *are* under him: he spreadeth sharp pointed things upon the mire.
31 He maketh the deep to boil like a pot:
he maketh the sea like a pot of ointment.
32 He maketh a path to shine after him; *one*
would think the deep *to be* hoary.
33 Upon earth there is not his like, who is
made without fear.
34 He beholdeth all high *things:* he *is* a king
over all the children of pride.

Job 42

1 Then Job answered the LORD, and said,
2 I know that thou canst do every *thing,*
and *that* no thought can be withholden
from thee.
3 Who *is* he that hideth counsel without
knowledge? therefore have I uttered that I
understood not; things too wonderful for
me, which I knew not.
4 Hear, I beseech thee, and I will speak: I will
demand of thee, and declare thou unto me.
5 I have heard of thee by the hearing of the
ear: but now mine eye seeth thee.
6 Wherefore I abhor *myself,* and repent in
dust and ashes.
7 ¶ And it was *so,* that after the LORD had
spoken these words unto Job, the LORD said
to Eliphaz the Temanite, My wrath is kindled
against thee, and against thy two friends:
for ye have not spoken of me *the thing that*
is right, as my servant Job *hath.*
8 Therefore take unto you now seven bullocks and seven rams, and go to my servant
Job, and offer up for yourselves a burnt
offering; and my servant Job shall pray for
you: for him will I accept: lest I deal with
you *after your* folly, in that ye have not
spoken of me *the thing which is* right, like
my servant Job.
9 So Eliphaz the Temanite and Bildad the
Shuhite *and* Zophar the Naamathite went,
and did according as the LORD commanded
them: the LORD also accepted Job.
10 And the LORD turned the captivity of
Job, when he prayed for his friends: also
the LORD gave Job twice as much as he
had before.
11 Then came there unto him all his brethren, and all his sisters, and all they that had
been of his acquaintance before, and did
eat bread with him in his house: and they
bemoaned him, and comforted him over all
the evil that the LORD had brought upon him:
every man also gave him a piece of money,
and every one an earring of gold.
12 So the LORD blessed the latter end of
Job more than his beginning: for he had
fourteen thousand sheep, and six thousand
camels, and a thousand yoke of oxen, and
a thousand she asses.
13 He had also seven sons and three daughters.
14 And he called the name of the first,
Jemima; and the name of the second, Kezia;
and the name of the third, Keren-happuch.
15 And in all the land were no women
found *so* fair as the daughters of Job: and
their father gave them inheritance among
their brethren.
16 After this lived Job an hundred and forty
years, and saw his sons, and his sons' sons,
even four generations.
17 So Job died, *being* old and full of days.

The Book Of

Psalms

Psalm 1

1 Blessed *is* the man that walketh not in the counsel of the ungodly, nor standeth in the way of sinners, nor sitteth in the seat of the scornful.

2 But his delight *is* in the law of the LORD; and in his law doth he meditate day and night.

3 And he shall be like a tree planted by the rivers of water, that bringeth forth his fruit in his season; his leaf also shall not wither; and whatsoever he doeth shall prosper.

4 The ungodly *are* not so: but *are* like the chaff which the wind driveth away.

5 Therefore the ungodly shall not stand in the judgment, nor sinners in the congregation of the righteous.

6 For the LORD knoweth the way of the righteous: but the way of the ungodly shall perish.

Psalm 2

1 Why do the heathen rage, and the people imagine a vain thing?

2 The kings of the earth set themselves, and the rulers take counsel together, against the LORD, and against his anointed, *saying,*

3 Let us break their bands asunder, and cast away their cords from us.

4 He that sitteth in the heavens shall laugh: the Lord shall have them in derision.

5 Then shall he speak unto them in his wrath, and vex them in his sore displeasure.

6 Yet have I set my king upon my holy hill of Zion.

7 I will declare the decree: the LORD hath said unto me, Thou *art* my Son; this day have I begotten thee.

8 Ask of me, and I shall give *thee* the heathen *for* thine inheritance, and the uttermost parts of the earth *for* thy possession.

9 Thou shalt break them with a rod of iron; thou shalt dash them in pieces like a potter's vessel.

10 Be wise now therefore, O ye kings: be instructed, ye judges of the earth.

11 Serve the LORD with fear, and rejoice with trembling.

12 Kiss the Son, lest he be angry, and ye perish *from* the way, when his wrath is kindled but a little. Blessed *are* all they that put their trust in him.

Psalm 3

A Psalm of David, when he fled from Absalom his son.

1 Lord, how are they increased that trouble me! many *are* they that rise up against me.

2 Many *there be* which say of my soul, *There is* no help for him in God. Selah.

3 But thou, O LORD, *art* a shield for me; my glory, and the lifter up of mine head.

4 I cried unto the LORD with my voice, and he heard me out of his holy hill. Selah.

5 I laid me down and slept; I awaked; for the LORD sustained me.

6 I will not be afraid of ten thousands of people, that have set *themselves* against me round about.

7 Arise, O LORD; save me, O my God: for thou hast smitten all mine enemies *upon* the cheek bone; thou hast broken the teeth of the ungodly.

8 Salvation *belongeth* unto the LORD: thy blessing *is* upon thy people. Selah.

Psalm 4

To the chief Musician on Neginoth, A Psalm of David.

1 Hear me when I call, O God of my righteousness: thou hast enlarged me *when I was* in distress; have mercy upon me, and hear my prayer.

2 O ye sons of men, how long *will ye turn* my glory into shame? *how long* will ye love vanity, *and* seek after leasing? Selah.

3 But know that the LORD hath set apart him that is godly for himself: the LORD will hear when I call unto him.

4 Stand in awe, and sin not: commune with your own heart upon your bed, and be still. Selah.

5 Offer the sacrifices of righteousness, and put your trust in the LORD.
6 *There be* many that say, Who will shew us *any* good? LORD, lift thou up the light of thy countenance upon us.
7 Thou hast put gladness in my heart, more than in the time *that* their corn and their wine increased.
8 I will both lay me down in peace, and sleep: for thou, LORD, only makest me dwell in safety.

Psalm 5

To the chief Musician upon Nehiloth, A Psalm of David.

1 Give ear to my words, O LORD, consider my meditation.
2 Hearken unto the voice of my cry, my King, and my God: for unto thee will I pray.
3 My voice shalt thou hear in the morning, O LORD; in the morning will I direct *my prayer* unto thee, and will look up.
4 For thou *art* not a God that hath pleasure in wickedness: neither shall evil dwell with thee.
5 The foolish shall not stand in thy sight: thou hatest all workers of iniquity.
6 Thou shalt destroy them that speak leasing: the LORD will abhor the bloody and deceitful man.
7 But as for me, I will come *into* thy house in the multitude of thy mercy: *and* in thy fear will I worship toward thy holy temple.
8 Lead me, O LORD, in thy righteousness because of mine enemies; make thy way straight before my face.
9 For *there is* no faithfulness in their mouth; their inward part *is* very wickedness; their throat *is* an open sepulchre; they flatter with their tongue.
10 Destroy thou them, O God; let them fall by their own counsels; cast them out in the multitude of their transgressions; for they have rebelled against thee.
11 But let all those that put their trust in thee rejoice: let them ever shout for joy, because thou defendest them: let them also that love thy name be joyful in thee.
12 For thou, LORD, wilt bless the righteous; with favour wilt thou compass him as *with* a shield.

Psalm 6

To the chief Musician on Neginoth upon Sheminith, A Psalm of David.

1 O Lord, rebuke me not in thine anger, neither chasten me in thy hot displeasure.
2 Have mercy upon me, O LORD; for I *am* weak: O LORD, heal me; for my bones are vexed.
3 My soul is also sore vexed: but thou, O LORD, how long?
4 Return, O LORD, deliver my soul: oh save me for thy mercies' sake.
5 For in death *there is* no remembrance of thee: in the grave who shall give thee thanks?
6 I am weary with my groaning; all the night make I my bed to swim; I water my couch with my tears.
7 Mine eye is consumed because of grief; it waxeth old because of all mine enemies.
8 Depart from me, all ye workers of iniquity; for the LORD hath heard the voice of my weeping.
9 The LORD hath heard my supplication; the LORD will receive my prayer.
10 Let all mine enemies be ashamed and sore vexed: let them return *and* be ashamed suddenly.

Psalm 7

Shiggaion of David, which he sang unto the LORD, concerning the words of Cush the Benjamite.

1 O Lord my God, in thee do I put my trust: save me from all them that persecute me, and deliver me:
2 Lest he tear my soul like a lion, rending *it* in pieces, while *there is* none to deliver.
3 O LORD my God, if I have done this; if there be iniquity in my hands;
4 If I have rewarded evil unto him that was at peace with me; (yea, I have delivered him that without cause is mine enemy:)
5 Let the enemy persecute my soul, and take *it;* yea, let him tread down my life upon the earth, and lay mine honour in the dust. Selah.
6 Arise, O LORD, in thine anger, lift up thyself because of the rage of mine enemies: and awake for me *to* the judgment *that* thou hast commanded.
7 So shall the congregation of the people

compass thee about: for their sakes therefore return thou on high.
8 The LORD shall judge the people: judge me,
O LORD, according to my righteousness, and
according to mine integrity *that is* in me.
9 Oh let the wickedness of the wicked come
to an end; but establish the just: for the
righteous God trieth the hearts and reins.
10 My defence *is* of God, which saveth the
upright in heart.
11 God judgeth the righteous, and God is
angry *with the wicked* every day.
12 If he turn not, he will whet his sword;
he hath bent his bow, and made it ready.
13 He hath also prepared for him the instruments of death; he ordaineth his arrows
against the persecutors.
14 Behold, he travaileth with iniquity, and
hath conceived mischief, and brought forth
falsehood.
15 He made a pit, and digged it, and is fallen
into the ditch *which* he made.
16 His mischief shall return upon his own
head, and his violent dealing shall come
down upon his own pate.
17 I will praise the LORD according to his
righteousness: and will sing praise to the
name of the LORD most high.

Psalm 8

To the chief Musician upon Gittith, A Psalm of David.

1 O Lord our Lord, how excellent *is* thy name
in all the earth! who hast set thy glory above
the heavens.
2 Out of the mouth of babes and sucklings
hast thou ordained strength because of
thine enemies, that thou mightest still the
enemy and the avenger.
3 When I consider thy heavens, the work of
thy fingers, the moon and the stars, which
thou hast ordained;
4 What is man, that thou art mindful of him?
and the son of man, that thou visitest him?
5 For thou hast made him a little lower than
the angels, and hast crowned him with glory
and honour.
6 Thou madest him to have dominion over
the works of thy hands; thou hast put all
things under his feet:
7 All sheep and oxen, yea, and the beasts
of the field;
8 The fowl of the air, and the fish of the sea,
and whatsoever passeth through the paths
of the seas.
9 O LORD our Lord, how excellent *is* thy name
in all the earth!

Psalm 9

To the chief Musician upon Muth-labben, A Psalm of David.

1 I will praise *thee*, O LORD, with my whole
heart; I will shew forth all thy marvellous
works.
2 I will be glad and rejoice in thee: I will sing
praise to thy name, O thou most High.
3 When mine enemies are turned back, they
shall fall and perish at thy presence.
4 For thou hast maintained my right and
my cause; thou satest in the throne judging right.
5 Thou hast rebuked the heathen, thou hast
destroyed the wicked, thou hast put out
their name for ever and ever.
6 O thou enemy, destructions are come to
a perpetual end: and thou hast destroyed
cities; their memorial is perished with them.
7 But the LORD shall endure for ever: he hath
prepared his throne for judgment.
8 And he shall judge the world in righteousness, he shall minister judgment to the
people in uprightness.
9 The LORD also will be a refuge for the
oppressed, a refuge in times of trouble.
10 And they that know thy name will put
their trust in thee: for thou, LORD, hast not
forsaken them that seek thee.
11 Sing praises to the LORD, which dwelleth in Zion: declare among the people his
doings.
12 When he maketh inquisition for blood,
he remembereth them: he forgetteth not
the cry of the humble.
13 Have mercy upon me, O LORD; consider
my trouble *which I suffer* of them that hate
me, thou that liftest me up from the gates
of death:
14 That I may shew forth all thy praise in the
gates of the daughter of Zion: I will rejoice
in thy salvation.
15 The heathen are sunk down in the pit
that they made: in the net which they hid
is their own foot taken.
16 The LORD is known *by* the judgment
which he executeth: the wicked is snared in
the work of his own hands. Higgaion. Selah.

17 The wicked shall be turned into hell, *and*
all the nations that forget God.
18 For the needy shall not alway be forgotten: the expectation of the poor shall *not*
perish for ever.
19 Arise, O LORD; let not man prevail: let the
heathen be judged in thy sight.
20 Put them in fear, O LORD: *that* the nations
may know themselves *to be but* men. Selah.

Psalm 10

1 Why standest thou afar off, O LORD? *why*
hidest thou *thyself* in times of trouble?
2 The wicked in *his* pride doth persecute
the poor: let them be taken in the devices
that they have imagined.
3 For the wicked boasteth of his heart's
desire, and blesseth the covetous, *whom*
the LORD abhorreth.
4 The wicked, through the pride of his countenance, will not seek *after God:* God *is* not
in all his thoughts.
5 His ways are always grievous; thy judgments *are* far above out of his sight: *as for*
all his enemies, he puffeth at them.
6 He hath said in his heart, I shall not be
moved: for *I shall* never *be* in adversity.
7 His mouth is full of cursing and deceit
and fraud: under his tongue *is* mischief
and vanity.
8 He sitteth in the lurking places of the villages: in the secret places doth he murder
the innocent: his eyes are privily set against
the poor.
9 He lieth in wait secretly as a lion in his
den: he lieth in wait to catch the poor: he
doth catch the poor, when he draweth him
into his net.
10 He croucheth, *and* humbleth himself,
that the poor may fall by his strong ones.
11 He hath said in his heart, God hath forgotten: he hideth his face; he will never see *it*.
12 Arise, O LORD; O God, lift up thine hand:
forget not the humble.
13 Wherefore doth the wicked contemn
God? he hath said in his heart, Thou wilt
not require *it*.
14 Thou hast seen *it;* for thou beholdest
mischief and spite, to requite *it* with thy
hand: the poor committeth himself unto
thee; thou art the helper of the fatherless.
15 Break thou the arm of the wicked and
the evil *man:* seek out his wickedness *till*
thou find none.
16 The LORD *is* King for ever and ever: the
heathen are perished out of his land.
17 LORD, thou hast heard the desire of the
humble: thou wilt prepare their heart, thou
wilt cause thine ear to hear:
18 To judge the fatherless and the
oppressed, that the man of the earth may
no more oppress.

Psalm 11

To the chief Musician,
A Psalm of David.

1 In the LORD put I my trust: how say ye to
my soul, Flee *as* a bird to your mountain?
2 For, lo, the wicked bend *their* bow, they
make ready their arrow upon the string,
that they may privily shoot at the upright
in heart.
3 If the foundations be destroyed, what can
the righteous do?
4 The LORD *is* in his holy temple, the LORD's
throne *is* in heaven: his eyes behold, his
eyelids try, the children of men.
5 The LORD trieth the righteous: but the
wicked and him that loveth violence his
soul hateth.
6 Upon the wicked he shall rain snares, fire
and brimstone, and an horrible tempest: *this*
shall be the portion of their cup.
7 For the righteous LORD loveth righteousness; his countenance doth behold the
upright.

Psalm 12

To the chief Musician upon
Sheminith, A Psalm of David.

1 Help, LORD; for the godly man ceaseth;
for the faithful fail from among the children of men.
2 They speak vanity every one with his
neighbour: *with* flattering lips *and* with a
double heart do they speak.
3 The LORD shall cut off all flattering lips,
and the tongue that speaketh proud things:
4 Who have said, With our tongue will we
prevail; our lips *are* our own: who *is* lord
over us?
5 For the oppression of the poor, for the
sighing of the needy, now will I arise, saith
the LORD; I will set *him* in safety *from him*
that puffeth at him.

6 The words of the LORD *are* pure words: *as* silver tried in a furnace of earth, purified seven times.
7 Thou shalt keep them, O LORD, thou shalt preserve them from this generation for ever.
8 The wicked walk on every side, when the vilest men are exalted.

Psalm 13

To the chief Musician,
A Psalm of David.

1 How long wilt thou forget me, O LORD? for ever? how long wilt thou hide thy face from me?
2 How long shall I take counsel in my soul, *having* sorrow in my heart daily? how long shall mine enemy be exalted over me?
3 Consider *and* hear me, O LORD my God: lighten mine eyes, lest I sleep the *sleep of* death;
4 Lest mine enemy say, I have prevailed against him; *and* those that trouble me rejoice when I am moved.
5 But I have trusted in thy mercy; my heart shall rejoice in thy salvation.
6 I will sing unto the LORD, because he hath dealt bountifully with me.

Psalm 14

To the chief Musician,
A Psalm of David.

1 The fool hath said in his heart, *There is* no God. They are corrupt, they have done abominable works, *there is* none that doeth good.
2 The LORD looked down from heaven upon the children of men, to see if there were any that did understand, *and* seek God.
3 They are all gone aside, they are *all* together become filthy: *there is* none that doeth good, no, not one.
4 Have all the workers of iniquity no knowledge? who eat up my people *as* they eat bread, and call not upon the LORD.
5 There were they in great fear: for God *is* in the generation of the righteous.
6 Ye have shamed the counsel of the poor, because the LORD *is* his refuge.
7 Oh that the salvation of Israel *were come* out of Zion! when the LORD bringeth back the captivity of his people, Jacob shall rejoice, *and* Israel shall be glad.

Psalm 15

A Psalm of David.

1 Lord, who shall abide in thy tabernacle? who shall dwell in thy holy hill?
2 He that walketh uprightly, and worketh righteousness, and speaketh the truth in his heart.
3 *He that* backbiteth not with his tongue, nor doeth evil to his neighbour, nor taketh up a reproach against his neighbour.
4 In whose eyes a vile person is contemned; but he honoureth them that fear the LORD. *He that* sweareth to *his own* hurt, and changeth not.
5 *He that* putteth not out his money to usury, nor taketh reward against the innocent. He that doeth these *things* shall never be moved.

Psalm 16

Michtam of David.

1 Preserve me, O God: for in thee do I put my trust.
2 *O my soul,* thou hast said unto the LORD, Thou *art* my Lord: my goodness *extendeth* not to thee;
3 *But* to the saints that *are* in the earth, and *to* the excellent, in whom *is* all my delight.
4 Their sorrows shall be multiplied *that* hasten *after* another *god:* their drink offerings of blood will I not offer, nor take up their names into my lips.
5 The LORD *is* the portion of mine inheritance and of my cup: thou maintainest my lot.
6 The lines are fallen unto me in pleasant *places;* yea, I have a goodly heritage.
7 I will bless the LORD, who hath given me counsel: my reins also instruct me in the night seasons.
8 I have set the LORD always before me: because *he is* at my right hand, I shall not be moved.
9 Therefore my heart is glad, and my glory rejoiceth: my flesh also shall rest in hope.
10 For thou wilt not leave my soul in hell; neither wilt thou suffer thine Holy One to see corruption.
11 Thou wilt shew me the path of life: in thy presence *is* fulness of joy; at thy right hand *there are* pleasures for evermore.

Psalm 17

A Prayer of David.

1 Hear the right, O LORD, attend unto my
cry, give ear unto my prayer, *that goeth* not
out of feigned lips.
2 Let my sentence come forth from thy
presence; let thine eyes behold the things
that are equal.
3 Thou hast proved mine heart; thou hast
visited *me* in the night; thou hast tried me,
and shalt find nothing; I am purposed *that*
my mouth shall not transgress.
4 Concerning the works of men, by the word
of thy lips I have kept *me from* the paths of
the destroyer.
5 Hold up my goings in thy paths, *that* my
footsteps slip not.
6 I have called upon thee, for thou wilt hear
me, O God: incline thine ear unto me, *and*
hear my speech.
7 Shew thy marvellous lovingkindness, O
thou that savest by thy right hand them
which put their trust *in thee* from those that
rise up *against them*.
8 Keep me as the apple of the eye, hide me
under the shadow of thy wings,
9 From the wicked that oppress me, *from*
my deadly enemies, *who* compass me about.
10 They are inclosed in their own fat: with
their mouth they speak proudly.
11 They have now compassed us in our
steps: they have set their eyes bowing down
to the earth;
12 Like as a lion *that* is greedy of his prey,
and as it were a young lion lurking in secret
places.
13 Arise, O LORD, disappoint him, cast him
down: deliver my soul from the wicked,
which is thy sword:
14 From men *which are* thy hand, O LORD,
from men of the world, *which have* their
portion in *this* life, and whose belly thou
fillest with thy hid *treasure:* they are full
of children, and leave the rest of their *sub-*
stance to their babes.
15 As for me, I will behold thy face in righteousness: I shall be satisfied, when I awake,
with thy likeness.

Psalm 18

To the chief Musician, A Psalm of David, the servant of the LORD, who spake unto the LORD the words of this song in the day that the LORD delivered him from the hand of all his enemies, and from the hand of Saul: And he said,

1 I will love thee, O LORD, my strength.
2 The LORD *is* my rock, and my fortress, and
my deliverer; my God, my strength, in whom
I will trust; my buckler, and the horn of my
salvation, *and* my high tower.
3 I will call upon the LORD, *who is worthy* to
be praised: so shall I be saved from mine
enemies.
4 The sorrows of death compassed me, and
the floods of ungodly men made me afraid.
5 The sorrows of hell compassed me about:
the snares of death prevented me.
6 In my distress I called upon the LORD, and
cried unto my God: he heard my voice out
of his temple, and my cry came before him,
even into his ears.
7 Then the earth shook and trembled; the
foundations also of the hills moved and were
shaken, because he was wroth.
8 There went up a smoke out of his nostrils,
and fire out of his mouth devoured: coals
were kindled by it.
9 He bowed the heavens also, and came
down: and darkness *was* under his feet.
10 And he rode upon a cherub, and did fly:
yea, he did fly upon the wings of the wind.
11 He made darkness his secret place; his
pavilion round about him *were* dark waters
and thick clouds of the skies.
12 At the brightness *that was* before him
his thick clouds passed, hail *stones* and
coals of fire.
13 The LORD also thundered in the heavens,
and the Highest gave his voice; hail *stones*
and coals of fire.
14 Yea, he sent out his arrows, and scattered
them; and he shot out lightnings, and discomfited them.
15 Then the channels of waters were seen,
and the foundations of the world were discovered at thy rebuke, O LORD, at the blast
of the breath of thy nostrils.
16 He sent from above, he took me, he drew
me out of many waters.
17 He delivered me from my strong enemy,

and from them which hated me: for they
were too strong for me.
18 They prevented me in the day of my
calamity: but the LORD was my stay.
19 He brought me forth also into a large
place; he delivered me, because he
delighted in me.
20 The LORD rewarded me according to my
righteousness; according to the cleanness of
my hands hath he recompensed me.
21 For I have kept the ways of the LORD, and
have not wickedly departed from my God.
22 For all his judgments *were* before me,
and I did not put away his statutes from me.
23 I was also upright before him, and I kept
myself from mine iniquity.
24 Therefore hath the LORD recompensed
me according to my righteousness, according to the cleanness of my hands in his
eyesight.
25 With the merciful thou wilt shew thyself
merciful; with an upright man thou wilt
shew thyself upright;
26 With the pure thou wilt shew thyself
pure; and with the froward thou wilt shew
thyself froward.
27 For thou wilt save the afflicted people;
but wilt bring down high looks.
28 For thou wilt light my candle: the LORD
my God will enlighten my darkness.
29 For by thee I have run through a troop;
and by my God have I leaped over a wall.
30 *As for* God, his way *is* perfect: the word
of the LORD is tried: he *is* a buckler to all
those that trust in him.
31 For who *is* God save the LORD? or who *is*
a rock save our God?
32 *It is* God that girdeth me with strength,
and maketh my way perfect.
33 He maketh my feet like hinds' *feet*, and
setteth me upon my high places.
34 He teacheth my hands to war, so that a
bow of steel is broken by mine arms.
35 Thou hast also given me the shield of thy
salvation: and thy right hand hath holden me
up, and thy gentleness hath made me great.
36 Thou hast enlarged my steps under me,
that my feet did not slip.
37 I have pursued mine enemies, and overtaken them: neither did I turn again till they
were consumed.
38 I have wounded them that they were not
able to rise: they are fallen under my feet.
39 For thou hast girded me with strength
unto the battle: thou hast subdued under
me those that rose up against me.
40 Thou hast also given me the necks of
mine enemies; that I might destroy them
that hate me.
41 They cried, but *there was* none to save
them: even unto the LORD, but he answered
them not.
42 Then did I beat them small as the dust
before the wind: I did cast them out as the
dirt in the streets.
43 Thou hast delivered me from the strivings
of the people; *and* thou hast made me the
head of the heathen: a people *whom* I have
not known shall serve me.
44 As soon as they hear of me, they shall
obey me: the strangers shall submit themselves unto me.
45 The strangers shall fade away, and be
afraid out of their close places.
46 The LORD liveth; and blessed *be* my rock;
and let the God of my salvation be exalted.
47 *It is* God that avengeth me, and subdueth
the people under me.
48 He delivereth me from mine enemies:
yea, thou liftest me up above those that
rise up against me: thou hast delivered me
from the violent man.
49 Therefore will I give thanks unto thee, O
LORD, among the heathen, and sing praises
unto thy name.
50 Great deliverance giveth he to his king;
and sheweth mercy to his anointed, to
David, and to his seed for evermore.

Psalm 19

To the chief Musician,
A Psalm of David.

1 The heavens declare the glory of God;
and the firmament sheweth his handywork.
2 Day unto day uttereth speech, and night
unto night sheweth knowledge.
3 *There is* no speech nor language, *where*
their voice is not heard.
4 Their line is gone out through all the earth,
and their words to the end of the world. In
them hath he set a tabernacle for the sun,
5 Which *is* as a bridegroom coming out of
his chamber, *and* rejoiceth as a strong man
to run a race.
6 His going forth *is* from the end of the
heaven, and his circuit unto the ends of

it: and there is nothing hid from the heat
thereof.
7 The law of the LORD *is* perfect, converting
the soul: the testimony of the LORD *is* sure,
making wise the simple.
8 The statutes of the LORD *are* right, rejoicing
the heart: the commandment of the LORD
is pure, enlightening the eyes.
9 The fear of the LORD *is* clean, enduring for
ever: the judgments of the LORD *are* true
and righteous altogether.
10 More to be desired *are they* than gold,
yea, than much fine gold: sweeter also than
honey and the honeycomb.
11 Moreover by them is thy servant warned:
and in keeping of them *there is* great reward.
12 Who can understand *his* errors? cleanse
thou me from secret *faults.*
13 Keep back thy servant also from presumptuous *sins;* let them not have dominion
over me: then shall I be upright, and I shall
be innocent from the great transgression.
14 Let the words of my mouth, and the
meditation of my heart, be acceptable in
thy sight, O LORD, my strength, and my
redeemer.

Psalm 20

To the chief Musician,
A Psalm of David.

1 The LORD hear thee in the day of trouble;
the name of the God of Jacob defend thee;
2 Send thee help from the sanctuary, and
strengthen thee out of Zion;
3 Remember all thy offerings, and accept
thy burnt sacrifice; Selah.
4 Grant thee according to thine own heart,
and fulfil all thy counsel.
5 We will rejoice in thy salvation, and in the
name of our God we will set up *our* banners:
the LORD fulfil all thy petitions.
6 Now know I that the LORD saveth his
anointed; he will hear him from his holy
heaven with the saving strength of his
right hand.
7 Some *trust* in chariots, and some in horses:
but we will remember the name of the
LORD our God.
8 They are brought down and fallen: but we
are risen, and stand upright.
9 Save, LORD: let the king hear us when
we call.

Psalm 21

To the chief Musician,
A Psalm of David.

1 The king shall joy in thy strength, O LORD;
and in thy salvation how greatly shall he
rejoice!
2 Thou hast given him his heart's desire,
and hast not withholden the request of his
lips. Selah.
3 For thou preventest him with the blessings
of goodness: thou settest a crown of pure
gold on his head.
4 He asked life of thee, *and* thou gavest *it*
him, *even* length of days for ever and ever.
5 His glory *is* great in thy salvation: honour
and majesty hast thou laid upon him.
6 For thou hast made him most blessed for
ever: thou hast made him exceeding glad
with thy countenance.
7 For the king trusteth in the LORD, and
through the mercy of the most High he shall
not be moved.
8 Thine hand shall find out all thine enemies: thy right hand shall find out those
that hate thee.
9 Thou shalt make them as a fiery oven
in the time of thine anger: the LORD shall
swallow them up in his wrath, and the fire
shall devour them.
10 Their fruit shalt thou destroy from the
earth, and their seed from among the children of men.
11 For they intended evil against thee: they
imagined a mischievous device, *which* they
are not able *to perform.*
12 Therefore shalt thou make them turn
their back, *when* thou shalt make ready
thine arrows upon thy strings against the
face of them.
13 Be thou exalted, LORD, in thine own
strength: *so* will we sing and praise thy
power.

Psalm 22

To the chief Musician upon Aijeleth
Shahar, A Psalm of David.

1 My God, my God, why hast thou forsaken
me? *why art thou so* far from helping me,
and from the words of my roaring?
2 O my God, I cry in the daytime, but thou
hearest not; and in the night season, and
am not silent.

3 But thou *art* holy, *O thou* that inhabitest the praises of Israel.
4 Our fathers trusted in thee: they trusted, and thou didst deliver them.
5 They cried unto thee, and were delivered: they trusted in thee, and were not confounded.
6 But I *am* a worm, and no man; a reproach of men, and despised of the people.
7 All they that see me laugh me to scorn: they shoot out the lip, they shake the head, *saying,*
8 He trusted on the LORD *that* he would deliver him: let him deliver him, seeing he delighted in him.
9 But thou *art* he that took me out of the womb: thou didst make me hope *when I was* upon my mother's breasts.
10 I was cast upon thee from the womb: thou *art* my God from my mother's belly.
11 Be not far from me; for trouble *is* near; for *there is* none to help.
12 Many bulls have compassed me: strong *bulls* of Bashan have beset me round.
13 They gaped upon me *with* their mouths, *as* a ravening and a roaring lion.
14 I am poured out like water, and all my bones are out of joint: my heart is like wax; it is melted in the midst of my bowels.
15 My strength is dried up like a potsherd; and my tongue cleaveth to my jaws; and thou hast brought me into the dust of death.
16 For dogs have compassed me: the assembly of the wicked have inclosed me: they pierced my hands and my feet.
17 I may tell all my bones: they look *and* stare upon me.
18 They part my garments among them, and cast lots upon my vesture.
19 But be not thou far from me, O LORD: O my strength, haste thee to help me.
20 Deliver my soul from the sword; my darling from the power of the dog.
21 Save me from the lion's mouth: for thou hast heard me from the horns of the unicorns.
22 I will declare thy name unto my brethren: in the midst of the congregation will I praise thee.
23 Ye that fear the LORD, praise him; all ye the seed of Jacob, glorify him; and fear him, all ye the seed of Israel.
24 For he hath not despised nor abhorred the affliction of the afflicted; neither hath he hid his face from him; but when he cried unto him, he heard.
25 My praise *shall be* of thee in the great congregation: I will pay my vows before them that fear him.
26 The meek shall eat and be satisfied: they shall praise the LORD that seek him: your heart shall live for ever.
27 All the ends of the world shall remember and turn unto the LORD: and all the kindreds of the nations shall worship before thee.
28 For the kingdom *is* the LORD's: and he *is* the governor among the nations.
29 All *they that be* fat upon earth shall eat and worship: all they that go down to the dust shall bow before him: and none can keep alive his own soul.
30 A seed shall serve him; it shall be accounted to the Lord for a generation.
31 They shall come, and shall declare his righteousness unto a people that shall be born, that he hath done *this.*

Psalm 23

A Psalm of David.

1 The LORD *is* my shepherd; I shall not want.
2 He maketh me to lie down in green pastures: he leadeth me beside the still waters.
3 He restoreth my soul: he leadeth me in the paths of righteousness for his name's sake.
4 Yea, though I walk through the valley of the shadow of death, I will fear no evil: for thou *art* with me; thy rod and thy staff they comfort me.
5 Thou preparest a table before me in the presence of mine enemies: thou anointest my head with oil; my cup runneth over.
6 Surely goodness and mercy shall follow me all the days of my life: and I will dwell in the house of the LORD for ever.

Psalm 24

A Psalm of David.

1 The earth *is* the LORD's, and the fulness thereof; the world, and they that dwell therein.
2 For he hath founded it upon the seas, and established it upon the floods.
3 Who shall ascend into the hill of the LORD? or who shall stand in his holy place?
4 He that hath clean hands, and a pure

heart; who hath not lifted up his soul unto vanity, nor sworn deceitfully.

5 He shall receive the blessing from the LORD, and righteousness from the God of his salvation.

6 This *is* the generation of them that seek him, that seek thy face, O Jacob. Selah.

7 Lift up your heads, O ye gates; and be ye lift up, ye everlasting doors; and the King of glory shall come in.

8 Who *is* this King of glory? The LORD strong and mighty, the LORD mighty in battle.

9 Lift up your heads, O ye gates; even lift *them* up, ye everlasting doors; and the King of glory shall come in.

10 Who is this King of glory? The LORD of hosts, he *is* the King of glory. Selah.

Psalm 25

A Psalm of David.

1 Unto thee, O LORD, do I lift up my soul.

2 O my God, I trust in thee: let me not be ashamed, let not mine enemies triumph over me.

3 Yea, let none that wait on thee be ashamed: let them be ashamed which transgress without cause.

4 Shew me thy ways, O LORD; teach me thy paths.

5 Lead me in thy truth, and teach me: for thou *art* the God of my salvation; on thee do I wait all the day.

6 Remember, O LORD, thy tender mercies and thy lovingkindnesses; for they *have been* ever of old.

7 Remember not the sins of my youth, nor my transgressions: according to thy mercy remember thou me for thy goodness' sake, O LORD.

8 Good and upright *is* the LORD: therefore will he teach sinners in the way.

9 The meek will he guide in judgment: and the meek will he teach his way.

10 All the paths of the LORD *are* mercy and truth unto such as keep his covenant and his testimonies.

11 For thy name's sake, O LORD, pardon mine iniquity; for it *is* great.

12 What man *is* he that feareth the LORD? him shall he teach in the way *that* he shall choose.

13 His soul shall dwell at ease; and his seed shall inherit the earth.

14 The secret of the LORD *is* with them that fear him; and he will shew them his covenant.

15 Mine eyes *are* ever toward the LORD; for he shall pluck my feet out of the net.

16 Turn thee unto me, and have mercy upon me; for I *am* desolate and afflicted.

17 The troubles of my heart are enlarged: *O* bring thou me out of my distresses.

18 Look upon mine affliction and my pain; and forgive all my sins.

19 Consider mine enemies; for they are many; and they hate me with cruel hatred.

20 O keep my soul, and deliver me: let me not be ashamed; for I put my trust in thee.

21 Let integrity and uprightness preserve me; for I wait on thee.

22 Redeem Israel, O God, out of all his troubles.

Psalm 26

A Psalm of David.

1 Judge me, O LORD; for I have walked in mine integrity: I have trusted also in the LORD; *therefore* I shall not slide.

2 Examine me, O LORD, and prove me; try my reins and my heart.

3 For thy lovingkindness *is* before mine eyes: and I have walked in thy truth.

4 I have not sat with vain persons, neither will I go in with dissemblers.

5 I have hated the congregation of evil doers; and will not sit with the wicked.

6 I will wash mine hands in innocency: so will I compass thine altar, O LORD:

7 That I may publish with the voice of thanksgiving, and tell of all thy wondrous works.

8 LORD, I have loved the habitation of thy house, and the place where thine honour dwelleth.

9 Gather not my soul with sinners, nor my life with bloody men:

10 In whose hands *is* mischief, and their right hand is full of bribes.

11 But as for me, I will walk in mine integrity: redeem me, and be merciful unto me.

12 My foot standeth in an even place: in the congregations will I bless the LORD.

Psalm 27

A Psalm of David.

1 The LORD *is* my light and my salvation;

whom shall I fear? the LORD *is* the strength
of my life; of whom shall I be afraid?
2 When the wicked, *even* mine enemies and
my foes, came upon me to eat up my flesh,
they stumbled and fell.
3 Though an host should encamp against
me, my heart shall not fear: though war
should rise against me, in this *will* I *be*
confident.
4 One *thing* have I desired of the LORD, that
will I seek after; that I may dwell in the house
of the LORD all the days of my life, to behold
the beauty of the LORD, and to inquire in
his temple.
5 For in the time of trouble he shall hide
me in his pavilion: in the secret of his tabernacle shall he hide me; he shall set me
up upon a rock.
6 And now shall mine head be lifted up
above mine enemies round about me:
therefore will I offer in his tabernacle sacrifices of joy; I will sing, yea, I will sing praises
unto the LORD.
7 Hear, O LORD, *when* I cry with my voice:
have mercy also upon me, and answer me.
8 *When thou saidst,* Seek ye my face; my
heart said unto thee, Thy face, LORD, will
I seek.
9 Hide not thy face *far* from me; put not thy
servant away in anger: thou hast been my
help; leave me not, neither forsake me, O
God of my salvation.
10 When my father and my mother forsake
me, then the LORD will take me up.
11 Teach me thy way, O LORD, and lead me
in a plain path, because of mine enemies.
12 Deliver me not over unto the will of mine
enemies: for false witnesses are risen up
against me, and such as breathe out cruelty.
13 *I had fainted,* unless I had believed to
see the goodness of the LORD in the land
of the living.
14 Wait on the LORD: be of good courage,
and he shall strengthen thine heart: wait, I
say, on the LORD.

Psalm 28

A Psalm of David.

1 Unto thee will I cry, O LORD my rock; be not
silent to me: lest, *if* thou be silent to me, I
become like them that go down into the pit.
2 Hear the voice of my supplications, when
I cry unto thee, when I lift up my hands
toward thy holy oracle.
3 Draw me not away with the wicked, and
with the workers of iniquity, which speak
peace to their neighbours, but mischief *is*
in their hearts.
4 Give them according to their deeds,
and according to the wickedness of their
endeavours: give them after the work of
their hands; render to them their desert.
5 Because they regard not the works of the
LORD, nor the operation of his hands, he
shall destroy them, and not build them up.
6 Blessed *be* the LORD, because he hath
heard the voice of my supplications.
7 The LORD *is* my strength and my shield;
my heart trusted in him, and I am helped:
therefore my heart greatly rejoiceth; and
with my song will I praise him.
8 The LORD *is* their strength, and he *is* the
saving strength of his anointed.
9 Save thy people, and bless thine inheritance: feed them also, and lift them up
for ever.

Psalm 29

A Psalm of David.

1 Give unto the LORD, O ye mighty, give unto
the LORD glory and strength.
2 Give unto the LORD the glory due unto
his name; worship the LORD in the beauty
of holiness.
3 The voice of the LORD *is* upon the waters:
the God of glory thundereth: the LORD *is*
upon many waters.
4 The voice of the LORD *is* powerful; the
voice of the LORD *is* full of majesty.
5 The voice of the LORD breaketh the cedars;
yea, the LORD breaketh the cedars of Lebanon.
6 He maketh them also to skip like a calf;
Lebanon and Sirion like a young unicorn.
7 The voice of the LORD divideth the flames
of fire.
8 The voice of the LORD shaketh the wilderness; the LORD shaketh the wilderness
of Kadesh.
9 The voice of the LORD maketh the hinds to
calve, and discovereth the forests: and in his
temple doth every one speak of *his* glory.
10 The LORD sitteth upon the flood; yea, the
LORD sitteth King for ever.
11 The LORD will give strength unto his

people; the LORD will bless his people with peace.

Psalm 30

A Psalm and Song at the dedication of the house of David.

1 I will extol thee, O LORD; for thou hast lifted me up, and hast not made my foes to rejoice over me.
2 O LORD my God, I cried unto thee, and thou hast healed me.
3 O LORD, thou hast brought up my soul from the grave: thou hast kept me alive, that I should not go down to the pit.
4 Sing unto the LORD, O ye saints of his, and give thanks at the remembrance of his holiness.
5 For his anger *endureth but* a moment; in his favour *is* life: weeping may endure for a night, but joy *cometh* in the morning.
6 And in my prosperity I said, I shall never be moved.
7 LORD, by thy favour thou hast made my mountain to stand strong: thou didst hide thy face, *and* I was troubled.
8 I cried to thee, O LORD; and unto the LORD I made supplication.
9 What profit *is there* in my blood, when I go down to the pit? Shall the dust praise thee? shall it declare thy truth?
10 Hear, O LORD, and have mercy upon me: LORD, be thou my helper.
11 Thou hast turned for me my mourning into dancing: thou hast put off my sackcloth, and girded me with gladness;
12 To the end that *my* glory may sing praise to thee, and not be silent. O LORD my God, I will give thanks unto thee for ever.

Psalm 31

To the chief Musician, A Psalm of David.

1 In thee, O LORD, do I put my trust; let me never be ashamed: deliver me in thy righteousness.
2 Bow down thine ear to me; deliver me speedily: be thou my strong rock, for an house of defence to save me.
3 For thou *art* my rock and my fortress; therefore for thy name's sake lead me, and guide me.
4 Pull me out of the net that they have laid privily for me: for thou *art* my strength.
5 Into thine hand I commit my spirit: thou hast redeemed me, O LORD God of truth.
6 I have hated them that regard lying vanities: but I trust in the LORD.
7 I will be glad and rejoice in thy mercy: for thou hast considered my trouble; thou hast known my soul in adversities;
8 And hast not shut me up into the hand of the enemy: thou hast set my feet in a large room.
9 Have mercy upon me, O LORD, for I am in trouble: mine eye is consumed with grief, *yea,* my soul and my belly.
10 For my life is spent with grief, and my years with sighing: my strength faileth because of mine iniquity, and my bones are consumed.
11 I was a reproach among all mine enemies, but especially among my neighbours, and a fear to mine acquaintance: they that did see me without fled from me.
12 I am forgotten as a dead man out of mind: I am like a broken vessel.
13 For I have heard the slander of many: fear *was* on every side: while they took counsel together against me, they devised to take away my life.
14 But I trusted in thee, O LORD: I said, Thou *art* my God.
15 My times *are* in thy hand: deliver me from the hand of mine enemies, and from them that persecute me.
16 Make thy face to shine upon thy servant: save me for thy mercies' sake.
17 Let me not be ashamed, O LORD; for I have called upon thee: let the wicked be ashamed, *and* let them be silent in the grave.
18 Let the lying lips be put to silence; which speak grievous things proudly and contemptuously against the righteous.
19 *Oh* how great *is* thy goodness, which thou hast laid up for them that fear thee; *which* thou hast wrought for them that trust in thee before the sons of men!
20 Thou shalt hide them in the secret of thy presence from the pride of man: thou shalt keep them secretly in a pavilion from the strife of tongues.
21 Blessed *be* the LORD: for he hath shewed me his marvellous kindness in a strong city.
22 For I said in my haste, I am cut off from before thine eyes: nevertheless thou heard-

est the voice of my supplications when I
cried unto thee.
23 O love the LORD, all ye his saints: *for* the
LORD preserveth the faithful, and plentifully
rewardeth the proud doer.
24 Be of good courage, and he shall
strengthen your heart, all ye that hope in
the LORD.

Psalm 32

A Psalm of David, Maschil.

1 Blessed *is he whose* transgression *is* forgiven, *whose* sin *is* covered.
2 Blessed *is* the man unto whom the LORD
imputeth not iniquity, and in whose spirit
there is no guile.
3 When I kept silence, my bones waxed old
through my roaring all the day long.
4 For day and night thy hand was heavy
upon me: my moisture is turned into the
drought of summer. Selah.
5 I acknowledged my sin unto thee, and
mine iniquity have I not hid. I said, I will confess my transgressions unto the LORD; and
thou forgavest the iniquity of my sin. Selah.
6 For this shall every one that is godly pray
unto thee in a time when thou mayest be
found: surely in the floods of great waters
they shall not come nigh unto him.
7 Thou *art* my hiding place; thou shalt preserve me from trouble; thou shalt compass
me about with songs of deliverance. Selah.
8 I will instruct thee and teach thee in the
way which thou shalt go: I will guide thee
with mine eye.
9 Be ye not as the horse, *or* as the mule,
which have no understanding: whose mouth
must be held in with bit and bridle, lest they
come near unto thee.
10 Many sorrows *shall be* to the wicked: but
he that trusteth in the LORD, mercy shall
compass him about.
11 Be glad in the LORD, and rejoice, ye
righteous: and shout for joy, all *ye that are*
upright in heart.

Psalm 33

1 Rejoice in the LORD, O ye righteous: *for*
praise is comely for the upright.
2 Praise the LORD with harp: sing unto him
with the psaltery *and* an instrument of ten
strings.
3 Sing unto him a new song; play skilfully
with a loud noise.
4 For the word of the LORD *is* right; and all
his works *are done* in truth.
5 He loveth righteousness and judgment:
the earth is full of the goodness of the LORD.
6 By the word of the LORD were the heavens made; and all the host of them by the
breath of his mouth.
7 He gathereth the waters of the sea
together as an heap: he layeth up the depth
in storehouses.
8 Let all the earth fear the LORD: let all the
inhabitants of the world stand in awe of him.
9 For he spake, and it was *done;* he commanded, and it stood fast.
10 The LORD bringeth the counsel of the
heathen to nought: he maketh the devices
of the people of none effect.
11 The counsel of the LORD standeth for
ever, the thoughts of his heart to all generations.
12 Blessed *is* the nation whose God *is* the
LORD; *and* the people *whom* he hath chosen
for his own inheritance.
13 The LORD looketh from heaven; he beholdeth all the sons of men.
14 From the place of his habitation he
looketh upon all the inhabitants of the earth.
15 He fashioneth their hearts alike; he considereth all their works.
16 There is no king saved by the multitude
of an host: a mighty man is not delivered
by much strength.
17 An horse *is* a vain thing for safety: neither
shall he deliver *any* by his great strength.
18 Behold, the eye of the LORD *is* upon
them that fear him, upon them that hope
in his mercy;
19 To deliver their soul from death, and to
keep them alive in famine.
20 Our soul waiteth for the LORD: he *is* our
help and our shield.
21 For our heart shall rejoice in him, because
we have trusted in his holy name.
22 Let thy mercy, O LORD, be upon us,
according as we hope in thee.

Psalm 34

A Psalm of David, when he changed his behaviour before Abimelech; who drove him away, and he departed.

1 I will bless the LORD at all times: his praise
shall continually *be* in my mouth.
2 My soul shall make her boast in the LORD:
the humble shall hear *thereof*, and be glad.
3 O magnify the LORD with me, and let us
exalt his name together.
4 I sought the LORD, and he heard me, and
delivered me from all my fears.
5 They looked unto him, and were lightened:
and their faces were not ashamed.
6 This poor man cried, and the LORD heard
him, and saved him out of all his troubles.
7 The angel of the LORD encampeth round
about them that fear him, and delivereth
them.
8 O taste and see that the LORD *is* good:
blessed *is* the man *that* trusteth in him.
9 O fear the LORD, ye his saints: for *there is*
no want to them that fear him.
10 The young lions do lack, and suffer hunger: but they that seek the LORD shall not
want any good *thing*.
11 Come, ye children, hearken unto me: I
will teach you the fear of the LORD.
12 What man *is he that* desireth life, *and*
loveth *many* days, that he may see good?
13 Keep thy tongue from evil, and thy lips
from speaking guile.
14 Depart from evil, and do good; seek
peace, and pursue it.
15 The eyes of the LORD *are* upon the righteous, and his ears *are open* unto their cry.
16 The face of the LORD *is* against them that
do evil, to cut off the remembrance of them
from the earth.
17 *The righteous* cry, and the LORD heareth,
and delivereth them out of all their troubles.
18 The LORD *is* nigh unto them that are of
a broken heart; and saveth such as be of a
contrite spirit.
19 Many *are* the afflictions of the righteous:
but the LORD delivereth him out of them all.
20 He keepeth all his bones: not one of
them is broken.
21 Evil shall slay the wicked: and they that
hate the righteous shall be desolate.
22 The LORD redeemeth the soul of his servants: and none of them that trust in him
shall be desolate.

Psalm 35

A Psalm of David.

1 Plead *my cause*, O LORD, with them that
strive with me: fight against them that fight
against me.
2 Take hold of shield and buckler, and stand
up for mine help.
3 Draw out also the spear, and stop *the way*
against them that persecute me: say unto
my soul, I *am* thy salvation.
4 Let them be confounded and put to shame
that seek after my soul: let them be turned
back and brought to confusion that devise
my hurt.
5 Let them be as chaff before the wind: and
let the angel of the LORD chase *them*.
6 Let their way be dark and slippery: and
let the angel of the LORD persecute them.
7 For without cause have they hid for me
their net *in* a pit, *which* without cause they
have digged for my soul.
8 Let destruction come upon him at
unawares; and let his net that he hath hid
catch himself: into that very destruction
let him fall.
9 And my soul shall be joyful in the LORD: it
shall rejoice in his salvation.
10 All my bones shall say, LORD, who *is* like
unto thee, which deliverest the poor from
him that is too strong for him, yea, the poor
and the needy from him that spoileth him?
11 False witnesses did rise up; they laid to
my charge *things* that I knew not.
12 They rewarded me evil for good *to* the
spoiling of my soul.
13 But as for me, when they were sick, my
clothing *was* sackcloth: I humbled my soul
with fasting; and my prayer returned into
mine own bosom.
14 I behaved myself as though *he had been*
my friend *or* brother: I bowed down heavily,
as one that mourneth *for his* mother.
15 But in mine adversity they rejoiced,
and gathered themselves together: *yea*,
the abjects gathered themselves together
against me, and I knew *it* not; they did tear
me, and ceased not:
16 With hypocritical mockers in feasts, they
gnashed upon me with their teeth.
17 Lord, how long wilt thou look on? rescue

my soul from their destructions, my darling
from the lions.
18 I will give thee thanks in the great congregation: I will praise thee among much
people.
19 Let not them that are mine enemies
wrongfully rejoice over me: *neither* let them
wink with the eye that hate me without a
cause.
20 For they speak not peace: but they devise
deceitful matters against *them that are*
quiet in the land.
21 Yea, they opened their mouth wide
against me, *and* said, Aha, aha, our eye
hath seen *it*.
22 *This* thou hast seen, O LORD: keep not
silence: O Lord, be not far from me.
23 Stir up thyself, and awake to my judgment, *even* unto my cause, my God and
my Lord.
24 Judge me, O LORD my God, according to
thy righteousness; and let them not rejoice
over me.
25 Let them not say in their hearts, Ah, so
would we have it: let them not say, We have
swallowed him up.
26 Let them be ashamed and brought to
confusion together that rejoice at mine hurt:
let them be clothed with shame and dishonour that magnify *themselves* against me.
27 Let them shout for joy, and be glad, that
favour my righteous cause: yea, let them
say continually, Let the LORD be magnified,
which hath pleasure in the prosperity of
his servant.
28 And my tongue shall speak of thy righteousness *and* of thy praise all the day long.

Psalm 36

To the chief Musician, A Psalm of David the servant of the LORD.

1 The transgression of the wicked saith
within my heart, *that there is* no fear of God
before his eyes.
2 For he flattereth himself in his own eyes,
until his iniquity be found to be hateful.
3 The words of his mouth *are* iniquity and
deceit: he hath left off to be wise, *and* to
do good.
4 He deviseth mischief upon his bed; he
setteth himself in a way *that is* not good;
he abhorreth not evil.
5 Thy mercy, O LORD, *is* in the heavens; *and*
thy faithfulness *reacheth* unto the clouds.
6 Thy righteousness *is* like the great mountains; thy judgments *are* a great deep: O
LORD, thou preservest man and beast.
7 How excellent *is* thy lovingkindness, O
God! therefore the children of men put
their trust under the shadow of thy wings.
8 They shall be abundantly satisfied with the
fatness of thy house; and thou shalt make
them drink of the river of thy pleasures.
9 For with thee *is* the fountain of life: in thy
light shall we see light.
10 O continue thy lovingkindness unto them
that know thee; and thy righteousness to
the upright in heart.
11 Let not the foot of pride come against
me, and let not the hand of the wicked
remove me.
12 There are the workers of iniquity fallen:
they are cast down, and shall not be able
to rise.

Psalm 37

A Psalm of David.

1 Fret not thyself because of evildoers, neither be thou envious against the workers
of iniquity.
2 For they shall soon be cut down like the
grass, and wither as the green herb.
3 Trust in the LORD, and do good; *so* shalt
thou dwell in the land, and verily thou shalt
be fed.
4 Delight thyself also in the LORD; and he
shall give thee the desires of thine heart.
5 Commit thy way unto the LORD; trust also
in him; and he shall bring *it* to pass.
6 And he shall bring forth thy righteousness as the light, and thy judgment as the
noonday.
7 Rest in the LORD, and wait patiently for
him: fret not thyself because of him who
prospereth in his way, because of the man
who bringeth wicked devices to pass.
8 Cease from anger, and forsake wrath: fret
not thyself in any wise to do evil.
9 For evildoers shall be cut off: but those
that wait upon the LORD, they shall inherit
the earth.
10 For yet a little while, and the wicked *shall*
not *be*: yea, thou shalt diligently consider his
place, and it *shall* not *be*.
11 But the meek shall inherit the earth; and

shall delight themselves in the abundance of peace.
12 The wicked plotteth against the just, and gnasheth upon him with his teeth.
13 The Lord shall laugh at him: for he seeth that his day is coming.
14 The wicked have drawn out the sword, and have bent their bow, to cast down the poor and needy, *and* to slay such as be of upright conversation.
15 Their sword shall enter into their own heart, and their bows shall be broken.
16 A little that a righteous man hath *is* better than the riches of many wicked.
17 For the arms of the wicked shall be broken: but the LORD upholdeth the righteous.
18 The LORD knoweth the days of the upright: and their inheritance shall be for ever.
19 They shall not be ashamed in the evil time: and in the days of famine they shall be satisfied.
20 But the wicked shall perish, and the enemies of the LORD *shall be* as the fat of lambs: they shall consume; into smoke shall they consume away.
21 The wicked borroweth, and payeth not again: but the righteous sheweth mercy, and giveth.
22 For *such as be* blessed of him shall inherit the earth; and *they that be* cursed of him shall be cut off.
23 The steps of a *good* man are ordered by the LORD: and he delighteth in his way.
24 Though he fall, he shall not be utterly cast down: for the LORD upholdeth *him with* his hand.
25 I have been young, and *now* am old; yet have I not seen the righteous forsaken, nor his seed begging bread.
26 *He is* ever merciful, and lendeth; and his seed *is* blessed.
27 Depart from evil, and do good; and dwell for evermore.
28 For the LORD loveth judgment, and forsaketh not his saints; they are preserved for ever: but the seed of the wicked shall be cut off.
29 The righteous shall inherit the land, and dwell therein for ever.
30 The mouth of the righteous speaketh wisdom, and his tongue talketh of judgment.
31 The law of his God *is* in his heart; none of his steps shall slide.
32 The wicked watcheth the righteous, and seeketh to slay him.
33 The LORD will not leave him in his hand, nor condemn him when he is judged.
34 Wait on the LORD, and keep his way, and he shall exalt thee to inherit the land: when the wicked are cut off, thou shalt see *it*.
35 I have seen the wicked in great power, and spreading himself like a green bay tree.
36 Yet he passed away, and, lo, he *was* not: yea, I sought him, but he could not be found.
37 Mark the perfect *man*, and behold the upright: for the end of *that* man *is* peace.
38 But the transgressors shall be destroyed together: the end of the wicked shall be cut off.
39 But the salvation of the righteous *is* of the LORD: *he is* their strength in the time of trouble.
40 And the LORD shall help them, and deliver them: he shall deliver them from the wicked, and save them, because they trust in him.

Psalm 38

A Psalm of David, to bring to remembrance.

1 O Lord, rebuke me not in thy wrath: neither chasten me in thy hot displeasure.
2 For thine arrows stick fast in me, and thy hand presseth me sore.
3 *There is* no soundness in my flesh because of thine anger; neither *is there any* rest in my bones because of my sin.
4 For mine iniquities are gone over mine head: as an heavy burden they are too heavy for me.
5 My wounds stink *and* are corrupt because of my foolishness.
6 I am troubled; I am bowed down greatly; I go mourning all the day long.
7 For my loins are filled with a loathsome *disease:* and *there is* no soundness in my flesh.
8 I am feeble and sore broken: I have roared by reason of the disquietness of my heart.
9 Lord, all my desire *is* before thee; and my groaning is not hid from thee.
10 My heart panteth, my strength faileth me: as for the light of mine eyes, it also is gone from me.
11 My lovers and my friends stand aloof

from my sore; and my kinsmen stand afar
off.
12 They also that seek after my life lay snares
for me: and they that seek my hurt speak
mischievous things, and imagine deceits all
the day long.
13 But I, as a deaf *man*, heard not; and *I was*
as a dumb man *that* openeth not his mouth.
14 Thus I was as a man that heareth not, and
in whose mouth *are* no reproofs.
15 For in thee, O LORD, do I hope: thou wilt
hear, O Lord my God.
16 For I said, *Hear me*, lest *otherwise* they
should rejoice over me: when my foot slippeth, they magnify *themselves* against me.
17 For I *am* ready to halt, and my sorrow *is*
continually before me.
18 For I will declare mine iniquity; I will be
sorry for my sin.
19 But mine enemies *are* lively, *and* they are
strong: and they that hate me wrongfully
are multiplied.
20 They also that render evil for good are
mine adversaries; because I follow *the thing*
that good *is*.
21 Forsake me not, O LORD: O my God, be
not far from me.
22 Make haste to help me, O Lord my salvation.

Psalm 39

To the chief Musician, even to Jeduthun, A Psalm of David.

1 I said, I will take heed to my ways, that I sin
not with my tongue: I will keep my mouth
with a bridle, while the wicked is before me.
2 I was dumb with silence, I held my peace,
even from good; and my sorrow was stirred.
3 My heart was hot within me, while I was
musing the fire burned: *then* spake I with
my tongue,
4 LORD, make me to know mine end, and
the measure of my days, what it *is; that* I
may know how frail I *am*.
5 Behold, thou hast made my days *as* an
handbreadth; and mine age *is* as nothing
before thee: verily every man at his best
state *is* altogether vanity. Selah.
6 Surely every man walketh in a vain shew:
surely they are disquieted in vain: he
heapeth up *riches*, and knoweth not who
shall gather them.
7 And now, Lord, what wait I for? my hope
is in thee.
8 Deliver me from all my transgressions:
make me not the reproach of the foolish.
9 I was dumb, I opened not my mouth;
because thou didst *it*.
10 Remove thy stroke away from me: I am
consumed by the blow of thine hand.
11 When thou with rebukes dost correct
man for iniquity, thou makest his beauty
to consume away like a moth: surely every
man *is* vanity. Selah.
12 Hear my prayer, O LORD, and give ear
unto my cry; hold not thy peace at my
tears: for I *am* a stranger with thee, *and* a
sojourner, as all my fathers *were*.
13 O spare me, that I may recover strength,
before I go hence, and be no more.

Psalm 40

To the chief Musician, A Psalm of David.

1 I waited patiently for the LORD; and he
inclined unto me, and heard my cry.
2 He brought me up also out of an horrible
pit, out of the miry clay, and set my feet
upon a rock, *and* established my goings.
3 And he hath put a new song in my mouth,
even praise unto our God: many shall see *it*,
and fear, and shall trust in the LORD.
4 Blessed *is* that man that maketh the LORD
his trust, and respecteth not the proud, nor
such as turn aside to lies.
5 Many, O LORD my God, *are* thy wonderful works *which* thou hast done, and thy
thoughts *which are* to us-ward: they cannot
be reckoned up in order unto thee: *if* I would
declare and speak *of them*, they are more
than can be numbered.
6 Sacrifice and offering thou didst not desire;
mine ears hast thou opened: burnt offering
and sin offering hast thou not required.
7 Then said I, Lo, I come: in the volume of
the book *it is* written of me,
8 I delight to do thy will, O my God: yea, thy
law *is* within my heart.
9 I have preached righteousness in the great
congregation: lo, I have not refrained my
lips, O LORD, thou knowest.
10 I have not hid thy righteousness within
my heart; I have declared thy faithfulness
and thy salvation: I have not concealed thy

lovingkindness and thy truth from the great
congregation.
11 Withhold not thou thy tender mercies
from me, O LORD: let thy lovingkindness and
thy truth continually preserve me.
12 For innumerable evils have compassed
me about: mine iniquities have taken hold
upon me, so that I am not able to look up;
they are more than the hairs of mine head:
therefore my heart faileth me.
13 Be pleased, O LORD, to deliver me: O
LORD, make haste to help me.
14 Let them be ashamed and confounded
together that seek after my soul to destroy
it; let them be driven backward and put to
shame that wish me evil.
15 Let them be desolate for a reward of their
shame that say unto me, Aha, aha.
16 Let all those that seek thee rejoice and
be glad in thee: let such as love thy salvation
say continually, The LORD be magnified.
17 But I *am* poor and needy; *yet* the Lord
thinketh upon me: thou *art* my help and
my deliverer; make no tarrying, O my God.

Psalm 41

To the chief Musician,
A Psalm of David.

1 Blessed *is* he that considereth the poor:
the LORD will deliver him in time of trouble.
2 The LORD will preserve him, and keep
him alive; *and* he shall be blessed upon the
earth: and thou wilt not deliver him unto
the will of his enemies.
3 The LORD will strengthen him upon the
bed of languishing: thou wilt make all his
bed in his sickness.
4 I said, LORD, be merciful unto me: heal my
soul; for I have sinned against thee.
5 Mine enemies speak evil of me, When
shall he die, and his name perish?
6 And if he come to see *me*, he speaketh
vanity: his heart gathereth iniquity to itself;
when he goeth abroad, he telleth *it*.
7 All that hate me whisper together against
me: against me do they devise my hurt.
8 An evil disease, *say they*, cleaveth fast
unto him: and *now* that he lieth he shall
rise up no more.
9 Yea, mine own familiar friend, in whom
I trusted, which did eat of my bread, hath
lifted up *his* heel against me.
10 But thou, O LORD, be merciful unto me,
and raise me up, that I may requite them.
11 By this I know that thou favourest me,
because mine enemy doth not triumph
over me.
12 And as for me, thou upholdest me in
mine integrity, and settest me before thy
face for ever.
13 Blessed *be* the LORD God of Israel from
everlasting, and to everlasting. Amen, and
Amen.

Psalm 42

To the chief Musician, Maschil,
for the sons of Korah.

1 As the hart panteth after the water brooks,
so panteth my soul after thee, O God.
2 My soul thirsteth for God, for the living
God: when shall I come and appear before
God?
3 My tears have been my meat day and
night, while they continually say unto me,
Where *is* thy God?
4 When I remember these *things*, I pour
out my soul in me: for I had gone with the
multitude, I went with them to the house of
God, with the voice of joy and praise, with
a multitude that kept holyday.
5 Why art thou cast down, O my soul? and
why art thou disquieted in me? hope thou
in God: for I shall yet praise him *for* the help
of his countenance.
6 O my God, my soul is cast down within
me: therefore will I remember thee from
the land of Jordan, and of the Hermonites,
from the hill Mizar.
7 Deep calleth unto deep at the noise of thy
waterspouts: all thy waves and thy billows
are gone over me.
8 *Yet* the LORD will command his lovingkindness in the daytime, and in the night his
song *shall be* with me, *and* my prayer unto
the God of my life.
9 I will say unto God my rock, Why hast thou
forgotten me? why go I mourning because
of the oppression of the enemy?
10 *As* with a sword in my bones, mine enemies reproach me; while they say daily unto
me, Where *is* thy God?
11 Why art thou cast down, O my soul? and
why art thou disquieted within me? hope
thou in God: for I shall yet praise him, *who is*
the health of my countenance, and my God.

Psalm 43

1 Judge me, O God, and plead my cause
against an ungodly nation: O deliver me
from the deceitful and unjust man.
2 For thou *art* the God of my strength: why
dost thou cast me off? why go I mourning
because of the oppression of the enemy?
3 O send out thy light and thy truth: let them
lead me; let them bring me unto thy holy
hill, and to thy tabernacles.
4 Then will I go unto the altar of God, unto
God my exceeding joy: yea, upon the harp
will I praise thee, O God my God.
5 Why art thou cast down, O my soul? and
why art thou disquieted within me? hope
in God: for I shall yet praise him, *who is* the
health of my countenance, and my God.

Psalm 44

To the chief Musician for the sons of Korah, Maschil.

1 We have heard with our ears, O God, our
fathers have told us, *what* work thou didst
in their days, in the times of old.
2 *How* thou didst drive out the heathen with
thy hand, and plantedst them; *how* thou
didst afflict the people, and cast them out.
3 For they got not the land in possession
by their own sword, neither did their own
arm save them: but thy right hand, and
thine arm, and the light of thy countenance,
because thou hadst a favour unto them.
4 Thou art my King, O God: command deliv-
erances for Jacob.
5 Through thee will we push down our enemies: through thy name will we tread them
under that rise up against us.
6 For I will not trust in my bow, neither shall
my sword save me.
7 But thou hast saved us from our enemies,
and hast put them to shame that hated us.
8 In God we boast all the day long, and
praise thy name for ever. Selah.
9 But thou hast cast off, and put us to
shame; and goest not forth with our armies.
10 Thou makest us to turn back from the
enemy: and they which hate us spoil for
themselves.
11 Thou hast given us like sheep *appointed*
for meat; and hast scattered us among the
heathen.
12 Thou sellest thy people for nought, and
dost not increase *thy wealth* by their price.
13 Thou makest us a reproach to our neighbours, a scorn and a derision to them that
are round about us.
14 Thou makest us a byword among the
heathen, a shaking of the head among the
people.
15 My confusion *is* continually before me,
and the shame of my face hath covered me,
16 For the voice of him that reproacheth
and blasphemeth; by reason of the enemy
and avenger.
17 All this is come upon us; yet have we not
forgotten thee, neither have we dealt falsely
in thy covenant.
18 Our heart is not turned back, neither
have our steps declined from thy way;
19 Though thou hast sore broken us in the
place of dragons, and covered us with the
shadow of death.
20 If we have forgotten the name of our
God, or stretched out our hands to a strange
god;
21 Shall not God search this out? for he
knoweth the secrets of the heart.
22 Yea, for thy sake are we killed all the
day long; we are counted as sheep for the
slaughter.
23 Awake, why sleepest thou, O Lord? arise,
cast *us* not off for ever.
24 Wherefore hidest thou thy face, *and*
forgettest our affliction and our oppression?
25 For our soul is bowed down to the dust:
our belly cleaveth unto the earth.
26 Arise for our help, and redeem us for thy
mercies' sake.

Psalm 45

To the chief Musician upon Shoshannim, for the sons of Korah, Maschil, A Song of loves.

1 My heart is inditing a good matter: I speak
of the things which I have made touching the
king: my tongue *is* the pen of a ready writer.
2 Thou art fairer than the children of men:
grace is poured into thy lips: therefore God
hath blessed thee for ever.
3 Gird thy sword upon *thy* thigh, O *most*
mighty, with thy glory and thy majesty.
4 And in thy majesty ride prosperously
because of truth and meekness *and* righteousness; and thy right hand shall teach
thee terrible things.
5 Thine arrows *are* sharp in the heart of

the king's enemies; *whereby* the people
fall under thee.
6 Thy throne, O God, *is* for ever and ever:
the sceptre of thy kingdom *is* a right sceptre.
7 Thou lovest righteousness, and hatest
wickedness: therefore God, thy God, hath
anointed thee with the oil of gladness above
thy fellows.
8 All thy garments *smell* of myrrh, and aloes,
and cassia, out of the ivory palaces, whereby
they have made thee glad.
9 Kings' daughters *were* among thy honourable women: upon thy right hand did stand
the queen in gold of Ophir.
10 Hearken, O daughter, and consider, and
incline thine ear; forget also thine own people, and thy father's house;
11 So shall the king greatly desire thy beauty:
for he *is* thy Lord; and worship thou him.
12 And the daughter of Tyre *shall be there*
with a gift; *even* the rich among the people
shall intreat thy favour.
13 The king's daughter *is* all glorious within:
her clothing *is* of wrought gold.
14 She shall be brought unto the king in
raiment of needlework: the virgins her
companions that follow her shall be brought
unto thee.
15 With gladness and rejoicing shall they
be brought: they shall enter into the king's
palace.
16 Instead of thy fathers shall be thy children, whom thou mayest make princes in
all the earth.
17 I will make thy name to be remembered
in all generations: therefore shall the people
praise thee for ever and ever.

Psalm 46

To the chief Musician for the sons of Korah, A Song upon Alamoth.

1 God *is* our refuge and strength, a very
present help in trouble.
2 Therefore will not we fear, though the
earth be removed, and though the mountains be carried into the midst of the sea;
3 *Though* the waters thereof roar *and* be
troubled, *though* the mountains shake with
the swelling thereof. Selah.
4 *There is* a river, the streams whereof shall
make glad the city of God, the holy *place* of
the tabernacles of the most High.
5 God *is* in the midst of her; she shall not
be moved: God shall help her, *and that*
right early.
6 The heathen raged, the kingdoms were
moved: he uttered his voice, the earth
melted.
7 The LORD of hosts *is* with us; the God of
Jacob *is* our refuge. Selah.
8 Come, behold the works of the LORD, what
desolations he hath made in the earth.
9 He maketh wars to cease unto the end of
the earth; he breaketh the bow, and cutteth
the spear in sunder; he burneth the chariot
in the fire.
10 Be still, and know that I *am* God: I will be
exalted among the heathen, I will be exalted
in the earth.
11 The LORD of hosts *is* with us; the God of
Jacob *is* our refuge. Selah.

Psalm 47

To the chief Musician, A Psalm for the sons of Korah.

1 O clap your hands, all ye people; shout
unto God with the voice of triumph.
2 For the LORD most high *is* terrible; *he is* a
great King over all the earth.
3 He shall subdue the people under us, and
the nations under our feet.
4 He shall choose our inheritance for us, the
excellency of Jacob whom he loved. Selah.
5 God is gone up with a shout, the LORD with
the sound of a trumpet.
6 Sing praises to God, sing praises: sing
praises unto our King, sing praises.
7 For God *is* the King of all the earth: sing
ye praises with understanding.
8 God reigneth over the heathen: God sitteth upon the throne of his holiness.
9 The princes of the people are gathered
together, *even* the people of the God of
Abraham: for the shields of the earth *belong*
unto God: he is greatly exalted.

Psalm 48

A Song and Psalm for the sons of Korah.

1 Great *is* the LORD, and greatly to be praised
in the city of our God, *in* the mountain of
his holiness.
2 Beautiful for situation, the joy of the whole
earth, *is* mount Zion, *on* the sides of the
north, the city of the great King.
3 God is known in her palaces for a refuge.

4 For, lo, the kings were assembled, they passed by together.
5 They saw *it, and* so they marvelled; they were troubled, *and* hasted away.
6 Fear took hold upon them there, *and* pain, as of a woman in travail.
7 Thou breakest the ships of Tarshish with an east wind.
8 As we have heard, so have we seen in the city of the LORD of hosts, in the city of our God: God will establish it for ever. Selah.
9 We have thought of thy lovingkindness, O God, in the midst of thy temple.
10 According to thy name, O God, so *is* thy praise unto the ends of the earth: thy right hand is full of righteousness.
11 Let mount Zion rejoice, let the daughters of Judah be glad, because of thy judgments.
12 Walk about Zion, and go round about her: tell the towers thereof.
13 Mark ye well her bulwarks, consider her palaces; that ye may tell *it* to the generation following.
14 For this God *is* our God for ever and ever: he will be our guide *even* unto death.

Psalm 49

To the chief Musician, A Psalm for the sons of Korah.

1 Hear this, all *ye* people; give ear, all *ye* inhabitants of the world:
2 Both low and high, rich and poor, together.
3 My mouth shall speak of wisdom; and the meditation of my heart *shall be* of understanding.
4 I will incline mine ear to a parable: I will open my dark saying upon the harp.
5 Wherefore should I fear in the days of evil, *when* the iniquity of my heels shall compass me about?
6 They that trust in their wealth, and boast themselves in the multitude of their riches;
7 None *of them* can by any means redeem his brother, nor give to God a ransom for him:
8 (For the redemption of their soul *is* precious, and it ceaseth for ever:)
9 That he should still live for ever, *and* not see corruption.
10 For he seeth *that* wise men die, likewise the fool and the brutish person perish, and leave their wealth to others.
11 Their inward thought *is, that* their houses *shall continue* for ever, *and* their dwelling places to all generations; they call *their* lands after their own names.
12 Nevertheless man *being* in honour abideth not: he is like the beasts *that* perish.
13 This their way *is* their folly: yet their posterity approve their sayings. Selah.
14 Like sheep they are laid in the grave; death shall feed on them; and the upright shall have dominion over them in the morning; and their beauty shall consume in the grave from their dwelling.
15 But God will redeem my soul from the power of the grave: for he shall receive me. Selah.
16 Be not thou afraid when one is made rich, when the glory of his house is increased;
17 For when he dieth he shall carry nothing away: his glory shall not descend after him.
18 Though while he lived he blessed his soul: and *men* will praise thee, when thou doest well to thyself.
19 He shall go to the generation of his fathers; they shall never see light.
20 Man *that is* in honour, and understandeth not, is like the beasts *that* perish.

Psalm 50

A Psalm of Asaph.

1 The mighty God, *even* the LORD, hath spoken, and called the earth from the rising of the sun unto the going down thereof.
2 Out of Zion, the perfection of beauty, God hath shined.
3 Our God shall come, and shall not keep silence: a fire shall devour before him, and it shall be very tempestuous round about him.
4 He shall call to the heavens from above, and to the earth, that he may judge his people.
5 Gather my saints together unto me; those that have made a covenant with me by sacrifice.
6 And the heavens shall declare his righteousness: for God *is* judge himself. Selah.
7 Hear, O my people, and I will speak; O Israel, and I will testify against thee: I *am* God, *even* thy God.
8 I will not reprove thee for thy sacrifices or thy burnt offerings, *to have been* continually before me.
9 I will take no bullock out of thy house, *nor* he goats out of thy folds.

10 For every beast of the forest *is* mine, *and* the cattle upon a thousand hills.

11 I know all the fowls of the mountains: and the wild beasts of the field *are* mine.

12 If I were hungry, I would not tell thee: for the world *is* mine, and the fulness thereof.

13 Will I eat the flesh of bulls, or drink the blood of goats?

14 Offer unto God thanksgiving; and pay thy vows unto the most High:

15 And call upon me in the day of trouble: I will deliver thee, and thou shalt glorify me.

16 But unto the wicked God saith, What hast thou to do to declare my statutes, or *that* thou shouldest take my covenant in thy mouth?

17 Seeing thou hatest instruction, and castest my words behind thee.

18 When thou sawest a thief, then thou consentedst with him, and hast been partaker with adulterers.

19 Thou givest thy mouth to evil, and thy tongue frameth deceit.

20 Thou sittest *and* speakest against thy brother; thou slanderest thine own mother's son.

21 These *things* hast thou done, and I kept silence; thou thoughtest that I was altogether *such an one* as thyself: *but* I will reprove thee, and set *them* in order before thine eyes.

22 Now consider this, ye that forget God, lest I tear *you* in pieces, and *there be* none to deliver.

23 Whoso offereth praise glorifieth me: and to him that ordereth *his* conversation *aright* will I shew the salvation of God.

Psalm 51

To the chief Musician, A Psalm of David, when Nathan the prophet came unto him, after he had gone in to Bath-sheba.

1 Have mercy upon me, O God, according to thy lovingkindness: according unto the multitude of thy tender mercies blot out my transgressions.

2 Wash me throughly from mine iniquity, and cleanse me from my sin.

3 For I acknowledge my transgressions: and my sin *is* ever before me.

4 Against thee, thee only, have I sinned, and done *this* evil in thy sight: that thou mightest be justified when thou speakest, *and* be clear when thou judgest.

5 Behold, I was shapen in iniquity; and in sin did my mother conceive me.

6 Behold, thou desirest truth in the inward parts: and in the hidden *part* thou shalt make me to know wisdom.

7 Purge me with hyssop, and I shall be clean: wash me, and I shall be whiter than snow.

8 Make me to hear joy and gladness; *that* the bones *which* thou hast broken may rejoice.

9 Hide thy face from my sins, and blot out all mine iniquities.

10 Create in me a clean heart, O God; and renew a right spirit within me.

11 Cast me not away from thy presence; and take not thy holy spirit from me.

12 Restore unto me the joy of thy salvation; and uphold me *with thy* free spirit.

13 *Then* will I teach transgressors thy ways; and sinners shall be converted unto thee.

14 Deliver me from bloodguiltiness, O God, thou God of my salvation: *and* my tongue shall sing aloud of thy righteousness.

15 O Lord, open thou my lips; and my mouth shall shew forth thy praise.

16 For thou desirest not sacrifice; else would I give *it:* thou delightest not in burnt offering.

17 The sacrifices of God *are* a broken spirit: a broken and a contrite heart, O God, thou wilt not despise.

18 Do good in thy good pleasure unto Zion: build thou the walls of Jerusalem.

19 Then shalt thou be pleased with the sacrifices of righteousness, with burnt offering and whole burnt offering: then shall they offer bullocks upon thine altar.

Psalm 52

To the chief Musician, Maschil, A Psalm of David, when Doeg the Edomite came and told Saul, and said unto him, David is come to the house of Ahimelech.

1 Why boastest thou thyself in mischief, O mighty man? the goodness of God *endureth* continually.

2 Thy tongue deviseth mischiefs; like a sharp rasor, working deceitfully.

3 Thou lovest evil more than good; *and* lying rather than to speak righteousness. Selah.

4 Thou lovest all devouring words, O *thou* deceitful tongue.

5 God shall likewise destroy thee for ever,
he shall take thee away, and pluck thee out
of *thy* dwelling place, and root thee out of
the land of the living. Selah.
6 The righteous also shall see, and fear, and
shall laugh at him:
7 Lo, *this is* the man *that* made not God his
strength; but trusted in the abundance of
his riches, *and* strengthened himself in his
wickedness.
8 But I *am* like a green olive tree in the
house of God: I trust in the mercy of God
for ever and ever.
9 I will praise thee for ever, because thou
hast done *it:* and I will wait on thy name;
for *it is* good before thy saints.

Psalm 53

To the chief Musician upon Mahalath, Maschil, A Psalm of David.

1 The fool hath said in his heart, *There is*
no God. Corrupt are they, and have done
abominable iniquity: *there is* none that
doeth good.
2 God looked down from heaven upon the
children of men, to see if there were *any*
that did understand, that did seek God.
3 Every one of them is gone back: they are
altogether become filthy; *there is* none that
doeth good, no, not one.
4 Have the workers of iniquity no knowledge? who eat up my people *as* they eat
bread: they have not called upon God.
5 There were they in great fear, *where* no
fear was: for God hath scattered the bones
of him that encampeth *against* thee: thou
hast put *them* to shame, because God hath
despised them.
6 Oh that the salvation of Israel *were come*
out of Zion! When God bringeth back the
captivity of his people, Jacob shall rejoice,
and Israel shall be glad.

Psalm 54

To the chief Musician on Neginoth, Maschil, A Psalm of David, when the Ziphims came and said to Saul, Doth not David hide himself with us?

1 Save me, O God, by thy name, and judge
me by thy strength.
2 Hear my prayer, O God; give ear to the
words of my mouth.
3 For strangers are risen up against me, and
oppressors seek after my soul: they have
not set God before them. Selah.
4 Behold, God *is* mine helper: the Lord *is*
with them that uphold my soul.
5 He shall reward evil unto mine enemies:
cut them off in thy truth.
6 I will freely sacrifice unto thee: I will praise
thy name, O LORD; for *it is* good.
7 For he hath delivered me out of all trouble: and mine eye hath seen *his desire* upon
mine enemies.

Psalm 55

To the chief Musician on Neginoth, Maschil, A Psalm of David.

1 Give ear to my prayer, O God; and hide
not thyself from my supplication.
2 Attend unto me, and hear me: I mourn in
my complaint, and make a noise;
3 Because of the voice of the enemy,
because of the oppression of the wicked:
for they cast iniquity upon me, and in wrath
they hate me.
4 My heart is sore pained within me: and
the terrors of death are fallen upon me.
5 Fearfulness and trembling are come upon
me, and horror hath overwhelmed me.
6 And I said, Oh that I had wings like a dove!
for then would I fly away, and be at rest.
7 Lo, *then* would I wander far off, *and* remain
in the wilderness. Selah.
8 I would hasten my escape from the windy
storm *and* tempest.
9 Destroy, O Lord, *and* divide their tongues:
for I have seen violence and strife in the city.
10 Day and night they go about it upon the
walls thereof: mischief also and sorrow *are*
in the midst of it.
11 Wickedness *is* in the midst thereof: deceit
and guile depart not from her streets.
12 For *it was* not an enemy *that* reproached
me; then I could have borne *it:* neither *was*
it he that hated me *that* did magnify *himself*
against me; then I would have hid myself
from him:
13 But *it was* thou, a man mine equal, my
guide, and mine acquaintance.
14 We took sweet counsel together, *and*
walked unto the house of God in company.
15 Let death seize upon them, *and* let them
go down quick into hell: for wickedness *is* in
their dwellings, *and* among them.

16 As for me, I will call upon God; and the
LORD shall save me.
17 Evening, and morning, and at noon, will
I pray, and cry aloud: and he shall hear my
voice.
18 He hath delivered my soul in peace from
the battle *that was* against me: for there
were many with me.
19 God shall hear, and afflict them, even he
that abideth of old. Selah. Because they have
no changes, therefore they fear not God.
20 He hath put forth his hands against such
as be at peace with him: he hath broken
his covenant.
21 *The words* of his mouth were smoother
than butter, but war *was* in his heart: his
words were softer than oil, yet *were* they
drawn swords.
22 Cast thy burden upon the LORD, and he
shall sustain thee: he shall never suffer the
righteous to be moved.
23 But thou, O God, shalt bring them down
into the pit of destruction: bloody and
deceitful men shall not live out half their
days; but I will trust in thee.

Psalm 56

*To the chief Musician upon
Jonath-elem-rechokim,
Michtam of David, when the
Philistines took him in Gath.*

1 Be merciful unto me, O God: for man
would swallow me up; he fighting daily
oppresseth me.
2 Mine enemies would daily swallow *me*
up: for *they be* many that fight against me,
O thou most High.
3 What time I am afraid, I will trust in thee.
4 In God I will praise his word, in God I have
put my trust; I will not fear what flesh can
do unto me.
5 Every day they wrest my words: all their
thoughts *are* against me for evil.
6 They gather themselves together, they
hide themselves, they mark my steps, when
they wait for my soul.
7 Shall they escape by iniquity? in *thine*
anger cast down the people, O God.
8 Thou tellest my wanderings: put thou
my tears into thy bottle: *are they* not in
thy book?
9 When I cry *unto thee,* then shall mine
enemies turn back: this I know; for God
is for me.
10 In God will I praise *his* word: in the LORD
will I praise *his* word.
11 In God have I put my trust: I will not be
afraid what man can do unto me.
12 Thy vows *are* upon me, O God: I will
render praises unto thee.
13 For thou hast delivered my soul from
death: *wilt* not *thou deliver* my feet from
falling, that I may walk before God in the
light of the living?

Psalm 57

*To the chief Musician, Al-taschith,
Michtam of David, when he
fled from Saul in the cave.*

1 Be merciful unto me, O God, be merciful
unto me: for my soul trusteth in thee: yea,
in the shadow of thy wings will I make my
refuge, until *these* calamities be overpast.
2 I will cry unto God most high; unto God
that performeth *all things* for me.
3 He shall send from heaven, and save me
from the reproach of him that would swallow me up. Selah. God shall send forth his
mercy and his truth.
4 My soul *is* among lions: *and* I lie *even
among* them that are set on fire, *even* the
sons of men, whose teeth *are* spears and
arrows, and their tongue a sharp sword.
5 Be thou exalted, O God, above the heavens; *let* thy glory *be* above all the earth.
6 They have prepared a net for my steps;
my soul is bowed down: they have digged a
pit before me, into the midst whereof they
are fallen *themselves*. Selah.
7 My heart is fixed, O God, my heart is fixed:
I will sing and give praise.
8 Awake up, my glory; awake, psaltery and
harp: I *myself* will awake early.
9 I will praise thee, O Lord, among the people: I will sing unto thee among the nations.
10 For thy mercy *is* great unto the heavens,
and thy truth unto the clouds.
11 Be thou exalted, O God, above the heavens: *let* thy glory *be* above all the earth.

Psalm 58

*To the chief Musician, Al-taschith,
Michtam of David.*

1 Do ye indeed speak righteousness, O

congregation? do ye judge uprightly, O ye
sons of men?
2 Yea, in heart ye work wickedness; ye weigh
the violence of your hands in the earth.
3 The wicked are estranged from the womb:
they go astray as soon as they be born,
speaking lies.
4 Their poison *is* like the poison of a serpent:
they are like the deaf adder *that* stoppeth
her ear;
5 Which will not hearken to the voice of
charmers, charming never so wisely.
6 Break their teeth, O God, in their mouth:
break out the great teeth of the young
lions, O LORD.
7 Let them melt away as waters *which*
run continually: *when* he bendeth *his bow*
to shoot his arrows, let them be as cut in
pieces.
8 As a snail *which* melteth, let *every one of*
them pass away: *like* the untimely birth of
a woman, *that* they may not see the sun.
9 Before your pots can feel the thorns, he
shall take them away as with a whirlwind,
both living, and in *his* wrath.
10 The righteous shall rejoice when he seeth
the vengeance: he shall wash his feet in the
blood of the wicked.
11 So that a man shall say, Verily *there is* a
reward for the righteous: verily he is a God
that judgeth in the earth.

Psalm 59

To the chief Musician, Al-taschith,
Michtam of David; when
Saul sent, and they watched
the house to kill him.

1 Deliver me from mine enemies, O my
God: defend me from them that rise up
against me.
2 Deliver me from the workers of iniquity,
and save me from bloody men.
3 For, lo, they lie in wait for my soul: the
mighty are gathered against me; not *for*
my transgression, nor *for* my sin, O LORD.
4 They run and prepare themselves without
my fault: awake to help me, and behold.
5 Thou therefore, O LORD God of hosts, the
God of Israel, awake to visit all the heathen:
be not merciful to any wicked transgressors. Selah.
6 They return at evening: they make a noise
like a dog, and go round about the city.
7 Behold, they belch out with their mouth:
swords *are* in their lips: for who, *say they,*
doth hear?
8 But thou, O LORD, shalt laugh at them;
thou shalt have all the heathen in derision.
9 *Because of* his strength will I wait upon
thee: for God *is* my defence.
10 The God of my mercy shall prevent me:
God shall let me see *my desire* upon mine
enemies.
11 Slay them not, lest my people forget:
scatter them by thy power; and bring them
down, O Lord our shield.
12 *For* the sin of their mouth *and* the words
of their lips let them even be taken in their
pride: and for cursing and lying *which* they
speak.
13 Consume *them* in wrath, consume *them,*
that they *may* not *be:* and let them know
that God ruleth in Jacob unto the ends of
the earth. Selah.
14 And at evening let them return; *and* let
them make a noise like a dog, and go round
about the city.
15 Let them wander up and down for meat,
and grudge if they be not satisfied.
16 But I will sing of thy power; yea, I will
sing aloud of thy mercy in the morning: for
thou hast been my defence and refuge in
the day of my trouble.
17 Unto thee, O my strength, will I sing:
for God *is* my defence, *and* the God of my
mercy.

Psalm 60

To the chief Musician upon Shushan-
eduth, Michtam of David, to teach;
when he strove with Aram-naharaim
and with Aram-zobah, when Joab
returned, and smote of Edom in
the valley of salt twelve thousand.

1 O God, thou hast cast us off, thou hast
scattered us, thou hast been displeased; O
turn thyself to us again.
2 Thou hast made the earth to tremble; thou
hast broken it: heal the breaches thereof;
for it shaketh.
3 Thou hast shewed thy people hard things:
thou hast made us to drink the wine of
astonishment.
4 Thou hast given a banner to them that
fear thee, that it may be displayed because
of the truth. Selah.

5 That thy beloved may be delivered; save
with thy right hand, and hear me.
6 God hath spoken in his holiness; I will
rejoice, I will divide Shechem, and mete out
the valley of Succoth.
7 Gilead *is* mine, and Manasseh *is* mine;
Ephraim also *is* the strength of mine head;
Judah *is* my lawgiver;
8 Moab *is* my washpot; over Edom will I
cast out my shoe: Philistia, triumph thou
because of me.
9 Who will bring me *into* the strong city?
who will lead me into Edom?
10 *Wilt* not thou, O God, *which* hadst cast
us off? and *thou*, O God, *which* didst not go
out with our armies?
11 Give us help from trouble: for vain *is* the
help of man.
12 Through God we shall do valiantly: for
he *it is that* shall tread down our enemies.

Psalm 61

To the chief Musician upon Neginah, A Psalm of David.

1 Hear my cry, O God; attend unto my
prayer.
2 From the end of the earth will I cry unto
thee, when my heart is overwhelmed: lead
me to the rock *that* is higher than I.
3 For thou hast been a shelter for me, *and*
a strong tower from the enemy.
4 I will abide in thy tabernacle for ever: I
will trust in the covert of thy wings. Selah.
5 For thou, O God, hast heard my vows:
thou hast given *me* the heritage of those
that fear thy name.
6 Thou wilt prolong the king's life: *and* his
years as many generations.
7 He shall abide before God for ever: O
prepare mercy and truth, *which* may preserve him.
8 So will I sing praise unto thy name for ever,
that I may daily perform my vows.

Psalm 62

To the chief Musician, to Jeduthun, A Psalm of David.

1 Truly my soul waiteth upon God: from him
cometh my salvation.
2 He only *is* my rock and my salvation; *he is*
my defence; I shall not be greatly moved.
3 How long will ye imagine mischief against a
man? ye shall be slain all of you: as a bowing
wall *shall ye be, and as* a tottering fence.
4 They only consult to cast *him* down from
his excellency: they delight in lies: they bless
with their mouth, but they curse inwardly.
Selah.
5 My soul, wait thou only upon God; for my
expectation *is* from him.
6 He only *is* my rock and my salvation: *he is*
my defence; I shall not be moved.
7 In God *is* my salvation and my glory: the
rock of my strength, *and* my refuge, *is* in
God.
8 Trust in him at all times; ye people, pour
out your heart before him: God *is* a refuge
for us. Selah.
9 Surely men of low degree *are* vanity, *and*
men of high degree *are* a lie: to be laid in
the balance, they *are* altogether *lighter*
than vanity.
10 Trust not in oppression, and become not
vain in robbery: if riches increase, set not
your heart *upon them*.
11 God hath spoken once; twice have I heard
this; that power *belongeth* unto God.
12 Also unto thee, O Lord, *belongeth* mercy:
for thou renderest to every man according
to his work.

Psalm 63

A Psalm of David, when he was in the wilderness of Judah.

1 O God, thou *art* my God; early will I seek
thee: my soul thirsteth for thee, my flesh
longeth for thee in a dry and thirsty land,
where no water is;
2 To see thy power and thy glory, so *as* I
have seen thee in the sanctuary.
3 Because thy lovingkindness *is* better than
life, my lips shall praise thee.
4 Thus will I bless thee while I live: I will lift
up my hands in thy name.
5 My soul shall be satisfied as *with* marrow
and fatness; and my mouth shall praise *thee*
with joyful lips:
6 When I remember thee upon my bed,
and meditate on thee in the *night* watches.
7 Because thou hast been my help, therefore in the shadow of thy wings will I rejoice.
8 My soul followeth hard after thee: thy
right hand upholdeth me.
9 But those *that* seek my soul, to destroy *it*,
shall go into the lower parts of the earth.

10 They shall fall by the sword: they shall be a portion for foxes.

11 But the king shall rejoice in God; every one that sweareth by him shall glory: but the mouth of them that speak lies shall be stopped.

Psalm 64

To the chief Musician,
A Psalm of David.

1 Hear my voice, O God, in my prayer: preserve my life from fear of the enemy.

2 Hide me from the secret counsel of the wicked; from the insurrection of the workers of iniquity:

3 Who whet their tongue like a sword, *and* bend *their bows to shoot* their arrows, *even* bitter words:

4 That they may shoot in secret at the perfect: suddenly do they shoot at him, and fear not.

5 They encourage themselves *in* an evil matter: they commune of laying snares privily; they say, Who shall see them?

6 They search out iniquities; they accomplish a diligent search: both the inward *thought* of every one *of them*, and the heart, *is* deep.

7 But God shall shoot at them *with* an arrow; suddenly shall they be wounded.

8 So they shall make their own tongue to fall upon themselves: all that see them shall flee away.

9 And all men shall fear, and shall declare the work of God; for they shall wisely consider of his doing.

10 The righteous shall be glad in the LORD, and shall trust in him; and all the upright in heart shall glory.

Psalm 65

To the chief Musician, A
Psalm and Song of David.

1 Praise waiteth for thee, O God, in Sion: and unto thee shall the vow be performed.

2 O thou that hearest prayer, unto thee shall all flesh come.

3 Iniquities prevail against me: *as for* our transgressions, thou shalt purge them away.

4 Blessed *is the man whom* thou choosest, and causest to approach *unto thee, that* he may dwell in thy courts: we shall be satisfied with the goodness of thy house, *even* of thy holy temple.

5 *By* terrible things in righteousness wilt thou answer us, O God of our salvation; *who art* the confidence of all the ends of the earth, and of them that are afar off *upon* the sea:

6 Which by his strength setteth fast the mountains; *being* girded with power:

7 Which stilleth the noise of the seas, the noise of their waves, and the tumult of the people.

8 They also that dwell in the uttermost parts are afraid at thy tokens: thou makest the outgoings of the morning and evening to rejoice.

9 Thou visitest the earth, and waterest it: thou greatly enrichest it with the river of God, *which* is full of water: thou preparest them corn, when thou hast so provided for it.

10 Thou waterest the ridges thereof abundantly: thou settlest the furrows thereof: thou makest it soft with showers: thou blessest the springing thereof.

11 Thou crownest the year with thy goodness; and thy paths drop fatness.

12 They drop *upon* the pastures of the wilderness: and the little hills rejoice on every side.

13 The pastures are clothed with flocks; the valleys also are covered over with corn; they shout for joy, they also sing.

Psalm 66

To the chief Musician,
A Song or Psalm.

1 Make a joyful noise unto God, all ye lands:

2 Sing forth the honour of his name: make his praise glorious.

3 Say unto God, How terrible *art thou in* thy works! through the greatness of thy power shall thine enemies submit themselves unto thee.

4 All the earth shall worship thee, and shall sing unto thee; they shall sing *to* thy name. Selah.

5 Come and see the works of God: *he is* terrible *in his* doing toward the children of men.

6 He turned the sea into dry *land:* they went through the flood on foot: there did we rejoice in him.

7 He ruleth by his power for ever; his eyes behold the nations: let not the rebellious exalt themselves. Selah.

8 O bless our God, ye people, and make the
voice of his praise to be heard:
9 Which holdeth our soul in life, and suffereth not our feet to be moved.
10 For thou, O God, hast proved us: thou
hast tried us, as silver is tried.
11 Thou broughtest us into the net; thou
laidst affliction upon our loins.
12 Thou hast caused men to ride over our
heads; we went through fire and through
water: but thou broughtest us out into a
wealthy *place*.
13 I will go into thy house with burnt offerings: I will pay thee my vows,
14 Which my lips have uttered, and my
mouth hath spoken, when I was in trouble.
15 I will offer unto thee burnt sacrifices of
fatlings, with the incense of rams; I will offer
bullocks with goats. Selah.
16 Come *and* hear, all ye that fear God, and
I will declare what he hath done for my soul.
17 I cried unto him with my mouth, and he
was extolled with my tongue.
18 If I regard iniquity in my heart, the Lord
will not hear *me:*
19 *But* verily God hath heard *me;* he hath
attended to the voice of my prayer.
20 Blessed *be* God, which hath not turned
away my prayer, nor his mercy from me.

Psalm 67

To the chief Musician on
Neginoth, A Psalm or Song.

1 God be merciful unto us, and bless us;
and cause his face to shine upon us; Selah.
2 That thy way may be known upon earth,
thy saving health among all nations.
3 Let the people praise thee, O God; let all
the people praise thee.
4 O let the nations be glad and sing for joy:
for thou shalt judge the people righteously,
and govern the nations upon earth. Selah.
5 Let the people praise thee, O God; let all
the people praise thee.
6 *Then* shall the earth yield her increase;
and God, *even* our own God, shall bless us.
7 God shall bless us; and all the ends of the
earth shall fear him.

Psalm 68

To the chief Musician, A
Psalm or Song of David.

1 Let God arise, let his enemies be scattered:
let them also that hate him flee before him.
2 As smoke is driven away, *so* drive *them*
away: as wax melteth before the fire, *so* let
the wicked perish at the presence of God.
3 But let the righteous be glad; let them
rejoice before God: yea, let them exceedingly rejoice.
4 Sing unto God, sing praises to his name:
extol him that rideth upon the heavens by
his name JAH, and rejoice before him.
5 A father of the fatherless, and a judge of
the widows, *is* God in his holy habitation.
6 God setteth the solitary in families: he
bringeth out those which are bound with
chains: but the rebellious dwell in a dry *land*.
7 O God, when thou wentest forth before
thy people, when thou didst march through
the wilderness; Selah:
8 The earth shook, the heavens also dropped
at the presence of God: *even* Sinai itself *was*
moved at the presence of God, the God of
Israel.
9 Thou, O God, didst send a plentiful rain,
whereby thou didst confirm thine inheritance, when it was weary.
10 Thy congregation hath dwelt therein:
thou, O God, hast prepared of thy goodness
for the poor.
11 The Lord gave the word: great *was* the
company of those that published *it*.
12 Kings of armies did flee apace: and she
that tarried at home divided the spoil.
13 Though ye have lien among the pots, *yet*
shall ye be as the wings of a dove covered
with silver, and her feathers with yellow
gold.
14 When the Almighty scattered kings in it,
it was *white* as snow in Salmon.
15 The hill of God *is as* the hill of Bashan;
an high hill *as* the hill of Bashan.
16 Why leap ye, ye high hills? *this is* the hill
which God desireth to dwell in; yea, the
LORD will dwell *in it* for ever.
17 The chariots of God *are* twenty thousand,
even thousands of angels: the Lord *is* among
them, *as in* Sinai, in the holy *place*.
18 Thou hast ascended on high, thou hast
led captivity captive: thou hast received

gifts for men; yea, *for* the rebellious also,
that the LORD God might dwell *among them.*
19 Blessed *be* the Lord, *who* daily loadeth
us *with benefits, even* the God of our salvation. Selah.
20 *He that is* our God *is* the God of salvation;
and unto GOD the Lord *belong* the issues
from death.
21 But God shall wound the head of his
enemies, *and* the hairy scalp of such an one
as goeth on still in his trespasses.
22 The Lord said, I will bring again from
Bashan, I will bring *my people* again from
the depths of the sea:
23 That thy foot may be dipped in the blood
of *thine* enemies, *and* the tongue of thy dogs
in the same.
24 They have seen thy goings, O God;
even the goings of my God, my King, in the
sanctuary.
25 The singers went before, the players on
instruments *followed* after; among *them*
were the damsels playing with timbrels.
26 Bless ye God in the congregations, *even*
the Lord, from the fountain of Israel.
27 There *is* little Benjamin *with* their ruler,
the princes of Judah *and* their council,
the princes of Zebulun, *and* the princes of
Naphtali.
28 Thy God hath commanded thy strength:
strengthen, O God, that which thou hast
wrought for us.
29 Because of thy temple at Jerusalem shall
kings bring presents unto thee.
30 Rebuke the company of spearmen, the
multitude of the bulls, with the calves of the
people, *till every one* submit himself with
pieces of silver: scatter thou the people
that delight in war.
31 Princes shall come out of Egypt; Ethiopia
shall soon stretch out her hands unto God.
32 Sing unto God, ye kingdoms of the earth;
O sing praises unto the Lord; Selah:
33 To him that rideth upon the heavens
of heavens, *which were* of old; lo, he doth
send out his voice, *and that* a mighty voice.
34 Ascribe ye strength unto God: his excellency *is* over Israel, and his strength *is* in
the clouds.
35 O God, *thou art* terrible out of thy holy
places: the God of Israel *is* he that giveth
strength and power unto *his* people. Blessed
be God.

Psalm 69

To the chief Musician upon
Shoshannim, A Psalm of David.

1 Save me, O God; for the waters are come
in unto *my* soul.
2 I sink in deep mire, where *there is* no
standing: I am come into deep waters,
where the floods overflow me.
3 I am weary of my crying: my throat is
dried: mine eyes fail while I wait for my God.
4 They that hate me without a cause are
more than the hairs of mine head: they
that would destroy me, *being* mine enemies
wrongfully, are mighty: then I restored *that*
which I took not away.
5 O God, thou knowest my foolishness; and
my sins are not hid from thee.
6 Let not them that wait on thee, O Lord
GOD of hosts, be ashamed for my sake: let
not those that seek thee be confounded for
my sake, O God of Israel.
7 Because for thy sake I have borne
reproach; shame hath covered my face.
8 I am become a stranger unto my brethren,
and an alien unto my mother's children.
9 For the zeal of thine house hath eaten
me up; and the reproaches of them that
reproached thee are fallen upon me.
10 When I wept, *and chastened* my soul with
fasting, that was to my reproach.
11 I made sackcloth also my garment; and
I became a proverb to them.
12 They that sit in the gate speak against
me; and I *was* the song of the drunkards.
13 But as for me, my prayer *is* unto thee, O
LORD, *in* an acceptable time: O God, in the
multitude of thy mercy hear me, in the truth
of thy salvation.
14 Deliver me out of the mire, and let me
not sink: let me be delivered from them
that hate me, and out of the deep waters.
15 Let not the waterflood overflow me,
neither let the deep swallow me up, and
let not the pit shut her mouth upon me.
16 Hear me, O LORD; for thy lovingkindness
is good: turn unto me according to the multitude of thy tender mercies.
17 And hide not thy face from thy servant;
for I am in trouble: hear me speedily.
18 Draw nigh unto my soul, *and* redeem it:
deliver me because of mine enemies.
19 Thou hast known my reproach, and my

shame, and my dishonour: mine adversaries
are all before thee.
20 Reproach hath broken my heart; and I
am full of heaviness: and I looked *for some*
to take pity, but *there was* none; and for
comforters, but I found none.
21 They gave me also gall for my meat; and
in my thirst they gave me vinegar to drink.
22 Let their table become a snare before
them: and *that which should have been* for
their welfare, *let it become* a trap.
23 Let their eyes be darkened, that they
see not; and make their loins continually
to shake.
24 Pour out thine indignation upon them,
and let thy wrathful anger take hold of them.
25 Let their habitation be desolate; *and* let
none dwell in their tents.
26 For they persecute *him* whom thou hast
smitten; and they talk to the grief of those
whom thou hast wounded.
27 Add iniquity unto their iniquity: and let
them not come into thy righteousness.
28 Let them be blotted out of the book
of the living, and not be written with the
righteous.
29 But I *am* poor and sorrowful: let thy salvation, O God, set me up on high.
30 I will praise the name of God with a song,
and will magnify him with thanksgiving.
31 *This* also shall please the LORD better than
an ox *or* bullock that hath horns and hoofs.
32 The humble shall see *this, and* be glad:
and your heart shall live that seek God.
33 For the LORD heareth the poor, and
despiseth not his prisoners.
34 Let the heaven and earth praise him, the
seas, and every thing that moveth therein.
35 For God will save Zion, and will build the
cities of Judah: that they may dwell there,
and have it in possession.
36 The seed also of his servants shall inherit
it: and they that love his name shall dwell
therein.

Psalm 70

To the chief Musician, A Psalm of David, to bring to remembrance.

1 *Make haste,* O God, to deliver me; make
haste to help me, O LORD.
2 Let them be ashamed and confounded
that seek after my soul: let them be turned
backward, and put to confusion, that desire
my hurt.
3 Let them be turned back for a reward of
their shame that say, Aha, aha.
4 Let all those that seek thee rejoice and be
glad in thee: and let such as love thy salvation say continually, Let God be magnified.
5 But I *am* poor and needy: make haste
unto me, O God: thou *art* my help and my
deliverer; O LORD, make no tarrying.

Psalm 71

1 In thee, O LORD, do I put my trust: let me
never be put to confusion.
2 Deliver me in thy righteousness, and cause
me to escape: incline thine ear unto me,
and save me.
3 Be thou my strong habitation, whereunto
I may continually resort: thou hast given
commandment to save me; for thou *art* my
rock and my fortress.
4 Deliver me, O my God, out of the hand of
the wicked, out of the hand of the unrighteous and cruel man.
5 For thou *art* my hope, O Lord GOD: *thou*
art my trust from my youth.
6 By thee have I been holden up from the
womb: thou art he that took me out of my
mother's bowels: my praise *shall be* continually of thee.
7 I am as a wonder unto many; but thou *art*
my strong refuge.
8 Let my mouth be filled *with* thy praise *and*
with thy honour all the day.
9 Cast me not off in the time of old age;
forsake me not when my strength faileth.
10 For mine enemies speak against me; and
they that lay wait for my soul take counsel
together,
11 Saying, God hath forsaken him: persecute and take him; for *there is* none to
deliver *him*.
12 O God, be not far from me: O my God,
make haste for my help.
13 Let them be confounded *and* consumed
that are adversaries to my soul; let them be
covered *with* reproach and dishonour that
seek my hurt.
14 But I will hope continually, and will yet
praise thee more and more.
15 My mouth shall shew forth thy righteousness *and* thy salvation all the day; for I know
not the numbers *thereof*.

16 I will go in the strength of the Lord GOD:
I will make mention of thy righteousness,
even of thine only.
17 O God, thou hast taught me from my
youth: and hitherto have I declared thy
wondrous works.
18 Now also when I am old and grayheaded,
O God, forsake me not; until I have shewed
thy strength unto *this* generation, *and* thy
power to every one *that* is to come.
19 Thy righteousness also, O God, *is* very
high, who hast done great things: O God,
who *is* like unto thee!
20 *Thou,* which hast shewed me great and
sore troubles, shalt quicken me again, and
shalt bring me up again from the depths
of the earth.
21 Thou shalt increase my greatness, and
comfort me on every side.
22 I will also praise thee with the psaltery,
even thy truth, O my God: unto thee will I
sing with the harp, O thou Holy One of Israel.
23 My lips shall greatly rejoice when I sing
unto thee; and my soul, which thou hast
redeemed.
24 My tongue also shall talk of thy righteousness all the day long: for they are confounded, for they are brought unto shame,
that seek my hurt.

Psalm 72

A Psalm for Solomon.

1 Give the king thy judgments, O God, and
thy righteousness unto the king's son.
2 He shall judge thy people with righteousness, and thy poor with judgment.
3 The mountains shall bring peace to the
people, and the little hills, by righteousness.
4 He shall judge the poor of the people, he
shall save the children of the needy, and
shall break in pieces the oppressor.
5 They shall fear thee as long as the sun and
moon endure, throughout all generations.
6 He shall come down like rain upon the
mown grass: as showers *that* water the
earth.
7 In his days shall the righteous flourish;
and abundance of peace so long as the
moon endureth.
8 He shall have dominion also from sea to
sea, and from the river unto the ends of
the earth.
9 They that dwell in the wilderness shall
bow before him; and his enemies shall lick
the dust.
10 The kings of Tarshish and of the isles shall
bring presents: the kings of Sheba and Seba
shall offer gifts.
11 Yea, all kings shall fall down before him:
all nations shall serve him.
12 For he shall deliver the needy when he
crieth; the poor also, and *him* that hath no
helper.
13 He shall spare the poor and needy, and
shall save the souls of the needy.
14 He shall redeem their soul from deceit
and violence: and precious shall their blood
be in his sight.
15 And he shall live, and to him shall be
given of the gold of Sheba: prayer also shall
be made for him continually; *and* daily shall
he be praised.
16 There shall be an handful of corn in the
earth upon the top of the mountains; the
fruit thereof shall shake like Lebanon: an
they of the city shall flourish like grass o
the earth.
17 His name shall endure for ever: his nam
shall be continued as long as the sun: an
men shall be blessed in him: all nations sha
call him blessed.
18 Blessed *be* the LORD God, the God o
Israel, who only doeth wondrous things.
19 And blessed *be* his glorious name for
ever: and let the whole earth be filled *with*
his glory; Amen, and Amen.
20 The prayers of David the son of Jesse
are ended.

Psalm 73

A Psalm of Asaph.

1 Truly God *is* good to Israel, *even* to such
as are of a clean heart.
2 But as for me, my feet were almost gone;
my steps had well nigh slipped.
3 For I was envious at the foolish, *when* I
saw the prosperity of the wicked.
4 For *there are* no bands in their death: but
their strength *is* firm.
5 They *are* not in trouble *as other* men;
neither are they plagued like *other* men.
6 Therefore pride compasseth them about
as a chain; violence covereth them *as* a
garment.
7 Their eyes stand out with fatness: they
have more than heart could wish.

8 They are corrupt, and speak wickedly
concerning oppression: they speak loftily.
9 They set their mouth against the heavens,
and their tongue walketh through the earth.
10 Therefore his people return hither: and
waters of a full *cup* are wrung out to them.
11 And they say, How doth God know? and
is there knowledge in the most High?
12 Behold, these *are* the ungodly, who
prosper in the world; they increase *in* riches.
13 Verily I have cleansed my heart *in* vain,
and washed my hands in innocency.
14 For all the day long have I been plagued,
and chastened every morning.
15 If I say, I will speak thus; behold, I should
offend *against* the generation of thy children.
16 When I thought to know this, it *was* too
painful for me;
17 Until I went into the sanctuary of God;
then understood I their end.
18 Surely thou didst set them in slippery
places: thou castedst them down into
destruction.
19 How are they *brought* into desolation,
as in a moment! they are utterly consumed
with terrors.
20 As a dream when *one* awaketh; *so,* O
Lord, when thou awakest, thou shalt despise
their image.
21 Thus my heart was grieved, and I was
pricked in my reins.
22 So foolish *was* I, and ignorant: I was *as*
a beast before thee.
23 Nevertheless I *am* continually with thee:
thou hast holden *me* by my right hand.
24 Thou shalt guide me with thy counsel,
and afterward receive me *to* glory.
25 Whom have I in heaven *but thee?* and
there is none upon earth *that* I desire beside
thee.
26 My flesh and my heart faileth: *but* God
is the strength of my heart, and my portion
for ever.
27 For, lo, they that are far from thee shall
perish: thou hast destroyed all them that
go a whoring from thee.
28 But *it is* good for me to draw near to God:
I have put my trust in the Lord GOD, that I
may declare all thy works.

Psalm 74

Maschil of Asaph.

1 O God, why hast thou cast *us* off for ever?
why doth thine anger smoke against the
sheep of thy pasture?
2 Remember thy congregation, *which* thou
hast purchased of old; the rod of thine
inheritance, *which* thou hast redeemed;
this mount Zion, wherein thou hast dwelt.
3 Lift up thy feet unto the perpetual desolations;
even all *that* the enemy hath done
wickedly in the sanctuary.
4 Thine enemies roar in the midst of thy
congregations; they set up their ensigns
for signs.
5 *A man* was famous according as he had
lifted up axes upon the thick trees.
6 But now they break down the carved work
thereof at once with axes and hammers.
7 They have cast fire into thy sanctuary, they
have defiled *by casting down* the dwelling
place of thy name to the ground.
8 They said in their hearts, Let us destroy
them together: they have burned up all the
synagogues of God in the land.
9 We see not our signs: *there is* no more any
prophet: neither *is there* among us any that
knoweth how long.
10 O God, how long shall the adversary
reproach? shall the enemy blaspheme thy
name for ever?
11 Why withdrawest thou thy hand, even
thy right hand? pluck *it* out of thy bosom.
12 For God *is* my King of old, working salvation
in the midst of the earth.
13 Thou didst divide the sea by thy strength:
thou brakest the heads of the dragons in
the waters.
14 Thou brakest the heads of leviathan in
pieces, *and* gavest him *to be* meat to the
people inhabiting the wilderness.
15 Thou didst cleave the fountain and the
flood: thou driedst up mighty rivers.
16 The day *is* thine, the night also *is* thine:
thou hast prepared the light and the sun.
17 Thou hast set all the borders of the earth:
thou hast made summer and winter.
18 Remember this, *that* the enemy hath
reproached, O LORD, and *that* the foolish
people have blasphemed thy name.
19 O deliver not the soul of thy turtledove
unto the multitude *of the wicked:* forget
not the congregation of thy poor for ever.

20 Have respect unto the covenant: for the dark places of the earth are full of the habitations of cruelty.
21 O let not the oppressed return ashamed: let the poor and needy praise thy name.
22 Arise, O God, plead thine own cause: remember how the foolish man reproacheth thee daily.
23 Forget not the voice of thine enemies: the tumult of those that rise up against thee increaseth continually.

Psalm 75

To the chief Musician, Al-taschith, A Psalm or Song of Asaph.

1 Unto thee, O God, do we give thanks, *unto thee* do we give thanks: for *that* thy name is near thy wondrous works declare.
2 When I shall receive the congregation I will judge uprightly.
3 The earth and all the inhabitants thereof are dissolved: I bear up the pillars of it. Selah.
4 I said unto the fools, Deal not foolishly: and to the wicked, Lift not up the horn:
5 Lift not up your horn on high: speak *not with* a stiff neck.
6 For promotion *cometh* neither from the east, nor from the west, nor from the south.
7 But God *is* the judge: he putteth down one, and setteth up another.
8 For in the hand of the LORD *there is* a cup, and the wine is red; it is full of mixture; and he poureth out of the same: but the dregs thereof, all the wicked of the earth shall wring *them* out, *and* drink *them*.
9 But I will declare for ever; I will sing praises to the God of Jacob.
10 All the horns of the wicked also will I cut off; *but* the horns of the righteous shall be exalted.

Psalm 76

To the chief Musician on Neginoth, A Psalm or Song of Asaph.

1 In Judah *is* God known: his name *is* great in Israel.
2 In Salem also is his tabernacle, and his dwelling place in Zion.
3 There brake he the arrows of the bow, the shield, and the sword, and the battle. Selah.
4 Thou *art* more glorious *and* excellent than the mountains of prey.
5 The stouthearted are spoiled, they have slept their sleep: and none of the men of might have found their hands.
6 At thy rebuke, O God of Jacob, both the chariot and horse are cast into a dead sleep.
7 Thou, *even* thou, *art* to be feared: and who may stand in thy sight when once thou art angry?
8 Thou didst cause judgment to be heard from heaven; the earth feared, and was still,
9 When God arose to judgment, to save all the meek of the earth. Selah.
10 Surely the wrath of man shall praise thee: the remainder of wrath shalt thou restrain.
11 Vow, and pay unto the LORD your God: let all that be round about him bring presents unto him that ought to be feared.
12 He shall cut off the spirit of princes: *he is* terrible to the kings of the earth.

Psalm 77

To the chief Musician, to Jeduthun, A Psalm of Asaph.

1 I cried unto God with my voice, *even* unto God with my voice; and he gave ear unto me.
2 In the day of my trouble I sought the Lord: my sore ran in the night, and ceased not: my soul refused to be comforted.
3 I remembered God, and was troubled: I complained, and my spirit was overwhelmed. Selah.
4 Thou holdest mine eyes waking: I am so troubled that I cannot speak.
5 I have considered the days of old, the years of ancient times.
6 I call to remembrance my song in the night: I commune with mine own heart: and my spirit made diligent search.
7 Will the Lord cast off for ever? and will he be favourable no more?
8 Is his mercy clean gone for ever? doth *his* promise fail for evermore?
9 Hath God forgotten to be gracious? hath he in anger shut up his tender mercies? Selah.
10 And I said, This *is* my infirmity: *but I will remember* the years of the right hand of the most High.
11 I will remember the works of the LORD: surely I will remember thy wonders of old.
12 I will meditate also of all thy work, and talk of thy doings.

13 Thy way, O God, *is* in the sanctuary: who
is so great a God as *our* God?
14 Thou *art* the God that doest wonders:
thou hast declared thy strength among
the people.
15 Thou hast with *thine* arm redeemed thy
people, the sons of Jacob and Joseph. Selah.
16 The waters saw thee, O God, the waters
saw thee; they were afraid: the depths also
were troubled.
17 The clouds poured out water: the skies
sent out a sound: thine arrows also went
abroad.
18 The voice of thy thunder *was* in the
heaven: the lightnings lightened the world:
the earth trembled and shook.
19 Thy way *is* in the sea, and thy path in
the great waters, and thy footsteps are
not known.
20 Thou leddest thy people like a flock by
the hand of Moses and Aaron.

Psalm 78

Maschil of Asaph.

1 Give ear, O my people, *to* my law: incline
your ears to the words of my mouth.
2 I will open my mouth in a parable: I will
utter dark sayings of old:
3 Which we have heard and known, and our
fathers have told us.
4 We will not hide *them* from their children, shewing to the generation to come
the praises of the LORD, and his strength,
and his wonderful works that he hath done.
5 For he established a testimony in Jacob,
and appointed a law in Israel, which he
commanded our fathers, that they should
make them known to their children:
6 That the generation to come might know
them, even the children *which* should be
born; *who* should arise and declare *them*
to their children:
7 That they might set their hope in God, and
not forget the works of God, but keep his
commandments:
8 And might not be as their fathers, a stubborn and rebellious generation; a generation
that set not their heart aright, and whose
spirit was not stedfast with God.
9 The children of Ephraim, *being* armed,
and carrying bows, turned back in the day
of battle.
10 They kept not the covenant of God, and
refused to walk in his law;
11 And forgat his works, and his wonders
that he had shewed them.
12 Marvellous things did he in the sight of
their fathers, in the land of Egypt, *in* the
field of Zoan.
13 He divided the sea, and caused them to
pass through; and he made the waters to
stand as an heap.
14 In the daytime also he led them with a
cloud, and all the night with a light of fire.
15 He clave the rocks in the wilderness, and
gave *them* drink as *out of* the great depths.
16 He brought streams also out of the rock,
and caused waters to run down like rivers.
17 And they sinned yet more against him by
provoking the most High in the wilderness.
18 And they tempted God in their heart by
asking meat for their lust.
19 Yea, they spake against God; they said,
Can God furnish a table in the wilderness?
20 Behold, he smote the rock, that the
waters gushed out, and the streams overflowed; can he give bread also? can he
provide flesh for his people?
21 Therefore the LORD heard *this*, and was
wroth: so a fire was kindled against Jacob,
and anger also came up against Israel;
22 Because they believed not in God, and
trusted not in his salvation:
23 Though he had commanded the clouds
from above, and opened the doors of
heaven,
24 And had rained down manna upon them
to eat, and had given them of the corn of
heaven.
25 Man did eat angels' food: he sent them
meat to the full.
26 He caused an east wind to blow in the
heaven: and by his power he brought in the
south wind.
27 He rained flesh also upon them as dust,
and feathered fowls like as the sand of
the sea:
28 And he let *it* fall in the midst of their
camp, round about their habitations.
29 So they did eat, and were well filled: for
he gave them their own desire;
30 They were not estranged from their
lust. But while their meat *was* yet in their
mouths,
31 The wrath of God came upon them, and

slew the fattest of them, and smote down
the chosen *men* of Israel.
32 For all this they sinned still, and believed
not for his wondrous works.
33 Therefore their days did he consume in
vanity, and their years in trouble.
34 When he slew them, then they sought
him: and they returned and inquired early
after God.
35 And they remembered that God *was*
their rock, and the high God their redeemer.
36 Nevertheless they did flatter him with
their mouth, and they lied unto him with
their tongues.
37 For their heart was not right with him,
neither were they stedfast in his covenant.
38 But he, *being* full of compassion, forgave
their iniquity, and destroyed *them* not: yea,
many a time turned he his anger away, and
did not stir up all his wrath.
39 For he remembered that they *were but*
flesh; a wind that passeth away, and cometh not again.
40 How oft did they provoke him in the
wilderness, *and* grieve him in the desert!
41 Yea, they turned back and tempted God,
and limited the Holy One of Israel.
42 They remembered not his hand, *nor*
the day when he delivered them from the
enemy.
43 How he had wrought his signs in Egypt,
and his wonders in the field of Zoan:
44 And had turned their rivers into blood;
and their floods, that they could not drink.
45 He sent divers sorts of flies among them,
which devoured them; and frogs, which
destroyed them.
46 He gave also their increase unto the
caterpiller, and their labour unto the locust.
47 He destroyed their vines with hail, and
their sycomore trees with frost.
48 He gave up their cattle also to the hail,
and their flocks to hot thunderbolts.
49 He cast upon them the fierceness of his
anger, wrath, and indignation, and trouble,
by sending evil angels *among them*.
50 He made a way to his anger; he spared
not their soul from death, but gave their life
over to the pestilence;
51 And smote all the firstborn in Egypt; the
chief of *their* strength in the tabernacles
of Ham:
52 But made his own people to go forth like
sheep, and guided them in the wilderness
like a flock.
53 And he led them on safely, so that they
feared not: but the sea overwhelmed their
enemies.
54 And he brought them to the border of
his sanctuary, *even to* this mountain, *which*
his right hand had purchased.
55 He cast out the heathen also before
them, and divided them an inheritance by
line, and made the tribes of Israel to dwell
in their tents.
56 Yet they tempted and provoked the most
high God, and kept not his testimonies:
57 But turned back, and dealt unfaithfully
like their fathers: they were turned aside
like a deceitful bow.
58 For they provoked him to anger with their
high places, and moved him to jealousy with
their graven images.
59 When God heard *this*, he was wroth, and
greatly abhorred Israel:
60 So that he forsook the tabernacle of Shiloh, the tent *which* he placed among men;
61 And delivered his strength into captivity,
and his glory into the enemy's hand.
62 He gave his people over also unto the
sword; and was wroth with his inheritance.
63 The fire consumed their young men; and
their maidens were not given to marriage.
64 Their priests fell by the sword; and their
widows made no lamentation.
65 Then the Lord awaked as one out of
sleep, *and* like a mighty man that shouteth
by reason of wine.
66 And he smote his enemies in the hinder
parts: he put them to a perpetual reproach.
67 Moreover he refused the tabernacle of
Joseph, and chose not the tribe of Ephraim:
68 But chose the tribe of Judah, the mount
Zion which he loved.
69 And he built his sanctuary like high *palaces*, like the earth which he hath established for ever.
70 He chose David also his servant, and took
him from the sheepfolds:
71 From following the ewes great with
young he brought him to feed Jacob his
people, and Israel his inheritance.
72 So he fed them according to the integrity of his heart; and guided them by the
skilfulness of his hands.

Psalm 79

A Psalm of Asaph.

1 O God, the heathen are come into thine
inheritance; thy holy temple have they
defiled; they have laid Jerusalem on heaps.
2 The dead bodies of thy servants have
they given *to be* meat unto the fowls of
the heaven, the flesh of thy saints unto the
beasts of the earth.
3 Their blood have they shed like water
round about Jerusalem; and *there was* none
to bury *them*.
4 We are become a reproach to our neighbours, a scorn and derision to them that are
round about us.
5 How long, LORD? wilt thou be angry for
ever? shall thy jealousy burn like fire?
6 Pour out thy wrath upon the heathen that
have not known thee, and upon the kingdoms that have not called upon thy name.
7 For they have devoured Jacob, and laid
waste his dwelling place.
8 O remember not against us former iniquities: let thy tender mercies speedily prevent
us: for we are brought very low.
9 Help us, O God of our salvation, for the
glory of thy name: and deliver us, and purge
away our sins, for thy name's sake.
10 Wherefore should the heathen say,
Where *is* their God? let him be known
among the heathen in our sight *by* the
revenging of the blood of thy servants
which is shed.
11 Let the sighing of the prisoner come
before thee; according to the greatness
of thy power preserve thou those that are
appointed to die;
12 And render unto our neighbours sevenfold into their bosom their reproach, wherewith they have reproached thee, O Lord.
13 So we thy people and sheep of thy pasture will give thee thanks for ever: we will
shew forth thy praise to all generations.

Psalm 80

To the chief Musician upon Shoshannim-Eduth, A Psalm of Asaph.

1 Give ear, O Shepherd of Israel, thou that
leadest Joseph like a flock; thou that dwellest *between* the cherubims, shine forth.
2 Before Ephraim and Benjamin and
Manasseh stir up thy strength, and come
and save us.
3 Turn us again, O God, and cause thy face
to shine; and we shall be saved.
4 O LORD God of hosts, how long wilt thou
be angry against the prayer of thy people?
5 Thou feedest them with the bread of
tears; and givest them tears to drink in
great measure.
6 Thou makest us a strife unto our neighbours: and our enemies laugh among themselves.
7 Turn us again, O God of hosts, and cause
thy face to shine; and we shall be saved.
8 Thou hast brought a vine out of Egypt:
thou hast cast out the heathen, and planted
it.
9 Thou preparedst *room* before it, and
didst cause it to take deep root, and it filled
the land.
10 The hills were covered with the shadow
of it, and the boughs thereof *were like* the
goodly cedars.
11 She sent out her boughs unto the sea,
and her branches unto the river.
12 Why hast thou *then* broken down her
hedges, so that all they which pass by the
way do pluck her?
13 The boar out of the wood doth waste
it, and the wild beast of the field doth
devour it.
14 Return, we beseech thee, O God of hosts:
look down from heaven, and behold, and
visit this vine;
15 And the vineyard which thy right hand
hath planted, and the branch *that* thou
madest strong for thyself.
16 *It is* burned with fire, *it is* cut down: they
perish at the rebuke of thy countenance.
17 Let thy hand be upon the man of thy
right hand, upon the son of man *whom* thou
madest strong for thyself.
18 So will not we go back from thee: quicken
us, and we will call upon thy name.
19 Turn us again, O LORD God of hosts, cause
thy face to shine; and we shall be saved.

Psalm 81

To the chief Musician upon Gittith, A Psalm of Asaph.

1 Sing aloud unto God our strength: make a
joyful noise unto the God of Jacob.

2 Take a psalm, and bring hither the timbrel, the pleasant harp with the psaltery.
3 Blow up the trumpet in the new moon, in the time appointed, on our solemn feast day.
4 For this *was* a statute for Israel, *and* a law of the God of Jacob.
5 This he ordained in Joseph *for* a testimony, when he went out through the land of Egypt: *where* I heard a language *that* I understood not.
6 I removed his shoulder from the burden: his hands were delivered from the pots.
7 Thou calledst in trouble, and I delivered thee; I answered thee in the secret place of thunder: I proved thee at the waters of Meribah. Selah.
8 Hear, O my people, and I will testify unto thee: O Israel, if thou wilt hearken unto me;
9 There shall no strange god be in thee; neither shalt thou worship any strange god.
10 I *am* the LORD thy God, which brought thee out of the land of Egypt: open thy mouth wide, and I will fill it.
11 But my people would not hearken to my voice; and Israel would none of me.
12 So I gave them up unto their own hearts' lust: *and* they walked in their own counsels.
13 Oh that my people had hearkened unto me, *and* Israel had walked in my ways!
14 I should soon have subdued their enemies, and turned my hand against their adversaries.
15 The haters of the LORD should have submitted themselves unto him: but their time should have endured for ever.
16 He should have fed them also with the finest of the wheat: and with honey out of the rock should I have satisfied thee.

Psalm 82

A Psalm of Asaph.

1 God standeth in the congregation of the mighty; he judgeth among the gods.
2 How long will ye judge unjustly, and accept the persons of the wicked? Selah.
3 Defend the poor and fatherless: do justice to the afflicted and needy.
4 Deliver the poor and needy: rid *them* out of the hand of the wicked.
5 They know not, neither will they understand; they walk on in darkness: all the foundations of the earth are out of course.
6 I have said, Ye *are* gods; and all of you *are* children of the most High.
7 But ye shall die like men, and fall like one of the princes.
8 Arise, O God, judge the earth: for thou shalt inherit all nations.

Psalm 83

A Song or Psalm of Asaph.

1 Keep not thou silence, O God: hold not thy peace, and be not still, O God.
2 For, lo, thine enemies make a tumult: and they that hate thee have lifted up the head.
3 They have taken crafty counsel against thy people, and consulted against thy hidden ones.
4 They have said, Come, and let us cut them off from *being* a nation; that the name of Israel may be no more in remembrance.
5 For they have consulted together with one consent: they are confederate against thee:
6 The tabernacles of Edom, and the Ishmaelites; of Moab, and the Hagarenes;
7 Gebal, and Ammon, and Amalek; the Philistines with the inhabitants of Tyre;
8 Assur also is joined with them: they have holpen the children of Lot. Selah.
9 Do unto them as *unto* the Midianites; as *to* Sisera, as *to* Jabin, at the brook of Kison:
10 *Which* perished at En-dor: they became *as* dung for the earth.
11 Make their nobles like Oreb, and like Zeeb: yea, all their princes as Zebah, and as Zalmunna:
12 Who said, Let us take to ourselves the houses of God in possession.
13 O my God, make them like a wheel; as the stubble before the wind.
14 As the fire burneth a wood, and as the flame setteth the mountains on fire;
15 So persecute them with thy tempest, and make them afraid with thy storm.
16 Fill their faces with shame; that they may seek thy name, O LORD.
17 Let them be confounded and troubled for ever; yea, let them be put to shame, and perish:
18 That *men* may know that thou, whose name alone *is* JEHOVAH, *art* the most high over all the earth.

Psalm 84

To the chief Musician upon Gittith,
A Psalm for the sons of Korah.

1 How amiable *are* thy tabernacles, O LORD
of hosts!
2 My soul longeth, yea, even fainteth for the
courts of the LORD: my heart and my flesh
crieth out for the living God.
3 Yea, the sparrow hath found an house,
and the swallow a nest for herself, where
she may lay her young, *even* thine altars, O
LORD of hosts, my King, and my God.
4 Blessed *are* they that dwell in thy house:
they will be still praising thee. Selah.
5 Blessed *is* the man whose strength *is* in
thee; in whose heart *are* the ways *of them*.
6 *Who* passing through the valley of Baca
make it a well; the rain also filleth the pools.
7 They go from strength to strength, *every
one of them* in Zion appeareth before God.
8 O LORD God of hosts, hear my prayer: give
ear, O God of Jacob. Selah.
9 Behold, O God our shield, and look upon
the face of thine anointed.
10 For a day in thy courts *is* better than a
thousand. I had rather be a doorkeeper in
the house of my God, than to dwell in the
tents of wickedness.
11 For the LORD God *is* a sun and shield:
the LORD will give grace and glory: no good
thing will he withhold from them that walk
uprightly.
12 O LORD of hosts, blessed *is* the man that
trusteth in thee.

Psalm 85

To the chief Musician, A Psalm
for the sons of Korah.

1 Lord, thou hast been favourable unto thy
land: thou hast brought back the captivity
of Jacob.
2 Thou hast forgiven the iniquity of thy people, thou hast covered all their sin. Selah.
3 Thou hast taken away all thy wrath: thou
hast turned *thyself* from the fierceness of
thine anger.
4 Turn us, O God of our salvation, and cause
thine anger toward us to cease.
5 Wilt thou be angry with us for ever? wilt
thou draw out thine anger to all generations?
6 Wilt thou not revive us again: that thy
people may rejoice in thee?
7 Shew us thy mercy, O LORD, and grant us
thy salvation.
8 I will hear what God the LORD will speak:
for he will speak peace unto his people,
and to his saints: but let them not turn
again to folly.
9 Surely his salvation *is* nigh them that fear
him; that glory may dwell in our land.
10 Mercy and truth are met together; righteousness and peace have kissed *each other*.
11 Truth shall spring out of the earth; and
righteousness shall look down from heaven.
12 Yea, the LORD shall give *that which is*
good; and our land shall yield her increase.
13 Righteousness shall go before him; and
shall set *us* in the way of his steps.

Psalm 86

A Prayer of David.

1 Bow down thine ear, O LORD, hear me: for
I *am* poor and needy.
2 Preserve my soul; for I *am* holy: O thou my
God, save thy servant that trusteth in thee.
3 Be merciful unto me, O Lord: for I cry
unto thee daily.
4 Rejoice the soul of thy servant: for unto
thee, O Lord, do I lift up my soul.
5 For thou, Lord, *art* good, and ready to
forgive; and plenteous in mercy unto all
them that call upon thee.
6 Give ear, O LORD, unto my prayer; and
attend to the voice of my supplications.
7 In the day of my trouble I will call upon
thee: for thou wilt answer me.
8 Among the gods *there is* none like unto
thee, O Lord; neither *are there any works*
like unto thy works.
9 All nations whom thou hast made shall
come and worship before thee, O Lord; and
shall glorify thy name.
10 For thou *art* great, and doest wondrous
things: thou *art* God alone.
11 Teach me thy way, O LORD; I will walk in
thy truth: unite my heart to fear thy name.
12 I will praise thee, O Lord my God, with
all my heart: and I will glorify thy name for
evermore.
13 For great *is* thy mercy toward me: and
thou hast delivered my soul from the lowest hell.
14 O God, the proud are risen against me,
and the assemblies of violent *men* have

sought after my soul; and have not set thee
before them.
15 But thou, O Lord, *art* a God full of compassion, and gracious, longsuffering, and
plenteous in mercy and truth.
16 O turn unto me, and have mercy upon
me; give thy strength unto thy servant, and
save the son of thine handmaid.
17 Shew me a token for good; that they
which hate me may see *it*, and be ashamed:
because thou, LORD, hast holpen me, and
comforted me.

Psalm 87

A Psalm or Song for the sons of Korah.

1 His foundation *is* in the holy mountains.
2 The LORD loveth the gates of Zion more
than all the dwellings of Jacob.
3 Glorious things are spoken of thee, O city
of God. Selah.
4 I will make mention of Rahab and Babylon
to them that know me: behold Philistia, and
Tyre, with Ethiopia; this *man* was born there.
5 And of Zion it shall be said, This and that
man was born in her: and the highest himself shall establish her.
6 The LORD shall count, when he writeth
up the people, *that* this *man* was born
there. Selah.
7 As well the singers as the players on
instruments *shall be there:* all my springs
are in thee.

Psalm 88

A Song or Psalm for the sons of Korah, to the chief Musician upon Mahalath Leannoth, Maschil of Heman the Ezrahite.

1 O Lord God of my salvation, I have cried
day *and* night before thee:
2 Let my prayer come before thee: incline
thine ear unto my cry;
3 For my soul is full of troubles: and my life
draweth nigh unto the grave.
4 I am counted with them that go down into
the pit: I am as a man *that hath* no strength:
5 Free among the dead, like the slain that lie
in the grave, whom thou rememberest no
more: and they are cut off from thy hand.
6 Thou hast laid me in the lowest pit, in
darkness, in the deeps.
7 Thy wrath lieth hard upon me, and thou
hast afflicted *me* with all thy waves. Selah.
8 Thou hast put away mine acquaintance far
from me; thou hast made me an abomination unto them: *I am* shut up, and I cannot
come forth.
9 Mine eye mourneth by reason of affliction:
LORD, I have called daily upon thee, I have
stretched out my hands unto thee.
10 Wilt thou shew wonders to the dead?
shall the dead arise *and* praise thee? Selah.
11 Shall thy lovingkindness be declared in
the grave? *or* thy faithfulness in destruction?
12 Shall thy wonders be known in the
dark? and thy righteousness in the land of
forgetfulness?
13 But unto thee have I cried, O LORD; and
in the morning shall my prayer prevent thee.
14 LORD, why castest thou off my soul? *why*
hidest thou thy face from me?
15 I *am* afflicted and ready to die from *my*
youth up: *while* I suffer thy terrors I am
distracted.
16 Thy fierce wrath goeth over me; thy terrors have cut me off.
17 They came round about me daily like
water; they compassed me about together.
18 Lover and friend hast thou put far from
me, *and* mine acquaintance into darkness.

Psalm 89

Maschil of Ethan the Ezrahite.

1 I will sing of the mercies of the LORD for
ever: with my mouth will I make known thy
faithfulness to all generations.
2 For I have said, Mercy shall be built up for
ever: thy faithfulness shalt thou establish in
the very heavens.
3 I have made a covenant with my chosen, I
have sworn unto David my servant,
4 Thy seed will I establish for ever, and build
up thy throne to all generations. Selah.
5 And the heavens shall praise thy wonders,
O LORD: thy faithfulness also in the congregation of the saints.
6 For who in the heaven can be compared
unto the LORD? *who* among the sons of the
mighty can be likened unto the LORD?
7 God is greatly to be feared in the assembly
of the saints, and to be had in reverence of
all *them that are* about him.
8 O LORD God of hosts, who *is* a strong LORD

like unto thee? or to thy faithfulness round
about thee?
9 Thou rulest the raging of the sea: when
the waves thereof arise, thou stillest them.
10 Thou hast broken Rahab in pieces, as
one that is slain; thou hast scattered thine
enemies with thy strong arm.
11 The heavens *are* thine, the earth also
is thine: *as for* the world and the fulness
thereof, thou hast founded them.
12 The north and the south thou hast created them: Tabor and Hermon shall rejoice
in thy name.
13 Thou hast a mighty arm: strong is thy
hand, *and* high is thy right hand.
14 Justice and judgment *are* the habitation
of thy throne: mercy and truth shall go
before thy face.
15 Blessed *is* the people that know the joyful
sound: they shall walk, O LORD, in the light
of thy countenance.
16 In thy name shall they rejoice all the
day: and in thy righteousness shall they
be exalted.
17 For thou *art* the glory of their strength:
and in thy favour our horn shall be exalted.
18 For the LORD *is* our defence; and the Holy
One of Israel *is* our king.
19 Then thou spakest in vision to thy holy
one, and saidst, I have laid help upon *one*
that is mighty; I have exalted *one* chosen
out of the people.
20 I have found David my servant; with my
holy oil have I anointed him:
21 With whom my hand shall be established:
mine arm also shall strengthen him.
22 The enemy shall not exact upon him; nor
the son of wickedness afflict him.
23 And I will beat down his foes before his
face, and plague them that hate him.
24 But my faithfulness and my mercy *shall*
be with him: and in my name shall his horn
be exalted.
25 I will set his hand also in the sea, and his
right hand in the rivers.
26 He shall cry unto me, Thou *art* my father,
my God, and the rock of my salvation.
27 Also I will make him *my* firstborn, higher
than the kings of the earth.
28 My mercy will I keep for him for evermore, and my covenant shall stand fast
with him.
29 His seed also will I make *to endure* for
ever, and his throne as the days of heaven.
30 If his children forsake my law, and walk
not in my judgments;
31 If they break my statutes, and keep not
my commandments;
32 Then will I visit their transgression with
the rod, and their iniquity with stripes.
33 Nevertheless my lovingkindness will I
not utterly take from him, nor suffer my
faithfulness to fail.
34 My covenant will I not break, nor alter
the thing that is gone out of my lips.
35 Once have I sworn by my holiness that I
will not lie unto David.
36 His seed shall endure for ever, and his
throne as the sun before me.
37 It shall be established for ever as the
moon, and *as* a faithful witness in heaven.
Selah.
38 But thou hast cast off and abhorred,
thou hast been wroth with thine anointed.
39 Thou hast made void the covenant of
thy servant: thou hast profaned his crown
by casting it to the ground.
40 Thou hast broken down all his hedges;
thou hast brought his strong holds to ruin.
41 All that pass by the way spoil him: he is
a reproach to his neighbours.
42 Thou hast set up the right hand of his
adversaries; thou hast made all his enemies
to rejoice.
43 Thou hast also turned the edge of his
sword, and hast not made him to stand in
the battle.
44 Thou hast made his glory to cease, and
cast his throne down to the ground.
45 The days of his youth hast thou shortened: thou hast covered him with shame.
Selah.
46 How long, LORD? wilt thou hide thyself
for ever? shall thy wrath burn like fire?
47 Remember how short my time is: wherefore hast thou made all men in vain?
48 What man *is he that* liveth, and shall not
see death? shall he deliver his soul from the
hand of the grave? Selah.
49 Lord, where *are* thy former lovingkindnesses, *which* thou swarest unto David in
thy truth?
50 Remember, Lord, the reproach of thy
servants; *how* I do bear in my bosom *the*
reproach of all the mighty people;

51 Wherewith thine enemies have
reproached, O LORD; wherewith they have
reproached the footsteps of thine anointed.
52 Blessed *be* the LORD for evermore. Amen,
and Amen.

Psalm 90

A Prayer of Moses the man of God.

1 Lord, thou hast been our dwelling place
in all generations.
2 Before the mountains were brought forth,
or ever thou hadst formed the earth and the
world, even from everlasting to everlasting,
thou *art* God.
3 Thou turnest man to destruction; and
sayest, Return, ye children of men.
4 For a thousand years in thy sight *are but*
as yesterday when it is past, and *as* a watch
in the night.
5 Thou carriest them away as with a flood;
they are *as* a sleep: in the morning *they are*
like grass *which* groweth up.
6 In the morning it flourisheth, and groweth
up; in the evening it is cut down, and withereth.
7 For we are consumed by thine anger, and
by thy wrath are we troubled.
8 Thou hast set our iniquities before thee,
our secret *sins* in the light of thy countenance.
9 For all our days are passed away in thy
wrath: we spend our years as a tale *that
is told*.
10 The days of our years *are* threescore
years and ten; and if by reason of strength
they be fourscore years, yet *is* their strength
labour and sorrow; for it is soon cut off, and
we fly away.
11 Who knoweth the power of thine anger?
even according to thy fear, *so is* thy wrath.
12 So teach *us* to number our days, that we
may apply *our* hearts unto wisdom.
13 Return, O LORD, how long? and let it
repent thee concerning thy servants.
14 O satisfy us early with thy mercy; that
we may rejoice and be glad all our days.
15 Make us glad according to the days
wherein thou hast afflicted us, *and* the years
wherein we have seen evil.
16 Let thy work appear unto thy servants,
and thy glory unto their children.
17 And let the beauty of the LORD our God
be upon us: and establish thou the work
of our hands upon us; yea, the work of our
hands establish thou it.

Psalm 91

1 He that dwelleth in the secret place of the
most High shall abide under the shadow of
the Almighty.
2 I will say of the LORD, *He is* my refuge and
my fortress: my God; in him will I trust.
3 Surely he shall deliver thee from the
snare of the fowler, *and* from the noisome
pestilence.
4 He shall cover thee with his feathers, and
under his wings shalt thou trust: his truth
shall be thy shield and buckler.
5 Thou shalt not be afraid for the terror by
night; *nor* for the arrow *that* flieth by day;
6 *Nor* for the pestilence *that* walketh in darkness; *nor* for the destruction *that* wasteth
at noonday.
7 A thousand shall fall at thy side, and ten
thousand at thy right hand; *but* it shall not
come nigh thee.
8 Only with thine eyes shalt thou behold
and see the reward of the wicked.
9 Because thou hast made the LORD, *which
is* my refuge, *even* the most High, thy habitation;
10 There shall no evil befall thee, neither
shall any plague come nigh thy dwelling.
11 For he shall give his angels charge over
thee, to keep thee in all thy ways.
12 They shall bear thee up in *their* hands,
lest thou dash thy foot against a stone.
13 Thou shalt tread upon the lion and adder:
the young lion and the dragon shalt thou
trample under feet.
14 Because he hath set his love upon me,
therefore will I deliver him: I will set him
on high, because he hath known my name.
15 He shall call upon me, and I will answer
him: I *will be* with him in trouble; I will
deliver him, and honour him.
16 With long life will I satisfy him, and shew
him my salvation.

Psalm 92

A Psalm or Song for the sabbath day.

1 *It is a* good *thing* to give thanks unto the
LORD, and to sing praises unto thy name,
O most High:
2 To shew forth thy lovingkindness in the
morning, and thy faithfulness every night,

3 Upon an instrument of ten strings, and
upon the psaltery; upon the harp with a
solemn sound.
4 For thou, LORD, hast made me glad
through thy work: I will triumph in the
works of thy hands.
5 O LORD, how great are thy works! *and* thy
thoughts are very deep.
6 A brutish man knoweth not; neither doth
a fool understand this.
7 When the wicked spring as the grass, and
when all the workers of iniquity do flourish;
it is that they shall be destroyed for ever:
8 But thou, LORD, *art most* high for evermore.
9 For, lo, thine enemies, O LORD, for, lo,
thine enemies shall perish; all the workers
of iniquity shall be scattered.
10 But my horn shalt thou exalt like *the
horn of* an unicorn: I shall be anointed with
fresh oil.
11 Mine eye also shall see *my desire* on mine
enemies, *and* mine ears shall hear *my desire*
of the wicked that rise up against me.
12 The righteous shall flourish like the palm
tree: he shall grow like a cedar in Lebanon.
13 Those that be planted in the house of the
LORD shall flourish in the courts of our God.
14 They shall still bring forth fruit in old age;
they shall be fat and flourishing;
15 To shew that the LORD *is* upright: *he is* my
rock, and *there is* no unrighteousness in him.

Psalm 93

1 The LORD reigneth, he is clothed with
majesty; the LORD is clothed with strength,
wherewith he hath girded himself: the world
also is stablished, that it cannot be moved.
2 Thy throne *is* established of old: thou *art*
from everlasting.
3 The floods have lifted up, O LORD, the
floods have lifted up their voice; the floods
lift up their waves.
4 The LORD on high *is* mightier than the
noise of many waters, *yea, than* the mighty
waves of the sea.
5 Thy testimonies are very sure: holiness
becometh thine house, O LORD, for ever.

Psalm 94

1 O Lord God, to whom vengeance belongeth; O God, to whom vengeance belongeth,
shew thyself.
2 Lift up thyself, thou judge of the earth:
render a reward to the proud.
3 LORD, how long shall the wicked, how long
shall the wicked triumph?
4 *How long* shall they utter *and* speak hard
things? *and* all the workers of iniquity boast
themselves?
5 They break in pieces thy people, O LORD,
and afflict thine heritage.
6 They slay the widow and the stranger, and
murder the fatherless.
7 Yet they say, The LORD shall not see, neither shall the God of Jacob regard *it*.
8 Understand, ye brutish among the people:
and *ye* fools, when will ye be wise?
9 He that planted the ear, shall he not hear?
he that formed the eye, shall he not see?
10 He that chastiseth the heathen, shall not
he correct? he that teacheth man knowledge, *shall not he know*?
11 The LORD knoweth the thoughts of man,
that they *are* vanity.
12 Blessed *is* the man whom thou chasten-
est, O LORD, and teachest him out of thy law;
13 That thou mayest give him rest from the
days of adversity, until the pit be digged for
the wicked.
14 For the LORD will not cast off his people,
neither will he forsake his inheritance.
15 But judgment shall return unto righteousness: and all the upright in heart shall
follow it.
16 Who will rise up for me against the evildoers? *or* who will stand up for me against
the workers of iniquity?
17 Unless the LORD *had been* my help, my
soul had almost dwelt in silence.
18 When I said, My foot slippeth; thy mercy,
O LORD, held me up.
19 In the multitude of my thoughts within
me thy comforts delight my soul.
20 Shall the throne of iniquity have fellowship with thee, which frameth mischief by
a law?
21 They gather themselves together against
the soul of the righteous, and condemn the
innocent blood.
22 But the LORD is my defence; and my God
is the rock of my refuge.
23 And he shall bring upon them their own
iniquity, and shall cut them off in their own
wickedness; *yea*, the LORD our God shall
cut them off.

Psalm 95

1 O come, let us sing unto the LORD: let us make a joyful noise to the rock of our salvation.
2 Let us come before his presence with thanksgiving, and make a joyful noise unto him with psalms.
3 For the LORD *is* a great God, and a great King above all gods.
4 In his hand *are* the deep places of the earth: the strength of the hills *is* his also.
5 The sea *is* his, and he made it: and his hands formed the dry *land*.
6 O come, let us worship and bow down: let us kneel before the LORD our maker.
7 For he *is* our God; and we *are* the people of his pasture, and the sheep of his hand. To day if ye will hear his voice,
8 Harden not your heart, as in the provocation, *and* as *in* the day of temptation in the wilderness:
9 When your fathers tempted me, proved me, and saw my work.
10 Forty years long was I grieved with *this* generation, and said, It *is* a people that do err in their heart, and they have not known my ways:
11 Unto whom I sware in my wrath that they should not enter into my rest.

Psalm 96

1 O sing unto the LORD a new song: sing unto the LORD, all the earth.
2 Sing unto the LORD, bless his name; shew forth his salvation from day to day.
3 Declare his glory among the heathen, his wonders among all people.
4 For the LORD *is* great, and greatly to be praised: he *is* to be feared above all gods.
5 For all the gods of the nations *are* idols: but the LORD made the heavens.
6 Honour and majesty *are* before him: strength and beauty *are* in his sanctuary.
7 Give unto the LORD, O ye kindreds of the people, give unto the LORD glory and strength.
8 Give unto the LORD the glory *due unto* his name: bring an offering, and come into his courts.
9 O worship the LORD in the beauty of holiness: fear before him, all the earth.
10 Say among the heathen *that* the LORD reigneth: the world also shall be established that it shall not be moved: he shall judge the people righteously.
11 Let the heavens rejoice, and let the earth be glad; let the sea roar, and the fulness thereof.
12 Let the field be joyful, and all that *is* therein: then shall all the trees of the wood rejoice
13 Before the LORD: for he cometh, for he cometh to judge the earth: he shall judge the world with righteousness, and the people with his truth.

Psalm 97

1 The LORD reigneth; let the earth rejoice; let the multitude of isles be glad *thereof*.
2 Clouds and darkness *are* round about him: righteousness and judgment *are* the habitation of his throne.
3 A fire goeth before him, and burneth up his enemies round about.
4 His lightnings enlightened the world: the earth saw, and trembled.
5 The hills melted like wax at the presence of the LORD, at the presence of the Lord of the whole earth.
6 The heavens declare his righteousness, and all the people see his glory.
7 Confounded be all they that serve graven images, that boast themselves of idols: worship him, all *ye* gods.
8 Zion heard, and was glad; and the daughters of Judah rejoiced because of thy judgments, O LORD.
9 For thou, LORD, *art* high above all the earth: thou art exalted far above all gods.
10 Ye that love the LORD, hate evil: he preserveth the souls of his saints; he delivereth them out of the hand of the wicked.
11 Light is sown for the righteous, and gladness for the upright in heart.
12 Rejoice in the LORD, ye righteous; and give thanks at the remembrance of his holiness.

Psalm 98

A Psalm.

1 O sing unto the LORD a new song; for he hath done marvellous things: his right hand, and his holy arm, hath gotten him the victory.
2 The LORD hath made known his salvation:

his righteousness hath he openly shewed in
the sight of the heathen.
3 He hath remembered his mercy and his
truth toward the house of Israel: all the
ends of the earth have seen the salvation
of our God.
4 Make a joyful noise unto the LORD, all the
earth: make a loud noise, and rejoice, and
sing praise.
5 Sing unto the LORD with the harp; with the
harp, and the voice of a psalm.
6 With trumpets and sound of cornet make
a joyful noise before the LORD, the King.
7 Let the sea roar, and the fulness thereof;
the world, and they that dwell therein.
8 Let the floods clap *their* hands: let the hills
be joyful together
9 Before the LORD; for he cometh to judge
the earth: with righteousness shall he judge
the world, and the people with equity.

Psalm 99

1 The LORD reigneth; let the people tremble:
he sitteth *between* the cherubims; let the
earth be moved.
2 The LORD *is* great in Zion; and he *is* high
above all the people.
3 Let them praise thy great and terrible
name; *for* it *is* holy.
4 The king's strength also loveth judgment;
thou dost establish equity, thou executest
judgment and righteousness in Jacob.
5 Exalt ye the LORD our God, and worship
at his footstool; *for* he *is* holy.
6 Moses and Aaron among his priests, and
Samuel among them that call upon his
name; they called upon the LORD, and he
answered them.
7 He spake unto them in the cloudy pillar:
they kept his testimonies, and the ordinance
that he gave them.
8 Thou answeredst them, O LORD our God:
thou wast a God that forgavest them,
though thou tookest vengeance of their
inventions.
9 Exalt the LORD our God, and worship at
his holy hill; for the LORD our God *is* holy.

Psalm 100

A Psalm of praise.

1 Make a joyful noise unto the LORD, all
ye lands.
2 Serve the LORD with gladness: come
before his presence with singing.
3 Know ye that the LORD he *is* God: *it is* he
that hath made us, and not we ourselves; *we*
are his people, and the sheep of his pasture.
4 Enter into his gates with thanksgiving, *and*
into his courts with praise: be thankful unto
him, *and* bless his name.
5 For the LORD *is* good; his mercy *is* everlasting; and his truth *endureth* to all generations.

Psalm 101

A Psalm of David.

1 I will sing of mercy and judgment: unto
thee, O LORD, will I sing.
2 I will behave myself wisely in a perfect
way. O when wilt thou come unto me? I will
walk within my house with a perfect heart.
3 I will set no wicked thing before mine eyes:
I hate the work of them that turn aside; *it*
shall not cleave to me.
4 A froward heart shall depart from me: I
will not know a wicked *person*.
5 Whoso privily slandereth his neighbour,
him will I cut off: him that hath an high look
and a proud heart will not I suffer.
6 Mine eyes *shall be* upon the faithful of the
land, that they may dwell with me: he that
walketh in a perfect way, he shall serve me.
7 He that worketh deceit shall not dwell
within my house: he that telleth lies shall
not tarry in my sight.
8 I will early destroy all the wicked of the
land; that I may cut off all wicked doers from
the city of the LORD.

Psalm 102

A Prayer of the afflicted, when he is overwhelmed, and poureth out his complaint before the LORD.

1 Hear my prayer, O LORD, and let my cry
come unto thee.
2 Hide not thy face from me in the day *when*
I am in trouble; incline thine ear unto me:
in the day *when* I call answer me speedily.
3 For my days are consumed like smoke, and
my bones are burned as an hearth.
4 My heart is smitten, and withered like
grass; so that I forget to eat my bread.
5 By reason of the voice of my groaning my
bones cleave to my skin.

6 I am like a pelican of the wilderness: I am
like an owl of the desert.
7 I watch, and am as a sparrow alone upon
the house top.
8 Mine enemies reproach me all the day;
and they that are mad against me are sworn
against me.
9 For I have eaten ashes like bread, and
mingled my drink with weeping,
10 Because of thine indignation and thy
wrath: for thou hast lifted me up, and cast
me down.
11 My days *are* like a shadow that declineth;
and I am withered like grass.
12 But thou, O LORD, shalt endure for ever;
and thy remembrance unto all generations.
13 Thou shalt arise, *and* have mercy upon
Zion: for the time to favour her, yea, the set
time, is come.
14 For thy servants take pleasure in her
stones, and favour the dust thereof.
15 So the heathen shall fear the name of the
LORD, and all the kings of the earth thy glory.
16 When the LORD shall build up Zion, he
shall appear in his glory.
17 He will regard the prayer of the destitute,
and not despise their prayer.
18 This shall be written for the generation
to come: and the people which shall be
created shall praise the LORD.
19 For he hath looked down from the height
of his sanctuary; from heaven did the LORD
behold the earth;
20 To hear the groaning of the prisoner; to
loose those that are appointed to death;
21 To declare the name of the LORD in Zion,
and his praise in Jerusalem;
22 When the people are gathered together,
and the kingdoms, to serve the LORD.
23 He weakened my strength in the way;
he shortened my days.
24 I said, O my God, take me not away in the
midst of my days: thy years *are* throughout
all generations.
25 Of old hast thou laid the foundation of
the earth: and the heavens *are* the work
of thy hands.
26 They shall perish, but thou shalt endure:
yea, all of them shall wax old like a garment;
as a vesture shalt thou change them, and
they shall be changed:
27 But thou *art* the same, and thy years
shall have no end.
28 The children of thy servants shall continue, and their seed shall be established
before thee.

Psalm 103

A Psalm of David.

1 Bless the LORD, O my soul: and all that is
within me, *bless* his holy name.
2 Bless the LORD, O my soul, and forget not
all his benefits:
3 Who forgiveth all thine iniquities; who
healeth all thy diseases;
4 Who redeemeth thy life from destruction;
who crowneth thee with lovingkindness and
tender mercies;
5 Who satisfieth thy mouth with good
things; so that thy youth is renewed like
the eagle's.
6 The LORD executeth righteousness and
judgment for all that are oppressed.
7 He made known his ways unto Moses, his
acts unto the children of Israel.
8 The LORD *is* merciful and gracious, slow
to anger, and plenteous in mercy.
9 He will not always chide: neither will he
keep *his anger* for ever.
10 He hath not dealt with us after our sins;
nor rewarded us according to our iniquities.
11 For as the heaven is high above the
earth, *so* great is his mercy toward them
that fear him.
12 As far as the east is from the west, *so*
far hath he removed our transgressions
from us.
13 Like as a father pitieth *his* children, *so* the
LORD pitieth them that fear him.
14 For he knoweth our frame; he remembereth that we *are* dust.
15 *As for* man, his days *are* as grass: as a
flower of the field, so he flourisheth.
16 For the wind passeth over it, and it is
gone; and the place thereof shall know it
no more.
17 But the mercy of the LORD *is* from everlasting to everlasting upon them that fear
him, and his righteousness unto children's
children;
18 To such as keep his covenant, and to
those that remember his commandments
to do them.
19 The LORD hath prepared his throne in the
heavens; and his kingdom ruleth over all.
20 Bless the LORD, ye his angels, that excel

in strength, that do his commandments,
hearkening unto the voice of his word.
21 Bless ye the LORD, all *ye* his hosts; *ye*
ministers of his, that do his pleasure.
22 Bless the LORD, all his works in all places
of his dominion: bless the LORD, O my soul.

Psalm 104

1 Bless the LORD, O my soul. O LORD my God,
thou art very great; thou art clothed with
honour and majesty.
2 Who coverest *thyself* with light as *with* a
garment: who stretchest out the heavens
like a curtain:
3 Who layeth the beams of his chambers
in the waters: who maketh the clouds his
chariot: who walketh upon the wings of
the wind:
4 Who maketh his angels spirits; his ministers a flaming fire:
5 *Who* laid the foundations of the earth, *that*
it should not be removed for ever.
6 Thou coveredst it with the deep as *with*
a garment: the waters stood above the
mountains.
7 At thy rebuke they fled; at the voice of thy
thunder they hasted away.
8 They go up by the mountains; they go
down by the valleys unto the place which
thou hast founded for them.
9 Thou hast set a bound that they may not
pass over; that they turn not again to cover
the earth.
10 He sendeth the springs into the valleys,
which run among the hills.
11 They give drink to every beast of the field:
the wild asses quench their thirst.
12 By them shall the fowls of the heaven
have their habitation, *which* sing among
the branches.
13 He watereth the hills from his chambers: the earth is satisfied with the fruit of
thy works.
14 He causeth the grass to grow for the
cattle, and herb for the service of man: that
he may bring forth food out of the earth;
15 And wine *that* maketh glad the heart of
man, *and* oil to make *his* face to shine, and
bread *which* strengtheneth man's heart.
16 The trees of the LORD are full *of sap;* the
cedars of Lebanon, which he hath planted;
17 Where the birds make their nests: *as for*
the stork, the fir trees *are* her house.
18 The high hills *are* a refuge for the wild
goats; *and* the rocks for the conies.
19 He appointed the moon for seasons: the
sun knoweth his going down.
20 Thou makest darkness, and it is night:
wherein all the beasts of the forest do
creep *forth*.
21 The young lions roar after their prey, and
seek their meat from God.
22 The sun ariseth, they gather themselves
together, and lay them down in their dens.
23 Man goeth forth unto his work and to
his labour until the evening.
24 O LORD, how manifold are thy works! in
wisdom hast thou made them all: the earth
is full of thy riches.
25 *So is* this great and wide sea, wherein
are things creeping innumerable, both small
and great beasts.
26 There go the ships: *there is* that leviathan,
whom thou hast made to play therein.
27 These wait all upon thee; that thou
mayest give *them* their meat in due season.
28 *That* thou givest them they gather:
thou openest thine hand, they are filled
with good.
29 Thou hidest thy face, they are troubled:
thou takest away their breath, they die, and
return to their dust.
30 Thou sendest forth thy spirit, they are
created: and thou renewest the face of
the earth.
31 The glory of the LORD shall endure for
ever: the LORD shall rejoice in his works.
32 He looketh on the earth, and it trembleth:
he toucheth the hills, and they smoke.
33 I will sing unto the LORD as long as I live:
I will sing praise to my God while I have
my being.
34 My meditation of him shall be sweet: I
will be glad in the LORD.
35 Let the sinners be consumed out of
the earth, and let the wicked be no more.
Bless thou the LORD, O my soul. Praise ye
the LORD.

Psalm 105

1 O give thanks unto the LORD; call upon
his name: make known his deeds among
the people.
2 Sing unto him, sing psalms unto him: talk
ye of all his wondrous works.

3 Glory ye in his holy name: let the heart of
them rejoice that seek the LORD.
4 Seek the LORD, and his strength: seek his
face evermore.
5 Remember his marvellous works that he
hath done; his wonders, and the judgments
of his mouth;
6 O ye seed of Abraham his servant, ye
children of Jacob his chosen.
7 He *is* the LORD our God: his judgments *are*
in all the earth.
8 He hath remembered his covenant for
ever, the word *which* he commanded to a
thousand generations.
9 Which *covenant* he made with Abraham,
and his oath unto Isaac;
10 And confirmed the same unto Jacob
for a law, *and* to Israel *for* an everlasting
covenant:
11 Saying, Unto thee will I give the land of
Canaan, the lot of your inheritance:
12 When they were *but* a few men in number; yea, very few, and strangers in it.
13 When they went from one nation to
another, from *one* kingdom to another
people;
14 He suffered no man to do them wrong:
yea, he reproved kings for their sakes;
15 *Saying,* Touch not mine anointed, and
do my prophets no harm.
16 Moreover he called for a famine upon
the land: he brake the whole staff of bread.
17 He sent a man before them, *even* Joseph,
who was sold for a servant:
18 Whose feet they hurt with fetters: he
was laid in iron:
19 Until the time that his word came: the
word of the LORD tried him.
20 The king sent and loosed him; *even* the
ruler of the people, and let him go free.
21 He made him lord of his house, and ruler
of all his substance:
22 To bind his princes at his pleasure; and
teach his senators wisdom.
23 Israel also came into Egypt; and Jacob
sojourned in the land of Ham.
24 And he increased his people greatly; and
made them stronger than their enemies.
25 He turned their heart to hate his people,
to deal subtilly with his servants.
26 He sent Moses his servant; *and* Aaron
whom he had chosen.
27 They shewed his signs among them, and
wonders in the land of Ham.
28 He sent darkness, and made it dark; and
they rebelled not against his word.
29 He turned their waters into blood, and
slew their fish.
30 Their land brought forth frogs in abundance, in the chambers of their kings.
31 He spake, and there came divers sorts
of flies, *and* lice in all their coasts.
32 He gave them hail for rain, *and* flaming
fire in their land.
33 He smote their vines also and their fig
trees; and brake the trees of their coasts.
34 He spake, and the locusts came, and caterpillers, and that without number,
35 And did eat up all the herbs in their land,
and devoured the fruit of their ground.
36 He smote also all the firstborn in their
land, the chief of all their strength.
37 He brought them forth also with silver
and gold: and *there was* not one feeble
person among their tribes.
38 Egypt was glad when they departed: for
the fear of them fell upon them.
39 He spread a cloud for a covering; and fire
to give light in the night.
40 *The people* asked, and he brought quails,
and satisfied them with the bread of heaven.
41 He opened the rock, and the waters
gushed out; they ran in the dry places *like*
a river.
42 For he remembered his holy promise,
and Abraham his servant.
43 And he brought forth his people with joy,
and his chosen with gladness:
44 And gave them the lands of the heathen:
and they inherited the labour of the people;
45 That they might observe his statutes, and
keep his laws. Praise ye the LORD.

Psalm 106

1 Praise ye the LORD. O give thanks unto the
LORD; for *he is* good: for his mercy *endureth*
for ever.
2 Who can utter the mighty acts of the
LORD? *who* can shew forth all his praise?
3 Blessed *are* they that keep judgment, *and*
he that doeth righteousness at all times.
4 Remember me, O LORD, with the favour
that thou bearest unto thy people: O visit
me with thy salvation;
5 That I may see the good of thy chosen, that

I may rejoice in the gladness of thy nation,
that I may glory with thine inheritance.
6 We have sinned with our fathers, we have
committed iniquity, we have done wickedly.
7 Our fathers understood not thy wonders in
Egypt; they remembered not the multitude
of thy mercies; but provoked *him* at the sea,
even at the Red sea.
8 Nevertheless he saved them for his name's
sake, that he might make his mighty power
to be known.
9 He rebuked the Red sea also, and it was
dried up: so he led them through the depths,
as through the wilderness.
10 And he saved them from the hand of him
that hated *them*, and redeemed them from
the hand of the enemy.
11 And the waters covered their enemies:
there was not one of them left.
12 Then believed they his words; they sang
his praise.
13 They soon forgat his works; they waited
not for his counsel:
14 But lusted exceedingly in the wilderness,
and tempted God in the desert.
15 And he gave them their request; but sent
leanness into their soul.
16 They envied Moses also in the camp, *and*
Aaron the saint of the LORD.
17 The earth opened and swallowed up
Dathan, and covered the company of Abiram.
18 And a fire was kindled in their company;
the flame burned up the wicked.
19 They made a calf in Horeb, and worshipped the molten image.
20 Thus they changed their glory into the
similitude of an ox that eateth grass.
21 They forgat God their saviour, which had
done great things in Egypt;
22 Wondrous works in the land of Ham, *and*
terrible things by the Red sea.
23 Therefore he said that he would destroy
them, had not Moses his chosen stood
before him in the breach, to turn away his
wrath, lest he should destroy *them*.
24 Yea, they despised the pleasant land,
they believed not his word:
25 But murmured in their tents, *and* hearkened not unto the voice of the LORD.
26 Therefore he lifted up his hand against
them, to overthrow them in the wilderness:
27 To overthrow their seed also among the
nations, and to scatter them in the lands.
28 They joined themselves also unto Baal-
peor, and ate the sacrifices of the dead.
29 Thus they provoked *him* to anger with
their inventions: and the plague brake in
upon them.
30 Then stood up Phinehas, and executed
judgment: and *so* the plague was stayed.
31 And that was counted unto him for
righteousness unto all generations for
evermore.
32 They angered *him* also at the waters
of strife, so that it went ill with Moses for
their sakes:
33 Because they provoked his spirit, so that
he spake unadvisedly with his lips.
34 They did not destroy the nations, concerning whom the LORD commanded them:
35 But were mingled among the heathen,
and learned their works.
36 And they served their idols: which were
a snare unto them.
37 Yea, they sacrificed their sons and their
daughters unto devils,
38 And shed innocent blood, *even* the blood
of their sons and of their daughters, whom
they sacrificed unto the idols of Canaan: and
the land was polluted with blood.
39 Thus were they defiled with their own
works, and went a whoring with their own
inventions.
40 Therefore was the wrath of the LORD
kindled against his people, insomuch that
he abhorred his own inheritance.
41 And he gave them into the hand of the
heathen; and they that hated them ruled
over them.
42 Their enemies also oppressed them, and
they were brought into subjection under
their hand.
43 Many times did he deliver them; but they
provoked *him* with their counsel, and were
brought low for their iniquity.
44 Nevertheless he regarded their affliction,
when he heard their cry:
45 And he remembered for them his covenant, and repented according to the multitude of his mercies.
46 He made them also to be pitied of all
those that carried them captives.
47 Save us, O LORD our God, and gather us
from among the heathen, to give thanks

unto thy holy name, *and* to triumph in thy
praise.
48 Blessed *be* the LORD God of Israel from
everlasting to everlasting: and let all the
people say, Amen. Praise ye the LORD.

Psalm 107

1 O give thanks unto the LORD, for *he is* good:
for his mercy *endureth* for ever.
2 Let the redeemed of the LORD say *so*,
whom he hath redeemed from the hand
of the enemy;
3 And gathered them out of the lands, from
the east, and from the west, from the north,
and from the south.
4 They wandered in the wilderness in a
solitary way; they found no city to dwell in.
5 Hungry and thirsty, their soul fainted in
them.
6 Then they cried unto the LORD in their
trouble, *and* he delivered them out of their
distresses.
7 And he led them forth by the right way,
that they might go to a city of habitation.
8 Oh that *men* would praise the LORD *for*
his goodness, and *for* his wonderful works
to the children of men!
9 For he satisfieth the longing soul, and filleth the hungry soul with goodness.
10 Such as sit in darkness and in the shadow
of death, *being* bound in affliction and iron;
11 Because they rebelled against the words
of God, and contemned the counsel of the
most High:
12 Therefore he brought down their heart
with labour; they fell down, and *there was*
none to help.
13 Then they cried unto the LORD in their
trouble, *and* he saved them out of their
distresses.
14 He brought them out of darkness and
the shadow of death, and brake their bands
in sunder.
15 Oh that *men* would praise the LORD *for*
his goodness, and *for* his wonderful works
to the children of men!
16 For he hath broken the gates of brass,
and cut the bars of iron in sunder.
17 Fools because of their transgression, and
because of their iniquities, are afflicted.
18 Their soul abhorreth all manner of meat;
and they draw near unto the gates of death.
19 Then they cry unto the LORD in their
trouble, *and* he saveth them out of their
distresses.
20 He sent his word, and healed them, and
delivered *them* from their destructions.
21 Oh that *men* would praise the LORD *for*
his goodness, and *for* his wonderful works
to the children of men!
22 And let them sacrifice the sacrifices of
thanksgiving, and declare his works with
rejoicing.
23 They that go down to the sea in ships,
that do business in great waters;
24 These see the works of the LORD, and his
wonders in the deep.
25 For he commandeth, and raiseth the
stormy wind, which lifteth up the waves
thereof.
26 They mount up to the heaven, they
go down again to the depths: their soul is
melted because of trouble.
27 They reel to and fro, and stagger like a
drunken man, and are at their wits' end.
28 Then they cry unto the LORD in their
trouble, and he bringeth them out of their
distresses.
29 He maketh the storm a calm, so that the
waves thereof are still.
30 Then are they glad because they be quiet;
so he bringeth them unto their desired
haven.
31 Oh that *men* would praise the LORD *for*
his goodness, and *for* his wonderful works
to the children of men!
32 Let them exalt him also in the congregation of the people, and praise him in the
assembly of the elders.
33 He turneth rivers into a wilderness, and
the watersprings into dry ground;
34 A fruitful land into barrenness, for the
wickedness of them that dwell therein.
35 He turneth the wilderness into a standing
water, and dry ground into watersprings.
36 And there he maketh the hungry to dwell,
that they may prepare a city for habitation;
37 And sow the fields, and plant vineyards,
which may yield fruits of increase.
38 He blesseth them also, so that they are
multiplied greatly; and suffereth not their
cattle to decrease.
39 Again, they are minished and brought low
through oppression, affliction, and sorrow.
40 He poureth contempt upon princes, and

causeth them to wander in the wilderness, *where there is* no way.
41 Yet setteth he the poor on high from affliction, and maketh *him* families like a flock.
42 The righteous shall see *it*, and rejoice: and all iniquity shall stop her mouth.
43 Whoso *is* wise, and will observe these *things*, even they shall understand the lovingkindness of the LORD.

Psalm 108

A Song or Psalm of David.

1 O God, my heart is fixed; I will sing and give praise, even with my glory.
2 Awake, psaltery and harp: I *myself* will awake early.
3 I will praise thee, O LORD, among the people: and I will sing praises unto thee among the nations.
4 For thy mercy *is* great above the heavens: and thy truth *reacheth* unto the clouds.
5 Be thou exalted, O God, above the heavens: and thy glory above all the earth;
6 That thy beloved may be delivered: save *with* thy right hand, and answer me.
7 God hath spoken in his holiness; I will rejoice, I will divide Shechem, and mete out the valley of Succoth.
8 Gilead *is* mine; Manasseh *is* mine; Ephraim also *is* the strength of mine head; Judah *is* my lawgiver;
9 Moab *is* my washpot; over Edom will I cast out my shoe; over Philistia will I triumph.
10 Who will bring me into the strong city? who will lead me into Edom?
11 *Wilt* not *thou*, O God, *who* hast cast us off? and wilt not thou, O God, go forth with our hosts?
12 Give us help from trouble: for vain *is* the help of man.
13 Through God we shall do valiantly: for he *it is that* shall tread down our enemies.

Psalm 109

To the chief Musician,
A Psalm of David.

1 Hold not thy peace, O God of my praise;
2 For the mouth of the wicked and the mouth of the deceitful are opened against me: they have spoken against me with a lying tongue.
3 They compassed me about also with words of hatred; and fought against me without a cause.
4 For my love they are my adversaries: but I *give myself unto* prayer.
5 And they have rewarded me evil for good, and hatred for my love.
6 Set thou a wicked man over him: and let Satan stand at his right hand.
7 When he shall be judged, let him be condemned: and let his prayer become sin.
8 Let his days be few; *and* let another take his office.
9 Let his children be fatherless, and his wife a widow.
10 Let his children be continually vagabonds, and beg: let them seek *their bread* also out of their desolate places.
11 Let the extortioner catch all that he hath; and let the strangers spoil his labour.
12 Let there be none to extend mercy unto him: neither let there be any to favour his fatherless children.
13 Let his posterity be cut off; *and* in the generation following let their name be blotted out.
14 Let the iniquity of his fathers be remembered with the LORD; and let not the sin of his mother be blotted out.
15 Let them be before the LORD continually, that he may cut off the memory of them from the earth.
16 Because that he remembered not to shew mercy, but persecuted the poor and needy man, that he might even slay the broken in heart.
17 As he loved cursing, so let it come unto him: as he delighted not in blessing, so let it be far from him.
18 As he clothed himself with cursing like as with his garment, so let it come into his bowels like water, and like oil into his bones.
19 Let it be unto him as the garment *which* covereth him, and for a girdle wherewith he is girded continually.
20 *Let* this *be* the reward of mine adversaries from the LORD, and of them that speak evil against my soul.
21 But do thou for me, O GOD the Lord, for thy name's sake: because thy mercy *is* good, deliver thou me.
22 For I *am* poor and needy, and my heart is wounded within me.
23 I am gone like the shadow when it

declineth: I am tossed up and down as the
locust.
24 My knees are weak through fasting; and
my flesh faileth of fatness.
25 I became also a reproach unto them:
when they looked upon me they shaked
their heads.
26 Help me, O LORD my God: O save me
according to thy mercy:
27 That they may know that this *is* thy hand;
that thou, LORD, hast done it.
28 Let them curse, but bless thou: when
they arise, let them be ashamed; but let
thy servant rejoice.
29 Let mine adversaries be clothed with
shame, and let them cover themselves with
their own confusion, as with a mantle.
30 I will greatly praise the LORD with my
mouth; yea, I will praise him among the
multitude.
31 For he shall stand at the right hand of
the poor, to save *him* from those that condemn his soul.

Psalm 110

A Psalm of David.

1 The LORD said unto my Lord, Sit thou at
my right hand, until I make thine enemies
thy footstool.
2 The LORD shall send the rod of thy strength
out of Zion: rule thou in the midst of thine
enemies.
3 Thy people *shall be* willing in the day of
thy power, in the beauties of holiness from
the womb of the morning: thou hast the
dew of thy youth.
4 The LORD hath sworn, and will not repent,
Thou *art* a priest for ever after the order of
Melchizedek.
5 The Lord at thy right hand shall strike
through kings in the day of his wrath.
6 He shall judge among the heathen, he
shall fill *the places* with the dead bodies; he
shall wound the heads over many countries.
7 He shall drink of the brook in the way:
therefore shall he lift up the head.

Psalm 111

1 Praise ye the LORD. I will praise the LORD
with *my* whole heart, in the assembly of the
upright, and *in* the congregation.
2 The works of the LORD *are* great, sought
out of all them that have pleasure therein.
3 His work *is* honourable and glorious: and
his righteousness endureth for ever.
4 He hath made his wonderful works to be
remembered: the LORD *is* gracious and full
of compassion.
5 He hath given meat unto them that fear
him: he will ever be mindful of his covenant.
6 He hath shewed his people the power of
his works, that he may give them the heritage of the heathen.
7 The works of his hands *are* verity and
judgment; all his commandments *are* sure.
8 They stand fast for ever and ever, *and are*
done in truth and uprightness.
9 He sent redemption unto his people: he
hath commanded his covenant for ever:
holy and reverend *is* his name.
10 The fear of the LORD *is* the beginning
of wisdom: a good understanding have all
they that do *his commandments:* his praise
endureth for ever.

Psalm 112

1 Praise ye the LORD. Blessed *is* the man *that*
feareth the LORD, *that* delighteth greatly in
his commandments.
2 His seed shall be mighty upon earth: the
generation of the upright shall be blessed.
3 Wealth and riches *shall be* in his house:
and his righteousness endureth for ever.
4 Unto the upright there ariseth light in the
darkness: *he is* gracious, and full of compassion, and righteous.
5 A good man sheweth favour, and lendeth:
he will guide his affairs with discretion.
6 Surely he shall not be moved for ever: the
righteous shall be in everlasting remembrance.
7 He shall not be afraid of evil tidings: his
heart is fixed, trusting in the LORD.
8 His heart *is* established, he shall not
be afraid, until he see *his desire* upon his
enemies.
9 He hath dispersed, he hath given to the
poor; his righteousness endureth for ever;
his horn shall be exalted with honour.
10 The wicked shall see *it*, and be grieved;
he shall gnash with his teeth, and melt away:
the desire of the wicked shall perish.

Psalm 113

1 Praise ye the LORD. Praise, O ye servants
of the LORD, praise the name of the LORD.

2 Blessed be the name of the LORD from this
time forth and for evermore.
3 From the rising of the sun unto the going
down of the same the LORD's name *is* to
be praised.
4 The LORD *is* high above all nations, *and* his
glory above the heavens.
5 Who *is* like unto the LORD our God, who
dwelleth on high,
6 Who humbleth *himself* to behold *the
things that are* in heaven, and in the earth!
7 He raiseth up the poor out of the dust,
and lifteth the needy out of the dunghill;
8 That he may set *him* with princes, *even*
with the princes of his people.
9 He maketh the barren woman to keep
house, *and to be* a joyful mother of children.
Praise ye the LORD.

Psalm 114

1 When Israel went out of Egypt, the house
of Jacob from a people of strange language;
2 Judah was his sanctuary, *and* Israel his
dominion.
3 The sea saw *it*, and fled: Jordan was
driven back.
4 The mountains skipped like rams, *and* the
little hills like lambs.
5 What *ailed* thee, O thou sea, that thou
fleddest? thou Jordan, *that* thou wast
driven back?
6 Ye mountains, *that* ye skipped like rams;
and ye little hills, like lambs?
7 Tremble, thou earth, at the presence of the
Lord, at the presence of the God of Jacob;
8 Which turned the rock *into* a standing
water, the flint into a fountain of waters.

Psalm 115

1 Not unto us, O LORD, not unto us, but unto
thy name give glory, for thy mercy, *and* for
thy truth's sake.
2 Wherefore should the heathen say, Where
is now their God?
3 But our God *is* in the heavens: he hath
done whatsoever he hath pleased.
4 Their idols *are* silver and gold, the work
of men's hands.
5 They have mouths, but they speak not:
eyes have they, but they see not:
6 They have ears, but they hear not: noses
have they, but they smell not:
7 They have hands, but they handle not:
feet have they, but they walk not: neither
speak they through their throat.
8 They that make them are like unto them;
so is every one that trusteth in them.
9 O Israel, trust thou in the LORD: he *is* their
help and their shield.
10 O house of Aaron, trust in the LORD: he
is their help and their shield.
11 Ye that fear the LORD, trust in the LORD:
he *is* their help and their shield.
12 The LORD hath been mindful of us: he will
bless *us;* he will bless the house of Israel; he
will bless the house of Aaron.
13 He will bless them that fear the LORD,
both small and great.
14 The LORD shall increase you more and
more, you and your children.
15 Ye *are* blessed of the LORD which made
heaven and earth.
16 The heaven, *even* the heavens, *are* the
LORD's: but the earth hath he given to the
children of men.
17 The dead praise not the LORD, neither
any that go down into silence.
18 But we will bless the LORD from this time
forth and for evermore. Praise the LORD.

Psalm 116

1 I love the LORD, because he hath heard
my voice *and* my supplications.
2 Because he hath inclined his ear unto me,
therefore will I call upon *him* as long as I live.
3 The sorrows of death compassed me, and
the pains of hell gat hold upon me: I found
trouble and sorrow.
4 Then called I upon the name of the LORD;
O LORD, I beseech thee, deliver my soul.
5 Gracious *is* the LORD, and righteous; yea,
our God *is* merciful.
6 The LORD preserveth the simple: I was
brought low, and he helped me.
7 Return unto thy rest, O my soul; for the
LORD hath dealt bountifully with thee.
8 For thou hast delivered my soul from
death, mine eyes from tears, *and* my feet
from falling.
9 I will walk before the LORD in the land of
the living.
10 I believed, therefore have I spoken: I was
greatly afflicted:
11 I said in my haste, All men *are* liars.
12 What shall I render unto the LORD *for* all
his benefits toward me?

13 I will take the cup of salvation, and call upon the name of the LORD.

14 I will pay my vows unto the LORD now in the presence of all his people.

15 Precious in the sight of the LORD *is* the death of his saints.

16 O LORD, truly I *am* thy servant; I *am* thy servant, *and* the son of thine handmaid: thou hast loosed my bonds.

17 I will offer to thee the sacrifice of thanksgiving, and will call upon the name of the LORD.

18 I will pay my vows unto the LORD now in the presence of all his people,

19 In the courts of the LORD's house, in the midst of thee, O Jerusalem. Praise ye the LORD.

Psalm 117

1 O praise the LORD, all ye nations: praise him, all ye people.

2 For his merciful kindness is great toward us: and the truth of the LORD *endureth* for ever. Praise ye the LORD.

Psalm 118

1 O give thanks unto the LORD; for *he is* good: because his mercy *endureth* for ever.

2 Let Israel now say, that his mercy *endureth* for ever.

3 Let the house of Aaron now say, that his mercy *endureth* for ever.

4 Let them now that fear the LORD say, that his mercy *endureth* for ever.

5 I called upon the LORD in distress: the LORD answered me, *and set me* in a large place.

6 The LORD *is* on my side; I will not fear: what can man do unto me?

7 The LORD taketh my part with them that help me: therefore shall I see *my desire* upon them that hate me.

8 *It is* better to trust in the LORD than to put confidence in man.

9 *It is* better to trust in the LORD than to put confidence in princes.

10 All nations compassed me about: but in the name of the LORD will I destroy them.

11 They compassed me about; yea, they compassed me about: but in the name of the LORD I will destroy them.

12 They compassed me about like bees; they are quenched as the fire of thorns: for in the name of the LORD I will destroy them.

13 Thou hast thrust sore at me that I might fall: but the LORD helped me.

14 The LORD *is* my strength and song, and is become my salvation.

15 The voice of rejoicing and salvation *is* in the tabernacles of the righteous: the right hand of the LORD doeth valiantly.

16 The right hand of the LORD is exalted: the right hand of the LORD doeth valiantly.

17 I shall not die, but live, and declare the works of the LORD.

18 The LORD hath chastened me sore: but he hath not given me over unto death.

19 Open to me the gates of righteousness: I will go into them, *and* I will praise the LORD:

20 This gate of the LORD, into which the righteous shall enter.

21 I will praise thee: for thou hast heard me, and art become my salvation.

22 The stone *which* the builders refused is become the head *stone* of the corner.

23 This is the LORD's doing; it *is* marvellous in our eyes.

24 This *is* the day *which* the LORD hath made; we will rejoice and be glad in it.

25 Save now, I beseech thee, O LORD: O LORD, I beseech thee, send now prosperity.

26 Blessed *be* he that cometh in the name of the LORD: we have blessed you out of the house of the LORD.

27 God *is* the LORD, which hath shewed us light: bind the sacrifice with cords, *even* unto the horns of the altar.

28 Thou *art* my God, and I will praise thee: *thou art* my God, I will exalt thee.

29 O give thanks unto the LORD; for *he is* good: for his mercy *endureth* for ever.

Psalm 119

א ALEPH

1 Blessed *are* the undefiled in the way, who walk in the law of the LORD.

2 Blessed *are* they that keep his testimonies, *and that* seek him with the whole heart.

3 They also do no iniquity: they walk in his ways.

4 Thou hast commanded *us* to keep thy precepts diligently.

5 O that my ways were directed to keep thy statutes!

6 Then shall I not be ashamed, when I have respect unto all thy commandments.

7 I will praise thee with uprightness of heart,

when I shall have learned thy righteous judgments.
8 I will keep thy statutes: O forsake me not utterly.

ב BETH

9 Wherewithal shall a young man cleanse his way? by taking heed *thereto* according to thy word.
10 With my whole heart have I sought thee: O let me not wander from thy commandments.
11 Thy word have I hid in mine heart, that I might not sin against thee.
12 Blessed *art* thou, O LORD: teach me thy statutes.
13 With my lips have I declared all the judgments of thy mouth.
14 I have rejoiced in the way of thy testimonies, as *much as* in all riches.
15 I will meditate in thy precepts, and have respect unto thy ways.
16 I will delight myself in thy statutes: I will not forget thy word.

ג GIMEL

17 Deal bountifully with thy servant, *that* I may live, and keep thy word.
18 Open thou mine eyes, that I may behold wondrous things out of thy law.
19 I *am* a stranger in the earth: hide not thy commandments from me.
20 My soul breaketh for the longing *that it hath* unto thy judgments at all times.
21 Thou hast rebuked the proud *that are* cursed, which do err from thy commandments.
22 Remove from me reproach and contempt; for I have kept thy testimonies.
23 Princes also did sit *and* speak against me: *but* thy servant did meditate in thy statutes.
24 Thy testimonies also *are* my delight *and* my counsellers.

ד DALETH

25 My soul cleaveth unto the dust: quicken thou me according to thy word.
26 I have declared my ways, and thou heardest me: teach me thy statutes.
27 Make me to understand the way of thy precepts: so shall I talk of thy wondrous works.
28 My soul melteth for heaviness: strengthen thou me according unto thy word.
29 Remove from me the way of lying: and grant me thy law graciously.
30 I have chosen the way of truth: thy judgments have I laid *before me*.
31 I have stuck unto thy testimonies: O LORD, put me not to shame.
32 I will run the way of thy commandments, when thou shalt enlarge my heart.

ה HE

33 Teach me, O LORD, the way of thy statutes; and I shall keep it *unto* the end.
34 Give me understanding, and I shall keep thy law; yea, I shall observe it with *my* whole heart.
35 Make me to go in the path of thy commandments; for therein do I delight.
36 Incline my heart unto thy testimonies, and not to covetousness.
37 Turn away mine eyes from beholding vanity; *and* quicken thou me in thy way.
38 Stablish thy word unto thy servant, who *is devoted* to thy fear.
39 Turn away my reproach which I fear: for thy judgments *are* good.
40 Behold, I have longed after thy precepts: quicken me in thy righteousness.

ו VAU

41 Let thy mercies come also unto me, O LORD, *even* thy salvation, according to thy word.
42 So shall I have wherewith to answer him that reproacheth me: for I trust in thy word.
43 And take not the word of truth utterly out of my mouth; for I have hoped in thy judgments.
44 So shall I keep thy law continually for ever and ever.
45 And I will walk at liberty: for I seek thy precepts.
46 I will speak of thy testimonies also before kings, and will not be ashamed.
47 And I will delight myself in thy commandments, which I have loved.
48 My hands also will I lift up unto thy commandments, which I have loved; and I will meditate in thy statutes.

ז ZAIN

49 Remember the word unto thy servant, upon which thou hast caused me to hope.
50 This *is* my comfort in my affliction: for thy word hath quickened me.
51 The proud have had me greatly in derision: *yet* have I not declined from thy law.
52 I remembered thy judgments of old, O LORD; and have comforted myself.
53 Horror hath taken hold upon me because of the wicked that forsake thy law.
54 Thy statutes have been my songs in the house of my pilgrimage.
55 I have remembered thy name, O LORD, in the night, and have kept thy law.
56 This I had, because I kept thy precepts.

ח CHETH

57 *Thou art* my portion, O LORD: I have said that I would keep thy words.
58 I intreated thy favour with *my* whole heart: be merciful unto me according to thy word.
59 I thought on my ways, and turned my feet unto thy testimonies.
60 I made haste, and delayed not to keep thy commandments.
61 The bands of the wicked have robbed me: *but* I have not forgotten thy law.
62 At midnight I will rise to give thanks unto thee because of thy righteous judgments.
63 I *am* a companion of all *them* that fear thee, and of them that keep thy precepts.
64 The earth, O LORD, is full of thy mercy: teach me thy statutes.

ט TETH

65 Thou hast dealt well with thy servant, O LORD, according unto thy word.
66 Teach me good judgment and knowledge: for I have believed thy commandments.
67 Before I was afflicted I went astray: but now have I kept thy word.
68 Thou *art* good, and doest good; teach me thy statutes.
69 The proud have forged a lie against me: *but* I will keep thy precepts with *my* whole heart.
70 Their heart is as fat as grease; *but* I delight in thy law.
71 *It is* good for me that I have been afflicted; that I might learn thy statutes.
72 The law of thy mouth *is* better unto me than thousands of gold and silver.

י JOD

73 Thy hands have made me and fashioned me: give me understanding, that I may learn thy commandments.
74 They that fear thee will be glad when they see me; because I have hoped in thy word.
75 I know, O LORD, that thy judgments *are* right, and *that* thou in faithfulness hast afflicted me.
76 Let, I pray thee, thy merciful kindness be for my comfort, according to thy word unto thy servant.
77 Let thy tender mercies come unto me, that I may live: for thy law *is* my delight.
78 Let the proud be ashamed; for they dealt perversely with me without a cause: *but* I will meditate in thy precepts.
79 Let those that fear thee turn unto me, and those that have known thy testimonies.
80 Let my heart be sound in thy statutes; that I be not ashamed.

כ CAPH

81 My soul fainteth for thy salvation: *but* I hope in thy word.
82 Mine eyes fail for thy word, saying, When wilt thou comfort me?
83 For I am become like a bottle in the smoke; *yet* do I not forget thy statutes.
84 How many *are* the days of thy servant? when wilt thou execute judgment on them that persecute me?
85 The proud have digged pits for me, which *are* not after thy law.
86 All thy commandments *are* faithful: they persecute me wrongfully; help thou me.
87 They had almost consumed me upon earth; but I forsook not thy precepts.
88 Quicken me after thy lovingkindness; so shall I keep the testimony of thy mouth.

ל LAMED

89 For ever, O LORD, thy word is settled in heaven.
90 Thy faithfulness *is* unto all generations: thou hast established the earth, and it abideth.
91 They continue this day according to thine ordinances: for all *are* thy servants.

92 Unless thy law *had been* my delights, I should then have perished in mine affliction.
93 I will never forget thy precepts: for with them thou hast quickened me.
94 I *am* thine, save me; for I have sought thy precepts.
95 The wicked have waited for me to destroy me: *but* I will consider thy testimonies.
96 I have seen an end of all perfection: *but* thy commandment *is* exceeding broad.

מ MEM

97 O how love I thy law! it *is* my meditation all the day.
98 Thou through thy commandments hast made me wiser than mine enemies: for they *are* ever with me.
99 I have more understanding than all my teachers: for thy testimonies *are* my meditation.
100 I understand more than the ancients, because I keep thy precepts.
101 I have refrained my feet from every evil way, that I might keep thy word.
102 I have not departed from thy judgments: for thou hast taught me.
103 How sweet are thy words unto my taste! *yea, sweeter* than honey to my mouth!
104 Through thy precepts I get understanding: therefore I hate every false way.

נ NUN

105 Thy word *is* a lamp unto my feet, and a light unto my path.
106 I have sworn, and I will perform *it*, that I will keep thy righteous judgments.
107 I am afflicted very much: quicken me, O LORD, according unto thy word.
108 Accept, I beseech thee, the freewill offerings of my mouth, O LORD, and teach me thy judgments.
109 My soul *is* continually in my hand: yet do I not forget thy law.
110 The wicked have laid a snare for me: yet I erred not from thy precepts.
111 Thy testimonies have I taken as an heritage for ever: for they *are* the rejoicing of my heart.
112 I have inclined mine heart to perform thy statutes alway, *even unto* the end.

ס SAMECH

113 I hate *vain* thoughts: but thy law do I love.
114 Thou *art* my hiding place and my shield: I hope in thy word.
115 Depart from me, ye evildoers: for I will keep the commandments of my God.
116 Uphold me according unto thy word, that I may live: and let me not be ashamed of my hope.
117 Hold thou me up, and I shall be safe: and I will have respect unto thy statutes continually.
118 Thou hast trodden down all them that err from thy statutes: for their deceit *is* falsehood.
119 Thou puttest away all the wicked of the earth *like* dross: therefore I love thy testimonies.
120 My flesh trembleth for fear of thee; and I am afraid of thy judgments.

ע AIN

121 I have done judgment and justice: leave me not to mine oppressors.
122 Be surety for thy servant for good: let not the proud oppress me.
123 Mine eyes fail for thy salvation, and for the word of thy righteousness.
124 Deal with thy servant according unto thy mercy, and teach me thy statutes.
125 I *am* thy servant; give me understanding, that I may know thy testimonies.
126 *It is* time for *thee*, LORD, to work: *for* they have made void thy law.
127 Therefore I love thy commandments above gold; yea, above fine gold.
128 Therefore I esteem all *thy* precepts *concerning* all *things to be* right; *and* I hate every false way.

פ PE

129 Thy testimonies *are* wonderful: therefore doth my soul keep them.
130 The entrance of thy words giveth light; it giveth understanding unto the simple.
131 I opened my mouth, and panted: for I longed for thy commandments.
132 Look thou upon me, and be merciful unto me, as thou usest to do unto those that love thy name.

133 Order my steps in thy word: and let not any iniquity have dominion over me.
134 Deliver me from the oppression of man: so will I keep thy precepts.
135 Make thy face to shine upon thy servant; and teach me thy statutes.
136 Rivers of waters run down mine eyes, because they keep not thy law.

צ TZADDI

137 Righteous *art* thou, O LORD, and upright *are* thy judgments.
138 Thy testimonies *that* thou hast commanded *are* righteous and very faithful.
139 My zeal hath consumed me, because mine enemies have forgotten thy words.
140 Thy word *is* very pure: therefore thy servant loveth it.
141 I *am* small and despised: *yet* do not I forget thy precepts.
142 Thy righteousness *is* an everlasting righteousness, and thy law *is* the truth.
143 Trouble and anguish have taken hold on me: *yet* thy commandments *are* my delights.
144 The righteousness of thy testimonies *is* everlasting: give me understanding, and I shall live.

ק KOPH

145 I cried with *my* whole heart; hear me, O LORD: I will keep thy statutes.
146 I cried unto thee; save me, and I shall keep thy testimonies.
147 I prevented the dawning of the morning, and cried: I hoped in thy word.
148 Mine eyes prevent the *night* watches, that I might meditate in thy word.
149 Hear my voice according unto thy lovingkindness: O LORD, quicken me according to thy judgment.
150 They draw nigh that follow after mischief: they are far from thy law.
151 Thou *art* near, O LORD; and all thy commandments *are* truth.
152 Concerning thy testimonies, I have known of old that thou hast founded them for ever.

ר RESH

153 Consider mine affliction, and deliver me: for I do not forget thy law.
154 Plead my cause, and deliver me: quicken me according to thy word.
155 Salvation *is* far from the wicked: for they seek not thy statutes.
156 Great *are* thy tender mercies, O LORD: quicken me according to thy judgments.
157 Many *are* my persecutors and mine enemies; *yet* do I not decline from thy testimonies.
158 I beheld the transgressors, and was grieved; because they kept not thy word.
159 Consider how I love thy precepts: quicken me, O LORD, according to thy lovingkindness.
160 Thy word *is* true *from* the beginning: and every one of thy righteous judgments *endureth* for ever.

ש SCHIN

161 Princes have persecuted me without a cause: but my heart standeth in awe of thy word.
162 I rejoice at thy word, as one that findeth great spoil.
163 I hate and abhor lying: *but* thy law do I love.
164 Seven times a day do I praise thee because of thy righteous judgments.
165 Great peace have they which love thy law: and nothing shall offend them.
166 LORD, I have hoped for thy salvation, and done thy commandments.
167 My soul hath kept thy testimonies; and I love them exceedingly.
168 I have kept thy precepts and thy testimonies: for all my ways *are* before thee.

ת TAU

169 Let my cry come near before thee, O LORD: give me understanding according to thy word.
170 Let my supplication come before thee: deliver me according to thy word.
171 My lips shall utter praise, when thou hast taught me thy statutes.
172 My tongue shall speak of thy word: for all thy commandments *are* righteousness.
173 Let thine hand help me; for I have chosen thy precepts.
174 I have longed for thy salvation, O LORD; and thy law *is* my delight.

175 Let my soul live, and it shall praise thee; and let thy judgments help me.
176 I have gone astray like a lost sheep; seek thy servant; for I do not forget thy commandments.

Psalm 120

A Song of degrees.

1 In my distress I cried unto the LORD, and he heard me.
2 Deliver my soul, O LORD, from lying lips, *and* from a deceitful tongue.
3 What shall be given unto thee? or what shall be done unto thee, thou false tongue?
4 Sharp arrows of the mighty, with coals of juniper.
5 Woe is me, that I sojourn in Mesech, *that* I dwell in the tents of Kedar!
6 My soul hath long dwelt with him that hateth peace.
7 I *am for* peace: but when I speak, they *are* for war.

Psalm 121

A Song of degrees.

1 I will lift up mine eyes unto the hills, from whence cometh my help.
2 My help *cometh* from the LORD, which made heaven and earth.
3 He will not suffer thy foot to be moved: he that keepeth thee will not slumber.
4 Behold, he that keepeth Israel shall neither slumber nor sleep.
5 The LORD *is* thy keeper: the LORD *is* thy shade upon thy right hand.
6 The sun shall not smite thee by day, nor the moon by night.
7 The LORD shall preserve thee from all evil: he shall preserve thy soul.
8 The LORD shall preserve thy going out and thy coming in from this time forth, and even for evermore.

Psalm 122

A Song of degrees of David.

1 I was glad when they said unto me, Let us go into the house of the LORD.
2 Our feet shall stand within thy gates, O Jerusalem.
3 Jerusalem is builded as a city that is compact together:
4 Whither the tribes go up, the tribes of the LORD, unto the testimony of Israel, to give thanks unto the name of the LORD.
5 For there are set thrones of judgment, the thrones of the house of David.
6 Pray for the peace of Jerusalem: they shall prosper that love thee.
7 Peace be within thy walls, *and* prosperity within thy palaces.
8 For my brethren and companions' sakes, I will now say, Peace *be* within thee.
9 Because of the house of the LORD our God I will seek thy good.

Psalm 123

A Song of degrees.

1 Unto thee lift I up mine eyes, O thou that dwellest in the heavens.
2 Behold, as the eyes of servants *look* unto the hand of their masters, *and* as the eyes of a maiden unto the hand of her mistress; so our eyes *wait* upon the LORD our God, until that he have mercy upon us.
3 Have mercy upon us, O LORD, have mercy upon us: for we are exceedingly filled with contempt.
4 Our soul is exceedingly filled with the scorning of those that are at ease, *and* with the contempt of the proud.

Psalm 124

A Song of degrees of David.

1 If *it had* not *been* the LORD who was on our side, now may Israel say;
2 If *it had* not *been* the LORD who was on our side, when men rose up against us:
3 Then they had swallowed us up quick, when their wrath was kindled against us:
4 Then the waters had overwhelmed us, the stream had gone over our soul:
5 Then the proud waters had gone over our soul.
6 Blessed *be* the LORD, who hath not given us *as* a prey to their teeth.
7 Our soul is escaped as a bird out of the snare of the fowlers: the snare is broken, and we are escaped.
8 Our help *is* in the name of the LORD, who made heaven and earth.

Psalm 125

A Song of degrees.

1 They that trust in the LORD *shall be* as

mount Zion, *which* cannot be removed, *but*
abideth for ever.
2 *As* the mountains *are* round about Jerusalem, so the LORD *is* round about his people
from henceforth even for ever.
3 For the rod of the wicked shall not rest
upon the lot of the righteous; lest the righteous put forth their hands unto iniquity.
4 Do good, O LORD, unto *those that be* good,
and to *them that are* upright in their hearts.
5 As for such as turn aside unto their crooked
ways, the LORD shall lead them forth with
the workers of iniquity: *but* peace *shall be*
upon Israel.

Psalm 126

A Song of degrees.

1 When the LORD turned again the captivity of Zion, we were like them that dream.
2 Then was our mouth filled with laughter,
and our tongue with singing: then said they
among the heathen, The LORD hath done
great things for them.
3 The LORD hath done great things for us;
whereof we are glad.
4 Turn again our captivity, O LORD, as the
streams in the south.
5 They that sow in tears shall reap in joy.
6 He that goeth forth and weepeth, bearing
precious seed, shall doubtless come again
with rejoicing, bringing his sheaves *with him*.

Psalm 127

A Song of degrees for Solomon.

1 Except the LORD build the house, they
labour in vain that build it: except the LORD
keep the city, the watchman waketh *but*
in vain.
2 *It is* vain for you to rise up early, to sit up
late, to eat the bread of sorrows: *for* so he
giveth his beloved sleep.
3 Lo, children *are* an heritage of the LORD:
and the fruit of the womb *is his* reward.
4 As arrows *are* in the hand of a mighty man;
so *are* children of the youth.
5 Happy *is* the man that hath his quiver full
of them: they shall not be ashamed, but they
shall speak with the enemies in the gate.

Psalm 128

A Song of degrees.

1 Blessed *is* every one that feareth the LORD;
that walketh in his ways.
2 For thou shalt eat the labour of thine
hands: happy *shalt* thou *be*, and *it shall be*
well with thee.
3 Thy wife *shall be* as a fruitful vine by the
sides of thine house: thy children like olive
plants round about thy table.
4 Behold, that thus shall the man be blessed
that feareth the LORD.
5 The LORD shall bless thee out of Zion: and
thou shalt see the good of Jerusalem all the
days of thy life.
6 Yea, thou shalt see thy children's children,
and peace upon Israel.

Psalm 129

A Song of degrees.

1 Many a time have they afflicted me from
my youth, may Israel now say:
2 Many a time have they afflicted me from
my youth: yet they have not prevailed
against me.
3 The plowers plowed upon my back: they
made long their furrows.
4 The LORD *is* righteous: he hath cut asunder
the cords of the wicked.
5 Let them all be confounded and turned
back that hate Zion.
6 Let them be as the grass *upon* the housetops, which withereth afore it groweth up:
7 Wherewith the mower filleth not his hand;
nor he that bindeth sheaves his bosom.
8 Neither do they which go by say, The
blessing of the LORD *be* upon you: we bless
you in the name of the LORD.

Psalm 130

A Song of degrees.

1 Out of the depths have I cried unto thee,
O LORD.
2 Lord, hear my voice: let thine ears be
attentive to the voice of my supplications.
3 If thou, LORD, shouldest mark iniquities,
O Lord, who shall stand?
4 But *there is* forgiveness with thee, that
thou mayest be feared.
5 I wait for the LORD, my soul doth wait, and
in his word do I hope.
6 My soul *waiteth* for the Lord more than
they that watch for the morning: *I say, more*
than they that watch for the morning.
7 Let Israel hope in the LORD: for with the
LORD *there is* mercy, and with him *is* plenteous redemption.

8 And he shall redeem Israel from all his iniquities.

Psalm 131

A Song of degrees of David.

1 Lord, my heart is not haughty, nor mine eyes lofty: neither do I exercise myself in great matters, or in things too high for me.
2 Surely I have behaved and quieted myself, as a child that is weaned of his mother: my soul *is* even as a weaned child.
3 Let Israel hope in the LORD from henceforth and for ever.

Psalm 132

A Song of degrees.

1 Lord, remember David, *and* all his afflictions:
2 How he sware unto the LORD, *and* vowed unto the mighty *God* of Jacob;
3 Surely I will not come into the tabernacle of my house, nor go up into my bed;
4 I will not give sleep to mine eyes, *or* slumber to mine eyelids,
5 Until I find out a place for the LORD, an habitation for the mighty *God* of Jacob.
6 Lo, we heard of it at Ephratah: we found it in the fields of the wood.
7 We will go into his tabernacles: we will worship at his footstool.
8 Arise, O LORD, into thy rest; thou, and the ark of thy strength.
9 Let thy priests be clothed with righteousness; and let thy saints shout for joy.
10 For thy servant David's sake turn not away the face of thine anointed.
11 The LORD hath sworn *in* truth unto David; he will not turn from it; Of the fruit of thy body will I set upon thy throne.
12 If thy children will keep my covenant and my testimony that I shall teach them, their children shall also sit upon thy throne for evermore.
13 For the LORD hath chosen Zion; he hath desired *it* for his habitation.
14 This *is* my rest for ever: here will I dwell; for I have desired it.
15 I will abundantly bless her provision: I will satisfy her poor with bread.
16 I will also clothe her priests with salvation: and her saints shall shout aloud for joy.
17 There will I make the horn of David to bud: I have ordained a lamp for mine anointed.
18 His enemies will I clothe with shame: but upon himself shall his crown flourish.

Psalm 133

A Song of degrees of David.

1 Behold, how good and how pleasant *it is* for brethren to dwell together in unity!
2 *It is* like the precious ointment upon the head, that ran down upon the beard, *even* Aaron's beard: that went down to the skirts of his garments;
3 As the dew of Hermon, *and as the dew* that descended upon the mountains of Zion: for there the LORD commanded the blessing, *even* life for evermore.

Psalm 134

A Song of degrees.

1 Behold, bless ye the LORD, all *ye* servants of the LORD, which by night stand in the house of the LORD.
2 Lift up your hands *in* the sanctuary, and bless the LORD.
3 The LORD that made heaven and earth bless thee out of Zion.

Psalm 135

1 Praise ye the LORD. Praise ye the name of the LORD; praise *him*, O ye servants of the LORD.
2 Ye that stand in the house of the LORD, in the courts of the house of our God,
3 Praise the LORD; for the LORD *is* good: sing praises unto his name; for *it is* pleasant.
4 For the LORD hath chosen Jacob unto himself, *and* Israel for his peculiar treasure.
5 For I know that the LORD *is* great, and *that* our Lord *is* above all gods.
6 Whatsoever the LORD pleased, *that* did he in heaven, and in earth, in the seas, and all deep places.
7 He causeth the vapours to ascend from the ends of the earth; he maketh lightnings for the rain; he bringeth the wind out of his treasuries.
8 Who smote the firstborn of Egypt, both of man and beast.
9 *Who* sent tokens and wonders into the midst of thee, O Egypt, upon Pharaoh, and upon all his servants.

10 Who smote great nations, and slew
mighty kings;
11 Sihon king of the Amorites, and Og king
of Bashan, and all the kingdoms of Canaan:
12 And gave their land *for* an heritage, an
heritage unto Israel his people.
13 Thy name, O LORD, *endureth* for ever;
and thy memorial, O LORD, throughout all
generations.
14 For the LORD will judge his people, and he
will repent himself concerning his servants.
15 The idols of the heathen *are* silver and
gold, the work of men's hands.
16 They have mouths, but they speak not;
eyes have they, but they see not;
17 They have ears, but they hear not; neither
is there *any* breath in their mouths.
18 They that make them are like unto them:
so is every one that trusteth in them.
19 Bless the LORD, O house of Israel: bless
the LORD, O house of Aaron:
20 Bless the LORD, O house of Levi: ye that
fear the LORD, bless the LORD.
21 Blessed be the LORD out of Zion, which
dwelleth at Jerusalem. Praise ye the LORD.

Psalm 136

1 O give thanks unto the LORD; for *he is*
good: for his mercy *endureth* for ever.
2 O give thanks unto the God of gods: for
his mercy *endureth* for ever.
3 O give thanks to the Lord of lords: for his
mercy *endureth* for ever.
4 To him who alone doeth great wonders:
for his mercy *endureth* for ever.
5 To him that by wisdom made the heavens:
for his mercy *endureth* for ever.
6 To him that stretched out the earth above
the waters: for his mercy *endureth* for ever.
7 To him that made great lights: for his
mercy *endureth* for ever:
8 The sun to rule by day: for his mercy
endureth for ever:
9 The moon and stars to rule by night: for
his mercy *endureth* for ever.
10 To him that smote Egypt in their firstborn:
for his mercy *endureth* for ever:
11 And brought out Israel from among them:
for his mercy *endureth* for ever:
12 With a strong hand, and with a stretched
out arm: for his mercy *endureth* for ever.
13 To him which divided the Red sea into
parts: for his mercy *endureth* for ever:
14 And made Israel to pass through the
midst of it: for his mercy *endureth* for ever:
15 But overthrew Pharaoh and his host in
the Red sea: for his mercy *endureth* for ever.
16 To him which led his people through the
wilderness: for his mercy *endureth* for ever.
17 To him which smote great kings: for his
mercy *endureth* for ever:
18 And slew famous kings: for his mercy
endureth for ever:
19 Sihon king of the Amorites: for his mercy
endureth for ever:
20 And Og the king of Bashan: for his mercy
endureth for ever:
21 And gave their land for an heritage: for
his mercy *endureth* for ever:
22 *Even* an heritage unto Israel his servant:
for his mercy *endureth* for ever.
23 Who remembered us in our low estate:
for his mercy *endureth* for ever:
24 And hath redeemed us from our enemies: for his mercy *endureth* for ever.
25 Who giveth food to all flesh: for his mercy
endureth for ever.
26 O give thanks unto the God of heaven:
for his mercy *endureth* for ever.

Psalm 137

1 By the rivers of Babylon, there we sat
down, yea, we wept, when we remembered Zion.
2 We hanged our harps upon the willows in
the midst thereof.
3 For there they that carried us away captive
required of us a song; and they that wasted
us *required of us* mirth, *saying*, Sing us *one*
of the songs of Zion.
4 How shall we sing the LORD's song in a
strange land?
5 If I forget thee, O Jerusalem, let my right
hand forget *her cunning*.
6 If I do not remember thee, let my tongue
cleave to the roof of my mouth; if I prefer
not Jerusalem above my chief joy.
7 Remember, O LORD, the children of Edom
in the day of Jerusalem; who said, Rase *it*,
rase *it*, *even* to the foundation thereof.
8 O daughter of Babylon, who art to be
destroyed; happy *shall he be*, that rewardeth
thee as thou hast served us.
9 Happy *shall he be*, that taketh and dasheth
thy little ones against the stones.

Psalm 138

A Psalm of David.

1 I will praise thee with my whole heart:
before the gods will I sing praise unto thee.
2 I will worship toward thy holy temple, and
praise thy name for thy lovingkindness and
for thy truth: for thou hast magnified thy
word above all thy name.
3 In the day when I cried thou answeredst
me, *and* strengthenedst me *with* strength
in my soul.
4 All the kings of the earth shall praise thee,
O LORD, when they hear the words of thy
mouth.
5 Yea, they shall sing in the ways of the LORD:
for great *is* the glory of the LORD.
6 Though the LORD *be* high, yet hath he
respect unto the lowly: but the proud he
knoweth afar off.
7 Though I walk in the midst of trouble, thou
wilt revive me: thou shalt stretch forth thine
hand against the wrath of mine enemies,
and thy right hand shall save me.
8 The LORD will perfect *that which* concerneth me: thy mercy, O LORD, *endureth* for
ever: forsake not the works of thine own
hands.

Psalm 139

To the chief Musician,
A Psalm of David.

1 O Lord, thou hast searched me, and
known *me*.
2 Thou knowest my downsitting and mine
uprising, thou understandest my thought
afar off.
3 Thou compassest my path and my lying
down, and art acquainted *with* all my ways.
4 For *there is* not a word in my tongue, *but*,
lo, O LORD, thou knowest it altogether.
5 Thou hast beset me behind and before,
and laid thine hand upon me.
6 *Such* knowledge *is* too wonderful for me;
it is high, I cannot *attain* unto it.
7 Whither shall I go from thy spirit? or
whither shall I flee from thy presence?
8 If I ascend up into heaven, thou *art* there: if
I make my bed in hell, behold, thou *art there.*
9 *If* I take the wings of the morning, *and*
dwell in the uttermost parts of the sea;
10 Even there shall thy hand lead me, and
thy right hand shall hold me.
11 If I say, Surely the darkness shall cover
me; even the night shall be light about me.
12 Yea, the darkness hideth not from thee;
but the night shineth as the day: the darkness and the light *are* both alike *to thee.*
13 For thou hast possessed my reins: thou
hast covered me in my mother's womb.
14 I will praise thee; for I am fearfully *and*
wonderfully made: marvellous *are* thy
works; and *that* my soul knoweth right well.
15 My substance was not hid from thee,
when I was made in secret, *and* curiously
wrought in the lowest parts of the earth.
16 Thine eyes did see my substance, yet
being unperfect; and in thy book all *my*
members were written, *which* in continuance were fashioned, when *as yet there*
was none of them.
17 How precious also are thy thoughts unto
me, O God! how great is the sum of them!
18 *If* I should count them, they are more in
number than the sand: when I awake, I am
still with thee.
19 Surely thou wilt slay the wicked, O God:
depart from me therefore, ye bloody men.
20 For they speak against thee wickedly,
and thine enemies take *thy name* in vain.
21 Do not I hate them, O LORD, that hate
thee? and am not I grieved with those that
rise up against thee?
22 I hate them with perfect hatred: I count
them mine enemies.
23 Search me, O God, and know my heart:
try me, and know my thoughts:
24 And see if *there be any* wicked way in me,
and lead me in the way everlasting.

Psalm 140

To the chief Musician,
A Psalm of David.

1 Deliver me, O LORD, from the evil man:
preserve me from the violent man;
2 Which imagine mischiefs in *their* heart;
continually are they gathered together
for war.
3 They have sharpened their tongues like
a serpent; adders' poison *is* under their
lips. Selah.
4 Keep me, O LORD, from the hands of the
wicked; preserve me from the violent man;
who have purposed to overthrow my goings.
5 The proud have hid a snare for me, and

cords; they have spread a net by the wayside; they have set gins for me. Selah.
6 I said unto the LORD, Thou *art* my God:
hear the voice of my supplications, O LORD.
7 O GOD the Lord, the strength of my salvation, thou hast covered my head in the
day of battle.
8 Grant not, O LORD, the desires of the
wicked: further not his wicked device; *lest*
they exalt themselves. Selah.
9 *As for* the head of those that compass
me about, let the mischief of their own lips
cover them.
10 Let burning coals fall upon them: let them
be cast into the fire; into deep pits, that they
rise not up again.
11 Let not an evil speaker be established in
the earth: evil shall hunt the violent man to
overthrow *him*.
12 I know that the LORD will maintain the
cause of the afflicted, *and* the right of the
poor.
13 Surely the righteous shall give thanks
unto thy name: the upright shall dwell in
thy presence.

Psalm 141

A Psalm of David.

1 Lord, I cry unto thee: make haste unto me;
give ear unto my voice, when I cry unto thee.
2 Let my prayer be set forth before thee *as*
incense; *and* the lifting up of my hands *as*
the evening sacrifice.
3 Set a watch, O LORD, before my mouth;
keep the door of my lips.
4 Incline not my heart to *any* evil thing, to
practise wicked works with men that work
iniquity: and let me not eat of their dainties.
5 Let the righteous smite me; *it shall be* a
kindness: and let him reprove me; *it shall
be* an excellent oil, *which* shall not break
my head: for yet my prayer also *shall be* in
their calamities.
6 When their judges are overthrown in
stony places, they shall hear my words; for
they are sweet.
7 Our bones are scattered at the grave's
mouth, as when one cutteth and cleaveth
wood upon the earth.
8 But mine eyes *are* unto thee, O GOD the
Lord: in thee is my trust; leave not my soul
destitute.
9 Keep me from the snares *which* they have
laid for me, and the gins of the workers of
iniquity.
10 Let the wicked fall into their own nets,
whilst that I withal escape.

Psalm 142

*Maschil of David; A Prayer
when he was in the cave.*

1 I cried unto the LORD with my voice; with
my voice unto the LORD did I make my
supplication.
2 I poured out my complaint before him; I
shewed before him my trouble.
3 When my spirit was overwhelmed within
me, then thou knewest my path. In the way
wherein I walked have they privily laid a
snare for me.
4 I looked on *my* right hand, and beheld,
but *there was* no man that would know me:
refuge failed me; no man cared for my soul.
5 I cried unto thee, O LORD: I said, Thou
art my refuge *and* my portion in the land
of the living.
6 Attend unto my cry; for I am brought very
low: deliver me from my persecutors; for
they are stronger than I.
7 Bring my soul out of prison, that I may
praise thy name: the righteous shall compass me about; for thou shalt deal bountifully with me.

Psalm 143

A Psalm of David.

1 Hear my prayer, O LORD, give ear to my
supplications: in thy faithfulness answer me,
and in thy righteousness.
2 And enter not into judgment with thy
servant: for in thy sight shall no man living
be justified.
3 For the enemy hath persecuted my soul;
he hath smitten my life down to the ground;
he hath made me to dwell in darkness, as
those that have been long dead.
4 Therefore is my spirit overwhelmed within
me; my heart within me is desolate.
5 I remember the days of old; I meditate
on all thy works; I muse on the work of
thy hands.
6 I stretch forth my hands unto thee: my soul
thirsteth after thee, as a thirsty land. Selah.
7 Hear me speedily, O LORD: my spirit faileth:
hide not thy face from me, lest I be like unto
them that go down into the pit.

8 Cause me to hear thy lovingkindness in the morning; for in thee do I trust: cause me to know the way wherein I should walk; for I lift up my soul unto thee.

9 Deliver me, O LORD, from mine enemies: I flee unto thee to hide me.

10 Teach me to do thy will; for thou *art* my God: thy spirit *is* good; lead me into the land of uprightness.

11 Quicken me, O LORD, for thy name's sake: for thy righteousness' sake bring my soul out of trouble.

12 And of thy mercy cut off mine enemies, and destroy all them that afflict my soul: for I *am* thy servant.

Psalm 144

A Psalm of David.

1 Blessed *be* the LORD my strength, which teacheth my hands to war, *and* my fingers to fight:

2 My goodness, and my fortress; my high tower, and my deliverer; my shield, and *he* in whom I trust; who subdueth my people under me.

3 LORD, what *is* man, that thou takest knowledge of him! *or* the son of man, that thou makest account of him!

4 Man is like to vanity: his days *are* as a shadow that passeth away.

5 Bow thy heavens, O LORD, and come down: touch the mountains, and they shall smoke.

6 Cast forth lightning, and scatter them: shoot out thine arrows, and destroy them.

7 Send thine hand from above; rid me, and deliver me out of great waters, from the hand of strange children;

8 Whose mouth speaketh vanity, and their right hand *is* a right hand of falsehood.

9 I will sing a new song unto thee, O God: upon a psaltery *and* an instrument of ten strings will I sing praises unto thee.

10 *It is he* that giveth salvation unto kings: who delivereth David his servant from the hurtful sword.

11 Rid me, and deliver me from the hand of strange children, whose mouth speaketh vanity, and their right hand *is* a right hand of falsehood:

12 That our sons *may be* as plants grown up in their youth; *that* our daughters *may be* as corner stones, polished *after* the similitude of a palace:

13 *That* our garners *may be* full, affording all manner of store: *that* our sheep may bring forth thousands and ten thousands in our streets:

14 *That* our oxen *may be* strong to labour; *that there be* no breaking in, nor going out; that *there be* no complaining in our streets.

15 Happy *is that* people, that is in such a case: *yea*, happy *is that* people, whose God *is* the LORD.

Psalm 145

David's Psalm of praise.

1 I will extol thee, my God, O king; and I will bless thy name for ever and ever.

2 Every day will I bless thee; and I will praise thy name for ever and ever.

3 Great *is* the LORD, and greatly to be praised; and his greatness *is* unsearchable.

4 One generation shall praise thy works to another, and shall declare thy mighty acts.

5 I will speak of the glorious honour of thy majesty, and of thy wondrous works.

6 And *men* shall speak of the might of thy terrible acts: and I will declare thy greatness.

7 They shall abundantly utter the memory of thy great goodness, and shall sing of thy righteousness.

8 The LORD *is* gracious, and full of compassion; slow to anger, and of great mercy.

9 The LORD *is* good to all: and his tender mercies *are* over all his works.

10 All thy works shall praise thee, O LORD; and thy saints shall bless thee.

11 They shall speak of the glory of thy kingdom, and talk of thy power;

12 To make known to the sons of men his mighty acts, and the glorious majesty of his kingdom.

13 Thy kingdom *is* an everlasting kingdom, and thy dominion *endureth* throughout all generations.

14 The LORD upholdeth all that fall, and raiseth up all *those that be* bowed down.

15 The eyes of all wait upon thee; and thou givest them their meat in due season.

16 Thou openest thine hand, and satisfiest the desire of every living thing.

17 The LORD *is* righteous in all his ways, and holy in all his works.

18 The LORD *is* nigh unto all them that call upon him, to all that call upon him in truth.

19 He will fulfil the desire of them that fear

him: he also will hear their cry, and will save them.

20 The LORD preserveth all them that love him: but all the wicked will he destroy.

21 My mouth shall speak the praise of the LORD: and let all flesh bless his holy name for ever and ever.

Psalm 146

1 Praise ye the LORD. Praise the LORD, O my soul.

2 While I live will I praise the LORD: I will sing praises unto my God while I have any being.

3 Put not your trust in princes, *nor* in the son of man, in whom *there is* no help.

4 His breath goeth forth, he returneth to his earth; in that very day his thoughts perish.

5 Happy *is he* that *hath* the God of Jacob for his help, whose hope *is* in the LORD his God:

6 Which made heaven, and earth, the sea, and all that therein *is:* which keepeth truth for ever:

7 Which executeth judgment for the oppressed: which giveth food to the hungry. The LORD looseth the prisoners:

8 The LORD openeth *the eyes of* the blind: the LORD raiseth them that are bowed down: the LORD loveth the righteous:

9 The LORD preserveth the strangers; he relieveth the fatherless and widow: but the way of the wicked he turneth upside down.

10 The LORD shall reign for ever, *even* thy God, O Zion, unto all generations. Praise ye the LORD.

Psalm 147

1 Praise ye the LORD: for *it is* good to sing praises unto our God; for *it is* pleasant; *and* praise is comely.

2 The LORD doth build up Jerusalem: he gathereth together the outcasts of Israel.

3 He healeth the broken in heart, and bindeth up their wounds.

4 He telleth the number of the stars; he calleth them all by *their* names.

5 Great *is* our Lord, and of great power: his understanding *is* infinite.

6 The LORD lifteth up the meek: he casteth the wicked down to the ground.

7 Sing unto the LORD with thanksgiving; sing praise upon the harp unto our God:

8 Who covereth the heaven with clouds, who prepareth rain for the earth, who maketh grass to grow upon the mountains.

9 He giveth to the beast his food, *and* to the young ravens which cry.

10 He delighteth not in the strength of the horse: he taketh not pleasure in the legs of a man.

11 The LORD taketh pleasure in them that fear him, in those that hope in his mercy.

12 Praise the LORD, O Jerusalem; praise thy God, O Zion.

13 For he hath strengthened the bars of thy gates; he hath blessed thy children within thee.

14 He maketh peace *in* thy borders, *and* filleth thee with the finest of the wheat.

15 He sendeth forth his commandment *upon* earth: his word runneth very swiftly.

16 He giveth snow like wool: he scattereth the hoarfrost like ashes.

17 He casteth forth his ice like morsels: who can stand before his cold?

18 He sendeth out his word, and melteth them: he causeth his wind to blow, *and* the waters flow.

19 He sheweth his word unto Jacob, his statutes and his judgments unto Israel.

20 He hath not dealt so with any nation: and *as for his* judgments, they have not known them. Praise ye the LORD.

Psalm 148

1 Praise ye the LORD. Praise ye the LORD from the heavens: praise him in the heights.

2 Praise ye him, all his angels: praise ye him, all his hosts.

3 Praise ye him, sun and moon: praise him, all ye stars of light.

4 Praise him, ye heavens of heavens, and ye waters that *be* above the heavens.

5 Let them praise the name of the LORD: for he commanded, and they were created.

6 He hath also stablished them for ever and ever: he hath made a decree which shall not pass.

7 Praise the LORD from the earth, ye dragons, and all deeps:

8 Fire, and hail; snow, and vapour; stormy wind fulfilling his word:

9 Mountains, and all hills; fruitful trees, and all cedars:

10 Beasts, and all cattle; creeping things, and flying fowl:

11 Kings of the earth, and all people; princes,
and all judges of the earth:
12 Both young men, and maidens; old men,
and children:
13 Let them praise the name of the LORD:
for his name alone is excellent; his glory *is*
above the earth and heaven.
14 He also exalteth the horn of his people, the praise of all his saints; *even* of the
children of Israel, a people near unto him.
Praise ye the LORD.

Psalm 149

1 Praise ye the LORD. Sing unto the LORD a
new song, *and* his praise in the congregation of saints.
2 Let Israel rejoice in him that made him: let
the children of Zion be joyful in their King.
3 Let them praise his name in the dance:
let them sing praises unto him with the
timbrel and harp.
4 For the LORD taketh pleasure in his people:
he will beautify the meek with salvation.
5 Let the saints be joyful in glory: let them
sing aloud upon their beds.
6 *Let* the high *praises* of God *be* in their
mouth, and a twoedged sword in their hand;
7 To execute vengeance upon the heathen,
and punishments upon the people;
8 To bind their kings with chains, and their
nobles with fetters of iron;
9 To execute upon them the judgment written: this honour have all his saints. Praise
ye the LORD.

Psalm 150

1 Praise ye the LORD. Praise God in his
sanctuary: praise him in the firmament of
his power.
2 Praise him for his mighty acts: praise him
according to his excellent greatness.
3 Praise him with the sound of the trumpet:
praise him with the psaltery and harp.
4 Praise him with the timbrel and dance:
praise him with stringed instruments and
organs.
5 Praise him upon the loud cymbals: praise
him upon the high sounding cymbals.
6 Let every thing that hath breath praise
the LORD. Praise ye the LORD.

The Proverbs

Proverbs 1

1 The proverbs of Solomon the son of David,
king of Israel;
2 To know wisdom and instruction; to perceive the words of understanding;
3 To receive the instruction of wisdom, justice, and judgment, and equity;
4 To give subtilty to the simple, to the young
man knowledge and discretion.
5 A wise *man* will hear, and will increase
learning; and a man of understanding shall
attain unto wise counsels:
6 To understand a proverb, and the interpretation; the words of the wise, and their
dark sayings.
7 ¶ The fear of the LORD *is* the beginning of
knowledge: *but* fools despise wisdom and
instruction.
8 My son, hear the instruction of thy father,
and forsake not the law of thy mother:
9 For they *shall be* an ornament of grace
unto thy head, and chains about thy neck.
10 ¶ My son, if sinners entice thee, consent
thou not.
11 If they say, Come with us, let us lay wait
for blood, let us lurk privily for the innocent
without cause:
12 Let us swallow them up alive as the
grave; and whole, as those that go down
into the pit:
13 We shall find all precious substance, we
shall fill our houses with spoil:
14 Cast in thy lot among us; let us all have
one purse:
15 My son, walk not thou in the way with
them; refrain thy foot from their path:

16 For their feet run to evil, and make haste to shed blood.
17 Surely in vain the net is spread in the sight of any bird.
18 And they lay wait for their *own* blood; they lurk privily for their *own* lives.
19 So *are* the ways of every one that is greedy of gain; *which* taketh away the life of the owners thereof.
20 ¶ Wisdom crieth without; she uttereth her voice in the streets:
21 She crieth in the chief place of concourse, in the openings of the gates: in the city she uttereth her words, *saying*,
22 How long, ye simple ones, will ye love simplicity? and the scorners delight in their scorning, and fools hate knowledge?
23 Turn you at my reproof: behold, I will pour out my spirit unto you, I will make known my words unto you.
24 ¶ Because I have called, and ye refused; I have stretched out my hand, and no man regarded;
25 But ye have set at nought all my counsel, and would none of my reproof:
26 I also will laugh at your calamity; I will mock when your fear cometh;
27 When your fear cometh as desolation, and your destruction cometh as a whirlwind; when distress and anguish cometh upon you.
28 Then shall they call upon me, but I will not answer; they shall seek me early, but they shall not find me:
29 For that they hated knowledge, and did not choose the fear of the LORD:
30 They would none of my counsel: they despised all my reproof.
31 Therefore shall they eat of the fruit of their own way, and be filled with their own devices.
32 For the turning away of the simple shall slay them, and the prosperity of fools shall destroy them.
33 But whoso hearkeneth unto me shall dwell safely, and shall be quiet from fear of evil.

Proverbs 2

1 My son, if thou wilt receive my words, and hide my commandments with thee;
2 So that thou incline thine ear unto wisdom, *and* apply thine heart to understanding;
3 Yea, if thou criest after knowledge, *and* liftest up thy voice for understanding;
4 If thou seekest her as silver, and searchest for her as *for* hid treasures;
5 Then shalt thou understand the fear of the LORD, and find the knowledge of God.
6 For the LORD giveth wisdom: out of his mouth *cometh* knowledge and understanding.
7 He layeth up sound wisdom for the righteous: *he is* a buckler to them that walk uprightly.
8 He keepeth the paths of judgment, and preserveth the way of his saints.
9 Then shalt thou understand righteousness, and judgment, and equity; *yea*, every good path.
10 ¶ When wisdom entereth into thine heart, and knowledge is pleasant unto thy soul;
11 Discretion shall preserve thee, understanding shall keep thee:
12 To deliver thee from the way of the evil *man*, from the man that speaketh froward things;
13 Who leave the paths of uprightness, to walk in the ways of darkness;
14 Who rejoice to do evil, *and* delight in the frowardness of the wicked;
15 Whose ways *are* crooked, and *they* froward in their paths:
16 To deliver thee from the strange woman, *even* from the stranger *which* flattereth with her words;
17 Which forsaketh the guide of her youth, and forgetteth the covenant of her God.
18 For her house inclineth unto death, and her paths unto the dead.
19 None that go unto her return again, neither take they hold of the paths of life.
20 That thou mayest walk in the way of good *men*, and keep the paths of the righteous.
21 For the upright shall dwell in the land, and the perfect shall remain in it.
22 But the wicked shall be cut off from the earth, and the transgressors shall be rooted out of it.

Proverbs 3

1 My son, forget not my law; but let thine heart keep my commandments:
2 For length of days, and long life, and peace, shall they add to thee.

3 Let not mercy and truth forsake thee: bind them about thy neck; write them upon the table of thine heart:

4 So shalt thou find favour and good understanding in the sight of God and man.

5 ¶ Trust in the LORD with all thine heart; and lean not unto thine own understanding.

6 In all thy ways acknowledge him, and he shall direct thy paths.

7 ¶ Be not wise in thine own eyes: fear the LORD, and depart from evil.

8 It shall be health to thy navel, and marrow to thy bones.

9 Honour the LORD with thy substance, and with the firstfruits of all thine increase:

10 So shall thy barns be filled with plenty, and thy presses shall burst out with new wine.

11 ¶ My son, despise not the chastening of the LORD; neither be weary of his correction:

12 For whom the LORD loveth he correcteth; even as a father the son *in whom* he delighteth.

13 ¶ Happy *is* the man *that* findeth wisdom, and the man *that* getteth understanding.

14 For the merchandise of it *is* better than the merchandise of silver, and the gain thereof than fine gold.

15 She *is* more precious than rubies: and all the things thou canst desire are not to be compared unto her.

16 Length of days *is* in her right hand; *and* in her left hand riches and honour.

17 Her ways *are* ways of pleasantness, and all her paths *are* peace.

18 She *is* a tree of life to them that lay hold upon her: and happy *is every one* that retaineth her.

19 The LORD by wisdom hath founded the earth; by understanding hath he established the heavens.

20 By his knowledge the depths are broken up, and the clouds drop down the dew.

21 ¶ My son, let not them depart from thine eyes: keep sound wisdom and discretion:

22 So shall they be life unto thy soul, and grace to thy neck.

23 Then shalt thou walk in thy way safely, and thy foot shall not stumble.

24 When thou liest down, thou shalt not be afraid: yea, thou shalt lie down, and thy sleep shall be sweet.

25 Be not afraid of sudden fear, neither of the desolation of the wicked, when it cometh.

26 For the LORD shall be thy confidence, and shall keep thy foot from being taken.

27 ¶ Withhold not good from them to whom it is due, when it is in the power of thine hand to do *it*.

28 Say not unto thy neighbour, Go, and come again, and to morrow I will give; when thou hast it by thee.

29 Devise not evil against thy neighbour, seeing he dwelleth securely by thee.

30 ¶ Strive not with a man without cause, if he have done thee no harm.

31 ¶ Envy thou not the oppressor, and choose none of his ways.

32 For the froward *is* abomination to the LORD: but his secret *is* with the righteous.

33 ¶ The curse of the LORD *is* in the house of the wicked: but he blesseth the habitation of the just.

34 Surely he scorneth the scorners: but he giveth grace unto the lowly.

35 The wise shall inherit glory: but shame shall be the promotion of fools.

Proverbs 4

1 Hear, ye children, the instruction of a father, and attend to know understanding.

2 For I give you good doctrine, forsake ye not my law.

3 For I was my father's son, tender and only *beloved* in the sight of my mother.

4 He taught me also, and said unto me, Let thine heart retain my words: keep my commandments, and live.

5 Get wisdom, get understanding: forget *it* not; neither decline from the words of my mouth.

6 Forsake her not, and she shall preserve thee: love her, and she shall keep thee.

7 Wisdom *is* the principal thing; *therefore* get wisdom: and with all thy getting get understanding.

8 Exalt her, and she shall promote thee: she shall bring thee to honour, when thou dost embrace her.

9 She shall give to thine head an ornament of grace: a crown of glory shall she deliver to thee.

10 Hear, O my son, and receive my sayings; and the years of thy life shall be many.

11 I have taught thee in the way of wisdom;
I have led thee in right paths.
12 When thou goest, thy steps shall not be
straitened; and when thou runnest, thou
shalt not stumble.
13 Take fast hold of instruction; let *her* not
go: keep her; for she *is* thy life.
14 ¶ Enter not into the path of the wicked,
and go not in the way of evil *men*.
15 Avoid it, pass not by it, turn from it, and
pass away.
16 For they sleep not, except they have
done mischief; and their sleep is taken away,
unless they cause *some* to fall.
17 For they eat the bread of wickedness,
and drink the wine of violence.
18 But the path of the just *is* as the shining
light, that shineth more and more unto the
perfect day.
19 The way of the wicked *is* as darkness:
they know not at what they stumble.
20 ¶ My son, attend to my words; incline
thine ear unto my sayings.
21 Let them not depart from thine eyes;
keep them in the midst of thine heart.
22 For they *are* life unto those that find
them, and health to all their flesh.
23 ¶ Keep thy heart with all diligence; for
out of it *are* the issues of life.
24 Put away from thee a froward mouth,
and perverse lips put far from thee.
25 Let thine eyes look right on, and let thine
eyelids look straight before thee.
26 Ponder the path of thy feet, and let all
thy ways be established.
27 Turn not to the right hand nor to the left:
remove thy foot from evil.

Proverbs 5

1 My son, attend unto my wisdom, *and* bow
thine ear to my understanding:
2 That thou mayest regard discretion, and
that thy lips may keep knowledge.
3 ¶ For the lips of a strange woman drop *as*
an honeycomb, and her mouth *is* smoother
than oil:
4 But her end is bitter as wormwood, sharp
as a twoedged sword.
5 Her feet go down to death; her steps take
hold on hell.
6 Lest thou shouldest ponder the path of
life, her ways are moveable, *that* thou canst
not know *them*.
7 Hear me now therefore, O ye children, and
depart not from the words of my mouth.
8 Remove thy way far from her, and come
not nigh the door of her house:
9 Lest thou give thine honour unto others,
and thy years unto the cruel:
10 Lest strangers be filled with thy wealth;
and thy labours *be* in the house of a stranger;
11 And thou mourn at the last, when thy
flesh and thy body are consumed,
12 And say, How have I hated instruction,
and my heart despised reproof;
13 And have not obeyed the voice of my
teachers, nor inclined mine ear to them
that instructed me!
14 I was almost in all evil in the midst of the
congregation and assembly.
15 ¶ Drink waters out of thine own cistern,
and running waters out of thine own well.
16 Let thy fountains be dispersed abroad,
and rivers of waters in the streets.
17 Let them be only thine own, and not
strangers' with thee.
18 Let thy fountain be blessed: and rejoice
with the wife of thy youth.
19 *Let her be as* the loving hind and pleasant
roe; let her breasts satisfy thee at all times;
and be thou ravished always with her love.
20 And why wilt thou, my son, be ravished
with a strange woman, and embrace the
bosom of a stranger?
21 For the ways of man *are* before the eyes
of the LORD, and he pondereth all his goings.
22 ¶ His own iniquities shall take the wicked
himself, and he shall be holden with the
cords of his sins.
23 He shall die without instruction; and in
the greatness of his folly he shall go astray.

Proverbs 6

1 My son, if thou be surety for thy friend, *if*
thou hast stricken thy hand with a stranger,
2 Thou art snared with the words of thy
mouth, thou art taken with the words of
thy mouth.
3 Do this now, my son, and deliver thyself,
when thou art come into the hand of thy
friend; go, humble thyself, and make sure
thy friend.
4 Give not sleep to thine eyes, nor slumber
to thine eyelids.
5 Deliver thyself as a roe from the hand *of*

the hunter, and as a bird from the hand of
the fowler.
6 ¶ Go to the ant, thou sluggard; consider
her ways, and be wise:
7 Which having no guide, overseer, or ruler,
8 Provideth her meat in the summer, *and*
gathereth her food in the harvest.
9 How long wilt thou sleep, O sluggard?
when wilt thou arise out of thy sleep?
10 *Yet* a little sleep, a little slumber, a little
folding of the hands to sleep:
11 So shall thy poverty come as one that
travelleth, and thy want as an armed man.
12 ¶ A naughty person, a wicked man,
walketh with a froward mouth.
13 He winketh with his eyes, he speaketh
with his feet, he teacheth with his fingers;
14 Frowardness *is* in his heart, he deviseth
mischief continually; he soweth discord.
15 Therefore shall his calamity come suddenly; suddenly shall he be broken without
remedy.
16 ¶ These six *things* doth the LORD hate:
yea, seven *are* an abomination unto him:
17 A proud look, a lying tongue, and hands
that shed innocent blood,
18 An heart that deviseth wicked imaginations, feet that be swift in running to
mischief,
19 A false witness *that* speaketh lies, and
he that soweth discord among brethren.
20 ¶ My son, keep thy father's commandment, and forsake not the law of thy mother:
21 Bind them continually upon thine heart,
and tie them about thy neck.
22 When thou goest, it shall lead thee; when
thou sleepest, it shall keep thee; and *when*
thou awakest, it shall talk with thee.
23 For the commandment *is* a lamp; and
the law *is* light; and reproofs of instruction
are the way of life:
24 To keep thee from the evil woman,
from the flattery of the tongue of a strange
woman.
25 Lust not after her beauty in thine heart;
neither let her take thee with her eyelids.
26 For by means of a whorish woman *a*
man is brought to a piece of bread: and the
adulteress will hunt for the precious life.
27 Can a man take fire in his bosom, and his
clothes not be burned?
28 Can one go upon hot coals, and his feet
not be burned?
29 So he that goeth in to his neighbour's
wife; whosoever toucheth her shall not be
innocent.
30 *Men* do not despise a thief, if he steal to
satisfy his soul when he is hungry;
31 But *if* he be found, he shall restore sevenfold; he shall give all the substance of
his house.
32 *But* whoso committeth adultery with
a woman lacketh understanding: he *that*
doeth it destroyeth his own soul.
33 A wound and dishonour shall he get;
and his reproach shall not be wiped away.
34 For jealousy *is* the rage of a man: therefore he will not spare in the day of vengeance.
35 He will not regard any ransom; neither
will he rest content, though thou givest
many gifts.

Proverbs 7

1 My son, keep my words, and lay up my
commandments with thee.
2 Keep my commandments, and live; and
my law as the apple of thine eye.
3 Bind them upon thy fingers, write them
upon the table of thine heart.
4 Say unto wisdom, Thou *art* my sister; and
call understanding *thy* kinswoman:
5 That they may keep thee from the strange
woman, from the stranger *which* flattereth
with her words.
6 ¶ For at the window of my house I looked
through my casement,
7 And beheld among the simple ones, I
discerned among the youths, a young man
void of understanding,
8 Passing through the street near her corner;
and he went the way to her house,
9 In the twilight, in the evening, in the black
and dark night:
10 And, behold, there met him a woman
with the attire of an harlot, and subtil of
heart.
11 (She *is* loud and stubborn; her feet abide
not in her house:
12 Now *is she* without, now in the streets,
and lieth in wait at every corner.)
13 So she caught him, and kissed him, *and*
with an impudent face said unto him,
14 *I have* peace offerings with me; this day
have I payed my vows.
15 Therefore came I forth to meet thee,

diligently to seek thy face, and I have found thee.

16 I have decked my bed with coverings of tapestry, with carved *works*, with fine linen of Egypt.

17 I have perfumed my bed with myrrh, aloes, and cinnamon.

18 Come, let us take our fill of love until the morning: let us solace ourselves with loves.

19 For the goodman *is* not at home, he is gone a long journey:

20 He hath taken a bag of money with him, *and* will come home at the day appointed.

21 With her much fair speech she caused him to yield, with the flattering of her lips she forced him.

22 He goeth after her straightway, as an ox goeth to the slaughter, or as a fool to the correction of the stocks;

23 Till a dart strike through his liver; as a bird hasteth to the snare, and knoweth not that it *is* for his life.

24 ¶ Hearken unto me now therefore, O ye children, and attend to the words of my mouth.

25 Let not thine heart decline to her ways, go not astray in her paths.

26 For she hath cast down many wounded: yea, many strong *men* have been slain by her.

27 Her house *is* the way to hell, going down to the chambers of death.

Proverbs 8

1 Doth not wisdom cry? and understanding put forth her voice?

2 She standeth in the top of high places, by the way in the places of the paths.

3 She crieth at the gates, at the entry of the city, at the coming in at the doors.

4 Unto you, O men, I call; and my voice *is* to the sons of man.

5 O ye simple, understand wisdom: and, ye fools, be ye of an understanding heart.

6 Hear; for I will speak of excellent things; and the opening of my lips *shall be* right things.

7 For my mouth shall speak truth; and wickedness *is* an abomination to my lips.

8 All the words of my mouth *are* in righteousness; *there is* nothing froward or perverse in them.

9 They *are* all plain to him that understandeth, and right to them that find knowledge.

10 Receive my instruction, and not silver; and knowledge rather than choice gold.

11 For wisdom *is* better than rubies; and all the things that may be desired are not to be compared to it.

12 I wisdom dwell with prudence, and find out knowledge of witty inventions.

13 The fear of the LORD *is* to hate evil: pride, and arrogancy, and the evil way, and the froward mouth, do I hate.

14 Counsel *is* mine, and sound wisdom: I *am* understanding; I have strength.

15 By me kings reign, and princes decree justice.

16 By me princes rule, and nobles, *even* all the judges of the earth.

17 I love them that love me; and those that seek me early shall find me.

18 Riches and honour *are* with me; *yea*, durable riches and righteousness.

19 My fruit *is* better than gold, yea, than fine gold; and my revenue than choice silver.

20 I lead in the way of righteousness, in the midst of the paths of judgment:

21 That I may cause those that love me to inherit substance; and I will fill their treasures.

22 The LORD possessed me in the beginning of his way, before his works of old.

23 I was set up from everlasting, from the beginning, or ever the earth was.

24 When *there were* no depths, I was brought forth; when *there were* no fountains abounding with water.

25 Before the mountains were settled, before the hills was I brought forth:

26 While as yet he had not made the earth, nor the fields, nor the highest part of the dust of the world.

27 When he prepared the heavens, I *was* there: when he set a compass upon the face of the depth:

28 When he established the clouds above: when he strengthened the fountains of the deep:

29 When he gave to the sea his decree, that the waters should not pass his commandment: when he appointed the foundations of the earth:

30 Then I was by him, *as* one brought up

with him: and I was daily *his* delight, rejoicing
always before him;
31 Rejoicing in the habitable part of his
earth; and my delights *were* with the sons
of men.
32 Now therefore hearken unto me, O ye
children: for blessed *are they that* keep
my ways.
33 Hear instruction, and be wise, and refuse
it not.
34 Blessed *is* the man that heareth me,
watching daily at my gates, waiting at the
posts of my doors.
35 For whoso findeth me findeth life, and
shall obtain favour of the LORD.
36 But he that sinneth against me wrong-
eth his own soul: all they that hate me
love death.

Proverbs 9

1 Wisdom hath builded her house, she hath
hewn out her seven pillars:
2 She hath killed her beasts; she hath mingled her wine; she hath also furnished her
table.
3 She hath sent forth her maidens: she crieth
upon the highest places of the city,
4 Whoso *is* simple, let him turn in hither:
as for him that wanteth understanding,
she saith to him,
5 Come, eat of my bread, and drink of the
wine *which* I have mingled.
6 Forsake the foolish, and live; and go in the
way of understanding.
7 He that reproveth a scorner getteth to
himself shame: and he that rebuketh a
wicked *man getteth* himself a blot.
8 Reprove not a scorner, lest he hate thee:
rebuke a wise man, and he will love thee.
9 Give *instruction* to a wise *man*, and he will
be yet wiser: teach a just *man*, and he will
increase in learning.
10 The fear of the LORD *is* the beginning of
wisdom: and the knowledge of the holy *is*
understanding.
11 For by me thy days shall be multiplied,
and the years of thy life shall be increased.
12 If thou be wise, thou shalt be wise for
thyself: but *if* thou scornest, thou alone
shalt bear *it*.
13 ¶ A foolish woman *is* clamorous: *she is*
simple, and knoweth nothing.
14 For she sitteth at the door of her house,
on a seat in the high places of the city,
15 To call passengers who go right on their
ways:
16 Whoso *is* simple, let him turn in hither:
and *as for* him that wanteth understanding,
she saith to him,
17 Stolen waters are sweet, and bread *eaten*
in secret is pleasant.
18 But he knoweth not that the dead *are*
there; *and that* her guests *are* in the depths
of hell.

Proverbs 10

1 The proverbs of Solomon. A wise son
maketh a glad father: but a foolish son *is*
the heaviness of his mother.
2 Treasures of wickedness profit nothing:
but righteousness delivereth from death.
3 The LORD will not suffer the soul of the
righteous to famish: but he casteth away
the substance of the wicked.
4 He becometh poor that dealeth *with* a
slack hand: but the hand of the diligent
maketh rich.
5 He that gathereth in summer *is* a wise son:
but he that sleepeth in harvest *is* a son that
causeth shame.
6 Blessings *are* upon the head of the just: but
violence covereth the mouth of the wicked.
7 The memory of the just *is* blessed: but the
name of the wicked shall rot.
8 The wise in heart will receive commandments: but a prating fool shall fall.
9 He that walketh uprightly walketh surely:
but he that perverteth his ways shall be
known.
10 He that winketh with the eye causeth
sorrow: but a prating fool shall fall.
11 The mouth of a righteous *man is* a well
of life: but violence covereth the mouth of
the wicked.
12 Hatred stirreth up strifes: but love covereth all sins.
13 In the lips of him that hath understanding
wisdom is found: but a rod *is* for the back of
him that is void of understanding.
14 Wise *men* lay up knowledge: but the
mouth of the foolish *is* near destruction.
15 The rich man's wealth *is* his strong city:
the destruction of the poor *is* their poverty.
16 The labour of the righteous *tendeth* to
life: the fruit of the wicked to sin.

17 He *is in* the way of life that keepeth instruction: but he that refuseth reproof erreth.

18 He that hideth hatred *with* lying lips, and he that uttereth a slander, *is* a fool.

19 In the multitude of words there wanteth not sin: but he that refraineth his lips *is* wise.

20 The tongue of the just *is as* choice silver: the heart of the wicked *is* little worth.

21 The lips of the righteous feed many: but fools die for want of wisdom.

22 The blessing of the LORD, it maketh rich, and he addeth no sorrow with it.

23 *It is* as sport to a fool to do mischief: but a man of understanding hath wisdom.

24 The fear of the wicked, it shall come upon him: but the desire of the righteous shall be granted.

25 As the whirlwind passeth, so *is* the wicked no *more:* but the righteous *is* an everlasting foundation.

26 As vinegar to the teeth, and as smoke to the eyes, so *is* the sluggard to them that send him.

27 The fear of the LORD prolongeth days: but the years of the wicked shall be shortened.

28 The hope of the righteous *shall be* gladness: but the expectation of the wicked shall perish.

29 The way of the LORD *is* strength to the upright: but destruction *shall be* to the workers of iniquity.

30 The righteous shall never be removed: but the wicked shall not inhabit the earth.

31 The mouth of the just bringeth forth wisdom: but the froward tongue shall be cut out.

32 The lips of the righteous know what is acceptable: but the mouth of the wicked *speaketh* frowardness.

Proverbs 11

1 A false balance *is* abomination to the LORD: but a just weight *is* his delight.

2 *When* pride cometh, then cometh shame: but with the lowly *is* wisdom.

3 The integrity of the upright shall guide them: but the perverseness of transgressors shall destroy them.

4 Riches profit not in the day of wrath: but righteousness delivereth from death.

5 The righteousness of the perfect shall direct his way: but the wicked shall fall by his own wickedness.

6 The righteousness of the upright shall deliver them: but transgressors shall be taken in *their own* naughtiness.

7 When a wicked man dieth, *his* expectation shall perish: and the hope of unjust *men* perisheth.

8 The righteous is delivered out of trouble, and the wicked cometh in his stead.

9 An hypocrite with *his* mouth destroyeth his neighbour: but through knowledge shall the just be delivered.

10 When it goeth well with the righteous, the city rejoiceth: and when the wicked perish, *there is* shouting.

11 By the blessing of the upright the city is exalted: but it is overthrown by the mouth of the wicked.

12 He that is void of wisdom despiseth his neighbour: but a man of understanding holdeth his peace.

13 A talebearer revealeth secrets: but he that is of a faithful spirit concealeth the matter.

14 Where no counsel *is,* the people fall: but in the multitude of counsellers *there is* safety.

15 He that is surety for a stranger shall smart *for it:* and he that hateth suretiship is sure.

16 A gracious woman retaineth honour: and strong *men* retain riches.

17 The merciful man doeth good to his own soul: but *he that is* cruel troubleth his own flesh.

18 The wicked worketh a deceitful work: but to him that soweth righteousness *shall be* a sure reward.

19 As righteousness *tendeth* to life: so he that pursueth evil *pursueth it* to his own death.

20 They that are of a froward heart *are* abomination to the LORD: but *such as are* upright in *their* way *are* his delight.

21 *Though* hand *join* in hand, the wicked shall not be unpunished: but the seed of the righteous shall be delivered.

22 *As* a jewel of gold in a swine's snout, *so is* a fair woman which is without discretion.

23 The desire of the righteous *is* only good: *but* the expectation of the wicked *is* wrath.

24 There is that scattereth, and yet

increaseth; and *there is* that withholdeth
more than is meet, but *it tendeth* to poverty.
25 The liberal soul shall be made fat: and he
that watereth shall be watered also himself.
26 He that withholdeth corn, the people
shall curse him: but blessing *shall be* upon
the head of him that selleth *it*.
27 He that diligently seeketh good procureth
favour: but he that seeketh mischief, it shall
come unto him.
28 He that trusteth in his riches shall fall:
but the righteous shall flourish as a branch.
29 He that troubleth his own house shall
inherit the wind: and the fool *shall be* servant to the wise of heart.
30 The fruit of the righteous *is* a tree of life;
and he that winneth souls *is* wise.
31 Behold, the righteous shall be recompensed in the earth: much more the wicked
and the sinner.

Proverbs 12

1 Whoso loveth instruction loveth knowledge: but he that hateth reproof *is* brutish.
2 A good *man* obtaineth favour of the
LORD: but a man of wicked devices will he
condemn.
3 A man shall not be established by wickedness: but the root of the righteous shall
not be moved.
4 A virtuous woman *is* a crown to her husband: but she that maketh ashamed *is* as
rottenness in his bones.
5 The thoughts of the righteous *are* right:
but the counsels of the wicked *are* deceit.
6 The words of the wicked *are* to lie in wait
for blood: but the mouth of the upright shall
deliver them.
7 The wicked are overthrown, and *are* not:
but the house of the righteous shall stand.
8 A man shall be commended according
to his wisdom: but he that is of a perverse
heart shall be despised.
9 *He that is* despised, and hath a servant, *is*
better than he that honoureth himself, and
lacketh bread.
10 A righteous *man* regardeth the life of
his beast: but the tender mercies of the
wicked *are* cruel.
11 He that tilleth his land shall be satisfied
with bread: but he that followeth vain *persons is* void of understanding.
12 The wicked desireth the net of evil *men:*
but the root of the righteous yieldeth *fruit*.
13 The wicked is snared by the transgression of *his* lips: but the just shall come out
of trouble.
14 A man shall be satisfied with good by the
fruit of *his* mouth: and the recompence of
a man's hands shall be rendered unto him.
15 The way of a fool *is* right in his own eyes:
but he that hearkeneth unto counsel *is* wise.
16 A fool's wrath is presently known: but a
prudent *man* covereth shame.
17 *He that* speaketh truth sheweth forth
righteousness: but a false witness deceit.
18 There is that speaketh like the piercings
of a sword: but the tongue of the wise *is*
health.
19 The lip of truth shall be established for
ever: but a lying tongue *is* but for a moment.
20 Deceit *is* in the heart of them that imagine evil: but to the counsellers of peace *is*
joy.
21 There shall no evil happen to the just:
but the wicked shall be filled with mischief.
22 Lying lips *are* abomination to the LORD:
but they that deal truly *are* his delight.
23 A prudent man concealeth knowledge:
but the heart of fools proclaimeth foolishness.
24 The hand of the diligent shall bear rule:
but the slothful shall be under tribute.
25 Heaviness in the heart of man maketh
it stoop: but a good word maketh it glad.
26 The righteous *is* more excellent than
his neighbour: but the way of the wicked
seduceth them.
27 The slothful *man* roasteth not that which
he took in hunting: but the substance of a
diligent man *is* precious.
28 In the way of righteousness *is* life; and
in the pathway *thereof there is* no death.

Proverbs 13

1 A wise son *heareth* his father's instruction:
but a scorner heareth not rebuke.
2 A man shall eat good by the fruit of *his*
mouth: but the soul of the transgressors
shall eat violence.
3 He that keepeth his mouth keepeth his
life: *but* he that openeth wide his lips shall
have destruction.
4 The soul of the sluggard desireth, and

hath nothing: but the soul of the diligent
shall be made fat.
5 A righteous *man* hateth lying: but a wicked
man is loathsome, and cometh to shame.
6 Righteousness keepeth *him that is* upright
in the way: but wickedness overthroweth
the sinner.
7 There is that maketh himself rich, yet *hath*
nothing: *there is* that maketh himself poor,
yet *hath* great riches.
8 The ransom of a man's life *are* his riches:
but the poor heareth not rebuke.
9 The light of the righteous rejoiceth: but
the lamp of the wicked shall be put out.
10 Only by pride cometh contention: but
with the well advised *is* wisdom.
11 Wealth *gotten* by vanity shall be diminished: but he that gathereth by labour shall
increase.
12 Hope deferred maketh the heart sick: but
when the desire cometh, *it is* a tree of life.
13 Whoso despiseth the word shall be
destroyed: but he that feareth the commandment shall be rewarded.
14 The law of the wise *is* a fountain of life,
to depart from the snares of death.
15 Good understanding giveth favour: but
the way of transgressors *is* hard.
16 Every prudent *man* dealeth with knowledge: but a fool layeth open *his* folly.
17 A wicked messenger falleth into mischief:
but a faithful ambassador *is* health.
18 Poverty and shame *shall be to* him that
refuseth instruction: but he that regardeth
reproof shall be honoured.
19 The desire accomplished is sweet to
the soul: but *it is* abomination to fools to
depart from evil.
20 He that walketh with wise *men* shall
be wise: but a companion of fools shall be
destroyed.
21 Evil pursueth sinners: but to the righteous
good shall be repayed.
22 A good *man* leaveth an inheritance to
his children's children: and the wealth of
the sinner *is* laid up for the just.
23 Much food *is in* the tillage of the poor:
but there is *that is* destroyed for want of
judgment.
24 He that spareth his rod hateth his son:
but he that loveth him chasteneth him
betimes.
25 The righteous eateth to the satisfying
of his soul: but the belly of the wicked shall
want.

Proverbs 14

1 Every wise woman buildeth her house: but
the foolish plucketh it down with her hands.
2 He that walketh in his uprightness feareth
the LORD: but *he that is* perverse in his ways
despiseth him.
3 In the mouth of the foolish *is* a rod of pride:
but the lips of the wise shall preserve them.
4 Where no oxen *are*, the crib *is* clean: but
much increase *is* by the strength of the ox.
5 A faithful witness will not lie: but a false
witness will utter lies.
6 A scorner seeketh wisdom, and *findeth it*
not: but knowledge *is* easy unto him that
understandeth.
7 Go from the presence of a foolish man,
when thou perceivest not *in him* the lips of
knowledge.
8 The wisdom of the prudent *is* to understand his way: but the folly of fools *is* deceit.
9 Fools make a mock at sin: but among the
righteous *there is* favour.
10 The heart knoweth his own bitterness;
and a stranger doth not intermeddle with
his joy.
11 The house of the wicked shall be overthrown: but the tabernacle of the upright
shall flourish.
12 There is a way which seemeth right unto
a man, but the end thereof *are* the ways
of death.
13 Even in laughter the heart is sorrowful;
and the end of that mirth *is* heaviness.
14 The backslider in heart shall be filled
with his own ways: and a good man *shall
be satisfied* from himself.
15 The simple believeth every word: but
the prudent *man* looketh well to his going.
16 A wise *man* feareth, and departeth from
evil: but the fool rageth, and is confident.
17 *He that is* soon angry dealeth foolishly:
and a man of wicked devices is hated.
18 The simple inherit folly: but the prudent
are crowned with knowledge.
19 The evil bow before the good; and the
wicked at the gates of the righteous.
20 The poor is hated even of his own neighbour: but the rich *hath* many friends.
21 He that despiseth his neighbour sin-

neth: but he that hath mercy on the poor,
happy *is* he.
22 Do they not err that devise evil? but
mercy and truth *shall be* to them that
devise good.
23 In all labour there is profit: but the talk
of the lips *tendeth* only to penury.
24 The crown of the wise *is* their riches: *but*
the foolishness of fools *is* folly.
25 A true witness delivereth souls: but a
deceitful *witness* speaketh lies.
26 In the fear of the LORD *is* strong confidence: and his children shall have a place
of refuge.
27 The fear of the LORD *is* a fountain of life,
to depart from the snares of death.
28 In the multitude of people *is* the king's
honour: but in the want of people *is* the
destruction of the prince.
29 *He that is* slow to wrath *is* of great
understanding: but *he that is* hasty of spirit
exalteth folly.
30 A sound heart *is* the life of the flesh: but
envy the rottenness of the bones.
31 He that oppresseth the poor reproacheth
his Maker: but he that honoureth him hath
mercy on the poor.
32 The wicked is driven away in his wickedness: but the righteous hath hope in
his death.
33 Wisdom resteth in the heart of him that
hath understanding: but *that which is* in the
midst of fools is made known.
34 Righteousness exalteth a nation: but sin
is a reproach to any people.
35 The king's favour *is* toward a wise servant: but his wrath is *against* him that
causeth shame.

Proverbs 15

1 A soft answer turneth away wrath: but
grievous words stir up anger.
2 The tongue of the wise useth knowledge
aright: but the mouth of fools poureth out
foolishness.
3 The eyes of the LORD *are* in every place,
beholding the evil and the good.
4 A wholesome tongue *is* a tree of life: but
perverseness therein *is* a breach in the spirit.
5 A fool despiseth his father's instruction:
but he that regardeth reproof is prudent.
6 In the house of the righteous *is* much
treasure: but in the revenues of the wicked
is trouble.
7 The lips of the wise disperse knowledge:
but the heart of the foolish *doeth* not so.
8 The sacrifice of the wicked *is* an abomination to the LORD: but the prayer of the
upright *is* his delight.
9 The way of the wicked *is* an abomination
unto the LORD: but he loveth him that followeth after righteousness.
10 Correction *is* grievous unto him that forsaketh the way: *and* he that hateth reproof
shall die.
11 Hell and destruction *are* before the
LORD: how much more then the hearts of
the children of men?
12 A scorner loveth not one that reproveth
him: neither will he go unto the wise.
13 A merry heart maketh a cheerful countenance: but by sorrow of the heart the
spirit is broken.
14 The heart of him that hath understanding
seeketh knowledge: but the mouth of fools
feedeth on foolishness.
15 All the days of the afflicted *are* evil: but
he that is of a merry heart *hath* a continual feast.
16 Better *is* little with the fear of the LORD
than great treasure and trouble therewith.
17 Better *is* a dinner of herbs where love
is, than a stalled ox and hatred therewith.
18 A wrathful man stirreth up strife: but *he*
that is slow to anger appeaseth strife.
19 The way of the slothful *man is* as an
hedge of thorns: but the way of the righteous *is* made plain.
20 A wise son maketh a glad father: but a
foolish man despiseth his mother.
21 Folly *is* joy to *him that is* destitute of wisdom: but a man of understanding walketh
uprightly.
22 Without counsel purposes are disap-
pointed: but in the multitude of counsellers
they are established.
23 A man hath joy by the answer of his
mouth: and a word *spoken* in due season,
how good *is it!*
24 The way of life *is* above to the wise, that
he may depart from hell beneath.
25 The LORD will destroy the house of the
proud: but he will establish the border of
the widow.
26 The thoughts of the wicked *are* an abom-

ination to the LORD: but *the words* of the
pure *are* pleasant words.
27 He that is greedy of gain troubleth his
own house; but he that hateth gifts shall live.
28 The heart of the righteous studieth
to answer: but the mouth of the wicked
poureth out evil things.
29 The LORD *is* far from the wicked: but he
heareth the prayer of the righteous.
30 The light of the eyes rejoiceth the heart:
and a good report maketh the bones fat.
31 The ear that heareth the reproof of life
abideth among the wise.
32 He that refuseth instruction despiseth
his own soul: but he that heareth reproof
getteth understanding.
33 The fear of the LORD *is* the instruction
of wisdom; and before honour *is* humility.

Proverbs 16

1 The preparations of the heart in man, and
the answer of the tongue, *is* from the LORD.
2 All the ways of a man *are* clean in his own
eyes; but the LORD weigheth the spirits.
3 Commit thy works unto the LORD, and thy
thoughts shall be established.
4 The LORD hath made all *things* for himself:
yea, even the wicked for the day of evil.
5 Every one *that is* proud in heart *is* an
abomination to the LORD: *though* hand *join*
in hand, he shall not be unpunished.
6 By mercy and truth iniquity is purged: and
by the fear of the LORD *men* depart from evil.
7 When a man's ways please the LORD, he
maketh even his enemies to be at peace
with him.
8 Better *is* a little with righteousness than
great revenues without right.
9 A man's heart deviseth his way: but the
LORD directeth his steps.
10 A divine sentence *is* in the lips of the king:
his mouth transgresseth not in judgment.
11 A just weight and balance *are* the LORD's:
all the weights of the bag *are* his work.
12 *It is* an abomination to kings to commit
wickedness: for the throne is established
by righteousness.
13 Righteous lips *are* the delight of kings;
and they love him that speaketh right.
14 The wrath of a king *is as* messengers of
death: but a wise man will pacify it.
15 In the light of the king's countenance
is life; and his favour *is* as a cloud of the
latter rain.
16 How much better *is it* to get wisdom than
gold! and to get understanding rather to be
chosen than silver!
17 The highway of the upright *is* to depart
from evil: he that keepeth his way preserveth his soul.
18 Pride *goeth* before destruction, and an
haughty spirit before a fall.
19 Better *it is to be* of an humble spirit with
the lowly, than to divide the spoil with the
proud.
20 He that handleth a matter wisely shall
find good: and whoso trusteth in the LORD,
happy *is* he.
21 The wise in heart shall be called prudent:
and the sweetness of the lips increaseth
learning.
22 Understanding *is* a wellspring of life
unto him that hath it: but the instruction
of fools *is* folly.
23 The heart of the wise teacheth his mouth,
and addeth learning to his lips.
24 Pleasant words *are as* an honeycomb,
sweet to the soul, and health to the bones.
25 There is a way that seemeth right unto
a man, but the end thereof *are* the ways
of death.
26 He that laboureth laboureth for himself;
for his mouth craveth it of him.
27 An ungodly man diggeth up evil: and in
his lips *there is* as a burning fire.
28 A froward man soweth strife: and a whis-
perer separateth chief friends.
29 A violent man enticeth his neighbour, and
leadeth him into the way *that is* not good.
30 He shutteth his eyes to devise froward
things: moving his lips he bringeth evil to
pass.
31 The hoary head *is* a crown of glory, *if* it
be found in the way of righteousness.
32 *He that is* slow to anger *is* better than the
mighty; and he that ruleth his spirit than he
that taketh a city.
33 The lot is cast into the lap; but the whole
disposing thereof *is* of the LORD.

Proverbs 17

1 Better *is* a dry morsel, and quietness
therewith, than an house full of sacrifices
with strife.
2 A wise servant shall have rule over a son

that causeth shame, and shall have part of the inheritance among the brethren.
3 The fining pot *is* for silver, and the furnace for gold: but the LORD trieth the hearts.
4 A wicked doer giveth heed to false lips; *and* a liar giveth ear to a naughty tongue.
5 Whoso mocketh the poor reproacheth his Maker: *and* he that is glad at calamities shall not be unpunished.
6 Children's children *are* the crown of old men; and the glory of children *are* their fathers.
7 Excellent speech becometh not a fool: much less do lying lips a prince.
8 A gift *is as* a precious stone in the eyes of him that hath it: whithersoever it turneth, it prospereth.
9 He that covereth a transgression seeketh love; but he that repeateth a matter separateth *very* friends.
10 A reproof entereth more into a wise man than an hundred stripes into a fool.
11 An evil *man* seeketh only rebellion: therefore a cruel messenger shall be sent against him.
12 Let a bear robbed of her whelps meet a man, rather than a fool in his folly.
13 Whoso rewardeth evil for good, evil shall not depart from his house.
14 The beginning of strife *is as* when one letteth out water: therefore leave off contention, before it be meddled with.
15 He that justifieth the wicked, and he that condemneth the just, even they both *are* abomination to the LORD.
16 Wherefore *is there* a price in the hand of a fool to get wisdom, seeing *he hath* no heart *to it?*
17 A friend loveth at all times, and a brother is born for adversity.
18 A man void of understanding striketh hands, *and* becometh surety in the presence of his friend.
19 He loveth transgression that loveth strife: *and* he that exalteth his gate seeketh destruction.
20 He that hath a froward heart findeth no good: and he that hath a perverse tongue falleth into mischief.
21 He that begetteth a fool *doeth it* to his sorrow: and the father of a fool hath no joy.
22 A merry heart doeth good *like* a medicine: but a broken spirit drieth the bones.
23 A wicked *man* taketh a gift out of the bosom to pervert the ways of judgment.
24 Wisdom *is* before him that hath understanding; but the eyes of a fool *are* in the ends of the earth.
25 A foolish son *is* a grief to his father, and bitterness to her that bare him.
26 Also to punish the just *is* not good, *nor* to strike princes for equity.
27 He that hath knowledge spareth his words: *and* a man of understanding is of an excellent spirit.
28 Even a fool, when he holdeth his peace, is counted wise: *and* he that shutteth his lips *is esteemed* a man of understanding.

Proverbs 18

1 Through desire a man, having separated himself, seeketh *and* intermeddleth with all wisdom.
2 A fool hath no delight in understanding, but that his heart may discover itself.
3 When the wicked cometh, *then* cometh also contempt, and with ignominy reproach.
4 The words of a man's mouth *are as* deep waters, *and* the wellspring of wisdom *as* a flowing brook.
5 *It is* not good to accept the person of the wicked, to overthrow the righteous in judgment.
6 A fool's lips enter into contention, and his mouth calleth for strokes.
7 A fool's mouth *is* his destruction, and his lips *are* the snare of his soul.
8 The words of a talebearer *are* as wounds, and they go down into the innermost parts of the belly.
9 He also that is slothful in his work is brother to him that is a great waster.
10 The name of the LORD *is* a strong tower: the righteous runneth into it, and is safe.
11 The rich man's wealth *is* his strong city, and as an high wall in his own conceit.
12 Before destruction the heart of man is haughty, and before honour *is* humility.
13 He that answereth a matter before he heareth *it*, it *is* folly and shame unto him.
14 The spirit of a man will sustain his infirmity; but a wounded spirit who can bear?
15 The heart of the prudent getteth knowledge; and the ear of the wise seeketh knowledge.

16 A man's gift maketh room for him, and
bringeth him before great men.
17 *He that is* first in his own cause *seemeth*
just; but his neighbour cometh and searcheth him.
18 The lot causeth contentions to cease,
and parteth between the mighty.
19 A brother offended *is harder to be won*
than a strong city: and *their* contentions *are*
like the bars of a castle.
20 A man's belly shall be satisfied with the
fruit of his mouth; *and* with the increase of
his lips shall he be filled.
21 Death and life *are* in the power of the
tongue: and they that love it shall eat the
fruit thereof.
22 *Whoso* findeth a wife findeth a good
thing, and obtaineth favour of the LORD.
23 The poor useth intreaties; but the rich
answereth roughly.
24 A man *that hath* friends must shew
himself friendly: and there is a friend *that*
sticketh closer than a brother.

Proverbs 19

1 Better *is* the poor that walketh in his
integrity, than *he that is* perverse in his lips,
and is a fool.
2 Also, *that* the soul *be* without knowledge,
it is not good; and he that hasteth with *his*
feet sinneth.
3 The foolishness of man perverteth his
way: and his heart fretteth against the LORD.
4 Wealth maketh many friends; but the poor
is separated from his neighbour.
5 A false witness shall not be unpunished,
and *he that* speaketh lies shall not escape.
6 Many will intreat the favour of the prince:
and every man *is* a friend to him that giveth
gifts.
7 All the brethren of the poor do hate him:
how much more do his friends go far from
him? he pursueth *them with* words, *yet* they
are wanting *to him.*
8 He that getteth wisdom loveth his own
soul: he that keepeth understanding shall
find good.
9 A false witness shall not be unpunished,
and *he that* speaketh lies shall perish.
10 Delight is not seemly for a fool; much
less for a servant to have rule over princes.
11 The discretion of a man deferreth his
anger; and *it is* his glory to pass over a
transgression.
12 The king's wrath *is* as the roaring of a
lion; but his favour *is* as dew upon the grass.
13 A foolish son *is* the calamity of his father:
and the contentions of a wife *are* a continual dropping.
14 House and riches *are* the inheritance of
fathers: and a prudent wife *is* from the LORD.
15 Slothfulness casteth into a deep sleep;
and an idle soul shall suffer hunger.
16 He that keepeth the commandment
keepeth his own soul; *but* he that despiseth
his ways shall die.
17 He that hath pity upon the poor lendeth
unto the LORD; and that which he hath given
will he pay him again.
18 Chasten thy son while there is hope, and
let not thy soul spare for his crying.
19 A man of great wrath shall suffer punishment: for if thou deliver *him,* yet thou
must do it again.
20 Hear counsel, and receive instruction,
that thou mayest be wise in thy latter end.
21 *There are* many devices in a man's heart;
nevertheless the counsel of the LORD, that
shall stand.
22 The desire of a man *is* his kindness: and
a poor man *is* better than a liar.
23 The fear of the LORD *tendeth* to life: and
he that hath it shall abide satisfied; he shall
not be visited with evil.
24 A slothful *man* hideth his hand in *his*
bosom, and will not so much as bring it to
his mouth again.
25 Smite a scorner, and the simple will
beware: and reprove one that hath understanding, *and* he will understand knowledge.
26 He that wasteth *his* father, *and* chaseth
away *his* mother, *is* a son that causeth
shame, and bringeth reproach.
27 Cease, my son, to hear the instruction
that causeth to err from the words of
knowledge.
28 An ungodly witness scorneth judgment:
and the mouth of the wicked devoureth
iniquity.
29 Judgments are prepared for scorners,
and stripes for the back of fools.

Proverbs 20

1 Wine *is* a mocker, strong drink *is* raging:

and whosoever is deceived thereby is not wise.

2 The fear of a king *is* as the roaring of a lion: *whoso* provoketh him to anger sinneth *against* his own soul.

3 *It is* an honour for a man to cease from strife: but every fool will be meddling.

4 The sluggard will not plow by reason of the cold; *therefore* shall he beg in harvest, and *have* nothing.

5 Counsel in the heart of man *is like* deep water; but a man of understanding will draw it out.

6 Most men will proclaim every one his own goodness: but a faithful man who can find?

7 The just *man* walketh in his integrity: his children *are* blessed after him.

8 A king that sitteth in the throne of judgment scattereth away all evil with his eyes.

9 Who can say, I have made my heart clean, I am pure from my sin?

10 Divers weights, *and* divers measures, both of them *are* alike abomination to the LORD.

11 Even a child is known by his doings, whether his work *be* pure, and whether *it be* right.

12 The hearing ear, and the seeing eye, the LORD hath made even both of them.

13 Love not sleep, lest thou come to poverty; open thine eyes, *and* thou shalt be satisfied with bread.

14 *It is* naught, *it is* naught, saith the buyer: but when he is gone his way, then he boasteth.

15 There is gold, and a multitude of rubies: but the lips of knowledge *are* a precious jewel.

16 Take his garment that is surety *for* a stranger: and take a pledge of him for a strange woman.

17 Bread of deceit *is* sweet to a man; but afterwards his mouth shall be filled with gravel.

18 *Every* purpose is established by counsel: and with good advice make war.

19 He that goeth about *as* a talebearer revealeth secrets: therefore meddle not with him that flattereth with his lips.

20 Whoso curseth his father or his mother, his lamp shall be put out in obscure darkness.

21 An inheritance *may be* gotten hastily at the beginning; but the end thereof shall not be blessed.

22 Say not thou, I will recompense evil; *but* wait on the LORD, and he shall save thee.

23 Divers weights *are* an abomination unto the LORD; and a false balance *is* not good.

24 Man's goings *are* of the LORD; how can a man then understand his own way?

25 *It is* a snare to the man *who* devoureth *that which is* holy, and after vows to make inquiry.

26 A wise king scattereth the wicked, and bringeth the wheel over them.

27 The spirit of man *is* the candle of the LORD, searching all the inward parts of the belly.

28 Mercy and truth preserve the king: and his throne is upholden by mercy.

29 The glory of young men *is* their strength: and the beauty of old men *is* the gray head.

30 The blueness of a wound cleanseth away evil: so *do* stripes the inward parts of the belly.

Proverbs 21

1 The king's heart *is* in the hand of the LORD, *as* the rivers of water: he turneth it whithersoever he will.

2 Every way of a man *is* right in his own eyes: but the LORD pondereth the hearts.

3 To do justice and judgment *is* more acceptable to the LORD than sacrifice.

4 An high look, and a proud heart, *and* the plowing of the wicked, *is* sin.

5 The thoughts of the diligent *tend* only to plenteousness; but of every one *that is* hasty only to want.

6 The getting of treasures by a lying tongue *is* a vanity tossed to and fro of them that seek death.

7 The robbery of the wicked shall destroy them; because they refuse to do judgment.

8 The way of man *is* froward and strange: but *as for* the pure, his work *is* right.

9 *It is* better to dwell in a corner of the housetop, than with a brawling woman in a wide house.

10 The soul of the wicked desireth evil: his neighbour findeth no favour in his eyes.

11 When the scorner is punished, the simple is made wise: and when the wise is instructed, he receiveth knowledge.

12 The righteous *man* wisely considereth

the house of the wicked: *but God* overthroweth the wicked for *their* wickedness.
13 Whoso stoppeth his ears at the cry of the poor, he also shall cry himself, but shall not be heard.
14 A gift in secret pacifieth anger: and a reward in the bosom strong wrath.
15 *It is* joy to the just to do judgment: but destruction *shall be* to the workers of iniquity.
16 The man that wandereth out of the way of understanding shall remain in the congregation of the dead.
17 He that loveth pleasure *shall be* a poor man: he that loveth wine and oil shall not be rich.
18 The wicked *shall be* a ransom for the righteous, and the transgressor for the upright.
19 *It is* better to dwell in the wilderness, than with a contentious and an angry woman.
20 *There is* treasure to be desired and oil in the dwelling of the wise; but a foolish man spendeth it up.
21 He that followeth after righteousness and mercy findeth life, righteousness, and honour.
22 A wise *man* scaleth the city of the mighty, and casteth down the strength of the confidence thereof.
23 Whoso keepeth his mouth and his tongue keepeth his soul from troubles.
24 Proud *and* haughty scorner *is* his name, who dealeth in proud wrath.
25 The desire of the slothful killeth him; for his hands refuse to labour.
26 He coveteth greedily all the day long: but the righteous giveth and spareth not.
27 The sacrifice of the wicked *is* abomination: how much more, *when* he bringeth it with a wicked mind?
28 A false witness shall perish: but the man that heareth speaketh constantly.
29 A wicked man hardeneth his face: but *as for* the upright, he directeth his way.
30 *There is* no wisdom nor understanding nor counsel against the LORD.
31 The horse *is* prepared against the day of battle: but safety *is* of the LORD.

Proverbs 22

1 A *good* name *is* rather to be chosen than great riches, *and* loving favour rather than silver and gold.
2 The rich and poor meet together: the LORD *is* the maker of them all.
3 A prudent *man* foreseeth the evil, and hideth himself: but the simple pass on, and are punished.
4 By humility *and* the fear of the LORD *are* riches, and honour, and life.
5 Thorns *and* snares *are* in the way of the froward: he that doth keep his soul shall be far from them.
6 Train up a child in the way he should go: and when he is old, he will not depart from it.
7 The rich ruleth over the poor, and the borrower *is* servant to the lender.
8 He that soweth iniquity shall reap vanity: and the rod of his anger shall fail.
9 He that hath a bountiful eye shall be blessed; for he giveth of his bread to the poor.
10 Cast out the scorner, and contention shall go out; yea, strife and reproach shall cease.
11 He that loveth pureness of heart, *for* the grace of his lips the king *shall be* his friend.
12 The eyes of the LORD preserve knowledge, and he overthroweth the words of the transgressor.
13 The slothful *man* saith, *There is* a lion without, I shall be slain in the streets.
14 The mouth of strange women *is* a deep pit: he that is abhorred of the LORD shall fall therein.
15 Foolishness *is* bound in the heart of a child; *but* the rod of correction shall drive it far from him.
16 He that oppresseth the poor to increase his *riches, and* he that giveth to the rich, *shall* surely *come* to want.
17 Bow down thine ear, and hear the words of the wise, and apply thine heart unto my knowledge.
18 For *it is* a pleasant thing if thou keep them within thee; they shall withal be fitted in thy lips.
19 That thy trust may be in the LORD, I have made known to thee this day, even to thee.
20 Have not I written to thee excellent things in counsels and knowledge,
21 That I might make thee know the certainty of the words of truth; that thou mightest answer the words of truth to them that send unto thee?

22 Rob not the poor, because he *is* poor:
neither oppress the afflicted in the gate:
23 For the LORD will plead their cause, and
spoil the soul of those that spoiled them.
24 Make no friendship with an angry man;
and with a furious man thou shalt not go:
25 Lest thou learn his ways, and get a snare
to thy soul.
26 Be not thou *one* of them that strike
hands, *or* of them that are sureties for debts.
27 If thou hast nothing to pay, why should
he take away thy bed from under thee?
28 Remove not the ancient landmark, which
thy fathers have set.
29 Seest thou a man diligent in his business?
he shall stand before kings; he shall not
stand before mean *men*.

Proverbs 23

1 When thou sittest to eat with a ruler, consider diligently what *is* before thee:
2 And put a knife to thy throat, if thou *be* a
man given to appetite.
3 Be not desirous of his dainties: for they
are deceitful meat.
4 Labour not to be rich: cease from thine
own wisdom.
5 Wilt thou set thine eyes upon that which
is not? for *riches* certainly make themselves
wings; they fly away as an eagle toward
heaven.
6 Eat thou not the bread of *him that hath*
an evil eye, neither desire thou his dainty
meats:
7 For as he thinketh in his heart, so *is* he:
Eat and drink, saith he to thee; but his heart
is not with thee.
8 The morsel *which* thou hast eaten shalt
thou vomit up, and lose thy sweet words.
9 Speak not in the ears of a fool: for he will
despise the wisdom of thy words.
10 Remove not the old landmark; and enter
not into the fields of the fatherless:
11 For their redeemer *is* mighty; he shall
plead their cause with thee.
12 Apply thine heart unto instruction, and
thine ears to the words of knowledge.
13 Withhold not correction from the child:
for *if* thou beatest him with the rod, he
shall not die.
14 Thou shalt beat him with the rod, and
shalt deliver his soul from hell.
15 My son, if thine heart be wise, my heart
shall rejoice, even mine.
16 Yea, my reins shall rejoice, when thy lips
speak right things.
17 Let not thine heart envy sinners: but *be*
thou in the fear of the LORD all the day long.
18 For surely there is an end; and thine
expectation shall not be cut off.
19 Hear thou, my son, and be wise, and
guide thine heart in the way.
20 Be not among winebibbers; among riotous eaters of flesh:
21 For the drunkard and the glutton shall
come to poverty: and drowsiness shall
clothe *a man* with rags.
22 Hearken unto thy father that begat thee,
and despise not thy mother when she is old.
23 Buy the truth, and sell *it* not; *also* wisdom, and instruction, and understanding.
24 The father of the righteous shall greatly
rejoice: and he that begetteth a wise *child*
shall have joy of him.
25 Thy father and thy mother shall be glad,
and she that bare thee shall rejoice.
26 My son, give me thine heart, and let thine
eyes observe my ways.
27 For a whore *is* a deep ditch; and a strange
woman *is* a narrow pit.
28 She also lieth in wait as *for* a prey, and
increaseth the transgressors among men.
29 Who hath woe? who hath sorrow? who
hath contentions? who hath babbling? who
hath wounds without cause? who hath
redness of eyes?
30 They that tarry long at the wine; they
that go to seek mixed wine.
31 Look not thou upon the wine when it
is red, when it giveth his colour in the cup,
when it moveth itself aright.
32 At the last it biteth like a serpent, and
stingeth like an adder.
33 Thine eyes shall behold strange women,
and thine heart shall utter perverse things.
34 Yea, thou shalt be as he that lieth down
in the midst of the sea, or as he that lieth
upon the top of a mast.
35 They have stricken me, *shalt thou say,*
and I was not sick; they have beaten me,
and I felt *it* not: when shall I awake? I will
seek it yet again.

Proverbs 24

1 Be not thou envious against evil men, neither desire to be with them.
2 For their heart studieth destruction, and their lips talk of mischief.
3 Through wisdom is an house builded; and by understanding it is established:
4 And by knowledge shall the chambers be filled with all precious and pleasant riches.
5 A wise man *is* strong; yea, a man of knowledge increaseth strength.
6 For by wise counsel thou shalt make thy war: and in multitude of counsellers *there is* safety.
7 Wisdom *is* too high for a fool: he openeth not his mouth in the gate.
8 He that deviseth to do evil shall be called a mischievous person.
9 The thought of foolishness *is* sin: and the scorner *is* an abomination to men.
10 *If* thou faint in the day of adversity, thy strength *is* small.
11 If thou forbear to deliver *them that are* drawn unto death, and *those that are* ready to be slain;
12 If thou sayest, Behold, we knew it not; doth not he that pondereth the heart consider *it?* and he that keepeth thy soul, doth *not* he know *it?* and shall *not* he render to *every* man according to his works?
13 My son, eat thou honey, because *it is* good; and the honeycomb, *which is* sweet to thy taste:
14 So *shall* the knowledge of wisdom *be* unto thy soul: when thou hast found *it,* then there shall be a reward, and thy expectation shall not be cut off.
15 Lay not wait, O wicked *man,* against the dwelling of the righteous; spoil not his resting place:
16 For a just *man* falleth seven times, and riseth up again: but the wicked shall fall into mischief.
17 Rejoice not when thine enemy falleth, and let not thine heart be glad when he stumbleth:
18 Lest the LORD see *it,* and it displease him, and he turn away his wrath from him.
19 Fret not thyself because of evil *men,* neither be thou envious at the wicked;
20 For there shall be no reward to the evil *man;* the candle of the wicked shall be put out.
21 My son, fear thou the LORD and the king: *and* meddle not with them that are given to change:
22 For their calamity shall rise suddenly; and who knoweth the ruin of them both?
23 These *things* also *belong* to the wise. *It is* not good to have respect of persons in judgment.
24 He that saith unto the wicked, Thou *art* righteous; him shall the people curse, nations shall abhor him:
25 But to them that rebuke *him* shall be delight, and a good blessing shall come upon them.
26 *Every man* shall kiss *his* lips that giveth a right answer.
27 Prepare thy work without, and make it fit for thyself in the field; and afterwards build thine house.
28 Be not a witness against thy neighbour without cause; and deceive *not* with thy lips.
29 Say not, I will do so to him as he hath done to me: I will render to the man according to his work.
30 I went by the field of the slothful, and by the vineyard of the man void of understanding;
31 And, lo, it was all grown over with thorns, *and* nettles had covered the face thereof, and the stone wall thereof was broken down.
32 Then I saw, *and* considered *it* well: I looked upon *it, and* received instruction.
33 *Yet* a little sleep, a little slumber, a little folding of the hands to sleep:
34 So shall thy poverty come *as* one that travelleth; and thy want as an armed man.

Proverbs 25

1 These *are* also proverbs of Solomon, which the men of Hezekiah king of Judah copied out.
2 *It is* the glory of God to conceal a thing: but the honour of kings *is* to search out a matter.
3 The heaven for height, and the earth for depth, and the heart of kings *is* unsearchable.
4 Take away the dross from the silver, and there shall come forth a vessel for the finer.
5 Take away the wicked *from* before the king, and his throne shall be established in righteousness.
6 Put not forth thyself in the presence

of the king, and stand not in the place of
great *men:*
7 For better *it is* that it be said unto thee,
Come up hither; than that thou shouldest
be put lower in the presence of the prince
whom thine eyes have seen.
8 Go not forth hastily to strive, lest *thou*
know not what to do in the end thereof,
when thy neighbour hath put thee to shame.
9 Debate thy cause with thy neighbour *him-*
self; and discover not a secret to another:
10 Lest he that heareth *it* put thee to shame,
and thine infamy turn not away.
11 A word fitly spoken *is like* apples of gold
in pictures of silver.
12 *As* an earring of gold, and an ornament
of fine gold, *so is* a wise reprover upon an
obedient ear.
13 As the cold of snow in the time of harvest, *so is* a faithful messenger to them
that send him: for he refresheth the soul
of his masters.
14 Whoso boasteth himself of a false gift *is*
like clouds and wind without rain.
15 By long forbearing is a prince persuaded,
and a soft tongue breaketh the bone.
16 Hast thou found honey? eat so much
as is sufficient for thee, lest thou be filled
therewith, and vomit it.
17 Withdraw thy foot from thy neighbour's
house; lest he be weary of thee, and *so*
hate thee.
18 A man that beareth false witness against
his neighbour *is* a maul, and a sword, and
a sharp arrow.
19 Confidence in an unfaithful man in time
of trouble *is like* a broken tooth, and a foot
out of joint.
20 *As* he that taketh away a garment in cold
weather, *and as* vinegar upon nitre, so *is* he
that singeth songs to an heavy heart.
21 If thine enemy be hungry, give him bread
to eat; and if he be thirsty, give him water
to drink:
22 For thou shalt heap coals of fire upon
his head, and the LORD shall reward thee.
23 The north wind driveth away rain: so *doth*
an angry countenance a backbiting tongue.
24 *It is* better to dwell in the corner of the
housetop, than with a brawling woman and
in a wide house.
25 *As* cold waters to a thirsty soul, so *is* good
news from a far country.
26 A righteous man falling down before
the wicked *is as* a troubled fountain, and a
corrupt spring.
27 *It is* not good to eat much honey: so *for*
men to search their own glory *is not* glory.
28 He that *hath* no rule over his own spirit
is like a city *that is* broken down, *and* without walls.

Proverbs 26

1 As snow in summer, and as rain in harvest,
so honour is not seemly for a fool.
2 As the bird by wandering, as the swallow
by flying, so the curse causeless shall not
come.
3 A whip for the horse, a bridle for the ass,
and a rod for the fool's back.
4 Answer not a fool according to his folly,
lest thou also be like unto him.
5 Answer a fool according to his folly, lest
he be wise in his own conceit.
6 He that sendeth a message by the hand
of a fool cutteth off the feet, *and* drinketh
damage.
7 The legs of the lame are not equal: so *is* a
parable in the mouth of fools.
8 As he that bindeth a stone in a sling, so *is*
he that giveth honour to a fool.
9 *As* a thorn goeth up into the hand of a
drunkard, so *is* a parable in the mouth of
fools.
10 The great *God* that formed all *things*
both rewardeth the fool, and rewardeth
transgressors.
11 As a dog returneth to his vomit, *so* a fool
returneth to his folly.
12 Seest thou a man wise in his own conceit?
there is more hope of a fool than of him.
13 The slothful *man* saith, *There is* a lion in
the way; a lion *is* in the streets.
14 *As* the door turneth upon his hinges, so
doth the slothful upon his bed.
15 The slothful hideth his hand in *his* bosom;
it grieveth him to bring it again to his mouth.
16 The sluggard *is* wiser in his own conceit
than seven men that can render a reason.
17 He that passeth by, *and* meddleth with
strife *belonging* not to him, *is like* one that
taketh a dog by the ears.
18 As a mad *man* who casteth firebrands,
arrows, and death,
19 So *is* the man *that* deceiveth his neighbour, and saith, Am not I in sport?

20 Where no wood is, *there* the fire goeth
out: so where *there is* no talebearer, the
strife ceaseth.
21 *As* coals *are* to burning coals, and wood
to fire; so *is* a contentious man to kindle
strife.
22 The words of a talebearer *are* as wounds,
and they go down into the innermost parts
of the belly.
23 Burning lips and a wicked heart *are like* a
potsherd covered with silver dross.
24 He that hateth dissembleth with his lips,
and layeth up deceit within him;
25 When he speaketh fair, believe him
not: for *there are* seven abominations in
his heart.
26 *Whose* hatred is covered by deceit, his
wickedness shall be shewed before the
whole congregation.
27 Whoso diggeth a pit shall fall therein:
and he that rolleth a stone, it will return
upon him.
28 A lying tongue hateth *those that are*
afflicted by it; and a flattering mouth worketh ruin.

Proverbs 27

1 Boast not thyself of to morrow; for thou
knowest not what a day may bring forth.
2 Let another man praise thee, and not
thine own mouth; a stranger, and not thine
own lips.
3 A stone *is* heavy, and the sand weighty;
but a fool's wrath *is* heavier than them both.
4 Wrath *is* cruel, and anger *is* outrageous;
but who *is* able to stand before envy?
5 Open rebuke *is* better than secret love.
6 Faithful *are* the wounds of a friend; but
the kisses of an enemy *are* deceitful.
7 The full soul loatheth an honeycomb;
but to the hungry soul every bitter thing
is sweet.
8 As a bird that wandereth from her nest,
so *is* a man that wandereth from his place.
9 Ointment and perfume rejoice the heart:
so *doth* the sweetness of a man's friend by
hearty counsel.
10 Thine own friend, and thy father's friend,
forsake not; neither go into thy brother's
house in the day of thy calamity: *for* better
is a neighbour *that is* near than a brother
far off.
11 My son, be wise, and make my heart glad,
that I may answer him that reproacheth me.
12 A prudent *man* foreseeth the evil, *and*
hideth himself; *but* the simple pass on, *and*
are punished.
13 Take his garment that is surety for a
stranger, and take a pledge of him for a
strange woman.
14 He that blesseth his friend with a loud
voice, rising early in the morning, it shall be
counted a curse to him.
15 A continual dropping in a very rainy day
and a contentious woman are alike.
16 Whosoever hideth her hideth the wind,
and the ointment of his right hand, *which*
bewrayeth *itself*.
17 Iron sharpeneth iron; so a man sharpeneth the countenance of his friend.
18 Whoso keepeth the fig tree shall eat
the fruit thereof: so he that waiteth on his
master shall be honoured.
19 As in water face *answereth* to face, so
the heart of man to man.
20 Hell and destruction are never full; so the
eyes of man are never satisfied.
21 *As* the fining pot for silver, and the furnace for gold; so *is* a man to his praise.
22 Though thou shouldest bray a fool in a
mortar among wheat with a pestle, *yet* will
not his foolishness depart from him.
23 Be thou diligent to know the state of thy
flocks, *and* look well to thy herds.
24 For riches *are* not for ever: and doth the
crown *endure* to every generation?
25 The hay appeareth, and the tender grass
sheweth itself, and herbs of the mountains
are gathered.
26 The lambs *are* for thy clothing, and the
goats *are* the price of the field.
27 And *thou shalt have* goats' milk enough
for thy food, for the food of thy household,
and *for* the maintenance for thy maidens.

Proverbs 28

1 The wicked flee when no man pursueth:
but the righteous are bold as a lion.
2 For the transgression of a land many *are*
the princes thereof: but by a man of understanding *and* knowledge the state *thereof*
shall be prolonged.
3 A poor man that oppresseth the poor *is*
like a sweeping rain which leaveth no food.
4 They that forsake the law praise the

wicked: but such as keep the law contend
with them.
5 Evil men understand not judgment: but
they that seek the LORD understand all
things.
6 Better *is* the poor that walketh in his
uprightness, than *he that is* perverse *in his*
ways, though he *be* rich.
7 Whoso keepeth the law *is* a wise son:
but he that is a companion of riotous *men*
shameth his father.
8 He that by usury and unjust gain increaseth
his substance, he shall gather it for him that
will pity the poor.
9 He that turneth away his ear from hearing
the law, even his prayer *shall be* abomination.
10 Whoso causeth the righteous to go astray
in an evil way, he shall fall himself into his
own pit: but the upright shall have good
things in possession.
11 The rich man *is* wise in his own conceit;
but the poor that hath understanding searcheth him out.
12 When righteous *men* do rejoice, *there*
is great glory: but when the wicked rise, a
man is hidden.
13 He that covereth his sins shall not prosper: but whoso confesseth and forsaketh
them shall have mercy.
14 Happy *is* the man that feareth alway:
but he that hardeneth his heart shall fall
into mischief.
15 *As* a roaring lion, and a ranging bear;
so is a wicked ruler over the poor people.
16 The prince that wanteth understanding
is also a great oppressor: *but* he that hateth
covetousness shall prolong *his* days.
17 A man that doeth violence to the blood
of *any* person shall flee to the pit; let no
man stay him.
18 Whoso walketh uprightly shall be saved:
but *he that is* perverse *in his* ways shall fall
at once.
19 He that tilleth his land shall have plenty
of bread: but he that followeth after vain
persons shall have poverty enough.
20 A faithful man shall abound with blessings: but he that maketh haste to be rich
shall not be innocent.
21 To have respect of persons *is* not good:
for for a piece of bread *that* man will transgress.
22 He that hasteth to be rich *hath* an evil
eye, and considereth not that poverty shall
come upon him.
23 He that rebuketh a man afterwards shall
find more favour than he that flattereth
with the tongue.
24 Whoso robbeth his father or his mother,
and saith, *It is* no transgression; the same *is*
the companion of a destroyer.
25 He that is of a proud heart stirreth up
strife: but he that putteth his trust in the
LORD shall be made fat.
26 He that trusteth in his own heart is a
fool: but whoso walketh wisely, he shall
be delivered.
27 He that giveth unto the poor shall not
lack: but he that hideth his eyes shall have
many a curse.
28 When the wicked rise, men hide themselves: but when they perish, the righteous
increase.

Proverbs 29

1 He, that being often reproved hardeneth
his neck, shall suddenly be destroyed, and
that without remedy.
2 When the righteous are in authority, the
people rejoice: but when the wicked beareth
rule, the people mourn.
3 Whoso loveth wisdom rejoiceth his father:
but he that keepeth company with harlots
spendeth *his* substance.
4 The king by judgment establisheth the
land: but he that receiveth gifts overthroweth it.
5 A man that flattereth his neighbour spreadeth a net for his feet.
6 In the transgression of an evil man *there*
is a snare: but the righteous doth sing and
rejoice.
7 The righteous considereth the cause of
the poor: *but* the wicked regardeth not to
know *it*.
8 Scornful men bring a city into a snare: but
wise *men* turn away wrath.
9 *If* a wise man contendeth with a foolish
man, whether he rage or laugh, *there is*
no rest.
10 The bloodthirsty hate the upright: but
the just seek his soul.
11 A fool uttereth all his mind: but a wise
man keepeth it in till afterwards.

12 If a ruler hearken to lies, all his servants
are wicked.
13 The poor and the deceitful man meet
together: the LORD lighteneth both their
eyes.
14 The king that faithfully judgeth the poor,
his throne shall be established for ever.
15 The rod and reproof give wisdom: but
a child left *to himself* bringeth his mother
to shame.
16 When the wicked are multiplied, transgression increaseth: but the righteous shall
see their fall.
17 Correct thy son, and he shall give thee
rest; yea, he shall give delight unto thy soul.
18 Where *there is* no vision, the people perish: but he that keepeth the law, happy *is* he.
19 A servant will not be corrected by
words: for though he understand he will
not answer.
20 Seest thou a man *that is* hasty in his
words? *there is* more hope of a fool than
of him.
21 He that delicately bringeth up his servant
from a child shall have him become *his* son
at the length.
22 An angry man stirreth up strife, and a
furious man aboundeth in transgression.
23 A man's pride shall bring him low: but
honour shall uphold the humble in spirit.
24 Whoso is partner with a thief hateth his
own soul: he heareth cursing, and bewrayeth *it* not.
25 The fear of man bringeth a snare: but
whoso putteth his trust in the LORD shall
be safe.
26 Many seek the ruler's favour; but *every*
man's judgment *cometh* from the LORD.
27 An unjust man *is* an abomination to the
just: and *he that is* upright in the way *is*
abomination to the wicked.

Proverbs 30

1 The words of Agur the son of Jakeh, *even*
the prophecy: the man spake unto Ithiel,
even unto Ithiel and Ucal,
2 Surely I *am* more brutish than *any* man,
and have not the understanding of a man.
3 I neither learned wisdom, nor have the
knowledge of the holy.
4 Who hath ascended up into heaven, or
descended? who hath gathered the wind
in his fists? who hath bound the waters in a
garment? who hath established all the ends
of the earth? what *is* his name, and what *is*
his son's name, if thou canst tell?
5 Every word of God *is* pure: he *is* a shield
unto them that put their trust in him.
6 Add thou not unto his words, lest he
reprove thee, and thou be found a liar.
7 Two *things* have I required of thee; deny
me *them* not before I die:
8 Remove far from me vanity and lies: give
me neither poverty nor riches; feed me with
food convenient for me:
9 Lest I be full, and deny *thee*, and say, Who
is the LORD? or lest I be poor, and steal, and
take the name of my God *in vain*.
10 Accuse not a servant unto his master,
lest he curse thee, and thou be found guilty.
11 *There is* a generation *that* curseth their
father, and doth not bless their mother.
12 *There is* a generation *that are* pure in
their own eyes, and *yet* is not washed from
their filthiness.
13 *There is* a generation, O how lofty are
their eyes! and their eyelids are lifted up.
14 *There is* a generation, whose teeth *are*
as swords, and their jaw teeth *as* knives, to
devour the poor from off the earth, and the
needy from *among* men.
15 The horseleach hath two daughters,
crying, Give, give. There are three *things*
that are never satisfied, *yea*, four *things* say
not, *It is* enough:
16 The grave; and the barren womb; the
earth *that* is not filled with water; and the
fire *that* saith not, *It is* enough.
17 The eye *that* mocketh at *his* father, and
despiseth to obey *his* mother, the ravens of
the valley shall pick it out, and the young
eagles shall eat it.
18 There be three *things which* are too wonderful for me, yea, four which I know not:
19 The way of an eagle in the air; the way
of a serpent upon a rock; the way of a ship
in the midst of the sea; and the way of a
man with a maid.
20 Such *is* the way of an adulterous woman;
she eateth, and wipeth her mouth, and
saith, I have done no wickedness.
21 For three *things* the earth is disquieted,
and for four *which* it cannot bear:
22 For a servant when he reigneth; and a
fool when he is filled with meat;
23 For an odious *woman* when she is mar-

ried; and an handmaid that is heir to her
mistress.
24 There be four *things which are* little upon
the earth, but they *are* exceeding wise:
25 The ants *are* a people not strong, yet they
prepare their meat in the summer;
26 The conies *are but* a feeble folk, yet make
they their houses in the rocks;
27 The locusts have no king, yet go they
forth all of them by bands;
28 The spider taketh hold with her hands,
and is in kings' palaces.
29 There be three *things* which go well, yea,
four are comely in going:
30 A lion *which is* strongest among beasts,
and turneth not away for any;
31 A greyhound; an he goat also; and a king,
against whom *there is* no rising up.
32 If thou hast done foolishly in lifting up
thyself, or if thou hast thought evil, *lay* thine
hand upon thy mouth.
33 Surely the churning of milk bringeth
forth butter, and the wringing of the nose
bringeth forth blood: so the forcing of wrath
bringeth forth strife.

Proverbs 31

1 The words of king Lemuel, the prophecy
that his mother taught him.
2 What, my son? and what, the son of my
womb? and what, the son of my vows?
3 Give not thy strength unto women, nor
thy ways to that which destroyeth kings.
4 *It is* not for kings, O Lemuel, *it is* not for
kings to drink wine; nor for princes strong
drink:
5 Lest they drink, and forget the law, and
pervert the judgment of any of the afflicted.
6 Give strong drink unto him that is ready
to perish, and wine unto those that be of
heavy hearts.
7 Let him drink, and forget his poverty, and
remember his misery no more.
8 Open thy mouth for the dumb in the cause
of all such as are appointed to destruction.
9 Open thy mouth, judge righteously, and
plead the cause of the poor and needy.
10 ¶ Who can find a virtuous woman? for
her price *is* far above rubies.
11 The heart of her husband doth safely
trust in her, so that he shall have no need
of spoil.
12 She will do him good and not evil all the
days of her life.
13 She seeketh wool, and flax, and worketh
willingly with her hands.
14 She is like the merchants' ships; she
bringeth her food from afar.
15 She riseth also while it is yet night, and
giveth meat to her household, and a portion
to her maidens.
16 She considereth a field, and buyeth it:
with the fruit of her hands she planteth a
vineyard.
17 She girdeth her loins with strength, and
strengtheneth her arms.
18 She perceiveth that her merchandise *is*
good: her candle goeth not out by night.
19 She layeth her hands to the spindle, and
her hands hold the distaff.
20 She stretcheth out her hand to the
poor; yea, she reacheth forth her hands
to the needy.
21 She is not afraid of the snow for her
household: for all her household *are* clothed
with scarlet.
22 She maketh herself coverings of tapestry;
her clothing *is* silk and purple.
23 Her husband is known in the gates, when
he sitteth among the elders of the land.
24 She maketh fine linen, and selleth *it;* and
delivereth girdles unto the merchant.
25 Strength and honour *are* her clothing;
and she shall rejoice in time to come.
26 She openeth her mouth with wisdom;
and in her tongue *is* the law of kindness.
27 She looketh well to the ways of her
household, and eateth not the bread of
idleness.
28 Her children arise up, and call her blessed;
her husband *also*, and he praiseth her.
29 Many daughters have done virtuously,
but thou excellest them all.
30 Favour *is* deceitful, and beauty *is* vain:
but a woman *that* feareth the LORD, she
shall be praised.
31 Give her of the fruit of her hands; and
let her own works praise her in the gates.

Ecclesiastes

Or, The Preacher

Ecclesiastes 1

1 The words of the Preacher, the son of David, king in Jerusalem.

2 Vanity of vanities, saith the Preacher, vanity of vanities; all *is* vanity.

3 What profit hath a man of all his labour which he taketh under the sun?

4 *One* generation passeth away, and *another* generation cometh: but the earth abideth for ever.

5 The sun also ariseth, and the sun goeth down, and hasteth to his place where he arose.

6 The wind goeth toward the south, and turneth about unto the north; it whirleth about continually, and the wind returneth again according to his circuits.

7 All the rivers run into the sea; yet the sea *is* not full; unto the place from whence the rivers come, thither they return again.

8 All things *are* full of labour; man cannot utter *it:* the eye is not satisfied with seeing, nor the ear filled with hearing.

9 The thing that hath been, it *is that* which shall be; and that which is done *is* that which shall be done: and *there is* no new *thing* under the sun.

10 Is there *any* thing whereof it may be said, See, this *is* new? it hath been already of old time, which was before us.

11 *There is* no remembrance of former *things;* neither shall there be *any* remembrance of *things* that are to come with *those* that shall come after.

12 ¶ I the Preacher was king over Israel in Jerusalem.

13 And I gave my heart to seek and search out by wisdom concerning all *things* that are done under heaven: this sore travail hath God given to the sons of man to be exercised therewith.

14 I have seen all the works that are done under the sun; and, behold, all *is* vanity and vexation of spirit.

15 *That which is* crooked cannot be made straight: and that which is wanting cannot be numbered.

16 I communed with mine own heart, saying, Lo, I am come to great estate, and have gotten more wisdom than all *they* that have been before me in Jerusalem: yea, my heart had great experience of wisdom and knowledge.

17 And I gave my heart to know wisdom, and to know madness and folly: I perceived that this also is vexation of spirit.

18 For in much wisdom *is* much grief: and he that increaseth knowledge increaseth sorrow.

Ecclesiastes 2

1 I said in mine heart, Go to now, I will prove thee with mirth, therefore enjoy pleasure: and, behold, this also *is* vanity.

2 I said of laughter, *It is* mad: and of mirth, What doeth it?

3 I sought in mine heart to give myself unto wine, yet acquainting mine heart with wisdom; and to lay hold on folly, till I might see what *was* that good for the sons of men, which they should do under the heaven all the days of their life.

4 I made me great works; I builded me houses; I planted me vineyards:

5 I made me gardens and orchards, and I planted trees in them of all *kind of* fruits:

6 I made me pools of water, to water therewith the wood that bringeth forth trees:

7 I got *me* servants and maidens, and had servants born in my house; also I had great possessions of great and small cattle above all that were in Jerusalem before me:

8 I gathered me also silver and gold, and the peculiar treasure of kings and of the provinces: I gat me men singers and women singers, and the delights of the sons of men, *as* musical instruments, and that of all sorts.

9 So I was great, and increased more than all that were before me in Jerusalem: also my wisdom remained with me.

10 And whatsoever mine eyes desired I kept not from them, I withheld not my heart from any joy; for my heart rejoiced in all my labour: and this was my portion of all my labour.

11 Then I looked on all the works that my

hands had wrought, and on the labour that
I had laboured to do: and, behold, all *was*
vanity and vexation of spirit, and *there was*
no profit under the sun.
12 ¶ And I turned myself to behold wisdom,
and madness, and folly: for what *can* the
man *do* that cometh after the king? *even*
that which hath been already done.
13 Then I saw that wisdom excelleth folly,
as far as light excelleth darkness.
14 The wise man's eyes *are* in his head; but
the fool walketh in darkness: and I myself
perceived also that one event happeneth
to them all.
15 Then said I in my heart, As it happeneth
to the fool, so it happeneth even to me; and
why was I then more wise? Then I said in
my heart, that this also *is* vanity.
16 For *there is* no remembrance of the wise
more than of the fool for ever; seeing that
which now *is* in the days to come shall all
be forgotten. And how dieth the wise *man*?
as the fool.
17 Therefore I hated life; because the work
that is wrought under the sun *is* grievous
unto me: for all *is* vanity and vexation of
spirit.
18 ¶ Yea, I hated all my labour which I had
taken under the sun: because I should leave
it unto the man that shall be after me.
19 And who knoweth whether he shall be
a wise *man* or a fool? yet shall he have rule
over all my labour wherein I have laboured,
and wherein I have shewed myself wise
under the sun. This *is* also vanity.
20 Therefore I went about to cause my
heart to despair of all the labour which I
took under the sun.
21 For there is a man whose labour *is* in
wisdom, and in knowledge, and in equity;
yet to a man that hath not laboured therein
shall he leave it *for* his portion. This also *is*
vanity and a great evil.
22 For what hath man of all his labour, and
of the vexation of his heart, wherein he hath
laboured under the sun?
23 For all his days *are* sorrows, and his travail
grief; yea, his heart taketh not rest in the
night. This is also vanity.
24 ¶ *There is* nothing better for a man,
than that he should eat and drink, and *that*
he should make his soul enjoy good in his
labour. This also I saw, that it *was* from the
hand of God.
25 For who can eat, or who else can hasten
hereunto, more than I?
26 For *God* giveth to a man that *is* good in
his sight wisdom, and knowledge, and joy:
but to the sinner he giveth travail, to gather
and to heap up, that he may give to *him that*
is good before God. This also *is* vanity and
vexation of spirit.

Ecclesiastes 3

1 To every *thing there is* a season, and a
time to every purpose under the heaven:
2 A time to be born, and a time to die; a
time to plant, and a time to pluck up *that*
which is planted;
3 A time to kill, and a time to heal; a time to
break down, and a time to build up;
4 A time to weep, and a time to laugh; a time
to mourn, and a time to dance;
5 A time to cast away stones, and a time to
gather stones together; a time to embrace,
and a time to refrain from embracing;
6 A time to get, and a time to lose; a time
to keep, and a time to cast away;
7 A time to rend, and a time to sew; a time
to keep silence, and a time to speak;
8 A time to love, and a time to hate; a time
of war, and a time of peace.
9 What profit hath he that worketh in that
wherein he laboureth?
10 I have seen the travail, which God hath
given to the sons of men to be exercised
in it.
11 He hath made every *thing* beautiful in
his time: also he hath set the world in their
heart, so that no man can find out the
work that God maketh from the beginning
to the end.
12 I know that *there is* no good in them,
but for *a man* to rejoice, and to do good
in his life.
13 And also that every man should eat and
drink, and enjoy the good of all his labour,
it *is* the gift of God.
14 I know that, whatsoever God doeth, it
shall be for ever: nothing can be put to it,
nor any thing taken from it: and God doeth
it, that *men* should fear before him.
15 That which hath been is now; and that
which is to be hath already been; and God
requireth that which is past.

16 ¶ And moreover I saw under the sun the
place of judgment, *that* wickedness *was*
there; and the place of righteousness, *that*
iniquity *was* there.
17 I said in mine heart, God shall judge the
righteous and the wicked: for *there is* a time
there for every purpose and for every work.
18 I said in mine heart concerning the estate
of the sons of men, that God might manifest
them, and that they might see that they
themselves are beasts.
19 For that which befalleth the sons of men
befalleth beasts; even one thing befalleth
them: as the one dieth, so dieth the other;
yea, they have all one breath; so that a man
hath no preeminence above a beast: for all
is vanity.
20 All go unto one place; all are of the dust,
and all turn to dust again.
21 Who knoweth the spirit of man that
goeth upward, and the spirit of the beast
that goeth downward to the earth?
22 Wherefore I perceive that *there is* nothing better, than that a man should rejoice
in his own works; for that *is* his portion:
for who shall bring him to see what shall
be after him?

Ecclesiastes 4

1 So I returned, and considered all the
oppressions that are done under the sun:
and behold the tears of *such as were*
oppressed, and they had no comforter;
and on the side of their oppressors *there*
was power; but they had no comforter.
2 Wherefore I praised the dead which are
already dead more than the living which
are yet alive.
3 Yea, better *is he* than both they, which
hath not yet been, who hath not seen the
evil work that is done under the sun.
4 ¶ Again, I considered all travail, and every
right work, that for this a man is envied of
his neighbour. This *is* also vanity and vexation of spirit.
5 The fool foldeth his hands together, and
eateth his own flesh.
6 Better *is* an handful *with* quietness, than
both the hands full *with* travail and vexation of spirit.
7 ¶ Then I returned, and I saw vanity under
the sun.
8 There is one *alone*, and *there is* not a second; yea, he hath neither child nor brother:
yet *is there* no end of all his labour; neither
is his eye satisfied with riches; neither *saith*
he, For whom do I labour, and bereave my
soul of good? This *is* also vanity, yea, it *is* a
sore travail.
9 ¶ Two *are* better than one; because they
have a good reward for their labour.
10 For if they fall, the one will lift up his
fellow: but woe to him *that is* alone when
he falleth; for *he hath* not another to help
him up.
11 Again, if two lie together, then they have
heat: but how can one be warm *alone?*
12 And if one prevail against him, two shall
withstand him; and a threefold cord is not
quickly broken.
13 ¶ Better *is* a poor and a wise child than
an old and foolish king, who will no more
be admonished.
14 For out of prison he cometh to reign;
whereas also *he that is* born in his kingdom
becometh poor.
15 I considered all the living which walk
under the sun, with the second child that
shall stand up in his stead.
16 *There is* no end of all the people, *even*
of all that have been before them: they
also that come after shall not rejoice in
him. Surely this also *is* vanity and vexation
of spirit.

Ecclesiastes 5

1 Keep thy foot when thou goest to the
house of God, and be more ready to hear,
than to give the sacrifice of fools: for they
consider not that they do evil.
2 Be not rash with thy mouth, and let not
thine heart be hasty to utter *any* thing
before God: for God *is* in heaven, and thou
upon earth: therefore let thy words be few.
3 For a dream cometh through the multitude
of business; and a fool's voice *is known* by
multitude of words.
4 When thou vowest a vow unto God, defer
not to pay it; for *he hath* no pleasure in fools:
pay that which thou hast vowed.
5 Better *is it* that thou shouldest not vow,
than that thou shouldest vow and not pay.
6 Suffer not thy mouth to cause thy flesh to
sin; neither say thou before the angel, that
it *was* an error: wherefore should God be

angry at thy voice, and destroy the work of
thine hands?
7 For in the multitude of dreams and many
words *there are* also *divers* vanities: but
fear thou God.
8 ¶ If thou seest the oppression of the
poor, and violent perverting of judgment
and justice in a province, marvel not at the
matter: for *he that is* higher than the highest
regardeth; and *there be* higher than they.
9 ¶ Moreover the profit of the earth is for
all: the king *himself* is served by the field.
10 He that loveth silver shall not be satisfied
with silver; nor he that loveth abundance
with increase: this *is* also vanity.
11 When goods increase, they are increased
that eat them: and what good *is there* to
the owners thereof, saving the beholding
of them with their eyes?
12 The sleep of a labouring man *is* sweet,
whether he eat little or much: but the abundance of the rich will not suffer him to sleep.
13 There is a sore evil *which* I have seen
under the sun, *namely*, riches kept for the
owners thereof to their hurt.
14 But those riches perish by evil travail:
and he begetteth a son, and *there is* nothing in his hand.
15 As he came forth of his mother's womb,
naked shall he return to go as he came, and
shall take nothing of his labour, which he
may carry away in his hand.
16 And this also *is* a sore evil, *that* in all
points as he came, so shall he go: and
what profit hath he that hath laboured for
the wind?
17 All his days also he eateth in darkness,
and *he hath* much sorrow and wrath with
his sickness.
18 ¶ Behold *that* which I have seen: *it is* good
and comely *for one* to eat and to drink, and
to enjoy the good of all his labour that he
taketh under the sun all the days of his life,
which God giveth him: for it *is* his portion.
19 Every man also to whom God hath given
riches and wealth, and hath given him power
to eat thereof, and to take his portion, and
to rejoice in his labour; this *is* the gift of God.
20 For he shall not much remember the days
of his life; because God answereth *him* in
the joy of his heart.

Ecclesiastes 6

1 There is an evil which I have seen under
the sun, and it *is* common among men:
2 A man to whom God hath given riches,
wealth, and honour, so that he wanteth
nothing for his soul of all that he desireth,
yet God giveth him not power to eat thereof,
but a stranger eateth it: this *is* vanity, and it
is an evil disease.
3 ¶ If a man beget an hundred *children*,
and live many years, so that the days of his
years be many, and his soul be not filled
with good, and also *that* he have no burial; I
say, *that* an untimely birth *is* better than he.
4 For he cometh in with vanity, and departeth in darkness, and his name shall be
covered with darkness.
5 Moreover he hath not seen the sun, nor
known *any thing:* this hath more rest than
the other.
6 ¶ Yea, though he live a thousand years
twice *told*, yet hath he seen no good: do
not all go to one place?
7 All the labour of man *is* for his mouth, and
yet the appetite is not filled.
8 For what hath the wise more than the
fool? what hath the poor, that knoweth to
walk before the living?
9 ¶ Better *is* the sight of the eyes than the
wandering of the desire: this *is* also vanity
and vexation of spirit.
10 That which hath been is named already,
and it is known that it *is* man: neither may he
contend with him that is mightier than he.
11 ¶ Seeing there be many things that
increase vanity, what *is* man the better?
12 For who knoweth what *is* good for man
in *this* life, all the days of his vain life which
he spendeth as a shadow? for who can tell a
man what shall be after him under the sun?

Ecclesiastes 7

1 A good name *is* better than precious ointment; and the day of death than the day of
one's birth.
2 ¶ *It is* better to go to the house of mourning, than to go to the house of feasting: for
that *is* the end of all men; and the living will
lay *it* to his heart.
3 Sorrow *is* better than laughter: for by the
sadness of the countenance the heart is
made better.
4 The heart of the wise *is* in the house of

mourning; but the heart of fools *is* in the house of mirth.

5 *It is* better to hear the rebuke of the wise, than for a man to hear the song of fools.

6 For as the crackling of thorns under a pot, so *is* the laughter of the fool: this also *is* vanity.

7 ¶ Surely oppression maketh a wise man mad; and a gift destroyeth the heart.

8 Better *is* the end of a thing than the beginning thereof: *and* the patient in spirit *is* better than the proud in spirit.

9 Be not hasty in thy spirit to be angry: for anger resteth in the bosom of fools.

10 Say not thou, What is *the cause* that the former days were better than these? for thou dost not inquire wisely concerning this.

11 ¶ Wisdom *is* good with an inheritance: and *by it there is* profit to them that see the sun.

12 For wisdom *is* a defence, *and* money *is* a defence: but the excellency of knowledge *is, that* wisdom giveth life to them that have it.

13 Consider the work of God: for who can make *that* straight, which he hath made crooked?

14 In the day of prosperity be joyful, but in the day of adversity consider: God also hath set the one over against the other, to the end that man should find nothing after him.

15 All *things* have I seen in the days of my vanity: there is a just *man* that perisheth in his righteousness, and there is a wicked *man* that prolongeth *his life* in his wickedness.

16 Be not righteous over much; neither make thyself over wise: why shouldest thou destroy thyself?

17 Be not over much wicked, neither be thou foolish: why shouldest thou die before thy time?

18 *It is* good that thou shouldest take hold of this; yea, also from this withdraw not thine hand: for he that feareth God shall come forth of them all.

19 Wisdom strengtheneth the wise more than ten mighty *men* which are in the city.

20 For *there is* not a just man upon earth, that doeth good, and sinneth not.

21 Also take no heed unto all words that are spoken; lest thou hear thy servant curse thee:

22 For oftentimes also thine own heart knoweth that thou thyself likewise hast cursed others.

23 ¶ All this have I proved by wisdom: I said, I will be wise; but it *was* far from me.

24 That which is far off, and exceeding deep, who can find it out?

25 I applied mine heart to know, and to search, and to seek out wisdom, and the reason *of things*, and to know the wickedness of folly, even of foolishness *and* madness:

26 And I find more bitter than death the woman, whose heart *is* snares and nets, *and* her hands *as* bands: whoso pleaseth God shall escape from her; but the sinner shall be taken by her.

27 Behold, this have I found, saith the preacher, *counting* one by one, to find out the account:

28 Which yet my soul seeketh, but I find not: one man among a thousand have I found; but a woman among all those have I not found.

29 Lo, this only have I found, that God hath made man upright; but they have sought out many inventions.

Ecclesiastes 8

1 Who *is* as the wise *man?* and who knoweth the interpretation of a thing? a man's wisdom maketh his face to shine, and the boldness of his face shall be changed.

2 I *counsel thee* to keep the king's commandment, and *that* in regard of the oath of God.

3 Be not hasty to go out of his sight: stand not in an evil thing; for he doeth whatsoever pleaseth him.

4 Where the word of a king *is, there is* power: and who may say unto him, What doest thou?

5 Whoso keepeth the commandment shall feel no evil thing: and a wise man's heart discerneth both time and judgment.

6 ¶ Because to every purpose there is time and judgment, therefore the misery of man *is* great upon him.

7 For he knoweth not that which shall be: for who can tell him when it shall be?

8 *There is* no man that hath power over the spirit to retain the spirit; neither *hath he* power in the day of death: and *there is* no discharge in *that* war; neither shall wickedness deliver those that are given to it.

9 All this have I seen, and applied my heart

unto every work that is done under the sun:
there is a time wherein one man ruleth over
another to his own hurt.
10 And so I saw the wicked buried, who had
come and gone from the place of the holy,
and they were forgotten in the city where
they had so done: this *is* also vanity.
11 Because sentence against an evil work is
not executed speedily, therefore the heart
of the sons of men is fully set in them to
do evil.
12 ¶ Though a sinner do evil an hundred
times, and his *days* be prolonged, yet surely
I know that it shall be well with them that
fear God, which fear before him:
13 But it shall not be well with the wicked,
neither shall he prolong *his* days, *which
are* as a shadow; because he feareth not
before God.
14 There is a vanity which is done upon the
earth; that there be just *men*, unto whom
it happeneth according to the work of the
wicked; again, there be wicked *men*, to
whom it happeneth according to the work
of the righteous: I said that this also *is* vanity.
15 Then I commended mirth, because a
man hath no better thing under the sun,
than to eat, and to drink, and to be merry:
for that shall abide with him of his labour
the days of his life, which God giveth him
under the sun.
16 ¶ When I applied mine heart to know
wisdom, and to see the business that is done
upon the earth: (for also *there is that* neither
day nor night seeth sleep with his eyes:)
17 Then I beheld all the work of God, that a
man cannot find out the work that is done
under the sun: because though a man labour
to seek *it* out, yet he shall not find *it;* yea
further; though a wise *man* think to know
it, yet shall he not be able to find *it*.

Ecclesiastes 9

1 For all this I considered in my heart even
to declare all this, that the righteous, and
the wise, and their works, *are* in the hand of
God: no man knoweth either love or hatred
by all *that is* before them.
2 All *things come* alike to all: *there is* one
event to the righteous, and to the wicked;
to the good and to the clean, and to the
unclean; to him that sacrificeth, and to him
that sacrificeth not: as *is* the good, so *is* the
sinner; *and* he that sweareth, as *he* that
feareth an oath.
3 This *is* an evil among all *things* that are
done under the sun, that *there is* one event
unto all: yea, also the heart of the sons of
men is full of evil, and madness *is* in their
heart while they live, and after that *they
go* to the dead.
4 ¶ For to him that is joined to all the living
there is hope: for a living dog is better than
a dead lion.
5 For the living know that they shall die: but
the dead know not any thing, neither have
they any more a reward; for the memory
of them is forgotten.
6 Also their love, and their hatred, and their
envy, is now perished; neither have they any
more a portion for ever in any *thing* that is
done under the sun.
7 ¶ Go thy way, eat thy bread with joy, and
drink thy wine with a merry heart; for God
now accepteth thy works.
8 Let thy garments be always white; and let
thy head lack no ointment.
9 Live joyfully with the wife whom thou
lovest all the days of the life of thy vanity,
which he hath given thee under the sun, all
the days of thy vanity: for that *is* thy portion
in *this* life, and in thy labour which thou
takest under the sun.
10 Whatsoever thy hand findeth to do, do
it with thy might; for *there is* no work, nor
device, nor knowledge, nor wisdom, in the
grave, whither thou goest.
11 ¶ I returned, and saw under the sun, that
the race *is* not to the swift, nor the battle to
the strong, neither yet bread to the wise,
nor yet riches to men of understanding,
nor yet favour to men of skill; but time and
chance happeneth to them all.
12 For man also knoweth not his time: as
the fishes that are taken in an evil net, and
as the birds that are caught in the snare; so
are the sons of men snared in an evil time,
when it falleth suddenly upon them.
13 ¶ This wisdom have I seen also under the
sun, and it *seemed* great unto me:
14 *There was* a little city, and few men within
it; and there came a great king against it,
and besieged it, and built great bulwarks
against it:
15 Now there was found in it a poor wise
man, and he by his wisdom delivered the

city; yet no man remembered that same
poor man.
16 Then said I, Wisdom *is* better than
strength: nevertheless the poor man's
wisdom *is* despised, and his words are not
heard.
17 The words of wise *men are* heard in
quiet more than the cry of him that ruleth
among fools.
18 Wisdom *is* better than weapons of war:
but one sinner destroyeth much good.

Ecclesiastes 10

1 Dead flies cause the ointment of the
apothecary to send forth a stinking savour:
so doth a little folly him that is in reputation
for wisdom *and* honour.
2 A wise man's heart *is* at his right hand; but
a fool's heart at his left.
3 Yea also, when he that is a fool walketh
by the way, his wisdom faileth *him*, and he
saith to every one *that* he *is* a fool.
4 If the spirit of the ruler rise up against thee,
leave not thy place; for yielding pacifieth
great offences.
5 There is an evil *which* I have seen under
the sun, as an error *which* proceedeth from
the ruler:
6 Folly is set in great dignity, and the rich
sit in low place.
7 I have seen servants upon horses, and
princes walking as servants upon the earth.
8 He that diggeth a pit shall fall into it; and
whoso breaketh an hedge, a serpent shall
bite him.
9 Whoso removeth stones shall be hurt
therewith; *and* he that cleaveth wood shall
be endangered thereby.
10 If the iron be blunt, and he do not
whet the edge, then must he put to more
strength: but wisdom *is* profitable to direct.
11 Surely the serpent will bite without
enchantment; and a babbler is no better.
12 The words of a wise man's mouth *are*
gracious; but the lips of a fool will swallow
up himself.
13 The beginning of the words of his mouth
is foolishness: and the end of his talk *is* mischievous madness.
14 A fool also is full of words: a man cannot
tell what shall be; and what shall be after
him, who can tell him?
15 The labour of the foolish wearieth every
one of them, because he knoweth not how
to go to the city.
16 ¶ Woe to thee, O land, when thy king *is*
a child, and thy princes eat in the morning!
17 Blessed *art* thou, O land, when thy king
is the son of nobles, and thy princes eat
in due season, for strength, and not for
drunkenness!
18 ¶ By much slothfulness the building
decayeth; and through idleness of the hands
the house droppeth through.
19 ¶ A feast is made for laughter, and wine
maketh merry: but money answereth all
things.
20 ¶ Curse not the king, no not in thy
thought; and curse not the rich in thy bedchamber: for a bird of the air shall carry
the voice, and that which hath wings shall
tell the matter.

Ecclesiastes 11

1 Cast thy bread upon the waters: for thou
shalt find it after many days.
2 Give a portion to seven, and also to eight;
for thou knowest not what evil shall be
upon the earth.
3 If the clouds be full of rain, they empty
themselves upon the earth: and if the tree
fall toward the south, or toward the north,
in the place where the tree falleth, there
it shall be.
4 He that observeth the wind shall not sow;
and he that regardeth the clouds shall not
reap.
5 As thou knowest not what *is* the way of
the spirit, *nor* how the bones *do grow* in
the womb of her that is with child: even so
thou knowest not the works of God who
maketh all.
6 In the morning sow thy seed, and in the
evening withhold not thine hand: for thou
knowest not whether shall prosper, either
this or that, or whether they both *shall be*
alike good.
7 ¶ Truly the light *is* sweet, and a pleasant
thing it is for the eyes to behold the sun:
8 But if a man live many years, *and* rejoice
in them all; yet let him remember the days
of darkness; for they shall be many. All that
cometh *is* vanity.
9 ¶ Rejoice, O young man, in thy youth; and
let thy heart cheer thee in the days of thy
youth, and walk in the ways of thine heart,

and in the sight of thine eyes: but know thou, that for all these *things* God will bring thee into judgment.
10 Therefore remove sorrow from thy heart, and put away evil from thy flesh: for childhood and youth *are* vanity.

Ecclesiastes 12

1 Remember now thy Creator in the days of thy youth, while the evil days come not, nor the years draw nigh, when thou shalt say, I have no pleasure in them;
2 While the sun, or the light, or the moon, or the stars, be not darkened, nor the clouds return after the rain:
3 In the day when the keepers of the house shall tremble, and the strong men shall bow themselves, and the grinders cease because they are few, and those that look out of the windows be darkened,
4 And the doors shall be shut in the streets, when the sound of the grinding is low, and he shall rise up at the voice of the bird, and all the daughters of musick shall be brought low;
5 Also *when* they shall be afraid of *that which is* high, and fears *shall be* in the way, and the almond tree shall flourish, and the grasshopper shall be a burden, and desire shall fail: because man goeth to his long home, and the mourners go about the streets:
6 Or ever the silver cord be loosed, or the golden bowl be broken, or the pitcher be broken at the fountain, or the wheel broken at the cistern.
7 Then shall the dust return to the earth as it was: and the spirit shall return unto God who gave it.
8 ¶ Vanity of vanities, saith the preacher; all *is* vanity.
9 And moreover, because the preacher was wise, he still taught the people knowledge; yea, he gave good heed, and sought out, *and* set in order many proverbs.
10 The preacher sought to find out acceptable words: and *that which was* written *was* upright, *even* words of truth.
11 The words of the wise *are* as goads, and as nails fastened *by* the masters of assemblies, *which* are given from one shepherd.
12 And further, by these, my son, be admonished: of making many books *there is* no end; and much study *is* a weariness of the flesh.
13 ¶ Let us hear the conclusion of the whole matter: Fear God, and keep his commandments: for this *is* the whole *duty* of man.
14 For God shall bring every work into judgment, with every secret thing, whether *it be* good, or whether *it be* evil.

The Song Of Solomon

Song of Solomon 1

1 The song of songs, which *is* Solomon's.
2 Let him kiss me with the kisses of his mouth: for thy love *is* better than wine.
3 Because of the savour of thy good ointments thy name *is as* ointment poured forth, therefore do the virgins love thee.
4 Draw me, we will run after thee: the king hath brought me into his chambers: we will be glad and rejoice in thee, we will remember thy love more than wine: the upright love thee.
5 I *am* black, but comely, O ye daughters of Jerusalem, as the tents of Kedar, as the curtains of Solomon.
6 Look not upon me, because I *am* black, because the sun hath looked upon me: my mother's children were angry with me; they made me the keeper of the vineyards; *but* mine own vineyard have I not kept.
7 Tell me, O thou whom my soul loveth, where thou feedest, where thou makest *thy flock* to rest at noon: for why should I be as one that turneth aside by the flocks of thy companions?
8 ¶ If thou know not, O thou fairest among women, go thy way forth by the footsteps

of the flock, and feed thy kids beside the
shepherds' tents.
9 I have compared thee, O my love, to a
company of horses in Pharaoh's chariots.
10 Thy cheeks are comely with rows *of jewels*, thy neck with chains *of gold*.
11 We will make thee borders of gold with
studs of silver.
12 ¶ While the king *sitteth* at his table, my
spikenard sendeth forth the smell thereof.
13 A bundle of myrrh *is* my wellbeloved unto
me; he shall lie all night betwixt my breasts.
14 My beloved *is* unto me *as* a cluster of
camphire in the vineyards of En-gedi.
15 Behold, thou *art* fair, my love; behold,
thou *art* fair; thou *hast* doves' eyes.
16 Behold, thou *art* fair, my beloved, yea,
pleasant: also our bed *is* green.
17 The beams of our house *are* cedar, *and*
our rafters of fir.

Song of Solomon 2

1 I *am* the rose of Sharon, *and* the lily of
the valleys.
2 As the lily among thorns, so *is* my love
among the daughters.
3 As the apple tree among the trees of the
wood, so *is* my beloved among the sons. I sat
down under his shadow with great delight,
and his fruit *was* sweet to my taste.
4 He brought me to the banqueting house,
and his banner over me *was* love.
5 Stay me with flagons, comfort me with
apples: for I *am* sick of love.
6 His left hand *is* under my head, and his
right hand doth embrace me.
7 I charge you, O ye daughters of Jerusalem,
by the roes, and by the hinds of the field,
that ye stir not up, nor awake *my* love, till
he please.
8 ¶ The voice of my beloved! behold, he
cometh leaping upon the mountains, skip-
ping upon the hills.
9 My beloved is like a roe or a young hart:
behold, he standeth behind our wall, he
looketh forth at the windows, shewing
himself through the lattice.
10 My beloved spake, and said unto me, Rise
up, my love, my fair one, and come away.
11 For, lo, the winter is past, the rain is over
and gone;
12 The flowers appear on the earth; the time
of the singing *of birds* is come, and the voice
of the turtle is heard in our land;
13 The fig tree putteth forth her green figs,
and the vines *with* the tender grape give a
good smell. Arise, my love, my fair one, and
come away.
14 ¶ O my dove, *that art* in the clefts of the
rock, in the secret *places* of the stairs, let
me see thy countenance, let me hear thy
voice; for sweet *is* thy voice, and thy countenance *is* comely.
15 Take us the foxes, the little foxes, that
spoil the vines: for our vines *have* tender
grapes.
16 ¶ My beloved *is* mine, and I *am* his: he
feedeth among the lilies.
17 Until the day break, and the shadows
flee away, turn, my beloved, and be thou
like a roe or a young hart upon the mountains of Bether.

Song of Solomon 3

1 By night on my bed I sought him whom
my soul loveth: I sought him, but I found
him not.
2 I will rise now, and go about the city in the
streets, and in the broad ways I will seek
him whom my soul loveth: I sought him,
but I found him not.
3 The watchmen that go about the city
found me: *to whom I said*, Saw ye him whom
my soul loveth?
4 *It was* but a little that I passed from them,
but I found him whom my soul loveth: I held
him, and would not let him go, until I had
brought him into my mother's house, and
into the chamber of her that conceived me.
5 I charge you, O ye daughters of Jerusalem,
by the roes, and by the hinds of the field,
that ye stir not up, nor awake *my* love, till
he please.
6 ¶ Who *is* this that cometh out of the wilderness like pillars of smoke, perfumed with
myrrh and frankincense, with all powders
of the merchant?
7 Behold his bed, which *is* Solomon's; threescore valiant men *are* about it, of the valiant
of Israel.
8 They all hold swords, *being* expert in war:
every man *hath* his sword upon his thigh
because of fear in the night.
9 King Solomon made himself a chariot of
the wood of Lebanon.

10 He made the pillars thereof *of* silver, the
bottom thereof *of* gold, the covering of it *of*
purple, the midst thereof being paved *with*
love, for the daughters of Jerusalem.
11 Go forth, O ye daughters of Zion, and
behold king Solomon with the crown wherewith his mother crowned him in the day of
his espousals, and in the day of the gladness
of his heart.

Song of Solomon 4

1 Behold, thou *art* fair, my love; behold,
thou *art* fair; thou *hast* doves' eyes within
thy locks: thy hair *is* as a flock of goats, that
appear from mount Gilead.
2 Thy teeth *are* like a flock *of sheep that*
are even shorn, which came up from the
washing; whereof every one bear twins,
and none *is* barren among them.
3 Thy lips *are* like a thread of scarlet, and
thy speech *is* comely: thy temples *are* like
a piece of a pomegranate within thy locks.
4 Thy neck *is* like the tower of David builded
for an armoury, whereon there hang a thousand bucklers, all shields of mighty men.
5 Thy two breasts *are* like two young roes
that are twins, which feed among the lilies.
6 Until the day break, and the shadows flee
away, I will get me to the mountain of myrrh,
and to the hill of frankincense.
7 Thou *art* all fair, my love; *there is* no spot
in thee.
8 ¶ Come with me from Lebanon, *my*
spouse, with me from Lebanon: look from
the top of Amana, from the top of Shenir
and Hermon, from the lions' dens, from the
mountains of the leopards.
9 Thou hast ravished my heart, my sister,
my spouse; thou hast ravished my heart
with one of thine eyes, with one chain of
thy neck.
10 How fair is thy love, my sister, *my* spouse!
how much better is thy love than wine! and
the smell of thine ointments than all spices!
11 Thy lips, O *my* spouse, drop *as* the honeycomb: honey and milk *are* under thy
tongue; and the smell of thy garments *is*
like the smell of Lebanon.
12 A garden inclosed *is* my sister, *my* spouse;
a spring shut up, a fountain sealed.
13 Thy plants *are* an orchard of pomegranates, with pleasant fruits; camphire, with
spikenard,
14 Spikenard and saffron; calamus and
cinnamon, with all trees of frankincense;
myrrh and aloes, with all the chief spices:
15 A fountain of gardens, a well of living
waters, and streams from Lebanon.
16 ¶ Awake, O north wind; and come, thou
south; blow upon my garden, *that* the spices
thereof may flow out. Let my beloved come
into his garden, and eat his pleasant fruits.

Song of Solomon 5

1 I am come into my garden, my sister, *my*
spouse: I have gathered my myrrh with my
spice; I have eaten my honeycomb with my
honey; I have drunk my wine with my milk:
eat, O friends; drink, yea, drink abundantly,
O beloved.
2 ¶ I sleep, but my heart waketh: *it is* the
voice of my beloved that knocketh, *saying,*
Open to me, my sister, my love, my dove,
my undefiled: for my head is filled with dew,
and my locks with the drops of the night.
3 I have put off my coat; how shall I put
it on? I have washed my feet; how shall I
defile them?
4 My beloved put in his hand by the hole
of the door, and my bowels were moved
for him.
5 I rose up to open to my beloved; and my
hands dropped *with* myrrh, and my fingers
with sweet smelling myrrh, upon the han-
dles of the lock.
6 I opened to my beloved; but my beloved
had withdrawn himself, *and* was gone: my
soul failed when he spake: I sought him,
but I could not find him; I called him, but
he gave me no answer.
7 The watchmen that went about the city
found me, they smote me, they wounded
me; the keepers of the walls took away my
veil from me.
8 I charge you, O daughters of Jerusalem,
if ye find my beloved, that ye tell him, that
I *am* sick of love.
9 ¶ What *is* thy beloved more than *another*
beloved, O thou fairest among women?
what *is* thy beloved more than *another*
beloved, that thou dost so charge us?
10 My beloved *is* white and ruddy, the chiefest among ten thousand.
11 His head *is as* the most fine gold, his locks
are bushy, *and* black as a raven.
12 His eyes *are* as *the eyes* of doves by the

rivers of waters, washed with milk, *and*
fitly set.
13 His cheeks *are* as a bed of spices, *as*
sweet flowers: his lips *like* lilies, dropping
sweet smelling myrrh.
14 His hands *are as* gold rings set with the
beryl: his belly *is as* bright ivory overlaid
with sapphires.
15 His legs *are as* pillars of marble, set upon
sockets of fine gold: his countenance *is* as
Lebanon, excellent as the cedars.
16 His mouth *is* most sweet: yea, he *is* altogether lovely. This *is* my beloved, and this *is*
my friend, O daughters of Jerusalem.

Song of Solomon 6

1 Whither is thy beloved gone, O thou fairest among women? whither is thy beloved
turned aside? that we may seek him with
thee.
2 My beloved is gone down into his garden,
to the beds of spices, to feed in the gardens,
and to gather lilies.
3 I *am* my beloved's, and my beloved *is*
mine: he feedeth among the lilies.
4 ¶ Thou *art* beautiful, O my love, as Tirzah,
comely as Jerusalem, terrible as *an army*
with banners.
5 Turn away thine eyes from me, for they
have overcome me: thy hair *is* as a flock of
goats that appear from Gilead.
6 Thy teeth *are* as a flock of sheep which go
up from the washing, whereof every one
beareth twins, and *there is* not one barren
among them.
7 As a piece of a pomegranate *are* thy temples within thy locks.
8 There are threescore queens, and fourscore concubines, and virgins without
number.
9 My dove, my undefiled is *but* one; she *is*
the *only* one of her mother, she *is* the choice
one of her that bare her. The daughters saw
her, and blessed her; *yea*, the queens and
the concubines, and they praised her.
10 ¶ Who *is* she *that* looketh forth as the
morning, fair as the moon, clear as the sun,
and terrible as *an army* with banners?
11 I went down into the garden of nuts
to see the fruits of the valley, *and* to see
whether the vine flourished, *and* the pomegranates budded.
12 Or ever I was aware, my soul made me
like the chariots of Amminadib.
13 Return, return, O Shulamite; return,
return, that we may look upon thee. What
will ye see in the Shulamite? As it were the
company of two armies.

Song of Solomon 7

1 How beautiful are thy feet with shoes, O
prince's daughter! the joints of thy thighs
are like jewels, the work of the hands of a
cunning workman.
2 Thy navel *is like* a round goblet, *which*
wanteth not liquor: thy belly *is like* an heap
of wheat set about with lilies.
3 Thy two breasts *are* like two young roes
that are twins.
4 Thy neck *is* as a tower of ivory; thine eyes
like the fishpools in Heshbon, by the gate
of Bath-rabbim: thy nose *is* as the tower of
Lebanon which looketh toward Damascus.
5 Thine head upon thee *is* like Carmel, and
the hair of thine head like purple; the king
is held in the galleries.
6 How fair and how pleasant art thou, O
love, for delights!
7 This thy stature is like to a palm tree, and
thy breasts to clusters *of grapes*.
8 I said, I will go up to the palm tree, I will
take hold of the boughs thereof: now also
thy breasts shall be as clusters of the vine,
and the smell of thy nose like apples;
9 And the roof of thy mouth like the best
wine for my beloved, that goeth *down*
sweetly, causing the lips of those that are
asleep to speak.
10 ¶ I *am* my beloved's, and his desire *is*
toward me.
11 Come, my beloved, let us go forth into
the field; let us lodge in the villages.
12 Let us get up early to the vineyards; let us
see if the vine flourish, *whether* the tender
grape appear, *and* the pomegranates bud
forth: there will I give thee my loves.
13 The mandrakes give a smell, and at our
gates *are* all manner of pleasant *fruits*, new
and old, *which* I have laid up for thee, O my
beloved.

Song of Solomon 8

1 O that thou *wert* as my brother, that
sucked the breasts of my mother! *when* I

should find thee without, I would kiss thee;
yea, I should not be despised.
2 I would lead thee, *and* bring thee into my
mother's house, *who* would instruct me: I
would cause thee to drink of spiced wine of
the juice of my pomegranate.
3 His left hand *should be* under my head, and
his right hand should embrace me.
4 I charge you, O daughters of Jerusalem,
that ye stir not up, nor awake *my* love, until
he please.
5 Who *is* this that cometh up from the
wilderness, leaning upon her beloved? I
raised thee up under the apple tree: there
thy mother brought thee forth: there she
brought thee forth *that* bare thee.
6 ¶ Set me as a seal upon thine heart, as a
seal upon thine arm: for love *is* strong as
death; jealousy *is* cruel as the grave: the
coals thereof *are* coals of fire, *which hath*
a most vehement flame.
7 Many waters cannot quench love, neither
can the floods drown it: if a man would give
all the substance of his house for love, it
would utterly be contemned.
8 ¶ We have a little sister, and she hath no
breasts: what shall we do for our sister in
the day when she shall be spoken for?
9 If she *be* a wall, we will build upon her a
palace of silver: and if she *be* a door, we will
inclose her with boards of cedar.
10 I *am* a wall, and my breasts like towers:
then was I in his eyes as one that found
favour.
11 Solomon had a vineyard at Baal-hamon;
he let out the vineyard unto keepers; every
one for the fruit thereof was to bring a
thousand *pieces* of silver.
12 My vineyard, which *is* mine, *is* before
me: thou, O Solomon, *must have* a thousand, and those that keep the fruit thereof
two hundred.
13 Thou that dwellest in the gardens, the
companions hearken to thy voice: cause
me to hear *it*.
14 ¶ Make haste, my beloved, and be thou
like to a roe or to a young hart upon the
mountains of spices.

The Book Of

Isaiah

Isaiah 1

1 The vision of Isaiah the son of Amoz, which
he saw concerning Judah and Jerusalem
in the days of Uzziah, Jotham, Ahaz, *and*
Hezekiah, kings of Judah.
2 Hear, O heavens, and give ear, O earth: for
the LORD hath spoken, I have nourished and
brought up children, and they have rebelled
against me.
3 The ox knoweth his owner, and the ass his
master's crib: *but* Israel doth not know, my
people doth not consider.
4 Ah sinful nation, a people laden with iniquity, a seed of evildoers, children that are
corrupters: they have forsaken the LORD,
they have provoked the Holy One of Israel
unto anger, they are gone away backward.
5 ¶ Why should ye be stricken any more? ye
will revolt more and more: the whole head
is sick, and the whole heart faint.
6 From the sole of the foot even unto the
head *there is* no soundness in it; *but* wounds,
and bruises, and putrifying sores: they have
not been closed, neither bound up, neither
mollified with ointment.
7 Your country *is* desolate, your cities
are burned with fire: your land, strangers
devour it in your presence, and *it is* desolate,
as overthrown by strangers.
8 And the daughter of Zion is left as a cot-
tage in a vineyard, as a lodge in a garden of
cucumbers, as a besieged city.
9 Except the LORD of hosts had left unto
us a very small remnant, we should have
been as Sodom, *and* we should have been
like unto Gomorrah.
10 ¶ Hear the word of the LORD, ye rulers

of Sodom; give ear unto the law of our God,
ye people of Gomorrah.
11 To what purpose *is* the multitude of your
sacrifices unto me? saith the LORD: I am full
of the burnt offerings of rams, and the fat of
fed beasts; and I delight not in the blood of
bullocks, or of lambs, or of he goats.
12 When ye come to appear before me,
who hath required this at your hand, to
tread my courts?
13 Bring no more vain oblations; incense is
an abomination unto me; the new moons
and sabbaths, the calling of assemblies, I
cannot away with; *it is* iniquity, even the
solemn meeting.
14 Your new moons and your appointed
feasts my soul hateth: they are a trouble
unto me; I am weary to bear *them*.
15 And when ye spread forth your hands,
I will hide mine eyes from you: yea, when
ye make many prayers, I will not hear: your
hands are full of blood.
16 ¶ Wash you, make you clean; put away
the evil of your doings from before mine
eyes; cease to do evil;
17 Learn to do well; seek judgment, relieve
the oppressed, judge the fatherless, plead
for the widow.
18 Come now, and let us reason together,
saith the LORD: though your sins be as
scarlet, they shall be as white as snow;
though they be red like crimson, they shall
be as wool.
19 If ye be willing and obedient, ye shall eat
the good of the land:
20 But if ye refuse and rebel, ye shall be
devoured with the sword: for the mouth
of the LORD hath spoken *it*.
21 ¶ How is the faithful city become an harlot! it was full of judgment; righteousness
lodged in it; but now murderers.
22 Thy silver is become dross, thy wine
mixed with water:
23 Thy princes *are* rebellious, and companions of thieves: every one loveth gifts, and
followeth after rewards: they judge not the
fatherless, neither doth the cause of the
widow come unto them.
24 Therefore saith the Lord, the LORD of
hosts, the mighty One of Israel, Ah, I will
ease me of mine adversaries, and avenge
me of mine enemies:
25 ¶ And I will turn my hand upon thee,
and purely purge away thy dross, and take
away all thy tin:
26 And I will restore thy judges as at the
first, and thy counsellers as at the beginning:
afterward thou shalt be called, The city of
righteousness, the faithful city.
27 Zion shall be redeemed with judgment,
and her converts with righteousness.
28 ¶ And the destruction of the transgressors and of the sinners *shall be* together,
and they that forsake the LORD shall be
consumed.
29 For they shall be ashamed of the oaks
which ye have desired, and ye shall be
confounded for the gardens that ye have
chosen.
30 For ye shall be as an oak whose leaf
fadeth, and as a garden that hath no water.
31 And the strong shall be as tow, and the
maker of it as a spark, and they shall both
burn together, and none shall quench *them*.

Isaiah 2

1 The word that Isaiah the son of Amoz saw
concerning Judah and Jerusalem.
2 And it shall come to pass in the last days,
that the mountain of the LORD's house shall
be established in the top of the mountains,
and shall be exalted above the hills; and all
nations shall flow unto it.
3 And many people shall go and say, Come
ye, and let us go up to the mountain of the
LORD, to the house of the God of Jacob;
and he will teach us of his ways, and we
will walk in his paths: for out of Zion shall
go forth the law, and the word of the LORD
from Jerusalem.
4 And he shall judge among the nations, and
shall rebuke many people: and they shall
beat their swords into plowshares, and their
spears into pruninghooks: nation shall not
lift up sword against nation, neither shall
they learn war any more.
5 O house of Jacob, come ye, and let us walk
in the light of the LORD.
6 ¶ Therefore thou hast forsaken thy people
the house of Jacob, because they be replenished from the east, and *are* soothsayers like
the Philistines, and they please themselves
in the children of strangers.
7 Their land also is full of silver and gold,
neither *is there any* end of their treasures;

their land is also full of horses, neither *is*
there any end of their chariots:
8 Their land also is full of idols; they worship
the work of their own hands, that which
their own fingers have made:
9 And the mean man boweth down, and
the great man humbleth himself: therefore
forgive them not.
10 ¶ Enter into the rock, and hide thee in
the dust, for fear of the LORD, and for the
glory of his majesty.
11 The lofty looks of man shall be humbled,
and the haughtiness of men shall be bowed
down, and the LORD alone shall be exalted
in that day.
12 For the day of the LORD of hosts *shall be*
upon every *one that is* proud and lofty, and
upon every *one that is* lifted up; and he shall
be brought low:
13 And upon all the cedars of Lebanon, *that*
are high and lifted up, and upon all the oaks
of Bashan,
14 And upon all the high mountains, and
upon all the hills *that are* lifted up,
15 And upon every high tower, and upon
every fenced wall,
16 And upon all the ships of Tarshish, and
upon all pleasant pictures.
17 And the loftiness of man shall be bowed
down, and the haughtiness of men shall
be made low: and the LORD alone shall be
exalted in that day.
18 And the idols he shall utterly abolish.
19 And they shall go into the holes of the
rocks, and into the caves of the earth, for
fear of the LORD, and for the glory of his
majesty, when he ariseth to shake terribly
the earth.
20 In that day a man shall cast his idols
of silver, and his idols of gold, which they
made *each one* for himself to worship, to
the moles and to the bats;
21 To go into the clefts of the rocks, and
into the tops of the ragged rocks, for fear
of the LORD, and for the glory of his majesty,
when he ariseth to shake terribly the earth.
22 Cease ye from man, whose breath *is* in his
nostrils: for wherein is he to be accounted
of?

Isaiah 3

1 For, behold, the Lord, the LORD of hosts,
doth take away from Jerusalem and from
Judah the stay and the staff, the whole stay
of bread, and the whole stay of water,
2 The mighty man, and the man of war, the
judge, and the prophet, and the prudent,
and the ancient,
3 The captain of fifty, and the honourable
man, and the counseller, and the cunning
artificer, and the eloquent orator.
4 And I will give children *to be* their princes,
and babes shall rule over them.
5 And the people shall be oppressed, every
one by another, and every one by his neighbour: the child shall behave himself proudly
against the ancient, and the base against
the honourable.
6 When a man shall take hold of his brother
of the house of his father, *saying,* Thou hast
clothing, be thou our ruler, and *let* this ruin
be under thy hand:
7 In that day shall he swear, saying, I will
not be an healer; for in my house *is* neither
bread nor clothing: make me not a ruler of
the people.
8 For Jerusalem is ruined, and Judah is fallen:
because their tongue and their doings *are*
against the LORD, to provoke the eyes of
his glory.
9 ¶ The shew of their countenance doth
witness against them; and they declare
their sin as Sodom, they hide *it* not. Woe
unto their soul! for they have rewarded evil
unto themselves.
10 Say ye to the righteous, that *it shall be*
well *with him:* for they shall eat the fruit of
their doings.
11 Woe unto the wicked! *it shall be* ill *with*
him: for the reward of his hands shall be
given him.
12 ¶ *As for* my people, children *are* their
oppressors, and women rule over them. O
my people, they which lead thee cause *thee*
to err, and destroy the way of thy paths.
13 The LORD standeth up to plead, and
standeth to judge the people.
14 The LORD will enter into judgment with
the ancients of his people, and the princes
thereof: for ye have eaten up the vineyard;
the spoil of the poor *is* in your houses.
15 What mean ye *that* ye beat my people
to pieces, and grind the faces of the poor?
saith the Lord GOD of hosts.
16 ¶ Moreover the LORD saith, Because the
daughters of Zion are haughty, and walk

with stretched forth necks and wanton eyes, walking and mincing *as* they go, and making a tinkling with their feet:

17 Therefore the Lord will smite with a scab the crown of the head of the daughters of Zion, and the LORD will discover their secret parts.

18 In that day the Lord will take away the bravery of *their* tinkling ornaments *about their feet*, and *their* cauls, and *their* round tires like the moon,

19 The chains, and the bracelets, and the mufflers,

20 The bonnets, and the ornaments of the legs, and the headbands, and the tablets, and the earrings,

21 The rings, and nose jewels,

22 The changeable suits of apparel, and the mantles, and the wimples, and the crisping pins,

23 The glasses, and the fine linen, and the hoods, and the vails.

24 And it shall come to pass, *that* instead of sweet smell there shall be stink; and instead of a girdle a rent; and instead of well set hair baldness; and instead of a stomacher a girding of sackcloth; *and* burning instead of beauty.

25 Thy men shall fall by the sword, and thy mighty in the war.

26 And her gates shall lament and mourn; and she *being* desolate shall sit upon the ground.

Isaiah 4

1 And in that day seven women shall take hold of one man, saying, We will eat our own bread, and wear our own apparel: only let us be called by thy name, to take away our reproach.

2 In that day shall the branch of the LORD be beautiful and glorious, and the fruit of the earth *shall be* excellent and comely for them that are escaped of Israel.

3 And it shall come to pass, *that he that is* left in Zion, and *he that* remaineth in Jerusalem, shall be called holy, *even* every one that is written among the living in Jerusalem:

4 When the Lord shall have washed away the filth of the daughters of Zion, and shall have purged the blood of Jerusalem from the midst thereof by the spirit of judgment, and by the spirit of burning.

5 And the LORD will create upon every dwelling place of mount Zion, and upon her assemblies, a cloud and smoke by day, and the shining of a flaming fire by night: for upon all the glory *shall be* a defence.

6 And there shall be a tabernacle for a shadow in the daytime from the heat, and for a place of refuge, and for a covert from storm and from rain.

Isaiah 5

1 Now will I sing to my wellbeloved a song of my beloved touching his vineyard. My wellbeloved hath a vineyard in a very fruitful hill:

2 And he fenced it, and gathered out the stones thereof, and planted it with the choicest vine, and built a tower in the midst of it, and also made a winepress therein: and he looked that it should bring forth grapes, and it brought forth wild grapes.

3 And now, O inhabitants of Jerusalem, and men of Judah, judge, I pray you, betwixt me and my vineyard.

4 What could have been done more to my vineyard, that I have not done in it? wherefore, when I looked that it should bring forth grapes, brought it forth wild grapes?

5 And now go to; I will tell you what I will do to my vineyard: I will take away the hedge thereof, and it shall be eaten up; *and* break down the wall thereof, and it shall be trodden down:

6 And I will lay it waste: it shall not be pruned, nor digged; but there shall come up briers and thorns: I will also command the clouds that they rain no rain upon it.

7 For the vineyard of the LORD of hosts *is* the house of Israel, and the men of Judah his pleasant plant: and he looked for judgment, but behold oppression; for righteousness, but behold a cry.

8 ¶ Woe unto them that join house to house, *that* lay field to field, till *there be* no place, that they may be placed alone in the midst of the earth!

9 In mine ears *said* the LORD of hosts, Of a truth many houses shall be desolate, *even* great and fair, without inhabitant.

10 Yea, ten acres of vineyard shall yield one bath, and the seed of an homer shall yield an ephah.

11 ¶ Woe unto them that rise up early in the morning, *that* they may follow strong

drink; that continue until night, *till* wine
inflame them!
12 And the harp, and the viol, the tabret,
and pipe, and wine, are in their feasts: but
they regard not the work of the LORD, neither consider the operation of his hands.
13 ¶ Therefore my people are gone into
captivity, because *they have* no knowledge:
and their honourable men *are* famished, and
their multitude dried up with thirst.
14 Therefore hell hath enlarged herself,
and opened her mouth without measure:
and their glory, and their multitude, and
their pomp, and he that rejoiceth, shall
descend into it.
15 And the mean man shall be brought
down, and the mighty man shall be humbled, and the eyes of the lofty shall be
humbled:
16 But the LORD of hosts shall be exalted
in judgment, and God that is holy shall be
sanctified in righteousness.
17 Then shall the lambs feed after their
manner, and the waste places of the fat
ones shall strangers eat.
18 Woe unto them that draw iniquity with
cords of vanity, and sin as it were with a
cart rope:
19 That say, Let him make speed, *and* hasten his work, that we may see *it:* and let the
counsel of the Holy One of Israel draw nigh
and come, that we may know *it!*
20 ¶ Woe unto them that call evil good, and
good evil; that put darkness for light, and
light for darkness; that put bitter for sweet,
and sweet for bitter!
21 Woe unto *them that are* wise in their
own eyes, and prudent in their own sight!
22 Woe unto *them that are* mighty to drink
wine, and men of strength to mingle strong
drink:
23 Which justify the wicked for reward,
and take away the righteousness of the
righteous from him!
24 Therefore as the fire devoureth the
stubble, and the flame consumeth the chaff,
so their root shall be as rottenness, and
their blossom shall go up as dust: because
they have cast away the law of the LORD of
hosts, and despised the word of the Holy
One of Israel.
25 Therefore is the anger of the LORD
kindled against his people, and he hath
stretched forth his hand against them, and
hath smitten them: and the hills did tremble, and their carcases *were* torn in the
midst of the streets. For all this his anger is
not turned away, but his hand *is* stretched
out still.
26 ¶ And he will lift up an ensign to the
nations from far, and will hiss unto them
from the end of the earth: and, behold, they
shall come with speed swiftly:
27 None shall be weary nor stumble among
them; none shall slumber nor sleep; neither
shall the girdle of their loins be loosed, nor
the latchet of their shoes be broken:
28 Whose arrows *are* sharp, and all their
bows bent, their horses' hoofs shall be
counted like flint, and their wheels like a
whirlwind:
29 Their roaring *shall be* like a lion, they shall
roar like young lions: yea, they shall roar, and
lay hold of the prey, and shall carry *it* away
safe, and none shall deliver *it*.
30 And in that day they shall roar against
them like the roaring of the sea: and if *one*
look unto the land, behold darkness *and*
sorrow, and the light is darkened in the
heavens thereof.

Isaiah 6

1 In the year that king Uzziah died I saw
also the Lord sitting upon a throne, high
and lifted up, and his train filled the temple.
2 Above it stood the seraphims: each one
had six wings; with twain he covered his
face, and with twain he covered his feet,
and with twain he did fly.
3 And one cried unto another, and said, Holy,
holy, holy, *is* the LORD of hosts: the whole
earth *is* full of his glory.
4 And the posts of the door moved at the
voice of him that cried, and the house was
filled with smoke.
5 ¶ Then said I, Woe *is* me! for I am undone;
because I *am* a man of unclean lips, and I
dwell in the midst of a people of unclean
lips: for mine eyes have seen the King, the
LORD of hosts.
6 Then flew one of the seraphims unto me,
having a live coal in his hand, *which* he had
taken with the tongs from off the altar:
7 And he laid *it* upon my mouth, and said,
Lo, this hath touched thy lips; and thine
iniquity is taken away, and thy sin purged.

8 Also I heard the voice of the Lord, saying,
Whom shall I send, and who will go for us?
Then said I, Here *am* I; send me.
9 ¶ And he said, Go, and tell this people,
Hear ye indeed, but understand not; and
see ye indeed, but perceive not.
10 Make the heart of this people fat, and
make their ears heavy, and shut their eyes;
lest they see with their eyes, and hear with
their ears, and understand with their heart,
and convert, and be healed.
11 Then said I, Lord, how long? And he
answered, Until the cities be wasted without
inhabitant, and the houses without man,
and the land be utterly desolate,
12 And the LORD have removed men far
away, and *there be* a great forsaking in the
midst of the land.
13 ¶ But yet in it *shall be* a tenth, and *it* shall
return, and shall be eaten: as a teil tree, and
as an oak, whose substance *is* in them, when
they cast *their leaves: so* the holy seed *shall*
be the substance thereof.

Isaiah 7

1 And it came to pass in the days of Ahaz
the son of Jotham, the son of Uzziah, king
of Judah, *that* Rezin the king of Syria, and
Pekah the son of Remaliah, king of Israel,
went up toward Jerusalem to war against
it, but could not prevail against it.
2 And it was told the house of David, saying, Syria is confederate with Ephraim. And
his heart was moved, and the heart of his
people, as the trees of the wood are moved
with the wind.
3 Then said the LORD unto Isaiah, Go forth
now to meet Ahaz, thou, and Shear-jashub
thy son, at the end of the conduit of the
upper pool in the highway of the fuller's
field;
4 And say unto him, Take heed, and be
quiet; fear not, neither be fainthearted for
the two tails of these smoking firebrands,
for the fierce anger of Rezin with Syria, and
of the son of Remaliah.
5 Because Syria, Ephraim, and the son of
Remaliah, have taken evil counsel against
thee, saying,
6 Let us go up against Judah, and vex it, and
let us make a breach therein for us, and set a
king in the midst of it, *even* the son of Tabeal:
7 Thus saith the Lord GOD, It shall not stand,
neither shall it come to pass.
8 For the head of Syria *is* Damascus, and
the head of Damascus *is* Rezin; and within
threescore and five years shall Ephraim be
broken, that it be not a people.
9 And the head of Ephraim *is* Samaria, and
the head of Samaria *is* Remaliah's son. If
ye will not believe, surely ye shall not be
established.
10 ¶ Moreover the LORD spake again unto
Ahaz, saying,
11 Ask thee a sign of the LORD thy God; ask
it either in the depth, or in the height above.
12 But Ahaz said, I will not ask, neither will
I tempt the LORD.
13 And he said, Hear ye now, O house of
David; *Is it* a small thing for you to weary
men, but will ye weary my God also?
14 Therefore the Lord himself shall give
you a sign; Behold, a virgin shall conceive,
and bear a son, and shall call his name
Immanuel.
15 Butter and honey shall he eat, that he
may know to refuse the evil, and choose
the good.
16 For before the child shall know to refuse
the evil, and choose the good, the land that
thou abhorrest shall be forsaken of both
her kings.
17 ¶ The LORD shall bring upon thee, and
upon thy people, and upon thy father's
house, days that have not come, from the
day that Ephraim departed from Judah; *even*
the king of Assyria.
18 And it shall come to pass in that day, *that*
the LORD shall hiss for the fly that *is* in the
uttermost part of the rivers of Egypt, and
for the bee that *is* in the land of Assyria.
19 And they shall come, and shall rest all
of them in the desolate valleys, and in the
holes of the rocks, and upon all thorns, and
upon all bushes.
20 In the same day shall the Lord shave
with a rasor that is hired, *namely*, by them
beyond the river, by the king of Assyria, the
head, and the hair of the feet: and it shall
also consume the beard.
21 And it shall come to pass in that day,
that a man shall nourish a young cow, and
two sheep;
22 And it shall come to pass, for the abundance of milk *that* they shall give he shall

eat butter: for butter and honey shall every one eat that is left in the land.

23 And it shall come to pass in that day, *that* every place shall be, where there were a thousand vines at a thousand silverlings, it shall *even* be for briers and thorns.

24 With arrows and with bows shall *men* come thither; because all the land shall become briers and thorns.

25 And *on* all hills that shall be digged with the mattock, there shall not come thither the fear of briers and thorns: but it shall be for the sending forth of oxen, and for the treading of lesser cattle.

Isaiah 8

1 Moreover the LORD said unto me, Take thee a great roll, and write in it with a man's pen concerning Maher-shalal-hash-baz.

2 And I took unto me faithful witnesses to record, Uriah the priest, and Zechariah the son of Jeberechiah.

3 And I went unto the prophetess; and she conceived, and bare a son. Then said the LORD to me, Call his name Maher-shalal-hash-baz.

4 For before the child shall have knowledge to cry, My father, and my mother, the riches of Damascus and the spoil of Samaria shall be taken away before the king of Assyria.

5 ¶ The LORD spake also unto me again, saying,

6 Forasmuch as this people refuseth the waters of Shiloah that go softly, and rejoice in Rezin and Remaliah's son;

7 Now therefore, behold, the Lord bringeth up upon them the waters of the river, strong and many, *even* the king of Assyria, and all his glory: and he shall come up over all his channels, and go over all his banks:

8 And he shall pass through Judah; he shall overflow and go over, he shall reach *even* to the neck; and the stretching out of his wings shall fill the breadth of thy land, O Immanuel.

9 ¶ Associate yourselves, O ye people, and ye shall be broken in pieces; and give ear, all ye of far countries: gird yourselves, and ye shall be broken in pieces; gird yourselves, and ye shall be broken in pieces.

10 Take counsel together, and it shall come to nought; speak the word, and it shall not stand: for God *is* with us.

11 ¶ For the LORD spake thus to me with a strong hand, and instructed me that I should not walk in the way of this people, saying,

12 Say ye not, A confederacy, to all *them to* whom this people shall say, A confederacy; neither fear ye their fear, nor be afraid.

13 Sanctify the LORD of hosts himself; and *let* him *be* your fear, and *let* him *be* your dread.

14 And he shall be for a sanctuary; but for a stone of stumbling and for a rock of offence to both the houses of Israel, for a gin and for a snare to the inhabitants of Jerusalem.

15 And many among them shall stumble, and fall, and be broken, and be snared, and be taken.

16 Bind up the testimony, seal the law among my disciples.

17 And I will wait upon the LORD, that hideth his face from the house of Jacob, and I will look for him.

18 Behold, I and the children whom the LORD hath given me *are* for signs and for wonders in Israel from the LORD of hosts, which dwelleth in mount Zion.

19 ¶ And when they shall say unto you, Seek unto them that have familiar spirits, and unto wizards that peep, and that mutter: should not a people seek unto their God? for the living to the dead?

20 To the law and to the testimony: if they speak not according to this word, *it is* because *there is* no light in them.

21 And they shall pass through it, hardly bestead and hungry: and it shall come to pass, that when they shall be hungry, they shall fret themselves, and curse their king and their God, and look upward.

22 And they shall look unto the earth; and behold trouble and darkness, dimness of anguish; and *they shall be* driven to darkness.

Isaiah 9

1 Nevertheless the dimness *shall* not *be* such as *was* in her vexation, when at the first he lightly afflicted the land of Zebulun and the land of Naphtali, and afterward did more grievously afflict *her by* the way of the sea, beyond Jordan, in Galilee of the nations.

2 The people that walked in darkness have seen a great light: they that dwell in the land of the shadow of death, upon them hath the light shined.

3 Thou hast multiplied the nation, *and* not
increased the joy: they joy before thee
according to the joy in harvest, *and* as *men*
rejoice when they divide the spoil.
4 For thou hast broken the yoke of his burden, and the staff of his shoulder, the rod
of his oppressor, as in the day of Midian.
5 For every battle of the warrior *is* with con-
fused noise, and garments rolled in blood;
but *this* shall be with burning *and* fuel of fire.
6 For unto us a child is born, unto us a son
is given: and the government shall be upon
his shoulder: and his name shall be called
Wonderful, Counseller, The mighty God,
The everlasting Father, The Prince of Peace.
7 Of the increase of *his* government and
peace *there shall be* no end, upon the throne
of David, and upon his kingdom, to order it,
and to establish it with judgment and with
justice from henceforth even for ever. The
zeal of the LORD of hosts will perform this.
8 ¶ The Lord sent a word into Jacob, and it
hath lighted upon Israel.
9 And all the people shall know, *even*
Ephraim and the inhabitant of Samaria,
that say in the pride and stoutness of heart,
10 The bricks are fallen down, but we will
build with hewn stones: the sycomores
are cut down, but we will change *them*
into cedars.
11 Therefore the LORD shall set up the
adversaries of Rezin against him, and join
his enemies together;
12 The Syrians before, and the Philistines
behind; and they shall devour Israel with
open mouth. For all this his anger is not
turned away, but his hand *is* stretched
out still.
13 ¶ For the people turneth not unto him
that smiteth them, neither do they seek the
LORD of hosts.
14 Therefore the LORD will cut off from Israel
head and tail, branch and rush, in one day.
15 The ancient and honourable, he *is* the
head; and the prophet that teacheth lies,
he *is* the tail.
16 For the leaders of this people cause
them to err; and *they that are* led of them
are destroyed.
17 Therefore the Lord shall have no joy in
their young men, neither shall have mercy
on their fatherless and widows: for every
one *is* an hypocrite and an evildoer, and
every mouth speaketh folly. For all this his
anger is not turned away, but his hand *is*
stretched out still.
18 ¶ For wickedness burneth as the fire: it
shall devour the briers and thorns, and shall
kindle in the thickets of the forest, and they
shall mount up *like* the lifting up of smoke.
19 Through the wrath of the LORD of hosts
is the land darkened, and the people shall
be as the fuel of the fire: no man shall spare
his brother.
20 And he shall snatch on the right hand,
and be hungry; and he shall eat on the left
hand, and they shall not be satisfied: they
shall eat every man the flesh of his own arm:
21 Manasseh, Ephraim; and Ephraim,
Manasseh: *and* they together *shall be*
against Judah. For all this his anger is not
turned away, but his hand *is* stretched
out still.

Isaiah 10

1 Woe unto them that decree unrighteous
decrees, and that write grievousness *which*
they have prescribed;
2 To turn aside the needy from judgment,
and to take away the right from the poor
of my people, that widows may be their
prey, and *that* they may rob the fatherless!
3 And what will ye do in the day of visitation, and in the desolation *which* shall come
from far? to whom will ye flee for help? and
where will ye leave your glory?
4 Without me they shall bow down under
the prisoners, and they shall fall under the
slain. For all this his anger is not turned away,
but his hand *is* stretched out still.
5 ¶ O Assyrian, the rod of mine anger, and
the staff in their hand is mine indignation.
6 I will send him against an hypocritical
nation, and against the people of my wrath
will I give him a charge, to take the spoil, and
to take the prey, and to tread them down
like the mire of the streets.
7 Howbeit he meaneth not so, neither doth
his heart think so; but *it is* in his heart to
destroy and cut off nations not a few.
8 For he saith, *Are* not my princes altogether kings?
9 *Is* not Calno as Carchemish? *is* not Hamath
as Arpad? *is* not Samaria as Damascus?
10 As my hand hath found the kingdoms

of the idols, and whose graven images did
excel them of Jerusalem and of Samaria;
11 Shall I not, as I have done unto Samaria
and her idols, so do to Jerusalem and her
idols?
12 Wherefore it shall come to pass, *that*
when the Lord hath performed his whole
work upon mount Zion and on Jerusalem,
I will punish the fruit of the stout heart of
the king of Assyria, and the glory of his
high looks.
13 For he saith, By the strength of my hand
I have done *it*, and by my wisdom; for I am
prudent: and I have removed the bounds of
the people, and have robbed their treasures,
and I have put down the inhabitants like a
valiant *man:*
14 And my hand hath found as a nest the
riches of the people: and as one gathereth
eggs *that are* left, have I gathered all the
earth; and there was none that moved the
wing, or opened the mouth, or peeped.
15 Shall the axe boast itself against him that
heweth therewith? *or* shall the saw magnify
itself against him that shaketh it? as if the
rod should shake *itself* against them that lift
it up, *or* as if the staff should lift up *itself, as
if it were* no wood.
16 Therefore shall the Lord, the Lord of
hosts, send among his fat ones leanness;
and under his glory he shall kindle a burning
like the burning of a fire.
17 And the light of Israel shall be for a fire,
and his Holy One for a flame: and it shall
burn and devour his thorns and his briers
in one day;
18 And shall consume the glory of his forest,
and of his fruitful field, both soul and body:
and they shall be as when a standardbearer
fainteth.
19 And the rest of the trees of his forest
shall be few, that a child may write them.
20 ¶ And it shall come to pass in that day,
that the remnant of Israel, and such as are
escaped of the house of Jacob, shall no more
again stay upon him that smote them; but
shall stay upon the LORD, the Holy One of
Israel, in truth.
21 The remnant shall return, *even* the remnant of Jacob, unto the mighty God.
22 For though thy people Israel be as the
sand of the sea, *yet* a remnant of them
shall return: the consumption decreed shall
overflow with righteousness.
23 For the Lord GOD of hosts shall make a
consumption, even determined, in the midst
of all the land.
24 ¶ Therefore thus saith the Lord GOD of
hosts, O my people that dwellest in Zion,
be not afraid of the Assyrian: he shall smite
thee with a rod, and shall lift up his staff
against thee, after the manner of Egypt.
25 For yet a very little while, and the indignation shall cease, and mine anger in their
destruction.
26 And the LORD of hosts shall stir up a
scourge for him according to the slaughter
of Midian at the rock of Oreb: and *as* his rod
was upon the sea, so shall he lift it up after
the manner of Egypt.
27 And it shall come to pass in that day, *that*
his burden shall be taken away from off thy
shoulder, and his yoke from off thy neck,
and the yoke shall be destroyed because
of the anointing.
28 He is come to Aiath, he is passed to
Migron; at Michmash he hath laid up his
carriages:
29 They are gone over the passage: they
have taken up their lodging at Geba; Ramah
is afraid; Gibeah of Saul is fled.
30 Lift up thy voice, O daughter of Gallim:
cause it to be heard unto Laish, O poor
Anathoth.
31 Madmenah is removed; the inhabitants
of Gebim gather themselves to flee.
32 As yet shall he remain at Nob that day:
he shall shake his hand *against* the mount of
the daughter of Zion, the hill of Jerusalem.
33 Behold, the Lord, the LORD of hosts, shall
lop the bough with terror: and the high
ones of stature *shall be* hewn down, and
the haughty shall be humbled.
34 And he shall cut down the thickets of
the forest with iron, and Lebanon shall fall
by a mighty one.

Isaiah 11

1 And there shall come forth a rod out of
the stem of Jesse, and a Branch shall grow
out of his roots:
2 And the spirit of the LORD shall rest upon
him, the spirit of wisdom and understanding, the spirit of counsel and might, the spirit
of knowledge and of the fear of the LORD;

3 And shall make him of quick understanding in the fear of the LORD: and he shall not
judge after the sight of his eyes, neither
reprove after the hearing of his ears:
4 But with righteousness shall he judge the
poor, and reprove with equity for the meek
of the earth: and he shall smite the earth
with the rod of his mouth, and with the
breath of his lips shall he slay the wicked.
5 And righteousness shall be the girdle of his
loins, and faithfulness the girdle of his reins.
6 The wolf also shall dwell with the lamb,
and the leopard shall lie down with the
kid; and the calf and the young lion and
the fatling together; and a little child shall
lead them.
7 And the cow and the bear shall feed; their
young ones shall lie down together: and the
lion shall eat straw like the ox.
8 And the sucking child shall play on the hole
of the asp, and the weaned child shall put
his hand on the cockatrice' den.
9 They shall not hurt nor destroy in all my
holy mountain: for the earth shall be full of
the knowledge of the LORD, as the waters
cover the sea.
10 ¶ And in that day there shall be a root of
Jesse, which shall stand for an ensign of the
people; to it shall the Gentiles seek: and his
rest shall be glorious.
11 And it shall come to pass in that day, *that*
the Lord shall set his hand again the second
time to recover the remnant of his people,
which shall be left, from Assyria, and from
Egypt, and from Pathros, and from Cush,
and from Elam, and from Shinar, and from
Hamath, and from the islands of the sea.
12 And he shall set up an ensign for the
nations, and shall assemble the outcasts of
Israel, and gather together the dispersed of
Judah from the four corners of the earth.
13 The envy also of Ephraim shall depart,
and the adversaries of Judah shall be cut
off: Ephraim shall not envy Judah, and Judah
shall not vex Ephraim.
14 But they shall fly upon the shoulders of
the Philistines toward the west; they shall
spoil them of the east together: they shall
lay their hand upon Edom and Moab; and
the children of Ammon shall obey them.
15 And the LORD shall utterly destroy the
tongue of the Egyptian sea; and with his
mighty wind shall he shake his hand over
the river, and shall smite it in the seven
streams, and make *men* go over dryshod.
16 And there shall be an highway for the
remnant of his people, which shall be left,
from Assyria; like as it was to Israel in the
day that he came up out of the land of Egypt.

Isaiah 12

1 And in that day thou shalt say, O LORD, I
will praise thee: though thou wast angry
with me, thine anger is turned away, and
thou comfortedst me.
2 Behold, God *is* my salvation; I will trust,
and not be afraid: for the LORD JEHOVAH *is*
my strength and *my* song; he also is become
my salvation.
3 Therefore with joy shall ye draw water
out of the wells of salvation.
4 And in that day shall ye say, Praise the
LORD, call upon his name, declare his doings
among the people, make mention that his
name is exalted.
5 Sing unto the LORD; for he hath done excellent things: this *is* known in all the earth.
6 Cry out and shout, thou inhabitant of
Zion: for great *is* the Holy One of Israel in
the midst of thee.

Isaiah 13

1 The burden of Babylon, which Isaiah the
son of Amoz did see.
2 Lift ye up a banner upon the high mountain, exalt the voice unto them, shake the
hand, that they may go into the gates of
the nobles.
3 I have commanded my sanctified ones, I
have also called my mighty ones for mine
anger, *even* them that rejoice in my highness.
4 The noise of a multitude in the mountains,
like as of a great people; a tumultuous
noise of the kingdoms of nations gathered
together: the LORD of hosts mustereth the
host of the battle.
5 They come from a far country, from the
end of heaven, *even* the LORD, and the
weapons of his indignation, to destroy the
whole land.
6 ¶ Howl ye; for the day of the LORD *is* at
hand; it shall come as a destruction from
the Almighty.
7 Therefore shall all hands be faint, and
every man's heart shall melt:

8 And they shall be afraid: pangs and sorrows shall take hold of them; they shall be
in pain as a woman that travaileth: they shall
be amazed one at another; their faces *shall
be as* flames.
9 Behold, the day of the LORD cometh, cruel
both with wrath and fierce anger, to lay
the land desolate: and he shall destroy the
sinners thereof out of it.
10 For the stars of heaven and the constel-
lations thereof shall not give their light: the
sun shall be darkened in his going forth, and
the moon shall not cause her light to shine.
11 And I will punish the world for *their*
evil, and the wicked for their iniquity; and
I will cause the arrogancy of the proud to
cease, and will lay low the haughtiness of
the terrible.
12 I will make a man more precious than
fine gold; even a man than the golden
wedge of Ophir.
13 Therefore I will shake the heavens, and
the earth shall remove out of her place, in
the wrath of the LORD of hosts, and in the
day of his fierce anger.
14 And it shall be as the chased roe, and as
a sheep that no man taketh up: they shall
every man turn to his own people, and flee
every one into his own land.
15 Every one that is found shall be thrust
through; and every one that is joined *unto
them* shall fall by the sword.
16 Their children also shall be dashed to
pieces before their eyes; their houses shall
be spoiled, and their wives ravished.
17 Behold, I will stir up the Medes against
them, which shall not regard silver; and *as
for* gold, they shall not delight in it.
18 *Their* bows also shall dash the young
men to pieces; and they shall have no pity
on the fruit of the womb; their eye shall not
spare children.
19 ¶ And Babylon, the glory of kingdoms,
the beauty of the Chaldees' excellency,
shall be as when God overthrew Sodom
and Gomorrah.
20 It shall never be inhabited, neither shall
it be dwelt in from generation to generation: neither shall the Arabian pitch tent
there; neither shall the shepherds make
their fold there.
21 But wild beasts of the desert shall lie
there; and their houses shall be full of doleful creatures; and owls shall dwell there, and
satyrs shall dance there.
22 And the wild beasts of the islands shall
cry in their desolate houses, and dragons
in *their* pleasant palaces: and her time *is*
near to come, and her days shall not be
prolonged.

Isaiah 14

1 For the LORD will have mercy on Jacob,
and will yet choose Israel, and set them in
their own land: and the strangers shall be
joined with them, and they shall cleave to
the house of Jacob.
2 And the people shall take them, and bring
them to their place: and the house of Israel
shall possess them in the land of the LORD
for servants and handmaids: and they
shall take them captives, whose captives
they were; and they shall rule over their
oppressors.
3 And it shall come to pass in the day that
the LORD shall give thee rest from thy sorrow, and from thy fear, and from the hard
bondage wherein thou wast made to serve,
4 ¶ That thou shalt take up this proverb
against the king of Babylon, and say, How
hath the oppressor ceased! the golden city
ceased!
5 The LORD hath broken the staff of the
wicked, *and* the sceptre of the rulers.
6 He who smote the people in wrath with a
continual stroke, he that ruled the nations
in anger, is persecuted, *and* none hindereth.
7 The whole earth is at rest, *and* is quiet:
they break forth into singing.
8 Yea, the fir trees rejoice at thee, *and* the
cedars of Lebanon, *saying,* Since thou art
laid down, no feller is come up against us.
9 Hell from beneath is moved for thee to
meet *thee* at thy coming: it stirreth up the
dead for thee, *even* all the chief ones of the
earth; it hath raised up from their thrones
all the kings of the nations.
10 All they shall speak and say unto thee,
Art thou also become weak as we? art thou
become like unto us?
11 Thy pomp is brought down to the grave,
and the noise of thy viols: the worm is
spread under thee, and the worms cover
thee.
12 How art thou fallen from heaven, O Luci-
fer, son of the morning! *how* art thou cut

down to the ground, which didst weaken
the nations!
13 For thou hast said in thine heart, I will
ascend into heaven, I will exalt my throne
above the stars of God: I will sit also upon
the mount of the congregation, in the sides
of the north:
14 I will ascend above the heights of the
clouds; I will be like the most High.
15 Yet thou shalt be brought down to hell,
to the sides of the pit.
16 They that see thee shall narrowly look
upon thee, *and* consider thee, *saying, Is* this
the man that made the earth to tremble,
that did shake kingdoms;
17 *That* made the world as a wilderness, and
destroyed the cities thereof; *that* opened
not the house of his prisoners?
18 All the kings of the nations, *even* all of
them, lie in glory, every one in his own
house.
19 But thou art cast out of thy grave like an
abominable branch, *and as* the raiment of
those that are slain, thrust through with a
sword, that go down to the stones of the pit;
as a carcase trodden under feet.
20 Thou shalt not be joined with them in
burial, because thou hast destroyed thy
land, *and* slain thy people: the seed of evildoers shall never be renowned.
21 Prepare slaughter for his children for the
iniquity of their fathers; that they do not
rise, nor possess the land, nor fill the face
of the world with cities.
22 For I will rise up against them, saith the
LORD of hosts, and cut off from Babylon the
name, and remnant, and son, and nephew,
saith the LORD.
23 I will also make it a possession for the
bittern, and pools of water: and I will sweep
it with the besom of destruction, saith the
LORD of hosts.
24 ¶ The LORD of hosts hath sworn, saying,
Surely as I have thought, so shall it come
to pass; and as I have purposed, *so* shall
it stand:
25 That I will break the Assyrian in my land,
and upon my mountains tread him under
foot: then shall his yoke depart from off
them, and his burden depart from off their
shoulders.
26 This *is* the purpose that is purposed upon
the whole earth: and this *is* the hand that is
stretched out upon all the nations.
27 For the LORD of hosts hath purposed,
and who shall disannul *it?* and his hand *is*
stretched out, and who shall turn it back?
28 In the year that king Ahaz died was this
burden.
29 ¶ Rejoice not thou, whole Palestina,
because the rod of him that smote thee is
broken: for out of the serpent's root shall
come forth a cockatrice, and his fruit *shall
be* a fiery flying serpent.
30 And the firstborn of the poor shall feed,
and the needy shall lie down in safety: and
I will kill thy root with famine, and he shall
slay thy remnant.
31 Howl, O gate; cry, O city; thou, whole
Palestina, *art* dissolved: for there shall come
from the north a smoke, and none *shall be*
alone in his appointed times.
32 What shall *one* then answer the messengers of the nation? That the LORD hath
founded Zion, and the poor of his people
shall trust in it.

Isaiah 15

1 The burden of Moab. Because in the night
Ar of Moab is laid waste, *and* brought to
silence; because in the night Kir of Moab is
laid waste, *and* brought to silence;
2 He is gone up to Bajith, and to Dibon, the
high places, to weep: Moab shall howl over
Nebo, and over Medeba: on all their heads
shall be baldness, *and* every beard cut off.
3 In their streets they shall gird themselves
with sackcloth: on the tops of their houses,
and in their streets, every one shall howl,
weeping abundantly.
4 And Heshbon shall cry, and Elealeh: their
voice shall be heard *even* unto Jahaz: therefore the armed soldiers of Moab shall cry
out; his life shall be grievous unto him.
5 My heart shall cry out for Moab; his fugitives *shall flee* unto Zoar, an heifer of three
years old: for by the mounting up of Luhith
with weeping shall they go it up; for in the
way of Horonaim they shall raise up a cry
of destruction.
6 For the waters of Nimrim shall be desolate: for the hay is withered away, the grass
faileth, there is no green thing.
7 Therefore the abundance they have got-

ten, and that which they have laid up, shall they carry away to the brook of the willows.
8 For the cry is gone round about the borders of Moab; the howling thereof unto Eglaim, and the howling thereof unto Beer-elim.
9 For the waters of Dimon shall be full of blood: for I will bring more upon Dimon, lions upon him that escapeth of Moab, and upon the remnant of the land.

Isaiah 16

1 Send ye the lamb to the ruler of the land from Sela to the wilderness, unto the mount of the daughter of Zion.
2 For it shall be, *that*, as a wandering bird cast out of the nest, *so* the daughters of Moab shall be at the fords of Arnon.
3 Take counsel, execute judgment; make thy shadow as the night in the midst of the noonday; hide the outcasts; bewray not him that wandereth.
4 Let mine outcasts dwell with thee, Moab; be thou a covert to them from the face of the spoiler: for the extortioner is at an end, the spoiler ceaseth, the oppressors are consumed out of the land.
5 And in mercy shall the throne be established: and he shall sit upon it in truth in the tabernacle of David, judging, and seeking judgment, and hasting righteousness.
6 ¶ We have heard of the pride of Moab; *he is* very proud: *even* of his haughtiness, and his pride, and his wrath: *but* his lies *shall* not *be* so.
7 Therefore shall Moab howl for Moab, every one shall howl: for the foundations of Kir-hareseth shall ye mourn; surely *they are* stricken.
8 For the fields of Heshbon languish, *and* the vine of Sibmah: the lords of the heathen have broken down the principal plants thereof, they are come *even* unto Jazer, they wandered *through* the wilderness: her branches are stretched out, they are gone over the sea.
9 ¶ Therefore I will bewail with the weeping of Jazer the vine of Sibmah: I will water thee with my tears, O Heshbon, and Elealeh: for the shouting for thy summer fruits and for thy harvest is fallen.
10 And gladness is taken away, and joy out of the plentiful field; and in the vineyards there shall be no singing, neither shall there be shouting: the treaders shall tread out no wine in *their* presses; I have made *their vintage* shouting to cease.
11 Wherefore my bowels shall sound like an harp for Moab, and mine inward parts for Kir-haresh.
12 ¶ And it shall come to pass, when it is seen that Moab is weary on the high place, that he shall come to his sanctuary to pray; but he shall not prevail.
13 This *is* the word that the LORD hath spoken concerning Moab since that time.
14 But now the LORD hath spoken, saying, Within three years, as the years of an hireling, and the glory of Moab shall be contemned, with all that great multitude; and the remnant *shall be* very small *and* feeble.

Isaiah 17

1 The burden of Damascus. Behold, Damascus is taken away from *being* a city, and it shall be a ruinous heap.
2 The cities of Aroer *are* forsaken: they shall be for flocks, which shall lie down, and none shall make *them* afraid.
3 The fortress also shall cease from Ephraim, and the kingdom from Damascus, and the remnant of Syria: they shall be as the glory of the children of Israel, saith the LORD of hosts.
4 And in that day it shall come to pass, *that* the glory of Jacob shall be made thin, and the fatness of his flesh shall wax lean.
5 And it shall be as when the harvestman gathereth the corn, and reapeth the ears with his arm; and it shall be as he that gathereth ears in the valley of Rephaim.
6 ¶ Yet gleaning grapes shall be left in it, as the shaking of an olive tree, two *or* three berries in the top of the uppermost bough, four *or* five in the outmost fruitful branches thereof, saith the LORD God of Israel.
7 At that day shall a man look to his Maker, and his eyes shall have respect to the Holy One of Israel.
8 And he shall not look to the altars, the work of his hands, neither shall respect *that* which his fingers have made, either the groves, or the images.
9 ¶ In that day shall his strong cities be as a forsaken bough, and an uppermost branch,

which they left because of the children of
Israel: and there shall be desolation.
10 Because thou hast forgotten the God of
thy salvation, and hast not been mindful
of the rock of thy strength, therefore shalt
thou plant pleasant plants, and shalt set it
with strange slips:
11 In the day shalt thou make thy plant to
grow, and in the morning shalt thou make
thy seed to flourish: *but* the harvest *shall*
be a heap in the day of grief and of desperate sorrow.
12 ¶ Woe to the multitude of many people,
which make a noise like the noise of the
seas; and to the rushing of nations, *that*
make a rushing like the rushing of mighty
waters!
13 The nations shall rush like the rushing of
many waters: but *God* shall rebuke them,
and they shall flee far off, and shall be
chased as the chaff of the mountains before
the wind, and like a rolling thing before the
whirlwind.
14 And behold at eveningtide trouble; *and*
before the morning he *is* not. This *is* the
portion of them that spoil us, and the lot
of them that rob us.

Isaiah 18

1 Woe to the land shadowing with wings,
which *is* beyond the rivers of Ethiopia:
2 That sendeth ambassadors by the sea,
even in vessels of bulrushes upon the
waters, *saying*, Go, ye swift messengers,
to a nation scattered and peeled, to a people terrible from their beginning hitherto; a
nation meted out and trodden down, whose
land the rivers have spoiled!
3 All ye inhabitants of the world, and dwellers on the earth, see ye, when he lifteth up
an ensign on the mountains; and when he
bloweth a trumpet, hear ye.
4 For so the LORD said unto me, I will take
my rest, and I will consider in my dwelling
place like a clear heat upon herbs, *and* like
a cloud of dew in the heat of harvest.
5 For afore the harvest, when the bud is
perfect, and the sour grape is ripening in
the flower, he shall both cut off the sprigs
with pruning hooks, and take away *and* cut
down the branches.
6 They shall be left together unto the fowls
of the mountains, and to the beasts of the
earth: and the fowls shall summer upon
them, and all the beasts of the earth shall
winter upon them.
7 ¶ In that time shall the present be brought
unto the LORD of hosts of a people scattered
and peeled, and from a people terrible from
their beginning hitherto; a nation meted
out and trodden under foot, whose land
the rivers have spoiled, to the place of the
name of the LORD of hosts, the mount Zion.

Isaiah 19

1 The burden of Egypt. Behold, the LORD
rideth upon a swift cloud, and shall come
into Egypt: and the idols of Egypt shall be
moved at his presence, and the heart of
Egypt shall melt in the midst of it.
2 And I will set the Egyptians against the
Egyptians: and they shall fight every one
against his brother, and every one against
his neighbour; city against city, *and* kingdom
against kingdom.
3 And the spirit of Egypt shall fail in the
midst thereof; and I will destroy the counsel thereof: and they shall seek to the idols,
and to the charmers, and to them that have
familiar spirits, and to the wizards.
4 And the Egyptians will I give over into the
hand of a cruel lord; and a fierce king shall
rule over them, saith the Lord, the LORD
of hosts.
5 And the waters shall fail from the sea,
and the river shall be wasted and dried up.
6 And they shall turn the rivers far away; *and*
the brooks of defence shall be emptied and
dried up: the reeds and flags shall wither.
7 The paper reeds by the brooks, by the
mouth of the brooks, and every thing sown
by the brooks, shall wither, be driven away,
and be no *more*.
8 The fishers also shall mourn, and all they
that cast angle into the brooks shall lament,
and they that spread nets upon the waters
shall languish.
9 Moreover they that work in fine flax,
and they that weave networks, shall be
confounded.
10 And they shall be broken in the purposes
thereof, all that make sluices *and* ponds
for fish.
11 ¶ Surely the princes of Zoan *are* fools,
the counsel of the wise counsellers of Pharaoh is become brutish: how say ye unto

Pharaoh, I *am* the son of the wise, the son of ancient kings?

12 Where *are* they? where *are* thy wise *men?* and let them tell thee now, and let them know what the LORD of hosts hath purposed upon Egypt.

13 The princes of Zoan are become fools, the princes of Noph are deceived; they have also seduced Egypt, *even they that are* the stay of the tribes thereof.

14 The LORD hath mingled a perverse spirit in the midst thereof: and they have caused Egypt to err in every work thereof, as a drunken *man* staggereth in his vomit.

15 Neither shall there be *any* work for Egypt, which the head or tail, branch or rush, may do.

16 In that day shall Egypt be like unto women: and it shall be afraid and fear because of the shaking of the hand of the LORD of hosts, which he shaketh over it.

17 And the land of Judah shall be a terror unto Egypt, every one that maketh mention thereof shall be afraid in himself, because of the counsel of the LORD of hosts, which he hath determined against it.

18 ¶ In that day shall five cities in the land of Egypt speak the language of Canaan, and swear to the LORD of hosts; one shall be called, The city of destruction.

19 In that day shall there be an altar to the LORD in the midst of the land of Egypt, and a pillar at the border thereof to the LORD.

20 And it shall be for a sign and for a witness unto the LORD of hosts in the land of Egypt: for they shall cry unto the LORD because of the oppressors, and he shall send them a saviour, and a great one, and he shall deliver them.

21 And the LORD shall be known to Egypt, and the Egyptians shall know the LORD in that day, and shall do sacrifice and oblation; yea, they shall vow a vow unto the LORD, and perform *it*.

22 And the LORD shall smite Egypt: he shall smite and heal *it:* and they shall return *even* to the LORD, and he shall be intreated of them, and shall heal them.

23 ¶ In that day shall there be a highway out of Egypt to Assyria, and the Assyrian shall come into Egypt, and the Egyptian into Assyria, and the Egyptians shall serve with the Assyrians.

24 In that day shall Israel be the third with Egypt and with Assyria, *even* a blessing in the midst of the land:

25 Whom the LORD of hosts shall bless, saying, Blessed *be* Egypt my people, and Assyria the work of my hands, and Israel mine inheritance.

Isaiah 20

1 In the year that Tartan came unto Ashdod, (when Sargon the king of Assyria sent him,) and fought against Ashdod, and took it;

2 At the same time spake the LORD by Isaiah the son of Amoz, saying, Go and loose the sackcloth from off thy loins, and put off thy shoe from thy foot. And he did so, walking naked and barefoot.

3 And the LORD said, Like as my servant Isaiah hath walked naked and barefoot three years *for* a sign and wonder upon Egypt and upon Ethiopia;

4 So shall the king of Assyria lead away the Egyptians prisoners, and the Ethiopians captives, young and old, naked and barefoot, even with *their* buttocks uncovered, to the shame of Egypt.

5 And they shall be afraid and ashamed of Ethiopia their expectation, and of Egypt their glory.

6 And the inhabitant of this isle shall say in that day, Behold, such *is* our expectation, whither we flee for help to be delivered from the king of Assyria: and how shall we escape?

Isaiah 21

1 The burden of the desert of the sea. As whirlwinds in the south pass through; *so* it cometh from the desert, from a terrible land.

2 A grievous vision is declared unto me; the treacherous dealer dealeth treacherously, and the spoiler spoileth. Go up, O Elam: besiege, O Media; all the sighing thereof have I made to cease.

3 Therefore are my loins filled with pain: pangs have taken hold upon me, as the pangs of a woman that travaileth: I was bowed down at the hearing *of it;* I was dismayed at the seeing *of it*.

4 My heart panted, fearfulness affrighted me: the night of my pleasure hath he turned into fear unto me.

5 Prepare the table, watch in the watchtower, eat, drink: arise, ye princes, *and* anoint the shield.

6 For thus hath the Lord said unto me, Go, set a watchman, let him declare what he seeth.

7 And he saw a chariot *with* a couple of horsemen, a chariot of asses, *and* a chariot of camels; and he hearkened diligently with much heed:

8 And he cried, A lion: My lord, I stand continually upon the watchtower in the daytime, and I am set in my ward whole nights:

9 And, behold, here cometh a chariot of men, *with* a couple of horsemen. And he answered and said, Babylon is fallen, is fallen; and all the graven images of her gods he hath broken unto the ground.

10 O my threshing, and the corn of my floor: that which I have heard of the LORD of hosts, the God of Israel, have I declared unto you.

11 ¶ The burden of Dumah. He calleth to me out of Seir, Watchman, what of the night? Watchman, what of the night?

12 The watchman said, The morning cometh, and also the night: if ye will inquire, inquire ye: return, come.

13 ¶ The burden upon Arabia. In the forest in Arabia shall ye lodge, O ye travelling companies of Dedanim.

14 The inhabitants of the land of Tema brought water to him that was thirsty, they prevented with their bread him that fled.

15 For they fled from the swords, from the drawn sword, and from the bent bow, and from the grievousness of war.

16 For thus hath the Lord said unto me, Within a year, according to the years of an hireling, and all the glory of Kedar shall fail:

17 And the residue of the number of archers, the mighty men of the children of Kedar, shall be diminished: for the LORD God of Israel hath spoken *it*.

Isaiah 22

1 The burden of the valley of vision. What aileth thee now, that thou art wholly gone up to the housetops?

2 Thou that art full of stirs, a tumultuous city, a joyous city: thy slain *men are* not slain with the sword, nor dead in battle.

3 All thy rulers are fled together, they are bound by the archers: all that are found in thee are bound together, *which* have fled from far.

4 Therefore said I, Look away from me; I will weep bitterly, labour not to comfort me, because of the spoiling of the daughter of my people.

5 For *it is* a day of trouble, and of treading down, and of perplexity by the Lord GOD of hosts in the valley of vision, breaking down the walls, and of crying to the mountains.

6 And Elam bare the quiver with chariots of men *and* horsemen, and Kir uncovered the shield.

7 And it shall come to pass, *that* thy choicest valleys shall be full of chariots, and the horsemen shall set themselves in array at the gate.

8 ¶ And he discovered the covering of Judah, and thou didst look in that day to the armour of the house of the forest.

9 Ye have seen also the breaches of the city of David, that they are many: and ye gathered together the waters of the lower pool.

10 And ye have numbered the houses of Jerusalem, and the houses have ye broken down to fortify the wall.

11 Ye made also a ditch between the two walls for the water of the old pool: but ye have not looked unto the maker thereof, neither had respect unto him that fashioned it long ago.

12 And in that day did the Lord GOD of hosts call to weeping, and to mourning, and to baldness, and to girding with sackcloth:

13 And behold joy and gladness, slaying oxen, and killing sheep, eating flesh, and drinking wine: let us eat and drink; for to morrow we shall die.

14 And it was revealed in mine ears by the LORD of hosts, Surely this iniquity shall not be purged from you till ye die, saith the Lord GOD of hosts.

15 ¶ Thus saith the Lord GOD of hosts, Go, get thee unto this treasurer, *even* unto Shebna, which *is* over the house, *and say*,

16 What hast thou here? and whom hast thou here, that thou hast hewed thee out a sepulchre here, *as* he that heweth him out a sepulchre on high, *and* that graveth an habitation for himself in a rock?

17 Behold, the LORD will carry thee away with a mighty captivity, and will surely cover thee.

18 He will surely violently turn and toss
thee *like* a ball into a large country: there
shalt thou die, and there the chariots of thy
glory *shall be* the shame of thy lord's house.
19 And I will drive thee from thy station,
and from thy state shall he pull thee down.
20 ¶ And it shall come to pass in that day,
that I will call my servant Eliakim the son
of Hilkiah:
21 And I will clothe him with thy robe, and
strengthen him with thy girdle, and I will
commit thy government into his hand: and
he shall be a father to the inhabitants of
Jerusalem, and to the house of Judah.
22 And the key of the house of David will
I lay upon his shoulder; so he shall open,
and none shall shut; and he shall shut, and
none shall open.
23 And I will fasten him *as* a nail in a sure
place; and he shall be for a glorious throne
to his father's house.
24 And they shall hang upon him all the
glory of his father's house, the offspring
and the issue, all vessels of small quantity,
from the vessels of cups, even to all the
vessels of flagons.
25 In that day, saith the LORD of hosts, shall
the nail that is fastened in the sure place be
removed, and be cut down, and fall; and the
burden that *was* upon it shall be cut off: for
the LORD hath spoken *it*.

Isaiah 23

1 The burden of Tyre. Howl, ye ships of
Tarshish; for it is laid waste, so that there is
no house, no entering in: from the land of
Chittim it is revealed to them.
2 Be still, ye inhabitants of the isle; thou
whom the merchants of Zidon, that pass
over the sea, have replenished.
3 And by great waters the seed of Sihor, the
harvest of the river, *is* her revenue; and she
is a mart of nations.
4 Be thou ashamed, O Zidon: for the sea
hath spoken, *even* the strength of the sea,
saying, I travail not, nor bring forth children,
neither do I nourish up young men, *nor*
bring up virgins.
5 As at the report concerning Egypt, *so* shall
they be sorely pained at the report of Tyre.
6 Pass ye over to Tarshish; howl, ye inhabitants of the isle.
7 *Is* this your joyous *city*, whose antiquity
is of ancient days? her own feet shall carry
her afar off to sojourn.
8 Who hath taken this counsel against Tyre,
the crowning *city*, whose merchants *are*
princes, whose traffickers *are* the honourable of the earth?
9 The LORD of hosts hath purposed it, to
stain the pride of all glory, *and* to bring into
contempt all the honourable of the earth.
10 Pass through thy land as a river, O daughter of Tarshish: *there is* no more strength.
11 He stretched out his hand over the sea,
he shook the kingdoms: the LORD hath given
a commandment against the merchant *city*,
to destroy the strong holds thereof.
12 And he said, Thou shalt no more rejoice,
O thou oppressed virgin, daughter of Zidon:
arise, pass over to Chittim; there also shalt
thou have no rest.
13 Behold the land of the Chaldeans; this
people was not, *till* the Assyrian founded it
for them that dwell in the wilderness: they
set up the towers thereof, they raised up the
palaces thereof; *and* he brought it to ruin.
14 Howl, ye ships of Tarshish: for your
strength is laid waste.
15 And it shall come to pass in that day,
that Tyre shall be forgotten seventy years,
according to the days of one king: after
the end of seventy years shall Tyre sing as
an harlot.
16 Take an harp, go about the city, thou
harlot that hast been forgotten; make sweet
melody, sing many songs, that thou mayest
be remembered.
17 ¶ And it shall come to pass after the end
of seventy years, that the LORD will visit Tyre,
and she shall turn to her hire, and shall commit fornication with all the kingdoms of the
world upon the face of the earth.
18 And her merchandise and her hire shall
be holiness to the LORD: it shall not be trea-
sured nor laid up; for her merchandise shall
be for them that dwell before the LORD, to
eat sufficiently, and for durable clothing.

Isaiah 24

1 Behold, the LORD maketh the earth empty,
and maketh it waste, and turneth it upside
down, and scattereth abroad the inhabitants thereof.
2 And it shall be, as with the people, so with
the priest; as with the servant, so with his

master; as with the maid, so with her mistress; as with the buyer, so with the seller;
as with the lender, so with the borrower; as
with the taker of usury, so with the giver of
usury to him.
3 The land shall be utterly emptied, and
utterly spoiled: for the LORD hath spoken
this word.
4 The earth mourneth *and* fadeth away,
the world languisheth *and* fadeth away, the
haughty people of the earth do languish.
5 The earth also is defiled under the inhabitants thereof; because they have transgressed the laws, changed the ordinance,
broken the everlasting covenant.
6 Therefore hath the curse devoured the
earth, and they that dwell therein are desolate: therefore the inhabitants of the earth
are burned, and few men left.
7 The new wine mourneth, the vine languisheth, all the merryhearted do sigh.
8 The mirth of tabrets ceaseth, the noise
of them that rejoice endeth, the joy of the
harp ceaseth.
9 They shall not drink wine with a song;
strong drink shall be bitter to them that
drink it.
10 The city of confusion is broken down:
every house is shut up, that no man may
come in.
11 *There is* a crying for wine in the streets; all
joy is darkened, the mirth of the land is gone.
12 In the city is left desolation, and the gate
is smitten with destruction.
13 ¶ When thus it shall be in the midst of
the land among the people, *there shall be*
as the shaking of an olive tree, *and* as the
gleaning grapes when the vintage is done.
14 They shall lift up their voice, they shall
sing for the majesty of the LORD, they shall
cry aloud from the sea.
15 Wherefore glorify ye the LORD in the fires,
even the name of the LORD God of Israel in
the isles of the sea.
16 ¶ From the uttermost part of the earth
have we heard songs, *even* glory to the righteous. But I said, My leanness, my leanness,
woe unto me! the treacherous dealers have
dealt treacherously; yea, the treacherous
dealers have dealt very treacherously.
17 Fear, and the pit, and the snare, *are* upon
thee, O inhabitant of the earth.
18 And it shall come to pass, *that* he who
fleeth from the noise of the fear shall fall
into the pit; and he that cometh up out of
the midst of the pit shall be taken in the
snare: for the windows from on high are
open, and the foundations of the earth
do shake.
19 The earth is utterly broken down, the
earth is clean dissolved, the earth is moved
exceedingly.
20 The earth shall reel to and fro like a
drunkard, and shall be removed like a cot-
tage; and the transgression thereof shall
be heavy upon it; and it shall fall, and not
rise again.
21 And it shall come to pass in that day, *that*
the LORD shall punish the host of the high
ones *that are* on high, and the kings of the
earth upon the earth.
22 And they shall be gathered together, *as*
prisoners are gathered in the pit, and shall
be shut up in the prison, and after many
days shall they be visited.
23 Then the moon shall be confounded, and
the sun ashamed, when the LORD of hosts
shall reign in mount Zion, and in Jerusalem,
and before his ancients gloriously.

Isaiah 25

1 O Lord, thou *art* my God; I will exalt thee,
I will praise thy name; for thou hast done
wonderful *things; thy* counsels of old *are*
faithfulness *and* truth.
2 For thou hast made of a city an heap; *of* a
defenced city a ruin: a palace of strangers
to be no city; it shall never be built.
3 Therefore shall the strong people glorify
thee, the city of the terrible nations shall
fear thee.
4 For thou hast been a strength to the poor,
a strength to the needy in his distress, a
refuge from the storm, a shadow from the
heat, when the blast of the terrible ones *is*
as a storm *against* the wall.
5 Thou shalt bring down the noise of strangers, as the heat in a dry place; *even* the heat
with the shadow of a cloud: the branch of
the terrible ones shall be brought low.
6 ¶ And in this mountain shall the LORD of
hosts make unto all people a feast of fat
things, a feast of wines on the lees, of fat
things full of marrow, of wines on the lees
well refined.
7 And he will destroy in this mountain the

face of the covering cast over all people,
and the vail that is spread over all nations.
8 He will swallow up death in victory; and
the LORD GOD will wipe away tears from off
all faces; and the rebuke of his people shall
he take away from off all the earth: for the
LORD hath spoken *it*.
9 ¶ And it shall be said in that day, Lo, this
is our God; we have waited for him, and
he will save us: this *is* the LORD; we have
waited for him, we will be glad and rejoice
in his salvation.
10 For in this mountain shall the hand of
the LORD rest, and Moab shall be trodden
down under him, even as straw is trodden
down for the dunghill.
11 And he shall spread forth his hands in
the midst of them, as he that swimmeth
spreadeth forth *his hands* to swim: and he
shall bring down their pride together with
the spoils of their hands.
12 And the fortress of the high fort of thy
walls shall he bring down, lay low, *and* bring
to the ground, *even* to the dust.

Isaiah 26

1 In that day shall this song be sung in the
land of Judah; We have a strong city; salvation will *God* appoint *for* walls and bulwarks.
2 Open ye the gates, that the righteous
nation which keepeth the truth may enter in.
3 Thou wilt keep *him* in perfect peace,
whose mind *is* stayed *on thee:* because he
trusteth in thee.
4 Trust ye in the LORD for ever: for in the
LORD JEHOVAH *is* everlasting strength:
5 ¶ For he bringeth down them that dwell
on high; the lofty city, he layeth it low; he
layeth it low, *even* to the ground; he bringeth
it *even* to the dust.
6 The foot shall tread it down, *even* the feet
of the poor, *and* the steps of the needy.
7 The way of the just *is* uprightness: thou,
most upright, dost weigh the path of the
just.
8 Yea, in the way of thy judgments, O LORD,
have we waited for thee; the desire of *our*
soul *is* to thy name, and to the remembrance of thee.
9 With my soul have I desired thee in the
night; yea, with my spirit within me will I
seek thee early: for when thy judgments *are*
in the earth, the inhabitants of the world
will learn righteousness.
10 Let favour be shewed to the wicked, *yet*
will he not learn righteousness: in the land
of uprightness will he deal unjustly, and will
not behold the majesty of the LORD.
11 LORD, *when* thy hand is lifted up, they will
not see: *but* they shall see, and be ashamed
for *their* envy at the people; yea, the fire of
thine enemies shall devour them.
12 ¶ LORD, thou wilt ordain peace for us: for
thou also hast wrought all our works in us.
13 O LORD our God, *other* lords beside thee
have had dominion over us: *but* by thee only
will we make mention of thy name.
14 *They are* dead, they shall not live; *they
are* deceased, they shall not rise: therefore
hast thou visited and destroyed them, and
made all their memory to perish.
15 Thou hast increased the nation, O LORD,
thou hast increased the nation: thou art
glorified: thou hadst removed *it* far *unto*
all the ends of the earth.
16 LORD, in trouble have they visited thee,
they poured out a prayer *when* thy chastening *was* upon them.
17 Like as a woman with child, *that* draweth
near the time of her delivery, is in pain, *and*
crieth out in her pangs; so have we been in
thy sight, O LORD.
18 We have been with child, we have been
in pain, we have as it were brought forth
wind; we have not wrought any deliverance
in the earth; neither have the inhabitants
of the world fallen.
19 Thy dead *men* shall live, *together with*
my dead body shall they arise. Awake and
sing, ye that dwell in dust: for thy dew *is as*
the dew of herbs, and the earth shall cast
out the dead.
20 ¶ Come, my people, enter thou into thy
chambers, and shut thy doors about thee:
hide thyself as it were for a little moment,
until the indignation be overpast.
21 For, behold, the LORD cometh out of his
place to punish the inhabitants of the earth
for their iniquity: the earth also shall disclose
her blood, and shall no more cover her slain.

Isaiah 27

1 In that day the LORD with his sore and
great and strong sword shall punish leviathan the piercing serpent, even leviathan

that crooked serpent; and he shall slay the
dragon that *is* in the sea.
2 In that day sing ye unto her, A vineyard
of red wine.
3 I the LORD do keep it; I will water it every
moment: lest *any* hurt it, I will keep it night
and day.
4 Fury *is* not in me: who would set the briers
and thorns against me in battle? I would go
through them, I would burn them together.
5 Or let him take hold of my strength, *that*
he may make peace with me; *and* he shall
make peace with me.
6 He shall cause them that come of Jacob to
take root: Israel shall blossom and bud, and
fill the face of the world with fruit.
7 ¶ Hath he smitten him, as he smote those
that smote him? *or* is he slain according to
the slaughter of them that are slain by him?
8 In measure, when it shooteth forth, thou
wilt debate with it: he stayeth his rough
wind in the day of the east wind.
9 By this therefore shall the iniquity of
Jacob be purged; and this *is* all the fruit to
take away his sin; when he maketh all the
stones of the altar as chalkstones that are
beaten in sunder, the groves and images
shall not stand up.
10 Yet the defenced city *shall be* desolate,
and the habitation forsaken, and left like a
wilderness: there shall the calf feed, and
there shall he lie down, and consume the
branches thereof.
11 When the boughs thereof are withered,
they shall be broken off: the women come,
and set them on fire: for it *is* a people of
no understanding: therefore he that made
them will not have mercy on them, and he
that formed them will shew them no favour.
12 ¶ And it shall come to pass in that day,
that the LORD shall beat off from the chan-
nel of the river unto the stream of Egypt,
and ye shall be gathered one by one, O ye
children of Israel.
13 And it shall come to pass in that day, *that*
the great trumpet shall be blown, and they
shall come which were ready to perish in
the land of Assyria, and the outcasts in the
land of Egypt, and shall worship the LORD
in the holy mount at Jerusalem.

Isaiah 28

1 Woe to the crown of pride, to the drunkards of Ephraim, whose glorious beauty *is*
a fading flower, which *are* on the head of
the fat valleys of them that are overcome
with wine!
2 Behold, the Lord hath a mighty and
strong one, *which* as a tempest of hail *and*
a destroying storm, as a flood of mighty
waters overflowing, shall cast down to the
earth with the hand.
3 The crown of pride, the drunkards of
Ephraim, shall be trodden under feet:
4 And the glorious beauty, which *is* on
the head of the fat valley, shall be a fading flower, *and* as the hasty fruit before
the summer; which *when* he that looketh
upon it seeth, while it is yet in his hand he
eateth it up.
5 ¶ In that day shall the LORD of hosts be for
a crown of glory, and for a diadem of beauty,
unto the residue of his people,
6 And for a spirit of judgment to him that
sitteth in judgment, and for strength to them
that turn the battle to the gate.
7 ¶ But they also have erred through wine,
and through strong drink are out of the
way; the priest and the prophet have erred
through strong drink, they are swallowed
up of wine, they are out of the way through
strong drink; they err in vision, they stumble
in judgment.
8 For all tables are full of vomit *and* filthiness, *so that there is* no place *clean*.
9 ¶ Whom shall he teach knowledge? and
whom shall he make to understand doctrine? *them that are* weaned from the milk,
and drawn from the breasts.
10 For precept *must be* upon precept, precept upon precept; line upon line, line upon
line; here a little, *and* there a little:
11 For with stammering lips and another
tongue will he speak to this people.
12 To whom he said, This *is* the rest *wherewith* ye may cause the weary to rest; and this
is the refreshing: yet they would not hear.
13 But the word of the LORD was unto
them precept upon precept, precept upon
precept; line upon line, line upon line; here
a little, *and* there a little; that they might
go, and fall backward, and be broken, and
snared, and taken.
14 ¶ Wherefore hear the word of the LORD,
ye scornful men, that rule this people which
is in Jerusalem.

15 Because ye have said, We have made a
covenant with death, and with hell are we at
agreement; when the overflowing scourge
shall pass through, it shall not come unto us:
for we have made lies our refuge, and under
falsehood have we hid ourselves:
16 ¶ Therefore thus saith the Lord GOD,
Behold, I lay in Zion for a foundation a stone,
a tried stone, a precious corner *stone*, a
sure foundation: he that believeth shall not
make haste.
17 Judgment also will I lay to the line, and
righteousness to the plummet: and the hail
shall sweep away the refuge of lies, and
the waters shall overflow the hiding place.
18 ¶ And your covenant with death shall
be disannulled, and your agreement with
hell shall not stand; when the overflowing
scourge shall pass through, then ye shall be
trodden down by it.
19 From the time that it goeth forth it shall
take you: for morning by morning shall it
pass over, by day and by night: and it shall
be a vexation only *to* understand the report.
20 For the bed is shorter than that *a man*
can stretch himself *on it:* and the covering
narrower than that he can wrap himself *in it.*
21 For the LORD shall rise up as *in* mount
Perazim, he shall be wroth as *in* the valley
of Gibeon, that he may do his work, his
strange work; and bring to pass his act, his
strange act.
22 Now therefore be ye not mockers, lest
your bands be made strong: for I have heard
from the Lord GOD of hosts a consumption,
even determined upon the whole earth.
23 ¶ Give ye ear, and hear my voice; hearken, and hear my speech.
24 Doth the plowman plow all day to sow?
doth he open and break the clods of his
ground?
25 When he hath made plain the face
thereof, doth he not cast abroad the fitches,
and scatter the cummin, and cast in the
principal wheat and the appointed barley
and the rie in their place?
26 For his God doth instruct him to discretion, *and* doth teach him.
27 For the fitches are not threshed with a
threshing instrument, neither is a cart wheel
turned about upon the cummin; but the
fitches are beaten out with a staff, and the
cummin with a rod.
28 Bread *corn* is bruised; because he will
not ever be threshing it, nor break *it with*
the wheel of his cart, nor bruise it *with* his
horsemen.
29 This also cometh forth from the LORD of
hosts, *which* is wonderful in counsel, *and*
excellent in working.

Isaiah 29

1 Woe to Ariel, to Ariel, the city *where*
David dwelt! add ye year to year; let them
kill sacrifices.
2 Yet I will distress Ariel, and there shall be
heaviness and sorrow: and it shall be unto
me as Ariel.
3 And I will camp against thee round about,
and will lay siege against thee with a mount,
and I will raise forts against thee.
4 And thou shalt be brought down, *and* shalt
speak out of the ground, and thy speech
shall be low out of the dust, and thy voice
shall be, as of one that hath a familiar spirit,
out of the ground, and thy speech shall
whisper out of the dust.
5 Moreover the multitude of thy strangers
shall be like small dust, and the multitude
of the terrible ones *shall be* as chaff that
passeth away: yea, it shall be at an instant
suddenly.
6 Thou shalt be visited of the LORD of hosts
with thunder, and with earthquake, and
great noise, with storm and tempest, and
the flame of devouring fire.
7 ¶ And the multitude of all the nations that
fight against Ariel, even all that fight against
her and her munition, and that distress her,
shall be as a dream of a night vision.
8 It shall even be as when an hungry *man*
dreameth, and, behold, he eateth; but he
awaketh, and his soul is empty: or as when
a thirsty man dreameth, and, behold, he
drinketh; but he awaketh, and, behold, *he*
is faint, and his soul hath appetite: so shall
the multitude of all the nations be, that fight
against mount Zion.
9 ¶ Stay yourselves, and wonder; cry ye
out, and cry: they are drunken, but not
with wine; they stagger, but not with strong
drink.
10 For the LORD hath poured out upon you
the spirit of deep sleep, and hath closed
your eyes: the prophets and your rulers,
the seers hath he covered.

11 And the vision of all is become unto you as the words of a book that is sealed, which *men* deliver to one that is learned, saying, Read this, I pray thee: and he saith, I cannot; for it *is* sealed:

12 And the book is delivered to him that is not learned, saying, Read this, I pray thee: and he saith, I am not learned.

13 ¶ Wherefore the Lord said, Forasmuch as this people draw near *me* with their mouth, and with their lips do honour me, but have removed their heart far from me, and their fear toward me is taught by the precept of men:

14 Therefore, behold, I will proceed to do a marvellous work among this people, *even* a marvellous work and a wonder: for the wisdom of their wise *men* shall perish, and the understanding of their prudent *men* shall be hid.

15 Woe unto them that seek deep to hide their counsel from the LORD, and their works are in the dark, and they say, Who seeth us? and who knoweth us?

16 Surely your turning of things upside down shall be esteemed as the potter's clay: for shall the work say of him that made it, He made me not? or shall the thing framed say of him that framed it, He had no understanding?

17 *Is* it not yet a very little while, and Lebanon shall be turned into a fruitful field, and the fruitful field shall be esteemed as a forest?

18 ¶ And in that day shall the deaf hear the words of the book, and the eyes of the blind shall see out of obscurity, and out of darkness.

19 The meek also shall increase *their* joy in the LORD, and the poor among men shall rejoice in the Holy One of Israel.

20 For the terrible one is brought to nought, and the scorner is consumed, and all that watch for iniquity are cut off:

21 That make a man an offender for a word, and lay a snare for him that reproveth in the gate, and turn aside the just for a thing of nought.

22 Therefore thus saith the LORD, who redeemed Abraham, concerning the house of Jacob, Jacob shall not now be ashamed, neither shall his face now wax pale.

23 But when he seeth his children, the work of mine hands, in the midst of him, they shall sanctify my name, and sanctify the Holy One of Jacob, and shall fear the God of Israel.

24 They also that erred in spirit shall come to understanding, and they that murmured shall learn doctrine.

Isaiah 30

1 Woe to the rebellious children, saith the LORD, that take counsel, but not of me; and that cover with a covering, but not of my spirit, that they may add sin to sin:

2 That walk to go down into Egypt, and have not asked at my mouth; to strengthen themselves in the strength of Pharaoh, and to trust in the shadow of Egypt!

3 Therefore shall the strength of Pharaoh be your shame, and the trust in the shadow of Egypt *your* confusion.

4 For his princes were at Zoan, and his ambassadors came to Hanes.

5 They were all ashamed of a people *that* could not profit them, nor be an help nor profit, but a shame, and also a reproach.

6 The burden of the beasts of the south: into the land of trouble and anguish, from whence *come* the young and old lion, the viper and fiery flying serpent, they will carry their riches upon the shoulders of young asses, and their treasures upon the bunches of camels, to a people *that* shall not profit *them*.

7 For the Egyptians shall help in vain, and to no purpose: therefore have I cried concerning this, Their strength *is* to sit still.

8 ¶ Now go, write it before them in a table, and note it in a book, that it may be for the time to come for ever and ever:

9 That this *is* a rebellious people, lying children, children *that* will not hear the law of the LORD:

10 Which say to the seers, See not; and to the prophets, Prophesy not unto us right things, speak unto us smooth things, prophesy deceits:

11 Get you out of the way, turn aside out of the path, cause the Holy One of Israel to cease from before us.

12 Wherefore thus saith the Holy One of Israel, Because ye despise this word, and trust in oppression and perverseness, and stay thereon:

13 Therefore this iniquity shall be to you as

a breach ready to fall, swelling out in a high wall, whose breaking cometh suddenly at an instant.

14 And he shall break it as the breaking of the potters' vessel that is broken in pieces; he shall not spare: so that there shall not be found in the bursting of it a sherd to take fire from the hearth, or to take water *withal* out of the pit.

15 For thus saith the Lord GOD, the Holy One of Israel; In returning and rest shall ye be saved; in quietness and in confidence shall be your strength: and ye would not.

16 But ye said, No; for we will flee upon horses; therefore shall ye flee: and, We will ride upon the swift; therefore shall they that pursue you be swift.

17 One thousand *shall flee* at the rebuke of one; at the rebuke of five shall ye flee: till ye be left as a beacon upon the top of a mountain, and as an ensign on an hill.

18 ¶ And therefore will the LORD wait, that he may be gracious unto you, and therefore will he be exalted, that he may have mercy upon you: for the LORD *is* a God of judgment: blessed *are* all they that wait for him.

19 For the people shall dwell in Zion at Jerusalem: thou shalt weep no more: he will be very gracious unto thee at the voice of thy cry; when he shall hear it, he will answer thee.

20 And *though* the Lord give you the bread of adversity, and the water of affliction, yet shall not thy teachers be removed into a corner any more, but thine eyes shall see thy teachers:

21 And thine ears shall hear a word behind thee, saying, This *is* the way, walk ye in it, when ye turn to the right hand, and when ye turn to the left.

22 Ye shall defile also the covering of thy graven images of silver, and the ornament of thy molten images of gold: thou shalt cast them away as a menstruous cloth; thou shalt say unto it, Get thee hence.

23 Then shall he give the rain of thy seed, that thou shalt sow the ground withal; and bread of the increase of the earth, and it shall be fat and plenteous: in that day shall thy cattle feed in large pastures.

24 The oxen likewise and the young asses that ear the ground shall eat clean provender, which hath been winnowed with the shovel and with the fan.

25 And there shall be upon every high mountain, and upon every high hill, rivers *and* streams of waters in the day of the great slaughter, when the towers fall.

26 Moreover the light of the moon shall be as the light of the sun, and the light of the sun shall be sevenfold, as the light of seven days, in the day that the LORD bindeth up the breach of his people, and healeth the stroke of their wound.

27 ¶ Behold, the name of the LORD cometh from far, burning *with* his anger, and the burden *thereof is* heavy: his lips are full of indignation, and his tongue as a devouring fire:

28 And his breath, as an overflowing stream, shall reach to the midst of the neck, to sift the nations with the sieve of vanity: and *there shall be* a bridle in the jaws of the people, causing *them* to err.

29 Ye shall have a song, as in the night *when* a holy solemnity is kept; and gladness of heart, as when one goeth with a pipe to come into the mountain of the LORD, to the mighty One of Israel.

30 And the LORD shall cause his glorious voice to be heard, and shall shew the lighting down of his arm, with the indignation of *his* anger, and *with* the flame of a devouring fire, *with* scattering, and tempest, and hailstones.

31 For through the voice of the LORD shall the Assyrian be beaten down, *which* smote with a rod.

32 And *in* every place where the grounded staff shall pass, which the LORD shall lay upon him, *it* shall be with tabrets and harps: and in battles of shaking will he fight with it.

33 For Tophet *is* ordained of old; yea, for the king it is prepared; he hath made *it* deep *and* large: the pile thereof *is* fire and much wood; the breath of the LORD, like a stream of brimstone, doth kindle it.

Isaiah 31

1 Woe to them that go down to Egypt for help; and stay on horses, and trust in chariots, because *they are* many; and in horsemen, because they are very strong; but they look not unto the Holy One of Israel, neither seek the LORD!

2 Yet he also *is* wise, and will bring evil, and

will not call back his words: but will arise
against the house of the evildoers, and
against the help of them that work iniquity.
3 Now the Egyptians *are* men, and not
God; and their horses flesh, and not spirit.
When the LORD shall stretch out his hand,
both he that helpeth shall fall, and he that
is holpen shall fall down, and they all shall
fail together.
4 For thus hath the LORD spoken unto me,
Like as the lion and the young lion roaring
on his prey, when a multitude of shepherds
is called forth against him, *he* will not be
afraid of their voice, nor abase himself for
the noise of them: so shall the LORD of hosts
come down to fight for mount Zion, and for
the hill thereof.
5 As birds flying, so will the LORD of hosts
defend Jerusalem; defending also he will
deliver *it; and* passing over he will preserve *it*.
6 ¶ Turn ye unto *him from* whom the children of Israel have deeply revolted.
7 For in that day every man shall cast away
his idols of silver, and his idols of gold,
which your own hands have made unto
you *for* a sin.
8 ¶ Then shall the Assyrian fall with the
sword, not of a mighty man; and the sword,
not of a mean man, shall devour him: but
he shall flee from the sword, and his young
men shall be discomfited.
9 And he shall pass over to his strong hold
for fear, and his princes shall be afraid of
the ensign, saith the LORD, whose fire *is* in
Zion, and his furnace in Jerusalem.

Isaiah 32

1 Behold, a king shall reign in righteousness,
and princes shall rule in judgment.
2 And a man shall be as an hiding place from
the wind, and a covert from the tempest; as
rivers of water in a dry place, as the shadow
of a great rock in a weary land.
3 And the eyes of them that see shall not
be dim, and the ears of them that hear
shall hearken.
4 The heart also of the rash shall understand
knowledge, and the tongue of the stammer-
ers shall be ready to speak plainly.
5 The vile person shall be no more called
liberal, nor the churl said *to be* bountiful.
6 For the vile person will speak villany,
and his heart will work iniquity, to practise hypocrisy, and to utter error against
the LORD, to make empty the soul of the
hungry, and he will cause the drink of the
thirsty to fail.
7 The instruments also of the churl *are* evil:
he deviseth wicked devices to destroy the
poor with lying words, even when the needy
speaketh right.
8 But the liberal deviseth liberal things; and
by liberal things shall he stand.
9 ¶ Rise up, ye women that are at ease;
hear my voice, ye careless daughters; give
ear unto my speech.
10 Many days and years shall ye be troubled,
ye careless women: for the vintage shall fail,
the gathering shall not come.
11 Tremble, ye women that are at ease; be
troubled, ye careless ones: strip you, and
make you bare, and gird *sackcloth* upon
your loins.
12 They shall lament for the teats, for the
pleasant fields, for the fruitful vine.
13 Upon the land of my people shall come
up thorns *and* briers; yea, upon all the
houses of joy *in* the joyous city:
14 Because the palaces shall be forsaken;
the multitude of the city shall be left; the
forts and towers shall be for dens for ever,
a joy of wild asses, a pasture of flocks;
15 Until the spirit be poured upon us from
on high, and the wilderness be a fruitful
field, and the fruitful field be counted for
a forest.
16 Then judgment shall dwell in the wilderness, and righteousness remain in the
fruitful field.
17 And the work of righteousness shall be
peace; and the effect of righteousness quietness and assurance for ever.
18 And my people shall dwell in a peaceable
habitation, and in sure dwellings, and in
quiet resting places;
19 When it shall hail, coming down on the
forest; and the city shall be low in a low
place.
20 Blessed *are* ye that sow beside all waters,
that send forth *thither* the feet of the ox
and the ass.

Isaiah 33

1 Woe to thee that spoilest, and thou *wast*
not spoiled; and dealest treacherously, and

they dealt not treacherously with thee!
when thou shalt cease to spoil, thou shalt
be spoiled; *and* when thou shalt make an
end to deal treacherously, they shall deal
treacherously with thee.
2 O LORD, be gracious unto us; we have
waited for thee: be thou their arm every
morning, our salvation also in the time of
trouble.
3 At the noise of the tumult the people
fled; at the lifting up of thyself the nations
were scattered.
4 And your spoil shall be gathered *like* the
gathering of the caterpiller: as the running
to and fro of locusts shall he run upon them.
5 The LORD is exalted; for he dwelleth on
high: he hath filled Zion with judgment and
righteousness.
6 And wisdom and knowledge shall be the
stability of thy times, *and* strength of salvation: the fear of the LORD *is* his treasure.
7 Behold, their valiant ones shall cry with-
ut: the ambassadors of peace shall weep
itterly.
The highways lie waste, the wayfaring
ian ceaseth: he hath broken the covenant,
e hath despised the cities, he regardeth
o man.
The earth mourneth *and* languisheth: Leb-
non is ashamed *and* hewn down: Sharon
; like a wilderness; and Bashan and Carmel
hake off *their fruits*.
10 Now will I rise, saith the LORD; now will I
be exalted; now will I lift up myself.
11 Ye shall conceive chaff, ye shall bring
forth stubble: your breath, *as* fire, shall
devour you.
12 And the people shall be *as* the burnings of
lime: *as* thorns cut up shall they be burned
in the fire.
13 ¶ Hear, ye *that are* far off, what I have
done; and, ye *that are* near, acknowledge
my might.
14 The sinners in Zion are afraid; fearfulness hath surprised the hypocrites. Who
among us shall dwell with the devouring
fire? who among us shall dwell with everlasting burnings?
15 He that walketh righteously, and speaketh uprightly; he that despiseth the gain
of oppressions, that shaketh his hands
from holding of bribes, that stoppeth his
ears from hearing of blood, and shutteth
his eyes from seeing evil;
16 He shall dwell on high: his place of
defence *shall be* the munitions of rocks:
bread shall be given him; his waters *shall
be* sure.
17 Thine eyes shall see the king in his beauty:
they shall behold the land that is very far off.
18 Thine heart shall meditate terror. Where
is the scribe? where *is* the receiver? where
is he that counted the towers?
19 Thou shalt not see a fierce people, a
people of a deeper speech than thou canst
perceive; of a stammering tongue, *that thou
canst* not understand.
20 Look upon Zion, the city of our solemnities: thine eyes shall see Jerusalem a quiet
habitation, a tabernacle *that* shall not be
taken down; not one of the stakes thereof
shall ever be removed, neither shall any of
the cords thereof be broken.
21 But there the glorious LORD *will be* unto
us a place of broad rivers *and* streams;
wherein shall go no galley with oars, neither
shall gallant ship pass thereby.
22 For the LORD *is* our judge, the LORD *is*
our lawgiver, the LORD *is* our king; he will
save us.
23 Thy tacklings are loosed; they could not
well strengthen their mast, they could not
spread the sail: then is the prey of a great
spoil divided; the lame take the prey.
24 And the inhabitant shall not say, I am
sick: the people that dwell therein *shall be*
forgiven *their* iniquity.

Isaiah 34

1 Come near, ye nations, to hear; and hearken, ye people: let the earth hear, and all
that is therein; the world, and all things that
come forth of it.
2 For the indignation of the LORD *is* upon all
nations, and *his* fury upon all their armies:
he hath utterly destroyed them, he hath
delivered them to the slaughter.
3 Their slain also shall be cast out, and their
stink shall come up out of their carcases,
and the mountains shall be melted with
their blood.
4 And all the host of heaven shall be dissolved, and the heavens shall be rolled
together as a scroll: and all their host shall

fall down, as the leaf falleth off from the
vine, and as a falling *fig* from the fig tree.
5 For my sword shall be bathed in heaven:
behold, it shall come down upon Idumea,
and upon the people of my curse, to judgment.
6 The sword of the LORD is filled with blood,
it is made fat with fatness, *and* with the
blood of lambs and goats, with the fat of
the kidneys of rams: for the LORD hath a
sacrifice in Bozrah, and a great slaughter in
the land of Idumea.
7 And the unicorns shall come down with
them, and the bullocks with the bulls; and
their land shall be soaked with blood, and
their dust made fat with fatness.
8 For *it is* the day of the LORD's vengeance,
and the year of recompences for the controversy of Zion.
9 And the streams thereof shall be turned
into pitch, and the dust thereof into brimstone, and the land thereof shall become
burning pitch.
10 It shall not be quenched night nor day;
the smoke thereof shall go up for ever: from
generation to generation it shall lie waste;
none shall pass through it for ever and ever.
11 ¶ But the cormorant and the bittern shall
possess it; the owl also and the raven shall
dwell in it: and he shall stretch out upon
it the line of confusion, and the stones of
emptiness.
12 They shall call the nobles thereof to the
kingdom, but none *shall be* there, and all
her princes shall be nothing.
13 And thorns shall come up in her palaces,
nettles and brambles in the fortresses
thereof: and it shall be an habitation of
dragons, *and* a court for owls.
14 The wild beasts of the desert shall also
meet with the wild beasts of the island, and
the satyr shall cry to his fellow; the screech
owl also shall rest there, and find for herself
a place of rest.
15 There shall the great owl make her nest,
and lay, and hatch, and gather under her
shadow: there shall the vultures also be
gathered, every one with her mate.
16 ¶ Seek ye out of the book of the LORD,
and read: no one of these shall fail, none
shall want her mate: for my mouth it hath
commanded, and his spirit it hath gathered
them.
17 And he hath cast the lot for them, and his
hand hath divided it unto them by line: they
shall possess it for ever, from generation to
generation shall they dwell therein.

Isaiah 35

1 The wilderness and the solitary place
shall be glad for them; and the desert shall
rejoice, and blossom as the rose.
2 It shall blossom abundantly, and rejoice
even with joy and singing: the glory of Lebanon shall be given unto it, the excellency of
Carmel and Sharon, they shall see the glory
of the LORD, *and* the excellency of our God.
3 ¶ Strengthen ye the weak hands, and
confirm the feeble knees.
4 Say to them *that are* of a fearful heart,
Be strong, fear not: behold, your God will
come *with* vengeance, *even* God *with* a
recompence; he will come and save you.
5 Then the eyes of the blind shall be opened,
and the ears of the deaf shall be unstopped.
6 Then shall the lame *man* leap as an hart,
and the tongue of the dumb sing: for in
the wilderness shall waters break out, and
streams in the desert.
7 And the parched ground shall become a
pool, and the thirsty land springs of water:
in the habitation of dragons, where each
lay, *shall be* grass with reeds and rushes.
8 And an highway shall be there, and a way,
and it shall be called The way of holiness; the
unclean shall not pass over it; but it *shall be*
for those: the wayfaring men, though fools,
shall not err *therein*.
9 No lion shall be there, nor *any* ravenous
beast shall go up thereon, it shall not be
found there; but the redeemed shall walk
there:
10 And the ransomed of the LORD shall
return, and come to Zion with songs and
everlasting joy upon their heads: they shall
obtain joy and gladness, and sorrow and
sighing shall flee away.

Isaiah 36

1 Now it came to pass in the fourteenth year
of king Hezekiah, *that* Sennacherib king of
Assyria came up against all the defenced
cities of Judah, and took them.
2 And the king of Assyria sent Rabshakeh
from Lachish to Jerusalem unto king Hezekiah with a great army. And he stood by the

conduit of the upper pool in the highway of
the fuller's field.
3 Then came forth unto him Eliakim, Hilkiah's son, which was over the house, and
Shebna the scribe, and Joah, Asaph's son,
the recorder.
4 ¶ And Rabshakeh said unto them, Say ye
now to Hezekiah, Thus saith the great king,
the king of Assyria, What confidence *is* this
wherein thou trustest?
5 I say, *sayest thou*, (but *they are but* vain
words) *I have* counsel and strength for war:
now on whom dost thou trust, that thou
rebellest against me?
6 Lo, thou trustest in the staff of this broken
reed, on Egypt; whereon if a man lean, it will
go into his hand, and pierce it: so *is* Pharaoh
king of Egypt to all that trust in him.
7 But if thou say to me, We trust in the LORD
our God: *is it* not he, whose high places and
whose altars Hezekiah hath taken away,
and said to Judah and to Jerusalem, Ye shall
worship before this altar?
8 Now therefore give pledges, I pray thee,
to my master the king of Assyria, and I will
give thee two thousand horses, if thou be
able on thy part to set riders upon them.
9 How then wilt thou turn away the face
of one captain of the least of my master's
servants, and put thy trust on Egypt for
chariots and for horsemen?
10 And am I now come up without the LORD
against this land to destroy it? the LORD
said unto me, Go up against this land, and
destroy it.
11 ¶ Then said Eliakim and Shebna and Joah
unto Rabshakeh, Speak, I pray thee, unto
thy servants in the Syrian language; for we
understand *it:* and speak not to us in the
Jews' language, in the ears of the people
that *are* on the wall.
12 ¶ But Rabshakeh said, Hath my master
sent me to thy master and to thee to speak
these words? *hath he* not *sent me* to the
men that sit upon the wall, that they may
eat their own dung, and drink their own
piss with you?
13 Then Rabshakeh stood, and cried with a
loud voice in the Jews' language, and said,
Hear ye the words of the great king, the
king of Assyria.
14 Thus saith the king, Let not Hezekiah
deceive you: for he shall not be able to
deliver you.
15 Neither let Hezekiah make you trust in
the LORD, saying, The LORD will surely deliver
us: this city shall not be delivered into the
hand of the king of Assyria.
16 Hearken not to Hezekiah: for thus saith
the king of Assyria, Make *an agreement* with
me *by* a present, and come out to me: and
eat ye every one of his vine, and every one
of his fig tree, and drink ye every one the
waters of his own cistern;
17 Until I come and take you away to a land
like your own land, a land of corn and wine,
a land of bread and vineyards.
18 *Beware* lest Hezekiah persuade you, saying, The LORD will deliver us. Hath any of the
gods of the nations delivered his land out of
the hand of the king of Assyria?
19 Where *are* the gods of Hamath and
Arphad? where *are* the gods of Sepharvaim? and have they delivered Samaria out
of my hand?
20 Who *are they* among all the gods of these
lands, that have delivered their land out
of my hand, that the LORD should deliver
Jerusalem out of my hand?
21 But they held their peace, and answered
him not a word: for the king's commandment was, saying, Answer him not.
22 ¶ Then came Eliakim, the son of Hilkiah,
that *was* over the household, and Shebna
the scribe, and Joah, the son of Asaph, the
recorder, to Hezekiah with *their* clothes
rent, and told him the words of Rabshakeh.

Isaiah 37

1 And it came to pass, when king Hezekiah
heard *it*, that he rent his clothes, and covered himself with sackcloth, and went into
the house of the LORD.
2 And he sent Eliakim, who *was* over the
household, and Shebna the scribe, and the
elders of the priests covered with sackcloth,
unto Isaiah the prophet the son of Amoz.
3 And they said unto him, Thus saith Hezekiah, This day *is* a day of trouble, and of
rebuke, and of blasphemy: for the children
are come to the birth, and *there is* not
strength to bring forth.
4 It may be the LORD thy God will hear the
words of Rabshakeh, whom the king of
Assyria his master hath sent to reproach the

living God, and will reprove the words which
the LORD thy God hath heard: wherefore lift
up *thy* prayer for the remnant that is left.
5 So the servants of king Hezekiah came
to Isaiah.
6 ¶ And Isaiah said unto them, Thus shall ye
say unto your master, Thus saith the LORD,
Be not afraid of the words that thou hast
heard, wherewith the servants of the king
of Assyria have blasphemed me.
7 Behold, I will send a blast upon him, and
he shall hear a rumour, and return to his
own land; and I will cause him to fall by the
sword in his own land.
8 ¶ So Rabshakeh returned, and found the
king of Assyria warring against Libnah: for
he had heard that he was departed from
Lachish.
9 And he heard say concerning Tirhakah king
of Ethiopia, He is come forth to make war
with thee. And when he heard *it*, he sent
messengers to Hezekiah, saying,
10 Thus shall ye speak to Hezekiah king of
Judah, saying, Let not thy God, in whom
thou trustest, deceive thee, saying, Jerusalem shall not be given into the hand of the
king of Assyria.
11 Behold, thou hast heard what the kings of
Assyria have done to all lands by destroying
them utterly; and shalt thou be delivered?
12 Have the gods of the nations delivered
them which my fathers have destroyed,
as Gozan, and Haran, and Rezeph, and the
children of Eden which *were* in Telassar?
13 Where *is* the king of Hamath, and the
king of Arphad, and the king of the city of
Sepharvaim, Hena, and Ivah?
14 ¶ And Hezekiah received the letter from
the hand of the messengers, and read it:
and Hezekiah went up unto the house of
the LORD, and spread it before the LORD.
15 And Hezekiah prayed unto the LORD,
saying,
16 O LORD of hosts, God of Israel, that dwellest *between* the cherubims, thou *art* the
God, *even* thou alone, of all the kingdoms of
the earth: thou hast made heaven and earth.
17 Incline thine ear, O LORD, and hear; open
thine eyes, O LORD, and see: and hear all the
words of Sennacherib, which hath sent to
reproach the living God.
18 Of a truth, LORD, the kings of Assyria
have laid waste all the nations, and their
countries,
19 And have cast their gods into the fire: for
they *were* no gods, but the work of men's
hands, wood and stone: therefore they have
destroyed them.
20 Now therefore, O LORD our God, save
us from his hand, that all the kingdoms of
the earth may know that thou *art* the LORD,
even thou only.
21 ¶ Then Isaiah the son of Amoz sent unto
Hezekiah, saying, Thus saith the LORD God
of Israel, Whereas thou hast prayed to me
against Sennacherib king of Assyria:
22 This *is* the word which the LORD hath spoken concerning him; The virgin, the daughter
of Zion, hath despised thee, *and* laughed
thee to scorn; the daughter of Jerusalem
hath shaken her head at thee.
23 Whom hast thou reproached and blasphemed? and against whom hast thou
exalted *thy* voice, and lifted up thine eyes
on high? *even* against the Holy One of Israel.
24 By thy servants hast thou reproached
the Lord, and hast said, By the multitude
of my chariots am I come up to the height
of the mountains, to the sides of Lebanon;
and I will cut down the tall cedars thereof,
and the choice fir trees thereof: and I will
enter into the height of his border, *and* the
forest of his Carmel.
25 I have digged, and drunk water; and with
the sole of my feet have I dried up all the
rivers of the besieged places.
26 Hast thou not heard long ago, *how* I
have done it; *and* of ancient times, that I
have formed it? now have I brought it to
pass, that thou shouldest be to lay waste
defenced cities *into* ruinous heaps.
27 Therefore their inhabitants *were* of
small power, they were dismayed and confounded: they were *as* the grass of the field,
and *as* the green herb, *as* the grass on the
housetops, and *as corn* blasted before it
be grown up.
28 But I know thy abode, and thy going out,
and thy coming in, and thy rage against me.
29 Because thy rage against me, and thy
tumult, is come up into mine ears, therefore
will I put my hook in thy nose, and my bridle
in thy lips, and I will turn thee back by the
way by which thou camest.
30 And this *shall be* a sign unto thee, Ye

shall eat *this* year such as groweth of itself;
and the second year that which springeth
of the same: and in the third year sow ye,
and reap, and plant vineyards, and eat the
fruit thereof.
31 And the remnant that is escaped of the
house of Judah shall again take root downward, and bear fruit upward:
32 For out of Jerusalem shall go forth
a remnant, and they that escape out of
mount Zion: the zeal of the LORD of hosts
shall do this.
33 Therefore thus saith the LORD concerning the king of Assyria, He shall not come
into this city, nor shoot an arrow there,
nor come before it with shields, nor cast a
bank against it.
34 By the way that he came, by the same
shall he return, and shall not come into this
city, saith the LORD.
35 For I will defend this city to save it for
mine own sake, and for my servant David's
sake.
36 Then the angel of the LORD went forth,
and smote in the camp of the Assyrians a
hundred and fourscore and five thousand:
and when they arose early in the morning,
behold, they *were* all dead corpses.
37 ¶ So Sennacherib king of Assyria
departed, and went and returned, and
dwelt at Nineveh.
38 And it came to pass, as he was worshipping in the house of Nisroch his god, that
Adrammelech and Sharezer his sons smote
him with the sword; and they escaped into
the land of Armenia: and Esar-haddon his
son reigned in his stead.

Isaiah 38

1 In those days was Hezekiah sick unto
death. And Isaiah the prophet the son of
Amoz came unto him, and said unto him,
Thus saith the LORD, Set thine house in
order: for thou shalt die, and not live.
2 Then Hezekiah turned his face toward the
wall, and prayed unto the LORD,
3 And said, Remember now, O LORD, I
beseech thee, how I have walked before
thee in truth and with a perfect heart, and
have done *that which is* good in thy sight.
And Hezekiah wept sore.
4 ¶ Then came the word of the LORD to
Isaiah, saying,
5 Go, and say to Hezekiah, Thus saith the
LORD, the God of David thy father, I have
heard thy prayer, I have seen thy tears:
behold, I will add unto thy days fifteen years.
6 And I will deliver thee and this city out of
the hand of the king of Assyria: and I will
defend this city.
7 And this *shall be* a sign unto thee from the
LORD, that the LORD will do this thing that
he hath spoken;
8 Behold, I will bring again the shadow of
the degrees, which is gone down in the sun
dial of Ahaz, ten degrees backward. So the
sun returned ten degrees, by which degrees
it was gone down.
9 ¶ The writing of Hezekiah king of Judah,
when he had been sick, and was recovered
of his sickness:
10 I said in the cutting off of my days, I shall
go to the gates of the grave: I am deprived
of the residue of my years.
11 I said, I shall not see the LORD, *even*
the LORD, in the land of the living: I shall
behold man no more with the inhabitants
of the world.
12 Mine age is departed, and is removed
from me as a shepherd's tent: I have cut off
like a weaver my life: he will cut me off with
pining sickness: from day *even* to night wilt
thou make an end of me.
13 I reckoned till morning, *that*, as a lion, so
will he break all my bones: from day *even* to
night wilt thou make an end of me.
14 Like a crane *or* a swallow, so did I chatter:
I did mourn as a dove: mine eyes fail *with
looking* upward: O LORD, I am oppressed;
undertake for me.
15 What shall I say? he hath both spoken
unto me, and himself hath done *it:* I shall
go softly all my years in the bitterness of
my soul.
16 O Lord, by these *things men* live, and in
all these *things is* the life of my spirit: so
wilt thou recover me, and make me to live.
17 Behold, for peace I had great bitterness:
but thou hast in love to my soul *delivered
it* from the pit of corruption: for thou hast
cast all my sins behind thy back.
18 For the grave cannot praise thee, death
can *not* celebrate thee: they that go down
into the pit cannot hope for thy truth.
19 The living, the living, he shall praise thee,

as I *do* this day: the father to the children
shall make known thy truth.
20 The LORD *was ready* to save me: therefore we will sing my songs to the stringed
instruments all the days of our life in the
house of the LORD.
21 For Isaiah had said, Let them take a lump
of figs, and lay *it* for a plaister upon the boil,
and he shall recover.
22 Hezekiah also had said, What *is* the sign
that I shall go up to the house of the LORD?

Isaiah 39

1 At that time Merodach-baladan, the son
of Baladan, king of Babylon, sent letters
and a present to Hezekiah: for he had heard
that he had been sick, and was recovered.
2 And Hezekiah was glad of them, and
shewed them the house of his precious
things, the silver, and the gold, and the
spices, and the precious ointment, and all
the house of his armour, and all that was
found in his treasures: there was nothing
in his house, nor in all his dominion, that
Hezekiah shewed them not.
3 ¶ Then came Isaiah the prophet unto
king Hezekiah, and said unto him, What
said these men? and from whence came
they unto thee? And Hezekiah said, They
are come from a far country unto me, *even*
from Babylon.
4 Then said he, What have they seen in
thine house? And Hezekiah answered, All
that *is* in mine house have they seen: there
is nothing among my treasures that I have
not shewed them.
5 Then said Isaiah to Hezekiah, Hear the
word of the LORD of hosts:
6 Behold, the days come, that all that *is* in
thine house, and *that* which thy fathers
have laid up in store until this day, shall be
carried to Babylon: nothing shall be left,
saith the LORD.
7 And of thy sons that shall issue from thee,
which thou shalt beget, shall they take away;
and they shall be eunuchs in the palace of
the king of Babylon.
8 Then said Hezekiah to Isaiah, Good *is* the
word of the LORD which thou hast spoken.
He said moreover, For there shall be peace
and truth in my days.

Isaiah 40

1 Comfort ye, comfort ye my people, saith
your God.
2 Speak ye comfortably to Jerusalem, and
cry unto her, that her warfare is accomplished, that her iniquity is pardoned: for
she hath received of the LORD's hand double
for all her sins.
3 ¶ The voice of him that crieth in the wilderness, Prepare ye the way of the LORD, make
straight in the desert a highway for our God.
4 Every valley shall be exalted, and every
mountain and hill shall be made low: and
the crooked shall be made straight, and the
rough places plain:
5 And the glory of the LORD shall be
revealed, and all flesh shall see *it* together:
for the mouth of the LORD hath spoken *it*.
6 The voice said, Cry. And he said, What shall
I cry? All flesh *is* grass, and all the goodliness
thereof *is* as the flower of the field:
7 The grass withereth, the flower fadeth:
because the spirit of the LORD bloweth upon
it: surely the people *is* grass.
8 The grass withereth, the flower fadeth:
but the word of our God shall stand for ever.
9 ¶ O Zion, that bringest good tidings, get
thee up into the high mountain; O Jerusalem, that bringest good tidings, lift up
thy voice with strength; lift *it* up, be not
afraid; say unto the cities of Judah, Behold
your God!
10 Behold, the Lord GOD will come with
strong *hand*, and his arm shall rule for him:
behold, his reward *is* with him, and his work
before him.
11 He shall feed his flock like a shepherd:
he shall gather the lambs with his arm, and
carry *them* in his bosom, *and* shall gently
lead those that are with young.
12 ¶ Who hath measured the waters in the
hollow of his hand, and meted out heaven
with the span, and comprehended the dust
of the earth in a measure, and weighed
the mountains in scales, and the hills in a
balance?
13 Who hath directed the Spirit of the LORD,
or *being* his counseller hath taught him?
14 With whom took he counsel, and *who*
instructed him, and taught him in the path of
judgment, and taught him knowledge, and
shewed to him the way of understanding?
15 Behold, the nations *are* as a drop of a

bucket, and are counted as the small dust
of the balance: behold, he taketh up the
isles as a very little thing.
16 And Lebanon *is* not sufficient to burn,
nor the beasts thereof sufficient for a burnt
offering.
17 All nations before him *are* as nothing; and
they are counted to him less than nothing,
and vanity.
18 ¶ To whom then will ye liken God? or
what likeness will ye compare unto him?
19 The workman melteth a graven image,
and the goldsmith spreadeth it over with
gold, and casteth silver chains.
20 He that *is* so impoverished that he hath
no oblation chooseth a tree *that* will not
rot; he seeketh unto him a cunning workman to prepare a graven image, *that* shall
not be moved.
21 Have ye not known? have ye not heard?
hath it not been told you from the beginning? have ye not understood from the
foundations of the earth?
22 *It is* he that sitteth upon the circle of
the earth, and the inhabitants thereof *are*
as grasshoppers; that stretcheth out the
heavens as a curtain, and spreadeth them
out as a tent to dwell in:
23 That bringeth the princes to nothing; he
maketh the judges of the earth as vanity.
24 Yea, they shall not be planted; yea, they
shall not be sown: yea, their stock shall not
take root in the earth: and he shall also blow
upon them, and they shall wither, and the
whirlwind shall take them away as stubble.
25 To whom then will ye liken me, or shall
I be equal? saith the Holy One.
26 Lift up your eyes on high, and behold who
hath created these *things*, that bringeth out
their host by number: he calleth them all
by names by the greatness of his might, for
that *he is* strong in power; not one faileth.
27 Why sayest thou, O Jacob, and speakest,
O Israel, My way is hid from the LORD, and
my judgment is passed over from my God?
28 ¶ Hast thou not known? hast thou not
heard, *that* the everlasting God, the LORD,
the Creator of the ends of the earth, fainteth
not, neither is weary? *there is* no searching
of his understanding.
29 He giveth power to the faint; and to *them
that have* no might he increaseth strength.
30 Even the youths shall faint and be weary,
and the young men shall utterly fall:
31 But they that wait upon the LORD shall
renew *their* strength; they shall mount up
with wings as eagles; they shall run, and not
be weary; *and* they shall walk, and not faint.

Isaiah 41

1 Keep silence before me, O islands; and let
the people renew *their* strength: let them
come near; then let them speak: let us come
near together to judgment.
2 Who raised up the righteous *man* from the
east, called him to his foot, gave the nations
before him, and made *him* rule over kings?
he gave *them* as the dust to his sword, *and*
as driven stubble to his bow.
3 He pursued them, *and* passed safely;
even by the way *that* he had not gone with
his feet.
4 Who hath wrought and done *it*, calling
the generations from the beginning? I the
LORD, the first, and with the last; I *am* he.
5 The isles saw *it*, and feared; the ends of
the earth were afraid, drew near, and came.
6 They helped every one his neighbour;
and *every one* said to his brother, Be of
good courage.
7 So the carpenter encouraged the goldsmith, *and* he that smootheth *with* the
hammer him that smote the anvil, saying,
It *is* ready for the sodering: and he fastened
it with nails, *that* it should not be moved.
8 But thou, Israel, *art* my servant, Jacob
whom I have chosen, the seed of Abraham
my friend.
9 *Thou* whom I have taken from the ends
of the earth, and called thee from the chief
men thereof, and said unto thee, Thou *art*
my servant; I have chosen thee, and not
cast thee away.
10 ¶ Fear thou not; for I *am* with thee:
be not dismayed; for I *am* thy God: I will
strengthen thee; yea, I will help thee; yea,
I will uphold thee with the right hand of my
righteousness.
11 Behold, all they that were incensed
against thee shall be ashamed and confounded: they shall be as nothing; and they
that strive with thee shall perish.
12 Thou shalt seek them, and shalt not
find them, *even* them that contended with

thee: they that war against thee shall be as nothing, and as a thing of nought.

13 For I the LORD thy God will hold thy right hand, saying unto thee, Fear not; I will help thee.

14 Fear not, thou worm Jacob, *and* ye men of Israel; I will help thee, saith the LORD, and thy redeemer, the Holy One of Israel.

15 Behold, I will make thee a new sharp threshing instrument having teeth: thou shalt thresh the mountains, and beat *them* small, and shalt make the hills as chaff.

16 Thou shalt fan them, and the wind shall carry them away, and the whirlwind shall scatter them: and thou shalt rejoice in the LORD, *and* shalt glory in the Holy One of Israel.

17 *When* the poor and needy seek water, and *there is* none, *and* their tongue faileth for thirst, I the LORD will hear them, *I* the God of Israel will not forsake them.

18 I will open rivers in high places, and fountains in the midst of the valleys: I will make the wilderness a pool of water, and the dry land springs of water.

19 I will plant in the wilderness the cedar, the shittah tree, and the myrtle, and the oil tree; I will set in the desert the fir tree, *and* the pine, and the box tree together:

20 That they may see, and know, and consider, and understand together, that the hand of the LORD hath done this, and the Holy One of Israel hath created it.

21 Produce your cause, saith the LORD; bring forth your strong *reasons*, saith the King of Jacob.

22 Let them bring *them* forth, and shew us what shall happen: let them shew the former things, what they *be*, that we may consider them, and know the latter end of them; or declare us things for to come.

23 Shew the things that are to come hereafter, that we may know that ye *are* gods: yea, do good, or do evil, that we may be dismayed, and behold *it* together.

24 Behold, ye *are* of nothing, and your work of nought: an abomination *is he that* chooseth you.

25 I have raised up *one* from the north, and he shall come: from the rising of the sun shall he call upon my name: and he shall come upon princes as *upon* morter, and as the potter treadeth clay.

26 Who hath declared from the beginning, that we may know? and beforetime, that we may say, *He is* righteous? yea, *there is* none that sheweth, yea, *there is* none that declareth, yea, *there is* none that heareth your words.

27 The first *shall say* to Zion, Behold, behold them: and I will give to Jerusalem one that bringeth good tidings.

28 For I beheld, and *there was* no man; even among them, and *there was* no counseller, that, when I asked of them, could answer a word.

29 Behold, they *are* all vanity; their works *are* nothing: their molten images *are* wind and confusion.

Isaiah 42

1 Behold my servant, whom I uphold; mine elect, *in whom* my soul delighteth; I have put my spirit upon him: he shall bring forth judgment to the Gentiles.

2 He shall not cry, nor lift up, nor cause his voice to be heard in the street.

3 A bruised reed shall he not break, and the smoking flax shall he not quench: he shall bring forth judgment unto truth.

4 He shall not fail nor be discouraged, till he have set judgment in the earth: and the isles shall wait for his law.

5 ¶ Thus saith God the LORD, he that created the heavens, and stretched them out; he that spread forth the earth, and that which cometh out of it; he that giveth breath unto the people upon it, and spirit to them that walk therein:

6 I the LORD have called thee in righteousness, and will hold thine hand, and will keep thee, and give thee for a covenant of the people, for a light of the Gentiles;

7 To open the blind eyes, to bring out the prisoners from the prison, *and* them that sit in darkness out of the prison house.

8 I *am* the LORD: that *is* my name: and my glory will I not give to another, neither my praise to graven images.

9 Behold, the former things are come to pass, and new things do I declare: before they spring forth I tell you of them.

10 Sing unto the LORD a new song, *and* his praise from the end of the earth, ye that go down to the sea, and all that is therein; the isles, and the inhabitants thereof.

11 Let the wilderness and the cities thereof lift up *their voice*, the villages *that* Kedar doth inhabit: let the inhabitants of the rock sing, let them shout from the top of the mountains.
12 Let them give glory unto the LORD, and declare his praise in the islands.
13 The LORD shall go forth as a mighty man, he shall stir up jealousy like a man of war: he shall cry, yea, roar; he shall prevail against his enemies.
14 I have long time holden my peace; I have been still, *and* refrained myself: *now* will I cry like a travailing woman; I will destroy and devour at once.
15 I will make waste mountains and hills, and dry up all their herbs; and I will make the rivers islands, and I will dry up the pools.
16 And I will bring the blind by a way *that* they knew not; I will lead them in paths *that* they have not known: I will make darkness light before them, and crooked things straight. These things will I do unto them, and not forsake them.
17 ¶ They shall be turned back, they shall be greatly ashamed, that trust in graven images, that say to the molten images, Ye *are* our gods.
18 Hear, ye deaf; and look, ye blind, that ye may see.
19 Who *is* blind, but my servant? or deaf, as my messenger *that* I sent? who *is* blind as *he that is* perfect, and blind as the LORD's servant?
20 Seeing many things, but thou observest not; opening the ears, but he heareth not.
21 The LORD is well pleased for his righteousness' sake; he will magnify the law, and make *it* honourable.
22 But this *is* a people robbed and spoiled; *they are* all of them snared in holes, and they are hid in prison houses: they are for a prey, and none delivereth; for a spoil, and none saith, Restore.
23 Who among you will give ear to this? *who* will hearken and hear for the time to come?
24 Who gave Jacob for a spoil, and Israel to the robbers? did not the LORD, he against whom we have sinned? for they would not walk in his ways, neither were they obedient unto his law.
25 Therefore he hath poured upon him the fury of his anger, and the strength of battle: and it hath set him on fire round about, yet he knew not; and it burned him, yet he laid *it* not to heart.

Isaiah 43

1 But now thus saith the LORD that created thee, O Jacob, and he that formed thee, O Israel, Fear not: for I have redeemed thee, I have called *thee* by thy name; thou *art* mine.
2 When thou passest through the waters, I *will be* with thee; and through the rivers, they shall not overflow thee: when thou walkest through the fire, thou shalt not be burned; neither shall the flame kindle upon thee.
3 For I *am* the LORD thy God, the Holy One of Israel, thy Saviour: I gave Egypt *for* thy ransom, Ethiopia and Seba for thee.
4 Since thou wast precious in my sight, thou hast been honourable, and I have loved thee: therefore will I give men for thee, and people for thy life.
5 Fear not: for I *am* with thee: I will bring thy seed from the east, and gather thee from the west;
6 I will say to the north, Give up; and to the south, Keep not back: bring my sons from far, and my daughters from the ends of the earth;
7 *Even* every one that is called by my name: for I have created him for my glory, I have formed him; yea, I have made him.
8 ¶ Bring forth the blind people that have eyes, and the deaf that have ears.
9 Let all the nations be gathered together, and let the people be assembled: who among them can declare this, and shew us former things? let them bring forth their witnesses, that they may be justified: or let them hear, and say, *It is* truth.
10 Ye *are* my witnesses, saith the LORD, and my servant whom I have chosen: that ye may know and believe me, and understand that I *am* he: before me there was no God formed, neither shall there be after me.
11 I, *even* I, *am* the LORD; and beside me *there is* no saviour.
12 I have declared, and have saved, and I have shewed, when *there was* no strange *god* among you: therefore ye *are* my witnesses, saith the LORD, that I *am* God.
13 Yea, before the day *was* I *am* he; and

there is none that can deliver out of my
hand: I will work, and who shall let it?
14 ¶ Thus saith the LORD, your redeemer,
the Holy One of Israel; For your sake I have
sent to Babylon, and have brought down
all their nobles, and the Chaldeans, whose
cry *is* in the ships.
15 I *am* the LORD, your Holy One, the creator
of Israel, your King.
16 Thus saith the LORD, which maketh a way
in the sea, and a path in the mighty waters;
17 Which bringeth forth the chariot and
horse, the army and the power; they shall
lie down together, they shall not rise: they
are extinct, they are quenched as tow.
18 ¶ Remember ye not the former things,
neither consider the things of old.
19 Behold, I will do a new thing; now it shall
spring forth; shall ye not know it? I will even
make a way in the wilderness, *and* rivers in
the desert.
20 The beast of the field shall honour me,
the dragons and the owls: because I give
waters in the wilderness, *and* rivers in
the desert, to give drink to my people, my
chosen.
21 This people have I formed for myself;
they shall shew forth my praise.
22 ¶ But thou hast not called upon me, O
Jacob; but thou hast been weary of me,
O Israel.
23 Thou hast not brought me the small cattle of thy burnt offerings; neither hast thou
honoured me with thy sacrifices. I have not
caused thee to serve with an offering, nor
wearied thee with incense.
24 Thou hast bought me no sweet cane with
money, neither hast thou filled me with the
fat of thy sacrifices: but thou hast made me
to serve with thy sins, thou hast wearied me
with thine iniquities.
25 I, *even* I, *am* he that blotteth out thy
transgressions for mine own sake, and will
not remember thy sins.
26 Put me in remembrance: let us plead
together: declare thou, that thou mayest
be justified.
27 Thy first father hath sinned, and thy
teachers have transgressed against me.
28 Therefore I have profaned the princes of
the sanctuary, and have given Jacob to the
curse, and Israel to reproaches.

Isaiah 44

1 Yet now hear, O Jacob my servant; and
Israel, whom I have chosen:
2 Thus saith the LORD that made thee, and
formed thee from the womb, *which* will
help thee; Fear not, O Jacob, my servant;
and thou, Jesurun, whom I have chosen.
3 For I will pour water upon him that is
thirsty, and floods upon the dry ground: I
will pour my spirit upon thy seed, and my
blessing upon thine offspring:
4 And they shall spring up *as* among the
grass, as willows by the water courses.
5 One shall say, I *am* the LORD's; and another
shall call *himself* by the name of Jacob; and
another shall subscribe *with* his hand unto
the LORD, and surname *himself* by the name
of Israel.
6 Thus saith the LORD the King of Israel,
and his redeemer the LORD of hosts; I *am*
the first, and I *am* the last; and beside me
there is no God.
7 And who, as I, shall call, and shall declare it,
and set it in order for me, since I appointed
the ancient people? and the things that
are coming, and shall come, let them shew
unto them.
8 Fear ye not, neither be afraid: have not I
told thee from that time, and have declared
it? ye *are* even my witnesses. Is there a God
beside me? yea, *there is* no God; I know
not *any.*
9 ¶ They that make a graven image *are* all
of them vanity; and their delectable things
shall not profit; and they *are* their own witnesses; they see not, nor know; that they
may be ashamed.
10 Who hath formed a god, or molten a
graven image *that* is profitable for nothing?
11 Behold, all his fellows shall be ashamed:
and the workmen, they *are* of men: let them
all be gathered together, let them stand
up; *yet* they shall fear, *and* they shall be
ashamed together.
12 The smith with the tongs both worketh in
the coals, and fashioneth it with hammers,
and worketh it with the strength of his arms:
yea, he is hungry, and his strength faileth:
he drinketh no water, and is faint.
13 The carpenter stretcheth out *his* rule;
he marketh it out with a line; he fitteth it
with planes, and he marketh it out with the
compass, and maketh it after the figure of

a man, according to the beauty of a man; that it may remain in the house.

14 He heweth him down cedars, and taketh the cypress and the oak, which he strengtheneth for himself among the trees of the forest: he planteth an ash, and the rain doth nourish *it*.

15 Then shall it be for a man to burn: for he will take thereof, and warm himself; yea, he kindleth *it*, and baketh bread; yea, he maketh a god, and worshippeth *it;* he maketh it a graven image, and falleth down thereto.

16 He burneth part thereof in the fire; with part thereof he eateth flesh; he roasteth roast, and is satisfied: yea, he warmeth *himself*, and saith, Aha, I am warm, I have seen the fire:

17 And the residue thereof he maketh a god, *even* his graven image: he falleth down unto it, and worshippeth *it*, and prayeth unto it, and saith, Deliver me; for thou *art* my god.

18 They have not known nor understood: for he hath shut their eyes, that they cannot see; *and* their hearts, that they cannot understand.

19 And none considereth in his heart, neither *is there* knowledge nor understanding to say, I have burned part of it in the fire; yea, also I have baked bread upon the coals thereof; I have roasted flesh, and eaten *it:* and shall I make the residue thereof an abomination? shall I fall down to the stock of a tree?

20 He feedeth on ashes: a deceived heart hath turned him aside, that he cannot deliver his soul, nor say, *Is there* not a lie in my right hand?

21 ¶ Remember these, O Jacob and Israel; for thou *art* my servant: I have formed thee; thou *art* my servant: O Israel, thou shalt not be forgotten of me.

22 I have blotted out, as a thick cloud, thy transgressions, and, as a cloud, thy sins: return unto me; for I have redeemed thee.

23 Sing, O ye heavens; for the LORD hath done *it:* shout, ye lower parts of the earth: break forth into singing, ye mountains, O forest, and every tree therein: for the LORD hath redeemed Jacob, and glorified himself in Israel.

24 Thus saith the LORD, thy redeemer, and he that formed thee from the womb, I *am* the LORD that maketh all *things;* that stretcheth forth the heavens alone; that spreadeth abroad the earth by myself;

25 That frustrateth the tokens of the liars, and maketh diviners mad; that turneth wise *men* backward, and maketh their knowledge foolish;

26 That confirmeth the word of his servant, and performeth the counsel of his messengers; that saith to Jerusalem, Thou shalt be inhabited; and to the cities of Judah, Ye shall be built, and I will raise up the decayed places thereof:

27 That saith to the deep, Be dry, and I will dry up thy rivers:

28 That saith of Cyrus, *He is* my shepherd, and shall perform all my pleasure: even saying to Jerusalem, Thou shalt be built; and to the temple, Thy foundation shall be laid.

Isaiah 45

1 Thus saith the LORD to his anointed, to Cyrus, whose right hand I have holden, to subdue nations before him; and I will loose the loins of kings, to open before him the two leaved gates; and the gates shall not be shut;

2 I will go before thee, and make the crooked places straight: I will break in pieces the gates of brass, and cut in sunder the bars of iron:

3 And I will give thee the treasures of darkness, and hidden riches of secret places, that thou mayest know that I, the LORD, which call *thee* by thy name, *am* the God of Israel.

4 For Jacob my servant's sake, and Israel mine elect, I have even called thee by thy name: I have surnamed thee, though thou hast not known me.

5 ¶ I *am* the LORD, and *there is* none else, *there is* no God beside me: I girded thee, though thou hast not known me:

6 That they may know from the rising of the sun, and from the west, that *there is* none beside me. I *am* the LORD, and *there is* none else.

7 I form the light, and create darkness: I make peace, and create evil: I the LORD do all these *things*.

8 Drop down, ye heavens, from above, and let the skies pour down righteousness: let the earth open, and let them bring forth

salvation, and let righteousness spring up together; I the LORD have created it.

9 Woe unto him that striveth with his Maker! *Let* the potsherd *strive* with the potsherds of the earth. Shall the clay say to him that fashioneth it, What makest thou? or thy work, He hath no hands?

10 Woe unto him that saith unto *his* father, What begettest thou? or to the woman, What hast thou brought forth?

11 Thus saith the LORD, the Holy One of Israel, and his Maker, Ask me of things to come concerning my sons, and concerning the work of my hands command ye me.

12 I have made the earth, and created man upon it: I, *even* my hands, have stretched out the heavens, and all their host have I commanded.

13 I have raised him up in righteousness, and I will direct all his ways: he shall build my city, and he shall let go my captives, not for price nor reward, saith the LORD of hosts.

14 Thus saith the LORD, The labour of Egypt, and merchandise of Ethiopia and of the Sabeans, men of stature, shall come over unto thee, and they shall be thine: they shall come after thee; in chains they shall come over, and they shall fall down unto thee, they shall make supplication unto thee, *saying*, Surely God *is* in thee; and *there is* none else, *there is* no God.

15 Verily thou *art* a God that hidest thyself, O God of Israel, the Saviour.

16 They shall be ashamed, and also confounded, all of them: they shall go to confusion together *that are* makers of idols.

17 *But* Israel shall be saved in the LORD with an everlasting salvation: ye shall not be ashamed nor confounded world without end.

18 For thus saith the LORD that created the heavens; God himself that formed the earth and made it; he hath established it, he created it not in vain, he formed it to be inhabited: I *am* the LORD; and *there is* none else.

19 I have not spoken in secret, in a dark place of the earth: I said not unto the seed of Jacob, Seek ye me in vain: I the LORD speak righteousness, I declare things that are right.

20 ¶ Assemble yourselves and come; draw near together, ye *that are* escaped of the nations: they have no knowledge that set up the wood of their graven image, and pray unto a god *that* cannot save.

21 Tell ye, and bring *them* near; yea, let them take counsel together: who hath declared this from ancient time? *who* hath told it from that time? *have* not I the LORD? and *there is* no God else beside me; a just God and a Saviour; *there is* none beside me.

22 Look unto me, and be ye saved, all the ends of the earth: for I *am* God, and *there is* none else.

23 I have sworn by myself, the word is gone out of my mouth *in* righteousness, and shall not return, That unto me every knee shall bow, every tongue shall swear.

24 Surely, shall *one* say, in the LORD have I righteousness and strength: *even* to him shall *men* come; and all that are incensed against him shall be ashamed.

25 In the LORD shall all the seed of Israel be justified, and shall glory.

Isaiah 46

1 Bel boweth down, Nebo stoopeth, their idols were upon the beasts, and upon the cattle: your carriages *were* heavy loaden; *they are* a burden to the weary *beast*.

2 They stoop, they bow down together; they could not deliver the burden, but themselves are gone into captivity.

3 ¶ Hearken unto me, O house of Jacob, and all the remnant of the house of Israel, which are borne *by me* from the belly, which are carried from the womb:

4 And *even* to *your* old age I *am* he; and *even* to hoar hairs will I carry *you:* I have made, and I will bear; even I will carry, and will deliver *you*.

5 ¶ To whom will ye liken me, and make *me* equal, and compare me, that we may be like?

6 They lavish gold out of the bag, and weigh silver in the balance, *and* hire a goldsmith; and he maketh it a god: they fall down, yea, they worship.

7 They bear him upon the shoulder, they carry him, and set him in his place, and he standeth; from his place shall he not remove: yea, *one* shall cry unto him, yet can he not answer, nor save him out of his trouble.

8 Remember this, and shew yourselves men: bring *it* again to mind, O ye transgressors.

9 Remember the former things of old: for I *am* God, and *there is* none else; *I am* God, and *there is* none like me,

10 Declaring the end from the beginning, and from ancient times *the things* that are not *yet* done, saying, My counsel shall stand, and I will do all my pleasure:

11 Calling a ravenous bird from the east, the man that executeth my counsel from a far country: yea, I have spoken *it*, I will also bring it to pass; I have purposed *it*, I will also do it.

12 ¶ Hearken unto me, ye stouthearted, that *are* far from righteousness:

13 I bring near my righteousness; it shall not be far off, and my salvation shall not tarry: and I will place salvation in Zion for Israel my glory.

Isaiah 47

1 Come down, and sit in the dust, O virgin daughter of Babylon, sit on the ground: *there is* no throne, O daughter of the Chaldeans: for thou shalt no more be called tender and delicate.

2 Take the millstones, and grind meal: uncover thy locks, make bare the leg, uncover the thigh, pass over the rivers.

3 Thy nakedness shall be uncovered, yea, thy shame shall be seen: I will take vengeance, and I will not meet *thee as* a man.

4 *As for* our redeemer, the LORD of hosts *is* his name, the Holy One of Israel.

5 Sit thou silent, and get thee into darkness, O daughter of the Chaldeans: for thou shalt no more be called, The lady of kingdoms.

6 ¶ I was wroth with my people, I have polluted mine inheritance, and given them into thine hand: thou didst shew them no mercy; upon the ancient hast thou very heavily laid thy yoke.

7 ¶ And thou saidst, I shall be a lady for ever: *so* that thou didst not lay these *things* to thy heart, neither didst remember the latter end of it.

8 Therefore hear now this, *thou that art* given to pleasures, that dwellest carelessly, that sayest in thine heart, I *am*, and none else beside me; I shall not sit *as* a widow, neither shall I know the loss of children:

9 But these two *things* shall come to thee in a moment in one day, the loss of children, and widowhood: they shall come upon thee in their perfection for the multitude of thy sorceries, *and* for the great abundance of thine enchantments.

10 ¶ For thou hast trusted in thy wickedness: thou hast said, None seeth me. Thy wisdom and thy knowledge, it hath perverted thee; and thou hast said in thine heart, I *am*, and none else beside me.

11 ¶ Therefore shall evil come upon thee; thou shalt not know from whence it riseth: and mischief shall fall upon thee; thou shalt not be able to put it off: and desolation shall come upon thee suddenly, *which* thou shalt not know.

12 Stand now with thine enchantments, and with the multitude of thy sorceries, wherein thou hast laboured from thy youth; if so be thou shalt be able to profit, if so be thou mayest prevail.

13 Thou art wearied in the multitude of thy counsels. Let now the astrologers, the stargazers, the monthly prognosticators, stand up, and save thee from *these things* that shall come upon thee.

14 Behold, they shall be as stubble; the fire shall burn them; they shall not deliver themselves from the power of the flame: *there shall* not *be* a coal to warm at, *nor* fire to sit before it.

15 Thus shall they be unto thee with whom thou hast laboured, *even* thy merchants, from thy youth: they shall wander every one to his quarter; none shall save thee.

Isaiah 48

1 Hear ye this, O house of Jacob, which are called by the name of Israel, and are come forth out of the waters of Judah, which swear by the name of the LORD, and make mention of the God of Israel, *but* not in truth, nor in righteousness.

2 For they call themselves of the holy city, and stay themselves upon the God of Israel; The LORD of hosts *is* his name.

3 I have declared the former things from the beginning; and they went forth out of my mouth, and I shewed them; I did *them* suddenly, and they came to pass.

4 Because I knew that thou *art* obstinate, and thy neck *is* an iron sinew, and thy brow brass;

5 I have even from the beginning declared *it* to thee; before it came to pass I shewed

it thee: lest thou shouldest say, Mine idol hath done them, and my graven image, and my molten image, hath commanded them.

6 Thou hast heard, see all this; and will not ye declare *it?* I have shewed thee new things from this time, even hidden things, and thou didst not know them.

7 They are created now, and not from the beginning; even before the day when thou heardest them not; lest thou shouldest say, Behold, I knew them.

8 Yea, thou heardest not; yea, thou knewest not; yea, from that time *that* thine ear was not opened: for I knew that thou wouldest deal very treacherously, and wast called a transgressor from the womb.

9 ¶ For my name's sake will I defer mine anger, and for my praise will I refrain for thee, that I cut thee not off.

10 Behold, I have refined thee, but not with silver; I have chosen thee in the furnace of affliction.

11 For mine own sake, *even* for mine own sake, will I do *it:* for how should *my name* be polluted? and I will not give my glory unto another.

12 ¶ Hearken unto me, O Jacob and Israel, my called; I *am* he; I *am* the first, I also *am* the last.

13 Mine hand also hath laid the foundation of the earth, and my right hand hath spanned the heavens: *when* I call unto them, they stand up together.

14 All ye, assemble yourselves, and hear; which among them hath declared these *things?* The LORD hath loved him: he will do his pleasure on Babylon, and his arm *shall be on* the Chaldeans.

15 I, *even* I, have spoken; yea, I have called him: I have brought him, and he shall make his way prosperous.

16 ¶ Come ye near unto me, hear ye this; I have not spoken in secret from the beginning; from the time that it was, there *am* I: and now the Lord GOD, and his Spirit, hath sent me.

17 Thus saith the LORD, thy Redeemer, the Holy One of Israel; I *am* the LORD thy God which teacheth thee to profit, which leadeth thee by the way *that* thou shouldest go.

18 O that thou hadst hearkened to my commandments! then had thy peace been as a river, and thy righteousness as the waves of the sea:

19 Thy seed also had been as the sand, and the offspring of thy bowels like the gravel thereof; his name should not have been cut off nor destroyed from before me.

20 ¶ Go ye forth of Babylon, flee ye from the Chaldeans, with a voice of singing declare ye, tell this, utter it *even* to the end of the earth; say ye, The LORD hath redeemed his servant Jacob.

21 And they thirsted not *when* he led them through the deserts: he caused the waters to flow out of the rock for them: he clave the rock also, and the waters gushed out.

22 *There is* no peace, saith the LORD, unto the wicked.

Isaiah 49

1 Listen, O isles, unto me; and hearken, ye people, from far; The LORD hath called me from the womb; from the bowels of my mother hath he made mention of my name.

2 And he hath made my mouth like a sharp sword; in the shadow of his hand hath he hid me, and made me a polished shaft; in his quiver hath he hid me;

3 And said unto me, Thou *art* my servant, O Israel, in whom I will be glorified.

4 Then I said, I have laboured in vain, I have spent my strength for nought, and in vain: *yet* surely my judgment *is* with the LORD, and my work with my God.

5 ¶ And now, saith the LORD that formed me from the womb *to be* his servant, to bring Jacob again to him, Though Israel be not gathered, yet shall I be glorious in the eyes of the LORD, and my God shall be my strength.

6 And he said, It is a light thing that thou shouldest be my servant to raise up the tribes of Jacob, and to restore the preserved of Israel: I will also give thee for a light to the Gentiles, that thou mayest be my salvation unto the end of the earth.

7 Thus saith the LORD, the Redeemer of Israel, *and* his Holy One, to him whom man despiseth, to him whom the nation abhorreth, to a servant of rulers, Kings shall see and arise, princes also shall worship, because of the LORD that is faithful, *and* the Holy One of Israel, and he shall choose thee.

8 Thus saith the LORD, In an acceptable time

have I heard thee, and in a day of salvation
have I helped thee: and I will preserve thee,
and give thee for a covenant of the people,
to establish the earth, to cause to inherit
the desolate heritages;
9 That thou mayest say to the prisoners, Go
forth; to them that *are* in darkness, Shew
yourselves. They shall feed in the ways, and
their pastures *shall be* in all high places.
10 They shall not hunger nor thirst; neither
shall the heat nor sun smite them: for he
that hath mercy on them shall lead them,
even by the springs of water shall he guide
them.
11 And I will make all my mountains a way,
and my highways shall be exalted.
12 Behold, these shall come from far: and,
lo, these from the north and from the west;
and these from the land of Sinim.
13 ¶ Sing, O heavens; and be joyful, O earth;
and break forth into singing, O mountains:
for the LORD hath comforted his people, and
will have mercy upon his afflicted.
14 But Zion said, The LORD hath forsaken
me, and my Lord hath forgotten me.
15 Can a woman forget her sucking child,
that she should not have compassion on the
son of her womb? yea, they may forget, yet
will I not forget thee.
16 Behold, I have graven thee upon the
palms of *my* hands; thy walls *are* continually
before me.
17 Thy children shall make haste; thy
destroyers and they that made thee waste
shall go forth of thee.
18 ¶ Lift up thine eyes round about,
and behold: all these gather themselves
together, *and* come to thee. *As* I live, saith
the LORD, thou shalt surely clothe thee with
them all, as with an ornament, and bind
them *on thee*, as a bride *doeth*.
19 For thy waste and thy desolate places,
and the land of thy destruction, shall even
now be too narrow by reason of the inhabitants, and they that swallowed thee up shall
be far away.
20 The children which thou shalt have, after
thou hast lost the other, shall say again in
thine ears, The place *is* too strait for me:
give place to me that I may dwell.
21 Then shalt thou say in thine heart, Who
hath begotten me these, seeing I have lost
my children, and am desolate, a captive,
and removing to and fro? and who hath
brought up these? Behold, I was left alone;
these, where *had* they *been*?
22 Thus saith the Lord GOD, Behold, I will
lift up mine hand to the Gentiles, and set up
my standard to the people: and they shall
bring thy sons in *their* arms, and thy daughters shall be carried upon *their* shoulders.
23 And kings shall be thy nursing fathers,
and their queens thy nursing mothers:
they shall bow down to thee with *their* face
toward the earth, and lick up the dust of
thy feet; and thou shalt know that I *am* the
LORD: for they shall not be ashamed that
wait for me.
24 ¶ Shall the prey be taken from the
mighty, or the lawful captive delivered?
25 But thus saith the LORD, Even the captives
of the mighty shall be taken away, and the
prey of the terrible shall be delivered: for I
will contend with him that contendeth with
thee, and I will save thy children.
26 And I will feed them that oppress thee
with their own flesh; and they shall be
drunken with their own blood, as with
sweet wine: and all flesh shall know that I
the LORD *am* thy Saviour and thy Redeemer,
the mighty One of Jacob.

Isaiah 50

1 Thus saith the LORD, Where *is* the bill of
your mother's divorcement, whom I have
put away? or which of my creditors *is it* to
whom I have sold you? Behold, for your iniquities have ye sold yourselves, and for your
transgressions is your mother put away.
2 Wherefore, when I came, *was there* no
man? when I called, *was there* none to
answer? Is my hand shortened at all, that
it cannot redeem? or have I no power to
deliver? behold, at my rebuke I dry up the
sea, I make the rivers a wilderness: their
fish stinketh, because *there is* no water, and
dieth for thirst.
3 I clothe the heavens with blackness, and
I make sackcloth their covering.
4 The Lord GOD hath given me the tongue
of the learned, that I should know how to
speak a word in season to *him that is* weary:
he wakeneth morning by morning, he wakeneth mine ear to hear as the learned.
5 ¶ The Lord GOD hath opened mine ear,

and I was not rebellious, neither turned
away back.
6 I gave my back to the smiters, and my
cheeks to them that plucked off the hair:
I hid not my face from shame and spitting.
7 ¶ For the Lord GOD will help me; therefore
shall I not be confounded: therefore have
I set my face like a flint, and I know that I
shall not be ashamed.
8 *He is* near that justifieth me; who will contend with me? let us stand together: who *is*
mine adversary? let him come near to me.
9 Behold, the Lord GOD will help me; who
is he *that* shall condemn me? lo, they all
shall wax old as a garment; the moth shall
eat them up.
10 ¶ Who *is* among you that feareth the
LORD, that obeyeth the voice of his servant,
that walketh *in* darkness, and hath no light?
let him trust in the name of the LORD, and
stay upon his God.
11 Behold, all ye that kindle a fire, that compass *yourselves* about with sparks: walk in
the light of your fire, and in the sparks *that*
ye have kindled. This shall ye have of mine
hand; ye shall lie down in sorrow.

Isaiah 51

1 Hearken to me, ye that follow after righteousness, ye that seek the LORD: look unto
the rock *whence* ye are hewn, and to the
hole of the pit *whence* ye are digged.
2 Look unto Abraham your father, and unto
Sarah *that* bare you: for I called him alone,
and blessed him, and increased him.
3 For the LORD shall comfort Zion: he will
comfort all her waste places; and he will
make her wilderness like Eden, and her
desert like the garden of the LORD; joy and
gladness shall be found therein, thanksgiving, and the voice of melody.
4 ¶ Hearken unto me, my people; and give
ear unto me, O my nation: for a law shall
proceed from me, and I will make my judgment to rest for a light of the people.
5 My righteousness *is* near; my salvation is
gone forth, and mine arms shall judge the
people; the isles shall wait upon me, and on
mine arm shall they trust.
6 Lift up your eyes to the heavens, and look
upon the earth beneath: for the heavens
shall vanish away like smoke, and the earth
shall wax old like a garment, and they that
dwell therein shall die in like manner: but
my salvation shall be for ever, and my righteousness shall not be abolished.
7 ¶ Hearken unto me, ye that know righteousness, the people in whose heart *is* my
law; fear ye not the reproach of men, neither
be ye afraid of their revilings.
8 For the moth shall eat them up like a
garment, and the worm shall eat them like
wool: but my righteousness shall be for
ever, and my salvation from generation to
generation.
9 ¶ Awake, awake, put on strength, O arm
of the LORD; awake, as in the ancient days,
in the generations of old. *Art* thou not it that
hath cut Rahab, *and* wounded the dragon?
10 *Art* thou not it which hath dried the sea,
the waters of the great deep; that hath
made the depths of the sea a way for the
ransomed to pass over?
11 Therefore the redeemed of the LORD
shall return, and come with singing unto
Zion; and everlasting joy *shall be* upon their
head: they shall obtain gladness and joy;
and sorrow and mourning shall flee away.
12 I, *even* I, *am* he that comforteth you: who
art thou, that thou shouldest be afraid of
a man *that* shall die, and of the son of man
which shall be made *as* grass;
13 And forgettest the LORD thy maker,
that hath stretched forth the heavens,
and laid the foundations of the earth; and
hast feared continually every day because
of the fury of the oppressor, as if he were
ready to destroy? and where *is* the fury of
the oppressor?
14 The captive exile hasteneth that he may
be loosed, and that he should not die in the
pit, nor that his bread should fail.
15 But I *am* the LORD thy God, that divided
the sea, whose waves roared: The LORD of
hosts *is* his name.
16 And I have put my words in thy mouth,
and I have covered thee in the shadow of
mine hand, that I may plant the heavens,
and lay the foundations of the earth, and
say unto Zion, Thou *art* my people.
17 ¶ Awake, awake, stand up, O Jerusalem,
which hast drunk at the hand of the LORD
the cup of his fury; thou hast drunken the
dregs of the cup of trembling, *and* wrung
them out.
18 *There is* none to guide her among all the

sons *whom* she hath brought forth; neither
is there any that taketh her by the hand of
all the sons *that* she hath brought up.
19 These two *things* are come unto thee;
who shall be sorry for thee? desolation, and
destruction, and the famine, and the sword:
by whom shall I comfort thee?
20 Thy sons have fainted, they lie at the
head of all the streets, as a wild bull in a
net: they are full of the fury of the LORD,
the rebuke of thy God.
21 ¶ Therefore hear now this, thou afflicted,
and drunken, but not with wine:
22 Thus saith thy Lord the LORD, and thy
God *that* pleadeth the cause of his people,
Behold, I have taken out of thine hand the
cup of trembling, *even* the dregs of the cup
of my fury; thou shalt no more drink it again:
23 But I will put it into the hand of them
that afflict thee; which have said to thy soul,
Bow down, that we may go over: and thou
hast laid thy body as the ground, and as the
street, to them that went over.

Isaiah 52

1 Awake, awake; put on thy strength, O Zion;
put on thy beautiful garments, O Jerusalem,
the holy city: for henceforth there shall no
more come into thee the uncircumcised
and the unclean.
2 Shake thyself from the dust; arise, *and*
sit down, O Jerusalem: loose thyself from
the bands of thy neck, O captive daughter
of Zion.
3 For thus saith the LORD, Ye have sold yourselves for nought; and ye shall be redeemed
without money.
4 For thus saith the Lord GOD, My people
went down aforetime into Egypt to sojourn
there; and the Assyrian oppressed them
without cause.
5 Now therefore, what have I here, saith
the LORD, that my people is taken away
for nought? they that rule over them make
them to howl, saith the LORD; and my name
continually every day *is* blasphemed.
6 Therefore my people shall know my name:
therefore *they shall know* in that day that I
am he that doth speak: behold, *it is* I.
7 ¶ How beautiful upon the mountains are
the feet of him that bringeth good tidings,
that publisheth peace; that bringeth good
tidings of good, that publisheth salvation;
that saith unto Zion, Thy God reigneth!
8 Thy watchmen shall lift up the voice; with
the voice together shall they sing: for they
shall see eye to eye, when the LORD shall
bring again Zion.
9 ¶ Break forth into joy, sing together, ye
waste places of Jerusalem: for the LORD hath
comforted his people, he hath redeemed
Jerusalem.
10 The LORD hath made bare his holy arm in
the eyes of all the nations; and all the ends of
the earth shall see the salvation of our God.
11 ¶ Depart ye, depart ye, go ye out from
thence, touch no unclean *thing;* go ye out
of the midst of her; be ye clean, that bear
the vessels of the LORD.
12 For ye shall not go out with haste, nor
go by flight: for the LORD will go before you;
and the God of Israel *will be* your rereward.
13 ¶ Behold, my servant shall deal pru-
dently, he shall be exalted and extolled,
and be very high.
14 As many were astonied at thee; his visage
was so marred more than any man, and his
form more than the sons of men:
15 So shall he sprinkle many nations; the
kings shall shut their mouths at him: for
that which had not been told them shall
they see; and *that* which they had not heard
shall they consider.

Isaiah 53

1 Who hath believed our report? and to
whom is the arm of the LORD revealed?
2 For he shall grow up before him as a tender plant, and as a root out of a dry ground:
he hath no form nor comeliness; and when
we shall see him, *there is* no beauty that we
should desire him.
3 He is despised and rejected of men; a man
of sorrows, and acquainted with grief: and
we hid as it were *our* faces from him; he
was despised, and we esteemed him not.
4 ¶ Surely he hath borne our griefs, and
carried our sorrows: yet we did esteem
him stricken, smitten of God, and afflicted.
5 But he *was* wounded for our transgressions, *he was* bruised for our iniquities: the
chastisement of our peace *was* upon him;
and with his stripes we are healed.
6 All we like sheep have gone astray; we
have turned every one to his own way;

and the LORD hath laid on him the iniquity
of us all.
7 He was oppressed, and he was afflicted,
yet he opened not his mouth: he is brought
as a lamb to the slaughter, and as a sheep
before her shearers is dumb, so he openeth
not his mouth.
8 He was taken from prison and from judgment: and who shall declare his generation?
for he was cut off out of the land of the
living: for the transgression of my people
was he stricken.
9 And he made his grave with the wicked,
and with the rich in his death; because he
had done no violence, neither *was any*
deceit in his mouth.
10 ¶ Yet it pleased the LORD to bruise him;
he hath put *him* to grief: when thou shalt
make his soul an offering for sin, he shall
see *his* seed, he shall prolong *his* days, and
the pleasure of the LORD shall prosper in
his hand.
11 He shall see of the travail of his soul, *and*
shall be satisfied: by his knowledge shall my
righteous servant justify many; for he shall
bear their iniquities.
12 Therefore will I divide him *a portion* with
the great, and he shall divide the spoil with
the strong; because he hath poured out
his soul unto death: and he was numbered
with the transgressors; and he bare the
sin of many, and made intercession for the
transgressors.

Isaiah 54

1 Sing, O barren, thou *that* didst not bear;
break forth into singing, and cry aloud, thou
that didst not travail with child: for more
are the children of the desolate than the
children of the married wife, saith the LORD.
2 Enlarge the place of thy tent, and let them
stretch forth the curtains of thine habitations: spare not, lengthen thy cords, and
strengthen thy stakes;
3 For thou shalt break forth on the right
hand and on the left; and thy seed shall
inherit the Gentiles, and make the desolate
cities to be inhabited.
4 Fear not; for thou shalt not be ashamed:
neither be thou confounded; for thou shalt
not be put to shame: for thou shalt forget
the shame of thy youth, and shalt not
remember the reproach of thy widowhood
any more.
5 For thy Maker *is* thine husband; the LORD
of hosts *is* his name; and thy Redeemer the
Holy One of Israel; The God of the whole
earth shall he be called.
6 For the LORD hath called thee as a woman
forsaken and grieved in spirit, and a wife
of youth, when thou wast refused, saith
thy God.
7 For a small moment have I forsaken thee;
but with great mercies will I gather thee.
8 In a little wrath I hid my face from thee
for a moment; but with everlasting kindness
will I have mercy on thee, saith the LORD
thy Redeemer.
9 For this *is as* the waters of Noah unto me:
for *as* I have sworn that the waters of Noah
should no more go over the earth; so have I
sworn that I would not be wroth with thee,
nor rebuke thee.
10 For the mountains shall depart, and the
hills be removed; but my kindness shall not
depart from thee, neither shall the covenant
of my peace be removed, saith the LORD that
hath mercy on thee.
11 ¶ O thou afflicted, tossed with tempest,
and not comforted, behold, I will lay thy
stones with fair colours, and lay thy foundations with sapphires.
12 And I will make thy windows of agates,
and thy gates of carbuncles, and all thy
borders of pleasant stones.
13 And all thy children *shall be* taught of
the LORD; and great *shall be* the peace of
thy children.
14 In righteousness shalt thou be established: thou shalt be far from oppression;
for thou shalt not fear: and from terror; for
it shall not come near thee.
15 Behold, they shall surely gather together,
but not by me: whosoever shall gather
together against thee shall fall for thy sake.
16 Behold, I have created the smith that
bloweth the coals in the fire, and that bringeth forth an instrument for his work; and
I have created the waster to destroy.
17 ¶ No weapon that is formed against thee
shall prosper; and every tongue *that* shall
rise against thee in judgment thou shalt condemn. This *is* the heritage of the servants
of the LORD, and their righteousness *is* of
me, saith the LORD.

Isaiah 55

1 Ho, every one that thirsteth, come ye to
the waters, and he that hath no money;
come ye, buy, and eat; yea, come, buy wine
and milk without money and without price.
2 Wherefore do ye spend money for *that*
which is not bread? and your labour for *that*
which satisfieth not? hearken diligently unto
me, and eat ye *that which is* good, and let
your soul delight itself in fatness.
3 Incline your ear, and come unto me: hear,
and your soul shall live; and I will make an
everlasting covenant with you, *even* the sure
mercies of David.
4 Behold, I have given him *for* a witness to
the people, a leader and commander to
the people.
5 Behold, thou shalt call a nation *that* thou
knowest not, and nations *that* knew not
thee shall run unto thee because of the LORD
thy God, and for the Holy One of Israel; for
he hath glorified thee.
6 ¶ Seek ye the LORD while he may be found,
call ye upon him while he is near:
7 Let the wicked forsake his way, and the
unrighteous man his thoughts: and let him
return unto the LORD, and he will have
mercy upon him; and to our God, for he
will abundantly pardon.
8 ¶ For my thoughts *are* not your thoughts,
neither *are* your ways my ways, saith the
LORD.
9 For *as* the heavens are higher than the
earth, so are my ways higher than your
ways, and my thoughts than your thoughts.
10 For as the rain cometh down, and the
snow from heaven, and returneth not
thither, but watereth the earth, and maketh
it bring forth and bud, that it may give seed
to the sower, and bread to the eater:
11 So shall my word be that goeth forth
out of my mouth: it shall not return unto
me void, but it shall accomplish that which
I please, and it shall prosper *in the thing*
whereto I sent it.
12 For ye shall go out with joy, and be led
forth with peace: the mountains and the
hills shall break forth before you into singing, and all the trees of the field shall clap
their hands.
13 Instead of the thorn shall come up the fir
tree, and instead of the brier shall come up
the myrtle tree: and it shall be to the LORD
for a name, for an everlasting sign *that* shall
not be cut off.

Isaiah 56

1 Thus saith the LORD, Keep ye judgment,
and do justice: for my salvation *is* near to
come, and my righteousness to be revealed.
2 Blessed *is* the man *that* doeth this, and
the son of man *that* layeth hold on it; that
keepeth the sabbath from polluting it, and
keepeth his hand from doing any evil.
3 ¶ Neither let the son of the stranger, that
hath joined himself to the LORD, speak,
saying, The LORD hath utterly separated
me from his people: neither let the eunuch
say, Behold, I *am* a dry tree.
4 For thus saith the LORD unto the eunuchs
that keep my sabbaths, and choose *the*
things that please me, and take hold of my
covenant;
5 Even unto them will I give in mine house
and within my walls a place and a name
better than of sons and of daughters: I will
give them an everlasting name, that shall
not be cut off.
6 Also the sons of the stranger, that join
themselves to the LORD, to serve him, and
to love the name of the LORD, to be his
servants, every one that keepeth the sabbath from polluting it, and taketh hold of
my covenant;
7 Even them will I bring to my holy mountain, and make them joyful in my house of
prayer: their burnt offerings and their sacrifices *shall be* accepted upon mine altar;
for mine house shall be called an house of
prayer for all people.
8 The Lord GOD which gathereth the outcasts of Israel saith, Yet will I gather *others*
to him, beside those that are gathered
unto him.
9 ¶ All ye beasts of the field, come to devour,
yea, all ye beasts in the forest.
10 His watchmen *are* blind: they are all
ignorant, they *are* all dumb dogs, they
cannot bark; sleeping, lying down, loving
to slumber.
11 Yea, *they are* greedy dogs *which* can
never have enough, and they *are* shepherds
that cannot understand: they all look to
their own way, every one for his gain, from
his quarter.
12 Come ye, *say they*, I will fetch wine, and

we will fill ourselves with strong drink; and to morrow shall be as this day, *and* much more abundant.

Isaiah 57

1 The righteous perisheth, and no man layeth *it* to heart: and merciful men *are* taken away, none considering that the righteous is taken away from the evil *to come*.
2 He shall enter into peace: they shall rest in their beds, *each one* walking *in* his uprightness.
3 ¶ But draw near hither, ye sons of the sorceress, the seed of the adulterer and the whore.
4 Against whom do ye sport yourselves? against whom make ye a wide mouth, *and* draw out the tongue? *are* ye not children of transgression, a seed of falsehood,
5 Enflaming yourselves with idols under every green tree, slaying the children in the valleys under the clifts of the rocks?
6 Among the smooth *stones* of the stream *is* thy portion; they, they *are* thy lot: even to them hast thou poured a drink offering, thou hast offered a meat offering. Should I receive comfort in these?
7 Upon a lofty and high mountain hast thou set thy bed: even thither wentest thou up to offer sacrifice.
8 Behind the doors also and the posts hast thou set up thy remembrance: for thou hast discovered *thyself to another* than me, and art gone up; thou hast enlarged thy bed, and made thee *a covenant* with them; thou lovedst their bed where thou sawest *it*.
9 And thou wentest to the king with ointment, and didst increase thy perfumes, and didst send thy messengers far off, and didst debase *thyself even* unto hell.
10 Thou art wearied in the greatness of thy way; *yet* saidst thou not, There is no hope: thou hast found the life of thine hand; therefore thou wast not grieved.
11 And of whom hast thou been afraid or feared, that thou hast lied, and hast not remembered me, nor laid *it* to thy heart? have not I held my peace even of old, and thou fearest me not?
12 I will declare thy righteousness, and thy works; for they shall not profit thee.
13 ¶ When thou criest, let thy companies deliver thee; but the wind shall carry them all away; vanity shall take *them:* but he that putteth his trust in me shall possess the land, and shall inherit my holy mountain;
14 And shall say, Cast ye up, cast ye up, prepare the way, take up the stumblingblock out of the way of my people.
15 For thus saith the high and lofty One that inhabiteth eternity, whose name *is* Holy; I dwell in the high and holy *place*, with him also *that is* of a contrite and humble spirit, to revive the spirit of the humble, and to revive the heart of the contrite ones.
16 For I will not contend for ever, neither will I be always wroth: for the spirit should fail before me, and the souls *which* I have made.
17 For the iniquity of his covetousness was I wroth, and smote him: I hid me, and was wroth, and he went on frowardly in the way of his heart.
18 I have seen his ways, and will heal him: I will lead him also, and restore comforts unto him and to his mourners.
19 I create the fruit of the lips; Peace, peace to *him that is* far off, and to *him that is* near, saith the LORD; and I will heal him.
20 But the wicked *are* like the troubled sea, when it cannot rest, whose waters cast up mire and dirt.
21 *There is* no peace, saith my God, to the wicked.

Isaiah 58

1 Cry aloud, spare not, lift up thy voice like a trumpet, and shew my people their transgression, and the house of Jacob their sins.
2 Yet they seek me daily, and delight to know my ways, as a nation that did righteousness, and forsook not the ordinance of their God: they ask of me the ordinances of justice; they take delight in approaching to God.
3 ¶ Wherefore have we fasted, *say they,* and thou seest not? *wherefore* have we afflicted our soul, and thou takest no knowledge? Behold, in the day of your fast ye find pleasure, and exact all your labours.
4 Behold, ye fast for strife and debate, and to smite with the fist of wickedness: ye shall not fast as *ye do this* day, to make your voice to be heard on high.
5 Is it such a fast that I have chosen? a day for a man to afflict his soul? *is it* to bow down his head as a bulrush, and to spread sackcloth and ashes *under him?* wilt thou

call this a fast, and an acceptable day to
the LORD?
6 *Is* not this the fast that I have chosen? to
loose the bands of wickedness, to undo the
heavy burdens, and to let the oppressed go
free, and that ye break every yoke?
7 *Is it* not to deal thy bread to the hungry,
and that thou bring the poor that are cast
out to thy house? when thou seest the
naked, that thou cover him; and that thou
hide not thyself from thine own flesh?
8 ¶ Then shall thy light break forth as the
morning, and thine health shall spring forth
speedily: and thy righteousness shall go
before thee; the glory of the LORD shall be
thy rereward.
9 Then shalt thou call, and the LORD shall
answer; thou shalt cry, and he shall say, Here
I *am*. If thou take away from the midst of
thee the yoke, the putting forth of the finger,
and speaking vanity;
10 And *if* thou draw out thy soul to the hungry, and satisfy the afflicted soul; then shall
thy light rise in obscurity, and thy darkness
be as the noonday:
11 And the LORD shall guide thee continually,
and satisfy thy soul in drought, and make fat
thy bones: and thou shalt be like a watered
garden, and like a spring of water, whose
waters fail not.
12 And *they that shall be* of thee shall build
the old waste places: thou shalt raise up the
foundations of many generations; and thou
shalt be called, The repairer of the breach,
The restorer of paths to dwell in.
13 ¶ If thou turn away thy foot from the
sabbath, *from* doing thy pleasure on my
holy day; and call the sabbath a delight,
the holy of the LORD, honourable; and shalt
honour him, not doing thine own ways, nor
finding thine own pleasure, nor speaking
thine own words:
14 Then shalt thou delight thyself in the
LORD; and I will cause thee to ride upon
the high places of the earth, and feed thee
with the heritage of Jacob thy father: for the
mouth of the LORD hath spoken *it*.

Isaiah 59

1 Behold, the LORD's hand is not shortened,
that it cannot save; neither his ear heavy,
that it cannot hear:
2 But your iniquities have separated
between you and your God, and your sins
have hid *his* face from you, that he will
not hear.
3 For your hands are defiled with blood, and
your fingers with iniquity; your lips have
spoken lies, your tongue hath muttered
perverseness.
4 None calleth for justice, nor *any* pleadeth
for truth: they trust in vanity, and speak
lies; they conceive mischief, and bring forth
iniquity.
5 They hatch cockatrice' eggs, and weave
the spider's web: he that eateth of their eggs
dieth, and that which is crushed breaketh
out into a viper.
6 Their webs shall not become garments,
neither shall they cover themselves with
their works: their works *are* works of iniquity, and the act of violence *is* in their hands.
7 Their feet run to evil, and they make haste
to shed innocent blood: their thoughts *are*
thoughts of iniquity; wasting and destruction *are* in their paths.
8 The way of peace they know not; and
there is no judgment in their goings: they
have made them crooked paths: whosoever
goeth therein shall not know peace.
9 ¶ Therefore is judgment far from us, neither doth justice overtake us: we wait for
light, but behold obscurity; for brightness,
but we walk in darkness.
10 We grope for the wall like the blind, and
we grope as if *we had* no eyes: we stumble
at noonday as in the night; *we are* in desolate places as dead *men*.
11 We roar all like bears, and mourn sore
like doves: we look for judgment, but *there
is* none; for salvation, *but* it is far off from us.
12 For our transgressions are multiplied
before thee, and our sins testify against us:
for our transgressions *are* with us; and *as
for* our iniquities, we know them;
13 In transgressing and lying against the
LORD, and departing away from our God,
speaking oppression and revolt, conceiv-
ing and uttering from the heart words of
falsehood.
14 And judgment is turned away backward,
and justice standeth afar off: for truth is
fallen in the street, and equity cannot enter.
15 Yea, truth faileth; and he *that* departeth
from evil maketh himself a prey: and the

LORD saw *it*, and it displeased him that *there*
was no judgment.
16 ¶ And he saw that *there was* no man, and
wondered that *there was* no intercessor:
therefore his arm brought salvation unto
him; and his righteousness, it sustained him.
17 For he put on righteousness as a breastplate, and an helmet of salvation upon
his head; and he put on the garments of
vengeance *for* clothing, and was clad with
zeal as a cloke.
18 According to *their* deeds, accordingly he
will repay, fury to his adversaries, recompence to his enemies; to the islands he will
repay recompence.
19 So shall they fear the name of the LORD
from the west, and his glory from the rising
of the sun. When the enemy shall come in
like a flood, the Spirit of the LORD shall lift
up a standard against him.
20 ¶ And the Redeemer shall come to Zion,
and unto them that turn from transgression
in Jacob, saith the LORD.
21 As for me, this *is* my covenant with them,
saith the LORD; My spirit that *is* upon thee,
and my words which I have put in thy mouth,
shall not depart out of thy mouth, nor out
of the mouth of thy seed, nor out of the
mouth of thy seed's seed, saith the LORD,
from henceforth and for ever.

Isaiah 60

1 Arise, shine; for thy light is come, and the
glory of the LORD is risen upon thee.
2 For, behold, the darkness shall cover the
earth, and gross darkness the people: but
the LORD shall arise upon thee, and his glory
shall be seen upon thee.
3 And the Gentiles shall come to thy light,
and kings to the brightness of thy rising.
4 Lift up thine eyes round about, and see: all
they gather themselves together, they come
to thee: thy sons shall come from far, and
thy daughters shall be nursed at *thy* side.
5 Then thou shalt see, and flow together,
and thine heart shall fear, and be enlarged;
because the abundance of the sea shall
be converted unto thee, the forces of the
Gentiles shall come unto thee.
6 The multitude of camels shall cover thee,
the dromedaries of Midian and Ephah; all
they from Sheba shall come: they shall bring
gold and incense; and they shall shew forth
the praises of the LORD.
7 All the flocks of Kedar shall be gathered
together unto thee, the rams of Nebaioth
shall minister unto thee: they shall come
up with acceptance on mine altar, and I will
glorify the house of my glory.
8 Who *are* these *that* fly as a cloud, and as
the doves to their windows?
9 Surely the isles shall wait for me, and the
ships of Tarshish first, to bring thy sons from
far, their silver and their gold with them,
unto the name of the LORD thy God, and
to the Holy One of Israel, because he hath
glorified thee.
10 And the sons of strangers shall build up
thy walls, and their kings shall minister unto
thee: for in my wrath I smote thee, but in my
favour have I had mercy on thee.
11 Therefore thy gates shall be open continually; they shall not be shut day nor night;
that *men* may bring unto thee the forces
of the Gentiles, and *that* their kings *may*
be brought.
12 For the nation and kingdom that will not
serve thee shall perish; yea, *those* nations
shall be utterly wasted.
13 The glory of Lebanon shall come unto
thee, the fir tree, the pine tree, and the
box together, to beautify the place of my
sanctuary; and I will make the place of my
feet glorious.
14 The sons also of them that afflicted thee
shall come bending unto thee; and all they
that despised thee shall bow themselves
down at the soles of thy feet; and they shall
call thee, The city of the LORD, The Zion of
the Holy One of Israel.
15 Whereas thou hast been forsaken and
hated, so that no man went through *thee*, I
will make thee an eternal excellency, a joy
of many generations.
16 Thou shalt also suck the milk of the
Gentiles, and shalt suck the breast of kings:
and thou shalt know that I the LORD *am*
thy Saviour and thy Redeemer, the mighty
One of Jacob.
17 For brass I will bring gold, and for iron
I will bring silver, and for wood brass, and
for stones iron: I will also make thy officers
peace, and thine exactors righteousness.
18 Violence shall no more be heard in thy
land, wasting nor destruction within thy

borders; but thou shalt call thy walls Salvation, and thy gates Praise.
19 The sun shall be no more thy light by
day; neither for brightness shall the moon
give light unto thee: but the LORD shall be
unto thee an everlasting light, and thy God
thy glory.
20 Thy sun shall no more go down; neither
shall thy moon withdraw itself: for the LORD
shall be thine everlasting light, and the days
of thy mourning shall be ended.
21 Thy people also *shall be* all righteous:
they shall inherit the land for ever, the
branch of my planting, the work of my
hands, that I may be glorified.
22 A little one shall become a thousand, and
a small one a strong nation: I the LORD will
hasten it in his time.

Isaiah 61

1 The Spirit of the Lord GOD *is* upon me;
because the LORD hath anointed me to
preach good tidings unto the meek; he hath
sent me to bind up the brokenhearted, to
proclaim liberty to the captives, and the
opening of the prison to *them that are*
bound;
2 To proclaim the acceptable year of the
LORD, and the day of vengeance of our God;
to comfort all that mourn;
3 To appoint unto them that mourn in Zion,
to give unto them beauty for ashes, the oil
of joy for mourning, the garment of praise
for the spirit of heaviness; that they might
be called trees of righteousness, the planting of the LORD, that he might be glorified.
4 ¶ And they shall build the old wastes,
they shall raise up the former desolations,
and they shall repair the waste cities, the
desolations of many generations.
5 And strangers shall stand and feed your
flocks, and the sons of the alien *shall be* your
plowmen and your vinedressers.
6 But ye shall be named the Priests of the
LORD: *men* shall call you the Ministers of our
God: ye shall eat the riches of the Gentiles,
and in their glory shall ye boast yourselves.
7 ¶ For your shame *ye shall have* double;
and *for* confusion they shall rejoice in their
portion: therefore in their land they shall
possess the double: everlasting joy shall
be unto them.
8 For I the LORD love judgment, I hate robbery for burnt offering; and I will direct their
work in truth, and I will make an everlasting
covenant with them.
9 And their seed shall be known among
the Gentiles, and their offspring among the
people: all that see them shall acknowledge
them, that they *are* the seed *which* the LORD
hath blessed.
10 I will greatly rejoice in the LORD, my soul
shall be joyful in my God; for he hath clothed
me with the garments of salvation, he hath
covered me with the robe of righteousness,
as a bridegroom decketh *himself* with ornaments, and as a bride adorneth *herself* with
her jewels.
11 For as the earth bringeth forth her bud,
and as the garden causeth the things that
are sown in it to spring forth; so the Lord
GOD will cause righteousness and praise to
spring forth before all the nations.

Isaiah 62

1 For Zion's sake will I not hold my peace,
and for Jerusalem's sake I will not rest,
until the righteousness thereof go forth as
brightness, and the salvation thereof as a
lamp *that* burneth.
2 And the Gentiles shall see thy righteousness, and all kings thy glory: and thou shalt
be called by a new name, which the mouth
of the LORD shall name.
3 Thou shalt also be a crown of glory in the
hand of the LORD, and a royal diadem in the
hand of thy God.
4 Thou shalt no more be termed Forsaken;
neither shall thy land any more be termed
Desolate: but thou shalt be called Hephzi-bah, and thy land Beulah: for the LORD
delighteth in thee, and thy land shall be
married.
5 ¶ For *as* a young man marrieth a virgin, *so*
shall thy sons marry thee: and *as* the bridegroom rejoiceth over the bride, *so* shall thy
God rejoice over thee.
6 I have set watchmen upon thy walls, O
Jerusalem, *which* shall never hold their
peace day nor night: ye that make mention
of the LORD, keep not silence,
7 And give him no rest, till he establish, and
till he make Jerusalem a praise in the earth.
8 The LORD hath sworn by his right hand,
and by the arm of his strength, Surely I will
no more give thy corn *to be* meat for thine

enemies; and the sons of the stranger shall
not drink thy wine, for the which thou hast
laboured:
9 But they that have gathered it shall eat
it, and praise the LORD; and they that have
brought it together shall drink it in the courts
of my holiness.
10 ¶ Go through, go through the gates;
prepare ye the way of the people; cast up,
cast up the highway; gather out the stones;
lift up a standard for the people.
11 Behold, the LORD hath proclaimed unto
the end of the world, Say ye to the daughter of Zion, Behold, thy salvation cometh;
behold, his reward *is* with him, and his work
before him.
12 And they shall call them, The holy people,
The redeemed of the LORD: and thou shalt
be called, Sought out, A city not forsaken.

Isaiah 63

1 Who *is* this that cometh from Edom, with
dyed garments from Bozrah? this *that is*
glorious in his apparel, travelling in the
greatness of his strength? I that speak in
righteousness, mighty to save.
2 Wherefore *art thou* red in thine apparel,
and thy garments like him that treadeth in
the winefat?
3 I have trodden the winepress alone; and
of the people *there was* none with me: for
I will tread them in mine anger, and trample them in my fury; and their blood shall
be sprinkled upon my garments, and I will
stain all my raiment.
4 For the day of vengeance *is* in mine heart,
and the year of my redeemed is come.
5 And I looked, and *there was* none to help;
and I wondered that *there was* none to
uphold: therefore mine own arm brought
salvation unto me; and my fury, it upheld
me.
6 And I will tread down the people in mine
anger, and make them drunk in my fury, and
I will bring down their strength to the earth.
7 ¶ I will mention the lovingkindnesses
of the LORD, *and* the praises of the LORD,
according to all that the LORD hath bestowed
on us, and the great goodness toward the
house of Israel, which he hath bestowed on
them according to his mercies, and according to the multitude of his lovingkindnesses.
8 For he said, Surely they *are* my people,
children *that* will not lie: so he was their
Saviour.
9 In all their affliction he was afflicted, and
the angel of his presence saved them: in
his love and in his pity he redeemed them;
and he bare them, and carried them all the
days of old.
10 ¶ But they rebelled, and vexed his holy
Spirit: therefore he was turned to be their
enemy, *and* he fought against them.
11 Then he remembered the days of old,
Moses, *and* his people, *saying*, Where *is* he
that brought them up out of the sea with
the shepherd of his flock? where *is* he that
put his holy Spirit within him?
12 That led *them* by the right hand of Moses
with his glorious arm, dividing the water
before them, to make himself an everlasting name?
13 That led them through the deep, as an
horse in the wilderness, *that* they should
not stumble?
14 As a beast goeth down into the valley,
the Spirit of the LORD caused him to rest: so
didst thou lead thy people, to make thyself
a glorious name.
15 ¶ Look down from heaven, and behold
from the habitation of thy holiness and of
thy glory: where *is* thy zeal and thy strength,
the sounding of thy bowels and of thy mercies toward me? are they restrained?
16 Doubtless thou *art* our father, though
Abraham be ignorant of us, and Israel
acknowledge us not: thou, O LORD, *art* our
father, our redeemer; thy name *is* from
everlasting.
17 ¶ O LORD, why hast thou made us to err
from thy ways, *and* hardened our heart from
thy fear? Return for thy servants' sake, the
tribes of thine inheritance.
18 The people of thy holiness have possessed *it* but a little while: our adversaries
have trodden down thy sanctuary.
19 We are *thine:* thou never barest rule over
them; they were not called by thy name.

Isaiah 64

1 Oh that thou wouldest rend the heavens,
that thou wouldest come down, that the
mountains might flow down at thy presence,
2 As *when* the melting fire burneth, the
fire causeth the waters to boil, to make

thy name known to thine adversaries, *that*
the nations may tremble at thy presence!
3 When thou didst terrible things *which*
we looked not for, thou camest down, the
mountains flowed down at thy presence.
4 For since the beginning of the world *men*
have not heard, nor perceived by the ear,
neither hath the eye seen, O God, beside
thee, *what* he hath prepared for him that
waiteth for him.
5 Thou meetest him that rejoiceth and worketh righteousness, *those that* remember
thee in thy ways: behold, thou art wroth;
for we have sinned: in those is continuance,
and we shall be saved.
6 But we are all as an unclean *thing*, and all
our righteousnesses *are* as filthy rags; and
we all do fade as a leaf; and our iniquities,
like the wind, have taken us away.
7 And *there is* none that calleth upon thy
name, that stirreth up himself to take hold of
thee: for thou hast hid thy face from us, and
hast consumed us, because of our iniquities.
8 But now, O LORD, thou *art* our father; we
are the clay, and thou our potter; and we
all *are* the work of thy hand.
9 ¶ Be not wroth very sore, O LORD, neither
remember iniquity for ever: behold, see, we
beseech thee, we *are* all thy people.
10 Thy holy cities are a wilderness, Zion is a
wilderness, Jerusalem a desolation.
11 Our holy and our beautiful house, where
our fathers praised thee, is burned up with
fire: and all our pleasant things are laid
waste.
12 Wilt thou refrain thyself for these *things*,
O LORD? wilt thou hold thy peace, and afflict
us very sore?

Isaiah 65

1 I am sought of *them that* asked not *for me;*
I am found of *them that* sought me not: I
said, Behold me, behold me, unto a nation
that was not called by my name.
2 I have spread out my hands all the day
unto a rebellious people, which walketh in
a way *that was* not good, after their own
thoughts;
3 A people that provoketh me to anger
continually to my face; that sacrificeth in
gardens, and burneth incense upon altars
of brick;
4 Which remain among the graves, and
lodge in the monuments, which eat swine's
flesh, and broth of abominable *things is in*
their vessels;
5 Which say, Stand by thyself, come not
near to me; for I am holier than thou. These
are a smoke in my nose, a fire that burneth
all the day.
6 Behold, *it is* written before me: I will not
keep silence, but will recompense, even
recompense into their bosom,
7 Your iniquities, and the iniquities of your
fathers together, saith the LORD, which have
burned incense upon the mountains, and
blasphemed me upon the hills: therefore
will I measure their former work into their
bosom.
8 ¶ Thus saith the LORD, As the new wine is
found in the cluster, and *one* saith, Destroy
it not; for a blessing *is* in it: so will I do for
my servants' sakes, that I may not destroy
them all.
9 And I will bring forth a seed out of Jacob,
and out of Judah an inheritor of my mountains: and mine elect shall inherit it, and my
servants shall dwell there.
10 And Sharon shall be a fold of flocks, and
the valley of Achor a place for the herds
to lie down in, for my people that have
sought me.
11 ¶ But ye *are* they that forsake the LORD,
that forget my holy mountain, that prepare
a table for that troop, and that furnish the
drink offering unto that number.
12 Therefore will I number you to the sword,
and ye shall all bow down to the slaughter:
because when I called, ye did not answer;
when I spake, ye did not hear; but did evil
before mine eyes, and did choose *that*
wherein I delighted not.
13 Therefore thus saith the Lord GOD,
Behold, my servants shall eat, but ye shall
be hungry: behold, my servants shall drink,
but ye shall be thirsty: behold, my servants
shall rejoice, but ye shall be ashamed:
14 Behold, my servants shall sing for joy of
heart, but ye shall cry for sorrow of heart,
and shall howl for vexation of spirit.
15 And ye shall leave your name for a curse
unto my chosen: for the Lord GOD shall slay
thee, and call his servants by another name:
16 That he who blesseth himself in the earth
shall bless himself in the God of truth; and
he that sweareth in the earth shall swear

by the God of truth; because the former
troubles are forgotten, and because they
are hid from mine eyes.
17 ¶ For, behold, I create new heavens and
a new earth: and the former shall not be
remembered, nor come into mind.
18 But be ye glad and rejoice for ever *in*
that which I create: for, behold, I create
Jerusalem a rejoicing, and her people a joy.
19 And I will rejoice in Jerusalem, and joy in
my people: and the voice of weeping shall
be no more heard in her, nor the voice of
crying.
20 There shall be no more thence an infant
of days, nor an old man that hath not filled
his days: for the child shall die an hundred
years old; but the sinner *being* an hundred
years old shall be accursed.
21 And they shall build houses, and inhabit
them; and they shall plant vineyards, and
eat the fruit of them.
22 They shall not build, and another inhabit;
they shall not plant, and another eat: for as
the days of a tree *are* the days of my people,
and mine elect shall long enjoy the work of
their hands.
23 They shall not labour in vain, nor bring
forth for trouble; for they *are* the seed of
the blessed of the LORD, and their offspring
with them.
24 And it shall come to pass, that before
they call, I will answer; and while they are
yet speaking, I will hear.
25 The wolf and the lamb shall feed together,
and the lion shall eat straw like the bullock:
and dust *shall be* the serpent's meat. They
shall not hurt nor destroy in all my holy
mountain, saith the LORD.

Isaiah 66

1 Thus saith the LORD, The heaven *is* my
throne, and the earth *is* my footstool: where
is the house that ye build unto me? and
where *is* the place of my rest?
2 For all those *things* hath mine hand made,
and all those *things* have been, saith the
LORD: but to this *man* will I look, *even* to
him that is poor and of a contrite spirit, and
trembleth at my word.
3 He that killeth an ox *is as if* he slew a man;
he that sacrificeth a lamb, *as if* he cut off a
dog's neck; he that offereth an oblation, *as*
if he offered swine's blood; he that burneth
incense, *as if* he blessed an idol. Yea, they
have chosen their own ways, and their soul
delighteth in their abominations.
4 I also will choose their delusions, and
will bring their fears upon them; because
when I called, none did answer; when I
spake, they did not hear: but they did evil
before mine eyes, and chose *that* in which
I delighted not.
5 ¶ Hear the word of the LORD, ye that
tremble at his word; Your brethren that
hated you, that cast you out for my name's
sake, said, Let the LORD be glorified: but
he shall appear to your joy, and they shall
be ashamed.
6 A voice of noise from the city, a voice
from the temple, a voice of the LORD that
rendereth recompence to his enemies.
7 Before she travailed, she brought forth;
before her pain came, she was delivered
of a man child.
8 Who hath heard such a thing? who hath
seen such things? Shall the earth be made to
bring forth in one day? *or* shall a nation be
born at once? for as soon as Zion travailed,
she brought forth her children.
9 Shall I bring to the birth, and not cause
to bring forth? saith the LORD: shall I cause
to bring forth, and shut *the womb?* saith
thy God.
10 Rejoice ye with Jerusalem, and be glad
with her, all ye that love her: rejoice for joy
with her, all ye that mourn for her:
11 That ye may suck, and be satisfied with
the breasts of her consolations; that ye may
milk out, and be delighted with the abundance of her glory.
12 For thus saith the LORD, Behold, I will
extend peace to her like a river, and the
glory of the Gentiles like a flowing stream:
then shall ye suck, ye shall be borne upon
her sides, and be dandled upon *her* knees.
13 As one whom his mother comforteth, so
will I comfort you; and ye shall be comforted
in Jerusalem.
14 And when ye see *this*, your heart shall
rejoice, and your bones shall flourish like
an herb: and the hand of the LORD shall be
known toward his servants, and *his* indignation toward his enemies.
15 For, behold, the LORD will come with fire,
and with his chariots like a whirlwind, to

15 Then answered Peter and said unto him,
Declare unto us this parable.
16 And Jesus said, Are ye also yet without
understanding?
17 Do not ye yet understand, that whatsoever entereth in at the mouth goeth into
the belly, and is cast out into the draught?
18 But those things which proceed out of
the mouth come forth from the heart; and
they defile the man.
19 For out of the heart proceed evil
thoughts, murders, adulteries, fornications,
thefts, false witness, blasphemies:
20 These are *the things* which defile a man:
but to eat with unwashen hands defileth
not a man.
21 ¶ Then Jesus went thence, and departed
into the coasts of Tyre and Sidon.
22 And, behold, a woman of Canaan came
out of the same coasts, and cried unto him,
saying, Have mercy on me, O Lord, *thou* Son
of David; my daughter is grievously vexed
with a devil.
23 But he answered her not a word. And his
disciples came and besought him, saying,
Send her away; for she crieth after us.
24 But he answered and said, I am not
sent but unto the lost sheep of the house
of Israel.
25 Then came she and worshipped him,
saying, Lord, help me.
26 But he answered and said, It is not meet
to take the children's bread, and to cast *it*
to dogs.
27 And she said, Truth, Lord: yet the dogs
eat of the crumbs which fall from their
masters' table.
28 Then Jesus answered and said unto her,
O woman, great *is* thy faith: be it unto thee
even as thou wilt. And her daughter was
made whole from that very hour.
29 And Jesus departed from thence, and
came nigh unto the sea of Galilee; and went
up into a mountain, and sat down there.
30 And great multitudes came unto him,
having with them *those that were* lame,
blind, dumb, maimed, and many others,
and cast them down at Jesus' feet; and he
healed them:
31 Insomuch that the multitude wondered,
when they saw the dumb to speak, the
maimed to be whole, the lame to walk,
and the blind to see: and they glorified the
God of Israel.
32 ¶ Then Jesus called his disciples *unto
him*, and said, I have compassion on the
multitude, because they continue with me
now three days, and have nothing to eat:
and I will not send them away fasting, lest
they faint in the way.
33 And his disciples say unto him, Whence
should we have so much bread in the wilderness, as to fill so great a multitude?
34 And Jesus saith unto them, How many
loaves have ye? And they said, Seven, and
a few little fishes.
35 And he commanded the multitude to sit
down on the ground.
36 And he took the seven loaves and the
fishes, and gave thanks, and brake *them*,
and gave to his disciples, and the disciples
to the multitude.
37 And they did all eat, and were filled: and
they took up of the broken *meat* that was
left seven baskets full.
38 And they that did eat were four thousand
men, beside women and children.
39 And he sent away the multitude, and took
ship, and came into the coasts of Magdala.

Matthew 16

1 The Pharisees also with the Sadducees
came, and tempting desired him that he
would shew them a sign from heaven.
2 He answered and said unto them, When
it is evening, ye say, *It will be* fair weather:
for the sky is red.
3 And in the morning, *It will be* foul weather
to day: for the sky is red and lowring. O *ye*
hypocrites, ye can discern the face of the
sky; but can ye not *discern* the signs of the
times?
4 A wicked and adulterous generation
seeketh after a sign; and there shall no sign
be given unto it, but the sign of the prophet
Jonas. And he left them, and departed.
5 And when his disciples were come to the
other side, they had forgotten to take bread.
6 ¶ Then Jesus said unto them, Take heed
and beware of the leaven of the Pharisees
and of the Sadducees.
7 And they reasoned among themselves,
saying, *It is* because we have taken no bread.
8 *Which* when Jesus perceived, he said
unto them, O ye of little faith, why reason

ye among yourselves, because ye have
brought no bread?
9 Do ye not yet understand, neither remember the five loaves of the five thousand, and
how many baskets ye took up?
10 Neither the seven loaves of the four thousand, and how many baskets ye took up?
11 How is it that ye do not understand that
I spake *it* not to you concerning bread, that
ye should beware of the leaven of the Pharisees and of the Sadducees?
12 Then understood they how that he bade
them not beware of the leaven of bread,
but of the doctrine of the Pharisees and of
the Sadducees.
13 ¶ When Jesus came into the coasts of
Cæsarea Philippi, he asked his disciples,
saying, Whom do men say that I the Son
of man am?
14 And they said, Some *say that thou art*
John the Baptist: some, Elias; and others,
Jeremias, or one of the prophets.
15 He saith unto them, But whom say ye
that I am?
16 And Simon Peter answered and said,
Thou art the Christ, the Son of the living
God.
17 And Jesus answered and said unto him,
Blessed art thou, Simon Bar-jona: for flesh
and blood hath not revealed *it* unto thee,
but my Father which is in heaven.
18 And I say also unto thee, That thou art
Peter, and upon this rock I will build my
church; and the gates of hell shall not prevail against it.
19 And I will give unto thee the keys of the
kingdom of heaven: and whatsoever thou
shalt bind on earth shall be bound in heaven:
and whatsoever thou shalt loose on earth
shall be loosed in heaven.
20 Then charged he his disciples that they
should tell no man that he was Jesus the
Christ.
21 ¶ From that time forth began Jesus to
shew unto his disciples, how that he must go
unto Jerusalem, and suffer many things of
the elders and chief priests and scribes, and
be killed, and be raised again the third day.
22 Then Peter took him, and began to
rebuke him, saying, Be it far from thee, Lord:
this shall not be unto thee.
23 But he turned, and said unto Peter, Get
thee behind me, Satan: thou art an offence
unto me: for thou savourest not the things
that be of God, but those that be of men.
24 ¶ Then said Jesus unto his disciples, If any
man will come after me, let him deny himself, and take up his cross, and follow me.
25 For whosoever will save his life shall lose
it: and whosoever will lose his life for my
sake shall find it.
26 For what is a man profited, if he shall
gain the whole world, and lose his own
soul? or what shall a man give in exchange
for his soul?
27 For the Son of man shall come in the
glory of his Father with his angels; and
then he shall reward every man according
to his works.
28 Verily I say unto you, There be some
standing here, which shall not taste of
death, till they see the Son of man coming
in his kingdom.

Matthew 17

1 And after six days Jesus taketh Peter,
James, and John his brother, and bringeth
them up into an high mountain apart,
2 And was transfigured before them: and
his face did shine as the sun, and his raiment
was white as the light.
3 And, behold, there appeared unto them
Moses and Elias talking with him.
4 Then answered Peter, and said unto Jesus,
Lord, it is good for us to be here: if thou wilt,
let us make here three tabernacles; one for
thee, and one for Moses, and one for Elias.
5 While he yet spake, behold, a bright cloud
overshadowed them: and behold a voice out
of the cloud, which said, This is my beloved
Son, in whom I am well pleased; hear ye him.
6 And when the disciples heard *it*, they fell
on their face, and were sore afraid.
7 And Jesus came and touched them, and
said, Arise, and be not afraid.
8 And when they had lifted up their eyes,
they saw no man, save Jesus only.
9 And as they came down from the mountain, Jesus charged them, saying, Tell the
vision to no man, until the Son of man be
risen again from the dead.
10 And his disciples asked him, saying,
Why then say the scribes that Elias must
first come?
11 And Jesus answered and said unto them,

to cease; and the sound of thy harps shall
be no more heard.
14 And I will make thee like the top of a rock:
thou shalt be *a place* to spread nets upon;
thou shalt be built no more: for I the LORD
have spoken *it*, saith the Lord GOD.
15 ¶ Thus saith the Lord GOD to Tyrus; Shall
not the isles shake at the sound of thy fall,
when the wounded cry, when the slaughter
is made in the midst of thee?
16 Then all the princes of the sea shall come
down from their thrones, and lay away
their robes, and put off their broidered
garments: they shall clothe themselves with
trembling; they shall sit upon the ground,
and shall tremble at *every* moment, and be
astonished at thee.
17 And they shall take up a lamentation
for thee, and say to thee, How art thou
destroyed, *that wast* inhabited of seafaring
men, the renowned city, which wast strong
in the sea, she and her inhabitants, which
cause their terror *to be* on all that haunt it!
18 Now shall the isles tremble in the day of
thy fall; yea, the isles that *are* in the sea shall
be troubled at thy departure.
19 For thus saith the Lord GOD; When I shall
make thee a desolate city, like the cities
that are not inhabited; when I shall bring
up the deep upon thee, and great waters
shall cover thee;
20 When I shall bring thee down with them
that descend into the pit, with the people of
old time, and shall set thee in the low parts
of the earth, in places desolate of old, with
them that go down to the pit, that thou be
not inhabited; and I shall set glory in the
land of the living;
21 I will make thee a terror, and thou *shalt
be* no *more:* though thou be sought for, yet
shalt thou never be found again, saith the
Lord GOD.

Ezekiel 27

1 The word of the LORD came again unto
me, saying,
2 Now, thou son of man, take up a lamentation for Tyrus;
3 And say unto Tyrus, O thou that art situate
at the entry of the sea, *which art* a merchant
of the people for many isles, Thus saith the
Lord GOD; O Tyrus, thou hast said, I *am* of
perfect beauty.
4 Thy borders *are* in the midst of the seas,
thy builders have perfected thy beauty.
5 They have made all thy *ship* boards of fir
trees of Senir: they have taken cedars from
Lebanon to make masts for thee.
6 *Of* the oaks of Bashan have they made
thine oars; the company of the Ashurites
have made thy benches *of* ivory, *brought*
out of the isles of Chittim.
7 Fine linen with broidered work from Egypt
was that which thou spreadest forth to be
thy sail; blue and purple from the isles of
Elishah was that which covered thee.
8 The inhabitants of Zidon and Arvad were
thy mariners: thy wise *men*, O Tyrus, *that*
were in thee, were thy pilots.
9 The ancients of Gebal and the wise *men*
thereof were in thee thy calkers: all the ships
of the sea with their mariners were in thee
to occupy thy merchandise.
10 They of Persia and of Lud and of Phut
were in thine army, thy men of war: they
hanged the shield and helmet in thee; they
set forth thy comeliness.
11 The men of Arvad with thine army *were*
upon thy walls round about, and the Gam-
madims were in thy towers: they hanged
their shields upon thy walls round about;
they have made thy beauty perfect.
12 Tarshish *was* thy merchant by reason of
the multitude of all *kind of* riches; with silver,
iron, tin, and lead, they traded in thy fairs.
13 Javan, Tubal, and Meshech, they *were*
thy merchants: they traded the persons
of men and vessels of brass in thy market.
14 They of the house of Togarmah traded
in thy fairs with horses and horsemen and
mules.
15 The men of Dedan *were* thy merchants;
many isles *were* the merchandise of thine
hand: they brought thee *for* a present horns
of ivory and ebony.
16 Syria *was* thy merchant by reason of the
multitude of the wares of thy making: they
occupied in thy fairs with emeralds, purple,
and broidered work, and fine linen, and
coral, and agate.
17 Judah, and the land of Israel, they *were*
thy merchants: they traded in thy market
wheat of Minnith, and Pannag, and honey,
and oil, and balm.
18 Damascus *was* thy merchant in the multitude of the wares of thy making, for the

multitude of all riches; in the wine of Helbon,
and white wool.
19 Dan also and Javan going to and fro
occupied in thy fairs: bright iron, cassia, and
calamus, were in thy market.
20 Dedan *was* thy merchant in precious
clothes for chariots.
21 Arabia, and all the princes of Kedar, they
occupied with thee in lambs, and rams, and
goats: in these *were they* thy merchants.
22 The merchants of Sheba and Raamah,
they *were* thy merchants: they occupied in
thy fairs with chief of all spices, and with all
precious stones, and gold.
23 Haran, and Canneh, and Eden, the merchants of Sheba, Asshur, *and* Chilmad, *were*
thy merchants.
24 These *were* thy merchants in all sorts
of things, in blue clothes, and broidered
work, and in chests of rich apparel, bound
with cords, and made of cedar, among thy
merchandise.
25 The ships of Tarshish did sing of thee in
thy market: and thou wast replenished, and
made very glorious in the midst of the seas.
26 ¶ Thy rowers have brought thee into
great waters: the east wind hath broken
thee in the midst of the seas.
27 Thy riches, and thy fairs, thy merchandise, thy mariners, and thy pilots, thy calkers, and the occupiers of thy merchandise,
and all thy men of war, that *are* in thee, and
in all thy company which *is* in the midst of
thee, shall fall into the midst of the seas in
the day of thy ruin.
28 The suburbs shall shake at the sound of
the cry of thy pilots.
29 And all that handle the oar, the mariners,
and all the pilots of the sea, shall come
down from their ships, they shall stand
upon the land;
30 And shall cause their voice to be heard
against thee, and shall cry bitterly, and shall
cast up dust upon their heads, they shall
wallow themselves in the ashes:
31 And they shall make themselves utterly
bald for thee, and gird them with sackcloth,
and they shall weep for thee with bitterness
of heart *and* bitter wailing.
32 And in their wailing they shall take up
a lamentation for thee, and lament over
thee, *saying*, What *city is* like Tyrus, like the
destroyed in the midst of the sea?
33 When thy wares went forth out of the
seas, thou filledst many people; thou didst
enrich the kings of the earth with the multitude of thy riches and of thy merchandise.
34 In the time *when* thou shalt be broken
by the seas in the depths of the waters thy
merchandise and all thy company in the
midst of thee shall fall.
35 All the inhabitants of the isles shall be
astonished at thee, and their kings shall be
sore afraid, they shall be troubled in *their*
countenance.
36 The merchants among the people shall
hiss at thee; thou shalt be a terror, and never
shalt be any more.

Ezekiel 28

1 The word of the LORD came again unto
me, saying,
2 Son of man, say unto the prince of Tyrus,
Thus saith the Lord GOD; Because thine
heart *is* lifted up, and thou hast said, I *am*
a God, I sit *in* the seat of God, in the midst
of the seas; yet thou *art* a man, and not
God, though thou set thine heart as the
heart of God:
3 Behold, thou *art* wiser than Daniel; there
is no secret that they can hide from thee:
4 With thy wisdom and with thine understanding thou hast gotten thee riches,
and hast gotten gold and silver into thy
treasures:
5 By thy great wisdom *and* by thy traffick
hast thou increased thy riches, and thine
heart is lifted up because of thy riches:
6 Therefore thus saith the Lord GOD;
Because thou hast set thine heart as the
heart of God;
7 Behold, therefore I will bring strangers
upon thee, the terrible of the nations: and
they shall draw their swords against the
beauty of thy wisdom, and they shall defile
thy brightness.
8 They shall bring thee down to the pit, and
thou shalt die the deaths of *them that are*
slain in the midst of the seas.
9 Wilt thou yet say before him that slayeth
thee, I *am* God? but thou *shalt be* a man, and
no God, in the hand of him that slayeth thee.
10 Thou shalt die the deaths of the uncircumcised by the hand of strangers: for I have
spoken *it*, saith the Lord GOD.

11 ¶ Moreover the word of the LORD came
unto me, saying,
12 Son of man, take up a lamentation upon
the king of Tyrus, and say unto him, Thus
saith the Lord GOD; Thou sealest up the
sum, full of wisdom, and perfect in beauty.
13 Thou hast been in Eden the garden of
God; every precious stone *was* thy covering,
the sardius, topaz, and the diamond, the
beryl, the onyx, and the jasper, the sapphire,
the emerald, and the carbuncle, and gold:
the workmanship of thy tabrets and of thy
pipes was prepared in thee in the day that
thou wast created.
14 Thou *art* the anointed cherub that covereth; and I have set thee *so:* thou wast
upon the holy mountain of God; thou hast
walked up and down in the midst of the
stones of fire.
15 Thou *wast* perfect in thy ways from the
day that thou wast created, till iniquity was
found in thee.
16 By the multitude of thy merchandise they
have filled the midst of thee with violence,
and thou hast sinned: therefore I will cast
thee as profane out of the mountain of God:
and I will destroy thee, O covering cherub,
from the midst of the stones of fire.
17 Thine heart was lifted up because of thy
beauty, thou hast corrupted thy wisdom by
reason of thy brightness: I will cast thee to
the ground, I will lay thee before kings, that
they may behold thee.
18 Thou hast defiled thy sanctuaries by
the multitude of thine iniquities, by the
iniquity of thy traffick; therefore will I bring
forth a fire from the midst of thee, it shall
devour thee, and I will bring thee to ashes
upon the earth in the sight of all them that
behold thee.
19 All they that know thee among the people shall be astonished at thee: thou shalt be
a terror, and never *shalt* thou *be* any more.
20 ¶ Again the word of the LORD came unto
me, saying,
21 Son of man, set thy face against Zidon,
and prophesy against it,
22 And say, Thus saith the Lord GOD; Behold,
I *am* against thee, O Zidon; and I will be
glorified in the midst of thee: and they shall
know that I *am* the LORD, when I shall have
executed judgments in her, and shall be
sanctified in her.
23 For I will send into her pestilence, and
blood into her streets; and the wounded
shall be judged in the midst of her by the
sword upon her on every side; and they shall
know that I *am* the LORD.
24 ¶ And there shall be no more a prick-
ing brier unto the house of Israel, nor *any*
grieving thorn of all *that are* round about
them, that despised them; and they shall
know that I *am* the Lord GOD.
25 Thus saith the Lord GOD; When I shall
have gathered the house of Israel from the
people among whom they are scattered,
and shall be sanctified in them in the sight
of the heathen, then shall they dwell in their
land that I have given to my servant Jacob.
26 And they shall dwell safely therein, and
shall build houses, and plant vineyards; yea,
they shall dwell with confidence, when I
have executed judgments upon all those
that despise them round about them; and
they shall know that I *am* the LORD their
God.

Ezekiel 29

1 In the tenth year, in the tenth *month*, in
the twelfth *day* of the month, the word of
the LORD came unto me, saying,
2 Son of man, set thy face against Pharaoh
king of Egypt, and prophesy against him,
and against all Egypt:
3 Speak, and say, Thus saith the Lord GOD;
Behold, I *am* against thee, Pharaoh king of
Egypt, the great dragon that lieth in the
midst of his rivers, which hath said, My river
is mine own, and I have made *it* for myself.
4 But I will put hooks in thy jaws, and I will
cause the fish of thy rivers to stick unto thy
scales, and I will bring thee up out of the
midst of thy rivers, and all the fish of thy
rivers shall stick unto thy scales.
5 And I will leave thee *thrown* into the wilderness, thee and all the fish of thy rivers:
thou shalt fall upon the open fields; thou
shalt not be brought together, nor gathered:
I have given thee for meat to the beasts of
the field and to the fowls of the heaven.
6 And all the inhabitants of Egypt shall know
that I *am* the LORD, because they have been
a staff of reed to the house of Israel.
7 When they took hold of thee by thy hand,
thou didst break, and rend all their shoulder: and when they leaned upon thee, thou

brakest, and madest all their loins to be at
a stand.
8 ¶ Therefore thus saith the Lord GOD;
Behold, I will bring a sword upon thee, and
cut off man and beast out of thee.
9 And the land of Egypt shall be desolate
and waste; and they shall know that I *am*
the LORD: because he hath said, The river
is mine, and I have made *it*.
10 Behold, therefore I *am* against thee, and
against thy rivers, and I will make the land
of Egypt utterly waste *and* desolate, from
the tower of Syene even unto the border
of Ethiopia.
11 No foot of man shall pass through it, nor
foot of beast shall pass through it, neither
shall it be inhabited forty years.
12 And I will make the land of Egypt desolate in the midst of the countries *that are*
desolate, and her cities among the cities
that are laid waste shall be desolate forty
years: and I will scatter the Egyptians among
the nations, and will disperse them through
the countries.
13 ¶ Yet thus saith the Lord GOD; At the
end of forty years will I gather the Egyptians from the people whither they were
scattered:
14 And I will bring again the captivity of
Egypt, and will cause them to return *into*
the land of Pathros, into the land of their
habitation; and they shall be there a base
kingdom.
15 It shall be the basest of the kingdoms;
neither shall it exalt itself any more above
the nations: for I will diminish them, that
they shall no more rule over the nations.
16 And it shall be no more the confidence
of the house of Israel, which bringeth *their*
iniquity to remembrance, when they shall
look after them: but they shall know that I
am the Lord GOD.
17 ¶ And it came to pass in the seven and
twentieth year, in the first *month*, in the
first *day* of the month, the word of the LORD
came unto me, saying,
18 Son of man, Nebuchadrezzar king of
Babylon caused his army to serve a great
service against Tyrus: every head *was* made
bald, and every shoulder *was* peeled: yet
had he no wages, nor his army, for Tyrus,
for the service that he had served against it:
19 Therefore thus saith the Lord GOD;
Behold, I will give the land of Egypt unto
Nebuchadrezzar king of Babylon; and he
shall take her multitude, and take her spoil,
and take her prey; and it shall be the wages
for his army.
20 I have given him the land of Egypt *for*
his labour wherewith he served against
it, because they wrought for me, saith the
Lord GOD.
21 ¶ In that day will I cause the horn of
the house of Israel to bud forth, and I will
give thee the opening of the mouth in the
midst of them; and they shall know that I
am the LORD.

Ezekiel 30

1 The word of the LORD came again unto
me, saying,
2 Son of man, prophesy and say, Thus saith
the Lord GOD; Howl ye, Woe worth the day!
3 For the day *is* near, even the day of the
LORD *is* near, a cloudy day; it shall be the
time of the heathen.
4 And the sword shall come upon Egypt,
and great pain shall be in Ethiopia, when the
slain shall fall in Egypt, and they shall take
away her multitude, and her foundations
shall be broken down.
5 Ethiopia, and Libya, and Lydia, and all the
mingled people, and Chub, and the men
of the land that is in league, shall fall with
them by the sword.
6 Thus saith the LORD; They also that uphold
Egypt shall fall; and the pride of her power
shall come down: from the tower of Syene
shall they fall in it by the sword, saith the
Lord GOD.
7 And they shall be desolate in the midst
of the countries *that are* desolate, and her
cities shall be in the midst of the cities *that
are* wasted.
8 And they shall know that I *am* the LORD,
when I have set a fire in Egypt, and *when*
all her helpers shall be destroyed.
9 In that day shall messengers go forth from
me in ships to make the careless Ethiopians
afraid, and great pain shall come upon them,
as in the day of Egypt: for, lo, it cometh.
10 Thus saith the Lord GOD; I will also make
the multitude of Egypt to cease by the hand
of Nebuchadrezzar king of Babylon.
11 He and his people with him, the terrible
of the nations, shall be brought to destroy

the land: and they shall draw their swords
against Egypt, and fill the land with the slain.
12 And I will make the rivers dry, and sell
the land into the hand of the wicked: and
I will make the land waste, and all that is
therein, by the hand of strangers: I the LORD
have spoken *it*.
13 Thus saith the Lord GOD; I will also
destroy the idols, and I will cause *their*
images to cease out of Noph; and there shall
be no more a prince of the land of Egypt:
and I will put a fear in the land of Egypt.
14 And I will make Pathros desolate, and
will set fire in Zoan, and will execute judgments in No.
15 And I will pour my fury upon Sin, the
strength of Egypt; and I will cut off the
multitude of No.
16 And I will set fire in Egypt: Sin shall have
great pain, and No shall be rent asunder, and
Noph *shall have* distresses daily.
17 The young men of Aven and of Pi-beseth
shall fall by the sword: and these *cities* shall
go into captivity.
18 At Tehaphnehes also the day shall be
darkened, when I shall break there the yokes
of Egypt: and the pomp of her strength shall
cease in her: as for her, a cloud shall cover
her, and her daughters shall go into captivity.
19 Thus will I execute judgments in Egypt:
and they shall know that I *am* the LORD.
20 ¶ And it came to pass in the eleventh
year, in the first *month*, in the seventh *day*
of the month, *that* the word of the LORD
came unto me, saying,
21 Son of man, I have broken the arm of
Pharaoh king of Egypt; and, lo, it shall not
be bound up to be healed, to put a roller to
bind it, to make it strong to hold the sword.
22 Therefore thus saith the Lord GOD;
Behold, I *am* against Pharaoh king of Egypt,
and will break his arms, the strong, and that
which was broken; and I will cause the sword
to fall out of his hand.
23 And I will scatter the Egyptians among
the nations, and will disperse them through
the countries.
24 And I will strengthen the arms of the king
of Babylon, and put my sword in his hand:
but I will break Pharaoh's arms, and he shall
groan before him with the groanings of a
deadly wounded *man*.
25 But I will strengthen the arms of the king
of Babylon, and the arms of Pharaoh shall
fall down; and they shall know that I *am* the
LORD, when I shall put my sword into the
hand of the king of Babylon, and he shall
stretch it out upon the land of Egypt.
26 And I will scatter the Egyptians among
the nations, and disperse them among the
countries; and they shall know that I *am*
the LORD.

Ezekiel 31

1 And it came to pass in the eleventh year,
in the third *month*, in the first *day* of the
month, *that* the word of the LORD came
unto me, saying,
2 Son of man, speak unto Pharaoh king of
Egypt, and to his multitude; Whom art thou
like in thy greatness?
3 ¶ Behold, the Assyrian *was* a cedar in
Lebanon with fair branches, and with a
shadowing shroud, and of an high stature;
and his top was among the thick boughs.
4 The waters made him great, the deep set
him up on high with her rivers running round
about his plants, and sent out her little rivers
unto all the trees of the field.
5 Therefore his height was exalted above all
the trees of the field, and his boughs were
multiplied, and his branches became long
because of the multitude of waters, when
he shot forth.
6 All the fowls of heaven made their nests
in his boughs, and under his branches did
all the beasts of the field bring forth their
young, and under his shadow dwelt all
great nations.
7 Thus was he fair in his greatness, in the
length of his branches: for his root was by
great waters.
8 The cedars in the garden of God could
not hide him: the fir trees were not like his
boughs, and the chesnut trees were not like
his branches; nor any tree in the garden of
God was like unto him in his beauty.
9 I have made him fair by the multitude of
his branches: so that all the trees of Eden,
that *were* in the garden of God, envied him.
10 ¶ Therefore thus saith the Lord GOD;
Because thou hast lifted up thyself in height,
and he hath shot up his top among the
thick boughs, and his heart is lifted up in
his height;
11 I have therefore delivered him into the

hand of the mighty one of the heathen; he
shall surely deal with him: I have driven him
out for his wickedness.
12 And strangers, the terrible of the nations,
have cut him off, and have left him: upon the
mountains and in all the valleys his branches
are fallen, and his boughs are broken by all
the rivers of the land; and all the people of
the earth are gone down from his shadow,
and have left him.
13 Upon his ruin shall all the fowls of the
heaven remain, and all the beasts of the
field shall be upon his branches:
14 To the end that none of all the trees by
the waters exalt themselves for their height,
neither shoot up their top among the thick
boughs, neither their trees stand up in their
height, all that drink water: for they are all
delivered unto death, to the nether parts
of the earth, in the midst of the children
of men, with them that go down to the pit.
15 Thus saith the Lord GOD; In the day
when he went down to the grave I caused a
mourning: I covered the deep for him, and I
restrained the floods thereof, and the great
waters were stayed: and I caused Lebanon
to mourn for him, and all the trees of the
field fainted for him.
16 I made the nations to shake at the sound
of his fall, when I cast him down to hell with
them that descend into the pit: and all the
trees of Eden, the choice and best of Lebanon, all that drink water, shall be comforted
in the nether parts of the earth.
17 They also went down into hell with him
unto *them that be* slain with the sword; and
they that were his arm, *that* dwelt under his
shadow in the midst of the heathen.
18 ¶ To whom art thou thus like in glory and
in greatness among the trees of Eden? yet
shalt thou be brought down with the trees
of Eden unto the nether parts of the earth:
thou shalt lie in the midst of the uncircumcised with *them that be* slain by the sword.
This *is* Pharaoh and all his multitude, saith
the Lord GOD.

Ezekiel 32

1 And it came to pass in the twelfth year,
in the twelfth month, in the first *day* of the
month, *that* the word of the LORD came
unto me, saying,
2 Son of man, take up a lamentation for
Pharaoh king of Egypt, and say unto him,
Thou art like a young lion of the nations,
and thou *art* as a whale in the seas: and
thou camest forth with thy rivers, and
troubledst the waters with thy feet, and
fouledst their rivers.
3 Thus saith the Lord GOD; I will therefore
spread out my net over thee with a company
of many people; and they shall bring thee
up in my net.
4 Then will I leave thee upon the land, I will
cast thee forth upon the open field, and will
cause all the fowls of the heaven to remain
upon thee, and I will fill the beasts of the
whole earth with thee.
5 And I will lay thy flesh upon the mountains,
and fill the valleys with thy height.
6 I will also water with thy blood the land
wherein thou swimmest, *even* to the mountains; and the rivers shall be full of thee.
7 And when I shall put thee out, I will cover
the heaven, and make the stars thereof
dark; I will cover the sun with a cloud, and
the moon shall not give her light.
8 All the bright lights of heaven will I make
dark over thee, and set darkness upon thy
land, saith the Lord GOD.
9 I will also vex the hearts of many people,
when I shall bring thy destruction among
the nations, into the countries which thou
hast not known.
10 Yea, I will make many people amazed at
thee, and their kings shall be horribly afraid
for thee, when I shall brandish my sword
before them; and they shall tremble at *every*
moment, every man for his own life, in the
day of thy fall.
11 ¶ For thus saith the Lord GOD; The sword
of the king of Babylon shall come upon thee.
12 By the swords of the mighty will I cause
thy multitude to fall, the terrible of the
nations, all of them: and they shall spoil
the pomp of Egypt, and all the multitude
thereof shall be destroyed.
13 I will destroy also all the beasts thereof
from beside the great waters; neither shall
the foot of man trouble them any more, nor
the hoofs of beasts trouble them.
14 Then will I make their waters deep, and
cause their rivers to run like oil, saith the
Lord GOD.
15 When I shall make the land of Egypt desolate, and the country shall be destitute of

that whereof it was full, when I shall smite
all them that dwell therein, then shall they
know that I *am* the LORD.
16 This *is* the lamentation wherewith they
shall lament her: the daughters of the
nations shall lament her: they shall lament
for her, *even* for Egypt, and for all her multitude, saith the Lord GOD.
17 ¶ It came to pass also in the twelfth year,
in the fifteenth *day* of the month, *that* the
word of the LORD came unto me, saying,
18 Son of man, wail for the multitude of
Egypt, and cast them down, *even* her, and
the daughters of the famous nations, unto
the nether parts of the earth, with them
that go down into the pit.
19 Whom dost thou pass in beauty? go
down, and be thou laid with the uncircumcised.
20 They shall fall in the midst of *them that
are* slain by the sword: she is delivered to
the sword: draw her and all her multitudes.
21 The strong among the mighty shall speak
to him out of the midst of hell with them
that help him: they are gone down, they lie
uncircumcised, slain by the sword.
22 Asshur *is* there and all her company:
his graves *are* about him: all of them slain,
fallen by the sword:
23 Whose graves are set in the sides of the
pit, and her company is round about her
grave: all of them slain, fallen by the sword,
which caused terror in the land of the living.
24 There *is* Elam and all her multitude round
about her grave, all of them slain, fallen by
the sword, which are gone down uncircumcised into the nether parts of the earth,
which caused their terror in the land of the
living; yet have they borne their shame with
them that go down to the pit.
25 They have set her a bed in the midst of
the slain with all her multitude: her graves
are round about him: all of them uncircumcised, slain by the sword: though their terror
was caused in the land of the living, yet have
they borne their shame with them that go
down to the pit: he is put in the midst of
them that be slain.
26 There *is* Meshech, Tubal, and all her multitude: her graves *are* round about him: all
of them uncircumcised, slain by the sword,
though they caused their terror in the land
of the living.
27 And they shall not lie with the mighty
that are fallen of the uncircumcised, which
are gone down to hell with their weapons of
war: and they have laid their swords under
their heads, but their iniquities shall be upon
their bones, though *they were* the terror of
the mighty in the land of the living.
28 Yea, thou shalt be broken in the midst of
the uncircumcised, and shalt lie with *them
that are* slain with the sword.
29 There *is* Edom, her kings, and all her
princes, which with their might are laid by
them that were slain by the sword: they shall
lie with the uncircumcised, and with them
that go down to the pit.
30 There *be* the princes of the north, all
of them, and all the Zidonians, which are
gone down with the slain; with their terror
they are ashamed of their might; and they
lie uncircumcised with *them that be* slain
by the sword, and bear their shame with
them that go down to the pit.
31 Pharaoh shall see them, and shall be comforted over all his multitude, *even* Pharaoh
and all his army slain by the sword, saith
the Lord GOD.
32 For I have caused my terror in the land of
the living: and he shall be laid in the midst
of the uncircumcised with *them that are*
slain with the sword, *even* Pharaoh and all
his multitude, saith the Lord GOD.

Ezekiel 33

1 Again the word of the LORD came unto
me, saying,
2 Son of man, speak to the children of thy
people, and say unto them, When I bring
the sword upon a land, if the people of the
land take a man of their coasts, and set him
for their watchman:
3 If when he seeth the sword come upon
the land, he blow the trumpet, and warn
the people;
4 Then whosoever heareth the sound of
the trumpet, and taketh not warning; if the
sword come, and take him away, his blood
shall be upon his own head.
5 He heard the sound of the trumpet, and
took not warning; his blood shall be upon
him. But he that taketh warning shall deliver
his soul.
6 But if the watchman see the sword come,
and blow not the trumpet, and the people

be not warned; if the sword come, and take
any person from among them, he is taken
away in his iniquity; but his blood will I
require at the watchman's hand.
7 ¶ So thou, O son of man, I have set thee a
watchman unto the house of Israel; therefore thou shalt hear the word at my mouth,
and warn them from me.
8 When I say unto the wicked, O wicked
man, thou shalt surely die; if thou dost not
speak to warn the wicked from his way, that
wicked *man* shall die in his iniquity; but his
blood will I require at thine hand.
9 Nevertheless, if thou warn the wicked
of his way to turn from it; if he do not turn
from his way, he shall die in his iniquity; but
thou hast delivered thy soul.
10 Therefore, O thou son of man, speak unto
the house of Israel; Thus ye speak, saying,
If our transgressions and our sins *be* upon
us, and we pine away in them, how should
we then live?
11 Say unto them, *As* I live, saith the Lord
GOD, I have no pleasure in the death of the
wicked; but that the wicked turn from his
way and live: turn ye, turn ye from your evil
ways; for why will ye die, O house of Israel?
12 Therefore, thou son of man, say unto
the children of thy people, The righteousness of the righteous shall not deliver him
in the day of his transgression: as for the
wickedness of the wicked, he shall not fall
thereby in the day that he turneth from his
wickedness; neither shall the righteous be
able to live for his *righteousness* in the day
that he sinneth.
13 When I shall say to the righteous, *that*
he shall surely live; if he trust to his own
righteousness, and commit iniquity, all his
righteousnesses shall not be remembered;
but for his iniquity that he hath committed,
he shall die for it.
14 Again, when I say unto the wicked, Thou
shalt surely die; if he turn from his sin, and
do that which is lawful and right;
15 *If* the wicked restore the pledge, give
again that he had robbed, walk in the statutes of life, without committing iniquity; he
shall surely live, he shall not die.
16 None of his sins that he hath committed shall be mentioned unto him: he hath
done that which is lawful and right; he shall
surely live.
17 ¶ Yet the children of thy people say, The
way of the Lord is not equal: but as for them,
their way is not equal.
18 When the righteous turneth from his
righteousness, and committeth iniquity, he
shall even die thereby.
19 But if the wicked turn from his wickedness, and do that which is lawful and right,
he shall live thereby.
20 ¶ Yet ye say, The way of the Lord is not
equal. O ye house of Israel, I will judge you
every one after his ways.
21 ¶ And it came to pass in the twelfth year
of our captivity, in the tenth *month*, in the
fifth *day* of the month, *that* one that had
escaped out of Jerusalem came unto me,
saying, The city is smitten.
22 Now the hand of the LORD was upon me
in the evening, afore he that was escaped
came; and had opened my mouth, until he
came to me in the morning; and my mouth
was opened, and I was no more dumb.
23 Then the word of the LORD came unto
me, saying,
24 Son of man, they that inhabit those
wastes of the land of Israel speak, saying,
Abraham was one, and he inherited the
land: but we *are* many; the land is given us
for inheritance.
25 Wherefore say unto them, Thus saith the
Lord GOD; Ye eat with the blood, and lift up
your eyes toward your idols, and shed blood:
and shall ye possess the land?
26 Ye stand upon your sword, ye work
abomination, and ye defile every one his
neighbour's wife: and shall ye possess the
land?
27 Say thou thus unto them, Thus saith the
Lord GOD; *As* I live, surely they that *are* in the
wastes shall fall by the sword, and him that
is in the open field will I give to the beasts to
be devoured, and they that *be* in the forts
and in the caves shall die of the pestilence.
28 For I will lay the land most desolate, and
the pomp of her strength shall cease; and
the mountains of Israel shall be desolate,
that none shall pass through.
29 Then shall they know that I *am* the LORD,
when I have laid the land most desolate
because of all their abominations which
they have committed.
30 ¶ Also, thou son of man, the children of
thy people still are talking against thee by

the walls and in the doors of the houses,
and speak one to another, every one to
his brother, saying, Come, I pray you, and
hear what is the word that cometh forth
from the LORD.
31 And they come unto thee as the people
cometh, and they sit before thee *as* my
people, and they hear thy words, but they
will not do them: for with their mouth they
shew much love, *but* their heart goeth after
their covetousness.
32 And, lo, thou *art* unto them as a very
lovely song of one that hath a pleasant voice,
and can play well on an instrument: for they
hear thy words, but they do them not.
33 And when this cometh to pass, (lo, it will
come,) then shall they know that a prophet
hath been among them.

Ezekiel 34

1 And the word of the LORD came unto
me, saying,
2 Son of man, prophesy against the shepherds of Israel, prophesy, and say unto
them, Thus saith the Lord GOD unto the
shepherds; Woe *be* to the shepherds of
Israel that do feed themselves! should not
the shepherds feed the flocks?
3 Ye eat the fat, and ye clothe you with the
wool, ye kill them that are fed: *but* ye feed
not the flock.
4 The diseased have ye not strengthened,
neither have ye healed that which was sick,
neither have ye bound up *that which was*
broken, neither have ye brought again that
which was driven away, neither have ye
sought that which was lost; but with force
and with cruelty have ye ruled them.
5 And they were scattered, because *there*
is no shepherd: and they became meat to
all the beasts of the field, when they were
scattered.
6 My sheep wandered through all the mountains, and upon every high hill: yea, my flock
was scattered upon all the face of the earth,
and none did search or seek *after them*.
7 ¶ Therefore, ye shepherds, hear the word
of the LORD;
8 *As* I live, saith the Lord GOD, surely because
my flock became a prey, and my flock
became meat to every beast of the field,
because *there was* no shepherd, neither
did my shepherds search for my flock, but
the shepherds fed themselves, and fed not
my flock;
9 Therefore, O ye shepherds, hear the word
of the LORD;
10 Thus saith the Lord GOD; Behold, I *am*
against the shepherds; and I will require
my flock at their hand, and cause them to
cease from feeding the flock; neither shall
the shepherds feed themselves any more;
for I will deliver my flock from their mouth,
that they may not be meat for them.
11 ¶ For thus saith the Lord GOD; Behold,
I, *even* I, will both search my sheep, and
seek them out.
12 As a shepherd seeketh out his flock in
the day that he is among his sheep *that are*
scattered; so will I seek out my sheep, and
will deliver them out of all places where
they have been scattered in the cloudy
and dark day.
13 And I will bring them out from the people, and gather them from the countries,
and will bring them to their own land, and
feed them upon the mountains of Israel by
the rivers, and in all the inhabited places
of the country.
14 I will feed them in a good pasture, and
upon the high mountains of Israel shall their
fold be: there shall they lie in a good fold,
and *in* a fat pasture shall they feed upon the
mountains of Israel.
15 I will feed my flock, and I will cause them
to lie down, saith the Lord GOD.
16 I will seek that which was lost, and bring
again that which was driven away, and will
bind up *that which was* broken, and will
strengthen that which was sick: but I will
destroy the fat and the strong; I will feed
them with judgment.
17 And *as for* you, O my flock, thus saith
the Lord GOD; Behold, I judge between
cattle and cattle, between the rams and
the he goats.
18 *Seemeth it* a small thing unto you to have
eaten up the good pasture, but ye must
tread down with your feet the residue of
your pastures? and to have drunk of the
deep waters, but ye must foul the residue
with your feet?
19 And *as for* my flock, they eat that which
ye have trodden with your feet; and they
drink that which ye have fouled with your
feet.

20 ¶ Therefore thus saith the Lord GOD unto
them; Behold, I, *even* I, will judge between
the fat cattle and between the lean cattle.
21 Because ye have thrust with side and
with shoulder, and pushed all the diseased
with your horns, till ye have scattered them
abroad;
22 Therefore will I save my flock, and they
shall no more be a prey; and I will judge
between cattle and cattle.
23 And I will set up one shepherd over them,
and he shall feed them, *even* my servant
David; he shall feed them, and he shall be
their shepherd.
24 And I the LORD will be their God, and my
servant David a prince among them; I the
LORD have spoken *it*.
25 And I will make with them a covenant of
peace, and will cause the evil beasts to cease
out of the land: and they shall dwell safely
in the wilderness, and sleep in the woods.
26 And I will make them and the places
round about my hill a blessing; and I will
cause the shower to come down in his
season; there shall be showers of blessing.
27 And the tree of the field shall yield her
fruit, and the earth shall yield her increase,
and they shall be safe in their land, and shall
know that I *am* the LORD, when I have broken the bands of their yoke, and delivered
them out of the hand of those that served
themselves of them.
28 And they shall no more be a prey to the
heathen, neither shall the beast of the land
devour them; but they shall dwell safely, and
none shall make *them* afraid.
29 And I will raise up for them a plant of
renown, and they shall be no more consumed with hunger in the land, neither
bear the shame of the heathen any more.
30 Thus shall they know that I the LORD their
God *am* with them, and *that* they, *even* the
house of Israel, *are* my people, saith the
Lord GOD.
31 And ye my flock, the flock of my pasture, *are* men, *and* I *am* your God, saith
the Lord GOD.

Ezekiel 35

1 Moreover the word of the LORD came
unto me, saying,
2 Son of man, set thy face against mount
Seir, and prophesy against it,
3 And say unto it, Thus saith the Lord GOD;
Behold, O mount Seir, I *am* against thee,
and I will stretch out mine hand against
thee, and I will make thee most desolate.
4 I will lay thy cities waste, and thou shalt
be desolate, and thou shalt know that I *am*
the LORD.
5 Because thou hast had a perpetual hatred,
and hast shed *the blood of* the children of
Israel by the force of the sword in the time
of their calamity, in the time *that their* iniquity *had* an end:
6 Therefore, *as* I live, saith the Lord GOD,
I will prepare thee unto blood, and blood
shall pursue thee: sith thou hast not hated
blood, even blood shall pursue thee.
7 Thus will I make mount Seir most desolate,
and cut off from it him that passeth out and
him that returneth.
8 And I will fill his mountains with his slain
men: in thy hills, and in thy valleys, and in
all thy rivers, shall they fall that are slain
with the sword.
9 I will make thee perpetual desolations,
and thy cities shall not return: and ye shall
know that I *am* the LORD.
10 Because thou hast said, These two
nations and these two countries shall be
mine, and we will possess it; whereas the
LORD was there:
11 Therefore, *as* I live, saith the Lord GOD,
I will even do according to thine anger, and
according to thine envy which thou hast
used out of thy hatred against them; and I
will make myself known among them, when
I have judged thee.
12 And thou shalt know that I *am* the LORD,
and that I have heard all thy blasphemies
which thou hast spoken against the mountains of Israel, saying, They are laid desolate,
they are given us to consume.
13 Thus with your mouth ye have boasted
against me, and have multiplied your words
against me: I have heard *them*.
14 Thus saith the Lord GOD; When the whole
earth rejoiceth, I will make thee desolate.
15 As thou didst rejoice at the inheritance of
the house of Israel, because it was desolate,
so will I do unto thee: thou shalt be desolate,
O mount Seir, and all Idumea, *even* all of
it: and they shall know that I *am* the LORD.

Ezekiel 36

1 Also, thou son of man, prophesy unto the
mountains of Israel, and say, Ye mountains
of Israel, hear the word of the LORD:
2 Thus saith the Lord GOD; Because the
enemy hath said against you, Aha, even the
ancient high places are ours in possession:
3 Therefore prophesy and say, Thus saith
the Lord GOD; Because they have made *you*
desolate, and swallowed you up on every
side, that ye might be a possession unto the
residue of the heathen, and ye are taken
up in the lips of talkers, and *are* an infamy
of the people:
4 Therefore, ye mountains of Israel, hear the
word of the Lord GOD; Thus saith the Lord
GOD to the mountains, and to the hills, to
the rivers, and to the valleys, to the desolate
wastes, and to the cities that are forsaken,
which became a prey and derision to the
residue of the heathen that *are* round about;
5 Therefore thus saith the Lord GOD; Surely
in the fire of my jealousy have I spoken
against the residue of the heathen, and
against all Idumea, which have appointed
my land into their possession with the joy
of all *their* heart, with despiteful minds, to
cast it out for a prey.
6 Prophesy therefore concerning the land
of Israel, and say unto the mountains, and
to the hills, to the rivers, and to the valleys,
Thus saith the Lord GOD; Behold, I have spoken in my jealousy and in my fury, because
ye have borne the shame of the heathen:
7 Therefore thus saith the Lord GOD; I have
lifted up mine hand, Surely the heathen that
are about you, they shall bear their shame.
8 ¶ But ye, O mountains of Israel, ye shall
shoot forth your branches, and yield your
fruit to my people of Israel; for they are at
hand to come.
9 For, behold, I *am* for you, and I will turn
unto you, and ye shall be tilled and sown:
10 And I will multiply men upon you, all the
house of Israel, *even* all of it: and the cities
shall be inhabited, and the wastes shall be
builded:
11 And I will multiply upon you man and
beast; and they shall increase and bring
fruit: and I will settle you after your old
estates, and will do better *unto you* than
at your beginnings: and ye shall know that
I *am* the LORD.
12 Yea, I will cause men to walk upon you,
even my people Israel; and they shall possess
thee, and thou shalt be their inheritance,
and thou shalt no more henceforth bereave
them *of men*.
13 Thus saith the Lord GOD; Because they
say unto you, Thou *land* devourest up men,
and hast bereaved thy nations;
14 Therefore thou shalt devour men no
more, neither bereave thy nations any more,
saith the Lord GOD.
15 Neither will I cause *men* to hear in thee
the shame of the heathen any more, neither
shalt thou bear the reproach of the people
any more, neither shalt thou cause thy
nations to fall any more, saith the Lord GOD.
16 ¶ Moreover the word of the LORD came
unto me, saying,
17 Son of man, when the house of Israel
dwelt in their own land, they defiled it by
their own way and by their doings: their
way was before me as the uncleanness of
a removed woman.
18 Wherefore I poured my fury upon them
for the blood that they had shed upon the
land, and for their idols *wherewith* they had
polluted it:
19 And I scattered them among the heathen,
and they were dispersed through the countries: according to their way and according
to their doings I judged them.
20 And when they entered unto the heathen, whither they went, they profaned my
holy name, when they said to them, These
are the people of the LORD, and are gone
forth out of his land.
21 ¶ But I had pity for mine holy name,
which the house of Israel had profaned
among the heathen, whither they went.
22 Therefore say unto the house of Israel,
Thus saith the Lord GOD; I do not *this* for
your sakes, O house of Israel, but for mine
holy name's sake, which ye have profaned
among the heathen, whither ye went.
23 And I will sanctify my great name, which
was profaned among the heathen, which ye
have profaned in the midst of them; and the
heathen shall know that I *am* the LORD, saith
the Lord GOD, when I shall be sanctified in
you before their eyes.
24 For I will take you from among the heathen, and gather you out of all countries, and
will bring you into your own land.

25 ¶ Then will I sprinkle clean water upon
you, and ye shall be clean: from all your
filthiness, and from all your idols, will I
cleanse you.
26 A new heart also will I give you, and a
new spirit will I put within you: and I will take
away the stony heart out of your flesh, and
I will give you an heart of flesh.
27 And I will put my spirit within you, and
cause you to walk in my statutes, and ye
shall keep my judgments, and do *them*.
28 And ye shall dwell in the land that I gave
to your fathers; and ye shall be my people,
and I will be your God.
29 I will also save you from all your unclean-
nesses: and I will call for the corn, and will
increase it, and lay no famine upon you.
30 And I will multiply the fruit of the tree,
and the increase of the field, that ye shall
receive no more reproach of famine among
the heathen.
31 Then shall ye remember your own evil
ways, and your doings that *were* not good,
and shall lothe yourselves in your own sight
for your iniquities and for your abominations.
32 Not for your sakes do I *this*, saith the Lord
GOD, be it known unto you: be ashamed
and confounded for your own ways, O
house of Israel.
33 Thus saith the Lord GOD; In the day that I
shall have cleansed you from all your iniquities I will also cause *you* to dwell in the cities,
and the wastes shall be builded.
34 And the desolate land shall be tilled,
whereas it lay desolate in the sight of all
that passed by.
35 And they shall say, This land that was
desolate is become like the garden of Eden;
and the waste and desolate and ruined cities *are become* fenced, *and* are inhabited.
36 Then the heathen that are left round
about you shall know that I the LORD build
the ruined *places, and* plant that that was
desolate: I the LORD have spoken *it*, and I
will do *it*.
37 Thus saith the Lord GOD; I will yet *for*
this be inquired of by the house of Israel,
to do *it* for them; I will increase them with
men like a flock.
38 As the holy flock, as the flock of Jerusalem in her solemn feasts; so shall the waste
cities be filled with flocks of men: and they
shall know that I *am* the LORD.

Ezekiel 37

1 The hand of the LORD was upon me, and
carried me out in the spirit of the LORD, and
set me down in the midst of the valley which
was full of bones,
2 And caused me to pass by them round
about: and, behold, *there were* very many in
the open valley; and, lo, *they were* very dry.
3 And he said unto me, Son of man, can
these bones live? And I answered, O Lord
GOD, thou knowest.
4 Again he said unto me, Prophesy upon
these bones, and say unto them, O ye dry
bones, hear the word of the LORD.
5 Thus saith the Lord GOD unto these bones;
Behold, I will cause breath to enter into you,
and ye shall live:
6 And I will lay sinews upon you, and will
bring up flesh upon you, and cover you with
skin, and put breath in you, and ye shall live;
and ye shall know that I *am* the LORD.
7 So I prophesied as I was commanded:
and as I prophesied, there was a noise,
and behold a shaking, and the bones came
together, bone to his bone.
8 And when I beheld, lo, the sinews and
the flesh came up upon them, and the skin
covered them above: but *there was* no
breath in them.
9 Then said he unto me, Prophesy unto the
wind, prophesy, son of man, and say to the
wind, Thus saith the Lord GOD; Come from
the four winds, O breath, and breathe upon
these slain, that they may live.
10 So I prophesied as he commanded me,
and the breath came into them, and they
lived, and stood up upon their feet, an
exceeding great army.
11 ¶ Then he said unto me, Son of man,
these bones are the whole house of Israel:
behold, they say, Our bones are dried, and
our hope is lost: we are cut off for our parts.
12 Therefore prophesy and say unto them,
Thus saith the Lord GOD; Behold, O my people, I will open your graves, and cause you
to come up out of your graves, and bring
you into the land of Israel.
13 And ye shall know that I *am* the LORD,
when I have opened your graves, O my people, and brought you up out of your graves,

14 And shall put my spirit in you, and ye
shall live, and I shall place you in your own
land: then shall ye know that I the LORD have
spoken *it*, and performed *it*, saith the LORD.
15 ¶ The word of the LORD came again unto
me, saying,
16 Moreover, thou son of man, take thee
one stick, and write upon it, For Judah, and
for the children of Israel his companions:
then take another stick, and write upon it,
For Joseph, the stick of Ephraim, and *for* all
the house of Israel his companions:
17 And join them one to another into one
stick; and they shall become one in thine
hand.
18 ¶ And when the children of thy people
shall speak unto thee, saying, Wilt thou not
shew us what thou *meanest* by these?
19 Say unto them, Thus saith the Lord GOD;
Behold, I will take the stick of Joseph, which
is in the hand of Ephraim, and the tribes of
Israel his fellows, and will put them with
him, *even* with the stick of Judah, and make
them one stick, and they shall be one in
mine hand.
20 ¶ And the sticks whereon thou writest
shall be in thine hand before their eyes.
21 And say unto them, Thus saith the Lord
GOD; Behold, I will take the children of Israel
from among the heathen, whither they be
gone, and will gather them on every side,
and bring them into their own land:
22 And I will make them one nation in the
land upon the mountains of Israel; and
one king shall be king to them all: and they
shall be no more two nations, neither shall
they be divided into two kingdoms any
more at all:
23 Neither shall they defile themselves
any more with their idols, nor with their
detestable things, nor with any of their
transgressions: but I will save them out of
all their dwellingplaces, wherein they have
sinned, and will cleanse them: so shall they
be my people, and I will be their God.
24 And David my servant *shall be* king over
them; and they all shall have one shepherd:
they shall also walk in my judgments, and
observe my statutes, and do them.
25 And they shall dwell in the land that I
have given unto Jacob my servant, wherein
your fathers have dwelt; and they shall dwell
therein, *even* they, and their children, and
their children's children for ever: and my
servant David *shall be* their prince for ever.
26 Moreover I will make a covenant of peace
with them; it shall be an everlasting covenant with them: and I will place them, and
multiply them, and will set my sanctuary in
the midst of them for evermore.
27 My tabernacle also shall be with them:
yea, I will be their God, and they shall be
my people.
28 And the heathen shall know that I the
LORD do sanctify Israel, when my sanctuary
shall be in the midst of them for evermore.

Ezekiel 38

1 And the word of the LORD came unto
me, saying,
2 Son of man, set thy face against Gog, the
land of Magog, the chief prince of Meshech
and Tubal, and prophesy against him,
3 And say, Thus saith the Lord GOD; Behold,
I *am* against thee, O Gog, the chief prince
of Meshech and Tubal:
4 And I will turn thee back, and put hooks
into thy jaws, and I will bring thee forth, and
all thine army, horses and horsemen, all of
them clothed with all sorts *of armour, even*
a great company *with* bucklers and shields,
all of them handling swords:
5 Persia, Ethiopia, and Libya with them; all
of them with shield and helmet:
6 Gomer, and all his bands; the house of
Togarmah of the north quarters, and all his
bands: *and* many people with thee.
7 Be thou prepared, and prepare for thyself, thou, and all thy company that are
assembled unto thee, and be thou a guard
unto them.
8 ¶ After many days thou shalt be visited:
in the latter years thou shalt come into the
land *that is* brought back from the sword,
and is gathered out of many people, against
the mountains of Israel, which have been
always waste: but it is brought forth out
of the nations, and they shall dwell safely
all of them.
9 Thou shalt ascend and come like a storm,
thou shalt be like a cloud to cover the land,
thou, and all thy bands, and many people
with thee.
10 Thus saith the Lord GOD; It shall also
come to pass, *that* at the same time shall

things come into thy mind, and thou shalt think an evil thought:

11 And thou shalt say, I will go up to the land of unwalled villages; I will go to them that are at rest, that dwell safely, all of them dwelling without walls, and having neither bars nor gates,

12 To take a spoil, and to take a prey; to turn thine hand upon the desolate places *that are now* inhabited, and upon the people *that are* gathered out of the nations, which have gotten cattle and goods, that dwell in the midst of the land.

13 Sheba, and Dedan, and the merchants of Tarshish, with all the young lions thereof, shall say unto thee, Art thou come to take a spoil? hast thou gathered thy company to take a prey? to carry away silver and gold, to take away cattle and goods, to take a great spoil?

14 ¶ Therefore, son of man, prophesy and say unto Gog, Thus saith the Lord GOD; In that day when my people of Israel dwelleth safely, shalt thou not know *it?*

15 And thou shalt come from thy place out of the north parts, thou, and many people with thee, all of them riding upon horses, a great company, and a mighty army:

16 And thou shalt come up against my people of Israel, as a cloud to cover the land; it shall be in the latter days, and I will bring thee against my land, that the heathen may know me, when I shall be sanctified in thee, O Gog, before their eyes.

17 Thus saith the Lord GOD; *Art* thou he of whom I have spoken in old time by my servants the prophets of Israel, which prophesied in those days *many* years that I would bring thee against them?

18 And it shall come to pass at the same time when Gog shall come against the land of Israel, saith the Lord GOD, *that* my fury shall come up in my face.

19 For in my jealousy *and* in the fire of my wrath have I spoken, Surely in that day there shall be a great shaking in the land of Israel;

20 So that the fishes of the sea, and the fowls of the heaven, and the beasts of the field, and all creeping things that creep upon the earth, and all the men that *are* upon the face of the earth, shall shake at my presence, and the mountains shall be thrown down, and the steep places shall fall, and every wall shall fall to the ground.

21 And I will call for a sword against him throughout all my mountains, saith the Lord GOD: every man's sword shall be against his brother.

22 And I will plead against him with pestilence and with blood; and I will rain upon him, and upon his bands, and upon the many people that *are* with him, an overflowing rain, and great hailstones, fire, and brimstone.

23 Thus will I magnify myself, and sanctify myself; and I will be known in the eyes of many nations, and they shall know that I *am* the LORD.

Ezekiel 39

1 Therefore, thou son of man, prophesy against Gog, and say, Thus saith the Lord GOD; Behold, I *am* against thee, O Gog, the chief prince of Meshech and Tubal:

2 And I will turn thee back, and leave but the sixth part of thee, and will cause thee to come up from the north parts, and will bring thee upon the mountains of Israel:

3 And I will smite thy bow out of thy left hand, and will cause thine arrows to fall out of thy right hand.

4 Thou shalt fall upon the mountains of Israel, thou, and all thy bands, and the people that *is* with thee: I will give thee unto the ravenous birds of every sort, and *to* the beasts of the field to be devoured.

5 Thou shalt fall upon the open field: for I have spoken *it*, saith the Lord GOD.

6 And I will send a fire on Magog, and among them that dwell carelessly in the isles: and they shall know that I *am* the LORD.

7 So will I make my holy name known in the midst of my people Israel; and I will not *let them* pollute my holy name any more: and the heathen shall know that I *am* the LORD, the Holy One in Israel.

8 ¶ Behold, it is come, and it is done, saith the Lord GOD; this *is* the day whereof I have spoken.

9 And they that dwell in the cities of Israel shall go forth, and shall set on fire and burn the weapons, both the shields and the bucklers, the bows and the arrows, and the handstaves, and the spears, and they shall burn them with fire seven years:

10 So that they shall take no wood out of the field, neither cut down *any* out of the forests; for they shall burn the weapons with fire: and they shall spoil those that spoiled them, and rob those that robbed them, saith the Lord GOD.
11 ¶ And it shall come to pass in that day, *that* I will give unto Gog a place there of graves in Israel, the valley of the passengers on the east of the sea: and it shall stop the *noses* of the passengers: and there shall they bury Gog and all his multitude: and they shall call *it* The valley of Hamon-gog.
12 And seven months shall the house of Israel be burying of them, that they may cleanse the land.
13 Yea, all the people of the land shall bury *them;* and it shall be to them a renown the day that I shall be glorified, saith the Lord GOD.
14 And they shall sever out men of continual employment, passing through the land to bury with the passengers those that remain upon the face of the earth, to cleanse it: after the end of seven months shall they search.
15 And the passengers *that* pass through the land, when *any* seeth a man's bone, then shall he set up a sign by it, till the buriers have buried it in the valley of Hamon-gog.
16 And also the name of the city *shall be* Hamonah. Thus shall they cleanse the land.
17 ¶ And, thou son of man, thus saith the Lord GOD; Speak unto every feathered fowl, and to every beast of the field, Assemble yourselves, and come; gather yourselves on every side to my sacrifice that I do sacrifice for you, *even* a great sacrifice upon the mountains of Israel, that ye may eat flesh, and drink blood.
18 Ye shall eat the flesh of the mighty, and drink the blood of the princes of the earth, of rams, of lambs, and of goats, of bullocks, all of them fatlings of Bashan.
19 And ye shall eat fat till ye be full, and drink blood till ye be drunken, of my sacrifice which I have sacrificed for you.
20 Thus ye shall be filled at my table with horses and chariots, with mighty men, and with all men of war, saith the Lord GOD.
21 And I will set my glory among the heathen, and all the heathen shall see my judgment that I have executed, and my hand that I have laid upon them.
22 So the house of Israel shall know that I *am* the LORD their God from that day and forward.
23 ¶ And the heathen shall know that the house of Israel went into captivity for their iniquity: because they trespassed against me, therefore hid I my face from them, and gave them into the hand of their enemies: so fell they all by the sword.
24 According to their uncleanness and according to their transgressions have I done unto them, and hid my face from them.
25 Therefore thus saith the Lord GOD; Now will I bring again the captivity of Jacob, and have mercy upon the whole house of Israel, and will be jealous for my holy name;
26 After that they have borne their shame, and all their trespasses whereby they have trespassed against me, when they dwelt safely in their land, and none made *them* afraid.
27 When I have brought them again from the people, and gathered them out of their enemies' lands, and am sanctified in them in the sight of many nations;
28 Then shall they know that I *am* the LORD their God, which caused them to be led into captivity among the heathen: but I have gathered them unto their own land, and have left none of them any more there.
29 Neither will I hide my face any more from them: for I have poured out my spirit upon the house of Israel, saith the Lord GOD.

Ezekiel 40

1 In the five and twentieth year of our captivity, in the beginning of the year, in the tenth *day* of the month, in the fourteenth year after that the city was smitten, in the selfsame day the hand of the LORD was upon me, and brought me thither.
2 In the visions of God brought he me into the land of Israel, and set me upon a very high mountain, by which *was* as the frame of a city on the south.
3 And he brought me thither, and, behold, *there was* a man, whose appearance *was* like the appearance of brass, with a line of flax in his hand, and a measuring reed; and he stood in the gate.
4 And the man said unto me, Son of man,

behold with thine eyes, and hear with thine
ears, and set thine heart upon all that I shall
shew thee; for to the intent that I might
shew *them* unto thee *art* thou brought
hither: declare all that thou seest to the
house of Israel.
5 And behold a wall on the outside of the
house round about, and in the man's hand
a measuring reed of six cubits *long* by the
cubit and an hand breadth: so he measured
the breadth of the building, one reed; and
the height, one reed.
6 ¶ Then came he unto the gate which
looketh toward the east, and went up the
stairs thereof, and measured the threshold
of the gate, *which was* one reed broad; and
the other threshold *of the gate, which was*
one reed broad.
7 And *every* little chamber *was* one reed
long, and one reed broad; and between
the little chambers *were* five cubits; and
the threshold of the gate by the porch of
the gate within *was* one reed.
8 He measured also the porch of the gate
within, one reed.
9 Then measured he the porch of the
gate, eight cubits; and the posts thereof,
two cubits; and the porch of the gate *was*
inward.
10 And the little chambers of the gate eastward *were* three on this side, and three on
that side; they three *were* of one measure:
and the posts had one measure on this side
and on that side.
11 And he measured the breadth of the
entry of the gate, ten cubits; *and* the length
of the gate, thirteen cubits.
12 The space also before the little chambers
was one cubit *on this side*, and the space
was one cubit on that side: and the little
chambers *were* six cubits on this side, and
six cubits on that side.
13 He measured then the gate from the
roof of *one* little chamber to the roof of
another: the breadth *was* five and twenty
cubits, door against door.
14 He made also posts of threescore cubits,
even unto the post of the court round about
the gate.
15 And from the face of the gate of the
entrance unto the face of the porch of the
inner gate *were* fifty cubits.
16 And *there were* narrow windows to the
little chambers, and to their posts within
the gate round about, and likewise to the
arches: and windows *were* round about
inward: and upon *each* post *were* palm
trees.
17 Then brought he me into the outward
court, and, lo, *there were* chambers, and a
pavement made for the court round about:
thirty chambers *were* upon the pavement.
18 And the pavement by the side of the
gates over against the length of the gates
was the lower pavement.
19 Then he measured the breadth from the
forefront of the lower gate unto the forefront of the inner court without, an hundred
cubits eastward and northward.
20 ¶ And the gate of the outward court that
looked toward the north, he measured the
length thereof, and the breadth thereof.
21 And the little chambers thereof *were*
three on this side and three on that side;
and the posts thereof and the arches thereof
were after the measure of the first gate:
the length thereof *was* fifty cubits, and the
breadth five and twenty cubits.
22 And their windows, and their arches, and
their palm trees, *were* after the measure of
the gate that looketh toward the east; and
they went up unto it by seven steps; and the
arches thereof *were* before them.
23 And the gate of the inner court *was* over
against the gate toward the north, and
toward the east; and he measured from
gate to gate an hundred cubits.
24 ¶ After that he brought me toward the
south, and behold a gate toward the south:
and he measured the posts thereof and the
arches thereof according to these measures.
25 And *there were* windows in it and in the
arches thereof round about, like those windows: the length *was* fifty cubits, and the
breadth five and twenty cubits.
26 And *there were* seven steps to go up
to it, and the arches thereof *were* before
them: and it had palm trees, one on this
side, and another on that side, upon the
posts thereof.
27 And *there was* a gate in the inner court
toward the south: and he measured from
gate to gate toward the south an hundred
cubits.
28 And he brought me to the inner court by

the south gate: and he measured the south gate according to these measures;

29 And the little chambers thereof, and the posts thereof, and the arches thereof, according to these measures: and *there were* windows in it and in the arches thereof round about: *it was* fifty cubits long, and five and twenty cubits broad.

30 And the arches round about *were* five and twenty cubits long, and five cubits broad.

31 And the arches thereof *were* toward the utter court; and palm trees *were* upon the posts thereof: and the going up to it *had* eight steps.

32 ¶ And he brought me into the inner court toward the east: and he measured the gate according to these measures.

33 And the little chambers thereof, and the posts thereof, and the arches thereof, *were* according to these measures: and *there were* windows therein and in the arches thereof round about: *it was* fifty cubits long, and five and twenty cubits broad.

34 And the arches thereof *were* toward the outward court; and palm trees *were* upon the posts thereof, on this side, and on that side: and the going up to it *had* eight steps.

35 ¶ And he brought me to the north gate, and measured *it* according to these measures;

36 The little chambers thereof, the posts thereof, and the arches thereof, and the windows to it round about: the length *was* fifty cubits, and the breadth five and twenty cubits.

37 And the posts thereof *were* toward the utter court; and palm trees *were* upon the posts thereof, on this side, and on that side: and the going up to it *had* eight steps.

38 And the chambers and the entries thereof *were* by the posts of the gates, where they washed the burnt offering.

39 ¶ And in the porch of the gate *were* two tables on this side, and two tables on that side, to slay thereon the burnt offering and the sin offering and the trespass offering.

40 And at the side without, as one goeth up to the entry of the north gate, *were* two tables; and on the other side, which *was* at the porch of the gate, *were* two tables.

41 Four tables *were* on this side, and four tables on that side, by the side of the gate; eight tables, whereupon they slew *their sacrifices*.

42 And the four tables *were* of hewn stone for the burnt offering, of a cubit and an half long, and a cubit and an half broad, and one cubit high: whereupon also they laid the instruments wherewith they slew the burnt offering and the sacrifice.

43 And within *were* hooks, an hand broad, fastened round about: and upon the tables *was* the flesh of the offering.

44 ¶ And without the inner gate *were* the chambers of the singers in the inner court, which *was* at the side of the north gate; and their prospect *was* toward the south: one at the side of the east gate *having* the prospect toward the north.

45 And he said unto me, This chamber, whose prospect *is* toward the south, *is* for the priests, the keepers of the charge of the house.

46 And the chamber whose prospect *is* toward the north *is* for the priests, the keepers of the charge of the altar: these *are* the sons of Zadok among the sons of Levi, which come near to the LORD to minister unto him.

47 So he measured the court, an hundred cubits long, and an hundred cubits broad, foursquare; and the altar *that was* before the house.

48 ¶ And he brought me to the porch of the house, and measured *each* post of the porch, five cubits on this side, and five cubits on that side: and the breadth of the gate *was* three cubits on this side, and three cubits on that side.

49 The length of the porch *was* twenty cubits, and the breadth eleven cubits; and *he brought me* by the steps whereby they went up to it: and *there were* pillars by the posts, one on this side, and another on that side.

Ezekiel 41

1 Afterward he brought me to the temple, and measured the posts, six cubits broad on the one side, and six cubits broad on the other side, *which was* the breadth of the tabernacle.

2 And the breadth of the door *was* ten cubits; and the sides of the door *were* five cubits on the one side, and five cubits on the other side: and he measured the length

thereof, forty cubits: and the breadth,
twenty cubits.
3 Then went he inward, and measured the
post of the door, two cubits; and the door,
six cubits; and the breadth of the door,
seven cubits.
4 So he measured the length thereof, twenty
cubits; and the breadth, twenty cubits,
before the temple: and he said unto me,
This *is* the most holy *place*.
5 After he measured the wall of the house,
six cubits; and the breadth of *every* side
chamber, four cubits, round about the house
on every side.
6 And the side chambers *were* three, one
over another, and thirty in order; and they
entered into the wall which *was* of the
house for the side chambers round about,
that they might have hold, but they had not
hold in the wall of the house.
7 And *there was* an enlarging, and a winding
about still upward to the side chambers: for
the winding about of the house went still
upward round about the house: therefore
the breadth of the house *was still* upward,
and so increased *from* the lowest *chamber*
to the highest by the midst.
8 I saw also the height of the house round
about: the foundations of the side chambers
were a full reed of six great cubits.
9 The thickness of the wall, which *was* for
the side chamber without, *was* five cubits:
and *that* which *was* left *was* the place of the
side chambers that *were* within.
10 And between the chambers *was* the
wideness of twenty cubits round about the
house on every side.
11 And the doors of the side chambers *were*
toward *the place that was* left, one door
toward the north, and another door toward
the south: and the breadth of the place that
was left *was* five cubits round about.
12 Now the building that *was* before the
separate place at the end toward the west
was seventy cubits broad; and the wall of
the building *was* five cubits thick round
about, and the length thereof ninety cubits.
13 So he measured the house, an hundred
cubits long; and the separate place, and the
building, with the walls thereof, an hundred
cubits long;
14 Also the breadth of the face of the house,
and of the separate place toward the east,
an hundred cubits.
15 And he measured the length of the building over against the separate place which
was behind it, and the galleries thereof on
the one side and on the other side, an hundred cubits, with the inner temple, and the
porches of the court;
16 The door posts, and the narrow windows,
and the galleries round about on their three
stories, over against the door, cieled with
wood round about, and from the ground
up to the windows, and the windows *were*
covered;
17 To that above the door, even unto the
inner house, and without, and by all the
wall round about within and without, by
measure.
18 And *it was* made with cherubims and
palm trees, so that a palm tree *was* between
a cherub and a cherub; and *every* cherub
had two faces;
19 So that the face of a man *was* toward
the palm tree on the one side, and the face
of a young lion toward the palm tree on
the other side: *it was* made through all the
house round about.
20 From the ground unto above the door
were cherubims and palm trees made, and
on the wall of the temple.
21 The posts of the temple *were* squared,
and the face of the sanctuary; the appearance *of the one* as the appearance *of the
other.*
22 The altar of wood *was* three cubits high,
and the length thereof two cubits; and the
corners thereof, and the length thereof,
and the walls thereof, *were* of wood: and
he said unto me, This *is* the table that *is*
before the LORD.
23 And the temple and the sanctuary had
two doors.
24 And the doors had two leaves *apiece*, two
turning leaves; two *leaves* for the one door,
and two leaves for the other *door.*
25 And *there were* made on them, on the
doors of the temple, cherubims and palm
trees, like as *were* made upon the walls;
and *there were* thick planks upon the face
of the porch without.
26 And *there were* narrow windows and
palm trees on the one side and on the
other side, on the sides of the porch, and

upon the side chambers of the house, and
thick planks.

Ezekiel 42

1 Then he brought me forth into the utter
court, the way toward the north: and he
brought me into the chamber that *was*
over against the separate place, and which
was before the building toward the north.
2 Before the length of an hundred cubits
was the north door, and the breadth *was*
fifty cubits.
3 Over against the twenty *cubits* which *were*
for the inner court, and over against the
pavement which *was* for the utter court,
was gallery against gallery in three *stories*.
4 And before the chambers *was* a walk of
ten cubits breadth inward, a way of one
cubit; and their doors toward the north.
5 Now the upper chambers *were* shorter:
for the galleries were higher than these,
than the lower, and than the middlemost
of the building.
6 For they *were* in three *stories*, but had
not pillars as the pillars of the courts: therefore *the building* was straitened more than
the lowest and the middlemost from the
ground.
7 And the wall that *was* without over against
the chambers, toward the utter court on
the forepart of the chambers, the length
thereof *was* fifty cubits.
8 For the length of the chambers that *were*
in the utter court *was* fifty cubits: and, lo,
before the temple *were* an hundred cubits.
9 And from under these chambers *was* the
entry on the east side, as one goeth into
them from the utter court.
10 The chambers *were* in the thickness of
the wall of the court toward the east, over
against the separate place, and over against
the building.
11 And the way before them *was* like the
appearance of the chambers which *were*
toward the north, as long as they, *and*
as broad as they: and all their goings out
were both according to their fashions, and
according to their doors.
12 And according to the doors of the chambers that *were* toward the south *was* a
door in the head of the way, *even* the way
directly before the wall toward the east, as
one entereth into them.
13 ¶ Then said he unto me, The north
chambers *and* the south chambers, which
are before the separate place, they *be* holy
chambers, where the priests that approach
unto the LORD shall eat the most holy things:
there shall they lay the most holy things, and
the meat offering, and the sin offering, and
the trespass offering; for the place *is* holy.
14 When the priests enter therein, then
shall they not go out of the holy *place* into
the utter court, but there they shall lay their
garments wherein they minister; for they
are holy; and shall put on other garments,
and shall approach to *those things* which
are for the people.
15 Now when he had made an end of measuring the inner house, he brought me forth
toward the gate whose prospect *is* toward
the east, and measured it round about.
16 He measured the east side with the
measuring reed, five hundred reeds, with
the measuring reed round about.
17 He measured the north side, five hundred reeds, with the measuring reed round
about.
18 He measured the south side, five hundred
reeds, with the measuring reed.
19 ¶ He turned about to the west side,
and measured five hundred reeds with the
measuring reed.
20 He measured it by the four sides: it had
a wall round about, five hundred *reeds*
long, and five hundred broad, to make a
separation between the sanctuary and the
profane place.

Ezekiel 43

1 Afterward he brought me to the gate,
even the gate that looketh toward the east:
2 And, behold, the glory of the God of Israel
came from the way of the east: and his voice
was like a noise of many waters: and the
earth shined with his glory.
3 And *it was* according to the appearance
of the vision which I saw, *even* according to
the vision that I saw when I came to destroy
the city: and the visions *were* like the vision
that I saw by the river Chebar; and I fell
upon my face.
4 And the glory of the LORD came into the
house by the way of the gate whose prospect *is* toward the east.
5 So the spirit took me up, and brought me

into the inner court; and, behold, the glory
of the LORD filled the house.
6 And I heard *him* speaking unto me out of
the house; and the man stood by me.
7 ¶ And he said unto me, Son of man, the
place of my throne, and the place of the
soles of my feet, where I will dwell in the
midst of the children of Israel for ever, and
my holy name, shall the house of Israel no
more defile, *neither* they, nor their kings,
by their whoredom, nor by the carcases of
their kings in their high places.
8 In their setting of their threshold by my
thresholds, and their post by my posts, and
the wall between me and them, they have
even defiled my holy name by their abominations that they have committed: wherefore I have consumed them in mine anger.
9 Now let them put away their whoredom,
and the carcases of their kings, far from me,
and I will dwell in the midst of them for ever.
10 ¶ Thou son of man, shew the house
to the house of Israel, that they may be
ashamed of their iniquities: and let them
measure the pattern.
11 And if they be ashamed of all that they
have done, shew them the form of the
house, and the fashion thereof, and the
goings out thereof, and the comings in
thereof, and all the forms thereof, and all
the ordinances thereof, and all the forms
thereof, and all the laws thereof: and write *it*
in their sight, that they may keep the whole
form thereof, and all the ordinances thereof,
and do them.
12 This *is* the law of the house; Upon the
top of the mountain the whole limit thereof
round about *shall be* most holy. Behold, this
is the law of the house.
13 ¶ And these *are* the measures of the
altar after the cubits: The cubit *is* a cubit
and an hand breadth; even the bottom *shall*
be a cubit, and the breadth a cubit, and the
border thereof by the edge thereof round
about *shall be* a span: and this *shall be* the
higher place of the altar.
14 And from the bottom *upon* the ground
even to the lower settle *shall be* two cubits,
and the breadth one cubit; and from the
lesser settle *even* to the greater settle *shall*
be four cubits, and the breadth *one* cubit.
15 So the altar *shall be* four cubits; and from
the altar and upward *shall be* four horns.
16 And the altar *shall be* twelve *cubits* long,
twelve broad, square in the four squares
thereof.
17 And the settle *shall be* fourteen *cubits*
long and fourteen broad in the four squares
thereof; and the border about it *shall be*
half a cubit; and the bottom thereof *shall*
be a cubit about; and his stairs shall look
toward the east.
18 ¶ And he said unto me, Son of man,
thus saith the Lord GOD; These *are* the
ordinances of the altar in the day when
they shall make it, to offer burnt offerings
thereon, and to sprinkle blood thereon.
19 And thou shalt give to the priests the
Levites that be of the seed of Zadok, which
approach unto me, to minister unto me,
saith the Lord GOD, a young bullock for a
sin offering.
20 And thou shalt take of the blood thereof,
and put *it* on the four horns of it, and on
the four corners of the settle, and upon the
border round about: thus shalt thou cleanse
and purge it.
21 Thou shalt take the bullock also of the
sin offering, and he shall burn it in the
appointed place of the house, without the
sanctuary.
22 And on the second day thou shalt offer
a kid of the goats without blemish for a sin
offering; and they shall cleanse the altar, as
they did cleanse *it* with the bullock.
23 When thou hast made an end of cleansing *it*, thou shalt offer a young bullock
without blemish, and a ram out of the flock
without blemish.
24 And thou shalt offer them before the
LORD, and the priests shall cast salt upon
them, and they shall offer them up *for* a
burnt offering unto the LORD.
25 Seven days shalt thou prepare every
day a goat *for* a sin offering: they shall also
prepare a young bullock, and a ram out of
the flock, without blemish.
26 Seven days shall they purge the altar
and purify it; and they shall consecrate
themselves.
27 And when these days are expired, it
shall be, *that* upon the eighth day, and *so*
forward, the priests shall make your burnt
offerings upon the altar, and your peace
offerings; and I will accept you, saith the
Lord GOD.

Ezekiel 44

1 Then he brought me back the way of
the gate of the outward sanctuary which
looketh toward the east; and it *was* shut.
2 Then said the LORD unto me; This gate
shall be shut, it shall not be opened, and
no man shall enter in by it; because the
LORD, the God of Israel, hath entered in by
it, therefore it shall be shut.
3 *It is* for the prince; the prince, he shall sit
in it to eat bread before the LORD; he shall
enter by the way of the porch of *that* gate,
and shall go out by the way of the same.
4 ¶ Then brought he me the way of the
north gate before the house: and I looked,
and, behold, the glory of the LORD filled the
house of the LORD: and I fell upon my face.
5 And the LORD said unto me, Son of man,
mark well, and behold with thine eyes, and
hear with thine ears all that I say unto thee
concerning all the ordinances of the house
of the LORD, and all the laws thereof; and
mark well the entering in of the house, with
every going forth of the sanctuary.
6 And thou shalt say to the rebellious, *even*
to the house of Israel, Thus saith the Lord
GOD; O ye house of Israel, let it suffice you
of all your abominations,
7 In that ye have brought *into my sanctuary*
strangers, uncircumcised in heart, and
uncircumcised in flesh, to be in my sanctuary, to pollute it, *even* my house, when ye
offer my bread, the fat and the blood, and
they have broken my covenant because of
all your abominations.
8 And ye have not kept the charge of mine
holy things: but ye have set keepers of my
charge in my sanctuary for yourselves.
9 ¶ Thus saith the Lord GOD; No stranger,
uncircumcised in heart, nor uncircumcised
in flesh, shall enter into my sanctuary, of any
stranger that *is* among the children of Israel.
10 And the Levites that are gone away far
from me, when Israel went astray, which
went astray away from me after their idols;
they shall even bear their iniquity.
11 Yet they shall be ministers in my sanctuary, *having* charge at the gates of the house,
and ministering to the house: they shall slay
the burnt offering and the sacrifice for the
people, and they shall stand before them
to minister unto them.
12 Because they ministered unto them
before their idols, and caused the house of
Israel to fall into iniquity; therefore have I
lifted up mine hand against them, saith the
Lord GOD, and they shall bear their iniquity.
13 And they shall not come near unto me,
to do the office of a priest unto me, nor to
come near to any of my holy things, in the
most holy *place:* but they shall bear their
shame, and their abominations which they
have committed.
14 But I will make them keepers of the
charge of the house, for all the service
thereof, and for all that shall be done
therein.
15 ¶ But the priests the Levites, the sons of
Zadok, that kept the charge of my sanctuary
when the children of Israel went astray from
me, they shall come near to me to minister
unto me, and they shall stand before me to
offer unto me the fat and the blood, saith
the Lord GOD:
16 They shall enter into my sanctuary, and
they shall come near to my table, to minister
unto me, and they shall keep my charge.
17 ¶ And it shall come to pass, *that* when
they enter in at the gates of the inner court,
they shall be clothed with linen garments;
and no wool shall come upon them, whiles
they minister in the gates of the inner court,
and within.
18 They shall have linen bonnets upon their
heads, and shall have linen breeches upon
their loins; they shall not gird *themselves*
with any thing that causeth sweat.
19 And when they go forth into the utter
court, *even* into the utter court to the
people, they shall put off their garments
wherein they ministered, and lay them in
the holy chambers, and they shall put on
other garments; and they shall not sanctify
the people with their garments.
20 Neither shall they shave their heads, nor
suffer their locks to grow long; they shall
only poll their heads.
21 Neither shall any priest drink wine, when
they enter into the inner court.
22 Neither shall they take for their wives a
widow, nor her that is put away: but they
shall take maidens of the seed of the house
of Israel, or a widow that had a priest before.
23 And they shall teach my people *the difference* between the holy and profane, and

cause them to discern between the unclean
and the clean.
24 And in controversy they shall stand in
judgment; *and* they shall judge it according
to my judgments: and they shall keep my
laws and my statutes in all mine assemblies;
and they shall hallow my sabbaths.
25 And they shall come at no dead person
to defile themselves: but for father, or for
mother, or for son, or for daughter, for
brother, or for sister that hath had no husband, they may defile themselves.
26 And after he is cleansed, they shall reckon
unto him seven days.
27 And in the day that he goeth into the
sanctuary, unto the inner court, to minister in the sanctuary, he shall offer his sin
offering, saith the Lord GOD.
28 And it shall be unto them for an inheritance: I *am* their inheritance: and ye shall
give them no possession in Israel: I *am* their
possession.
29 They shall eat the meat offering, and
the sin offering, and the trespass offering;
and every dedicated thing in Israel shall
be theirs.
30 And the first of all the firstfruits of all
things, and every oblation of all, of every
sort of your oblations, shall be the priest's:
ye shall also give unto the priest the first of
your dough, that he may cause the blessing
to rest in thine house.
31 The priests shall not eat of any thing
that is dead of itself, or torn, whether it be
fowl or beast.

Ezekiel 45

1 Moreover, when ye shall divide by lot
the land for inheritance, ye shall offer an
oblation unto the LORD, an holy portion of
the land: the length *shall be* the length of
five and twenty thousand *reeds*, and the
breadth *shall be* ten thousand. This *shall be*
holy in all the borders thereof round about.
2 Of this there shall be for the sanctuary
five hundred *in length*, with five hundred
in breadth, square round about; and fifty
cubits round about for the suburbs thereof.
3 And of this measure shalt thou measure
the length of five and twenty thousand, and
the breadth of ten thousand: and in it shall
be the sanctuary *and* the most holy *place*.
4 The holy *portion* of the land shall be for
the priests the ministers of the sanctuary,
which shall come near to minister unto the
LORD: and it shall be a place for their houses,
and an holy place for the sanctuary.
5 And the five and twenty thousand of
length, and the ten thousand of breadth,
shall also the Levites, the ministers of the
house, have for themselves, for a possession
for twenty chambers.
6 ¶ And ye shall appoint the possession of
the city five thousand broad, and five and
twenty thousand long, over against the
oblation of the holy *portion*: it shall be for
the whole house of Israel.
7 ¶ And *a portion shall be* for the prince on
the one side and on the other side of the
oblation of the holy *portion*, and of the possession of the city, before the oblation of the
holy *portion*, and before the possession of
the city, from the west side westward, and
from the east side eastward: and the length
shall be over against one of the portions,
from the west border unto the east border.
8 In the land shall be his possession in Israel:
and my princes shall no more oppress my
people; and *the rest of* the land shall they
give to the house of Israel according to
their tribes.
9 ¶ Thus saith the Lord GOD; Let it suffice
you, O princes of Israel: remove violence
and spoil, and execute judgment and justice,
take away your exactions from my people,
saith the Lord GOD.
10 Ye shall have just balances, and a just
ephah, and a just bath.
11 The ephah and the bath shall be of one
measure, that the bath may contain the
tenth part of an homer, and the ephah the
tenth part of an homer: the measure thereof
shall be after the homer.
12 And the shekel *shall be* twenty gerahs:
twenty shekels, five and twenty shekels,
fifteen shekels, shall be your maneh.
13 This *is* the oblation that ye shall offer;
the sixth part of an ephah of an homer of
wheat, and ye shall give the sixth part of an
ephah of an homer of barley:
14 Concerning the ordinance of oil, the bath
of oil, *ye shall offer* the tenth part of a bath
out of the cor, *which is* an homer of ten
baths; for ten baths *are* an homer:
15 And one lamb out of the flock, out of
two hundred, out of the fat pastures of

Israel; for a meat offering, and for a burnt
offering, and for peace offerings, to make
reconciliation for them, saith the Lord GOD.
16 All the people of the land shall give this
oblation for the prince in Israel.
17 And it shall be the prince's part *to give*
burnt offerings, and meat offerings, and
drink offerings, in the feasts, and in the
new moons, and in the sabbaths, in all
solemnities of the house of Israel: he shall
prepare the sin offering, and the meat
offering, and the burnt offering, and the
peace offerings, to make reconciliation for
the house of Israel.
18 Thus saith the Lord GOD; In the first
month, in the first *day* of the month, thou
shalt take a young bullock without blemish,
and cleanse the sanctuary:
19 And the priest shall take of the blood of
the sin offering, and put *it* upon the posts
of the house, and upon the four corners of
the settle of the altar, and upon the posts
of the gate of the inner court.
20 And so thou shalt do the seventh *day* of
the month for every one that erreth, and
for *him that is* simple: so shall ye reconcile
the house.
21 In the first *month*, in the fourteenth day
of the month, ye shall have the passover,
a feast of seven days; unleavened bread
shall be eaten.
22 And upon that day shall the prince prepare for himself and for all the people of the
land a bullock *for* a sin offering.
23 And seven days of the feast he shall
prepare a burnt offering to the LORD, seven
bullocks and seven rams without blemish
daily the seven days; and a kid of the goats
daily *for* a sin offering.
24 And he shall prepare a meat offering of
an ephah for a bullock, and an ephah for a
ram, and an hin of oil for an ephah.
25 In the seventh *month*, in the fifteenth
day of the month, shall he do the like in the
feast of the seven days, according to the sin
offering, according to the burnt offering,
and according to the meat offering, and
according to the oil.

Ezekiel 46

1 Thus saith the Lord GOD; The gate of the
inner court that looketh toward the east
shall be shut the six working days; but on
the sabbath it shall be opened, and in the
day of the new moon it shall be opened.
2 And the prince shall enter by the way of
the porch of *that* gate without, and shall
stand by the post of the gate, and the
priests shall prepare his burnt offering and
his peace offerings, and he shall worship at
the threshold of the gate: then he shall go
forth; but the gate shall not be shut until
the evening.
3 Likewise the people of the land shall
worship at the door of this gate before the
LORD in the sabbaths and in the new moons.
4 And the burnt offering that the prince shall
offer unto the LORD in the sabbath day *shall
be* six lambs without blemish, and a ram
without blemish.
5 And the meat offering *shall be* an ephah
for a ram, and the meat offering for the
lambs as he shall be able to give, and an hin
of oil to an ephah.
6 And in the day of the new moon *it shall
be* a young bullock without blemish, and
six lambs, and a ram: they shall be without
blemish.
7 And he shall prepare a meat offering, an
ephah for a bullock, and an ephah for a ram,
and for the lambs according as his hand shall
attain unto, and an hin of oil to an ephah.
8 And when the prince shall enter, he shall
go in by the way of the porch of *that* gate,
and he shall go forth by the way thereof.
9 ¶ But when the people of the land shall
come before the LORD in the solemn feasts,
he that entereth in by the way of the north
gate to worship shall go out by the way of
the south gate; and he that entereth by the
way of the south gate shall go forth by the
way of the north gate: he shall not return
by the way of the gate whereby he came in,
but shall go forth over against it.
10 And the prince in the midst of them,
when they go in, shall go in; and when they
go forth, shall go forth.
11 And in the feasts and in the solemnities
the meat offering shall be an ephah to a
bullock, and an ephah to a ram, and to the
lambs as he is able to give, and an hin of oil
to an ephah.
12 Now when the prince shall prepare a
voluntary burnt offering or peace offerings
voluntarily unto the LORD, *one* shall then
open him the gate that looketh toward the

east, and he shall prepare his burnt offering
and his peace offerings, as he did on the
sabbath day: then he shall go forth; and
after his going forth *one* shall shut the gate.
13 Thou shalt daily prepare a burnt offering unto the LORD *of* a lamb of the first
year without blemish: thou shalt prepare
it every morning.
14 And thou shalt prepare a meat offering
for it every morning, the sixth part of an
ephah, and the third part of an hin of oil, to
temper with the fine flour; a meat offering
continually by a perpetual ordinance unto
the LORD.
15 Thus shall they prepare the lamb, and the
meat offering, and the oil, every morning
for a continual burnt offering.
16 ¶ Thus saith the Lord GOD; If the prince
give a gift unto any of his sons, the inheritance thereof shall be his sons'; it *shall be*
their possession by inheritance.
17 But if he give a gift of his inheritance to
one of his servants, then it shall be his to
the year of liberty; after it shall return to
the prince: but his inheritance shall be his
sons' for them.
18 Moreover the prince shall not take of
the people's inheritance by oppression, to
thrust them out of their possession; *but* he
shall give his sons inheritance out of his own
possession: that my people be not scattered
every man from his possession.
19 ¶ After he brought me through the entry,
which *was* at the side of the gate, into the
holy chambers of the priests, which looked
toward the north: and, behold, there *was* a
place on the two sides westward.
20 Then said he unto me, This *is* the place
where the priests shall boil the trespass
offering and the sin offering, where they
shall bake the meat offering; that they bear
them not out into the utter court, to sanctify
the people.
21 Then he brought me forth into the utter
court, and caused me to pass by the four
corners of the court; and, behold, in every
corner of the court *there was* a court.
22 In the four corners of the court *there*
were courts joined of forty *cubits* long and
thirty broad: these four corners *were* of
one measure.
23 And *there was* a row *of building* round
about in them, round about them four, and
it was made with boiling places under the
rows round about.
24 Then said he unto me, These *are* the
places of them that boil, where the ministers of the house shall boil the sacrifice of
the people.

Ezekiel 47

1 Afterward he brought me again unto the
door of the house; and, behold, waters
issued out from under the threshold of the
house eastward: for the forefront of the
house *stood toward* the east, and the waters
came down from under from the right side
of the house, at the south *side* of the altar.
2 Then brought he me out of the way of the
gate northward, and led me about the way
without unto the utter gate by the way that
looketh eastward; and, behold, there ran
out waters on the right side.
3 And when the man that had the line in
his hand went forth eastward, he measured a thousand cubits, and he brought
me through the waters; the waters *were*
to the ancles.
4 Again he measured a thousand, and
brought me through the waters; the waters
were to the knees. Again he measured a
thousand, and brought me through; the
waters *were* to the loins.
5 Afterward he measured a thousand; *and*
it was a river that I could not pass over: for
the waters were risen, waters to swim in, a
river that could not be passed over.
6 ¶ And he said unto me, Son of man, hast
thou seen *this?* Then he brought me, and
caused me to return to the brink of the river.
7 Now when I had returned, behold, at the
bank of the river *were* very many trees on
the one side and on the other.
8 Then said he unto me, These waters issue
out toward the east country, and go down
into the desert, and go into the sea: *which*
being brought forth into the sea, the waters
shall be healed.
9 And it shall come to pass, *that* every thing
that liveth, which moveth, whithersoever
the rivers shall come, shall live: and there
shall be a very great multitude of fish,
because these waters shall come thither:
for they shall be healed; and every thing
shall live whither the river cometh.
10 And it shall come to pass, *that* the fishers

shall stand upon it from En-gedi even unto
En-eglaim; they shall be a *place* to spread
forth nets; their fish shall be according to
their kinds, as the fish of the great sea,
exceeding many.
11 But the miry places thereof and the mar-
ishes thereof shall not be healed; they shall
be given to salt.
12 And by the river upon the bank thereof,
on this side and on that side, shall grow all
trees for meat, whose leaf shall not fade,
neither shall the fruit thereof be consumed:
it shall bring forth new fruit according to his
months, because their waters they issued
out of the sanctuary: and the fruit thereof
shall be for meat, and the leaf thereof for
medicine.
13 ¶ Thus saith the Lord GOD; This *shall be*
the border, whereby ye shall inherit the
land according to the twelve tribes of Israel:
Joseph *shall have two* portions.
14 And ye shall inherit it, one as well as
another: *concerning* the which I lifted up
mine hand to give it unto your fathers: and
this land shall fall unto you for inheritance.
15 And this *shall be* the border of the land
toward the north side, from the great sea,
the way of Hethlon, as men go to Zedad;
16 Hamath, Berothah, Sibraim, which *is*
between the border of Damascus and the
border of Hamath; Hazar-hatticon, which *is*
by the coast of Hauran.
17 And the border from the sea shall be
Hazar-enan, the border of Damascus, and
the north northward, and the border of
Hamath. And *this is* the north side.
18 And the east side ye shall measure from
Hauran, and from Damascus, and from Gilead, and from the land of Israel *by* Jordan,
from the border unto the east sea. And *this*
is the east side.
19 And the south side southward, from
Tamar *even* to the waters of strife *in* Kadesh,
the river to the great sea. And *this is* the
south side southward.
20 The west side also *shall be* the great
sea from the border, till a man come over
against Hamath. This *is* the west side.
21 So shall ye divide this land unto you
according to the tribes of Israel.
22 ¶ And it shall come to pass, *that* ye shall
divide it by lot for an inheritance unto you,
and to the strangers that sojourn among
you, which shall beget children among you:
and they shall be unto you as born in the
country among the children of Israel; they
shall have inheritance with you among the
tribes of Israel.
23 And it shall come to pass, *that* in what
tribe the stranger sojourneth, there shall ye
give *him* his inheritance, saith the Lord GOD.

Ezekiel 48

1 Now these *are* the names of the tribes.
From the north end to the coast of the
way of Hethlon, as one goeth to Hamath,
Hazar-enan, the border of Damascus northward, to the coast of Hamath; for these are
his sides east *and* west; a *portion for* Dan.
2 And by the border of Dan, from the east
side unto the west side, a *portion for* Asher.
3 And by the border of Asher, from the east
side even unto the west side, a *portion for*
Naphtali.
4 And by the border of Naphtali, from the
east side unto the west side, a *portion for*
Manasseh.
5 And by the border of Manasseh, from
the east side unto the west side, a *portion*
for Ephraim.
6 And by the border of Ephraim, from the
east side even unto the west side, a *portion*
for Reuben.
7 And by the border of Reuben, from the
east side unto the west side, a *portion for*
Judah.
8 ¶ And by the border of Judah, from the
east side unto the west side, shall be the
offering which ye shall offer of five and
twenty thousand *reeds in* breadth, and *in*
length as one of the *other* parts, from the
east side unto the west side: and the sanctuary shall be in the midst of it.
9 The oblation that ye shall offer unto the
LORD *shall be* of five and twenty thousand
in length, and of ten thousand in breadth.
10 And for them, *even* for the priests, shall
be *this* holy oblation; toward the north five
and twenty thousand *in length*, and toward
the west ten thousand in breadth, and
toward the east ten thousand in breadth,
and toward the south five and twenty thousand in length: and the sanctuary of the
LORD shall be in the midst thereof.
11 *It shall be* for the priests that are sanctified of the sons of Zadok; which have kept

my charge, which went not astray when the children of Israel went astray, as the Levites went astray.
12 And *this* oblation of the land that is offered shall be unto them a thing most holy by the border of the Levites.
13 And over against the border of the priests the Levites *shall have* five and twenty thousand in length, and ten thousand in breadth: all the length *shall be* five and twenty thousand, and the breadth ten thousand.
14 And they shall not sell of it, neither exchange, nor alienate the firstfruits of the land: for *it is* holy unto the LORD.
15 ¶ And the five thousand, that are left in the breadth over against the five and twenty thousand, shall be a profane *place* for the city, for dwelling, and for suburbs: and the city shall be in the midst thereof.
16 And these *shall be* the measures thereof; the north side four thousand and five hundred, and the south side four thousand and five hundred, and on the east side four thousand and five hundred, and the west side four thousand and five hundred.
17 And the suburbs of the city shall be toward the north two hundred and fifty, and toward the south two hundred and fifty, and toward the east two hundred and fifty, and toward the west two hundred and fifty.
18 And the residue in length over against the oblation of the holy *portion shall be* ten thousand eastward, and ten thousand westward: and it shall be over against the oblation of the holy *portion;* and the increase thereof shall be for food unto them that serve the city.
19 And they that serve the city shall serve it out of all the tribes of Israel.
20 All the oblation *shall be* five and twenty thousand by five and twenty thousand: ye shall offer the holy oblation foursquare, with the possession of the city.
21 ¶ And the residue *shall be* for the prince, on the one side and on the other of the holy oblation, and of the possession of the city, over against the five and twenty thousand of the oblation toward the east border, and westward over against the five and twenty thousand toward the west border, over against the portions for the prince: and it shall be the holy oblation; and the sanctuary of the house *shall be* in the midst thereof.
22 Moreover from the possession of the Levites, and from the possession of the city, *being* in the midst *of that* which is the prince's, between the border of Judah and the border of Benjamin, shall be for the prince.
23 As for the rest of the tribes, from the east side unto the west side, Benjamin *shall have* a *portion*.
24 And by the border of Benjamin, from the east side unto the west side, Simeon *shall have* a *portion*.
25 And by the border of Simeon, from the east side unto the west side, Issachar a *portion*.
26 And by the border of Issachar, from the east side unto the west side, Zebulun a *portion*.
27 And by the border of Zebulun, from the east side unto the west side, Gad a *portion*.
28 And by the border of Gad, at the south side southward, the border shall be even from Tamar *unto* the waters of strife *in* Kadesh, *and* to the river toward the great sea.
29 This *is* the land which ye shall divide by lot unto the tribes of Israel for inheritance, and these *are* their portions, saith the Lord GOD.
30 ¶ And these *are* the goings out of the city on the north side, four thousand and five hundred measures.
31 And the gates of the city *shall be* after the names of the tribes of Israel: three gates northward; one gate of Reuben, one gate of Judah, one gate of Levi.
32 And at the east side four thousand and five hundred: and three gates; and one gate of Joseph, one gate of Benjamin, one gate of Dan.
33 And at the south side four thousand and five hundred measures: and three gates; one gate of Simeon, one gate of Issachar, one gate of Zebulun.
34 At the west side four thousand and five hundred, *with* their three gates; one gate of Gad, one gate of Asher, one gate of Naphtali.
35 *It was* round about eighteen thousand *measures:* and the name of the city from *that* day *shall be,* The LORD *is* there.

The Book Of Daniel

Daniel 1

1 In the third year of the reign of Jehoiakim king of Judah came Nebuchadnezzar king of Babylon unto Jerusalem, and besieged it.

2 And the Lord gave Jehoiakim king of Judah into his hand, with part of the vessels of the house of God: which he carried into the land of Shinar to the house of his god; and he brought the vessels into the treasure house of his god.

3 ¶ And the king spake unto Ashpenaz the master of his eunuchs, that he should bring *certain* of the children of Israel, and of the king's seed, and of the princes;

4 Children in whom *was* no blemish, but well favoured, and skilful in all wisdom, and cunning in knowledge, and understanding science, and such as *had* ability in them to stand in the king's palace, and whom they might teach the learning and the tongue of the Chaldeans.

5 And the king appointed them a daily provision of the king's meat, and of the wine which he drank: so nourishing them three years, that at the end thereof they might stand before the king.

6 Now among these were of the children of Judah, Daniel, Hananiah, Mishael, and Azariah:

7 Unto whom the prince of the eunuchs gave names: for he gave unto Daniel *the name* of Belteshazzar; and to Hananiah, of Shadrach; and to Mishael, of Meshach; and to Azariah, of Abed-nego.

8 ¶ But Daniel purposed in his heart that he would not defile himself with the portion of the king's meat, nor with the wine which he drank: therefore he requested of the prince of the eunuchs that he might not defile himself.

9 Now God had brought Daniel into favour and tender love with the prince of the eunuchs.

10 And the prince of the eunuchs said unto Daniel, I fear my lord the king, who hath appointed your meat and your drink: for why should he see your faces worse liking than the children which *are* of your sort? then shall ye make *me* endanger my head to the king.

11 Then said Daniel to Melzar, whom the prince of the eunuchs had set over Daniel, Hananiah, Mishael, and Azariah,

12 Prove thy servants, I beseech thee, ten days; and let them give us pulse to eat, and water to drink.

13 Then let our countenances be looked upon before thee, and the countenance of the children that eat of the portion of the king's meat: and as thou seest, deal with thy servants.

14 So he consented to them in this matter, and proved them ten days.

15 And at the end of ten days their countenances appeared fairer and fatter in flesh than all the children which did eat the portion of the king's meat.

16 Thus Melzar took away the portion of their meat, and the wine that they should drink; and gave them pulse.

17 ¶ As for these four children, God gave them knowledge and skill in all learning and wisdom: and Daniel had understanding in all visions and dreams.

18 Now at the end of the days that the king had said he should bring them in, then the prince of the eunuchs brought them in before Nebuchadnezzar.

19 And the king communed with them; and among them all was found none like Daniel, Hananiah, Mishael, and Azariah: therefore stood they before the king.

20 And in all matters of wisdom *and* understanding, that the king inquired of them, he found them ten times better than all the magicians *and* astrologers that *were* in all his realm.

21 And Daniel continued *even* unto the first year of king Cyrus.

Daniel 2

1 And in the second year of the reign of Nebuchadnezzar Nebuchadnezzar dreamed

dreams, wherewith his spirit was troubled, and his sleep brake from him.

2 Then the king commanded to call the magicians, and the astrologers, and the sorcerers, and the Chaldeans, for to shew the king his dreams. So they came and stood before the king.

3 And the king said unto them, I have dreamed a dream, and my spirit was troubled to know the dream.

4 Then spake the Chaldeans to the king in Syriack, O king, live for ever: tell thy servants the dream, and we will shew the interpretation.

5 The king answered and said to the Chaldeans, The thing is gone from me: if ye will not make known unto me the dream, with the interpretation thereof, ye shall be cut in pieces, and your houses shall be made a dunghill.

6 But if ye shew the dream, and the interpretation thereof, ye shall receive of me gifts and rewards and great honour: therefore shew me the dream, and the interpretation thereof.

7 They answered again and said, Let the king tell his servants the dream, and we will shew the interpretation of it.

8 The king answered and said, I know of certainty that ye would gain the time, because ye see the thing is gone from me.

9 But if ye will not make known unto me the dream, *there is but* one decree for you: for ye have prepared lying and corrupt words to speak before me, till the time be changed: therefore tell me the dream, and I shall know that ye can shew me the interpretation thereof.

10 ¶ The Chaldeans answered before the king, and said, There is not a man upon the earth that can shew the king's matter: therefore *there is* no king, lord, nor ruler, *that* asked such things at any magician, or astrologer, or Chaldean.

11 And *it is* a rare thing that the king requireth, and there is none other that can shew it before the king, except the gods, whose dwelling is not with flesh.

12 For this cause the king was angry and very furious, and commanded to destroy all the wise *men* of Babylon.

13 And the decree went forth that the wise *men* should be slain; and they sought Daniel and his fellows to be slain.

14 ¶ Then Daniel answered with counsel and wisdom to Arioch the captain of the king's guard, which was gone forth to slay the wise *men* of Babylon:

15 He answered and said to Arioch the king's captain, Why *is* the decree *so* hasty from the king? Then Arioch made the thing known to Daniel.

16 Then Daniel went in, and desired of the king that he would give him time, and that he would shew the king the interpretation.

17 Then Daniel went to his house, and made the thing known to Hananiah, Mishael, and Azariah, his companions:

18 That they would desire mercies of the God of heaven concerning this secret; that Daniel and his fellows should not perish with the rest of the wise *men* of Babylon.

19 ¶ Then was the secret revealed unto Daniel in a night vision. Then Daniel blessed the God of heaven.

20 Daniel answered and said, Blessed be the name of God for ever and ever: for wisdom and might are his:

21 And he changeth the times and the seasons: he removeth kings, and setteth up kings: he giveth wisdom unto the wise, and knowledge to them that know understanding:

22 He revealeth the deep and secret things: he knoweth what *is* in the darkness, and the light dwelleth with him.

23 I thank thee, and praise thee, O thou God of my fathers, who hast given me wisdom and might, and hast made known unto me now what we desired of thee: for thou hast *now* made known unto us the king's matter.

24 ¶ Therefore Daniel went in unto Arioch, whom the king had ordained to destroy the wise *men* of Babylon: he went and said thus unto him; Destroy not the wise *men* of Babylon: bring me in before the king, and I will shew unto the king the interpretation.

25 Then Arioch brought in Daniel before the king in haste, and said thus unto him, I have found a man of the captives of Judah, that will make known unto the king the interpretation.

26 The king answered and said to Daniel, whose name *was* Belteshazzar, Art thou able

to make known unto me the dream which I
have seen, and the interpretation thereof?
27 Daniel answered in the presence of the
king, and said, The secret which the king
hath demanded cannot the wise *men*, the
astrologers, the magicians, the soothsayers,
shew unto the king;
28 But there is a God in heaven that
revealeth secrets, and maketh known to
the king Nebuchadnezzar what shall be in
the latter days. Thy dream, and the visions
of thy head upon thy bed, are these;
29 As for thee, O king, thy thoughts came
into thy mind upon thy bed, what should
come to pass hereafter: and he that
revealeth secrets maketh known to thee
what shall come to pass.
30 But as for me, this secret is not revealed
to me for *any* wisdom that I have more than
any living, but for *their* sakes that shall make
known the interpretation to the king, and
that thou mightest know the thoughts of
thy heart.
31 ¶ Thou, O king, sawest, and behold a
great image. This great image, whose brightness *was* excellent, stood before thee; and
the form thereof *was* terrible.
32 This image's head *was* of fine gold, his
breast and his arms of silver, his belly and
his thighs of brass,
33 His legs of iron, his feet part of iron and
part of clay.
34 Thou sawest till that a stone was cut out
without hands, which smote the image upon
his feet *that were* of iron and clay, and brake
them to pieces.
35 Then was the iron, the clay, the brass,
the silver, and the gold, broken to pieces
together, and became like the chaff of the
summer threshingfloors; and the wind carried them away, that no place was found for
them: and the stone that smote the image
became a great mountain, and filled the
whole earth.
36 ¶ This *is* the dream; and we will tell the
interpretation thereof before the king.
37 Thou, O king, *art* a king of kings: for the
God of heaven hath given thee a kingdom,
power, and strength, and glory.
38 And wheresoever the children of men
dwell, the beasts of the field and the fowls
of the heaven hath he given into thine hand,
and hath made thee ruler over them all.
Thou *art* this head of gold.
39 And after thee shall arise another kingdom inferior to thee, and another third
kingdom of brass, which shall bear rule over
all the earth.
40 And the fourth kingdom shall be strong
as iron: forasmuch as iron breaketh in pieces
and subdueth all *things:* and as iron that
breaketh all these, shall it break in pieces
and bruise.
41 And whereas thou sawest the feet and
toes, part of potters' clay, and part of iron,
the kingdom shall be divided; but there
shall be in it of the strength of the iron,
forasmuch as thou sawest the iron mixed
with miry clay.
42 And *as* the toes of the feet *were* part of
iron, and part of clay, *so* the kingdom shall
be partly strong, and partly broken.
43 And whereas thou sawest iron mixed
with miry clay, they shall mingle themselves
with the seed of men: but they shall not
cleave one to another, even as iron is not
mixed with clay.
44 And in the days of these kings shall the
God of heaven set up a kingdom, which shall
never be destroyed: and the kingdom shall
not be left to other people, *but* it shall break
in pieces and consume all these kingdoms,
and it shall stand for ever.
45 Forasmuch as thou sawest that the stone
was cut out of the mountain without hands,
and that it brake in pieces the iron, the brass,
the clay, the silver, and the gold; the great
God hath made known to the king what shall
come to pass hereafter: and the dream *is*
certain, and the interpretation thereof sure.
46 ¶ Then the king Nebuchadnezzar fell
upon his face, and worshipped Daniel, and
commanded that they should offer an oblation and sweet odours unto him.
47 The king answered unto Daniel, and
said, Of a truth *it is,* that your God *is* a God
of gods, and a Lord of kings, and a revealer
of secrets, seeing thou couldest reveal this
secret.
48 Then the king made Daniel a great man,
and gave him many great gifts, and made
him ruler over the whole province of Babylon, and chief of the governors over all the
wise *men* of Babylon.
49 Then Daniel requested of the king, and

he set Shadrach, Meshach, and Abed-nego,
over the affairs of the province of Babylon:
but Daniel *sat* in the gate of the king.

Daniel 3

1 Nebuchadnezzar the king made an image
of gold, whose height *was* threescore cubits,
and the breadth thereof six cubits: he set
it up in the plain of Dura, in the province
of Babylon.
2 Then Nebuchadnezzar the king sent to
gather together the princes, the governors,
and the captains, the judges, the treasurers,
the counsellers, the sheriffs, and all the
rulers of the provinces, to come to the dedication of the image which Nebuchadnezzar
the king had set up.
3 Then the princes, the governors, and
captains, the judges, the treasurers, the
counsellers, the sheriffs, and all the rulers of
the provinces, were gathered together unto
the dedication of the image that Nebuchadnezzar the king had set up; and they stood
before the image that Nebuchadnezzar
had set up.
4 Then an herald cried aloud, To you it is
commanded, O people, nations, and languages,
5 *That* at what time ye hear the sound of
the cornet, flute, harp, sackbut, psaltery,
dulcimer, and all kinds of musick, ye fall
down and worship the golden image that
Nebuchadnezzar the king hath set up:
6 And whoso falleth not down and worshippeth shall the same hour be cast into the
midst of a burning fiery furnace.
7 Therefore at that time, when all the people
heard the sound of the cornet, flute, harp,
sackbut, psaltery, and all kinds of musick, all
the people, the nations, and the languages,
fell down *and* worshipped the golden image
that Nebuchadnezzar the king had set up.
8 ¶ Wherefore at that time certain Chaldeans came near, and accused the Jews.
9 They spake and said to the king Nebuchadnezzar, O king, live for ever.
10 Thou, O king, hast made a decree, that
every man that shall hear the sound of the
cornet, flute, harp, sackbut, psaltery, and
dulcimer, and all kinds of musick, shall fall
down and worship the golden image:
11 And whoso falleth not down and worshippeth, *that* he should be cast into the
midst of a burning fiery furnace.
12 There are certain Jews whom thou hast
set over the affairs of the province of Babylon, Shadrach, Meshach, and Abed-nego;
these men, O king, have not regarded thee:
they serve not thy gods, nor worship the
golden image which thou hast set up.
13 ¶ Then Nebuchadnezzar in *his* rage
and fury commanded to bring Shadrach,
Meshach, and Abed-nego. Then they
brought these men before the king.
14 Nebuchadnezzar spake and said unto
them, *Is it* true, O Shadrach, Meshach, and
Abed-nego, do not ye serve my gods, nor
worship the golden image which I have
set up?
15 Now if ye be ready that at what time ye
hear the sound of the cornet, flute, harp,
sackbut, psaltery, and dulcimer, and all
kinds of musick, ye fall down and worship
the image which I have made; *well:* but if ye
worship not, ye shall be cast the same hour
into the midst of a burning fiery furnace;
and who *is* that God that shall deliver you
out of my hands?
16 Shadrach, Meshach, and Abed-nego,
answered and said to the king, O Nebuchadnezzar, we *are* not careful to answer
thee in this matter.
17 If it be *so*, our God whom we serve is
able to deliver us from the burning fiery
furnace, and he will deliver *us* out of thine
hand, O king.
18 But if not, be it known unto thee, O king,
that we will not serve thy gods, nor worship
the golden image which thou hast set up.
19 ¶ Then was Nebuchadnezzar full of fury,
and the form of his visage was changed
against Shadrach, Meshach, and Abed-nego:
therefore he spake, and commanded that
they should heat the furnace one seven
times more than it was wont to be heated.
20 And he commanded the most mighty
men that *were* in his army to bind Shadrach,
Meshach, and Abed-nego, *and* to cast *them*
into the burning fiery furnace.
21 Then these men were bound in their
coats, their hosen, and their hats, and their
other garments, and were cast into the
midst of the burning fiery furnace.
22 Therefore because the king's commandment was urgent, and the furnace exceed-

ing hot, the flame of the fire slew those men that took up Shadrach, Meshach, and Abed-nego.

23 And these three men, Shadrach, Meshach, and Abed-nego, fell down bound into the midst of the burning fiery furnace.

24 Then Nebuchadnezzar the king was astonied, and rose up in haste, *and* spake, and said unto his counsellers, Did not we cast three men bound into the midst of the fire? They answered and said unto the king, True, O king.

25 He answered and said, Lo, I see four men loose, walking in the midst of the fire, and they have no hurt; and the form of the fourth is like the Son of God.

26 ¶ Then Nebuchadnezzar came near to the mouth of the burning fiery furnace, *and* spake, and said, Shadrach, Meshach, and Abed-nego, ye servants of the most high God, come forth, and come *hither.* Then Shadrach, Meshach, and Abed-nego, came forth of the midst of the fire.

27 And the princes, governors, and captains, and the king's counsellers, being gathered together, saw these men, upon whose bodies the fire had no power, nor was an hair of their head singed, neither were their coats changed, nor the smell of fire had passed on them.

28 *Then* Nebuchadnezzar spake, and said, Blessed *be* the God of Shadrach, Meshach, and Abed-nego, who hath sent his angel, and delivered his servants that trusted in him, and have changed the king's word, and yielded their bodies, that they might not serve nor worship any god, except their own God.

29 Therefore I make a decree, That every people, nation, and language, which speak any thing amiss against the God of Shadrach, Meshach, and Abed-nego, shall be cut in pieces, and their houses shall be made a dunghill: because there is no other God that can deliver after this sort.

30 Then the king promoted Shadrach, Meshach, and Abed-nego, in the province of Babylon.

Daniel 4

1 Nebuchadnezzar the king, unto all people, nations, and languages, that dwell in all the earth; Peace be multiplied unto you.

2 I thought it good to shew the signs and wonders that the high God hath wrought toward me.

3 How great *are* his signs! and how mighty *are* his wonders! his kingdom *is* an everlasting kingdom, and his dominion *is* from generation to generation.

4 ¶ I Nebuchadnezzar was at rest in mine house, and flourishing in my palace:

5 I saw a dream which made me afraid, and the thoughts upon my bed and the visions of my head troubled me.

6 Therefore made I a decree to bring in all the wise *men* of Babylon before me, that they might make known unto me the interpretation of the dream.

7 Then came in the magicians, the astrologers, the Chaldeans, and the soothsayers: and I told the dream before them; but they did not make known unto me the interpretation thereof.

8 ¶ But at the last Daniel came in before me, whose name *was* Belteshazzar, according to the name of my god, and in whom *is* the spirit of the holy gods: and before him I told the dream, *saying*,

9 O Belteshazzar, master of the magicians, because I know that the spirit of the holy gods *is* in thee, and no secret troubleth thee, tell me the visions of my dream that I have seen, and the interpretation thereof.

10 Thus *were* the visions of mine head in my bed; I saw, and behold a tree in the midst of the earth, and the height thereof *was* great.

11 The tree grew, and was strong, and the height thereof reached unto heaven, and the sight thereof to the end of all the earth:

12 The leaves thereof *were* fair, and the fruit thereof much, and in it *was* meat for all: the beasts of the field had shadow under it, and the fowls of the heaven dwelt in the boughs thereof, and all flesh was fed of it.

13 I saw in the visions of my head upon my bed, and, behold, a watcher and an holy one came down from heaven;

14 He cried aloud, and said thus, Hew down the tree, and cut off his branches, shake off his leaves, and scatter his fruit: let the beasts get away from under it, and the fowls from his branches:

15 Nevertheless leave the stump of his roots in the earth, even with a band of iron and brass, in the tender grass of the field; and

let it be wet with the dew of heaven, and *let*
his portion *be* with the beasts in the grass
of the earth:
16 Let his heart be changed from man's, and
let a beast's heart be given unto him; and
let seven times pass over him.
17 This matter *is* by the decree of the watchers, and the demand by the word of the holy
ones: to the intent that the living may know
that the most High ruleth in the kingdom of
men, and giveth it to whomsoever he will,
and setteth up over it the basest of men.
18 This dream I king Nebuchadnezzar have
seen. Now thou, O Belteshazzar, declare the
interpretation thereof, forasmuch as all the
wise *men* of my kingdom are not able to
make known unto me the interpretation:
but thou *art* able; for the spirit of the holy
gods *is* in thee.
19 ¶ Then Daniel, whose name *was* Belteshazzar, was astonied for one hour, and
his thoughts troubled him. The king spake,
and said, Belteshazzar, let not the dream,
or the interpretation thereof, trouble thee.
Belteshazzar answered and said, My lord,
the dream *be* to them that hate thee, and
the interpretation thereof to thine enemies.
20 The tree that thou sawest, which grew,
and was strong, whose height reached
unto the heaven, and the sight thereof to
all the earth;
21 Whose leaves *were* fair, and the fruit
thereof much, and in it *was* meat for all;
under which the beasts of the field dwelt,
and upon whose branches the fowls of the
heaven had their habitation:
22 It *is* thou, O king, that art grown and
become strong: for thy greatness is grown,
and reacheth unto heaven, and thy dominion to the end of the earth.
23 And whereas the king saw a watcher and
an holy one coming down from heaven, and
saying, Hew the tree down, and destroy it;
yet leave the stump of the roots thereof
in the earth, even with a band of iron and
brass, in the tender grass of the field; and
let it be wet with the dew of heaven, and *let*
his portion *be* with the beasts of the field,
till seven times pass over him;
24 This *is* the interpretation, O king, and
this *is* the decree of the most High, which
is come upon my lord the king:
25 That they shall drive thee from men, and
thy dwelling shall be with the beasts of the
field, and they shall make thee to eat grass
as oxen, and they shall wet thee with the
dew of heaven, and seven times shall pass
over thee, till thou know that the most High
ruleth in the kingdom of men, and giveth it
to whomsoever he will.
26 And whereas they commanded to leave
the stump of the tree roots; thy kingdom
shall be sure unto thee, after that thou
shalt have known that the heavens do rule.
27 Wherefore, O king, let my counsel be
acceptable unto thee, and break off thy
sins by righteousness, and thine iniquities
by shewing mercy to the poor; if it may be
a lengthening of thy tranquillity.
28 ¶ All this came upon the king Nebuchadnezzar.
29 At the end of twelve months he walked
in the palace of the kingdom of Babylon.
30 The king spake, and said, Is not this great
Babylon, that I have built for the house of
the kingdom by the might of my power, and
for the honour of my majesty?
31 While the word *was* in the king's mouth,
there fell a voice from heaven, *saying*, O king
Nebuchadnezzar, to thee it is spoken; The
kingdom is departed from thee.
32 And they shall drive thee from men, and
thy dwelling *shall be* with the beasts of the
field: they shall make thee to eat grass as
oxen, and seven times shall pass over thee,
until thou know that the most High ruleth
in the kingdom of men, and giveth it to
whomsoever he will.
33 The same hour was the thing fulfilled
upon Nebuchadnezzar: and he was driven
from men, and did eat grass as oxen, and his
body was wet with the dew of heaven, till
his hairs were grown like eagles' *feathers*,
and his nails like birds' *claws*.
34 And at the end of the days I Nebuchadnezzar lifted up mine eyes unto heaven, and
mine understanding returned unto me, and
I blessed the most High, and I praised and
honoured him that liveth for ever, whose
dominion *is* an everlasting dominion, and his
kingdom *is* from generation to generation:
35 And all the inhabitants of the earth *are*
reputed as nothing: and he doeth according to his will in the army of heaven, and
among the inhabitants of the earth: and

none can stay his hand, or say unto him,
What doest thou?
36 At the same time my reason returned
unto me; and for the glory of my kingdom,
mine honour and brightness returned
unto me; and my counsellers and my lords
sought unto me; and I was established in
my kingdom, and excellent majesty was
added unto me.
37 Now I Nebuchadnezzar praise and extol
and honour the King of heaven, all whose
works *are* truth, and his ways judgment: and
those that walk in pride he is able to abase.

Daniel 5

1 Belshazzar the king made a great feast
to a thousand of his lords, and drank wine
before the thousand.
2 Belshazzar, whiles he tasted the wine,
commanded to bring the golden and silver
vessels which his father Nebuchadnezzar
had taken out of the temple which *was* in
Jerusalem; that the king, and his princes,
his wives, and his concubines, might drink
therein.
3 Then they brought the golden vessels
that were taken out of the temple of the
house of God which *was* at Jerusalem; and
the king, and his princes, his wives, and his
concubines, drank in them.
4 They drank wine, and praised the gods of
gold, and of silver, of brass, of iron, of wood,
and of stone.
5 ¶ In the same hour came forth fingers of
a man's hand, and wrote over against the
candlestick upon the plaister of the wall of
the king's palace: and the king saw the part
of the hand that wrote.
6 Then the king's countenance was changed,
and his thoughts troubled him, so that the
joints of his loins were loosed, and his knees
smote one against another.
7 The king cried aloud to bring in the astrologers, the Chaldeans, and the soothsayers.
And the king spake, and said to the wise
men of Babylon, Whosoever shall read this
writing, and shew me the interpretation
thereof, shall be clothed with scarlet, and
have a chain of gold about his neck, and shall
be the third ruler in the kingdom.
8 Then came in all the king's wise *men:*
but they could not read the writing, nor
make known to the king the interpretation
thereof.
9 Then was king Belshazzar greatly troubled,
and his countenance was changed in him,
and his lords were astonied.
10 ¶ *Now* the queen, by reason of the words
of the king and his lords, came into the banquet house: *and* the queen spake and said,
O king, live for ever: let not thy thoughts
trouble thee, nor let thy countenance be
changed:
11 There is a man in thy kingdom, in whom
is the spirit of the holy gods; and in the days
of thy father light and understanding and
wisdom, like the wisdom of the gods, was
found in him; whom the king Nebuchadnezzar thy father, the king, *I say*, thy father,
made master of the magicians, astrologers,
Chaldeans, *and* soothsayers;
12 Forasmuch as an excellent spirit, and
knowledge, and understanding, interpreting
of dreams, and shewing of hard sentences,
and dissolving of doubts, were found in the
same Daniel, whom the king named Belteshazzar: now let Daniel be called, and he
will shew the interpretation.
13 Then was Daniel brought in before the
king. *And* the king spake and said unto Daniel, *Art* thou that Daniel, which *art* of the
children of the captivity of Judah, whom
the king my father brought out of Jewry?
14 I have even heard of thee, that the spirit
of the gods *is* in thee, and *that* light and
understanding and excellent wisdom is
found in thee.
15 And now the wise *men*, the astrologers,
have been brought in before me, that they
should read this writing, and make known
unto me the interpretation thereof: but
they could not shew the interpretation of
the thing:
16 And I have heard of thee, that thou canst
make interpretations, and dissolve doubts:
now if thou canst read the writing, and make
known to me the interpretation thereof,
thou shalt be clothed with scarlet, and *have*
a chain of gold about thy neck, and shalt be
the third ruler in the kingdom.
17 ¶ Then Daniel answered and said before
the king, Let thy gifts be to thyself, and give
thy rewards to another; yet I will read the
writing unto the king, and make known to
him the interpretation.

18 O thou king, the most high God gave
Nebuchadnezzar thy father a kingdom, and
majesty, and glory, and honour:
19 And for the majesty that he gave him, all
people, nations, and languages, trembled
and feared before him: whom he would he
slew; and whom he would he kept alive; and
whom he would he set up; and whom he
would he put down.
20 But when his heart was lifted up, and his
mind hardened in pride, he was deposed
from his kingly throne, and they took his
glory from him:
21 And he was driven from the sons of men;
and his heart was made like the beasts, and
his dwelling *was* with the wild asses: they
fed him with grass like oxen, and his body
was wet with the dew of heaven; till he
knew that the most high God ruled in the
kingdom of men, and *that* he appointeth
over it whomsoever he will.
22 And thou his son, O Belshazzar, hast not
humbled thine heart, though thou knewest
all this;
23 But hast lifted up thyself against the
Lord of heaven; and they have brought the
vessels of his house before thee, and thou,
and thy lords, thy wives, and thy concubines, have drunk wine in them; and thou
hast praised the gods of silver, and gold, of
brass, iron, wood, and stone, which see not,
nor hear, nor know: and the God in whose
hand thy breath *is*, and whose *are* all thy
ways, hast thou not glorified:
24 Then was the part of the hand sent from
him; and this writing was written.
25 ¶ And this *is* the writing that was written,
MENE, MENE, TEKEL, UPHARSIN.
26 This *is* the interpretation of the thing:
MENE; God hath numbered thy kingdom,
and finished it.
27 TEKEL; Thou art weighed in the balances,
and art found wanting.
28 PERES; Thy kingdom is divided, and given
to the Medes and Persians.
29 Then commanded Belshazzar, and they
clothed Daniel with scarlet, and *put* a chain
of gold about his neck, and made a proclamation concerning him, that he should be
the third ruler in the kingdom.
30 ¶ In that night was Belshazzar the king
of the Chaldeans slain.
31 And Darius the Median took the kingdom,
being about threescore and two years old.

Daniel 6

1 It pleased Darius to set over the kingdom
an hundred and twenty princes, which
should be over the whole kingdom;
2 And over these three presidents; of whom
Daniel *was* first: that the princes might give
accounts unto them, and the king should
have no damage.
3 Then this Daniel was preferred above the
presidents and princes, because an excellent
spirit *was* in him; and the king thought to
set him over the whole realm.
4 ¶ Then the presidents and princes sought
to find occasion against Daniel concerning
the kingdom; but they could find none
occasion nor fault; forasmuch as he *was*
faithful, neither was there any error or fault
found in him.
5 Then said these men, We shall not find any
occasion against this Daniel, except we find
it against him concerning the law of his God.
6 Then these presidents and princes assembled together to the king, and said thus unto
him, King Darius, live for ever.
7 All the presidents of the kingdom, the
governors, and the princes, the counsellers,
and the captains, have consulted together
to establish a royal statute, and to make
a firm decree, that whosoever shall ask a
petition of any God or man for thirty days,
save of thee, O king, he shall be cast into
the den of lions.
8 Now, O king, establish the decree, and sign
the writing, that it be not changed, according to the law of the Medes and Persians,
which altereth not.
9 Wherefore king Darius signed the writing
and the decree.
10 ¶ Now when Daniel knew that the writing
was signed, he went into his house; and his
windows being open in his chamber toward
Jerusalem, he kneeled upon his knees three
times a day, and prayed, and gave thanks
before his God, as he did aforetime.
11 Then these men assembled, and found
Daniel praying and making supplication
before his God.
12 Then they came near, and spake before
the king concerning the king's decree; Hast
thou not signed a decree, that every man

that shall ask *a petition* of any God or man within thirty days, save of thee, O king, shall be cast into the den of lions? The king answered and said, The thing *is* true, according to the law of the Medes and Persians, which altereth not.

13 Then answered they and said before the king, That Daniel, which *is* of the children of the captivity of Judah, regardeth not thee, O king, nor the decree that thou hast signed, but maketh his petition three times a day.

14 Then the king, when he heard *these* words, was sore displeased with himself, and set *his* heart on Daniel to deliver him: and he laboured till the going down of the sun to deliver him.

15 Then these men assembled unto the king, and said unto the king, Know, O king, that the law of the Medes and Persians *is*, That no decree nor statute which the king establisheth may be changed.

16 Then the king commanded, and they brought Daniel, and cast *him* into the den of lions. *Now* the king spake and said unto Daniel, Thy God whom thou servest continually, he will deliver thee.

17 And a stone was brought, and laid upon the mouth of the den; and the king sealed it with his own signet, and with the signet of his lords; that the purpose might not be changed concerning Daniel.

18 ¶ Then the king went to his palace, and passed the night fasting: neither were instruments of musick brought before him: and his sleep went from him.

19 Then the king arose very early in the morning, and went in haste unto the den of lions.

20 And when he came to the den, he cried with a lamentable voice unto Daniel: *and* the king spake and said to Daniel, O Daniel, servant of the living God, is thy God, whom thou servest continually, able to deliver thee from the lions?

21 Then said Daniel unto the king, O king, live for ever.

22 My God hath sent his angel, and hath shut the lions' mouths, that they have not hurt me: forasmuch as before him innocency was found in me; and also before thee, O king, have I done no hurt.

23 Then was the king exceeding glad for him, and commanded that they should take Daniel up out of the den. So Daniel was taken up out of the den, and no manner of hurt was found upon him, because he believed in his God.

24 ¶ And the king commanded, and they brought those men which had accused Daniel, and they cast *them* into the den of lions, them, their children, and their wives; and the lions had the mastery of them, and brake all their bones in pieces or ever they came at the bottom of the den.

25 ¶ Then king Darius wrote unto all people, nations, and languages, that dwell in all the earth; Peace be multiplied unto you.

26 I make a decree, That in every dominion of my kingdom men tremble and fear before the God of Daniel: for he *is* the living God, and stedfast for ever, and his kingdom *that* which shall not be destroyed, and his dominion *shall be even* unto the end.

27 He delivereth and rescueth, and he worketh signs and wonders in heaven and in earth, who hath delivered Daniel from the power of the lions.

28 So this Daniel prospered in the reign of Darius, and in the reign of Cyrus the Persian.

Daniel 7

1 In the first year of Belshazzar king of Babylon Daniel had a dream and visions of his head upon his bed: then he wrote the dream, *and* told the sum of the matters.

2 Daniel spake and said, I saw in my vision by night, and, behold, the four winds of the heaven strove upon the great sea.

3 And four great beasts came up from the sea, diverse one from another.

4 The first *was* like a lion, and had eagle's wings: I beheld till the wings thereof were plucked, and it was lifted up from the earth, and made stand upon the feet as a man, and a man's heart was given to it.

5 And behold another beast, a second, like to a bear, and it raised up itself on one side, and *it had* three ribs in the mouth of it between the teeth of it: and they said thus unto it, Arise, devour much flesh.

6 After this I beheld, and lo another, like a leopard, which had upon the back of it four wings of a fowl; the beast had also four heads; and dominion was given to it.

7 After this I saw in the night visions, and behold a fourth beast, dreadful and terrible,

and strong exceedingly; and it had great iron
teeth: it devoured and brake in pieces, and
stamped the residue with the feet of it: and
it *was* diverse from all the beasts that *were*
before it; and it had ten horns.
8 I considered the horns, and, behold, there
came up among them another little horn,
before whom there were three of the first
horns plucked up by the roots: and, behold,
in this horn *were* eyes like the eyes of man,
and a mouth speaking great things.
9 ¶ I beheld till the thrones were cast down,
and the Ancient of days did sit, whose
garment *was* white as snow, and the hair
of his head like the pure wool: his throne
was like the fiery flame, *and* his wheels *as*
burning fire.
10 A fiery stream issued and came forth
from before him: thousand thousands ministered unto him, and ten thousand times ten
thousand stood before him: the judgment
was set, and the books were opened.
11 I beheld then because of the voice of the
great words which the horn spake: I beheld
even till the beast was slain, and his body
destroyed, and given to the burning flame.
12 As concerning the rest of the beasts, they
had their dominion taken away: yet their
lives were prolonged for a season and time.
13 I saw in the night visions, and, behold,
one like the Son of man came with the
clouds of heaven, and came to the Ancient
of days, and they brought him near before
him.
14 And there was given him dominion,
and glory, and a kingdom, that all people,
nations, and languages, should serve him:
his dominion *is* an everlasting dominion,
which shall not pass away, and his kingdom
that which shall not be destroyed.
15 ¶ I Daniel was grieved in my spirit in the
midst of *my* body, and the visions of my
head troubled me.
16 I came near unto one of them that stood
by, and asked him the truth of all this. So he
told me, and made me know the interpretation of the things.
17 These great beasts, which are four, *are*
four kings, *which* shall arise out of the earth.
18 But the saints of the most High shall take
the kingdom, and possess the kingdom for
ever, even for ever and ever.
19 Then I would know the truth of the fourth
beast, which was diverse from all the others,
exceeding dreadful, whose teeth *were of*
iron, and his nails *of* brass; *which* devoured,
brake in pieces, and stamped the residue
with his feet;
20 And of the ten horns that *were* in his
head, and *of* the other which came up, and
before whom three fell; even *of* that horn
that had eyes, and a mouth that spake very
great things, whose look *was* more stout
than his fellows.
21 I beheld, and the same horn made war
with the saints, and prevailed against them;
22 Until the Ancient of days came, and judgment was given to the saints of the most
High; and the time came that the saints
possessed the kingdom.
23 Thus he said, The fourth beast shall be
the fourth kingdom upon earth, which shall
be diverse from all kingdoms, and shall
devour the whole earth, and shall tread it
down, and break it in pieces.
24 And the ten horns out of this kingdom *are*
ten kings *that* shall arise: and another shall
rise after them; and he shall be diverse from
the first, and he shall subdue three kings.
25 And he shall speak *great* words against
the most High, and shall wear out the saints
of the most High, and think to change times
and laws: and they shall be given into his
hand until a time and times and the dividing of time.
26 But the judgment shall sit, and they shall
take away his dominion, to consume and to
destroy *it* unto the end.
27 And the kingdom and dominion, and the
greatness of the kingdom under the whole
heaven, shall be given to the people of the
saints of the most High, whose kingdom *is*
an everlasting kingdom, and all dominions
shall serve and obey him.
28 Hitherto *is* the end of the matter. As for
me Daniel, my cogitations much troubled
me, and my countenance changed in me:
but I kept the matter in my heart.

Daniel 8

1 In the third year of the reign of king
Belshazzar a vision appeared unto me, *even*
unto me Daniel, after that which appeared
unto me at the first.
2 And I saw in a vision; and it came to pass,
when I saw, that I *was* at Shushan *in* the pal-

ace, which *is* in the province of Elam; and I
saw in a vision, and I was by the river of Ulai.
3 Then I lifted up mine eyes, and saw, and,
behold, there stood before the river a ram
which had *two* horns: and the *two* horns
were high; but one *was* higher than the
other, and the higher came up last.
4 I saw the ram pushing westward, and
northward, and southward; so that no
beasts might stand before him, neither
was there any that could deliver out of his
hand; but he did according to his will, and
became great.
5 And as I was considering, behold, an he
goat came from the west on the face of the
whole earth, and touched not the ground:
and the goat *had* a notable horn between
his eyes.
6 And he came to the ram that had *two*
horns, which I had seen standing before
the river, and ran unto him in the fury of
his power.
7 And I saw him come close unto the ram,
and he was moved with choler against
him, and smote the ram, and brake his two
horns: and there was no power in the ram
to stand before him, but he cast him down
to the ground, and stamped upon him: and
there was none that could deliver the ram
out of his hand.
8 Therefore the he goat waxed very great:
and when he was strong, the great horn was
broken; and for it came up four notable ones
toward the four winds of heaven.
9 And out of one of them came forth a little
horn, which waxed exceeding great, toward
the south, and toward the east, and toward
the pleasant *land*.
10 And it waxed great, *even* to the host of
heaven; and it cast down *some* of the host
and of the stars to the ground, and stamped
upon them.
11 Yea, he magnified *himself* even to the
prince of the host, and by him the daily
sacrifice was taken away, and the place of
his sanctuary was cast down.
12 And an host was given *him* against the
daily *sacrifice* by reason of transgression,
and it cast down the truth to the ground;
and it practised, and prospered.
13 ¶ Then I heard one saint speaking, and
another saint said unto that certain *saint*
which spake, How long *shall be* the vision
concerning the daily *sacrifice*, and the
transgression of desolation, to give both
the sanctuary and the host to be trodden
under foot?
14 And he said unto me, Unto two thousand and three hundred days; then shall
the sanctuary be cleansed.
15 ¶ And it came to pass, when I, *even* I Daniel, had seen the vision, and sought for the
meaning, then, behold, there stood before
me as the appearance of a man.
16 And I heard a man's voice between *the
banks of* Ulai, which called, and said, Gabriel,
make this *man* to understand the vision.
17 So he came near where I stood: and
when he came, I was afraid, and fell upon
my face: but he said unto me, Understand,
O son of man: for at the time of the end
shall be the vision.
18 Now as he was speaking with me, I was in
a deep sleep on my face toward the ground:
but he touched me, and set me upright.
19 And he said, Behold, I will make thee
know what shall be in the last end of the
indignation: for at the time appointed the
end *shall be*.
20 The ram which thou sawest having *two*
horns *are* the kings of Media and Persia.
21 And the rough goat *is* the king of Grecia:
and the great horn that *is* between his eyes
is the first king.
22 Now that being broken, whereas four
stood up for it, four kingdoms shall stand
up out of the nation, but not in his power.
23 And in the latter time of their kingdom,
when the transgressors are come to the full,
a king of fierce countenance, and understanding dark sentences, shall stand up.
24 And his power shall be mighty, but not
by his own power: and he shall destroy
wonderfully, and shall prosper, and practise, and shall destroy the mighty and the
holy people.
25 And through his policy also he shall cause
craft to prosper in his hand; and he shall
magnify *himself* in his heart, and by peace
shall destroy many: he shall also stand up
against the Prince of princes; but he shall
be broken without hand.
26 And the vision of the evening and the
morning which was told *is* true: wherefore
shut thou up the vision; for it *shall be* for
many days.

27 And I Daniel fainted, and was sick *certain* days; afterward I rose up, and did the king's business; and I was astonished at the vision, but none understood *it*.

Daniel 9

1 In the first year of Darius the son of Ahasuerus, of the seed of the Medes, which was made king over the realm of the Chaldeans;

2 In the first year of his reign I Daniel understood by books the number of the years, whereof the word of the LORD came to Jeremiah the prophet, that he would accomplish seventy years in the desolations of Jerusalem.

3 ¶ And I set my face unto the Lord God, to seek by prayer and supplications, with fasting, and sackcloth, and ashes:

4 And I prayed unto the LORD my God, and made my confession, and said, O Lord, the great and dreadful God, keeping the covenant and mercy to them that love him, and to them that keep his commandments;

5 We have sinned, and have committed iniquity, and have done wickedly, and have rebelled, even by departing from thy precepts and from thy judgments:

6 Neither have we hearkened unto thy servants the prophets, which spake in thy name to our kings, our princes, and our fathers, and to all the people of the land.

7 O Lord, righteousness *belongeth* unto thee, but unto us confusion of faces, as at this day; to the men of Judah, and to the inhabitants of Jerusalem, and unto all Israel, *that are* near, and *that are* far off, through all the countries whither thou hast driven them, because of their trespass that they have trespassed against thee.

8 O Lord, to us *belongeth* confusion of face, to our kings, to our princes, and to our fathers, because we have sinned against thee.

9 To the Lord our God *belong* mercies and forgivenesses, though we have rebelled against him;

10 Neither have we obeyed the voice of the LORD our God, to walk in his laws, which he set before us by his servants the prophets.

11 Yea, all Israel have transgressed thy law, even by departing, that they might not obey thy voice; therefore the curse is poured upon us, and the oath that *is* written in the law of Moses the servant of God, because we have sinned against him.

12 And he hath confirmed his words, which he spake against us, and against our judges that judged us, by bringing upon us a great evil: for under the whole heaven hath not been done as hath been done upon Jerusalem.

13 As *it is* written in the law of Moses, all this evil is come upon us: yet made we not our prayer before the LORD our God, that we might turn from our iniquities, and understand thy truth.

14 Therefore hath the LORD watched upon the evil, and brought it upon us: for the LORD our God *is* righteous in all his works which he doeth: for we obeyed not his voice.

15 And now, O Lord our God, that hast brought thy people forth out of the land of Egypt with a mighty hand, and hast gotten thee renown, as at this day; we have sinned, we have done wickedly.

16 ¶ O Lord, according to all thy righteousness, I beseech thee, let thine anger and thy fury be turned away from thy city Jerusalem, thy holy mountain: because for our sins, and for the iniquities of our fathers, Jerusalem and thy people *are become* a reproach to all *that are* about us.

17 Now therefore, O our God, hear the prayer of thy servant, and his supplications, and cause thy face to shine upon thy sanctuary that is desolate, for the Lord's sake.

18 O my God, incline thine ear, and hear; open thine eyes, and behold our desolations, and the city which is called by thy name: for we do not present our supplications before thee for our righteousnesses, but for thy great mercies.

19 O Lord, hear; O Lord, forgive; O Lord, hearken and do; defer not, for thine own sake, O my God: for thy city and thy people are called by thy name.

20 ¶ And whiles I *was* speaking, and praying, and confessing my sin and the sin of my people Israel, and presenting my supplication before the LORD my God for the holy mountain of my God;

21 Yea, whiles I *was* speaking in prayer, even the man Gabriel, whom I had seen in the vision at the beginning, being caused to fly swiftly, touched me about the time of the evening oblation.

22 And he informed *me,* and talked with me,
and said, O Daniel, I am now come forth to
give thee skill and understanding.
23 At the beginning of thy supplications the
commandment came forth, and I am come
to shew *thee;* for thou *art* greatly beloved:
therefore understand the matter, and consider the vision.
24 Seventy weeks are determined upon thy
people and upon thy holy city, to finish the
transgression, and to make an end of sins,
and to make reconciliation for iniquity, and
to bring in everlasting righteousness, and
to seal up the vision and prophecy, and to
anoint the most Holy.
25 Know therefore and understand, *that*
from the going forth of the commandment
to restore and to build Jerusalem unto the
Messiah the Prince *shall be* seven weeks,
and threescore and two weeks: the street
shall be built again, and the wall, even in
troublous times.
26 And after threescore and two weeks shall
Messiah be cut off, but not for himself: and
the people of the prince that shall come
shall destroy the city and the sanctuary;
and the end thereof *shall be* with a flood,
and unto the end of the war desolations
are determined.
27 And he shall confirm the covenant with
many for one week: and in the midst of
the week he shall cause the sacrifice and
the oblation to cease, and for the overspreading of abominations he shall make
it desolate, even until the consummation,
and that determined shall be poured upon
the desolate.

Daniel 10

1 In the third year of Cyrus king of Persia
a thing was revealed unto Daniel, whose
name was called Belteshazzar; and the
thing *was* true, but the time appointed *was*
long: and he understood the thing, and had
understanding of the vision.
2 In those days I Daniel was mourning three
full weeks.
3 I ate no pleasant bread, neither came
flesh nor wine in my mouth, neither did I
anoint myself at all, till three whole weeks
were fulfilled.
4 And in the four and twentieth day of the
first month, as I was by the side of the great
river, which *is* Hiddekel;
5 Then I lifted up mine eyes, and looked,
and behold a certain man clothed in linen,
whose loins *were* girded with fine gold of
Uphaz:
6 His body also *was* like the beryl, and his
face as the appearance of lightning, and
his eyes as lamps of fire, and his arms and
his feet like in colour to polished brass,
and the voice of his words like the voice of
a multitude.
7 And I Daniel alone saw the vision: for the
men that were with me saw not the vision;
but a great quaking fell upon them, so that
they fled to hide themselves.
8 Therefore I was left alone, and saw this
great vision, and there remained no strength
in me: for my comeliness was turned in me
into corruption, and I retained no strength.
9 Yet heard I the voice of his words: and
when I heard the voice of his words, then
was I in a deep sleep on my face, and my
face toward the ground.
10 ¶ And, behold, an hand touched me,
which set me upon my knees and *upon* the
palms of my hands.
11 And he said unto me, O Daniel, a man
greatly beloved, understand the words that
I speak unto thee, and stand upright: for
unto thee am I now sent. And when he had
spoken this word unto me, I stood trembling.
12 Then said he unto me, Fear not, Daniel:
for from the first day that thou didst set
thine heart to understand, and to chasten
thyself before thy God, thy words were
heard, and I am come for thy words.
13 But the prince of the kingdom of Persia
withstood me one and twenty days: but,
lo, Michael, one of the chief princes, came
to help me; and I remained there with the
kings of Persia.
14 Now I am come to make thee understand
what shall befall thy people in the latter
days: for yet the vision *is* for *many* days.
15 And when he had spoken such words
unto me, I set my face toward the ground,
and I became dumb.
16 And, behold, *one* like the similitude of
the sons of men touched my lips: then I
opened my mouth, and spake, and said
unto him that stood before me, O my lord,

by the vision my sorrows are turned upon
me, and I have retained no strength.
17 For how can the servant of this my
lord talk with this my lord? for as for me,
straightway there remained no strength in
me, neither is there breath left in me.
18 Then there came again and touched me
one like the appearance of a man, and he
strengthened me,
19 And said, O man greatly beloved, fear
not: peace *be* unto thee, be strong, yea,
be strong. And when he had spoken unto
me, I was strengthened, and said, Let my
lord speak; for thou hast strengthened me.
20 Then said he, Knowest thou wherefore
I come unto thee? and now will I return to
fight with the prince of Persia: and when
I am gone forth, lo, the prince of Grecia
shall come.
21 But I will shew thee that which is noted
in the scripture of truth: and *there is* none
that holdeth with me in these things, but
Michael your prince.

Daniel 11

1 Also I in the first year of Darius the Mede,
even I, stood to confirm and to strengthen
him.
2 And now will I shew thee the truth. Behold,
there shall stand up yet three kings in Persia;
and the fourth shall be far richer than *they*
all: and by his strength through his riches he
shall stir up all against the realm of Grecia.
3 And a mighty king shall stand up, that shall
rule with great dominion, and do according
to his will.
4 And when he shall stand up, his kingdom
shall be broken, and shall be divided toward
the four winds of heaven; and not to his posterity, nor according to his dominion which
he ruled: for his kingdom shall be plucked
up, even for others beside those.
5 ¶ And the king of the south shall be strong,
and *one* of his princes; and he shall be strong
above him, and have dominion; his dominion *shall be* a great dominion.
6 And in the end of years they shall join
themselves together; for the king's daughter
of the south shall come to the king of the
north to make an agreement: but she shall
not retain the power of the arm; neither
shall he stand, nor his arm: but she shall be
given up, and they that brought her, and he
that begat her, and he that strengthened
her in *these* times.
7 But out of a branch of her roots shall *one*
stand up in his estate, which shall come with
an army, and shall enter into the fortress of
the king of the north, and shall deal against
them, and shall prevail:
8 And shall also carry captives into Egypt
their gods, with their princes, *and* with their
precious vessels of silver and of gold; and
he shall continue *more* years than the king
of the north.
9 So the king of the south shall come into *his*
kingdom, and shall return into his own land.
10 But his sons shall be stirred up, and shall
assemble a multitude of great forces: and
one shall certainly come, and overflow, and
pass through: then shall he return, and be
stirred up, *even* to his fortress.
11 And the king of the south shall be moved
with choler, and shall come forth and fight
with him, *even* with the king of the north:
and he shall set forth a great multitude; but
the multitude shall be given into his hand.
12 *And* when he hath taken away the multitude, his heart shall be lifted up; and he
shall cast down *many* ten thousands: but
he shall not be strengthened *by it*.
13 For the king of the north shall return,
and shall set forth a multitude greater than
the former, and shall certainly come after
certain years with a great army and with
much riches.
14 And in those times there shall many stand
up against the king of the south: also the
robbers of thy people shall exalt themselves
to establish the vision; but they shall fall.
15 So the king of the north shall come,
and cast up a mount, and take the most
fenced cities: and the arms of the south
shall not withstand, neither his chosen
people, neither *shall there be any* strength
to withstand.
16 But he that cometh against him shall do
according to his own will, and none shall
stand before him: and he shall stand in the
glorious land, which by his hand shall be
consumed.
17 He shall also set his face to enter with
the strength of his whole kingdom, and
upright ones with him; thus shall he do: and
he shall give him the daughter of women,

corrupting her: but she shall not stand *on*
his side, neither be for him.
18 After this shall he turn his face unto the
isles, and shall take many: but a prince for
his own behalf shall cause the reproach
offered by him to cease; without his own
reproach he shall cause *it* to turn upon him.
19 Then he shall turn his face toward the
fort of his own land: but he shall stumble
and fall, and not be found.
20 Then shall stand up in his estate a raiser
of taxes *in* the glory of the kingdom: but
within few days he shall be destroyed, neither in anger, nor in battle.
21 And in his estate shall stand up a vile
person, to whom they shall not give the
honour of the kingdom: but he shall come
in peaceably, and obtain the kingdom by
flatteries.
22 And with the arms of a flood shall they
be overflown from before him, and shall be
broken; yea, also the prince of the covenant.
23 And after the league *made* with him he
shall work deceitfully: for he shall come
up, and shall become strong with a small
people.
24 He shall enter peaceably even upon the
fattest places of the province; and he shall
do *that* which his fathers have not done, nor
his fathers' fathers; he shall scatter among
them the prey, and spoil, and riches: *yea*,
and he shall forecast his devices against the
strong holds, even for a time.
25 And he shall stir up his power and his
courage against the king of the south with
a great army; and the king of the south shall
be stirred up to battle with a very great and
mighty army; but he shall not stand: for they
shall forecast devices against him.
26 Yea, they that feed of the portion of his
meat shall destroy him, and his army shall
overflow: and many shall fall down slain.
27 And both these kings' hearts *shall be* to
do mischief, and they shall speak lies at one
table; but it shall not prosper: for yet the end
shall be at the time appointed.
28 Then shall he return into his land with
great riches; and his heart *shall be* against
the holy covenant; and he shall do *exploits*,
and return to his own land.
29 At the time appointed he shall return,
and come toward the south; but it shall not
be as the former, or as the latter.
30 ¶ For the ships of Chittim shall come
against him: therefore he shall be grieved,
and return, and have indignation against the
holy covenant: so shall he do; he shall even
return, and have intelligence with them that
forsake the holy covenant.
31 And arms shall stand on his part, and they
shall pollute the sanctuary of strength, and
shall take away the daily *sacrifice*, and they
shall place the abomination that maketh
desolate.
32 And such as do wickedly against the
covenant shall he corrupt by flatteries: but
the people that do know their God shall be
strong, and do *exploits*.
33 And they that understand among the
people shall instruct many: yet they shall
fall by the sword, and by flame, by captivity,
and by spoil, *many* days.
34 Now when they shall fall, they shall be
holpen with a little help: but many shall
cleave to them with flatteries.
35 And *some* of them of understanding
shall fall, to try them, and to purge, and to
make *them* white, *even* to the time of the
end: because *it is* yet for a time appointed.
36 And the king shall do according to his
will; and he shall exalt himself, and magnify
himself above every god, and shall speak
marvellous things against the God of gods,
and shall prosper till the indignation be
accomplished: for that that is determined
shall be done.
37 Neither shall he regard the God of his
fathers, nor the desire of women, nor
regard any god: for he shall magnify himself above all.
38 But in his estate shall he honour the God
of forces: and a god whom his fathers knew
not shall he honour with gold, and silver, and
with precious stones, and pleasant things.
39 Thus shall he do in the most strong
holds with a strange god, whom he shall
acknowledge *and* increase with glory: and
he shall cause them to rule over many, and
shall divide the land for gain.
40 And at the time of the end shall the king
of the south push at him: and the king of the
north shall come against him like a whirlwind, with chariots, and with horsemen, and
with many ships; and he shall enter into the
countries, and shall overflow and pass over.
41 He shall enter also into the glorious land,

and many *countries* shall be overthrown:
but these shall escape out of his hand, *even*
Edom, and Moab, and the chief of the children of Ammon.
42 He shall stretch forth his hand also upon
the countries: and the land of Egypt shall
not escape.
43 But he shall have power over the treasures of gold and of silver, and over all the
precious things of Egypt: and the Libyans
and the Ethiopians *shall be* at his steps.
44 But tidings out of the east and out of the
north shall trouble him: therefore he shall go
forth with great fury to destroy, and utterly
to make away many.
45 And he shall plant the tabernacles of his
palace between the seas in the glorious holy
mountain; yet he shall come to his end, and
none shall help him.

Daniel 12

1 And at that time shall Michael stand up,
the great prince which standeth for the
children of thy people: and there shall be
a time of trouble, such as never was since
there was a nation *even* to that same time:
and at that time thy people shall be delivered, every one that shall be found written
in the book.
2 And many of them that sleep in the dust
of the earth shall awake, some to everlasting life, and some to shame *and* everlasting
contempt.
3 And they that be wise shall shine as the
brightness of the firmament; and they that
turn many to righteousness as the stars for
ever and ever.
4 But thou, O Daniel, shut up the words, and
seal the book, *even* to the time of the end:
many shall run to and fro, and knowledge
shall be increased.
5 ¶ Then I Daniel looked, and, behold, there
stood other two, the one on this side of the
bank of the river, and the other on that side
of the bank of the river.
6 And *one* said to the man clothed in linen,
which *was* upon the waters of the river, How
long *shall it be to* the end of these wonders?
7 And I heard the man clothed in linen,
which *was* upon the waters of the river,
when he held up his right hand and his
left hand unto heaven, and sware by him
that liveth for ever that *it shall be* for a
time, times, and an half; and when he shall
have accomplished to scatter the power
of the holy people, all these *things* shall
be finished.
8 And I heard, but I understood not: then
said I, O my Lord, what *shall be* the end of
these *things?*
9 And he said, Go thy way, Daniel: for the
words *are* closed up and sealed till the time
of the end.
10 Many shall be purified, and made white,
and tried; but the wicked shall do wickedly:
and none of the wicked shall understand;
but the wise shall understand.
11 And from the time *that* the daily *sacrifice*
shall be taken away, and the abomination
that maketh desolate set up, *there shall be*
a thousand two hundred and ninety days.
12 Blessed *is* he that waiteth, and cometh
to the thousand three hundred and five
and thirty days.
13 But go thou thy way till the end *be:* for
thou shalt rest, and stand in thy lot at the
end of the days.

The Book Of

Hosea

Hosea 1

1 The word of the LORD that came unto
Hosea, the son of Beeri, in the days of
Uzziah, Jotham, Ahaz, *and* Hezekiah, kings
of Judah, and in the days of Jeroboam the
son of Joash, king of Israel.
2 The beginning of the word of the LORD by
Hosea. And the LORD said to Hosea, Go, take
unto thee a wife of whoredoms and children

of whoredoms: for the land hath committed
great whoredom, *departing* from the LORD.
3 So he went and took Gomer the daughter of Diblaim; which conceived, and bare
him a son.
4 And the LORD said unto him, Call his name
Jezreel; for yet a little *while*, and I will avenge
the blood of Jezreel upon the house of Jehu,
and will cause to cease the kingdom of the
house of Israel.
5 And it shall come to pass at that day, that
I will break the bow of Israel in the valley
of Jezreel.
6 ¶ And she conceived again, and bare a
daughter. And *God* said unto him, Call her
name Lo-ruhamah: for I will no more have
mercy upon the house of Israel; but I will
utterly take them away.
7 But I will have mercy upon the house
of Judah, and will save them by the LORD
their God, and will not save them by bow,
nor by sword, nor by battle, by horses, nor
by horsemen.
8 ¶ Now when she had weaned Lo-ruhamah,
she conceived, and bare a son.
9 Then said *God*, Call his name Lo-ammi:
for ye *are* not my people, and I will not be
your *God*.
10 ¶ Yet the number of the children of
Israel shall be as the sand of the sea, which
cannot be measured nor numbered; and it
shall come to pass, *that* in the place where
it was said unto them, Ye *are* not my people,
there it shall be said unto them, *Ye are* the
sons of the living God.
11 Then shall the children of Judah and the
children of Israel be gathered together, and
appoint themselves one head, and they shall
come up out of the land: for great *shall be*
the day of Jezreel.

Hosea 2

1 Say ye unto your brethren, Ammi; and to
your sisters, Ru-hamah.
2 Plead with your mother, plead: for she *is*
not my wife, neither *am* I her husband: let
her therefore put away her whoredoms
out of her sight, and her adulteries from
between her breasts;
3 Lest I strip her naked, and set her as in the
day that she was born, and make her as a
wilderness, and set her like a dry land, and
slay her with thirst.
4 And I will not have mercy upon her children; for they *be* the children of whoredoms.
5 For their mother hath played the harlot:
she that conceived them hath done shamefully: for she said, I will go after my lovers,
that give *me* my bread and my water, my
wool and my flax, mine oil and my drink.
6 ¶ Therefore, behold, I will hedge up thy
way with thorns, and make a wall, that she
shall not find her paths.
7 And she shall follow after her lovers, but
she shall not overtake them; and she shall
seek them, but shall not find *them:* then
shall she say, I will go and return to my first
husband; for then *was it* better with me
than now.
8 For she did not know that I gave her corn,
and wine, and oil, and multiplied her silver
and gold, *which* they prepared for Baal.
9 Therefore will I return, and take away my
corn in the time thereof, and my wine in the
season thereof, and will recover my wool
and my flax *given* to cover her nakedness.
10 And now will I discover her lewdness in
the sight of her lovers, and none shall deliver
her out of mine hand.
11 I will also cause all her mirth to cease,
her feast days, her new moons, and her
sabbaths, and all her solemn feasts.
12 And I will destroy her vines and her fig
trees, whereof she hath said, These *are* my
rewards that my lovers have given me: and
I will make them a forest, and the beasts of
the field shall eat them.
13 And I will visit upon her the days of Baalim, wherein she burned incense to them,
and she decked herself with her earrings and
her jewels, and she went after her lovers,
and forgat me, saith the LORD.
14 ¶ Therefore, behold, I will allure her, and
bring her into the wilderness, and speak
comfortably unto her.
15 And I will give her her vineyards from
thence, and the valley of Achor for a door
of hope: and she shall sing there, as in the
days of her youth, and as in the day when
she came up out of the land of Egypt.
16 And it shall be at that day, saith the LORD,
that thou shalt call me Ishi; and shalt call me
no more Baali.
17 For I will take away the names of Baalim

out of her mouth, and they shall no more be remembered by their name.

18 And in that day will I make a covenant for them with the beasts of the field, and with the fowls of heaven, and *with* the creeping things of the ground: and I will break the bow and the sword and the battle out of the earth, and will make them to lie down safely.

19 And I will betroth thee unto me for ever; yea, I will betroth thee unto me in righteousness, and in judgment, and in lovingkindness, and in mercies.

20 I will even betroth thee unto me in faithfulness: and thou shalt know the LORD.

21 And it shall come to pass in that day, I will hear, saith the LORD, I will hear the heavens, and they shall hear the earth;

22 And the earth shall hear the corn, and the wine, and the oil; and they shall hear Jezreel.

23 And I will sow her unto me in the earth; and I will have mercy upon her that had not obtained mercy; and I will say to *them which were* not my people, Thou *art* my people; and they shall say, *Thou art* my God.

Hosea 3

1 Then said the LORD unto me, Go yet, love a woman beloved of *her* friend, yet an adulteress, according to the love of the LORD toward the children of Israel, who look to other gods, and love flagons of wine.

2 So I bought her to me for fifteen *pieces* of silver, and *for* an homer of barley, and an half homer of barley:

3 And I said unto her, Thou shalt abide for me many days; thou shalt not play the harlot, and thou shalt not be for *another* man: so *will* I also *be* for thee.

4 For the children of Israel shall abide many days without a king, and without a prince, and without a sacrifice, and without an image, and without an ephod, and *without* teraphim:

5 Afterward shall the children of Israel return, and seek the LORD their God, and David their king; and shall fear the LORD and his goodness in the latter days.

Hosea 4

1 Hear the word of the LORD, ye children of Israel: for the LORD hath a controversy with the inhabitants of the land, because *there is* no truth, nor mercy, nor knowledge of God in the land.

2 By swearing, and lying, and killing, and stealing, and committing adultery, they break out, and blood toucheth blood.

3 Therefore shall the land mourn, and every one that dwelleth therein shall languish, with the beasts of the field, and with the fowls of heaven; yea, the fishes of the sea also shall be taken away.

4 Yet let no man strive, nor reprove another: for thy people *are* as they that strive with the priest.

5 Therefore shalt thou fall in the day, and the prophet also shall fall with thee in the night, and I will destroy thy mother.

6 ¶ My people are destroyed for lack of knowledge: because thou hast rejected knowledge, I will also reject thee, that thou shalt be no priest to me: seeing thou hast forgotten the law of thy God, I will also forget thy children.

7 As they were increased, so they sinned against me: *therefore* will I change their glory into shame.

8 They eat up the sin of my people, and they set their heart on their iniquity.

9 And there shall be, like people, like priest: and I will punish them for their ways, and reward them their doings.

10 For they shall eat, and not have enough: they shall commit whoredom, and shall not increase: because they have left off to take heed to the LORD.

11 Whoredom and wine and new wine take away the heart.

12 ¶ My people ask counsel at their stocks, and their staff declareth unto them: for the spirit of whoredoms hath caused *them* to err, and they have gone a whoring from under their God.

13 They sacrifice upon the tops of the mountains, and burn incense upon the hills, under oaks and poplars and elms, because the shadow thereof *is* good: therefore your daughters shall commit whoredom, and your spouses shall commit adultery.

14 I will not punish your daughters when they commit whoredom, nor your spouses when they commit adultery: for themselves are separated with whores, and they sacrifice with harlots: therefore the people *that* doth not understand shall fall.

15 ¶ Though thou, Israel, play the harlot,
yet let not Judah offend; and come not ye
unto Gilgal, neither go ye up to Beth-aven,
nor swear, The LORD liveth.
16 For Israel slideth back as a backsliding
heifer: now the LORD will feed them as a
lamb in a large place.
17 Ephraim *is* joined to idols: let him alone.
18 Their drink is sour: they have committed whoredom continually: her rulers *with*
shame do love, Give ye.
19 The wind hath bound her up in her wings,
and they shall be ashamed because of their
sacrifices.

Hosea 5

1 Hear ye this, O priests; and hearken, ye
house of Israel; and give ye ear, O house
of the king; for judgment *is* toward you,
because ye have been a snare on Mizpah,
and a net spread upon Tabor.
2 And the revolters are profound to make
slaughter, though I *have been* a rebuker of
them all.
3 I know Ephraim, and Israel is not hid from
me: for now, O Ephraim, thou committest
whoredom, *and* Israel is defiled.
4 They will not frame their doings to turn
unto their God: for the spirit of whoredoms
is in the midst of them, and they have not
known the LORD.
5 And the pride of Israel doth testify to his
face: therefore shall Israel and Ephraim
fall in their iniquity; Judah also shall fall
with them.
6 They shall go with their flocks and with
their herds to seek the LORD; but they shall
not find *him;* he hath withdrawn himself
from them.
7 They have dealt treacherously against
the LORD: for they have begotten strange
children: now shall a month devour them
with their portions.
8 Blow ye the cornet in Gibeah, *and* the
trumpet in Ramah: cry aloud *at* Beth-aven,
after thee, O Benjamin.
9 Ephraim shall be desolate in the day of
rebuke: among the tribes of Israel have I
made known that which shall surely be.
10 The princes of Judah were like them that
remove the bound: *therefore* I will pour out
my wrath upon them like water.
11 Ephraim *is* oppressed *and* broken in judgment, because he willingly walked after the
commandment.
12 Therefore *will* I *be* unto Ephraim as a
moth, and to the house of Judah as rottenness.
13 When Ephraim saw his sickness, and
Judah *saw* his wound, then went Ephraim
to the Assyrian, and sent to king Jareb: yet
could he not heal you, nor cure you of your
wound.
14 For I *will be* unto Ephraim as a lion, and
as a young lion to the house of Judah: I, *even*
I, will tear and go away; I will take away, and
none shall rescue *him*.
15 ¶ I will go *and* return to my place, till
they acknowledge their offence, and seek
my face: in their affliction they will seek
me early.

Hosea 6

1 Come, and let us return unto the LORD: for
he hath torn, and he will heal us; he hath
smitten, and he will bind us up.
2 After two days will he revive us: in the
third day he will raise us up, and we shall
live in his sight.
3 Then shall we know, *if* we follow on to
know the LORD: his going forth is prepared
as the morning; and he shall come unto us
as the rain, as the latter *and* former rain
unto the earth.
4 ¶ O Ephraim, what shall I do unto thee? O
Judah, what shall I do unto thee? for your
goodness *is* as a morning cloud, and as the
early dew it goeth away.
5 Therefore have I hewed *them* by the
prophets; I have slain them by the words
of my mouth: and thy judgments *are as* the
light *that* goeth forth.
6 For I desired mercy, and not sacrifice; and
the knowledge of God more than burnt
offerings.
7 But they like men have transgressed the
covenant: there have they dealt treacherously against me.
8 Gilead *is* a city of them that work iniquity,
and is polluted with blood.
9 And as troops of robbers wait for a man,
so the company of priests murder in the
way by consent: for they commit lewdness.
10 I have seen an horrible thing in the house
of Israel: there *is* the whoredom of Ephraim,
Israel is defiled.

11 Also, O Judah, he hath set an harvest
for thee, when I returned the captivity of
my people.

Hosea 7

1 When I would have healed Israel, then
the iniquity of Ephraim was discovered, and
the wickedness of Samaria: for they commit
falsehood; and the thief cometh in, *and* the
troop of robbers spoileth without.
2 And they consider not in their hearts *that*
I remember all their wickedness: now their
own doings have beset them about; they
are before my face.
3 They make the king glad with their wickedness, and the princes with their lies.
4 They *are* all adulterers, as an oven heated
by the baker, *who* ceaseth from raising
after he hath kneaded the dough, until it
be leavened.
5 In the day of our king the princes have
made *him* sick with bottles of wine; he
stretched out his hand with scorners.
6 For they have made ready their heart like
an oven, whiles they lie in wait: their baker
sleepeth all the night; in the morning it
burneth as a flaming fire.
7 They are all hot as an oven, and have
devoured their judges; all their kings are
fallen: *there is* none among them that calleth unto me.
8 Ephraim, he hath mixed himself among
the people; Ephraim is a cake not turned.
9 Strangers have devoured his strength, and
he knoweth *it* not: yea, gray hairs are here
and there upon him, yet he knoweth not.
10 And the pride of Israel testifieth to his
face: and they do not return to the LORD
their God, nor seek him for all this.
11 ¶ Ephraim also is like a silly dove without
heart: they call to Egypt, they go to Assyria.
12 When they shall go, I will spread my net
upon them; I will bring them down as the
fowls of the heaven; I will chastise them, as
their congregation hath heard.
13 Woe unto them! for they have fled from
me: destruction unto them! because they
have transgressed against me: though I have
redeemed them, yet they have spoken lies
against me.
14 And they have not cried unto me with
their heart, when they howled upon their
beds: they assemble themselves for corn
and wine, *and* they rebel against me.
15 Though I have bound *and* strengthened
their arms, yet do they imagine mischief
against me.
16 They return, *but* not to the most High:
they are like a deceitful bow: their princes
shall fall by the sword for the rage of their
tongue: this *shall be* their derision in the
land of Egypt.

Hosea 8

1 *Set* the trumpet to thy mouth. *He shall
come* as an eagle against the house of the
LORD, because they have transgressed my
covenant, and trespassed against my law.
2 Israel shall cry unto me, My God, we
know thee.
3 Israel hath cast off *the thing that is* good:
the enemy shall pursue him.
4 They have set up kings, but not by me:
they have made princes, and I knew *it* not:
of their silver and their gold have they made
them idols, that they may be cut off.
5 ¶ Thy calf, O Samaria, hath cast *thee* off;
mine anger is kindled against them: how
long *will it be* ere they attain to innocency?
6 For from Israel *was* it also: the workman
made it; therefore it *is* not God: but the calf
of Samaria shall be broken in pieces.
7 For they have sown the wind, and they
shall reap the whirlwind: it hath no stalk:
the bud shall yield no meal: if so be it yield,
the strangers shall swallow it up.
8 Israel is swallowed up: now shall they be
among the Gentiles as a vessel wherein *is*
no pleasure.
9 For they are gone up to Assyria, a wild ass
alone by himself: Ephraim hath hired lovers.
10 Yea, though they have hired among the
nations, now will I gather them, and they
shall sorrow a little for the burden of the
king of princes.
11 Because Ephraim hath made many altars
to sin, altars shall be unto him to sin.
12 I have written to him the great things
of my law, *but* they were counted as a
strange thing.
13 They sacrifice flesh *for* the sacrifices
of mine offerings, and eat *it; but* the LORD
accepteth them not; now will he remember
their iniquity, and visit their sins: they shall
return to Egypt.

14 For Israel hath forgotten his Maker, and
buildeth temples; and Judah hath multiplied
fenced cities: but I will send a fire upon
his cities, and it shall devour the palaces
thereof.

Hosea 9

1 Rejoice not, O Israel, for joy, as *other*
people: for thou hast gone a whoring from
thy God, thou hast loved a reward upon
every cornfloor.
2 The floor and the winepress shall not feed
them, and the new wine shall fail in her.
3 They shall not dwell in the LORD's land; but
Ephraim shall return to Egypt, and they shall
eat unclean *things* in Assyria.
4 They shall not offer wine *offerings* to the
LORD, neither shall they be pleasing unto
him: their sacrifices *shall be* unto them as
the bread of mourners; all that eat thereof
shall be polluted: for their bread for their
soul shall not come into the house of the
LORD.
5 What will ye do in the solemn day, and in
the day of the feast of the LORD?
6 For, lo, they are gone because of destruction: Egypt shall gather them up, Memphis
shall bury them: the pleasant *places* for their
silver, nettles shall possess them: thorns
shall be in their tabernacles.
7 The days of visitation are come, the days
of recompence are come; Israel shall know
it: the prophet *is* a fool, the spiritual man
is mad, for the multitude of thine iniquity,
and the great hatred.
8 The watchman of Ephraim *was* with my
God: *but* the prophet *is* a snare of a fowler
in all his ways, *and* hatred in the house of
his God.
9 They have deeply corrupted *themselves*,
as in the days of Gibeah: *therefore* he will
remember their iniquity, he will visit their
sins.
10 I found Israel like grapes in the wilderness; I saw your fathers as the firstripe in
the fig tree at her first time: *but* they went
to Baal-peor, and separated themselves
unto *that* shame; and *their* abominations
were according as they loved.
11 *As for* Ephraim, their glory shall fly away
like a bird, from the birth, and from the
womb, and from the conception.
12 Though they bring up their children, yet
will I bereave them, *that there shall* not *be*
a man *left:* yea, woe also to them when I
depart from them!
13 Ephraim, as I saw Tyrus, *is* planted in a
pleasant place: but Ephraim shall bring forth
his children to the murderer.
14 Give them, O LORD: what wilt thou
give? give them a miscarrying womb and
dry breasts.
15 All their wickedness *is* in Gilgal: for there
I hated them: for the wickedness of their
doings I will drive them out of mine house,
I will love them no more: all their princes
are revolters.
16 Ephraim is smitten, their root is dried up,
they shall bear no fruit: yea, though they
bring forth, yet will I slay *even* the beloved
fruit of their womb.
17 My God will cast them away, because
they did not hearken unto him: and they
shall be wanderers among the nations.

Hosea 10

1 Israel *is* an empty vine, he bringeth forth
fruit unto himself: according to the multitude of his fruit he hath increased the altars;
according to the goodness of his land they
have made goodly images.
2 Their heart is divided; now shall they be
found faulty: he shall break down their
altars, he shall spoil their images.
3 For now they shall say, We have no king,
because we feared not the LORD; what then
should a king do to us?
4 They have spoken words, swearing falsely
in making a covenant: thus judgment springeth up as hemlock in the furrows of the
field.
5 The inhabitants of Samaria shall fear
because of the calves of Beth-aven: for the
people thereof shall mourn over it, and the
priests thereof *that* rejoiced on it, for the
glory thereof, because it is departed from it.
6 It shall be also carried unto Assyria *for* a
present to king Jareb: Ephraim shall receive
shame, and Israel shall be ashamed of his
own counsel.
7 *As for* Samaria, her king is cut off as the
foam upon the water.
8 The high places also of Aven, the sin of
Israel, shall be destroyed: the thorn and
the thistle shall come up on their altars;

and they shall say to the mountains, Cover
us; and to the hills, Fall on us.
9 O Israel, thou hast sinned from the days
of Gibeah: there they stood: the battle in
Gibeah against the children of iniquity did
not overtake them.
10 *It is* in my desire that I should chastise
them; and the people shall be gathered
against them, when they shall bind themselves in their two furrows.
11 And Ephraim *is as* an heifer *that is* taught,
and loveth to tread out *the corn;* but I passed
over upon her fair neck: I will make Ephraim
to ride; Judah shall plow, *and* Jacob shall
break his clods.
12 Sow to yourselves in righteousness, reap
in mercy; break up your fallow ground: for
it is time to seek the LORD, till he come and
rain righteousness upon you.
13 Ye have plowed wickedness, ye have
reaped iniquity; ye have eaten the fruit of
lies: because thou didst trust in thy way, in
the multitude of thy mighty men.
14 Therefore shall a tumult arise among
thy people, and all thy fortresses shall be
spoiled, as Shalman spoiled Beth-arbel in
the day of battle: the mother was dashed
in pieces upon *her* children.
15 So shall Beth-el do unto you because of
your great wickedness: in a morning shall
the king of Israel utterly be cut off.

Hosea 11

1 When Israel *was* a child, then I loved him,
and called my son out of Egypt.
2 *As* they called them, so they went from
them: they sacrificed unto Baalim, and
burned incense to graven images.
3 I taught Ephraim also to go, taking them
by their arms; but they knew not that I
healed them.
4 I drew them with cords of a man, with
bands of love: and I was to them as they
that take off the yoke on their jaws, and I
laid meat unto them.
5 ¶ He shall not return into the land of Egypt,
but the Assyrian shall be his king, because
they refused to return.
6 And the sword shall abide on his cities,
and shall consume his branches, and devour
them, because of their own counsels.
7 And my people are bent to backsliding
from me: though they called them to the
most High, none at all would exalt *him.*
8 How shall I give thee up, Ephraim? *how*
shall I deliver thee, Israel? how shall I make
thee as Admah? *how* shall I set thee as
Zeboim? mine heart is turned within me,
my repentings are kindled together.
9 I will not execute the fierceness of mine
anger, I will not return to destroy Ephraim:
for I *am* God, and not man; the Holy One
in the midst of thee: and I will not enter
into the city.
10 They shall walk after the LORD: he shall
roar like a lion: when he shall roar, then the
children shall tremble from the west.
11 They shall tremble as a bird out of Egypt,
and as a dove out of the land of Assyria:
and I will place them in their houses, saith
the LORD.
12 Ephraim compasseth me about with
lies, and the house of Israel with deceit: but
Judah yet ruleth with God, and is faithful
with the saints.

Hosea 12

1 Ephraim feedeth on wind, and followeth
after the east wind: he daily increaseth lies
and desolation; and they do make a covenant with the Assyrians, and oil is carried
into Egypt.
2 The LORD hath also a controversy with
Judah, and will punish Jacob according to
his ways; according to his doings will he
recompense him.
3 ¶ He took his brother by the heel in the
womb, and by his strength he had power
with God:
4 Yea, he had power over the angel, and
prevailed: he wept, and made supplication
unto him: he found him *in* Beth-el, and there
he spake with us;
5 Even the LORD God of hosts; the LORD *is*
his memorial.
6 Therefore turn thou to thy God: keep
mercy and judgment, and wait on thy God
continually.
7 ¶ *He is* a merchant, the balances of deceit
are in his hand: he loveth to oppress.
8 And Ephraim said, Yet I am become rich,
I have found me out substance: *in* all my
labours they shall find none iniquity in me
that *were* sin.
9 And I *that am* the LORD thy God from the

land of Egypt will yet make thee to dwell in
tabernacles, as in the days of the solemn
feast.
10 I have also spoken by the prophets, and
I have multiplied visions, and used simili-
tudes, by the ministry of the prophets.
11 *Is there* iniquity *in* Gilead? surely they
are vanity: they sacrifice bullocks in Gilgal;
yea, their altars *are* as heaps in the furrows
of the fields.
12 And Jacob fled into the country of Syria,
and Israel served for a wife, and for a wife
he kept *sheep*.
13 And by a prophet the LORD brought
Israel out of Egypt, and by a prophet was
he preserved.
14 Ephraim provoked *him* to anger most
bitterly: therefore shall he leave his blood
upon him, and his reproach shall his Lord
return unto him.

Hosea 13

1 When Ephraim spake trembling, he exalted
himself in Israel; but when he offended in
Baal, he died.
2 And now they sin more and more, and
have made them molten images of their
silver, *and* idols according to their own
understanding, all of it the work of the
craftsmen: they say of them, Let the men
that sacrifice kiss the calves.
3 Therefore they shall be as the morning
cloud, and as the early dew that passeth
away, as the chaff *that* is driven with the
whirlwind out of the floor, and as the smoke
out of the chimney.
4 Yet I *am* the LORD thy God from the land of
Egypt, and thou shalt know no god but me:
for *there is* no saviour beside me.
5 ¶ I did know thee in the wilderness, in the
land of great drought.
6 According to their pasture, so were they
filled; they were filled, and their heart was
exalted; therefore have they forgotten me.
7 Therefore I will be unto them as a lion: as
a leopard by the way will I observe *them*:
8 I will meet them as a bear *that is* bereaved
of her whelps, and will rend the caul of their
heart, and there will I devour them like a
lion: the wild beast shall tear them.
9 ¶ O Israel, thou hast destroyed thyself;
but in me *is* thine help.
10 I will be thy king: where *is any other*
that may save thee in all thy cities? and thy
judges of whom thou saidst, Give me a king
and princes?
11 I gave thee a king in mine anger, and took
him away in my wrath.
12 The iniquity of Ephraim *is* bound up; his
sin *is* hid.
13 The sorrows of a travailing woman shall
come upon him: he *is* an unwise son; for
he should not stay long in *the place of* the
breaking forth of children.
14 I will ransom them from the power of
the grave; I will redeem them from death:
O death, I will be thy plagues; O grave, I will
be thy destruction: repentance shall be hid
from mine eyes.
15 ¶ Though he be fruitful among *his* brethren, an east wind shall come, the wind of the
LORD shall come up from the wilderness, and
his spring shall become dry, and his fountain
shall be dried up: he shall spoil the treasure
of all pleasant vessels.
16 Samaria shall become desolate; for she
hath rebelled against her God: they shall fall
by the sword: their infants shall be dashed
in pieces, and their women with child shall
be ripped up.

Hosea 14

1 O Israel, return unto the LORD thy God; for
thou hast fallen by thine iniquity.
2 Take with you words, and turn to the
LORD: say unto him, Take away all iniquity,
and receive *us* graciously: so will we render
the calves of our lips.
3 Asshur shall not save us; we will not ride
upon horses: neither will we say any more
to the work of our hands, *Ye are* our gods:
for in thee the fatherless findeth mercy.
4 ¶ I will heal their backsliding, I will love
them freely: for mine anger is turned away
from him.
5 I will be as the dew unto Israel: he shall
grow as the lily, and cast forth his roots as
Lebanon.
6 His branches shall spread, and his beauty
shall be as the olive tree, and his smell as
Lebanon.
7 They that dwell under his shadow shall
return; they shall revive *as* the corn, and
grow as the vine: the scent thereof *shall be*
as the wine of Lebanon.
8 Ephraim *shall say*, What have I to do any

more with idols? I have heard *him*, and
observed him: I *am* like a green fir tree.
From me is thy fruit found.
9 Who *is* wise, and he shall understand these
things? prudent, and he shall know them?
for the ways of the LORD *are* right, and the
just shall walk in them: but the transgressors
shall fall therein.

The Book Of

Joel

Joel 1

1 The word of the LORD that came to Joel
the son of Pethuel.
2 Hear this, ye old men, and give ear, all
ye inhabitants of the land. Hath this been
in your days, or even in the days of your
fathers?
3 Tell ye your children of it, and *let* your
children *tell* their children, and their children
another generation.
4 That which the palmerworm hath left hath
the locust eaten; and that which the locust
hath left hath the cankerworm eaten; and
that which the cankerworm hath left hath
the caterpiller eaten.
5 Awake, ye drunkards, and weep; and howl,
all ye drinkers of wine, because of the new
wine; for it is cut off from your mouth.
6 For a nation is come up upon my land,
strong, and without number, whose teeth
are the teeth of a lion, and he hath the cheek
teeth of a great lion.
7 He hath laid my vine waste, and barked
my fig tree: he hath made it clean bare,
and cast *it* away; the branches thereof are
made white.
8 ¶ Lament like a virgin girded with sackcloth
for the husband of her youth.
9 The meat offering and the drink offering
is cut off from the house of the LORD; the
priests, the LORD's ministers, mourn.
10 The field is wasted, the land mourneth;
for the corn is wasted: the new wine is dried
up, the oil languisheth.
11 Be ye ashamed, O ye husbandmen; howl,
O ye vinedressers, for the wheat and for the
barley; because the harvest of the field is
perished.
12 The vine is dried up, and the fig tree languisheth; the pomegranate tree, the palm
tree also, and the apple tree, *even* all the
trees of the field, are withered: because
joy is withered away from the sons of men.
13 Gird yourselves, and lament, ye priests:
howl, ye ministers of the altar: come, lie all
night in sackcloth, ye ministers of my God:
for the meat offering and the drink offering
is withholden from the house of your God.
14 ¶ Sanctify ye a fast, call a solemn assembly, gather the elders *and* all the inhabitants
of the land *into* the house of the LORD your
God, and cry unto the LORD,
15 Alas for the day! for the day of the LORD
is at hand, and as a destruction from the
Almighty shall it come.
16 Is not the meat cut off before our eyes,
yea, joy and gladness from the house of
our God?
17 The seed is rotten under their clods, the
garners are laid desolate, the barns are broken down; for the corn is withered.
18 How do the beasts groan! the herds of
cattle are perplexed, because they have no
pasture; yea, the flocks of sheep are made
desolate.
19 O LORD, to thee will I cry: for the fire hath
devoured the pastures of the wilderness,
and the flame hath burned all the trees of
the field.
20 The beasts of the field cry also unto
thee: for the rivers of waters are dried up,
and the fire hath devoured the pastures of
the wilderness.

Joel 2

1 Blow ye the trumpet in Zion, and sound
an alarm in my holy mountain: let all the
inhabitants of the land tremble: for the day
of the LORD cometh, for *it is* nigh at hand;
2 A day of darkness and of gloominess, a

day of clouds and of thick darkness, as the morning spread upon the mountains: a great people and a strong; there hath not been ever the like, neither shall be any more after it, *even* to the years of many generations.

3 A fire devoureth before them; and behind them a flame burneth: the land *is* as the garden of Eden before them, and behind them a desolate wilderness; yea, and nothing shall escape them.

4 The appearance of them *is* as the appearance of horses; and as horsemen, so shall they run.

5 Like the noise of chariots on the tops of mountains shall they leap, like the noise of a flame of fire that devoureth the stubble, as a strong people set in battle array.

6 Before their face the people shall be much pained: all faces shall gather blackness.

7 They shall run like mighty men; they shall climb the wall like men of war; and they shall march every one on his ways, and they shall not break their ranks:

8 Neither shall one thrust another; they shall walk every one in his path: and *when* they fall upon the sword, they shall not be wounded.

9 They shall run to and fro in the city; they shall run upon the wall, they shall climb up upon the houses; they shall enter in at the windows like a thief.

10 The earth shall quake before them; the heavens shall tremble: the sun and the moon shall be dark, and the stars shall withdraw their shining:

11 And the LORD shall utter his voice before his army: for his camp *is* very great: for *he is* strong that executeth his word: for the day of the LORD *is* great and very terrible; and who can abide it?

12 ¶ Therefore also now, saith the LORD, turn ye *even* to me with all your heart, and with fasting, and with weeping, and with mourning:

13 And rend your heart, and not your garments, and turn unto the LORD your God: for he *is* gracious and merciful, slow to anger, and of great kindness, and repenteth him of the evil.

14 Who knoweth *if* he will return and repent, and leave a blessing behind him; *even* a meat offering and a drink offering unto the LORD your God?

15 ¶ Blow the trumpet in Zion, sanctify a fast, call a solemn assembly:

16 Gather the people, sanctify the congregation, assemble the elders, gather the children, and those that suck the breasts: let the bridegroom go forth of his chamber, and the bride out of her closet.

17 Let the priests, the ministers of the LORD, weep between the porch and the altar, and let them say, Spare thy people, O LORD, and give not thine heritage to reproach, that the heathen should rule over them: wherefore should they say among the people, Where *is* their God?

18 ¶ Then will the LORD be jealous for his land, and pity his people.

19 Yea, the LORD will answer and say unto his people, Behold, I will send you corn, and wine, and oil, and ye shall be satisfied therewith: and I will no more make you a reproach among the heathen:

20 But I will remove far off from you the northern *army*, and will drive him into a land barren and desolate, with his face toward the east sea, and his hinder part toward the utmost sea, and his stink shall come up, and his ill savour shall come up, because he hath done great things.

21 ¶ Fear not, O land; be glad and rejoice: for the LORD will do great things.

22 Be not afraid, ye beasts of the field: for the pastures of the wilderness do spring, for the tree beareth her fruit, the fig tree and the vine do yield their strength.

23 Be glad then, ye children of Zion, and rejoice in the LORD your God: for he hath given you the former rain moderately, and he will cause to come down for you the rain, the former rain, and the latter rain in the first *month*.

24 And the floors shall be full of wheat, and the fats shall overflow with wine and oil.

25 And I will restore to you the years that the locust hath eaten, the cankerworm, and the caterpiller, and the palmerworm, my great army which I sent among you.

26 And ye shall eat in plenty, and be satisfied, and praise the name of the LORD your God, that hath dealt wondrously with you: and my people shall never be ashamed.

27 And ye shall know that I *am* in the midst of Israel, and *that* I *am* the LORD your God,

and none else: and my people shall never
be ashamed.
28 ¶ And it shall come to pass afterward,
that I will pour out my spirit upon all flesh;
and your sons and your daughters shall
prophesy, your old men shall dream dreams,
your young men shall see visions:
29 And also upon the servants and upon
the handmaids in those days will I pour
out my spirit.
30 And I will shew wonders in the heavens
and in the earth, blood, and fire, and pillars
of smoke.
31 The sun shall be turned into darkness,
and the moon into blood, before the great
and the terrible day of the LORD come.
32 And it shall come to pass, *that* whosoever
shall call on the name of the LORD shall be
delivered: for in mount Zion and in Jerusalem shall be deliverance, as the LORD hath
said, and in the remnant whom the LORD
shall call.

Joel 3

1 For, behold, in those days, and in that
time, when I shall bring again the captivity
of Judah and Jerusalem,
2 I will also gather all nations, and will bring
them down into the valley of Jehoshaphat,
and will plead with them there for my people and *for* my heritage Israel, whom they
have scattered among the nations, and
parted my land.
3 And they have cast lots for my people; and
have given a boy for an harlot, and sold a
girl for wine, that they might drink.
4 Yea, and what have ye to do with me, O
Tyre, and Zidon, and all the coasts of Pales-
tine? will ye render me a recompence? and
if ye recompense me, swiftly *and* speedily
will I return your recompence upon your
own head;
5 Because ye have taken my silver and my
gold, and have carried into your temples my
goodly pleasant things:
6 The children also of Judah and the children of Jerusalem have ye sold unto the
Grecians, that ye might remove them far
from their border.
7 Behold, I will raise them out of the place
whither ye have sold them, and will return
your recompence upon your own head:
8 And I will sell your sons and your daughters into the hand of the children of Judah,
and they shall sell them to the Sabeans, to a
people far off: for the LORD hath spoken *it*.
9 ¶ Proclaim ye this among the Gentiles;
Prepare war, wake up the mighty men,
let all the men of war draw near; let them
come up:
10 Beat your plowshares into swords, and
your pruninghooks into spears: let the weak
say, I *am* strong.
11 Assemble yourselves, and come, all ye
heathen, and gather yourselves together
round about: thither cause thy mighty ones
to come down, O LORD.
12 Let the heathen be wakened, and come
up to the valley of Jehoshaphat: for there
will I sit to judge all the heathen round
about.
13 Put ye in the sickle, for the harvest is ripe:
come, get you down; for the press is full, the
fats overflow; for their wickedness *is* great.
14 Multitudes, multitudes in the valley of
decision: for the day of the LORD *is* near in
the valley of decision.
15 The sun and the moon shall be darkened,
and the stars shall withdraw their shining.
16 The LORD also shall roar out of Zion, and
utter his voice from Jerusalem; and the
heavens and the earth shall shake: but the
LORD *will be* the hope of his people, and the
strength of the children of Israel.
17 So shall ye know that I *am* the LORD your
God dwelling in Zion, my holy mountain:
then shall Jerusalem be holy, and there shall
no strangers pass through her any more.
18 ¶ And it shall come to pass in that day,
that the mountains shall drop down new
wine, and the hills shall flow with milk,
and all the rivers of Judah shall flow with
waters, and a fountain shall come forth of
the house of the LORD, and shall water the
valley of Shittim.
19 Egypt shall be a desolation, and Edom
shall be a desolate wilderness, for the violence *against* the children of Judah, because
they have shed innocent blood in their land.
20 But Judah shall dwell for ever, and Jerusalem from generation to generation.
21 For I will cleanse their blood *that* I have
not cleansed: for the LORD dwelleth in Zion.

The Book Of
Amos

Amos 1

1 The words of Amos, who was among the
herdmen of Tekoa, which he saw concerning
Israel in the days of Uzziah king of Judah,
and in the days of Jeroboam the son of
Joash king of Israel, two years before the
earthquake.
2 And he said, The LORD will roar from Zion,
and utter his voice from Jerusalem; and the
habitations of the shepherds shall mourn,
and the top of Carmel shall wither.
3 Thus saith the LORD; For three transgressions of Damascus, and for four, I will not
turn away *the punishment* thereof; because
they have threshed Gilead with threshing
instruments of iron:
4 But I will send a fire into the house of
Hazael, which shall devour the palaces of
Ben-hadad.
5 I will break also the bar of Damascus, and
cut off the inhabitant from the plain of Aven,
and him that holdeth the sceptre from the
house of Eden: and the people of Syria shall
go into captivity unto Kir, saith the LORD.
6 ¶ Thus saith the LORD; For three transgressions of Gaza, and for four, I will not turn
away *the punishment* thereof; because they
carried away captive the whole captivity, to
deliver *them* up to Edom:
7 But I will send a fire on the wall of Gaza,
which shall devour the palaces thereof:
8 And I will cut off the inhabitant from Ashdod, and him that holdeth the sceptre from
Ashkelon, and I will turn mine hand against
Ekron: and the remnant of the Philistines
shall perish, saith the Lord GOD.
9 ¶ Thus saith the LORD; For three transgressions of Tyrus, and for four, I will not
turn away *the punishment* thereof; because
they delivered up the whole captivity to
Edom, and remembered not the brotherly
covenant:
10 But I will send a fire on the wall of Tyrus,
which shall devour the palaces thereof.
11 ¶ Thus saith the LORD; For three transgressions of Edom, and for four, I will not
turn away *the punishment* thereof; because
he did pursue his brother with the sword,
and did cast off all pity, and his anger did
tear perpetually, and he kept his wrath
for ever:
12 But I will send a fire upon Teman, which
shall devour the palaces of Bozrah.
13 ¶ Thus saith the LORD; For three transgressions of the children of Ammon, and
for four, I will not turn away *the punishment*
thereof; because they have ripped up the
women with child of Gilead, that they might
enlarge their border:
14 But I will kindle a fire in the wall of Rabbah, and it shall devour the palaces thereof,
with shouting in the day of battle, with a
tempest in the day of the whirlwind:
15 And their king shall go into captivity, he
and his princes together, saith the LORD.

Amos 2

1 Thus saith the LORD; For three transgressions of Moab, and for four, I will not turn
away *the punishment* thereof; because
he burned the bones of the king of Edom
into lime:
2 But I will send a fire upon Moab, and it
shall devour the palaces of Kerioth: and
Moab shall die with tumult, with shouting,
and with the sound of the trumpet:
3 And I will cut off the judge from the midst
thereof, and will slay all the princes thereof
with him, saith the LORD.
4 ¶ Thus saith the LORD; For three transgressions of Judah, and for four, I will not turn
away *the punishment* thereof; because they
have despised the law of the LORD, and have
not kept his commandments, and their lies
caused them to err, after the which their
fathers have walked:
5 But I will send a fire upon Judah, and it
shall devour the palaces of Jerusalem.
6 ¶ Thus saith the LORD; For three transgressions of Israel, and for four, I will not turn
away *the punishment* thereof; because they
sold the righteous for silver, and the poor
for a pair of shoes;
7 That pant after the dust of the earth on

the head of the poor, and turn aside the
way of the meek: and a man and his father
will go in unto the *same* maid, to profane
my holy name:
8 And they lay *themselves* down upon
clothes laid to pledge by every altar, and
they drink the wine of the condemned *in*
the house of their god.
9 ¶ Yet destroyed I the Amorite before
them, whose height *was* like the height of
the cedars, and he *was* strong as the oaks;
yet I destroyed his fruit from above, and his
roots from beneath.
10 Also I brought you up from the land
of Egypt, and led you forty years through
the wilderness, to possess the land of the
Amorite.
11 And I raised up of your sons for prophets, and of your young men for Nazarites.
Is it not even thus, O ye children of Israel?
saith the LORD.
12 But ye gave the Nazarites wine to drink;
and commanded the prophets, saying,
Prophesy not.
13 Behold, I am pressed under you, as a cart
is pressed *that is* full of sheaves.
14 Therefore the flight shall perish from the
swift, and the strong shall not strengthen
his force, neither shall the mighty deliver
himself:
15 Neither shall he stand that handleth the
bow; and *he that is* swift of foot shall not
deliver *himself:* neither shall he that rideth
the horse deliver himself.
16 And *he that is* courageous among the
mighty shall flee away naked in that day,
saith the LORD.

Amos 3

1 Hear this word that the LORD hath spoken
against you, O children of Israel, against the
whole family which I brought up from the
land of Egypt, saying,
2 You only have I known of all the families
of the earth: therefore I will punish you for
all your iniquities.
3 Can two walk together, except they be
agreed?
4 Will a lion roar in the forest, when he hath
no prey? will a young lion cry out of his den,
if he have taken nothing?
5 Can a bird fall in a snare upon the earth,
where no gin *is* for him? shall *one* take up
a snare from the earth, and have taken
nothing at all?
6 Shall a trumpet be blown in the city, and
the people not be afraid? shall there be evil
in a city, and the LORD hath not done *it?*
7 Surely the Lord GOD will do nothing, but
he revealeth his secret unto his servants
the prophets.
8 The lion hath roared, who will not fear?
the Lord GOD hath spoken, who can but
prophesy?
9 ¶ Publish in the palaces at Ashdod, and
in the palaces in the land of Egypt, and say,
Assemble yourselves upon the mountains
of Samaria, and behold the great tumults
in the midst thereof, and the oppressed in
the midst thereof.
10 For they know not to do right, saith the
LORD, who store up violence and robbery
in their palaces.
11 Therefore thus saith the Lord GOD;
An adversary *there shall be* even round
about the land; and he shall bring down
thy strength from thee, and thy palaces
shall be spoiled.
12 Thus saith the LORD; As the shepherd
taketh out of the mouth of the lion two legs,
or a piece of an ear; so shall the children of
Israel be taken out that dwell in Samaria
in the corner of a bed, and in Damascus
in a couch.
13 Hear ye, and testify in the house of Jacob,
saith the Lord GOD, the God of hosts,
14 That in the day that I shall visit the transgressions of Israel upon him I will also visit
the altars of Beth-el: and the horns of the
altar shall be cut off, and fall to the ground.
15 And I will smite the winter house with
the summer house; and the houses of ivory
shall perish, and the great houses shall have
an end, saith the LORD.

Amos 4

1 Hear this word, ye kine of Bashan, that *are*
in the mountain of Samaria, which oppress
the poor, which crush the needy, which say
to their masters, Bring, and let us drink.
2 The Lord GOD hath sworn by his holiness,
that, lo, the days shall come upon you, that
he will take you away with hooks, and your
posterity with fishhooks.
3 And ye shall go out at the breaches, every

cow at that which is before her; and ye shall
cast *them* into the palace, saith the LORD.
4 ¶ Come to Beth-el, and transgress; at Gilgal multiply transgression; and bring your
sacrifices every morning, *and* your tithes
after three years:
5 And offer a sacrifice of thanksgiving with
leaven, and proclaim *and* publish the free
offerings: for this liketh you, O ye children
of Israel, saith the Lord GOD.
6 ¶ And I also have given you cleanness of
teeth in all your cities, and want of bread
in all your places: yet have ye not returned
unto me, saith the LORD.
7 And also I have withholden the rain from
you, when *there were* yet three months to
the harvest: and I caused it to rain upon one
city, and caused it not to rain upon another
city: one piece was rained upon, and the
piece whereupon it rained not withered.
8 So two *or* three cities wandered unto
one city, to drink water; but they were not
satisfied: yet have ye not returned unto me,
saith the LORD.
9 I have smitten you with blasting and
mildew: when your gardens and your vineyards and your fig trees and your olive trees
increased, the palmerworm devoured *them:*
yet have ye not returned unto me, saith
the LORD.
10 I have sent among you the pestilence
after the manner of Egypt: your young men
have I slain with the sword, and have taken
away your horses; and I have made the
stink of your camps to come up unto your
nostrils: yet have ye not returned unto me,
saith the LORD.
11 I have overthrown *some* of you, as God
overthrew Sodom and Gomorrah, and ye
were as a firebrand plucked out of the
burning: yet have ye not returned unto me,
saith the LORD.
12 Therefore thus will I do unto thee, O
Israel: *and* because I will do this unto thee,
prepare to meet thy God, O Israel.
13 For, lo, he that formeth the mountains,
and createth the wind, and declareth unto
man what *is* his thought, that maketh the
morning darkness, and treadeth upon the
high places of the earth, The LORD, The God
of hosts, *is* his name.

Amos 5

1 Hear ye this word which I take up against
you, *even* a lamentation, O house of Israel.
2 The virgin of Israel is fallen; she shall no
more rise: she is forsaken upon her land;
there is none to raise her up.
3 For thus saith the Lord GOD; The city that
went out *by* a thousand shall leave an hundred, and that which went forth *by* an hundred shall leave ten, to the house of Israel.
4 ¶ For thus saith the LORD unto the house
of Israel, Seek ye me, and ye shall live:
5 But seek not Beth-el, nor enter into Gilgal,
and pass not to Beer-sheba: for Gilgal shall
surely go into captivity, and Beth-el shall
come to nought.
6 Seek the LORD, and ye shall live; lest he
break out like fire in the house of Joseph,
and devour *it*, and *there be* none to quench
it in Beth-el.
7 Ye who turn judgment to wormwood, and
leave off righteousness in the earth,
8 *Seek him* that maketh the seven stars and
Orion, and turneth the shadow of death into
the morning, and maketh the day dark with
night: that calleth for the waters of the sea,
and poureth them out upon the face of the
earth: The LORD *is* his name:
9 That strengtheneth the spoiled against
the strong, so that the spoiled shall come
against the fortress.
10 They hate him that rebuketh in the gate,
and they abhor him that speaketh uprightly.
11 Forasmuch therefore as your treading
is upon the poor, and ye take from him
burdens of wheat: ye have built houses of
hewn stone, but ye shall not dwell in them;
ye have planted pleasant vineyards, but ye
shall not drink wine of them.
12 For I know your manifold transgressions
and your mighty sins: they afflict the just,
they take a bribe, and they turn aside the
poor in the gate *from their right.*
13 Therefore the prudent shall keep silence
in that time; for it *is* an evil time.
14 Seek good, and not evil, that ye may live:
and so the LORD, the God of hosts, shall be
with you, as ye have spoken.
15 Hate the evil, and love the good, and
establish judgment in the gate: it may be
that the LORD God of hosts will be gracious
unto the remnant of Joseph.
16 Therefore the LORD, the God of hosts,

the Lord, saith thus; Wailing *shall be* in all
streets; and they shall say in all the highways, Alas! alas! and they shall call the
husbandman to mourning, and such as are
skilful of lamentation to wailing.
17 And in all vineyards *shall be* wailing: for
I will pass through thee, saith the LORD.
18 Woe unto you that desire the day of the
LORD! to what end *is* it for you? the day of
the LORD *is* darkness, and not light.
19 As if a man did flee from a lion, and a bear
met him; or went into the house, and leaned
his hand on the wall, and a serpent bit him.
20 *Shall* not the day of the LORD *be* darkness, and not light? even very dark, and no
brightness in it?
21 ¶ I hate, I despise your feast days, and
I will not smell in your solemn assemblies.
22 Though ye offer me burnt offerings and
your meat offerings, I will not accept *them:*
neither will I regard the peace offerings of
your fat beasts.
23 Take thou away from me the noise of
thy songs; for I will not hear the melody
of thy viols.
24 But let judgment run down as waters, and
righteousness as a mighty stream.
25 Have ye offered unto me sacrifices and
offerings in the wilderness forty years, O
house of Israel?
26 But ye have borne the tabernacle of your
Moloch and Chiun your images, the star of
your god, which ye made to yourselves.
27 Therefore will I cause you to go into
captivity beyond Damascus, saith the LORD,
whose name *is* The God of hosts.

Amos 6

1 Woe to them *that are* at ease in Zion, and
trust in the mountain of Samaria, *which are*
named chief of the nations, to whom the
house of Israel came!
2 Pass ye unto Calneh, and see; and from
thence go ye to Hamath the great: then go
down to Gath of the Philistines: *be they*
better than these kingdoms? or their border
greater than your border?
3 Ye that put far away the evil day, and cause
the seat of violence to come near;
4 That lie upon beds of ivory, and stretch
themselves upon their couches, and eat the
lambs out of the flock, and the calves out
of the midst of the stall;
5 That chant to the sound of the viol, *and*
invent to themselves instruments of musick,
like David;
6 That drink wine in bowls, and anoint themselves with the chief ointments: but they
are not grieved for the affliction of Joseph.
7 ¶ Therefore now shall they go captive with
the first that go captive, and the banquet
of them that stretched themselves shall
be removed.
8 The Lord GOD hath sworn by himself,
saith the LORD the God of hosts, I abhor the
excellency of Jacob, and hate his palaces:
therefore will I deliver up the city with all
that is therein.
9 And it shall come to pass, if there remain
ten men in one house, that they shall die.
10 And a man's uncle shall take him up, and
he that burneth him, to bring out the bones
out of the house, and shall say unto him that
is by the sides of the house, *Is there* yet *any*
with thee? and he shall say, No. Then shall he
say, Hold thy tongue: for we may not make
mention of the name of the LORD.
11 For, behold, the LORD commandeth, and
he will smite the great house with breaches,
and the little house with clefts.
12 ¶ Shall horses run upon the rock? will
one plow *there* with oxen? for ye have
turned judgment into gall, and the fruit of
righteousness into hemlock:
13 Ye which rejoice in a thing of nought,
which say, Have we not taken to us horns
by our own strength?
14 But, behold, I will raise up against you
a nation, O house of Israel, saith the LORD
the God of hosts; and they shall afflict you
from the entering in of Hemath unto the
river of the wilderness.

Amos 7

1 Thus hath the Lord GOD shewed unto me;
and, behold, he formed grasshoppers in the
beginning of the shooting up of the latter
growth; and, lo, *it was* the latter growth
after the king's mowings.
2 And it came to pass, *that* when they had
made an end of eating the grass of the land,
then I said, O Lord GOD, forgive, I beseech
thee: by whom shall Jacob arise? for he *is*
small.
3 The LORD repented for this: It shall not be,
saith the LORD.

4 ¶ Thus hath the Lord GOD shewed unto me: and, behold, the Lord GOD called to contend by fire, and it devoured the great deep, and did eat up a part.
5 Then said I, O Lord GOD, cease, I beseech thee: by whom shall Jacob arise? for he *is* small.
6 The LORD repented for this: This also shall not be, saith the Lord GOD.
7 ¶ Thus he shewed me: and, behold, the Lord stood upon a wall *made* by a plumbline, with a plumbline in his hand.
8 And the LORD said unto me, Amos, what seest thou? And I said, A plumbline. Then said the Lord, Behold, I will set a plumbline in the midst of my people Israel: I will not again pass by them any more:
9 And the high places of Isaac shall be desolate, and the sanctuaries of Israel shall be laid waste; and I will rise against the house of Jeroboam with the sword.
10 ¶ Then Amaziah the priest of Beth-el sent to Jeroboam king of Israel, saying, Amos hath conspired against thee in the midst of the house of Israel: the land is not able to bear all his words.
11 For thus Amos saith, Jeroboam shall die by the sword, and Israel shall surely be led away captive out of their own land.
12 Also Amaziah said unto Amos, O thou seer, go, flee thee away into the land of Judah, and there eat bread, and prophesy there:
13 But prophesy not again any more at Beth-el: for it *is* the king's chapel, and it *is* the king's court.
14 ¶ Then answered Amos, and said to Amaziah, I *was* no prophet, neither *was* I a prophet's son; but I *was* an herdman, and a gatherer of sycomore fruit:
15 And the LORD took me as I followed the flock, and the LORD said unto me, Go, prophesy unto my people Israel.
16 ¶ Now therefore hear thou the word of the LORD: Thou sayest, Prophesy not against Israel, and drop not *thy word* against the house of Isaac.
17 Therefore thus saith the LORD; Thy wife shall be an harlot in the city, and thy sons and thy daughters shall fall by the sword, and thy land shall be divided by line; and thou shalt die in a polluted land: and Israel shall surely go into captivity forth of his land.

Amos 8

1 Thus hath the Lord GOD shewed unto me: and behold a basket of summer fruit.
2 And he said, Amos, what seest thou? And I said, A basket of summer fruit. Then said the LORD unto me, The end is come upon my people of Israel; I will not again pass by them any more.
3 And the songs of the temple shall be howlings in that day, saith the Lord GOD: *there shall be* many dead bodies in every place; they shall cast *them* forth with silence.
4 ¶ Hear this, O ye that swallow up the needy, even to make the poor of the land to fail,
5 Saying, When will the new moon be gone, that we may sell corn? and the sabbath, that we may set forth wheat, making the ephah small, and the shekel great, and falsifying the balances by deceit?
6 That we may buy the poor for silver, and the needy for a pair of shoes; *yea*, and sell the refuse of the wheat?
7 The LORD hath sworn by the excellency of Jacob, Surely I will never forget any of their works.
8 Shall not the land tremble for this, and every one mourn that dwelleth therein? and it shall rise up wholly as a flood; and it shall be cast out and drowned, as *by* the flood of Egypt.
9 And it shall come to pass in that day, saith the Lord GOD, that I will cause the sun to go down at noon, and I will darken the earth in the clear day:
10 And I will turn your feasts into mourning, and all your songs into lamentation; and I will bring up sackcloth upon all loins, and baldness upon every head; and I will make it as the mourning of an only *son*, and the end thereof as a bitter day.
11 ¶ Behold, the days come, saith the Lord GOD, that I will send a famine in the land, not a famine of bread, nor a thirst for water, but of hearing the words of the LORD:
12 And they shall wander from sea to sea, and from the north even to the east, they shall run to and fro to seek the word of the LORD, and shall not find *it*.
13 In that day shall the fair virgins and young men faint for thirst.
14 They that swear by the sin of Samaria, and say, Thy god, O Dan, liveth; and, The

manner of Beer-sheba liveth; even they shall
fall, and never rise up again.

Amos 9

1 I saw the Lord standing upon the altar: and
he said, Smite the lintel of the door, that the
posts may shake: and cut them in the head,
all of them; and I will slay the last of them
with the sword: he that fleeth of them shall
not flee away, and he that escapeth of them
shall not be delivered.
2 Though they dig into hell, thence shall
mine hand take them; though they climb up
to heaven, thence will I bring them down:
3 And though they hide themselves in the
top of Carmel, I will search and take them
out thence; and though they be hid from
my sight in the bottom of the sea, thence
will I command the serpent, and he shall
bite them:
4 And though they go into captivity before
their enemies, thence will I command the
sword, and it shall slay them: and I will set
mine eyes upon them for evil, and not for
good.
5 And the Lord GOD of hosts *is* he that
toucheth the land, and it shall melt, and
all that dwell therein shall mourn: and it
shall rise up wholly like a flood; and shall be
drowned, as *by* the flood of Egypt.
6 *It is* he that buildeth his stories in the
heaven, and hath founded his troop in the
earth; he that calleth for the waters of the
sea, and poureth them out upon the face
of the earth: The LORD *is* his name.
7 *Are* ye not as children of the Ethiopians
unto me, O children of Israel? saith the LORD.
Have not I brought up Israel out of the land
of Egypt? and the Philistines from Caphtor,
and the Syrians from Kir?
8 Behold, the eyes of the Lord GOD *are*
upon the sinful kingdom, and I will destroy
it from off the face of the earth; saving that
I will not utterly destroy the house of Jacob,
saith the LORD.
9 For, lo, I will command, and I will sift the
house of Israel among all nations, like as
corn is sifted in a sieve, yet shall not the
least grain fall upon the earth.
10 All the sinners of my people shall die
by the sword, which say, The evil shall not
overtake nor prevent us.
11 ¶ In that day will I raise up the tabernacle of David that is fallen, and close up the
breaches thereof; and I will raise up his
ruins, and I will build it as in the days of old:
12 That they may possess the remnant of
Edom, and of all the heathen, which are
called by my name, saith the LORD that
doeth this.
13 Behold, the days come, saith the LORD,
that the plowman shall overtake the reaper,
and the treader of grapes him that soweth
seed; and the mountains shall drop sweet
wine, and all the hills shall melt.
14 And I will bring again the captivity of my
people of Israel, and they shall build the
waste cities, and inhabit *them;* and they
shall plant vineyards, and drink the wine
thereof; they shall also make gardens, and
eat the fruit of them.
15 And I will plant them upon their land,
and they shall no more be pulled up out of
their land which I have given them, saith
the LORD thy God.

The Book Of

Obadiah

Obadiah 1

1 The vision of Obadiah. Thus saith the Lord
GOD concerning Edom; We have heard a
rumour from the LORD, and an ambassador
is sent among the heathen, Arise ye, and let
us rise up against her in battle.
2 Behold, I have made thee small among the
heathen: thou art greatly despised.
3 ¶ The pride of thine heart hath deceived
thee, thou that dwellest in the clefts of the
rock, whose habitation *is* high; that saith

in his heart, Who shall bring me down to
the ground?
4 Though thou exalt *thyself* as the eagle, and
though thou set thy nest among the stars,
thence will I bring thee down, saith the LORD.
5 If thieves came to thee, if robbers by
night, (how art thou cut off!) would they
not have stolen till they had enough? if the
grapegatherers came to thee, would they
not leave *some* grapes?
6 How are *the things* of Esau searched out!
how are his hidden things sought up!
7 All the men of thy confederacy have
brought thee *even* to the border: the men
that were at peace with thee have deceived
thee, *and* prevailed against thee; *they that*
eat thy bread have laid a wound under thee:
there is none understanding in him.
8 Shall I not in that day, saith the LORD, even
destroy the wise *men* out of Edom, and
understanding out of the mount of Esau?
9 And thy mighty *men*, O Teman, shall be
dismayed, to the end that every one of the
mount of Esau may be cut off by slaughter.
10 ¶ For *thy* violence against thy brother
Jacob shame shall cover thee, and thou shalt
be cut off for ever.
11 In the day that thou stoodest on the
other side, in the day that the strangers carried away captive his forces, and foreigners
entered into his gates, and cast lots upon
Jerusalem, even thou *wast* as one of them.
12 But thou shouldest not have looked on
the day of thy brother in the day that he
became a stranger; neither shouldest thou
have rejoiced over the children of Judah in
the day of their destruction; neither shouldest thou have spoken proudly in the day
of distress.
13 Thou shouldest not have entered into the
gate of my people in the day of their calamity; yea, thou shouldest not have looked on
their affliction in the day of their calamity,
nor have laid *hands* on their substance in
the day of their calamity;
14 Neither shouldest thou have stood in
the crossway, to cut off those of his that
did escape; neither shouldest thou have
delivered up those of his that did remain
in the day of distress.
15 For the day of the LORD *is* near upon all
the heathen: as thou hast done, it shall be
done unto thee: thy reward shall return
upon thine own head.
16 For as ye have drunk upon my holy
mountain, *so* shall all the heathen drink
continually, yea, they shall drink, and they
shall swallow down, and they shall be as
though they had not been.
17 ¶ But upon mount Zion shall be deliverance, and there shall be holiness; and
the house of Jacob shall possess their
possessions.
18 And the house of Jacob shall be a fire, and
the house of Joseph a flame, and the house
of Esau for stubble, and they shall kindle in
them, and devour them; and there shall not
be *any* remaining of the house of Esau; for
the LORD hath spoken *it*.
19 And *they of* the south shall possess the
mount of Esau; and *they of* the plain the
Philistines: and they shall possess the fields
of Ephraim, and the fields of Samaria: and
Benjamin *shall possess* Gilead.
20 And the captivity of this host of the
children of Israel *shall possess* that of the
Canaanites, *even* unto Zarephath; and the
captivity of Jerusalem, which *is* in Sepharad,
shall possess the cities of the south.
21 And saviours shall come up on mount
Zion to judge the mount of Esau; and the
kingdom shall be the LORD's.

The Book Of

Jonah

Jonah 1

1 Now the word of the LORD came unto
Jonah the son of Amittai, saying,
2 Arise, go to Nineveh, that great city, and
cry against it; for their wickedness is come
up before me.

3 But Jonah rose up to flee unto Tarshish
from the presence of the LORD, and went
down to Joppa; and he found a ship going
to Tarshish: so he paid the fare thereof, and
went down into it, to go with them unto
Tarshish from the presence of the LORD.
4 ¶ But the LORD sent out a great wind into
the sea, and there was a mighty tempest
in the sea, so that the ship was like to be
broken.
5 Then the mariners were afraid, and cried
every man unto his god, and cast forth the
wares that *were* in the ship into the sea,
to lighten *it* of them. But Jonah was gone
down into the sides of the ship; and he lay,
and was fast asleep.
6 So the shipmaster came to him, and said
unto him, What meanest thou, O sleeper?
arise, call upon thy God, if so be that God
will think upon us, that we perish not.
7 And they said every one to his fellow,
Come, and let us cast lots, that we may
know for whose cause this evil *is* upon us.
So they cast lots, and the lot fell upon Jonah.
8 Then said they unto him, Tell us, we pray
thee, for whose cause this evil *is* upon us;
What *is* thine occupation? and whence
comest thou? what *is* thy country? and of
what people *art* thou?
9 And he said unto them, I *am* an Hebrew;
and I fear the LORD, the God of heaven,
which hath made the sea and the dry *land*.
10 Then were the men exceedingly afraid,
and said unto him, Why hast thou done
this? For the men knew that he fled from
the presence of the LORD, because he had
told them.
11 ¶ Then said they unto him, What shall
we do unto thee, that the sea may be calm
unto us? for the sea wrought, and was
tempestuous.
12 And he said unto them, Take me up, and
cast me forth into the sea; so shall the sea be
calm unto you: for I know that for my sake
this great tempest *is* upon you.
13 Nevertheless the men rowed hard to
bring *it* to the land; but they could not: for
the sea wrought, and was tempestuous
against them.
14 Wherefore they cried unto the LORD, and
said, We beseech thee, O LORD, we beseech
thee, let us not perish for this man's life, and
lay not upon us innocent blood: for thou, O
LORD, hast done as it pleased thee.
15 So they took up Jonah, and cast him
forth into the sea: and the sea ceased from
her raging.
16 Then the men feared the LORD exceedingly, and offered a sacrifice unto the LORD,
and made vows.
17 ¶ Now the LORD had prepared a great fish
to swallow up Jonah. And Jonah was in the
belly of the fish three days and three nights.

Jonah 2

1 Then Jonah prayed unto the LORD his God
out of the fish's belly,
2 And said, I cried by reason of mine affliction unto the LORD, and he heard me; out of
the belly of hell cried I, *and* thou heardest
my voice.
3 For thou hadst cast me into the deep, in
the midst of the seas; and the floods compassed me about: all thy billows and thy
waves passed over me.
4 Then I said, I am cast out of thy sight; yet
I will look again toward thy holy temple.
5 The waters compassed me about, *even* to
the soul: the depth closed me round about,
the weeds were wrapped about my head.
6 I went down to the bottoms of the mountains; the earth with her bars *was* about me
for ever: yet hast thou brought up my life
from corruption, O LORD my God.
7 When my soul fainted within me I remembered the LORD: and my prayer came in unto
thee, into thine holy temple.
8 They that observe lying vanities forsake
their own mercy.
9 But I will sacrifice unto thee with the voice
of thanksgiving; I will pay *that* that I have
vowed. Salvation *is* of the LORD.
10 ¶ And the LORD spake unto the fish, and
it vomited out Jonah upon the dry *land*.

Jonah 3

1 And the word of the LORD came unto
Jonah the second time, saying,
2 Arise, go unto Nineveh, that great city, and
preach unto it the preaching that I bid thee.
3 So Jonah arose, and went unto Nineveh,
according to the word of the LORD. Now
Nineveh was an exceeding great city of
three days' journey.
4 And Jonah began to enter into the city

a day's journey, and he cried, and said,
Yet forty days, and Nineveh shall be overthrown.
5 ¶ So the people of Nineveh believed God,
and proclaimed a fast, and put on sackcloth,
from the greatest of them even to the least
of them.
6 For word came unto the king of Nineveh,
and he arose from his throne, and he laid
his robe from him, and covered *him* with
sackcloth, and sat in ashes.
7 And he caused *it* to be proclaimed and
published through Nineveh by the decree of
the king and his nobles, saying, Let neither
man nor beast, herd nor flock, taste any
thing: let them not feed, nor drink water:
8 But let man and beast be covered with
sackcloth, and cry mightily unto God: yea,
let them turn every one from his evil way,
and from the violence that *is* in their hands.
9 Who can tell *if* God will turn and repent,
and turn away from his fierce anger, that
we perish not?
10 ¶ And God saw their works, that they
turned from their evil way; and God
repented of the evil, that he had said that
he would do unto them; and he did *it* not.

Jonah 4

1 But it displeased Jonah exceedingly, and
he was very angry.
2 And he prayed unto the LORD, and said, I
pray thee, O LORD, *was* not this my saying,
when I was yet in my country? Therefore I
fled before unto Tarshish: for I knew that
thou *art* a gracious God, and merciful,
slow to anger, and of great kindness, and
repentest thee of the evil.
3 Therefore now, O LORD, take, I beseech
thee, my life from me; for *it is* better for me
to die than to live.
4 ¶ Then said the LORD, Doest thou well to
be angry?
5 So Jonah went out of the city, and sat on
the east side of the city, and there made him
a booth, and sat under it in the shadow, till
he might see what would become of the city.
6 And the LORD God prepared a gourd, and
made *it* to come up over Jonah, that it might
be a shadow over his head, to deliver him
from his grief. So Jonah was exceeding glad
of the gourd.
7 But God prepared a worm when the
morning rose the next day, and it smote
the gourd that it withered.
8 And it came to pass, when the sun did
arise, that God prepared a vehement east
wind; and the sun beat upon the head of
Jonah, that he fainted, and wished in himself to die, and said, *It is* better for me to
die than to live.
9 And God said to Jonah, Doest thou well
to be angry for the gourd? And he said, I do
well to be angry, *even* unto death.
10 Then said the LORD, Thou hast had pity
on the gourd, for the which thou hast not
laboured, neither madest it grow; which
came up in a night, and perished in a night:
11 And should not I spare Nineveh, that
great city, wherein are more than sixscore
thousand persons that cannot discern
between their right hand and their left hand;
and *also* much cattle?

The Book Of

Micah

Micah 1

1 The word of the LORD that came to Micah
the Morasthite in the days of Jotham, Ahaz,
and Hezekiah, kings of Judah, which he saw
concerning Samaria and Jerusalem.
2 Hear, all ye people; hearken, O earth, and
all that therein is: and let the Lord GOD be
witness against you, the Lord from his holy
temple.
3 For, behold, the LORD cometh forth out
of his place, and will come down, and tread
upon the high places of the earth.
4 And the mountains shall be molten under
him, and the valleys shall be cleft, as wax

before the fire, *and* as the waters *that are*
poured down a steep place.
5 For the transgression of Jacob *is* all this,
and for the sins of the house of Israel.
What *is* the transgression of Jacob? *is it* not
Samaria? and what *are* the high places of
Judah? *are they* not Jerusalem?
6 Therefore I will make Samaria as an heap
of the field, *and* as plantings of a vineyard:
and I will pour down the stones thereof
into the valley, and I will discover the foundations thereof.
7 And all the graven images thereof shall be
beaten to pieces, and all the hires thereof
shall be burned with the fire, and all the idols
thereof will I lay desolate: for she gathered *it*
of the hire of an harlot, and they shall return
to the hire of an harlot.
8 Therefore I will wail and howl, I will go
stripped and naked: I will make a wailing
like the dragons, and mourning as the owls.
9 For her wound *is* incurable; for it is come
unto Judah; he is come unto the gate of my
people, *even* to Jerusalem.
10 ¶ Declare ye *it* not at Gath, weep ye not
at all: in the house of Aphrah roll thyself
in the dust.
11 Pass ye away, thou inhabitant of Saphir,
having thy shame naked: the inhabitant of
Zaanan came not forth in the mourning
of Beth-ezel; he shall receive of you his
standing.
12 For the inhabitant of Maroth waited carefully for good: but evil came down from the
LORD unto the gate of Jerusalem.
13 O thou inhabitant of Lachish, bind the
chariot to the swift beast: she *is* the beginning of the sin to the daughter of Zion: for
the transgressions of Israel were found in
thee.
14 Therefore shalt thou give presents to
Moresheth-gath: the houses of Achzib *shall*
be a lie to the kings of Israel.
15 Yet will I bring an heir unto thee, O
inhabitant of Mareshah: he shall come unto
Adullam the glory of Israel.
16 Make thee bald, and poll thee for thy
delicate children; enlarge thy baldness as
the eagle; for they are gone into captivity
from thee.

Micah 2

1 Woe to them that devise iniquity, and
work evil upon their beds! when the morning is light, they practise it, because it is in
the power of their hand.
2 And they covet fields, and take *them* by
violence; and houses, and take *them* away:
so they oppress a man and his house, even
a man and his heritage.
3 Therefore thus saith the LORD; Behold,
against this family do I devise an evil, from
which ye shall not remove your necks; neither shall ye go haughtily: for this time *is* evil.
4 ¶ In that day shall *one* take up a parable
against you, and lament with a doleful lamentation, *and* say, We be utterly spoiled: he
hath changed the portion of my people: how
hath he removed *it* from me! turning away
he hath divided our fields.
5 Therefore thou shalt have none that shall
cast a cord by lot in the congregation of
the LORD.
6 Prophesy ye not, *say they to them that*
prophesy: they shall not prophesy to them,
that they shall not take shame.
7 ¶ O *thou that art* named the house of
Jacob, is the spirit of the LORD straitened?
are these his doings? do not my words do
good to him that walketh uprightly?
8 Even of late my people is risen up as an
enemy: ye pull off the robe with the garment
from them that pass by securely as men
averse from war.
9 The women of my people have ye cast out
from their pleasant houses; from their children have ye taken away my glory for ever.
10 Arise ye, and depart; for this *is* not *your*
rest: because it is polluted, it shall destroy
you, even with a sore destruction.
11 If a man walking in the spirit and falsehood do lie, *saying*, I will prophesy unto thee
of wine and of strong drink; he shall even
be the prophet of this people.
12 ¶ I will surely assemble, O Jacob, all of
thee; I will surely gather the remnant of
Israel; I will put them together as the sheep
of Bozrah, as the flock in the midst of their
fold: they shall make great noise by reason
of *the multitude of* men.
13 The breaker is come up before them: they
have broken up, and have passed through
the gate, and are gone out by it: and their
king shall pass before them, and the LORD
on the head of them.

Micah 3

1 And I said, Hear, I pray you, O heads of
Jacob, and ye princes of the house of Israel;
Is it not for you to know judgment?
2 Who hate the good, and love the evil; who
pluck off their skin from off them, and their
flesh from off their bones;
3 Who also eat the flesh of my people, and
flay their skin from off them; and they break
their bones, and chop them in pieces, as
for the pot, and as flesh within the caldron.
4 Then shall they cry unto the LORD, but
he will not hear them: he will even hide his
face from them at that time, as they have
behaved themselves ill in their doings.
5 ¶ Thus saith the LORD concerning the
prophets that make my people err, that
bite with their teeth, and cry, Peace; and
he that putteth not into their mouths, they
even prepare war against him.
6 Therefore night *shall be* unto you, that ye
shall not have a vision; and it shall be dark
unto you, that ye shall not divine; and the
sun shall go down over the prophets, and
the day shall be dark over them.
7 Then shall the seers be ashamed, and the
diviners confounded: yea, they shall all cover
their lips; for *there is* no answer of God.
8 ¶ But truly I am full of power by the spirit
of the LORD, and of judgment, and of might,
to declare unto Jacob his transgression, and
to Israel his sin.
9 Hear this, I pray you, ye heads of the house
of Jacob, and princes of the house of Israel,
that abhor judgment, and pervert all equity.
10 They build up Zion with blood, and Jerusalem with iniquity.
11 The heads thereof judge for reward,
and the priests thereof teach for hire, and
the prophets thereof divine for money:
yet will they lean upon the LORD, and say,
Is not the LORD among us? none evil can
come upon us.
12 Therefore shall Zion for your sake be
plowed *as* a field, and Jerusalem shall
become heaps, and the mountain of the
house as the high places of the forest.

Micah 4

1 But in the last days it shall come to pass,
that the mountain of the house of the LORD
shall be established in the top of the mountains, and it shall be exalted above the hills;
and people shall flow unto it.
2 And many nations shall come, and say,
Come, and let us go up to the mountain of
the LORD, and to the house of the God of
Jacob; and he will teach us of his ways, and
we will walk in his paths: for the law shall
go forth of Zion, and the word of the LORD
from Jerusalem.
3 ¶ And he shall judge among many people,
and rebuke strong nations afar off; and they
shall beat their swords into plowshares, and
their spears into pruninghooks: nation shall
not lift up a sword against nation, neither
shall they learn war any more.
4 But they shall sit every man under his vine
and under his fig tree; and none shall make
them afraid: for the mouth of the LORD of
hosts hath spoken *it*.
5 For all people will walk every one in the
name of his god, and we will walk in the
name of the LORD our God for ever and ever.
6 In that day, saith the LORD, will I assemble
her that halteth, and I will gather her that
is driven out, and her that I have afflicted;
7 And I will make her that halted a remnant,
and her that was cast far off a strong nation:
and the LORD shall reign over them in mount
Zion from henceforth, even for ever.
8 ¶ And thou, O tower of the flock, the
strong hold of the daughter of Zion, unto
thee shall it come, even the first dominion;
the kingdom shall come to the daughter of
Jerusalem.
9 Now why dost thou cry out aloud? *is there*
no king in thee? is thy counseller perished?
for pangs have taken thee as a woman in
travail.
10 Be in pain, and labour to bring forth, O
daughter of Zion, like a woman in travail:
for now shalt thou go forth out of the city,
and thou shalt dwell in the field, and thou
shalt go *even* to Babylon; there shalt thou
be delivered; there the LORD shall redeem
thee from the hand of thine enemies.
11 ¶ Now also many nations are gathered
against thee, that say, Let her be defiled,
and let our eye look upon Zion.
12 But they know not the thoughts of the
LORD, neither understand they his counsel:
for he shall gather them as the sheaves into
the floor.
13 Arise and thresh, O daughter of Zion: for I

will make thine horn iron, and I will make thy
hoofs brass: and thou shalt beat in pieces
many people: and I will consecrate their gain
unto the LORD, and their substance unto the
Lord of the whole earth.

Micah 5

1 Now gather thyself in troops, O daughter
of troops: he hath laid siege against us: they
shall smite the judge of Israel with a rod
upon the cheek.
2 But thou, Beth-lehem Ephratah, *though*
thou be little among the thousands of
Judah, *yet* out of thee shall he come forth
unto me *that is* to be ruler in Israel; whose
goings forth *have been* from of old, from
everlasting.
3 Therefore will he give them up, until the
time *that* she which travaileth hath brought
forth: then the remnant of his brethren shall
return unto the children of Israel.
4 ¶ And he shall stand and feed in the
strength of the LORD, in the majesty of the
name of the LORD his God; and they shall
abide: for now shall he be great unto the
ends of the earth.
5 And this *man* shall be the peace, when
the Assyrian shall come into our land: and
when he shall tread in our palaces, then shall
we raise against him seven shepherds, and
eight principal men.
6 And they shall waste the land of Assyria
with the sword, and the land of Nimrod in
the entrances thereof: thus shall he deliver
us from the Assyrian, when he cometh into
our land, and when he treadeth within our
borders.
7 And the remnant of Jacob shall be in the
midst of many people as a dew from the
LORD, as the showers upon the grass, that
tarrieth not for man, nor waiteth for the
sons of men.
8 ¶ And the remnant of Jacob shall be
among the Gentiles in the midst of many
people as a lion among the beasts of the
forest, as a young lion among the flocks of
sheep: who, if he go through, both treadeth
down, and teareth in pieces, and none can
deliver.
9 Thine hand shall be lifted up upon thine
adversaries, and all thine enemies shall be
cut off.
10 And it shall come to pass in that day,
saith the LORD, that I will cut off thy horses
out of the midst of thee, and I will destroy
thy chariots:
11 And I will cut off the cities of thy land, and
throw down all thy strong holds:
12 And I will cut off witchcrafts out of
thine hand; and thou shalt have no *more*
soothsayers:
13 Thy graven images also will I cut off, and
thy standing images out of the midst of thee;
and thou shalt no more worship the work
of thine hands.
14 And I will pluck up thy groves out of the
midst of thee: so will I destroy thy cities.
15 And I will execute vengeance in anger
and fury upon the heathen, such as they
have not heard.

Micah 6

1 Hear ye now what the LORD saith; Arise,
contend thou before the mountains, and
let the hills hear thy voice.
2 Hear ye, O mountains, the LORD's controversy, and ye strong foundations of the
earth: for the LORD hath a controversy with
his people, and he will plead with Israel.
3 O my people, what have I done unto thee?
and wherein have I wearied thee? testify
against me.
4 For I brought thee up out of the land of
Egypt, and redeemed thee out of the house
of servants; and I sent before thee Moses,
Aaron, and Miriam.
5 O my people, remember now what Balak
king of Moab consulted, and what Balaam
the son of Beor answered him from Shittim
unto Gilgal; that ye may know the righteousness of the LORD.
6 ¶ Wherewith shall I come before the LORD,
and bow myself before the high God? shall I
come before him with burnt offerings, with
calves of a year old?
7 Will the LORD be pleased with thousands
of rams, *or* with ten thousands of rivers of
oil? shall I give my firstborn *for* my transgression, the fruit of my body *for* the sin
of my soul?
8 He hath shewed thee, O man, what *is*
good; and what doth the LORD require of
thee, but to do justly, and to love mercy,
and to walk humbly with thy God?
9 The LORD's voice crieth unto the city, and

the man of wisdom shall see thy name: hear
ye the rod, and who hath appointed it.
10 ¶ Are there yet the treasures of wickedness in the house of the wicked, and the
scant measure *that is* abominable?
11 Shall I count *them* pure with the wicked
balances, and with the bag of deceitful
weights?
12 For the rich men thereof are full of violence, and the inhabitants thereof have
spoken lies, and their tongue *is* deceitful
in their mouth.
13 Therefore also will I make *thee* sick
in smiting thee, in making *thee* desolate
because of thy sins.
14 Thou shalt eat, but not be satisfied; and
thy casting down *shall be* in the midst of
thee; and thou shalt take hold, but shalt
not deliver; and *that* which thou deliverest
will I give up to the sword.
15 Thou shalt sow, but thou shalt not reap;
thou shalt tread the olives, but thou shalt
not anoint thee with oil; and sweet wine,
but shalt not drink wine.
16 ¶ For the statutes of Omri are kept, and
all the works of the house of Ahab, and ye
walk in their counsels; that I should make
thee a desolation, and the inhabitants
thereof an hissing: therefore ye shall bear
the reproach of my people.

Micah 7

1 Woe is me! for I am as when they
have gathered the summer fruits, as the
grapegleanings of the vintage: *there is* no
cluster to eat: my soul desired the firstripe
fruit.
2 The good *man* is perished out of the earth:
and *there is* none upright among men: they
all lie in wait for blood; they hunt every man
his brother with a net.
3 ¶ That they may do evil with both hands
earnestly, the prince asketh, and the judge
asketh for a reward; and the great *man*, he
uttereth his mischievous desire: so they
wrap it up.
4 The best of them *is* as a brier: the most
upright *is sharper* than a thorn hedge: the
day of thy watchmen *and* thy visitation cometh; now shall be their perplexity.
5 ¶ Trust ye not in a friend, put ye not confidence in a guide: keep the doors of thy
mouth from her that lieth in thy bosom.
6 For the son dishonoureth the father, the
daughter riseth up against her mother, the
daughter in law against her mother in law;
a man's enemies *are* the men of his own
house.
7 Therefore I will look unto the LORD; I will
wait for the God of my salvation: my God
will hear me.
8 ¶ Rejoice not against me, O mine enemy:
when I fall, I shall arise; when I sit in darkness, the LORD *shall be* a light unto me.
9 I will bear the indignation of the LORD,
because I have sinned against him, until he
plead my cause, and execute judgment for
me: he will bring me forth to the light, *and*
I shall behold his righteousness.
10 Then *she that is* mine enemy shall see *it*,
and shame shall cover her which said unto
me, Where is the LORD thy God? mine eyes
shall behold her: now shall she be trodden
down as the mire of the streets.
11 *In* the day that thy walls are to be built,
in that day shall the decree be far removed.
12 *In* that day *also* he shall come even to
thee from Assyria, and *from* the fortified
cities, and from the fortress even to the
river, and from sea to sea, and *from* mountain to mountain.
13 Notwithstanding the land shall be desolate because of them that dwell therein,
for the fruit of their doings.
14 ¶ Feed thy people with thy rod, the flock
of thine heritage, which dwell solitarily *in* the
wood, in the midst of Carmel: let them feed
in Bashan and Gilead, as in the days of old.
15 According to the days of thy coming out
of the land of Egypt will I shew unto him
marvellous *things*.
16 ¶ The nations shall see and be confounded at all their might: they shall lay
their hand upon *their* mouth, their ears
shall be deaf.
17 They shall lick the dust like a serpent, they
shall move out of their holes like worms of
the earth: they shall be afraid of the LORD
our God, and shall fear because of thee.
18 Who *is* a God like unto thee, that par-
doneth iniquity, and passeth by the transgression of the remnant of his heritage? he
retaineth not his anger for ever, because he
delighteth *in* mercy.
19 He will turn again, he will have compassion upon us; he will subdue our iniquities;

and thou wilt cast all their sins into the
depths of the sea.
20 Thou wilt perform the truth to Jacob,
and the mercy to Abraham, which thou hast
sworn unto our fathers from the days of old.

The Book Of

Nahum

Nahum 1

1 The burden of Nineveh. The book of the
vision of Nahum the Elkoshite.
2 God *is* jealous, and the LORD revengeth;
the LORD revengeth, and *is* furious; the LORD
will take vengeance on his adversaries, and
he reserveth *wrath* for his enemies.
3 The LORD *is* slow to anger, and great in
power, and will not at all acquit *the wicked:*
the LORD *hath* his way in the whirlwind and
in the storm, and the clouds *are* the dust
of his feet.
4 He rebuketh the sea, and maketh it dry,
and drieth up all the rivers: Bashan languisheth, and Carmel, and the flower of
Lebanon languisheth.
5 The mountains quake at him, and the
hills melt, and the earth is burned at his
presence, yea, the world, and all that dwell
therein.
6 Who can stand before his indignation?
and who can abide in the fierceness of his
anger? his fury is poured out like fire, and
the rocks are thrown down by him.
7 The LORD *is* good, a strong hold in the
day of trouble; and he knoweth them that
trust in him.
8 But with an overrunning flood he will
make an utter end of the place thereof, and
darkness shall pursue his enemies.
9 What do ye imagine against the LORD? he
will make an utter end: affliction shall not
rise up the second time.
10 For while *they be* folden together *as*
thorns, and while they are drunken *as*
drunkards, they shall be devoured as stubble fully dry.
11 There is *one* come out of thee, that
imagineth evil against the LORD, a wicked
counseller.
12 Thus saith the LORD; Though *they be*
quiet, and likewise many, yet thus shall they
be cut down, when he shall pass through.
Though I have afflicted thee, I will afflict
thee no more.
13 For now will I break his yoke from off
thee, and will burst thy bonds in sunder.
14 And the LORD hath given a commandment concerning thee, *that* no more of
thy name be sown: out of the house of thy
gods will I cut off the graven image and the
molten image: I will make thy grave; for
thou art vile.
15 Behold upon the mountains the feet of
him that bringeth good tidings, that publisheth peace! O Judah, keep thy solemn
feasts, perform thy vows: for the wicked
shall no more pass through thee; he is
utterly cut off.

Nahum 2

1 He that dasheth in pieces is come up
before thy face: keep the munition, watch
the way, make *thy* loins strong, fortify *thy*
power mightily.
2 For the LORD hath turned away the excellency of Jacob, as the excellency of Israel:
for the emptiers have emptied them out,
and marred their vine branches.
3 The shield of his mighty men is made red,
the valiant men *are* in scarlet: the chariots
shall be with flaming torches in the day of
his preparation, and the fir trees shall be
terribly shaken.
4 The chariots shall rage in the streets, they
shall justle one against another in the broad
ways: they shall seem like torches, they shall
run like the lightnings.
5 He shall recount his worthies: they shall
stumble in their walk; they shall make haste
to the wall thereof, and the defence shall
be prepared.

6 The gates of the rivers shall be opened,
and the palace shall be dissolved.
7 And Huzzab shall be led away captive, she
shall be brought up, and her maids shall lead
her as with the voice of doves, tabering upon
their breasts.
8 But Nineveh *is* of old like a pool of water:
yet they shall flee away. Stand, stand, *shall
they cry;* but none shall look back.
9 Take ye the spoil of silver, take the spoil
of gold: for *there is* none end of the store
and glory out of all the pleasant furniture.
10 She is empty, and void, and waste: and
the heart melteth, and the knees smite
together, and much pain *is* in all loins, and
the faces of them all gather blackness.
11 Where *is* the dwelling of the lions, and
the feedingplace of the young lions, where
the lion, *even* the old lion, walked, *and* the
lion's whelp, and none made *them* afraid?
12 The lion did tear in pieces enough for
his whelps, and strangled for his lionesses,
and filled his holes with prey, and his dens
with ravin.
13 Behold, I *am* against thee, saith the LORD
of hosts, and I will burn her chariots in the
smoke, and the sword shall devour thy
young lions: and I will cut off thy prey from
the earth, and the voice of thy messengers
shall no more be heard.

Nahum 3

1 Woe to the bloody city! it *is* all full of lies
and robbery; the prey departeth not;
2 The noise of a whip, and the noise of the
rattling of the wheels, and of the pransing
horses, and of the jumping chariots.
3 The horseman lifteth up both the bright
sword and the glittering spear: and *there
is* a multitude of slain, and a great number
of carcases; and *there is* none end of *their*
corpses; they stumble upon their corpses:
4 Because of the multitude of the whoredoms of the wellfavoured harlot, the mistress of witchcrafts, that selleth nations
through her whoredoms, and families
through her witchcrafts.
5 Behold, I *am* against thee, saith the LORD
of hosts; and I will discover thy skirts upon
thy face, and I will shew the nations thy
nakedness, and the kingdoms thy shame.
6 And I will cast abominable filth upon thee,
and make thee vile, and will set thee as a
gazingstock.
7 And it shall come to pass, *that* all they that
look upon thee shall flee from thee, and say,
Nineveh is laid waste: who will bemoan her?
whence shall I seek comforters for thee?
8 Art thou better than populous No, that
was situate among the rivers, *that had* the
waters round about it, whose rampart *was*
the sea, *and* her wall *was* from the sea?
9 Ethiopia and Egypt *were* her strength,
and *it was* infinite; Put and Lubim were
thy helpers.
10 Yet *was* she carried away, she went into
captivity: her young children also were
dashed in pieces at the top of all the streets:
and they cast lots for her honourable men,
and all her great men were bound in chains.
11 Thou also shalt be drunken: thou shalt be
hid, thou also shalt seek strength because
of the enemy.
12 All thy strong holds *shall be like* fig trees
with the firstripe figs: if they be shaken, they
shall even fall into the mouth of the eater.
13 Behold, thy people in the midst of thee
are women: the gates of thy land shall be
set wide open unto thine enemies: the fire
shall devour thy bars.
14 Draw thee waters for the siege, fortify
thy strong holds: go into clay, and tread the
morter, make strong the brickkiln.
15 There shall the fire devour thee; the
sword shall cut thee off, it shall eat thee up
like the cankerworm: make thyself many
as the cankerworm, make thyself many as
the locusts.
16 Thou hast multiplied thy merchants
above the stars of heaven: the cankerworm
spoileth, and flieth away.
17 Thy crowned *are* as the locusts, and thy
captains as the great grasshoppers, which
camp in the hedges in the cold day, *but*
when the sun ariseth they flee away, and
their place is not known where they *are*.
18 Thy shepherds slumber, O king of Assyria:
thy nobles shall dwell *in the dust:* thy people
is scattered upon the mountains, and no
man gathereth *them*.
19 *There is* no healing of thy bruise; thy
wound is grievous: all that hear the bruit
of thee shall clap the hands over thee: for
upon whom hath not thy wickedness passed
continually?

The Book Of

Habakkuk

Habakkuk 1

1 The burden which Habakkuk the prophet
did see.
2 O LORD, how long shall I cry, and thou wilt
not hear! *even* cry out unto thee *of* violence,
and thou wilt not save!
3 Why dost thou shew me iniquity, and
cause *me* to behold grievance? for spoiling
and violence *are* before me: and there are
that raise up strife and contention.
4 Therefore the law is slacked, and judgment
doth never go forth: for the wicked doth
compass about the righteous; therefore
wrong judgment proceedeth.
5 ¶ Behold ye among the heathen, and
regard, and wonder marvellously: for *I* will
work a work in your days, *which* ye will not
believe, though it be told *you*.
6 For, lo, I raise up the Chaldeans, *that* bitter
and hasty nation, which shall march through
the breadth of the land, to possess the
dwellingplaces *that are* not theirs.
7 They *are* terrible and dreadful: their
judgment and their dignity shall proceed
of themselves.
8 Their horses also are swifter than the
leopards, and are more fierce than the
evening wolves: and their horsemen shall
spread themselves, and their horsemen
shall come from far; they shall fly as the
eagle *that* hasteth to eat.
9 They shall come all for violence: their faces
shall sup up *as* the east wind, and they shall
gather the captivity as the sand.
10 And they shall scoff at the kings, and the
princes shall be a scorn unto them: they shall
deride every strong hold; for they shall heap
dust, and take it.
11 Then shall *his* mind change, and he shall
pass over, and offend, *imputing* this his
power unto his god.
12 ¶ *Art* thou not from everlasting, O LORD
my God, mine Holy One? we shall not die.
O LORD, thou hast ordained them for judgment; and, O mighty God, thou hast established them for correction.
13 *Thou art* of purer eyes than to behold
evil, and canst not look on iniquity: wherefore lookest thou upon them that deal
treacherously, *and* holdest thy tongue when
the wicked devoureth *the man that is* more
righteous than he?
14 And makest men as the fishes of the sea,
as the creeping things, *that have* no ruler
over them?
15 They take up all of them with the angle,
they catch them in their net, and gather
them in their drag: therefore they rejoice
and are glad.
16 Therefore they sacrifice unto their net,
and burn incense unto their drag; because
by them their portion *is* fat, and their meat
plenteous.
17 Shall they therefore empty their net, and
not spare continually to slay the nations?

Habakkuk 2

1 I will stand upon my watch, and set me
upon the tower, and will watch to see what
he will say unto me, and what I shall answer
when I am reproved.
2 And the LORD answered me, and said,
Write the vision, and make *it* plain upon
tables, that he may run that readeth it.
3 For the vision *is* yet for an appointed time,
but at the end it shall speak, and not lie:
though it tarry, wait for it; because it will
surely come, it will not tarry.
4 Behold, his soul *which* is lifted up is not
upright in him: but the just shall live by his
faith.
5 ¶ Yea also, because he transgresseth by
wine, *he is* a proud man, neither keepeth
at home, who enlargeth his desire as hell,
and *is* as death, and cannot be satisfied, but
gathereth unto him all nations, and heapeth
unto him all people:
6 Shall not all these take up a parable against
him, and a taunting proverb against him, and
say, Woe to him that increaseth *that which
is* not his! how long? and to him that ladeth
himself with thick clay!
7 Shall they not rise up suddenly that shall

bite thee, and awake that shall vex thee, and thou shalt be for booties unto them?

8 Because thou hast spoiled many nations, all the remnant of the people shall spoil thee; because of men's blood, and *for* the violence of the land, of the city, and of all that dwell therein.

9 ¶ Woe to him that coveteth an evil covetousness to his house, that he may set his nest on high, that he may be delivered from the power of evil!

10 Thou hast consulted shame to thy house by cutting off many people, and hast sinned *against* thy soul.

11 For the stone shall cry out of the wall, and the beam out of the timber shall answer it.

12 ¶ Woe to him that buildeth a town with blood, and stablisheth a city by iniquity!

13 Behold, *is it* not of the LORD of hosts that the people shall labour in the very fire, and the people shall weary themselves for very vanity?

14 For the earth shall be filled with the knowledge of the glory of the LORD, as the waters cover the sea.

15 ¶ Woe unto him that giveth his neighbour drink, that puttest thy bottle to *him*, and makest *him* drunken also, that thou mayest look on their nakedness!

16 Thou art filled with shame for glory: drink thou also, and let thy foreskin be uncovered: the cup of the LORD's right hand shall be turned unto thee, and shameful spewing *shall be* on thy glory.

17 For the violence of Lebanon shall cover thee, and the spoil of beasts, *which* made them afraid, because of men's blood, and for the violence of the land, of the city, and of all that dwell therein.

18 ¶ What profiteth the graven image that the maker thereof hath graven it; the molten image, and a teacher of lies, that the maker of his work trusteth therein, to make dumb idols?

19 Woe unto him that saith to the wood, Awake; to the dumb stone, Arise, it shall teach! Behold, it *is* laid over with gold and silver, and *there is* no breath at all in the midst of it.

20 But the LORD *is* in his holy temple: let all the earth keep silence before him.

Habakkuk 3

1 A prayer of Habakkuk the prophet upon Shigionoth.

2 O LORD, I have heard thy speech, *and* was afraid: O LORD, revive thy work in the midst of the years, in the midst of the years make known; in wrath remember mercy.

3 God came from Teman, and the Holy One from mount Paran. Selah. His glory covered the heavens, and the earth was full of his praise.

4 And *his* brightness was as the light; he had horns *coming* out of his hand: and there *was* the hiding of his power.

5 Before him went the pestilence, and burning coals went forth at his feet.

6 He stood, and measured the earth: he beheld, and drove asunder the nations; and the everlasting mountains were scattered, the perpetual hills did bow: his ways *are* everlasting.

7 I saw the tents of Cushan in affliction: *and* the curtains of the land of Midian did tremble.

8 Was the LORD displeased against the rivers? *was* thine anger against the rivers? *was* thy wrath against the sea, that thou didst ride upon thine horses *and* thy chariots of salvation?

9 Thy bow was made quite naked, *according* to the oaths of the tribes, *even thy* word. Selah. Thou didst cleave the earth with rivers.

10 The mountains saw thee, *and* they trembled: the overflowing of the water passed by: the deep uttered his voice, *and* lifted up his hands on high.

11 The sun *and* moon stood still in their habitation: at the light of thine arrows they went, *and* at the shining of thy glittering spear.

12 Thou didst march through the land in indignation, thou didst thresh the heathen in anger.

13 Thou wentest forth for the salvation of thy people, *even* for salvation with thine anointed; thou woundedst the head out of the house of the wicked, by discovering the foundation unto the neck. Selah.

14 Thou didst strike through with his staves the head of his villages: they came out as a whirlwind to scatter me: their rejoicing *was* as to devour the poor secretly.

15 Thou didst walk through the sea with
thine horses, *through* the heap of great
waters.
16 When I heard, my belly trembled; my lips
quivered at the voice: rottenness entered
into my bones, and I trembled in myself, that
I might rest in the day of trouble: when he
cometh up unto the people, he will invade
them with his troops.
17 ¶ Although the fig tree shall not blossom,
neither *shall* fruit *be* in the vines; the labour
of the olive shall fail, and the fields shall yield
no meat; the flock shall be cut off from the
fold, and *there shall be* no herd in the stalls:
18 Yet I will rejoice in the LORD, I will joy in
the God of my salvation.
19 The LORD God *is* my strength, and he will
make my feet like hinds' *feet*, and he will
make me to walk upon mine high places. To
the chief singer on my stringed instruments.

The Book Of

Zephaniah

Zephaniah 1

1 The word of the LORD which came unto
Zephaniah the son of Cushi, the son of
Gedaliah, the son of Amariah, the son of
Hizkiah, in the days of Josiah the son of
Amon, king of Judah.
2 I will utterly consume all *things* from off
the land, saith the LORD.
3 I will consume man and beast; I will consume the fowls of the heaven, and the fishes
of the sea, and the stumblingblocks with the
wicked; and I will cut off man from off the
land, saith the LORD.
4 I will also stretch out mine hand upon
Judah, and upon all the inhabitants of
Jerusalem; and I will cut off the remnant of
Baal from this place, *and* the name of the
Chemarims with the priests;
5 And them that worship the host of heaven
upon the housetops; and them that worship
and that swear by the LORD, and that swear
by Malcham;
6 And them that are turned back from the
LORD; and *those* that have not sought the
LORD, nor inquired for him.
7 Hold thy peace at the presence of the Lord
GOD: for the day of the LORD *is* at hand: for
the LORD hath prepared a sacrifice, he hath
bid his guests.
8 And it shall come to pass in the day of
the LORD's sacrifice, that I will punish the
princes, and the king's children, and all such
as are clothed with strange apparel.
9 In the same day also will I punish all those
that leap on the threshold, which fill their
masters' houses with violence and deceit.
10 And it shall come to pass in that day,
saith the LORD, *that there shall be* the noise
of a cry from the fish gate, and an howling
from the second, and a great crashing from
the hills.
11 Howl, ye inhabitants of Maktesh, for all
the merchant people are cut down; all they
that bear silver are cut off.
12 And it shall come to pass at that time,
that I will search Jerusalem with candles,
and punish the men that are settled on their
lees: that say in their heart, The LORD will
not do good, neither will he do evil.
13 Therefore their goods shall become a
booty, and their houses a desolation: they
shall also build houses, but not inhabit *them;*
and they shall plant vineyards, but not drink
the wine thereof.
14 The great day of the LORD *is* near, *it is*
near, and hasteth greatly, *even* the voice of
the day of the LORD: the mighty man shall
cry there bitterly.
15 That day *is* a day of wrath, a day of trouble and distress, a day of wasteness and desolation, a day of darkness and gloominess,
a day of clouds and thick darkness,
16 A day of the trumpet and alarm against
the fenced cities, and against the high
towers.
17 And I will bring distress upon men, that
they shall walk like blind men, because they
have sinned against the LORD: and their

blood shall be poured out as dust, and their
flesh as the dung.
18 Neither their silver nor their gold shall
be able to deliver them in the day of the
LORD's wrath; but the whole land shall be
devoured by the fire of his jealousy: for he
shall make even a speedy riddance of all
them that dwell in the land.

Zephaniah 2

1 Gather yourselves together, yea, gather
together, O nation not desired;
2 Before the decree bring forth, *before* the
day pass as the chaff, before the fierce anger
of the LORD come upon you, before the day
of the LORD's anger come upon you.
3 Seek ye the LORD, all ye meek of the earth,
which have wrought his judgment; seek
righteousness, seek meekness: it may be ye
shall be hid in the day of the LORD's anger.
4 ¶ For Gaza shall be forsaken, and Ashkelon
a desolation: they shall drive out Ashdod at
the noon day, and Ekron shall be rooted up.
5 Woe unto the inhabitants of the sea coast,
the nation of the Cherethites! the word of
the LORD *is* against you; O Canaan, the land
of the Philistines, I will even destroy thee,
that there shall be no inhabitant.
6 And the sea coast shall be dwellings *and*
cottages for shepherds, and folds for flocks.
7 And the coast shall be for the remnant of
the house of Judah; they shall feed thereupon: in the houses of Ashkelon shall they
lie down in the evening: for the LORD their
God shall visit them, and turn away their
captivity.
8 ¶ I have heard the reproach of Moab,
and the revilings of the children of Ammon,
whereby they have reproached my people,
and magnified *themselves* against their
border.
9 Therefore *as* I live, saith the LORD of hosts,
the God of Israel, Surely Moab shall be as
Sodom, and the children of Ammon as
Gomorrah, *even* the breeding of nettles, and
saltpits, and a perpetual desolation: the residue of my people shall spoil them, and the
remnant of my people shall possess them.
10 This shall they have for their pride,
because they have reproached and magnified *themselves* against the people of the
LORD of hosts.
11 The LORD *will be* terrible unto them: for
he will famish all the gods of the earth; and
men shall worship him, every one from his
place, *even* all the isles of the heathen.
12 ¶ Ye Ethiopians also, ye *shall be* slain by
my sword.
13 And he will stretch out his hand against
the north, and destroy Assyria; and will
make Nineveh a desolation, *and* dry like a
wilderness.
14 And flocks shall lie down in the midst of
her, all the beasts of the nations: both the
cormorant and the bittern shall lodge in the
upper lintels of it; *their* voice shall sing in the
windows; desolation *shall be* in the thresholds: for he shall uncover the cedar work.
15 This *is* the rejoicing city that dwelt carelessly, that said in her heart, I *am*, and *there*
is none beside me: how is she become a
desolation, a place for beasts to lie down
in! every one that passeth by her shall hiss,
and wag his hand.

Zephaniah 3

1 Woe to her that is filthy and polluted, to
the oppressing city!
2 She obeyed not the voice; she received
not correction; she trusted not in the LORD;
she drew not near to her God.
3 Her princes within her *are* roaring lions;
her judges *are* evening wolves; they gnaw
not the bones till the morrow.
4 Her prophets *are* light *and* treacherous
persons: her priests have polluted the sanctuary, they have done violence to the law.
5 The just LORD *is* in the midst thereof; he
will not do iniquity: every morning doth he
bring his judgment to light, he faileth not;
but the unjust knoweth no shame.
6 I have cut off the nations: their towers are
desolate; I made their streets waste, that
none passeth by: their cities are destroyed,
so that there is no man, that there is none
inhabitant.
7 I said, Surely thou wilt fear me, thou wilt
receive instruction; so their dwelling should
not be cut off, howsoever I punished them:
but they rose early, *and* corrupted all their
doings.
8 ¶ Therefore wait ye upon me, saith the
LORD, until the day that I rise up to the
prey: for my determination *is* to gather the
nations, that I may assemble the kingdoms,
to pour upon them mine indignation, *even*

all my fierce anger: for all the earth shall be devoured with the fire of my jealousy.
9 For then will I turn to the people a pure language, that they may all call upon the name of the LORD, to serve him with one consent.
10 From beyond the rivers of Ethiopia my suppliants, *even* the daughter of my dispersed, shall bring mine offering.
11 In that day shalt thou not be ashamed for all thy doings, wherein thou hast transgressed against me: for then I will take away out of the midst of thee them that rejoice in thy pride, and thou shalt no more be haughty because of my holy mountain.
12 I will also leave in the midst of thee an afflicted and poor people, and they shall trust in the name of the LORD.
13 The remnant of Israel shall not do iniquity, nor speak lies; neither shall a deceitful tongue be found in their mouth: for they shall feed and lie down, and none shall make *them* afraid.
14 ¶ Sing, O daughter of Zion; shout, O Israel; be glad and rejoice with all the heart, O daughter of Jerusalem.
15 The LORD hath taken away thy judgments, he hath cast out thine enemy: the king of Israel, *even* the LORD, *is* in the midst of thee: thou shalt not see evil any more.
16 In that day it shall be said to Jerusalem, Fear thou not: *and to* Zion, Let not thine hands be slack.
17 The LORD thy God in the midst of thee *is* mighty; he will save, he will rejoice over thee with joy; he will rest in his love, he will joy over thee with singing.
18 I will gather *them that are* sorrowful for the solemn assembly, *who* are of thee, *to whom* the reproach of it *was* a burden.
19 Behold, at that time I will undo all that afflict thee: and I will save her that halteth, and gather her that was driven out; and I will get them praise and fame in every land where they have been put to shame.
20 At that time will I bring you *again*, even in the time that I gather you: for I will make you a name and a praise among all people of the earth, when I turn back your captivity before your eyes, saith the LORD.

The Book Of

Haggai

Haggai 1

1 In the second year of Darius the king, in the sixth month, in the first day of the month, came the word of the LORD by Haggai the prophet unto Zerubbabel the son of Shealtiel, governor of Judah, and to Joshua the son of Josedech, the high priest, saying,
2 Thus speaketh the LORD of hosts, saying, This people say, The time is not come, the time that the LORD's house should be built.
3 Then came the word of the LORD by Haggai the prophet, saying,
4 *Is it* time for you, O ye, to dwell in your cieled houses, and this house *lie* waste?
5 Now therefore thus saith the LORD of hosts; Consider your ways.
6 Ye have sown much, and bring in little; ye eat, but ye have not enough; ye drink, but ye are not filled with drink; ye clothe you, but there is none warm; and he that earneth wages earneth wages *to put it* into a bag with holes.
7 ¶ Thus saith the LORD of hosts; Consider your ways.
8 Go up to the mountain, and bring wood, and build the house; and I will take pleasure in it, and I will be glorified, saith the LORD.
9 Ye looked for much, and, lo, *it came* to little; and when ye brought *it* home, I did blow upon it. Why? saith the LORD of hosts. Because of mine house that *is* waste, and ye run every man unto his own house.
10 Therefore the heaven over you is stayed from dew, and the earth is stayed *from* her fruit.
11 And I called for a drought upon the land,

and upon the mountains, and upon the corn,
and upon the new wine, and upon the oil,
and upon *that* which the ground bringeth
forth, and upon men, and upon cattle, and
upon all the labour of the hands.
12 ¶ Then Zerubbabel the son of Shealtiel,
and Joshua the son of Josedech, the high
priest, with all the remnant of the people,
obeyed the voice of the LORD their God,
and the words of Haggai the prophet, as
the LORD their God had sent him, and the
people did fear before the LORD.
13 Then spake Haggai the LORD's messenger
in the LORD's message unto the people, saying, I *am* with you, saith the LORD.
14 And the LORD stirred up the spirit of
Zerubbabel the son of Shealtiel, governor
of Judah, and the spirit of Joshua the son
of Josedech, the high priest, and the spirit
of all the remnant of the people; and they
came and did work in the house of the LORD
of hosts, their God,
15 In the four and twentieth day of the sixth
month, in the second year of Darius the king.

Haggai 2

1 In the seventh *month*, in the one and
twentieth *day* of the month, came the word
of the LORD by the prophet Haggai, saying,
2 Speak now to Zerubbabel the son of Shealtiel, governor of Judah, and to Joshua the
son of Josedech, the high priest, and to the
residue of the people, saying,
3 Who *is* left among you that saw this house
in her first glory? and how do ye see it now?
is it not in your eyes in comparison of it as
nothing?
4 Yet now be strong, O Zerubbabel, saith the
LORD; and be strong, O Joshua, son of Josedech, the high priest; and be strong, all ye
people of the land, saith the LORD, and work:
for I *am* with you, saith the LORD of hosts:
5 *According to* the word that I covenanted
with you when ye came out of Egypt, so my
spirit remaineth among you: fear ye not.
6 For thus saith the LORD of hosts; Yet
once, it *is* a little while, and I will shake the
heavens, and the earth, and the sea, and
the dry *land;*
7 And I will shake all nations, and the desire
of all nations shall come: and I will fill this
house with glory, saith the LORD of hosts.
8 The silver *is* mine, and the gold *is* mine,
saith the LORD of hosts.
9 The glory of this latter house shall be
greater than of the former, saith the LORD
of hosts: and in this place will I give peace,
saith the LORD of hosts.
10 ¶ In the four and twentieth *day* of the
ninth *month*, in the second year of Darius,
came the word of the LORD by Haggai the
prophet, saying,
11 Thus saith the LORD of hosts; Ask now the
priests *concerning* the law, saying,
12 If one bear holy flesh in the skirt of his
garment, and with his skirt do touch bread,
or pottage, or wine, or oil, or any meat,
shall it be holy? And the priests answered
and said, No.
13 Then said Haggai, If *one that is* unclean
by a dead body touch any of these, shall it
be unclean? And the priests answered and
said, It shall be unclean.
14 Then answered Haggai, and said, So *is*
this people, and so *is* this nation before
me, saith the LORD; and so *is* every work
of their hands; and that which they offer
there *is* unclean.
15 And now, I pray you, consider from this
day and upward, from before a stone was
laid upon a stone in the temple of the LORD:
16 Since those *days* were, when *one* came
to an heap of twenty *measures*, there were
but ten: when *one* came to the pressfat for
to draw out fifty *vessels* out of the press,
there were *but* twenty.
17 I smote you with blasting and with
mildew and with hail in all the labours of
your hands; yet ye *turned* not to me, saith
the LORD.
18 Consider now from this day and upward,
from the four and twentieth day of the
ninth *month*, *even* from the day that the
foundation of the LORD's temple was laid,
consider *it*.
19 Is the seed yet in the barn? yea, as yet the
vine, and the fig tree, and the pomegranate,
and the olive tree, hath not brought forth:
from this day will I bless *you*.
20 ¶ And again the word of the LORD came
unto Haggai in the four and twentieth *day*
of the month, saying,
21 Speak to Zerubbabel, governor of Judah,
saying, I will shake the heavens and the
earth;

22 And I will overthrow the throne of kingdoms, and I will destroy the strength of the kingdoms of the heathen; and I will overthrow the chariots, and those that ride in them; and the horses and their riders shall come down, every one by the sword of his brother.

23 In that day, saith the LORD of hosts, will I take thee, O Zerubbabel, my servant, the son of Shealtiel, saith the LORD, and will make thee as a signet: for I have chosen thee, saith the LORD of hosts.

The Book Of

Zechariah

Zechariah 1

1 In the eighth month, in the second year of Darius, came the word of the LORD unto Zechariah, the son of Berechiah, the son of Iddo the prophet, saying,

2 The LORD hath been sore displeased with your fathers.

3 Therefore say thou unto them, Thus saith the LORD of hosts; Turn ye unto me, saith the LORD of hosts, and I will turn unto you, saith the LORD of hosts.

4 Be ye not as your fathers, unto whom the former prophets have cried, saying, Thus saith the LORD of hosts; Turn ye now from your evil ways, and *from* your evil doings: but they did not hear, nor hearken unto me, saith the LORD.

5 Your fathers, where *are* they? and the prophets, do they live for ever?

6 But my words and my statutes, which I commanded my servants the prophets, did they not take hold of your fathers? and they returned and said, Like as the LORD of hosts thought to do unto us, according to our ways, and according to our doings, so hath he dealt with us.

7 ¶ Upon the four and twentieth day of the eleventh month, which *is* the month Sebat, in the second year of Darius, came the word of the LORD unto Zechariah, the son of Berechiah, the son of Iddo the prophet, saying,

8 I saw by night, and behold a man riding upon a red horse, and he stood among the myrtle trees that *were* in the bottom; and behind him *were there* red horses, speckled, and white.

9 Then said I, O my lord, what *are* these? And the angel that talked with me said unto me, I will shew thee what these *be*.

10 And the man that stood among the myrtle trees answered and said, These *are they* whom the LORD hath sent to walk to and fro through the earth.

11 And they answered the angel of the LORD that stood among the myrtle trees, and said, We have walked to and fro through the earth, and, behold, all the earth sitteth still, and is at rest.

12 ¶ Then the angel of the LORD answered and said, O LORD of hosts, how long wilt thou not have mercy on Jerusalem and on the cities of Judah, against which thou hast had indignation these threescore and ten years?

13 And the LORD answered the angel that talked with me *with* good words *and* comfortable words.

14 So the angel that communed with me said unto me, Cry thou, saying, Thus saith the LORD of hosts; I am jealous for Jerusalem and for Zion with a great jealousy.

15 And I am very sore displeased with the heathen *that are* at ease: for I was but a little displeased, and they helped forward the affliction.

16 Therefore thus saith the LORD; I am returned to Jerusalem with mercies: my house shall be built in it, saith the LORD of hosts, and a line shall be stretched forth upon Jerusalem.

17 Cry yet, saying, Thus saith the LORD of hosts; My cities through prosperity shall yet be spread abroad; and the LORD shall yet comfort Zion, and shall yet choose Jerusalem.

18 ¶ Then lifted I up mine eyes, and saw,
and behold four horns.
19 And I said unto the angel that talked with
me, What *be* these? And he answered me,
These *are* the horns which have scattered
Judah, Israel, and Jerusalem.
20 And the LORD shewed me four carpenters.
21 Then said I, What come these to do? And
he spake, saying, These *are* the horns which
have scattered Judah, so that no man did
lift up his head: but these are come to fray
them, to cast out the horns of the Gentiles,
which lifted up *their* horn over the land of
Judah to scatter it.

Zechariah 2

1 I lifted up mine eyes again, and looked,
and behold a man with a measuring line
in his hand.
2 Then said I, Whither goest thou? And he
said unto me, To measure Jerusalem, to see
what *is* the breadth thereof, and what *is* the
length thereof.
3 And, behold, the angel that talked with
me went forth, and another angel went
out to meet him,
4 And said unto him, Run, speak to this
young man, saying, Jerusalem shall be
inhabited *as* towns without walls for the
multitude of men and cattle therein:
5 For I, saith the LORD, will be unto her a wall
of fire round about, and will be the glory in
the midst of her.
6 ¶ Ho, ho, *come forth*, and flee from the
land of the north, saith the LORD: for I have
spread you abroad as the four winds of the
heaven, saith the LORD.
7 Deliver thyself, O Zion, that dwellest *with*
the daughter of Babylon.
8 For thus saith the LORD of hosts; After
the glory hath he sent me unto the nations
which spoiled you: for he that toucheth you
toucheth the apple of his eye.
9 For, behold, I will shake mine hand upon
them, and they shall be a spoil to their servants: and ye shall know that the LORD of
hosts hath sent me.
10 ¶ Sing and rejoice, O daughter of Zion:
for, lo, I come, and I will dwell in the midst
of thee, saith the LORD.
11 And many nations shall be joined to the
LORD in that day, and shall be my people:
and I will dwell in the midst of thee, and thou
shalt know that the LORD of hosts hath sent
me unto thee.
12 And the LORD shall inherit Judah his
portion in the holy land, and shall choose
Jerusalem again.
13 Be silent, O all flesh, before the LORD: for
he is raised up out of his holy habitation.

Zechariah 3

1 And he shewed me Joshua the high priest
standing before the angel of the LORD, and
Satan standing at his right hand to resist
him.
2 And the LORD said unto Satan, The LORD
rebuke thee, O Satan; even the LORD that
hath chosen Jerusalem rebuke thee: *is* not
this a brand plucked out of the fire?
3 Now Joshua was clothed with filthy garments, and stood before the angel.
4 And he answered and spake unto those
that stood before him, saying, Take away the
filthy garments from him. And unto him he
said, Behold, I have caused thine iniquity to
pass from thee, and I will clothe thee with
change of raiment.
5 And I said, Let them set a fair mitre upon
his head. So they set a fair mitre upon his
head, and clothed him with garments. And
the angel of the LORD stood by.
6 And the angel of the LORD protested unto
Joshua, saying,
7 Thus saith the LORD of hosts; If thou wilt
walk in my ways, and if thou wilt keep
my charge, then thou shalt also judge my
house, and shalt also keep my courts, and
I will give thee places to walk among these
that stand by.
8 Hear now, O Joshua the high priest, thou,
and thy fellows that sit before thee: for they
are men wondered at: for, behold, I will
bring forth my servant the BRANCH.
9 For behold the stone that I have laid before
Joshua; upon one stone *shall be* seven eyes:
behold, I will engrave the graving thereof,
saith the LORD of hosts, and I will remove
the iniquity of that land in one day.
10 In that day, saith the LORD of hosts, shall
ye call every man his neighbour under the
vine and under the fig tree.

Zechariah 4

1 And the angel that talked with me came

again, and waked me, as a man that is wakened out of his sleep,
2 And said unto me, What seest thou? And I
said, I have looked, and behold a candlestick
all *of* gold, with a bowl upon the top of it,
and his seven lamps thereon, and seven
pipes to the seven lamps, which *are* upon
the top thereof:
3 And two olive trees by it, one upon the
right *side* of the bowl, and the other upon
the left *side* thereof.
4 So I answered and spake to the angel that
talked with me, saying, What *are* these,
my lord?
5 Then the angel that talked with me
answered and said unto me, Knowest thou
not what these be? And I said, No, my lord.
6 Then he answered and spake unto me,
saying, This *is* the word of the LORD unto
Zerubbabel, saying, Not by might, nor by
power, but by my spirit, saith the LORD of
hosts.
7 Who *art* thou, O great mountain? before
Zerubbabel *thou shalt become* a plain: and
he shall bring forth the headstone *thereof*
with shoutings, *crying*, Grace, grace unto it.
8 Moreover the word of the LORD came
unto me, saying,
9 The hands of Zerubbabel have laid the
foundation of this house; his hands shall also
finish it; and thou shalt know that the LORD
of hosts hath sent me unto you.
10 For who hath despised the day of small
things? for they shall rejoice, and shall see
the plummet in the hand of Zerubbabel
with those seven; they *are* the eyes of the
LORD, which run to and fro through the
whole earth.
11 ¶ Then answered I, and said unto him,
What *are* these two olive trees upon the
right *side* of the candlestick and upon the
left *side* thereof?
12 And I answered again, and said unto him,
What *be these* two olive branches which
through the two golden pipes empty the
golden *oil* out of themselves?
13 And he answered me and said, Knowest
thou not what these *be?* And I said, No,
my lord.
14 Then said he, These *are* the two anointed
ones, that stand by the Lord of the whole
earth.

Zechariah 5

1 Then I turned, and lifted up mine eyes, and
looked, and behold a flying roll.
2 And he said unto me, What seest thou?
And I answered, I see a flying roll; the length
thereof *is* twenty cubits, and the breadth
thereof ten cubits.
3 Then said he unto me, This *is* the curse
that goeth forth over the face of the whole
earth: for every one that stealeth shall be
cut off *as* on this side according to it; and
every one that sweareth shall be cut off *as*
on that side according to it.
4 I will bring it forth, saith the LORD of hosts,
and it shall enter into the house of the thief,
and into the house of him that sweareth
falsely by my name: and it shall remain in the
midst of his house, and shall consume it with
the timber thereof and the stones thereof.
5 ¶ Then the angel that talked with me went
forth, and said unto me, Lift up now thine
eyes, and see what *is* this that goeth forth.
6 And I said, What *is* it? And he said, This *is*
an ephah that goeth forth. He said more-
over, This *is* their resemblance through all
the earth.
7 And, behold, there was lifted up a talent
of lead: and this *is* a woman that sitteth in
the midst of the ephah.
8 And he said, This *is* wickedness. And he
cast it into the midst of the ephah; and he
cast the weight of lead upon the mouth
thereof.
9 Then lifted I up mine eyes, and looked,
and, behold, there came out two women,
and the wind *was* in their wings; for they
had wings like the wings of a stork: and they
lifted up the ephah between the earth and
the heaven.
10 Then said I to the angel that talked with
me, Whither do these bear the ephah?
11 And he said unto me, To build it an house
in the land of Shinar: and it shall be established, and set there upon her own base.

Zechariah 6

1 And I turned, and lifted up mine eyes, and
looked, and, behold, there came four chariots out from between two mountains; and
the mountains *were* mountains of brass.
2 In the first chariot *were* red horses; and in
the second chariot black horses;

3 And in the third chariot white horses; and
in the fourth chariot grisled and bay horses.
4 Then I answered and said unto the angel
that talked with me, What *are* these, my
lord?
5 And the angel answered and said unto me,
These *are* the four spirits of the heavens,
which go forth from standing before the
Lord of all the earth.
6 The black horses which *are* therein go
forth into the north country; and the white
go forth after them; and the grisled go forth
toward the south country.
7 And the bay went forth, and sought to go
that they might walk to and fro through the
earth: and he said, Get you hence, walk to
and fro through the earth. So they walked
to and fro through the earth.
8 Then cried he upon me, and spake unto
me, saying, Behold, these that go toward
the north country have quieted my spirit
in the north country.
9 ¶ And the word of the LORD came unto
me, saying,
10 Take of *them of* the captivity, *even* of
Heldai, of Tobijah, and of Jedaiah, which
are come from Babylon, and come thou the
same day, and go into the house of Josiah
the son of Zephaniah;
11 Then take silver and gold, and make
crowns, and set *them* upon the head of
Joshua the son of Josedech, the high priest;
12 And speak unto him, saying, Thus speaketh the LORD of hosts, saying, Behold the
man whose name *is* The BRANCH; and he
shall grow up out of his place, and he shall
build the temple of the LORD:
13 Even he shall build the temple of the
LORD; and he shall bear the glory, and shall
sit and rule upon his throne; and he shall be
a priest upon his throne: and the counsel of
peace shall be between them both.
14 And the crowns shall be to Helem, and to
Tobijah, and to Jedaiah, and to Hen the son
of Zephaniah, for a memorial in the temple
of the LORD.
15 And they *that are* far off shall come and
build in the temple of the LORD, and ye shall
know that the LORD of hosts hath sent me
unto you. And *this* shall come to pass, if ye
will diligently obey the voice of the LORD
your God.

Zechariah 7

1 And it came to pass in the fourth year of
king Darius, *that* the word of the LORD came
unto Zechariah in the fourth *day* of the ninth
month, *even* in Chisleu;
2 When they had sent unto the house of
God Sherezer and Regem-melech, and their
men, to pray before the LORD,
3 *And* to speak unto the priests which *were*
in the house of the LORD of hosts, and to the
prophets, saying, Should I weep in the fifth
month, separating myself, as I have done
these so many years?
4 ¶ Then came the word of the LORD of hosts
unto me, saying,
5 Speak unto all the people of the land, and
to the priests, saying, When ye fasted and
mourned in the fifth and seventh *month*,
even those seventy years, did ye at all fast
unto me, *even* to me?
6 And when ye did eat, and when ye did
drink, did not ye eat *for yourselves*, and
drink *for yourselves?*
7 *Should ye* not *hear* the words which the
LORD hath cried by the former prophets,
when Jerusalem was inhabited and in prosperity, and the cities thereof round about
her, when *men* inhabited the south and
the plain?
8 ¶ And the word of the LORD came unto
Zechariah, saying,
9 Thus speaketh the LORD of hosts, saying,
Execute true judgment, and shew mercy
and compassions every man to his brother:
10 And oppress not the widow, nor the
fatherless, the stranger, nor the poor; and
let none of you imagine evil against his
brother in your heart.
11 But they refused to hearken, and pulled
away the shoulder, and stopped their ears,
that they should not hear.
12 Yea, they made their hearts *as* an adamant stone, lest they should hear the law,
and the words which the LORD of hosts hath
sent in his spirit by the former prophets:
therefore came a great wrath from the
LORD of hosts.
13 Therefore it is come to pass, *that* as he
cried, and they would not hear; so they
cried, and I would not hear, saith the LORD
of hosts:
14 But I scattered them with a whirlwind
among all the nations whom they knew not.

Thus the land was desolate after them, that
no man passed through nor returned: for
they laid the pleasant land desolate.

Zechariah 8

1 Again the word of the LORD of hosts came
to me, saying,
2 Thus saith the LORD of hosts; I was jealous for Zion with great jealousy, and I was
jealous for her with great fury.
3 Thus saith the LORD; I am returned unto
Zion, and will dwell in the midst of Jerusalem: and Jerusalem shall be called a city of
truth; and the mountain of the LORD of hosts
the holy mountain.
4 Thus saith the LORD of hosts; There shall
yet old men and old women dwell in the
streets of Jerusalem, and every man with
his staff in his hand for very age.
5 And the streets of the city shall be full of
boys and girls playing in the streets thereof.
6 Thus saith the LORD of hosts; If it be marvellous in the eyes of the remnant of this
people in these days, should it also be marvellous in mine eyes? saith the LORD of hosts.
7 Thus saith the LORD of hosts; Behold, I will
save my people from the east country, and
from the west country;
8 And I will bring them, and they shall dwell
in the midst of Jerusalem: and they shall be
my people, and I will be their God, in truth
and in righteousness.
9 ¶ Thus saith the LORD of hosts; Let your
hands be strong, ye that hear in these days
these words by the mouth of the prophets,
which *were* in the day *that* the foundation
of the house of the LORD of hosts was laid,
that the temple might be built.
10 For before these days there was no hire
for man, nor any hire for beast; neither *was
there any* peace to him that went out or
came in because of the affliction: for I set
all men every one against his neighbour.
11 But now I *will* not *be* unto the residue of
this people as in the former days, saith the
LORD of hosts.
12 For the seed *shall be* prosperous; the vine
shall give her fruit, and the ground shall give
her increase, and the heavens shall give their
dew; and I will cause the remnant of this
people to possess all these *things*.
13 And it shall come to pass, *that* as ye
were a curse among the heathen, O house
of Judah, and house of Israel; so will I save
you, and ye shall be a blessing: fear not, *but*
let your hands be strong.
14 For thus saith the LORD of hosts; As I
thought to punish you, when your fathers
provoked me to wrath, saith the LORD of
hosts, and I repented not:
15 So again have I thought in these days to
do well unto Jerusalem and to the house of
Judah: fear ye not.
16 ¶ These *are* the things that ye shall do;
Speak ye every man the truth to his neighbour; execute the judgment of truth and
peace in your gates:
17 And let none of you imagine evil in your
hearts against his neighbour; and love no
false oath: for all these *are things* that I hate,
saith the LORD.
18 ¶ And the word of the LORD of hosts
came unto me, saying,
19 Thus saith the LORD of hosts; The fast of
the fourth *month*, and the fast of the fifth,
and the fast of the seventh, and the fast of
the tenth, shall be to the house of Judah joy
and gladness, and cheerful feasts; therefore
love the truth and peace.
20 Thus saith the LORD of hosts; *It shall* yet
come to pass, that there shall come people,
and the inhabitants of many cities:
21 And the inhabitants of one *city* shall go
to another, saying, Let us go speedily to pray
before the LORD, and to seek the LORD of
hosts: I will go also.
22 Yea, many people and strong nations
shall come to seek the LORD of hosts in
Jerusalem, and to pray before the LORD.
23 Thus saith the LORD of hosts; In those
days *it shall come to pass*, that ten men shall
take hold out of all languages of the nations,
even shall take hold of the skirt of him that
is a Jew, saying, We will go with you: for we
have heard *that* God *is* with you.

Zechariah 9

1 The burden of the word of the LORD in the
land of Hadrach, and Damascus *shall be* the
rest thereof: when the eyes of man, as of all
the tribes of Israel, *shall be* toward the LORD.
2 And Hamath also shall border thereby;
Tyrus, and Zidon, though it be very wise.
3 And Tyrus did build herself a strong hold,
and heaped up silver as the dust, and fine
gold as the mire of the streets.

4 Behold, the Lord will cast her out, and he
will smite her power in the sea; and she shall
be devoured with fire.
5 Ashkelon shall see *it*, and fear; Gaza also
shall see it, and be very sorrowful, and
Ekron; for her expectation shall be ashamed;
and the king shall perish from Gaza, and
Ashkelon shall not be inhabited.
6 And a bastard shall dwell in Ashdod, and I
will cut off the pride of the Philistines.
7 And I will take away his blood out of his
mouth, and his abominations from between
his teeth: but he that remaineth, even he,
shall be for our God, and he shall be as a
governor in Judah, and Ekron as a Jebusite.
8 And I will encamp about mine house
because of the army, because of him that
passeth by, and because of him that returneth: and no oppressor shall pass through
them any more: for now have I seen with
mine eyes.
9 ¶ Rejoice greatly, O daughter of Zion;
shout, O daughter of Jerusalem: behold,
thy King cometh unto thee: he *is* just, and
having salvation; lowly, and riding upon an
ass, and upon a colt the foal of an ass.
10 And I will cut off the chariot from
Ephraim, and the horse from Jerusalem,
and the battle bow shall be cut off: and he
shall speak peace unto the heathen: and his
dominion *shall be* from sea *even* to sea, and
from the river *even* to the ends of the earth.
11 As for thee also, by the blood of thy covenant I have sent forth thy prisoners out of
the pit wherein *is* no water.
12 ¶ Turn you to the strong hold, ye prisoners of hope: even to day do I declare *that* I
will render double unto thee;
13 When I have bent Judah for me, filled the
bow with Ephraim, and raised up thy sons, O
Zion, against thy sons, O Greece, and made
thee as the sword of a mighty man.
14 And the LORD shall be seen over them,
and his arrow shall go forth as the lightning:
and the Lord GOD shall blow the trumpet,
and shall go with whirlwinds of the south.
15 The LORD of hosts shall defend them;
and they shall devour, and subdue with
sling stones; and they shall drink, *and* make
a noise as through wine; and they shall be
filled like bowls, *and* as the corners of the
altar.
16 And the LORD their God shall save them
in that day as the flock of his people: for *they*
shall be as the stones of a crown, lifted up
as an ensign upon his land.
17 For how great *is* his goodness, and how
great *is* his beauty! corn shall make the
young men cheerful, and new wine the
maids.

Zechariah 10

1 Ask ye of the LORD rain in the time of the
latter rain; *so* the LORD shall make bright
clouds, and give them showers of rain, to
every one grass in the field.
2 For the idols have spoken vanity, and the
diviners have seen a lie, and have told false
dreams; they comfort in vain: therefore
they went their way as a flock, they were
troubled, because *there was* no shepherd.
3 Mine anger was kindled against the shepherds, and I punished the goats: for the LORD
of hosts hath visited his flock the house of
Judah, and hath made them as his goodly
horse in the battle.
4 Out of him came forth the corner, out of
him the nail, out of him the battle bow, out
of him every oppressor together.
5 ¶ And they shall be as mighty *men*, which
tread down *their enemies* in the mire of the
streets in the battle: and they shall fight,
because the LORD *is* with them, and the
riders on horses shall be confounded.
6 And I will strengthen the house of Judah,
and I will save the house of Joseph, and I
will bring them again to place them; for I
have mercy upon them: and they shall be
as though I had not cast them off: for I *am*
the LORD their God, and will hear them.
7 And *they of* Ephraim shall be like a mighty
man, and their heart shall rejoice as through
wine: yea, their children shall see *it*, and be
glad; their heart shall rejoice in the LORD.
8 I will hiss for them, and gather them;
for I have redeemed them: and they shall
increase as they have increased.
9 And I will sow them among the people:
and they shall remember me in far countries; and they shall live with their children,
and turn again.
10 I will bring them again also out of the land
of Egypt, and gather them out of Assyria;
and I will bring them into the land of Gilead
and Lebanon; and *place* shall not be found
for them.

11 And he shall pass through the sea with
affliction, and shall smite the waves in the
sea, and all the deeps of the river shall
dry up: and the pride of Assyria shall be
brought down, and the sceptre of Egypt
shall depart away.
12 And I will strengthen them in the LORD;
and they shall walk up and down in his name,
saith the LORD.

Zechariah 11

1 Open thy doors, O Lebanon, that the fire
may devour thy cedars.
2 Howl, fir tree; for the cedar is fallen;
because the mighty are spoiled: howl, O ye
oaks of Bashan; for the forest of the vintage
is come down.
3 ¶ *There is* a voice of the howling of the
shepherds; for their glory is spoiled: a voice
of the roaring of young lions; for the pride
of Jordan is spoiled.
4 Thus saith the LORD my God; Feed the
flock of the slaughter;
5 Whose possessors slay them, and hold
themselves not guilty: and they that sell
them say, Blessed *be* the LORD; for I am rich:
and their own shepherds pity them not.
6 For I will no more pity the inhabitants of
the land, saith the LORD: but, lo, I will deliver
the men every one into his neighbour's
hand, and into the hand of his king: and
they shall smite the land, and out of their
hand I will not deliver *them*.
7 And I will feed the flock of slaughter, *even*
you, O poor of the flock. And I took unto me
two staves; the one I called Beauty, and the
other I called Bands; and I fed the flock.
8 Three shepherds also I cut off in one
month; and my soul lothed them, and their
soul also abhorred me.
9 Then said I, I will not feed you: that that
dieth, let it die; and that that is to be cut off,
let it be cut off; and let the rest eat every
one the flesh of another.
10 ¶ And I took my staff, *even* Beauty, and
cut it asunder, that I might break my covenant which I had made with all the people.
11 And it was broken in that day: and so the
poor of the flock that waited upon me knew
that it *was* the word of the LORD.
12 And I said unto them, If ye think good,
give *me* my price; and if not, forbear. So they
weighed for my price thirty *pieces* of silver.
13 And the LORD said unto me, Cast it unto
the potter: a goodly price that I was prised
at of them. And I took the thirty *pieces* of
silver, and cast them to the potter in the
house of the LORD.
14 Then I cut asunder mine other staff, *even*
Bands, that I might break the brotherhood
between Judah and Israel.
15 ¶ And the LORD said unto me, Take
unto thee yet the instruments of a foolish
shepherd.
16 For, lo, I will raise up a shepherd in the
land, *which* shall not visit those that be cut
off, neither shall seek the young one, nor
heal that that is broken, nor feed that that
standeth still: but he shall eat the flesh of
the fat, and tear their claws in pieces.
17 Woe to the idol shepherd that leaveth
the flock! the sword *shall be* upon his arm,
and upon his right eye: his arm shall be
clean dried up, and his right eye shall be
utterly darkened.

Zechariah 12

1 The burden of the word of the LORD for
Israel, saith the LORD, which stretcheth forth
the heavens, and layeth the foundation of
the earth, and formeth the spirit of man
within him.
2 Behold, I will make Jerusalem a cup of
trembling unto all the people round about,
when they shall be in the siege both against
Judah *and* against Jerusalem.
3 ¶ And in that day will I make Jerusalem
a burdensome stone for all people: all that
burden themselves with it shall be cut in
pieces, though all the people of the earth
be gathered together against it.
4 In that day, saith the LORD, I will smite
every horse with astonishment, and his
rider with madness: and I will open mine
eyes upon the house of Judah, and will smite
every horse of the people with blindness.
5 And the governors of Judah shall say in
their heart, The inhabitants of Jerusalem
shall be my strength in the LORD of hosts
their God.
6 ¶ In that day will I make the governors of
Judah like an hearth of fire among the wood,
and like a torch of fire in a sheaf; and they
shall devour all the people round about, on
the right hand and on the left: and Jerusalem

shall be inhabited again in her own place,
even in Jerusalem.
7 The LORD also shall save the tents of Judah
first, that the glory of the house of David and
the glory of the inhabitants of Jerusalem
do not magnify *themselves* against Judah.
8 In that day shall the LORD defend the
inhabitants of Jerusalem; and he that is
feeble among them at that day shall be as
David; and the house of David *shall be* as
God, as the angel of the LORD before them.
9 ¶ And it shall come to pass in that day,
that I will seek to destroy all the nations
that come against Jerusalem.
10 And I will pour upon the house of David,
and upon the inhabitants of Jerusalem, the
spirit of grace and of supplications: and
they shall look upon me whom they have
pierced, and they shall mourn for him, as
one mourneth for *his* only *son*, and shall
be in bitterness for him, as one that is in
bitterness for *his* firstborn.
11 In that day shall there be a great mourning in Jerusalem, as the mourning of
Hadadrimmon in the valley of Megiddon.
12 And the land shall mourn, every family
apart; the family of the house of David
apart, and their wives apart; the family
of the house of Nathan apart, and their
wives apart;
13 The family of the house of Levi apart,
and their wives apart; the family of Shimei
apart, and their wives apart;
14 All the families that remain, every family
apart, and their wives apart.

Zechariah 13

1 In that day there shall be a fountain
opened to the house of David and to the
inhabitants of Jerusalem for sin and for
uncleanness.
2 ¶ And it shall come to pass in that day,
saith the LORD of hosts, *that* I will cut off
the names of the idols out of the land, and
they shall no more be remembered: and also
I will cause the prophets and the unclean
spirit to pass out of the land.
3 And it shall come to pass, *that* when any
shall yet prophesy, then his father and his
mother that begat him shall say unto him,
Thou shalt not live; for thou speakest lies in
the name of the LORD: and his father and
his mother that begat him shall thrust him
through when he prophesieth.
4 And it shall come to pass in that day, *that*
the prophets shall be ashamed every one of
his vision, when he hath prophesied; neither
shall they wear a rough garment to deceive:
5 But he shall say, I *am* no prophet, I *am* an
husbandman; for man taught me to keep
cattle from my youth.
6 And *one* shall say unto him, What *are*
these wounds in thine hands? Then he shall
answer, *Those* with which I was wounded
in the house of my friends.
7 ¶ Awake, O sword, against my shepherd,
and against the man *that is* my fellow, saith
the LORD of hosts: smite the shepherd, and
the sheep shall be scattered: and I will turn
mine hand upon the little ones.
8 And it shall come to pass, *that* in all the
land, saith the LORD, two parts therein
shall be cut off *and* die; but the third shall
be left therein.
9 And I will bring the third part through the
fire, and will refine them as silver is refined,
and will try them as gold is tried: they shall
call on my name, and I will hear them: I will
say, It *is* my people: and they shall say, The
LORD *is* my God.

Zechariah 14

1 Behold, the day of the LORD cometh,
and thy spoil shall be divided in the midst
of thee.
2 For I will gather all nations against Jerusalem to battle; and the city shall be taken,
and the houses rifled, and the women ravished; and half of the city shall go forth into
captivity, and the residue of the people shall
not be cut off from the city.
3 Then shall the LORD go forth, and fight
against those nations, as when he fought
in the day of battle.
4 ¶ And his feet shall stand in that day upon
the mount of Olives, which *is* before Jerusalem on the east, and the mount of Olives
shall cleave in the midst thereof toward the
east and toward the west, *and there shall be*
a very great valley; and half of the mountain
shall remove toward the north, and half of
it toward the south.
5 And ye shall flee *to* the valley of the mountains; for the valley of the mountains shall
reach unto Azal: yea, ye shall flee, like as ye

fled from before the earthquake in the days
of Uzziah king of Judah: and the LORD my
God shall come, *and* all the saints with thee.
6 And it shall come to pass in that day, *that*
the light shall not be clear, *nor* dark:
7 But it shall be one day which shall be
known to the LORD, not day, nor night: but
it shall come to pass, *that* at evening time
it shall be light.
8 And it shall be in that day, *that* living
waters shall go out from Jerusalem; half
of them toward the former sea, and half
of them toward the hinder sea: in summer
and in winter shall it be.
9 And the LORD shall be king over all the
earth: in that day shall there be one LORD,
and his name one.
10 All the land shall be turned as a plain
from Geba to Rimmon south of Jerusalem:
and it shall be lifted up, and inhabited in her
place, from Benjamin's gate unto the place
of the first gate, unto the corner gate, and
from the tower of Hananeel unto the king's
winepresses.
11 And *men* shall dwell in it, and there shall
be no more utter destruction; but Jerusalem
shall be safely inhabited.
12 ¶ And this shall be the plague wherewith
the LORD will smite all the people that have
fought against Jerusalem; Their flesh shall
consume away while they stand upon their
feet, and their eyes shall consume away in
their holes, and their tongue shall consume
away in their mouth.
13 And it shall come to pass in that day, *that*
a great tumult from the LORD shall be among
them; and they shall lay hold every one on
the hand of his neighbour, and his hand shall
rise up against the hand of his neighbour.
14 And Judah also shall fight at Jerusalem;
and the wealth of all the heathen round
about shall be gathered together, gold,
and silver, and apparel, in great abundance.
15 And so shall be the plague of the horse,
of the mule, of the camel, and of the ass,
and of all the beasts that shall be in these
tents, as this plague.
16 ¶ And it shall come to pass, *that* every
one that is left of all the nations which came
against Jerusalem shall even go up from year
to year to worship the King, the LORD of
hosts, and to keep the feast of tabernacles.
17 And it shall be, *that* whoso will not come
up of *all* the families of the earth unto
Jerusalem to worship the King, the LORD
of hosts, even upon them shall be no rain.
18 And if the family of Egypt go not up, and
come not, that *have* no *rain;* there shall be
the plague, wherewith the LORD will smite
the heathen that come not up to keep the
feast of tabernacles.
19 This shall be the punishment of Egypt,
and the punishment of all nations that come
not up to keep the feast of tabernacles.
20 ¶ In that day shall there be upon the bells
of the horses, HOLINESS UNTO THE LORD;
and the pots in the LORD's house shall be
like the bowls before the altar.
21 Yea, every pot in Jerusalem and in Judah
shall be holiness unto the LORD of hosts: and
all they that sacrifice shall come and take of
them, and seethe therein: and in that day
there shall be no more the Canaanite in the
house of the LORD of hosts.

The Book Of

Malachi

Malachi 1

1 The burden of the word of the LORD to Israel by Malachi.

2 I have loved you, saith the LORD. Yet ye say, Wherein hast thou loved us? *Was* not Esau Jacob's brother? saith the LORD: yet I loved Jacob,

3 And I hated Esau, and laid his mountains and his heritage waste for the dragons of the wilderness.

4 Whereas Edom saith, We are impoverished, but we will return and build the desolate places; thus saith the LORD of hosts, They shall build, but I will throw down; and they shall call them, The border of wickedness, and, The people against whom the LORD hath indignation for ever.

5 And your eyes shall see, and ye shall say, The LORD will be magnified from the border of Israel.

6 ¶ A son honoureth *his* father, and a servant his master: if then I *be* a father, where *is* mine honour? and if I *be* a master, where *is* my fear? saith the LORD of hosts unto you, O priests, that despise my name. And ye say, Wherein have we despised thy name?

7 Ye offer polluted bread upon mine altar; and ye say, Wherein have we polluted thee? In that ye say, The table of the LORD *is* contemptible.

8 And if ye offer the blind for sacrifice, *is it* not evil? and if ye offer the lame and sick, *is it* not evil? offer it now unto thy governor; will he be pleased with thee, or accept thy person? saith the LORD of hosts.

9 And now, I pray you, beseech God that he will be gracious unto us: this hath been by your means: will he regard your persons? saith the LORD of hosts.

10 Who *is there* even among you that would shut the doors *for nought?* neither do ye kindle *fire* on mine altar for nought. I have no pleasure in you, saith the LORD of hosts, neither will I accept an offering at your hand.

11 For from the rising of the sun even unto the going down of the same my name *shall be* great among the Gentiles; and in every place incense *shall be* offered unto my name, and a pure offering: for my name *shall be* great among the heathen, saith the LORD of hosts.

12 ¶ But ye have profaned it, in that ye say, The table of the LORD *is* polluted; and the fruit thereof, *even* his meat, *is* contemptible.

13 Ye said also, Behold, what a weariness *is it!* and ye have snuffed at it, saith the LORD of hosts; and ye brought *that which was* torn, and the lame, and the sick; thus ye brought an offering: should I accept this of your hand? saith the LORD.

14 But cursed *be* the deceiver, which hath in his flock a male, and voweth, and sacrificeth unto the Lord a corrupt thing: for I *am* a great King, saith the LORD of hosts, and my name *is* dreadful among the heathen.

Malachi 2

1 And now, O ye priests, this commandment *is* for you.

2 If ye will not hear, and if ye will not lay *it* to heart, to give glory unto my name, saith the LORD of hosts, I will even send a curse upon you, and I will curse your blessings: yea, I have cursed them already, because ye do not lay *it* to heart.

3 Behold, I will corrupt your seed, and spread dung upon your faces, *even* the dung of your solemn feasts; and *one* shall take you away with it.

4 And ye shall know that I have sent this commandment unto you, that my covenant might be with Levi, saith the LORD of hosts.

5 My covenant was with him of life and peace; and I gave them to him *for* the fear wherewith he feared me, and was afraid before my name.

6 The law of truth was in his mouth, and iniquity was not found in his lips: he walked with me in peace and equity, and did turn many away from iniquity.

7 For the priest's lips should keep knowledge, and they should seek the law at his mouth: for he *is* the messenger of the LORD of hosts.

8 But ye are departed out of the way; ye
have caused many to stumble at the law; ye
have corrupted the covenant of Levi, saith
the LORD of hosts.
9 Therefore have I also made you contemptible and base before all the people,
according as ye have not kept my ways, but
have been partial in the law.
10 Have we not all one father? hath not one
God created us? why do we deal treacherously every man against his brother, by
profaning the covenant of our fathers?
11 ¶ Judah hath dealt treacherously, and
an abomination is committed in Israel and
in Jerusalem; for Judah hath profaned the
holiness of the LORD which he loved, and
hath married the daughter of a strange god.
12 The LORD will cut off the man that doeth
this, the master and the scholar, out of the
tabernacles of Jacob, and him that offereth
an offering unto the LORD of hosts.
13 And this have ye done again, covering the
altar of the LORD with tears, with weeping,
and with crying out, insomuch that he regardeth not the offering any more, or receiveth
it with good will at your hand.
14 ¶ Yet ye say, Wherefore? Because the
LORD hath been witness between thee and
the wife of thy youth, against whom thou
hast dealt treacherously: yet *is* she thy
companion, and the wife of thy covenant.
15 And did not he make one? Yet had he the
residue of the spirit. And wherefore one?
That he might seek a godly seed. Therefore
take heed to your spirit, and let none deal
treacherously against the wife of his youth.
16 For the LORD, the God of Israel, saith that
he hateth putting away: for *one* covereth
violence with his garment, saith the LORD
of hosts: therefore take heed to your spirit,
that ye deal not treacherously.
17 ¶ Ye have wearied the LORD with your
words. Yet ye say, Wherein have we wearied
him? When ye say, Every one that doeth
evil *is* good in the sight of the LORD, and he
delighteth in them; or, Where *is* the God
of judgment?

Malachi 3

1 Behold, I will send my messenger, and he
shall prepare the way before me: and the
Lord, whom ye seek, shall suddenly come
to his temple, even the messenger of the
covenant, whom ye delight in: behold, he
shall come, saith the LORD of hosts.
2 But who may abide the day of his coming?
and who shall stand when he appeareth? for
he *is* like a refiner's fire, and like fullers' soap:
3 And he shall sit *as* a refiner and purifier of
silver: and he shall purify the sons of Levi,
and purge them as gold and silver, that
they may offer unto the LORD an offering
in righteousness.
4 Then shall the offering of Judah and Jerusalem be pleasant unto the LORD, as in the
days of old, and as in former years.
5 And I will come near to you to judgment;
and I will be a swift witness against the
sorcerers, and against the adulterers, and
against false swearers, and against those
that oppress the hireling in *his* wages, the
widow, and the fatherless, and that turn
aside the stranger *from his right*, and fear
not me, saith the LORD of hosts.
6 For I *am* the LORD, I change not; therefore
ye sons of Jacob are not consumed.
7 ¶ Even from the days of your fathers ye
are gone away from mine ordinances, and
have not kept *them*. Return unto me, and I
will return unto you, saith the LORD of hosts.
But ye said, Wherein shall we return?
8 ¶ Will a man rob God? Yet ye have robbed
me. But ye say, Wherein have we robbed
thee? In tithes and offerings.
9 Ye *are* cursed with a curse: for ye have
robbed me, *even* this whole nation.
10 Bring ye all the tithes into the storehouse,
that there may be meat in mine house, and
prove me now herewith, saith the LORD of
hosts, if I will not open you the windows of
heaven, and pour you out a blessing, that
there shall not *be room* enough *to receive it*.
11 And I will rebuke the devourer for your
sakes, and he shall not destroy the fruits of
your ground; neither shall your vine cast her
fruit before the time in the field, saith the
LORD of hosts.
12 And all nations shall call you blessed: for
ye shall be a delightsome land, saith the
LORD of hosts.
13 ¶ Your words have been stout against
me, saith the LORD. Yet ye say, What have
we spoken *so much* against thee?
14 Ye have said, It *is* vain to serve God: and
what profit *is it* that we have kept his ordi-

nance, and that we have walked mournfully
before the LORD of hosts?
15 And now we call the proud happy; yea,
they that work wickedness are set up; yea,
they that tempt God are even delivered.
16 ¶ Then they that feared the LORD spake
often one to another: and the LORD hearkened, and heard *it*, and a book of remembrance was written before him for them
that feared the LORD, and that thought
upon his name.
17 And they shall be mine, saith the LORD of
hosts, in that day when I make up my jewels;
and I will spare them, as a man spareth his
own son that serveth him.
18 Then shall ye return, and discern
between the righteous and the wicked,
between him that serveth God and him that
serveth him not.

Malachi 4

1 For, behold, the day cometh, that shall
burn as an oven; and all the proud, yea, and
all that do wickedly, shall be stubble: and the
day that cometh shall burn them up, saith
the LORD of hosts, that it shall leave them
neither root nor branch.
2 ¶ But unto you that fear my name shall
the Sun of righteousness arise with healing
in his wings; and ye shall go forth, and grow
up as calves of the stall.
3 And ye shall tread down the wicked; for
they shall be ashes under the soles of your
feet in the day that I shall do *this*, saith the
LORD of hosts.
4 ¶ Remember ye the law of Moses my
servant, which I commanded unto him in
Horeb for all Israel, *with* the statutes and
judgments.
5 ¶ Behold, I will send you Elijah the prophet
before the coming of the great and dreadful
day of the LORD:
6 And he shall turn the heart of the fathers
to the children, and the heart of the children
to their fathers, lest I come and smite the
earth with a curse.

The
New Testament

The Gospel According To

Matthew

Matthew 1

1 The book of the generation of Jesus Christ,
the son of David, the son of Abraham.
2 Abraham begat Isaac; and Isaac begat
Jacob; and Jacob begat Judas and his brethren;
3 And Judas begat Phares and Zara of
Thamar; and Phares begat Esrom; and Esrom
begat Aram;
4 And Aram begat Aminadab; and Aminadab
begat Naasson; and Naasson begat Salmon;
5 And Salmon begat Booz of Rachab; and
Booz begat Obed of Ruth; and Obed begat
Jesse;
6 And Jesse begat David the king; and David
the king begat Solomon of her *that had been
the wife* of Urias;
7 And Solomon begat Roboam; and Roboam
begat Abia; and Abia begat Asa;
8 And Asa begat Josaphat; and Josaphat
begat Joram; and Joram begat Ozias;
9 And Ozias begat Joatham; and Joatham
begat Achaz; and Achaz begat Ezekias;
10 And Ezekias begat Manasses; and
Manasses begat Amon; and Amon begat
Josias;
11 And Josias begat Jechonias and his brethren, about the time they were carried away
to Babylon:
12 And after they were brought to Babylon,
Jechonias begat Salathiel; and Salathiel
begat Zorobabel;
13 And Zorobabel begat Abiud; and Abiud
begat Eliakim; and Eliakim begat Azor;
14 And Azor begat Sadoc; and Sadoc begat
Achim; and Achim begat Eliud;
15 And Eliud begat Eleazar; and Eleazar
begat Matthan; and Matthan begat Jacob;
16 And Jacob begat Joseph the husband
of Mary, of whom was born Jesus, who is
called Christ.
17 So all the generations from Abraham to
David *are* fourteen generations; and from
David until the carrying away into Babylon
are fourteen generations; and from the
carrying away into Babylon unto Christ *are*
fourteen generations.
18 ¶ Now the birth of Jesus Christ was on
this wise: When as his mother Mary was
espoused to Joseph, before they came
together, she was found with child of the
Holy Spirit.
19 Then Joseph her husband, being a just
man, and not willing to make her a publick
example, was minded to put her away
privily.
20 But while he thought on these things,
behold, the angel of the Lord appeared unto
him in a dream, saying, Joseph, thou son of
David, fear not to take unto thee Mary thy
wife: for that which is conceived in her is of
the Holy Spirit.
21 And she shall bring forth a son, and thou
shalt call his name JESUS: for he shall save
his people from their sins.
22 Now all this was done, that it might be
fulfilled which was spoken of the Lord by
the prophet, saying,
23 Behold, a virgin shall be with child, and
shall bring forth a son, and they shall call his
name Emmanuel, which being interpreted
is, God with us.
24 Then Joseph being raised from sleep did
as the angel of the Lord had bidden him, and
took unto him his wife:
25 And knew her not till she had brought
forth her firstborn son: and he called his
name JESUS.

Matthew 2

1 Now when Jesus was born in Bethlehem of Judæa in the days of Herod the king, behold, there came wise men from the east to Jerusalem,

2 Saying, Where is he that is born King of the Jews? for we have seen his star in the east, and are come to worship him.

3 When Herod the king had heard *these things*, he was troubled, and all Jerusalem with him.

4 And when he had gathered all the chief priests and scribes of the people together, he demanded of them where Christ should be born.

5 And they said unto him, In Bethlehem of Judæa: for thus it is written by the prophet,

6 And thou Bethlehem, *in* the land of Juda, art not the least among the princes of Juda: for out of thee shall come a Governor, that shall rule my people Israel.

7 Then Herod, when he had privily called the wise men, inquired of them diligently what time the star appeared.

8 And he sent them to Bethlehem, and said, Go and search diligently for the young child; and when ye have found *him*, bring me word again, that I may come and worship him also.

9 When they had heard the king, they departed; and, lo, the star, which they saw in the east, went before them, till it came and stood over where the young child was.

10 When they saw the star, they rejoiced with exceeding great joy.

11 ¶ And when they were come into the house, they saw the young child with Mary his mother, and fell down, and worshipped him: and when they had opened their treasures, they presented unto him gifts; gold, and frankincense, and myrrh.

12 And being warned of God in a dream that they should not return to Herod, they departed into their own country another way.

13 And when they were departed, behold, the angel of the Lord appeareth to Joseph in a dream, saying, Arise, and take the young child and his mother, and flee into Egypt, and be thou there until I bring thee word: for Herod will seek the young child to destroy him.

14 When he arose, he took the young child and his mother by night, and departed into Egypt:

15 And was there until the death of Herod: that it might be fulfilled which was spoken of the Lord by the prophet, saying, Out of Egypt have I called my son.

16 ¶ Then Herod, when he saw that he was mocked of the wise men, was exceeding wroth, and sent forth, and slew all the children that were in Bethlehem, and in all the coasts thereof, from two years old and under, according to the time which he had diligently inquired of the wise men.

17 Then was fulfilled that which was spoken by Jeremy the prophet, saying,

18 In Rama was there a voice heard, lamentation, and weeping, and great mourning, Rachel weeping *for* her children, and would not be comforted, because they are not.

19 ¶ But when Herod was dead, behold, an angel of the Lord appeareth in a dream to Joseph in Egypt,

20 Saying, Arise, and take the young child and his mother, and go into the land of Israel: for they are dead which sought the young child's life.

21 And he arose, and took the young child and his mother, and came into the land of Israel.

22 But when he heard that Archelaus did reign in Judæa in the room of his father Herod, he was afraid to go thither: notwithstanding, being warned of God in a dream, he turned aside into the parts of Galilee:

23 And he came and dwelt in a city called Nazareth: that it might be fulfilled which was spoken by the prophets, He shall be called a Nazarene.

Matthew 3

1 In those days came John the Baptist, preaching in the wilderness of Judæa,

2 And saying, Repent ye: for the kingdom of heaven is at hand.

3 For this is he that was spoken of by the prophet Esaias, saying, The voice of one crying in the wilderness, Prepare ye the way of the Lord, make his paths straight.

4 And the same John had his raiment of camel's hair, and a leathern girdle about his loins; and his meat was locusts and wild honey.

5 Then went out to him Jerusalem, and

all Judæa, and all the region round about
Jordan,
6 And were baptized of him in Jordan, confessing their sins.
7 ¶ But when he saw many of the Pharisees
and Sadducees come to his baptism, he said
unto them, O generation of vipers, who hath
warned you to flee from the wrath to come?
8 Bring forth therefore fruits meet for
repentance:
9 And think not to say within yourselves,
We have Abraham to *our* father: for I say
unto you, that God is able of these stones
to raise up children unto Abraham.
10 And now also the axe is laid unto the
root of the trees: therefore every tree which
bringeth not forth good fruit is hewn down,
and cast into the fire.
11 I indeed baptize you with water unto
repentance: but he that cometh after me
is mightier than I, whose shoes I am not
worthy to bear: he shall baptize you with
the Holy Spirit, and *with* fire:
12 Whose fan *is* in his hand, and he will
throughly purge his floor, and gather his
wheat into the garner; but he will burn up
the chaff with unquenchable fire.
13 ¶ Then cometh Jesus from Galilee to
Jordan unto John, to be baptized of him.
14 But John forbad him, saying, I have
need to be baptized of thee, and comest
thou to me?
15 And Jesus answering said unto him,
Suffer *it to be so* now: for thus it becometh us to fulfil all righteousness. Then he
suffered him.
16 And Jesus, when he was baptized, went
up straightway out of the water: and, lo,
the heavens were opened unto him, and
he saw the Spirit of God descending like a
dove, and lighting upon him:
17 And lo a voice from heaven, saying, This is
my beloved Son, in whom I am well pleased.

Matthew 4

1 Then was Jesus led up of the Spirit into
the wilderness to be tempted of the devil.
2 And when he had fasted forty days and
forty nights, he was afterward an hungred.
3 And when the tempter came to him, he
said, If thou be the Son of God, command
that these stones be made bread.
4 But he answered and said, It is written,
Man shall not live by bread alone, but by
every word that proceedeth out of the
mouth of God.
5 Then the devil taketh him up into the
holy city, and setteth him on a pinnacle of
the temple,
6 And saith unto him, If thou be the Son of
God, cast thyself down: for it is written, He
shall give his angels charge concerning thee:
and in *their* hands they shall bear thee up,
lest at any time thou dash thy foot against
a stone.
7 Jesus said unto him, It is written again,
Thou shalt not tempt the Lord thy God.
8 Again, the devil taketh him up into an
exceeding high mountain, and sheweth
him all the kingdoms of the world, and the
glory of them;
9 And saith unto him, All these things will
I give thee, if thou wilt fall down and worship me.
10 Then saith Jesus unto him, Get thee
hence, Satan: for it is written, Thou shalt
worship the Lord thy God, and him only
shalt thou serve.
11 Then the devil leaveth him, and, behold,
angels came and ministered unto him.
12 ¶ Now when Jesus had heard that John
was cast into prison, he departed into
Galilee;
13 And leaving Nazareth, he came and dwelt
in Capernaum, which is upon the sea coast,
in the borders of Zabulon and Nephthalim:
14 That it might be fulfilled which was spoken by Esaias the prophet, saying,
15 The land of Zabulon, and the land of
Nephthalim, *by* the way of the sea, beyond
Jordan, Galilee of the Gentiles;
16 The people which sat in darkness saw
great light; and to them which sat in the
region and shadow of death light is sprung
up.
17 ¶ From that time Jesus began to preach,
and to say, Repent: for the kingdom of
heaven is at hand.
18 ¶ And Jesus, walking by the sea of Galilee,
saw two brethren, Simon called Peter, and
Andrew his brother, casting a net into the
sea: for they were fishers.
19 And he saith unto them, Follow me, and
I will make you fishers of men.
20 And they straightway left *their* nets, and
followed him.

21 And going on from thence, he saw other two brethren, James *the son* of Zebedee, and John his brother, in a ship with Zebedee their father, mending their nets; and he called them.
22 And they immediately left the ship and their father, and followed him.
23 ¶ And Jesus went about all Galilee, teaching in their synagogues, and preaching the gospel of the kingdom, and healing all manner of sickness and all manner of disease among the people.
24 And his fame went throughout all Syria: and they brought unto him all sick people that were taken with divers diseases and torments, and those which were possessed with devils, and those which were lunatick, and those that had the palsy; and he healed them.
25 And there followed him great multitudes of people from Galilee, and *from* Decapolis, and *from* Jerusalem, and *from* Judæa, and *from* beyond Jordan.

Matthew 5

1 And seeing the multitudes, he went up into a mountain: and when he was set, his disciples came unto him:
2 And he opened his mouth, and taught them, saying,
3 Blessed *are* the poor in spirit: for theirs is the kingdom of heaven.
4 Blessed *are* they that mourn: for they shall be comforted.
5 Blessed *are* the meek: for they shall inherit the earth.
6 Blessed *are* they which do hunger and thirst after righteousness: for they shall be filled.
7 Blessed *are* the merciful: for they shall obtain mercy.
8 Blessed *are* the pure in heart: for they shall see God.
9 Blessed *are* the peacemakers: for they shall be called the children of God.
10 Blessed *are* they which are persecuted for righteousness' sake: for theirs is the kingdom of heaven.
11 Blessed are ye, when *men* shall revile you, and persecute *you*, and shall say all manner of evil against you falsely, for my sake.
12 Rejoice, and be exceeding glad: for great *is* your reward in heaven: for so persecuted they the prophets which were before you.
13 ¶ Ye are the salt of the earth: but if the salt have lost his savour, wherewith shall it be salted? it is thenceforth good for nothing, but to be cast out, and to be trodden under foot of men.
14 Ye are the light of the world. A city that is set on an hill cannot be hid.
15 Neither do men light a candle, and put it under a bushel, but on a candlestick; and it giveth light unto all that are in the house.
16 Let your light so shine before men, that they may see your good works, and glorify your Father which is in heaven.
17 ¶ Think not that I am come to destroy the law, or the prophets: I am not come to destroy, but to fulfil.
18 For verily I say unto you, Till heaven and earth pass, one jot or one tittle shall in no wise pass from the law, till all be fulfilled.
19 Whosoever therefore shall break one of these least commandments, and shall teach men so, he shall be called the least in the kingdom of heaven: but whosoever shall do and teach *them*, the same shall be called great in the kingdom of heaven.
20 For I say unto you, That except your righteousness shall exceed *the righteousness* of the scribes and Pharisees, ye shall in no case enter into the kingdom of heaven.
21 ¶ Ye have heard that it was said by them of old time, Thou shalt not kill; and whosoever shall kill shall be in danger of the judgment:
22 But I say unto you, That whosoever is angry with his brother without a cause shall be in danger of the judgment: and whosoever shall say to his brother, Raca, shall be in danger of the council: but whosoever shall say, Thou fool, shall be in danger of hell fire.
23 Therefore if thou bring thy gift to the altar, and there rememberest that thy brother hath ought against thee;
24 Leave there thy gift before the altar, and go thy way; first be reconciled to thy brother, and then come and offer thy gift.
25 Agree with thine adversary quickly, whiles thou art in the way with him; lest at any time the adversary deliver thee to the judge, and the judge deliver thee to the officer, and thou be cast into prison.
26 Verily I say unto thee, Thou shalt by no

means come out thence, till thou hast paid
the uttermost farthing.
27 ¶ Ye have heard that it was said by them
of old time, Thou shalt not commit adultery:
28 But I say unto you, That whosoever
looketh on a woman to lust after her hath
committed adultery with her already in
his heart.
29 And if thy right eye offend thee, pluck it
out, and cast *it* from thee: for it is profitable
for thee that one of thy members should
perish, and not *that* thy whole body should
be cast into hell.
30 And if thy right hand offend thee, cut it
off, and cast *it* from thee: for it is profitable
for thee that one of thy members should
perish, and not *that* thy whole body should
be cast into hell.
31 It hath been said, Whosoever shall put
away his wife, let him give her a writing of
divorcement:
32 But I say unto you, That whosoever shall
put away his wife, saving for the cause of
fornication, causeth her to commit adultery: and whosoever shall marry her that
is divorced committeth adultery.
33 ¶ Again, ye have heard that it hath been
said by them of old time, Thou shalt not
forswear thyself, but shalt perform unto
the Lord thine oaths:
34 But I say unto you, Swear not at all; neither by heaven; for it is God's throne:
35 Nor by the earth; for it is his footstool:
neither by Jerusalem; for it is the city of
the great King.
36 Neither shalt thou swear by thy head,
because thou canst not make one hair
white or black.
37 But let your communication be, Yea, yea;
Nay, nay: for whatsoever is more than these
cometh of evil.
38 ¶ Ye have heard that it hath been said,
An eye for an eye, and a tooth for a tooth:
39 But I say unto you, That ye resist not evil:
but whosoever shall smite thee on thy right
cheek, turn to him the other also.
40 And if any man will sue thee at the law,
and take away thy coat, let him have *thy*
cloke also.
41 And whosoever shall compel thee to go
a mile, go with him twain.
42 Give to him that asketh thee, and from
him that would borrow of thee turn not
thou away.
43 ¶ Ye have heard that it hath been said,
Thou shalt love thy neighbour, and hate
thine enemy.
44 But I say unto you, Love your enemies,
bless them that curse you, do good to them
that hate you, and pray for them which
despitefully use you, and persecute you;
45 That ye may be the children of your
Father which is in heaven: for he maketh his
sun to rise on the evil and on the good, and
sendeth rain on the just and on the unjust.
46 For if ye love them which love you, what
reward have ye? do not even the publicans
the same?
47 And if ye salute your brethren only, what
do ye more *than others?* do not even the
publicans so?
48 Be ye therefore perfect, even as your
Father which is in heaven is perfect.

Matthew 6

1 Take heed that ye do not your alms before
men, to be seen of them: otherwise ye have
no reward of your Father which is in heaven.
2 Therefore when thou doest *thine* alms,
do not sound a trumpet before thee, as the
hypocrites do in the synagogues and in the
streets, that they may have glory of men.
Verily I say unto you, They have their reward.
3 But when thou doest alms, let not thy
left hand know what thy right hand doeth:
4 That thine alms may be in secret: and thy
Father which seeth in secret himself shall
reward thee openly.
5 ¶ And when thou prayest, thou shalt not
be as the hypocrites *are:* for they love to
pray standing in the synagogues and in the
corners of the streets, that they may be
seen of men. Verily I say unto you, They
have their reward.
6 But thou, when thou prayest, enter into
thy closet, and when thou hast shut thy
door, pray to thy Father which is in secret;
and thy Father which seeth in secret shall
reward thee openly.
7 But when ye pray, use not vain repetitions,
as the heathen *do:* for they think that they
shall be heard for their much speaking.
8 Be not ye therefore like unto them: for
your Father knoweth what things ye have
need of, before ye ask him.

9 After this manner therefore pray ye: Our
Father which art in heaven, Hallowed be
thy name.
10 Thy kingdom come. Thy will be done in
earth, as *it is* in heaven.
11 Give us this day our daily bread.
12 And forgive us our debts, as we forgive
our debtors.
13 And lead us not into temptation, but
deliver us from evil: For thine is the kingdom, and the power, and the glory, for
ever. Amen.
14 For if ye forgive men their trespasses,
your heavenly Father will also forgive you:
15 But if ye forgive not men their trespasses, neither will your Father forgive your
trespasses.
16 ¶ Moreover when ye fast, be not, as the
hypocrites, of a sad countenance: for they
disfigure their faces, that they may appear
unto men to fast. Verily I say unto you, They
have their reward.
17 But thou, when thou fastest, anoint thine
head, and wash thy face;
18 That thou appear not unto men to fast,
but unto thy Father which is in secret: and
thy Father, which seeth in secret, shall
reward thee openly.
19 ¶ Lay not up for yourselves treasures
upon earth, where moth and rust doth
corrupt, and where thieves break through
and steal:
20 But lay up for yourselves treasures in
heaven, where neither moth nor rust doth
corrupt, and where thieves do not break
through nor steal:
21 For where your treasure is, there will
your heart be also.
22 The light of the body is the eye: if therefore thine eye be single, thy whole body
shall be full of light.
23 But if thine eye be evil, thy whole body
shall be full of darkness. If therefore the
light that is in thee be darkness, how great
is that darkness!
24 ¶ No man can serve two masters: for
either he will hate the one, and love the
other; or else he will hold to the one, and
despise the other. Ye cannot serve God and
mammon.
25 Therefore I say unto you, Take no thought
for your life, what ye shall eat, or what ye
shall drink; nor yet for your body, what ye
shall put on. Is not the life more than meat,
and the body than raiment?
26 Behold the fowls of the air: for they sow
not, neither do they reap, nor gather into
barns; yet your heavenly Father feedeth
them. Are ye not much better than they?
27 Which of you by taking thought can add
one cubit unto his stature?
28 And why take ye thought for raiment?
Consider the lilies of the field, how they
grow; they toil not, neither do they spin:
29 And yet I say unto you, That even Solomon in all his glory was not arrayed like
one of these.
30 Wherefore, if God so clothe the grass of
the field, which to day is, and to morrow is
cast into the oven, *shall he* not much more
clothe you, O ye of little faith?
31 Therefore take no thought, saying, What
shall we eat? or, What shall we drink? or,
Wherewithal shall we be clothed?
32 (For after all these things do the Gentiles
seek:) for your heavenly Father knoweth that
ye have need of all these things.
33 But seek ye first the kingdom of God, and
his righteousness; and all these things shall
be added unto you.
34 Take therefore no thought for the morrow: for the morrow shall take thought for
the things of itself. Sufficient unto the day
is the evil thereof.

Matthew 7

1 Judge not, that ye be not judged.
2 For with what judgment ye judge, ye shall
be judged: and with what measure ye mete,
it shall be measured to you again.
3 And why beholdest thou the mote that is
in thy brother's eye, but considerest not the
beam that is in thine own eye?
4 Or how wilt thou say to thy brother, Let
me pull out the mote out of thine eye; and,
behold, a beam *is* in thine own eye?
5 Thou hypocrite, first cast out the beam
out of thine own eye; and then shalt thou
see clearly to cast out the mote out of thy
brother's eye.
6 ¶ Give not that which is holy unto the
dogs, neither cast ye your pearls before
swine, lest they trample them under their
feet, and turn again and rend you.
7 ¶ Ask, and it shall be given you; seek, and

ye shall find; knock, and it shall be opened unto you:

8 For every one that asketh receiveth; and he that seeketh findeth; and to him that knocketh it shall be opened.

9 Or what man is there of you, whom if his son ask bread, will he give him a stone?

10 Or if he ask a fish, will he give him a serpent?

11 If ye then, being evil, know how to give good gifts unto your children, how much more shall your Father which is in heaven give good things to them that ask him?

12 Therefore all things whatsoever ye would that men should do to you, do ye even so to them: for this is the law and the prophets.

13 ¶ Enter ye in at the strait gate: for wide *is* the gate, and broad *is* the way, that leadeth to destruction, and many there be which go in thereat:

14 Because strait *is* the gate, and narrow *is* the way, which leadeth unto life, and few there be that find it.

15 ¶ Beware of false prophets, which come to you in sheep's clothing, but inwardly they are ravening wolves.

16 Ye shall know them by their fruits. Do men gather grapes of thorns, or figs of thistles?

17 Even so every good tree bringeth forth good fruit; but a corrupt tree bringeth forth evil fruit.

18 A good tree cannot bring forth evil fruit, neither *can* a corrupt tree bring forth good fruit.

19 Every tree that bringeth not forth good fruit is hewn down, and cast into the fire.

20 Wherefore by their fruits ye shall know them.

21 ¶ Not every one that saith unto me, Lord, Lord, shall enter into the kingdom of heaven; but he that doeth the will of my Father which is in heaven.

22 Many will say to me in that day, Lord, Lord, have we not prophesied in thy name? and in thy name have cast out devils? and in thy name done many wonderful works?

23 And then will I profess unto them, I never knew you: depart from me, ye that work iniquity.

24 ¶ Therefore whosoever heareth these sayings of mine, and doeth them, I will liken him unto a wise man, which built his house upon a rock:

25 And the rain descended, and the floods came, and the winds blew, and beat upon that house; and it fell not: for it was founded upon a rock.

26 And every one that heareth these sayings of mine, and doeth them not, shall be likened unto a foolish man, which built his house upon the sand:

27 And the rain descended, and the floods came, and the winds blew, and beat upon that house; and it fell: and great was the fall of it.

28 And it came to pass, when Jesus had ended these sayings, the people were astonished at his doctrine:

29 For he taught them as *one* having authority, and not as the scribes.

Matthew 8

1 When he was come down from the mountain, great multitudes followed him.

2 And, behold, there came a leper and worshipped him, saying, Lord, if thou wilt, thou canst make me clean.

3 And Jesus put forth *his* hand, and touched him, saying, I will; be thou clean. And immediately his leprosy was cleansed.

4 And Jesus saith unto him, See thou tell no man; but go thy way, shew thyself to the priest, and offer the gift that Moses commanded, for a testimony unto them.

5 ¶ And when Jesus was entered into Capernaum, there came unto him a centurion, beseeching him,

6 And saying, Lord, my servant lieth at home sick of the palsy, grievously tormented.

7 And Jesus saith unto him, I will come and heal him.

8 The centurion answered and said, Lord, I am not worthy that thou shouldest come under my roof: but speak the word only, and my servant shall be healed.

9 For I am a man under authority, having soldiers under me: and I say to this *man*, Go, and he goeth; and to another, Come, and he cometh; and to my servant, Do this, and he doeth *it*.

10 When Jesus heard *it*, he marvelled, and said to them that followed, Verily I say unto you, I have not found so great faith, no, not in Israel.

11 And I say unto you, That many shall come from the east and west, and shall sit down with Abraham, and Isaac, and Jacob, in the kingdom of heaven.

12 But the children of the kingdom shall be cast out into outer darkness: there shall be weeping and gnashing of teeth.

13 And Jesus said unto the centurion, Go thy way; and as thou hast believed, *so* be it done unto thee. And his servant was healed in the selfsame hour.

14 ¶ And when Jesus was come into Peter's house, he saw his wife's mother laid, and sick of a fever.

15 And he touched her hand, and the fever left her: and she arose, and ministered unto them.

16 ¶ When the even was come, they brought unto him many that were possessed with devils: and he cast out the spirits with *his* word, and healed all that were sick:

17 That it might be fulfilled which was spoken by Esaias the prophet, saying, Himself took our infirmities, and bare *our* sicknesses.

18 ¶ Now when Jesus saw great multitudes about him, he gave commandment to depart unto the other side.

19 And a certain scribe came, and said unto him, Master, I will follow thee whithersoever thou goest.

20 And Jesus saith unto him, The foxes have holes, and the birds of the air *have* nests; but the Son of man hath not where to lay *his* head.

21 And another of his disciples said unto him, Lord, suffer me first to go and bury my father.

22 But Jesus said unto him, Follow me; and let the dead bury their dead.

23 ¶ And when he was entered into a ship, his disciples followed him.

24 And, behold, there arose a great tempest in the sea, insomuch that the ship was covered with the waves: but he was asleep.

25 And his disciples came to *him*, and awoke him, saying, Lord, save us: we perish.

26 And he saith unto them, Why are ye fearful, O ye of little faith? Then he arose, and rebuked the winds and the sea; and there was a great calm.

27 But the men marvelled, saying, What manner of man is this, that even the winds and the sea obey him!

28 ¶ And when he was come to the other side into the country of the Gergesenes, there met him two possessed with devils, coming out of the tombs, exceeding fierce, so that no man might pass by that way.

29 And, behold, they cried out, saying, What have we to do with thee, Jesus, thou Son of God? art thou come hither to torment us before the time?

30 And there was a good way off from them an herd of many swine feeding.

31 So the devils besought him, saying, If thou cast us out, suffer us to go away into the herd of swine.

32 And he said unto them, Go. And when they were come out, they went into the herd of swine: and, behold, the whole herd of swine ran violently down a steep place into the sea, and perished in the waters.

33 And they that kept them fled, and went their ways into the city, and told every thing, and what was befallen to the possessed of the devils.

34 And, behold, the whole city came out to meet Jesus: and when they saw him, they besought *him* that he would depart out of their coasts.

Matthew 9

1 And he entered into a ship, and passed over, and came into his own city.

2 And, behold, they brought to him a man sick of the palsy, lying on a bed: and Jesus seeing their faith said unto the sick of the palsy; Son, be of good cheer; thy sins be forgiven thee.

3 And, behold, certain of the scribes said within themselves, This *man* blasphemeth.

4 And Jesus knowing their thoughts said, Wherefore think ye evil in your hearts?

5 For whether is easier, to say, *Thy* sins be forgiven thee; or to say, Arise, and walk?

6 But that ye may know that the Son of man hath power on earth to forgive sins, (then saith he to the sick of the palsy,) Arise, take up thy bed, and go unto thine house.

7 And he arose, and departed to his house.

8 But when the multitudes saw *it*, they marvelied, and glorified God, which had given such power unto men.

9 ¶ And as Jesus passed forth from thence, he saw a man, named Matthew, sitting at

the receipt of custom: and he saith unto him,
Follow me. And he arose, and followed him.
10 ¶ And it came to pass, as Jesus sat at
meat in the house, behold, many publicans
and sinners came and sat down with him
and his disciples.
11 And when the Pharisees saw *it*, they said
unto his disciples, Why eateth your Master
with publicans and sinners?
12 But when Jesus heard *that*, he said unto
them, They that be whole need not a physician, but they that are sick.
13 But go ye and learn what *that* meaneth,
I will have mercy, and not sacrifice: for I am
not come to call the righteous, but sinners
to repentance.
14 ¶ Then came to him the disciples of John,
saying, Why do we and the Pharisees fast
oft, but thy disciples fast not?
15 And Jesus said unto them, Can the children of the bridechamber mourn, as long as
the bridegroom is with them? but the days
will come, when the bridegroom shall be
taken from them, and then shall they fast.
16 No man putteth a piece of new cloth
unto an old garment, for that which is put
in to fill it up taketh from the garment, and
the rent is made worse.
17 Neither do men put new wine into old
bottles: else the bottles break, and the wine
runneth out, and the bottles perish: but they
put new wine into new bottles, and both
are preserved.
18 ¶ While he spake these things unto
them, behold, there came a certain ruler,
and worshipped him, saying, My daughter is
even now dead: but come and lay thy hand
upon her, and she shall live.
19 And Jesus arose, and followed him, and
so did his disciples.
20 ¶ And, behold, a woman, which was diseased with an issue of blood twelve years,
came behind *him*, and touched the hem of
his garment:
21 For she said within herself, If I may but
touch his garment, I shall be whole.
22 But Jesus turned him about, and when
he saw her, he said, Daughter, be of good
comfort; thy faith hath made thee whole.
And the woman was made whole from
that hour.
23 And when Jesus came into the ruler's
house, and saw the minstrels and the people
making a noise,
24 He said unto them, Give place: for the
maid is not dead, but sleepeth. And they
laughed him to scorn.
25 But when the people were put forth, he
went in, and took her by the hand, and the
maid arose.
26 And the fame hereof went abroad into
all that land.
27 ¶ And when Jesus departed thence, two
blind men followed him, crying, and saying,
Thou Son of David, have mercy on us.
28 And when he was come into the house,
the blind men came to him: and Jesus saith
unto them, Believe ye that I am able to do
this? They said unto him, Yea, Lord.
29 Then touched he their eyes, saying,
According to your faith be it unto you.
30 And their eyes were opened; and Jesus
straitly charged them, saying, See *that* no
man know *it*.
31 But they, when they were departed,
spread abroad his fame in all that country.
32 ¶ As they went out, behold, they brought
to him a dumb man possessed with a devil.
33 And when the devil was cast out, the
dumb spake: and the multitudes marvelled,
saying, It was never so seen in Israel.
34 But the Pharisees said, He casteth out
devils through the prince of the devils.
35 And Jesus went about all the cities and
villages, teaching in their synagogues, and
preaching the gospel of the kingdom, and
healing every sickness and every disease
among the people.
36 ¶ But when he saw the multitudes, he
was moved with compassion on them,
because they fainted, and were scattered
abroad, as sheep having no shepherd.
37 Then saith he unto his disciples, The
harvest truly *is* plenteous, but the labourers *are* few;
38 Pray ye therefore the Lord of the harvest, that he will send forth labourers into
his harvest.

Matthew 10

1 And when he had called unto *him* his
twelve disciples, he gave them power
against unclean spirits, to cast them out,
and to heal all manner of sickness and all
manner of disease.

2 Now the names of the twelve apostles are
these; The first, Simon, who is called Peter,
and Andrew his brother; James *the son* of
Zebedee, and John his brother;
3 Philip, and Bartholomew; Thomas, and
Matthew the publican; James *the son* of
Alphæus, and Lebbæus, whose surname
was Thaddæus;
4 Simon the Canaanite, and Judas Iscariot,
who also betrayed him.
5 These twelve Jesus sent forth, and commanded them, saying, Go not into the way
of the Gentiles, and into *any* city of the
Samaritans enter ye not:
6 But go rather to the lost sheep of the
house of Israel.
7 And as ye go, preach, saying, The kingdom
of heaven is at hand.
8 Heal the sick, cleanse the lepers, raise
the dead, cast out devils: freely ye have
received, freely give.
9 Provide neither gold, nor silver, nor brass
in your purses,
10 Nor scrip for *your* journey, neither two
coats, neither shoes, nor yet staves: for the
workman is worthy of his meat.
11 And into whatsoever city or town ye shall
enter, inquire who in it is worthy; and there
abide till ye go thence.
12 And when ye come into an house, salute
it.
13 And if the house be worthy, let your
peace come upon it: but if it be not worthy,
let your peace return to you.
14 And whosoever shall not receive you,
nor hear your words, when ye depart out
of that house or city, shake off the dust of
your feet.
15 Verily I say unto you, It shall be more tolerable for the land of Sodom and Gomorrha
in the day of judgment, than for that city.
16 ¶ Behold, I send you forth as sheep in
the midst of wolves: be ye therefore wise
as serpents, and harmless as doves.
17 But beware of men: for they will deliver
you up to the councils, and they will scourge
you in their synagogues;
18 And ye shall be brought before governors and kings for my sake, for a testimony
against them and the Gentiles.
19 But when they deliver you up, take no
thought how or what ye shall speak: for it
shall be given you in that same hour what
ye shall speak.
20 For it is not ye that speak, but the Spirit
of your Father which speaketh in you.
21 And the brother shall deliver up the
brother to death, and the father the child:
and the children shall rise up against *their*
parents, and cause them to be put to death.
22 And ye shall be hated of all *men* for my
name's sake: but he that endureth to the
end shall be saved.
23 But when they persecute you in this city,
flee ye into another: for verily I say unto
you, Ye shall not have gone over the cities
of Israel, till the Son of man be come.
24 The disciple is not above *his* master, nor
the servant above his lord.
25 It is enough for the disciple that he be
as his master, and the servant as his lord.
If they have called the master of the house
Beelzebub, how much more *shall they call*
them of his household?
26 Fear them not therefore: for there is
nothing covered, that shall not be revealed;
and hid, that shall not be known.
27 What I tell you in darkness, *that* speak
ye in light: and what ye hear in the ear, *that*
preach ye upon the housetops.
28 And fear not them which kill the body,
but are not able to kill the soul: but rather
fear him which is able to destroy both soul
and body in hell.
29 Are not two sparrows sold for a farthing?
and one of them shall not fall on the ground
without your Father.
30 But the very hairs of your head are all
numbered.
31 Fear ye not therefore, ye are of more
value than many sparrows.
32 Whosoever therefore shall confess me
before men, him will I confess also before
my Father which is in heaven.
33 But whosoever shall deny me before
men, him will I also deny before my Father
which is in heaven.
34 Think not that I am come to send peace
on earth: I came not to send peace, but a
sword.
35 For I am come to set a man at variance
against his father, and the daughter against
her mother, and the daughter in law against
her mother in law.

36 And a man's foes *shall be* they of his own
household.
37 He that loveth father or mother more
than me is not worthy of me: and he that
loveth son or daughter more than me is not
worthy of me.
38 And he that taketh not his cross, and
followeth after me, is not worthy of me.
39 He that findeth his life shall lose it: and he
that loseth his life for my sake shall find it.
40 ¶ He that receiveth you receiveth me,
and he that receiveth me receiveth him
that sent me.
41 He that receiveth a prophet in the name
of a prophet shall receive a prophet's
reward; and he that receiveth a righteous
man in the name of a righteous man shall
receive a righteous man's reward.
42 And whosoever shall give to drink unto
one of these little ones a cup of cold *water*
only in the name of a disciple, verily I say
unto you, he shall in no wise lose his reward.

Matthew 11

1 And it came to pass, when Jesus had made
an end of commanding his twelve disciples,
he departed thence to teach and to preach
in their cities.
2 Now when John had heard in the prison
the works of Christ, he sent two of his
disciples,
3 And said unto him, Art thou he that should
come, or do we look for another?
4 Jesus answered and said unto them, Go
and shew John again those things which ye
do hear and see:
5 The blind receive their sight, and the lame
walk, the lepers are cleansed, and the deaf
hear, the dead are raised up, and the poor
have the gospel preached to them.
6 And blessed is *he*, whosoever shall not be
offended in me.
7 ¶ And as they departed, Jesus began to
say unto the multitudes concerning John,
What went ye out into the wilderness to
see? A reed shaken with the wind?
8 But what went ye out for to see? A man
clothed in soft raiment? behold, they that
wear soft *clothing* are in kings' houses.
9 But what went ye out for to see? A
prophet? yea, I say unto you, and more
than a prophet.
10 For this is *he*, of whom it is written,
Behold, I send my messenger before thy
face, which shall prepare thy way before
thee.
11 Verily I say unto you, Among them that
are born of women there hath not risen a
greater than John the Baptist: notwithstanding he that is least in the kingdom of heaven
is greater than he.
12 And from the days of John the Baptist
until now the kingdom of heaven suffereth
violence, and the violent take it by force.
13 For all the prophets and the law prophesied until John.
14 And if ye will receive *it*, this is Elias, which
was for to come.
15 He that hath ears to hear, let him hear.
16 ¶ But whereunto shall I liken this generation? It is like unto children sitting in
the markets, and calling unto their fellows,
17 And saying, We have piped unto you, and
ye have not danced; we have mourned unto
you, and ye have not lamented.
18 For John came neither eating nor drinking, and they say, He hath a devil.
19 The Son of man came eating and drinking, and they say, Behold a man gluttonous,
and a winebibber, a friend of publicans
and sinners. But wisdom is justified of her
children.
20 ¶ Then began he to upbraid the cities
wherein most of his mighty works were
done, because they repented not:
21 Woe unto thee, Chorazin! woe unto thee,
Bethsaida! for if the mighty works, which
were done in you, had been done in Tyre
and Sidon, they would have repented long
ago in sackcloth and ashes.
22 But I say unto you, It shall be more
tolerable for Tyre and Sidon at the day of
judgment, than for you.
23 And thou, Capernaum, which art exalted
unto heaven, shalt be brought down to hell:
for if the mighty works, which have been
done in thee, had been done in Sodom, it
would have remained until this day.
24 But I say unto you, That it shall be more
tolerable for the land of Sodom in the day
of judgment, than for thee.
25 ¶ At that time Jesus answered and said,
I thank thee, O Father, Lord of heaven
and earth, because thou hast hid these
things from the wise and prudent, and hast
revealed them unto babes.

26 Even so, Father: for so it seemed good
in thy sight.
27 All things are delivered unto me of my
Father: and no man knoweth the Son, but
the Father; neither knoweth any man the
Father, save the Son, and *he* to whomsoever
the Son will reveal *him*.
28 ¶ Come unto me, all *ye* that labour and
are heavy laden, and I will give you rest.
29 Take my yoke upon you, and learn of
me; for I am meek and lowly in heart: and
ye shall find rest unto your souls.
30 For my yoke *is* easy, and my burden is
light.

Matthew 12

1 At that time Jesus went on the sabbath
day through the corn; and his disciples were
an hungred, and began to pluck the ears of
corn, and to eat.
2 But when the Pharisees saw *it*, they said
unto him, Behold, thy disciples do that which
is not lawful to do upon the sabbath day.
3 But he said unto them, Have ye not read
what David did, when he was an hungred,
and they that were with him;
4 How he entered into the house of God,
and did eat the shewbread, which was not
lawful for him to eat, neither for them which
were with him, but only for the priests?
5 Or have ye not read in the law, how that on
the sabbath days the priests in the temple
profane the sabbath, and are blameless?
6 But I say unto you, That in this place is *one*
greater than the temple.
7 But if ye had known what *this* meaneth, I
will have mercy, and not sacrifice, ye would
not have condemned the guiltless.
8 For the Son of man is Lord even of the
sabbath day.
9 And when he was departed thence, he
went into their synagogue:
10 ¶ And, behold, there was a man which
had *his* hand withered. And they asked him,
saying, Is it lawful to heal on the sabbath
days? that they might accuse him.
11 And he said unto them, What man shall
there be among you, that shall have one
sheep, and if it fall into a pit on the sabbath
day, will he not lay hold on it, and lift *it* out?
12 How much then is a man better than a
sheep? Wherefore it is lawful to do well on
the sabbath days.
13 Then saith he to the man, Stretch forth
thine hand. And he stretched *it* forth; and
it was restored whole, like as the other.
14 ¶ Then the Pharisees went out, and
held a council against him, how they might
destroy him.
15 But when Jesus knew *it*, he withdrew
himself from thence: and great multitudes
followed him, and he healed them all;
16 And charged them that they should not
make him known:
17 That it might be fulfilled which was spoken by Esaias the prophet, saying,
18 Behold my servant, whom I have chosen; my beloved, in whom my soul is well
pleased: I will put my spirit upon him, and
he shall shew judgment to the Gentiles.
19 He shall not strive, nor cry; neither shall
any man hear his voice in the streets.
20 A bruised reed shall he not break, and
smoking flax shall he not quench, till he send
forth judgment unto victory.
21 And in his name shall the Gentiles trust.
22 ¶ Then was brought unto him one possessed with a devil, blind, and dumb: and
he healed him, insomuch that the blind and
dumb both spake and saw.
23 And all the people were amazed, and
said, Is not this the son of David?
24 But when the Pharisees heard *it*, they
said, This *fellow* doth not cast out devils,
but by Beelzebub the prince of the devils.
25 And Jesus knew their thoughts, and said
unto them, Every kingdom divided against
itself is brought to desolation; and every
city or house divided against itself shall
not stand:
26 And if Satan cast out Satan, he is divided
against himself; how shall then his kingdom
stand?
27 And if I by Beelzebub cast out devils,
by whom do your children cast *them* out?
therefore they shall be your judges.
28 But if I cast out devils by the Spirit of God,
then the kingdom of God is come unto you.
29 Or else how can one enter into a strong
man's house, and spoil his goods, except he
first bind the strong man? and then he will
spoil his house.
30 He that is not with me is against me; and
he that gathereth not with me scattereth
abroad.
31 ¶ Wherefore I say unto you, All manner

of sin and blasphemy shall be forgiven unto men: but the blasphemy *against* the *Holy* Spirit shall not be forgiven unto men.

32 And whosoever speaketh a word against the Son of man, it shall be forgiven him: but whosoever speaketh against the Holy Spirit, it shall not be forgiven him, neither in this world, neither in the *world* to come.

33 Either make the tree good, and his fruit good; or else make the tree corrupt, and his fruit corrupt: for the tree is known by *his* fruit.

34 O generation of vipers, how can ye, being evil, speak good things? for out of the abundance of the heart the mouth speaketh.

35 A good man out of the good treasure of the heart bringeth forth good things: and an evil man out of the evil treasure bringeth forth evil things.

36 But I say unto you, That every idle word that men shall speak, they shall give account thereof in the day of judgment.

37 For by thy words thou shalt be justified, and by thy words thou shalt be condemned.

38 ¶ Then certain of the scribes and of the Pharisees answered, saying, Master, we would see a sign from thee.

39 But he answered and said unto them, An evil and adulterous generation seeketh after a sign; and there shall no sign be given to it, but the sign of the prophet Jonas:

40 For as Jonas was three days and three nights in the whale's belly; so shall the Son of man be three days and three nights in the heart of the earth.

41 The men of Nineveh shall rise in judgment with this generation, and shall condemn it: because they repented at the preaching of Jonas; and, behold, a greater than Jonas *is* here.

42 The queen of the south shall rise up in the judgment with this generation, and shall condemn it: for she came from the uttermost parts of the earth to hear the wisdom of Solomon; and, behold, a greater than Solomon *is* here.

43 When the unclean spirit is gone out of a man, he walketh through dry places, seeking rest, and findeth none.

44 Then he saith, I will return into my house from whence I came out; and when he is come, he findeth *it* empty, swept, and garnished.

45 Then goeth he, and taketh with himself seven other spirits more wicked than himself, and they enter in and dwell there: and the last *state* of that man is worse than the first. Even so shall it be also unto this wicked generation.

46 ¶ While he yet talked to the people, behold, *his* mother and his brethren stood without, desiring to speak with him.

47 Then one said unto him, Behold, thy mother and thy brethren stand without, desiring to speak with thee.

48 But he answered and said unto him that told him, Who is my mother? and who are my brethren?

49 And he stretched forth his hand toward his disciples, and said, Behold my mother and my brethren!

50 For whosoever shall do the will of my Father which is in heaven, the same is my brother, and sister, and mother.

Matthew 13

1 The same day went Jesus out of the house, and sat by the sea side.

2 And great multitudes were gathered together unto him, so that he went into a ship, and sat; and the whole multitude stood on the shore.

3 And he spake many things unto them in parables, saying, Behold, a sower went forth to sow;

4 And when he sowed, some *seeds* fell by the way side, and the fowls came and devoured them up:

5 Some fell upon stony places, where they had not much earth: and forthwith they sprung up, because they had no deepness of earth:

6 And when the sun was up, they were scorched; and because they had no root, they withered away.

7 And some fell among thorns; and the thorns sprung up, and choked them:

8 But other fell into good ground, and brought forth fruit, some an hundredfold, some sixtyfold, some thirtyfold.

9 Who hath ears to hear, let him hear.

10 And the disciples came, and said unto him, Why speakest thou unto them in parables?

11 He answered and said unto them, Because it is given unto you to know the

mysteries of the kingdom of heaven, but
to them it is not given.
12 For whosoever hath, to him shall be
given, and he shall have more abundance:
but whosoever hath not, from him shall be
taken away even that he hath.
13 Therefore speak I to them in parables:
because they seeing see not; and hearing
they hear not, neither do they understand.
14 And in them is fulfilled the prophecy of
Esaias, which saith, By hearing ye shall hear,
and shall not understand; and seeing ye shall
see, and shall not perceive:
15 For this people's heart is waxed gross,
and *their* ears are dull of hearing, and their
eyes they have closed; lest at any time they
should see with *their* eyes, and hear with
their ears, and should understand with
their heart, and should be converted, and I
should heal them.
16 But blessed *are* your eyes, for they see:
and your ears, for they hear.
17 For verily I say unto you, That many
prophets and righteous *men* have desired
to see *those things* which ye see, and have
not seen *them;* and to hear *those things*
which ye hear, and have not heard *them.*
18 ¶ Hear ye therefore the parable of the
sower.
19 When any one heareth the word of the
kingdom, and understandeth *it* not, then
cometh the wicked *one*, and catcheth away
that which was sown in his heart. This is he
which received seed by the way side.
20 But he that received the seed into stony
places, the same is he that heareth the
word, and anon with joy receiveth it;
21 Yet hath he not root in himself, but
dureth for a while: for when tribulation or
persecution ariseth because of the word,
by and by he is offended.
22 He also that received seed among the
thorns is he that heareth the word; and the
care of this world, and the deceitfulness of
riches, choke the word, and he becometh
unfruitful.
23 But he that received seed into the good
ground is he that heareth the word, and
understandeth *it;* which also beareth fruit,
and bringeth forth, some an hundredfold,
some sixty, some thirty.
24 ¶ Another parable put he forth unto
them, saying, The kingdom of heaven is
likened unto a man which sowed good seed
in his field:
25 But while men slept, his enemy came
and sowed tares among the wheat, and
went his way.
26 But when the blade was sprung up, and
brought forth fruit, then appeared the
tares also.
27 So the servants of the householder came
and said unto him, Sir, didst not thou sow
good seed in thy field? from whence then
hath it tares?
28 He said unto them, An enemy hath done
this. The servants said unto him, Wilt thou
then that we go and gather them up?
29 But he said, Nay; lest while ye gather
up the tares, ye root up also the wheat
with them.
30 Let both grow together until the harvest:
and in the time of harvest I will say to the
reapers, Gather ye together first the tares,
and bind them in bundles to burn them: but
gather the wheat into my barn.
31 ¶ Another parable put he forth unto
them, saying, The kingdom of heaven is like
to a grain of mustard seed, which a man
took, and sowed in his field:
32 Which indeed is the least of all seeds:
but when it is grown, it is the greatest
among herbs, and becometh a tree, so that
the birds of the air come and lodge in the
branches thereof.
33 ¶ Another parable spake he unto them;
The kingdom of heaven is like unto leaven,
which a woman took, and hid in three measures of meal, till the whole was leavened.
34 All these things spake Jesus unto the
multitude in parables; and without a parable
spake he not unto them:
35 That it might be fulfilled which was spoken by the prophet, saying, I will open my
mouth in parables; I will utter things which
have been kept secret from the foundation
of the world.
36 Then Jesus sent the multitude away,
and went into the house: and his disciples
came unto him, saying, Declare unto us the
parable of the tares of the field.
37 He answered and said unto them, He that
soweth the good seed is the Son of man;
38 The field is the world; the good seed are
the children of the kingdom; but the tares
are the children of the wicked *one;*

39 The enemy that sowed them is the devil;
the harvest is the end of the world; and the
reapers are the angels.
40 As therefore the tares are gathered and
burned in the fire; so shall it be in the end
of this world.
41 The Son of man shall send forth his
angels, and they shall gather out of his
kingdom all things that offend, and them
which do iniquity;
42 And shall cast them into a furnace of fire:
there shall be wailing and gnashing of teeth.
43 Then shall the righteous shine forth as
the sun in the kingdom of their Father. Who
hath ears to hear, let him hear.
44 ¶ Again, the kingdom of heaven is like
unto treasure hid in a field; the which when
a man hath found, he hideth, and for joy
thereof goeth and selleth all that he hath,
and buyeth that field.
45 ¶ Again, the kingdom of heaven is like
unto a merchant man, seeking goodly pearls:
46 Who, when he had found one pearl of
great price, went and sold all that he had,
and bought it.
47 ¶ Again, the kingdom of heaven is like
unto a net, that was cast into the sea, and
gathered of every kind:
48 Which, when it was full, they drew to
shore, and sat down, and gathered the good
into vessels, but cast the bad away.
49 So shall it be at the end of the world:
the angels shall come forth, and sever the
wicked from among the just,
50 And shall cast them into the furnace of
fire: there shall be wailing and gnashing
of teeth.
51 Jesus saith unto them, Have ye understood all these things? They say unto him,
Yea, Lord.
52 Then said he unto them, Therefore
every scribe *which is* instructed unto the
kingdom of heaven is like unto a man *that*
is an householder, which bringeth forth out
of his treasure *things* new and old.
53 ¶ And it came to pass, *that* when Jesus
had finished these parables, he departed
thence.
54 And when he was come into his own
country, he taught them in their synagogue,
insomuch that they were astonished, and
said, Whence hath this *man* this wisdom,
and *these* mighty works?
55 Is not this the carpenter's son? is not
his mother called Mary? and his brethren,
James, and Joses, and Simon, and Judas?
56 And his sisters, are they not all with us?
Whence then hath this *man* all these things?
57 And they were offended in him. But Jesus
said unto them, A prophet is not without
honour, save in his own country, and in his
own house.
58 And he did not many mighty works there
because of their unbelief.

Matthew 14

1 At that time Herod the tetrarch heard of
the fame of Jesus,
2 And said unto his servants, This is John
the Baptist; he is risen from the dead; and
therefore mighty works do shew forth
themselves in him.
3 ¶ For Herod had laid hold on John, and
bound him, and put *him* in prison for Herodias' sake, his brother Philip's wife.
4 For John said unto him, It is not lawful for
thee to have her.
5 And when he would have put him to
death, he feared the multitude, because
they counted him as a prophet.
6 But when Herod's birthday was kept, the
daughter of Herodias danced before them,
and pleased Herod.
7 Whereupon he promised with an oath to
give her whatsoever she would ask.
8 And she, being before instructed of her
mother, said, Give me here John Baptist's
head in a charger.
9 And the king was sorry: nevertheless for
the oath's sake, and them which sat with him
at meat, he commanded *it* to be given *her*.
10 And he sent, and beheaded John in the
prison.
11 And his head was brought in a charger,
and given to the damsel: and she brought
it to her mother.
12 And his disciples came, and took up the
body, and buried it, and went and told Jesus.
13 ¶ When Jesus heard *of it*, he departed
thence by ship into a desert place apart:
and when the people had heard *thereof*,
they followed him on foot out of the cities.
14 And Jesus went forth, and saw a great
multitude, and was moved with compassion
toward them, and he healed their sick.
15 ¶ And when it was evening, his disciples

came to him, saying, This is a desert place, and the time is now past; send the multitude away, that they may go into the villages, and buy themselves victuals.

16 But Jesus said unto them, They need not depart; give ye them to eat.

17 And they say unto him, We have here but five loaves, and two fishes.

18 He said, Bring them hither to me.

19 And he commanded the multitude to sit down on the grass, and took the five loaves, and the two fishes, and looking up to heaven, he blessed, and brake, and gave the loaves to *his* disciples, and the disciples to the multitude.

20 And they did all eat, and were filled: and they took up of the fragments that remained twelve baskets full.

21 And they that had eaten were about five thousand men, beside women and children.

22 ¶ And straightway Jesus constrained his disciples to get into a ship, and to go before him unto the other side, while he sent the multitudes away.

23 And when he had sent the multitudes away, he went up into a mountain apart to pray: and when the evening was come, he was there alone.

24 But the ship was now in the midst of the sea, tossed with waves: for the wind was contrary.

25 And in the fourth watch of the night Jesus went unto them, walking on the sea.

26 And when the disciples saw him walking on the sea, they were troubled, saying, It is a spirit; and they cried out for fear.

27 But straightway Jesus spake unto them, saying, Be of good cheer; it is I; be not afraid.

28 And Peter answered him and said, Lord, if it be thou, bid me come unto thee on the water.

29 And he said, Come. And when Peter was come down out of the ship, he walked on the water, to go to Jesus.

30 But when he saw the wind boisterous, he was afraid; and beginning to sink, he cried, saying, Lord, save me.

31 And immediately Jesus stretched forth *his* hand, and caught him, and said unto him, O thou of little faith, wherefore didst thou doubt?

32 And when they were come into the ship, the wind ceased.

33 Then they that were in the ship came and worshipped him, saying, Of a truth thou art the Son of God.

34 ¶ And when they were gone over, they came into the land of Gennesaret.

35 And when the men of that place had knowledge of him, they sent out into all that country round about, and brought unto him all that were diseased;

36 And besought him that they might only touch the hem of his garment: and as many as touched were made perfectly whole.

Matthew 15

1 Then came to Jesus scribes and Pharisees, which were of Jerusalem, saying,

2 Why do thy disciples transgress the tradition of the elders? for they wash not their hands when they eat bread.

3 But he answered and said unto them, Why do ye also transgress the commandment of God by your tradition?

4 For God commanded, saying, Honour thy father and mother: and, He that curseth father or mother, let him die the death.

5 But ye say, Whosoever shall say to *his* father or *his* mother, *It is* a gift, by whatsoever thou mightest be profited by me;

6 And honour not his father or his mother, *he shall be free*. Thus have ye made the commandment of God of none effect by your tradition.

7 *Ye* hypocrites, well did Esaias prophesy of you, saying,

8 This people draweth nigh unto me with their mouth, and honoureth me with *their* lips; but their heart is far from me.

9 But in vain they do worship me, teaching *for* doctrines the commandments of men.

10 ¶ And he called the multitude, and said unto them, Hear, and understand:

11 Not that which goeth into the mouth defileth a man; but that which cometh out of the mouth, this defileth a man.

12 Then came his disciples, and said unto him, Knowest thou that the Pharisees were offended, after they heard this saying?

13 But he answered and said, Every plant, which my heavenly Father hath not planted, shall be rooted up.

14 Let them alone: they be blind leaders of the blind. And if the blind lead the blind, both shall fall into the ditch.

render his anger with fury, and his rebuke
with flames of fire.
16 For by fire and by his sword will the LORD
plead with all flesh: and the slain of the LORD
shall be many.
17 They that sanctify themselves, and purify
themselves in the gardens behind one *tree*
in the midst, eating swine's flesh, and the
abomination, and the mouse, shall be consumed together, saith the LORD.
18 For I *know* their works and their thoughts:
it shall come, that I will gather all nations
and tongues; and they shall come, and see
my glory.
19 And I will set a sign among them, and I
will send those that escape of them unto
the nations, *to* Tarshish, Pul, and Lud, that
draw the bow, *to* Tubal, and Javan, *to* the
isles afar off, that have not heard my fame,
neither have seen my glory; and they shall
declare my glory among the Gentiles.
20 And they shall bring all your brethren *for*
an offering unto the LORD out of all nations
upon horses, and in chariots, and in litters,
and upon mules, and upon swift beasts, to
my holy mountain Jerusalem, saith the LORD,
as the children of Israel bring an offering in
a clean vessel into the house of the LORD.
21 And I will also take of them for priests
and for Levites, saith the LORD.
22 For as the new heavens and the new
earth, which I will make, shall remain before
me, saith the LORD, so shall your seed and
your name remain.
23 And it shall come to pass, *that* from
one new moon to another, and from one
sabbath to another, shall all flesh come to
worship before me, saith the LORD.
24 And they shall go forth, and look upon the
carcases of the men that have transgressed
against me: for their worm shall not die,
neither shall their fire be quenched; and
they shall be an abhorring unto all flesh.

The Book Of

Jeremiah

Jeremiah 1

1 The words of Jeremiah the son of Hilkiah,
of the priests that *were* in Anathoth in the
land of Benjamin:
2 To whom the word of the LORD came in
the days of Josiah the son of Amon king of
Judah, in the thirteenth year of his reign.
3 It came also in the days of Jehoiakim the
son of Josiah king of Judah, unto the end
of the eleventh year of Zedekiah the son of
Josiah king of Judah, unto the carrying away
of Jerusalem captive in the fifth month.
4 Then the word of the LORD came unto
me, saying,
5 Before I formed thee in the belly I knew
thee; and before thou camest forth out of
the womb I sanctified thee, *and* I ordained
thee a prophet unto the nations.
6 Then said I, Ah, Lord GOD! behold, I cannot
speak: for I *am* a child.
7 ¶ But the LORD said unto me, Say not, I
am a child: for thou shalt go to all that I shall
send thee, and whatsoever I command thee
thou shalt speak.
8 Be not afraid of their faces: for I *am* with
thee to deliver thee, saith the LORD.
9 Then the LORD put forth his hand, and
touched my mouth. And the LORD said
unto me, Behold, I have put my words in
thy mouth.
10 See, I have this day set thee over the
nations and over the kingdoms, to root out,
and to pull down, and to destroy, and to
throw down, to build, and to plant.
11 ¶ Moreover the word of the LORD came
unto me, saying, Jeremiah, what seest thou?
And I said, I see a rod of an almond tree.
12 Then said the LORD unto me, Thou hast
well seen: for I will hasten my word to
perform it.
13 And the word of the LORD came unto me
the second time, saying, What seest thou?
And I said, I see a seething pot; and the face
thereof *is* toward the north.

14 Then the LORD said unto me, Out of the
north an evil shall break forth upon all the
inhabitants of the land.
15 For, lo, I will call all the families of the
kingdoms of the north, saith the LORD; and
they shall come, and they shall set every
one his throne at the entering of the gates
of Jerusalem, and against all the walls
thereof round about, and against all the
cities of Judah.
16 And I will utter my judgments against
them touching all their wickedness, who
have forsaken me, and have burned incense
unto other gods, and worshipped the works
of their own hands.
17 ¶ Thou therefore gird up thy loins, and
arise, and speak unto them all that I command thee: be not dismayed at their faces,
lest I confound thee before them.
18 For, behold, I have made thee this day a
defenced city, and an iron pillar, and brasen
walls against the whole land, against the
kings of Judah, against the princes thereof,
against the priests thereof, and against the
people of the land.
19 And they shall fight against thee; but
they shall not prevail against thee; for I *am*
with thee, saith the LORD, to deliver thee.

Jeremiah 2

1 Moreover the word of the LORD came to
me, saying,
2 Go and cry in the ears of Jerusalem, saying, Thus saith the LORD; I remember thee,
the kindness of thy youth, the love of thine
espousals, when thou wentest after me in
the wilderness, in a land *that was* not sown.
3 Israel *was* holiness unto the LORD, *and*
the firstfruits of his increase: all that devour
him shall offend; evil shall come upon them,
saith the LORD.
4 Hear ye the word of the LORD, O house
of Jacob, and all the families of the house
of Israel:
5 ¶ Thus saith the LORD, What iniquity have
your fathers found in me, that they are gone
far from me, and have walked after vanity,
and are become vain?
6 Neither said they, Where *is* the LORD that
brought us up out of the land of Egypt, that
led us through the wilderness, through a
land of deserts and of pits, through a land
of drought, and of the shadow of death,
through a land that no man passed through,
and where no man dwelt?
7 And I brought you into a plentiful country,
to eat the fruit thereof and the goodness
thereof; but when ye entered, ye defiled
my land, and made mine heritage an abomination.
8 The priests said not, Where *is* the LORD?
and they that handle the law knew me not:
the pastors also transgressed against me,
and the prophets prophesied by Baal, and
walked after *things that* do not profit.
9 ¶ Wherefore I will yet plead with you, saith
the LORD, and with your children's children
will I plead.
10 For pass over the isles of Chittim, and
see; and send unto Kedar, and consider
diligently, and see if there be such a thing.
11 Hath a nation changed *their* gods,
which *are* yet no gods? but my people
have changed their glory for *that which*
doth not profit.
12 Be astonished, O ye heavens, at this,
and be horribly afraid, be ye very desolate,
saith the LORD.
13 For my people have committed two evils;
they have forsaken me the fountain of living waters, *and* hewed them out cisterns,
broken cisterns, that can hold no water.
14 ¶ *Is* Israel a servant? *is* he a homeborn
slave? why is he spoiled?
15 The young lions roared upon him, *and*
yelled, and they made his land waste: his
cities are burned without inhabitant.
16 Also the children of Noph and Tahapanes
have broken the crown of thy head.
17 Hast thou not procured this unto thyself,
in that thou hast forsaken the LORD thy God,
when he led thee by the way?
18 And now what hast thou to do in the way
of Egypt, to drink the waters of Sihor? or
what hast thou to do in the way of Assyria,
to drink the waters of the river?
19 Thine own wickedness shall correct thee,
and thy backslidings shall reprove thee:
know therefore and see that *it is* an evil
thing and bitter, that thou hast forsaken
the LORD thy God, and that my fear *is* not in
thee, saith the Lord GOD of hosts.
20 ¶ For of old time I have broken thy yoke,
and burst thy bands; and thou saidst, I will
not transgress; when upon every high hill

and under every green tree thou wanderest,
playing the harlot.
21 Yet I had planted thee a noble vine,
wholly a right seed: how then art thou
turned into the degenerate plant of a
strange vine unto me?
22 For though thou wash thee with nitre,
and take thee much soap, *yet* thine iniquity
is marked before me, saith the Lord GOD.
23 How canst thou say, I am not polluted, I
have not gone after Baalim? see thy way in
the valley, know what thou hast done: *thou*
art a swift dromedary traversing her ways;
24 A wild ass used to the wilderness, *that*
snuffeth up the wind at her pleasure; in her
occasion who can turn her away? all they
that seek her will not weary themselves; in
her month they shall find her.
25 Withhold thy foot from being unshod,
and thy throat from thirst: but thou saidst,
There is no hope: no; for I have loved strangers, and after them will I go.
26 As the thief is ashamed when he is found,
so is the house of Israel ashamed; they, their
kings, their princes, and their priests, and
their prophets,
27 Saying to a stock, Thou *art* my father; and
to a stone, Thou hast brought me forth: for
they have turned *their* back unto me, and
not *their* face: but in the time of their trouble
they will say, Arise, and save us.
28 But where *are* thy gods that thou hast
made thee? let them arise, if they can save
thee in the time of thy trouble: for *accord-*
ing to the number of thy cities are thy gods,
O Judah.
29 Wherefore will ye plead with me? ye
all have transgressed against me, saith
the LORD.
30 In vain have I smitten your children;
they received no correction: your own
sword hath devoured your prophets, like a
destroying lion.
31 ¶ O generation, see ye the word of
the LORD. Have I been a wilderness unto
Israel? a land of darkness? wherefore say
my people, We are lords; we will come no
more unto thee?
32 Can a maid forget her ornaments, *or* a
bride her attire? yet my people have forgotten me days without number.
33 Why trimmest thou thy way to seek love?
therefore hast thou also taught the wicked
ones thy ways.
34 Also in thy skirts is found the blood of
the souls of the poor innocents: I have not
found it by secret search, but upon all these.
35 Yet thou sayest, Because I am innocent,
surely his anger shall turn from me. Behold,
I will plead with thee, because thou sayest,
I have not sinned.
36 Why gaddest thou about so much to
change thy way? thou also shalt be ashamed
of Egypt, as thou wast ashamed of Assyria.
37 Yea, thou shalt go forth from him, and
thine hands upon thine head: for the LORD
hath rejected thy confidences, and thou
shalt not prosper in them.

Jeremiah 3

1 They say, If a man put away his wife, and
she go from him, and become another
man's, shall he return unto her again? shall
not that land be greatly polluted? but thou
hast played the harlot with many lovers; yet
return again to me, saith the LORD.
2 Lift up thine eyes unto the high places,
and see where thou hast not been lien with.
In the ways hast thou sat for them, as the
Arabian in the wilderness; and thou hast
polluted the land with thy whoredoms and
with thy wickedness.
3 Therefore the showers have been withholden, and there hath been no latter rain;
and thou hadst a whore's forehead, thou
refusedst to be ashamed.
4 Wilt thou not from this time cry unto me,
My father, thou *art* the guide of my youth?
5 Will he reserve *his anger* for ever? will he
keep *it* to the end? Behold, thou hast spoken and done evil things as thou couldest.
6 ¶ The LORD said also unto me in the days
of Josiah the king, Hast thou seen *that* which
backsliding Israel hath done? she is gone up
upon every high mountain and under every
green tree, and there hath played the harlot.
7 And I said after she had done all these
things, Turn thou unto me. But she returned
not. And her treacherous sister Judah saw *it*.
8 And I saw, when for all the causes whereby
backsliding Israel committed adultery I had
put her away, and given her a bill of divorce;
yet her treacherous sister Judah feared not,
but went and played the harlot also.
9 And it came to pass through the lightness

of her whoredom, that she defiled the land, and committed adultery with stones and with stocks.

10 And yet for all this her treacherous sister Judah hath not turned unto me with her whole heart, but feignedly, saith the LORD.

11 And the LORD said unto me, The backsliding Israel hath justified herself more than treacherous Judah.

12 ¶ Go and proclaim these words toward the north, and say, Return, thou backsliding Israel, saith the LORD; *and* I will not cause mine anger to fall upon you: for I *am* merciful, saith the LORD, *and* I will not keep *anger* for ever.

13 Only acknowledge thine iniquity, that thou hast transgressed against the LORD thy God, and hast scattered thy ways to the strangers under every green tree, and ye have not obeyed my voice, saith the LORD.

14 Turn, O backsliding children, saith the LORD; for I am married unto you: and I will take you one of a city, and two of a family, and I will bring you to Zion:

15 And I will give you pastors according to mine heart, which shall feed you with knowledge and understanding.

16 And it shall come to pass, when ye be multiplied and increased in the land, in those days, saith the LORD, they shall say no more, The ark of the covenant of the LORD: neither shall it come to mind: neither shall they remember it; neither shall they visit *it;* neither shall *that* be done any more.

17 At that time they shall call Jerusalem the throne of the LORD; and all the nations shall be gathered unto it, to the name of the LORD, to Jerusalem: neither shall they walk any more after the imagination of their evil heart.

18 In those days the house of Judah shall walk with the house of Israel, and they shall come together out of the land of the north to the land that I have given for an inheritance unto your fathers.

19 But I said, How shall I put thee among the children, and give thee a pleasant land, a goodly heritage of the hosts of nations? and I said, Thou shalt call me, My father; and shalt not turn away from me.

20 ¶ Surely *as* a wife treacherously departeth from her husband, so have ye dealt treacherously with me, O house of Israel, saith the LORD.

21 A voice was heard upon the high places, weeping *and* supplications of the children of Israel: for they have perverted their way, *and* they have forgotten the LORD their God.

22 Return, ye backsliding children, *and* I will heal your backslidings. Behold, we come unto thee; for thou *art* the LORD our God.

23 Truly in vain *is salvation hoped for* from the hills, *and from* the multitude of mountains: truly in the LORD our God *is* the salvation of Israel.

24 For shame hath devoured the labour of our fathers from our youth; their flocks and their herds, their sons and their daughters.

25 We lie down in our shame, and our confusion covereth us: for we have sinned against the LORD our God, we and our fathers, from our youth even unto this day, and have not obeyed the voice of the LORD our God.

Jeremiah 4

1 If thou wilt return, O Israel, saith the LORD, return unto me: and if thou wilt put away thine abominations out of my sight, then shalt thou not remove.

2 And thou shalt swear, The LORD liveth, in truth, in judgment, and in righteousness; and the nations shall bless themselves in him, and in him shall they glory.

3 ¶ For thus saith the LORD to the men of Judah and Jerusalem, Break up your fallow ground, and sow not among thorns.

4 Circumcise yourselves to the LORD, and take away the foreskins of your heart, ye men of Judah and inhabitants of Jerusalem: lest my fury come forth like fire, and burn that none can quench *it,* because of the evil of your doings.

5 Declare ye in Judah, and publish in Jerusalem; and say, Blow ye the trumpet in the land: cry, gather together, and say, Assemble yourselves, and let us go into the defenced cities.

6 Set up the standard toward Zion: retire, stay not: for I will bring evil from the north, and a great destruction.

7 The lion is come up from his thicket, and the destroyer of the Gentiles is on his way; he is gone forth from his place to make thy land desolate; *and* thy cities shall be laid waste, without an inhabitant.

8 For this gird you with sackcloth, lament
and howl: for the fierce anger of the LORD
is not turned back from us.
9 And it shall come to pass at that day, saith
the LORD, *that* the heart of the king shall
perish, and the heart of the princes; and
the priests shall be astonished, and the
prophets shall wonder.
10 Then said I, Ah, Lord GOD! surely thou
hast greatly deceived this people and Jerusalem, saying, Ye shall have peace; whereas
the sword reacheth unto the soul.
11 At that time shall it be said to this people
and to Jerusalem, A dry wind of the high
places in the wilderness toward the daughter of my people, not to fan, nor to cleanse,
12 *Even* a full wind from those *places* shall
come unto me: now also will I give sentence
against them.
13 Behold, he shall come up as clouds, and
his chariots *shall be* as a whirlwind: his
horses are swifter than eagles. Woe unto
us! for we are spoiled.
14 O Jerusalem, wash thine heart from
wickedness, that thou mayest be saved.
How long shall thy vain thoughts lodge
within thee?
15 For a voice declareth from Dan, and
publisheth affliction from mount Ephraim.
16 Make ye mention to the nations; behold,
publish against Jerusalem, *that* watchers
come from a far country, and give out their
voice against the cities of Judah.
17 As keepers of a field, are they against
her round about; because she hath been
rebellious against me, saith the LORD.
18 Thy way and thy doings have procured
these *things* unto thee; this *is* thy wickedness, because it is bitter, because it reacheth
unto thine heart.
19 ¶ My bowels, my bowels! I am pained at
my very heart; my heart maketh a noise in
me; I cannot hold my peace, because thou
hast heard, O my soul, the sound of the
trumpet, the alarm of war.
20 Destruction upon destruction is cried; for
the whole land is spoiled: suddenly are my
tents spoiled, *and* my curtains in a moment.
21 How long shall I see the standard, *and*
hear the sound of the trumpet?
22 For my people *is* foolish, they have not
known me; they *are* sottish children, and
they have none understanding: they *are*
wise to do evil, but to do good they have
no knowledge.
23 I beheld the earth, and, lo, *it was* without
form, and void; and the heavens, and they
had no light.
24 I beheld the mountains, and, lo, they
trembled, and all the hills moved lightly.
25 I beheld, and, lo, *there was* no man, and
all the birds of the heavens were fled.
26 I beheld, and, lo, the fruitful place *was* a
wilderness, and all the cities thereof were
broken down at the presence of the LORD,
and by his fierce anger.
27 For thus hath the LORD said, The whole
land shall be desolate; yet will I not make
a full end.
28 For this shall the earth mourn, and the
heavens above be black: because I have
spoken *it*, I have purposed *it*, and will not
repent, neither will I turn back from it.
29 The whole city shall flee for the noise of
the horsemen and bowmen; they shall go
into thickets, and climb up upon the rocks:
every city *shall be* forsaken, and not a man
dwell therein.
30 And *when* thou *art* spoiled, what wilt
thou do? Though thou clothest thyself with
crimson, though thou deckest thee with
ornaments of gold, though thou rentest thy
face with painting, in vain shalt thou make
thyself fair; *thy* lovers will despise thee, they
will seek thy life.
31 For I have heard a voice as of a woman
in travail, *and* the anguish as of her that
bringeth forth her first child, the voice of
the daughter of Zion, *that* bewaileth herself,
that spreadeth her hands, *saying*, Woe *is*
me now! for my soul is wearied because
of murderers.

Jeremiah 5

1 Run ye to and fro through the streets of
Jerusalem, and see now, and know, and
seek in the broad places thereof, if ye can
find a man, if there be *any* that executeth
judgment, that seeketh the truth; and I will
pardon it.
2 And though they say, The LORD liveth;
surely they swear falsely.
3 O LORD, *are* not thine eyes upon the truth?
thou hast stricken them, but they have not
grieved; thou hast consumed them, *but* they
have refused to receive correction: they

have made their faces harder than a rock;
they have refused to return.
4 Therefore I said, Surely these *are* poor;
they are foolish: for they know not the way
of the LORD, *nor* the judgment of their God.
5 I will get me unto the great men, and will
speak unto them; for they have known the
way of the LORD, *and* the judgment of their
God: but these have altogether broken the
yoke, *and* burst the bonds.
6 Wherefore a lion out of the forest shall
slay them, *and* a wolf of the evenings shall
spoil them, a leopard shall watch over their
cities: every one that goeth out thence shall
be torn in pieces: because their transgressions are many, *and* their backslidings are
increased.
7 ¶ How shall I pardon thee for this? thy
children have forsaken me, and sworn by
them that are no gods: when I had fed them
to the full, they then committed adultery,
and assembled themselves by troops in the
harlots' houses.
8 They were *as* fed horses in the morning:
every one neighed after his neighbour's
wife.
9 Shall I not visit for these *things?* saith the
LORD: and shall not my soul be avenged on
such a nation as this?
10 ¶ Go ye up upon her walls, and destroy;
but make not a full end: take away her bat-
tlements; for they *are* not the LORD's.
11 For the house of Israel and the house of
Judah have dealt very treacherously against
me, saith the LORD.
12 They have belied the LORD, and said, *It*
is not he; neither shall evil come upon us;
neither shall we see sword nor famine:
13 And the prophets shall become wind,
and the word *is* not in them: thus shall it
be done unto them.
14 Wherefore thus saith the LORD God of
hosts, Because ye speak this word, behold,
I will make my words in thy mouth fire, and
this people wood, and it shall devour them.
15 Lo, I will bring a nation upon you from
far, O house of Israel, saith the LORD: it *is*
a mighty nation, it *is* an ancient nation, a
nation whose language thou knowest not,
neither understandest what they say.
16 Their quiver *is* as an open sepulchre, they
are all mighty men.
17 And they shall eat up thine harvest, and
thy bread, *which* thy sons and thy daughters should eat: they shall eat up thy flocks
and thine herds: they shall eat up thy vines
and thy fig trees: they shall impoverish thy
fenced cities, wherein thou trustedst, with
the sword.
18 Nevertheless in those days, saith the
LORD, I will not make a full end with you.
19 ¶ And it shall come to pass, when ye shall
say, Wherefore doeth the LORD our God all
these *things* unto us? then shalt thou answer
them, Like as ye have forsaken me, and
served strange gods in your land, so shall ye
serve strangers in a land *that is* not yours.
20 Declare this in the house of Jacob, and
publish it in Judah, saying,
21 Hear now this, O foolish people, and
without understanding; which have eyes,
and see not; which have ears, and hear not:
22 Fear ye not me? saith the LORD: will ye
not tremble at my presence, which have
placed the sand *for* the bound of the sea by a
perpetual decree, that it cannot pass it: and
though the waves thereof toss themselves,
yet can they not prevail; though they roar,
yet can they not pass over it?
23 But this people hath a revolting and a
rebellious heart; they are revolted and gone.
24 Neither say they in their heart, Let us now
fear the LORD our God, that giveth rain, both
the former and the latter, in his season: he
reserveth unto us the appointed weeks of
the harvest.
25 ¶ Your iniquities have turned away these
things, and your sins have withholden good
things from you.
26 For among my people are found wicked
men: they lay wait, as he that setteth snares;
they set a trap, they catch men.
27 As a cage is full of birds, so *are* their
houses full of deceit: therefore they are
become great, and waxen rich.
28 They are waxen fat, they shine: yea,
they overpass the deeds of the wicked:
they judge not the cause, the cause of the
fatherless, yet they prosper; and the right
of the needy do they not judge.
29 Shall I not visit for these *things?* saith the
LORD: shall not my soul be avenged on such
a nation as this?
30 ¶ A wonderful and horrible thing is committed in the land;
31 The prophets prophesy falsely, and the

priests bear rule by their means; and my people love *to have it* so: and what will ye do in the end thereof?

Jeremiah 6

1 O ye children of Benjamin, gather yourselves to flee out of the midst of Jerusalem, and blow the trumpet in Tekoa, and set up a sign of fire in Beth-haccerem: for evil appeareth out of the north, and great destruction.
2 I have likened the daughter of Zion to a comely and delicate *woman*.
3 The shepherds with their flocks shall come unto her; they shall pitch *their* tents against her round about; they shall feed every one in his place.
4 Prepare ye war against her; arise, and let us go up at noon. Woe unto us! for the day goeth away, for the shadows of the evening are stretched out.
5 Arise, and let us go by night, and let us destroy her palaces.
6 ¶ For thus hath the LORD of hosts said, Hew ye down trees, and cast a mount against Jerusalem: this *is* the city to be visited; she *is* wholly oppression in the midst of her.
7 As a fountain casteth out her waters, so she casteth out her wickedness: violence and spoil is heard in her; before me continually *is* grief and wounds.
8 Be thou instructed, O Jerusalem, lest my soul depart from thee; lest I make thee desolate, a land not inhabited.
9 ¶ Thus saith the LORD of hosts, They shall throughly glean the remnant of Israel as a vine: turn back thine hand as a grapegatherer into the baskets.
10 To whom shall I speak, and give warning, that they may hear? behold, their ear *is* uncircumcised, and they cannot hearken: behold, the word of the LORD is unto them a reproach; they have no delight in it.
11 Therefore I am full of the fury of the LORD; I am weary with holding in: I will pour it out upon the children abroad, and upon the assembly of young men together: for even the husband with the wife shall be taken, the aged with *him that is* full of days.
12 And their houses shall be turned unto others, *with their* fields and wives together: for I will stretch out my hand upon the inhabitants of the land, saith the LORD.
13 For from the least of them even unto the greatest of them every one *is* given to covetousness; and from the prophet even unto the priest every one dealeth falsely.
14 They have healed also the hurt *of the daughter* of my people slightly, saying, Peace, peace; when *there is* no peace.
15 Were they ashamed when they had committed abomination? nay, they were not at all ashamed, neither could they blush: therefore they shall fall among them that fall: at the time *that* I visit them they shall be cast down, saith the LORD.
16 Thus saith the LORD, Stand ye in the ways, and see, and ask for the old paths, where *is* the good way, and walk therein, and ye shall find rest for your souls. But they said, We will not walk *therein*.
17 Also I set watchmen over you, *saying*, Hearken to the sound of the trumpet. But they said, We will not hearken.
18 ¶ Therefore hear, ye nations, and know, O congregation, what *is* among them.
19 Hear, O earth: behold, I will bring evil upon this people, *even* the fruit of their thoughts, because they have not hearkened unto my words, nor to my law, but rejected it.
20 To what purpose cometh there to me incense from Sheba, and the sweet cane from a far country? your burnt offerings *are* not acceptable, nor your sacrifices sweet unto me.
21 Therefore thus saith the LORD, Behold, I will lay stumblingblocks before this people, and the fathers and the sons together shall fall upon them; the neighbour and his friend shall perish.
22 Thus saith the LORD, Behold, a people cometh from the north country, and a great nation shall be raised from the sides of the earth.
23 They shall lay hold on bow and spear; they *are* cruel, and have no mercy; their voice roareth like the sea; and they ride upon horses, set in array as men for war against thee, O daughter of Zion.
24 We have heard the fame thereof: our hands wax feeble: anguish hath taken hold of us, *and* pain, as of a woman in travail.
25 Go not forth into the field, nor walk by

the way; for the sword of the enemy *and*
fear *is* on every side.
26 ¶ O daughter of my people, gird *thee*
with sackcloth, and wallow thyself in ashes:
make thee mourning, *as for* an only son,
most bitter lamentation: for the spoiler shall
suddenly come upon us.
27 I have set thee *for* a tower *and* a fortress
among my people, that thou mayest know
and try their way.
28 They *are* all grievous revolters, walking
with slanders: *they are* brass and iron; they
are all corrupters.
29 The bellows are burned, the lead is consumed of the fire; the founder melteth in
vain: for the wicked are not plucked away.
30 Reprobate silver shall *men* call them,
because the LORD hath rejected them.

Jeremiah 7

1 The word that came to Jeremiah from the
LORD, saying,
2 Stand in the gate of the LORD's house, and
proclaim there this word, and say, Hear the
word of the LORD, all *ye of* Judah, that enter
in at these gates to worship the LORD.
3 Thus saith the LORD of hosts, the God of
Israel, Amend your ways and your doings,
and I will cause you to dwell in this place.
4 Trust ye not in lying words, saying, The
temple of the LORD, The temple of the LORD,
The temple of the LORD, *are* these.
5 For if ye throughly amend your ways and
your doings; if ye throughly execute judgment between a man and his neighbour;
6 *If* ye oppress not the stranger, the fatherless, and the widow, and shed not innocent
blood in this place, neither walk after other
gods to your hurt:
7 Then will I cause you to dwell in this place,
in the land that I gave to your fathers, for
ever and ever.
8 ¶ Behold, ye trust in lying words, that
cannot profit.
9 Will ye steal, murder, and commit adultery, and swear falsely, and burn incense
unto Baal, and walk after other gods whom
ye know not;
10 And come and stand before me in this
house, which is called by my name, and
say, We are delivered to do all these abominations?
11 Is this house, which is called by my name,
become a den of robbers in your eyes?
Behold, even I have seen *it*, saith the LORD.
12 But go ye now unto my place which *was*
in Shiloh, where I set my name at the first,
and see what I did to it for the wickedness
of my people Israel.
13 And now, because ye have done all these
works, saith the LORD, and I spake unto you,
rising up early and speaking, but ye heard
not; and I called you, but ye answered not;
14 Therefore will I do unto *this* house, which
is called by my name, wherein ye trust, and
unto the place which I gave to you and to
your fathers, as I have done to Shiloh.
15 And I will cast you out of my sight, as I
have cast out all your brethren, *even* the
whole seed of Ephraim.
16 Therefore pray not thou for this people, neither lift up cry nor prayer for them,
neither make intercession to me: for I will
not hear thee.
17 ¶ Seest thou not what they do in the cities of Judah and in the streets of Jerusalem?
18 The children gather wood, and the
fathers kindle the fire, and the women
knead *their* dough, to make cakes to the
queen of heaven, and to pour out drink
offerings unto other gods, that they may
provoke me to anger.
19 Do they provoke me to anger? saith the
LORD: *do they* not *provoke* themselves to
the confusion of their own faces?
20 Therefore thus saith the Lord GOD;
Behold, mine anger and my fury shall be
poured out upon this place, upon man, and
upon beast, and upon the trees of the field,
and upon the fruit of the ground; and it shall
burn, and shall not be quenched.
21 ¶ Thus saith the LORD of hosts, the God
of Israel; Put your burnt offerings unto your
sacrifices, and eat flesh.
22 For I spake not unto your fathers, nor
commanded them in the day that I brought
them out of the land of Egypt, concerning
burnt offerings or sacrifices:
23 But this thing commanded I them, saying, Obey my voice, and I will be your God,
and ye shall be my people: and walk ye in
all the ways that I have commanded you,
that it may be well unto you.
24 But they hearkened not, nor inclined
their ear, but walked in the counsels *and*

in the imagination of their evil heart, and
went backward, and not forward.
25 Since the day that your fathers came
forth out of the land of Egypt unto this day
I have even sent unto you all my servants
the prophets, daily rising up early and
sending *them:*
26 Yet they hearkened not unto me, nor
inclined their ear, but hardened their neck:
they did worse than their fathers.
27 Therefore thou shalt speak all these
words unto them; but they will not hearken
to thee: thou shalt also call unto them; but
they will not answer thee.
28 But thou shalt say unto them, This *is* a
nation that obeyeth not the voice of the
LORD their God, nor receiveth correction:
truth is perished, and is cut off from their
mouth.
29 ¶ Cut off thine hair, *O Jerusalem*, and
cast *it* away, and take up a lamentation on
high places; for the LORD hath rejected and
forsaken the generation of his wrath.
30 For the children of Judah have done evil
in my sight, saith the LORD: they have set
their abominations in the house which is
called by my name, to pollute it.
31 And they have built the high places of
Tophet, which *is* in the valley of the son of
Hinnom, to burn their sons and their daughters in the fire; which I commanded *them*
not, neither came it into my heart.
32 ¶ Therefore, behold, the days come,
saith the LORD, that it shall no more be
called Tophet, nor the valley of the son of
Hinnom, but the valley of slaughter: for they
shall bury in Tophet, till there be no place.
33 And the carcases of this people shall be
meat for the fowls of the heaven, and for
the beasts of the earth; and none shall fray
them away.
34 Then will I cause to cease from the cities
of Judah, and from the streets of Jerusalem,
the voice of mirth, and the voice of gladness,
the voice of the bridegroom, and the voice
of the bride: for the land shall be desolate.

Jeremiah 8

1 At that time, saith the LORD, they shall
bring out the bones of the kings of Judah,
and the bones of his princes, and the bones
of the priests, and the bones of the prophets, and the bones of the inhabitants of
Jerusalem, out of their graves:
2 And they shall spread them before the sun,
and the moon, and all the host of heaven,
whom they have loved, and whom they have
served, and after whom they have walked,
and whom they have sought, and whom
they have worshipped: they shall not be
gathered, nor be buried; they shall be for
dung upon the face of the earth.
3 And death shall be chosen rather than
life by all the residue of them that remain
of this evil family, which remain in all the
places whither I have driven them, saith
the LORD of hosts.
4 ¶ Moreover thou shalt say unto them,
Thus saith the LORD; Shall they fall, and not
arise? shall he turn away, and not return?
5 Why *then* is this people of Jerusalem
slidden back by a perpetual backsliding?
they hold fast deceit, they refuse to return.
6 I hearkened and heard, *but* they spake not
aright: no man repented him of his wickedness, saying, What have I done? every one
turned to his course, as the horse rusheth
into the battle.
7 Yea, the stork in the heaven knoweth her
appointed times; and the turtle and the
crane and the swallow observe the time of
their coming; but my people know not the
judgment of the LORD.
8 How do ye say, We *are* wise, and the law
of the LORD *is* with us? Lo, certainly in vain
made he *it;* the pen of the scribes *is* in vain.
9 The wise *men* are ashamed, they are dismayed and taken: lo, they have rejected
the word of the LORD; and what wisdom
is in them?
10 Therefore will I give their wives unto
others, *and* their fields to them that shall
inherit *them:* for every one from the least
even unto the greatest is given to covetousness, from the prophet even unto the priest
every one dealeth falsely.
11 For they have healed the hurt of the
daughter of my people slightly, saying,
Peace, peace; when *there is* no peace.
12 Were they ashamed when they had
committed abomination? nay, they were
not at all ashamed, neither could they blush:
therefore shall they fall among them that
fall: in the time of their visitation they shall
be cast down, saith the LORD.

13 ¶ I will surely consume them, saith the
LORD: *there shall be* no grapes on the vine,
nor figs on the fig tree, and the leaf shall
fade; and *the things that* I have given them
shall pass away from them.
14 Why do we sit still? assemble yourselves,
and let us enter into the defenced cities, and
let us be silent there: for the LORD our God
hath put us to silence, and given us water
of gall to drink, because we have sinned
against the LORD.
15 We looked for peace, but no good *came;*
and for a time of health, and behold trouble!
16 The snorting of his horses was heard
from Dan: the whole land trembled at the
sound of the neighing of his strong ones;
for they are come, and have devoured the
land, and all that is in it; the city, and those
that dwell therein.
17 For, behold, I will send serpents, cock-
atrices, among you, which *will* not *be*
charmed, and they shall bite you, saith
the LORD.
18 ¶ *When* I would comfort myself against
sorrow, my heart *is* faint in me.
19 Behold the voice of the cry of the daughter of my people because of them that dwell
in a far country: *Is* not the LORD in Zion? *is*
not her king in her? Why have they provoked
me to anger with their graven images, *and*
with strange vanities?
20 The harvest is past, the summer is ended,
and we are not saved.
21 For the hurt of the daughter of my people
am I hurt; I am black; astonishment hath
taken hold on me.
22 *Is there* no balm in Gilead; *is there* no
physician there? why then is not the health
of the daughter of my people recovered?

Jeremiah 9

1 Oh that my head were waters, and mine
eyes a fountain of tears, that I might weep
day and night for the slain of the daughter
of my people!
2 Oh that I had in the wilderness a lodging
place of wayfaring men; that I might leave
my people, and go from them! for they *be* all
adulterers, an assembly of treacherous men.
3 And they bend their tongues *like* their bow
for lies: but they are not valiant for the truth
upon the earth; for they proceed from evil to
evil, and they know not me, saith the LORD.
4 Take ye heed every one of his neighbour,
and trust ye not in any brother: for every
brother will utterly supplant, and every
neighbour will walk with slanders.
5 And they will deceive every one his neighbour, and will not speak the truth: they have
taught their tongue to speak lies, *and* weary
themselves to commit iniquity.
6 Thine habitation *is* in the midst of deceit;
through deceit they refuse to know me,
saith the LORD.
7 Therefore thus saith the LORD of hosts,
Behold, I will melt them, and try them;
for how shall I do for the daughter of my
people?
8 Their tongue *is as* an arrow shot out; it
speaketh deceit: *one* speaketh peaceably to
his neighbour with his mouth, but in heart
he layeth his wait.
9 ¶ Shall I not visit them for these *things?*
saith the LORD: shall not my soul be avenged
on such a nation as this?
10 For the mountains will I take up a weeping and wailing, and for the habitations
of the wilderness a lamentation, because
they are burned up, so that none can pass
through *them;* neither can *men* hear the
voice of the cattle; both the fowl of the heavens and the beast are fled; they are gone.
11 And I will make Jerusalem heaps, *and* a
den of dragons; and I will make the cities
of Judah desolate, without an inhabitant.
12 ¶ Who *is* the wise man, that may understand this? and *who is he* to whom the
mouth of the LORD hath spoken, that he
may declare it, for what the land perisheth
and is burned up like a wilderness, that none
passeth through?
13 And the LORD saith, Because they have
forsaken my law which I set before them,
and have not obeyed my voice, neither
walked therein;
14 But have walked after the imagination
of their own heart, and after Baalim, which
their fathers taught them:
15 Therefore thus saith the LORD of hosts,
the God of Israel; Behold, I will feed them,
even this people, with wormwood, and give
them water of gall to drink.
16 I will scatter them also among the heathen, whom neither they nor their fathers
have known: and I will send a sword after
them, till I have consumed them.

17 ¶ Thus saith the LORD of hosts, Consider ye, and call for the mourning women, that they may come; and send for cunning *women*, that they may come:
18 And let them make haste, and take up a wailing for us, that our eyes may run down with tears, and our eyelids gush out with waters.
19 For a voice of wailing is heard out of Zion, How are we spoiled! we are greatly confounded, because we have forsaken the land, because our dwellings have cast *us* out.
20 Yet hear the word of the LORD, O ye women, and let your ear receive the word of his mouth, and teach your daughters wailing, and every one her neighbour lamentation.
21 For death is come up into our windows, *and* is entered into our palaces, to cut off the children from without, *and* the young men from the streets.
22 Speak, Thus saith the LORD, Even the carcases of men shall fall as dung upon the open field, and as the handful after the harvestman, and none shall gather *them*.
23 ¶ Thus saith the LORD, Let not the wise *man* glory in his wisdom, neither let the mighty *man* glory in his might, let not the rich *man* glory in his riches:
24 But let him that glorieth glory in this, that he understandeth and knoweth me, that I *am* the LORD which exercise lovingkindness, judgment, and righteousness, in the earth: for in these *things* I delight, saith the LORD.
25 ¶ Behold, the days come, saith the LORD, that I will punish all *them which are* circumcised with the uncircumcised;
26 Egypt, and Judah, and Edom, and the children of Ammon, and Moab, and all *that are* in the utmost corners, that dwell in the wilderness: for all *these* nations *are* uncircumcised, and all the house of Israel *are* uncircumcised in the heart.

Jeremiah 10

1 Hear ye the word which the LORD speaketh unto you, O house of Israel:
2 Thus saith the LORD, Learn not the way of the heathen, and be not dismayed at the signs of heaven; for the heathen are dismayed at them.
3 For the customs of the people *are* vain: for *one* cutteth a tree out of the forest, the work of the hands of the workman, with the axe.
4 They deck it with silver and with gold; they fasten it with nails and with hammers, that it move not.
5 They *are* upright as the palm tree, but speak not: they must needs be borne, because they cannot go. Be not afraid of them; for they cannot do evil, neither also *is it* in them to do good.
6 Forasmuch as *there is* none like unto thee, O LORD; thou *art* great, and thy name *is* great in might.
7 Who would not fear thee, O King of nations? for to thee doth it appertain: forasmuch as among all the wise *men* of the nations, and in all their kingdoms, *there is* none like unto thee.
8 But they are altogether brutish and foolish: the stock *is* a doctrine of vanities.
9 Silver spread into plates is brought from Tarshish, and gold from Uphaz, the work of the workman, and of the hands of the founder: blue and purple *is* their clothing: they *are* all the work of cunning *men*.
10 But the LORD *is* the true God, he *is* the living God, and an everlasting king: at his wrath the earth shall tremble, and the nations shall not be able to abide his indignation.
11 Thus shall ye say unto them, The gods that have not made the heavens and the earth, *even* they shall perish from the earth, and from under these heavens.
12 He hath made the earth by his power, he hath established the world by his wisdom, and hath stretched out the heavens by his discretion.
13 When he uttereth his voice, *there is* a multitude of waters in the heavens, and he causeth the vapours to ascend from the ends of the earth; he maketh lightnings with rain, and bringeth forth the wind out of his treasures.
14 Every man is brutish in *his* knowledge: every founder is confounded by the graven image: for his molten image *is* falsehood, and *there is* no breath in them.
15 They *are* vanity, *and* the work of errors: in the time of their visitation they shall perish.
16 The portion of Jacob *is* not like them: for he *is* the former of all *things;* and Israel *is* the rod of his inheritance: The LORD of hosts *is* his name.

17 ¶ Gather up thy wares out of the land, O inhabitant of the fortress.

18 For thus saith the LORD, Behold, I will sling out the inhabitants of the land at this once, and will distress them, that they may find *it so*.

19 ¶ Woe is me for my hurt! my wound is grievous: but I said, Truly this *is* a grief, and I must bear it.

20 My tabernacle is spoiled, and all my cords are broken: my children are gone forth of me, and they *are* not: *there is* none to stretch forth my tent any more, and to set up my curtains.

21 For the pastors are become brutish, and have not sought the LORD: therefore they shall not prosper, and all their flocks shall be scattered.

22 Behold, the noise of the bruit is come, and a great commotion out of the north country, to make the cities of Judah desolate, *and* a den of dragons.

23 ¶ O LORD, I know that the way of man *is* not in himself: *it is* not in man that walketh to direct his steps.

24 O LORD, correct me, but with judgment; not in thine anger, lest thou bring me to nothing.

25 Pour out thy fury upon the heathen that know thee not, and upon the families that call not on thy name: for they have eaten up Jacob, and devoured him, and consumed him, and have made his habitation desolate.

Jeremiah 11

1 The word that came to Jeremiah from the LORD, saying,

2 Hear ye the words of this covenant, and speak unto the men of Judah, and to the inhabitants of Jerusalem;

3 And say thou unto them, Thus saith the LORD God of Israel; Cursed *be* the man that obeyeth not the words of this covenant,

4 Which I commanded your fathers in the day *that* I brought them forth out of the land of Egypt, from the iron furnace, saying, Obey my voice, and do them, according to all which I command you: so shall ye be my people, and I will be your God:

5 That I may perform the oath which I have sworn unto your fathers, to give them a land flowing with milk and honey, as *it is* this day. Then answered I, and said, So be it, O LORD.

6 Then the LORD said unto me, Proclaim all these words in the cities of Judah, and in the streets of Jerusalem, saying, Hear ye the words of this covenant, and do them.

7 For I earnestly protested unto your fathers in the day *that* I brought them up out of the land of Egypt, *even* unto this day, rising early and protesting, saying, Obey my voice.

8 Yet they obeyed not, nor inclined their ear, but walked every one in the imagination of their evil heart: therefore I will bring upon them all the words of this covenant, which I commanded *them* to do; but they did *them* not.

9 And the LORD said unto me, A conspiracy is found among the men of Judah, and among the inhabitants of Jerusalem.

10 They are turned back to the iniquities of their forefathers, which refused to hear my words; and they went after other gods to serve them: the house of Israel and the house of Judah have broken my covenant which I made with their fathers.

11 ¶ Therefore thus saith the LORD, Behold, I will bring evil upon them, which they shall not be able to escape; and though they shall cry unto me, I will not hearken unto them.

12 Then shall the cities of Judah and inhabitants of Jerusalem go, and cry unto the gods unto whom they offer incense: but they shall not save them at all in the time of their trouble.

13 For *according to* the number of thy cities were thy gods, O Judah; and *according to* the number of the streets of Jerusalem have ye set up altars to *that* shameful thing, *even* altars to burn incense unto Baal.

14 Therefore pray not thou for this people, neither lift up a cry or prayer for them: for I will not hear *them* in the time that they cry unto me for their trouble.

15 What hath my beloved to do in mine house, *seeing* she hath wrought lewdness with many, and the holy flesh is passed from thee? when thou doest evil, then thou rejoicest.

16 The LORD called thy name, A green olive tree, fair, *and* of goodly fruit: with the noise of a great tumult he hath kindled fire upon it, and the branches of it are broken.

17 For the LORD of hosts, that planted thee, hath pronounced evil against thee, for the evil of the house of Israel and of the house of

Judah, which they have done against themselves to provoke me to anger in offering incense unto Baal.
18 ¶ And the LORD hath given me knowledge *of it*, and I know *it:* then thou shewedst me their doings.
19 But I *was* like a lamb *or* an ox *that* is brought to the slaughter; and I knew not that they had devised devices against me, *saying*, Let us destroy the tree with the fruit thereof, and let us cut him off from the land of the living, that his name may be no more remembered.
20 But, O LORD of hosts, that judgest righteously, that triest the reins and the heart, let me see thy vengeance on them: for unto thee have I revealed my cause.
21 Therefore thus saith the LORD of the men of Anathoth, that seek thy life, saying, Prophesy not in the name of the LORD, that thou die not by our hand:
22 Therefore thus saith the LORD of hosts, Behold, I will punish them: the young men shall die by the sword; their sons and their daughters shall die by famine:
23 And there shall be no remnant of them: for I will bring evil upon the men of Anathoth, *even* the year of their visitation.

Jeremiah 12

1 Righteous *art* thou, O LORD, when I plead with thee: yet let me talk with thee of *thy* judgments: Wherefore doth the way of the wicked prosper? *wherefore* are all they happy that deal very treacherously?
2 Thou hast planted them, yea, they have taken root: they grow, yea, they bring forth fruit: thou *art* near in their mouth, and far from their reins.
3 But thou, O LORD, knowest me: thou hast seen me, and tried mine heart toward thee: pull them out like sheep for the slaughter, and prepare them for the day of slaughter.
4 How long shall the land mourn, and the herbs of every field wither, for the wickedness of them that dwell therein? the beasts are consumed, and the birds; because they said, He shall not see our last end.
5 ¶ If thou hast run with the footmen, and they have wearied thee, then how canst thou contend with horses? and *if* in the land of peace, *wherein* thou trustedst, *they* *wearied thee*, then how wilt thou do in the swelling of Jordan?
6 For even thy brethren, and the house of thy father, even they have dealt treacherously with thee; yea, they have called a multitude after thee: believe them not, though they speak fair words unto thee.
7 ¶ I have forsaken mine house, I have left mine heritage; I have given the dearly beloved of my soul into the hand of her enemies.
8 Mine heritage is unto me as a lion in the forest; it crieth out against me: therefore have I hated it.
9 Mine heritage *is* unto me *as* a speckled bird, the birds round about *are* against her; come ye, assemble all the beasts of the field, come to devour.
10 Many pastors have destroyed my vineyard, they have trodden my portion under foot, they have made my pleasant portion a desolate wilderness.
11 They have made it desolate, *and being* desolate it mourneth unto me; the whole land is made desolate, because no man layeth *it* to heart.
12 The spoilers are come upon all high places through the wilderness: for the sword of the LORD shall devour from the *one* end of the land even to the *other* end of the land: no flesh shall have peace.
13 They have sown wheat, but shall reap thorns: they have put themselves to pain, *but* shall not profit: and they shall be ashamed of your revenues because of the fierce anger of the LORD.
14 ¶ Thus saith the LORD against all mine evil neighbours, that touch the inheritance which I have caused my people Israel to inherit; Behold, I will pluck them out of their land, and pluck out the house of Judah from among them.
15 And it shall come to pass, after that I have plucked them out I will return, and have compassion on them, and will bring them again, every man to his heritage, and every man to his land.
16 And it shall come to pass, if they will diligently learn the ways of my people, to swear by my name, The LORD liveth; as they taught my people to swear by Baal; then shall they be built in the midst of my people.
17 But if they will not obey, I will utterly

pluck up and destroy that nation, saith the LORD.

Jeremiah 13

1 Thus saith the LORD unto me, Go and get thee a linen girdle, and put it upon thy loins, and put it not in water.

2 So I got a girdle according to the word of the LORD, and put *it* on my loins.

3 And the word of the LORD came unto me the second time, saying,

4 Take the girdle that thou hast got, which *is* upon thy loins, and arise, go to Euphrates, and hide it there in a hole of the rock.

5 So I went, and hid it by Euphrates, as the LORD commanded me.

6 And it came to pass after many days, that the LORD said unto me, Arise, go to Euphrates, and take the girdle from thence, which I commanded thee to hide there.

7 Then I went to Euphrates, and digged, and took the girdle from the place where I had hid it: and, behold, the girdle was marred, it was profitable for nothing.

8 Then the word of the LORD came unto me, saying,

9 Thus saith the LORD, After this manner will I mar the pride of Judah, and the great pride of Jerusalem.

10 This evil people, which refuse to hear my words, which walk in the imagination of their heart, and walk after other gods, to serve them, and to worship them, shall even be as this girdle, which is good for nothing.

11 For as the girdle cleaveth to the loins of a man, so have I caused to cleave unto me the whole house of Israel and the whole house of Judah, saith the LORD; that they might be unto me for a people, and for a name, and for a praise, and for a glory: but they would not hear.

12 ¶ Therefore thou shalt speak unto them this word; Thus saith the LORD God of Israel, Every bottle shall be filled with wine: and they shall say unto thee, Do we not certainly know that every bottle shall be filled with wine?

13 Then shalt thou say unto them, Thus saith the LORD, Behold, I will fill all the inhabitants of this land, even the kings that sit upon David's throne, and the priests, and the prophets, and all the inhabitants of Jerusalem, with drunkenness.

14 And I will dash them one against another, even the fathers and the sons together, saith the LORD: I will not pity, nor spare, nor have mercy, but destroy them.

15 ¶ Hear ye, and give ear; be not proud: for the LORD hath spoken.

16 Give glory to the LORD your God, before he cause darkness, and before your feet stumble upon the dark mountains, and, while ye look for light, he turn it into the shadow of death, *and* make *it* gross darkness.

17 But if ye will not hear it, my soul shall weep in secret places for *your* pride; and mine eye shall weep sore, and run down with tears, because the LORD's flock is carried away captive.

18 Say unto the king and to the queen, Humble yourselves, sit down: for your principalities shall come down, *even* the crown of your glory.

19 The cities of the south shall be shut up, and none shall open *them:* Judah shall be carried away captive all of it, it shall be wholly carried away captive.

20 Lift up your eyes, and behold them that come from the north: where *is* the flock *that* was given thee, thy beautiful flock?

21 What wilt thou say when he shall punish thee? for thou hast taught them *to be* captains, *and* as chief over thee: shall not sorrows take thee, as a woman in travail?

22 ¶ And if thou say in thine heart, Wherefore come these things upon me? For the greatness of thine iniquity are thy skirts discovered, *and* thy heels made bare.

23 Can the Ethiopian change his skin, or the leopard his spots? *then* may ye also do good, that are accustomed to do evil.

24 Therefore will I scatter them as the stubble that passeth away by the wind of the wilderness.

25 This *is* thy lot, the portion of thy measures from me, saith the LORD; because thou hast forgotten me, and trusted in falsehood.

26 Therefore will I discover thy skirts upon thy face, that thy shame may appear.

27 I have seen thine adulteries, and thy neighings, the lewdness of thy whoredom, *and* thine abominations on the hills in the fields. Woe unto thee, O Jerusalem! wilt thou not be made clean? when *shall it* once *be?*

Jeremiah 14

1 The word of the LORD that came to Jeremiah concerning the dearth.

2 Judah mourneth, and the gates thereof languish; they are black unto the ground; and the cry of Jerusalem is gone up.

3 And their nobles have sent their little ones to the waters: they came to the pits, *and* found no water; they returned with their vessels empty; they were ashamed and confounded, and covered their heads.

4 Because the ground is chapt, for there was no rain in the earth, the plowmen were ashamed, they covered their heads.

5 Yea, the hind also calved in the field, and forsook *it*, because there was no grass.

6 And the wild asses did stand in the high places, they snuffed up the wind like dragons; their eyes did fail, because *there was* no grass.

7 ¶ O LORD, though our iniquities testify against us, do thou *it* for thy name's sake: for our backslidings are many; we have sinned against thee.

8 O the hope of Israel, the saviour thereof in time of trouble, why shouldest thou be as a stranger in the land, and as a wayfaring man *that* turneth aside to tarry for a night?

9 Why shouldest thou be as a man astonied, as a mighty man *that* cannot save? yet thou, O LORD, *art* in the midst of us, and we are called by thy name; leave us not.

10 ¶ Thus saith the LORD unto this people, Thus have they loved to wander, they have not refrained their feet, therefore the LORD doth not accept them; he will now remember their iniquity, and visit their sins.

11 Then said the LORD unto me, Pray not for this people for *their* good.

12 When they fast, I will not hear their cry; and when they offer burnt offering and an oblation, I will not accept them: but I will consume them by the sword, and by the famine, and by the pestilence.

13 ¶ Then said I, Ah, Lord GOD! behold, the prophets say unto them, Ye shall not see the sword, neither shall ye have famine; but I will give you assured peace in this place.

14 Then the LORD said unto me, The prophets prophesy lies in my name: I sent them not, neither have I commanded them, neither spake unto them: they prophesy unto you a false vision and divination, and a thing of nought, and the deceit of their heart.

15 Therefore thus saith the LORD concerning the prophets that prophesy in my name, and I sent them not, yet they say, Sword and famine shall not be in this land; By sword and famine shall those prophets be consumed.

16 And the people to whom they prophesy shall be cast out in the streets of Jerusalem because of the famine and the sword; and they shall have none to bury them, them, their wives, nor their sons, nor their daughters: for I will pour their wickedness upon them.

17 ¶ Therefore thou shalt say this word unto them; Let mine eyes run down with tears night and day, and let them not cease: for the virgin daughter of my people is broken with a great breach, with a very grievous blow.

18 If I go forth into the field, then behold the slain with the sword! and if I enter into the city, then behold them that are sick with famine! yea, both the prophet and the priest go about into a land that they know not.

19 Hast thou utterly rejected Judah? hath thy soul lothed Zion? why hast thou smitten us, and *there is* no healing for us? we looked for peace, and *there is* no good; and for the time of healing, and behold trouble!

20 We acknowledge, O LORD, our wickedness, *and* the iniquity of our fathers: for we have sinned against thee.

21 Do not abhor *us*, for thy name's sake, do not disgrace the throne of thy glory: remember, break not thy covenant with us.

22 Are there *any* among the vanities of the Gentiles that can cause rain? or can the heavens give showers? *art* not thou he, O LORD our God? therefore we will wait upon thee: for thou hast made all these *things*.

Jeremiah 15

1 Then said the LORD unto me, Though Moses and Samuel stood before me, *yet* my mind *could* not *be* toward this people: cast *them* out of my sight, and let them go forth.

2 And it shall come to pass, if they say unto thee, Whither shall we go forth? then thou shalt tell them, Thus saith the LORD; Such as *are* for death, to death; and such as *are* for the sword, to the sword; and such as *are* for

the famine, to the famine; and such as *are*
for the captivity, to the captivity.
3 And I will appoint over them four kinds,
saith the LORD: the sword to slay, and the
dogs to tear, and the fowls of the heaven,
and the beasts of the earth, to devour and
destroy.
4 And I will cause them to be removed
into all kingdoms of the earth, because of
Manasseh the son of Hezekiah king of Judah,
for *that* which he did in Jerusalem.
5 For who shall have pity upon thee, O
Jerusalem? or who shall bemoan thee? or
who shall go aside to ask how thou doest?
6 Thou hast forsaken me, saith the LORD,
thou art gone backward: therefore will
I stretch out my hand against thee, and
destroy thee; I am weary with repenting.
7 And I will fan them with a fan in the gates
of the land; I will bereave *them* of children,
I will destroy my people, *since* they return
not from their ways.
8 Their widows are increased to me above
the sand of the seas: I have brought upon
them against the mother of the young men a
spoiler at noonday: I have caused *him* to fall
upon it suddenly, and terrors upon the city.
9 She that hath borne seven languisheth:
she hath given up the ghost; her sun is gone
down while *it was* yet day: she hath been
ashamed and confounded: and the residue
of them will I deliver to the sword before
their enemies, saith the LORD.
10 ¶ Woe is me, my mother, that thou hast
borne me a man of strife and a man of contention to the whole earth! I have neither
lent on usury, nor men have lent to me on
usury; *yet* every one of them doth curse me.
11 The LORD said, Verily it shall be well with
thy remnant; verily I will cause the enemy
to entreat thee *well* in the time of evil and
in the time of affliction.
12 Shall iron break the northern iron and
the steel?
13 Thy substance and thy treasures will I
give to the spoil without price, and *that* for
all thy sins, even in all thy borders.
14 And I will make *thee* to pass with thine
enemies into a land *which* thou knowest
not: for a fire is kindled in mine anger, *which*
shall burn upon you.
15 ¶ O LORD, thou knowest: remember
me, and visit me, and revenge me of my
persecutors; take me not away in thy longsuffering: know that for thy sake I have
suffered rebuke.
16 Thy words were found, and I did eat
them; and thy word was unto me the joy
and rejoicing of mine heart: for I am called
by thy name, O LORD God of hosts.
17 I sat not in the assembly of the mockers,
nor rejoiced; I sat alone because of thy hand:
for thou hast filled me with indignation.
18 Why is my pain perpetual, and my wound
incurable, *which* refuseth to be healed? wilt
thou be altogether unto me as a liar, *and as*
waters *that* fail?
19 ¶ Therefore thus saith the LORD, If thou
return, then will I bring thee again, *and* thou
shalt stand before me: and if thou take forth
the precious from the vile, thou shalt be as
my mouth: let them return unto thee; but
return not thou unto them.
20 And I will make thee unto this people
a fenced brasen wall: and they shall fight
against thee, but they shall not prevail
against thee: for I *am* with thee to save thee
and to deliver thee, saith the LORD.
21 And I will deliver thee out of the hand
of the wicked, and I will redeem thee out
of the hand of the terrible.

Jeremiah 16

1 The word of the LORD came also unto
me, saying,
2 Thou shalt not take thee a wife, neither
shalt thou have sons or daughters in this
place.
3 For thus saith the LORD concerning the
sons and concerning the daughters that
are born in this place, and concerning their
mothers that bare them, and concerning
their fathers that begat them in this land;
4 They shall die of grievous deaths; they shall
not be lamented; neither shall they be buried; *but* they shall be as dung upon the face
of the earth: and they shall be consumed by
the sword, and by famine; and their carcases
shall be meat for the fowls of heaven, and
for the beasts of the earth.
5 For thus saith the LORD, Enter not into the
house of mourning, neither go to lament
nor bemoan them: for I have taken away
my peace from this people, saith the LORD,
even lovingkindness and mercies.
6 Both the great and the small shall die in

this land: they shall not be buried, neither
shall *men* lament for them, nor cut themselves, nor make themselves bald for them:
7 Neither shall *men* tear *themselves* for
them in mourning, to comfort them for the
dead; neither shall *men* give them the cup
of consolation to drink for their father or
for their mother.
8 Thou shalt not also go into the house of
feasting, to sit with them to eat and to drink.
9 For thus saith the LORD of hosts, the God
of Israel; Behold, I will cause to cease out
of this place in your eyes, and in your days,
the voice of mirth, and the voice of gladness,
the voice of the bridegroom, and the voice
of the bride.
10 ¶ And it shall come to pass, when thou
shalt shew this people all these words, and
they shall say unto thee, Wherefore hath the
LORD pronounced all this great evil against
us? or what *is* our iniquity? or what *is* our
sin that we have committed against the
LORD our God?
11 Then shalt thou say unto them, Because
your fathers have forsaken me, saith the
LORD, and have walked after other gods, and
have served them, and have worshipped
them, and have forsaken me, and have not
kept my law;
12 And ye have done worse than your
fathers; for, behold, ye walk every one after
the imagination of his evil heart, that they
may not hearken unto me:
13 Therefore will I cast you out of this land
into a land that ye know not, *neither* ye nor
your fathers; and there shall ye serve other
gods day and night; where I will not shew
you favour.
14 ¶ Therefore, behold, the days come, saith
the LORD, that it shall no more be said, The
LORD liveth, that brought up the children of
Israel out of the land of Egypt;
15 But, The LORD liveth, that brought up the
children of Israel from the land of the north,
and from all the lands whither he had driven
them: and I will bring them again into their
land that I gave unto their fathers.
16 ¶ Behold, I will send for many fishers,
saith the LORD, and they shall fish them;
and after will I send for many hunters, and
they shall hunt them from every mountain,
and from every hill, and out of the holes of
the rocks.
17 For mine eyes *are* upon all their ways:
they are not hid from my face, neither is
their iniquity hid from mine eyes.
18 And first I will recompense their iniquity
and their sin double; because they have
defiled my land, they have filled mine inheritance with the carcases of their detestable
and abominable things.
19 O LORD, my strength, and my fortress,
and my refuge in the day of affliction, the
Gentiles shall come unto thee from the
ends of the earth, and shall say, Surely our
fathers have inherited lies, vanity, and *things*
wherein *there is* no profit.
20 Shall a man make gods unto himself, and
they *are* no gods?
21 Therefore, behold, I will this once cause
them to know, I will cause them to know
mine hand and my might; and they shall
know that my name *is* The LORD.

Jeremiah 17

1 The sin of Judah *is* written with a pen of
iron, *and* with the point of a diamond: *it is*
graven upon the table of their heart, and
upon the horns of your altars;
2 Whilst their children remember their
altars and their groves by the green trees
upon the high hills.
3 O my mountain in the field, I will give thy
substance *and* all thy treasures to the spoil,
and thy high places for sin, throughout all
thy borders.
4 And thou, even thyself, shalt discontinue
from thine heritage that I gave thee; and I
will cause thee to serve thine enemies in
the land which thou knowest not: for ye
have kindled a fire in mine anger, *which*
shall burn for ever.
5 ¶ Thus saith the LORD; Cursed *be* the man
that trusteth in man, and maketh flesh his
arm, and whose heart departeth from the
LORD.
6 For he shall be like the heath in the desert, and shall not see when good cometh;
but shall inhabit the parched places in the
wilderness, *in* a salt land and not inhabited.
7 Blessed *is* the man that trusteth in the
LORD, and whose hope the LORD is.
8 For he shall be as a tree planted by the
waters, and *that* spreadeth out her roots
by the river, and shall not see when heat
cometh, but her leaf shall be green; and

shall not be careful in the year of drought, neither shall cease from yielding fruit.
9 ¶ The heart *is* deceitful above all *things*, and desperately wicked: who can know it?
10 I the LORD search the heart, *I* try the reins, even to give every man according to his ways, *and* according to the fruit of his doings.
11 *As* the partridge sitteth *on eggs*, and hatcheth *them* not; *so* he that getteth riches, and not by right, shall leave them in the midst of his days, and at his end shall be a fool.
12 ¶ A glorious high throne from the beginning *is* the place of our sanctuary.
13 O LORD, the hope of Israel, all that forsake thee shall be ashamed, *and* they that depart from me shall be written in the earth, because they have forsaken the LORD, the fountain of living waters.
14 Heal me, O LORD, and I shall be healed; save me, and I shall be saved: for thou *art* my praise.
15 ¶ Behold, they say unto me, Where *is* the word of the LORD? let it come now.
16 As for me, I have not hastened from *being* a pastor to follow thee: neither have I desired the woeful day; thou knowest: that which came out of my lips was *right* before thee.
17 Be not a terror unto me: thou *art* my hope in the day of evil.
18 Let them be confounded that persecute me, but let not me be confounded: let them be dismayed, but let not me be dismayed: bring upon them the day of evil, and destroy them with double destruction.
19 ¶ Thus said the LORD unto me; Go and stand in the gate of the children of the people, whereby the kings of Judah come in, and by the which they go out, and in all the gates of Jerusalem;
20 And say unto them, Hear ye the word of the LORD, ye kings of Judah, and all Judah, and all the inhabitants of Jerusalem, that enter in by these gates:
21 Thus saith the LORD; Take heed to yourselves, and bear no burden on the sabbath day, nor bring *it* in by the gates of Jerusalem;
22 Neither carry forth a burden out of your houses on the sabbath day, neither do ye any work, but hallow ye the sabbath day, as I commanded your fathers.
23 But they obeyed not, neither inclined their ear, but made their neck stiff, that they might not hear, nor receive instruction.
24 And it shall come to pass, if ye diligently hearken unto me, saith the LORD, to bring in no burden through the gates of this city on the sabbath day, but hallow the sabbath day, to do no work therein;
25 Then shall there enter into the gates of this city kings and princes sitting upon the throne of David, riding in chariots and on horses, they, and their princes, the men of Judah, and the inhabitants of Jerusalem: and this city shall remain for ever.
26 And they shall come from the cities of Judah, and from the places about Jerusalem, and from the land of Benjamin, and from the plain, and from the mountains, and from the south, bringing burnt offerings, and sacrifices, and meat offerings, and incense, and bringing sacrifices of praise, unto the house of the LORD.
27 But if ye will not hearken unto me to hallow the sabbath day, and not to bear a burden, even entering in at the gates of Jerusalem on the sabbath day; then will I kindle a fire in the gates thereof, and it shall devour the palaces of Jerusalem, and it shall not be quenched.

Jeremiah 18

1 The word which came to Jeremiah from the LORD, saying,
2 Arise, and go down to the potter's house, and there I will cause thee to hear my words.
3 Then I went down to the potter's house, and, behold, he wrought a work on the wheels.
4 And the vessel that he made of clay was marred in the hand of the potter: so he made it again another vessel, as seemed good to the potter to make *it*.
5 Then the word of the LORD came to me, saying,
6 O house of Israel, cannot I do with you as this potter? saith the LORD. Behold, as the clay *is* in the potter's hand, so *are* ye in mine hand, O house of Israel.
7 *At what* instant I shall speak concerning a nation, and concerning a kingdom, to pluck up, and to pull down, and to destroy *it;*
8 If that nation, against whom I have pro-

nounced, turn from their evil, I will repent
of the evil that I thought to do unto them.
9 And *at what* instant I shall speak concerning a nation, and concerning a kingdom, to
build and to plant *it;*
10 If it do evil in my sight, that it obey not
my voice, then I will repent of the good,
wherewith I said I would benefit them.
11 ¶ Now therefore go to, speak to the men
of Judah, and to the inhabitants of Jerusalem, saying, Thus saith the LORD; Behold, I
frame evil against you, and devise a device
against you: return ye now every one from
his evil way, and make your ways and your
doings good.
12 And they said, There is no hope: but we
will walk after our own devices, and we
will every one do the imagination of his
evil heart.
13 Therefore thus saith the LORD; Ask ye
now among the heathen, who hath heard
such things: the virgin of Israel hath done
a very horrible thing.
14 Will *a man* leave the snow of Lebanon
which cometh from the rock of the field?
or shall the cold flowing waters that come
from another place be forsaken?
15 Because my people hath forgotten me,
they have burned incense to vanity, and they
have caused them to stumble in their ways
from the ancient paths, to walk in paths, *in*
a way not cast up;
16 To make their land desolate, *and* a
perpetual hissing; every one that passeth
thereby shall be astonished, and wag his
head.
17 I will scatter them as with an east wind
before the enemy; I will shew them the back,
and not the face, in the day of their calamity.
18 ¶ Then said they, Come, and let us devise
devices against Jeremiah; for the law shall
not perish from the priest, nor counsel from
the wise, nor the word from the prophet.
Come, and let us smite him with the tongue,
and let us not give heed to any of his words.
19 Give heed to me, O LORD, and hearken
to the voice of them that contend with me.
20 Shall evil be recompensed for good? for
they have digged a pit for my soul. Remember that I stood before thee to speak good
for them, *and* to turn away thy wrath from
them.
21 Therefore deliver up their children to
the famine, and pour out their *blood* by the
force of the sword; and let their wives be
bereaved of their children, and *be* widows;
and let their men be put to death; *let* their
young men *be* slain by the sword in battle.
22 Let a cry be heard from their houses,
when thou shalt bring a troop suddenly
upon them: for they have digged a pit to
take me, and hid snares for my feet.
23 Yet, LORD, thou knowest all their counsel against me to slay *me:* forgive not their
iniquity, neither blot out their sin from thy
sight, but let them be overthrown before
thee; deal *thus* with them in the time of
thine anger.

Jeremiah 19

1 Thus saith the LORD, Go and get a potter's
earthen bottle, and *take* of the ancients
of the people, and of the ancients of the
priests;
2 And go forth unto the valley of the son of
Hinnom, which *is* by the entry of the east
gate, and proclaim there the words that I
shall tell thee,
3 And say, Hear ye the word of the LORD, O
kings of Judah, and inhabitants of Jerusalem; Thus saith the LORD of hosts, the God
of Israel; Behold, I will bring evil upon this
place, the which whosoever heareth, his
ears shall tingle.
4 Because they have forsaken me, and
have estranged this place, and have burned
incense in it unto other gods, whom neither
they nor their fathers have known, nor the
kings of Judah, and have filled this place
with the blood of innocents;
5 They have built also the high places of
Baal, to burn their sons with fire *for* burnt
offerings unto Baal, which I commanded not,
nor spake *it*, neither came *it* into my mind:
6 Therefore, behold, the days come, saith
the LORD, that this place shall no more be
called Tophet, nor The valley of the son of
Hinnom, but The valley of slaughter.
7 And I will make void the counsel of Judah
and Jerusalem in this place; and I will cause
them to fall by the sword before their enemies, and by the hands of them that seek
their lives: and their carcases will I give to
be meat for the fowls of the heaven, and
for the beasts of the earth.
8 And I will make this city desolate, and an

hissing; every one that passeth thereby
shall be astonished and hiss because of all
the plagues thereof.
9 And I will cause them to eat the flesh of
their sons and the flesh of their daughters,
and they shall eat every one the flesh of his
friend in the siege and straitness, wherewith
their enemies, and they that seek their lives,
shall straiten them.
10 Then shalt thou break the bottle in the
sight of the men that go with thee,
11 And shalt say unto them, Thus saith the
LORD of hosts; Even so will I break this people and this city, as *one* breaketh a potter's
vessel, that cannot be made whole again:
and they shall bury *them* in Tophet, till *there*
be no place to bury.
12 Thus will I do unto this place, saith the
LORD, and to the inhabitants thereof, and
even make this city as Tophet:
13 And the houses of Jerusalem, and the
houses of the kings of Judah, shall be defiled
as the place of Tophet, because of all the
houses upon whose roofs they have burned
incense unto all the host of heaven, and
have poured out drink offerings unto other
gods.
14 Then came Jeremiah from Tophet,
whither the LORD had sent him to prophesy; and he stood in the court of the LORD's
house; and said to all the people,
15 Thus saith the LORD of hosts, the God of
Israel; Behold, I will bring upon this city and
upon all her towns all the evil that I have
pronounced against it, because they have
hardened their necks, that they might not
hear my words.

Jeremiah 20

1 Now Pashur the son of Immer the priest,
who *was* also chief governor in the house of
the LORD, heard that Jeremiah prophesied
these things.
2 Then Pashur smote Jeremiah the prophet,
and put him in the stocks that *were* in the
high gate of Benjamin, which *was* by the
house of the LORD.
3 And it came to pass on the morrow, that
Pashur brought forth Jeremiah out of the
stocks. Then said Jeremiah unto him, The
LORD hath not called thy name Pashur, but
Magor-missabib.
4 For thus saith the LORD, Behold, I will
make thee a terror to thyself, and to all thy
friends: and they shall fall by the sword of
their enemies, and thine eyes shall behold
it: and I will give all Judah into the hand of
the king of Babylon, and he shall carry them
captive into Babylon, and shall slay them
with the sword.
5 Moreover I will deliver all the strength of
this city, and all the labours thereof, and
all the precious things thereof, and all the
treasures of the kings of Judah will I give
into the hand of their enemies, which shall
spoil them, and take them, and carry them
to Babylon.
6 And thou, Pashur, and all that dwell in
thine house shall go into captivity: and
thou shalt come to Babylon, and there
thou shalt die, and shalt be buried there,
thou, and all thy friends, to whom thou hast
prophesied lies.
7 ¶ O LORD, thou hast deceived me, and I
was deceived: thou art stronger than I, and
hast prevailed: I am in derision daily, every
one mocketh me.
8 For since I spake, I cried out, I cried violence and spoil; because the word of the
LORD was made a reproach unto me, and a
derision, daily.
9 Then I said, I will not make mention of
him, nor speak any more in his name. But
his word was in mine heart as a burning fire
shut up in my bones, and I was weary with
forbearing, and I could not *stay.*
10 ¶ For I heard the defaming of many, fear
on every side. Report, *say they,* and we will
report it. All my familiars watched for my
halting, *saying,* Peradventure he will be
enticed, and we shall prevail against him,
and we shall take our revenge on him.
11 But the LORD *is* with me as a mighty terrible one: therefore my persecutors shall
stumble, and they shall not prevail: they
shall be greatly ashamed; for they shall not
prosper: *their* everlasting confusion shall
never be forgotten.
12 But, O LORD of hosts, that triest the righteous, *and* seest the reins and the heart, let
me see thy vengeance on them: for unto
thee have I opened my cause.
13 Sing unto the LORD, praise ye the LORD:
for he hath delivered the soul of the poor
from the hand of evildoers.
14 ¶ Cursed *be* the day wherein I was born:

let not the day wherein my mother bare me be blessed.

15 Cursed *be* the man who brought tidings to my father, saying, A man child is born unto thee; making him very glad.

16 And let that man be as the cities which the LORD overthrew, and repented not: and let him hear the cry in the morning, and the shouting at noontide;

17 Because he slew me not from the womb; or that my mother might have been my grave, and her womb *to be* always great *with me*.

18 Wherefore came I forth out of the womb to see labour and sorrow, that my days should be consumed with shame?

Jeremiah 21

1 The word which came unto Jeremiah from the LORD, when king Zedekiah sent unto him Pashur the son of Melchiah, and Zephaniah the son of Maaseiah the priest, saying,

2 Inquire, I pray thee, of the LORD for us; for Nebuchadrezzar king of Babylon maketh war against us; if so be that the LORD will deal with us according to all his wondrous works, that he may go up from us.

3 ¶ Then said Jeremiah unto them, Thus shall ye say to Zedekiah:

4 Thus saith the LORD God of Israel; Behold, I will turn back the weapons of war that *are* in your hands, wherewith ye fight against the king of Babylon, and *against* the Chaldeans, which besiege you without the walls, and I will assemble them into the midst of this city.

5 And I myself will fight against you with an outstretched hand and with a strong arm, even in anger, and in fury, and in great wrath.

6 And I will smite the inhabitants of this city, both man and beast: they shall die of a great pestilence.

7 And afterward, saith the LORD, I will deliver Zedekiah king of Judah, and his servants, and the people, and such as are left in this city from the pestilence, from the sword, and from the famine, into the hand of Nebuchadrezzar king of Babylon, and into the hand of their enemies, and into the hand of those that seek their life: and he shall smite them with the edge of the sword; he shall not spare them, neither have pity, nor have mercy.

8 ¶ And unto this people thou shalt say, Thus saith the LORD; Behold, I set before you the way of life, and the way of death.

9 He that abideth in this city shall die by the sword, and by the famine, and by the pestilence: but he that goeth out, and falleth to the Chaldeans that besiege you, he shall live, and his life shall be unto him for a prey.

10 For I have set my face against this city for evil, and not for good, saith the LORD: it shall be given into the hand of the king of Babylon, and he shall burn it with fire.

11 ¶ And touching the house of the king of Judah, *say*, Hear ye the word of the LORD;

12 O house of David, thus saith the LORD; Execute judgment in the morning, and deliver *him that is* spoiled out of the hand of the oppressor, lest my fury go out like fire, and burn that none can quench *it*, because of the evil of your doings.

13 Behold, I *am* against thee, O inhabitant of the valley, *and* rock of the plain, saith the LORD; which say, Who shall come down against us? or who shall enter into our habitations?

14 But I will punish you according to the fruit of your doings, saith the LORD: and I will kindle a fire in the forest thereof, and it shall devour all things round about it.

Jeremiah 22

1 Thus saith the LORD; Go down to the house of the king of Judah, and speak there this word,

2 And say, Hear the word of the LORD, O king of Judah, that sittest upon the throne of David, thou, and thy servants, and thy people that enter in by these gates:

3 Thus saith the LORD; Execute ye judgment and righteousness, and deliver the spoiled out of the hand of the oppressor: and do no wrong, do no violence to the stranger, the fatherless, nor the widow, neither shed innocent blood in this place.

4 For if ye do this thing indeed, then shall there enter in by the gates of this house kings sitting upon the throne of David, riding in chariots and on horses, he, and his servants, and his people.

5 But if ye will not hear these words, I swear

by myself, saith the LORD, that this house
shall become a desolation.
6 For thus saith the LORD unto the king's
house of Judah; Thou *art* Gilead unto me,
and the head of Lebanon: *yet* surely I will
make thee a wilderness, *and* cities *which*
are not inhabited.
7 And I will prepare destroyers against thee,
every one with his weapons: and they shall
cut down thy choice cedars, and cast *them*
into the fire.
8 And many nations shall pass by this city,
and they shall say every man to his neighbour, Wherefore hath the LORD done thus
unto this great city?
9 Then they shall answer, Because they
have forsaken the covenant of the LORD
their God, and worshipped other gods, and
served them.
10 ¶ Weep ye not for the dead, neither
bemoan him: *but* weep sore for him that
goeth away: for he shall return no more,
nor see his native country.
11 For thus saith the LORD touching Shallum the son of Josiah king of Judah, which
reigned instead of Josiah his father, which
went forth out of this place; He shall not
return thither any more:
12 But he shall die in the place whither they
have led him captive, and shall see this land
no more.
13 ¶ Woe unto him that buildeth his house
by unrighteousness, and his chambers by
wrong; *that* useth his neighbour's service
without wages, and giveth him not for his
work;
14 That saith, I will build me a wide house
and large chambers, and cutteth him out
windows; and *it is* cieled with cedar, and
painted with vermilion.
15 Shalt thou reign, because thou closest
thyself in cedar? did not thy father eat and
drink, and do judgment and justice, *and*
then *it was* well with him?
16 He judged the cause of the poor and
needy; then *it was* well *with him: was* not
this to know me? saith the LORD.
17 But thine eyes and thine heart *are* not
but for thy covetousness, and for to shed
innocent blood, and for oppression, and for
violence, to do *it*.
18 Therefore thus saith the LORD concerning
Jehoiakim the son of Josiah king of Judah;
They shall not lament for him, *saying*, Ah my
brother! or, Ah sister! they shall not lament
for him, *saying*, Ah lord! or, Ah his glory!
19 He shall be buried with the burial of an
ass, drawn and cast forth beyond the gates
of Jerusalem.
20 ¶ Go up to Lebanon, and cry; and lift
up thy voice in Bashan, and cry from the
passages: for all thy lovers are destroyed.
21 I spake unto thee in thy prosperity; *but*
thou saidst, I will not hear. This *hath been*
thy manner from thy youth, that thou obeyedst not my voice.
22 The wind shall eat up all thy pastors, and
thy lovers shall go into captivity: surely then
shalt thou be ashamed and confounded for
all thy wickedness.
23 O inhabitant of Lebanon, that makest
thy nest in the cedars, how gracious shalt
thou be when pangs come upon thee, the
pain as of a woman in travail!
24 *As* I live, saith the LORD, though Coniah
the son of Jehoiakim king of Judah were
the signet upon my right hand, yet would I
pluck thee thence;
25 And I will give thee into the hand of them
that seek thy life, and into the hand *of them*
whose face thou fearest, even into the hand
of Nebuchadrezzar king of Babylon, and into
the hand of the Chaldeans.
26 And I will cast thee out, and thy mother
that bare thee, into another country, where
ye were not born; and there shall ye die.
27 But to the land whereunto they desire to
return, thither shall they not return.
28 *Is* this man Coniah a despised broken
idol? *is he* a vessel wherein *is* no pleasure?
wherefore are they cast out, he and his
seed, and are cast into a land which they
know not?
29 O earth, earth, earth, hear the word of
the LORD.
30 Thus saith the LORD, Write ye this man
childless, a man *that* shall not prosper in his
days: for no man of his seed shall prosper,
sitting upon the throne of David, and ruling
any more in Judah.

Jeremiah 23

1 Woe be unto the pastors that destroy
and scatter the sheep of my pasture! saith
the LORD.
2 Therefore thus saith the LORD God of Israel

against the pastors that feed my people; Ye
have scattered my flock, and driven them
away, and have not visited them: behold, I
will visit upon you the evil of your doings,
saith the LORD.
3 And I will gather the remnant of my flock
out of all countries whither I have driven
them, and will bring them again to their
folds; and they shall be fruitful and increase.
4 And I will set up shepherds over them
which shall feed them: and they shall fear
no more, nor be dismayed, neither shall
they be lacking, saith the LORD.
5 ¶ Behold, the days come, saith the LORD,
that I will raise unto David a righteous
Branch, and a King shall reign and prosper,
and shall execute judgment and justice in
the earth.
6 In his days Judah shall be saved, and
Israel shall dwell safely: and this *is* his name
whereby he shall be called, THE LORD OUR
RIGHTEOUSNESS.
7 Therefore, behold, the days come, saith
the LORD, that they shall no more say, The
LORD liveth, which brought up the children
of Israel out of the land of Egypt;
8 But, The LORD liveth, which brought up and
which led the seed of the house of Israel out
of the north country, and from all countries
whither I had driven them; and they shall
dwell in their own land.
9 ¶ Mine heart within me is broken because
of the prophets; all my bones shake; I am
like a drunken man, and like a man whom
wine hath overcome, because of the LORD,
and because of the words of his holiness.
10 For the land is full of adulterers; for
because of swearing the land mourneth;
the pleasant places of the wilderness are
dried up, and their course is evil, and their
force *is* not right.
11 For both prophet and priest are profane;
yea, in my house have I found their wickedness, saith the LORD.
12 Wherefore their way shall be unto them
as slippery *ways* in the darkness: they shall
be driven on, and fall therein: for I will bring
evil upon them, *even* the year of their visitation, saith the LORD.
13 And I have seen folly in the prophets
of Samaria; they prophesied in Baal, and
caused my people Israel to err.
14 I have seen also in the prophets of Jerusalem an horrible thing: they commit adultery,
and walk in lies: they strengthen also the
hands of evildoers, that none doth return
from his wickedness: they are all of them
unto me as Sodom, and the inhabitants
thereof as Gomorrah.
15 Therefore thus saith the LORD of hosts
concerning the prophets; Behold, I will feed
them with wormwood, and make them drink
the water of gall: for from the prophets of
Jerusalem is profaneness gone forth into
all the land.
16 Thus saith the LORD of hosts, Hearken
not unto the words of the prophets that
prophesy unto you: they make you vain:
they speak a vision of their own heart, *and*
not out of the mouth of the LORD.
17 They say still unto them that despise me,
The LORD hath said, Ye shall have peace; and
they say unto every one that walketh after
the imagination of his own heart, No evil
shall come upon you.
18 For who hath stood in the counsel of
the LORD, and hath perceived and heard
his word? who hath marked his word, and
heard *it?*
19 Behold, a whirlwind of the LORD is gone
forth in fury, even a grievous whirlwind: it
shall fall grievously upon the head of the
wicked.
20 The anger of the LORD shall not return,
until he have executed, and till he have
performed the thoughts of his heart: in
the latter days ye shall consider it perfectly.
21 I have not sent these prophets, yet they
ran: I have not spoken to them, yet they
prophesied.
22 But if they had stood in my counsel, and
had caused my people to hear my words,
then they should have turned them from
their evil way, and from the evil of their
doings.
23 *Am* I a God at hand, saith the LORD, and
not a God afar off?
24 Can any hide himself in secret places
that I shall not see him? saith the LORD. Do
not I fill heaven and earth? saith the LORD.
25 I have heard what the prophets said, that
prophesy lies in my name, saying, I have
dreamed, I have dreamed.
26 How long shall *this* be in the heart of the
prophets that prophesy lies? yea, *they are*
prophets of the deceit of their own heart;

27 Which think to cause my people to forget
my name by their dreams which they tell
every man to his neighbour, as their fathers
have forgotten my name for Baal.
28 The prophet that hath a dream, let him
tell a dream; and he that hath my word, let
him speak my word faithfully. What *is* the
chaff to the wheat? saith the LORD.
29 *Is* not my word like as a fire? saith the
LORD; and like a hammer *that* breaketh the
rock in pieces?
30 Therefore, behold, I *am* against the
prophets, saith the LORD, that steal my
words every one from his neighbour.
31 Behold, I *am* against the prophets, saith
the LORD, that use their tongues, and say,
He saith.
32 Behold, I *am* against them that prophesy false dreams, saith the LORD, and do
tell them, and cause my people to err by
their lies, and by their lightness; yet I sent
them not, nor commanded them: therefore
they shall not profit this people at all, saith
the LORD.
33 ¶ And when this people, or the prophet,
or a priest, shall ask thee, saying, What *is*
the burden of the LORD? thou shalt then say
unto them, What burden? I will even forsake
you, saith the LORD.
34 And *as for* the prophet, and the priest,
and the people, that shall say, The burden
of the LORD, I will even punish that man
and his house.
35 Thus shall ye say every one to his neighbour, and every one to his brother, What
hath the LORD answered? and, What hath
the LORD spoken?
36 And the burden of the LORD shall ye
mention no more: for every man's word
shall be his burden; for ye have perverted
the words of the living God, of the LORD of
hosts our God.
37 Thus shalt thou say to the prophet, What
hath the LORD answered thee? and, What
hath the LORD spoken?
38 But since ye say, The burden of the LORD;
therefore thus saith the LORD; Because ye
say this word, The burden of the LORD, and
I have sent unto you, saying, Ye shall not
say, The burden of the LORD;
39 Therefore, behold, I, even I, will utterly
forget you, and I will forsake you, and the
city that I gave you and your fathers, *and
cast you* out of my presence:
40 And I will bring an everlasting reproach
upon you, and a perpetual shame, which
shall not be forgotten.

Jeremiah 24

1 The LORD shewed me, and, behold, two
baskets of figs *were* set before the temple of
the LORD, after that Nebuchadrezzar king of
Babylon had carried away captive Jeconiah
the son of Jehoiakim king of Judah, and the
princes of Judah, with the carpenters and
smiths, from Jerusalem, and had brought
them to Babylon.
2 One basket *had* very good figs, *even* like
the figs *that are* first ripe: and the other
basket *had* very naughty figs, which could
not be eaten, they were so bad.
3 Then said the LORD unto me, What seest
thou, Jeremiah? And I said, Figs; the good
figs, very good; and the evil, very evil, that
cannot be eaten, they are so evil.
4 ¶ Again the word of the LORD came unto
me, saying,
5 Thus saith the LORD, the God of Israel;
Like these good figs, so will I acknowledge
them that are carried away captive of Judah,
whom I have sent out of this place into the
land of the Chaldeans for *their* good.
6 For I will set mine eyes upon them for
good, and I will bring them again to this
land: and I will build them, and not pull
them down; and I will plant them, and not
pluck *them* up.
7 And I will give them an heart to know
me, that I *am* the LORD: and they shall be
my people, and I will be their God: for they
shall return unto me with their whole heart.
8 ¶ And as the evil figs, which cannot be
eaten, they are so evil; surely thus saith
the LORD, So will I give Zedekiah the king
of Judah, and his princes, and the residue
of Jerusalem, that remain in this land, and
them that dwell in the land of Egypt:
9 And I will deliver them to be removed into
all the kingdoms of the earth for *their* hurt,
to be a reproach and a proverb, a taunt and a
curse, in all places whither I shall drive them.
10 And I will send the sword, the famine,
and the pestilence, among them, till they
be consumed from off the land that I gave
unto them and to their fathers.

Jeremiah 25

1 The word that came to Jeremiah concerning all the people of Judah in the fourth year
of Jehoiakim the son of Josiah king of Judah,
that *was* the first year of Nebuchadrezzar
king of Babylon;
2 The which Jeremiah the prophet spake
unto all the people of Judah, and to all the
inhabitants of Jerusalem, saying,
3 From the thirteenth year of Josiah the
son of Amon king of Judah, even unto this
day, that *is* the three and twentieth year,
the word of the LORD hath come unto me,
and I have spoken unto you, rising early
and speaking; but ye have not hearkened.
4 And the LORD hath sent unto you all his
servants the prophets, rising early and
sending *them;* but ye have not hearkened,
nor inclined your ear to hear.
5 They said, Turn ye again now every one
from his evil way, and from the evil of your
doings, and dwell in the land that the LORD
hath given unto you and to your fathers for
ever and ever:
6 And go not after other gods to serve them,
and to worship them, and provoke me not
to anger with the works of your hands; and
I will do you no hurt.
7 Yet ye have not hearkened unto me,
saith the LORD; that ye might provoke me
to anger with the works of your hands to
your own hurt.
8 ¶ Therefore thus saith the LORD of hosts;
Because ye have not heard my words,
9 Behold, I will send and take all the families
of the north, saith the LORD, and Nebuchadrezzar the king of Babylon, my servant, and will bring them against this land,
and against the inhabitants thereof, and
against all these nations round about, and
will utterly destroy them, and make them
an astonishment, and an hissing, and perpetual desolations.
10 Moreover I will take from them the voice
of mirth, and the voice of gladness, the
voice of the bridegroom, and the voice of
the bride, the sound of the millstones, and
the light of the candle.
11 And this whole land shall be a desolation,
and an astonishment; and these nations
shall serve the king of Babylon seventy
years.
12 ¶ And it shall come to pass, when seventy
years are accomplished, *that* I will punish
the king of Babylon, and that nation, saith
the LORD, for their iniquity, and the land of
the Chaldeans, and will make it perpetual
desolations.
13 And I will bring upon that land all my
words which I have pronounced against it,
even all that is written in this book, which
Jeremiah hath prophesied against all the
nations.
14 For many nations and great kings shall
serve themselves of them also: and I will
recompense them according to their deeds,
and according to the works of their own
hands.
15 ¶ For thus saith the LORD God of Israel
unto me; Take the wine cup of this fury at
my hand, and cause all the nations, to whom
I send thee, to drink it.
16 And they shall drink, and be moved, and
be mad, because of the sword that I will
send among them.
17 Then took I the cup at the LORD's hand,
and made all the nations to drink, unto
whom the LORD had sent me:
18 *To wit*, Jerusalem, and the cities of Judah,
and the kings thereof, and the princes
thereof, to make them a desolation, an
astonishment, an hissing, and a curse; as
it is this day;
19 Pharaoh king of Egypt, and his servants,
and his princes, and all his people;
20 And all the mingled people, and all the
kings of the land of Uz, and all the kings of
the land of the Philistines, and Ashkelon,
and Azzah, and Ekron, and the remnant
of Ashdod,
21 Edom, and Moab, and the children of
Ammon,
22 And all the kings of Tyrus, and all the kings
of Zidon, and the kings of the isles which *are*
beyond the sea,
23 Dedan, and Tema, and Buz, and all *that*
are in the utmost corners,
24 And all the kings of Arabia, and all the
kings of the mingled people that dwell in
the desert,
25 And all the kings of Zimri, and all the
kings of Elam, and all the kings of the Medes,
26 And all the kings of the north, far and
near, one with another, and all the kingdoms
of the world, which *are* upon the face of the

earth: and the king of Sheshach shall drink after them.
27 Therefore thou shalt say unto them, Thus saith the LORD of hosts, the God of Israel; Drink ye, and be drunken, and spue, and fall, and rise no more, because of the sword which I will send among you.
28 And it shall be, if they refuse to take the cup at thine hand to drink, then shalt thou say unto them, Thus saith the LORD of hosts; Ye shall certainly drink.
29 For, lo, I begin to bring evil on the city which is called by my name, and should ye be utterly unpunished? Ye shall not be unpunished: for I will call for a sword upon all the inhabitants of the earth, saith the LORD of hosts.
30 Therefore prophesy thou against them all these words, and say unto them, The LORD shall roar from on high, and utter his voice from his holy habitation; he shall mightily roar upon his habitation; he shall give a shout, as they that tread *the grapes*, against all the inhabitants of the earth.
31 A noise shall come *even* to the ends of the earth; for the LORD hath a controversy with the nations, he will plead with all flesh; he will give them *that are* wicked to the sword, saith the LORD.
32 Thus saith the LORD of hosts, Behold, evil shall go forth from nation to nation, and a great whirlwind shall be raised up from the coasts of the earth.
33 And the slain of the LORD shall be at that day from *one* end of the earth even unto the *other* end of the earth: they shall not be lamented, neither gathered, nor buried; they shall be dung upon the ground.
34 ¶ Howl, ye shepherds, and cry; and wallow yourselves *in the ashes*, ye principal of the flock: for the days of your slaughter and of your dispersions are accomplished; and ye shall fall like a pleasant vessel.
35 And the shepherds shall have no way to flee, nor the principal of the flock to escape.
36 A voice of the cry of the shepherds, and an howling of the principal of the flock, *shall be heard:* for the LORD hath spoiled their pasture.
37 And the peaceable habitations are cut down because of the fierce anger of the LORD.
38 He hath forsaken his covert, as the lion: for their land is desolate because of the fierceness of the oppressor, and because of his fierce anger.

Jeremiah 26

1 In the beginning of the reign of Jehoiakim the son of Josiah king of Judah came this word from the LORD, saying,
2 Thus saith the LORD; Stand in the court of the LORD's house, and speak unto all the cities of Judah, which come to worship in the LORD's house, all the words that I command thee to speak unto them; diminish not a word:
3 If so be they will hearken, and turn every man from his evil way, that I may repent me of the evil, which I purpose to do unto them because of the evil of their doings.
4 And thou shalt say unto them, Thus saith the LORD; If ye will not hearken to me, to walk in my law, which I have set before you,
5 To hearken to the words of my servants the prophets, whom I sent unto you, both rising up early, and sending *them*, but ye have not hearkened;
6 Then will I make this house like Shiloh, and will make this city a curse to all the nations of the earth.
7 So the priests and the prophets and all the people heard Jeremiah speaking these words in the house of the LORD.
8 ¶ Now it came to pass, when Jeremiah had made an end of speaking all that the LORD had commanded *him* to speak unto all the people, that the priests and the prophets and all the people took him, saying, Thou shalt surely die.
9 Why hast thou prophesied in the name of the LORD, saying, This house shall be like Shiloh, and this city shall be desolate without an inhabitant? And all the people were gathered against Jeremiah in the house of the LORD.
10 ¶ When the princes of Judah heard these things, then they came up from the king's house unto the house of the LORD, and sat down in the entry of the new gate of the LORD's *house*.
11 Then spake the priests and the prophets unto the princes and to all the people, saying, This man *is* worthy to die; for he hath prophesied against this city, as ye have heard with your ears.

12 ¶ Then spake Jeremiah unto all the
princes and to all the people, saying, The
LORD sent me to prophesy against this house
and against this city all the words that ye
have heard.
13 Therefore now amend your ways and
your doings, and obey the voice of the
LORD your God; and the LORD will repent
him of the evil that he hath pronounced
against you.
14 As for me, behold, I *am* in your hand:
do with me as seemeth good and meet
unto you.
15 But know ye for certain, that if ye put
me to death, ye shall surely bring innocent
blood upon yourselves, and upon this city,
and upon the inhabitants thereof: for of a
truth the LORD hath sent me unto you to
speak all these words in your ears.
16 ¶ Then said the princes and all the people
unto the priests and to the prophets; This
man *is* not worthy to die: for he hath spoken to us in the name of the LORD our God.
17 Then rose up certain of the elders of the
land, and spake to all the assembly of the
people, saying,
18 Micah the Morasthite prophesied in the
days of Hezekiah king of Judah, and spake
to all the people of Judah, saying, Thus saith
the LORD of hosts; Zion shall be plowed *like*
a field, and Jerusalem shall become heaps,
and the mountain of the house as the high
places of a forest.
19 Did Hezekiah king of Judah and all Judah
put him at all to death? did he not fear
the LORD, and besought the LORD, and the
LORD repented him of the evil which he had
pronounced against them? Thus might we
procure great evil against our souls.
20 And there was also a man that prophesied in the name of the LORD, Urijah the
son of Shemaiah of Kirjath-jearim, who
prophesied against this city and against this
land according to all the words of Jeremiah:
21 And when Jehoiakim the king, with all his
mighty men, and all the princes, heard his
words, the king sought to put him to death:
but when Urijah heard it, he was afraid, and
fled, and went into Egypt;
22 And Jehoiakim the king sent men into
Egypt, *namely*, Elnathan the son of Achbor,
and *certain* men with him into Egypt.
23 And they fetched forth Urijah out of
Egypt, and brought him unto Jehoiakim
the king; who slew him with the sword,
and cast his dead body into the graves of
the common people.
24 Nevertheless the hand of Ahikam the
son of Shaphan was with Jeremiah, that
they should not give him into the hand of
the people to put him to death.

Jeremiah 27

1 In the beginning of the reign of Jehoiakim
the son of Josiah king of Judah came this
word unto Jeremiah from the LORD, saying,
2 Thus saith the LORD to me; Make thee
bonds and yokes, and put them upon thy
neck,
3 And send them to the king of Edom, and
to the king of Moab, and to the king of the
Ammonites, and to the king of Tyrus, and
to the king of Zidon, by the hand of the
messengers which come to Jerusalem unto
Zedekiah king of Judah;
4 And command them to say unto their masters, Thus saith the LORD of hosts, the God of
Israel; Thus shall ye say unto your masters;
5 I have made the earth, the man and the
beast that *are* upon the ground, by my
great power and by my outstretched arm,
and have given it unto whom it seemed
meet unto me.
6 And now have I given all these lands into
the hand of Nebuchadnezzar the king of
Babylon, my servant; and the beasts of the
field have I given him also to serve him.
7 And all nations shall serve him, and his
son, and his son's son, until the very time of
his land come: and then many nations and
great kings shall serve themselves of him.
8 And it shall come to pass, *that* the nation
and kingdom which will not serve the same
Nebuchadnezzar the king of Babylon, and
that will not put their neck under the yoke of
the king of Babylon, that nation will I punish,
saith the LORD, with the sword, and with the
famine, and with the pestilence, until I have
consumed them by his hand.
9 Therefore hearken not ye to your prophets, nor to your diviners, nor to your dreamers, nor to your enchanters, nor to your
sorcerers, which speak unto you, saying, Ye
shall not serve the king of Babylon:
10 For they prophesy a lie unto you, to

remove you far from your land; and that I should drive you out, and ye should perish.

11 But the nations that bring their neck under the yoke of the king of Babylon, and serve him, those will I let remain still in their own land, saith the LORD; and they shall till it, and dwell therein.

12 ¶ I spake also to Zedekiah king of Judah according to all these words, saying, Bring your necks under the yoke of the king of Babylon, and serve him and his people, and live.

13 Why will ye die, thou and thy people, by the sword, by the famine, and by the pestilence, as the LORD hath spoken against the nation that will not serve the king of Babylon?

14 Therefore hearken not unto the words of the prophets that speak unto you, saying, Ye shall not serve the king of Babylon: for they prophesy a lie unto you.

15 For I have not sent them, saith the LORD, yet they prophesy a lie in my name; that I might drive you out, and that ye might perish, ye, and the prophets that prophesy unto you.

16 Also I spake to the priests and to all this people, saying, Thus saith the LORD; Hearken not to the words of your prophets that prophesy unto you, saying, Behold, the vessels of the LORD's house shall now shortly be brought again from Babylon: for they prophesy a lie unto you.

17 Hearken not unto them; serve the king of Babylon, and live: wherefore should this city be laid waste?

18 But if they *be* prophets, and if the word of the LORD be with them, let them now make intercession to the LORD of hosts, that the vessels which are left in the house of the LORD, and *in* the house of the king of Judah, and at Jerusalem, go not to Babylon.

19 ¶ For thus saith the LORD of hosts concerning the pillars, and concerning the sea, and concerning the bases, and concerning the residue of the vessels that remain in this city,

20 Which Nebuchadnezzar king of Babylon took not, when he carried away captive Jeconiah the son of Jehoiakim king of Judah from Jerusalem to Babylon, and all the nobles of Judah and Jerusalem;

21 Yea, thus saith the LORD of hosts, the God of Israel, concerning the vessels that remain *in* the house of the LORD, and *in* the house of the king of Judah and of Jerusalem;

22 They shall be carried to Babylon, and there shall they be until the day that I visit them, saith the LORD; then will I bring them up, and restore them to this place.

Jeremiah 28

1 And it came to pass the same year, in the beginning of the reign of Zedekiah king of Judah, in the fourth year, *and* in the fifth month, *that* Hananiah the son of Azur the prophet, which *was* of Gibeon, spake unto me in the house of the LORD, in the presence of the priests and of all the people, saying,

2 Thus speaketh the LORD of hosts, the God of Israel, saying, I have broken the yoke of the king of Babylon.

3 Within two full years will I bring again into this place all the vessels of the LORD's house, that Nebuchadnezzar king of Babylon took away from this place, and carried them to Babylon:

4 And I will bring again to this place Jeconiah the son of Jehoiakim king of Judah, with all the captives of Judah, that went into Babylon, saith the LORD: for I will break the yoke of the king of Babylon.

5 ¶ Then the prophet Jeremiah said unto the prophet Hananiah in the presence of the priests, and in the presence of all the people that stood in the house of the LORD,

6 Even the prophet Jeremiah said, Amen: the LORD do so: the LORD perform thy words which thou hast prophesied, to bring again the vessels of the LORD's house, and all that is carried away captive, from Babylon into this place.

7 Nevertheless hear thou now this word that I speak in thine ears, and in the ears of all the people;

8 The prophets that have been before me and before thee of old prophesied both against many countries, and against great kingdoms, of war, and of evil, and of pestilence.

9 The prophet which prophesieth of peace, when the word of the prophet shall come to pass, *then* shall the prophet be known, that the LORD hath truly sent him.

10 ¶ Then Hananiah the prophet took the

yoke from off the prophet Jeremiah's neck,
and brake it.
11 And Hananiah spake in the presence of
all the people, saying, Thus saith the LORD;
Even so will I break the yoke of Nebuchadnezzar king of Babylon from the neck of all
nations within the space of two full years.
And the prophet Jeremiah went his way.
12 ¶ Then the word of the LORD came unto
Jeremiah *the prophet*, after that Hananiah
the prophet had broken the yoke from off
the neck of the prophet Jeremiah, saying,
13 Go and tell Hananiah, saying, Thus saith
the LORD; Thou hast broken the yokes of
wood; but thou shalt make for them yokes
of iron.
14 For thus saith the LORD of hosts, the God
of Israel; I have put a yoke of iron upon the
neck of all these nations, that they may
serve Nebuchadnezzar king of Babylon; and
they shall serve him: and I have given him
the beasts of the field also.
15 ¶ Then said the prophet Jeremiah unto
Hananiah the prophet, Hear now, Hananiah;
The LORD hath not sent thee; but thou makest this people to trust in a lie.
16 Therefore thus saith the LORD; Behold, I
will cast thee from off the face of the earth:
this year thou shalt die, because thou hast
taught rebellion against the LORD.
17 So Hananiah the prophet died the same
year in the seventh month.

Jeremiah 29

1 Now these *are* the words of the letter that
Jeremiah the prophet sent from Jerusalem
unto the residue of the elders which were
carried away captives, and to the priests,
and to the prophets, and to all the people
whom Nebuchadnezzar had carried away
captive from Jerusalem to Babylon;
2 (After that Jeconiah the king, and the
queen, and the eunuchs, the princes of
Judah and Jerusalem, and the carpenters,
and the smiths, were departed from Jerusalem;)
3 By the hand of Elasah the son of Shaphan,
and Gemariah the son of Hilkiah, (whom
Zedekiah king of Judah sent unto Babylon
to Nebuchadnezzar king of Babylon) saying,
4 Thus saith the LORD of hosts, the God of
Israel, unto all that are carried away captives, whom I have caused to be carried
away from Jerusalem unto Babylon;
5 Build ye houses, and dwell *in them;* and
plant gardens, and eat the fruit of them;
6 Take ye wives, and beget sons and daughters; and take wives for your sons, and give
your daughters to husbands, that they may
bear sons and daughters; that ye may be
increased there, and not diminished.
7 And seek the peace of the city whither I
have caused you to be carried away captives, and pray unto the LORD for it: for in
the peace thereof shall ye have peace.
8 ¶ For thus saith the LORD of hosts, the
God of Israel; Let not your prophets and
your diviners, that *be* in the midst of you,
deceive you, neither hearken to your dreams
which ye cause to be dreamed.
9 For they prophesy falsely unto you in my
name: I have not sent them, saith the LORD.
10 ¶ For thus saith the LORD, That after seventy years be accomplished at Babylon I will
visit you, and perform my good word toward
you, in causing you to return to this place.
11 For I know the thoughts that I think
toward you, saith the LORD, thoughts
of peace, and not of evil, to give you an
expected end.
12 Then shall ye call upon me, and ye shall
go and pray unto me, and I will hearken
unto you.
13 And ye shall seek me, and find *me*, when
ye shall search for me with all your heart.
14 And I will be found of you, saith the LORD:
and I will turn away your captivity, and I will
gather you from all the nations, and from
all the places whither I have driven you,
saith the LORD; and I will bring you again
into the place whence I caused you to be
carried away captive.
15 ¶ Because ye have said, The LORD hath
raised us up prophets in Babylon;
16 *Know* that thus saith the LORD of the king
that sitteth upon the throne of David, and
of all the people that dwelleth in this city,
and of your brethren that are not gone forth
with you into captivity;
17 Thus saith the LORD of hosts; Behold, I will
send upon them the sword, the famine, and
the pestilence, and will make them like vile
figs, that cannot be eaten, they are so evil.
18 And I will persecute them with the sword,
with the famine, and with the pestilence,

and will deliver them to be removed to all
the kingdoms of the earth, to be a curse,
and an astonishment, and an hissing, and
a reproach, among all the nations whither
I have driven them:
19 Because they have not hearkened to my
words, saith the LORD, which I sent unto
them by my servants the prophets, rising
up early and sending *them;* but ye would
not hear, saith the LORD.
20 ¶ Hear ye therefore the word of the
LORD, all ye of the captivity, whom I have
sent from Jerusalem to Babylon:
21 Thus saith the LORD of hosts, the God
of Israel, of Ahab the son of Kolaiah, and
of Zedekiah the son of Maaseiah, which
prophesy a lie unto you in my name; Behold,
I will deliver them into the hand of Nebuchadrezzar king of Babylon; and he shall slay
them before your eyes;
22 And of them shall be taken up a curse
by all the captivity of Judah which *are* in
Babylon, saying, The LORD make thee like
Zedekiah and like Ahab, whom the king of
Babylon roasted in the fire;
23 Because they have committed villany in
Israel, and have committed adultery with
their neighbours' wives, and have spoken
lying words in my name, which I have not
commanded them; even I know, and *am* a
witness, saith the LORD.
24 ¶ *Thus* shalt thou also speak to Shemaiah
the Nehelamite, saying,
25 Thus speaketh the LORD of hosts, the
God of Israel, saying, Because thou hast
sent letters in thy name unto all the people
that *are* at Jerusalem, and to Zephaniah the
son of Maaseiah the priest, and to all the
priests, saying,
26 The LORD hath made thee priest in the
stead of Jehoiada the priest, that ye should
be officers in the house of the LORD, for
every man *that is* mad, and maketh himself
a prophet, that thou shouldest put him in
prison, and in the stocks.
27 Now therefore why hast thou not
reproved Jeremiah of Anathoth, which
maketh himself a prophet to you?
28 For therefore he sent unto us *in* Babylon,
saying, This *captivity is* long: build ye houses,
and dwell *in them;* and plant gardens, and
eat the fruit of them.
29 And Zephaniah the priest read this letter
in the ears of Jeremiah the prophet.
30 ¶ Then came the word of the LORD unto
Jeremiah, saying,
31 Send to all them of the captivity, saying,
Thus saith the LORD concerning Shemaiah
the Nehelamite; Because that Shemaiah
hath prophesied unto you, and I sent him
not, and he caused you to trust in a lie:
32 Therefore thus saith the LORD; Behold, I
will punish Shemaiah the Nehelamite, and
his seed: he shall not have a man to dwell
among this people; neither shall he behold
the good that I will do for my people, saith
the LORD; because he hath taught rebellion
against the LORD.

Jeremiah 30

1 The word that came to Jeremiah from the
LORD, saying,
2 Thus speaketh the LORD God of Israel,
saying, Write thee all the words that I have
spoken unto thee in a book.
3 For, lo, the days come, saith the LORD, that
I will bring again the captivity of my people
Israel and Judah, saith the LORD: and I will
cause them to return to the land that I gave
to their fathers, and they shall possess it.
4 ¶ And these *are* the words that the LORD
spake concerning Israel and concerning
Judah.
5 For thus saith the LORD; We have heard a
voice of trembling, of fear, and not of peace.
6 Ask ye now, and see whether a man
doth travail with child? wherefore do I see
every man with his hands on his loins, as a
woman in travail, and all faces are turned
into paleness?
7 Alas! for that day *is* great, so that none *is*
like it: it *is* even the time of Jacob's trouble;
but he shall be saved out of it.
8 For it shall come to pass in that day, saith
the LORD of hosts, *that* I will break his yoke
from off thy neck, and will burst thy bonds,
and strangers shall no more serve themselves of him:
9 But they shall serve the LORD their God,
and David their king, whom I will raise up
unto them.
10 ¶ Therefore fear thou not, O my servant
Jacob, saith the LORD; neither be dismayed,
O Israel: for, lo, I will save thee from afar, and
thy seed from the land of their captivity; and

Jacob shall return, and shall be in rest, and
be quiet, and none shall make *him* afraid.
11 For I *am* with thee, saith the LORD, to
save thee: though I make a full end of all
nations whither I have scattered thee, yet
will I not make a full end of thee: but I will
correct thee in measure, and will not leave
thee altogether unpunished.
12 For thus saith the LORD, Thy bruise *is*
incurable, *and* thy wound *is* grievous.
13 *There is* none to plead thy cause, that
thou mayest be bound up: thou hast no
healing medicines.
14 All thy lovers have forgotten thee; they
seek thee not; for I have wounded thee
with the wound of an enemy, with the
chastisement of a cruel one, for the multitude of thine iniquity; *because* thy sins
were increased.
15 Why criest thou for thine affliction?
thy sorrow *is* incurable for the multitude
of thine iniquity: *because* thy sins were
increased, I have done these things unto
thee.
16 Therefore all they that devour thee shall
be devoured; and all thine adversaries,
every one of them, shall go into captivity;
and they that spoil thee shall be a spoil, and
all that prey upon thee will I give for a prey.
17 For I will restore health unto thee, and I
will heal thee of thy wounds, saith the LORD;
because they called thee an Outcast, *saying*,
This *is* Zion, whom no man seeketh after.
18 ¶ Thus saith the LORD; Behold, I will
bring again the captivity of Jacob's tents,
and have mercy on his dwellingplaces;
and the city shall be builded upon her own
heap, and the palace shall remain after the
manner thereof.
19 And out of them shall proceed thanksgiving and the voice of them that make merry:
and I will multiply them, and they shall not
be few; I will also glorify them, and they
shall not be small.
20 Their children also shall be as aforetime,
and their congregation shall be established
before me, and I will punish all that oppress
them.
21 And their nobles shall be of themselves,
and their governor shall proceed from
the midst of them; and I will cause him to
draw near, and he shall approach unto me:
for who *is* this that engaged his heart to
approach unto me? saith the LORD.
22 And ye shall be my people, and I will be
your God.
23 Behold, the whirlwind of the LORD goeth
forth with fury, a continuing whirlwind: it
shall fall with pain upon the head of the
wicked.
24 The fierce anger of the LORD shall not
return, until he have done *it*, and until he
have performed the intents of his heart: in
the latter days ye shall consider it.

Jeremiah 31

1 At the same time, saith the LORD, will I be
the God of all the families of Israel, and they
shall be my people.
2 Thus saith the LORD, The people *which*
were left of the sword found grace in the
wilderness; *even* Israel, when I went to
cause him to rest.
3 The LORD hath appeared of old unto me,
saying, Yea, I have loved thee with an everlasting love: therefore with lovingkindness
have I drawn thee.
4 Again I will build thee, and thou shalt be
built, O virgin of Israel: thou shalt again be
adorned with thy tabrets, and shalt go forth
in the dances of them that make merry.
5 Thou shalt yet plant vines upon the mountains of Samaria: the planters shall plant, and
shall eat *them* as common things.
6 For there shall be a day, *that* the watchmen upon the mount Ephraim shall cry,
Arise ye, and let us go up to Zion unto the
LORD our God.
7 For thus saith the LORD; Sing with gladness
for Jacob, and shout among the chief of the
nations: publish ye, praise ye, and say, O
LORD, save thy people, the remnant of Israel.
8 Behold, I will bring them from the north
country, and gather them from the coasts
of the earth, *and* with them the blind and
the lame, the woman with child and her
that travaileth with child together: a great
company shall return thither.
9 They shall come with weeping, and with
supplications will I lead them: I will cause
them to walk by the rivers of waters in a
straight way, wherein they shall not stumble: for I am a father to Israel, and Ephraim
is my firstborn.
10 ¶ Hear the word of the LORD, O ye

nations, and declare *it* in the isles afar off,
and say, He that scattered Israel will gather
him, and keep him, as a shepherd *doth* his
flock.
11 For the LORD hath redeemed Jacob, and
ransomed him from the hand of *him that*
was stronger than he.
12 Therefore they shall come and sing in
the height of Zion, and shall flow together
to the goodness of the LORD, for wheat,
and for wine, and for oil, and for the young
of the flock and of the herd: and their soul
shall be as a watered garden; and they shall
not sorrow any more at all.
13 Then shall the virgin rejoice in the dance,
both young men and old together: for I
will turn their mourning into joy, and will
comfort them, and make them rejoice from
their sorrow.
14 And I will satiate the soul of the priests
with fatness, and my people shall be satisfied with my goodness, saith the LORD.
15 ¶ Thus saith the LORD; A voice was heard
in Ramah, lamentation, *and* bitter weeping;
Rahel weeping for her children refused to
be comforted for her children, because
they *were* not.
16 Thus saith the LORD; Refrain thy voice
from weeping, and thine eyes from tears:
for thy work shall be rewarded, saith the
LORD; and they shall come again from the
land of the enemy.
17 And there is hope in thine end, saith the
LORD, that thy children shall come again to
their own border.
18 ¶ I have surely heard Ephraim bemoaning
himself *thus;* Thou hast chastised me, and I
was chastised, as a bullock unaccustomed *to*
the yoke: turn thou me, and I shall be turned;
for thou *art* the LORD my God.
19 Surely after that I was turned, I repented;
and after that I was instructed, I smote upon
my thigh: I was ashamed, yea, even confounded, because I did bear the reproach
of my youth.
20 *Is* Ephraim my dear son? *is he* a pleasant
child? for since I spake against him, I do
earnestly remember him still: therefore my
bowels are troubled for him; I will surely
have mercy upon him, saith the LORD.
21 Set thee up waymarks, make thee high
heaps: set thine heart toward the highway,
even the way *which* thou wentest: turn
again, O virgin of Israel, turn again to these
thy cities.
22 ¶ How long wilt thou go about, O thou
backsliding daughter? for the LORD hath
created a new thing in the earth, A woman
shall compass a man.
23 Thus saith the LORD of hosts, the God of
Israel; As yet they shall use this speech in
the land of Judah and in the cities thereof,
when I shall bring again their captivity; The
LORD bless thee, O habitation of justice, *and*
mountain of holiness.
24 And there shall dwell in Judah itself, and
in all the cities thereof together, husbandmen, and they *that* go forth with flocks.
25 For I have satiated the weary soul, and
I have replenished every sorrowful soul.
26 Upon this I awaked, and beheld; and my
sleep was sweet unto me.
27 ¶ Behold, the days come, saith the LORD,
that I will sow the house of Israel and the
house of Judah with the seed of man, and
with the seed of beast.
28 And it shall come to pass, *that* like as I
have watched over them, to pluck up, and
to break down, and to throw down, and to
destroy, and to afflict; so will I watch over
them, to build, and to plant, saith the LORD.
29 In those days they shall say no more, The
fathers have eaten a sour grape, and the
children's teeth are set on edge.
30 But every one shall die for his own iniquity: every man that eateth the sour grape,
his teeth shall be set on edge.
31 ¶ Behold, the days come, saith the LORD,
that I will make a new covenant with the
house of Israel, and with the house of Judah:
32 Not according to the covenant that I
made with their fathers in the day *that* I
took them by the hand to bring them out
of the land of Egypt; which my covenant
they brake, although I was an husband unto
them, saith the LORD:
33 But this *shall be* the covenant that I will
make with the house of Israel; After those
days, saith the LORD, I will put my law in
their inward parts, and write it in their
hearts; and will be their God, and they shall
be my people.
34 And they shall teach no more every man
his neighbour, and every man his brother,
saying, Know the LORD: for they shall all
know me, from the least of them unto the

greatest of them, saith the LORD: for I will forgive their iniquity, and I will remember their sin no more.
35 ¶ Thus saith the LORD, which giveth the sun for a light by day, *and* the ordinances of the moon and of the stars for a light by night, which divideth the sea when the waves thereof roar; The LORD of hosts *is* his name:
36 If those ordinances depart from before me, saith the LORD, *then* the seed of Israel also shall cease from being a nation before me for ever.
37 Thus saith the LORD; If heaven above can be measured, and the foundations of the earth searched out beneath, I will also cast off all the seed of Israel for all that they have done, saith the LORD.
38 ¶ Behold, the days come, saith the LORD, that the city shall be built to the LORD from the tower of Hananeel unto the gate of the corner.
39 And the measuring line shall yet go forth over against it upon the hill Gareb, and shall compass about to Goath.
40 And the whole valley of the dead bodies, and of the ashes, and all the fields unto the brook of Kidron, unto the corner of the horse gate toward the east, *shall be* holy unto the LORD; it shall not be plucked up, nor thrown down any more for ever.

Jeremiah 32

1 The word that came to Jeremiah from the LORD in the tenth year of Zedekiah king of Judah, which *was* the eighteenth year of Nebuchadrezzar.
2 For then the king of Babylon's army besieged Jerusalem: and Jeremiah the prophet was shut up in the court of the prison, which *was* in the king of Judah's house.
3 For Zedekiah king of Judah had shut him up, saying, Wherefore dost thou prophesy, and say, Thus saith the LORD, Behold, I will give this city into the hand of the king of Babylon, and he shall take it;
4 And Zedekiah king of Judah shall not escape out of the hand of the Chaldeans, but shall surely be delivered into the hand of the king of Babylon, and shall speak with him mouth to mouth, and his eyes shall behold his eyes;
5 And he shall lead Zedekiah to Babylon, and there shall he be until I visit him, saith the LORD: though ye fight with the Chaldeans, ye shall not prosper?
6 ¶ And Jeremiah said, The word of the LORD came unto me, saying,
7 Behold, Hanameel the son of Shallum thine uncle shall come unto thee, saying, Buy thee my field that *is* in Anathoth: for the right of redemption *is* thine to buy *it*.
8 So Hanameel mine uncle's son came to me in the court of the prison according to the word of the LORD, and said unto me, Buy my field, I pray thee, that *is* in Anathoth, which *is* in the country of Benjamin: for the right of inheritance *is* thine, and the redemption *is* thine; buy *it* for thyself. Then I knew that this *was* the word of the LORD.
9 And I bought the field of Hanameel my uncle's son, that *was* in Anathoth, and weighed him the money, *even* seventeen shekels of silver.
10 And I subscribed the evidence, and sealed *it*, and took witnesses, and weighed *him* the money in the balances.
11 So I took the evidence of the purchase, *both* that which was sealed *according* to the law and custom, and that which was open:
12 And I gave the evidence of the purchase unto Baruch the son of Neriah, the son of Maaseiah, in the sight of Hanameel mine uncle's *son*, and in the presence of the witnesses that subscribed the book of the purchase, before all the Jews that sat in the court of the prison.
13 ¶ And I charged Baruch before them, saying,
14 Thus saith the LORD of hosts, the God of Israel; Take these evidences, this evidence of the purchase, both which is sealed, and this evidence which is open; and put them in an earthen vessel, that they may continue many days.
15 For thus saith the LORD of hosts, the God of Israel; Houses and fields and vineyards shall be possessed again in this land.
16 ¶ Now when I had delivered the evidence of the purchase unto Baruch the son of Neriah, I prayed unto the LORD, saying,
17 Ah Lord GOD! behold, thou hast made the heaven and the earth by thy great power and stretched out arm, *and* there is nothing too hard for thee:
18 Thou shewest lovingkindness unto thou-

sands, and recompensest the iniquity of the
fathers into the bosom of their children after
them: the Great, the Mighty God, the LORD
of hosts, *is* his name,
19 Great in counsel, and mighty in work: for
thine eyes *are* open upon all the ways of the
sons of men: to give every one according
to his ways, and according to the fruit of
his doings:
20 Which hast set signs and wonders in
the land of Egypt, *even* unto this day, and
in Israel, and among *other* men; and hast
made thee a name, as at this day;
21 And hast brought forth thy people Israel
out of the land of Egypt with signs, and with
wonders, and with a strong hand, and with
a stretched out arm, and with great terror;
22 And hast given them this land, which thou
didst swear to their fathers to give them, a
land flowing with milk and honey;
23 And they came in, and possessed it; but
they obeyed not thy voice, neither walked
in thy law; they have done nothing of all
that thou commandedst them to do: therefore thou hast caused all this evil to come
upon them:
24 Behold the mounts, they are come unto
the city to take it; and the city is given into
the hand of the Chaldeans, that fight against
it, because of the sword, and of the famine,
and of the pestilence: and what thou hast
spoken is come to pass; and, behold, thou
seest *it*.
25 And thou hast said unto me, O Lord GOD,
Buy thee the field for money, and take witnesses; for the city is given into the hand of
the Chaldeans.
26 ¶ Then came the word of the LORD unto
Jeremiah, saying,
27 Behold, I *am* the LORD, the God of all
flesh: is there any thing too hard for me?
28 Therefore thus saith the LORD; Behold, I
will give this city into the hand of the Chaldeans, and into the hand of Nebuchadrezzar
king of Babylon, and he shall take it:
29 And the Chaldeans, that fight against
this city, shall come and set fire on this city,
and burn it with the houses, upon whose
roofs they have offered incense unto Baal,
and poured out drink offerings unto other
gods, to provoke me to anger.
30 For the children of Israel and the children
of Judah have only done evil before me from
their youth: for the children of Israel have
only provoked me to anger with the work
of their hands, saith the LORD.
31 For this city hath been to me *as* a provocation of mine anger and of my fury from
the day that they built it even unto this day;
that I should remove it from before my face,
32 Because of all the evil of the children of
Israel and of the children of Judah, which
they have done to provoke me to anger,
they, their kings, their princes, their priests,
and their prophets, and the men of Judah,
and the inhabitants of Jerusalem.
33 And they have turned unto me the back,
and not the face: though I taught them,
rising up early and teaching *them*, yet they
have not hearkened to receive instruction.
34 But they set their abominations in the
house, which is called by my name, to
defile it.
35 And they built the high places of Baal,
which *are* in the valley of the son of Hinnom,
to cause their sons and their daughters to
pass through *the fire* unto Molech; which I
commanded them not, neither came it into
my mind, that they should do this abomination, to cause Judah to sin.
36 ¶ And now therefore thus saith the
LORD, the God of Israel, concerning this city,
whereof ye say, It shall be delivered into the
hand of the king of Babylon by the sword,
and by the famine, and by the pestilence;
37 Behold, I will gather them out of all countries, whither I have driven them in mine
anger, and in my fury, and in great wrath;
and I will bring them again unto this place,
and I will cause them to dwell safely:
38 And they shall be my people, and I will
be their God:
39 And I will give them one heart, and one
way, that they may fear me for ever, for
the good of them, and of their children
after them:
40 And I will make an everlasting covenant
with them, that I will not turn away from
them, to do them good; but I will put my
fear in their hearts, that they shall not
depart from me.
41 Yea, I will rejoice over them to do them
good, and I will plant them in this land
assuredly with my whole heart and with
my whole soul.
42 For thus saith the LORD; Like as I have

brought all this great evil upon this people,
so will I bring upon them all the good that
I have promised them.
43 And fields shall be bought in this land,
whereof ye say, *It is* desolate without man
or beast; it is given into the hand of the
Chaldeans.
44 Men shall buy fields for money, and subscribe evidences, and seal *them*, and take
witnesses in the land of Benjamin, and in the
places about Jerusalem, and in the cities of
Judah, and in the cities of the mountains,
and in the cities of the valley, and in the
cities of the south: for I will cause their
captivity to return, saith the LORD.

Jeremiah 33

1 Moreover the word of the LORD came unto
Jeremiah the second time, while he was yet
shut up in the court of the prison, saying,
2 Thus saith the LORD the maker thereof,
the LORD that formed it, to establish it; the
LORD *is* his name;
3 Call unto me, and I will answer thee, and
shew thee great and mighty things, which
thou knowest not.
4 For thus saith the LORD, the God of Israel,
concerning the houses of this city, and concerning the houses of the kings of Judah,
which are thrown down by the mounts,
and by the sword;
5 They come to fight with the Chaldeans,
but *it is* to fill them with the dead bodies of
men, whom I have slain in mine anger and
in my fury, and for all whose wickedness I
have hid my face from this city.
6 Behold, I will bring it health and cure, and
I will cure them, and will reveal unto them
the abundance of peace and truth.
7 And I will cause the captivity of Judah and
the captivity of Israel to return, and will build
them, as at the first.
8 And I will cleanse them from all their iniquity, whereby they have sinned against me;
and I will pardon all their iniquities, whereby
they have sinned, and whereby they have
transgressed against me.
9 ¶ And it shall be to me a name of joy, a
praise and an honour before all the nations
of the earth, which shall hear all the good
that I do unto them: and they shall fear and
tremble for all the goodness and for all the
prosperity that I procure unto it.
10 Thus saith the LORD; Again there shall be
heard in this place, which ye say *shall be* desolate without man and without beast, *even*
in the cities of Judah, and in the streets of
Jerusalem, that are desolate, without man,
and without inhabitant, and without beast,
11 The voice of joy, and the voice of gladness, the voice of the bridegroom, and the
voice of the bride, the voice of them that
shall say, Praise the LORD of hosts: for the
LORD *is* good; for his mercy *endureth* for
ever: *and* of them that shall bring the sacrifice of praise into the house of the LORD.
For I will cause to return the captivity of the
land, as at the first, saith the LORD.
12 Thus saith the LORD of hosts; Again in this
place, which is desolate without man and
without beast, and in all the cities thereof,
shall be an habitation of shepherds causing
their flocks to lie down.
13 In the cities of the mountains, in the cities
of the vale, and in the cities of the south, and
in the land of Benjamin, and in the places
about Jerusalem, and in the cities of Judah,
shall the flocks pass again under the hands
of him that telleth *them*, saith the LORD.
14 Behold, the days come, saith the LORD,
that I will perform that good thing which I
have promised unto the house of Israel and
to the house of Judah.
15 ¶ In those days, and at that time, will I
cause the Branch of righteousness to grow
up unto David; and he shall execute judgment and righteousness in the land.
16 In those days shall Judah be saved, and
Jerusalem shall dwell safely: and this *is the
name* wherewith she shall be called, The
LORD our righteousness.
17 ¶ For thus saith the LORD; David shall
never want a man to sit upon the throne
of the house of Israel;
18 Neither shall the priests the Levites want
a man before me to offer burnt offerings,
and to kindle meat offerings, and to do
sacrifice continually.
19 ¶ And the word of the LORD came unto
Jeremiah, saying,
20 Thus saith the LORD; If ye can break my
covenant of the day, and my covenant of
the night, and that there should not be day
and night in their season;
21 *Then* may also my covenant be broken
with David my servant, that he should not

have a son to reign upon his throne; and
with the Levites the priests, my ministers.
22 As the host of heaven cannot be numbered, neither the sand of the sea measured: so will I multiply the seed of David
my servant, and the Levites that minister
unto me.
23 Moreover the word of the LORD came to
Jeremiah, saying,
24 Considerest thou not what this people
have spoken, saying, The two families which
the LORD hath chosen, he hath even cast
them off? thus they have despised my people, that they should be no more a nation
before them.
25 Thus saith the LORD; If my covenant *be*
not with day and night, *and if* I have not
appointed the ordinances of heaven and
earth;
26 Then will I cast away the seed of Jacob,
and David my servant, *so* that I will not take
any of his seed *to be* rulers over the seed of
Abraham, Isaac, and Jacob: for I will cause
their captivity to return, and have mercy
on them.

Jeremiah 34

1 The word which came unto Jeremiah from
the LORD, when Nebuchadnezzar king of
Babylon, and all his army, and all the kingdoms of the earth of his dominion, and all
the people, fought against Jerusalem, and
against all the cities thereof, saying,
2 Thus saith the LORD, the God of Israel; Go
and speak to Zedekiah king of Judah, and tell
him, Thus saith the LORD; Behold, I will give
this city into the hand of the king of Babylon,
and he shall burn it with fire:
3 And thou shalt not escape out of his hand,
but shalt surely be taken, and delivered into
his hand; and thine eyes shall behold the
eyes of the king of Babylon, and he shall
speak with thee mouth to mouth, and thou
shalt go to Babylon.
4 Yet hear the word of the LORD, O Zedekiah
king of Judah; Thus saith the LORD of thee,
Thou shalt not die by the sword:
5 *But* thou shalt die in peace: and with the
burnings of thy fathers, the former kings
which were before thee, so shall they burn
odours for thee; and they will lament thee,
saying, Ah lord! for I have pronounced the
word, saith the LORD.
6 Then Jeremiah the prophet spake all
these words unto Zedekiah king of Judah
in Jerusalem,
7 When the king of Babylon's army fought
against Jerusalem, and against all the cities
of Judah that were left, against Lachish, and
against Azekah: for these defenced cities
remained of the cities of Judah.
8 ¶ *This is* the word that came unto Jeremiah
from the LORD, after that the king Zedekiah
had made a covenant with all the people
which *were* at Jerusalem, to proclaim liberty unto them;
9 That every man should let his manservant,
and every man his maidservant, *being* an
Hebrew or an Hebrewess, go free; that
none should serve himself of them, *to wit*,
of a Jew his brother.
10 Now when all the princes, and all the
people, which had entered into the covenant, heard that every one should let his
manservant, and every one his maidservant,
go free, that none should serve themselves
of them any more, then they obeyed, and
let *them* go.
11 But afterward they turned, and caused
the servants and the handmaids, whom
they had let go free, to return, and brought
them into subjection for servants and for
handmaids.
12 ¶ Therefore the word of the LORD came
to Jeremiah from the LORD, saying,
13 Thus saith the LORD, the God of Israel; I
made a covenant with your fathers in the
day that I brought them forth out of the
land of Egypt, out of the house of bondmen, saying,
14 At the end of seven years let ye go every
man his brother an Hebrew, which hath
been sold unto thee; and when he hath
served thee six years, thou shalt let him go
free from thee: but your fathers hearkened
not unto me, neither inclined their ear.
15 And ye were now turned, and had done
right in my sight, in proclaiming liberty every
man to his neighbour; and ye had made a
covenant before me in the house which is
called by my name:
16 But ye turned and polluted my name,
and caused every man his servant, and
every man his handmaid, whom ye had set
at liberty at their pleasure, to return, and

brought them into subjection, to be unto
you for servants and for handmaids.
17 Therefore thus saith the LORD; Ye have
not hearkened unto me, in proclaiming
liberty, every one to his brother, and every
man to his neighbour: behold, I proclaim a
liberty for you, saith the LORD, to the sword,
to the pestilence, and to the famine; and I
will make you to be removed into all the
kingdoms of the earth.
18 And I will give the men that have transgressed my covenant, which have not performed the words of the covenant which
they had made before me, when they cut
the calf in twain, and passed between the
parts thereof,
19 The princes of Judah, and the princes of
Jerusalem, the eunuchs, and the priests,
and all the people of the land, which passed
between the parts of the calf;
20 I will even give them into the hand of
their enemies, and into the hand of them
that seek their life: and their dead bodies
shall be for meat unto the fowls of the
heaven, and to the beasts of the earth.
21 And Zedekiah king of Judah and his
princes will I give into the hand of their
enemies, and into the hand of them that
seek their life, and into the hand of the
king of Babylon's army, which are gone up
from you.
22 Behold, I will command, saith the LORD,
and cause them to return to this city; and
they shall fight against it, and take it, and
burn it with fire: and I will make the cities of
Judah a desolation without an inhabitant.

Jeremiah 35

1 The word which came unto Jeremiah from
the LORD in the days of Jehoiakim the son
of Josiah king of Judah, saying,
2 Go unto the house of the Rechabites, and
speak unto them, and bring them into the
house of the LORD, into one of the chambers,
and give them wine to drink.
3 Then I took Jaazaniah the son of Jeremiah,
the son of Habaziniah, and his brethren,
and all his sons, and the whole house of
the Rechabites;
4 And I brought them into the house of
the LORD, into the chamber of the sons of
Hanan, the son of Igdaliah, a man of God,
which *was* by the chamber of the princes,
which *was* above the chamber of Maaseiah
the son of Shallum, the keeper of the door:
5 And I set before the sons of the house of
the Rechabites pots full of wine, and cups,
and I said unto them, Drink ye wine.
6 But they said, We will drink no wine: for
Jonadab the son of Rechab our father commanded us, saying, Ye shall drink no wine,
neither ye, nor your sons for ever:
7 Neither shall ye build house, nor sow
seed, nor plant vineyard, nor have *any:* but
all your days ye shall dwell in tents; that ye
may live many days in the land where ye
be strangers.
8 Thus have we obeyed the voice of Jonadab
the son of Rechab our father in all that he
hath charged us, to drink no wine all our
days, we, our wives, our sons, nor our
daughters;
9 Nor to build houses for us to dwell in: neither have we vineyard, nor field, nor seed:
10 But we have dwelt in tents, and have
obeyed, and done according to all that
Jonadab our father commanded us.
11 But it came to pass, when Nebuchadrezzar king of Babylon came up into the land,
that we said, Come, and let us go to Jerusalem for fear of the army of the Chaldeans,
and for fear of the army of the Syrians: so
we dwell at Jerusalem.
12 ¶ Then came the word of the LORD unto
Jeremiah, saying,
13 Thus saith the LORD of hosts, the God
of Israel; Go and tell the men of Judah and
the inhabitants of Jerusalem, Will ye not
receive instruction to hearken to my words?
saith the LORD.
14 The words of Jonadab the son of Rechab,
that he commanded his sons not to drink
wine, are performed; for unto this day they
drink none, but obey their father's commandment: notwithstanding I have spoken
unto you, rising early and speaking; but ye
hearkened not unto me.
15 I have sent also unto you all my servants
the prophets, rising up early and sending
them, saying, Return ye now every man from
his evil way, and amend your doings, and go
not after other gods to serve them, and ye
shall dwell in the land which I have given
to you and to your fathers: but ye have not
inclined your ear, nor hearkened unto me.
16 Because the sons of Jonadab the son of

Rechab have performed the commandment
of their father, which he commanded them;
but this people hath not hearkened unto me:
17 Therefore thus saith the LORD God of
hosts, the God of Israel; Behold, I will bring
upon Judah and upon all the inhabitants
of Jerusalem all the evil that I have pronounced against them: because I have
spoken unto them, but they have not heard;
and I have called unto them, but they have
not answered.
18 ¶ And Jeremiah said unto the house of
the Rechabites, Thus saith the LORD of hosts,
the God of Israel; Because ye have obeyed
the commandment of Jonadab your father,
and kept all his precepts, and done according unto all that he hath commanded you:
19 Therefore thus saith the LORD of hosts,
the God of Israel; Jonadab the son of Rechab
shall not want a man to stand before me
for ever.

Jeremiah 36

1 And it came to pass in the fourth year of
Jehoiakim the son of Josiah king of Judah,
that this word came unto Jeremiah from
the LORD, saying,
2 Take thee a roll of a book, and write
therein all the words that I have spoken
unto thee against Israel, and against Judah,
and against all the nations, from the day I
spake unto thee, from the days of Josiah,
even unto this day.
3 It may be that the house of Judah will
hear all the evil which I purpose to do unto
them; that they may return every man from
his evil way; that I may forgive their iniquity
and their sin.
4 Then Jeremiah called Baruch the son of
Neriah: and Baruch wrote from the mouth of
Jeremiah all the words of the LORD, which he
had spoken unto him, upon a roll of a book.
5 And Jeremiah commanded Baruch, saying,
I *am* shut up; I cannot go into the house of
the LORD:
6 Therefore go thou, and read in the roll,
which thou hast written from my mouth, the
words of the LORD in the ears of the people
in the LORD's house upon the fasting day:
and also thou shalt read them in the ears
of all Judah that come out of their cities.
7 It may be they will present their supplication before the LORD, and will return every
one from his evil way: for great *is* the anger
and the fury that the LORD hath pronounced
against this people.
8 And Baruch the son of Neriah did according to all that Jeremiah the prophet commanded him, reading in the book the words
of the LORD in the LORD's house.
9 And it came to pass in the fifth year of
Jehoiakim the son of Josiah king of Judah,
in the ninth month, *that* they proclaimed
a fast before the LORD to all the people in
Jerusalem, and to all the people that came
from the cities of Judah unto Jerusalem.
10 Then read Baruch in the book the words
of Jeremiah in the house of the LORD, in the
chamber of Gemariah the son of Shaphan
the scribe, in the higher court, at the entry
of the new gate of the LORD's house, in the
ears of all the people.
11 ¶ When Michaiah the son of Gemariah,
the son of Shaphan, had heard out of the
book all the words of the LORD,
12 Then he went down into the king's
house, into the scribe's chamber: and, lo,
all the princes sat there, *even* Elishama the
scribe, and Delaiah the son of Shemaiah, and
Elnathan the son of Achbor, and Gemariah
the son of Shaphan, and Zedekiah the son
of Hananiah, and all the princes.
13 Then Michaiah declared unto them all
the words that he had heard, when Baruch
read the book in the ears of the people.
14 Therefore all the princes sent Jehudi the
son of Nethaniah, the son of Shelemiah, the
son of Cushi, unto Baruch, saying, Take in
thine hand the roll wherein thou hast read in
the ears of the people, and come. So Baruch
the son of Neriah took the roll in his hand,
and came unto them.
15 And they said unto him, Sit down now,
and read it in our ears. So Baruch read *it*
in their ears.
16 Now it came to pass, when they had
heard all the words, they were afraid both
one and other, and said unto Baruch, We
will surely tell the king of all these words.
17 And they asked Baruch, saying, Tell us
now, How didst thou write all these words
at his mouth?
18 Then Baruch answered them, He pronounced all these words unto me with his
mouth, and I wrote *them* with ink in the
book.

19 Then said the princes unto Baruch, Go,
hide thee, thou and Jeremiah; and let no
man know where ye be.
20 ¶ And they went in to the king into the
court, but they laid up the roll in the chamber of Elishama the scribe, and told all the
words in the ears of the king.
21 So the king sent Jehudi to fetch the roll:
and he took it out of Elishama the scribe's
chamber. And Jehudi read it in the ears of
the king, and in the ears of all the princes
which stood beside the king.
22 Now the king sat in the winterhouse in
the ninth month: and *there was a fire* on
the hearth burning before him.
23 And it came to pass, *that* when Jehudi
had read three or four leaves, he cut it with
the penknife, and cast *it* into the fire that
was on the hearth, until all the roll was consumed in the fire that *was* on the hearth.
24 Yet they were not afraid, nor rent their
garments, *neither* the king, nor any of his
servants that heard all these words.
25 Nevertheless Elnathan and Delaiah and
Gemariah had made intercession to the
king that he would not burn the roll: but
he would not hear them.
26 But the king commanded Jerahmeel the
son of Hammelech, and Seraiah the son of
Azriel, and Shelemiah the son of Abdeel,
to take Baruch the scribe and Jeremiah the
prophet: but the LORD hid them.
27 ¶ Then the word of the LORD came to
Jeremiah, after that the king had burned
the roll, and the words which Baruch wrote
at the mouth of Jeremiah, saying,
28 Take thee again another roll, and write
in it all the former words that were in the
first roll, which Jehoiakim the king of Judah
hath burned.
29 And thou shalt say to Jehoiakim king
of Judah, Thus saith the LORD; Thou hast
burned this roll, saying, Why hast thou
written therein, saying, The king of Babylon
shall certainly come and destroy this land,
and shall cause to cease from thence man
and beast?
30 Therefore thus saith the LORD of
Jehoiakim king of Judah; He shall have
none to sit upon the throne of David: and
his dead body shall be cast out in the day
to the heat, and in the night to the frost.
31 And I will punish him and his seed and
his servants for their iniquity; and I will
bring upon them, and upon the inhabitants
of Jerusalem, and upon the men of Judah,
all the evil that I have pronounced against
them; but they hearkened not.
32 ¶ Then took Jeremiah another roll, and
gave it to Baruch the scribe, the son of Neriah; who wrote therein from the mouth of
Jeremiah all the words of the book which
Jehoiakim king of Judah had burned in the
fire: and there were added besides unto
them many like words.

Jeremiah 37

1 And king Zedekiah the son of Josiah
reigned instead of Coniah the son of
Jehoiakim, whom Nebuchadrezzar king of
Babylon made king in the land of Judah.
2 But neither he, nor his servants, nor the
people of the land, did hearken unto the
words of the LORD, which he spake by the
prophet Jeremiah.
3 And Zedekiah the king sent Jehucal the
son of Shelemiah and Zephaniah the son
of Maaseiah the priest to the prophet Jeremiah, saying, Pray now unto the LORD our
God for us.
4 Now Jeremiah came in and went out
among the people: for they had not put
him into prison.
5 Then Pharaoh's army was come forth
out of Egypt: and when the Chaldeans that
besieged Jerusalem heard tidings of them,
they departed from Jerusalem.
6 ¶ Then came the word of the LORD unto
the prophet Jeremiah, saying,
7 Thus saith the LORD, the God of Israel; Thus
shall ye say to the king of Judah, that sent
you unto me to inquire of me; Behold, Pharaoh's army, which is come forth to help you,
shall return to Egypt into their own land.
8 And the Chaldeans shall come again, and
fight against this city, and take it, and burn
it with fire.
9 Thus saith the LORD; Deceive not yourselves, saying, The Chaldeans shall surely
depart from us: for they shall not depart.
10 For though ye had smitten the whole
army of the Chaldeans that fight against
you, and there remained *but* wounded men
among them, *yet* should they rise up every
man in his tent, and burn this city with fire.
11 ¶ And it came to pass, that when the

army of the Chaldeans was broken up from
Jerusalem for fear of Pharaoh's army,
12 Then Jeremiah went forth out of Jerusalem to go into the land of Benjamin, to
separate himself thence in the midst of
the people.
13 And when he was in the gate of Benjamin, a captain of the ward *was* there, whose
name *was* Irijah, the son of Shelemiah, the
son of Hananiah; and he took Jeremiah the
prophet, saying, Thou fallest away to the
Chaldeans.
14 Then said Jeremiah, *It is* false; I fall not
away to the Chaldeans. But he hearkened
not to him: so Irijah took Jeremiah, and
brought him to the princes.
15 Wherefore the princes were wroth with
Jeremiah, and smote him, and put him in
prison in the house of Jonathan the scribe:
for they had made that the prison.
16 ¶ When Jeremiah was entered into the
dungeon, and into the cabins, and Jeremiah
had remained there many days;
17 Then Zedekiah the king sent, and took
him out: and the king asked him secretly in
his house, and said, Is there *any* word from
the LORD? And Jeremiah said, There is: for,
said he, thou shalt be delivered into the
hand of the king of Babylon.
18 Moreover Jeremiah said unto king
Zedekiah, What have I offended against
thee, or against thy servants, or against
this people, that ye have put me in prison?
19 Where *are* now your prophets which
prophesied unto you, saying, The king of
Babylon shall not come against you, nor
against this land?
20 Therefore hear now, I pray thee, O my
lord the king: let my supplication, I pray
thee, be accepted before thee; that thou
cause me not to return to the house of
Jonathan the scribe, lest I die there.
21 Then Zedekiah the king commanded
that they should commit Jeremiah into the
court of the prison, and that they should
give him daily a piece of bread out of the
bakers' street, until all the bread in the city
were spent. Thus Jeremiah remained in the
court of the prison.

Jeremiah 38

1 Then Shephatiah the son of Mattan, and
Gedaliah the son of Pashur, and Jucal the
son of Shelemiah, and Pashur the son of
Malchiah, heard the words that Jeremiah
had spoken unto all the people, saying,
2 Thus saith the LORD, He that remaineth
in this city shall die by the sword, by the
famine, and by the pestilence: but he that
goeth forth to the Chaldeans shall live; for
he shall have his life for a prey, and shall live.
3 Thus saith the LORD, This city shall surely
be given into the hand of the king of Babylon's army, which shall take it.
4 Therefore the princes said unto the king,
We beseech thee, let this man be put to
death: for thus he weakeneth the hands of
the men of war that remain in this city, and
the hands of all the people, in speaking such
words unto them: for this man seeketh not
the welfare of this people, but the hurt.
5 Then Zedekiah the king said, Behold, he
is in your hand: for the king *is* not *he that*
can do *any* thing against you.
6 Then took they Jeremiah, and cast him into
the dungeon of Malchiah the son of Hammelech, that *was* in the court of the prison:
and they let down Jeremiah with cords. And
in the dungeon *there was* no water, but
mire: so Jeremiah sunk in the mire.
7 ¶ Now when Ebed-melech the Ethiopian,
one of the eunuchs which was in the king's
house, heard that they had put Jeremiah
in the dungeon; the king then sitting in the
gate of Benjamin;
8 Ebed-melech went forth out of the king's
house, and spake to the king, saying,
9 My lord the king, these men have done
evil in all that they have done to Jeremiah
the prophet, whom they have cast into the
dungeon; and he is like to die for hunger in
the place where he is: for *there is* no more
bread in the city.
10 Then the king commanded Ebed-melech
the Ethiopian, saying, Take from hence thirty
men with thee, and take up Jeremiah the
prophet out of the dungeon, before he die.
11 So Ebed-melech took the men with him,
and went into the house of the king under
the treasury, and took thence old cast clouts
and old rotten rags, and let them down by
cords into the dungeon to Jeremiah.
12 And Ebed-melech the Ethiopian said unto
Jeremiah, Put now *these* old cast clouts and
rotten rags under thine armholes under the
cords. And Jeremiah did so.

13 So they drew up Jeremiah with cords, and took him up out of the dungeon: and Jeremiah remained in the court of the prison.

14 ¶ Then Zedekiah the king sent, and took Jeremiah the prophet unto him into the third entry that *is* in the house of the LORD: and the king said unto Jeremiah, I will ask thee a thing; hide nothing from me.

15 Then Jeremiah said unto Zedekiah, If I declare *it* unto thee, wilt thou not surely put me to death? and if I give thee counsel, wilt thou not hearken unto me?

16 So Zedekiah the king sware secretly unto Jeremiah, saying, *As* the LORD liveth, that made us this soul, I will not put thee to death, neither will I give thee into the hand of these men that seek thy life.

17 Then said Jeremiah unto Zedekiah, Thus saith the LORD, the God of hosts, the God of Israel; If thou wilt assuredly go forth unto the king of Babylon's princes, then thy soul shall live, and this city shall not be burned with fire; and thou shalt live, and thine house:

18 But if thou wilt not go forth to the king of Babylon's princes, then shall this city be given into the hand of the Chaldeans, and they shall burn it with fire, and thou shalt not escape out of their hand.

19 And Zedekiah the king said unto Jeremiah, I am afraid of the Jews that are fallen to the Chaldeans, lest they deliver me into their hand, and they mock me.

20 But Jeremiah said, They shall not deliver *thee*. Obey, I beseech thee, the voice of the LORD, which I speak unto thee: so it shall be well unto thee, and thy soul shall live.

21 But if thou refuse to go forth, this *is* the word that the LORD hath shewed me:

22 And, behold, all the women that are left in the king of Judah's house *shall be* brought forth to the king of Babylon's princes, and those *women* shall say, Thy friends have set thee on, and have prevailed against thee: thy feet are sunk in the mire, *and* they are turned away back.

23 So they shall bring out all thy wives and thy children to the Chaldeans: and thou shalt not escape out of their hand, but shalt be taken by the hand of the king of Babylon: and thou shalt cause this city to be burned with fire.

24 ¶ Then said Zedekiah unto Jeremiah, Let no man know of these words, and thou shalt not die.

25 But if the princes hear that I have talked with thee, and they come unto thee, and say unto thee, Declare unto us now what thou hast said unto the king, hide it not from us, and we will not put thee to death; also what the king said unto thee:

26 Then thou shalt say unto them, I presented my supplication before the king, that he would not cause me to return to Jonathan's house, to die there.

27 Then came all the princes unto Jeremiah, and asked him: and he told them according to all these words that the king had commanded. So they left off speaking with him; for the matter was not perceived.

28 So Jeremiah abode in the court of the prison until the day that Jerusalem was taken: and he was *there* when Jerusalem was taken.

Jeremiah 39

1 In the ninth year of Zedekiah king of Judah, in the tenth month, came Nebuchadrezzar king of Babylon and all his army against Jerusalem, and they besieged it.

2 *And* in the eleventh year of Zedekiah, in the fourth month, the ninth *day* of the month, the city was broken up.

3 And all the princes of the king of Babylon came in, and sat in the middle gate, *even* Nergal-sharezer, Samgar-nebo, Sarsechim, Rab-saris, Nergal-sharezer, Rab-mag, with all the residue of the princes of the king of Babylon.

4 ¶ And it came to pass, *that* when Zedekiah the king of Judah saw them, and all the men of war, then they fled, and went forth out of the city by night, by the way of the king's garden, by the gate betwixt the two walls: and he went out the way of the plain.

5 But the Chaldeans' army pursued after them, and overtook Zedekiah in the plains of Jericho: and when they had taken him, they brought him up to Nebuchadnezzar king of Babylon to Riblah in the land of Hamath, where he gave judgment upon him.

6 Then the king of Babylon slew the sons of Zedekiah in Riblah before his eyes: also the king of Babylon slew all the nobles of Judah.

7 Moreover he put out Zedekiah's eyes,

and bound him with chains, to carry him
to Babylon.
8 ¶ And the Chaldeans burned the king's
house, and the houses of the people, with
fire, and brake down the walls of Jerusalem.
9 Then Nebuzar-adan the captain of the
guard carried away captive into Babylon the
remnant of the people that remained in the
city, and those that fell away, that fell to him,
with the rest of the people that remained.
10 But Nebuzar-adan the captain of the
guard left of the poor of the people, which
had nothing, in the land of Judah, and gave
them vineyards and fields at the same time.
11 ¶ Now Nebuchadrezzar king of Babylon
gave charge concerning Jeremiah to Nebuzar-adan the captain of the guard, saying,
12 Take him, and look well to him, and do
him no harm; but do unto him even as he
shall say unto thee.
13 So Nebuzar-adan the captain of the
guard sent, and Nebushasban, Rab-saris,
and Nergal-sharezer, Rab-mag, and all the
king of Babylon's princes;
14 Even they sent, and took Jeremiah out of
the court of the prison, and committed him
unto Gedaliah the son of Ahikam the son of
Shaphan, that he should carry him home:
so he dwelt among the people.
15 ¶ Now the word of the LORD came unto
Jeremiah, while he was shut up in the court
of the prison, saying,
16 Go and speak to Ebed-melech the Ethiopian, saying, Thus saith the LORD of hosts,
the God of Israel; Behold, I will bring my
words upon this city for evil, and not for
good; and they shall be *accomplished* in
that day before thee.
17 But I will deliver thee in that day, saith the
LORD: and thou shalt not be given into the
hand of the men of whom thou *art* afraid.
18 For I will surely deliver thee, and thou
shalt not fall by the sword, but thy life shall
be for a prey unto thee: because thou hast
put thy trust in me, saith the LORD.

Jeremiah 40

1 The word that came to Jeremiah from the
LORD, after that Nebuzar-adan the captain of
the guard had let him go from Ramah, when
he had taken him being bound in chains
among all that were carried away captive
of Jerusalem and Judah, which were carried
away captive unto Babylon.
2 And the captain of the guard took Jeremiah, and said unto him, The LORD thy God
hath pronounced this evil upon this place.
3 Now the LORD hath brought *it*, and done
according as he hath said: because ye have
sinned against the LORD, and have not
obeyed his voice, therefore this thing is
come upon you.
4 And now, behold, I loose thee this day
from the chains which *were* upon thine
hand. If it seem good unto thee to come
with me into Babylon, come; and I will look
well unto thee: but if it seem ill unto thee
to come with me into Babylon, forbear:
behold, all the land *is* before thee: whither
it seemeth good and convenient for thee
to go, thither go.
5 Now while he was not yet gone back, *he
said,* Go back also to Gedaliah the son of
Ahikam the son of Shaphan, whom the king
of Babylon hath made governor over the
cities of Judah, and dwell with him among
the people: or go wheresoever it seemeth
convenient unto thee to go. So the captain
of the guard gave him victuals and a reward,
and let him go.
6 Then went Jeremiah unto Gedaliah the son
of Ahikam to Mizpah; and dwelt with him
among the people that were left in the land.
7 ¶ Now when all the captains of the forces
which *were* in the fields, *even* they and their
men, heard that the king of Babylon had
made Gedaliah the son of Ahikam governor
in the land, and had committed unto him
men, and women, and children, and of the
poor of the land, of them that were not
carried away captive to Babylon;
8 Then they came to Gedaliah to Mizpah,
even Ishmael the son of Nethaniah, and
Johanan and Jonathan the sons of Kareah,
and Seraiah the son of Tanhumeth, and
the sons of Ephai the Netophathite, and
Jezaniah the son of a Maachathite, they
and their men.
9 And Gedaliah the son of Ahikam the son
of Shaphan sware unto them and to their
men, saying, Fear not to serve the Chaldeans: dwell in the land, and serve the king
of Babylon, and it shall be well with you.
10 As for me, behold, I will dwell at Mizpah
to serve the Chaldeans, which will come

unto us: but ye, gather ye wine, and summer
fruits, and oil, and put *them* in your vessels,
and dwell in your cities that ye have taken.
11 Likewise when all the Jews that *were* in
Moab, and among the Ammonites, and in
Edom, and that *were* in all the countries,
heard that the king of Babylon had left a
remnant of Judah, and that he had set over
them Gedaliah the son of Ahikam the son
of Shaphan;
12 Even all the Jews returned out of all
places whither they were driven, and came
to the land of Judah, to Gedaliah, unto Mizpah, and gathered wine and summer fruits
very much.
13 ¶ Moreover Johanan the son of Kareah,
and all the captains of the forces that *were*
in the fields, came to Gedaliah to Mizpah,
14 And said unto him, Dost thou certainly
know that Baalis the king of the Ammonites
hath sent Ishmael the son of Nethaniah to
slay thee? But Gedaliah the son of Ahikam
believed them not.
15 Then Johanan the son of Kareah spake
to Gedaliah in Mizpah secretly, saying, Let
me go, I pray thee, and I will slay Ishmael
the son of Nethaniah, and no man shall
know *it:* wherefore should he slay thee,
that all the Jews which are gathered unto
thee should be scattered, and the remnant
in Judah perish?
16 But Gedaliah the son of Ahikam said
unto Johanan the son of Kareah, Thou shalt
not do this thing: for thou speakest falsely
of Ishmael.

Jeremiah 41

1 Now it came to pass in the seventh month,
that Ishmael the son of Nethaniah the son of
Elishama, of the seed royal, and the princes
of the king, even ten men with him, came
unto Gedaliah the son of Ahikam to Mizpah; and there they did eat bread together
in Mizpah.
2 Then arose Ishmael the son of Nethaniah,
and the ten men that were with him, and
smote Gedaliah the son of Ahikam the son
of Shaphan with the sword, and slew him,
whom the king of Babylon had made governor over the land.
3 Ishmael also slew all the Jews that were
with him, *even* with Gedaliah, at Mizpah,
and the Chaldeans that were found there,
and the men of war.
4 And it came to pass the second day after
he had slain Gedaliah, and no man knew *it*,
5 That there came certain from Shechem,
from Shiloh, and from Samaria, *even* fourscore men, having their beards shaven, and
their clothes rent, and having cut themselves, with offerings and incense in their
hand, to bring *them* to the house of the
LORD.
6 And Ishmael the son of Nethaniah went
forth from Mizpah to meet them, weeping
all along as he went: and it came to pass,
as he met them, he said unto them, Come
to Gedaliah the son of Ahikam.
7 And it was *so*, when they came into the
midst of the city, that Ishmael the son of
Nethaniah slew them, *and cast them* into
the midst of the pit, he, and the men that
were with him.
8 But ten men were found among them that
said unto Ishmael, Slay us not: for we have
treasures in the field, of wheat, and of barley, and of oil, and of honey. So he forbare,
and slew them not among their brethren.
9 Now the pit wherein Ishmael had cast all
the dead bodies of the men, whom he had
slain because of Gedaliah, *was* it which Asa
the king had made for fear of Baasha king
of Israel: *and* Ishmael the son of Nethaniah
filled it with *them that were* slain.
10 Then Ishmael carried away captive all
the residue of the people that *were* in Mizpah, *even* the king's daughters, and all the
people that remained in Mizpah, whom
Nebuzar-adan the captain of the guard had
committed to Gedaliah the son of Ahikam:
and Ishmael the son of Nethaniah carried
them away captive, and departed to go over
to the Ammonites.
11 ¶ But when Johanan the son of Kareah,
and all the captains of the forces that *were*
with him, heard of all the evil that Ishmael
the son of Nethaniah had done,
12 Then they took all the men, and went
to fight with Ishmael the son of Nethaniah,
and found him by the great waters that *are*
in Gibeon.
13 Now it came to pass, *that* when all
the people which *were* with Ishmael saw
Johanan the son of Kareah, and all the cap-

tains of the forces that *were* with him, then
they were glad.
14 So all the people that Ishmael had carried away captive from Mizpah cast about
and returned, and went unto Johanan the
son of Kareah.
15 But Ishmael the son of Nethaniah
escaped from Johanan with eight men,
and went to the Ammonites.
16 Then took Johanan the son of Kareah,
and all the captains of the forces that *were*
with him, all the remnant of the people
whom he had recovered from Ishmael the
son of Nethaniah, from Mizpah, after *that*
he had slain Gedaliah the son of Ahikam,
even mighty men of war, and the women,
and the children, and the eunuchs, whom
he had brought again from Gibeon:
17 And they departed, and dwelt in the habitation of Chimham, which is by Beth-lehem,
to go to enter into Egypt,
18 Because of the Chaldeans: for they were
afraid of them, because Ishmael the son of
Nethaniah had slain Gedaliah the son of
Ahikam, whom the king of Babylon made
governor in the land.

Jeremiah 42

1 Then all the captains of the forces, and
Johanan the son of Kareah, and Jezaniah
the son of Hoshaiah, and all the people from
the least even unto the greatest, came near,
2 And said unto Jeremiah the prophet,
Let, we beseech thee, our supplication be
accepted before thee, and pray for us unto
the LORD thy God, *even* for all this remnant;
(for we are left *but* a few of many, as thine
eyes do behold us:)
3 That the LORD thy God may shew us the
way wherein we may walk, and the thing
that we may do.
4 Then Jeremiah the prophet said unto
them, I have heard *you;* behold, I will pray
unto the LORD your God according to your
words; and it shall come to pass, *that* whatsoever thing the LORD shall answer you, I
will declare *it* unto you; I will keep nothing
back from you.
5 Then they said to Jeremiah, The LORD
be a true and faithful witness between us,
if we do not even according to all things
for the which the LORD thy God shall send
thee to us.
6 Whether *it be* good, or whether *it be* evil,
we will obey the voice of the LORD our God,
to whom we send thee; that it may be well
with us, when we obey the voice of the
LORD our God.
7 ¶ And it came to pass after ten days, that
the word of the LORD came unto Jeremiah.
8 Then called he Johanan the son of Kareah,
and all the captains of the forces which *were*
with him, and all the people from the least
even to the greatest,
9 And said unto them, Thus saith the LORD,
the God of Israel, unto whom ye sent me
to present your supplication before him;
10 If ye will still abide in this land, then will I
build you, and not pull *you* down, and I will
plant you, and not pluck *you* up: for I repent
me of the evil that I have done unto you.
11 Be not afraid of the king of Babylon, of
whom ye are afraid; be not afraid of him,
saith the LORD: for I *am* with you to save you,
and to deliver you from his hand.
12 And I will shew mercies unto you, that
he may have mercy upon you, and cause
you to return to your own land.
13 ¶ But if ye say, We will not dwell in this
land, neither obey the voice of the LORD
your God,
14 Saying, No; but we will go into the land of
Egypt, where we shall see no war, nor hear
the sound of the trumpet, nor have hunger
of bread; and there will we dwell:
15 And now therefore hear the word of the
LORD, ye remnant of Judah; Thus saith the
LORD of hosts, the God of Israel; If ye wholly
set your faces to enter into Egypt, and go
to sojourn there;
16 Then it shall come to pass, *that* the
sword, which ye feared, shall overtake you
there in the land of Egypt, and the famine, whereof ye were afraid, shall follow
close after you there in Egypt; and there
ye shall die.
17 So shall it be with all the men that set
their faces to go into Egypt to sojourn there;
they shall die by the sword, by the famine,
and by the pestilence: and none of them
shall remain or escape from the evil that I
will bring upon them.
18 For thus saith the LORD of hosts, the God
of Israel; As mine anger and my fury hath
been poured forth upon the inhabitants of
Jerusalem; so shall my fury be poured forth

upon you, when ye shall enter into Egypt:
and ye shall be an execration, and an astonishment, and a curse, and a reproach; and
ye shall see this place no more.
19 ¶ The LORD hath said concerning you, O
ye remnant of Judah; Go ye not into Egypt:
know certainly that I have admonished
you this day.
20 For ye dissembled in your hearts, when
ye sent me unto the LORD your God, saying, Pray for us unto the LORD our God;
and according unto all that the LORD our
God shall say, so declare unto us, and we
will do *it*.
21 And *now* I have this day declared *it* to
you; but ye have not obeyed the voice of
the LORD your God, nor any *thing* for the
which he hath sent me unto you.
22 Now therefore know certainly that ye
shall die by the sword, by the famine, and
by the pestilence, in the place whither ye
desire to go *and* to sojourn.

Jeremiah 43

1 And it came to pass, *that* when Jeremiah
had made an end of speaking unto all the
people all the words of the LORD their God,
for which the LORD their God had sent him
to them, *even* all these words,
2 Then spake Azariah the son of Hoshaiah,
and Johanan the son of Kareah, and all the
proud men, saying unto Jeremiah, Thou
speakest falsely: the LORD our God hath
not sent thee to say, Go not into Egypt to
sojourn there:
3 But Baruch the son of Neriah setteth thee
on against us, for to deliver us into the hand
of the Chaldeans, that they might put us
to death, and carry us away captives into
Babylon.
4 So Johanan the son of Kareah, and all the
captains of the forces, and all the people,
obeyed not the voice of the LORD, to dwell
in the land of Judah.
5 But Johanan the son of Kareah, and all
the captains of the forces, took all the remnant of Judah, that were returned from all
nations, whither they had been driven, to
dwell in the land of Judah;
6 *Even* men, and women, and children, and
the king's daughters, and every person that
Nebuzar-adan the captain of the guard had
left with Gedaliah the son of Ahikam the son
of Shaphan, and Jeremiah the prophet, and
Baruch the son of Neriah.
7 So they came into the land of Egypt: for
they obeyed not the voice of the LORD: thus
came they *even* to Tahpanhes.
8 ¶ Then came the word of the LORD unto
Jeremiah in Tahpanhes, saying,
9 Take great stones in thine hand, and hide
them in the clay in the brickkiln, which *is* at
the entry of Pharaoh's house in Tahpanhes,
in the sight of the men of Judah;
10 And say unto them, Thus saith the LORD
of hosts, the God of Israel; Behold, I will
send and take Nebuchadrezzar the king of
Babylon, my servant, and will set his throne
upon these stones that I have hid; and he
shall spread his royal pavilion over them.
11 And when he cometh, he shall smite the
land of Egypt, *and deliver* such *as are* for
death to death; and such *as are* for captivity
to captivity; and such *as are* for the sword
to the sword.
12 And I will kindle a fire in the houses of
the gods of Egypt; and he shall burn them,
and carry them away captives: and he shall
array himself with the land of Egypt, as a
shepherd putteth on his garment; and he
shall go forth from thence in peace.
13 He shall break also the images of Beth-
shemesh, that *is* in the land of Egypt; and
the houses of the gods of the Egyptians shall
he burn with fire.

Jeremiah 44

1 The word that came to Jeremiah concerning all the Jews which dwell in the land of
Egypt, which dwell at Migdol, and at Tahpanhes, and at Noph, and in the country of
Pathros, saying,
2 Thus saith the LORD of hosts, the God of
Israel; Ye have seen all the evil that I have
brought upon Jerusalem, and upon all the
cities of Judah; and, behold, this day they *are*
a desolation, and no man dwelleth therein,
3 Because of their wickedness which they
have committed to provoke me to anger, in
that they went to burn incense, *and* to serve
other gods, whom they knew not, *neither*
they, ye, nor your fathers.
4 Howbeit I sent unto you all my servants
the prophets, rising early and sending *them*,
saying, Oh, do not this abominable thing
that I hate.

5 But they hearkened not, nor inclined their
ear to turn from their wickedness, to burn
no incense unto other gods.
6 Wherefore my fury and mine anger was
poured forth, and was kindled in the cities
of Judah and in the streets of Jerusalem; and
they are wasted *and* desolate, as at this day.
7 Therefore now thus saith the LORD, the
God of hosts, the God of Israel; Wherefore
commit ye *this* great evil against your souls,
to cut off from you man and woman, child
and suckling, out of Judah, to leave you
none to remain;
8 In that ye provoke me unto wrath with the
works of your hands, burning incense unto
other gods in the land of Egypt, whither ye
be gone to dwell, that ye might cut yourselves off, and that ye might be a curse and a
reproach among all the nations of the earth?
9 Have ye forgotten the wickedness of
your fathers, and the wickedness of the
kings of Judah, and the wickedness of their
wives, and your own wickedness, and the
wickedness of your wives, which they have
committed in the land of Judah, and in the
streets of Jerusalem?
10 They are not humbled *even* unto this day,
neither have they feared, nor walked in my
law, nor in my statutes, that I set before you
and before your fathers.
11 ¶ Therefore thus saith the LORD of hosts,
the God of Israel; Behold, I will set my face
against you for evil, and to cut off all Judah.
12 And I will take the remnant of Judah,
that have set their faces to go into the land
of Egypt to sojourn there, and they shall all
be consumed, *and* fall in the land of Egypt;
they shall *even* be consumed by the sword
and by the famine: they shall die, from the
least even unto the greatest, by the sword
and by the famine: and they shall be an execration, *and* an astonishment, and a curse,
and a reproach.
13 For I will punish them that dwell in the
land of Egypt, as I have punished Jerusalem, by the sword, by the famine, and by
the pestilence:
14 So that none of the remnant of Judah,
which are gone into the land of Egypt to
sojourn there, shall escape or remain, that
they should return into the land of Judah,
to the which they have a desire to return to
dwell there: for none shall return but such
as shall escape.
15 ¶ Then all the men which knew that their
wives had burned incense unto other gods,
and all the women that stood by, a great
multitude, even all the people that dwelt
in the land of Egypt, in Pathros, answered
Jeremiah, saying,
16 *As for* the word that thou hast spoken
unto us in the name of the LORD, we will not
hearken unto thee.
17 But we will certainly do whatsoever thing
goeth forth out of our own mouth, to burn
incense unto the queen of heaven, and to
pour out drink offerings unto her, as we have
done, we, and our fathers, our kings, and
our princes, in the cities of Judah, and in the
streets of Jerusalem: for *then* had we plenty
of victuals, and were well, and saw no evil.
18 But since we left off to burn incense
to the queen of heaven, and to pour out
drink offerings unto her, we have wanted
all *things*, and have been consumed by the
sword and by the famine.
19 And when we burned incense to the
queen of heaven, and poured out drink
offerings unto her, did we make her cakes
to worship her, and pour out drink offerings
unto her, without our men?
20 ¶ Then Jeremiah said unto all the people, to the men, and to the women, and
to all the people which had given him *that*
answer, saying,
21 The incense that ye burned in the cities
of Judah, and in the streets of Jerusalem,
ye, and your fathers, your kings, and your
princes, and the people of the land, did not
the LORD remember them, and came it *not*
into his mind?
22 So that the LORD could no longer bear,
because of the evil of your doings, *and*
because of the abominations which ye
have committed; therefore is your land a
desolation, and an astonishment, and a
curse, without an inhabitant, as at this day.
23 Because ye have burned incense, and
because ye have sinned against the LORD,
and have not obeyed the voice of the LORD,
nor walked in his law, nor in his statutes,
nor in his testimonies; therefore this evil is
happened unto you, as at this day.
24 Moreover Jeremiah said unto all the
people, and to all the women, Hear the

word of the LORD, all Judah that *are* in the
land of Egypt:
25 Thus saith the LORD of hosts, the God of
Israel, saying; Ye and your wives have both
spoken with your mouths, and fulfilled with
your hand, saying, We will surely perform
our vows that we have vowed, to burn
incense to the queen of heaven, and to pour
out drink offerings unto her: ye will surely
accomplish your vows, and surely perform
your vows.
26 Therefore hear ye the word of the LORD,
all Judah that dwell in the land of Egypt;
Behold, I have sworn by my great name,
saith the LORD, that my name shall no more
be named in the mouth of any man of Judah
in all the land of Egypt, saying, The Lord
GOD liveth.
27 Behold, I will watch over them for evil,
and not for good: and all the men of Judah
that *are* in the land of Egypt shall be consumed by the sword and by the famine, until
there be an end of them.
28 Yet a small number that escape the sword
shall return out of the land of Egypt into
the land of Judah, and all the remnant of
Judah, that are gone into the land of Egypt
to sojourn there, shall know whose words
shall stand, mine, or theirs.
29 ¶ And this *shall be* a sign unto you, saith
the LORD, that I will punish you in this place,
that ye may know that my words shall surely
stand against you for evil:
30 Thus saith the LORD; Behold, I will give
Pharaoh-hophra king of Egypt into the hand
of his enemies, and into the hand of them
that seek his life; as I gave Zedekiah king
of Judah into the hand of Nebuchadrezzar
king of Babylon, his enemy, and that sought
his life.

Jeremiah 45

1 The word that Jeremiah the prophet spake
unto Baruch the son of Neriah, when he had
written these words in a book at the mouth
of Jeremiah, in the fourth year of Jehoiakim
the son of Josiah king of Judah, saying,
2 Thus saith the LORD, the God of Israel,
unto thee, O Baruch;
3 Thou didst say, Woe is me now! for the
LORD hath added grief to my sorrow; I
fainted in my sighing, and I find no rest.
4 ¶ Thus shalt thou say unto him, The LORD
saith thus; Behold, *that* which I have built
will I break down, and that which I have
planted I will pluck up, even this whole land.
5 And seekest thou great things for thyself?
seek *them* not: for, behold, I will bring evil
upon all flesh, saith the LORD: but thy life
will I give unto thee for a prey in all places
whither thou goest.

Jeremiah 46

1 The word of the LORD which came to
Jeremiah the prophet against the Gentiles;
2 Against Egypt, against the army of Pha-
raoh-necho king of Egypt, which was by
the river Euphrates in Carchemish, which
Nebuchadrezzar king of Babylon smote
in the fourth year of Jehoiakim the son of
Josiah king of Judah.
3 Order ye the buckler and shield, and draw
near to battle.
4 Harness the horses; and get up, ye horsemen, and stand forth with *your* helmets; fur-
bish the spears, *and* put on the brigandines.
5 Wherefore have I seen them dismayed
and turned away back? and their mighty
ones are beaten down, and are fled apace,
and look not back: *for* fear *was* round about,
saith the LORD.
6 Let not the swift flee away, nor the mighty
man escape; they shall stumble, and fall
toward the north by the river Euphrates.
7 Who *is* this *that* cometh up as a flood,
whose waters are moved as the rivers?
8 Egypt riseth up like a flood, and *his* waters
are moved like the rivers; and he saith, I will
go up, *and* will cover the earth; I will destroy
the city and the inhabitants thereof.
9 Come up, ye horses; and rage, ye chariots; and let the mighty men come forth;
the Ethiopians and the Libyans, that handle
the shield; and the Lydians, that handle *and*
bend the bow.
10 For this *is* the day of the Lord GOD of
hosts, a day of vengeance, that he may
avenge him of his adversaries: and the
sword shall devour, and it shall be satiate
and made drunk with their blood: for the
Lord GOD of hosts hath a sacrifice in the
north country by the river Euphrates.
11 Go up into Gilead, and take balm, O
virgin, the daughter of Egypt: in vain shalt
thou use many medicines; *for* thou shalt
not be cured.

12 The nations have heard of thy shame, and
thy cry hath filled the land: for the mighty
man hath stumbled against the mighty, *and*
they are fallen both together.
13 ¶ The word that the LORD spake to Jeremiah the prophet, how Nebuchadrezzar
king of Babylon should come *and* smite the
land of Egypt.
14 Declare ye in Egypt, and publish in
Migdol, and publish in Noph and in Tahpanhes: say ye, Stand fast, and prepare thee; for
the sword shall devour round about thee.
15 Why are thy valiant *men* swept away?
they stood not, because the LORD did drive
them.
16 He made many to fall, yea, one fell upon
another: and they said, Arise, and let us go
again to our own people, and to the land
of our nativity, from the oppressing sword.
17 They did cry there, Pharaoh king of
Egypt *is but* a noise; he hath passed the
time appointed.
18 *As* I live, saith the King, whose name *is*
the LORD of hosts, Surely as Tabor *is* among
the mountains, and as Carmel by the sea,
so shall he come.
19 O thou daughter dwelling in Egypt, furnish thyself to go into captivity: for Noph
shall be waste and desolate without an
inhabitant.
20 Egypt *is like* a very fair heifer, *but* destruction cometh; it cometh out of the north.
21 Also her hired men *are* in the midst of
her like fatted bullocks; for they also are
turned back, *and* are fled away together:
they did not stand, because the day of their
calamity was come upon them, *and* the time
of their visitation.
22 The voice thereof shall go like a serpent;
for they shall march with an army, and come
against her with axes, as hewers of wood.
23 They shall cut down her forest, saith the
LORD, though it cannot be searched; because
they are more than the grasshoppers, and
are innumerable.
24 The daughter of Egypt shall be confounded; she shall be delivered into the
hand of the people of the north.
25 The LORD of hosts, the God of Israel,
saith; Behold, I will punish the multitude
of No, and Pharaoh, and Egypt, with their
gods, and their kings; even Pharaoh, and *all*
them that trust in him:
26 And I will deliver them into the hand of
those that seek their lives, and into the hand
of Nebuchadrezzar king of Babylon, and into
the hand of his servants: and afterward it
shall be inhabited, as in the days of old,
saith the LORD.
27 ¶ But fear not thou, O my servant Jacob,
and be not dismayed, O Israel: for, behold,
I will save thee from afar off, and thy seed
from the land of their captivity; and Jacob
shall return, and be in rest and at ease, and
none shall make *him* afraid.
28 Fear thou not, O Jacob my servant, saith
the LORD: for I *am* with thee; for I will make
a full end of all the nations whither I have
driven thee: but I will not make a full end of
thee, but correct thee in measure; yet will I
not leave thee wholly unpunished.

Jeremiah 47

1 The word of the LORD that came to Jeremiah the prophet against the Philistines,
before that Pharaoh smote Gaza.
2 Thus saith the LORD; Behold, waters rise up
out of the north, and shall be an overflowing
flood, and shall overflow the land, and all
that is therein; the city, and them that dwell
therein: then the men shall cry, and all the
inhabitants of the land shall howl.
3 At the noise of the stamping of the hoofs
of his strong *horses*, at the rushing of his
chariots, *and at* the rumbling of his wheels,
the fathers shall not look back to *their* children for feebleness of hands;
4 Because of the day that cometh to spoil all
the Philistines, *and* to cut off from Tyrus and
Zidon every helper that remaineth: for the
LORD will spoil the Philistines, the remnant
of the country of Caphtor.
5 Baldness is come upon Gaza; Ashkelon is
cut off *with* the remnant of their valley: how
long wilt thou cut thyself?
6 O thou sword of the LORD, how long *will
it be* ere thou be quiet? put up thyself into
thy scabbard, rest, and be still.
7 How can it be quiet, seeing the LORD
hath given it a charge against Ashkelon,
and against the sea shore? there hath he
appointed it.

Jeremiah 48

1 Against Moab thus saith the LORD of hosts,
the God of Israel; Woe unto Nebo! for it is

spoiled: Kiriathaim is confounded *and* taken:
Misgab is confounded and dismayed.
2 *There shall be* no more praise of Moab:
in Heshbon they have devised evil against
it; come, and let us cut it off from *being* a
nation. Also thou shalt be cut down, O Mad-
men; the sword shall pursue thee.
3 A voice of crying *shall be* from Horonaim,
spoiling and great destruction.
4 Moab is destroyed; her little ones have
caused a cry to be heard.
5 For in the going up of Luhith continual
weeping shall go up; for in the going down
of Horonaim the enemies have heard a cry
of destruction.
6 Flee, save your lives, and be like the heath
in the wilderness.
7 ¶ For because thou hast trusted in thy
works and in thy treasures, thou shalt also
be taken: and Chemosh shall go forth into
captivity *with* his priests and his princes
together.
8 And the spoiler shall come upon every city,
and no city shall escape: the valley also shall
perish, and the plain shall be destroyed, as
the LORD hath spoken.
9 Give wings unto Moab, that it may flee
and get away: for the cities thereof shall
be desolate, without any to dwell therein.
10 Cursed *be* he that doeth the work of
the LORD deceitfully, and cursed *be* he that
keepeth back his sword from blood.
11 ¶ Moab hath been at ease from his youth,
and he hath settled on his lees, and hath not
been emptied from vessel to vessel, neither
hath he gone into captivity: therefore his
taste remained in him, and his scent is not
changed.
12 Therefore, behold, the days come, saith
the LORD, that I will send unto him wanderers, that shall cause him to wander, and shall
empty his vessels, and break their bottles.
13 And Moab shall be ashamed of Chemosh, as the house of Israel was ashamed
of Beth-el their confidence.
14 ¶ How say ye, We *are* mighty and strong
men for the war?
15 Moab is spoiled, and gone up *out of* her
cities, and his chosen young men are gone
down to the slaughter, saith the King, whose
name *is* the LORD of hosts.
16 The calamity of Moab *is* near to come,
and his affliction hasteth fast.
17 All ye that are about him, bemoan him;
and all ye that know his name, say, How is
the strong staff broken, *and* the beautiful
rod!
18 Thou daughter that dost inhabit Dibon,
come down from *thy* glory, and sit in thirst;
for the spoiler of Moab shall come upon
thee, *and* he shall destroy thy strong holds.
19 O inhabitant of Aroer, stand by the way,
and espy; ask him that fleeth, and her that
escapeth, *and* say, What is done?
20 Moab is confounded; for it is broken
down: howl and cry; tell ye it in Arnon, that
Moab is spoiled,
21 And judgment is come upon the plain
country; upon Holon, and upon Jahazah,
and upon Mephaath,
22 And upon Dibon, and upon Nebo, and
upon Beth-diblathaim,
23 And upon Kiriathaim, and upon Beth-
gamul, and upon Beth-meon,
24 And upon Kerioth, and upon Bozrah,
and upon all the cities of the land of Moab,
far or near.
25 The horn of Moab is cut off, and his arm
is broken, saith the LORD.
26 ¶ Make ye him drunken: for he magnified *himself* against the LORD: Moab also
shall wallow in his vomit, and he also shall
be in derision.
27 For was not Israel a derision unto thee?
was he found among thieves? for since thou
spakest of him, thou skippedst for joy.
28 O ye that dwell in Moab, leave the cities,
and dwell in the rock, and be like the dove
that maketh her nest in the sides of the
hole's mouth.
29 We have heard the pride of Moab, (he
is exceeding proud) his loftiness, and his
arrogancy, and his pride, and the haughtiness of his heart.
30 I know his wrath, saith the LORD; but *it*
shall not *be* so; his lies shall not so effect *it*.
31 Therefore will I howl for Moab, and I will
cry out for all Moab; *mine heart* shall mourn
for the men of Kir-heres.
32 O vine of Sibmah, I will weep for thee
with the weeping of Jazer: thy plants are
gone over the sea, they reach *even* to the
sea of Jazer: the spoiler is fallen upon thy
summer fruits and upon thy vintage.
33 And joy and gladness is taken from the
plentiful field, and from the land of Moab;

and I have caused wine to fail from the
winepresses: none shall tread with shouting;
their shouting *shall be* no shouting.
34 From the cry of Heshbon *even* unto Elealeh, *and even* unto Jahaz, have they uttered
their voice, from Zoar *even* unto Horonaim,
as an heifer of three years old: for the waters
also of Nimrim shall be desolate.
35 Moreover I will cause to cease in Moab,
saith the LORD, him that offereth in the
high places, and him that burneth incense
to his gods.
36 Therefore mine heart shall sound for
Moab like pipes, and mine heart shall sound
like pipes for the men of Kir-heres: because
the riches *that* he hath gotten are perished.
37 For every head *shall be* bald, and every
beard clipped: upon all the hands *shall be*
cuttings, and upon the loins sackcloth.
38 *There shall be* lamentation generally
upon all the housetops of Moab, and in
the streets thereof: for I have broken Moab
like a vessel wherein *is* no pleasure, saith
the LORD.
39 They shall howl, *saying*, How is it broken
down! how hath Moab turned the back with
shame! so shall Moab be a derision and a
dismaying to all them about him.
40 For thus saith the LORD; Behold, he shall
fly as an eagle, and shall spread his wings
over Moab.
41 Kerioth is taken, and the strong holds are
surprised, and the mighty men's hearts in
Moab at that day shall be as the heart of a
woman in her pangs.
42 And Moab shall be destroyed from *being*
a people, because he hath magnified *himself*
against the LORD.
43 Fear, and the pit, and the snare, *shall
be* upon thee, O inhabitant of Moab, saith
the LORD.
44 He that fleeth from the fear shall fall into
the pit; and he that getteth up out of the pit
shall be taken in the snare: for I will bring
upon it, *even* upon Moab, the year of their
visitation, saith the LORD.
45 They that fled stood under the shadow
of Heshbon because of the force: but a
fire shall come forth out of Heshbon, and
a flame from the midst of Sihon, and shall
devour the corner of Moab, and the crown
of the head of the tumultuous ones.
46 Woe be unto thee, O Moab! the people
of Chemosh perisheth: for thy sons are
taken captives, and thy daughters captives.
47 ¶ Yet will I bring again the captivity of
Moab in the latter days, saith the LORD. Thus
far *is* the judgment of Moab.

Jeremiah 49

1 Concerning the Ammonites, thus saith the
LORD; Hath Israel no sons? hath he no heir?
why *then* doth their king inherit Gad, and
his people dwell in his cities?
2 Therefore, behold, the days come, saith
the LORD, that I will cause an alarm of war
to be heard in Rabbah of the Ammonites;
and it shall be a desolate heap, and her
daughters shall be burned with fire: then
shall Israel be heir unto them that were his
heirs, saith the LORD.
3 Howl, O Heshbon, for Ai is spoiled: cry, ye
daughters of Rabbah, gird you with sackcloth; lament, and run to and fro by the
hedges; for their king shall go into captivity,
and his priests and his princes together.
4 Wherefore gloriest thou in the valleys,
thy flowing valley, O backsliding daughter?
that trusted in her treasures, *saying*, Who
shall come unto me?
5 Behold, I will bring a fear upon thee, saith
the Lord GOD of hosts, from all those that
be about thee; and ye shall be driven out
every man right forth; and none shall gather
up him that wandereth.
6 And afterward I will bring again the captivity of the children of Ammon, saith the LORD.
7 ¶ Concerning Edom, thus saith the LORD
of hosts; *Is* wisdom no more in Teman? is
counsel perished from the prudent? is their
wisdom vanished?
8 Flee ye, turn back, dwell deep, O inhabitants of Dedan; for I will bring the calamity
of Esau upon him, the time *that* I will visit
him.
9 If grapegatherers come to thee, would
they not leave *some* gleaning grapes? if
thieves by night, they will destroy till they
have enough.
10 But I have made Esau bare, I have uncovered his secret places, and he shall not be
able to hide himself: his seed is spoiled,
and his brethren, and his neighbours, and
he *is* not.
11 Leave thy fatherless children, I will pre-

serve *them* alive; and let thy widows trust
in me.
12 For thus saith the LORD; Behold, they
whose judgment *was* not to drink of the
cup have assuredly drunken; and *art* thou
he *that* shall altogether go unpunished?
thou shalt not go unpunished, but thou shalt
surely drink *of it*.
13 For I have sworn by myself, saith the
LORD, that Bozrah shall become a desolation,
a reproach, a waste, and a curse; and all the
cities thereof shall be perpetual wastes.
14 I have heard a rumour from the LORD,
and an ambassador is sent unto the heathen, *saying*, Gather ye together, and come
against her, and rise up to the battle.
15 For, lo, I will make thee small among the
heathen, *and* despised among men.
16 Thy terribleness hath deceived thee,
and the pride of thine heart, O thou that
dwellest in the clefts of the rock, that
holdest the height of the hill: though thou
shouldest make thy nest as high as the
eagle, I will bring thee down from thence,
saith the LORD.
17 Also Edom shall be a desolation: every
one that goeth by it shall be astonished, and
shall hiss at all the plagues thereof.
18 As in the overthrow of Sodom and
Gomorrah and the neighbour *cities* thereof,
saith the LORD, no man shall abide there,
neither shall a son of man dwell in it.
19 Behold, he shall come up like a lion from
the swelling of Jordan against the habitation
of the strong: but I will suddenly make him
run away from her: and who *is* a chosen
man, *that* I may appoint over her? for who
is like me? and who will appoint me the
time? and who *is* that shepherd that will
stand before me?
20 Therefore hear the counsel of the LORD,
that he hath taken against Edom; and his
purposes, that he hath purposed against
the inhabitants of Teman: Surely the least of
the flock shall draw them out: surely he shall
make their habitations desolate with them.
21 The earth is moved at the noise of their
fall, at the cry the noise thereof was heard
in the Red sea.
22 Behold, he shall come up and fly as the
eagle, and spread his wings over Bozrah:
and at that day shall the heart of the mighty
men of Edom be as the heart of a woman
in her pangs.
23 ¶ Concerning Damascus. Hamath is confounded, and Arpad: for they have heard
evil tidings: they are fainthearted; *there is*
sorrow on the sea; it cannot be quiet.
24 Damascus is waxed feeble, *and* turneth
herself to flee, and fear hath seized on *her*:
anguish and sorrows have taken her, as a
woman in travail.
25 How is the city of praise not left, the
city of my joy!
26 Therefore her young men shall fall in
her streets, and all the men of war shall be
cut off in that day, saith the LORD of hosts.
27 And I will kindle a fire in the wall of
Damascus, and it shall consume the palaces
of Ben-hadad.
28 ¶ Concerning Kedar, and concerning the
kingdoms of Hazor, which Nebuchadrezzar
king of Babylon shall smite, thus saith the
LORD; Arise ye, go up to Kedar, and spoil the
men of the east.
29 Their tents and their flocks shall they
take away: they shall take to themselves
their curtains, and all their vessels, and their
camels; and they shall cry unto them, Fear
is on every side.
30 ¶ Flee, get you far off, dwell deep, O ye
inhabitants of Hazor, saith the LORD; for
Nebuchadrezzar king of Babylon hath taken
counsel against you, and hath conceived a
purpose against you.
31 Arise, get you up unto the wealthy nation,
that dwelleth without care, saith the LORD,
which have neither gates nor bars, *which*
dwell alone.
32 And their camels shall be a booty, and
the multitude of their cattle a spoil: and I will
scatter into all winds them *that are* in the
utmost corners; and I will bring their calamity from all sides thereof, saith the LORD.
33 And Hazor shall be a dwelling for dragons,
and a desolation for ever: there shall no man
abide there, nor *any* son of man dwell in it.
34 ¶ The word of the LORD that came to
Jeremiah the prophet against Elam in the
beginning of the reign of Zedekiah king of
Judah, saying,
35 Thus saith the LORD of hosts; Behold,
I will break the bow of Elam, the chief of
their might.
36 And upon Elam will I bring the four winds

from the four quarters of heaven, and will scatter them toward all those winds; and there shall be no nation whither the outcasts of Elam shall not come.

37 For I will cause Elam to be dismayed before their enemies, and before them that seek their life: and I will bring evil upon them, *even* my fierce anger, saith the LORD; and I will send the sword after them, till I have consumed them:

38 And I will set my throne in Elam, and will destroy from thence the king and the princes, saith the LORD.

39 ¶ But it shall come to pass in the latter days, *that* I will bring again the captivity of Elam, saith the LORD.

Jeremiah 50

1 The word that the LORD spake against Babylon *and* against the land of the Chaldeans by Jeremiah the prophet.

2 Declare ye among the nations, and publish, and set up a standard; publish, *and* conceal not: say, Babylon is taken, Bel is confounded, Merodach is broken in pieces; her idols are confounded, her images are broken in pieces.

3 For out of the north there cometh up a nation against her, which shall make her land desolate, and none shall dwell therein: they shall remove, they shall depart, both man and beast.

4 ¶ In those days, and in that time, saith the LORD, the children of Israel shall come, they and the children of Judah together, going and weeping: they shall go, and seek the LORD their God.

5 They shall ask the way to Zion with their faces thitherward, *saying*, Come, and let us join ourselves to the LORD in a perpetual covenant *that* shall not be forgotten.

6 My people hath been lost sheep: their shepherds have caused them to go astray, they have turned them away *on* the mountains: they have gone from mountain to hill, they have forgotten their restingplace.

7 All that found them have devoured them: and their adversaries said, We offend not, because they have sinned against the LORD, the habitation of justice, even the LORD, the hope of their fathers.

8 Remove out of the midst of Babylon, and go forth out of the land of the Chaldeans, and be as the he goats before the flocks.

9 ¶ For, lo, I will raise and cause to come up against Babylon an assembly of great nations from the north country: and they shall set themselves in array against her; from thence she shall be taken: their arrows *shall be* as of a mighty expert man; none shall return in vain.

10 And Chaldea shall be a spoil: all that spoil her shall be satisfied, saith the LORD.

11 Because ye were glad, because ye rejoiced, O ye destroyers of mine heritage, because ye are grown fat as the heifer at grass, and bellow as bulls;

12 Your mother shall be sore confounded; she that bare you shall be ashamed: behold, the hindermost of the nations *shall be* a wilderness, a dry land, and a desert.

13 Because of the wrath of the LORD it shall not be inhabited, but it shall be wholly desolate: every one that goeth by Babylon shall be astonished, and hiss at all her plagues.

14 Put yourselves in array against Babylon round about: all ye that bend the bow, shoot at her, spare no arrows: for she hath sinned against the LORD.

15 Shout against her round about: she hath given her hand: her foundations are fallen, her walls are thrown down: for it *is* the vengeance of the LORD: take vengeance upon her; as she hath done, do unto her.

16 Cut off the sower from Babylon, and him that handleth the sickle in the time of harvest: for fear of the oppressing sword they shall turn every one to his people, and they shall flee every one to his own land.

17 ¶ Israel *is* a scattered sheep; the lions have driven *him* away: first the king of Assyria hath devoured him; and last this Nebuchadrezzar king of Babylon hath broken his bones.

18 Therefore thus saith the LORD of hosts, the God of Israel; Behold, I will punish the king of Babylon and his land, as I have punished the king of Assyria.

19 And I will bring Israel again to his habitation, and he shall feed on Carmel and Bashan, and his soul shall be satisfied upon mount Ephraim and Gilead.

20 In those days, and in that time, saith the LORD, the iniquity of Israel shall be sought for, and *there shall be* none; and the sins of

Judah, and they shall not be found: for I will pardon them whom I reserve.

21 ¶ Go up against the land of Merathaim, *even* against it, and against the inhabitants of Pekod: waste and utterly destroy after them, saith the LORD, and do according to all that I have commanded thee.

22 A sound of battle *is* in the land, and of great destruction.

23 How is the hammer of the whole earth cut asunder and broken! how is Babylon become a desolation among the nations!

24 I have laid a snare for thee, and thou art also taken, O Babylon, and thou wast not aware: thou art found, and also caught, because thou hast striven against the LORD.

25 The LORD hath opened his armoury, and hath brought forth the weapons of his indignation: for this *is* the work of the Lord GOD of hosts in the land of the Chaldeans.

26 Come against her from the utmost border, open her storehouses: cast her up as heaps, and destroy her utterly: let nothing of her be left.

27 Slay all her bullocks; let them go down to the slaughter: woe unto them! for their day is come, the time of their visitation.

28 The voice of them that flee and escape out of the land of Babylon, to declare in Zion the vengeance of the LORD our God, the vengeance of his temple.

29 Call together the archers against Babylon: all ye that bend the bow, camp against it round about; let none thereof escape: recompense her according to her work; according to all that she hath done, do unto her: for she hath been proud against the LORD, against the Holy One of Israel.

30 Therefore shall her young men fall in the streets, and all her men of war shall be cut off in that day, saith the LORD.

31 Behold, I *am* against thee, *O thou* most proud, saith the Lord GOD of hosts: for thy day is come, the time *that* I will visit thee.

32 And the most proud shall stumble and fall, and none shall raise him up: and I will kindle a fire in his cities, and it shall devour all round about him.

33 ¶ Thus saith the LORD of hosts; The children of Israel and the children of Judah *were* oppressed together: and all that took them captives held them fast; they refused to let them go.

34 Their Redeemer *is* strong; the LORD of hosts *is* his name: he shall throughly plead their cause, that he may give rest to the land, and disquiet the inhabitants of Babylon.

35 ¶ A sword *is* upon the Chaldeans, saith the LORD, and upon the inhabitants of Babylon, and upon her princes, and upon her wise *men*.

36 A sword *is* upon the liars; and they shall dote: a sword *is* upon her mighty men; and they shall be dismayed.

37 A sword *is* upon their horses, and upon their chariots, and upon all the mingled people that *are* in the midst of her; and they shall become as women: a sword *is* upon her treasures; and they shall be robbed.

38 A drought *is* upon her waters; and they shall be dried up: for it *is* the land of graven images, and they are mad upon *their* idols.

39 Therefore the wild beasts of the desert with the wild beasts of the islands shall dwell *there*, and the owls shall dwell therein: and it shall be no more inhabited for ever; neither shall it be dwelt in from generation to generation.

40 As God overthrew Sodom and Gomorrah and the neighbour *cities* thereof, saith the LORD; *so* shall no man abide there, neither shall any son of man dwell therein.

41 Behold, a people shall come from the north, and a great nation, and many kings shall be raised up from the coasts of the earth.

42 They shall hold the bow and the lance: they *are* cruel, and will not shew mercy: their voice shall roar like the sea, and they shall ride upon horses, *every one* put in array, like a man to the battle, against thee, O daughter of Babylon.

43 The king of Babylon hath heard the report of them, and his hands waxed feeble: anguish took hold of him, *and* pangs as of a woman in travail.

44 Behold, he shall come up like a lion from the swelling of Jordan unto the habitation of the strong: but I will make them suddenly run away from her: and who *is* a chosen *man, that* I may appoint over her? for who *is* like me? and who will appoint me the time? and who *is* that shepherd that will stand before me?

45 Therefore hear ye the counsel of the LORD, that he hath taken against Babylon;

and his purposes, that he hath purposed against the land of the Chaldeans: Surely the least of the flock shall draw them out: surely he shall make *their* habitation desolate with them.

46 At the noise of the taking of Babylon the earth is moved, and the cry is heard among the nations.

Jeremiah 51

1 Thus saith the LORD; Behold, I will raise up against Babylon, and against them that dwell in the midst of them that rise up against me, a destroying wind;

2 And will send unto Babylon fanners, that shall fan her, and shall empty her land: for in the day of trouble they shall be against her round about.

3 Against *him that* bendeth let the archer bend his bow, and against *him that* lifteth himself up in his brigandine: and spare ye not her young men; destroy ye utterly all her host.

4 Thus the slain shall fall in the land of the Chaldeans, and *they that are* thrust through in her streets.

5 For Israel *hath* not *been* forsaken, nor Judah of his God, of the LORD of hosts; though their land was filled with sin against the Holy One of Israel.

6 Flee out of the midst of Babylon, and deliver every man his soul: be not cut off in her iniquity; for this *is* the time of the LORD's vengeance; he will render unto her a recompence.

7 Babylon *hath been* a golden cup in the LORD's hand, that made all the earth drunken: the nations have drunken of her wine; therefore the nations are mad.

8 Babylon is suddenly fallen and destroyed: howl for her; take balm for her pain, if so be she may be healed.

9 We would have healed Babylon, but she is not healed: forsake her, and let us go every one into his own country: for her judgment reacheth unto heaven, and is lifted up *even* to the skies.

10 The LORD hath brought forth our righteousness: come, and let us declare in Zion the work of the LORD our God.

11 Make bright the arrows; gather the shields: the LORD hath raised up the spirit of the kings of the Medes: for his device *is* against Babylon, to destroy it; because it *is* the vengeance of the LORD, the vengeance of his temple.

12 Set up the standard upon the walls of Babylon, make the watch strong, set up the watchmen, prepare the ambushes: for the LORD hath both devised and done that which he spake against the inhabitants of Babylon.

13 O thou that dwellest upon many waters, abundant in treasures, thine end is come, *and* the measure of thy covetousness.

14 The LORD of hosts hath sworn by himself, *saying*, Surely I will fill thee with men, as with caterpillers; and they shall lift up a shout against thee.

15 He hath made the earth by his power, he hath established the world by his wisdom, and hath stretched out the heaven by his understanding.

16 When he uttereth *his* voice, *there is* a multitude of waters in the heavens; and he causeth the vapours to ascend from the ends of the earth: he maketh lightnings with rain, and bringeth forth the wind out of his treasures.

17 Every man is brutish by *his* knowledge; every founder is confounded by the graven image: for his molten image *is* falsehood, and *there is* no breath in them.

18 They *are* vanity, the work of errors: in the time of their visitation they shall perish.

19 The portion of Jacob *is* not like them; for he *is* the former of all things: and *Israel is* the rod of his inheritance: the LORD of hosts *is* his name.

20 Thou *art* my battle axe *and* weapons of war: for with thee will I break in pieces the nations, and with thee will I destroy kingdoms;

21 And with thee will I break in pieces the horse and his rider; and with thee will I break in pieces the chariot and his rider;

22 With thee also will I break in pieces man and woman; and with thee will I break in pieces old and young; and with thee will I break in pieces the young man and the maid;

23 I will also break in pieces with thee the shepherd and his flock; and with thee will I break in pieces the husbandman and his yoke of oxen; and with thee will I break in pieces captains and rulers.

24 And I will render unto Babylon and to all the inhabitants of Chaldea all their evil

that they have done in Zion in your sight, saith the LORD.
25 Behold, I *am* against thee, O destroying mountain, saith the LORD, which destroyest all the earth: and I will stretch out mine hand upon thee, and roll thee down from the rocks, and will make thee a burnt mountain.
26 And they shall not take of thee a stone for a corner, nor a stone for foundations; but thou shalt be desolate for ever, saith the LORD.
27 Set ye up a standard in the land, blow the trumpet among the nations, prepare the nations against her, call together against her the kingdoms of Ararat, Minni, and Ashchenaz; appoint a captain against her; cause the horses to come up as the rough caterpillers.
28 Prepare against her the nations with the kings of the Medes, the captains thereof, and all the rulers thereof, and all the land of his dominion.
29 And the land shall tremble and sorrow: for every purpose of the LORD shall be performed against Babylon, to make the land of Babylon a desolation without an inhabitant.
30 The mighty men of Babylon have forborn to fight, they have remained in *their* holds: their might hath failed; they became as women: they have burned her dwellingplaces; her bars are broken.
31 One post shall run to meet another, and one messenger to meet another, to shew the king of Babylon that his city is taken at *one* end,
32 And that the passages are stopped, and the reeds they have burned with fire, and the men of war are affrighted.
33 For thus saith the LORD of hosts, the God of Israel; The daughter of Babylon *is* like a threshingfloor, *it is* time to thresh her: yet a little while, and the time of her harvest shall come.
34 Nebuchadrezzar the king of Babylon hath devoured me, he hath crushed me, he hath made me an empty vessel, he hath swallowed me up like a dragon, he hath filled his belly with my delicates, he hath cast me out.
35 The violence done to me and to my flesh *be* upon Babylon, shall the inhabitant of Zion say; and my blood upon the inhabitants of Chaldea, shall Jerusalem say.
36 Therefore thus saith the LORD; Behold, I will plead thy cause, and take vengeance for thee; and I will dry up her sea, and make her springs dry.
37 And Babylon shall become heaps, a dwellingplace for dragons, an astonishment, and an hissing, without an inhabitant.
38 They shall roar together like lions: they shall yell as lions' whelps.
39 In their heat I will make their feasts, and I will make them drunken, that they may rejoice, and sleep a perpetual sleep, and not wake, saith the LORD.
40 I will bring them down like lambs to the slaughter, like rams with he goats.
41 How is Sheshach taken! and how is the praise of the whole earth surprised! how is Babylon become an astonishment among the nations!
42 The sea is come up upon Babylon: she is covered with the multitude of the waves thereof.
43 Her cities are a desolation, a dry land, and a wilderness, a land wherein no man dwelleth, neither doth *any* son of man pass thereby.
44 And I will punish Bel in Babylon, and I will bring forth out of his mouth that which he hath swallowed up: and the nations shall not flow together any more unto him: yea, the wall of Babylon shall fall.
45 My people, go ye out of the midst of her, and deliver ye every man his soul from the fierce anger of the LORD.
46 And lest your heart faint, and ye fear for the rumour that shall be heard in the land; a rumour shall both come *one* year, and after that in *another* year *shall come* a rumour, and violence in the land, ruler against ruler.
47 Therefore, behold, the days come, that I will do judgment upon the graven images of Babylon: and her whole land shall be confounded, and all her slain shall fall in the midst of her.
48 Then the heaven and the earth, and all that *is* therein, shall sing for Babylon: for the spoilers shall come unto her from the north, saith the LORD.
49 As Babylon *hath caused* the slain of Israel to fall, so at Babylon shall fall the slain of all the earth.
50 Ye that have escaped the sword, go away, stand not still: remember the LORD afar off, and let Jerusalem come into your mind.

51 We are confounded, because we have heard reproach: shame hath covered our faces: for strangers are come into the sanctuaries of the LORD's house.

52 Wherefore, behold, the days come, saith the LORD, that I will do judgment upon her graven images: and through all her land the wounded shall groan.

53 Though Babylon should mount up to heaven, and though she should fortify the height of her strength, *yet* from me shall spoilers come unto her, saith the LORD.

54 A sound of a cry *cometh* from Babylon, and great destruction from the land of the Chaldeans:

55 Because the LORD hath spoiled Babylon, and destroyed out of her the great voice; when her waves do roar like great waters, a noise of their voice is uttered:

56 Because the spoiler is come upon her, *even* upon Babylon, and her mighty men are taken, every one of their bows is broken: for the LORD God of recompences shall surely requite.

57 And I will make drunk her princes, and her wise *men*, her captains, and her rulers, and her mighty men: and they shall sleep a perpetual sleep, and not wake, saith the King, whose name *is* the LORD of hosts.

58 Thus saith the LORD of hosts; The broad walls of Babylon shall be utterly broken, and her high gates shall be burned with fire; and the people shall labour in vain, and the folk in the fire, and they shall be weary.

59 ¶ The word which Jeremiah the prophet commanded Seraiah the son of Neriah, the son of Maaseiah, when he went with Zedekiah the king of Judah into Babylon in the fourth year of his reign. And *this* Seraiah *was* a quiet prince.

60 So Jeremiah wrote in a book all the evil that should come upon Babylon, *even* all these words that are written against Babylon.

61 And Jeremiah said to Seraiah, When thou comest to Babylon, and shalt see, and shalt read all these words;

62 Then shalt thou say, O LORD, thou hast spoken against this place, to cut it off, that none shall remain in it, neither man nor beast, but that it shall be desolate for ever.

63 And it shall be, when thou hast made an end of reading this book, *that* thou shalt bind a stone to it, and cast it into the midst of Euphrates:

64 And thou shalt say, Thus shall Babylon sink, and shall not rise from the evil that I will bring upon her: and they shall be weary. Thus far *are* the words of Jeremiah.

Jeremiah 52

1 Zedekiah *was* one and twenty years old when he began to reign, and he reigned eleven years in Jerusalem. And his mother's name *was* Hamutal the daughter of Jeremiah of Libnah.

2 And he did *that which was* evil in the eyes of the LORD, according to all that Jehoiakim had done.

3 For through the anger of the LORD it came to pass in Jerusalem and Judah, till he had cast them out from his presence, that Zedekiah rebelled against the king of Babylon.

4 ¶ And it came to pass in the ninth year of his reign, in the tenth month, in the tenth *day* of the month, *that* Nebuchadrezzar king of Babylon came, he and all his army, against Jerusalem, and pitched against it, and built forts against it round about.

5 So the city was besieged unto the eleventh year of king Zedekiah.

6 And in the fourth month, in the ninth *day* of the month, the famine was sore in the city, so that there was no bread for the people of the land.

7 Then the city was broken up, and all the men of war fled, and went forth out of the city by night by the way of the gate between the two walls, which *was* by the king's garden; (now the Chaldeans *were* by the city round about:) and they went by the way of the plain.

8 ¶ But the army of the Chaldeans pursued after the king, and overtook Zedekiah in the plains of Jericho; and all his army was scattered from him.

9 Then they took the king, and carried him up unto the king of Babylon to Riblah in the land of Hamath; where he gave judgment upon him.

10 And the king of Babylon slew the sons of Zedekiah before his eyes: he slew also all the princes of Judah in Riblah.

11 Then he put out the eyes of Zedekiah; and the king of Babylon bound him in chains,

and carried him to Babylon, and put him in
prison till the day of his death.
12 ¶ Now in the fifth month, in the tenth *day*
of the month, which *was* the nineteenth year
of Nebuchadrezzar king of Babylon, came
Nebuzar-adan, captain of the guard, *which*
served the king of Babylon, into Jerusalem,
13 And burned the house of the LORD, and
the king's house; and all the houses of Jerusalem, and all the houses of the great *men*,
burned he with fire:
14 And all the army of the Chaldeans, that
were with the captain of the guard, brake
down all the walls of Jerusalem round about.
15 Then Nebuzar-adan the captain of the
guard carried away captive *certain* of the
poor of the people, and the residue of the
people that remained in the city, and those
that fell away, that fell to the king of Babylon, and the rest of the multitude.
16 But Nebuzar-adan the captain of the
guard left *certain* of the poor of the land for
vinedressers and for husbandmen.
17 Also the pillars of brass that *were* in the
house of the LORD, and the bases, and the
brasen sea that *was* in the house of the
LORD, the Chaldeans brake, and carried all
the brass of them to Babylon.
18 The caldrons also, and the shovels, and
the snuffers, and the bowls, and the spoons,
and all the vessels of brass wherewith they
ministered, took they away.
19 And the basons, and the firepans, and
the bowls, and the caldrons, and the candlesticks, and the spoons, and the cups; *that*
which *was* of gold *in* gold, and *that* which
was of silver *in* silver, took the captain of
the guard away.
20 The two pillars, one sea, and twelve
brasen bulls that *were* under the bases,
which king Solomon had made in the house
of the LORD: the brass of all these vessels
was without weight.
21 And *concerning* the pillars, the height of
one pillar *was* eighteen cubits; and a fillet of
twelve cubits did compass it; and the thickness thereof *was* four fingers: *it was* hollow.
22 And a chapiter of brass *was* upon it; and
the height of one chapiter *was* five cubits,
with network and pomegranates upon the
chapiters round about, all *of* brass. The
second pillar also and the pomegranates
were like unto these.
23 And there were ninety and six pomegranates on a side; *and* all the pomegranates upon the network *were* an hundred
round about.
24 ¶ And the captain of the guard took
Seraiah the chief priest, and Zephaniah
the second priest, and the three keepers
of the door:
25 He took also out of the city an eunuch,
which had the charge of the men of war;
and seven men of them that were near
the king's person, which were found in the
city; and the principal scribe of the host,
who mustered the people of the land; and
threescore men of the people of the land,
that were found in the midst of the city.
26 So Nebuzar-adan the captain of the guard
took them, and brought them to the king of
Babylon to Riblah.
27 And the king of Babylon smote them,
and put them to death in Riblah in the land
of Hamath. Thus Judah was carried away
captive out of his own land.
28 This *is* the people whom Nebuchadrezzar
carried away captive: in the seventh year
three thousand Jews and three and twenty:
29 In the eighteenth year of Nebuchadrezzar he carried away captive from Jerusalem
eight hundred thirty and two persons:
30 In the three and twentieth year of Nebuchadrezzar Nebuzar-adan the captain of
the guard carried away captive of the Jews
seven hundred forty and five persons: all
the persons *were* four thousand and six
hundred.
31 ¶ And it came to pass in the seven and
thirtieth year of the captivity of Jehoiachin
king of Judah, in the twelfth month, in the
five and twentieth *day* of the month, *that*
Evil-merodach king of Babylon in the *first*
year of his reign lifted up the head of Jehoiachin king of Judah, and brought him forth
out of prison,
32 And spake kindly unto him, and set his
throne above the throne of the kings that
were with him in Babylon,
33 And changed his prison garments: and
he did continually eat bread before him all
the days of his life.
34 And *for* his diet, there was a continual
diet given him of the king of Babylon, every
day a portion until the day of his death, all
the days of his life.

The Lamentations
Of Jeremiah

Lamentations 1

1 How doth the city sit solitary, *that was* full of people! *how* is she become as a widow! she *that was* great among the nations, *and* princess among the provinces, *how* is she become tributary!

2 She weepeth sore in the night, and her tears *are* on her cheeks: among all her lovers she hath none to comfort *her:* all her friends have dealt treacherously with her, they are become her enemies.

3 Judah is gone into captivity because of affliction, and because of great servitude: she dwelleth among the heathen, she findeth no rest: all her persecutors overtook her between the straits.

4 The ways of Zion do mourn, because none come to the solemn feasts: all her gates are desolate: her priests sigh, her virgins are afflicted, and she *is* in bitterness.

5 Her adversaries are the chief, her enemies prosper; for the LORD hath afflicted her for the multitude of her transgressions: her children are gone into captivity before the enemy.

6 And from the daughter of Zion all her beauty is departed: her princes are become like harts *that* find no pasture, and they are gone without strength before the pursuer.

7 Jerusalem remembered in the days of her affliction and of her miseries all her pleasant things that she had in the days of old, when her people fell into the hand of the enemy, and none did help her: the adversaries saw her, *and* did mock at her sabbaths.

8 Jerusalem hath grievously sinned; therefore she is removed: all that honoured her despise her, because they have seen her nakedness: yea, she sigheth, and turneth backward.

9 Her filthiness *is* in her skirts; she remembereth not her last end; therefore she came down wonderfully: she had no comforter. O LORD, behold my affliction: for the enemy hath magnified *himself.*

10 The adversary hath spread out his hand upon all her pleasant things: for she hath seen *that* the heathen entered into her sanctuary, whom thou didst command *that* they should not enter into thy congregation.

11 All her people sigh, they seek bread; they have given their pleasant things for meat to relieve the soul: see, O LORD, and consider; for I am become vile.

12 ¶ *Is it* nothing to you, all ye that pass by? behold, and see if there be any sorrow like unto my sorrow, which is done unto me, wherewith the LORD hath afflicted *me* in the day of his fierce anger.

13 From above hath he sent fire into my bones, and it prevaileth against them: he hath spread a net for my feet, he hath turned me back: he hath made me desolate *and* faint all the day.

14 The yoke of my transgressions is bound by his hand: they are wreathed, *and* come up upon my neck: he hath made my strength to fall, the Lord hath delivered me into *their* hands, *from whom* I am not able to rise up.

15 The Lord hath trodden under foot all my mighty *men* in the midst of me: he hath called an assembly against me to crush my young men: the Lord hath trodden the virgin, the daughter of Judah, *as* in a winepress.

16 For these *things* I weep; mine eye, mine eye runneth down with water, because the comforter that should relieve my soul is far from me: my children are desolate, because the enemy prevailed.

17 Zion spreadeth forth her hands, *and there is* none to comfort her: the LORD hath commanded concerning Jacob, *that* his adversaries *should be* round about him: Jerusalem is as a menstruous woman among them.

18 ¶ The LORD is righteous; for I have rebelled against his commandment: hear, I pray you, all people, and behold my sorrow: my virgins and my young men are gone into captivity.

19 I called for my lovers, *but* they deceived me: my priests and mine elders gave up the ghost in the city, while they sought their meat to relieve their souls.

20 Behold, O LORD; for I *am* in distress: my bowels are troubled; mine heart is turned within me; for I have grievously rebelled:

abroad the sword bereaveth, at home *there*
is as death.
21 They have heard that I sigh: *there is* none
to comfort me: all mine enemies have heard
of my trouble; they are glad that thou hast
done *it:* thou wilt bring the day *that* thou
hast called, and they shall be like unto me.
22 Let all their wickedness come before
thee; and do unto them, as thou hast done
unto me for all my transgressions: for my
sighs *are* many, and my heart *is* faint.

Lamentations 2

1 How hath the Lord covered the daughter of Zion with a cloud in his anger, *and*
cast down from heaven unto the earth the
beauty of Israel, and remembered not his
footstool in the day of his anger!
2 The Lord hath swallowed up all the habitations of Jacob, and hath not pitied: he hath
thrown down in his wrath the strong holds
of the daughter of Judah; he hath brought
them down to the ground: he hath polluted
the kingdom and the princes thereof.
3 He hath cut off in *his* fierce anger all the
horn of Israel: he hath drawn back his right
hand from before the enemy, and he burned
against Jacob like a flaming fire, *which* devoureth round about.
4 He hath bent his bow like an enemy: he
stood with his right hand as an adversary,
and slew all *that were* pleasant to the eye
in the tabernacle of the daughter of Zion:
he poured out his fury like fire.
5 The Lord was as an enemy: he hath swallowed up Israel, he hath swallowed up all
her palaces: he hath destroyed his strong
holds, and hath increased in the daughter
of Judah mourning and lamentation.
6 And he hath violently taken away his tabernacle, as *if it were of* a garden: he hath
destroyed his places of the assembly: the
LORD hath caused the solemn feasts and
sabbaths to be forgotten in Zion, and hath
despised in the indignation of his anger the
king and the priest.
7 The Lord hath cast off his altar, he hath
abhorred his sanctuary, he hath given up
into the hand of the enemy the walls of
her palaces; they have made a noise in
the house of the LORD, as in the day of a
solemn feast.
8 The LORD hath purposed to destroy
the wall of the daughter of Zion: he hath
stretched out a line, he hath not withdrawn
his hand from destroying: therefore he
made the rampart and the wall to lament;
they languished together.
9 Her gates are sunk into the ground; he
hath destroyed and broken her bars: her
king and her princes *are* among the Gentiles:
the law *is* no *more;* her prophets also find
no vision from the LORD.
10 The elders of the daughter of Zion sit
upon the ground, *and* keep silence: they
have cast up dust upon their heads; they
have girded themselves with sackcloth: the
virgins of Jerusalem hang down their heads
to the ground.
11 Mine eyes do fail with tears, my bowels
are troubled, my liver is poured upon the
earth, for the destruction of the daughter
of my people; because the children and the
sucklings swoon in the streets of the city.
12 They say to their mothers, Where *is*
corn and wine? when they swooned as the
wounded in the streets of the city, when
their soul was poured out into their mothers' bosom.
13 What thing shall I take to witness for
thee? what thing shall I liken to thee, O
daughter of Jerusalem? what shall I equal
to thee, that I may comfort thee, O virgin
daughter of Zion? for thy breach *is* great like
the sea: who can heal thee?
14 Thy prophets have seen vain and foolish
things for thee: and they have not discovered thine iniquity, to turn away thy captivity; but have seen for thee false burdens
and causes of banishment.
15 All that pass by clap *their* hands at thee;
they hiss and wag their head at the daughter of Jerusalem, *saying, Is* this the city that
men call The perfection of beauty, The joy
of the whole earth?
16 All thine enemies have opened their
mouth against thee: they hiss and gnash the
teeth: they say, We have swallowed *her* up:
certainly this *is* the day that we looked for;
we have found, we have seen *it*.
17 The LORD hath done *that* which he had
devised; he hath fulfilled his word that he
had commanded in the days of old: he
hath thrown down, and hath not pitied:
and he hath caused *thine* enemy to rejoice

over thee, he hath set up the horn of thine
adversaries.
18 Their heart cried unto the Lord, O wall
of the daughter of Zion, let tears run down
like a river day and night: give thyself no
rest; let not the apple of thine eye cease.
19 Arise, cry out in the night: in the beginning of the watches pour out thine heart
like water before the face of the Lord: lift
up thy hands toward him for the life of thy
young children, that faint for hunger in the
top of every street.
20 ¶ Behold, O LORD, and consider to whom
thou hast done this. Shall the women eat
their fruit, *and* children of a span long? shall
the priest and the prophet be slain in the
sanctuary of the Lord?
21 The young and the old lie on the ground
in the streets: my virgins and my young men
are fallen by the sword; thou hast slain *them*
in the day of thine anger; thou hast killed,
and not pitied.
22 Thou hast called as in a solemn day my
terrors round about, so that in the day of the
LORD's anger none escaped nor remained:
those that I have swaddled and brought up
hath mine enemy consumed.

Lamentations 3

1 I *am* the man *that* hath seen affliction by
the rod of his wrath.
2 He hath led me, and brought *me into*
darkness, but not *into* light.
3 Surely against me is he turned; he turneth
his hand *against me* all the day.
4 My flesh and my skin hath he made old;
he hath broken my bones.
5 He hath builded against me, and compassed *me* with gall and travail.
6 He hath set me in dark places, as *they that*
be dead of old.
7 He hath hedged me about, that I cannot
get out: he hath made my chain heavy.
8 Also when I cry and shout, he shutteth
out my prayer.
9 He hath inclosed my ways with hewn
stone, he hath made my paths crooked.
10 He *was* unto me *as* a bear lying in wait,
and as a lion in secret places.
11 He hath turned aside my ways, and pulled
me in pieces: he hath made me desolate.
12 He hath bent his bow, and set me as a
mark for the arrow.
13 He hath caused the arrows of his quiver
to enter into my reins.
14 I was a derision to all my people; *and*
their song all the day.
15 He hath filled me with bitterness, he
hath made me drunken with wormwood.
16 He hath also broken my teeth with gravel
stones, he hath covered me with ashes.
17 And thou hast removed my soul far off
from peace: I forgat prosperity.
18 And I said, My strength and my hope is
perished from the LORD:
19 Remembering mine affliction and my
misery, the wormwood and the gall.
20 My soul hath *them* still in remembrance,
and is humbled in me.
21 This I recall to my mind, therefore have
I hope.
22 ¶ *It is of* the LORD's mercies that we are
not consumed, because his compassions
fail not.
23 *They are* new every morning: great *is*
thy faithfulness.
24 The LORD *is* my portion, saith my soul;
therefore will I hope in him.
25 The LORD *is* good unto them that wait for
him, to the soul *that* seeketh him.
26 *It is* good that *a man* should both hope
and quietly wait for the salvation of the
LORD.
27 *It is* good for a man that he bear the yoke
in his youth.
28 He sitteth alone and keepeth silence,
because he hath borne *it* upon him.
29 He putteth his mouth in the dust; if so
be there may be hope.
30 He giveth *his* cheek to him that smiteth
him: he is filled full with reproach.
31 For the Lord will not cast off for ever:
32 But though he cause grief, yet will he
have compassion according to the multitude
of his mercies.
33 For he doth not afflict willingly nor grieve
the children of men.
34 To crush under his feet all the prisoners
of the earth,
35 To turn aside the right of a man before
the face of the most High,
36 To subvert a man in his cause, the Lord
approveth not.
37 ¶ Who *is* he *that* saith, and it cometh to
pass, *when* the Lord commandeth *it* not?

38 Out of the mouth of the most High proceedeth not evil and good?
39 Wherefore doth a living man complain, a man for the punishment of his sins?
40 Let us search and try our ways, and turn again to the LORD.
41 Let us lift up our heart with *our* hands unto God in the heavens.
42 We have transgressed and have rebelled: thou hast not pardoned.
43 Thou hast covered with anger, and persecuted us: thou hast slain, thou hast not pitied.
44 Thou hast covered thyself with a cloud, that *our* prayer should not pass through.
45 Thou hast made us *as* the offscouring and refuse in the midst of the people.
46 All our enemies have opened their mouths against us.
47 Fear and a snare is come upon us, desolation and destruction.
48 Mine eye runneth down with rivers of water for the destruction of the daughter of my people.
49 Mine eye trickleth down, and ceaseth not, without any intermission,
50 Till the LORD look down, and behold from heaven.
51 Mine eye affecteth mine heart because of all the daughters of my city.
52 Mine enemies chased me sore, like a bird, without cause.
53 They have cut off my life in the dungeon, and cast a stone upon me.
54 Waters flowed over mine head; *then* I said, I am cut off.
55 ¶ I called upon thy name, O LORD, out of the low dungeon.
56 Thou hast heard my voice: hide not thine ear at my breathing, at my cry.
57 Thou drewest near in the day *that* I called upon thee: thou saidst, Fear not.
58 O Lord, thou hast pleaded the causes of my soul; thou hast redeemed my life.
59 O LORD, thou hast seen my wrong: judge thou my cause.
60 Thou hast seen all their vengeance *and* all their imaginations against me.
61 Thou hast heard their reproach, O LORD, *and* all their imaginations against me;
62 The lips of those that rose up against me, and their device against me all the day.
63 Behold their sitting down, and their rising up; I *am* their musick.
64 ¶ Render unto them a recompence, O LORD, according to the work of their hands.
65 Give them sorrow of heart, thy curse unto them.
66 Persecute and destroy them in anger from under the heavens of the LORD.

Lamentations 4

1 How is the gold become dim! *how* is the most fine gold changed! the stones of the sanctuary are poured out in the top of every street.
2 The precious sons of Zion, comparable to fine gold, how are they esteemed as earthen pitchers, the work of the hands of the potter!
3 Even the sea monsters draw out the breast, they give suck to their young ones: the daughter of my people *is become* cruel, like the ostriches in the wilderness.
4 The tongue of the sucking child cleaveth to the roof of his mouth for thirst: the young children ask bread, *and* no man breaketh *it* unto them.
5 They that did feed delicately are desolate in the streets: they that were brought up in scarlet embrace dunghills.
6 For the punishment of the iniquity of the daughter of my people is greater than the punishment of the sin of Sodom, that was overthrown as in a moment, and no hands stayed on her.
7 Her Nazarites were purer than snow, they were whiter than milk, they were more ruddy in body than rubies, their polishing *was* of sapphire:
8 Their visage is blacker than a coal; they are not known in the streets: their skin cleaveth to their bones; it is withered, it is become like a stick.
9 *They that be* slain with the sword are better than *they that be* slain with hunger: for these pine away, stricken through for *want of* the fruits of the field.
10 The hands of the pitiful women have sodden their own children: they were their meat in the destruction of the daughter of my people.
11 The LORD hath accomplished his fury; he hath poured out his fierce anger, and hath

kindled a fire in Zion, and it hath devoured
the foundations thereof.
12 The kings of the earth, and all the inhabitants of the world, would not have believed
that the adversary and the enemy should
have entered into the gates of Jerusalem.
13 ¶ For the sins of her prophets, *and* the
iniquities of her priests, that have shed the
blood of the just in the midst of her,
14 They have wandered *as* blind *men* in
the streets, they have polluted themselves
with blood, so that men could not touch
their garments.
15 They cried unto them, Depart ye; *it is*
unclean; depart, depart, touch not: when
they fled away and wandered, they said
among the heathen, They shall no more
sojourn *there*.
16 The anger of the LORD hath divided them;
he will no more regard them: they respected
not the persons of the priests, they favoured
not the elders.
17 As for us, our eyes as yet failed for our
vain help: in our watching we have watched
for a nation *that* could not save *us*.
18 They hunt our steps, that we cannot go
in our streets: our end is near, our days are
fulfilled; for our end is come.
19 Our persecutors are swifter than the
eagles of the heaven: they pursued us upon
the mountains, they laid wait for us in the
wilderness.
20 The breath of our nostrils, the anointed
of the LORD, was taken in their pits, of whom
we said, Under his shadow we shall live
among the heathen.
21 ¶ Rejoice and be glad, O daughter of
Edom, that dwellest in the land of Uz; the
cup also shall pass through unto thee: thou
shalt be drunken, and shalt make thyself
naked.
22 ¶ The punishment of thine iniquity is
accomplished, O daughter of Zion; he will
no more carry thee away into captivity: he
will visit thine iniquity, O daughter of Edom;
he will discover thy sins.

Lamentations 5

1 Remember, O LORD, what is come upon us:
consider, and behold our reproach.
2 Our inheritance is turned to strangers, our
houses to aliens.
3 We are orphans and fatherless, our mothers *are* as widows.
4 We have drunken our water for money;
our wood is sold unto us.
5 Our necks *are* under persecution: we
labour, *and* have no rest.
6 We have given the hand *to* the Egyptians,
and to the Assyrians, to be satisfied with
bread.
7 Our fathers have sinned, *and are* not; and
we have borne their iniquities.
8 Servants have ruled over us: *there is* none
that doth deliver *us* out of their hand.
9 We gat our bread with *the peril of* our lives
because of the sword of the wilderness.
10 Our skin was black like an oven because
of the terrible famine.
11 They ravished the women in Zion, *and*
the maids in the cities of Judah.
12 Princes are hanged up by their hand: the
faces of elders were not honoured.
13 They took the young men to grind, and
the children fell under the wood.
14 The elders have ceased from the gate,
the young men from their musick.
15 The joy of our heart is ceased; our dance
is turned into mourning.
16 The crown is fallen *from* our head: woe
unto us, that we have sinned!
17 For this our heart is faint; for these *things*
our eyes are dim.
18 Because of the mountain of Zion, which
is desolate, the foxes walk upon it.
19 Thou, O LORD, remainest for ever; thy
throne from generation to generation.
20 Wherefore dost thou forget us for ever,
and forsake us so long time?
21 Turn thou us unto thee, O LORD, and we
shall be turned; renew our days as of old.
22 But thou hast utterly rejected us; thou
art very wroth against us.

The Book Of
Ezekiel

Ezekiel 1

1 Now it came to pass in the thirtieth year,
in the fourth *month*, in the fifth *day* of the
month, as I *was* among the captives by
the river of Chebar, *that* the heavens were
opened, and I saw visions of God.
2 In the fifth *day* of the month, which *was*
the fifth year of king Jehoiachin's captivity,
3 The word of the LORD came expressly unto
Ezekiel the priest, the son of Buzi, in the land
of the Chaldeans by the river Chebar; and
the hand of the LORD was there upon him.
4 ¶ And I looked, and, behold, a whirlwind
came out of the north, a great cloud, and
a fire infolding itself, and a brightness *was*
about it, and out of the midst thereof as the
colour of amber, out of the midst of the fire.
5 Also out of the midst thereof *came* the
likeness of four living creatures. And this
was their appearance; they had the likeness of a man.
6 And every one had four faces, and every
one had four wings.
7 And their feet *were* straight feet; and the
sole of their feet *was* like the sole of a calf's
foot: and they sparkled like the colour of
burnished brass.
8 And *they had* the hands of a man under
their wings on their four sides; and they four
had their faces and their wings.
9 Their wings *were* joined one to another;
they turned not when they went; they went
every one straight forward.
10 As for the likeness of their faces, they
four had the face of a man, and the face of
a lion, on the right side: and they four had
the face of an ox on the left side; they four
also had the face of an eagle.
11 Thus *were* their faces: and their wings
were stretched upward; two *wings* of every
one *were* joined one to another, and two
covered their bodies.
12 And they went every one straight forward: whither the spirit was to go, they
went; *and* they turned not when they went.
13 As for the likeness of the living creatures,
their appearance *was* like burning coals of
fire, *and* like the appearance of lamps: it
went up and down among the living creatures; and the fire was bright, and out of
the fire went forth lightning.
14 And the living creatures ran and returned
as the appearance of a flash of lightning.
15 ¶ Now as I beheld the living creatures,
behold one wheel upon the earth by the
living creatures, with his four faces.
16 The appearance of the wheels and their
work *was* like unto the colour of a beryl:
and they four had one likeness: and their
appearance and their work *was* as it were
a wheel in the middle of a wheel.
17 When they went, they went upon their
four sides: *and* they turned not when they
went.
18 As for their rings, they were so high that
they were dreadful; and their rings *were* full
of eyes round about them four.
19 And when the living creatures went, the
wheels went by them: and when the living
creatures were lifted up from the earth, the
wheels were lifted up.
20 Whithersoever the spirit was to go, they
went, thither *was their* spirit to go; and the
wheels were lifted up over against them:
for the spirit of the living creature *was* in
the wheels.
21 When those went, *these* went; and
when those stood, *these* stood; and when
those were lifted up from the earth, the
wheels were lifted up over against them:
for the spirit of the living creature *was* in
the wheels.
22 And the likeness of the firmament upon
the heads of the living creature *was* as the
colour of the terrible crystal, stretched forth
over their heads above.
23 And under the firmament *were* their
wings straight, the one toward the other:
every one had two, which covered on this
side, and every one had two, which covered
on that side, their bodies.
24 And when they went, I heard the noise
of their wings, like the noise of great waters,
as the voice of the Almighty, the voice of

speech, as the noise of an host: when they
stood, they let down their wings.
25 And there was a voice from the firmament that *was* over their heads, when they
stood, *and* had let down their wings.
26 ¶ And above the firmament that *was* over
their heads *was* the likeness of a throne,
as the appearance of a sapphire stone:
and upon the likeness of the throne *was*
the likeness as the appearance of a man
above upon it.
27 And I saw as the colour of amber, as
the appearance of fire round about within
it, from the appearance of his loins even
upward, and from the appearance of his
loins even downward, I saw as it were the
appearance of fire, and it had brightness
round about.
28 As the appearance of the bow that is
in the cloud in the day of rain, so *was* the
appearance of the brightness round about.
This *was* the appearance of the likeness of
the glory of the LORD. And when I saw *it*,
I fell upon my face, and I heard a voice of
one that spake.

Ezekiel 2

1 And he said unto me, Son of man, stand
upon thy feet, and I will speak unto thee.
2 And the spirit entered into me when he
spake unto me, and set me upon my feet,
that I heard him that spake unto me.
3 And he said unto me, Son of man, I send
thee to the children of Israel, to a rebellious
nation that hath rebelled against me: they
and their fathers have transgressed against
me, *even* unto this very day.
4 For *they are* impudent children and stiff-
hearted. I do send thee unto them; and
thou shalt say unto them, Thus saith the
Lord GOD.
5 And they, whether they will hear, or
whether they will forbear, (for they *are* a
rebellious house,) yet shall know that there
hath been a prophet among them.
6 ¶ And thou, son of man, be not afraid
of them, neither be afraid of their words,
though briers and thorns *be* with thee,
and thou dost dwell among scorpions: be
not afraid of their words, nor be dismayed
at their looks, though they *be* a rebellious
house.
7 And thou shalt speak my words unto them,
whether they will hear, or whether they will
forbear: for they *are* most rebellious.
8 But thou, son of man, hear what I say
unto thee; Be not thou rebellious like that
rebellious house: open thy mouth, and eat
that I give thee.
9 ¶ And when I looked, behold, an hand
was sent unto me; and, lo, a roll of a book
was therein;
10 And he spread it before me; and it *was*
written within and without: and *there was*
written therein lamentations, and mourning, and woe.

Ezekiel 3

1 Moreover he said unto me, Son of man,
eat that thou findest; eat this roll, and go
speak unto the house of Israel.
2 So I opened my mouth, and he caused me
to eat that roll.
3 And he said unto me, Son of man, cause
thy belly to eat, and fill thy bowels with this
roll that I give thee. Then did I eat *it;* and it
was in my mouth as honey for sweetness.
4 ¶ And he said unto me, Son of man, go,
get thee unto the house of Israel, and speak
with my words unto them.
5 For thou *art* not sent to a people of a
strange speech and of an hard language,
but to the house of Israel;
6 Not to many people of a strange speech
and of an hard language, whose words thou
canst not understand. Surely, had I sent
thee to them, they would have hearkened
unto thee.
7 But the house of Israel will not hearken
unto thee; for they will not hearken unto
me: for all the house of Israel *are* impudent
and hardhearted.
8 Behold, I have made thy face strong
against their faces, and thy forehead strong
against their foreheads.
9 As an adamant harder than flint have I
made thy forehead: fear them not, neither
be dismayed at their looks, though they *be*
a rebellious house.
10 Moreover he said unto me, Son of man,
all my words that I shall speak unto thee
receive in thine heart, and hear with thine
ears.
11 And go, get thee to them of the captivity, unto the children of thy people, and
speak unto them, and tell them, Thus saith

the Lord GOD; whether they will hear, or
whether they will forbear.
12 Then the spirit took me up, and I heard
behind me a voice of a great rushing, *saying*, Blessed *be* the glory of the LORD from
his place.
13 *I heard* also the noise of the wings of the
living creatures that touched one another,
and the noise of the wheels over against
them, and a noise of a great rushing.
14 So the spirit lifted me up, and took me
away, and I went in bitterness, in the heat
of my spirit; but the hand of the LORD was
strong upon me.
15 ¶ Then I came to them of the captivity
at Tel-abib, that dwelt by the river of Chebar, and I sat where they sat, and remained
there astonished among them seven days.
16 And it came to pass at the end of seven
days, that the word of the LORD came unto
me, saying,
17 Son of man, I have made thee a watchman unto the house of Israel: therefore
hear the word at my mouth, and give them
warning from me.
18 When I say unto the wicked, Thou shalt
surely die; and thou givest him not warning,
nor speakest to warn the wicked from his
wicked way, to save his life; the same wicked
man shall die in his iniquity; but his blood
will I require at thine hand.
19 Yet if thou warn the wicked, and he
turn not from his wickedness, nor from his
wicked way, he shall die in his iniquity; but
thou hast delivered thy soul.
20 Again, When a righteous *man* doth turn
from his righteousness, and commit iniquity,
and I lay a stumblingblock before him, he
shall die: because thou hast not given him
warning, he shall die in his sin, and his righteousness which he hath done shall not be
remembered; but his blood will I require
at thine hand.
21 Nevertheless if thou warn the righteous
man, that the righteous sin not, and he doth
not sin, he shall surely live, because he is
warned; also thou hast delivered thy soul.
22 ¶ And the hand of the LORD was there
upon me; and he said unto me, Arise, go
forth into the plain, and I will there talk
with thee.
23 Then I arose, and went forth into the
plain: and, behold, the glory of the LORD
stood there, as the glory which I saw by
the river of Chebar: and I fell on my face.
24 Then the spirit entered into me, and
set me upon my feet, and spake with me,
and said unto me, Go, shut thyself within
thine house.
25 But thou, O son of man, behold, they
shall put bands upon thee, and shall bind
thee with them, and thou shalt not go out
among them:
26 And I will make thy tongue cleave to the
roof of thy mouth, that thou shalt be dumb,
and shalt not be to them a reprover: for they
are a rebellious house.
27 But when I speak with thee, I will open
thy mouth, and thou shalt say unto them,
Thus saith the Lord GOD; He that heareth,
let him hear; and he that forbeareth, let
him forbear: for they *are* a rebellious house.

Ezekiel 4

1 Thou also, son of man, take thee a tile,
and lay it before thee, and pourtray upon
it the city, *even* Jerusalem:
2 And lay siege against it, and build a fort
against it, and cast a mount against it; set
the camp also against it, and set *battering*
rams against it round about.
3 Moreover take thou unto thee an iron
pan, and set it *for* a wall of iron between
thee and the city: and set thy face against
it, and it shall be besieged, and thou shalt
lay siege against it. This *shall be* a sign to
the house of Israel.
4 Lie thou also upon thy left side, and lay
the iniquity of the house of Israel upon it:
according to the number of the days that
thou shalt lie upon it thou shalt bear their
iniquity.
5 For I have laid upon thee the years of
their iniquity, according to the number of
the days, three hundred and ninety days:
so shalt thou bear the iniquity of the house
of Israel.
6 And when thou hast accomplished them,
lie again on thy right side, and thou shalt
bear the iniquity of the house of Judah
forty days: I have appointed thee each day
for a year.
7 Therefore thou shalt set thy face toward
the siege of Jerusalem, and thine arm *shall
be* uncovered, and thou shalt prophesy
against it.

8 And, behold, I will lay bands upon thee,
and thou shalt not turn thee from one side
to another, till thou hast ended the days
of thy siege.
9 ¶ Take thou also unto thee wheat, and
barley, and beans, and lentiles, and millet,
and fitches, and put them in one vessel,
and make thee bread thereof, *according*
to the number of the days that thou shalt
lie upon thy side, three hundred and ninety
days shalt thou eat thereof.
10 And thy meat which thou shalt eat *shall*
be by weight, twenty shekels a day: from
time to time shalt thou eat it.
11 Thou shalt drink also water by measure,
the sixth part of an hin: from time to time
shalt thou drink.
12 And thou shalt eat it *as* barley cakes, and
thou shalt bake it with dung that cometh
out of man, in their sight.
13 And the LORD said, Even thus shall the
children of Israel eat their defiled bread
among the Gentiles, whither I will drive
them.
14 Then said I, Ah Lord GOD! behold, my
soul hath not been polluted: for from my
youth up even till now have I not eaten of
that which dieth of itself, or is torn in pieces;
neither came there abominable flesh into
my mouth.
15 Then he said unto me, Lo, I have given
thee cow's dung for man's dung, and thou
shalt prepare thy bread therewith.
16 Moreover he said unto me, Son of man,
behold, I will break the staff of bread in Jerusalem: and they shall eat bread by weight,
and with care; and they shall drink water by
measure, and with astonishment:
17 That they may want bread and water, and
be astonied one with another, and consume
away for their iniquity.

Ezekiel 5

1 And thou, son of man, take thee a sharp
knife, take thee a barber's rasor, and cause
it to pass upon thine head and upon thy
beard: then take thee balances to weigh,
and divide the *hair*.
2 Thou shalt burn with fire a third part in
the midst of the city, when the days of the
siege are fulfilled: and thou shalt take a third
part, *and* smite about it with a knife: and a
third part thou shalt scatter in the wind; and
I will draw out a sword after them.
3 Thou shalt also take thereof a few in number, and bind them in thy skirts.
4 Then take of them again, and cast them
into the midst of the fire, and burn them in
the fire; *for* thereof shall a fire come forth
into all the house of Israel.
5 ¶ Thus saith the Lord GOD; This *is* Jerusalem: I have set it in the midst of the nations
and countries *that are* round about her.
6 And she hath changed my judgments into
wickedness more than the nations, and my
statutes more than the countries that *are*
round about her: for they have refused my
judgments and my statutes, they have not
walked in them.
7 Therefore thus saith the Lord GOD;
Because ye multiplied more than the nations
that *are* round about you, *and* have not
walked in my statutes, neither have kept
my judgments, neither have done according
to the judgments of the nations that *are*
round about you;
8 Therefore thus saith the Lord GOD; Behold,
I, even I, *am* against thee, and will execute
judgments in the midst of thee in the sight
of the nations.
9 And I will do in thee that which I have not
done, and whereunto I will not do any more
the like, because of all thine abominations.
10 Therefore the fathers shall eat the sons
in the midst of thee, and the sons shall eat
their fathers; and I will execute judgments
in thee, and the whole remnant of thee will
I scatter into all the winds.
11 Wherefore, *as* I live, saith the Lord GOD;
Surely, because thou hast defiled my sanctuary with all thy detestable things, and
with all thine abominations, therefore will
I also diminish *thee;* neither shall mine eye
spare, neither will I have any pity.
12 ¶ A third part of thee shall die with the
pestilence, and with famine shall they be
consumed in the midst of thee: and a third
part shall fall by the sword round about
thee; and I will scatter a third part into
all the winds, and I will draw out a sword
after them.
13 Thus shall mine anger be accomplished,
and I will cause my fury to rest upon them,
and I will be comforted: and they shall know

that I the LORD have spoken *it* in my zeal, when I have accomplished my fury in them.

14 Moreover I will make thee waste, and a reproach among the nations that *are* round about thee, in the sight of all that pass by.

15 So it shall be a reproach and a taunt, an instruction and an astonishment unto the nations that *are* round about thee, when I shall execute judgments in thee in anger and in fury and in furious rebukes. I the LORD have spoken *it*.

16 When I shall send upon them the evil arrows of famine, which shall be for *their* destruction, *and* which I will send to destroy you: and I will increase the famine upon you, and will break your staff of bread:

17 So will I send upon you famine and evil beasts, and they shall bereave thee; and pestilence and blood shall pass through thee; and I will bring the sword upon thee. I the LORD have spoken *it*.

Ezekiel 6

1 And the word of the LORD came unto me, saying,

2 Son of man, set thy face toward the mountains of Israel, and prophesy against them,

3 And say, Ye mountains of Israel, hear the word of the Lord GOD; Thus saith the Lord GOD to the mountains, and to the hills, to the rivers, and to the valleys; Behold, I, *even* I, will bring a sword upon you, and I will destroy your high places.

4 And your altars shall be desolate, and your images shall be broken: and I will cast down your slain *men* before your idols.

5 And I will lay the dead carcases of the children of Israel before their idols; and I will scatter your bones round about your altars.

6 In all your dwellingplaces the cities shall be laid waste, and the high places shall be desolate; that your altars may be laid waste and made desolate, and your idols may be broken and cease, and your images may be cut down, and your works may be abolished.

7 And the slain shall fall in the midst of you, and ye shall know that I *am* the LORD.

8 ¶ Yet will I leave a remnant, that ye may have *some* that shall escape the sword among the nations, when ye shall be scattered through the countries.

9 And they that escape of you shall remember me among the nations whither they shall be carried captives, because I am broken with their whorish heart, which hath departed from me, and with their eyes, which go a whoring after their idols: and they shall lothe themselves for the evils which they have committed in all their abominations.

10 And they shall know that I *am* the LORD, *and that* I have not said in vain that I would do this evil unto them.

11 ¶ Thus saith the Lord GOD; Smite with thine hand, and stamp with thy foot, and say, Alas for all the evil abominations of the house of Israel! for they shall fall by the sword, by the famine, and by the pestilence.

12 He that is far off shall die of the pestilence; and he that is near shall fall by the sword; and he that remaineth and is besieged shall die by the famine: thus will I accomplish my fury upon them.

13 Then shall ye know that I *am* the LORD, when their slain *men* shall be among their idols round about their altars, upon every high hill, in all the tops of the mountains, and under every green tree, and under every thick oak, the place where they did offer sweet savour to all their idols.

14 So will I stretch out my hand upon them, and make the land desolate, yea, more desolate than the wilderness toward Diblath, in all their habitations: and they shall know that I *am* the LORD.

Ezekiel 7

1 Moreover the word of the LORD came unto me, saying,

2 Also, thou son of man, thus saith the Lord GOD unto the land of Israel; An end, the end is come upon the four corners of the land.

3 Now *is* the end *come* upon thee, and I will send mine anger upon thee, and will judge thee according to thy ways, and will recompense upon thee all thine abominations.

4 And mine eye shall not spare thee, neither will I have pity: but I will recompense thy ways upon thee, and thine abominations shall be in the midst of thee: and ye shall know that I *am* the LORD.

5 Thus saith the Lord GOD; An evil, an only evil, behold, is come.

6 An end is come, the end is come: it watcheth for thee; behold, it is come.

7 The morning is come unto thee, O thou

that dwellest in the land: the time is come,
the day of trouble *is* near, and not the sounding again of the mountains.
8 Now will I shortly pour out my fury upon
thee, and accomplish mine anger upon
thee: and I will judge thee according to thy
ways, and will recompense thee for all thine
abominations.
9 And mine eye shall not spare, neither will I
have pity: I will recompense thee according
to thy ways and thine abominations *that* are
in the midst of thee; and ye shall know that
I *am* the LORD that smiteth.
10 Behold the day, behold, it is come: the
morning is gone forth; the rod hath blos-
somed, pride hath budded.
11 Violence is risen up into a rod of wickedness: none of them *shall remain*, nor of
their multitude, nor of any of theirs: neither
shall there be wailing for them.
12 The time is come, the day draweth near:
let not the buyer rejoice, nor the seller
mourn: for wrath *is* upon all the multitude
thereof.
13 For the seller shall not return to that
which is sold, although they were yet alive:
for the vision *is* touching the whole multitude thereof, *which* shall not return; neither
shall any strengthen himself in the iniquity
of his life.
14 They have blown the trumpet, even to
make all ready; but none goeth to the battle: for my wrath *is* upon all the multitude
thereof.
15 The sword *is* without, and the pestilence
and the famine within: he that *is* in the field
shall die with the sword; and he that *is* in the
city, famine and pestilence shall devour him.
16 ¶ But they that escape of them shall
escape, and shall be on the mountains like
doves of the valleys, all of them mourning,
every one for his iniquity.
17 All hands shall be feeble, and all knees
shall be weak *as* water.
18 They shall also gird *themselves* with
sackcloth, and horror shall cover them; and
shame *shall be* upon all faces, and baldness
upon all their heads.
19 They shall cast their silver in the streets,
and their gold shall be removed: their silver
and their gold shall not be able to deliver
them in the day of the wrath of the LORD:
they shall not satisfy their souls, neither fill
their bowels: because it is the stumblingblock of their iniquity.
20 ¶ As for the beauty of his ornament, he
set it in majesty: but they made the images
of their abominations *and* of their detestable things therein: therefore have I set it
far from them.
21 And I will give it into the hands of the
strangers for a prey, and to the wicked of
the earth for a spoil; and they shall pollute it.
22 My face will I turn also from them, and
they shall pollute my secret *place:* for the
robbers shall enter into it, and defile it.
23 ¶ Make a chain: for the land is full of
bloody crimes, and the city is full of violence.
24 Wherefore I will bring the worst of
the heathen, and they shall possess their
houses: I will also make the pomp of the
strong to cease; and their holy places shall
be defiled.
25 Destruction cometh; and they shall seek
peace, and *there shall be* none.
26 Mischief shall come upon mischief, and
rumour shall be upon rumour; then shall
they seek a vision of the prophet; but the
law shall perish from the priest, and counsel
from the ancients.
27 The king shall mourn, and the prince shall
be clothed with desolation, and the hands
of the people of the land shall be troubled:
I will do unto them after their way, and
according to their deserts will I judge them;
and they shall know that I *am* the LORD.

Ezekiel 8

1 And it came to pass in the sixth year, in the
sixth *month*, in the fifth *day* of the month,
as I sat in mine house, and the elders of
Judah sat before me, that the hand of the
Lord GOD fell there upon me.
2 Then I beheld, and lo a likeness as the
appearance of fire: from the appearance
of his loins even downward, fire; and from
his loins even upward, as the appearance of
brightness, as the colour of amber.
3 And he put forth the form of an hand, and
took me by a lock of mine head; and the
spirit lifted me up between the earth and
the heaven, and brought me in the visions
of God to Jerusalem, to the door of the inner
gate that looketh toward the north; where
was the seat of the image of jealousy, which
provoketh to jealousy.

4 And, behold, the glory of the God of Israel *was* there, according to the vision that I saw in the plain.

5 ¶ Then said he unto me, Son of man, lift up thine eyes now the way toward the north. So I lifted up mine eyes the way toward the north, and behold northward at the gate of the altar this image of jealousy in the entry.

6 He said furthermore unto me, Son of man, seest thou what they do? *even* the great abominations that the house of Israel committeth here, that I should go far off from my sanctuary? but turn thee yet again, *and* thou shalt see greater abominations.

7 ¶ And he brought me to the door of the court; and when I looked, behold a hole in the wall.

8 Then said he unto me, Son of man, dig now in the wall: and when I had digged in the wall, behold a door.

9 And he said unto me, Go in, and behold the wicked abominations that they do here.

10 So I went in and saw; and behold every form of creeping things, and abominable beasts, and all the idols of the house of Israel, pourtrayed upon the wall round about.

11 And there stood before them seventy men of the ancients of the house of Israel, and in the midst of them stood Jaazaniah the son of Shaphan, with every man his censer in his hand; and a thick cloud of incense went up.

12 Then said he unto me, Son of man, hast thou seen what the ancients of the house of Israel do in the dark, every man in the chambers of his imagery? for they say, The LORD seeth us not; the LORD hath forsaken the earth.

13 ¶ He said also unto me, Turn thee yet again, *and* thou shalt see greater abominations that they do.

14 Then he brought me to the door of the gate of the LORD's house which *was* toward the north; and, behold, there sat women weeping for Tammuz.

15 ¶ Then said he unto me, Hast thou seen *this*, O son of man? turn thee yet again, *and* thou shalt see greater abominations than these.

16 And he brought me into the inner court of the LORD's house, and, behold, at the door of the temple of the LORD, between the porch and the altar, *were* about five and twenty men, with their backs toward the temple of the LORD, and their faces toward the east; and they worshipped the sun toward the east.

17 ¶ Then he said unto me, Hast thou seen *this*, O son of man? Is it a light thing to the house of Judah that they commit the abominations which they commit here? for they have filled the land with violence, and have returned to provoke me to anger: and, lo, they put the branch to their nose.

18 Therefore will I also deal in fury: mine eye shall not spare, neither will I have pity: and though they cry in mine ears with a loud voice, *yet* will I not hear them.

Ezekiel 9

1 He cried also in mine ears with a loud voice, saying, Cause them that have charge over the city to draw near, even every man *with* his destroying weapon in his hand.

2 And, behold, six men came from the way of the higher gate, which lieth toward the north, and every man a slaughter weapon in his hand; and one man among them *was* clothed with linen, with a writer's inkhorn by his side: and they went in, and stood beside the brasen altar.

3 And the glory of the God of Israel was gone up from the cherub, whereupon he was, to the threshold of the house. And he called to the man clothed with linen, which *had* the writer's inkhorn by his side;

4 And the LORD said unto him, Go through the midst of the city, through the midst of Jerusalem, and set a mark upon the foreheads of the men that sigh and that cry for all the abominations that be done in the midst thereof.

5 ¶ And to the others he said in mine hearing, Go ye after him through the city, and smite: let not your eye spare, neither have ye pity:

6 Slay utterly old *and* young, both maids, and little children, and women: but come not near any man upon whom *is* the mark; and begin at my sanctuary. Then they began at the ancient men which *were* before the house.

7 And he said unto them, Defile the house, and fill the courts with the slain: go ye forth. And they went forth, and slew in the city.

8 ¶ And it came to pass, while they were
slaying them, and I was left, that I fell upon
my face, and cried, and said, Ah Lord GOD!
wilt thou destroy all the residue of Israel in
thy pouring out of thy fury upon Jerusalem?
9 Then said he unto me, The iniquity of the
house of Israel and Judah *is* exceeding great,
and the land is full of blood, and the city full
of perverseness: for they say, The LORD hath
forsaken the earth, and the LORD seeth not.
10 And as for me also, mine eye shall not
spare, neither will I have pity, *but* I will recompense their way upon their head.
11 And, behold, the man clothed with linen,
which *had* the inkhorn by his side, reported
the matter, saying, I have done as thou hast
commanded me.

Ezekiel 10

1 Then I looked, and, behold, in the firmament that was above the head of the
cherubims there appeared over them as it
were a sapphire stone, as the appearance
of the likeness of a throne.
2 And he spake unto the man clothed with
linen, and said, Go in between the wheels,
even under the cherub, and fill thine hand
with coals of fire from between the cherubims, and scatter *them* over the city. And
he went in in my sight.
3 Now the cherubims stood on the right side
of the house, when the man went in; and
the cloud filled the inner court.
4 Then the glory of the LORD went up from
the cherub, *and stood* over the threshold of
the house; and the house was filled with the
cloud, and the court was full of the brightness of the LORD's glory.
5 And the sound of the cherubims' wings
was heard *even* to the outer court, as the
voice of the Almighty God when he speaketh.
6 And it came to pass, *that* when he had
commanded the man clothed with linen,
saying, Take fire from between the wheels,
from between the cherubims; then he went
in, and stood beside the wheels.
7 And *one* cherub stretched forth his hand
from between the cherubims unto the fire
that *was* between the cherubims, and took
thereof, and put *it* into the hands of *him
that was* clothed with linen: who took *it*,
and went out.
8 ¶ And there appeared in the cherubims
the form of a man's hand under their wings.
9 And when I looked, behold the four wheels
by the cherubims, one wheel by one cherub,
and another wheel by another cherub: and
the appearance of the wheels *was* as the
colour of a beryl stone.
10 And *as for* their appearances, they four
had one likeness, as if a wheel had been in
the midst of a wheel.
11 When they went, they went upon their
four sides; they turned not as they went, but
to the place whither the head looked they
followed it; they turned not as they went.
12 And their whole body, and their backs,
and their hands, and their wings, and the
wheels, *were* full of eyes round about, *even*
the wheels that they four had.
13 As for the wheels, it was cried unto them
in my hearing, O wheel.
14 And every one had four faces: the first
face *was* the face of a cherub, and the second face *was* the face of a man, and the
third the face of a lion, and the fourth the
face of an eagle.
15 And the cherubims were lifted up. This
is the living creature that I saw by the river
of Chebar.
16 And when the cherubims went, the
wheels went by them: and when the cherubims lifted up their wings to mount up from
the earth, the same wheels also turned not
from beside them.
17 When they stood, *these* stood; and
when they were lifted up, *these* lifted up
themselves *also:* for the spirit of the living
creature *was* in them.
18 Then the glory of the LORD departed from
off the threshold of the house, and stood
over the cherubims.
19 And the cherubims lifted up their wings,
and mounted up from the earth in my sight:
when they went out, the wheels also *were*
beside them, and *every one* stood at the
door of the east gate of the LORD's house;
and the glory of the God of Israel *was* over
them above.
20 This *is* the living creature that I saw under
the God of Israel by the river of Chebar; and
I knew that they *were* the cherubims.
21 Every one had four faces apiece, and
every one four wings; and the likeness of
the hands of a man *was* under their wings.

22 And the likeness of their faces *was* the
same faces which I saw by the river of Chebar, their appearances and themselves: they
went every one straight forward.

Ezekiel 11

1 Moreover the spirit lifted me up, and
brought me unto the east gate of the LORD's
house, which looketh eastward: and behold
at the door of the gate five and twenty
men; among whom I saw Jaazaniah the son
of Azur, and Pelatiah the son of Benaiah,
princes of the people.
2 Then said he unto me, Son of man, these
are the men that devise mischief, and give
wicked counsel in this city:
3 Which say, *It is* not near; let us build
houses: this *city is* the caldron, and we *be*
the flesh.
4 ¶ Therefore prophesy against them,
prophesy, O son of man.
5 And the Spirit of the LORD fell upon me,
and said unto me, Speak; Thus saith the
LORD; Thus have ye said, O house of Israel:
for I know the things that come into your
mind, *every one of* them.
6 Ye have multiplied your slain in this city,
and ye have filled the streets thereof with
the slain.
7 Therefore thus saith the Lord GOD; Your
slain whom ye have laid in the midst of it,
they *are* the flesh, and this *city is* the caldron: but I will bring you forth out of the
midst of it.
8 Ye have feared the sword; and I will bring
a sword upon you, saith the Lord GOD.
9 And I will bring you out of the midst
thereof, and deliver you into the hands
of strangers, and will execute judgments
among you.
10 Ye shall fall by the sword; I will judge you
in the border of Israel; and ye shall know
that I *am* the LORD.
11 This *city* shall not be your caldron, neither
shall ye be the flesh in the midst thereof;
but I will judge you in the border of Israel:
12 And ye shall know that I *am* the LORD: for
ye have not walked in my statutes, neither
executed my judgments, but have done
after the manners of the heathen that *are*
round about you.
13 ¶ And it came to pass, when I prophesied,
that Pelatiah the son of Benaiah died. Then
fell I down upon my face, and cried with a
loud voice, and said, Ah Lord GOD! wilt thou
make a full end of the remnant of Israel?
14 Again the word of the LORD came unto
me, saying,
15 Son of man, thy brethren, *even* thy
brethren, the men of thy kindred, and all
the house of Israel wholly, *are* they unto
whom the inhabitants of Jerusalem have
said, Get you far from the LORD: unto us is
this land given in possession.
16 Therefore say, Thus saith the Lord GOD;
Although I have cast them far off among
the heathen, and although I have scattered
them among the countries, yet will I be to
them as a little sanctuary in the countries
where they shall come.
17 Therefore say, Thus saith the Lord GOD;
I will even gather you from the people, and
assemble you out of the countries where ye
have been scattered, and I will give you the
land of Israel.
18 And they shall come thither, and they
shall take away all the detestable things
thereof and all the abominations thereof
from thence.
19 And I will give them one heart, and I will
put a new spirit within you; and I will take
the stony heart out of their flesh, and will
give them an heart of flesh:
20 That they may walk in my statutes, and
keep mine ordinances, and do them: and
they shall be my people, and I will be their
God.
21 But *as for them* whose heart walketh
after the heart of their detestable things
and their abominations, I will recompense
their way upon their own heads, saith the
Lord GOD.
22 ¶ Then did the cherubims lift up their
wings, and the wheels beside them; and
the glory of the God of Israel *was* over
them above.
23 And the glory of the LORD went up from
the midst of the city, and stood upon the
mountain which *is* on the east side of the
city.
24 ¶ Afterwards the spirit took me up, and
brought me in a vision by the Spirit of God
into Chaldea, to them of the captivity. So
the vision that I had seen went up from me.
25 Then I spake unto them of the captivity
all the things that the LORD had shewed me.

Ezekiel 12

1 The word of the LORD also came unto
me, saying,
2 Son of man, thou dwellest in the midst of
a rebellious house, which have eyes to see,
and see not; they have ears to hear, and
hear not: for they *are* a rebellious house.
3 Therefore, thou son of man, prepare thee
stuff for removing, and remove by day in
their sight; and thou shalt remove from
thy place to another place in their sight: it
may be they will consider, though they *be*
a rebellious house.
4 Then shalt thou bring forth thy stuff by
day in their sight, as stuff for removing: and
thou shalt go forth at even in their sight, as
they that go forth into captivity.
5 Dig thou through the wall in their sight,
and carry out thereby.
6 In their sight shalt thou bear *it* upon *thy*
shoulders, *and* carry *it* forth in the twilight:
thou shalt cover thy face, that thou see not
the ground: for I have set thee *for* a sign
unto the house of Israel.
7 And I did so as I was commanded: I
brought forth my stuff by day, as stuff for
captivity, and in the even I digged through
the wall with mine hand; I brought *it* forth in
the twilight, *and* I bare *it* upon *my* shoulder
in their sight.
8 ¶ And in the morning came the word of
the LORD unto me, saying,
9 Son of man, hath not the house of Israel,
the rebellious house, said unto thee, What
doest thou?
10 Say thou unto them, Thus saith the Lord
GOD; This burden *concerneth* the prince in
Jerusalem, and all the house of Israel that
are among them.
11 Say, I *am* your sign: like as I have done,
so shall it be done unto them: they shall
remove *and* go into captivity.
12 And the prince that *is* among them shall
bear upon *his* shoulder in the twilight, and
shall go forth: they shall dig through the wall
to carry out thereby: he shall cover his face,
that he see not the ground with *his* eyes.
13 My net also will I spread upon him, and
he shall be taken in my snare: and I will
bring him to Babylon *to* the land of the
Chaldeans; yet shall he not see it, though
he shall die there.
14 And I will scatter toward every wind all
that *are* about him to help him, and all his
bands; and I will draw out the sword after
them.
15 And they shall know that I *am* the LORD,
when I shall scatter them among the nations,
and disperse them in the countries.
16 But I will leave a few men of them from
the sword, from the famine, and from the
pestilence; that they may declare all their
abominations among the heathen whither
they come; and they shall know that I *am*
the LORD.
17 ¶ Moreover the word of the LORD came
to me, saying,
18 Son of man, eat thy bread with quaking,
and drink thy water with trembling and with
carefulness;
19 And say unto the people of the land,
Thus saith the Lord GOD of the inhabitants
of Jerusalem, *and* of the land of Israel; They
shall eat their bread with carefulness, and
drink their water with astonishment, that
her land may be desolate from all that is
therein, because of the violence of all them
that dwell therein.
20 And the cities that are inhabited shall be
laid waste, and the land shall be desolate;
and ye shall know that I *am* the LORD.
21 ¶ And the word of the LORD came unto
me, saying,
22 Son of man, what *is* that proverb *that* ye
have in the land of Israel, saying, The days
are prolonged, and every vision faileth?
23 Tell them therefore, Thus saith the Lord
GOD; I will make this proverb to cease, and
they shall no more use it as a proverb in
Israel; but say unto them, The days are at
hand, and the effect of every vision.
24 For there shall be no more any vain
vision nor flattering divination within the
house of Israel.
25 For I *am* the LORD: I will speak, and the
word that I shall speak shall come to pass; it
shall be no more prolonged: for in your days,
O rebellious house, will I say the word, and
will perform it, saith the Lord GOD.
26 ¶ Again the word of the LORD came to
me, saying,
27 Son of man, behold, *they of* the house
of Israel say, The vision that he seeth *is* for
many days *to come*, and he prophesieth of
the times *that are* far off.
28 Therefore say unto them, Thus saith the

Lord GOD; There shall none of my words be
prolonged any more, but the word which I
have spoken shall be done, saith the Lord
GOD.

Ezekiel 13

1 And the word of the LORD came unto
me, saying,
2 Son of man, prophesy against the prophets
of Israel that prophesy, and say thou unto
them that prophesy out of their own hearts,
Hear ye the word of the LORD;
3 Thus saith the Lord GOD; Woe unto the
foolish prophets, that follow their own spirit,
and have seen nothing!
4 O Israel, thy prophets are like the foxes
in the deserts.
5 Ye have not gone up into the gaps, neither
made up the hedge for the house of Israel
to stand in the battle in the day of the LORD.
6 They have seen vanity and lying divination,
saying, The LORD saith: and the LORD hath
not sent them: and they have made *others*
to hope that they would confirm the word.
7 Have ye not seen a vain vision, and have
ye not spoken a lying divination, whereas
ye say, The LORD saith *it;* albeit I have not
spoken?
8 Therefore thus saith the Lord GOD;
Because ye have spoken vanity, and seen
lies, therefore, behold, I *am* against you,
saith the Lord GOD.
9 And mine hand shall be upon the prophets
that see vanity, and that divine lies: they
shall not be in the assembly of my people,
neither shall they be written in the writing
of the house of Israel, neither shall they
enter into the land of Israel; and ye shall
know that I *am* the Lord GOD.
10 ¶ Because, even because they have
seduced my people, saying, Peace; and
there was no peace; and one built up a wall,
and, lo, others daubed it with untempered
morter:
11 Say unto them which daub *it* with untempered *morter,* that it shall fall: there shall
be an overflowing shower; and ye, O great
hailstones, shall fall; and a stormy wind
shall rend *it.*
12 Lo, when the wall is fallen, shall it not
be said unto you, Where *is* the daubing
wherewith ye have daubed *it?*
13 Therefore thus saith the Lord GOD; I will
even rend *it* with a stormy wind in my fury;
and there shall be an overflowing shower in
mine anger, and great hailstones in *my* fury
to consume *it.*
14 So will I break down the wall that ye
have daubed with untempered *morter,*
and bring it down to the ground, so that
the foundation thereof shall be discovered,
and it shall fall, and ye shall be consumed in
the midst thereof: and ye shall know that
I *am* the LORD.
15 Thus will I accomplish my wrath upon
the wall, and upon them that have daubed
it with untempered *morter,* and will say
unto you, The wall *is* no *more,* neither they
that daubed it;
16 *To wit,* the prophets of Israel which
prophesy concerning Jerusalem, and which
see visions of peace for her, and *there is* no
peace, saith the Lord GOD.
17 ¶ Likewise, thou son of man, set thy
face against the daughters of thy people,
which prophesy out of their own heart; and
prophesy thou against them,
18 And say, Thus saith the Lord GOD; Woe to
the *women* that sew pillows to all armholes,
and make kerchiefs upon the head of every
stature to hunt souls! Will ye hunt the souls
of my people, and will ye save the souls alive
that come unto you?
19 And will ye pollute me among my people for handfuls of barley and for pieces of
bread, to slay the souls that should not die,
and to save the souls alive that should not
live, by your lying to my people that hear
your lies?
20 Wherefore thus saith the Lord GOD;
Behold, I *am* against your pillows, wherewith ye there hunt the souls to make *them*
fly, and I will tear them from your arms, and
will let the souls go, *even* the souls that ye
hunt to make *them* fly.
21 Your kerchiefs also will I tear, and deliver
my people out of your hand, and they shall
be no more in your hand to be hunted; and
ye shall know that I *am* the LORD.
22 Because with lies ye have made the heart
of the righteous sad, whom I have not made
sad; and strengthened the hands of the
wicked, that he should not return from his
wicked way, by promising him life:
23 Therefore ye shall see no more vanity,
nor divine divinations: for I will deliver my

people out of your hand: and ye shall know
that I *am* the LORD.

Ezekiel 14

1 Then came certain of the elders of Israel
unto me, and sat before me.
2 And the word of the LORD came unto
me, saying,
3 Son of man, these men have set up their
idols in their heart, and put the stumblingblock of their iniquity before their face:
should I be inquired of at all by them?
4 Therefore speak unto them, and say unto
them, Thus saith the Lord GOD; Every man of
the house of Israel that setteth up his idols
in his heart, and putteth the stumblingblock
of his iniquity before his face, and cometh
to the prophet; I the LORD will answer him
that cometh according to the multitude of
his idols;
5 That I may take the house of Israel in their
own heart, because they are all estranged
from me through their idols.
6 ¶ Therefore say unto the house of Israel,
Thus saith the Lord GOD; Repent, and turn
yourselves from your idols; and turn away
your faces from all your abominations.
7 For every one of the house of Israel, or of
the stranger that sojourneth in Israel, which
separateth himself from me, and setteth
up his idols in his heart, and putteth the
stumblingblock of his iniquity before his
face, and cometh to a prophet to inquire of
him concerning me; I the LORD will answer
him by myself:
8 And I will set my face against that man,
and will make him a sign and a proverb, and
I will cut him off from the midst of my people; and ye shall know that I *am* the LORD.
9 And if the prophet be deceived when
he hath spoken a thing, I the LORD have
deceived that prophet, and I will stretch
out my hand upon him, and will destroy him
from the midst of my people Israel.
10 And they shall bear the punishment
of their iniquity: the punishment of the
prophet shall be even as the punishment
of him that seeketh *unto him;*
11 That the house of Israel may go no more
astray from me, neither be polluted any
more with all their transgressions; but that
they may be my people, and I may be their
God, saith the Lord GOD.
12 ¶ The word of the LORD came again to
me, saying,
13 Son of man, when the land sinneth
against me by trespassing grievously, then
will I stretch out mine hand upon it, and will
break the staff of the bread thereof, and will
send famine upon it, and will cut off man
and beast from it:
14 Though these three men, Noah, Daniel,
and Job, were in it, they should deliver *but*
their own souls by their righteousness, saith
the Lord GOD.
15 ¶ If I cause noisome beasts to pass
through the land, and they spoil it, so that it
be desolate, that no man may pass through
because of the beasts:
16 *Though* these three men *were* in it, *as* I
live, saith the Lord GOD, they shall deliver
neither sons nor daughters; they only shall
be delivered, but the land shall be desolate.
17 ¶ Or *if* I bring a sword upon that land,
and say, Sword, go through the land; so that
I cut off man and beast from it:
18 Though these three men *were* in it, *as* I
live, saith the Lord GOD, they shall deliver
neither sons nor daughters, but they only
shall be delivered themselves.
19 ¶ Or *if* I send a pestilence into that land,
and pour out my fury upon it in blood, to
cut off from it man and beast:
20 Though Noah, Daniel, and Job, *were* in
it, *as* I live, saith the Lord GOD, they shall
deliver neither son nor daughter; they
shall *but* deliver their own souls by their
righteousness.
21 For thus saith the Lord GOD; How much
more when I send my four sore judgments
upon Jerusalem, the sword, and the famine,
and the noisome beast, and the pestilence,
to cut off from it man and beast?
22 ¶ Yet, behold, therein shall be left a
remnant that shall be brought forth, *both*
sons and daughters: behold, they shall come
forth unto you, and ye shall see their way
and their doings: and ye shall be comforted
concerning the evil that I have brought upon
Jerusalem, *even* concerning all that I have
brought upon it.
23 And they shall comfort you, when ye see
their ways and their doings: and ye shall
know that I have not done without cause
all that I have done in it, saith the Lord GOD.

Ezekiel 15

1 And the word of the LORD came unto
me, saying,
2 Son of man, What is the vine tree more
than any tree, *or than* a branch which is
among the trees of the forest?
3 Shall wood be taken thereof to do any
work? or will *men* take a pin of it to hang
any vessel thereon?
4 Behold, it is cast into the fire for fuel; the
fire devoureth both the ends of it, and the
midst of it is burned. Is it meet for *any* work?
5 Behold, when it was whole, it was meet for
no work: how much less shall it be meet yet
for *any* work, when the fire hath devoured
it, and it is burned?
6 ¶ Therefore thus saith the Lord GOD; As
the vine tree among the trees of the forest,
which I have given to the fire for fuel, so will
I give the inhabitants of Jerusalem.
7 And I will set my face against them; they
shall go out from *one* fire, and *another* fire
shall devour them; and ye shall know that
I *am* the LORD, when I set my face against
them.
8 And I will make the land desolate, because
they have committed a trespass, saith the
Lord GOD.

Ezekiel 16

1 Again the word of the LORD came unto
me, saying,
2 Son of man, cause Jerusalem to know her
abominations,
3 And say, Thus saith the Lord GOD unto
Jerusalem; Thy birth and thy nativity *is* of the
land of Canaan; thy father *was* an Amorite,
and thy mother an Hittite.
4 And *as for* thy nativity, in the day thou
wast born thy navel was not cut, neither
wast thou washed in water to supple *thee;*
thou wast not salted at all, nor swaddled
at all.
5 None eye pitied thee, to do any of these
unto thee, to have compassion upon thee;
but thou wast cast out in the open field, to
the lothing of thy person, in the day that
thou wast born.
6 ¶ And when I passed by thee, and saw thee
polluted in thine own blood, I said unto thee
when thou wast in thy blood, Live; yea, I said
unto thee *when thou wast* in thy blood, Live.
7 I have caused thee to multiply as the bud
of the field, and thou hast increased and
waxen great, and thou art come to excellent ornaments: *thy* breasts are fashioned,
and thine hair is grown, whereas thou *wast*
naked and bare.
8 Now when I passed by thee, and looked
upon thee, behold, thy time *was* the time
of love; and I spread my skirt over thee,
and covered thy nakedness: yea, I sware
unto thee, and entered into a covenant
with thee, saith the Lord GOD, and thou
becamest mine.
9 Then washed I thee with water; yea, I
throughly washed away thy blood from
thee, and I anointed thee with oil.
10 I clothed thee also with broidered work,
and shod thee with badgers' skin, and I
girded thee about with fine linen, and I
covered thee with silk.
11 I decked thee also with ornaments, and
I put bracelets upon thy hands, and a chain
on thy neck.
12 And I put a jewel on thy forehead, and
earrings in thine ears, and a beautiful crown
upon thine head.
13 Thus wast thou decked with gold and
silver; and thy raiment *was of* fine linen,
and silk, and broidered work; thou didst
eat fine flour, and honey, and oil: and thou
wast exceeding beautiful, and thou didst
prosper into a kingdom.
14 And thy renown went forth among the
heathen for thy beauty: for it *was* perfect
through my comeliness, which I had put
upon thee, saith the Lord GOD.
15 ¶ But thou didst trust in thine own
beauty, and playedst the harlot because of
thy renown, and pouredst out thy fornications on every one that passed by; his it was.
16 And of thy garments thou didst take, and
deckedst thy high places with divers colours,
and playedst the harlot thereupon: *the like
things* shall not come, neither shall it be *so.*
17 Thou hast also taken thy fair jewels of
my gold and of my silver, which I had given
thee, and madest to thyself images of men,
and didst commit whoredom with them,
18 And tookest thy broidered garments, and
coveredst them: and thou hast set mine oil
and mine incense before them.
19 My meat also which I gave thee, fine
flour, and oil, and honey, *wherewith* I fed
thee, thou hast even set it before them for

a sweet savour: and *thus* it was, saith the
Lord GOD.
20 Moreover thou hast taken thy sons and
thy daughters, whom thou hast borne unto
me, and these hast thou sacrificed unto
them to be devoured. *Is this* of thy whoredoms a small matter,
21 That thou hast slain my children, and
delivered them to cause them to pass
through *the fire* for them?
22 And in all thine abominations and thy
whoredoms thou hast not remembered the
days of thy youth, when thou wast naked
and bare, *and* wast polluted in thy blood.
23 And it came to pass after all thy wickedness, (woe, woe unto thee! saith the
Lord GOD;)
24 *That* thou hast also built unto thee an
eminent place, and hast made thee an high
place in every street.
25 Thou hast built thy high place at every
head of the way, and hast made thy beauty
to be abhorred, and hast opened thy feet
to every one that passed by, and multiplied
thy whoredoms.
26 Thou hast also committed fornication
with the Egyptians thy neighbours, great of
flesh; and hast increased thy whoredoms,
to provoke me to anger.
27 Behold, therefore I have stretched out my
hand over thee, and have diminished thine
ordinary *food*, and delivered thee unto the
will of them that hate thee, the daughters
of the Philistines, which are ashamed of
thy lewd way.
28 Thou hast played the whore also with the
Assyrians, because thou wast unsatiable;
yea, thou hast played the harlot with them,
and yet couldest not be satisfied.
29 Thou hast moreover multiplied thy fornication in the land of Canaan unto Chaldea;
and yet thou wast not satisfied herewith.
30 How weak is thine heart, saith the Lord
GOD, seeing thou doest all these *things*,
the work of an imperious whorish woman;
31 In that thou buildest thine eminent place
in the head of every way, and makest thine
high place in every street; and hast not been
as an harlot, in that thou scornest hire;
32 *But as* a wife that committeth adultery,
which taketh strangers instead of her husband!
33 They give gifts to all whores: but thou
givest thy gifts to all thy lovers, and hirest
them, that they may come unto thee on
every side for thy whoredom.
34 And the contrary is in thee from *other*
women in thy whoredoms, whereas none
followeth thee to commit whoredoms:
and in that thou givest a reward, and no
reward is given unto thee, therefore thou
art contrary.
35 ¶ Wherefore, O harlot, hear the word
of the LORD:
36 Thus saith the Lord GOD; Because thy
filthiness was poured out, and thy nakedness discovered through thy whoredoms
with thy lovers, and with all the idols of
thy abominations, and by the blood of thy
children, which thou didst give unto them;
37 Behold, therefore I will gather all thy lovers, with whom thou hast taken pleasure,
and all *them* that thou hast loved, with all
them that thou hast hated; I will even gather
them round about against thee, and will
discover thy nakedness unto them, that
they may see all thy nakedness.
38 And I will judge thee, as women that
break wedlock and shed blood are judged;
and I will give thee blood in fury and jealousy.
39 And I will also give thee into their hand,
and they shall throw down thine eminent
place, and shall break down thy high places:
they shall strip thee also of thy clothes, and
shall take thy fair jewels, and leave thee
naked and bare.
40 They shall also bring up a company
against thee, and they shall stone thee
with stones, and thrust thee through with
their swords.
41 And they shall burn thine houses with
fire, and execute judgments upon thee in
the sight of many women: and I will cause
thee to cease from playing the harlot, and
thou also shalt give no hire any more.
42 So will I make my fury toward thee to
rest, and my jealousy shall depart from
thee, and I will be quiet, and will be no
more angry.
43 Because thou hast not remembered the
days of thy youth, but hast fretted me in all
these *things;* behold, therefore I also will
recompense thy way upon *thine* head, saith
the Lord GOD: and thou shalt not commit
this lewdness above all thine abominations.

44 ¶ Behold, every one that useth proverbs
shall use *this* proverb against thee, saying,
As *is* the mother, *so is* her daughter.
45 Thou *art* thy mother's daughter, that
lotheth her husband and her children; and
thou *art* the sister of thy sisters, which
lothed their husbands and their children:
your mother *was* an Hittite, and your father
an Amorite.
46 And thine elder sister *is* Samaria, she and
her daughters that dwell at thy left hand:
and thy younger sister, that dwelleth at thy
right hand, *is* Sodom and her daughters.
47 Yet hast thou not walked after their ways,
nor done after their abominations: but, as
if that were a very little *thing*, thou wast
corrupted more than they in all thy ways.
48 *As* I live, saith the Lord GOD, Sodom thy
sister hath not done, she nor her daughters,
as thou hast done, thou and thy daughters.
49 Behold, this was the iniquity of thy
sister Sodom, pride, fulness of bread, and
abundance of idleness was in her and in her
daughters, neither did she strengthen the
hand of the poor and needy.
50 And they were haughty, and committed
abomination before me: therefore I took
them away as I saw *good*.
51 Neither hath Samaria committed half
of thy sins; but thou hast multiplied thine
abominations more than they, and hast
justified thy sisters in all thine abominations
which thou hast done.
52 Thou also, which hast judged thy sisters,
bear thine own shame for thy sins that thou
hast committed more abominable than
they: they are more righteous than thou:
yea, be thou confounded also, and bear thy
shame, in that thou hast justified thy sisters.
53 When I shall bring again their captivity,
the captivity of Sodom and her daughters,
and the captivity of Samaria and her daughters, then *will I bring again* the captivity of
thy captives in the midst of them:
54 That thou mayest bear thine own shame,
and mayest be confounded in all that thou
hast done, in that thou art a comfort unto
them.
55 When thy sisters, Sodom and her daughters, shall return to their former estate, and
Samaria and her daughters shall return
to their former estate, then thou and thy
daughters shall return to your former estate.
56 For thy sister Sodom was not mentioned
by thy mouth in the day of thy pride,
57 Before thy wickedness was discovered,
as at the time of *thy* reproach of the daughters of Syria, and all *that are* round about
her, the daughters of the Philistines, which
despise thee round about.
58 Thou hast borne thy lewdness and thine
abominations, saith the LORD.
59 For thus saith the Lord GOD; I will even
deal with thee as thou hast done, which hast
despised the oath in breaking the covenant.
60 ¶ Nevertheless I will remember my covenant with thee in the days of thy youth,
and I will establish unto thee an everlasting
covenant.
61 Then thou shalt remember thy ways, and
be ashamed, when thou shalt receive thy
sisters, thine elder and thy younger: and I
will give them unto thee for daughters, but
not by thy covenant.
62 And I will establish my covenant with
thee; and thou shalt know that I *am* the
LORD:
63 That thou mayest remember, and be
confounded, and never open thy mouth
any more because of thy shame, when I am
pacified toward thee for all that thou hast
done, saith the Lord GOD.

Ezekiel 17

1 And the word of the LORD came unto
me, saying,
2 Son of man, put forth a riddle, and speak
a parable unto the house of Israel;
3 And say, Thus saith the Lord GOD; A great
eagle with great wings, longwinged, full of
feathers, which had divers colours, came
unto Lebanon, and took the highest branch
of the cedar:
4 He cropped off the top of his young twigs,
and carried it into a land of traffick; he set
it in a city of merchants.
5 He took also of the seed of the land, and
planted it in a fruitful field; he placed *it* by
great waters, *and* set it *as* a willow tree.
6 And it grew, and became a spreading
vine of low stature, whose branches turned
toward him, and the roots thereof were
under him: so it became a vine, and brought
forth branches, and shot forth sprigs.
7 There was also another great eagle with
great wings and many feathers: and, behold,

this vine did bend her roots toward him,
and shot forth her branches toward him,
that he might water it by the furrows of
her plantation.
8 It was planted in a good soil by great
waters, that it might bring forth branches,
and that it might bear fruit, that it might be
a goodly vine.
9 Say thou, Thus saith the Lord GOD; Shall
it prosper? shall he not pull up the roots
thereof, and cut off the fruit thereof, that it
wither? it shall wither in all the leaves of her
spring, even without great power or many
people to pluck it up by the roots thereof.
10 Yea, behold, *being* planted, shall it prosper? shall it not utterly wither, when the
east wind toucheth it? it shall wither in the
furrows where it grew.
11 ¶ Moreover the word of the LORD came
unto me, saying,
12 Say now to the rebellious house, Know
ye not what these *things mean?* tell *them*,
Behold, the king of Babylon is come to
Jerusalem, and hath taken the king thereof,
and the princes thereof, and led them with
him to Babylon;
13 And hath taken of the king's seed, and
made a covenant with him, and hath taken
an oath of him: he hath also taken the
mighty of the land:
14 That the kingdom might be base, that it
might not lift itself up, *but* that by keeping
of his covenant it might stand.
15 But he rebelled against him in sending
his ambassadors into Egypt, that they might
give him horses and much people. Shall he
prosper? shall he escape that doeth such
things? or shall he break the covenant, and
be delivered?
16 *As* I live, saith the Lord GOD, surely in the
place *where* the king *dwelleth* that made him
king, whose oath he despised, and whose
covenant he brake, *even* with him in the
midst of Babylon he shall die.
17 Neither shall Pharaoh with *his* mighty
army and great company make for him in
the war, by casting up mounts, and building
forts, to cut off many persons:
18 Seeing he despised the oath by breaking
the covenant, when, lo, he had given his
hand, and hath done all these *things*, he
shall not escape.
19 Therefore thus saith the Lord GOD; *As* I
live, surely mine oath that he hath despised,
and my covenant that he hath broken, even
it will I recompense upon his own head.
20 And I will spread my net upon him, and
he shall be taken in my snare, and I will
bring him to Babylon, and will plead with
him there for his trespass that he hath trespassed against me.
21 And all his fugitives with all his bands
shall fall by the sword, and they that remain
shall be scattered toward all winds: and ye
shall know that I the LORD have spoken *it*.
22 ¶ Thus saith the Lord GOD; I will also take
of the highest branch of the high cedar, and
will set *it;* I will crop off from the top of his
young twigs a tender one, and will plant *it*
upon an high mountain and eminent:
23 In the mountain of the height of Israel
will I plant it: and it shall bring forth boughs,
and bear fruit, and be a goodly cedar: and
under it shall dwell all fowl of every wing;
in the shadow of the branches thereof shall
they dwell.
24 And all the trees of the field shall know
that I the LORD have brought down the high
tree, have exalted the low tree, have dried
up the green tree, and have made the dry
tree to flourish: I the LORD have spoken and
have done *it*.

Ezekiel 18

1 The word of the LORD came unto me
again, saying,
2 What mean ye, that ye use this proverb
concerning the land of Israel, saying, The
fathers have eaten sour grapes, and the
children's teeth are set on edge?
3 *As* I live, saith the Lord GOD, ye shall not
have *occasion* any more to use this proverb
in Israel.
4 Behold, all souls are mine; as the soul of
the father, so also the soul of the son is mine:
the soul that sinneth, it shall die.
5 ¶ But if a man be just, and do that which
is lawful and right,
6 *And* hath not eaten upon the mountains,
neither hath lifted up his eyes to the idols of
the house of Israel, neither hath defiled his
neighbour's wife, neither hath come near
to a menstruous woman,
7 And hath not oppressed any, *but* hath
restored to the debtor his pledge, hath
spoiled none by violence, hath given his

bread to the hungry, and hath covered the naked with a garment;
8 He *that* hath not given forth upon usury, neither hath taken any increase, *that* hath withdrawn his hand from iniquity, hath executed true judgment between man and man,
9 Hath walked in my statutes, and hath kept my judgments, to deal truly; he *is* just, he shall surely live, saith the Lord GOD.
10 ¶ If he beget a son *that is* a robber, a shedder of blood, and *that* doeth the like to *any* one of these *things*,
11 And that doeth not any of those *duties*, but even hath eaten upon the mountains, and defiled his neighbour's wife,
12 Hath oppressed the poor and needy, hath spoiled by violence, hath not restored the pledge, and hath lifted up his eyes to the idols, hath committed abomination,
13 Hath given forth upon usury, and hath taken increase: shall he then live? he shall not live: he hath done all these abominations; he shall surely die; his blood shall be upon him.
14 ¶ Now, lo, *if* he beget a son, that seeth all his father's sins which he hath done, and considereth, and doeth not such like,
15 *That* hath not eaten upon the mountains, neither hath lifted up his eyes to the idols of the house of Israel, hath not defiled his neighbour's wife,
16 Neither hath oppressed any, hath not withholden the pledge, neither hath spoiled by violence, *but* hath given his bread to the hungry, and hath covered the naked with a garment,
17 *That* hath taken off his hand from the poor, *that* hath not received usury nor increase, hath executed my judgments, hath walked in my statutes; he shall not die for the iniquity of his father, he shall surely live.
18 *As for* his father, because he cruelly oppressed, spoiled his brother by violence, and did *that* which *is* not good among his people, lo, even he shall die in his iniquity.
19 ¶ Yet say ye, Why? doth not the son bear the iniquity of the father? When the son hath done that which is lawful and right, *and* hath kept all my statutes, and hath done them, he shall surely live.
20 The soul that sinneth, it shall die. The son shall not bear the iniquity of the father, neither shall the father bear the iniquity of the son: the righteousness of the righteous shall be upon him, and the wickedness of the wicked shall be upon him.
21 But if the wicked will turn from all his sins that he hath committed, and keep all my statutes, and do that which is lawful and right, he shall surely live, he shall not die.
22 All his transgressions that he hath committed, they shall not be mentioned unto him: in his righteousness that he hath done he shall live.
23 Have I any pleasure at all that the wicked should die? saith the Lord GOD: *and* not that he should return from his ways, and live?
24 ¶ But when the righteous turneth away from his righteousness, and committeth iniquity, *and* doeth according to all the abominations that the wicked *man* doeth, shall he live? All his righteousness that he hath done shall not be mentioned: in his trespass that he hath trespassed, and in his sin that he hath sinned, in them shall he die.
25 ¶ Yet ye say, The way of the Lord is not equal. Hear now, O house of Israel; Is not my way equal? are not your ways unequal?
26 When a righteous *man* turneth away from his righteousness, and committeth iniquity, and dieth in them; for his iniquity that he hath done shall he die.
27 Again, when the wicked *man* turneth away from his wickedness that he hath committed, and doeth that which is lawful and right, he shall save his soul alive.
28 Because he considereth, and turneth away from all his transgressions that he hath committed, he shall surely live, he shall not die.
29 Yet saith the house of Israel, The way of the Lord is not equal. O house of Israel, are not my ways equal? are not your ways unequal?
30 Therefore I will judge you, O house of Israel, every one according to his ways, saith the Lord GOD. Repent, and turn *yourselves* from all your transgressions; so iniquity shall not be your ruin.
31 ¶ Cast away from you all your transgressions, whereby ye have transgressed; and make you a new heart and a new spirit: for why will ye die, O house of Israel?
32 For I have no pleasure in the death of him

that dieth, saith the Lord GOD: wherefore
turn *yourselves*, and live ye.

Ezekiel 19

1 Moreover take thou up a lamentation for
the princes of Israel,
2 And say, What *is* thy mother? A lioness:
she lay down among lions, she nourished
her whelps among young lions.
3 And she brought up one of her whelps: it
became a young lion, and it learned to catch
the prey; it devoured men.
4 The nations also heard of him; he was
taken in their pit, and they brought him with
chains unto the land of Egypt.
5 Now when she saw that she had waited,
and her hope was lost, then she took
another of her whelps, *and* made him a
young lion.
6 And he went up and down among the
lions, he became a young lion, and learned
to catch the prey, *and* devoured men.
7 And he knew their desolate palaces, and
he laid waste their cities; and the land was
desolate, and the fulness thereof, by the
noise of his roaring.
8 Then the nations set against him on every
side from the provinces, and spread their
net over him: he was taken in their pit.
9 And they put him in ward in chains, and
brought him to the king of Babylon: they
brought him into holds, that his voice should
no more be heard upon the mountains of
Israel.
10 ¶ Thy mother *is* like a vine in thy blood,
planted by the waters: she was fruitful and
full of branches by reason of many waters.
11 And she had strong rods for the sceptres
of them that bare rule, and her stature was
exalted among the thick branches, and she
appeared in her height with the multitude
of her branches.
12 But she was plucked up in fury, she was
cast down to the ground, and the east wind
dried up her fruit: her strong rods were broken and withered; the fire consumed them.
13 And now she *is* planted in the wilderness,
in a dry and thirsty ground.
14 And fire is gone out of a rod of her
branches, *which* hath devoured her fruit, so
that she hath no strong rod *to be* a sceptre
to rule. This *is* a lamentation, and shall be
for a lamentation.

Ezekiel 20

1 And it came to pass in the seventh year, in
the fifth *month*, the tenth *day* of the month,
that certain of the elders of Israel came to
inquire of the LORD, and sat before me.
2 Then came the word of the LORD unto
me, saying,
3 Son of man, speak unto the elders of
Israel, and say unto them, Thus saith the
Lord GOD; Are ye come to inquire of me?
As I live, saith the Lord GOD, I will not be
inquired of by you.
4 Wilt thou judge them, son of man, wilt
thou judge *them?* cause them to know the
abominations of their fathers:
5 ¶ And say unto them, Thus saith the Lord
GOD; In the day when I chose Israel, and
lifted up mine hand unto the seed of the
house of Jacob, and made myself known
unto them in the land of Egypt, when I lifted
up mine hand unto them, saying, I *am* the
LORD your God;
6 In the day *that* I lifted up mine hand unto
them, to bring them forth of the land of
Egypt into a land that I had espied for them,
flowing with milk and honey, which *is* the
glory of all lands:
7 Then said I unto them, Cast ye away every
man the abominations of his eyes, and defile
not yourselves with the idols of Egypt: I *am*
the LORD your God.
8 But they rebelled against me, and would
not hearken unto me: they did not every
man cast away the abominations of their
eyes, neither did they forsake the idols of
Egypt: then I said, I will pour out my fury
upon them, to accomplish my anger against
them in the midst of the land of Egypt.
9 But I wrought for my name's sake, that it
should not be polluted before the heathen,
among whom they *were*, in whose sight I
made myself known unto them, in bringing
them forth out of the land of Egypt.
10 ¶ Wherefore I caused them to go forth
out of the land of Egypt, and brought them
into the wilderness.
11 And I gave them my statutes, and shewed
them my judgments, which *if* a man do, he
shall even live in them.
12 Moreover also I gave them my sabbaths,
to be a sign between me and them, that
they might know that I *am* the LORD that
sanctify them.

13 But the house of Israel rebelled against
me in the wilderness: they walked not in my
statutes, and they despised my judgments,
which *if* a man do, he shall even live in them;
and my sabbaths they greatly polluted: then
I said, I would pour out my fury upon them
in the wilderness, to consume them.
14 But I wrought for my name's sake, that it
should not be polluted before the heathen,
in whose sight I brought them out.
15 Yet also I lifted up my hand unto them
in the wilderness, that I would not bring
them into the land which I had given *them*,
flowing with milk and honey, which *is* the
glory of all lands;
16 Because they despised my judgments,
and walked not in my statutes, but polluted
my sabbaths: for their heart went after
their idols.
17 Nevertheless mine eye spared them from
destroying them, neither did I make an end
of them in the wilderness.
18 But I said unto their children in the wilderness, Walk ye not in the statutes of your
fathers, neither observe their judgments,
nor defile yourselves with their idols:
19 I *am* the LORD your God; walk in my statutes, and keep my judgments, and do them;
20 And hallow my sabbaths; and they shall
be a sign between me and you, that ye may
know that I *am* the LORD your God.
21 Notwithstanding the children rebelled
against me: they walked not in my statutes, neither kept my judgments to do
them, which *if* a man do, he shall even live
in them; they polluted my sabbaths: then I
said, I would pour out my fury upon them,
to accomplish my anger against them in
the wilderness.
22 Nevertheless I withdrew mine hand, and
wrought for my name's sake, that it should
not be polluted in the sight of the heathen,
in whose sight I brought them forth.
23 I lifted up mine hand unto them also in
the wilderness, that I would scatter them
among the heathen, and disperse them
through the countries;
24 Because they had not executed my judgments, but had despised my statutes, and
had polluted my sabbaths, and their eyes
were after their fathers' idols.
25 Wherefore I gave them also statutes *that*
were not good, and judgments whereby
they should not live;
26 And I polluted them in their own gifts, in
that they caused to pass through *the fire* all
that openeth the womb, that I might make
them desolate, to the end that they might
know that I *am* the LORD.
27 ¶ Therefore, son of man, speak unto the
house of Israel, and say unto them, Thus
saith the Lord GOD; Yet in this your fathers
have blasphemed me, in that they have
committed a trespass against me.
28 *For* when I had brought them into the
land, *for* the which I lifted up mine hand to
give it to them, then they saw every high
hill, and all the thick trees, and they offered
there their sacrifices, and there they presented the provocation of their offering:
there also they made their sweet savour,
and poured out there their drink offerings.
29 Then I said unto them, What *is* the high
place whereunto ye go? And the name
thereof is called Bamah unto this day.
30 Wherefore say unto the house of Israel,
Thus saith the Lord GOD; Are ye polluted
after the manner of your fathers? and commit ye whoredom after their abominations?
31 For when ye offer your gifts, when ye
make your sons to pass through the fire, ye
pollute yourselves with all your idols, even
unto this day: and shall I be inquired of by
you, O house of Israel? *As* I live, saith the
Lord GOD, I will not be inquired of by you.
32 And that which cometh into your mind
shall not be at all, that ye say, We will be as
the heathen, as the families of the countries,
to serve wood and stone.
33 ¶ *As* I live, saith the Lord GOD, surely
with a mighty hand, and with a stretched
out arm, and with fury poured out, will I
rule over you:
34 And I will bring you out from the people,
and will gather you out of the countries
wherein ye are scattered, with a mighty
hand, and with a stretched out arm, and
with fury poured out.
35 And I will bring you into the wilderness
of the people, and there will I plead with
you face to face.
36 Like as I pleaded with your fathers in
the wilderness of the land of Egypt, so will
I plead with you, saith the Lord GOD.
37 And I will cause you to pass under the

rod, and I will bring you into the bond of
the covenant:
38 And I will purge out from among you the
rebels, and them that transgress against
me: I will bring them forth out of the country where they sojourn, and they shall not
enter into the land of Israel: and ye shall
know that I *am* the LORD.
39 As for you, O house of Israel, thus saith
the Lord GOD; Go ye, serve ye every one his
idols, and hereafter *also*, if ye will not hearken unto me: but pollute ye my holy name
no more with your gifts, and with your idols.
40 For in mine holy mountain, in the mountain of the height of Israel, saith the Lord
GOD, there shall all the house of Israel, all
of them in the land, serve me: there will I
accept them, and there will I require your
offerings, and the firstfruits of your oblations, with all your holy things.
41 I will accept you with your sweet savour,
when I bring you out from the people, and
gather you out of the countries wherein ye
have been scattered; and I will be sanctified
in you before the heathen.
42 And ye shall know that I *am* the LORD,
when I shall bring you into the land of Israel,
into the country *for* the which I lifted up
mine hand to give it to your fathers.
43 And there shall ye remember your ways,
and all your doings, wherein ye have been
defiled; and ye shall lothe yourselves in
your own sight for all your evils that ye have
committed.
44 And ye shall know that I *am* the LORD,
when I have wrought with you for my
name's sake, not according to your wicked
ways, nor according to your corrupt doings,
O ye house of Israel, saith the Lord GOD.
45 ¶ Moreover the word of the LORD came
unto me, saying,
46 Son of man, set thy face toward the
south, and drop *thy word* toward the south,
and prophesy against the forest of the
south field;
47 And say to the forest of the south, Hear
the word of the LORD; Thus saith the Lord
GOD; Behold, I will kindle a fire in thee, and
it shall devour every green tree in thee, and
every dry tree: the flaming flame shall not
be quenched, and all faces from the south
to the north shall be burned therein.
48 And all flesh shall see that I the LORD
have kindled it: it shall not be quenched.
49 Then said I, Ah Lord GOD! they say of me,
Doth he not speak parables?

Ezekiel 21

1 And the word of the LORD came unto
me, saying,
2 Son of man, set thy face toward Jerusalem,
and drop *thy word* toward the holy places,
and prophesy against the land of Israel,
3 And say to the land of Israel, Thus saith
the LORD; Behold, I *am* against thee, and
will draw forth my sword out of his sheath,
and will cut off from thee the righteous and
the wicked.
4 Seeing then that I will cut off from thee the
righteous and the wicked, therefore shall my
sword go forth out of his sheath against all
flesh from the south to the north:
5 That all flesh may know that I the LORD
have drawn forth my sword out of his
sheath: it shall not return any more.
6 Sigh therefore, thou son of man, with the
breaking of *thy* loins; and with bitterness
sigh before their eyes.
7 And it shall be, when they say unto thee,
Wherefore sighest thou? that thou shalt
answer, For the tidings; because it cometh:
and every heart shall melt, and all hands
shall be feeble, and every spirit shall faint,
and all knees shall be weak *as* water: behold,
it cometh, and shall be brought to pass, saith
the Lord GOD.
8 ¶ Again the word of the LORD came unto
me, saying,
9 Son of man, prophesy, and say, Thus saith
the LORD; Say, A sword, a sword is sharpened, and also furbished:
10 It is sharpened to make a sore slaughter;
it is furbished that it may glitter: should we
then make mirth? it contemneth the rod of
my son, *as* every tree.
11 And he hath given it to be furbished, that
it may be handled: this sword is sharpened,
and it is furbished, to give it into the hand
of the slayer.
12 Cry and howl, son of man: for it shall
be upon my people, it *shall be* upon all
the princes of Israel: terrors by reason of
the sword shall be upon my people: smite
therefore upon *thy* thigh.
13 Because *it is* a trial, and what if *the sword*

contemn even the rod? it shall be no *more*,
saith the Lord GOD.
14 Thou therefore, son of man, prophesy,
and smite *thine* hands together, and let the
sword be doubled the third time, the sword
of the slain: it *is* the sword of the great *men*
that are slain, which entereth into their
privy chambers.
15 I have set the point of the sword against
all their gates, that *their* heart may faint,
and *their* ruins be multiplied: ah! *it is* made
bright, *it is* wrapped up for the slaughter.
16 Go thee one way or other, *either* on the
right hand, *or* on the left, whithersoever
thy face *is* set.
17 I will also smite mine hands together,
and I will cause my fury to rest: I the LORD
have said *it*.
18 ¶ The word of the LORD came unto me
again, saying,
19 Also, thou son of man, appoint thee two
ways, that the sword of the king of Babylon
may come: both twain shall come forth out
of one land: and choose thou a place, choose
it at the head of the way to the city.
20 Appoint a way, that the sword may come
to Rabbath of the Ammonites, and to Judah
in Jerusalem the defenced.
21 For the king of Babylon stood at the
parting of the way, at the head of the two
ways, to use divination: he made *his* arrows
bright, he consulted with images, he looked
in the liver.
22 At his right hand was the divination for
Jerusalem, to appoint captains, to open the
mouth in the slaughter, to lift up the voice
with shouting, to appoint *battering* rams
against the gates, to cast a mount, *and* to
build a fort.
23 And it shall be unto them as a false divination in their sight, to them that have sworn
oaths: but he will call to remembrance the
iniquity, that they may be taken.
24 Therefore thus saith the Lord GOD;
Because ye have made your iniquity to be
remembered, in that your transgressions are
discovered, so that in all your doings your
sins do appear; because, *I say*, that ye are
come to remembrance, ye shall be taken
with the hand.
25 ¶ And thou, profane wicked prince of
Israel, whose day is come, when iniquity
shall have an end,
26 Thus saith the Lord GOD; Remove the
diadem, and take off the crown: this *shall*
not *be* the same: exalt *him that is* low, and
abase *him that is* high.
27 I will overturn, overturn, overturn, it: and
it shall be no *more*, until he come whose
right it is; and I will give it *him*.
28 ¶ And thou, son of man, prophesy and
say, Thus saith the Lord GOD concerning the
Ammonites, and concerning their reproach;
even say thou, The sword, the sword *is*
drawn: for the slaughter *it is* furbished, to
consume because of the glittering:
29 Whiles they see vanity unto thee, whiles
they divine a lie unto thee, to bring thee
upon the necks of *them that are* slain, of
the wicked, whose day is come, when their
iniquity *shall have* an end.
30 Shall I cause *it* to return into his sheath? I
will judge thee in the place where thou wast
created, in the land of thy nativity.
31 And I will pour out mine indignation upon
thee, I will blow against thee in the fire of
my wrath, and deliver thee into the hand of
brutish men, *and* skilful to destroy.
32 Thou shalt be for fuel to the fire; thy
blood shall be in the midst of the land; thou
shalt be no *more* remembered: for I the
LORD have spoken *it*.

Ezekiel 22

1 Moreover the word of the LORD came
unto me, saying,
2 Now, thou son of man, wilt thou judge,
wilt thou judge the bloody city? yea, thou
shalt shew her all her abominations.
3 Then say thou, Thus saith the Lord GOD,
The city sheddeth blood in the midst of it,
that her time may come, and maketh idols
against herself to defile herself.
4 Thou art become guilty in thy blood that
thou hast shed; and hast defiled thyself in
thine idols which thou hast made; and thou
hast caused thy days to draw near, and art
come *even* unto thy years: therefore have
I made thee a reproach unto the heathen,
and a mocking to all countries.
5 *Those that be* near, and *those that be* far
from thee, shall mock thee, *which art* infa-
mous *and* much vexed.
6 Behold, the princes of Israel, every one
were in thee to their power to shed blood.
7 In thee have they set light by father and

mother: in the midst of thee have they
dealt by oppression with the stranger: in
thee have they vexed the fatherless and
the widow.
8 Thou hast despised mine holy things, and
hast profaned my sabbaths.
9 In thee are men that carry tales to shed
blood: and in thee they eat upon the mountains: in the midst of thee they commit
lewdness.
10 In thee have they discovered their
fathers' nakedness: in thee have they humbled her that was set apart for pollution.
11 And one hath committed abomination
with his neighbour's wife; and another
hath lewdly defiled his daughter in law; and
another in thee hath humbled his sister, his
father's daughter.
12 In thee have they taken gifts to shed
blood; thou hast taken usury and increase,
and thou hast greedily gained of thy neighbours by extortion, and hast forgotten me,
saith the Lord GOD.
13 ¶ Behold, therefore I have smitten mine
hand at thy dishonest gain which thou hast
made, and at thy blood which hath been in
the midst of thee.
14 Can thine heart endure, or can thine
hands be strong, in the days that I shall
deal with thee? I the LORD have spoken *it*,
and will do *it*.
15 And I will scatter thee among the heathen, and disperse thee in the countries,
and will consume thy filthiness out of thee.
16 And thou shalt take thine inheritance in
thyself in the sight of the heathen, and thou
shalt know that I *am* the LORD.
17 And the word of the LORD came unto
me, saying,
18 Son of man, the house of Israel is to
me become dross: all they *are* brass, and
tin, and iron, and lead, in the midst of the
furnace; they are *even* the dross of silver.
19 Therefore thus saith the Lord GOD;
Because ye are all become dross, behold,
therefore I will gather you into the midst
of Jerusalem.
20 *As* they gather silver, and brass, and
iron, and lead, and tin, into the midst of the
furnace, to blow the fire upon it, to melt *it;*
so will I gather *you* in mine anger and in my
fury, and I will leave *you there,* and melt you.
21 Yea, I will gather you, and blow upon
you in the fire of my wrath, and ye shall be
melted in the midst thereof.
22 As silver is melted in the midst of the
furnace, so shall ye be melted in the midst
thereof; and ye shall know that I the LORD
have poured out my fury upon you.
23 ¶ And the word of the LORD came unto
me, saying,
24 Son of man, say unto her, Thou *art* the
land that is not cleansed, nor rained upon
in the day of indignation.
25 *There is* a conspiracy of her prophets in
the midst thereof, like a roaring lion ravening the prey; they have devoured souls;
they have taken the treasure and precious
things; they have made her many widows
in the midst thereof.
26 Her priests have violated my law, and
have profaned mine holy things: they have
put no difference between the holy and
profane, neither have they shewed *difference* between the unclean and the clean,
and have hid their eyes from my sabbaths,
and I am profaned among them.
27 Her princes in the midst thereof *are* like
wolves ravening the prey, to shed blood,
and to destroy souls, to get dishonest gain.
28 And her prophets have daubed them
with untempered *morter*, seeing vanity,
and divining lies unto them, saying, Thus
saith the Lord GOD, when the LORD hath
not spoken.
29 The people of the land have used oppression, and exercised robbery, and have
vexed the poor and needy: yea, they have
oppressed the stranger wrongfully.
30 And I sought for a man among them, that
should make up the hedge, and stand in the
gap before me for the land, that I should not
destroy it: but I found none.
31 Therefore have I poured out mine indignation upon them; I have consumed them
with the fire of my wrath: their own way
have I recompensed upon their heads, saith
the Lord GOD.

Ezekiel 23

1 The word of the LORD came again unto
me, saying,
2 Son of man, there were two women, the
daughters of one mother:
3 And they committed whoredoms in Egypt;
they committed whoredoms in their youth:

there were their breasts pressed, and there
they bruised the teats of their virginity.
4 And the names of them *were* Aholah the
elder, and Aholibah her sister: and they were
mine, and they bare sons and daughters.
Thus *were* their names; Samaria *is* Aholah,
and Jerusalem Aholibah.
5 And Aholah played the harlot when she
was mine; and she doted on her lovers, on
the Assyrians *her* neighbours,
6 *Which were* clothed with blue, captains
and rulers, all of them desirable young men,
horsemen riding upon horses.
7 Thus she committed her whoredoms with
them, with all them *that were* the chosen
men of Assyria, and with all on whom she
doted: with all their idols she defiled herself.
8 Neither left she her whoredoms *brought*
from Egypt: for in her youth they lay with
her, and they bruised the breasts of her
virginity, and poured their whoredom
upon her.
9 Wherefore I have delivered her into the
hand of her lovers, into the hand of the
Assyrians, upon whom she doted.
10 These discovered her nakedness: they
took her sons and her daughters, and slew
her with the sword: and she became famous
among women; for they had executed judgment upon her.
11 And when her sister Aholibah saw *this*,
she was more corrupt in her inordinate love
than she, and in her whoredoms more than
her sister in *her* whoredoms.
12 She doted upon the Assyrians *her* neighbours, captains and rulers clothed most
gorgeously, horsemen riding upon horses,
all of them desirable young men.
13 Then I saw that she was defiled, *that* they
took both one way,
14 And *that* she increased her whoredoms:
for when she saw men pourtrayed upon the
wall, the images of the Chaldeans pourtrayed with vermilion,
15 Girded with girdles upon their loins,
exceeding in dyed attire upon their heads,
all of them princes to look to, after the
manner of the Babylonians of Chaldea, the
land of their nativity:
16 And as soon as she saw them with her
eyes, she doted upon them, and sent messengers unto them into Chaldea.
17 And the Babylonians came to her into the
bed of love, and they defiled her with their
whoredom, and she was polluted with them,
and her mind was alienated from them.
18 So she discovered her whoredoms, and
discovered her nakedness: then my mind
was alienated from her, like as my mind was
alienated from her sister.
19 Yet she multiplied her whoredoms, in
calling to remembrance the days of her
youth, wherein she had played the harlot
in the land of Egypt.
20 For she doted upon their paramours,
whose flesh *is as* the flesh of asses, and
whose issue *is like* the issue of horses.
21 Thus thou calledst to remembrance the
lewdness of thy youth, in bruising thy teats
by the Egyptians for the paps of thy youth.
22 ¶ Therefore, O Aholibah, thus saith the
Lord GOD; Behold, I will raise up thy lovers
against thee, from whom thy mind is alienated, and I will bring them against thee on
every side;
23 The Babylonians, and all the Chaldeans,
Pekod, and Shoa, and Koa, *and* all the Assyrians with them: all of them desirable young
men, captains and rulers, great lords and
renowned, all of them riding upon horses.
24 And they shall come against thee with
chariots, wagons, and wheels, and with an
assembly of people, *which* shall set against
thee buckler and shield and helmet round
about: and I will set judgment before them,
and they shall judge thee according to their
judgments.
25 And I will set my jealousy against thee,
and they shall deal furiously with thee: they
shall take away thy nose and thine ears; and
thy remnant shall fall by the sword: they
shall take thy sons and thy daughters; and
thy residue shall be devoured by the fire.
26 They shall also strip thee out of thy
clothes, and take away thy fair jewels.
27 Thus will I make thy lewdness to cease
from thee, and thy whoredom *brought* from
the land of Egypt: so that thou shalt not lift
up thine eyes unto them, nor remember
Egypt any more.
28 For thus saith the Lord GOD; Behold, I will
deliver thee into the hand *of them* whom
thou hatest, into the hand *of them* from
whom thy mind is alienated:
29 And they shall deal with thee hatefully,
and shall take away all thy labour, and shall

leave thee naked and bare: and the nakedness of thy whoredoms shall be discovered, both thy lewdness and thy whoredoms.
30 I will do these *things* unto thee, because thou hast gone a whoring after the heathen, *and* because thou art polluted with their idols.
31 Thou hast walked in the way of thy sister; therefore will I give her cup into thine hand.
32 Thus saith the Lord GOD; Thou shalt drink of thy sister's cup deep and large: thou shalt be laughed to scorn and had in derision; it containeth much.
33 Thou shalt be filled with drunkenness and sorrow, with the cup of astonishment and desolation, with the cup of thy sister Samaria.
34 Thou shalt even drink it and suck *it* out, and thou shalt break the sherds thereof, and pluck off thine own breasts: for I have spoken *it*, saith the Lord GOD.
35 Therefore thus saith the Lord GOD; Because thou hast forgotten me, and cast me behind thy back, therefore bear thou also thy lewdness and thy whoredoms.
36 ¶ The LORD said moreover unto me; Son of man, wilt thou judge Aholah and Aholibah? yea, declare unto them their abominations;
37 That they have committed adultery, and blood *is* in their hands, and with their idols have they committed adultery, and have also caused their sons, whom they bare unto me, to pass for them through *the fire*, to devour *them*.
38 Moreover this they have done unto me: they have defiled my sanctuary in the same day, and have profaned my sabbaths.
39 For when they had slain their children to their idols, then they came the same day into my sanctuary to profane it; and, lo, thus have they done in the midst of mine house.
40 And furthermore, that ye have sent for men to come from far, unto whom a messenger *was* sent; and, lo, they came: for whom thou didst wash thyself, paintedst thy eyes, and deckedst thyself with ornaments,
41 And satest upon a stately bed, and a table prepared before it, whereupon thou hast set mine incense and mine oil.
42 And a voice of a multitude being at ease *was* with her: and with the men of the common sort *were* brought Sabeans from the wilderness, which put bracelets upon their hands, and beautiful crowns upon their heads.
43 Then said I unto *her that was* old in adulteries, Will they now commit whoredoms with her, and she *with them?*
44 Yet they went in unto her, as they go in unto a woman that playeth the harlot: so went they in unto Aholah and unto Aholibah, the lewd women.
45 ¶ And the righteous men, they shall judge them after the manner of adulteresses, and after the manner of women that shed blood; because they *are* adulteresses, and blood *is* in their hands.
46 For thus saith the Lord GOD; I will bring up a company upon them, and will give them to be removed and spoiled.
47 And the company shall stone them with stones, and dispatch them with their swords; they shall slay their sons and their daughters, and burn up their houses with fire.
48 Thus will I cause lewdness to cease out of the land, that all women may be taught not to do after your lewdness.
49 And they shall recompense your lewdness upon you, and ye shall bear the sins of your idols: and ye shall know that I *am* the Lord GOD.

Ezekiel 24

1 Again in the ninth year, in the tenth month, in the tenth *day* of the month, the word of the LORD came unto me, saying,
2 Son of man, write thee the name of the day, *even* of this same day: the king of Babylon set himself against Jerusalem this same day.
3 And utter a parable unto the rebellious house, and say unto them, Thus saith the Lord GOD; Set on a pot, set *it* on, and also pour water into it:
4 Gather the pieces thereof into it, *even* every good piece, the thigh, and the shoulder; fill *it* with the choice bones.
5 Take the choice of the flock, and burn also the bones under it, *and* make it boil well, and let them seethe the bones of it therein.
6 ¶ Wherefore thus saith the Lord GOD; Woe to the bloody city, to the pot whose scum *is* therein, and whose scum is not gone out

of it! bring it out piece by piece; let no lot
fall upon it.
7 For her blood is in the midst of her; she
set it upon the top of a rock; she poured it
not upon the ground, to cover it with dust;
8 That it might cause fury to come up to take
vengeance; I have set her blood upon the
top of a rock, that it should not be covered.
9 Therefore thus saith the Lord GOD; Woe
to the bloody city! I will even make the pile
for fire great.
10 Heap on wood, kindle the fire, consume
the flesh, and spice it well, and let the bones
be burned.
11 Then set it empty upon the coals thereof,
that the brass of it may be hot, and may
burn, and *that* the filthiness of it may be
molten in it, *that* the scum of it may be
consumed.
12 She hath wearied *herself* with lies, and
her great scum went not forth out of her:
her scum *shall be* in the fire.
13 In thy filthiness *is* lewdness: because
I have purged thee, and thou wast not
purged, thou shalt not be purged from thy
filthiness any more, till I have caused my
fury to rest upon thee.
14 I the LORD have spoken *it:* it shall come
to pass, and I will do *it;* I will not go back,
neither will I spare, neither will I repent;
according to thy ways, and according to
thy doings, shall they judge thee, saith the
Lord GOD.
15 ¶ Also the word of the LORD came unto
me, saying,
16 Son of man, behold, I take away from
thee the desire of thine eyes with a stroke:
yet neither shalt thou mourn nor weep,
neither shall thy tears run down.
17 Forbear to cry, make no mourning for
the dead, bind the tire of thine head upon
thee, and put on thy shoes upon thy feet,
and cover not *thy* lips, and eat not the
bread of men.
18 So I spake unto the people in the morning: and at even my wife died; and I did in
the morning as I was commanded.
19 ¶ And the people said unto me, Wilt thou
not tell us what these *things are* to us, that
thou doest *so?*
20 Then I answered them, The word of the
LORD came unto me, saying,
21 Speak unto the house of Israel, Thus saith
the Lord GOD; Behold, I will profane my
sanctuary, the excellency of your strength,
the desire of your eyes, and that which
your soul pitieth; and your sons and your
daughters whom ye have left shall fall by
the sword.
22 And ye shall do as I have done: ye shall
not cover *your* lips, nor eat the bread of
men.
23 And your tires *shall be* upon your heads,
and your shoes upon your feet: ye shall not
mourn nor weep; but ye shall pine away
for your iniquities, and mourn one toward
another.
24 Thus Ezekiel is unto you a sign: according to all that he hath done shall ye do: and
when this cometh, ye shall know that I *am*
the Lord GOD.
25 Also, thou son of man, *shall it* not *be*
in the day when I take from them their
strength, the joy of their glory, the desire
of their eyes, and that whereupon they set
their minds, their sons and their daughters,
26 *That* he that escapeth in that day shall
come unto thee, to cause *thee* to hear *it*
with *thine* ears?
27 In that day shall thy mouth be opened to
him which is escaped, and thou shalt speak,
and be no more dumb: and thou shalt be
a sign unto them; and they shall know that
I *am* the LORD.

Ezekiel 25

1 The word of the LORD came again unto
me, saying,
2 Son of man, set thy face against the
Ammonites, and prophesy against them;
3 And say unto the Ammonites, Hear the
word of the Lord GOD; Thus saith the Lord
GOD; Because thou saidst, Aha, against
my sanctuary, when it was profaned; and
against the land of Israel, when it was desolate; and against the house of Judah, when
they went into captivity;
4 Behold, therefore I will deliver thee to the
men of the east for a possession, and they
shall set their palaces in thee, and make
their dwellings in thee: they shall eat thy
fruit, and they shall drink thy milk.
5 And I will make Rabbah a stable for camels, and the Ammonites a couchingplace for
flocks: and ye shall know that I *am* the LORD.
6 For thus saith the Lord GOD; Because thou

hast clapped *thine* hands, and stamped with
the feet, and rejoiced in heart with all thy
despite against the land of Israel;
7 Behold, therefore I will stretch out mine
hand upon thee, and will deliver thee for a
spoil to the heathen; and I will cut thee off
from the people, and I will cause thee to perish out of the countries: I will destroy thee;
and thou shalt know that I *am* the LORD.
8 ¶ Thus saith the Lord GOD; Because that
Moab and Seir do say, Behold, the house of
Judah *is* like unto all the heathen;
9 Therefore, behold, I will open the side of
Moab from the cities, from his cities *which
are* on his frontiers, the glory of the country,
Beth-jeshimoth, Baal-meon, and Kiriathaim,
10 Unto the men of the east with the Ammonites, and will give them in possession, that
the Ammonites may not be remembered
among the nations.
11 And I will execute judgments upon Moab;
and they shall know that I *am* the LORD.
12 ¶ Thus saith the Lord GOD; Because
that Edom hath dealt against the house of
Judah by taking vengeance, and hath greatly
offended, and revenged himself upon them;
13 Therefore thus saith the Lord GOD; I will
also stretch out mine hand upon Edom, and
will cut off man and beast from it; and I will
make it desolate from Teman; and they of
Dedan shall fall by the sword.
14 And I will lay my vengeance upon Edom
by the hand of my people Israel: and they
shall do in Edom according to mine anger
and according to my fury; and they shall
know my vengeance, saith the Lord GOD.
15 ¶ Thus saith the Lord GOD; Because the
Philistines have dealt by revenge, and have
taken vengeance with a despiteful heart, to
destroy *it* for the old hatred;
16 Therefore thus saith the Lord GOD;
Behold, I will stretch out mine hand upon
the Philistines, and I will cut off the Chere-
thims, and destroy the remnant of the sea
coast.
17 And I will execute great vengeance upon
them with furious rebukes; and they shall
know that I *am* the LORD, when I shall lay
my vengeance upon them.

Ezekiel 26

1 And it came to pass in the eleventh year,
in the first *day* of the month, *that* the word
of the LORD came unto me, saying,
2 Son of man, because that Tyrus hath said
against Jerusalem, Aha, she is broken *that
was* the gates of the people: she is turned
unto me: I shall be replenished, *now* she is
laid waste:
3 Therefore thus saith the Lord GOD; Behold,
I *am* against thee, O Tyrus, and will cause
many nations to come up against thee, as
the sea causeth his waves to come up.
4 And they shall destroy the walls of Tyrus,
and break down her towers: I will also scrape
her dust from her, and make her like the
top of a rock.
5 It shall be *a place for* the spreading of nets
in the midst of the sea: for I have spoken *it*,
saith the Lord GOD: and it shall become a
spoil to the nations.
6 And her daughters which *are* in the field
shall be slain by the sword; and they shall
know that I *am* the LORD.
7 ¶ For thus saith the Lord GOD; Behold,
I will bring upon Tyrus Nebuchadrezzar
king of Babylon, a king of kings, from the
north, with horses, and with chariots, and
with horsemen, and companies, and much
people.
8 He shall slay with the sword thy daughters
in the field: and he shall make a fort against
thee, and cast a mount against thee, and lift
up the buckler against thee.
9 And he shall set engines of war against
thy walls, and with his axes he shall break
down thy towers.
10 By reason of the abundance of his horses
their dust shall cover thee: thy walls shall
shake at the noise of the horsemen, and of
the wheels, and of the chariots, when he
shall enter into thy gates, as men enter into
a city wherein is made a breach.
11 With the hoofs of his horses shall he tread
down all thy streets: he shall slay thy people
by the sword, and thy strong garrisons shall
go down to the ground.
12 And they shall make a spoil of thy riches,
and make a prey of thy merchandise: and
they shall break down thy walls, and destroy
thy pleasant houses: and they shall lay thy
stones and thy timber and thy dust in the
midst of the water.
13 And I will cause the noise of thy songs

Elias truly shall first come, and restore all
things.
12 But I say unto you, That Elias is come
already, and they knew him not, but have
done unto him whatsoever they listed.
Likewise shall also the Son of man suffer
of them.
13 Then the disciples understood that he
spake unto them of John the Baptist.
14 ¶ And when they were come to the multitude, there came to him a *certain* man,
kneeling down to him, and saying,
15 Lord, have mercy on my son: for he is
lunatick, and sore vexed: for ofttimes he
falleth into the fire, and oft into the water.
16 And I brought him to thy disciples, and
they could not cure him.
17 Then Jesus answered and said, O faithless
and perverse generation, how long shall I be
with you? how long shall I suffer you? bring
him hither to me.
18 And Jesus rebuked the devil; and he
departed out of him: and the child was cured
from that very hour.
19 Then came the disciples to Jesus apart,
and said, Why could not we cast him out?
20 And Jesus said unto them, Because of
your unbelief: for verily I say unto you, If
ye have faith as a grain of mustard seed,
ye shall say unto this mountain, Remove
hence to yonder place; and it shall remove;
and nothing shall be impossible unto you.
21 Howbeit this kind goeth not out but by
prayer and fasting.
22 ¶ And while they abode in Galilee, Jesus
said unto them, The Son of man shall be
betrayed into the hands of men:
23 And they shall kill him, and the third day
he shall be raised again. And they were
exceeding sorry.
24 ¶ And when they were come to Capernaum, they that received tribute *money*
came to Peter, and said, Doth not your
master pay tribute?
25 He saith, Yes. And when he was come
into the house, Jesus prevented him, saying,
What thinkest thou, Simon? of whom do the
kings of the earth take custom or tribute? of
their own children, or of strangers?
26 Peter saith unto him, Of strangers. Jesus
saith unto him, Then are the children free.
27 Notwithstanding, lest we should offend
them, go thou to the sea, and cast an hook,
and take up the fish that first cometh up;
and when thou hast opened his mouth, thou
shalt find a piece of money: that take, and
give unto them for me and thee.

Matthew 18

1 At the same time came the disciples unto
Jesus, saying, Who is the greatest in the
kingdom of heaven?
2 And Jesus called a little child unto him,
and set him in the midst of them,
3 And said, Verily I say unto you, Except
ye be converted, and become as little children, ye shall not enter into the kingdom
of heaven.
4 Whosoever therefore shall humble himself
as this little child, the same is greatest in the
kingdom of heaven.
5 And whoso shall receive one such little
child in my name receiveth me.
6 But whoso shall offend one of these little
ones which believe in me, it were better for
him that a millstone were hanged about
his neck, and *that* he were drowned in the
depth of the sea.
7 ¶ Woe unto the world because of offences!
for it must needs be that offences come;
but woe to that man by whom the offence
cometh!
8 Wherefore if thy hand or thy foot offend
thee, cut them off, and cast *them* from thee:
it is better for thee to enter into life halt or
maimed, rather than having two hands or
two feet to be cast into everlasting fire.
9 And if thine eye offend thee, pluck it out,
and cast *it* from thee: it is better for thee
to enter into life with one eye, rather than
having two eyes to be cast into hell fire.
10 Take heed that ye despise not one of
these little ones; for I say unto you, That in
heaven their angels do always behold the
face of my Father which is in heaven.
11 For the Son of man is come to save that
which was lost.
12 How think ye? if a man have an hundred
sheep, and one of them be gone astray, doth
he not leave the ninety and nine, and goeth
into the mountains, and seeketh that which
is gone astray?
13 And if so be that he find it, verily I say
unto you, he rejoiceth more of that *sheep*,
than of the ninety and nine which went
not astray.

14 Even so it is not the will of your Father which is in heaven, that one of these little ones should perish.

15 ¶ Moreover if thy brother shall trespass against thee, go and tell him his fault between thee and him alone: if he shall hear thee, thou hast gained thy brother.

16 But if he will not hear *thee, then* take with thee one or two more, that in the mouth of two or three witnesses every word may be established.

17 And if he shall neglect to hear them, tell *it* unto the church: but if he neglect to hear the church, let him be unto thee as an heathen man and a publican.

18 Verily I say unto you, Whatsoever ye shall bind on earth shall be bound in heaven: and whatsoever ye shall loose on earth shall be loosed in heaven.

19 Again I say unto you, That if two of you shall agree on earth as touching any thing that they shall ask, it shall be done for them of my Father which is in heaven.

20 For where two or three are gathered together in my name, there am I in the midst of them.

21 ¶ Then came Peter to him, and said, Lord, how oft shall my brother sin against me, and I forgive him? till seven times?

22 Jesus saith unto him, I say not unto thee, Until seven times: but, Until seventy times seven.

23 ¶ Therefore is the kingdom of heaven likened unto a certain king, which would take account of his servants.

24 And when he had begun to reckon, one was brought unto him, which owed him ten thousand talents.

25 But forasmuch as he had not to pay, his lord commanded him to be sold, and his wife, and children, and all that he had, and payment to be made.

26 The servant therefore fell down, and worshipped him, saying, Lord, have patience with me, and I will pay thee all.

27 Then the lord of that servant was moved with compassion, and loosed him, and forgave him the debt.

28 But the same servant went out, and found one of his fellowservants, which owed him an hundred pence: and he laid hands on him, and took *him* by the throat, saying, Pay me that thou owest.

29 And his fellowservant fell down at his feet, and besought him, saying, Have patience with me, and I will pay thee all.

30 And he would not: but went and cast him into prison, till he should pay the debt.

31 So when his fellowservants saw what was done, they were very sorry, and came and told unto their lord all that was done.

32 Then his lord, after that he had called him, said unto him, O thou wicked servant, I forgave thee all that debt, because thou desiredst me:

33 Shouldest not thou also have had compassion on thy fellowservant, even as I had pity on thee?

34 And his lord was wroth, and delivered him to the tormentors, till he should pay all that was due unto him.

35 So likewise shall my heavenly Father do also unto you, if ye from your hearts forgive not every one his brother their trespasses.

Matthew 19

1 And it came to pass, *that* when Jesus had finished these sayings, he departed from Galilee, and came into the coasts of Judæa beyond Jordan;

2 And great multitudes followed him; and he healed them there.

3 ¶ The Pharisees also came unto him, tempting him, and saying unto him, Is it lawful for a man to put away his wife for every cause?

4 And he answered and said unto them, Have ye not read, that he which made *them* at the beginning made them male and female,

5 And said, For this cause shall a man leave father and mother, and shall cleave to his wife: and they twain shall be one flesh?

6 Wherefore they are no more twain, but one flesh. What therefore God hath joined together, let not man put asunder.

7 They say unto him, Why did Moses then command to give a writing of divorcement, and to put her away?

8 He saith unto them, Moses because of the hardness of your hearts suffered you to put away your wives: but from the beginning it was not so.

9 And I say unto you, Whosoever shall put away his wife, except *it be* for fornication, and shall marry another, committeth adul-

tery: and whoso marrieth her which is put
away doth commit adultery.
10 ¶ His disciples say unto him, If the case
of the man be so with *his* wife, it is not
good to marry.
11 But he said unto them, All *men* cannot
receive this saying, save *they* to whom it
is given.
12 For there are some eunuchs, which were
so born from *their* mother's womb: and
there are some eunuchs, which were made
eunuchs of men: and there be eunuchs,
which have made themselves eunuchs for
the kingdom of heaven's sake. He that is
able to receive *it*, let him receive *it*.
13 ¶ Then were there brought unto him little
children, that he should put *his* hands on
them, and pray: and the disciples rebuked
them.
14 But Jesus said, Suffer little children, and
forbid them not, to come unto me: for of
such is the kingdom of heaven.
15 And he laid *his* hands on them, and
departed thence.
16 ¶ And, behold, one came and said unto
him, Good Master, what good thing shall I
do, that I may have eternal life?
17 And he said unto him, Why callest thou
me good? *there is* none good but one, *that
is*, God: but if thou wilt enter into life, keep
the commandments.
18 He saith unto him, Which? Jesus said,
Thou shalt do no murder, Thou shalt not
commit adultery, Thou shalt not steal, Thou
shalt not bear false witness,
19 Honour thy father and *thy* mother: and,
Thou shalt love thy neighbour as thyself.
20 The young man saith unto him, All these
things have I kept from my youth up: what
lack I yet?
21 Jesus said unto him, If thou wilt be perfect, go *and* sell that thou hast, and give to
the poor, and thou shalt have treasure in
heaven: and come *and* follow me.
22 But when the young man heard that
saying, he went away sorrowful: for he had
great possessions.
23 ¶ Then said Jesus unto his disciples, Verily
I say unto you, That a rich man shall hardly
enter into the kingdom of heaven.
24 And again I say unto you, It is easier for
a camel to go through the eye of a needle,
than for a rich man to enter into the kingdom of God.
25 When his disciples heard *it*, they were
exceedingly amazed, saying, Who then can
be saved?
26 But Jesus beheld *them*, and said unto
them, With men this is impossible; but with
God all things are possible.
27 ¶ Then answered Peter and said unto
him, Behold, we have forsaken all, and followed thee; what shall we have therefore?
28 And Jesus said unto them, Verily I say
unto you, That ye which have followed me,
in the regeneration when the Son of man
shall sit in the throne of his glory, ye also
shall sit upon twelve thrones, judging the
twelve tribes of Israel.
29 And every one that hath forsaken houses,
or brethren, or sisters, or father, or mother,
or wife, or children, or lands, for my name's
sake, shall receive an hundredfold, and shall
inherit everlasting life.
30 But many *that are* first shall be last; and
the last *shall be* first.

Matthew 20

1 For the kingdom of heaven is like unto a
man *that is* an householder, which went
out early in the morning to hire labourers
into his vineyard.
2 And when he had agreed with the labourers for a penny a day, he sent them into his
vineyard.
3 And he went out about the third hour, and
saw others standing idle in the marketplace,
4 And said unto them; Go ye also into the
vineyard, and whatsoever is right I will give
you. And they went their way.
5 Again he went out about the sixth and
ninth hour, and did likewise.
6 And about the eleventh hour he went
out, and found others standing idle, and
saith unto them, Why stand ye here all the
day idle?
7 They say unto him, Because no man hath
hired us. He saith unto them, Go ye also into
the vineyard; and whatsoever is right, *that*
shall ye receive.
8 So when even was come, the lord of the
vineyard saith unto his steward, Call the
labourers, and give them *their* hire, beginning from the last unto the first.
9 And when they came that *were hired*

about the eleventh hour, they received
every man a penny.
10 But when the first came, they supposed
that they should have received more; and
they likewise received every man a penny.
11 And when they had received *it*, they murmured against the goodman of the house,
12 Saying, These last have wrought *but* one
hour, and thou hast made them equal unto
us, which have borne the burden and heat
of the day.
13 But he answered one of them, and said,
Friend, I do thee no wrong: didst not thou
agree with me for a penny?
14 Take *that* thine *is*, and go thy way: I will
give unto this last, even as unto thee.
15 Is it not lawful for me to do what I will
with mine own? Is thine eye evil, because
I am good?
16 So the last shall be first, and the first last:
for many be called, but few chosen.
17 ¶ And Jesus going up to Jerusalem took
the twelve disciples apart in the way, and
said unto them,
18 Behold, we go up to Jerusalem; and the
Son of man shall be betrayed unto the chief
priests and unto the scribes, and they shall
condemn him to death,
19 And shall deliver him to the Gentiles to
mock, and to scourge, and to crucify *him:*
and the third day he shall rise again.
20 ¶ Then came to him the mother of Zebedee's children with her sons, worshipping
him, and desiring a certain thing of him.
21 And he said unto her, What wilt thou?
She saith unto him, Grant that these my two
sons may sit, the one on thy right hand, and
the other on the left, in thy kingdom.
22 But Jesus answered and said, Ye know
not what ye ask. Are ye able to drink of the
cup that I shall drink of, and to be baptized
with the baptism that I am baptized with?
They say unto him, We are able.
23 And he saith unto them, Ye shall drink
indeed of my cup, and be baptized with the
baptism that I am baptized with: but to sit on
my right hand, and on my left, is not mine to
give, but *it shall be given to them* for whom
it is prepared of my Father.
24 And when the ten heard *it*, they were
moved with indignation against the two
brethren.
25 But Jesus called them *unto him*, and said,
Ye know that the princes of the Gentiles
exercise dominion over them, and they that
are great exercise authority upon them.
26 But it shall not be so among you: but
whosoever will be great among you, let him
be your minister;
27 And whosoever will be chief among you,
let him be your servant:
28 Even as the Son of man came not to be
ministered unto, but to minister, and to give
his life a ransom for many.
29 And as they departed from Jericho, a
great multitude followed him.
30 ¶ And, behold, two blind men sitting by
the way side, when they heard that Jesus
passed by, cried out, saying, Have mercy on
us, O Lord, *thou* Son of David.
31 And the multitude rebuked them,
because they should hold their peace: but
they cried the more, saying, Have mercy on
us, O Lord, *thou* Son of David.
32 And Jesus stood still, and called them,
and said, What will ye that I shall do unto
you?
33 They say unto him, Lord, that our eyes
may be opened.
34 So Jesus had compassion *on them*, and
touched their eyes: and immediately their
eyes received sight, and they followed him.

Matthew 21

1 And when they drew nigh unto Jerusalem, and were come to Bethphage, unto
the mount of Olives, then sent Jesus two
disciples,
2 Saying unto them, Go into the village over
against you, and straightway ye shall find an
ass tied, and a colt with her: loose *them*, and
bring *them* unto me.
3 And if any *man* say ought unto you, ye
shall say, The Lord hath need of them; and
straightway he will send them.
4 All this was done, that it might be fulfilled
which was spoken by the prophet, saying,
5 Tell ye the daughter of Sion, Behold, thy
King cometh unto thee, meek, and sitting
upon an ass, and a colt the foal of an ass.
6 And the disciples went, and did as Jesus
commanded them,
7 And brought the ass, and the colt, and
put on them their clothes, and they set
him thereon.
8 And a very great multitude spread their

garments in the way; others cut down
branches from the trees, and strawed *them*
in the way.
9 And the multitudes that went before,
and that followed, cried, saying, Hosanna
to the Son of David: Blessed *is* he that
cometh in the name of the Lord; Hosanna
in the highest.
10 And when he was come into Jerusalem,
all the city was moved, saying, Who is this?
11 And the multitude said, This is Jesus the
prophet of Nazareth of Galilee.
12 ¶ And Jesus went into the temple of God,
and cast out all them that sold and bought
in the temple, and overthrew the tables of
the moneychangers, and the seats of them
that sold doves,
13 And said unto them, It is written, My
house shall be called the house of prayer;
but ye have made it a den of thieves.
14 And the blind and the lame came to him
in the temple; and he healed them.
15 And when the chief priests and scribes
saw the wonderful things that he did, and
the children crying in the temple, and saying, Hosanna to the Son of David; they were
sore displeased,
16 And said unto him, Hearest thou what
these say? And Jesus saith unto them, Yea;
have ye never read, Out of the mouth of
babes and sucklings thou hast perfected
praise?
17 ¶ And he left them, and went out of the
city into Bethany; and he lodged there.
18 Now in the morning as he returned into
the city, he hungered.
19 And when he saw a fig tree in the way,
he came to it, and found nothing thereon,
but leaves only, and said unto it, Let no fruit
grow on thee henceforward for ever. And
presently the fig tree withered away.
20 And when the disciples saw *it*, they
marvelled, saying, How soon is the fig tree
withered away!
21 Jesus answered and said unto them,
Verily I say unto you, If ye have faith, and
doubt not, ye shall not only do this *which is*
done to the fig tree, but also if ye shall say
unto this mountain, Be thou removed, and
be thou cast into the sea; it shall be done.
22 And all things, whatsoever ye shall ask in
prayer, believing, ye shall receive.
23 ¶ And when he was come into the temple, the chief priests and the elders of the
people came unto him as he was teaching,
and said, By what authority doest thou these
things? and who gave thee this authority?
24 And Jesus answered and said unto them,
I also will ask you one thing, which if ye
tell me, I in like wise will tell you by what
authority I do these things.
25 The baptism of John, whence was it?
from heaven, or of men? And they reasoned
with themselves, saying, If we shall say,
From heaven; he will say unto us, Why did
ye not then believe him?
26 But if we shall say, Of men; we fear the
people; for all hold John as a prophet.
27 And they answered Jesus, and said, We
cannot tell. And he said unto them, Neither
tell I you by what authority I do these things.
28 ¶ But what think ye? A *certain* man had
two sons; and he came to the first, and said,
Son, go work to day in my vineyard.
29 He answered and said, I will not: but
afterward he repented, and went.
30 And he came to the second, and said
likewise. And he answered and said, I *go*,
sir: and went not.
31 Whether of them twain did the will of *his*
father? They say unto him, The first. Jesus
saith unto them, Verily I say unto you, That
the publicans and the harlots go into the
kingdom of God before you.
32 For John came unto you in the way of
righteousness, and ye believed him not:
but the publicans and the harlots believed
him: and ye, when ye had seen *it*, repented
not afterward, that ye might believe him.
33 ¶ Hear another parable: There was
a certain householder, which planted a
vineyard, and hedged it round about, and
digged a winepress in it, and built a tower,
and let it out to husbandmen, and went into
a far country:
34 And when the time of the fruit drew near,
he sent his servants to the husbandmen,
that they might receive the fruits of it.
35 And the husbandmen took his servants,
and beat one, and killed another, and stoned
another.
36 Again, he sent other servants more than
the first: and they did unto them likewise.
37 But last of all he sent unto them his son,
saying, They will reverence my son.
38 But when the husbandmen saw the son,

they said among themselves, This is the heir;
come, let us kill him, and let us seize on his
inheritance.
39 And they caught him, and cast *him* out
of the vineyard, and slew *him*.
40 When the lord therefore of the vineyard cometh, what will he do unto those
husbandmen?
41 They say unto him, He will miserably
destroy those wicked men, and will let out
his vineyard unto other husbandmen, which
shall render him the fruits in their seasons.
42 Jesus saith unto them, Did ye never
read in the scriptures, The stone which the
builders rejected, the same is become the
head of the corner: this is the Lord's doing,
and it is marvellous in our eyes?
43 Therefore say I unto you, The kingdom
of God shall be taken from you, and given
to a nation bringing forth the fruits thereof.
44 And whosoever shall fall on this stone
shall be broken: but on whomsoever it shall
fall, it will grind him to powder.
45 And when the chief priests and Pharisees
had heard his parables, they perceived that
he spake of them.
46 But when they sought to lay hands on
him, they feared the multitude, because
they took him for a prophet.

Matthew 22

1 And Jesus answered and spake unto them
again by parables, and said,
2 The kingdom of heaven is like unto a certain king, which made a marriage for his son,
3 And sent forth his servants to call them
that were bidden to the wedding: and they
would not come.
4 Again, he sent forth other servants, saying, Tell them which are bidden, Behold, I
have prepared my dinner: my oxen and *my*
fatlings *are* killed, and all things *are* ready:
come unto the marriage.
5 But they made light of *it*, and went their
ways, one to his farm, another to his merchandise:
6 And the remnant took his servants, and
entreated *them* spitefully, and slew *them*.
7 But when the king heard *thereof*, he was
wroth: and he sent forth his armies, and
destroyed those murderers, and burned
up their city.
8 Then saith he to his servants, The wedding
is ready, but they which were bidden were
not worthy.
9 Go ye therefore into the highways, and as
many as ye shall find, bid to the marriage.
10 So those servants went out into the
highways, and gathered together all as many
as they found, both bad and good: and the
wedding was furnished with guests.
11 ¶ And when the king came in to see the
guests, he saw there a man which had not
on a wedding garment:
12 And he saith unto him, Friend, how
camest thou in hither not having a wedding
garment? And he was speechless.
13 Then said the king to the servants, Bind
him hand and foot, and take him away, and
cast *him* into outer darkness; there shall be
weeping and gnashing of teeth.
14 For many are called, but few *are* chosen.
15 ¶ Then went the Pharisees, and took
counsel how they might entangle him in
his talk.
16 And they sent out unto him their disciples with the Herodians, saying, Master, we
know that thou art true, and teachest the
way of God in truth, neither carest thou
for any *man:* for thou regardest not the
person of men.
17 Tell us therefore, What thinkest thou? Is
it lawful to give tribute unto Cæsar, or not?
18 But Jesus perceived their wickedness,
and said, Why tempt ye me, *ye* hypocrites?
19 Shew me the tribute money. And they
brought unto him a penny.
20 And he saith unto them, Whose *is* this
image and superscription?
21 They say unto him, Cæsar's. Then saith
he unto them, Render therefore unto Cæsar
the things which are Cæsar's; and unto God
the things that are God's.
22 When they had heard *these words*, they
marvelled, and left him, and went their way.
23 ¶ The same day came to him the Sadducees, which say that there is no resurrection,
and asked him,
24 Saying, Master, Moses said, If a man die,
having no children, his brother shall marry
his wife, and raise up seed unto his brother.
25 Now there were with us seven brethren:
and the first, when he had married a wife,
deceased, and, having no issue, left his wife
unto his brother:

26 Likewise the second also, and the third, unto the seventh.
27 And last of all the woman died also.
28 Therefore in the resurrection whose wife shall she be of the seven? for they all had her.
29 Jesus answered and said unto them, Ye do err, not knowing the scriptures, nor the power of God.
30 For in the resurrection they neither marry, nor are given in marriage, but are as the angels of God in heaven.
31 But as touching the resurrection of the dead, have ye not read that which was spoken unto you by God, saying,
32 I am the God of Abraham, and the God of Isaac, and the God of Jacob? God is not the God of the dead, but of the living.
33 And when the multitude heard *this*, they were astonished at his doctrine.
34 ¶ But when the Pharisees had heard that he had put the Sadducees to silence, they were gathered together.
35 Then one of them, *which was* a lawyer, asked *him a question*, tempting him, and saying,
36 Master, which *is* the great commandment in the law?
37 Jesus said unto him, Thou shalt love the Lord thy God with all thy heart, and with all thy soul, and with all thy mind.
38 This is the first and great commandment.
39 And the second *is* like unto it, Thou shalt love thy neighbour as thyself.
40 On these two commandments hang all the law and the prophets.
41 ¶ While the Pharisees were gathered together, Jesus asked them,
42 Saying, What think ye of Christ? whose son is he? They say unto him, *The Son* of David.
43 He saith unto them, How then doth David in spirit call him Lord, saying,
44 The LORD said unto my Lord, Sit thou on my right hand, till I make thine enemies thy footstool?
45 If David then call him Lord, how is he his son?
46 And no man was able to answer him a word, neither durst any *man* from that day forth ask him any more *questions*.

Matthew 23

1 Then spake Jesus to the multitude, and to his disciples,
2 Saying, The scribes and the Pharisees sit in Moses' seat:
3 All therefore whatsoever they bid you observe, *that* observe and do; but do not ye after their works: for they say, and do not.
4 For they bind heavy burdens and grievous to be borne, and lay *them* on men's shoulders; but they *themselves* will not move them with one of their fingers.
5 But all their works they do for to be seen of men: they make broad their phylacteries, and enlarge the borders of their garments,
6 And love the uppermost rooms at feasts, and the chief seats in the synagogues,
7 And greetings in the markets, and to be called of men, Rabbi, Rabbi.
8 But be not ye called Rabbi: for one is your Master, *even* Christ; and all ye are brethren.
9 And call no *man* your father upon the earth: for one is your Father, which is in heaven.
10 Neither be ye called masters: for one is your Master, *even* Christ.
11 But he that is greatest among you shall be your servant.
12 And whosoever shall exalt himself shall be abased; and he that shall humble himself shall be exalted.
13 ¶ But woe unto you, scribes and Pharisees, hypocrites! for ye shut up the kingdom of heaven against men: for ye neither go in *yourselves*, neither suffer ye them that are entering to go in.
14 Woe unto you, scribes and Pharisees, hypocrites! for ye devour widows' houses, and for a pretence make long prayer: therefore ye shall receive the greater damnation.
15 Woe unto you, scribes and Pharisees, hypocrites! for ye compass sea and land to make one proselyte, and when he is made, ye make him twofold more the child of hell than yourselves.
16 Woe unto you, *ye* blind guides, which say, Whosoever shall swear by the temple, it is nothing; but whosoever shall swear by the gold of the temple, he is a debtor!
17 *Ye* fools and blind: for whether is greater, the gold, or the temple that sanctifieth the gold?
18 And, Whosoever shall swear by the altar,

it is nothing; but whosoever sweareth by the
gift that is upon it, he is guilty.
19 *Ye* fools and blind: for whether *is* greater,
the gift, or the altar that sanctifieth the gift?
20 Whoso therefore shall swear by the altar,
sweareth by it, and by all things thereon.
21 And whoso shall swear by the temple,
sweareth by it, and by him that dwelleth
therein.
22 And he that shall swear by heaven,
sweareth by the throne of God, and by him
that sitteth thereon.
23 Woe unto you, scribes and Pharisees,
hypocrites! for ye pay tithe of mint and
anise and cummin, and have omitted the
weightier *matters* of the law, judgment,
mercy, and faith: these ought ye to have
done, and not to leave the other undone.
24 *Ye* blind guides, which strain at a gnat,
and swallow a camel.
25 Woe unto you, scribes and Pharisees,
hypocrites! for ye make clean the outside
of the cup and of the platter, but within they
are full of extortion and excess.
26 *Thou* blind Pharisee, cleanse first that
which is within the cup and platter, that the
outside of them may be clean also.
27 Woe unto you, scribes and Pharisees,
hypocrites! for ye are like unto whited
sepulchres, which indeed appear beautiful
outward, but are within full of dead *men's*
bones, and of all uncleanness.
28 Even so ye also outwardly appear righteous unto men, but within ye are full of
hypocrisy and iniquity.
29 Woe unto you, scribes and Pharisees,
hypocrites! because ye build the tombs of
the prophets, and garnish the sepulchres
of the righteous,
30 And say, If we had been in the days of our
fathers, we would not have been partakers
with them in the blood of the prophets.
31 Wherefore ye be witnesses unto yourselves, that ye are the children of them
which killed the prophets.
32 Fill ye up then the measure of your
fathers.
33 *Ye* serpents, *ye* generation of vipers,
how can ye escape the damnation of hell?
34 ¶ Wherefore, behold, I send unto you
prophets, and wise men, and scribes: and
some of them ye shall kill and crucify; and
some of them shall ye scourge in your synagogues, and persecute *them* from city
to city:
35 That upon you may come all the righteous blood shed upon the earth, from the
blood of righteous Abel unto the blood of
Zacharias son of Barachias, whom ye slew
between the temple and the altar.
36 Verily I say unto you, All these things shall
come upon this generation.
37 O Jerusalem, Jerusalem, *thou* that killest
the prophets, and stonest them which are
sent unto thee, how often would I have
gathered thy children together, even as a
hen gathereth her chickens under *her* wings,
and ye would not!
38 Behold, your house is left unto you
desolate.
39 For I say unto you, Ye shall not see me
henceforth, till ye shall say, Blessed *is* he that
cometh in the name of the Lord.

Matthew 24

1 And Jesus went out, and departed from
the temple: and his disciples came to *him*
for to shew him the buildings of the temple.
2 And Jesus said unto them, See ye not all
these things? verily I say unto you, There
shall not be left here one stone upon
another, that shall not be thrown down.
3 ¶ And as he sat upon the mount of Olives,
the disciples came unto him privately, saying, Tell us, when shall these things be? and
what *shall be* the sign of thy coming, and of
the end of the world?
4 And Jesus answered and said unto them,
Take heed that no man deceive you.
5 For many shall come in my name, saying,
I am Christ; and shall deceive many.
6 And ye shall hear of wars and rumours
of wars: see that ye be not troubled: for
all *these things* must come to pass, but the
end is not yet.
7 For nation shall rise against nation, and
kingdom against kingdom: and there shall be
famines, and pestilences, and earthquakes,
in divers places.
8 All these *are* the beginning of sorrows.
9 Then shall they deliver you up to be
afflicted, and shall kill you: and ye shall be
hated of all nations for my name's sake.
10 And then shall many be offended, and
shall betray one another, and shall hate
one another.

11 And many false prophets shall rise, and
shall deceive many.
12 And because iniquity shall abound, the
love of many shall wax cold.
13 But he that shall endure unto the end,
the same shall be saved.
14 And this gospel of the kingdom shall be
preached in all the world for a witness unto
all nations; and then shall the end come.
15 When ye therefore shall see the abomination of desolation, spoken of by Daniel
the prophet, stand in the holy place, (whoso
readeth, let him understand:)
16 Then let them which be in Judæa flee
into the mountains:
17 Let him which is on the housetop not
come down to take any thing out of his
house:
18 Neither let him which is in the field return
back to take his clothes.
19 And woe unto them that are with child,
and to them that give suck in those days!
20 But pray ye that your flight be not in the
winter, neither on the sabbath day:
21 For then shall be great tribulation, such
as was not since the beginning of the world
to this time, no, nor ever shall be.
22 And except those days should be shortened, there should no flesh be saved: but
for the elect's sake those days shall be
shortened.
23 Then if any man shall say unto you, Lo,
here *is* Christ, or there; believe *it* not.
24 For there shall arise false Christs, and
false prophets, and shall shew great signs
and wonders; insomuch that, if *it were*
possible, they shall deceive the very elect.
25 Behold, I have told you before.
26 Wherefore if they shall say unto you,
Behold, he is in the desert; go not forth:
behold, *he is* in the secret chambers; believe
it not.
27 For as the lightning cometh out of the
east, and shineth even unto the west; so
shall also the coming of the Son of man be.
28 For wheresoever the carcase is, there will
the eagles be gathered together.
29 ¶ Immediately after the tribulation of
those days shall the sun be darkened, and
the moon shall not give her light, and the
stars shall fall from heaven, and the powers
of the heavens shall be shaken:
30 And then shall appear the sign of the
Son of man in heaven: and then shall all the
tribes of the earth mourn, and they shall
see the Son of man coming in the clouds of
heaven with power and great glory.
31 And he shall send his angels with a great
sound of a trumpet, and they shall gather
together his elect from the four winds, from
one end of heaven to the other.
32 Now learn a parable of the fig tree; When
his branch is yet tender, and putteth forth
leaves, ye know that summer *is* nigh:
33 So likewise ye, when ye shall see all
these things, know that it is near, *even* at
the doors.
34 Verily I say unto you, This generation
shall not pass, till all these things be fulfilled.
35 Heaven and earth shall pass away, but
my words shall not pass away.
36 ¶ But of that day and hour knoweth no
man, no, not the angels of heaven, but my
Father only.
37 But as the days of Noe *were*, so shall also
the coming of the Son of man be.
38 For as in the days that were before the
flood they were eating and drinking, marrying and giving in marriage, until the day
that Noe entered into the ark,
39 And knew not until the flood came, and
took them all away; so shall also the coming
of the Son of man be.
40 Then shall two be in the field; the one
shall be taken, and the other left.
41 Two *women shall be* grinding at the mill;
the one shall be taken, and the other left.
42 ¶ Watch therefore: for ye know not what
hour your Lord doth come.
43 But know this, that if the goodman of
the house had known in what watch the
thief would come, he would have watched,
and would not have suffered his house to
be broken up.
44 Therefore be ye also ready: for in such an
hour as ye think not the Son of man cometh.
45 Who then is a faithful and wise servant, whom his lord hath made ruler over
his household, to give them meat in due
season?
46 Blessed *is* that servant, whom his lord
when he cometh shall find so doing.
47 Verily I say unto you, That he shall make
him ruler over all his goods.
48 But and if that evil servant shall say in his
heart, My lord delayeth his coming;

49 And shall begin to smite *his* fellowservants, and to eat and drink with the drunken;

50 The lord of that servant shall come in a day when he looketh not for *him*, and in an hour that he is not aware of,

51 And shall cut him asunder, and appoint *him* his portion with the hypocrites: there shall be weeping and gnashing of teeth.

Matthew 25

1 Then shall the kingdom of heaven be likened unto ten virgins, which took their lamps, and went forth to meet the bridegroom.

2 And five of them were wise, and five *were* foolish.

3 They that *were* foolish took their lamps, and took no oil with them:

4 But the wise took oil in their vessels with their lamps.

5 While the bridegroom tarried, they all slumbered and slept.

6 And at midnight there was a cry made, Behold, the bridegroom cometh; go ye out to meet him.

7 Then all those virgins arose, and trimmed their lamps.

8 And the foolish said unto the wise, Give us of your oil; for our lamps are gone out.

9 But the wise answered, saying, *Not so;* lest there be not enough for us and you: but go ye rather to them that sell, and buy for yourselves.

10 And while they went to buy, the bridegroom came; and they that were ready went in with him to the marriage: and the door was shut.

11 Afterward came also the other virgins, saying, Lord, Lord, open to us.

12 But he answered and said, Verily I say unto you, I know you not.

13 Watch therefore, for ye know neither the day nor the hour wherein the Son of man cometh.

14 ¶ For *the kingdom of heaven is* as a man travelling into a far country, *who* called his own servants, and delivered unto them his goods.

15 And unto one he gave five talents, to another two, and to another one; to every man according to his several ability; and straightway took his journey.

16 Then he that had received the five talents went and traded with the same, and made *them* other five talents.

17 And likewise he that *had received* two, he also gained other two.

18 But he that had received one went and digged in the earth, and hid his lord's money.

19 After a long time the lord of those servants cometh, and reckoneth with them.

20 And so he that had received five talents came and brought other five talents, saying, Lord, thou deliveredst unto me five talents: behold, I have gained beside them five talents more.

21 His lord said unto him, Well done, *thou* good and faithful servant: thou hast been faithful over a few things, I will make thee ruler over many things: enter thou into the joy of thy lord.

22 He also that had received two talents came and said, Lord, thou deliveredst unto me two talents: behold, I have gained two other talents beside them.

23 His lord said unto him, Well done, good and faithful servant; thou hast been faithful over a few things, I will make thee ruler over many things: enter thou into the joy of thy lord.

24 Then he which had received the one talent came and said, Lord, I knew thee that thou art an hard man, reaping where thou hast not sown, and gathering where thou hast not strawed:

25 And I was afraid, and went and hid thy talent in the earth: lo, *there* thou hast *that is* thine.

26 His lord answered and said unto him, *Thou* wicked and slothful servant, thou knewest that I reap where I sowed not, and gather where I have not strawed:

27 Thou oughtest therefore to have put my money to the exchangers, and *then* at my coming I should have received mine own with usury.

28 Take therefore the talent from him, and give *it* unto him which hath ten talents.

29 For unto every one that hath shall be given, and he shall have abundance: but from him that hath not shall be taken away even that which he hath.

30 And cast ye the unprofitable servant into outer darkness: there shall be weeping and gnashing of teeth.

31 ¶ When the Son of man shall come in his

glory, and all the holy angels with him, then
shall he sit upon the throne of his glory:
32 And before him shall be gathered all
nations: and he shall separate them one
from another, as a shepherd divideth *his*
sheep from the goats:
33 And he shall set the sheep on his right
hand, but the goats on the left.
34 Then shall the King say unto them on his
right hand, Come, ye blessed of my Father,
inherit the kingdom prepared for you from
the foundation of the world:
35 For I was an hungred, and ye gave me
meat: I was thirsty, and ye gave me drink: I
was a stranger, and ye took me in:
36 Naked, and ye clothed me: I was sick,
and ye visited me: I was in prison, and ye
came unto me.
37 Then shall the righteous answer him,
saying, Lord, when saw we thee an hungred,
and fed *thee?* or thirsty, and gave *thee* drink?
38 When saw we thee a stranger, and took
thee in? or naked, and clothed *thee?*
39 Or when saw we thee sick, or in prison,
and came unto thee?
40 And the King shall answer and say unto
them, Verily I say unto you, Inasmuch as ye
have done *it* unto one of the least of these
my brethren, ye have done *it* unto me.
41 Then shall he say also unto them on the
left hand, Depart from me, ye cursed, into
everlasting fire, prepared for the devil and
his angels:
42 For I was an hungred, and ye gave me no
meat: I was thirsty, and ye gave me no drink:
43 I was a stranger, and ye took me not in:
naked, and ye clothed me not: sick, and in
prison, and ye visited me not.
44 Then shall they also answer him, saying,
Lord, when saw we thee an hungred, or
athirst, or a stranger, or naked, or sick, or
in prison, and did not minister unto thee?
45 Then shall he answer them, saying, Verily
I say unto you, Inasmuch as ye did *it* not to
one of the least of these, ye did *it* not to me.
46 And these shall go away into everlasting punishment: but the righteous into life
eternal.

Matthew 26

1 And it came to pass, when Jesus had
finished all these sayings, he said unto his
disciples,
2 Ye know that after two days is *the feast of*
the passover, and the Son of man is betrayed
to be crucified.
3 Then assembled together the chief priests,
and the scribes, and the elders of the people, unto the palace of the high priest, who
was called Caiaphas,
4 And consulted that they might take Jesus
by subtilty, and kill *him*.
5 But they said, Not on the feast *day*, lest
there be an uproar among the people.
6 ¶ Now when Jesus was in Bethany, in the
house of Simon the leper,
7 There came unto him a woman having an
alabaster box of very precious ointment,
and poured it on his head, as he sat *at meat*.
8 But when his disciples saw *it*, they had
indignation, saying, To what purpose *is*
this waste?
9 For this ointment might have been sold
for much, and given to the poor.
10 When Jesus understood *it*, he said unto
them, Why trouble ye the woman? for she
hath wrought a good work upon me.
11 For ye have the poor always with you;
but me ye have not always.
12 For in that she hath poured this ointment
on my body, she did *it* for my burial.
13 Verily I say unto you, Wheresoever this
gospel shall be preached in the whole world,
there shall also this, that this woman hath
done, be told for a memorial of her.
14 ¶ Then one of the twelve, called Judas
Iscariot, went unto the chief priests,
15 And said *unto them*, What will ye give
me, and I will deliver him unto you? And
they covenanted with him for thirty pieces
of silver.
16 And from that time he sought opportunity to betray him.
17 ¶ Now the first *day* of the *feast of* unleavened bread the disciples came to Jesus,
saying unto him, Where wilt thou that we
prepare for thee to eat the passover?
18 And he said, Go into the city to such a
man, and say unto him, The Master saith,
My time is at hand; I will keep the passover
at thy house with my disciples.
19 And the disciples did as Jesus had
appointed them; and they made ready the
passover.
20 Now when the even was come, he sat
down with the twelve.

21 And as they did eat, he said, Verily I say unto you, that one of you shall betray me.
22 And they were exceeding sorrowful, and began every one of them to say unto him, Lord, is it I?
23 And he answered and said, He that dippeth *his* hand with me in the dish, the same shall betray me.
24 The Son of man goeth as it is written of him: but woe unto that man by whom the Son of man is betrayed! it had been good for that man if he had not been born.
25 Then Judas, which betrayed him, answered and said, Master, is it I? He said unto him, Thou hast said.
26 ¶ And as they were eating, Jesus took bread, and blessed *it*, and brake *it*, and gave *it* to the disciples, and said, Take, eat; this is my body.
27 And he took the cup, and gave thanks, and gave *it* to them, saying, Drink ye all of it;
28 For this is my blood of the new testament, which is shed for many for the remission of sins.
29 But I say unto you, I will not drink henceforth of this fruit of the vine, until that day when I drink it new with you in my Father's kingdom.
30 And when they had sung an hymn, they went out into the mount of Olives.
31 Then saith Jesus unto them, All ye shall be offended because of me this night: for it is written, I will smite the shepherd, and the sheep of the flock shall be scattered abroad.
32 But after I am risen again, I will go before you into Galilee.
33 Peter answered and said unto him, Though all *men* shall be offended because of thee, *yet* will I never be offended.
34 Jesus said unto him, Verily I say unto thee, That this night, before the cock crow, thou shalt deny me thrice.
35 Peter said unto him, Though I should die with thee, yet will I not deny thee. Likewise also said all the disciples.
36 ¶ Then cometh Jesus with them unto a place called Gethsemane, and saith unto the disciples, Sit ye here, while I go and pray yonder.
37 And he took with him Peter and the two sons of Zebedee, and began to be sorrowful and very heavy.
38 Then saith he unto them, My soul is exceeding sorrowful, even unto death: tarry ye here, and watch with me.
39 And he went a little further, and fell on his face, and prayed, saying, O my Father, if it be possible, let this cup pass from me: nevertheless not as I will, but as thou *wilt*.
40 And he cometh unto the disciples, and findeth them asleep, and saith unto Peter, What, could ye not watch with me one hour?
41 Watch and pray, that ye enter not into temptation: the spirit indeed *is* willing, but the flesh *is* weak.
42 He went away again the second time, and prayed, saying, O my Father, if this cup may not pass away from me, except I drink it, thy will be done.
43 And he came and found them asleep again: for their eyes were heavy.
44 And he left them, and went away again, and prayed the third time, saying the same words.
45 Then cometh he to his disciples, and saith unto them, Sleep on now, and take *your* rest: behold, the hour is at hand, and the Son of man is betrayed into the hands of sinners.
46 Rise, let us be going: behold, he is at hand that doth betray me.
47 ¶ And while he yet spake, lo, Judas, one of the twelve, came, and with him a great multitude with swords and staves, from the chief priests and elders of the people.
48 Now he that betrayed him gave them a sign, saying, Whomsoever I shall kiss, that same is he: hold him fast.
49 And forthwith he came to Jesus, and said, Hail, master; and kissed him.
50 And Jesus said unto him, Friend, wherefore art thou come? Then came they, and laid hands on Jesus, and took him.
51 And, behold, one of them which were with Jesus stretched out *his* hand, and drew his sword, and struck a servant of the high priest's, and smote off his ear.
52 Then said Jesus unto him, Put up again thy sword into his place: for all they that take the sword shall perish with the sword.
53 Thinkest thou that I cannot now pray to my Father, and he shall presently give me more than twelve legions of angels?
54 But how then shall the scriptures be fulfilled, that thus it must be?
55 In that same hour said Jesus to the multitudes, Are ye come out as against a thief

with swords and staves for to take me? I sat
daily with you teaching in the temple, and
ye laid no hold on me.
56 But all this was done, that the scriptures
of the prophets might be fulfilled. Then all
the disciples forsook him, and fled.
57 ¶ And they that had laid hold on Jesus led
him away to Caiaphas the high priest, where
the scribes and the elders were assembled.
58 But Peter followed him afar off unto the
high priest's palace, and went in, and sat
with the servants, to see the end.
59 Now the chief priests, and elders, and
all the council, sought false witness against
Jesus, to put him to death;
60 But found none: yea, though many false
witnesses came, *yet* found they none. At the
last came two false witnesses,
61 And said, This *fellow* said, I am able to
destroy the temple of God, and to build it
in three days.
62 And the high priest arose, and said unto
him, Answerest thou nothing? what *is it*
which these witness against thee?
63 But Jesus held his peace. And the high
priest answered and said unto him, I adjure
thee by the living God, that thou tell us
whether thou be the Christ, the Son of God.
64 Jesus saith unto him, Thou hast said:
nevertheless I say unto you, Hereafter shall
ye see the Son of man sitting on the right
hand of power, and coming in the clouds
of heaven.
65 Then the high priest rent his clothes,
saying, He hath spoken blasphemy; what
further need have we of witnesses? behold,
now ye have heard his blasphemy.
66 What think ye? They answered and said,
He is guilty of death.
67 Then did they spit in his face, and buffeted him; and others smote *him* with the
palms of their hands,
68 Saying, Prophesy unto us, thou Christ,
Who is he that smote thee?
69 ¶ Now Peter sat without in the palace:
and a damsel came unto him, saying, Thou
also wast with Jesus of Galilee.
70 But he denied before *them* all, saying, I
know not what thou sayest.
71 And when he was gone out into the
porch, another *maid* saw him, and said unto
them that were there, This *fellow* was also
with Jesus of Nazareth.
72 And again he denied with an oath, I do
not know the man.
73 And after a while came unto *him* they
that stood by, and said to Peter, Surely
thou also art *one* of them; for thy speech
bewrayeth thee.
74 Then began he to curse and to swear,
saying, I know not the man. And immediately the cock crew.
75 And Peter remembered the word of
Jesus, which said unto him, Before the cock
crow, thou shalt deny me thrice. And he
went out, and wept bitterly.

Matthew 27

1 When the morning was come, all the
chief priests and elders of the people took
counsel against Jesus to put him to death:
2 And when they had bound him, they led
him away, and delivered him to Pontius
Pilate the governor.
3 ¶ Then Judas, which had betrayed him,
when he saw that he was condemned,
repented himself, and brought again the
thirty pieces of silver to the chief priests
and elders,
4 Saying, I have sinned in that I have
betrayed the innocent blood. And they
said, What *is that* to us? see thou *to that*.
5 And he cast down the pieces of silver in
the temple, and departed, and went and
hanged himself.
6 And the chief priests took the silver pieces,
and said, It is not lawful for to put them into
the treasury, because it is the price of blood.
7 And they took counsel, and bought with
them the potter's field, to bury strangers in.
8 Wherefore that field was called, The field
of blood, unto this day.
9 Then was fulfilled that which was spoken
by Jeremy the prophet, saying, And they
took the thirty pieces of silver, the price
of him that was valued, whom they of the
children of Israel did value;
10 And gave them for the potter's field, as
the Lord appointed me.
11 And Jesus stood before the governor:
and the governor asked him, saying, Art
thou the King of the Jews? And Jesus said
unto him, Thou sayest.
12 And when he was accused of the chief
priests and elders, he answered nothing.
13 Then said Pilate unto him, Hearest thou

not how many things they witness against
thee?
14 And he answered him to never a word;
insomuch that the governor marvelled
greatly.
15 Now at *that* feast the governor was wont
to release unto the people a prisoner, whom
they would.
16 And they had then a notable prisoner,
called Barabbas.
17 Therefore when they were gathered
together, Pilate said unto them, Whom
will ye that I release unto you? Barabbas,
or Jesus which is called Christ?
18 For he knew that for envy they had
delivered him.
19 ¶ When he was set down on the judgment seat, his wife sent unto him, saying,
Have thou nothing to do with that just man:
for I have suffered many things this day in a
dream because of him.
20 But the chief priests and elders persuaded the multitude that they should ask
Barabbas, and destroy Jesus.
21 The governor answered and said unto
them, Whether of the twain will ye that
I release unto you? They said, Barabbas.
22 Pilate saith unto them, What shall I do
then with Jesus which is called Christ? *They*
all say unto him, Let him be crucified.
23 And the governor said, Why, what evil
hath he done? But they cried out the more,
saying, Let him be crucified.
24 ¶ When Pilate saw that he could prevail
nothing, but *that* rather a tumult was made,
he took water, and washed *his* hands before
the multitude, saying, I am innocent of the
blood of this just person: see ye *to it*.
25 Then answered all the people, and said,
His blood *be* on us, and on our children.
26 ¶ Then released he Barabbas unto them:
and when he had scourged Jesus, he delivered *him* to be crucified.
27 Then the soldiers of the governor took
Jesus into the common hall, and gathered
unto him the whole band *of soldiers*.
28 And they stripped him, and put on him
a scarlet robe.
29 ¶ And when they had platted a crown
of thorns, they put *it* upon his head, and a
reed in his right hand: and they bowed the
knee before him, and mocked him, saying,
Hail, King of the Jews!
30 And they spit upon him, and took the
reed, and smote him on the head.
31 And after that they had mocked him,
they took the robe off from him, and put
his own raiment on him, and led him away
to crucify *him*.
32 And as they came out, they found a man
of Cyrene, Simon by name: him they compelled to bear his cross.
33 And when they were come unto a place
called Golgotha, that is to say, a place of
a skull,
34 ¶ They gave him vinegar to drink mingled
with gall: and when he had tasted *thereof*,
he would not drink.
35 And they crucified him, and parted his
garments, casting lots: that it might be
fulfilled which was spoken by the prophet,
They parted my garments among them, and
upon my vesture did they cast lots.
36 And sitting down they watched him
there;
37 And set up over his head his accusation
written, THIS IS JESUS THE KING OF THE
JEWS.
38 Then were there two thieves crucified
with him, one on the right hand, and another
on the left.
39 ¶ And they that passed by reviled him,
wagging their heads,
40 And saying, Thou that destroyest the
temple, and buildest *it* in three days, save
thyself. If thou be the Son of God, come
down from the cross.
41 Likewise also the chief priests mocking
him, with the scribes and elders, said,
42 He saved others; himself he cannot
save. If he be the King of Israel, let him
now come down from the cross, and we
will believe him.
43 He trusted in God; let him deliver him
now, if he will have him: for he said, I am
the Son of God.
44 The thieves also, which were crucified
with him, cast the same in his teeth.
45 Now from the sixth hour there was darkness over all the land unto the ninth hour.
46 And about the ninth hour Jesus cried with
a loud voice, saying, Eli, Eli, lama sabach-
thani? that is to say, My God, my God, why
hast thou forsaken me?
47 Some of them that stood there, when

they heard *that*, said, This *man* calleth for Elias.
48 And straightway one of them ran, and took a spunge, and filled *it* with vinegar, and put *it* on a reed, and gave him to drink.
49 The rest said, Let be, let us see whether Elias will come to save him.
50 ¶ Jesus, when he had cried again with a loud voice, yielded up the ghost.
51 And, behold, the veil of the temple was rent in twain from the top to the bottom; and the earth did quake, and the rocks rent;
52 And the graves were opened; and many bodies of the saints which slept arose,
53 And came out of the graves after his resurrection, and went into the holy city, and appeared unto many.
54 Now when the centurion, and they that were with him, watching Jesus, saw the earthquake, and those things that were done, they feared greatly, saying, Truly this was the Son of God.
55 And many women were there beholding afar off, which followed Jesus from Galilee, ministering unto him:
56 Among which was Mary Magdalene, and Mary the mother of James and Joses, and the mother of Zebedee's children.
57 When the even was come, there came a rich man of Arimathæa, named Joseph, who also himself was Jesus' disciple:
58 He went to Pilate, and begged the body of Jesus. Then Pilate commanded the body to be delivered.
59 And when Joseph had taken the body, he wrapped it in a clean linen cloth,
60 And laid it in his own new tomb, which he had hewn out in the rock: and he rolled a great stone to the door of the sepulchre, and departed.
61 And there was Mary Magdalene, and the other Mary, sitting over against the sepulchre.
62 ¶ Now the next day, that followed the day of the preparation, the chief priests and Pharisees came together unto Pilate,
63 Saying, Sir, we remember that that deceiver said, while he was yet alive, After three days I will rise again.
64 Command therefore that the sepulchre be made sure until the third day, lest his disciples come by night, and steal him away, and say unto the people, He is risen from the dead: so the last error shall be worse than the first.
65 Pilate said unto them, Ye have a watch: go your way, make *it* as sure as ye can.
66 So they went, and made the sepulchre sure, sealing the stone, and setting a watch.

Matthew 28

1 In the end of the sabbath, as it began to dawn toward the first *day* of the week, came Mary Magdalene and the other Mary to see the sepulchre.
2 And, behold, there was a great earthquake: for the angel of the Lord descended from heaven, and came and rolled back the stone from the door, and sat upon it.
3 His countenance was like lightning, and his raiment white as snow:
4 And for fear of him the keepers did shake, and became as dead *men*.
5 And the angel answered and said unto the women, Fear not ye: for I know that ye seek Jesus, which was crucified.
6 He is not here: for he is risen, as he said. Come, see the place where the Lord lay.
7 And go quickly, and tell his disciples that he is risen from the dead; and, behold, he goeth before you into Galilee; there shall ye see him: lo, I have told you.
8 And they departed quickly from the sepulchre with fear and great joy; and did run to bring his disciples word.
9 ¶ And as they went to tell his disciples, behold, Jesus met them, saying, All hail. And they came and held him by the feet, and worshipped him.
10 Then said Jesus unto them, Be not afraid: go tell my brethren that they go into Galilee, and there shall they see me.
11 ¶ Now when they were going, behold, some of the watch came into the city, and shewed unto the chief priests all the things that were done.
12 And when they were assembled with the elders, and had taken counsel, they gave large money unto the soldiers,
13 Saying, Say ye, His disciples came by night, and stole him *away* while we slept.
14 And if this come to the governor's ears, we will persuade him, and secure you.
15 So they took the money, and did as they were taught: and this saying is commonly reported among the Jews until this day.

16 ¶ Then the eleven disciples went away
into Galilee, into a mountain where Jesus
had appointed them.
17 And when they saw him, they worshipped
him: but some doubted.
18 And Jesus came and spake unto them,
saying, All power is given unto me in heaven
and in earth.
19 ¶ Go ye therefore, and teach all nations,
baptizing them in the name of the Father,
and of the Son, and of the Holy Spirit:
20 Teaching them to observe all things
whatsoever I have commanded you: and,
lo, I am with you alway, *even* unto the end
of the world. Amen.

The Gospel According To

Mark

Mark 1

1 The beginning of the gospel of Jesus Christ,
the Son of God;
2 As it is written in the prophets, Behold, I
send my messenger before thy face, which
shall prepare thy way before thee.
3 The voice of one crying in the wilderness,
Prepare ye the way of the Lord, make his
paths straight.
4 John did baptize in the wilderness, and
preach the baptism of repentance for the
remission of sins.
5 And there went out unto him all the land
of Judæa, and they of Jerusalem, and were
all baptized of him in the river of Jordan,
confessing their sins.
6 And John was clothed with camel's hair,
and with a girdle of a skin about his loins;
and he did eat locusts and wild honey;
7 And preached, saying, There cometh
one mightier than I after me, the latchet
of whose shoes I am not worthy to stoop
down and unloose.
8 I indeed have baptized you with water:
but he shall baptize you with the Holy Spirit.
9 And it came to pass in those days, that
Jesus came from Nazareth of Galilee, and
was baptized of John in Jordan.
10 And straightway coming up out of the
water, he saw the heavens opened, and
the Spirit like a dove descending upon him:
11 And there came a voice from heaven,
saying, Thou art my beloved Son, in whom
I am well pleased.
12 And immediately the Spirit driveth him
into the wilderness.
13 And he was there in the wilderness forty
days, tempted of Satan; and was with the
wild beasts; and the angels ministered
unto him.
14 Now after that John was put in prison,
Jesus came into Galilee, preaching the gospel of the kingdom of God,
15 And saying, The time is fulfilled, and the
kingdom of God is at hand: repent ye, and
believe the gospel.
16 Now as he walked by the sea of Galilee,
he saw Simon and Andrew his brother casting a net into the sea: for they were fishers.
17 And Jesus said unto them, Come ye after
me, and I will make you to become fishers
of men.
18 And straightway they forsook their nets,
and followed him.
19 And when he had gone a little further
thence, he saw James the *son* of Zebedee,
and John his brother, who also were in the
ship mending their nets.
20 And straightway he called them: and
they left their father Zebedee in the ship
with the hired servants, and went after him.
21 And they went into Capernaum; and
straightway on the sabbath day he entered
into the synagogue, and taught.
22 And they were astonished at his doctrine:
for he taught them as one that had authority, and not as the scribes.
23 And there was in their synagogue a man
with an unclean spirit; and he cried out,
24 Saying, Let *us* alone; what have we to do
with thee, thou Jesus of Nazareth? art thou

come to destroy us? I know thee who thou
art, the Holy One of God.
25 And Jesus rebuked him, saying, Hold thy
peace, and come out of him.
26 And when the unclean spirit had torn
him, and cried with a loud voice, he came
out of him.
27 And they were all amazed, insomuch that
they questioned among themselves, saying,
What thing is this? what new doctrine *is* this?
for with authority commandeth he even
the unclean spirits, and they do obey him.
28 And immediately his fame spread abroad
throughout all the region round about
Galilee.
29 And forthwith, when they were come
out of the synagogue, they entered into the
house of Simon and Andrew, with James
and John.
30 But Simon's wife's mother lay sick of a
fever, and anon they tell him of her.
31 And he came and took her by the hand,
and lifted her up; and immediately the fever
left her, and she ministered unto them.
32 And at even, when the sun did set, they
brought unto him all that were diseased,
and them that were possessed with devils.
33 And all the city was gathered together
at the door.
34 And he healed many that were sick of divers diseases, and cast out many devils; and
suffered not the devils to speak, because
they knew him.
35 And in the morning, rising up a great
while before day, he went out, and departed
into a solitary place, and there prayed.
36 And Simon and they that were with him
followed after him.
37 And when they had found him, they said
unto him, All *men* seek for thee.
38 And he said unto them, Let us go into the
next towns, that I may preach there also: for
therefore came I forth.
39 And he preached in their synagogues
throughout all Galilee, and cast out devils.
40 And there came a leper to him, beseeching him, and kneeling down to him, and
saying unto him, If thou wilt, thou canst
make me clean.
41 And Jesus, moved with compassion, put
forth *his* hand, and touched him, and saith
unto him, I will; be thou clean.
42 And as soon as he had spoken, immediately the leprosy departed from him, and
he was cleansed.
43 And he straitly charged him, and forthwith sent him away;
44 And saith unto him, See thou say nothing
to any man: but go thy way, shew thyself to
the priest, and offer for thy cleansing those
things which Moses commanded, for a testimony unto them.
45 But he went out, and began to publish
it much, and to blaze abroad the matter,
insomuch that Jesus could no more openly
enter into the city, but was without in
desert places: and they came to him from
every quarter.

Mark 2

1 And again he entered into Capernaum,
after *some* days; and it was noised that he
was in the house.
2 And straightway many were gathered
together, insomuch that there was no
room to receive *them*, no, not so much as
about the door: and he preached the word
unto them.
3 And they come unto him, bringing one
sick of the palsy, which was borne of four.
4 And when they could not come nigh unto
him for the press, they uncovered the roof
where he was: and when they had broken
it up, they let down the bed wherein the
sick of the palsy lay.
5 When Jesus saw their faith, he said unto
the sick of the palsy, Son, thy sins be forgiven thee.
6 But there were certain of the scribes sitting
there, and reasoning in their hearts,
7 Why doth this *man* thus speak blasphemies? who can forgive sins but God only?
8 And immediately when Jesus perceived
in his spirit that they so reasoned within
themselves, he said unto them, Why reason
ye these things in your hearts?
9 Whether is it easier to say to the sick of
the palsy, *Thy* sins be forgiven thee; or to
say, Arise, and take up thy bed, and walk?
10 But that ye may know that the Son of
man hath power on earth to forgive sins,
(he saith to the sick of the palsy,)
11 I say unto thee, Arise, and take up thy
bed, and go thy way into thine house.
12 And immediately he arose, took up
the bed, and went forth before them all;

insomuch that they were all amazed, and
glorified God, saying, We never saw it on
this fashion.
13 And he went forth again by the sea side;
and all the multitude resorted unto him, and
he taught them.
14 And as he passed by, he saw Levi the *son*
of Alphæus sitting at the receipt of custom,
and said unto him, Follow me. And he arose
and followed him.
15 And it came to pass, that, as Jesus sat
at meat in his house, many publicans and
sinners sat also together with Jesus and his
disciples: for there were many, and they
followed him.
16 And when the scribes and Pharisees saw
him eat with publicans and sinners, they said
unto his disciples, How is it that he eateth
and drinketh with publicans and sinners?
17 When Jesus heard *it*, he saith unto them,
They that are whole have no need of the
physician, but they that are sick: I came
not to call the righteous, but sinners to
repentance.
18 And the disciples of John and of the
Pharisees used to fast: and they come and
say unto him, Why do the disciples of John
and of the Pharisees fast, but thy disciples
fast not?
19 And Jesus said unto them, Can the
children of the bridechamber fast, while
the bridegroom is with them? as long as
they have the bridegroom with them, they
cannot fast.
20 But the days will come, when the bridegroom shall be taken away from them, and
then shall they fast in those days.
21 No man also seweth a piece of new cloth
on an old garment: else the new piece that
filled it up taketh away from the old, and
the rent is made worse.
22 And no man putteth new wine into old
bottles: else the new wine doth burst the
bottles, and the wine is spilled, and the
bottles will be marred: but new wine must
be put into new bottles.
23 And it came to pass, that he went through
the corn fields on the sabbath day; and his
disciples began, as they went, to pluck the
ears of corn.
24 And the Pharisees said unto him, Behold,
why do they on the sabbath day that which
is not lawful?
25 And he said unto them, Have ye never
read what David did, when he had need,
and was an hungred, he, and they that
were with him?
26 How he went into the house of God in
the days of Abiathar the high priest, and
did eat the shewbread, which is not lawful
to eat but for the priests, and gave also to
them which were with him?
27 And he said unto them, The sabbath was
made for man, and not man for the sabbath:
28 Therefore the Son of man is Lord also
of the sabbath.

Mark 3

1 And he entered again into the synagogue;
and there was a man there which had a
withered hand.
2 And they watched him, whether he would
heal him on the sabbath day; that they might
accuse him.
3 And he saith unto the man which had the
withered hand, Stand forth.
4 And he saith unto them, Is it lawful to do
good on the sabbath days, or to do evil? to
save life, or to kill? But they held their peace.
5 And when he had looked round about
on them with anger, being grieved for the
hardness of their hearts, he saith unto
the man, Stretch forth thine hand. And he
stretched *it* out: and his hand was restored
whole as the other.
6 And the Pharisees went forth, and straightway took counsel with the Herodians against
him, how they might destroy him.
7 But Jesus withdrew himself with his disciples to the sea: and a great multitude from
Galilee followed him, and from Judæa,
8 And from Jerusalem, and from Idumæa,
and *from* beyond Jordan; and they about
Tyre and Sidon, a great multitude, when
they had heard what great things he did,
came unto him.
9 And he spake to his disciples, that a small
ship should wait on him because of the multitude, lest they should throng him.
10 For he had healed many; insomuch that
they pressed upon him for to touch him, as
many as had plagues.
11 And unclean spirits, when they saw him,
fell down before him, and cried, saying,
Thou art the Son of God.

12 And he straitly charged them that they should not make him known.
13 And he goeth up into a mountain, and calleth *unto him* whom he would: and they came unto him.
14 And he ordained twelve, that they should be with him, and that he might send them forth to preach,
15 And to have power to heal sicknesses, and to cast out devils:
16 And Simon he surnamed Peter;
17 And James the *son* of Zebedee, and John the brother of James; and he surnamed them Boanerges, which is, The sons of thunder:
18 And Andrew, and Philip, and Bartholomew, and Matthew, and Thomas, and James the *son* of Alphæus, and Thaddæus, and Simon the Canaanite,
19 And Judas Iscariot, which also betrayed him: and they went into an house.
20 And the multitude cometh together again, so that they could not so much as eat bread.
21 And when his friends heard *of it*, they went out to lay hold on him: for they said, He is beside himself.
22 ¶ And the scribes which came down from Jerusalem said, He hath Beelzebub, and by the prince of the devils casteth he out devils.
23 And he called them *unto him*, and said unto them in parables, How can Satan cast out Satan?
24 And if a kingdom be divided against itself, that kingdom cannot stand.
25 And if a house be divided against itself, that house cannot stand.
26 And if Satan rise up against himself, and be divided, he cannot stand, but hath an end.
27 No man can enter into a strong man's house, and spoil his goods, except he will first bind the strong man; and then he will spoil his house.
28 Verily I say unto you, All sins shall be forgiven unto the sons of men, and blasphemies wherewith soever they shall blaspheme:
29 But he that shall blaspheme against the Holy Spirit hath never forgiveness, but is in danger of eternal damnation:
30 Because they said, He hath an unclean spirit.
31 ¶ There came then his brethren and his mother, and, standing without, sent unto him, calling him.
32 And the multitude sat about him, and they said unto him, Behold, thy mother and thy brethren without seek for thee.
33 And he answered them, saying, Who is my mother, or my brethren?
34 And he looked round about on them which sat about him, and said, Behold my mother and my brethren!
35 For whosoever shall do the will of God, the same is my brother, and my sister, and mother.

Mark 4

1 And he began again to teach by the sea side: and there was gathered unto him a great multitude, so that he entered into a ship, and sat in the sea; and the whole multitude was by the sea on the land.
2 And he taught them many things by parables, and said unto them in his doctrine,
3 Hearken; Behold, there went out a sower to sow:
4 And it came to pass, as he sowed, some fell by the way side, and the fowls of the air came and devoured it up.
5 And some fell on stony ground, where it had not much earth; and immediately it sprang up, because it had no depth of earth:
6 But when the sun was up, it was scorched; and because it had no root, it withered away.
7 And some fell among thorns, and the thorns grew up, and choked it, and it yielded no fruit.
8 And other fell on good ground, and did yield fruit that sprang up and increased; and brought forth, some thirty, and some sixty, and some an hundred.
9 And he said unto them, He that hath ears to hear, let him hear.
10 And when he was alone, they that were about him with the twelve asked of him the parable.
11 And he said unto them, Unto you it is given to know the mystery of the kingdom of God: but unto them that are without, all *these* things are done in parables:
12 That seeing they may see, and not perceive; and hearing they may hear, and not understand; lest at any time they should

be converted, and *their* sins should be forgiven them.
13 And he said unto them, Know ye not this parable? and how then will ye know all parables?
14 ¶ The sower soweth the word.
15 And these are they by the way side, where the word is sown; but when they have heard, Satan cometh immediately, and taketh away the word that was sown in their hearts.
16 And these are they likewise which are sown on stony ground; who, when they have heard the word, immediately receive it with gladness;
17 And have no root in themselves, and so endure but for a time: afterward, when affliction or persecution ariseth for the word's sake, immediately they are offended.
18 And these are they which are sown among thorns; such as hear the word,
19 And the cares of this world, and the deceitfulness of riches, and the lusts of other things entering in, choke the word, and it becometh unfruitful.
20 And these are they which are sown on good ground; such as hear the word, and receive *it*, and bring forth fruit, some thirtyfold, some sixty, and some an hundred.
21 ¶ And he said unto them, Is a candle brought to be put under a bushel, or under a bed? and not to be set on a candlestick?
22 For there is nothing hid, which shall not be manifested; neither was any thing kept secret, but that it should come abroad.
23 If any man have ears to hear, let him hear.
24 And he said unto them, Take heed what ye hear: with what measure ye mete, it shall be measured to you: and unto you that hear shall more be given.
25 For he that hath, to him shall be given: and he that hath not, from him shall be taken even that which he hath.
26 ¶ And he said, So is the kingdom of God, as if a man should cast seed into the ground;
27 And should sleep, and rise night and day, and the seed should spring and grow up, he knoweth not how.
28 For the earth bringeth forth fruit of herself; first the blade, then the ear, after that the full corn in the ear.
29 But when the fruit is brought forth, immediately he putteth in the sickle, because the harvest is come.
30 ¶ And he said, Whereunto shall we liken the kingdom of God? or with what comparison shall we compare it?
31 *It is* like a grain of mustard seed, which, when it is sown in the earth, is less than all the seeds that be in the earth:
32 But when it is sown, it groweth up, and becometh greater than all herbs, and shooteth out great branches; so that the fowls of the air may lodge under the shadow of it.
33 And with many such parables spake he the word unto them, as they were able to hear *it*.
34 But without a parable spake he not unto them: and when they were alone, he expounded all things to his disciples.
35 And the same day, when the even was come, he saith unto them, Let us pass over unto the other side.
36 And when they had sent away the multitude, they took him even as he was in the ship. And there were also with him other little ships.
37 And there arose a great storm of wind, and the waves beat into the ship, so that it was now full.
38 And he was in the hinder part of the ship, asleep on a pillow: and they awake him, and say unto him, Master, carest thou not that we perish?
39 And he arose, and rebuked the wind, and said unto the sea, Peace, be still. And the wind ceased, and there was a great calm.
40 And he said unto them, Why are ye so fearful? how is it that ye have no faith?
41 And they feared exceedingly, and said one to another, What manner of man is this, that even the wind and the sea obey him?

Mark 5

1 And they came over unto the other side of the sea, into the country of the Gadarenes.
2 And when he was come out of the ship, immediately there met him out of the tombs a man with an unclean spirit,
3 Who had *his* dwelling among the tombs; and no man could bind him, no, not with chains:
4 Because that he had been often bound with fetters and chains, and the chains had been plucked asunder by him, and the

fetters broken in pieces: neither could any
man tame him.
5 And always, night and day, he was in the
mountains, and in the tombs, crying, and
cutting himself with stones.
6 But when he saw Jesus afar off, he ran and
worshipped him,
7 And cried with a loud voice, and said, What
have I to do with thee, Jesus, *thou* Son of
the most high God? I adjure thee by God,
that thou torment me not.
8 For he said unto him, Come out of the
man, *thou* unclean spirit.
9 And he asked him, What *is* thy name? And
he answered, saying, My name *is* Legion:
for we are many.
10 And he besought him much that he would
not send them away out of the country.
11 Now there was there nigh unto the
mountains a great herd of swine feeding.
12 And all the devils besought him, saying,
Send us into the swine, that we may enter
into them.
13 And forthwith Jesus gave them leave. And
the unclean spirits went out, and entered
into the swine: and the herd ran violently
down a steep place into the sea, (they were
about two thousand;) and were choked in
the sea.
14 And they that fed the swine fled, and told
it in the city, and in the country. And they
went out to see what it was that was done.
15 And they come to Jesus, and see him that
was possessed with the devil, and had the
legion, sitting, and clothed, and in his right
mind: and they were afraid.
16 And they that saw *it* told them how it
befell to him that was possessed with the
devil, and *also* concerning the swine.
17 And they began to pray him to depart
out of their coasts.
18 And when he was come into the ship,
he that had been possessed with the devil
prayed him that he might be with him.
19 Howbeit Jesus suffered him not, but saith
unto him, Go home to thy friends, and tell
them how great things the Lord hath done
for thee, and hath had compassion on thee.
20 And he departed, and began to publish in
Decapolis how great things Jesus had done
for him: and all *men* did marvel.
21 And when Jesus was passed over again
by ship unto the other side, much people
gathered unto him: and he was nigh unto
the sea.
22 And, behold, there cometh one of the
rulers of the synagogue, Jairus by name;
and when he saw him, he fell at his feet,
23 And besought him greatly, saying, My
little daughter lieth at the point of death: *I*
pray thee, come and lay thy hands on her,
that she may be healed; and she shall live.
24 And *Jesus* went with him; and much
people followed him, and thronged him.
25 And a certain woman, which had an issue
of blood twelve years,
26 And had suffered many things of many
physicians, and had spent all that she had,
and was nothing bettered, but rather grew
worse,
27 When she had heard of Jesus, came in
the press behind, and touched his garment.
28 For she said, If I may touch but his
clothes, I shall be whole.
29 And straightway the fountain of her
blood was dried up; and she felt in *her* body
that she was healed of that plague.
30 And Jesus, immediately knowing in
himself that virtue had gone out of him,
turned him about in the press, and said,
Who touched my clothes?
31 And his disciples said unto him, Thou
seest the multitude thronging thee, and
sayest thou, Who touched me?
32 And he looked round about to see her
that had done this thing.
33 But the woman fearing and trembling,
knowing what was done in her, came and fell
down before him, and told him all the truth.
34 And he said unto her, Daughter, thy faith
hath made thee whole; go in peace, and be
whole of thy plague.
35 While he yet spake, there came from the
ruler of the synagogue's *house certain* which
said, Thy daughter is dead: why troublest
thou the Master any further?
36 As soon as Jesus heard the word that
was spoken, he saith unto the ruler of the
synagogue, Be not afraid, only believe.
37 And he suffered no man to follow him,
save Peter, and James, and John the brother
of James.
38 And he cometh to the house of the ruler
of the synagogue, and seeth the tumult, and
them that wept and wailed greatly.
39 And when he was come in, he saith unto

them, Why make ye this ado, and weep? the
damsel is not dead, but sleepeth.
40 And they laughed him to scorn. But when
he had put them all out, he taketh the father
and the mother of the damsel, and them
that were with him, and entereth in where
the damsel was lying.
41 And he took the damsel by the hand, and
said unto her, Talitha cumi; which is, being
interpreted, Damsel, I say unto thee, arise.
42 And straightway the damsel arose, and
walked; for she was *of the age* of twelve
years. And they were astonished with a
great astonishment.
43 And he charged them straitly that no
man should know it; and commanded that
something should be given her to eat.

Mark 6

1 And he went out from thence, and came
into his own country; and his disciples follow him.
2 And when the sabbath day was come, he
began to teach in the synagogue: and many
hearing *him* were astonished, saying, From
whence hath this *man* these things? and
what wisdom *is* this which is given unto him,
that even such mighty works are wrought
by his hands?
3 Is not this the carpenter, the son of Mary,
the brother of James, and Joses, and of Juda,
and Simon? and are not his sisters here with
us? And they were offended at him.
4 But Jesus said unto them, A prophet is not
without honour, but in his own country, and
among his own kin, and in his own house.
5 And he could there do no mighty work,
save that he laid his hands upon a few sick
folk, and healed *them*.
6 And he marvelled because of their unbelief. And he went round about the villages,
teaching.
7 ¶ And he called *unto him* the twelve, and
began to send them forth by two and two;
and gave them power over unclean spirits;
8 And commanded them that they should
take nothing for *their* journey, save a staff
only; no scrip, no bread, no money in *their*
purse:
9 But *be* shod with sandals; and not put on
two coats.
10 And he said unto them, In what place
soever ye enter into an house, there abide
till ye depart from that place.
11 And whosoever shall not receive you,
nor hear you, when ye depart thence, shake
off the dust under your feet for a testimony
against them. Verily I say unto you, It shall
be more tolerable for Sodom and Gomorrha
in the day of judgment, than for that city.
12 And they went out, and preached that
men should repent.
13 And they cast out many devils, and
anointed with oil many that were sick, and
healed *them*.
14 And king Herod heard *of him;* (for his
name was spread abroad:) and he said, That
John the Baptist was risen from the dead,
and therefore mighty works do shew forth
themselves in him.
15 Others said, That it is Elias. And others
said, That it is a prophet, or as one of the
prophets.
16 But when Herod heard *thereof*, he said,
It is John, whom I beheaded: he is risen
from the dead.
17 For Herod himself had sent forth and laid
hold upon John, and bound him in prison
for Herodias' sake, his brother Philip's wife:
for he had married her.
18 For John had said unto Herod, It is not
lawful for thee to have thy brother's wife.
19 Therefore Herodias had a quarrel against
him, and would have killed him; but she
could not:
20 For Herod feared John, knowing that he
was a just man and an holy, and observed
him; and when he heard him, he did many
things, and heard him gladly.
21 And when a convenient day was come,
that Herod on his birthday made a supper
to his lords, high captains, and chief *estates*
of Galilee;
22 And when the daughter of the said
Herodias came in, and danced, and pleased
Herod and them that sat with him, the king
said unto the damsel, Ask of me whatsoever
thou wilt, and I will give *it* thee.
23 And he sware unto her, Whatsoever thou
shalt ask of me, I will give *it* thee, unto the
half of my kingdom.
24 And she went forth, and said unto her
mother, What shall I ask? And she said, The
head of John the Baptist.
25 And she came in straightway with haste

unto the king, and asked, saying, I will that
thou give me by and by in a charger the head
of John the Baptist.
26 And the king was exceeding sorry; *yet* for
his oath's sake, and for their sakes which sat
with him, he would not reject her.
27 And immediately the king sent an executioner, and commanded his head to be
brought: and he went and beheaded him
in the prison,
28 And brought his head in a charger, and
gave it to the damsel: and the damsel gave
it to her mother.
29 And when his disciples heard *of it*, they
came and took up his corpse, and laid it in
a tomb.
30 And the apostles gathered themselves
together unto Jesus, and told him all things,
both what they had done, and what they
had taught.
31 And he said unto them, Come ye yourselves apart into a desert place, and rest
a while: for there were many coming and
going, and they had no leisure so much as
to eat.
32 And they departed into a desert place
by ship privately.
33 And the people saw them departing, and
many knew him, and ran afoot thither out
of all cities, and outwent them, and came
together unto him.
34 And Jesus, when he came out, saw much
people, and was moved with compassion
toward them, because they were as sheep
not having a shepherd: and he began to
teach them many things.
35 And when the day was now far spent, his
disciples came unto him, and said, This is a
desert place, and now the time *is* far passed:
36 Send them away, that they may go into
the country round about, and into the villages, and buy themselves bread: for they
have nothing to eat.
37 He answered and said unto them, Give
ye them to eat. And they say unto him, Shall
we go and buy two hundred pennyworth of
bread, and give them to eat?
38 He saith unto them, How many loaves
have ye? go and see. And when they knew,
they say, Five, and two fishes.
39 And he commanded them to make all sit
down by companies upon the green grass.
40 And they sat down in ranks, by hundreds,
and by fifties.
41 And when he had taken the five loaves
and the two fishes, he looked up to heaven,
and blessed, and brake the loaves, and gave
them to his disciples to set before them; and
the two fishes divided he among them all.
42 And they did all eat, and were filled.
43 And they took up twelve baskets full of
the fragments, and of the fishes.
44 And they that did eat of the loaves were
about five thousand men.
45 And straightway he constrained his disciples to get into the ship, and to go to the
other side before unto Bethsaida, while he
sent away the people.
46 And when he had sent them away, he
departed into a mountain to pray.
47 And when even was come, the ship was
in the midst of the sea, and he alone on
the land.
48 And he saw them toiling in rowing; for the
wind was contrary unto them: and about the
fourth watch of the night he cometh unto
them, walking upon the sea, and would have
passed by them.
49 But when they saw him walking upon
the sea, they supposed it had been a spirit,
and cried out:
50 For they all saw him, and were troubled.
And immediately he talked with them, and
saith unto them, Be of good cheer: it is I;
be not afraid.
51 And he went up unto them into the ship;
and the wind ceased: and they were sore
amazed in themselves beyond measure,
and wondered.
52 For they considered not *the miracle* of
the loaves: for their heart was hardened.
53 And when they had passed over, they
came into the land of Gennesaret, and drew
to the shore.
54 And when they were come out of the
ship, straightway they knew him,
55 And ran through that whole region
round about, and began to carry about
in beds those that were sick, where they
heard he was.
56 And whithersoever he entered, into
villages, or cities, or country, they laid the
sick in the streets, and besought him that
they might touch if it were but the border

of his garment: and as many as touched him
were made whole.

Mark 7

1 Then came together unto him the Pharisees, and certain of the scribes, which came
from Jerusalem.
2 And when they saw some of his disciples
eat bread with defiled, that is to say, with
unwashen, hands, they found fault.
3 For the Pharisees, and all the Jews, except
they wash *their* hands oft, eat not, holding
the tradition of the elders.
4 And *when they come* from the market,
except they wash, they eat not. And many
other things there be, which they have
received to hold, *as* the washing of cups, and
pots, brasen vessels, and of tables.
5 Then the Pharisees and scribes asked him,
Why walk not thy disciples according to the
tradition of the elders, but eat bread with
unwashen hands?
6 He answered and said unto them, Well
hath Esaias prophesied of you hypocrites,
as it is written, This people honoureth me
with *their* lips, but their heart is far from me.
7 Howbeit in vain do they worship me,
teaching *for* doctrines the commandments
of men.
8 For laying aside the commandment of
God, ye hold the tradition of men, *as* the
washing of pots and cups: and many other
such like things ye do.
9 And he said unto them, Full well ye reject
the commandment of God, that ye may keep
your own tradition.
10 For Moses said, Honour thy father and
thy mother; and, Whoso curseth father or
mother, let him die the death:
11 But ye say, If a man shall say to his father
or mother, *It is* Corban, that is to say, a gift,
by whatsoever thou mightest be profited
by me; *he shall be free*.
12 And ye suffer him no more to do ought
for his father or his mother;
13 Making the word of God of none effect
through your tradition, which ye have
delivered: and many such like things do ye.
14 ¶ And when he had called all the people
unto him, he said unto them, Hearken unto
me every one *of you*, and understand:
15 There is nothing from without a man,
that entering into him can defile him: but
the things which come out of him, those are
they that defile the man.
16 If any man have ears to hear, let him hear.
17 And when he was entered into the house
from the people, his disciples asked him
concerning the parable.
18 And he saith unto them, Are ye so without understanding also? Do ye not perceive,
that whatsoever thing from without entereth into the man, *it* cannot defile him;
19 Because it entereth not into his heart,
but into the belly, and goeth out into the
draught, purging all meats?
20 And he said, That which cometh out of
the man, that defileth the man.
21 For from within, out of the heart of men,
proceed evil thoughts, adulteries, fornications, murders,
22 Thefts, covetousness, wickedness, deceit,
lasciviousness, an evil eye, blasphemy, pride,
foolishness:
23 All these evil things come from within,
and defile the man.
24 ¶ And from thence he arose, and went
into the borders of Tyre and Sidon, and
entered into an house, and would have no
man know *it:* but he could not be hid.
25 For a *certain* woman, whose young
daughter had an unclean spirit, heard of
him, and came and fell at his feet:
26 The woman was a Greek, a Syropheni-
cian by nation; and she besought him that
he would cast forth the devil out of her
daughter.
27 But Jesus said unto her, Let the children
first be filled: for it is not meet to take the
children's bread, and to cast *it* unto the dogs.
28 And she answered and said unto him,
Yes, Lord: yet the dogs under the table eat
of the children's crumbs.
29 And he said unto her, For this saying
go thy way; the devil is gone out of thy
daughter.
30 And when she was come to her house,
she found the devil gone out, and her daughter laid upon the bed.
31 ¶ And again, departing from the coasts
of Tyre and Sidon, he came unto the sea of
Galilee, through the midst of the coasts of
Decapolis.
32 And they bring unto him one that was
deaf, and had an impediment in his speech;

and they beseech him to put his hand upon
him.
33 And he took him aside from the multitude, and put his fingers into his ears, and
he spit, and touched his tongue;
34 And looking up to heaven, he sighed,
and saith unto him, Ephphatha, that is, Be
opened.
35 And straightway his ears were opened,
and the string of his tongue was loosed, and
he spake plain.
36 And he charged them that they should
tell no man: but the more he charged
them, so much the more a great deal they
published *it;*
37 And were beyond measure astonished,
saying, He hath done all things well: he
maketh both the deaf to hear, and the
dumb to speak.

Mark 8

1 In those days the multitude being very
great, and having nothing to eat, Jesus called
his disciples *unto him*, and saith unto them,
2 I have compassion on the multitude,
because they have now been with me three
days, and have nothing to eat:
3 And if I send them away fasting to their
own houses, they will faint by the way: for
divers of them came from far.
4 And his disciples answered him, From
whence can a man satisfy these *men* with
bread here in the wilderness?
5 And he asked them, How many loaves
have ye? And they said, Seven.
6 And he commanded the people to sit
down on the ground: and he took the seven
loaves, and gave thanks, and brake, and gave
to his disciples to set before *them;* and they
did set *them* before the people.
7 And they had a few small fishes: and he
blessed, and commanded to set them also
before *them*.
8 So they did eat, and were filled: and they
took up of the broken *meat* that was left
seven baskets.
9 And they that had eaten were about four
thousand: and he sent them away.
10 ¶ And straightway he entered into a ship
with his disciples, and came into the parts
of Dalmanutha.
11 And the Pharisees came forth, and began
to question with him, seeking of him a sign
from heaven, tempting him.
12 And he sighed deeply in his spirit, and
saith, Why doth this generation seek after
a sign? verily I say unto you, There shall no
sign be given unto this generation.
13 And he left them, and entering into the
ship again departed to the other side.
14 ¶ Now *the disciples* had forgotten to take
bread, neither had they in the ship with
them more than one loaf.
15 And he charged them, saying, Take heed,
beware of the leaven of the Pharisees, and
of the leaven of Herod.
16 And they reasoned among themselves,
saying, *It is* because we have no bread.
17 And when Jesus knew *it*, he saith unto
them, Why reason ye, because ye have no
bread? perceive ye not yet, neither understand? have ye your heart yet hardened?
18 Having eyes, see ye not? and having ears,
hear ye not? and do ye not remember?
19 When I brake the five loaves among
five thousand, how many baskets full of
fragments took ye up? They say unto him,
Twelve.
20 And when the seven among four thousand, how many baskets full of fragments
took ye up? And they said, Seven.
21 And he said unto them, How is it that ye
do not understand?
22 ¶ And he cometh to Bethsaida; and they
bring a blind man unto him, and besought
him to touch him.
23 And he took the blind man by the hand,
and led him out of the town; and when he
had spit on his eyes, and put his hands upon
him, he asked him if he saw ought.
24 And he looked up, and said, I see men
as trees, walking.
25 After that he put *his* hands again upon
his eyes, and made him look up: and he was
restored, and saw every man clearly.
26 And he sent him away to his house, saying, Neither go into the town, nor tell *it* to
any in the town.
27 ¶ And Jesus went out, and his disciples,
into the towns of Cæsarea Philippi: and by
the way he asked his disciples, saying unto
them, Whom do men say that I am?
28 And they answered, John the Baptist:
but some *say*, Elias; and others, One of the
prophets.

29 And he saith unto them, But whom say
ye that I am? And Peter answereth and saith
unto him, Thou art the Christ.
30 And he charged them that they should
tell no man of him.
31 And he began to teach them, that the
Son of man must suffer many things, and
be rejected of the elders, and *of* the chief
priests, and scribes, and be killed, and after
three days rise again.
32 And he spake that saying openly. And
Peter took him, and began to rebuke him.
33 But when he had turned about and
looked on his disciples, he rebuked Peter,
saying, Get thee behind me, Satan: for thou
savourest not the things that be of God, but
the things that be of men.
34 ¶ And when he had called the people
unto him with his disciples also, he said
unto them, Whosoever will come after me,
let him deny himself, and take up his cross,
and follow me.
35 For whosoever will save his life shall lose
it; but whosoever shall lose his life for my
sake and the gospel's, the same shall save it.
36 For what shall it profit a man, if he shall
gain the whole world, and lose his own soul?
37 Or what shall a man give in exchange
for his soul?
38 Whosoever therefore shall be ashamed
of me and of my words in this adulterous
and sinful generation; of him also shall the
Son of man be ashamed, when he cometh in
the glory of his Father with the holy angels.

Mark 9

1 And he said unto them, Verily I say unto
you, That there be some of them that stand
here, which shall not taste of death, till
they have seen the kingdom of God come
with power.
2 ¶ And after six days Jesus taketh *with*
him Peter, and James, and John, and leadeth them up into an high mountain apart
by themselves: and he was transfigured
before them.
3 And his raiment became shining, exceeding white as snow; so as no fuller on earth
can white them.
4 And there appeared unto them Elias with
Moses: and they were talking with Jesus.
5 And Peter answered and said to Jesus,
Master, it is good for us to be here: and let
us make three tabernacles; one for thee, and
one for Moses, and one for Elias.
6 For he wist not what to say; for they were
sore afraid.
7 And there was a cloud that overshadowed
them: and a voice came out of the cloud,
saying, This is my beloved Son: hear him.
8 And suddenly, when they had looked
round about, they saw no man any more,
save Jesus only with themselves.
9 And as they came down from the mountain, he charged them that they should tell
no man what things they had seen, till the
Son of man were risen from the dead.
10 And they kept that saying with themselves, questioning one with another what
the rising from the dead should mean.
11 ¶ And they asked him, saying, Why say
the scribes that Elias must first come?
12 And he answered and told them, Elias
verily cometh first, and restoreth all things;
and how it is written of the Son of man,
that he must suffer many things, and be
set at nought.
13 But I say unto you, That Elias is indeed
come, and they have done unto him whatsoever they listed, as it is written of him.
14 ¶ And when he came to *his* disciples, he
saw a great multitude about them, and the
scribes questioning with them.
15 And straightway all the people, when
they beheld him, were greatly amazed, and
running to *him* saluted him.
16 And he asked the scribes, What question
ye with them?
17 And one of the multitude answered and
said, Master, I have brought unto thee my
son, which hath a dumb spirit;
18 And wheresoever he taketh him, he
teareth him: and he foameth, and gnasheth
with his teeth, and pineth away: and I spake
to thy disciples that they should cast him
out; and they could not.
19 He answereth him, and saith, O faithless generation, how long shall I be with
you? how long shall I suffer you? bring him
unto me.
20 And they brought him unto him: and
when he saw him, straightway the spirit
tare him; and he fell on the ground, and
wallowed foaming.
21 And he asked his father, How long is it

ago since this came unto him? And he said,
Of a child.
22 And ofttimes it hath cast him into the fire,
and into the waters, to destroy him: but if
thou canst do any thing, have compassion
on us, and help us.
23 Jesus said unto him, If thou canst believe,
all things *are* possible to him that believeth.
24 And straightway the father of the child
cried out, and said with tears, Lord, I believe;
help thou mine unbelief.
25 When Jesus saw that the people came
running together, he rebuked the foul spirit,
saying unto him, *Thou* dumb and deaf spirit,
I charge thee, come out of him, and enter
no more into him.
26 And *the spirit* cried, and rent him sore,
and came out of him: and he was as one
dead; insomuch that many said, He is dead.
27 But Jesus took him by the hand, and lifted
him up; and he arose.
28 And when he was come into the house,
his disciples asked him privately, Why could
not we cast him out?
29 And he said unto them, This kind can
come forth by nothing, but by prayer and
fasting.
30 ¶ And they departed thence, and passed
through Galilee; and he would not that any
man should know *it*.
31 For he taught his disciples, and said
unto them, The Son of man is delivered
into the hands of men, and they shall kill
him; and after that he is killed, he shall rise
the third day.
32 But they understood not that saying, and
were afraid to ask him.
33 ¶ And he came to Capernaum: and
being in the house he asked them, What
was it that ye disputed among yourselves
by the way?
34 But they held their peace: for by the way
they had disputed among themselves, who
should be the greatest.
35 And he sat down, and called the twelve,
and saith unto them, If any man desire to
be first, *the same* shall be last of all, and
servant of all.
36 And he took a child, and set him in the
midst of them: and when he had taken him
in his arms, he said unto them,
37 Whosoever shall receive one of such
children in my name, receiveth me: and
whosoever shall receive me, receiveth not
me, but him that sent me.
38 ¶ And John answered him, saying, Master, we saw one casting out devils in thy
name, and he followeth not us: and we
forbad him, because he followeth not us.
39 But Jesus said, Forbid him not: for there is
no man which shall do a miracle in my name,
that can lightly speak evil of me.
40 For he that is not against us is on our part.
41 For whosoever shall give you a cup of
water to drink in my name, because ye
belong to Christ, verily I say unto you, he
shall not lose his reward.
42 And whosoever shall offend one of *these*
little ones that believe in me, it is better for
him that a millstone were hanged about his
neck, and he were cast into the sea.
43 And if thy hand offend thee, cut it off: it
is better for thee to enter into life maimed,
than having two hands to go into hell, into
the fire that never shall be quenched:
44 Where their worm dieth not, and the fire
is not quenched.
45 And if thy foot offend thee, cut it off: it
is better for thee to enter halt into life, than
having two feet to be cast into hell, into the
fire that never shall be quenched:
46 Where their worm dieth not, and the fire
is not quenched.
47 And if thine eye offend thee, pluck it out:
it is better for thee to enter into the kingdom
of God with one eye, than having two eyes
to be cast into hell fire:
48 Where their worm dieth not, and the fire
is not quenched.
49 For every one shall be salted with fire,
and every sacrifice shall be salted with salt.
50 Salt *is* good: but if the salt have lost his
saltness, wherewith will ye season it? Have
salt in yourselves, and have peace one with
another.

Mark 10

1 And he arose from thence, and cometh
into the coasts of Judæa by the farther
side of Jordan: and the people resort unto
him again; and, as he was wont, he taught
them again.
2 ¶ And the Pharisees came to him, and
asked him, Is it lawful for a man to put away
his wife? tempting him.

3 And he answered and said unto them,
What did Moses command you?
4 And they said, Moses suffered to write a
bill of divorcement, and to put *her* away.
5 And Jesus answered and said unto them,
For the hardness of your heart he wrote
you this precept.
6 But from the beginning of the creation
God made them male and female.
7 For this cause shall a man leave his father
and mother, and cleave to his wife;
8 And they twain shall be one flesh: so then
they are no more twain, but one flesh.
9 What therefore God hath joined together,
let not man put asunder.
10 And in the house his disciples asked him
again of the same *matter*.
11 And he saith unto them, Whosoever
shall put away his wife, and marry another,
committeth adultery against her.
12 And if a woman shall put away her
husband, and be married to another, she
committeth adultery.
13 ¶ And they brought young children to
him, that he should touch them: and *his*
disciples rebuked those that brought *them*.
14 But when Jesus saw *it*, he was much
displeased, and said unto them, Suffer the
little children to come unto me, and forbid
them not: for of such is the kingdom of God.
15 Verily I say unto you, Whosoever shall
not receive the kingdom of God as a little
child, he shall not enter therein.
16 And he took them up in his arms, put *his*
hands upon them, and blessed them.
17 ¶ And when he was gone forth into the
way, there came one running, and kneeled
to him, and asked him, Good Master, what
shall I do that I may inherit eternal life?
18 And Jesus said unto him, Why callest
thou me good? *there is* none good but one,
that is, God.
19 Thou knowest the commandments, Do
not commit adultery, Do not kill, Do not
steal, Do not bear false witness, Defraud
not, Honour thy father and mother.
20 And he answered and said unto him,
Master, all these have I observed from my
youth.
21 Then Jesus beholding him loved him,
and said unto him, One thing thou lackest:
go thy way, sell whatsoever thou hast, and
give to the poor, and thou shalt have treasure in heaven: and come, take up the cross,
and follow me.
22 And he was sad at that saying, and went
away grieved: for he had great possessions.
23 ¶ And Jesus looked round about, and
saith unto his disciples, How hardly shall
they that have riches enter into the kingdom of God!
24 And the disciples were astonished at
his words. But Jesus answereth again, and
saith unto them, Children, how hard is it for
them that trust in riches to enter into the
kingdom of God!
25 It is easier for a camel to go through the
eye of a needle, than for a rich man to enter
into the kingdom of God.
26 And they were astonished out of measure, saying among themselves, Who then
can be saved?
27 And Jesus looking upon them saith, With
men *it is* impossible, but not with God: for
with God all things are possible.
28 ¶ Then Peter began to say unto him, Lo,
we have left all, and have followed thee.
29 And Jesus answered and said, Verily I
say unto you, There is no man that hath left
house, or brethren, or sisters, or father, or
mother, or wife, or children, or lands, for
my sake, and the gospel's,
30 But he shall receive an hundredfold now
in this time, houses, and brethren, and sisters, and mothers, and children, and lands,
with persecutions; and in the world to come
eternal life.
31 But many *that are* first shall be last; and
the last first.
32 ¶ And they were in the way going up to
Jerusalem; and Jesus went before them: and
they were amazed; and as they followed,
they were afraid. And he took again the
twelve, and began to tell them what things
should happen unto him,
33 *Saying*, Behold, we go up to Jerusalem;
and the Son of man shall be delivered unto
the chief priests, and unto the scribes; and
they shall condemn him to death, and shall
deliver him to the Gentiles:
34 And they shall mock him, and shall
scourge him, and shall spit upon him, and
shall kill him: and the third day he shall
rise again.
35 ¶ And James and John, the sons of
Zebedee, come unto him, saying, Master,

we would that thou shouldest do for us
whatsoever we shall desire.
36 And he said unto them, What would ye
that I should do for you?
37 They said unto him, Grant unto us that
we may sit, one on thy right hand, and the
other on thy left hand, in thy glory.
38 But Jesus said unto them, Ye know not
what ye ask: can ye drink of the cup that I
drink of? and be baptized with the baptism
that I am baptized with?
39 And they said unto him, We can. And
Jesus said unto them, Ye shall indeed drink
of the cup that I drink of; and with the
baptism that I am baptized withal shall ye
be baptized:
40 But to sit on my right hand and on my
left hand is not mine to give; but *it shall be
given to them* for whom it is prepared.
41 And when the ten heard *it*, they began to
be much displeased with James and John.
42 But Jesus called them *to him*, and saith
unto them, Ye know that they which are
accounted to rule over the Gentiles exercise
lordship over them; and their great ones
exercise authority upon them.
43 But so shall it not be among you: but
whosoever will be great among you, shall
be your minister:
44 And whosoever of you will be the chiefest, shall be servant of all.
45 For even the Son of man came not to be
ministered unto, but to minister, and to give
his life a ransom for many.
46 ¶ And they came to Jericho: and as he
went out of Jericho with his disciples and a
great number of people, blind Bartimæus,
the son of Timæus, sat by the highway side
begging.
47 And when he heard that it was Jesus
of Nazareth, he began to cry out, and say,
Jesus, *thou* Son of David, have mercy on me.
48 And many charged him that he should
hold his peace: but he cried the more a great
deal, *Thou* Son of David, have mercy on me.
49 And Jesus stood still, and commanded
him to be called. And they call the blind
man, saying unto him, Be of good comfort,
rise; he calleth thee.
50 And he, casting away his garment, rose,
and came to Jesus.
51 And Jesus answered and said unto him,
What wilt thou that I should do unto thee?
The blind man said unto him, Lord, that I
might receive my sight.
52 And Jesus said unto him, Go thy way; thy
faith hath made thee whole. And immediately he received his sight, and followed
Jesus in the way.

Mark 11

1 And when they came nigh to Jerusalem, unto Bethphage and Bethany, at the
mount of Olives, he sendeth forth two of
his disciples,
2 And saith unto them, Go your way into
the village over against you: and as soon
as ye be entered into it, ye shall find a colt
tied, whereon never man sat; loose him,
and bring *him*.
3 And if any man say unto you, Why do ye
this? say ye that the Lord hath need of him;
and straightway he will send him hither.
4 And they went their way, and found the
colt tied by the door without in a place
where two ways met; and they loose him.
5 And certain of them that stood there said
unto them, What do ye, loosing the colt?
6 And they said unto them even as Jesus had
commanded: and they let them go.
7 And they brought the colt to Jesus, and
cast their garments on him; and he sat
upon him.
8 And many spread their garments in the
way: and others cut down branches off the
trees, and strawed *them* in the way.
9 And they that went before, and they that
followed, cried, saying, Hosanna; Blessed
is he that cometh in the name of the Lord:
10 Blessed *be* the kingdom of our father
David, that cometh in the name of the Lord:
Hosanna in the highest.
11 And Jesus entered into Jerusalem, and
into the temple: and when he had looked
round about upon all things, and now the
eventide was come, he went out unto Bethany with the twelve.
12 ¶ And on the morrow, when they were
come from Bethany, he was hungry:
13 And seeing a fig tree afar off having
leaves, he came, if haply he might find any
thing thereon: and when he came to it, he
found nothing but leaves; for the time of
figs was not *yet*.
14 And Jesus answered and said unto it, No

man eat fruit of thee hereafter for ever. And
his disciples heard *it*.
15 ¶ And they come to Jerusalem: and
Jesus went into the temple, and began to
cast out them that sold and bought in the
temple, and overthrew the tables of the
moneychangers, and the seats of them
that sold doves;
16 And would not suffer that any man
should carry *any* vessel through the temple.
17 And he taught, saying unto them, Is it
not written, My house shall be called of all
nations the house of prayer? but ye have
made it a den of thieves.
18 And the scribes and chief priests heard
it, and sought how they might destroy him:
for they feared him, because all the people
was astonished at his doctrine.
19 And when even was come, he went out
of the city.
20 ¶ And in the morning, as they passed
by, they saw the fig tree dried up from the
roots.
21 And Peter calling to remembrance saith
unto him, Master, behold, the fig tree which
thou cursedst is withered away.
22 And Jesus answering saith unto them,
Have faith in God.
23 For verily I say unto you, That whosoever shall say unto this mountain, Be thou
removed, and be thou cast into the sea; and
shall not doubt in his heart, but shall believe
that those things which he saith shall come
to pass; he shall have whatsoever he saith.
24 Therefore I say unto you, What things
soever ye desire, when ye pray, believe that
ye receive *them*, and ye shall have *them*.
25 And when ye stand praying, forgive, if
ye have ought against any: that your Father
also which is in heaven may forgive you
your trespasses.
26 But if ye do not forgive, neither will
your Father which is in heaven forgive your
trespasses.
27 ¶ And they come again to Jerusalem: and
as he was walking in the temple, there come
to him the chief priests, and the scribes,
and the elders,
28 And say unto him, By what authority
doest thou these things? and who gave thee
this authority to do these things?
29 And Jesus answered and said unto them, I
will also ask of you one question, and answer
me, and I will tell you by what authority I
do these things.
30 The baptism of John, was *it* from heaven,
or of men? answer me.
31 And they reasoned with themselves, saying, If we shall say, From heaven; he will say,
Why then did ye not believe him?
32 But if we shall say, Of men; they feared
the people: for all *men* counted John, that
he was a prophet indeed.
33 And they answered and said unto Jesus,
We cannot tell. And Jesus answering saith
unto them, Neither do I tell you by what
authority I do these things.

Mark 12

1 And he began to speak unto them by parables. A *certain* man planted a vineyard, and
set an hedge about *it*, and digged *a place for*
the winefat, and built a tower, and let it out
to husbandmen, and went into a far country.
2 And at the season he sent to the husbandmen a servant, that he might receive from
the husbandmen of the fruit of the vineyard.
3 And they caught *him*, and beat him, and
sent *him* away empty.
4 And again he sent unto them another
servant; and at him they cast stones, and
wounded *him* in the head, and sent *him*
away shamefully handled.
5 And again he sent another; and him they
killed, and many others; beating some, and
killing some.
6 Having yet therefore one son, his wellbeloved, he sent him also last unto them,
saying, They will reverence my son.
7 But those husbandmen said among themselves, This is the heir; come, let us kill him,
and the inheritance shall be ours.
8 And they took him, and killed *him*, and
cast *him* out of the vineyard.
9 What shall therefore the lord of the
vineyard do? he will come and destroy the
husbandmen, and will give the vineyard
unto others.
10 And have ye not read this scripture; The
stone which the builders rejected is become
the head of the corner:
11 This was the Lord's doing, and it is marvellous in our eyes?
12 And they sought to lay hold on him, but
feared the people: for they knew that he

had spoken the parable against them: and
they left him, and went their way.
13 ¶ And they send unto him certain of the
Pharisees and of the Herodians, to catch
him in *his* words.
14 And when they were come, they say unto
him, Master, we know that thou art true,
and carest for no man: for thou regardest
not the person of men, but teachest the way
of God in truth: Is it lawful to give tribute to
Cæsar, or not?
15 Shall we give, or shall we not give? But
he, knowing their hypocrisy, said unto them,
Why tempt ye me? bring me a penny, that
I may see *it*.
16 And they brought *it*. And he saith unto
them, Whose *is* this image and superscription? And they said unto him, Cæsar's.
17 And Jesus answering said unto them,
Render to Cæsar the things that are Cæsar's,
and to God the things that are God's. And
they marvelled at him.
18 ¶ Then come unto him the Sadducees,
which say there is no resurrection; and they
asked him, saying,
19 Master, Moses wrote unto us, If a man's
brother die, and leave *his* wife *behind him*,
and leave no children, that his brother
should take his wife, and raise up seed unto
his brother.
20 Now there were seven brethren: and
the first took a wife, and dying left no seed.
21 And the second took her, and died, neither left he any seed: and the third likewise.
22 And the seven had her, and left no seed:
last of all the woman died also.
23 In the resurrection therefore, when they
shall rise, whose wife shall she be of them?
for the seven had her to wife.
24 And Jesus answering said unto them, Do
ye not therefore err, because ye know not
the scriptures, neither the power of God?
25 For when they shall rise from the dead,
they neither marry, nor are given in marriage; but are as the angels which are in
heaven.
26 And as touching the dead, that they rise:
have ye not read in the book of Moses, how
in the bush God spake unto him, saying, I
am the God of Abraham, and the God of
Isaac, and the God of Jacob?
27 He is not the God of the dead, but the
God of the living: ye therefore do greatly err.
28 ¶ And one of the scribes came, and
having heard them reasoning together, and
perceiving that he had answered them well,
asked him, Which is the first commandment of all?
29 And Jesus answered him, The first of all
the commandments *is*, Hear, O Israel; The
Lord our God is one Lord:
30 And thou shalt love the Lord thy God with
all thy heart, and with all thy soul, and with
all thy mind, and with all thy strength: this
is the first commandment.
31 And the second *is* like, *namely* this, Thou
shalt love thy neighbour as thyself. There
is none other commandment greater than
these.
32 And the scribe said unto him, Well, Master, thou hast said the truth: for there is one
God; and there is none other but he:
33 And to love him with all the heart, and
with all the understanding, and with all the
soul, and with all the strength, and to love
his neighbour as himself, is more than all
whole burnt offerings and sacrifices.
34 And when Jesus saw that he answered
discreetly, he said unto him, Thou art not
far from the kingdom of God. And no man
after that durst ask him *any question*.
35 ¶ And Jesus answered and said, while he
taught in the temple, How say the scribes
that Christ is the Son of David?
36 For David himself said by the Holy Spirit,
The LORD said to my Lord, Sit thou on my
right hand, till I make thine enemies thy
footstool.
37 David therefore himself calleth him Lord;
and whence is he *then* his son? And the
common people heard him gladly.
38 ¶ And he said unto them in his doctrine,
Beware of the scribes, which love to go in
long clothing, and *love* salutations in the
marketplaces,
39 And the chief seats in the synagogues,
and the uppermost rooms at feasts:
40 Which devour widows' houses, and for
a pretence make long prayers: these shall
receive greater damnation.
41 ¶ And Jesus sat over against the treasury,
and beheld how the people cast money
into the treasury: and many that were rich
cast in much.
42 And there came a certain poor widow,

and she threw in two mites, which make
a farthing.
43 And he called *unto him* his disciples, and
saith unto them, Verily I say unto you, That
this poor widow hath cast more in, than
all they which have cast into the treasury:
44 For all *they* did cast in of their abundance;
but she of her want did cast in all that she
had, *even* all her living.

Mark 13

1 And as he went out of the temple, one
of his disciples saith unto him, Master, see
what manner of stones and what buildings
are here!
2 And Jesus answering said unto him, Seest
thou these great buildings? there shall not
be left one stone upon another, that shall
not be thrown down.
3 And as he sat upon the mount of Olives
over against the temple, Peter and James
and John and Andrew asked him privately,
4 Tell us, when shall these things be? and
what *shall be* the sign when all these things
shall be fulfilled?
5 And Jesus answering them began to say,
Take heed lest any *man* deceive you:
6 For many shall come in my name, saying,
I am *Christ;* and shall deceive many.
7 And when ye shall hear of wars and
rumours of wars, be ye not troubled: for
such things must needs be; but the end
shall not *be* yet.
8 For nation shall rise against nation, and
kingdom against kingdom: and there shall
be earthquakes in divers places, and there
shall be famines and troubles: these *are* the
beginnings of sorrows.
9 ¶ But take heed to yourselves: for they
shall deliver you up to councils; and in the
synagogues ye shall be beaten: and ye shall
be brought before rulers and kings for my
sake, for a testimony against them.
10 And the gospel must first be published
among all nations.
11 But when they shall lead *you*, and deliver
you up, take no thought beforehand what ye
shall speak, neither do ye premeditate: but
whatsoever shall be given you in that hour,
that speak ye: for it is not ye that speak, but
the Holy Spirit.
12 Now the brother shall betray the brother
to death, and the father the son; and children shall rise up against *their* parents, and
shall cause them to be put to death.
13 And ye shall be hated of all *men* for my
name's sake: but he that shall endure unto
the end, the same shall be saved.
14 ¶ But when ye shall see the abomination of desolation, spoken of by Daniel the
prophet, standing where it ought not, (let
him that readeth understand,) then let them
that be in Judæa flee to the mountains:
15 And let him that is on the housetop
not go down into the house, neither enter
therein, to take any thing out of his house:
16 And let him that is in the field not turn
back again for to take up his garment.
17 But woe to them that are with child, and
to them that give suck in those days!
18 And pray ye that your flight be not in
the winter.
19 For *in* those days shall be affliction,
such as was not from the beginning of the
creation which God created unto this time,
neither shall be.
20 And except that the Lord had shortened
those days, no flesh should be saved: but
for the elect's sake, whom he hath chosen,
he hath shortened the days.
21 And then if any man shall say to you,
Lo, here *is* Christ; or, lo, *he is* there; believe
him not:
22 For false Christs and false prophets shall
rise, and shall shew signs and wonders, to
seduce, if *it were* possible, even the elect.
23 But take ye heed: behold, I have foretold
you all things.
24 ¶ But in those days, after that tribulation,
the sun shall be darkened, and the moon
shall not give her light,
25 And the stars of heaven shall fall, and the
powers that are in heaven shall be shaken.
26 And then shall they see the Son of man
coming in the clouds with great power
and glory.
27 And then shall he send his angels, and
shall gather together his elect from the four
winds, from the uttermost part of the earth
to the uttermost part of heaven.
28 Now learn a parable of the fig tree; When
her branch is yet tender, and putteth forth
leaves, ye know that summer is near:
29 So ye in like manner, when ye shall see
these things come to pass, know that it is
nigh, *even* at the doors.

30 Verily I say unto you, that this generation
shall not pass, till all these things be done.
31 Heaven and earth shall pass away: but
my words shall not pass away.
32 ¶ But of that day and *that* hour knoweth
no man, no, not the angels which are in
heaven, neither the Son, but the Father.
33 Take ye heed, watch and pray: for ye
know not when the time is.
34 *For the Son of man is* as a man taking a
far journey, who left his house, and gave
authority to his servants, and to every
man his work, and commanded the porter
to watch.
35 Watch ye therefore: for ye know not
when the master of the house cometh, at
even, or at midnight, or at the cockcrowing,
or in the morning:
36 Lest coming suddenly he find you sleeping.
37 And what I say unto you I say unto all,
Watch.

Mark 14

1 After two days was *the feast of* the passover, and of unleavened bread: and the
chief priests and the scribes sought how
they might take him by craft, and put *him*
to death.
2 But they said, Not on the feast *day*, lest
there be an uproar of the people.
3 ¶ And being in Bethany in the house of
Simon the leper, as he sat at meat, there
came a woman having an alabaster box of
ointment of spikenard very precious; and
she brake the box, and poured *it* on his head.
4 And there were some that had indignation
within themselves, and said, Why was this
waste of the ointment made?
5 For it might have been sold for more than
three hundred pence, and have been given
to the poor. And they murmured against her.
6 And Jesus said, Let her alone; why trouble ye her? she hath wrought a good work
on me.
7 For ye have the poor with you always, and
whensoever ye will ye may do them good:
but me ye have not always.
8 She hath done what she could: she is come
aforehand to anoint my body to the burying.
9 Verily I say unto you, Wheresoever this
gospel shall be preached throughout the
whole world, *this* also that she hath done
shall be spoken of for a memorial of her.
10 ¶ And Judas Iscariot, one of the twelve,
went unto the chief priests, to betray him
unto them.
11 And when they heard *it*, they were glad,
and promised to give him money. And he
sought how he might conveniently betray
him.
12 ¶ And the first day of unleavened bread,
when they killed the passover, his disciples
said unto him, Where wilt thou that we
go and prepare that thou mayest eat the
passover?
13 And he sendeth forth two of his disciples,
and saith unto them, Go ye into the city,
and there shall meet you a man bearing a
pitcher of water: follow him.
14 And wheresoever he shall go in, say ye
to the goodman of the house, The Master
saith, Where is the guestchamber, where
I shall eat the passover with my disciples?
15 And he will shew you a large upper
room furnished *and* prepared: there make
ready for us.
16 And his disciples went forth, and came
into the city, and found as he had said unto
them: and they made ready the passover.
17 And in the evening he cometh with the
twelve.
18 And as they sat and did eat, Jesus said,
Verily I say unto you, One of you which eateth with me shall betray me.
19 And they began to be sorrowful, and to
say unto him one by one, *Is* it I? and another
said, *Is* it I?
20 And he answered and said unto them,
It is one of the twelve, that dippeth with
me in the dish.
21 The Son of man indeed goeth, as it is written of him: but woe to that man by whom
the Son of man is betrayed! good were it for
that man if he had never been born.
22 ¶ And as they did eat, Jesus took bread,
and blessed, and brake *it*, and gave to them,
and said, Take, eat: this is my body.
23 And he took the cup, and when he had
given thanks, he gave *it* to them: and they
all drank of it.
24 And he said unto them, This is my blood
of the new testament, which is shed for
many.
25 Verily I say unto you, I will drink no more

of the fruit of the vine, until that day that I
drink it new in the kingdom of God.
26 ¶ And when they had sung an hymn, they
went out into the mount of Olives.
27 And Jesus saith unto them, All ye shall
be offended because of me this night: for
it is written, I will smite the shepherd, and
the sheep shall be scattered.
28 But after that I am risen, I will go before
you into Galilee.
29 But Peter said unto him, Although all
shall be offended, yet *will* not I.
30 And Jesus saith unto him, Verily I say
unto thee, That this day, *even* in this night,
before the cock crow twice, thou shalt deny
me thrice.
31 But he spake the more vehemently, If I
should die with thee, I will not deny thee in
any wise. Likewise also said they all.
32 And they came to a place which was
named Gethsemane: and he saith to his
disciples, Sit ye here, while I shall pray.
33 And he taketh with him Peter and James
and John, and began to be sore amazed, and
to be very heavy;
34 And saith unto them, My soul is exceeding sorrowful unto death: tarry ye here,
and watch.
35 And he went forward a little, and fell
on the ground, and prayed that, if it were
possible, the hour might pass from him.
36 And he said, Abba, Father, all things *are*
possible unto thee; take away this cup from
me: nevertheless not what I will, but what
thou wilt.
37 And he cometh, and findeth them sleeping, and saith unto Peter, Simon, sleepest
thou? couldest not thou watch one hour?
38 Watch ye and pray, lest ye enter into
temptation. The spirit truly *is* ready, but
the flesh *is* weak.
39 And again he went away, and prayed,
and spake the same words.
40 And when he returned, he found them
asleep again, (for their eyes were heavy,)
neither wist they what to answer him.
41 And he cometh the third time, and saith
unto them, Sleep on now, and take *your*
rest: it is enough, the hour is come; behold,
the Son of man is betrayed into the hands
of sinners.
42 Rise up, let us go; lo, he that betrayeth
me is at hand.
43 ¶ And immediately, while he yet spake,
cometh Judas, one of the twelve, and with
him a great multitude with swords and
staves, from the chief priests and the scribes
and the elders.
44 And he that betrayed him had given
them a token, saying, Whomsoever I shall
kiss, that same is he; take him, and lead *him*
away safely.
45 And as soon as he was come, he goeth
straightway to him, and saith, Master, master; and kissed him.
46 ¶ And they laid their hands on him, and
took him.
47 And one of them that stood by drew
a sword, and smote a servant of the high
priest, and cut off his ear.
48 And Jesus answered and said unto them,
Are ye come out, as against a thief, with
swords and *with* staves to take me?
49 I was daily with you in the temple teaching, and ye took me not: but the scriptures
must be fulfilled.
50 And they all forsook him, and fled.
51 And there followed him a certain young
man, having a linen cloth cast about *his*
naked *body;* and the young men laid hold
on him:
52 And he left the linen cloth, and fled from
them naked.
53 ¶ And they led Jesus away to the high
priest: and with him were assembled all the
chief priests and the elders and the scribes.
54 And Peter followed him afar off, even
into the palace of the high priest: and he
sat with the servants, and warmed himself
at the fire.
55 And the chief priests and all the council
sought for witness against Jesus to put him
to death; and found none.
56 For many bare false witness against him,
but their witness agreed not together.
57 And there arose certain, and bare false
witness against him, saying,
58 We heard him say, I will destroy this
temple that is made with hands, and within
three days I will build another made without hands.
59 But neither so did their witness agree
together.
60 And the high priest stood up in the midst,
and asked Jesus, saying, Answerest thou

nothing? what *is it which* these witness
against thee?
61 But he held his peace, and answered
nothing. Again the high priest asked him,
and said unto him, Art thou the Christ, the
Son of the Blessed?
62 And Jesus said, I am: and ye shall see
the Son of man sitting on the right hand of
power, and coming in the clouds of heaven.
63 Then the high priest rent his clothes, and
saith, What need we any further witnesses?
64 Ye have heard the blasphemy: what
think ye? And they all condemned him to
be guilty of death.
65 And some began to spit on him, and to
cover his face, and to buffet him, and to say
unto him, Prophesy: and the servants did
strike him with the palms of their hands.
66 ¶ And as Peter was beneath in the palace, there cometh one of the maids of the
high priest:
67 And when she saw Peter warming himself, she looked upon him, and said, And
thou also wast with Jesus of Nazareth.
68 But he denied, saying, I know not, neither understand I what thou sayest. And he
went out into the porch; and the cock crew.
69 And a maid saw him again, and began
to say to them that stood by, This is *one*
of them.
70 And he denied it again. And a little after,
they that stood by said again to Peter,
Surely thou art *one* of them: for thou art a
Galilæan, and thy speech agreeth *thereto*.
71 But he began to curse and to swear, *saying*, I know not this man of whom ye speak.
72 And the second time the cock crew. And
Peter called to mind the word that Jesus said
unto him, Before the cock crow twice, thou
shalt deny me thrice. And when he thought
thereon, he wept.

Mark 15

1 And straightway in the morning the chief
priests held a consultation with the elders
and scribes and the whole council, and
bound Jesus, and carried *him* away, and
delivered *him* to Pilate.
2 And Pilate asked him, Art thou the King of
the Jews? And he answering said unto him,
Thou sayest *it*.
3 And the chief priests accused him of many
things: but he answered nothing.
4 And Pilate asked him again, saying,
Answerest thou nothing? behold how many
things they witness against thee.
5 But Jesus yet answered nothing; so that
Pilate marvelled.
6 Now at *that* feast he released unto them
one prisoner, whomsoever they desired.
7 And there was *one* named Barabbas,
which lay bound with them that had made
insurrection with him, who had committed
murder in the insurrection.
8 And the multitude crying aloud began
to desire *him to do* as he had ever done
unto them.
9 But Pilate answered them, saying, Will ye
that I release unto you the King of the Jews?
10 For he knew that the chief priests had
delivered him for envy.
11 But the chief priests moved the people,
that he should rather release Barabbas
unto them.
12 And Pilate answered and said again unto
them, What will ye then that I shall do *unto
him* whom ye call the King of the Jews?
13 And they cried out again, Crucify him.
14 Then Pilate said unto them, Why, what
evil hath he done? And they cried out the
more exceedingly, Crucify him.
15 ¶ And *so* Pilate, willing to content the
people, released Barabbas unto them, and
delivered Jesus, when he had scourged *him*,
to be crucified.
16 And the soldiers led him away into
the hall, called Prætorium; and they call
together the whole band.
17 And they clothed him with purple, and
platted a crown of thorns, and put it about
his *head*,
18 And began to salute him, Hail, King of
the Jews!
19 And they smote him on the head with
a reed, and did spit upon him, and bowing
their knees worshipped him.
20 And when they had mocked him, they
took off the purple from him, and put his
own clothes on him, and led him out to
crucify him.
21 And they compel one Simon a Cyrenian,
who passed by, coming out of the country,
the father of Alexander and Rufus, to bear
his cross.
22 And they bring him unto the place Gol-

gotha, which is, being interpreted, The
place of a skull.
23 And they gave him to drink wine mingled
with myrrh: but he received *it* not.
24 And when they had crucified him, they
parted his garments, casting lots upon them,
what every man should take.
25 And it was the third hour, and they crucified him.
26 And the superscription of his accusation
was written over, THE KING OF THE JEWS.
27 And with him they crucify two thieves;
the one on his right hand, and the other
on his left.
28 And the scripture was fulfilled, which
saith, And he was numbered with the
transgressors.
29 And they that passed by railed on him,
wagging their heads, and saying, Ah, thou
that destroyest the temple, and buildest *it*
in three days,
30 Save thyself, and come down from the
cross.
31 Likewise also the chief priests mocking
said among themselves with the scribes,
He saved others; himself he cannot save.
32 Let Christ the King of Israel descend
now from the cross, that we may see and
believe. And they that were crucified with
him reviled him.
33 And when the sixth hour was come, there
was darkness over the whole land until the
ninth hour.
34 And at the ninth hour Jesus cried with a
loud voice, saying, Eloi, Eloi, lama sabach-
thani? which is, being interpreted, My God,
my God, why hast thou forsaken me?
35 And some of them that stood by, when
they heard *it*, said, Behold, he calleth Elias.
36 And one ran and filled a spunge full of
vinegar, and put *it* on a reed, and gave him to
drink, saying, Let alone; let us see whether
Elias will come to take him down.
37 And Jesus cried with a loud voice, and
gave up the ghost.
38 And the veil of the temple was rent in
twain from the top to the bottom.
39 ¶ And when the centurion, which stood
over against him, saw that he so cried out,
and gave up the ghost, he said, Truly this
man was the Son of God.
40 There were also women looking on afar
off: among whom was Mary Magdalene,
and Mary the mother of James the less and
of Joses, and Salome;
41 (Who also, when he was in Galilee, followed him, and ministered unto him;) and
many other women which came up with
him unto Jerusalem.
42 ¶ And now when the even was come,
because it was the preparation, that is, the
day before the sabbath,
43 Joseph of Arimathæa, an honourable
counseller, which also waited for the kingdom of God, came, and went in boldly unto
Pilate, and craved the body of Jesus.
44 And Pilate marvelled if he were already
dead: and calling *unto him* the centurion,
he asked him whether he had been any
while dead.
45 And when he knew *it* of the centurion,
he gave the body to Joseph.
46 And he bought fine linen, and took him
down, and wrapped him in the linen, and
laid him in a sepulchre which was hewn out
of a rock, and rolled a stone unto the door
of the sepulchre.
47 And Mary Magdalene and Mary *the
mother* of Joses beheld where he was laid.

Mark 16

1 And when the sabbath was past, Mary
Magdalene, and Mary the *mother* of James,
and Salome, had bought sweet spices, that
they might come and anoint him.
2 And very early in the morning the first *day*
of the week, they came unto the sepulchre
at the rising of the sun.
3 And they said among themselves, Who
shall roll us away the stone from the door
of the sepulchre?
4 And when they looked, they saw that the
stone was rolled away: for it was very great.
5 And entering into the sepulchre, they
saw a young man sitting on the right side,
clothed in a long white garment; and they
were affrighted.
6 And he saith unto them, Be not affrighted:
Ye seek Jesus of Nazareth, which was crucified: he is risen; he is not here: behold the
place where they laid him.
7 But go your way, tell his disciples and Peter
that he goeth before you into Galilee: there
shall ye see him, as he said unto you.
8 And they went out quickly, and fled from
the sepulchre; for they trembled and were

amazed: neither said they any thing to any
man; for they were afraid.
9 ¶ Now when *Jesus* was risen early the
first *day* of the week, he appeared first to
Mary Magdalene, out of whom he had cast
seven devils.
10 *And* she went and told them that had
been with him, as they mourned and wept.
11 And they, when they had heard that
he was alive, and had been seen of her,
believed not.
12 ¶ After that he appeared in another form
unto two of them, as they walked, and went
into the country.
13 And they went and told *it* unto the residue: neither believed they them.
14 ¶ Afterward he appeared unto the eleven
as they sat at meat, and upbraided them
with their unbelief and hardness of heart,
because they believed not them which had
seen him after he was risen.
15 And he said unto them, Go ye into all
the world, and preach the gospel to every
creature.
16 He that believeth and is baptized shall
be saved; but he that believeth not shall
be damned.
17 And these signs shall follow them that
believe; In my name shall they cast out
devils; they shall speak with new tongues;
18 They shall take up serpents; and if they
drink any deadly thing, it shall not hurt
them; they shall lay hands on the sick, and
they shall recover.
19 ¶ So then after the Lord had spoken unto
them, he was received up into heaven, and
sat on the right hand of God.
20 And they went forth, and preached every
where, the Lord working with *them*, and
confirming the word with signs following.
Amen.

The Gospel According To

Luke

Luke 1

1 Forasmuch as many have taken in hand
to set forth in order a declaration of those
things which are most surely believed
among us,
2 Even as they delivered them unto us,
which from the beginning were eyewitnesses, and ministers of the word;
3 It seemed good to me also, having had
perfect understanding of all things from
the very first, to write unto thee in order,
most excellent Theophilus,
4 That thou mightest know the certainty
of those things, wherein thou hast been
instructed.
5 ¶ THERE was in the days of Herod, the king
of Judæa, a certain priest named Zacharias,
of the course of Abia: and his wife *was* of
the daughters of Aaron, and her name *was*
Elisabeth.
6 And they were both righteous before
God, walking in all the commandments and
ordinances of the Lord blameless.
7 And they had no child, because that Elisabeth was barren, and they both were *now*
well stricken in years.
8 And it came to pass, that while he executed the priest's office before God in the
order of his course,
9 According to the custom of the priest's
office, his lot was to burn incense when he
went into the temple of the Lord.
10 And the whole multitude of the people
were praying without at the time of incense.
11 And there appeared unto him an angel
of the Lord standing on the right side of the
altar of incense.
12 And when Zacharias saw *him*, he was
troubled, and fear fell upon him.
13 But the angel said unto him, Fear not,
Zacharias: for thy prayer is heard; and thy
wife Elisabeth shall bear thee a son, and
thou shalt call his name John.
14 And thou shalt have joy and gladness;
and many shall rejoice at his birth.
15 For he shall be great in the sight of the

Lord, and shall drink neither wine nor strong
drink; and he shall be filled with the Holy
Spirit, even from his mother's womb.
16 And many of the children of Israel shall
he turn to the Lord their God.
17 And he shall go before him in the spirit
and power of Elias, to turn the hearts of the
fathers to the children, and the disobedient
to the wisdom of the just; to make ready a
people prepared for the Lord.
18 And Zacharias said unto the angel,
Whereby shall I know this? for I am an old
man, and my wife well stricken in years.
19 And the angel answering said unto him,
I am Gabriel, that stand in the presence of
God; and am sent to speak unto thee, and
to shew thee these glad tidings.
20 And, behold, thou shalt be dumb, and
not able to speak, until the day that these
things shall be performed, because thou
believest not my words, which shall be fulfilled in their season.
21 And the people waited for Zacharias,
and marvelled that he tarried so long in
the temple.
22 And when he came out, he could not
speak unto them: and they perceived that he
had seen a vision in the temple: for he beckoned unto them, and remained speechless.
23 And it came to pass, that, as soon as the
days of his ministration were accomplished,
he departed to his own house.
24 And after those days his wife Elisabeth
conceived, and hid herself five months,
saying,
25 Thus hath the Lord dealt with me in the
days wherein he looked on *me*, to take away
my reproach among men.
26 And in the sixth month the angel Gabriel
was sent from God unto a city of Galilee,
named Nazareth,
27 To a virgin espoused to a man whose
name was Joseph, of the house of David;
and the virgin's name *was* Mary.
28 And the angel came in unto her, and
said, Hail, *thou that art* highly favoured, the
Lord *is* with thee: blessed *art* thou among
women.
29 And when she saw *him*, she was troubled
at his saying, and cast in her mind what
manner of salutation this should be.
30 And the angel said unto her, Fear not,
Mary: for thou hast found favour with God.
31 And, behold, thou shalt conceive in thy
womb, and bring forth a son, and shalt call
his name JESUS.
32 He shall be great, and shall be called the
Son of the Highest: and the Lord God shall
give unto him the throne of his father David:
33 And he shall reign over the house of
Jacob for ever; and of his kingdom there
shall be no end.
34 Then said Mary unto the angel, How shall
this be, seeing I know not a man?
35 And the angel answered and said unto
her, The Holy Spirit shall come upon thee,
and the power of the Highest shall overshadow thee: therefore also that holy thing
which shall be born of thee shall be called
the Son of God.
36 And, behold, thy cousin Elisabeth, she
hath also conceived a son in her old age:
and this is the sixth month with her, who
was called barren.
37 For with God nothing shall be impossible.
38 And Mary said, Behold the handmaid
of the Lord; be it unto me according to thy
word. And the angel departed from her.
39 And Mary arose in those days, and went
into the hill country with haste, into a city
of Juda;
40 And entered into the house of Zacharias,
and saluted Elisabeth.
41 And it came to pass, that, when Elisabeth
heard the salutation of Mary, the babe
leaped in her womb; and Elisabeth was filled
with the Holy Spirit:
42 And she spake out with a loud voice, and
said, Blessed *art* thou among women, and
blessed *is* the fruit of thy womb.
43 And whence *is* this to me, that the
mother of my Lord should come to me?
44 For, lo, as soon as the voice of thy salutation sounded in mine ears, the babe leaped
in my womb for joy.
45 And blessed *is* she that believed: for there
shall be a performance of those things which
were told her from the Lord.
46 And Mary said, My soul doth magnify
the Lord,
47 And my spirit hath rejoiced in God my
Saviour.
48 For he hath regarded the low estate of
his handmaiden: for, behold, from henceforth all generations shall call me blessed.

49 For he that is mighty hath done to me
great things; and holy *is* his name.
50 And his mercy *is* on them that fear him
from generation to generation.
51 He hath shewed strength with his arm; he
hath scattered the proud in the imagination
of their hearts.
52 He hath put down the mighty from *their*
seats, and exalted them of low degree.
53 He hath filled the hungry with good
things; and the rich he hath sent empty
away.
54 He hath holpen his servant Israel, in
remembrance of *his* mercy;
55 As he spake to our fathers, to Abraham,
and to his seed for ever.
56 And Mary abode with her about three
months, and returned to her own house.
57 Now Elisabeth's full time came that
she should be delivered; and she brought
forth a son.
58 And her neighbours and her cousins
heard how the Lord had shewed great mercy
upon her; and they rejoiced with her.
59 And it came to pass, that on the eighth
day they came to circumcise the child; and
they called him Zacharias, after the name
of his father.
60 And his mother answered and said, Not
so; but he shall be called John.
61 And they said unto her, There is none
of thy kindred that is called by this name.
62 And they made signs to his father, how
he would have him called.
63 And he asked for a writing table, and
wrote, saying, His name is John. And they
marvelled all.
64 And his mouth was opened immediately,
and his tongue *loosed*, and he spake, and
praised God.
65 And fear came on all that dwelt round
about them: and all these sayings were
noised abroad throughout all the hill country of Judæa.
66 And all they that heard *them* laid *them*
up in their hearts, saying, What manner of
child shall this be! And the hand of the Lord
was with him.
67 And his father Zacharias was filled with
the Holy Spirit, and prophesied, saying,
68 Blessed *be* the Lord God of Israel; for
he hath visited and redeemed his people,
69 And hath raised up an horn of salvation
for us in the house of his servant David;
70 As he spake by the mouth of his holy
prophets, which have been since the world
began:
71 That we should be saved from our enemies, and from the hand of all that hate us;
72 To perform the mercy *promised* to our
fathers, and to remember his holy covenant;
73 The oath which he sware to our father
Abraham,
74 That he would grant unto us, that we
being delivered out of the hand of our enemies might serve him without fear,
75 In holiness and righteousness before him,
all the days of our life.
76 And thou, child, shalt be called the
prophet of the Highest: for thou shalt go
before the face of the Lord to prepare his
ways;
77 To give knowledge of salvation unto his
people by the remission of their sins,
78 Through the tender mercy of our God;
whereby the dayspring from on high hath
visited us,
79 To give light to them that sit in darkness
and *in* the shadow of death, to guide our
feet into the way of peace.
80 And the child grew, and waxed strong in
spirit, and was in the deserts till the day of
his shewing unto Israel.

Luke 2

1 And it came to pass in those days, that
there went out a decree from Cæsar Augustus, that all the world should be taxed.
2 (*And* this taxing was first made when
Cyrenius was governor of Syria.)
3 And all went to be taxed, every one into
his own city.
4 And Joseph also went up from Galilee, out
of the city of Nazareth, into Judæa, unto the
city of David, which is called Bethlehem;
(because he was of the house and lineage
of David:)
5 To be taxed with Mary his espoused wife,
being great with child.
6 And so it was, that, while they were there,
the days were accomplished that she should
be delivered.
7 And she brought forth her firstborn son,
and wrapped him in swaddling clothes, and

laid him in a manger; because there was no
room for them in the inn.
8 And there were in the same country shepherds abiding in the field, keeping watch
over their flock by night.
9 And, lo, the angel of the Lord came upon
them, and the glory of the Lord shone round
about them: and they were sore afraid.
10 And the angel said unto them, Fear not:
for, behold, I bring you good tidings of great
joy, which shall be to all people.
11 For unto you is born this day in the city
of David a Saviour, which is Christ the Lord.
12 And this *shall be* a sign unto you; Ye shall
find the babe wrapped in swaddling clothes,
lying in a manger.
13 And suddenly there was with the angel
a multitude of the heavenly host praising
God, and saying,
14 Glory to God in the highest, and on earth
peace, good will toward men.
15 And it came to pass, as the angels were
gone away from them into heaven, the
shepherds said one to another, Let us now
go even unto Bethlehem, and see this thing
which is come to pass, which the Lord hath
made known unto us.
16 And they came with haste, and found
Mary, and Joseph, and the babe lying in
a manger.
17 And when they had seen *it*, they made
known abroad the saying which was told
them concerning this child.
18 And all they that heard *it* wondered at
those things which were told them by the
shepherds.
19 But Mary kept all these things, and pon-
dered *them* in her heart.
20 And the shepherds returned, glorifying
and praising God for all the things that
they had heard and seen, as it was told
unto them.
21 And when eight days were accomplished
for the circumcising of the child, his name
was called JESUS, which was so named of
the angel before he was conceived in the
womb.
22 And when the days of her purification
according to the law of Moses were accomplished, they brought him to Jerusalem, to
present *him* to the Lord;
23 (As it is written in the law of the Lord,
Every male that openeth the womb shall be
called holy to the Lord;)
24 And to offer a sacrifice according to that
which is said in the law of the Lord, A pair of
turtledoves, or two young pigeons.
25 And, behold, there was a man in Jerusalem, whose name *was* Simeon; and the
same man *was* just and devout, waiting for
the consolation of Israel: and the Holy Spirit
was upon him.
26 And it was revealed unto him by the Holy
Spirit, that he should not see death, before
he had seen the Lord's Christ.
27 And he came by the Spirit into the temple: and when the parents brought in the
child Jesus, to do for him after the custom
of the law,
28 Then took he him up in his arms, and
blessed God, and said,
29 Lord, now lettest thou thy servant depart
in peace, according to thy word:
30 For mine eyes have seen thy salvation,
31 Which thou hast prepared before the
face of all people;
32 A light to lighten the Gentiles, and the
glory of thy people Israel.
33 And Joseph and his mother marvelled
at those things which were spoken of him.
34 And Simeon blessed them, and said unto
Mary his mother, Behold, this *child* is set for
the fall and rising again of many in Israel;
and for a sign which shall be spoken against;
35 (Yea, a sword shall pierce through thy
own soul also,) that the thoughts of many
hearts may be revealed.
36 And there was one Anna, a prophetess,
the daughter of Phanuel, of the tribe of Aser:
she was of a great age, and had lived with
an husband seven years from her virginity;
37 And she *was* a widow of about fourscore
and four years, which departed not from
the temple, but served *God* with fastings
and prayers night and day.
38 And she coming in that instant gave
thanks likewise unto the Lord, and spake of
him to all them that looked for redemption
in Jerusalem.
39 And when they had performed all things
according to the law of the Lord, they
returned into Galilee, to their own city
Nazareth.
40 And the child grew, and waxed strong in

spirit, filled with wisdom: and the grace of
God was upon him.
41 Now his parents went to Jerusalem every
year at the feast of the passover.
42 And when he was twelve years old, they
went up to Jerusalem after the custom of
the feast.
43 And when they had fulfilled the days, as
they returned, the child Jesus tarried behind
in Jerusalem; and Joseph and his mother
knew not *of it*.
44 But they, supposing him to have been
in the company, went a day's journey; and
they sought him among *their* kinsfolk and
acquaintance.
45 And when they found him not, they
turned back again to Jerusalem, seeking
him.
46 And it came to pass, that after three days
they found him in the temple, sitting in the
midst of the doctors, both hearing them,
and asking them questions.
47 And all that heard him were astonished
at his understanding and answers.
48 And when they saw him, they were
amazed: and his mother said unto him, Son,
why hast thou thus dealt with us? behold,
thy father and I have sought thee sorrowing.
49 And he said unto them, How is it that ye
sought me? wist ye not that I must be about
my Father's business?
50 And they understood not the saying
which he spake unto them.
51 And he went down with them, and came
to Nazareth, and was subject unto them:
but his mother kept all these sayings in
her heart.
52 And Jesus increased in wisdom and
stature, and in favour with God and man.

Luke 3

1 Now in the fifteenth year of the reign of
Tiberius Cæsar, Pontius Pilate being governor of Judæa, and Herod being tetrarch of
Galilee, and his brother Philip tetrarch of
Ituræa and of the region of Trachonitis, and
Lysanias the tetrarch of Abilene,
2 Annas and Caiaphas being the high priests,
the word of God came unto John the son of
Zacharias in the wilderness.
3 And he came into all the country about
Jordan, preaching the baptism of repentance for the remission of sins;
4 As it is written in the book of the words
of Esaias the prophet, saying, The voice of
one crying in the wilderness, Prepare ye the
way of the Lord, make his paths straight.
5 Every valley shall be filled, and every
mountain and hill shall be brought low; and
the crooked shall be made straight, and the
rough ways *shall be* made smooth;
6 And all flesh shall see the salvation of God.
7 Then said he to the multitude that came
forth to be baptized of him, O generation of
vipers, who hath warned you to flee from
the wrath to come?
8 Bring forth therefore fruits worthy of
repentance, and begin not to say within
yourselves, We have Abraham to *our* father:
for I say unto you, That God is able of these
stones to raise up children unto Abraham.
9 And now also the axe is laid unto the root
of the trees: every tree therefore which
bringeth not forth good fruit is hewn down,
and cast into the fire.
10 And the people asked him, saying, What
shall we do then?
11 He answereth and saith unto them, He
that hath two coats, let him impart to him
that hath none; and he that hath meat, let
him do likewise.
12 Then came also publicans to be baptized,
and said unto him, Master, what shall we do?
13 And he said unto them, Exact no more
than that which is appointed you.
14 And the soldiers likewise demanded of
him, saying, And what shall we do? And he
said unto them, Do violence to no man,
neither accuse *any* falsely; and be content
with your wages.
15 And as the people were in expectation,
and all men mused in their hearts of John,
whether he were the Christ, or not;
16 John answered, saying unto *them* all,
I indeed baptize you with water; but one
mightier than I cometh, the latchet of
whose shoes I am not worthy to unloose:
he shall baptize you with the Holy Spirit
and with fire:
17 Whose fan *is* in his hand, and he will
throughly purge his floor, and will gather
the wheat into his garner; but the chaff he
will burn with fire unquenchable.
18 And many other things in his exhortation
preached he unto the people.
19 But Herod the tetrarch, being reproved

by him for Herodias his brother Philip's wife,
and for all the evils which Herod had done,
20 Added yet this above all, that he shut up
John in prison.
21 Now when all the people were baptized,
it came to pass, that Jesus also being baptized, and praying, the heaven was opened,
22 And the Holy Spirit descended in a bodily
shape like a dove upon him, and a voice
came from heaven, which said, Thou art
my beloved Son; in thee I am well pleased.
23 And Jesus himself began to be about
thirty years of age, being (as was supposed)
the son of Joseph, which was *the son* of Heli,
24 Which was *the son* of Matthat, which
was *the son* of Levi, which was *the son* of
Melchi, which was *the son* of Janna, which
was *the son* of Joseph,
25 Which was *the son* of Mattathias, which
was *the son* of Amos, which was *the son* of
Naum, which was *the son* of Esli, which was
the son of Nagge,
26 Which was *the son* of Maath, which was
the son of Mattathias, which was *the son* of
Semei, which was *the son* of Joseph, which
was *the son* of Juda,
27 Which was *the son* of Joanna, which
was *the son* of Rhesa, which was *the son* of
Zorobabel, which was *the son* of Salathiel,
which was *the son* of Neri,
28 Which was *the son* of Melchi, which was
the son of Addi, which was *the son* of Cosam,
which was *the son* of Elmodam, which was
the son of Er,
29 Which was *the son* of Jose, which was *the
son* of Eliezer, which was *the son* of Jorim,
which was *the son* of Matthat, which was
the son of Levi,
30 Which was *the son* of Simeon, which
was *the son* of Juda, which was *the son* of
Joseph, which was *the son* of Jonan, which
was *the son* of Eliakim,
31 Which was *the son* of Melea, which was
the son of Menan, which was *the son* of
Mattatha, which was *the son* of Nathan,
which was *the son* of David,
32 Which was *the son* of Jesse, which was
the son of Obed, which was *the son* of Booz,
which was *the son* of Salmon, which was *the
son* of Naasson,
33 Which was *the son* of Aminadab, which
was *the son* of Aram, which was *the son* of
Esrom, which was *the son* of Phares, which
was *the son* of Juda,
34 Which was *the son* of Jacob, which was
the son of Isaac, which was *the son* of Abraham, which was *the son* of Thara, which was
the son of Nachor,
35 Which was *the son* of Saruch, which
was *the son* of Ragau, which was *the son* of
Phalec, which was *the son* of Heber, which
was *the son* of Sala,
36 Which was *the son* of Cainan, which was
the son of Arphaxad, which was *the son* of
Sem, which was *the son* of Noe, which was
the son of Lamech,
37 Which was *the son* of Mathusala, which
was *the son* of Enoch, which was *the son* of
Jared, which was *the son* of Maleleel, which
was *the son* of Cainan,
38 Which was *the son* of Enos, which was
the son of Seth, which was *the son* of Adam,
which was *the son* of God.

Luke 4

1 And Jesus being full of the Holy Spirit
returned from Jordan, and was led by the
Spirit into the wilderness,
2 Being forty days tempted of the devil. And
in those days he did eat nothing: and when
they were ended, he afterward hungered.
3 And the devil said unto him, If thou be
the Son of God, command this stone that
it be made bread.
4 And Jesus answered him, saying, It is written, That man shall not live by bread alone,
but by every word of God.
5 And the devil, taking him up into an high
mountain, shewed unto him all the kingdoms of the world in a moment of time.
6 And the devil said unto him, All this power
will I give thee, and the glory of them: for
that is delivered unto me; and to whomsoever I will I give it.
7 If thou therefore wilt worship me, all shall
be thine.
8 And Jesus answered and said unto him,
Get thee behind me, Satan: for it is written,
Thou shalt worship the Lord thy God, and
him only shalt thou serve.
9 And he brought him to Jerusalem, and set
him on a pinnacle of the temple, and said
unto him, If thou be the Son of God, cast
thyself down from hence:

10 For it is written, He shall give his angels
charge over thee, to keep thee:
11 And in *their* hands they shall bear thee
up, lest at any time thou dash thy foot
against a stone.
12 And Jesus answering said unto him, It is
said, Thou shalt not tempt the Lord thy God.
13 And when the devil had ended all the
temptation, he departed from him for a
season.
14 ¶ And Jesus returned in the power of the
Spirit into Galilee: and there went out a fame
of him through all the region round about.
15 And he taught in their synagogues, being
glorified of all.
16 ¶ And he came to Nazareth, where he
had been brought up: and, as his custom
was, he went into the synagogue on the
sabbath day, and stood up for to read.
17 And there was delivered unto him the
book of the prophet Esaias. And when he
had opened the book, he found the place
where it was written,
18 The Spirit of the Lord *is* upon me, because
he hath anointed me to preach the gospel
to the poor; he hath sent me to heal the
brokenhearted, to preach deliverance to
the captives, and recovering of sight to the
blind, to set at liberty them that are bruised,
19 To preach the acceptable year of the
Lord.
20 And he closed the book, and he gave *it*
again to the minister, and sat down. And the
eyes of all them that were in the synagogue
were fastened on him.
21 And he began to say unto them, This day
is this scripture fulfilled in your ears.
22 And all bare him witness, and wondered
at the gracious words which proceeded
out of his mouth. And they said, Is not this
Joseph's son?
23 And he said unto them, Ye will surely
say unto me this proverb, Physician, heal
thyself: whatsoever we have heard done
in Capernaum, do also here in thy country.
24 And he said, Verily I say unto you, No
prophet is accepted in his own country.
25 But I tell you of a truth, many widows
were in Israel in the days of Elias, when the
heaven was shut up three years and six
months, when great famine was throughout all the land;
26 But unto none of them was Elias sent,
save unto Sarepta, *a city* of Sidon, unto a
woman *that was* a widow.
27 And many lepers were in Israel in the
time of Eliseus the prophet; and none of
them was cleansed, saving Naaman the
Syrian.
28 And all they in the synagogue, when they
heard these things, were filled with wrath,
29 And rose up, and thrust him out of the
city, and led him unto the brow of the hill
whereon their city was built, that they might
cast him down headlong.
30 But he passing through the midst of them
went his way,
31 And came down to Capernaum, a city
of Galilee, and taught them on the sabbath days.
32 And they were astonished at his doctrine:
for his word was with power.
33 ¶ And in the synagogue there was a man,
which had a spirit of an unclean devil, and
cried out with a loud voice,
34 Saying, Let *us* alone; what have we to do
with thee, *thou* Jesus of Nazareth? art thou
come to destroy us? I know thee who thou
art; the Holy One of God.
35 And Jesus rebuked him, saying, Hold thy
peace, and come out of him. And when the
devil had thrown him in the midst, he came
out of him, and hurt him not.
36 And they were all amazed, and spake
among themselves, saying, What a word
is this! for with authority and power he
commandeth the unclean spirits, and they
come out.
37 And the fame of him went out into every
place of the country round about.
38 ¶ And he arose out of the synagogue, and
entered into Simon's house. And Simon's
wife's mother was taken with a great fever;
and they besought him for her.
39 And he stood over her, and rebuked the
fever; and it left her: and immediately she
arose and ministered unto them.
40 ¶ Now when the sun was setting, all
they that had any sick with divers diseases
brought them unto him; and he laid his
hands on every one of them, and healed
them.
41 And devils also came out of many, crying
out, and saying, Thou art Christ the Son of
God. And he rebuking *them* suffered them

not to speak: for they knew that he was
Christ.
42 And when it was day, he departed and
went into a desert place: and the people
sought him, and came unto him, and stayed
him, that he should not depart from them.
43 And he said unto them, I must preach
the kingdom of God to other cities also: for
therefore am I sent.
44 And he preached in the synagogues of
Galilee.

Luke 5

1 And it came to pass, that, as the people
pressed upon him to hear the word of God,
he stood by the lake of Gennesaret,
2 And saw two ships standing by the lake:
but the fishermen were gone out of them,
and were washing *their* nets.
3 And he entered into one of the ships,
which was Simon's, and prayed him that
he would thrust out a little from the land.
And he sat down, and taught the people
out of the ship.
4 Now when he had left speaking, he said
unto Simon, Launch out into the deep, and
let down your nets for a draught.
5 And Simon answering said unto him, Master, we have toiled all the night, and have
taken nothing: nevertheless at thy word I
will let down the net.
6 And when they had this done, they
inclosed a great multitude of fishes: and
their net brake.
7 And they beckoned unto *their* partners,
which were in the other ship, that they
should come and help them. And they
came, and filled both the ships, so that they
began to sink.
8 When Simon Peter saw *it*, he fell down at
Jesus' knees, saying, Depart from me; for I
am a sinful man, O Lord.
9 For he was astonished, and all that were
with him, at the draught of the fishes which
they had taken:
10 And so *was* also James, and John, the
sons of Zebedee, which were partners with
Simon. And Jesus said unto Simon, Fear
not; from henceforth thou shalt catch men.
11 And when they had brought their ships
to land, they forsook all, and followed him.
12 ¶ And it came to pass, when he was
in a certain city, behold a man full of leprosy: who seeing Jesus fell on *his* face, and
besought him, saying, Lord, if thou wilt, thou
canst make me clean.
13 And he put forth *his* hand, and touched
him, saying, I will: be thou clean. And immediately the leprosy departed from him.
14 And he charged him to tell no man: but
go, and shew thyself to the priest, and offer
for thy cleansing, according as Moses commanded, for a testimony unto them.
15 But so much the more went there a fame
abroad of him: and great multitudes came
together to hear, and to be healed by him
of their infirmities.
16 ¶ And he withdrew himself into the wilderness, and prayed.
17 And it came to pass on a certain day, as
he was teaching, that there were Pharisees
and doctors of the law sitting by, which
were come out of every town of Galilee,
and Judæa, and Jerusalem: and the power
of the Lord was *present* to heal them.
18 ¶ And, behold, men brought in a bed
a man which was taken with a palsy: and
they sought *means* to bring him in, and to
lay *him* before him.
19 And when they could not find by what
way they might bring him in because of the
multitude, they went upon the housetop,
and let him down through the tiling with *his*
couch into the midst before Jesus.
20 And when he saw their faith, he said
unto him, Man, thy sins are forgiven thee.
21 And the scribes and the Pharisees began
to reason, saying, Who is this which speaketh blasphemies? Who can forgive sins,
but God alone?
22 But when Jesus perceived their thoughts,
he answering said unto them, What reason
ye in your hearts?
23 Whether is easier, to say, Thy sins be
forgiven thee; or to say, Rise up and walk?
24 But that ye may know that the Son of
man hath power upon earth to forgive sins,
(he said unto the sick of the palsy,) I say unto
thee, Arise, and take up thy couch, and go
into thine house.
25 And immediately he rose up before
them, and took up that whereon he lay, and
departed to his own house, glorifying God.
26 And they were all amazed, and they glorified God, and were filled with fear, saying,
We have seen strange things to day.

27 ¶ And after these things he went forth,
and saw a publican, named Levi, sitting at
the receipt of custom: and he said unto
him, Follow me.
28 And he left all, rose up, and followed him.
29 And Levi made him a great feast in his
own house: and there was a great company
of publicans and of others that sat down
with them.
30 But their scribes and Pharisees murmured against his disciples, saying, Why do
ye eat and drink with publicans and sinners?
31 And Jesus answering said unto them,
They that are whole need not a physician;
but they that are sick.
32 I came not to call the righteous, but sinners to repentance.
33 ¶ And they said unto him, Why do the disciples of John fast often, and make prayers,
and likewise *the disciples* of the Pharisees;
but thine eat and drink?
34 And he said unto them, Can ye make the
children of the bridechamber fast, while the
bridegroom is with them?
35 But the days will come, when the bridegroom shall be taken away from them, and
then shall they fast in those days.
36 ¶ And he spake also a parable unto them;
No man putteth a piece of a new garment
upon an old; if otherwise, then both the new
maketh a rent, and the piece that was *taken*
out of the new agreeth not with the old.
37 And no man putteth new wine into old
bottles; else the new wine will burst the
bottles, and be spilled, and the bottles
shall perish.
38 But new wine must be put into new
bottles; and both are preserved.
39 No man also having drunk old *wine*
straightway desireth new: for he saith, The
old is better.

Luke 6

1 And it came to pass on the second sabbath after the first, that he went through
the corn fields; and his disciples plucked
the ears of corn, and did eat, rubbing *them*
in *their* hands.
2 And certain of the Pharisees said unto
them, Why do ye that which is not lawful
to do on the sabbath days?
3 And Jesus answering them said, Have ye
not read so much as this, what David did,
when himself was an hungred, and they
which were with him;
4 How he went into the house of God, and
did take and eat the shewbread, and gave
also to them that were with him; which it is
not lawful to eat but for the priests alone?
5 And he said unto them, That the Son of
man is Lord also of the sabbath.
6 And it came to pass also on another sabbath, that he entered into the synagogue
and taught: and there was a man whose
right hand was withered.
7 And the scribes and Pharisees watched
him, whether he would heal on the sabbath
day; that they might find an accusation
against him.
8 But he knew their thoughts, and said to the
man which had the withered hand, Rise up,
and stand forth in the midst. And he arose
and stood forth.
9 Then said Jesus unto them, I will ask you
one thing; Is it lawful on the sabbath days
to do good, or to do evil? to save life, or to
destroy *it?*
10 And looking round about upon them
all, he said unto the man, Stretch forth
thy hand. And he did so: and his hand was
restored whole as the other.
11 And they were filled with madness; and
communed one with another what they
might do to Jesus.
12 And it came to pass in those days, that
he went out into a mountain to pray, and
continued all night in prayer to God.
13 ¶ And when it was day, he called *unto him*
his disciples: and of them he chose twelve,
whom also he named apostles;
14 Simon, (whom he also named Peter,) and
Andrew his brother, James and John, Philip
and Bartholomew,
15 Matthew and Thomas, James the *son* of
Alphæus, and Simon called Zelotes,
16 And Judas *the brother* of James, and
Judas Iscariot, which also was the traitor.
17 ¶ And he came down with them, and
stood in the plain, and the company of his
disciples, and a great multitude of people
out of all Judæa and Jerusalem, and from the
sea coast of Tyre and Sidon, which came to
hear him, and to be healed of their diseases;
18 And they that were vexed with unclean
spirits: and they were healed.
19 And the whole multitude sought to touch

him: for there went virtue out of him, and
healed *them* all.
20 ¶ And he lifted up his eyes on his disciples, and said, Blessed *be ye* poor: for yours
is the kingdom of God.
21 Blessed *are ye* that hunger now: for ye
shall be filled. Blessed *are ye* that weep now:
for ye shall laugh.
22 Blessed are ye, when men shall hate
you, and when they shall separate you *from
their company*, and shall reproach *you*, and
cast out your name as evil, for the Son of
man's sake.
23 Rejoice ye in that day, and leap for joy:
for, behold, your reward *is* great in heaven:
for in the like manner did their fathers unto
the prophets.
24 But woe unto you that are rich! for ye
have received your consolation.
25 Woe unto you that are full! for ye shall
hunger. Woe unto you that laugh now! for
ye shall mourn and weep.
26 Woe unto you, when all men shall speak
well of you! for so did their fathers to the
false prophets.
27 ¶ But I say unto you which hear, Love
your enemies, do good to them which
hate you,
28 Bless them that curse you, and pray for
them which despitefully use you.
29 And unto him that smiteth thee on the
one cheek offer also the other; and him
that taketh away thy cloke forbid not *to
take thy* coat also.
30 Give to every man that asketh of thee;
and of him that taketh away thy goods ask
them not again.
31 And as ye would that men should do to
you, do ye also to them likewise.
32 For if ye love them which love you, what
thank have ye? for sinners also love those
that love them.
33 And if ye do good to them which do good
to you, what thank have ye? for sinners also
do even the same.
34 And if ye lend *to them* of whom ye
hope to receive, what thank have ye? for
sinners also lend to sinners, to receive as
much again.
35 But love ye your enemies, and do good,
and lend, hoping for nothing again; and your
reward shall be great, and ye shall be the
children of the Highest: for he is kind unto
the unthankful and *to* the evil.
36 Be ye therefore merciful, as your Father
also is merciful.
37 Judge not, and ye shall not be judged:
condemn not, and ye shall not be condemned: forgive, and ye shall be forgiven:
38 Give, and it shall be given unto you;
good measure, pressed down, and shaken
together, and running over, shall men give
into your bosom. For with the same measure
that ye mete withal it shall be measured to
you again.
39 And he spake a parable unto them, Can
the blind lead the blind? shall they not both
fall into the ditch?
40 The disciple is not above his master:
but every one that is perfect shall be as
his master.
41 And why beholdest thou the mote that
is in thy brother's eye, but perceivest not
the beam that is in thine own eye?
42 Either how canst thou say to thy brother,
Brother, let me pull out the mote that is in
thine eye, when thou thyself beholdest not
the beam that is in thine own eye? Thou hypocrite, cast out first the beam out of thine
own eye, and then shalt thou see clearly to
pull out the mote that is in thy brother's eye.
43 For a good tree bringeth not forth corrupt fruit; neither doth a corrupt tree bring
forth good fruit.
44 For every tree is known by his own fruit.
For of thorns men do not gather figs, nor of
a bramble bush gather they grapes.
45 A good man out of the good treasure of
his heart bringeth forth that which is good;
and an evil man out of the evil treasure of
his heart bringeth forth that which is evil:
for of the abundance of the heart his mouth
speaketh.
46 ¶ And why call ye me, Lord, Lord, and do
not the things which I say?
47 Whosoever cometh to me, and heareth
my sayings, and doeth them, I will shew you
to whom he is like:
48 He is like a man which built an house,
and digged deep, and laid the foundation
on a rock: and when the flood arose, the
stream beat vehemently upon that house,
and could not shake it: for it was founded
upon a rock.
49 But he that heareth, and doeth not, is

like a man that without a foundation built an house upon the earth; against which the stream did beat vehemently, and immediately it fell; and the ruin of that house was great.

Luke 7

1 Now when he had ended all his sayings in the audience of the people, he entered into Capernaum.
2 And a certain centurion's servant, who was dear unto him, was sick, and ready to die.
3 And when he heard of Jesus, he sent unto him the elders of the Jews, beseeching him that he would come and heal his servant.
4 And when they came to Jesus, they besought him instantly, saying, That he was worthy for whom he should do this:
5 For he loveth our nation, and he hath built us a synagogue.
6 Then Jesus went with them. And when he was now not far from the house, the centurion sent friends to him, saying unto him, Lord, trouble not thyself: for I am not worthy that thou shouldest enter under my roof:
7 Wherefore neither thought I myself worthy to come unto thee: but say in a word, and my servant shall be healed.
8 For I also am a man set under authority, having under me soldiers, and I say unto one, Go, and he goeth; and to another, Come, and he cometh; and to my servant, Do this, and he doeth *it*.
9 When Jesus heard these things, he marvelled at him, and turned him about, and said unto the people that followed him, I say unto you, I have not found so great faith, no, not in Israel.
10 And they that were sent, returning to the house, found the servant whole that had been sick.
11 ¶ And it came to pass the day after, that he went into a city called Nain; and many of his disciples went with him, and much people.
12 Now when he came nigh to the gate of the city, behold, there was a dead man carried out, the only son of his mother, and she was a widow: and much people of the city was with her.
13 And when the Lord saw her, he had compassion on her, and said unto her, Weep not.
14 And he came and touched the bier: and they that bare *him* stood still. And he said, Young man, I say unto thee, Arise.
15 And he that was dead sat up, and began to speak. And he delivered him to his mother.
16 And there came a fear on all: and they glorified God, saying, That a great prophet is risen up among us; and, That God hath visited his people.
17 And this rumour of him went forth throughout all Judæa, and throughout all the region round about.
18 And the disciples of John shewed him of all these things.
19 ¶ And John calling *unto him* two of his disciples sent *them* to Jesus, saying, Art thou he that should come? or look we for another?
20 When the men were come unto him, they said, John Baptist hath sent us unto thee, saying, Art thou he that should come? or look we for another?
21 And in that same hour he cured many of *their* infirmities and plagues, and of evil spirits; and unto many *that were* blind he gave sight.
22 Then Jesus answering said unto them, Go your way, and tell John what things ye have seen and heard; how that the blind see, the lame walk, the lepers are cleansed, the deaf hear, the dead are raised, to the poor the gospel is preached.
23 And blessed is *he*, whosoever shall not be offended in me.
24 ¶ And when the messengers of John were departed, he began to speak unto the people concerning John, What went ye out into the wilderness for to see? A reed shaken with the wind?
25 But what went ye out for to see? A man clothed in soft raiment? Behold, they which are gorgeously apparelled, and live delicately, are in kings' courts.
26 But what went ye out for to see? A prophet? Yea, I say unto you, and much more than a prophet.
27 This is *he*, of whom it is written, Behold, I send my messenger before thy face, which shall prepare thy way before thee.
28 For I say unto you, Among those that are born of women there is not a greater prophet than John the Baptist: but he that

is least in the kingdom of God is greater
than he.
29 And all the people that heard *him*, and
the publicans, justified God, being baptized
with the baptism of John.
30 But the Pharisees and lawyers rejected
the counsel of God against themselves,
being not baptized of him.
31 ¶ And the Lord said, Whereunto then
shall I liken the men of this generation? and
to what are they like?
32 They are like unto children sitting in the
marketplace, and calling one to another,
and saying, We have piped unto you, and
ye have not danced; we have mourned to
you, and ye have not wept.
33 For John the Baptist came neither eating bread nor drinking wine; and ye say, He
hath a devil.
34 The Son of man is come eating and
drinking; and ye say, Behold a gluttonous
man, and a winebibber, a friend of publicans
and sinners!
35 But wisdom is justified of all her children.
36 ¶ And one of the Pharisees desired him
that he would eat with him. And he went
into the Pharisee's house, and sat down
to meat.
37 And, behold, a woman in the city, which
was a sinner, when she knew that *Jesus* sat
at meat in the Pharisee's house, brought an
alabaster box of ointment,
38 And stood at his feet behind *him* weeping, and began to wash his feet with tears,
and did wipe *them* with the hairs of her
head, and kissed his feet, and anointed *them*
with the ointment.
39 Now when the Pharisee which had bidden him saw *it*, he spake within himself,
saying, This man, if he were a prophet,
would have known who and what manner
of woman *this is* that toucheth him: for she
is a sinner.
40 And Jesus answering said unto him,
Simon, I have somewhat to say unto thee.
And he saith, Master, say on.
41 There was a certain creditor which had
two debtors: the one owed five hundred
pence, and the other fifty.
42 And when they had nothing to pay, he
frankly forgave them both. Tell me therefore, which of them will love him most?
43 Simon answered and said, I suppose that
he, to whom he forgave most. And he said
unto him, Thou hast rightly judged.
44 And he turned to the woman, and said
unto Simon, Seest thou this woman? I
entered into thine house, thou gavest me
no water for my feet: but she hath washed
my feet with tears, and wiped *them* with
the hairs of her head.
45 Thou gavest me no kiss: but this woman
since the time I came in hath not ceased to
kiss my feet.
46 My head with oil thou didst not anoint:
but this woman hath anointed my feet with
ointment.
47 Wherefore I say unto thee, Her sins,
which are many, are forgiven; for she loved
much: but to whom little is forgiven, *the
same* loveth little.
48 And he said unto her, Thy sins are forgiven.
49 And they that sat at meat with him began
to say within themselves, Who is this that
forgiveth sins also?
50 And he said to the woman, Thy faith hath
saved thee; go in peace.

Luke 8

1 And it came to pass afterward, that he
went throughout every city and village,
preaching and shewing the glad tidings of
the kingdom of God: and the twelve *were*
with him,
2 And certain women, which had been
healed of evil spirits and infirmities, Mary
called Magdalene, out of whom went seven
devils,
3 And Joanna the wife of Chuza Herod's
steward, and Susanna, and many others,
which ministered unto him of their substance.
4 ¶ And when much people were gathered
together, and were come to him out of every
city, he spake by a parable:
5 A sower went out to sow his seed: and as
he sowed, some fell by the way side; and
it was trodden down, and the fowls of the
air devoured it.
6 And some fell upon a rock; and as soon as
it was sprung up, it withered away, because
it lacked moisture.
7 And some fell among thorns; and the
thorns sprang up with it, and choked it.
8 And other fell on good ground, and sprang

up, bare fruit an hundredfold. And when
he had said these things, he cried, He that
hath ears to hear, let him hear.
9 And his disciples asked him, saying, What
might this parable be?
10 And he said, Unto you it is given to know
the mysteries of the kingdom of God: but
to others in parables; that seeing they
might not see, and hearing they might not
understand.
11 Now the parable is this: The seed is the
word of God.
12 Those by the way side are they that hear;
then cometh the devil, and taketh away the
word out of their hearts, lest they should
believe and be saved.
13 They on the rock *are they*, which, when
they hear, receive the word with joy; and
these have no root, which for a while
believe, and in time of temptation fall away.
14 And that which fell among thorns are
they, which, when they have heard, go forth,
and are choked with cares and riches and
pleasures of *this* life, and bring no fruit to
perfection.
15 But that on the good ground are they,
which in an honest and good heart, having
heard the word, keep *it*, and bring forth fruit
with patience.
16 ¶ No man, when he hath lighted a candle, covereth it with a vessel, or putteth *it*
under a bed; but setteth *it* on a candlestick,
that they which enter in may see the light.
17 For nothing is secret, that shall not be
made manifest; neither *any thing* hid, that
shall not be known and come abroad.
18 Take heed therefore how ye hear: for
whosoever hath, to him shall be given; and
whosoever hath not, from him shall be taken
even that which he seemeth to have.
19 ¶ Then came to him *his* mother and his
brethren, and could not come at him for
the press.
20 And it was told him *by certain* which said,
Thy mother and thy brethren stand without,
desiring to see thee.
21 And he answered and said unto them, My
mother and my brethren are these which
hear the word of God, and do it.
22 ¶ Now it came to pass on a certain day,
that he went into a ship with his disciples:
and he said unto them, Let us go over
unto the other side of the lake. And they
launched forth.
23 But as they sailed he fell asleep: and
there came down a storm of wind on the
lake; and they were filled *with water*, and
were in jeopardy.
24 And they came to him, and awoke him,
saying, Master, master, we perish. Then he
arose, and rebuked the wind and the raging
of the water: and they ceased, and there
was a calm.
25 And he said unto them, Where is your
faith? And they being afraid wondered, saying one to another, What manner of man
is this! for he commandeth even the winds
and water, and they obey him.
26 ¶ And they arrived at the country of the
Gadarenes, which is over against Galilee.
27 And when he went forth to land, there
met him out of the city a certain man,
which had devils long time, and ware no
clothes, neither abode in *any* house, but
in the tombs.
28 When he saw Jesus, he cried out, and
fell down before him, and with a loud voice
said, What have I to do with thee, Jesus,
thou Son of God most high? I beseech thee,
torment me not.
29 (For he had commanded the unclean
spirit to come out of the man. For oftentimes it had caught him: and he was kept
bound with chains and in fetters; and he
brake the bands, and was driven of the devil
into the wilderness.)
30 And Jesus asked him, saying, What is thy
name? And he said, Legion: because many
devils were entered into him.
31 And they besought him that he would
not command them to go out into the deep.
32 And there was there an herd of many
swine feeding on the mountain: and they
besought him that he would suffer them
to enter into them. And he suffered them.
33 Then went the devils out of the man,
and entered into the swine: and the herd
ran violently down a steep place into the
lake, and were choked.
34 When they that fed *them* saw what was
done, they fled, and went and told *it* in the
city and in the country.
35 Then they went out to see what was
done; and came to Jesus, and found the
man, out of whom the devils were departed,

sitting at the feet of Jesus, clothed, and in his right mind: and they were afraid.

36 They also which saw *it* told them by what means he that was possessed of the devils was healed.

37 ¶ Then the whole multitude of the country of the Gadarenes round about besought him to depart from them; for they were taken with great fear: and he went up into the ship, and returned back again.

38 Now the man out of whom the devils were departed besought him that he might be with him: but Jesus sent him away, saying,

39 Return to thine own house, and shew how great things God hath done unto thee. And he went his way, and published throughout the whole city how great things Jesus had done unto him.

40 And it came to pass, that, when Jesus was returned, the people *gladly* received him: for they were all waiting for him.

41 ¶ And, behold, there came a man named Jairus, and he was a ruler of the synagogue: and he fell down at Jesus' feet, and besought him that he would come into his house:

42 For he had one only daughter, about twelve years of age, and she lay a dying. But as he went the people thronged him.

43 ¶ And a woman having an issue of blood twelve years, which had spent all her living upon physicians, neither could be healed of any,

44 Came behind *him*, and touched the border of his garment: and immediately her issue of blood stanched.

45 And Jesus said, Who touched me? When all denied, Peter and they that were with him said, Master, the multitude throng thee and press *thee*, and sayest thou, Who touched me?

46 And Jesus said, Somebody hath touched me: for I perceive that virtue is gone out of me.

47 And when the woman saw that she was not hid, she came trembling, and falling down before him, she declared unto him before all the people for what cause she had touched him, and how she was healed immediately.

48 And he said unto her, Daughter, be of good comfort: thy faith hath made thee whole; go in peace.

49 ¶ While he yet spake, there cometh one from the ruler of the synagogue's *house*, saying to him, Thy daughter is dead; trouble not the Master.

50 But when Jesus heard *it*, he answered him, saying, Fear not: believe only, and she shall be made whole.

51 And when he came into the house, he suffered no man to go in, save Peter, and James, and John, and the father and the mother of the maiden.

52 And all wept, and bewailed her: but he said, Weep not; she is not dead, but sleepeth.

53 And they laughed him to scorn, knowing that she was dead.

54 And he put them all out, and took her by the hand, and called, saying, Maid, arise.

55 And her spirit came again, and she arose straightway: and he commanded to give her meat.

56 And her parents were astonished: but he charged them that they should tell no man what was done.

Luke 9

1 Then he called his twelve disciples together, and gave them power and authority over all devils, and to cure diseases.

2 And he sent them to preach the kingdom of God, and to heal the sick.

3 And he said unto them, Take nothing for *your* journey, neither staves, nor scrip, neither bread, neither money; neither have two coats apiece.

4 And whatsoever house ye enter into, there abide, and thence depart.

5 And whosoever will not receive you, when ye go out of that city, shake off the very dust from your feet for a testimony against them.

6 And they departed, and went through the towns, preaching the gospel, and healing every where.

7 ¶ Now Herod the tetrarch heard of all that was done by him: and he was perplexed, because that it was said of some, that John was risen from the dead;

8 And of some, that Elias had appeared; and of others, that one of the old prophets was risen again.

9 And Herod said, John have I beheaded: but who is this, of whom I hear such things? And he desired to see him.

10 ¶ And the apostles, when they were
returned, told him all that they had done.
And he took them, and went aside privately
into a desert place belonging to the city
called Bethsaida.
11 And the people, when they knew *it*,
followed him: and he received them, and
spake unto them of the kingdom of God,
and healed them that had need of healing.
12 And when the day began to wear away,
then came the twelve, and said unto him,
Send the multitude away, that they may go
into the towns and country round about,
and lodge, and get victuals: for we are here
in a desert place.
13 But he said unto them, Give ye them to
eat. And they said, We have no more but
five loaves and two fishes; except we should
go and buy meat for all this people.
14 For they were about five thousand men.
And he said to his disciples, Make them sit
down by fifties in a company.
15 And they did so, and made them all sit
down.
16 Then he took the five loaves and the two
fishes, and looking up to heaven, he blessed
them, and brake, and gave to the disciples
to set before the multitude.
17 And they did eat, and were all filled:
and there was taken up of fragments that
remained to them twelve baskets.
18 ¶ And it came to pass, as he was alone
praying, his disciples were with him: and he
asked them, saying, Whom say the people
that I am?
19 They answering said, John the Baptist;
but some *say*, Elias; and others *say*, that one
of the old prophets is risen again.
20 He said unto them, But whom say ye
that I am? Peter answering said, The Christ
of God.
21 And he straitly charged them, and commanded *them* to tell no man that thing;
22 Saying, The Son of man must suffer many
things, and be rejected of the elders and
chief priests and scribes, and be slain, and
be raised the third day.
23 ¶ And he said to *them* all, If any *man*
will come after me, let him deny himself,
and take up his cross daily, and follow me.
24 For whosoever will save his life shall lose
it: but whosoever will lose his life for my
sake, the same shall save it.
25 For what is a man advantaged, if he gain
the whole world, and lose himself, or be
cast away?
26 For whosoever shall be ashamed of me
and of my words, of him shall the Son of
man be ashamed, when he shall come in
his own glory, and *in his* Father's, and of
the holy angels.
27 But I tell you of a truth, there be some
standing here, which shall not taste of death,
till they see the kingdom of God.
28 ¶ And it came to pass about an eight
days after these sayings, he took Peter and
John and James, and went up into a mountain to pray.
29 And as he prayed, the fashion of his
countenance was altered, and his raiment
was white *and* glistering.
30 And, behold, there talked with him two
men, which were Moses and Elias:
31 Who appeared in glory, and spake of
his decease which he should accomplish
at Jerusalem.
32 But Peter and they that were with him
were heavy with sleep: and when they were
awake, they saw his glory, and the two men
that stood with him.
33 And it came to pass, as they departed
from him, Peter said unto Jesus, Master, it
is good for us to be here: and let us make
three tabernacles; one for thee, and one
for Moses, and one for Elias: not knowing
what he said.
34 While he thus spake, there came a cloud,
and overshadowed them: and they feared
as they entered into the cloud.
35 And there came a voice out of the cloud,
saying, This is my beloved Son: hear him.
36 And when the voice was past, Jesus was
found alone. And they kept *it* close, and told
no man in those days any of those things
which they had seen.
37 ¶ And it came to pass, that on the next
day, when they were come down from the
hill, much people met him.
38 And, behold, a man of the company
cried out, saying, Master, I beseech thee,
look upon my son: for he is mine only child.
39 And, lo, a spirit taketh him, and he suddenly crieth out; and it teareth him that
he foameth again, and bruising him hardly
departeth from him.

40 And I besought thy disciples to cast him out; and they could not.

41 And Jesus answering said, O faithless and perverse generation, how long shall I be with you, and suffer you? Bring thy son hither.

42 And as he was yet a coming, the devil threw him down, and tare *him*. And Jesus rebuked the unclean spirit, and healed the child, and delivered him again to his father.

43 ¶ And they were all amazed at the mighty power of God. But while they wondered every one at all things which Jesus did, he said unto his disciples,

44 Let these sayings sink down into your ears: for the Son of man shall be delivered into the hands of men.

45 But they understood not this saying, and it was hid from them, that they perceived it not: and they feared to ask him of that saying.

46 ¶ Then there arose a reasoning among them, which of them should be greatest.

47 And Jesus, perceiving the thought of their heart, took a child, and set him by him,

48 And said unto them, Whosoever shall receive this child in my name receiveth me: and whosoever shall receive me receiveth him that sent me: for he that is least among you all, the same shall be great.

49 ¶ And John answered and said, Master, we saw one casting out devils in thy name; and we forbad him, because he followeth not with us.

50 And Jesus said unto him, Forbid *him* not: for he that is not against us is for us.

51 ¶ And it came to pass, when the time was come that he should be received up, he stedfastly set his face to go to Jerusalem,

52 And sent messengers before his face: and they went, and entered into a village of the Samaritans, to make ready for him.

53 And they did not receive him, because his face was as though he would go to Jerusalem.

54 And when his disciples James and John saw *this*, they said, Lord, wilt thou that we command fire to come down from heaven, and consume them, even as Elias did?

55 But he turned, and rebuked them, and said, Ye know not what manner of spirit ye are of.

56 For the Son of man is not come to destroy men's lives, but to save *them*. And they went to another village.

57 ¶ And it came to pass, that, as they went in the way, a certain *man* said unto him, Lord, I will follow thee whithersoever thou goest.

58 And Jesus said unto him, Foxes have holes, and birds of the air *have* nests; but the Son of man hath not where to lay *his* head.

59 And he said unto another, Follow me. But he said, Lord, suffer me first to go and bury my father.

60 Jesus said unto him, Let the dead bury their dead: but go thou and preach the kingdom of God.

61 And another also said, Lord, I will follow thee; but let me first go bid them farewell, which are at home at my house.

62 And Jesus said unto him, No man, having put his hand to the plough, and looking back, is fit for the kingdom of God.

Luke 10

1 After these things the Lord appointed other seventy also, and sent them two and two before his face into every city and place, whither he himself would come.

2 Therefore said he unto them, The harvest truly *is* great, but the labourers *are* few: pray ye therefore the Lord of the harvest, that he would send forth labourers into his harvest.

3 Go your ways: behold, I send you forth as lambs among wolves.

4 Carry neither purse, nor scrip, nor shoes: and salute no man by the way.

5 And into whatsoever house ye enter, first say, Peace *be* to this house.

6 And if the son of peace be there, your peace shall rest upon it: if not, it shall turn to you again.

7 And in the same house remain, eating and drinking such things as they give: for the labourer is worthy of his hire. Go not from house to house.

8 And into whatsoever city ye enter, and they receive you, eat such things as are set before you:

9 And heal the sick that are therein, and say unto them, The kingdom of God is come nigh unto you.

10 But into whatsoever city ye enter, and they receive you not, go your ways out into the streets of the same, and say,

11 Even the very dust of your city, which cleaveth on us, we do wipe off against you: notwithstanding be ye sure of this, that the kingdom of God is come nigh unto you.

12 But I say unto you, that it shall be more tolerable in that day for Sodom, than for that city.

13 Woe unto thee, Chorazin! woe unto thee, Bethsaida! for if the mighty works had been done in Tyre and Sidon, which have been done in you, they had a great while ago repented, sitting in sackcloth and ashes.

14 But it shall be more tolerable for Tyre and Sidon at the judgment, than for you.

15 And thou, Capernaum, which art exalted to heaven, shalt be thrust down to hell.

16 He that heareth you heareth me; and he that despiseth you despiseth me; and he that despiseth me despiseth him that sent me.

17 ¶ And the seventy returned again with joy, saying, Lord, even the devils are subject unto us through thy name.

18 And he said unto them, I beheld Satan as lightning fall from heaven.

19 Behold, I give unto you power to tread on serpents and scorpions, and over all the power of the enemy: and nothing shall by any means hurt you.

20 Notwithstanding in this rejoice not, that the spirits are subject unto you; but rather rejoice, because your names are written in heaven.

21 ¶ In that hour Jesus rejoiced in spirit, and said, I thank thee, O Father, Lord of heaven and earth, that thou hast hid these things from the wise and prudent, and hast revealed them unto babes: even so, Father; for so it seemed good in thy sight.

22 All things are delivered to me of my Father: and no man knoweth who the Son is, but the Father; and who the Father is, but the Son, and *he* to whom the Son will reveal *him*.

23 ¶ And he turned him unto *his* disciples, and said privately, Blessed *are* the eyes which see the things that ye see:

24 For I tell you, that many prophets and kings have desired to see those things which ye see, and have not seen *them;* and to hear those things which ye hear, and have not heard *them*.

25 ¶ And, behold, a certain lawyer stood up, and tempted him, saying, Master, what shall I do to inherit eternal life?

26 He said unto him, What is written in the law? how readest thou?

27 And he answering said, Thou shalt love the Lord thy God with all thy heart, and with all thy soul, and with all thy strength, and with all thy mind; and thy neighbour as thyself.

28 And he said unto him, Thou hast answered right: this do, and thou shalt live.

29 But he, willing to justify himself, said unto Jesus, And who is my neighbour?

30 And Jesus answering said, A certain *man* went down from Jerusalem to Jericho, and fell among thieves, which stripped him of his raiment, and wounded *him*, and departed, leaving *him* half dead.

31 And by chance there came down a certain priest that way: and when he saw him, he passed by on the other side.

32 And likewise a Levite, when he was at the place, came and looked *on him*, and passed by on the other side.

33 But a certain Samaritan, as he journeyed, came where he was: and when he saw him, he had compassion *on him*,

34 And went to *him*, and bound up his wounds, pouring in oil and wine, and set him on his own beast, and brought him to an inn, and took care of him.

35 And on the morrow when he departed, he took out two pence, and gave *them* to the host, and said unto him, Take care of him; and whatsoever thou spendest more, when I come again, I will repay thee.

36 Which now of these three, thinkest thou, was neighbour unto him that fell among the thieves?

37 And he said, He that shewed mercy on him. Then said Jesus unto him, Go, and do thou likewise.

38 ¶ Now it came to pass, as they went, that he entered into a certain village: and a certain woman named Martha received him into her house.

39 And she had a sister called Mary, which also sat at Jesus' feet, and heard his word.

40 But Martha was cumbered about much serving, and came to him, and said, Lord, dost thou not care that my sister hath left me to serve alone? bid her therefore that she help me.

41 And Jesus answered and said unto her, Martha, Martha, thou art careful and troubled about many things:
42 But one thing is needful: and Mary hath chosen that good part, which shall not be taken away from her.

Luke 11

1 And it came to pass, that, as he was praying in a certain place, when he ceased, one of his disciples said unto him, Lord, teach us to pray, as John also taught his disciples.
2 And he said unto them, When ye pray, say, Our Father which art in heaven, Hallowed be thy name. Thy kingdom come. Thy will be done, as in heaven, so in earth.
3 Give us day by day our daily bread.
4 And forgive us our sins; for we also forgive every one that is indebted to us. And lead us not into temptation; but deliver us from evil.
5 And he said unto them, Which of you shall have a friend, and shall go unto him at midnight, and say unto him, Friend, lend me three loaves;
6 For a friend of mine in his journey is come to me, and I have nothing to set before him?
7 And he from within shall answer and say, Trouble me not: the door is now shut, and my children are with me in bed; I cannot rise and give thee.
8 I say unto you, Though he will not rise and give him, because he is his friend, yet because of his importunity he will rise and give him as many as he needeth.
9 And I say unto you, Ask, and it shall be given you; seek, and ye shall find; knock, and it shall be opened unto you.
10 For every one that asketh receiveth; and he that seeketh findeth; and to him that knocketh it shall be opened.
11 If a son shall ask bread of any of you that is a father, will he give him a stone? or if *he ask* a fish, will he for a fish give him a serpent?
12 Or if he shall ask an egg, will he offer him a scorpion?
13 If ye then, being evil, know how to give good gifts unto your children: how much more shall *your* heavenly Father give the Holy Spirit to them that ask him?
14 ¶ And he was casting out a devil, and it was dumb. And it came to pass, when the devil was gone out, the dumb spake; and the people wondered.
15 But some of them said, He casteth out devils through Beelzebub the chief of the devils.
16 And others, tempting *him*, sought of him a sign from heaven.
17 But he, knowing their thoughts, said unto them, Every kingdom divided against itself is brought to desolation; and a house *divided* against a house falleth.
18 If Satan also be divided against himself, how shall his kingdom stand? because ye say that I cast out devils through Beelzebub.
19 And if I by Beelzebub cast out devils, by whom do your sons cast *them* out? therefore shall they be your judges.
20 But if I with the finger of God cast out devils, no doubt the kingdom of God is come upon you.
21 When a strong man armed keepeth his palace, his goods are in peace:
22 But when a stronger than he shall come upon him, and overcome him, he taketh from him all his armour wherein he trusted, and divideth his spoils.
23 He that is not with me is against me: and he that gathereth not with me scattereth.
24 When the unclean spirit is gone out of a man, he walketh through dry places, seeking rest; and finding none, he saith, I will return unto my house whence I came out.
25 And when he cometh, he findeth *it* swept and garnished.
26 Then goeth he, and taketh *to him* seven other spirits more wicked than himself; and they enter in, and dwell there: and the last *state* of that man is worse than the first.
27 ¶ And it came to pass, as he spake these things, a certain woman of the company lifted up her voice, and said unto him, Blessed *is* the womb that bare thee, and the paps which thou hast sucked.
28 But he said, Yea rather, blessed *are* they that hear the word of God, and keep it.
29 ¶ And when the people were gathered thick together, he began to say, This is an evil generation: they seek a sign; and there shall no sign be given it, but the sign of Jonas the prophet.
30 For as Jonas was a sign unto the Ninevites, so shall also the Son of man be to this generation.

31 The queen of the south shall rise up in
the judgment with the men of this generation, and condemn them: for she came from
the utmost parts of the earth to hear the
wisdom of Solomon; and, behold, a greater
than Solomon *is* here.
32 The men of Nineve shall rise up in the
judgment with this generation, and shall
condemn it: for they repented at the preaching of Jonas; and, behold, a greater than
Jonas *is* here.
33 No man, when he hath lighted a candle,
putteth *it* in a secret place, neither under a
bushel, but on a candlestick, that they which
come in may see the light.
34 The light of the body is the eye: therefore
when thine eye is single, thy whole body also
is full of light; but when *thine eye* is evil, thy
body also *is* full of darkness.
35 Take heed therefore that the light which
is in thee be not darkness.
36 If thy whole body therefore *be* full of
light, having no part dark, the whole shall
be full of light, as when the bright shining
of a candle doth give thee light.
37 ¶ And as he spake, a certain Pharisee
besought him to dine with him: and he went
in, and sat down to meat.
38 And when the Pharisee saw *it,* he marvelled that he had not first washed before
dinner.
39 And the Lord said unto him, Now do ye
Pharisees make clean the outside of the cup
and the platter; but your inward part is full
of ravening and wickedness.
40 *Ye* fools, did not he that made that which
is without make that which is within also?
41 But rather give alms of such things as
ye have; and, behold, all things are clean
unto you.
42 But woe unto you, Pharisees! for ye tithe
mint and rue and all manner of herbs, and
pass over judgment and the love of God:
these ought ye to have done, and not to
leave the other undone.
43 Woe unto you, Pharisees! for ye love the
uppermost seats in the synagogues, and
greetings in the markets.
44 Woe unto you, scribes and Pharisees,
hypocrites! for ye are as graves which
appear not, and the men that walk over
them are not aware *of them.*
45 ¶ Then answered one of the lawyers,
and said unto him, Master, thus saying thou
reproachest us also.
46 And he said, Woe unto you also, *ye* lawyers! for ye lade men with burdens grievous
to be borne, and ye yourselves touch not the
burdens with one of your fingers.
47 Woe unto you! for ye build the sepulchres of the prophets, and your fathers
killed them.
48 Truly ye bear witness that ye allow the
deeds of your fathers: for they indeed killed
them, and ye build their sepulchres.
49 Therefore also said the wisdom of God, I
will send them prophets and apostles, and
some of them they shall slay and persecute:
50 That the blood of all the prophets, which
was shed from the foundation of the world,
may be required of this generation;
51 From the blood of Abel unto the blood
of Zacharias, which perished between the
altar and the temple: verily I say unto you,
It shall be required of this generation.
52 Woe unto you, lawyers! for ye have taken
away the key of knowledge: ye entered not
in yourselves, and them that were entering
in ye hindered.
53 And as he said these things unto them,
the scribes and the Pharisees began to urge
him vehemently, and to provoke him to
speak of many things:
54 Laying wait for him, and seeking to catch
something out of his mouth, that they might
accuse him.

Luke 12

1 In the mean time, when there were gathered together an innumerable multitude of
people, insomuch that they trode one upon
another, he began to say unto his disciples
first of all, Beware ye of the leaven of the
Pharisees, which is hypocrisy.
2 For there is nothing covered, that shall
not be revealed; neither hid, that shall not
be known.
3 Therefore whatsoever ye have spoken in
darkness shall be heard in the light; and that
which ye have spoken in the ear in closets
shall be proclaimed upon the housetops.
4 And I say unto you my friends, Be not
afraid of them that kill the body, and after
that have no more that they can do.
5 But I will forewarn you whom ye shall
fear: Fear him, which after he hath killed

hath power to cast into hell; yea, I say unto
you, Fear him.
6 Are not five sparrows sold for two far-
things, and not one of them is forgotten
before God?
7 But even the very hairs of your head are
all numbered. Fear not therefore: ye are of
more value than many sparrows.
8 Also I say unto you, Whosoever shall confess me before men, him shall the Son of
man also confess before the angels of God:
9 But he that denieth me before men shall
be denied before the angels of God.
10 And whosoever shall speak a word
against the Son of man, it shall be forgiven
him: but unto him that blasphemeth against
the Holy Spirit it shall not be forgiven.
11 And when they bring you unto the synagogues, and *unto* magistrates, and powers,
take ye no thought how or what thing ye
shall answer, or what ye shall say:
12 For the Holy Spirit shall teach you in the
same hour what ye ought to say.
13 ¶ And one of the company said unto him,
Master, speak to my brother, that he divide
the inheritance with me.
14 And he said unto him, Man, who made
me a judge or a divider over you?
15 And he said unto them, Take heed, and
beware of covetousness: for a man's life
consisteth not in the abundance of the
things which he possesseth.
16 And he spake a parable unto them,
saying, The ground of a certain rich man
brought forth plentifully:
17 And he thought within himself, saying,
What shall I do, because I have no room
where to bestow my fruits?
18 And he said, This will I do: I will pull down
my barns, and build greater; and there will I
bestow all my fruits and my goods.
19 And I will say to my soul, Soul, thou hast
much goods laid up for many years; take
thine ease, eat, drink, *and* be merry.
20 But God said unto him, *Thou* fool, this
night thy soul shall be required of thee: then
whose shall those things be, which thou
hast provided?
21 So *is* he that layeth up treasure for himself, and is not rich toward God.
22 ¶ And he said unto his disciples, Therefore I say unto you, Take no thought for your
life, what ye shall eat; neither for the body,
what ye shall put on.
23 The life is more than meat, and the body
is more than raiment.
24 Consider the ravens: for they neither sow
nor reap; which neither have storehouse nor
barn; and God feedeth them: how much
more are ye better than the fowls?
25 And which of you with taking thought
can add to his stature one cubit?
26 If ye then be not able to do that thing
which is least, why take ye thought for
the rest?
27 Consider the lilies how they grow: they
toil not, they spin not; and yet I say unto
you, that Solomon in all his glory was not
arrayed like one of these.
28 If then God so clothe the grass, which
is to day in the field, and to morrow is cast
into the oven; how much more *will he clothe*
you, O ye of little faith?
29 And seek not ye what ye shall eat, or
what ye shall drink, neither be ye of doubtful mind.
30 For all these things do the nations of the
world seek after: and your Father knoweth
that ye have need of these things.
31 ¶ But rather seek ye the kingdom of God;
and all these things shall be added unto you.
32 Fear not, little flock; for it is your Father's
good pleasure to give you the kingdom.
33 Sell that ye have, and give alms; provide yourselves bags which wax not old,
a treasure in the heavens that faileth not,
where no thief approacheth, neither moth
corrupteth.
34 For where your treasure is, there will
your heart be also.
35 Let your loins be girded about, and *your*
lights burning;
36 And ye yourselves like unto men that wait
for their lord, when he will return from the
wedding; that when he cometh and knocketh, they may open unto him immediately.
37 Blessed *are* those servants, whom the
lord when he cometh shall find watching:
verily I say unto you, that he shall gird himself, and make them to sit down to meat,
and will come forth and serve them.
38 And if he shall come in the second watch,
or come in the third watch, and find *them*
so, blessed are those servants.
39 And this know, that if the goodman of

the house had known what hour the thief
would come, he would have watched, and
not have suffered his house to be broken
through.
40 Be ye therefore ready also: for the Son of
man cometh at an hour when ye think not.
41 ¶ Then Peter said unto him, Lord, speakest thou this parable unto us, or even to all?
42 And the Lord said, Who then is that
faithful and wise steward, whom *his* lord
shall make ruler over his household, to give
them their portion of meat in due season?
43 Blessed *is* that servant, whom his lord
when he cometh shall find so doing.
44 Of a truth I say unto you, that he will
make him ruler over all that he hath.
45 But and if that servant say in his heart,
My lord delayeth his coming; and shall begin
to beat the menservants and maidens, and
to eat and drink, and to be drunken;
46 The lord of that servant will come in a
day when he looketh not for *him*, and at an
hour when he is not aware, and will cut him
in sunder, and will appoint him his portion
with the unbelievers.
47 And that servant, which knew his lord's
will, and prepared not *himself*, neither did
according to his will, shall be beaten with
many *stripes*.
48 But he that knew not, and did commit
things worthy of stripes, shall be beaten with
few *stripes*. For unto whomsoever much is
given, of him shall be much required: and to
whom men have committed much, of him
they will ask the more.
49 ¶ I am come to send fire on the earth; and
what will I, if it be already kindled?
50 But I have a baptism to be baptized
with; and how am I straitened till it be
accomplished!
51 Suppose ye that I am come to give peace
on earth? I tell you, Nay; but rather division:
52 For from henceforth there shall be five in
one house divided, three against two, and
two against three.
53 The father shall be divided against the
son, and the son against the father; the
mother against the daughter, and the daughter against the mother; the mother in law
against her daughter in law, and the daughter in law against her mother in law.
54 ¶ And he said also to the people, When
ye see a cloud rise out of the west, straightway ye say, There cometh a shower; and
so it is.
55 And when *ye see* the south wind blow,
ye say, There will be heat; and it cometh
to pass.
56 *Ye* hypocrites, ye can discern the face of
the sky and of the earth; but how is it that
ye do not discern this time?
57 Yea, and why even of yourselves judge
ye not what is right?
58 ¶ When thou goest with thine adversary
to the magistrate, *as thou art* in the way,
give diligence that thou mayest be delivered
from him; lest he hale thee to the judge, and
the judge deliver thee to the officer, and the
officer cast thee into prison.
59 I tell thee, thou shalt not depart thence,
till thou hast paid the very last mite.

Luke 13

1 There were present at that season some
that told him of the Galilæans, whose blood
Pilate had mingled with their sacrifices.
2 And Jesus answering said unto them,
Suppose ye that these Galilæans were sinners above all the Galilæans, because they
suffered such things?
3 I tell you, Nay: but, except ye repent, ye
shall all likewise perish.
4 Or those eighteen, upon whom the tower
in Siloam fell, and slew them, think ye that
they were sinners above all men that dwelt
in Jerusalem?
5 I tell you, Nay: but, except ye repent, ye
shall all likewise perish.
6 ¶ He spake also this parable; A certain
man had a fig tree planted in his vineyard;
and he came and sought fruit thereon, and
found none.
7 Then said he unto the dresser of his
vineyard, Behold, these three years I come
seeking fruit on this fig tree, and find none:
cut it down; why cumbereth it the ground?
8 And he answering said unto him, Lord, let
it alone this year also, till I shall dig about
it, and dung *it*:
9 And if it bear fruit, *well*: and if not, *then*
after that thou shalt cut it down.
10 And he was teaching in one of the synagogues on the sabbath.
11 ¶ And, behold, there was a woman which
had a spirit of infirmity eighteen years, and

was bowed together, and could in no wise
lift up *herself*.
12 And when Jesus saw her, he called *her*
to him, and said unto her, Woman, thou art
loosed from thine infirmity.
13 And he laid *his* hands on her: and immediately she was made straight, and glorified
God.
14 And the ruler of the synagogue answered
with indignation, because that Jesus had
healed on the sabbath day, and said unto
the people, There are six days in which men
ought to work: in them therefore come and
be healed, and not on the sabbath day.
15 The Lord then answered him, and said,
Thou hypocrite, doth not each one of you
on the sabbath loose his ox or *his* ass from
the stall, and lead *him* away to watering?
16 And ought not this woman, being a
daughter of Abraham, whom Satan hath
bound, lo, these eighteen years, be loosed
from this bond on the sabbath day?
17 And when he had said these things, all
his adversaries were ashamed: and all the
people rejoiced for all the glorious things
that were done by him.
18 ¶ Then said he, Unto what is the kingdom of God like? and whereunto shall I
resemble it?
19 It is like a grain of mustard seed, which
a man took, and cast into his garden; and
it grew, and waxed a great tree; and the
fowls of the air lodged in the branches of it.
20 And again he said, Whereunto shall I liken
the kingdom of God?
21 It is like leaven, which a woman took and
hid in three measures of meal, till the whole
was leavened.
22 And he went through the cities and
villages, teaching, and journeying toward
Jerusalem.
23 Then said one unto him, Lord, are there
few that be saved? And he said unto them,
24 ¶ Strive to enter in at the strait gate: for
many, I say unto you, will seek to enter in,
and shall not be able.
25 When once the master of the house is
risen up, and hath shut to the door, and ye
begin to stand without, and to knock at the
door, saying, Lord, Lord, open unto us; and
he shall answer and say unto you, I know
you not whence ye are:
26 Then shall ye begin to say, We have eaten
and drunk in thy presence, and thou hast
taught in our streets.
27 But he shall say, I tell you, I know you
not whence ye are; depart from me, all *ye*
workers of iniquity.
28 There shall be weeping and gnashing of
teeth, when ye shall see Abraham, and Isaac,
and Jacob, and all the prophets, in the kingdom of God, and you *yourselves* thrust out.
29 And they shall come from the east, and
from the west, and from the north, and
from the south, and shall sit down in the
kingdom of God.
30 And, behold, there are last which shall be
first, and there are first which shall be last.
31 ¶ The same day there came certain of
the Pharisees, saying unto him, Get thee out,
and depart hence: for Herod will kill thee.
32 And he said unto them, Go ye, and tell
that fox, Behold, I cast out devils, and I do
cures to day and to morrow, and the third
day I shall be perfected.
33 Nevertheless I must walk to day, and to
morrow, and the *day* following: for it cannot
be that a prophet perish out of Jerusalem.
34 O Jerusalem, Jerusalem, which killest
the prophets, and stonest them that are
sent unto thee; how often would I have
gathered thy children together, as a hen
doth gather her brood under *her* wings,
and ye would not!
35 Behold, your house is left unto you desolate: and verily I say unto you, Ye shall not
see me, until *the time* come when ye shall
say, Blessed *is* he that cometh in the name
of the Lord.

Luke 14

1 And it came to pass, as he went into
the house of one of the chief Pharisees to
eat bread on the sabbath day, that they
watched him.
2 And, behold, there was a certain man
before him which had the dropsy.
3 And Jesus answering spake unto the lawyers and Pharisees, saying, Is it lawful to
heal on the sabbath day?
4 And they held their peace. And he took
him, and healed him, and let him go;
5 And answered them, saying, Which of you
shall have an ass or an ox fallen into a pit,
and will not straightway pull him out on the
sabbath day?

6 And they could not answer him again to
these things.
7 ¶ And he put forth a parable to those
which were bidden, when he marked how
they chose out the chief rooms; saying
unto them,
8 When thou art bidden of any *man* to a
wedding, sit not down in the highest room;
lest a more honourable man than thou be
bidden of him;
9 And he that bade thee and him come and
say to thee, Give this man place; and thou
begin with shame to take the lowest room.
10 But when thou art bidden, go and sit
down in the lowest room; that when he that
bade thee cometh, he may say unto thee,
Friend, go up higher: then shalt thou have
worship in the presence of them that sit at
meat with thee.
11 For whosoever exalteth himself shall be
abased; and he that humbleth himself shall
be exalted.
12 ¶ Then said he also to him that bade him,
When thou makest a dinner or a supper, call
not thy friends, nor thy brethren, neither
thy kinsmen, nor *thy* rich neighbours; lest
they also bid thee again, and a recompence
be made thee.
13 But when thou makest a feast, call the
poor, the maimed, the lame, the blind:
14 And thou shalt be blessed; for they cannot recompense thee: for thou shalt be
recompensed at the resurrection of the just.
15 ¶ And when one of them that sat at meat
with him heard these things, he said unto
him, Blessed *is* he that shall eat bread in the
kingdom of God.
16 Then said he unto him, A certain man
made a great supper, and bade many:
17 And sent his servant at supper time to
say to them that were bidden, Come; for all
things are now ready.
18 And they all with one *consent* began to
make excuse. The first said unto him, I have
bought a piece of ground, and I must needs
go and see it: I pray thee have me excused.
19 And another said, I have bought five yoke
of oxen, and I go to prove them: I pray thee
have me excused.
20 And another said, I have married a wife,
and therefore I cannot come.
21 So that servant came, and shewed his
lord these things. Then the master of the
house being angry said to his servant, Go
out quickly into the streets and lanes of the
city, and bring in hither the poor, and the
maimed, and the halt, and the blind.
22 And the servant said, Lord, it is done
as thou hast commanded, and yet there
is room.
23 And the lord said unto the servant, Go
out into the highways and hedges, and
compel *them* to come in, that my house
may be filled.
24 For I say unto you, That none of those
men which were bidden shall taste of my
supper.
25 ¶ And there went great multitudes with
him: and he turned, and said unto them,
26 If any *man* come to me, and hate not his
father, and mother, and wife, and children,
and brethren, and sisters, yea, and his own
life also, he cannot be my disciple.
27 And whosoever doth not bear his cross,
and come after me, cannot be my disciple.
28 For which of you, intending to build a
tower, sitteth not down first, and counteth the cost, whether he have *sufficient*
to finish *it?*
29 Lest haply, after he hath laid the foundation, and is not able to finish *it*, all that
behold *it* begin to mock him,
30 Saying, This man began to build, and was
not able to finish.
31 Or what king, going to make war against
another king, sitteth not down first, and
consulteth whether he be able with ten
thousand to meet him that cometh against
him with twenty thousand?
32 Or else, while the other is yet a great way
off, he sendeth an ambassage, and desireth
conditions of peace.
33 So likewise, whosoever he be of you that
forsaketh not all that he hath, he cannot be
my disciple.
34 ¶ Salt *is* good: but if the salt have lost
his savour, wherewith shall it be seasoned?
35 It is neither fit for the land, nor yet for
the dunghill; *but* men cast it out. He that
hath ears to hear, let him hear.

Luke 15

1 Then drew near unto him all the publicans
and sinners for to hear him.
2 And the Pharisees and scribes murmured,

saying, This man receiveth sinners, and
eateth with them.
3 ¶ And he spake this parable unto them,
saying,
4 What man of you, having an hundred
sheep, if he lose one of them, doth not leave
the ninety and nine in the wilderness, and
go after that which is lost, until he find it?
5 And when he hath found *it*, he layeth *it*
on his shoulders, rejoicing.
6 And when he cometh home, he calleth
together *his* friends and neighbours, saying
unto them, Rejoice with me; for I have found
my sheep which was lost.
7 I say unto you, that likewise joy shall be
in heaven over one sinner that repenteth,
more than over ninety and nine just persons,
which need no repentance.
8 ¶ Either what woman having ten pieces
of silver, if she lose one piece, doth not light
a candle, and sweep the house, and seek
diligently till she find *it?*
9 And when she hath found *it*, she calleth
her friends and *her* neighbours together,
saying, Rejoice with me; for I have found
the piece which I had lost.
10 Likewise, I say unto you, there is joy in
the presence of the angels of God over one
sinner that repenteth.
11 ¶ And he said, A certain man had two
sons:
12 And the younger of them said to *his*
father, Father, give me the portion of goods
that falleth *to me*. And he divided unto
them *his* living.
13 And not many days after the younger son
gathered all together, and took his journey
into a far country, and there wasted his
substance with riotous living.
14 And when he had spent all, there arose
a mighty famine in that land; and he began
to be in want.
15 And he went and joined himself to a citizen of that country; and he sent him into
his fields to feed swine.
16 And he would fain have filled his belly
with the husks that the swine did eat: and
no man gave unto him.
17 And when he came to himself, he said,
How many hired servants of my father's
have bread enough and to spare, and I
perish with hunger!
18 I will arise and go to my father, and will
say unto him, Father, I have sinned against
heaven, and before thee,
19 And am no more worthy to be called thy
son: make me as one of thy hired servants.
20 And he arose, and came to his father. But
when he was yet a great way off, his father
saw him, and had compassion, and ran, and
fell on his neck, and kissed him.
21 And the son said unto him, Father, I have
sinned against heaven, and in thy sight, and
am no more worthy to be called thy son.
22 But the father said to his servants, Bring
forth the best robe, and put *it* on him; and
put a ring on his hand, and shoes on *his* feet:
23 And bring hither the fatted calf, and kill
it; and let us eat, and be merry:
24 For this my son was dead, and is alive
again; he was lost, and is found. And they
began to be merry.
25 Now his elder son was in the field: and
as he came and drew nigh to the house, he
heard musick and dancing.
26 And he called one of the servants, and
asked what these things meant.
27 And he said unto him, Thy brother is
come; and thy father hath killed the fatted
calf, because he hath received him safe
and sound.
28 And he was angry, and would not go
in: therefore came his father out, and
intreated him.
29 And he answering said to *his* father, Lo,
these many years do I serve thee, neither
transgressed I at any time thy commandment: and yet thou never gavest me a kid,
that I might make merry with my friends:
30 But as soon as this thy son was come,
which hath devoured thy living with harlots, thou hast killed for him the fatted calf.
31 And he said unto him, Son, thou art ever
with me, and all that I have is thine.
32 It was meet that we should make merry,
and be glad: for this thy brother was dead,
and is alive again; and was lost, and is found.

Luke 16

1 And he said also unto his disciples, There
was a certain rich man, which had a steward;
and the same was accused unto him that he
had wasted his goods.
2 And he called him, and said unto him, How
is it that I hear this of thee? give an account

of thy stewardship; for thou mayest be no
longer steward.
3 Then the steward said within himself,
What shall I do? for my lord taketh away
from me the stewardship: I cannot dig; to
beg I am ashamed.
4 I am resolved what to do, that, when I am
put out of the stewardship, they may receive
me into their houses.
5 So he called every one of his lord's debtors
unto him, and said unto the first, How much
owest thou unto my lord?
6 And he said, An hundred measures of oil.
And he said unto him, Take thy bill, and sit
down quickly, and write fifty.
7 Then said he to another, And how much
owest thou? And he said, An hundred measures
of wheat. And he said unto him, Take
thy bill, and write fourscore.
8 And the lord commended the unjust steward,
because he had done wisely: for the
children of this world are in their generation
wiser than the children of light.
9 And I say unto you, Make to yourselves
friends of the mammon of unrighteousness;
that, when ye fail, they may receive you into
everlasting habitations.
10 He that is faithful in that which is least is
faithful also in much: and he that is unjust
in the least is unjust also in much.
11 If therefore ye have not been faithful in
the unrighteous mammon, who will commit
to your trust the true *riches*?
12 And if ye have not been faithful in that
which is another man's, who shall give you
that which is your own?
13 ¶ No servant can serve two masters:
for either he will hate the one, and love
the other; or else he will hold to the one,
and despise the other. Ye cannot serve God
and mammon.
14 And the Pharisees also, who were covetous,
heard all these things: and they
derided him.
15 And he said unto them, Ye are they
which justify yourselves before men; but
God knoweth your hearts: for that which is
highly esteemed among men is abomination
in the sight of God.
16 The law and the prophets *were* until
John: since that time the kingdom of God is
preached, and every man presseth into it.
17 And it is easier for heaven and earth to
pass, than one tittle of the law to fail.
18 Whosoever putteth away his wife, and
marrieth another, committeth adultery: and
whosoever marrieth her that is put away
from *her* husband committeth adultery.
19 ¶ There was a certain rich man, which
was clothed in purple and fine linen, and
fared sumptuously every day:
20 And there was a certain beggar named
Lazarus, which was laid at his gate, full of
sores,
21 And desiring to be fed with the crumbs
which fell from the rich man's table: moreover
the dogs came and licked his sores.
22 And it came to pass, that the beggar
died, and was carried by the angels into
Abraham's bosom: the rich man also died,
and was buried;
23 And in hell he lift up his eyes, being in
torments, and seeth Abraham afar off, and
Lazarus in his bosom.
24 And he cried and said, Father Abraham,
have mercy on me, and send Lazarus, that
he may dip the tip of his finger in water,
and cool my tongue; for I am tormented
in this flame.
25 But Abraham said, Son, remember that
thou in thy lifetime receivedst thy good
things, and likewise Lazarus evil things:
but now he is comforted, and thou art
tormented.
26 And beside all this, between us and you
there is a great gulf fixed: so that they which
would pass from hence to you cannot; neither
can they pass to us, that *would come*
from thence.
27 Then he said, I pray thee therefore,
father, that thou wouldest send him to my
father's house:
28 For I have five brethren; that he may
testify unto them, lest they also come into
this place of torment.
29 Abraham saith unto him, They have
Moses and the prophets; let them hear
them.
30 And he said, Nay, father Abraham: but
if one went unto them from the dead, they
will repent.
31 And he said unto him, If they hear not
Moses and the prophets, neither will they be
persuaded, though one rose from the dead.

Luke 17

1 Then said he unto the disciples, It is impossible but that offences will come: but woe
unto him, through whom they come!
2 It were better for him that a millstone
were hanged about his neck, and he cast
into the sea, than that he should offend one
of these little ones.
3 ¶ Take heed to yourselves: If thy brother
trespass against thee, rebuke him; and if he
repent, forgive him.
4 And if he trespass against thee seven
times in a day, and seven times in a day
turn again to thee, saying, I repent; thou
shalt forgive him.
5 And the apostles said unto the Lord,
Increase our faith.
6 And the Lord said, If ye had faith as a grain
of mustard seed, ye might say unto this
sycamine tree, Be thou plucked up by the
root, and be thou planted in the sea; and it
should obey you.
7 But which of you, having a servant plowing
or feeding cattle, will say unto him by and
by, when he is come from the field, Go and
sit down to meat?
8 And will not rather say unto him, Make
ready wherewith I may sup, and gird thyself,
and serve me, till I have eaten and drunken;
and afterward thou shalt eat and drink?
9 Doth he thank that servant because he
did the things that were commanded him?
I trow not.
10 So likewise ye, when ye shall have done
all those things which are commanded you,
say, We are unprofitable servants: we have
done that which was our duty to do.
11 ¶ And it came to pass, as he went to Jerusalem, that he passed through the midst of
Samaria and Galilee.
12 And as he entered into a certain village,
there met him ten men that were lepers,
which stood afar off:
13 And they lifted up *their* voices, and said,
Jesus, Master, have mercy on us.
14 And when he saw *them*, he said unto
them, Go shew yourselves unto the priests.
And it came to pass, that, as they went, they
were cleansed.
15 And one of them, when he saw that he
was healed, turned back, and with a loud
voice glorified God,
16 And fell down on *his* face at his feet,
giving him thanks: and he was a Samaritan.
17 And Jesus answering said, Were there
not ten cleansed? but where *are* the nine?
18 There are not found that returned to give
glory to God, save this stranger.
19 And he said unto him, Arise, go thy way:
thy faith hath made thee whole.
20 ¶ And when he was demanded of the
Pharisees, when the kingdom of God should
come, he answered them and said, The kingdom of God cometh not with observation:
21 Neither shall they say, Lo here! or, lo
there! for, behold, the kingdom of God is
within you.
22 And he said unto the disciples, The days
will come, when ye shall desire to see one
of the days of the Son of man, and ye shall
not see *it*.
23 And they shall say to you, See here; or,
see there: go not after *them*, nor follow
them.
24 For as the lightning, that lighteneth out
of the one *part* under heaven, shineth unto
the other *part* under heaven; so shall also
the Son of man be in his day.
25 But first must he suffer many things, and
be rejected of this generation.
26 And as it was in the days of Noe, so shall
it be also in the days of the Son of man.
27 They did eat, they drank, they married
wives, they were given in marriage, until the
day that Noe entered into the ark, and the
flood came, and destroyed them all.
28 Likewise also as it was in the days of Lot;
they did eat, they drank, they bought, they
sold, they planted, they builded;
29 But the same day that Lot went out of
Sodom it rained fire and brimstone from
heaven, and destroyed *them* all.
30 Even thus shall it be in the day when the
Son of man is revealed.
31 In that day, he which shall be upon the
housetop, and his stuff in the house, let
him not come down to take it away: and
he that is in the field, let him likewise not
return back.
32 Remember Lot's wife.
33 Whosoever shall seek to save his life
shall lose it; and whosoever shall lose his
life shall preserve it.
34 I tell you, in that night there shall be two

men in one bed; the one shall be taken, and
the other shall be left.
35 Two *women* shall be grinding together;
the one shall be taken, and the other left.
36 Two *men* shall be in the field; the one
shall be taken, and the other left.
37 And they answered and said unto him,
Where, Lord? And he said unto them,
Wheresoever the body *is*, thither will the
eagles be gathered together.

Luke 18

1 And he spake a parable unto them *to this*
end, that men ought always to pray, and
not to faint;
2 Saying, There was in a city a judge, which
feared not God, neither regarded man:
3 And there was a widow in that city; and
she came unto him, saying, Avenge me of
mine adversary.
4 And he would not for a while: but afterward he said within himself, Though I fear
not God, nor regard man;
5 Yet because this widow troubleth me, I
will avenge her, lest by her continual coming
she weary me.
6 And the Lord said, Hear what the unjust
judge saith.
7 And shall not God avenge his own elect,
which cry day and night unto him, though
he bear long with them?
8 I tell you that he will avenge them speedily.
Nevertheless when the Son of man cometh,
shall he find faith on the earth?
9 And he spake this parable unto certain
which trusted in themselves that they were
righteous, and despised others:
10 Two men went up into the temple to
pray; the one a Pharisee, and the other a
publican.
11 The Pharisee stood and prayed thus with
himself, God, I thank thee, that I am not as
other men *are*, extortioners, unjust, adulterers, or even as this publican.
12 I fast twice in the week, I give tithes of
all that I possess.
13 And the publican, standing afar off, would
not lift up so much as *his* eyes unto heaven,
but smote upon his breast, saying, God be
merciful to me a sinner.
14 I tell you, this man went down to his
house justified *rather* than the other: for
every one that exalteth himself shall be
abased; and he that humbleth himself shall
be exalted.
15 And they brought unto him also infants,
that he would touch them: but when *his*
disciples saw *it*, they rebuked them.
16 But Jesus called them *unto him*, and said,
Suffer little children to come unto me, and
forbid them not: for of such is the kingdom
of God.
17 Verily I say unto you, Whosoever shall
not receive the kingdom of God as a little
child shall in no wise enter therein.
18 And a certain ruler asked him, saying,
Good Master, what shall I do to inherit
eternal life?
19 And Jesus said unto him, Why callest
thou me good? none *is* good, save one,
that is, God.
20 Thou knowest the commandments, Do
not commit adultery, Do not kill, Do not
steal, Do not bear false witness, Honour
thy father and thy mother.
21 And he said, All these have I kept from
my youth up.
22 Now when Jesus heard these things, he
said unto him, Yet lackest thou one thing:
sell all that thou hast, and distribute unto
the poor, and thou shalt have treasure in
heaven: and come, follow me.
23 And when he heard this, he was very
sorrowful: for he was very rich.
24 And when Jesus saw that he was very sorrowful, he said, How hardly shall they that
have riches enter into the kingdom of God!
25 For it is easier for a camel to go through
a needle's eye, than for a rich man to enter
into the kingdom of God.
26 And they that heard *it* said, Who then
can be saved?
27 And he said, The things which are impossible with men are possible with God.
28 Then Peter said, Lo, we have left all, and
followed thee.
29 And he said unto them, Verily I say unto
you, There is no man that hath left house,
or parents, or brethren, or wife, or children,
for the kingdom of God's sake,
30 Who shall not receive manifold more in
this present time, and in the world to come
life everlasting.
31 ¶ Then he took *unto him* the twelve,
and said unto them, Behold, we go up to
Jerusalem, and all things that are written

by the prophets concerning the Son of man
shall be accomplished.
32 For he shall be delivered unto the Gentiles, and shall be mocked, and spitefully
entreated, and spitted on:
33 And they shall scourge *him*, and put
him to death: and the third day he shall
rise again.
34 And they understood none of these
things: and this saying was hid from them,
neither knew they the things which were
spoken.
35 ¶ And it came to pass, that as he was
come nigh unto Jericho, a certain blind man
sat by the way side begging:
36 And hearing the multitude pass by, he
asked what it meant.
37 And they told him, that Jesus of Nazareth
passeth by.
38 And he cried, saying, Jesus, *thou* Son of
David, have mercy on me.
39 And they which went before rebuked
him, that he should hold his peace: but he
cried so much the more, *Thou* Son of David,
have mercy on me.
40 And Jesus stood, and commanded him
to be brought unto him: and when he was
come near, he asked him,
41 Saying, What wilt thou that I shall do
unto thee? And he said, Lord, that I may
receive my sight.
42 And Jesus said unto him, Receive thy
sight: thy faith hath saved thee.
43 And immediately he received his sight,
and followed him, glorifying God: and all
the people, when they saw *it*, gave praise
unto God.

Luke 19

1 And *Jesus* entered and passed through
Jericho.
2 And, behold, *there was* a man named
Zacchæus, which was the chief among the
publicans, and he was rich.
3 And he sought to see Jesus who he was;
and could not for the press, because he was
little of stature.
4 And he ran before, and climbed up into
a sycomore tree to see him: for he was to
pass that *way*.
5 And when Jesus came to the place, he
looked up, and saw him, and said unto him,
Zacchæus, make haste, and come down; for
to day I must abide at thy house.
6 And he made haste, and came down, and
received him joyfully.
7 And when they saw *it*, they all murmured,
saying, That he was gone to be guest with
a man that is a sinner.
8 And Zacchæus stood, and said unto the
Lord; Behold, Lord, the half of my goods
I give to the poor; and if I have taken any
thing from any man by false accusation, I
restore *him* fourfold.
9 And Jesus said unto him, This day is salvation come to this house, forsomuch as he
also is a son of Abraham.
10 For the Son of man is come to seek and
to save that which was lost.
11 And as they heard these things, he added
and spake a parable, because he was nigh
to Jerusalem, and because they thought
that the kingdom of God should immediately appear.
12 He said therefore, A certain nobleman
went into a far country to receive for himself
a kingdom, and to return.
13 And he called his ten servants, and delivered them ten pounds, and said unto them,
Occupy till I come.
14 But his citizens hated him, and sent a
message after him, saying, We will not have
this *man* to reign over us.
15 And it came to pass, that when he was
returned, having received the kingdom, then
he commanded these servants to be called
unto him, to whom he had given the money,
that he might know how much every man
had gained by trading.
16 Then came the first, saying, Lord, thy
pound hath gained ten pounds.
17 And he said unto him, Well, thou good
servant: because thou hast been faithful
in a very little, have thou authority over
ten cities.
18 And the second came, saying, Lord, thy
pound hath gained five pounds.
19 And he said likewise to him, Be thou also
over five cities.
20 And another came, saying, Lord, behold,
here is thy pound, which I have kept laid up
in a napkin:
21 For I feared thee, because thou art an
austere man: thou takest up that thou

layedst not down, and reapest that thou
didst not sow.
22 And he saith unto him, Out of thine own
mouth will I judge thee, *thou* wicked servant. Thou knewest that I was an austere
man, taking up that I laid not down, and
reaping that I did not sow:
23 Wherefore then gavest not thou my
money into the bank, that at my coming I
might have required mine own with usury?
24 And he said unto them that stood by,
Take from him the pound, and give *it* to him
that hath ten pounds.
25 (And they said unto him, Lord, he hath
ten pounds.)
26 For I say unto you, That unto every one
which hath shall be given; and from him that
hath not, even that he hath shall be taken
away from him.
27 But those mine enemies, which would
not that I should reign over them, bring
hither, and slay *them* before me.
28 ¶ And when he had thus spoken, he went
before, ascending up to Jerusalem.
29 And it came to pass, when he was come
nigh to Bethphage and Bethany, at the
mount called *the mount* of Olives, he sent
two of his disciples,
30 Saying, Go ye into the village over against
you; in the which at your entering ye shall
find a colt tied, whereon yet never man sat:
loose him, and bring *him hither.*
31 And if any man ask you, Why do ye loose
him? thus shall ye say unto him, Because the
Lord hath need of him.
32 And they that were sent went their way,
and found even as he had said unto them.
33 And as they were loosing the colt, the
owners thereof said unto them, Why loose
ye the colt?
34 And they said, The Lord hath need of him.
35 And they brought him to Jesus: and they
cast their garments upon the colt, and they
set Jesus thereon.
36 And as he went, they spread their clothes
in the way.
37 And when he was come nigh, even now
at the descent of the mount of Olives, the
whole multitude of the disciples began to
rejoice and praise God with a loud voice for
all the mighty works that they had seen;
38 Saying, Blessed *be* the King that cometh
in the name of the Lord: peace in heaven,
and glory in the highest.
39 And some of the Pharisees from among
the multitude said unto him, Master, rebuke
thy disciples.
40 And he answered and said unto them,
I tell you that, if these should hold their
peace, the stones would immediately cry
out.
41 ¶ And when he was come near, he beheld
the city, and wept over it,
42 Saying, If thou hadst known, even thou,
at least in this thy day, the things *which*
belong unto thy peace! but now they are
hid from thine eyes.
43 For the days shall come upon thee, that
thine enemies shall cast a trench about thee,
and compass thee round, and keep thee in
on every side,
44 And shall lay thee even with the ground,
and thy children within thee; and they shall
not leave in thee one stone upon another;
because thou knewest not the time of thy
visitation.
45 And he went into the temple, and began
to cast out them that sold therein, and them
that bought;
46 Saying unto them, It is written, My house
is the house of prayer: but ye have made it
a den of thieves.
47 And he taught daily in the temple. But
the chief priests and the scribes and the
chief of the people sought to destroy him,
48 And could not find what they might do:
for all the people were very attentive to
hear him.

Luke 20

1 And it came to pass, *that* on one of those
days, as he taught the people in the temple,
and preached the gospel, the chief priests
and the scribes came upon *him* with the
elders,
2 And spake unto him, saying, Tell us, by
what authority doest thou these things?
or who is he that gave thee this authority?
3 And he answered and said unto them, I
will also ask you one thing; and answer me:
4 The baptism of John, was it from heaven,
or of men?
5 And they reasoned with themselves, saying, If we shall say, From heaven; he will say,
Why then believed ye him not?

6 But and if we say, Of men; all the people
will stone us: for they be persuaded that
John was a prophet.
7 And they answered, that they could not
tell whence *it was*.
8 And Jesus said unto them, Neither tell I
you by what authority I do these things.
9 Then began he to speak to the people this
parable; A certain man planted a vineyard,
and let it forth to husbandmen, and went
into a far country for a long time.
10 And at the season he sent a servant to
the husbandmen, that they should give him
of the fruit of the vineyard: but the husbandmen beat him, and sent *him* away empty.
11 And again he sent another servant:
and they beat him also, and entreated *him*
shamefully, and sent *him* away empty.
12 And again he sent a third: and they
wounded him also, and cast *him* out.
13 Then said the lord of the vineyard, What
shall I do? I will send my beloved son: it
may be they will reverence *him* when they
see him.
14 But when the husbandmen saw him,
they reasoned among themselves, saying,
This is the heir: come, let us kill him, that
the inheritance may be ours.
15 So they cast him out of the vineyard, and
killed *him*. What therefore shall the lord of
the vineyard do unto them?
16 He shall come and destroy these husbandmen, and shall give the vineyard to
others. And when they heard *it*, they said,
God forbid.
17 And he beheld them, and said, What is
this then that is written, The stone which
the builders rejected, the same is become
the head of the corner?
18 Whosoever shall fall upon that stone shall
be broken; but on whomsoever it shall fall,
it will grind him to powder.
19 ¶ And the chief priests and the scribes
the same hour sought to lay hands on
him; and they feared the people: for they
perceived that he had spoken this parable
against them.
20 And they watched *him*, and sent forth
spies, which should feign themselves just
men, that they might take hold of his words,
that so they might deliver him unto the
power and authority of the governor.
21 And they asked him, saying, Master, we
know that thou sayest and teachest rightly,
neither acceptest thou the person *of any*,
but teachest the way of God truly:
22 Is it lawful for us to give tribute unto
Cæsar, or no?
23 But he perceived their craftiness, and
said unto them, Why tempt ye me?
24 Shew me a penny. Whose image and
superscription hath it? They answered and
said, Cæsar's.
25 And he said unto them, Render therefore
unto Cæsar the things which be Cæsar's,
and unto God the things which be God's.
26 And they could not take hold of his words
before the people: and they marvelled at
his answer, and held their peace.
27 ¶ Then came to *him* certain of the Sadducees, which deny that there is any resurrection; and they asked him,
28 Saying, Master, Moses wrote unto us, If
any man's brother die, having a wife, and
he die without children, that his brother
should take his wife, and raise up seed unto
his brother.
29 There were therefore seven brethren:
and the first took a wife, and died without
children.
30 And the second took her to wife, and he
died childless.
31 And the third took her; and in like manner
the seven also: and they left no children,
and died.
32 Last of all the woman died also.
33 Therefore in the resurrection whose wife
of them is she? for seven had her to wife.
34 And Jesus answering said unto them,
The children of this world marry, and are
given in marriage:
35 But they which shall be accounted worthy
to obtain that world, and the resurrection
from the dead, neither marry, nor are given
in marriage:
36 Neither can they die any more: for they
are equal unto the angels; and are the
children of God, being the children of the
resurrection.
37 Now that the dead are raised, even
Moses shewed at the bush, when he calleth
the Lord the God of Abraham, and the God
of Isaac, and the God of Jacob.
38 For he is not a God of the dead, but of
the living: for all live unto him.

39 ¶ Then certain of the scribes answering said, Master, thou hast well said.
40 And after that they durst not ask him any *question at all*.
41 And he said unto them, How say they that Christ is David's son?
42 And David himself saith in the book of Psalms, The LORD said unto my Lord, Sit thou on my right hand,
43 Till I make thine enemies thy footstool.
44 David therefore calleth him Lord, how is he then his son?
45 ¶ Then in the audience of all the people he said unto his disciples,
46 Beware of the scribes, which desire to walk in long robes, and love greetings in the markets, and the highest seats in the synagogues, and the chief rooms at feasts;
47 Which devour widows' houses, and for a shew make long prayers: the same shall receive greater damnation.

Luke 21

1 And he looked up, and saw the rich men casting their gifts into the treasury.
2 And he saw also a certain poor widow casting in thither two mites.
3 And he said, Of a truth I say unto you, that this poor widow hath cast in more than they all:
4 For all these have of their abundance cast in unto the offerings of God: but she of her penury hath cast in all the living that she had.
5 ¶ And as some spake of the temple, how it was adorned with goodly stones and gifts, he said,
6 *As for* these things which ye behold, the days will come, in the which there shall not be left one stone upon another, that shall not be thrown down.
7 And they asked him, saying, Master, but when shall these things be? and what sign *will there be* when these things shall come to pass?
8 And he said, Take heed that ye be not deceived: for many shall come in my name, saying, I am *Christ;* and the time draweth near: go ye not therefore after them.
9 But when ye shall hear of wars and commotions, be not terrified: for these things must first come to pass; but the end *is* not by and by.
10 Then said he unto them, Nation shall rise against nation, and kingdom against kingdom:
11 And great earthquakes shall be in divers places, and famines, and pestilences; and fearful sights and great signs shall there be from heaven.
12 But before all these, they shall lay their hands on you, and persecute *you*, delivering *you* up to the synagogues, and into prisons, being brought before kings and rulers for my name's sake.
13 And it shall turn to you for a testimony.
14 Settle *it* therefore in your hearts, not to meditate before what ye shall answer:
15 For I will give you a mouth and wisdom, which all your adversaries shall not be able to gainsay nor resist.
16 And ye shall be betrayed both by parents, and brethren, and kinsfolks, and friends; and *some* of you shall they cause to be put to death.
17 And ye shall be hated of all *men* for my name's sake.
18 But there shall not an hair of your head perish.
19 In your patience possess ye your souls.
20 And when ye shall see Jerusalem compassed with armies, then know that the desolation thereof is nigh.
21 Then let them which are in Judæa flee to the mountains; and let them which are in the midst of it depart out; and let not them that are in the countries enter thereinto.
22 For these be the days of vengeance, that all things which are written may be fulfilled.
23 But woe unto them that are with child, and to them that give suck, in those days! for there shall be great distress in the land, and wrath upon this people.
24 And they shall fall by the edge of the sword, and shall be led away captive into all nations: and Jerusalem shall be trodden down of the Gentiles, until the times of the Gentiles be fulfilled.
25 ¶ And there shall be signs in the sun, and in the moon, and in the stars; and upon the earth distress of nations, with perplexity; the sea and the waves roaring;
26 Men's hearts failing them for fear, and for looking after those things which are coming on the earth: for the powers of heaven shall be shaken.

27 And then shall they see the Son of man coming in a cloud with power and great glory.

28 And when these things begin to come to pass, then look up, and lift up your heads; for your redemption draweth nigh.

29 And he spake to them a parable; Behold the fig tree, and all the trees;

30 When they now shoot forth, ye see and know of your own selves that summer is now nigh at hand.

31 So likewise ye, when ye see these things come to pass, know ye that the kingdom of God is nigh at hand.

32 Verily I say unto you, This generation shall not pass away, till all be fulfilled.

33 Heaven and earth shall pass away: but my words shall not pass away.

34 ¶ And take heed to yourselves, lest at any time your hearts be overcharged with surfeiting, and drunkenness, and cares of this life, and *so* that day come upon you unawares.

35 For as a snare shall it come on all them that dwell on the face of the whole earth.

36 Watch ye therefore, and pray always, that ye may be accounted worthy to escape all these things that shall come to pass, and to stand before the Son of man.

37 And in the day time he was teaching in the temple; and at night he went out, and abode in the mount that is called *the mount* of Olives.

38 And all the people came early in the morning to him in the temple, for to hear him.

Luke 22

1 Now the feast of unleavened bread drew nigh, which is called the Passover.

2 And the chief priests and scribes sought how they might kill him; for they feared the people.

3 ¶ Then entered Satan into Judas surnamed Iscariot, being of the number of the twelve.

4 And he went his way, and communed with the chief priests and captains, how he might betray him unto them.

5 And they were glad, and covenanted to give him money.

6 And he promised, and sought opportunity to betray him unto them in the absence of the multitude.

7 ¶ Then came the day of unleavened bread, when the passover must be killed.

8 And he sent Peter and John, saying, Go and prepare us the passover, that we may eat.

9 And they said unto him, Where wilt thou that we prepare?

10 And he said unto them, Behold, when ye are entered into the city, there shall a man meet you, bearing a pitcher of water; follow him into the house where he entereth in.

11 And ye shall say unto the goodman of the house, The Master saith unto thee, Where is the guestchamber, where I shall eat the passover with my disciples?

12 And he shall shew you a large upper room furnished: there make ready.

13 And they went, and found as he had said unto them: and they made ready the passover.

14 And when the hour was come, he sat down, and the twelve apostles with him.

15 And he said unto them, With desire I have desired to eat this passover with you before I suffer:

16 For I say unto you, I will not any more eat thereof, until it be fulfilled in the kingdom of God.

17 And he took the cup, and gave thanks, and said, Take this, and divide *it* among yourselves:

18 For I say unto you, I will not drink of the fruit of the vine, until the kingdom of God shall come.

19 ¶ And he took bread, and gave thanks, and brake *it*, and gave unto them, saying, This is my body which is given for you: this do in remembrance of me.

20 Likewise also the cup after supper, saying, This cup *is* the new testament in my blood, which is shed for you.

21 ¶ But, behold, the hand of him that betrayeth me *is* with me on the table.

22 And truly the Son of man goeth, as it was determined: but woe unto that man by whom he is betrayed!

23 And they began to inquire among themselves, which of them it was that should do this thing.

24 ¶ And there was also a strife among them, which of them should be accounted the greatest.

25 And he said unto them, The kings of the Gentiles exercise lordship over them; and

they that exercise authority upon them are
called benefactors.
26 But ye *shall* not *be* so: but he that is greatest among you, let him be as the younger;
and he that is chief, as he that doth serve.
27 For whether *is* greater, he that sitteth
at meat, or he that serveth? *is* not he that
sitteth at meat? but I am among you as he
that serveth.
28 Ye are they which have continued with
me in my temptations.
29 And I appoint unto you a kingdom, as my
Father hath appointed unto me;
30 That ye may eat and drink at my table
in my kingdom, and sit on thrones judging
the twelve tribes of Israel.
31 ¶ And the Lord said, Simon, Simon,
behold, Satan hath desired *to have* you,
that he may sift *you* as wheat:
32 But I have prayed for thee, that thy faith
fail not: and when thou art converted,
strengthen thy brethren.
33 And he said unto him, Lord, I am ready to
go with thee, both into prison, and to death.
34 And he said, I tell thee, Peter, the cock
shall not crow this day, before that thou
shalt thrice deny that thou knowest me.
35 And he said unto them, When I sent you
without purse, and scrip, and shoes, lacked
ye any thing? And they said, Nothing.
36 Then said he unto them, But now, he that
hath a purse, let him take *it*, and likewise *his*
scrip: and he that hath no sword, let him sell
his garment, and buy one.
37 For I say unto you, that this that is written must yet be accomplished in me, And
he was reckoned among the transgressors:
for the things concerning me have an end.
38 And they said, Lord, behold, here *are* two
swords. And he said unto them, It is enough.
39 ¶ And he came out, and went, as he
was wont, to the mount of Olives; and his
disciples also followed him.
40 And when he was at the place, he said
unto them, Pray that ye enter not into
temptation.
41 And he was withdrawn from them about
a stone's cast, and kneeled down, and
prayed,
42 Saying, Father, if thou be willing, remove
this cup from me: nevertheless not my will,
but thine, be done.
43 And there appeared an angel unto him
from heaven, strengthening him.
44 And being in an agony he prayed more
earnestly: and his sweat was as it were great
drops of blood falling down to the ground.
45 And when he rose up from prayer, and
was come to his disciples, he found them
sleeping for sorrow,
46 And said unto them, Why sleep ye? rise
and pray, lest ye enter into temptation.
47 ¶ And while he yet spake, behold a multitude, and he that was called Judas, one of
the twelve, went before them, and drew
near unto Jesus to kiss him.
48 But Jesus said unto him, Judas, betrayest
thou the Son of man with a kiss?
49 When they which were about him saw
what would follow, they said unto him, Lord,
shall we smite with the sword?
50 ¶ And one of them smote the servant
of the high priest, and cut off his right ear.
51 And Jesus answered and said, Suffer
ye thus far. And he touched his ear, and
healed him.
52 Then Jesus said unto the chief priests,
and captains of the temple, and the elders,
which were come to him, Be ye come out,
as against a thief, with swords and staves?
53 When I was daily with you in the temple,
ye stretched forth no hands against me: but
this is your hour, and the power of darkness.
54 ¶ Then took they him, and led *him*, and
brought him into the high priest's house.
And Peter followed afar off.
55 And when they had kindled a fire in
the midst of the hall, and were set down
together, Peter sat down among them.
56 But a certain maid beheld him as he sat
by the fire, and earnestly looked upon him,
and said, This man was also with him.
57 And he denied him, saying, Woman, I
know him not.
58 And after a little while another saw him,
and said, Thou art also of them. And Peter
said, Man, I am not.
59 And about the space of one hour after
another confidently affirmed, saying, Of a
truth this *fellow* also was with him: for he
is a Galilæan.
60 And Peter said, Man, I know not what
thou sayest. And immediately, while he yet
spake, the cock crew.
61 And the Lord turned, and looked upon

Peter. And Peter remembered the word of the Lord, how he had said unto him, Before the cock crow, thou shalt deny me thrice.

62 And Peter went out, and wept bitterly.

63 ¶ And the men that held Jesus mocked him, and smote *him*.

64 And when they had blindfolded him, they struck him on the face, and asked him, saying, Prophesy, who is it that smote thee?

65 And many other things blasphemously spake they against him.

66 ¶ And as soon as it was day, the elders of the people and the chief priests and the scribes came together, and led him into their council, saying,

67 Art thou the Christ? tell us. And he said unto them, If I tell you, ye will not believe:

68 And if I also ask *you*, ye will not answer me, nor let *me* go.

69 Hereafter shall the Son of man sit on the right hand of the power of God.

70 Then said they all, Art thou then the Son of God? And he said unto them, Ye say that I am.

71 And they said, What need we any further witness? for we ourselves have heard of his own mouth.

Luke 23

1 And the whole multitude of them arose, and led him unto Pilate.

2 And they began to accuse him, saying, We found this *fellow* perverting the nation, and forbidding to give tribute to Cæsar, saying that he himself is Christ a King.

3 And Pilate asked him, saying, Art thou the King of the Jews? And he answered him and said, Thou sayest *it*.

4 Then said Pilate to the chief priests and *to* the people, I find no fault in this man.

5 And they were the more fierce, saying, He stirreth up the people, teaching throughout all Jewry, beginning from Galilee to this place.

6 When Pilate heard of Galilee, he asked whether the man were a Galilæan.

7 And as soon as he knew that he belonged unto Herod's jurisdiction, he sent him to Herod, who himself also was at Jerusalem at that time.

8 ¶ And when Herod saw Jesus, he was exceeding glad: for he was desirous to see him of a long *season*, because he had heard many things of him; and he hoped to have seen some miracle done by him.

9 Then he questioned with him in many words; but he answered him nothing.

10 And the chief priests and scribes stood and vehemently accused him.

11 And Herod with his men of war set him at nought, and mocked *him*, and arrayed him in a gorgeous robe, and sent him again to Pilate.

12 ¶ And the same day Pilate and Herod were made friends together: for before they were at enmity between themselves.

13 ¶ And Pilate, when he had called together the chief priests and the rulers and the people,

14 Said unto them, Ye have brought this man unto me, as one that perverteth the people: and, behold, I, having examined *him* before you, have found no fault in this man touching those things whereof ye accuse him:

15 No, nor yet Herod: for I sent you to him; and, lo, nothing worthy of death is done unto him.

16 I will therefore chastise him, and release *him*.

17 (For of necessity he must release one unto them at the feast.)

18 And they cried out all at once, saying, Away with this *man*, and release unto us Barabbas:

19 (Who for a certain sedition made in the city, and for murder, was cast into prison.)

20 Pilate therefore, willing to release Jesus, spake again to them.

21 But they cried, saying, Crucify *him*, crucify him.

22 And he said unto them the third time, Why, what evil hath he done? I have found no cause of death in him: I will therefore chastise him, and let *him* go.

23 And they were instant with loud voices, requiring that he might be crucified. And the voices of them and of the chief priests prevailed.

24 And Pilate gave sentence that it should be as they required.

25 And he released unto them him that for sedition and murder was cast into prison, whom they had desired; but he delivered Jesus to their will.

26 And as they led him away, they laid hold upon one Simon, a Cyrenian, coming out of

the country, and on him they laid the cross,
that he might bear *it* after Jesus.
27 ¶ And there followed him a great company of people, and of women, which also
bewailed and lamented him.
28 But Jesus turning unto them said, Daughters of Jerusalem, weep not for me, but
weep for yourselves, and for your children.
29 For, behold, the days are coming, in the
which they shall say, Blessed *are* the barren,
and the wombs that never bare, and the
paps which never gave suck.
30 Then shall they begin to say to the mountains, Fall on us; and to the hills, Cover us.
31 For if they do these things in a green tree,
what shall be done in the dry?
32 And there were also two other, malefactors, led with him to be put to death.
33 And when they were come to the place,
which is called Calvary, there they crucified
him, and the malefactors, one on the right
hand, and the other on the left.
34 ¶ Then said Jesus, Father, forgive them;
for they know not what they do. And they
parted his raiment, and cast lots.
35 And the people stood beholding. And the
rulers also with them derided *him*, saying,
He saved others; let him save himself, if he
be Christ, the chosen of God.
36 And the soldiers also mocked him, coming to him, and offering him vinegar,
37 And saying, If thou be the king of the
Jews, save thyself.
38 And a superscription also was written
over him in letters of Greek, and Latin, and
Hebrew, THIS IS THE KING OF THE JEWS.
39 ¶ And one of the malefactors which
were hanged railed on him, saying, If thou
be Christ, save thyself and us.
40 But the other answering rebuked him,
saying, Dost not thou fear God, seeing thou
art in the same condemnation?
41 And we indeed justly; for we receive the
due reward of our deeds: but this man hath
done nothing amiss.
42 And he said unto Jesus, Lord, remember
me when thou comest into thy kingdom.
43 And Jesus said unto him, Verily I say
unto thee, To day shalt thou be with me
in paradise.
44 And it was about the sixth hour, and
there was a darkness over all the earth until
the ninth hour.
45 And the sun was darkened, and the veil
of the temple was rent in the midst.
46 ¶ And when Jesus had cried with a loud
voice, he said, Father, into thy hands I commend my spirit: and having said thus, he
gave up the ghost.
47 Now when the centurion saw what was
done, he glorified God, saying, Certainly this
was a righteous man.
48 And all the people that came together to
that sight, beholding the things which were
done, smote their breasts, and returned.
49 And all his acquaintance, and the women
that followed him from Galilee, stood afar
off, beholding these things.
50 ¶ And, behold, *there was* a man named
Joseph, a counseller; *and he was* a good
man, and a just:
51 (The same had not consented to the
counsel and deed of them;) *he was* of Arimathæa, a city of the Jews: who also himself
waited for the kingdom of God.
52 This *man* went unto Pilate, and begged
the body of Jesus.
53 And he took it down, and wrapped it
in linen, and laid it in a sepulchre that was
hewn in stone, wherein never man before
was laid.
54 And that day was the preparation, and
the sabbath drew on.
55 And the women also, which came with
him from Galilee, followed after, and beheld
the sepulchre, and how his body was laid.
56 And they returned, and prepared spices
and ointments; and rested the sabbath day
according to the commandment.

Luke 24

1 Now upon the first *day* of the week, very
early in the morning, they came unto the
sepulchre, bringing the spices which they
had prepared, and certain *others* with them.
2 And they found the stone rolled away
from the sepulchre.
3 And they entered in, and found not the
body of the Lord Jesus.
4 And it came to pass, as they were much
perplexed thereabout, behold, two men
stood by them in shining garments:
5 And as they were afraid, and bowed down
their faces to the earth, they said unto them,
Why seek ye the living among the dead?
6 He is not here, but is risen: remember

how he spake unto you when he was yet
in Galilee,
7 Saying, The Son of man must be delivered
into the hands of sinful men, and be crucified, and the third day rise again.
8 And they remembered his words,
9 And returned from the sepulchre, and
told all these things unto the eleven, and
to all the rest.
10 It was Mary Magdalene, and Joanna,
and Mary *the mother* of James, and other
women that were with them, which told
these things unto the apostles.
11 And their words seemed to them as idle
tales, and they believed them not.
12 Then arose Peter, and ran unto the
sepulchre; and stooping down, he beheld
the linen clothes laid by themselves, and
departed, wondering in himself at that
which was come to pass.
13 ¶ And, behold, two of them went that
same day to a village called Emmaus, which
was from Jerusalem *about* threescore
furlongs.
14 And they talked together of all these
things which had happened.
15 And it came to pass, that, while they
communed *together* and reasoned, Jesus
himself drew near, and went with them.
16 But their eyes were holden that they
should not know him.
17 And he said unto them, What manner of
communications *are* these that ye have one
to another, as ye walk, and are sad?
18 And the one of them, whose name was
Cleopas, answering said unto him, Art thou
only a stranger in Jerusalem, and hast not
known the things which are come to pass
there in these days?
19 And he said unto them, What things? And
they said unto him, Concerning Jesus of Nazareth, which was a prophet mighty in deed
and word before God and all the people:
20 And how the chief priests and our rulers
delivered him to be condemned to death,
and have crucified him.
21 But we trusted that it had been he which
should have redeemed Israel: and beside
all this, to day is the third day since these
things were done.
22 Yea, and certain women also of our company made us astonished, which were early
at the sepulchre;
23 And when they found not his body, they
came, saying, that they had also seen a
vision of angels, which said that he was alive.
24 And certain of them which were with us
went to the sepulchre, and found *it* even
so as the women had said: but him they
saw not.
25 Then he said unto them, O fools, and
slow of heart to believe all that the prophets
have spoken:
26 Ought not Christ to have suffered these
things, and to enter into his glory?
27 And beginning at Moses and all the
prophets, he expounded unto them in all
the scriptures the things concerning himself.
28 And they drew nigh unto the village,
whither they went: and he made as though
he would have gone further.
29 But they constrained him, saying, Abide
with us: for it is toward evening, and the
day is far spent. And he went in to tarry
with them.
30 And it came to pass, as he sat at meat
with them, he took bread, and blessed *it*,
and brake, and gave to them.
31 And their eyes were opened, and they
knew him; and he vanished out of their sight.
32 And they said one to another, Did not
our heart burn within us, while he talked
with us by the way, and while he opened
to us the scriptures?
33 And they rose up the same hour, and
returned to Jerusalem, and found the
eleven gathered together, and them that
were with them,
34 Saying, The Lord is risen indeed, and hath
appeared to Simon.
35 And they told what things *were done* in
the way, and how he was known of them
in breaking of bread.
36 ¶ And as they thus spake, Jesus himself
stood in the midst of them, and saith unto
them, Peace *be* unto you.
37 But they were terrified and affrighted,
and supposed that they had seen a spirit.
38 And he said unto them, Why are ye
troubled? and why do thoughts arise in
your hearts?
39 Behold my hands and my feet, that it is I
myself: handle me, and see; for a spirit hath
not flesh and bones, as ye see me have.
40 And when he had thus spoken, he
shewed them *his* hands and *his* feet.

41 And while they yet believed not for joy,
and wondered, he said unto them, Have ye
here any meat?
42 And they gave him a piece of a broiled
fish, and of an honeycomb.
43 And he took *it*, and did eat before them.
44 And he said unto them, These *are* the
words which I spake unto you, while I was
yet with you, that all things must be fulfilled,
which were written in the law of Moses,
and *in* the prophets, and *in* the psalms,
concerning me.
45 Then opened he their understanding,
that they might understand the scriptures,
46 And said unto them, Thus it is written,
and thus it behoved Christ to suffer, and to
rise from the dead the third day:
47 And that repentance and remission of
sins should be preached in his name among
all nations, beginning at Jerusalem.
48 And ye are witnesses of these things.
49 ¶ And, behold, I send the promise of my
Father upon you: but tarry ye in the city of
Jerusalem, until ye be endued with power
from on high.
50 ¶ And he led them out as far as to
Bethany, and he lifted up his hands, and
blessed them.
51 And it came to pass, while he blessed
them, he was parted from them, and carried
up into heaven.
52 And they worshipped him, and returned
to Jerusalem with great joy:
53 And were continually in the temple,
praising and blessing God. Amen.

The Gospel According To

John

John 1

1 In the beginning was the Word, and the
Word was with God, and the Word was God.
2 The same was in the beginning with God.
3 All things were made by him; and without
him was not any thing made that was made.
4 In him was life; and the life was the light
of men.
5 And the light shineth in darkness; and the
darkness comprehended it not.
6 ¶ There was a man sent from God, whose
name *was* John.
7 The same came for a witness, to bear
witness of the Light, that all *men* through
him might believe.
8 He was not that Light, but *was sent* to bear
witness of that Light.
9 *That* was the true Light, which lighteth
every man that cometh into the world.
10 He was in the world, and the world was
made by him, and the world knew him not.
11 He came unto his own, and his own
received him not.
12 But as many as received him, to them
gave he power to become the sons of God,
even to them that believe on his name:
13 Which were born, not of blood, nor of
the will of the flesh, nor of the will of man,
but of God.
14 And the Word was made flesh, and dwelt
among us, (and we beheld his glory, the
glory as of the only begotten of the Father,)
full of grace and truth.
15 ¶ John bare witness of him, and cried,
saying, This was he of whom I spake, He
that cometh after me is preferred before
me: for he was before me.
16 And of his fulness have all we received,
and grace for grace.
17 For the law was given by Moses, *but* grace
and truth came by Jesus Christ.
18 No man hath seen God at any time; the
only begotten Son, which is in the bosom of
the Father, he hath declared *him*.
19 ¶ And this is the record of John, when the
Jews sent priests and Levites from Jerusalem
to ask him, Who art thou?
20 And he confessed, and denied not; but
confessed, I am not the Christ.
21 And they asked him, What then? Art thou
Elias? And he saith, I am not. Art thou that
prophet? And he answered, No.

22 Then said they unto him, Who art thou?
that we may give an answer to them that
sent us. What sayest thou of thyself?
23 He said, I *am* the voice of one crying in
the wilderness, Make straight the way of the
Lord, as said the prophet Esaias.
24 And they which were sent were of the
Pharisees.
25 And they asked him, and said unto him,
Why baptizest thou then, if thou be not
that Christ, nor Elias, neither that prophet?
26 John answered them, saying, I baptize
with water: but there standeth one among
you, whom ye know not;
27 He it is, who coming after me is preferred
before me, whose shoe's latchet I am not
worthy to unloose.
28 These things were done in Bethabara
beyond Jordan, where John was baptizing.
29 ¶ The next day John seeth Jesus coming
unto him, and saith, Behold the Lamb of
God, which taketh away the sin of the world.
30 This is he of whom I said, After me cometh a man which is preferred before me: for
he was before me.
31 And I knew him not: but that he should
be made manifest to Israel, therefore am I
come baptizing with water.
32 And John bare record, saying, I saw the
Spirit descending from heaven like a dove,
and it abode upon him.
33 And I knew him not: but he that sent me
to baptize with water, the same said unto
me, Upon whom thou shalt see the Spirit
descending, and remaining on him, the same
is he which baptizeth with the Holy Spirit.
34 And I saw, and bare record that this is
the Son of God.
35 ¶ Again the next day after John stood,
and two of his disciples;
36 And looking upon Jesus as he walked, he
saith, Behold the Lamb of God!
37 And the two disciples heard him speak,
and they followed Jesus.
38 Then Jesus turned, and saw them following, and saith unto them, What seek
ye? They said unto him, Rabbi, (which is
to say, being interpreted, Master,) where
dwellest thou?
39 He saith unto them, Come and see.
They came and saw where he dwelt, and
abode with him that day: for it was about
the tenth hour.
40 One of the two which heard John *speak*,
and followed him, was Andrew, Simon
Peter's brother.
41 He first findeth his own brother Simon,
and saith unto him, We have found the Messias, which is, being interpreted, the Christ.
42 And he brought him to Jesus. And when
Jesus beheld him, he said, Thou art Simon
the son of Jona: thou shalt be called Cephas,
which is by interpretation, A stone.
43 ¶ The day following Jesus would go forth
into Galilee, and findeth Philip, and saith
unto him, Follow me.
44 Now Philip was of Bethsaida, the city of
Andrew and Peter.
45 Philip findeth Nathanael, and saith unto
him, We have found him, of whom Moses in
the law, and the prophets, did write, Jesus
of Nazareth, the son of Joseph.
46 And Nathanael said unto him, Can there
any good thing come out of Nazareth? Philip
saith unto him, Come and see.
47 Jesus saw Nathanael coming to him, and
saith of him, Behold an Israelite indeed, in
whom is no guile!
48 Nathanael saith unto him, Whence knowest thou me? Jesus answered and said unto
him, Before that Philip called thee, when
thou wast under the fig tree, I saw thee.
49 Nathanael answered and saith unto him,
Rabbi, thou art the Son of God; thou art the
King of Israel.
50 Jesus answered and said unto him,
Because I said unto thee, I saw thee under
the fig tree, believest thou? thou shalt see
greater things than these.
51 And he saith unto him, Verily, verily, I
say unto you, Hereafter ye shall see heaven
open, and the angels of God ascending and
descending upon the Son of man.

John 2

1 And the third day there was a marriage
in Cana of Galilee; and the mother of Jesus
was there:
2 And both Jesus was called, and his disciples, to the marriage.
3 And when they wanted wine, the mother
of Jesus saith unto him, They have no wine.
4 Jesus saith unto her, Woman, what have I
to do with thee? mine hour is not yet come.
5 His mother saith unto the servants, Whatsoever he saith unto you, do *it*.

6 And there were set there six waterpots
of stone, after the manner of the purifying
of the Jews, containing two or three firkins
apiece.
7 Jesus saith unto them, Fill the waterpots
with water. And they filled them up to the
brim.
8 And he saith unto them, Draw out now,
and bear unto the governor of the feast.
And they bare *it*.
9 When the ruler of the feast had tasted
the water that was made wine, and knew
not whence it was: (but the servants which
drew the water knew;) the governor of the
feast called the bridegroom,
10 And saith unto him, Every man at the
beginning doth set forth good wine; and
when men have well drunk, then that which
is worse: *but* thou hast kept the good wine
until now.
11 This beginning of miracles did Jesus in
Cana of Galilee, and manifested forth his
glory; and his disciples believed on him.
12 ¶ After this he went down to Capernaum,
he, and his mother, and his brethren, and
his disciples: and they continued there not
many days.
13 ¶ And the Jews' passover was at hand,
and Jesus went up to Jerusalem,
14 And found in the temple those that sold
oxen and sheep and doves, and the changers
of money sitting:
15 And when he had made a scourge of
small cords, he drove them all out of the
temple, and the sheep, and the oxen; and
poured out the changers' money, and overthrew the tables;
16 And said unto them that sold doves, Take
these things hence; make not my Father's
house an house of merchandise.
17 And his disciples remembered that it
was written, The zeal of thine house hath
eaten me up.
18 ¶ Then answered the Jews and said unto
him, What sign shewest thou unto us, seeing
that thou doest these things?
19 Jesus answered and said unto them,
Destroy this temple, and in three days I
will raise it up.
20 Then said the Jews, Forty and six years
was this temple in building, and wilt thou
rear it up in three days?
21 But he spake of the temple of his body.
22 When therefore he was risen from the
dead, his disciples remembered that he
had said this unto them; and they believed
the scripture, and the word which Jesus
had said.
23 ¶ Now when he was in Jerusalem at the
passover, in the feast *day*, many believed
in his name, when they saw the miracles
which he did.
24 But Jesus did not commit himself unto
them, because he knew all *men*,
25 And needed not that any should testify
of man: for he knew what was in man.

John 3

1 There was a man of the Pharisees, named
Nicodemus, a ruler of the Jews:
2 The same came to Jesus by night, and said
unto him, Rabbi, we know that thou art a
teacher come from God: for no man can
do these miracles that thou doest, except
God be with him.
3 Jesus answered and said unto him, Verily,
verily, I say unto thee, Except a man be born
again, he cannot see the kingdom of God.
4 Nicodemus saith unto him, How can a
man be born when he is old? can he enter
the second time into his mother's womb,
and be born?
5 Jesus answered, Verily, verily, I say unto
thee, Except a man be born of water and
of the Spirit, he cannot enter into the kingdom of God.
6 That which is born of the flesh is flesh;
and that which is born of the Spirit is spirit.
7 Marvel not that I said unto thee, Ye must
be born again.
8 The wind bloweth where it listeth, and
thou hearest the sound thereof, but canst
not tell whence it cometh, and whither it
goeth: so is every one that is born of the
Spirit.
9 Nicodemus answered and said unto him,
How can these things be?
10 Jesus answered and said unto him, Art
thou a master of Israel, and knowest not
these things?
11 Verily, verily, I say unto thee, We speak
that we do know, and testify that we have
seen; and ye receive not our witness.
12 If I have told you earthly things, and ye
believe not, how shall ye believe, if I tell you
of heavenly things?

13 And no man hath ascended up to heaven,
but he that came down from heaven, *even*
the Son of man which is in heaven.
14 ¶ And as Moses lifted up the serpent
in the wilderness, even so must the Son of
man be lifted up:
15 That whosoever believeth in him should
not perish, but have eternal life.
16 ¶ For God so loved the world, that he
gave his only begotten Son, that whosoever
believeth in him should not perish, but have
everlasting life.
17 For God sent not his Son into the world
to condemn the world; but that the world
through him might be saved.
18 ¶ He that believeth on him is not condemned:
but he that believeth not is condemned
already, because he hath not
believed in the name of the only begotten
Son of God.
19 And this is the condemnation, that light
is come into the world, and men loved
darkness rather than light, because their
deeds were evil.
20 For every one that doeth evil hateth the
light, neither cometh to the light, lest his
deeds should be reproved.
21 But he that doeth truth cometh to the
light, that his deeds may be made manifest,
that they are wrought in God.
22 ¶ After these things came Jesus and his
disciples into the land of Judæa; and there
he tarried with them, and baptized.
23 ¶ And John also was baptizing in Ænon
near to Salim, because there was much
water there: and they came, and were
baptized.
24 For John was not yet cast into prison.
25 ¶ Then there arose a question between
some of John's disciples and the Jews about
purifying.
26 And they came unto John, and said unto
him, Rabbi, he that was with thee beyond
Jordan, to whom thou barest witness,
behold, the same baptizeth, and all *men*
come to him.
27 John answered and said, A man can
receive nothing, except it be given him
from heaven.
28 Ye yourselves bear me witness, that I
said, I am not the Christ, but that I am sent
before him.
29 He that hath the bride is the bridegroom:
but the friend of the bridegroom, which
standeth and heareth him, rejoiceth greatly
because of the bridegroom's voice: this my
joy therefore is fulfilled.
30 He must increase, but I *must* decrease.
31 He that cometh from above is above
all: he that is of the earth is earthly, and
speaketh of the earth: he that cometh from
heaven is above all.
32 And what he hath seen and heard, that
he testifieth; and no man receiveth his
testimony.
33 He that hath received his testimony hath
set to his seal that God is true.
34 For he whom God hath sent speaketh
the words of God: for God giveth not the
Spirit by measure *unto him*.
35 The Father loveth the Son, and hath given
all things into his hand.
36 He that believeth on the Son hath everlasting
life: and he that believeth not the
Son shall not see life; but the wrath of God
abideth on him.

John 4

1 When therefore the Lord knew how the
Pharisees had heard that Jesus made and
baptized more disciples than John,
2 (Though Jesus himself baptized not, but
his disciples,)
3 He left Judæa, and departed again into
Galilee.
4 And he must needs go through Samaria.
5 Then cometh he to a city of Samaria, which
is called Sychar, near to the parcel of ground
that Jacob gave to his son Joseph.
6 Now Jacob's well was there. Jesus therefore,
being wearied with *his* journey, sat thus
on the well: *and* it was about the sixth hour.
7 There cometh a woman of Samaria to
draw water: Jesus saith unto her, Give me
to drink.
8 (For his disciples were gone away unto the
city to buy meat.)
9 Then saith the woman of Samaria unto
him, How is it that thou, being a Jew, askest
drink of me, which am a woman of Samaria?
for the Jews have no dealings with the
Samaritans.
10 Jesus answered and said unto her, If
thou knewest the gift of God, and who it is
that saith to thee, Give me to drink; thou

wouldest have asked of him, and he would
have given thee living water.
11 The woman saith unto him, Sir, thou
hast nothing to draw with, and the well
is deep: from whence then hast thou that
living water?
12 Art thou greater than our father Jacob,
which gave us the well, and drank thereof
himself, and his children, and his cattle?
13 Jesus answered and said unto her, Whosoever drinketh of this water shall thirst
again:
14 But whosoever drinketh of the water
that I shall give him shall never thirst; but
the water that I shall give him shall be in
him a well of water springing up into everlasting life.
15 The woman saith unto him, Sir, give me
this water, that I thirst not, neither come
hither to draw.
16 Jesus saith unto her, Go, call thy husband,
and come hither.
17 The woman answered and said, I have
no husband. Jesus said unto her, Thou hast
well said, I have no husband:
18 For thou hast had five husbands; and he
whom thou now hast is not thy husband: in
that saidst thou truly.
19 The woman saith unto him, Sir, I perceive
that thou art a prophet.
20 Our fathers worshipped in this mountain;
and ye say, that in Jerusalem is the place
where men ought to worship.
21 Jesus saith unto her, Woman, believe me,
the hour cometh, when ye shall neither in
this mountain, nor yet at Jerusalem, worship the Father.
22 Ye worship ye know not what: we know
what we worship: for salvation is of the
Jews.
23 But the hour cometh, and now is, when
the true worshippers shall worship the
Father in spirit and in truth: for the Father
seeketh such to worship him.
24 God *is* a Spirit: and they that worship
him must worship *him* in spirit and in truth.
25 The woman saith unto him, I know that
Messias cometh, which is called Christ:
when he is come, he will tell us all things.
26 Jesus saith unto her, I that speak unto
thee am *he*.
27 ¶ And upon this came his disciples, and
marvelled that he talked with the woman:
yet no man said, What seekest thou? or,
Why talkest thou with her?
28 The woman then left her waterpot,
and went her way into the city, and saith
to the men,
29 Come, see a man, which told me all things
that ever I did: is not this the Christ?
30 Then they went out of the city, and came
unto him.
31 ¶ In the mean while his disciples prayed
him, saying, Master, eat.
32 But he said unto them, I have meat to
eat that ye know not of.
33 Therefore said the disciples one to
another, Hath any man brought him *ought*
to eat?
34 Jesus saith unto them, My meat is to do
the will of him that sent me, and to finish
his work.
35 Say not ye, There are yet four months,
and *then* cometh harvest? behold, I say
unto you, Lift up your eyes, and look on the
fields; for they are white already to harvest.
36 And he that reapeth receiveth wages,
and gathereth fruit unto life eternal: that
both he that soweth and he that reapeth
may rejoice together.
37 And herein is that saying true, One
soweth, and another reapeth.
38 I sent you to reap that whereon ye
bestowed no labour: other men laboured,
and ye are entered into their labours.
39 ¶ And many of the Samaritans of that
city believed on him for the saying of the
woman, which testified, He told me all that
ever I did.
40 So when the Samaritans were come unto
him, they besought him that he would tarry
with them: and he abode there two days.
41 And many more believed because of his
own word;
42 And said unto the woman, Now we
believe, not because of thy saying: for we
have heard *him* ourselves, and know that
this is indeed the Christ, the Saviour of the
world.
43 ¶ Now after two days he departed
thence, and went into Galilee.
44 For Jesus himself testified, that a prophet
hath no honour in his own country.
45 Then when he was come into Galilee, the
Galilæans received him, having seen all the

things that he did at Jerusalem at the feast:
for they also went unto the feast.
46 So Jesus came again into Cana of Galilee,
where he made the water wine. And there
was a certain nobleman, whose son was
sick at Capernaum.
47 When he heard that Jesus was come out
of Judæa into Galilee, he went unto him,
and besought him that he would come
down, and heal his son: for he was at the
point of death.
48 Then said Jesus unto him, Except ye see
signs and wonders, ye will not believe.
49 The nobleman saith unto him, Sir, come
down ere my child die.
50 Jesus saith unto him, Go thy way; thy
son liveth. And the man believed the word
that Jesus had spoken unto him, and he
went his way.
51 And as he was now going down, his servants met him, and told *him*, saying, Thy
son liveth.
52 Then inquired he of them the hour when
he began to amend. And they said unto
him, Yesterday at the seventh hour the
fever left him.
53 So the father knew that *it was* at the
same hour, in the which Jesus said unto
him, Thy son liveth: and himself believed,
and his whole house.
54 This *is* again the second miracle *that*
Jesus did, when he was come out of Judæa
into Galilee.

John 5

1 After this there was a feast of the Jews;
and Jesus went up to Jerusalem.
2 Now there is at Jerusalem by the sheep
market a pool, which is called in the Hebrew
tongue Bethesda, having five porches.
3 In these lay a great multitude of impotent
folk, of blind, halt, withered, waiting for the
moving of the water.
4 For an angel went down at a certain season into the pool, and troubled the water:
whosoever then first after the troubling of
the water stepped in was made whole of
whatsoever disease he had.
5 And a certain man was there, which had
an infirmity thirty and eight years.
6 When Jesus saw him lie, and knew that he
had been now a long time *in that case*, he
saith unto him, Wilt thou be made whole?
7 The impotent man answered him, Sir, I
have no man, when the water is troubled, to
put me into the pool: but while I am coming,
another steppeth down before me.
8 Jesus saith unto him, Rise, take up thy
bed, and walk.
9 And immediately the man was made
whole, and took up his bed, and walked: and
on the same day was the sabbath.
10 ¶ The Jews therefore said unto him that
was cured, It is the sabbath day: it is not
lawful for thee to carry *thy* bed.
11 He answered them, He that made me
whole, the same said unto me, Take up thy
bed, and walk.
12 Then asked they him, What man is that
which said unto thee, Take up thy bed, and
walk?
13 And he that was healed wist not who it
was: for Jesus had conveyed himself away,
a multitude being in *that* place.
14 Afterward Jesus findeth him in the temple, and said unto him, Behold, thou art
made whole: sin no more, lest a worse thing
come unto thee.
15 The man departed, and told the Jews that
it was Jesus, which had made him whole.
16 And therefore did the Jews persecute
Jesus, and sought to slay him, because he
had done these things on the sabbath day.
17 ¶ But Jesus answered them, My Father
worketh hitherto, and I work.
18 Therefore the Jews sought the more to
kill him, because he not only had broken
the sabbath, but said also that God was
his Father, making himself equal with God.
19 Then answered Jesus and said unto them,
Verily, verily, I say unto you, The Son can do
nothing of himself, but what he seeth the
Father do: for what things soever he doeth,
these also doeth the Son likewise.
20 For the Father loveth the Son, and
sheweth him all things that himself doeth:
and he will shew him greater works than
these, that ye may marvel.
21 For as the Father raiseth up the dead,
and quickeneth *them;* even so the Son
quickeneth whom he will.
22 For the Father judgeth no man, but hath
committed all judgment unto the Son:
23 That all *men* should honour the Son,
even as they honour the Father. He that

honoureth not the Son honoureth not the
Father which hath sent him.
24 Verily, verily, I say unto you, He that
heareth my word, and believeth on him
that sent me, hath everlasting life, and shall
not come into condemnation; but is passed
from death unto life.
25 Verily, verily, I say unto you, The hour is
coming, and now is, when the dead shall
hear the voice of the Son of God: and they
that hear shall live.
26 For as the Father hath life in himself;
so hath he given to the Son to have life in
himself;
27 And hath given him authority to execute judgment also, because he is the Son
of man.
28 Marvel not at this: for the hour is coming,
in the which all that are in the graves shall
hear his voice,
29 And shall come forth; they that have
done good, unto the resurrection of life;
and they that have done evil, unto the resurrection of damnation.
30 I can of mine own self do nothing: as
I hear, I judge: and my judgment is just;
because I seek not mine own will, but the
will of the Father which hath sent me.
31 If I bear witness of myself, my witness
is not true.
32 ¶ There is another that beareth witness
of me; and I know that the witness which
he witnesseth of me is true.
33 Ye sent unto John, and he bare witness
unto the truth.
34 But I receive not testimony from man:
but these things I say, that ye might be
saved.
35 He was a burning and a shining light:
and ye were willing for a season to rejoice
in his light.
36 ¶ But I have greater witness than *that* of
John: for the works which the Father hath
given me to finish, the same works that
I do, bear witness of me, that the Father
hath sent me.
37 And the Father himself, which hath sent
me, hath borne witness of me. Ye have neither heard his voice at any time, nor seen
his shape.
38 And ye have not his word abiding in you:
for whom he hath sent, him ye believe not.
39 ¶ Search the scriptures; for in them ye
think ye have eternal life: and they are they
which testify of me.
40 And ye will not come to me, that ye
might have life.
41 I receive not honour from men.
42 But I know you, that ye have not the love
of God in you.
43 I am come in my Father's name, and ye
receive me not: if another shall come in his
own name, him ye will receive.
44 How can ye believe, which receive honour one of another, and seek not the honour
that *cometh* from God only?
45 Do not think that I will accuse you to the
Father: there is *one* that accuseth you, *even*
Moses, in whom ye trust.
46 For had ye believed Moses, ye would
have believed me: for he wrote of me.
47 But if ye believe not his writings, how
shall ye believe my words?

John 6

1 After these things Jesus went over the
sea of Galilee, which is *the sea* of Tiberias.
2 And a great multitude followed him,
because they saw his miracles which he did
on them that were diseased.
3 And Jesus went up into a mountain, and
there he sat with his disciples.
4 And the passover, a feast of the Jews,
was nigh.
5 ¶ When Jesus then lifted up *his* eyes,
and saw a great company come unto him,
he saith unto Philip, Whence shall we buy
bread, that these may eat?
6 And this he said to prove him: for he himself knew what he would do.
7 Philip answered him, Two hundred pennyworth of bread is not sufficient for them,
that every one of them may take a little.
8 One of his disciples, Andrew, Simon Peter's
brother, saith unto him,
9 There is a lad here, which hath five barley
loaves, and two small fishes: but what are
they among so many?
10 And Jesus said, Make the men sit down.
Now there was much grass in the place. So
the men sat down, in number about five
thousand.
11 And Jesus took the loaves; and when he
had given thanks, he distributed to the disciples, and the disciples to them that were

set down; and likewise of the fishes as much
as they would.
12 When they were filled, he said unto his
disciples, Gather up the fragments that
remain, that nothing be lost.
13 Therefore they gathered *them* together,
and filled twelve baskets with the fragments
of the five barley loaves, which remained
over and above unto them that had eaten.
14 Then those men, when they had seen
the miracle that Jesus did, said, This is of a
truth that prophet that should come into
the world.
15 ¶ When Jesus therefore perceived that
they would come and take him by force, to
make him a king, he departed again into a
mountain himself alone.
16 And when even was *now* come, his disciples went down unto the sea,
17 And entered into a ship, and went over
the sea toward Capernaum. And it was now
dark, and Jesus was not come to them.
18 And the sea arose by reason of a great
wind that blew.
19 So when they had rowed about five and
twenty or thirty furlongs, they see Jesus
walking on the sea, and drawing nigh unto
the ship: and they were afraid.
20 But he saith unto them, It is I; be not
afraid.
21 Then they willingly received him into the
ship: and immediately the ship was at the
land whither they went.
22 ¶ The day following, when the people
which stood on the other side of the sea
saw that there was none other boat there,
save that one whereinto his disciples were
entered, and that Jesus went not with his
disciples into the boat, but *that* his disciples
were gone away alone;
23 (Howbeit there came other boats from
Tiberias nigh unto the place where they
did eat bread, after that the Lord had given
thanks:)
24 When the people therefore saw that
Jesus was not there, neither his disciples,
they also took shipping, and came to Capernaum, seeking for Jesus.
25 And when they had found him on the
other side of the sea, they said unto him,
Rabbi, when camest thou hither?
26 Jesus answered them and said, Verily, verily, I say unto you, Ye seek me, not
because ye saw the miracles, but because
ye did eat of the loaves, and were filled.
27 Labour not for the meat which perisheth, but for that meat which endureth
unto everlasting life, which the Son of man
shall give unto you: for him hath God the
Father sealed.
28 Then said they unto him, What shall we
do, that we might work the works of God?
29 Jesus answered and said unto them, This
is the work of God, that ye believe on him
whom he hath sent.
30 They said therefore unto him, What sign
shewest thou then, that we may see, and
believe thee? what dost thou work?
31 Our fathers did eat manna in the desert;
as it is written, He gave them bread from
heaven to eat.
32 Then Jesus said unto them, Verily, verily,
I say unto you, Moses gave you not that
bread from heaven; but my Father giveth
you the true bread from heaven.
33 For the bread of God is he which cometh
down from heaven, and giveth life unto
the world.
34 Then said they unto him, Lord, evermore
give us this bread.
35 And Jesus said unto them, I am the bread
of life: he that cometh to me shall never
hunger; and he that believeth on me shall
never thirst.
36 But I said unto you, That ye also have
seen me, and believe not.
37 All that the Father giveth me shall come
to me; and him that cometh to me I will in
no wise cast out.
38 For I came down from heaven, not to
do mine own will, but the will of him that
sent me.
39 And this is the Father's will which hath
sent me, that of all which he hath given me
I should lose nothing, but should raise it up
again at the last day.
40 And this is the will of him that sent me,
that every one which seeth the Son, and
believeth on him, may have everlasting life:
and I will raise him up at the last day.
41 The Jews then murmured at him, because
he said, I am the bread which came down
from heaven.
42 And they said, Is not this Jesus, the son
of Joseph, whose father and mother we

know? how is it then that he saith, I came down from heaven?
43 Jesus therefore answered and said unto them, Murmur not among yourselves.
44 No man can come to me, except the Father which hath sent me draw him: and I will raise him up at the last day.
45 It is written in the prophets, And they shall be all taught of God. Every man therefore that hath heard, and hath learned of the Father, cometh unto me.
46 Not that any man hath seen the Father, save he which is of God, he hath seen the Father.
47 Verily, verily, I say unto you, He that believeth on me hath everlasting life.
48 I am that bread of life.
49 Your fathers did eat manna in the wilderness, and are dead.
50 This is the bread which cometh down from heaven, that a man may eat thereof, and not die.
51 I am the living bread which came down from heaven: if any man eat of this bread, he shall live for ever: and the bread that I will give is my flesh, which I will give for the life of the world.
52 The Jews therefore strove among themselves, saying, How can this man give us *his* flesh to eat?
53 Then Jesus said unto them, Verily, verily, I say unto you, Except ye eat the flesh of the Son of man, and drink his blood, ye have no life in you.
54 Whoso eateth my flesh, and drinketh my blood, hath eternal life; and I will raise him up at the last day.
55 For my flesh is meat indeed, and my blood is drink indeed.
56 He that eateth my flesh, and drinketh my blood, dwelleth in me, and I in him.
57 As the living Father hath sent me, and I live by the Father: so he that eateth me, even he shall live by me.
58 This is that bread which came down from heaven: not as your fathers did eat manna, and are dead: he that eateth of this bread shall live for ever.
59 These things said he in the synagogue, as he taught in Capernaum.
60 Many therefore of his disciples, when they had heard *this*, said, This is an hard saying; who can hear it?
61 When Jesus knew in himself that his disciples murmured at it, he said unto them, Doth this offend you?
62 *What* and if ye shall see the Son of man ascend up where he was before?
63 It is the spirit that quickeneth; the flesh profiteth nothing: the words that I speak unto you, *they* are spirit, and *they* are life.
64 But there are some of you that believe not. For Jesus knew from the beginning who they were that believed not, and who should betray him.
65 And he said, Therefore said I unto you, that no man can come unto me, except it were given unto him of my Father.
66 ¶ From that *time* many of his disciples went back, and walked no more with him.
67 Then said Jesus unto the twelve, Will ye also go away?
68 Then Simon Peter answered him, Lord, to whom shall we go? thou hast the words of eternal life.
69 And we believe and are sure that thou art that Christ, the Son of the living God.
70 Jesus answered them, Have not I chosen you twelve, and one of you is a devil?
71 He spake of Judas Iscariot *the son* of Simon: for he it was that should betray him, being one of the twelve.

John 7

1 After these things Jesus walked in Galilee: for he would not walk in Jewry, because the Jews sought to kill him.
2 Now the Jews' feast of tabernacles was at hand.
3 His brethren therefore said unto him, Depart hence, and go into Judæa, that thy disciples also may see the works that thou doest.
4 For *there is* no man *that* doeth any thing in secret, and he himself seeketh to be known openly. If thou do these things, shew thyself to the world.
5 For neither did his brethren believe in him.
6 Then Jesus said unto them, My time is not yet come: but your time is alway ready.
7 The world cannot hate you; but me it hateth, because I testify of it, that the works thereof are evil.
8 Go ye up unto this feast: I go not up yet unto this feast; for my time is not yet full come.

9 When he had said these words unto them,
he abode *still* in Galilee.
10 ¶ But when his brethren were gone up,
then went he also up unto the feast, not
openly, but as it were in secret.
11 Then the Jews sought him at the feast,
and said, Where is he?
12 And there was much murmuring among
the people concerning him: for some said,
He is a good man: others said, Nay; but he
deceiveth the people.
13 Howbeit no man spake openly of him for
fear of the Jews.
14 ¶ Now about the midst of the feast Jesus
went up into the temple, and taught.
15 And the Jews marvelled, saying, How
knoweth this man letters, having never
learned?
16 Jesus answered them, and said, My
doctrine is not mine, but his that sent me.
17 If any man will do his will, he shall know
of the doctrine, whether it be of God, or
whether I speak of myself.
18 He that speaketh of himself seeketh his
own glory: but he that seeketh his glory that
sent him, the same is true, and no unrighteousness is in him.
19 Did not Moses give you the law, and *yet*
none of you keepeth the law? Why go ye
about to kill me?
20 The people answered and said, Thou
hast a devil: who goeth about to kill thee?
21 Jesus answered and said unto them, I
have done one work, and ye all marvel.
22 Moses therefore gave unto you circumcision; (not because it is of Moses, but of
the fathers;) and ye on the sabbath day
circumcise a man.
23 If a man on the sabbath day receive
circumcision, that the law of Moses should
not be broken; are ye angry at me, because
I have made a man every whit whole on the
sabbath day?
24 Judge not according to the appearance,
but judge righteous judgment.
25 Then said some of them of Jerusalem, Is
not this he, whom they seek to kill?
26 But, lo, he speaketh boldly, and they
say nothing unto him. Do the rulers know
indeed that this is the very Christ?
27 Howbeit we know this man whence he is:
but when Christ cometh, no man knoweth
whence he is.
28 Then cried Jesus in the temple as he
taught, saying, Ye both know me, and ye
know whence I am: and I am not come of
myself, but he that sent me is true, whom
ye know not.
29 But I know him: for I am from him, and
he hath sent me.
30 Then they sought to take him: but no
man laid hands on him, because his hour
was not yet come.
31 And many of the people believed on
him, and said, When Christ cometh, will
he do more miracles than these which this
man hath done?
32 ¶ The Pharisees heard that the people
murmured such things concerning him;
and the Pharisees and the chief priests sent
officers to take him.
33 Then said Jesus unto them, Yet a little
while am I with you, and *then* I go unto him
that sent me.
34 Ye shall seek me, and shall not find *me:*
and where I am, *thither* ye cannot come.
35 Then said the Jews among themselves,
Whither will he go, that we shall not find
him? will he go unto the dispersed among
the Gentiles, and teach the Gentiles?
36 What *manner of* saying is this that he
said, Ye shall seek me, and shall not find *me:*
and where I am, *thither* ye cannot come?
37 In the last day, that great *day* of the feast,
Jesus stood and cried, saying, If any man
thirst, let him come unto me, and drink.
38 He that believeth on me, as the scripture
hath said, out of his belly shall flow rivers
of living water.
39 (But this spake he of the Spirit, which they
that believe on him should receive: for the
Holy Spirit was not yet *given;* because that
Jesus was not yet glorified.)
40 ¶ Many of the people therefore, when
they heard this saying, said, Of a truth this
is the Prophet.
41 Others said, This is the Christ. But some
said, Shall Christ come out of Galilee?
42 Hath not the scripture said, That Christ
cometh of the seed of David, and out of
the town of Bethlehem, where David was?
43 So there was a division among the people
because of him.
44 And some of them would have taken him;
but no man laid hands on him.
45 ¶ Then came the officers to the chief

priests and Pharisees; and they said unto
them, Why have ye not brought him?
46 The officers answered, Never man spake
like this man.
47 Then answered them the Pharisees, Are
ye also deceived?
48 Have any of the rulers or of the Pharisees
believed on him?
49 But this people who knoweth not the
law are cursed.
50 Nicodemus saith unto them, (he that
came to Jesus by night, being one of them,)
51 Doth our law judge *any* man, before it
hear him, and know what he doeth?
52 They answered and said unto him, Art
thou also of Galilee? Search, and look: for
out of Galilee ariseth no prophet.
53 And every man went unto his own house.

John 8

1 Jesus went unto the mount of Olives.
2 And early in the morning he came again
into the temple, and all the people came
unto him; and he sat down, and taught
them.
3 And the scribes and Pharisees brought
unto him a woman taken in adultery; and
when they had set her in the midst,
4 They say unto him, Master, this woman
was taken in adultery, in the very act.
5 Now Moses in the law commanded us,
that such should be stoned: but what sayest thou?
6 This they said, tempting him, that they
might have to accuse him. But Jesus stooped
down, and with *his* finger wrote on the
ground, *as though he heard them not*.
7 So when they continued asking him, he
lifted up himself, and said unto them, He
that is without sin among you, let him first
cast a stone at her.
8 And again he stooped down, and wrote
on the ground.
9 And they which heard *it*, being convicted
by *their own* conscience, went out one by
one, beginning at the eldest, *even* unto
the last: and Jesus was left alone, and the
woman standing in the midst.
10 When Jesus had lifted up himself, and
saw none but the woman, he said unto her,
Woman, where are those thine accusers?
hath no man condemned thee?
11 She said, No man, Lord. And Jesus said
unto her, Neither do I condemn thee: go,
and sin no more.
12 ¶ Then spake Jesus again unto them,
saying, I am the light of the world: he that
followeth me shall not walk in darkness, but
shall have the light of life.
13 The Pharisees therefore said unto him,
Thou bearest record of thyself; thy record
is not true.
14 Jesus answered and said unto them,
Though I bear record of myself, *yet* my
record is true: for I know whence I came,
and whither I go; but ye cannot tell whence
I come, and whither I go.
15 Ye judge after the flesh; I judge no man.
16 And yet if I judge, my judgment is true:
for I am not alone, but I and the Father that
sent me.
17 It is also written in your law, that the
testimony of two men is true.
18 I am one that bear witness of myself,
and the Father that sent me beareth witness of me.
19 Then said they unto him, Where is thy
Father? Jesus answered, Ye neither know
me, nor my Father: if ye had known me, ye
should have known my Father also.
20 These words spake Jesus in the treasury,
as he taught in the temple: and no man laid
hands on him; for his hour was not yet come.
21 Then said Jesus again unto them, I go
my way, and ye shall seek me, and shall die
in your sins: whither I go, ye cannot come.
22 Then said the Jews, Will he kill himself?
because he saith, Whither I go, ye cannot
come.
23 And he said unto them, Ye are from
beneath; I am from above: ye are of this
world; I am not of this world.
24 I said therefore unto you, that ye shall
die in your sins: for if ye believe not that I
am *he*, ye shall die in your sins.
25 Then said they unto him, Who art thou?
And Jesus saith unto them, Even *the same*
that I said unto you from the beginning.
26 I have many things to say and to judge
of you: but he that sent me is true; and I
speak to the world those things which I
have heard of him.
27 They understood not that he spake to
them of the Father.
28 Then said Jesus unto them, When ye
have lifted up the Son of man, then shall ye

know that I am *he*, and *that* I do nothing of
myself; but as my Father hath taught me, I
speak these things.
29 And he that sent me is with me: the
Father hath not left me alone; for I do always
those things that please him.
30 As he spake these words, many believed
on him.
31 Then said Jesus to those Jews which
believed on him, If ye continue in my word,
then are ye my disciples indeed;
32 And ye shall know the truth, and the truth
shall make you free.
33 ¶ They answered him, We be Abraham's seed, and were never in bondage
to any man: how sayest thou, Ye shall be
made free?
34 Jesus answered them, Verily, verily, I say
unto you, Whosoever committeth sin is the
servant of sin.
35 And the servant abideth not in the house
for ever: *but* the Son abideth ever.
36 If the Son therefore shall make you free,
ye shall be free indeed.
37 I know that ye are Abraham's seed; but
ye seek to kill me, because my word hath
no place in you.
38 I speak that which I have seen with my
Father: and ye do that which ye have seen
with your father.
39 They answered and said unto him, Abraham is our father. Jesus saith unto them, If
ye were Abraham's children, ye would do
the works of Abraham.
40 But now ye seek to kill me, a man that
hath told you the truth, which I have heard
of God: this did not Abraham.
41 Ye do the deeds of your father. Then said
they to him, We be not born of fornication;
we have one Father, *even* God.
42 Jesus said unto them, If God were your
Father, ye would love me: for I proceeded
forth and came from God; neither came I
of myself, but he sent me.
43 Why do ye not understand my speech?
even because ye cannot hear my word.
44 Ye are of *your* father the devil, and the
lusts of your father ye will do. He was a
murderer from the beginning, and abode
not in the truth, because there is no truth in
him. When he speaketh a lie, he speaketh of
his own: for he is a liar, and the father of it.
45 And because I tell *you* the truth, ye
believe me not.
46 Which of you convinceth me of sin? And
if I say the truth, why do ye not believe me?
47 He that is of God heareth God's words:
ye therefore hear *them* not, because ye are
not of God.
48 Then answered the Jews, and said unto
him, Say we not well that thou art a Samaritan, and hast a devil?
49 Jesus answered, I have not a devil; but I
honour my Father, and ye do dishonour me.
50 And I seek not mine own glory: there is
one that seeketh and judgeth.
51 Verily, verily, I say unto you, If a man keep
my saying, he shall never see death.
52 Then said the Jews unto him, Now we
know that thou hast a devil. Abraham is
dead, and the prophets; and thou sayest,
If a man keep my saying, he shall never
taste of death.
53 Art thou greater than our father Abraham, which is dead? and the prophets are
dead: whom makest thou thyself?
54 Jesus answered, If I honour myself,
my honour is nothing: it is my Father that
honoureth me; of whom ye say, that he is
your God:
55 Yet ye have not known him; but I know
him: and if I should say, I know him not, I
shall be a liar like unto you: but I know him,
and keep his saying.
56 Your father Abraham rejoiced to see my
day: and he saw *it*, and was glad.
57 Then said the Jews unto him, Thou art
not yet fifty years old, and hast thou seen
Abraham?
58 Jesus said unto them, Verily, verily, I say
unto you, Before Abraham was, I am.
59 Then took they up stones to cast at him:
but Jesus hid himself, and went out of the
temple, going through the midst of them,
and so passed by.

John 9

1 And as *Jesus* passed by, he saw a man
which was blind from *his* birth.
2 And his disciples asked him, saying, Master, who did sin, this man, or his parents,
that he was born blind?
3 Jesus answered, Neither hath this man
sinned, nor his parents: but that the works
of God should be made manifest in him.

4 I must work the works of him that sent
me, while it is day: the night cometh, when
no man can work.
5 As long as I am in the world, I am the light
of the world.
6 When he had thus spoken, he spat on
the ground, and made clay of the spittle,
and he anointed the eyes of the blind man
with the clay,
7 And said unto him, Go, wash in the pool
of Siloam, (which is by interpretation, Sent.)
He went his way therefore, and washed,
and came seeing.
8 ¶ The neighbours therefore, and they
which before had seen him that he was
blind, said, Is not this he that sat and
begged?
9 Some said, This is he: others *said*, He is
like him: *but* he said, I am *he*.
10 Therefore said they unto him, How were
thine eyes opened?
11 He answered and said, A man that is
called Jesus made clay, and anointed mine
eyes, and said unto me, Go to the pool of
Siloam, and wash: and I went and washed,
and I received sight.
12 Then said they unto him, Where is he?
He said, I know not.
13 ¶ They brought to the Pharisees him that
aforetime was blind.
14 And it was the sabbath day when Jesus
made the clay, and opened his eyes.
15 Then again the Pharisees also asked him
how he had received his sight. He said unto
them, He put clay upon mine eyes, and I
washed, and do see.
16 Therefore said some of the Pharisees,
This man is not of God, because he keepeth
not the sabbath day. Others said, How can a
man that is a sinner do such miracles? And
there was a division among them.
17 They say unto the blind man again, What
sayest thou of him, that he hath opened
thine eyes? He said, He is a prophet.
18 But the Jews did not believe concerning
him, that he had been blind, and received
his sight, until they called the parents of him
that had received his sight.
19 And they asked them, saying, Is this your
son, who ye say was born blind? how then
doth he now see?
20 His parents answered them and said,
We know that this is our son, and that he
was born blind:
21 But by what means he now seeth, we
know not; or who hath opened his eyes,
we know not: he is of age; ask him: he shall
speak for himself.
22 These *words* spake his parents, because
they feared the Jews: for the Jews had
agreed already, that if any man did confess
that he was Christ, he should be put out of
the synagogue.
23 Therefore said his parents, He is of age;
ask him.
24 Then again called they the man that
was blind, and said unto him, Give God the
praise: we know that this man is a sinner.
25 He answered and said, Whether he be a
sinner *or no*, I know not: one thing I know,
that, whereas I was blind, now I see.
26 Then said they to him again, What did he
to thee? how opened he thine eyes?
27 He answered them, I have told you
already, and ye did not hear: wherefore
would ye hear *it* again? will ye also be his
disciples?
28 Then they reviled him, and said, Thou
art his disciple; but we are Moses' disciples.
29 We know that God spake unto Moses: *as*
for this *fellow*, we know not from whence
he is.
30 The man answered and said unto them,
Why herein is a marvellous thing, that ye
know not from whence he is, and *yet* he
hath opened mine eyes.
31 Now we know that God heareth not
sinners: but if any man be a worshipper of
God, and doeth his will, him he heareth.
32 Since the world began was it not heard
that any man opened the eyes of one that
was born blind.
33 If this man were not of God, he could
do nothing.
34 They answered and said unto him, Thou
wast altogether born in sins, and dost thou
teach us? And they cast him out.
35 Jesus heard that they had cast him out;
and when he had found him, he said unto
him, Dost thou believe on the Son of God?
36 He answered and said, Who is he, Lord,
that I might believe on him?
37 And Jesus said unto him, Thou hast both
seen him, and it is he that talketh with thee.

38 And he said, Lord, I believe. And he worshipped him.
39 ¶ And Jesus said, For judgment I am come
into this world, that they which see not
might see; and that they which see might
be made blind.
40 And *some* of the Pharisees which were
with him heard these words, and said unto
him, Are we blind also?
41 Jesus said unto them, If ye were blind,
ye should have no sin: but now ye say, We
see; therefore your sin remaineth.

John 10

1 Verily, verily, I say unto you, He that entereth not by the door into the sheepfold, but
climbeth up some other way, the same is a
thief and a robber.
2 But he that entereth in by the door is the
shepherd of the sheep.
3 To him the porter openeth; and the sheep
hear his voice: and he calleth his own sheep
by name, and leadeth them out.
4 And when he putteth forth his own sheep,
he goeth before them, and the sheep follow
him: for they know his voice.
5 And a stranger will they not follow, but
will flee from him: for they know not the
voice of strangers.
6 This parable spake Jesus unto them: but
they understood not what things they were
which he spake unto them.
7 Then said Jesus unto them again, Verily,
verily, I say unto you, I am the door of the
sheep.
8 All that ever came before me are thieves
and robbers: but the sheep did not hear
them.
9 I am the door: by me if any man enter in,
he shall be saved, and shall go in and out,
and find pasture.
10 The thief cometh not, but for to steal,
and to kill, and to destroy: I am come that
they might have life, and that they might
have *it* more abundantly.
11 I am the good shepherd: the good shepherd giveth his life for the sheep.
12 But he that is an hireling, and not the
shepherd, whose own the sheep are not,
seeth the wolf coming, and leaveth the
sheep, and fleeth: and the wolf catcheth
them, and scattereth the sheep.
13 The hireling fleeth, because he is an hireling, and careth not for the sheep.
14 I am the good shepherd, and know my
sheep, and am known of mine.
15 As the Father knoweth me, even so
know I the Father: and I lay down my life
for the sheep.
16 And other sheep I have, which are not of
this fold: them also I must bring, and they
shall hear my voice; and there shall be one
fold, *and* one shepherd.
17 Therefore doth my Father love me,
because I lay down my life, that I might
take it again.
18 No man taketh it from me, but I lay it
down of myself. I have power to lay it down,
and I have power to take it again. This commandment have I received of my Father.
19 ¶ There was a division therefore again
among the Jews for these sayings.
20 And many of them said, He hath a devil,
and is mad; why hear ye him?
21 Others said, These are not the words of
him that hath a devil. Can a devil open the
eyes of the blind?
22 ¶ And it was at Jerusalem the feast of
the dedication, and it was winter.
23 And Jesus walked in the temple in Solomon's porch.
24 Then came the Jews round about him,
and said unto him, How long dost thou
make us to doubt? If thou be the Christ,
tell us plainly.
25 Jesus answered them, I told you, and
ye believed not: the works that I do in my
Father's name, they bear witness of me.
26 But ye believe not, because ye are not
of my sheep, as I said unto you.
27 My sheep hear my voice, and I know
them, and they follow me:
28 And I give unto them eternal life; and
they shall never perish, neither shall any
man pluck them out of my hand.
29 My Father, which gave *them* me, is
greater than all; and no *man* is able to pluck
them out of my Father's hand.
30 I and *my* Father are one.
31 Then the Jews took up stones again to
stone him.
32 Jesus answered them, Many good works
have I shewed you from my Father; for
which of those works do ye stone me?
33 The Jews answered him, saying, For

a good work we stone thee not; but for blasphemy; and because that thou, being a man, makest thyself God.

34 Jesus answered them, Is it not written in your law, I said, Ye are gods?

35 If he called them gods, unto whom the word of God came, and the scripture cannot be broken;

36 Say ye of him, whom the Father hath sanctified, and sent into the world, Thou blasphemest; because I said, I am the Son of God?

37 If I do not the works of my Father, believe me not.

38 But if I do, though ye believe not me, believe the works: that ye may know, and believe, that the Father *is* in me, and I in him.

39 Therefore they sought again to take him: but he escaped out of their hand,

40 And went away again beyond Jordan into the place where John at first baptized; and there he abode.

41 And many resorted unto him, and said, John did no miracle: but all things that John spake of this man were true.

42 And many believed on him there.

John 11

1 Now a certain *man* was sick, *named* Lazarus, of Bethany, the town of Mary and her sister Martha.

2 (It was *that* Mary which anointed the Lord with ointment, and wiped his feet with her hair, whose brother Lazarus was sick.)

3 Therefore his sisters sent unto him, saying, Lord, behold, he whom thou lovest is sick.

4 When Jesus heard *that*, he said, This sickness is not unto death, but for the glory of God, that the Son of God might be glorified thereby.

5 Now Jesus loved Martha, and her sister, and Lazarus.

6 When he had heard therefore that he was sick, he abode two days still in the same place where he was.

7 Then after that saith he to *his* disciples, Let us go into Judæa again.

8 *His* disciples say unto him, Master, the Jews of late sought to stone thee; and goest thou thither again?

9 Jesus answered, Are there not twelve hours in the day? If any man walk in the day, he stumbleth not, because he seeth the light of this world.

10 But if a man walk in the night, he stumbleth, because there is no light in him.

11 These things said he: and after that he saith unto them, Our friend Lazarus sleepeth; but I go, that I may awake him out of sleep.

12 Then said his disciples, Lord, if he sleep, he shall do well.

13 Howbeit Jesus spake of his death: but they thought that he had spoken of taking of rest in sleep.

14 Then said Jesus unto them plainly, Lazarus is dead.

15 And I am glad for your sakes that I was not there, to the intent ye may believe; nevertheless let us go unto him.

16 Then said Thomas, which is called Didymus, unto his fellowdisciples, Let us also go, that we may die with him.

17 Then when Jesus came, he found that he had *lain* in the grave four days already.

18 Now Bethany was nigh unto Jerusalem, about fifteen furlongs off:

19 And many of the Jews came to Martha and Mary, to comfort them concerning their brother.

20 Then Martha, as soon as she heard that Jesus was coming, went and met him: but Mary sat *still* in the house.

21 Then said Martha unto Jesus, Lord, if thou hadst been here, my brother had not died.

22 But I know, that even now, whatsoever thou wilt ask of God, God will give *it* thee.

23 Jesus saith unto her, Thy brother shall rise again.

24 Martha saith unto him, I know that he shall rise again in the resurrection at the last day.

25 Jesus said unto her, I am the resurrection, and the life: he that believeth in me, though he were dead, yet shall he live:

26 And whosoever liveth and believeth in me shall never die. Believest thou this?

27 She saith unto him, Yea, Lord: I believe that thou art the Christ, the Son of God, which should come into the world.

28 And when she had so said, she went her way, and called Mary her sister secretly, saying, The Master is come, and calleth for thee.

29 As soon as she heard *that*, she arose
quickly, and came unto him.
30 Now Jesus was not yet come into the
town, but was in that place where Martha
met him.
31 The Jews then which were with her in
the house, and comforted her, when they
saw Mary, that she rose up hastily and went
out, followed her, saying, She goeth unto
the grave to weep there.
32 Then when Mary was come where Jesus
was, and saw him, she fell down at his feet,
saying unto him, Lord, if thou hadst been
here, my brother had not died.
33 When Jesus therefore saw her weeping,
and the Jews also weeping which came
with her, he groaned in the spirit, and was
troubled,
34 And said, Where have ye laid him? They
said unto him, Lord, come and see.
35 Jesus wept.
36 Then said the Jews, Behold how he
loved him!
37 And some of them said, Could not this
man, which opened the eyes of the blind,
have caused that even this man should not
have died?
38 Jesus therefore again groaning in himself
cometh to the grave. It was a cave, and a
stone lay upon it.
39 Jesus said, Take ye away the stone. Martha, the sister of him that was dead, saith
unto him, Lord, by this time he stinketh: for
he hath been *dead* four days.
40 Jesus saith unto her, Said I not unto thee,
that, if thou wouldest believe, thou shouldest see the glory of God?
41 Then they took away the stone *from the
place* where the dead was laid. And Jesus
lifted up *his* eyes, and said, Father, I thank
thee that thou hast heard me.
42 And I knew that thou hearest me always:
but because of the people which stand by
I said *it*, that they may believe that thou
hast sent me.
43 And when he thus had spoken, he cried
with a loud voice, Lazarus, come forth.
44 And he that was dead came forth, bound
hand and foot with graveclothes: and his
face was bound about with a napkin. Jesus
saith unto them, Loose him, and let him go.
45 Then many of the Jews which came to
Mary, and had seen the things which Jesus
did, believed on him.
46 But some of them went their ways to
the Pharisees, and told them what things
Jesus had done.
47 ¶ Then gathered the chief priests and the
Pharisees a council, and said, What do we?
for this man doeth many miracles.
48 If we let him thus alone, all *men* will
believe on him: and the Romans shall come
and take away both our place and nation.
49 And one of them, *named* Caiaphas, being
the high priest that same year, said unto
them, Ye know nothing at all,
50 Nor consider that it is expedient for us,
that one man should die for the people, and
that the whole nation perish not.
51 And this spake he not of himself: but
being high priest that year, he prophesied
that Jesus should die for that nation;
52 And not for that nation only, but that
also he should gather together in one the
children of God that were scattered abroad.
53 Then from that day forth they took counsel together for to put him to death.
54 Jesus therefore walked no more openly
among the Jews; but went thence unto a
country near to the wilderness, into a city
called Ephraim, and there continued with
his disciples.
55 ¶ And the Jews' passover was nigh at
hand: and many went out of the country
up to Jerusalem before the passover, to
purify themselves.
56 Then sought they for Jesus, and spake
among themselves, as they stood in the
temple, What think ye, that he will not come
to the feast?
57 Now both the chief priests and the Pharisees had given a commandment, that, if any
man knew where he were, he should shew
it, that they might take him.

John 12

1 Then Jesus six days before the passover
came to Bethany, where Lazarus was which
had been dead, whom he raised from the
dead.
2 There they made him a supper; and Martha served: but Lazarus was one of them
that sat at the table with him.
3 Then took Mary a pound of ointment of
spikenard, very costly, and anointed the feet

of Jesus, and wiped his feet with her hair:
and the house was filled with the odour of
the ointment.
4 Then saith one of his disciples, Judas Iscariot, Simon's *son*, which should betray him,
5 Why was not this ointment sold for three
hundred pence, and given to the poor?
6 This he said, not that he cared for the poor;
but because he was a thief, and had the bag,
and bare what was put therein.
7 Then said Jesus, Let her alone: against the
day of my burying hath she kept this.
8 For the poor always ye have with you; but
me ye have not always.
9 Much people of the Jews therefore knew
that he was there: and they came not for
Jesus' sake only, but that they might see
Lazarus also, whom he had raised from
the dead.
10 ¶ But the chief priests consulted that they
might put Lazarus also to death;
11 Because that by reason of him many of
the Jews went away, and believed on Jesus.
12 ¶ On the next day much people that
were come to the feast, when they heard
that Jesus was coming to Jerusalem,
13 Took branches of palm trees, and went
forth to meet him, and cried, Hosanna:
Blessed *is* the King of Israel that cometh in
the name of the Lord.
14 And Jesus, when he had found a young
ass, sat thereon; as it is written,
15 Fear not, daughter of Sion: behold, thy
King cometh, sitting on an ass's colt.
16 These things understood not his disciples
at the first: but when Jesus was glorified,
then remembered they that these things
were written of him, and *that* they had done
these things unto him.
17 The people therefore that was with him
when he called Lazarus out of his grave,
and raised him from the dead, bare record.
18 For this cause the people also met him,
for that they heard that he had done this
miracle.
19 The Pharisees therefore said among
themselves, Perceive ye how ye prevail
nothing? behold, the world is gone after him.
20 ¶ And there were certain Greeks among
them that came up to worship at the feast:
21 The same came therefore to Philip, which
was of Bethsaida of Galilee, and desired him,
saying, Sir, we would see Jesus.
22 Philip cometh and telleth Andrew: and
again Andrew and Philip tell Jesus.
23 ¶ And Jesus answered them, saying, The
hour is come, that the Son of man should
be glorified.
24 Verily, verily, I say unto you, Except a
corn of wheat fall into the ground and die,
it abideth alone: but if it die, it bringeth
forth much fruit.
25 He that loveth his life shall lose it; and he
that hateth his life in this world shall keep
it unto life eternal.
26 If any man serve me, let him follow me;
and where I am, there shall also my servant
be: if any man serve me, him will *my* Father
honour.
27 Now is my soul troubled; and what shall
I say? Father, save me from this hour: but
for this cause came I unto this hour.
28 Father, glorify thy name. Then came
there a voice from heaven, *saying*, I have
both glorified *it*, and will glorify *it* again.
29 The people therefore, that stood by, and
heard *it*, said that it thundered: others said,
An angel spake to him.
30 Jesus answered and said, This voice came
not because of me, but for your sakes.
31 Now is the judgment of this world: now
shall the prince of this world be cast out.
32 And I, if I be lifted up from the earth, will
draw all *men* unto me.
33 This he said, signifying what death he
should die.
34 The people answered him, We have
heard out of the law that Christ abideth for
ever: and how sayest thou, The Son of man
must be lifted up? who is this Son of man?
35 Then Jesus said unto them, Yet a little
while is the light with you. Walk while ye
have the light, lest darkness come upon you:
for he that walketh in darkness knoweth not
whither he goeth.
36 While ye have light, believe in the light,
that ye may be the children of light. These
things spake Jesus, and departed, and did
hide himself from them.
37 ¶ But though he had done so many
miracles before them, yet they believed
not on him:
38 That the saying of Esaias the prophet
might be fulfilled, which he spake, Lord,
who hath believed our report? and to whom
hath the arm of the Lord been revealed?

39 Therefore they could not believe,
because that Esaias said again,
40 He hath blinded their eyes, and hardened
their heart; that they should not see with
their eyes, nor understand with *their* heart,
and be converted, and I should heal them.
41 These things said Esaias, when he saw
his glory, and spake of him.
42 ¶ Nevertheless among the chief rulers
also many believed on him; but because of
the Pharisees they did not confess *him*, lest
they should be put out of the synagogue:
43 For they loved the praise of men more
than the praise of God.
44 ¶ Jesus cried and said, He that believeth
on me, believeth not on me, but on him
that sent me.
45 And he that seeth me seeth him that
sent me.
46 I am come a light into the world, that
whosoever believeth on me should not
abide in darkness.
47 And if any man hear my words, and
believe not, I judge him not: for I came not
to judge the world, but to save the world.
48 He that rejecteth me, and receiveth not
my words, hath one that judgeth him: the
word that I have spoken, the same shall
judge him in the last day.
49 For I have not spoken of myself; but the
Father which sent me, he gave me a commandment, what I should say, and what I
should speak.
50 And I know that his commandment is life
everlasting: whatsoever I speak therefore,
even as the Father said unto me, so I speak.

John 13

1 Now before the feast of the passover,
when Jesus knew that his hour was come
that he should depart out of this world unto
the Father, having loved his own which were
in the world, he loved them unto the end.
2 And supper being ended, the devil having
now put into the heart of Judas Iscariot,
Simon's *son*, to betray him;
3 Jesus knowing that the Father had given
all things into his hands, and that he was
come from God, and went to God;
4 He riseth from supper, and laid aside his
garments; and took a towel, and girded
himself.
5 After that he poureth water into a bason,
and began to wash the disciples' feet, and
to wipe *them* with the towel wherewith he
was girded.
6 Then cometh he to Simon Peter: and
Peter saith unto him, Lord, dost thou wash
my feet?
7 Jesus answered and said unto him, What
I do thou knowest not now; but thou shalt
know hereafter.
8 Peter saith unto him, Thou shalt never
wash my feet. Jesus answered him, If I wash
thee not, thou hast no part with me.
9 Simon Peter saith unto him, Lord, not my
feet only, but also *my* hands and *my* head.
10 Jesus saith to him, He that is washed needeth not save to wash *his* feet, but is clean
every whit: and ye are clean, but not all.
11 For he knew who should betray him;
therefore said he, Ye are not all clean.
12 So after he had washed their feet, and
had taken his garments, and was set down
again, he said unto them, Know ye what I
have done to you?
13 Ye call me Master and Lord: and ye say
well; for *so* I am.
14 If I then, *your* Lord and Master, have
washed your feet; ye also ought to wash
one another's feet.
15 For I have given you an example, that ye
should do as I have done to you.
16 Verily, verily, I say unto you, The servant
is not greater than his lord; neither he that
is sent greater than he that sent him.
17 If ye know these things, happy are ye if
ye do them.
18 ¶ I speak not of you all: I know whom I
have chosen: but that the scripture may be
fulfilled, He that eateth bread with me hath
lifted up his heel against me.
19 Now I tell you before it come, that,
when it is come to pass, ye may believe
that I am *he*.
20 Verily, verily, I say unto you, He that
receiveth whomsoever I send receiveth
me; and he that receiveth me receiveth
him that sent me.
21 When Jesus had thus said, he was troubled in spirit, and testified, and said, Verily,
verily, I say unto you, that one of you shall
betray me.
22 Then the disciples looked one on another,
doubting of whom he spake.

23 Now there was leaning on Jesus' bosom
one of his disciples, whom Jesus loved.
24 Simon Peter therefore beckoned to
him, that he should ask who it should be
of whom he spake.
25 He then lying on Jesus' breast saith unto
him, Lord, who is it?
26 Jesus answered, He it is, to whom I shall
give a sop, when I have dipped *it*. And when
he had dipped the sop, he gave *it* to Judas
Iscariot, *the son* of Simon.
27 And after the sop Satan entered into
him. Then said Jesus unto him, That thou
doest, do quickly.
28 Now no man at the table knew for what
intent he spake this unto him.
29 For some *of them* thought, because
Judas had the bag, that Jesus had said unto
him, Buy *those things* that we have need
of against the feast; or, that he should give
something to the poor.
30 He then having received the sop went
immediately out: and it was night.
31 ¶ Therefore, when he was gone out, Jesus
said, Now is the Son of man glorified, and
God is glorified in him.
32 If God be glorified in him, God shall also
glorify him in himself, and shall straightway
glorify him.
33 Little children, yet a little while I am with
you. Ye shall seek me: and as I said unto the
Jews, Whither I go, ye cannot come; so now
I say to you.
34 A new commandment I give unto you,
That ye love one another; as I have loved
you, that ye also love one another.
35 By this shall all *men* know that ye are my
disciples, if ye have love one to another.
36 ¶ Simon Peter said unto him, Lord,
whither goest thou? Jesus answered him,
Whither I go, thou canst not follow me now;
but thou shalt follow me afterwards.
37 Peter said unto him, Lord, why cannot
I follow thee now? I will lay down my life
for thy sake.
38 Jesus answered him, Wilt thou lay down
thy life for my sake? Verily, verily, I say unto
thee, The cock shall not crow, till thou hast
denied me thrice.

John 14

1 Let not your heart be troubled: ye believe
in God, believe also in me.
2 In my Father's house are many mansions:
if *it were* not *so*, I would have told you. I go
to prepare a place for you.
3 And if I go and prepare a place for you,
I will come again, and receive you unto
myself; that where I am, *there* ye may be
also.
4 And whither I go ye know, and the way
ye know.
5 Thomas saith unto him, Lord, we know
not whither thou goest; and how can we
know the way?
6 Jesus saith unto him, I am the way, the
truth, and the life: no man cometh unto the
Father, but by me.
7 If ye had known me, ye should have known
my Father also: and from henceforth ye
know him, and have seen him.
8 Philip saith unto him, Lord, shew us the
Father, and it sufficeth us.
9 Jesus saith unto him, Have I been so long
time with you, and yet hast thou not known
me, Philip? he that hath seen me hath seen
the Father; and how sayest thou *then*, Shew
us the Father?
10 Believest thou not that I am in the Father,
and the Father in me? the words that I
speak unto you I speak not of myself: but
the Father that dwelleth in me, he doeth
the works.
11 Believe me that I *am* in the Father, and
the Father in me: or else believe me for the
very works' sake.
12 Verily, verily, I say unto you, He that believeth on me, the works that I do shall he do
also; and greater *works* than these shall he
do; because I go unto my Father.
13 And whatsoever ye shall ask in my name,
that will I do, that the Father may be glorified in the Son.
14 If ye shall ask any thing in my name, I
will do *it*.
15 ¶ If ye love me, keep my commandments.
16 And I will pray the Father, and he shall
give you another Comforter, that he may
abide with you for ever;
17 *Even* the Spirit of truth; whom the world
cannot receive, because it seeth him not,
neither knoweth him: but ye know him; for
he dwelleth with you, and shall be in you.
18 I will not leave you comfortless: I will
come to you.
19 Yet a little while, and the world seeth

me no more; but ye see me: because I live, ye shall live also.
20 At that day ye shall know that I *am* in my Father, and ye in me, and I in you.
21 He that hath my commandments, and keepeth them, he it is that loveth me: and he that loveth me shall be loved of my Father, and I will love him, and will manifest myself to him.
22 Judas saith unto him, not Iscariot, Lord, how is it that thou wilt manifest thyself unto us, and not unto the world?
23 Jesus answered and said unto him, If a man love me, he will keep my words: and my Father will love him, and we will come unto him, and make our abode with him.
24 He that loveth me not keepeth not my sayings: and the word which ye hear is not mine, but the Father's which sent me.
25 These things have I spoken unto you, being *yet* present with you.
26 But the Comforter, *which is* the Holy Spirit, whom the Father will send in my name, he shall teach you all things, and bring all things to your remembrance, whatsoever I have said unto you.
27 Peace I leave with you, my peace I give unto you: not as the world giveth, give I unto you. Let not your heart be troubled, neither let it be afraid.
28 Ye have heard how I said unto you, I go away, and come *again* unto you. If ye loved me, ye would rejoice, because I said, I go unto the Father: for my Father is greater than I.
29 And now I have told you before it come to pass, that, when it is come to pass, ye might believe.
30 Hereafter I will not talk much with you: for the prince of this world cometh, and hath nothing in me.
31 But that the world may know that I love the Father; and as the Father gave me commandment, even so I do. Arise, let us go hence.

John 15

1 I am the true vine, and my Father is the husbandman.
2 Every branch in me that beareth not fruit he taketh away: and every *branch* that beareth fruit, he purgeth it, that it may bring forth more fruit.
3 Now ye are clean through the word which I have spoken unto you.
4 Abide in me, and I in you. As the branch cannot bear fruit of itself, except it abide in the vine; no more can ye, except ye abide in me.
5 I am the vine, ye *are* the branches: He that abideth in me, and I in him, the same bringeth forth much fruit: for without me ye can do nothing.
6 If a man abide not in me, he is cast forth as a branch, and is withered; and men gather them, and cast *them* into the fire, and they are burned.
7 If ye abide in me, and my words abide in you, ye shall ask what ye will, and it shall be done unto you.
8 Herein is my Father glorified, that ye bear much fruit; so shall ye be my disciples.
9 As the Father hath loved me, so have I loved you: continue ye in my love.
10 If ye keep my commandments, ye shall abide in my love; even as I have kept my Father's commandments, and abide in his love.
11 These things have I spoken unto you, that my joy might remain in you, and *that* your joy might be full.
12 This is my commandment, That ye love one another, as I have loved you.
13 Greater love hath no man than this, that a man lay down his life for his friends.
14 Ye are my friends, if ye do whatsoever I command you.
15 Henceforth I call you not servants; for the servant knoweth not what his lord doeth: but I have called you friends; for all things that I have heard of my Father I have made known unto you.
16 Ye have not chosen me, but I have chosen you, and ordained you, that ye should go and bring forth fruit, and *that* your fruit should remain: that whatsoever ye shall ask of the Father in my name, he may give it you.
17 These things I command you, that ye love one another.
18 If the world hate you, ye know that it hated me before *it hated* you.
19 If ye were of the world, the world would love his own: but because ye are not of the world, but I have chosen you out of the world, therefore the world hateth you.
20 Remember the word that I said unto you,

The servant is not greater than his lord. If
they have persecuted me, they will also
persecute you; if they have kept my saying,
they will keep yours also.
21 But all these things will they do unto you
for my name's sake, because they know not
him that sent me.
22 If I had not come and spoken unto them,
they had not had sin: but now they have no
cloke for their sin.
23 He that hateth me hateth my Father also.
24 If I had not done among them the works
which none other man did, they had not had
sin: but now have they both seen and hated
both me and my Father.
25 But *this cometh to pass*, that the word
might be fulfilled that is written in their law,
They hated me without a cause.
26 But when the Comforter is come, whom
I will send unto you from the Father, *even*
the Spirit of truth, which proceedeth from
the Father, he shall testify of me:
27 And ye also shall bear witness, because
ye have been with me from the beginning.

John 16

1 These things have I spoken unto you, that
ye should not be offended.
2 They shall put you out of the synagogues:
yea, the time cometh, that whosoever killeth
you will think that he doeth God service.
3 And these things will they do unto you,
because they have not known the Father,
nor me.
4 But these things have I told you, that when
the time shall come, ye may remember that
I told you of them. And these things I said
not unto you at the beginning, because I
was with you.
5 But now I go my way to him that sent
me; and none of you asketh me, Whither
goest thou?
6 But because I have said these things unto
you, sorrow hath filled your heart.
7 Nevertheless I tell you the truth; It is
expedient for you that I go away: for if I go
not away, the Comforter will not come unto
you; but if I depart, I will send him unto you.
8 And when he is come, he will reprove the
world of sin, and of righteousness, and of
judgment:
9 Of sin, because they believe not on me;
10 Of righteousness, because I go to my
Father, and ye see me no more;
11 Of judgment, because the prince of this
world is judged.
12 I have yet many things to say unto you,
but ye cannot bear them now.
13 Howbeit when he, the Spirit of truth, is
come, he will guide you into all truth: for he
shall not speak of himself; but whatsoever
he shall hear, *that* shall he speak: and he
will shew you things to come.
14 He shall glorify me: for he shall receive
of mine, and shall shew *it* unto you.
15 All things that the Father hath are mine:
therefore said I, that he shall take of mine,
and shall shew *it* unto you.
16 A little while, and ye shall not see me:
and again, a little while, and ye shall see
me, because I go to the Father.
17 Then said *some* of his disciples among
themselves, What is this that he saith unto
us, A little while, and ye shall not see me:
and again, a little while, and ye shall see me:
and, Because I go to the Father?
18 They said therefore, What is this that
he saith, A little while? we cannot tell what
he saith.
19 Now Jesus knew that they were desirous to ask him, and said unto them, Do ye
inquire among yourselves of that I said, A
little while, and ye shall not see me: and
again, a little while, and ye shall see me?
20 Verily, verily, I say unto you, That ye
shall weep and lament, but the world shall
rejoice: and ye shall be sorrowful, but your
sorrow shall be turned into joy.
21 A woman when she is in travail hath
sorrow, because her hour is come: but as
soon as she is delivered of the child, she
remembereth no more the anguish, for joy
that a man is born into the world.
22 And ye now therefore have sorrow:
but I will see you again, and your heart
shall rejoice, and your joy no man taketh
from you.
23 And in that day ye shall ask me nothing.
Verily, verily, I say unto you, Whatsoever
ye shall ask the Father in my name, he will
give *it* you.
24 Hitherto have ye asked nothing in my
name: ask, and ye shall receive, that your
joy may be full.
25 These things have I spoken unto you in

proverbs: but the time cometh, when I shall
no more speak unto you in proverbs, but I
shall shew you plainly of the Father.
26 At that day ye shall ask in my name:
and I say not unto you, that I will pray the
Father for you:
27 For the Father himself loveth you,
because ye have loved me, and have
believed that I came out from God.
28 I came forth from the Father, and am
come into the world: again, I leave the
world, and go to the Father.
29 His disciples said unto him, Lo, now
speakest thou plainly, and speakest no
proverb.
30 Now are we sure that thou knowest all
things, and needest not that any man should
ask thee: by this we believe that thou camest
forth from God.
31 Jesus answered them, Do ye now believe?
32 Behold, the hour cometh, yea, is now
come, that ye shall be scattered, every
man to his own, and shall leave me alone:
and yet I am not alone, because the Father
is with me.
33 These things I have spoken unto you, that
in me ye might have peace. In the world ye
shall have tribulation: but be of good cheer;
I have overcome the world.

John 17

1 These words spake Jesus, and lifted up his
eyes to heaven, and said, Father, the hour
is come; glorify thy Son, that thy Son also
may glorify thee:
2 As thou hast given him power over all
flesh, that he should give eternal life to as
many as thou hast given him.
3 And this is life eternal, that they might
know thee the only true God, and Jesus
Christ, whom thou hast sent.
4 I have glorified thee on the earth: I have
finished the work which thou gavest me
to do.
5 And now, O Father, glorify thou me with
thine own self with the glory which I had
with thee before the world was.
6 I have manifested thy name unto the men
which thou gavest me out of the world:
thine they were, and thou gavest them me;
and they have kept thy word.
7 Now they have known that all things
whatsoever thou hast given me are of thee.
8 For I have given unto them the words
which thou gavest me; and they have
received *them*, and have known surely
that I came out from thee, and they have
believed that thou didst send me.
9 I pray for them: I pray not for the world,
but for them which thou hast given me; for
they are thine.
10 And all mine are thine, and thine are
mine; and I am glorified in them.
11 And now I am no more in the world, but
these are in the world, and I come to thee.
Holy Father, keep through thine own name
those whom thou hast given me, that they
may be one, as we *are*.
12 While I was with them in the world, I kept
them in thy name: those that thou gavest
me I have kept, and none of them is lost,
but the son of perdition; that the scripture
might be fulfilled.
13 And now come I to thee; and these things
I speak in the world, that they might have
my joy fulfilled in themselves.
14 I have given them thy word; and the
world hath hated them, because they are
not of the world, even as I am not of the
world.
15 I pray not that thou shouldest take them
out of the world, but that thou shouldest
keep them from the evil.
16 They are not of the world, even as I am
not of the world.
17 Sanctify them through thy truth: thy
word is truth.
18 As thou hast sent me into the world,
even so have I also sent them into the world.
19 And for their sakes I sanctify myself,
that they also might be sanctified through
the truth.
20 Neither pray I for these alone, but for
them also which shall believe on me through
their word;
21 That they all may be one; as thou, Father,
art in me, and I in thee, that they also may
be one in us: that the world may believe
that thou hast sent me.
22 And the glory which thou gavest me I
have given them; that they may be one,
even as we are one:
23 I in them, and thou in me, that they may
be made perfect in one; and that the world
may know that thou hast sent me, and hast
loved them, as thou hast loved me.

24 Father, I will that they also, whom thou
hast given me, be with me where I am; that
they may behold my glory, which thou hast
given me: for thou lovedst me before the
foundation of the world.
25 O righteous Father, the world hath not
known thee: but I have known thee, and
these have known that thou hast sent me.
26 And I have declared unto them thy name,
and will declare *it:* that the love wherewith
thou hast loved me may be in them, and I
in them.

John 18

1 When Jesus had spoken these words, he
went forth with his disciples over the brook
Cedron, where was a garden, into the which
he entered, and his disciples.
2 And Judas also, which betrayed him, knew
the place: for Jesus ofttimes resorted thither
with his disciples.
3 Judas then, having received a band *of
men* and officers from the chief priests and
Pharisees, cometh thither with lanterns and
torches and weapons.
4 Jesus therefore, knowing all things that
should come upon him, went forth, and
said unto them, Whom seek ye?
5 They answered him, Jesus of Nazareth.
Jesus saith unto them, I am *he.* And Judas
also, which betrayed him, stood with them.
6 As soon then as he had said unto them,
I am *he*, they went backward, and fell to
the ground.
7 Then asked he them again, Whom seek
ye? And they said, Jesus of Nazareth.
8 Jesus answered, I have told you that I
am *he:* if therefore ye seek me, let these
go their way:
9 That the saying might be fulfilled, which
he spake, Of them which thou gavest me
have I lost none.
10 Then Simon Peter having a sword drew
it, and smote the high priest's servant, and
cut off his right ear. The servant's name
was Malchus.
11 Then said Jesus unto Peter, Put up thy
sword into the sheath: the cup which my
Father hath given me, shall I not drink it?
12 Then the band and the captain and officers of the Jews took Jesus, and bound him,
13 And led him away to Annas first; for he
was father in law to Caiaphas, which was
the high priest that same year.
14 Now Caiaphas was he, which gave counsel to the Jews, that it was expedient that
one man should die for the people.
15 ¶ And Simon Peter followed Jesus, and
so did another disciple: that disciple was
known unto the high priest, and went in
with Jesus into the palace of the high priest.
16 But Peter stood at the door without.
Then went out that other disciple, which was
known unto the high priest, and spake unto
her that kept the door, and brought in Peter.
17 Then saith the damsel that kept the door
unto Peter, Art not thou also *one* of this
man's disciples? He saith, I am not.
18 And the servants and officers stood
there, who had made a fire of coals; for it
was cold: and they warmed themselves: and
Peter stood with them, and warmed himself.
19 ¶ The high priest then asked Jesus of his
disciples, and of his doctrine.
20 Jesus answered him, I spake openly to
the world; I ever taught in the synagogue,
and in the temple, whither the Jews always
resort; and in secret have I said nothing.
21 Why askest thou me? ask them which
heard me, what I have said unto them:
behold, they know what I said.
22 And when he had thus spoken, one of
the officers which stood by struck Jesus with
the palm of his hand, saying, Answerest thou
the high priest so?
23 Jesus answered him, If I have spoken
evil, bear witness of the evil: but if well, why
smitest thou me?
24 Now Annas had sent him bound unto
Caiaphas the high priest.
25 And Simon Peter stood and warmed
himself. They said therefore unto him, Art
not thou also *one* of his disciples? He denied
it, and said, I am not.
26 One of the servants of the high priest,
being *his* kinsman whose ear Peter cut
off, saith, Did not I see thee in the garden
with him?
27 Peter then denied again: and immediately
the cock crew.
28 ¶ Then led they Jesus from Caiaphas unto
the hall of judgment: and it was early; and
they themselves went not into the judgment
hall, lest they should be defiled; but that
they might eat the passover.

29 Pilate then went out unto them, and said,
What accusation bring ye against this man?
30 They answered and said unto him, If he
were not a malefactor, we would not have
delivered him up unto thee.
31 Then said Pilate unto them, Take ye him,
and judge him according to your law. The
Jews therefore said unto him, It is not lawful
for us to put any man to death:
32 That the saying of Jesus might be fulfilled,
which he spake, signifying what death he
should die.
33 Then Pilate entered into the judgment
hall again, and called Jesus, and said unto
him, Art thou the King of the Jews?
34 Jesus answered him, Sayest thou this
thing of thyself, or did others tell it thee
of me?
35 Pilate answered, Am I a Jew? Thine own
nation and the chief priests have delivered
thee unto me: what hast thou done?
36 Jesus answered, My kingdom is not of
this world: if my kingdom were of this world,
then would my servants fight, that I should
not be delivered to the Jews: but now is my
kingdom not from hence.
37 Pilate therefore said unto him, Art thou
a king then? Jesus answered, Thou sayest
that I am a king. To this end was I born, and
for this cause came I into the world, that I
should bear witness unto the truth. Every
one that is of the truth heareth my voice.
38 Pilate saith unto him, What is truth? And
when he had said this, he went out again
unto the Jews, and saith unto them, I find
in him no fault *at all*.
39 But ye have a custom, that I should
release unto you one at the passover: will
ye therefore that I release unto you the
King of the Jews?
40 Then cried they all again, saying, Not
this man, but Barabbas. Now Barabbas
was a robber.

John 19

1 Then Pilate therefore took Jesus, and
scourged *him*.
2 And the soldiers platted a crown of thorns,
and put *it* on his head, and they put on him
a purple robe,
3 And said, Hail, King of the Jews! and they
smote him with their hands.
4 Pilate therefore went forth again, and saith
unto them, Behold, I bring him forth to you,
that ye may know that I find no fault in him.
5 Then came Jesus forth, wearing the crown
of thorns, and the purple robe. And *Pilate*
saith unto them, Behold the man!
6 When the chief priests therefore and
officers saw him, they cried out, saying,
Crucify *him*, crucify *him*. Pilate saith unto
them, Take ye him, and crucify *him:* for I
find no fault in him.
7 The Jews answered him, We have a law,
and by our law he ought to die, because he
made himself the Son of God.
8 ¶ When Pilate therefore heard that saying,
he was the more afraid;
9 And went again into the judgment hall,
and saith unto Jesus, Whence art thou? But
Jesus gave him no answer.
10 Then saith Pilate unto him, Speakest thou
not unto me? knowest thou not that I have
power to crucify thee, and have power to
release thee?
11 Jesus answered, Thou couldest have
no power *at all* against me, except it were
given thee from above: therefore he that
delivered me unto thee hath the greater sin.
12 And from thenceforth Pilate sought to
release him: but the Jews cried out, saying,
If thou let this man go, thou art not Cæsar's
friend: whosoever maketh himself a king
speaketh against Cæsar.
13 ¶ When Pilate therefore heard that saying, he brought Jesus forth, and sat down in
the judgment seat in a place that is called
the Pavement, but in the Hebrew, Gabbatha.
14 And it was the preparation of the passover, and about the sixth hour: and he saith
unto the Jews, Behold your King!
15 But they cried out, Away with *him*, away
with *him*, crucify him. Pilate saith unto them,
Shall I crucify your King? The chief priests
answered, We have no king but Cæsar.
16 Then delivered he him therefore unto
them to be crucified. And they took Jesus,
and led *him* away.
17 And he bearing his cross went forth into
a place called *the place* of a skull, which is
called in the Hebrew Golgotha:
18 Where they crucified him, and two other
with him, on either side one, and Jesus in
the midst.
19 ¶ And Pilate wrote a title, and put *it* on

the cross. And the writing was, JESUS OF
NAZARETH THE KING OF THE JEWS.
20 This title then read many of the Jews: for
the place where Jesus was crucified was nigh
to the city: and it was written in Hebrew,
and Greek, *and* Latin.
21 Then said the chief priests of the Jews to
Pilate, Write not, The King of the Jews; but
that he said, I am King of the Jews.
22 Pilate answered, What I have written I
have written.
23 ¶ Then the soldiers, when they had crucified Jesus, took his garments, and made
four parts, to every soldier a part; and also
his coat: now the coat was without seam,
woven from the top throughout.
24 They said therefore among themselves,
Let us not rend it, but cast lots for it, whose
it shall be: that the scripture might be fulfilled, which saith, They parted my raiment
among them, and for my vesture they did
cast lots. These things therefore the soldiers did.
25 ¶ Now there stood by the cross of Jesus
his mother, and his mother's sister, Mary
the *wife* of Cleophas, and Mary Magdalene.
26 When Jesus therefore saw his mother,
and the disciple standing by, whom he
loved, he saith unto his mother, Woman,
behold thy son!
27 Then saith he to the disciple, Behold thy
mother! And from that hour that disciple
took her unto his own *home*.
28 ¶ After this, Jesus knowing that all things
were now accomplished, that the scripture
might be fulfilled, saith, I thirst.
29 Now there was set a vessel full of vinegar:
and they filled a spunge with vinegar, and
put *it* upon hyssop, and put *it* to his mouth.
30 When Jesus therefore had received the
vinegar, he said, It is finished: and he bowed
his head, and gave up the ghost.
31 The Jews therefore, because it was the
preparation, that the bodies should not
remain upon the cross on the sabbath day,
(for that sabbath day was an high day,)
besought Pilate that their legs might be
broken, and *that* they might be taken away.
32 Then came the soldiers, and brake the
legs of the first, and of the other which was
crucified with him.
33 But when they came to Jesus, and saw
that he was dead already, they brake not
his legs:
34 But one of the soldiers with a spear
pierced his side, and forthwith came there
out blood and water.
35 And he that saw *it* bare record, and his
record is true: and he knoweth that he saith
true, that ye might believe.
36 For these things were done, that the
scripture should be fulfilled, A bone of him
shall not be broken.
37 And again another scripture saith, They
shall look on him whom they pierced.
38 ¶ And after this Joseph of Arimathæa,
being a disciple of Jesus, but secretly for fear
of the Jews, besought Pilate that he might
take away the body of Jesus: and Pilate gave
him leave. He came therefore, and took the
body of Jesus.
39 And there came also Nicodemus, which
at the first came to Jesus by night, and
brought a mixture of myrrh and aloes, about
an hundred pound *weight*.
40 Then took they the body of Jesus, and
wound it in linen clothes with the spices, as
the manner of the Jews is to bury.
41 Now in the place where he was crucified
there was a garden; and in the garden a new
sepulchre, wherein was never man yet laid.
42 There laid they Jesus therefore because
of the Jews' preparation *day;* for the sepulchre was nigh at hand.

John 20

1 The first *day* of the week cometh Mary
Magdalene early, when it was yet dark, unto
the sepulchre, and seeth the stone taken
away from the sepulchre.
2 Then she runneth, and cometh to Simon
Peter, and to the other disciple, whom Jesus
loved, and saith unto them, They have taken
away the Lord out of the sepulchre, and we
know not where they have laid him.
3 Peter therefore went forth, and that other
disciple, and came to the sepulchre.
4 So they ran both together: and the other
disciple did outrun Peter, and came first to
the sepulchre.
5 And he stooping down, *and looking in*, saw
the linen clothes lying; yet went he not in.
6 Then cometh Simon Peter following him,
and went into the sepulchre, and seeth the
linen clothes lie,

7 And the napkin, that was about his head,
not lying with the linen clothes, but wrapped
together in a place by itself.
8 Then went in also that other disciple,
which came first to the sepulchre, and he
saw, and believed.
9 For as yet they knew not the scripture, that
he must rise again from the dead.
10 Then the disciples went away again unto
their own home.
11 ¶ But Mary stood without at the sepulchre weeping: and as she wept, she stooped
down, *and looked* into the sepulchre,
12 And seeth two angels in white sitting, the
one at the head, and the other at the feet,
where the body of Jesus had lain.
13 And they say unto her, Woman, why
weepest thou? She saith unto them,
Because they have taken away my Lord,
and I know not where they have laid him.
14 And when she had thus said, she turned
herself back, and saw Jesus standing, and
knew not that it was Jesus.
15 Jesus saith unto her, Woman, why weepest thou? whom seekest thou? She, supposing him to be the gardener, saith unto him,
Sir, if thou have borne him hence, tell me
where thou hast laid him, and I will take
him away.
16 Jesus saith unto her, Mary. She turned
herself, and saith unto him, Rabboni; which
is to say, Master.
17 Jesus saith unto her, Touch me not; for I
am not yet ascended to my Father: but go
to my brethren, and say unto them, I ascend
unto my Father, and your Father; and *to* my
God, and your God.
18 Mary Magdalene came and told the
disciples that she had seen the Lord, and
that he had spoken these things unto her.
19 ¶ Then the same day at evening, being
the first *day* of the week, when the doors
were shut where the disciples were assembled for fear of the Jews, came Jesus and
stood in the midst, and saith unto them,
Peace *be* unto you.
20 And when he had so said, he shewed
unto them *his* hands and his side. Then were
the disciples glad, when they saw the Lord.
21 Then said Jesus to them again, Peace *be*
unto you: as *my* Father hath sent me, even
so send I you.
22 And when he had said this, he breathed
on *them*, and saith unto them, Receive ye
the Holy Spirit:
23 Whose soever sins ye remit, they are
remitted unto them; *and* whose soever *sins*
ye retain, they are retained.
24 ¶ But Thomas, one of the twelve, called
Didymus, was not with them when Jesus
came.
25 The other disciples therefore said unto
him, We have seen the Lord. But he said
unto them, Except I shall see in his hands
the print of the nails, and put my finger into
the print of the nails, and thrust my hand
into his side, I will not believe.
26 ¶ And after eight days again his disciples
were within, and Thomas with them: *then*
came Jesus, the doors being shut, and stood
in the midst, and said, Peace *be* unto you.
27 Then saith he to Thomas, Reach hither
thy finger, and behold my hands; and reach
hither thy hand, and thrust *it* into my side:
and be not faithless, but believing.
28 And Thomas answered and said unto
him, My Lord and my God.
29 Jesus saith unto him, Thomas, because
thou hast seen me, thou hast believed:
blessed *are* they that have not seen, and
yet have believed.
30 ¶ And many other signs truly did Jesus
in the presence of his disciples, which are
not written in this book:
31 But these are written, that ye might
believe that Jesus is the Christ, the Son of
God; and that believing ye might have life
through his name.

John 21

1 After these things Jesus shewed himself
again to the disciples at the sea of Tiberias;
and on this wise shewed he *himself*.
2 There were together Simon Peter, and
Thomas called Didymus, and Nathanael of
Cana in Galilee, and the *sons* of Zebedee,
and two other of his disciples.
3 Simon Peter saith unto them, I go a fishing.
They say unto him, We also go with thee.
They went forth, and entered into a ship
immediately; and that night they caught
nothing.
4 But when the morning was now come,
Jesus stood on the shore: but the disciples
knew not that it was Jesus.

5 Then Jesus saith unto them, Children,
have ye any meat? They answered him, No.
6 And he said unto them, Cast the net on
the right side of the ship, and ye shall find.
They cast therefore, and now they were not
able to draw it for the multitude of fishes.
7 Therefore that disciple whom Jesus loved
saith unto Peter, It is the Lord. Now when
Simon Peter heard that it was the Lord, he
girt *his* fisher's coat *unto him*, (for he was
naked,) and did cast himself into the sea.
8 And the other disciples came in a little
ship; (for they were not far from land, but
as it were two hundred cubits,) dragging
the net with fishes.
9 As soon then as they were come to land,
they saw a fire of coals there, and fish laid
thereon, and bread.
10 Jesus saith unto them, Bring of the fish
which ye have now caught.
11 Simon Peter went up, and drew the net
to land full of great fishes, an hundred and
fifty and three: and for all there were so
many, yet was not the net broken.
12 Jesus saith unto them, Come *and* dine.
And none of the disciples durst ask him,
Who art thou? knowing that it was the Lord.
13 Jesus then cometh, and taketh bread,
and giveth them, and fish likewise.
14 This is now the third time that Jesus
shewed himself to his disciples, after that
he was risen from the dead.
15 ¶ So when they had dined, Jesus saith
to Simon Peter, Simon, *son* of Jonas, lovest
thou me more than these? He saith unto
him, Yea, Lord; thou knowest that I love
thee. He saith unto him, Feed my lambs.
16 He saith to him again the second time,
Simon, *son* of Jonas, lovest thou me? He
saith unto him, Yea, Lord; thou knowest
that I love thee. He saith unto him, Feed
my sheep.
17 He saith unto him the third time, Simon,
son of Jonas, lovest thou me? Peter was
grieved because he said unto him the third
time, Lovest thou me? And he said unto
him, Lord, thou knowest all things; thou
knowest that I love thee. Jesus saith unto
him, Feed my sheep.
18 Verily, verily, I say unto thee, When
thou wast young, thou girdedst thyself,
and walkedst whither thou wouldest: but
when thou shalt be old, thou shalt stretch
forth thy hands, and another shall gird thee,
and carry *thee* whither thou wouldest not.
19 This spake he, signifying by what death
he should glorify God. And when he had
spoken this, he saith unto him, Follow me.
20 Then Peter, turning about, seeth the
disciple whom Jesus loved following; which
also leaned on his breast at supper, and
said, Lord, which is he that betrayeth thee?
21 Peter seeing him saith to Jesus, Lord, and
what *shall* this man *do?*
22 Jesus saith unto him, If I will that he
tarry till I come, what *is that* to thee? follow thou me.
23 Then went this saying abroad among the
brethren, that that disciple should not die:
yet Jesus said not unto him, He shall not die;
but, If I will that he tarry till I come, what
is that to thee?
24 This is the disciple which testifieth of
these things, and wrote these things: and
we know that his testimony is true.
25 And there are also many other things
which Jesus did, the which, if they should
be written every one, I suppose that even
the world itself could not contain the books
that should be written. Amen.

The

Acts Of The Apostles

Acts 1

1 The former treatise have I made, O Theophilus, of all that Jesus began both to do
and teach,
2 Until the day in which he was taken up,
after that he through the Holy Spirit had
given commandments unto the apostles
whom he had chosen:
3 To whom also he shewed himself alive
after his passion by many infallible proofs,
being seen of them forty days, and speaking of the things pertaining to the kingdom
of God:
4 And, being assembled together with
them, commanded them that they should
not depart from Jerusalem, but wait for the
promise of the Father, which, *saith he*, ye
have heard of me.
5 For John truly baptized with water; but
ye shall be baptized with the Holy Spirit not
many days hence.
6 When they therefore were come together,
they asked of him, saying, Lord, wilt thou
at this time restore again the kingdom to
Israel?
7 And he said unto them, It is not for you to
know the times or the seasons, which the
Father hath put in his own power.
8 But ye shall receive power, after that the
Holy Spirit is come upon you: and ye shall
be witnesses unto me both in Jerusalem,
and in all Judæa, and in Samaria, and unto
the uttermost part of the earth.
9 And when he had spoken these things,
while they beheld, he was taken up; and a
cloud received him out of their sight.
10 And while they looked stedfastly toward
heaven as he went up, behold, two men
stood by them in white apparel;
11 Which also said, Ye men of Galilee, why
stand ye gazing up into heaven? this same
Jesus, which is taken up from you into
heaven, shall so come in like manner as ye
have seen him go into heaven.
12 Then returned they unto Jerusalem from
the mount called Olivet, which is from Jerusalem a sabbath day's journey.
13 And when they were come in, they went
up into an upper room, where abode both
Peter, and James, and John, and Andrew,
Philip, and Thomas, Bartholomew, and Matthew, James *the son* of Alphæus, and Simon
Zelotes, and Judas *the brother* of James.
14 These all continued with one accord in
prayer and supplication, with the women,
and Mary the mother of Jesus, and with
his brethren.
15 ¶ And in those days Peter stood up in
the midst of the disciples, and said, (the
number of names together were about an
hundred and twenty,)
16 Men *and* brethren, this scripture must
needs have been fulfilled, which the Holy
Spirit by the mouth of David spake before
concerning Judas, which was guide to them
that took Jesus.
17 For he was numbered with us, and had
obtained part of this ministry.
18 Now this man purchased a field with the
reward of iniquity; and falling headlong,
he burst asunder in the midst, and all his
bowels gushed out.
19 And it was known unto all the dwellers at
Jerusalem; insomuch as that field is called
in their proper tongue, Aceldama, that is to
say, The field of blood.
20 For it is written in the book of Psalms,
Let his habitation be desolate, and let no
man dwell therein: and his bishoprick let
another take.
21 Wherefore of these men which have
companied with us all the time that the Lord
Jesus went in and out among us,
22 Beginning from the baptism of John, unto
that same day that he was taken up from
us, must one be ordained to be a witness
with us of his resurrection.
23 And they appointed two, Joseph called
Barsabas, who was surnamed Justus, and
Matthias.
24 And they prayed, and said, Thou, Lord,
which knowest the hearts of all *men*, shew
whether of these two thou hast chosen,
25 That he may take part of this ministry and

apostleship, from which Judas by transgression fell, that he might go to his own place.
26 And they gave forth their lots; and the lot fell upon Matthias; and he was numbered with the eleven apostles.

Acts 2

1 And when the day of Pentecost was fully come, they were all with one accord in one place.
2 And suddenly there came a sound from heaven as of a rushing mighty wind, and it filled all the house where they were sitting.
3 And there appeared unto them cloven tongues like as of fire, and it sat upon each of them.
4 And they were all filled with the Holy Spirit, and began to speak with other tongues, as the Spirit gave them utterance.
5 And there were dwelling at Jerusalem Jews, devout men, out of every nation under heaven.
6 Now when this was noised abroad, the multitude came together, and were confounded, because that every man heard them speak in his own language.
7 And they were all amazed and marvelled, saying one to another, Behold, are not all these which speak Galilæans?
8 And how hear we every man in our own tongue, wherein we were born?
9 Parthians, and Medes, and Elamites, and the dwellers in Mesopotamia, and in Judæa, and Cappadocia, in Pontus, and Asia,
10 Phrygia, and Pamphylia, in Egypt, and in the parts of Libya about Cyrene, and strangers of Rome, Jews and proselytes,
11 Cretes and Arabians, we do hear them speak in our tongues the wonderful works of God.
12 And they were all amazed, and were in doubt, saying one to another, What meaneth this?
13 Others mocking said, These men are full of new wine.
14 ¶ But Peter, standing up with the eleven, lifted up his voice, and said unto them, Ye men of Judæa, and all *ye* that dwell at Jerusalem, be this known unto you, and hearken to my words:
15 For these are not drunken, as ye suppose, seeing it is *but* the third hour of the day.
16 But this is that which was spoken by the prophet Joel;
17 And it shall come to pass in the last days, saith God, I will pour out of my Spirit upon all flesh: and your sons and your daughters shall prophesy, and your young men shall see visions, and your old men shall dream dreams:
18 And on my servants and on my handmaidens I will pour out in those days of my Spirit; and they shall prophesy:
19 And I will shew wonders in heaven above, and signs in the earth beneath; blood, and fire, and vapour of smoke:
20 The sun shall be turned into darkness, and the moon into blood, before that great and notable day of the Lord come:
21 And it shall come to pass, *that* whosoever shall call on the name of the Lord shall be saved.
22 Ye men of Israel, hear these words; Jesus of Nazareth, a man approved of God among you by miracles and wonders and signs, which God did by him in the midst of you, as ye yourselves also know:
23 Him, being delivered by the determinate counsel and foreknowledge of God, ye have taken, and by wicked hands have crucified and slain:
24 Whom God hath raised up, having loosed the pains of death: because it was not possible that he should be holden of it.
25 For David speaketh concerning him, I foresaw the Lord always before my face, for he is on my right hand, that I should not be moved:
26 Therefore did my heart rejoice, and my tongue was glad; moreover also my flesh shall rest in hope:
27 Because thou wilt not leave my soul in hell, neither wilt thou suffer thine Holy One to see corruption.
28 Thou hast made known to me the ways of life; thou shalt make me full of joy with thy countenance.
29 Men *and* brethren, let me freely speak unto you of the patriarch David, that he is both dead and buried, and his sepulchre is with us unto this day.
30 Therefore being a prophet, and knowing that God had sworn with an oath to him, that of the fruit of his loins, according to

the flesh, he would raise up Christ to sit on
his throne;
31 He seeing this before spake of the resurrection of Christ, that his soul was not left
in hell, neither his flesh did see corruption.
32 This Jesus hath God raised up, whereof
we all are witnesses.
33 Therefore being by the right hand of God
exalted, and having received of the Father
the promise of the Holy Spirit, he hath shed
forth this, which ye now see and hear.
34 For David is not ascended into the heavens: but he saith himself, The LORD said unto
my Lord, Sit thou on my right hand,
35 Until I make thy foes thy footstool.
36 Therefore let all the house of Israel know
assuredly, that God hath made that same
Jesus, whom ye have crucified, both Lord
and Christ.
37 ¶ Now when they heard *this*, they were
pricked in their heart, and said unto Peter
and to the rest of the apostles, Men *and*
brethren, what shall we do?
38 Then Peter said unto them, Repent, and
be baptized every one of you in the name
of Jesus Christ for the remission of sins, and
ye shall receive the gift of the Holy Spirit.
39 For the promise is unto you, and to your
children, and to all that are afar off, *even* as
many as the Lord our God shall call.
40 And with many other words did he testify
and exhort, saying, Save yourselves from
this untoward generation.
41 ¶ Then they that gladly received his
word were baptized: and the same day
there were added *unto them* about three
thousand souls.
42 And they continued stedfastly in the
apostles' doctrine and fellowship, and in
breaking of bread, and in prayers.
43 And fear came upon every soul: and
many wonders and signs were done by the
apostles.
44 And all that believed were together, and
had all things common;
45 And sold their possessions and goods,
and parted them to all *men*, as every man
had need.
46 And they, continuing daily with one
accord in the temple, and breaking bread
from house to house, did eat their meat with
gladness and singleness of heart,
47 Praising God, and having favour with
all the people. And the Lord added to the
church daily such as should be saved.

Acts 3

1 Now Peter and John went up together
into the temple at the hour of prayer, *being*
the ninth *hour*.
2 And a certain man lame from his mother's
womb was carried, whom they laid daily
at the gate of the temple which is called
Beautiful, to ask alms of them that entered
into the temple;
3 Who seeing Peter and John about to go
into the temple asked an alms.
4 And Peter, fastening his eyes upon him
with John, said, Look on us.
5 And he gave heed unto them, expecting
to receive something of them.
6 Then Peter said, Silver and gold have I
none; but such as I have give I thee: In the
name of Jesus Christ of Nazareth rise up
and walk.
7 And he took him by the right hand, and
lifted *him* up: and immediately his feet and
ancle bones received strength.
8 And he leaping up stood, and walked, and
entered with them into the temple, walking,
and leaping, and praising God.
9 And all the people saw him walking and
praising God:
10 And they knew that it was he which sat
for alms at the Beautiful gate of the temple: and they were filled with wonder and
amazement at that which had happened
unto him.
11 And as the lame man which was healed
held Peter and John, all the people ran
together unto them in the porch that is
called Solomon's, greatly wondering.
12 ¶ And when Peter saw *it*, he answered
unto the people, Ye men of Israel, why marvel ye at this? or why look ye so earnestly on
us, as though by our own power or holiness
we had made this man to walk?
13 The God of Abraham, and of Isaac, and of
Jacob, the God of our fathers, hath glorified
his Son Jesus; whom ye delivered up, and
denied him in the presence of Pilate, when
he was determined to let *him* go.
14 But ye denied the Holy One and the
Just, and desired a murderer to be granted
unto you;
15 And killed the Prince of life, whom God

hath raised from the dead; whereof we are
witnesses.
16 And his name through faith in his name
hath made this man strong, whom ye see
and know: yea, the faith which is by him
hath given him this perfect soundness in
the presence of you all.
17 And now, brethren, I wot that through
ignorance ye did *it*, as *did* also your rulers.
18 But those things, which God before had
shewed by the mouth of all his prophets,
that Christ should suffer, he hath so fulfilled.
19 ¶ Repent ye therefore, and be converted,
that your sins may be blotted out, when
the times of refreshing shall come from the
presence of the Lord;
20 And he shall send Jesus Christ, which
before was preached unto you:
21 Whom the heaven must receive until the
times of restitution of all things, which God
hath spoken by the mouth of all his holy
prophets since the world began.
22 For Moses truly said unto the fathers,
A prophet shall the Lord your God raise up
unto you of your brethren, like unto me;
him shall ye hear in all things whatsoever
he shall say unto you.
23 And it shall come to pass, *that* every soul,
which will not hear that prophet, shall be
destroyed from among the people.
24 Yea, and all the prophets from Samuel
and those that follow after, as many as have
spoken, have likewise foretold of these days.
25 Ye are the children of the prophets, and
of the covenant which God made with our
fathers, saying unto Abraham, And in thy
seed shall all the kindreds of the earth be
blessed.
26 Unto you first God, having raised up his
Son Jesus, sent him to bless you, in turning
away every one of you from his iniquities.

Acts 4

1 And as they spake unto the people, the
priests, and the captain of the temple, and
the Sadducees, came upon them,
2 Being grieved that they taught the people,
and preached through Jesus the resurrection from the dead.
3 And they laid hands on them, and put
them in hold unto the next day: for it was
now eventide.
4 Howbeit many of them which heard the
word believed; and the number of the men
was about five thousand.
5 ¶ And it came to pass on the morrow, that
their rulers, and elders, and scribes,
6 And Annas the high priest, and Caiaphas,
and John, and Alexander, and as many as
were of the kindred of the high priest, were
gathered together at Jerusalem.
7 And when they had set them in the midst,
they asked, By what power, or by what
name, have ye done this?
8 Then Peter, filled with the Holy Spirit, said
unto them, Ye rulers of the people, and
elders of Israel,
9 If we this day be examined of the good
deed done to the impotent man, by what
means he is made whole;
10 Be it known unto you all, and to all the
people of Israel, that by the name of Jesus
Christ of Nazareth, whom ye crucified,
whom God raised from the dead, *even* by
him doth this man stand here before you
whole.
11 This is the stone which was set at nought
of you builders, which is become the head
of the corner.
12 Neither is there salvation in any other:
for there is none other name under heaven
given among men, whereby we must be
saved.
13 ¶ Now when they saw the boldness of
Peter and John, and perceived that they
were unlearned and ignorant men, they
marvelled; and they took knowledge of
them, that they had been with Jesus.
14 And beholding the man which was healed
standing with them, they could say nothing
against it.
15 But when they had commanded them to
go aside out of the council, they conferred
among themselves,
16 Saying, What shall we do to these men?
for that indeed a notable miracle hath been
done by them *is* manifest to all them that
dwell in Jerusalem; and we cannot deny *it*.
17 But that it spread no further among
the people, let us straitly threaten them,
that they speak henceforth to no man in
this name.
18 And they called them, and commanded
them not to speak at all nor teach in the
name of Jesus.
19 But Peter and John answered and said

unto them, Whether it be right in the sight
of God to hearken unto you more than unto
God, judge ye.
20 For we cannot but speak the things which
we have seen and heard.
21 So when they had further threatened
them, they let them go, finding nothing
how they might punish them, because of
the people: for all *men* glorified God for
that which was done.
22 For the man was above forty years
old, on whom this miracle of healing was
shewed.
23 ¶ And being let go, they went to their
own company, and reported all that the
chief priests and elders had said unto them.
24 And when they heard that, they lifted
up their voice to God with one accord, and
said, Lord, thou *art* God, which hast made
heaven, and earth, and the sea, and all that
in them is:
25 Who by the mouth of thy servant David
hast said, Why did the heathen rage, and
the people imagine vain things?
26 The kings of the earth stood up, and the
rulers were gathered together against the
Lord, and against his Christ.
27 For of a truth against thy holy child Jesus,
whom thou hast anointed, both Herod, and
Pontius Pilate, with the Gentiles, and the
people of Israel, were gathered together,
28 For to do whatsoever thy hand and thy
counsel determined before to be done.
29 And now, Lord, behold their threatenings:
and grant unto thy servants, that with all
boldness they may speak thy word,
30 By stretching forth thine hand to heal;
and that signs and wonders may be done
by the name of thy holy child Jesus.
31 ¶ And when they had prayed, the place
was shaken where they were assembled
together; and they were all filled with the
Holy Spirit, and they spake the word of God
with boldness.
32 And the multitude of them that believed
were of one heart and of one soul: neither
said any *of them* that ought of the things
which he possessed was his own; but they
had all things common.
33 And with great power gave the apostles
witness of the resurrection of the Lord Jesus:
and great grace was upon them all.
34 Neither was there any among them that
lacked: for as many as were possessors of
lands or houses sold them, and brought the
prices of the things that were sold,
35 And laid *them* down at the apostles' feet:
and distribution was made unto every man
according as he had need.
36 And Joses, who by the apostles was
surnamed Barnabas, (which is, being interpreted, The son of consolation,) a Levite,
and of the country of Cyprus,
37 Having land, sold *it*, and brought the
money, and laid *it* at the apostles' feet.

Acts 5

1 But a certain man named Ananias, with
Sapphira his wife, sold a possession,
2 And kept back *part* of the price, his wife
also being privy *to it*, and brought a certain
part, and laid *it* at the apostles' feet.
3 But Peter said, Ananias, why hath Satan
filled thine heart to lie to the Holy Spirit, and
to keep back *part* of the price of the land?
4 Whiles it remained, was it not thine own?
and after it was sold, was it not in thine own
power? why hast thou conceived this thing
in thine heart? thou hast not lied unto men,
but unto God.
5 And Ananias hearing these words fell
down, and gave up the ghost: and great fear
came on all them that heard these things.
6 And the young men arose, wound him up,
and carried *him* out, and buried *him*.
7 And it was about the space of three hours
after, when his wife, not knowing what was
done, came in.
8 And Peter answered unto her, Tell me
whether ye sold the land for so much? And
she said, Yea, for so much.
9 Then Peter said unto her, How is it that ye
have agreed together to tempt the Spirit of
the Lord? behold, the feet of them which
have buried thy husband *are* at the door,
and shall carry thee out.
10 Then fell she down straightway at his
feet, and yielded up the ghost: and the
young men came in, and found her dead,
and, carrying *her* forth, buried *her* by her
husband.
11 And great fear came upon all the church,
and upon as many as heard these things.
12 ¶ And by the hands of the apostles were
many signs and wonders wrought among

the people; (and they were all with one
accord in Solomon's porch.
13 And of the rest durst no man join himself
to them: but the people magnified them.
14 And believers were the more added
to the Lord, multitudes both of men and
women.)
15 Insomuch that they brought forth the
sick into the streets, and laid *them* on beds
and couches, that at the least the shadow
of Peter passing by might overshadow some
of them.
16 There came also a multitude *out* of the
cities round about unto Jerusalem, bringing sick folks, and them which were vexed
with unclean spirits: and they were healed
every one.
17 ¶ Then the high priest rose up, and all
they that were with him, (which is the sect
of the Sadducees,) and were filled with
indignation,
18 And laid their hands on the apostles, and
put them in the common prison.
19 But the angel of the Lord by night opened
the prison doors, and brought them forth,
and said,
20 Go, stand and speak in the temple to the
people all the words of this life.
21 And when they heard *that*, they entered
into the temple early in the morning, and
taught. But the high priest came, and they
that were with him, and called the council
together, and all the senate of the children
of Israel, and sent to the prison to have
them brought.
22 But when the officers came, and found
them not in the prison, they returned, and
told,
23 Saying, The prison truly found we shut
with all safety, and the keepers standing
without before the doors: but when we had
opened, we found no man within.
24 Now when the high priest and the captain of the temple and the chief priests
heard these things, they doubted of them
whereunto this would grow.
25 Then came one and told them, saying,
Behold, the men whom ye put in prison
are standing in the temple, and teaching
the people.
26 Then went the captain with the officers,
and brought them without violence: for
they feared the people, lest they should
have been stoned.
27 And when they had brought them, they
set *them* before the council: and the high
priest asked them,
28 Saying, Did not we straitly command
you that ye should not teach in this name?
and, behold, ye have filled Jerusalem with
your doctrine, and intend to bring this man's
blood upon us.
29 ¶ Then Peter and the *other* apostles
answered and said, We ought to obey God
rather than men.
30 The God of our fathers raised up Jesus,
whom ye slew and hanged on a tree.
31 Him hath God exalted with his right hand
to be a Prince and a Saviour, for to give
repentance to Israel, and forgiveness of sins.
32 And we are his witnesses of these things;
and *so is* also the Holy Spirit, whom God
hath given to them that obey him.
33 ¶ When they heard *that*, they were cut
to the heart, and took counsel to slay them.
34 Then stood there up one in the council,
a Pharisee, named Gamaliel, a doctor of the
law, had in reputation among all the people,
and commanded to put the apostles forth
a little space;
35 And said unto them, Ye men of Israel,
take heed to yourselves what ye intend to
do as touching these men.
36 For before these days rose up Theudas,
boasting himself to be somebody; to whom
a number of men, about four hundred,
joined themselves: who was slain; and all,
as many as obeyed him, were scattered, and
brought to nought.
37 After this man rose up Judas of Galilee
in the days of the taxing, and drew away
much people after him: he also perished;
and all, *even* as many as obeyed him, were
dispersed.
38 And now I say unto you, Refrain from
these men, and let them alone: for if this
counsel or this work be of men, it will come
to nought:
39 But if it be of God, ye cannot overthrow
it; lest haply ye be found even to fight
against God.
40 And to him they agreed: and when they
had called the apostles, and beaten *them*,
they commanded that they should not speak
in the name of Jesus, and let them go.

41 ¶ And they departed from the presence
of the council, rejoicing that they were
counted worthy to suffer shame for his
name.
42 And daily in the temple, and in every
house, they ceased not to teach and preach
Jesus Christ.

Acts 6

1 And in those days, when the number of the
disciples was multiplied, there arose a murmuring of the Grecians against the Hebrews,
because their widows were neglected in the
daily ministration.
2 Then the twelve called the multitude of
the disciples *unto them*, and said, It is not
reason that we should leave the word of
God, and serve tables.
3 Wherefore, brethren, look ye out among
you seven men of honest report, full of
the Holy Spirit and wisdom, whom we may
appoint over this business.
4 But we will give ourselves continually to
prayer, and to the ministry of the word.
5 ¶ And the saying pleased the whole multitude: and they chose Stephen, a man full of
faith and of the Holy Spirit, and Philip, and
Prochorus, and Nicanor, and Timon, and Par-
menas, and Nicolas a proselyte of Antioch:
6 Whom they set before the apostles: and
when they had prayed, they laid *their* hands
on them.
7 And the word of God increased; and the
number of the disciples multiplied in Jerusalem greatly; and a great company of the
priests were obedient to the faith.
8 And Stephen, full of faith and power, did
great wonders and miracles among the
people.
9 ¶ Then there arose certain of the synagogue, which is called *the synagogue* of the
Libertines, and Cyrenians, and Alexandrians,
and of them of Cilicia and of Asia, disputing
with Stephen.
10 And they were not able to resist the
wisdom and the spirit by which he spake.
11 Then they suborned men, which said, We
have heard him speak blasphemous words
against Moses, and *against* God.
12 And they stirred up the people, and the
elders, and the scribes, and came upon
him, and caught him, and brought *him* to
the council,
13 And set up false witnesses, which said,
This man ceaseth not to speak blasphemous
words against this holy place, and the law:
14 For we have heard him say, that this
Jesus of Nazareth shall destroy this place,
and shall change the customs which Moses
delivered us.
15 And all that sat in the council, looking
stedfastly on him, saw his face as it had
been the face of an angel.

Acts 7

1 Then said the high priest, Are these things
so?
2 And he said, Men, brethren, and fathers,
hearken; The God of glory appeared unto
our father Abraham, when he was in Mesopotamia, before he dwelt in Charran,
3 And said unto him, Get thee out of thy
country, and from thy kindred, and come
into the land which I shall shew thee.
4 Then came he out of the land of the
Chaldæans, and dwelt in Charran: and
from thence, when his father was dead,
he removed him into this land, wherein ye
now dwell.
5 And he gave him none inheritance in it,
no, not *so much as* to set his foot on: yet he
promised that he would give it to him for a
possession, and to his seed after him, when
as yet he had no child.
6 And God spake on this wise, That his seed
should sojourn in a strange land; and that
they should bring them into bondage, and
entreat *them* evil four hundred years.
7 And the nation to whom they shall be in
bondage will I judge, said God: and after
that shall they come forth, and serve me
in this place.
8 And he gave him the covenant of circumcision: and so *Abraham* begat Isaac, and
circumcised him the eighth day; and Isaac
begat Jacob; and Jacob *begat* the twelve
patriarchs.
9 And the patriarchs, moved with envy, sold
Joseph into Egypt: but God was with him,
10 And delivered him out of all his afflictions,
and gave him favour and wisdom in the sight
of Pharaoh king of Egypt; and he made him
governor over Egypt and all his house.
11 Now there came a dearth over all the
land of Egypt and Chanaan, and great affliction: and our fathers found no sustenance.

12 But when Jacob heard that there was
corn in Egypt, he sent out our fathers first.
13 And at the second *time* Joseph was made
known to his brethren; and Joseph's kindred
was made known unto Pharaoh.
14 Then sent Joseph, and called his father
Jacob to *him*, and all his kindred, threescore
and fifteen souls.
15 So Jacob went down into Egypt, and died,
he, and our fathers,
16 And were carried over into Sychem, and
laid in the sepulchre that Abraham bought
for a sum of money of the sons of Emmor
the father of Sychem.
17 But when the time of the promise drew
nigh, which God had sworn to Abraham,
the people grew and multiplied in Egypt,
18 Till another king arose, which knew not
Joseph.
19 The same dealt subtilly with our kindred,
and evil entreated our fathers, so that they
cast out their young children, to the end
they might not live.
20 In which time Moses was born, and
was exceeding fair, and nourished up in his
father's house three months:
21 And when he was cast out, Pharaoh's
daughter took him up, and nourished him
for her own son.
22 And Moses was learned in all the wisdom
of the Egyptians, and was mighty in words
and in deeds.
23 And when he was full forty years old, it
came into his heart to visit his brethren the
children of Israel.
24 And seeing one *of them* suffer wrong, he
defended *him*, and avenged him that was
oppressed, and smote the Egyptian:
25 For he supposed his brethren would have
understood how that God by his hand would
deliver them: but they understood not.
26 And the next day he shewed himself
unto them as they strove, and would have
set them at one again, saying, Sirs, ye are
brethren; why do ye wrong one to another?
27 But he that did his neighbour wrong
thrust him away, saying, Who made thee a
ruler and a judge over us?
28 Wilt thou kill me, as thou diddest the
Egyptian yesterday?
29 Then fled Moses at this saying, and was
a stranger in the land of Madian, where he
begat two sons.
30 And when forty years were expired,
there appeared to him in the wilderness of
mount Sina an angel of the Lord in a flame
of fire in a bush.
31 When Moses saw *it*, he wondered at the
sight: and as he drew near to behold *it*, the
voice of the Lord came unto him,
32 *Saying*, I *am* the God of thy fathers, the
God of Abraham, and the God of Isaac, and
the God of Jacob. Then Moses trembled,
and durst not behold.
33 Then said the Lord to him, Put off thy
shoes from thy feet: for the place where
thou standest is holy ground.
34 I have seen, I have seen the affliction
of my people which is in Egypt, and I have
heard their groaning, and am come down
to deliver them. And now come, I will send
thee into Egypt.
35 This Moses whom they refused, saying, Who made thee a ruler and a judge?
the same did God send *to be* a ruler and
a deliverer by the hand of the angel which
appeared to him in the bush.
36 He brought them out, after that he had
shewed wonders and signs in the land of
Egypt, and in the Red sea, and in the wilderness forty years.
37 ¶ This is that Moses, which said unto the
children of Israel, A prophet shall the Lord
your God raise up unto you of your brethren,
like unto me; him shall ye hear.
38 This is he, that was in the church in the
wilderness with the angel which spake
to him in the mount Sina, and *with* our
fathers: who received the lively oracles to
give unto us:
39 To whom our fathers would not obey, but
thrust *him* from them, and in their hearts
turned back again into Egypt,
40 Saying unto Aaron, Make us gods to
go before us: for *as for* this Moses, which
brought us out of the land of Egypt, we wot
not what is become of him.
41 And they made a calf in those days, and
offered sacrifice unto the idol, and rejoiced
in the works of their own hands.
42 Then God turned, and gave them up to
worship the host of heaven; as it is written
in the book of the prophets, O ye house of
Israel, have ye offered to me slain beasts
and sacrifices *by the space of* forty years in
the wilderness?

43 Yea, ye took up the tabernacle of Moloch,
and the star of your god Remphan, figures
which ye made to worship them: and I will
carry you away beyond Babylon.
44 Our fathers had the tabernacle of witness in the wilderness, as he had appointed,
speaking unto Moses, that he should make
it according to the fashion that he had seen.
45 Which also our fathers that came after
brought in with Jesus into the possession of
the Gentiles, whom God drave out before
the face of our fathers, unto the days of
David;
46 Who found favour before God, and
desired to find a tabernacle for the God
of Jacob.
47 But Solomon built him an house.
48 Howbeit the most High dwelleth not
in temples made with hands; as saith the
prophet,
49 Heaven *is* my throne, and earth *is* my
footstool: what house will ye build me? saith
the Lord: or what *is* the place of my rest?
50 Hath not my hand made all these things?
51 ¶ Ye stiffnecked and uncircumcised in
heart and ears, ye do always resist the Holy
Spirit: as your fathers *did*, so *do* ye.
52 Which of the prophets have not your
fathers persecuted? and they have slain
them which shewed before of the coming
of the Just One; of whom ye have been now
the betrayers and murderers:
53 Who have received the law by the dispo-
sition of angels, and have not kept *it*.
54 ¶ When they heard these things, they
were cut to the heart, and they gnashed
on him with *their* teeth.
55 But he, being full of the Holy Spirit,
looked up stedfastly into heaven, and saw
the glory of God, and Jesus standing on the
right hand of God,
56 And said, Behold, I see the heavens
opened, and the Son of man standing on
the right hand of God.
57 Then they cried out with a loud voice,
and stopped their ears, and ran upon him
with one accord,
58 And cast *him* out of the city, and stoned
him: and the witnesses laid down their
clothes at a young man's feet, whose name
was Saul.
59 And they stoned Stephen, calling upon
God, and saying, Lord Jesus, receive my
spirit.
60 And he kneeled down, and cried with
a loud voice, Lord, lay not this sin to their
charge. And when he had said this, he fell
asleep.

Acts 8

1 And Saul was consenting unto his death.
And at that time there was a great persecution against the church which was
at Jerusalem; and they were all scattered
abroad throughout the regions of Judæa
and Samaria, except the apostles.
2 And devout men carried Stephen *to his
burial*, and made great lamentation over
him.
3 As for Saul, he made havock of the church,
entering into every house, and haling men
and women committed *them* to prison.
4 Therefore they that were scattered abroad
went every where preaching the word.
5 Then Philip went down to the city of
Samaria, and preached Christ unto them.
6 And the people with one accord gave heed
unto those things which Philip spake, hearing and seeing the miracles which he did.
7 For unclean spirits, crying with loud voice,
came out of many that were possessed *with
them:* and many taken with palsies, and that
were lame, were healed.
8 And there was great joy in that city.
9 But there was a certain man, called Simon,
which beforetime in the same city used sor-
cery, and bewitched the people of Samaria,
giving out that himself was some great one:
10 To whom they all gave heed, from the
least to the greatest, saying, This man is the
great power of God.
11 And to him they had regard, because
that of long time he had bewitched them
with sorceries.
12 But when they believed Philip preaching
the things concerning the kingdom of God,
and the name of Jesus Christ, they were
baptized, both men and women.
13 Then Simon himself believed also: and
when he was baptized, he continued with
Philip, and wondered, beholding the miracles and signs which were done.
14 Now when the apostles which were at
Jerusalem heard that Samaria had received

the word of God, they sent unto them Peter
and John:
15 Who, when they were come down,
prayed for them, that they might receive
the Holy Spirit:
16 (For as yet he was fallen upon none of
them: only they were baptized in the name
of the Lord Jesus.)
17 Then laid they *their* hands on them, and
they received the Holy Spirit.
18 And when Simon saw that through laying
on of the apostles' hands the Holy Spirit was
given, he offered them money,
19 Saying, Give me also this power, that on
whomsoever I lay hands, he may receive
the Holy Spirit.
20 But Peter said unto him, Thy money perish
with thee, because thou hast thought
that the gift of God may be purchased with
money.
21 Thou hast neither part nor lot in this
matter: for thy heart is not right in the
sight of God.
22 Repent therefore of this thy wickedness,
and pray God, if perhaps the thought of
thine heart may be forgiven thee.
23 For I perceive that thou art in the gall
of bitterness, and *in* the bond of iniquity.
24 Then answered Simon, and said, Pray
ye to the Lord for me, that none of these
things which ye have spoken come upon me.
25 And they, when they had testified and
preached the word of the Lord, returned
to Jerusalem, and preached the gospel in
many villages of the Samaritans.
26 And the angel of the Lord spake unto
Philip, saying, Arise, and go toward the
south unto the way that goeth down from
Jerusalem unto Gaza, which is desert.
27 And he arose and went: and, behold, a
man of Ethiopia, an eunuch of great authority
under Candace queen of the Ethiopians,
who had the charge of all her treasure, and
had come to Jerusalem for to worship,
28 Was returning, and sitting in his chariot
read Esaias the prophet.
29 Then the Spirit said unto Philip, Go near,
and join thyself to this chariot.
30 And Philip ran thither to *him*, and heard
him read the prophet Esaias, and said,
Understandest thou what thou readest?
31 And he said, How can I, except some man
should guide me? And he desired Philip that
he would come up and sit with him.
32 The place of the scripture which he
read was this, He was led as a sheep to the
slaughter; and like a lamb dumb before his
shearer, so opened he not his mouth:
33 In his humiliation his judgment was taken
away: and who shall declare his generation?
for his life is taken from the earth.
34 And the eunuch answered Philip, and
said, I pray thee, of whom speaketh the
prophet this? of himself, or of some other
man?
35 Then Philip opened his mouth, and began
at the same scripture, and preached unto
him Jesus.
36 And as they went on *their* way, they came
unto a certain water: and the eunuch said,
See, *here is* water; what doth hinder me to
be baptized?
37 And Philip said, If thou believest with all
thine heart, thou mayest. And he answered
and said, I believe that Jesus Christ is the
Son of God.
38 And he commanded the chariot to stand
still: and they went down both into the
water, both Philip and the eunuch; and he
baptized him.
39 And when they were come up out of the
water, the Spirit of the Lord caught away
Philip, that the eunuch saw him no more:
and he went on his way rejoicing.
40 But Philip was found at Azotus: and passing
through he preached in all the cities, till
he came to Cæsarea.

Acts 9

1 And Saul, yet breathing out threatenings
and slaughter against the disciples of the
Lord, went unto the high priest,
2 And desired of him letters to Damascus to
the synagogues, that if he found any of this
way, whether they were men or women, he
might bring them bound unto Jerusalem.
3 And as he journeyed, he came near
Damascus: and suddenly there shined round
about him a light from heaven:
4 And he fell to the earth, and heard a voice
saying unto him, Saul, Saul, why persecutest
thou me?
5 And he said, Who art thou, Lord? And
the Lord said, I am Jesus whom thou per-

secutest: *it is* hard for thee to kick against
the pricks.
6 And he trembling and astonished said,
Lord, what wilt thou have me to do? And
the Lord *said* unto him, Arise, and go into
the city, and it shall be told thee what thou
must do.
7 And the men which journeyed with him
stood speechless, hearing a voice, but seeing no man.
8 And Saul arose from the earth; and when
his eyes were opened, he saw no man: but
they led him by the hand, and brought *him*
into Damascus.
9 And he was three days without sight, and
neither did eat nor drink.
10 ¶ And there was a certain disciple at
Damascus, named Ananias; and to him said
the Lord in a vision, Ananias. And he said,
Behold, I *am here*, Lord.
11 And the Lord *said* unto him, Arise, and go
into the street which is called Straight, and
inquire in the house of Judas for *one* called
Saul, of Tarsus: for, behold, he prayeth,
12 And hath seen in a vision a man named
Ananias coming in, and putting *his* hand on
him, that he might receive his sight.
13 Then Ananias answered, Lord, I have
heard by many of this man, how much evil
he hath done to thy saints at Jerusalem:
14 And here he hath authority from the
chief priests to bind all that call on thy name.
15 But the Lord said unto him, Go thy way:
for he is a chosen vessel unto me, to bear
my name before the Gentiles, and kings,
and the children of Israel:
16 For I will shew him how great things he
must suffer for my name's sake.
17 And Ananias went his way, and entered
into the house; and putting his hands on him
said, Brother Saul, the Lord, *even* Jesus, that
appeared unto thee in the way as thou camest, hath sent me, that thou mightest receive
thy sight, and be filled with the Holy Spirit.
18 And immediately there fell from his eyes
as it had been scales: and he received sight
forthwith, and arose, and was baptized.
19 And when he had received meat, he was
strengthened. Then was Saul certain days
with the disciples which were at Damascus.
20 And straightway he preached Christ in
the synagogues, that he is the Son of God.
21 But all that heard *him* were amazed,
and said; Is not this he that destroyed them
which called on this name in Jerusalem, and
came hither for that intent, that he might
bring them bound unto the chief priests?
22 But Saul increased the more in strength,
and confounded the Jews which dwelt at
Damascus, proving that this is very Christ.
23 ¶ And after that many days were fulfilled,
the Jews took counsel to kill him:
24 But their laying await was known of Saul.
And they watched the gates day and night
to kill him.
25 Then the disciples took him by night, and
let *him* down by the wall in a basket.
26 And when Saul was come to Jerusalem,
he assayed to join himself to the disciples:
but they were all afraid of him, and believed
not that he was a disciple.
27 But Barnabas took him, and brought *him*
to the apostles, and declared unto them
how he had seen the Lord in the way, and
that he had spoken to him, and how he
had preached boldly at Damascus in the
name of Jesus.
28 And he was with them coming in and
going out at Jerusalem.
29 And he spake boldly in the name of
the Lord Jesus, and disputed against the
Grecians: but they went about to slay him.
30 *Which* when the brethren knew, they
brought him down to Cæsarea, and sent
him forth to Tarsus.
31 Then had the churches rest throughout
all Judæa and Galilee and Samaria, and were
edified; and walking in the fear of the Lord,
and in the comfort of the Holy Spirit, were
multiplied.
32 ¶ And it came to pass, as Peter passed
throughout all *quarters*, he came down also
to the saints which dwelt at Lydda.
33 And there he found a certain man named
Æneas, which had kept his bed eight years,
and was sick of the palsy.
34 And Peter said unto him, Æneas, Jesus
Christ maketh thee whole: arise, and make
thy bed. And he arose immediately.
35 And all that dwelt at Lydda and Saron
saw him, and turned to the Lord.
36 ¶ Now there was at Joppa a certain disciple named Tabitha, which by interpretation
is called Dorcas: this woman was full of good
works and almsdeeds which she did.
37 And it came to pass in those days, that

she was sick, and died: whom when they had
washed, they laid *her* in an upper chamber.
38 And forasmuch as Lydda was nigh to
Joppa, and the disciples had heard that
Peter was there, they sent unto him two
men, desiring *him* that he would not delay
to come to them.
39 Then Peter arose and went with them.
When he was come, they brought him into
the upper chamber: and all the widows
stood by him weeping, and shewing the
coats and garments which Dorcas made,
while she was with them.
40 But Peter put them all forth, and kneeled
down, and prayed; and turning *him* to the
body said, Tabitha, arise. And she opened
her eyes: and when she saw Peter, she
sat up.
41 And he gave her *his* hand, and lifted her
up, and when he had called the saints and
widows, presented her alive.
42 And it was known throughout all Joppa;
and many believed in the Lord.
43 And it came to pass, that he tarried many
days in Joppa with one Simon a tanner.

Acts 10

1 There was a certain man in Cæsarea called
Cornelius, a centurion of the band called
the Italian *band*,
2 *A* devout *man*, and one that feared God
with all his house, which gave much alms
to the people, and prayed to God alway.
3 He saw in a vision evidently about the
ninth hour of the day an angel of God coming in to him, and saying unto him, Cornelius.
4 And when he looked on him, he was afraid,
and said, What is it, Lord? And he said unto
him, Thy prayers and thine alms are come
up for a memorial before God.
5 And now send men to Joppa, and call for
one Simon, whose surname is Peter:
6 He lodgeth with one Simon a tanner,
whose house is by the sea side: he shall tell
thee what thou oughtest to do.
7 And when the angel which spake unto
Cornelius was departed, he called two of his
household servants, and a devout soldier of
them that waited on him continually;
8 And when he had declared all *these* things
unto them, he sent them to Joppa.
9 ¶ On the morrow, as they went on their
journey, and drew nigh unto the city, Peter
went up upon the housetop to pray about
the sixth hour:
10 And he became very hungry, and would
have eaten: but while they made ready, he
fell into a trance,
11 And saw heaven opened, and a certain
vessel descending unto him, as it had been
a great sheet knit at the four corners, and
let down to the earth:
12 Wherein were all manner of fourfooted
beasts of the earth, and wild beasts, and
creeping things, and fowls of the air.
13 And there came a voice to him, Rise,
Peter; kill, and eat.
14 But Peter said, Not so, Lord; for I have
never eaten any thing that is common or
unclean.
15 And the voice *spake* unto him again the
second time, What God hath cleansed, *that*
call not thou common.
16 This was done thrice: and the vessel was
received up again into heaven.
17 Now while Peter doubted in himself what
this vision which he had seen should mean,
behold, the men which were sent from Cornelius had made inquiry for Simon's house,
and stood before the gate,
18 And called, and asked whether Simon,
which was surnamed Peter, were lodged
there.
19 ¶ While Peter thought on the vision,
the Spirit said unto him, Behold, three men
seek thee.
20 Arise therefore, and get thee down, and
go with them, doubting nothing: for I have
sent them.
21 Then Peter went down to the men which
were sent unto him from Cornelius; and said,
Behold, I am he whom ye seek: what *is* the
cause wherefore ye are come?
22 And they said, Cornelius the centurion,
a just man, and one that feareth God, and
of good report among all the nation of the
Jews, was warned from God by an holy angel
to send for thee into his house, and to hear
words of thee.
23 Then called he them in, and lodged *them*.
And on the morrow Peter went away with
them, and certain brethren from Joppa
accompanied him.
24 And the morrow after they entered into
Cæsarea. And Cornelius waited for them,

and had called together his kinsmen and
near friends.
25 And as Peter was coming in, Cornelius
met him, and fell down at his feet, and
worshipped *him*.
26 But Peter took him up, saying, Stand up;
I myself also am a man.
27 And as he talked with him, he went in,
and found many that were come together.
28 And he said unto them, Ye know how
that it is an unlawful thing for a man that is
a Jew to keep company, or come unto one
of another nation; but God hath shewed
me that I should not call any man common
or unclean.
29 Therefore came I *unto you* without gainsaying, as soon as I was sent for: I ask therefore for what intent ye have sent for me?
30 And Cornelius said, Four days ago I was
fasting until this hour; and at the ninth hour
I prayed in my house, and, behold, a man
stood before me in bright clothing,
31 And said, Cornelius, thy prayer is heard,
and thine alms are had in remembrance in
the sight of God.
32 Send therefore to Joppa, and call hither
Simon, whose surname is Peter; he is lodged
in the house of *one* Simon a tanner by the
sea side: who, when he cometh, shall speak
unto thee.
33 Immediately therefore I sent to thee;
and thou hast well done that thou art
come. Now therefore are we all here present before God, to hear all things that are
commanded thee of God.
34 ¶ Then Peter opened *his* mouth, and
said, Of a truth I perceive that God is no
respecter of persons:
35 But in every nation he that feareth him,
and worketh righteousness, is accepted
with him.
36 The word which *God* sent unto the children of Israel, preaching peace by Jesus
Christ: (he is Lord of all:)
37 That word, *I say*, ye know, which was
published throughout all Judæa, and began
from Galilee, after the baptism which John
preached;
38 How God anointed Jesus of Nazareth
with the Holy Spirit and with power: who
went about doing good, and healing all
that were oppressed of the devil; for God
was with him.
39 And we are witnesses of all things which
he did both in the land of the Jews, and in
Jerusalem; whom they slew and hanged
on a tree:
40 Him God raised up the third day, and
shewed him openly;
41 Not to all the people, but unto witnesses
chosen before of God, *even* to us, who did
eat and drink with him after he rose from
the dead.
42 And he commanded us to preach unto
the people, and to testify that it is he which
was ordained of God *to be* the Judge of
quick and dead.
43 To him give all the prophets witness, that
through his name whosoever believeth in
him shall receive remission of sins.
44 ¶ While Peter yet spake these words,
the Holy Spirit fell on all them which heard
the word.
45 And they of the circumcision which
believed were astonished, as many as came
with Peter, because that on the Gentiles also
was poured out the gift of the Holy Spirit.
46 For they heard them speak with tongues,
and magnify God. Then answered Peter,
47 Can any man forbid water, that these
should not be baptized, which have received
the Holy Spirit as well as we?
48 And he commanded them to be baptized
in the name of the Lord. Then prayed they
him to tarry certain days.

Acts 11

1 And the apostles and brethren that were
in Judæa heard that the Gentiles had also
received the word of God.
2 And when Peter was come up to Jerusalem, they that were of the circumcision
contended with him,
3 Saying, Thou wentest in to men uncircumcised, and didst eat with them.
4 But Peter rehearsed *the matter* from the
beginning, and expounded *it* by order unto
them, saying,
5 I was in the city of Joppa praying: and
in a trance I saw a vision, A certain vessel
descend, as it had been a great sheet, let
down from heaven by four corners; and it
came even to me:
6 Upon the which when I had fastened mine
eyes, I considered, and saw fourfooted

beasts of the earth, and wild beasts, and
creeping things, and fowls of the air.
7 And I heard a voice saying unto me, Arise,
Peter; slay and eat.
8 But I said, Not so, Lord: for nothing common or unclean hath at any time entered
into my mouth.
9 But the voice answered me again from
heaven, What God hath cleansed, *that* call
not thou common.
10 And this was done three times: and all
were drawn up again into heaven.
11 And, behold, immediately there were
three men already come unto the house
where I was, sent from Cæsarea unto me.
12 And the spirit bade me go with them,
nothing doubting. Moreover these six brethren accompanied me, and we entered into
the man's house:
13 And he shewed us how he had seen an
angel in his house, which stood and said
unto him, Send men to Joppa, and call for
Simon, whose surname is Peter;
14 Who shall tell thee words, whereby thou
and all thy house shall be saved.
15 And as I began to speak, the Holy Spirit
fell on them, as on us at the beginning.
16 Then remembered I the word of the
Lord, how that he said, John indeed baptized with water; but ye shall be baptized
with the Holy Spirit.
17 Forasmuch then as God gave them the
like gift as *he did* unto us, who believed on
the Lord Jesus Christ; what was I, that I could
withstand God?
18 When they heard these things, they
held their peace, and glorified God, saying,
Then hath God also to the Gentiles granted
repentance unto life.
19 ¶ Now they which were scattered abroad
upon the persecution that arose about Stephen travelled as far as Phenice, and Cyprus,
and Antioch, preaching the word to none
but unto the Jews only.
20 And some of them were men of Cyprus
and Cyrene, which, when they were come to
Antioch, spake unto the Grecians, preaching
the Lord Jesus.
21 And the hand of the Lord was with them:
and a great number believed, and turned
unto the Lord.
22 ¶ Then tidings of these things came unto
the ears of the church which was in Jerusalem: and they sent forth Barnabas, that he
should go as far as Antioch.
23 Who, when he came, and had seen the
grace of God, was glad, and exhorted them
all, that with purpose of heart they would
cleave unto the Lord.
24 For he was a good man, and full of the
Holy Spirit and of faith: and much people
was added unto the Lord.
25 Then departed Barnabas to Tarsus, for
to seek Saul:
26 And when he had found him, he brought
him unto Antioch. And it came to pass, that
a whole year they assembled themselves
with the church, and taught much people.
And the disciples were called Christians
first in Antioch.
27 ¶ And in these days came prophets from
Jerusalem unto Antioch.
28 And there stood up one of them named
Agabus, and signified by the spirit that there
should be great dearth throughout all the
world: which came to pass in the days of
Claudius Cæsar.
29 Then the disciples, every man according
to his ability, determined to send relief unto
the brethren which dwelt in Judæa:
30 Which also they did, and sent it to the
elders by the hands of Barnabas and Saul.

Acts 12

1 Now about that time Herod the king
stretched forth *his* hands to vex certain of
the church.
2 And he killed James the brother of John
with the sword.
3 And because he saw it pleased the Jews,
he proceeded further to take Peter also.
(Then were the days of unleavened bread.)
4 And when he had apprehended him, he
put *him* in prison, and delivered *him* to
four quaternions of soldiers to keep him;
intending after Easter to bring him forth
to the people.
5 Peter therefore was kept in prison: but
prayer was made without ceasing of the
church unto God for him.
6 And when Herod would have brought
him forth, the same night Peter was sleeping between two soldiers, bound with two
chains: and the keepers before the door
kept the prison.
7 And, behold, the angel of the Lord came

upon *him*, and a light shined in the prison:
and he smote Peter on the side, and raised
him up, saying, Arise up quickly. And his
chains fell off from *his* hands.
8 And the angel said unto him, Gird thyself,
and bind on thy sandals. And so he did. And
he saith unto him, Cast thy garment about
thee, and follow me.
9 And he went out, and followed him; and
wist not that it was true which was done
by the angel; but thought he saw a vision.
10 When they were past the first and the
second ward, they came unto the iron gate
that leadeth unto the city; which opened
to them of his own accord: and they went
out, and passed on through one street; and
forthwith the angel departed from him.
11 And when Peter was come to himself, he
said, Now I know of a surety, that the Lord
hath sent his angel, and hath delivered me
out of the hand of Herod, and *from* all the
expectation of the people of the Jews.
12 And when he had considered *the thing*,
he came to the house of Mary the mother
of John, whose surname was Mark; where
many were gathered together praying.
13 And as Peter knocked at the door of the
gate, a damsel came to hearken, named
Rhoda.
14 And when she knew Peter's voice, she
opened not the gate for gladness, but ran in,
and told how Peter stood before the gate.
15 And they said unto her, Thou art mad.
But she constantly affirmed that it was even
so. Then said they, It is his angel.
16 But Peter continued knocking: and when
they had opened *the door*, and saw him,
they were astonished.
17 But he, beckoning unto them with the
hand to hold their peace, declared unto
them how the Lord had brought him out
of the prison. And he said, Go shew these
things unto James, and to the brethren. And
he departed, and went into another place.
18 Now as soon as it was day, there was
no small stir among the soldiers, what was
become of Peter.
19 And when Herod had sought for him, and
found him not, he examined the keepers,
and commanded that *they* should be put to
death. And he went down from Judæa to
Cæsarea, and *there* abode.
20 ¶ And Herod was highly displeased with
them of Tyre and Sidon: but they came with
one accord to him, and, having made Blastus
the king's chamberlain their friend, desired
peace; because their country was nourished
by the king's *country*.
21 And upon a set day Herod, arrayed in
royal apparel, sat upon his throne, and made
an oration unto them.
22 And the people gave a shout, *saying, It is*
the voice of a god, and not of a man.
23 And immediately the angel of the Lord
smote him, because he gave not God the
glory: and he was eaten of worms, and gave
up the ghost.
24 ¶ But the word of God grew and multiplied.
25 And Barnabas and Saul returned from
Jerusalem, when they had fulfilled *their*
ministry, and took with them John, whose
surname was Mark.

Acts 13

1 Now there were in the church that was
at Antioch certain prophets and teachers;
as Barnabas, and Simeon that was called
Niger, and Lucius of Cyrene, and Manaen,
which had been brought up with Herod the
tetrarch, and Saul.
2 As they ministered to the Lord, and fasted,
the Holy Spirit said, Separate me Barnabas
and Saul for the work whereunto I have
called them.
3 And when they had fasted and prayed,
and laid *their* hands on them, they sent
them away.
4 ¶ So they, being sent forth by the Holy
Spirit, departed unto Seleucia; and from
thence they sailed to Cyprus.
5 And when they were at Salamis, they
preached the word of God in the synagogues
of the Jews: and they had also John to *their*
minister.
6 And when they had gone through the isle
unto Paphos, they found a certain sorcerer,
a false prophet, a Jew, whose name *was*
Bar-jesus:
7 Which was with the deputy of the country,
Sergius Paulus, a prudent man; who called
for Barnabas and Saul, and desired to hear
the word of God.
8 But Elymas the sorcerer (for so is his name
by interpretation) withstood them, seeking
to turn away the deputy from the faith.

9 Then Saul, (who also *is called* Paul,) filled
with the Holy Spirit, set his eyes on him,
10 And said, O full of all subtilty and all mischief, *thou* child of the devil, *thou* enemy
of all righteousness, wilt thou not cease to
pervert the right ways of the Lord?
11 And now, behold, the hand of the Lord
is upon thee, and thou shalt be blind, not
seeing the sun for a season. And immediately there fell on him a mist and a darkness;
and he went about seeking some to lead
him by the hand.
12 Then the deputy, when he saw what
was done, believed, being astonished at
the doctrine of the Lord.
13 Now when Paul and his company loosed
from Paphos, they came to Perga in Pamphylia: and John departing from them
returned to Jerusalem.
14 ¶ But when they departed from Perga,
they came to Antioch in Pisidia, and went
into the synagogue on the sabbath day,
and sat down.
15 And after the reading of the law and the
prophets the rulers of the synagogue sent
unto them, saying, *Ye* men *and* brethren,
if ye have any word of exhortation for the
people, say on.
16 Then Paul stood up, and beckoning with
his hand said, Men of Israel, and ye that fear
God, give audience.
17 The God of this people of Israel chose our
fathers, and exalted the people when they
dwelt as strangers in the land of Egypt, and
with an high arm brought he them out of it.
18 And about the time of forty years suffered he their manners in the wilderness.
19 And when he had destroyed seven
nations in the land of Chanaan, he divided
their land to them by lot.
20 And after that he gave *unto them* judges
about the space of four hundred and fifty
years, until Samuel the prophet.
21 And afterward they desired a king: and
God gave unto them Saul the son of Cis, a
man of the tribe of Benjamin, by the space
of forty years.
22 And when he had removed him, he
raised up unto them David to be their king;
to whom also he gave testimony, and said,
I have found David the *son* of Jesse, a man
after mine own heart, which shall fulfil all
my will.
23 Of this man's seed hath God according
to *his* promise raised unto Israel a Saviour,
Jesus:
24 When John had first preached before his
coming the baptism of repentance to all the
people of Israel.
25 And as John fulfilled his course, he said,
Whom think ye that I am? I am not *he*. But,
behold, there cometh one after me, whose
shoes of *his* feet I am not worthy to loose.
26 Men *and* brethren, children of the stock
of Abraham, and whosoever among you
feareth God, to you is the word of this salvation sent.
27 For they that dwell at Jerusalem, and
their rulers, because they knew him not,
nor yet the voices of the prophets which are
read every sabbath day, they have fulfilled
them in condemning *him*.
28 And though they found no cause of
death *in him*, yet desired they Pilate that
he should be slain.
29 And when they had fulfilled all that was
written of him, they took *him* down from
the tree, and laid *him* in a sepulchre.
30 But God raised him from the dead:
31 And he was seen many days of them
which came up with him from Galilee to
Jerusalem, who are his witnesses unto the
people.
32 And we declare unto you glad tidings,
how that the promise which was made
unto the fathers,
33 God hath fulfilled the same unto us their
children, in that he hath raised up Jesus
again; as it is also written in the second
psalm, Thou art my Son, this day have I
begotten thee.
34 And as concerning that he raised him up
from the dead, *now* no more to return to
corruption, he said on this wise, I will give
you the sure mercies of David.
35 Wherefore he saith also in another *psalm*,
Thou shalt not suffer thine Holy One to see
corruption.
36 For David, after he had served his own
generation by the will of God, fell on sleep,
and was laid unto his fathers, and saw
corruption:
37 But he, whom God raised again, saw no
corruption.
38 ¶ Be it known unto you therefore, men

and brethren, that through this man is
preached unto you the forgiveness of sins:
39 And by him all that believe are justified
from all things, from which ye could not be
justified by the law of Moses.
40 Beware therefore, lest that come upon
you, which is spoken of in the prophets;
41 Behold, ye despisers, and wonder, and
perish: for I work a work in your days, a work
which ye shall in no wise believe, though a
man declare it unto you.
42 And when the Jews were gone out of
the synagogue, the Gentiles besought that
these words might be preached to them
the next sabbath.
43 Now when the congregation was broken up, many of the Jews and religious
proselytes followed Paul and Barnabas:
who, speaking to them, persuaded them
to continue in the grace of God.
44 ¶ And the next sabbath day came almost
the whole city together to hear the word
of God.
45 But when the Jews saw the multitudes,
they were filled with envy, and spake against
those things which were spoken by Paul,
contradicting and blaspheming.
46 Then Paul and Barnabas waxed bold,
and said, It was necessary that the word of
God should first have been spoken to you:
but seeing ye put it from you, and judge
yourselves unworthy of everlasting life, lo,
we turn to the Gentiles.
47 For so hath the Lord commanded us,
saying, I have set thee to be a light of the
Gentiles, that thou shouldest be for salvation unto the ends of the earth.
48 And when the Gentiles heard this, they
were glad, and glorified the word of the
Lord: and as many as were ordained to
eternal life believed.
49 And the word of the Lord was published
throughout all the region.
50 But the Jews stirred up the devout and
honourable women, and the chief men of
the city, and raised persecution against
Paul and Barnabas, and expelled them out
of their coasts.
51 But they shook off the dust of their feet
against them, and came unto Iconium.
52 And the disciples were filled with joy,
and with the Holy Spirit.

Acts 14

1 And it came to pass in Iconium, that they
went both together into the synagogue
of the Jews, and so spake, that a great
multitude both of the Jews and also of the
Greeks believed.
2 But the unbelieving Jews stirred up the
Gentiles, and made their minds evil affected
against the brethren.
3 Long time therefore abode they speaking
boldly in the Lord, which gave testimony
unto the word of his grace, and granted signs
and wonders to be done by their hands.
4 But the multitude of the city was divided:
and part held with the Jews, and part with
the apostles.
5 And when there was an assault made both
of the Gentiles, and also of the Jews with
their rulers, to use *them* despitefully, and
to stone them,
6 They were ware of *it*, and fled unto Lystra
and Derbe, cities of Lycaonia, and unto the
region that lieth round about:
7 And there they preached the gospel.
8 ¶ And there sat a certain man at Lystra,
impotent in his feet, being a cripple from
his mother's womb, who never had walked:
9 The same heard Paul speak: who stedfastly
beholding him, and perceiving that he had
faith to be healed,
10 Said with a loud voice, Stand upright on
thy feet. And he leaped and walked.
11 And when the people saw what Paul had
done, they lifted up their voices, saying in
the speech of Lycaonia, The gods are come
down to us in the likeness of men.
12 And they called Barnabas, Jupiter; and
Paul, Mercurius, because he was the chief
speaker.
13 Then the priest of Jupiter, which was
before their city, brought oxen and garlands
unto the gates, and would have done sacrifice with the people.
14 *Which* when the apostles, Barnabas and
Paul, heard *of*, they rent their clothes, and
ran in among the people, crying out,
15 And saying, Sirs, why do ye these things?
We also are men of like passions with you,
and preach unto you that ye should turn
from these vanities unto the living God,
which made heaven, and earth, and the sea,
and all things that are therein:

16 Who in times past suffered all nations to walk in their own ways.
17 Nevertheless he left not himself without witness, in that he did good, and gave us rain from heaven, and fruitful seasons, filling our hearts with food and gladness.
18 And with these sayings scarce restrained they the people, that they had not done sacrifice unto them.
19 ¶ And there came thither *certain* Jews from Antioch and Iconium, who persuaded the people, and, having stoned Paul, drew *him* out of the city, supposing he had been dead.
20 Howbeit, as the disciples stood round about him, he rose up, and came into the city: and the next day he departed with Barnabas to Derbe.
21 And when they had preached the gospel to that city, and had taught many, they returned again to Lystra, and *to* Iconium, and Antioch,
22 Confirming the souls of the disciples, *and* exhorting them to continue in the faith, and that we must through much tribulation enter into the kingdom of God.
23 And when they had ordained them elders in every church, and had prayed with fasting, they commended them to the Lord, on whom they believed.
24 And after they had passed throughout Pisidia, they came to Pamphylia.
25 And when they had preached the word in Perga, they went down into Attalia:
26 And thence sailed to Antioch, from whence they had been recommended to the grace of God for the work which they fulfilled.
27 And when they were come, and had gathered the church together, they rehearsed all that God had done with them, and how he had opened the door of faith unto the Gentiles.
28 And there they abode long time with the disciples.

Acts 15

1 And certain men which came down from Judæa taught the brethren, *and said,* Except ye be circumcised after the manner of Moses, ye cannot be saved.
2 When therefore Paul and Barnabas had no small dissension and disputation with them, they determined that Paul and Barnabas, and certain other of them, should go up to Jerusalem unto the apostles and elders about this question.
3 And being brought on their way by the church, they passed through Phenice and Samaria, declaring the conversion of the Gentiles: and they caused great joy unto all the brethren.
4 And when they were come to Jerusalem, they were received of the church, and *of* the apostles and elders, and they declared all things that God had done with them.
5 But there rose up certain of the sect of the Pharisees which believed, saying, That it was needful to circumcise them, and to command *them* to keep the law of Moses.
6 ¶ And the apostles and elders came together for to consider of this matter.
7 And when there had been much disputing, Peter rose up, and said unto them, Men *and* brethren, ye know how that a good while ago God made choice among us, that the Gentiles by my mouth should hear the word of the gospel, and believe.
8 And God, which knoweth the hearts, bare them witness, giving them the Holy Spirit, even as *he did* unto us;
9 And put no difference between us and them, purifying their hearts by faith.
10 Now therefore why tempt ye God, to put a yoke upon the neck of the disciples, which neither our fathers nor we were able to bear?
11 But we believe that through the grace of the Lord Jesus Christ we shall be saved, even as they.
12 ¶ Then all the multitude kept silence, and gave audience to Barnabas and Paul, declaring what miracles and wonders God had wrought among the Gentiles by them.
13 ¶ And after they had held their peace, James answered, saying, Men *and* brethren, hearken unto me:
14 Simeon hath declared how God at the first did visit the Gentiles, to take out of them a people for his name.
15 And to this agree the words of the prophets; as it is written,
16 After this I will return, and will build again the tabernacle of David, which is fallen down; and I will build again the ruins thereof, and I will set it up:

17 That the residue of men might seek after
the Lord, and all the Gentiles, upon whom
my name is called, saith the Lord, who doeth
all these things.
18 Known unto God are all his works from
the beginning of the world.
19 Wherefore my sentence is, that we
trouble not them, which from among the
Gentiles are turned to God:
20 But that we write unto them, that they
abstain from pollutions of idols, and *from*
fornication, and *from* things strangled, and
from blood.
21 For Moses of old time hath in every city
them that preach him, being read in the
synagogues every sabbath day.
22 Then pleased it the apostles and elders,
with the whole church, to send chosen men
of their own company to Antioch with Paul
and Barnabas; *namely*, Judas surnamed
Barsabas, and Silas, chief men among the
brethren:
23 And they wrote *letters* by them after
this manner; The apostles and elders and
brethren *send* greeting unto the brethren
which are of the Gentiles in Antioch and
Syria and Cilicia:
24 Forasmuch as we have heard, that certain
which went out from us have troubled you
with words, subverting your souls, saying,
Ye must be circumcised, and keep the law:
to whom we gave no *such* commandment:
25 It seemed good unto us, being assembled
with one accord, to send chosen men unto
you with our beloved Barnabas and Paul,
26 Men that have hazarded their lives for
the name of our Lord Jesus Christ.
27 We have sent therefore Judas and Silas,
who shall also tell *you* the same things by
mouth.
28 For it seemed good to the Holy Spirit,
and to us, to lay upon you no greater burden
than these necessary things;
29 That ye abstain from meats offered to
idols, and from blood, and from things
strangled, and from fornication: from which
if ye keep yourselves, ye shall do well. Fare
ye well.
30 So when they were dismissed, they came
to Antioch: and when they had gathered
the multitude together, they delivered the
epistle:
31 *Which* when they had read, they rejoiced
for the consolation.
32 And Judas and Silas, being prophets also
themselves, exhorted the brethren with
many words, and confirmed *them*.
33 And after they had tarried *there* a space,
they were let go in peace from the brethren
unto the apostles.
34 Notwithstanding it pleased Silas to abide
there still.
35 Paul also and Barnabas continued in
Antioch, teaching and preaching the word
of the Lord, with many others also.
36 ¶ And some days after Paul said unto
Barnabas, Let us go again and visit our brethren in every city where we have preached
the word of the Lord, *and see* how they do.
37 And Barnabas determined to take with
them John, whose surname was Mark.
38 But Paul thought not good to take him
with them, who departed from them from
Pamphylia, and went not with them to the
work.
39 And the contention was so sharp
between them, that they departed asunder one from the other: and so Barnabas
took Mark, and sailed unto Cyprus;
40 And Paul chose Silas, and departed,
being recommended by the brethren unto
the grace of God.
41 And he went through Syria and Cilicia,
confirming the churches.

Acts 16

1 Then came he to Derbe and Lystra: and,
behold, a certain disciple was there, named
Timotheus, the son of a certain woman,
which was a Jewess, and believed; but his
father *was* a Greek:
2 Which was well reported of by the brethren that were at Lystra and Iconium.
3 Him would Paul have to go forth with him;
and took and circumcised him because of
the Jews which were in those quarters: for
they knew all that his father was a Greek.
4 And as they went through the cities, they
delivered them the decrees for to keep, that
were ordained of the apostles and elders
which were at Jerusalem.
5 And so were the churches established in
the faith, and increased in number daily.
6 Now when they had gone throughout
Phrygia and the region of Galatia, and were

forbidden of the Holy Spirit to preach the
word in Asia,
7 After they were come to Mysia, they
assayed to go into Bithynia: but the Spirit
suffered them not.
8 And they passing by Mysia came down
to Troas.
9 And a vision appeared to Paul in the
night; There stood a man of Macedonia,
and prayed him, saying, Come over into
Macedonia, and help us.
10 And after he had seen the vision, immediately
we endeavoured to go into Macedonia,
assuredly gathering that the Lord had called
us for to preach the gospel unto them.
11 Therefore loosing from Troas, we came
with a straight course to Samothracia, and
the next *day* to Neapolis;
12 And from thence to Philippi, which is the
chief city of that part of Macedonia, *and* a
colony: and we were in that city abiding
certain days.
13 And on the sabbath we went out of the
city by a river side, where prayer was wont
to be made; and we sat down, and spake
unto the women which resorted *thither.*
14 ¶ And a certain woman named Lydia,
a seller of purple, of the city of Thyatira,
which worshipped God, heard *us:* whose
heart the Lord opened, that she attended
unto the things which were spoken of Paul.
15 And when she was baptized, and her
household, she besought *us*, saying, If ye
have judged me to be faithful to the Lord,
come into my house, and abide *there*. And
she constrained us.
16 ¶ And it came to pass, as we went to
prayer, a certain damsel possessed with a
spirit of divination met us, which brought
her masters much gain by soothsaying:
17 The same followed Paul and us, and
cried, saying, These men are the servants
of the most high God, which shew unto us
the way of salvation.
18 And this did she many days. But Paul,
being grieved, turned and said to the spirit,
I command thee in the name of Jesus Christ
to come out of her. And he came out the
same hour.
19 ¶ And when her masters saw that the
hope of their gains was gone, they caught
Paul and Silas, and drew *them* into the marketplace
unto the rulers,
20 And brought them to the magistrates,
saying, These men, being Jews, do exceedingly
trouble our city,
21 And teach customs, which are not lawful
for us to receive, neither to observe, being
Romans.
22 And the multitude rose up together
against them: and the magistrates rent off
their clothes, and commanded to beat *them.*
23 And when they had laid many stripes
upon them, they cast *them* into prison,
charging the jailor to keep them safely:
24 Who, having received such a charge,
thrust them into the inner prison, and made
their feet fast in the stocks.
25 ¶ And at midnight Paul and Silas prayed,
and sang praises unto God: and the prisoners
heard them.
26 And suddenly there was a great earthquake,
so that the foundations of the prison
were shaken: and immediately all the doors
were opened, and every one's bands were
loosed.
27 And the keeper of the prison awaking
out of his sleep, and seeing the prison
doors open, he drew out his sword, and
would have killed himself, supposing that
the prisoners had been fled.
28 But Paul cried with a loud voice, saying,
Do thyself no harm: for we are all here.
29 Then he called for a light, and sprang in,
and came trembling, and fell down before
Paul and Silas,
30 And brought them out, and said, Sirs,
what must I do to be saved?
31 And they said, Believe on the Lord Jesus
Christ, and thou shalt be saved, and thy
house.
32 And they spake unto him the word of
the Lord, and to all that were in his house.
33 And he took them the same hour of the
night, and washed *their* stripes; and was
baptized, he and all his, straightway.
34 And when he had brought them into
his house, he set meat before them, and
rejoiced, believing in God with all his house.
35 And when it was day, the magistrates
sent the serjeants, saying, Let those men go.
36 And the keeper of the prison told this
saying to Paul, The magistrates have sent
to let you go: now therefore depart, and
go in peace.
37 But Paul said unto them, They have

beaten us openly uncondemned, being
Romans, and have cast *us* into prison;
and now do they thrust us out privily? nay
verily; but let them come themselves and
fetch us out.
38 And the serjeants told these words unto
the magistrates: and they feared, when they
heard that they were Romans.
39 And they came and besought them,
and brought *them* out, and desired *them*
to depart out of the city.
40 And they went out of the prison, and
entered into *the house of* Lydia: and when
they had seen the brethren, they comforted
them, and departed.

Acts 17

1 Now when they had passed through
Amphipolis and Apollonia, they came to
Thessalonica, where was a synagogue of
the Jews:
2 And Paul, as his manner was, went in unto
them, and three sabbath days reasoned with
them out of the scriptures,
3 Opening and alleging, that Christ must
needs have suffered, and risen again from
the dead; and that this Jesus, whom I preach
unto you, is Christ.
4 And some of them believed, and con-
sorted with Paul and Silas; and of the devout
Greeks a great multitude, and of the chief
women not a few.
5 ¶ But the Jews which believed not, moved
with envy, took unto them certain lewd fellows of the baser sort, and gathered a company, and set all the city on an uproar, and
assaulted the house of Jason, and sought
to bring them out to the people.
6 And when they found them not, they drew
Jason and certain brethren unto the rulers
of the city, crying, These that have turned
the world upside down are come hither also;
7 Whom Jason hath received: and these all
do contrary to the decrees of Cæsar, saying
that there is another king, *one* Jesus.
8 And they troubled the people and the rulers of the city, when they heard these things.
9 And when they had taken security of
Jason, and of the other, they let them go.
10 ¶ And the brethren immediately sent
away Paul and Silas by night unto Berea:
who coming *thither* went into the synagogue
of the Jews.
11 These were more noble than those in
Thessalonica, in that they received the word
with all readiness of mind, and searched
the scriptures daily, whether those things
were so.
12 Therefore many of them believed; also
of honourable women which were Greeks,
and of men, not a few.
13 But when the Jews of Thessalonica
had knowledge that the word of God was
preached of Paul at Berea, they came thither
also, and stirred up the people.
14 And then immediately the brethren sent
away Paul to go as it were to the sea: but
Silas and Timotheus abode there still.
15 And they that conducted Paul brought
him unto Athens: and receiving a commandment unto Silas and Timotheus for to come
to him with all speed, they departed.
16 ¶ Now while Paul waited for them at
Athens, his spirit was stirred in him, when
he saw the city wholly given to idolatry.
17 Therefore disputed he in the synagogue
with the Jews, and with the devout persons,
and in the market daily with them that met
with him.
18 Then certain philosophers of the Epicu-
reans, and of the Stoicks, encountered him.
And some said, What will this babbler say?
other some, He seemeth to be a setter forth
of strange gods: because he preached unto
them Jesus, and the resurrection.
19 And they took him, and brought him unto
Areopagus, saying, May we know what this
new doctrine, whereof thou speakest, *is?*
20 For thou bringest certain strange things
to our ears: we would know therefore what
these things mean.
21 (For all the Athenians and strangers
which were there spent their time in nothing else, but either to tell, or to hear some
new thing.)
22 ¶ Then Paul stood in the midst of Mars'
hill, and said, *Ye* men of Athens, I perceive
that in all things ye are too superstitious.
23 For as I passed by, and beheld your devo-
tions, I found an altar with this inscription,
TO THE UNKNOWN GOD. Whom therefore
ye ignorantly worship, him declare I unto
you.
24 God that made the world and all things
therein, seeing that he is Lord of heaven

and earth, dwelleth not in temples made
with hands;
25 Neither is worshipped with men's hands,
as though he needed any thing, seeing he
giveth to all life, and breath, and all things;
26 And hath made of one blood all nations
of men for to dwell on all the face of the
earth, and hath determined the times
before appointed, and the bounds of their
habitation;
27 That they should seek the Lord, if haply
they might feel after him, and find him,
though he be not far from every one of us:
28 For in him we live, and move, and have
our being; as certain also of your own poets
have said, For we are also his offspring.
29 Forasmuch then as we are the offspring
of God, we ought not to think that the Godhead is like unto gold, or silver, or stone,
graven by art and man's device.
30 And the times of this ignorance God
winked at; but now commandeth all men
every where to repent:
31 Because he hath appointed a day, in the
which he will judge the world in righteousness by *that* man whom he hath ordained;
whereof he hath given assurance unto all
men, in that he hath raised him from the
dead.
32 ¶ And when they heard of the resurrection of the dead, some mocked: and others
said, We will hear thee again of this *matter*.
33 So Paul departed from among them.
34 Howbeit certain men clave unto him, and
believed: among the which *was* Dionysius
the Areopagite, and a woman named Dam-
aris, and others with them.

Acts 18

1 After these things Paul departed from
Athens, and came to Corinth;
2 And found a certain Jew named Aquila,
born in Pontus, lately come from Italy, with
his wife Priscilla; (because that Claudius had
commanded all Jews to depart from Rome:)
and came unto them.
3 And because he was of the same craft, he
abode with them, and wrought: for by their
occupation they were tentmakers.
4 And he reasoned in the synagogue every
sabbath, and persuaded the Jews and the
Greeks.
5 And when Silas and Timotheus were come
from Macedonia, Paul was pressed in the
spirit, and testified to the Jews *that* Jesus
was Christ.
6 And when they opposed themselves, and
blasphemed, he shook *his* raiment, and said
unto them, Your blood *be* upon your own
heads; I *am* clean: from henceforth I will go
unto the Gentiles.
7 ¶ And he departed thence, and entered
into a certain *man's* house, named Justus,
one that worshipped God, whose house
joined hard to the synagogue.
8 And Crispus, the chief ruler of the synagogue, believed on the Lord with all his
house; and many of the Corinthians hearing
believed, and were baptized.
9 Then spake the Lord to Paul in the night
by a vision, Be not afraid, but speak, and
hold not thy peace:
10 For I am with thee, and no man shall
set on thee to hurt thee: for I have much
people in this city.
11 And he continued *there* a year and six
months, teaching the word of God among
them.
12 ¶ And when Gallio was the deputy of
Achaia, the Jews made insurrection with
one accord against Paul, and brought him
to the judgment seat,
13 Saying, This *fellow* persuadeth men to
worship God contrary to the law.
14 And when Paul was now about to open
his mouth, Gallio said unto the Jews, If it
were a matter of wrong or wicked lewdness,
O *ye* Jews, reason would that I should bear
with you:
15 But if it be a question of words and
names, and *of* your law, look ye *to it;* for I
will be no judge of such *matters*.
16 And he drave them from the judgment
seat.
17 Then all the Greeks took Sosthenes, the
chief ruler of the synagogue, and beat *him*
before the judgment seat. And Gallio cared
for none of those things.
18 ¶ And Paul *after this* tarried *there* yet a
good while, and then took his leave of the
brethren, and sailed thence into Syria, and
with him Priscilla and Aquila; having shorn
his head in Cenchrea: for he had a vow.
19 And he came to Ephesus, and left them
there: but he himself entered into the synagogue, and reasoned with the Jews.

20 When they desired *him* to tarry longer
time with them, he consented not;
21 But bade them farewell, saying, I must
by all means keep this feast that cometh in
Jerusalem: but I will return again unto you,
if God will. And he sailed from Ephesus.
22 And when he had landed at Cæsarea,
and gone up, and saluted the church, he
went down to Antioch.
23 And after he had spent some time *there*,
he departed, and went over *all* the country
of Galatia and Phrygia in order, strengthening all the disciples.
24 ¶ And a certain Jew named Apollos, born
at Alexandria, an eloquent man, *and* mighty
in the scriptures, came to Ephesus.
25 This man was instructed in the way of
the Lord; and being fervent in the spirit, he
spake and taught diligently the things of
the Lord, knowing only the baptism of John.
26 And he began to speak boldly in the
synagogue: whom when Aquila and Priscilla had heard, they took him unto *them*,
and expounded unto him the way of God
more perfectly.
27 And when he was disposed to pass into
Achaia, the brethren wrote, exhorting the
disciples to receive him: who, when he
was come, helped them much which had
believed through grace:
28 For he mightily convinced the Jews, *and*
that publickly, shewing by the scriptures that
Jesus was Christ.

Acts 19

1 And it came to pass, that, while Apollos
was at Corinth, Paul having passed through
the upper coasts came to Ephesus: and
finding certain disciples,
2 He said unto them, Have ye received the
Holy Spirit since ye believed? And they said
unto him, We have not so much as heard
whether there be any Holy Spirit.
3 And he said unto them, Unto what then
were ye baptized? And they said, Unto
John's baptism.
4 Then said Paul, John verily baptized with
the baptism of repentance, saying unto the
people, that they should believe on him
which should come after him, that is, on
Christ Jesus.
5 When they heard *this*, they were baptized
in the name of the Lord Jesus.
6 And when Paul had laid *his* hands upon
them, the Holy Spirit came on them; and
they spake with tongues, and prophesied.
7 And all the men were about twelve.
8 And he went into the synagogue, and
spake boldly for the space of three months,
disputing and persuading the things concerning the kingdom of God.
9 But when divers were hardened, and
believed not, but spake evil of that way
before the multitude, he departed from
them, and separated the disciples, disputing
daily in the school of one Tyrannus.
10 And this continued by the space of two
years; so that all they which dwelt in Asia
heard the word of the Lord Jesus, both Jews
and Greeks.
11 And God wrought special miracles by
the hands of Paul:
12 So that from his body were brought unto
the sick handkerchiefs or aprons, and the
diseases departed from them, and the evil
spirits went out of them.
13 ¶ Then certain of the vagabond Jews,
exorcists, took upon them to call over them
which had evil spirits the name of the Lord
Jesus, saying, We adjure you by Jesus whom
Paul preacheth.
14 And there were seven sons of *one* Sceva,
a Jew, *and* chief of the priests, which did so.
15 And the evil spirit answered and said,
Jesus I know, and Paul I know; but who
are ye?
16 And the man in whom the evil spirit was
leaped on them, and overcame them, and
prevailed against them, so that they fled out
of that house naked and wounded.
17 And this was known to all the Jews and
Greeks also dwelling at Ephesus; and fear
fell on them all, and the name of the Lord
Jesus was magnified.
18 And many that believed came, and confessed, and shewed their deeds.
19 Many of them also which used curious
arts brought their books together, and
burned them before all *men:* and they
counted the price of them, and found *it* fifty
thousand *pieces* of silver.
20 So mightily grew the word of God and
prevailed.
21 ¶ After these things were ended, Paul
purposed in the spirit, when he had passed
through Macedonia and Achaia, to go to

Jerusalem, saying, After I have been there,
I must also see Rome.
22 So he sent into Macedonia two of them
that ministered unto him, Timotheus and
Erastus; but he himself stayed in Asia for
a season.
23 And the same time there arose no small
stir about that way.
24 For a certain *man* named Demetrius,
a silversmith, which made silver shrines
for Diana, brought no small gain unto the
craftsmen;
25 Whom he called together with the workmen of like occupation, and said, Sirs, ye
know that by this craft we have our wealth.
26 Moreover ye see and hear, that not alone
at Ephesus, but almost throughout all Asia,
this Paul hath persuaded and turned away
much people, saying that they be no gods,
which are made with hands:
27 So that not only this our craft is in danger to be set at nought; but also that the
temple of the great goddess Diana should
be despised, and her magnificence should
be destroyed, whom all Asia and the world
worshippeth.
28 And when they heard *these sayings*, they
were full of wrath, and cried out, saying,
Great *is* Diana of the Ephesians.
29 And the whole city was filled with confusion: and having caught Gaius and Aristarchus, men of Macedonia, Paul's companions in travel, they rushed with one accord
into the theatre.
30 And when Paul would have entered
in unto the people, the disciples suffered
him not.
31 And certain of the chief of Asia, which
were his friends, sent unto him, desiring
him that he would not adventure himself
into the theatre.
32 Some therefore cried one thing, and
some another: for the assembly was con-
fused; and the more part knew not wherefore they were come together.
33 And they drew Alexander out of the
multitude, the Jews putting him forward.
And Alexander beckoned with the hand,
and would have made his defence unto
the people.
34 But when they knew that he was a Jew, all
with one voice about the space of two hours
cried out, Great *is* Diana of the Ephesians.
35 And when the townclerk had appeased
the people, he said, *Ye* men of Ephesus, what
man is there that knoweth not how that
the city of the Ephesians is a worshipper of
the great goddess Diana, and of the *image*
which fell down from Jupiter?
36 Seeing then that these things cannot be
spoken against, ye ought to be quiet, and
to do nothing rashly.
37 For ye have brought hither these men,
which are neither robbers of churches, nor
yet blasphemers of your goddess.
38 Wherefore if Demetrius, and the craftsmen which are with him, have a matter
against any man, the law is open, and there
are deputies: let them implead one another.
39 But if ye inquire any thing concerning
other matters, it shall be determined in a
lawful assembly.
40 For we are in danger to be called in
question for this day's uproar, there being
no cause whereby we may give an account
of this concourse.
41 And when he had thus spoken, he dismissed the assembly.

Acts 20

1 And after the uproar was ceased, Paul
called unto *him* the disciples, and embraced
them, and departed for to go into Macedonia.
2 And when he had gone over those parts,
and had given them much exhortation, he
came into Greece,
3 And *there* abode three months. And when
the Jews laid wait for him, as he was about
to sail into Syria, he purposed to return
through Macedonia.
4 And there accompanied him into Asia
Sopater of Berea; and of the Thessalonians,
Aristarchus and Secundus; and Gaius of
Derbe, and Timotheus; and of Asia, Tychicus
and Trophimus.
5 These going before tarried for us at Troas.
6 And we sailed away from Philippi after
the days of unleavened bread, and came
unto them to Troas in five days; where we
abode seven days.
7 And upon the first *day* of the week, when
the disciples came together to break bread,
Paul preached unto them, ready to depart
on the morrow; and continued his speech
until midnight.

8 And there were many lights in the upper
chamber, where they were gathered
together.
9 And there sat in a window a certain young
man named Eutychus, being fallen into a
deep sleep: and as Paul was long preaching,
he sunk down with sleep, and fell down
from the third loft, and was taken up dead.
10 And Paul went down, and fell on him, and
embracing *him* said, Trouble not yourselves;
for his life is in him.
11 When he therefore was come up again,
and had broken bread, and eaten, and
talked a long while, even till break of day,
so he departed.
12 And they brought the young man alive,
and were not a little comforted.
13 ¶ And we went before to ship, and sailed
unto Assos, there intending to take in Paul:
for so had he appointed, minding himself
to go afoot.
14 And when he met with us at Assos, we
took him in, and came to Mitylene.
15 And we sailed thence, and came the next
day over against Chios; and the next *day* we
arrived at Samos, and tarried at Trogyllium;
and the next *day* we came to Miletus.
16 For Paul had determined to sail by Ephesus, because he would not spend the time
in Asia: for he hasted, if it were possible for
him, to be at Jerusalem the day of Pentecost.
17 ¶ And from Miletus he sent to Ephesus,
and called the elders of the church.
18 And when they were come to him, he
said unto them, Ye know, from the first day
that I came into Asia, after what manner I
have been with you at all seasons,
19 Serving the Lord with all humility of
mind, and with many tears, and temptations, which befell me by the lying in wait
of the Jews:
20 *And* how I kept back nothing that was
profitable *unto you*, but have shewed you,
and have taught you publickly, and from
house to house,
21 Testifying both to the Jews, and also to
the Greeks, repentance toward God, and
faith toward our Lord Jesus Christ.
22 And now, behold, I go bound in the spirit
unto Jerusalem, not knowing the things that
shall befall me there:
23 Save that the Holy Spirit witnesseth in
every city, saying that bonds and afflictions
abide me.
24 But none of these things move me,
neither count I my life dear unto myself,
so that I might finish my course with joy,
and the ministry, which I have received of
the Lord Jesus, to testify the gospel of the
grace of God.
25 And now, behold, I know that ye all,
among whom I have gone preaching the
kingdom of God, shall see my face no more.
26 Wherefore I take you to record this day,
that I *am* pure from the blood of all *men*.
27 For I have not shunned to declare unto
you all the counsel of God.
28 ¶ Take heed therefore unto yourselves,
and to all the flock, over the which the Holy
Spirit hath made you overseers, to feed the
church of God, which he hath purchased
with his own blood.
29 For I know this, that after my departing
shall grievous wolves enter in among you,
not sparing the flock.
30 Also of your own selves shall men arise,
speaking perverse things, to draw away
disciples after them.
31 Therefore watch, and remember, that
by the space of three years I ceased not to
warn every one night and day with tears.
32 And now, brethren, I commend you to
God, and to the word of his grace, which
is able to build you up, and to give you
an inheritance among all them which are
sanctified.
33 I have coveted no man's silver, or gold,
or apparel.
34 Yea, ye yourselves know, that these
hands have ministered unto my necessities,
and to them that were with me.
35 I have shewed you all things, how that
so labouring ye ought to support the weak,
and to remember the words of the Lord
Jesus, how he said, It is more blessed to
give than to receive.
36 ¶ And when he had thus spoken, he
kneeled down, and prayed with them all.
37 And they all wept sore, and fell on Paul's
neck, and kissed him,
38 Sorrowing most of all for the words
which he spake, that they should see his
face no more. And they accompanied him
unto the ship.

Acts 21

1 And it came to pass, that after we were
gotten from them, and had launched, we
came with a straight course unto Coos, and
the *day* following unto Rhodes, and from
thence unto Patara:
2 And finding a ship sailing over unto Phenicia, we went aboard, and set forth.
3 Now when we had discovered Cyprus, we
left it on the left hand, and sailed into Syria,
and landed at Tyre: for there the ship was
to unlade her burden.
4 And finding disciples, we tarried there
seven days: who said to Paul through the
Spirit, that he should not go up to Jerusalem.
5 And when we had accomplished those
days, we departed and went our way; and
they all brought us on our way, with wives
and children, till *we were* out of the city: and
we kneeled down on the shore, and prayed.
6 And when we had taken our leave one of
another, we took ship; and they returned
home again.
7 And when we had finished *our* course from
Tyre, we came to Ptolemais, and saluted the
brethren, and abode with them one day.
8 And the next *day* we that were of Paul's
company departed, and came unto Cæsarea:
and we entered into the house of Philip the
evangelist, which was *one* of the seven; and
abode with him.
9 And the same man had four daughters,
virgins, which did prophesy.
10 And as we tarried *there* many days, there
came down from Judæa a certain prophet,
named Agabus.
11 And when he was come unto us, he took
Paul's girdle, and bound his own hands and
feet, and said, Thus saith the Holy Spirit, So
shall the Jews at Jerusalem bind the man
that owneth this girdle, and shall deliver
him into the hands of the Gentiles.
12 And when we heard these things, both
we, and they of that place, besought him
not to go up to Jerusalem.
13 Then Paul answered, What mean ye to
weep and to break mine heart? for I am
ready not to be bound only, but also to die
at Jerusalem for the name of the Lord Jesus.
14 And when he would not be persuaded,
we ceased, saying, The will of the Lord be
done.
15 And after those days we took up our
carriages, and went up to Jerusalem.
16 There went with us also *certain* of the
disciples of Cæsarea, and brought with them
one Mnason of Cyprus, an old disciple, with
whom we should lodge.
17 And when we were come to Jerusalem,
the brethren received us gladly.
18 And the *day* following Paul went in with
us unto James; and all the elders were
present.
19 And when he had saluted them, he
declared particularly what things God had
wrought among the Gentiles by his ministry.
20 And when they heard *it*, they glorified
the Lord, and said unto him, Thou seest,
brother, how many thousands of Jews there
are which believe; and they are all zealous
of the law:
21 And they are informed of thee, that thou
teachest all the Jews which are among the
Gentiles to forsake Moses, saying that they
ought not to circumcise *their* children, neither to walk after the customs.
22 What is it therefore? the multitude must
needs come together: for they will hear that
thou art come.
23 Do therefore this that we say to thee: We
have four men which have a vow on them;
24 Them take, and purify thyself with them,
and be at charges with them, that they may
shave *their* heads: and all may know that
those things, whereof they were informed
concerning thee, are nothing; but *that* thou
thyself also walkest orderly, and keepest
the law.
25 As touching the Gentiles which believe,
we have written *and* concluded that they
observe no such thing, save only that they
keep themselves from *things* offered to
idols, and from blood, and from strangled,
and from fornication.
26 Then Paul took the men, and the next
day purifying himself with them entered into
the temple, to signify the accomplishment of
the days of purification, until that an offering
should be offered for every one of them.
27 And when the seven days were almost
ended, the Jews which were of Asia, when
they saw him in the temple, stirred up all
the people, and laid hands on him,
28 Crying out, Men of Israel, help: This
is the man, that teacheth all *men* every

where against the people, and the law,
and this place: and further brought Greeks
also into the temple, and hath polluted this
holy place.
29 (For they had seen before with him in
the city Trophimus an Ephesian, whom
they supposed that Paul had brought into
the temple.)
30 And all the city was moved, and the people ran together: and they took Paul, and
drew him out of the temple: and forthwith
the doors were shut.
31 And as they went about to kill him, tidings
came unto the chief captain of the band,
that all Jerusalem was in an uproar.
32 Who immediately took soldiers and centurions, and ran down unto them: and when
they saw the chief captain and the soldiers,
they left beating of Paul.
33 Then the chief captain came near, and
took him, and commanded *him* to be bound
with two chains; and demanded who he
was, and what he had done.
34 And some cried one thing, some another,
among the multitude: and when he could
not know the certainty for the tumult, he
commanded him to be carried into the
castle.
35 And when he came upon the stairs, so it
was, that he was borne of the soldiers for
the violence of the people.
36 For the multitude of the people followed
after, crying, Away with him.
37 And as Paul was to be led into the castle, he said unto the chief captain, May I
speak unto thee? Who said, Canst thou
speak Greek?
38 Art not thou that Egyptian, which before
these days madest an uproar, and leddest
out into the wilderness four thousand men
that were murderers?
39 But Paul said, I am a man *which am* a
Jew of Tarsus, *a city* in Cilicia, a citizen of
no mean city: and, I beseech thee, suffer
me to speak unto the people.
40 And when he had given him licence, Paul
stood on the stairs, and beckoned with the
hand unto the people. And when there was
made a great silence, he spake unto *them*
in the Hebrew tongue, saying,

Acts 22

1 Men, brethren, and fathers, hear ye my
defence *which I make* now unto you.
2 (And when they heard that he spake in
the Hebrew tongue to them, they kept the
more silence: and he saith,)
3 I am verily a man *which am* a Jew, born
in Tarsus, *a city* in Cilicia, yet brought up in
this city at the feet of Gamaliel, *and* taught
according to the perfect manner of the law
of the fathers, and was zealous toward God,
as ye all are this day.
4 And I persecuted this way unto the death,
binding and delivering into prisons both
men and women.
5 As also the high priest doth bear me witness, and all the estate of the elders: from
whom also I received letters unto the brethren, and went to Damascus, to bring them
which were there bound unto Jerusalem,
for to be punished.
6 And it came to pass, that, as I made my
journey, and was come nigh unto Damascus
about noon, suddenly there shone from
heaven a great light round about me.
7 And I fell unto the ground, and heard a
voice saying unto me, Saul, Saul, why persecutest thou me?
8 And I answered, Who art thou, Lord? And
he said unto me, I am Jesus of Nazareth,
whom thou persecutest.
9 And they that were with me saw indeed
the light, and were afraid; but they heard
not the voice of him that spake to me.
10 And I said, What shall I do, Lord? And
the Lord said unto me, Arise, and go into
Damascus; and there it shall be told thee of
all things which are appointed for thee to do.
11 And when I could not see for the glory
of that light, being led by the hand of them
that were with me, I came into Damascus.
12 And one Ananias, a devout man according to the law, having a good report of all
the Jews which dwelt *there*,
13 Came unto me, and stood, and said unto
me, Brother Saul, receive thy sight. And the
same hour I looked up upon him.
14 And he said, The God of our fathers hath
chosen thee, that thou shouldest know his
will, and see that Just One, and shouldest
hear the voice of his mouth.
15 For thou shalt be his witness unto all men
of what thou hast seen and heard.

16 And now why tarriest thou? arise, and
be baptized, and wash away thy sins, calling
on the name of the Lord.
17 And it came to pass, that, when I was
come again to Jerusalem, even while I
prayed in the temple, I was in a trance;
18 And saw him saying unto me, Make
haste, and get thee quickly out of Jerusalem: for they will not receive thy testimony
concerning me.
19 And I said, Lord, they know that I impris-
oned and beat in every synagogue them that
believed on thee:
20 And when the blood of thy martyr Stephen was shed, I also was standing by, and
consenting unto his death, and kept the
raiment of them that slew him.
21 And he said unto me, Depart: for I will
send thee far hence unto the Gentiles.
22 And they gave him audience unto this
word, and *then* lifted up their voices, and
said, Away with such a *fellow* from the earth:
for it is not fit that he should live.
23 And as they cried out, and cast off *their*
clothes, and threw dust into the air,
24 The chief captain commanded him to
be brought into the castle, and bade that
he should be examined by scourging; that
he might know wherefore they cried so
against him.
25 And as they bound him with thongs,
Paul said unto the centurion that stood by,
Is it lawful for you to scourge a man that is
a Roman, and uncondemned?
26 When the centurion heard *that*, he went
and told the chief captain, saying, Take heed
what thou doest: for this man is a Roman.
27 Then the chief captain came, and said
unto him, Tell me, art thou a Roman? He
said, Yea.
28 And the chief captain answered, With
a great sum obtained I this freedom. And
Paul said, But I was *free* born.
29 Then straightway they departed from
him which should have examined him: and
the chief captain also was afraid, after he
knew that he was a Roman, and because
he had bound him.
30 On the morrow, because he would have
known the certainty wherefore he was
accused of the Jews, he loosed him from
his bands, and commanded the chief priests
and all their council to appear, and brought
Paul down, and set him before them.

Acts 23

1 And Paul, earnestly beholding the council,
said, Men *and* brethren, I have lived in all
good conscience before God until this day.
2 And the high priest Ananias commanded
them that stood by him to smite him on
the mouth.
3 Then said Paul unto him, God shall smite
thee, *thou* whited wall: for sittest thou to
judge me after the law, and commandest me
to be smitten contrary to the law?
4 And they that stood by said, Revilest thou
God's high priest?
5 Then said Paul, I wist not, brethren, that
he was the high priest: for it is written,
Thou shalt not speak evil of the ruler of
thy people.
6 But when Paul perceived that the one part
were Sadducees, and the other Pharisees,
he cried out in the council, Men *and* brethren, I am a Pharisee, the son of a Pharisee:
of the hope and resurrection of the dead I
am called in question.
7 And when he had so said, there arose a
dissension between the Pharisees and the
Sadducees: and the multitude was divided.
8 For the Sadducees say that there is no
resurrection, neither angel, nor spirit: but
the Pharisees confess both.
9 And there arose a great cry: and the
scribes *that were* of the Pharisees' part
arose, and strove, saying, We find no evil
in this man: but if a spirit or an angel hath
spoken to him, let us not fight against God.
10 And when there arose a great dissension, the chief captain, fearing lest Paul
should have been pulled in pieces of them,
commanded the soldiers to go down, and
to take him by force from among them, and
to bring *him* into the castle.
11 And the night following the Lord stood
by him, and said, Be of good cheer, Paul: for
as thou hast testified of me in Jerusalem,
so must thou bear witness also at Rome.
12 And when it was day, certain of the Jews
banded together, and bound themselves
under a curse, saying that they would neither eat nor drink till they had killed Paul.
13 And they were more than forty which
had made this conspiracy.

14 And they came to the chief priests and
elders, and said, We have bound ourselves
under a great curse, that we will eat nothing
until we have slain Paul.
15 Now therefore ye with the council signify to the chief captain that he bring him
down unto you to morrow, as though ye
would inquire something more perfectly
concerning him: and we, or ever he come
near, are ready to kill him.
16 And when Paul's sister's son heard of
their lying in wait, he went and entered into
the castle, and told Paul.
17 Then Paul called one of the centurions
unto *him*, and said, Bring this young man
unto the chief captain: for he hath a certain
thing to tell him.
18 So he took him, and brought *him* to the
chief captain, and said, Paul the prisoner
called me unto *him*, and prayed me to bring
this young man unto thee, who hath something to say unto thee.
19 Then the chief captain took him by the
hand, and went *with him* aside privately, and
asked *him*, What is that thou hast to tell me?
20 And he said, The Jews have agreed to
desire thee that thou wouldest bring down
Paul to morrow into the council, as though
they would inquire somewhat of him more
perfectly.
21 But do not thou yield unto them: for
there lie in wait for him of them more than
forty men, which have bound themselves
with an oath, that they will neither eat nor
drink till they have killed him: and now are
they ready, looking for a promise from thee.
22 So the chief captain *then* let the young
man depart, and charged *him*, *See thou*
tell no man that thou hast shewed these
things to me.
23 And he called unto *him* two centurions,
saying, Make ready two hundred soldiers to
go to Cæsarea, and horsemen threescore
and ten, and spearmen two hundred, at the
third hour of the night;
24 And provide *them* beasts, that they may
set Paul on, and bring *him* safe unto Felix
the governor.
25 And he wrote a letter after this manner:
26 Claudius Lysias unto the most excellent
governor Felix *sendeth* greeting.
27 This man was taken of the Jews, and
should have been killed of them: then came
I with an army, and rescued him, having
understood that he was a Roman.
28 And when I would have known the cause
wherefore they accused him, I brought him
forth into their council:
29 Whom I perceived to be accused of questions of their law, but to have nothing laid
to his charge worthy of death or of bonds.
30 And when it was told me how that the
Jews laid wait for the man, I sent straightway to thee, and gave commandment to his
accusers also to say before thee what *they
had* against him. Farewell.
31 Then the soldiers, as it was commanded
them, took Paul, and brought *him* by night
to Antipatris.
32 On the morrow they left the horsemen
to go with him, and returned to the castle:
33 Who, when they came to Cæsarea, and
delivered the epistle to the governor, presented Paul also before him.
34 And when the governor had read *the letter*, he asked of what province he was. And
when he understood that *he was* of Cilicia;
35 I will hear thee, said he, when thine
accusers are also come. And he commanded
him to be kept in Herod's judgment hall.

Acts 24

1 And after five days Ananias the high priest
descended with the elders, and *with* a certain orator *named* Tertullus, who informed
the governor against Paul.
2 And when he was called forth, Tertullus
began to accuse *him*, saying, Seeing that by
thee we enjoy great quietness, and that very
worthy deeds are done unto this nation by
thy providence,
3 We accept *it* always, and in all places, most
noble Felix, with all thankfulness.
4 Notwithstanding, that I be not further
tedious unto thee, I pray thee that thou
wouldest hear us of thy clemency a few
words.
5 For we have found this man *a* pestilent
fellow, and a mover of sedition among all the
Jews throughout the world, and a ringleader
of the sect of the Nazarenes:
6 Who also hath gone about to profane the
temple: whom we took, and would have
judged according to our law.
7 But the chief captain Lysias came *upon*

us, and with great violence took *him* away
out of our hands,
8 Commanding his accusers to come unto
thee: by examining of whom thyself mayest
take knowledge of all these things, whereof
we accuse him.
9 And the Jews also assented, saying that
these things were so.
10 Then Paul, after that the governor had
beckoned unto him to speak, answered,
Forasmuch as I know that thou hast been
of many years a judge unto this nation, I
do the more cheerfully answer for myself:
11 Because that thou mayest understand,
that there are yet but twelve days since I
went up to Jerusalem for to worship.
12 And they neither found me in the temple
disputing with any man, neither raising up
the people, neither in the synagogues, nor
in the city:
13 Neither can they prove the things
whereof they now accuse me.
14 But this I confess unto thee, that after the
way which they call heresy, so worship I the
God of my fathers, believing all things which
are written in the law and in the prophets:
15 And have hope toward God, which they
themselves also allow, that there shall be
a resurrection of the dead, both of the just
and unjust.
16 And herein do I exercise myself, to have
always a conscience void of offence toward
God, and *toward* men.
17 Now after many years I came to bring
alms to my nation, and offerings.
18 Whereupon certain Jews from Asia
found me purified in the temple, neither
with multitude, nor with tumult.
19 Who ought to have been here before
thee, and object, if they had ought against
me.
20 Or else let these same *here* say, if they
have found any evil doing in me, while I
stood before the council,
21 Except it be for this one voice, that I cried
standing among them, Touching the resurrection of the dead I am called in question
by you this day.
22 And when Felix heard these things, having more perfect knowledge of *that* way, he
deferred them, and said, When Lysias the
chief captain shall come down, I will know
the uttermost of your matter.
23 And he commanded a centurion to keep
Paul, and to let *him* have liberty, and that
he should forbid none of his acquaintance
to minister or come unto him.
24 And after certain days, when Felix came
with his wife Drusilla, which was a Jewess,
he sent for Paul, and heard him concerning
the faith in Christ.
25 And as he reasoned of righteousness,
temperance, and judgment to come, Felix
trembled, and answered, Go thy way for
this time; when I have a convenient season,
I will call for thee.
26 He hoped also that money should have
been given him of Paul, that he might loose
him: wherefore he sent for him the oftener,
and communed with him.
27 But after two years Porcius Festus came
into Felix' room: and Felix, willing to shew
the Jews a pleasure, left Paul bound.

Acts 25

1 Now when Festus was come into the
province, after three days he ascended from
Cæsarea to Jerusalem.
2 Then the high priest and the chief of
the Jews informed him against Paul, and
besought him,
3 And desired favour against him, that he
would send for him to Jerusalem, laying wait
in the way to kill him.
4 But Festus answered, that Paul should be
kept at Cæsarea, and that he himself would
depart shortly *thither.*
5 Let them therefore, said he, which among
you are able, go down with *me*, and accuse
this man, if there be any wickedness in him.
6 And when he had tarried among them
more than ten days, he went down unto
Cæsarea; and the next day sitting on the
judgment seat commanded Paul to be
brought.
7 And when he was come, the Jews which
came down from Jerusalem stood round
about, and laid many and grievous com-
plaints against Paul, which they could not
prove.
8 While he answered for himself, Neither
against the law of the Jews, neither against
the temple, nor yet against Cæsar, have I
offended any thing at all.
9 But Festus, willing to do the Jews a pleasure, answered Paul, and said, Wilt thou

go up to Jerusalem, and there be judged of
these things before me?
10 Then said Paul, I stand at Cæsar's judgment seat, where I ought to be judged: to
the Jews have I done no wrong, as thou very
well knowest.
11 For if I be an offender, or have committed any thing worthy of death, I refuse not
to die: but if there be none of these things
whereof these accuse me, no man may
deliver me unto them. I appeal unto Cæsar.
12 Then Festus, when he had conferred with
the council, answered, Hast thou appealed
unto Cæsar? unto Cæsar shalt thou go.
13 And after certain days king Agrippa and
Bernice came unto Cæsarea to salute Festus.
14 And when they had been there many
days, Festus declared Paul's cause unto the
king, saying, There is a certain man left in
bonds by Felix:
15 About whom, when I was at Jerusalem,
the chief priests and the elders of the Jews
informed *me*, desiring *to have* judgment
against him.
16 To whom I answered, It is not the manner of the Romans to deliver any man to
die, before that he which is accused have
the accusers face to face, and have licence
to answer for himself concerning the crime
laid against him.
17 Therefore, when they were come hither,
without any delay on the morrow I sat on
the judgment seat, and commanded the
man to be brought forth.
18 Against whom when the accusers stood
up, they brought none accusation of such
things as I supposed:
19 But had certain questions against him
of their own superstition, and of one Jesus,
which was dead, whom Paul affirmed to
be alive.
20 And because I doubted of such manner
of questions, I asked *him* whether he would
go to Jerusalem, and there be judged of
these matters.
21 But when Paul had appealed to be
reserved unto the hearing of Augustus, I
commanded him to be kept till I might send
him to Cæsar.
22 Then Agrippa said unto Festus, I would
also hear the man myself. To morrow, said
he, thou shalt hear him.
23 And on the morrow, when Agrippa was
come, and Bernice, with great pomp, and
was entered into the place of hearing, with
the chief captains, and principal men of the
city, at Festus' commandment Paul was
brought forth.
24 And Festus said, King Agrippa, and all
men which are here present with us, ye see
this man, about whom all the multitude of
the Jews have dealt with me, both at Jerusalem, and *also* here, crying that he ought
not to live any longer.
25 But when I found that he had committed nothing worthy of death, and that he
himself hath appealed to Augustus, I have
determined to send him.
26 Of whom I have no certain thing to write
unto my lord. Wherefore I have brought him
forth before you, and specially before thee,
O king Agrippa, that, after examination had,
I might have somewhat to write.
27 For it seemeth to me unreasonable to
send a prisoner, and not withal to signify
the crimes *laid* against him.

Acts 26

1 Then Agrippa said unto Paul, Thou art
permitted to speak for thyself. Then Paul
stretched forth the hand, and answered
for himself:
2 I think myself happy, king Agrippa, because
I shall answer for myself this day before
thee touching all the things whereof I am
accused of the Jews:
3 Especially *because I know* thee to be
expert in all customs and questions which
are among the Jews: wherefore I beseech
thee to hear me patiently.
4 My manner of life from my youth, which
was at the first among mine own nation at
Jerusalem, know all the Jews;
5 Which knew me from the beginning, if
they would testify, that after the most strait-
est sect of our religion I lived a Pharisee.
6 And now I stand and am judged for the
hope of the promise made of God unto
our fathers:
7 Unto which *promise* our twelve tribes,
instantly serving *God* day and night, hope to
come. For which hope's sake, king Agrippa,
I am accused of the Jews.
8 Why should it be thought a thing incredible
with you, that God should raise the dead?
9 I verily thought with myself, that I ought

to do many things contrary to the name of
Jesus of Nazareth.
10 Which thing I also did in Jerusalem: and
many of the saints did I shut up in prison,
having received authority from the chief
priests; and when they were put to death,
I gave my voice against *them*.
11 And I punished them oft in every synagogue, and compelled *them* to blaspheme;
and being exceedingly mad against them, I
persecuted *them* even unto strange cities.
12 Whereupon as I went to Damascus with
authority and commission from the chief
priests,
13 At midday, O king, I saw in the way a
light from heaven, above the brightness of
the sun, shining round about me and them
which journeyed with me.
14 And when we were all fallen to the earth,
I heard a voice speaking unto me, and saying in the Hebrew tongue, Saul, Saul, why
persecutest thou me? *it is* hard for thee to
kick against the pricks.
15 And I said, Who art thou, Lord? And he
said, I am Jesus whom thou persecutest.
16 But rise, and stand upon thy feet: for I
have appeared unto thee for this purpose,
to make thee a minister and a witness both
of these things which thou hast seen, and
of those things in the which I will appear
unto thee;
17 Delivering thee from the people, and
from the Gentiles, unto whom now I send
thee,
18 To open their eyes, *and* to turn *them*
from darkness to light, and *from* the power
of Satan unto God, that they may receive
forgiveness of sins, and inheritance among
them which are sanctified by faith that is
in me.
19 Whereupon, O king Agrippa, I was not
disobedient unto the heavenly vision:
20 But shewed first unto them of Damascus,
and at Jerusalem, and throughout all the
coasts of Judæa, and *then* to the Gentiles,
that they should repent and turn to God,
and do works meet for repentance.
21 For these causes the Jews caught me
in the temple, and went about to kill *me*.
22 Having therefore obtained help of God,
I continue unto this day, witnessing both to
small and great, saying none other things
than those which the prophets and Moses
did say should come:
23 That Christ should suffer, *and* that he
should be the first that should rise from
the dead, and should shew light unto the
people, and to the Gentiles.
24 And as he thus spake for himself, Festus
said with a loud voice, Paul, thou art beside
thyself; much learning doth make thee mad.
25 But he said, I am not mad, most noble
Festus; but speak forth the words of truth
and soberness.
26 For the king knoweth of these things,
before whom also I speak freely: for I am
persuaded that none of these things are
hidden from him; for this thing was not
done in a corner.
27 King Agrippa, believest thou the prophets? I know that thou believest.
28 Then Agrippa said unto Paul, Almost thou
persuadest me to be a Christian.
29 And Paul said, I would to God, that not
only thou, but also all that hear me this day,
were both almost, and altogether such as I
am, except these bonds.
30 And when he had thus spoken, the king
rose up, and the governor, and Bernice, and
they that sat with them:
31 And when they were gone aside, they
talked between themselves, saying, This
man doeth nothing worthy of death or of
bonds.
32 Then said Agrippa unto Festus, This man
might have been set at liberty, if he had not
appealed unto Cæsar.

Acts 27

1 And when it was determined that we
should sail into Italy, they delivered Paul
and certain other prisoners unto *one* named
Julius, a centurion of Augustus' band.
2 And entering into a ship of Adramyttium,
we launched, meaning to sail by the coasts
of Asia; *one* Aristarchus, a Macedonian of
Thessalonica, being with us.
3 And the next *day* we touched at Sidon.
And Julius courteously entreated Paul, and
gave *him* liberty to go unto his friends to
refresh himself.
4 And when we had launched from thence,
we sailed under Cyprus, because the winds
were contrary.
5 And when we had sailed over the sea of

Cilicia and Pamphylia, we came to Myra, *a*
city of Lycia.
6 And there the centurion found a ship of
Alexandria sailing into Italy; and he put us
therein.
7 And when we had sailed slowly many days,
and scarce were come over against Cnidus,
the wind not suffering us, we sailed under
Crete, over against Salmone;
8 And, hardly passing it, came unto a place
which is called The fair havens; nigh whereunto was the city *of* Lasea.
9 Now when much time was spent, and
when sailing was now dangerous, because
the fast was now already past, Paul admonished *them*,
10 And said unto them, Sirs, I perceive that
this voyage will be with hurt and much
damage, not only of the lading and ship,
but also of our lives.
11 Nevertheless the centurion believed the
master and the owner of the ship, more than
those things which were spoken by Paul.
12 And because the haven was not commo-
dious to winter in, the more part advised to
depart thence also, if by any means they
might attain to Phenice, *and there* to winter;
which is an haven of Crete, and lieth toward
the south west and north west.
13 And when the south wind blew softly,
supposing that they had obtained *their*
purpose, loosing *thence*, they sailed close
by Crete.
14 But not long after there arose against
it a tempestuous wind, called Euroclydon.
15 And when the ship was caught, and could
not bear up into the wind, we let *her* drive.
16 And running under a certain island which
is called Claude, we had much work to come
by the boat:
17 Which when they had taken up, they used
helps, undergirding the ship; and, fearing
lest they should fall into the quicksands,
strake sail, and so were driven.
18 And we being exceedingly tossed with
a tempest, the next *day* they lightened
the ship;
19 And the third *day* we cast out with our
own hands the tackling of the ship.
20 And when neither sun nor stars in many
days appeared, and no small tempest lay on
us, all hope that we should be saved was
then taken away.
21 But after long abstinence Paul stood
forth in the midst of them, and said, Sirs,
ye should have hearkened unto me, and
not have loosed from Crete, and to have
gained this harm and loss.
22 And now I exhort you to be of good
cheer: for there shall be no loss of *any man's*
life among you, but of the ship.
23 For there stood by me this night the
angel of God, whose I am, and whom I serve,
24 Saying, Fear not, Paul; thou must be
brought before Cæsar: and, lo, God hath
given thee all them that sail with thee.
25 Wherefore, sirs, be of good cheer: for I
believe God, that it shall be even as it was
told me.
26 Howbeit we must be cast upon a certain island.
27 But when the fourteenth night was come,
as we were driven up and down in Adria,
about midnight the shipmen deemed that
they drew near to some country;
28 And sounded, and found *it* twenty fathoms: and when they had gone a little further,
they sounded again, and found *it* fifteen
fathoms.
29 Then fearing lest we should have fallen
upon rocks, they cast four anchors out of
the stern, and wished for the day.
30 And as the shipmen were about to flee
out of the ship, when they had let down the
boat into the sea, under colour as though
they would have cast anchors out of the
foreship,
31 Paul said to the centurion and to the
soldiers, Except these abide in the ship, ye
cannot be saved.
32 Then the soldiers cut off the ropes of the
boat, and let her fall off.
33 And while the day was coming on, Paul
besought *them* all to take meat, saying,
This day is the fourteenth day that ye have
tarried and continued fasting, having taken
nothing.
34 Wherefore I pray you to take *some* meat:
for this is for your health: for there shall not
an hair fall from the head of any of you.
35 And when he had thus spoken, he took
bread, and gave thanks to God in presence
of them all: and when he had broken *it*, he
began to eat.
36 Then were they all of good cheer, and
they also took *some* meat.

37 And we were in all in the ship two hundred threescore and sixteen souls.
38 And when they had eaten enough, they
lightened the ship, and cast out the wheat
into the sea.
39 And when it was day, they knew not
the land: but they discovered a certain
creek with a shore, into the which they
were minded, if it were possible, to thrust
in the ship.
40 And when they had taken up the anchors,
they committed *themselves* unto the sea,
and loosed the rudder bands, and hoised
up the mainsail to the wind, and made
toward shore.
41 And falling into a place where two seas
met, they ran the ship aground; and the
forepart stuck fast, and remained unmoveable, but the hinder part was broken with
the violence of the waves.
42 And the soldiers' counsel was to kill the
prisoners, lest any of them should swim
out, and escape.
43 But the centurion, willing to save Paul,
kept them from *their* purpose; and commanded that they which could swim should
cast *themselves* first *into the sea*, and get
to land:
44 And the rest, some on boards, and some
on *broken pieces* of the ship. And so it came
to pass, that they escaped all safe to land.

Acts 28

1 And when they were escaped, then they
knew that the island was called Melita.
2 And the barbarous people shewed us no
little kindness: for they kindled a fire, and
received us every one, because of the present rain, and because of the cold.
3 And when Paul had gathered a bundle
of sticks, and laid *them* on the fire, there
came a viper out of the heat, and fastened
on his hand.
4 And when the barbarians saw the *ven-
omous* beast hang on his hand, they said
among themselves, No doubt this man is a
murderer, whom, though he hath escaped
the sea, yet vengeance suffereth not to live.
5 And he shook off the beast into the fire,
and felt no harm.
6 Howbeit they looked when he should have
swollen, or fallen down dead suddenly: but
after they had looked a great while, and saw
no harm come to him, they changed their
minds, and said that he was a god.
7 In the same quarters were possessions
of the chief man of the island, whose name
was Publius; who received us, and lodged
us three days courteously.
8 And it came to pass, that the father of
Publius lay sick of a fever and of a bloody
flux: to whom Paul entered in, and prayed,
and laid his hands on him, and healed him.
9 So when this was done, others also, which
had diseases in the island, came, and were
healed:
10 Who also honoured us with many hon-
ours; and when we departed, they laded *us*
with such things as were necessary.
11 And after three months we departed in
a ship of Alexandria, which had wintered in
the isle, whose sign was Castor and Pollux.
12 And landing at Syracuse, we tarried *there*
three days.
13 And from thence we fetched a compass,
and came to Rhegium: and after one day
the south wind blew, and we came the next
day to Puteoli:
14 Where we found brethren, and were
desired to tarry with them seven days: and
so we went toward Rome.
15 And from thence, when the brethren
heard of us, they came to meet us as far as
Appii forum, and The three taverns: whom
when Paul saw, he thanked God, and took
courage.
16 And when we came to Rome, the centurion delivered the prisoners to the captain of
the guard: but Paul was suffered to dwell by
himself with a soldier that kept him.
17 And it came to pass, that after three days
Paul called the chief of the Jews together:
and when they were come together, he said
unto them, Men *and* brethren, though I have
committed nothing against the people, or
customs of our fathers, yet was I delivered
prisoner from Jerusalem into the hands of
the Romans.
18 Who, when they had examined me,
would have let *me* go, because there was
no cause of death in me.
19 But when the Jews spake against *it*, I was
constrained to appeal unto Cæsar; not that
I had ought to accuse my nation of.
20 For this cause therefore have I called
for you, to see *you*, and to speak with *you*:

because that for the hope of Israel I am
bound with this chain.
21 And they said unto him, We neither
received letters out of Judæa concerning
thee, neither any of the brethren that came
shewed or spake any harm of thee.
22 But we desire to hear of thee what thou
thinkest: for as concerning this sect, we
know that every where it is spoken against.
23 And when they had appointed him a day,
there came many to him into *his* lodging; to
whom he expounded and testified the kingdom of God, persuading them concerning
Jesus, both out of the law of Moses, and *out
of* the prophets, from morning till evening.
24 And some believed the things which were
spoken, and some believed not.
25 And when they agreed not among themselves, they departed, after that Paul had
spoken one word, Well spake the Holy Spirit
by Esaias the prophet unto our fathers,
26 Saying, Go unto this people, and say,
Hearing ye shall hear, and shall not understand; and seeing ye shall see, and not
perceive:
27 For the heart of this people is waxed
gross, and their ears are dull of hearing, and
their eyes have they closed; lest they should
see with *their* eyes, and hear with *their* ears,
and understand with *their* heart, and should
be converted, and I should heal them.
28 Be it known therefore unto you, that the
salvation of God is sent unto the Gentiles,
and *that* they will hear it.
29 And when he had said these words, the
Jews departed, and had great reasoning
among themselves.
30 And Paul dwelt two whole years in his
own hired house, and received all that came
in unto him,
31 Preaching the kingdom of God, and
teaching those things which concern the
Lord Jesus Christ, with all confidence, no
man forbidding him.

The Epistle Of Paul To The

Romans

Romans 1

1 Paul, a servant of Jesus Christ, called *to
be* an apostle, separated unto the gospel
of God,
2 (Which he had promised afore by his
prophets in the holy scriptures,)
3 Concerning his Son Jesus Christ our Lord,
which was made of the seed of David
according to the flesh;
4 And declared *to be* the Son of God with
power, according to the spirit of holiness,
by the resurrection from the dead:
5 By whom we have received grace and
apostleship, for obedience to the faith
among all nations, for his name:
6 Among whom are ye also the called of
Jesus Christ:
7 To all that be in Rome, beloved of God,
called *to be* saints: Grace to you and peace
from God our Father, and the Lord Jesus
Christ.
8 First, I thank my God through Jesus Christ
for you all, that your faith is spoken of
throughout the whole world.
9 For God is my witness, whom I serve with
my spirit in the gospel of his Son, that without ceasing I make mention of you always
in my prayers;
10 Making request, if by any means now at
length I might have a prosperous journey by
the will of God to come unto you.
11 For I long to see you, that I may impart
unto you some spiritual gift, to the end ye
may be established;
12 That is, that I may be comforted together
with you by the mutual faith both of you
and me.
13 Now I would not have you ignorant,
brethren, that oftentimes I purposed to
come unto you, (but was let hitherto,) that
I might have some fruit among you also,
even as among other Gentiles.
14 I am debtor both to the Greeks, and to

the Barbarians; both to the wise, and to
the unwise.
15 So, as much as in me is, I am ready to
preach the gospel to you that are at Rome
also.
16 For I am not ashamed of the gospel of
Christ: for it is the power of God unto salvation to every one that believeth; to the
Jew first, and also to the Greek.
17 For therein is the righteousness of God
revealed from faith to faith: as it is written,
The just shall live by faith.
18 For the wrath of God is revealed from
heaven against all ungodliness and unrighteousness of men, who hold the truth in
unrighteousness;
19 Because that which may be known of God
is manifest in them; for God hath shewed
it unto them.
20 For the invisible things of him from the
creation of the world are clearly seen, being
understood by the things that are made,
even his eternal power and Godhead; so
that they are without excuse:
21 Because that, when they knew God,
they glorified *him* not as God, neither were
thankful; but became vain in their imaginations, and their foolish heart was darkened.
22 Professing themselves to be wise, they
became fools,
23 And changed the glory of the uncorrupt-
ible God into an image made like to corruptible man, and to birds, and fourfooted
beasts, and creeping things.
24 Wherefore God also gave them up to
uncleanness through the lusts of their
own hearts, to dishonour their own bodies
between themselves:
25 Who changed the truth of God into a lie,
and worshipped and served the creature
more than the Creator, who is blessed for
ever. Amen.
26 For this cause God gave them up unto
vile affections: for even their women did
change the natural use into that which is
against nature:
27 And likewise also the men, leaving the
natural use of the woman, burned in their
lust one toward another; men with men
working that which is unseemly, and receiving in themselves that recompence of their
error which was meet.
28 And even as they did not like to retain
God in *their* knowledge, God gave them
over to a reprobate mind, to do those things
which are not convenient;
29 Being filled with all unrighteousness,
fornication, wickedness, covetousness,
maliciousness; full of envy, murder, debate,
deceit, malignity; whisperers,
30 Backbiters, haters of God, despiteful,
proud, boasters, inventors of evil things,
disobedient to parents,
31 Without understanding, covenantbreak-
ers, without natural affection, implacable,
unmerciful:
32 Who knowing the judgment of God, that
they which commit such things are worthy
of death, not only do the same, but have
pleasure in them that do them.

Romans 2

1 Therefore thou art inexcusable, O man,
whosoever thou art that judgest: for
wherein thou judgest another, thou con-
demnest thyself; for thou that judgest doest
the same things.
2 But we are sure that the judgment of God
is according to truth against them which
commit such things.
3 And thinkest thou this, O man, that judgest
them which do such things, and doest the
same, that thou shalt escape the judgment
of God?
4 Or despisest thou the riches of his goodness and forbearance and longsuffering; not
knowing that the goodness of God leadeth
thee to repentance?
5 But after thy hardness and impenitent
heart treasurest up unto thyself wrath
against the day of wrath and revelation of
the righteous judgment of God;
6 Who will render to every man according
to his deeds:
7 To them who by patient continuance in
well doing seek for glory and honour and
immortality, eternal life:
8 But unto them that are contentious, and
do not obey the truth, but obey unrighteousness, indignation and wrath,
9 Tribulation and anguish, upon every soul
of man that doeth evil, of the Jew first, and
also of the Gentile;
10 But glory, honour, and peace, to every
man that worketh good, to the Jew first,
and also to the Gentile:

11 For there is no respect of persons with
God.
12 For as many as have sinned without law
shall also perish without law: and as many
as have sinned in the law shall be judged
by the law;
13 (For not the hearers of the law *are* just
before God, but the doers of the law shall
be justified.
14 For when the Gentiles, which have not
the law, do by nature the things contained
in the law, these, having not the law, are a
law unto themselves:
15 Which shew the work of the law written
in their hearts, their conscience also bearing
witness, and *their* thoughts the mean while
accusing or else excusing one another;)
16 In the day when God shall judge the
secrets of men by Jesus Christ according
to my gospel.
17 Behold, thou art called a Jew, and restest
in the law, and makest thy boast of God,
18 And knowest *his* will, and approvest
the things that are more excellent, being
instructed out of the law;
19 And art confident that thou thyself art
a guide of the blind, a light of them which
are in darkness,
20 An instructor of the foolish, a teacher of
babes, which hast the form of knowledge
and of the truth in the law.
21 Thou therefore which teachest another,
teachest thou not thyself? thou that
preachest a man should not steal, dost
thou steal?
22 Thou that sayest a man should not commit adultery, dost thou commit adultery?
thou that abhorrest idols, dost thou commit
sacrilege?
23 Thou that makest thy boast of the law,
through breaking the law dishonourest
thou God?
24 For the name of God is blasphemed
among the Gentiles through you, as it is
written.
25 For circumcision verily profiteth, if thou
keep the law: but if thou be a breaker of
the law, thy circumcision is made uncircumcision.
26 Therefore if the uncircumcision keep
the righteousness of the law, shall not his
uncircumcision be counted for circumcision?
27 And shall not uncircumcision which is by
nature, if it fulfil the law, judge thee, who
by the letter and circumcision dost transgress the law?
28 For he is not a Jew, which is one outwardly; neither *is that* circumcision, which
is outward in the flesh:
29 But he *is* a Jew, which is one inwardly;
and circumcision *is that* of the heart, in the
spirit, *and* not in the letter; whose praise *is*
not of men, but of God.

Romans 3

1 What advantage then hath the Jew? or
what profit *is there* of circumcision?
2 Much every way: chiefly, because that
unto them were committed the oracles
of God.
3 For what if some did not believe? shall
their unbelief make the faith of God without effect?
4 God forbid: yea, let God be true, but every
man a liar; as it is written, That thou mightest be justified in thy sayings, and mightest
overcome when thou art judged.
5 But if our unrighteousness commend the
righteousness of God, what shall we say? *Is*
God unrighteous who taketh vengeance? (I
speak as a man)
6 God forbid: for then how shall God judge
the world?
7 For if the truth of God hath more abounded
through my lie unto his glory; why yet am I
also judged as a sinner?
8 And not *rather*, (as we be slanderously
reported, and as some affirm that we say,)
Let us do evil, that good may come? whose
damnation is just.
9 What then? are we better *than they?*
No, in no wise: for we have before proved
both Jews and Gentiles, that they are all
under sin;
10 As it is written, There is none righteous,
no, not one:
11 There is none that understandeth, there
is none that seeketh after God.
12 They are all gone out of the way, they
are together become unprofitable; there is
none that doeth good, no, not one.
13 Their throat *is* an open sepulchre; with
their tongues they have used deceit; the
poison of asps *is* under their lips:
14 Whose mouth *is* full of cursing and bitterness:

15 Their feet *are* swift to shed blood:
16 Destruction and misery *are* in their ways:
17 And the way of peace have they not
known:
18 There is no fear of God before their eyes.
19 Now we know that what things soever
the law saith, it saith to them who are
under the law: that every mouth may be
stopped, and all the world may become
guilty before God.
20 Therefore by the deeds of the law there
shall no flesh be justified in his sight: for by
the law *is* the knowledge of sin.
21 But now the righteousness of God without the law is manifested, being witnessed
by the law and the prophets;
22 Even the righteousness of God *which is*
by faith of Jesus Christ unto all and upon all
them that believe: for there is no difference:
23 For all have sinned, and come short of
the glory of God;
24 Being justified freely by his grace through
the redemption that is in Christ Jesus:
25 Whom God hath set forth *to be* a propitiation through faith in his blood, to declare
his righteousness for the remission of sins
that are past, through the forbearance of
God;
26 To declare, *I say*, at this time his righteousness: that he might be just, and the
justifier of him which believeth in Jesus.
27 Where *is* boasting then? It is excluded.
By what law? of works? Nay: but by the
law of faith.
28 Therefore we conclude that a man is justified by faith without the deeds of the law.
29 *Is he* the God of the Jews only? *is he* not
also of the Gentiles? Yes, of the Gentiles also:
30 Seeing *it is* one God, which shall justify
the circumcision by faith, and uncircumcision through faith.
31 Do we then make void the law through
faith? God forbid: yea, we establish the law.

Romans 4

1 What shall we say then that Abraham
our father, as pertaining to the flesh, hath
found?
2 For if Abraham were justified by works, he
hath *whereof* to glory; but not before God.
3 For what saith the scripture? Abraham
believed God, and it was counted unto him
for righteousness.
4 Now to him that worketh is the reward
not reckoned of grace, but of debt.
5 But to him that worketh not, but believeth
on him that justifieth the ungodly, his faith
is counted for righteousness.
6 Even as David also describeth the blessedness of the man, unto whom God imputeth
righteousness without works,
7 *Saying*, Blessed *are* they whose iniquities
are forgiven, and whose sins are covered.
8 Blessed *is* the man to whom the Lord will
not impute sin.
9 *Cometh* this blessedness then upon the
circumcision *only*, or upon the uncircumcision also? for we say that faith was reckoned
to Abraham for righteousness.
10 How was it then reckoned? when he
was in circumcision, or in uncircumcision?
Not in circumcision, but in uncircumcision.
11 And he received the sign of circumcision,
a seal of the righteousness of the faith which
he had yet being uncircumcised: that he
might be the father of all them that believe,
though they be not circumcised; that righteousness might be imputed unto them also:
12 And the father of circumcision to them
who are not of the circumcision only, but
who also walk in the steps of that faith of
our father Abraham, which *he had* being
yet uncircumcised.
13 For the promise, that he should be the
heir of the world, *was* not to Abraham, or
to his seed, through the law, but through
the righteousness of faith.
14 For if they which are of the law *be* heirs,
faith is made void, and the promise made
of none effect:
15 Because the law worketh wrath: for
where no law is, *there is* no transgression.
16 Therefore *it is* of faith, that *it might be*
by grace; to the end the promise might be
sure to all the seed; not to that only which
is of the law, but to that also which is of the
faith of Abraham; who is the father of us all,
17 (As it is written, I have made thee a
father of many nations,) before him whom
he believed, *even* God, who quickeneth the
dead, and calleth those things which be not
as though they were.
18 Who against hope believed in hope,
that he might become the father of many
nations; according to that which was spoken, So shall thy seed be.

19 And being not weak in faith, he considered not his own body now dead, when he
was about an hundred years old, neither
yet the deadness of Sara's womb:
20 He staggered not at the promise of God
through unbelief; but was strong in faith,
giving glory to God;
21 And being fully persuaded that, what he
had promised, he was able also to perform.
22 And therefore it was imputed to him for
righteousness.
23 Now it was not written for his sake alone,
that it was imputed to him;
24 But for us also, to whom it shall be
imputed, if we believe on him that raised
up Jesus our Lord from the dead;
25 Who was delivered for our offences, and
was raised again for our justification.

Romans 5

1 Therefore being justified by faith, we
have peace with God through our Lord
Jesus Christ:
2 By whom also we have access by faith into
this grace wherein we stand, and rejoice in
hope of the glory of God.
3 And not only *so*, but we glory in tribulations also: knowing that tribulation worketh
patience;
4 And patience, experience; and experience, hope:
5 And hope maketh not ashamed; because
the love of God is shed abroad in our hearts
by the Holy Spirit which is given unto us.
6 For when we were yet without strength,
in due time Christ died for the ungodly.
7 For scarcely for a righteous man will one
die: yet peradventure for a good man some
would even dare to die.
8 But God commendeth his love toward us,
in that, while we were yet sinners, Christ
died for us.
9 Much more then, being now justified by
his blood, we shall be saved from wrath
through him.
10 For if, when we were enemies, we were
reconciled to God by the death of his Son,
much more, being reconciled, we shall be
saved by his life.
11 And not only *so*, but we also joy in God
through our Lord Jesus Christ, by whom we
have now received the atonement.
12 Wherefore, as by one man sin entered
into the world, and death by sin; and so
death passed upon all men, for that all
have sinned:
13 (For until the law sin was in the world:
but sin is not imputed when there is no law.
14 Nevertheless death reigned from Adam
to Moses, even over them that had not
sinned after the similitude of Adam's transgression, who is the figure of him that was
to come.
15 But not as the offence, so also *is* the free
gift. For if through the offence of one many
be dead, much more the grace of God, and
the gift by grace, *which is* by one man, Jesus
Christ, hath abounded unto many.
16 And not as *it was* by one that sinned, *so*
is the gift: for the judgment *was* by one to
condemnation, but the free gift *is* of many
offences unto justification.
17 For if by one man's offence death reigned
by one; much more they which receive
abundance of grace and of the gift of righteousness shall reign in life by one, Jesus
Christ.)
18 Therefore as by the offence of one *judg-*
ment came upon all men to condemnation;
even so by the righteousness of one *the*
free gift came upon all men unto justification of life.
19 For as by one man's disobedience many
were made sinners, so by the obedience of
one shall many be made righteous.
20 Moreover the law entered, that the
offence might abound. But where sin
abounded, grace did much more abound:
21 That as sin hath reigned unto death, even
so might grace reign through righteousness
unto eternal life by Jesus Christ our Lord.

Romans 6

1 What shall we say then? Shall we continue
in sin, that grace may abound?
2 God forbid. How shall we, that are dead
to sin, live any longer therein?
3 Know ye not, that so many of us as were
baptized into Jesus Christ were baptized
into his death?
4 Therefore we are buried with him by
baptism into death: that like as Christ was
raised up from the dead by the glory of
the Father, even so we also should walk in
newness of life.
5 For if we have been planted together in

the likeness of his death, we shall be also *in the likeness* of *his* resurrection:
6 Knowing this, that our old man is crucified with *him*, that the body of sin might be destroyed, that henceforth we should not serve sin.
7 For he that is dead is freed from sin.
8 Now if we be dead with Christ, we believe that we shall also live with him:
9 Knowing that Christ being raised from the dead dieth no more; death hath no more dominion over him.
10 For in that he died, he died unto sin once: but in that he liveth, he liveth unto God.
11 Likewise reckon ye also yourselves to be dead indeed unto sin, but alive unto God through Jesus Christ our Lord.
12 Let not sin therefore reign in your mortal body, that ye should obey it in the lusts thereof.
13 Neither yield ye your members *as* instruments of unrighteousness unto sin: but yield yourselves unto God, as those that are alive from the dead, and your members *as* instruments of righteousness unto God.
14 For sin shall not have dominion over you: for ye are not under the law, but under grace.
15 What then? shall we sin, because we are not under the law, but under grace? God forbid.
16 Know ye not, that to whom ye yield yourselves servants to obey, his servants ye are to whom ye obey; whether of sin unto death, or of obedience unto righteousness?
17 But God be thanked, that ye were the servants of sin, but ye have obeyed from the heart that form of doctrine which was delivered you.
18 Being then made free from sin, ye became the servants of righteousness.
19 I speak after the manner of men because of the infirmity of your flesh: for as ye have yielded your members servants to uncleanness and to iniquity unto iniquity; even so now yield your members servants to righteousness unto holiness.
20 For when ye were the servants of sin, ye were free from righteousness.
21 What fruit had ye then in those things whereof ye are now ashamed? for the end of those things *is* death.
22 But now being made free from sin, and become servants to God, ye have your fruit unto holiness, and the end everlasting life.
23 For the wages of sin *is* death; but the gift of God *is* eternal life through Jesus Christ our Lord.

Romans 7

1 Know ye not, brethren, (for I speak to them that know the law,) how that the law hath dominion over a man as long as he liveth?
2 For the woman which hath an husband is bound by the law to *her* husband so long as he liveth; but if the husband be dead, she is loosed from the law of *her* husband.
3 So then if, while *her* husband liveth, she be married to another man, she shall be called an adulteress: but if her husband be dead, she is free from that law; so that she is no adulteress, though she be married to another man.
4 Wherefore, my brethren, ye also are become dead to the law by the body of Christ; that ye should be married to another, *even* to him who is raised from the dead, that we should bring forth fruit unto God.
5 For when we were in the flesh, the motions of sins, which were by the law, did work in our members to bring forth fruit unto death.
6 But now we are delivered from the law, that being dead wherein we were held; that we should serve in newness of spirit, and not *in* the oldness of the letter.
7 What shall we say then? *Is* the law sin? God forbid. Nay, I had not known sin, but by the law: for I had not known lust, except the law had said, Thou shalt not covet.
8 But sin, taking occasion by the commandment, wrought in me all manner of concupiscence. For without the law sin *was* dead.
9 For I was alive without the law once: but when the commandment came, sin revived, and I died.
10 And the commandment, which *was ordained* to life, I found *to be* unto death.
11 For sin, taking occasion by the commandment, deceived me, and by it slew *me*.
12 Wherefore the law *is* holy, and the commandment holy, and just, and good.
13 Was then that which is good made death unto me? God forbid. But sin, that it might appear sin, working death in me by that which is good; that sin by the commandment might become exceeding sinful.

14 For we know that the law is spiritual: but
I am carnal, sold under sin.
15 For that which I do I allow not: for what
I would, that do I not; but what I hate, that
do I.
16 If then I do that which I would not, I consent unto the law that *it is* good.
17 Now then it is no more I that do it, but
sin that dwelleth in me.
18 For I know that in me (that is, in my flesh,)
dwelleth no good thing: for to will is present
with me; but *how* to perform that which is
good I find not.
19 For the good that I would I do not: but
the evil which I would not, that I do.
20 Now if I do that I would not, it is no more
I that do it, but sin that dwelleth in me.
21 I find then a law, that, when I would do
good, evil is present with me.
22 For I delight in the law of God after the
inward man:
23 But I see another law in my members,
warring against the law of my mind, and
bringing me into captivity to the law of sin
which is in my members.
24 O wretched man that I am! who shall
deliver me from the body of this death?
25 I thank God through Jesus Christ our Lord.
So then with the mind I myself serve the law
of God; but with the flesh the law of sin.

Romans 8

1 *There is* therefore now no condemnation
to them which are in Christ Jesus, who walk
not after the flesh, but after the Spirit.
2 For the law of the Spirit of life in Christ
Jesus hath made me free from the law of
sin and death.
3 For what the law could not do, in that it
was weak through the flesh, God sending his
own Son in the likeness of sinful flesh, and
for sin, condemned sin in the flesh:
4 That the righteousness of the law might be
fulfilled in us, who walk not after the flesh,
but after the Spirit.
5 For they that are after the flesh do mind
the things of the flesh; but they that are after
the Spirit the things of the Spirit.
6 For to be carnally minded *is* death; but
to be spiritually minded *is* life and peace.
7 Because the carnal mind *is* enmity against
God: for it is not subject to the law of God,
neither indeed can be.
8 So then they that are in the flesh cannot
please God.
9 But ye are not in the flesh, but in the Spirit,
if so be that the Spirit of God dwell in you.
Now if any man have not the Spirit of Christ,
he is none of his.
10 And if Christ *be* in you, the body *is* dead
because of sin; but the Spirit *is* life because
of righteousness.
11 But if the Spirit of him that raised up
Jesus from the dead dwell in you, he that
raised up Christ from the dead shall also
quicken your mortal bodies by his Spirit
that dwelleth in you.
12 Therefore, brethren, we are debtors, not
to the flesh, to live after the flesh.
13 For if ye live after the flesh, ye shall die:
but if ye through the Spirit do mortify the
deeds of the body, ye shall live.
14 For as many as are led by the Spirit of
God, they are the sons of God.
15 For ye have not received the spirit of
bondage again to fear; but ye have received
the Spirit of adoption, whereby we cry,
Abba, Father.
16 The Spirit itself beareth witness with
our spirit, that we are the children of God:
17 And if children, then heirs; heirs of God,
and joint-heirs with Christ; if so be that we
suffer with *him*, that we may be also glorified together.
18 For I reckon that the sufferings of this
present time *are* not worthy *to be compared*
with the glory which shall be revealed in us.
19 For the earnest expectation of the creature waiteth for the manifestation of the
sons of God.
20 For the creature was made subject to
vanity, not willingly, but by reason of him
who hath subjected *the same* in hope,
21 Because the creature itself also shall be
delivered from the bondage of corruption
into the glorious liberty of the children of
God.
22 For we know that the whole creation
groaneth and travaileth in pain together
until now.
23 And not only *they*, but ourselves also,
which have the firstfruits of the Spirit, even
we ourselves groan within ourselves, waiting for the adoption, *to wit*, the redemption
of our body.
24 For we are saved by hope: but hope that

is seen is not hope: for what a man seeth,
why doth he yet hope for?
25 But if we hope for that we see not, *then*
do we with patience wait for *it*.
26 Likewise the Spirit also helpeth our infirmities: for we know not what we should
pray for as we ought: but the Spirit itself
maketh intercession for us with groanings
which cannot be uttered.
27 And he that searcheth the hearts
knoweth what *is* the mind of the Spirit,
because he maketh intercession for the
saints according to *the will of* God.
28 And we know that all things work
together for good to them that love God,
to them who are the called according to
his purpose.
29 For whom he did foreknow, he also did
predestinate *to be* conformed to the image
of his Son, that he might be the firstborn
among many brethren.
30 Moreover whom he did predestinate,
them he also called: and whom he called,
them he also justified: and whom he justified, them he also glorified.
31 What shall we then say to these things?
If God *be* for us, who *can be* against us?
32 He that spared not his own Son, but
delivered him up for us all, how shall he
not with him also freely give us all things?
33 Who shall lay any thing to the charge of
God's elect? *It is* God that justifieth.
34 Who *is* he that condemneth? *It is* Christ
that died, yea rather, that is risen again, who
is even at the right hand of God, who also
maketh intercession for us.
35 Who shall separate us from the love
of Christ? *shall* tribulation, or distress, or
persecution, or famine, or nakedness, or
peril, or sword?
36 As it is written, For thy sake we are killed
all the day long; we are accounted as sheep
for the slaughter.
37 Nay, in all these things we are more than
conquerors through him that loved us.
38 For I am persuaded, that neither death,
nor life, nor angels, nor principalities, nor
powers, nor things present, nor things to
come,
39 Nor height, nor depth, nor any other
creature, shall be able to separate us from
the love of God, which is in Christ Jesus
our Lord.

Romans 9

1 I say the truth in Christ, I lie not, my
conscience also bearing me witness in the
Holy Spirit,
2 That I have great heaviness and continual
sorrow in my heart.
3 For I could wish that myself were accursed
from Christ for my brethren, my kinsmen
according to the flesh:
4 Who are Israelites; to whom *pertaineth*
the adoption, and the glory, and the covenants, and the giving of the law, and the
service *of God*, and the promises;
5 Whose *are* the fathers, and of whom as
concerning the flesh Christ *came*, who is
over all, God blessed for ever. Amen.
6 Not as though the word of God hath taken
none effect. For they *are* not all Israel, which
are of Israel:
7 Neither, because they are the seed of
Abraham, *are they* all children: but, In Isaac
shall thy seed be called.
8 That is, They which are the children of the
flesh, these *are* not the children of God: but
the children of the promise are counted
for the seed.
9 For this *is* the word of promise, At this
time will I come, and Sara shall have a son.
10 And not only *this;* but when Rebecca
also had conceived by one, *even* by our
father Isaac;
11 (For *the children* being not yet born, neither having done any good or evil, that the
purpose of God according to election might
stand, not of works, but of him that calleth;)
12 It was said unto her, The elder shall serve
the younger.
13 As it is written, Jacob have I loved, but
Esau have I hated.
14 What shall we say then? *Is there* unrighteousness with God? God forbid.
15 For he saith to Moses, I will have mercy
on whom I will have mercy, and I will have
compassion on whom I will have compassion.
16 So then *it is* not of him that willeth,
nor of him that runneth, but of God that
sheweth mercy.
17 For the scripture saith unto Pharaoh,
Even for this same purpose have I raised
thee up, that I might shew my power in
thee, and that my name might be declared
throughout all the earth.

18 Therefore hath he mercy on whom he will *have mercy*, and whom he will he hardeneth.

19 Thou wilt say then unto me, Why doth he yet find fault? For who hath resisted his will?

20 Nay but, O man, who art thou that repliest against God? Shall the thing formed say to him that formed *it*, Why hast thou made me thus?

21 Hath not the potter power over the clay, of the same lump to make one vessel unto honour, and another unto dishonour?

22 *What* if God, willing to shew *his* wrath, and to make his power known, endured with much longsuffering the vessels of wrath fitted to destruction:

23 And that he might make known the riches of his glory on the vessels of mercy, which he had afore prepared unto glory,

24 Even us, whom he hath called, not of the Jews only, but also of the Gentiles?

25 As he saith also in Osee, I will call them my people, which were not my people; and her beloved, which was not beloved.

26 And it shall come to pass, *that* in the place where it was said unto them, Ye *are* not my people; there shall they be called the children of the living God.

27 Esaias also crieth concerning Israel, Though the number of the children of Israel be as the sand of the sea, a remnant shall be saved:

28 For he will finish the work, and cut *it* short in righteousness: because a short work will the Lord make upon the earth.

29 And as Esaias said before, Except the Lord of Sabaoth had left us a seed, we had been as Sodoma, and been made like unto Gomorrha.

30 What shall we say then? That the Gentiles, which followed not after righteousness, have attained to righteousness, even the righteousness which is of faith.

31 But Israel, which followed after the law of righteousness, hath not attained to the law of righteousness.

32 Wherefore? Because *they sought it* not by faith, but as it were by the works of the law. For they stumbled at that stumblingstone;

33 As it is written, Behold, I lay in Sion a stumblingstone and rock of offence: and whosoever believeth on him shall not be ashamed.

Romans 10

1 Brethren, my heart's desire and prayer to God for Israel is, that they might be saved.

2 For I bear them record that they have a zeal of God, but not according to knowledge.

3 For they being ignorant of God's righteousness, and going about to establish their own righteousness, have not submitted themselves unto the righteousness of God.

4 For Christ *is* the end of the law for righteousness to every one that believeth.

5 For Moses describeth the righteousness which is of the law, That the man which doeth those things shall live by them.

6 But the righteousness which is of faith speaketh on this wise, Say not in thine heart, Who shall ascend into heaven? (that is, to bring Christ down *from above:*)

7 Or, Who shall descend into the deep? (that is, to bring up Christ again from the dead.)

8 But what saith it? The word is nigh thee, *even* in thy mouth, and in thy heart: that is, the word of faith, which we preach;

9 That if thou shalt confess with thy mouth the Lord Jesus, and shalt believe in thine heart that God hath raised him from the dead, thou shalt be saved.

10 For with the heart man believeth unto righteousness; and with the mouth confession is made unto salvation.

11 For the scripture saith, Whosoever believeth on him shall not be ashamed.

12 For there is no difference between the Jew and the Greek: for the same Lord over all is rich unto all that call upon him.

13 For whosoever shall call upon the name of the Lord shall be saved.

14 How then shall they call on him in whom they have not believed? and how shall they believe in him of whom they have not heard? and how shall they hear without a preacher?

15 And how shall they preach, except they be sent? as it is written, How beautiful are the feet of them that preach the gospel of peace, and bring glad tidings of good things!

16 But they have not all obeyed the gospel. For Esaias saith, Lord, who hath believed our report?

17 So then faith *cometh* by hearing, and hearing by the word of God.

18 But I say, Have they not heard? Yes verily,

their sound went into all the earth, and their
words unto the ends of the world.
19 But I say, Did not Israel know? First Moses
saith, I will provoke you to jealousy by *them*
that are no people, *and* by a foolish nation
I will anger you.
20 But Esaias is very bold, and saith, I was
found of them that sought me not; I was
made manifest unto them that asked not
after me.
21 But to Israel he saith, All day long I have
stretched forth my hands unto a disobedient
and gainsaying people.

Romans 11

1 I say then, Hath God cast away his people?
God forbid. For I also am an Israelite, of the
seed of Abraham, *of* the tribe of Benjamin.
2 God hath not cast away his people which
he foreknew. Wot ye not what the scripture
saith of Elias? how he maketh intercession
to God against Israel, saying,
3 Lord, they have killed thy prophets, and
digged down thine altars; and I am left
alone, and they seek my life.
4 But what saith the answer of God unto
him? I have reserved to myself seven thousand men, who have not bowed the knee
to *the image of* Baal.
5 Even so then at this present time also
there is a remnant according to the election of grace.
6 And if by grace, then *is it* no more of works:
otherwise grace is no more grace. But if *it*
be of works, then is it no more grace: otherwise work is no more work.
7 What then? Israel hath not obtained that
which he seeketh for; but the election hath
obtained it, and the rest were blinded
8 (According as it is written, God hath given
them the spirit of slumber, eyes that they
should not see, and ears that they should
not hear;) unto this day.
9 And David saith, Let their table be made
a snare, and a trap, and a stumblingblock,
and a recompence unto them:
10 Let their eyes be darkened, that they may
not see, and bow down their back alway.
11 I say then, Have they stumbled that they
should fall? God forbid: but *rather* through
their fall salvation *is come* unto the Gentiles,
for to provoke them to jealousy.
12 Now if the fall of them *be* the riches of
the world, and the diminishing of them
the riches of the Gentiles; how much more
their fulness?
13 For I speak to you Gentiles, inasmuch as
I am the apostle of the Gentiles, I magnify
mine office:
14 If by any means I may provoke to emu-
lation *them which are* my flesh, and might
save some of them.
15 For if the casting away of them *be* the
reconciling of the world, what *shall* the
receiving *of them be*, but life from the dead?
16 For if the firstfruit *be* holy, the lump *is*
also *holy:* and if the root *be* holy, so *are* the
branches.
17 And if some of the branches be broken
off, and thou, being a wild olive tree, wert
graffed in among them, and with them
partakest of the root and fatness of the
olive tree;
18 Boast not against the branches. But if
thou boast, thou bearest not the root, but
the root thee.
19 Thou wilt say then, The branches were
broken off, that I might be graffed in.
20 Well; because of unbelief they were
broken off, and thou standest by faith. Be
not highminded, but fear:
21 For if God spared not the natural
branches, *take heed* lest he also spare not
thee.
22 Behold therefore the goodness and
severity of God: on them which fell, severity;
but toward thee, goodness, if thou continue
in *his* goodness: otherwise thou also shalt
be cut off.
23 And they also, if they abide not still in
unbelief, shall be graffed in: for God is able
to graff them in again.
24 For if thou wert cut out of the olive tree
which is wild by nature, and wert graffed
contrary to nature into a good olive tree:
how much more shall these, which be the
natural *branches*, be graffed into their own
olive tree?
25 For I would not, brethren, that ye should
be ignorant of this mystery, lest ye should be
wise in your own conceits; that blindness in
part is happened to Israel, until the fulness
of the Gentiles be come in.
26 And so all Israel shall be saved: as it is
written, There shall come out of Sion the

Deliverer, and shall turn away ungodliness
from Jacob:
27 For this *is* my covenant unto them, when
I shall take away their sins.
28 As concerning the gospel, *they are* enemies for your sakes: but as touching the
election, *they are* beloved for the fathers'
sakes.
29 For the gifts and calling of God *are* without repentance.
30 For as ye in times past have not believed
God, yet have now obtained mercy through
their unbelief:
31 Even so have these also now not believed,
that through your mercy they also may
obtain mercy.
32 For God hath concluded them all in
unbelief, that he might have mercy upon all.
33 O the depth of the riches both of the wisdom and knowledge of God! how unsearchable *are* his judgments, and his ways past
finding out!
34 For who hath known the mind of the
Lord? or who hath been his counseller?
35 Or who hath first given to him, and it shall
be recompensed unto him again?
36 For of him, and through him, and to
him, *are* all things: to whom *be* glory for
ever. Amen.

Romans 12

1 I beseech you therefore, brethren, by the
mercies of God, that ye present your bodies
a living sacrifice, holy, acceptable unto God,
which is your reasonable service.
2 And be not conformed to this world: but
be ye transformed by the renewing of your
mind, that ye may prove what *is* that good,
and acceptable, and perfect, will of God.
3 For I say, through the grace given unto
me, to every man that is among you, not to
think *of himself* more highly than he ought
to think; but to think soberly, according as
God hath dealt to every man the measure
of faith.
4 For as we have many members in one
body, and all members have not the same
office:
5 So we, *being* many, are one body in Christ,
and every one members one of another.
6 Having then gifts differing according to the
grace that is given to us, whether prophecy,
let us prophesy according to the proportion
of faith;
7 Or ministry, *let us wait* on *our* ministering:
or he that teacheth, on teaching;
8 Or he that exhorteth, on exhortation: he
that giveth, *let him do it* with simplicity; he
that ruleth, with diligence; he that sheweth
mercy, with cheerfulness.
9 *Let* love be without dissimulation. Abhor
that which is evil; cleave to that which is
good.
10 *Be* kindly affectioned one to another
with brotherly love; in honour preferring
one another;
11 Not slothful in business; fervent in spirit;
serving the Lord;
12 Rejoicing in hope; patient in tribulation;
continuing instant in prayer;
13 Distributing to the necessity of saints;
given to hospitality.
14 Bless them which persecute you: bless,
and curse not.
15 Rejoice with them that do rejoice, and
weep with them that weep.
16 *Be* of the same mind one toward another.
Mind not high things, but condescend to
men of low estate. Be not wise in your own
conceits.
17 Recompense to no man evil for evil. Provide things honest in the sight of all men.
18 If it be possible, as much as lieth in you,
live peaceably with all men.
19 Dearly beloved, avenge not yourselves,
but *rather* give place unto wrath: for it is
written, Vengeance *is* mine; I will repay,
saith the Lord.
20 Therefore if thine enemy hunger, feed
him; if he thirst, give him drink: for in so
doing thou shalt heap coals of fire on his
head.
21 Be not overcome of evil, but overcome
evil with good.

Romans 13

1 Let every soul be subject unto the higher
powers. For there is no power but of God:
the powers that be are ordained of God.
2 Whosoever therefore resisteth the power,
resisteth the ordinance of God: and they
that resist shall receive to themselves
damnation.
3 For rulers are not a terror to good works,
but to the evil. Wilt thou then not be afraid

of the power? do that which is good, and thou shalt have praise of the same:

4 For he is the minister of God to thee for good. But if thou do that which is evil, be afraid; for he beareth not the sword in vain: for he is the minister of God, a revenger to *execute* wrath upon him that doeth evil.

5 Wherefore *ye* must needs be subject, not only for wrath, but also for conscience sake.

6 For for this cause pay ye tribute also: for they are God's ministers, attending continually upon this very thing.

7 Render therefore to all their dues: tribute to whom tribute *is due;* custom to whom custom; fear to whom fear; honour to whom honour.

8 Owe no man any thing, but to love one another: for he that loveth another hath fulfilled the law.

9 For this, Thou shalt not commit adultery, Thou shalt not kill, Thou shalt not steal, Thou shalt not bear false witness, Thou shalt not covet; and if *there be* any other commandment, it is briefly comprehended in this saying, namely, Thou shalt love thy neighbour as thyself.

10 Love worketh no ill to his neighbour: therefore love *is* the fulfilling of the law.

11 And that, knowing the time, that now *it is* high time to awake out of sleep: for now *is* our salvation nearer than when we believed.

12 The night is far spent, the day is at hand: let us therefore cast off the works of darkness, and let us put on the armour of light.

13 Let us walk honestly, as in the day; not in rioting and drunkenness, not in chambering and wantonness, not in strife and envying.

14 But put ye on the Lord Jesus Christ, and make not provision for the flesh, to *fulfil* the lusts *thereof.*

Romans 14

1 Him that is weak in the faith receive ye, *but* not to doubtful disputations.

2 For one believeth that he may eat all things: another, who is weak, eateth herbs.

3 Let not him that eateth despise him that eateth not; and let not him which eateth not judge him that eateth: for God hath received him.

4 Who art thou that judgest another man's servant? to his own master he standeth or falleth. Yea, he shall be holden up: for God is able to make him stand.

5 One man esteemeth one day above another: another esteemeth every day *alike.* Let every man be fully persuaded in his own mind.

6 He that regardeth the day, regardeth *it* unto the Lord; and he that regardeth not the day, to the Lord he doth not regard *it.* He that eateth, eateth to the Lord, for he giveth God thanks; and he that eateth not, to the Lord he eateth not, and giveth God thanks.

7 For none of us liveth to himself, and no man dieth to himself.

8 For whether we live, we live unto the Lord; and whether we die, we die unto the Lord: whether we live therefore, or die, we are the Lord's.

9 For to this end Christ both died, and rose, and revived, that he might be Lord both of the dead and living.

10 But why dost thou judge thy brother? or why dost thou set at nought thy brother? for we shall all stand before the judgment seat of Christ.

11 For it is written, *As* I live, saith the Lord, every knee shall bow to me, and every tongue shall confess to God.

12 So then every one of us shall give account of himself to God.

13 Let us not therefore judge one another any more: but judge this rather, that no man put a stumblingblock or an occasion to fall in *his* brother's way.

14 I know, and am persuaded by the Lord Jesus, that *there is* nothing unclean of itself: but to him that esteemeth any thing to be unclean, to him *it is* unclean.

15 But if thy brother be grieved with *thy* meat, now walkest thou not charitably. Destroy not him with thy meat, for whom Christ died.

16 Let not then your good be evil spoken of:

17 For the kingdom of God is not meat and drink; but righteousness, and peace, and joy in the Holy Spirit.

18 For he that in these things serveth Christ *is* acceptable to God, and approved of men.

19 Let us therefore follow after the things which make for peace, and things wherewith one may edify another.

20 For meat destroy not the work of God.

All things indeed *are* pure; but *it is* evil for
that man who eateth with offence.
21 *It is* good neither to eat flesh, nor to drink
wine, nor *any thing* whereby thy brother
stumbleth, or is offended, or is made weak.
22 Hast thou faith? have *it* to thyself before
God. Happy *is* he that condemneth not himself in that thing which he alloweth.
23 And he that doubteth is damned if he
eat, because *he eateth* not of faith: for
whatsoever *is* not of faith is sin.

Romans 15

1 We then that are strong ought to bear the
infirmities of the weak, and not to please
ourselves.
2 Let every one of us please *his* neighbour
for *his* good to edification.
3 For even Christ pleased not himself; but,
as it is written, The reproaches of them that
reproached thee fell on me.
4 For whatsoever things were written
aforetime were written for our learning,
that we through patience and comfort of
the scriptures might have hope.
5 Now the God of patience and consolation
grant you to be likeminded one toward
another according to Christ Jesus:
6 That ye may with one mind *and* one
mouth glorify God, even the Father of our
Lord Jesus Christ.
7 Wherefore receive ye one another, as
Christ also received us to the glory of God.
8 Now I say that Jesus Christ was a minister of the circumcision for the truth of
God, to confirm the promises *made* unto
the fathers:
9 And that the Gentiles might glorify God
for *his* mercy; as it is written, For this cause
I will confess to thee among the Gentiles,
and sing unto thy name.
10 And again he saith, Rejoice, ye Gentiles,
with his people.
11 And again, Praise the Lord, all ye Gentiles;
and laud him, all ye people.
12 And again, Esaias saith, There shall be
a root of Jesse, and he that shall rise to
reign over the Gentiles; in him shall the
Gentiles trust.
13 Now the God of hope fill you with all
joy and peace in believing, that ye may
abound in hope, through the power of the
Holy Spirit.
14 And I myself also am persuaded of you,
my brethren, that ye also are full of goodness, filled with all knowledge, able also to
admonish one another.
15 Nevertheless, brethren, I have written
the more boldly unto you in some sort, as
putting you in mind, because of the grace
that is given to me of God,
16 That I should be the minister of Jesus
Christ to the Gentiles, ministering the gospel
of God, that the offering up of the Gentiles
might be acceptable, being sanctified by
the Holy Spirit.
17 I have therefore whereof I may glory
through Jesus Christ in those things which
pertain to God.
18 For I will not dare to speak of any of
those things which Christ hath not wrought
by me, to make the Gentiles obedient, by
word and deed,
19 Through mighty signs and wonders, by
the power of the Spirit of God; so that from
Jerusalem, and round about unto Illyricum,
I have fully preached the gospel of Christ.
20 Yea, so have I strived to preach the
gospel, not where Christ was named, lest
I should build upon another man's foundation:
21 But as it is written, To whom he was not
spoken of, they shall see: and they that have
not heard shall understand.
22 For which cause also I have been much
hindered from coming to you.
23 But now having no more place in these
parts, and having a great desire these many
years to come unto you;
24 Whensoever I take my journey into Spain,
I will come to you: for I trust to see you in
my journey, and to be brought on my way
thitherward by you, if first I be somewhat
filled with your *company*.
25 But now I go unto Jerusalem to minister
unto the saints.
26 For it hath pleased them of Macedonia
and Achaia to make a certain contribution
for the poor saints which are at Jerusalem.
27 It hath pleased them verily; and their
debtors they are. For if the Gentiles have
been made partakers of their spiritual
things, their duty is also to minister unto
them in carnal things.
28 When therefore I have performed this,

and have sealed to them this fruit, I will
come by you into Spain.
29 And I am sure that, when I come unto
you, I shall come in the fulness of the blessing of the gospel of Christ.
30 Now I beseech you, brethren, for the
Lord Jesus Christ's sake, and for the love of
the Spirit, that ye strive together with me
in *your* prayers to God for me;
31 That I may be delivered from them that
do not believe in Judæa; and that my service
which *I have* for Jerusalem may be accepted
of the saints;
32 That I may come unto you with joy by the
will of God, and may with you be refreshed.
33 Now the God of peace *be* with you all.
Amen.

Romans 16

1 I commend unto you Phebe our sister,
which is a servant of the church which is
at Cenchrea:
2 That ye receive her in the Lord, as becometh saints, and that ye assist her in whatsoever business she hath need of you: for
she hath been a succourer of many, and of
myself also.
3 Greet Priscilla and Aquila my helpers in
Christ Jesus:
4 Who have for my life laid down their own
necks: unto whom not only I give thanks,
but also all the churches of the Gentiles.
5 Likewise *greet* the church that is in their
house. Salute my wellbeloved Epænetus,
who is the firstfruits of Achaia unto Christ.
6 Greet Mary, who bestowed much labour
on us.
7 Salute Andronicus and Junia, my kinsmen,
and my fellowprisoners, who are of note
among the apostles, who also were in Christ
before me.
8 Greet Amplias my beloved in the Lord.
9 Salute Urbane, our helper in Christ, and
Stachys my beloved.
10 Salute Apelles approved in Christ. Salute
them which are of Aristobulus' *household*.
11 Salute Herodion my kinsman. Greet them
that be of the *household* of Narcissus, which
are in the Lord.
12 Salute Tryphena and Tryphosa, who
labour in the Lord. Salute the beloved Persis,
which laboured much in the Lord.
13 Salute Rufus chosen in the Lord, and his
mother and mine.
14 Salute Asyncritus, Phlegon, Hermas,
Patrobas, Hermes, and the brethren which
are with them.
15 Salute Philologus, and Julia, Nereus, and
his sister, and Olympas, and all the saints
which are with them.
16 Salute one another with an holy kiss. The
churches of Christ salute you.
17 Now I beseech you, brethren, mark them
which cause divisions and offences contrary
to the doctrine which ye have learned; and
avoid them.
18 For they that are such serve not our Lord
Jesus Christ, but their own belly; and by
good words and fair speeches deceive the
hearts of the simple.
19 For your obedience is come abroad unto
all *men*. I am glad therefore on your behalf:
but yet I would have you wise unto that
which is good, and simple concerning evil.
20 And the God of peace shall bruise Satan
under your feet shortly. The grace of our
Lord Jesus Christ *be* with you. Amen.
21 Timotheus my workfellow, and Lucius,
and Jason, and Sosipater, my kinsmen,
salute you.
22 I Tertius, who wrote *this* epistle, salute
you in the Lord.
23 Gaius mine host, and of the whole
church, saluteth you. Erastus the chamberlain of the city saluteth you, and Quartus
a brother.
24 The grace of our Lord Jesus Christ *be*
with you all. Amen.
25 Now to him that is of power to stablish you according to my gospel, and the
preaching of Jesus Christ, according to the
revelation of the mystery, which was kept
secret since the world began,
26 But now is made manifest, and by the
scriptures of the prophets, according to
the commandment of the everlasting God,
made known to all nations for the obedience of faith:
27 To God only wise, *be* glory through Jesus
Christ for ever. Amen.

The First Epistle Of Paul To The

Corinthians

1 Corinthians 1

1 Paul, called *to be* an apostle of Jesus Christ through the will of God, and Sosthenes *our* brother,

2 Unto the church of God which is at Corinth, to them that are sanctified in Christ Jesus, called *to be* saints, with all that in every place call upon the name of Jesus Christ our Lord, both theirs and ours:

3 Grace *be* unto you, and peace, from God our Father, and *from* the Lord Jesus Christ.

4 I thank my God always on your behalf, for the grace of God which is given you by Jesus Christ;

5 That in every thing ye are enriched by him, in all utterance, and *in* all knowledge;

6 Even as the testimony of Christ was confirmed in you:

7 So that ye come behind in no gift; waiting for the coming of our Lord Jesus Christ:

8 Who shall also confirm you unto the end, *that ye may be* blameless in the day of our Lord Jesus Christ.

9 God *is* faithful, by whom ye were called unto the fellowship of his Son Jesus Christ our Lord.

10 Now I beseech you, brethren, by the name of our Lord Jesus Christ, that ye all speak the same thing, and *that* there be no divisions among you; but *that* ye be perfectly joined together in the same mind and in the same judgment.

11 For it hath been declared unto me of you, my brethren, by them *which are of the house* of Chloe, that there are contentions among you.

12 Now this I say, that every one of you saith, I am of Paul; and I of Apollos; and I of Cephas; and I of Christ.

13 Is Christ divided? was Paul crucified for you? or were ye baptized in the name of Paul?

14 I thank God that I baptized none of you, but Crispus and Gaius;

15 Lest any should say that I had baptized in mine own name.

16 And I baptized also the household of Stephanas: besides, I know not whether I baptized any other.

17 For Christ sent me not to baptize, but to preach the gospel: not with wisdom of words, lest the cross of Christ should be made of none effect.

18 For the preaching of the cross is to them that perish foolishness; but unto us which are saved it is the power of God.

19 For it is written, I will destroy the wisdom of the wise, and will bring to nothing the understanding of the prudent.

20 Where *is* the wise? where *is* the scribe? where *is* the disputer of this world? hath not God made foolish the wisdom of this world?

21 For after that in the wisdom of God the world by wisdom knew not God, it pleased God by the foolishness of preaching to save them that believe.

22 For the Jews require a sign, and the Greeks seek after wisdom:

23 But we preach Christ crucified, unto the Jews a stumblingblock, and unto the Greeks foolishness;

24 But unto them which are called, both Jews and Greeks, Christ the power of God, and the wisdom of God.

25 Because the foolishness of God is wiser than men; and the weakness of God is stronger than men.

26 For ye see your calling, brethren, how that not many wise men after the flesh, not many mighty, not many noble, *are called:*

27 But God hath chosen the foolish things of the world to confound the wise; and God hath chosen the weak things of the world to confound the things which are mighty;

28 And base things of the world, and things which are despised, hath God chosen, *yea,* and things which are not, to bring to nought things that are:

29 That no flesh should glory in his presence.

30 But of him are ye in Christ Jesus, who of God is made unto us wisdom, and righteousness, and sanctification, and redemption:

31 That, according as it is written, He that glorieth, let him glory in the Lord.

1 Corinthians 2

1 And I, brethren, when I came to you, came
not with excellency of speech or of wisdom,
declaring unto you the testimony of God.
2 For I determined not to know any thing
among you, save Jesus Christ, and him
crucified.
3 And I was with you in weakness, and in
fear, and in much trembling.
4 And my speech and my preaching *was* not
with enticing words of man's wisdom, but in
demonstration of the Spirit and of power:
5 That your faith should not stand in the
wisdom of men, but in the power of God.
6 Howbeit we speak wisdom among them
that are perfect: yet not the wisdom of this
world, nor of the princes of this world, that
come to nought:
7 But we speak the wisdom of God in a mystery, *even* the hidden *wisdom*, which God
ordained before the world unto our glory:
8 Which none of the princes of this world
knew: for had they known *it*, they would not
have crucified the Lord of glory.
9 But as it is written, Eye hath not seen, nor
ear heard, neither have entered into the
heart of man, the things which God hath
prepared for them that love him.
10 But God hath revealed *them* unto us by
his Spirit: for the Spirit searcheth all things,
yea, the deep things of God.
11 For what man knoweth the things of a
man, save the spirit of man which is in him?
even so the things of God knoweth no man,
but the Spirit of God.
12 Now we have received, not the spirit of
the world, but the spirit which is of God; that
we might know the things that are freely
given to us of God.
13 Which things also we speak, not in the
words which man's wisdom teacheth, but
which the Holy Spirit teacheth; comparing
spiritual things with spiritual.
14 But the natural man receiveth not the
things of the Spirit of God: for they are
foolishness unto him: neither can he know
them, because they are spiritually discerned.
15 But he that is spiritual judgeth all things,
yet he himself is judged of no man.
16 For who hath known the mind of the
Lord, that he may instruct him? But we have
the mind of Christ.

1 Corinthians 3

1 And I, brethren, could not speak unto you
as unto spiritual, but as unto carnal, *even* as
unto babes in Christ.
2 I have fed you with milk, and not with
meat: for hitherto ye were not able *to bear*
it, neither yet now are ye able.
3 For ye are yet carnal: for whereas *there is*
among you envying, and strife, and divisions,
are ye not carnal, and walk as men?
4 For while one saith, I am of Paul; and
another, I *am* of Apollos; are ye not carnal?
5 Who then is Paul, and who *is* Apollos, but
ministers by whom ye believed, even as the
Lord gave to every man?
6 I have planted, Apollos watered; but God
gave the increase.
7 So then neither is he that planteth any
thing, neither he that watereth; but God
that giveth the increase.
8 Now he that planteth and he that watereth are one: and every man shall receive his
own reward according to his own labour.
9 For we are labourers together with God: ye
are God's husbandry, *ye are* God's building.
10 According to the grace of God which is
given unto me, as a wise masterbuilder, I
have laid the foundation, and another buildeth thereon. But let every man take heed
how he buildeth thereupon.
11 For other foundation can no man lay than
that is laid, which is Jesus Christ.
12 Now if any man build upon this foundation gold, silver, precious stones, wood,
hay, stubble;
13 Every man's work shall be made manifest:
for the day shall declare it, because it shall
be revealed by fire; and the fire shall try
every man's work of what sort it is.
14 If any man's work abide which he hath
built thereupon, he shall receive a reward.
15 If any man's work shall be burned, he
shall suffer loss: but he himself shall be
saved; yet so as by fire.
16 Know ye not that ye are the temple of
God, and *that* the Spirit of God dwelleth
in you?
17 If any man defile the temple of God, him
shall God destroy; for the temple of God is
holy, which *temple* ye are.
18 Let no man deceive himself. If any man
among you seemeth to be wise in this world,
let him become a fool, that he may be wise.

19 For the wisdom of this world is foolishness with God. For it is written, He taketh
the wise in their own craftiness.
20 And again, The Lord knoweth the
thoughts of the wise, that they are vain.
21 Therefore let no man glory in men. For
all things are yours;
22 Whether Paul, or Apollos, or Cephas, or
the world, or life, or death, or things present,
or things to come; all are yours;
23 And ye are Christ's; and Christ *is* God's.

1 Corinthians 4

1 Let a man so account of us, as of the
ministers of Christ, and stewards of the
mysteries of God.
2 Moreover it is required in stewards, that
a man be found faithful.
3 But with me it is a very small thing that I
should be judged of you, or of man's judgment: yea, I judge not mine own self.
4 For I know nothing by myself; yet am I
not hereby justified: but he that judgeth
me is the Lord.
5 Therefore judge nothing before the time,
until the Lord come, who both will bring to
light the hidden things of darkness, and will
make manifest the counsels of the hearts:
and then shall every man have praise of God.
6 And these things, brethren, I have in a
figure transferred to myself and *to* Apollos
for your sakes; that ye might learn in us not
to think *of men* above that which is written,
that no one of you be puffed up for one
against another.
7 For who maketh thee to differ *from
another?* and what hast thou that thou
didst not receive? now if thou didst receive
it, why dost thou glory, as if thou hadst not
received *it?*
8 Now ye are full, now ye are rich, ye have
reigned as kings without us: and I would to
God ye did reign, that we also might reign
with you.
9 For I think that God hath set forth us the
apostles last, as it were appointed to death:
for we are made a spectacle unto the world,
and to angels, and to men.
10 We *are* fools for Christ's sake, but ye
are wise in Christ; we *are* weak, but ye
are strong; ye *are* honourable, but we *are*
despised.
11 Even unto this present hour we both
hunger, and thirst, and are naked, and are
buffeted, and have no certain dwellingplace;
12 And labour, working with our own hands:
being reviled, we bless; being persecuted,
we suffer it:
13 Being defamed, we intreat: we are
made as the filth of the world, *and are* the
offscouring of all things unto this day.
14 I write not these things to shame you,
but as my beloved sons I warn *you*.
15 For though ye have ten thousand instruc-
tors in Christ, yet *have ye* not many fathers:
for in Christ Jesus I have begotten you
through the gospel.
16 Wherefore I beseech you, be ye followers of me.
17 For this cause have I sent unto you Timotheus, who is my beloved son, and faithful
in the Lord, who shall bring you into remembrance of my ways which be in Christ, as I
teach every where in every church.
18 Now some are puffed up, as though I
would not come to you.
19 But I will come to you shortly, if the Lord
will, and will know, not the speech of them
which are puffed up, but the power.
20 For the kingdom of God *is* not in word,
but in power.
21 What will ye? shall I come unto you with a
rod, or in love, and *in* the spirit of meekness?

1 Corinthians 5

1 It is reported commonly *that there is* fornication among you, and such fornication as is
not so much as named among the Gentiles,
that one should have his father's wife.
2 And ye are puffed up, and have not rather
mourned, that he that hath done this deed
might be taken away from among you.
3 For I verily, as absent in body, but present
in spirit, have judged already, as though I
were present, *concerning* him that hath so
done this deed,
4 In the name of our Lord Jesus Christ, when
ye are gathered together, and my spirit, with
the power of our Lord Jesus Christ,
5 To deliver such an one unto Satan for the
destruction of the flesh, that the spirit may
be saved in the day of the Lord Jesus.
6 Your glorying *is* not good. Know ye not that
a little leaven leaveneth the whole lump?
7 Purge out therefore the old leaven, that ye
may be a new lump, as ye are unleavened.

For even Christ our passover is sacrificed
for us:
8 Therefore let us keep the feast, not with
old leaven, neither with the leaven of malice
and wickedness; but with the unleavened
bread of sincerity and truth.
9 I wrote unto you in an epistle not to company with fornicators:
10 Yet not altogether with the fornicators of
this world, or with the covetous, or extortioners, or with idolaters; for then must ye
needs go out of the world.
11 But now I have written unto you not to
keep company, if any man that is called a
brother be a fornicator, or covetous, or an
idolater, or a railer, or a drunkard, or an
extortioner; with such an one no not to eat.
12 For what have I to do to judge them also
that are without? do not ye judge them that
are within?
13 But them that are without God judgeth.
Therefore put away from among yourselves
that wicked person.

1 Corinthians 6

1 Dare any of you, having a matter against
another, go to law before the unjust, and
not before the saints?
2 Do ye not know that the saints shall judge
the world? and if the world shall be judged
by you, are ye unworthy to judge the smallest matters?
3 Know ye not that we shall judge angels?
how much more things that pertain to
this life?
4 If then ye have judgments of things pertaining to this life, set them to judge who
are least esteemed in the church.
5 I speak to your shame. Is it so, that there is
not a wise man among you? no, not one that
shall be able to judge between his brethren?
6 But brother goeth to law with brother,
and that before the unbelievers.
7 Now therefore there is utterly a fault
among you, because ye go to law one with
another. Why do ye not rather take wrong?
why do ye not rather *suffer yourselves to*
be defrauded?
8 Nay, ye do wrong, and defraud, and that
your brethren.
9 Know ye not that the unrighteous shall
not inherit the kingdom of God? Be not
deceived: neither fornicators, nor idolaters,
nor adulterers, nor effeminate, nor abusers
of themselves with mankind,
10 Nor thieves, nor covetous, nor drunkards,
nor revilers, nor extortioners, shall inherit
the kingdom of God.
11 And such were some of you: but ye are
washed, but ye are sanctified, but ye are
justified in the name of the Lord Jesus, and
by the Spirit of our God.
12 All things are lawful unto me, but all
things are not expedient: all things are lawful for me, but I will not be brought under
the power of any.
13 Meats for the belly, and the belly for
meats: but God shall destroy both it and
them. Now the body *is* not for fornication,
but for the Lord; and the Lord for the body.
14 And God hath both raised up the Lord,
and will also raise up us by his own power.
15 Know ye not that your bodies are the
members of Christ? shall I then take the
members of Christ, and make *them* the
members of an harlot? God forbid.
16 What? know ye not that he which is
joined to an harlot is one body? for two,
saith he, shall be one flesh.
17 But he that is joined unto the Lord is
one spirit.
18 Flee fornication. Every sin that a man
doeth is without the body; but he that
committeth fornication sinneth against his
own body.
19 What? know ye not that your body is
the temple of the Holy Spirit *which is* in
you, which ye have of God, and ye are not
your own?
20 For ye are bought with a price: therefore
glorify God in your body, and in your spirit,
which are God's.

1 Corinthians 7

1 Now concerning the things whereof ye
wrote unto me: *It is* good for a man not to
touch a woman.
2 Nevertheless, *to avoid* fornication, let
every man have his own wife, and let every
woman have her own husband.
3 Let the husband render unto the wife due
benevolence: and likewise also the wife unto
the husband.
4 The wife hath not power of her own body,
but the husband: and likewise also the

husband hath not power of his own body, but the wife.
5 Defraud ye not one the other, except *it be* with consent for a time, that ye may give yourselves to fasting and prayer; and come together again, that Satan tempt you not for your incontinency.
6 But I speak this by permission, *and* not of commandment.
7 For I would that all men were even as I myself. But every man hath his proper gift of God, one after this manner, and another after that.
8 I say therefore to the unmarried and widows, It is good for them if they abide even as I.
9 But if they cannot contain, let them marry: for it is better to marry than to burn.
10 And unto the married I command, *yet* not I, but the Lord, Let not the wife depart from *her* husband:
11 But and if she depart, let her remain unmarried, or be reconciled to *her* husband: and let not the husband put away *his* wife.
12 But to the rest speak I, not the Lord: If any brother hath a wife that believeth not, and she be pleased to dwell with him, let him not put her away.
13 And the woman which hath an husband that believeth not, and if he be pleased to dwell with her, let her not leave him.
14 For the unbelieving husband is sanctified by the wife, and the unbelieving wife is sanctified by the husband: else were your children unclean; but now are they holy.
15 But if the unbelieving depart, let him depart. A brother or a sister is not under bondage in such *cases:* but God hath called us to peace.
16 For what knowest thou, O wife, whether thou shalt save *thy* husband? or how knowest thou, O man, whether thou shalt save *thy* wife?
17 But as God hath distributed to every man, as the Lord hath called every one, so let him walk. And so ordain I in all churches.
18 Is any man called being circumcised? let him not become uncircumcised. Is any called in uncircumcision? let him not be circumcised.
19 Circumcision is nothing, and uncircumcision is nothing, but the keeping of the commandments of God.
20 Let every man abide in the same calling wherein he was called.
21 Art thou called *being* a servant? care not for it: but if thou mayest be made free, use *it* rather.
22 For he that is called in the Lord, *being* a servant, is the Lord's freeman: likewise also he that is called, *being* free, is Christ's servant.
23 Ye are bought with a price; be not ye the servants of men.
24 Brethren, let every man, wherein he is called, therein abide with God.
25 Now concerning virgins I have no commandment of the Lord: yet I give my judgment, as one that hath obtained mercy of the Lord to be faithful.
26 I suppose therefore that this is good for the present distress, *I say,* that *it is* good for a man so to be.
27 Art thou bound unto a wife? seek not to be loosed. Art thou loosed from a wife? seek not a wife.
28 But and if thou marry, thou hast not sinned; and if a virgin marry, she hath not sinned. Nevertheless such shall have trouble in the flesh: but I spare you.
29 But this I say, brethren, the time *is* short: it remaineth, that both they that have wives be as though they had none;
30 And they that weep, as though they wept not; and they that rejoice, as though they rejoiced not; and they that buy, as though they possessed not;
31 And they that use this world, as not abusing *it:* for the fashion of this world passeth away.
32 But I would have you without carefulness. He that is unmarried careth for the things that belong to the Lord, how he may please the Lord:
33 But he that is married careth for the things that are of the world, how he may please *his* wife.
34 There is difference *also* between a wife and a virgin. The unmarried woman careth for the things of the Lord, that she may be holy both in body and in spirit: but she that is married careth for the things of the world, how she may please *her* husband.
35 And this I speak for your own profit; not that I may cast a snare upon you, but

for that which is comely, and that ye may
attend upon the Lord without distraction.
36 But if any man think that he behaveth
himself uncomely toward his virgin, if she
pass the flower of *her* age, and need so
require, let him do what he will, he sinneth
not: let them marry.
37 Nevertheless he that standeth stedfast in his heart, having no necessity, but
hath power over his own will, and hath so
decreed in his heart that he will keep his
virgin, doeth well.
38 So then he that giveth *her* in marriage
doeth well; but he that giveth *her* not in
marriage doeth better.
39 The wife is bound by the law as long as
her husband liveth; but if her husband be
dead, she is at liberty to be married to whom
she will; only in the Lord.
40 But she is happier if she so abide, after
my judgment: and I think also that I have
the Spirit of God.

1 Corinthians 8

1 Now as touching things offered unto
idols, we know that we all have knowledge.
Knowledge puffeth up, but charity edifieth.
2 And if any man think that he knoweth
any thing, he knoweth nothing yet as he
ought to know.
3 But if any man love God, the same is
known of him.
4 As concerning therefore the eating of
those things that are offered in sacrifice
unto idols, we know that an idol *is* nothing
in the world, and that *there is* none other
God but one.
5 For though there be that are called gods,
whether in heaven or in earth, (as there be
gods many, and lords many,)
6 But to us *there is but* one God, the Father,
of whom *are* all things, and we in him; and
one Lord Jesus Christ, by whom *are* all
things, and we by him.
7 Howbeit *there is* not in every man that
knowledge: for some with conscience of the
idol unto this hour eat *it* as a thing offered
unto an idol; and their conscience being
weak is defiled.
8 But meat commendeth us not to God: for
neither, if we eat, are we the better; neither,
if we eat not, are we the worse.
9 But take heed lest by any means this liberty of yours become a stumblingblock to
them that are weak.
10 For if any man see thee which hast knowledge sit at meat in the idol's temple, shall
not the conscience of him which is weak be
emboldened to eat those things which are
offered to idols;
11 And through thy knowledge shall the
weak brother perish, for whom Christ died?
12 But when ye sin so against the brethren,
and wound their weak conscience, ye sin
against Christ.
13 Wherefore, if meat make my brother to
offend, I will eat no flesh while the world
standeth, lest I make my brother to offend.

1 Corinthians 9

1 Am I not an apostle? am I not free? have
I not seen Jesus Christ our Lord? are not ye
my work in the Lord?
2 If I be not an apostle unto others, yet
doubtless I am to you: for the seal of mine
apostleship are ye in the Lord.
3 Mine answer to them that do examine
me is this,
4 Have we not power to eat and to drink?
5 Have we not power to lead about a sister,
a wife, as well as other apostles, and *as* the
brethren of the Lord, and Cephas?
6 Or I only and Barnabas, have not we power
to forbear working?
7 Who goeth a warfare any time at his
own charges? who planteth a vineyard,
and eateth not of the fruit thereof? or who
feedeth a flock, and eateth not of the milk
of the flock?
8 Say I these things as a man? or saith not
the law the same also?
9 For it is written in the law of Moses, Thou
shalt not muzzle the mouth of the ox that
treadeth out the corn. Doth God take care
for oxen?
10 Or saith he *it* altogether for our sakes?
For our sakes, no doubt, *this* is written: that
he that ploweth should plow in hope; and
that he that thresheth in hope should be
partaker of his hope.
11 If we have sown unto you spiritual things,
is it a great thing if we shall reap your carnal things?
12 If others be partakers of *this* power
over you, *are* not we rather? Nevertheless
we have not used this power; but suffer all

things, lest we should hinder the gospel
of Christ.
13 Do ye not know that they which minister
about holy things live *of the things* of the
temple? and they which wait at the altar
are partakers with the altar?
14 Even so hath the Lord ordained that
they which preach the gospel should live
of the gospel.
15 But I have used none of these things:
neither have I written these things, that it
should be so done unto me: for *it were* better for me to die, than that any man should
make my glorying void.
16 For though I preach the gospel, I have
nothing to glory of: for necessity is laid
upon me; yea, woe is unto me, if I preach
not the gospel!
17 For if I do this thing willingly, I have a
reward: but if against my will, a dispensation
of the gospel is committed unto me.
18 What is my reward then? *Verily* that,
when I preach the gospel, I may make the
gospel of Christ without charge, that I abuse
not my power in the gospel.
19 For though I be free from all *men*, yet
have I made myself servant unto all, that I
might gain the more.
20 And unto the Jews I became as a Jew,
that I might gain the Jews; to them that are
under the law, as under the law, that I might
gain them that are under the law;
21 To them that are without law, as without law, (being not without law to God, but
under the law to Christ,) that I might gain
them that are without law.
22 To the weak became I as weak, that I
might gain the weak: I am made all things to
all *men*, that I might by all means save some.
23 And this I do for the gospel's sake, that I
might be partaker thereof with *you*.
24 Know ye not that they which run in a race
run all, but one receiveth the prize? So run,
that ye may obtain.
25 And every man that striveth for the mastery is temperate in all things. Now they *do*
it to obtain a corruptible crown; but we an
incorruptible.
26 I therefore so run, not as uncertainly;
so fight I, not as one that beateth the air:
27 But I keep under my body, and bring
it into subjection: lest that by any means,
when I have preached to others, I myself
should be a castaway.

1 Corinthians 10

1 Moreover, brethren, I would not that
ye should be ignorant, how that all our
fathers were under the cloud, and all passed
through the sea;
2 And were all baptized unto Moses in the
cloud and in the sea;
3 And did all eat the same spiritual meat;
4 And did all drink the same spiritual drink:
for they drank of that spiritual Rock that
followed them: and that Rock was Christ.
5 But with many of them God was not well
pleased: for they were overthrown in the
wilderness.
6 Now these things were our examples,
to the intent we should not lust after evil
things, as they also lusted.
7 Neither be ye idolaters, as *were* some of
them; as it is written, The people sat down
to eat and drink, and rose up to play.
8 Neither let us commit fornication, as some
of them committed, and fell in one day three
and twenty thousand.
9 Neither let us tempt Christ, as some of
them also tempted, and were destroyed
of serpents.
10 Neither murmur ye, as some of them
also murmured, and were destroyed of
the destroyer.
11 Now all these things happened unto
them for ensamples: and they are written
for our admonition, upon whom the ends
of the world are come.
12 Wherefore let him that thinketh he standeth take heed lest he fall.
13 There hath no temptation taken you but
such as is common to man: but God *is* faithful, who will not suffer you to be tempted
above that ye are able; but will with the
temptation also make a way to escape, that
ye may be able to bear *it*.
14 Wherefore, my dearly beloved, flee
from idolatry.
15 I speak as to wise men; judge ye what
I say.
16 The cup of blessing which we bless, is it
not the communion of the blood of Christ?
The bread which we break, is it not the
communion of the body of Christ?
17 For we *being* many are one bread, *and*

one body: for we are all partakers of that
one bread.
18 Behold Israel after the flesh: are not
they which eat of the sacrifices partakers
of the altar?
19 What say I then? that the idol is any thing,
or that which is offered in sacrifice to idols
is any thing?
20 But *I say*, that the things which the Gentiles sacrifice, they sacrifice to devils, and
not to God: and I would not that ye should
have fellowship with devils.
21 Ye cannot drink the cup of the Lord, and
the cup of devils: ye cannot be partakers of
the Lord's table, and of the table of devils.
22 Do we provoke the Lord to jealousy? are
we stronger than he?
23 All things are lawful for me, but all things
are not expedient: all things are lawful for
me, but all things edify not.
24 Let no man seek his own, but every man
another's *wealth*.
25 Whatsoever is sold in the shambles, *that*
eat, asking no question for conscience sake:
26 For the earth *is* the Lord's, and the fulness thereof.
27 If any of them that believe not bid you
to a feast, and ye be disposed to go; whatsoever is set before you, eat, asking no
question for conscience sake.
28 But if any man say unto you, This is
offered in sacrifice unto idols, eat not for
his sake that shewed it, and for conscience
sake: for the earth *is* the Lord's, and the
fulness thereof:
29 Conscience, I say, not thine own, but of
the other: for why is my liberty judged of
another *man's* conscience?
30 For if I by grace be a partaker, why am
I evil spoken of for that for which I give
thanks?
31 Whether therefore ye eat, or drink, or
whatsoever ye do, do all to the glory of God.
32 Give none offence, neither to the Jews,
nor to the Gentiles, nor to the church of
God:
33 Even as I please all *men* in all *things*, not
seeking mine own profit, but the *profit* of
many, that they may be saved.

1 Corinthians 11

1 Be ye followers of me, even as I also *am*
of Christ.
2 Now I praise you, brethren, that ye
remember me in all things, and keep the
ordinances, as I delivered *them* to you.
3 But I would have you know, that the head
of every man is Christ; and the head of the
woman *is* the man; and the head of Christ
is God.
4 Every man praying or prophesying, having
his head covered, dishonoureth his head.
5 But every woman that prayeth or prophesieth with *her* head uncovered dishonoureth
her head: for that is even all one as if she
were shaven.
6 For if the woman be not covered, let her
also be shorn: but if it be a shame for a
woman to be shorn or shaven, let her be
covered.
7 For a man indeed ought not to cover *his*
head, forasmuch as he is the image and
glory of God: but the woman is the glory
of the man.
8 For the man is not of the woman; but the
woman of the man.
9 Neither was the man created for the
woman; but the woman for the man.
10 For this cause ought the woman to have
power on *her* head because of the angels.
11 Nevertheless neither is the man without
the woman, neither the woman without the
man, in the Lord.
12 For as the woman *is* of the man, even
so *is* the man also by the woman; but all
things of God.
13 Judge in yourselves: is it comely that a
woman pray unto God uncovered?
14 Doth not even nature itself teach you,
that, if a man have long hair, it is a shame
unto him?
15 But if a woman have long hair, it is a glory
to her: for *her* hair is given her for a covering.
16 But if any man seem to be conten-
tious, we have no such custom, neither the
churches of God.
17 Now in this that I declare *unto you* I praise
you not, that ye come together not for the
better, but for the worse.
18 For first of all, when ye come together
in the church, I hear that there be divisions
among you; and I partly believe it.
19 For there must be also heresies among
you, that they which are approved may be
made manifest among you.

20 When ye come together therefore into one place, *this* is not to eat the Lord's supper.
21 For in eating every one taketh before *other* his own supper: and one is hungry, and another is drunken.
22 What? have ye not houses to eat and to drink in? or despise ye the church of God, and shame them that have not? What shall I say to you? shall I praise you in this? I praise *you* not.
23 For I have received of the Lord that which also I delivered unto you, That the Lord Jesus the *same* night in which he was betrayed took bread:
24 And when he had given thanks, he brake *it*, and said, Take, eat: this is my body, which is broken for you: this do in remembrance of me.
25 After the same manner also *he took* the cup, when he had supped, saying, This cup is the new testament in my blood: this do ye, as oft as ye drink *it*, in remembrance of me.
26 For as often as ye eat this bread, and drink this cup, ye do shew the Lord's death till he come.
27 Wherefore whosoever shall eat this bread, and drink *this* cup of the Lord, unworthily, shall be guilty of the body and blood of the Lord.
28 But let a man examine himself, and so let him eat of *that* bread, and drink of *that* cup.
29 For he that eateth and drinketh unworthily, eateth and drinketh damnation to himself, not discerning the Lord's body.
30 For this cause many *are* weak and sickly among you, and many sleep.
31 For if we would judge ourselves, we should not be judged.
32 But when we are judged, we are chastened of the Lord, that we should not be condemned with the world.
33 Wherefore, my brethren, when ye come together to eat, tarry one for another.
34 And if any man hunger, let him eat at home; that ye come not together unto condemnation. And the rest will I set in order when I come.

1 Corinthians 12

1 Now concerning spiritual *gifts*, brethren, I would not have you ignorant.
2 Ye know that ye were Gentiles, carried away unto these dumb idols, even as ye were led.
3 Wherefore I give you to understand, that no man speaking by the Spirit of God calleth Jesus accursed: and *that* no man can say that Jesus is the Lord, but by the Holy Spirit.
4 Now there are diversities of gifts, but the same Spirit.
5 And there are differences of administrations, but the same Lord.
6 And there are diversities of operations, but it is the same God which worketh all in all.
7 But the manifestation of the Spirit is given to every man to profit withal.
8 For to one is given by the Spirit the word of wisdom; to another the word of knowledge by the same Spirit;
9 To another faith by the same Spirit; to another the gifts of healing by the same Spirit;
10 To another the working of miracles; to another prophecy; to another discerning of spirits; to another *divers* kinds of tongues; to another the interpretation of tongues:
11 But all these worketh that one and the selfsame Spirit, dividing to every man severally as he will.
12 For as the body is one, and hath many members, and all the members of that one body, being many, are one body: so also *is* Christ.
13 For by one Spirit are we all baptized into one body, whether *we be* Jews or Gentiles, whether *we be* bond or free; and have been all made to drink into one Spirit.
14 For the body is not one member, but many.
15 If the foot shall say, Because I am not the hand, I am not of the body; is it therefore not of the body?
16 And if the ear shall say, Because I am not the eye, I am not of the body; is it therefore not of the body?
17 If the whole body *were* an eye, where *were* the hearing? If the whole *were* hearing, where *were* the smelling?
18 But now hath God set the members every one of them in the body, as it hath pleased him.
19 And if they were all one member, where *were* the body?
20 But now *are they* many members, yet but one body.

21 And the eye cannot say unto the hand,
I have no need of thee: nor again the head
to the feet, I have no need of you.
22 Nay, much more those members of the
body, which seem to be more feeble, are
necessary:
23 And those *members* of the body, which
we think to be less honourable, upon these
we bestow more abundant honour; and
our uncomely *parts* have more abundant
comeliness.
24 For our comely *parts* have no need: but
God hath tempered the body together,
having given more abundant honour to that
part which lacked:
25 That there should be no schism in the
body; but *that* the members should have
the same care one for another.
26 And whether one member suffer, all the
members suffer with it; or one member be
honoured, all the members rejoice with it.
27 Now ye are the body of Christ, and members in particular.
28 And God hath set some in the church,
first apostles, secondarily prophets, thirdly
teachers, after that miracles, then gifts of
healings, helps, governments, diversities
of tongues.
29 *Are* all apostles? *are* all prophets? *are*
all teachers? *are* all workers of miracles?
30 Have all the gifts of healing? do all speak
with tongues? do all interpret?
31 But covet earnestly the best gifts: and
yet shew I unto you a more excellent way.

1 Corinthians 13

1 Though I speak with the tongues of men
and of angels, and have not charity, I am
become *as* sounding brass, or a tinkling
cymbal.
2 And though I have *the gift of* prophecy, and
understand all mysteries, and all knowledge;
and though I have all faith, so that I could
remove mountains, and have not charity, I
am nothing.
3 And though I bestow all my goods to feed
the poor, and though I give my body to be
burned, and have not charity, it profiteth
me nothing.
4 Charity suffereth long, *and* is kind; charity
envieth not; charity vaunteth not itself, is
not puffed up,
5 Doth not behave itself unseemly, seeketh
not her own, is not easily provoked, thinketh no evil;
6 Rejoiceth not in iniquity, but rejoiceth in
the truth;
7 Beareth all things, believeth all things,
hopeth all things, endureth all things.
8 Charity never faileth: but whether *there
be* prophecies, they shall fail; whether *there
be* tongues, they shall cease; whether *there
be* knowledge, it shall vanish away.
9 For we know in part, and we prophesy
in part.
10 But when that which is perfect is come,
then that which is in part shall be done away.
11 When I was a child, I spake as a child, I
understood as a child, I thought as a child:
but when I became a man, I put away child-
ish things.
12 For now we see through a glass, darkly;
but then face to face: now I know in part; but
then shall I know even as also I am known.
13 And now abideth faith, hope, charity,
these three; but the greatest of these *is*
charity.

1 Corinthians 14

1 Follow after charity, and desire spiritual
gifts, but rather that ye may prophesy.
2 For he that speaketh in an *unknown*
tongue speaketh not unto men, but unto
God: for no man understandeth *him;* howbeit in the spirit he speaketh mysteries.
3 But he that prophesieth speaketh unto
men *to* edification, and exhortation, and
comfort.
4 He that speaketh in an *unknown* tongue
edifieth himself; but he that prophesieth
edifieth the church.
5 I would that ye all spake with tongues,
but rather that ye prophesied: for greater *is*
he that prophesieth than he that speaketh
with tongues, except he interpret, that the
church may receive edifying.
6 Now, brethren, if I come unto you speaking
with tongues, what shall I profit you, except
I shall speak to you either by revelation, or
by knowledge, or by prophesying, or by
doctrine?
7 And even things without life giving sound,
whether pipe or harp, except they give a
distinction in the sounds, how shall it be
known what is piped or harped?

8 For if the trumpet give an uncertain sound,
who shall prepare himself to the battle?
9 So likewise ye, except ye utter by the
tongue words easy to be understood, how
shall it be known what is spoken? for ye shall
speak into the air.
10 There are, it may be, so many kinds of
voices in the world, and none of them *is*
without signification.
11 Therefore if I know not the meaning of
the voice, I shall be unto him that speaketh
a barbarian, and he that speaketh *shall be*
a barbarian unto me.
12 Even so ye, forasmuch as ye are zealous
of spiritual *gifts*, seek that ye may excel to
the edifying of the church.
13 Wherefore let him that speaketh in an
unknown tongue pray that he may interpret.
14 For if I pray in an *unknown* tongue, my
spirit prayeth, but my understanding is
unfruitful.
15 What is it then? I will pray with the spirit,
and I will pray with the understanding also:
I will sing with the spirit, and I will sing with
the understanding also.
16 Else when thou shalt bless with the spirit,
how shall he that occupieth the room of
the unlearned say Amen at thy giving of
thanks, seeing he understandeth not what
thou sayest?
17 For thou verily givest thanks well, but
the other is not edified.
18 I thank my God, I speak with tongues
more than ye all:
19 Yet in the church I had rather speak five
words with my understanding, that *by my
voice* I might teach others also, than ten
thousand words in an *unknown* tongue.
20 Brethren, be not children in understanding: howbeit in malice be ye children, but in
understanding be men.
21 In the law it is written, With *men of* other
tongues and other lips will I speak unto this
people; and yet for all that will they not hear
me, saith the Lord.
22 Wherefore tongues are for a sign, not to
them that believe, but to them that believe
not: but prophesying *serveth* not for them
that believe not, but for them which believe.
23 If therefore the whole church be come
together into one place, and all speak with
tongues, and there come in *those that are*
unlearned, or unbelievers, will they not say
that ye are mad?
24 But if all prophesy, and there come in one
that believeth not, or *one* unlearned, he is
convinced of all, he is judged of all:
25 And thus are the secrets of his heart
made manifest; and so falling down on *his*
face he will worship God, and report that
God is in you of a truth.
26 How is it then, brethren? when ye come
together, every one of you hath a psalm,
hath a doctrine, hath a tongue, hath a revelation, hath an interpretation. Let all things
be done unto edifying.
27 If any man speak in an *unknown* tongue,
let it be by two, or at the most *by* three, and
that by course; and let one interpret.
28 But if there be no interpreter, let him
keep silence in the church; and let him speak
to himself, and to God.
29 Let the prophets speak two or three, and
let the other judge.
30 If *any thing* be revealed to another that
sitteth by, let the first hold his peace.
31 For ye may all prophesy one by one, that
all may learn, and all may be comforted.
32 And the spirits of the prophets are subject to the prophets.
33 For God is not *the author* of confusion,
but of peace, as in all churches of the saints.
34 Let your women keep silence in the
churches: for it is not permitted unto them
to speak; but *they are commanded* to be
under obedience, as also saith the law.
35 And if they will learn any thing, let them
ask their husbands at home: for it is a shame
for women to speak in the church.
36 What? came the word of God out from
you? or came it unto you only?
37 If any man think himself to be a prophet,
or spiritual, let him acknowledge that the
things that I write unto you are the commandments of the Lord.
38 But if any man be ignorant, let him be
ignorant.
39 Wherefore, brethren, covet to prophesy,
and forbid not to speak with tongues.
40 Let all things be done decently and in
order.

1 Corinthians 15

1 Moreover, brethren, I declare unto you

the gospel which I preached unto you, which
also ye have received, and wherein ye stand;
2 By which also ye are saved, if ye keep in
memory what I preached unto you, unless
ye have believed in vain.
3 For I delivered unto you first of all that
which I also received, how that Christ died
for our sins according to the scriptures;
4 And that he was buried, and that he
rose again the third day according to the
scriptures:
5 And that he was seen of Cephas, then of
the twelve:
6 After that, he was seen of above five hundred brethren at once; of whom the greater
part remain unto this present, but some are
fallen asleep.
7 After that, he was seen of James; then of
all the apostles.
8 And last of all he was seen of me also, as
of one born out of due time.
9 For I am the least of the apostles, that am
not meet to be called an apostle, because I
persecuted the church of God.
10 But by the grace of God I am what I am:
and his grace which *was bestowed* upon
me was not in vain; but I laboured more
abundantly than they all: yet not I, but the
grace of God which was with me.
11 Therefore whether *it were* I or they, so
we preach, and so ye believed.
12 Now if Christ be preached that he rose
from the dead, how say some among you
that there is no resurrection of the dead?
13 But if there be no resurrection of the
dead, then is Christ not risen:
14 And if Christ be not risen, then *is* our
preaching vain, and your faith *is* also vain.
15 Yea, and we are found false witnesses of
God; because we have testified of God that
he raised up Christ: whom he raised not up,
if so be that the dead rise not.
16 For if the dead rise not, then is not Christ
raised:
17 And if Christ be not raised, your faith *is*
vain; ye are yet in your sins.
18 Then they also which are fallen asleep
in Christ are perished.
19 If in this life only we have hope in Christ,
we are of all men most miserable.
20 But now is Christ risen from the dead, *and*
become the firstfruits of them that slept.
21 For since by man *came* death, by man
came also the resurrection of the dead.
22 For as in Adam all die, even so in Christ
shall all be made alive.
23 But every man in his own order: Christ
the firstfruits; afterward they that are
Christ's at his coming.
24 Then *cometh* the end, when he shall have
delivered up the kingdom to God, even the
Father; when he shall have put down all rule
and all authority and power.
25 For he must reign, till he hath put all
enemies under his feet.
26 The last enemy *that* shall be destroyed
is death.
27 For he hath put all things under his feet.
But when he saith, all things are put under
him, it is manifest that he is excepted, which
did put all things under him.
28 And when all things shall be subdued
unto him, then shall the Son also himself be
subject unto him that put all things under
him, that God may be all in all.
29 Else what shall they do which are baptized for the dead, if the dead rise not at all?
why are they then baptized for the dead?
30 And why stand we in jeopardy every
hour?
31 I protest by your rejoicing which I have
in Christ Jesus our Lord, I die daily.
32 If after the manner of men I have fought
with beasts at Ephesus, what advantageth
it me, if the dead rise not? let us eat and
drink; for to morrow we die.
33 Be not deceived: evil communications
corrupt good manners.
34 Awake to righteousness, and sin not;
for some have not the knowledge of God: I
speak *this* to your shame.
35 But some *man* will say, How are the
dead raised up? and with what body do
they come?
36 *Thou* fool, that which thou sowest is not
quickened, except it die:
37 And that which thou sowest, thou sowest not that body that shall be, but bare
grain, it may chance of wheat, or of some
other *grain:*
38 But God giveth it a body as it hath pleased
him, and to every seed his own body.
39 All flesh *is* not the same flesh: but *there*
is one *kind of* flesh of men, another flesh

of beasts, another of fishes, *and* another
of birds.
40 *There are* also celestial bodies, and bodies terrestrial: but the glory of the celestial
is one, and the *glory* of the terrestrial *is*
another.
41 *There is* one glory of the sun, and another
glory of the moon, and another glory of the
stars: for *one* star differeth from *another*
star in glory.
42 So also *is* the resurrection of the dead.
It is sown in corruption; it is raised in incorruption:
43 It is sown in dishonour; it is raised in
glory: it is sown in weakness; it is raised
in power:
44 It is sown a natural body; it is raised a
spiritual body. There is a natural body, and
there is a spiritual body.
45 And so it is written, The first man Adam
was made a living soul; the last Adam *was*
made a quickening spirit.
46 Howbeit that *was* not first which is spiritual, but that which is natural; and afterward
that which is spiritual.
47 The first man *is* of the earth, earthy: the
second man *is* the Lord from heaven.
48 As *is* the earthy, such *are* they also that
are earthy: and as *is* the heavenly, such *are*
they also that are heavenly.
49 And as we have borne the image of the
earthy, we shall also bear the image of the
heavenly.
50 Now this I say, brethren, that flesh and
blood cannot inherit the kingdom of God;
neither doth corruption inherit incorruption.
51 Behold, I shew you a mystery; We shall
not all sleep, but we shall all be changed,
52 In a moment, in the twinkling of an eye, at
the last trump: for the trumpet shall sound,
and the dead shall be raised incorruptible,
and we shall be changed.
53 For this corruptible must put on incorruption, and this mortal *must* put on immortality.
54 So when this corruptible shall have put
on incorruption, and this mortal shall have
put on immortality, then shall be brought
to pass the saying that is written, Death is
swallowed up in victory.
55 O death, where *is* thy sting? O grave,
where *is* thy victory?
56 The sting of death *is* sin; and the strength
of sin *is* the law.
57 But thanks *be* to God, which giveth us
the victory through our Lord Jesus Christ.
58 Therefore, my beloved brethren, be ye
stedfast, unmoveable, always abounding in
the work of the Lord, forasmuch as ye know
that your labour is not in vain in the Lord.

1 Corinthians 16

1 Now concerning the collection for the
saints, as I have given order to the churches
of Galatia, even so do ye.
2 Upon the first *day* of the week let every
one of you lay by him in store, as *God* hath
prospered him, that there be no gatherings
when I come.
3 And when I come, whomsoever ye shall
approve by *your* letters, them will I send to
bring your liberality unto Jerusalem.
4 And if it be meet that I go also, they shall
go with me.
5 Now I will come unto you, when I shall pass
through Macedonia: for I do pass through
Macedonia.
6 And it may be that I will abide, yea, and
winter with you, that ye may bring me on
my journey whithersoever I go.
7 For I will not see you now by the way;
but I trust to tarry a while with you, if the
Lord permit.
8 But I will tarry at Ephesus until Pentecost.
9 For a great door and effectual is opened
unto me, and *there are* many adversaries.
10 Now if Timotheus come, see that he may
be with you without fear: for he worketh
the work of the Lord, as I also *do*.
11 Let no man therefore despise him: but
conduct him forth in peace, that he may
come unto me: for I look for him with the
brethren.
12 As touching *our* brother Apollos, I greatly
desired him to come unto you with the
brethren: but his will was not at all to come
at this time; but he will come when he shall
have convenient time.
13 Watch ye, stand fast in the faith, quit you
like men, be strong.
14 Let all your things be done with charity.
15 I beseech you, brethren, (ye know the
house of Stephanas, that it is the firstfruits
of Achaia, and *that* they have addicted
themselves to the ministry of the saints,)

16 That ye submit yourselves unto such,
and to every one that helpeth with *us*, and
laboureth.
17 I am glad of the coming of Stephanas and
Fortunatus and Achaicus: for that which was
lacking on your part they have supplied.
18 For they have refreshed my spirit and
yours: therefore acknowledge ye them
that are such.
19 The churches of Asia salute you. Aquila
and Priscilla salute you much in the Lord,
with the church that is in their house.
20 All the brethren greet you. Greet ye one
another with an holy kiss.
21 The salutation of *me* Paul with mine
own hand.
22 If any man love not the Lord Jesus Christ,
let him be Anathema Maran-atha.
23 The grace of our Lord Jesus Christ *be*
with you.
24 My love *be* with you all in Christ Jesus.
Amen.

The Second Epistle Of Paul To The

Corinthians

2 Corinthians 1

1 Paul, an apostle of Jesus Christ by the will
of God, and Timothy *our* brother, unto the
church of God which is at Corinth, with all
the saints which are in all Achaia:
2 Grace *be* to you and peace from God our
Father, and *from* the Lord Jesus Christ.
3 Blessed *be* God, even the Father of our
Lord Jesus Christ, the Father of mercies,
and the God of all comfort;
4 Who comforteth us in all our tribulation,
that we may be able to comfort them which
are in any trouble, by the comfort wherewith we ourselves are comforted of God.
5 For as the sufferings of Christ abound in us,
so our consolation also aboundeth by Christ.
6 And whether we be afflicted, *it is* for your
consolation and salvation, which is effectual
in the enduring of the same sufferings which
we also suffer: or whether we be comforted,
it is for your consolation and salvation.
7 And our hope of you *is* stedfast, knowing,
that as ye are partakers of the sufferings, so
shall ye be also of the consolation.
8 For we would not, brethren, have you
ignorant of our trouble which came to us in
Asia, that we were pressed out of measure,
above strength, insomuch that we despaired
even of life:
9 But we had the sentence of death in ourselves, that we should not trust in ourselves,
but in God which raiseth the dead:
10 Who delivered us from so great a death,
and doth deliver: in whom we trust that he
will yet deliver *us;*
11 Ye also helping together by prayer for
us, that for the gift *bestowed* upon us by
the means of many persons thanks may be
given by many on our behalf.
12 For our rejoicing is this, the testimony of
our conscience, that in simplicity and godly
sincerity, not with fleshly wisdom, but by
the grace of God, we have had our conversation in the world, and more abundantly
to you-ward.
13 For we write none other things unto you,
than what ye read or acknowledge; and I
trust ye shall acknowledge even to the end;
14 As also ye have acknowledged us in part,
that we are your rejoicing, even as ye also
are ours in the day of the Lord Jesus.
15 And in this confidence I was minded to
come unto you before, that ye might have
a second benefit;
16 And to pass by you into Macedonia,
and to come again out of Macedonia unto
you, and of you to be brought on my way
toward Judæa.
17 When I therefore was thus minded, did I
use lightness? or the things that I purpose,
do I purpose according to the flesh, that with
me there should be yea yea, and nay nay?
18 But *as* God *is* true, our word toward you
was not yea and nay.

19 For the Son of God, Jesus Christ, who was preached among you by us, *even* by me and Silvanus and Timotheus, was not yea and nay, but in him was yea.

20 For all the promises of God in him *are* yea, and in him Amen, unto the glory of God by us.

21 Now he which stablisheth us with you in Christ, and hath anointed us, *is* God;

22 Who hath also sealed us, and given the earnest of the Spirit in our hearts.

23 Moreover I call God for a record upon my soul, that to spare you I came not as yet unto Corinth.

24 Not for that we have dominion over your faith, but are helpers of your joy: for by faith ye stand.

2 Corinthians 2

1 But I determined this with myself, that I would not come again to you in heaviness.

2 For if I make you sorry, who is he then that maketh me glad, but the same which is made sorry by me?

3 And I wrote this same unto you, lest, when I came, I should have sorrow from them of whom I ought to rejoice; having confidence in you all, that my joy is *the joy* of you all.

4 For out of much affliction and anguish of heart I wrote unto you with many tears; not that ye should be grieved, but that ye might know the love which I have more abundantly unto you.

5 But if any have caused grief, he hath not grieved me, but in part: that I may not overcharge you all.

6 Sufficient to such a man *is* this punishment, which *was inflicted* of many.

7 So that contrariwise ye *ought* rather to forgive *him*, and comfort *him*, lest perhaps such a one should be swallowed up with overmuch sorrow.

8 Wherefore I beseech you that ye would confirm *your* love toward him.

9 For to this end also did I write, that I might know the proof of you, whether ye be obedient in all things.

10 To whom ye forgive any thing, I *forgive* also: for if I forgave any thing, to whom I forgave *it*, for your sakes *forgave I it* in the person of Christ;

11 Lest Satan should get an advantage of us: for we are not ignorant of his devices.

12 Furthermore, when I came to Troas to *preach* Christ's gospel, and a door was opened unto me of the Lord,

13 I had no rest in my spirit, because I found not Titus my brother: but taking my leave of them, I went from thence into Macedonia.

14 Now thanks *be* unto God, which always causeth us to triumph in Christ, and maketh manifest the savour of his knowledge by us in every place.

15 For we are unto God a sweet savour of Christ, in them that are saved, and in them that perish:

16 To the one *we are* the savour of death unto death; and to the other the savour of life unto life. And who *is* sufficient for these things?

17 For we are not as many, which corrupt the word of God: but as of sincerity, but as of God, in the sight of God speak we in Christ.

2 Corinthians 3

1 Do we begin again to commend ourselves? or need we, as some *others*, epistles of commendation to you, or *letters* of commendation from you?

2 Ye are our epistle written in our hearts, known and read of all men:

3 *Forasmuch as ye are* manifestly declared to be the epistle of Christ ministered by us, written not with ink, but with the Spirit of the living God; not in tables of stone, but in fleshy tables of the heart.

4 And such trust have we through Christ to God-ward:

5 Not that we are sufficient of ourselves to think any thing as of ourselves; but our sufficiency *is* of God;

6 Who also hath made us able ministers of the new testament; not of the letter, but of the spirit: for the letter killeth, but the spirit giveth life.

7 But if the ministration of death, written *and* engraven in stones, was glorious, so that the children of Israel could not stedfastly behold the face of Moses for the glory of his countenance; which *glory* was to be done away:

8 How shall not the ministration of the spirit be rather glorious?

9 For if the ministration of condemnation *be* glory, much more doth the ministration of righteousness exceed in glory.

10 For even that which was made glorious
had no glory in this respect, by reason of
the glory that excelleth.
11 For if that which is done away *was* glorious, much more that which remaineth *is*
glorious.
12 Seeing then that we have such hope, we
use great plainness of speech:
13 And not as Moses, *which* put a vail over
his face, that the children of Israel could not
stedfastly look to the end of that which is
abolished:
14 But their minds were blinded: for until
this day remaineth the same vail untaken
away in the reading of the old testament;
which *vail* is done away in Christ.
15 But even unto this day, when Moses is
read, the vail is upon their heart.
16 Nevertheless when it shall turn to the
Lord, the vail shall be taken away.
17 Now the Lord is that Spirit: and where the
Spirit of the Lord *is*, there *is* liberty.
18 But we all, with open face beholding as
in a glass the glory of the Lord, are changed
into the same image from glory to glory,
even as by the Spirit of the Lord.

2 Corinthians 4

1 Therefore seeing we have this ministry,
as we have received mercy, we faint not;
2 But have renounced the hidden things of
dishonesty, not walking in craftiness, nor
handling the word of God deceitfully; but
by manifestation of the truth commending
ourselves to every man's conscience in the
sight of God.
3 But if our gospel be hid, it is hid to them
that are lost:
4 In whom the god of this world hath blinded
the minds of them which believe not, lest
the light of the glorious gospel of Christ, who
is the image of God, should shine unto them.
5 For we preach not ourselves, but Christ
Jesus the Lord; and ourselves your servants
for Jesus' sake.
6 For God, who commanded the light to
shine out of darkness, hath shined in our
hearts, to *give* the light of the knowledge of
the glory of God in the face of Jesus Christ.
7 But we have this treasure in earthen vessels, that the excellency of the power may
be of God, and not of us.
8 *We are* troubled on every side, yet not
distressed; *we are* perplexed, but not in
despair;
9 Persecuted, but not forsaken; cast down,
but not destroyed;
10 Always bearing about in the body the
dying of the Lord Jesus, that the life also of
Jesus might be made manifest in our body.
11 For we which live are alway delivered
unto death for Jesus' sake, that the life
also of Jesus might be made manifest in
our mortal flesh.
12 So then death worketh in us, but life
in you.
13 We having the same spirit of faith,
according as it is written, I believed, and
therefore have I spoken; we also believe,
and therefore speak;
14 Knowing that he which raised up the
Lord Jesus shall raise up us also by Jesus,
and shall present *us* with you.
15 For all things *are* for your sakes, that the
abundant grace might through the thanksgiving of many redound to the glory of God.
16 For which cause we faint not; but though
our outward man perish, yet the inward
man is renewed day by day.
17 For our light affliction, which is but for a
moment, worketh for us a far more exceeding *and* eternal weight of glory;
18 While we look not at the things which
are seen, but at the things which are not
seen: for the things which are seen *are*
temporal; but the things which are not seen
are eternal.

2 Corinthians 5

1 For we know that if our earthly house of
this tabernacle were dissolved, we have a
building of God, an house not made with
hands, eternal in the heavens.
2 For in this we groan, earnestly desiring
to be clothed upon with our house which
is from heaven:
3 If so be that being clothed we shall not
be found naked.
4 For we that are in *this* tabernacle do groan,
being burdened: not for that we would be
unclothed, but clothed upon, that mortality
might be swallowed up of life.
5 Now he that hath wrought us for the
selfsame thing *is* God, who also hath given
unto us the earnest of the Spirit.
6 Therefore *we are* always confident, know-

ing that, whilst we are at home in the body,
we are absent from the Lord:
7 (For we walk by faith, not by sight:)
8 We are confident, *I say*, and willing rather
to be absent from the body, and to be present with the Lord.
9 Wherefore we labour, that, whether present or absent, we may be accepted of him.
10 For we must all appear before the judgment seat of Christ; that every one may receive the things *done* in *his* body, according to that he hath done, whether *it be* good or bad.
11 Knowing therefore the terror of the Lord, we persuade men; but we are made manifest unto God; and I trust also are made manifest in your consciences.
12 For we commend not ourselves again unto you, but give you occasion to glory on our behalf, that ye may have somewhat to *answer* them which glory in appearance, and not in heart.
13 For whether we be beside ourselves, *it is* to God: or whether we be sober, *it is* for your cause.
14 For the love of Christ constraineth us; because we thus judge, that if one died for all, then were all dead:
15 And *that* he died for all, that they which live should not henceforth live unto themselves, but unto him which died for them, and rose again.
16 Wherefore henceforth know we no man after the flesh: yea, though we have known Christ after the flesh, yet now henceforth know we *him* no more.
17 Therefore if any man *be* in Christ, *he is* a new creature: old things are passed away; behold, all things are become new.
18 And all things *are* of God, who hath reconciled us to himself by Jesus Christ, and hath given to us the ministry of reconciliation;
19 To wit, that God was in Christ, reconciling the world unto himself, not imputing their trespasses unto them; and hath committed unto us the word of reconciliation.
20 Now then we are ambassadors for Christ, as though God did beseech *you* by us: we pray *you* in Christ's stead, be ye reconciled to God.
21 For he hath made him *to be* sin for us,
who knew no sin; that we might be made the righteousness of God in him.

2 Corinthians 6

1 We then, *as* workers together *with him*, beseech *you* also that ye receive not the grace of God in vain.
2 (For he saith, I have heard thee in a time accepted, and in the day of salvation have I succoured thee: behold, now *is* the accepted time; behold, now *is* the day of salvation.)
3 Giving no offence in any thing, that the ministry be not blamed:
4 But in all *things* approving ourselves as the ministers of God, in much patience, in afflictions, in necessities, in distresses,
5 In stripes, in imprisonments, in tumults, in labours, in watchings, in fastings;
6 By pureness, by knowledge, by longsuffering, by kindness, by the Holy Spirit, by love unfeigned,
7 By the word of truth, by the power of God, by the armour of righteousness on the right hand and on the left,
8 By honour and dishonour, by evil report and good report: as deceivers, and *yet* true;
9 As unknown, and *yet* well known; as dying, and, behold, we live; as chastened, and not killed;
10 As sorrowful, yet alway rejoicing; as poor, yet making many rich; as having nothing, and *yet* possessing all things.
11 O *ye* Corinthians, our mouth is open unto you, our heart is enlarged.
12 Ye are not straitened in us, but ye are straitened in your own bowels.
13 Now for a recompence in the same, (I speak as unto *my* children,) be ye also enlarged.
14 Be ye not unequally yoked together with unbelievers: for what fellowship hath righteousness with unrighteousness? and what communion hath light with darkness?
15 And what concord hath Christ with Belial? or what part hath he that believeth with an infidel?
16 And what agreement hath the temple of God with idols? for ye are the temple of the living God; as God hath said, I will dwell in them, and walk in *them;* and I will be their God, and they shall be my people.
17 Wherefore come out from among them, and be ye separate, saith the Lord, and

touch not the unclean *thing;* and I will
receive you,
18 And will be a Father unto you, and ye
shall be my sons and daughters, saith the
Lord Almighty.

2 Corinthians 7

1 Having therefore these promises, dearly
beloved, let us cleanse ourselves from all
filthiness of the flesh and spirit, perfecting
holiness in the fear of God.
2 Receive us; we have wronged no man, we
have corrupted no man, we have defrauded
no man.
3 I speak not *this* to condemn *you:* for I have
said before, that ye are in our hearts to die
and live with *you.*
4 Great *is* my boldness of speech toward
you, great *is* my glorying of you: I am filled
with comfort, I am exceeding joyful in all
our tribulation.
5 For, when we were come into Macedonia,
our flesh had no rest, but we were troubled
on every side; without *were* fightings, within
were fears.
6 Nevertheless God, that comforteth those
that are cast down, comforted us by the
coming of Titus;
7 And not by his coming only, but by the
consolation wherewith he was comforted
in you, when he told us your earnest desire,
your mourning, your fervent mind toward
me; so that I rejoiced the more.
8 For though I made you sorry with a letter,
I do not repent, though I did repent: for I
perceive that the same epistle hath made
you sorry, though *it were* but for a season.
9 Now I rejoice, not that ye were made sorry,
but that ye sorrowed to repentance: for ye
were made sorry after a godly manner, that
ye might receive damage by us in nothing.
10 For godly sorrow worketh repentance
to salvation not to be repented of: but the
sorrow of the world worketh death.
11 For behold this selfsame thing, that ye
sorrowed after a godly sort, what carefulness it wrought in you, yea, *what* clearing
of yourselves, yea, *what* indignation, yea,
what fear, yea, *what* vehement desire, yea,
what zeal, yea, *what* revenge! In all *things*
ye have approved yourselves to be clear in
this matter.
12 Wherefore, though I wrote unto you, *I did*
it not for his cause that had done the wrong,
nor for his cause that suffered wrong, but
that our care for you in the sight of God
might appear unto you.
13 Therefore we were comforted in your
comfort: yea, and exceedingly the more
joyed we for the joy of Titus, because his
spirit was refreshed by you all.
14 For if I have boasted any thing to him of
you, I am not ashamed; but as we spake all
things to you in truth, even so our boasting,
which *I made* before Titus, is found a truth.
15 And his inward affection is more abundant toward you, whilst he remembereth
the obedience of you all, how with fear and
trembling ye received him.
16 I rejoice therefore that I have confidence
in you in all *things.*

2 Corinthians 8

1 Moreover, brethren, we do you to wit of
the grace of God bestowed on the churches
of Macedonia;
2 How that in a great trial of affliction the
abundance of their joy and their deep
poverty abounded unto the riches of their
liberality.
3 For to *their* power, I bear record, yea,
and beyond *their* power *they were* willing
of themselves;
4 Praying us with much intreaty that we
would receive the gift, and *take upon us* the
fellowship of the ministering to the saints.
5 And *this they did,* not as we hoped, but
first gave their own selves to the Lord, and
unto us by the will of God.
6 Insomuch that we desired Titus, that as
he had begun, so he would also finish in you
the same grace also.
7 Therefore, as ye abound in every *thing, in*
faith, and utterance, and knowledge, and *in*
all diligence, and *in* your love to us, *see* that
ye abound in this grace also.
8 I speak not by commandment, but by
occasion of the forwardness of others, and
to prove the sincerity of your love.
9 For ye know the grace of our Lord Jesus
Christ, that, though he was rich, yet for your
sakes he became poor, that ye through his
poverty might be rich.
10 And herein I give *my* advice: for this is
expedient for you, who have begun before,

not only to do, but also to be forward a
year ago.
11 Now therefore perform the doing *of
it;* that as *there was* a readiness to will, so
there may be a performance also out of that
which ye have.
12 For if there be first a willing mind, *it is*
accepted according to that a man hath, *and*
not according to that he hath not.
13 For *I mean* not that other men be eased,
and ye burdened:
14 But by an equality, *that* now at this time
your abundance *may be a supply* for their
want, that their abundance also may be *a
supply* for your want: that there may be
equality:
15 As it is written, He that *had gathered*
much had nothing over; and he that *had
gathered* little had no lack.
16 But thanks *be* to God, which put the same
earnest care into the heart of Titus for you.
17 For indeed he accepted the exhortation;
but being more forward, of his own accord
he went unto you.
18 And we have sent with him the brother,
whose praise *is* in the gospel throughout
all the churches;
19 And not *that* only, but who was also chosen of the churches to travel with us with
this grace, which is administered by us to
the glory of the same Lord, and *declaration
of* your ready mind:
20 Avoiding this, that no man should blame
us in this abundance which is administered
by us:
21 Providing for honest things, not only in
the sight of the Lord, but also in the sight
of men.
22 And we have sent with them our brother,
whom we have oftentimes proved diligent
in many things, but now much more diligent, upon the great confidence which *I
have* in you.
23 Whether *any do inquire* of Titus, *he is*
my partner and fellowhelper concerning
you: or our brethren *be inquired of, they
are* the messengers of the churches, *and*
the glory of Christ.
24 Wherefore shew ye to them, and before
the churches, the proof of your love, and of
our boasting on your behalf.

2 Corinthians 9

1 For as touching the ministering to the
saints, it is superfluous for me to write to
you:
2 For I know the forwardness of your mind,
for which I boast of you to them of Macedonia, that Achaia was ready a year ago; and
your zeal hath provoked very many.
3 Yet have I sent the brethren, lest our boasting of you should be in vain in this behalf;
that, as I said, ye may be ready:
4 Lest haply if they of Macedonia come with
me, and find you unprepared, we (that we
say not, ye) should be ashamed in this same
confident boasting.
5 Therefore I thought it necessary to exhort
the brethren, that they would go before
unto you, and make up beforehand your
bounty, whereof ye had notice before, that
the same might be ready, as *a matter of*
bounty, and not as *of* covetousness.
6 But this *I say,* He which soweth sparingly
shall reap also sparingly; and he which
soweth bountifully shall reap also bountifully.
7 Every man according as he purposeth in
his heart, *so let him give;* not grudgingly, or
of necessity: for God loveth a cheerful giver.
8 And God *is* able to make all grace abound
toward you; that ye, always having all sufficiency in all *things,* may abound to every
good work:
9 (As it is written, He hath dispersed abroad;
he hath given to the poor: his righteousness
remaineth for ever.
10 Now he that ministereth seed to the
sower both minister bread for *your* food,
and multiply your seed sown, and increase
the fruits of your righteousness;)
11 Being enriched in every thing to all
bountifulness, which causeth through us
thanksgiving to God.
12 For the administration of this service
not only supplieth the want of the saints,
but is abundant also by many thanksgivings
unto God;
13 Whiles by the experiment of this ministration they glorify God for your professed
subjection unto the gospel of Christ, and
for *your* liberal distribution unto them, and
unto all *men;*
14 And by their prayer for you, which long

after you for the exceeding grace of God
in you.
15 Thanks *be* unto God for his unspeakable gift.

2 Corinthians 10

1 Now I Paul myself beseech you by the
meekness and gentleness of Christ, who in
presence *am* base among you, but being
absent am bold toward you:
2 But I beseech *you*, that I may not be bold
when I am present with that confidence,
wherewith I think to be bold against some,
which think of us as if we walked according
to the flesh.
3 For though we walk in the flesh, we do
not war after the flesh:
4 (For the weapons of our warfare *are* not
carnal, but mighty through God to the pulling down of strong holds;)
5 Casting down imaginations, and every high
thing that exalteth itself against the knowledge of God, and bringing into captivity
every thought to the obedience of Christ;
6 And having in a readiness to revenge
all disobedience, when your obedience is
fulfilled.
7 Do ye look on things after the outward
appearance? If any man trust to himself
that he is Christ's, let him of himself think
this again, that, as he *is* Christ's, even so
are we Christ's.
8 For though I should boast somewhat more
of our authority, which the Lord hath given
us for edification, and not for your destruction, I should not be ashamed:
9 That I may not seem as if I would terrify
you by letters.
10 For *his* letters, say they, *are* weighty and
powerful; but *his* bodily presence *is* weak,
and *his* speech contemptible.
11 Let such an one think this, that, such
as we are in word by letters when we are
absent, such *will we be* also in deed when
we are present.
12 For we dare not make ourselves of
the number, or compare ourselves with
some that commend themselves: but they
measuring themselves by themselves, and
comparing themselves among themselves,
are not wise.
13 But we will not boast of things without
our measure, but according to the measure
of the rule which God hath distributed to us,
a measure to reach even unto you.
14 For we stretch not ourselves beyond *our*
measure, as though we reached not unto
you: for we are come as far as to you also
in *preaching* the gospel of Christ:
15 Not boasting of things without *our* measure, *that is*, of other men's labours; but
having hope, when your faith is increased,
that we shall be enlarged by you according
to our rule abundantly,
16 To preach the gospel in the *regions*
beyond you, *and* not to boast in another
man's line of things made ready to our hand.
17 But he that glorieth, let him glory in
the Lord.
18 For not he that commendeth himself is
approved, but whom the Lord commendeth.

2 Corinthians 11

1 Would to God ye could bear with me a
little in *my* folly: and indeed bear with me.
2 For I am jealous over you with godly
jealousy: for I have espoused you to one
husband, that I may present *you as* a chaste
virgin to Christ.
3 But I fear, lest by any means, as the serpent beguiled Eve through his subtilty, so
your minds should be corrupted from the
simplicity that is in Christ.
4 For if he that cometh preacheth another
Jesus, whom we have not preached, or *if*
ye receive another spirit, which ye have not
received, or another gospel, which ye have
not accepted, ye might well bear with *him*.
5 For I suppose I was not a whit behind the
very chiefest apostles.
6 But though *I be* rude in speech, yet not
in knowledge; but we have been throughly
made manifest among you in all things.
7 Have I committed an offence in abasing
myself that ye might be exalted, because
I have preached to you the gospel of God
freely?
8 I robbed other churches, taking wages *of*
them, to do you service.
9 And when I was present with you, and
wanted, I was chargeable to no man: for
that which was lacking to me the brethren
which came from Macedonia supplied:
and in all *things* I have kept myself from
being burdensome unto you, and *so* will I
keep *myself*.

10 As the truth of Christ is in me, no man
shall stop me of this boasting in the regions
of Achaia.
11 Wherefore? because I love you not?
God knoweth.
12 But what I do, that I will do, that I may
cut off occasion from them which desire
occasion; that wherein they glory, they may
be found even as we.
13 For such *are* false apostles, deceitful
workers, transforming themselves into the
apostles of Christ.
14 And no marvel; for Satan himself is transformed into an angel of light.
15 Therefore *it is* no great thing if his ministers also be transformed as the ministers of
righteousness; whose end shall be according
to their works.
16 I say again, Let no man think me a fool;
if otherwise, yet as a fool receive me, that
I may boast myself a little.
17 That which I speak, I speak *it* not after
the Lord, but as it were foolishly, in this
confidence of boasting.
18 Seeing that many glory after the flesh, I
will glory also.
19 For ye suffer fools gladly, seeing ye *yourselves* are wise.
20 For ye suffer, if a man bring you into
bondage, if a man devour *you*, if a man take
of you, if a man exalt himself, if a man smite
you on the face.
21 I speak as concerning reproach, as though
we had been weak. Howbeit whereinsoever
any is bold, (I speak foolishly,) I am bold also.
22 Are they Hebrews? so *am* I. Are they
Israelites? so *am* I. Are they the seed of
Abraham? so *am* I.
23 Are they ministers of Christ? (I speak as a
fool) I *am* more; in labours more abundant,
in stripes above measure, in prisons more
frequent, in deaths oft.
24 Of the Jews five times received I forty
stripes save one.
25 Thrice was I beaten with rods, once was
I stoned, thrice I suffered shipwreck, a night
and a day I have been in the deep;
26 *In* journeyings often, *in* perils of waters, *in*
perils of robbers, *in* perils by *mine own* countrymen, *in* perils by the heathen, *in* perils in
the city, *in* perils in the wilderness, *in* perils
in the sea, *in* perils among false brethren;
27 In weariness and painfulness, in watchings often, in hunger and thirst, in fastings
often, in cold and nakedness.
28 Beside those things that are without,
that which cometh upon me daily, the care
of all the churches.
29 Who is weak, and I am not weak? who
is offended, and I burn not?
30 If I must needs glory, I will glory of the
things which concern mine infirmities.
31 The God and Father of our Lord Jesus
Christ, which is blessed for evermore,
knoweth that I lie not.
32 In Damascus the governor under Aretas
the king kept the city of the Damascenes
with a garrison, desirous to apprehend me:
33 And through a window in a basket was I
let down by the wall, and escaped his hands.

2 Corinthians 12

1 It is not expedient for me doubtless to
glory. I will come to visions and revelations
of the Lord.
2 I knew a man in Christ above fourteen
years ago, (whether in the body, I cannot
tell; or whether out of the body, I cannot
tell: God knoweth;) such an one caught up
to the third heaven.
3 And I knew such a man, (whether in the
body, or out of the body, I cannot tell: God
knoweth;)
4 How that he was caught up into paradise,
and heard unspeakable words, which it is
not lawful for a man to utter.
5 Of such an one will I glory: yet of myself I
will not glory, but in mine infirmities.
6 For though I would desire to glory, I shall
not be a fool; for I will say the truth: but
now I forbear, lest any man should think of
me above that which he seeth me *to be*, or
that he heareth of me.
7 And lest I should be exalted above measure through the abundance of the revelations, there was given to me a thorn in the
flesh, the messenger of Satan to buffet me,
lest I should be exalted above measure.
8 For this thing I besought the Lord thrice,
that it might depart from me.
9 And he said unto me, My grace is sufficient
for thee: for my strength is made perfect in
weakness. Most gladly therefore will I rather
glory in my infirmities, that the power of
Christ may rest upon me.
10 Therefore I take pleasure in infirmities, in

reproaches, in necessities, in persecutions,
in distresses for Christ's sake: for when I am
weak, then am I strong.
11 I am become a fool in glorying; ye have
compelled me: for I ought to have been
commended of you: for in nothing am I
behind the very chiefest apostles, though
I be nothing.
12 Truly the signs of an apostle were
wrought among you in all patience, in signs,
and wonders, and mighty deeds.
13 For what is it wherein ye were inferior
to other churches, except *it be* that I myself
was not burdensome to you? forgive me
this wrong.
14 Behold, the third time I am ready to come
to you; and I will not be burdensome to you:
for I seek not yours, but you: for the children
ought not to lay up for the parents, but the
parents for the children.
15 And I will very gladly spend and be spent
for you; though the more abundantly I love
you, the less I be loved.
16 But be it so, I did not burden you: nevertheless, being crafty, I caught you with guile.
17 Did I make a gain of you by any of them
whom I sent unto you?
18 I desired Titus, and with *him* I sent a
brother. Did Titus make a gain of you?
walked we not in the same spirit? *walked
we* not in the same steps?
19 Again, think ye that we excuse ourselves
unto you? we speak before God in Christ:
but *we do* all things, dearly beloved, for
your edifying.
20 For I fear, lest, when I come, I shall not
find you such as I would, and *that* I shall be
found unto you such as ye would not: lest
there be debates, envyings, wraths, strifes,
backbitings, whisperings, swellings, tumults:
21 *And* lest, when I come again, my God
will humble me among you, and *that* I shall
bewail many which have sinned already, and
have not repented of the uncleanness and
fornication and lasciviousness which they
have committed.

2 Corinthians 13

1 This *is* the third *time* I am coming to you.
In the mouth of two or three witnesses shall
every word be established.
2 I told you before, and foretell you, as if I
were present, the second time; and being
absent now I write to them which heretofore have sinned, and to all other, that, if I
come again, I will not spare:
3 Since ye seek a proof of Christ speaking
in me, which to you-ward is not weak, but
is mighty in you.
4 For though he was crucified through weakness, yet he liveth by the power of God. For
we also are weak in him, but we shall live
with him by the power of God toward you.
5 Examine yourselves, whether ye be in the
faith; prove your own selves. Know ye not
your own selves, how that Jesus Christ is in
you, except ye be reprobates?
6 But I trust that ye shall know that we are
not reprobates.
7 Now I pray to God that ye do no evil; not
that we should appear approved, but that
ye should do that which is honest, though
we be as reprobates.
8 For we can do nothing against the truth,
but for the truth.
9 For we are glad, when we are weak, and
ye are strong: and this also we wish, *even*
your perfection.
10 Therefore I write these things being
absent, lest being present I should use
sharpness, according to the power which
the Lord hath given me to edification, and
not to destruction.
11 Finally, brethren, farewell. Be perfect,
be of good comfort, be of one mind, live in
peace; and the God of love and peace shall
be with you.
12 Greet one another with an holy kiss.
13 All the saints salute you.
14 The grace of the Lord Jesus Christ, and
the love of God, and the communion of the
Holy Spirit, *be* with you all. Amen.

The Epistle Of Paul To The

Galatians

Galatians 1

1 Paul, an apostle, (not of men, neither by
man, but by Jesus Christ, and God the Father,
who raised him from the dead;)
2 And all the brethren which are with me,
unto the churches of Galatia:
3 Grace *be* to you and peace from God the
Father, and *from* our Lord Jesus Christ,
4 Who gave himself for our sins, that he
might deliver us from this present evil world,
according to the will of God and our Father:
5 To whom *be* glory for ever and ever. Amen.
6 I marvel that ye are so soon removed from
him that called you into the grace of Christ
unto another gospel:
7 Which is not another; but there be some
that trouble you, and would pervert the
gospel of Christ.
8 But though we, or an angel from heaven,
preach any other gospel unto you than that
which we have preached unto you, let him
be accursed.
9 As we said before, so say I now again, If any
man preach any other gospel unto you than
that ye have received, let him be accursed.
10 For do I now persuade men, or God? or
do I seek to please men? for if I yet pleased
men, I should not be the servant of Christ.
11 But I certify you, brethren, that the
gospel which was preached of me is not
after man.
12 For I neither received it of man, neither
was I taught *it*, but by the revelation of
Jesus Christ.
13 For ye have heard of my conversation
in time past in the Jews' religion, how that
beyond measure I persecuted the church
of God, and wasted it:
14 And profited in the Jews' religion above
many my equals in mine own nation, being
more exceedingly zealous of the traditions
of my fathers.
15 But when it pleased God, who separated
me from my mother's womb, and called *me*
by his grace,
16 To reveal his Son in me, that I might
preach him among the heathen; immediately I conferred not with flesh and blood:
17 Neither went I up to Jerusalem to them
which were apostles before me; but I went
into Arabia, and returned again unto Damascus.
18 Then after three years I went up to Jerusalem to see Peter, and abode with him
fifteen days.
19 But other of the apostles saw I none,
save James the Lord's brother.
20 Now the things which I write unto you,
behold, before God, I lie not.
21 Afterwards I came into the regions of
Syria and Cilicia;
22 And was unknown by face unto the
churches of Judæa which were in Christ:
23 But they had heard only, That he which
persecuted us in times past now preacheth
the faith which once he destroyed.
24 And they glorified God in me.

Galatians 2

1 Then fourteen years after I went up again
to Jerusalem with Barnabas, and took Titus
with *me* also.
2 And I went up by revelation, and communicated unto them that gospel which I
preach among the Gentiles, but privately
to them which were of reputation, lest by
any means I should run, or had run, in vain.
3 But neither Titus, who was with me, being
a Greek, was compelled to be circumcised:
4 And that because of false brethren
unawares brought in, who came in privily to
spy out our liberty which we have in Christ
Jesus, that they might bring us into bondage:
5 To whom we gave place by subjection, no,
not for an hour; that the truth of the gospel
might continue with you.
6 But of these who seemed to be somewhat,
(whatsoever they were, it maketh no matter
to me: God accepteth no man's person:)
for they who seemed *to be somewhat* in
conference added nothing to me:
7 But contrariwise, when they saw that the
gospel of the uncircumcision was committed

unto me, as *the gospel* of the circumcision
was unto Peter;
8 (For he that wrought effectually in Peter
to the apostleship of the circumcision,
the same was mighty in me toward the
Gentiles:)
9 And when James, Cephas, and John, who
seemed to be pillars, perceived the grace
that was given unto me, they gave to me and
Barnabas the right hands of fellowship; that
we *should go* unto the heathen, and they
unto the circumcision.
10 Only *they would* that we should remember the poor; the same which I also was
forward to do.
11 But when Peter was come to Antioch, I
withstood him to the face, because he was
to be blamed.
12 For before that certain came from James,
he did eat with the Gentiles: but when they
were come, he withdrew and separated
himself, fearing them which were of the
circumcision.
13 And the other Jews dissembled likewise
with him; insomuch that Barnabas also was
carried away with their dissimulation.
14 But when I saw that they walked not
uprightly according to the truth of the
gospel, I said unto Peter before *them* all, If
thou, being a Jew, livest after the manner
of Gentiles, and not as do the Jews, why
compellest thou the Gentiles to live as do
the Jews?
15 We *who are* Jews by nature, and not
sinners of the Gentiles,
16 Knowing that a man is not justified by
the works of the law, but by the faith of
Jesus Christ, even we have believed in Jesus
Christ, that we might be justified by the faith
of Christ, and not by the works of the law:
for by the works of the law shall no flesh
be justified.
17 But if, while we seek to be justified by
Christ, we ourselves also are found sinners,
is therefore Christ the minister of sin? God
forbid.
18 For if I build again the things which I
destroyed, I make myself a transgressor.
19 For I through the law am dead to the law,
that I might live unto God.
20 I am crucified with Christ: nevertheless
I live; yet not I, but Christ liveth in me: and
the life which I now live in the flesh I live by
the faith of the Son of God, who loved me,
and gave himself for me.
21 I do not frustrate the grace of God: for if
righteousness *come* by the law, then Christ
is dead in vain.

Galatians 3

1 O foolish Galatians, who hath bewitched
you, that ye should not obey the truth,
before whose eyes Jesus Christ hath been
evidently set forth, crucified among you?
2 This only would I learn of you, Received
ye the Spirit by the works of the law, or by
the hearing of faith?
3 Are ye so foolish? having begun in the
Spirit, are ye now made perfect by the flesh?
4 Have ye suffered so many things in vain?
if *it be* yet in vain.
5 He therefore that ministereth to you the
Spirit, and worketh miracles among you,
doeth he it by the works of the law, or by
the hearing of faith?
6 Even as Abraham believed God, and it was
accounted to him for righteousness.
7 Know ye therefore that they which are of
faith, the same are the children of Abraham.
8 And the scripture, foreseeing that God
would justify the heathen through faith,
preached before the gospel unto Abraham,
saying, In thee shall all nations be blessed.
9 So then they which be of faith are blessed
with faithful Abraham.
10 For as many as are of the works of the
law are under the curse: for it is written,
Cursed *is* every one that continueth not in
all things which are written in the book of
the law to do them.
11 But that no man is justified by the law in
the sight of God, *it is* evident: for, The just
shall live by faith.
12 And the law is not of faith: but, The man
that doeth them shall live in them.
13 Christ hath redeemed us from the curse
of the law, being made a curse for us: for it
is written, Cursed *is* every one that hangeth
on a tree:
14 That the blessing of Abraham might come
on the Gentiles through Jesus Christ; that
we might receive the promise of the Spirit
through faith.
15 Brethren, I speak after the manner of
men; Though *it be* but a man's covenant,

yet *if it be* confirmed, no man disannulleth,
or addeth thereto.
16 Now to Abraham and his seed were the
promises made. He saith not, And to seeds,
as of many; but as of one, And to thy seed,
which is Christ.
17 And this I say, *that* the covenant, that was
confirmed before of God in Christ, the law,
which was four hundred and thirty years
after, cannot disannul, that it should make
the promise of none effect.
18 For if the inheritance *be* of the law, *it*
is no more of promise: but God gave *it* to
Abraham by promise.
19 Wherefore then *serveth* the law? It was
added because of transgressions, till the
seed should come to whom the promise
was made; *and it was* ordained by angels
in the hand of a mediator.
20 Now a mediator is not *a mediator* of one,
but God is one.
21 *Is* the law then against the promises of
God? God forbid: for if there had been a
law given which could have given life, verily
righteousness should have been by the law.
22 But the scripture hath concluded all
under sin, that the promise by faith of Jesus
Christ might be given to them that believe.
23 But before faith came, we were kept
under the law, shut up unto the faith which
should afterwards be revealed.
24 Wherefore the law was our schoolmaster
to bring us unto Christ, that we might be
justified by faith.
25 But after that faith is come, we are no
longer under a schoolmaster.
26 For ye are all the children of God by faith
in Christ Jesus.
27 For as many of you as have been baptized
into Christ have put on Christ.
28 There is neither Jew nor Greek, there is
neither bond nor free, there is neither male
nor female: for ye are all one in Christ Jesus.
29 And if ye *be* Christ's, then are ye Abraham's seed, and heirs according to the
promise.

Galatians 4

1 Now I say, *That* the heir, as long as he is
a child, differeth nothing from a servant,
though he be lord of all;
2 But is under tutors and governors until
the time appointed of the father.
3 Even so we, when we were children, were
in bondage under the elements of the world:
4 But when the fulness of the time was
come, God sent forth his Son, made of a
woman, made under the law,
5 To redeem them that were under the law,
that we might receive the adoption of sons.
6 And because ye are sons, God hath sent
forth the Spirit of his Son into your hearts,
crying, Abba, Father.
7 Wherefore thou art no more a servant,
but a son; and if a son, then an heir of God
through Christ.
8 Howbeit then, when ye knew not God,
ye did service unto them which by nature
are no gods.
9 But now, after that ye have known God,
or rather are known of God, how turn ye
again to the weak and beggarly elements,
whereunto ye desire again to be in bondage?
10 Ye observe days, and months, and times,
and years.
11 I am afraid of you, lest I have bestowed
upon you labour in vain.
12 Brethren, I beseech you, be as I *am;* for I
am as ye *are:* ye have not injured me at all.
13 Ye know how through infirmity of the
flesh I preached the gospel unto you at
the first.
14 And my temptation which was in my flesh
ye despised not, nor rejected; but received
me as an angel of God, *even* as Christ Jesus.
15 Where is then the blessedness ye spake
of? for I bear you record, that, if *it had been*
possible, ye would have plucked out your
own eyes, and have given them to me.
16 Am I therefore become your enemy,
because I tell you the truth?
17 They zealously affect you, *but* not well;
yea, they would exclude you, that ye might
affect them.
18 But *it is* good to be zealously affected
always in *a* good *thing,* and not only when
I am present with you.
19 My little children, of whom I travail in
birth again until Christ be formed in you,
20 I desire to be present with you now, and
to change my voice; for I stand in doubt
of you.
21 Tell me, ye that desire to be under the
law, do ye not hear the law?
22 For it is written, that Abraham had two

sons, the one by a bondmaid, the other by
a freewoman.
23 But he *who was* of the bondwoman was
born after the flesh; but he of the freewoman *was* by promise.
24 Which things are an allegory: for these
are the two covenants; the one from the
mount Sinai, which gendereth to bondage,
which is Agar.
25 For this Agar is mount Sinai in Arabia, and
answereth to Jerusalem which now is, and
is in bondage with her children.
26 But Jerusalem which is above is free,
which is the mother of us all.
27 For it is written, Rejoice, *thou* barren
that bearest not; break forth and cry, thou
that travailest not: for the desolate hath
many more children than she which hath
an husband.
28 Now we, brethren, as Isaac was, are the
children of promise.
29 But as then he that was born after the
flesh persecuted him *that was born* after
the Spirit, even so *it is* now.
30 Nevertheless what saith the scripture?
Cast out the bondwoman and her son: for
the son of the bondwoman shall not be heir
with the son of the freewoman.
31 So then, brethren, we are not children of
the bondwoman, but of the free.

Galatians 5

1 Stand fast therefore in the liberty wherewith Christ hath made us free, and be not
entangled again with the yoke of bondage.
2 Behold, I Paul say unto you, that if ye be
circumcised, Christ shall profit you nothing.
3 For I testify again to every man that is
circumcised, that he is a debtor to do the
whole law.
4 Christ is become of no effect unto you,
whosoever of you are justified by the law;
ye are fallen from grace.
5 For we through the Spirit wait for the hope
of righteousness by faith.
6 For in Jesus Christ neither circumcision
availeth any thing, nor uncircumcision; but
faith which worketh by love.
7 Ye did run well; who did hinder you that
ye should not obey the truth?
8 This persuasion *cometh* not of him that
calleth you.
9 A little leaven leaveneth the whole lump.
10 I have confidence in you through the
Lord, that ye will be none otherwise minded:
but he that troubleth you shall bear his
judgment, whosoever he be.
11 And I, brethren, if I yet preach circumcision, why do I yet suffer persecution? then
is the offence of the cross ceased.
12 I would they were even cut off which
trouble you.
13 For, brethren, ye have been called unto
liberty; only *use* not liberty for an occasion
to the flesh, but by love serve one another.
14 For all the law is fulfilled in one word,
even in this; Thou shalt love thy neighbour
as thyself.
15 But if ye bite and devour one another,
take heed that ye be not consumed one
of another.
16 *This* I say then, Walk in the Spirit, and ye
shall not fulfil the lust of the flesh.
17 For the flesh lusteth against the Spirit,
and the Spirit against the flesh: and these
are contrary the one to the other: so that ye
cannot do the things that ye would.
18 But if ye be led of the Spirit, ye are not
under the law.
19 Now the works of the flesh are manifest, which are *these;* Adultery, fornication,
uncleanness, lasciviousness,
20 Idolatry, witchcraft, hatred, variance,
emulations, wrath, strife, seditions, heresies,
21 Envyings, murders, drunkenness, revellings, and such like: of the which I tell you
before, as I have also told *you* in time past,
that they which do such things shall not
inherit the kingdom of God.
22 But the fruit of the Spirit is love, joy,
peace, longsuffering, gentleness, goodness, faith,
23 Meekness, temperance: against such
there is no law.
24 And they that are Christ's have crucified
the flesh with the affections and lusts.
25 If we live in the Spirit, let us also walk
in the Spirit.
26 Let us not be desirous of vain glory, provoking one another, envying one another.

Galatians 6

1 Brethren, if a man be overtaken in a fault,
ye which are spiritual, restore such an one in

the spirit of meekness; considering thyself,
lest thou also be tempted.
2 Bear ye one another's burdens, and so
fulfil the law of Christ.
3 For if a man think himself to be something,
when he is nothing, he deceiveth himself.
4 But let every man prove his own work,
and then shall he have rejoicing in himself
alone, and not in another.
5 For every man shall bear his own burden.
6 Let him that is taught in the word communicate unto him that teacheth in all
good things.
7 Be not deceived; God is not mocked: for
whatsoever a man soweth, that shall he
also reap.
8 For he that soweth to his flesh shall of the
flesh reap corruption; but he that soweth
to the Spirit shall of the Spirit reap life
everlasting.
9 And let us not be weary in well doing: for
in due season we shall reap, if we faint not.
10 As we have therefore opportunity, let us
do good unto all *men*, especially unto them
who are of the household of faith.
11 Ye see how large a letter I have written
unto you with mine own hand.
12 As many as desire to make a fair shew in
the flesh, they constrain you to be circumcised; only lest they should suffer persecution for the cross of Christ.
13 For neither they themselves who are
circumcised keep the law; but desire to
have you circumcised, that they may glory
in your flesh.
14 But God forbid that I should glory, save
in the cross of our Lord Jesus Christ, by
whom the world is crucified unto me, and
I unto the world.
15 For in Christ Jesus neither circumcision
availeth any thing, nor uncircumcision, but
a new creature.
16 And as many as walk according to this
rule, peace *be* on them, and mercy, and
upon the Israel of God.
17 From henceforth let no man trouble
me: for I bear in my body the marks of the
Lord Jesus.
18 Brethren, the grace of our Lord Jesus
Christ *be* with your spirit. Amen.

The Epistle Of Paul To The

Ephesians

Ephesians 1

1 Paul, an apostle of Jesus Christ by the will
of God, to the saints which are at Ephesus,
and to the faithful in Christ Jesus:
2 Grace *be* to you, and peace, from God
our Father, and *from* the Lord Jesus Christ.
3 Blessed *be* the God and Father of our
Lord Jesus Christ, who hath blessed us with
all spiritual blessings in heavenly *places* in
Christ:
4 According as he hath chosen us in him
before the foundation of the world, that we
should be holy and without blame before
him in love:
5 Having predestinated us unto the adoption of children by Jesus Christ to himself,
according to the good pleasure of his will,
6 To the praise of the glory of his grace,
wherein he hath made us accepted in the
beloved.
7 In whom we have redemption through his
blood, the forgiveness of sins, according to
the riches of his grace;
8 Wherein he hath abounded toward us in
all wisdom and prudence;
9 Having made known unto us the mystery
of his will, according to his good pleasure
which he hath purposed in himself:
10 That in the dispensation of the fulness
of times he might gather together in one all
things in Christ, both which are in heaven,
and which are on earth; *even* in him:
11 In whom also we have obtained an inheritance, being predestinated according to the
purpose of him who worketh all things after
the counsel of his own will:

12 That we should be to the praise of his
glory, who first trusted in Christ.
13 In whom ye also *trusted*, after that ye
heard the word of truth, the gospel of
your salvation: in whom also after that ye
believed, ye were sealed with that holy
Spirit of promise,
14 Which is the earnest of our inheritance
until the redemption of the purchased possession, unto the praise of his glory.
15 Wherefore I also, after I heard of your
faith in the Lord Jesus, and love unto all
the saints,
16 Cease not to give thanks for you, making
mention of you in my prayers;
17 That the God of our Lord Jesus Christ,
the Father of glory, may give unto you
the spirit of wisdom and revelation in the
knowledge of him:
18 The eyes of your understanding being
enlightened; that ye may know what is the
hope of his calling, and what the riches of
the glory of his inheritance in the saints,
19 And what *is* the exceeding greatness of
his power to us-ward who believe, according
to the working of his mighty power,
20 Which he wrought in Christ, when he
raised him from the dead, and set *him* at
his own right hand in the heavenly *places*,
21 Far above all principality, and power, and
might, and dominion, and every name that
is named, not only in this world, but also in
that which is to come:
22 And hath put all *things* under his feet,
and gave him *to be* the head over all *things*
to the church,
23 Which is his body, the fulness of him that
filleth all in all.

Ephesians 2

1 And you *hath he quickened*, who were
dead in trespasses and sins;
2 Wherein in time past ye walked according to the course of this world, according
to the prince of the power of the air, the
spirit that now worketh in the children of
disobedience:
3 Among whom also we all had our conversation in times past in the lusts of our flesh,
fulfilling the desires of the flesh and of the
mind; and were by nature the children of
wrath, even as others.
4 But God, who is rich in mercy, for his great
love wherewith he loved us,
5 Even when we were dead in sins, hath
quickened us together with Christ, (by grace
ye are saved;)
6 And hath raised *us* up together, and made
us sit together in heavenly *places* in Christ
Jesus:
7 That in the ages to come he might shew
the exceeding riches of his grace in *his* kindness toward us through Christ Jesus.
8 For by grace are ye saved through faith;
and that not of yourselves: *it is* the gift of
God:
9 Not of works, lest any man should boast.
10 For we are his workmanship, created in
Christ Jesus unto good works, which God
hath before ordained that we should walk
in them.
11 Wherefore remember, that ye *being*
in time past Gentiles in the flesh, who are
called Uncircumcision by that which is called
the Circumcision in the flesh made by hands;
12 That at that time ye were without Christ,
being aliens from the commonwealth of
Israel, and strangers from the covenants
of promise, having no hope, and without
God in the world:
13 But now in Christ Jesus ye who sometimes were far off are made nigh by the
blood of Christ.
14 For he is our peace, who hath made both
one, and hath broken down the middle wall
of partition *between us;*
15 Having abolished in his flesh the enmity,
even the law of commandments *contained*
in ordinances; for to make in himself of
twain one new man, *so* making peace;
16 And that he might reconcile both unto
God in one body by the cross, having slain
the enmity thereby:
17 And came and preached peace to you
which were afar off, and to them that
were nigh.
18 For through him we both have access by
one Spirit unto the Father.
19 Now therefore ye are no more strangers
and foreigners, but fellowcitizens with the
saints, and of the household of God;
20 And are built upon the foundation of the
apostles and prophets, Jesus Christ himself
being the chief corner *stone;*
21 In whom all the building fitly framed

together groweth unto an holy temple in
the Lord:
22 In whom ye also are builded together
for an habitation of God through the Spirit.

Ephesians 3

1 For this cause I Paul, the prisoner of Jesus
Christ for you Gentiles,
2 If ye have heard of the dispensation of the
grace of God which is given me to you-ward:
3 How that by revelation he made known
unto me the mystery; (as I wrote afore in
few words,
4 Whereby, when ye read, ye may understand my knowledge in the mystery of
Christ)
5 Which in other ages was not made known
unto the sons of men, as it is now revealed
unto his holy apostles and prophets by
the Spirit;
6 That the Gentiles should be fellowheirs,
and of the same body, and partakers of his
promise in Christ by the gospel:
7 Whereof I was made a minister, according
to the gift of the grace of God given unto
me by the effectual working of his power.
8 Unto me, who am less than the least of
all saints, is this grace given, that I should
preach among the Gentiles the unsearchable riches of Christ;
9 And to make all *men* see what *is* the
fellowship of the mystery, which from the
beginning of the world hath been hid in
God, who created all things by Jesus Christ:
10 To the intent that now unto the principalities and powers in heavenly *places*
might be known by the church the manifold
wisdom of God,
11 According to the eternal purpose which
he purposed in Christ Jesus our Lord:
12 In whom we have boldness and access
with confidence by the faith of him.
13 Wherefore I desire that ye faint not at
my tribulations for you, which is your glory.
14 For this cause I bow my knees unto the
Father of our Lord Jesus Christ,
15 Of whom the whole family in heaven and
earth is named,
16 That he would grant you, according to
the riches of his glory, to be strengthened
with might by his Spirit in the inner man;
17 That Christ may dwell in your hearts by
faith; that ye, being rooted and grounded
in love,
18 May be able to comprehend with all
saints what *is* the breadth, and length, and
depth, and height;
19 And to know the love of Christ, which
passeth knowledge, that ye might be filled
with all the fulness of God.
20 Now unto him that is able to do exceeding abundantly above all that we ask or
think, according to the power that worketh in us,
21 Unto him *be* glory in the church by Christ
Jesus throughout all ages, world without
end. Amen.

Ephesians 4

1 I therefore, the prisoner of the Lord,
beseech you that ye walk worthy of the
vocation wherewith ye are called,
2 With all lowliness and meekness, with
longsuffering, forbearing one another in
love;
3 Endeavouring to keep the unity of the
Spirit in the bond of peace.
4 *There is* one body, and one Spirit, even
as ye are called in one hope of your calling;
5 One Lord, one faith, one baptism,
6 One God and Father of all, who *is* above
all, and through all, and in you all.
7 But unto every one of us is given grace
according to the measure of the gift of
Christ.
8 Wherefore he saith, When he ascended
up on high, he led captivity captive, and
gave gifts unto men.
9 (Now that he ascended, what is it but that
he also descended first into the lower parts
of the earth?
10 He that descended is the same also that
ascended up far above all heavens, that he
might fill all things.)
11 And he gave some, apostles; and some,
prophets; and some, evangelists; and some,
pastors and teachers;
12 For the perfecting of the saints, for the
work of the ministry, for the edifying of the
body of Christ:
13 Till we all come in the unity of the faith,
and of the knowledge of the Son of God,
unto a perfect man, unto the measure of
the stature of the fulness of Christ:
14 That we *henceforth* be no more children,

tossed to and fro, and carried about with
every wind of doctrine, by the sleight of
men, *and* cunning craftiness, whereby they
lie in wait to deceive;
15 But speaking the truth in love, may grow
up into him in all things, which is the head,
even Christ:
16 From whom the whole body fitly joined
together and compacted by that which
every joint supplieth, according to the
effectual working in the measure of every
part, maketh increase of the body unto the
edifying of itself in love.
17 This I say therefore, and testify in the
Lord, that ye henceforth walk not as other
Gentiles walk, in the vanity of their mind,
18 Having the understanding darkened,
being alienated from the life of God through
the ignorance that is in them, because of
the blindness of their heart:
19 Who being past feeling have given themselves over unto lasciviousness, to work all
uncleanness with greediness.
20 But ye have not so learned Christ;
21 If so be that ye have heard him, and have
been taught by him, as the truth is in Jesus:
22 That ye put off concerning the former
conversation the old man, which is corrupt
according to the deceitful lusts;
23 And be renewed in the spirit of your
mind;
24 And that ye put on the new man, which
after God is created in righteousness and
true holiness.
25 Wherefore putting away lying, speak
every man truth with his neighbour: for we
are members one of another.
26 Be ye angry, and sin not: let not the sun
go down upon your wrath:
27 Neither give place to the devil.
28 Let him that stole steal no more: but
rather let him labour, working with *his* hands
the thing which is good, that he may have
to give to him that needeth.
29 Let no corrupt communication proceed
out of your mouth, but that which is good
to the use of edifying, that it may minister
grace unto the hearers.
30 And grieve not the holy Spirit of God,
whereby ye are sealed unto the day of
redemption.
31 Let all bitterness, and wrath, and anger,
and clamour, and evil speaking, be put away
from you, with all malice:
32 And be ye kind one to another, tenderhearted, forgiving one another, even as God
for Christ's sake hath forgiven you.

Ephesians 5

1 Be ye therefore followers of God, as dear
children;
2 And walk in love, as Christ also hath loved
us, and hath given himself for us an offering
and a sacrifice to God for a sweetsmelling
savour.
3 But fornication, and all uncleanness, or
covetousness, let it not be once named
among you, as becometh saints;
4 Neither filthiness, nor foolish talking, nor
jesting, which are not convenient: but rather
giving of thanks.
5 For this ye know, that no whoremonger,
nor unclean person, nor covetous man, who
is an idolater, hath any inheritance in the
kingdom of Christ and of God.
6 Let no man deceive you with vain words:
for because of these things cometh the
wrath of God upon the children of disobedience.
7 Be not ye therefore partakers with them.
8 For ye were sometimes darkness, but
now *are ye* light in the Lord: walk as children of light:
9 (For the fruit of the Spirit *is* in all goodness
and righteousness and truth;)
10 Proving what is acceptable unto the Lord.
11 And have no fellowship with the unfruitful works of darkness, but rather reprove
them.
12 For it is a shame even to speak of those
things which are done of them in secret.
13 But all things that are reproved are made
manifest by the light: for whatsoever doth
make manifest is light.
14 Wherefore he saith, Awake thou that
sleepest, and arise from the dead, and Christ
shall give thee light.
15 See then that ye walk circumspectly, not
as fools, but as wise,
16 Redeeming the time, because the days
are evil.
17 Wherefore be ye not unwise, but understanding what the will of the Lord *is*.
18 And be not drunk with wine, wherein is
excess; but be filled with the Spirit;

19 Speaking to yourselves in psalms and
hymns and spiritual songs, singing and
making melody in your heart to the Lord;
20 Giving thanks always for all things unto
God and the Father in the name of our Lord
Jesus Christ;
21 Submitting yourselves one to another in
the fear of God.
22 Wives, submit yourselves unto your own
husbands, as unto the Lord.
23 For the husband is the head of the wife,
even as Christ is the head of the church: and
he is the saviour of the body.
24 Therefore as the church is subject unto
Christ, so *let* the wives *be* to their own husbands in every thing.
25 Husbands, love your wives, even as
Christ also loved the church, and gave
himself for it;
26 That he might sanctify and cleanse it with
the washing of water by the word,
27 That he might present it to himself a
glorious church, not having spot, or wrinkle,
or any such thing; but that it should be holy
and without blemish.
28 So ought men to love their wives as
their own bodies. He that loveth his wife
loveth himself.
29 For no man ever yet hated his own flesh;
but nourisheth and cherisheth it, even as
the Lord the church:
30 For we are members of his body, of his
flesh, and of his bones.
31 For this cause shall a man leave his father
and mother, and shall be joined unto his
wife, and they two shall be one flesh.
32 This is a great mystery: but I speak concerning Christ and the church.
33 Nevertheless let every one of you in particular so love his wife even as himself; and
the wife *see* that she reverence *her* husband.

Ephesians 6

1 Children, obey your parents in the Lord:
for this is right.
2 Honour thy father and mother; (which
is the first commandment with promise;)
3 That it may be well with thee, and thou
mayest live long on the earth.
4 And, ye fathers, provoke not your children
to wrath: but bring them up in the nurture
and admonition of the Lord.
5 Servants, be obedient to them that are
your masters according to the flesh, with
fear and trembling, in singleness of your
heart, as unto Christ;
6 Not with eyeservice, as menpleasers; but
as the servants of Christ, doing the will of
God from the heart;
7 With good will doing service, as to the
Lord, and not to men:
8 Knowing that whatsoever good thing any
man doeth, the same shall he receive of the
Lord, whether *he be* bond or free.
9 And, ye masters, do the same things unto
them, forbearing threatening: knowing that
your Master also is in heaven; neither is
there respect of persons with him.
10 Finally, my brethren, be strong in the
Lord, and in the power of his might.
11 Put on the whole armour of God, that
ye may be able to stand against the wiles
of the devil.
12 For we wrestle not against flesh and
blood, but against principalities, against
powers, against the rulers of the darkness
of this world, against spiritual wickedness
in high *places*.
13 Wherefore take unto you the whole
armour of God, that ye may be able to
withstand in the evil day, and having done
all, to stand.
14 Stand therefore, having your loins girt
about with truth, and having on the breastplate of righteousness;
15 And your feet shod with the preparation
of the gospel of peace;
16 Above all, taking the shield of faith,
wherewith ye shall be able to quench all
the fiery darts of the wicked.
17 And take the helmet of salvation, and
the sword of the Spirit, which is the word
of God:
18 Praying always with all prayer and supplication in the Spirit, and watching thereunto
with all perseverance and supplication for
all saints;
19 And for me, that utterance may be given
unto me, that I may open my mouth boldly,
to make known the mystery of the gospel,
20 For which I am an ambassador in bonds:
that therein I may speak boldly, as I ought
to speak.
21 But that ye also may know my affairs,
and how I do, Tychicus, a beloved brother

and faithful minister in the Lord, shall make
known to you all things:
22 Whom I have sent unto you for the same
purpose, that ye might know our affairs, and
that he might comfort your hearts.
23 Peace *be* to the brethren, and love with
faith, from God the Father and the Lord
Jesus Christ.
24 Grace *be* with all them that love our Lord
Jesus Christ in sincerity. Amen.

The Epistle Of Paul To The

Philippians

Philippians 1

1 Paul and Timotheus, the servants of
Jesus Christ, to all the saints in Christ Jesus
which are at Philippi, with the bishops and
deacons:
2 Grace *be* unto you, and peace, from God
our Father, and *from* the Lord Jesus Christ.
3 I thank my God upon every remembrance
of you,
4 Always in every prayer of mine for you all
making request with joy,
5 For your fellowship in the gospel from the
first day until now;
6 Being confident of this very thing, that
he which hath begun a good work in you
will perform *it* until the day of Jesus Christ:
7 Even as it is meet for me to think this of
you all, because I have you in my heart;
inasmuch as both in my bonds, and in the
defence and confirmation of the gospel, ye
all are partakers of my grace.
8 For God is my record, how greatly I long
after you all in the bowels of Jesus Christ.
9 And this I pray, that your love may abound
yet more and more in knowledge and *in* all
judgment;
10 That ye may approve things that are
excellent; that ye may be sincere and without offence till the day of Christ;
11 Being filled with the fruits of righteousness, which are by Jesus Christ, unto the
glory and praise of God.
12 But I would ye should understand, brethren, that the things *which happened* unto
me have fallen out rather unto the furtherance of the gospel;
13 So that my bonds in Christ are manifest
in all the palace, and in all other *places;*
14 And many of the brethren in the Lord,
waxing confident by my bonds, are much
more bold to speak the word without fear.
15 Some indeed preach Christ even of envy
and strife; and some also of good will:
16 The one preach Christ of contention,
not sincerely, supposing to add affliction
to my bonds:
17 But the other of love, knowing that I am
set for the defence of the gospel.
18 What then? notwithstanding, every way,
whether in pretence, or in truth, Christ is
preached; and I therein do rejoice, yea, and
will rejoice.
19 For I know that this shall turn to my salvation through your prayer, and the supply
of the Spirit of Jesus Christ,
20 According to my earnest expectation and
my hope, that in nothing I shall be ashamed,
but *that* with all boldness, as always, *so* now
also Christ shall be magnified in my body,
whether *it be* by life, or by death.
21 For to me to live *is* Christ, and to die *is*
gain.
22 But if I live in the flesh, this *is* the fruit of
my labour: yet what I shall choose I wot not.
23 For I am in a strait betwixt two, having
a desire to depart, and to be with Christ;
which is far better:
24 Nevertheless to abide in the flesh *is* more
needful for you.
25 And having this confidence, I know that
I shall abide and continue with you all for
your furtherance and joy of faith;
26 That your rejoicing may be more abundant in Jesus Christ for me by my coming
to you again.
27 Only let your conversation be as it
becometh the gospel of Christ: that whether
I come and see you, or else be absent, I may

hear of your affairs, that ye stand fast in one
spirit, with one mind striving together for
the faith of the gospel;
28 And in nothing terrified by your adversaries: which is to them an evident token
of perdition, but to you of salvation, and
that of God.
29 For unto you it is given in the behalf of
Christ, not only to believe on him, but also
to suffer for his sake;
30 Having the same conflict which ye saw
in me, and now hear *to be* in me.

Philippians 2

1 If *there be* therefore any consolation in
Christ, if any comfort of love, if any fellowship of the Spirit, if any bowels and mercies,
2 Fulfil ye my joy, that ye be likeminded,
having the same love, *being* of one accord,
of one mind.
3 *Let* nothing *be done* through strife or
vainglory; but in lowliness of mind let each
esteem other better than themselves.
4 Look not every man on his own things,
but every man also on the things of others.
5 Let this mind be in you, which was also
in Christ Jesus:
6 Who, being in the form of God, thought it
not robbery to be equal with God:
7 But made himself of no reputation, and
took upon him the form of a servant, and
was made in the likeness of men:
8 And being found in fashion as a man, he
humbled himself, and became obedient
unto death, even the death of the cross.
9 Wherefore God also hath highly exalted
him, and given him a name which is above
every name:
10 That at the name of Jesus every knee
should bow, of *things* in heaven, and *things*
in earth, and *things* under the earth;
11 And *that* every tongue should confess
that Jesus Christ *is* Lord, to the glory of God
the Father.
12 Wherefore, my beloved, as ye have
always obeyed, not as in my presence
only, but now much more in my absence,
work out your own salvation with fear and
trembling.
13 For it is God which worketh in you both
to will and to do of *his* good pleasure.
14 Do all things without murmurings and
disputings:
15 That ye may be blameless and harmless,
the sons of God, without rebuke, in the
midst of a crooked and perverse nation,
among whom ye shine as lights in the world;
16 Holding forth the word of life; that I may
rejoice in the day of Christ, that I have not
run in vain, neither laboured in vain.
17 Yea, and if I be offered upon the sacrifice
and service of your faith, I joy, and rejoice
with you all.
18 For the same cause also do ye joy, and
rejoice with me.
19 But I trust in the Lord Jesus to send Timotheus shortly unto you, that I also may be
of good comfort, when I know your state.
20 For I have no man likeminded, who will
naturally care for your state.
21 For all seek their own, not the things
which are Jesus Christ's.
22 But ye know the proof of him, that, as
a son with the father, he hath served with
me in the gospel.
23 Him therefore I hope to send presently,
so soon as I shall see how it will go with me.
24 But I trust in the Lord that I also myself
shall come shortly.
25 Yet I supposed it necessary to send to you
Epaphroditus, my brother, and companion
in labour, and fellowsoldier, but your messenger, and he that ministered to my wants.
26 For he longed after you all, and was full
of heaviness, because that ye had heard
that he had been sick.
27 For indeed he was sick nigh unto death:
but God had mercy on him; and not on him
only, but on me also, lest I should have sorrow upon sorrow.
28 I sent him therefore the more carefully,
that, when ye see him again, ye may rejoice,
and that I may be the less sorrowful.
29 Receive him therefore in the Lord with
all gladness; and hold such in reputation:
30 Because for the work of Christ he was
nigh unto death, not regarding his life, to
supply your lack of service toward me.

Philippians 3

1 Finally, my brethren, rejoice in the Lord. To
write the same things to you, to me indeed
is not grievous, but for you *it is* safe.
2 Beware of dogs, beware of evil workers,
beware of the concision.
3 For we are the circumcision, which wor-

ship God in the spirit, and rejoice in Christ
Jesus, and have no confidence in the flesh.
4 Though I might also have confidence in the
flesh. If any other man thinketh that he hath
whereof he might trust in the flesh, I more:
5 Circumcised the eighth day, of the stock of
Israel, *of* the tribe of Benjamin, an Hebrew
of the Hebrews; as touching the law, a
Pharisee;
6 Concerning zeal, persecuting the church;
touching the righteousness which is in the
law, blameless.
7 But what things were gain to me, those I
counted loss for Christ.
8 Yea doubtless, and I count all things *but*
loss for the excellency of the knowledge
of Christ Jesus my Lord: for whom I have
suffered the loss of all things, and do count
them *but* dung, that I may win Christ,
9 And be found in him, not having mine
own righteousness, which is of the law, but
that which is through the faith of Christ,
the righteousness which is of God by faith:
10 That I may know him, and the power of
his resurrection, and the fellowship of his
sufferings, being made conformable unto
his death;
11 If by any means I might attain unto the
resurrection of the dead.
12 Not as though I had already attained,
either were already perfect: but I follow
after, if that I may apprehend that for which
also I am apprehended of Christ Jesus.
13 Brethren, I count not myself to have
apprehended: but *this* one thing *I do*, for-
getting those things which are behind, and
reaching forth unto those things which are
before,
14 I press toward the mark for the prize of
the high calling of God in Christ Jesus.
15 Let us therefore, as many as be perfect,
be thus minded: and if in any thing ye be
otherwise minded, God shall reveal even
this unto you.
16 Nevertheless, whereto we have already
attained, let us walk by the same rule, let
us mind the same thing.
17 Brethren, be followers together of me,
and mark them which walk so as ye have us
for an ensample.
18 (For many walk, of whom I have told you
often, and now tell you even weeping, *that
they are* the enemies of the cross of Christ:
19 Whose end *is* destruction, whose God *is
their* belly, and *whose* glory *is* in their shame,
who mind earthly things.)
20 For our conversation is in heaven; from
whence also we look for the Saviour, the
Lord Jesus Christ:
21 Who shall change our vile body, that it
may be fashioned like unto his glorious body,
according to the working whereby he is
able even to subdue all things unto himself.

Philippians 4

1 Therefore, my brethren dearly beloved
and longed for, my joy and crown, so stand
fast in the Lord, *my* dearly beloved.
2 I beseech Euodias, and beseech Syntyche,
that they be of the same mind in the Lord.
3 And I intreat thee also, true yokefellow,
help those women which laboured with me
in the gospel, with Clement also, and *with*
other my fellowlabourers, whose names *are*
in the book of life.
4 Rejoice in the Lord alway: *and* again I
say, Rejoice.
5 Let your moderation be known unto all
men. The Lord *is* at hand.
6 Be careful for nothing; but in every thing
by prayer and supplication with thanksgiving
let your requests be made known unto God.
7 And the peace of God, which passeth all
understanding, shall keep your hearts and
minds through Christ Jesus.
8 Finally, brethren, whatsoever things are
true, whatsoever things *are* honest, whatsoever things *are* just, whatsoever things *are*
pure, whatsoever things *are* lovely, whatsoever things *are* of good report; if *there be*
any virtue, and if *there be* any praise, think
on these things.
9 Those things, which ye have both learned,
and received, and heard, and seen in me,
do: and the God of peace shall be with you.
10 But I rejoiced in the Lord greatly, that now
at the last your care of me hath flourished
again; wherein ye were also careful, but ye
lacked opportunity.
11 Not that I speak in respect of want: for
I have learned, in whatsoever state I am,
therewith to be content.
12 I know both how to be abased, and I
know how to abound: every where and
in all things I am instructed both to be full

and to be hungry, both to abound and to
suffer need.
13 I can do all things through Christ which
strengtheneth me.
14 Notwithstanding ye have well done, that
ye did communicate with my affliction.
15 Now ye Philippians know also, that in the
beginning of the gospel, when I departed
from Macedonia, no church communicated
with me as concerning giving and receiving,
but ye only.
16 For even in Thessalonica ye sent once
and again unto my necessity.
17 Not because I desire a gift: but I desire
fruit that may abound to your account.
18 But I have all, and abound: I am full,
having received of Epaphroditus the things
which were sent from you, an odour of a
sweet smell, a sacrifice acceptable, wellpleasing to God.
19 But my God shall supply all your need
according to his riches in glory by Christ
Jesus.
20 Now unto God and our Father *be* glory
for ever and ever. Amen.
21 Salute every saint in Christ Jesus. The
brethren which are with me greet you.
22 All the saints salute you, chiefly they that
are of Cæsar's household.
23 The grace of our Lord Jesus Christ *be*
with you all. Amen.

The Epistle Of Paul To The

Colossians

Colossians 1

1 Paul, an apostle of Jesus Christ by the will
of God, and Timotheus *our* brother,
2 To the saints and faithful brethren in Christ
which are at Colosse: Grace *be* unto you,
and peace, from God our Father and the
Lord Jesus Christ.
3 We give thanks to God and the Father of
our Lord Jesus Christ, praying always for you,
4 Since we heard of your faith in Christ
Jesus, and of the love *which ye have* to all
the saints,
5 For the hope which is laid up for you in
heaven, whereof ye heard before in the
word of the truth of the gospel;
6 Which is come unto you, as *it is* in all the
world; and bringeth forth fruit, as *it doth*
also in you, since the day ye heard *of it*, and
knew the grace of God in truth:
7 As ye also learned of Epaphras our dear
fellowservant, who is for you a faithful
minister of Christ;
8 Who also declared unto us your love in
the Spirit.
9 For this cause we also, since the day we
heard *it*, do not cease to pray for you, and
to desire that ye might be filled with the
knowledge of his will in all wisdom and
spiritual understanding;
10 That ye might walk worthy of the Lord
unto all pleasing, being fruitful in every
good work, and increasing in the knowledge of God;
11 Strengthened with all might, according
to his glorious power, unto all patience and
longsuffering with joyfulness;
12 Giving thanks unto the Father, which
hath made us meet to be partakers of the
inheritance of the saints in light:
13 Who hath delivered us from the power
of darkness, and hath translated *us* into the
kingdom of his dear Son:
14 In whom we have redemption through
his blood, *even* the forgiveness of sins:
15 Who is the image of the invisible God,
the firstborn of every creature:
16 For by him were all things created, that
are in heaven, and that are in earth, visible
and invisible, whether *they be* thrones, or
dominions, or principalities, or powers: all
things were created by him, and for him:
17 And he is before all things, and by him
all things consist.
18 And he is the head of the body, the
church: who is the beginning, the firstborn

from the dead; that in all *things* he might
have the preeminence.
19 For it pleased *the Father* that in him
should all fulness dwell;
20 And, having made peace through the
blood of his cross, by him to reconcile all
things unto himself; by him, *I say*, whether
they be things in earth, or things in heaven.
21 And you, that were sometime alienated
and enemies in *your* mind by wicked works,
yet now hath he reconciled
22 In the body of his flesh through death,
to present you holy and unblameable and
unreproveable in his sight:
23 If ye continue in the faith grounded and
settled, and *be* not moved away from the
hope of the gospel, which ye have heard,
and which was preached to every creature
which is under heaven; whereof I Paul am
made a minister;
24 Who now rejoice in my sufferings for
you, and fill up that which is behind of the
afflictions of Christ in my flesh for his body's
sake, which is the church:
25 Whereof I am made a minister, according
to the dispensation of God which is given to
me for you, to fulfil the word of God;
26 *Even* the mystery which hath been hid
from ages and from generations, but now
is made manifest to his saints:
27 To whom God would make known what
is the riches of the glory of this mystery
among the Gentiles; which is Christ in you,
the hope of glory:
28 Whom we preach, warning every man,
and teaching every man in all wisdom;
that we may present every man perfect in
Christ Jesus:
29 Whereunto I also labour, striving according to his working, which worketh in me
mightily.

Colossians 2

1 For I would that ye knew what great conflict I have for you, and *for* them at Laodicea,
and *for* as many as have not seen my face
in the flesh;
2 That their hearts might be comforted,
being knit together in love, and unto all
riches of the full assurance of understanding, to the acknowledgement of the mystery
of God, and of the Father, and of Christ;
3 In whom are hid all the treasures of wisdom and knowledge.
4 And this I say, lest any man should beguile
you with enticing words.
5 For though I be absent in the flesh, yet am
I with you in the spirit, joying and beholding
your order, and the stedfastness of your
faith in Christ.
6 As ye have therefore received Christ Jesus
the Lord, *so* walk ye in him:
7 Rooted and built up in him, and stablished
in the faith, as ye have been taught, abounding therein with thanksgiving.
8 Beware lest any man spoil you through
philosophy and vain deceit, after the tradition of men, after the rudiments of the
world, and not after Christ.
9 For in him dwelleth all the fulness of the
Godhead bodily.
10 And ye are complete in him, which is the
head of all principality and power:
11 In whom also ye are circumcised with
the circumcision made without hands, in
putting off the body of the sins of the flesh
by the circumcision of Christ:
12 Buried with him in baptism, wherein also
ye are risen with *him* through the faith of
the operation of God, who hath raised him
from the dead.
13 And you, being dead in your sins and
the uncircumcision of your flesh, hath he
quickened together with him, having forgiven you all trespasses;
14 Blotting out the handwriting of ordinances that was against us, which was
contrary to us, and took it out of the way,
nailing it to his cross;
15 *And* having spoiled principalities and
powers, he made a shew of them openly,
triumphing over them in it.
16 Let no man therefore judge you in meat,
or in drink, or in respect of an holyday, or
of the new moon, or of the sabbath *days:*
17 Which are a shadow of things to come;
but the body *is* of Christ.
18 Let no man beguile you of your reward
in a voluntary humility and worshipping of
angels, intruding into those things which
he hath not seen, vainly puffed up by his
fleshly mind,
19 And not holding the Head, from which
all the body by joints and bands having

nourishment ministered, and knit together, increaseth with the increase of God.
20 Wherefore if ye be dead with Christ from the rudiments of the world, why, as though living in the world, are ye subject to ordinances,
21 (Touch not; taste not; handle not;
22 Which all are to perish with the using;) after the commandments and doctrines of men?
23 Which things have indeed a shew of wisdom in will worship, and humility, and neglecting of the body; not in any honour to the satisfying of the flesh.

Colossians 3

1 If ye then be risen with Christ, seek those things which are above, where Christ sitteth on the right hand of God.
2 Set your affection on things above, not on things on the earth.
3 For ye are dead, and your life is hid with Christ in God.
4 When Christ, *who is* our life, shall appear, then shall ye also appear with him in glory.
5 Mortify therefore your members which are upon the earth; fornication, uncleanness, inordinate affection, evil concupiscence, and covetousness, which is idolatry:
6 For which things' sake the wrath of God cometh on the children of disobedience:
7 In the which ye also walked some time, when ye lived in them.
8 But now ye also put off all these; anger, wrath, malice, blasphemy, filthy communication out of your mouth.
9 Lie not one to another, seeing that ye have put off the old man with his deeds;
10 And have put on the new *man*, which is renewed in knowledge after the image of him that created him:
11 Where there is neither Greek nor Jew, circumcision nor uncircumcision, Barbarian, Scythian, bond *nor* free: but Christ *is* all, and in all.
12 Put on therefore, as the elect of God, holy and beloved, bowels of mercies, kindness, humbleness of mind, meekness, longsuffering;
13 Forbearing one another, and forgiving one another, if any man have a quarrel against any: even as Christ forgave you, so also *do* ye.
14 And above all these things *put on* charity, which is the bond of perfectness.
15 And let the peace of God rule in your hearts, to the which also ye are called in one body; and be ye thankful.
16 Let the word of Christ dwell in you richly in all wisdom; teaching and admonishing one another in psalms and hymns and spiritual songs, singing with grace in your hearts to the Lord.
17 And whatsoever ye do in word or deed, *do* all in the name of the Lord Jesus, giving thanks to God and the Father by him.
18 Wives, submit yourselves unto your own husbands, as it is fit in the Lord.
19 Husbands, love *your* wives, and be not bitter against them.
20 Children, obey *your* parents in all things: for this is well pleasing unto the Lord.
21 Fathers, provoke not your children *to anger*, lest they be discouraged.
22 Servants, obey in all things *your* masters according to the flesh; not with eyeservice, as menpleasers; but in singleness of heart, fearing God:
23 And whatsoever ye do, do *it* heartily, as to the Lord, and not unto men;
24 Knowing that of the Lord ye shall receive the reward of the inheritance: for ye serve the Lord Christ.
25 But he that doeth wrong shall receive for the wrong which he hath done: and there is no respect of persons.

Colossians 4

1 Masters, give unto *your* servants that which is just and equal; knowing that ye also have a Master in heaven.
2 Continue in prayer, and watch in the same with thanksgiving;
3 Withal praying also for us, that God would open unto us a door of utterance, to speak the mystery of Christ, for which I am also in bonds:
4 That I may make it manifest, as I ought to speak.
5 Walk in wisdom toward them that are without, redeeming the time.
6 Let your speech *be* alway with grace, seasoned with salt, that ye may know how ye ought to answer every man.
7 All my state shall Tychicus declare unto

you, *who is* a beloved brother, and a faithful minister and fellowservant in the Lord:
8 Whom I have sent unto you for the same
purpose, that he might know your estate,
and comfort your hearts;
9 With Onesimus, a faithful and beloved
brother, who is *one* of you. They shall make
known unto you all things which *are done*
here.
10 Aristarchus my fellowprisoner saluteth
you, and Marcus, sister's son to Barnabas,
(touching whom ye received commandments: if he come unto you, receive him;)
11 And Jesus, which is called Justus, who
are of the circumcision. These only *are my*
fellowworkers unto the kingdom of God,
which have been a comfort unto me.
12 Epaphras, who is *one* of you, a servant of
Christ, saluteth you, always labouring fervently for you in prayers, that ye may stand
perfect and complete in all the will of God.
13 For I bear him record, that he hath a great
zeal for you, and them *that are* in Laodicea,
and them in Hierapolis.
14 Luke, the beloved physician, and Demas,
greet you.
15 Salute the brethren which are in Laodicea, and Nymphas, and the church which
is in his house.
16 And when this epistle is read among you,
cause that it be read also in the church of
the Laodiceans; and that ye likewise read
the *epistle* from Laodicea.
17 And say to Archippus, Take heed to the
ministry which thou hast received in the
Lord, that thou fulfil it.
18 The salutation by the hand of me Paul.
Remember my bonds. Grace *be* with you.
Amen.

The First Epistle Of Paul To The

Thessalonians

1 Thessalonians 1

1 Paul, and Silvanus, and Timotheus, unto
the church of the Thessalonians *which is* in
God the Father and *in* the Lord Jesus Christ:
Grace *be* unto you, and peace, from God our
Father, and the Lord Jesus Christ.
2 We give thanks to God always for you
all, making mention of you in our prayers;
3 Remembering without ceasing your work
of faith, and labour of love, and patience of
hope in our Lord Jesus Christ, in the sight of
God and our Father;
4 Knowing, brethren beloved, your election
of God.
5 For our gospel came not unto you in word
only, but also in power, and in the Holy
Spirit, and in much assurance; as ye know
what manner of men we were among you
for your sake.
6 And ye became followers of us, and of
the Lord, having received the word in much
affliction, with joy of the Holy Spirit:
7 So that ye were ensamples to all that
believe in Macedonia and Achaia.
8 For from you sounded out the word of the
Lord not only in Macedonia and Achaia, but
also in every place your faith to God-ward
is spread abroad; so that we need not to
speak any thing.
9 For they themselves shew of us what
manner of entering in we had unto you, and
how ye turned to God from idols to serve
the living and true God;
10 And to wait for his Son from heaven,
whom he raised from the dead, *even* Jesus,
which delivered us from the wrath to come.

1 Thessalonians 2

1 For yourselves, brethren, know our
entrance in unto you, that it was not in vain:
2 But even after that we had suffered
before, and were shamefully entreated, as
ye know, at Philippi, we were bold in our
God to speak unto you the gospel of God
with much contention.
3 For our exhortation *was* not of deceit, nor
of uncleanness, nor in guile:
4 But as we were allowed of God to be put

in trust with the gospel, even so we speak;
not as pleasing men, but God, which trieth
our hearts.
5 For neither at any time used we flattering
words, as ye know, nor a cloke of covetousness; God *is* witness:
6 Nor of men sought we glory, neither of
you, nor *yet* of others, when we might have
been burdensome, as the apostles of Christ.
7 But we were gentle among you, even as
a nurse cherisheth her children:
8 So being affectionately desirous of you,
we were willing to have imparted unto you,
not the gospel of God only, but also our own
souls, because ye were dear unto us.
9 For ye remember, brethren, our labour
and travail: for labouring night and day,
because we would not be chargeable unto
any of you, we preached unto you the gospel of God.
10 Ye *are* witnesses, and God *also*, how
holily and justly and unblameably we
behaved ourselves among you that believe:
11 As ye know how we exhorted and comforted and charged every one of you, as a
father *doth* his children,
12 That ye would walk worthy of God, who
hath called you unto his kingdom and glory.
13 For this cause also thank we God without ceasing, because, when ye received
the word of God which ye heard of us, ye
received *it* not *as* the word of men, but as it
is in truth, the word of God, which effectually worketh also in you that believe.
14 For ye, brethren, became followers of
the churches of God which in Judæa are in
Christ Jesus: for ye also have suffered like
things of your own countrymen, even as
they *have* of the Jews:
15 Who both killed the Lord Jesus, and their
own prophets, and have persecuted us;
and they please not God, and are contrary
to all men:
16 Forbidding us to speak to the Gentiles
that they might be saved, to fill up their sins
alway: for the wrath is come upon them to
the uttermost.
17 But we, brethren, being taken from you
for a short time in presence, not in heart,
endeavoured the more abundantly to see
your face with great desire.
18 Wherefore we would have come unto
you, even I Paul, once and again; but Satan
hindered us.
19 For what *is* our hope, or joy, or crown of
rejoicing? *Are* not even ye in the presence of
our Lord Jesus Christ at his coming?
20 For ye are our glory and joy.

1 Thessalonians 3

1 Wherefore when we could no longer
forbear, we thought it good to be left at
Athens alone;
2 And sent Timotheus, our brother, and
minister of God, and our fellowlabourer in
the gospel of Christ, to establish you, and to
comfort you concerning your faith:
3 That no man should be moved by these
afflictions: for yourselves know that we are
appointed thereunto.
4 For verily, when we were with you, we told
you before that we should suffer tribulation;
even as it came to pass, and ye know.
5 For this cause, when I could no longer
forbear, I sent to know your faith, lest by
some means the tempter have tempted
you, and our labour be in vain.
6 But now when Timotheus came from you
unto us, and brought us good tidings of your
faith and charity, and that ye have good
remembrance of us always, desiring greatly
to see us, as we also *to see* you:
7 Therefore, brethren, we were comforted
over you in all our affliction and distress by
your faith:
8 For now we live, if ye stand fast in the Lord.
9 For what thanks can we render to God
again for you, for all the joy wherewith we
joy for your sakes before our God;
10 Night and day praying exceedingly that
we might see your face, and might perfect
that which is lacking in your faith?
11 Now God himself and our Father, and our
Lord Jesus Christ, direct our way unto you.
12 And the Lord make you to increase and
abound in love one toward another, and
toward all *men*, even as we *do* toward you:
13 To the end he may stablish your hearts
unblameable in holiness before God, even
our Father, at the coming of our Lord Jesus
Christ with all his saints.

1 Thessalonians 4

1 Furthermore then we beseech you, brethren, and exhort *you* by the Lord Jesus, that

as ye have received of us how ye ought to
walk and to please God, *so* ye would abound
more and more.
2 For ye know what commandments we
gave you by the Lord Jesus.
3 For this is the will of God, *even* your
sanctification, that ye should abstain from
fornication:
4 That every one of you should know how
to possess his vessel in sanctification and
honour;
5 Not in the lust of concupiscence, even as
the Gentiles which know not God:
6 That no *man* go beyond and defraud his
brother in *any* matter: because that the Lord
is the avenger of all such, as we also have
forewarned you and testified.
7 For God hath not called us unto uncleanness, but unto holiness.
8 He therefore that despiseth, despiseth not
man, but God, who hath also given unto us
his holy Spirit.
9 But as touching brotherly love ye need not
that I write unto you: for ye yourselves are
taught of God to love one another.
10 And indeed ye do it toward all the brethren which are in all Macedonia: but we
beseech you, brethren, that ye increase
more and more;
11 And that ye study to be quiet, and to do
your own business, and to work with your
own hands, as we commanded you;
12 That ye may walk honestly toward them
that are without, and *that* ye may have lack
of nothing.
13 But I would not have you to be ignorant, brethren, concerning them which are
asleep, that ye sorrow not, even as others
which have no hope.
14 For if we believe that Jesus died and
rose again, even so them also which sleep
in Jesus will God bring with him.
15 For this we say unto you by the word
of the Lord, that we which are alive *and*
remain unto the coming of the Lord shall
not prevent them which are asleep.
16 For the Lord himself shall descend from
heaven with a shout, with the voice of the
archangel, and with the trump of God: and
the dead in Christ shall rise first:
17 Then we which are alive *and* remain
shall be caught up together with them in
the clouds, to meet the Lord in the air: and
so shall we ever be with the Lord.
18 Wherefore comfort one another with
these words.

1 Thessalonians 5

1 But of the times and the seasons, brethren, ye have no need that I write unto you.
2 For yourselves know perfectly that the day
of the Lord so cometh as a thief in the night.
3 For when they shall say, Peace and safety;
then sudden destruction cometh upon
them, as travail upon a woman with child;
and they shall not escape.
4 But ye, brethren, are not in darkness, that
that day should overtake you as a thief.
5 Ye are all the children of light, and the
children of the day: we are not of the night,
nor of darkness.
6 Therefore let us not sleep, as *do* others;
but let us watch and be sober.
7 For they that sleep sleep in the night;
and they that be drunken are drunken in
the night.
8 But let us, who are of the day, be sober,
putting on the breastplate of faith and love;
and for an helmet, the hope of salvation.
9 For God hath not appointed us to wrath,
but to obtain salvation by our Lord Jesus
Christ,
10 Who died for us, that, whether we wake
or sleep, we should live together with him.
11 Wherefore comfort yourselves together,
and edify one another, even as also ye do.
12 And we beseech you, brethren, to know
them which labour among you, and are over
you in the Lord, and admonish you;
13 And to esteem them very highly in love
for their work's sake. *And* be at peace among
yourselves.
14 Now we exhort you, brethren, warn
them that are unruly, comfort the fee-
bleminded, support the weak, be patient
toward all *men*.
15 See that none render evil for evil unto
any *man;* but ever follow that which is good,
both among yourselves, and to all *men*.
16 Rejoice evermore.
17 Pray without ceasing.
18 In every thing give thanks: for this is the
will of God in Christ Jesus concerning you.
19 Quench not the Spirit.
20 Despise not prophesyings.

21 Prove all things; hold fast that which
is good.
22 Abstain from all appearance of evil.
23 And the very God of peace sanctify you
wholly; and *I pray God* your whole spirit and
soul and body be preserved blameless unto
the coming of our Lord Jesus Christ.
24 Faithful *is* he that calleth you, who also
will do *it*.
25 Brethren, pray for us.
26 Greet all the brethren with an holy kiss.
27 I charge you by the Lord that this epistle
be read unto all the holy brethren.
28 The grace of our Lord Jesus Christ *be*
with you. Amen.

The Second Epistle Of Paul To The

Thessalonians

2 Thessalonians 1

1 Paul, and Silvanus, and Timotheus, unto
the church of the Thessalonians in God our
Father and the Lord Jesus Christ:
2 Grace unto you, and peace, from God our
Father and the Lord Jesus Christ.
3 We are bound to thank God always for
you, brethren, as it is meet, because that
your faith groweth exceedingly, and the
charity of every one of you all toward each
other aboundeth;
4 So that we ourselves glory in you in the
churches of God for your patience and faith
in all your persecutions and tribulations
that ye endure:
5 *Which is* a manifest token of the righteous
judgment of God, that ye may be counted
worthy of the kingdom of God, for which
ye also suffer:
6 Seeing *it is* a righteous thing with God
to recompense tribulation to them that
trouble you;
7 And to you who are troubled rest with us,
when the Lord Jesus shall be revealed from
heaven with his mighty angels,
8 In flaming fire taking vengeance on them
that know not God, and that obey not the
gospel of our Lord Jesus Christ:
9 Who shall be punished with everlasting
destruction from the presence of the Lord,
and from the glory of his power;
10 When he shall come to be glorified in his
saints, and to be admired in all them that
believe (because our testimony among you
was believed) in that day.
11 Wherefore also we pray always for you,
that our God would count you worthy of *this*
calling, and fulfil all the good pleasure of *his*
goodness, and the work of faith with power:
12 That the name of our Lord Jesus Christ
may be glorified in you, and ye in him,
according to the grace of our God and the
Lord Jesus Christ.

2 Thessalonians 2

1 Now we beseech you, brethren, by the
coming of our Lord Jesus Christ, and *by* our
gathering together unto him,
2 That ye be not soon shaken in mind, or
be troubled, neither by spirit, nor by word,
nor by letter as from us, as that the day of
Christ is at hand.
3 Let no man deceive you by any means: for
that day shall not come, except there come
a falling away first, and that man of sin be
revealed, the son of perdition;
4 Who opposeth and exalteth himself above
all that is called God, or that is worshipped;
so that he as God sitteth in the temple of
God, shewing himself that he is God.
5 Remember ye not, that, when I was yet
with you, I told you these things?
6 And now ye know what withholdeth that
he might be revealed in his time.
7 For the mystery of iniquity doth already
work: only he who now letteth *will let*, until
he be taken out of the way.
8 And then shall that Wicked be revealed,
whom the Lord shall consume with the
spirit of his mouth, and shall destroy with
the brightness of his coming:
9 *Even him*, whose coming is after the work-

ing of Satan with all power and signs and
lying wonders,
10 And with all deceivableness of unrighteousness in them that perish; because they
received not the love of the truth, that they
might be saved.
11 And for this cause God shall send them
strong delusion, that they should believe
a lie:
12 That they all might be damned who
believed not the truth, but had pleasure in
unrighteousness.
13 But we are bound to give thanks alway to
God for you, brethren beloved of the Lord,
because God hath from the beginning chosen you to salvation through sanctification
of the Spirit and belief of the truth:
14 Whereunto he called you by our gospel,
to the obtaining of the glory of our Lord
Jesus Christ.
15 Therefore, brethren, stand fast, and hold
the traditions which ye have been taught,
whether by word, or our epistle.
16 Now our Lord Jesus Christ himself, and
God, even our Father, which hath loved us,
and hath given *us* everlasting consolation
and good hope through grace,
17 Comfort your hearts, and stablish you in
every good word and work.

2 Thessalonians 3

1 Finally, brethren, pray for us, that the word
of the Lord may have *free* course, and be
glorified, even as *it is* with you:
2 And that we may be delivered from
unreasonable and wicked men: for all *men*
have not faith.
3 But the Lord is faithful, who shall stablish
you, and keep *you* from evil.
4 And we have confidence in the Lord
touching you, that ye both do and will do
the things which we command you.
5 And the Lord direct your hearts into the
love of God, and into the patient waiting
for Christ.
6 Now we command you, brethren, in
the name of our Lord Jesus Christ, that ye
withdraw yourselves from every brother
that walketh disorderly, and not after the
tradition which he received of us.
7 For yourselves know how ye ought to
follow us: for we behaved not ourselves
disorderly among you;
8 Neither did we eat any man's bread for
nought; but wrought with labour and travail
night and day, that we might not be chargeable to any of you:
9 Not because we have not power, but to
make ourselves an ensample unto you to
follow us.
10 For even when we were with you, this
we commanded you, that if any would not
work, neither should he eat.
11 For we hear that there are some which
walk among you disorderly, working not at
all, but are busybodies.
12 Now them that are such we command
and exhort by our Lord Jesus Christ, that
with quietness they work, and eat their
own bread.
13 But ye, brethren, be not weary in well
doing.
14 And if any man obey not our word by this
epistle, note that man, and have no company with him, that he may be ashamed.
15 Yet count *him* not as an enemy, but
admonish *him* as a brother.
16 Now the Lord of peace himself give you
peace always by all means. The Lord *be*
with you all.
17 The salutation of Paul with mine own
hand, which is the token in every epistle:
so I write.
18 The grace of our Lord Jesus Christ *be*
with you all. Amen.

The First Epistle Of Paul To

Timothy

1 Timothy 1

1 Paul, an apostle of Jesus Christ by the commandment of God our Saviour, and Lord Jesus Christ, *which is* our hope;
2 Unto Timothy, *my* own son in the faith: Grace, mercy, *and* peace, from God our Father and Jesus Christ our Lord.
3 As I besought thee to abide still at Ephesus, when I went into Macedonia, that thou mightest charge some that they teach no other doctrine,
4 Neither give heed to fables and endless genealogies, which minister questions, rather than godly edifying which is in faith: *so do.*
5 Now the end of the commandment is charity out of a pure heart, and *of* a good conscience, and *of* faith unfeigned:
6 From which some having swerved have turned aside unto vain jangling;
7 Desiring to be teachers of the law; understanding neither what they say, nor whereof they affirm.
8 But we know that the law *is* good, if a man use it lawfully;
9 Knowing this, that the law is not made for a righteous man, but for the lawless and disobedient, for the ungodly and for sinners, for unholy and profane, for murderers of fathers and murderers of mothers, for manslayers,
10 For whoremongers, for them that defile themselves with mankind, for menstealers, for liars, for perjured persons, and if there be any other thing that is contrary to sound doctrine;
11 According to the glorious gospel of the blessed God, which was committed to my trust.
12 And I thank Christ Jesus our Lord, who hath enabled me, for that he counted me faithful, putting me into the ministry;
13 Who was before a blasphemer, and a persecutor, and injurious: but I obtained mercy, because I did *it* ignorantly in unbelief.
14 And the grace of our Lord was exceeding abundant with faith and love which is in Christ Jesus.
15 This *is* a faithful saying, and worthy of all acceptation, that Christ Jesus came into the world to save sinners; of whom I am chief.
16 Howbeit for this cause I obtained mercy, that in me first Jesus Christ might shew forth all longsuffering, for a pattern to them which should hereafter believe on him to life everlasting.
17 Now unto the King eternal, immortal, invisible, the only wise God, *be* honour and glory for ever and ever. Amen.
18 This charge I commit unto thee, son Timothy, according to the prophecies which went before on thee, that thou by them mightest war a good warfare;
19 Holding faith, and a good conscience; which some having put away concerning faith have made shipwreck:
20 Of whom is Hymenæus and Alexander; whom I have delivered unto Satan, that they may learn not to blaspheme.

1 Timothy 2

1 I exhort therefore, that, first of all, supplications, prayers, intercessions, *and* giving of thanks, be made for all men;
2 For kings, and *for* all that are in authority; that we may lead a quiet and peaceable life in all godliness and honesty.
3 For this *is* good and acceptable in the sight of God our Saviour;
4 Who will have all men to be saved, and to come unto the knowledge of the truth.
5 For *there is* one God, and one mediator between God and men, the man Christ Jesus;
6 Who gave himself a ransom for all, to be testified in due time.
7 Whereunto I am ordained a preacher, and an apostle, (I speak the truth in Christ, *and* lie not;) a teacher of the Gentiles in faith and verity.
8 I will therefore that men pray every where, lifting up holy hands, without wrath and doubting.

9 In like manner also, that women adorn
themselves in modest apparel, with shame-
facedness and sobriety; not with broided
hair, or gold, or pearls, or costly array;
10 But (which becometh women professing
godliness) with good works.
11 Let the woman learn in silence with all
subjection.
12 But I suffer not a woman to teach, nor
to usurp authority over the man, but to be
in silence.
13 For Adam was first formed, then Eve.
14 And Adam was not deceived, but the
woman being deceived was in the transgression.
15 Notwithstanding she shall be saved in
childbearing, if they continue in faith and
charity and holiness with sobriety.

1 Timothy 3

1 This *is* a true saying, If a man desire the
office of a bishop, he desireth a good work.
2 A bishop then must be blameless, the
husband of one wife, vigilant, sober, of good
behaviour, given to hospitality, apt to teach;
3 Not given to wine, no striker, not greedy
of filthy lucre; but patient, not a brawler,
not covetous;
4 One that ruleth well his own house, having
his children in subjection with all gravity;
5 (For if a man know not how to rule his
own house, how shall he take care of the
church of God?)
6 Not a novice, lest being lifted up with pride
he fall into the condemnation of the devil.
7 Moreover he must have a good report
of them which are without; lest he fall into
reproach and the snare of the devil.
8 Likewise *must* the deacons *be* grave, not
doubletongued, not given to much wine,
not greedy of filthy lucre;
9 Holding the mystery of the faith in a pure
conscience.
10 And let these also first be proved; then
let them use the office of a deacon, being
found blameless.
11 Even so *must their* wives *be* grave, not
slanderers, sober, faithful in all things.
12 Let the deacons be the husbands of one
wife, ruling their children and their own
houses well.
13 For they that have used the office of a
deacon well purchase to themselves a good
degree, and great boldness in the faith
which is in Christ Jesus.
14 These things write I unto thee, hoping
to come unto thee shortly:
15 But if I tarry long, that thou mayest know
how thou oughtest to behave thyself in the
house of God, which is the church of the
living God, the pillar and ground of the truth.
16 And without controversy great is the
mystery of godliness: God was manifest
in the flesh, justified in the Spirit, seen of
angels, preached unto the Gentiles, believed
on in the world, received up into glory.

1 Timothy 4

1 Now the Spirit speaketh expressly, that in
the latter times some shall depart from the
faith, giving heed to seducing spirits, and
doctrines of devils;
2 Speaking lies in hypocrisy; having their
conscience seared with a hot iron;
3 Forbidding to marry, *and commanding* to
abstain from meats, which God hath created
to be received with thanksgiving of them
which believe and know the truth.
4 For every creature of God *is* good, and
nothing to be refused, if it be received with
thanksgiving:
5 For it is sanctified by the word of God
and prayer.
6 If thou put the brethren in remembrance
of these things, thou shalt be a good minister of Jesus Christ, nourished up in the words
of faith and of good doctrine, whereunto
thou hast attained.
7 But refuse profane and old wives' fables,
and exercise thyself *rather* unto godliness.
8 For bodily exercise profiteth little: but
godliness is profitable unto all things, having
promise of the life that now is, and of that
which is to come.
9 This *is* a faithful saying and worthy of all
acceptation.
10 For therefore we both labour and suffer
reproach, because we trust in the living God,
who is the Saviour of all men, specially of
those that believe.
11 These things command and teach.
12 Let no man despise thy youth; but be
thou an example of the believers, in word,
in conversation, in charity, in spirit, in faith,
in purity.

13 Till I come, give attendance to reading, to exhortation, to doctrine.

14 Neglect not the gift that is in thee, which was given thee by prophecy, with the laying on of the hands of the presbytery.

15 Meditate upon these things; give thyself wholly to them; that thy profiting may appear to all.

16 Take heed unto thyself, and unto the doctrine; continue in them: for in doing this thou shalt both save thyself, and them that hear thee.

1 Timothy 5

1 Rebuke not an elder, but intreat *him* as a father; *and* the younger men as brethren;

2 The elder women as mothers; the younger as sisters, with all purity.

3 Honour widows that are widows indeed.

4 But if any widow have children or nephews, let them learn first to shew piety at home, and to requite their parents: for that is good and acceptable before God.

5 Now she that is a widow indeed, and desolate, trusteth in God, and continueth in supplications and prayers night and day.

6 But she that liveth in pleasure is dead while she liveth.

7 And these things give in charge, that they may be blameless.

8 But if any provide not for his own, and specially for those of his own house, he hath denied the faith, and is worse than an infidel.

9 Let not a widow be taken into the number under threescore years old, having been the wife of one man,

10 Well reported of for good works; if she have brought up children, if she have lodged strangers, if she have washed the saints' feet, if she have relieved the afflicted, if she have diligently followed every good work.

11 But the younger widows refuse: for when they have begun to wax wanton against Christ, they will marry;

12 Having damnation, because they have cast off their first faith.

13 And withal they learn *to be* idle, wandering about from house to house; and not only idle, but tattlers also and busybodies, speaking things which they ought not.

14 I will therefore that the younger women marry, bear children, guide the house, give none occasion to the adversary to speak reproachfully.

15 For some are already turned aside after Satan.

16 If any man or woman that believeth have widows, let them relieve them, and let not the church be charged; that it may relieve them that are widows indeed.

17 Let the elders that rule well be counted worthy of double honour, especially they who labour in the word and doctrine.

18 For the scripture saith, Thou shalt not muzzle the ox that treadeth out the corn. And, The labourer *is* worthy of his reward.

19 Against an elder receive not an accusation, but before two or three witnesses.

20 Them that sin rebuke before all, that others also may fear.

21 I charge *thee* before God, and the Lord Jesus Christ, and the elect angels, that thou observe these things without preferring one before another, doing nothing by partiality.

22 Lay hands suddenly on no man, neither be partaker of other men's sins: keep thyself pure.

23 Drink no longer water, but use a little wine for thy stomach's sake and thine often infirmities.

24 Some men's sins are open beforehand, going before to judgment; and some *men* they follow after.

25 Likewise also the good works *of some* are manifest beforehand; and they that are otherwise cannot be hid.

1 Timothy 6

1 Let as many servants as are under the yoke count their own masters worthy of all honour, that the name of God and *his* doctrine be not blasphemed.

2 And they that have believing masters, let them not despise *them*, because they are brethren; but rather do *them* service, because they are faithful and beloved, partakers of the benefit. These things teach and exhort.

3 If any man teach otherwise, and consent not to wholesome words, *even* the words of our Lord Jesus Christ, and to the doctrine which is according to godliness;

4 He is proud, knowing nothing, but doting about questions and strifes of words,

whereof cometh envy, strife, railings, evil
surmisings,
5 Perverse disputings of men of corrupt
minds, and destitute of the truth, supposing
that gain is godliness: from such withdraw
thyself.
6 But godliness with contentment is great
gain.
7 For we brought nothing into *this* world,
and it is certain we can carry nothing out.
8 And having food and raiment let us be
therewith content.
9 But they that will be rich fall into temptation and a snare, and *into* many foolish and
hurtful lusts, which drown men in destruction and perdition.
10 For the love of money is the root of all
evil: which while some coveted after, they
have erred from the faith, and pierced
themselves through with many sorrows.
11 But thou, O man of God, flee these things;
and follow after righteousness, godliness,
faith, love, patience, meekness.
12 Fight the good fight of faith, lay hold on
eternal life, whereunto thou art also called,
and hast professed a good profession before
many witnesses.
13 I give thee charge in the sight of God,
who quickeneth all things, and *before* Christ
Jesus, who before Pontius Pilate witnessed
a good confession;
14 That thou keep *this* commandment without spot, unrebukeable, until the appearing
of our Lord Jesus Christ:
15 Which in his times he shall shew, *who is*
the blessed and only Potentate, the King of
kings, and Lord of lords;
16 Who only hath immortality, dwelling in
the light which no man can approach unto;
whom no man hath seen, nor can see: to
whom *be* honour and power everlasting.
Amen.
17 Charge them that are rich in this world,
that they be not highminded, nor trust in
uncertain riches, but in the living God, who
giveth us richly all things to enjoy;
18 That they do good, that they be rich in
good works, ready to distribute, willing to
communicate;
19 Laying up in store for themselves a good
foundation against the time to come, that
they may lay hold on eternal life.
20 O Timothy, keep that which is committed to thy trust, avoiding profane *and* vain
babblings, and oppositions of science falsely
so called:
21 Which some professing have erred concerning the faith. Grace *be* with thee. Amen.

The Second Epistle Of Paul To

Timothy

2 Timothy 1

1 Paul, an apostle of Jesus Christ by the will
of God, according to the promise of life
which is in Christ Jesus,
2 To Timothy, *my* dearly beloved son: Grace,
mercy, *and* peace, from God the Father and
Christ Jesus our Lord.
3 I thank God, whom I serve from *my* forefathers with pure conscience, that without
ceasing I have remembrance of thee in my
prayers night and day;
4 Greatly desiring to see thee, being mindful
of thy tears, that I may be filled with joy;
5 When I call to remembrance the unfeigned
faith that is in thee, which dwelt first in thy
grandmother Lois, and thy mother Eunice;
and I am persuaded that in thee also.
6 Wherefore I put thee in remembrance that
thou stir up the gift of God, which is in thee
by the putting on of my hands.
7 For God hath not given us the spirit of
fear; but of power, and of love, and of a
sound mind.
8 Be not thou therefore ashamed of the testimony of our Lord, nor of me his prisoner:
but be thou partaker of the afflictions of
the gospel according to the power of God;
9 Who hath saved us, and called *us* with an
holy calling, not according to our works, but
according to his own purpose and grace,

which was given us in Christ Jesus before
the world began,
10 But is now made manifest by the appearing of our Saviour Jesus Christ, who hath
abolished death, and hath brought life and
immortality to light through the gospel:
11 Whereunto I am appointed a preacher,
and an apostle, and a teacher of the Gentiles.
12 For the which cause I also suffer these
things: nevertheless I am not ashamed: for
I know whom I have believed, and am persuaded that he is able to keep that which I
have committed unto him against that day.
13 Hold fast the form of sound words, which
thou hast heard of me, in faith and love
which is in Christ Jesus.
14 That good thing which was committed
unto thee keep by the Holy Spirit which
dwelleth in us.
15 This thou knowest, that all they which are
in Asia be turned away from me; of whom
are Phygellus and Hermogenes.
16 The Lord give mercy unto the house of
Onesiphorus; for he oft refreshed me, and
was not ashamed of my chain:
17 But, when he was in Rome, he sought me
out very diligently, and found *me*.
18 The Lord grant unto him that he may
find mercy of the Lord in that day: and in
how many things he ministered unto me at
Ephesus, thou knowest very well.

2 Timothy 2

1 Thou therefore, my son, be strong in the
grace that is in Christ Jesus.
2 And the things that thou hast heard of me
among many witnesses, the same commit
thou to faithful men, who shall be able to
teach others also.
3 Thou therefore endure hardness, as a
good soldier of Jesus Christ.
4 No man that warreth entangleth himself
with the affairs of *this* life; that he may
please him who hath chosen him to be a
soldier.
5 And if a man also strive for masteries, *yet*
is he not crowned, except he strive lawfully.
6 The husbandman that laboureth must be
first partaker of the fruits.
7 Consider what I say; and the Lord give
thee understanding in all things.
8 Remember that Jesus Christ of the seed of
David was raised from the dead according
to my gospel:
9 Wherein I suffer trouble, as an evil doer,
even unto bonds; but the word of God is
not bound.
10 Therefore I endure all things for the
elect's sakes, that they may also obtain
the salvation which is in Christ Jesus with
eternal glory.
11 *It is* a faithful saying: For if we be dead
with *him*, we shall also live with *him:*
12 If we suffer, we shall also reign with *him:*
if we deny *him*, he also will deny us:
13 If we believe not, *yet* he abideth faithful:
he cannot deny himself.
14 Of these things put *them* in remembrance, charging *them* before the Lord that
they strive not about words to no profit, *but*
to the subverting of the hearers.
15 Study to shew thyself approved unto
God, a workman that needeth not to be
ashamed, rightly dividing the word of truth.
16 But shun profane *and* vain babblings: for
they will increase unto more ungodliness.
17 And their word will eat as doth a canker:
of whom is Hymenæus and Philetus;
18 Who concerning the truth have erred,
saying that the resurrection is past already;
and overthrow the faith of some.
19 Nevertheless the foundation of God
standeth sure, having this seal, The Lord
knoweth them that are his. And, Let every
one that nameth the name of Christ depart
from iniquity.
20 But in a great house there are not only
vessels of gold and of silver, but also of
wood and of earth; and some to honour,
and some to dishonour.
21 If a man therefore purge himself from
these, he shall be a vessel unto honour,
sanctified, and meet for the master's use,
and prepared unto every good work.
22 Flee also youthful lusts: but follow righteousness, faith, charity, peace, with them
that call on the Lord out of a pure heart.
23 But foolish and unlearned questions
avoid, knowing that they do gender strifes.
24 And the servant of the Lord must not
strive; but be gentle unto all *men*, apt to
teach, patient,
25 In meekness instructing those that
oppose themselves; if God peradventure

will give them repentance to the acknowledging of the truth;
26 And *that* they may recover themselves
out of the snare of the devil, who are taken
captive by him at his will.

2 Timothy 3

1 This know also, that in the last days per-
ilous times shall come.
2 For men shall be lovers of their own selves,
covetous, boasters, proud, blasphemers,
disobedient to parents, unthankful, unholy,
3 Without natural affection, trucebreakers,
false accusers, incontinent, fierce, despisers
of those that are good,
4 Traitors, heady, highminded, lovers of
pleasures more than lovers of God;
5 Having a form of godliness, but denying
the power thereof: from such turn away.
6 For of this sort are they which creep into
houses, and lead captive silly women laden
with sins, led away with divers lusts,
7 Ever learning, and never able to come to
the knowledge of the truth.
8 Now as Jannes and Jambres withstood
Moses, so do these also resist the truth:
men of corrupt minds, reprobate concerning the faith.
9 But they shall proceed no further: for
their folly shall be manifest unto all *men*,
as theirs also was.
10 But thou hast fully known my doctrine,
manner of life, purpose, faith, longsuffering,
charity, patience,
11 Persecutions, afflictions, which came
unto me at Antioch, at Iconium, at Lystra;
what persecutions I endured: but out of
them all the Lord delivered me.
12 Yea, and all that will live godly in Christ
Jesus shall suffer persecution.
13 But evil men and seducers shall wax
worse and worse, deceiving, and being
deceived.
14 But continue thou in the things which
thou hast learned and hast been assured of,
knowing of whom thou hast learned *them;*
15 And that from a child thou hast known
the holy scriptures, which are able to make
thee wise unto salvation through faith which
is in Christ Jesus.
16 All scripture *is* given by inspiration of God,
and *is* profitable for doctrine, for reproof, for
correction, for instruction in righteousness:
17 That the man of God may be perfect,
throughly furnished unto all good works.

2 Timothy 4

1 I charge *thee* therefore before God, and
the Lord Jesus Christ, who shall judge the
quick and the dead at his appearing and
his kingdom;
2 Preach the word; be instant in season, out
of season; reprove, rebuke, exhort with all
longsuffering and doctrine.
3 For the time will come when they will not
endure sound doctrine; but after their own
lusts shall they heap to themselves teachers,
having itching ears;
4 And they shall turn away *their* ears from
the truth, and shall be turned unto fables.
5 But watch thou in all things, endure afflictions, do the work of an evangelist, make
full proof of thy ministry.
6 For I am now ready to be offered, and the
time of my departure is at hand.
7 I have fought a good fight, I have finished
my course, I have kept the faith:
8 Henceforth there is laid up for me a crown
of righteousness, which the Lord, the righteous judge, shall give me at that day: and
not to me only, but unto all them also that
love his appearing.
9 Do thy diligence to come shortly unto me:
10 For Demas hath forsaken me, having
loved this present world, and is departed
unto Thessalonica; Crescens to Galatia, Titus
unto Dalmatia.
11 Only Luke is with me. Take Mark, and
bring him with thee: for he is profitable to
me for the ministry.
12 And Tychicus have I sent to Ephesus.
13 The cloke that I left at Troas with Carpus,
when thou comest, bring *with thee*, and
the books, *but* especially the parchments.
14 Alexander the coppersmith did me
much evil: the Lord reward him according
to his works:
15 Of whom be thou ware also; for he hath
greatly withstood our words.
16 At my first answer no man stood with
me, but all *men* forsook me: *I pray God* that
it may not be laid to their charge.
17 Notwithstanding the Lord stood with
me, and strengthened me; that by me the
preaching might be fully known, and *that* all

the Gentiles might hear: and I was delivered
out of the mouth of the lion.
18 And the Lord shall deliver me from every
evil work, and will preserve *me* unto his
heavenly kingdom: to whom *be* glory for
ever and ever. Amen.
19 Salute Prisca and Aquila, and the household of Onesiphorus.
20 Erastus abode at Corinth: but Trophimus
have I left at Miletum sick.
21 Do thy diligence to come before winter.
Eubulus greeteth thee, and Pudens, and
Linus, and Claudia, and all the brethren.
22 The Lord Jesus Christ *be* with thy spirit.
Grace *be* with you. Amen.

The Epistle Of Paul To

Titus

Titus 1

1 Paul, a servant of God, and an apostle of
Jesus Christ, according to the faith of God's
elect, and the acknowledging of the truth
which is after godliness;
2 In hope of eternal life, which God, that cannot lie, promised before the world began;
3 But hath in due times manifested his word
through preaching, which is committed unto
me according to the commandment of God
our Saviour;
4 To Titus, *mine* own son after the common
faith: Grace, mercy, *and* peace, from God
the Father and the Lord Jesus Christ our
Saviour.
5 For this cause left I thee in Crete, that thou
shouldest set in order the things that are
wanting, and ordain elders in every city, as
I had appointed thee:
6 If any be blameless, the husband of one
wife, having faithful children not accused
of riot or unruly.
7 For a bishop must be blameless, as the
steward of God; not selfwilled, not soon
angry, not given to wine, no striker, not
given to filthy lucre;
8 But a lover of hospitality, a lover of good
men, sober, just, holy, temperate;
9 Holding fast the faithful word as he hath
been taught, that he may be able by sound
doctrine both to exhort and to convince
the gainsayers.
10 For there are many unruly and vain
talkers and deceivers, specially they of the
circumcision:
11 Whose mouths must be stopped, who
subvert whole houses, teaching things which
they ought not, for filthy lucre's sake.
12 One of themselves, *even* a prophet of
their own, said, The Cretians *are* alway liars,
evil beasts, slow bellies.
13 This witness is true. Wherefore rebuke
them sharply, that they may be sound in
the faith;
14 Not giving heed to Jewish fables, and
commandments of men, that turn from
the truth.
15 Unto the pure all things *are* pure: but
unto them that are defiled and unbelieving
is nothing pure; but even their mind and
conscience is defiled.
16 They profess that they know God; but
in works they deny *him*, being abominable,
and disobedient, and unto every good work
reprobate.

Titus 2

1 But speak thou the things which become
sound doctrine:
2 That the aged men be sober, grave, temperate, sound in faith, in charity, in patience.
3 The aged women likewise, that *they be* in
behaviour as becometh holiness, not false
accusers, not given to much wine, teachers
of good things;
4 That they may teach the young women
to be sober, to love their husbands, to love
their children,
5 *To be* discreet, chaste, keepers at home,
good, obedient to their own husbands, that
the word of God be not blasphemed.

6 Young men likewise exhort to be sober minded.

7 In all things shewing thyself a pattern of good works: in doctrine *shewing* uncorruptness, gravity, sincerity,

8 Sound speech, that cannot be condemned; that he that is of the contrary part may be ashamed, having no evil thing to say of you.

9 *Exhort* servants to be obedient unto their own masters, *and* to please *them* well in all *things;* not answering again;

10 Not purloining, but shewing all good fidelity; that they may adorn the doctrine of God our Saviour in all things.

11 For the grace of God that bringeth salvation hath appeared to all men,

12 Teaching us that, denying ungodliness and worldly lusts, we should live soberly, righteously, and godly, in this present world;

13 Looking for that blessed hope, and the glorious appearing of the great God and our Saviour Jesus Christ;

14 Who gave himself for us, that he might redeem us from all iniquity, and purify unto himself a peculiar people, zealous of good works.

15 These things speak, and exhort, and rebuke with all authority. Let no man despise thee.

Titus 3

1 Put them in mind to be subject to principalities and powers, to obey magistrates, to be ready to every good work,

2 To speak evil of no man, to be no brawlers, *but* gentle, shewing all meekness unto all men.

3 For we ourselves also were sometimes foolish, disobedient, deceived, serving divers lusts and pleasures, living in malice and envy, hateful, *and* hating one another.

4 But after that the kindness and love of God our Saviour toward man appeared,

5 Not by works of righteousness which we have done, but according to his mercy he saved us, by the washing of regeneration, and renewing of the Holy Spirit;

6 Which he shed on us abundantly through Jesus Christ our Saviour;

7 That being justified by his grace, we should be made heirs according to the hope of eternal life.

8 *This is* a faithful saying, and these things I will that thou affirm constantly, that they which have believed in God might be careful to maintain good works. These things are good and profitable unto men.

9 But avoid foolish questions, and genealogies, and contentions, and strivings about the law; for they are unprofitable and vain.

10 A man that is an heretick after the first and second admonition reject;

11 Knowing that he that is such is subverted, and sinneth, being condemned of himself.

12 When I shall send Artemas unto thee, or Tychicus, be diligent to come unto me to Nicopolis: for I have determined there to winter.

13 Bring Zenas the lawyer and Apollos on their journey diligently, that nothing be wanting unto them.

14 And let ours also learn to maintain good works for necessary uses, that they be not unfruitful.

15 All that are with me salute thee. Greet them that love us in the faith. Grace *be* with you all. Amen.

The Epistle Of Paul To

Philemon

Philemon 1

1 Paul, a prisoner of Jesus Christ, and Timothy *our* brother, unto Philemon our dearly beloved, and fellowlabourer,

2 And to *our* beloved Apphia, and Archippus our fellowsoldier, and to the church in thy house:

3 Grace to you, and peace, from God our Father and the Lord Jesus Christ.

4 I thank my God, making mention of thee always in my prayers,

5 Hearing of thy love and faith, which thou hast toward the Lord Jesus, and toward all saints;

6 That the communication of thy faith may become effectual by the acknowledging of every good thing which is in you in Christ Jesus.

7 For we have great joy and consolation in thy love, because the bowels of the saints are refreshed by thee, brother.

8 Wherefore, though I might be much bold in Christ to enjoin thee that which is convenient,

9 Yet for love's sake I rather beseech *thee*, being such an one as Paul the aged, and now also a prisoner of Jesus Christ.

10 I beseech thee for my son Onesimus, whom I have begotten in my bonds:

11 Which in time past was to thee unprofitable, but now profitable to thee and to me:

12 Whom I have sent again: thou therefore receive him, that is, mine own bowels:

13 Whom I would have retained with me, that in thy stead he might have ministered unto me in the bonds of the gospel:

14 But without thy mind would I do nothing; that thy benefit should not be as it were of necessity, but willingly.

15 For perhaps he therefore departed for a season, that thou shouldest receive him for ever;

16 Not now as a servant, but above a servant, a brother beloved, specially to me, but how much more unto thee, both in the flesh, and in the Lord?

17 If thou count me therefore a partner, receive him as myself.

18 If he hath wronged thee, or oweth *thee* ought, put that on mine account;

19 I Paul have written *it* with mine own hand, I will repay *it:* albeit I do not say to thee how thou owest unto me even thine own self besides.

20 Yea, brother, let me have joy of thee in the Lord: refresh my bowels in the Lord.

21 Having confidence in thy obedience I wrote unto thee, knowing that thou wilt also do more than I say.

22 But withal prepare me also a lodging: for I trust that through your prayers I shall be given unto you.

23 There salute thee Epaphras, my fellowprisoner in Christ Jesus;

24 Marcus, Aristarchus, Demas, Lucas, my fellowlabourers.

25 The grace of our Lord Jesus Christ *be* with your spirit. Amen.

The Epistle Of Paul To The

Hebrews

Hebrews 1

1 God, who at sundry times and in divers manners spake in time past unto the fathers by the prophets,

2 Hath in these last days spoken unto us by *his* Son, whom he hath appointed heir of all things, by whom also he made the worlds;

3 Who being the brightness of *his* glory, and the express image of his person, and upholding all things by the word of his power, when he had by himself purged our sins, sat down on the right hand of the Majesty on high;

4 Being made so much better than the angels, as he hath by inheritance obtained a more excellent name than they.

5 For unto which of the angels said he at any time, Thou art my Son, this day have I begotten thee? And again, I will be to him a Father, and he shall be to me a Son?

6 And again, when he bringeth in the firstbegotten into the world, he saith, And let all the angels of God worship him.

7 And of the angels he saith, Who maketh his angels spirits, and his ministers a flame of fire.

8 But unto the Son *he saith*, Thy throne, O

God, *is* for ever and ever: a sceptre of righteousness *is* the sceptre of thy kingdom.
9 Thou hast loved righteousness, and hated
iniquity; therefore God, *even* thy God, hath anointed thee with the oil of gladness above thy fellows.
10 And, Thou, Lord, in the beginning hast
laid the foundation of the earth; and the heavens are the works of thine hands:
11 They shall perish; but thou remainest;
and they all shall wax old as doth a garment;
12 And as a vesture shalt thou fold them up,
and they shall be changed: but thou art the same, and thy years shall not fail.
13 But to which of the angels said he at any
time, Sit on my right hand, until I make thine enemies thy footstool?
14 Are they not all ministering spirits, sent
forth to minister for them who shall be heirs of salvation?

Hebrews 2

1 Therefore we ought to give the more
earnest heed to the things which we have heard, lest at any time we should let *them* slip.
2 For if the word spoken by angels was sted-
fast, and every transgression and disobedience received a just recompence of reward;
3 How shall we escape, if we neglect so
great salvation; which at the first began to be spoken by the Lord, and was confirmed unto us by them that heard *him;*
4 God also bearing *them* witness, both with
signs and wonders, and with divers miracles, and gifts of the Holy Spirit, according to his own will?
5 For unto the angels hath he not put in
subjection the world to come, whereof we speak.
6 But one in a certain place testified, saying,
What is man, that thou art mindful of him? or the son of man, that thou visitest him?
7 Thou madest him a little lower than the
angels; thou crownedst him with glory and honour, and didst set him over the works of thy hands:
8 Thou hast put all things in subjection under
his feet. For in that he put all in subjection under him, he left nothing *that is* not put under him. But now we see not yet all things put under him.
9 But we see Jesus, who was made a little
lower than the angels for the suffering of death, crowned with glory and honour; that he by the grace of God should taste death for every man.
10 For it became him, for whom *are* all
things, and by whom *are* all things, in bringing many sons unto glory, to make the captain of their salvation perfect through sufferings.
11 For both he that sanctifieth and they who
are sanctified *are* all of one: for which cause he is not ashamed to call them brethren,
12 Saying, I will declare thy name unto my
brethren, in the midst of the church will I sing praise unto thee.
13 And again, I will put my trust in him. And
again, Behold I and the children which God hath given me.
14 Forasmuch then as the children are par-
takers of flesh and blood, he also himself likewise took part of the same; that through death he might destroy him that had the power of death, that is, the devil;
15 And deliver them who through fear
of death were all their lifetime subject to bondage.
16 For verily he took not on *him the nature*
of angels; but he took on *him* the seed of Abraham.
17 Wherefore in all things it behoved him
to be made like unto *his* brethren, that he might be a merciful and faithful high priest in things *pertaining* to God, to make reconciliation for the sins of the people.
18 For in that he himself hath suffered being
tempted, he is able to succour them that are tempted.

Hebrews 3

1 Wherefore, holy brethren, partakers of the
heavenly calling, consider the Apostle and High Priest of our profession, Christ Jesus;
2 Who was faithful to him that appointed
him, as also Moses *was faithful* in all his house.
3 For this *man* was counted worthy of more
glory than Moses, inasmuch as he who hath builded the house hath more honour than the house.
4 For every house is builded by some *man;*
but he that built all things *is* God.
5 And Moses verily *was* faithful in all his

house, as a servant, for a testimony of those things which were to be spoken after;

6 But Christ as a son over his own house; whose house are we, if we hold fast the confidence and the rejoicing of the hope firm unto the end.

7 Wherefore (as the Holy Spirit saith, To day if ye will hear his voice,

8 Harden not your hearts, as in the provocation, in the day of temptation in the wilderness:

9 When your fathers tempted me, proved me, and saw my works forty years.

10 Wherefore I was grieved with that generation, and said, They do alway err in *their* heart; and they have not known my ways.

11 So I sware in my wrath, They shall not enter into my rest.)

12 Take heed, brethren, lest there be in any of you an evil heart of unbelief, in departing from the living God.

13 But exhort one another daily, while it is called To day; lest any of you be hardened through the deceitfulness of sin.

14 For we are made partakers of Christ, if we hold the beginning of our confidence stedfast unto the end;

15 While it is said, To day if ye will hear his voice, harden not your hearts, as in the provocation.

16 For some, when they had heard, did provoke: howbeit not all that came out of Egypt by Moses.

17 But with whom was he grieved forty years? *was it* not with them that had sinned, whose carcases fell in the wilderness?

18 And to whom sware he that they should not enter into his rest, but to them that believed not?

19 So we see that they could not enter in because of unbelief.

Hebrews 4

1 Let us therefore fear, lest, a promise being left *us* of entering into his rest, any of you should seem to come short of it.

2 For unto us was the gospel preached, as well as unto them: but the word preached did not profit them, not being mixed with faith in them that heard *it*.

3 For we which have believed do enter into rest, as he said, As I have sworn in my wrath, if they shall enter into my rest: although the works were finished from the foundation of the world.

4 For he spake in a certain place of the seventh *day* on this wise, And God did rest the seventh day from all his works.

5 And in this *place* again, If they shall enter into my rest.

6 Seeing therefore it remaineth that some must enter therein, and they to whom it was first preached entered not in because of unbelief:

7 Again, he limiteth a certain day, saying in David, To day, after so long a time; as it is said, To day if ye will hear his voice, harden not your hearts.

8 For if Jesus had given them rest, then would he not afterward have spoken of another day.

9 There remaineth therefore a rest to the people of God.

10 For he that is entered into his rest, he also hath ceased from his own works, as God *did* from his.

11 Let us labour therefore to enter into that rest, lest any man fall after the same example of unbelief.

12 For the word of God *is* quick, and powerful, and sharper than any twoedged sword, piercing even to the dividing asunder of soul and spirit, and of the joints and marrow, and *is* a discerner of the thoughts and intents of the heart.

13 Neither is there any creature that is not manifest in his sight: but all things *are* naked and opened unto the eyes of him with whom we have to do.

14 Seeing then that we have a great high priest, that is passed into the heavens, Jesus the Son of God, let us hold fast *our* profession.

15 For we have not an high priest which cannot be touched with the feeling of our infirmities; but was in all points tempted like as *we are, yet* without sin.

16 Let us therefore come boldly unto the throne of grace, that we may obtain mercy, and find grace to help in time of need.

Hebrews 5

1 For every high priest taken from among men is ordained for men in things *pertaining* to God, that he may offer both gifts and sacrifices for sins:

2 Who can have compassion on the ignorant, and on them that are out of the way;
for that he himself also is compassed with
infirmity.
3 And by reason hereof he ought, as for the
people, so also for himself, to offer for sins.
4 And no man taketh this honour unto
himself, but he that is called of God, as
was Aaron.
5 So also Christ glorified not himself to
be made an high priest; but he that said
unto him, Thou art my Son, to day have I
begotten thee.
6 As he saith also in another *place*, Thou
art a priest for ever after the order of
Melchisedec.
7 Who in the days of his flesh, when he had
offered up prayers and supplications with
strong crying and tears unto him that was
able to save him from death, and was heard
in that he feared;
8 Though he were a Son, yet learned he
obedience by the things which he suffered;
9 And being made perfect, he became the
author of eternal salvation unto all them
that obey him;
10 Called of God an high priest after the
order of Melchisedec.
11 Of whom we have many things to say,
and hard to be uttered, seeing ye are dull
of hearing.
12 For when for the time ye ought to be
teachers, ye have need that one teach you
again which *be* the first principles of the
oracles of God; and are become such as
have need of milk, and not of strong meat.
13 For every one that useth milk *is* unskil-
ful in the word of righteousness: for he is
a babe.
14 But strong meat belongeth to them that
are of full age, *even* those who by reason of
use have their senses exercised to discern
both good and evil.

Hebrews 6

1 Therefore leaving the principles of the
doctrine of Christ, let us go on unto perfection; not laying again the foundation of
repentance from dead works, and of faith
toward God,
2 Of the doctrine of baptisms, and of laying
on of hands, and of resurrection of the dead,
and of eternal judgment.
3 And this will we do, if God permit.
4 For *it is* impossible for those who were
once enlightened, and have tasted of the
heavenly gift, and were made partakers of
the Holy Spirit,
5 And have tasted the good word of God,
and the powers of the world to come,
6 If they shall fall away, to renew them
again unto repentance; seeing they crucify
to themselves the Son of God afresh, and
put *him* to an open shame.
7 For the earth which drinketh in the rain
that cometh oft upon it, and bringeth forth
herbs meet for them by whom it is dressed,
receiveth blessing from God:
8 But that which beareth thorns and briers
is rejected, and *is* nigh unto cursing; whose
end *is* to be burned.
9 But, beloved, we are persuaded better
things of you, and things that accompany
salvation, though we thus speak.
10 For God *is* not unrighteous to forget your
work and labour of love, which ye have
shewed toward his name, in that ye have
ministered to the saints, and do minister.
11 And we desire that every one of you do
shew the same diligence to the full assurance of hope unto the end:
12 That ye be not slothful, but followers of
them who through faith and patience inherit
the promises.
13 For when God made promise to Abraham, because he could swear by no greater,
he sware by himself,
14 Saying, Surely blessing I will bless thee,
and multiplying I will multiply thee.
15 And so, after he had patiently endured,
he obtained the promise.
16 For men verily swear by the greater: and
an oath for confirmation *is* to them an end
of all strife.
17 Wherein God, willing more abundantly to
shew unto the heirs of promise the immuta-
bility of his counsel, confirmed *it* by an oath:
18 That by two immutable things, in which
it was impossible for God to lie, we might
have a strong consolation, who have fled
for refuge to lay hold upon the hope set
before us:
19 Which *hope* we have as an anchor of
the soul, both sure and stedfast, and which
entereth into that within the veil;
20 Whither the forerunner is for us entered,

even Jesus, made an high priest for ever after the order of Melchisedec.

Hebrews 7

1 For this Melchisedec, king of Salem, priest of the most high God, who met Abraham returning from the slaughter of the kings, and blessed him;
2 To whom also Abraham gave a tenth part of all; first being by interpretation King of righteousness, and after that also King of Salem, which is, King of peace;
3 Without father, without mother, without descent, having neither beginning of days, nor end of life; but made like unto the Son of God; abideth a priest continually.
4 Now consider how great this man *was*, unto whom even the patriarch Abraham gave the tenth of the spoils.
5 And verily they that are of the sons of Levi, who receive the office of the priesthood, have a commandment to take tithes of the people according to the law, that is, of their brethren, though they come out of the loins of Abraham:
6 But he whose descent is not counted from them received tithes of Abraham, and blessed him that had the promises.
7 And without all contradiction the less is blessed of the better.
8 And here men that die receive tithes; but there he *receiveth them*, of whom it is witnessed that he liveth.
9 And as I may so say, Levi also, who receiveth tithes, payed tithes in Abraham.
10 For he was yet in the loins of his father, when Melchisedec met him.
11 If therefore perfection were by the Levitical priesthood, (for under it the people received the law,) what further need *was there* that another priest should rise after the order of Melchisedec, and not be called after the order of Aaron?
12 For the priesthood being changed, there is made of necessity a change also of the law.
13 For he of whom these things are spoken pertaineth to another tribe, of which no man gave attendance at the altar.
14 For *it is* evident that our Lord sprang out of Juda; of which tribe Moses spake nothing concerning priesthood.
15 And it is yet far more evident: for that after the similitude of Melchisedec there ariseth another priest,
16 Who is made, not after the law of a carnal commandment, but after the power of an endless life.
17 For he testifieth, Thou *art* a priest for ever after the order of Melchisedec.
18 For there is verily a disannulling of the commandment going before for the weakness and unprofitableness thereof.
19 For the law made nothing perfect, but the bringing in of a better hope *did;* by the which we draw nigh unto God.
20 And inasmuch as not without an oath *he was made priest:*
21 (For those priests were made without an oath; but this with an oath by him that said unto him, The Lord sware and will not repent, Thou *art* a priest for ever after the order of Melchisedec:)
22 By so much was Jesus made a surety of a better testament.
23 And they truly were many priests, because they were not suffered to continue by reason of death:
24 But this *man*, because he continueth ever, hath an unchangeable priesthood.
25 Wherefore he is able also to save them to the uttermost that come unto God by him, seeing he ever liveth to make intercession for them.
26 For such an high priest became us, *who is* holy, harmless, undefiled, separate from sinners, and made higher than the heavens;
27 Who needeth not daily, as those high priests, to offer up sacrifice, first for his own sins, and then for the people's: for this he did once, when he offered up himself.
28 For the law maketh men high priests which have infirmity; but the word of the oath, which was since the law, *maketh* the Son, who is consecrated for evermore.

Hebrews 8

1 Now of the things which we have spoken *this is* the sum: We have such an high priest, who is set on the right hand of the throne of the Majesty in the heavens;
2 A minister of the sanctuary, and of the true tabernacle, which the Lord pitched, and not man.
3 For every high priest is ordained to offer gifts and sacrifices: wherefore *it is* of neces-

sity that this man have somewhat also to
offer.
4 For if he were on earth, he should not be
a priest, seeing that there are priests that
offer gifts according to the law:
5 Who serve unto the example and shadow
of heavenly things, as Moses was admonished of God when he was about to make
the tabernacle: for, See, saith he, *that* thou
make all things according to the pattern
shewed to thee in the mount.
6 But now hath he obtained a more excellent ministry, by how much also he is the
mediator of a better covenant, which was
established upon better promises.
7 For if that first *covenant* had been fault-
less, then should no place have been sought
for the second.
8 For finding fault with them, he saith,
Behold, the days come, saith the Lord, when
I will make a new covenant with the house
of Israel and with the house of Judah:
9 Not according to the covenant that I made
with their fathers in the day when I took
them by the hand to lead them out of the
land of Egypt; because they continued not
in my covenant, and I regarded them not,
saith the Lord.
10 For this *is* the covenant that I will make
with the house of Israel after those days,
saith the Lord; I will put my laws into their
mind, and write them in their hearts: and I
will be to them a God, and they shall be to
me a people:
11 And they shall not teach every man his
neighbour, and every man his brother, saying, Know the Lord: for all shall know me,
from the least to the greatest.
12 For I will be merciful to their unrighteousness, and their sins and their iniquities will
I remember no more.
13 In that he saith, A new *covenant*, he hath
made the first old. Now that which decayeth
and waxeth old *is* ready to vanish away.

Hebrews 9

1 Then verily the first *covenant* had also
ordinances of divine service, and a worldly
sanctuary.
2 For there was a tabernacle made; the
first, wherein *was* the candlestick, and the
table, and the shewbread; which is called
the sanctuary.
3 And after the second veil, the tabernacle
which is called the Holiest of all;
4 Which had the golden censer, and the ark
of the covenant overlaid round about with
gold, wherein *was* the golden pot that had
manna, and Aaron's rod that budded, and
the tables of the covenant;
5 And over it the cherubims of glory shadowing the mercyseat; of which we cannot
now speak particularly.
6 Now when these things were thus
ordained, the priests went always into the
first tabernacle, accomplishing the service
of God.
7 But into the second *went* the high priest
alone once every year, not without blood,
which he offered for himself, and *for* the
errors of the people:
8 The Holy Spirit this signifying, that the
way into the holiest of all was not yet made
manifest, while as the first tabernacle was
yet standing:
9 Which *was* a figure for the time then
present, in which were offered both gifts
and sacrifices, that could not make him
that did the service perfect, as pertaining
to the conscience;
10 *Which stood* only in meats and drinks,
and divers washings, and carnal ordinances,
imposed *on them* until the time of refor-
mation.
11 But Christ being come an high priest of
good things to come, by a greater and more
perfect tabernacle, not made with hands,
that is to say, not of this building;
12 Neither by the blood of goats and calves,
but by his own blood he entered in once
into the holy place, having obtained eternal
redemption *for us*.
13 For if the blood of bulls and of goats, and
the ashes of an heifer sprinkling the unclean,
sanctifieth to the purifying of the flesh:
14 How much more shall the blood of Christ,
who through the eternal Spirit offered
himself without spot to God, purge your
conscience from dead works to serve the
living God?
15 And for this cause he is the mediator of
the new testament, that by means of death,
for the redemption of the transgressions
that were under the first testament, they
which are called might receive the promise
of eternal inheritance.

16 For where a testament *is*, there must also of necessity be the death of the testator.

17 For a testament *is* of force after men are dead: otherwise it is of no strength at all while the testator liveth.

18 Whereupon neither the first *testament* was dedicated without blood.

19 For when Moses had spoken every precept to all the people according to the law, he took the blood of calves and of goats, with water, and scarlet wool, and hyssop, and sprinkled both the book, and all the people,

20 Saying, This *is* the blood of the testament which God hath enjoined unto you.

21 Moreover he sprinkled with blood both the tabernacle, and all the vessels of the ministry.

22 And almost all things are by the law purged with blood; and without shedding of blood is no remission.

23 *It was* therefore necessary that the patterns of things in the heavens should be purified with these; but the heavenly things themselves with better sacrifices than these.

24 For Christ is not entered into the holy places made with hands, *which are* the figures of the true; but into heaven itself, now to appear in the presence of God for us:

25 Nor yet that he should offer himself often, as the high priest entereth into the holy place every year with blood of others;

26 For then must he often have suffered since the foundation of the world: but now once in the end of the world hath he appeared to put away sin by the sacrifice of himself.

27 And as it is appointed unto men once to die, but after this the judgment:

28 So Christ was once offered to bear the sins of many; and unto them that look for him shall he appear the second time without sin unto salvation.

Hebrews 10

1 For the law having a shadow of good things to come, *and* not the very image of the things, can never with those sacrifices which they offered year by year continually make the comers thereunto perfect.

2 For then would they not have ceased to be offered? because that the worshippers once purged should have had no more conscience of sins.

3 But in those *sacrifices there is* a remembrance again *made* of sins every year.

4 For *it is* not possible that the blood of bulls and of goats should take away sins.

5 Wherefore when he cometh into the world, he saith, Sacrifice and offering thou wouldest not, but a body hast thou prepared me:

6 In burnt offerings and *sacrifices* for sin thou hast had no pleasure.

7 Then said I, Lo, I come (in the volume of the book it is written of me,) to do thy will, O God.

8 Above when he said, Sacrifice and offering and burnt offerings and *offering* for sin thou wouldest not, neither hadst pleasure *therein;* which are offered by the law;

9 Then said he, Lo, I come to do thy will, O God. He taketh away the first, that he may establish the second.

10 By the which will we are sanctified through the offering of the body of Jesus Christ once *for all.*

11 And every priest standeth daily ministering and offering oftentimes the same sacrifices, which can never take away sins:

12 But this man, after he had offered one sacrifice for sins for ever, sat down on the right hand of God;

13 From henceforth expecting till his enemies be made his footstool.

14 For by one offering he hath perfected for ever them that are sanctified.

15 *Whereof* the Holy Spirit also is a witness to us: for after that he had said before,

16 This *is* the covenant that I will make with them after those days, saith the Lord, I will put my laws into their hearts, and in their minds will I write them;

17 And their sins and iniquities will I remember no more.

18 Now where remission of these *is, there is* no more offering for sin.

19 Having therefore, brethren, boldness to enter into the holiest by the blood of Jesus,

20 By a new and living way, which he hath consecrated for us, through the veil, that is to say, his flesh;

21 And *having* an high priest over the house of God;

22 Let us draw near with a true heart in

full assurance of faith, having our hearts
sprinkled from an evil conscience, and our
bodies washed with pure water.
23 Let us hold fast the profession of *our*
faith without wavering; (for he *is* faithful
that promised;)
24 And let us consider one another to provoke unto love and to good works:
25 Not forsaking the assembling of ourselves together, as the manner of some *is;*
but exhorting *one another:* and so much
the more, as ye see the day approaching.
26 For if we sin wilfully after that we have
received the knowledge of the truth, there
remaineth no more sacrifice for sins,
27 But a certain fearful looking for of judgment and fiery indignation, which shall
devour the adversaries.
28 He that despised Moses' law died without mercy under two or three witnesses:
29 Of how much sorer punishment, suppose
ye, shall he be thought worthy, who hath
trodden under foot the Son of God, and hath
counted the blood of the covenant, wherewith he was sanctified, an unholy thing, and
hath done despite unto the Spirit of grace?
30 For we know him that hath said, Vengeance *belongeth* unto me, I will recompense, saith the Lord. And again, The Lord
shall judge his people.
31 *It is* a fearful thing to fall into the hands
of the living God.
32 But call to remembrance the former
days, in which, after ye were illuminated, ye
endured a great fight of afflictions;
33 Partly, whilst ye were made a gazingstock both by reproaches and afflictions;
and partly, whilst ye became companions
of them that were so used.
34 For ye had compassion of me in my
bonds, and took joyfully the spoiling of your
goods, knowing in yourselves that ye have in
heaven a better and an enduring substance.
35 Cast not away therefore your confidence,
which hath great recompence of reward.
36 For ye have need of patience, that, after
ye have done the will of God, ye might
receive the promise.
37 For yet a little while, and he that shall
come will come, and will not tarry.
38 Now the just shall live by faith: but if
any man draw back, my soul shall have no
pleasure in him.
39 But we are not of them who draw back
unto perdition; but of them that believe to
the saving of the soul.

Hebrews 11

1 Now faith is the substance of things hoped
for, the evidence of things not seen.
2 For by it the elders obtained a good report.
3 Through faith we understand that the
worlds were framed by the word of God, so
that things which are seen were not made
of things which do appear.
4 By faith Abel offered unto God a more
excellent sacrifice than Cain, by which he
obtained witness that he was righteous,
God testifying of his gifts: and by it he being
dead yet speaketh.
5 By faith Enoch was translated that he
should not see death; and was not found,
because God had translated him: for before
his translation he had this testimony, that
he pleased God.
6 But without faith *it is* impossible to please
him: for he that cometh to God must believe
that he is, and *that* he is a rewarder of them
that diligently seek him.
7 By faith Noah, being warned of God of
things not seen as yet, moved with fear,
prepared an ark to the saving of his house;
by the which he condemned the world, and
became heir of the righteousness which is
by faith.
8 By faith Abraham, when he was called to
go out into a place which he should after
receive for an inheritance, obeyed; and he
went out, not knowing whither he went.
9 By faith he sojourned in the land of promise, as *in* a strange country, dwelling in
tabernacles with Isaac and Jacob, the heirs
with him of the same promise:
10 For he looked for a city which hath foundations, whose builder and maker *is* God.
11 Through faith also Sara herself received
strength to conceive seed, and was delivered of a child when she was past age,
because she judged him faithful who had
promised.
12 Therefore sprang there even of one, and
him as good as dead, *so many* as the stars of
the sky in multitude, and as the sand which
is by the sea shore innumerable.
13 These all died in faith, not having received
the promises, but having seen them afar off,

and were persuaded of *them*, and embraced
them, and confessed that they were strangers and pilgrims on the earth.
14 For they that say such things declare
plainly that they seek a country.
15 And truly, if they had been mindful of
that *country* from whence they came out,
they might have had opportunity to have
returned.
16 But now they desire a better *country*,
that is, an heavenly: wherefore God is not
ashamed to be called their God: for he hath
prepared for them a city.
17 By faith Abraham, when he was tried,
offered up Isaac: and he that had received
the promises offered up his only begotten
son,
18 Of whom it was said, That in Isaac shall
thy seed be called:
19 Accounting that God *was* able to raise
him up, even from the dead; from whence
also he received him in a figure.
20 By faith Isaac blessed Jacob and Esau
concerning things to come.
21 By faith Jacob, when he was a dying,
blessed both the sons of Joseph; and worshipped, *leaning* upon the top of his staff.
22 By faith Joseph, when he died, made
mention of the departing of the children of
Israel; and gave commandment concerning
his bones.
23 By faith Moses, when he was born, was
hid three months of his parents, because
they saw *he was* a proper child; and they
were not afraid of the king's commandment.
24 By faith Moses, when he was come to
years, refused to be called the son of Pharaoh's daughter;
25 Choosing rather to suffer affliction with
the people of God, than to enjoy the pleasures of sin for a season;
26 Esteeming the reproach of Christ greater
riches than the treasures in Egypt: for he had
respect unto the recompence of the reward.
27 By faith he forsook Egypt, not fearing the
wrath of the king: for he endured, as seeing
him who is invisible.
28 Through faith he kept the passover,
and the sprinkling of blood, lest he that
destroyed the firstborn should touch them.
29 By faith they passed through the Red sea
as by dry *land:* which the Egyptians assaying
to do were drowned.
30 By faith the walls of Jericho fell down,
after they were compassed about seven
days.
31 By faith the harlot Rahab perished not
with them that believed not, when she had
received the spies with peace.
32 And what shall I more say? for the time
would fail me to tell of Gedeon, and *of*
Barak, and *of* Samson, and *of* Jephthae; *of*
David also, and Samuel, and *of* the prophets:
33 Who through faith subdued kingdoms,
wrought righteousness, obtained promises,
stopped the mouths of lions,
34 Quenched the violence of fire, escaped
the edge of the sword, out of weakness were
made strong, waxed valiant in fight, turned
to flight the armies of the aliens.
35 Women received their dead raised to
life again: and others were tortured, not
accepting deliverance; that they might
obtain a better resurrection:
36 And others had trial of *cruel* mockings
and scourgings, yea, moreover of bonds and
imprisonment:
37 They were stoned, they were sawn
asunder, were tempted, were slain with the
sword: they wandered about in sheepskins
and goatskins; being destitute, afflicted,
tormented;
38 (Of whom the world was not worthy:)
they wandered in deserts, and *in* mountains,
and *in* dens and caves of the earth.
39 And these all, having obtained a good
report through faith, received not the
promise:
40 God having provided some better thing
for us, that they without us should not be
made perfect.

Hebrews 12

1 Wherefore seeing we also are compassed
about with so great a cloud of witnesses, let
us lay aside every weight, and the sin which
doth so easily beset *us*, and let us run with
patience the race that is set before us,
2 Looking unto Jesus the author and finisher
of *our* faith; who for the joy that was set
before him endured the cross, despising the
shame, and is set down at the right hand of
the throne of God.
3 For consider him that endured such contradiction of sinners against himself, lest ye
be wearied and faint in your minds.

4 Ye have not yet resisted unto blood, striving against sin.
5 And ye have forgotten the exhortation
which speaketh unto you as unto children,
My son, despise not thou the chastening of
the Lord, nor faint when thou art rebuked
of him:
6 For whom the Lord loveth he chasteneth, and scourgeth every son whom
he receiveth.
7 If ye endure chastening, God dealeth with
you as with sons; for what son is he whom
the father chasteneth not?
8 But if ye be without chastisement, whereof
all are partakers, then are ye bastards, and
not sons.
9 Furthermore we have had fathers of
our flesh which corrected *us*, and we gave
them reverence: shall we not much rather
be in subjection unto the Father of spirits,
and live?
10 For they verily for a few days chastened
us after their own pleasure; but he for *our*
profit, that *we* might be partakers of his
holiness.
11 Now no chastening for the present
seemeth to be joyous, but grievous: nevertheless afterward it yieldeth the peaceable
fruit of righteousness unto them which are
exercised thereby.
12 Wherefore lift up the hands which hang
down, and the feeble knees;
13 And make straight paths for your feet,
lest that which is lame be turned out of the
way; but let it rather be healed.
14 Follow peace with all *men*, and holiness,
without which no man shall see the Lord:
15 Looking diligently lest any man fail of
the grace of God; lest any root of bitterness
springing up trouble *you*, and thereby many
be defiled;
16 Lest there *be* any fornicator, or profane
person, as Esau, who for one morsel of meat
sold his birthright.
17 For ye know how that afterward, when
he would have inherited the blessing, he
was rejected: for he found no place of
repentance, though he sought it carefully
with tears.
18 For ye are not come unto the mount
that might be touched, and that burned
with fire, nor unto blackness, and darkness,
and tempest,
19 And the sound of a trumpet, and the
voice of words; which *voice* they that heard
intreated that the word should not be spoken to them any more:
20 (For they could not endure that which
was commanded, And if so much as a beast
touch the mountain, it shall be stoned, or
thrust through with a dart:
21 And so terrible was the sight, *that* Moses
said, I exceedingly fear and quake:)
22 But ye are come unto mount Sion, and
unto the city of the living God, the heavenly
Jerusalem, and to an innumerable company
of angels,
23 To the general assembly and church of
the firstborn, which are written in heaven,
and to God the Judge of all, and to the spirits
of just men made perfect,
24 And to Jesus the mediator of the new
covenant, and to the blood of sprinkling,
that speaketh better things than *that of*
Abel.
25 See that ye refuse not him that speaketh.
For if they escaped not who refused him
that spake on earth, much more *shall not*
we *escape*, if we turn away from him that
speaketh from heaven:
26 Whose voice then shook the earth: but
now he hath promised, saying, Yet once
more I shake not the earth only, but also
heaven.
27 And this *word*, Yet once more, signifi-
eth the removing of those things that are
shaken, as of things that are made, that
those things which cannot be shaken may
remain.
28 Wherefore we receiving a kingdom
which cannot be moved, let us have grace,
whereby we may serve God acceptably with
reverence and godly fear:
29 For our God *is* a consuming fire.

Hebrews 13

1 Let brotherly love continue.
2 Be not forgetful to entertain strangers:
for thereby some have entertained angels
unawares.
3 Remember them that are in bonds, as
bound with them; *and* them which suffer
adversity, as being yourselves also in the
body.
4 Marriage *is* honourable in all, and the bed

undefiled: but whoremongers and adulterers God will judge.

5 *Let your* conversation *be* without covetousness; *and be* content with such things as ye have: for he hath said, I will never leave thee, nor forsake thee.

6 So that we may boldly say, The Lord *is* my helper, and I will not fear what man shall do unto me.

7 Remember them which have the rule over you, who have spoken unto you the word of God: whose faith follow, considering the end of *their* conversation.

8 Jesus Christ the same yesterday, and to day, and for ever.

9 Be not carried about with divers and strange doctrines. For *it is* a good thing that the heart be established with grace; not with meats, which have not profited them that have been occupied therein.

10 We have an altar, whereof they have no right to eat which serve the tabernacle.

11 For the bodies of those beasts, whose blood is brought into the sanctuary by the high priest for sin, are burned without the camp.

12 Wherefore Jesus also, that he might sanctify the people with his own blood, suffered without the gate.

13 Let us go forth therefore unto him without the camp, bearing his reproach.

14 For here have we no continuing city, but we seek one to come.

15 By him therefore let us offer the sacrifice of praise to God continually, that is, the fruit of *our* lips giving thanks to his name.

16 But to do good and to communicate forget not: for with such sacrifices God is well pleased.

17 Obey them that have the rule over you, and submit yourselves: for they watch for your souls, as they that must give account, that they may do it with joy, and not with grief: for that *is* unprofitable for you.

18 Pray for us: for we trust we have a good conscience, in all things willing to live honestly.

19 But I beseech *you* the rather to do this, that I may be restored to you the sooner.

20 Now the God of peace, that brought again from the dead our Lord Jesus, that great shepherd of the sheep, through the blood of the everlasting covenant,

21 Make you perfect in every good work to do his will, working in you that which is wellpleasing in his sight, through Jesus Christ; to whom *be* glory for ever and ever. Amen.

22 And I beseech you, brethren, suffer the word of exhortation: for I have written a letter unto you in few words.

23 Know ye that *our* brother Timothy is set at liberty; with whom, if he come shortly, I will see you.

24 Salute all them that have the rule over you, and all the saints. They of Italy salute you.

25 Grace *be* with you all. Amen.

The Epistle Of

James

James 1

1 James, a servant of God and of the Lord Jesus Christ, to the twelve tribes which are scattered abroad, greeting.

2 My brethren, count it all joy when ye fall into divers temptations;

3 Knowing *this*, that the trying of your faith worketh patience.

4 But let patience have *her* perfect work, that ye may be perfect and entire, wanting nothing.

5 If any of you lack wisdom, let him ask of God, that giveth to all *men* liberally, and upbraideth not; and it shall be given him.

6 But let him ask in faith, nothing wavering. For he that wavereth is like a wave of the sea driven with the wind and tossed.

7 For let not that man think that he shall receive any thing of the Lord.

8 A double minded man *is* unstable in all
his ways.
9 Let the brother of low degree rejoice in
that he is exalted:
10 But the rich, in that he is made low:
because as the flower of the grass he shall
pass away.
11 For the sun is no sooner risen with a
burning heat, but it withereth the grass, and
the flower thereof falleth, and the grace of
the fashion of it perisheth: so also shall the
rich man fade away in his ways.
12 Blessed *is* the man that endureth temptation: for when he is tried, he shall receive the
crown of life, which the Lord hath promised
to them that love him.
13 Let no man say when he is tempted, I am
tempted of God: for God cannot be tempted
with evil, neither tempteth he any man:
14 But every man is tempted, when he is
drawn away of his own lust, and enticed.
15 Then when lust hath conceived, it bringeth forth sin: and sin, when it is finished,
bringeth forth death.
16 Do not err, my beloved brethren.
17 Every good gift and every perfect gift is
from above, and cometh down from the
Father of lights, with whom is no variable-
ness, neither shadow of turning.
18 Of his own will begat he us with the word
of truth, that we should be a kind of firstfruits of his creatures.
19 Wherefore, my beloved brethren, let
every man be swift to hear, slow to speak,
slow to wrath:
20 For the wrath of man worketh not the
righteousness of God.
21 Wherefore lay apart all filthiness and
superfluity of naughtiness, and receive with
meekness the engrafted word, which is able
to save your souls.
22 But be ye doers of the word, and not
hearers only, deceiving your own selves.
23 For if any be a hearer of the word, and
not a doer, he is like unto a man beholding
his natural face in a glass:
24 For he beholdeth himself, and goeth his
way, and straightway forgetteth what manner of man he was.
25 But whoso looketh into the perfect law
of liberty, and continueth *therein*, he being
not a forgetful hearer, but a doer of the
work, this man shall be blessed in his deed.
26 If any man among you seem to be religious, and bridleth not his tongue, but
deceiveth his own heart, this man's religion
is vain.
27 Pure religion and undefiled before God
and the Father is this, To visit the fatherless
and widows in their affliction, *and* to keep
himself unspotted from the world.

James 2

1 My brethren, have not the faith of our Lord
Jesus Christ, *the Lord* of glory, with respect
of persons.
2 For if there come unto your assembly a
man with a gold ring, in goodly apparel,
and there come in also a poor man in vile
raiment;
3 And ye have respect to him that weareth
the gay clothing, and say unto him, Sit thou
here in a good place; and say to the poor,
Stand thou there, or sit here under my
footstool:
4 Are ye not then partial in yourselves, and
are become judges of evil thoughts?
5 Hearken, my beloved brethren, Hath not
God chosen the poor of this world rich in
faith, and heirs of the kingdom which he hath
promised to them that love him?
6 But ye have despised the poor. Do not rich
men oppress you, and draw you before the
judgment seats?
7 Do not they blaspheme that worthy name
by the which ye are called?
8 If ye fulfil the royal law according to the
scripture, Thou shalt love thy neighbour as
thyself, ye do well:
9 But if ye have respect to persons, ye
commit sin, and are convinced of the law
as transgressors.
10 For whosoever shall keep the whole law,
and yet offend in one *point*, he is guilty of all.
11 For he that said, Do not commit adultery,
said also, Do not kill. Now if thou commit no
adultery, yet if thou kill, thou art become a
transgressor of the law.
12 So speak ye, and so do, as they that shall
be judged by the law of liberty.
13 For he shall have judgment without
mercy, that hath shewed no mercy; and
mercy rejoiceth against judgment.
14 What *doth it* profit, my brethren, though
a man say he hath faith, and have not works?
can faith save him?

15 If a brother or sister be naked, and destitute of daily food,
16 And one of you say unto them, Depart
in peace, be *ye* warmed and filled; notwithstanding ye give them not those things which
are needful to the body; what *doth it* profit?
17 Even so faith, if it hath not works, is dead,
being alone.
18 Yea, a man may say, Thou hast faith, and
I have works: shew me thy faith without
thy works, and I will shew thee my faith by
my works.
19 Thou believest that there is one God;
thou doest well: the devils also believe,
and tremble.
20 But wilt thou know, O vain man, that faith
without works is dead?
21 Was not Abraham our father justified by
works, when he had offered Isaac his son
upon the altar?
22 Seest thou how faith wrought with his
works, and by works was faith made perfect?
23 And the scripture was fulfilled which
saith, Abraham believed God, and it was
imputed unto him for righteousness: and
he was called the Friend of God.
24 Ye see then how that by works a man is
justified, and not by faith only.
25 Likewise also was not Rahab the harlot
justified by works, when she had received
the messengers, and had sent *them* out
another way?
26 For as the body without the spirit is dead,
so faith without works is dead also.

James 3

1 My brethren, be not many masters, knowing that we shall receive the greater condemnation.
2 For in many things we offend all. If any man
offend not in word, the same *is* a perfect
man, *and* able also to bridle the whole body.
3 Behold, we put bits in the horses' mouths,
that they may obey us; and we turn about
their whole body.
4 Behold also the ships, which though *they
be* so great, and *are* driven of fierce winds,
yet are they turned about with a very small
helm, whithersoever the governor listeth.
5 Even so the tongue is a little member, and
boasteth great things. Behold, how great a
matter a little fire kindleth!
6 And the tongue *is* a fire, a world of iniquity: so is the tongue among our members,
that it defileth the whole body, and setteth
on fire the course of nature; and it is set on
fire of hell.
7 For every kind of beasts, and of birds,
and of serpents, and of things in the sea, is
tamed, and hath been tamed of mankind:
8 But the tongue can no man tame; *it is* an
unruly evil, full of deadly poison.
9 Therewith bless we God, even the Father;
and therewith curse we men, which are
made after the similitude of God.
10 Out of the same mouth proceedeth blessing and cursing. My brethren, these things
ought not so to be.
11 Doth a fountain send forth at the same
place sweet *water* and bitter?
12 Can the fig tree, my brethren, bear olive
berries? either a vine, figs? so *can* no fountain both yield salt water and fresh.
13 Who *is* a wise man and endued with
knowledge among you? let him shew out of
a good conversation his works with meekness of wisdom.
14 But if ye have bitter envying and strife in
your hearts, glory not, and lie not against
the truth.
15 This wisdom descendeth not from above,
but *is* earthly, sensual, devilish.
16 For where envying and strife *is*, there *is*
confusion and every evil work.
17 But the wisdom that is from above is first
pure, then peaceable, gentle, *and* easy to
be intreated, full of mercy and good fruits,
without partiality, and without hypocrisy.
18 And the fruit of righteousness is sown in
peace of them that make peace.

James 4

1 From whence *come* wars and fightings
among you? *come they* not hence, *even* of
your lusts that war in your members?
2 Ye lust, and have not: ye kill, and desire to
have, and cannot obtain: ye fight and war,
yet ye have not, because ye ask not.
3 Ye ask, and receive not, because ye ask
amiss, that ye may consume *it* upon your
lusts.
4 Ye adulterers and adulteresses, know ye
not that the friendship of the world is enmity
with God? whosoever therefore will be a
friend of the world is the enemy of God.

5 Do ye think that the scripture saith in vain,
The spirit that dwelleth in us lusteth to envy?
6 But he giveth more grace. Wherefore he
saith, God resisteth the proud, but giveth
grace unto the humble.
7 Submit yourselves therefore to God. Resist
the devil, and he will flee from you.
8 Draw nigh to God, and he will draw nigh
to you. Cleanse *your* hands, *ye* sinners; and
purify *your* hearts, *ye* double minded.
9 Be afflicted, and mourn, and weep: let your
laughter be turned to mourning, and *your*
joy to heaviness.
10 Humble yourselves in the sight of the
Lord, and he shall lift you up.
11 Speak not evil one of another, brethren.
He that speaketh evil of *his* brother, and judgeth his brother, speaketh evil of the law, and
judgeth the law: but if thou judge the law,
thou art not a doer of the law, but a judge.
12 There is one lawgiver, who is able to save
and to destroy: who art thou that judgest
another?
13 Go to now, ye that say, To day or to morrow we will go into such a city, and continue
there a year, and buy and sell, and get gain:
14 Whereas ye know not what *shall be* on
the morrow. For what *is* your life? It is even
a vapour, that appeareth for a little time,
and then vanisheth away.
15 For that ye *ought* to say, If the Lord will,
we shall live, and do this, or that.
16 But now ye rejoice in your boastings: all
such rejoicing is evil.
17 Therefore to him that knoweth to do
good, and doeth *it* not, to him it is sin.

James 5

1 Go to now, *ye* rich men, weep and howl
for your miseries that shall come upon *you*.
2 Your riches are corrupted, and your garments are motheaten.
3 Your gold and silver is cankered; and the
rust of them shall be a witness against you,
and shall eat your flesh as it were fire. Ye
have heaped treasure together for the last
days.
4 Behold, the hire of the labourers who have
reaped down your fields, which is of you kept
back by fraud, crieth: and the cries of them
which have reaped are entered into the ears
of the Lord of sabaoth.
5 Ye have lived in pleasure on the earth,
and been wanton; ye have nourished your
hearts, as in a day of slaughter.
6 Ye have condemned *and* killed the just;
and he doth not resist you.
7 Be patient therefore, brethren, unto the
coming of the Lord. Behold, the husbandman
waiteth for the precious fruit of the earth,
and hath long patience for it, until he receive
the early and latter rain.
8 Be ye also patient; stablish your hearts:
for the coming of the Lord draweth nigh.
9 Grudge not one against another, brethren,
lest ye be condemned: behold, the judge
standeth before the door.
10 Take, my brethren, the prophets, who
have spoken in the name of the Lord, for
an example of suffering affliction, and of
patience.
11 Behold, we count them happy which
endure. Ye have heard of the patience of
Job, and have seen the end of the Lord; that
the Lord is very pitiful, and of tender mercy.
12 But above all things, my brethren, swear
not, neither by heaven, neither by the earth,
neither by any other oath: but let your yea
be yea; and *your* nay, nay; lest ye fall into
condemnation.
13 Is any among you afflicted? let him pray.
Is any merry? let him sing psalms.
14 Is any sick among you? let him call for
the elders of the church; and let them pray
over him, anointing him with oil in the name
of the Lord:
15 And the prayer of faith shall save the
sick, and the Lord shall raise him up; and
if he have committed sins, they shall be
forgiven him.
16 Confess *your* faults one to another, and
pray one for another, that ye may be healed.
The effectual fervent prayer of a righteous
man availeth much.
17 Elias was a man subject to like passions
as we are, and he prayed earnestly that it
might not rain: and it rained not on the earth
by the space of three years and six months.
18 And he prayed again, and the heaven gave
rain, and the earth brought forth her fruit.
19 Brethren, if any of you do err from the
truth, and one convert him;
20 Let him know, that he which converteth
the sinner from the error of his way shall
save a soul from death, and shall hide a
multitude of sins.

The First Epistle Of

Peter

1 Peter 1

1 Peter, an apostle of Jesus Christ, to the
strangers scattered throughout Pontus,
Galatia, Cappadocia, Asia, and Bithynia,
2 Elect according to the foreknowledge of
God the Father, through sanctification of the
Spirit, unto obedience and sprinkling of the
blood of Jesus Christ: Grace unto you, and
peace, be multiplied.
3 Blessed *be* the God and Father of our Lord
Jesus Christ, which according to his abundant mercy hath begotten us again unto
a lively hope by the resurrection of Jesus
Christ from the dead,
4 To an inheritance incorruptible, and undefiled, and that fadeth not away, reserved in
heaven for you,
5 Who are kept by the power of God through
faith unto salvation ready to be revealed in
the last time.
6 Wherein ye greatly rejoice, though now
for a season, if need be, ye are in heaviness
through manifold temptations:
7 That the trial of your faith, being much
more precious than of gold that perisheth,
though it be tried with fire, might be found
unto praise and honour and glory at the
appearing of Jesus Christ:
8 Whom having not seen, ye love; in whom,
though now ye see *him* not, yet believing,
ye rejoice with joy unspeakable and full
of glory:
9 Receiving the end of your faith, *even* the
salvation of *your* souls.
10 Of which salvation the prophets have
inquired and searched diligently, who prophesied of the grace *that should come* unto
you:
11 Searching what, or what manner of
time the Spirit of Christ which was in them
did signify, when it testified beforehand
the sufferings of Christ, and the glory that
should follow.
12 Unto whom it was revealed, that not unto
themselves, but unto us they did minister
the things, which are now reported unto
you by them that have preached the gospel
unto you with the Holy Spirit sent down
from heaven; which things the angels desire
to look into.
13 Wherefore gird up the loins of your mind,
be sober, and hope to the end for the grace
that is to be brought unto you at the revelation of Jesus Christ;
14 As obedient children, not fashioning
yourselves according to the former lusts in
your ignorance:
15 But as he which hath called you is holy,
so be ye holy in all manner of conversation;
16 Because it is written, Be ye holy; for I
am holy.
17 And if ye call on the Father, who without
respect of persons judgeth according to
every man's work, pass the time of your
sojourning *here* in fear:
18 Forasmuch as ye know that ye were not
redeemed with corruptible things, *as* silver and gold, from your vain conversation
received by tradition from your fathers;
19 But with the precious blood of Christ, as
of a lamb without blemish and without spot:
20 Who verily was foreordained before the
foundation of the world, but was manifest
in these last times for you,
21 Who by him do believe in God, that raised
him up from the dead, and gave him glory;
that your faith and hope might be in God.
22 Seeing ye have purified your souls in
obeying the truth through the Spirit unto
unfeigned love of the brethren, *see that
ye* love one another with a pure heart
fervently:
23 Being born again, not of corruptible seed,
but of incorruptible, by the word of God,
which liveth and abideth for ever.
24 For all flesh *is* as grass, and all the glory of
man as the flower of grass. The grass withereth, and the flower thereof falleth away:
25 But the word of the Lord endureth for
ever. And this is the word which by the gospel is preached unto you.

1 Peter 2

1 Wherefore laying aside all malice, and all

guile, and hypocrisies, and envies, and all
evil speakings,
2 As newborn babes, desire the sincere
milk of the word, that ye may grow thereby:
3 If so be ye have tasted that the Lord *is*
gracious.
4 To whom coming, *as unto* a living stone,
disallowed indeed of men, but chosen of
God, *and* precious,
5 Ye also, as lively stones, are built up a
spiritual house, an holy priesthood, to offer
up spiritual sacrifices, acceptable to God by
Jesus Christ.
6 Wherefore also it is contained in the
scripture, Behold, I lay in Sion a chief corner
stone, elect, precious: and he that believeth
on him shall not be confounded.
7 Unto you therefore which believe *he is*
precious: but unto them which be disobedient, the stone which the builders disallowed,
the same is made the head of the corner,
8 And a stone of stumbling, and a rock of
offence, *even to them* which stumble at the
word, being disobedient: whereunto also
they were appointed.
9 But ye *are* a chosen generation, a royal
priesthood, an holy nation, a peculiar people; that ye should shew forth the praises
of him who hath called you out of darkness
into his marvellous light:
10 Which in time past *were* not a people,
but *are* now the people of God: which had
not obtained mercy, but now have obtained
mercy.
11 Dearly beloved, I beseech *you* as strangers and pilgrims, abstain from fleshly lusts,
which war against the soul;
12 Having your conversation honest among
the Gentiles: that, whereas they speak
against you as evildoers, they may by *your*
good works, which they shall behold, glorify
God in the day of visitation.
13 Submit yourselves to every ordinance
of man for the Lord's sake: whether it be
to the king, as supreme;
14 Or unto governors, as unto them that are
sent by him for the punishment of evildoers,
and for the praise of them that do well.
15 For so is the will of God, that with well
doing ye may put to silence the ignorance
of foolish men:
16 As free, and not using *your* liberty for a
cloke of maliciousness, but as the servants
of God.
17 Honour all *men*. Love the brotherhood.
Fear God. Honour the king.
18 Servants, *be* subject to *your* masters with
all fear; not only to the good and gentle, but
also to the froward.
19 For this *is* thankworthy, if a man for conscience toward God endure grief, suffering
wrongfully.
20 For what glory *is it*, if, when ye be
buffeted for your faults, ye shall take it
patiently? but if, when ye do well, and suffer
for it, ye take it patiently, this *is* acceptable
with God.
21 For even hereunto were ye called:
because Christ also suffered for us, leaving us an example, that ye should follow
his steps:
22 Who did no sin, neither was guile found
in his mouth:
23 Who, when he was reviled, reviled not
again; when he suffered, he threatened not;
but committed *himself* to him that judgeth
righteously:
24 Who his own self bare our sins in his
own body on the tree, that we, being dead
to sins, should live unto righteousness: by
whose stripes ye were healed.
25 For ye were as sheep going astray; but
are now returned unto the Shepherd and
Bishop of your souls.

1 Peter 3

1 Likewise, ye wives, *be* in subjection to
your own husbands; that, if any obey not
the word, they also may without the word
be won by the conversation of the wives;
2 While they behold your chaste conversation *coupled* with fear.
3 Whose adorning let it not be that outward
adorning of plaiting the hair, and of wearing
of gold, or of putting on of apparel;
4 But *let it be* the hidden man of the heart,
in that which is not corruptible, *even the*
ornament of a meek and quiet spirit, which
is in the sight of God of great price.
5 For after this manner in the old time
the holy women also, who trusted in God,
adorned themselves, being in subjection
unto their own husbands:
6 Even as Sara obeyed Abraham, calling
him lord: whose daughters ye are, as long

as ye do well, and are not afraid with any
amazement.
7 Likewise, ye husbands, dwell with *them*
according to knowledge, giving honour unto
the wife, as unto the weaker vessel, and as
being heirs together of the grace of life; that
your prayers be not hindered.
8 Finally, *be ye* all of one mind, having compassion one of another, love as brethren, *be*
pitiful, *be* courteous:
9 Not rendering evil for evil, or railing for
railing: but contrariwise blessing; knowing
that ye are thereunto called, that ye should
inherit a blessing.
10 For he that will love life, and see good
days, let him refrain his tongue from evil,
and his lips that they speak no guile:
11 Let him eschew evil, and do good; let him
seek peace, and ensue it.
12 For the eyes of the Lord *are* over the
righteous, and his ears *are open* unto their
prayers: but the face of the Lord *is* against
them that do evil.
13 And who *is* he that will harm you, if ye
be followers of that which is good?
14 But and if ye suffer for righteousness'
sake, happy *are ye:* and be not afraid of
their terror, neither be troubled;
15 But sanctify the Lord God in your hearts:
and *be* ready always to *give* an answer to
every man that asketh you a reason of the
hope that is in you with meekness and fear:
16 Having a good conscience; that, whereas
they speak evil of you, as of evildoers, they
may be ashamed that falsely accuse your
good conversation in Christ.
17 For *it is* better, if the will of God be so,
that ye suffer for well doing, than for evil
doing.
18 For Christ also hath once suffered for
sins, the just for the unjust, that he might
bring us to God, being put to death in the
flesh, but quickened by the Spirit:
19 By which also he went and preached unto
the spirits in prison;
20 Which sometime were disobedient,
when once the longsuffering of God waited
in the days of Noah, while the ark was a
preparing, wherein few, that is, eight souls
were saved by water.
21 The like figure whereunto *even* baptism
doth also now save us (not the putting away
of the filth of the flesh, but the answer of a
good conscience toward God,) by the resurrection of Jesus Christ:
22 Who is gone into heaven, and is on the
right hand of God; angels and authorities
and powers being made subject unto him.

1 Peter 4

1 Forasmuch then as Christ hath suffered for
us in the flesh, arm yourselves likewise with
the same mind: for he that hath suffered in
the flesh hath ceased from sin;
2 That he no longer should live the rest of
his time in the flesh to the lusts of men, but
to the will of God.
3 For the time past of *our* life may suffice
us to have wrought the will of the Gentiles,
when we walked in lasciviousness, lusts,
excess of wine, revellings, banquetings, and
abominable idolatries:
4 Wherein they think it strange that ye run
not with *them* to the same excess of riot,
speaking evil of *you:*
5 Who shall give account to him that is ready
to judge the quick and the dead.
6 For for this cause was the gospel preached
also to them that are dead, that they might
be judged according to men in the flesh, but
live according to God in the spirit.
7 But the end of all things is at hand: be ye
therefore sober, and watch unto prayer.
8 And above all things have fervent charity
among yourselves: for charity shall cover
the multitude of sins.
9 Use hospitality one to another without
grudging.
10 As every man hath received the gift, *even*
so minister the same one to another, as
good stewards of the manifold grace of God.
11 If any man speak, *let him speak* as the
oracles of God; if any man minister, *let him*
do it as of the ability which God giveth: that
God in all things may be glorified through
Jesus Christ, to whom be praise and dominion for ever and ever. Amen.
12 Beloved, think it not strange concerning
the fiery trial which is to try you, as though
some strange thing happened unto you:
13 But rejoice, inasmuch as ye are partakers
of Christ's sufferings; that, when his glory
shall be revealed, ye may be glad also with
exceeding joy.
14 If ye be reproached for the name of
Christ, happy *are ye;* for the spirit of glory

and of God resteth upon you: on their part
he is evil spoken of, but on your part he is
glorified.
15 But let none of you suffer as a murderer,
or *as* a thief, or *as* an evildoer, or as a busy-
body in other men's matters.
16 Yet if *any man suffer* as a Christian, let
him not be ashamed; but let him glorify God
on this behalf.
17 For the time *is come* that judgment must
begin at the house of God: and if *it* first
begin at us, what shall the end *be* of them
that obey not the gospel of God?
18 And if the righteous scarcely be saved,
where shall the ungodly and the sinner
appear?
19 Wherefore let them that suffer according to the will of God commit the keeping
of their souls *to him* in well doing, as unto
a faithful Creator.

1 Peter 5

1 The elders which are among you I exhort,
who am also an elder, and a witness of the
sufferings of Christ, and also a partaker of
the glory that shall be revealed:
2 Feed the flock of God which is among
you, taking the oversight *thereof*, not by
constraint, but willingly; not for filthy lucre,
but of a ready mind;
3 Neither as being lords over *God's* heritage,
but being ensamples to the flock.
4 And when the chief Shepherd shall appear,
ye shall receive a crown of glory that fadeth
not away.
5 Likewise, ye younger, submit yourselves
unto the elder. Yea, all *of you* be subject one
to another, and be clothed with humility: for
God resisteth the proud, and giveth grace
to the humble.
6 Humble yourselves therefore under the
mighty hand of God, that he may exalt you
in due time:
7 Casting all your care upon him; for he
careth for you.
8 Be sober, be vigilant; because your adversary the devil, as a roaring lion, walketh
about, seeking whom he may devour:
9 Whom resist stedfast in the faith, knowing
that the same afflictions are accomplished
in your brethren that are in the world.
10 But the God of all grace, who hath called
us unto his eternal glory by Christ Jesus,
after that ye have suffered a while, make
you perfect, stablish, strengthen, settle *you*.
11 To him *be* glory and dominion for ever
and ever. Amen.
12 By Silvanus, a faithful brother unto you,
as I suppose, I have written briefly, exhorting, and testifying that this is the true grace
of God wherein ye stand.
13 The *church that is* at Babylon, elected
together with *you*, saluteth you; and *so doth*
Marcus my son.
14 Greet ye one another with a kiss of charity. Peace *be* with you all that are in Christ
Jesus. Amen.

The Second Epistle Of

Peter

2 Peter 1

1 Simon Peter, a servant and an apostle of
Jesus Christ, to them that have obtained like
precious faith with us through the righteousness of God and our Saviour Jesus Christ:
2 Grace and peace be multiplied unto you
through the knowledge of God, and of Jesus
our Lord,
3 According as his divine power hath given
unto us all things that *pertain* unto life and
godliness, through the knowledge of him that
hath called us to glory and virtue:
4 Whereby are given unto us exceeding
great and precious promises: that by these
ye might be partakers of the divine nature,
having escaped the corruption that is in the
world through lust.
5 And beside this, giving all diligence, add to
your faith virtue; and to virtue knowledge;

6 And to knowledge temperance; and to temperance patience; and to patience godliness;
7 And to godliness brotherly kindness; and to brotherly kindness charity.
8 For if these things be in you, and abound, they make *you that ye shall* neither *be* barren nor unfruitful in the knowledge of our Lord Jesus Christ.
9 But he that lacketh these things is blind, and cannot see afar off, and hath forgotten that he was purged from his old sins.
10 Wherefore the rather, brethren, give diligence to make your calling and election sure: for if ye do these things, ye shall never fall:
11 For so an entrance shall be ministered unto you abundantly into the everlasting kingdom of our Lord and Saviour Jesus Christ.
12 Wherefore I will not be negligent to put you always in remembrance of these things, though ye know *them*, and be established in the present truth.
13 Yea, I think it meet, as long as I am in this tabernacle, to stir you up by putting *you* in remembrance;
14 Knowing that shortly I must put off *this* my tabernacle, even as our Lord Jesus Christ hath shewed me.
15 Moreover I will endeavour that ye may be able after my decease to have these things always in remembrance.
16 For we have not followed cunningly devised fables, when we made known unto you the power and coming of our Lord Jesus Christ, but were eyewitnesses of his majesty.
17 For he received from God the Father honour and glory, when there came such a voice to him from the excellent glory, This is my beloved Son, in whom I am well pleased.
18 And this voice which came from heaven we heard, when we were with him in the holy mount.
19 We have also a more sure word of prophecy; whereunto ye do well that ye take heed, as unto a light that shineth in a dark place, until the day dawn, and the day star arise in your hearts:
20 Knowing this first, that no prophecy of the scripture is of any private interpretation.
21 For the prophecy came not in old time by the will of man: but holy men of God spake *as they were* moved by the Holy Spirit.

2 Peter 2

1 But there were false prophets also among the people, even as there shall be false teachers among you, who privily shall bring in damnable heresies, even denying the Lord that bought them, and bring upon themselves swift destruction.
2 And many shall follow their pernicious ways; by reason of whom the way of truth shall be evil spoken of.
3 And through covetousness shall they with feigned words make merchandise of you: whose judgment now of a long time lingereth not, and their damnation slumbereth not.
4 For if God spared not the angels that sinned, but cast *them* down to hell, and delivered *them* into chains of darkness, to be reserved unto judgment;
5 And spared not the old world, but saved Noah the eighth *person*, a preacher of righteousness, bringing in the flood upon the world of the ungodly;
6 And turning the cities of Sodom and Gomorrha into ashes condemned *them* with an overthrow, making *them* an ensample unto those that after should live ungodly;
7 And delivered just Lot, vexed with the filthy conversation of the wicked:
8 (For that righteous man dwelling among them, in seeing and hearing, vexed *his* righteous soul from day to day with *their* unlawful deeds;)
9 The Lord knoweth how to deliver the godly out of temptations, and to reserve the unjust unto the day of judgment to be punished:
10 But chiefly them that walk after the flesh in the lust of uncleanness, and despise government. Presumptuous *are they*, selfwilled, they are not afraid to speak evil of dignities.
11 Whereas angels, which are greater in power and might, bring not railing accusation against them before the Lord.
12 But these, as natural brute beasts, made to be taken and destroyed, speak evil of the things that they understand not; and shall utterly perish in their own corruption;
13 And shall receive the reward of unrighteousness, *as* they that count it pleasure to riot in the day time. Spots *they are* and blemishes, sporting themselves with their own deceivings while they feast with you;
14 Having eyes full of adultery, and that cannot cease from sin; beguiling unstable souls:

an heart they have exercised with covetous
practices; cursed children:
15 Which have forsaken the right way, and
are gone astray, following the way of Balaam
the son of Bosor, who loved the wages of
unrighteousness;
16 But was rebuked for his iniquity: the
dumb ass speaking with man's voice forbad
the madness of the prophet.
17 These are wells without water, clouds that
are carried with a tempest; to whom the mist
of darkness is reserved for ever.
18 For when they speak great swelling *words*
of vanity, they allure through the lusts of
the flesh, *through much* wantonness, those
that were clean escaped from them who
live in error.
19 While they promise them liberty, they
themselves are the servants of corruption:
for of whom a man is overcome, of the same
is he brought in bondage.
20 For if after they have escaped the pollutions of the world through the knowledge
of the Lord and Saviour Jesus Christ, they
are again entangled therein, and overcome,
the latter end is worse with them than the
beginning.
21 For it had been better for them not to
have known the way of righteousness, than,
after they have known *it*, to turn from the
holy commandment delivered unto them.
22 But it is happened unto them according
to the true proverb, The dog *is* turned to
his own vomit again; and the sow that was
washed to her wallowing in the mire.

2 Peter 3

1 This second epistle, beloved, I now write
unto you; in *both* which I stir up your pure
minds by way of remembrance:
2 That ye may be mindful of the words which
were spoken before by the holy prophets,
and of the commandment of us the apostles
of the Lord and Saviour:
3 Knowing this first, that there shall come
in the last days scoffers, walking after their
own lusts,
4 And saying, Where is the promise of his
coming? for since the fathers fell asleep,
all things continue as *they were* from the
beginning of the creation.
5 For this they willingly are ignorant of, that
by the word of God the heavens were of old,
and the earth standing out of the water and
in the water:
6 Whereby the world that then was, being
overflowed with water, perished:
7 But the heavens and the earth, which are
now, by the same word are kept in store,
reserved unto fire against the day of judgment and perdition of ungodly men.
8 But, beloved, be not ignorant of this one
thing, that one day *is* with the Lord as a thousand years, and a thousand years as one day.
9 The Lord is not slack concerning his promise, as some men count slackness; but is
longsuffering to us-ward, not willing that
any should perish, but that all should come
to repentance.
10 But the day of the Lord will come as a
thief in the night; in the which the heavens
shall pass away with a great noise, and the
elements shall melt with fervent heat, the
earth also and the works that are therein
shall be burned up.
11 *Seeing* then *that* all these things shall be
dissolved, what manner *of persons* ought ye
to be in *all* holy conversation and godliness,
12 Looking for and hasting unto the coming
of the day of God, wherein the heavens being
on fire shall be dissolved, and the elements
shall melt with fervent heat?
13 Nevertheless we, according to his promise, look for new heavens and a new earth,
wherein dwelleth righteousness.
14 Wherefore, beloved, seeing that ye look
for such things, be diligent that ye may be
found of him in peace, without spot, and
blameless.
15 And account *that* the longsuffering of our
Lord *is* salvation; even as our beloved brother
Paul also according to the wisdom given unto
him hath written unto you;
16 As also in all *his* epistles, speaking in them
of these things; in which are some things
hard to be understood, which they that are
unlearned and unstable wrest, as *they do*
also the other scriptures, unto their own
destruction.
17 Ye therefore, beloved, seeing ye know
these things before, beware lest ye also,
being led away with the error of the wicked,
fall from your own stedfastness.
18 But grow in grace, and *in* the knowledge
of our Lord and Saviour Jesus Christ. To him
be glory both now and for ever. Amen.

The First Epistle Of

John

1 John 1

1 That which was from the beginning, which
we have heard, which we have seen with
our eyes, which we have looked upon, and
our hands have handled, of the Word of life;
2 (For the life was manifested, and we have
seen *it*, and bear witness, and shew unto you
that eternal life, which was with the Father,
and was manifested unto us;)
3 That which we have seen and heard
declare we unto you, that ye also may have
fellowship with us: and truly our fellowship
is with the Father, and with his Son Jesus
Christ.
4 And these things write we unto you, that
your joy may be full.
5 This then is the message which we have
heard of him, and declare unto you, that
God is light, and in him is no darkness at all.
6 If we say that we have fellowship with
him, and walk in darkness, we lie, and do
not the truth:
7 But if we walk in the light, as he is in
the light, we have fellowship one with
another, and the blood of Jesus Christ his
Son cleanseth us from all sin.
8 If we say that we have no sin, we deceive
ourselves, and the truth is not in us.
9 If we confess our sins, he is faithful and
just to forgive us *our* sins, and to cleanse us
from all unrighteousness.
10 If we say that we have not sinned, we
make him a liar, and his word is not in us.

1 John 2

1 My little children, these things write I unto
you, that ye sin not. And if any man sin, we
have an advocate with the Father, Jesus
Christ the righteous:
2 And he is the propitiation for our sins: and
not for ours only, but also for *the sins of* the
whole world.
3 And hereby we do know that we know
him, if we keep his commandments.
4 He that saith, I know him, and keepeth
not his commandments, is a liar, and the
truth is not in him.
5 But whoso keepeth his word, in him verily
is the love of God perfected: hereby know
we that we are in him.
6 He that saith he abideth in him ought
himself also so to walk, even as he walked.
7 Brethren, I write no new commandment
unto you, but an old commandment which
ye had from the beginning. The old commandment is the word which ye have heard
from the beginning.
8 Again, a new commandment I write unto
you, which thing is true in him and in you:
because the darkness is past, and the true
light now shineth.
9 He that saith he is in the light, and hateth
his brother, is in darkness even until now.
10 He that loveth his brother abideth in the
light, and there is none occasion of stumbling in him.
11 But he that hateth his brother is in darkness, and walketh in darkness, and knoweth
not whither he goeth, because that darkness
hath blinded his eyes.
12 I write unto you, little children, because
your sins are forgiven you for his name's
sake.
13 I write unto you, fathers, because ye
have known him *that is* from the beginning.
I write unto you, young men, because ye
have overcome the wicked one. I write
unto you, little children, because ye have
known the Father.
14 I have written unto you, fathers, because
ye have known him *that is* from the beginning. I have written unto you, young men,
because ye are strong, and the word of God
abideth in you, and ye have overcome the
wicked one.
15 Love not the world, neither the things
that are in the world. If any man love the
world, the love of the Father is not in him.
16 For all that *is* in the world, the lust of
the flesh, and the lust of the eyes, and the
pride of life, is not of the Father, but is of
the world.
17 And the world passeth away, and the lust

thereof: but he that doeth the will of God
abideth for ever.
18 Little children, it is the last time: and as ye
have heard that antichrist shall come, even
now are there many antichrists; whereby
we know that it is the last time.
19 They went out from us, but they were not
of us; for if they had been of us, they would
no doubt have continued with us: but *they
went out*, that they might be made manifest
that they were not all of us.
20 But ye have an unction from the Holy
One, and ye know all things.
21 I have not written unto you because ye
know not the truth, but because ye know
it, and that no lie is of the truth.
22 Who is a liar but he that denieth that
Jesus is the Christ? He is antichrist, that
denieth the Father and the Son.
23 Whosoever denieth the Son, the same
hath not the Father: [*but*] *he that acknowl-
edgeth the Son hath the Father also.*
24 Let that therefore abide in you, which
ye have heard from the beginning. If that
which ye have heard from the beginning
shall remain in you, ye also shall continue
in the Son, and in the Father.
25 And this is the promise that he hath
promised us, *even* eternal life.
26 These *things* have I written unto you
concerning them that seduce you.
27 But the anointing which ye have received
of him abideth in you, and ye need not that
any man teach you: but as the same anointing teacheth you of all things, and is truth,
and is no lie, and even as it hath taught you,
ye shall abide in him.
28 And now, little children, abide in him;
that, when he shall appear, we may have
confidence, and not be ashamed before
him at his coming.
29 If ye know that he is righteous, ye know
that every one that doeth righteousness is
born of him.

1 John 3

1 Behold, what manner of love the Father
hath bestowed upon us, that we should be
called the sons of God: therefore the world
knoweth us not, because it knew him not.
2 Beloved, now are we the sons of God, and
it doth not yet appear what we shall be: but
we know that, when he shall appear, we
shall be like him; for we shall see him as he is.
3 And every man that hath this hope in him
purifieth himself, even as he is pure.
4 Whosoever committeth sin transgresseth
also the law: for sin is the transgression of
the law.
5 And ye know that he was manifested to
take away our sins; and in him is no sin.
6 Whosoever abideth in him sinneth not:
whosoever sinneth hath not seen him,
neither known him.
7 Little children, let no man deceive you: he
that doeth righteousness is righteous, even
as he is righteous.
8 He that committeth sin is of the devil; for
the devil sinneth from the beginning. For
this purpose the Son of God was manifested,
that he might destroy the works of the devil.
9 Whosoever is born of God doth not commit sin; for his seed remaineth in him: and
he cannot sin, because he is born of God.
10 In this the children of God are manifest,
and the children of the devil: whosoever
doeth not righteousness is not of God, neither he that loveth not his brother.
11 For this is the message that ye heard
from the beginning, that we should love
one another.
12 Not as Cain, *who* was of that wicked one,
and slew his brother. And wherefore slew
he him? Because his own works were evil,
and his brother's righteous.
13 Marvel not, my brethren, if the world
hate you.
14 We know that we have passed from
death unto life, because we love the brethren. He that loveth not *his* brother abideth
in death.
15 Whosoever hateth his brother is a murderer: and ye know that no murderer hath
eternal life abiding in him.
16 Hereby perceive we the love *of God*,
because he laid down his life for us: and we
ought to lay down *our* lives for the brethren.
17 But whoso hath this world's good, and
seeth his brother have need, and shutteth
up his bowels *of compassion* from him, how
dwelleth the love of God in him?
18 My little children, let us not love in word,
neither in tongue; but in deed and in truth.
19 And hereby we know that we are of the

truth, and shall assure our hearts before
him.
20 For if our heart condemn us, God is
greater than our heart, and knoweth all
things.
21 Beloved, if our heart condemn us not,
then have we confidence toward God.
22 And whatsoever we ask, we receive of
him, because we keep his commandments,
and do those things that are pleasing in
his sight.
23 And this is his commandment, That we
should believe on the name of his Son Jesus
Christ, and love one another, as he gave us
commandment.
24 And he that keepeth his commandments
dwelleth in him, and he in him. And hereby
we know that he abideth in us, by the Spirit
which he hath given us.

1 John 4

1 Beloved, believe not every spirit, but
try the spirits whether they are of God:
because many false prophets are gone out
into the world.
2 Hereby know ye the Spirit of God: Every
spirit that confesseth that Jesus Christ is
come in the flesh is of God:
3 And every spirit that confesseth not that
Jesus Christ is come in the flesh is not of
God: and this is that *spirit* of antichrist,
whereof ye have heard that it should come;
and even now already is it in the world.
4 Ye are of God, little children, and have
overcome them: because greater is he that
is in you, than he that is in the world.
5 They are of the world: therefore speak
they of the world, and the world heareth
them.
6 We are of God: he that knoweth God
heareth us; he that is not of God heareth
not us. Hereby know we the spirit of truth,
and the spirit of error.
7 Beloved, let us love one another: for love
is of God; and every one that loveth is born
of God, and knoweth God.
8 He that loveth not knoweth not God; for
God is love.
9 In this was manifested the love of God
toward us, because that God sent his only
begotten Son into the world, that we might
live through him.
10 Herein is love, not that we loved God,
but that he loved us, and sent his Son *to be*
the propitiation for our sins.
11 Beloved, if God so loved us, we ought
also to love one another.
12 No man hath seen God at any time. If we
love one another, God dwelleth in us, and
his love is perfected in us.
13 Hereby know we that we dwell in him,
and he in us, because he hath given us of
his Spirit.
14 And we have seen and do testify that
the Father sent the Son *to be* the Saviour
of the world.
15 Whosoever shall confess that Jesus is
the Son of God, God dwelleth in him, and
he in God.
16 And we have known and believed the
love that God hath to us. God is love; and
he that dwelleth in love dwelleth in God,
and God in him.
17 Herein is our love made perfect, that we
may have boldness in the day of judgment:
because as he is, so are we in this world.
18 There is no fear in love; but perfect love
casteth out fear: because fear hath torment.
He that feareth is not made perfect in love.
19 We love him, because he first loved us.
20 If a man say, I love God, and hateth his
brother, he is a liar: for he that loveth not
his brother whom he hath seen, how can he
love God whom he hath not seen?
21 And this commandment have we from
him, That he who loveth God love his
brother also.

1 John 5

1 Whosoever believeth that Jesus is the
Christ is born of God: and every one that
loveth him that begat loveth him also that
is begotten of him.
2 By this we know that we love the children
of God, when we love God, and keep his
commandments.
3 For this is the love of God, that we keep his
commandments: and his commandments
are not grievous.
4 For whatsoever is born of God overcometh
the world: and this is the victory that overcometh the world, *even* our faith.
5 Who is he that overcometh the world,
but he that believeth that Jesus is the Son
of God?
6 This is he that came by water and blood,

even Jesus Christ; not by water only, but
by water and blood. And it is the Spirit that
beareth witness, because the Spirit is truth.
7 For there are three that bear record in
heaven, the Father, the Word, and the Holy
Spirit: and these three are one.
8 And there are three that bear witness
in earth, the spirit, and the water, and the
blood: and these three agree in one.
9 If we receive the witness of men, the witness of God is greater: for this is the witness
of God which he hath testified of his Son.
10 He that believeth on the Son of God hath
the witness in himself: he that believeth not
God hath made him a liar; because he believeth not the record that God gave of his Son.
11 And this is the record, that God hath
given to us eternal life, and this life is in
his Son.
12 He that hath the Son hath life; *and* he
that hath not the Son of God hath not life.
13 These things have I written unto you that
believe on the name of the Son of God; that
ye may know that ye have eternal life, and
that ye may believe on the name of the
Son of God.
14 And this is the confidence that we have
in him, that, if we ask any thing according
to his will, he heareth us:
15 And if we know that he hear us, whatsoever we ask, we know that we have the
petitions that we desired of him.
16 If any man see his brother sin a sin *which*
is not unto death, he shall ask, and he shall
give him life for them that sin not unto
death. There is a sin unto death: I do not
say that he shall pray for it.
17 All unrighteousness is sin: and there is a
sin not unto death.
18 We know that whosoever is born of
God sinneth not; but he that is begotten of
God keepeth himself, and that wicked one
toucheth him not.
19 *And* we know that we are of God, and the
whole world lieth in wickedness.
20 And we know that the Son of God is
come, and hath given us an understanding,
that we may know him that is true, and we
are in him that is true, *even* in his Son Jesus
Christ. This is the true God, and eternal life.
21 Little children, keep yourselves from
idols. Amen.

The Second Epistle Of

John

2 John 1

1 The elder unto the elect lady and her
children, whom I love in the truth; and not
I only, but also all they that have known
the truth;
2 For the truth's sake, which dwelleth in us,
and shall be with us for ever.
3 Grace be with you, mercy, *and* peace,
from God the Father, and from the Lord
Jesus Christ, the Son of the Father, in truth
and love.
4 I rejoiced greatly that I found of thy children walking in truth, as we have received
a commandment from the Father.
5 And now I beseech thee, lady, not as
though I wrote a new commandment unto
thee, but that which we had from the beginning, that we love one another.
6 And this is love, that we walk after his
commandments. This is the commandment,
That, as ye have heard from the beginning,
ye should walk in it.
7 For many deceivers are entered into the
world, who confess not that Jesus Christ is
come in the flesh. This is a deceiver and an
antichrist.
8 Look to yourselves, that we lose not those
things which we have wrought, but that we
receive a full reward.
9 Whosoever transgresseth, and abideth
not in the doctrine of Christ, hath not God.
He that abideth in the doctrine of Christ, he
hath both the Father and the Son.
10 If there come any unto you, and bring
not this doctrine, receive him not into *your*
house, neither bid him God speed:

11 For he that biddeth him God speed is
partaker of his evil deeds.
12 Having many things to write unto you,
I would not *write* with paper and ink: but I
trust to come unto you, and speak face to
face, that our joy may be full.
13 The children of thy elect sister greet
thee. Amen.

The Third Epistle Of

John

3 John 1

1 The elder unto the wellbeloved Gaius,
whom I love in the truth.
2 Beloved, I wish above all things that thou
mayest prosper and be in health, even as
thy soul prospereth.
3 For I rejoiced greatly, when the brethren
came and testified of the truth that is in
thee, even as thou walkest in the truth.
4 I have no greater joy than to hear that my
children walk in truth.
5 Beloved, thou doest faithfully whatsoever
thou doest to the brethren, and to strangers;
6 Which have borne witness of thy charity
before the church: whom if thou bring forward on their journey after a godly sort,
thou shalt do well:
7 Because that for his name's sake they
went forth, taking nothing of the Gentiles.
8 We therefore ought to receive such, that
we might be fellowhelpers to the truth.
9 I wrote unto the church: but Diotrephes,
who loveth to have the preeminence among
them, receiveth us not.
10 Wherefore, if I come, I will remember
his deeds which he doeth, prating against
us with malicious words: and not content
therewith, neither doth he himself receive
the brethren, and forbiddeth them that
would, and casteth *them* out of the church.
11 Beloved, follow not that which is evil,
but that which is good. He that doeth good
is of God: but he that doeth evil hath not
seen God.
12 Demetrius hath good report of all *men*,
and of the truth itself: yea, and we *also* bear
record; and ye know that our record is true.
13 I had many things to write, but I will not
with ink and pen write unto thee:
14 But I trust I shall shortly see thee, and we
shall speak face to face. Peace *be* to thee.
Our friends salute thee. Greet the friends
by name.

The Epistle Of

Jude

Jude 1

1 Jude, the servant of Jesus Christ, and
brother of James, to them that are sanctified
by God the Father, and preserved in Jesus
Christ, *and* called:
2 Mercy unto you, and peace, and love, be
multiplied.
3 Beloved, when I gave all diligence to write
unto you of the common salvation, it was
needful for me to write unto you, and exhort
you that ye should earnestly contend for
the faith which was once delivered unto
the saints.
4 For there are certain men crept in
unawares, who were before of old ordained
to this condemnation, ungodly men, turning
the grace of our God into lasciviousness,

and denying the only Lord God, and our
Lord Jesus Christ.
5 I will therefore put you in remembrance,
though ye once knew this, how that the
Lord, having saved the people out of the
land of Egypt, afterward destroyed them
that believed not.
6 And the angels which kept not their first
estate, but left their own habitation, he hath
reserved in everlasting chains under darkness unto the judgment of the great day.
7 Even as Sodom and Gomorrha, and the
cities about them in like manner, giving
themselves over to fornication, and going
after strange flesh, are set forth for an example, suffering the vengeance of eternal fire.
8 Likewise also these *filthy* dreamers defile
the flesh, despise dominion, and speak evil
of dignities.
9 Yet Michael the archangel, when con-
tending with the devil he disputed about
the body of Moses, durst not bring against
him a railing accusation, but said, The Lord
rebuke thee.
10 But these speak evil of those things
which they know not: but what they know
naturally, as brute beasts, in those things
they corrupt themselves.
11 Woe unto them! for they have gone in
the way of Cain, and ran greedily after the
error of Balaam for reward, and perished
in the gainsaying of Core.
12 These are spots in your feasts of charity,
when they feast with you, feeding themselves without fear: clouds *they are* without
water, carried about of winds; trees whose
fruit withereth, without fruit, twice dead,
plucked up by the roots;
13 Raging waves of the sea, foaming out
their own shame; wandering stars, to whom
is reserved the blackness of darkness for
ever.
14 And Enoch also, the seventh from Adam,
prophesied of these, saying, Behold, the
Lord cometh with ten thousands of his
saints,
15 To execute judgment upon all, and to
convince all that are ungodly among them
of all their ungodly deeds which they have
ungodly committed, and of all their hard
speeches which ungodly sinners have spoken against him.
16 These are murmurers, complainers,
walking after their own lusts; and their
mouth speaketh great swelling *words*, having men's persons in admiration because
of advantage.
17 But, beloved, remember ye the words
which were spoken before of the apostles
of our Lord Jesus Christ;
18 How that they told you there should be
mockers in the last time, who should walk
after their own ungodly lusts.
19 These be they who separate themselves,
sensual, having not the Spirit.
20 But ye, beloved, building up yourselves
on your most holy faith, praying in the
Holy Spirit,
21 Keep yourselves in the love of God, looking for the mercy of our Lord Jesus Christ
unto eternal life.
22 And of some have compassion, making
a difference:
23 And others save with fear, pulling *them*
out of the fire; hating even the garment
spotted by the flesh.
24 Now unto him that is able to keep you
from falling, and to present *you* fault-
less before the presence of his glory with
exceeding joy,
25 To the only wise God our Saviour, *be*
glory and majesty, dominion and power,
both now and ever. Amen.

The Revelation

To John

Revelation 1

1 The Revelation of Jesus Christ, which God
gave unto him, to shew unto his servants
things which must shortly come to pass; and
he sent and signified *it* by his angel unto his
servant John:
2 Who bare record of the word of God, and
of the testimony of Jesus Christ, and of all
things that he saw.
3 Blessed *is* he that readeth, and they that
hear the words of this prophecy, and keep
those things which are written therein: for
the time *is* at hand.
4 JOHN to the seven churches which are in
Asia: Grace *be* unto you, and peace, from
him which is, and which was, and which is
to come; and from the seven Spirits which
are before his throne;
5 And from Jesus Christ, *who is* the faithful
witness, *and* the first begotten of the dead,
and the prince of the kings of the earth.
Unto him that loved us, and washed us from
our sins in his own blood,
6 And hath made us kings and priests unto
God and his Father; to him *be* glory and
dominion for ever and ever. Amen.
7 Behold, he cometh with clouds; and every
eye shall see him, and they *also* which
pierced him: and all kindreds of the earth
shall wail because of him. Even so, Amen.
8 I am Alpha and Omega, the beginning
and the ending, saith the Lord, which is,
and which was, and which is to come, the
Almighty.
9 I John, who also am your brother, and
companion in tribulation, and in the kingdom and patience of Jesus Christ, was in the
isle that is called Patmos, for the word of
God, and for the testimony of Jesus Christ.
10 I was in the Spirit on the Lord's day,
and heard behind me a great voice, as of
a trumpet,
11 Saying, I am Alpha and Omega, the first
and the last: and, What thou seest, write in
a book, and send *it* unto the seven churches
which are in Asia; unto Ephesus, and unto
Smyrna, and unto Pergamos, and unto Thyatira, and unto Sardis, and unto Philadelphia,
and unto Laodicea.
12 And I turned to see the voice that spake
with me. And being turned, I saw seven
golden candlesticks;
13 And in the midst of the seven candlesticks *one* like unto the Son of man, clothed
with a garment down to the foot, and girt
about the paps with a golden girdle.
14 His head and *his* hairs *were* white like
wool, as white as snow; and his eyes *were*
as a flame of fire;
15 And his feet like unto fine brass, as if
they burned in a furnace; and his voice as
the sound of many waters.
16 And he had in his right hand seven
stars: and out of his mouth went a sharp
twoedged sword: and his countenance *was*
as the sun shineth in his strength.
17 And when I saw him, I fell at his feet as
dead. And he laid his right hand upon me,
saying unto me, Fear not; I am the first and
the last:
18 *I am* he that liveth, and was dead; and,
behold, I am alive for evermore, Amen; and
have the keys of hell and of death.
19 Write the things which thou hast seen,
and the things which are, and the things
which shall be hereafter;
20 The mystery of the seven stars which
thou sawest in my right hand, and the seven
golden candlesticks. The seven stars are
the angels of the seven churches: and the
seven candlesticks which thou sawest are
the seven churches.

Revelation 2

1 Unto the angel of the church of Ephesus
write; These things saith he that holdeth the
seven stars in his right hand, who walketh in
the midst of the seven golden candlesticks;
2 I know thy works, and thy labour, and thy
patience, and how thou canst not bear them
which are evil: and thou hast tried them
which say they are apostles, and are not,
and hast found them liars:
3 And hast borne, and hast patience, and

for my name's sake hast laboured, and hast
not fainted.
4 Nevertheless I have *somewhat* against
thee, because thou hast left thy first love.
5 Remember therefore from whence thou
art fallen, and repent, and do the first works;
or else I will come unto thee quickly, and
will remove thy candlestick out of his place,
except thou repent.
6 But this thou hast, that thou hatest the
deeds of the Nicolaitans, which I also hate.
7 He that hath an ear, let him hear what the
Spirit saith unto the churches; To him that
overcometh will I give to eat of the tree of
life, which is in the midst of the paradise
of God.
8 And unto the angel of the church in
Smyrna write; These things saith the first
and the last, which was dead, and is alive;
9 I know thy works, and tribulation, and
poverty, (but thou art rich) and *I know* the
blasphemy of them which say they are Jews,
and are not, but *are* the synagogue of Satan.
10 Fear none of those things which thou
shalt suffer: behold, the devil shall cast *some*
of you into prison, that ye may be tried; and
ye shall have tribulation ten days: be thou
faithful unto death, and I will give thee a
crown of life.
11 He that hath an ear, let him hear what
the Spirit saith unto the churches; He that
overcometh shall not be hurt of the second death.
12 And to the angel of the church in Pergamos write; These things saith he which hath
the sharp sword with two edges;
13 I know thy works, and where thou dwellest, *even* where Satan's seat *is:* and thou
holdest fast my name, and hast not denied
my faith, even in those days wherein Anti-
pas *was* my faithful martyr, who was slain
among you, where Satan dwelleth.
14 But I have a few things against thee,
because thou hast there them that hold
the doctrine of Balaam, who taught Balac
to cast a stumblingblock before the children
of Israel, to eat things sacrificed unto idols,
and to commit fornication.
15 So hast thou also them that hold the doctrine of the Nicolaitans, which thing I hate.
16 Repent; or else I will come unto thee
quickly, and will fight against them with the
sword of my mouth.
17 He that hath an ear, let him hear what the
Spirit saith unto the churches; To him that
overcometh will I give to eat of the hidden
manna, and will give him a white stone, and
in the stone a new name written, which no
man knoweth saving he that receiveth *it.*
18 And unto the angel of the church in
Thyatira write; These things saith the Son
of God, who hath his eyes like unto a flame
of fire, and his feet *are* like fine brass;
19 I know thy works, and charity, and service, and faith, and thy patience, and thy
works; and the last *to be* more than the first.
20 Notwithstanding I have a few things
against thee, because thou sufferest that
woman Jezebel, which calleth herself a
prophetess, to teach and to seduce my
servants to commit fornication, and to eat
things sacrificed unto idols.
21 And I gave her space to repent of her
fornication; and she repented not.
22 Behold, I will cast her into a bed, and
them that commit adultery with her into
great tribulation, except they repent of
their deeds.
23 And I will kill her children with death;
and all the churches shall know that I am he
which searcheth the reins and hearts: and
I will give unto every one of you according
to your works.
24 But unto you I say, and unto the rest in
Thyatira, as many as have not this doctrine,
and which have not known the depths of
Satan, as they speak; I will put upon you
none other burden.
25 But that which ye have *already* hold fast
till I come.
26 And he that overcometh, and keepeth
my works unto the end, to him will I give
power over the nations:
27 And he shall rule them with a rod of
iron; as the vessels of a potter shall they
be broken to shivers: even as I received of
my Father.
28 And I will give him the morning star.
29 He that hath an ear, let him hear what
the Spirit saith unto the churches.

Revelation 3

1 And unto the angel of the church in Sardis
write; These things saith he that hath the
seven Spirits of God, and the seven stars; I

know thy works, that thou hast a name that
thou livest, and art dead.
2 Be watchful, and strengthen the things
which remain, that are ready to die: for I
have not found thy works perfect before
God.
3 Remember therefore how thou hast
received and heard, and hold fast, and
repent. If therefore thou shalt not watch, I
will come on thee as a thief, and thou shalt
not know what hour I will come upon thee.
4 Thou hast a few names even in Sardis
which have not defiled their garments; and
they shall walk with me in white: for they
are worthy.
5 He that overcometh, the same shall be
clothed in white raiment; and I will not blot
out his name out of the book of life, but I
will confess his name before my Father, and
before his angels.
6 He that hath an ear, let him hear what the
Spirit saith unto the churches.
7 And to the angel of the church in Philadelphia write; These things saith he that is holy,
he that is true, he that hath the key of David,
he that openeth, and no man shutteth; and
shutteth, and no man openeth;
8 I know thy works: behold, I have set before
thee an open door, and no man can shut it:
for thou hast a little strength, and hast kept
my word, and hast not denied my name.
9 Behold, I will make them of the synagogue
of Satan, which say they are Jews, and are
not, but do lie; behold, I will make them to
come and worship before thy feet, and to
know that I have loved thee.
10 Because thou hast kept the word of my
patience, I also will keep thee from the
hour of temptation, which shall come upon
all the world, to try them that dwell upon
the earth.
11 Behold, I come quickly: hold that fast
which thou hast, that no man take thy
crown.
12 Him that overcometh will I make a pillar
in the temple of my God, and he shall go
no more out: and I will write upon him the
name of my God, and the name of the city
of my God, *which is* new Jerusalem, which
cometh down out of heaven from my God:
and *I will write upon him* my new name.
13 He that hath an ear, let him hear what
the Spirit saith unto the churches.
14 And unto the angel of the church of the
Laodiceans write; These things saith the
Amen, the faithful and true witness, the
beginning of the creation of God;
15 I know thy works, that thou art neither
cold nor hot: I would thou wert cold or hot.
16 So then because thou art lukewarm, and
neither cold nor hot, I will spue thee out of
my mouth.
17 Because thou sayest, I am rich, and
increased with goods, and have need of
nothing; and knowest not that thou art
wretched, and miserable, and poor, and
blind, and naked:
18 I counsel thee to buy of me gold tried in
the fire, that thou mayest be rich; and white
raiment, that thou mayest be clothed, and
that the shame of thy nakedness do not
appear; and anoint thine eyes with eyesalve,
that thou mayest see.
19 As many as I love, I rebuke and chasten:
be zealous therefore, and repent.
20 Behold, I stand at the door, and knock: if
any man hear my voice, and open the door,
I will come in to him, and will sup with him,
and he with me.
21 To him that overcometh will I grant to sit
with me in my throne, even as I also overcame, and am set down with my Father in
his throne.
22 He that hath an ear, let him hear what
the Spirit saith unto the churches.

Revelation 4

1 After this I looked, and, behold, a door
was opened in heaven: and the first voice
which I heard *was* as it were of a trumpet
talking with me; which said, Come up hither,
and I will shew thee things which must be
hereafter.
2 And immediately I was in the spirit: and,
behold, a throne was set in heaven, and *one*
sat on the throne.
3 And he that sat was to look upon like a
jasper and a sardine stone: and *there was*
a rainbow round about the throne, in sight
like unto an emerald.
4 And round about the throne *were* four
and twenty seats: and upon the seats I saw
four and twenty elders sitting, clothed in
white raiment; and they had on their heads
crowns of gold.
5 And out of the throne proceeded light-

nings and thunderings and voices: and *there*
were seven lamps of fire burning before the
throne, which are the seven Spirits of God.
6 And before the throne *there was* a sea of
glass like unto crystal: and in the midst of the
throne, and round about the throne, *were*
four beasts full of eyes before and behind.
7 And the first beast *was* like a lion, and the
second beast like a calf, and the third beast
had a face as a man, and the fourth beast
was like a flying eagle.
8 And the four beasts had each of them six
wings about *him;* and *they were* full of eyes
within: and they rest not day and night,
saying, Holy, holy, holy, Lord God Almighty,
which was, and is, and is to come.
9 And when those beasts give glory and
honour and thanks to him that sat on the
throne, who liveth for ever and ever,
10 The four and twenty elders fall down
before him that sat on the throne, and worship him that liveth for ever and ever, and
cast their crowns before the throne, saying,
11 Thou art worthy, O Lord, to receive glory
and honour and power: for thou hast created all things, and for thy pleasure they are
and were created.

Revelation 5

1 And I saw in the right hand of him that sat
on the throne a book written within and on
the backside, sealed with seven seals.
2 And I saw a strong angel proclaiming with a
loud voice, Who is worthy to open the book,
and to loose the seals thereof?
3 And no man in heaven, nor in earth, neither under the earth, was able to open the
book, neither to look thereon.
4 And I wept much, because no man was
found worthy to open and to read the book,
neither to look thereon.
5 And one of the elders saith unto me, Weep
not: behold, the Lion of the tribe of Juda, the
Root of David, hath prevailed to open the
book, and to loose the seven seals thereof.
6 And I beheld, and, lo, in the midst of the
throne and of the four beasts, and in the
midst of the elders, stood a Lamb as it had
been slain, having seven horns and seven
eyes, which are the seven Spirits of God sent
forth into all the earth.
7 And he came and took the book out of the
right hand of him that sat upon the throne.
8 And when he had taken the book, the four
beasts and four *and* twenty elders fell down
before the Lamb, having every one of them
harps, and golden vials full of odours, which
are the prayers of saints.
9 And they sung a new song, saying, Thou
art worthy to take the book, and to open
the seals thereof: for thou wast slain, and
hast redeemed us to God by thy blood out
of every kindred, and tongue, and people,
and nation;
10 And hast made us unto our God kings
and priests: and we shall reign on the earth.
11 And I beheld, and I heard the voice of
many angels round about the throne and
the beasts and the elders: and the number
of them was ten thousand times ten thousand, and thousands of thousands;
12 Saying with a loud voice, Worthy is the
Lamb that was slain to receive power, and
riches, and wisdom, and strength, and honour, and glory, and blessing.
13 And every creature which is in heaven,
and on the earth, and under the earth, and
such as are in the sea, and all that are in
them, heard I saying, Blessing, and honour,
and glory, and power, *be* unto him that sitteth upon the throne, and unto the Lamb
for ever and ever.
14 And the four beasts said, Amen. And the
four *and* twenty elders fell down and worshipped him that liveth for ever and ever.

Revelation 6

1 And I saw when the Lamb opened one of
the seals, and I heard, as it were the noise
of thunder, one of the four beasts saying,
Come and see.
2 And I saw, and behold a white horse: and
he that sat on him had a bow; and a crown
was given unto him: and he went forth
conquering, and to conquer.
3 And when he had opened the second seal,
I heard the second beast say, Come and see.
4 And there went out another horse *that*
was red: and *power* was given to him that
sat thereon to take peace from the earth,
and that they should kill one another: and
there was given unto him a great sword.
5 And when he had opened the third seal,
I heard the third beast say, Come and see.
And I beheld, and lo a black horse; and he

that sat on him had a pair of balances in
his hand.
6 And I heard a voice in the midst of the four
beasts say, A measure of wheat for a penny,
and three measures of barley for a penny;
and *see* thou hurt not the oil and the wine.
7 And when he had opened the fourth seal,
I heard the voice of the fourth beast say,
Come and see.
8 And I looked, and behold a pale horse:
and his name that sat on him was Death,
and Hell followed with him. And power
was given unto them over the fourth part
of the earth, to kill with sword, and with
hunger, and with death, and with the beasts
of the earth.
9 And when he had opened the fifth seal, I
saw under the altar the souls of them that
were slain for the word of God, and for the
testimony which they held:
10 And they cried with a loud voice, saying,
How long, O Lord, holy and true, dost thou
not judge and avenge our blood on them
that dwell on the earth?
11 And white robes were given unto every
one of them; and it was said unto them, that
they should rest yet for a little season, until
their fellowservants also and their brethren,
that should be killed as they *were*, should
be fulfilled.
12 And I beheld when he had opened
the sixth seal, and, lo, there was a great
earthquake; and the sun became black as
sackcloth of hair, and the moon became
as blood;
13 And the stars of heaven fell unto the
earth, even as a fig tree casteth her untimely
figs, when she is shaken of a mighty wind.
14 And the heaven departed as a scroll when
it is rolled together; and every mountain
and island were moved out of their places.
15 And the kings of the earth, and the great
men, and the rich men, and the chief captains, and the mighty men, and every bondman, and every free man, hid themselves in
the dens and in the rocks of the mountains;
16 And said to the mountains and rocks, Fall
on us, and hide us from the face of him that
sitteth on the throne, and from the wrath
of the Lamb:
17 For the great day of his wrath is come;
and who shall be able to stand?

Revelation 7

1 And after these things I saw four angels
standing on the four corners of the earth,
holding the four winds of the earth, that the
wind should not blow on the earth, nor on
the sea, nor on any tree.
2 And I saw another angel ascending from
the east, having the seal of the living God:
and he cried with a loud voice to the four
angels, to whom it was given to hurt the
earth and the sea,
3 Saying, Hurt not the earth, neither the
sea, nor the trees, till we have sealed the
servants of our God in their foreheads.
4 And I heard the number of them which
were sealed: *and there were* sealed an hundred *and* forty *and* four thousand of all the
tribes of the children of Israel.
5 Of the tribe of Juda *were* sealed twelve
thousand. Of the tribe of Reuben *were*
sealed twelve thousand. Of the tribe of Gad
were sealed twelve thousand.
6 Of the tribe of Aser *were* sealed twelve
thousand. Of the tribe of Nepthalim *were*
sealed twelve thousand. Of the tribe of
Manasses *were* sealed twelve thousand.
7 Of the tribe of Simeon *were* sealed twelve
thousand. Of the tribe of Levi *were* sealed
twelve thousand. Of the tribe of Issachar
were sealed twelve thousand.
8 Of the tribe of Zabulon *were* sealed twelve
thousand. Of the tribe of Joseph *were* sealed
twelve thousand. Of the tribe of Benjamin
were sealed twelve thousand.
9 After this I beheld, and, lo, a great multitude, which no man could number, of all
nations, and kindreds, and people, and
tongues, stood before the throne, and
before the Lamb, clothed with white robes,
and palms in their hands;
10 And cried with a loud voice, saying, Salvation to our God which sitteth upon the
throne, and unto the Lamb.
11 And all the angels stood round about the
throne, and *about* the elders and the four
beasts, and fell before the throne on their
faces, and worshipped God,
12 Saying, Amen: Blessing, and glory, and
wisdom, and thanksgiving, and honour, and
power, and might, *be* unto our God for ever
and ever. Amen.
13 And one of the elders answered, saying

unto me, What are these which are arrayed
in white robes? and whence came they?
14 And I said unto him, Sir, thou knowest.
And he said to me, These are they which
came out of great tribulation, and have
washed their robes, and made them white
in the blood of the Lamb.
15 Therefore are they before the throne
of God, and serve him day and night in his
temple: and he that sitteth on the throne
shall dwell among them.
16 They shall hunger no more, neither thirst
any more; neither shall the sun light on
them, nor any heat.
17 For the Lamb which is in the midst of the
throne shall feed them, and shall lead them
unto living fountains of waters: and God
shall wipe away all tears from their eyes.

Revelation 8

1 And when he had opened the seventh
seal, there was silence in heaven about the
space of half an hour.
2 And I saw the seven angels which stood
before God; and to them were given seven
trumpets.
3 And another angel came and stood at the
altar, having a golden censer; and there was
given unto him much incense, that he should
offer *it* with the prayers of all saints upon the
golden altar which was before the throne.
4 And the smoke of the incense, *which came*
with the prayers of the saints, ascended up
before God out of the angel's hand.
5 And the angel took the censer, and filled
it with fire of the altar, and cast *it* into the
earth: and there were voices, and thunderings, and lightnings, and an earthquake.
6 And the seven angels which had the seven
trumpets prepared themselves to sound.
7 The first angel sounded, and there followed hail and fire mingled with blood, and
they were cast upon the earth: and the third
part of trees was burnt up, and all green
grass was burnt up.
8 And the second angel sounded, and as
it were a great mountain burning with fire
was cast into the sea: and the third part of
the sea became blood;
9 And the third part of the creatures which
were in the sea, and had life, died; and the
third part of the ships were destroyed.
10 And the third angel sounded, and there
fell a great star from heaven, burning as it
were a lamp, and it fell upon the third part of
the rivers, and upon the fountains of waters;
11 And the name of the star is called Wormwood: and the third part of the waters
became wormwood; and many men died of
the waters, because they were made bitter.
12 And the fourth angel sounded, and the
third part of the sun was smitten, and the
third part of the moon, and the third part of
the stars; so as the third part of them was
darkened, and the day shone not for a third
part of it, and the night likewise.
13 And I beheld, and heard an angel flying
through the midst of heaven, saying with a
loud voice, Woe, woe, woe, to the inhabiters
of the earth by reason of the other voices
of the trumpet of the three angels, which
are yet to sound!

Revelation 9

1 And the fifth angel sounded, and I saw a
star fall from heaven unto the earth: and to
him was given the key of the bottomless pit.
2 And he opened the bottomless pit; and
there arose a smoke out of the pit, as the
smoke of a great furnace; and the sun and
the air were darkened by reason of the
smoke of the pit.
3 And there came out of the smoke locusts
upon the earth: and unto them was given
power, as the scorpions of the earth have
power.
4 And it was commanded them that they
should not hurt the grass of the earth, neither any green thing, neither any tree; but
only those men which have not the seal of
God in their foreheads.
5 And to them it was given that they should
not kill them, but that they should be tormented five months: and their torment
was as the torment of a scorpion, when he
striketh a man.
6 And in those days shall men seek death,
and shall not find it; and shall desire to die,
and death shall flee from them.
7 And the shapes of the locusts *were* like
unto horses prepared unto battle; and on
their heads *were* as it were crowns like gold,
and their faces *were* as the faces of men.
8 And they had hair as the hair of women,
and their teeth were as *the teeth* of lions.
9 And they had breastplates, as it were

breastplates of iron; and the sound of their wings *was* as the sound of chariots of many horses running to battle.
10 And they had tails like unto scorpions, and there were stings in their tails: and their power *was* to hurt men five months.
11 And they had a king over them, *which is* the angel of the bottomless pit, whose name in the Hebrew tongue *is* Abaddon, but in the Greek tongue hath *his* name Apollyon.
12 One woe is past; *and*, behold, there come two woes more hereafter.
13 And the sixth angel sounded, and I heard a voice from the four horns of the golden altar which is before God,
14 Saying to the sixth angel which had the trumpet, Loose the four angels which are bound in the great river Euphrates.
15 And the four angels were loosed, which were prepared for an hour, and a day, and a month, and a year, for to slay the third part of men.
16 And the number of the army of the horsemen *were* two hundred thousand thousand: and I heard the number of them.
17 And thus I saw the horses in the vision, and them that sat on them, having breastplates of fire, and of jacinth, and brimstone: and the heads of the horses *were* as the heads of lions; and out of their mouths issued fire and smoke and brimstone.
18 By these three was the third part of men killed, by the fire, and by the smoke, and by the brimstone, which issued out of their mouths.
19 For their power is in their mouth, and in their tails: for their tails *were* like unto serpents, and had heads, and with them they do hurt.
20 And the rest of the men which were not killed by these plagues yet repented not of the works of their hands, that they should not worship devils, and idols of gold, and silver, and brass, and stone, and of wood: which neither can see, nor hear, nor walk:
21 Neither repented they of their murders, nor of their sorceries, nor of their fornication, nor of their thefts.

Revelation 10

1 And I saw another mighty angel come down from heaven, clothed with a cloud: and a rainbow *was* upon his head, and his face *was* as it were the sun, and his feet as pillars of fire:
2 And he had in his hand a little book open: and he set his right foot upon the sea, and *his* left *foot* on the earth,
3 And cried with a loud voice, as *when* a lion roareth: and when he had cried, seven thunders uttered their voices.
4 And when the seven thunders had uttered their voices, I was about to write: and I heard a voice from heaven saying unto me, Seal up those things which the seven thunders uttered, and write them not.
5 And the angel which I saw stand upon the sea and upon the earth lifted up his hand to heaven,
6 And sware by him that liveth for ever and ever, who created heaven, and the things that therein are, and the earth, and the things that therein are, and the sea, and the things which are therein, that there should be time no longer:
7 But in the days of the voice of the seventh angel, when he shall begin to sound, the mystery of God should be finished, as he hath declared to his servants the prophets.
8 And the voice which I heard from heaven spake unto me again, and said, Go *and* take the little book which is open in the hand of the angel which standeth upon the sea and upon the earth.
9 And I went unto the angel, and said unto him, Give me the little book. And he said unto me, Take *it*, and eat it up; and it shall make thy belly bitter, but it shall be in thy mouth sweet as honey.
10 And I took the little book out of the angel's hand, and ate it up; and it was in my mouth sweet as honey: and as soon as I had eaten it, my belly was bitter.
11 And he said unto me, Thou must prophesy again before many peoples, and nations, and tongues, and kings.

Revelation 11

1 And there was given me a reed like unto a rod: and the angel stood, saying, Rise, and measure the temple of God, and the altar, and them that worship therein.
2 But the court which is without the temple leave out, and measure it not; for it is given unto the Gentiles: and the holy city shall they tread under foot forty *and* two months.

3 And I will give *power* unto my two witnesses, and they shall prophesy a thousand
two hundred *and* threescore days, clothed
in sackcloth.
4 These are the two olive trees, and the
two candlesticks standing before the God
of the earth.
5 And if any man will hurt them, fire proceedeth out of their mouth, and devoureth
their enemies: and if any man will hurt them,
he must in this manner be killed.
6 These have power to shut heaven, that
it rain not in the days of their prophecy:
and have power over waters to turn them
to blood, and to smite the earth with all
plagues, as often as they will.
7 And when they shall have finished their
testimony, the beast that ascendeth out of
the bottomless pit shall make war against
them, and shall overcome them, and kill
them.
8 And their dead bodies *shall lie* in the street
of the great city, which spiritually is called
Sodom and Egypt, where also our Lord was
crucified.
9 And they of the people and kindreds and
tongues and nations shall see their dead
bodies three days and an half, and shall not
suffer their dead bodies to be put in graves.
10 And they that dwell upon the earth shall
rejoice over them, and make merry, and
shall send gifts one to another; because
these two prophets tormented them that
dwelt on the earth.
11 And after three days and an half the Spirit
of life from God entered into them, and
they stood upon their feet; and great fear
fell upon them which saw them.
12 And they heard a great voice from heaven
saying unto them, Come up hither. And they
ascended up to heaven in a cloud; and their
enemies beheld them.
13 And the same hour was there a great
earthquake, and the tenth part of the city
fell, and in the earthquake were slain of
men seven thousand: and the remnant
were affrighted, and gave glory to the God
of heaven.
14 The second woe is past; *and*, behold, the
third woe cometh quickly.
15 And the seventh angel sounded; and
there were great voices in heaven, saying,
The kingdoms of this world are become *the*
kingdoms of our Lord, and of his Christ; and
he shall reign for ever and ever.
16 And the four and twenty elders, which
sat before God on their seats, fell upon their
faces, and worshipped God,
17 Saying, We give thee thanks, O Lord God
Almighty, which art, and wast, and art to
come; because thou hast taken to thee thy
great power, and hast reigned.
18 And the nations were angry, and thy
wrath is come, and the time of the dead,
that they should be judged, and that thou
shouldest give reward unto thy servants the
prophets, and to the saints, and them that
fear thy name, small and great; and shouldest destroy them which destroy the earth.
19 And the temple of God was opened in
heaven, and there was seen in his temple
the ark of his testament: and there were
lightnings, and voices, and thunderings, and
an earthquake, and great hail.

Revelation 12

1 And there appeared a great wonder in
heaven; a woman clothed with the sun, and
the moon under her feet, and upon her head
a crown of twelve stars:
2 And she being with child cried, travailing
in birth, and pained to be delivered.
3 And there appeared another wonder in
heaven; and behold a great red dragon,
having seven heads and ten horns, and
seven crowns upon his heads.
4 And his tail drew the third part of the stars
of heaven, and did cast them to the earth:
and the dragon stood before the woman
which was ready to be delivered, for to
devour her child as soon as it was born.
5 And she brought forth a man child, who
was to rule all nations with a rod of iron:
and her child was caught up unto God, and
to his throne.
6 And the woman fled into the wilderness,
where she hath a place prepared of God,
that they should feed her there a thousand
two hundred *and* threescore days.
7 And there was war in heaven: Michael and
his angels fought against the dragon; and
the dragon fought and his angels,
8 And prevailed not; neither was their place
found any more in heaven.
9 And the great dragon was cast out, that
old serpent, called the Devil, and Satan,

which deceiveth the whole world: he was
cast out into the earth, and his angels were
cast out with him.
10 And I heard a loud voice saying in heaven,
Now is come salvation, and strength, and
the kingdom of our God, and the power of
his Christ: for the accuser of our brethren
is cast down, which accused them before
our God day and night.
11 And they overcame him by the blood
of the Lamb, and by the word of their testimony; and they loved not their lives unto
the death.
12 Therefore rejoice, *ye* heavens, and ye that
dwell in them. Woe to the inhabiters of the
earth and of the sea! for the devil is come
down unto you, having great wrath, because
he knoweth that he hath but a short time.
13 And when the dragon saw that he was
cast unto the earth, he persecuted the
woman which brought forth the man *child*.
14 And to the woman were given two wings
of a great eagle, that she might fly into the
wilderness, into her place, where she is
nourished for a time, and times, and half a
time, from the face of the serpent.
15 And the serpent cast out of his mouth
water as a flood after the woman, that he
might cause her to be carried away of the
flood.
16 And the earth helped the woman, and
the earth opened her mouth, and swallowed
up the flood which the dragon cast out of
his mouth.
17 And the dragon was wroth with the
woman, and went to make war with the
remnant of her seed, which keep the commandments of God, and have the testimony
of Jesus Christ.

Revelation 13

1 And I stood upon the sand of the sea, and
saw a beast rise up out of the sea, having
seven heads and ten horns, and upon his
horns ten crowns, and upon his heads the
name of blasphemy.
2 And the beast which I saw was like unto
a leopard, and his feet were as *the feet* of a
bear, and his mouth as the mouth of a lion:
and the dragon gave him his power, and his
seat, and great authority.
3 And I saw one of his heads as it were
wounded to death; and his deadly wound
was healed: and all the world wondered
after the beast.
4 And they worshipped the dragon which
gave power unto the beast: and they worshipped the beast, saying, Who *is* like unto
the beast? who is able to make war with
him?
5 And there was given unto him a mouth
speaking great things and blasphemies; and
power was given unto him to continue forty
and two months.
6 And he opened his mouth in blasphemy
against God, to blaspheme his name, and his
tabernacle, and them that dwell in heaven.
7 And it was given unto him to make war
with the saints, and to overcome them: and
power was given him over all kindreds, and
tongues, and nations.
8 And all that dwell upon the earth shall
worship him, whose names are not written
in the book of life of the Lamb slain from
the foundation of the world.
9 If any man have an ear, let him hear.
10 He that leadeth into captivity shall go
into captivity: he that killeth with the sword
must be killed with the sword. Here is the
patience and the faith of the saints.
11 And I beheld another beast coming up
out of the earth; and he had two horns like
a lamb, and he spake as a dragon.
12 And he exerciseth all the power of the
first beast before him, and causeth the earth
and them which dwell therein to worship
the first beast, whose deadly wound was
healed.
13 And he doeth great wonders, so that he
maketh fire come down from heaven on
the earth in the sight of men,
14 And deceiveth them that dwell on the
earth by *the means of* those miracles which
he had power to do in the sight of the beast;
saying to them that dwell on the earth,
that they should make an image to the
beast, which had the wound by a sword,
and did live.
15 And he had power to give life unto the
image of the beast, that the image of the
beast should both speak, and cause that as
many as would not worship the image of the
beast should be killed.
16 And he causeth all, both small and great,
rich and poor, free and bond, to receive a

mark in their right hand, or in their foreheads:
17 And that no man might buy or sell, save
he that had the mark, or the name of the
beast, or the number of his name.
18 Here is wisdom. Let him that hath understanding count the number of the beast: for
it is the number of a man; and his number
is Six hundred threescore *and* six.

Revelation 14

1 And I looked, and, lo, a Lamb stood on the
mount Sion, and with him an hundred forty
and four thousand, having his Father's name
written in their foreheads.
2 And I heard a voice from heaven, as the
voice of many waters, and as the voice of
a great thunder: and I heard the voice of
harpers harping with their harps:
3 And they sung as it were a new song
before the throne, and before the four
beasts, and the elders: and no man could
learn that song but the hundred *and* forty
and four thousand, which were redeemed
from the earth.
4 These are they which were not defiled
with women; for they are virgins. These
are they which follow the Lamb whithersoever he goeth. These were redeemed from
among men, *being* the firstfruits unto God
and to the Lamb.
5 And in their mouth was found no guile:
for they are without fault before the throne
of God.
6 And I saw another angel fly in the midst
of heaven, having the everlasting gospel to
preach unto them that dwell on the earth,
and to every nation, and kindred, and
tongue, and people,
7 Saying with a loud voice, Fear God, and
give glory to him; for the hour of his judgment is come: and worship him that made
heaven, and earth, and the sea, and the
fountains of waters.
8 And there followed another angel, saying,
Babylon is fallen, is fallen, that great city,
because she made all nations drink of the
wine of the wrath of her fornication.
9 And the third angel followed them, saying
with a loud voice, If any man worship the
beast and his image, and receive *his* mark
in his forehead, or in his hand,
10 The same shall drink of the wine of the
wrath of God, which is poured out without
mixture into the cup of his indignation; and
he shall be tormented with fire and brimstone in the presence of the holy angels,
and in the presence of the Lamb:
11 And the smoke of their torment ascendeth up for ever and ever: and they have no
rest day nor night, who worship the beast
and his image, and whosoever receiveth the
mark of his name.
12 Here is the patience of the saints: here
are they that keep the commandments of
God, and the faith of Jesus.
13 And I heard a voice from heaven saying
unto me, Write, Blessed *are* the dead which
die in the Lord from henceforth: Yea, saith
the Spirit, that they may rest from their
labours; and their works do follow them.
14 And I looked, and behold a white cloud,
and upon the cloud *one* sat like unto the Son
of man, having on his head a golden crown,
and in his hand a sharp sickle.
15 And another angel came out of the temple, crying with a loud voice to him that sat
on the cloud, Thrust in thy sickle, and reap:
for the time is come for thee to reap; for the
harvest of the earth is ripe.
16 And he that sat on the cloud thrust in
his sickle on the earth; and the earth was
reaped.
17 And another angel came out of the
temple which is in heaven, he also having
a sharp sickle.
18 And another angel came out from the
altar, which had power over fire; and cried
with a loud cry to him that had the sharp
sickle, saying, Thrust in thy sharp sickle, and
gather the clusters of the vine of the earth;
for her grapes are fully ripe.
19 And the angel thrust in his sickle into the
earth, and gathered the vine of the earth,
and cast *it* into the great winepress of the
wrath of God.
20 And the winepress was trodden without the city, and blood came out of the
winepress, even unto the horse bridles, by
the space of a thousand *and* six hundred
furlongs.

Revelation 15

1 And I saw another sign in heaven, great
and marvellous, seven angels having the

seven last plagues; for in them is filled up
the wrath of God.
2 And I saw as it were a sea of glass mingled
with fire: and them that had gotten the
victory over the beast, and over his image,
and over his mark, *and* over the number of
his name, stand on the sea of glass, having
the harps of God.
3 And they sing the song of Moses the
servant of God, and the song of the Lamb,
saying, Great and marvellous *are* thy works,
Lord God Almighty; just and true *are* thy
ways, thou King of saints.
4 Who shall not fear thee, O Lord, and glorify thy name? for *thou* only *art* holy: for
all nations shall come and worship before
thee; for thy judgments are made manifest.
5 And after that I looked, and, behold, the
temple of the tabernacle of the testimony
in heaven was opened:
6 And the seven angels came out of the
temple, having the seven plagues, clothed
in pure and white linen, and having their
breasts girded with golden girdles.
7 And one of the four beasts gave unto the
seven angels seven golden vials full of the
wrath of God, who liveth for ever and ever.
8 And the temple was filled with smoke from
the glory of God, and from his power; and
no man was able to enter into the temple,
till the seven plagues of the seven angels
were fulfilled.

Revelation 16

1 And I heard a great voice out of the temple
saying to the seven angels, Go your ways,
and pour out the vials of the wrath of God
upon the earth.
2 And the first went, and poured out his vial
upon the earth; and there fell a noisome and
grievous sore upon the men which had the
mark of the beast, and *upon* them which
worshipped his image.
3 And the second angel poured out his vial
upon the sea; and it became as the blood
of a dead *man:* and every living soul died
in the sea.
4 And the third angel poured out his vial
upon the rivers and fountains of waters;
and they became blood.
5 And I heard the angel of the waters say,
Thou art righteous, O Lord, which art, and
wast, and shalt be, because thou hast
judged thus.
6 For they have shed the blood of saints and
prophets, and thou hast given them blood
to drink; for they are worthy.
7 And I heard another out of the altar say,
Even so, Lord God Almighty, true and righteous *are* thy judgments.
8 And the fourth angel poured out his vial
upon the sun; and power was given unto
him to scorch men with fire.
9 And men were scorched with great heat,
and blasphemed the name of God, which
hath power over these plagues: and they
repented not to give him glory.
10 And the fifth angel poured out his vial
upon the seat of the beast; and his kingdom
was full of darkness; and they gnawed their
tongues for pain,
11 And blasphemed the God of heaven
because of their pains and their sores, and
repented not of their deeds.
12 And the sixth angel poured out his vial
upon the great river Euphrates; and the
water thereof was dried up, that the way
of the kings of the east might be prepared.
13 And I saw three unclean spirits like frogs
come out of the mouth of the dragon, and
out of the mouth of the beast, and out of
the mouth of the false prophet.
14 For they are the spirits of devils, working
miracles, *which* go forth unto the kings of
the earth and of the whole world, to gather
them to the battle of that great day of God
Almighty.
15 Behold, I come as a thief. Blessed *is* he
that watcheth, and keepeth his garments,
lest he walk naked, and they see his shame.
16 And he gathered them together into a
place called in the Hebrew tongue Arma-
geddon.
17 And the seventh angel poured out his vial
into the air; and there came a great voice out
of the temple of heaven, from the throne,
saying, It is done.
18 And there were voices, and thunders,
and lightnings; and there was a great earthquake, such as was not since men were
upon the earth, so mighty an earthquake,
and so great.
19 And the great city was divided into three
parts, and the cities of the nations fell: and
great Babylon came in remembrance before

God, to give unto her the cup of the wine of
the fierceness of his wrath.
20 And every island fled away, and the
mountains were not found.
21 And there fell upon men a great hail out
of heaven, *every stone* about the weight of
a talent: and men blasphemed God because
of the plague of the hail; for the plague
thereof was exceeding great.

Revelation 17

1 And there came one of the seven angels
which had the seven vials, and talked with
me, saying unto me, Come hither; I will shew
unto thee the judgment of the great whore
that sitteth upon many waters:
2 With whom the kings of the earth have
committed fornication, and the inhabitants
of the earth have been made drunk with the
wine of her fornication.
3 So he carried me away in the spirit into the
wilderness: and I saw a woman sit upon a
scarlet coloured beast, full of names of blasphemy, having seven heads and ten horns.
4 And the woman was arrayed in purple
and scarlet colour, and decked with gold
and precious stones and pearls, having a
golden cup in her hand full of abominations
and filthiness of her fornication:
5 And upon her forehead *was* a name written, MYSTERY, BABYLON THE GREAT, THE
MOTHER OF HARLOTS AND ABOMINATIONS
OF THE EARTH.
6 And I saw the woman drunken with the
blood of the saints, and with the blood of
the martyrs of Jesus: and when I saw her, I
wondered with great admiration.
7 And the angel said unto me, Wherefore
didst thou marvel? I will tell thee the mystery of the woman, and of the beast that
carrieth her, which hath the seven heads
and ten horns.
8 The beast that thou sawest was, and is not;
and shall ascend out of the bottomless pit,
and go into perdition: and they that dwell
on the earth shall wonder, whose names
were not written in the book of life from the
foundation of the world, when they behold
the beast that was, and is not, and yet is.
9 And here *is* the mind which hath wisdom.
The seven heads are seven mountains, on
which the woman sitteth.
10 And there are seven kings: five are fallen,
and one is, *and* the other is not yet come;
and when he cometh, he must continue a
short space.
11 And the beast that was, and is not, even
he is the eighth, and is of the seven, and
goeth into perdition.
12 And the ten horns which thou sawest are
ten kings, which have received no kingdom
as yet; but receive power as kings one hour
with the beast.
13 These have one mind, and shall give their
power and strength unto the beast.
14 These shall make war with the Lamb,
and the Lamb shall overcome them: for he
is Lord of lords, and King of kings: and they
that are with him *are* called, and chosen,
and faithful.
15 And he saith unto me, The waters which
thou sawest, where the whore sitteth, are
peoples, and multitudes, and nations, and
tongues.
16 And the ten horns which thou sawest
upon the beast, these shall hate the whore,
and shall make her desolate and naked, and
shall eat her flesh, and burn her with fire.
17 For God hath put in their hearts to fulfil
his will, and to agree, and give their kingdom
unto the beast, until the words of God shall
be fulfilled.
18 And the woman which thou sawest is
that great city, which reigneth over the
kings of the earth.

Revelation 18

1 And after these things I saw another
angel come down from heaven, having
great power; and the earth was lightened
with his glory.
2 And he cried mightily with a strong voice,
saying, Babylon the great is fallen, is fallen,
and is become the habitation of devils, and
the hold of every foul spirit, and a cage of
every unclean and hateful bird.
3 For all nations have drunk of the wine of
the wrath of her fornication, and the kings
of the earth have committed fornication
with her, and the merchants of the earth
are waxed rich through the abundance of
her delicacies.
4 And I heard another voice from heaven,
saying, Come out of her, my people, that
ye be not partakers of her sins, and that ye
receive not of her plagues.

5 For her sins have reached unto heaven,
and God hath remembered her iniquities.
6 Reward her even as she rewarded you,
and double unto her double according to
her works: in the cup which she hath filled
fill to her double.
7 How much she hath glorified herself,
and lived deliciously, so much torment and
sorrow give her: for she saith in her heart,
I sit a queen, and am no widow, and shall
see no sorrow.
8 Therefore shall her plagues come in one
day, death, and mourning, and famine;
and she shall be utterly burned with fire:
for strong *is* the Lord God who judgeth her.
9 And the kings of the earth, who have
committed fornication and lived deliciously
with her, shall bewail her, and lament for
her, when they shall see the smoke of her
burning,
10 Standing afar off for the fear of her
torment, saying, Alas, alas, that great city
Babylon, that mighty city! for in one hour
is thy judgment come.
11 And the merchants of the earth shall
weep and mourn over her; for no man buyeth their merchandise any more:
12 The merchandise of gold, and silver,
and precious stones, and of pearls, and
fine linen, and purple, and silk, and scarlet, and all thyine wood, and all manner
vessels of ivory, and all manner vessels of
most precious wood, and of brass, and iron,
and marble,
13 And cinnamon, and odours, and ointments, and frankincense, and wine, and oil,
and fine flour, and wheat, and beasts, and
sheep, and horses, and chariots, and slaves,
and souls of men.
14 And the fruits that thy soul lusted after
are departed from thee, and all things which
were dainty and goodly are departed from
thee, and thou shalt find them no more
at all.
15 The merchants of these things, which
were made rich by her, shall stand afar off
for the fear of her torment, weeping and
wailing,
16 And saying, Alas, alas, that great city, that
was clothed in fine linen, and purple, and
scarlet, and decked with gold, and precious
stones, and pearls!
17 For in one hour so great riches is come to
nought. And every shipmaster, and all the
company in ships, and sailors, and as many
as trade by sea, stood afar off,
18 And cried when they saw the smoke of
her burning, saying, What *city is* like unto
this great city!
19 And they cast dust on their heads, and
cried, weeping and wailing, saying, Alas,
alas, that great city, wherein were made
rich all that had ships in the sea by reason
of her costliness! for in one hour is she
made desolate.
20 Rejoice over her, *thou* heaven, and *ye*
holy apostles and prophets; for God hath
avenged you on her.
21 And a mighty angel took up a stone like
a great millstone, and cast *it* into the sea,
saying, Thus with violence shall that great
city Babylon be thrown down, and shall be
found no more at all.
22 And the voice of harpers, and musi-
cians, and of pipers, and trumpeters, shall
be heard no more at all in thee; and no
craftsman, of whatsoever craft *he be*, shall
be found any more in thee; and the sound
of a millstone shall be heard no more at
all in thee;
23 And the light of a candle shall shine no
more at all in thee; and the voice of the
bridegroom and of the bride shall be heard
no more at all in thee: for thy merchants
were the great men of the earth; for by thy
sorceries were all nations deceived.
24 And in her was found the blood of prophets, and of saints, and of all that were slain
upon the earth.

Revelation 19

1 And after these things I heard a great voice
of much people in heaven, saying, Alleluia;
Salvation, and glory, and honour, and power,
unto the Lord our God:
2 For true and righteous *are* his judgments:
for he hath judged the great whore, which
did corrupt the earth with her fornication,
and hath avenged the blood of his servants
at her hand.
3 And again they said, Alleluia. And her
smoke rose up for ever and ever.
4 And the four and twenty elders and the
four beasts fell down and worshipped
God that sat on the throne, saying, Amen;
Alleluia.

5 And a voice came out of the throne, saying,
Praise our God, all ye his servants, and ye
that fear him, both small and great.
6 And I heard as it were the voice of a great
multitude, and as the voice of many waters,
and as the voice of mighty thunderings,
saying, Alleluia: for the Lord God omnipo-
tent reigneth.
7 Let us be glad and rejoice, and give honour to him: for the marriage of the Lamb is
come, and his wife hath made herself ready.
8 And to her was granted that she should
be arrayed in fine linen, clean and white: for
the fine linen is the righteousness of saints.
9 And he saith unto me, Write, Blessed *are*
they which are called unto the marriage
supper of the Lamb. And he saith unto me,
These are the true sayings of God.
10 And I fell at his feet to worship him. And
he said unto me, See *thou do it* not: I am thy
fellowservant, and of thy brethren that have
the testimony of Jesus: worship God: for the
testimony of Jesus is the spirit of prophecy.
11 And I saw heaven opened, and behold a
white horse; and he that sat upon him *was*
called Faithful and True, and in righteousness he doth judge and make war.
12 His eyes *were* as a flame of fire, and on his
head *were* many crowns; and he had a name
written, that no man knew, but he himself.
13 And he *was* clothed with a vesture dipped
in blood: and his name is called The Word
of God.
14 And the armies *which were* in heaven
followed him upon white horses, clothed
in fine linen, white and clean.
15 And out of his mouth goeth a sharp
sword, that with it he should smite the
nations: and he shall rule them with a rod
of iron: and he treadeth the winepress of
the fierceness and wrath of Almighty God.
16 And he hath on *his* vesture and on his
thigh a name written, KING OF KINGS, AND
LORD OF LORDS.
17 And I saw an angel standing in the sun;
and he cried with a loud voice, saying to all
the fowls that fly in the midst of heaven,
Come and gather yourselves together unto
the supper of the great God;
18 That ye may eat the flesh of kings, and
the flesh of captains, and the flesh of mighty
men, and the flesh of horses, and of them
that sit on them, and the flesh of all *men*,
both free and bond, both small and great.
19 And I saw the beast, and the kings of the
earth, and their armies, gathered together
to make war against him that sat on the
horse, and against his army.
20 And the beast was taken, and with him
the false prophet that wrought miracles
before him, with which he deceived them
that had received the mark of the beast, and
them that worshipped his image. These both
were cast alive into a lake of fire burning
with brimstone.
21 And the remnant were slain with the
sword of him that sat upon the horse, which
sword proceeded out of his mouth: and all
the fowls were filled with their flesh.

Revelation 20

1 And I saw an angel come down from
heaven, having the key of the bottomless
pit and a great chain in his hand.
2 And he laid hold on the dragon, that old
serpent, which is the Devil, and Satan, and
bound him a thousand years,
3 And cast him into the bottomless pit, and
shut him up, and set a seal upon him, that
he should deceive the nations no more, till
the thousand years should be fulfilled: and
after that he must be loosed a little season.
4 And I saw thrones, and they sat upon
them, and judgment was given unto them:
and *I saw* the souls of them that were
beheaded for the witness of Jesus, and
for the word of God, and which had not
worshipped the beast, neither his image,
neither had received *his* mark upon their
foreheads, or in their hands; and they lived
and reigned with Christ a thousand years.
5 But the rest of the dead lived not again
until the thousand years were finished. This
is the first resurrection.
6 Blessed and holy *is* he that hath part in the
first resurrection: on such the second death
hath no power, but they shall be priests of
God and of Christ, and shall reign with him
a thousand years.
7 And when the thousand years are expired,
Satan shall be loosed out of his prison,
8 And shall go out to deceive the nations
which are in the four quarters of the earth,
Gog and Magog, to gather them together

to battle: the number of whom *is* as the
sand of the sea.
9 And they went up on the breadth of the
earth, and compassed the camp of the
saints about, and the beloved city: and fire
came down from God out of heaven, and
devoured them.
10 And the devil that deceived them was
cast into the lake of fire and brimstone,
where the beast and the false prophet *are*,
and shall be tormented day and night for
ever and ever.
11 And I saw a great white throne, and him
that sat on it, from whose face the earth
and the heaven fled away; and there was
found no place for them.
12 And I saw the dead, small and great,
stand before God; and the books were
opened: and another book was opened,
which is *the book* of life: and the dead were
judged out of those things which were written in the books, according to their works.
13 And the sea gave up the dead which were
in it; and death and hell delivered up the
dead which were in them: and they were
judged every man according to their works.
14 And death and hell were cast into the
lake of fire. This is the second death.
15 And whosoever was not found written in
the book of life was cast into the lake of fire.

Revelation 21

1 And I saw a new heaven and a new earth:
for the first heaven and the first earth were
passed away; and there was no more sea.
2 And I John saw the holy city, new Jerusalem, coming down from God out of
heaven, prepared as a bride adorned for
her husband.
3 And I heard a great voice out of heaven
saying, Behold, the tabernacle of God *is* with
men, and he will dwell with them, and they
shall be his people, and God himself shall
be with them, *and be* their God.
4 And God shall wipe away all tears from
their eyes; and there shall be no more
death, neither sorrow, nor crying, neither
shall there be any more pain: for the former
things are passed away.
5 And he that sat upon the throne said,
Behold, I make all things new. And he said
unto me, Write: for these words are true
and faithful.
6 And he said unto me, It is done. I am Alpha
and Omega, the beginning and the end. I will
give unto him that is athirst of the fountain
of the water of life freely.
7 He that overcometh shall inherit all things;
and I will be his God, and he shall be my son.
8 But the fearful, and unbelieving, and the
abominable, and murderers, and whoremongers, and sorcerers, and idolaters,
and all liars, shall have their part in the lake
which burneth with fire and brimstone:
which is the second death.
9 And there came unto me one of the seven
angels which had the seven vials full of the
seven last plagues, and talked with me,
saying, Come hither, I will shew thee the
bride, the Lamb's wife.
10 And he carried me away in the spirit to
a great and high mountain, and shewed me
that great city, the holy Jerusalem, descending out of heaven from God,
11 Having the glory of God: and her light
was like unto a stone most precious, even
like a jasper stone, clear as crystal;
12 And had a wall great and high, *and* had
twelve gates, and at the gates twelve angels,
and names written thereon, which are *the
names* of the twelve tribes of the children
of Israel:
13 On the east three gates; on the north
three gates; on the south three gates; and
on the west three gates.
14 And the wall of the city had twelve
foundations, and in them the names of the
twelve apostles of the Lamb.
15 And he that talked with me had a golden
reed to measure the city, and the gates
thereof, and the wall thereof.
16 And the city lieth foursquare, and the
length is as large as the breadth: and he
measured the city with the reed, twelve
thousand furlongs. The length and the
breadth and the height of it are equal.
17 And he measured the wall thereof, an
hundred *and* forty *and* four cubits, *according to* the measure of a man, that is, of the
angel.
18 And the building of the wall of it was *of*
jasper: and the city *was* pure gold, like unto
clear glass.
19 And the foundations of the wall of the
city *were* garnished with all manner of
precious stones. The first foundation *was*

jasper; the second, sapphire; the third, a
chalcedony; the fourth, an emerald;
20 The fifth, sardonyx; the sixth, sardius; the
seventh, chrysolite; the eighth, beryl; the
ninth, a topaz; the tenth, a chrysoprasus; the
eleventh, a jacinth; the twelfth, an amethyst.
21 And the twelve gates *were* twelve pearls;
every several gate was of one pearl: and the
street of the city *was* pure gold, as it were
transparent glass.
22 And I saw no temple therein: for the
Lord God Almighty and the Lamb are the
temple of it.
23 And the city had no need of the sun,
neither of the moon, to shine in it: for the
glory of God did lighten it, and the Lamb *is*
the light thereof.
24 And the nations of them which are
saved shall walk in the light of it: and the
kings of the earth do bring their glory and
honour into it.
25 And the gates of it shall not be shut at
all by day: for there shall be no night there.
26 And they shall bring the glory and honour
of the nations into it.
27 And there shall in no wise enter into it any
thing that defileth, neither *whatsoever* worketh abomination, or *maketh* a lie: but they
which are written in the Lamb's book of life.

Revelation 22

1 And he shewed me a pure river of water
of life, clear as crystal, proceeding out of the
throne of God and of the Lamb.
2 In the midst of the street of it, and on
either side of the river, *was there* the tree
of life, which bare twelve *manner of* fruits,
and yielded her fruit every month: and the
leaves of the tree *were* for the healing of
the nations.
3 And there shall be no more curse: but the
throne of God and of the Lamb shall be in
it; and his servants shall serve him:
4 And they shall see his face; and his name
shall be in their foreheads.
5 And there shall be no night there; and they
need no candle, neither light of the sun; for
the Lord God giveth them light: and they
shall reign for ever and ever.
6 And he said unto me, These sayings *are*
faithful and true: and the Lord God of the
holy prophets sent his angel to shew unto
his servants the things which must shortly
be done.
7 Behold, I come quickly: blessed *is* he that
keepeth the sayings of the prophecy of
this book.
8 And I John saw these things, and heard
them. And when I had heard and seen, I fell
down to worship before the feet of the angel
which shewed me these things.
9 Then saith he unto me, See *thou do it*
not: for I am thy fellowservant, and of thy
brethren the prophets, and of them which
keep the sayings of this book: worship God.
10 And he saith unto me, Seal not the sayings of the prophecy of this book: for the
time is at hand.
11 He that is unjust, let him be unjust still:
and he which is filthy, let him be filthy still:
and he that is righteous, let him be righteous
still: and he that is holy, let him be holy still.
12 And, behold, I come quickly; and my
reward *is* with me, to give every man according as his work shall be.
13 I am Alpha and Omega, the beginning
and the end, the first and the last.
14 Blessed *are* they that do his commandments, that they may have right to the tree
of life, and may enter in through the gates
into the city.
15 For without *are* dogs, and sorcerers, and
whoremongers, and murderers, and idolaters, and whosoever loveth and maketh a lie.
16 I Jesus have sent mine angel to testify
unto you these things in the churches. I am
the root and the offspring of David, *and* the
bright and morning star.
17 And the Spirit and the bride say, Come.
And let him that heareth say, Come. And
let him that is athirst come. And whosoever
will, let him take the water of life freely.
18 For I testify unto every man that heareth
the words of the prophecy of this book, If
any man shall add unto these things, God
shall add unto him the plagues that are
written in this book:
19 And if any man shall take away from the
words of the book of this prophecy, God
shall take away his part out of the book of
life, and out of the holy city, and *from* the
things which are written in this book.
20 He which testifieth these things saith,
Surely I come quickly. Amen. Even so, come,
Lord Jesus.
21 The grace of our Lord Jesus Christ *be*
with you all. Amen.

Prayers

And this is the confidence that we have in him, that, if we ask any thing according to his will, he heareth us: And if we know that he hear us, whatsoever we ask, we know that we have the petitions that we desired of him.
– 1 John 5:14-15

Prayer	Date Answered

20 But Samson's wife was *given* to his companion, whom he had used as his friend.

Judges 15

1 But it came to pass within a while after,
in the time of wheat harvest, that Samson
visited his wife with a kid; and he said, I will
go in to my wife into the chamber. But her
father would not suffer him to go in.
2 And her father said, I verily thought that
thou hadst utterly hated her; therefore
I gave her to thy companion: *is* not her
younger sister fairer than she? take her, I
pray thee, instead of her.
3 ¶ And Samson said concerning them,
Now shall I be more blameless than the
Philistines, though I do them a displeasure.
4 And Samson went and caught three hundred foxes, and took firebrands, and turned
tail to tail, and put a firebrand in the midst
between two tails.
5 And when he had set the brands on fire,
he let *them* go into the standing corn of the
Philistines, and burnt up both the shocks,
and also the standing corn, with the vineyards *and* olives.
6 ¶ Then the Philistines said, Who hath done
this? And they answered, Samson, the son
in law of the Timnite, because he had taken
his wife, and given her to his companion.
And the Philistines came up, and burnt her
and her father with fire.
7 ¶ And Samson said unto them, Though ye
have done this, yet will I be avenged of you,
and after that I will cease.
8 And he smote them hip and thigh with
a great slaughter: and he went down and
dwelt in the top of the rock Etam.
9 ¶ Then the Philistines went up, and pitched
in Judah, and spread themselves in Lehi.
10 And the men of Judah said, Why are ye
come up against us? And they answered, To
bind Samson are we come up, to do to him
as he hath done to us.
11 Then three thousand men of Judah
went to the top of the rock Etam, and said
to Samson, Knowest thou not that the Philistines *are* rulers over us? what *is* this *that*
thou hast done unto us? And he said unto
them, As they did unto me, so have I done
unto them.
12 And they said unto him, We are come
down to bind thee, that we may deliver thee
into the hand of the Philistines. And Samson
said unto them, Swear unto me, that ye will
not fall upon me yourselves.
13 And they spake unto him, saying, No; but
we will bind thee fast, and deliver thee into
their hand: but surely we will not kill thee.
And they bound him with two new cords,
and brought him up from the rock.
14 ¶ *And* when he came unto Lehi, the Philistines shouted against him: and the Spirit of
the LORD came mightily upon him, and the
cords that *were* upon his arms became as
flax that was burnt with fire, and his bands
loosed from off his hands.
15 And he found a new jawbone of an ass,
and put forth his hand, and took it, and slew
a thousand men therewith.
16 And Samson said, With the jawbone of
an ass, heaps upon heaps, with the jaw of
an ass have I slain a thousand men.
17 And it came to pass, when he had made
an end of speaking, that he cast away the
jawbone out of his hand, and called that
place Ramath-lehi.
18 ¶ And he was sore athirst, and called
on the LORD, and said, Thou hast given this
great deliverance into the hand of thy servant: and now shall I die for thirst, and fall
into the hand of the uncircumcised?
19 But God clave an hollow place that *was*
in the jaw, and there came water thereout;
and when he had drunk, his spirit came
again, and he revived: wherefore he called
the name thereof En-hakkore, which *is* in
Lehi unto this day.
20 And he judged Israel in the days of the
Philistines twenty years.

Judges 16

1 Then went Samson to Gaza, and saw there
an harlot, and went in unto her.
2 *And it was told* the Gazites, saying, Samson is come hither. And they compassed
him in, and laid wait for him all night in the
gate of the city, and were quiet all the night,
saying, In the morning, when it is day, we
shall kill him.
3 And Samson lay till midnight, and arose at
midnight, and took the doors of the gate of
the city, and the two posts, and went away
with them, bar and all, and put *them* upon
his shoulders, and carried them up to the
top of an hill that *is* before Hebron.

4 ¶ And it came to pass afterward, that he
loved a woman in the valley of Sorek, whose
name *was* Delilah.
5 And the lords of the Philistines came up
unto her, and said unto her, Entice him, and
see wherein his great strength *lieth*, and by
what *means* we may prevail against him,
that we may bind him to afflict him: and
we will give thee every one of us eleven
hundred *pieces* of silver.
6 ¶ And Delilah said to Samson, Tell me, I
pray thee, wherein thy great strength *lieth*,
and wherewith thou mightest be bound to
afflict thee.
7 And Samson said unto her, If they bind
me with seven green withs that were
never dried, then shall I be weak, and be
as another man.
8 Then the lords of the Philistines brought
up to her seven green withs which had not
been dried, and she bound him with them.
9 Now *there were* men lying in wait, abiding
with her in the chamber. And she said unto
him, The Philistines *be* upon thee, Samson.
And he brake the withs, as a thread of tow
is broken when it toucheth the fire. So his
strength was not known.
10 And Delilah said unto Samson, Behold,
thou hast mocked me, and told me lies:
now tell me, I pray thee, wherewith thou
mightest be bound.
11 And he said unto her, If they bind me fast
with new ropes that never were occupied,
then shall I be weak, and be as another man.
12 Delilah therefore took new ropes, and
bound him therewith, and said unto him,
The Philistines *be* upon thee, Samson. And
there were liers in wait abiding in the chamber. And he brake them from off his arms
like a thread.
13 And Delilah said unto Samson, Hitherto
thou hast mocked me, and told me lies: tell
me wherewith thou mightest be bound. And
he said unto her, If thou weavest the seven
locks of my head with the web.
14 And she fastened *it* with the pin, and
said unto him, The Philistines *be* upon thee,
Samson. And he awaked out of his sleep,
and went away with the pin of the beam,
and with the web.
15 ¶ And she said unto him, How canst
thou say, I love thee, when thine heart *is*
not with me? thou hast mocked me these
three times, and hast not told me wherein
thy great strength *lieth*.
16 And it came to pass, when she pressed
him daily with her words, and urged him, so
that his soul was vexed unto death;
17 That he told her all his heart, and said
unto her, There hath not come a rasor upon
mine head; for I *have been* a Nazarite unto
God from my mother's womb: if I be shaven,
then my strength will go from me, and I shall
become weak, and be like any *other* man.
18 And when Delilah saw that he had told
her all his heart, she sent and called for the
lords of the Philistines, saying, Come up this
once, for he hath shewed me all his heart.
Then the lords of the Philistines came up
unto her, and brought money in their hand.
19 And she made him sleep upon her knees,
and she called for a man, and she caused
him to shave off the seven locks of his
head; and she began to afflict him, and his
strength went from him.
20 And she said, The Philistines *be* upon
thee, Samson. And he awoke out of his
sleep, and said, I will go out as at other
times before, and shake myself. And he wist
not that the LORD was departed from him.
21 ¶ But the Philistines took him, and put
out his eyes, and brought him down to Gaza,
and bound him with fetters of brass; and he
did grind in the prison house.
22 Howbeit the hair of his head began to
grow again after he was shaven.
23 Then the lords of the Philistines gathered
them together for to offer a great sacrifice
unto Dagon their god, and to rejoice: for
they said, Our god hath delivered Samson
our enemy into our hand.
24 And when the people saw him, they
praised their god: for they said, Our god
hath delivered into our hands our enemy,
and the destroyer of our country, which
slew many of us.
25 And it came to pass, when their hearts
were merry, that they said, Call for Samson, that he may make us sport. And they
called for Samson out of the prison house;
and he made them sport: and they set him
between the pillars.
26 And Samson said unto the lad that held
him by the hand, Suffer me that I may feel
the pillars whereupon the house standeth,
that I may lean upon them.

Prayer	Date Answered

Prayer	Date Answered